The Great
Contemporary
Issues

THE
MASS MEDIA
AND
POLITICS

**The Great
Contemporary
Issues**

James F. Fixx
General Editor

THE
MASS MEDIA
AND
POLITICS

𝕿𝖍𝖊 𝕹𝖊𝖜 𝖄𝖔𝖗𝖐 𝕿𝖎𝖒𝖊𝖘
Arno Press
New York/1972

The editors express special thanks to The Associated Press, United Press International, and Reuters for permission to include in this series of books a number of dispatches originally distributed by those news services.

Series Designer: Emil Micha
Research Assistant and Indexer: Donald Murk

"A Necessity, Not a Duty"
A Note About This Series

It would take even an accomplished speed-reader, moving at full throttle, some three and a half solid hours a day to work his way through all the news THE NEW YORK TIMES prints. The sad irony, of course, is that even such indefatigable devotion to life's carnival would scarcely assure a decent understanding of what it was really all about. For even the most dutiful reader might easily overlook an occasional long-range trend of importance, or perhaps some of the fragile, elusive relationships between events that sometimes turn out to be more significant than the events themselves.

This is why "The Great Contemporary Issues" was created—to help make sense out of some of the major forces and counterforces at large in today's world. The philosophical conviction behind the series is a simple one: that the past not only can illuminate the present but must. ("Continuity with the past," declared Oliver Wendell Holmes, "is a necessity, not a duty.") Each book in the series, therefore, has as its subject some central issue of our time that needs to be viewed in the context of its antecedents if it is to be fully understood. By showing, through a substantial selection of contemporary accounts from THE NEW YORK TIMES, the evolution of a subject and its significance, each book in the series offers a perspective that is available in no other way. For while most books on contemporary affairs specialize, for excellent reasons, in predigested facts and neatly drawn conclusions, the books in this series allow the reader to draw his own conclusions on the basis of the facts as they appeared at virtually the moment of their occurrence. This is not to argue that there is no place for events recollected in tranquility; it is simply to say that when fresh, raw truths are allowed to speak for themselves, some quite distinct values often emerge.

For this reason, most of the articles in "The Great Contemporary Issues" are reprinted in their entirety, even in those cases where portions are not central to a given book's theme. Editing has been done only rarely, and in all such cases it is clearly indicated. (Such an excision occasionally occurs, for example, in the case of a Presidential State of the Union Message, where only brief portions are germane to a particular volume, and in the case of some names, where for legal reasons or reasons of taste it is preferable not to republish specific identifications.) Similarly, typographical errors, where they occur, have been allowed to stand as originally printed.

"The Great Contemporary Issues" inevitably encompasses a substantial amount of history. In order to explore their subjects fully, some of the books go back a century or more. Yet their fundamental theme is not the past but the present. In this series the past is of significance insofar as it suggests how we got where we are today. These books, therefore, do not always treat a subject in a purely chronological way. Rather, their material is arranged to point up trends and interrelationships that the editors believe are more illuminating that a chronological listing would be.

Each volume in this series contains an index, compiled by NEW YORK TIMES indexers. Cumulative indexes to the entire series will be issued from time to time.

Each volume also contains a selective bibliography, prepared by the research staff of THE NEW YORK TIMES.

"The Great Contemporary Issues" series will ultimately constitute an encyclopedic library of today's major issues. Long before editorial work on the first volume had even begun, some fifty specific titles had already been either scheduled for definite publication or listed as candidates. Since then, events have prompted the inclusion of a number of additional titles, and the editors are, moreover, alert not only for new issues as they emerge but also for issues whose development may call for the publication of sequel volumes. We will, of course, also welcome readers' suggestions for future topics.

James F. Fixx, General Editor

Contents

A Note About This Series   v

Introduction, by Walter Cronkite   ix

1. Defining the Issues—The main themes in the
relationship of the mass media and politics.   1

2. Looking at Politics—How the media have covered
political events. Changes in political procedures
brought about by television. The political convention
and rally. "Underground newspapers."   61

3. The Use and Abuse of the Media—Politicians as
they have made use of—and sometimes tried to
manipulate—newspapers, radio, and television. The
press conference. Attacks on the media. Political
advertising and its costs.   107

4. The Fight for Fairness—The equal-time debate.
The fairness doctrine. Attempts to limit political
spending and assure fair access to the media. 203

5. Regulating the Media—Government information
policies. National security. Freedom of information.

Censorship and news management. Intimidation
of reporters. 289

Appendix: Cases in Point—Seven historic examples
of the ways the media and politics interact: President
Truman's walks with the press. Richard M. Nixon's
"Checkers" speech. Political debates. Goldwater and
Fact magazine. Spiro T. Agnew's criticisms of the
media. CBS-TV's "The Selling of the Pentagon"
show. Vietnam and the press 361

Suggested Reading 611

Index 613

Introduction
Disturbing the Politicians' Peace

Politics and the media are inseparable. It is only politicians and the media that are incompatible.

One might even say that in a very real sense politics is the media and the media is politics. For whether a nation's news is censored and disseminated only with official sanction or is as free as ours, the media are still as essential to government and the act of governing as a third leg is essential to a stool.

Newspapers and broadcasting stations are to politicians as heavy guns are to generals—weapons to be used or neutralized in the continuing battle for favorable public opinion.

There used to be—perhaps there still is—a sign on the police station on the island of Malta that said, as I recall: "Weapons registration office. All firearms, explosives and printing presses must be registered here."

How other nations control, marshal, and mass the artillery of the press is not our concern here. How politicians in our democracy attempt to, and how we of the media respond, is the subject of this book.

Part of the question to be considered here is whether the media are fair to politicians, whether they are performing their essential role in the democratic process with responsibility. Here the incompatibility factor makes its appearance. For the answer to the question of responsibility depends almost entirely upon who defines it. The politician seeking only a favorable image is likely to brand as irresponsible any reporting that disagrees with his point of view or even holds him up to the sharp light of critical appraisal.

There has scarcely been a president who has not registered his distaste for press criticism.

George Washington complained: "We have some infamous papers *calculated* for disturbing, if not absolutely *intended,* to disturb the peace."

Thomas Jefferson, in a letter, complained: "Even the least informed of the people have learnt that nothing in a newspaper is to be believed."

Woodrow Wilson said the papers "impede the public business by playing up controversy and difficulties."

Franklin Roosevelt and Harry Truman complained about the "one-party press"—by which *they,* of course, meant Republican.

President Lyndon Johnson asserted that the press twisted, imagined and magnified his viewpoint and that it was not his but the press's credibility gap that should be in question.

And what the Nixon administration thinks of the press has been set forth in abundant detail—duly reported, it might be noted, by that same press.

The press has been accused of being hypersensitive when it responds to criticism leveled against it. We are accused of not being able to take the same medicine that we dish out.

There may be an element of truth in that. Perhaps at times we have indeed overreacted to criticism. But if so, we have erred on the side of prudence. The press must be continually vigilant against those who would chip away at its freedoms, for if it does not rise to its own defense there are few others who will man the barricades for it.

Most journalists I know believe that this issue of the relationship of the press to the government—*i.e.,* to politics —is one that needs to be kept under constant review. This book is just such a review, and in it the new role of television plays an important part.

Television and politics flirted in 1948. They were wed in 1952. Whether or not the marriage was made in heaven, it is destined to endure for the life of the partners.

The first meeting at the political conventions in Philadelphia in 1948 had all the charm, finesse and sophistication of a schoolboy romance. The gropings and fumblings were accentuated by the June-December nature of the event. Here was Television, fresh of face and virginal in her innocence about her potential power. And here was Politics, its ash-strewn vest hanging open over a belly fat with power and, perhaps, even corruption.

Circumstances held the shotgun when this unlikely couple were united four years later at the conventions in Chicago. They have bickered and fought ever since but, as with some other marriages, even though the participants are not always happy together, they can no longer live apart.

Nor, of course, should they. The wonderful scientific achievement that is television has brought closer a true, full participation of the people in their government. The question, of course, is what use men make of this marvelous tool —whether they utilize it to its full benefit or pervert it to their own advantage.

The political problems presented by television are unique and may require unique answers.

One of these is access to television—the "equal time" debate discussed in Part 4 of this volume.

Another is the politicians' use of television as an advertising medium. Cost and the relative financial resources of candidates are important factors here, but a closely related question and an even more complex one is the nature of the advertising. A tendency has been growing to use twenty-second, thirty-second, and one-minute commercials to sell candidates like soap. These slick mini-presentations by advertising agencies do little to elucidate issues or expose the candidates as they really are.

As long as the press is alert it seems unlikely that this technique, even exercised with an unlimited budget, could elect a candidate whose face and philosophy were unknown to the public. But it is at least conceivable. For this reason, it presents a potential threat to the democratic process.

These are typical of problems that can exist only in a democratic nation. Any infringement of a candidate's right to use the media in any way he feels fit and proper might be interpreted as an infringement on his rights of free speech and press, and we are understandably nervous about that.

Clearly any attempt to legislate the manner of the media's coverage of matters political *is* such an infringement, and so would be government attempts to investigate, *ex post facto*, the media's performance, particularly in the world of politics with its inherent biases and prejudices.

Since it is elemental to the entire democratic process that the public have confidence in its news media, it is important that it understand the highly sophisticated and complex relationship between the media and the government. The greater that understanding, the greater the assurance that politicians will not successfully manipulate the media, and that the media will be left free to discharge their role as independent and fearless monitors of the public's servants.

This book is a contribution toward such understanding.

Walter Cronkite

1 DEFINING THE ISSUES

Newspapers clattering off a press by night

HOW IT ALL STARTED

November and National Election Recall 1920 Fad That Turned Into Big Idea

By ORRIN E. DUNLAP JR.

WHEN November arrives, thoughts of the broadcasters turn to election returns, and this always recalls that radio milestone in 1920, when the Harding-Cox election bulletins were broadcast through Pittsburgh's smoky air.

It was a pioneer radio program, although there had been previous experimental radiophone broadcasts from a number of other stations. The importance of this early KDKA election broadcast, however, lies in the fact that it opened the eyes of the experimentalists to the tremendous possibilities of the instruments with which they were talking through space.

Pioneering stations in New York and Detroit may have kindled the spark but the 1920 election broadcast fanned the radio flame into a "craze" that spread with amazing rapidity into a vast new industry giving employment to thousands and thousands of people. They came from sundry fields into this promised land of wireless wonders.

Electrical engineers and wireless amateurs became radio experts; elocutionists and singers became announcers, college graduates turned playwrights while others led bands up to the "mike." Tin Pan Alley worked overtime to turn out new songs which radio quickly gobbled, while clever arrangers dusted off the old masterpieces and dressed them up for the watts and waves.

Receivers Total 21,000,000

The industry and its many branches have grown with unabated fury ever since. Now there are 21,000,000 receiving sets in the United States; 600 broadcast transmitters, and instead of a 100-watt "voice" a Cincinnati giant of the air boasts 500,000 watts of superpower.

No one in 1920 seemed to surmise who might be called upon to finance the "show." Commercial sponsors were never suspected until 1922, but in 1936 it is estimated that the gross advertising volume on the air will total more than $100,000,000; it was $87,523,848 in 1935.

In 1920-21 the artists of distinction and the screen stars frowned upon the microphone as an instrument of the devil as far as their art was concerned; it could never do justice to their golden tones. Today radio has made them famous; it publicizes them nation-wide and pays high salaries for even thirty minutes of song or banter. Now Presidential nominees campaign by radio; kings talk across the globe to their colonies more quickly than a fly can crawl around an orange. The voices of Europeans are as loud in New York as New Yorkers themselves, and Big Ben striking the hours atop the House of Parliament in London echoes around the world. Wonders undreamed of in 1920 are now commonplace things, for all the world is radio-minded.

A Product of the War

Today, when technicians and artisans are busy studying television and spending thousands of dollars in research in an effort to offer telecasts to the public, it is interesting to recall how broadcasting "grew like Topsy."

The radiophone was a product of the World War. In Pittsburgh two stations had been built by the Westinghouse Electric and Manufacturing Company. One transmitter was at the East Pittsburgh plant and the other, about five miles away, was at the home of Dr. Frank Conrad, radio engineer. What to do with these stations at the end of the war was a problem. Dr. Conrad continued his experiments and from time to time broadcast phonograph music which was picked up by wireless amateurs. They comprised the "audience." The station's call letters 8XX became widely known because of the melodies and voices linked with it in space.

Birth of an Idea

"We were watching this activity very closely," recalled the late H. P. Davis, who was then vice president of the Westinghouse Electric and Manufacturing Company. "In the early part of the following year the thought came which led to the initiation of a regular broadcast service.

"An advertisement of a local department store in a Pittsburgh newspaper, calling attention to a stock of radio receivers which could be used to receive the programs sent out by Dr. Conrad, caused the thought to come to me that the efforts that were then being made to develop radio telephony as a confidential means of communication were wrong, and that instead its field was really one of wide publicity; in fact the only means of instantaneous collective communication ever devised. Right in our grasp, therefore, we had that service which we had been thinking about and endeavoring to formulate.

"Here was an idea of limitless opportunity if it could be 'put across.' A little study of this thought developed great possibilities. It was felt that here was something that would make a new public service of a kind certain to create epochal changes in the then accepted everyday affairs, quite as vital as had the introduction of the telephone and telegraph or the application of electricity to lighting and to power.

"We became convinced that we had in our hands, in this idea, the instrument that would prove to be the greatest and most direct mass communicational and mass educational means that had ever appeared. The natural fascination of its mystery, coupled with its ability to annihilate distance, would attract, interest and open many avenues to bring ease and happiness into human lives. It was obviously a form of service of universal application, that could be rendered without favor and without price."

The main objectives which were laid down as a basis to guide broadcasting at KDKA were:

1. To work hand and hand with the press, recognizing that only by published programs could the public fully appreciate a broadcasting service.

2. To provide a type of program that would be of interest and benefit to the greatest number, touching the lives of young and old.

3. To avoid monotony by introducing variety in music and talks.

4. To have distinctive features so timed as to assure their coming on at regular periods every evening.

5. To be continuous; that is, operate every day of the year.

"In our discussion the subject of the first program was a matter of very careful deliberation," continued Mr. Davis. "We wanted to do something unusual — we wanted to make it spectacular; we wanted it to attract attention. So the Harding-Cox election bulletins were selected for the historic broadcast."

Quite in contrast with this simple beginning is ultra-short wave television, the product of big laboratories and nurtured by million-dollar field tests under private enterprise in America and subsidized by governments in Europe. Television is being planned on an international scale, and there is no thought that it is to be a mere fad, toy or fancy. Every one knows too much about the wonders of radio to doubt that sound-sight in combination will be a much more powerful force in space than sound alone, yet sound has worked miracles, scientifically and socially, since 1920's election day.

Simple Formula Is Guide

Once broadcasting was a hit-or-miss affair, on the air only a few hours a day; now it is an eighteen-hour performance. There was a time when the "mike" dared not leave its pedestal in the studio, but in 1936 it goes far afield.

Program acts are picked up from various cities, across the continent and across the seas, to be dovetailed with split-second precision without the slightest clue, except for the announcement that the entertainers are separated by a thousand miles or more. Programs may be staged in aircraft or on ocean liners, while in 1920 no one thought of such "fantastic" acts. To the globe-girdling short wave goes credit for these broadcasts.

The big show costs money to stage, and the broadcasters, while they have no definite figures, estimate the "talent and material expenses" incurred in a year of broadcasting amounts to between twenty and thirty million dollars. It is believed that from 100 million to 150 million dollars are invested in broadcasting stations.

And the simple keynote of the gigantic set-up is summarized in the law which warns the broadcaster he must perform according to the formula of "public interest, convenience and necessity."

A SUBTLE ART

'Leather Lungs' of Spellbinders Have No Place on the Air, Says Reed

THERE will be no place in the 1936 national political campaign for the old-time spellbinder, according to Dr. Thomas H. Reed, chairman of the Committee on Civic Education by Radio, who asserts in a report to the Radio Institute of Audible Arts that one of radio's greatest achievements has been "to put leather lungs out of business." He contends that the mere strength of wind and nasal resonance have ceased to be factors in politics to the manifest advantage of democracy.

"The radio audience not being a mass audience is not to be influenced by bellowing, arm waving, or even by any of the subtler physical arts by which a speaker sways a crowd," said Dr. Reed. "The radio audience is made up of myriads of individuals and small family groups. No one likes violent noises in his living room, and even small noises reach portentous volume as they emerge from a loud-speaker.

"The man at the controls, too, can and does step up the weakest voice to tones that suggest power and confidence.

"Today any man who has something to say, and can get a chance on the air, can say it to his countrymen without regard to whether his voice is a light tenor or a rumbling bass. The difficulties in the way of his success as a radio speaker will be purely intellectual, and these may be overcome, even in a case most obstinately inarticulate, by employing a ghost writer and a production expert."

Demeanor Still Concealed

Dr. Reed explains, however, this does not mean that discussion of public questions has been elevated to that exalted plane for which idealists long. Good radio technique, he asserts, is not always an accompaniment of political virtue. Until television supplies the lack, there can be no accurate appraisal of the demeanor of a radio speaker.

"One may lie over the radio without blushing, for it can be done without catching a single skeptical eye. In addition, heckling, an informal sort of cross-examination

much relied on in public assemblies for deflating conceit and exposing ignorance and falsehoods, is impossible. It required courage to take the tribune in the Roman Forum, but a radio debate is necessarily a prearranged and stilted affair in which no interruptions are possible. A nation, therefore, which listens avidly to crooners must be doubly on its guard against the blandishments of political self-advertisers.

Access Is Usually Purchased

"Access to the air is not determined, or for that matter determinable, on a merit basis," said Dr. Reed. "It is primarily obtainable by purchase. This means that all the best periods, with rare and mostly accidental exceptions, are acquired for long stretches of time by advertisers. . . . Political parties, or other organizations interested in propaganda of one sort and another, also buy radio time—a good deal of it in the heat of campaigns and very little of it at other times.

"Obviously, there is little opportunity in this scheme for the isolated individual—discoverer, scholar, patriot, whatever he may be—to launch his voice into the ether.

"Wisdom in the field of government and politics may have to be dumb as far as the radio is concerned, unless its possessor is asked to speak by a political party, by a broadcasting company or by some voluntary organization. He will not be invited to speak by a political party, except to make a partisan address. He will probably not be invited at all by a broadcasting company, because while very generous in initiating educational programs in such fields as music, science, &c., such companies, subject to regulation by the Federal government, naturally shrink from assuming responsibility for the political views which may be poured into their microphones."

Civic education by radio has just begun, according to Dr. Reed. He sees American radio in a formative period, groping for means of calling young and old to listen to wisdom and experience instead of recklessness and folly. One thing he believes is certain, that the public will listen —to whom is the question.

A STUDY IN VOICES

Presidential Nominees Use Plain Words— Their Radio Personalities Differ

By ORRIN E. DUNLAP Jr.

TWO contrasting radio personalities are in the race for the Presidency. Mr. Roosevelt is generally recognized as a master in the art of broadcasting; that mysterious element called "microphone technique" comes naturally to him.

Governor Landon is described as the average American at the "mike." The Republicans boast that he introduces "a new style of political broadcasting, direct and factual." His speech is simple and straightforward; his tone calm and temper even. He is credited so far in the campaign with "plain talking that reveals the true anatomy of an issue."

Mr. Roosevelt is an expert vocal showman with the talents of an actor, whose voice is as vibrant with enthusiasm and stamina at the end as in the beginning of the speech. A number of critics have observed that to date Mr. Landon has not mastered the art of reading a radio speech, of injecting what the broadcasters call "punch" into his delivery. He seems to lack the instinct of timing his words to dovetail with applause and vital pauses which is part of the artistry in radio speechmaking.

Mr. Landon, however, has been heard in the most difficult broadcasting, that of addressing a visible and invisible audience at the same time. He has yet to be heard in a "fireside chat" type of talk microphoned in the quiet of his own study. The more peaceful and less distracting conditions may help to improve his radio technique.

How the Voices Differ

Landon's radio voice is described as "plain"; Roosevelt's "plain, but lively, colored by a Harvard accent." Landon's voice is undramatic; Roosevelt's is dramatic. Those who hear Landon on the air, however, are in tune with a man whom they recognize as they know their neighbors; they understand and trust him, and his associates further believe that listeners are impressed with his "homely, grassroots common sense, modesty and fairness."

Those who hear Roosevelt are in tune with a man who knows to perfection how to dress up his speech in all the habiliments of stage setting. While he may resort to what some call "vocal gymnastics of an elocutionary expert," yet no one of ordinary intelligence can have any difficulty in understanding what he says.

Both Landon and Roosevelt are men of plain speech, but it is in delivery and voice personality that they are vastly different. Both have

high ideals, but whether the solemn Hoover-like speech of Landon can hold an unseen audience for an hour, as can the more dramatic, forceful Roosevelt, is yet to be determined. Landon as "the Kansas Coolidge" seems to need some of Roosevelt's rhetorical but subtle flourishes, although it may be inconsistent with his rôle of the plain, average man.

Two Schools of Thought

There are two schools of thought on this subject, even in radio circles. One group believes that radio, being a medium of entertainment, calls for showmanship in speechmaking, and asserts the speech must be sugarcoated with more than common sense and candid talk. This group favors "vocal gymnastics," deftly handled, whether the speaker is a Presidential nominee or a gardener talking on green peas or petunias. On the other hand are those who insist that the people are in the mood to welcome "plain, unassuming exposition of a subject" spoken by "a horse and buggy" voice without the slightest trace of radio-announcerial style.

The neighbors, as the politicians like to call the radio audience, can understand both Landon and Roosevelt, but some of the radio showmen wonder if they are more likely to listen longer to Roosevelt because his voice is more entertaining. Landon has been noted to slur diction and neglect pauses. Roosevelt is a perfectionist in both; he is a radio strategist. Landon at times talks too quickly, although he has slowed his pace in more recent broadcasts. Roosevelt adheres to a pace which permits his message to "sink in," but he does so with such skill that the listener is never conscious of it.

Roosevelt knows tricks about broadcasting that Landon still must learn. Simple straightforward language is not always enough; delivery with oratorical ease counts. To date Landon misses this mark; Roosevelt strikes it. Radio's forum is no place for dullness, although it is said "dullness does not always damn an oration." This does not mean radio is no place for "plain talk," for there is a difference between dullness and plainness.

A Photographer's Observation

George W. Harris, photographer of notables, once said that a plain picture of a man wore better than that of one animated and smiling.

"You like the latter at first, but after you look at it a few times you get tired of the smiles," Mr. Harris added.

April 12, 1936

3

Recalling the photographer's comment, a Washington political observer asserts, "This is probably just as true of a voice over the radio. Landon's voice is as plain as an old shoe. Yet it is clear and natural, easy to understand and, aided by his simple language and by newspaper pictures and movies, really seems to bring the man himself into your presence. * * * The Governor easily measures up as a star in a great broadcast and really looms as a foe worthy of President Roosevelt's ethereal steel."

Radio personality, too, may be developed. Former President Hoover proved this is possible in his recent speeches. He so improved his radio delivery that he has been called "the new Hoover."

Mr. Landon's natural voice may exactly fit the rôle of "the Kansas Coolidge" that has been assigned to him, and it may not be the desire of the strategists in his camp to change the ethereal personality through rhetorical frills. His radio associates must be well aware of the tricks, and no doubt could apply them through his delivery, but by such coaching they would change his character on the air. They apparently seek to win through what he has to say rather than how he says it.

There are voice critics, however, who contend that a "quiet" man runs the chance of obscuring the vital significance of his speech by adhering too faithfully to the rôle of the plain man. Oddly enough, the sound of a voice "paints" a picture of a radio singer, actor or speaker in the listener's mind. The imagination fed by radio creates a character based on sound alone.

Broadcasting, being essentially show business electrified, is one reason why a dramatic, not necessarily a thunder-and-lightning orator, is more likely to attract and grip an audience. The quiet speaker is a man of mere words; a dramatic broadcaster is one who cleverly injects showmanship into his speech, yet without destroying its meaning by too much "sugarcoating."

"Coloring" Has a Limit

Given the same speech, Roosevelt and Landon would make it sound entirely different on the radio.

There is a limit to "coloring" beyond which the voice dominates the words. For example, American radio announcers are far more colorful than the British announcers because in England it is the belief that sober thoughts must be first and voice personality secondary; otherwise the man overrides the message. In politics it is slightly different; there is a happy medium in which both words and personality go across on the air. Roosevelt seems to have the secret, for he is as much a part of the broadcast as his message, yet he does not permit his ethereal personality to "run ahead" of his words.

Soon after President Roosevelt introduced his historic "fireside chats" in 1932 a representative of the Columbia Broadcasting Company remarked: "Radio has been generously thanked for the part which it played in the President's direct attack upon a national crisis. It remains, it seems to us, for radio to thank the President. For history has repeated its pattern with a new hero and a new sword—and both the power of the man and the power of the weapon which he wields are suddenly, sweepingly revealed."

Status of the Silver Tongue

Now radio has this same effective voice pitted in a campaign against a plain voice. There are some who argue that sixteen years of broadcasting has educated the populace to devote little attention to everyday speech. But on the other side of the case is the listener who points to the fact that this is a campaign in which the man and the issues count more than the sound of a voice. To substantiate this theory, those favoring the "plain voice" call attention to William Jennings Bryan, whose silver tongue surpassed all others of his day, but the great orator failed in three attempts to enter the White House as President.

Whether the "homey talk, couched in short, quotable Coolidge-like sentences," will overpower the plain but dramatic speech is yet to be seen; November will tell.

MAYOR SAYS RADIO 'DEBUNKS' POLITICS

Tells 25 Foreign Officials That Broadcasts Extend Spirit of Democracy.

Radio has elevated political campaigns by "debunking" them and forcing candidates to stick to the campaign issues, Mayor La Guardia told twenty-five foreign radio officials when he welcomed them at City Hall yesterday in connection with the tenth anniversary of the National Broadcasting Company.

"The radio is doing a great deal in our country in extending the real spirit of Democracy," the Mayor told the visitors. "Perhaps some of you have heard that we had an election a few days ago. The radio has changed and elevated the technique of political campaigns. And what is more important, it has done a great deal to debunk, and to compel political parties to state the facts and stick to the issues."

The Mayor told his guests that the time was not far distant when interchange of international programs would be a commonplace instead of a special feature of broadcasting. In its relatively short life, he said radio had passed quickly through several stages; the experimental, then the artistic and finally the present-day commercial stage where entertainment was coupled with advertising.

The radio executives from abroad are all members of the International Broadcasting Union. Headed by Maurice Rambert, they were introduced to the Mayor by Dr. Max Jordan, European commentator for the system. The Mayor showed he was a versatile linguist by greeting various members of the party in tongues they understood, using German, Italian, French, Serbian and English.

The reception was held in the Aldermanic chamber, and was broadcast abroad and in this country.

Topics of The Times

Their Master's Voice

F. P. A., ruminating in his Conning Tower on the lessons of last Tuesday, observes, "They are saying that the radio was more effective than the newspapers." Well, naturally, they would say some such thing. It will take a great many landslides to undermine one of the most cherished of post-war superstitions. This is the fond belief that national majorities are always the product of manipulation. Somebody is always pulling the strings from the outside.

The thought that a popular majority may express the natural sentiments of the voters is abhorrent to the Manipulationists. They have been educated to the theory of conditioned reflexes and the irresistible might of Propaganda. By this doctrine the masses automatically believe what is told them. If they are not conditioned by the newspapers they are conditioned by the radio. If they are not under the spell of Mr. Hearst and Father Coughlin they are under the spell of President Roosevelt.

One hypothesis which the Manipulationists never consider is that the people might be under nobody's spell. They might be guided by what they think is their own best interest. A simple motive, almost an elementary animal motive, but the people's own.

Behind the Words

The effectiveness of the press in last Tuesday's happenings will some day repay a little closer examination. But it is extraordinary that any one should choose to speak of the effectiveness of the radio after a campaign in which the radio failed so signally to come up to expectations.

Father Coughlin, the Radio Priest himself, has bid a mournful farewell to the political arena, thoroughly deflated. Socialists and Communists for the first time in a Presidential campaign had fair representation on the radio, and both parties are now in the hospital. Republicans spent twice as much money as Democrats, of which a good deal must have gone into radio time; and much good it did them.

Apparently, then, it comes down to Mr. Roosevelt and his magnificent radio voice. For the Manipulationists it will be the fireside talks from the White House that explain a 10,000,000 plurality. Most of us know that Mr. Roosevelt might have spoken over the radio with the tongues of men and of angels, but if he had not business recovery and Government relief on his side his efforts would have been wasted.

ACT II BEGINS

Roosevelt's Second Inaugural Finds Radio Stage Set for a Vast Audience

By ORRIN E. DUNLAP Jr.

RADIO'S outstanding event this week is the second inaugural · of Franklin D. Roosevelt as President of the United States. Washington will be the center of broadcasting from early morning on Wednesday until late afternoon.

Special wire lines will run in all directions to broadcast transmitters everywhere so that the coverage of this quadrennial event will be the most elaborate ever attempted by the broadcasters. More than 300 stations in the United States will be linked in the vast copper web that will form the record-breaking hook-up.

This will be radio's fourth inaugural program. The first was in March, 1925, when it was heralded as a wonder of scientific magic that twenty-four stations could be chained by wire to enable a coast-to-coast audience to eavesdrop on the inauguration of Calvin Coolidge as the thirtieth President of the United States.

Two dozen stations comprised a record-breaking hook-up twelve years ago. In this day and age, however, with the stations counted by hundreds and powerful short waves flashing to every corner of the globe, a description of the history-making scene on the portico of the nation's Capitol and the President's inaugural message slide around the earth as easily as a fly crawls around an orange. With so many stentorian stations handling the event the ethereal envelope of the earth will pulse with the electrified words of this inaugural so a vast audience may listen.

HOW many may be in tune is only a guess, for radio still has no definite yardstick with which to gauge the size of the unseen audiences. But it is safe to say that a greater multitude will be within tuning range this year than when Mr. Coolidge was inaugurated, or Mr. Hoover in 1929. The size of the radio audience has grown. In 1924 the count was 3,000,000 radios in the United States; and the international short waves were merely experimental. The overseas audience in those days was insignificant, and if any listeners on foreign shores heard the Coolidge inaugural they may have been experimenters who intercepted stray waves abetted by freak atmospherics.

Today the estimates place the number of home receivers in this country at 21,000,000, while at the time of the 1933 inaugural the count was 16,000,000. Now, with millions of additional sets, more powerful stations and short-wave outfits, radio offers a record-breaking audience an opportunity to listen in. For instance, as an indication of radio's remarkable advance, there is one station in the United States today, namely WLW, Cincinnati, a 500,000-watt transmitter, which is more powerful than all of the twenty-four transmitters put together for the Coolidge inauguration.

With space so powerfully electrified and with foreign stations re-broadcasting, it seems that Mr. Roosevelt will have at least 100,-000,000 persons in the international audience that hears the Presidential oath administered to him for the second time by the Chief Justice of the Supreme Court, Charles Evans Hughes.

THE first Roosevelt inaugural is still fresh in the memories of the broadcasters. They recall those crucial days in 1933 and how they rushed to Washington with all the broadcasting paraphernalia they could muster to make the event the greatest of its kind ever put on the air.

Drama was the keynote. The aim was to tell the nation and the world that the turning point had been reached in the depression. The inaugural signalized victory. There was no place for gloom on this program; all was to be sunshine. And evidence that the announcers succeeded was found in the mail from listeners, some of whom protested that the commentators were too enthusiastic; they were accused of painting too "rosy" a picture. But America was at the crossroads, and whether radio put "the sunshine" on too thick in 1933 has never been decided; the point is that Americans everywhere were more cheerful when the sun went down that night. The inaugural message of "the radio President," so called because of his magnificent voice, had lifted high the banners in a fight to banish fear. The world heard the voice of a new leadership. The battle for recovery was on with vigor and America rallied to end the disastrous depression, which had only the day before caused the closing of all the banks in the land.

The Rooseveltian voice has lost none of the power and fighting spirit it revealed on that March day, while thousands in Washington watched the historic scene and millions listened to the battle-cry that inaugurated the New Deal. The man and the voice have both gained in power and influence. On Wednesday Mr. Roosevelt will send forth into space another electromagnetic message: the keynote for another four years.

A most intricate network has been woven throughout Washington. Announcers will be at strategic points everywhere; in transport planes, atop the Washington monument and the Capitol dome. They will be along the streets, in the Capitol corridors and on the plaza, while observers equipped with portable pack transmitters roam around for interviews with celebrities attending the colorful Rooseveltian pageant.

Broadcasting will begin at approximately 8:30 A. M., Eastern standard time. From special booths along the line of march, from mobile transmitters and from traffic towers announcers will describe the parade on Pennsylvania Avenue. The "mike" has also been invited to enter the official reviewing stand, a few feet from the President and Mrs. Roosevelt.

Although time for the broadcasts from various points has not been fixed, it is expected that the President will leave the White House at about 11:30 A. M., Eastern standard time. At noon, the Rev. Z. B. Phillips, chaplain of the Senate, is scheduled to begin the formal inaugural ceremonies with a prayer. Then Senator Joseph T. Robinson of Arkansas will administer the oath of office to Vice President Garner.

The Presidential oath will be administered and the inaugural address will be broadcast between noon and 1 o'clock, at which hour the parade is scheduled to begin.

MOBILIZATION of the radio facilities represents a big engineering task which began in November. For example, the Columbia Broadcasting system estimates the installation and testing of the apparatus will have consumed 1,000 hours of the engineering department's time. Vacuum tubes required for the CBS part of the broadcast will number more than 150, and at least thirty microphones will be in the circuit. Twenty engineers will man the controls during the broadcast. Six special transmitters have been installed "to make use of short waves to an extent never before attempted."

The "cue" transmitter, assigned the call W10XGJ, is located in the peak of the Washington Monument, from which site a control operator will relay instructions to other short-wave "voices"—a blimp, two radio-equipped limousines and two roving announcers carrying pack sets. Four short-wave receivers in the dome of the Capitol will intercept the messages from these mobile stations and relay to the master control booth near the steps of the Capitol, where, tucked out of sight of the proceedings, the main control man will direct and coordinate the program and route it to the far-flung hook-up.

During the entire broadcast listeners will never be "out of sight" of the main protagonist of the drama. Announcers will keep an eye on Mr. Roosevelt. First, from the White House, they will describe his departure for the ceremonies. Radio-equipped cars will follow the Presidential party up Pennsylvania to the Capitol. Then, inside the Senate door, observers will describe Mr. Roosevelt's arrival. Commentators alongside the platform and in booths directly behind the speakers' stand will tell the story of the President's approach. A battery of microphones will eavesdrop as the oath is administered, and then will follow the inaugural address.

The New York outlets affiliated with the major networks for the broadcasts will be WEAF, WJZ, WABC, WOR, WMCA and WHN. The majority of regularly scheduled programs from 8:30 A. M. to 4 P. M. will be canceled.

Contrary to hopes and predictions of days gone by, no plans have been announced to televise the inauguration, so that dream of scientific achievement is now passed along to January, 1941.

CHARMING TONGUES

Analysis of Voices on the Air Reveals Roosevelt Has 'Amenity Beyond Price'

By ORRIN E. DUNLAP Jr.

AMERICAN voices are heard calling across the world for peace, while the rumble of armed forces echoes in news bulletins from Europe, the Orient and the Near East. Short-wave beams "searchlight" President Roosevelt's voice through space in notification to the world that Uncle Sam will not stand idly by if domination of Canadian soil should be threatened by a foreign power. Secretary of State Cordell Hull's Southern voice is heard in a plea for international law and order.

A radio listener recently observed that the power of broadcast speech to express the range and variety of human character is boundless, but it is not always attained. He criticized dull talks, also the falsely bright and chatty talks as "falling flat." But he confessed "it is remarkable how many radio speakers have by voice alone impressed their distinctive personalities upon the listening public."

And to this it is not surprising in this day and age, when broadcasts glide so easily across the Atlantic, to read of an English listener saying:

"We all know the bustling, high-pressure friendliness of the American radio announcers who seemingly lie in wait with impatient and unwinking vigilance until the song is ended and then put over to the folks a little neighborly salesmanship. These methods are infinitely remote from the true expression of personality."

* * *

FOR many a listener, according to their criticism, American radio announcing has become too stately. For example, here are several other adjectives used to describe the average announcer's voice as it resounds from the loudspeaker: "pompous, ingratiating, ironical, halting, fluent, raucous and truculent." Tongues that wag and lash through space at sunlight's speed to merit such adjectives cause listeners to lose interest in the man. Generally, in attracting and holding attention voice personality is first; what is said is second in importance. There is no better proof of this than in the history of political

broadcasting in the United States.

Perfection in speech, however, is not enough; there must be that natural timbre of friendliness in the voice. Every word must ring with true sincerity. Showmanship is also part of the act. Simplicity and a choice of words which the multitudes understand are other elements in the "golden technique."

The successful broadcast speaker, for example, Mr. Roosevelt or Mr. Hull, is described as one who does not lecture or preach, but one whose personality unconsciously and automatically registers its impression on the unseen audience. If the voice vibrates with confidence and sincerity, uncannily radio transmits it and listners detect it. If the soft-voiced tone is timid or the speaker an egoist, the listeners detect that just as easily.

The triumphant speaker on the air is one who seems to be reasoning in a friendly way; he does not assume an "I'm telling you" attitude.

* * *

IT is surprising, and this is revealed by reading fan letters, how much listeners have come to regard broadcast voices as old friends.

The charm of these invisible friendships formed by listening almost daily to a disembodied voice is said to be "the unforced, personal intimacy." To the lonely, especially the sick and shut-ins, this ethereal sense of familiarity is recognized as "an amenity beyond price."

In the tone of a voice, in the rhythm of spoken words is the unseen power of companionship and friendship. Broadcasters with this magic power of joining the family circle drop in daily for what becomes a neighborly chat. Every one, however, does not possess this captivating power.

The question arises: who among the thousands of broadcasters on the American air have so impressed their personalities on the public by the very sound of their voices?

Certainly no one has "dropped in for a chat" by an electrical slide down the antenna wire with greater mastery for neighborliness than Franklin D. Roosevelt, recognized by political friend and foe as the

ace among friend-makers on the radio. His opponents have found no one to equal him in campaigning or in "chatting" from the "fireside" to the hearth. They admit his voice is "magic without a flaw," never sounding thin or dry.

* * *

MR. ROOSEVELT has found that qualification which the trained announcers say is essential: he has found or created a radio version of himself—the radio quintessence of himself—and then writes for it and goes to the "mike" to act it with sincerity.

With a flair for showmanship, he knows exactly where to put the pauses, the jabs and catchwords such as "copperheads," which live to flash across the headlines. The radio listener, it is observed, does not hear a speech as a sequence of words, but chunks of words. The trick seems to be to throw just the right number of words in bunches and pause just long enough to let the listener pull in the bunch.

This is a sample of the Rooseveltian style à la "fireside chat:

Never in our lifetime has such a concerted campaign of defeatism been thrown at the heads of the President and Senators and Congressmen as in the case of this seventy-fifth Congress. Never before have we had so many copperheads—and you will remember that it was the copperheads who, in the days of the War between the States, tried their best to make Lincoln and his Congress give up the fight, let the nation remain split in two and return to peace—peace at any price.

* * *

"MANY explanations of President Roosevelt's overwhelming victory at the polls have been offered," said Hamilton Fyfe, British journalist, in The Radio Times. "He swept the country. He did so because he was able to talk to the country as no candidate ever talked before. It used to be said (the other President Roosevelt told me this) that any man who got his portrait into the homes of two-thirds the voters could count on winning a Presidential election. To get your voice into the homes of almost the whole electorate—that is better still.

"If it is the right kind of voice, it establishes a feeling of intimacy. That is all-important. The personal

touch is immensely useful. I remember once asking a member of Parliament who had won a sensational contest, beating a Cabinet Minister, how he did it. He said grimly, clenching his fist, 'I shook hands with 20,000 people.'

"What a vastly greater influence than a mere handshake must twenty minutes' talk have (twenty minutes is quite enough)! How hard to resist a pleasant friendly voice which tells you several times where your interest lies, in a tone which sounds as if its owner might be chatting with you from the other side of the room! That is the essential—to chat, not to make speeches; to use everyday language, all the better if a little slangy; to drop in a little homely humor; to sink your voice to a confidence now and then; to talk exactly as if you were on the other side of the room. The blind judge people by their voices, and scarcely ever misjudge them."

* * *

MR. FYFE contends that of all speakers President Roosevelt has adapted "the other side of the room" technique to politics and "made it a complete success." He finds that too many broadcast speakers orate; some fail by reading at breakneck speed, while others are too statistical. Lloyd George on the air is described as "too emphatic." But it is equally ineffective at the microphone to sound "too cocksure" or "resolutely political."

Turning to an analysis of Hitler's broadcasting Mr. Fyfe points out that he rouses Germans to rage or patriotic fervor by having masses of people sitting or standing close together, thus creating in some degree the mass-psychology which a speaker requires. He adds, "The speeches on the air do not cause one-tenth of the excitement they create in a hall."

Whether a man who appeals successfully to the masses of a nation will be better qualified to lead in difficult times than a man who is given command by a small number who have watched and really know him, is doubtful, Mr. Fyfe fears. He believes that the great leader must carry both the good opinion of the few and the devotion of the many.

Radio's Standing in America

CBS Official Points to Record for Truth,
"Working Side by Side" With Press

To THE EDITOR OF THE NEW YORK TIMES:

In your issue of Aug. 23 there appears a brief editorial commenting upon the high position of radio in official Washington's esteem. The editorial concludes with this astonishing paragraph:

"Like most fashions, this anti-newspaper fashion in Washington had its day. Perhaps in the last two years it has not been so easy to exalt the radio over the press as an instrument of truth, in view of what the Central European radios have been doing in the service of truth and justice."

Without attempting to assay the relative merits of American radio and the American press in disseminating the truth, there still seems to be no possible analogy between radio reports in Central Europe and news programs in this country.

Do you mean to imply, for instance, that radio abroad has a monopoly on falsehoods? Is it your belief that the government-owned press associations and the government-controlled press throughout Central Europe are innocent of spreading lies and distorting facts?

Or is it THE TIMES'S contention that radio in the United States has in some strange manner decided to operate along totalitarian lines, thus forsaking a very cherished heritage of freedom of speech and abandoning a young but sturdy tradition of accuracy?

I rather think that, with a little more examination of the subject, it will occur to you that American broadcasting, operating along truly democratic lines, is working strenuously side by side with American newspapers and American press associations to present daily the whole truth, or such of it as is known. Our record in that regard is open and available to every one. Surely care should be exercised before any medium of public information performs a public disservice by any imputation to the contrary.   PAUL W. WHITE,
Director, Department of Public Affairs,
Columbia Broadcasting System.

New York, Aug. 26, 1940.

[We believe, with Mr. White, that American broadcasting, operating along democratic lines, is working side by side with the American press to present the daily truth. Our reference to what the Central European radios have been doing was intended simply to make the point that the radio is not ipso facto a more reliable instrument than the press. Some Washington officials have spoken as if they thought it was.—Editor, THE TIMES.]

Topics of The Times

Facts in the Papers
"Yes, I believe in a free press, but a free press can only exist if it is a truthful press. I do not think the free press gives any one the right to distort facts."—Mayor La Guardia.

The subject is a difficult one. The argument developed in the lines that follow is pretty sure to be distorted— in some quarters. It will be said, for example, that we defend the thesis that it is not necessary for the press to tell the truth. Nevertheless, the general welfare demands that Mr. La Guardia's dictum about freedom and truth in the newspapers be more closely examined. So here goes, and let the chips fall where they may.

Free and Distorted
We begin, then, by denying that a free press can "only" exist if it is a truthful press. As a matter of record, ever since there has been a free press there have been newspapers that have been very free with the truth, so to speak. How truthful were some of the journalists and the journals who made President Washington cry out that he would sooner be in his grave than continue to be subjected to their vituperation?

It was the Father of his Country whom a free press assailed in "such exaggerated and indecent terms as could scarcely be applied to a Nero, a notorious defaulter, or even to a common pickpocket." We may be sure that no such language dealing with the head of the state is to be found today in the Berlin, Rome, Tokyo newspapers.

Part of the Trade
Freedom of the press obviously does not carry with it the right to distort facts. But in the exercise of such freedom, the press, being only a human institution, cannot help now and then sinning against the facts, with the best will in the world. The better papers will do everything in their power to serve the truth and tell the truth, but in the course of human events the thing will happen.

The thing will happen the more often because the daily newspaper comes out every day; it is not published once every two years from a scholar's study or a scientist's laboratory. A margin of deviation from the truth is an occupational hazard in a free press which we cannot abolish without abolishing the occupation. Freedom of the press is like other freedoms. It has to be paid for; and part of the price we pay for liberty of the press is the abuse of that liberty, as other freedoms are abused.

Men of good-will naturally try to live up to the full responsibilities of a free press; but if they set themselves perfection as a standard, there won't be any free press, because there won't be any press at all.

Hazard of Office
And especially will the press refuse to shrink from the hazard of occasionally tripping over the facts when the press is dealing with public persons. The private citizen who suffers from bad reporting and bad editing has a right to feel aggrieved, even when the error has been committed in good faith and after the exercise of due care. The public official has no claim on 100 per cent perfection in the newspaper offices.

One of the occupational hazards of public office is to be misunderstood and misrepresented. It will happen often in the yellow or the partisan press. It will happen occasionally in the very best newspapers. So it must be, or the press, acting for the people, must give up all attempts to watch the people's rulers. And that is among the primary duties of a free press—to keep an eye on the rulers, so that the people may remain free.

Print Is Cheap
If the newspapers, with all their errors and sins, are not to keep the people informed and on guard, who or what will do the job? "Well, I have the radio," says Mr. La Guardia. In still higher official places the superior worth of the radio over the press as a truth-telling agency has been periodically stressed. Well, the Mayor of a great city and the head of a government have radio facilities. It will take a lot of private citizens to build themselves a broadcasting station and get a hearing. But it is perfectly feasible for a few private citizens to pass around the hat and print something. It may be William Lloyd Garrison's Liberator, or Nikolai Lenin's Pravda, or the onion-paper underground press in the conquered populations under Hitler's heel.

RADIO RECORD HELD NO SIGN OF WISDOM

Special to THE NEW YORK TIMES.

CHICAGO, April 17 — Although the United States has more radios than the rest of the world combined, its people are misinformed on many vital questions, Herman W. Steinkraus, president of the United States Chamber of Commerce, told the convention of the National Association of Broadcasters today.

"For one thing," Mr. Steinkraus said, "they are grossly misinformed relative to the distribution of the national income. The majority believe that 2 per cent of the people get 80 per cent of the wealth. The truth is that 88 per cent of the national income is paid to people who earn $5,000 a year or less."

A recent poll disclosed, he said, that 69 per cent of the people did not know anything about the Government reorganization plan recommended by Herbert Hoover's commission, although the plan was aimed at saving the taxpayers $5,000,000,000 a year.

Washington Pressure Group

"Also," he said, "the public knows very little about legislation resulting from pressure groups in Washington. The greatest pressure group in Washington today is the Administration, which has organized the greatest public relations group in the world's history. The function of this group is to maintain the Administration in power.

"I wonder if we should not have a lobby for the people in Washington today?"

Another recent poll disclosed, Mr. Steinkraus said, that 69 per cent of the people thought socialism would be bad for the country.

"But although socialism cannot come in the front door, it could come in the back door, because the people are not thoroughly informed of the machinations of their government," he said.

"The American people are the best informed in the world on baseball, popular songs and the movies, yet on such subjects as government service, and responsibilities of each person as a citizen, they are uninformed.

Too Few Persons Vote

"Forty-nine persons out of every 100 in the United States failed to vote in the 1948 election, although this election placed in office officials who are spending billions of tax dollars."

Mr. Steinkraus pointed out that in the recent British election 82 per cent of the people voted; in Belgium, 90 per cent voted, and in Italy, 95 per cent.

"The American public does not consider its citizenship as highly as it ought to," he declared.

Warren Austin, United States delegate to the United Nations and former Republic Senator from Vermont, told the convention that the world needed to be liberated from ignorance, hunger, poverty, disease and fear. He said that 200,000,000 of the world's children faced death from starvation.

THE CRIME HEARINGS

Television Provides Both a Lively Show And a Notable Public Service

By JACK GOULD

LAST week's all-star television revue with Frank Erickson, Joe Adonis and Frank Costello, the man with the fascinating hands, marked an epoch for television and gangsterdom alike.

The reluctant trio from the underworld were forced to leave the privacy of their favorite restaurants and barbershops and let millions watch them try to get off the spot. The big boys who always preferred to stay in the background suddenly found themselves in the center of the stage, the most popular act in town.

In turn, television displayed a social impact of such enormous potentialities that undoubtedly the politicians, broadcasters and educators will be studying and debating its implications for days to come. Housewives have left the housework undone and husbands have slipped away from their jobs to watch. The city has been under a hypnotic spell, absorbed, fascinated, angered and amused. It has been a rare community experience.

Timely

From the standpoint of public enlightenment the union of television and the Senate Crime Investigating Committee, headed by the lean and soft-spoken Southerner, Senator Estes W. Kefauver, Democrat of Tennessee, has been uniquely timely and beneficial.

In the committee there has been the will to bring into the open the seamy side of the shadowy figures who live on both sides of the law and permeate even the highest levels of society. In television there has been the means to make the story come alive in the minds of millions.

It has been an almost incredible cast of characters that have made their entrance on the screen. The poker-faced Erickson, the suavely arrogant Adonis, the shy Costello and the jocose Virginia Hill might have been hired from Hollywood's Central Casting Bureau. The committee's counsel, Rudolph Halley of the dry, flat sandpaper voice, has been the relentless inquisitor of tradition.

Both the principals and the bit players have made a capital show and the hearings have had all the elements of drama—suspense, conflict, varied motivation and contrasting personalities—so dear to the impresario's heart. Yet underneath has lain the hard core of harsh reality which has kept one glued to the screen hour after hour.

Narcotic

The human equation has been so strongly invoked that often a viewer could not help but be preoccupied with individual performances. Watching personalities who were real yet had all the appeal of characters straight out of a mystery thriller had a narcotic fascination on the viewer at home.

But to conclude that television by itself was responsible for the theatrical overtones to the hearings would be a serious mistake. With such a list of witnesses the hearings would have been just as dramatic had the cameras not been there, as was true of any number of similar investigations before the day of TV. It may be recalled that it was no television camera which put the famous midget on the lap of the late J. P. Morgan.

Television is a new and complementary medium of mass communication which in the case of actuality broadcasts, such as last week's hearings, mirrors the scene as it exists. The committee and the witnesses put on the show, not TV. For years the press has had to cope with those who either could not or would not see the distinction between making news and reporting news. If television is to have its rightful freedom as a reportorial medium, it now faces the same task.

Certainly, it is of the utmost importance that such hearings be conducted with scrupulous regard for the rights of a witness, but Costello's objections first to having his face shown on camera and then to the lighting were tenuous to say the least.

Veteran reporters at the hearing say that the lighting is far less troublesome than is experienced at national political conventions. The members of the committee and in particular Mr. Halley, who has been "on camera" more than any other individual, also have not appeared bothered.

Actually, "live" television was the victim of a case of discrimination which should not be allowed to stand as a precedent. Although television was forced to take its cameras off Costello's face, the newsreel cameras continued on and some films were shown over video. An underworld leader's frantic search for reasons not to answer questions must not be allowed to become a permanent hobble on TV.

What is so new and strange to Costello — and many others who have not yet thoroughly grasped the true meaning of television's advent—is that video takes away the walls around the hearing room. It makes the public hearing more public than it ever was before.

In this fact lies the true measure of the importance of television's coverage of the hearings. It has shown that it can arouse public interest to a degree which virtually beggars immediate description.

Through the medium of the camera's perceptive eye the individual has had a liberal education in government and morality. Television's qualities of intimacy and immediacy have made the experience so personal that the TV viewer actually is closer to the scene than the spectator in the courtroom.

What television has done is to provide the implementation for the goal of Senator Kefauver's committee. Once the set has been tuned in to the proceedings in the Federal Building it has taken extraordinary will power to turn the receiver off. Whether sitting at home, in an office or at a bar, the viewer becomes a participant to see with his own eyes, to hear with his own ears, and to form his own opinion at first-hand.

The power to elicit this public participation is a priceless asset at a time when democracy is facing one of its severest tests. To use the power selfishly or solely for commercial expediency would represent an inexcusable waste of a national resource. To employ the power wisely and progressively can bring benefits and gains far transcending television itself.

The hearings of Senator Kefauver's committee have provided a wonderful show. But as they draw to a close the telecasts also should make the public, broadcasters and legislators a little humble. The last week has demonstrated with awesome vividness what television can do to enlighten, to educate and to drive home a lesson. It will take the best efforts of all of us to see that TV truly rises to its own opportunity.

TV TRANSFORMING U. S. SOCIAL SCENE;   CHALLENGES FILMS

Its Impact on Leisure, Politics, Reading, Culture Unparalleled Since Advent of the Auto

MOVIE TRADE OFF 20-40%

By JACK GOULD

Television, in commercial use for only a little more than five years, is influencing the social and economic habits of the nation to a degree unparalleled since the advent of the automobile.

The now familiar dipole aerial perched on the rooftop symbolizes a fundamental change in national behavior: The home has become a new center of interest for the most gregarious people on earth.

Reports by correspondents of THE NEW YORK TIMES in more than 100 cities, towns and villages over the country show that the impact of pictures sent into the living room is being felt in almost every phase of endeavor.

The ability of television to conquer time and distance together, permitting millions of persons to see and hear the same person simultaneously, is having its effect on the way the public passes its leisure time, how it feels and acts about politics and government, how much it reads, how it rears its children and how it charts its cultural future. The country never has experienced anything quite like it.

Inflation Plays a Role

The rise of television also has put the spotlight on corollary factors that are contributing to a shifting pattern of preferences in diversion. The inflationary spiral, especially the high cost of food, is working to the advantage of television as almost every community, even those without TV, reports a major decline in spending for "luxury" items.

The immediate consequence is increased activity, ranging from frantic self-appraisal to costly promotional outlay, among those who are competing for a share of the individual's budget of time and money. And the catalyst in the new era of intensified competition is society's powerful unknown: The continuous free show available upon the flicking of the switch of a television set.

What happens when the screen lights up in the home and the public curtails its spending is demonstrated graphically in the case of motion pictures.

Attendance at theatres has dropped 20 to 40 per cent since the introduction of television, according to reports from THE

TIMES correspondents. Many film distributors believe the national decline is roughly 35 per cent.

In contrast, representative cities that do not have television report business is holding up well and attribute at most a 10 per cent decline to the higher cost of living.

There have been theatre closings—seventy in Eastern Pennsylvania, 134 in Southern California, sixty-one in Massachusetts, sixty-four in the Chicago area and at least fifty-five in metropolitan New York. The New York Film Board of Trade said that in the last six weeks there had been perhaps thirty closings, some only for varying periods in the warm-weather season.

Many cities reported film houses going on part-time schedules to a far greater extent than in any other summer.

But any assumption that the film industry faces extinction is contradicted by numerous other considerations.

Many of the theatres that were closed were outmoded buildings in distressed neighborhoods and could be considered normal business casualties. In addition, there have been many new houses that, in some cases at least, actually have added to the total seating capacity in a community.

Especially significant, however, is the number of drive-in theatres, where customers can avoid parking charges, baby-sitter fees and traffic congestion, and can dress as they please. These have increased by 800 in the last year, bringing the total to about 3,000. And almost all report a booming trade.

Quality Films Stressed

Exhibitors in every part of the country emphasized that pictures of quality or those boasting a fresh personality were doing a good business and were immune to TV's inroads. "The Great Caruso," "Born Yesterday" and "All About Eve" were among those repeatedly cited.

In pleading with Hollywood for an improved product, exhibitors lost much of the hesitancy that had marked their answers on the status of business at the box-office. Here are some sample observations:

Washington: "You can't charge for mediocrity any more when everybody can get it at home for nothing."

San Francisco: "Quality counts. That's the story."

New Orleans: "The good picture still packs 'em in."

Richmond: "Before the war movie-going was a habit. Now people come when they really want to see a picture."

The plight of the theatre owners is borne out by specific reports of TIMES correspondents. TV was

mentioned invariably as a contributory cause, but living costs and picture quality also received strong emphasis.

TV's Effect on Theatres

Here are representative reports from cities having television stations:

EAST

City	Effect on Box-office Since TV
Boston (2 stations)	25-40% off
Providence (1)	25-40% off
New Haven (1)	10-40% off
New York (7)	10% on Broadway, 20-40% in neighborhood
Philadelphia (3)	"Definite inroads"; "bad"
Wilmington (1)	"Slump in business"
Baltimore (3)	"Off sharply"
Washington (4)	"Definite drop"
Syracuse (2)	50% off
Schenectady (1)	"TV unquestionably hurt"
Binghamton (1)	"Badly hurt"
Utica (1)	30% off
Rochester (1)	"Drop in attendance"
Buffalo (1)	"Hit hard"
Pittsburgh (1)	15% off
Lancaster (1)	"At least 25%"
Johnstown (1)	"Big drop"

MIDWEST

City	Effect
Cleveland (3)	25-35% off
Columbus (3)	"Noticeable drop"
Detroit (3)	18-25% off
Grand Rapids (1)	12-20% off
Lansing (1)	20-40% off
Milwaukee (1)	"Poor attendance"
Minneapolis-St. Paul (2)	20% off
Chicago (4)	20-40% off
Kansas City (1)	15% off
St. Louis (1)	"Definite effect, cutting attendance"

SOUTH

City	Effect
Richmond (1)	"Downward trend"
Atlanta (2)	"Operators blame TV"
Birmingham (2)	"Badly hurt"
Jacksonville (1)	5% off
New Orleans (1)	"Not noticeable—only one station"
Memphis (1)	10-20% off
Nashville (1)	"Decline in attendance"

SOUTHWEST

City	Effect
Houston (1)	"Slight crimp"
San Antonio (2)	"Very definitely cut"
Fort Worth (1)	"Fallen off sharply"
Oklahoma City (1)	"Effects uncertain"

WEST

City	Effect
Los Angeles (7)	25-40% off
San Francisco (3)	5-10% off
San Diego (1)	40% off
Seattle (1)	15-20% off
Salt Lake City (2)	"Sluggish box office"
Phoenix (1)	"Not much effect"
Albuquerque (1)	"No sustained cut"

Business in the suburbs outside the major cities reflected the general trend, except in the case of drive-ins. Population shifts—new housing developments having a preponderance of young families with no teen-agers to baby-sit—and parking facilities were factors. In the New York area, Stamford, Conn., reported a decline running up to 50 per cent; Passaic-Clifton, N. J., 25 per cent; Patchogue, L. I., 20 per cent; Peekskill, N. Y., 25 per cent, and Englewood, N. J., 10 to 25 per cent.

Non-Video Areas Report

By contrast with returns from cities with television, the box-office situation in non-video cities varies substantially. For example:

City	Box-office Business
Portland, Me.	"Attendance o. k."
Portland, Ore.	"Same as last year—some cases perhaps off 10 per cent"

Austin, Tex.	"Same as year ago"
Fargo, N. D.	"Business down slightly, but still good"
Denver	"Slightly higher"
Little Rock	"Virtually no change"

That the American public is feeling the "squeeze" between rising costs and rising taxes likewise is borne out in reports from local theatre owners and business men:

Oklahoma City: "An occasional sirloin steak for the whole family is a hell of a lot more entertainment than it used to be."

Newark: "We're in some kind of a recession; people haven't got the money."

Seattle: "It costs about $5 for a couple to attend a movie. Two 94-cent tickets with all the taxes, parking expense, cup of coffee or dish of ice cream and then the baby-sitter."

Memphis: "The people are fearful; they don't know what's going to happen."

Chicago: "A lot of people are still paying for the hard goods bought during the rush after the start of the Korean war."

Isolated and highly tentative reports—from Erie, Pa.; New Brunswick, N. J.; Miami, Syracuse, White Plains, N. Y., and Dallas—give the first hints that veteran video viewers are beginning to resume the movie-going habit after a steady dose of TV. Business shows signs of leveling off, it is reported, and in some instances there is a slight upward trend at the box office.

"The housewife sooner or later is going to get fed up staying in the house day and night," remarked one exhibitor in Westchester County.

But the average theatre owner across the country has his fingers crossed and many correspondents reported persistent rumors that more closings could be expected. Granting that inflation is an important influence adversely affecting attendance, it was noted that many persons now were looking at television as a replacement for "movie night." That is what is new.

Hollywood's Big Problem

If the local theatre is acutely aware of television, the capital of the film industry, Hollywood, thinks of little else at the moment. Though a variety of causes are responsible, the gross revenues of the eight major film companies have declined from $952,000,000 in 1947 to $861,000,000 in 1950. Retrenchment is the order of the day on the West Coast.

In 1947 the average craft union employment in the Hollywood film industry was 18,400 persons and the average monthly payroll was $7,000,000. By 1950, the average employment was down to 13,600 and the payroll to $5,600,000, but some of the slack has been taken up in production of films for video. Reductions in executive personnel as well as among actors, writers and directors appear inevitable, it was noted, and there will be further economies in production schedules. All indications, how-

HOW MOVIES ARE HIT BY TV AND ONE ANSWER TO THE CHALLENGE

A neighborhood motion picture theatre on Broadway that has been closed for many months.

A former movie house at Sixty-fifth Street and Broadway, now a C. B. S. studio.

Cars parked in a drive-in theatre in the Bronx where customers avoid parking charges, baby-sitter fees and traffic congestion.

The New York Times

ever, point to maintenance of the volume of picture output.

Production of films especially for television is a growing business in Hollywood, and seems certain to increase. According to one source, film footage for TV was being produced in May at a rate of 988 hours a year, compared with 855 hours of feature films for theatre showing.

Hollywood's difficulty is that it isn't geared to what the television sponsor can pay for a film. In this connection several of the smaller companies — Republic, Monogram and Lippert—have made arrangements to release their backlog of films by agreeing to make a new musical sound track that will benefit the American Federation of Musicians. Other producers have hesitated to release their old films lest they offend their primary customers, the theatre exhibitors.

Of increasing importance to both Hollywood and its exhibitors is theatre television, whereby video images are projected directly on the large-size screen. The recent box-office success in theatre television's pick-up of the Joe Louis-Lee Savold fight, which the home TV audience did not see as it happened, has stimulated interest. By fall perhaps more than 100 houses will have theatre TV equipment and will be in a position to outbid an advertising sponsor on home video.

Theatre TV, in turn, has led to a consideration of subscription television for the home, a system under which the viewer would have to pay if he wished to view "unscrambled" pictures. Paramount Pictures has invested in one coin-operated device and, with some reluctance, other producers have cooperated with the Zenith Radio Corporation's box-office method known as "Phonevision." In New York later this year there may be further tests of another method called "Skiatron."

Speculation on "Marriage"

A matter for major speculation has been the possibility of "a marriage" between TV and Hollywood. While many deals have been rumored periodically, the only concrete development has been the contemplated merger of the American Broadcasting Company with United Paramount Theatres, which is a theatre chain and is not to be confused with the producing concern, Paramount Pictures, Inc.

But overshadowing all other considerations in the relationship between television and the motion-picture world is the fact that television is still only in its relatively early stages of development.

Today 107 stations are operating in sixty-three cities, within range of roughly 62 per cent of the country's population. Of the sixty-three cities, however, only twenty-four have between two and seven stations, and a choice of TV programs generally has been a prerequisite for the medium to exercise its full impact on competitive media. The remaining thirty-nine TV cities have only one station each.

For the last two years there has been a "freeze" on the construction of new television stations, which to some extent has provided the film industry with a chance to catch its breath. But the plans of the Federal Communications Commission envisage ultimately perhaps 2,000 stations serving several hundred communities.

Military priorities and many other factors may affect TV's expansion, but the motion picture business none the less has reason to worry. Television's major strides still lie ahead.

Waiting Across 1,500 Miles

Milton Buhr of Saskatoon, Sask., in the western part of Canada, has a 100-foot television aerial in his backyard and a modern set. His only trouble so far is that he hasn't seen a program; the nearest station is 1,500 miles away.

"I'm going to be ready," he explained.

Reaffirming of "Progress"

Twenty-five years ago Volmer Dahlstrand, president of the Milwaukee Federation of Musicians, complained to a theatre owner about the movies hurting the employment of pit orchestras.

"This is progress," replied the operator, curtly.

A few weeks ago the two men met and the theatre owner complained about television hurting his business.

"That's progress," replied Mr. Dahlstrand happily.

As One Medium to Another

In Kansas City, Mo., movie houses are plugging their pictures on television while knocking the medium in their advertising statements.

A typical "ad" will describe the picture to be shown and close with this sort of announcement:

"Only the giant motion picture screen can present the true grandeur and magnificence of . . . etc."

June 24, 1951

Political Leaders Acclaim TV But Warn Against Its Misuse

Truman and Dewey View It as Constructive Campaign Adjunct, Yet Say It Should Not Publicize Congressional Inquiries

By JACK GOULD

President Truman believes that television is essential in modern political life and insists on its full use for major speeches, according to a White House spokesman, but is sharply critical of the televising of Congressional investigations on the ground that such action invites "Roman holidays."

The President's views on television in government, made known in some detail for the first time, are shared by Governor Dewey, who has declared that video is a constructive political force but that the recent telecasts of the Senate crime inquiry were of "very doubtful legitimacy."

The opinions of the titular heads of the Democratic and Republican parties were obtained as part of a NEW YORK TIMES reportorial canvass on effects of the TV medium on politics and government. Participating in the canvass were this newspaper's regular political reporters in New York, Washington and Albany, as well as correspondents in each of the sixty-three cities that now have television service.

Evidence of the impact of television on the voting public came from virtually every city. In Oklahoma City, where the State Legislature has been televised, it was said that interest in local and public issues had been greatly stimulated.

Discussion programs and interviews with figures in public life were credited uniformly with contributing to a more enlightened public opinion. Several communities said television had been of decisive help in meeting lagging Red Cross quotas.

City after city reported that the touring Senate crime inquiry had aroused widespread public reaction, virtually paralyzing normal social activity, and had had direct political repercussions.

In New York, the Liberal party's nomination of Rudolph Halley, committee counsel, for President of the City Council was attributed largely to television. Mr. Halley, whose "fan mail" during the inquiry rivaled that of a film star, was "on camera" for more consecutive hours than any other person in the new medium's short history.

Political figures in all sections of the country agreed that no individual running for office could afford to ignore television's influence, but there was substantial division of opinion on whether this influence always would be socially desirable.

One thought receiving wide expression was that the politician of tomorrow must become an "actor" and that a premium might be placed on personality rather than competence. A contrary opinion was that the "political hack" faced difficult days because he could not survive the penetrating eye of the electronic camera.

President Truman's stand on the subject of Congressional hearings was regarded by some political observers as reflecting his feelings about recent investigations, a number of which have been directed against the Administration. In the case of the Senate committee's crime inquiry, headed by Senator Estes W. Kefauver, Democrat of Tennessee, one of the committee's principal targets was William O'Dwyer, former Mayor of New York, who since has enjoyed Presidential support in his post as Ambassador to Mexico.

Statement from White House

The text of the White House statement made available to the Washington Bureau of THE TIMES follows:

"In general it is pretty obvious that the President thinks highly of television. He insists on full use of it in all of his major speeches.

"The President has real misgivings, however, about the use of television at hearings because of the tendency to make Roman holidays of them.

"One day he observed that one of the major factors in the weakening of the governments of Athens and of other democratic Greek states was the adoption of trial by mass jury. In that way emotions sway over reason. Socrates was tried in that way and the result was most unfair.

"On this the President is most seriously concerned. The trouble with television hearings, he said, is that a man is held before cameras and 40,000,000 people more or less hear him charged with so and so, and the public, untrained generally with evaluating the presentation of evidence, is inclined to think him guilty just because he is charged.

"Then the pressure begins mounting on the committee and the result can be that the witness is pushed around. It is the very negation of judicial process, with the committee acting as prosecutor and defense, and the public acting as the jury."

Governor Dewey's Views

Governor Dewey, who pioneered in the political use of television with his informal chats and "man-in-the-street" interviews during the last Gubernatorial contest, declared that video "definitely should be very useful in assessing some of the qualities of candidates for office."

"Politically, television is an X-ray," he told THE TIMES. "If a man doesn't know the business of government, he cannot long stand its piercing lights and stark realism. It should make a constructive advance in political campaigning."

But the Governor, who first entered the political limelight as a special prosecutor, left no doubt of his stand on the televising of the Kefauver crime inquiry, which, among other things, put the spotlight on the New York State Police and gambling in Saratoga.

"The use of television and radio to broadcast testimony of witnesses is of very doubtful legitimacy," he asserted. "To use the power of government to subpoena individuals, put them under the piercing glare of kleig lights and question them smacks too much of the Russian method to fit in with our institutions and respect for the dignity of the judicial process and the rights of individuals."

Many other prominent figures agreed that TV was important in politics.

Senator Robert A. Taft, Republican policy leader in the Senate, said TV favored "the man of sincerity," and eliminated "the false value of the sweetness of the voice and, I think, makes a better medium for the truth." He said TV could reach people not reached by radios or newspapers.

Had there been television in the campaign of William Jennings Bryan and William McKinley, according to Senator William Benton, Democrat of Connecticut, Bryan would have been elected.

"The potentialities of television are so great they will revolutionize politics," Senator Benton said. "The terrifying aspect is the high cost, the expenses of which could well determine election or defeat."

Representative John W. McCormack, Democrat of Massachusetts, majority floor leader in the House, said TV would have an "outstanding effect" on politics, but that he also was worried about the high cost of time on the air. Senator Everett L. Dirksen, Republican of Illinois, said television had helped him in his last campaign.

Should Congress be Shown?

The idea of televising the proceedings of Congress drew little support in Washington.

Representative Sam Rayburn, Democrat of Texas, Speaker of the House, remarked: "Televise sessions of the House? Hell, no! Not while I'm around here are they going to do that televising."

"Can I quote you on that, Mr. Speaker?" asked a reporter for THE TIMES.

"Hell, yes," the Speaker replied. "I've said it often enough around here. Everybody knows where I stand on that."

Senators Taft and Harry F.

The Impact of the Television Camera on Politics in the United States

President Truman, who insists on TV's full use for major speeches, making one of his telecasts in the White House.

Byrd, Democrat of Virginia, also opposed televising Congress on the ground that it would prove a distracting factor, as did Representative McCormack. Senators Benton and Dirksen favored telecasts of Congress on the ground that they would prove an educational force in demonstrating the workings of a democracy. However, Senator Benton added: "The opposition to it is very great."

The practical effect of television on politics and government today takes many different forms and is noticeable in almost every city where TV has been established sufficiently long to be effective.

One striking example was in the New York area during the speech before Congress of General of the Army Douglas MacArthur. The consumption of electricity during the daylight hour when he was on the air took a spectacular upward jump, according to charts of the Consolidated Edison Company.

Political Rally Seen Doomed

In New York and New Jersey, the Republican party has made surveys that attest to the demise of the political rally in the wake of video. According to the surveys the effectiveness of various methods to reach the public ranked as follows last fall: Publicity and advertising in newspapers; television; radio; mail circulars; rallies and posters and billboards.

Although it is only a temporary effect, television is a factor in dictating the site of political meetings. Because of technical reasons the video network at present goes only northward and westward through New York State, and cannot be reversed to bring programs

Governor Dewey, who also says the video is a constructive political force, is shown appearing before the camera.

southward. Therefore, important meetings for which publicity is desired must be held in this city, though in many cases it would be more convenient for most participants to meet midway upstate.

Availability of TV facilities for all practical purposes also limits national conventions to Philadelphia and Chicago. To make possible economies in TV equipment installation, both Republicans and Democrats meet in the same city.

Some of the most vivid illustrations of television's potency in the realm of politics and government, however, are to be found away from the larger cities on the Eastern seaboard. Here are some examples reported by correspondents of THE TIMES:

Oklahoma City: The Oklahoma State Legislature has been televised, and Wendell Barnes, State Representative from Tulsa County, summed up the results as follows:

"The most outstanding effect was on the Legislature itself. Whenever it knew the cameras were running, it stuck strictly to business. During that hour, you wouldn't see a single pair of feet on a desk on the House floor; not a single House member was reading a newspaper while someone was speaking, and attendance was excellent.

The hearing of the Kefauver Senate Committee as it came into the homes of millions throughout the country.

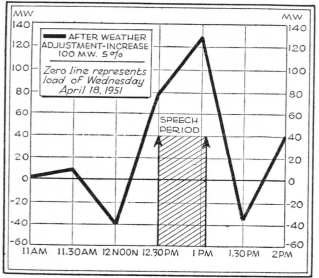

AFTER WEATHER ADJUSTMENT-INCREASE 100 MW. 5%

Zero line represents load of Wednesday April 18, 1951

SPEECH PERIOD

June 25, 1951

A chart prepared by the Consolidated Edison system showing how the use of electricity increased during General MacArthur's address before Congress. The MW indicates megawatts.

factor in politics, either because the local station had not been on the air long; the city was not linked to the co-axial cable and could not transmit Washington events immediately, or local officials were still awkward before the cameras.

Until audiences grow larger, local party officials in many cities believed, television's costs were excessive.

The national political campaign of 1952, the correspondents in a number of communities agreed, would give a fuller delineation of television's varied impact on the world of politics.

Governor Dewey has a television set in the antechamber of his private suite in the Roosevelt Hotel in New York. His aides say that while he does not profess to use the set himself, he feels that it is valuable in keeping some of his callers occupied while waiting for an audience, and in some instances "cools them down."

Peekskill, N. Y., reports that television appears to be a "must" in vacation homes. Nearly all summer houses in the area are topped with TV antennas. In most instances sets are brought up in the family car when the household leaves New York, and are returned in the fall.

Nassau County Welfare Commissioner Edwin Wallace, faced last year with the incongruous situation of television antennas being installed on the homes of many of his welfare families, directed that the owners either get rid of the sets or get off the relief rolls.

One woman told Mr. Wallace she would give up her relief checks before getting rid of her television.

"She kept the set, got a job and we have heard nothing more from her," the commissioner said.

Soon after the Bridgeport, Conn., Housing Authority issued a similar order banning sets in a low rent project, its agents found a violator.

The tenant who felt he had to have TV was putting up an aerial after dark and taking it down before going to bed.

Erie, Pa., is regarded as a devout, rather pious city, and a surprising number of people—the elder ones in particular—will have nothing to do with television.

"We're afraid of the thing," one couple explained. "The devil's playing around."

Navy personnel at Norfolk, Va., make up part of the television audience, both on land and at sea. Most of the larger training vessels operating off the Virginia Capes have sets with an adjustable antenna that brings in the signal from any angle.

his appearance on TV," according to city politicians.

Memphis: When Representative Clifford Davis, Democrat, was campaigning for re-election to Congress last fall, he appeared in a living room setting before the cameras. At his "home" he was visited by a workingman, a banker, a merchant and a farmer who dutifully asked the candidate's views on subjects of interest to them. Representative Davis gave "almost a professional, a convincing performance," the correspondent said.

Albany: While most political figures agree that television was in large measure responsible in giving Governor Dewey a plurality of 586,000 over Walter A. Lynch—advance estimates before the Governor's TV appearances indicated a margin of 150,000—not many state politicians are exactly enthusiastic over video.

"Generally, they are afraid that TV could easily break down the power of the local machines that roll them back into office each year by exposing the fact that their hand-picked men are not always entirely prepossessing," the Albany bureau of THE TIMES reported.

Chicago: Use of theatrical terminology in discussing public figures appearing on television promises to add a little liveliness to political writing. In mentioning the election last fall of John E. Babb, Republican, to the office of Sheriff of Cook County, the Chicago Bureau of THE TIMES described him as "the telegenic G. O. P. nominee."

From many TV cities throughout the country came reports that video was not yet an important

"Sure, there was some ham acting, obviously for the benefit of the TV audience, but you must expect things like that."

San Diego: Television is credited largely with the recent election of San Diego's new Mayor, John D. Butler. He is a young, handsome bachelor and has "a youthful and fresh appearance." His opponent, Gerald Crary, an older man, "was handicapped by

TV MAKES INROADS ON BIG RADIO CHAINS

Network Programs Lose Much of Audience—Local Business of Stations Stands Up Well

By JACK GOULD

Established evening habits of the American people are undergoing drastic revision in the wake of television's upward surge. Playing an almost equal part, however, is the rising cost of living.

Major radio network programs have lost a sizable proportion of their after-dark audiences and this loss has caused a substantial revision in the business operations of the four principal chains.

Business at night clubs, bars and restaurants has shown a general decline.

Schedules of civic and community meetings have been altered to avoid competition with video's stars.

Bus, trolley and taxicab concerns report slackening trade as more families remain at home.

Conversely, retail clothing stores report increased sale of lounging apparel for use in the home, particularly women's robes and "TV slacks." Furniture manufacturers also say they have benefited from the "back-to-home" movement as viewers decided to "dress up the living room."

In the case of radio, the lure of being able to watch, as well as hear, a performer on TV, has led to a severe drop in popularity ratings for major network attractions, prompted slashes in network charges for time, and caused reductions in fees for most artists on chain shows.

In contrast to the economic reverses of the networks, however, local business of radio stations continues at a good level all over the country, according to reports from correspondents of THE NEW YORK TIMES.

Few individual stations have cut rates for programs originating in their own studios, and several have announced increases. Daytime shows, which on the radio can be enjoyed without neglecting work or household chores, still have a strong following. Straight musical presentations, both popular and classical, and news programs — the two fields in which television is weakest—are growing in acceptance.

The extent of the decline in network radio bears an almost direct relationship to the rise in video. Where the volume of TV sets begins to approach the saturation point in a community, the chain radio programs suffer most heavily. Where TV is still a pastime for a minority, radio holds its own. In cities where there is no television, radio in many instances is advancing.

The deterioration of the network radio situation in New York, where TV has been in existence the longest, where one of every two families has a video receiver and where there is the widest choice of new programs, is startlingly illustrated in new statistics made public today by C. E. Hooper, Inc.

The figures, which in themselves may set off a new controversy over TV's impact, compare the relative popularity of major network shows among New York listeners during the late winter and early spring of 1948 and 1951. The Hooper tabulation follows:

Program	1948 Rating	1951 Rating
Jack Benny	26.5	4.8
"Amos 'n Andy"	13.6	5.9
Arthur Godfrey's Talent Scouts	20.3	5.9
Radio Theatre	25.3	8.4
"My Friend Irma"	18.8	6.6
Bob Hope	16	3.2
"Fibber McGee and Molly"	17.2	5
"Big Town"	12.7	2.2
Groucho Marx	12	5
Bing Crosby	18	3.8

Some Still Shun TV

Of the programs cited, the Godfrey and Marx features are now regular video attractions, and "Radio Theatre" and "Big Town" have video versions. Bob Hope and Jack Benny appear at irregular intervals. "Amos 'n Andy" will have its TV debut tomorrow night, and "My Friend Irma" is mentioned for the fall. Bing Crosby and "Fibber McGee and Molly" thus far have shunned TV.

Next Sunday all the four radio chains—the National Broadcasting Company, the Columbia Broadcasting System, American Broadcasting Company and Mutual Broadcasting System—will put into effect a rate cut of 10 to 15 per cent, covering afternoon and evening hours. The move, incidentally, had been opposed vigorously by the affiliated stations.

The contrast in relative costs of radio and television is indicated in a comparison of the local charges for an hour's best broadcasting time in the New York City area:

	N. Y. TV Stations	N. Y. Radio Stations
N. B. C.	$3,250	$1,200
C. B. S.	3,250	1,350
A. B. C.	3,100	1,200

Several broadcasters expressed the view that while radio and TV were now compared economically, the growing disparity in rates soon would make radio virtually a "new low-priced medium" that could stand on its own.

In this connection the networks are paring down program costs. Attractions running into five figures a week, which were commonplace five years ago, are now out of the question. The emphasis on reduced costs was evidenced by Tallulah Bankhead's "Big Show,"

which was the hit of radio last season but could not obtain a sponsor at $8,820 for a half hour.

By contrast, hour-long television shows costing between $30,000 and $50,000, such as the Jimmy Durante, Eddie Cantor and Robert Montgomery programs, have been almost a nightly occurence during the past season.

Radio officials outside the New York area also voiced the belief that many persons soon would tire of giving the complete concentration that television requires and go back to just listening. Here are reports on the TV-radio situation from widely scattered areas:

Philadelphia: Evening radio listening is off 25 per cent or more, but daytime listening has increased. Philadelphia stations have not followed network rate cuts.

New Haven: Stations are stressing programs with local appeal. No rate cuts.

Pittsburgh: Radio news shows and sportscasters are holding their own.

Providence: To date TV has not caused revenue of stations to drop.

Boston: Television has just about flattened evening radio listening. Independent stations are offering music and have gained new listeners from TV viewers satiated with variety shows. No local rate cuts.

Rochester: Stations say they're holding their own, but audience for frequency modulation stations has been affected.

Schenectady: Director of WSNY says, "TV viewer is same person given to watching soap opera" and "music, news and local approach" have proved successful.

Minneapolis: Stations find that daytime shows, except for soap operas, do well. This means chiefly news programs and music.

Grand Rapids: No rate cuts and some increase in radio revenue reported.

Cleveland: No trade secret that radio stations have been hit hard. Asking price for one large station has skidded from $3,000,000 to $1,250,000 in a year. Among programs holding up well are those in the afternoon dealing with preparation of foods and care of home.

Detroit: Harry Bannister, operator of radio and television stations, says audience has fallen off 60 per cent at night and 30 to 35 per cent before 6 P. M. He reduced his nighttime rate but had increased daytime rates six months previously.

Chicago: Stations have not cut their local rates. Station WEFM, whose programs are devoted to good music, says subscriptions to its programs have shown biggest increase in eighteen months. This is attributed to decline of good music on radio networks.

Los Angeles: Southern California Broadcasters Association reports stations are maintaining their local rates.

Houston: Only one TV station here, and too early to determine effects.

Seattle: Local sales are up about 5 per cent, spot sales to national advertisers 8 per cent.

Tulsa: One station increased its rates 12 per cent recently.

Birmingham: No local rate cuts contemplated.

Richmond: Local stations agree network rate cuts were "dead wrong" and were accepted with reluctance.

VIEWING A TELECAST IN A LOCAL TAVERN

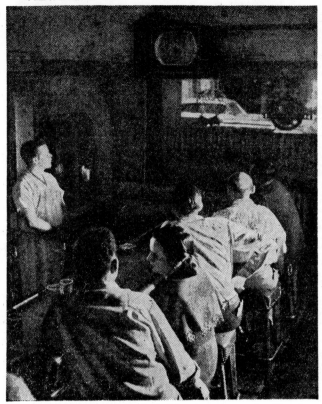

Customers watching the television in a bar and grill, where this medium of entertainment was once a boon and is now a bane.

The New York Times

Memphis: Radio has increased right along with television.

Washington: WINX was sold two weeks ago for $120,000; in 1944 it was purchased for $500,-000.

From the standpoint of statistics, radio also can make itself a case. The number of radio homes is in excess of 44,000,000, compared with 14,000,000 for TV. And as TV has grown, the number of radio stations also has risen. According to the Federal Communications Commission in Washington, there were 931 licensed stations in June, 1945. Now there are 2,235. The number of licensed frequency modulation outlets has grown in the same period from forty-six to 519.

NIGHT CLUBS, BARS, RESTAURANTS

If television once was a boon to bars and saloons, today it is a bane. From all over the country come reports that trade in bars is off, while package-store sales of beer and stronger spirits have remained steady or substantially improved. Night clubs also sing a sad business refrain and, with the drop in movie-going, many transportation concerns—buses and cabs—report a slump in after-dark traffic.

But where the "night out" is concerned, television by no means is solely responsible for the trend. As in the attendance at movies, the inflationary cycle—food costs, heavy installment-buying and rising prices for most essentials—is having a pronounced effect, perhaps far more than has been generally realized. This is borne out by reports from cities not having television.

Monte Proser, a leader in the New York night club field, expressed the belief that the day of the large night club may be over and that more intimate spots will become the general vogue. One exception in New York, however, is the Latin Quarter, which is holding up well, but probably has been aided by the closing of a number of its large rivals, notably Billy Rose's Diamond Horseshoe. The Copacabana and Riviera also often have done excellent business with major TV stars.

Cabaret proprietors acknowledge one interesting social development that has a direct bearing on their trade. Television viewers are now seeing so many stars and variety acts that they've become more demanding. Where once only the professional critic saw everything in town, now virtually everybody does.

In New York, the lessening availability of one of the staples of the night club business — the pretty girl—is giving owners some concern. On television a chorus girl can get $112.50 for a half-hour show once a week, the fee including rehearsals. Leading night clubs pay $100 to a chorus girl and she must do eighteen shows a week. Agents with new acts also are slighting the club in favor of TV: a guest appearance on a video program introduces the new act more quickly.

Away from the Broadway area, the effects of television and inflation on the individual's night out varies sharply with local conditions. The following are representative reports:

Chicago: George T. Drake, president of the Chicago Restaurant Association, reports a 25 per cent drop in evening trade. The Chicago Transit Authority believes decline in evening traffic on trolleys and elevated trains is due in part to TV.

White Plains: Westchester Restaurant Association says there has been a 20 per cent drop decline because of TV.

San Francisco: Night clubs are "taking a beating."

Hartford: When Sid Caesar is on TV on Saturday nights, says one proprietor, people eat early and rush home.

Detroit: Most restaurants say decline is due to inflation rather than to TV.

Atlanta: Economic conditions have hurt night clubs.

Columbus, Ohio: Trolley and bus patronage off, but this could be attributed to factors other than TV.

Greenwich, Conn.: Evening bus schedules reduced; television held "definitely" responsible.

Lansing, Mich.: Marked decline in evening traffic owing to TV, say local transportation companies.

Kansas City, Mo.: Public Service Company thinks TV is reducing fare receipts.

Perth Amboy, N. J.: Cab drivers say there has been a 15 per cent drop.

Babylon, L. I.: Cab companies say money is "tight" and is being used to pay off installments on TV sets.

Denver: No TV here, and a general increase in patronage at restaurants.

Portland, Ore.: There's no television, but night clubs are ailing and "free-spending of war boom period is waning or gone."

CIVIC MEETINGS

Reports from a number of localities suggest that community leaders are worried over television's impact on attendance at community meetings.

In Peekskill, N. Y., it was said that fraternal organizations were waging a losing battle, "but that ladies' auxiliaries did better." It was reported that if 10 per cent of the resident membership of lodges show up, officers were surprised. In Milwaukee, officials of the city's labor unions said "the screen has been playing hob with meeting attendance."

LEGITIMATE THEATRE

The Broadway theatre, which in late years has been operating increasingly on a "hit-or-flop" basis, apparently has suffered little from TV's advent in so far as attendance is concerned, but there have been behind-the-scenes repercussions, some good and some bad.

Gilbert Miller, the producer, currently is surveying theatre patrons' habits generally, including their interest in TV shows. Preliminary indications are that those who can afford orchestra seats are apt to be most selective and critical where TV is concerned. Kermit Bloomgarden, producer, believes TV may have hurt window-sale of tickets on inclement nights.

As for the summer theatres, which are just starting up, Lewis Harmon, operator of the Chapel Theatre at Guilford, Conn., observed: "I don't think any shadows on a screen will hurt my box-office."

Stage actors have welcomed TV as a new field of employment and the performer who does not work before the video camera from time to time is becoming a rarity. Many stars also are enthusiastic about TV because it enables them to indulge their first love—the theatre —and, through occasional video appearances, to keep themselves in the national eye.

Where television has been a costly burden to the theatre is in the matter of scenery and set-building. Many of the set-building concerns, finding a vast new volume of business, are inclined to give TV preference because it affords a year-round income. The opening of the recent theatre production of "Romeo and Juliet" was held up two weeks because the set manufacturers could not get around to the assignment. The stagehands' union, which controls both stagehands and carpenters, is a closed union and, according to theatre producers, there is a shortage of skilled and younger men to meet the combined needs of the theatre and television.

Victor Samrock, general manager of the Playwrights Company, said that with added competition for the services of actors and TV's demand for scenery, the long-range ffect on the theatre pointed to further increased costs of production.

Seven Broadway houses have been taken over by the television networks—the Adelphi, Belasco, International, Mansfield, Hudson, Centre and Little. Twenty years ago there were sixty-eight houses for the living stage; today, with movies, demolition, radio and now TV, there are thirty.

OTHER BUSINESS

According to officials of clothing stores, the volume of sale of women's lounging apparel has increased steadily with the rise of sets, though no definite figures are available.

Both stores and manufacturers reported that TV had had a "marked effect" in stimulating sales of living room furniture. As they stayed home, families were said to be more conscious of the condition and appearance of sofas and chairs. What were known as modern occasional chairs now are advertised frequently as "TV chairs." "TV lamps," reflecting the light away from the video screen, also made their bow in early 1950.

Television has been a primary factor in "tie-in" merchandise sales based on "characters," notably "Hopalong Cassidy" and "Howdy Doody." Endorsements of foods, clothing, jewelry, toys, savings plans in banks, and comic books, as well as many other sources of royalty fees, run into very high figures. The combined commercial value of "Hopalong" and "Howdy" was estimated last year at more than $1,750,000,000.

In Bridgeport, Conn., an official of the restaurant owners association said that evening trade had fallen off except for "hand-holding young couples." Romance, he observed, manages to survive TV.

A Greenwich, Conn., bartender said that he had found a substitute for TV.

"A shuffleboard table now is a better business booster than a television set," he said.

From Chicago came a report that the juke boxes are feeling the effects of TV. "It has definitely curtailed our revenue," said Ray Cunliffe, president of the Recorded Music Service Association.

In Fargo, N. D., a non-television community, a bar proprietor said his trade was drinking more beer and less bourbon and scotch. "It may reflect a wholesome condition among the customers," he added.

A radio station operator in Tulsa has infinite faith in his 'public.'

"Sure," he says, "TV is competing for the public's attention with radio, but the public seems able to absorb everything you can throw at it, or how do you explain the better business radio is having here?"

RELATIONS OF PRESIDENT AND PRESS

Decline in Contacts Is Attributed to Nature of News and Fear of Officials

By JAMES RESTON
Special to THE NEW YORK TIMES.

WASHINGTON, Dec. 22—Ever since George Washington complained to the Congress during the War of Independence that the newspapers were giving valuable information to the enemy, the President and the press of this country have been bickering about what to print in times of crisis.

General Washington was a reasonable man who was able to write to Gouverneur Morris that in a free Government "allowances must be made for occasional effervescences" on the part of the press. But he also wrote the President of the Congress in 1777: "It is much to be wished that our printers were more discreet in many of their publications."

There have been quite a few indiscretions since then, to say nothing of one or two "effervescences," but President Harry S. Truman was making more or less the same complaints to the press this week.

"I want to refer again," he wrote to The Associated Press Managing Editors' Association, "to the matter of protecting secrets from the enemy and to say: this is your country as well as mine. We can only win in the present world struggle if we all work together."

Confidence Declining

This is, of course, an incontestible principle, but it is difficult to apply at the present time because the contacts between the Executive Branch of the Government and the reporters are declining all the time and the confidence between the Executive and the press is not very high on either side.

In his 147 months in office (as Dr. James E. Pollard of Ohio State University has recently pointed out), the late President Franklin D. Roosevelt held 998 press conferences, an average of a little more than nine every six weeks.

Mr. Truman held 256 press conferences in his first six years in office, or as at present, about five every six weeks, most of them lasting less time than Mr. Roosevelt's. Indeed, Mr. Truman has frequently submitted himself to the critical questioning of the reporters but he has explained less than Mr. Roosevelt and has not used the press conference to illuminate complex problems nearly so much nor so adroitly as his predecessor.

The record of the Truman Cabinet is not only worse than the Roosevelt Cabinets, but is worse than Mr. Truman's record. In the Roosevelt era, Cabinet officers held regular and frequent press conferences, with the result that the press performed, under the American system of government, a func-

tion very much like the so-called "question hour" in the British House of Commons, where the heads of the executive departments are obliged almost every day to answer the questions of any Member of Parliament.

Over the past few years, however, the habit of regular and frequent press conferences by Cabinet officers has slackened and in some cases it has been abandoned. This is partly due to the increase in the flow of foreign news, and Congressional news; partly due to the change in personalities in the Cabinet, and partly due to the increasing dangers of free-wheeling public questioning in a time of world crisis.

Nevertheless, the facts today are quite different. Secretary of the Treasury John W. Snyder has held fourteen press conferences in Washington this year, few of which were illuminating. Instead of the well-attended weekly conferences at the Department of Interior under Harold Ickes, Secretary Chapman has held only nine conferences here this year. And at the Commerce and Justice Departments the trend is even more marked, for while Secretary of Commerce Sawyer has made many public speeches throughout the country he has abandoned the regular press conference, and Attorney General Howard McGrath has not had a single press conference in the capital since he entered the Cabinet.

These facts are not evidence of any planned assault on the principle of freedom of information, and they need to be qualified. For example, Mr. McGrath, Mr. Sawyer and Mr. Chapman are available to the press on a private basis. Secretary of State Acheson holds a weekly press conference, and when he's in the mood—which he sometimes is—he can make available more information in half an hour than former Secretary of State Cordell Hull did in a week of daily conferences.

Change in Relations

As a generalization, however, the main point is valid: contacts between press and the President and the Cabinet have declined to a marked degree; the free and regular open questioning of top officials, a useful and even valuable instrument of inquiry and education, has dropped off. And the interesting thing about it is that neither the White House nor the Cabinet officers are conscious of the fact that the change has taken place.

Personalities and certain events have contributed to this widening gap between the Executive and the reporters. The main flow of foreign news, currently so large a

percentage of the news budget out of Washington, is now in the hands of Secretary Acheson, Secretary of Defense Robert A. Lovett, and Mutual Security Administrator W. Averell Harriman—three of the most cautious men in the history of the public press conference.

In a gathering of not more than five men after 8 o'clock in the evening, Mr. Harriman can explain almost anything, maybe even the machinery of the North Atlantic Treaty, but in a press conference he is nervous and obscure —and nobody konws whether this is by accident or design.

With Mr. Acheson and Mr. Lovett no doubt arises. Unlike most men, they have the gift of being precisely as clear or obscure as they want to be, and there's never any doubt about it. The question of whether their calculated obscurity is justified is a matter of judgment.

Hazards of the Time

Certainly, the hazards of our time overseas and the atmosphere of easy ethics which affects both officials and reporters at home contribute a great deal to the lack of contact and of confidence between those who make and those who report the news.

Every official statement made here under the sharp questioning of reporters at press conferences is read now all over the world, and the fear of saying the wrong thing or giving away something to the Russians or upsetting one of our Allies paralyzes many an official.

The United States is now part of a coalition of nations engaged in a partial war which jeopardizes the security of some other nations more than our own, and, therefore, officials conscious of the hazards, take refuge either in being unavailable or in being obscure.

Worse, they take refuge today in the direct lie, or the half-truth, or the technical denial much more than they did a year or so ago. And they blame this—when they are caught—on the hazards of events overseas. But many things contribute to the decline—the bitterness of the political battle at home, the atmosphere of the impending Presidential election, the violence and unfairness of much criticism of public officials, and the general intellectual corruption of the period.

The President and the Associated Press managing editors have not got anywhere in their current argument because they are not arguing about the main issue. The press cannot define what should be put in various security categories; for it does not and cannot have all the facts necessary to make such definitions.

All the problems that exist now, between the Executive and the press existed before the President's recent security information order was announced, because fear is dominating the activities of many of our officials—fear of the Russians, fear of the Congress, fear of the press, fear of unfair investigation, fear of upsetting our Allies, fear of talking openly to all reporters and fear of the possible political consequences of separating the responsible reporters from the irresponsible.

As the prestige of the civilian branch of the Government has declined the prestige of the military has gone up, and the rise of military prestige has never been accompanied by an increase in the flow of public information.

As responsible criticism in the Congress and the press has declined, the Executive has increased the tendency, which was always strong, to play up the good things and play down or censor the bad things. Thus, the press agent's view of government public relations is now very much to the fore, with the press conference looked upon by officials more as an opportunity to "put over" an idea than as an institution to provide answers to the questions that are in the public mind.

Principles and Practice

This problem cannot be solved by writing new definitions of what should be classified information and what shouldn't, no matter who writes them. The problem is to get officials to carry out the admirable principles laid down by the President himself, namely, to keep bona fide military secrets from the enemy and "to provide that information shall not be withheld from the public on the ground that it affects the national security unless it is in fact actually necessary to protect such information in the interests of national security."

The President and the press and the Congress, which is so upset by the new security information regulations, can all cooperate to remove the atmosphere of fear which now dominates so many aspects of American policy.

Specifically, the old contacts between the press and top Government officials can be re-established in the hope that confidence, which has declined with the contacts, can be restored.

But until higher standards of political conduct and criticism are established by all branches of the Government and by the press, it is doubtful whether the objectives agreed upon by both the President and the editors can be achieved.

December 23, 1951

VIDEO AND POLITICS

New Hampshire Primary Voting Coverage
May Change Campaigning Techniques

By JACK GOULD

THE New Hampshire preferential primary has raised a number of provocative questions regarding the use of television in political campaigns. On the basis of what a viewer saw prior to the victories of General of the Army Dwight D. Eisenhower and Senator Estes W. Kefauver, the impact of the medium may be felt in several ways not heretofore fully appreciated.

In New Hampshire, television tried its reportorial wings and found it could fly. In consequence both the politician and the voting viewer may find it necessary to re-appraise the medium's role and influence on government.

The direct effect of video on those who voted in the New England state, it must be emphasized, was practically nil; there are no television receivers to speak of in New Hampshire. But there was undoubtedly a very great effect on citizens hundreds of miles from New Hampshire. That is the new and unknown wrinkle in politics in 1952.

Documentary Reporting

For last week's primary the camera men and commentators of the networks, especially those of the Columbia Broadcasting System and the National Broadcasting Company, swarmed over the state and by means of film did a generally fine job of documentary reporting on the activities of the candidates and the reaction of local residents.

In fact, it was this demonstration of original journalistic enterprise on the part of television that may constitute one of the most important and heartening developments in video in many years. For the broadcasters showed that they really can dig into a story on their own initiative and by visual means provide millions of persons with a new and illuminating insight into men and events.

The New Hampshire primary more than bore this out. If a viewer watched a reasonable percentage of the nightly newsreel programs, the discussion forums and special primary presentations, the chances are that he saw a great deal more of the principal campaigners than the New Hampshire resident without TV.

But, more pertinently, the home viewer had a better understanding of the mechanics of the campaign as a whole. And it is on this score that the New Hampshire primary has provided the hot stove leagues in both television and politics with some intriguing grounds for speculation.

If one fact stood out in TV's political coverage of the last two weeks, it was the fantastically high degree of repetition in what the candidates said and did. Since there are no television receivers in New Hampshire the candidates admittedly had scant alternative but to do door-to-door campaigning and give speeches in town after town.

But in this television era of instantaneous and far-flung communications this traditional technique may soon prove to have critical drawbacks and limitations. For in the areas with television there was a new factor of which the politicians might not have been fully aware but the viewers at home were.

Only the Start

The candidates who toured the snow-covered roads and stopped at every crossroads may have been under the impression that they were speaking chiefly to the local residents who came out to see what all the excitement was about. But actually through television the candidates were speaking to untold millions across the country.

And New Hampshire was just the beginning. In the next five weeks primaries are coming up in Minnesota (next Tuesday), Nebraska and Wisconsin (April 1); Illinois (April 8); New Jersey (April 15); New York and Pennsylvania (April 22) and Massachusetts (April 29). The politicians have just begun their road tours so far as TV is concerned.

Under these circumstances it may be well for the political figures to recognize that television could develop into a double-edged sword, just as it has for the entertainers, producers and writers who work in the medium. TV can boom a candidate into overnight prominence but once it does TV demands more of him.

In the New Hampshire primary a viewer heard certain pat phrases until he almost knew them by heart. In short, after a few days the "material" became pretty familiar and lost much of its freshness. To hear a politician make a joke the first time is fun; the fourth or fifth time it seems just like an act.

But in politics the familiarity of the candidate's "routine" has implications extending beyond the backstage gossip of the show business. To see a man make the same speech in a succession of communities inevitably detracts from the element of sincerity; the spectacle takes on the overtones of an impersonal, almost automatic "act."

Let it be repeated often enough—this, after all, is only the month of March and November is a long way off—and it will be interesting to see what will be the viewer's reaction to old-fashioned machine politics.

Far from lengthening political campaigns, as might now seem to be the case, television could just as easily shorten them in the future. Nobody knows, to be sure, but the coming months should provide an interesting test of whether candidates who jump into campaigning at a late date may not have a television advantage over those making an early start.

Indeed, the politicians' concept of the role of television will require substantial revision. Up to now they have thought of TV primarily in terms of guest appearances or in the purchase of time over which they would have control. Boiled down to its essentials, TV has been envisioned as a political advertising medium.

But the New Hampshire primary showed that television's complementary role of the independent reporter may be of even greater significance. For much the most rewarding and absorbing film "shots" from New Hampshire were the informal and unprepared scenes which caught the human equation in the raw and told their own stories in terms of character and personality.

Lesson

There was the brilliant and amusing example of journalistic acumen on the Ed Murrow show during which the campaigners all explained how much they loved New Hampshire. Or the sidelight on Senator Kefauver, unaware that he was in camera range, bemoaning his delivery of a particular speech. Or the rising indignation of Senator Taft as he insisted repeatedly that he was a winner, not a loser, in politics.

The vivid lesson of the New Hampshire primary is that campaigns in the TV age are going to be conducted in a goldfish bowl. Heretofore the individual voter only saw the political show staged for his benefit in his own community. Now, with television, he is going to have a glimpse of the succession of shows across the country. Where once only political correspondents accompanied the candidates on their cross-country junkets, now millions of persons also will make the trip. That may very well mean surprises for candidates and voters alike.

March 16, 1952

TV AUDIENCE SEES HISTORY IN MAKING

Gets Close-Up View of Truman Revealing He Will Not Run —Held Lesson for Video

By JACK GOULD

If ever there was a striking example of television's power to enable millions of persons to sit in on history in the making, it came with President Truman's surprise announcement that he would not be a candidate for re-election.

The set owner at home had a far better view of the event than those in attendance at the Jefferson-Jackson Day dinner Saturday night in Washington. He saw in close-up what already has been described as one of the truly remarkable "deadpan" performances in political history. It certainly was on TV.

In making his surprise announcement, the President also gave most of the television industry a long-overdue lesson on how its policies in regard to news coverage stand in urgent need of basic revision and much more reportorial flexibility and alertness.

From the moment of his introduction, the President obviously knew he was on the verge of a moment of high drama, and he played it to the hilt. Little personal gestures, which at the time seemed devoid of any special significance, acquired in retrospect a new meaning after the announcement. The President masterfully filled in the many sides to his part in preparation for the climax.

A viewer was struck at the outset by the President's relaxed manner, joviality and broad smile. But since for the evening he was in politics, which always has brought out the true Truman personality, this did not seem too unusual. When the opening applause did not subside quickly, the President laughingly pointed to his wrist watch. He was on the air and time was precious.

The President's mood swiftly changed in accordance with the contents of his address. He amusingly baited the trap with the observation that he expected to attend future Jefferson-Jackson Day dinners "in one capacity or another." On domestic politics, he went to the attack with relish and humor, even employing in spots the language of show business, and in his recapitulation of the Democratic party's role on the international scene he was deadly serious.

Then, viewers saw what proved to be the climactic moment. The President was using a prepared manuscript but for the first time he was seen to turn over a page without reading it. The next page brought his succinct, one-paragraph statement on his decision. In a minute or two, he had finished, and the camera revealed that the two most composed persons on the rostrum were the Pres-

17

ident and Mrs. Truman. Everyone else stood in stunned silence.

Being the only television network to carry the speech, the Columbia Broadcasting System scored a notable "beat," of which it has reason to be proud. But the fact that the three other chains were caught napping, which means that at least some cities did not see the President at all, points up the need for the broadcasters to re-orient their thinking in news matters.

As a general rule the broadcasting industry gets cold feet when an event is "political," as the Jefferson-Jackson Day dinner certainly is. If it covers such an event, it worries over the fact that it must give equal time to an opposing party. Equally often, the industry doesn't want to disturb a commercial show.

This thinking, of course, primarily reflects a concept of television as a dispenser of time, not as an indigenous news medium. Unfortunately, from the standpoint of TV's convenience, news is news no matter what the source of its "sponsorship" and front-page events cannot be neatly catalogued or anticipated in advance.

In this connection not even C. B. S. fully capitalized on its opportunity. Important as was the President's decision, just as important was the reaction to it. C. B. S. had its cameras right on the scene and also an able commentator, but did the network do a round-up of comment of the many prominent figures at the dinner, which could have made unusually dramatic and absorbing viewing? No, as a matter of habit it went back to its New York studio and followed its schedule as originally planned.

CAMPAIGN ON TV WILL BE GREATEST

But It Will Run Into Money if the Party Leaders Try to Cover the Country

Special to THE NEW YORK TIMES.
WASHINGTON, April 19— Thanks to television, the people of the United States are going to see and hear more of a national political campaign this year than at any time in history.

But members of a Senate Elections subcommittee, delving into this new medium with the 1952 campaign in mind, have discovered that there are several flies in the ointment—not the least of which is the matter of cost.

A half-hour of Class A on N. B. C.'s sixty-station national network after July 1 will cost $30,365, exclusive of any other costs that may accrue because of the displacement of a regularly scheduled commercial program. Class A time runs from 6 to 11 o'clock each night and all of Saturday and Sunday afternoons.

Even a half-hour of TV time on individual stations runs into money. It comes to $2,700 in New York, $1,320 in Chicago, $1,260 in Philadelphia. The television people assert that they can deliver a good audience in a spirited campaign for "about three-tenths of a cent for each person of voting age reached." The politicians, who know the effectiveness of TV campaigning from 1950, agree this may be so but ruefully point to the fact that there are an awful lot of people of voting age in the United States.

RADIO AND TELEVISION

By JACK GOULD

The Columbia Broadcasting System has announced a school of television technique for politicians. According to the network, candidates who are afraid that they might offend will be taught how to talk, walk, sit down and get up in front of the cameras. Obviously, this means that the campaign speech of tomorrow will have to be presented in the TV way.

The setting for the speech, of course, will be Studio One, with the convention hall in Chicago being used to store scenery. As the curtain rises, the camera will dolly in on an orchestra of seventy-five pieces. The ward heelers will appear on stage under the direction of Agnes de Mille. There will follow a moment's silence with Gladys Gooding at the organ. On cue, everyone will rise. Sound off for Chesterfields!

The candidate will plunge through a paper billboard bearing his picture and, to the measured refrain of "The Strutaway," will move down stage front and center. When the applause has subsided, the candidate will look straight at the camera and raise his voice in the standard test for a video appearance: "If your sweetheart sends a letter. * * *"

The opening of the campaign speech will now serve a useful purpose.

CANDIDATE: Fellow Americans. It is a privilege * * *

ANNOUNCER: Yes, you are, you know, fellow Americans. And it is a privilege to show you the latest de luxe television receiver. After years of scientific research our engineers have produced a set that does away with both the aerial and the picture.

CANDIDATE: Yes, if you are troubled by the current inflationary tendencies in our national economy, act now. If you live in New York, call MUrray Hill 9-9999; if you live in New Jersey, call MArket 9-9999. Don't be half safe.

ANNOUNCER: Before we go any further, let's not forget: This is Channel Two. Throat cool? Smoke Hots.

CANDIDATE: Yes, the North Atlantic Treaty Organization is definitely milder. Independent tests show that four out of five chiropractors believe that the Solid South will tell why in twenty-five words or less.

ANNOUNCER: And now we have come to the big moment that you have all been waiting for. Write in for your free copy of our platform in its original vacuum-sealed container. It's the only platform with no unpleasant aftertaste. With 99 per cent of the issues removed, you, too, can enjoy this summer.

CANDIDATE: "If your sweetheart sends a letter. * * *"

ANNOUNCER: The opinions expressed on this program are not necessarily those of the speaker.

Memo to C. B. S.: For this you've got to go to school?

March 31, 1952

April 20, 1952

May 12, 1952

VIDEO COVERAGE OF THE CONVENTIONS

By LARRY WOLTERS

CHICAGO.

THREE days after the Fourth of July, television will set off its biggest fireworks to date. The Republican national convention opens July 7 at Convention Hall (International Amphitheatre) and will be followed by the Democratic convention at the same place on July 21.

With the 1948 video coverage of the conventions limited largely to the northeastern corner of the nation, these political meetings will be the first to reach coast-to-coast proportions. Some 60 million viewers, looking on 17 million sets, are ready to watch every move of the political merry-go-round this summer. Mindful that these millions are concentrated in the most populous states, the party managers are giving the greatest consideration to television, for they are convinced that opinions will be molded by the actions and performances on the flickering TV screens throughout the conventions. And after they are over, television will be used as a major stumping medium by national, state and, in some cases, local political aspirants.

Convention Hall was chosen over the much larger Chicago Stadium largely because of its ample working space for television; and a new air-conditioning system was another factor. The Stadium is several miles farther from the Loop. In picking Convention Hall the party chieftains had to give up thousands of seats, since the Stadium can accommodate 18,000 against the hall's 12,000. The seats allotted to the public have been reduced from 9,000 at the Stadium to about 3,000 at the hall.

Surrendering large blocks of tickets for politicians is roughly the equivalent of having to donate a pint of blood apiece, according to Sig Mickelson, C. B. S. director of public events.

New Look

Television and radio actually will require more space at the conventions than the delegates—and will get it. TV and radio will have almost as much manpower on hand to cover the meetings as there are delegates. The Republicans will have 1,205 and the Democrats, 1,230. N.B.C. alone is moving in a caravan of 300

The Broadcasters Agree With the Politicians On Its Importance

commentators, analysts, cameramen, engineers and assorted technicians and $1,500,000 worth of equipment. C.B.S. will have 250 men. A.B.C. and DuMont may have nearly as many and numerous independent stations will be represented.

Westinghouse is picking up the C.B.S. bill of $3,000,000; Philco is spending $2,400,000 with N.B.C.; Admiral, $2,000,000 on A.B.C. The committees, however, have made it perfectly clear that sponsors will have no voice in conducting the conventions or campaigns.

Nevertheless, the conventions are going to have a new look because of television. The changes may be subtle, but definite. There are expected to be some alterations in convention procedures. The arrangements committees of the two parties are considering scheduling most of their major sessions at night so they can reach the maximum audiences.

"The eyes and ears of America will literally be turned toward Chicago," said Edward T. Ingle, radio-TV director for the Republican committee. "Millions of televiewers will see for the first time a major political party in action. No door bell ringer can ever hope to enjoy such a ready reception. It is up to us to make the most of this opportunity."

Kenneth D. Fry, radio-TV director for the Democratic committee, holds similar views: "Certainly there can be no doubt that television has more impact on any given audience than any other mass medium yet devised. * * * Through television properly and conscientiously used by candidates and political parties, more people will know more about their political leaders, their ideas and issues in these vital times than ever before in history."

Technique

The technicians and party chieftains responsible for these big shows cannot dictate how the conventions will proceed, but they expect to do a lot toward streamlining activities and making them more dignified—they hope.

The video experts, retained by the politicians, are counseling simplicity and earnestness. Old-fashioned bombast and hand-flailing oratory are out for TV. What is sought is the quiet, pleasant but firm technique of the door-to-door salesman.

The pros are cautioning politicians to remember that they may not be out of the camera's range when they step down from the rostrum. The prying eye may catch them in moments of inattention, or casting a gleaming eye on some glamor puss when they should be paying attention to the keynoter.

The conventions are to be covered by a new device, a walkie-lookie, which is enough to give party leaders the jitters. This gimmick, a portable video camera and transmitter, will be carried piggy-back upon the floor of the convention. The fear is that delegates may be caught reading the Racing Form or in other forms of unseemly conduct.

While the party chieftains are wrestling with strategy, the technicians, especially those from the Illinois Bell Telephone Company, are grappling with logistics. These conventions, because of the vastly extended coverage, call for 50 per cent more in electric and electronic equipment than was needed in 1948.

Microwave equipment has been installed to beam the TV programs from atop Convention Hall to headquarters at the downtown Hilton Hotel and to the television stations in the Loop area.

Two new cables, each carrying 1,414 wires, have been installed to connect Hilton headquarters and the hall. Fifty-five special phone circuits have been installed to serve television alone. Some 215 circuits are being put in service for radio. About 1,000 telephones will be added to existing facilities.

Whether all these preparations and expenses will pay off is yet to be determined. Anyway the party bosses and all major candidates are taking TV with the utmost seriousness. They have been persuaded that one-eyed video giant. And for votes they are prepared to expend big money.

A SIGN OF MATURITY

TV Fights for Rights as A Journalistic Medium

By JACK GOULD

TELEVISION'S coverage of General Eisenhower's press conference in Abilene, Kan., may rank as one of the milestones in the developing maturity of the medium. For the first time, in Abilene, the video industry stood up for its rights as a new arm of journalism and refused to be locked out of an important news event. And it won!

For reasons never completely explained the leaders of the Eisenhower campaign originally decided that they did not want the TV cameras present at the general's first meeting with the press after the opening of his campaign. Some newspaper men reportedly objected because they would be "scooped" by TV before they could get their stories into print. The motion picture newsreels also were said to feel that they deserved to get an edge.

In any case, the Columbia Broadcasting System, largely at the instigation of William S. Paley, chairman of the network's board, decided to force a showdown. It advised the campaign leaders that the video cameras would be in place come what may and that the responsibility for censoring the TV medium would rest with them. The National Broadcasting Company also stood firm.

The outcome was that TV did cover the conference, reportedly after General Eisenhower himself so approved.

Turning Point

The importance of the Abilene incident can hardly be overemphasized because it marks a turning point in what up to now has been the shamefully wishy-washy attitude of the video broadcasters toward their new role in journalism.

Except for a few pathetic regrets expressed by the National Association of Radio and Television Broadcasters, the TV stations largely have just stood by and watched while their rights as reporters were steadily whittled away, compromised or ignored.

Access to legislative chambers, including the House and probably the Senate, has been denied on the flimsiest of pretexts and stations quietly have acquiesced in this denial of the public's stake in knowing what is happening—or isn't happening—in their government. Until Abilene television's policy in spot news coverage was appeasement at all costs, which, as it always does, meant a succession of defeats.

The sudden acquisition of cour-

June 15, 1952

The X of the Campaign— TV 'Personality'

How candidates impress video audiences adds an imponderable to this election.

By JACK GOULD

SEVENTY MILLION Americans are expected to be in the nation-wide audience when our greatest recurring drama—the nomination and election of a President—opens this year in Chicago. In two weeks one out of every two persons in the country will pull up a chair in front of a TV set and personally witness the first of the sessions that will pick standard-bearers for the Republican and Democratic parties.

The question on the minds of politicians and voters alike is: What is television going to do to American politics? In the last Presidential year, 1948, there were not enough sets to provide a test. This year the 18,000,000 receivers installed in homes will turn the nation into a gigantic town meeting, and perhaps supply a definitive answer.

If General Eisenhower and Senator Taft are deadlocked in the balloting, will the country experience a form of video fever like that which accompanied the Senate Crime Committee's quizzing of Frank Costello—only greater? If the methods of the smoke-filled room are brought into the cold and penetrating light of the cameras, will voters deluge the delegates with a flood of telegrams and phone calls? The persons who affect to know about television and politics are agreed on only one thing: anything can happen.

There is no dispute, however, that television is going to wield a major and perhaps determining influence this year over both the conventions and the campaign to follow. Deliberately or not, the political leader must think in new and strange terms, because with television he faces the same fundamental task as any impresario—to attract and hold the attention of millions.

The basic elements of showmanship are being introduced into the American political scene. The rival candidates are the stars of the show, and the delegates are the supporting cast who can make or break the headliner. The convention sessions themselves, followed by the campaign, are the production and setting.

JACK GOULD, The Times radio-TV editor, has covered this field for over a decade.

---

age and determination by television in a journalistic matter comes in the nick of time. Whether they knew or not, the broadcasters were being jockeyed into a highly dangerous position where politicians were beginning to assume that they could call the turn as to what TV would or would not cover.

The emergence of television as a full-fledged journalistic medium of independence and integrity can have incalculably beneficial effects on video as a whole and also on the older reportorial media such as the press.

The one thing which the television industry most desperately needs is self confidence and a true awareness of its own strength. Ninety per cent of its troubles have arisen from a timidity and fear that it may get in trouble. What broadcasting has failed to recognize is that this course is no guarantee of a sure and easy life but can lead only to constantly increasing difficulties.

Handicap

Television's great handicap is that it has suffered from a colossal inferiority complex and that advertisers, pressure groups and politicians have known it was an easy mark. Let television taste of the stimulating fresh air that goes with journalistic independence and it will find that those who have tried to bend the medium to their way will keep their distance. Television must continue to recognize, as it did at Abilene, that respect and freedom are not available for the asking; they must be earned.

For its part the press should aid and encourage the newcomer into journalism and not dissipate its energies in worrying about competition. Television and the newspaper are complementary media serving the public in different ways and performing different functions.

The newspaper can't beat the television station in speed in covering a press conference, but it can and does in providing evaluation, background and completeness. The great strength of the newspaper is that it is a permanent record to be read at the convenience of the individual. Television is subject to the tyranny of time.

In a very real sense television coverage of a press conference can be of inestimable aid to the Fourth Estate. Video can vividly impress upon the public the day-to-day role of the reporter in making the country's leaders offer an accounting of their thoughts and actions.

At the same time television can provide an incentive for constant improvement of the efforts of the Fourth Estate. To know that millions of "reporters" sitting at home are watching the same event as the professional newspaper men is a new disciplining agent to assure objectivity, accuracy and alertness. No harm can come from that.

If television is to sit at the journalistic table, however, it must accept the obligations that go with it. Television must not rely so much on announcers reading scripts prepared by rewrite men just combing press association reports; it must develop its own staff of specialists and leg men who go out into the field. TV cannot just poach on the training and experience of others.

The important point is that the more media which can further the public's understanding of today's many critical issues, the greater the gain for all. And if in the future TV is in doubt of its role, let it just do one thing: Remember Abilene!

THE greatest election change to be wrought by television is likely to revolve around the factor of personality. In 1952 a TV-aware electorate is not going to be voting for a man merely on the basis of his reputation, or his thoughts as recorded in the printed word, or his disembodied voice as it comes out of a loudspeaker. Television makes the candidate of today a human being at one's elbow, who is going to be judged on the same terms as a man greets any new acquaintance. The candidate's mannerisms, gestures, looks, reactions and behavior under varying conditions—most of them trying—will be plain for all to see and evaluate. Millions of American voters will feel that they personally know the candidate and this circumstance is going to help determine their vote as perhaps no other single factor will.

What goes to make an ideal television personality? Is there a formula that will assure the aspirant for office that he will be liked for what he is as well as for what he says or thinks?

Before these questions can be answered it should be said that television also poses a new challenge to the public. Never before have all the people of any land been in a position to see a candidate simultaneously and under exactly the same circumstances and then been asked to rate his capabilities for office at the ballot box. If television is new for the politician, it is equally new for the voter.

Theoretically, it might seem the attainment of ideal democracy that everyone should know for whom he is voting. Television may indeed prove that this is so.

On the other hand, the best and soundest mind is not always the flashiest or most winning on stage. The merely clever and inferior politician with a well-polished "act" might sweep the emotions of the TV audience. Or will the public, through the X-ray lens of the video camera, unerringly pick the soundest public servant? Time and TV will tell.

If the type of person who will catch the people's fancy and vote is still in doubt, there are certain qualities which experience has already shown that the political candidate must have to be seen to the best advantage over TV. The most important—and the hardest to attain—is the quality of naturalness. Whatever the candidate may be, he must be himself. Politicians who have tried to adopt tricks of the stage—and most of them already have tried in the last few months—have uniformly flopped. Their discomfort in trying to remember cues, or in affecting a calculated pose, comes across the screen only too vividly.

switched to "I Love Lucy."

Facial appearances — "good looks" — have not proved as critical a factor on video as all the to-do over the use of make-up once suggested. If there is a minor disfigurement, a touch of pancake powder, will disguise it. But handsomeness by itself is not nearly as important as the "interesting" face —the face which for reasons no one can pin down holds attention. In this connection perhaps the acid test is whether the candidate's facial expressions complement his spoken words. It is often a revealing clue to personality when they do—and don't.

BUT even if all these desirable qualities are put together in one candidate, he must still face another hazard peculiar to the television medium. This is the inherent fragility—TV's "law of diminishing returns"—of the most attractive

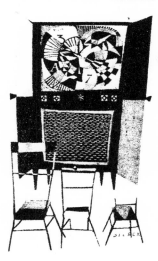

personality when it is seen day after day on a screen. Put another way, will the candidate who makes the appearances necessary to a political campaign wear out his welcome and overstay his visit in the home? Can he lose his appeal through too many TV performances?

Already television can count many stage folk who have shortened their careers by too frequent appearances, and some of the industry's countless "experts" believe that politicians may face the same dilemma.

The odds are probably against it, for the reason that the forward march of events tends to provide the political candidate with at least some changes in his script—something the professional come-

CLOSELY related to the quality of naturalness is the quality of spontaneity. The candidate who hopes to get by on a prepared script is at a decided disadvantage beside a rival who is willing to answer any and all questions freely. The viewer instinctively knows when a speech is staged. It is like hearing a vacuum-cleaner salesman giving a prepared pitch in one's own living room. What the viewer wants—and what television does best—is to convey actuality.

Both the foregoing factors measure, by TV standards, a candidate's sincerity. A third attribute worth its weight in ballots on TV is a sense of humor. By necessity and right most of the millions of words heard in a campaign must be serious, but here too the viewing voter tends to liken a visitor on the screen to a visitor in his home. There must be some measure of relief or the next time the candidate is on the air the dial may be

dian, for example, cannot always find. Nevertheless, if the individual politician repeats himself too often, he may find his Gallup rating markedly going down as the campaign lengthens. Nobody who appears on television—including the office-seeker—is any better than his material.

THE principal figures in the current political drama constitute a casting director's delight. There is a remarkable diversification of personalities and certainly there is no lack of ready-made conflict, which is the core of compelling TV. Here would seem to be some of the distinguishing characteristics of the cast which has assembled for the 1952 political show:

SENATOR ROBERT A. TAFT— The Ohio Senator has shown marked improvement in his video deportment over four years ago. He's not so stiff, formal and professorial on the screen but much more of a human being.

The Senator is severely handicapped in one particular by a lack of warmth in his delivery and he adheres too closely to a single level of expression. His willingness to answer questions specifically is good TV, but after repeated performances he shows some tendency to do it a little automatically. That, however, is getting to be a problem for several politicos who are on television a great deal.

GENERAL DWIGHT D. EISENHOWER—The general has the distinction, at least on television, of being a "new act" as compared with his rivals and so enjoys a major advantage in front of the cameras. His delivery is perhaps the best of those candidates now in the spotlight—forceful, varied and sincere.

General Eisenhower's handicap is that, because his exact position on many matters is still unknown, he is under great pressure to give specific answers on a large number of questions in short order. He can't afford to be vague.

GENERAL DOUGLAS MacARTHUR—The man who is to be keynoter of the Republican convention exemplifies the old-style orator and stands out in marked contrast to all others in the field of politics. His vocabulary is the richest by far and his phrasing is always in the grand manner. His gestures are somewhat overly dramatic and they sometimes detract from the impact of what he says, but by any standards he is a compelling figure.

GOVERNOR EARL WARREN—California's chief executive scores on amiability and, like General Eisenhower and Senator Taft, handles himself well with the press. He also is videogenic, with the best smile of all candidates. His delivery is warm if not spectacular.

HAROLD E. STASSEN — The president of the University of Pennsylvania showed an early foot on TV but after the New Hampshire primary rapidly faded. He formerly used the artificial technique of being interviewed by two hired actors posing as a typical young couple. Their planted questions didn't ring true and Mr. Stassen was a little too anxious in his political pitches.

AVERELL HARRIMAN — Mr. Harriman obviously is new to Presidential politics and it comes through on the screen. He is almost painfully self-conscious as a candidate but is showing signs of gaining in poise and confidence. Perhaps because he entered the campaign at a late date compared with his Democratic rivals and is not an old hand at stumping the countryside and studios, he seems a lonely and too reserved figure before the cameras.

SENATOR ESTES W. KEFAUVER—The Tennessee Senator is virtually a product of TV, in so far as his national prominence is concerned. His conduct of the Senate crime inquiry made him a video knight in armor. He is relaxed and keeps himself under control, but sometimes—fairly or not—a viewer senses that his calm approach is planned. Mrs. Kefauver, incidentally, is the belle of political TV.

SENATOR RICHARD RUSSELL—The Georgia Senator is perhaps the most facile debater of the Presidential hopefuls. As a dark horse he may tend to lack some authority in the presentation of his case but his fund of factual information is impressive on TV.

GOVERNOR ADLAI E. STEVENSON—The Illinois chief executive handily moves to the head of the Democratic class from the standpoint of humor. His wit is dry and original and he is undoubtedly the ablest speaker in the Democratic camp.

WHATEVER the attractions of the personalities of the principals in the campaign, all of them need the aid of competent production assistance. Most of all they need to be protected against the evil of "over-production," which conjures up the thought of planned artificiality in the viewer's mind. On television a voter can tell for himself whether actions ring true and sound effects—and applause—are real.

How a seemingly small detail can upset the best-laid plans was shown during General Eisenhower's speech in Abilene. Sitting directly behind the general was a man wearing a wide-brimmed hat. Periodically he applauded and yelled, "Hooray!" His lack of sincerity detracted seriously from the earnestness of Eisenhower's words. It was like having a stage walk-on fidget nervously during the star's soliloquy.

TELEVISION will lead to some national convention reforms that will be most welcome. The National Committees are planning to have as many major speeches as possible come in the evening hours—when the maximum TV audience is available—and so far as possible to cut down on the length of addresses. The politician's idea of what constitutes a "short" address, however, probably doesn't warrant too much optimism in this regard.

The convention directors also have their fingers crossed in the matter of demonstrations. In the 1948 conventions it was pretty dull TV watching perspiring delegates parade around hour after hour to see if they could stay on their feet longer than the supporters of other candidates. Once a burst of genuine enthusiasm has spent itself the TV audience knows it. It must be hoped that the delegates will, too.

Whatever the delegates decide to do, the television networks are ready with the greatest amount of TV equipment ever massed in one place. They await only the fall of the gavel to open a show the like of which most of the country has never seen.

Coverage of the Republican Convention Shows Advantages and Limitations

By JACK GOULD

TELEVISION'S coverage of the Republican National Convention has afforded an unusual opportunity to study both the remarkable advantages and the very real limitations of the video medium as the newest arm of journalism.

The most important development from a long-range standpoint is that within a period of two weeks the TV medium faced and met a serious challenge to its independence and, thanks in no small measure to a coincidental political issue, emerged with colors flying as an accepted partner of the press.

Originally, as so often had been the case in the past until the TV industry stood its ground in covering the press conference of General Eisenhower in Abilene, Kan., there were ominous indications that video was to be treated as a stepchild in Chicago. The supporters of Senator Robert A. Taft voted to exclude the video cameras from the meetings of the Republican National Committee when that body was hearing the pre-convention rows over the seating of contested delegates.

Reversal

This decision played directly into the hands of General Eisenhower's supporters, who had made a free and open convention their major battle cry. The blackout of TV led to allegations that "somebody had something to hide," as indeed it so appeared on home screens.

In the matter of days the situation with regard to television was completely reversed. After the Eisenhower forces won their "fair play amendment" on the convention rules, the Taft supporters capitulated and television was permitted to cover the sessions of the Credentials Committee. What's more, the committee broke with tradition and even allowed coverage of its actual voting on the contests. Television had successfully invaded at least one "smoke-filled room."

What gaining access to the committee sessions meant was quickly apparent with the telecasts of these deliberations. In many ways these programs provided the most enlightening insight into the workings of politics at the grass-roots level and underscored the significance of even the smallest precinct political meetings which so often fail to arouse the slightest public interest.

Through TV a viewer could see for himself the chain of events through which a participant in a small county meeting can have a direct voice in the choice of a party's Presidential nominee. What appeared on the screen was a vivid and unrivaled lesson in democracy at work.

Participation

As all the specific and detailed evidence in the local contests was heard and seen from coast to coast, a viewer could sense the future implications of TV in the world of politics. Actions which politicians once regarded as primarily matters of local concern became a topic of national conversation. The many predictions that TV would turn the country into a gigantic town meeting during the conventions were not wrong.

In the larger sense, what TV did was personalize the convention's proceedings so that for the person many miles away there was a very genuine sense of participation. Fleeting moments caught by the untiring camera—a lady clapping her hands during the demonstration for Hoover, the difference in ages and personalities of the supporters of Taft and Eisenhower, and the hilarious roll call of the Puerto Rican delegation—painted a memorable panorama.

As the convention progressed, however, a viewer also suddenly realized that the eyes of TV suffer from the same inherent handicap as the eyes of the individual: they can only watch one thing at a time.

During the summing up of the exciting contest in the Credentials Committee over the Texas delegation, TV switched away to the convention floor for the speech of Senator Joseph McCarthy. Why all the networks had to carry the speech instead of dividing their facilities between the two concurrent running stories was an unexplained mystery, albeit probably no network wanted to run the chance of being accused of "censoring" the controversial senator.

The same conflict of attractions arose during other periods of the convention and on a number of occasions television could not fully satisfy a viewer's curiosity as to what was happening elsewhere while on the screen there was only oratory.

Significantly, too, at least during the early parts of the convention, many of the most interesting events, especially the first test of strength between Eisenhower and Taft, came at hours when most persons had to be at work.

In short, what the television coverage of the convention has demonstrated conclusively is that video is one more means for conveying understanding and information of today's issues, but that, contrary to the periodic fears and alarums, it is not going to replace the older media.

The comprehensive round-up in the newspapers, with their distillation of all and not just part of the action in Chicago, was, if anything, made more interesting because the individual reader had a personal familiarity with the events and personalities mentioned in the news columns. The background of the developments, which television, so seldom has time to explore, also acquired a new interest for the viewing reader.

Similarly, the advantage of being able to absorb the news of the convention at one's own convenience, which only the printed record makes possible, was even more fully appreciated after catching snatches of the TV coverage.

All in all, the exciting implication of the first coast-to-coast televising of a political convention is that the forward march of science is enabling the American public, at a time when it is most needed, to take a deeper and more active interest in the vital job of government.

The spectacular medium of TV last week really won its spurs as an original and creative reporter willing to stand on its own feet and not be pushed around. As such, it is a vital and welcome addition to the ranks of the Fourth Estate. Each doing its own job in its own way, the television station and the newspaper will find their respective efforts will benefit each other.

As for the detailed aspects of the television coverage per se, the networks by and large have reason to be proud. The images were clear and varied and there was no restless shifting about of the cameras just for the sake of visual action.

The principal commentators—Walter Cronkite, of C. B. S.; Bill Henry of N. B. C. and John Daly and Martin Agronsky of A. B. C.—turned in workmanlike jobs. However, in one respect they were careless. That was their habit of frequently interrupting the proceedings, even roll-call votes, to contribute their own summaries or observations. As a general rule the commentators would be well advised to stay away from the microphone when the camera shows someone else speaking.

The commercial announcements were not always handled too well. Several of the advertising plugs conflicted with action at the convention itself and a viewer almost instinctively found himself turning to an alternate channel. Under such circumstances it would be better to sacrifice a few of the commercials. When the plugs intrude they only annoy the prospective customer and don't sell the product.

But none of these relatively minor faults, which should be easily corrected during the Democratic convention, can take away from television's big achievement. Millions had the best seats in the house for a show that lived up to its advance billing.

July 13, 1952

RADIO AND TELEVISION

'Forgotten Media' Becomes 'Forgotten Man' of Convention, but Radio Still Gets a Lot of Votes

By JACK GOULD

In the understandable preoccupation with television's coverage of the national conventions, the job done by radio has been all but ignored. In fact, according to emissaries returning from Chicago, the radio broadcaster has been the forgotten man during the last three weeks in the Windy City.

Just for the records, therefore, it should be noted that the radio contingent by and large has done itself proud and in some ways, especially in the handling of incidental commentary, has an edge over the TV boys. There also are some further advantages that give substance to the contention that the two media, which so often are competitive, also can be complementary.

Hard as it may be for the proponents of radio to accept, candor does compel the observation that under normal circumstances there can be no question over the relative attractions of TV and the older aural medium. Instinctively, one feels he is missing a lot in not being able to watch the goings-on. And radio might as well face it: that handicap is lasting.

But the conventions did point up how none the less radio still can perform useful service in the television-equipped home. Basically, it has been a real blessing in its role of watchdog. When the TV viewer's eyes started to droop or he wanted to be freed from the bondage of the visual screen, radio has been the ideal means to ride out the convention lulls yet be alerted if any excitement materialized.

Top honors in the radio coverage probably go to two veterans: Bob Trout, who has provided the running account for C. B. S. radio, and George Hicks, who has performed the same task for N. B. C. While perhaps a shade flowery on

occasion, Mr. Trout's word picture of the proceedings often has been very vivid and perceptive and nicely relieved by humorous observations. A combination of TV's picture and Mr. Trout's "sound track" was suggested to this corner by several "viewing listeners" as an ideal mixture of reportorial media. Often it has been.

As usual, Mr. Hicks during the conventions has been the reporter's reporter in the radio field. His calm and detached approach to the often bizarre doings on the floor have been a welcome relief to the recurrent note of breathlessness that frequently crept into other running accounts, both on radio and TV.

Where radio has topped television has been in the interpretive commentary and analysis provided by such "old pros" as H. V. Kaltenborn, Lowell Thomas, Ed Murrow and Elmer Davis, the latter two, of course, having doubled to some extent on TV.

What these commentators did was offer illuminating appraisals of the major addresses and weigh the significance, or lack of it, of the developments on and off the floor. Without intruding on the proceedings themselves, they did manage better than their TV colleagues to explain the meaning of events as well as the events themselves.

The task of convention reporting is not only the unedited recording of the story per se. Also important is the reaction of the disinterested observer on the scene, if only because the person at home is interested in learning whether the commentator's reaction checks with his own. And old-fashioned radio has been far more deft than TV in doing this at opportune moments that did not interrupt the straight coverage of the convention but complemented it.

AFTER CHICAGO

By JACK GOULD

SECOND-GUESSING on the long-range implications of television's coverage of the Republican and Democratic National Conventions undoubtedly will prove a popular pastime for a long time to come. With two such inherently volatile and unpredictable topics for debate as video and politics there is bound to be an almost unlimited number of opinions on what their future relationship will be.

Up to now most of the emphasis has been on the more vivid and obvious aspects of television's impact on the political scene, which assuredly has been great. Many millions have gone through a unique and unprecedented educational experience that in one way or another undoubtedly will be reflected in the voting booth in November.

But at the same time the debut of coast-to-coast TV at the conventions also had some ramifications which received scant notice. While not susceptible to definitive proof one way or another these ramifications do raise several points which, to say the least, are rather intriguing.

Although it could hardly be guessed from all the excitement over TV in Chicago, actually the video coverage did not attract anything like the audiences that had been anticipated. While the ratings were good by summer standards, there was no duplication of the practical paralysis of normal social activity that marked the Senate crime hearings which had Frank Costello as star.

Smaller Audience

Available statistics indicate that the peak audiences for the conventions did not match the figures achieved during the winter season by the top entertainment shows.

There were a variety of factors responsible. Many of the most interesting moments in the conventions came during off hours for TV—in the daytime or very late at night. Vacations, week-end trips and the oppressive heat reduced the audience's size as well.

A further interesting development was the experience of the motion picture industry during the conventions. The theatres had been prepared for the worst by way of an attendance drop. Instead the box-office receipts not only held up well but, according to some exhibitors, actually showed an increase. The appeal of spending the evening in an air-conditioned theatre probably explains the attendance figures to some extent.

But this is not the whole story. The theatre managers also have noted for a couple of seasons that

July 25, 1952

23

when the major shows go off television for the summer their houses enjoy an increase in business. In this connection they advance the thought that the political conventions may have lent added impetus to the trend.

Pertinent to TV's audience figures was the quality of viewing fare of the convention sessions. Under the pooled coverage plans of the TV industry they were the only programs on the air in most cities and it hardly can be denied that many of the proceedings were heavy going. Unrelieved oratory is not ordinarily regarded as the best way of attracting a maximum audience.

But the corollary question is whether after several years of TV sizable segments of the American public are so addicted to entertainment that they can't do without it for even a few days. If television admittedly has whetted public interest in politics, may it not have whetted an equal or greater interest in continuous escapist diversion?

Decision

Put another way, as the public increasingly takes video in stride, both broadcasters and political leaders may have to take into account the inevitable law of diminishing returns that will apply to political telecasts just as certainly as it has to other types of programming.

What remains to be determined is the point beyond which the use of television may not further arouse the voter's interest but only contribute unintentionally to inertia among the electorate. To abuse or overextend the individual's power to absorb any given subject could be as ill-advised as not making sufficient effort to obtain his participation.

Similarly, the experience of the last few weeks suggests that while television is now part and parcel of the political scene its judicious use is becoming more important for the aspirant to office.

A week ago, just before the opening of the Democratic convention, five of the avowed candidates at the time— Vice President Barkley, Averell Harriman and Senators Kefauver, Kerr and Russell— appeared as a troupe on the TV circuit. One performance by the touring quintet provided an opportunity for a study of the contrasting personalities, but upon repetition it was hard to down the thought that here was primarily an "act" for video's benefit.

Granting that these appearances accorded the candidates a generous measure of publicity, was it altogether good publicity or good politics? Certainly, some viewers must have sensed a sacrifice in dignity which participation in such a patent stunt entailed. The mad scramble of the candidates to keep in front of the camera was at times difficult to reconcile with the element of personal stature that would seem desirable for a man anxious to be President.

That constant TV appearances over a long period of time are not essential for success in politics is borne out by the appeal of General Eisenhower and Gov. Adlai E. Stevenson. Of all the figures on the political horizon this summer, they have been on television the least.

If a highly tentative conclusion can be reached, it is that it may be wise to temper some of the excitement over the role of television in politics and recognize that as the novelty of the marriage between the two fields wears off there will be a greater sense of perspective by both the broadcaster and the politician. A good rule of thumb for both would be that television's job is to report the show, not produce it.

ANYHOW, GADGETS CAN'T VOTE

The wise men who sat down in Philadelphia 165 years ago last May to draw up a Constitution for "the people of the United States" couldn't foresee the technology of a Presidential campaign in the year 1952. Anybody who thinks they should be blamed for this might like to tell us what a campaign in the year 2116 will be like. He will find this hard, because what has changed has not been the basic concept of self-government but the machinery —the real machinery, the gadgets—by which governing gets done. Can anybody imagine what television will be like 165 years from now? Or how we will travel? Or whether it will be necessary for Congress or any other body to meet at a particular place in order to debate? Maybe all this will come down to button-pressing. Maybe something will be invented that will supersede the button.

Today we have astounding contrivances for moving candidates around and sending their voices and faces to the four winds. These contrivances are not new in this election but they are being more effectively used—especially in the case of television—than ever before. Nearly everybody in the country can find out what a candidate looks like, how his expressions change, what his gestures are like. More people can see him in the flesh, because he can get around faster and easier, by air, than he could even four years ago. Four years from now he will be riding jets, but that is another story.

But gadgets cannot alter principles. They cannot make the false true or the true false. It is possible that television may give the edge to a candidate whose voice and facial planes are adapted to the medium; it is possible, but one doubts it. The decision still lies with the beholder, listener and voter. Democracy is served, but the machine does not decide.

Has TV Changed Campaigning?

It has brought candidates and issues 'into the home,' greatly stimulated registration and altered traditional stumping techniques.

By ROBERT BENDINER

FAR into 1953 the experts will be calculating the extent to which television helped to elect the next President of the United States. Armed with slide-rules, past statistics, and comparative voting records for areas with and without TV, they will come up with judgments on the role of the new medium in its first big year in national politics. Until then we can hardly do more than speculate on its impact on the voters, but its impact on the ancient business of campaigning is no longer a matter of guesswork. Clearly in this area its effects have been considerable, costly and contradictory.

Of the $30,000,000 which, by the most modest estimates, the two major parties have sunk into the campaign this year, more than one-fourth has been spent on radio and TV. This does not count, of course, the roughly $8,000,000 paid to the networks by commercial enterprises—Westinghouse, Philco and Admiral—for sponsoring TV coverage of the party conventions and of election-night returns. Nor does it include money spent for Pick the Winner, Meet the Press, Keep Posted, and other commercially sponsored shows on which the issues of the campaign have been ventilated.

On this financial score alone the coming of TV has altered the normal course of campaigning. Even with all the generous loopholes in the Federal Corrupt Practices Act and the Hatch Act, there are limits to the amount of money that can be poured into a campaign. With a half-hour on a single television network running from $50,-000 to $60,000, and even a twenty-second spot announcement coming to $600, it has been necessary to divert funds from more traditional campaign investments, such as billboards, advertising and even, to some extent, travel. The Stevenson strategists have deliberately sacrificed touring to television and have had a hard time making payments at that. According to George Ball, executive director of Volunteers for Stevenson, the $55,000 needed for one telecast was raised only minutes before the deadline.

HAVE the prospects been hopeful enough to warrant the huge expenditures and the feverish effort? Yes and no. Probably TV can be credited, using the word in terms of effectiveness, with

ROBERT BENDINER, a free lance who frequently writes on political affairs, based this story on legwork and television eyework.

"Television is an extremely important adjunct to traditional American electioneering and its reporting by a vigilant press"—TV cameramen covering a convention.

at least three major campaign achievements, no matter how the election itself turns out.

First, it enabled Adlai Stevenson, until the eve of the Democratic convention virtually the Great Unknown of American politics, to establish himself in three months as a figure of authentic stature. Politics aside, his eloquence, wit and unique personality, all conceded by the opposition, were impressed on the country to an extent that would hardly have been possible in so short a time by any other means, radio included.

Second, television must be rated a major factor in the remarkable comeback of Richard Nixon after revelations concerning his private finances seriously threatened to force him off the Republican ticket. Radio alone might have saved the day for Nixon, but there is no question that he proved himself a master of television technique and that the new medium counted very heavily in his rescue from impending disaster.

Third, though there is no way of proving it, television should probably be given a good share of credit for the unexpectedly high registration throughout the country. Not only did TV indirectly stimulate a big turnout by the political interest it aroused, but, along with radio, it very directly pounded away at the theme through spot announcements, "Get Out the Vote" shows, and other devices. The saturation campaign put on by WGAR of Cleveland, for example, has been credited with a 30 per cent registration increase in that area.

Nevertheless, there is a feeling in both radio-TV and political circles that television has not yet played, if indeed it ever will, the decisive campaign role that some enthusiasts predicted for it early in the year. Those were the days when "experts," awed by what TV had done for the political fortunes of Estes Kefauver and Rudolph Halley, were saying that the Democrats could not nominate Chief Justice Vinson simply because he was not "telegenic."

THE fact appears to be that far too much was expected of an untried and still experimental medium, and inevitably it fell short. At its peak of interest the Republican Convention earned a Hooper rating of 36 in New York City, as compared, say, with the 62 recorded for "I Love Lucy," which just might have been a more diverting show. In their drearier stretches the conventions naturally rated far worse, dropping to a low of 17. What is even more to the point, reliable estimates indicate that in October, with the campaign reaching a crescendo, only 10 to 15 per cent of the people were even listening to the radio and TV speeches of the major Presidential candidates.

For these figures some of the blame must be attributed to mistakes of judgment. It is generally agreed, for example, that in its initial enthusiasm the

networks were too extensive and too indiscriminate in their convention coverage, giving more than their sponsors had paid for and more than their viewers could take. Hours of vapid oratory and meaningless shots of bored delegates unquestionably drove viewers away in droves. Done out of programs which they normally enjoyed and which had been preempted for the conventions, many went to the movies instead —box-office figures for the month unexpectedly picked up—and in some cases they wrote resentful letters to the networks.

SIMILAR mistakes were made during the campaign itself, this time by the politicians rather than the networks. People who regularly watched boxing bouts, say, on Tuesday evening, did not relish the substitution of General Eisenhower or Governor Stevenson for more professional sluggers, and they either provided no audience to speak of or a very grudging one. Television viewers in one-channel towns, virtually captive audiences, were presumably even less enthusiastic.

Camera technique, too, often proved unsatisfactory or worse. Whether the fault lay in uneven lighting or poor makeup,

"It enabled Adlai Stevenson, virtually the Great Unknown of American politics, to establish himself as a man of authentic stature."

Eisenhower on several occasions appeared considerably older and less attractive than he does in person. And politicians, policemen and other platform habitués, all milling about, chatting, and mugging, were frequently allowed to steal the scene from the speaker and distract the audience. Everyone who watched Stevenson accepting the nomination must remember how the camera dwelt on President Truman, who was so engrossed in conversation that he absentmindedly joined the audience in applauding himself.

MORE important than these technical flaws, all susceptible of correction, is the revelation that TV is far from evenhanded in its blessings. Governor Stevenson, a poised and excellent speaker in any case, had for some time been making monthly television reports to the people of Illinois and even answering letters on TV. His lively and witty show regularly attracted a half million viewers, and the experience served him well.

Eisenhower, on the other hand, had only one pre-campaign try at television and knew almost nothing of its demands. Although he improved rapidly as the campaign developed, he is by nature neither an urbane nor a rousing speaker, and when extemporizing he is apt at any moment to sink down in a bog of sticky syntax. Where a $50,000 investment in a televised half hour for Stevenson undoubtedly paid off, there is reason to doubt that, beyond a few speeches, this form of campaigning was helpful to the Eisenhower cause, especially since the General, unlike the Governor, was in no need of familiarizing the country with his personality.

Even when the techniques of television are perfected, there is good reason to hope and assume it will never monopolize campaigning to the point of eliminating the grand tour, with all its old-fashioned fevers and follies. For, granting the powerful advantages television has already introduced, it has also brought with it exceedingly tricky problems.

Foremost among these is the obvious danger involved in this

costliest of all types of campaigning. Government-imposed ceilings on expenditures, which meant little enough before, owing to gaps in the law, are now wholly absurd. Theoretically a national committee is limited to an outlay of $3,000,000 for an entire campaign, but volunteer committees for Eisenhower are reliably reported to be spending $2,000,000 just for spot announcements in these final two weeks of the battle. Congress can raise the ceilings, of course, but what can it do to assure an equitable balance of expenditures on this scale between two parties of unequal resources, not to mention the hardship that would be worked on a new party just coming into being?

PAUL PORTER, former chairman of the Federal Communications Commission, was recently moved to advise the networks that by allowing one party to dominate the airwaves in the closing days of the campaign, simply because it had the money to pay for it, they would invite "legislative reprisal." And Governor Stevenson himself has warned that "The problem of financing these costly campaigns presents to political parties the temptation to concentrate on large donations from a few individuals or private interests, which does not always serve the public interest best."

Private sponsorship of such public affairs as the Presidential conventions and election returns is another delicate problem raised by TV. Why, it has reasonably been asked, should a voter's most pressing business be brought to him, over his own airwaves, by courtesy of Westinghouse, or Philco, or Admiral? This mixing of business and politics is clearly hazardous, but if private sponsors don't foot the bill, who will? For all the $7,750,000 paid out by these three corporations, the networks are still believed to have lost $2,000,000 on the deal.

OBVIOUSLY such problems as these will be intensified to the degree that television tends to replace other forms of campaigning. But there are factors other than financial that serve to keep any such tendency in check.

Repetition, for example, is the life of politics, as it is of advertising, but it makes extremely poor television. If you happen to be at the railroad station when your candidate's train stops at Wappingers Falls, you expect to hear from

"It must be rated a major factor in the remarkable comeback staged by Richard Nixon after revelations concerning his private finances."

him the same catchwords and stock arguments you have already absorbed from your newspaper reading, from billboards, and from campaign literature. The chances are that you don't resent hearing them again.

But if, on your TV screen, you should subsequently hear and see your candidate put on precisely the same show at Yaphank, Owl's Head and East Sciatica with the same trumped-up air of spontaneity—your enthusiasm would chill in short order. On the other hand, if you were to watch him change his tune from one section of the country to another, your enthusiasm would chill even faster. None of this seamier aspect of campaigning is suitable to television.

With its constant demand for freshness, TV poses for politicians the same problem it poses for the entertainer. It consumes material at a prohibitive rate. If it were ever to replace the traditional forms of campaigning, a candidate would either require a regiment of speech writers or he would have to limit his campaign to something like a month—which might be a good idea at that.

The fireside type of television campaign presents a danger all its own. At first glance nothing could be more democratic than this direct contact between a candidate and his television audience, with no distracting scene stealers and no audience to sway the viewer with either partisan applause or catcalls. Perhaps it is the most satisfactory way of presenting a political argument, but if it is allowed to stand alone, without the

wholesome questioning of the press or the chance of heckling, it can be an invitation to the demagogue.

The viewer himself has neither the opportunity to demand clarification nor, often, the store of information on which such questioning must be based. Specifically, the emotional kind of telecast that Senator Nixon made in connection with his finances can be seriously misleading if the speaker subsequently seals himself off from legitimate requests for more information.

To cite these hazards and shortcomings of television as a political instrument is simply to suggest that, in spite of its enthusiasts, it is neither qualified nor destined to replace the traditional forms of American electioneering and its active reporting by a vigilant press. As an adjunct to these, however, it is already extremely valuable and will doubtless become more so.

Given a role in keeping with its power, its nature, and its demands, TV can serve to distill the essentials of campaign debate from the mass of flummery and empty rhetoric. It can establish a greater rapport between the nation and its potential leaders. It can arouse and sustain a wholesome public interest in the public business. And it can give a democracy a more intimate feel for its political machinery than it can hope to get from years of civics courses in school or from a desultory reading of the daily paper. All of which should provide justification enough, reward enough and glory enough for any institution.

November 2, 1952

PALEY DECLARES TV CAN CUT CAMPAIGNS

PHILADELPHIA, Jan. 17 (UP)—William S. Paley, chairman of the board of the Columbia Broadcasting System, called tonight for shorter Presidential campaigns to ease the strain on both the candidates and the voters.

Mr. Paley said that effective use of television and other communications media should make it possible to hold conventions in September, instead of July. Whistle-stop train tours could be reduced to a minimum and campaigns could be limited to seven weeks, instead of twelve or fifteen.

He made the proposal in a speech to the Poor Richard Club, which presented its Gold Achievement Medal to him for his contributions to the nation through Government service, most recently as chairman of the President's Materials Policy Commission.

Mr. Paley received the club's medal in 1933 for his contribution to the progress of radio broadcasting.

"It seems to me that one of the central and major contributions which television can make to our political life is to shorten the campaigning process by a considerable length of time," Mr. Paley said.

"The effective use of television and other media of communication, combined with the basic minimum traveling demands required by political necessity, would, in my judgment, enable the candidates to register a deep and pervasive impact on the electorate."

January 18, 1953

PUBLIC PROPERTY

Through TV, President's Press Conference

By JACK GOULD

SOME time ago the White House reported that it had under consideration the idea of occasionally televising President Eisenhower's press conference. Since then the proposal has languished. It deserves reconsideration.

There has been strong opposition, especially among members of the Fourth Estate, to the televising of a Presidential press conference and for reasons that merit careful and serious study. But many of the objections, it is to be feared, are rooted in prejudice that purposely dwells more on the problems of TV than on its enlightened use in the field of reporting government. Indeed, it is ironic that those who so often criticize TV for not doing enough public service programming are the same ones who find excuses for handcuffing the medium.

The importance and integrity of the press conference, of course, must be upheld. The conference represents the only regular give-and-take between the nation's Chief Executive and representatives of the public at large, and is the American equivalent of the House of Commons session wherein the British Prime Minister must give an accounting of his stewardship and undergo a cross-examination.

The chief objection to televising the press conference is the fear that the presence of the cameras would turn this vital instrument of democracy into a show. Both the President and the reporters might tend to freeze up from camera shyness. Perhaps some reporters would want to "ham it up" and impress their bosses back home that they were on the job. With the whole world watching every word and gesture, it is argued, neither the President nor the reporters would be at ease and would tend to pull their punches.

This line of reasoning is misleading because it is based on a fundamental misunderstanding of what was suggested in televising the White House's press conference. It also reflects an outmoded concept of journalism and a denial of the public's interest in what transpires in Washington.

Whenever the subject of televising a press conference is raised, opponents of the idea automatically leap to the conclusion that this would mean the end of

27

the conference as it is now known. Nothing could be further from the truth. The press conference of today would continue to be held exactly as in the past.

What is proposed is a supplementary press conference intended for TV, some further service that we do not now have. At stated intervals—perhaps once every six weeks or so—there would be a press conference to which the public would be admitted through the means of television. And why not?

The newspaper reporters and columnists who object to this supplementary service seem to forget two things: (1) the true nature of their craft and (2) that times have changed.

The reporter may think of himself as a representative of the press, but in the larger sense he is a representative of the public. Until the advent of electronic communications, there was no way for the public itself to be present physically at a press conference. The public's agent was and is the reporter, who is the servant of the millions who read his account of what transpired.

The coming of TV never will lessen this reportorial function. To separate the important from the trivial and to provide the background that gives meaning to news, will always require the talents of the trained reporter.

No Justification

But now that television does provide the means whereby millions of persons can witness for themselves the news conference, there can be no justification for trying to exclude this public. The press conference is not the property of the press; it is the property of the public. If a reporter insists—and altogether properly —on his right to put questions to the President, how can he logically deny the public, whose servant he is, the right to hear the answers directly?

The arguments about a televised press conference becoming "a show" conveniently overlook a number of factors. Much of the confusion that comes from the presence of TV at a public event is technical in origin and can be readily corrected. In a room built for TV all the maze of equipment can be hidden away and no one made unduly conscious of the cameras. The excellent installation at the United Nations shows this can be done.

Similarly, the bright lights are not necessary. TV does not really need them; they are required by the newsreels.

As for the personal factor, the fear of reporters "hamming" it up seems far-fetched. This has not been true on "Meet the Press." If some prima donna wants to act up in the presence of the President, let us see who she is. The public reaction to a display of bad manners by a show-off might in itself take care of the situation. Once sensible technical arrangements are made and TV is accepted as a matter of course, the fear of "a show" would disappear.

The advantages of the televised press conference would be many. Presented at a good evening hour, such a program would have enormous informational and educational value. Not to use TV to help simplify and personalize government is a needless waste of a valuable resource.

Even more, the press conference would give President Eisenhower the maximum opportunity to appear to best advantage. His recent broadcasts, with all their meticulous regard for lighting, shadows, reflections, etc., have tended to show the President in the awkward light of a student actor trying to remember all his cues.

Reasonable Trial

There always will be many occasions, to be sure, when the formal address will be the only proper method for the President to speak to the country. But, at periodic intervals, let him get away from the desks and the Teleprompters. Let him move about comfortably as he takes on questions from newsmen. Let's see, once again, President Eisenhower, the human being, speaking in his own way. He did just that on his return from Europe and, without the help of experts, it was by far the most successful television appearance he has yet made.

If in practice the televised press conference does not work out satisfactorily, no great harm will have been done. It can always be stopped. But the idea should not be dropped without at least a reasonable trial.

Washington

No News Is Bad News Sometimes

By JAMES RESTON

WASHINGTON, Nov. 13 — This morning's headlines illustrate a serious national problem. They are dominated once more by McCarthy, by Dixon-Yates, and by the petty dissensions of state and national politics.

This is a problem because the people and issues that command the headlines dominate the atmosphere at home and misrepresent the true image of America abroad.

The Government spends most of its time behind the scenes trying to do good things and most of the time before the public trying to stop bad things. It has the power to make news—a greater power than McCarthy ever had—but it does not exploit its possibilities.

President Eisenhower demonstrated what could be done to capitalize on the news-making capacity of the Presidency in the last ten days of the campaign, but any fair analysis of the news during the rest of the year illustrates the triumph of the negative.

A Dismal Catalogue

In January the headlines were dominated by the Democrats' cries of "recession," by the efforts of the United States Government to block a Big Four meeting on Indochina, and by Secretary of State Dulles' threats of "massive retaliation."

In February, they were overwhelmed by the Bricker Amendment debate, by Senator McCarthy's "twenty years of treason" speeches during the Lincoln's Birthday political rallies, and by the start of the Wisconsin Senator's feud with the Army.

March was all McCarthy when it wasn't Cohn and Schine. April dramatized the interesting fact that an H-bomb could produce total destruction over an area of fifty square miles, but even this was blotted out later in the month by Mr. Dulles' differences with the British over Southeast Asia, by the security hearing of Dr. J. Robert Oppenheimer, and by the formal opening of the Army-McCarthy hearings.

In midsummer, it was the French crisis over the defeat of the European Defense Community, Senator Knowland's threat to quit as Majority Leader if Red China were brought into the United Nations, and Senator Flanders' move for the formal censure of Senator McCarthy.

There was a period of solid achievement in September and October, when Mr. Dulles reverted to the role of statesman and helped unify the alliance at both the London and Manila Conferences, but by that time the midterm election campaign was on, and everybody knows how much light

that produced.

A Few Neglected Assets

There is nothing in the Constitution that grants the privilege of the Sunday evening fireside chat to one President and denies it to another. Roosevelt employed it with great effect, not only for his party but for the general enlightenment of the public. Eisenhower does not choose to do it, except on very rare occasions, partly because he hasn't got around to it, and partly because he does not have the staff in the White House to do it effectively.

Nor is there anything to prevent the President from coming into his news conference every week with an illuminating statement on some positive aspect of his many policies. Merely to throw the meeting open to questions, as he usually does, is to assure that politics will dominate the transcript.

The Eisenhower Cabinet is another wasted asset. Mr. Dulles is almost the only member who looks on the reporters as an opportunity as well as a problem. The others come into the news rarely, and though health, education and welfare would seem to be subjects of considerable interest to the general public, Mrs. Oveta Culp Hobby (a newspaper publisher, incidentally) runs the department as if it were the Atomic Energy Commission.

The Vacuum McCarthy Fills

Meanwhile, the permanent officials of the Government, who know more about what is going on here and elsewhere in the world than the Cabinet members, have been steadily discouraged over the last year from talking to reporters.

In his dismissal of John Paton Davies from the Foreign Service, partly for expressing his opinions to reporters, Mr. Dulles, consciously or unconsciously, has put every State Department and Foreign Service employe on notice that it is a dangerous thing to express dissents from the State Department line.

If his object was to shut off a source of positive information, the Secretary of State can be reassured that he has been fairly successful. The inevitable result, however, is that the vacuum gets larger and in the end is filled by precisely the kind of news he most deplores. McCarthy loves this vacuum. He is a student of the competitive press, radio and television. He knows precisely when to release his thunderbolts to hit the best edition times and the largest radio and TV audiences.

The Administration, however, has many ways of redressing the balance between negative and positive information. It does not have to "answer" McCarthy. All it has to do is recognize what is happening and use the instruments at its command to correct the situation. As Secretary of the Treasury Humphrey puts it: "We have a pretty good production department, but our sales department is awful."

Q. & A. on the Press Conference

Televising that unique institution, the President's encounter with the press, reopens debate over its value and the way it is handled.

By CABELL PHILLIPS

WASHINGTON.

THE Presidential press conference, one of Washington's cherished institutions, has now become a center of debate as the result of the advent of television into the meetings. Some fundamental questions are being asked: What is the basic value of the conference anyway? And in the light of developments, what is TV likely to do to it? The conference is a mechanism unique among the political systems of the world and it has come to be looked upon as one of the important hallmarks of our Land of the Free. To obtain some light on the questions raised in this debate, it is useful to have the background of the conference.

At a little after 10 o'clock on most Wednesday mornings when the President is in town, a line of reporters begins to queue up outside a pair of tall mahogany doors in the musty, shadowy fourth-floor corridor of the old State Department Building, a few steps across West Executive Avenue from the White House. It is a cosmopolitan group, predominantly masculine, numbering between 150 and 200. There is a liberal sprinkling of the more celebrated names in contemporary journalism—through the crowd of comparatively anonymous correspondents who serve, directly or indirectly, about 90 per cent of the nation's press and networks.

Promptly at 10:20 the doors swing open and the line surges forward through a gantlet of Secret Service men and White House police to debouch into a gloomy, cube-shaped room reaching about forty feet in each of its dimensions and about a century backward in time. Known officially as the Indian Treaty Room, it is an architectural museum piece in dull red and black marble, muted goldleaf, grotesque bronze cherubim clutching clusters of frosted light globes, and crowned about halfway up by an ornate balcony railing.

IN grating contrast to this staid elegance are the bleakly utilitarian furnishings at floor level. Gray chairs are set in tight, austere ranks on either side of a narrow center aisle. At precise intervals polished microphones poke incisively above the chair

CABELL PHILLIPS has attended many Presidential press conferences as Washington representative of The Times Sunday Department.

tops. At the head of the room, flanked by two parade-sized flags, is a severely business-like desk which is also topped with microphones.

Off to one side, two Army Signal Corps men sit at the controls of a tape recorder, and down in front of the desk a pair of stenographers tend their silent dictating machines. And now, for the first time, arrayed along the back wall and looking almost insolently anachronistic, are the hypnotic eyes of newsreel and television cameras.

Usually on the dot of 10:30, there is a sudden hush of conversation; the reporters, packed shoulder to shoulder in their narrow seats, get noisily to their feet, and the President strides purposefully in from a side entrance.

On most mornings he starts the proceedings by reading one or two prepared statements or by making some oral announcement. By custom, the first question is pre-empted by one of the press association men regularly assigned to the White House. The question usually seeks Presidential clarification on whatever the chief topic of news interest that day happens to be. With the first question out of the way, the privilege of gaining the floor is up for grabs. A dozen reporters sit tensely on the edge of their chairs, hoping to be the first on their feet when the President stops speaking.

The questions cover the whole field of national and international affairs, of local problems and politics, of the

President's philosophy and his hopes and his personal affairs. Many of the questions are trivial and of narrow interest, at best. Others are designed to pry out of him factual information bearing on some larger issues of the day. Finally, there are the probing, carefully calculated questions designed to expose the President's thinking and feeling about certain basic problems and issues. Occasionally questions are loaded, with the intention either of smoking the President out of a previously prepared position of obscurity or of putting him on record with a revelatory "No comment."

The institution of the press conference was begun by that most unconventional and democratic of twentieth-century Presidents, Theodore Roosevelt, and was brought to its highest state of perfection by his equally unconventional and democratic second cousin, Franklin D. Roosevelt.

THEODORE ROOSEVELT, with the natural public relations sense that seems to run in the bloodstream of that distinguished family, was the first to recognize the far greater value of the news columns over the editorial columns as a medium of swaying public opinion. When he entered the White House, he inaugurated the practice of regular weekly conferences with the reporters and provided them with a small workroom in the White House itself. He also established the basic rule of anonymity for the President

A newspaper man poses a question for the President at a press conference photographed for television.

that is still observed: no direct quotation of anything he says except with special permission.

Woodrow Wilson was too aloof to make good use of the press, but he faithfully continued the press conference practice until the declaration of war with Germany in 1917. Coolidge held only infrequent press conferences. He required that all questions be submitted in writing in advance, and that such answers as were granted be attributed only to an anonymous "White House spokesman."

HERBERT HOOVER held a total of sixty-six press conferences during his four-year term in the White House. Franklin D. Roosevelt held 337 during his first term, 374 during his second, 279 during his third and eight in the three months of his fourth term—a total of 998 meetings with the press corps in twelve years, usually on a twice-a-week basis. F. D. R. and President Truman both got the maximum use out of the press conference because they made it a busy and efficient two-way channel for the exchange of information.

President Eisenhower's handling of this tricky and difficult assignment has improved quite markedly over the last two years. At first, he was uncertain of himself and ill at ease; he often betrayed a surprising lack of information on subjects about which he should have been well informed. Today, his manner is more confident and his grasp of facts somewhat more trustworthy.

He tries quite conscientiously, it appears, to give the best answer he can to each question. Where a positive answer proves elusive, he is likely to ad lib around it, and not always with happy results. A few weeks ago, in discussing the security controversy over Wolf Ladejinsky, his off-the-cuff peroration wound up in a bewildering tangle of ambiguities. On the other hand, these asides sometimes yield little homilies of striking simplicity and significance.

The press conference, as it has now developed, has great support, but there is also some questioning. There is no longer any serious dispute about its value, though at times its handling, and more important, its results, may be unfortunate.

The greatest advantage of the press conference is that the President does express himself on important subjects, and by so doing illustrates how democracy functions. The press conference is a window through which the public may observe and criticize the workings of the Executive; a protective device against the evils of bureaucratic secrecy and even of inefficiency. Any future President who seriously attempted to curtail this window would immediately become the object of suspicion.

FROM the standpoint of the Administration in power, the press conference is invaluable as a sounding board from which to explain its objectives and its accomplishments to the people. Whatever a President says to the assembled reporters becomes, almost automatically, headline news before nightfall. Moreover, it goes out just about the way he says it.

Finally, the press conference is a source of intelligence to the President. Not only do the questions themselves reveal to him significant trends in public opinion, but the necessity of preparing himself for the weekly inquisition requires him, and particularly his staff, to anticipate those trends.

The questionings of the press conference revolve around the issue of whether the President should talk extemporaneously about important problems. Presidents have seriously imperiled some pending program or diplomatic negotiation by hasty, ill-considered answers they have given to press-conference inquiries.

A classic example occurred in Mr. Truman's press conference of Nov. 30, 1951. Confusion over his statement about the possibilities of using the atomic bomb against targets in Manchuria led many reporters to bulletin their papers that Gen. Douglas MacArthur had been granted authority to use the weapon at his own discretion.

THERE was an immediate uproar around the world. The news created political panic in Paris, Rome and Tokyo. Prime Minister Clement Attlee rushed to Washington forty-eight hours later for a face-to-face discussion with the President over his intentions. The White House Press Secretary issued a "clarifying statement" saying the President had not meant at all what he had seemed to say. But it was a week before Western diplomats got over their jitters.

It is, of course, a frightening burden to realize that one's slightest opinion or most off-hand remark can go ricocheting around the world leaving consternation, and even disaster, in its wake. But such is the responsibility of a President, and it is an inhibiting dread he must live with constantly.

"We had a hell of a time during the first few months," an aide of former President Truman's recalled recently, "because the old man had a habit of shooting from the hip whether he was sure of the answer or not. After some pretty embarrassing bobbles, Charlie Ross (then Press Secretary) hit on the idea of having a preconference briefing. From then on we had a lot less trouble."

James C. Hagerty, Mr. Eisenhower's capable Press Secretary, installed the briefing session at the outset of this Administration. For about half an hour before each press conference he and one or two other top Presidential advisers run over with the President the questions they think are most likely to be asked and the direction which the answers should take. The briefing session cannot supply all the answers but it can and does tend to minimize the inadvertent gaffes.

WHAT, then, does the introduction of television do to the Presidential press conference? Does it, as some are now arguing, put an overlay of artificiality, of self-conscious restraint upon the proceedings? Or does it, as it is also being argued from a contrary point of view, give it a vast new dimension and usefulness?

Mr. Hagerty has spent a good part of his time the last couple of weeks arguing these points back and forth. He says, first of all, that he will, under no circumstances, permit a "live" instantaneous telecast of the press conference proceedings. (They are now filmed and the portions deemed not privileged for showing or direct quotation are excised before release to the public.)

"The White House must have control over the spoken word of the President," he explains. "There are too many unpredictable consequences that can flow from the slightest off-hand remark." Mr. Hagerty adds that all future press conferences will be covered by the television and newsreel cameras, and that he will censor only two types of material: (A) That which might, by direct quote, in some way endanger national security or efficient Government operations, and (B) that which is merely repetitive or of purely local interest.

AS to the criteria that will govern cuts in the first category, he says: "I can't lay down any hard rules about it and I won't try. We'll just have to decide in each case whether to cut or not to cut.

I know that's going to raise the cry of 'censorship,' but I can take that, too. I am sure that, in the long run, the people are going to be a lot better served by getting out, say, three-fourths of what the President says on television than they will be hurt by what we cut out."

This is one important score, however, on which criticism of the new move is based. The argument runs to this effect: the compulsion upon a Press Secretary to make his chief "look good" under all circumstances is a tremendous one. Thus, when there is an embarrassing bobble of speech, or when the President gets entangled in a subject on which he is improperly informed—and Mr. Eisenhower falls into such traps on occasion—the temptation to kill that sequence will be strong. To do so, however, it is contended, would be to prostitute the press conference into a huckstering device for the President's own publicity build-up.

MOREOVER, the mere knowledge that the press conference is being subjected to some form of regulation will, in the view of some, tend to undermine public confidence in the institution. Why, it will be asked, was the President unwilling to be quoted or shown in such and such a situation? Was it something he thought the public could not be trusted with? Such questions, it is argued by some, could raise serious doubts in the public's mind about the integrity of the whole press conference procedure.

To these doubts, this answer is made: Newspapers are permitted to run the full and uncensored transcript of the press conferences, using the President's own first person language where such permission is granted, and paraphrasing the remainder in the third person. Nothing substantial, so far as meaning is concerned, is lost in this process. Similarly, the television companies are free to report in *the third person* everything the President said in the excised portion of his discussion. The only stricture is that they may not show him saying it or use his direct language.

THE general prohibition against quoting the President directly is based, of course, on the grounds that he must have an escape hatch for words that develop an explosive potential after they are uttered. If some press conference statement proves wrong or troublesome it is always possible to say that he was either misquoted or inaccurately interpreted. The fact that the public can read these words back only in paraphrase provides a thin veil of verisimilitude for such a charge. When the rule is abrogated to permit direct quotation, it is usually to underline some point to which the President, for reasons of state, wishes to give particular emphasis.

Another argument being heard is that the mere presence of the television cameras will rob the press conference of much of its informality and spontaneity. "Everyone," it is being said, "will be self-conscious about the impression he will make that night on twenty million home television screens." But so far as can be observed from the two performances that have been held there has been no pronounced tendency on the part of either the President or the reporters to "ham it up." The cameras are pretty well ignored.

What is much more likely, however, is a sharply stepped-up pressure on the President to be cautious and studied in his replies. A wrong answer, a misleading comment, an unfortunate grimace, once it is caught on film, cannot be retrieved without recourse to the censor's shears—which Mr. Hagerty is sworn to avoid save in the direst emergency. But he, and possibly the President too, will scrutinize every foot of film taken with the appraising eye of a theatre critic. The lags and the low spots will be noted, thus making the President increasingly tense and on guard.

THIS, it is argued, could lead ultimately to reviving the Coolidge-Hoover system of requiring written questions in advance, or even to limiting all use of the press conference transcript, for newspapers and television alike, to those portions cleared for direct quotes.

The case for preserving the integrity of the press conference against all efforts to alter or delimit it was succinctly put by President Roosevelt during the first New Deal Administration. The House passed a resolution requesting that the President furnish it with a transcript of one of his conferences for inclusion in The Congressional Record. The President refused to do it on the grounds that he wanted to preserve "the free and open basis" on which his conferences were conducted, and that if he did as the House requested, "it would bring to me a consciousness of restraint as well as a necessity for constant preparation of my remarks."

A's to the Q's—The camera records a variety of Eisenhower facial expressions as the President frames replies to newsmen's questions.

Dilemma of the White House Q & A

It is this: how to modify procedure at the Presidential press conference and at the same time preserve that unique institution.

By JAMES RESTON

WASHINGTON.

FOR the first time since he came back from Europe six years ago today to seek the Republican Presidential nomination, Dwight D. Eisenhower is facing a skeptical and critical Washington press corps. He has been spared this ordeal for longer than any other President of this century, and he still retains the support of the vast majority of United States editors. But the Washington reporters are now questioning him more sharply than ever before in the Presidential news conferences, and this is resented much of the time by his White House

associates and sometimes by the President himself.

Accordingly, a generation of Americans who have watched reporters questioning public figures on the television screen are now asking why a President, in addition to all his other anxieties, has to go into this shooting gallery every week or so. And reporters here also are analyzing the strengths and

---

JAMES RESTON is the Washington correspondent of The New York Times and the author of the weekly column "Washington."

weaknesses of the Presidential press conference.

WHAT has produced this change of atmosphere between the President and the Washington press corps? How do Eisenhower's relations compare with those of recent Presidents? And finally, is the institution of the Presidential press conference, as now conducted, compatible with the Presidential responsibilities of this era?

The atmosphere has changed in these conferences in recent months because the times have changed. Reporters in

Washington do not create atmosphere by their questions so much as they reflect the atmosphere created elsewhere. If the country seems prosperous, if the scientific and technological race with the Russians seems to be going well, and if Allied relations appear to be going smoothly, even those reporters who question the validity of these appearances cannot easily make a dent on the complacency of the public and the politicians.

If, however, prosperity, peace, inter-Allied tranquillity and the prestige of the nation are threatened, the public and the politicians begin asking sharp and critical questions, and these questions are reflected in the questions of the reporters at the Presidential press conference. This is one major reason why the institution exists.

WHEN President Eisenhower was asked on the forty-third anniversary of the White House news conference what he thought of it, he replied that he thought it was a "wonderful institution," and added: "I rather like to get the questions because frequently I think they represent the kind of thinking that is going on."

This is probably the main cause of the recent change of atmosphere. The "kind of thinking that is going on" in the nation, in the Congress and in the world about the state of our affairs is more critical
of the White House than before the Soviet sputniks went up and the American economy went down. And the reporters mirror this change.

The President has gone through three distinct phases in his relations with the Washington reporters. Until he left his North Atlantic Treaty command six years ago after forty spectacularly successful years in the Army, he was accustomed to the formality and protection of an Army command headquarters. He was surrounded by a respectful and obedient staff. He was never quoted unless he wanted to be. An immensely attractive and successful human being, he was not obliged to explain policy or tolerate personal questions, for he was not then, as now, the initiator, but merely the administrator, of policy made elsewhere.

WHEN General Eisenhower took off his Army uniform and sought the Presidency, he expected that his friends in the press, of whom there were and are many, would apply to a political headquarters the same ground rules that had prevailed at his military headquarters. He was soon disillusioned.

The day after he arrived, at the beginning of June, 1952, he held a press conference at the Pentagon. A political reporter interrupted a discussion on the defense of Europe with a blunt question: "What's the matter with your eye?"

The general was startled. He explained that he had had an eye infection in Paris, that the eye had been dilated just before he left but that it was all right.

The first Presidential campaign produced more evidence that the days of controlled Army press relations were gone. He held a background press conference with the reporters at his headquarters in Denver. Eddie Lahey of

THEODORE ROOSEVELT, seen with reporters at his Long Island estate, Sagamore Hill, in 1912, belonged to the era of haphazard Presidential press relations. In office, he feuded often with the press and consigned his critics to "The Ananias Club."

FRANKLIN D. ROOSEVELT, shown holding his first Presidential press conference, in March, 1933, gave the news conference its modern form and used it shrewdly as a political weapon. He sometimes bore down hard on correspondents who displeased him.

The Chicago Daily News asked him what he thought of Senator Robert A. Taft, who was then his leading competitor for the Republican nomination. "He's just a ——— isolationist," remarked the general.

The ground rules of the conference were that the material could be used but not attributed to him. Lahey did not break the confidence but somebody else outside the meeting heard about the remark and printed it. Eisenhower was furious.

On another occasion, Eisenhower allowed reporters into his headquarters at the Blackstone Hotel in Chicago while he was talking to some Republicans from Nebraska. They reported, accurately, that he had made some derogatory remarks about the "immorality" of the French people. This, like the Taft remark, caused him acute political embarrassment, and thereafter he kept the reporters at a distance.

This, then, was the first phase of his political experience with the press and
it was rough. After he was elected, Russell Wiggins of The Washington Post went around and asked him whether he intended to hold Presidential news conferences. He indicated that he did but he was still bridling about the questions put to him in the campaign. "Some of these fellows," he remarked, "are not reporters but district attorneys."

THE second phase lasted from his first inauguration until the Soviets launched their first earth satellite in October of 1957—probably the longest honeymoon any President ever had with the Washington press corps. This was a pleasant surprise to the President.

He had not realized that, just as reporters draw a distinction between a general and a Presidential candidate so do they differentiate between a Presidential candidate and a President. Once he was surrounded by the majesty of the Presidency, he was questioned with
much more caution, courtesy and respect.

There were difficult times over the McCarthy issue, the budget, the internal security policy of the Government and various other things. But, on the whole, the questions put to him were general and lent themselves to general answers. Moreover, the President developed an effective technique for dealing with his questioners.

He paid everyone the compliment of taking seriously the questions asked. At no time did he ever use the vast power and authority of his position to embarrass a questioner. Even when he was asked a vague or even silly question, he tried to make some sense out of it. He was often imprecise and ungrammatical, but he was usually responsive and fair and unfailingly courteous.

It is only recently that the third or critical phase has set in. Since the turn of the year, the questions have centered on the recession, foreign economic

WOODROW WILSON, shown receiving congratulations on his 1912 nomination, started the formal White House press conference shortly after his inauguration. But later on, harried and ill, he cut himself off from newsmen.

HARRY TRUMAN faced the capital press corps regularly, beginning, above, on April 17, 1945, five days after he became President. He was outspoken, as when he denounced by personal letter a critic of his daughter's singing.

policy, his correspondence with the Russians about a "summit meeting" and the reorganization of the Pentagon. By the nature of developments in these fields, the questions have undoubtedly been more direct and specific. They have therefore brought up, in a public forum, embarrassing issues the President wanted to avoid if he could. Almost for the first time he has reacted with considerable annoyance and occasionally with anger. He is now back where he started in his conversation with Mr. Wiggins, resenting hard questions as the inquiries, not of reporters, but of district attorneys.

THE surprising thing about all of this is not that it has happened now but that it has been delayed for so long. The history of the relationships between Presidents and the press is as consistently combative as the history of cats and dogs. When the Founding

Fathers forbade the Congress in the first article of the Bill of Rights to pass any laws abridging the freedom of the press, they did not intend that the press should act like a band of cheer leaders for the Chief Executive or any other public official. Their intention was that the press would be skeptical of power and that their skepticism would increase as the power of any man or institution increased. Whenever the press has been faithful to this obligation, it has found itself in conflict with the President.

The Presidential press conference has merely dramatized this natural situation by producing periodic confrontations between the President and the reporters. It brings the fox into contact with the hunters in a shooting gallery, and the result under Eisenhower has been surprisingly tame as compared with past foxes.

Until the Administration of President Taft, most news of the White House

was gathered on Capitol Hill. President Washington avoided contact with the press unless he was advertising for a cook. Only when he retired did he seek out the press and then merely to ask the editor of The Pennsylvania Packet and Daily Advertiser to run the text of his Farewell Address.

Most Presidents, if they dealt with reporters at all, called in a few tame and friendly scribes and used them as a channel for favorable publicity. President Taft started what he called White House "town meetings," in which he summoned the chief correspondents of the news agencies and principal papers and talked to them periodically in the White House Cabinet Room. These, however, were primarily friendly story-telling sessions, designed mainly to win the allegiance of the correspondents for a genial man.

Teddy Roosevelt was constantly feuding with the press and developed the habit of consigning his newspaper

critics to what he called "The Ananias Club." Woodrow Wilson started the formal Presidential news conference. Eleven days after his first inauguration, he called in the reporters.

"I feel," he told them, "that a large part of the success of public affairs depends on newspaper men—not so much on the editorial writers, because we can live down what they say, as upon news writers, because the news is the atmosphere of public affairs."

THIS experiment did not run smoothly for long. When a few reporters printed rumors of the romantic association of Wilson's daughter Margaret, he reacted almost as violently as Harry Truman did when Paul Hume of The Washington Post wrote that Margaret Truman was not the finest singer in Christendom.

"This must stop," Wilson warned the reporters. "On the next offense, I shall do what any other indignant father would do. I will punch the man who prints it in the nose." This was the first modification of his avowed policy of "pitiless publicity." He carried on the formal Presidential press conferences for years but gradually, under the influence of the war, illness and mounting criticism, he cut himself away from the reporters entirely.

President Harding instituted, and demonstrated the foolishness of, chumminess between the President and the reporters. During his campaign against James M. Cox — another newspaper publisher—he established a press headquarters in a three-room bungalow on the grounds of his neighbor, George B. Christian, in Marion, Ohio. There he would visit them once or twice a day in what they called their "shack," "bum" a chew of tobacco from one of them, and answer their questions without evasion.

When Harding tried to apply in the White House the same casual jolliness that worked to his advantage in the campaign, he came to grief. He took the Washington press corps behind the scenes in the White House more than any of his predecessors, but neglected to create behind the scenes the kind of honesty, efficiency and purpose that correspondents instinctively expect of the Presidency. Also, he was casual with his facts and, ironically, failed by trying to be friendly instead of being accurate.

In a press conference during the Washington naval conference, Harding undertook to explain something he knew little about. His Secretary of State, Charles Evans Hughes, had told several correspondents that the naval limitation treaty, under negotiation at the time, permitted Japan to maintain some defenses on her main islands, although the treaty was purposely vague on this important point. A reporter asked President Harding about this, and he strongly denied that Japan had any such authority.

THIS blunder produced a sharp protest from the Secretary of State to the White House and led to a new rule in Presidential press conferences: not only that the President's off-the-record remarks could not be discussed outside the White House, not only that he could not be quoted verbatim, but that in future all questions to the President had to be submitted in writing and in advance.

This system carried over into the Coolidge and Hoover Administrations, both of which had their share of anguish with the press. Like Eisenhower in his first term, Coolidge enjoyed prosperity and discovered, like Eisenhower, that when things are going well, the President can rely on public indifference and need have no fear of the press.

He produced little news. He operated on the principle of "judicious leaving alone" and even when he announced, "I do not choose to run," he was indifferent to the reporters' judgment that this was an ambiguous statement probably indicating that he could be had. The White House correspondents pressed him hard for a clarification of this statement but he would not respond. Finally, under the White House rule requiring written questions, they all got together before one press conference there were twenty-two reporters then as compared with 302 at a recent Eisenhower conference—and handed in the same question, designed to persuade him to elaborate on his "I do not choose to run" remark. No other question on any other subject was asked.

Coolidge came into the conference, leafed through the twenty-two questions patiently, and then said: "I am asked to explain the condition of the children of Puerto Rico." Whereupon he recited on that subject for fifteen minutes, made no reference to the twenty-two questions and left the correspondents angry but helpless.

It was Franklin D. Roosevelt, however, who really established the modern Presidential press conference, and who understood what Coolidge demonstrated in the Puerto Rico story, namely, that a shrewd President is always in command of the press conference, no matter how clever or even hostile his questioners may be.

Unlike his predecessors, who generally came into these conferences with a combination of fear and enmity, Roosevelt regarded them as a game and an opportunity. He knew that the main objective of a reporter was not to pass judgment on a policy but to gather

HERBERT HOOVER, second from left, talked with reporters as President-elect early in 1929. But in the White House, he adopted the practice, established under Harding and continued by Coolidge, of receiving reporters' questions only in writing and in advance.

DWIGHT D. EISENHOWER has added two innovations to the news conference: admitting television cameras and allowing direct quotation of all his remarks. After a long honeymoon with the press, he recently began encountering more critical lines of questioning.

news, and he gave it to them in abundance. That is to say, he kept them so busy reporting what he had to say that they had very little time to think about what they wanted to say.

Golf is fun and relaxation to Eisenhower; the Presidential press conference was Roosevelt's personal recreation. It was his golf. He knew where all the traps lay. His strategy was to use the conference for his own political advantage and he used every tactic to stay on the offensive. Flattery, irony, satire, special favors for cooperative correspondents, sharp and embarrassing comment for critics—all these were part of his arsenal and he used them ruthlessly.

When John O'Donnell of The New York Daily News wrote in April of 1941 that charges were about to be made in the Senate that Roosevelt was permitting the United States Navy to convoy ships to England before we were in the war, Roosevelt denounced this as a "deliberate lie" and conferred a German Iron Cross on O'Donnell in a press conference in recognition of what he proclaimed to be O'Donnell's services to Hitler. (As a matter of fact, O'Donnell's report was right, for Senator Tobey of New Hampshire made the charge in the Senate the next day.)

He also pinned the title of "liar" on Drew Pearson for printing that Secretary of State Hull was an anti-Communist who wanted to see the Soviet Union bled white by Germany. And when Robert Post of The New York Times printed something he did not like, Roosevelt provided him in a press conference with a dunce cap and instructed him to go stand in a corner of the office.

Once, in February of 1939, F. D. R. was asked about reports in the papers that he had told members of the Senate Military Affairs Committee that the Rhine River in Germany was now the United States frontier in defense of the democratic nations. This was before the war, and again he denounced the report as a "deliberate lie." Afterward some of his most loyal supporters on the committee confirmed the report, but this did not trouble the President or change his tactics.

In historic terms, therefore, this recent flurry about Eisenhower's troubles with the press is comparatively tame and insignificant. Harding once threatened to bar from the White House press conference a reporter who complained in print that the President's pants were too long. Once Roosevelt disappeared in a voting machine booth at Hyde Park and, running into trouble with the machine, was reported by Time magazine as saying "The goddam thing won't work." The clergy protested; Roosevelt insisted that he had merely said, "The damn thing won't work," and had to be dissuaded by his press secretary, Steve Early, from lifting the reporter's White House pass.

THE question remains whether the Presidential press conference, as now conducted, can be reconciled with the complexity and menace of the events of today. This is the age of the reporter-specialist in Washington. Many men who attend these conferences have been concentrating for years on specific aspects of domestic and foreign affairs. The President is often asked questions on labor, farm, economic or disarmament matters, and is asked them by men who undoubtedly know more about the subjects than the President. This is, of course, embarrassing, especially since his general answers are then studied in the Congress and abroad by other experts who also concentrate more and know more about the subject than he does.

Some officials can field these questions without a bobble—Secretary of State Dulles is a case in point—but Eisenhower is not a scholar; he uses the staff system of administration and relies more than any other President of this century on his Cabinet and their subordinates. Therefore, when he muffs or evades a question with an oblique generality, he exposes weakness and damages his prestige.

IT does not follow from this, however, that the institution of the press conference

should be abandoned, though it probably does follow that it should be modified to meet the qualities of the President of the day and the requirements of the time. If fairly used by both the reporters and the President, it can be a useful instrument of education in an age when public understanding is both difficult to achieve and necessary for support. If unfairly used by the reporters, it can mislead and confuse the public by emphasizing the trivial and the personal. If unfairly used by the President, it can flood the channels of communication with one-sided propaganda.

The problem, therefore, is to strike a just balance. If all questions were prepared in advance, the President could have the answers prepared in advance and press and public would have little or no means of estimating the President's qualities or judging whether his answers represented his ideas or merely the views of some unknown official.

Eisenhower introduced the television camera into the Presidential press conference and he has not abused the opportunity provided by that powerful new political instrument. The opportunity, however, exists and ought to be recognized.

For example, it should not be assumed that the present inadequate facilities for the Presidential press conference will prevail through another Administration. Before many years pass, there will undoubtedly be a small theatre attached to the Executive offices, complete with modern sound-proof television rooms, probably similar to those now in the Security Council chamber of the United Nations.

Then it will be possible to "shoot" the press conference from all angles and provide perfect reproduction. This will be both an opportunity and a danger. There will then be an opportunity for more effective dissemination of Presidential views. There will be, however, nothing to prevent the President from having a press conference a day, if he likes, and flooding the television screens with prepared answers to questions written in advance. Thus, while that other "equal" branch of the Govern-

ment, the Congress, is arguing its case to virtually empty seats, the President would be in a position to use the carefully prepared and televised conference to overwhelm the weaker voice of the Congress.

PRESUMABLY, any calculated attempt to unbalance the American system of checks and balances in such a way would create its own counterpressures, but while the present problems of the press conference are under study, the future dangers have to be considered.

The present problems are not serious and corrective measures can be adopted next week, if desired. There is nothing in the Constitution that commands the President to attempt off-the-cuff answers to intricate and dangerous

questions. It is not necessary to eliminate all extemporaneous questions in order to protect the President, nor is it necessary for him to answer all questions in order to meet the requirements of a free press. A blend of the two is possible and probably advisable.

FOR some reason or other, the idea has been adopted that somehow a question is a personal challenge and that the President is obliged to answer it in order to demonstrate his courage and knowledge of everything. In this day of endless paradoxes and dilemmas, when questions involve everything from the price of lead to the density of outer space, the expectation of clear and careful answers is pre-

posterous on the face of it.

There is no reason why the President cannot reply that the question is fair but requires a studied answer which will be provided in writing later in the week. This is not only common sense but good politics, for one of the technical problems of the press conference for the average Washington news bureau is that the President provides so many answers on so many questions each press conference day that nothing but a large staff can do justice to them. The delayed answer on at least some questions would thus enable the President to space his statements over a longer period and assure better coverage and more front-page copy on more days of the week.

Also, if there were a fifteen-minute or half-hour moratorium on distribution of press conference news after the close of the conference, the President's staff would have time to catch and correct any grievous error before it was broadcast. Even the lowest freshman Representative on the Congressional totem pole has the right to revise and correct his remarks after he makes them on the floor of the House. Surely the President is entitled to equal treatment.

IN short, the Presidential press conference, like most of our political institutions today, has not kept pace with the changing requirements of the times. It was started in the days of the Model T, and is now trying to operate unchanged in the age of the Jupiter C. In fact, if anything, it has become more open and casual as the elements of accident, danger and risk have increased.

The remedy, however, is not to withdraw the President behind a paper curtain of carefully prepared handouts: that has happened already to such a degree that it is only in the give-and-take of the Presidential press conference that he appears as a genuine human being speaking what is in his mind. The remedy is simply to modify the present procedure so as to protect the President while preserving the spontaneity of a useful and uniquely American institution.

Torchlight, Train, Television

By CABELL PHILLIPS

WASHINGTON.

FOR the first time in political history, it is going to take a conscious effort this year on the part of practically any resident of the North American continent to avoid listening to a campaign speech. Since time out of mind politicians have argued plaintively that if they could just get their "message" to enough people they would win their elections in a walk. Now, in 1960, their problem is not going to be how to reach the people; it is going to be how not to saturate them to the point of angry boredom.

This historic circumstance is occasioned, of course, by the unprecedented use the candidates plan to make this year of television, the highlights of which will be all-network confrontations between the two candidates in what are being billed as "the great debates." The first of these will be seen a week from tomorrow night. On some 46,000,000 television sets with perhaps some 80,000,000 people watching, candidates Nixon and Kennedy will present their arguments as to why each thinks he should be elected to the White House.

There will be no Westerns or soap operas competing for the public's attention; it will look at the candidates or nothing for a whole hour at a time, like it or not. It will constitute the biggest political audience ever amassed. And what all this will do to the type and technology of the political campaign of the future nobody knows.

ALMOST every campaign is notable in one way or another for producing a "first"—some new stratagem or tactic or whoop-de-do that had not been thought of before. The battle of 1956 saw the burgeoning of the "Madison Avenue Era" and the "hard sell." And a century and a quarter earlier, when campaigning as we know it today first blossomed, John Quincy Adams was moved to this moody observation: "Here is a revolution in the habits and manners of the people. Electioneering for the Presidency has spread its contagion to the President himself. * * * Where will it end?"

Looking back, one finds that the basic script of the political campaign has changed scarcely at all in its fundamentals, only in its embellishments. Its essential purpose is, and always has been, to persuade as many people as possible that the candidate is (1) wise, (2) honest, and (3) concerned about "you." If a

CABELL PHILLIPS is the Washington correspondent for The Times Sunday Department.

candidate can't show these prerequisites all the wiles of a Jim Farley or the massed brainpower of the hidden persuaders can't fake them for him. The most that campaign managers can do is to provide the stage setting and the hospitable frame of mind in which the candidate can do his stuff.

Over the years, campaigning has gone through a number of styles and transformations. The rite as we know it today got its start under the progenitor of political "pros," Andy Jackson, who, to dramatize his fight against the United States Bank in 1832, fathered the torchlight parade. As a means of stirring up the voters' interest in political issues, the torchlight parade and its many variants remained the staple of the political campaign for fifty years.

YET an old tradition held that active campaigning on the part of a Presidential candidate was unseemly. Abe Lincoln, for example, refused to budge from his front porch and law office in Springfield, Ill., in the months preceding his first election—he left the "canvassing," as the process was known in those days, to his backers. But this tradition of modesty crumbled away in later years as the fires of partisan competition grew hotter: only an incumbent President seeking a second term felt a hesitancy about taking his case to the voters in person.

The spread of the railroads in the decades after the Civil War worked as big a revolution in campaigning as the advent of television did in the Nineteen Fifties, for it gave the candidates a new and exciting means of mobility—the "whistle stop" tour. William Jennings Bryan was its first great practitioner, and in his second campaign of 1900 against McKinley he made more than 600 speeches in twenty-four states in a little less than three months. Thereafter, the "campaign special" became a factor in political life for the next fifty years.

BUT there never was any substitute, in the days before radio and television, for seeing the candidate in person if you wanted to know what he was like. Hence, the rally—personal appearance cum oratory— was the most durable of all the campaign techniques.

Rallies came in a wide assortment of sizes, shapes, colors and smells and a big one in any fair-sized community was an event to cherish and remember, a spectacle that often outdrew and outshone a Billy Sunday revival or a Ringling Brothers Circus. Weeks of effort went into the preparations and the affair often took on the quality of a nonpartisan community enterprise. People for miles around closed their shops or quit their farms to be on hand for the great event.

Main Street would be draped in flags and bunting and welcoming banners. Church ladies and lodge sisters would prepare tubs of potato salad and fried chicken to be sold at two bits a plate, or perhaps there would be a barbecue or fish fry. There might be a ball game or a mule race to fill in the waiting time, and sometimes an itinerant carnival, dispensing sin and frivolity, would pitch its tents near by. The serious business began when the candidate's train puffed into the depot, and the great man stepped down to be paraded through the city to the fair grounds or the ball park.

A big political speech was a one-time experience for most people forty and fifty years ago: if their voting preferences were to be changed, the candidate had to do it then or never. He rarely got a second shot at the same audience. He had to move and persuade all in one operation, so his oratory was as important as his logic.

Generally speaking, two or three set speeches would serve a candidate for a whole campaign. They were always memorized (a script would have been an unpardonable solecism) so he could turn his conscious energies to matters of style, intonation, gesture—and volume. William Jennings Bryan's famous "Cross-of-Gold" speech had been delivered countless times in bits and pieces on the Chautauqua circuit before he welded it into a bombshell with which to startle the Democratic convention of 1896.

Local political organizations played a more important role in campaign strategy in past decades than they have in recent years. Those were the days of the "bosses," and they functioned with varying degrees of efficiency in almost every state and city in the country, and in many populous counties as well.

BEHIND the bosses were loyal and disciplined cohorts, banded together by ties both fraternal and pecuniary; their local organizations were often social clubs in the off-seasons, and many of the members gained their livelihood from patronage jobs dispensed by the "boss." So he could turn out a crowd—and in many cases he could "deliver the vote" —and accordingly was welcome aboard the candidate's train and had a seat of honor on the platform when the great man spoke.

Both the rally and the whistle stop carried over into the first half of the twentieth century; in fact, the climax and the end of the era of the "campaign special" occurred in 1948 when President Truman clocked 31,700 miles by rail and delivered 556 prepared and "off-the-cuff" speeches, many of them at rallies with a distinctive old-time flavor. But both devices were already headed for the scrap heap.

One notable turning point in campaign techniques occurred in 1924, when radio, for the first time, carried the voices of the Presidential candidates into thousands of homes across the country. Another occurred in 1932 when Franklin D. Roosevelt, breaking all the traditions of decorum, flew from Albany to Chicago to accept the nomination from the rostrum of the Democratic convention. In years past, the notification of the candidate at his home or office had been observed as a great ceremonial function and as a major campaign gambit. The impetuous Roosevelt kicked that out the window and, except for the Willkie notification, at his Indiana farm in 1940, it has not been observed since.

IN the opinion of such present-day experts in the business as Leonard W. Hall, former Republican chairman and now general director of the Nixon campaign, it was F. D. R. and Farley who set the contemporary pattern of Presidential campaigning.

"Farley and Roosevelt," he said recently, "brought more system and careful planning into the campaign effort than had ever been used before. They just didn't leave things to chance, or to the whims of a lot of unknown politicians around the country. They decided what needed to happen to get Roosevelt the Presidency in 1932 and then they set about deliberately and meticulously making those things happen. That's the way a campaign is run today, and it's the only way for a winning campaign to be run."

But 1952 brought more radical and profound changes in campaign techniques than had ever occurred in any single campaign before. These were the first substantial use on a nation-wide basis of television: the substitution of the "prop stop" (or airplane tour) for the "whistle stop," and the widespread employment of public opinion polls to test out voter sentiment and campaign tactics.

THE all-but-total disappearance of the campaign train in that year took a lot of the fun and drama out of campaigning. An airborne campaign, first of all, has to operate on a tighter, more businesslike schedule; its whole mood is geared to speed and efficiency. For another thing, there is little comparison in either the size or the spirit of the crowds who will drive miles out of town to the airport and those who would flock to the near-by railroad station to see the candidate and his party come in.

But planes get the candidate around the country farther and faster than would the train, and this year's switch to jets adds still more distance and speed. (It is worth noting, however, that Kennedy's brief and experimental whistle-stop invasion of California a couple of weeks ago was so successful that he has promised to try to fit others like it into his tight campaign schedule.)

The addiction of both parties to public opinion surveys is increasing rapidly, and one informed official has estimated that more than $1,000,000 will have been invested in them by the Nixon and Kennedy forces before Election Day. They are used to detect the trends and shiftings of political sentiment in key states and localities, to pre-test voter reaction to campaign themes and issues, and to check back on the candidate's performance.

ROBERT KENNEDY, the Democratic candidate's brother

and campaign manager, remarked recently that setting up a campaign organization today, "is like putting U. S. Steel together to run at top speed for eight weeks, and then dismantling it." The analogy is not a bad one.

Political organizations have become inordinately complex and high-pressured, and the skills of a host of specialists are needed to keep them going — historians, economists, lawyers, scientific advisers, communications specialists, transportation specialists, publicity and advertising specialists, advance men, accountants and a lot of durable, patient jacks-of-all-trades to pitch in whenever and wherever they are needed.

What the total cost of the 1960 campaign will be is anybody's guess. One estimate of the direct expenditures by national committees only in behalf of the two Presidential tickets in 1956 is $12,000,000. All that any one will hazard with respect to 1960 is that this campaign will cost "a lot" more.

THE chief casualty of the stepped-up, automated modern campaign is, of course, the old-fashioned rally. It has been on the way out for the last twenty years, anyway, and its last rites probably were sealed with the decision this year by both camps to leave their fate chiefly to the television cameras. Not that some sizable crowds won't be attracted to halls and stadiums this fall when the candidates come to town, but, as one veteran campaigner said the other day "they'll be the converted, not the sinners."

"All you look for in a turn-out of that kind today," he went, "is a window dressing for the candidate; enough bodies to cheer and make a lot of noise so it goes out over the radio and television like a stampede. If people have seen these fellows on their television screens two or three times a week—and often cutting into their favorite programs—they haven't enough curiosity about them left to go to see them in some lodge hall or baseball park.

"The ones who do turn out are likely to be those who are going to vote for him anyway. The audience you are really aiming at is sitting before his television set at home with a cold can of beer in his hand."

TV and the Campaign

Its Use Has Increased the Audience And Added Some Unique Problems

By ARTHUR KROCK

WASHINGTON, Oct. 15—The joint appearance of Vice President Nixon and Senator Kennedy on the same video screen, to state their views on current public issues, has produced several effects new to national political campaigns. It has projected the personalities of the candidates for President for appraisal by more millions of people than ever had this opportunity. It has provided a basis, not previously available, for simultaneous comparison of their personalities, physical and mental, and of the capacity of each to expound his views under the immediate and constant challenge of the other.

The size of the public audiences these programs have attracted, and the nation-wide discussion of the leadership qualities the candidates may have revealed, support the general opinion that the public will demand these joint appearances in all future Presidential campaigns. If this is a sound forecast, then even an incumbent President of the future will find it difficult, if not impossible, to refuse to meet his challenger in person.

Defects, Too

The new form of campaigning, therefore, may become an institution in contests for the Presidency. But the defects in the format of the Nixon-Kennedy programs have been so widely noted, and commented on so unfavorably, that in 1964 and thereafter the arrangements perhaps will more nearly resemble the formula which assures a true and responsible debate. Under those rules, which especially demonstrated their soundness and informative value in the exchanges between Abraham Lincoln and Stephen A. Douglas in 1858, the candidates:

Agree on the issues they will discuss. Decide by lot the order in which they will speak. Ask each other questions pertinent to the discussion. And allow sufficient time for orderly and comprehensive rebuttal and surrebuttal.

In the Nixon-Kennedy discussions the topics discussed have been decided by questions that have occurred to members of panels composed of newspaper and television reporters. Since the panelists must share the programs equitably, and there are time limits on each candidate for his answers and for comments on the answers of his rival, most of the responses are fragmentary. Under this arrangement when an answer requires more time than the format allows, or a principal wants to evade a specific response, the

Ivey in The San Francisco Examiner
"... the truth lies somewhere in between."

question is left hanging in the air.

The result has been a Q. and A. series that roves from the important to the trivial, depending entirely on what subject interests the member of the panel who has the floor. That is why Vice President Nixon and Senator Kennedy became embroiled on a subject which has no proper place in a political campaign because it concerns a most delicate matter of United States foreign-military policy in the most dangerous of the areas where international communism threatens the free world — the Taiwan Strait.

The intrusion of this subject, and the decision of the candidates to discuss it, are excellent illustrations of the irresponsibility generated by the panel format and the lure of television's gift of widespread and photographic publicity. The deplorable incident began on the night of Oct. 1 when the fol-

37

lowing question occurred to Chet Huntley of N. B. C. during a two-man panel interview with Kennedy:

Do you agree • • • with the present policy with which it seems to me we are committed now to the defense of the tiny islands off the coast of China, Quemoy and Matsu?

Kennedy quickly substituted for these words an accurate statement of U. S. policy toward these possessions of Nationalist China. Our commitment, he pointed out, is conditional: "We would defend Quemoy and Matsu if it [an attack on the islands] was part of an attack on Formosa." But then he added comments which amounted to public notice that in his judgment the islands are not a necessary part of the defenses of Taiwan (Formosa). And he made it plain that if elected President his policy will be to eliminate the islands from the defense pattern in the strait.

This brought up to date, and into the Presidential campaign, his Senate support in 1955 of a proposal by Senator Lehman that, in the Senate resolution affirming Presidential authority and responsibility to determine what military tactic was essential to the defense of Taiwan and the Pescadores, Matsu and Quemoy be specifically named as outside the defense perimeter. The Senate rejected this proposal, and also omitted mention of the islands from its resolution so that the President could keep the Taiwan defense tactic flexible and leave the

Chinese Communists to guess what the zone of military reaction would be.

Nixon was quick to challenge Kennedy on this comment as the kind of "woolly" thinking that, he said, had brought on the Communist attack on South Korea and the terrible war into which this drew the United States. He would never, said Nixon, "surrender" even a rock of the free world to the Communist nations. This Kennedy pounced on to represent Nixon as "trigger-happy." And since these events had flowed from the Huntley question on Oct. 1 and Kennedy's answer, there was bound to be another question on it at the subsequent joint appearance of the candidates. By the time they finished their responses, the Chinese Communists had guidance as to the foreign-military policy tactic each as President would employ toward an attack on Quemoy and Matsu.

In subsequent statements both candidates have drawn back somewhat from the haste and imprudence of their original positions and this may repair some of the damage inflicted on our international relations by an aspect of the urge for votes that has appalled the diplomats of friendly nations. And the 1964 campaign is far enough away to justify the hope that the format of the television joint appearances of Presidential candidates then no longer will invite such incidents.

TV MAY DOMINATE 1964 CAMPAIGNING

Kennedy's Stand on Debates and Equal-Time Change Could Curtail Stumping

By TOM WICKER
Special to The New York Times

WASHINGTON, Feb. 4—It appeared possible this week that television might bring a merciful end to the coast-to-coast, jet-powered scramble that Presidential campaigning became in 1960.

For one thing, President Kennedy committed himself to meet in televised debates with the Republican challenger if the President is the Democratic nominee in 1964.

That could set a precedent no future President could ignore, and make such discussions the cornerstone of all campaigns.

For another thing, Congress appeared ready to modify or even eliminate the equal-time requirement that has limited the usefulness of broadcast campaigning almost since its beginning.

Spending Hit Peak

Frederick W. Ford, the retiring chairman of the Federal Communications Commission, disclosed a report on the 1960 campaign that showed the two parties had relied more on broadcast appeals—paid programs as well as free—than ever before.

Television and radio executives, who testified before a Senate subcommittee studying the equal-time matter, pointed out that in 1960 the four Nixon-Kennedy debates reached 120,-000,000 separate Americans, a number larger than the electorate.

They did not hesitate, moreover, to declare that this coverage had been a major factor in bringing 65 per cent of the electorate to the polls, the highest percentage ever.

Thus, broadcasting made a case for itself as the best instrument of modern campaigning. Mr. Kennedy and the Congress seemed to be moving to capitalize on it.

14.6 Million Paid Out

Mr. Ford's figures showed that all paid political broadcasts for all parties in 1960 totaled $11,650,000. He said this was "substantially higher" than expenditures in 1956, which he did not total.

This spending, moreover, was an addition to the greatest amount of free time—thirty-nine hours and twenty-two minutes—ever made available by the networks.

This time, plus the forty-three hours and fourteen minutes provided free by the radio networks and the thousands of additional free hours on individual stations, was made possible largely by the temporary suspension of the equal-time requirement.

Ordinarily, this rule requires that the same amount of time be given to all candidates for an office as is given to any one. Because of the many minor-party candidates, broadcasters used to solve the problem by giving free time to none.

The suspension in 1960 solved that one, but the parties and their supporters kept buying more and more time in addition.

Radio Sales Decrease

Radio suffered, however, in sales of political time.

To the four amplitude-modulation (AM) networks, the Republicans paid for all broadcasts only $44,546, compared with the $144,645 they spent on this medium in 1956.

The Democrats bought only $34,321 worth of radio time in 1960. In 1956, they bought time valued at $176,295.

Mr. Ford's report was based on a questionnaire sent to all radio and television stations and networks and answered by all except what he called a "handful." It turned up some interesting sidelights on political broadcasting.

In 1960, for instance, radio stations began to move into editorializing. Fifty AM stations, six AM-FM (frequency modulation) stations and four FM stations broadcast editorials for or against political candidates, compared with only two television stations that did so.

Twenty-seven of the radio stations also broadcast replies from the candidates they had opposed.

Washington

The Arts of Black Magic and the Press

By JAMES RESTON

WASHINGTON, April 25 — Part of the official inquiry here into the Cuban fiasco will deal with the problems of a free press in a cold war.

To put it bluntly the question is: How can the United States compete effectively against the Communists in the black arts of subversion when it has to put up with a lot of nosey reporters who snoop out and publish every dirty trick they discover?

It would be easy to answer: "Throw them all in the Potomac," and this would undoubtedly have wide popular support, except that there are one or two other aspects of the problem.

Even if all the reporters had been drowned at dawn three weeks before the inglorious landings, the bearded legions in Havana and their Russian accomplices would not have been denied much information.

Castro had his agents in the refugee recruiting and training camps. The Cuban radio was broadcasting all about these camps and the U. S. Government's part in them weeks before they were discussed in the American press. The official line in Washington was that this was a "secret" operation, but it was about as secret as opening day in Yankee Stadium.

In fact the only people who knew very little about what was happening back in the early planning stages of the exercise were the American people who were unknowingly picking up the tab and may yet have to redeem the promises to chase the bearded bully boy into the Caribbean.

Nevertheless, there is a problem and the President's investigating committee is wise to look into it, for nobody in government, or in the press, for that matter, has really thought through where the press' responsibility to speak begins in this kind of subversive warfare and where it ends.

The Sad Record

There is nothing in the Government's handling of the Cuban affair to suggest that the press should just look the other way and let officials do what they like in this field. Likewise, the handling of the U-2 spy plane case is not exactly a recommendation for the infinite wisdom of the bureaucracy.

Nor is there much in the post-war record of the C. I. A. to prove its infallibility and therefore its right to unquestioned confidence. The Communist invasion of South Korea in 1950, Red China's entrance into that war, Moscow's sudden and spectacular advances in atomic science, technology and rocketry, the Soviet attack on Hungary, etc., etc. —all of these reduced the confidence in the intelligence agency.

Yet it is true that the balance of power in the world is more likely to shift back and forth through acts of limited war, subversion, infiltration, economic penetration than it is through a big splashy war with atomic and hydrogen bombs. And these maneuvers are not always fit to print.

President Kennedy is well aware of this. "We dare not fail to see the insidious nature of this new and deeper struggle," he told the American Society of Newspaper Editors here last week. "We intend to re-examine and reorient our forces of all kinds: our tactics, and our institutions * * *."

Time for Review

The problem is to put this part of his speech together with his opening in the same speech: "The President of a great democracy such as ours," he said, "and the editors of great newspapers such as yours owe a common obligation to present the facts, to present them with candor, and to present them in perspective."

This, of course, is one of those grand noble generalizations usually heard once a year during Newspaper Week. It is always nice to hear and, if you don't inhale it, it is fairly harmless. The trouble is that it isn't as true as it used to be.

Neither the President nor the press could present all the facts with candor, and if they had, the mess would be even worse than it is. Nevertheless, the White House press secretary, Pierre Salinger, was probably right in suggesting today that a re-examination is due all around.

The cold war has created a long catalogue of new problems for all American institutions, both the Presidency and the press included. Cuba has made this clear once more. It was generous in this respect: it provided enough blame for everybody.

April 26, 1961

An issue fundamental to the security and to the freedom of the American people was raised last night by the President of the United States in his speech to the Bureau of Advertising of the American Newspaper Publishers Association. It is an issue that most immediately and directly affects the press in our free democratic society and it is an issue that, especially since American participation in the fiasco of the Cuban landings became publicly known, has been deeply troubling thoughtful newspaper men throughout the country.

It is the question of how to reconcile, in the context of cold war and of the Communist technique of fighting that war, the basic American principle of the public's right to know with the basic necessity of maintaining the national security. In time of open and declared war the question is regularly posed, but the solution is relatively simple. Under such circumstances, the need for censorship, even if it is self-censorship, as it was in this country during the last war, is universally recognized and generally observed.

But cold war is different, and we are living in a period of cold war. It is a kind of war, and yet it is not war. For the preservation of our democratic society in this time of "clear and present danger" it is more essential than ever that the people be fully informed of the problems and of the perils confronting them. This is a responsibility as much of the press as of the President. But it is equally essential that the secrets of military technique and—as the President said—of "covert preparations to counter the enemy's covert operations"—be kept inviolate. On matters affecting policy the people must know so that the people in the last analysis can decide; but the terrible difficulty arises in that twilight zone where the revelation of military secrets might affect immediately and adversely the security of the country, and yet where the withholding of information might involve deception of the public. This is a problem that no society but our kind of open democracy faces; and it is because the maintenance of our kind of open society is so precious that the dilemma is so terrible.

Naturally, when "secret" activities become matters of general knowledge in the community, there is no longer a secret—as to a large extent was the case in connection with the Cuban landings. But to dismiss the problem with that observation is to beg the question. For there are often real secrets, and they are often discovered. The President did not attempt to solve the problem, but he did ask American journalists to apply something more than the mere test of "is it news?" He asked that we also apply the test of "is it in the national interest?"—an unsatisfactory test because it is so subjective, and yet one that in the context of the present day must also be applied.

No formula can be entirely satisfactory. Certainly censorship is not, and complete license is not, either. The best for the moment is to take seriously the President's request for self-restraint. Along with this ought to go greater accessibility of officials, so that newspaper men may have frank and informed advice on the harm that might come from revelation of a discovered secret. No responsible newspaper would knowingly damage the national interest; and the greater candor in government promised by the President will materially help protect that interest.

Freedom and the Press

April 28, 1961

Los Angeles

How to Overbalance the Political Scales

By JAMES RESTON

LOS ANGELES, May 8—The increasing power of nationwide mass communications is obviously working to the political advantage of the Kennedys.

Not only is the President dominating the political news on national television, but his only competition in the national magazines seems to be his wife, Jacqueline.

The big, colorful magazine racks in the streets of Los Angeles today illustrate the point. Harper's Magazine proclaims from its front cover "The Kennedys Move In on Dixie." The cover on McCall's carries a picture of Mrs. Kennedy and her two children, and The Saturday Evening Post advertises "A Feminine Chat With Jackie." In fact Mrs. Kennedy's only competition at the moment seems to come from Gov. Nelson Rockefeller of New York on the cover of Newsweek, and from Nikolai Lenin, of all people, on the cover of Look.

On top of all this, the advent of a nation lly circulated daily and weekly press is clearly adding to this trend. The Wall Street Journal is already publishing five days a week on the Pacific Coast and circulating The National Observer on Sunday. The New York Times will start publishing six days a week in Los Angeles in the autumn, and this is already having a visible effect on the Pacific Coast daily press.

They are increasing their coverage of national and international news. They are adding more nationally syndicated columns, most of them originating in Washington, and all this gives the President an even wider audience than he had before.

Kennedy's Techniques

This is something new in American political life. Franklin Roosevelt had national radio and the will and ability to use it effectively. But he didn't have television. Harry Truman and Dwight D. Eisenhower had both radio and television but used them sparingly and kept the Washington press corps in formal channels.

President Kennedy, however, is exploiting all the new mass communications. He had an audience of 85,000 for a speech at the University of California the other day. Over 200,000 turned out to see him in New Orleans last week. He was all over the TV screens from Atlantic City today. Tomorrow his press conference will be televised nationally, and after that it will be a big Presidential rally in Madison Square Garden, with many of the stars of Hollywood and the New York theatre as his supporting cast.

This conscious policy of dominating the news is apparent enough in Washington, but it is even more striking out here—especially in the absence of a popular national figure in the political opposition.

Former President Eisenhower has receded into the well-earned and agreeable shadows of retirement. Governor Rockefeller is still a remote regional figure at this distance, and even former Vice President Richard M. Nixon, showing off his new house to the press here last night, seemed less of a national figure than he did when he came to within 100,000 votes of the Presidency a little over a year ago.

This is a serious problem for the Republican party. It is being overwhelmed in the field of publicity, which is the battleground of Presidential politics. The Democrats have passed power from the men born in the nineteenth century to the new generation born in the twentieth, and the G. O. P. has not. Also, the Republicans have to deal not only with an articulate young President in the White House but with the whole Kennedy clan.

Not since the days of Teddy Roosevelt and his "Princess Alice" has there been anything like it, and the Teddy Roosevelts didn't have instant communication with the whole continent. But now the Kennedys are getting more publicity than the Prime Minister and the Queen of England combined.

Some of this publicity is of course adverse, particularly in the national business and financial papers, and especially since the steel price controversy. But the mass circulation magazines are treating the Kennedys like a royal family and overwhelming the voice of the smaller critical journals.

It is true, of course, that the President has usually dominated the news in all generations. What he says and does command the front pages, even if he does not open the White House and its staff to the press and TV reporters, but there is a new dimension now.

As the daily newspaper goes national, many of the large city newspapers that used to concentrate on local news have to move into the world to meet their competition. And Kennedy, being an astute politician, is exploiting the trend as much as he can.

As this trend continues, the dangers are obvious. The opposition can continue to express its feelings on the floor of the Congress, probably in the presence of a handful of members and spectators, but the President has an audience of millions at his command any day he likes. It is not a situation that promises to maintain a political balance of power in the United States.

May 9, 1962

Q's and A's About the Press Conference

By TOM WICKER

WASHINGTON.

AT each of President Kennedy's news conferences, a large bus arrives a few minutes before the proceedings begin at the State Department Auditorium on 23d Street. Out of the bus come dozens of reporters, all of whom maintain offices in the National Press Club building 10 blocks away and who charter the bus as their answer to Washington's traffic and parking problems.

Behind them at the Press Club they leave a number of colleagues in a special part of the east lounge, equipped with television and bar. This has been set aside by the club management for those reporters who wish to cover Presidential news conferences in gentlemanly fashion, glass as well as pencil in hand.

These customs reflect the major problems of the new, giant economy-size Presidential news conference. What is wrong with it, according to the critics,

TOM WICKER of The Times Washington bureau is assigned to the White House beat.

can be summed up under two major points: First, it has become more an instrument of Presidential power than a useful tool of the press. Second, it is too big; too many reporters try to ask too many questions on too many subjects, and too little useful and coherent information results.

It is the first point that most disturbs thoughtful newspapermen, many of whom fear that, too often during the half-hour sessions in the State Department Auditorium, they have been playing minor roles in a bit of show biz that might be called: "See Kennedy Run, or A Young President Makes Good." They wonder whether they have really been questioning the President usefully, or merely holding him up for all the world to admire.

Doubts of this nature first arose during the administration of Dwight D. Eisenhower, the first President to allow his remarks to be quoted directly and to let himself be televised (on tape and film, but not live) answering questions.

GENERAL EISENHOWER con-

veyed the impression of calm, fatherly competence, Main Street common sense, and a soldier's steel. With such a man in the White House, it was easy to conclude, Americans could make a buck, live it up and stop worrying about the world. Everything was taken care of. Even the General's nomadic syntax was familiar and reassuring, like that of the Rotary Club treasurer.

Mr. Kennedy, going his predecessor one better by holding his news conferences before live television cameras, makes a different but also effective impression. He is the keen executive of the computer generation. Never at a loss for relevant statistics or apt quotations, briefed on every known problem of the civilized world and a few in outer space, he emerges on 6,000,000 home screens every week or so as the cool, business-like manager of the national enterprise, the pace-setter for a generation that believes in living well, looking sharp and knowing all the answers. It is an impression that destroyed the eager-to-please and uncool Richard M. Nixon in the televised debates of 1960—an impression that well

THE PRESS FACES THE PRESIDENT—Reporters criticize today's news conference because they find it less a source of information for themselves than a rostrum for the President, because it is impossible to pursue a reasoned inquiry in the welter of questioning, and because too often, they fear, bland predictable queries yield bland predictable answers.

may be Mr. Kennedy's prime asset for 1964.

That the news conference has become more nearly an instrument of Presidential policy than of usefulness to the press is suggested by the pattern of the Kennedy regime. When Congress is in session and there is an almost constant political need for Mr. Kennedy to convey his personal force and his views on pending issues both to Capitol Hill and to the country, the frequency of his news conferences is sharply increased.

"It gives him a chance," concedes Pierre Salinger, the President's press secretary, "to dominate the news at least once a week."

When, for example, he found himself in deadly conflict with Big Steel, with public opinion as the arbiter, the President somehow found in his tight schedule a free half hour when he could answer questions. To make sure they would be the right questions, he opened his news conference with the most scathing attack any President has made on anybody since Harry Truman called Drew Pearson an S.O.B. The timing was so propitious, the opening state-

ment so sensational, that that news conference of April 11, 1962, was one of the few ever devoted almost entirely to one subject—steel. It was the public pressure Mr. Kennedy generated that day, with reporters as his involuntary helpers, that was the major factor in the ultimate surrender of Roger Blough and the steel companies.

BUT when there are delicate matters afoot in the world of diplomacy, about which reporters would like to inquire, Mr. Kennedy can suddenly find himself much too busy to meet the press. In 1961, after his Vienna meeting with Nikita Khrushchev and the sharpening of the Berlin crisis, he deliberately stayed out of the State Department Auditorium for nearly seven weeks. In 1962, after putting down Mr. Khrushchev in the second Cuban crisis, Mr. Kennedy just as deliberately delayed holding a news conference for about a month. Reporters had no recourse, since no law requires a President to hold news conferences or to answer anybody's questions.

When they discuss the second criti-

cism—that today's news conferences are so big that no one can hope to pursue a reasoned line of inquiry at them —reporters often ask themselves: Didn't the old intimate sessions of Q. & A. between Presidents and a few reporters really serve the public better?

Reporters who used to gather around Franklin Roosevelt's desk believe they did, that they had a better chance in that close situation to drive home a question or a series of questions and thus a better chance to get useful information.

They saw F.D.R. at close range, relaxed one day and under great pressure the next, and they believe they learned a lot about him from the intense scrutiny they were afforded.

Harry Truman moved the news conference into larger quarters but it was still of manageable size and without live radio or television to inhibit the salty Truman responses that often were highly revealing of man, events and policies.

Today, the cavernous State Department Auditorium affords little more

THE PRESIDENT FACES THE PRESS—Mr. Kennedy is critical of today's big news conference because of its aimlessness and because questions that are not first-rate limit the chances to give first-rate answers.

intimacy than would Yankee Stadium, and under the baleful eye of the television camera President and inquisitors alike are all too often given to bland predictable questions and bland predictable answers.

To the conscientious reporter, honestly seeking vital information, these affairs can be maddening. Among 300 to 400 clamoring newsmen, he probably cannot get recognition; after all, fewer than 30 questions can be asked and answered in a half-hour session. Some other reporter may ask the question he has in mind—and phrase it so ineptly as to make the answer useless or incomplete. If the President does call on him, and if he does get in a well-conceived and carefully worded question, Mr. Kennedy—ever conscious of the omnipresent cameras—may retreat into cloudy generalities, counter with a parrying stroke rather than an answer, or simply answer some other, unasked question on the same subject.

Thus, when Mr. Kennedy was asked if he agreed with General Eisenhower that the terms of members of Congress ought to be limited, he cast a wary eye at Capitol Hill and sidestepped the trap, as follows:

"It is the sort of proposal which I may advance in a post-Presidential period, but not right now."

HOW easily the most forthright question can be ducked without really running from it was illustrated in the following exchange:

Q. Mr. President, can you say whether the four Americans who died in the Bay of Pigs invasion were employes of the Government or the C.I.A.?

A. Let me just say about these four men: They were serving their country. The flight that cost them their lives was a volunteer flight and that while, because of the nature of their work, it has not been a matter of public record, as it might be in the case of soldiers or sailors, I can say that they were

serving their country. As I say, their work was volunteer.

A number of reporters' news conference problems, of course, are created by the reporters—alas, many of them with one eye on the television camera and the other on their cocktail-party status. All too many questions turn into speeches. Some even turn into debates—as when Mrs. May Craig importuned the President to put up a statue of Sir Winston Churchill somewhere around town.

Other questions are nit-picking, localized or in the have-you-stopped-beating-Caroline vein. There is virtually no continuity. The answer to one question may suggest another question, but the follow-up is seldom asked, for most reporters come to the news conference with a fixed idea (if any) of what they intend to put to Mr. Kennedy.

These failures among reporters create most of the complaints that have been voiced by the viewing audience: The questions are not good enough, there is no organized approach to, say, questions on Cuba; too many subjects are raised and too little is said about any one; the reporters show disrespect by yelling at the President or implying that he makes deals with Khrushchev and favors the national debt; who cares whether the President thinks modern dancing should be part of the training of combat soldiers?

Questions on the order of the latter, understandably enough, often have caused the public, and Presidents themselves, to wonder whether the news conference is as vital a part of freedom of the press as is frequently claimed.

MR. KENNEDY, for his part, is reported to believe that the questions are not always first-rate, cutting down his opportunity for first-rate answers. He and Mr. Salinger think the aimlessness of a news conference makes it inferior (as an instrument of education, propaganda — and show biz) to something like the President's televised interview with three reporters last winter, an effort sure to be repeated.

Faulty though the modern news conference may be, however, some strong arguments can be made in its defense. If the impression of Mr. Kennedy conveyed by his televised sessions is useful to him politically, it may be equally useful in helping him to do his job. The news conference gives him one of his best opportunities to create public confidence in himself, in his ideas, style and manner—a public confidence without which no President could lead the nation.

As for the supposed advantages of the Roosevelt-Truman years, the intimate news conferences of that period had definite limitations in comparison with those of today. The Presidents could not be quoted directly; only reporters' para-

President Kennedy at four moments during a recent press conference.

phrases of their words reached the public. And voters could not sit in their living rooms in Coon Rapids and Walla Walla, watching the President of the United States barely conceal his anger at de Gaulle or his pride in brother Teddy.

In short, what has been lost *to the reporter* may have been compensated for by what has been gained *by the public*. A rough average of 18,000,000 people now sit before TV sets and watch John F. Kennedy meet the press. Eight major newspapers scattered across the continent regularly publish the complete transcripts of all the President's remarks; others do so occasionally, or publish lengthy excerpts. And those remarks come to the viewer and the reader not in paraphrase but exactly as the great man utters them—split infinitives, Boston accent, diplomatic dodging and all.

TODAY'S conference is bound to have provided a new and insistent source of education for the American people. For if there is less information in today's news conferences— and that is not always true— what there is goes, in its most precise form, to an infinitely larger number of people and in an infinitely more impressive manner.

For every reporter who misses his chance to spot the egg on the President's tie or to share a private Presidential joke, for every hopeful who finds himself unable to gain Presidential recognition for some cosmic question—for each of these, there may be untold numbers of Americans newly aware of the problems

of foreign policy, the dilemma of the domestic economy, the character and style of the man in the White House.

Nor is the reporter on the spot really reduced to being just another spectator. No television set could convey to the home viewer the electric tingle of Mr. Kennedy's anger at the steel companies in April of 1962; the man in the front-row seat can catch an occasional *sotto voce* witticism or word that no one else hears; for many non-White House reporters the press conference still provides the best opportunity for a valuable look at the President in the flesh, or a valuable estimate of the President in personal action. Reporters still largely control news-conference subject matter. And what other reporters of what other major nations have better—or even equal—access to the head of the government?

IS there an answer to the real and imagined ills of the news conference? Mr. Salinger has under consideration only two possible remedies. One is the one-subject-only news conference. "The President will discuss," it would be announced in advance, "the economy and taxation." Or, "The President will accept questions on Soviet-American relations only."

This would produce a greater depth of information on the chosen subject. It would eliminate many localized questions and impose some continuity on the questioners. But if choice of subject were left to the White House, that would be "managing the news"

in an extreme form — a sort of advance censorship. One has only to imagine the outcry that would have gone up if a news conference limited to Soviet-American relations had been scheduled following the desegregation riots at Ole Miss last year.

(Yet, at the first Presidential news conference following the riots, held about six weeks later, not a single question was put to Mr. Kennedy on that subject.)

THE other possibility is that of confining the first ten minutes of a news conference to giving prepared answers to written questions submitted in advance. There is precedent for this. Warren G. Harding, who had blundered with an off-the-cuff answer, thereafter required reporters' questions to be submitted in advance and in writing. So did Calvin Coolidge—with the result that his news conferences still are remembered as the deadliest bores of a deadly boring era in Washington.

Written questions might enable the President to answer more precisely, but a reporter usually prefers to torture his victims directly. There could be cross-examination later in the conference, but the element of surprise would be lost; and surprise and audacity are the only weapons a reporter has in confronting a President before the television camera.

A danger for the President would lie in the editorial decision of selecting which questions to answer; the whole world might wonder why he *didn't* respond to a query on, say, Adenauer's retirement.

thus creating more furor than if he had owned right up that he was for it.

THIS reform might also produce the non-story. That is, a reporter whose question had not been answered might write a non-story about the non-answer: "President Kennedy refused today to say whether he had stopped beating Caroline."

Mr. Salinger already ranks as a major news conference innovator for opening the peculiar institution to live television. His predecessor, James Hagerty, took an equally significant step when he put President Eisenhower's actual words "on the record" and abandoned the paraphrase. Both these developments brought the news conference to more people more accurately. The two steps Mr. Salinger is considering but only half-heartedly — not only would take the news conference back to the arid days of Coolidge and Harding rather than to the intimacy of the F.D.R. years; they also would tend to give the President even more control of content and even greater opportunity to turn the news conference to his advantage.

That is why these reforms are sure to anger the press if adopted. Already most reporters at a Presidential news conference feel too much like spear-carriers in "Cyrano de Bergerac." They will not welcome anything that turns their most direct access to the President into more of a one-man show than it already is.

Washington

On Presidential Politics and World Responsibilities

By JAMES RESTON

WASHINGTON, Sept. 12—The Presidential press conference is both a thermometer and a calendar. It registers the political temperature of the moment and it measures the time to the next election.

This was fairly obvious today at President Kennedy's meeting with the reporters. Most of the questions reflected some criticism of the President or his policies, and all of them together gave notice that the Presidential election is already under way.

One day, hopefully, the United States will find a better way to reconcile its internal political processes with its world responsibilities.

The British, who carried the burden for so long, gradually cut down the length of their election campaigns to three weeks. This produced some domestic tranquillity and left the Prime Minister free to deal with the great questions of the day, but that time has not arrived here yet.

The Political Dilemma

The President has to deal with domestic and world politics at the same time and for a longer time than anybody's patience can endure. For at least one whole year out of every four, everything he says about the world has its impact on the election, and many of the things he says about the election have their impact on the world.

Thus, when he was asked today about Senator Goldwater's criticisms of his Cuban, Vietnamese and test-ban policies, the President had to keep in mind the implications of his reply on his own political fortunes and on Cuba, Vietnam and the Soviet Union.

Thus, too, when he was asked about Governor Rockefeller's criticisms of the Administration's economic policy, he had to find words to put Rockefeller on the defensive politically without lowering confidence in the country's economy.

Kennedy is adept at this kind of political juggling. Any question with even a vague political twist arouses his defensive wit. He seems to welcome domestic politics as a relief from world problems and usually manages to find some pleasant phrase to reconcile the two.

Nevertheless, his problems in this campaign are much more complicated than in the last. He was the challenger in 1960 and could say anything he liked. He had no responsibility then for the troubles in the world, but now he has responsibility and he has to explain things, not merely as a candidate, but as the President of the United States.

Also, the easier postwar days are over for an American President. From 1945 until about 1955, the rest of the free world depended so completely on the United States that allied governments felt obliged to be civil and uncritical of Washington. Now seldom a day goes past without some Prime Minister of a so-called friendly government charging Kennedy with handing over some continent to the Communists.

If it isn't de Gaulle or Adenauer, then it is Chiang Kai-shek or some Nhu from Vietnam, usually female, who is blaming Kennedy for something, and if the offshore chorus subsides even momentarily, there's always Governor Wallace standing in some doorway in Alabama shaking his fist.

Advantages—Disadvantages

All this provides ammunition for the political opposition and questions for the Presidential press conference. The reporters reflected them all today: Was he really misinformed about Vietnam, as the flower of the Orient had charged? Had he made any secret deals with Khrushchev about the test-ban treaty or Cuba? How about the mess in Pakistan and India? And in Cuba?

Somehow nobody asked him, maybe because this was his tenth wedding anniversary, what he thought about America's "prestige" abroad now, and what about the "missile gap"? But otherwise most of the old questions he leveled at Eisenhower in 1960 are now being hurled at him.

If they annoyed him, he didn't show it today. He thought it was a good idea to put the President in "the eye of the target," he said, and, he added, he had been called so many things lately that even Fidel Castro's latest insults seemed mild.

Later it may be different, but at this point in the campaign he seems fairly relaxed, surrounded as he is by the authority of the Presidency. This makes a big difference. For while he carries more responsibility into his campaign and has to speak more carefully, he enjoys the privileges and courtesies of his office and can use the White House as his campaign headquarters, and the Air Force as his convoy.

Advertising: Does It Have a Role in Politics?

By PETER BART

Several days ago the Republican Club of Manhattan's Ninth Assembly District invited two advertising agency executives to a meeting and asked them some tough—if predictable—questions.

"Can professional ad men really change the image of a candidate?" the club wanted to know. "Does the professional ad man have a legitimate role to play in American politics?"

Some club members were surprised to find that the ad men themselves differed on some key questions—that indeed Madison Avenue is as divided as the rest of the nation about the role of advertising in politics.

The club's invitations came at a propitious time, for the debate over political advertising is starting to simmer once again as it does every four years. The two parties have begun to ponder their advertising plans for the 1964 Presidential election and the leading candidates are lining up their Madison Avenue strategists.

Emotions Rise

And whenever politicians confer with ad men, emotions start to rise. Opposition to the ad men's intervention generally follows two contradictory schools of thought. There are those who say that advertising men know nothing about politics and should stick to their soap and toothpaste. And there are those who say that ad men know so much about how to manipulate mass emotions that they endanger democratic processes.

The debate has taken an ironic twist in Britain where the Labor Party for the first time is gearing up for a major advertising campaign prior to the general election. Four years ago when the Conservatives made extensive use of advertising, Alice Bacon, chairman of Labor's publicity subcommittee, demanded a parliamentary investigation into "Madison Avenue's intervention" into British politics. Now Labor is dusting off the slogan, "Let's GO with Labor" to counter the Conservatives' "Life's better with the Conservatives."

In this country campaign slogans have not as yet been developed, but both the Democrats and the supporters of Senator Barry Goldwater are busily hunting for agencies. The Republicans broke off their long association with Batten, Barton, Durstine & Osborn, Inc., last January to sign a two-year contract with the Leo Burnett Company of Chicago.

The Republicans, in signing up the Burnett agency so far in advance, met a criticism that has long been levied against the political parties by ad men. "An advertising agency's greatest contribution can be in advance research and planning," Carroll P. Newton, a vice president at B.B.D.O. who has long been active in politics, told the Manhattan Republican Club.

When a party lines up its agency only a month or so before the campaign, as has generally been done in the past, its role is limited to the prosaic task of turning out a few ads, Mr. Newton said.

More Data Available

If given more time, Mr. Newton added, an agency can tell the party what the voters are thinking, how to appeal to them and where the key districts are situated. "It also can translate phrases that few people understand—such as free enterprise—into words that carry a wider meaning," he continued.

Mr. Newton essentially is arguing for a total involvement of ad men in the political process—a proposal that would raise the hackles of many both in politics and advertising. Opponents of this proposal got fresh ammunition last month when the Republicans' new agency, Leo Burnett, apparently stubbed its toe over its first experimental campaign.

The Burnett agency had initiated a series of test ads to run in local newspapers and regional editions of news magazines that were designed to be self-sustaining—that is, each ad was supposed to bring in enough campaign contributions to pay its way.

One ad in the series, for example, showed three rocking chairs and asked readers to contribute to the "Kennedy Retirement Fund."

Much to the disappointment of the Republicans, the ads produced only about half the money that had been invested. All this was ammunition for those political old-timers who maintain, "Madison Avenue doesn't really know much about politics."

While some people oppose Madison Avenue's intervention on the ground of ignorance, still others have just the opposite concern. They fear that ad men have attained such proficiency at the art of mass persuasion that they may put an ineffectual or evil candidate over on the American people.

If given free rein, wrote Dr. Joost A. M. Meerloo, ad men will "knead man's mental dough with all the tools of communication available to them. They may water down the spontaneity and creativity of thoughts into sterile and streamlined clichés."

Critics commonly point to the spot television commercials used in 1952 on behalf of Gen. Dwight D. Eisenhower as proof that Madison Avenue believes it can sell candidates like toothpaste through the hypnotic repetition of a prescribed set of slogans.

Professional ad men deny these omniscient powers. In his talk before the Republican Club, Julian Koenig, president of Papert, Koenig, Lois, Inc., asserted that ad men have no magic formula for influencing the mass mind—that all they could do was present a candidate as honestly and forthrightly as possible and hope for the best.

"Whether we're talking toothpaste, cigarettes or Senators, I think agencies today have the responsibility of looking for uncommon denominators, of doing a job we can have pride in as well as profit," Mr. Koenig said.

In taking over Senator Jacob Javits's Senatorial campaign in 1962, Mr. Koenig added, the agency set as its goal the task of presenting the New York Republican "as he is." Hence the agency videotaped a series of informal street-corner question-and-answer sessions between the Senator and his constituents. The "commercials" were mostly of five-minute duration backed up by one-minute spots.

"The problem with 15 or 30-minute political presentations is that they hold no interest—no one stays with it," Mr. Koenig said. "We felt the one and five-minute segments were just right."

Good Ratings

The Senator's spots generally received favorable comment and good ratings—and, of course, he won by a landslide. The basic device used, however, certainly did not represent any form of mass hypnosis or hidden persuasion, Mr. Koenig noted. It was simply a matter of "revealing a candidate as he is, and doing it vividly, memorably and honestly."

Mr. Koenig's reassuring remarks will not allay the fears of many people about the dangers inherent in Madison Avenue's encroachment in politics. Nor will it convince the political professionals that ad men really know enough to be taken into the inner councils.

But one thing is clear: Now that television has become the critical medium in political warfare, politicians increasingly will have to seek the technical aid of advertising men who presumably know and understand the complex medium. To some degree, at least, candidates from now on will be "sold" like toothpaste, and people hungry for political power will doubtless bear in mind that Madison Avenue knows a great deal about toothpaste.

October 27, 1963

JOHNSON SEEKS POLICY ON PRESS

By TOM WICKER
Special to The New York Times

WASHINGTON, Feb. 8—"The news," Woodrow Wilson said, "is the atmosphere of events." And most modern Presidents, including Wilson, have devoted considerable time and effort to creating an atmosphere in which events might unfold to their liking.

Wilson, in fact, invented the modern news conference by inviting reporters into his office for question-and-answer sessions, although he would not allow himself to be quoted directly. Warren Harding tried the same method, committed an embarrassing goof, and thereafter required reporters to submit questions in writing; naturally, he answered only those he chose.

Calvin Coolidge and Herbert Hoover followed much the same cautious course and it remained for F. D. R. to resurrect the Wilsonian model and turn it into a highly successful source of publicity for himself and for the American people. Harry S. Truman found the peppery news conferences so well-attended that he moved them out of his office into an auditorium in the nearby Executive Office Building.

Cautious Course

Dwight D. Eisenhower and his press secretary, James C. Hagerty, were responsible for two major innovations in the developing institution of the news conference. They put General Eisenhower's remarks "on the record," permitting direct quotation, and they allowed the event to be photographed for later televising in full.

John F. Kennedy went a daring step further: he appeared in the spacious State Department auditorium, before hundreds of reporters, with live television cameras in action.

Despite these developments, there was nothing ordained, statutory or permanently established about the news conference as Mr. Kennedy practiced it. Nothing except custom and public pressure required a President to submit himself to the questioning of the press; nothing dictated to him the manner in which he had to undergo the ordeal.

That is why President Johnson has been able to alter sharply what had been the Kennedy and even the Eisenhower pattern; and it is also why some reporters and the television networks have been able to urge upon him—with creeping success—that he return to a news conference format that they

like, rather than one that he likes.

Consultations

Mr. Johnson was deeply concerned from the start to find ways and means of dealing with the press—knowing well the importance of "the atmosphere of events." A reporter who talked to him his first week in office was asked for advice on the matter; there were anxious consultations with Pierre Salinger, the White House news secretary, and with Johnson confidants.

The rather typically Johnsonian solution hit upon consisted of unannounced and informal news conferences held in the President's office and attended by whichever reporters happened to be in the White House at the time, but unlike the similar news conference of F. D. R.'s day, Mr. Johnson's remarks were placed on the record.

The President held a number of these news conferences. Last Saturday, partly because of pressure from reporters and the networks for regularly announced and televised news conferences, Mr. Johnson gave two hours' notice, then met reporters before film cameras in the White House screening room. The half-hour film was available for later televising.

White House sources say Mr. Johnson, sooner or later, will appear before live cameras as Mr. Kennedy did. The primary reason he has not done so, they say, is not that he is particularly afraid of a fluff but because he wishes to avoid situations in which he can be directly compared to President Kennedy. And there was no situation in which Mr. Kennedy appeared to better advantage than his news conference.

At his more formal news conference of last week, Mr. Johnson offered answers on General de Gaulle's Asian policies that seemed to be contradictory; this enhanced the belief in Washington that Mr. Johnson was uncomfortable before the cameras and therefore liable to error or slipshod performance.

Nevertheless, Mr. Johnson has seemed much more at home in the "quickie" news conference around his desk—and in one memorable instance over a bale of hay at the LBJ Ranch. In such circumstances, he seems to feel that he is among friends, that he is in control of the situation, that he is not so directly exposed to the public glare as he composes his thoughts and forms his words.

In his 32 years in Washing-

ton, the President has dealt with with the press countless times. He knows literally dozens of reporters by their first names, counts a small number as close personal friends, and has a friendly personal regard for a larger circle. In addition, the President is not without a politician's perception that those who create "the atmosphere of events" have a great power to advance or retard his fortunes. He has no wish deliberately to offend them.

As President, he has found time for a large number of private interviews with reporters—more than Mr. Kennedy was granting in the last months of his Presidency. In a number of other ways, Mr. Johnson has provided the press with more access to him than they had been accustomed to.

For instance, he personally briefed them on the contents of his State of the Union message. On most Presidential flights, he has talked with the pool of reporters flying with him. On Christmas Day, he combined an impromptu news conference with a tour of his ranch house.

In addition, Mr. Johnson has provided more information than is customary about his Cabinet meetings and conferences with other officials. He has even taken the unusual step of authorizing visitors to quote him to the press.

His relations with reporters have not been, however, entirely happy. As was the case with Mr. Kennedy, criticism gets under his skin and he is likely to telephone a reporter to argue about a piece he thinks unfriendly. His sensitivity to press criticism caused him to make the remarks—considered ill-advised by some of his supporters—about the Bobby Baker case. It was in response to press pressures that, against the advice of aides like Theodore C. Sorensen, he held his more formal news conference last Saturday.

On the other hand, some reporters believe that Mr. Johnson has sought to "use" the press on some occasions—for instance, by making it seem that it would be impossible to keep the budget under $102 or $103 billion, then cutting it to $97.9 billion in an apparent show of sleight-of-hand.

Thus, two months after Mr. Johnson took office, he and the press are still circling each other warily, each apparently willing to make friends but not quite sure the other is sincere about it.

February 9, 1964

President's TV Ordeal

By JAMES RESTON
Special to The New York Times

WASHINGTON, Feb. 29 — President Johnson achieved his major objective in his first live televised news conference today: He survived.

He approached this ordeal like a man going to the gallows. He insisted, from the first day he entered the White House, that the TV was not his medium, and he was right. But he got through today's assignment in good order: No runs, no hits, no errors—and several issues left stranded. Lyndon Johnson is a talker rather than a performer. The more natural he is, the more impressive he is, and the smaller the room the better. So he was out of his natural element today.

The New State Department building, where the conference was held, is as antiseptic as a hospital. When you go into it, you almost expect to hear somebody say on the loud-speaker: "Dr. Johnson wanted in surgery, please."

News Analysis

Sound Piped In

And the International Conference Room, where the President recited, is one of those big square half-acre, windowless I.B.M. rooms where the air, the sound and everything else comes out of a pipe.

President Johnson, who used to charge through the swinging doors of the Senate, scattering page boys in his wake, almost slipped into this operating chamber today. He was dressed in television blue—suit, shirt and striped tie—and he came prepared.

First, a sheaf of appointments: Bill Bundy, a favorite of reporters, to be Assistant Secretary of State for Far Eastern affairs; John T. McNaughton to replace Mr. Bundy as Assistant Secretary of Defense; Daniel M. Luevano to be Assistant Secretary of the Army; Mrs. Frankie Muse Freeman, a lawyer, to be on the Civil Rights Commission.

And then a surprise.

One of this country's closest held secrets has been the development of a high-flying, extremely fast successor to the famous U-2 sky spy plane.

Subjected to Pressure

When Secretary of Defense Robert S. McNamara began to be criticized as a big rocket man who hated manned aeroplanes, there was pressure to disclose the fact that this new plane, the A-11, had been tested successfully.

Such disclosure was opposed on the ground that one day, in a crisis, the country might use such a plane to the surprise of any enemy, so why tell the world about it? Why, indeed? But the President announced it anyway, explanation undisclosed.

All this he read out in a drone,

as if he were determined to be slow and casual about the whole affair. Besides, as every President knows, the more you talk in these journalistic inquisitions, the fewer questions you have to answer. He took his time.

It was the same with his answers to questions. When a man's name was mentioned, he gave you the fellow's biography. The President is a cautious man with a sure instinct for danger: He didn't exactly filibuster at the conference, but he managed to give a maximum of background and a minimum of news.

Technique Displayed

Nevertheless, the conference indicated a number of things, including just how far a politician will go to keep the television networks happy. It also demonstrated the Johnson political technique.

This is, primarily, to minimize or evade trouble. One reporter mentioned those two terrible words, "Bobby Baker." Mr. Johnson quickly tossed Bobby to the Senators, remembering to express confidence that they, in some mysterious fashion, would take "proper action."

Another reporter mentioned all the speculation about carrying the war to North Vietnam, which the Administration itself had inspired. Mr. Johnson thought speculation was "a great disservice" and pessimism even worse.

Panama? All he wanted was to be fair. Southeast Asia? All we wanted was peace. The outlook for the future?

"I am an optimist . . . I am encouraged and I'm not pessimistic."

Would he debate with his opponent in the Presidential election, and was it true that he had speculated on Richard Nixon as his opponent?

No, said he, he hadn't speculated on whether he'd run for President or even who he'd run against "if I do run." This he said without even a flicker or a smile.

What did he mean by saying last week that the Communists were playing a "dangerous game" in Vietnam, and what had he intended by that phrase?

He intended, by saying it was a dangerous game, to imply that it was a dangerous game. "That's what I said, and that's what I meant."

He was patient, courteous, cautious and verbose, and though he concentrated most of the time on what everybody knew, he made a better impression on the reporters in the room than he apparently did on those who saw him on television.

Nevertheless, he is now over an ordeal he dreaded, and can now return to his small spontaneous conferences, where he is usually more effective.

When the Client Is a Candidate

By PETE HAMILL

LAST Sept. 7, during NBC-TV's "Monday Night at the Movies," a rather tepid spear-and-sandal epic called "David and Bathsheba" was interrupted, as usual, by a commercial. It is not known how many viewers fled the celluloid travail of Gregory Peck at that point to grab a beer from the refrigerator, but among those who stayed were a good number of Republicans. At the end of one minute, they had been transformed into angry Republicans. The commercial they saw was the first of the campaign sponsored by the Democratic National Committee, and despite the subject of the interrupted film, it was not about slingshots or even about the ingredients of a palace bubble bath.

Instead, a little girl with wind-tossed hair was shown in a sunny field, picking daisies. As she plucks the petals of one daisy, she counts. On the sound track, coming in stronger and stronger, a male voice counts backwards. When the girl reaches 10, the man's voice, in the doom-filled cadences of the countdown, reaches zero. The screen is rent with an atomic explosion. "These are the stakes," says the voice of Lyndon Baines Johnson. "To make a world in which all of God's children can live, or go into the dark. We must either love each other, or we must die." The doom-voice returns, urging viewers to vote for President Johnson Nov. 3: "The stakes are too high for you to stay home."

WITHIN days of its first showing, "the little girl with the daisies" had become what is probably the most controversial TV commercial of all time. Newspapers were bombarded with letters from angry Republicans, and from some dismayed Democrats. Telephone calls were made to TV stations in protest. Mail piled up in the offices of the Democratic National Committee in Washington. The little girl became part of the rhetoric of the campaign. Democratic Vice-Presidential candidate Hubert Humphrey said he thought the commercial was "unfortunate." The little girl was part of a Time cover on "The Nuclear Issue." Nearly three weeks after its first showing, Republican candidate Barry Goldwater was moved to say: "The homes of America are horrified and the intelligence of Americans is insulted by weird television advertising by which this Administration threatens the end of the world unless

PETE HAMILL worked in an advertising agency (but never on a political account) for four years before he became a writer.

all-wise Lyndon is given the nation for his very own." For the first time in history, the use of advertising had become a campaign issue in an American Presidential election.

The sound and fury over that little girl and her daisies (the commercial disappeared from home screens in early October), also managed to focus attention on a fact of political life that went past the immediate issue of nuclear responsibility. Its very appearance, and the reaction which followed, dramatized the fact that to an almost overwhelming degree American political campaigns are being fought on the TV channels of this country through the use of advertising. Neither major party will release exact figures, but a reliable source in the advertising business estimates that each party will spend about $12,000,000 trying to get its candidate elected, almost half of which will be spent on advertising placed through agencies. The Republicans are emphasizing commercials in which Senator Goldwater speaks softly and confidently while answering the questions put to him by voters. The Democrats run a wider gamut. As a case history, let's take a look at how the agency chosen by the Democrats — Doyle Dane Bernbach Inc.—is handling its end of the campaign.

FIRST, it should be mentioned that D.D.B. is, in the judgment of its peers, one of the best in the business. At this year's annual exhibition of the Art Directors' Club of New York, the agency won five of 11 gold medals (no other agency received more than one). The Outdoor Advertising Association of America awarded D.D.B. first, second and third prizes this year for ads appearing in markets of over 750,000.

At the 1964 American Television Commercials Festival, the agency took down seven bests out of 38. Of seven gold medals awarded by the Advertising Writers Association of New York this year, D.D.B. won two. Last year, the advertising trade publication Printers' Ink chose four D.D.B. ads for the 22 best of "all time" going back more than half a century. No other agency had more than two.

The agency is noted for its dramatic graphic presentation (under the supervision of award-laden art director Robert Gage), its catholicity of clients (El Al Israel Airlines and Volkswagen, the Lincoln Center for the Performing Arts and the Cracker Jack Company) and its reputation

---

for good taste. It has yet to run an ad showing a cross section of a stomach.

"The little girl commercial was deplored on absolutely erroneous grounds," says 53-year-old William Bernbach, who is president of the agency he founded in 1949 with Ned Doyle and Maxwell Dane. "The central theme of this campaign—whether you like it or not—is nuclear responsibility. Perhaps that theme is not a tasteful one; there is no way to make death pleasant. But I am satisfied that our presentation of the issue was done dramatically, truthfully, and with taste. We built an agency on taste."

ONE man's taste, of course, may be another's heartburn, but the Democrats insist they were drawn to Doyle Dane Bernbach specifically because of its reputation for good taste and dramatic impact. The agency had never before handled a political account.

"I think it was President Kennedy who suggested we contact them," said a staffer with the Democratic National Committee. "He saw a Volkswagen ad with the headline 'Think Small.' It was the kind of thing that appealed to his sense of humor."

Negotiations for handling the Democratic National Committee had already begun about six weeks before President Kennedy was assassinated. They were completed in mid-February, and Bernbach, who supervises all creative activities in the agency, immediately began assembling a unit to work on the account. He drew entirely on the company's 800 employes, the only catch being that those he chose had to be dedicated Democrats.

By April, he had assembled 40 people, including art directors, copywriters, TV production men and assorted secretaries. They were to function as a separate, self-contained advertising agency, leaning on the full company only for help with media (selection of outlets and placing of advertising), market research and, of course, the payroll department.

At the head of this agency-within-an-agency, vice-president Doyle placed a tall, curly-haired 41-year-old recruit from Benton & Bowles named James Graham. "I had just joined Doyle Dane Bernbach," says Graham, an affable, articulate fellow who does not look much like the Madison Avenue stereotype. "But I wasn't brought in especially for this account, like a gunslinger or something. I was simply asked if I would like to head this unit working with the Democrats, and I said I'd love to."

SINCE then, Graham has been working a six- and sometimes seven-day week, up to 18 hours a day, out of a block of 20 cubicle-offices specially rented by the agency on the seventh floor of 20 West 43d Street.

The main offices of Doyle Dane Bernbach occupy the 20th to the 29th floors of the same building. Graham's chief associates on the account are Sidney Myers, senior art director; Aaron Ehrlich, TV executive producer; and Stanley Lee, copy supervisor. They work well together, and none could remember precisely who came up with the little girl and the daisies idea. "It was a kind of joint effort," Graham says.

The experience thus far, all agree has been highly educational. "The very first thing I did was to start reading," Graham remembers. "I had never worked on an account like this before and had really never been involved in politics. Politics had interested me, of course, the way it does anyone who reads newspapers and magazines. But when I came to this, I realized how little I knew. I learned more in two months about American history, political institutions and government than I had in the previous 40 years."

THE unit decided to start completely fresh (to this day none of the executives has looked at any advertising used in the Kennedy-Nixon campaign of 1960). "We felt the campaign was different from almost any other in recent years," Graham says. "For one thing, L.B.J. took over from a martyred President. Therefore, the ideas and styles of two men had to be indicated. For another, it has been many years since the lines of American political arguments have been drawn so sharply. And yet, there are hazards involved. The lines can shift suddenly and sharply.

"Back in April and the early summer, for example, it looked as if civil rights would be a big issue. The Civil Rights Bill had not been passed, and to some of us it seemed as if Johnson had an awful lot to lose by pushing it through. I was frankly awed by his courage. We had prepared a lot of material on civil rights then, expecting it to be a big issue. But frankly, it looks now as if we'll never use it."

THE first step Graham took was to set up liaison with the Democratic National Committee. Lloyd Wright, a three-year-veteran of the Peace Corps headquarters in Washington had been chosen by the Committee as media coordinator. Wright reported directly to Bill Moyers, another alumnus of the Peace Corps, now a special assistant to President Johnson. Doyle Dane Bernbach opened an office in Washington, headed by a copy executive named George Abra-

ham, located in the subheadquarters of the Democratic National Committee at 1907 K Street.

It was Wright's responsibility to inform Graham of any major changes or shifts in emphasis in the campaign as determined by the professional politicians. To that end, Graham spent considerable time in Washington, working at the highest levels. "I know this sounds corny," he says, "but the first time I walked into that White House to see the President of the United States, I got a hell of a tingle."

"The way an agency functions with a political party is not much different from the way it functions with any other account," says Graham. "They know what they want to say, and we know how to say it."

Basically, the upper echelon decided initially to hammer away at the following points: Nuclear responsibility, Social Security (while a voice speaks of Republican William Miller as "admitting" Goldwater's advocacy of voluntary Social Security would wreck the present system, a Social Security card is torn in half on the screen) and anti-Goldwater Republicanism.

THE agency has also prepared commercials stressing Johnson's experience, the War on Poverty program and what one agency member called "the inconsistency bit." The last was illustrated by a commercial quoting Goldwater's repeated opposition to public power projects like T.V.A., and his advocacy of a huge Federal irrigation project in his home state of Arizona.

"Almost all of these ideas come from within the unit itself," Graham says. "The client does not interfere, although he ultimately has the final say. We get plenty of outside suggestions, mostly through the mail, but we never use them. The one thing I learned from working with serious politicians is that you have to know the terrain yourself. You can't wing it. It has to be your own baby, all the way down the line, or the consistency and the general impact suffers."

"It's sort of like a commando squad," Graham says, laughing. "I'm just afraid that when this is over we'll all slow down. This is like a two-year campaign being done in two months, and I'm afraid that when the group is broken up, we'll have to go through a decompression period."

GRAHAM denies that the little girl with the daisies was withdrawn under protest, or under orders from Washington. "We just felt that it had outlived its usefulness," he says. "Some things we did four weeks ago now look to us as if we had done them 12 years ago. They lose impact after too much viewing, and that's when we change them. But we might run our little girl again before Nov. 3."

In at least one important respect, the agency treats its client like any other. It collects its fee through the standard agency procedure of the 15 per cent media discount. Under this system, advertising media ranging from TV to daily, newspapers allow a 15 per cent discount on advertising placed through agencies. But the agency charges the amount the client would have paid anyway, and pockets the discount money as its fee.

THE bulk of the advertising budget was channeled into radio and TV commercials, mainly of a duration of one minute, with a good number of special five-minute spots (a special length made available to political parties during election campaigns). A series of half-hour shows, featuring speeches by President Johnson, was also prepared and an election eve special is in the works. It is an indication of how audiences for political messages have changed that no print advertising is included in the budget of the Democratic National Committee. Such advertising is handled by local groups supporting the Democratic ticket. The agency has prepared a local advertising kit for use in these local groups in newspapers and magazines, but the cost of such advertising must be borne at the local level.

"The choice of where we advertise is based on sound media considerations," says Graham. "We want to reach the most people, most effectively. And we want to reach a broad audience. The switch voter could be in any audience. The only shows we avoid are those for children or those with high teen audiences. They can't vote."

THE choice of media is in the hands of the Media, Research and Marketing Division of the agency, but it is doubtful that the research department has ever had to answer anything like the questions put to it on this particular account. Among other bits of research done in the past few weeks: Everything there is to know about right-to-work laws; everything Barry Goldwater has ever said about nuclear weaponry, Social Security, public power; everything Scranton, Rockefeller and Romney have ever said about Barry Goldwater; everything Barry Goldwater has ever said about Barry Goldwater's fitness for the nation's highest office; everything William Miller has ever said about the ethics of public men.

SO far, there have been no advertisements prepared that are being slanted to particular audiences. But Graham did say that it is possible that certain advertisements seen in the North might not be seen in the South. And all of the commercials so far shown have omitted the name of President Johnson's running mate, Senator Humphrey. Graham says that his omission has a purpose, but it does not involve a fear that Humphrey's name will hurt the ticket (actually, pre-convention polls of the South showed Johnson running best with no running mate at all).

"We just don't feel that people vote for Vice-Presidential candidates," Graham explains. "We're selling the President of the United States."

It is precisely this conception of the President-as-commodity that frightens many people—including some in the advertising business — about the relationship between advertising and politics. All admit that Americans are the best salesmen in the world, but critics fear that their enormously clever and sophisticated techniques could be placed in the service of unscrupulous, or totalitarian, types and that advertising could thus contribute to the destruction of the democratic system. One critic, Joseph H.

Murphy, New York State Commissioner of Taxation and Finance, said in a radio address recently: "A political candidate needs all the assistance he can get, and a qualified public relations or advertising agency is of assistance in guiding him. But he should not be a slave to the agency."

Murphy and other panelists agreed that the real danger occurs when issues are sidetracked in favor of emotional appeals and the creation of a spurious "image." "We see candidates very nearly packaged like soap," he said, adding that agencies "should not take so primary a role."

The defenders of advertising seem to feel that most of the criticism is based on an exaggerated idea of the importance of the agency, and that the forebodings about dark results are highly improbable, mostly impossible and generally ludicrous.

"Advertising is just an intelligent way for a free political party in a free country to get the issues across," says Graham. "Besides, we have a free press in this country and if unscrupulous types ever did get involved, they wouldn't get very far. The real problem is that too many people think of advertising in stereotypes. It's chic to knock Madison Avenue."

IN Washington, none of those involved is doing any knocking. "We expected a flock of guys in nine-button suits," said one highly placed Democrat. "But instead, we got first-rate professionals. We have nothing against advertising in general. As a matter of fact, George Reedy [Presidential press secretary] is the biggest press agent in this country."

Graham has been leading a hermitlike existence, broken

only by sprints to Washington and long hours in viewing rooms. Most of his time is spent in his small half-office on the seventh floor. The walls are covered with maps of the United States broken into election districts, signs saying "ALL THE WAY WITH LBJ" and four sensitively drawn casein portraits: three of John Kennedy and one of Lyndon Johnson, by an artist friend named Bernie Fuchs.

IN one drawer of his cluttered desk he keeps clean shirts and in another his dirty laundry; his suits are cleaned and pressed at a nearby one-day cleaner's. He takes lunch and dinner on the run, but he doesn't seem to mind. Instead, one recognizes all the symptoms of the disease of political fever. "It's the greatest experience of my career," he says, his face beaming. In the hall, there is a hand-lettered calendar with the days crossed off with red grease pencil. The calender goes to Nov. 5 "because it makes a full line," but the important date is Nov. 4. That has been blacked out, with a photostat of a crowd scene replacing it. A member of the crowd is seen carrying a sign with one word written on it: "PEACE."

"I actually got home last weekend," Graham said, on this late afternoon in his office. "And my wife told me what happened to my 9-year-old son Michael. He goes to St. Joseph's in Bronxville, and one afternoon his teacher asked all the kids to get up and tell the class what their fathers did for a living. Michael got up and said 'My father's a politician. I don't see him any more.'"

The phone rang and Graham picked it up. The client wanted to see the rough cut of the War on Poverty commercial.

October 25, 1964

In The Nation: The Mirrors of 1600 Pennsylvania Avenue

By ARTHUR KROCK

WASHINGTON, Feb. 17— The White House Press Secretary is what the President makes him or allows him to make himself. On this choice depends whether he will be the President's principal and authoritative deputy for disclosing those actions and reactions to events and speculations that the President chooses not to convey in person.

Authoritative Channels

Stephen T. Early, James C. Hagerty and Pierre Salinger, Press Secretaries of Presidents F. D. Roosevelt, Eisenhower and Kennedy, were the principal and authoritative channels of such information to the public. For no fault or desire of his own, George E. Reedy, who serves President Johnson in the same capacity, definitely is not. Instead, the President is making unexampled use of special writers in the press, as distinguished from straight news reporters, to provide (with a positiveness and identification of the source that also is unexampled) the answers to questions of legitimate public concern that Reedy apparently is restrained from giving.

The result is that, while the practice has obvious advantages for the President and the special writers, the same cannot be said for the public interest. Vital information is transferred from the news columns, where the prevailing press standards require that it be presented with cold objectivity. Lacking the official imprimatur of statements made by the White House or the President in person, the product at any time can be minimized as hearsay or an honest misunderstanding. Even though there can be no question of the professional competence and integrity of those whom Mr. Johnson is authorizing to give answers to vital questions that his press secretary perforce evades, they do not subject him to the accountability imposed by a public record.

A Bumper Crop

The last three weeks have yielded a bumper crop of information which even intense cultivation of official areas could not produce. For example, when Washington was buzzing with speculation why the then-ailing President did not send the Vice President as the chief representative of the United States at the funeral of Winston Churchill, and Mr. Johnson was keeping his own counsel, the following appeared in a syndicated column on Feb. 5:

It's Only Gossip

The President is strong in his reaction against the cocktail circuit gossip here that his failure to send Vice President Humphrey . . . indicates friction with Humphrey. Johnson didn't pick Humphrey as Vice President to go to funerals; he needs him and is using him to put through the legislative program.

On Feb. 10 and 15, respectively, the President was clearly the direct source of descriptions of his irritation with a 'too demanding press" by two syndicated columnists. "Mr. Johnson feels," wrote one, "that most of the criticism directed at him is not only petty but contradictory. . . . He recites chapter and verse, at the same time declining to say that they do, in fact, get under his skin."

"The President laughs," cozily confided the other to his readers, "and with every justification, when he hears it said he is afraid of a formal press conference. Most of these . . . are in fact rather laughable. . . ."

Last week the vigor with which Press Secretary Reedy rejected rumors—growing out of the promotion of Thomas Mann to Under Secretary—that Secretary of State Rusk was on his way out demonstrated that, in this matter at least, he was sure of his ground. But much more emphatic assurance came in two syndicated columns published today, with every mark of Presidential authority. "It may be stated, on the highest possible authority," asserted the author of one, "that Mr. Johnson is determined to keep Dean Rusk as Secretary of State just so long as a man named Lyndon Johnson is President and Rusk is willing to stay." "It is impossible," declared the other, "to overstate the confidence that Johnson has in Rusk. . . . All reports and rumors [of a breach] are false. . . ."

These indeed are words with the bark on, affixed with the brand "L.B.J." But they are as evanescent as breath on a mirror, in comparison with those spoken in reply to questions by the President himself at the formal news conferences now so few and far between.

February 18, 1965

Johnson News Aide Finds Some Danger In Unfettered Press

WASHINGTON, Oct. 23 (UPI) —A free and unfettered press is a "necessity, but sometimes a dangerous necessity" in a democratic society, Bill D. Moyers, Presidential press secretary, declared today.

It is necessary, he said, "because the people need to be informed; dangerous because it is people who do the informing, and people are always susceptible to mistakes and misinterpretations and errors of judgment."

Mr. Moyers made the statement in a transcribed radio interview for the Storer Broadcasting Company's program, "Report to the People."

There is always the risk, he said, that the information the public gets is not "the fact as it actually happened, but the fact as one other person saw it."

Mr. Moyers conceded that news reporters were not deliberately inaccurate or deceptive. They are just human beings, he said, adding:

"Reporters are like pointers. If they get off in a direction from which a scent came, but where there's no quarry, they may run around all day looking for something that isn't there."

He also said in reply to questions that he did not think the press was overly critical of President Johnson and his actions, but he added:

"They are too picayune from time to time, and too inaccurate about what they are picayune about."

Among illustrations Mr. Moyers gave was a newspaper report saying the President had installed a Muzak system in the White House. He said the Muzak was in fact installed by another President several years ago.

"Here, about something in which the public wasn't interested," he said, "the erroneous impression was given that the President had spent the taxpayer's money to install a Muzak in the White House."

October 24, 1965

The President and the Press: Their Relationship Continues to Be Uneasy

By JOHN D. POMFRET
Special to The New York Times

WASHINGTON, Feb. 27 — "Mr. President," the reporter began, "there have been reports that there may be a change—"

"What reports?" President Johnson interrupted. "I don't want to deny just rumors."

"There have been newspaper reports," the reporter began again.

"What newspaper?" bristled Mr. Johnson.

"Several newspapers, including The Washington Post, including The New York Herald Tribune, and others, that Ambassador Goldberg may be replacing Secretary of State Rusk sometime this summer. Would you care to comment on it?"

"No," Mr. Johnson snapped. Then he went on: "I have not seen those reports. I would not believe that The Washington Post and The New York Herald Tribune would be in the business of either predicting or nominating my Secretary of State."

This exchange yesterday at Mr. Johnson's news conference indicated that relationships between the President and the press were about as usual—mutually testy.

Reasons for Friction

In part, this arises from the traditional conflict between Presidents and the press. Reporters invariably want to know more, particularly about policy while it is still in the formative stage, than Presidents are willing to divulge.

In part also, it arises from Mr. Johnson's own personality and political outlook. The President is sensitive to criticism, especially when it implies that because of his Texas background he is devoid of grace, insufficient in manners and intellect, and generally a country bumpkin.

More important, however, is Mr. Johnson's preoccupation with his political standing. To those who have asked him why he worried so about what was written about him, he has replied that he had to because these things influenced public opinion and the political leader who disregarded this factor did not remain a political leader for long.

Search for a Format

The President's concern with his public standing has led him into a seemingly restless search for a suitable platform from which to put his points across.

He has tried news conferences on live television from the East Room of the White House. Observers here feel that

Mr. Johnson handles himself well in these encounters, but they seem to make him uncomfortable and he has not held one since Aug. 25.

Mr. Johnson seems to prefer the less formal setting of his own office—the site of the news conference yesterday — where reporters cluster around his desk to ask questions.

Most of all, however, the President appears to prefer speaking directly to the American people on television.

It is regarded as significant that Mr. Johnson's new deputy press secretary, Robert H. Fleming, has spent the last nine years in the news end of the television business. He left his job as Washington bureau chief of the American Broadcasting Company last week to go to work at the White House.

An important part of Mr. Fleming's job will be to see to it that Mr. Johnson's television appearances are as polished and effective as possible.

Mr. Johnson's preference for talking directly with the American people over television is just one element in what seems to be an intensive effort to dominate what is disclosed about him and his Administration, and when it is disclosed.

All Presidents have been concerned with information policy. Mr. Johnson's preoccupation with it, however, appears to attract his attention to seemingly inconsequential things.

A few weeks ago, for example, when the President was in the process of deciding whether to resume United States air strikes against North Vietnam, he noticed a news ticker item that quoted Vice President Humphrey as saying that Mr. Johnson had left a White House dinner early because he had a cold. The President sent a message to Mr. Humphrey saying that he did not have a cold.

To those who wondered why such a detail was worthy of the President's notice, Mr. Johnson's aides replied that he did not want the American people to think that he was making important decisions when he was sick. The Vice President, by the way, denied that he had said that the President had a cold.

Mr. Johnson has a particularly intense dislike for unauthorized "leaks" about his plans.

Searches within the Administration for the sources of leaks sometimes reach such a pitch that some Government officials outside the White House have wondered whether Mr. Johnson did not prefer secrecy for its own sake.

White House aides reply that Mr. Johnson dislikes leaks and speculation because they reduce his "options."

One example they cite is the leak of a plan devised by Walter W. Heller when he was chairman of the President's Council of Economic Advisers. The plan called for distribution of Federal tax revenues directly to states to spend as needed.

When the plan was disclosed in The New York Times, George Meany, president of the American Federation of Labor and Congress of Industrial Organizations, told the President that he was firmly against it. It was sensitivity has made it difficult on occasion for reporters to get information not only while an event was in motion, but also afterward.

The entire story of the Administration's successful efforts late last year to roll back aluminum and structural steel price increases and particularly the degree of Mr. Johnson's own involvement has never been fully told.

In refusing to discuss these incidents, White House aides have made it clear that Mr. Johnson does not intend to make public any information that might provoke a quarrel with the business community. This continued secrecy is in sharp contrast to the large amount of information that was available after the event on how President Kennedy shortly before the 1964 election and Mr. Johnson needed labor's support politically and for legislation he intended to present to Congress. As a result, Mr. Johnson, according to aides, felt forced to shelve the plan, which he thought had merit and might have been put across had he been able to prepare the ground.

The President's political went about rolling back a steel price increase in the spring of 1962.

Some observers believe that Mr. Johnson essentially has a far less episodic view of events than Mr. Kennedy did. He seems unwilling to have officials in his Administration discuss sensitive actions even after the fact because he thinks that such revelations will impede his flexibility in the future.

So great was the Johnson Administration's effort to obscure what was happening dur-

ing the aluminum price increase battle that it denied that an announcement it would sell aluminum from Government surplus stocks had anything to do with the price increase, although it plainly did.

Such incidents have led some critics to question the credibility of the Administration's information.

The White House is acutely sensitive to these criticisms and, although it believes they are unwarranted, sometimes takes them into account in deciding what to do.

Thus, last December, when The St. Louis Post-Dispatch printed a partial account of an alleged peace feeler transmitted from Hanoi to the Government by two Italians, the White House ordered that an exchange of letters involving the incident be made public. The action may have ruled out any possibility that the contact might have borne fruit, but White House aides said that this was preferable to letting stand the newspaper's assertion that the United States had rejected the peace feeler out of hand.

The principal problem regarding credibility of information given out by the Administration has revolved around the war in Vietnam and involves essentially the question of whether the Administration has been candid with the people over the widening dimensions of that conflict.

The situation in Vietnam has raised a further basic question in the minds of some observers. In deciding what to tell, President Johnson must strike a balance between the right of people in a democracy to know what their Government is doing, the nation's own interest, which may not always be served by disclosure, and his own political self-interest.

Some reporters think the White House press secretary, Bill D. Moyers, would sometimes be better advised to simply say "no comment" in answer to some questions than to give partial answers that may lead reporters astray. Mr. Moyers seems to have swung toward this view. He recently has been saying less in public briefings and making himself available to reporters individually for more detailed discussions.

Mr. Fleming's arrival appears to portend an even more pronounced trend in this direction.

Dateline, Washington

THE ARTILLERY OF THE PRESS. Its Influence on American Foreign Policy. By James Reston. 116 pp. Published for the Council on Foreign Relations. New York: Harper & Row. $3.95.

By JOHN KENNETH GALBRAITH

SOME years ago I volunteered the estimate that for tedium, tendentious commitment to the clichés of the cold war and recurrent incompetence, the publications of the Council on Foreign Relations were among the worst in what speakers at the off-the-record sessions of that distinguished organization frequently refer to as the Free World. This expression of limited admiration extended to those articles in Foreign Affairs — "Canada Looks South," "Mexico Looks North," "Switzerland Looks Up," "Panama, Between Two Worlds" — by which foreign ministers in those lands demonstrated the limited literacy of their ghost writers.

The reaction to these gentle thoughts was generally favorable, with the exception of the staff and some officers of the Council, whose response closely paralleled that of the British Establishment to a treatise by Malcolm Muggeridge on the Royal household. I subsided into awed silence, but ever since I have been looking at the Council's publications, and if they are bad I take this as proof of my position, and if they are better I regard my indiscretion as having done good. If matters like this are well handled, it is hard to lose.

This book by James Reston is well on the credit side, even allowing for the tact that can easily temper the treatment of a very active news columnist and editor. It incorporates the substance of the most recent Elihu Root lectures at the Council, and is readable, informative and, by my standards at least, wise. It makes a great many points — from the fact that The New York Times earns more money from a half-interest in a paper mill in the wilds of Northern Ontario than it does on Times Square, to Reston's conviction that John Foster Dulles's talents as a lawyer were not transferable and that, by implication, the Washington International airport should now be equipped with a plaque identifying it with his services to the law firm of Sullivan & Cromwell. In consequence, in a fine old lecture tradition, the author rambles; but this he frankly concedes, and his main points come into clear focus.

One of these, in sharp contrast with some somber assessments by

MR. GALBRAITH, professor of economics at Harvard and a former Ambassador to India, wrote "The Affluent Society," "The Great Crash" and other books.

other Washington newspapermen of the terrible responsibilities they carry, is that in relation to the Presidency their power isn't much. Technology, the nature of modern armament and diplomacy, and the apparatus of the Welfare State have added enormously to the President's authority in modern times. The power of the press is diminished, along with that of the Congress and, presumably, also businessmen, bankers and the public at large.

The President cannot control what is written about him (though he can considerably influence those who are too close), but he can make the news that is written. This is a much greater source of power. Reston's conclusion, with which I devoutly agree, is that we hadn't better have any more limitations on the press in the interest of national security, national solidarity, national interest, the C.I.A., or general bureaucratic convenience. The press is already, relatively speaking, too weak and docile.

His other rather more orthodox point is that foreign policy is badly handled by the newspapers. The wire-service tradition puts the most arresting facts in the first paragraph, the next most needed information in the second, and so on down to the temperature that day. Most papers chop off after a paragraph or two. This is fine for football, murder, indecent assault, Stalin's daughter and even war, but utterly inadequate for a revolution in the Dominican Republic or a new move on the Common Market by Harold Wilson.

The columnists help to give body to this material, but for too select an audience. Reston hopes that one day these will be an audience — a "remnant," it was called by Matthew Arnold — large enough to support far more substantial and much more judicious and critical reporting on foreign affairs. He hopes that the newspapers, together with radio and television, will foster it. But he is not completely sanguine. "In the press the networks, politics, the church the schools and universities, and in commerce, the pressures today are running in favor of the conformist majority that offers the popular and easy answers to our problems. So great are these pressures and so alluring the rewards of conforming to them, that we see all around us the resignation and even the surrender of many of our very best men and women."

This is a fair warning, but it could be too pessimistic. There is certainly comfort in conformity and wonderful music in the applause of an audience which has heard precisely what it wants to hear, but there is also a great and perverse satisfaction in stating the truth, and it is a pleasure which those with a preference for candor are too inclined to think peculiar to themselves.

ODDLY enough, on reading Reston, I had another thought. Over the years he has learned to treat all people in the manner of a newspaperman who must one day go back and see them again. It is clear from any close reading of this volume that he has the gravest doubts about present policies in Vietnam and the wisdom in this grave matter of the President and the Secretary of State. But one must, on occasion, read between the lines. There are few newspapermen with a firmer, more dour instinct for the truth than Reston; my thought was that he should now indulge himself more often in the added pleasure of plain and candid and categorical speech.

April 2, 1967

White House Says Newsmen Eavesdrop on Johnson Talks

WASHINGTON, April 25 (UPI)—The White House accused reporters today of eavesdropping on President Johnson at social receptions.

"The press is impeding receptions, standing by the President and overhearing his conversation," Mrs. Elizabeth Carpenter, press secretary for Mrs. Johnson, told newswomen in explaining why they would be restricted to the receiving line at a diplomatic reception tomorrow night. Reporters have "more and more unfortunate ways of crowding about the President," she said.

Mrs. Carpenter said she was acting on the President's orders in ordering newsmen to withdraw to the receiving line.

April 26, 1967

Mr. Nixon and the Press

By JAMES RESTON

The candidates and the press are fussing at each other again and this is the way it should be. They have different jobs and in many ways they are natural enemies, like cats and dogs. The first job of the candidate is to win, and he usually says what he thinks will help him win. The job of the reporter is to report what happens and decontaminate as much of the political poison as he can. The conflict is obvious.

Richard Nixon has always understood this natural antagonism between the candidate and the reporter. He has studied it more than almost any man in American political life over the last generation, yet somehow he never managed to master the problem.

Presidents and Opinion

It is interesting to try to analyze why, because the thing that separates the really effective Presidents from the rest is that the effective ones did learn how to deal with public opinion while the others didn't.

Mr. Nixon has had more than the normal share of trouble with reporters because, like Lyndon Johnson, he has never really understood the function of a free press or the meaning of the First Amendment, which protects the freedom of the press.

Ever since he came into national politics he has seemed to think that a newspaper reporter should take down and transmit what he says, like a tape recorder or a Xerox machine. He has learned to live with interpretive journalism more comfortably in this campaign than he did in the campaign of 1960, but he still suffers from this old illusion that the press is a kind of inanimate transmission belt which should pass along anything he chooses to dump on to it.

Accordingly, he has been critical of the press ever since he gave the world Spiro Agnew of Maryland and the press concluded that maybe this was not the Republican party's greatest gift to the human race or even to the Vice-Presidency.

It is easy to understand Mr. Nixon's problem. The press is a nosy nuisance for a candidate, fallible, skeptical, often inaccurate, and a menace to his maneuvers and objectives.

There are really only three ways to deal with the press: The best way is to tell them everything: this keeps them busy and eventually exhausts and bores them. The next best way is to tell them nothing, which at least excites the cop in them and gives them the excitement of a mystery. The worst way, which is Mr. Nixon's and also Mr. Johnson's way, is to try to manipulate them, to pretend to be candid in private conversation, but to use every trick in the book to get them to fill the headlines and front pages with calculated trash.

Air of Total Sincerity

Maybe Mr. Nixon had to take this road. Mr. Humphrey is not unfamiliar with it. George Wallace is perfectly cynical about it and cuts up the press nightly and winks to the reporters with his off-camera eye, but the Republican candidate has tried to use the press with an air of total sincerity, and this is the heart of his trouble.

Nobody has seen the reporters privately in this campaign more than Mr. Nixon, or talked more freely, but usually on an off-the-record basis. His television performances are masterpieces of contrived candor. He seems to be telling everything with an air of reckless sincerity, but nearly always in a controlled situation, with the questioners carefully chosen, the questions solicited from whole states or regions, but carefully screened.

He is now complaining publicly about how he and Mr. Agnew are misrepresented in the columns of The New York Times, but he has been refusing to be questioned on the record by editors of The Times and most other major newspapers ever since the very beginning of the campaign.

Mr. Humphrey and Mr. Wallace submitted to questions by C.B.S., but Mr. Nixon sent tapes of replies made in his carefully prepared broadcasts. And his refusal to debate Mr. Humphrey on television is merely one more incident in a long campaign of packaged broadcasts.

It is easy to say that this is not a model of democratic discussion, but it is hard to say it has failed. It takes a natural, confident, experienced and even wise man to grapple with the hard and often unfair questioning of the press in public, and he decided to duck it and he is apparently doing all right.

Yet it is fairly clear at the end that more people are going to vote for him than believe in him, and more newspaper editors than newspaper reporters are going to endorse him. It has been true of Mr. Nixon ever since he came into public life, and it helps explain the anxiety in the country today even among the people who will probably put him in the White House.

October 30, 1968

Newsroom Intruders

By JACK GOULD

AS AN aftermath of television coverage of 1968's hectic events, including the assassinations of the Rev. Martin Luther King Jr. and Senator Robert F. Kennedy and the turmoil of the Democratic National Convention, there are a number of disquieting developments that underscore increasing governmental involvement in the content of news appearing on the home screen. Whatever ailments may exist in electronic journalism, implied or real control over the output of the media is far from the cure.

A mere list of the current instances of second-guessing about what TV news has or has not done illustrates both the diversity and the dimensions of the problem.

In a class by itself—and potentially the most constructive undertaking of them all—is the study being conducted by the President's Commission on Crime and Violence, headed by Dr. Milton S. Eisenhower. This project will include a review of the problem of depicting violence, mainly in news coverage but also in entertainment, and it is to be hoped that the commission will come up with a sober appraisal lending itself primarily to implementation by the broadcasters themselves.

The complaints and compliance division of the Federal Communications Commission has directed the networks to answer in detail protests voiced by viewers over the coverage of the Democratic convention. Under what statute the FCC implies a right to make a judgment, either by some form of overt action or by mere dismissal of viewer complaints, is certainly a hazy question from a legal viewpoint.

The House Interstate and Foreign Commerce Committee also has injected itself into the coverage of the Chicago convention and, according to reports out of Washington, may come out with a report dealing not only with what the networks did do but also with what they might have done. Richard S. Salant, president of CBS News, hinted in a speech last week that "some agency of government" wanted to see tapes and films that were not used as well as those that were.

The Attorney General's office of the state of Illinois also has taken upon itself an inquiry into TV coverage of events in Chicago, even though it clearly has the flimsiest sort of legal grounds for making an inquiry into a news medium over which it has no authority.

The FCC also has been holding hearings, always with the implied possibility of revoking or suspending the station's license, into a marijuana party photographed by WBBM-TV, the Chicago outlet of CBS. The question has been raised whether the televising of such a séance, necessarily involving some advance

51

preparation of lighting and position of cameras, constituted the staging of a felonious act. CBS contended its role was that of a legitimate investigative reporter and that to argue about the propriety of depicting the party was secondary to advising the public of the widespread use of marijuana on college campuses.

Still another pending case concerns the action of an employe of the National Broadcasting Company in concealing a microphone in the room of the Democratic National Convention platform committee. Such "bugging," if established in a court of law, is a Federal offense.

Experienced television newsmen are the first to admit that the mechanics of the medium do pose distinctive problems. If a network receives advance word, for instance, that a disturbance may break out in a given locale, is it an incitement to riot or a normal news precaution to send a mobile truck to the area? Certainly, the mere presence of the camera does invite "acting" on the part of those eager to gain attention, and not all TV reporters in the country have been above the fabrication of a scene, if only because "action" is so much more vivid on the home screen and under TV's economic rules may have a practical consequence in the reporter's take-home pay.

To some extent, the various Congressmen, committees, regulatory agencies and state officials are capitalizing on the almost pathological worry of some networks that their licenses may be in jeopardy — stations and networks will make all sorts of compromises before inviting the risk of · losing franchises worth millions. Within the TV world there is a very real degree of anticipatory censorship, and the networks simply do not undertake those journalistic ventures which might stir up a storm. None of the networks was notably aggressive in covering the Presidential campaign itself, and many individual stations were either privately delighted by or completely indifferent to the failure of Congress to pass enabling legislation allowing political debates. In the waning hours of the campaign, it was enlightening to see how the networks did manage to find ways of affording some appraisal of the candidates and issues after weeks of saying they couldn't. Political scientists could argue for years over whether television's passivity during much of the campaign did not coincide with the strategy of President-elect Richard M. Nixon, who agreed to appear on interview shows only when the late surge for Vice President Humphrey became evident.

The networks cannot wholly exempt themselves, in short, from inviting politicians to conclude that TV is a medium which can be effectively controlled either through campaign expenditures or hints of legal reprisals against those networks or outlets failing to toe a partisan line.

The problem of TV journalism is not that it has been too aggressive but that it has not been aggressive enough, most notably in its pussyfooting around major stories originating in Washington itself. If the morale and energies of the network news departments are ever to enjoy maximum application, they need managements which are not afraid of an ultimate court test on the First Amendment.

But the overriding question is not that electronic journalism, as with all media, can stand improvement and refinement of its methods or an awareness of its limitations. The far greater problem is that, under one guise or another, government is showing an inclination to intrude in the specifics of reportage, to reach a judgment on what is right or wrong to put on the screen, to assert itself with respect to program content. Private TV may have its faults, but they are insignificant in comparison with the possibility of government sitting in the editor's chair in television. For substantiation of such a consequence there is one place to look: French television under de Gaulle.

November 17, 1968

In The Nation: The Whole Truth and Nothing But?

By TOM WICKER

President Nixon said during his news conference Monday night that he was willing to take his chances on the press, "so long as the news media allows, as it does tonight, an opportunity for me to be heard directly by the people."

No one ever really disputed that right, or could, but Vice President Agnew did suggest in his celebrated dissertation on television news that the American people had "the right to make up their own minds and form their own opinions about a Presidential address without having a President's words and thoughts characterized through the prejudices of hostile critics before they can even be digested."

Informing the People

What, then, of the responsibility of Presidents to inform the American people accurately and fully? Not even Presidents, after all, can be infallible.

It was probably a pure slip of the tongue when Mr. Nixon said that the Marines had built this year "over 250,000 churches, pagodas and temples" in Vietnam; and the point was well-taken anyway, because the Marines have built 117 churches and 251 schools, no mean feat. And Mr. Nixon was not wrong, just not very clear or instructive, when he said that a $5,400 minimum income for every family of four in America would cost $70 to $80 billion a year.

Guaranteed Income

Actually, the Government could guarantee every family of four the difference between what its breadwinner now earns and $5,400 for perhaps $20 billion a year; it could, that is, if they all kept on working and earning as much as they do now. If, on the other hand, they all quit earning anything, and started taking the full $5,400 from the Government, the cost would zoom up to at least $40 or $50 billion, and probably more.

The figure Mr. Nixon used would apply to a program with a so-called "work incentive" which would reward people for earning more income, on a declining scale of assistance that would reach zero only when the family of four was actually earning about $11,000 annually.

The impression the President left on the subject of Laos was much more seriously misleading. There are, he said, no American "combat troops" in Laos, when the fact is that the most that should be said is that there are no American "ground combat troops" there, so far as we know. There are Air Force pilots who drop bombs, and plenty of C.I.A. agents and Army personnel who organize, train, accompany and support native armies.

Mr. Nixon went on to say that American involvement in Laos was "as a result of the Laos negotiations and accords" worked out by the Kennedy Administration. But those accords supposedly guaranteed the neutrality of Laos. In fact, both North Vietnam and the United States violate the accords every day.

The Thai Subsidy

The President was no less facile in discussing the subsidy being paid Thailand for its division in South Vietnam. He said this was similar to subsidizing Western Europe after World War II, when it could not afford its own defense.

In this case, however, members of the Thai expeditionary force in Vietnam are being paid twice what they would receive from their own Government for duty in Thailand, and subsidy is also being paid to Bangkok. The Thais would not be fighting in Vietnam at all if the cost · of their doing so were not being so underwritten. Neither would the forces of South Korea or the Philippines. To call these troops in these circumstances "volunteers," as Mr. Nixon did, is to misuse the word and mislead its hearers.

Frankness Preferred

There may be a good case to be made for the American part of the war in Laos, and for hiring friendly troops to fight in South Vietnam. After their experiences of the past few years, it is a good bet that the American people would rather hear the President make those cases frankly and honestly, rather than once again to be told that there is no real problem, no reason to ask serious questions or expect candid answers.

December 11, 1969

Since Spiro Agnew brought up the subject,

How Well <u>Does</u> TV Present The News?

By HERBERT J. GANS

Bissell in The Nashville Tennessean

"Don Spirote."

IN the old days monarchs sometimes beheaded messengers who brought bad tidings—and today's rulers, though shorn of the divine right of kings, occasionally still feel the same urges. When the Nixon Administration sent Vice President Agnew forth in November to attack the TV networks for their bad tidings, he asked the citizenry to cut them down to size with letters and wires.

In his speech, the Vice President depicted network evening news programs as the work of a small band of conspirators who choose news and commentary in a way designed to sell the liberal ideology of the New York-Washington axis. That Agnew is not alone in this view is suggested by the many favorable responses to his speech—and also by the applause drawn by George Wallace when he made the same charge in 1968.

However, network newsmen do not function the way Agnew said they do. I have been studying the networks as well as news magazines for the past several years, and insofar as there is bias in their product it stems, I find, far less from their own prejudices than from the nature of modern journalism. While for the most part my subject in this article will be network news, some of my observations also apply to the news magazines, and probably to the national press in general.

THE network newsmen's task is not an easy one. Although millions of events take place in the world every day, only a few can be reported in the 22½ minutes available for news in the half-hour evening news program. But since events can only become news if someone is there to cover them, the newsmen must first *anticipate* which events might be newsworthy, and then decide which they can cover with the always limited number of reporters and cameramen. (What events become news therefore depends in part on the size and locations of the news-gathering bureaus.)

Thus, millions of events are reduced to a few dozen filmed and so-called "tell" news stories every day. These are reviewed on a given network by the news program's executive producer and about three producers and news editors; by about 4:00 in the afternoon, the executive producer selects the 20 or so stories

HERBERT J. GANS, professor of sociology and planning at M.I.T., is writing a book on the national news media.

that will be shown and told that night.

The final selection process accordingly involves only one man, rather than "the no more than a dozen anchormen, commentators and executive producers" Vice President Agnew described as being in on the decision—and most anchormen and commentators do not participate regularly in it. However, the executive producer's choices are based on the judgments of his assistants, and these in turn rest on prior anticipation and selection by assignment editors who send crews out on a story, and by the crews themselves, who compete with each other to produce film that will get on the air, and so affect how a story is covered. So do the film editors who cut the film into a story—and all these participants in the process are constantly checking the wire services and other news media to see what *they* have selected. In reality, then, many hundreds of people take part in deciding what will be shown every evening.

Since their decisions must often be made in split-second time, newsmen use a number of easily and quickly applied criteria to determine what events will be broadcast as news, principally (1) media considerations, (2) professional judgments, (3) professional and personal values and (4) audience reaction.

●Media considerations are perhaps most important. Since the print and electronic news media are competing against one another for audiences, each medium favors stories which it can or thinks it can do best. Thus, TV newsmen look particularly for events which can be filmed, while news magazine men prefer those that can be described dramatically, and picture magazine men look for stories best told through still pictures. This rule is by no means ironclad; TV will not ignore important stories that do not lend themselves to filming. The heavy use of film on TV news shows is, however, also based on the assumption that the audience prefers film to a talking anchorman. (If the audience preferred getting all its news from Cronkite or Huntley and Brinkley, there would be no film, and the networks would happily save the expense of sending three- or four-man crews all over the globe.)

●The professional judgments of newsmen on what to report and how to report it are a close second in importance. These are based on assessments of a story's importance,

A NEWSCAST IS BORN—
(1) A.B.C. anchorman Frank Reynolds starts out the day by reading the papers. (2) This is the news desk that backs him up (with more animation than is evident here—it's still morning). A technician (3) excerpts a Dec. 12 Agnew talk for use on the show. (4) The newscast begins, Reynolds on camera.

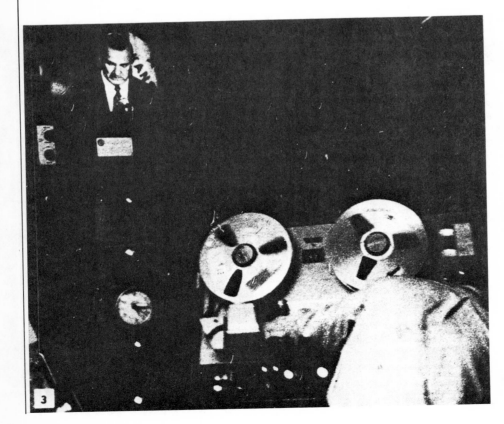

topicality, interest and dramatic quality.

On a national news show, stories are considered important if they are significant to the nation, by which is meant the Federal Government, or many people around the country. Important stories include almost all the public activities of the President (and Presidential candidates), major decisions by the Congress and its committees, changes of policy by agencies of the Federal Government, sharp changes in the economy, policy or personnel changes at the top levels of major foreign nations — especially if these affect American foreign policy —and wars, major disasters and occasional crimes involving many or famous people or large sums of money.

IN addition, there are always a number of continually important or "running" stories, and events relating to them are given frequent coverage. In recent years, the war in Vietnam, racial conflict, the youth rebellion and inflation have been running stories.

One of the most easily applied criteria for choosing

stories is topicality. Important stories are always told as quickly as they happen, partly because the possibility of scooping the competition, a hark-back to the days when news traveled more slowly, still excites almost every newsman.

Stories with high-interest content need not be topical; they are TV's equivalent of the newspaper feature and they are gathered both for use in case there are not enough important stories, and to vary the pace of the show. Such stories are those which interest the newsman. They may provide a detailed look at one part of a running story, at a new educational experiment in the ghetto, or at a new weapon being used in Vietnam. They can be human-interest stories about the poignant experience of an ordinary person, or they may take a nostalgic look at an old ship that has been retired—newsmen have a soft spot in their hearts for old ships, trains, cars and planes. Or they may be bizarre — what newsmen call man-bites-dog stories.

But above all, TV news films must have dramatic quality. This means action, people doing something, preferably involving disagreement, conflict or adventure. Thus films of an anti-war demonstration are more likely to get on the air than an interview—"talking heads," in the TV newsman's jargon, are considered dull. A violent

demonstration is rated more camera-worthy than a peaceful one, which is why TV will usually show whatever altercation takes place during a march, even if 99.9 per cent of the demonstrators did nothing more than walk. If the talking head belongs to the President, it will obviously be shown, but a more important statement by an underling is likely to be paraphrased by an anchorman in 20 or 25 seconds. Most of the decisions which the Vice President ascribed to the personal bias of the newsmen are actually based on the desire for exciting film.

● In making their selection, newsmen also apply values, most of which are professional — and are thus shared by most of their colleagues—and a few of which are personal. Newsmen prefer stories that report people rather than social processes. Nothing pleases a newsman more than to be able to tell an important story in terms of an individual — for example, the pacification program in Vietnam as it affects a Vietnamese peasant. The people newsmen seem to like best are individualists struggling against superhuman odds, a Chichester who conquers the oceans, or the astronauts, and people who can triumph over Big Technology and Bureaucracy.

SOME of the professional values are based on assumptions about how society

works. For example, while most sociologists would argue that leaders arise out of and in response to group needs, most journalists assume that leaders emerge independently and can transform their groups—that things only get done through "leadership," and that progress results from the availability of skilled, well-intentioned leaders. One result of this is that journalists place great importance on rooting out incompetent and ill-intentioned leaders, and the exposé that catches an officeholder with his fingers in the public till is many a newsman's dream.

The newsman's professional values regulate how he reports events. He sees himself as a detached outsider who does not try to inject himself into his story and never states an explicit personal opinion. Even the TV commentators, such as Eric Sevareid and Howard K. Smith, view themselves as analysts and interpreters, providing background information and possible explanations for the usually descriptive stories broadcast by their colleagues, and they offer personal opinions much less often than the Vice President suggested.

The newsman also attempts to be objective, and although he knows that his choice of stories and the way he covers them involve subjective considerations, he compensates by trying to be fair, especially on a controversial story. Fairness is achieved through balance, by giving both sides when reporting.

NEWSMEN's personal values are expressed mainly in choosing among interesting stories. One former TV executive producer, for ex-

66The approach of 'last resort' is Government subsidy of TV news.99

ample, was fond of features about children and nature. In recent years the anchormen have been given to expressing personal interests: for example, Cronkite's enthusiasm for the space program, Brinkley's for the showman tactics of the late Senator Dirksen and Huntley's and Smith's occasional editorializing in favor of the war in Vietnam.

Still, the impress of *explicit* personal values on news reports is far less important than Agnew charged, mainly because personal feelings are censored out by the professional emphasis on objectivity, but also because most newsmen do not have strong political inclinations or allegiances. They are not ideologists and their opinions change over time. A few years ago, I would guess, many newsmen favored the Vietnam war; today, the large majority are doves, although the percentage that favors unilateral withdrawal is probably no greater than it is among the citizens polled by Gallup or Harris.

Personal values do affect news presentation, however, but almost always unconsciously through the quick and intuitive choices of words and films picked to describe people and events. When newsmen describe the National Liberation Front as the Vietcong and then as the enemy, rebelling ghetto residents as rioters and mobs,

"Insofar as there is bias in TV newscasts, news magazines and newspapers, it stems far less from their own prejudices than from the nature of modern journalism."

"Who's Next?"

Feb in The Philadelphia Inquirer

55

draft resisters as draft dodgers; when they report democratic elections in South Vietnam and elsewhere but forget that candidates may have been nominated in a smoke-filled room; or when they smile with relief if the stock market goes up, they are making personal judgments.

Objectivity is nigh impossible here and, besides, the newsmen cannot be truly detached outsiders. Like most other professionals, they are a part of the middle-class culture that dominates America, accept most of the economic and social values of that culture, and often judge other societies by these values. Thus, they generally see what goes wrong in Socialist countries more easily than what goes right, are more aware of propaganda in Russian pronouncements than American ones, consider protesters more militant than insistent lobbyists, and deem marijuana-smoking more of a social problem than alcohol consumption.

By and large, the newsmen's personal values are not much different from those reflected in the majority opinions expressed in the polls, and if an accurate assessment were made of loaded adjectives and raised eyebrows on TV news shows, their implications would probably be more conservative, politically, than assumed. After all, until this year, the cameras watching antiwar demonstrators always seemed to focus on the bearded ones and on Vietcong flag carriers (although mainly because they provided the most dramatic film footage), and I doubt that any anchorman has yet chosen favorable words to describe a militant black-power advocate.

Still, newsmen are on the whole more liberal than their total audience, but this is probably because professionals are generally more liberal than laymen. Most newsmen consider themselves to be political independents, and if one looks closely at their unconscious value judgments, they will be liberal on some issues, conservative on others, and even radical on a few. (Although some viewers think that one network news show is more liberal than another, this is not really true; even the several correspondents reporting from Vietnam for the same news program differ in their views about the war.) However, few radicals, conservatives or even doctrinaire liberals go into journalism, for people with firm ideologies find it difficult to practice journalistic objectivity and fairness.

● Audience reaction is taken into account less in the selection of stories than in the way they are presented. Newsmen make sure that stories are told clearly, that difficult words are eschewed, that stories which might alarm people are told as calmly as possible, and that those which might raise false hopes are carefully hedged. (A report on a new development in cancer prevention will, for example, emphasize the experimental nature of the work.)

But when it comes to choosing stories, the newsmen believe firmly that if they like a story, the audience will like it, too, and they have no information about the audience to the contrary. Executive producers know the Nielsen ratings of their shows, but unless they are slipping, they pay little attention to them, and besides the ratings tell them nothing about what the audience is like or what it wants.

Moreover, TV newsmen do not want to know much about their audience, feeling that they are professionals who have a job to do, that the audience does not know how to cover the news, and that even if it did, audience opinions taken into account would restrict the professional's freedom to do a professional job. For example, most newsmen know that the audience has relatively little interest in foreign news, but they persist in presenting it because they are convinced that the audience needs to know what is going on in the world.

INDIRECTLY, however, the audience plays an infinitely greater role. Newsmen believe —and audience research tends to bear them out — that the audience, though massive, is not especially loyal or attentive and that it must constantly be attracted to the news show and the individual story. That is why TV newsmen rely on film more than on the anchorman, why they select the most dramatic film, why they leave room for interesting stories, and such. In the last analysis, this is why the riots, the war, the antiwar demonstrations, the opposition to the President and all of the political conflict that Agnew complained about being overplayed are covered so fully.

Newsmen need not consider audience reactions more than they do because the professional criteria which guide their journalistic decisions automatically make sure that a large audience will be attracted, and provided with a balanced viewpoint that alienates as few people as possible. The professional criteria thus fit in with the fact that newsmen are, after all, employed by profit-seeking businesses. Yet newsmen are also somewhat more than acquiescent servants of capitalism; few are happy about the commercials that interrupt the news, the little news they can provide in 22½ minutes, and about the small staffs and bureaus with which they must cover the world. Even so, the newsmen also want a large and attentive audience, and even in countries where government finances TV news, few producers deliberately choose an undramatic piece of film over a dramatic one, if they are free to choose.

ONE of the things that impressed me most when I began my study was how free American TV newsmen are to cover what they consider most important or interesting — and how little network management, sponsors and government officials interfere — or interfere effectively. Network management remains aloof—at least as long as the ratings do not slip precipitously. Executive producers, however, like magazine and newspaper editors, also know what stories will displease management: principally those detrimental to the firm's business interests. (This taboo rarely extends to parent companies, however, and N.B.C.'s coverage of war and space activities is not influenced by R.C.A.'s role in defense production.)

Sponsors do not interfere because they have no prior knowledge of what goes on the air. This is not true of all news programs; full-length documentaries now often have to be pre-sold, giving the sponsor some control at least over the topic of the documentary. But the evening news (though not the entire network news operation) is highly profitable for both network and sponsors, at least at N.B.C. and C.B.S., and an unhappy sponsor can be replaced from a long waiting list. Of course, executive producers do not go out of their way to antagonize sponsors; if a story on the relationship between smoking and cancer is scheduled, a cigarette sponsor will be informed that he is free to take his commercial out for the evening, and, in any case, the cancer story will not be placed immediately before or after a cigarette commercial.

Government tries to interfere far more often, and in several ways. One is by news management, forbidding the reporter access to information by stamping it secret, or by swamping him with official versions of the truth—a favorite method of the officers who put on the daily Saigon briefings known as the Five o'clock Follies. (Also, in Vietnam transportation may not be available for correspondents who want to film a battle that is being lost.)

Another method of Government interference is pressure, and both Presidents Kennedy and Johnson were known for their alacrity in calling network executives or newsmen to object to a story they had just seen on the evening news, and all Presidents use their press secretaries for this purpose, too. Network executives who receive such calls rarely pass them on to the offending newsman, for they want to protect his independence. At other times they may make sure that the attempt to pressure becomes public knowledge, in which case it boomerangs — and this discourages Presidents and other officials from complaining too often.

Newsmen who receive calls from unhappy politicians generally shrug them off. They know that by the next week the politician will have realized that he needs the newsman more than the newsman needs him. Of course, repeated pressure may make newsmen more careful in choosing words, but it will also leave a residue of ill will.

Politicians will also try to win a reporter to their side by wining and dining him, but the national newsman is much freer from political or commercial interference than his local colleague, who has less job security and prestige, and a less powerful employer as well. Sponsors can complain about the news coverage of a local station, and politicians can persuade friendly sponsors to do it for them, or send out building inspectors to find code violations in the studio.

National networks and sponsors are not so easily bullied. But another reason why the national newsman has so much freedom is that he rarely abuses it; he is reined in by his high visibility, his professionalism and by the sometimes terrifying feeling of responsibility that comes with broadcasting to an audience in the tens of millions.

CONSEQUENTLY, censorship is usually limited to matters of "taste." Anchormen never swear, of course, and until recent years even profanity uttered by an excited participant in a filmed news event was excised. Today what cuts are made are mostly in Vietnam film. Because the evening news is on at the dinner hour when children are watching, the bloodier battle footage is censored. As a result, TV has not, despite all claims to the contrary, shown the real war; few films have shown men dying or being wounded, and, in fact, print journalism has been more explicit about the bloodshed. (There are other reasons than taste for sanitizing the battle coverage; for one thing, networks don't like to ask their personnel to risk death by getting into the midst of a battle and only rarely do the South Vietnamese torture their prisoners or GI's cut ears off dead Vietcong when cameramen are around.)

Whether public protest results in self-censorship is difficult to determine. Coverage of ghetto rioting has been scarcer since the networks were blamed for publicizing Detroit and Newark, but the riots have been less severe since then, and newsmen say they are no longer so newsworthy.

Still, the battle footage from Vietnam seems more war-weary these days, although even in earlier years the war was not always covered so enthusiastically as people now think. But there is really little need for explicit self-censorship, for most newsmen are not inclined, professionally or personally, to see events and news stories from a radical perspective, of the left or the right. (Thus, radicals who believe that if newsmen were only liberated from their network restraints they would tell the truth as radicals see it are only deceiving themselves.)

DESPITE all the emphasis on objectivity and fairness, however, the criteria by which newsmen choose the news have political consequences for what becomes news and how American society is depicted. Displeased politicians and viewers find nothing easier than to attack that depiction as distortion, but because the newsmen do not purposely distort the news, and because one man's distortion is another man's truth, it is fairer to suggest that the news provides a *selective* picture of reality.

Consider the emphasis on topicality, for example, and how it affects the presentation of news. Topicality cuts reality into individual events and incidents and de-emphasizes the long-term processes of which these events are only a part. For example, because the Vietnam war has been covered in terms of daily battles and body counts, the nature and progress of the war was often lost from view until the Tet offensive in 1968. And although correspondents frequently ended their daily battle reports by warning that, in guerrilla warfare, the day's battle is not very significant, still they had to report a new battle the next evening.

The journalistic definition of what is important news also has a marked effect on the picture we get of society. A lot of attention is paid to governmental leaders and little to the less visible individuals and institutions that set the limits within which these leaders can act. For example, the President's actions and inactions with respect to inflation are depicted in much more detail than the economic institutions and policies, including the Government's, which have brought about inflation.

The prevailing definition of important news thus gives an inordinate amount of publicity to the President and other high Government officials—which they consider their due and take for granted—while more crucial activities by lesser known mortals may not be reported. Ordinary people appear in the news only when they commit major crimes; participate in strikes, riots and demonstrations; are victims of disaster—or happen to bite a dog. And since leaders tend to be of high income and advancing age, while newsworthy ordinary persons are often young or poor, the over-all picture of society that emerges is of responsible or at least respectable activities by an aging élite and not so respectable or unusual activities on the part of young lower-income groups.

But the major effect on the picture of society comes from a combination of these three things: media considerations, the choice of interesting stories, and the stress on dramatic quality. What most news media do, therefore, is over-emphasize unusual events. As one TV executive producer put it, "All journalists assume that the Boy Scouts and the churches are operating normally; our job is to cover what goes awry."

As a result of all this, we get a lot of selective glimpses. Vietnam coverage has mainly emphasized the dramatic side of the war, with just an occasional glance at the politics of South Vietnam. These politics, in turn, have been depicted mainly as a conflict between anti-democratic generals and democratic civilians, while little attention has been paid to the larger political and economic structure. Although quasifeudal landlords still have an inordinate amount of control over the South Vietnamese Government and economy, their activities and such basic problems as land reform have not often been dealt with on the TV screen or anywhere else in the major news media. But land reform is hard to put on film, and is not a very exciting subject to Americans in any case.

In domestic reporting, politicians are shown disagreeing with each other, but the compromises and what they compromise about are filmed more rarely. The college students who appear in news reports are usually protesters, or antiprotest protesters and drug users and the fact that differences still exist between management and labor becomes visible on the news front only when a strike is called and it becomes violent.

Even within the events that are covered, the scarcity of time and space allows the news media, particularly TV, to depict only the highlights, rather than a cross section of the action. What usually appears on film is only the most dramatic portion of a firefight, a riot or a demonstration. This may make the event look more alarming than it really is, and it may also leave out important aspects. For example, a group of radicals disrupted a medical convention in order to present their views but the film showed only the disruption and not the views they expressed. This happens frequently, irrespective of political position.

Newsmen's professional and personal values play a smaller role in shaping the media's picture of society. However, the journalistic theory that leaders are more important than followers sometimes results in too little information about the interest groups and larger constituencies leaders speak for even when they are national figures. And newsmen's personal beliefs enter in mostly to reinforce the middle-class values that pervade the news anyway.

The rules of objectivity and fairness have more impact on the image of society in the news. Objectivity can prevent the well-informed reporter from giving his conclusions about a topic he has investigated thoroughly; he can only report what various sides had to say. (Of course, reportorial analysis is also scarce because few news media provide the time or money for the investi-

One Man's Network

There is good reason to doubt that people get their picture of the world from the news reports. People develop their picture largely from other sources—especially from their own observations and by word of mouth from people they trust. That is, they rely mostly on an invisible network of amateur newsmen (their friends, neighbors and relatives) which intersects only occasionally with the professional networks.—H.J.G.

57

gative work that would allow a reporter to come to conclusions). As a result, a newsman who covers a speech that he knows to include some outright lies cannot, by the dictates of objectivity, tell what he knows; unless he can find a respected figure who will let himself be quoted to the effect that the speaker was lying, he must leave this task to the occasional commentator. But when the correction of lies is forced into the area of commentary, that correction is made to appear the commentator's personal opinion.

Even fairness in the press is not entirely fair to all sides. In a legislative controversy, the press believes it achieves balance by giving the Democratic and Republican views; no national news medium is likely to provide time for the S.D.S. and the John Birch Society to state their opinions. Perhaps more important, however, the press often only gives the view of the "other side" when it has a large or respectable constituency. For example, when antiwar demonstrations were in their infancy, many news media provided a platform for their opponents but saw little need to balance this with pro-demonstration rebuttals. Indeed, until a respectable Government figure, Senator Fulbright, came out against the Vietnam war, the national news media did not really consider the war a controversial issue requiring balanced treatment.

THAT the news, on TV and elsewhere, must present a selective picture of reality is inevitable, but the journalistic criteria now used for selecting news are not immutable and could be replaced. Despite their defects, however, they also have some virtues; for one thing, they have attracted a large audience and created interest in world events among a general public that only a generation ago knew almost nothing about them. Even the emphasis on dramatic conflict in the news may be desirable, for although the resulting picture of American society is overdrawn, anything else might attract even less public attention to the

conflicts that grip our society. Moreover, agreement on better criteria is difficult to reach, because all have political consequences and will result in the selection of news that seem distorted to somebody.

Consequently, the best criteria are probably those which maximize the diversity of news, giving all points of view a chance to be seen and heard. In this spirit, I would propose the following four additions to the current news fare:

"Representative" journalism. We need more descriptive and analytic reporting about, for, and by the poor, the not-so-affluent and other income classes; age, racial and ethnic groups; radicals and conservatives; and all groups whose activities and views are now covered only rarely, to inform them and to tell the rest of us what America and the world look like from their perspective.

"Unfair" and subjective analysis and commentary. However hard the newsmen try to be fair and objective, they cannot be fully detached observers. The only alternative is to have far more analysis and commentary, with commentators selected from *all* points on the political spectrum, age groups, income levels, etc., to interpret events and society from as many angles as possible. It would also be useful to hear regularly from foreign commentators who could tell us how America looks to the outsider and might puncture some of our more dangerous myths: for example, that we are a classless society, that we are less imperialistic than Russia or China, or that radicals and conservatives are usually ill-motivated and misled.

"Slice-of-life" journalism. In addition to what's going awry, the news ought also to present a cross section, in depth, of society's events and people. This type of news gathering would provide more information about the usual activities and problems of ordinary people, and, at the same time, seek to unearth the social, economic and political processes that really shape our life—and altogether try to reveal more of the iceberg that

is American society than just the tip that appears in the news today.

More news. We need a lot more news, particularly on TV, for even though it is no substitute for newspapers and magazines, it will have to be just that because it is the major source of national and international news for an increasingly larger majority of Americans all the time. More news means not only additional news broadcasts and longer one but also more investigative reporting and analysis.

These four* additions (the likes of which many newsmen have been proposing for some time) would provide more accurate and complete news coverage. Unfortunately, however, they would also be very expensive. For example, if news reports were to be more analytic, reporters would have to spend more time on every story and would need to be specialists. But more specialization would require more journalists, for specialists cannot produce as much as the present generalist, who can cover an amazingly wide variety of subjects without prior knowledge of them.

Whether anyone would be willing to pay the higher costs of these types of news is open to question. Many people seem satisfied with the present news fare and it is entirely possible that only by over-dramatizing reality can a large audience be attracted. Even so, people do not seem to be deeply involved in the news; audience studies show that only a minority of the 50 million reached by the network's evening news broadcasts watches every evening. National and international news is rarely of such direct relevance to people's daily lives that they cannot get along without it.

One may hope that more deeply realistic and representative journalism would arouse

* I would also propose a fifth addition: dramatic entertainment fare around topics and issues that appear in the news, similar to but more varied than the late lamented "East Side, West Side" and "The Defenders." For example, a TV series based on the idea of Upton Sinclair's Lanny Budd novels might attract more viewers to world events.

the interest of many persons now less attentive to the news, but most likely the only audience now willing to pay for more news is the highly educated group and it is already well supplied by various magazines, journals of opinion, educational TV and the few good newspapers. Where then, would the money come from? Certainly, existing TV stations and networks ought to devote a bigger portion of their profits from entertainment programing to the news, but viewers will have to exert considerable political pressure on the F.C.C. before it will stiffen the public-service requirements for broadcasters. And probably no one's news hunger is great enough to make pay-TV news financially feasible, or persuade Congress to establish TV-set license fees.

THEREFORE the approach of "last resort" is Government subsidy, at least until additions to the news fare can build an audience. Of course, this raises the danger of Government control—but so far, the Federal Government has had precious little success in controlling many activities it supports, including the print media which benefit from subsidized mailing rates. Still, one would have to find ways of making sure that Government support would not be denied to media, newsmen, and commentators who state unpopular ideas.

The subsidies should go not only to the networks (and other existing news media) but also to new journalistic enterprises, including non-profit ones. For example, why not a subsidy to allow journalists in the black or poor population to obtain TV stations and news programs, perhaps on a syndicated basis, to tell it like it is from their perspective? In fact, a major purpose of the subsidy would be to stimulate competition, for a society of more than 200-million people should be able to have access to more than three network news organizations and weekly news magazines. Ultimately, greater fairness and depth in news coverage can be brought about only by more diversity in the news. ∎

In The Nation: Tackling TV

By TOM WICKER

WASHINGTON, Aug. 12—It may well be that the House gave such thunderous approval to limiting campaign spending on television because members thought it would help protect them from rich challengers. It may also be that the Democratic Congress is moving this bill along because it clears the way for television debates between the Presidential contenders in 1972. Even so, the reform bill is a good day's work that will have far more important effects than these temporary and limited matters.

As for Presidential debates, Mr. Nixon will not always be in office and the removal of the equal-time restriction, which will make such debates almost certain, could come back to haunt the Democrats in the future. In 1964, after all, it was Lyndon B. Johnson who successfully restrained a Democratic Congress from making debates possible against a Republican challenger; this is obviously a cyclical advantage that will even out over the long haul.

The great thing is that House and Senate have now passed—although they have yet to agree on the scope of the measure—a bill that would drastically reduce the cost of television campaigning, while putting a virtually self-enforcing limitation on the amount any one candidate could spend. That amount would be determined at the rate of seven cents (three and a half in primaries) per vote cast for the same office in the previous election. It would have a self-enforcing effect because violations could be easily discerned by opposing candidates and the press; and because broadcasters would require candidates to affirm with each time purchase that they were not exceeding the ceiling—which would make a violation a deliberate deception.

Campaign Equalizer

This limitation on the rich candidate, combined with the bill's requirement that broadcasters sell political time at the lowest rate available to bulk commercial buyers, is likely to make it possible for more people to go into politics—which is the true reply to those who charge that this is an "incumbent defense bill."

Not all incumbents are poorer than their challengers, anyway. If the bill is given effect in time for the 1970 elections, for instance, Governor Rockefeller of New York would be sharply restricted in what otherwise, no doubt, he would spend on TV. It is a reasonable bet that an entrenched official like Governor Reagan of California is better heeled for the race than his challenger, Jesse M. Unruh, and the same is true of numerous important Senators and House members.

The recent trend, moreover, has been toward more and more TV campaigning at ever-rising cost, with no limit in sight, so that only the wealthy or those with ready access to the wallets of the wealthy could reasonably expect to win major office. Reopening the political arena to those without access to fat-cat money will be a major equalizer.

More to Be Done

Since the reform act also assures Presidential debates, it takes a long step toward full and fair utilization of television for political campaigning —which is to say, in the broadest sense, for political education. Nevertheless, a great deal more needs to be done.

The National Committee for an Effective Congress, a strong force in development of the present bill, is already at work on further legislation to strengthen requirements for disclosing the names of large political contributors, an area of persistent abuse. This is important, for although the limit on TV spending will sharply reduce campaign costs, huge sums still will be required and men with an interest will stand ready to provide them. And there remains the long-standing need for a program to encourage the small political contributor — perhaps through tax incentives.

Even more important, the door has barely been opened on the difficult area of equality of access to television—the question whether Congress or the opposition party or both, perhaps even others, should have the same general opportunity as the President to use this powerful medium. If that question is not settled quickly and responsibly, as Senator Muskie said the other day, "this phenomenon called television can virtually destroy the checks and balances so carefully established by our Constitution."

Exposing the President

By PIERRE SALINGER

LONDON—It is hard to realize, but it is still less than ten years since Presidents of the United States did away with the last safety controls over their words to the people of the United States and to the world.

Ten years ago, President Nixon's unfortunate words about the guilt of Charles Manson would surely not have been published if one can assume that Attorney General Mitchell and those with the President in Denver would have understood the import of his words on reading them in a typed transcript.

As late as the Administration of President Truman, a President could not be quoted directly without specific permission from the White House. The gradual evolution toward freedom to print a President's statements without allowing time for them to be scrutinized for possible grammatical or policy error began in the Administration of President Eisenhower.

He was the first to allow television cameras in his press conferences, but his press secretary, James Hagerty, maintained the right to a rapid review of the transcript. Only after such review was it available for direct quotation by the press or for transmission on radio or television news. The record shows that this prerogative was little utilized during the eight years of the Eisenhower Presidency, but the fact remains that this safety feature existed.

It was President Kennedy who first decided to permit free access to his words through the live television press conference. That decision was not taken without heated argument among his advisers. Dean Rusk, McGeorge Bundy and Theodore Sorensen all argued vehemently against such a step. Their view was that Presidents are likely, on occasion, to make statements that they will regret instants later. Such statements, they argued, could have the gravest implications for the Presidency and for the country.

The opposing argument, in which I participated with Arthur Schlesinger, Jr., and Kenneth O'Donnell — which was the basis for the position finally adopted by the President himself — was that in an era of ever more rapid communications, it was virtually impossible to protect a Chief Executive from himself. There was, on the other hand, much to be gained from the openness of a President with his people. With the growing mistrust of government—a phenomenon which has been accentuated over the past ten years——a President was more likely to be trusted if he showed his people he had nothing to hide from them.

Once President Kennedy had severed the umbilical cord with safety, it was exceedingly difficult, if not impossible, for his successors to change the ground rules without an assumption being drawn (fairly or unfairly) that they felt less sure of their ability to control their words than President Kennedy had.

President Johnson always felt particularly unhappy at having his press conference abilities compared unfavorably with those of President Kennedy. That is why, in the early days of the Johnson Administration, there was a conscious effort to change the format of the press conference. Many of President Johnson's early press gatherings were small informal meetings with the White House "regulars" held in the Presidential office without television cameras, where his own superb brand of informal persuasion with small groups could best be utilized.

The Manson case comments by President Nixon pose anew the central question of whether we should afford the President some protection — however minor in this day and age—from occasional spoken bloopers.

The subject is highly complex.

The idea that someday we could have a totally-programmed President — with all the human foibles well hidden from view—is not a far-fetched one. With the current cynicism and distrust of the institutions of government—and further than that of politicians in general — such a situation would seem to entail the greatest possible dangers for our democratic system.

The only logical way to combat such an attitude is with Presidential candor—even if such candor occasionally displeases or even repels a great many of his fellow citizens. The Manson case comments told us something about Mr. Nixon and it is far better that we know his breadth of character and his thoughts than to have them bottled up by advisers who may feel that some of the President's thoughts are not fit for consumption by the American people.

Presidents of today and of the future will have to live with their words, for better or for worse. This imposes a great responsibility on our Presidents, and to some lesser extent on their advisers. Certainly it will be legitimate in any future Presidential campaign to ask if the man we are being asked to elect to the Presidency is a man who is loose with his words.

As I believed in 1960 that it was advantageous to open the Presidency to greater public scrutiny, I believe today that once again to put a small protective muzzle on the words of Presidents would be a mistake—even if it were possible.

2 LOOKING AT POLITICS

On the television screen, the
1968 Democratic convention in Chicago
became vividly—at times alarmingly—alive

TELEFILMED FACES

Roosevelt and Landon Seen in Television Newsreel Test Across New York

By ORRIN E. DUNLAP Jr.

PRESIDENT ROOSEVELT and Governor Landon were telecast over the New York area a few days ago on the late evening air.

The few observers who have television receivers in their homes saw the two major nominees in the Presidential race talking to political gatherings as photographed by newsreel camera men. Mr. Roosevelt talked from the observation platform of a train. Mr. Landon addressed a crowd "somewhere in the East," according to those who looked in.

Pictures Clear on Long Island

The telefilm was run through the television transmitter atop the Empire State Building for broadcasting on tiny wave lengths. The "show" was so clear and the sound so loud on Long Island that it is believed the images were unreeled into space with sufficient power to overlap parts of at least three States, namely, New York, New Jersey and Connecticut.

A spectator described the quality of the images as excellent. In fact, he added that the reproduction was so "satisfactory" that there could be no doubt after seeing Mr. Roosevelt and Mr. Landon on the screen that political campaigning by television will be practical in the not-distant future.

The pictures were about six by seven inches in size and were screened without noticeable flicker.

The "show," which was on the air for more than an hour, also featured a film of the Spanish rebellion. The television "eye" was next turned on a large poster and several small objects, such as buttons on a dress, to demonstrate its ability in broadcasting all things which the electric camera "sees."

The pictures were telecast on the 49.75 megacycle channel and the associated sound on 52 megacycles. Both sight and sound leap from the same aerial rod simultaneously. The power of the ultra-short wave transmitter is rated at 10 kilowatts.

Improvements Are Expected

The pictures are broadcast at the speed of thirty a second and are comprised of 343 lines, the equivalent of the Electrical Musical Industries current television broadcasts from Alexandra Palace in London. The American engineers are understood to be developing a 441-line system, which will result in larger and clearer pictures.

The tests from the skyscraper have been under way since June 29. The engineers report that they have succeeded in "ironing the bugs" out of the transmitter and are now operating on a daily but irregular schedule.

The picture, as seen on the fourteen-control-knob set, has a greenish tint. The receiver is not as complicated to tune as the number of controls might indicate, for after the preliminary adjustments are made two or three knobs do the trick.

POLITICAL SPEAKING AND THE RADIO

From now on to election day the American people will have more than their fill of political speeches. Swarms of orators from both parties will be sent out to cover the land. It is to be feared that many of them will justify age-old criticisms and condemnations of political addresses. CARLYLE said that no man could make one, and tell the truth. He would be insensibly led into lying in order to please his immediate audience. GLADSTONE once remarked, in a somewhat similar vein, that the hearers had as much to do with the speech as the orator on the platform. They gave to him in vapor what he gave back to them in rain. But none of the old censors of this kind of public speaking could have foreseen what would be the effect upon it of the modern radio.

Some assert that it has killed political speaking. Certainly, it has destroyed the old fresh contact between the speaker and his audience, deprived him of the inspiration which comes from the sight of attentive and even fascinated listeners, and robbed him of the direct fire of flashing eyes and expressive features. Now he has written out his speech and talks it into a machine. When this new custom was beginning to come in, some one attempted to place a microphone in front of ELIHU ROOT. He exclaimed: "Take "that away. I can talk to a Democrat, "but I cannot speak into a dead "thing."

On the other hand, it may be contended that the radio has been almost the salvation of certain speakers. This was notably the case with President HOOVER. Before the advent of radio, it might have been said of him, as the Apostle PAUL said of himself, that he was in presence weak and in speech contemptible. But his voice went well over the radio, and by it he got the ear of millions who otherwise would not have heard him at all, or would have gone out from his audiences disappointed at his way of dropping his tones and speaking as if to himself alone. It is needless to dwell on the fact that President ROOSEVELT has made himself a technical master of the radio, so that by it his words have carried a charming personal quality all over the country and his voice rendered the most familiar in America.

Many political speakers are very poor over the radio. They think that they must shout in order to be emphatic. This is one of the natural and common offenses, committed by Colonel KNOX, among others. The easy conversational tones, with the instinctive sentence accents and cadences, which the radio makes it possible to convey, are quite beyond the conception or practice of many who make use of it. Then, of course, a radio speech has to be carefully timed. It must be written out and read with mechanical accuracy, which is fatal to the flashing inspiration of the old-time speaking face to face. In time, no doubt, speakers will have their imaginations cultivated to the point where they feel as if they saw their invisible audiences and could suit each phrase to the passing mood of listeners-in. At present, however, the whole practice of the art of political speaking over the radio is very much in a state of confusion. The masters of it are few and the misusers of it many. While in this field also knowledge comes but wisdom lingers, the machine which causes the trouble also affords the relief. One turn of the dial takes you instantly out of the presence of a speaker whom you no longer can bear to hear.

'BIAS' OF THE PRESS DEBATED ON RADIO

Irving Brandt Says Pro-Willkie Newspapers 'Distorted' News in Election Campaign

ARTHUR KROCK DIFFERS

Special to THE NEW YORK TIMES.

WASHINGTON, Nov. 17—The virtues and sins of the American press were debated by four well-known newspaper writers and editors here tonight in Theodore Granik's "American Forum of the Air," broadcast over a nation-wide network of the Mutual Broadcasting System.

The subject was "The Press and the Presidential Election," and the speakers were John W. Owens, editor in chief of The Baltimore Sun and Evening Sun; Herbert Agar, editor of The Louisville Courier-Journal; Irving Brandt, chief editorial writer of The St. Louis Star-Times, and Arthur Krock, chief Washington correspondent of THE NEW YORK TIMES.

Mr. Owens, replying to recent suggestions that newspapers which opposed President Roosevelt's re-election should fall into line, remarked that one might suppose, after an election in which the third-term tradition was abandoned, that all who believed in democracy would welcome an opposition press as one means of holding a balance in national life.

A Reply to Ickes

"Secretary Ickes argues that a newspaper has a constituency of readers which it must serve," said Mr. Owens. "When that constituency has definitely expressed its will at the polls the newspaper should obey. If Mr. Ickes is sound, the old New York World should have surrendered to Croker and Murphy, for New York City so repeatedly elected Tammany's candidates. Independent Democratic and Republican newspapers in Pennsylvania should have surrendered to Quay and Penrose. Chicago newspapers should have surrendered to 'Big Bill' Thompson. Kansas City newspapers should have surrendered to Tom Pendergast. Louisiana

newspapers should have surrendered to Huey Long. These machines were corrupt, but they won election after election. In the national field the Republicans won great popular victories in 1920, 1924 and 1928, the last one the most impressive of all. Under the Ickes rule Democratic newspapers should have surrendered to the Republican Old Guard. Needless to say, I do not think the Ickes theory is sound."

Agar Holds Press Timid

Mr. Agar admitted the justice of many accusations against the press. He declared, however, that it was not domination by advertisers or banks or other outside interests which injured our newspapers, but the newspaper publishers themselves.

"The press is not unfree, as in totalitarian States," said Mr. Agar. "It is merely timid. The press is not venal, as in pre-war France; it is merely conservative in the dullest sense of that word. This timidity and dullness are breaking the influence of the press, and may finally endanger its very existence.

"When a newspaper was very small business the press was bold and exciting. Modern inventions have made a newspaper bigger and bigger business, with an ever larger capital outlay. As the size of the enterprise grew, the boldness and the intellectual freedom diminished.

"So the trouble with the press is the publishers. As they became big business men most of them became timid business men."

Brandt Charges Bias

Mr. Brandt accused pro-Willkie newspapers, and specifically THE NEW YORK TIMES, of having been markedly unfair to Mr. Roosevelt in the recent Presidential campaign.

"The editorial position of newspapers is relatively unimportant if they print the news," said Mr. Brandt. "But in this campaign the pro-Willkie press turned itself inside out trying to elect its candidate. It gave the Republicans nearly four times as much news space as the Democrats. It played news up and played it down, suppressed news and distorted it, to aid Willkie and injure Roosevelt. That was the real reason why the President took to the stump.

"On Oct. 18 Arthur Krock published a column article in THE NEW YORK TIMES, defending the fairness of the press. I measured the news and feature space given by THE TIMES on that day and the next favorable to each party. Willkie got 71 per cent, Roosevelt 29 per cent.

"THE NEW YORK TIMES will rate among the fairest members of the Press-for-Willkie Club. Observe how this relatively fair newspaper

handled campaign news, and judge what the others were like. When Wendell Willkie dedicated a new building for his Consumers Power Company of Michigan his name appeared seven times in a NEW YORK TIMES story nearly a column long. Six days later the Federal courts found the Consumers Power Company guilty of violating the Wagner Act by fostering a company union and intimidating its employes. THE TIMES gave that story three inches, without Mr. Willkie's name. And what sort of a story? It said that the court had upheld the right of a Labor Board examiner to telephone to Washington. I could talk for ten hours giving similar instances of suppression and distortion of news by the free and impartial American press.

"A condition like this is a threat to the existence of our American democracy, for three reasons:

"1. Owing to the huge investment needed, it is practically impossible to establish new newspapers.

"2. The newspapers are permanently allied with reactionary financial interests whose lavish use of money in politics is in itself a threat to self-government.

"3. This combination of big newspapers and big money can be opposed successfully only by a glamorous personality, and sooner or later a choice between money and personality will lead to disaster."

Growth of Impartiality Traced

Mr. Krock traced the development of impartiality in the handling of news.

"Criticism of the press should always be welcomed by the press," said Mr. Krock. "Generally it is. An industry conducted by private persons which enjoys a constitutional guarantee of freedom has very special responsibilities. Among these must be candor in confessing its faults, honesty in seeking to correct them and all possible fairness in the news columns.

"More and more the daily press of the United States is discharging these responsibilities. I read many newspapers in the course of the recent campaign and the exceptions I noted were few. They were well-understood by the local reading public and steadily exposed by rival newspapers. So far as THE NEW YORK TIMES is concerned, as Mr. John Temple Graves 2d remarked in The Birmingham Age Herald, it was impossible for a reader who did not look at the editorial page to know which candidate THE NEW YORK TIMES was supporting.

"When I began newspaper work more than thirty years ago coloring the news columns with editorial bias was the usual thing. But, introduced to better journalism by a

few great publishers, the public began to demand it everywhere. Costs of providing the public with more news, and better editorials and features, grew great. Those papers which met the expensive demand necessarily became large commercial enterprises.

"But this expansion served as an automatic cleanser of the news columns. The papers which fell by the wayside were as often those which colored their news as those which were incompetently managed. The large news-gathering enterprises which have succeeded the small organs of personal journalism have, in most instances, discovered that existence depends on the honest presentation of the news. Their very size has nullified the pressure of advertisers and reader groups. The standards of publication have, I think, improved much more rapidly than political ones and those of other businesses.

"Wise and vigilant criticism, and brisk competition, have aided in producing this result."

Mr. Krock's Rebuttal

In the rebuttal following the main talks, Mr. Krock challenged Mr. Brandt's statement that THE NEW YORK TIMES had been unfair to the Democrats in its news coverage of the recent campaign. As to Mr. Brandt's statement that on Oct. 18 and 19 THE NEW YORK TIMES gave Mr. Willkie 71 per cent of news and feature space devoted to the Presidential campaign, compared with 29 per cent to Mr. Roosevelt, Mr. Krock asked Mr. Brandt what President Roosevelt was doing on that day and whether he had been campaigning.

"No," said Mr. Brandt.

"Then what do you think we should have done with the space—print what Mr. Roosevelt should have said?" asked Mr. Krock.

Mr. Brandt countered with the statement that he had kept score all week and that the average percentage of space given the Republicans was 69.5. He charged also that THE NEW YORK TIMES had sinned even more grievously in the amount of headline space on the front pages given to the Republicans.

"Is it your opinion," asked Mr. Krock, "that the ownership of THE NEW YORK TIMES gave orders to play down the Democrats and play up the Republicans?"

"I doubt if it was necessary," Mr. Brandt answered.

"Do you mean that the working newspaper men on THE TIMES themselves decided to give more space to the Willkie campaign than to Mr. Roosevelt?" asked Mr. Krock.

"Oh, no," said Mr. Brandt. "They were working under economic pressure."

November 18, 1940

Their Splendid Defeats

Mayor La Guardia at the Herald Square ceremonies day before yesterday found his thoughts straying back to the years of the James Gordon Bennetts. It was an age when newspapers "had a great influence in molding public opinion." American newspapers of fifty years ago will rise in their seats—or their graves—and give thanks for the compliment; but is it really deserved?

How much influence did the New York press have in fighting Tammany Hall through the years and into our own day? At long intervals, when the cup ran over, the populace rose against Tammany, and, after a brief spasm of virtue, forgot. The New York newspapers were almost unanimously against Tammany Hall, year in and year out, and the Tiger went its own happy way secure in the popular affection.

In Step With Whom?

Mr. La Guardia and his friends in Washington simply cannot get over the idea that newspaper editors are out of step with the voters today. But the newspapers in all the big cities have been regularly out of step with the municipal machines and the bosses. Through the years and the decades the newspapers went one way while the voting masses in the cities went the other way—the bosses' way.

This was the point made with such force the other night by John W. Owens of The Baltimore Sun; and it is a point which ought to find some merit in the eyes of a reform Mayor. If the newspapers had grown tired of keeping alive the torch of civic virtue through the long dark night, we should not have the saving intervals of good government we do have.

Radio Did Not Help

On this question of the relative influence and virtues of newspaper editors and radio voices Mr. La Guardia might have a look at a recent report by Bernard De Voto in Harper's Magazine. Traveling by auto across our great West and specifically across Kansas, it was borne in on Mr. De Voto that the radio has come to fill a long-felt want. These were for a long time the great empty spaces in newspaper coverage of world news. Practically, for the people of Kansas and surrounding territory, the outside world did not exist in their newspapers. But the radio has brought Europe and the world crisis to every lonely ranch house, filling station and lunchwagon; to every automobile equipped with an aerial.

And yet it is this section of our farther West that voted against President Roosevelt a couple of weeks ago. Four years ago and eight years ago, when the people were less generously supplied with radio news and presumably more dependent on their newspapers, the Far West voted solid for Mr. Roosevelt. This whole question of press, radio and folk behavior is not a simple one.

FREEDOM OF THE AIR

Mark Woods Discusses the Censorship of Commentators and the Reasons for It

By JACK GOULD

FREEDOM of speech on the radio has long ranked near the top of controversial issues in broadcasting and at the moment perhaps no one is more directly involved than Mark Woods, president of the Blue Network.

It is Mr. Woods who has believed it necessary on occasion to censor the Sunday night programs of Walter Winchell and Drew Pearson, thereby precipitating a lively ado in the world of commentators. Up to now Mr. Woods has not set forth his views on freedom of the air, but last week he agreed to outline the problem as seen from the standpoint of a broadcaster.

Mr. Woods said that the basic fact was that there was a tremendous difference between the exercise of freedom of the printed word and of the spoken word: The printed word is there for the reader to examine again and again, but the spoken word is heard only for a minute and gone.

Emphasis and Inflection

Added to this difference, Mr. Woods said, is the matter of reading. The placement of emphasis, the inflection and the tempo of a speaker's voice often determine the meaning which the listener attaches to a given set of words, he noted. One of the recent outstanding examples of reading was that done by William L. Shirer, the CBS correspondent, who outwitted the Nazi censors in Berlin largely by clever use of emphasis and inflection.

It is these factors, according to Mr. Woods, that make it incumbent upon radio to insure maximum clarity of a speaker's words. He explained that it was known many listeners gave only half-attention while listening, as witness the famed Orson Welles incident, and that unless this trait were recognized the consequences could easily be serious.

Mr. Woods said that it was generally conceded that a story told by word of mouth, the only means a listener has to relay something said by a commentator, is frequently distorted as it is passed along. For this reason, he said, radio has to guard against the circulation of an untruth, even though the commentator's purpose is to denounce it as an untruth. A listener is very apt to remember the original misstatement, which is frequently of the sensational order, rather than the exposure of it as such.

Recorded Comments?

Another problem is use of implication coupled with voice inflection, Mr. Woods said. A newspaper could state, for example, that a prohibitionist happened to live next door to a saloon. As spoken, Mr. Woods said, it could be suggested in the listener's mind either that it was an amusing coincidence or that there was some connection between the prohibitionist and the saloon.

Mr. Woods did not have any immediate solution for these problems, but he did venture the opinion that the day might come when it would be necessary to record such programs in advance and then play them on the air, assuring a check against innuendo and questionable taste.

Mr. Woods went on to say that another distinction between the newspaper and the radio network is that the latter does not have an editorial page. In the case of national political campaigns it is mandatory by FCC rule that both parties receive equal time, a policy which has also come to apply to other subjects of major national interest.

Controversy

In radio, the situation is complicated further by the fact that the commentator is generally sponsored. Too, Mr. Woods recognized that an aggrieved party cannot always be guaranteed the same audience or the same time, whereas the newspaper could guarantee that the counter-statement would be printed in the same number of papers and in the same position as the original.

Controversy on the air is vital to the future of broadcasting, according to Mr. Woods, and in this connection it might be noted that the Blue network, which has been the target of criticism, carries more commentators engaged in sundry controversies than any other network. Though Mr. Woods did not mention it himself, it is no secret in the radio industry that one chain flatly refused to carry, censored or otherwise, one of the Blue's present commentators.

Preservation of the freedom of the air, Mr. Woods said, can be achieved only through broadcasting a full amount of criticism that is completely fair. It is through protection of that freedom that commentator, network and listener can insure the larger liberties for which the nation as a whole is fighting, he said.

BIG STEP SEEN NEAR IN TELEVISION FIELD

Sarnoff Says 1947 May Be Its First Major Year if Flow of Materials Increases

POLITICAL VALUE STRESSED

RCA Head Says Video Could Be to 1948 What Radio Was to the 1924 Campaign

If industrial unrest is eliminated and the flow of raw materials increased, 1947 may become the country's first major year of television, Brig. Gen. David Sarnoff, president of the Radio Corporation of America, said yesterday in a review of the broadcasting industry.

The possibilities are such, General Sarnoff said, that the television camera may be ready to revolutionize the technique of a political campaign in 1948, the way the radio did in 1924 when Presidential candidates first used this medium.

"Television in 1947," he said,

"can make big strides in taking its place alongside the older arts, and in many instances visual communication can give them new and modern import.

"Although the television camera already has scanned national political conventions and Presidential candidates, it will be ready to play its first big role in the 1948 campaign.

"That year will be to television what 1924 was to broadcasting, when Coolidge, Davis, Dawes, Cox, Bryan and other orators picked up the microphone for the first time in a national campaign and marveled at its ability to reach the people.

"Political techniques were vastly changed in that era of the headphones and gooseneck loudspeaker horns. Similarly, in 1947, television will be studied as a new factor in politics as plans are laid for the '48 campaign of radio sound and sight."

General Sarnoff said it was possible that several hundred thousand American homes would be equipped with television in 1948, and possibly as many as 500,000.

The RCA president emphasized that in his opinion the amount of progress and prosperity in the new year "depend upon greater international cooperation for world peace and accelerated industrial production."

"In the achievement of these objectives," he said, "it is imperative that a free flow of information prevails throughout the world. It is also vital that scientific research be expanded to create new products, services and processes that continually will lead to full employment and rising standards of living."

ATOMIC BOMB SEEN WORLD NEWS GUIDE

Science Writer and Military Analyst Say Mighty Weapon Demands New Perspective

No proper evaluation of the news today can be made without the atomic bomb as the frame of reference, William L. Laurence, science reporter of THE NEW YORK TIMES, told 500 teachers yesterday.

"The worst thing we can do is to allow ourselves to be lulled to sleep behind an atomic 'Maginot Line'," Mr. Laurence said, speaking to teachers attending the course "Evaluating the News," sponsored by THE TIMES and the Board of Education, at Times Hall, 240 West Forty-fourth Street.

Hanson W. Baldwin, military analyst of THE TIMES, who shared the program with Mr. Laurence, declared that the atomic age had completely changed the problem of security.

"The paradox of American 'security' in the year 1947 is that there is no 'defense' — using the word in its narrow term," Mr. Baldwin said. "Never before has the old aphorism that a strong offense is the best defense been so true."

Mr. Laurence said that there could be no security unless the nations of the world could work out an effective method for the international control of atomic energy, a method that would make certain that no nation, great or small, could manufacture or possess atomic bombs or the fissionable materials in a form easily convertable into atomic bombs.

"Without such security there can be no peace, no matter what decisions are arrived at around the conference table in Moscow," he said.

Referring to Herbert Hoover's

suggestion that German industry be restored, Mr. Laurence asked what, in the absence of effective international control of atomic energy, would stop German industry from secretly importing fissionable materials from the outside and then surprising the world one day "with a super-Pearl Harbor from which there might be no recovery?"

"Mr. Hoover talks as though there were no atomic bombs," he declared.

Mr. Baldwin urged that the teachers, in trying to understand military news, do the following:

"Examine the source of the news, compare the news, beware of censorship, put the military news in perspective against the political and economic background and supplement the news with interpretation, commentary and opinion."

"Never consider military stories purely in the vacuum of that subject alone. Military action can, and often does, affect political action and vice versa, and influence economic trends. Look, not only for the military significance of a military story, but also for its political significance."

"Remember, particularly in military stories, that a War Department policy, as officially announced and released to the press, does not necessarily reflect the feelings or the opinions of all the people in the Army or even a full statement of the facts."

He listed as the two requirements for judging any story, military or otherwise, "a background of solid basic factual information, and an inquiring and even skeptical mind." He said, "Far too many people believe everything they read, with no critical evaluation of it."

James Russell Wiggins, assistant to the publisher of THE TIMES, was moderator. Next Tuesday's session at 4:15 will feature "The National Scene." Arthur Krock, chief Washington correspondent, will talk on "Washington" and Felix Belair Jr., member of the Washington bureau will discuss "The National Mood."

The Government Goes Into Journalism—Briefly

By ARTHUR KROCK

WASHINGTON, Dec. 8—The State Department last week became a competitor with the vehicles of public information which are operated under the guarantee of the Constitution by the daily and periodical press and, through government license, by the radio. Its "Voice of America," having been furnished by the routine processes of the department with a field report that Soviet citizens were on a buying spree in anticipation of a devaluation of the ruble, promptly went on the air with this interesting news.

By the time some one on the "Voice's" staff thought to notify the department's press officer, Mr. Lincoln White, the news was being officially broadcast. Mr. White, instantly realizing the implications, summoned reporters of the three press associations in an effort to have the news transmitted through the established channels in this republic, at least simultaneously. But before it could go out on the press wires and over the radio "The Voice of America" had finished its broadcast, and the government had scored what newspaper men call a "beat" and entered a new field of activity.

No Repeat Performance

For some cause the news from Moscow reached the staff of the "Voice" without the knowledge of the policy-making officials of the department and before any of them heard about it. Had it come to them first, or had they learned of the proposed official broadcast before it started, it is reasonably certain one of them would have silenced the "Voice" until the public heard the news in the established manner. This reasonable certainty makes it improbable the venture will be repeated, and the reasons for that are many.

In the first place the government properly cannot go into originating journalism, though it did for a few minutes last week. In that event, it would be adopting the practice of totalitarian states, it would be competing in an industry managed and supported by the citizens who have delegated authority to government and pay its costs; and the next logical steps would be an official newspaper and an official newscast.

Toward State Socialism

Should these steps be taken, the government would resemble those against which it has rallied the American people, and is now rallying them, as global threats to democracy, including our own. It might as properly enter any business as a rival of private ownership and management and as a bidder against industry for employes. The end would be state socialism, for clearly no industry could survive against the competition of the government.

Take the factor of news, as in this instance. The State Department every hour gets items of exclusive information from many places. This information becomes available to the department because it represents a great nation abroad and, by reason of unlimited means and international conventions, commands sources and facilities which the press cannot. By and large the press gives information to the public which is also fresh news to the government at Washington on many more occasions than otherwise. But government can pierce the iron curtain; and this gives it an advantage—very essential to its own legitimate functions, but not correctly or safely to be used outside the official area.

A Government Function

One function of the government is to pass on to the public through established channels of information the news its agents gather, subject to restrictions of policy and national security. When responsible officials decide what the White House or any department wishes to make known—whether this is news or opinion—a statement is issued or a press-and-radio conference is called. The information is released simultaneously to the representatives of the press and the radio, summoned for that purpose at a specified time, either to be attributed to official sources or named individuals, or authorized for use as "background." If by diligence, superior facilities or more acute reporting one unit of the press serves the public with this information better or more promptly than another, that is merely the operation of the system of free enterprise.

Only a Momentary Lapse

The point is that no favoritism is shown in this procedure, and the government is acting as a source and not a vehicle of information. Both limitations, founded in the very roots of American democracy, were exceeded when the "Voice of America" broadcast the State Department reports of the Moscow buying stampede the other day.

This sounds serious, and in active practice it would be. But the violation can be wholly ascribed, in the opinion of this correspondent, to zeal by members of the staff of the "Voice" that impelled a leap without a look. Those members of Congress who have been unfriendly to the State Department's broadcasts, vitally important in the waging of the "cold war," will distort the incident if they give it any greater significance. What the promoters of the official newscast did would have been most commendable in unofficial reporters, and it is likely they forgot for a moment they were not.

There seems to be no disposition among the policy-makers of the government, including the State Department, to set up a rival press.

December 9, 1947

FRIENDLY BIDS PRESS HELP U. S. CURB REDS

HARRISBURG, Pa., Oct. 7 (UP) —Edwin S. Friendly, president of the American Newspaper Publishers Association, urged today that the Government and the American press team up for the rigid control of Communists in the United States.

Mr. Friendly, vice president of The New York World-Telegram and Sun, applauded the new Communist control act (the Internal Security Act), in a speech at the annual convention of the Pennsylvania Newspaper Publishers Association.

"There will be Communist attempts to stymie the enforcement of this law," Mr. Friendly said. "I know that no alert publisher or editor will tolerate Government laxity or public apathy."

October 8, 1950

RADIO-TV CODE SET FOR CONVENTIONS

Major Networks and Political Parties Agree on Coverage by Commercial Sponsors

Special to The New York Times.

WASHINGTON, March 8 — A code covering commercial sponsorship of radio and television network broadcasting of the Republican and Democratic national conventions was made public here today.

The code was drawn up by representatives of both major parties after consultation and agreement with all major networks — the American Broadcasting Company, the Columbia Broadcasting System, the Dumont Television Network, the Liberty Broadcasting System, the Mutual Broadcasting System, and the National Broadcasting Company.

This will be the first time commercial sponsors have purchased the time from the networks for broadcasting and televising of the entire convention proceedings. The political parties agreed to commercial sponsoring of the broadcasts, but do not receive any of the funds.

The text of the code agreed to by the networks and the political parties is as follows:

"The two major political parties have no objections to sponsorship of the networks' television and radio coverage of the 1952 political conventions, under the following conditions:

"A. The type of sponsor shall be approved by the political parties.

"B. Commercial messages may be made only during recesses or during periods of long pauses during the actual convention proceedings.

"C. Commercial messages must meet the highest standards of dignity, good taste and length.

"D. No commercial announcements may be made from the floor of the convention.

"E. There shall be a disclaimer made at the beginning and end of each broadcast period. This disclaimer shall make perfectly clear two points: (1) that the client is sponsoring the network's coverage of the event; (2) that sponsorship by * * * company of the * * * network's coverage does not imply in any manner an endorsement of the product by the political party.

"All commercial announcements shall be written, programmed and delivered in such a way as to be clearly and completely separated from convention proceedings, political parties, issues and personalities."

March 9, 1952

In The Nation

Electronics Creates a New Political Problem

By ARTHUR KROCK

WASHINGTON, May 29—Those who are in charge of the physical arrangements for the July conventions of the Republican and Democratic parties are faced with a difficulty growing out of the modern developments in electronics that was unknown to their predecessors. Moreover, it cannot be worked out to general satisfaction until architecture has caught up with this branch of science and engineering.

The difficulty is how to carry on the business of the conventions and their committees with order and efficiency and at the same time admit to the proceedings the eyes of television and the ears of radio in numbers sufficient to give full electronic coverage of the events and fairly representative of its multiplying units.

If radio and television had not progressed with such speed the architecture of the rooms and buildings where public business is transacted might have kept pace with them. Then in every convention hall and committee room there would be partitions behind which motion-picture cameras and receiving sets could be operated without the distractions and confusions created by their mechanical processes. At loopholes in these partitions innumerable and mobile camera eyes and radio ears could be placed, and their records could be made and transmitted as unobtrusively as is that of the press in the section assigned to reporters.

But there are no such facilities for the political conventions and other large gatherings. In consequence the apparatuses of electronics must be accommodated in the committee rooms and on the platforms, floors and galleries of the convention halls. They are very tangible, often noisy, and for successful operation the cameras require blinding lights. Moreover, there are thousands of these apparatuses in 1952 where there were hundreds in 1948, and a consequent increase in the number of networks, stations and newsreel compilers.

As this means of public information has grown and been perfected it also has rivaled the press by making permanent records. Live television can be preserved in motion pictures. Radio networks regularly make transcripts of the spoken word. These are among the arguments for wider representation at the conventions that electronics is making and that the distracted committees on arrangements are trying to meet fairly in the public interest, at the same time enabling the delegates to concentrate on the business that calls them together.

But, though the arguments have merit, the press remains the only agency that can give complete coverage to such gatherings; assemble and report the events in the just proportion of one to the other; make a record that is more widely and promptly accessible and permanent as well; and do all this without disturbance to the scene. The press reporter, unimpeded by mechanical accessories, has complete mobility and can quietly acquire the news anywhere the authorities allow him to go. If his work confines him to his seat in the press sections he can do this also without coming into the consciousness of the convention, as spectators at these gatherings can testify. And, unlike viewers and listeners, the readers of the press have the whole record before them simultaneously.

However, electronic reporting to the public eyes and ears is dramatic and graphic. The power of television to bring a distant event and its physical components—sounds, people and backgrounds — to millions of people has made it an indispensable agent of public information. After the televising of the Senate crime inquiry this was established. And also established was the portentous fact that television can build a popular following, for a citizen who understands how to take advantage of it, more rapidly than any other channel through which personality is publicly projected. The swift rise of Senator Kefauver of Tennessee from a local to a national figure, with support for the Presidency that few thought possible a short time ago, is the outstanding demonstration.

Of this politicians and persons in any way ambitious for public support and recognition are fully aware. They gladly submit to the mechanical limitations on their appearances before the lens and the distractions to orderly and comfortable procedure that the modern miracle imposes. The public appetite for the product is vast and growing, stimulated by the circumstance that the viewer can see the show in his easy chair at home.

For these reasons alone the committees on arrangements of the two major party conventions must provide facilities that will satisfy the actors and the distant spectators, and this is giving them a problem to solve their predecessors never faced. How, for example, can it be met in the open meetings in comparatively small rooms that the credentials groups of the national committees will hold on contests over delegates? And will the quarrels in convention floor conferences that delegations call when a shift in support is afoot be seen and heard in detail by the listening and viewing millions—an alarming thought for politicians?

The arrangers have to find the answers somehow.

May 30, 1952

WHAT TELEVISION TELLS

Only a few more than 12,000 persons can get into the International Amphitheatre, down by the stockyards in Chicago, but sixty millions or more can see and hear a good deal of what is going on there. Many of these millions not only can but do. They may consider themselves part of a historic process, because television, though it existed in 1948, was just a baby then. Now it is all over the place.

Television doesn't explain what goes on. For that, words are needed. But what television tells it tells without restraint. It shows people going into huddles; it shows ladies (bless their hearts) being coy with the photographers and telecasters; it shows puzzled gentlemen, even those on the rostrum who ought to have had plenty of practice in parliamentary law, scratching their heads and rubbing their chins. It shows fat delegates hiking up their belts and thin delegates snapping their suspenders. It shows that even in an air-conditioned building where men change the course of history with their coats on a speaker may have to mop his fevered brow. It shows that some politicians are photogenic and others are not and raises a painful doubt as to whether the future may not lie with Hollywood.

Television does more than this. Television, when it is constant, catches many actors on the political stage in moments of forgetfulness. Nobody can be self-conscious all the time. Television may underline insincerity; it may catch an individual laughing at the wrong joke or yawning at some other person's eloquence; it may reveal some pretentious tub-thumper as the comic or tedious figure he actually is. Television, in short, gives democracy an all-seeing eye. Some day the results may startle us. They already do—a little.

July 8, 1952

HOW MUCH COMMENTARY IS NECESSARY?

By VAL ADAMS

ONE question not answered by the recent Republican National Convention was how much a television commentator should talk while proceedings from the convention floor are on view.

Bill Henry of the National Broadcasting Company believes he talked too much during the G. O. P. convention. Walter Cronkite of the Columbia Broadcasting System thinks he didn't talk enough. Ironically, neither commentator is in full agreement with the policy of his respective network as to the amount of explanatory matter he should present.

The two commentators, whose combined words are carried by roughly three-fourths of the inter-connected stations televising the two major political conventions, will resume their posts tomorrow when the Democrats gather in Chicago. The debate on how much commentary is required to augment the TV picture will be taken up again on two fronts: by television people behind the scenes and by viewers at home, the latter hoping to reap maximum fascination from the political big show and a minimum of irritation and boredom.

Both Mr. Henry and Mr. Cronkite agree that the most difficult part of their jobs in furnishing running commentary is to judge when to talk. Neither claims to have found the answer.

"If the television people directing the show in the studio would let me alone, I'd never talk except during a lull," says Mr. Henry, a staff member of The Los Angeles Times for forty years as reporter, sports editor and columnist and for twenty-nine of these years a radio news reporter and commentator. "But the television people want you to talk. It's a terrible hangover from radio."

During the balloting in the Republican convention, N. B. C. cameras superimposed a numerical tally showing the trend of voting as it progressed. This, Mr. Henry considered, required no explanation on his part, but his supervisors directed that he read the figures as they were presented on the screen.

Conversely, Mr. Cronkite of C. B. S., who covered World War II in the Atlantic and Europe for The United Press, was called down by his supervisors during the first convention for "talking too much."

Problem

"I would have liked to explain a little more during the last two days of the convention," says Mr. Cronkite, "but the powers that be

Walter Cronkite, top, and Bill Henry.

didn't think I should. The big problem in television is that you don't know your audience. Is it intelligent or is it made up of people who know nothing about political procedure? I received several telegrams from viewers asking, 'What is a caucus?' I explained it on the air but the people who already knew must have wondered why I didn't shut up."

To solve this dilemma, Mr. Cronkite and his C. B. S. associates even considered locating an "average man," sitting him at a monitor in the studio in Convention Hall and having him ask questions when he didn't understand what he saw. Theoretically, this would have been a cue for Mr. Cronkite to offer explanatory comment to his TV audience. The plan was dropped, however, because no one knew where to find the "average man."

Both Mr. Henry and Mr. Cronkite have been involved in news reporting of one kind or another, including politics, all of their professional lives. As a newspaper reporter, Mr. Henry covered his first national political convention in 1928 and has been on hand at such gatherings for radio, and now television, since 1940. This is the first convention year for Mr. Cronkite.

Athlete

Mr. Henry, 61, the son of a Baptist evangelist, was born in San Francisco. His formal schooling was gained in such widely scattered points as Chicago, Yonkers, N. Y., Switzerland, England and Australia. At Occidental College in Los Angeles, where he graduated, he became an all-round athlete, including participation in swimming, football, track, tennis basketball and baseball.

While a student at Occidental Mr. Henry reported campus sports for The Los Angeles Times, joining the regular staff upon graduation.

After his paper established radio station KHJ in 1922, Mr. Henry branched out as a sports and special events announcer. He served as technical director of the 1932 Olympic Games in Los Angeles and helped cover the 1936 Olympics in Berlin for C. B. S.

Mr. Henry became a war correspondent in 1939, attached to the Royal Air Force in France. He went to the South Pacific in 1942, but returned to Washington in 1943 to continue newspaper and radio reporting (C. B. S.) for the remainder of the war. He was hired by N. B. C. early this year for the convention job. For the last twelve years Mr. Henry has written a daily column entitled "By the Way" for The Los Angeles Times. He has freedom to write on any subject. In addition to television and the column, he has had to maintain a third job at the conventions—a nightly five-minute newscast heard over the Mutual radio network.

"I just stay up all night," says Mr. Henry.

Practical Politics

Mr. Cronkite, 35, was born in St. Joseph, Mo. He worked his way through the University of Texas by working simultaneously for the Scripps-Howard news bureau in Austin.

"I'd go to classes a couple of hours in the morning," says Mr. Cronkite, "and then go over to the capitol and cover the state legislature. I was held in awe by the professors because I'd tell them the inside of active, practical politics. They were teaching only theory. I didn't learn anything in school. I learned it in the legislature."

Upon receiving his college diploma, Mr. Cronkite went to work for The Houston Press in 1935. A year later he joined radio station KCMO, Kansas City, to cover football and then moved on to The United Press, opening a bureau in El Paso, Tex. Back to radio with WKY, Oklahoma City, he did football announcing in 1937, followed by a year with Braniff Airways in Kansas City. Early in 1939 he rejoined The United Press and went on to become a war correspondent.

Mr. Cronkite served as chief correspondent for The United Press in Moscow from 1946 to 1948. From Washington he broadcast news over a group of mid-Western radio stations until he joined C. B. S. two years ago as a member of the network's news staff in Washington.

July 20, 1952

Editors Report Press Is Under Criticism From Both Sides as Showing 'Favoritism'

WASHINGTON, Oct. 19 (AP)—Editors of some of the nation's leading newspapers agreed today that the press was under more pressure from both sides and subject to more criticism from partisan readers in its coverage of the 1952 Presidential campaign than in any other one in memory.

The editors, here for a week-end meeting of the directors of the American Society of Newspaper Editors, expressed their views in interviews.

Most of them agreed that a record vote was in prospect on Nov. 4 because of intense popular interest in the campaign between Gen. Dwight D. Eisenhower, Republican nominee, and Gov. Adlai E. Stevenson.

"The only other Presidential campaign I can recall which reached so high an emotional level was the Al Smith-Herbert Hoover campaign of 1928," said J. Donald Ferguson, president and editor of The Milwaukee Journal.

"The emotions aroused there were of one kind—religious. In this campaign we have numerous emotional currents, ranging from grievances against the Truman Administration to resentments within the Republican party because Senator Taft was not the nominee.

"Newspapers can only print the news as accurately as it comes to us. I suppose that so long as the shadow of Russia falls across the world and fear is in the minds of men, the public is going to be extremely edgy, suspicious, and angry temporarily at facts that do not please it."

"This is the roughest campaign we have ever experienced," said Felix R. McKnight, managing editor of The Dallas News. "We like to think it is healthy in one respect: that the people are interested and are doing something about it, even if the newspapers are the targets of their ire."

Virginius Dabney, editor of The Richmond, Va., Times Dispatch, which has come out for General Eisenhower, said: "Pro-Stevenson people feel that because the newspaper has editorially endorsed Ike, there is not and will not be fair treatment of Stevenson in the news columns, and they hunt for proof of their suspicions.

"The Eisenhower people, on the other hand, complain because we aren't crusading for Ike in our news columns."

Dwight Young, editor of The Dayton, Ohio, Journal Herald, which is supporting General Eisenhower, said most of The Journal Herald's criticism came from readers who "think we aren't Republican enough." The Journal Herald is owned by former Gov. James Cox of Ohio, Democratic Presidential nominee in 1920.

Stanley P. Barnett, managing editor of The Cleveland Plain Dealer, said he thought newspapers generally were giving so much space to the political campaign, in an effort to be complete and fair, that they were "too heavily weighted with politics."

Like most large papers, The Plain Dealer tries to carry texts of all major speeches, but Mr. Barnett expressed doubt that the percentage of readership justified devoting so much space to texts.

James S. Pope, executive editor of The Louisville Courier-Journal and Times, which are supporting Governor Stevenson, said:

"I have become convinced of one thing: Readers cannot judge the objectivity of a newspaper in a Presidential campaign for the simple reason that they cannot read objectively. Most of them do not want objectivity—they want their side favored.

"Some Democrats think we are trying to hurt Stevenson by putting on Page One accounts of Truman's attacks on Ike; but if we played Truman down, just as many Democrats would scream."

Mr. Pope added: "It is fairly easy to keep news even as between Adlai and Ike, but Truman throws things off balance."

October 20, 1952

THE PRESS AND THE CAMPAIGN

During and after the recent Presidential campaign there were many charges of political bias leveled against the American press. The accusations took two general forms: (1) A "one-party" press exists in the United States because an overwhelming majority of American newspapers editorially favored one candidate (General Eisenhower) and (2) the actual news coverage of the two candidates was unfair in that General Eisenhower received more favorable and fuller treatment than did Governor Stevenson.

So far as the first of these charges is concerned, we think it is erroneous to talk about a "one-party" press as long as newspapers are completely free to take—and do take—whichever side they choose in a political campaign. A "one-party" press exists, as in Russia, when it is permitted to express only one party's opinion, not when most of the opinion expressed happens to represent the views of one party. The prevailing newspaper opinion may or may not be in accordance with the prevailing views of the electorate. The point, however, is not that a majority of newspapers think thus and so, but that there is always a minority which thinks differently.

The critics of the so-called "one-party" press would surely not have newspaper management take an editorial position opposite to that which it honestly believes is the right one in order to balance out the political scales. Newspapers have the obligation and the privilege, as has each individual citizen, to express their own political views; and if they do so freely and honestly there is no real danger of a "one-party" press in the true meaning of the word.

It is the second charge—that the news columns in a large section of the American press were unfair to one of the candidates—that requires closer examination. Newspapers, we believe, are entitled to whatever editorial opinion they wish to express on their editorial page; but as purveyors of news newspapers have special responsibilities as well as rights. They have the responsibility of presenting to the public as fairly as possible the raw material on which they and their readers base political judgments. No one can force newspapers to accept this responsibility, and some newspapers that tend to ignore it have, unfortunately, been published with great financial success. Nevertheless, it would be a serious matter for American democracy as well as for the newspaper profession if the public should begin to lose confidence in the basic integrity of the news it reads in the newspapers.

No one really knows if the broad allegations of press distortion that were made during the campaign are justified or if they were founded on relatively few isolated instances. There have been various proposals for an impartial investigation of the matter; and Sigma Delta Chi, national journalistic fraternity, has named a committee of newspaper men to determine whether and how such an inquiry should be made. There is something to be said for having an investigation of this sort made by a foundation or other private body totally removed from any suspicion of partisanship. However it is done, such a study should be made so that both the newspapers and the public can know the facts. The newspapers of this country are touched with a great public interest and their responsibility should be as much a matter of public concern as is their freedom.

January 1, 1953

I. N. S. NOTES NEED TO EXPLAIN NEWS

Annual Report Says Public Is Skeptical Because of 'Cold War' Propaganda

Government propaganda has made the need for interpretive reporting greater than ever, the International News Service reported yesterday.

The agency's annual report, presented by Kingsbury Smith, stressed that people were skeptical of official news announcements and wanted to know not only what happened but what it meant.

Mr. Smith became vice president and general manager of the agency last year after a long career as a foreign and diplomatic correspondent.

He presented the report at a business meeting held at the International News Service offices, 235 East Forty-fifth Street. The meetings will continue today and tomorrow, coincident with Press Week.

"Cold war propaganda has made the people skeptical of official news announcements," Mr. Smith said. "They know there is a tendency by Government press departments to try to manage the news by presenting it in a light favorable to the policy of the Government concerned.

"Therefore, the need for accurate and objective interpretive reporting is greater today than ever before. Meeting that need is the purpose behind the editorial expansion program which has been launched by International News Service."

8 Correspondents Hired

Eight new correspondents have been hired in the last six months to strengthen the agency's coverage, Mr. Smith reported. He also said that staffs had been increased at a number of bureaus abroad, as well as in the foreign department in New York.

In the last year, he reported, the agency acquired 213 new clients for the news and photo divisions. Its television news film, he said, is now seen on more than 140 stations.

Barry Faris, associate general manager and editor in chief, presented a report on the news achievements of the agency in the last year, and praised a number of staff members for their work.

CONVENTION COVERAGE— A CHALLENGING TASK

By J. P. SHANLEY

TELEVISION and radio networks covering the political conventions next month face the most challenging assignment in the history of broadcasting.

In addition to the technical difficulties necessarily involved in reporting the activities at both conventions, there are unprecedented time and space problems to be considered.

The Democratic convention opens at the International Amphitheatre in Chicago on Aug. 13. The Republican delegates will convene in San Francisco's Cow Palace a week later.

Even if the Democratic convention were to conclude its business within three or four days—an unlikely possibility according to political experts—the movement of hundreds of network representatives and tons of electronic equipment from the Midwest to the West Coast would involve difficulties never before encountered. In 1952, for example, not only were both conventions held in Chicago, but there also was a week's lapse between them.

This year because of the likelihood of prolonged balloting before the Democratic convention ends, the networks are not overlooking the alarming possibility that the Republican gathering may begin before the Democrats have finished.

The networks, hoping fervently that simultaneous sessions will not confront them, have, nevertheless, made tentative plans for splitting their staffs to be ready to broadcast from either location. As one network executive said last week:

"We might even have to make a decision to pass up coverage of the keynote speech at the Republican convention in order to follow important balloting by the Democrats. It's a situation we don't like to think about, but we have to be ready for it."

Most of the heavy equipment is being duplicated in the two cities to facilitate continuous coverage if the conventions overlap.

The broadcasters are anticipating that the convention telecasts and radio programs will be beamed to the largest total audience ever reached. Unofficially, it was estimated that about 60,-000,000 viewers watched some part of the 1952 conventions on TV. Covering the conventions by both television and radio will be the American Broadcasting Company, the Columbia Broadcasting System and the National Broadcasting Company. Each of the networks plans to send a staff of more than 300 technicians, production specialists and broadcasters to Chicago. If the Democratic convention lasts less than a week, almost all of them will fly to San Francisco for the Republican meeting. Smaller advance parties also will be on hand in San Francisco the week before the convention opens there.

Also covering the conventions by radio will be the Mutual Broadcasting System, with a staff of 150.

Sponsorship of the convention broadcasts is in the realm of high finance. The manufacturers who will be paying for the programs on the three television-radio networks will spend a total of more than $14,000,000. This amount also will include coverage of returns on Election night, as well as some political programs between the time of the conventions and the elections.

Generally, these networks will be aiming for greater mobility in coverage than was achieved during the 1952 conventions. There will be some new devices in use, including portable television cameras, compact walkie-talkie-type equipment and transistor receivers, some of them no larger than cigarette lighters.

These devices will be used so that reporters on the convention floor will be able to communicate quickly with personnel at master-control panels and put important spontaneous developments on the air in a matter of seconds.

One network spokesman, who is concentrating on the television coverage of the convention said: "From the standpoint of mobility, radio was away ahead of TV at the 1952 conventions. We don't think it will happen this time. We're going to cobweb the halls with power lines and coaxial cables."

Convention rules limit to five the number of cameras on the floor. These will be operated in a "pool" arrangement, so that most of the pictures of convention activities will be the same for each network.

Occasionally, however, the networks will use long-range lenses on cameras off the floor to provide "exclusive" coverage from the floor. And each network plans to have cameras at a dozen key locations in both cities to cover important developments at the hotels to be used as convention headquarters and at other points where news may break.

Mobile TV units also will be utilized to take care of news breaks at airports, railroad stations and other locations.

It has been estimated that more than fifty tons of equipment will be used for the coverage of the two events.

Supervising the convention coverage will be Thomas Velotta for A. B. C., Sig Mickelson for C. B. S. and William R. McAndrew for N. B. C. The broadcasters will include John Daly for A. B. C., Walter Cronkite for C. B. S. and Chet Huntley for N. B. C.

They have been assigned as "anchor men" for their networks. Their task will be to coordinate and analyze important developments for viewers almost as soon as they occur.

ROUTINE SHOW

Convention on TV Lacks Real Excitement

By JACK GOULD

IF politicians persist in being dull, there's not much television can do about it. The Democratic National Convention certainly was often vapid fare on the home screen. The Republican conclave, with fewer prospects of disagreement, promises to be even more moderate viewing.

The audience figures undoubtedly have been disappointing to the networks, which went to so much effort and expense to report the Chicago proceedings. Far less than half of the country's viewers partook of much of the Democratic meeting. Former President Truman's decision to commit political hari-kari was the one unforeseen development; otherwise the convention was often a desultory affair on the home screen, undistinguished in much of its oratory and anticlimactic in its excitement.

The convention reaffirmed, of course, the acknowledged strengths of television as a journalistic force; the viewer who cared had an excellent seat at the proceedings. But mainly the convention highlighted the inherent weaknesses that TV does have as a reportorial medium. The convention just wasn't the type of story that lent itself to vivid visual treatment.

Remote

From the television standpoint too much of the convention took place out of the range of the cameras; the notion that electronics could penetrate smoke-filled rooms simply did not prove true. The jockeying over the Presidential nomination and the civil rights plank was done largely backstage. When the show did move out front much of the drama already had been drained out of the situation.

This combination of circumstances forced the networks to improvise their own show. Indeed, last week may be remembered chiefly as one in which more commentators talked to each other than ever before in broadcasting's history. When television is compelled to impart a sense of urgency to a vacuum, it rather stumbles over itself and sends viewers off to bed.

Television's handicap, of course, is its basic mode of operation. Journalistically, it does not have a newspaper's advantage of flexibility to adjust its behavior to the course of the news. Contractual arrangements are made months ahead and the networks are committed to giving so many hours of coverage, come what may.

Observers gifted in hindsight have suggested that the networks really overcovered the Democratic convention in its early stages and thereby invited some measure of viewer indifference. The point involves a ticklish problem in journalistic judgment for which there is no ready answer; the networks, after all, cannot know for certain what will happen next.

More realistically, the Democrats largely muffed their TV opportunities. With all that free time at their disposal, most of the major speeches up to the start of the actual nominating process certainly were not very invigorating.

Comparison

Sustained monitoring of the networks on three screens, with a switching arrangement permiting choice of any of the accompanying sound channels, led this corner to the conclusion that on the long pull there was perhaps not too much difference in the coverage of the three chains. Each had its share of fleeting "scoops," both visual and oral.

The American Broadcasting Company and John Daly merit initial commendation for intruding as little as possible under trying circumstances. They enabled a viewer to see perhaps more of what the delegate saw than the other chains. During the speeches of consequence A. B. C. was less restless with its cameras and special effects.

But the new television luminary of the convention was easily David Brinkley of the National Broadcasting Company. His succinct and wry observations were most welcome during periods of inactivity. Together with Chet Huntley Mr. Brinkley gave the N. B. C. news department what it has needed for nearly a quarter of a century, a sense of humor.

And surely there must be a word for the grand old man of them all, H. V. Kaltenborn. The passing years have robbed him of none of his power of direct analysis. N. B. C. could and should put him on the air more often.

For the C. B. S. network Walter Cronkite again was the astonishingly durable anchor man of old. His is indeed a remarkably smooth performance.

The C. B. S. network rather early found itself in the center of controversy over its decision not to show the Democratic film "The Pursuit of Happiness." Paul M. Butler, chairman of the Democratic National Committee, made a demand that it show the film at some other time.

Frank Stanton, C. B. S. president, altogether properly rejected the demand and made the sensible point that a journalistic medium must have the right to employ its own editorial discretion. If networks ever start bowing to the dictates of politicians, they might as well fold up.

But in the initial stages of the convention C. B. S. was guilty of too much smug masterminding. Its decision not to carry the film would have been more understandable if it had something more important. But, as it was, much of the time was given over to an exchange between Ed Murrow and Eric Sevareid and a visit by Lowell Thomas with Mr. Cronkite. These family tête-a-têtes easily could have waited.

Omission

On Tuesday C. B. S. grandly announced that another convention film, an excerpt from "The Best Years of Our Lives," was not up to its technical standard and hence was not presented. A. B. C. wisely decided that what was good enough for the convention delegates to see should be shown to the television audience.

Television is treading dangerous waters indeed if it applies show-business standards to news events. It may well be that as theatrical impresarios the Democrats leave much to be desired. But part of the fun of watching TV is to reach that conclusion for yourself, not have a network intervene in the role of a protective daddy.

The fate of a film or two manifestly is not of any lasting consequence in the light of television's enormous contribution in stimulating the nation's political consciousness through coverage of the conventions. But it does point to a problem that television should weigh much more seriously.

Every sensible viewer will agree that television must have maximum editorial freedom to cover a news story according to its own lights. But at the same time television must be careful to avoid what could be called a form of journalistic narcissism.

As the power and influence of the medium has grown, there has been an increasing tendency on the part of the medium's editors, commentators and restless directors to come between the viewer and the event. Some people in television try to improve on reality, to give actuality the special video treatment that presumably raises popularity ratings.

TV would be better off sometimes if it worried less about making history and more about reporting it. N. B. C. in particular is prone to re-invent television; some of its electronic gadgetry was more distracting than helpful. C. B. S. also seemed overly enamoured at times with its newest toys.

All in all, though, television acquitted itself well under circumstances hardly conducive to anything very spectacular. Four years ago, when both parties had king-sized donneybrooks, TV had a field day that showed off its potentialities. Perhaps this August, with the political scene less hectic, TV's job has been to learn to live without benefit of constant excitement. For video's eager hands this requirement may have come as quite a shock.

TV: Sweetness and Light

G. O. P. Harmony Session in San Francisco Leaves Commentators Frustrated

By JACK GOULD

THE sweetness and light in San Francisco inevitably crimped television's style yesterday. It was hard for the networks to be breathless over a telethon of harmony.

The American Broadcasting Company, Columbia Broadcasting System and National Broadcasting Company faithfully reported the major speeches in which, as every commentator duly noted, the speakers pointed with pride.

But in their pursuit of controversy the network reporters practically exhausted themselves in frustration. Day and night they boxed the compass on the Vice-Presidential situation, apparently being the last people on the West Coast to concede that Harold E. Stassen apparently wasn't going to sponsor a spectacular.

In almost pathetic desperation the video journalists tried to make stories where there weren't any; usually they wound up with only one more bulletin on Republican happiness or the attractiveness of San Francisco. Betty Furness must have been the envy of her TV colleagues; she knew what her important message was going to be.

Ethel Merman was a highlight of an evening otherwise devoted largely to predictable oratory. She introduced the Republicans' 1956 campaign song, a variation on "Alexander's Ragtime Band," with her usual energy. N. B. C. is not apt, however, to forget the song; during Miss Merman's performance it got caught with one of its commercials showing.

The technical coverage was generally smooth. Last evening Edward R. Murrow and Eric Sevareid had time for a leisurely post-session on C. B. S.; it was as interesting an interlude as a day of much commentary provided.

The policy of the networks with regard to fair coverage of both the Democratic and Republican conventions may be a subject of some discussion. Last night the three chains were on the air a half hour before the formal start of the Republican session. In Chicago a week ago they came on the air a half hour after the official opening of the first Democratic evening session.

Paul M. Butler, Democratic National Committee chairman, may be asking for equal time, but Leonard W. Hall, Republican National Committee chairman, was heard coast to coast last night.

August 21, 1956

ELECTION COVERAGE IS FOUND IMPROVED

Special to The New York Times.

LOUISVILLE, Ky., Nov. 29—News coverage of the recent national elections by communications media was called improved today at the opening session of the forty-seventh annual convention of Sigma Delta Chi, professional journalistic fraternity.

The consensus was that campaign reporting in terms of quantitative analysis and broader understanding was much better this year than in 1952. It was also agreed that there were "many imperfections" that could be ironed out only through experience.

The discussion was led by a five-member panel of Turner Catledge, managing editor of The New York Times, moderator; Davidson Taylor, vice president in charge of public affairs, National Broadcasting Company; Sig Mickelson, vice president in charge of news and public affairs, Columbia Broadcasting System; Julius Frandsen, news editor, Washington Bureau, United Press, and William L. Beale, Washington Bureau Chief, The Associated Press.

Mr. Catledge opened the meeting by noting that charges in 1952 of the existence of a 'one-party press," were taken into account in news coverage of this year's election.

"We did far from a perfect job," he said, "and a lot of things we would now do differently, but at this time I cannot recall any really substantial criticism of campaign coverage this year and I think that reflects our serious efforts."

ELECTIONS ON TELEVISION

By JACK GOULD

THE Columbia Broadcasting System took the television honors rather handily last Tuesday evening in covering the election returns. It was on its toes throughout the night, working with confidence and competence.

The C. B. S. edge derived primarily from the huge election board that fills a large room: there simply was no question that this afforded much the best method of following the returns.

The figures and photographs of candidates were clearly visible and very easy to read. The arrangement also had the advantage of making it simpler for the C. B. S. reporters to note changes in the returns. As a consequence, the commentators went about their work with a maximum sense of relaxation and their poise communicated itself to the viewer.

Complementing the studio set-up, which now has proved itself over a number of elections, was the sound editorial organization done behind the scenes. Redundancy, which can be a major plague in broadcasting returns, was held to a minimum and the evening's events reported with fine crispness.

Remote

C. B. S. also had excellent live remote pick-ups of Governor Harriman, Nelson A. Rockefeller and Senator William F. Knowland and Attorney General Edmund G. (Pat) Brown, the principals in the California Gubernatorial contest. Such coverage really shows TV at its best.

The C. B. S. coverage did precipitate a mite of intra-industry chit-chat, however. Edward R. Murrow, the network's traditional star in the news and commentary field, was assigned to the catwalk in front of the election board and reported on results in the Eastern states. He has done this before but usually he has been identified as a commentator on the broad national scene.

From time to time Mr. Murrow is known to want to "run copy," as it were, and get in the trenches with working video journalists. But Tuesday night he seemed far from happy and relaxed in being on his feet and ran through his assignment rather hurriedly and indifferently. To the viewer at home, unfamiliar with all the factors that apparently govern life at C. B. S. News, it appeared to be an odd bit of casting.

Change

In any event, Eric Sevareid was assigned the task of nursing the national perspective. Enjoying the luxury of a desk, he at one point actually broke out into a broad grin. A smiling Sevareid could be quite an innovation in television.

In contrast, the National Broadcasting Company did not have one of its more successful evenings. Its method of projecting merely names and figures on a dark screen was visually tiresome to watch; the intrusion of commercial billboards and props, most ill-advised, and the technical awkwardness, puzzling.

The physical layout of the studio also appeared very confused; when the camera panned around the election headquarters the scene was somewhat suggestive of a mild state of bedlam.

The N. B. C. reportorial staff, headed by Chet Huntley and David Brinkley, seemed noticeably ill at ease primarily because they were the victims of a cumbersome method of switching cues. Kenneth Banghart, doing the local results, also was called upon to do commercials and his desk was cluttered with the sponsor's product.

N. B. C. decided in advance not to do live remote pick-ups from the different party headquarters, which was a mistake. In the country's most important and interesting race—between Mr. Rockefeller and Mr. Harriman—it was certainly worthwhile to see the two men in person. After all, TV's great advantage is that it can humanize news in the making.

N. B. C. news covered the election adequately, to be sure, but not with any great style.

The American Broadcasting

November 30, 1956

Company did not take to the air until a full hour after its two television rivals; obviously this was not the fault of John Daly and his news department. Apparently A. B. C. decided that protection of Trendex ratings for regular-scheduled entertainment programs warranted priority over prompt public service.

Argument

Some industry figures aver that watching two networks covering the same event has its drawbacks, which it is not to be denied. But it also can be illuminating. At the moment when C. B. S. offered live coverage of Mr. Harriman's concession, N. B. C. hurriedly superimposed a bulletin on its own screen and Mr. Huntley and Mr. Brinkley noticeably paled. Apparently viewers weren't the only ones to sample more than one network.

To add to N. B. C.'s Tuesday agonies, C. B. S. also scored a scoop in the first showing of the films of the coronation of Pope John XXIII. C. B. S. attained the edge by the simple expedient of sending the necessary technical equipment out to the New York International Airport at Idlewild, Queens, rather than waiting for the films to be transported by motorcycle into the heart of Manhattan with all the attendant traffic problems.

To get back to politics, the victory of Mr. Rockefeller obviously was another example of the way in which television can shorten the time required to introduce a relatively unknown figure to the electorate. While Mr. Rockefeller had the qualities that bode well for campaigning without electronic assistance—personality, looks, a natural and forthright manner of speech, etc.—it was TV that undoubtedly played an instrumental role in making these assets known to the voting multitude. His formal TV campaign appearances actually ran less than six weeks.

Mr. Rockefeller's television consultant was Sylvester L. (Pat) Weaver, former chairman of N. B. C. and a Dartmouth classmate of the Republican winner. Since his TV protégé attained a good rating, undoubtedly other political figures now will be soliciting Mr. Weaver's advice. Mr. Weaver always has been a stout believer in injecting some excitement into TV; last week he wa associated with a political spectacular.

TV: Debate in Moscow
By JACK GOULD

THE taped telecast of the debate between Soviet Premier Nikita S. Khrushchev and Vice President Richard M. Nixon, seen Saturday evening and repeated again late yesterday, was certainly an item of unusual viewing.

Its first-hand glimpse of the two men engaged in their now celebrated tilt was a vivid supplement to the earlier newspaper accounts. The eagerness of the Premier to play up to the crowd and to adjust his hat for maximum laughs was revelation in itself. The Vice President at the outset seemed very unsteady in the extremely difficult situation but later regained his aplomb. Once again television showed how it could personalize a historic moment.

●

Made by the Ampex Corporation in Moscow, the tape was of excellent quality and reproduced well on all three networks. The use of American newscasters rather than official interpreters to give the translation of the Premier's remarks proved a boon. The translations not only reflected the substance of the statements in Russian but also the Premier's tone and attitude.

The networks had to reach a difficult yet proper decision in electing to go ahead with the telecasts despite a request from the United States Embassy in Moscow to withhold the program until the tape could be shown simultaneously on both United States and Soviet television.

The episode illustrated the recurring difficulty of a situation in which Soviet officials can determine when, where and how the press and TV may cover a story while American officials do not have such authority. As events turned out, the networks fulfilled Mr. Nixon's promise that the Premier's remarks would be heard fully on American TV while at the same time they did not put themselves in the position of being handmaidens of the State Department.

TV AND POLITICS

Interviews Should Try to Smoke Out Facts, Not Cover Guests With Soot

By JACK GOULD

TELEVISION commentators, newspaper men and politicians traditionally are enamored of the mechanics of politics; they are so close to the firing line that understandably every twist and turn in strategy takes on an absorbing fascination.

The most visible form of this professional preoccupation is in the game of cat-and-mouse that frequently passes for a political interview on television. For the questioners, the apparent goal is to induce a political figure to say what he doesn't want to say; for the politicians, the obvious riposte is to display the maximum versatility in evasion.

As parlor games go, this protracted duel of wits can have diverting consequences, particularly when politicians are asked to fight their way out of paper bags that they themselves have manufactured.

Admittedly no one would want to miss some of the more treasured moments that have occurred recently on the home screen: Adlai E. Stevenson's polished insistence that in effect a perennial bridesmaid doesn't want to become a bride; Governor Rockefeller's delicate explanation of how his disappointment in Vice President Nixon would not preclude his support of the man, and Senator Lyndon B. Johnson's inference that he is the best qualified Democrat to take President Eisenhower's place above interparty differences.

Trying to throw the wirewalker off balance is a familiar gambit in politics, long practiced both by rival candidates and those who must report the latest nuances in the behavior of political principals. But whether it is quite realized or not, either by journalists or politicians, such tactics are not notably attractive or fruitful in the age of television.

Impression

Certainly, members of the interviewing fraternity soon must realize that, however, inadvertently, they are stimulating a public impression of being Perry Masons who refuse to leave a program without obtaining a conviction.

If, for example, it becomes abundantly clear that a coy figure is neither going to announce his candidacy nor withdraw from the race, could not the matter be dropped rather than explored until every last possibility for redundancy has been exhausted?

It is serious enough that the institution of the interview has been debased on TV into a form of argumentative cross-examination. From the perspective of watching the screen at home there comes across a needlessly combative tone to the proceedings. Because TV is a form of exhibition, perhaps there has risen an understandable instinct to score a point that can be rather distantly removed from a questioner's more basic function to elicit information.

But actually the larger concern raised by political programs of this type is the inordinate waste of valuable television time that could, and should, be used for more constructive purposes.

No one will argue that the existence of differences between candidates must be adequately covered. But in an election of such crucial consequences as the November contest it would seem incumbent on both the press and television, in equal degree, to do whatever they can to keep public focus on basic issues, not to exploit fights as ends in themselves. How candidates may quarrel is not the primary issue; why they do is.

In this regard it is time that all candidates, not just a few, recognize how television has altered the ground rules by which they formerly played. A more unlikely political trio than former President Harry S. Truman, Senator John F. Kennedy and Governor Rockefeller might be hard to find, but the three are dead right in their plea that real problems be discussed openly and fully now, not later.

Attitude

Millions of viewers, especially young voters, are gaining an intimate glimpse of the intricacies of politics through TV. And for them it is not a very edifying sight to see men who aspire to national leadership playing a game of hide-and-seek with respect to their intentions.

Such an attitude reflects a serious misunderstanding of the power of television; the medium's power is not always beneficial and consistently affirmative. From the standpoint of both the politician and the country's well-being, the negative influence of TV must be equally recognized.

In olden political times it was not too difficult for candidates to skirt the issues until they were ready; they were not seen by too many persons. But with television, they are continually

73

"on," as the saying goes, and what they do or do not do has a direct effect on the interest of millions in politics and government.

If the viewer tunes in political programs and gets only a heavy dose of double talk, who is the historian or social student to complain that the electorate is passive or blasé? Much has been made of the point that viewers will tune in entertainment rather than politics. Some always will, to be sure. But are not some potential converts to a greater interest in government deterred by familiar Democratic and Republican platitudes voiced in an atmosphere of utmost caution?

Coverage

In recent Congressional hearings on the subject of television there has been considerable unanimity on both sides of the aisle that TV stations should do more in behalf of political candidates. There is some merit to their argument, and the prospects of more extensive coverage next fall are decidedly brighter.

But the candidates have a like obligation not to abuse a medium that, as they so repeatedly stressed, does belong to the public. Theirs is a companion obligation to take the voting audience into its confidence, not toy with it.

There can be no greater irony than, at a time when there are issues of unrivaled complexity, a matchless medium for making those issues better understood thus far has been only indifferently employed. Thoughtful viewers of every political persuasion have urged a greater measure of forthrightness and substance on the home screen, which is one way to describe the situation. Another way is to ask whether this is the time to have a stage wait.

TV-Manship Lesson for Politicians:
How to Project Sincerity Imagewise

By PHILIP BENJAMIN

Fifty politicians are getting cues on how to put their best face forward on TV.

A class was conducted Wednesday night by experts at WABC-TV, the local station of the American Broadcasting Company. The experts instructed the politicians, mostly candidates for the Legislature, in the techniques of dressing, talking, gesturing and looking sincere while reading a speech from a prompting device.

Joseph Stamler, vice president and general manager of WABC-TV, started things off at the studio at 7 West Sixty-sixth Street by telling the audience, with awe in his voice, that the "magic eye is a very penetrating device—it looks right through the candidate." The audience seemed impressed.

Bill Shadel, a news commentator, told the candidates that Vice President Nixon, the Republican Presidential candidate, had a masterly TV technique.

Mr. Shadel demonstrated formats for political image-projecting—for example, a desk (restrictive—holds the candidate down); an easy chair for that just-folks feeling (but it's hard to be forceful sprawled in an easy chair); the prepared-question interview. ("You'd be surprised how many men refuse to go on unless they know the questions in advance.")

Lou Volpicelli, a director, said: "The camera has an uncanny quality. It shows who you are, what you are and why you are. I can't explain it."

Scott Vincent, a reporter who like Mr. Shadel had his gray hair set off by a deep make-up tan, showed how to read from a prompter above the camera lens while seeming to be looking right into the lens and thus, of course, into the viewer's eye.

As for attire, the students were advised to eschew stripes in favor of plain gray suitings and to wear light blue or gray shirts, which show up well on the screen.

Some students were picked at random to see if they had learned anything. One, Alfred T. Correa, a Republican running for Assemblyman from the Bronx, also served as a make-up model. He sat suspiciously as a make-up man gave him a smooth, powdery tan.

Mr. Correa was told to read from the prompting device, which unrolled an encomium to Gen. Lyman L. Lemnitzer, the new chairman of the Joint Chiefs of Staff. Mr.

Lou Volpicelli, a director, gives instruction on how to read from prompting device without appearing to do so.

The New York Times (by Larry Morris)

Make-up is applied by Bert Roth to Alfred T. Correa, a Bronx Republican running for the State Assembly.

Correa read, scowling furiously. The director said he did not project enough.

"But this is a commentary," Mr. Correa said. "When I make a speech I'm not just going to comment."

The audience applauded.

KENNEDY PRIVACY URGED

Catholic Magazine Chides Press on Coverage

A Catholic magazine has urged the press to allow President-elect John F. Kennedy privacy in his Sunday attendance at religious services.

An editorial in the current issue of America, a national Catholic weekly review, notes that Senator Kennedy made known his preference for such privacy a month ago. But every Monday since then newspapers have carried pictures of him going to church or coming out, it said.

"If he regularly frequents the same church at the same hour, and if this fact is widely publicized," the editorial declares, "there will be unusual security problems for those charged with his protection."

"Why not just leave him alone on Sunday?" the editorial asks. "Reporters might simply take the day off—and even go to church themselves."

December 5, 1960

HAGERTY BERATES PRESS ON 'TRIVIA'

Charges Reporters Ask Silly Questions of President

By RICHARD F. SHEPARD

James C. Hagerty, a director of many Presidential press conferences in his time, chided newsmen yesterday for not being prepared for the conferences as well as the President and his staff.

"You get some of the most silly, trivial questions at a press conference," he told a gathering of Air Force information officers.

He recalled a recent press conference on a day when there was trouble in Laos and the Congo, with a news break over the diversion of five Navy ships in African waters.

"There was not one question on any of these subjects," he said. "I'm sure that the President and his staff were ready, willing and able to answer."

The former Presidential press secretary recalled that "President Eisenhower went for seven straight weeks before receiving a question on Suez" when the canal crisis was making headlines in 1956.

Mr. Hagerty, who is now an American Broadcasting Company executive, emphasized that his comments were not a "blanket indictment" of the press, in which he included radio and television as well as newspapers.

The Boiling Point

Mr. Hagerty reminisced on questions that had caused ill temper on his part. One such query was put when President Eisenhower was stricken in Denver and no one knew whether he would survive. The reporter wanted to know the color of the hospital room.

He criticized reporters for skipping about from one subject to another. There should be a way, he said, in which the President can dwell on one topic at a time so that a well-rounded opinion might be formulated.

Mr. Hagerty lamented an attitude that the press conference "belongs" to the press.

"It doesn't," he said. "It belongs to the President. He can hold it in Madison Square Garden or a telephone booth."

As vice president in charge of A. B. C.'s news and special events, Mr. Hagerty noted that he had instituted corrections of misstatements on the air. He has already made two corrections since he assumed his duties in January. It was learned later that one was on radio and the other on television.

"I would like to see the news media do what I do," he said, suggesting newspaper corrections on the same page that the error was made on and for broadcasting corrections on the same time period and program on which the errors occurred.

'A Two-Way Street'

He expressed confidence that the United States Government honestly tried to inform the news media and the free world of its activities with "the single exception of national security."

He urged the press to remember that "freedom of the press is a two-way street."

"I wish the American press had a little more responsibility to the American Government," he said. "All too often our country is wrong unless proven right. This is a quarrel I have with the press."

Mr. Hagerty was one of several speakers at the sixth annual World Wide Information Seminar sponsored by the 9215th Air Reserve Squadron of New York. The session was held at the Sheraton-Atlantic Hotel.

April 22, 1961

U.S. PRESS CRITICIZED

Salinger Blames It for Some Repercussions on Cuba

Pierre Salinger, Presidential news secretary, said yesterday he felt the American press must assume some responsibility for the repercussions of the unsuccessful rebel attack on Cuba.

Interviewed on the National Broadcasting Company's television show "Today," Mr. Salinger indicated that he felt some news reports on the attack had been "overinflated" and inaccurate.

"I was reading a copy of two of the news magazines today, where it showed that reporters who were attempting to write stories about what was going on in Cuba were just interviewing any Cuban they could find in Miami and quoting him as an authoritative source," he said.

Mr. Salinger said there had been "efforts in Washington" to correct inaccurate reports about the invasion.

April 26, 1961

Secrecy Threatens Democracy, State A. P. Editors Are Warned

ALBANY, Oct. 16 (AP)—The risk of too much secrecy "threatens democratic government, which depends directly on full information," Turner Catledge, managing editor of The New York Times, said tonight.

He declared secrecy also threatened to divide the nation "into an informed élite on the one hand and an ignorant mass on the other." He said that this would be exactly like the Soviet Union.

Mr. Catledge spoke at the annual meeting of the New York State Associated Press Association.

Earlier, Paul Miller, president of the Gannett Company of Rochester, told the A. P. editors that expansion of foreign news coverage was one of the most pressing problems facing newspapers.

Mr. Catledge said that there was no real source of independent, disinterested information in all the world except the free press of the United States and the countries that share the United States' ideals.

He criticized newspaper men for indulging in too much self-criticism. He said:

"I am hanging up the crying towel and I am asking you to do the same. Let's quit aimlessly cussing ourselves and make our criticisms constructive.

"If we are dissatisfied or uncertain or frightened, or even bored with what we are doing, there are others ways to do it."

Newspapers already have had their scare, he said, from a "new and terrifying device in the communications field — television."

"Far from destroying us," he went on, "television has given us an opportunity that we couldn't have dreamed of twenty years ago."

Criticism of the press by television, Mr. Catledge said, presents a challenge "to be more accurate and more responsible."

Earlier, Hamilton B. Mizer, managing editor of The Niagara Falls Gazette, was elected president of the state association.

He succeeded Davis Starr, associate editor of The Long Island Press, Jamaica, Queens.

Thomas E. Mullaney, assistant financial and business editor of The New York Times, was elected vice president. Norris Paxton, chief of the Albany Bureau of The Associated Press, was re-elected secretary.

Mr. Mullaney served as chairman of the group's continuing study committee in the last year.

The association, at its annual two-day meeting, also awarded citations for outstanding cooperation to member newspapers.

The citations, announced by Mr. Mullaney, went to The Staten Island Advance, The New York Journal-American, The Elmira Star-Gazette, Advertiser and Sunday Telegram, The Gloversville Leader-Herald, The Utica Press and Sunday Observer-Dispatch, and The Niagara Falls Gazette.

October 17, 1961

Hagerty Defends Hiss TV Interview

By RONALD SULLIVAN

James C. Hagerty, vice president in charge of news for the American Broadcasting Company, assailed Alger Hiss last night but defended A.B.C.'s right to interview him on a television program that examined the political career of Richard M. Nixon.

"Let's get one thing straight," Mr. Hagerty said. "I'm against Hiss and everything he stands for. I have no use for him—never had, and never will have.

"But that doesn't alter the fact that he did play an important part in the political career of Richard Nixon."

In a taped statement presented on TV, Mr. Hagerty asserted that the two-minute appearance of Mr. Hiss on a TV program of the network last Sunday, "brief as it was," was debatable. But, he continued:

"I cannot accept the charge that we used him deliberately to blacken or smear the patriotism and the integrity of Richard Nixon."

Mr. Hiss and others took part in a half-hour program conducted by Howard K. Smith. On the program, entitled "The Political Obituary of Richard M. Nixon," Mr. Hiss said in reply to questions:

"I can't but feel that political motivations played a very real part" in Mr. Nixon's activity as a member of the House Un-American Activities Committee.

It was a committee investigation in 1948, in which Mr. Nixon played a major role, that led to Mr. Hiss's conviction of perjury and subsequent prison term. He was convicted for having denied a role in a Communist espionage ring in 1938. The investigation advanced Mr. Nixon's political career.

Some Stations Rejected Show

A.B.C.'s decision to agree with Mr. Smith's interviewing of Mr. Hiss on his program was attacked even before the taped program appeared at 10:30 P.M. last Sunday. A number of A.B.C. affiliates refused to carry the show.

After the show, there were repercussions. Nixon associates charged that A.B.C. had allowed Mr. Hiss to "twist the life of a great American." The first deluge of messages received at A.B.C. offices here denounced the show.

Former President Dwight D. Eisenhower expressed astonishment, and a major sponsor of network shows on A.B.C. threatened to cancel a million-dollar contract.

There were even rumors—all denied by Mr. Hagerty— of a major shake-up in the A.B.C. news operation. One report had Mr. Hagerty moving to a new executive post within the company.

Before leaving on Saturday for a short vacation in the Bahamas, Mr. Nixon told a number of newspapers: "What does an attack by one convicted perjurer mean when weighed on the scale against thousands of wires and letters from patriotic Americans?"

Last night, Mr. Hagerty's six-minute defense preceded Mr. Smith's network program "The American Fighting Man." This show had been replaced last Sunday by Mr. Smith's program on Mr. Nixon.

Sees Issue of Free Speech

Mr. Hagerty said Mr. Nixon and Mr. Hiss were not the fundamental issues in the controversy.

"The issue deals with the basic American principle of freedom of the press, of exchange of ideas, free speech, free assent and dissent," he said.

"Perfectly aware of the background of Hiss, we sought neither to glorify him nor give him a forum to debate. Representing a chapter in Mr. Nixon's history, it seemed natural to put him on the program in historical context.

"Hiss was on the program for about two minutes out of the half hour. The appearance of Hiss, brief as it was, is debatable. Some of you feel that his appearance was a mistake, and I accept this as an honest and sincere position."

"To me it is just unthinkable," Mr. Hagerty said, "that Hiss, a convicted perjurer, could possibly damage Richard Nixon, whose credentials for public service and patriotism have national recognition. If I believed that—if I had any doubt as to that—I would never have permitted Hiss to appear on the program."

The Right to Disagree

Mr. Hagerty said that "any individual, any group, any company has the right to agree or disagree with anything that is presented on the air or printed in the press."

"But pressure in advance to force cancellation of a program and pressure after it by economic means to punish or intimidate is another matter," he declared. "It threatens not only the very existence of freedom of the press, but enterprise itself. It must be resisted."

Last Wednesday, the Schick Safety Razor Company, a division of Eversharp, Inc., tried to cancel a million-dollar advertising contract with A.B.C. But the network refused to cancel it.

Apparently referring to Schick and to the stations that refused to carry the show Mr. Hagerty said:

"To yield to prior censorship and the pressures of personal attack and economic boycott is to surrender the basic right of freedom of the press. This right we will never surrender—or compromise. To do so would be to betray our responsibility as a news medium.

"If we are weakened, you are weakened, for if through fear or intimidation we fail to provide all the news—good or bad, favorable or unfavorable—then you, the citizens of the nation, cannot be properly informed."

FEDERAL LEADERS ACCUSED ON NEWS

Papers' Witnesses Charge 'Lying' in Time of Crisis

By ROBERT C. TOTH
Special to The New York Times.

WASHINGTON, March 19—Newspaper officials accused the Government today of "lying" to the public in times of crisis, thereby causing, at present, "a really serious crisis in the credibility of Government pronouncements."

They called for repudiation of the "suggestion" that the Government had "a right to lie" under any circumstances. But they concede that it might be necessary to "withhold" or "censor" news affecting military security.

The newspaper representatives appeared before the House Subcommittee on Government Information. The group, according to its chairman, John E. Moss, Democrat of California, seeks to establish "guidelines" for separating the truly sensitive information from that which should legitimately be made public.

The hearing was conducted in the form of a symposium. The main participants, along with subcommittee members, included seven representatives of news media.

While the consensus of the group was generally condemnatory of the Administration's news policy, a somewhat more tolerant attitude was expressed by James Reston, chief of the Washington Bureau of The New York Times at the afternoon session.

Mr. Reston, who appeared as an invited witness, conceded that the problem of news management is a difficult and persistent one. But he did not believe that it was as bad today as it has been in the past.

"A good reporter can dig out more information today than he could when I came here 20 years ago," he said.

The crux of the issue, Mr. Reston declared, is whether, at a time of crisis, there is more or less access for the reporter to the informed Government official who can explain its meaning. His own experience has been that "the officials who are informed were not available, and the officials who were available were not informed.

"It is my own view that there has been an improvement in this situation in recent years."

A recurrent point in today's discussion was the action of Arthur Sylvester, Assistant Secretary of Defense for Public Information, in "the management of the news" in the Cuban crisis last October. Mr. Sylvester admitted then that certain information was withheld or slowed up in conformance, as he saw it, with the needs of national policy. He has since defended his action against many critics.

Associated Press Wirephoto

TESTIFY ON NEWS 'MANAGEMENT': Gene Robb, vice president of American Newspaper Publishers Association, gives his views at House hearing. At the right is Howard H. Bell, who is vice president of the National Association of Broadcasters, also a witness.

Washington

Lyndon Johnson's Driving and the Press

By JAMES RESTON

WASHINGTON, April 7 — Presidents always seem to be getting into trouble with automobiles, and now it is Lyndon Johnson's turn.

President Eisenhower was criticized several years ago for riding up to his Gettysburg farm at 90 miles an hour, and even Herbert Hoover, who was not generally regarded as a speedy type, ordered an investigation of the White House press in July of 1931 when they reported that he roared back from his Rapidan fishing camp at the outrageous clip of 50 miles an hour.

The report on President Johnson is that he recently drove a car over the roads near his Texas farm at 75, 80, or 85 miles an hour—it depends on whom you read—and the most interesting aspect of the incident is the President's reaction to the published reports.

He was in turn angry and hurt. He felt that some of the reporters had abused their privileges as his guests and, what is more important, that the big Eastern papers were taking a hostile attitude toward him because he is a Southerner.

The Reporters' Nightmare

This is an unfortunate and inaccurate conclusion. President Johnson has had a remarkably good press ever since he came into the White House, but the White House press corps has always been worried about the safety of the President and this is especially true since the assassination of President Kennedy.

Every serious White House correspondent is especially edgy when the President is away from the protective shield of the official residence. President Garfield was shot when he was leaving for an outing, Lincoln was murdered in a theater, McKinley was shot at a public reception away from Washington and so was Kennedy.

Most Presidents have dealt with their need for privacy simply by keeping reporters at a distance, but not President Johnson. He feels fenced in at the White House and is liberated at the ranch in Texas, but even then he has the reporters around night and day and acts in their presence precisely as he would act around old friends.

Usually this private relationship is respected, but much of the talk is about public matters and often there is confusion about what can and cannot be written. Also, when he leaves the privacy of his home and drives fast along the roads, with cars full of reporters who have not been guests in his house, reports of

Several spokesmen at today's hearings denounced any official news policy that involved "lying to, or deliberately misleading the public." Clark Mollenhoff, Washington correspondent for The Des Moines Register and Tribune, and a member of the panel, was particularly severe in his attacks on Mr. Sylvester, who is scheduled to appear before the subcommittee on Thursday.

Representative Henry Reuss, Democrat of Wisconsin, a member of the subcommittee, sought to draw out panel members on the implications of "the unidentified source" as the origin of many news stories. Did not the cloak of anonymity, he asked, open the way for many abuses either by Government officials or by reporters and editors?

The discussion drew a mixed response. Some defended it as a means of providing important background to the news that might not otherwise be available. Others denounced it as a particularly useful device for an official who wanted to manage the news by releasing it on his own most advantageous terms.

Gene Robb, vice president of the American Newspaper Publishers Association, told the hearing that there had been "several instances" of Government lying during crises. He cited the Bay of Pigs invasion attempt and the U-2 overflights of the Soviet Union.

"A government can successfully lie no more than once to its people," Mr. Robb, publisher of the Albany Times-Union and Knickerbocker News, said.

"Thereafter, everything it says and does becomes suspect.

All the more so when a high-ranking government officer makes speeches to justify these lies," he said.

Growth of Practice Seen

If the government can lie in one case, "there is the serious danger that this repugnant philosophy will be extended to more and more circumstances," said Charles S. Rowe, editor of the Fredericksburg, (Va.) Free Lance-Star, and chairman of the Freedom of Information Committee of the Associated Press Managing Editors Association.

Howard H. Bell, vice president of the National Association of Broadcasters, said "manipulation and control of the news must not be tolerated in time of peace or in time of crisis, and deliberate falsehoods should not be tolerated at any time."

Mr. Rowe complained that the Defense Department refused to release pictures of nuclear tests in the Pacific not to protect national security "but rather the 'image' the Administration wanted to present the world." Soviet ships were near the test site and could photograph the explosions.

Mr. Rowe also criticized the National Aeronautics and Space Administration for "doctoring its satellite reports by failing to list some Soviet launchings.

Mr. Robb asked for "a complete and categorical repudiation" of the suggestion that the Government had a right to lie. He called for an "affirmative statement" that news management was not a Government policy.

March 20, 1963

his driving inevitably are published, especially since on one of the recent rides in Texas he forced another car onto the shoulder of the road.

No Connection

Publication of such things, however, is no indication of hostility toward the President and certainly has nothing whatsoever to do with the fact that he is from Texas. As a matter of fact, probably the strongest support for President Johnson in the Washington press corps is coming from those who feel strongly that he may be able to reconcile the differences between North and South better than anybody else precisely because he is a Southerner.

This is also his own fondest hope. He has labored for years under the political handicap of not being a national but a regional figure. He has the reputation of being a hard man but is in truth a most sensitive man and does not feel that he can unify the nation unless he is accepted, respected and supported by the press in the North.

This is why he is so interested in the press and, paradoxically, why he likes to have reporters around and hates to have them criticize him when they come around.

His difficulty is that he wants to be liked and also to do what he likes. In some ways he is like President Truman. He does well with the big problems and has troubles with the little ones, and he wants to be both a private and a public figure at the same time.

This is all a typical part of the period of adjustment to the savage demands of the Presidency. A Senator or even a Vice President can have all kinds of freedom denied to a President. No matter where he goes outside the privacy of his family he is a public figure. He is expected to set the standards of the nation and to live by them in ways not demanded of other public figures.

No doubt he will slow down after the publicity given to his driving, but his problem with the press remains. For he is magnifying an incident of his own creation with the car into a feud of his own imagination with the press. And the misunderstandings between North and South are bad enough without this.

No doubt many people in the North do not admire the Johnson style, just as many courtly Southerners didn't like the Truman style, but this wasn't what worried the reporters. They were not concerned with his style but with his safety. They were not trying to tear down the President but to preserve him. In fact most of them were worrying mainly about the country and about the thought of John McCormack running it.

TV AND PRESS WED BY COMPUTERS

By JACK GOULD

TELEVISION'S coverage of the California primary election on Tuesday night will further mark the continuing change in journalism brought about by electronics. Not only will the massive network reportorial effort serve to apprise viewers of the winners in the Republican and Democratic contests, but it will constitute a major source of prompt information for most of the newspapers of the country.

Beginning with the races between Governor Rockefeller and Senator Barry Goldwater for California delegates to the Republican National Convention and between Pierre Salinger and Alan Cranston for the state's Democratic Senatorial nomination, the Fourth Estate in effect will openly acknowledge that TV can afford to do some things which the press cannot.

Under an agreement concluded by The Associated Press and the National Broadcasting Company, the country's largest press association will be using the network's analysis of returns as part of its service to newspapers.

The deal was concluded shortly after The New York Times made a similar agreement with the Columbia Broadcasting System to obtain its demographic date on how religious, educational, ethnic and economic factors may or may not influence voting. The Times step was followed by The Washington Post and The Los Angeles Times, which also acquired the C.B.S. information. The New York Herald Tribune signed up with N.B.C.

Election Night

Representatives of the press will be working on election night side-by-side with the reporters of N.B.C. and C.B.S. The results to the newspaper reader at first may seem a little strange. In some cases, and perhaps many, he will not be reading the material gleaned at first hand by the printed word medium but rather a report on the reporting of the electronic medium. If the marriage does not get out of hand by competitive excesses involving TV networks and newspapers alike, the union could be advantageous for both.

At all events, the wedding of the media on election nights was inevitable. The networks have an overriding incentive to obtain quick and complete information. Such is the battle for network prestige, which means an old-fashioned race for scoops, and the economic resources of TV that between the March primary in New Hampshire and Nov. 3, the date of the Presidential election, the three networks may spend a total of $27 million. On Tuesday night alone the outlay for N.B.C., C.B.S. and the American Broadcasting Company may run over $1 million.

Expensive Contest

That kind of contest is too expensive for the newspaper business. Moreover, it is futile. Broadcasting has the edge in speed and brevity; the press in permanence and depth. When radio first lifted its voice, the newspaper "extra" was dead. The added fascination of TV has merely underscored the fact that the two media are now complementary, not directly competitive.

The A.P. will go on collecting returns in the country, state, city and hamlet and the television networks will use them. But the networks will also have hordes of their own correspondents both in California and through-out the country on Nov. 3 and the network tallies will be what most of the country sees. Many newspapers subscribing to The Associated Press now quote in their last editions the latest network totals.

The incredible computing machines have led the revolution in election reporting. Whereas in olden times it was felt necessary to have substantial totals before predicting a race's outcome, now results from sample districts can be almost instantaneously compared with earlier elections and voting trends quickly detected. On Tuesday night, the California polls will close at 10, New York Time. Projections will soon follow.

Incredible Machines

If computers are so uncannily accurate in analyzing the meaning of returns before a good portion of the electorate has even gone to the polls, it poses the intriguing question of whether TV might encourage the stay-at-homes on the theory that their vote will not have much influence. Back in radio's heyday, however, much the same cry was raised that knowledge of the East's vote would lower the West's exercise of the franchise. It never worked out that way.

In some newspaper quarters, perhaps because of an understandable reluctance to depend on another medium for prime information, The A.P. has been criticized for "surrendering" to TV on election coverage. Actually, the course chosen by Wes Gallagher, general manager of the news service, may constitute a pattern which the networks themselves will come to adopt: cooperation.

Election returns are news for only a few days every two to four years. Any medium that would tax or drain its resources in blind competition for a scoop of a few minutes could be following a false sense of values. For what the networks will spend on Tuesday night alone, a number of documentaries could be prepared. Not even TV can afford indefinitely a wild scramble for what, after all, is the same set of figures.

A pooled effort to collect figures might be in the long-range interest of all media concerned so that the energies and economic resources of journalism can be used most constructively without needless waste. For those who chance to monitor the three networks during an election race, there is nothing quite so disheartening as the sight of the faces of those commentators who know they have been "beaten" by a matter of minutes. In each instance they became rattled and invariably are less effective. When competition leads to that end, its value to the public becomes somewhat obscure.

CURB ON TV ANALYSIS OF VOTES DEMANDED

WASHINGTON, June 7 (UPI) —A Republican Congressman called on the radio and television networks today to hold off announcing a winner in the November Presidential election until all polls in the country have closed.

Representative Oliver P. Bolton of Ohio said he would ask the Federal Communications Commission to step in if the networks failed to adopt such a policy voluntarily.

Leroy Collins, president of the National Association of Broadcasters, said the association would "resist any such action."

Mr. Bolton said projection of early results based on analysis by computers could influence voter attitudes in the Western part of the nation, where voting booths still would be open.

"We have always had that," Mr. Collins said in reply. "This is just a furtherance of technological competence. As long as the people understand that such projections are mechanically estimated, there can be no harm in that."

Representative Durward G. Hall, Republican of Missouri, called at the same time for a Congressional investigation of "polls and pollsters" in the same manner that Congress studied television rating services. He said many seemed intent on influencing an election outcome rather than predicting it.

June 8, 1964

100,000 TO GATHER ELECTION RETURNS

By JACK GOULD

A total of 100,000 persons will collect election returns Nov. 3 for a new reportorial pool established last night by the three television networks and The Associated Press. United Press International is expected to join the pool soon.

A major advance in the co-operation of news media, the pool will be known as the Network Election Service.

It will be administered by a board of directors representing the American Broadcasting Company, the Columbia Broadcasting System and the National Broadcasting Company. The press associations will be participating but non-voting members.

The pool will collect voting figures in the Presidential, senatorial and gubernatorial elections. Its budget will be $1,600,-000.

For the television viewer and newspaper reader, the chief effect of the pool will be to eliminate differences in incomplete vote results during the count. At each stage of the count, identical figures will be furnished to the networks and press associations.

Relay to New York

Plans call for 3,000 counties or precincts to be manned on Election Night by professional reporters, college students and members of civic organizations. Figures will be relayed to New York through tabulation headquarters in each state.

Under tentative arrangements, The Associated Press will collect returns in 16 states, while each of the networks will cover 11 or 12. The addition of the U.P.I. would alter the quotas.

Most of cost of the pool will be borne by the television networks. The outlay for A.P. was reported to be about $160,000, with the press association being credited with a like amount for the services of its regular staff.

In addition to participating in the pool, A.P. will, as usual, report returns for local and state offices, other than governorships.

Each of the networks will continue to offer its own analyses of the meaning of returns.

Each network will staff its own set of crucial precincts selected to give a quick indication of vote trends. On the basis of results from such precincts, the outcome of elections often can be predicted long before the full vote has been counted.

Directors of the Network Election Service will be Arnold Snyder, manager of election coverage for A.B.C. News; William Eames, editorial director of the C.B.S. News Election Unit, and Frank Jordan, manager of election coverage for N.B.C. News.

In a joint statement by the networks and The Associated Press, the pool was hailed as "a great step forward in the gathering and dissemination of news."

The statement was signed by Elmer W. Lower, president of A.B.C. News; Fred W. Friendly, president of C.B.S. News; William R. McAndrew, N.B.C. executive vice president in charge of news, and Wes Gallagher, general manager of A.P.

June 10, 1964

MARGIN FOR ERROR

Restraint Is Urged in Election Coverage

By JACK GOULD

WHEN television decides to make a move it is not a dawdling industry. In the California primary, the Columbia Broadcasting System caused some viewers to hold their breath with its overly quick call of Senator Barry Goldwater's narrow victory over Governor Rockefeller. Hours later, all the networks were rushing through an oft-suggested arrangement for pooling the collection of returns next November.

The chain of events should prove salutary. The pool had to come sooner or later because viewers were becoming baffled and annoyed by the sight of the three networks posting conflicting figures on the running vote totals.

Of greater significance, however, was the injection of a note of restraint into the competitive network scramble in journalism. It was the original chase for instant tallies that led directly to the reliance on pollsters and computers, a combination that offered a way to leapfrog over the traditional election mathematics and come up with winners before some citizens had gone to the polls.

The rivalry among networks, including their projections, declarations and demographic deductions, will continue to exist under the pool, which will only be concerned with compiling raw votes and will not supplant electronic punditry

Too Much Emphasis

But the California primary did underscore that too much emphasis on the end result in an election might obscure the means by which it came about. In declaring Goldwater the winner 22 minutes after the polls in Southern California had closed and 38 minutes before they closed in San Francisco, C.B.S. made the Senator's close triumph seem an easy sweep.

The C.B.S. declaration raised the question of whether television might be affecting the outcome of a vote by the manner in which the medium reported the event. If in the November election a candidate is declared a winner shortly after 6 o'clock, New York Time, not an impossibility, it would be only mid-afternoon on the West Coast. If TV, with its enormously influential impact, should dissuade citizens from going to the polls because it might appear that their vote was a useless gesture, the price of a fleeting scoop becomes too high.

Concern over the C.B.S. conduct certainly was justified. Under the operation set up by Bill Leonard, executive producer of the C.B.S. Election Unit, and Louis Harris, the pollster, the network relied on 42 precincts in California that had been chosen to represent "a microcosm of the state," both north and south. In California there is a total of 32,000 precincts.

Leonard's Comment

From this "microcosm" C.B.S. chose a "representative sampling" of 18 precincts. These precincts, Mr. Leonard said, showed "very clearly and unmistakably" that Senator Goldwater would get about 52.8 per cent. Such a projection, the C.B.S. executive added, meant the actual figure might fall somewhere between 54.8 and 50.8 per cent.

In addition to the 18 precinct returns, C.B.S. also had supporting evidence for its call from independent polling done by Mr. Harris, Mr. Leonard noted.

But if a projection were subject to the swing cited by Mr. Leonard, then the layman is bound to be puzzled by the figures that came in later for the full 42 sample precincts. This tally gave Mr. Goldwater a figure of 50.8. If this projection, in turn, meant that Mr. Goldwater might receive somewhere between 52.8 or 48.8 per cent, it certainly did appear that C.B.S. might be out on a limb.

C.B.S. reported the drop in the Goldwater margin to 50.8 but the fact was completely overshadowed by the earlier declaration of the winner. The same criteria by which the declaration was made clearly indicated a strong case for at least its temporary withdrawal. The final figures, incidentally, were 51.3 for Goldwater and 48.7 for Rockefeller.

Further, there was an additional element of confusion, one it is to be hoped that the pool coverage in November will alleviate. The C.B.S. declaration was based, the network said, on 2 per cent of the total vote of just over

2,000,000, or around 40,000 votes.

Yet, according to a picture in last week's issue of Broadcasting Magazine, the C.B.S. screen at the moment of the network's declaration — 10:22 P.M., New York Time—gave Goldwater a total of 13,423 votes and Rockefeller, 13,015, a difference of 408 votes with the city of San Francisco not yet finished voting.

Resolving Confusion

Surely, the lay viewer should not be imposed upon to the extent of resolving the confusion over what the eye sees and the ear hears. At the very least, all the networks, not merely C.B.S., must take the trouble to explain explicitly on the air—out in the open, as it were—exactly what they are doing in making projections and how big is the margin of possible error and why.

Both those working in the television news departments and those reporting on the medium, including this writer, may have been equally guilty in being drawn into a whirlpool of excessive preoccupation with TV's race for sensational scoop of a few minutes. The responsible caution exercised by the National Broadcasting Company in the California primary, which only declared itself at 12:51 A.M. after 75 per cent of the vote was counted, was a timely reminder for everyone that manmade restraint has a place in an age of speed.

Senate Gets Bill to Curb Election Return Broadcasts

WASHINGTON, June 19 (AP)—Senator Karl E. Mundt, Republican of South Dakota, introduced a bill today to prohibit broadcasting and telecasting of Presidential election returns until the polls have closed all over the country.

Mr. Mundt told the Senate that he was not certain that this was the answer to the problem of possible influence of Eastern election returns on voting in the West. But he urged it as a vehicle for Senate Commerce Committee hearings to get suggestions from the networks, the Federal Communications Commission and others.

The bill would prohibit any licensee to broadcast or telecast "the results, including any opinion, prediction, or other matter based on such results" of any Presidential election "in any state or part thereof until after the latest official closing time of any polling place for such an election in any other state on the same day." It also would prohibit broadcast of results of elections for members of the Senate and House until the polls were closed in all parts of a state.

PRESS RELATIONS OF SENATOR GOOD

But Columnists Sometimes Draw Goldwater Ire

By ANTHONY LEWIS
Special to The New York Times

SAN FRANCISCO, July 15 — Senator Barry Goldwater is on good personal terms with reporters—although his supporters sometimes show hostility toward news media.

Newsmen who cover Mr. Goldwater regularly say the Senator is less sensitive to press criticism than are some other national politicians, notably President Johnson. They do not believe he would blow up at the press as Richard M. Nixon did after his defeat in the campaign for the California Governorship in 1962.

However, they concede that not all is sweetness and light between the Senator and the press.

Senator Goldwater ordered Columbia Broadcasting System television cameras excluded the other day after a network correspondent, Daniel Schorr, reported that the Senator would meet with German rightists while on vacation in Berchtesgaden. Senator Goldwater called the report a lie and canceled his trip.

Senator Goldwater gives great weight to personal acquaintance with members of the press. He declined to let his wife, Peggy, appear on an American Broadcasting Company program recently unless the interviewer was the man who had been covering him, John Rolfson.

Floor Demonstration

The attitude of many Goldwater backers, newsmen have noted, is quite another thing. Many supporters at this convention — and at meetings around the country — have made clear their feeling that the press, radio and television treat him unfairly.

This attitude was dramatically evidenced on the convention floor last night during former President Dwight D. Eisenhower's speech.

"Let us particularly scorn," Mr. Eisenhower said, "the divisive efforts of those outside our family, including sensation-seeking columnists and commentators . . ."

A great shout went up from the crowd — by far the loudest cheer during the Eisenhower speech. There was more shouting and yelling and foot-stamping when he finished the sentence: "...because, my friends, I assure you that these are people who couldn't care less about the good of our party."

The Goldwater leaders felt that this demonstration of anti-press feeling was getting out of hand. They passed the word, through their efficient convention communications system, to cut it off.

Mr. Goldwater has often been asked by members of an audience whether the press is not prejudiced against him. The questioners expect to hear some criticism of the press.

The Senator almost always declines to please the audience with a free-swinging denunciation. He has been noted to remark: "I sometimes get bad treatment from columnists, but the reporters have been fair to me."

In Dallas on June 16, speaking to the State Republican Convention, he said "radical columnists" — Walter Lippmann, Joseph and Stewart Alsop, Roscoe Drummond and Marquis Childs — and "radical newspapers" — The New York Times and The Washington Post — opposed him "just like Izvestia."

Protest by C.B.S.

SAN FRANCISCO, July 15 (UPI)—The Columbia Broadcasting System lodged a "strong protest" with the Republican National Convention tonight over what it called restrictions on television newsmen and technicians.

In a telegram to the convention chairman, Senator Thruston B. Morton of Kentucky, Fred W. Friendly, C.B.S. News president, assailed "both for ourselves and for the other news media the unreasonable restrictions placed upon our personnel, in direct violation of standing agreements relating to coverage of the convention."

June 14, 1964

June 20, 1964

July 16, 1964

Nine Governors to Seek Election News Agreement

CARSON CITY, Nev. July 22 (AP)—Gov. Grant Sawyer of Nevada, chairman of the National Governors' Conference, today named a committee of nine governors to seek a voluntary agreement with the news media to withhold election projections until all polls are closed.

The committee, headed by Richard J. Hughes of New Jersey, includes Edmund G. Brown of California, vice chairman; John A. Burns of Hawaii, John P. Dempsy of Connecticut, Mark O. Hatfield of Oregon, Clifford P. Hansen of Wyoming, Farris Bryant of Florida, William W. Scranton of Pennsylvania and George W. Romney of Michigan.

Governor Rockefeller of New York was asked to be chairman but declined.

Governor Sawyer requested the group to meet as soon as possible with representatives of radio and television networks to discuss electronic predictions based on early returns before many polls are closed.

The committee was authorized by the governors' conference June 10 in Cleveland after Mr. Sawyer voiced fear that victory announcements could influence persons who had not yet voted.

July 23, 1964

N.B.C. Chief Opposes Curbs On Computer Vote Guessing

PROVIDENCE, R. I., July 24 (UPI)—Robert W. Sarnoff, Board Chairman of the National Broadcasting Company defended tonight the use on television of computer projections of election results. He called this a basic function of news in a free society.

Mr. Sarnoff, speaking at the 101st commencement at Bryant College, took issue with calls for Federal laws to regulate computer tabulation of election returns and projection of the outcome.

Gov. Grant Sawyer of Nevada, chairman of the National Governors' conference, appointed nine Governors this week to investigate the plan of television networks to declare election winners before polls have closed across the nation.

Mr. Sarnoff said that the call for legislative action "largely ignores the basic function of a news organization—of an open communications system—in a free society."

"It is," he said, "the obligation of radio and television, in common with all news media, to, present significant information to the public as soon as it is available, using all of the best tools at their command."

July 25, 1964

STANTON REJECTS CURB ON RETURNS

Finds No Proof That Early TV Tally Affects Elections

Dr. Frank Stanton, president of the Columbia Broadcasting System, yesterday condemned proposals to prevent the reporting of Presidential elections returns until the last polls close in the West.

He said there was no proof for theories that early reports would affect voting patterns in areas where the polls were still open. And he attacked any artificial delay in returns as a foolish and dangerous form of censorship.

Concern about the effects of early returns has grown with the development of new, swift techniques by the television networks to tabulate elections.

As a result, it has been suggested that the networks be forbidden to broadcast their computer tabulations on election night next November until the western vote is closed.

Dr. Stanton said this would mean "a banning of news, in no way involving national security, for a period of up to six hours." He spoke at a Waldorf-Astoria lunch of the National Institute of Bar Public Relations, held in connection with the American Bar Association meeting starting Monday.

Dr. Stanton criticized the "senselessness and inadequacy" of the sharply differing election laws of the various states. He said "the fragmentation and diversity of voting procedures in this country in what presumes to be a national election are almost unbelievable."

August 8, 1964

For Staggered Voting Hours

To THE EDITOR:

I note with interest, and I concur with, Senator Salinger's concern regarding the effect of electronic vote projections during this Presidential electoin.

Not only can a forecast deter voters from casting their votes; running forecasts can also influence voters to "get on the band wagon."

Either of the above indicates the undesirability of electronic forecasting while polls are open.

A worthwhile solution might be the institution of staggered polling hours from coast to coast, the Eastern areas opening their polling places later so that all polling places would open and close at exactly the same moment throughout the country.

CARL S. AUERBACH.
Syosset, L. I., Aug. 14, 1964.

August 22, 1964

NETWORKS SHARE COST OF PROJECT

Theater Will Be Converted —Move Bolsters Reports of Limited Campaign

By JACK GOULD

The motion-picture theater in the basement of the White House is to be converted to a television studio for the use of President Johnson.

Plans for the installation of electronic equipment were approved three weeks ago by the White House staff and officials of the American Broadcasting Company, the Columbia Broadcasting System and the National Broadcasting Company.

The studio will probably be put into operation in a few weeks. Specifications for the necessary equipment, including three cameras and a master control board, were sent to manufacturers yesterday. Bids were requested by tomorrow.

The three networks are sharing the cost of the conversion. The only formality remaining is their approval of a budget, after which construction will start, perhaps next week.

A full production and technical crew will be on duty at the White House every day except Sunday. The stand-by staff will enable the President to go on the air on short notice with a minimum of physical inconvenience.

When President Johnson was ready to announce the settlement of the railroad work-rules conflict, it was noted, he had to travel across Washington to a TV studio. He barely arrived in time for some of the evening TV newscasts.

The new White House studio will seat about 30 persons and will be intended primarily for Presidential announcements, statements and possibly interviews with small groups of reporters.

Better Access Long Sought

The networks have long sought improved access to news at the White House, particularly to cover the President's frequent impromptu news conferences on Saturday mornings. At present, the television industry must install and then remove cameras and related equipment each time the President speaks or holds a news conference.

Last winter there was talk of converting the Fish Room in the White House to a TV studio, but the plans were held in abeyance because of major construction problems, it was said. The Fish Room gained its name from President Franklin D. Roosevelt's use of the room to exhibit his tropical fish.

The decision to convert the basement theater was reported to have been made at the request of the White House. Accordingly, the action was regarded in some TV circles as confirmation of earlier suggestions that the President might be planning to stay close to the White House during much of the campaign. President Roosevelt, it was noted, campaigned over the radio from the White House.

The disclosure of the studio plans also led to speculation in some TV quarters as to whether the White House studio might invite new problems under the equal-time rules governing the appearance of political candidates on television and radio.

Proposal Killed in Senate

Last week Senate Democrats killed a proposed suspension of Section 315 of the Federal Communications Act under which the networks could have granted time to President Johnson and Senator Barry Goldwater of Arizona, the Republican Presidential candidate, without giving equal time to minority-party candidates.

While the major effect of the Democratic move was to eliminate the possibility of Presidential debates, other special political programing involving Mr. Johnson and Mr. Goldwater was also affected. The only current exemptions from the equal-time provision are regularly scheduled news programs.

It was reported yesterday that C.B.S. was considering asking the Federal Communications Commission whether irregularly scheduled news conferences with President Johnson, in his capacity as a candidate, and Mr. Goldwater might leave the network liable to interviewing minority and fringe candidates for the Presidency.

If the President decided to speak from the White House basement studio, it was suggested, there might be a question of whether he was appearing as a head of state or a party nominee.

At present the networks are aware of five other candidates who may be appealing to the commission for any consideration that might be accorded to President Johnson and Senator Goldwater.

They are Clifton DeBerry of the Socialist Workers Party; Eric Haas of the Socialist Labor party; Earl H. Munn of the Prohibition party; John Casper of the National States Rights party, and Joseph Lightburn of the Constitution party.

Other candidates may be put up by America's Unifying Movement, the Vegetarian party, the Industrial Government party, the Independent American party and the Independent Afro-American party.

Within the TV industry there is a growing conviction that President Johnson's staff might be developing a subtle strategy designed to minimize Senator Goldwater's opportunities for television exposure.

By declining to respond to invitations to appear on such programs as "Meet the Press" or "Face the Nation," the President in effect would also be denying the Senator free air time, it has been observed, since the networks would be hesitant to invite one Presidential candidate without an assurance that the other would also appear. The Senator's only recourse then would be to buy TV time, and run up his campaign costs, while the President might continue to enjoy the exposure that is the automatic advantage of an incumbent.

It was learned that as a consequence of Section 315 at least some extensive biographical programs on President Johnson and Senator Goldwater have either been dropped or substantially modified to avoid demands from other candidates for similar minute-by-minute attention.

To provide independent political reporting, it was understood, the networks will try to report the Republican and Democratic races with minimum recourse to words or pictures of President Johnson and Mr. Goldwater. Interviewing prominent Republicans and Democrats who are not running for office this year and hence would not be involved in the equal-time problem is one possible device, it was said.

No TV officials are talking publicly about their legal difficulties in trying to give away time to the President and Mr. Goldwater, but it is hardly an industry secret that they are concerned whether the equal-time philosophy in effect might lend itself to a widely publicized candidate's exercising a power of veto over the number of TV appearances by a less prominent rival.

The Voters and the Computers

A committee of state Governors has met with executives of news agencies and television networks to try to curb those awesome computers that supposedly make it possible to forecast the outcome of national elections down to the second decimal point on the basis of returns from the first few Eastern precincts. The Governors from the Far West fear these forecasts will discourage people in their states from voting at all in the late afternoon and evening.

But if we are to restrict the pretensions of the computers, what discipline are we going to impose on those publicity-wise Yankees in Vermont and New Hampshire villages who gather at 12:01 A.M. on Election Day to cast their ballots first in the nation and announce the results while the rest of us are still asleep? And, indeed, candor compels us to acknowledge that the judgments television now makes about the trend of an election differ only in precipitateness from those newspapers have been making for decades. Few news-gathering organizations, with or without the aid of computers, ever wait until all the polls are closed before beginning to publish or broadcast their decisions on who won.

As far back as 1916, California and other Western states voted for Woodrow Wilson, although the Eastern newspapers had already flashed the news that Charles Evans Hughes was "elected." Again, in 1948, the voters there as in many other states refused to be impressed by the news of Thomas E. Dewey's "victory." Both the newspapers and the computerized networks told California in 1960 that John F. Kennedy had won, but a majority of Californians insisted upon voting for Richard M. Nixon. With this tradition of independence behind them, the voters of the nation's most populous state will probably be able to go on resisting Eastern snares even in this electronic age.

September 7, 1964

The commission described the pressure of press, radio and television for information about Oswald. It told how police catered to the press and allowed newsmen to overrun the police and courts building.

The commission accused news media representatives of "regrettable lack of self-discipline." It emphasized that basic responsibility for the course of justice in Dallas in the two days that followed the assassination of President Kennedy lay with the police authorities.

The report rebuked the Dallas police on two counts: First, that its security precautions were inadequate; second, that statements by its members prejudiced Oswald's rights.

The report pointed out that Dallas police officials made no distinction between their customary efforts to accommodate the press and the special situation in which they found themselves.

As a consequence, the report said, Ruby was able to enter the basement of the Dallas police and court building and shoot-shoot Oswald in full view of the police, press, radio and TV men. Television cameras brought the scene to viewers throughout the nation.

The consequence of Oswald's death was that "it was no longer possible to arrive at the complete story of the assassination through normal judicial procedures during a trial of the alleged assassin," the commission said.

It declared that "the acceptance of inadequate press credentials posed a clear avenue for a one-man assault." It cited the "inadequacy of coordination" among the police authorities in arranging for the planned transfer of Oswald to the county jail. And it declared that "regardless of whether the press should have been allowed to witness the transfer, security measures in the basement for Oswald's protection could and should have been organized and more thorough."

"These additional deficiencies were directly related to the decision to admit newsmen to the basement," the report stated. "The commission concludes that the failure of the police to remove Oswald secretly or to control the crowd in the basement," the report transfer were the major causes of the security breakdown which led to Oswald's death."

Two members of the Dallas police at one point suggested to Capt. J. Will Fritz that Oswald be transferred surreptitiously to the county jail, leaving the press "waiting in the basement and on Commerce Street, and we could be to the county jail before anyone knew what was taking place," the report said.

However, Captain Fritz said that he did not think Chief Jesse E. Curry would agree to such a plan because he had promised that Oswald would be transferred at a time when newsmen could take pictures, the report continued.

Forrest Sorrels, a Secret Service agent, also suggested that Oswald be moved at an unannounced time when no one was around, but Capt.

Press and Dallas Police Blamed for Confusion

PANEL SUGGESTS A CODE OF ETHICS

Statements From Officials Are Called Prejudicial to Fair Trial for Assassin

By JACK RAYMOND
Special to The New York Times

WASHINGTON, Sept. 27—The Warren Commission declared today that news media must share with the Dallas police the responsibility for the breakdown of law enforcement that led to Jack L. Ruby's killing of Lee Harvey Oswald.

The commission noted that the prime responsibility was the police department's. However, the commission made a recommendation for a new code of professional conduct in the collection and presentation of information to the public.

The new code of "ethical standards," the commission said, is needed to that in the future "there will be no interference with pending criminal investigations, court proceedings, or the right of individuals to a fair trial."

Promulgation of such a code of ethics, the commission continued, should go beyond an expression of "general concern" in order to make clear "that the press had profited by the lesson of Dallas."

It proposed that representatives of the bar, law-enforcement associations and news media work out the suggested code.

August 26, 1964

J. Will Fritz told him, the report continued, that Chief Curry "wanted to go along with the press and not try to put anything over on them."

The commission cited interviews given by Dallas police officials during their detention of Oswald and said:

"The running commentary on investigations by the police inevitably carried with it the disclosure of many details that proved to be erroneous."

Fair Trial Endangered

The police furnished the press with opinions, hearsay items and erroneous information to the point where it not only endangered Oswald's constitutional right to a trial by an impartial jury but also "created a further risk of injuring innocent citizens by unfavorable publicity," the commission charged.

The commission devoted a substantial section of its report to newsmen in Dallas and what it termed "the responsibility of news media."

The commission said it recognized the "deep-felt interest" throughout the world in the events surrounding President Kennedy's death. It endorsed the public's right to know many of the developments surrounding the apprehension and detention of Oswald.

"However," the commission declared, "neither the press nor the public had a right to be contemporaneously informed by the police or prosecuting authorities of the details of the evidence being accumulated against Oswald."

"Undoubtedly," it went on, "the public was interested in these disclosures, but its curiosity should not have been satisfied at the expense of the accused's right to a trial by an impartial jury.

"The courtroom, not the newspaper or television screen, is the appropriate forum in our system for the trial of a man accused of a crime."

The commission called attention to the discussion among editors at the annual meeting of the American Society of Newspaper Editors in Washington last April in support of its criticism of the role of the press at Dallas.

"The discussion revealed the strong misgivings among the editors themselves about the role that the press had played and their desire that the press display more self-discipline and adhere to higher standards of conduct in the future," it said.

The commission's proposal for new ethical standards was similar to a proposal made by Associate Supreme Court Justice Arthur J. Goldberg at the April meeting of editors. Justice Goldberg, in a speech, called for an addition to the society's code of ethics that would "adequately safeguard the rights of an accused" in crime reporting.

The editors issued a statement by their society's Freedom of Information Committee warning of possible information curbs because of the events in Dallas. The committee said the curbs were probably aimed primarily at television but called upon newspapers to "re-examine our own shortcoming and rid our own house of irresponsibility."

The existing seven-point code of ethics of the editors' group contains references to the responsibility of newspapers to consider public welfare, to be truthful and to be cognizant of the requirements of fair play.

The section on fair play constrains a newspaper not to publish unofficial charges affecting the reputation or moral character of an individual without giving the accused an opportunity to be heard.

C.B.S. WILL DELAY FORECASTS NOV. 3

Acts to Answer Critics of Computer Projections

By JACK GOULD

The Columbia Broadcasting System announced a revision of its election night procedures yesterday to allay criticism that the voter is becoming subordinate to the computing machine.

Members of the network's staff have been instructed not to declare a winner in the race between Prsident Goldwater until it is clear that one has achieved the necessary majority of 270 electoral votes.

Projections and forecasts of the outcome will be made on the basis of early returns, but such analyses will be presented to the viewer "not as facts but only as well-informed judgments," according to Fred W. Friendly, president of C.B.S. News.

"We will not use the word 'declare' on Nov. 3," Mr. Friendly said. "We will speak of indicated winners,' 'apparent winners' or 'probable winners' until both our analysis of the vote and the vote itself leave no doubt of the result."

Before Polls Closed

Last June, the network declared Senator Goldwater the winner in the California Republican primary only 22 minutes after the first polls had closed and before some residents had cast their votes.

On that occasion, supporters of Governor Rockefeller, loser in the primary, hinted that some of his supporters might have concluded it was useless to go to the polls when a major network had stated flatly that the race was over.

The C.B.S. declaration was based on computer analyses of results in sample precincts supplemented by the judgment of Louis Harris, the poll-taker, and members of the network staff.

While the final outcome substantiated the declaration, fluctuations in the running vote totals invited doubts and confusion in the minds of some viewers and politicians watching the network's coverage.

It has been known for some time that C.B.S. believed its mistake in California did not lie with research techniques or tabulations but in the finality of the act of declaring a winner so early in the evening.

Both the National Broadcasting Company and the American Broadcasting Company said that they would use sample districts and computer processing to make projections of probable winners in the Presidential contest and other races.

In the California primary, A.B.C. did not declare Goldwater the winner until after all the polls had closed and N.B.C. waited for some hours after that.

During the early part of election night in the Eastern time zone, the networks are expected to stress that the polls on the West Coast have not closed and that many state and local issues depend on a strong voter turnout in that section of the country.

Should there be a landslide on Nov. 3, however, the choice of the next President could be known even before the West Coast polls close. This possibility explains why the networks feel they cannot agree to hold up returns until the last polling place has closed.

In a number of past elections West Coast politicians have complained that initial returns from the East may have had an influence on voting patterns in the West.

Mr. Friendly said that the role of the computers would be explained periodically during the election night coverage. The other networks also are expected to try to familiarize viewers with what the machines can and cannot do.

The election on Nov. 3 will mark the first time that the three networks and the two news services, The Associated Press and United Press International, will have a cooperative pool, called the Network Election Service, to collect and tabulate returns.

If the pool achieves its goal of speeding up the returns, some officials believe, the tallies could come in so quickly that the time advantage of projections from computers would be lessened.

Where the machines are expected to contribute chiefly to the election night coverage on TV is in providing fast analysis of how people in different economic and ethnic groups voted.

"That might be the most interesting story," one official observed.

October 21, 1964

A Correction

The Columbia Broadcasting System will make forecasts of the outcome of the Presidential election as early as possible on election night but will refrain from declaring a winner until it is clear that either President Johnson or Senator Barry Goldwater has obtained a majority of 270 electoral votes. A headline in yesterday's editions of The New York Times erroneously stated that the network planned to delay forecasts.

NEWS MEDIA POOL TO SPEED RETURNS

Major Networks and Wire Services Join to Tally and Report Vote Across U.S.

By WILL LISSNER

Next Tuesday evening, for the first time, the country's news media will pool their resources to report the Presidential election as fast and as comprehensively as modern high-speed communication makes possible.

About 130,000 men and women will collect the raw vote totals for President, Vice President, Governor, Senator and Representative in the precincts and report them to tabulating centers.

The cooperative effort combines the country's two major wire services, the Associated Press and United Press International, and the three major networks, the American Broadcasting Company, the Columbia Broadcasting System and the National Broadcasting Company. The pool organization is called the Network Election Service.

Most of the country's newspapers, news magazines, broadcasting stations and newsreels are affiliated with one or more of the wire services and networks.

Virtually every newspaper, news magazine, radio and television station in the United States will take part in reporting to the public the returns from the general election Nov 3 collected by this cooperative effort.

About 20,000 professional newsmen have been assigned to the election service to coordinate the work, supervise the effort and man key operations.

Even if the country's news-gathering organizations deployed their total staffs to the job, they could not handle it alone in so comprehensive a manner. The 20,000 they are providing are the nucleus of the working force.

A rapid count requires collection of the totals in the voting districts, the polling places, and passing them along by telephone to a central tabulation point in each state. From the state centers they must be transmitted to the national center.

The job is so vast no one has attempted it before on a comprehensive basis. What makes it possible for the first time this year is the cooperation of many of the country's civic, professional and fraternal organizations.

They are providing 130,000 persons of established reputation for accuracy, responsibility and integrity who will do the reporting from the country's 172,500 voting districts.

Everything from a Masonic temple to an insurance company headquarters is being used to collect the reports.

School Teachers Help

In 20 states the reporters will be school teachers. In others, young professional and businessmen of the Junior Chambers of Commerce; members of Civitans, a civic organization; the League of Women Voters; the National Association for the Advancement of Colored People, or the Catholic Youth Organization.

In Utah, California, Nevada and Oregon the well-organized Mormon Relief Society is cooperating. In Ohio, to cover one section, hunters and fishermen who belong to the Lorain County Conservation Society are serving.

Many would serve without payment being involved, as a civic duty. Bert Ivry of N.B.C., who is in charge of the operation, said.

"About 99 per cent of the precinct reporters will not accept pay for their work," Mr. Ivry said. "We are paying a lump sum to each of their organizations. What the organization does with it is the business of its members.

"Many of the organizations are using the payment to finance programs they couldn't afford before.

"State teachers' or state education associations are setting up scholarships for training the underprivileged in teaching, or for training teachers to work with the underprivileged or especially handicapped.

Scholarship Fund

"In New Jersey, the teachers are giving the payment to a scholarship fund and to a national disaster fund of the New Jersey Education Association."

The vote tabulation service will cover what politicians call the top of the ticket—Federal offices and Governors in states holding gubernatorial elections.

The rest of the ticket will be reported in the normal way by the wire services in an operation in which Board of Elections staffs and police departments cooperate.

The election service will only collect, tabulate and transmit total votes, precinct by precinct, in the major races. It will make no projections, "decide" no contests; it will not use computers even to count the votes.

Each of the five members has taken responsibility for the coverage in a specific number of the 51 voting areas. The responsible member in each state and the District of Columbia will report the totals to a combined tabulating center in New York at the Edison Hotel.

This center will compile the national Presidential vote and the state totals for President, Senator and Governor.

The totals will be transmitted simultaneously by teleprinter to the five members.

The wire services will put them on their wires for their subscribers. The networks will post them and announce them, and distribute them over their news service networks.

In addition, in each state, local representatives of the five members will operate in the state tabulating center of the responsible member. By teletype and telephone they will transmit state results to their subscribers.

Here are the assignments of pool members:

A.B.C.: Connecticut, Florida, Kansas, Kentucky, Michigan, North Carolina, Oklahoma, Washington, Wisconsin.

A.P.: Alaska, Arizona, Arkansas, Idaho, Iowa, Louisiana, Montana, New Mexico, North Dakota, Oregon, Vermont, Virginia.

C.B.S.: Colorado; District of Columbia, Indiana, Maryland, Missouri, New York, Rhode Island, Tennessee, Texas.

N.B.C.: California, Delaware, Illinois, Massachusetts, Minnesota, New Jersey, Ohio, Pennsylvania, South Carolina.

U.P.I.: Alabama, Georgia, Hawaii, Maine, Mississippi, Nebraska, Nevada, New Hampshire, South Dakota, Utah, West Virginia, Wyoming.

Most states have a single subcenter for tabulation. But N.B.C. has found that for California 14 centers and subcenters are needed.

The basic reporting will be from some 130,000 of the country's total of about 172,500 precincts. Some precincts are too remote to be covered or too small to make the effort worthwhile.

As a check on the operation, and to fill in any precinct gaps, 3,000 reporters will be assigned, one to a county. More than 10,000 persons will work in 75 state tabulation centers. Above the precinct level the reporters and workers will be professional news personnel.

In New York, the state manager for the service is Ted Kamp of C.B.S. In upstate New York, teachers of the New York State Teachers Association will report the results. In New York City various civic groups will be working. The teachers and the civic workers will cover 12,400 election districts. Their goal is to have most of the vote tabulated by 11 P.M.

The New York tabulating center at the New York Hilton Hotel plans to produce for members 62-county totals for President and Senator every 5 to 10 minutes. Congressional district totals are to be produced for each of the 41 contests for Congress every 10 minutes.

In New Jersey, Jerry Rosholt of N.B.C., who is state manager, is using 5,500 teacher members of the New Jersey Education Association to cover the state's 4,603 election districts. The organization's goal, with polls closing at 8 P.M., is to have 85 per cent of the vote in by 9.

Headquarters are in the association's building in Trenton.

In Connecticut, Miss Anne Morrissey of A.B.C. is state manager. The Connecticut Junior Chamber of Commerce is providing 1,000 reporters to staff 615 election districts. The returns will be tabulated at state headquarters in the Hartford National Bank Building at Hartford. With polls closing at 7 P.M., the organization's goal is to have a complete report in to the center by 7:30 P.M.

There are 546 races in this instant reporting operation.

To provide facilities for handling the flood of information, telephone companies have been involved in a crash program to install telephones, teleprinters, Data-Phone sets and switchboards.

About 600 telephone men and women, including secretaries and supervisors, are volunteering their services on election day.

In Manhattan, the service's special telephone system will be the equivalent of that for a city of 50,000. Similar systems are being set up for 74 other centers.

For the operation, the service has budgeted $1.5 million. But nobody knows what the total cost will be, as new expenses are still cropping up. The latest guess is $1.6 million.

Spokesmen say this cost will be much lower than that for a much less satisfactory operation by any of the members. Funds available would put a $1 million ceiling on an individual competitive collection one network executive has estimated.

For projections and other purposes, each network will collect raw votes in other states than those they are responsible for.

Setting up the organization and providing it with communications facilities has been only part of the job performed by Mr. Ivry and his group. The volunteers have had to be educated in the traditions of accuracy and speed as well.

Officials say that in 1960 A.P. had collected the vote from about half the precincts—88,121—by 1:21 A.M.

This was more than half of the popular vote. By 12:30 A.M. the A.P. tabulation covered 34,262,000 votes. U.P.I. ran neck and neck with A.P. tabulating 34,152,000 by 12:30 A.M.

November 1, 1964

EDITORS' DECISION ON CUBA RELATED

Kennedy LaterWishedTimes Had Printed All It Knew

ST. PAUL, June 1 (AP)— President Kennedy told an executive of The New York Times that if the paper had printed all it knew about preparations for the Bay of Pigs invasion the nation would have been saved from a "colossal mistake," a Times editor disclosed today.

The disclosure was made by Clifton Daniel, managing editor, in a speech at MacAlester College before a forum of the World Press Institute. The forum was held in honor of recent Pulitzer Prize winners and foreign journalists studying at the college.

Mr. Daniel recalled a number of difficult decisions at The Times, before both the Bay of Pigs invasion and the Cuban missile crisis a year later, as to whether the paper's responsibility to publish the news conflicted with national security.

He traced in detail some strong differences of opinion among Times executives that led to the toning down of a dispatch describing plans for the invasion of Cuba.

The dispatch, by Tad Szulc, appeared on Page 1 of The Times in the edition of Friday, April 7, 1961. Invasion forces landed in Cuba on Monday, April 17, 1961.

Kennedy of Two Minds

Mr. Daniel depicted President Kennedy as apparently torn in two directions by the course The Times took during the Bay of Pigs buildup.

At one point, meeting with a group of editors after the incident, President Kennedy "ran down a list of what he called premature disclosures of security information," mostly in The Times, Mr. Daniel said.

"While he scolded The New York Times," he went on, "the President said in an aside to Mr. Catledge, 'If you had printed more about the operation you would have saved us from a colossal mistake.'"

Turner Catledge was then managing editor of The Times. He is now executive editor.

"More than a year later," Mr. Daniel said, "President Kennedy was still talking the same way."

Mr. Daniel said that in a White House conversation on Sept. 13, 1962, never made public before, the President told the late Orvil Dryfoos, publisher of The Times:

"I wish you had run everything on Cuba. . . . I am just sorry you didn't tell it at the time."

A Historical Footnote

Mr. Daniel added another historical footnote to the Bay of Pigs invasion.

He recalled that in both a television interview on Meet the Press and in his own book, "A Thousand Days," Arthur M. Schlesinger Jr. said that The Times had suppressed an article giving "a fairly accurate account of the invasion plans."

Holding up a copy of the April 7, 1961, edition in which the article appeared, Mr. Daniel said:

"Mr. Schlesinger, was mistaken, both in his book and in his appearance on 'Meet the Press.'"

Mr. Daniel told of detailed and heated exchanges among Times executives before the decision was made to give the controversial dispatch a smaller headline, eliminate a reference to an "imminent" invasion, and drop a reference to participation of the Central Intelligence Agency in invasion preparations.

Mr. Daniel said his own view today was that the Bay of Pigs operation "might well have been canceled and the country would have been saved enormous embarrassment if The New York Times and other newspapers had been more diligent in the performance of their duty."

He added, however, that James Reston, then chief of The Times's Washington Bureau and now an associate editor, disagreed. He quoted Mr. Reston as saying:

"If I had it to do over, I would do exactly what we did at the time. It is ridiculous to think that publishing the fact that the invasion was imminent would have avoided' this disaster. I am quite sure the operation would have gone forward."

By contrast, Mr. Daniel said, when the Cuban missile crisis of 1962 reached a climax, The Times, at the personal request of President Kennedy, withheld an exclusive article on the presence of Russian missiles in Cuba until the news was announced by the Government.

Mr. Daniel also made public a letter from President Kennedy to Mrs. Dryfoos some time after the death of her husband in which the President praised the decision to withhold the article as having been in the interest of national security.

Excerpts From Speech on Coverage of Bay of Pigs Buildup

Following are excerpts from an address delivered yesterday by Clifton Daniel, managing editor of The New York Times, before the World Press Institute in St. Paul—an address that adds information about events preceding the Bay of Pigs to what has been presented before by Arthur M. Schlesinger Jr. and other observers:

This morning I am going to tell you a story—one that has never been told before— the inside story of The New York Times and the Bay of Pigs, something of a mystery story.

In its issue of Nov. 19, 1960, The Nation published an editorial under the heading, "Are We Training Cuban Guerrillas?"

I had never seen this editorial and had never heard it mentioned until a reader of The New York Times sent in a letter to the editor. He asked whether the allegations in the editorial were true, and, if so, why hadn't they been reported by The New York Times, whose resources for gathering information were much greater than those of a little magazine like The Nation.

The Nation said:

"Fidel Castro may have a sounder basis for his expressed fears of a U.S.-financed 'Guatemala-type' invasion than most of us realize. On a recent visit to Guatemala, Dr. Ronald Hilton, Director of the Institute of Hispanic-American Studies at Stanford University, was told:

"1. The United States Central Intelligence Agency has acquired a large tract of land, at an outlay in excess of $1-million, which is stoutly fenced and heavily guarded. . . . It is 'common knowledge' in Guatemala that the tract is being used as a training ground for Cuban counter-revolutionaries, who are preparing for an eventual landing in Cuba. . . . United States personnel and equipment are being used at the base. . . .

"2. Substantially all of the above was reported by a well-known Guatemalan journalist . . . in La Hora, a Guatemalan newspaper . . . .

"3. More recently, the President of Guatemala, forced to take cognizance of the persistent reports concerning the base, went on TV and admitted its existence, but refused to discuss its purpose or any other facts about it. . . .

". . . We believe the reports merit publication: they can, and should, be checked immediately by all U. S. news media with correspondents in Guatemala."

Off to Guatemala

With that last paragraph, The New York Times readily agreed. Paul Kennedy, our correspondent in Central America, was soon on his way to Guatemala.

He reported that intensive daily air training was taking place there on a partly hidden airfield. In the mountains, commando-like forces were being drilled in guerrilla warfare tactics by foreign personnel, mostly from the United States.

Guatemalan authorities insisted that the training operation was designed to meet an assault from Cuba. Opponents of the government said the preparations were for an offensive against the Cuban regime of Premier Fidel Castro. Mr. Kennedy actually penetrated two miles into the training area.

His article was published in The New York Times on Jan. 10, 1961.

The Nation also printed another article in its issue of Jan. 7, 1961, by Don Dwiggins, aviation editor of The Los Angeles Mirror.

And now Arthur M. Schlesinger, Jr. takes up the story in "A Thousand Days," his account of John F. Kennedy's years in the White House.

"On March 31," Mr. Schlesinger says, "Howard Handleman of U.S. News and World Report, returning from 10 days in Florida, said to me that the exiles were telling everyone that they would receive United States recognition as soon as they landed in Cuba, to be followed by the overt provision of arms and supplies.

"A few days later Gilbert Harrison of the New Republic sent over the galleys of a pseudonymous piece called 'Our Men in Miami,' asking whether there was any reason why it should not be published. It was a careful, accurate and devastating account of C.I.A. activities among the refugees, written, I learned later, by Karl Meyer. Obviously its publication in a responsible magazine would cause trouble, but could the Government properly ask an editor to suppress the truth? Defeated by the moral issue, I handed the article to the President, who instantly read it and expressed the hope that it could be stopped. Harrison accepted the suggestion and without questions — a patriotic act which left me oddly uncomfortable.

"About the same time Tad Szulc filed a story to The New York Times from Miami describing the recruitment drive and reporting that a landing on Cuba was imminent. Turner Catledge, the managing editor, called James Reston, who was in his weekend retreat in Virginia, to ask his advice. Reston counseled against publication: either the story would alert Castro, in which case The Times would be responsible for casualties on the beach, or else the expedition would be canceled, in which case The Times would be responsible for grave interference with national policy. This was another patriotic act; but in retrospect I have wondered whether, if the press had behaved irresponsibly, it would not have spared the country a disaster."

Article Was Not Suppressed

As recently as last November, Mr. Schlesinger was still telling the same story. In an appearance on "Meet the Press," he was asked about the article in The New York Times in which he was quoted as saying that he had lied to The Times in April, 1961, about the nature and size of the landing in the Bay of Pigs.

Mr. Schlesinger replied that, a few days before he misinformed The Times, the newspaper had suppressed a story by Tad Szulc from Miami, giving a fairly accurate account of the invasion plans.

"If," he said "I was reprehensible in misleading The Times by repeating the official cover story, The Times conceivably was just as reprehensible in misleading the American people by suppressing the Tad Szulc story from Miami. I, at least, had the excuse that I was working for the Government."

"I prefer to think," he said, "that both The Times and I were actuated by the same motives: that is, a sense, mistaken or not, that [it] was in the national interest to do so."

Mr. Schlesinger was mistaken, both in his book and in his appearance on "Meet the Press." The Times did not suppress the Tad Szulc article. We printed it, and here it is, on Page 1 of the issue of Friday, April 7, 1961.

What actually happened is, at this date, somewhat difficult to say.

None of those who took part in the incident described in Mr. Schlesinger's book kept records of what was said and done. That is unfortunate, and it should teach us a lesson. The Bay of Pigs was not only important in the history of United States relations with Latin America, the Soviet Union and world Communism; it was also important in the history of relations between the American press and the United States Government.

We owe a debt to history. We should try to reconstruct the event, and that is what I am attempting to do today.

Late in March and early in April, 1961, we were hearing rumors that the anti-Castro forces were organizing for an invasion. For example, the editor of The Miami Herald, Don Shoemaker, told me at lunch in New York one day, "They're drilling on the beaches all over southern Florida."

Tad Szulc, a veteran correspondent in Latin America with a well-deserved reputation for sniffing out plots and revolutions, came upon the Miami story quite accidentally.

He was being transferred from Rio de Janeiro to Washington and happened to stop in Miami to visit friends on his way north. He quickly discovered that an invasion force was indeed forming and that it was very largely financed and directed by the C.I.A. He asked for permission to come to New York to discuss the situation and was promptly assigned to cover the story.

His first article from Miami —the one I have just shown to you—began as follows:

"For nearly nine months Cuban exile military forces dedicated to the overthrow of Premier Fidel Castro have been in training in the United States as well as in Central America.

"An army of 5,000 to 6,000 men constitutes the external fighting arm of the anti-Castro Revolutionary Council, which was formed in the United States last month. Its purpose is the liberation of Cuba from what it describes as the Communist rule of the Castro regime."

His article, which was more than two columns long and very detailed, was scheduled to appear in the paper of Friday, April 7, 1961. It was dummied for Page 1 under a four-column head, leading the paper.

While the front-page dummy was being drawn up by the assistant managing editor, the news editor and the assistant news editor, Orvil Dryfoos, then the publisher of The New York Times, came down from the 14th floor to the office of Turner Catledge, the managing editor.

He was gravely troubled by the security implications of Szulc's story. He could envision failure for the invasion, and he could see The New York Times being blamed for a bloody fiasco.

He and the managing editor solicited the advice of Scotty Reston, who was then the Washington correspondent of The New York Times and is now an associate editor.

Recollections Conflict

At this point, the record becomes unclear. Mr. Reston distinctly recalls that Mr. Catledge's telephone call came on a Sunday, and that he was spending the weekend at his retreat in the Virginia mountains, as described by Arthur Schlesinger. As there was no telephone in his cabin, Mr. Reston had to return the call from a gas station in Marshall, Va. Mr. Catledge and others recall, with equal certainty, that the incident took place on Thursday and that Mr. Reston was reached in his office in Washington.

Whichever was the case, the managing editor told Mr. Reston about the Szulc dispatch, which said that a landing on Cuba was imminent.

Mr. Reston was asked what should be done with the dispatch.

"I told them not to run it," Mr. Reston says.

He did not advise against printing information about the forces gathering in Florida; that was already well known. He merely cautioned against printing any dispatch that would pinpoint the time of the landing.

Others agree that Szulc's dispatch did contain some phraseology to the effect that an invasion was imminent, and those words were eliminated.

Tad Szulc's own recollection, cabled to me from Madrid the other day, is that "in several instances the stories were considerably toned down, including the elimination of statements about the 'imminence' of an invasion.

"Specifically," Mr. Szulc

United Press International

TRAINING FOR BAY OF PIGS: Anti-Castro Cuban exiles as they took part in maneuvers in unidentified Caribbean country a few days before invasion of Cuba in April, 1961. Papers faced difficult decisions on reporting these activities at the time.

said, "a decision was made in New York not to mention the C.I.A.'s part in the invasion preparations, not to use the date of the invasion, and, on April 15, not to give away in detail the fact that the first air strike on Cuba was carried out from Guatemala."

After the dummy for the front page of The Times for Friday, April 7, 1961, was changed, Ted Bernstein, who was the assistant managing editor on night duty at The Times, and Lew Jordan, the news editor, sat in Mr. Bernstein's office fretting about it. They believed a colossal mistake was being made, and together they went into Mr. Catledge's office to appeal for reconsideration.

Mr. Catledge recalls that Mr. Jordan's face was dead white, and he was quivering with emotion. He and Mr. Bernstein told the managing editor that never before had the front-page play in The New York Times been changed for reasons of policy. They said they would like to hear from the publisher himself the reasons for the change.

Angry at Intervention

Lew Jordan later recalled that Mr. Catledge was "flaming mad" at this intervention. However, he turned around in his big swivel chair, picked up the telephone, and asked Mr. Dryfoos to come downstairs. By the time he arrived, Mr. Bernstein had gone to dinner, but Mr. Dryfoos spent 10 minutes patiently explaining to Mr. Jordan his reasons for wanting the story played down.

His reasons were those of national security, national interest and, above all, concern for the safety of the men who were preparing to offer their lives on the beaches of Cuba. He repeated the explanation in somewhat greater length to Mr. Bernstein the next day.

I describe the mood and behavior of the publisher and editors of The New York Times only to show how seriously and with what intensity of emotion they made their fateful decisions.

Mr. Bernstein and Mr. Jordan now say, five years later, that the change in play, not eliminating the reference to the imminence of the invasion, was the important thing done that night.

"It was important because a multi-column head in this paper means so much," Mr. Jordan told me the other day.

Mr. Reston, however, felt that the basic issue was the elimination of the statement that an invasion was imminent.

Ironically, although that fact was eliminated from our own dispatch, virtually the same information was printed in a shirttail on Tad Szulc's report. That was a report from the Columbia Broadcasting System. It said that plans for the invasion of Cuba were in their final stages. Ships and planes were carrying invasion units from Florida to their staging bases in preparation for the assault.

When the invasion actually took place 10 days later, the American Society of Newspaper Editors happened to be in session in Washington, and President Kennedy addressed the society. He devoted his speech entirely to the Cuban crisis. He said nothing at that time about press disclosures of invasion plans.

Appeal by President

However, a week later in New York, appearing before the Bureau of Advertising of the American Newspaper Publishers Association, the President asked members of the newspaper profession "to re-examine their own responsibilities."

He suggested that the circumstances of the cold war required newspapermen to show some of the same restraint they would exercise in a shooting war.

He went on to say, "Every newspaper now asks itself with respect to every story, 'Is it news?' All I suggest is that you add the question 'Is it in the interest of national security?'"

If the press should recommend voluntary measures to prevent the publication of material endangering the national security in peacetime, the President said, "the Government would cooperate whole-heartedly."

Turner Catledge, who was the retiring president of the A.S.N.E., Felix McKnight of The Dallas Times-Herald, the incoming president, and Lee Hills, executive editor of the Knight newspapers, took the President's statement as an invitation to talk.

Within two weeks, a delegation of editors, publishers and news agency executives was at the White House. They told President Kennedy they saw no need at that time for machinery to help prevent the disclosure of vital security information. They agreed that there should be another meeting in a few months. However, no further meeting was ever held.

That day in the White House, President Kennedy ran down a list of what he called premature disclosures of security information. His examples were mainly drawn from The New York Times.

He mentioned, for example, Paul Kennedy's story about the training of anti-Castro forces in Guatemala. Mr. Catledge pointed out that this information had been published in La Hora in Guatemala and in The Nation in this country before it was ever published in The New York Times.

"But it was not news until it appeared in The Times," the President replied.

While he scolded The New York Times, the President said in an aside to Mr. Catledge, "If you had printed more about the operation you would have saved us from a colossal mistake."

'Sorry You Didn't Tell it'

More than a year later, President Kennedy was still talking the same way. In a conversation with Orvil Dryfoos in the White House on Sept. 13, 1962, he said, "I wish you had run everything on Cuba. . . . I am just sorry you didn't tell it at the time."

Those words were echoed by Arthur Schlesinger when he wrote, "I have wondered whether, if the press had behaved irresponsibly, it would not have spared the country a disaster."

They are still echoing down the corridors of history. Just the other day in Washington, Senator Russell of Georgia confessed that, although he was chairman of the Senate Armed Forces Committee, he didn't know the timing of the Bay of Pigs operation.

"I only wish I had been consulted," he said in a speech to the Senate, "because I would have strongly advised against this kind of operation if I had been."

It is not so easy, it seems, even for Presidents, their most intimate advisers and distinguished United States Senators to know always what is really in the national interest. One is tempted to say that sometimes—sometimes—even a mere newspaperman knows better.

My own view is that the Bay of Pigs operation might well have been canceled and the country been saved enormous embarrassment if The New York Times and other newspapers had been more diligent in the performance of their duty—their duty to keep the public informed on matters vitally affecting our national honor and prestige, not to mention our national security.

Perhaps, as Mr. Reston believes, it was too late to stop the operation by the time we printed Tad Szulc's story on April 7.

"If I had it to do over, I would do exactly what we did at the time," Mr. Reston says. "It is ridiculous to think that publishing the fact that the invasion was imminent would have avoided this disaster. I am quite sure the operation would have gone forward.

"The thing had been cranked up too far. The C.I.A. would have had to disarm the anti-Castro forces physically. Jack Kennedy was in no mood to do anything like that."

Prelude to Graver Crisis

The Bay of Pigs, as it turned out, was the prelude to an even graver crisis—the Cuban missile crisis of 1962. In Arthur Schlesinger's opinion, failure in 1961 contributed to success in 1962. President Kennedy had learned from experience, and once again The New York Times was involved.

On May 28, 1963, the President sat at his desk in the White House and with his own hand wrote a letter to Mrs. Orvil Dryfoos, whose husband had just died at the age of 50. The letter was on White House stationery, and the President used both sides of the paper.

The existence of this letter has never been mentioned publicly before. I have the permission of Mr. Dryfoos's widow, now Mrs. Andrew Heiskell, to read it to you today:

"Dear Marian:

"I want you to know how sorry I was to hear the sad news of Orvil's untimely death.

"I had known him for a number of years and two experiences I had with him in the last two years gave me a clear insight into his unusual qualities of mind and heart. One involved a matter of national security—the other his decision to refrain from printing on October 21st the news, which only the man for The Times possessed, on the presence of Russian missiles in Cuba, upon my informing him that we needed twenty-four hours more to complete our preparations.

"This decision of his made far more effective our later actions and thereby contributed greatly to our national safety.

"All this means very little now, but I did want you to know that a good many people some distance away, had the same regard for Orvil's character as did those who knew him best.

"I know what a blow this is to you, and I hope you will accept Jackie's and my deepest sympathy.

"Sincerely, John F. Kennedy."

In the Cuban missile crisis, things were handled somewhat differently than in the previous year. The President telephoned directly to the publisher of The New York Times.

He had virtually been invited to do so in their conversation in the White House barely a month before.

That conversation had been on the subject of security leaks in the press and how to prevent them, and Mr. Dryfoos had told the President that what was needed was prior information and prior consultation. He said that, when there was danger of security uniformation getting into print, the thing to do was to call in the publishers and explain matters to them.

In the missile crisis, President Kennedy did exactly that.

Ten minutes before I was due on this platform this morning Mr. Reston telephoned me from Washington to give me further details of what happened that day.

"The President called me," Mr. Reston said. "He understood that I had been talking to Mac Bundy and he knew from the line of questioning that we knew the critical fact—that Russian missiles had indeed been emplaced in Cuba.

"The President told me," Mr. Reston continued, "that he was going on television on Monday evening to report to the American people. He said that if we published the news about the missiles Khrushchev could actually give him an ultimatum before he went on the air. Those were Kennedy's exact words.

"I told him I understood," Mr. Reston said this morning, "but I also told him I could not do anything about it. And this is an important thought that you should convey to those young reporters in your audience.

"I told the President I would report to my office in New York and if my advice were asked I would recommend that we not publish. It was not my duty to decide. My job was the same as that of an ambassador—to report to my superiors.

"I recommended to the President that he call New York. He did so."

That was the sequence of events as Mr. Reston recalled them this morning. The President telephoned the publisher of The New York Times; Mr. Dryfoos in turn put the issue up to Mr. Reston and his staff.

And the news that the Soviet Union had atomic missiles in Cuba only 90 miles from the coast of Florida was withheld until the Government announced it.

What conclusion do I reach from all these facts? What moral do I draw from my story?

My conclusion is this: Information is essential to people who propose to govern themselves. It is the responsibility of serious journalists to supply that information—whether in this country or in the countries from which our foreign colleagues come.

Still, the primary responsibility for safeguarding our national interest must rest always with our Government, as it did with President Kennedy in the two Cuban crises.

Up until the time we are actually at war or on the verge of war, it is not only permissible—it is our duty as journalists and citizens to be constantly questioning our leaders and our policy, and to be constantly informing the people, who are the masters of us all—both the press and the politicians.

TV: Emphasis on Scoops
Befogs Election Results

Viewers Bombarded by Computer-Bred Data

By JACK GOULD

THE television networks' coverage of the election returns, which had something to do with politics and a great deal to do with TV rivalry, contained elements of reassurance for the human being. The machines weren't right all the time.

The research systems that compute instant determinations of the fate of minority dogcatchers in swing precincts were off the beam with enough frequency to give the viewer a new game to replace the disappearance of the old election night races. The sport that's popular now is to wait and see whether a network is not only first but also right? For a sideline diversion there is the amusing spectacle of watching the oral footwork of commentators whose statistical caution or bravado has been gored by subsequent events.

The National Broadcasting Company did the best by this new rating system; it did not have to make any retractions of projections. But it paid for its conservatism in the New York contest. Governor Rockefeller had been re-elected by both the Columbia Broadcasting System and the American Broadcasting Company hours before N.B.C. felt he had a clear margin for victory.

But just as Walter Cronkite and his C.B.S. associates were savoring their New York scoop, along came N.B.C. with an almost instant declaration that Ronald Reagan had carried the California gubernatorial race. Apparently C.B.S. felt some of its viewers also were watching N.B.C because Mr Cronkite went to some pains to insist that the returns from sample precincts were too indecisive to warrant the early elevation of the film actor. N.B.C. had made the same type of argument with respect to the New York race.

The policy of utmost caution is one that deserves to be championed because it does not take many bloopers to give the viewer a sense of wider uneasiness about the whole projection razzle-dazzle.

C.B.S. came a cropper in trying to project the Maryland contest for Governor, failing to detect that Spiro T. Agnew, the Republican, would defeat George P. Mahoney, his Democratic opponent. On the air the network did not blame its own technique; it invited the conclusion that the race had taken a sudden turn.

In the early hours of Wednesday, A.B.C. ran a series of retractions on apparent winners who had actually proved to be losers, although earlier the network did have a high percentage of correct calls. A.B.C. did not pass the buck, however; it blamed its own "brain trust."

As journalists, the network staffs understandably feel that scoops are one way to win attention, but on Tuesday evening there was too much public emphasis on the intramural contest. The average viewer is not channel-hopping all night, and to boast on the air of having made a projection a half hour or an hour earlier is becoming a childishly tiresome procedure.

Moreover, the saturation point in probable, indicated, apparent and actual victory percentage margins may be approaching. The mind boggles at the flood of mathematical data and simply cannot keep up with the fantastic output of the computers. The problem is particularly acute in an off-year election with its multiplicity of local races and the absence of clean-cut countrywide decisions involving two national contenders.

On Tuesday night the deluge of machine-made analytical material often ran second in interest to the restrained musings of the commentators. Eric Sevareid

New Game: Who's Both First and Right?

of C.B.S., who enjoys the luxury of not having to double in reading bulletins, had a number of graciously phrased remarks that touched on the human factors behind the night's events and put evolving trends in a conversational form that was easily digested and understood.

Similarly, Howard K. Smith of A.B.C. at times wisely cautioned against oversimplification of the backlash factor. Chet Huntley and David Brinkley of N.B.C. detected diverting sidelights and other matters of significance not to be electronically registered.

Further refinement of vote-gathering techniques will come before the election of 1968, but in the interim the networks might strive to complement the know-it-all of computers and pollsters with greater emphasis on the fallible human judgment of mortal observers.

The speed in the collection of an election night's hard news now is almost staggering and necessarily of immediate importance. But ethnic breakdowns on the number of three-eyed aborigines voting an independent ticket in the Dakotas is a lot less satisfying than a few minutes of careful reflective commentary that gives shape and perspective to the meaning of the electorate's will.

The computers need to be kept in their place lest a torrent of information merely clog the channels of communication and defeat the growing journalistic urgency of achieving selective clarity.

Election Night Rivalry

By doing intensive research into typical voting districts and relying upon computers to make quick projections, the three major television networks have been able to accomplish astonishing feats of speed in determining probable winners on Election Night. The slow counting of ballots and the painstaking analysis of fragmentary returns used to take many hours or even days, but it is now possible to foretell the outcome in a matter of minutes.

The trouble is that the networks have become carried away by their fascination with this technical skill. As was evident in the recent elections, each of them is competing to see which can declare the largest number of winners in the shortest time. Inevitably errors occur because the research information on key precincts, while of excellent quality, is not infallible. Elections—like all events in which humans are involved—sometimes take an odd turn.

All the networks went wrong in proclaiming Democrat Lester Maddox the new Governor of Georgia, partly because they had not taken into account the write-in votes for a third candidate that prevented either Mr. Maddox or his Republican opponent from achieving the required majority.

The emphasis on speed has gone so far that the networks even predicted the outcome in certain states while the polls were still open. This is not in itself illogical since the laws of mathematical probability on which these computer projections work can take into account—as they do in public opinion polls—how those waiting in line are likely to vote. But there is justifiable concern that some voters may be deterred from taking part in the election or be influenced in the way they cast their vote if the networks have already proclaimed the winner.

* * *

This preoccupation with speed is part of the ratings game. Yet the accuracy of the information and the depth, coherence and style with which the information is presented and analyzed are probably more persuasive with most people than mere speed.

Unfortunately, William S. Paley, chairman of the Columbia Broadcasting System, has chosen to rebut the critics rather than examine the problem. He is silent on the Election Night errors, apparently incapable of admitting that speed and accuracy do not always go together. Instead of recognizing that potential voters may react in different ways to the news that a network has proclaimed the winner while the polls are still open, he blandly suggests that because the reactions are contradictory they did not occur at all. His only solution is to adapt elections to television, a classic example of exalting the means above the end.

If the television industry can rally to a more constructive attitude, the somewhat foolish Election Night competition can easily be regulated by industry self-discipline. A few ground rules would help. One might be that no election is to be "called" until after all the polls in that state have closed. Another would provide that no network proclaim a winner until at least 10 per cent of the votes have been tabulated. But mostly what is called for are those dull virtues, restraint and caution.

December 4, 1966

Networks Eager to Cover Conventions in Color

By HENRY RAYMONT

The three major television networks plan to offer coverage in color of the Republican and Democratic National Conventions next year, provided the two conventions are held in the same city.

The decision to supply the new technology to the conventions was disclosed in separate interviews yesterday with executives of the three networks. They agreed that the use of color instead of black and white might triple their convention coverage costs.

The conventions in 1964 cost $4.5-million each to the American Broadcasting Company, the Columbia Broadcasting System and the National Broadcasting Company to televise.

Elmer Lower, president of A.B.C. News, said the network had decided to provide color coverage of the conventions because the quadrennial political meeting had become "one of the most important and popular events in television."

For this reason, he said, the conventions merit the innovation, though only 20 per cent of America's estimated total of 55 million homes with television own color sets.

However, Mr. Lower and spokesmen for C.B.S. and N.B.C. said the decision to use color would probably be contingent on an agreement between the Republicans and Democrats on a single site.

If one party holds its convention in Chicago and the other in Miami, for example, the costs to the networks would be prohibitive, they said. Color coverage involves the moving of three times as much equipment and an expanded force of technical personnel, they said.

Representatives of the networks are reported to have emphasized these points last Feb. 20 in Washington at a closed hearing of the Republican National Committee's site panel. They plan to reiterate the argument in a similar meeting with the Democratic National Committee in Washington on Friday.

Ray C. Bliss, the Republican National Chairman, who has indicated he is not adverse to meeting in the same city as his rivals, said over the weekend that he might discuss the idea with the Democrats.

Democratic National Committee sources suggested yesterday that they would be receptive to such talks.

But G.O.P. Unit Is Told That Both Parties Must Meet in the Same City in '68

Confidence Expressed

Network representatives are expressing confidence in an agreement between the two parties. The assumption is that television has become an important factor in stimulating interest in the election issues and personalities.

Therefore, they see the needs of the networks as playing a decisive role on a site for the conventions.

Some television executives are dismissing any notion that they want to influence the National Committees.

"I certainly don't want to be in a position of dictating to the parties where they should meet," Richard Salant, president of the C.B.S. Network Division, said.

Mr. Salant explained that William Leonard, vice president of the Network Division in charge of news programs, had appeared before the Republican site committee "only because we were invited to testify."

Mr. Leonard said he had given the committee a detailed account of the network's requirements for the use of color, including increased lighting and air-conditioning facilities.

Much Lighting Needed

"We will need about double the lighting used for black and white," he said. "All that means is there'll be that much more heat, but that can be canceled by adding much more air-conditioning."

William R. McAndrew, president of N.B.C. News, said the network had been represented in Washington by Donald Meaney, a vice president.

"Mr. Meaney made the point strongly and urgently," Mr. McAndrew said, "that it would be almost impossible to obtain enough equipment for color if the two parties decided to have the conventions close to each other in time and far in distance."

Six cities have bid for the 1968 Republican National Convention and at least as many are expected to approach the Democratic National Committee this week. The applicants are Chicago, Miami Beach, Philadelphia, Houston, Los Angeles and San Francisco.

March 6, 1967

Actors Discuss Role of Actors in Politics

By GLADWIN HILL
Special to The New York Times

LOS ANGELES, Aug. 27—Do actors have an unfair advantage entering politics in the age of television?

Still smarting from the defeat they suffered in California last November in Ronald Reagan's election as Governor of California, 400 Democrats convoked a panel of actors this weekend to explore that question.

The scene was the annual Western States Democratic Conference. The panel comprised three party activists from the movie-television world: Barry Sullivan, Jill St. John and Joe Flynn—none of whom professed any personal political aspirations.

Their colloquy, moderated by a Los Angeles television newsman, Bill Brown, included the following observations:

Camera Press-Pix

Barry Sullivan   **Jill St. John**   **Joe Flynn**

BROWN: An actor is like a plumber or an attorney or anyone else. He has a right to get into politics. But the impact of an actor on television poses some very unusual problems. Perhaps it's an unfair advantage that a performer has over anyone else?

FLYNN: I don't think he necessarily does have an advantage. It depends on an actor's image. I don't think Richard Widmark—who had the image of pushing that old lady downstairs—would have beaten Ronald Reagan last year.

SULLIVAN: I don't think Eric Von Stroheim, who played so many Nazi types, would be a very electable candidate for anything. But I don't think any actor has any undue advantage. Maybe he's less nervous when he steps before a camera. But that's the size of the edge he has. If an actor doesn't have some idea of what he's talking about, all the slickness in the world won't help.

FLYNN: But what about Shirley Temple? The image everybody has of her is an 8-year-old moppet singing "On the Good Ship Lollipop." A lot of politicians are saying if she runs in that special Congressional election in Northern California [the forthcoming contest in San Mateo County to replace the late Representative J. Arthur Younger] that she's going to win. Is that the image people will be sending to Congress—an 8-year-old moppet?

SULLIVAN: I think she's aware of conditions in her area today. She's a person who's involved in the community. Therefore she has a right to run.

MISS ST. JOHN: I think the public's familiarity with actors creates an almost immediate dialogue, of the kind you don't get with an unknown candidate, and maybe that's something we need more of today.

'Tell It the Way It Is'

SULLIVAN: I agree with that. I think the whole dialogue of American society has altered considerably. As the kids say, "Tell it the way it is, baby." I think the Democratic Party's been telling it the way it was—talking about civil rights and Social Security and things like that as if it was still 1950. Somehow we've got to tell it the way it is, not the way it was in 1950. But there's a danger in an actor stepping out of the character that people know. Steve Allen is a very funny man. But when he was thinking of running for Congress and started making speeches, the shock was terrible. He didn't seem right, pontificating.

FLYNN: An incumbent has a great disadvantage because he has to tell it like it is. A challenger can tell you what you want to hear. Reagan said he'd lower taxes. Immediately he was elected he raised taxes. But a poll showed his popularity was higher than ever. Now how do you explain that?

BROWN: Is there a question of morality in this matter of "the way it is" versus what people want to hear? Is it a reflection on the intelligence of the voter?

MISS ST. JOHN: It must be. Those who think and care unfortunately are those who sit in armchairs theorizing.

BROWN: How about the way television projects the There's nothing wrong with presenting the best image you can. Politicians can't go on being disheveled in appearance in the age of television, because it indicates a mind that may be disheveled.

FLYNN: I think all America agrees that if Richard Nixon had had a better makeup man, he'd be President.

SULLIVAN: Over my dead body. . . .

FLYNN: Barry, you may still get a chance to lay that body down.

physical appeal of a candidate?

MISS ST. JOHN: I think women are the larger percentage of voters, although I'm not sure of these statistics. Anyway, a lot of them vote. But a lot of women are not politically oriented, and I think they tend to vote for the most attractive candidate, because he seems nice and is good to his mother. I'm all for attractive people, but I'm also for the statesman who can do the job. But to win elections we have to sell a product. And the material must be attractively packaged.

BROWN: What can a professional politician do to use these tools of the acting profession to advantage?

MISS ST. JOHN: I see nothing wrong with a politician seeking professional help, being taught how to use the camera, how to be made up. There's nothing wrong with presenting the best image you can. Politicians can't go on being disheveled in appearance in the age of television, because it indicates a mind that may be disheveled.

FLYNN: I think all America agrees that if Richard Nixon had had a better makeup man, he'd be President.

SULLIVAN: Over my dead body. . . .

FLYNN: Barry, you may still get a chance to lay that body down.

NETWORKS' IMPACT ON VOTERS DOUBTED

WASHINGTON, Aug. 31 (UPI)—The Senate Commerce Committee reported today that it had found no need at present for laws to change the current election system because of a possible impact on voting by the use of computers by networks to forecast election results.

The report was based on hearings into whether the projection of election returns could affect the behavior of voters in areas where polls were still open. The report said there was insufficient experience to call for a change "at this time."

Testimony was heard from representatives of the networks and broadcasters and the Federal Communications Commission and from persons who participated in research projects.

Without ruling out the possibility of future action, the report to the Senate said it was "satisfied that the networks and broadcasters will take appropriate steps to clearly label voting projections in a manner that the public will not be misled." The committee said that it found no evidence "of any discernible impact on voter behavior from such broadcasts," but added that it "expects to follow closely" future developments.

September 1, 1967

For 24-Hour Voting

To the Editor:

I am writing to raise two voices (my wife's and my own) in support of Dr. Frank Stanton's recent proposal that Election Day be declared a national holiday and that on that day polls be opened everywhere in the country at the same moment (regardless of local time differences) and for a 24-hour period.

Making Election Day a national holiday would avoid the necessity for voters' attempting to sandwich a visit to the polls between more pressing and "more important" obligations. It would dramatize and heighten the importance of Election Day, thereby encouraging more citizens to learn about candidates and familiarize themselves with issues.

Opening and closing the polls at the same time throughout the country would reduce the problem of election results being predicted by computers and announced while votes are still being cast in some states.

Keeping the polls open for 24 hours would assure all voters of the opportunity to find a convenient time to vote.

STEVEN H. BARUCH
White Plains, N. Y.
Oct. 12, 1967

October 29, 1967

Nixon Calls Makeup On TV a Big Factor In His 1960 Defeat

Former Vice President Richard M. Nixon said last night that bad television makeup during his 1960 debates with John F. Kennedy played a big part in his losing that Presidential election.

He made the statement on the Johnny Carson "Tonight" show televised by the National Broadcasting Company. A report circulated at the taping of that program that if Mr. Nixon announced his candidacy for the Republican Presidential nomination the makeup director on the "Tonight" program would join his staff.

The makeup director was identified as Roy Voege, 36 years old, of Edgewater, N. J., a member of the N.B.C. staff for 18 years. He was quoted as saying:

"Nothing's completely settled yet. I've worked with Nixon on some of his filming, and we get along fine. Now we have to wait for the formal announcement."

While Mr. Nixon was taping the Carson program, the Columbia Broadcasting System was reporting that its surveys had shown that he was virtually an assured winner of the Republican nomination if he won the New Hampshire and Wisconsin primaries.

The broadcasting chain's news correspondent, Mike Wallace, reported the results of the survey last night on the evening news program with Walter Cronkite.

November 23, 1967

Presidents' Relationship to TV Is Scrutinized

3 Former White House Press Aides on Panel

By JACK GOULD

THE relationship of the White House and the television medium was the ostensible subject of a live discussion last night on Channel 13, but the heart of the matter hardly came up until the closing moments of the 90-minute symposium. For some inexplicable reason the non-commercial station WNDT cut the program off just as the questioning began to get to the point. The flexibility of public broadcasting apparently was at the mercy of prior scheduling arrangements for the Eastern Educational Network; at times live interconnection of educational TV is an obvious disadvantage.

Three former White House press secretaries — Bill D. Moyers, who served President Johnson; Pierre Salinger, who served the late President Kennedy and President Johnson, and James C. Hagerty, who served former President Eisenhower, were the principal participants in the round table presented by the New York chapter of the National Academy of Television Arts and Sciences. The meeting was held at the Hilton Hotel.

●

In the waning moments of the live pickup Mr. Moyers raised the intriguing question of whether each succeeding President automatically had to bow to television precedents, or if he might work out his own means of communicating with the public. He said that President Kennedy was exceptionally adroit at the televised press conference, whereas President Johnson was more comfortable either speaking from the stump to a large audience or exercising his persuasive powers in small groups of three or four persons. President Johnson, he added, simply was not at ease with "the staged and set press conference."

Mr. Moyers went on to note that it was not possible for the television eye to penetrate a President's thinking at the fateful moment of an "inscrutable confluence of intel-

91

ligence and judgment." With this provocative suggestion that TV may not inherently be best suited to every President, surely a topic worthy of development on the air itself, the broadcast portion of the meeting came to a close.

●

Mr. Salinger contended that TV plays a key role in a whole variety of divisions between the people and their government. TV, he said, frequently goes to the fire without inquiring how the fire started, or whether a building was reconstructed after the blaze. He argued that had the Kennedy and Johnson Administrations displayed more candor in telling the people the perils of the Vietnamese involvement, there might now be less talk of a credibility gap.

Mr. Hagerty discussed his efforts to put the electronic media on an equal footing with the press, and reviewed the normal tensions between the Government and an aggressive press in a free society.

Frank McGee of the National Broadcasting Company and Dan Rather of the Columbia Broadcasting System asked questions in behalf of TV reporters, but their inquiries were something less than very searching.

●

In fact, the academy's forum filibustered too much over the history of the evolution of the relationship between TV and the White House and did not, as Mr. Moyers particularly stressed, deal with the present serious ramifications of those relations. Three men peculiarly qualified to see the issue from both the inside and outside of government were certainly not adequately challenged.

Edward P. Morgan, chief correspondent of the Public Broadcast Laboratory, acted as moderator. He noted jokingly that in Washington he had been accused in the past of asking very long questions. In that regard his reputation, was left intact last night. His protracted asides unfortunately accounted in part for the failure of the discussion to get down to hard facts until only a few minutes before Channel 13 elected to go about its business as usual.

Can the Conventions Compete With 'The Invaders'?

By JACK GOULD

THIS summer's political conventions may be facing a television surprise. For reasons of economy the American Broadcasting Company will be offering entertainment between 7:30 and 9:30 on convention nights and then picking up the political deliberations. The move conceivably could have a long-range influence on the other two networks and possibly on the structure of the conventions themselves.

If the National Broadcasting Company and Columbia Broadcasting System switch at 7:30 to the doings in Miami and Chicago and ABC is presenting theatrical diversion, there are many who feel that the ABC chain may run off with whopping ratings and that the politicos will be left with diminished audiences for their pronouncements.

One network executive last week noted that the problem is very real. Based on past conventions, he said, about 30 per cent of the television coverage of conventions was actually devoted to genuine business involving the speaker's rostrum and delegates, and 70 per cent was in the nature of a stage wait.

There does seem little doubt that television's fiercely competitive concern over the conventions—it has been in the nature of an electronic cause célèbre to which the chains look forward every four years—has contributed to the impression that the quadrennial parleys seemingly go on forever.

With hours of time to fill before the start of the convention sessions there has been almost a frenzy to achieve exclusive reports with this delegation or that one, with this possible candidate or another. The slightest incident can be blown out of substantive proportion, and the hapless anchorman must extemporaneously fill in to a point where his own sense of boredom is not very convincingly concealed.

Arguments for steamlining the convention process recur with monotonous regularity, but TV itself is by no means the chief cause of tedium. Part of it stems from the host cities, who call for at least four days of proceedings so that the hotels, restaurants and other businesses can recoup the outlays they may have made to attract the convention in the first place.

*

Moreover, the operating function of the convention may require more time than meets a viewer's eyes. It is the convention, after all, which does bring a nationwide multitude of party delegates into personal contact. Their deliberations and exchanges of view are not irrelevant to a political convention's importance. No other occasion affords quite the same opportunity for face-to-face meetings, and, in light of the extraordinarily complex issues facing the country today, the chance of such discussion can be of great value.

A convention is not intended as a television show but rather for the more serious business of selecting nominees and hammering out platforms. Unfortunately TV, in its desire to pad out inactive hours, may exaggerate small incidents or give over-emphasis to peripheral occurences. This problem is compounded in particular by the rivalry between NBC and CBS in their struggle to be the first with the most of every development.

No one in the political arena could have foreseen that last January's collapse of ABC's merger negotiations with the International Telephone and Telegraph Corporation would have economic repercussions affecting convention coverage.

With the crisis in the cities and the war in Vietnam it may well prove unrealistic for ABC to stick with entertainment for two hours while its rivals are going the gavel-to-gavel route. Conceivably, the thirst for theatrical escapism might dwindle away if more momentous developments affecting national survival were happening on alternate channels. Journalistic predictions of the country's future mood in wartime could be illusory, particularly if the painful realities of the Vietnamese conflict invade more and more homes because of mounting casualties and increased draft calls.

But ABC's contemplated step of providing entertainment and then switching to the conventions in itself could be a barometer of national attitude. Frankly, if the ABC posture should prevail, it may prove competitively more difficult for both NBC and CBS to run a contrary course. An erosion of commitment to public service can be disconcertingly contagious in the mass media.

But, by the same token, saturation coverage by all networks of the same event has evoked some criticism among viewers who do not have independent stations available as an alternative program choice. The forced feeding of dull political oratory, of which there is always some at any convention, conceivably could be self-defeating in terms of arousing a more active sense of citizenship, particularly when the commentators themselves turn away in favor of small talk.

At all events the summer conventions, barring changes in the interim, could shed some interesting sociological light on the depth of response of mass viewers to the conventions, whether there is a demand for cutting away the chaff and keeping only the wheat, or whether, in the anxiety of 1968, there will be an overriding interest in every scrap of news that can possibly be collected. Politicians and broadcasters alike could be affected by the outcome.

Dissent Is Not the Whole Story

By GEORGE GENT

THERE is a real danger that television may be contributing unwittingly to the growing irrationalism affecting American political and social life. This, at least, would be a reasonable conclusion for anyone watching the medium's coverage of the various movements of dissent in recent weeks. Television, for better or worse, is the way most Americans get their news and form opinions on the events shaping their times. How those events are presented to the TV viewing public will determine in large measure the nation's response to the challenges facing it. It should be obvious, therefore, that if television is presenting a distorted or superficial image of these forms of social protest, then the American public will respond by either over-reacting to these challenges to the status quo or by dismissing them as inconsequential.

*

Either response could be disastrous. Certainly there are vital social and moral issues involved in the Negro, student and anti-Vietnam protest movements, but there is much confusion and disharmony in the ranks of the protesters themselves, and it will not serve the public weal for television to do no more than mirror that confusion. Unfortunately, that is what it appears to be doing. Indeed, TV can be said to be adding to the confusion by giving voice to the strident dissenters without tackling the much tougher journalistic job of bringing clarity out of what seems to be chaos.

Three examples of TV's response to the journalistic challenge presented by dissenting Americans were offered to viewers in recent weeks. Two of them — on various aspects of the Negro-white confrontation — were presented on educational networks. The third, a sympathetic study of the growing resistance to military service by draft-age Americans, was carried on the National Broadcasting Company. All were interesting reports, but they left the really important questions unasked, much less unanswered, and thus contributed to the national confusion.

*

The first of these programs was "Color Us Black," a one-hour documentary on the recent student uprising at Howard University. The program, which was produced by National Educational Television and seen here on Channel 13, was an interesting but confused report on the growing self-consciousness among Negro students and intellectuals. The producers, however, apparently quickly tired of the rather restricting issue of university problems and allowed the students to voice their much more general indictment of American society, specifically white society, in what can only be termed the rhetoric of the new irrationalism.

It was disconcerting, to say the least, to watch young, middle-class Negro girls mouthing racist propaganda about the white man's rape of their great-grandmothers as though the sins of history will have to be avenged with a flaming sword on every white person living today. Nor was it conducive to racial understanding to have militant students referring to whites as "honkies." Another student— it was difficult to tell how representative he might have been — spoke elatedly of pulling down American society. That same young man — and others, as well — insisted that he would reject being incorporated into the existing social system, but no alternative system was proposed. And no one on the program even asked if an alternative had been considered.

*

The second program was "Blacks and Whites in Contact," a report on a Philadelphia interracial group that was carried on the Eastern Educational Network, including Channel 13. The participants, who were equally divided between Negroes and whites, were supposed to illustrate how racial cooperation between inner-city and suburb — in this case, the Northern Philadelphia area and the exclusive Chestnut Hill section — could achieve mutually satisfactory results.

Since the participants in the live discussion were all members of the interracial group, a certain minimal amount of goodwill might be assumed. Alas, that was not the case. Within minutes, the Negro militants, particularly one very bright and articulate young woman, took over the discussion and used it as a platform for the moral indictment of American society and for a vaguely metaphysical appeal for whites to become truly human. Needless to say, specifics on how to achieve this desirable goal were not forthcoming. By the hour's end, nothing concrete had been proposed and only the most absolute of optimists could say that there had been a meeting of minds.

The NBC program was "We Won't Go," a rather warmed-over and superficial report on the antidraft movements around the country. Its principal virtue was in conveying the high moral idealism that motivates many of the resisters who are propelled by conscience to defy the law and risk prison for their belief that the Vietnam war is immoral.

*

But it, like so many of the programs dealing with complex and emotion-charged issues, failed to clarify for the viewer the nature of the problem. The program captured the voices of dissent — defiant, sad, glad or mystical. However, the rationale by which the resisters arrived at their decision that the Vietnam war was so immoral that conscience forbade them to participate, in defiance of law and the opinion of the vast majority of their fellow citizens, was not even explored.

Many Americans have serious doubts about various aspects of the war but are not so convinced of the rightness of their judgments that they would refuse to serve.

The point is that these programs did not really serve the cause of viewer enlightenment, however noble their intentions. The often strident voice of dissent must be listened to, but it is best heard on the regular news programs. Documentaries and news specials should bring clarity and perspective to the issues and not be seduced by the easy journalistic victories of inflammatory rhetoric and harsh confrontations. Hard questions have to be asked if the public is to be well-served. Unsupported allegations and wild accusations should not pass unchallenged. Reporters should not accept without question general indictments of whole classes of people or of entire races, from whatever sources they emanate.

Negroes have substantive claims on American society and draft resisters have raised valid moral arguments about the Vietnamese war and war in general, but the television public must be presented with something more than generalized indictments of society if it is to respond meaningfully.

These are troubled times, and television provides a national forum for anyone who appears before its cameras. This affords the medium tremendous power, but also imposes upon it an enormous responsibility. The verbal grenade can be defused amid columns of newsprint, but on television it can explode with truly nuclear force. It behooves TV, therefore, to eschew the easy paths of controversy and conflict in its documentaries and take on the more responsible and more difficult role of interpretation and hard-nosed reporting that will not accept every statement at face value. The American public is desperately in need of light. It has had quite enough of rhetorical heat.

TV: Restrained, Thorough Coverage

Networks on Scene at Kennedy Shooting

By JACK GOULD

THE shooting of Senator Robert F. Kennedy constituted a bizarre and tragic television viewing experience—first the tension of the close primary race and then the numbing horror of yet another national figure violently struck down by a burst of bullets.

The networks, which chanced to have extensive equipment in Los Angeles for what they assumed would be one more chapter in the American political campaign, did a remarkably restrained and thorough job in covering the multiple facets of the story beset by confusion, hysteria, sorrow, grave medical speculation and unpredictable political implications.

●

The networks quickly acquired an amazing amount of vivid photographic material on the shooting, since their own cameras were not in place in the kitchen passageway of the Ambassador Hotel, scene of the assault. By means of interviews and other available film sources the networks supplemented their live coverage of Senator Kennedy's victory speech with close-ups of the tragedy that occurred minutes later.

There were pictures of Senator Kennedy lying on the floor of the passageway and then being lifted into an ambulance, as well as a briefer shots of the capture of the accused assailant. The tears and hysteria of some Kennedy supporters in the ballroom were shown but never in excessive detail. There was a glimpse of Mr. and Mrs. Pierre Salinger hitching a ride on a motor-cycle to get to Good Samaritan Hospital.

One of the most poignant network interviews was with the ambulance physician, who after Senator Kennedy's pulse appeared to have stopped, passed to Mrs. Kennedy his stethoscope so that she could hear for herself her husband's heartbeat.

The total visual effect was a segment of society suddenly thrown into disarray and reacting with all the variations of which bewildered humanity is capable. It was almost more than the eye and mind could comprehend over a period of 12 hours or more. It was a feeling of despairing exhaustion yet a determination to learn more details.

Ironically, the assassination of President Kennedy, the Senator's brother, had taught television and the police the virtue of caution. The accused assailant was carefully secreted from a three-ring journalistic circus and respect for his legal rights was repeatedly stressed. TV and radio, in turn, avoided deductions until they could be substantiated.

By curious coincidence the Columbia Broadcasting System's cockiness in projecting the final outcome of the primary, which proved substantially wide of the mark, caught C.B.S. with its guard down. The network, though not its affiliates in California, terminated primary coverage at 2:13 A.M., Eastern daylight time, slightly more than an hour before the shooting. The National Broadcasting Company and the American Broadcasting Company, which were much more conservative in their vote projections, stayed on the air longer and were prepared for the unexpected. C.B.S. came back at 3:30 A.M. with the shooting and at that hour in the Eastern section of the country the delay hardly rated as too serious.

●

Coverage by all three networks thereafter was continuous until either 12 noon or 1:30 P.M. yesterday. Regular scheduling remained subject to instant pre-emption as developments in Los Angeles warranted. For radio listeners, WCBS, WINS and WNEW, among others, turned in a highly commendable performance.

On TV, neurological surgeons by and large advanced a grim prognosis on Senator Kennedy's chances to survive without physical or mental impairment. Each network separately solicited the help of New York neurosurgeons to explain in lay terms the medical consequences of the shooting.

Reporters, some of whom were almost incoherent with fatigue or speechless shock, purposely said they did not want to get too far ahead of themselves in discussing what might be the political repercussions of Senator Kennedy's disability. But in adroit wordage they left no doubt that in 1968 the American scene once again had undergone incredible change, and that the indiscriminate selling of guns was a blight on a civilized country, to say nothing of the President's having to order protection for all candidates.

In a matter of hours, radio and television staged shows and commentaries on the national sickness of violence as a way of life. Eric Sevareid, the only consistently regular TV commentator, observed on C.B.S. in the afternoon that literature, movies and television all had played their part in profiteering on violence and encouraging disrespect for just authority.

Humphrey Charges Television Is a 'Catalyst' Spurring Riots

By VAL ADAMS

Vice President Humphrey charged yesterday that television "has spread the message of rioting and looting" and "has literally served as a catalyst to promote even more trouble."

His comment was contained in a profile of Mr. Humphrey published in the July 9 issue of Look magazine which goes on sale today. The article included his views on how to control civil disorders and the responsibility of television, radio and the press in reporting such events.

The Vice President's criticism that TV added fuel to civil disorders was much more unfavorable than the recent report by the President's National Advisory Commission on Civil Disorders, which analyzed the riots of last summer. That report, noting instances of sensationalism, inaccuracy and distortion by newspapers, radio and television, concluded that the media "on th whole tried to give a balanced, factual account of the 1967 disorders."

Asked to comment on Mr. Humphrey's charge, the National Broadcasting Company said it was essential to cover the news even if it were "unpleasant and unattractive." The American Broadcasting Company said it sought to televise balanced, objective reports that would not "inflame any situation."

The Columbia Broadcasting System declined direct comment but referred to an earlier statement of policy that it must report any "significant trends in our society."

Where the President's National Advisory Commission on Civil Disorders had said that "our criticisms, important as they are, do not lead us to conclude that the media are a cause of riots," the Vice President singled out television for criticism:

"I do know," Mr. Humphrey said in the Look article, "that TV in particular has spread the message of rioting and looting has displayed the carrying out of televisions, home appliances groceries, etc., and has literally served as a catalyst to promote even more trouble. The basic question is how do you report the news and at the same time not add fuel to the fire."

The Vice President said it

June 6, 1968

was essential that television in particular, "and radio and press secondarily," accept responsibility in riot situations.

"If the media are going to broadcast the emotional appeals of the Stokely Carmichaels and the other agitators," he said, "it is like throwing gasoline on the flames. I have discovered even in my campaign that Negro youth particularly likes to get on television. Half of the jumping, pushing and shoving that goes on in a campaign is a desire on the part of the youngster in the ghetto to have some publicity, to see his picture on television."

June 25, 1968

TV: A Chilling Spectacle in Chicago

Delegates See Tapes of Clashes in the Streets

By JACK GOULD

TELEVISION'S influence in covering the Democratic National Convention is likely to be a subject of study for years. Last night, untold millions of viewers, as well as the delegates in the hall, saw chilling TV tape recordings of Chicago policemen clearing the streets in front of the Conrad Hilton Hotel.

The tapes, relayed by motorcycle couriers to the headquarters of the networks in the International Amphitheater, showed girls being dragged across streets and young men being clubbed. How complete the visual accounts of the disturbance may have been could not be ascertained from only looking at the screen, but the pictures alone were enough to send a shudder down a viewer's spine.

August 29, 1968

Daley Defends His Police; Humphrey Scores Clashes

Criticism Angers Mayor

By R. W. APPLE Jr.
Special to The New York Times

CHICAGO, Aug. 29 — Infuriated by attacks upon himself, his city and his police force, Mayor Richard J. Daley defended today the manner in which antiwar, anti-Humphrey demonstrations were suppressed in downtown Chicago last night.

Mr. Daley described the demonstrators as "terrorists" and said they had come here determined to "assault, harass and taunt the police into reacting before television cameras."

The Mayor flushed deeply as he denounced the reports of newspapers, radio and television last night. He asserted that "the whole purpose of the city and the law enforcement agencies" had been "distorted and twisted."

"In the heat of emotion and riot," Mr. Daley said, "some policemen may have overreacted, but to judge the entire police force by the alleged action of a few would be just as unfair as to judge our entire younger generation by the actions of the mob."

In an interview tonight on the Columbia Broadcasting System television network, the Mayor said he had "intelligence reports" indicating that persons whom he did not identify had planned to assassinate him, the three leading Presidential contenders and others. He gave no further details.

Mr. Daley also commented bitterly on the program about remarks made by young men and women in the demonstrations. He said they had used "the foulest of language that you wouldn't hear in a brothel hall."

Mayor Daley appeared in the conference room adjacent to his office to read a two-minute statement at 1:20 P.M. He was cheered by members of his staff who gathered at the rear of the room minutes before.

When he finished his toughly worded, combative remarks, the 65-year-old Mayor said, "This is my statement, gentlemen it speaks for itself." Then stalked off the podium without giving newsmen an opportunity to ask questions.

Mr. Daley and his aides appeared to be aware that the Mayor had been singled out, both by the demonstrators and anti-Administration delegates on the floor of the Democratic National Convention, as a symbol of repression and old-line party leadership.

But they were prepared to concede almost nothing. Earl Bush, the Mayor's press secretary, volunteered the information that Mr. Daley was "determined to continue to do the right thing." And he said that telephone calls to City Hall were running 100-to-1 in support of Mr. Daley.

Mayor Daley met this morning with Vice President Humphrey, who has condemned what he called "storm trooper tactics," but no account of their conversation was available. It was also reliably reported that before Mr. Daley left the convention hall last night he was urged in telephone calls from party leaders to do what he could to restrain the police in the Loop district.

Cites Policemen's Injuries

The Mayor reported that 51 policemen had been injured, but he did not mention that from 100 to 200 demonstrators had been hurt. He also said that "60 per cent of those arrested did not live in Illinois."

"This administration and the people of Chicago," Mr. Daley went on, "have never condoned brutality at any time, but they will never permit a lawless, violent group of terrorists to menace the lives of millions of people, destroy the purpose of a national political convention, and take over the streets."

Reflecting his resentment at news coverage of the demonstrations, the Mayor began by saying that he expected his statement to "be given the same kind of distribution on press, radio and television as the mob of rioters was given yesterday."

"In every instance," he said, "the recommendation of the National Advisory Commission on Civil Disorders—'to use manpower instead of firepower'—had been followed.

Hard Line Is Taken

Attached to a copy of his statement that was handed to newsmen were copies of articles, favorable to the Mayor, from The Christian Science Monitor, The Chicago Tribune, Chicago's American and Barron's magazine, a weekly Wall Street publication.

Sources acquainted with Mr. Daley's thinking said that he was particularly angry at what he considered unfair aspersions cast upon the name of Chicago, a place he loves deeply and has often described as "the greatest city in the world."

Frank J. Sullivan, the police department's director of public information, took a similarly hard line at a news conference this morning.

Mr. Sullivan described the demonstrators as "revolutionaries" and called some of their leaders, including Tom Hayden and Rennie Davis, "Communists who are the allies of the men who are killing American soldiers."

"The intellectuals of America hate Richard J. Daley," Mr. Sullivan declared, "because he was elected by the people—unlike Walter Cronkite."

Besides Mr. Cronkite, the anchor man for the Columbia Broadcasting System's convention coverage, Mr. Sullivan denounced in general terms both C.B.S. and the National Broadcasting Company. He contended that they had conducted a "colossal propaganda campaign" against Chicago and the Chicago police.

The public relations officer insisted that there had been no "pattern of excessive force" in the clashes last night. His chief, Police Superintendent James B. Conlisk Jr., said, "The force used was the force necessary to repel the mob."

Mr. Sullivan made a point of denying published reports that the police had smashed a window in the Haymarket Lounge at the Conrad Hilton Hotel by pushing people, including bystanders, through the plate glass. He said that the window had been smashed by the protesters.

The New oYrk Times was among the newspapers that published accounts criticized by Mr. Sullivan. Its article was based on an eye-witness account by Earl Caldwell, one of its reporters.

Richard F. Salant, president of C.B.S. News, replied to Mr. Sullivan in a statement that said, "The pictures and sound of the Chicago police department in action speak for themselves—louder than any words ours or any attempt by them to find any scapegoats."

"If Mr. Sullivan feels that the unedited pictorial record showed excessive force," said Reuven Frank, president of N.B.C. News, "and therefore that the rules of his own department were being broken, that must be his conclusion. Anyone else in the country who watched and came to the same conclusion also did so on his own."

August 30, 1968

News Executives File Protest to Daley

The top executives of 10 of the nation's largest newspapers, news magazines and television networks yesterday sent a strong joint protest to Mayor Richard J. Daley of Chicago regarding police treatment of newsmen during the Democratic National Convention last week.

They sent Mayor Daley a telegram, the text of which follows:

"We strongly protest treatment of news reporters, photographers and cameramen by certain members of the Chicago police force during the Democratic convention. Newsmen were repeatedly singled out by policemen and deliberately beaten and harassed. Cameras were broken and film was destroyed. The obvious purpose was to discourage or prevent reporting of an important confrontation between police and demonstrators which the American public has the right to know about.

"An investigation by the F.B.I. is underway to ascertain whether this treatment of news personnel involved violation of Federal law. Regardless of the F.B.I. inquiry, we strongly urge that you yourself order an investigation by a responsible group of distinguished and disinterested citizens. This investigation should fix responsibility for the conduct of the members of the police force who participated in these incidents and see to it that suitable punishment is meted out as deserved.

If America is to survive, the freedom of our news media to observe and report must remain inviolate. The police must not be permitted to suppress this freedom by clubbing and intimidation.

Respectfully yours.

The telegram was signed by:

Leonard Goldenson, president of the American Broadcasting Company.

Bailey K. Howard, president of the newspaper division of Field Enterprises, Inc., publishing The Chicago Sun-Times and The Chicago Daily News.

Dr. Frank Stanton, president of the Columbia Broadcasting System.

Otis Chandler, publisher of The Los Angeles Times.

Julian Goodman, president of the National Broadcasting Company.

Arthur Ochs Sulzberger, president and publisher of The New York Times.

Hedley Donovan, editor-in-chief of Time magazine.

Mrs. Katharine Graham, president of The Washington Post Company, for The Washington Post and Newsweek magazine.

Politics Now the Focus of Underground Press

By JOHN LEO

The Underground Press, created to reflect and shape the withdrawn life style of hippies and dropouts, has taken a sharp turn toward radical politics.

Until recently, the formula for a successful underground paper was sex, drugs, rock music, Oriental religion and "the San Francisco look" in psychedelic art.

Now this material is yielding to coverage of student uprisings, the peace movement, guerrilla activities, draft resistance and muckraking attacks on the political and social Establishment.

The disruption in June by 20 people of a television panel discussion on the underground press, lavishly covered in underground papers, is regarded by many as symbolic of the shift toward confrontation. During the incident, which took place at the studios of Channel 13 while the "Newsfront" program was on the air, the invaders milled about in front of the camera, shouted and cursed the "Establishment media."

"We're not withdrawing," said one underground editor, speaking of the trend, "we're overturning."

There are perhaps 150 underground papers, almost all of them less than three years old and most of them published under shaky financial conditions in large cities or college towns.

By the standards of traditional journalism, much of the underground writing is freewheeling, lurid, superficial and sometimes indecipherable.

However, much of it is imaginative and impassioned coverage of events sometimes slighted by established media.

Range of the Genre

The underground journals range from the brash young political papers, like The Great Speckled Bird of Atlanta, to the solid affluence of The Los Angeles Free Press, an established part of that city's cultural scene; from the transcendental theory of Avatar to the "mind-blowing" visual effects and kinky sex ads of The East Village Other.

But the general trend is toward radical politics. The Free Press and Avatar (now published in separate Boston and New York editions)

have stepped up political coverage. The Oracle of San Francisco, perhaps the most influential of the papers promoting salvation through mysticism and drugs, has suspended publication.

Many other papers that grew out of the LSD and hippie culture, such as The East Village Other, are struggling for a new identity.

"The drug culture is dead," said Jeff Shero, editor of The Rat, which bills itself as "New York's muckraking subterranean newspaper."

"It's now impossible to believe in any kind of salvation from drugs. Kids get drafted or hit by cops on real or phony drug raids. The outside world keeps barging through your door and you've got to confront it."

Like many editors, Max Scherr of The Berkeley Barb believes that police "harassment" is the largest single factor in politicizing the alienated audience for underground papers.

"What the Germans used to call 'the inner exile' is over," he said. "When your friends and neighbors are getting hit on the head by police, running around in despair, you're involved whether you want to be or not. People are finding that they can't hide from society as they thought they could."

For many, prolonged living in a hippie area has come to mean danger, poverty, overcrowding, police raids and a slow brutalizing of the spirit.

"The concept of flower people in America today is absurd," said Peter Leggieri, publisher of The East Village Other.

Much of this disenchantment is now being channeled into political radicalism by the war in Vietnam, pressures from the draft and the recent student revolts at Columbia and the Sorbonne.

'Lenny Bruce in Print'

"The repressive aspects of society are just being seen more and more clearly," according to Paul Krassner, whose irreverent pre-underground journal, The Realist, has shifted from black humor ("it was Lenny Bruce in print," Mr. Krassner said) to equally antic but more political coverage.

Since the first of the year, the few older political papers, such as The Barb and The

San Francisco Free Press, have been joined by some 30 new radical underground papers, most of them heavily influenced by the leftist Students for a Democratic Society. Many of them, like S. D. S., consider American society hopelessly corrupt and advocate disruption of "the system."

Traditional coverage is politicized, not eliminated. The Paper, at Michigan State, has turned sports coverage of the university football team into a sociological indictment of America. In New York, The Rat covers rock music as "the language of the revolution."

"The point isn't to talk to people who are already radical," said The Rat's Mr. Shero, a member and former vice president of S.D.S. "We use the rock section, or an occasional nude on the cover, as a way of opening us up to people who are 17 and 18 and thinking about their own problems, not politics."

Columbia and Berkeley

Recently, The Rat published an exclusive story on a Mexican guerrilla band, first-person accounts and exclusive pictures of the Columbia turmoil, stories on the violence of the June demonstrations in Berkeley, Calif. ("the first off-campus white rebellion America has known in recent times"), and a "guide to survival" for demonstrators at the Democratic convention in Chicago.

In general, the underground papers keep a sharp watch for misconduct by the police ("psychopaths in blue"), anything dealing with Ernesto Che Guevara ("the saint who climbed mountains"), unflattering photographs of President Johnson (commonly touched up with swastikas) and for any evidence, however tenuous, that the United States is run by an interlocking directorate of the selfish and complacent.

The Black Panther party gets heavy coverage, but otherwise race is not usually a priority issue. ("Most of our readers have been through that," said Mr. Shero.) Timothy Leary and Alan Watts, heroes when drugs and religion reached their peak in the underground press, are now rarely mentioned.

Comics More Political

There are rambling personal essays laced with profanity and zany comic strips, both of which are becoming more and more political. "The San Francisco look"—basically the curved line of art nouveau in psychedelic color—seems to be yielding to "the New York look"—crowded and weird photo collages. ("The New York look creates tension," one editor said. "It's the perfect art for the politics of confrontation.")

There are perhaps 150 underground papers, mostly in large cities and college towns. Many editors of these publications attribute their shift in emphasis to police harassment.

News coverage is consciously subjective and one-sided; ("A growing revolt against the selfish and reactionary American Medical Association came to a head here," began a typical recent article in Open City, a Los Angeles paper.)

The theory is that truth is rooted in personal experience, and that the standard news media, by insisting on impartial and detached coverage, omit and distort the underlying reality of crucial news events. (In shorter form, the argument goes that no newspaper is objective— the underground papers are just the only ones acknowledging it.)

"Objectivity is a farce," said Thorne Dreyer of Liberation News Service, which serves many of the underground papers. Mr. Shero added: "We made our biases clear. That frees our writers to talk about their guts."

The papers are characteristically casual about checking facts before publication. One editor, who declined to be identified, when asked about a widely reprinted story about riots and murder at a Texas military base (actually no one was killed) replied: "Well, the straight press didn't print anything, and we printed too much. It all balances out in the end."

Another concern is that the goal of building a revolutionary movement can be endangered by turning down or questioning stories sent in by allies.

"We often print something for someone in the 'family,'" said Daniel McCauslin of Liberation News. "If you get someone sending you stuff from the Midwest, you just have to trust him. We're not held together by massive objectivity, but by trust."

This same trust led to the Underground Press Service, an agreement among some 60 underground editors to re-print from one another's newspapers without special permission, attribution or rechecking.

"The underground papers are not a quality press," Thomas Pepper, a former reporter and graduate student wrote recently in The Nation, "because they pander to their readers with a dexterity befitting the Establishment papers they criticize so bitterly. [They] offer nothing more than a stylized theory of protest."

Nevertheless, he adds, they "have awakened virtually all concerned to a real deficiency in American newspaper journalism. . .the fact that regular metropolitan dailies do not communicate with subcultures."

Paul Williams, 20-year-old Harvard dropout and publisher of Crawdaddy, the successful and highly regarded magazine of rock music, complains that the underground press generally covers the same subject matter as Look magazine.

"Very few are actually doing much work or original thinking, and the copy is getting sloppier," he said. "Many start with enthusiasm and are trapped by business — they owe people money and pretty soon they're on a treadmill, keeping the papers going by putting out what the readers are already interested in. There's no longer much difference between the underground and the regular press."

For most papers, financial pressures are heavy. Some editors who have lost their second-class mailing permits, usually for technical violations of the postal code, say they could be put out of business by a rapid subscription raise.

Eight out of ten papers would fail if a few phonograph record companies stopped advertising, according to John Walrus, business manager of The Seed in Chicago. His own paper, he said, receives $1,000 of its $1,400 in weekly advertising from record ads.

In talking about money problems and shifting reader tastes, an underground publisher can sound remarkably like an Establishment publisher. The East Village Other's Mr. Leggieri, who said it costs $18,000 a month to publish ("we're simply not geared to being an underground paper anymore") thinks that EVO must move away from the psychedelic scene, but rejects a switch toward radical politics.

"The times are changing and we have to change too, but we don't believe politics can lead to anything beneficial to mankind," he said. "This is a political year, but when it's over the political papers will be gone and we'll still be here." Mr. Leggieri said his astrologer, whom he consults regularly, reported that EVO's new approach will begin to take shape this month.

The advantage of the political papers is that they know exactly what their goal is, and a good deal of the credit for their rise is being assigned to Liberation News Service.

Liberation News was founded in Washington, in 1967 by Ray Mungo (Boston University, '67) and Marshall Bloom (Amherst, '66), both radical editors of their college papers. It provides inexpensive political coverage ($15 a month for two or three weekly packets) to 400 outlets, including 100 underground papers, and has reportedly persuaded many "drug culture" papers to emphasize politics.

C. B. S. a Subscriber

The agency has offered long reports from Hanoi, detailed round-ups of antidraft activities and a series on the latest chemical weapons stockpiled by the Pentagon. The Columbia Broadcasting System and Look magazine are among the agency's subscribers, and Doubleday has commissioned a book from Liberation News on the Columbia dispute.

Its basic belief is that a "new journalism" is taking shape in America, totally outside the province of established journalism, and that radicals are leading the movement. It also assumes that the established media are incapable of printing the truth about anything important.

"The media is the enemy," Mr. Mungo said. "I'd much rather put The Times out of business than the New York City police. It does much more damage."

Many underground editors who have come to rely heavily on Liberation News are apprehensive that it may go out of business. In a bitter dispute last month, the agency split into two factions, both of which are attempting to continue publication as the one and only Liberation News Service.

Mr. Mungo, Mr. Bloom and several other staffers are publishing from a farm in Montague, Mass. Thirteen other staff members are publishing from the Liberation News offices at 160 Claremont Avenue in New York. They moved there from Washington last spring.

Mr. Bloom suggested that the 13 staffers were too doctrinaire, narrow and prone to jargon-ridden prose. He in turn was accused of being authoritarian and insufficiently militant.

Liberation News and the underground press are part of a loose alliance sometimes referred to as "the alternative media." It includes high school and college papers (over 80 are served by Liberation (News), some prison and military papers, a string of 11 radical Spanish-language papers known as the Chicano press, a few "underground" TV and radio stations, and sympathetic "straight" journals such as Ramparts and The Village Voice.

This alliance is pugnaciously confident that it represents the wave of the future.

"We've educated a generation that no longer buys or needs daily papers," Mr. Mungo boasted. "They believe us, not you. We represent an idea whose time has come."

N.B.C. Admits Bugging
Democrat Platform Unit

By GEORGE GENT

The National Broadcasting Company acknowledged yesterday that "overzealous and over-eager employes, acting with-out authority," planted a microphone in a closed meeting of the Democratic platform committee in Chicago.

In a statement issued here, the network said that information obtained within the last 24 hours bearing on the microphone incident had been turned over to Federal authorities in Chicago, with whom the network has been cooperating in an investigation of the incident.

"Although no material obtained by this method was used in any way," the statement said, "N.B.C. deeply regrets this occurrence. No such action is condoned or encouraged by N.B.C. News or the management of the National Broadcasting Company."

N.B.C. officials refused to elaborate on the statement and it was understood that they had been advised by legal counsel not to make any statements beyond those officially sanctioned.

Microphone Discovered

The "bugging" incident took place Aug. 26 during a closed meeting of the executive committee of the Committee on Resolutions at the party's national convention.

The meeting was interrupted when one of the participants discovered the microphone in the meeting room at the Sheraton-Blackstone Hotel.

At the time, it was reported that the microphone was hidden inside a television set.

However, in replying yesterday to an earlier telegram from N.B.C. News, Representative Hale Boggs of Louisiana, the platform committee chairman, said the microphone had been discovered under a cushion behind a curtain.

"The microphone," he said in a statement released by his Washington office, "was attached to a cable leading directly to the recording facilities of the National Broadcasting Company in the same hotel."

Inquiry Asked by Boggs

A member of the platform committee said here last night that the proceeding had been interrupted "for about 15 or 20 minutes" and that there had been some "spoofing" of the security procedures.

"There was also some belief that an earlier meeting a day or two before had been bugged," the delegate said, "because the Chicago papers had such complete details of the closed meeting."

Such escapades are not new. At the Republican National Convention last month in Miami Beach, a Florida delegate concealed a tape recorder at a closed meeting in which Richard M. Nixon addressed Southern delegates and turned the tape over to The Miami Herald and The St. Petersburg Times.

And at the Democratic convention in Los Angeles eight years ago, a spokesman for the Stevenson-for-President committee charged that the group's telephone lines had been tapped.

Mr. Boggs said that he had requested an investigation of the "bugging" incident but that he had not planned to make any statement until the investigation was completed and he had a chance to confer with an N.B.C. officer who had requested a meeting.

The release of the telegram to him from Reuven Frank, president of N.B.C. News, had prompted his statement.

Representative Boggs said that the laws must apply equally to all men and that wiretapping, bugging and eavesdropping, except in matters of national security or organized crime, were direct violations of Federal and state stuatutes.

"The matter now is for determination by the appropriate Federal and state law enforcement agencies," he said.

In his telegram to Mr. Boggs, Mr. Frank said new information on the matter had been forwarded to the Chicago office of the Justice Department, adding that N.B.C. "intends to take stern disciplinary action against any personnel who acted improperly."

The Chicago office of the Justice Department said it had received "absolutely nothing" from N.B.C. on the incident but admitted that an investigation was under way.

The Chicago office of the Federal Bureau of Investigation declined to comment.

September 7, 1968

NEWSMEN ASSAIL CHICAGO PAPERS

Slanted Reporting to Help Daley's Image Is Alleged

By DONALD JANSON
Special to The New York Times

CHICAGO, Oct. 12—An association of newsmen has been organized here as a result of a conviction that Chicago papers slanted the news after the Democratic National Convention to improve the image of Mayor Richard J. Daley and the city's policemen.

The organization of reporters, photographers and copy editors is called the Association of the Working Press in Chicago. It published this week the first issue of a monthly called Chicago Journalism Review.

Newspaper and television reports during the convention made Mayor Daley seem to be the embodiment of a ruthless machine politician. Club-swinging policemen have been charged with injuring more than 600 antiwar and anti-establishment demonstrators and at least 34 newsmen.

Back 'to the Fold'

The newsletter-size, six-page Chicago Journalism Review charges that after reporting what happened, Chicago papers did an about-face and became apologists for the Mayor and his police force.

"Under the disinterested gaze of their colleagues from Washington and New York," said a page-one article in the review, "Chicago editors and publishers had nervously let their reporters set down uncomplimentary facts about the police and the Mayor . . .

"But when the cameras and conventioneers went home, the local media returned to the fold. Many of us, reporters in Chicago, could only watch what happened in silent frustration.

"Mayor Daley was permitted to take over the media. Our own editorialists told us that we didn't really see what we saw under those blue helmets. The violent scenes of police crowd dispersal became 'riots.' "

The review said the newspapers "accepted the idea that they had somehow distorted the coverage of the convention-in-the-streets and day after day they opened all that precious news space to the tedious re-telling of 'Daley's side of the story.' It was almost a standing headline."

Ronald Dorfman, a reporter for The Chicago American and temporary chairman of the new organization, said in an interview that about 100 newspaper, television and radio newsmen had attended one or more preliminary meetings. Membership, officers and programs may be announced at the next meeting, Oct. 30.

Fairness in News Sought

Henry de Zutter, education reporter for The Chicago Daily News, is editor of the review. The first issue says it will provide a continuing critique of media performance here and "explore problems created by official news management."

"Those who will benefit most from our activity are our employers, who really need and may secretly desire a counterweight against the pressures of the local establishment," the review says.

Listed objectives include insuring "the right of reporters and photographers to cover important events without interference from the police department or any other governmental agency," improving professional standards and fairness and accuracy in the media, and "publicly condemning obvious breaches of journalistic ethics."

None of the Chicago newspapers escaped criticism in unsigned articles by reporters for the papers in the first issue.

Editors who could be reached for comment today denied that there had been any pro-Daley shift in coverage and presentation after the convention.

"There was no retrenchment," said Lloyd Wendt, editor of The Chicago American. "The only instructions I ever gave anybody on my staff at any time was to tell it like it is."

Emmett Dedmon, then editor of The Sun-Times and now editorial director of both The Sun-Times and Chicago Daily News, said:

"There was no post-convention retrenchment. We felt our coverage was balanced and we have continued to keep it balanced. There was no change in policy before, during or after the convention."

The review devoted two columns to incidents it said Chicago newspapers failed to report at all, including a spree by policemen the first night of the convention that took place as Chicago Daily News and Washington Post men "watched from the 12th floor of the Lincoln Hotel."

After routing demonstrators from Lincoln Park, the report said, policemen slashed tires, broke aerials or shattered windows of "about 30" automobiles bearing stickers supporting Senator Eugene J. McCarthy of Minnesota for President.

"It happened after the demonstrators and cameramen had been chased from the intersection," the review said. "Officers on the scene later told other reporters that the damage was done by hippies."

October 13, 1968

C.B.S. MAN DOUBTS VIOLENCE THEORY

Tells Panel Studies Fail to Establish Link to TV

Special to The New York Times

WASHINGTON, Oct. 16—A network executive testified today that the belief that television violence stimulated real violence was not supported by any evidence he had been able to find.

Joseph T. Klapper, director of the office of social research of the Columbia Broadcasting System, told the National Commission on the Causes and Prevention of Violence that he had studied many surveys and experiments · bearing on the subject.

The surveys indicate, he said, that "mass media depictions of violence are not prime movers toward crime and delinquency." He continued:

"They suggest that certain personality traits lead to a taste for violent media material and that this material serves some sort of ill-understood psychological function — perhaps good, perhaps bad, and perhaps neither — for children with certain maladjustments.

"The surveys really do not tell us very much about whether such fare will render audiences more likely to behave violently."

Queried by Panel Member

Dr. W. Walter Menninger of Topeka, Kan., the psychiatrist, a member of the commission, remarked that the witness had given 19 pages of testimony about other research studies without indicating "what responsibility C.B.S. feels, what they have done and what they will do."

Mr. Klapper replied that C.B.S. spent more than $400,000 a year on social research but that any C.B.S. studies of the effect of television violence would be "sneered at or rejected purely because the money came from C.B.S."

Representatives of two other networks and of the newspaper industry will be heard tomorrow. Hearings are being held in a committee room of the New Senate Office Building.

Prof. Percy Tannenbaum, of the University of Pennsylvania, testified: "Every time Marshal Dillon pulls out his gun to kill the bad guy, it has, in effect, the N.A.B. [National Association of Broadcasters] seal of approval."

Another witness, Prof. Bradley S. Greenberg of the department of communication at Michigan State University, said that the urban poor were greatly dependent on television for their information and their image of the world outside themselves.

Five Hours a Day

"The adults in low-income homes watch TV for more than five hours each and every day," he said. "For low-income black Americans, this figure is closer to six hours every day." He said the same pattern was found among teen-agers.

Professor Greenberg also said that among adults generally, television was regarded as the principal information source for general news, world news and political news.

"At the same time, it is far and away favored as the most credible source," he said. "It is even more so regarded by low-income Americans."

In an aside, the witness said 90 per cent of these people identified with David Brinkley of the National Broadcasting Company, not with James Reston of The New York Times. Commission counsel, in another aside, announced a few minutes later that the commission's public information man had just polled the press tables and found that 90 per cent of the reporters identified with James Reston, not David Brinkley.

Dr. Menninger noted that Professor Greenberg's interviews with adults had been confined to about 200 families in Lansing, Mich., and suggested that this was a small sample that would not necessarily reflect national habits. Professor Greenberg said the data on teen-agers had been gathered in Philadelphia.

The commission was appointed by President Johnson after the assassination of Senator Robert F. Kennedy last June. Mr. Johnson instructed the 10-member commission to "look into the causes, the occurrence and the control of physical violence across the nation."

October 17, 1968

Nixon Now Backed By 483 Newspapers To Humphrey's 93

Richard M. Nixon has the editorial support of 483 daily newspapers, five times more than Vice President Humphrey enjoys, Editor & Publisher magazine said yesterday.

The weekly magazine added, however, that the number of newspapers supporting Mr. Nixon was fewer than the former Vice President had when he ran for the Presidency in 1960.

The magazine of the newspaper and advertising industries said the newspapers supporting Mr. Nixon have an aggregate circulation of 20.7 million copies.

Lined up for Mr. Humphrey are 93 daily newspapers, with total circulation of 3.9 million copies, while 10 daily newspapers, five of them in his home state, are supporting George C. Wallace.

The magazine said that 280 daily newspapers, with 9.4 million circulation, were still undeclared as of Oct. 15.

Inquiries were sent to the 1,749 daily newspapers in the United States, asking editors or publishers to check off candidates to whom their papers were giving editorial endorsement.

In endorsements yesterday, The Herkimer (N.Y.) Telegram, The Athens (Ga.) Banner-Herald, and The Maryville-Alcoa (Tenn.) Daily Times came out for Mr. Nixon, while The Suffolk Sun on Long Island backed Mr. Humphrey.

Mr. Nixon had the support of 731 dailies with 38 million circulation when he ran against Senator John F. Kennedy, who was backed by 208 papers with 8.4 million circulation. The magazine's final report will be published in the Nov. 2 issue.

TV Chains to Be Conservative in Projecting Vote

By JACK GOULD

The three national television networks plan a conservative approach in making any early projections of the winner in the Presidential race on election night.

If the returns do not show an irreversible landslide for Richard M. Nixon, the three presidents of the network news departments said yesterday, the "call" or "naming" of the successful nominee might not come until very late on the night of Nov. 5, or well into the next morning.

Elmer W. Lower, president of American Broadcasting Company news, and Reuven Frank, president of National Broadcasting Company news, said they were disturbed that a contest among Mr. Nixon, Vice President Humphrey and George C. Wallace might pose difficulties for computers that had been only stocked with data on the past two-candidate Presidential races.

But Richard S. Salant, president of the Columbia Broadcasting System news, said he saw no computer difficulties, noting that the machines had been suitably programed with respect to primaries for which there had been no precedent. One job of the computers is to report almost instantly voting trends that significantly depart from the results of previous elections.

The network news heads said their chains would stress throughout the evening that polls were still open in many Western states despite the receipt of earlier returns from the East.

This action is designed to allay criticism from some West Coast political figures who contend East Coast reports may induce voters to stay home on the assumption that the race is over. The networks have repeatedly argued that no research bears out such a conclusion.

Mr. Salant said that C.B.S. no longer would "declare a winner" in advance of actual voting figures but would merely say the election of one candidate over another was "a C.B.S. news estimate." Repeated mentions of "vote profile analysis" would be dropped, he added, in favor of a simpler explanation that selected sample precincts can give a clue to state or national trends.

October 18, 1968

100

Would Not Wait

The C.B.S. news president said the network would not hesitate to name the "estimated winner" as quickly as possible if its research so warranted. The polls in New York close at 9 P.M. and the California polls at 11 P.M., New York time. If a candidate already had a majority in the Electoral College before the California polls closed, Mr. Salant said the news could not be withheld. But, he said, Californians would be reminded that the importance of their vote in other contested offices, particularly for the Senate and House.

Mr. Lower said that there would be no projection of a state's total vote by A.B.C. until all the polls had closed in the state. Kansas normally releases partial results of voting before the closing of its polls.

The A.B.C. president said his network, too, would stress that the network's expectation that a given candidate would win should not be confused with an actual determination of the outcome by a complete count of the votes.

Mr. Frank said that N.B.C. would use two boards in the Presidential race, one carrying the actual vote and the other indicating how N.B.C. expected the race to come out. The second board, he said, would offer a variety of alternatives, such as signs indicating it was "too early" to make a projection or "too close" to do so.

Margin of Victory

If one candidate appeared to be a winner, the second board would indicate his probable margin of victory but no tentative checkmark would be placed beside his name, Mr. Frank said.

N.B.C. traditionally has been the most conservative network in making final calls on the Presidential race. Mr. Frank recalled it was nearly 7:30 in the morning after Election Day in 1960 that N.B.C. declared President Kennedy triumphant over Mr. Nixon.

All the network presidents maintained that computers and sampling methods could not be blamed for taking the fun out of election nights or spoiling the excitement of contests by early projections of probable winners. If the races are close enough, they said, neither computers nor human analysts are willing to go out on a limb.

One official projected his own hunch on the course of events on Nov. 5. "It'll be over either very early or we'll be lucky to get to sleep by noon on Nov. 6," he said.

The News Election Service, the cooperative organization of press associations and networks dividing the job of tabulating election results, is expected to operate with increased efficiency this year, the network heads said.

One bottleneck accompanying modernization of tallying votes, they said, was the result of some polling machines registering a voter's preference on cards. This method may require two or three hours to pick up all the cards and deliver them to a central counting headquarters. Los Angeles was plagued by this problem in 1964.

October 26, 1968

Paper Bars Comic Strip

BIRMINGHAM, Ala., Oct. 25 (UPI)—The Birmingham News said today it would not run Walt Kelly's "Pogo" comic strip through next week because it pokes "unfair" fun at George C. Wallace.

October 26, 1968

NEWS GROUP SCORES RECORD OF JOHNSON

ATLANTA, Nov. 19 (AP) — President Johnson will leave office with perhaps the worst record for credibility of any President in history, Sigma Delta Chi, the national journalism society, said today.

Mr. Johnson's secrecy policies "have periodically interfered with the operations of the Freedom of Information Law," said the society's report on freedom of information, released at the opening of the society's convention.

The report said that the "credibility gap" had reached "awesome proportions," making the Pentagon and the White House two of the most difficult news beats to cover.

"President Johnson has virtually abandoned the type of news conference which served the Washington press corps and the nation well from Franklin D. Roosevelt's time through the thousand days of John F. Kennedy," the report declared.

The report also said that the Reardon report of the American Bar Association had caused serious problems for the press.

The bar association's recommendations, prepared by a committee headed by Justice Paul C. Reardon of the Massachusetts Supreme Judicial Court, were designed to guide news coverage of trials.

November 20, 1968

F.C.C. CLEARS TV OF BIAS IN CHICAGO

Backs Convention Coverage but Doesn't Rule on 'Truth' or 'Staging' of Incidents

By WARREN WEAVER Jr.
Special to The New York Times

WASHINGTON, March 2 — The Federal Communications Commission declared today that national television coverage of the Democratic National Convention of 1968 in Chicago had given a "reasonable opportunity for presentation of contrasting viewpoints" on controversial issues there.

The agency thus cleared the three national networks on the general issue of "fairness," or offering time to both sides on such questions as the war in Vietnam and the civil disturbances in the convention city.

Quality Not Judged

The commission withheld judgment, however, as to whether the networks had distorted some news at Chicago by filming "staged" incidents. It said it was continuing its investigation in this area and asked for more details from the broadcasters.

In a letter to the three networks, the commission emphasized that its decision on the fairness question did not involve any judgment of the quality of convention coverage or any assessment of whether television had presented "the truth" on various events it showed.

The commissioners said they considered the "truth" about news events important but that an attempt to make such a subjective judgment by a Government agency would be "inconsistent with our concept of a free press."

"The Government would then be determining what is the 'truth' in each news situation —what actually occurred and whether the licensee deviated too substantially from that 'truth,'" the F.C.C. declared. "We do not sit as a review body of the 'truth' concerning news events."

Rumor-Spreading Rejected

Following this principle, it rejected complaints such as those that the networks spent too much time on the convention floor at the expense of the rostrum or helped "spread rumors" that a movement was under way to draft Senator Edward M. Kennedy for the Presidential nomination.

On the issue of fairness, the commission concluded from evidence submitted by the networks that they had presented evidence of provocation of the police by demonstrators and had given Mayor Richard J. Daley an opportunity to state the case for the Chicago police force.

The commission said it was still investigating four alleged examples of "staged" incidents. These involved:

¶A "girl hippy" with a bandaged forehead who walked up to National Guard troops and shouted "Don't hit me!" when a filming crew gave her a cue.

¶A fire set by "what appeared to be a newsman" into which he put a "Welcome to Chicago" sign, which cameramen then photographed as it burned.

¶A camera crew that apparently asked a young man in Grant Park to hold a bandage to his head while they shot film, although he had no visible injury.

¶Filming in Lincoln Park of a young man lying on the ground, being aided by girls in "white medical smocks;" he later got up and talked to the crew without apparent injury.

The last two episodes allegedly involved crews of the Columbia Broadcasting System, so identified by witnesses. No network was identified in the commission's description of the first two.

In its letter, the agency required all three networks to submit detailed reports of the four allegedly "staged" episodes by March 30.

Both the National Broadcasting System and Columbia Broadcasting System expressed criticism in the statements they submitted to the commission of the agency's requiring them to produce these "comments" in response to charges of unfairness.

Complaints Questioned

The C.B.S. reply said the network was "particularly concerned when the complaints to which comment is especially invited are complaints that a licensee has given insufficient attention to views of statements of Government officials or has displayed bias against the policies of the national Government."

In making a similar protest, N.B.C. declared:

"Few specters can be more frightening to a person concerned with the vitality of a free press than the vision of a television cameraman turning his camera to one aspect of a public event rather than another because of concern that a Government agency might want him to do so, or for fear of Government sanction if he did not."

The commission called these "puzzling assertions," adding: "We have made clear, in decision after decision, the right of broadcasters to be as outspoken as they wish, and that allowance must be made for honest mistakes on their part."

Nixon's Agency Returns to Normalcy

By PHILIP H. DOUGHERTY

Normalcy—or at least as close to normalcy as you can get in an ad agency — has returned to Fuller & Smith & Ross. And in its major offices in New York, Pittsburgh Cleveland and Chicago, some 335 employes are hard at work helping such clients as Alcoa, Grumman, Mobil, Heineken beer and the State Department of taxation and Finance to make a buck.

Up until last Nov. 5, they were also the agency for Richard M. Nixon and they helped him make the White House.

"It's a difficult thing for an agency, primarily because it keys everyone up — the importance of it transcends everything else. Everyone in the agency wants to be in on it. And it's an awful letdown when they can't get in on it and for those that do when it's over." That was Arthur E. Duram, one-time radio sportscaster turned agency president, and in his office near the top of 666 Fifth Avenue one day last week he went though some of the disruptive effects a political campaign can have on an agency. And when he got through he added, "We'd do it again."

Art Duram was in charge of the store that day since Robert E. Allen, the chairman and chief executive, was off doing his bit on jury duty.

●

His secretary was bringing in the coffee as he described the agency's effort in behalf of the Republican Presidential candidate as "the biggest consumer media problem that any agency has ever had in New York." He is not releasing any figures, but anyone who watched TV during the campaign just has to agree with him. Media problems are not new to the agency either, since it is the shop for the New York State Lottery, an account that carries with all sorts of interstate and broadcast advertising restrictions with it.

About 60 persons worked in the agency for Mr. Nixon —some were regular agency people, some were temporary workers and some were on loan from other shops.

"What they [the Nixon team] wanted," said Art Duram, "was an organization that could put an iron hand on the whole thing and run it rough and tough. And we did. We made up a chart in advance for every step of the way and we made them

stick to it." And look what happened.

Although F.S.R. did the pre-convention effort for Senator Barry Goldwater, this was the first full-fledged Presidential campaign the 62-year-old agency had been involved in, and you've got to admit they must have done something right. Maybe it's because they are, as Art Duram says, "the No. 1 agency in the whole field of talking to the businessman."

And the president adds with no little pride, "thirty-six clients on the Big Board and six of them with over $1-billion in sales."

The shop got started back in Cleveland as Fuller & Smith, an industrial advertising agency. Now it is about 60 per cent business advertising (a designation Mr. Duram prefers to industrial) and 40 per cent consumer. And as this man said, "The businessman is a tough market, a lot tougher than the consumer."

●

But the agency, which last year billed $54.7-million, is looking for more consumer accounts of the kind described by Mr. Duram as "not necessarily impulse items but along consumer lines." And the move in that direction can be understood better when Mr. Duram answered another question with "Conglomerates block out any expansion in the business world and it'll get worse and worse."

It was in 1913, before "conglomerate," or for that matter "make the world safe for democracy," became popular, that Art Duram made the scene out in Chicago. And because his father was a combustion engineer moving from job to job, young Art lived in 26 cities before he graduated from college — the University of Illinois to be specific, and 1935 to be exact. He was on the basketball and golf teams there and is still a bit of a sports nut — he'll admit it. Skiing, paddle tennis. That sort of thing.

Right after college, he went into broadcasting, covering the sports of the Big Ten "The Big Ten is all through the advertising business") and doing dramatic bits in soap operas. Then in World War II, of which you may have heard, he served overseas as an Army Air Forces intelligence officer. After the fracas he went to broadcasting but this time on the business side and stayed with it until 1953, when he left C.B.S. as national sales manager for black and white television to go to F.S.R. to be television director.

•

By that time, Bob Allen, now a 30-year-man with the agency, was manager of the New York office. He became president in 1955 and Art Duram replaced him as president in 1964.

Today, although it dropped about $4-million in billings last year, the agency that created the memorable line "This time vote like your whole world depended on it," is looking optimistically at 1969 since, as its president reports, the clients' attitude for the year is "very, very aggressive, very healthy."

Then taking a look at the broad agency scene, Mr. Duram comments, "All small agencies are saying 'Why do you want all that service for? All you want is a creative team.' With agencies like ours—full service agencies—our great stick is ways of finding information on which we build marketing concepts so that the creative guy can build his advertising against a real target. We believe this is really indispensable in today's market.

"Who's right? Who's wrong? The next five years will tell."

And while we wait for the answer — a thought. In a business where company names slide out of sight or change, Fuller & Smith & Ross is one of the oldest around. And whether or not you like to talk to businessmen or vote for Republicans, you've got to admire an agency with two ampersands. That's more than most.

Report Deplores Television's Uneven Treatment of the News

By FRED FERRETTI

When television covered major news events as they happened during the broadcasting year of 1968-69, it was "fascinating, beautiful, exciting, devastating, illuminating, or whatever other adjective of admiration one wished to apply."

But in the "no less essential and challenging chore of covering day-to-day news and public affairs . . . the picture was somewhat less dazzling."

Those are the findings of the first Alfred I. du Pont-Columbia University Survey of Broadcast Journalism, documented by a year of research into news and public affairs broadcasting throughout the United States and released yesterday.

Awards Coming Today

The survey was issued one day before presentation of the du Pont-Columbia Awards in Broadcast Journalism, which will be made today in ceremonies on the Columbia campus. Dean Burch, newly confirmed as chairman of the Federal Communications Commission, will speak.

The survey, which relied on protracted monitoring of television news and public affairs efforts; on 40 correspondents across the country; on the broadcasting industry itself and on the faculty of the Columbia Graduate School of Journalism, found little on which to congratulate television in the news field.

The survey jurors were Richard Baker, acting dean of the Journalism School; Edward W. Barrett, dean of the graduate School of Journalism from 1956 to 1968; Marya Mannes, critic and author; Michael Arlen, television critic for The New Yorker, and Sir William Haley, former director-general of the British Broadcasting Corporation and editor of The Times of London.

'Waste of Resources'

The survey indicted television. "Across vast distances, at enormous expense and with enormous ingenuity, shallow calls to shallow, morning, noon, and night. To any honest and objective eye . . . most broadcasting must appear —a hideous waste of one of the nation's most important resources."

"It was painfully ap-

parent," the jurors wrote, that in the summer of 1968, when the survey began, "electronic journalism was entering into a new phase, probably the most crucial in its history."

The assassinations of Dr. Martin Luther King and Robert F. Kennedy, and the drama and violence surrounding these events, the two political conventions and "the controversy surrounding their coverage all seemed to give the industry a new sense of dignity, an increased awareness of the importance of its journalistic functions."

'Dedication Has Flagged'

The report continues:

"Of course it was not so easy as that. In the months since, good intentions have been deplored and ridiculed where special interests were threatened, dedication has flagged in favor of profits, nerves have failed when stockholders have grown restive."

Singled out for criticism was the area of documentaries. The survey queried 500 television stations in the country's 100 largest television markets, asking them to list original documentary programing in 12 specific areas. Fewer than 50 stations replied.

The survey concluded that "documentary programing in the traditional sense of the term had hit a new low."

Many stations listed Sunday morning public affairs talk shows as documentaries; others asserted that extensive treatment of local events amounted to documentary coverage.

The survey said that of the 12 subjects it considered worthy of treatment as documentaries only politics, race and minorities, crime and youth received adequate coverage. Subjects such as international affairs, science and space, medicine, disarmament, birth control and environment received negligible or no local coverage.

The pattern that emerged, the survey said, was of greater time given to regular and expanded news programs, for which there was available sponsorship, and less time to documentary programs. Richard Salant, president of News for the Columbia Broadcasting System, told the survey:"We need an hour news show every night and an extra hour of prime time for news every week. We can't give stories

enough length or depth. Things are always left out."

The survey was also critical of investigative reporting on television: "Investigative efforts by news departments of commercial networks were disappointing—in contrast to the extensive, and often vigorous network coverage of such major news events as the Apollo flights and the national political conventions . . . and few appeared especially notable for the amount of subsurface probing required."

Convention Coverage Boring

It called television's coverage of the two national political conventions "profound journalistic ennui for purveyor and consumer alike." It criticized advertisers for not using more restraint when advertising on news programs. "Pitches . . . were presented with greater urgency and more technical expertise than the news items crushed between them. The more compelling and important the news, the more insufferable the intrusion."

The report criticized public and broadcasting officials for lobbying for the bill proposed by Senator John O. Pastore, Democrat of Rhode Island, which would effectively stifle challenges to commercial broadcast licenses.

Despite this, the survey found "the public's stake in broadcasting was dramatized, and the avenues through which it might influence broadcasting policy protected and broadened." It said the F.C.C. showed in 1968-69 "a decided increase in gumption by standing up to pressures from both Congress and the industry."

Politicians Are Satisfied

The survey found that politicians accepted television as necessary to American political life today, and were satisfied with television's treatment of them.

"Their misgivings about the broadcast media were largely centered," the survey reported, "on the high cost of television in view of its critical importance to success at the polls."

The survey said finally that the memory of the drama and technical proficiency displayed on "big stories" by television, "the memory of what was done and can be done again, coupled with the very real accomplishments of the year, give hope for the future."

STANTON WANTS TV TO COVER CONGRESS

Dr. Frank Stanton, president of the Columbia Broadcasting System, called last night for greater access by broadcasting to the significant proceedings of Congress and the Supreme Court.

Under current rules, the broadcast media are barred from House of Representative Committees, the floors of both houses of Congress and the Supreme Court.

Dr. Stanton's proposal was made in an address at the Waldorf-Astoria Hotel to the Advertising Council, which gave him its annual public service award.

"The only way we can keep the right to know alive is by expanding it," Dr. Stanton asserted, "making sure that our citizens know more about our Government and its actions, not less."

Noting that he was receiving the award on the 178th anniversary of the Bill of Rights, Dr. Stanton warned that those rights were being jeopardized by "Big Brother."

In an apparent reference to Vice President Agnew's recent criticisms of the press, Dr. Stanton said subsequent assurances that the purpose of the attacks was to further discussion "ring hollow when their sources and pattern, not to mention their language, are considered."

Opposition to Lowering Voting Age Laid to TV Coverage of College Unrest

Special to The New York Times

WASHINGTON, Feb. 16 — Television coverage of disruptive college students is a major factor in keeping states from granting the vote to 18-year-olds, according to witnesses who appeared today before a Senate Judiciary subcommittee considering a constitutional amendment to lower the voting age nationally.

Accusations of distortion and lack of perspective by the news media and especially television were supported by the two Senators at the hearing — Birch Bayh, Democrat of Indiana, and Marlow W. Cook, Republican of Kentucky.

Senator Cook was specifically critical of television news programs for creating what he termed an adult "backlash" that he felt was responsible for recent referendum defeats in Ohio and New Jersey for lower voting ages.

He pointed several times to the experience of his state, Kentucky, which gives the franchise at 18, to illustrate the voting maturity of adults between 18 and 21. He condemned the "cowboys and Indians shows at 6:30" that he said focused on an unruly minority in that age group.

All Back Amendment

All of the prominent witnesses testifying today were in favor of lowering the voting age and supported the amendment, which has been introduced by Senator Jennings Randolph, Democrat of West Virginia, along with 67 Senate co-sponsors.

The large audience, with many teen-age and young adult activists, obviously supported the lower voting age. Young people frequently crowded around witnesses and Senators to talk about plans in their states to lower the voting age.

As Senator Randolph, Theodore C. Sorensen, Dr. W. Walter Menninger, and Dr. S. I. Hayakawa testified, the audience and the Senators laughed at their light humor and even applauded when particularly significant statements were made.

Senator Randolph said that lowering the voting age was necessary "to expand the base of our democracy." Federal action is needed, he said, because state by state action would be too slow.

Mr. Sorensen, a New York City lawyer who was formerly a special counsel to President Kennedy, said he did not fully agree that meeting the physical and mental characteristics needed for the Army qualified a person to vote. But he asserted that there was a relevancy in the fact that "the brunt of fighting and dying in a prolonged and unpopular war falls with particular force on those between the ages of 18 and 21."

And he added: "If taxation without representation was tyranny, then conscription without representation is slavery."

He decried the coverage of this age group by the press which he said focused on the "comparatively few troublemakers in their midst."

"Campus disorders make sensational headlines," he said. "But nearly one-half of all 18-20-year-olds are not in college at all. Of the more than 2,300 colleges and universities in this country, less than 1 per cent have suffered serious disturbances. Of the seven million college students in this country, less than 2 per cent, according to a staff report to the Eisenhower violence commission, can be classified as militants or radicals."

His statements were underscored by Dr. Hayakawa, the president of San Francisco State University, who gained national notice when he calmed the campus with a stern approach to disruptions.

He said that of 18,000 students on the campus there were never more than 1,000 who actively participated in disorders. He said that of more than 700 arrested during the demonstrations, one-half were students and the average age of these was 23. Their leaders, he said, were 24 to 30.

Yet, he reported, when he tried to interest the networks and local television stations in covering some constructive actions by the remaining 17,000 students "there wasn't a single response."

In response to questions by Senator Cook, Dr. Hayakawa said that the nature of the campus had been hurt by "television distortion" and said that admissions applications from outside California had still not returned to levels prior to the demonstrations.

His only solution, he said, was "to sick Spiro Agnew on the networks again."

Dr. Menninger, the psychiatrist, who was here in his capacity as a member of the National Commission on the Causes and Prevention of Violence, told the subcommittee: "Today's youth are capable of exercising the right to vote. Statistically, they constitute the most highly educated group in our society."

He accused adults of treating young people as immature and thus provoking self-fulfilling prophecies. He called this "infantilization" and said the motives were rooted in adult fears and jealousies of the younger generation.

He insisted that it was important to "keep this population in perspective, since the attention of the news media on disruptive elements tends to obscure the character of the vast majority of these youth."

Editor Finds 'An Ugly Mood' Against the News Media

EL PASO, Tex., Feb. 16 (AP) — The head of the American Society of Newspaper Editors told Texas publishers today that "an ugly mood" against news media was sweeping the country. He predicted it would get worse.

Norman Isaacs, executive editor of The Louisville Courier-Journal, told delegates to the Texas Daily Newspapers Association that Vice President Agnew's criticism of news media "has tipped over a witch's caldron."

"We have more sick people in this country than we would like to admit—more people who would give up freedom of the press willingly than we have admitted," he said.

February 17, 1970

JOURNALISM UNIT CRITICAL OF NIXON

Sigma Delta Chi Suggests Reform of News Parleys

CHICAGO, Nov. 7 (AP)—The Freedom of Information Committee of Sigma Dela Chi, the professional journalism society, criticized the Nixon Administration today for the manner in which it communicates with the press and suggested experiments with a more detailed, nontelevised Presidential news conference.

A committee report was particularly critical of the President's news conferences, which, it said, have been reduced "essentially to a one-way proposition, convened when the President believes he has something to communicate."

Other Administration officials, including Vice President Agnew, Attorney General John N. Mitchell and Chief Justice Warren E. Burger, were criticized by the report.

Queries Limited

The report is to be presented at the society's annual convention opening Wednesday in Chicago.

"President Nixon's use of the news conference provides little to inspire confidence that he actually believes in full and free accountability to the public," the committee wrote.

A news conference, it said, should not be scheduled for the convenience of the President or the press but rather for the public convenience and interest.

The report said that Mr. Nixon's TV news conferences were not "wide open" and as informative as they seemed, noting that the President almost never allowed a reporter to ask a "follow-up" question that elicited a more complete answer and that not all reporters got to ask their questions.

"SDX therefore suggests that the President consider experimenting with a monthly, one-hour, on-the-record, sitdown, nontelevised news conference with no more than 20 reporters," the report stated.

Discussing Mr. Agnew's criticisms of television news and the press, the committee commented, "If this first year after his Des Moines, Iowa, speech is the beginning of the Age of Agnew in journalism, it does not portent to be a pleasant era for the journalist."

Burger Criticized

The report pointed out that Mr. Mitchell had reasserted the right of Federal judges to subpoena newsmen and their notes, a practice strongly criticized by SDX.

The committee, however, praised Mr. Mitchell for imposing restrictions on the use of subpoena power and for being willing to accept some form of reporter-informant privilege.

The report criticized Chief Justice Burger for occasionally barring radio-TV coverage of his public addresses, for attempting to control reprint rights to his "State of the Judiciary" address to the American Bar Association and for giving only two regular news service reporters background information on Supreme Court actions.

"It has been a disquieting year for the advancement of freedom of information," the report said.

November 8, 1970

Cronkite and Professor Differ on Press Freedom

By WALTER RUGABER
Special to The New York Times

WASHINGTON, Sept. 30 — Walter Cronkite, the television journalist, said today that the Government had too much power over the press, but a law professor asserted that the press had too much power over public expression

It was the first substantive clash in three days of hearings before the Senate Subcommittee on Constitutional Rights, which, under Senator Sam J. Ervin Jr., Democrat of North Carolina, has heard steady support of the press.

Mr. Cronkite, the longtime anchorman for the Columbia Broadcasting System's evening news program, joined earlier witnesses in describing radio and television as particularly threatened by hostile Government regulation.

"Broadcast news today is not free," Mr. Cronkite said. "Because it is operated by an industry that is beholden to Government for its right to exist, its freedom has been curtailed by fiat, by assumption, and by intimidation and harassment.

"We are at the mercy of the whim of politicians and bureaucrats and whether they choose to chop us down or not, the mere existence of their power is an intimidating and constraining threat in being," he contended.

Standing Room Only

Several Senators who had spent little or no time at the subcommittee's sessions earlier this week turned out for the newscaster's appearance and were joined in the Senate Caucus Room by a standing-room-only crowd.

Senator Roman L. Hruska, Republican of Nebraska, and Senator Hugh Scott of Pennsylvania, the minority leader, showed up for the first time this week. Senator Edward M. Kennedy, Democrat of Massachusetts, had attended less than an hour of the earlier sessions.

When Mr. Cronkite, the three Senators, and most of the crowd departed, Jerome A. Barron, a professor of law at George Washington University, appealed for restrictions on broadcasting and the newspapers.

The First Amendment guarantee of freedom of the press applies not just to the communications media, he said. It also gives the public a "right of access" to the media which is sometimes unfairly denied, he added.

Professor Barron proposed legislation, which the courts would enforce, requiring newspapers and broadcasters to accept paid advertising in support of views that receive little or no news coverage.

The contention of Mr. Cronkite and other witnesses that the press is sufficiently diverse to permit the airing of different views was also challenged by Mr. Barron. He said that broadcasters had not promoted diversity.

F.C.C. Ruling Opposed

They opposed a Federal Communications Commission ruling that requires television stations to offer some locally originated programs during prime-time evening hours, he said.

And while advocating an almost complete elimination of Federal regulation, the broadcasters are not suggesting that they "start all over again" with a new allocation of licenses to use the various frequencies, he continued.

Mr. Barron asserted that it was possible to establish "a procedure for dialogue" without the Government meddling with the content of the news, but Senator Ervin said he did not think "there would be much freedom in forcing a man to say what he doesn't want to say."

Mr. Cronkite had argued that access to an audience would not assure an audience. Special interest and minority groups could obtain half an hour of prime-time television, he said, but there would be "nothing to assure that a single viewer would still be with them at the end."

The newscaster, who called for an end to F.C.C. authority over broadcasting's content, acknowledged that radio and television were "a long way from perfection."

"But that is not the point," he continued. "How could we be improved by outside monitors without destroying the independence which is so essential to a free press?"

October 1, 1971

3 THE USE AND ABUSE OF THE MEDIA

Radio Campaigning Demands a Technique Of Its Own, but It Has Not Changed The Basic Rules of the Game

By FRANCIS BROWN.

THE party chieftains have marshaled their lieutenants before the microphone and the oratorical battles of 1936 are under way. To all who twirl the dials of a receiving set come the voices of political figures, praising, blaming, pleading, denouncing. Broadcasting has become a feature of political campaigning, but to what good? No one is quite sure, although probably the radio has altered not at all the fundamental nature of American politics—outward appearances to the contrary notwithstanding.

It is the outward appearances that have caught the imagination. The majority of voters recall campaigns before radio was known; after all, the first broadcasting station was not opened until the Fall of 1920—to crackle into the earphones of pioneer listeners the returns of the Harding-Cox Presidential election — and the first broadcasting of party conventions did not come until four years later.

When campaigning is mentioned the picture that comes to mind is of another era. William McKinley is speaking from his front porch at Canton or Warren G. Harding (also a front-porch campaigner) is shaking hands with the visitors to Marion. William Jennings Bryan is swinging about the circle, traveling 18,000 miles in a few weeks, speaking to perhaps 5,000,000 people and showing unbelievable endurance.

Or perhaps the picture is of the famous meeting at Cooper Union when Abraham Lincoln, in February, 1860, delivered before a few hundred distinguished Republicans, including the aging William Cullen Bryant, one of the most significant addresses in political history. Transparencies and torchlights are part of this tradition; so too is the baby-kissing of fond recollection. But it is all local and homely. It does not belong to the Nineteen Thirties.

* * *

RADIO, of course, tends to make a political rally, particularly one of any importance, a national matter. As the campaign of 1932 showed, whenever a candidate has something to say he wants to reach as wide an audience as possible. This means a national hook-up, and just because millions across the country may be listening the candidate must be careful what he says. He cannot tell San Franciscans something he does not want New Yorkers to hear. While at times the candidate or his lieutenants may be evasive, they cannot sidestep altogether the issues of the time and place.

Campaign speeches have not always been to the point. Garfield, for example, spoke a good deal in 1880, but, as one of his biographers has said, he used "the method of voluble silence," which included a talk at Chautauqua, N. Y., on "the significance of the Chautauqua educational ideal." The issues in 1880, to be sure, were neither as pressing nor as apparent as those of today, and it was easy to hold an audience with a speech wholly unrelated to politics. But if it had been possible to broadcast Garfield's address from Chautauqua, it is a safe guess that most of his listeners would have turned to another station.

Not all speakers were as pleasantly innocuous as Garfield. Some were spellbinders who won an audience as much by platform gymnastics as by words. Others were coldly intellectual, spouting figures and classical allusions. All depended a good deal on a personal magnetism that was not wholly a matter of vocal inflection. But the radio has brought a change, and ten years and more of experience have taught political broadcasters a good deal.

Speakers have thrown aside their sheaves of statistics and have forgotten their high-flown rhetoric. They have tried to solve the paradox of talking to the entire nation while actually speaking to the three or four gathered about the radio in a Chicago flat or a New England farmhouse. A speaker has learned that he must be able to dramatize national issues, to make radio listeners, whether men or women, believe that these issues are their own vital concerns. And in a fifteen or thirty minute talk the broadcaster must convince, possibly spur to action. Finally, he has to sell himself, especially if he is seeking office, to people who may have never seen him, who are unaware of his personal charm or the lack of it.

These are problems which men like Blaine and Cleveland and Harrison did not face, for never at any one time did they speak to more than a few thousand, while the crowds at their meetings could see them in all their impressiveness.

* * *

THE political broadcaster has to bear in mind still other things that did not bother his predecessors on the hustings. He must remember, for instance, that the radio makes possible the hearing of both sides of a political question and the deeper understanding of the issues dividing the parties. How much this opportunity means to the mass of voters is debatable, but it is present and must be taken into consideration, for the subtle influence of listening to a variety of political addresses has become one of the imponderables of modern politics.

Radio has thus helped to make politics ticklish for both campaigners and party strategists. Mark Hanna, back in that famous campaign of 1896, had his troubles, but he did not have to worry about radio programs. An organizer whose like has seldom been seen, he raised at least $3,500,000 for the Republicans, directed something like 1,400 campaigners in the field and saw to the distribution of about 120,000,000 pamphlets and broadsides. All his tricks have become rather commonplace now, and, while they have not been forgotten, they are supplemented by national hook-ups and local broadcasts.

A generation ago the party chairman

Harris & Ewing.

Political Broadcast—"The President Has the All-Important Asset of a 'Good Radio Personality.'"

spent his campaign funds for many things, and he always knew that the price of a vote was about $2 and a good cigar. Votes are no longer bought so easily, while radio forces the chairman to dip deeply into the party chest. In 1932, for example, the Republicans spent about $500,000 for broadcasts, and they have announced that this year they expect to allot $1,000,000 for this purpose. But money for radio time is not the only worry.

Whoever manages this part of the campaign must regulate the number of speeches given, the date of delivery, the nature of their subject, even as did Postmaster General Farley in 1934 when he drew up a code for Democratic broadcasts so that, as it was said, the country might have a "balanced diet of words." That was one way of expressing the fear that the party speakers might talk themselves to death. Too long a speech, it has been learned, is ineffective—and it is therefore a waste of money, something to guard against when contributions are neither large nor numerous. Finally, the chief of staff must constantly seek out the most able broadcasters in the party ranks, for too few have the all-important asset of a "good radio personality."

* * *

WHAT is a good radio personality? President Roosevelt is undoubtedly the example most often cited. His ability to be friendly yet dignified, to make complex questions seem simple, to speak slowly enough to make his ideas clear without becoming tiresome, and by homely illustration to awaken sympathetic responses in his listeners, goes far toward explaining his hold on the radio public. There is more than this, however. There is a confidential quality in voice and remarks; there is emphasis that gives a sense of the dramatic. A note of sincerity is never lacking, and a conversational element is injected by the use of a colloquial or slang phrase which the orator of another day would have gingerly avoided.

Naturally, few speakers combine all these qualities, nor would any one want them to, yet in greater or lesser degree this is the sort of man the party chairman wants on the air. Some spellbinders are as successful over the radio as they used to be on the stump, but they are the exceptions to prove the rule. And, in any event, these exceptions have no more to do now than in the past with the men who by talking endlessly and monotonously about vital subjects become both bores and political liabilities.

* * *

YET obviously all these matters, however important, touch only the surface of American political campaigning. And the fact that radio has given the demagogue a potentially greater audience than he could ever command in the past is less significant than at first appears. The radio makes it easier for the rabble-rouser to reach the people, but it cannot guarantee that he will be heard by many more people unless the public mood is sympathetic toward the ideas he is shouting.

Populism in the Eighties and Nineties might have had fairer treatment had its leaders been able to place their case before the nation as a whole. But one cannot be sure, for Easterners might have distorted the Populist position as easily by radio as they did by press and pamphlet. If Bryan in 1896 could have broadcast over a national network, he would have escaped the humiliating experience of being howled down by Yale undergraduates, but, on the other hand, he might have undergone the worse humiliation of not securing a radio audience. From the point of view of publicity, it would be far better to be booed in New Haven. Yet, radio or no radio, it is hard to say whether the net result to populism or Bryanism would have been different.

* * *

WHAT the radio means to American politics generally is likewise uncertain. It undoubtedly explains in part the rise of Father Coughlin; it helped to make Huey Long a national figure. And the radio can be used to make people act, as Father Coughlin showed when, by a radio appeal at the height of the fight against the World Court, he loosed a storm of telegrams upon the United States Senate. The radio has probably made the public more politi-

Times Wide World.

Political Rally—"People Always Want to See a Presidential Candidate."

cally conscious, more interested in what is happening in State and Federal capital, and yet, without discounting this claim too much, it has to be admitted that the great political use of radio has coincided with a social crisis when the public, if ever, would be interested in its government.

If the radio were the property of the party in power, as in Germany, its significance would be far greater than when broadcasting facilities are available to all parties, provided that during a campaign they have money or credit. It has probably helped to spread radical ideas which the press by and large would have been inclined to overlook. Once again the instance of Father Coughlin's gospel can be cited. But the radio so far has not upset American political methods or changed the traditional nature of campaigns.

Parties, in the final analysis, have always been dependent upon their local organizations in city wards and counties, organization built on patronage, favors of one sort and another, the personality of local leaders. Here the radio does not enter, nor has it entered to any great extent into the matters of local political interest, to which the daily press devotes a good deal of space.

On a single issue of municipal or State politics it is conceivable that the radio might aid in crystallizing public opinion quickly. But the examples are hard to find, and in those States where the Governors have made a practice of reporting regularly by radio on public affairs it is questionable whether much has been accomplished, except in the way of general political education. Even Huey Long did not rely solely upon the radio to oust Louisiana's old guard, although he found it at times a most valuable weapon.

In national politics the radio has had less effect, despite all that has been said, than might be expected. Here again organization is the important thing, and this goes on as before, building, reconstructing, on patronage and favors. Radio has not altered this imme-

morial custom. Nor has it measurably changed the well-known tactics of a political campaign.

* * *

THIS year again the parties will assemble in conventions; they will draft platforms, nominate candidates, enjoy the high jinks that to the delegates are almost as important as the business for which they were called together. The speeches, the balloting and the tomfoolery will be broadcast to the nation, which for its part will be periodically bored and amused by the performances at Cleveland and Philadelphia.

To the listener will come the flattering illusion that for the moment he is himself participating in what may be momentous events. His experience further quickens his interest in things political, and for it he can thank the radio. But the fact that the convention's proceedings are broadcast does not particularly affect the convention itself, while the convention's most important decisions are apt to be made, as always, in a "smoke-filled room" without benefit of microphone.

* * *

THE campaign launched, radio has, of course, its place. But organization remains first in importance. Then, despite broadcasts, printed speeches, clever publicity and the rest of the tricks in the political bag, comes the candidate. If possible, he must be seen, as well as heard, and a picture or newsreel is not enough. People always want to see a celebrity, a Presidential candidate above all others, whether he be speaking in a great auditorium or waving from the rear platform of a train.

Swings around the circle are still as necessary for the aspirant to the White House as for the Congressman who nurses an important constituency. Front-porch campaigns may serve sometimes, and today the radio would make such strategy even more effective than in Harding's campaign of 1920, but if the candidate is forceful he still does well to take his case directly to the country.

PHONE SURVEY 'COUNTS' EARS

Political Speeches Show The Advantages of Big Hook-Up

PRESIDENT ROOSEVELT had a larger radio audience in metropolitan centers than did former Governor Alfred E. Smith and Senator Joseph T. Robinson of Arkansas, in their recent broadcasts, according to a morning-after telephone survey conducted among listeners in thirty-three cities by the Cooperative Analysis of Broadcasting.

The day after President Roosevelt spoke at the Jackson Day dinner in Washington, 32.6 per cent of the set-owners contacted by telephone reported that they had listened.

Mr. Smith's Liberty League dinner speech on Jan. 25 was reported heard by 23 per cent of the listeners called by phone the next morning. Senator Robinson's reply to Mr. Smith on Jan. 28 was rated 19.4 per cent.

Governor Smith had comparatively more listeners in the East and Far West; the Midwest was third and the South a poor fourth, according to the telephone statistics. Senator Robinson rated highest in the Midwest, next highest in the East, with the Coast in third place, and the South a strong fourth.

In regard to the Roosevelt and Smith broadcasts, it is pointed out the number of stations handling the President's talk far exceeded the size of the network used by Mr. Smith; in fact, Mr. Roosevelt spoke through three major networks and several independent stations, while Mr. Smith used only one transcontinental hook-up of approximately ninety transmitters. The broadcasters estimate the Roosevelt Jackson-Day network totaled 200 stations.

Another special program which attracted a large number of listeners was the broadcast from England of the last part of the funeral services of King George V, from 8 to 9 A. M., New York time. The investigators found that 15.7 per cent of set-owners in the East, South and Midwest had tuned in.

An official of the analyzing bureau emphasized that the telephone survey covered no rural districts but was based on the listening habits of set-owners in large cities, including New York, Chicago, St. Louis, San Francisco and Los Angeles.

THE LANDON "INTERVIEW"

For the first time, if memory serves, a Presidential candidate has, before the National Convention meets, submitted to a long interview reported over the radio. It was a novel venture for Governor LANDON, but perhaps not so bold as it might appear. An effort was made to give his talk an air of spontaneity, but undoubtedly the questions had all been laid before him in advance and he had carefully written out his answers. Yet his direct and courageous statements on many controverted political subjects give a favorable impression of his vigor and readiness to let the public know what he thinks. Naturally, this unusual form of appeal will be taken as a fresh bid by him for the nomination at Cleveland. Those Republican rivals and leaders who are opposed to him will be quick to say that he fears his chances are waning and that he adopts this means to hearten his followers and draw to himself support from many who are in doubt about his opinions and his fitness for the Presidency.

Some of his utterances were very general in tone, as was inevitable, but he had specific things to say calculated to arrest attention. When he was asked what views he held about Government regulation of business, he made a discriminating reply. It is the duty of the authorities, Federal and State, to see to it that citizens are protected against monopolistic practices and abuses. Taking a leaf from his own experience, he recalled the fact that as an independent oil producer in Kansas he had found it necessary to fight monopoly in order to secure a fair market for his products. This was an indirect and ingenious way for Governor LANDON to seek to head off the attempt, already in the making, to "smear" him with Standard Oil. And his resolute stand against monopolies ought to please Senator BORAH, though it probably will not.

The most emphatic and significant answers by Governor LANDON had to do with relief of the unemployed. On this topic he spoke in concrete fashion, and with the positiveness of a man who knew what he was talking about. He agrees, of course, that men and women out of work and in need must be taken care of temporarily out of public funds. But he is disturbed, as are many others, by our lack of exact knowledge of the facts. To determine them should be the first object of any intelligent system of relief. Then the administration of it should be kept wholly free from waste and from politics. The work of administration should, as far as possible, be done by local agencies instead of by a centralized bureaucracy in Washington.

In these particulars it is evident that Governor LANDON's mind is working along with the best and most disinterested thought on the vexed question of relief. Such plans and methods as he indicates ought to be adopted whether he is nominated for the Presidency or not. And so far as concerns abhorrence at the idea of making political capital out of human misery, no one will dare publicly to challenge his hope that "the time may never come when "an American has to sell his vote for "bread."

RECORD AIR HOOK-UP SET FOR CONVENTION

Broadcast Will Start This Morning—Each Delegation to Have a Microphone.

Broadcasting from the Republican National Convention at Cleveland is scheduled to begin today at 11:30 A. M., Eastern daylight saving time, over a record-breaking hook-up of more than 200 transmitters. The New York outlets will be WEAF, WOR, WJZ and WABC.

The first broadcast from the Cleveland Auditorium today will be a description of the gathering of delegates and party leaders. Seventy-five microphones scattered throughout the hall will intercept the opening address by Chairman Fletcher and the subsequent proceedings.

Senator Frederick Steiwer's keynote address will be on the air tonight at about 10 o'clock, with the broadcast from the convention beginning at 9:30.

Each delegation will have a microphone, aside from those on the speaker's platform. Others will be in a special studio in a separate room adjoining the convention hall. The whole system will be correlated by a "push-button" control box, functioning as a kind of nerve center or link with the networks. During recesses and intermissions announcers and political commentators will present various angles of the conclave, aside from the actual proceedings. Provision has been made for picking up musical interludes from the band stand.

Several radio innovations will be utilized at the convention. The "photo-mike," a recent development by WABC engineers, will be tried out in political atmosphere for the first time. The device comprises a miniature portable transmitter, with self-contained batteries capable of operating several hours without renewal, also a small "candid" camera on which snap shots of the speaker can be taken as he talks. It is designed to afford the roving radio man complete freedom from trailing wires, &c., when interviews are being conducted. This machine operates on the 8.6 to 7.5-meter (ultra-short wave) channels and is said to be capable of covering distances up to four or five miles.

May 9, 1936

June 9, 1936

POLITICS AND MUSIC

A few of the millions who had listened in night after night at the Republican proceedings in Cleveland mechanically turned their radios on again Friday evening after the whole thing was ended. All that they heard was the weary patter of announcers and commentators snapping up a few stale and unprofitable trifles. It was very much like the cleaners coming in to sweep up the cigarette stubs on the floor, and the scrubwomen to put the auditorium in shape again. But those listeners-in who were lucky, suddenly passed into a crowded hour of glorious music. They caught selections from the familiar and ethereal works of MOZART and BEETHOVEN, BRAHMS and GRIEG and VERDI. What a contrast to the speeches and shoutings and marchings which had been going on for the previous four days! They had nothing to suggest a beautiful and lasting art, except in the ironic sense of the Spaniards who exclaim when some oration or writing is dull, pompous and insincere, " Música, música! "

A radio listener given to philosophic reflection might have fallen to wondering how little the politicians counted against the musicians. What man active in Cleveland will be remembered and praised a hundred years from now as one who had left something behind him for the permanent comfort and uplift of the human spirit? Creators of good government are very fine in their way, but how can they endure comparison with the master spirits who have poured their precious life-blood into the creation of immortal beauty? Such questions can never be answered, because the subjects to which they relate are not really comparable. We must go on letting the politicians have their little day upon the stage, knowing that only through such a medium can we attain the public reforms and social betterments which we crave. But at the same time it is a solace to turn from their sound and fury to the geniuses who are not for a day but for all time, and who have helped to heap up for mankind the store of " joy in widest commonalty spread."

DOUBT RADIO VALUE IN CONVENTION USE

Leaders Now Believe Old-Type Conclave Cannot Be Made Into an 'Air' Show.

MANY DELEGATES ANNOYED

Felt That They Were There Only to Make Noise in 'Mob Scene,' Not to Decide Issues.

By ANNE O'HARE McCORMICK
Special to THE NEW YORK TIMES.

PHILADELPHIA, June 27. — A very considerable proportion of the delegates to the convention did not stay for the climax, and on the platform during the closing session this morning misgivings were freely expressed by the political impresarios as to the net effect of holding a party conclave exclusively for the radio audience instead of for the delegates who have to organize and carry on the campaign.

Emil Hurja, for instance, scientific surveyor and chief political weather prophet for the administration, is of the opinion that the old type of convention cannot survive if given on the air.

A broadcast convention, he thinks after this experience, must be specifically prepared, abridged and dramatized for broadcasting. A new technique has to be developed. The issues shall be debated to interest the listening public, and to achieve this objective Mr. Hurja suggests the possibility of bringing to the floor, and hence to the microphone, condensed summaries of the discussions that take place in the resolutions committee.

Doubt on Convention's Effect

As the curtain falls, all those who had a hand in the production are a little dubious about the popular appeal of this show. They are not saying so for quotation, but privately the party leaders admit that the coming campaign is not going to be a walk-over. One of the shrewdest points out that only two Democratic Presidents have been re-elected, "Cleveland after a four-year vacation and Wilson by a narrow squeak in spite of the war issue."

This old campaigner believes that victory will not be so easy as yesterday's fifty-seven orators predicted.

"In the end it will come down to the relative force of two simple appeals," he said. "The ordinary citizen will vote for Roosevelt because he has gone ahead and done something, or he will vote for Landon to stop government spending.

"As a matter of salesmanship, I am not sure it was such a good idea as it seemed to put all the States on the air. The opportunity to address the nation from this platform caused too many heart-burnings among the unchosen. That would not have been felt if the speakers were merely addressing the convention.

"Senator Pittman of Nevada and Governor Cross of Connecticut were not the only ones who packed their bags and left because they were not the spokesmen for their States."

The political strategists realize that claptrap on the air may do more harm than good. Also they wonder if they gave too much tonight to the unseen audience and not enough to the delegates who leave here to carry on the campaign in their own States.

Not a "Delegates' Convention"

For the outstanding feature of this convention was that it was not a delegates' convention, and the delegates know it. In a radio convention, the representative of a Western State complained this morning, the delegates exist to supply scenery and sound effects so that the home audience can hear the animals roar.

So delegates stuck through twelve hours of oratorical bombardment yesterday because they will enjoy boasting at home that they suffered fifty-seven speeches in one day. A few were heard lamenting that there was no all-night session. They wanted to demonstrate for the President.

There was spontaneity in the wild hour following his nomination, and also in the uproar for Governor Lehman. It has penetrated even to the Virgin Islands that the party needs New York's Governor to win. But though the convention shouted and stampeded for Lehman with sincere fervor, nobody listened to his speech.

A round of the hall last night failed to discover a listener for any speech. The hum of conversation in the auditorium drowned out the loud-speakers. The delegates were visiting, telling funny stories, sleeping or collecting autographs. This is one of the chief businesses of a convention.

The white sombreros worn by the Texans were covered with signatures, the most prized being that of a Roosevelt, a Farley, Dizzy Dean or Governor Lehman. All the delegates seemed to be chewing gum.

In one corner, under the bandstand, a group of young Democrats danced to while the hours away.

"Ringers" at Last Session

A South Carolinian, with a robust voice, explained to all passers-by that Senator Smith had not taken a walk; he went home because his wife was sick.

Even that animation was exhausted in today's final session. Aside from Texas, the delegations demonstrating for Garner were sadly decimated. The nomination for Vice President was endorsed by listless alternates and "ringers," inheritors of tickets attending the convention for the first time.

The empty seats signified physical exhaustion, but also they betokened what may be called the devaluation of the delegate. He used to feel important. Maybe his sense of importance will revive the further he gets from this scene of his humiliation.

Here he felt that he did not count. He had himself reduced to the rôle of the mob in the mob scenes. To listen to his story as he goes is to conclude that Mr. Farley and his assistant stage managers are right in questioning whether a radio convention is the best way to build up party morale where it is needed most in a close campaign—in the county headquarters.

OPENING THE MAIL

Letters From Radio's Faithful Penmen Reveal Reaction to the Conventions

By ORRIN E. DUNLAP Jr.

WHILE the oratory, band music and bedlam of the national political conventions are rushing off into the emptiness of space toward other planets, the broadcasters who electrified the air are now discovering what the inhabitants of the earth thought about it all. Mail is the applause; it also contains brick-bats.

The postmarks reveal that many parts of the country were in tune at one time or another. Some thought the convention broadcasts "a grand lesson in civics"; others deplored the fact that the regular programs were cast aside for politics. But to such protests the broadcasters merely reply that they acted in "public interest, convenience and necessity."

Since the conclaves adjourned sine die a few faithful listeners have been writing, and now the broadcasters are reading the applause and criticism from afar.

The major networks report, however, that they are disappointed with the mail response, for it is much less than in 1932. Listeners, it seems, are not the letter-writers they once were, unless a contest or offer of something free inspires them to write. The current listener psychology is simple. They listen to what they enjoy; they snap the radio off when it displeases. The majority never write applause or report what irks them.

"I missed hearing the 'Show Boat' and the 'Music Hall' on Thursday night," wrote a Buffalonian. "In our neighborhood I noticed that none of the radios were turned on, and later I had occasion to visit in a large apartment. There, too, the majority of radios were silent, and the active ones were not tuned to the convention.

"What I am interested in particularly is to learn whether this was general or whether it was just a coincidence. Have you made any kind of a survey to determine whether the average listener is interested in this sort of thing? While a half hour or so might prove to be interesting, it becomes very monotonous to listen to speaking and noise for several hours and for three or four evenings out of a week."

Mail Tells the Story

All the broadcasters need do to realize they can never please all the people all of the time, no matter what is put on the air, is to read the mail. While a listener in Buffalo may "kick," some one in South Dakota may applaud. For example, from Huron a listener said:

"In the living room of my home I attended the conventions. I put in full time. Maybe I got more sleep than a majority of the delegates, but I was there just the same."

The plan of supplementing regular announcers with expert political commentators and analysts seems to have won favor among listeners.

The regular announcers were quite widely criticized for being too effervescent and too dramatic for attempting to dramatize insignificant happenings in an effort to "color" the show. Less artificial enthusiasm and more attention to sober thoughts is what several critics suggested.

The broadcasters found remarkably few complaints of favoritism, considering the size of the audience. The mail quite generally mentions the broadcasts of both conventions as "fair and unbiased." Some thought that every word of a party platform on the air sounded "clear and concise," and several listeners confessed "we now know what the platform is all about."

The Hope of a Listener

A listener in Ohio was grateful for the Republican convention broadcast, but when the microphone was switched to Topeka to pick up a talk by Governor Landon, that was called "a personal sense of the spiritual essence." And this same auditor turned prophet to say, "There can be no doubt the coming campaign will be intelligent and constructive."

A resident of Los Angeles who eavesdropped on the political arenas said: "We really believe we got a better picture than if we had been in the convention halls." He rated the announcers as brilliant, clear and very entertaining. He said the commentators were instructive and interesting; the show was grand.

But the next letter, from Mississippi, has a different tone; a listener in Tupelo describes the conventions as "tiresome proceedings, which merely make one appreciate the wonderful programs radio offers as regular fare." To which a Californian adds, on a postal card, "Please cast my vote against long political talks."

"Why, oh, why, do we have to forego our regular programs in favor of political conventions?" inquired a New Jersey listener. "Is it necessary for all stations to carry the conventions?"

From a listener in Connecticut: "Beside forcing the irksome noise of announcers on the public, why not at least give loyal listeners a break with their favorite programs instead of bunching up political ballyhoo on all stations?"

An auditor on the West Coast said she "would like to venture the opinion that there are many people who are not interested in listening to the conventions, and if so, for only a short time; they want music or some other entertainment."

Eight national political conclaves having been broadcast, some of the Old Guard still seem to be pondering whether or not radio is good or evil. They wonder if it might not be a good plan at least to follow the formula of Amos 'n' Andy and ban the "studio audience" which stirs all the noise and furor. The politicians are as much at sea on this question of "applause" as are comedians and opera stars.

There are strategists, however, who are firmly convinced that a noisy demonstration on the air, such as that which greeted President Roosevelt at Franklin Field, is worth as much as a speech; it creates what the politicians call "a grand psychology" among listeners. It is argued that the unseen millions catch the spirit of the occasion; they are made to feel the wave of popular enthusiasm, which, the politicians like to believe, is contagious.

Considering how carefully radio drama is planned and rehearsed, the showmen as well as old-time campaigners believe that the spontaneous political scene which at times gets out of control in the convention auditorium is not for radio because the folks back home resent the encroachment of such pandemonium on their regularly scheduled entertainment.

Delegates as "Sound Effects"

Some of the delegates are said to have gone home convinced they were merely in the arena for radio sound effects and to act in the scene which the announcers might describe. Then, too, the strategists assert that the "whooping-it-up" mitigates the business of the conventions because those in attendance cannot "hear themselves think" so uproarious is the clamor stirred up for "radio effect."

There is no charge for political convention broadcasting, and with the microphones of three major networks lined up in keen competition radio's precious time is "cast to the winds." Listeners insist it would be a sensible idea to have one major network handle the convention broadcasts while the others go about their business of entertaining.

Since 1924 every station that might possibly do so has gone to the convention, and no matter how dubious some of the old-timers may be about the value of broadcasting the radio men expect to be invited back in 1940, and by that time they may take television cameras along. In fact, the next convention cities may be selected because of available television facilities. If this holds true, New York may be able to bid strongly for a 1940 conclave, for at that time Manhattan Island is expected to be the center of radio-vision progress.

July 5, 1936

SAYS PRESIDENT LIKES TO OUTWIT THE PRESS

Krock Declares Roosevelt Was Delighted When Court Plan Came as Surprise

President Roosevelt was delighted when his plan for increasing the membership of the Supreme Court came as a complete surprise to the Washington newspaper men and "all anticipations were instantly transmuted into waste paper," Arthur Krock, Washington correspondent of THE NEW YORK TIMES, said last night in a lecture on news reporting at the New School for Social Research, 66 West Twelfth Street. Mr. Krock's lecture was the second in a series of fifteen on all phases of journalism.

When the President made public his plan, Mr. Krock said, "not one reporter could point to a line he had written that indicated real foreknowledge of the scheme; all speculations and situation stories had been proved worthless and went into the discard."

"That especially delighted the President," Mr. Krock continued. "He enjoys surprising the newspaper men and making them look absurd. He is greatly irritated whenever they flush one of his coveys."

He explained that in Washington censorship of primary news sources is incessant, "though censorship of the distributing medium—the newspaper—is, of course, something no American Government openly dares to attempt."

"The President is not always able to keep his secrets until they are ready to be served up with attractive publicity sauces," Mr. Krock asserted. "I remember two 'leaks' which dripped into the Washington Bureau of THE TIMES in April, 1933—two of many others which have forced into the open some of Mr. Roosevelt's dearest and shrewdest designs before he was ready. These two enabled us to forecast the abandonment of the gold standard and the birth of NRA."

Mr. Krock's advice to aspiring reporters was: "Have no heroes and no enemies in the news." The newspaper reporter must be a servant to truth he said, because the reporter is the norm and the archetype of the great newspaper.

February 9, 1937

PRESIDENT CHARGES MOST OF THE PRESS IS FOSTERING FEAR

Newspapers Promote a Spirit Responsible for Recession, He Tells Reporters

WONDERS WHAT THEY GAIN

Few Business Men Blamed, Too —Two Utility Officials Back 'Prudent' Valuation Basis

Special to THE NEW YORK TIMES.

WASHINGTON, Dec. 21.—President Roosevelt today accused a large percentage of the press and a small minority of business men of inculcating a psychology of fear which had had much to do with prevailing economic conditions in the country.

He told at a press conference of two business men with whom he had talked lately and declared that both had expressed themselves as in favor of New Deal principles but had said they were afraid to espouse them in public because of fear that their business associates would not approve.

The President emphasized his belief that the business recession was not the result of fear of what the government might do, but was largely the result of a psychology which he said was not only being inculcated but was being fostered by the minority of business men and a large percentage of newspapers.

The discussion which culminated in his accusations that the fear psychology was deliberately fostered came after he had conferred with two utility executives, Frank R. Phillips, president of the Duquesne Light Company of Pittsburgh, and William H. Taylor, president of the Philadelphia Light Company.

These officials came from the conference describing it as "very helpful" and declaring that they agreed with Mr. Roosevelt in his interpretation of the "prudent investment" principle of valuation for public utilities, as set forth in Justice Brandeis's dissenting opinion thirteen years ago in the rate case of the Southwestern Bell Telephone Company v. Missouri. The President has recently expressed favor for this prudent investment principle.

Brandeis Sentence Discussed

At the start of his press conference Mr. Roosevelt was asked about the utility conference. He said the whole Brandeis opinion had not been under discussion, but only a single sentence. This stated that the actual money put into a plant, less any items found after appropriate check-up to have been dishonestly or uselessly included, should be the basis for rate making.

The President went on to expound his own theory, saying that by such exceptions he meant graft paid to Aldermen for a franchise, or buying property at a figure above its worth, or not developing property bought at a low figure but waiting for the opportunity to write up its capital figure.

Such practices, the President said, are contrary to sound policies and should not be tolerated. Mr. Roosevelt added that he and the two utility executives agreed that the prudent investment theory was a pretty good rule of thumb and expressed the belief that a great many companies would act under it.

Mr. Roosevelt said Mr. Phillips and Mr. Taylor told him their need now was for money to expand their output, and that their difficulty was to get "junior" money. They could sell bonds, the President said they told him, but that would make their capital structures too heavy. People did not want to enter into junior investments. At this point the President said he asked them if the government was interfering, to which they replied it was not.

Tells of His Two Visitors

There was a general agreement, Mr. Roosevelt said, that a large part of the fear was caused by a small minority who were trying to create the impression that the government was waging war on the utilities. The President said he told them of two business men who recently came to see him, and he repeated the accounts for the correspondents.

One, he said, was an exceedingly successful Philadelphia business man who pays good wages and operates under a collective bargaining system. The President asked him if he favored raising purchasing power, to which the business man replied that he was in favor of a wages and hours bill.

Then, Mr. Roosevelt offered to get his friend fifteen minutes on the air to tell the country of his convictions on the subject. The man threw up his hands, said the President, and declared his directors would not permit him to broadcast such a speech.

The other case was that of a New England manufacturer, who told the President that his business, carried on almost exclusively in rural areas, fluctuated with crop prices. The visitor said he was in favor of a crop control law and to him also was extended the opportunity of going on the air to tell about it.

Mr. Roosevelt said the visitor declared he could not do it, not for fear of the government, but from fear of what his friends would think about him.

At this stage came Mr. Roosevelt's discussion of the newspapers. He was asked, after making the charge:

"What do you think the newspapers have to gain by fostering fear?"

The President replied that he and most of the country had been wondering the same thing.

On Capitol Hill the President's stand was criticized by Representative Fish, Republican, of New York, who declared:

"There is no reason for the present depression except the continued attacks by the President on business and on the Supreme Court and the fear of the future as a result of these attacks and an unbalanced budget. Confidence can be restored overnight if the President will balance the budget and stop his attacks on business."

Representative Boland, Democrat, of Pennsylvania, said:

"There is no doubt but that the press is engendering a lot of fear in people."

FEDERAL PROPAGANDA ASSAILED BY HANSON

Counsel Tells State Publishers Press Fights to Stay Free —Denies Mail 'Subsidy'

SYRACUSE, Jan. 11 (P).—Elisha Hanson of Washington, counsel to the American Newspaper Publishers Association, told New York State publishers today that "a constantly growing propaganda machine now operating in Washington * * * may result in the destruction of our democratic form of government."

He spoke before the annual meeting of the State Publishers Association.

Mr. Hanson said that a "vigilant and courageous press" had been able "by resisting the various aggressions" to uphold the "right of the people of this country to have a press free from official restraint."

He assailed the employment of "publicity experts" in Federal departments, saying that "every department of the government and every one of the alphabetical agencies has a publicity division busily engaged in grinding out official propaganda for public consumption."

Mr. Hanson commented on what he called "the misapprehension that the newspapers of this country receive a huge subsidy from the government each year in the nature of postal service rendered at less than cost." [The suggestion was made by President Roosevelt last Friday.]

If daily newspapers, "by further increased postal costs are driven from the mails," he said, "not they, but citizens of our rural areas will suffer, for the latter will have as their sources of information about the affairs of their government only what is dished up to them by our official propagandists."

"Can it be possible," he added, "that this is what the government in Washington is striving for?"

December 22, 1937

January 12, 1938

114

ROOSEVELT LAUDS PRESS CONFERENCE

Excerpts of Notes on 1935 Gathering Reveal His Views About Newspapers

ASSAILS 'COLORED STORIES'

He Declares Talks Result in Greater Accuracy in News of the Government

By CHARLES W. HURD
Special to THE NEW YORK TIMES.

WASHINGTON, April 27.—President Roosevelt's views about newspapers find expression in his excerpts from White House conference notes which were made public today.

His views are expressed in the partial transcript of a conference held on Dec. 27, 1935, for faculty members of schools of journalism.

At that time he outlined his favorable attitude toward the press conference system, and then attacked "colored stories" and alleged "control" of news by newspaper owners. There is no way of knowing whether other sides of the picture were presented during this conference because the original notes are in the custody of the President and not subject to review.

The excerpts are from notes of more than a dozen regular press conferences selected from the years 1934, 1935 and 1936.

Among the topics broached in the conferences were the Tennessee Valley Authority and the President's ideas about power generally, housing, wild-life preservation, soil conservation, the salvaging of operations stopped by Supreme Court decisions invalidating the NRA and the original Agricultural Adjustment Act, the death of the Passamaquoddy project, and numerous references to the flood and drought problems of the East and West respectively in 1936.

Holds to Original Aims

The general picture is that of reconstruction by the Administration on the basis of original experiments, with President Roosevelt still holding to his original plans to carry along his many ideas to promote the "more abundant life" by the creation of a planned economy.

All of these events have been reported in detail, except the matter of Mr. Roosevelt's attitude toward the press. In the same surroundings where he holds his "news" conferences he gave his views under the cloak of strict confidence, in reply to a question about his press gatherings.

A section of the White House transcript of that conference follows:

The President—I think it is a grand idea. I got my first training

in the old Navy Department days. We had a press conference—the Secretary or the Acting Secretary—once or twice a day, which was quite a strain. * * *

I think press conferences are very helpful. Of course, in Albany I carried on the same system. We had conferences there, not always twice a day, but sometimes; here we have them twice a week—on Tuesday afternoons for the morning-paper people and Friday mornings for the afternoon-paper people.

Method Called Effective

They ask all kinds of questions. I think it is very effective in straightening out a good deal in the way of misconception and lack of understanding that arise because of the infinite variety of new experiences in Washington.

Mr. Early (secretary to the President)—You might tell them about the Canadian trade conference and the special conference.

The President—Oh, yes. Occasionally we have special conferences, such as when we explain the textbook. The textbook every year is the budget; and at that time I have in the people primarily who are going to write the budget stories either the heads of bureaus here or the people who are interested in the financial picture. We go over the budget message that is to go up to Congress the following day, and take it apart. Anybody can ask any question he wants about it.

Of course, the budget message is a terribly difficult thing to write a good, accurate story about. The average of the newspaper profession knows less about dollars and cents—c-e-n-t-s—than almost any other profession — except possibly the clergy. That is the reason for a great many of these perfectly crazy, wild stories that come out of Washington about government finances, though I am trying all I can to keep the accuracy of these financial stories on a little higher level.

Sees Accuracy as Result

Q. Don't you think the conference as a whole leads toward accuracy?

The President: I think so, very much.

Q. Do you have any trouble at all with intentional violations?

The President: Only from a very small percentage of the press.

Q. You have to give a certain amount of background material that is "off the record"?

The President: Yes.

Q. Do these correspondents cause you quite a lot of trouble and put you "on the spot"?

The President: A great deal! Then, of course, here is another thing: they get a lot of queries sent to them from their own desks. Some are perfect fool questions. But they have to present them in order to retain their jobs. They do not want to. And they may get quite a tart answer from me, but they have to do it.

That is one of the great difficulties the average newspaper man labors under in this town and any other town—the orders from the desk. Of course the order from the desk isn't always the fault of the fellow who is running the desk; it nearly always traces back to the man who owns the paper.

Q.—You haven't found it necessary, as some previous administrations have done, to have the correspondents submit questions in writing?

The President: No. I take "pot luck" on that.

VEIL LIFTED ON PRESS CONFERENCES

By CHARLES W. HURD

WASHINGTON, May 14.—Recent publication by President Roosevelt of several thousand words of excerpts from stenographic notes of White House press conferences has served to place an official stamp on what heretofore has been considered the private forum of a man in a highly responsible position.

The first series of press conference notes were made public in advance of publication in a magazine to which they had been sold. These were handed to newspapers in mid-March. Another collection of selected and edited notes was issued within the last few weeks. Both series had to do with events that occurred in Mr. Roosevelt's first administration.

In neither case were the samples complete reports of White House press conferences. They were "excerpts" edited down by the President and his assistants so as to contain generally the statements he wished to make public, following in sequence after questions which gave him a peg for his exposition of policies.

His action makes available what might well become a textbook for political speeches by Administration adherents this Fall. Also, it removes, but only so far as the published material is concerned, restrictions which heretofore have made it impossible to quote the President directly or to give a completely accurate description of his press-conference technique.

A Precedent Set

It should be emphasized at once that the Roosevelt press conferences opened a new field of intimate contact between the President and newspaper representatives in Washington. Prior to March 4, 1933, a White House press conference was simply a formality, for questions had to be submitted in writing in advance, and as often as not these written questions did not receive replies. It was very exceptional when any President amplified orally whatever written reply he might make to a written question.

President Roosevelt never has invoked a rule requiring submission of questions in advance. He replies to scores of queries where any of his predecessors replied to single ones.

He receives newspaper men twice a week when in Washington and usually maintains that schedule when he travels.

The typical White House press conference hour finds a hundred or more newspaper men facing the President in his office. He sits be-

hind his desk, which is littered with its famous collection of souvenirs. A stenographer sits at his side. The atmosphere is friendly and cordial, with reservations on each side.

Most of the correspondents find Mr. Roosevelt affable, even charming, but there is an unavoidable air of restraint owing to the realization that, after all, he is President of the United States and, because of his responsible position, not subject to prodding or badgering if he is reluctant to discuss a question.

The President reserves the right, as a condition of his conferences, to reply only to such questions as he sees fit and to answer them in his own way. He may stipulate that his replies are for use as background; or he may make them entirely "off the record," which means that his statement must not be reported or referred to, but presumably only remembered for guidance in writing material originating elsewhere. He may never be quoted directly, unless he specifically authorizes the use of certain words.

The President obviously enjoys the press conferences, for, as he says, "taking it by and large, the run of the conference questions usually gives me a sense of public opinion—of how a subject is going to be treated."

On the other hand, he is avowedly suspicious of questions that may embarrass him, and he is convinced that there are newspaper editors who force their correspondents to ask questions of a type deliberately "planted" for the purpose of putting him "on the spot."

Two Fields Covered

Broadly speaking, the published excerpts cover two fields—the personal and the political.

In the first category are frequent passages containing an exchange of pleasantries, or "kidding," by the President—occasionally a pert question by a correspondent and a reply which caused laughter at the time, each such occasion being noted by the inclusion of the word "laughter" in parentheses.

In the other category, the political, are comments by the President on every major and most of the minor activities which he has initiated or in which he has participated.

Probably most interesting among the notes was the longest passage he ever spoke to newspaper men, his unbroken talk lasting more than an hour, in which he denounced the Supreme Court's decision invalidating the basic points of the National Industrial Recovery Act—the famous "horse-and-buggy" conference.

But most of the conference excerpts are arguments for propositions rather than denunciation of actions by others. In them are his original thoughts, expressed informally and in the loose form of English which characterizes Mr. Roosevelt's extemporaneous talks, on the whole gamut of subjects embraced in the New Deal.

Out of a clear sky, figuratively speaking, he announces his plans for forming the Civilian Conservation Corps and provides enough material for correspondents to write columns of "background." In the same manner, he uses the conferences to present basic arguments

THE INTERVIEWEE

Excerpts of his semi-weekly talks with newspaper men have been put into print by Mr. Roosevelt.

for the public works program and for reorganization of banking practices; to create sentiment favoring devaluation of the dollar, and to transmit to his enthusiastic following, in what might be termed the experimental years, all the points of his philosophy aimed at creating the "more abundant life."

Mental Facility Shown

The conference notes, far more than the President's formal speeches or even his "fireside chats," show the broad range of his thoughts and objectives and demonstrate the facility with which he could turn his enthusiasm from one important subject to another, often treating half a dozen in a single conference.

But the same excerpts which give the positive side of the picture of reporting White House news do not give another and equally significant one. The White House version of the press conferences does not convey the complete atmosphere of the conference system, because of the inability to read into old notes the importance of negative replies, silent shakes of the head or flashes of expression accompanying words.

There have been times when a jocular response that turned aside a question indicated highly important news to correspondents, although the President himself has protested on occasion against what he has termed interpretive writing. Likewise, the press conference of any one day has meaning and substance only when considered in relation to the events and conditions of the time in which it is held.

An Example Cited

For instance, on Jan. 15, 1934, President Roosevelt announced the sending to Congress on that day of his momentous message recommending devaluation of the dollar. But publication of excerpts of that press conference cannot re-create the feeling of suspense that had overhung business for a month prior to that time. It gives no idea of the crop of rumors and reports which had preceded the message, or of the suspicions or "leaks" which caused the business community to discount the message in advance, despite frequent and emphatic denials of the impending move by White House spokesmen in response to newspaper inquiries up to the very day the message to Congress was made public.

Neither do the notes record a large number of exchanges at press conferences in 1933 between President Roosevelt and a group of conservative correspondents who sought the President's views on a number of questions. To give examples of such questions is impossible, since quotation of them was forbidden at the time, and the only record is in the White House files.

The published transcript of excerpts, therefore, is a valuable record of the President's contemporary views on emergency problems, but as a historical record of newspaper reporting it gives only a fragment of the full picture of Washington news.

MR. ROOSEVELT COINS 'PLATE-SIDE CHAT' FOR BROADCASTS FROM DINNER TABLE

PRESIDENT ROOSEVELT gave radio a new designation for an after-dinner speech, when he referred to his good-humored talk at the $100-a-plate Jackson Day dinner as a "plate-side chat." This differentiates between the famous "fireside chats," which are recognized as a presidential broadcast from the President's study or the Oval Room of the White House, and directed from the Chief Executive's fireside to the firesides of American homes.

To Mr. Roosevelt goes the credit for coining "plate-side chat" although Stephen Early, Secretary to the President, has explained that the White House never catalogued any of the President's radio addresses as "fireside." Such a classification, he believed, was devised by either newswriters, broadcasters or commentators. Just where the term started no one seems to know, but it first came into being on March 12, 1933, when the Presi-

dent's nation-wide broadcast to explain the banking moratorium was described as his first "fireside chat."

The White House, however, has never drawn any distinctive lines between Presidential broadcasts. All are considered as "regular broadcasts." Now, for the sake of keeping the record straight, the first reference to a plate-side chat is credited to Mr. Roosevelt. After nineteen years of broadcasting, radio has a new definition for speeches picked up by the microphones that overlook the plates on a dinner table.

Governor Alfred E. Smith during the campaign of 1928 referred to the microphone as "the pie plate" and called radio "rad-dio," but none of these terms has survived as popular expressions as has "fireside," and now it is expected that "plate-side" will be picked up by the broadcasters for their diction-aries.

January 14, 1940

PRESIDENT PRAISES PRESS OF NATION

Credits Its Sense of Duty to Democracy for Keeping Faith in Liberty During War

Special to THE NEW YORK TIMES.
PHILADELPHIA, Dec. 13.— Thanks in part to an understanding by the working press of the United States of its obligations to democracy, President Roosevelt expressed today his "profound confidence" in the ability of the nation to meet the "bitter necessities of total war without losing any of its essential devotion to liberty."

The praise of the President for the manner in which the newspapers and newspaper men were recognizing their obligation to the nation was contained in a letter

sent to Harold J. Wiegand, president of the Pen and Pencil Club, which celebrates its fiftieth anniversary this week.

Mr. Wiegand is an editorial writer for The Philadelphia Inquirer and has been head of the newspaper man's club for several years.

"It was Benjamin Franklin, an old Philadelphia newspaper man, who said, 'we must all hang together or most assuredly we shall all hang separately,'" the President pointed out in his letter.

"This is as true today as it was in 1776, for freedom has always imposed upon those who would enjoy it an obligation to use that freedom for the purpose of democracy and liberty.

"The great body of our working press has shown a deep understanding of that obligation. In that understanding I find still another ground for my profound confidence in the ability of our democracy to grapple with the bitter necessities of total war without losing any of its essential devotion to liberty."

May 15, 1938

December 14, 1942

WASHINGTON, May 1—Congress has turned the spotlight on one of Washington's unique and colorful institutions—the press conference.

Administrative officials, lobbyists, politicians, feminists, laborites, actors, aviators, war heroes, channel swimmers, visiting sovereigns and diplomats, flagpole sitters, crackpots and just plain honest citizens trying to get along in Washington have used the press conference for years as a springboard from which to dive into the sea of publicity.

Distrust that some officials may be using the press conference to contravene the intents and purposes of Congress seems, however, to have been implanted in some Congressional minds. What Congress distrusts or doesn't understand, it investigates, so it has decided to find out if skullduggery goes on at these gatherings and to give itself the benefit long accruing to representatives of the press of hearing from the lips of bureaucrats words of bureaucratic wisdom.

Capital Conference

Last week, accordingly, the Senate Judiciary Committee provided a most unusual press-conference backdrop by having Elmer Davis, boss of the Office of War Information, hold a regular conference in its committee rooms. Next week, it hopes, Secretary Stimson will do likewise and after that Secretary Knox.

Just how far the scheme will be carried has not been revealed, but if the judiciary or any other committee, intends to go down the press-conference line it is in for a long trip. Washington may have a meatless day now and then but never a press-conferenceless day.

There are twenty-one regularly scheduled press conferences on the weekly list compiled by OWI. Thursday is the busiest day with six. Monday comes next with five. There are three each on Tuesday, Wednesday and Friday, and one regular gathering on Saturday.

Only the State Department schedules a press conference every day, except Sunday. Either Secretary Hull or Under-Secretary Welles meets with newspaper men each noon.

White House press conferences are held twice a week, on Tuesday and Friday, and Secretaries Morgenthau and Knox hold conferences on Monday and Thursday and Tuesday and Friday respectively.

Those Who Don't

Jesse Jones, Secretary of Commerce, and Frank Walker, Postmaster General, are the only members of the Cabinet who have no regularly scheduled conferences. They rarely hold one. Attorney General Biddle is down for a conference each Wednesday but he skips a lot of them. Secretary Perkins is scheduled to hold a Saturday conference once a month but frequently cancels it.

Aside from Cabinet members, James L. Fly, chairman of the Federal Communications Commission; Paul McNutt, War Manpower Commissioner; Mr. Davis of OWI, and Donald M. Nelson, chairman of the War Production Board, are the other officials on the official OWI list.

The only non-official conference on the official list is Mrs. Roosevelt's weekly gathering with the women writers.

But official press conferences are hardly a drop in the bucket. Impromptu, al fresco and irrelevant press conferences are tossed in by the dozen.

The impression that all Washington newspaper men do is sit around waiting for some one to hold a press conference seems to have gained wide currency in this country and abroad. So whether it is the head of the Retail Knot Hole Dealers Association or the Foreign Minister of Graustark, the first thing he does when he comes to Washington is call a press conference.

Fun and Facts

Some of these press conferences are genuinely informative and immensely valuable. Some are interesting, some amusing, some a pure waste of time. Some draw a full quota of top-notch reporters. Others attract only a few who have some special or regional interest in the topic to be discussed. Others are virtually ignored.

Most interesting, as a rule, and best attended and almost always the most productive of real news, are Mr. Roosevelt's conferences at the White House. Before wartime conditions caused limits and other restrictions to be imposed upon those who may attend, Mr. Roosevelt drew houses which packed his spacious office to the suffocation point. The President's talents as a ringmaster have lifted the Washington press conference to a high plane and everybody who can get in wants to see the show. In addition, White House press conferences produce more front-page headlines than any other news source except the battlefronts, and good reporters never stay away from a feast of news if they can help it.

Mr. Nelson's press conferences are usually well attended and almost always deal with important and interesting news. Secretary Ickes usually draws a good crowd and his seances are often very lively. They produce their fair share of news.

Elmer Davis, somewhat of a newcomer to the press-conference scene, was once a reporter so he meets the newsmen on common ground and usually makes good copy.

Restrictions imposed by the requirements of military secrecy detract quite a lot from the conferences of Secretaries Stimson and Knox but they are important, none the less, and well attended. Mr. Stimson is urbane and often a little dry. Mr. Knox imparts more vigor to his pronouncements and sometimes gets into a verbal sparring match with persistent questioners.

This writer wouldn't know, because males may not intrude upon Mrs. Roosevelt's press parleys, but the way the women writers often chatter when they come out indicates that the First Lady puts on a pretty good show even when she has nothing very important to impart.

THE PRESS CONFERENCE EVOLVES AS REAL ISSUE

Congress Wonders if Things Are Amiss And Takes a Look for Itself

By LUTHER HUSTON

AMERICA GETS THE NEWS

Doyle in The Philadelpha Record

The primary function of the press conference, of course, is to give news for publication. Adroit bureaucrats can use them, and have, to divert attention away from news they would rather not talk about. Top-ranking officials do not often resort to the device of using the press conference to dish out patent propaganda, but they never give their side the worst of it. The frequency with which some officials speak with utter frankness "off the record" is irksome to many news correspondents.

By and large, however, press conferences provide a convenient mechanism for the gathering of essential news and give newspaper men access in the mass to officials who never could find time to see all of them individually or in smaller groups. "Scoops," as such, do not come from press conferences, but often things that happen at these gatherings provide thoughtful, resourceful and industrious reporters with the seeds from which sprout important, exclusive stories.

PRESIDENT IS CRITICAL OF PRESS AND RADIO TOO

In Assigning Blame for Ward Case Opinion He Includes a Rebuke to The Latter for the First Time

CONGRESS FEELINGS SPARED

By ARTHUR KROCK

WASHINGTON, May 13—The President returned from a month's holiday this week, obviously displeased over the state of public opinion on the Montgomery Ward & Co. case; and to press and radio representatives he vigorously revealed his irritation. These were the first group outside the Government Mr. Roosevelt met after his vacation. But what he said is not to be explained by that fortuitous fact: the President many times before has blamed an unfavorable public attitude toward an administrative act on the attendants at his press conference and their editors and employers.

This time he included radio reporters and commentators as culprits who, through ignorance of the law and other failings, had, he said, misstated the facts to the people. That was new. Previously the President had implied that the faults he finds in the press are not apparent on the air waves.

His listeners, finding nothing in Mr. Roosevelt's account of the case that they had not fully grasped and stated, and noting the inclusion of the radio, decided the President was confusing his vexation over public reception of the episode with his general penchant to blame vehicles of public information for his official troubles. It was easy to recall many previous instances of this bent of Mr. Roosevelt's mind, some examples being:

On Dec. 21, 1937, the President accused a large percentage of the press and a small minority of business men of fostering a "psychology of fear," to which he attributed the unsatisfactory economic conditions then prevailing. When asked what he thought the newspapers had to gain by this, he replied that he and most of the country had been wondering about that, too.

Article Censures Press

The President wrote an article for Liberty Magazine in March, 1938, in which he said that "many hostile newspaper owners require their Washington correspondents to give their news dispatches a critical or unfriendly touch." That was a reflection on the integrity of many reporters who faced him, but he did not specify.

At Hyde Park, Nov. 4, 1938, Mr. Roosevelt said he had been misquoted by his press conference on a question concerning a poll of 5,000 Connecticut citizens who voted they were not better off than they had been two years before. He criticized an editorial based on that "misquotation," and said a "small group" (again not specifying) of newspapers steadily attempted to mislead the public with editorials based on inaccurate reports and deliberate misstatements of fact.

He was having trouble with Congress over his undistributed profits tax proposal in March, 1939, and on March 21 he charged the press with responsibility. The President said his position against any curtailment of corporate tax revenues had been "inadequately reported." He was challenged by those at the press conference to whom he made the statement. But the President's only conclusion was that, if his position had been properly reported, it must have been tacked on the end of the stories he had seen.

Borne Out by Events

These are but a few instances in a history that begins soon after the President took office in 1933. Generally the press has been able to refute Mr. Roosevelt's attacks on its veracity and character, both specific and otherwise, and much more often than not events have borne out the substance of news stories he has denounced as untrue. But the passage of time has increased rather than modified the President's disposition to blame his misadventures on the press, and now the radio has entered the area of his displeasure.

An interesting aspect of his home-coming mood, however, is that Mr. Roosevelt had no word of reproof for Congress, often a White House whipping-boy. When the President was lecturing the press and radio about the Montgomery Ward & Co. case Congress was well within the range of his complaint. This was, in effect, that the issue had been exaggerated and distorted; the facts were simple; the Government's tactics necessary and right; and the whole affair about to be settled anyhow by the outcome of Ward's union election.

Inquiries Are Launched

But as he spoke Congress was preparing to go ahead with two inquiries into the area of wartime Executive powers, whether they are (as Attorney General Francis Biddle told the Chicago Federal Court) unlimited except by the President's judgment as to what is an emergency bearing on the conduct of the war and what action is best calculated to meet it; or whether the precise limits of certain statutes, as in plant seizures, apply. No union election could settle this issue, but, since the President made it plain he wanted the Ward's case forgotten, Congress was clearly pursuing an objectionable course.

There were years in which, many observers think, Mr. Roosevelt would have launched criticism at a Congress which was looking into an issue he had said was about to be settled and should be publicly forgotten in the national interest. But the President had no views to express for Congress on the point, direct or indirect. Ever since his denunciation of Congress for the last tax bill aroused his majority leader, Senator Alben W. Barkley, to lead a successful movement to override the veto of this bill, and to evoke from the President an appeal that Mr. Barkley continue as leader, Mr. Roosevelt has adopted toward Congress a mild and respectful tone of address and has refrained from censure of its decisions. He maintained the latter this week, although Congress was compounding the Ward case troubles for which he blamed the radio and the press.

Attitude Toward Congress

On this front—Executive relations with Congress—it seems probable therefore that Mr. Roosevelt will continue to refrain from any disruptive act or word in so far as events and his own temperament will permit to do so. No objection was heard from the White House over the Senate amendment to lend-lease renewal that directed him to make no post-war commitment of funds or facilities. Up to this writing the President has not entered the deeply controversial Senate situation over an attempt to repeal State poll taxes by statute instead of by constitutional amendment. He said nothing about the Southern primaries in which his supporters were successful. And he nominated for Secretary of the Navy the overwhelming choice of Congress for the place, Under-Secretary James V. Forrestal.

Except on the proposal of universal service there is little visible occasion for any Presidential activity that may interrupt the armistice.

WALLACE ATTACKS NEWSPAPERS' VIEWS

He Charges That Publishers Don't Recognize Forces Pushing World Ahead

SCOLDS 'REACTIONARIES'

They Are Wrong in Wanting Restoration of 'Normalcy,' He Tells Chicago Gathering

Special to THE NEW YORK TIMES.

CHICAGO, Dec. 4—Vice President Wallace asserted here tonight that his "most serious criticism" of American newspaper publishers "is that they fail to realize the deep underlying forces which are remorselessly pushing the world ahead." He charged that north of the Ohio River the vast majority of the publishers of newspapers are either reactionary or Republican or both.

Addressing a civic testimonial dinner for Marshall Field, publisher and editor of The Chicago Sun, on the occasion of the paper's third anniversary, the Vice President said the "text" he "would urge on" all newspaper men at all times is, 'Can ye not discern the signs of the times?'"

Publishers, Mr. Wallace told the more than 1,000 dinner guests, "do not realize that the American Revolution, the Christian religion and modern science have combined to let the genie of world revolution out of the bottle."

He Praises Liberal Democrats

"The old-fashioned reactionaries think they can lure the genie back into the bottle again and put in the cork of normalcy," he said. "The liberal Democrats know that this cannot be done and therefore they strain themselves to the utmost in order that world-wide revolutionary forces may prove to be beneficient in terms of a well-fed, well-housed, highly productive humanity.

"Liberal Democrats know that these forces are world-wide and that after this war they will have as much influence in Africa, China and the Near East as they have in the United States and Europe."

Mr. Wallace said that 99 per cent of us in the United States had been given a totally false impression of Russia because of what had been published in newspapers or magazines.

"The people of the United States should have been taught the full truth about the Russian revolution from the very start," he said. "But we were not told the truth and as a result we nearly lost our national life. The lack of this knowledge of the true Russia could either have cost us our national life or the lives of millions of our boys."

No Training in Economy

Mr. Wallace charged that after World War I "the newspapers and magazines of the United States did not train the American people in the simple algebra of international relationships," when this country "suddenly shifted from a debtor to a creditor nation."

"This failure to discern the signs of the times was one of the main factors in costing the world nearly a trillion dollars, tens of millions of lives and the story of the full cost may just have begun."

Stating that "another terrible failure which can cost us tens of billions of dollars has to do with the algebra of the circuit flow of money," Mr. Wallace warned:

"Wage cutting and salary slashing can reduce our national income by $30,000,000,000 annually and can by reducing consumption cause such unemployment as to make the annual interest charge on the national debt almost impossible to pay.

"On the other hand, enlightened plans for the employment of 60,-000,000 people can produce a situation where the annual charge on the national debt can be carried almost as easily as in the decade of the Twenties."

In The Nation

'Contentious' Is the Very Word for It

BY ARTHUR KROCK

WASHINGTON, Dec. 20—The President told his press conference yesterday that during his stay at Warm Springs he learned a new word, "contentious," and he proceeded to put the word to immediate use. Several legitimate questions, the purpose of which was to obtain information on foreign policy, were rejected by Mr. Roosevelt as contentious inquiries, and, as usual, except when the President permits an impulse to overcome him, the reporters for the public got only what he intended.

Much is said about the press-conference system as a major process of democracy, and the regular meetings between the President and the news and radio reporters—continued even in wartime—are cited as an illustration of the great and beneficial difference between our form of government and any other. But in yield the press conferences of the White House do not supply in candor or information anything like as much as do the appearances of the British Ministers before the House of Commons. Press and radio representatives in London do not see the Prime Minister and his associates with any regularity and cannot as a matter of custom put them to the question. But the House can. And the result is that the British public is always far better informed on public facts and policies than the American, particularly since the White House press conferences were expanded under Mr. Roosevelt.

The reasons are plain. The British Ministers are Members of Parliament and directly responsible to it for their acts and their tenure. The House, except in the rare instances of executive sessions, is the forum and sounding-board of the British public. If members of the Cabinet are sly or evasive, if they attempt to be jocular about serious matters or deny legitimate information, they run an immediate risk of losing support. The House of Commons laughs at a sharp retort or a humorous observation just as the American people do. But it has dignity and responsibility and insists that these be respected.

Press Conferences

The press conference, especially at the White House, is very different. The President is the host; the meetings are held in his office; they begin and end at his pleasure; and he answers what he wishes to answer. He is responsible to his auditors only in the tenuous sense that they are the channels of public information. But they are not the only ones; the President is his own channel whenever he chooses; and if the people grumble over the paucity of information at press conferences, Mr. Roosevelt can always correct the situation by talking to them directly. He has often by-passed Congress in the same way. But even Mr. Churchill would not venture to make that a practice with the House of Commons.

The result of this is that the President uses the press conference primarily for his own end and not to account for his stewardship. There are some newspaper and radio men, as there are some citizens, who are flattered by the semblance of intimacy with the great, and these are represented at the conferences. They stand ready to ease Mr. Roosevelt out of tight places he sometimes, with all his advantages and cleverness, gets into. They roar with appreciative laughter at his feeblest jokes, the louder if these are launched at some earnest colleague who is trying to elicit facts. This undoubtedly stimulates the President to treat the entire audience as if it is composed of dim-witted or troublesome children who either can't understand what they are told or are prying into matters that don't concern them.

If Mr. Roosevelt answers a fair question by saying it is "iffy," or as it is now to be "contentious," these auditors appear to be satisfied. They give the tone to the press conferences unless Mr. Roosevelt happens to be communicative, and they watch carefully to be certain of getting the signal that brings from them the "Thank you, Mr. President" that concludes the proceedings. By this service they make it appear that Mr. Roosevelt's interviewers have ended the meeting on their own volition, which is only the case when he has revealed a total unwillingness to discuss any leading topic.

When the President came back from Warm Springs there were many subjects of legitimate inquiry by the public as represented by the press. Allied political controversies over Greece, Italy and Poland have disturbed great sections of American citizenship and blurred in Congress what seemed the only clear "mandate" in the President's election to a fourth term. The very people who voted for Mr. Roosevelt in the belief that this was the surest way to promote international cooperation during and after the war are among the most discouraged. But no form of questioning yesterday could bring any light for them from the President.

The German break-through is of most serious concern to the people, but the President made no effort to pierce the blackout instituted by SHAEF. He gave an interesting account of the physical genesis of the Atlantic Charter, but, by contrast with any of Mr. Churchill's recent reports to the Commons, the President's after three weeks of absence were very thin indeed.

Congress, including many of Mr. Roosevelt's most unswerving followers, appears to be in a mood to require more information from him. But it will never get that from the press conferences.

Truman Reduces Press Conferences; Limits Them to Making Announcements

Special to The New York Times.

WASHINGTON, April 17—President Truman announced today that he would hold press conferences only once a week instead of twice a week, as has been the rule for nearly twenty-five years in the White House.

The conference will be alternated between mornings and afternoons. They will be held on no set schedule, except that they will be on Tuesdays, Wednesdays or Thursdays. They will be called at such times as he has something to announce.

The rules that applied under President Roosevelt will govern the conferences. There will be no direct quotation of the President permitted unless specifically authorized.

Reduction of the number of press conferences presumably will reduce the spotlight just that much more on the White House at a time when the President is favoring the restoration of a more even balance between the Executive and the legislative.

Mr. Truman's decision to hold conferences for the purpose of making announcements is a departure from the rigid system followed by President Roosevelt, who adhered to the schedule of two conferences a week whether he had any announcements to make.

April 18, 1945

In The Nation

Some Capital "Leaks" and Their Consequences

By ARTHUR KROCK

WASHINGTON, Jan. 13—Like all other lesions in men and materials, Washington "leaks" come from all parts of the structure—top, side and bottom. But the leaks of the capital are unusual in that their source very seldom is the top. They usually appear lower down.

When information reaches the public before officials are ready to release it, or when it appears in print despite official efforts to suppress it, that is a leak. The latest instance concerned the resignation of the Secretary of State, Mr. Byrnes. But others have had important consequences, which this had not. And the subject of a famous leak of that sort was Mr. Byrnes' impending successor, Gen. George C. Marshall.

That came from the top or very near it. And since General Marshall's selection as Secretary of State has recalled the circumstances in various forms, some incorrect, this is a good time to review them and to deal with leaks generally.

After the revelation about General Marshall it was said and written that Winston S. Churchill had blocked the event which the revelation, in substance, foretold. From sources which, according to the general belief, were very high indeed, Kirke L. Simpson of The Associated Press got the information. It was that General Marshall, then Chief of Staff of the Army, was to be made generalissimo of all the anti-Axis forces in every land theatre of the war. It later developed that

this was a dressed-up version of the real plan to make him commander of the Second Front in Europe, but that was a detail: the dispatch was on the target.

Protests arose at once, the immediate consequences of this leak, which could hardly have been the intention of any of the sources agreed on as probable. These objections were made: (1) it was impossible for any General to command from Europe all front forces, including those in the Pacific areas; (2) the assignment, or even that of Second Front commander, would require the appointment of a successor as Chief of Staff, and this would make General Marshall his successor's subordinate; (3) persons interested in putting Gen. Brehon Somervell at the head of the Army were responsible, and this made it an inter-administration plot; (4) General Marshall was indispensable in the post he occupied.

The retired General of the Armies, John J. Pershing, to whom General Marshall had been an invaluable assistant in World War I, urged that he be retained as Chief of Staff. The Secretary of War, Mr. Stimson, was credited with a similar position. The plan was abandoned. But on its foundation the persistent story was laid that Mr. Churchill had made the objection which brought the substitution of General Eisenhower as Second Front commander.

But Mr. Churchill at the time made a statement to the British War Cabinet that disproves this account. He said

that, after the Second Front was de-
ided on, President Roosevelt and he
greed on General Sir Alan Brooke,
Chief of the Imperial General Staff,
as commander. But then Mr. Churchill
said he had a change of mind, based
on the reflections that the United
States Army would be far larger on
the front than any other and that the
designation of an American General
would deepen the interest of this nation in the European phase of the war.

He then asked Mr. Roosevelt to
name General Marshall, and this was
agreed on. However, there followed the
leak, the protests, and the eventual
substitution of General Eisenhower, for
which the British as well as the Americans are still grateful, without the
slightest implication of disparagement
of General Marshall.

That was an odd leak, considering
its eminent origin—or what is firmly
believed to have been that. For it
served to undo a revised and momentous decision of two chiefs of state
and launched the misinformation that
Mr. Churchill had vetoed General
Marshall.

But the disclosure of Secretary
Byrnes' resignation, and the probable
choice of the General to succeed him,
did no harm at all. It merely gave to
the public officially on the night of
Jan. 8 what it was not to have been
told until midday Jan. 10. And this
leak very decidedly came from below
the top, which is a far more porous
area.

As in nearly every instance, which
makes the AP story on General Marshall more unusual, the top has every
reason to keep its plans secret until an
agreed hour, or to suppress them entirely. But in every official group to
which a secret necessarily is entrusted
here are several who have neither this
interest nor this inclination. Someone
is a newcomer to inner councils and
not sufficiently indoctrinated to realize
the obligation of silence. Someone else
has a friend in the business of public
information whom he desires to favor,
occasionally on a basis of exchange. A
third person is very likely to be one
who wants to change the decision and
thinks premature publicity might accomplish this.

Hence the Washington leaks, which
were most infrequent when the government was small and the press gallery small and less enterprising. Those
restraining conditions have disappeared
from the capital.

There was nothing sinister in the
leak about Mr. Byrnes. Too many people knew of the plan and some who
got it at second hand were not sworn
to silence. Also it did no harm: that is
why Mr. Byrnes, when he became
assured the news was spreading, urged
the President to release it at once.

U. S. Gets News to Russians As Official Broadcasts Begin

Hour's Program Explains Our Government Set-Up, Offers Music—Soviet Listeners Find Script Wordy but Interesting

Special to THE NEW YORK TIMES.

WASHINGTON, Feb. 17—An
explanation of the structure of
government in the United States,
along with a few tips on its practical politics, and a news summary
were included in the State Department's first broadcast to the Soviet Union today.

The broadcast, in Russian, was
the beginning of a systematic effort by the United States Government to penetrate the "iron curtain" by radio with factual information about this country.

[Dispatches from Moscow indicated that it was difficult to
determine the number of persons
who listened to the broadcast.
Some Russians described the
wireless reception as "fair."
Some said the program was
wordy and did not give enough
entertainment, but added they
were glad to get the news. Others found the first effort generally interesting.]

The broadcast, which began at
9 P. M., Moscow time, and ran an
hour, will be a daily feature. The
program is sent out by the International Broadcasting Division of the
State Department. It is transmitted from New York and relayed by
Munich, Germany.

"The purpose of our broadcasts,"
the text explained, "is to give listeners in the U.S.S.R. a picture of
life in America, to explain our various problems and to point out how
we are trying to solve these problems. We will bring you the latest
world news of the day, feature
stories about life in the United
States and selections of serious and
light music."

The broadcast to Russia, along
with programs to other countries,
had encountered considerable opposition in Congress. Another obstacle, according to the State Department viewpoint, was the re-

fusal by The Associated Press and
The United Press to furnish news
for the broadcasts.

A considerable part of the broadcast, of which a translation was released by Kenneth D. Fry, chief of
the International Broadcasting Division, dealt with the relationship
between the Federal Government
and the governments of the States.
An attempt was made at illustrations that might be readily grasped
by listeners in the Soviet Union.

For example, it was explained
that a traveler undertaking a four-
day train trip from New York to
San Francisco passed through
twelve to fifteen State lines, "but
nowhere does he have to deal with
customs inspectors. He speaks the
same language the entire way and
eats the same kind of food, so it is
"no wonder he pays no attention
whatever to these borders."

So important are State governments, it was said, that a Governor gains great experience in office, and "it is not surprising that
both parties most often choose
their candidates for the Presidential election from among Governors who have distinguished themselves during their tenure of office."

"Americans do not fear individual power controlled by public
opinion and menaced by that sword
of Damocles, the possibility of losing the next election," the text
said.

Musical interludes in the program consisted of "The Battle
Hymn of the Republic," "Turkey
in the Straw," arranged by David
Guion, a medley of cowboy songs,
including "Sittin' Up Holler," "The
Old Chisholm Trail" and "Git
Along Little Dogie" (Harline arrangements), "Hoedown," from
Aaron Copland's ballet, "Rodeo,"
and Cole Porter's "Night and Day."

Envoys Watch Reaction

Special to THE NEW YORK TIMES.

MOSCOW, Feb. 17—Lieut. Gen.
W. Bedell Smith, United States
Ambassador, several Ministers and
First Secretaries of foreign mis-
sions, correspondents and Russians
gathered around radios tonight to

hear the first State Department
broadcast to Russia.

Russian friends telephoned news
men that the program was "just
fair."

Two Russians with whom a correspondent talked said there had
been "too much talk" in the broadcast and not enough entertainment. They added, however, that
they were happy to hear the news
summary.

The United States Embassy's recent press release announcing the
new program, has not been printed
in the Moscow press. Most of the
Russians who listened did so as a
result of word-of-mouth information passed on by employes of the
United States Embassy. It is impossible to say how many heard
the broadcast. The Soviet-made
Pioneer radio set can pick up the
broadcast, but it has been estimated that about one in 1,000 Russians has this type of set. It is
cheaper and easier in Moscow to
plug in on an apartment house
line and get the Moscow radio
twenty-four hours a day.

Russians feel that music, and
most of it jive, news and an interpretation of the earthier parts of
the American scene will reach most
Russians.

Blanketed by Other Stations

MOSCOW, Feb. 17 (AP)—The
State Department's broadcast was
marred somewhat by considerable
static and occasionally was mixed
up with European broadcasts.

Atmospherically, the night was
bad; all short-wave reception was
poor.

Three groups of Russians considered the program carefully and
gave their opinions to an American
correspondent. Some thought the
program too highbrow; others said
the announcers sounded amateur-
ish and put too much effort into
their inflections.

"The announcers sounded too
much like intelligent persons who
speak Russian perfectly but are
very conscious that they are speaking over the radio," one listener
declared. However, a number of
the Soviet citizens said the program generally was interesting.

Text of Translated First Broadcast to the Russians by Agency of the State Department

Following is a translation of the first broadcast, made yesterday, in the regular Russian-language program to be beamed to the Soviet Union by the State Department:

Announcer 1: Hello! This is New York calling. You are listening to "The Voice of the United States of America."

Music: Special Opening Theme. First bars of "The Battle Hymn of the Republic." In sustain and lose under.

Announcer 2: Good evening. It is now 1 P. M. here in New York City, 9 P. M. Moscow time. Tonight we inaugurate our American broadcasts in the Russian language. Until now, the United States has been broadcasting in twenty-four languages to countries within the range of our transmitters. An increase in the range of our radio network has widened the sphere of our broadcasts to all parts of the world and permits us to begin a daily one-hour program to listeners in the U.S.S.R. "The Voice of the United States of America" from New York may be heard in the U.S.S.R. daily from twenty-one to twenty-two hours [9 to 10 P. M.] Moscow time on the following wave lengths: 19.72, 19.65, 19.62, 19.57, 16.90, 16.83, and 13.91 meters. Our program is relayed by Munich on the following wave lengths: 48.62, 41.15, and 31.45 meters.

Aim to Mirror America

The purpose of our broadcasts is to give listeners in the U.S.S.R. a picture of life in America, to explain our various problems and to point out how we are trying to solve these problems. We will bring you the latest world news of the day, feature stories about life in the United States and selections of typical American music. "The Voice of the United States of America" is part of the informational service designed to tell the world about America and the American people. Secretary of State George Marshall in his first official press conference said that the United States, by means of radio broadcasts, would attempt to give the peoples of the world the pure and unadulterated truth. The Secretary of State emphasized that by such means America will continue its policy of disseminating the facts as best it is able to determine them. In this connection, the United States Ambassador to Russia, Lieut. Gen. Walter Bedell Smith, expressed the hope that these radio broadcasts will help broaden the base of understanding and friendship between the Russian and American people. Tonight, as on subsequent evenings at this time, "The Voice of the United States of America" begins its transmission with a complete review of the up-to-the-minute news from around the world. Here is the latest news—

Glossary of Radio Terms In Script of Broadcast

Technical broadcasting terms used in the State Department's script for the short-wave Russian-language program are defined as follows:

"In sustain and lose under"— The orchestra comes in with a blast for a sustained period at a sustained pitch and tempo and fades into background accompaniment when the announcer begins to talk.

"Bridge 0:15"—There will be an interlude of fifteen seconds of music or whatever else is specified.

"2:17"—Two minutes seventeen seconds.

"To tag"—The music continues until the next item on the program cuts in.

Announcer 1:

NANKING—In accordance with an order from the President of the Chinese Republic, Chiang Kai-shek, a series of military measures designed to fight inflation have been put into effect in China. The American dollar has been stabilized at 12,000 Chinese dollars. Strikes and the trade in foreign currency and gold have been prohibited. A sharp decrease in Government expenditures is also provided for.

LAKE SUCCESS—In a letter addressed to Trygve Lie, Secretary General of the United Nations, the United States delegate, Warren Austin, stated that the United States will place on the agenda of the Security Council a request to place under the permanent strategic guardianship of the United States the Pacific Islands formerly under Japanese mandates. These islands were taken by the United States armed forces during the war.

PRAGUE—According to a Prague dispatch, the President of the Czechoslovak Republic, Benes, has contacted the Slovak delegation and the President of the National Council of Slovakia with a warning of the necessity to abandon all plans for the formation of a Federated Central Europe. President Benes stated further: "Czechoslovakia must not be subjected to another crisis, since a new crisis would be equal to the death of the Republic of Czechoslovakia."

PARIS—According to the newspaper THE NEW YORK TIMES the French Government is continuing the struggle against the economic crisis and inflation by means of reductions in prices and the stabilization of wages at the existing level. There is fear that the economic situation may further deteriorate because of the unprecedented coldness of the weather, which endangers the planting of wheat. In the event that the planting is unsuccessful, it will become necessary to import millions of tons of grain.

LONDON—Despite the improved situation, England continues to feel a serious lack of coal. Yesterday, Sunday, thousands of English miners reported to work.

Customs Union Reported

According to a dispatch from Brussels in the newspaper THE NEW YORK TIMES, Holland, Belgium, and Luxembourg are prepared to establish a common customs union. This measure is the first step in the effort to achieve an economic unification of Belgium, Holland and Luxembourg.

LUXEMBOURG — Measures against German cartels, undertaken by the United States, are worrying Luxembourg industrialists. In their opinion, such measures are likewise directed against the Arbed, the largest steel works in Luxembourg.

In London, the deputies of the Foreign Ministers of the Four Governments have received the request of the Foreign Minister of Iran for the admission of that country to participate in the deliberations of the conditions of the German agreement.

JERUSALEM—According to the correspondent of THE NEW YORK TIMES, a British cruiser yesterday intercepted a transport vessel with 900 Jewish refugees within six miles of Tel Aviv. The refugees were endeavoring illegally to emigrate into Palestine. The refugees will be transported to the island of Cyprus. Many of the Jewish refugees offered resistance to the British forces, and several men jumped overboard.

BOGOTA—One of the most tragic catastrophes in the history of civil aviation took place in Colombia on Saturday, causing the death of fifty-four persons. Simultaneously, news comes from Cleveland, Ohio, of the death of Col. Earl Johnson in an explosion of a military plane. Colonel Johnson was chief of Civil Aviation Defense in the United States.

WASHINGTON—Sources close to the United States Senate report that the office of the Secretary of State has informed one of the Senate committees that from the point of view of the State Department the Government of the United States should fill remaining Soviet orders under lend-lease, to the amount of $25,000,000. In the opinion of the State Department, such orders constitute international agreements, which must be fulfilled regardless of the fact that Congress has prohibited further expenditures for transportation, insurance and other administrative costs connected with lend-lease contracts, effective Jan. 1, 1947. This question has arisen in discussion of legal problems related to the fulfillment of such orders, caused by the Congressional provisions under discussion.

WASHINGTON—The commander-in-chief of the American Navy, Admiral Nimitz, has issued a statement in which he expresses his belief in the ability of the United Nations to establish a stable peace. We must not be disappointed, Admiral Nimitz points out, by the lack of quick success. The problems of the United Nations are very great, and the obstacles in the path of their resolution are numerous. Therefore, Admiral Nimitz concludes, each step forward represents a great achievement.

Budget Procedure Explained

It is reported from Washington that there is a growing Congressional opposition to the proposed 18 per cent cut in the Federal budget for 1948-1949, as proposed by the Budget Committee of the Senate. As is well known, the Federal budget of the United States is drafted by the President and is put into effect only after its approval by both houses of Congress and after it has been signed by the President.

NEW YORK—The Association for the Administration of New York State Prisons has made public a report with an appeal for the coordination of all efforts for the rehabilitation of criminals.

Prison Report Mentioned

The report of the Administration of Prisons recommends particularly the creation of a central receiving station for all convicted persons where their classification should take place in accordance with the crimes they were convicted for. The report plans a rehabilitation program for alcoholics and those mentally affected. It stresses a program of productive activity in prisons.

The report praises in general the progressive management of prisons in the State of New York but underlines the necessity for more coordination among programs directed toward treatment of individual types of criminals.

WASHINGTON—The State Department reports that lively interest is shown in plans for the exchange of students and teachers between the United States and fifteen other countries. A special act of Congress voted necessary credits from amounts realized through the sale of war assets abroad. Nine hundred American citizens expressed their desire to participate in this exchange, but arrangements must await establishment of international agreements with respective countries. *(Pause.)*

The American Association of Newspaper Editors denies reports that many small papers are in danger of closing down because of lack of newsprint. The association says that an investigation shows that there is a sufficient supply of newsprint and adequate sources for increased distribution for large as well as small papers. The association points out that Canadian mills are cooperating toward impartial distribution of necessary newsprint to all American consumers.

The president of the American Automobile Dealers' Association states that during the current year, provided there are no strikes, the American automobile industry will be able to supply the market with 4,000,000 new cars.

An article by Charles Lindbergh, the famous American flyer, on the subject of safe passenger traffic appears today in THE NEW YORK TIMES and other papers. The article appeared in answer to public alarm aroused by the air crashes of the last month in the U.S.A. and abroad. It is the expansion of civilian aviation in the post-war period, says Lindbergh, that caused the increase in accidents. Lindbergh points out that American civilian aviation is safer than transportation by car, as far as statistics show.

Announcer 2: You have just heard the latest worldwide news. This is "The Voice of the United States of America." We now continue with our transmission to the Soviet Union—

Music: Bridge 0:15. Lose under

Announcer: The visitor to our shores often asks questions like these—

Voice: Why can one State of the Federal Union impose a higher tax than another of the forty-eight States?

Voice: Why must the motorist in one State of the United States observe traffic rules different from those in another?

Voice: Why is there a distinction between the criminal and civil laws of Pennsylvania, California and Nevada?

Announcer: Perhaps you, yourself, have asked such questions about our country. Tonight in the first of a series of talks on the structure of the American Government, we hope to answer some of these questions. Our subject this evening is the relationship between the Federal Government of the United States and the forty-eight individual States that make up the Union.

Narrator: In the field of foreign relations, the United States functions as a single unit. The President, as the head of the Government, or the Secretary of State, as the Foreign Minister, represents the United States before the entire world. For this reason foreigners are inclined to forget that the United States is not an integral state but a Union of forty-eight separate States.

A traveler, or a newspaper correspondent, for instance, during a four-day journey from New York to San Francisco, crosses twelve to fifteen State borders; but nowhere does he have to deal with customs inspectors. The passengers in his car speak the same English language, and in the dining car, during his entire journey, he is offered the same choice of meals. No wonder he pays no attention whatever to these borders. Nevertheless, American States are not only single administrative units with a wide autonomy in

local administration but are also living historical entities.

When America declared its independence from England in 1776, the representatives of the thirteen English Colonies signed the Declaration of Independence in Philadelphia. The Colonies renamed themselves States and declared their sovereignty. But the Union that fused them together was formed chiefly in order to wage war against England. The States preserved complete independence. Only ten years later was the Constitution formulated which unified the United States. The first sentence of the Constitution says that it has for its purpose "the creation of a more perfect union."

Some of the thirteen States which entered this Union, as, for example, Virginia and Massachusetts, had a historical record of over a hundred years, of which they were very proud. As the population moved west, the number of States increased; the last two States, Arizona and New Mexico, were admitted into the Union in 1912. But even to this day the citizens of the forty-eight States have their own State loyalties, which, of course, does not prevent them from being good Americans and ardent patriots of the United States.

States' Rights Fight Recalled

When the United States was formed, the separate States zealously defended their independence and were most reluctant to cede any rights to the newly formed Union. The Constitution of the United States was created as a result of a long struggle over the relationship between the individual States and the Union, and many of its resolutions bear the mark of compromise.

The principle of equality of rights was most clearly manifested in the Senate, that is, the upper chamber of the all-Union legislative organ. Each State, irrespective of its size or the number of citizens, has an equal number of representatives in the Senate, namely two Senators each. Without this guarantee, most of the States would have refused to join the Union, and such importance was attached to this provision that by a special resolution it can never be changed. The struggle between the State authorities and the central Government continued even after the formation of the Union. It reached its highest intensity in the middle of the nineteenth century. As is well known, eleven Southern States seceded from the Union in 1861, and formed a separate Confederation with its own President. A bloody civil war resulted from this secession of the Southern States—a civil war that lasted four years and ended with the capitulation of the South and the restoration of the Union.

Following the dramatic crisis, the acuteness of the struggle for the so-called States' rights slackened considerably, and in the ensuing years life itself gradually evolved a compromise acceptable to both sides. At the present time, as 150 years ago, the Federal Government in Washington has only those rights and authority that are directly granted to it by the Constitution. All the remaining rights belong to the Governments of the separate States, and, although the rights and functions of the Federal Government have greatly increased in comparison with what they were in the eigh-

teenth and nineteenth centuries, the autonomy of the States remains very great.

States' Structure Explained

Each State has its own Constitution, which is ratified by the direct vote of the whole population of the State. The State Constitutions are not subject to ratification by the Federal authority. The Constitution of the United States provides only that the States shall have a "republican form of government." Each State has its legislative organ, consisting of two Houses, its own State cabinet of ministers, headed by a Governor, who is elected by the population of the State for two or four years. It has its own army of state employes, its own system of courts, its own civil and criminal laws. A criminal who has committed a crime in one State cannot be tried in another. The first State must demand his "extradition."

Laws and regulations governing education, health, police, city government, etc., are entirely within the jurisdiction of the State. The majority of States have their own State universities and compete among themselves in giving large grants and appropriations for primary, intermediate and higher institutions of learning.

The brightest light on the political horizon of a State is the Governor. He is usually an outstanding political figure, and his prestige is heightened by the fact that he is the choice of the majority of the people of his State. Americans do not fear individual power controlled by public opinion and menaced by that sword of Damocles, the possibility of losing the next election. So the Governor of a State, like the President of the Republic, generally receives comparatively wide plenary powers. The Governor of a large State gains much political and administrative experience during his term of office, and his name often becomes known throughout the country. It is not surprising that both parties most often choose their candidate for the Presidential election from among Governors who have distinguished themselves during their tenure of office.

The individual States differ widely among themselves in area, population, cultural levels and the character of their economy. The State of Texas, for instance, is larger in area than Germany, while Rhode Island is smaller than Corsica. The State of New York has a population upward to 30,000,000, and its yearly budget reaches $1,000,000,000. Nevada, a Western State, has hardly more than 100,000 inhabitants.

In the East, a large part of the population consists of recent immigrants, their children and grandchildren. In the South there are many Negroes. In the State of Mississippi, for instance, more than half the population is Negro.

The economic life of the individual States likewise presents many contrasts, because of sharp divergencies in climate and soil. Nevertheless, the political life of all the forty-eight American States flows along the same general channels. The structure of State power is approximately the same throughout the land. The same two political parties are active in each State: the Republican and the Democratic. The representatives of each of these parties come to power depending upon the outcome of the elections. All States have universal

suffrage laws, with equal rights for women. This uniformity in political structure and political life in the States has been conditioned by historical factors. All the younger States have been founded by emigrants from the older ones; and those emigrants, in their march to the West, brought along with them their political customs and traditions. With the passing of time, the growing economic ties between the various parts of the country, the similarity of cultural, social and political interests as well as the swiftness of modern means of communications have all contributed to the eradication of special customs in the individual States.

History of Capital Site

In which State is the capital of the United States situated? In none of them. The keen sense of equality and the rivalry among the States would never permit the capital of the country to be located in State A rather than in State B. The authors of the Constitution found a shrewd solution to this problem. They decided that the future capital, Washington, was to be built on land contributed by two neighboring States, Maryland and Virginia, such land to be considered as part of no State.

This capital area, which lies along the banks of the Potomac River, was named the District of Columbia, and on it, during the ensuing one and a half centuries, the sparkling white marble city of Washington was built.

The capital is governed by a commission appointed by the Federal Congress, and, by an ancient paradox, its citizens have no right to vote in any election. In Washington is to be found the White House, which is the home and office of the President; the Congress, which is the Federal legislative organ; the Supreme Court, which is the highest court of the land, and the various Federal departments.

Under the jurisdiction of these central government organs fall the following functions: Foreign relations, Army and Navy, merchant marine, the postoffice, the printing of money, customs collections, etc.

The Constitution was intended to define precisely and limit rigidly the powers and privileges removed from the jurisdiction of the individual States and delegated to the Federal Government. Practice, however, proved stronger than the letter of the law. During 150 years of cultural and technical progress, new needs arose far beyond the ability and power of the individual State Governments to fulfill. These needs, as well as the decreasing fear of the so-called "despotism of central government," have contributed to the fact that the sphere of activity of the Federal Government in Washington has constantly grown. At the present time the Federal Government has taken on a number of functions that were not even envisaged by the founders of the United States. For instance, it now administers social security, supervises railroads and civil aviation, the building of dams, canals and power stations. Federal departments and special commissions have taken upon themselves many tasks in connection with agriculture, housing and public education. However, generally laws are executed through the medium of the appropriate State institutions.

Despite protests, the States have agreed to such an enlargement of the rights and functions of the central power. Yet in times of crises, when the States found themselves powerless to cope with the situation, they themselves often appealed to Washington for assistance.

Development Traced

The road of political development of the United States had led directly toward the gradual transfer of the center of gravity from the forty-eight State capitals to the National Capital on the Potomac. However, this does not mean, as some foreign observers believe, that the States have lost their "rajson d'etre" and must be reduced to mere administrative units, with limited powers of local government. American States are not artificial territorial fractions established for administrative expediency; they are healthy organisms created by historical forces. They will never voluntarily give up their status of fully equal members of the Union. And there never will be such a necessity, inasmuch as at the present time full harmony exists between States' rights and the expanded functions of the Federal Government.

Announcer 1: You have just heard the first in our series of talks on the structure of the Government of the United States.

Announcer 2: You are listening to "The Voice of the United States of America." *(Chime.)*

Announcer 2: "The Voice of the United States of America" from New York may be heard in the U.S.S.R. daily from 21 to 22 hours Moscow time on the following wave lengths: 19.72, 19.65, 19.62, 19.57, 16.90, 16.83 and 13.91 meters as well as on 48.62, 41.15 and 31.45 meters. *(Chime.)*

Announcer 1: We continue with our transmission from America. During the next few minutes we will bring to our listeners in the Soviet Union some music—folk music. Every country has its own folk music. One of the best-known of all our folk tunes is "Turkey in the Straw." It is what is called in America a "fiddler's tune" or country dance air. Although it probably originated in the South as part of a minstrel show, it is now known in all parts of the country. The arrangement you are about to hear is by the young American composer, David Guion. Here is, "Turkey in the Straw"—

Record: "Turkey in the Straw" (David Guion arrangement) 2:17.

Announcer 1: That was "Turkey in the Straw," a well-known American folk tune. Many of the popular folk tunes in America have their origin on the cattle ranches of the wide plains of the West. Here the cowboys in their solitude had to provide their own entertainment. So ·they sang, sometimes songs they had learned elsewhere and at other times songs they composed themselves. Some of their songs served another purpose: rhythmic yells to prod lagging cattle or lullabies to quiet the restless ani-

mals at night. The medley of cowboy tunes you are about to hear includes a sunrise song called "Gittin' up Holler," "The Old Chisholm Trail" and "Git-along Little Dogie."

Record: Medley of cowboy tunes (Harline Arrangement) 3:00.

Announcer 1: That was a medley of cowboy tunes. Songs like these and many others have in recent years received more and more the attention of contemporary American composers. One of these men, Aaron Copland, wrote a ballet about the Western part of the United States entitled "Rodeo." In it Mr. Copland makes use of the bright rhythms and tunes of the Western plains. Listen to the selection "Hoedown" from his ballet "Rodeo."

Record: "Hoedown," from "Rodeo" (Copland) 3:14.

Announcer 1: That was music from America, typical folk music that is known from one end of our country to the other. There will be more music after our next feature. *(Chime.)*

Announcer 2: Every week at this time we present a talk on recent scientific developments in the United States. Tonight you will hear a discussion of a new synthetic chemical substance called pyribenzamine, and we will also tell you of a new method of photographing infra-red rays.

Voice 1: At the end of last year, a regular conference of the American Society for the Encouragement of Science took place at Harvard University. This was the 113th conference since the time of the creation of the society 98 years ago. The program of the conference included more than 300 meetings and the presentation of about 1,500 scientific reports. It was attended by scientists from all parts of the United States as well as by many foreign guests. Prof. James Conant, president of Harvard University, was elected chairman. At one of the first meetings of the American Society for the Encouragement of Science a report was submitted by the pharmaceutical products corporation Ciba. It dealt with a new synthetic chemical substance, pyribenzamine. This substance has the property of being an intensive counteracting agent of histamine. It is an established fact that histamine is a chemical substance forming the basis of numerous phenomena of so-called allergies, particularly hay fever, nettle-rash and bronchial asthma. Observation shows that of one hundred patients suffering from hay or nettle fever, on the average ninety get immediate relief with pyribenzamine. With respect to bronchial asthma and chronic hay fever, positive results are not quite so good. Nevertheless, they do constitute a great step forward. The rarer forms of allergy likewise respond to treatment with pyribenzamine, with more or less success. The members of the conference at Harvard University were shown experiments and charts illustrating the

action of this new medicament on laboratory subjects, both animal and human. In a few cases only have there appeared parallel undesirable reactions, such as nausea, sleepiness, dryness of the mucous membrane of the mouth, weakness and headaches. Only in three or four of one hundred clinical cases has it become necessary to discontinue the pyribenzamine treatment because of the severity of parallel reactions.

The interest with which the new medicament is regarded is especially understandable when we consider that in the United States alone there are yearly more than 5,000,000 sufferers from hay fever. At the present time pyribenzamine is being produced in limited quantities and is released only on demand by a physician. *(Pause.)*

Participating in the recent scientific conference was the American Astronomical Society, which was marking the hundredth anniversary of the Harvard Observatory. At a meeting of the society the well-known astronomer of the Washburn Observatory of the University of Wisconsin, Dr. Whitford, presented a paper on the following interesting subject: The study of the infra-red spectrum of the stars was until recently complicated by the absence of sufficiently sensitive detectors. Today a method of constructing highly sensitive photo-elements has been discovered. Light emanating from the more distant stars is absorbed by these photo-elements and is transformed into electrical impulses, subject to great amplification and measurement. This method makes it possible to study stars of a brilliance fifteen times smaller than stars previously available to observation by us.

The details of this highly-sensitive photo-element were worked out during the war years by Dr. Cashman, professor of Northwestern University in the State of Illinois. Lead sulphate forms the basis of the photo-element. Because of its sensitivity, the new photo-element absorbs light waves five or six times longer than a wave of yellow light. The practical absorption ratio of the new photo-element is twice or three times greater than absorption by existing infra-red photographic film. As Professor Whitford points out, the water vapors of our atmosphere absorb a great part of the infra-red spectrum of the stars. However, observations made in regions of sufficiently clear atmospheric conditions have shown considerable practical results. It is well known that infra-red light has the characteristic of being able to penetrate through fog. This circumstance has been in the past exploited to observe the faintly perceptible contours of the distant nucleus of our star formation known as the Milky Way.

Greater Detail Found Possible

A detailed study of this nucleus has been almost impossible, inasmuch as the clouds of cosmic

dust, in inter-stellar space, swallowed the simple light rays of the nucleus. Now, thanks to the electronic photo-element, it has become possible to study the still more powerful cosmic rays. By the same token, it is now possible to study the Milky Way in considerably greater detail.

Thus, gradually, the human mind conquers the more and more distant spaces of the Universe.

Announcer 1: This ends our regular weekly talk on scientific developments in the United States. *(Chime.)*

Announcer 2: You are listening to "The Voice of the United States of America." Now for more music. One of the foremost American composers of light music is Cole Porter. His musical comedies during the past twenty years have been the toast of Broadway in New York City. The words and music of his songs long ago became the American scene. It would not be amiss to say that nearly every light musical program heard on the radio in our country contains at least one selection from the compositions of Cole Porter. The song you are about to hear is called "Night and Day." It was written in the 1930's and is still a popular favorite. Now Cole Porter's "Night and Day," played by an American radio orchestra—

Record: "Night and Day (Cole Porter)" 3:35.

Announcer 2: You have just heard Cole Porter's "Night and Day." This concludes the musical portion of our program from America. Tomorrow at this same time "The Voice of the United States of America" will bring you more music.

Announcer 1: For those who did not hear the beginning of our program, in a few minutes we will offer a brief resume of the main news of the day. Meanwhile you will hear a few short dispatches from today's American press.

WASHINGTON — The Sacred Cow, a plane especially built for the late President Roosevelt with an inside lift, will be shortly scrapped.

President Roosevelt used the Sacred Cow on all his flights, including the conferences in Teheran and Yalta. The Sacred Cow was often seen at the Moscow airfield, where it attracted considerable interest. Before concluding her distinguished career, the Sacred Cow will make a last flight, bringing back to Arabia after his three-week stay in the United States the Emir Ibn Saud, heir to the throne of Saudi Arabia.

The latest book by John Steinbeck, "The Wayward Bus," just published, describes conflicts between various human beings in a small bus, bogged in the mire of a California road. While the literary critic of THE NEW YORK TIMES gives a negative appraisal of this volume, which he considers flimsy and not original, the literary reviewer of The New York Herald Tribune writes on the same day that this is one of the subtlest works of Steinbeck.

The Metropolitan Opera of New York has decided to present Prokofieff's opera "War and Peace." Because of stage problems of a technical nature which will require more time than was expected at first, New York will not see Prokofieff's opera until next year.

And now for those who tuned in late, we repeat the news headlines:

NANKING—In order to fight inflation, Generalissimo Chiang Kai-shek reinstitutes war-time controls.

LAKE SUCCESS—The American delegate at the United Nations, Warren Austin, addressed a letter to Secretary General Trygve Lie asking to have placed on the agenda of the Security Council the American plan for perpetual strategic trusteeship over the Pacific islands. These islands, once under the Japanese mandate, were conquered by American forces.

PRAGUE—President Benes addressed the Slovak delegation warning them against projects for the creation of the Central European Federation as being impractical. The President points out that bringing out this question may provoke a new crisis that would be fatal for the Republic of Czechoslovakia.

PARIS — Exceptionally cold weather is threatening spring wheat sowing and may create a necessity for importing grain from abroad, which would complicate the country's economy.

WASHINGTON — The Department of State is of the opinion that, according to lend-lease agreements, the United States should deliver to the U.S.S.R. more goods, totaling $25,000,000.

WASHINGTON—Admiral Nimitz, commander-in-chief of the American Navy, declared yesterday that he has confidence in the United Nations ability to attain a solid perpetual peace.

WASHINGTON, again—In the American Congress the plan of the Budget Committee to cut 16 per cent from the budget meets serious opposition. The final decision on the question will be taken by the House and the Senate this week.

Announcer 1: This concludes the first broadcast to our listeners in the U.S.S.R. Tomorrow at 9 P. M., Moscow time, you will again hear "The Voice of the United States of America" on the following wave lengths: 19.72, 19.65, 19.62, 19.57, 16.90, 16.83 and 13.91 and in addition on 48.62, 41.15 and 31.45 meters. Now we wish our listeners in the Soviet Union good night.

Music: Theme, last bars of "The Battle Hymn of the Republic." *To tag.*

Announcer 1: This program came to you from the United States of America.

OUR RADIO HEARD BY FEW RUSSIANS

Audience of Voice of America Limited by Poor Reception, Want of Advance Notice

By DREW MIDDLETON
Special to THE NEW YORK TIMES.

MOSCOW, Feb. 22—The first drops of information were sprinkled this week by the "Voice of America" broadcasts to the Soviet Union.

There is avid interest here in news from the United States and news about American life, but at present the "Voice of America" program is struggling against two sizable difficulties.

One of these is poor reception here. The other is lack of advertisement.

Unless something can be done to strengthen the signals from Munich, where the program is retransmitted, many of its most interesting musical features will not reach the Russians in enjoyable form.

Officials See Improvement

This is a technical problem and officials of the Office of Information and Cultural Affairs attached to the United States Embassy here are confident that improvement will be made.

The Russians expect it. In fact this correspondent has heard a number of sly hints in the last few days to the effect that a nation that prides itself so much on its technical progress ought to be able to provide stronger transmission for its radio program.

Oddly enough, the British Broadcasting Corporation, the only real foreign rival of "Voice of America" in transmitting news to Russia's millions, has given the American program its widest publicity.

On Monday night the British broadcast an announcement of the American program on their Russian program, which meant that everyone who listened to the BBC news knows about the American broadcasts.

An official of the Office of Information and Cultural Affairs said Thursday that as yet the official news release sent by United States Ambassador W. Bedell Smith to the Moscow newspapers last Saturday, regarding the opening of the American broadcast, had not appeared in any newspaper.

A friend of this writer, discussing Wednesday night's program, praised the news section, which in-

Sharpe in The Glasgow Bulletin
Soviet Foreign Minister Molotov.

cluded Secretary of State Marshall's reply to Soviet Foreign Minister Molotov on the Acheson statement, Ambassador Smith's note to Mr. Molotov on American offers for increasing and strengthening scientific and cultural contact between the Soviet Union and the United States, and Rear Admiral Richard E. Byrd's invitation to Soviet scientists to visit his base at Little America and see what he is up to in the Antarctic.

This, said my friend, was "real news," since none of the items mentioned had by then appeared in Moscow newspapers.

What was the Soviet Union reading about the United States this week? The files in this office show that on Monday, Tuesday and Wednesday the Moscow press had fourteen items dealing with the United States.

Pravda on Monday published two news items from America. One of these cited an article in the newspaper PM to the effect that the Inter-American Defense Council had sent proposals to the twenty-one American republics, including a plan for representation of the General Staff of each nation on a permanent military board.

The other item dealt with a report on the sale of surplus American war equipment to the Philippines, France and Britain.

On Tuesday a Tass report from Rome said that an American specialist was to build airfields in Italy that would accommodate planes larger than the B-29 or B-36.

Another report from New York described Admiral Byrd's reconnaissance flights in Antarctica.

RADIO LISTENER?

THE AMERICAN WAY

Summers in The Buffalo Evening News

Trusteeship Issue Featured

On Wednesday all papers featured a Tass dispatch from New York quoting the Associated Press to the effect that the United States had asked Secretary General Trygve Lie of the United Nations to turn over trusteeship of the former Japanese mandated islands in the Pacific to the United States. A paragraph also appeared entitled "Lynch Law in South Carolina."

The six interpretive articles were naturally all longer than the news items. On Tuesday an article in Pravda dealt with the reported seizure of German patents by American and British monopolies, which Pravda characterized as the richest booty in history.

Two articles appeared in Izvestia, the Government newspaper. The first dealt with United States maneuvers in the Pacific, where Americans were viewed as attempting the economic and political infiltration of Australia; the other discussed the United States-Canadian agreement for joint security, which was criticized for its alleged aggressive intentions.

Wednesday brought three more articles in a critical vein. The first and most important, running a page and a quarter in Pravda, dealt with what it called American and British attacks on the sovereignty of western European nations.

Another in Red Star assailed the Dulles proposals as instigation to war. The third, in a Moscow evening newspaper, described aid given by United States occupational authorities to Japanese "reactionaries."

U.S. to Liven Broadcasts to Russia With Jazz Tunes and More News

Reception in Moscow Now Clear—Native Listeners Impressed by Announcers' Diction—Technical Feature Anchored

Special to THE NEW YORK TIMES.

WASHINGTON, Feb. 26 — Beginning tomorrow the State Department will rearrange its program of daily broadcasts of one hour to Russia to lighten and enliven them, as a result of criticisms received in the first nine days of the operations.

William Benton, Assistant Secretary of State, said today it had been found that the Russian audience had a "taste for the currently popular American jazz tunes." The music content of the programs, he added, is accordingly being veered away "from the turkey-in-the-straw type of folksong originally planned." The program tomorrow will feature "Jockey Up."

Other changes will be made in broadcasting news and features, so as not to weary the listeners. News of the day will be increased from fifteen to eighteen minutes. It will be given at the start of the program. Instead of attempting to cover high spots of all the world, it will concentrate on a few items that presumably will not appear in the Russian press. Those few items will be developed to provide the Russian listeners with a sufficient understanding of them.

Technical Feature to Be Last

The time given to technical features on a currently interesting subject will be reduced. This will be placed last on the program and will be introduced with clear warning of what is coming so that the uninterested listeners may turn off.

The program for tomorrow will be:
(1) News of the day (18 minutes)
(2) Music (10 minutes)
(3) Book review or other timely feature
(4) Popular music (10 minutes)
(5) Repeat of news in headline form
(6) Technical feature.
The changes have been decided upon in consequence of criticisms received from Lieut. Gen. W. Bedell Smith, United States Ambassador in Moscow, and members of his Embassy staff who not only have heard the programs but have obtained reactions of Russian listeners.

General Smith has been most frank. After the first broadcast he telegraphed:

"At the end of the first forty-five minutes you played 'Night and Day.' Everybody remarked that was what they had been waiting for."

He especially urged that the entire format be changed to make it easier for the Russian listener to know just when to tune in the part of the program in which he would be particularly interested.

There is as yet no way of knowing how many Russians have heard the broadcasts, but they have been advertised by the British Broadcasting Corporation over its well-established broadcasts, and the general reaction of the Russian listeners is described as "definitely favorable."

Later Reception Excellent

Poor atmospherics at first interfered with the clarity of the reception, but these conditions have cleared up and the reception thereafter has been declared excellent.

Russians have commented especially on the fine diction of the Russian-speaking American citizens, eight of whom were selected out of tests among 400 to conduct the broadcasting. This was regarded by Mr. Benton as high praise, since Russian announcers are noted for their diction.

It is the more noteworthy, Mr. Benton commented, in as much as he understands that the Russian language has changed a great deal in the past ten years, possibly as a result of the impact of the revolution.

February 27, 1947

News Coverage of ERP Bill Disappoints Washington

By JAMES RESTON
Special to The New York Times

WASHINGTON, Dec. 22—The White House and State Department are evidently not too happy about the attention given to the foreign policy pronouncements of President Truman and Secretary of State Marshall last Friday.

Officials there note that, except in the major newspapers, the texts of the President's message to Congress on the European Recovery Program and General Marshall's report on the London Conference were not published, and that the text of the Administration's ERP Bill, one of the most important to go to The Hill since HR 1776, has not yet appeared in any American daily newspaper.

Most observers in Washington agree that this is unfortunate, but those who have studied the public pronouncements of the Administration last Friday think the explanation is about as follows:

1. The Administration put out too much in a single day: (A) The President's message to Congress; (B) The Secretary of State's speech; (C) The text of the Administration's ERP Bill, and (D) A 227-page document explaining the Administration's policy on the European Recovery Program.

2 It is generally recognized, even by those who are in charge of public relations in the Government, that newspapers in the United States have their limits, and that the American reading public digests only one big story at a time. But neither Charles Ross, the President's press secretary, nor Michael McDermott, the State Department's press chief, endeavored to keep these announcements from coming out together on the last day before the Congressional recess.

3. The long ERP document of the State Department explaining the recovery policy, represented several months' work by a corps of experts in the Department, and had excellent news possibilities, but, it too, was released on Friday afternoon, and like the text of the bill, was crowded out of the papers and scarcely mentioned on the radio.

4. This is almost precisely what happened last June 5, when, after weeks of preparation, Secretary Marshall went to Cambridge to announce the plan that bears his name. On the day he spoke, the President called a press conference, denounced the Hungarian Communists and the economic views of Senator Robert A. Taft of Ohio, and thus crowded the Marshall announcement into a secondary position.

5. There was a good reason why the President's message had to be sent to Congress Friday afternoon. It was ready before then, but those in charge of the debate on the short-range European Relief Bill did not want it presented until after the interim debate.

In the opinion of most observers here, however, there was no reason why the Marshall speech, the text of the bill, or the long explanation of the measure had to be released when the wires and papers were already crowded with news of the Congressional recess.

On the contrary, many good reasons can be offered why these other announcements could have been postponed.

"I think," General Marshall said at the opening of his now famous Harvard speech last June, "one difficulty is that the program is one of such enormous complexity that the very mass of facts presented to the public by press and radio make it exceedingly difficult for the man in the street to reach a clear appraisal of the situation."

At the end of the address, the Secretary added:

"An essential part of any successful action (in Europe) on the part of the United States is an understanding on the part of the people of America of the character of the problem and the remedies to be applied."

There is the warmest support in Washington of these sentiments, but the feeling here is that both the White House and the State Department defied General Marshall's principle by the way in which they handled their material on Friday.

Secretary Marshall explained in simple terms "the character of the problem" and his Department in a monumental document explained "the remedies to be applied." But if ever—in Secretary Marshall's phrase—a "mass of facts" of "enormous complexity" were given precipitously to the public, this was it.

Officials in the Administration not only swamped the press and radio, but overwhelmed themselves. Although the report on the London conference and the official ERP were awaited by half the world, the State Department's own United States Information Service did not get sufficient time to handle the story. Indeed, the detailed State Department explanation has not yet been distributed to the main USIS outposts overseas, let alone to influential editors in this country, Britain and France.

Unfortunately it is not so easy to recapture, this week, the opportunity for education the Administration had last Friday morning.

Christmas week is a poor time for news. This week, however, the text of the bill, if released for the first time, would certainly have been printed in a few papers and widely reported. This week, too, with Congress demobilized, Administration spokesmen could have had a field day with their official explanations of the plan. But having shot its bolt on Friday, the State Department had only these two items to offer today:

1. A routine announcement about the date on which a United States-Cuban tariff agreement will take place; and

2. Confirmation of a report that Primo Carnera had finally received permission to stay in this country.

December 23, 1947

26

Press and President: No Holds Barred

The White House weekly conference is an exercise in democracy as well as a prime source of news.

By ANTHONY LEVIERO

TRUMAN PRAISES U. S. NEWSPAPERS

Country Has 'Many Wonderful' Publications, 22 German and Austrian Journalists Hear

Special to THE NEW YORK TIMES.

WASHINGTON, July 26—President Truman told a group of visiting German and Austrian journalists today that the United States had a "great many wonderful newspapers" and expressed hope that they had received some good out of them.

He addressed these remarks to the group, which included nineteen German and three Austrian newspaper men, in the Rose Garden outside his executive office and posed for photographs with them. The President said that he understood the visitors had heard it would not be possible to be photographed with the United States Chief Executive and he wanted to give them their opportunity to have this done.

In a brief talk the President said: "I understand that you have been taking a look at the press of the United States. We are glad to have you in this country, and hope that you will get some satisfaction out of your visit. There are a great many wonderful newspapers in this country, and I hope you will get some good out of them; and I am sure you will. When you get back to Germany, I hope you will be able to say that you have been cordially treated in this country and that we at least showed we were glad to have you pay us a visit."

The newspaper men were brought to the United States at the request of the American Military Government in Germany to observe the operations of a free press in a democracy. The Office of Education of the Federal Security Agency arranged the tour. They are concluding a two-month visit.

WASHINGTON.

ONCE a week the President of the United States faces the free press and endures a barrage of questions. It is the biggest show in Washington. It is also a great institution, uniquely American. It has become a factor in our checks-and-balances system of government. Nothing anywhere else in the world compares with it.

There, before a large assembly of correspondents, foreign as well as American, sits the Chief Executive of a great nation, subjecting himself to free-hand, no-holds-barred questioning. All the correspondents have the privilege of questioning him about pretty nearly any subject under the sun, and they often do. At his 193d conference recently they threw at Mr. Truman forty-two questions covering sixteen topics in a twenty-minute mass interview. At least a dozen were stinging questions about his friend and military aide, Maj. Gen. Harry H. Vaughan, and the "five per centers."

The President answered every question, the touchy and unbarbed alike, with a varying mood and demeanor—wit, laughter, firm "no comment," or challenge—and all with composure and courtesy. Imagine newsmen being permitted to question Prime Minister Clement Attlee of Britain, much less King George, that way!

Indeed, some have tried to compare this practice in the Oval Room of the White House—the "throne room"—with the question period in the British House of Commons. But how can a formal Parliamentary proceeding be compared with this free-wheeling affair of the press and the President? Members of Parliament submit questions in writing. They get their answers orally a week or two later, from Parliamentary secretaries and Ministers. Where is the resemblance when it is neither the press that asks nor the head of the nation that answers?

THE White House sessions have—despite their informality—a most serious background. Mr. Truman feels a deep sense of obligation toward his face-to-face relationship with the press, and prepares himself earnestly for the encounter. When he stands before the reporters he is really giving a repeat performance. He has already gone through a dress rehearsal of the drama of Q. and A. with his staff.

Three-quarters of an hour before the newsmen are admitted to the Oval Room, the members of the "Kitchen Cabinet" gather round to help the President prepare for his appearance before the greatest sounding board in the world. If some great national or international problem is likely to call for comment, the White House staff is augmented by an official of the State, Defense, or other pertinent department. In the group one specialist or another has data that will bring Mr. Truman up to date on such a problem.

The members of the staff question their chief sharply, and try to cover the range of current affairs, world and domestic, which the correspondents are apt to touch on. Charles G. Ross, the President's press secretary, who is an eminent newsman himself (a Pulitzer Prize man and for a long time chief of the Washington Bureau of The St. Louis Post-Dispatch), plays a leading role in trying to anticipate what questions will be asked.

Harry S. Truman, the man, gives the answers to his staff as they occur to him. He draws on his great knowledge of affairs, made possible by the continual flow of reports across his desk. Harry S. Truman, as President, then considers with his staff whether those answers should be uttered before the world. The problem of what to say is often secondary. Should it be said at all, and if so, should it be said now or at some more propitious moment? Timing, statesmanship, diplomacy, and political strategy are intermixed factors, and wise is the man who makes the right decision.

MR. TRUMAN himself usually decides. He has a ready capacity for making up his mind. He listens to advice, yet often differs with his aides, explains why and announces what he will do. They regard his reasoning and decisions as usually sound when viewed in the framework of his programs and policies.

Neither in the briefing nor in the news conference itself does Mr. Truman show signs of tension or nervousness. The reporter, more than Mr. Truman, is likely to regard the press conference as an ordeal. The public, however, has invested it with a certain amount of glamour. As

---

ANTHONY LEVIERO is a member of The Times Washington bureau who regularly covers the White House—and the Presidential conferences.

in most public affairs, the participant hardly savor the glamour. The press conference is hard work—for Mr. Truman a well as for most of the reporters.

Altogether 550 men and women are accredited to attend the weekly press conference, including a small number of Government press officers. But, unless great events are pending, usually between 100 and 200 are on hand. This corps will include reporters; nationally known news and radio commentators; columnists; chiefs of Washington bureaus of metropolitan dailies and of wire services that girdle the world; foreign newsmen, including a couple of correspondents of Tass, the official Soviet news agency, and the small group of White House correspondents proper who follow the President and what he does, day in, day out, no matter where he is.

I T is a Thursday morning, say, and about 125 correspondents are on hand. Some, perhaps, have told Mr. Ross of a question or so they intend to raise, and, as they gather in the spacious lobby of the White House executive offices, they chat informally about issues on which comment is likely to come from the President. But that is about as far as they go. There is no collaboration, no agreement beforehand to pursue a particular line of questioning.

At 10:30 o'clock (one week the conference is held in the morning, the next week at 4 in the afternoon to give afternoon and morning papers, respectively, a break on the news) a White House policeman opens the door to the Oval Room and the correspondents troop in. When all are there the door is closed, secret service men take their stations about the room, and the President greets the newsmen.

There is no "rank" here; Joe Beagle of The Podunk Bugle has as much standing with his question on an irrigation project in his district as Mr. Pundit of the big newspaper chain, who is eager to know from Mr. Truman's answers whether the next Big Four conference may be expected to bring a German settlement.

However, a comparative few reporters do the questioning. The others are content to listen and write. The main reason for this is the fact that it is hard to keep up with the fast pace of Q. and A. Mr. Truman is a rapid talker, and the reporters must scribble madly to catch not only what he says but also the question that started him talking, and the nuance and tone of his reply.

I F Mr. Truman has some news to give out he usually does not wait for a question.

Thus at the conference ten days ago which developed into a forty-two-question affair, Mr. Truman started off with the announcement that he (1) had sent a thank-you note (copies available as the newsmen left the conference) to Gen. Dwight D. Eisenhower for his services as presiding officer of the Joint Chiefs of Staff, and (2) that he had appointed Gen. Omar Bradley chairman of the Joint Chiefs of Staff and renamed Admiral Louis Denfeld Chief of Naval Operations for another two years.

T HIS in itself gave the conference a good news content. But the correspondents had many topics on their minds, and their ensuing questions demonstrated at once how closely they must follow world and domestic events, and how their questions leap from subject to subject like a grasshopper in a field.

After routine questions about whether the President

would sign the minimum wage bill passed by the House, and so on, one of the newsmen tossed the question that touched off this brisk exchange (presented in paraphrase in accordance with the White House rule):

Q. Mr. President, do you think it was within the realm of propriety for your military aide and veterans' affairs coordinator (General Vaughan) to assist a race track get a permit for scarce building materials when there was a serious shortage of these materials for veterans' housing?

A. I have no comment on that statement because I don't know whether your statement is a fact or not.

Q. Well, it was the * * * (President broke in)

A. I say I don't know whether it is a fact or not and you don't either.

Q. That was the testimony of your Housing Expediter under oath.

A. I have no comment to make on it.

Q. Is there any significance in the fact that General Vaughan isn't here today? We can't see him from the back row.

A. General Vaughan, I imagine, has some appointments in his office. It is always customary for him to be here when he is free. He's not afraid of you, don't worry about that. (Laughter.)

WHEN the questioning slows down, Merriman Smith of The United Press, the senior wire service man, says "Thank you, Mr. President." If the conference has been particularly rich Mr. Smith puts stress on the "you." The moment it is uttered Mr. Smith and three other wire service men rush out, and Mr. Truman, standing behind his desk, chuckles, as he watches them go. Through it all, with all the hard work, the news conference is by no means a grim affair. It is frequently punctuated with laughter. There are quips from both sides. The atmosphere is informal, yet a certain propriety toward the Chief Executive is observed. Rarely does the questioning get offensive, although it has happened that some indignant columnist has tried to

be sharp with Mr. Truman.

Mr. Truman is usually affable and the soul of courtesy. Even on the infrequent occasions when he tends to get testy he never humiliates a reporter. He never says, for instance, that he won't answer damn fool questions or tell a reporter to go stand in a corner and put on a dunce cap. Mr. Roosevelt used to do that.

The Presidential mass interview was essentially self-starting, although Theodore Roosevelt should be credited as its original sponsor. He let some reporters interview him while he was shaving. More important, he gave them a room to get them in out of the rain one nasty day, and they have been entrenched in the White House executive offices ever since.

WOODROW WILSON put the formal news conference on a regular weekly basis as we know it today. His successors continued it in a mediocre way until Franklin D. Roosevelt used it artfully for partisan, philosophical or statesmanlike expression.

Mr. Truman is carrying it forward conscientiously and with good-will. He has told editors he doesn't care much what they say about him on the editorial page so long as they keep the news columns accurate. Or as Mr. Ross put it recently: "The news conference is a necessary institution in our form of government and Mr. Truman feels the same way about it. It is not conducive to an orderly giving out of news. But it is a typically democratic institution, with all the virtues and all the faults of our democracy. You see them reflected there."

Yet the value of the news conference has been questioned. Some correspondents don't bother attending except on rare occasions. They consider them mostly a waste of time. Others feel that some more efficient, more comfortable means of interviewing the President should be worked out. Perhaps the most serious criticism heard is that in the rapid give-and-take of a press conference the President any President is likely to make boners that may have unfortunate repercussions at home and abroad. For this reason some say it should be abolished.

IT is true that many conferences produce little news and amount chiefly to exchange of pleasantries and "no-comment" sparring. But even if this is all that comes from a session, reporters there have performed one valuable service to this democracy. They have seen the President personally and can tell how he looks—healthy and cheerful or tired and worried, even ailing.

It should be borne in mind too, that the continual flow of White House press releases of the President's messages to Congress and statements on numerous issues obviate a lot of questioning that otherwise would make the news conferences seem more productive On May 9, this year, when he had been in office a little over four years, Mr. Truman's releases numbered an even 2,000. Mr. Roosevelt had been in office eight years and five months before he had issued that many.

It might be said that the mass interview suffers from bigness, an American characteristic. It should also be said, then, that this bigness is its strength, for no qualified Washington correspondent is barred. This is freedom of the press. In a time of deep conflict, with repressions multiplying abroad, such a uniquely free American institution is worth preserving for possible emulation some day elsewhere. It is a credit to the newsmen who kept siege at the White House gates in the old days, and a credit to the Presidents who have realized its value to them and to the electorate to which they are responsible.

IT is, as we have seen, a young institution. But it is in the long tradition of a free press. Jefferson, the sublime protagonist of this tradition, could contemplate only one form of censorship. He wrote to George Washington that no government should be free of censorship by a free press. The White House news conference is censorship of government at its source. Once a week it admits the essence of the body politic into the Oval Room to demand of its chosen man: "Mr. President, how is the state of the Union?"

Truman Likes Reporters; Their Bosses? Not Always

Special to THE NEW YORK TIMES.

WASHINGTON, Oct. 6—President Truman held his 200th press conference this morning and said that it was an institution that he liked. He also told reporters that he never got annoyed with them, but he did get annoyed sometimes with their bosses.

Mr. Truman opened his regular weekly news conference by remarking that it was the 200th in about 234 weeks that he has been President. Then he said he had no special announcement and invited questioning.

When he was asked to comment on his news conference as an institution the President said that he liked it. He added that he liked to answer reporters' questions straight from the shoulder, and when he could not tell the truth, he did not answer questions.

August 21, 1949

October 7, 1949

Truman Note Scolds Music Critic For 'Lousy Review' on Daughter

Special to THE NEW YORK TIMES.

WASHINGTON, Dec. 8—President Truman has threatened to beat up a critic who had criticized the singing of his daughter, Margaret, at a concert here Tuesday night. The story came out today in a Presidential letter that leaked out to the newspapers.

The missive, to Paul Hume, music critic of The Washington Post, caused almost as great a sensation as the letter Mr. Truman wrote to a member of Congress a few months ago in which he referred to the Marine Corps as the Navy's police force.

What was learned of the latest letter appeared as a bowdlerized version published by The Washington Daily News, a tabloid, in the following item:

"H. for hello
"S. for sweet
"T. for thing

"Margaret Truman sang here the other day. Paul Hume, The Washington Post's music critic, panned her unmercifully. He is now showing around a letter, on White House letterhead, which goes like this:

"'I have just read your lousy review buried in the back pages. You sound like a frustrated old man who never made a success, an eight-ulcer man on a four-ulcer job, and all four ulcers working.

"I never met you, but if I do you'll need a new nose and plenty of beefsteak and perhaps a supporter below. Westbrook Pegler, a guttersnipe, is a gentleman compared to you. You can take that as more of an insult than as a reflection on your ancestry.'

"The letter was initialed 'H. S. T.' and Mr. Hume, who once wanted a career as a singer himself, is wondering whether the initials stand for whom he thinks they might stand for, so to speak."

It was soon acknowledged at the White House that the letter had been written by Mr. Truman. The language was reported to be even earthier than the expurgated version. The letter was written in long-hand on a scratch pad bearing the White House imprint and it was sent in a bluish green envelope.

Mr. Hume, who is 34 years old and weighs 165 pounds, compared with the President's sixty-six years and 180 pounds or more, said in part in his review:

"She [Miss Truman] is extremely attractive on the stage. Her program is usually light in nature, designed to attract those who like the singing of Jeanette MacDonald and Nelson Eddy. Yet Miss Truman cannot sing very well. She is flat a good deal of the time—more last night than at any time we have heard her. She has learned about her diaphragm and its importance to her singing. She has learned that she must work in order to make something of her voice. But she still cannot sing with anything approaching professional finish.

"She communicates almost nothing of the music she presents. Schumann, Schubert and Mozart were on her program last night. Yet the performance of music by these composers was no more than a caricature of what it would be if sung by any one of a dozen artists today.

"And still the public goes and pays the same price it would for the world's finest singers.

"It is an extremely unpleasant duty to record such unhappy facts about so honestly appealing a personality. But as long as Miss Truman sings as she has for three years, and does today, we seem to have no recourse unless it is to omit comment on her programs altogether."

President Attended Recital

Mr. Truman attended his daughter's concert in Constitution Hall with Prime Minister Attlee of Great Britain. Before he did so he had to resolve a profound personal dilemma, however. His close friend and press secretary, Charles G. Ross, had died suddenly in the White House a few hours before the concert. Mr. Truman wanted to stay home but that would have meant his daughter would have learned of the death and perhaps have been unnerved. He decided to attend.

The Washington Post announced today that in tomorrow's issue it would reproduce The Washington News story and the following statement by Mr. Hume in his own column:

"The day after my review of Margaret Truman's concert I received a note on White House stationery signed 'H. S. T.' It was similar to, but not identical, to the quotation above. The letter was seen by office associates and by my editors, but I do not desire to publish it. Whether it was from the President I do not know.

"If it was, I can only say that a man suffering the loss of a close friend and carrying the terrible burden of the present world crisis ought to be indulged in an occasional outburst of temper."

Miss Truman Praises Critic

NASHVILLE, Tenn., Dec. 8 (UP)—Margaret Truman said tonight the music critic her father threatened "is a very fine critic."

"He has a right to write as he pleases," Miss Truman said of Paul Hume. At first Miss Truman, couldn't believe her father would "use language like that" when told what Mr. Truman had been reported to have written.

But when the White House confirmed that the President had indeed written such a letter, Miss Truman had "no comment." She was here tonight for a concert.

Pegler Says "Let Us Pray"

Westbrook Pegler, in New York, issued the following statement on the Truman letter:

"It is a great tragedy that in this awful hour the people of the United States must accept in lieu of leadership the nasty malice of a President whom Bernard Baruch in a similar incident called a rude, uncouth, ignorant man. Let us pray."

Mr. Pegler said Mr. Baruch had spoken of Mr. Truman in such a way after Mr. Truman had written the financier an angry letter about the time of the 1948 Presidential election.

RADIO AND TELEVISION

By JACK GOULD

General of the Army Dwight D. Eisenhower's chances of gaining the Republican nomination for President certainly are not going to be enhanced if there are many more telecasts such as last Friday night's from Madison Square Garden.

As a demonstration of popular support for the general, the feat of filling the Garden at the hour of midnight unquestionably had real political significance. But if judged solely from the standpoint of what could be seen on the screen, the rally was a disappointing show.

Tex McCrary and the Eisenhower Bandwagon Committee committed perhaps the most elementary mistake in the use of television for political purposes. They were so preoccupied with the near thousands in attendance at the Garden that they forgot the unseen millions sitting at home.

The rally should provide a good lesson for the managers of the forthcoming national conventions. The Eisenhower supporters on the floor of the arena apparently were content to entertain themselves by parading around with banners, waving placards and singing "I like Ike." No doubt they did have a sense of unity and excitement in launching the campaign for the general.

But on television the results were far different. For those at home, who after all were only spectators and not participants, the rally at times seemed like a ninety-minute stage wait of bewildering ineptitude, both politically and theatrically. By no means was enough said or done in front of the cameras to make for varied or stimulating viewing.

Sharing the center of the screen were Mr. McCrary and Bill Stern, the sportscaster. But neither of them, it is to be feared, has exactly the forceful type of personality needed to weld the crowd of some 18,000 persons into a purposeful and enthusiastic body. Mr. McCrary's contribution was limited largely to crying out, "Who likes Ike?" Mr. Stern spent most of the evening apologizing for talking so much because he was being heard simultaneously on both radio and TV.

Although limited in quantity, some of the straight entertainment was not bad—Ethel Merman singing "There's no business like show business" and Mary Martin singing in London while being accompanied by Richard Rodgers on a piano in the Garden. But Irving Berlin had difficulty in being heard above the din as he introduced his song called "I Like Ike"; Fred Waring couldn't resist a complicated business of trying to turn the whole Garden into a glee club and most of the other acts were lost in the general confusion.

The visiting celebrities, including Humphrey Bogart and Lauren Bacall, were shoved around like so many mute sheep as they were put on view in the prize ring in the center of the arena. It was not a very edifying or dignified experience for either the stars or their audience. Clark Gable brought a hush to the crowd when he was introduced but, where a few words for Eisenhower might have had an electrifying effect, he was permitted only to introduce Mr. Berlin.

Indeed, except for a few very hurried remarks from Senator Henry Cabot Lodge, Republican of Massachusetts, at the program's end, there was no truly inspirational message from General Eisenhower's supporters that the viewer—and voter—could retain and act upon. How the supporters felt was shown clearly on the screen; why they felt as they did, which was what really counted, was not shown.

The advent of television obviously is going to bring about many changes in politics and traditional campaign oratory, but it must be hoped that Friday night's rally does not augur an appeal to the electorate solely in terms of theatricalism and emotion. If TV's power for political good is to be realized, there must always be the essential appeal to the voter's mind. Those who most like Ike can only regret its omission from Friday night's rally.

MR. STEVENSON AND THE PRESS

In an address delivered yesterday in Portland, Ore., Governor Stevenson had some interesting things to say about the American press and its opportunities and responsibilities in the field of political action. He was, he said, "glad to pay * * * tribute to the press * * * for the impartiality and fullness" with which his own campaign activities have been reported in the news columns—which is, of course, as it should be. But at the same time he raised two points of criticism.

One of these is that we seem to be "developing a one-party press in a two-party country." Mr. Stevenson is referring here, of course, to the fact that in recent Presidential elections a very considerable majority of the press has chosen to support the Republican candidate. He thinks that this particularly holds great dangers both for the press itself and for our free society. For, as he puts it: "A free society means a society based on free competition and there is no more important competition than competition in ideas, competition in opinion. This form of competition is essential to the preservation of a free press." Indeed, I think the press should set an example to the nation in increasing opposition to uniformity."

But how does the press do this? Mr. Stevenson surely would not have publishers and editors who sincerely favor the election of a Republican candidate write instead in favor of the election of a Democratic candidate merely in order to create a diversity of opinion and for the sake of "increasing opposition to uniformity." It is the business of publishers and editors to say what they think. The essential safeguard against what Mr. Stevenson describes as a "one-party press" does not consist of an artificially balanced division of editorial opinion but rather of fair reporting of dissenting news and a free market for the publication of organs of dissenting opinion. We agree, however, with Governor Stevenson that editorial opinion itself should be based on something more than a mere automatic reflex to a party symbol and that it should reflect an independent judgment. We have sought, in our own case, to arrive at such judgments. In three of the last six Presidential elections (counting the present one) we have supported a Republican candidate

and in three we have supported a Democrat.

Governor Stevenson's other point of criticism is that some newspapers have been too precipitate in their choice of a candidate in the present case. Some of them, he says, "rushed to commit themselves to a candidate last spring, long before they knew what that candidate stood for, or what his party platform would be, or who his opponent was, or what would be the issues of the campaign."

If this criticism is meant to include our own newspaper, as it may be meant, since we declared our readiness last January to support General Eisenhower in the event of his nomination by the Republican party, let us say that while it is true that we could not then know who his opponent would be we did know what General Eisenhower stood for, including both a firm assertion of American leadership abroad and a middle-of-the-road policy in domestic matters; we knew that he could neither win nor accept nomination on a platform which repudiated these fundamental beliefs, and we knew that the issues of the campaign would turn, as they are turning now, on the record of the last four years.

Because we believed that only enlightened and responsible leadership could safeguard the American people in the face of the present threat from Russia we urged last January that the Republican party choose General Eisenhower as its candidate for President. At the same time we said that always provided, and only provided, such leadership was made available we believed that the time was ripe, after twenty years, for a change of party control in Washington. We continue to believe that this is true, because we believe that it is a healthy process in a democratic society to rotate the possession of political power; because we believe that a change of party control is the best guarantee that the "mess" which exists in Washington can be cleared up promptly, and because we believe that General Eisenhower, as President, would have bipartisan support both for a courageous foreign policy and for a middle-of-the-road domestic program under which the American system of private enterprise could once more prosper to full advantage.

'ONE-PARTY PRESS' STIRS TRUMAN IRE

But if News Columns Give Him Fair Deal He Doesn't Care a Hoot About Editorials

By ANTHONY LEVIERO
Special to The New York Times.

WASHINGTON, Sept. 11—President Truman asserted today that the nation's newspapers were "big business" and predominantly Republican and that therefore the public should read the news with a grain of salt in order to get a fair balance between Republican and Democratic political candidates.

The President's blast at the press was fired as a follow-up of the similar criticism made by Gov. Adlai E. Stevenson of Illinois, the Democratic Presidential candidate, in a speech to editors in Seattle on Monday.

Mr. Truman's censure of newspapers opened the weekly news conference at the White House. He first read a formal statement, enlarged on it with some off-the-cuff comments that somewhat mitigated the prepared statement and, in a later comment, asserted that the point of the statement was that a great many newspapers garbled the news.

President Truman quoted some figures to show that most newspapers were Republican in policy, or at least in their choice of candidates in 1948 and this year. His chief statistic was that only 10.3 per cent of the newspapers supported him for the Presidency in 1948.

While some conflict appeared in the aggregate of the President's comments, he acknowledged in reply to a question that the lesson of the statistics was that more persons read the news columns than the editorial columns.

In agreeing to this, Mr. Truman reiterated a favorite remark of his —that he didn't care a hoot about the editorials as long as he got a fair deal in the news columns.

Mr. Truman stressed that the "one-party press situation" was particularly tough for Democratic Congressional candidates, "who get even less opportunity to state their case in their local Republican papers than does the Democratic Presidential candidate." It was Governor Stevenson who had coined the phrase "one-party press."

If democracy is to work properly, said Mr. Truman, the people should be able to read the Democratic story as well as the Republican story. Newspapers, magazines, radio and television, he added, bear a great responsibility in political campaigns.

The President ended his formal statement on this note and then he went on to make extemporaneous comments, beginning by saying it did not matter what the newspapers did because in thirty years of political experience the metropolitan press of Missouri, as far as he could remember, never had supported him.

"I never needed it," he added.

Influence of Press 'Pitiful'

In these comments he also said the 1948 figures showed that the political influence of the "great free press" was "pitiful," and that fairness had been increasing since Governor Stevenson's talk.

The first question shot at the President was this:

"Mr. President, the Democrats have been winning for twenty years and I wonder if your figures mean that more readers read the news columns than read the editorial columns?"

Mr. Truman said he agreed, and he had always said that he did not give a hoot what was said in editorials as long as he got a fair deal in the news columns.

"When you said you don't give a hoot about the editorials, isn't that what your statement is aimed at?" asked another reporter.

No, replied Mr. Truman, his statement was principally aimed at garbling of the news. Some first class newspapers did not but a great many did, he added.

Mr. Truman gave a number of figures by states, among them being the fact that not one of Michigan's fifty-three newspapers supported him in 1948, while in New York only 4 per cent backed him.

An effort after the news conference to establish the research basis of the President's criticism brought this result: A White House aide said the basic figures came from the Democratic National Committee. The statistics quoted by the President were a handful of many used in a long article entitled "How Republican Is the Press," in the current issue of The New Republic.

The author of the article was Dr. Ralph Goldman, described in the weekly as "a political scientist presently serving as consultant with the Democratic National Committee." Reached on the telephone, Dr. Goldman said the primary source for both the White House and for his article were surveys by Editor and Publisher, a trade paper of American journalism.

Quoted Percentages Differ

The Associated Press this evening quoted current figures of Editor and Publisher which differed from the President's. While Mr. Truman said that he was supported by only 10.3 per cent of the dailies, the magazine said that in 1948 Governor Thomas E. Dewey was supported by 65.17 per cent of the dailies having 78.55 per cent of the circulation, while Mr. Truman was backed by 15.35 per cent having 10.03 per cent of the circulation.

Dr. Goldman's article agreed with Mr. Truman that only 10.3 per cent of the 1,769 had supported him. But his tables also showed that only 43.6 per cent were identified as Republican, while 43.4 per cent were uncommitted or had not reported their affiliation. The other 2.7 per cent had supported other candidates.

The treatment accorded to Governor Stevenson in Billings, Mont., last Monday was recalled today as an illustration of the President's criticism. When Governor Stevenson arrived there. The Billings Gazette had an exhaustive front-page account of the farm speech delivered by Gen. Dwight D. Eisenhower, the Republican Presidential candidate, at Kasson, Minn. Governor Stevenson also had made a farm speech there. The Gazette covered it entirely with this sentence:

"Governor Adlai Stevenson of Illinois also spoke."

Reporters traveling with Presidential candidates or political campaigners become aware of the idiosyncrasies of the metropolitan and grass roots papers in their treatment of politicians. One of these was noted during President Truman's Labor Day week-end trip to Milwaukee and was investigated today in the light of his criticism.

In a brief whistle stop at Clarksburg, W. Va., the reporters scanned the city's two newspapers. The Exponent, a morning newspaper, had a big story on the President's imminent visit. The Telegram, an evening paper, had not a word on Mr. Truman or Governor Stevenson.

Today's research brought this out: both The Exponent and The Telegram are owned by the Clarksburg Publishing Company, but the former is Democratic in its politics and the latter Republican. The Exponent's editor is Randal Strother, a Democrat, and The Telegram's is Frank E. Carpenter, a Republican.

On Sundays the same company publishes a paper called The Exponent - Telegram, with the two editors in charge. Reached by telephone today, Mr. Carpenter said:

"I saw no reason why I should help the Truman crowd."

"On Sundays I put out as non-partisan a paper as I possibly can," he added.

Mr. Carpenter went on to say, genially, that having refrained from advertising the President's visit, he noted it the following day in the lower section of a sort of two-part story in which Mr. Truman got fourteen lines.

The first part recalled the time eleven years ago when showmen arrived with an embalmed whale on two railroad flatcars and "stunk up" Clarksburg. The showmen asserted that 6,300 persons paid to see the whale, while the fact was only 630 saw it before the show was "run out of town."

The second part likened local Democrats to the showmen, for they declared that 16,000 turned out for Mr. Truman, as The Exponent reported. Others said only 160 turned out, while persons more experienced with crowds, the story explained, estimated 1,600. (This correspondent that day reported 2,500, a police estimate.)

Text of Truman Views on Press

WASHINGTON, Sept. 11 (UP) —Following is the text of President Truman's press conference statement today on the political leanings of the nation's newspapers:

The President has authorized direct quotation of the following statement made by him in today's news conference:

You know, at the Chicago convention, I said the Republicans have nearly all the newspapers and magazines on their side.

Governor Stevenson, the other day, in Oregon, had something to say on this situation. I agree with what he said, and would like to add just what I mean by Republican control of the press.

In 1948, only 10.3 per cent of the 1,769 daily papers in this country supported the Democratic candidate, and almost all the big circulation magazines were pro-Republican. I don't think the situation has changed much since then.

In Michigan, in 1948, for instance, not one of the fifty-three daily papers supported the Democratic ticket.

In New York, only 4 per cent of the papers were for the Democrats. In Pennsylvania, 1.5 per cent. In Illinois, 3.4 per cent. In Ohio, 4 per cent. In California, 4.8 per cent.

The one-party press situation is, of course, particularly tough for Democratic Congressional candidates, who get even less opportunity to state their case in their local Republican papers than does the Democratic Presidential candidate.

Now, I do not expect that listing these figures will result in any switches from the Republican to the Democratic party.

Newspapers — especially daily newspapers — have become big business, and big business traditionally has always been Republican.

I suggest that Americans bear this in mind, and add a dash of salt to every Republican helping of news, especially in those many papers and magazines which do not give a fair balance of news between the two major parties.

If democracy is to work properly, the people must be able to read and hear not only the Republican story but the Democratic as well. Our newspapers, magazines, radio and TV have a great responsibility to be fair in this and in all other campaigns.

This ended the formal statement; the following paragraphs were an off-the-cuff addition:

I want to add a comment to that, that I don't think it makes much difference what they do. I have had some experience with the situation for over thirty years, and as far as I can remember, I never had the support of the metropolitan press in Missouri when I was running for the Senate, and I never needed it.

In 1948 I read you the figures, and I think it is a rather pitiful situation—the small amount of political influence that the great free press of the United States has.

It is a good thing for the country, and I am not worried about the situation, but I am calling these things—nailing this thing down—for the simple reason that I am very anxious to see in the news columns a fair approach to this thing.

I will say this, that fairness has been increasing, since Governor Stevenson's speech.

Sparkman Calls Press Fair

SALT LAKE CITY, Sept. 11 (AP) —Senator John J. Sparkman of Alabama, Democratic Vice Presidential candidate, said today the nation's press had been fair to both major parties in its news columns.

Mr. Sparkman was in Utah for a series of talks in Salt Lake City and Ogden.

"Of course the press is heavily one-sided and has been for many, many years," Mr. Sparkman said. "I've been pleased to find a fair coverage in news columns. It's only in editorial policy that the press has been one-sided."

SMALL PAPERS FOR G. O. P.

Poll of Weeklies and Dailies Shows Eisenhower Is Favored

WASHINGTON, Sept. 11 (UP)— A grass roots poll of 3,511 weekly and small daily newspapers tended to show today that the Republican nominee, Gen. Dwight D. Eisenhower, was the personal choice of two thirds of the publishers for President.

By slightly smaller margins, the publishers said they would support General Eisenhower editorially and believed he was the man their readers wanted elected.

The mail poll of 3,062 weekly newspapers and 449 small-city dailies was conducted late last month by The Publishers' Auxiliary of Chicago, a weekly paper published by Western Newspaper Union. The concern said it mailed ballots to publishers of 8,570 weekly newspapers and 1,406 dailies with a top circulation of 25,000. Replies were received from all states except Arizona.

September 12, 1952

PRESIDENT AND PRESS: A NEW CHAPTER OPENS

Concern Is Felt Over Reports That
Eisenhower May Alter Conferences

By JAMES RESTON

Special to THE NEW YORK TIMES.

WASHINGTON, Jan. 17—Every President has had his share of troubles with the newspaper reporters, but General Eisenhower is having his troubles even before inauguration.

This is unfortunate, not only because every President needs and is entitled to a honeymoon free of unnecessary distractions but also because most of the trouble is based on an assumption that will probably not prove to be true.

This assumption, which started with a casual remark that the General might not have regular press conferences at the White House, and has been sustained by the fact that he has not actually had what could honestly be described as a press conference since the first week in September, is that he intends to abandon the weekly White House conference or change it substantially.

Even President Truman took note of this rumor on Thursday by asserting at his 324th and final White House press conference that he hoped the White House press conference would be continued.

There is no doubt that General Eisenhower's attitude and policy toward the reporters have changed considerably since he came home from Paris last June, and that he now feels uneasy about the problem of dealing with them after Tuesday.

Early Congeniality

When he returned at first, he was friendly and available. The day after he got back he held a large press conference at the Pentagon. Two days later in Abilene, Kan., he submitted to questions by more than 200 reporters before television cameras. The same day, on his special train en route to Kansas City, he invited several reporters back to his car for a private talk, then let them publish the substance of his remarks.

That same week in New York, then in Detroit, en route to his headquarters in Denver, he undertook to answer any and all questions, and when he got to Denver he was positively chummy.

Indeed, during one week in Denver, he dined with the reporters twice, held one hour-long press conference, and invited them to sit in on his question and answer sessions with various Republican convention delegates. Even at the convention in Chicago, reporters were in and out of his quarters at the Blackstone Hotel all the time.

Then the policy changed. When he returned to Denver after winning the nomination he seldom saw the reporters, and after he started campaigning in earnest he cut himself away almost entirely. Three or four times he came out into the press car on the campaign train,

once during the controversy over Senator Joseph R. McCarthy in Wisconsin and twice during the argument over Senator Richard M. Nixon's expense fund, but on each of these occasions he refused to be quoted directly or indirectly.

Thereafter, the only question and answer periods he held in public were with political supporters or with selected citizens whose questions were screened by Republican public relations experts in advance. Similarly, when he went to Korea, the rule was that only representatives of the three press associations could go along, and when he addressed the press there, it was on the explicit understanding that no questions were to be asked.

Finally, when he met with his Cabinet at the Commodore Hotel this week, he complained about a number of leaks in the press about his appointments and told his Cabinet officers they should be cautious in their private dealings with reporters. He also defended the idea that they should say nothing to a reporter, even in private, unless they wanted and expected what was said to be published.

Indeed, this is the principle that has been proposed to the General himself by his own official family: If you don't want to see it in print, don't mention it to a newspaperman, even in private.

Reasons for Shift

Several factors were involved in this sharp change of press policy. The first was that before the convention he regarded reporters' questions as an opportunity, and after he won the nomination he regarded them as a danger. Before the convention he was seeking public support, and one of the major complaints against his candidacy was that the delegates and the public did not know where he stood on a number of major public issues.

Consequently, he answered the questions. But after the nomination, he was engaged in a political battle, and he changed his tactics to conform to the objective of the battle, which was victory.

In June, he had disarmed many questioners by saying frankly that he didn't know the answer to this and that, but after he was nominated, his advisers told him that he was expected to know all the answers, and that he should concentrate on saying what he wanted to say rather than responding to what the reporters were asking. Incidentally, what was widely overlooked was that, during the campaign, his opponent, Adlai E. Stevenson, followed the same course.

One or two other things have contributed to this cautious policy toward the press. When the General went to Augusta, Ga., after his November victory, he decided

that, since President Truman still had the responsibility of governing, it was prudent, courteous and proper to say as little as possible between the election and the inauguration.

Also, General Eisenhower knew that his natural tendency was to be frank in private conversation, and that he had not yet mastered the details of many subjects. Therefore, he agreed with his counselors that a combination of frankness and limited knowledge was not exactly a formula for success.

Finally, the General was surprised and distressed by the contrast between press relations in the Army and press relations in a political campaign. He was able to control things when he was in the Army—he was protected there and always had the argument of security—but in the campaign he was an open target for a press corps which was, to put it mildly, somewhat less restrained than the reporters in Paris.

Since then General Eisenhower has been looking in on the television press shows, and these have apparently convinced him that he is up against, not a group of responsible men seeking information, but a multitude of well-informed and somewhat vindictive prosecuting attorneys.

Just as he has changed his tactics after the convention, however, and just as the reporters' tactics were different in the campaign from those at the North Atlantic Treaty headquarters in Paris, so it is likely that the General will change his tactics once more when he gets here.

Improvement Possible

The White House press conference is not like either a big political campaign press conference or a television "press conference." It is quite different. It is more orderly. It is infinitely more courteous and responsible, and while the reporters like it as it is, this does not mean that it cannot be changed for the better.

General Eisenhower has told Hugh Baillie of The United Press that the press conference will be continued, and that he is considering bringing Cabinet officers into it and asking that questions be written out by reporters in advance. If done with the objective of increasing the flow of information (an objective the Republicans have been demanding loudly for twenty years), both of these changes could be an improvement.

If, however, the General were to deny to reporters the right to question or follow up his written answers to written questions; if he were to try to put an end to the private talk between the responsible official and the respon-

sible reporter by imposing the rule that his officials should say nothing that could not be printed; or if he should decide—as he has indicated he might—that press conferences should be held only when he has something to announce, then something basic would have happened to the relations between the Government and the people.

Direct Tie to People

For while a lot of nonsense has been talked around the Press Club here about the rights and conveniences of reporters, the fact is that this is a question that goes well beyond the world of newspapering. The modern White House press conference is the only direct and regular contact between the people and their President, and it was devised not only as a means to enable him to make announcements—he can do that without press conferences—but also as a means by which reporters can bring questions direct from the people to the President.

The private talk between the responsible official and the responsible reporter is another indispensable device without which there would be even less understanding and faith between the Government and the people than there is today. Even more than most people, reporters distrust what they do not know and understand, and if the assumption is to be that they can be told nothing that cannot be printed, then "the eight millionaires and the plumber" of the President's Cabinet are in for some fun.

At the same time, the corollary—and maybe even the essential preliminary—of greater confidence between General Eisenhower and the press is more responsibility on the reporters' side. Rightly or not, his counselors in this field believe that there has been a decline in the good faith and dependability of reporters.

They feel that reporters are not protecting off-the-record confidences or sources of news as they used to do; specifically, they complain that reporters are now passing on confidences in private memoranda to their organizations, which in turn are casual with these confidences and even pass them across press association wires to hundreds of editors.

Thus the controversy over General Eisenhower and the press, even if it has started earlier than usual, may be useful, for it will give both sides an opportunity to think about and redefine their rights and obligations very early in the new Administration.

January 18, 1953

In The Nation

'Button Your Lips or Else' Is the Order

By ARTHUR KROCK

WASHINGTON, Jan. 26—Ever since 8:02 o'clock last Wednesday morning, when President Eisenhower began his first full day in office, those visitors who have not arrived and left by the side door, and hence eluded the White House reporters entirely, have been notably uncommunicative to the representatives of the press. It is customary for responsible persons who talk privately in the inner sanctum to refer questioning reporters in the White House lobby to the President for the answers. But some of these visitors to the new Chief Executive gave the impression of looking apprehensively over their shoulders when they said even that.

The explanation of their timidity seems to be that President Eisenhower has been greatly annoyed by publications of some of his decisions before he announced them formally and has taken steps toward the difficult goal of achieving a "no leak" Administration. The first of these steps, according to a member of Congress today, was the President's notice to whom it may concern that anyone (within the purview of his authority or range of his confidence) who gives information about matters reserved for White House release—so far virtually everything—may consider this tantamount to submitting his resignation, or being excluded from further confidential relationship, as the case may be.

The fact that this report of the President's attitude is in itself a leak suggests how difficult of attainment the goal will be. For some members of Congress will continue to keep newspaper reporters posted when this suits their purposes; others will do so out of personal amiability or a belief that such information provides one of the checks and balances on official action that is basic in the philosophy of the Constitution; and the reporters themselves will intensify their already intense effort to break through a curtain of secrecy between the people and the progressive stages of newsmaking.

Hard To Run Down

Presidents have tried and failed before to prevent these penetrations of the curtain, though the warning represented as coming from General Eisenhower suggests a more drastic enforcement method. And on numerous occasions when reporters have published accounts of important matters that an Administration wanted to announce later in its own words Presidents and their top subordinates have given orders to trace the source of the leaks. But seldom have the Executive bloodhounds tracked down the real offender. And the actual dismissal by a President of any important official as the source of leaking is an occurrence that is extremely rare.

The disclosures that appear to have annoyed the President have largely been of appointments decided on, including some that have run into snags on Capitol Hill. They could not conceivably have affected national security, even in the catch-all definition that is standard among the military. Perhaps General Eisenhower's long training in a service where an officer's sense of responsibility is heavily judged by the tightness of his lips has led him to rate this quality higher than it is or needs to be in the process of democratic, civilian government. Perhaps the fact that his Administration is new and he wants to set the opening scenes himself—a wish easy to comprehend with sympathy—has helped to produce the attitude described to this correspondent by a member of Congress today. But if it is maintained the President has a long prospect of similar annoyance, and, much as individuals in the press may not wish to vex him, their common duty is to procure and publish at all stages the accurate and legitimate news of government.

The President as Editor

If every Executive plan and decision could be excluded from public knowledge until a President was ready to announce it, the principle of the free press would disappear in the United States and the newspapers would become mere official gazettes. That is the arrangement in autocracies, logically attended by the regulation that the press not only publish the announcement as officially issued but also accept it fully at its face value. President Eisenhower, of course, has no thought of trying to move the press in any degree toward such a consummation. But his early visitors, even including today's group of Congressional leaders, reflect an unusual determination on his part to prevent publication of anything he may deem premature. And that, if true, would mean in effect that the President would at all times establish himself over the press as the judge of what among his activities is news and when its publication is legitimate and responsible.

In matters affecting national security, and in the course of negotiations calculated—if revealed—to give aid and comfort to the enemy, a President can act as a voluntary and effective censor with whom the overwhelming proportion of the American press fully cooperates. If he is not entirely successful the fault, as has repeatedly been proved, is with his subordinates. Often in recent years Presidents have complained about publications that were authorized by their own appointees, with Presidential directives to issue such information. If General Eisenhower can prevent this in such instances, if that is the extent of the effort attributed to him, a responsible press and the public it serves will approve and applaud it.

But until a President can do all his planning and deciding by himself certain kinds of leaks will continue. They are usually harmless; and the intolerable alternative is total secrecy.

January 27, 1953

WHITE HOUSE LAUDS PRESS

Aide Says That President Feels He Gets Fair Treatment

WASHINGTON, Oct. 21 (UP)—President Eisenhower feels that he is receiving "very fine, fair, accurate and impartial treatment" by the nation's press, radio and television.

James C. Hagerty, White House press secretary, said the President regarded the criticism of his Administration by columnists and commentators as "part of the business" of being President.

President Eisenhower considers his news conferences with reporters as a "50-50 proposition," Mr. Hagerty said. He declared the news conferences gave the President a cross-section of the questions in the minds of the American people and let him give out what he regarded as important news of his Administration.

October 22, 1953

Truman Admits He Enjoys Starring on TV; Likes to Watch It, Too, He Tells Executives

Harry S. Truman admitted yesterday that he was a two-way television fan. He likes to watch it and he likes to appear on it.

The former President spoke informally at a luncheon of the Radio and Television Executives Society in the Roosevelt Hotel. Displaying the attributes of any good performer who wants to please everybody, he divided his remarks between humor and inspiration, steering clear of political controversy.

"I enjoy viewing television," said Mr. Truman, smiling at his audience of 500 broadcasting representatives. "And I get some enjoyment from being on it once in a while."

Associated Press

THREE SPEAKERS: Former President Harry S. Truman, who addressed the Radio and Television Executives Society yesterday, talks to his daughter, Margaret, while George Shupert, president of the society, was delivering a speech.

Seated on the dais to Mr. Truman's left was his daughter, Margaret, an actress and singer.

"You can always be sure that you have two people in Independence, Mo., watching television when she is on," he commented.

Mr. Truman said that "television in the field of education can be the greatest asset this country or the world has ever had, if it is properly used." He called upon the broadcasters to use the medium with a concept of fairness to all.

In touching upon the job of a President of the United States, Mr. Truman spoke sympathetically of any one who filled the office. He said:

"No office ever had the powers or responsibilities of the Presidency, and you'll never hear me criticizing it. I may differ with policy, but I won't attack the office. No man can fill it in an ideal manner."

The former President answered several written questions sent to the dais. Some of them, with his answers, were:

Should meetings of Congress be televised?—"I wonder how many of you ever sat in the gallery and watched Congress at work." The audience laughed, and he added: "You can answer that question yourself."

Should White House press conferences be televised?—"That is up to the President of the United States."

What is your opinion of present economic trends?—"I am not an economist. I'm a public relations man—a politician, in other words, and I can't give you an answer on that."

Mr. Truman received a microphone from H. V. Kaltenborn that the commentator had used the night in 1948 when he erroneously speculated with confidence that "Thomas E. Dewey had been elected President of the United States."

Mr. Truman, mimicking Mr. Kaltenborn, said he would treasure it as long as he lived.

PRESIDENT PREPARES FOR PRESS WITH CARE

WASHINGTON, Feb. 14 (UP)—James C. Hagerty, White House Press Secretary, said today that President Eisenhower's news advisers spent two days preparing the President for each of his news conferences.

By the time the President steps up to meet the press, he has been briefed on every major question the reporters are likely to throw at him, Mr. Hagerty said.

In a radio interview, he gave this description of preparations for a Presidential news conference:

The day before the press conference, "I get up a list of questions that I think newspaper men are going to ask."

"We then have a staff meeting in the morning before the President has his press conference where we go over these proposed questions . . . and often we get additional material supporting statistics from departments as a result of our staff conference.

"I then go in a half an hour or forty minutes before a press conference and go over these questions with the President just to bring him up to date and refresh in his mind the decisions that have been made on these questions—the actual status of any one problem or any one major field, and by the time we leave we have gone over the main major questions."

Nixon Explains Talk

Denies Remarks on Indo-China Were 'Trial Balloon' for Intervention Policy

By JAMES RESTON
Special to The New York Times.

WASHINGTON, April 19—Vice President Richard M. Nixon is disturbed about some of the reaction to his recent controversial speech on the possibility of United States intervention in the Indo-China war. He makes these points:

¶He did not go to last Friday's meeting of the American Society of Newspaper Editors to launch a "trial balloon" for an interventionist policy.

¶He did not clear his notes in advance with anybody and specifically told his audience that only two men were authorized to define official United States foreign policy—President Eisenhower and the Secretary of State, John Foster Dulles.

¶He talked in the belief that his remarks would not be attributed to anybody. His mistake, as he now sees it, was in allowing the reporters to talk him into attributing the speech to a "high Administration official."

¶He thinks the editors and publishers will greatly reduce the flow of public information if they insist that all "talks" or speeches by Government officials to newspaper people be attributed.

Background of Meeting

Since the newspaper editors were the hosts Friday and many of them became highly critical of the guest of honor later, it is only fair that the background of the meeting be put on the record.

In the first place, the editors had not had one of their most successful conferences. Indeed, partly because most of the speakers who appeared before them took no chances on being quoted, the week was unexciting and sometimes not even very informative.

On Thursday, for example, the editors had gone to the Pentagon for a briefing and been treated to something that, more often than not, resembled a high school lecture on the geography and history of Asia.

Accordingly, when the Vice President went to the dais Friday noon, he was urged to talk frankly and to respond to questions from the floor. This he agreed to do.

When he was introduced, nobody defined the rules under which he was talking. However, he himself said he was going to talk not only about policies but also about personalities. He added that the editors could of course "plagiarize" him. This was his way of saying that his remarks were for the editors' information, to be used by them on their own authority if they wished but not to be pinned on anybody in the Administration.

Much of what the Vice President said had been said to many reporters in smaller private meetings in Washington before. Indeed, he had given the whole travelogue of his 1953 Asian trip to the Inland Press Association in Chicago several weeks before without having any leaks develop.

It was in the question period at the editors' meeting here that he expressed his private opinion about the loyalty of Dr. J. Robert Oppenheimer, whose case is now before the Atomic Energy Commission's Security Board, and said that while he did not anticipate that the French would quit in Indo-China, he thought the United States would have to replace them if necessary to prevent a Communist conquest of Southeast Asia.

These were the things that caught the reporters' eyes and when they urged him after the meeting to allow them to be attributed to a "high Administration source," he agreed.

The Vice President regrets that this has led to the "trial balloon" charge. He feels that this suggests he was trying to take advantage of his invitation to "put over" a policy the Administration was not prepared to announce.

His view is that the Administration has been trying to make clear since March 29 that a Communist victory in Southeast Asia would be a threat to the security of the United States and thus would justify intervention by United States ground troops, if necessary, to block another major Communist conquest.

All the Vice President intended to do Friday was to put this idea into words that everybody could understand. And the negative reaction to the possibility of using United States troops has convinced him all the more that public opinion is not yet aware of the nature of the threat to United States interests in that part of the world.

Finally, there is wide support among the newspaper reporters here for the Vice President's view that it would be wrong to insist that Government officials avoid such controversies by speaking only for attribution.

Few observers here think the Vice President was right in believing that he could keep such serious remarks quiet when he talked to the editors. Nor do they believe it was proper for him to comment on the Oppenheimer case while it was pending.

There is general agreement, however, that the Vice President was not alone to blame in this case; that the solution is for both hosts and guest to agree before any such speech on how it is to be handled by the press rather than adopting any extreme rule that all remarks by public officials must be subject to direct quotation.

The Problem of Orphan News Items

By ARTHUR KROCK

The circumstance that editors from all over the country were in Washington when the most recent parentless news item was produced, and in their very presence, has again concentrated the attention of the press on the problem presented by these orphans of public information. If they are to be totally banished from the channels of communication because their creators will not acknowledge them, a good deal of information the people have a right to know will remain concealed for the periods in which it could shape political action. But if the press opens its columns to give them indiscriminate shelter, many authors of their being who should take public responsibility for the orphans will escape it.

For example, there are the briefing officers at international conferences who serve the national interest by giving the press summaries of proceedings which necessarily are conducted behind closed doors, on the sound and reasonable condition that the briefing will not be attributed. Much important news is thus legitimately conveyed from other quarters also. But there is the politician who under the same condition tries to sell the press as an imminent fact what is as yet a mere gleam in his eye, hoping to discover how the public would receive it if it became a fact.

The Solution

The only apparent solution of the problem is for a reporter and his newspaper to handle it on an ad hoc basis—deciding whether or not to shelter an orphan news item each time it knocks at their doors. The probability is that the current revival of the issue, evoked by a celebrated recent incident in Washington, will produce no better method.

Ever since Hitler invaded Poland in 1939 small groups of Washington correspondents have met privately with important officials for the excellent purpose of getting background information to put the foreground news in its proper perspective. P, this means the reading and radio public has been getting more, and frequently more critical, news in better balance than before these meetings became an institution. Since non-attribution to the sources is inherent in such procedure, and this pledge cannot be assured of redemption in loosely screened mass press conferences, these groups have been and will remain small and self-selected.

How They Work

They are operated under clear rules which have been scrupulously followed. Those reporters present can publish as their own any information given them that is not specifically excluded from publication by the source, for instance: "The Administration will not compromise on the proposal in Congress to raise income tax exemptions in the lower brackets. All signs are that the President will fight this proposal to a finish."

And, in the opinion of this correspondent, no fact or situation has been misrepresented by any of the parents of the news orphans emerging from these meetings.

Some Abuses

But, on the other hand, ever since the phrase "off the record" came into vogue some officials have taken advantage of their right to lay down their press conference rules. They have suppressed what was plainly information due the public, and sometimes they have compounded the abuse by announcing the ban after instead of before they gave the information. The monotonous chant of "off the record," with its counterpoint of "no comment," became so absurd during the second World War that Gardner Cowles one night, addressing as Deputy Director of the Office of War Information a radio audience of national proportions, put his tongue in his cheek and said: "Now, off the record——." Another official, after solemnly announcing that his answer to a question must be off the record, said: "Off the record, no comment."

Non-Attribution

For various reasons, easily comprehensible, the rule of non-attribution is the favorite of certain news sources. Some propose it to escape the responsibility for fathering a smear; others to prevent their colleagues from finding and closing a valuable channel of information to a reporter who they feel has earned access to it by special diligence. Still others make the stipulation because they think legitimate news is being wrongfully suppressed and yet are not willing to risk reprisals for "not playing the game."

In these two latter instances the information is solid—it concerns something which has happened or is designed to happen. But when non-attribution is exacted for the expression of a view on high policy by an official whose very views are news, the rule proves unworkable. That was demonstrated by the incident in Washington last week of which the Vice President was the center. Manifestly, his opinion of what, in hypothetical circumstances, the United States would be obliged to do in Indo-China to redeem the President's pledge of "no retreat" from communism in Southeast Asia had to be hung on someone or be adopted by his hearers as their own editorial position. And the same was true of his expressed belief in the loyalty of J. Robert Oppenheimer.

They were news because of the importance of their source. And in such circumstances news just will get published.

OPPOSITE VIEWPOINT

A Political Candidate Talks of TV Artifice

SALEM, ORE.

RICHARD L. NEUBERGER, Democratic candidate for United States Senator from Oregon, recently took a different tack from most politicians regarding his appearances on television. He spoke out against use of any artificial devices to make him a theoretically more winning figure on the home screen.

"When I came to the studio tonight, a member of the staff wished to 'make me up' for my appearance on television," Mr. Neuberger said. "Paint was to be used to conceal the bald spot on my head. Any faint trace of beard on my chin and cheeks was to be camouflaged.

"Furthermore, it was suggested that I might desire to use a Teleprompter. This is a device—a clever device, I should add — which could deceive you into believing I was speaking extemporaneously, without benefit of manuscript or notes. The Teleprompter reveals the words to the speaker but out of range of vision of the audience. The speaker appears to be talking on his own, off the top of his head.

"I refused the make-up which the studio wanted to apply to my face and head. I am not using a Teleprompter. I should like to tell you why.

Real

"A campaign to decide who shall govern America is not a stage play or a movie. It is something real—or, at least, it should be real. It is all right to shoot blank cartridges in those Wild-West movie shows. It is fine to have actors using built-up shoes, stand-ins, wigs, false beards, facial make-up and prompters who sit in the wings.

"I doubt if these techniques should be applied to campaigns for high elective office. They are essentially the techniques of artifice, deception and the world of make-believe. This is fine for the escape world of the stage and the movies. We want to think, for a few fleeting hours, that some Hollywood playboy is actually a Canadian Mountie.

"But do we want fantasies to extend to men who seek to be Presidents and Senators and Governors?

"If a candidate will deliberately and calculatingly fool you as to whether or not he is reading from a manuscript or as to the actual condition of his complexion or beard, is there a chance that he might also fool you as to whether or not he intends to support the United Nations, or to conserve our timber and water-power resources, or to vote for a certain kind of policy regarding taxation?

"Truth, to me, is indivisible. If I use an instrument which will deceive you into thinking mistakenly that I can speak extemporaneously on complex and intricate subjects, what assurance do you have that what I am saying about those subjects is in itself true, to the best of my ability to make it true?

"During this campaign for the Senate, when I appear on television, I shall not use either facial make-up or a Teleprompter. If I have a bald spot or a trace of beard, you will know it. If I am reading from a manuscript, this fact will not be disguised or covered up. Although these things are, perhaps, of only passing merit, they are my assurance to you that I shall try to make an honest campaign."

The Eisenhower Riddle

A Study of How He Violates All Rules in Political Book and Gets Away With It

By JAMES RESTON
Special to The New York Times.

WASHINGTON, April 27— Amateur psychiatrists interested in Dwight D. Eisenhower as a person and amateur politicians interested in him as a political phenomenon would do well to study the President's performance at today's press conference.

For he returned to the TV arena after three weeks' absence this morning and broke almost every rule in the political book. Candor, which most politicians shun like the plague, was the rule of the day. And consistency, the politicians' favorite bugaboo, was openly defied.

He not only reversed the State Department's policy on negotiating with the Communists but also reversed himself. He was optimistic in a hive of professional pessimists. He differed with his old friend, Secretary of Defense Charles E. Wilson, and he criticized the Senate Republican Policy Committee.

All this, of course, was done indirectly and with the blandest air of innocence. Also, he split with the Republican right wing on several topics. And quite inadvertently he disclosed himself as a man counting the months— and knowing precisely how many there were—until the day he was liberated from office.

Moreover, if he was conscious that he was doing these things, he showed not the slightest trace of it. By the time the inevitable reaction came later in the day, he was off at Burning Tree, playing golf.

Who but President Eisenhower for example, could do these things and get away with them?:

¶Announce that he was carrying on a private correspondence with Marshal Georgi K. Zhukov, the Soviet Defense Minister, on improving United States-Russian relations and refuse to disclose anything more about it.

¶Approve a State Department statement of last Saturday saying the United States would "insist" on Nationalist China's being in on "any" conversations about the Formosa area, and announce that he was now for talking to the Chinese Communists about a cease-fire in the Formosa Strait without the participation of the Chinese Nationalists.

¶Contend at the opening of the press conference that this was no "reversal" of the Administration's position and later concede that maybe there was "an error of terminology."

¶Proclaim that the United States would not confer alone with the Communists "about the affairs of the Chinese Nationalists," but assert that "it is perfectly legitimate for us to talk to the Chicoms [Chinese Communists] about stopping firing."

¶Explain this by saying that the Communists were the only ones doing any firing; that a cease-fire therefore concerned only the Communists, and that, since the Nationalists were not attacking the China mainland, "a cease-fire on their side would be purely academic."

¶Criticize the Senate Republican Policy Committee's release of military information as a "blunder," differing in the process with his own Secretary of Defense, who said yesterday that no secret information had actually been released by the committee.

¶Differ from the right wing of the Republican party on (a) negotiating a cease-fire without the Nationalists, (b) lowering the tariffs in the reciprocal trade agreements legislation, (c) opposing the Bricker Amendment to the Constitution, and (d) amending the nation's refugee legislation.

All this the President did in the space of thirty-five minutes this morning. While there was an immediate cry of anguish from the Republican leader of the Senate, William F. Knowland, the reaction elsewhere was comparatively mild, and even Mr. Knowland did not mention the President in his criticism.

On the left, and among moderates of both parties, there was both pleasure and wonderment. How does he do it? they asked. What would have happened if Adlai Stevenson or any Democratic President had taken similar positions?

The answer to the first question seems to be that he does it merely by doing what comes naturally. He was as casual about supporting conversations with the Communists without the Nationalists today as he was last Saturday when he "insisted" that the Nationalists be in on "any" conversations concerning the Formosa area.

Both he and his Secretary of State were out of the capital when the first statement was made—a fact which in itself would have been the subject of criticism in any other circumstances. But this did not trouble the President.

He did what seemed right to him on Saturday, and though he reversed his field, he did what he thought was right today. And he got away with it because those who were most inclined to criticize him were precisely those who were most eager to see him switch.

As time goes on, he acts more and more in the role of President of all the people, a figure above party. He is strengthening his White House staff and delegating more and more responsibility, and in one revealing instant this morning he disclosed how keenly he is aware of the time when his term of office ends.

Talking about his hopes for retirement ten years ago on V-E Day, he said: "I saw a nice farm over the other side of the ocean, and it still is a long ways away. * * *"

The reporters, who are constantly fencing with him about whether he will run again, laughed heartily, believing that he had inadvertently indicated that he was reconciled to another term.

The President was visibly surprised, but he caught the point instantly, and blurted out that, at his age, "twenty-one months is still a long time."

The fact that he knew, during that surprising interruption in a serious discussion on another subject, that he still had twenty-one months to go, fascinated the reporters.

"He's thinking of his own liberation," one of them said leaving the conference. "He's like a guy in jail, tearing off the leaves of the calendar and counting the months."

TV TRAINING TO AID CANDIDATES IN '56

Station Will Offer Classes in Make-Up and Clothing for Color Appearances

By RICHARD F. SHEPARD

Color television school credits will be a prerequisite for the electoral college session next year.

Candidates for office will be able to buy air time on color TV and will be briefed on the best way to appear, according to William A. Berns, director of news and special events for WRCA and WRCA-TV.

Mr. Berns said the station would begin early next year to provide special classes for aspirants on how to use make-up and clothing for the medium.

MR. TRUMAN AND THE PRESS

Former President Truman gives full vent to his bitterness against the American press in the installment of his memoirs that we publish today. The overwhelming majority of American newspapers —Mr. Truman says "90 per cent of the press and radio"—opposed him during his successful campaign of 1948; and Mr. Truman has never forgiven them.

It is one thing for Mr. Truman to be angry at American journalism and journalists—after all, he was angry at many groups and individuals during his Presidential career; it is quite another for him to suggest that most American newspapers opposed him because they were owned, bought or bribed by sinister "private interests" with no concern for the common weal. He engages in the typical demagogy of denouncing publishers and writers for having "sold out to the special interests," without of course giving a single instance to substantiate this most serious accusation.

Mr. Truman's accusations fall into three general categories: (1) that most newspapers were against him for selfish or venal reasons; (2) that it was "commonplace practice" to distort the news; (3) that he fell out of favor in early 1948 not because of anything he did, but because of what the press did.

It is true that most newspapers were against him, but they had every right to make their own choice in a country with a free press. It is true that news and headlines were on occasion inexcusably distorted by some newspapers; but the practice was not "commonplace," and it is universally condemned by responsible newspaper men. It is true that Mr. Truman fell out of favor in 1948, but it is just as unrealistic for him to attribute his decline to misrepresentation by the press as it would be if he had attributed his subsequent electoral success to a build-up by the press.

Taken as a whole, the American press provides a mirror to what is going on in the country, and let those who do not like what they see in that mirror look first to the state of the nation.

President and the Press

A Study of the Differences in Reporting and Comment on His Two Illnesses

By JAMES RESTON
Special to The New York Times.

WASHINGTON, June 24 — There has been a marked change in the reporting and comment on President Eisenhower's illness during the last few weeks.

The general tendency still is to play up the Eisenhower side of the story, but the other side has been given far more play during the second illness than the first.

Part of the reason for this is that some doctors who disagreed with the optimistic official medical estimates of the President's future have spoken up since his abdominal operation.

It is fair to say that more doctors had more doubts about Dr. Paul Dudley White's comments on the President's heart attack than about Dr. Leonard Heaton's remarks about ileitis, but they made their remarks in private last fall. This summer at least a few of them have spoken up publicly about the second illness and this, of course, has been published.

Moreover, the reporters have been more willing to dig into the medical literature about the possible dangers of the recurrence of ileitis than they ever were about the life expectancy of heart patients. And editors, publishers and commentators have been much more outspoken this time against James C. Hagerty's efforts to create the impression that the President was back running the Government.

Publisher Changes View

For example, John S. Knight of the Knight papers (The Chicago Daily News, The Akron Beacon Journal, The Detroit Free Press, the Miami (Fla.) Herald), who was a strong supporter of the Eisenhower-Nixon ticket in 1952, has written an extremely sharp editorial condemning the official "Ike's-as-good-as-ever" thesis.

Walter Lippmann, the columnist, has emphasized the main point in the whole controversy— namely, that the election of 1956 is not merely a judgment on whether the President has done a good job in his first term, but on the selection of a President who can run the Government full-time for four and half more years after having sustained two major illnesses at the age of 65.

The Alsop brothers, who played the whole thing pianissimo in the first illness, have reported this time on the insurance statistics on patients who have had a heart attack and ileitis at the President's age.

And Doris Fleeson has led the way this time in reporting the differences between the official doctors' remarks on ileitis and the medical literature on the subject.

All this means is that some balance has been restored to the flow of information on an important political subject. It does not mean that the new balance will affect the President's decision. It is too late for that.

Were Candid in Private

Last fall and early winter, when the President was carefully considering his political future, the opinions of writers, editors and doctors might have influenced him if those opinions had been expressed as candidly in public as they were in private.

This did not happen, however. Most of the published opinions came from those who sincerely felt the President should seek a second term regardless of his heart attack, and these, of course, were shown to the President by aides who naturally agreed with them and used them in their arguments for a second term.

The other side of it was seldom written, and when it was, you may be sure nobody on the White House staff rushed it to the President.

That was the decisive period. It is too late now. The machinery of the election is in full swing. Movies of the President's Administration are being made every day and circulated to Re-

publican Senators and Representatives for use in their state and district campaigns. All the G.O.P. plans are being made on the assumption that the President and Vice President Richard M. Nixon will be the nominees.

The President knows all about this, so any statement reiterating his second-term candidacy is merely a formality. Just after the President announced his second-term plans last Feb. 29, Merriman Smith, the well-informed White House correspondent for The United Press, reported that General Eisenhower had said to an aide in the White House that he had made up his mind to run because he was told that there wasn't time to build up anybody who could win.

This was killed on the U. P. wire, but the President was later asked about it and he replied that if he said it, he must have been talking facetiously.

Nevertheless, that is about what the situation is today. It has been demonstrated that neither the President's own personal feelings about his health nor his doctors' estimates were able to foresee either of his illnesses. But he and his party have decided to take the gamble, and in fairness to them, it must be said that, in doing so, they seem to be responding to the wishes of the people.

Nobody here has any right to object to the President's making a second run provided all the facts are known, and provided everybody expresses his honest opinion on the matter.

There is room in all this for honest differences of opinion. The trouble was that the honest doubts about the wisdom of a second term were not expressed, and judgments were thus being formed on the basis of one-sided expressions of fact and opinion.

In short, the normal skeptical tradition under which the press consciously tries to decontaminate political announcements, from whatever source, or fill in the missing background was for a time abandoned, but fortunately it is now gradually being restored.

SHEPILOV HOPEFUL OF CLOSE U. S. TIE

By JACK RAYMOND
Special to The New York Times.

MOSCOW, July 5—Dmitri T. Shepilov said today that there was "a very broad basis" for not only "normalization" but also 'rapprochement" with the United States.

The new Foreign Minister, in an informal news conference, demanded a toning down of the United States press and radio as an essential condition.

But the "most important and urgent step to be taken," he declared, is for increased exchanges and contacts between the United States and the Soviet Union.

He said that he himself would seek to meet Secretary of State Dulles in the fall. Mr. Shepilov said that he would go to the United Nations General Assembly meeting in November.

Mr. Shepilov, former editor of Pravda, chief Soviet Communist party organ, who succeeded Vyacheslav M. Molotov as Foreign Minister last month, has just returned from an extended tour of the Middle East and Greece.

Shepilov's Major Points

He responded readily and seriously to questions put to him by correspondents at a diplomatic reception at which he was host to Dag Hammerskjold, Secretary General of the United Nations.

In the course of his responses, the Foreign Minister:

¶Declared the United Nations could not count on "'real respect and recognition" as long as Communist China was not a member.

¶Reaffirmed Soviet support for United Nations action in the Middle East strife.

¶Failed to respond to a question from what level the Soviet Union was reducing its forces by 1,200,000 troops, while urging that others take similar steps.

¶Expressed belief there had been "indications and steps" showing that the Soviet Union and the United States could find a path to improved relations.

He cited last year's visits by agricultural delegations and experts, war veterans and journalists of the two countries. He also noted this year's visits of artistic performers and military men, such as Gen. Nathan F. Twining, United States Air Force Chief of Staff.

"The most important and urgent task is to develop contacts all along the line, political, social, scientific, technical and cultural," declared Mr. Shepilov.

"I am convinced that such wide contacts will lead to overcoming many misunderstandings."

Reiterating the "importance" and "urgency" of the steps to be taken, Mr. Shepilov went on: "As for what one callls "normalization," or what I would call "rapprochement,' between the United States and the U. S. S. R., there is a very broad basis."

"We should work together to make it a reality," he continued. "In this way we can pass from words to deeds."

Criticizes U. S. Press

The former Pravda editor then turned to the subject of the United States press.

"An essential condition [for improved relations] is to muzzle the propagators of the cold war," he declared.

"I do not think you can accuse our press for a considerable period of time of unfounded attacks on the United States, whereas the United States press and radio is still a Niagara of all sorts of lies and slanders."

"These irresponsible elements, which poison the atmosphere, should be muzzled," Mr. Shepilov said. "True, they are fewer and fewer. Let us hope they will be still fewer."

Mr. Shepilov then joined his guest, Mr. Hammerskjold, before correspondents had a chance to pursue the subject with questions on the recent sharpening of the tone of the Soviet press toward the United States.

This is particularly true in the matter of Soviet accusations that United States agents are responsible for the rioting in Poznan, Poland. Pravda referred to "bloody provocations, such as the sally by American agents in Poznan."

Izvestia, Government newspaper, said: "Certain United States circles, compelled to take account of the general desire for the development of international contacts, are striving to use the very fact of the strengthening of international contacts for purposes of expanding espionage and subversive activity."

SHEPILOV UPHOLDS FREEDOM OF PRESS

Denies That He Advocated 'Muzzle' on Foreign Papers —Criticizes The Times

By JACK RAYMOND
Special to The New York Times.

MOSCOW, July 14—Dmitri T. Shepilov said today that he was ardently in favor of freedom of the press. The new Soviet Foreign Minister, who was editor of Pravda, said everyone had a right to his opinion after the publishing of the facts.

He raised strong objection to statements, published abroad, that he sought "muzzling" of the foreign press as the price of good relations with the Soviet Union.

Mr. Shepilov recalled a statement he made last week in a chat with foreign correspondents here during a reception for Dag Hammarskjold, United Nations Secretary General.

"I was badly impressed by the conversation," he complained to correspondents today at a French Bastille Day reception.

Mr. Shepilov recalled that he had denounced the "propagators of cold war" and had said that they were "an obstacle to rapprochement between the United States and the Soviet Union." However, he denied having suggested that the entire press was composed of such elements. He stressed that he had emphasized that they were comparatively few.

Accusation by Shepilov

Yet, Mr. Shepilov continued, certain newspapers had made it appear as if he wanted to "muzzle" the entire press by identifying the entire press with "propagators of the cold war."

Mr. Shepilov singled out The New York Times, accusing it of having asserted that he wanted to "muzzle" the entire press.

The Foreign Minister called a Times correspondent into the circle of newspaper men around him to demand whether, during last week's conversation, he had proposed such a condition for good relations. Mr. Shepilov, conceding he had not read the dispatch to The Times about the conversation, said he referred to an editorial on the subject.

[An editorial in The Times on July 8 said Mr. Shepilov had "rediscovered an old policy" that it was "easier to control subject populations if one begins by controlling the press." The editorial said Mr. Shepilov had called the American press and radio "these irresponsible elements that poison the atmosphere," and had said they should be "muzzled."]

The Soviet official said he hoped to establish friendly relations with newspaper men in Moscow. He added that he had been a newspaper man himself most of his life. He said he was a "devoted follower" of freedom of the press.

Mr. Shepilov broke off today's conversation as it warmed up.

There were several other news items at the reception whic was attended also by Nikita S. Khrushchev, Communist party chief, and Premier Nikolai A. Bulganin.

Mr. Khrushchev stressed Moscow's inability to purchase whaling ships from The Netherlands. This came up when a Dutch reporter raised the question of extended trade between the two countries. The Soviet leader referred to Western restrictions on the sale of strategic items to the Soviet bloc.

Mr. Khrushchev said he expected a big development program in the region of Birobidzhan because the soil was good there. He did not go into detail on this project, which has been mentioned before.

COVER-UP ON G.O.P. CHARGED TO PRESS

McNamara Says Newspapers and Hagerty Twist Facts on President's Health

WASHINGTON, July 18 (AP)—A charge that facts about President Eisenhower's health were being suppressed behind a "Hagerty curtain" stirred a bitter argument in the Senate tonight.

The charge was made by Senator Pat McNamara, Democrat of Michigan, who declared much of the press was at fault. He said it had failed to tell the people that President Eisenhower was under sedatives at a time when he was represented as making important decisions.

Senator William F. Knowland of California, Republican leader, said he was "greatly shocked" by McNamara's accusations. He interpreted them as an attack on the integrity of the President.

He said the Michigan Senator had sought to create the impression that the President "had deliberately set out to mislead" the American people about his capacity to serve another term.

Senator Knowland denied that United States newspapers had entered a conspiracy to suppress facts.

Mr. McNamara, in his speech to the Senate, attacked what he called "apparent manipulation of facts" in newspapers.

He said a "Hagerty curtain" had been erected to keep the public "from the truth in one of the most masterful suppressions of the facts ever put across by the advertising techniques of Madison Avenue." He referred to James C. Hagerty, the President's press secretary.

In criticizing the press, Mr. McNamara made several exceptions.

He said John S. Knight, publisher of five newspapers, "has had the courage to publish the truth." Doris Fleeson, a columnist, he said, has tried "to skim the whipped cream off the propaganda." And he said James Reston, Washington correspondent of The New York Times, had been forthright in reporting on the President's sickness and subsequent events.

Mr. McNamara also praised Drew Pearson, columnist, and Tom Donnelly, a writer for The Washington Daily News.

The Senator said newsmen in the Capital had been talking about what he termed Mr. Hagerty's "skillful cover-up."

"But few of them have been writing about it," he added. The only conclusion I can draw is that they are not allowed to."

Mr. McNamara said he was sure President Eisenhower "has not been a party to the shotgun medical bulletins and the hucksters' propaganda barrage from Madison Avenue that has been fired at the American public from his bedside."

At the White House, Murray Snyder, acting press secretary, said Senator McNamara's speech was "unworthy of comment." Mr. Hagerty left this morning for Panama, in connection with the President's trip there next week-end.

In commending Mr. Knight, Senator McNamara quoted the publisher's comment in his "Editor's Notebook" on June 16:

"The seriousness of the President's illness has been minimized by friendly editorialists * * * How idle and misleading it is to pretend that the President, a former heart case and chronic sufferer from gastric disturbance, can fully regain his old vigor.

"But in their anxiety over the future, the Republican strategists and the big guns in the business world are determined to have Ike run, even though he may not last through a second term under the pressures of the job."

Mr. Knight is president of Knight Newspapers, which publishes The Akron (Ohio) Beacon-Journal, Miami (Fla.) Herald, Chicago Daily News, Detroit Free Press and Charlotte (N. C.) Observer. The Senator said the papers were stanch supporters of the President.

Mr. McNamara said The Washington Post and Times-Herald recently "has been trying to put this health issue into greater perspective." But he said that on one occasion it had omitted a column by Mr. Pearson on President Eisenhower's illness.

On another, he said, the paper failed to carry remarks made in a speech by Mrs. Agnes Meyer, writer and lecturer. Mrs. Meyer is the wife of Eugene Meyer, chairman of the newspaper's board.

As reported by Mr. Donnelly, the Senator said, Mrs. Meyer declared there seemed to be "outright fear in this country of expressing any criticism of the President."

A spokesman for The Post and Times-Herald said the paper would have no comment.

Senator Barry Goldwater, Republican of Arizona, challenged Mr. McNamara to produce evidence that the press has been "covering up" for President Eisenhower.

The speech indicates, he said, that the Democrats have no issues and no candidate.

Senator Dennis Chavez, Democrat of New Mexico, rose to say he wanted to associate himself with the remarks of Mr. McNamara. He said he resented any effort to impugn Senator McNamara's "sincerity of purpose."

NEWS RULE ASKED ON ILL PRESIDENTS

Harvard Heart Expert Says Physicians Should Stick to the Medical Facts

BOSTON, July 30 (AP)—Dr. David B. Rutstein questions in a magazine article whether the American public is properly informed by medical men who care for our Presidents when they are stricken ill.

He is head of Harvard Medical School's Department of Preventive Medicine, and a vice president of the American Heart Association.

Dr. Rutstein previously has indicated that he feels some interpretive reports on the outlook for President Eisenhower's health after his heart attack and gain after his intestinal operation, were out of line with scientific medical literature on the diseases.

The White House press secretary, James C. Hagerty, has told news conferences that is no controversy "by the doctors in the case" over the President's operation. He declared reports following both the President's heart attack and his operation "have been honest and completely factual."

Informed of Dr. Rutstein's article, Mr. Hagerty said there would be no comment on it by the President's physicians.

Previous Illness Cited

Writing in the August Atlantic Monthly on "Doctors and Politics," Dr. Rutstein suggests that the proper role for a physician caring for a President or a Presidential candidate should be to stick to the medical facts and their precise interpretations.

"If the physician goes beyond this point, he then ceases to be an expert," Dr. Rutstein writes. "He becomes just an ordinary citizen subject to political influences in a field in which he has no expert qualifications * * * Political judgments by physicians have as little merit as medical judgments by politicians on the ability of a candidate to run for office."

Dr. Rutstein says the American public has fallen short of getting the best information in the illnesses of two previous Presidents—Woodrow Wilson and Franklin Delano Roosevelt.

"The occurrence of severe illness in three Presidents of the United States within a period of some forty years raises the important question of the responsibility to the public of the physicians attending the President," Dr. Rutstein asserts.

Dr. Rutstein concedes that news about President Eisenhower's heart attack "was handled in a strikingly different way," than the news of the illnesses of Presidents Wilson and Roosevelt.

News bulletins and conference, the article continues, "gave the appearance of a full disclosure of all pertinent medical information," but the public was not told about three researchers which showed "the five-year survival rate of such patients was approximately 50 per cent at the end of five years."

Dr. Rutstein asserts that when the physicians announced in February "The President should be able to carry on an active life satisfactorily for another five to ten years" the President had "no choice on medical grounds of refusing to run for re-election."

In connection with President Eisenhower's operation for intestinal obstruction — ileitis — Dr. Rutstein writes that within hours after the operation the physicians "apparently were perfectly willing to issue a statement "assuring the country that the President's health would in no way prevent him from carrying out his previous plans."

Recurrence of Ileitis

"At no time," he comments, "did they give any indication that ileitis is a chronic disease with a rate of recurrence varying between one-third and two-thirds of those on whom operation is performed, depending on the state of the disease, the type of surgery, and the duration of follow-up.

"Neither did they indicate that the majority of recurrence comes within the first year after operation."

Dr Rutstein makes this comment on the statement that patients of 65 do not have recurrences:

"At all ages where enough cases have been collected for analysis, as, for example, in the studies at the Mayo Clinic, age has had no effect on the recurrence rate."

Dr. Rutstein suggest that the physician to a President, or candidate, should inform him if the demands of the office exceed his physical capacity, "but if his patient were able to carry on, the physician would give the facts and indicate the documented scientific medical information which would justify his decision."

Thus, patient and public would be safeguarded, Dr. Rutstein declares.

TV FASHION ADVICE

Democratic Women Get Tips on Dress for Convention

Special to The New York Times.

CHICAGO, Aug. 3—Women delegates and visitors to the Democratic National Convention opening here Aug. 13 got their advice today on how to dress for the television cameras. Republican women got similar advice Wednesday.

Mrs. India Edwards, national co-director of the Harriman for President campaign and former vice-chairman of the Democratic National Committee, gave the advice to the Democratic women.

"Women often will be in the eye of the television camera, and may be interviewed at a moment's notice," Mrs. Edwards said.

To look their best on television the women were given these tips:

"Light colors add to a woman's size, small prints are apt to jump on the screen. And big hats are taboo—they obscure the woman as well as block out others."

August 4, 1956

Truman Airs a Word That Nobody Else Can

Former President Truman used a forbidden word over the radio last night and "got away with it."

The moment Adlai E. Stevenson received the votes of the Pennsylvania delegation that gave him the required majority for nomination, Richard C. Hottelot of the Columbia Broadcasting System approached Mr. Truman's box with a microphone and said:

"Well, Mr. President, what do you think? What are you going to do now."

Like a flash the man from Independence replied:

"Well, we're going to lick the hell out of the Republicans."

Robert Trout, interlocutor of the C. B. S. radio program, cut in to remark:

"I guess the ex-President of the United States is the only man who can get away with that word on radio."

August 17, 1956

G.O.P. Tells Nominees: Don't Lose Heads on TV

WASHINGTON, Sept. 26 (AP)—If you know a Republican nominee, chances are he's boning up on a handy little booklet put out today by the Republican National Committee:

"A Candidate's Primer on How to Utilize Radio and Television Effectively."

Television is intimate, says the booklet. Be simple, be sincere. Sitting behind a desk is stiff. Better to sit in an armchair—but don't lounge.

Once, and only once, says the booklet, get up and walk. Don't move too fast—the camera man has to keep aiming at you and if you pop up suddenly your head may jump right off the screen, an effect "disruptive, to say the least." Give the audience something to look at—a chart, maybe.

And, cheer up, viewers:

"Few people can keep a television audience interested for more than fifteen minutes. Don't ever speak for more than thirty."

September 27, 1956

President to Chat With People On TV by Use of Split Screen

National Citizens for Eisenhower is moving to bring the people to President Eisenhower. It will use the latest technological campaign weapons, network television, remote pick-ups and the split screen effect.

Sometime in October the President will face a succession of "little people" over a vast electronic no-man's land. Split screen telecasting, however, will suggest that the President and the people are physically close together.

During the half-hour telecast individuals typifying many economic and social groups will ask the President how his policies affect them.

Scouts are already seeking the individuals. These will be taken to television studios near their homes and put on the screen with the President. The program will be live and, its designers say, unrehearsed.

"We will have all kinds of people," a leader of the plan explained. "There will be garment workers and longshoremen and farmers and small business men. We will let them present their problems to the President of the United States."

The idea, this leader added, is to "make a fool of the Democratic charge that the President is the captive of big business."

Senator Estes Kefauver of Tennessee, the Democratic Vice-Presidential candidate, has accused the President of neglecting the "average family," the "plain, ordinary citizen."

Adlai E. Stevenson, the Democratic Presidential nominee, charges the Administration with "blindness" toward human values. It sees statistics, he says, where Democrats see people.

The President will not actually "see" people on the split screen telecast, except by television monitor. He will hear them and talk to them, however.

Citizens for Eisenhower hopes that this type of program will help overcome the disadvantages inherent in television as a medium of political campaigning. Foremost among these disadvantages is the distance of the audience from the speaker.

The Citizens group has also scheduled a series of telecasts featuring men and women who are strong in their admiration of the President.

Democrats who are switching to support of the Republican President in the election will explain why on coast-to-coast networks. On these programs will also appear persons in various fields of endeavor who intend to vote Republican.

There will be ten five-minute broadcasts of this sort, two half-hour broadcasts and one to take a full hour.

September 30, 1956

Reporters in 8 Cities To Query Nixon on TV

WASHINGTON, Oct. 2 (UP)—The Republican National Committee announced today that Vice President Richard M. Nixon would hold "the world's first transcontinental press conference" on Thursday.

Leonard W. Hall, chairman of the committee, said reporters in eight of the cities Mr. Nixon had visited would question the Vice President during a thirty-minute television program on the National Broadcasting Company network beginning at 8:30 P. M.

"The reporters will be free to ask any questions they choose and the program will be unrehearsed," Mr. Hall said. "This is the first time anything like this nation-wide conference has been attempted on a paid political broadcast."

He explained that sound wires would be open at all times so that reporters and the Vice President could talk with each other. It will be Mr. Nixon's first nation-wide TV appearance since the campaign opened.

October 3, 1956

PENTAGON GROUP
ASKS PRESS CURB

Advisory Unit Calls System of Classification Sound

By ALLEN DRURY
Special to The New York Times.

WASHINGTON, Nov. 13—A Defense Department advisory committee said today that the department's security classification system was "sound in concept." The House Government Information subcommittee resumed hearings designed to show that it was no such thing.

The advisory committee, headed by Charles A. Coolidge, a former Assistant Secretary of Defense, went so far as to suggest that reporters be haled before grand juries when they print information "which obviously gravely damages the security of the nation."

The Coolidge committee also recommended that when a department official is identified as the source of such a leak, "stern disciplinary action should be taken, and taken with the utmost promptness."

Charles E. Wilson, Secretary of Defense, in a letter to the committee, said he would have "serious reservations" about grand jury action against reporters.

The House subcommittee, headed by Representative John E. Moss, Democrat of California, meanwhile heard top officers of the military services reject the charge that security restrictions were so tight that they prevented exchange of scientific information needed for the development of new weapons.

The Coolidge committee admitted that it had found "overclassification" of secret material in the department. But it summed up its conclusion about the system as follows:

"Our examination leads us to conclude that there is no conscious attempt within the Department of Defense to withhold information which • • • the public should have; that the classification system is sound in concept, and while not operating satisfactorily in some respects, it has been and is essential to the security of the nation; and that further efforts should be made to cure the defects in its operation."

Secretary Wilson said he regarded with "serious reservations" a Coolidge committee recommendation that the department prepare and circulate widely to the press "a forceful statement outlining · the differences between ordinary peace and the present situation from the point of view of information security."

The committee also recommended that the department:

¶Make a determined attack on overclassification. This would include cutting down on the number of persons authorized to classify information as top secret, and make it clear to everyone in the department that information not vital to national security should not be classified.

¶Prohibit the use of the classification label for administrative matters.

¶"Cease attempts to do the impossible and stop classifying information which cannot be held secret."

¶Improve procedures to permit airing of differences between the services, allowing representatives to express the views of their particular service.

¶Educate industries not to give out too much classified technical information to trade and technical journals.

¶Edit the texts of Congressional hearings before they are released to the public to make sure they do not include classified information.

Representative Moss, opening his subcommittee's new series of hearings, said scientists who testified earlier in the year contended that restrictions hampered the free exchange of information.

He said there were complaints, for example, that a physicist working for the Army could not always discuss his problems informally with a scientist working for the Navy, even though both might have security clearance and be engaged on the same type of project.

Rear Admiral Rawson Bennett, Chief of Naval Research, said such complaints came from scientists who "just don't want to be bothered to fit themselves into the procedure."

Similar testimony came from Maj Gen. John P. Daley, special weapons director of the Army; Maj. Gen. J. S. Mills, assistant development chief of the Air Force, and S. E. Clements, director of planning for research and development in the Defense Department.

Mr. Clements said he knew of no case in which research and development suffered because red tape had prevented scientists from exchanging notes.

MAGAZINE FAVOR DENIED

Air Force Says B-52 Pictures Were Not Deliberate Leak

WASHINGTON, March 15 (UP) —The Air Force denied today that it had deliberately "leaked" military secrets to Life magazine or any other publication.

Representative B. F. Sisk, Democrat of California, said in the House recently that Life had received favorable treatment on pictures of January's round-the-world flight of B-52 bombers. Mr. Sisk described Henry R. Luce, Life's editor in chief, as an "ardent" Administration supporter.

An Air Force spokesman said that if Mr. Sisk meant to imply that Life was favored because Mr. Luce was a supporter of the Administration, "the supposition is without foundation."

The spokesman said that "through an error in judgment by a junior officer" Life had received photographs of the M-52's taking off, while other publications had not. He said the photographs had no captions and "were not identified as being connected with the then secret round-the-world operation."

MONRONEY SCORES
U. S. NEWS 'LEAKS'

Senator A. S. Mike Monroney assailed last night "the growing custom of government by leak." He called this a threat to the free flow of responsible information from the White House.

In an address here, the Oklahoma Democrat attributed the birth of the Eisenhower Doctrine to such a "not-for-attribution" story. He said that select groups "are sometimes assembled for the trial balloon launching of policy changes" to which the general press is barred.

No authority is given, he said, for the news that is "leaked" in this manner, as in the case of the Eisenhower Doctrine.

"The New York Times, in a story by James Reston, broke this big news," the Senator continued. "A day or two later, a few more top reporters were let in on the leak. Meanwhile, President Eisenhower was in Augusta and silent on the subject. At the same time, Speaker [Sam] Rayburn of the House and Democratic and Republican leaders of both the House and the Senate were waiting for the President's return to consult with him on what the policy was to be.

"They read about it in the newspapers in a 'not-for-attribution' manner. What Speaker Rayburn and others said also was 'not-for-attribution' in any family newspaper."

Senators Said to Be Angry

In an article published in The Times last Jan. 30, Mr. Reston reported that Senators were angry because they believed Middle East policy had been leaked. He went on:

"On this point, incidentally, the Senators have not taken the trouble to check the facts. The Secretary of State did not 'leak' the policy. The New York Times printed the story first. This newspaper reported the plan only because Mr. [John Foster] Dulles went to the White House to see the President on Dec. 26 and the White House announced that he and the President had discussed the future of Middle East policy. That was all that was put out at that time. The Times story was developed from this announcement and checked in official quarters, but it was not purposely put out, as the Senators still seem to believe."

Senator Monroney addressed the annual spring dinner-meeting of the National Editorial Association at the Commodore Hotel. The group's membership totals about 5,500 publishers and editors, mostly of small-town weeklies.

In a separate attack against the "cult of secrecy" in Government agencies and the "overclassifying" of innocuous documents, the Senator cited Mr. Reston's comments on the handling of information.

He noted that Mr. Reston,

Washington correspondent of The Times, had said that "free exchange of information between the responsible reporter and the responsible official of the Federal Government has seriously declined in the past two or three years."

Mr. Monroney, a former political writer for The Oklahoma News, asserted that a trend toward "news smothering" was hampering the flow of news about the Federal Government. He questioned to what extent the press should accept off-the-record information which, he said, "stifles digging for the truth."

The Senator contended that "only a vigorous press, a determined Congress and an awakened public can turn us away" from the cult of secrecy and "provide for birth control of classified documents."

Mr. Monroney observed also that the White House news conference "seems to be slipping, at least in frequency." He said the President and his Cabinet officers had held fewer news conferences than recent previous Administrations.

Senator Monroney deplored also the dissemination of news by "handouts." He said that, although the number of information officers employed by Government departments had continued to increase, the information from the genuine news sources "seems to diminish in direct proportion to the number of information specialists."

Press Is Called Republican

At an earlier session, Dr. John Tebbel, chairman of the Department of Journalism, New York University, declared that "only the most myopic partisan would deny that for the past twenty years the press has been overwhelmingly Republican."

Dr. Tebbel reported partial results of a study of political campaign coverage by the newspapers in seven cities. The study was made possible, he said, through a $5,000 grant from the Skinner Foundation, a Michigan fund.

Twenty-one newspapers published in New York, Providence, Chicago, Memphis, Houston, Kansas City, Mo., and Los Angeles were surveyed.

Dr. Tebbel said he had found little evidence of bias in the writing of news, but "considerable" bias in picture coverage. Also, "the general tendency was to give Mr. Eisenhower better position and more favorable headlines," he said.

"The device of the press conference, which Mr. Eisenhower used adroitly as a campaign weapon, was abetted by some newspapers through the common practice of splitting up the conference into special topic stories," Dr. Tebbel reported.

He criticized the "unfortunate tendency" by some newspapers to display in the news columns political stories by staff writers "which are really highly partisan editorials and columns."

March 23, 1957

U. S. Issues Clenched Handout

WASHINGTON, June 15 (UP)—In the pile of Government releases and press agents' hand-outs delivered by the mailman to the Washington Bureau of the United Press today was a document bearing this note: "Personal and confidential. This document is for extremely limited, wholly private, confidential circulation. Publication or divulging any of its contents, in whole or in part, or in abstract, is expressly forbidden."

June 16, 1957

The President's Health

An Analysis of His Remarks About It And His Bearing at News Conference

By JAMES RESTON
Special to The New York Times.

WASHINGTON, Jan. 15 — President Eisenhower was both optimistic and fatalistic about his health today.

"I feel very well indeed," he told reporters in his first news conference since last Oct. 30. "If I had sunlight this afternoon, and had two hours, I would like to be on the golf course right now."

As to his future, he remarked, a little wistfully:

"No one can tell what the physical future is. I am optimistic enough to say this: That as long as I am able, I am going to carry on just exactly as I have in the past, and with no thought of it, and from there on, it is in the lap of the gods —and that's that."

This was the President's first question-and-answer period with the reporters since before his cerebral occlusion of last Nov. 26. It was his first important effort at public extemporaneous speech since that time, and one of his associates in the White House reported that he had been nervous about it.

He spoke more slowly than before. He seemed at times to be groping for ideas, enunciating less clearly and rambling in his articulation more than usual. On these points, however, the reporters differed.

The Associated Press reported that he was "ruddy as of old, and the consensus of the 270 newsmen on hand was that he handled himself well."

The United Press, in contrast, reported, not that he was "ruddy," but that he was "pale," and added that he talked more slowly and "occasionally appeared to be having trouble finding the right word."

A Slowing-Down Seen

The Washington Star said: "It seemed indisputable that since his last illness, the President has slowed down."

At one point, he mispronounced the name of the Soviet Prime Minister, Mr. Bulganin, leaving off the first syllable. Later he referred to him as Mr. Bul-gain-in, and at another point, he seemed to be searching for the middle name of the Federal Reserve Board and finally let it go at "Federal Board."

The President responded to a question about the possibility of resigning, however, with the greatest calm and even good humor, though, paradoxically, he flushed with anger when asked about reports of Secretary of State Dulles' resignation.

A reporter asked the President if there were any truth in the stories that he had considered resigning last November and December. He said that he had not done so in "that particular illness." Then he added, with a charming smile:

"As a matter of fact, in a matter of a couple of hours, doctors were assuring me that there was at least no damage to whatever intellectual faculties I have."

Joining in the laughter that followed this sally, he told the audience in the crowded ornate Indian Treaty Room of the old State Department building:

"Any time that I believe or any group of doctors, eminent doctors, would say that I am not really up to doing my job, then I would personally, feeling as I do, I would have no recourse except to resign."

Another reporter referred to reports that Mr. Dulles had offered to resign and began to ask whether the President felt that the mounting criticism of the Secretary of State was in any way impairing the Secretary's usefulness. The President cut him off sharply:

GENERAL EISENHOWER—Have you seen that report or have you written it yourself?

REPORTER—No, sir; but it was in the newspapers.

GENERAL EISENHOWER—It was? Then I would say, I would class it as trash.

At this point, the President calmed down, and then, with almost a physical effort to control his temper, he said, very slowly that Mr. Dulles was the last man he would want to see resign, that Mr. Dulles was the "wisest, most dedicated man I know," and that "leading figures of the world" agreed with the President that Mr. Dulles should stay on the job.

Aside from this one flash of anger, the President seemed detached, both about his health and many of the major problems now before him.

Last week, in his State of the Union Message, he conveyed a sense of outrage about the open squabbling among service chiefs in the Pentagon, and sent the legislators away convinced that he was going to take this thing over and deal with it.

As a matter of fact his principal aides told reporters immediately after the President's appearance on Capitol Hill that he was taking personal charge of the Pentagon reorganization.

Today, however, his mood on this subject was quite different. He said that he had his own views on this subject (he had testified ten years ago for a single chief of staff and characterized the separate services as "obsolete," but that his personal convictions, no matter how strong, could not be the final answer.

He said he was going to be commander in chief for only three years and observed that there had to be a consensus with the Cabinet, the Congress and the people who have to run the Pentagon, on what should be done.

When he was asked whether he would request Prime Minister Bulganin to publish in the Soviet Union the President's latest letter on disarmament talks, he said he had already made and published such a request. Then after conferring with his press secretary, James C. Hagerty, he explained that the request had apparently been removed from the last draft.

"Sorry, I have apparently made a goof," he said.

For the rest, the President was erect and quick of step. He seemed a little thinner, and the old flashes of good humor were present. But unlike his trip to Paris and his visit to Capitol Hill, this public appearance provided many of his hearers with little reassurance.

The President's Temper

Anger Shown at News Conference Seen As Reaction to Opponents' New Attacks

By JAMES RESTON
Special to The New York Times.

WASHINGTON, April 23—The strain and pressure of the job began to show on President Eisenhower today for almost the first time in six years.

Ever since his heart attack in September of 1955, he has been keeping a tight rein on his temper, but he finally let it go today. The surprising thing is that it has not happened before.

News Analysis

Ever since the Anglo-French attack on Suez and the Soviet intervention in Hungary, he has been in the eye of the target.

After a long run of what had come to be known as "Eisenhower luck" in the first term, trouble with the Russians, trouble in the alliance, and finally trouble with the national economy have confronted him with one set of dilemmas after another.

These he has borne with good humor. But lately the criticism of his political opponents has prompted him to complain somewhat bitterly to one or two of his associates.

Recalls Boxing Days

Two weeks ago, he was still able to take a relaxed attitude about these criticisms. When a reporter asked him on April 9 whether he ever had felt the urge to take a "retaliatory poke" at his critics, he replied: "Look, I did a great deal of boxing as a young fellow, and that would probably be my natural reaction. I believe that there is a very great responsibility resting on a man in this office to preserve the dignity of this office."

Today, however, obviously angry about what he regarded as unfair and even stupid criticisms of his Pentagon reorganization plan, he fairly supttered with rage.

When Sarah McClendon of The San Antonio Light asked him about charges on Capitol Hill that his plan might make it possible for some other President or Secretary of Defense in the future to set up a kind of personal army, he took off like the Jupiter C.

"I've got one question to ask you," he remarked sharply. "Have you read the law?"

Miss McClendon replied that she had, and the President cut her off.

"No you haven't I don't think," he said. "Now look, Miss McClendon, it might be just as well, as sensible for you to say that the Congress is suddenly going nuts and completely abolishing the Defense Department, so why don't we do that instead of just giving a big personal army."

The next questioner referred to a speech made on the floor of the Senate by Senator Mike Mansfield of Montana, the Democratic whip, and one of the leading members of the Foreign Relations Committee. Senator Mansfield had said yesterday that the Eisenhower Administration was asserting that it had produced peace in the Far East, whereas, the Senator contended, no more than a tenuous truce exists in Korea, Taiwan [Formosa] and Vietnam.

"Would you comment on that, sir?" the reporter asked.

The President flushed, hesitated and then replied:

"No!"

When the next questioner asked him what he had bought recently to help buy the country out of the recession, General Eisenhower said sharply that he did not know and asked the reporter if he wanted to go and see his personal aide "who buys my things."

When the President was still replying to the next questioner with sharp questions of his own, it was obvious to the reporters that this was a wholly different Eisenhower mood.

Generous With Answers

In the last six years he has been uncommonly generous in his answers. A reporter questioning either President Truman or President Roosevelt was like a man pitching batting practice to the Yankees—every time he let go he had to be ready to duck.

Mr. Truman was blunt and caustic, Mr. Roosevelt sarcastic, but General Eisenhower has consistently tried to find some way of giving a responsive answer to any kind of question, no matter how vapid or critical.

Two years ago, when he was asked about the value of the press conference, he replied:

"As a matter of fact, I think this is a wonderful institution. I have seen all kinds of statements that Presidents have considered it a bore and a chore, but it does a lot of things for me personally.

"Moreover, I rather like to get the questions because frequently I think they represent the kind of thinking that is going on."

This, of course, is the problem today. The thinking that is going on around here is much more critical of the White House than whe nthe President made that statement in March of 1956. Almost from that date, the world situation has deteriorated. Coincidently, the White House than when the been blamed for the trend of events at home and abroad and he clearly reacted against that criticism today.

Eisenhower Calls News Parleys 'Fine'

By FELIX BELAIR Jr.
Special to The New York Times.

WASHINGTON, April 30—He really likes his news conferences, President Eisenhower said today. Then, after he had told why, for thirty minutes he proved his point in unruffled give and take with some of the 241 reporters present.

There was none of the supercharged atmosphere that resulted from the President's explosively curt replies to some questions at last week's conference. He recalled one of these questions today and remarked with a smile that, after all, there might be a good point in the suggestion that he should visit more small towns around the country. [Question 8, Page 14.]

The President talked about his job and part of the range of problems that comes across his desk. These included politics and candidates, nuclear weapons and Soviet intransigence, Indonesian strife and the era of Richard Harding Davis, recession and taxes and his controversial military modernization plan.

Sometimes the questions bordered on the personal—even after the President had remarked that he would be no more than human if he were irritated by them. But through it all he remained pleasantly calm.

The President conceded in answer to a question that he did experience a normal human irritation at questions he considered either inconsequential or a bit more personal than they need be. [Questions 5 and 7] but the news conference itself he considered "a very fine latter-day American institution."

The President's attitude toward the news conference came up when he was asked his opinion of a suggestion in a letter to the editor of The Washington Post and Times Herald that the President had more than enough serious questions confronting him every day without being "heckled by the press."

While he could appreciate the suggestion, the President said, it overlooked the fact that the Presidency, in the public mind, was a personality as well as an institution.

There is a natural curiosity, he went on, about his ability to handle the range of subjects that are fired at him.

The people, regardless of their geographic area, are interested in the President's thinking, General Eisenhower explained. They want to know that he is able to talk to the whole country in some way and they like the informal exchanges between the President and representatives of all sorts of publications from different areas.

It is just not good enough in modern America for reporters to submit questions in writing to be selected by some press officer along with suggested replies and then to call that a news conference. That is why he had approved the introduction of television and sound recording for radio broadcasts of the conferences, the President noted.

He concluded that it was "emphatically my view that the press conference is a very fine latter-day American institution."

Told that his show of irritation last week has been interpreted by some commentators as meaning that "the strain of office was beginning to tell on you," President Eisenhower at first remarked that it was a "presumption" that he was irritated. But he added quickly that those present were entitled to their own judgment on his disposition at the time.

It was then that the President observed that "I would be less than human if I were always a pollyanna, and I wouldn't suspect that anyone thinks or suspects that I am that kind of a person—and therefore, if something annoys me, I possibly show it a little bit."

The President went to remark that "I don't attempt to be a poker player before this crowd. I try to tell you exactly what I am thinking at the moment when the question is posed."

Last week, as a reporter put it today, the President appeared to show his "Dutch dander" when asked to comment on a criticism of his military reorganization program.

Today the President used logic and quiet persuasion to parry a similar question. By the same technique, he demolished a suggestion that his earlier show of acerbity had meant the burdens of his office were becoming onerous and that he might resign before the end of his term in favor of Vice President Nixon. [Question 9.]

President Eisenhower said without raising his voice:

"I just say this—I took on something last week that I think is a duty, and I'm going to perform that duty as long as I think I am capable of doing it."

Newsmen Are Called Greatest 'Free-Loaders'

WASHINGTON, June 17 (UPI)—A member of Congress voiced "dismay" today at the "obvious glee" he said newsmen showed at the difficulties confronting Sherman Adams over gifts.

Representative Charles S. Gubser, Republican of California, told the House that "there is no greater group of free-loaders in the world than the press."

Thus, he said, he "was dismayed to see members of the press in obvious glee because they were able to tell a story to the American public that an honest man was being made dishonest in the eyes of the public."

"I love the press," Mr. Gubser said. But, he said, the Adams case points up a "dual standard of conduct" for politicians in which good intentions "don't mean a thing."

"Let's not get this thing out of the proper perspective," he said amid scattered applause from Republican lawmakers.

Everyone at the hearing where Mr. Adams, the assistant to the President, testified on his gift exchanges with Boston industrialist, Bernard Goldfine, believed Mr. Adams was honest, Mr. Gubser declared.

June 18, 1958

PRESS CHARGE MODIFIED

Gubser Says All Newsmen Are Not 'Free-Loaders'

WASHINGTON, June 18 (AP) —Representative Charles S. Gubser, Republican of California said today his reference yesterday to members of the press as "free-loaders" had not been intended "as a blanket condemnation."

Mr. Gubser, after attending a subcommittee hearing at which the Presidential Assistant, Sherman Adams, was questioned, told the House "there was no greater group of free-loaders in the world than the press."

Today he said he had spoken "under great emotional stress" and had "made what could be interpreted as a blanket condemnation of our press corps. This was not intended."

The Anonymous Advisers

Little News Is Given Out on Vital Work Of President's Major Aides on Policy

By JAMES RESTON
Special to The New York Times.

WASHINGTON, June 25—The Adams case has focused attention on that largely anonymous but immensely powerful staff that serves the President in the White House.

Nevertheless, when Gen. Robert Cutler resigned yesterday and was replaced by Gordon Gray as Special Assistant to the President for National Security Affairs, the announcement created very little interest and was buried back in most newspapers among the shirt-sale ads.

News Analysis

This is one of the anomalies of Washington: Any personal misdemeanor by one of the President's assistants is a sensation, but conversely, there is very little interest in the work they do, or their capacity to do that work if they stay out of personal trouble.

For example, the President's ambassadors have to be confirmed by the Senate when it is in session before they are permitted to represent the President abroad. But men such as General Cutler and Gordon Gray, who have much greater responsibility, slip into the National Security Council without any review of their records or qualities.

Difficult to Judge

This is not to suggest that either General Cutler or Gordon Gray is unqualified for the job. On the contrary, the general impression here is that both were good appointments, but it is only an impression. Nobody outside the secret confines of the N. S. C. really knows whether or not General Cutler did a good job, any more than they have any means of judgment about how Sherman Adams exercises his power.

It is generally believed that the National Security Council is the most powerful body of Presidential advisers on foreign and defense policy in Washington. It is composed of the President, who presides as chairman, the Vice President, the Secretaries of State and Defense, and the director of the Office of Defense and Civilian Mobilization.

As the new Special Assistant to the President for National Security Affairs, Gordon Gray will present to this Cabinet committee many of the most important questions of world policy. He will circulate the

agenda and define the issues to be reviewed by the N. S. C. The President, of course, can accept or reject the recommendations of its members, but under the Eisenhower staff system, the men who define the issues and present them to the N. S. C. clearly have considerable authority.

Eisenhower's Views Recalled

This at least, is the theory, and General Eisenhower has placed great stress upon it During his first campaign for the Presidency, for example, he had this to say:

"I believe that membership in the National Security Council should not be limited to Cabinet officers and heads of administrative agencies. These men are already burdened by the duties of their own offices. The National Security Council as presently constituted is more a shadow agency than a really effective policy maker. That, I believe, can be corrected by appointing to it civilians of the highest capacity, integrity and dedication to public service. They should have no other official duties."

Is the N. S. C. so constituted today? The impression outside is that it is not, but again, it is only an impression, for there is no way to know how it is operating. The Congress cannot question it; its members are remote—perhaps necessarily so —from the press, but the outside impression is that the President's pledges of 1952 have not been kept.

President Eisenhower has brought more men into the N. S. C. from other departments and agencies, and it has met more regularly than during the Truman Administration, but the men who meet there are still "burdened by the duties of their own offices," and the N. S. C. is often either by-passed or dependent on the work of staff members who are not on the council.

For example, Secretary of State Dulles often operates outside the N. S. C., and it is his recommendations, rather than those of the council, that prevail in the field of foreign policy. This was true of the formulation of the mis-named Eisenhower Doctrine, which was not discussed in the N. S. C. before it was adopted as policy by Mr. Dulles and the President.

On another critical point of policy, many of the major budgetary questions, such as how much money is to be spent on missiles as distinct from conventional weapons, are often determined outside the N. S. C.

Maybe this is as the President wants it and as it should be, but the point is that these agencies of the Government and their members and staff operate in vital security fields without any outside information about the men concerned or how they are meeting their responsibilities.

For example, because the N. S. C. members are preoccupied with the affairs of their own departments, much of the N. S. C. work is done by the N. S. C. Planning Board, which is a mystery to even the most observant members of the Washington community.

Mr. Gray will preside over this board in his new job. The other members are:

Gerard Smith, head of the Policy Planning staff at the State Department; Mansfield Sprague, Assistant Secretary of Defense for International Security Affairs; Robert Finley of the Office of Defense and Civilian Mobilization; Frederick C. Scribner Jr., Under Secretary of the Treasury; Ralph W. E. Reid, assistant director of the Bureau of the Budget.

They are assisted by Robert Amory of the Central Intelligence Agency, Karl G. Harr Jr. of the Operations Coordinating Board and the President's staff, and Rear Admiral Charles O. Triebel, representing the Joint Chiefs of Staff.

No One Able to Say

How efficiently this board and the Operations Coordinating Board do their jobs nobody here knows. The Planning Board is supposed to prepare the work of the N. S. C., and the O. C. B. is supposed to see that the recommendations of the N. S. C. are carried out after they are approved by the President.

In theory they are responsibilities of primary importance. Their members, however, are largely unknown and even requests to take their photographs as a body are refused.

Thus, there is growing up around the President a large staff, which comes into the news only when one of them resigns, or as in the case of Mr. Adams, gets into trouble.

Master Manipulators?

The growing role of advertising agencies in the handling of political campaigns has caused some concern that people some day may be sold on candidates for public office in the same way they are sold soap.

This fear was rejected by Lloyd G. Whitebrook, executive vice president of Kastor, Hilton, Chesley & Clifford, and an experienced handler of Democratic party programs. In speaking before the American Political Science Association, he said:

"Television is an instrument. It can be used well or badly. It can help a candidate for political office or it can damage him. But it cannot create the candidate. At its best, it can show him clearly for what he is.

"We are only effective when we have a candidate and effective issues. The hard sell may peddle soap but it cannot peddle people. It is easy to underestimate the voter. He is usually badly informed, but he is a lot smarter than we think he is."

June 26, 1958

September 8, 1958

Faith, Hope and Hagerty

Briefings on Camp David Talks Fail To Fill the Public In on Berlin Crisis

By JAMES RESTON
Special to The New York Times.

WASHINGTON, March 23— There was considerable interest and some dismay here as a result of the disclosure in The New York Times this morning that 39 per cent of those questioned in a national spot check did not know that Berlin was an enclave in Communist East Germany 100 miles from the West German border. If this was even approximately accurate, officials here commented, something should be done to review the Government's information policies in the field of foreign affairs.

News Analysis

This conclusion was reinforced by complaints from members of the powerful Senate Foreign Relations Committee that even they had not been "briefed" on this week-end's conversations between President Eisenhower and Prime Minister Macmillan.

Part of the reason for the paucity of information about the State Department's policy for the forthcoming Big Four foreign ministers' meeting on Germany is that the policy itself has not been clearly formulated.

Another factor is the illness of Secretary of State Dulles, and the simultaneous illness of Andrew H. Berding, Assistant Secretary of State for Public Affairs, who is Mr. Dulles' principal spokesman.

When he was running the State Department, Mr. Dulles was not only the principal formulator and negotiator of foreign policy but the principal spokesman and witness on Capitol Hill as well.

He was interested in public information. Aside from his official appearances on the Hill and his weekly news conferences, he held many background meetings with legislators and reporters. These sessions nourished the general flow of diplomatic information from Washington to the country.

Everyone Is Considerate

With the Secretary seriously ill, everyone is being considerate and gentlemanly.

The President is being extremely considerate toward Mr. Dulles, saying that he himself must decide whether he can carry on his duties.

Mr. Dulles is being gentlemanly toward the President and the Acting Secretary of State, Christian A. Herter. He is talking daily with the State Department and he has had two sessions with his principal aides and the British on the Eisenhower-Macmillan talks, but he is not attempting to define policy or interfere with Mr. Herter's responsibilities.

Similarly Mr. Herter. He is avoiding news conferences and holding his appearances on Capitol Hill to a minimum. Even when he has been asked for personal information or background sessions on Berlin, he has explained that he wants to avoid doing anything that might give the impression that he is trying to "take over" the department in Mr. Dulles' absence.

Inevitably, this has reduced the flow, not of general information about the "firmness" of the United States position on Berlin, but of information on the increasingly important diplomatic negotiations concerning how the United States and its allies intend to implement their policy of firmness.

The task of informing the reporters during the Eisenhower-Macmillan talks was taken over by the White House press secretary, James C. Hagerty, and the British Foreign Office's spokesman, Peter Hope. The general impression since Mr. Macmillan arrived last week is that this procedure has not worked too well.

The Greatest Is Faith

It is a policy of faith, Hope and Hagerty, and of these the greatest is faith.

The reporters were kept in Gettysburg, miles away from Camp David. The reports of the meetings by Messrs. Hope and Hagerty were far from complete.

Indeed, Mr. Hagerty appears to have been persuaded more by the necessities of British internal politics than by the need to enlighten the American people.

There were sharp differences between him and Mr. Hope on the extent of the President's commitment to a summer summit meeting. While these were not allowed to show themselves in the briefings, they were no less real.

Thus, the British spokesman privately was describing the President's commitment as "unconditional" and without regard to results at a preliminary foreign ministers' conference and Mr. Hagerty was doing nothing to correct this impression. The result was that Mr. Macmillan has been credited with a great personal triumph and the President with having executed a complete about-face.

Those officials who had personal knowledge of what went on at Camp David were not available to the reporters, and those who were available either were not informed on important details of the conversations or were under instructions to avoid direct replies.

There is some justification for this at the moment. Differences still exist between London and Washington on some details of possible compromises with the Soviet Union and officials here feel there is no point in advertising them to the world.

Also, Moscow is taking advantage of every opportunity to blanket the Eisenhower-Macmillan talks with its own propaganda. The day before the British Prime Minister arrived here, Premier Nikita S. Khrushchev called an unusual news conference in Moscow and managed to dominate the news, even in this country, by agreeing to a May 11 foreign ministers' meeting before he had even received Western notes suggesting that date.

Officials here are concerned about the evidence that the public is not well informed on the crisis. There was some talk here today of having Mr. Herter and Mr. Macmillan hold background conferences to try to correct the situation.

PHONY-QUIZ ROLE LAID TO PRESIDENT

Democratic Digest Says He and G.O.P. Rigged Shows in '52 and '56 Drives

Special to The New York Times.

WASHINGTON, Nov. 15—The Democratic Digest, without tongue in cheek, made politics today out of revelations of rigged television quiz shows.

It said that President Eisenhower took part in a "phony" television program in the 1952 campaign.

The President's indignation at rigged shows is ironical, it said, considering that he is "the head of the political party which has made the rigged television show, even the phony quiz show, part of its everyday arsenal of campaign tools."

These comments were made in an article in the November issue of the magazine published monthly by the Democratic National Committee.

The Republican National Committee apparently did not receive an advance copy. Robert Humphreys, its campaign director, who was publicity director in the 1952 campaign, said the following when asked about the article:

"The Democratic Digest has been asking its own questions and supplying its own answers for six years now without contributing to the store of truth. It hasn't done any better job 'rigging' this story than it has done on the others."

The article took its text from the President's news conference of Oct. 23.

"Perhaps Ike has forgotten his famous blitz of spot commercials in the closing days of the 1952 campaign," it said. "They were rigged from beginning to end with glib, superficial answers to the most complex problems of the day."

It gave this example:

"Mr. Innes and wife: General, how would you clean up the mess in Washington?

"Eisenhower: My answer—it's not a one-agency mess, or even a one-department mess. It's a top-to-bottom mess. And I promise we'll clean it up, from top to bottom."

The Digest described how it said these "spots" had been rigged:

"On a single day in New York the President answered fifty questions in front of the television camera. The questions and answers were all hastily typed in a back room by Rosser Reeves, an adman with the Ted Bates advertising agency, then rushed to Milton Eisenhower [the President's brother] for approval, then on to Ike, who was sitting in front of the cameras.

"Reeves had twenty-two questions and answers prepared for the camera session, but when it was seen how fast Ike could rattle them off, Reeves batted out twenty-eight more while Ike was under the lights.

"A week later, people from geographic regions which the spots were intended to reach were recruited to ask matching questions. These were recorded and filmed and then fitted to the film containing Eisenhower's answers. Slick, eh."

Two in '56 Charged

The article declared that two "phony quiz shows" were also produced by the Republicans in the campaign of 1956. The first, it said, "had Ike before a group of Citizens for Eisenhower answering loaded questions, enabling him to give tranquilizing answers to such as this one, prompted by a question on housing for military personnel overseas":

" 'The big thing to do is to get things straightened out so we can bring our troops home.' "

"It was a refinement of the 'spontaneous' spots of 1952," The Digest commented.

The other "phony," it said, was an attempt to "reach the woman voter by cutting into the afternoon television fare of soap operas, old movies and, of all things, phony quiz programs.

"They did this by producing a phony quiz program of their own, starring Ike," it went on. "This one was a half-hour program in which the panel of seven women asked Ike pre-written questions. All the questions were set up to enable the President to repeat already stated positions on the issues of the campaign."

Nixon Appears on Television for 4 Hours

HE TERMS PEACE FOREMOST ISSUE

Subject Matter Ranges From Castro to Family Problems —Party Label Decried

DETROIT, Nov. 7 — Vice President Nixon appeared on a four-hour "Telethon" program today. The feat was unparalleled in Presidential campaigning.

Capping his campaign in all fifty states of the nation the Republican Presidential nominee appeared relaxed as he sat in a studio of WXYZ-TV here and answered questions telephoned from all sections of the country.

The subject-matter ranged from how to handle Cuba's Premier Fidel Castro to who made the decision that Mrs. Nixon should travel with her husband during the campaign.

Immediately after the Vice President left the air Senator John F. Kennedy, in hastily purchased time, appeared on the same network from Manchester, N. H., to challenge his rival's statements and to answer other questions phoned in to him.

His appearance was then countered by the Republicans, who pressed former Gov. Thomas E. Dewey into service from New York to answer the Democratic nominee's attacks on the Vice President.

Mr. Nixon told his television audience that everywhere he had traveled in the long campaign from Maine to Hawaii he had found the people concerned about the issue of keeping the peace, and extending freedom without war.

"If there's one thing I can emphasize above everything else," Mr. Nixon said, "it is that this is such an important election, since we are selecting not only the President of the United States but the leader of the free world, that it is vital, absolutely vital that we put America first rather than party first, that we put America first above every other consideration and that you, the voters of this country, think not in terms of, for example the party label I wear and you wear.

"If you are a Republican and I'm a republican, that isn't enough reason to vote for me, and the same is true of my opponent; if you are a Dem-

G. O. P. Running Mates Talk to the Nation in a Marathon TV Show

Vice President Nixon answers questions telephoned to him in Detroit during four-hour TV appearance. Sitting in the adjoining room are Robert Young, left, and Lloyd Nolan, actors, who served as moderators on nation-wide broadcast.

ocrat and he is Democrat, that isn't enough reason to vote for him. What we need is the best man that either party can produce in these times."

The program was carried over the American Broadcasting Company network.

According to telephone company officials, the response "swamped" the 100 telephone lines set up into the studio.

At one point during the program, an announcer declared in a burst of enthusiasm that "the response has been simply appalling."

The leading issue raised by the questioners dealt with "keeping the peace," according to a program announcer. The other principal questions were said to have dealt with "combating communism," personal life, and "human needs and welfare."

The program was not exclusively a question-and-answer period between the Presidential candidate and the voters.

Some of the questions were answered by Henry Cabot Lodge, the Vice-Presidential candidate, from Boston. The program was interrupted from time to time for films showing the careers of Mr. Nixon and Mr. Lodge, for parts of a speech by President Eisenhower endorsing the ticket and for statements by movie and television stars, in a studio in New York, praising the Republican ticket.

The program was put on, the Vice President said, to allow the American people for the first time in the history of American politics to question directly a candidate for the Presidency.

Associated Press Wirephotos

By means of a special hook-up, Henry Cabot Lodge, in Boston, assists Mr. Nixon with answers to some of queries.

The telephones installed in the studio were manned by about 200 Republican women volunteer workers from the Detroit area.

The calls, totaling more than 7,000, were paid for by the sponsors.

The questions screened by a panel, consisting of Dr. James Pollock of the University of Michigan, Prof. Tibor Payzs of the University of Detroit and Dr. James Miller, director of the Mental Health Research Institute at the University of Michigan.

They said that they processed the questions for good taste, intelligibility, and to avoid duplication.

Masters of ceremonies, who appeared with the Vice President and asked the questions, were Robert Young, Lloyd Noland and John Payne, actors.

At the beginning of the program the announcer said that voters could ask "any question under the sun." They very nearly did that.

The questions included one about the admission of Communist China to the United Nations (Mr. Nixon was opposed under "present circumstances" but did not preclude the possibility that eventually China might qualify) to whether the Vice President was a "strict father" (he said he was not and that he "spoils" his children).

The two Nixon daughters, Julie and Patricia, joined the campaign today, appearing with their father on a motorcade through downtown Detroit and at a rally in the Ford Auditorium.

They also made a brief appearance with their mother and Mr. Nixon on the telethon. Mr. Young asked the girls about their aims in life.

Patricia said that she would like to be a teacher and Julie that she once wanted to be an actress but wasn't so sure now. She emphasized, though, that she wanted to go to college.

At the beginning of the program, Mr. Nixon, who flew to Detroit overnight from Alaska, showed some irritation with photographers, who were busily snapping pictures just before he went on the air.

Later he told those assisting in processing questions that he wanted a full hour of questions without a break.

"Can everything but the question," he said.

But the telethon breaks continued, with switches to Mr. Lodge, film clips, interviews with movie stars supporting him, including Ginger Rogers, and even an occasional advertisement, including one for cranberry sauce.

For the most part, the questions produced no new positions by the Vice President but did give him an opportunity to restate positions taken throughout the campaign.

One of the rare moments of political spark during the program was generated when the Vice President was asked how it was that he found time to appear alone on a four-hour television program but could not find time to appear on a fifth televised debate with Senator Kennedy.

In reply the Vice President blamed the Kennedy camp for the collapse of negotiations for a fifth debate. He said that Senator Kennedy had undertaken a "calculated program" to break up the fifth debate because he did not want to appear on a nationally televised program with his running mate, Senator Lyndon B. Johnson of Texas.

The Vice President also took the occasion to get in a jab for what he described as the apparent reluctance of Senator Kennedy to have Senator Johnson appear with him in northern states. He emphasized that he was willing to have Senator Lodge appear any time any place with him in the United States.

At another point Mr. Nixon declined to comment on Senator Kennedy's tactics in the long campaign but said that Senator Johnson had been forced to take a back seat because Senator Kennedy had put him there. But he is not a back-seat driver, Mr. Nixon said, adding that the situation had become "quite embarrassing" to both of them.

Then the Vice President went on to say that he felt Senator Kennedy had distorted the record but that the Democratic nominee also felt that he, Mr. Nixon, had done the same.

"The voters will have to decide," Mr. Nixon said.

Another questioner inquired why the Vice President objected to Senator Kennedy's criticism of United States prestige and strength, since in 1942 Mr. Nixon was charging that the nation's military position had deteriorated.

"Then it was true." Mr. Nixon said. "Now it isn't."

Answer by Kennedy

Senator Kennedy interrupted a campaign swing through New Hampshire to go to a Manchester television station to answer the Vice President's telethon statements and to answer telephone questions.

He scoffed at Mr. Nixon's suggestion that the Democratic program would endanger the economy and call for an increase in taxes. He also pledged strong efforts to maintain the peace in his half-hour appearance.

In response to a question read to him on the program dealing with his position on the separation of church and state, the Senator, a Roman Catholic, pledged that he would "not let the Pope or anyone else in my church" influence him as President.

"If the Pope, or anyone else should attempt to bring improper influence, then I should tell that person that it was improper," he said. He added that he could be impeached if he permitted such interference in the conduct of his office.

Questions on the program were read to him by his three sisters, Mrs. Peter Lawford, Mrs. Stephen Smith and Mrs. R. Sargent Shriver Jr.

In caustic tones Mr. Dewey, who appeared on the same network, but from New York City, derided Senator Kennedy's assertion that he would be a full-time President.

The former New York Governor charged that Mr. Kennedy had not even been a full-time Senator. He said that Senator Kennedy, as chairman of a subcommittee on Africa, had never called a meeting of that body and had missed most of the meetings of other committees of which he was a member.

Questions Called 'Rigged'

DETROIT, Nov. 7 (AP)—Michigan's Democratic state chairman, Neil Staebler, charged tonight that Vice President Nixon's telethon had been rigged."

Mr. Staebler said "our switchboard at Democratic headquarters was flooded all afternoon with calls from people who were told that their questions could not be accepted."

He said, "This means only friendly questions were filtered through the screen of public relations monitors and passed on to Mr. Nixon to answer."

'Kennedy and Press' Seems a Hit; Star Shows Skill as Showman

By RUSSELL BAKER
Special to The New York Times.

WASHINGTON, Jan. 25—The new-style Presidential news conference, which replaced "Popeye the Sailor Man" at kiddie time on the home screen tonight, looks like a hit.

It has a new star with tremendous national appeal and the skill of a consummate showman, the President of the United States. At one point he flabbergasted his supporting cast by giving a questioner the precise location of the seized cruise liner Santa Maria.

At 4:10 this afternoon, he told his man, she was 600 miles north of the Amazon River, at 10 Degrees 35 Minutes North, 45 Degrees 32 Minutes West, proceeding on a course of 117 degrees at a speed of fifteen knots.

In line with the trend of panoramic, all-day movies, the Kennedy news conference is bigger, longer and, compared with the intimate conferences that President Dwight D. Eisenhower used to conduct, produced with a cast of thousands.

The setting is the auditorium of the New State Department Building, an amphitheatre done in the modern electronic mode and, except for coral-and-black trim on the cushioned seats, about as warm as an execution chamber.

Under Mr. Eisenhower, the conferences were held in the Indian Treaty room of the Old State Department Building adjoining the White House. There, in a cubicle that heated up like the Black Hole of Calcutta when the floodlights went on, baroque brass cherubs looked down on the President and the newsmen, pressed together in indescribable misery, sat close enough to reach his pulse or feel the heat when his temper blew.

Not in the new production. President Kennedy stands behind a lectern on a stage, a deep spacious well separating him from his antagonists, who rise in tier upon tier before him like the audience in a theatre balcony.

As usual in televised encounters of this sort, the people at home probably hear more of what happens than the people on the scene. There is some speculation here that eventually the reporters will simply stay by screenside to do their stories and that the President will have to rely on the cameramen and sundry frustrated hams among the press corps for questions.

If this is what the future holds there was no hint of it tonight. There were 418 persons in the auditorium when Mr. Kennedy, a study in bronze skin and sandy hair, strode onto the stage a moment after 6 P. M., wearing a blue pin-stripe suit and a white shirt.

From the beginning Mr. Kennedy clearly established himself as the star of the show. This was the result of a brilliant stroke executed Sunday by Pierre Salinger, Mr. Kennedy's press secretary.

Mr. Salinger simply announced that reporters questioning the President need not identify themselves and their organizations.

The requirement of identification had been in effect since the Truman Administration. Mr. Salinger's abandoning of it was a rending blow to theatrical types in the press corps who, presented with their first opportunity to share billing with the President before a national audience, learned that they would appear anonymously.

Nevertheless, at times there were as many as thirty persons on their feet shouting simultaneously for the President's attention.

Mr. Kennedy handled them, and some exceedingly delicate questions, with the controlled poise of a man who knew his brief. In his replies to difficult foreign policy questions, he was precise without permitting himself to say more than he wanted.

Replying to questions that he did not mean to answer, he avoided prolixity. The few questions that held a hook, he avoided. To one man whose premises seemed argumentative, he remarked that the question was a "statement," and finessed it graciously.

After thirty-eight minutes, Marvin Arrowsmith of The Associated Press called the traditional, "Thank you, Mr. President," and down in the front there was some minor scuffling for the door.

In the old days, the world did not know what the President had said until the room was opened at the end. Tonight, however, it was all public knowledge before the first reporter hit the exit.

In the old days, one of the dramatic highlights of every conference was the thundering crash of bodies against the exit as newsmen fought to be first to the telephone. There was no need for that tonight.

TV: Sensible Innovation

President's Decision to Hold His News Conference in the Evening Is Hailed

By JACK GOULD

PRESIDENT'S KENNEDY'S news conference was an altogether successful inovation for both Government and television.

Whatever the inconvenience to the networks or to Washington correspondents who may have a distaste for working the night shift, the President's decision to hold the conference at an evening hour was eminently sensible and constructive.

Not only was a far larger adult audience available for the program than has been the case with daytime news conferences but also it allowed untold numbers of youngsters to witness for themselves the governmental process at the Presidential level.

•

Any procedure that permits a closer liaison between the average citizen and Washington surely is desirable and last night in the living room there was a feeling of participation that had not existed before.

Part of this feeling derived from the President's preference for allowing the conference to be televised on a live basis. As with all live television, there was a reality and an immediacy that simply does not prevail with the use of tape recording.

From any standpoint it can only be hoped that further evening conferences will be scheduled with reasonable frequency and that the fourth estate will not become distressed over such accommodation of the electronic medium.

New conferences, after all, are held primarily for the public benefit and in 1961 that can best be served by permitting the largest number of people to attend at a convenient hour. The day when news conferences were scheduled with an eye on the deadlines of morning and afternoon newspapers is passing. Now the biggest number of reporters is made up of the folks sitting at home watching live TV.

But the volume of important news coming out of President Kennedy's conference illustrated the complementary nature of TV and the press. Many of the matters discussed by the President cried out for elaboration and expansion but two of the networks abruptly switched back to their regular schedules and a third gave only perfunctory footnotes. If anything, TV whetted the appetite for this morning's newspapers.

The live telecast was simply and effectively produced. There were front and profile closeups of the President as well as the usual long "shots." But the camera work was not too restless and there was no intrusion on substance. The microphones for the most part were well placed and practically all of the reporters were heard clearly.

•

The omission of the names of reporters and the organizations for which they work helped speed up the proceedings. The only billing some journalists received was to be recognized by name by the President.

The President's remarks were carried live on radio not only in this country but also over the facilities of the British Broadcasting Corporation, a precedent. The new Administration's use of "more direct communication," to quote the President's remark last night, could well be one of the more significant developments in the coming years.

January 26, 1961

Washington

How to Dissect Kennedy in Comfort

By JAMES RESTON

WASHINGTON, March 16—The Presidential press conference is getting bigger and noisier all the time and, under Kennedy, is turning into an exercise in physical fitness.

Every time the President stops to take a breath in one of these question-and-answer games at least forty-seven reporters bounce off sides and shout "Mr. President," thereby cutting the poor man down in midflight, and perpetuating the popular idea that reporters are not only unreadable but unspeakable.

Of course, we are actually as refined and gentle as Whistler's Mother, but since these conferences have been going out over the television networks, the TV audience, apparently unaccustomed to violence, has been complaining that we act like a pack of district attorneys working over a criminal.

There is a problem here, but it is primarily one of mathematics, and not of manners. Outside of the Government itself, the newspapers and periodicals are the biggest employers in Washington. There are more reporters here than lobbyists or even preachers and they no longer cover the President: they smother him.

Woodrow Wilson, who started the Presidential press conference with a cry for "pitiless publicity," could seat the whole White House press corps of those days around his fireside. Franklin Roosevelt stood them up around his desk in the Executive Office of the White House. Harry Truman and Dwight D. Eisenhower had to move them to the comparatively small if hideous Indian Treaty Room of the old State Department Building, but now the mob has got so large that Kennedy has them in an auditorium almost as big as Carnegie Hall.

This is a dandy place for a movie or a Patterson-Johansson championship fight, but asking questions in it is like making love in Grand Central Terminal. The President is confronted by a firing squad of television cameras. Behind him are two long-distance microphones that look like antitank guns, and between him and the reporters is a moat as wide as a canyon.

In the Indian Treaty Room you could see the whites of the President's eyes, and even if Mr. Eisenhower never finished a sentence, you knew when he was through. Then, too, the reporters jumped up and said "Mr. President," but he was close enough so that when he looked directly at a man, everybody knew which one he was recognizing for the next question.

The Loudest Win

This is no longer true. When Kennedy looks beyond the first couple of rows and indicates the next questioner, there are at least a dozen men in his line of vision, and the one who gets in is usually the character with the loudest voice and not necessarily the best question. Sometimes a shy and retiring fellow like William H. Lawrence of The New York Times will get in with a philosophic question, but not often.

There isn't much that can be done about all this. The President is the master-force of this Administration. He is the chief spokesman and newsmaker. He is releasing, not only important news of the White House, but, as a device to limit the questioning, secondary news of the departments as well. Accordingly, he is attracting at every conference many more reporters than Eisenhower's norm.

It is difficult to limit them: the small dailies have as much right as the big dailies to be represented. It is hard to go back to the Hoover system of written questions without losing spontaneity. And it is too much to expect the President to call the questioners by name, though he is tending to do that more and more.

Of course, it wouldn't hurt if the reporters learned from Kennedy the arts of brevity and precision of speech. Many of them are now following the example of the old lady who said, "How do I know what I think until I hear what I say?" And some of them are hogging the cameras to wow the folks back home.

Pending a revolutionary transformation of human nature, however, there are really only two practical ways to solve the problem. The first is to ban all reporters from The New York Times, or if that is too radical, cut The Times down to ten reporters. This would solve the crush at a single stroke.

The second is to build in the cellar of the Executive Office, or in the courtyard of the old State Department across the street, a small theatre-in-the-round, with steep sides like an operating theatre in a teaching hospital.

This might be regarded by the appropriations committee as an expensive substitute for good manners, but it would bring the President close to the reporters where we could whisper decorously and dissect him in comfort.

March 17, 1961

SALINGER SAYS G.O.P. MANIPULATED NEWS

WASHINGTON, March 20 (UPI)—Pierre Salinger, White House press secretary, accused the Eisenhower Administration today of manipulating the news during the 1960 Presidential campaign.

The American people, Mr. Salinger said, are "entitled to know what is going on when it's going on."

He told the Women's National Democratic Club that there was "nothing more vital in government than the freest possible flow of information."

Mr. Salinger said the Eisenhower Administration had manipulated news by withholding, or announcing ahead of time, Commerce and Labor Department figures. The objective, he said, was to paint a favorable picture of the Administration so that Vice President Nixon would be elected President.

Mr. Salinger said government policy was created out of healthy debate and that there was no reason that the people should not know the various viewpoints under discussion before a decision was made.

But once a policy decision is made, he said, Administration spokesmen have an obligation to support it.

Mr. Salinger said there were some government areas in which public disclosure of information had to be limited because of national security. But he said any such action had to clearly involve national security.

March 21, 1961

Washington

How to Make Life Worse Than It Actually Is

By JAMES RESTON

WASHINGTON, July 13—In the last few weeks the Kennedy Administration has been showing great sensitivity and even irritation about public criticism of its acts.

One reporter was called into the White House woodshed today for sending a detailed though factually accurate account about who helped pick up the tab for this week's party at Mount Vernon for President Mohammad Ayub Kahn of Pakistan.

A few days ago, President Kennedy himself spent over a half hour on the telephone complaining about a critical analysis of his administrative procedures in a weekly news magazine.

Two weeks ago, the F. B. I. was brought into a case at the Pentagon to investigate where a reporter had picked up a report about the Administration's plans for defending Berlin.

All this is fair enough: we criticize them, they criticize us; but lately there has been a tendency in Administration quarters to categorize reporters as either "for" or "against" the Administration, and in at least one case a refusal to cooperate with the representatives of a magazine assumed to be "hostile."

Dogs and Cats

Few Presidents have escaped similar responses to criticism. Late or soon Presidents and reporters usually develop a relationship like dogs and cats. George Washington conceded when he took office that "allowances must be made for occasional effervescences" in the press, but when Tom Paine wrote that Washington was "treacherous in private life and a hypocrite in public life," the General thought this was a little too effervescent and crossed him and most others off his list.

Mr. Jefferson started out by proclaiming that if he had to choose between government without newspapers or newspapers without government, he would choose the newspapers. By the time he left the White House, however, he refused to read anything but Thomas Ritchie's Richmond Enquirer and "that chiefly for the advertisements, for they contain the only truths to be relied on in a newspaper."

Dwight D. Eisenhower boasted after he left the White House that he seldom read the newspapers and wouldn't look at anything in The Washington Post except the sports pages; and, of course, Franklin D. Roosevelt, like "Teddy," had his "Ananias Club" and divided the White House press corps into heroes and villains.

The Kennedys and their principal aides in the White House are a different case. They drink printer's ink for breakfast instead of coffee. They read everything in sight and probably take it all more seriously than it deserves, and they are almost psychopathically concerned with that dreadful modern conception of "their image."

During the Presidential campaign, Mr. Kennedy took some savage personal criticism about his age and his religion in good grace, and in general the papers condemned this kind of personal attack. He has had a sympathetic press on the whole and is liked and respected by most of the men who cover him, but since Cuba, which was not an unqualified success, there has naturally been considerable analysis of what went wrong, and ever since he has been a little tender and peevish.

His latest flurry about the Mount Vernon party was actually inflamed by the White House itself. There were a few obscure comments about the lavishness of the affair in the society columns of Wednesday's papers, and a few telephone calls to Mount Vernon and Capitol Hill about the cost.

Nevertheless, most people here were commenting favorably about the originality of having a state dinner on the Mount Vernon lawn, about the grace and beauty of the affair, and it was not until the White House press secretary decided to make a statement on the occasion that it came out that private donations were made and even solicited to defray part of the expense.

This is what brought the incident to the fore. Some people said the Kennedys were doing no more than is done at a charity ball—getting friends to help foot the bill. Others said it was nobody's business anyway. But quite a few said it was the public's business and that, pretty as it all was, it didn't quite go with either the critical times or with the President's calls for sacrifice.

Much the same thing was said privately when the Kennedy entourage went to Europe last month, complete with dress designers and hair architects. There was no pretense in any of this, for these are young and attractive people accustomed to wealth, but, as in the days of Mary Todd Lincoln and Julia Tyler, there were mutterings about too much elegance amid a great deal of pride and satisfaction about the new "style" in the White House.

Now it has all been brought into the open, and the First Family, having benefited politically by all the glowing accounts of beauty in the past, is resentful of the opposite opinions.

They should read the history books and relax. Andy Jackson once got into more trouble in 1837 for bringing into the White House a free cheese four feet in diameter, and even Dolley Madison was described as "her majesty." But Dolley was smart. She just turned her pretty face the other way.

July 14, 1961

House Unit Finds Political Aim In Eisenhower's Secrecy Policy

WASHINGTON, July 29 (AP)—House investigators contended today that the Eisenhower Administration had kept certain records secret "for political purposes rather than in defense of the Constitution" in the Presidential campaign last year.

The observation came in a report by the House Government Operations Committee, which also said:

"Secrecy is not the exclusive property of any one political party. Secrecy is the handmaiden of bureaucracy, especially military bureaucracy."

The report covered activities of the Subcommittee on Government Information in the second half of 1960. It discussed a number of episodes already aired in Congress and elsewhere.

It gave special attention to the controversy over public-opinion polls made abroad for the United States Information Agency. These polls became an issue in the Presidential campaign between John F. Kennedy and Richard M. Nixon. Mr. Nixon contended that United States prestige was high. Mr. Kennedy said that it had fallen.

Request Is Turned Down

The Senate Foreign Relations Committee asked for the polls, which, according to unofficial published summaries, cast doubt on Mr. Nixon's contention. The information agency refused on the ground that the polls were staff reports and working papers and therefore were confidential.

The House committee said that this had been a claim of Executive privilege to hide "facts which would refute certain campaign statements."

The report also said:

"The Pentagon attempted to suppress some embarrassing research studies at election time. * * * One such study was withheld for an entire week—and was actually hand delivered the day after the election."

This referred to a research report on the air-raid warning system and one comparing economic growth rates of the United States and the Soviet Union.

Over all, the six months under study for progress in reducing Government secrecy produced a mixed record, the committee reported. It praised a quick turnabout by the Kennedy Administration that resulted in the release of previously withheld foreign-aid information to a subcommittee studying aid operations in Peru.

The report listed what it called both improvements and continued restrictions in the availability of information from July to December, 1960.

Listed among the improvements were these actions:

¶The Air Force made public, after previous refusals, the names of some 800 high-ranking officers designated to receive flight pay without actually flying.

¶Adverse entries were removed from the records of Navy Band members who had made statements after a plane crash in Rio de Janeiro.

...fusal to make public the prices paid for certain jet c....

The Labor Department released administrative decisions on violations of laws covering use of Mexican agricultural workers.

Listed among continued restrictions were there actions:

¶The Agriculture Department refused to make public certain cooperative contracts and minutes of an advisory committee meeting dealing with public land management.

¶The Army announced new helicopter records at an Army Aviation Association banquet, thirteen days after they had been set, and defended the delayed release as facilitating "greater public dissemination."

¶The Labor Department refused to disclose out-of-court settlements of wage-hour violations.

The Federal Aviation Agency was also criticized. While releasing transcripts of air-ground communications before a fatal aircraft accident, it would not permit broadcast of the actual tapes, the committee said.

Kennedy & Press

Since President Franklin D. Roosevelt began receiving groups of newspapermen in his office— usually twice a week — the Presidential news conference has developed into a Washington institution. President Truman held news conferences once a week; President Eisenhower's average was closer to once every two weeks. President Kennedy began at a rate of about once a week but since May has been averaging only one news conference a month.

When he held one last Wednesday a reporter asked why the conferences were not held more often, and whether there was "anything in particular you don't like about them."

"Well," the President replied, "I like them. Sort of." He then gave a reason cited by many a Prime Minister in postponing or turning off "question time" in Parliament. "We are involved in a number of very sensitive matters on the question of Berlin," he said, pointing out that his answers were closely followed not only at home but also abroad. Therefore, he said, "I feel that the schedule as we have had it is in the public interest."

Mr. Kennedy said he probably will return to a weekly schedule when Congress reconvenes in January and the focus of reporters' questions shifts from foreign policy to legislative matters.

November 12, 1961

WHITE HOUSE SEEKS BETTER TV COVERAGE

WASHINGTON, Feb. 8 (UPI) —The White House suggested yesterday to a group of Democratic legislative press aides that they could help encourage fuller television coverage of President Kennedy's news conferences and other appearances.

This occurred at a private meeting between Pierre Salinger, Presidential press secretary, and a group of press secretaries and other assistants serving Democratic Senators of Western states. Mr. Salinger, his assistant, Andrew T. Hatcher, and Mike Manatos and Claude Desautels, White House aides, took part in the briefing.

The press secretaries are loosely organized into a group called the "Demo-Hacks." The group is made up of assistants to Western legislators. It has no officers and no dues.

February 9, 1962

MORE TV COVERAGE OF PRESIDENT URGED

WASHINGTON, Feb. 9 (AP) —Pierre Salinger, White House press secretary, said today he considers it unfortunate that more television and radio stations do not carry President Kennedy's news conferences.

He said he had expressed this many times and had repeated it to a group of press aides and administrative assistants of Western Democratic Senators at a private meeting two days ago in the Capitol.

Reports emerging from that session described Mr. Salinger as suggesting that Congressional aides press for more hometown television coverage of the President to broaden support for Administration programs.

"One of the greatest tempests in a teapot I ever read about," he said of published accounts of the meeting.

He said he had told the Senatorial aides he was sure they received many letters asking why Mr. Kennedy's news conferences were not shown by their local TV and radio stations. He said he recommended that these people be told: "If you don't see the President on your television screen, write a letter to one of the networks or local outlet."

Mr. Salinger said he believed that President Kennedy would hold another news conference next week and that it would be open to simultaneous broadcast by both television and radio "if such a proposition is made to me."

February 10, 1962

SALINGER DENIES TIFF WITH PAPER

Tells Why Herald Tribune Was Dropped by Kennedy

By E. W. KENWORTHY
Special to The New York Times.

WASHINGTON, May 31 — The White House said today that it had canceled its subscriptions to The New York Herald Tribune to "diversify" President Kennedy's reading and not because of any "argument" with that paper.

"If we canceled all papers opposed to the Administration," Pierre Salinger, the White House press secretary, said, "there would be light reading around here."

Mr. Salinger noted that the White House was continuing to receive The Chicago Tribune, "which by no stretch of the imagination can be considered pro-Administration."

Yesterday Mr. Salinger confirmed reports that the White House had canceled last Monday the twenty-two copies of The Herald Tribune it had been receiving and would substitute the same number of copies of The St. Louis Post-Dispatch.

Reasons Are Outlined

In explaining the President's desire for "diversity," Mr. Salinger said that after all "he can read just so many newspapers."

"We get five New York newspapers now and that gives us quite a spread of opinion," he continued. "In fact, the people around here have been reading The Herald Tribune less and less. I suppose if they [The Herald Tribune] say anything significant, someone will ask us about it."

He named the five papers as The New York Times, The Wall Street Journal, The Daily News, The Journal-American and The New York Post.

Although Mr. Salinger insisted that displeasure with The Herald Tribune's editorial comment and news treatment had nothing to do with the cancellation, he said that the "culmination" came May 23 when The Herald Tribune "completely

July 30, 1961

ignored" the stockpile investigation conducted by a Senate subcommittee.

Stockpile Story Cited

On that day Government witnesses testified that in 1956 former Secretary of Commerce Sinclair Weeks and two other officials had decided to let Calumet and Hecla, Inc. "buy out" of a copper contract with the Government. As a consequence, these witnesses contended, the company received a "windfall" gain of $6,338,328.

In New York, a spokesman for the Herald Tribune said that the article did not appear in its City Edition but had been carried in the final edition, both in the page one news digest and on the financial page.

Commenting upon this explanation, Mr. Salinger said that the White House received both the City Edition and the First Late City, and that neither had the stockpiling article.

Statement by Whitney

SEATTLE, May 31 (UPI)— John Hay Whitney, editor in chief and publisher of The Herald Tribune, said tonight that the White House had canceled its subscriptions to his newspaper because the Presidential press secretary, Pierre Salinger, "got a little unhappy about certain pressures."

Mr. Whitney, former United States Ambassador to Britain, was here as United States chairman of the English-Speaking Union in connection with the visit of Prince Philip, Duke of Edinburgh, to the Seattle World's Fair.

Asked about the reasons given by the White House for The Herald Tribune cancellation, Mr. Whitney said:

"To ascribe a reason that the President has time to read just so many newspapers doesn't jibe with the fact that on the Eastern Seaboard The Tribune is the paper everyone is talking about. Our circulation increases have shown that.

"It has become clear to me that Mr. Salinger got a little unhappy about certain pressures and I can understand that, having been a P-R-O [public relations officer] myself. I don't think you can read any more into it that that."

Mr. Whitney was public relations officer for the Eighth Air Force in 1942 and 1943.

TV IS 'BARBARIC,' GOLDWATER SAYS

Senator Turns Critic in Talk to Greek-American Unit

By AUSTIN C. WEHRWEIN

Special to The New York Times.

CHICAGO, Aug. 22—Senator Barry Goldwater, in a new role as a theatre and television critic, said tonight that the Greeks would have had a hard word for American television: barbaric.

The Arizona Republican used ancient Hellenic culture as a standard for rating television in an address to a Greek-American audience.

Your ancestors, he told the Americans of Greek descent, provided a model against which to measure the theatre for all time.

"And what of the modern theatre?" Senator Goldwater asked rhetorically.

"Have you looked at your TV set lately?" he went on, "What wallowing in self-pity! What vast and contorted expressions of emotion over trifling problems! What meaningless violence and meaningless sex!" he declared.

"Comedy has become 'wisecracks,' very clever, sometimes even very witty. But the background of greatness is not there, so the savor, the depth of contrast, is gone. The surprise, the fast switch, the shock have taken its place," he continued.

"Your ancestors would look upon us with pity. To them, we would be truly barbarians," he said.

Minow Comment Recalled

Mr. Goldwater's attack on television was reminiscent of that made by Newton N. Minow, chairman of the Federal Communications Commission, who said it was a "vast wasteland."

The Senator's criticisms were in a context of praise for Greek contribution to civilization generally. Thus, he found Greek art serene, balanced, rational and with a sense of human dignity. By comparison, he said that modern art was often characterized by "confusion and distortion . . . tangled emotions, the cult of the ugly and commonplace . . ."

The Greek theatre, he went on, was created by men who drew the breath of greatness and even their comedies shared that sense.

"In the midst of even the wildest and most whimsical comedy there remained that breath of greatness and of freedom," he said.

"It is no surprise that the greatest writer of Greek comedy—Aristophanes—was also conservative," Senator Goldwater said.

"I wonder what he would have said about the humorless and self-righteous professional reformers of today? I wonder what he would have said about their cult of the common or mediocre man?" he asked.

Role of Tragedy

"Unless there is a belief in the potential greatness of man, there can no longer be tragedy; there can be only melodrama," Mr. Goldwater continued. "When man becomes trivial, tragedy becomes ludicrous. What is more, comedy also becomes a trifling thing—at best witty and clever, never carrying with it hints of the grandeur and depth of the tragic vision which must serve as the necessary vital contrast for truly great comedy.

"I do not believe, in our present social state, dominated as it is by a trivial conception of man—dominated as it is by superficial reformers who expect to save and to protect and to remake man through government action—I do not believe that either great tragedy or great comedy is possible in such an environment," Senator Goldwater declared.

The occasion for the speech was the Grant Banquet of the American Hellenic Educational Progressive Association, which is holding its fortieth annual convention here, in the Sherman House. A total of 25,000 persons are here for the convention, of whom 1,500 were at the dinner.

Others at the dinner included former President Harry S. Truman; Archbishop Iakovas, head of the Greek Orthodox Church of North and South America; Senators Paul H. Douglas, Illinois Democrat and Homer Capehart, Indiana Republican; Greek Ambassador Alexander Matsa, Greek Consul General Stephanas G. Rocanas, and Mayor Richard J. Daley.

NIXON DENOUNCES PRESS AS BIASED

In 'Last' News Conference He Attributes His Defeat to Crisis Over Cuba

BY GLADWIN HILL

Special to The New York Times

BEVERLY HILLS, Calif. Nov. 7—Richard M. Nixon conceded defeat today. He later devoted what many observers regard as the possible valedictory of his national political career to a bitter denunciation of the press.

He also made some acid remarks about his victorious gubernatorial opponent, Gov. Edmund G. Brown, in a statement to about 100 newsmen at the Beverly Hilton Hotel here. The statement was his first public utterance since the election yesterday, which dashed the former Vice President's hopes of a political comeback.

A failure to win his native state had been widely assessed before the election as impairing, probably irreparably, the 49-year-old Republican's viability in national politics.

His defeat came by a vote margin six times as large as the margin by which he carried California in 1960, when he lost the Presidential election to John F. Kennedy. The virtually unanimous opinion of political observers was that the defeat had obliterated the lingering possibility, despite his disclaimers, that he might figure in the Presidential race of 1964.

In his denunciation of the press, Mr. Nixon said to the newsmen today, "You won't have Nixon to kick around any more, because, gentlemen, this is my last press conference."

Mr. Nixon gave no hint of his plans. He has been a partner in a Los Angeles law firm. There has been speculation that he might run for the United States Senate against Senator Clair Engle, Democrat, in 1964.

The defeated candidate renounced any putative leadership of the Republican party in the state, saying that the party would have to be revitalized by others.

Blames Cuban Crisis

Mr. Nixon attributed this defeat principally to the Cuban crisis, which he said had cost his campaign impetus at a critical point. But in his denunciation of the press, he put strong emphasis on the newspapers' asserted failure to report his views fully.

This was an echo of complaints from the Nixon camp after his Presidential defeat in 1960.

Since yesterday afternoon, Mr. Nixon had been in a seventh floor suite of the hotel, scrutinizing election returns.

At 2:30 A. M. local time (5:30 A. M. Eastern Standard time), his press secretary, Herbert G. Klein, told a news conference that Mr. Nixon was going to bed without conceding because uncounted votes from Orange and San Diego counties could well offset a stated Brown advantage of only 90,000 votes at the time.

But within a few hours a margin of about 250,000 was apparent. About 10 A.M. Mr. Nixon sent this telegram to the Democratic Governor:

"Congratulations on your re-election as Governor. I wish you the best in your great honor and opportunity which you now have to lead the first state in the nation."

Changes His Plans

Mr. Klein then hurried downstairs for a news conference, stating that Mr. Nixon would make no appearance. The conference had been under way about 10 minutes when another aide descended to say that Mr. Nixon would appear immediately.

Mr. Nixon reportedly had made a last-minute change in plans, on the way to rejoin Mrs. Nixon and their two teen-age daughters at their home four miles away.

Mr. Nixon looked very tired. His voice quavered at several points in what turned out to be a 15-minute monologue.

He said that newspapers had attacked me" ever since the Alger Hiss case of 1948. He accused reporters of habitually planting articles toward "the candidate they think should win," and suggested, in seeming seriousness, that this was quite proper.

"Thank God we have television to keep our newspapers honest," he remarked.

"Just think how much you're going to be missing—you don't have Nixon to kick around any more," he said. He had opened his remarks with the assertion that "now that all the members of the press are so delighted that I have lost, I'd like to make a statement of my own."

He suggested that newspapers reporting on a future candidate should "give him the shaft," adding. "But if you do, put one lonely reporter on the campaign who will report what the candidate says now and then."

Mr. Nixon commended two of the hundreds of newsmen who have reported his doings. One was Carl Greenberg, of The Los Angeles Times. The other was Edwin Tetlow, New York correspondent of The London Daily Telegraph, who has been in California.

Mr. Nixon said that Mr. Greenberg "wrote every word I said."

"He felt he had an obligation to report the facts as he saw them, no matter how he felt personally," he said.

His denunciation of the press was interspersed with references to other aspects of the campaign.

Twice remarking that he had eschewed "personal considerations" in his contest with Governor Brown, he taxed the Governor with imputing to him "a lack of heart, a lack of patriotism."

"I am proud . . . that I defended the fact that he was a man of good motives," Mr. Nixon went on.

"You gentlemen didn't report it," he said.

"I would appreciate if you would write what I say," he said, adding. "I think it's very important that you write it in the lead," or beginning of a news article.

Governor Brown said later that Mr. Nixon had taken the asserted remarks out of context, "as he did so many other of my statements during the campaign."

The Governor, after watching Mr. Nixon's statement on television at his temporary residence in Los Angeles, was overheard to remark to Mrs. Brown:

"That's something that Nixon's going to regret all his life. The press is never going to let him forget it."

This comment was disseminated by a news agency. While stating that it had not been intended for public consumption, the Governor did not repudiate it. He said he would make no public comment on the Nixon statement.

Briefly referring to the Cuban crisis, Mr. Nixon mentioned speculatively the possibility that there might have been "a deal on NATO and the Warsaw Pact" — inferentially, between President Kennedy and Premier Khrushchev.

However, he said he thought **President Kennedy could deal with the situation adequately if he could just keep away "all of the woolly heads around him."**

Of the national picture, he commented: "I do feel that it is important that the economy get going again."

He said that Republican victories yesterday in New York, Pennsylvania, Ohio and Michigan boded well for the party in 1964.

In his criticism of the press, Mr. Nixon said:

"Among the great papers • • • people say that I should be concerned about—The Louisville Courier, The New York Post, The Milwaukee Journal, The Fresno and The Sacramento Bee—I couldn't be—disagree with that more. • • •

"I would hope that in the future, as a result of this campaign, that perhaps they would try . . . to see that what both candidates say is reported, that if they have questions to ask one candidate they ask the same questions of the other candidate."

Mr. Nixon in his campaign had the editorial support of many more of California's large newspapers than did Governor Brown, the state's press being traditionally heavily Republican.

Transcript of Nixon's Statement

Following is the text of Richard M. Nixon's news conference yesterday in Los Angeles, as recorded by The New York Times through the facilities of the A. B. C. Radio Network:

Good morsing, gentlemen, now that Mr. [Herbe rtG.] Klein [Nixon's press secretary] has made his statement, and now that all the members of the press are so delighted that I have lost, I'd like to make a statement of my own.

I appreciate the press coverage in this campaign. I think each of you covered it the way you saw it. You had to write it in the way according to your velief on how it would go. I don't believe publishers should tell reporters to write one way or another. I want them all to be free. I don't believe the F.C.C. [Federal Communications Commission] or anybody else should silence [word lost in transmission].

I have no complaints about the press coverage. I think each of you was writing it as you believed it.

I congratulate Governor Brown, as Herb Klein has already indicated, for his victory. He has, I think, the greatest honor and the greatest esponsibility of any Governor in the United States.

And if he has this honor and this responsibility, I think that he will now have certainly a position of tremendous interest for America and as well as for the people of California.

I wish him well. I wish him well not only from the personal standpoint, because there were never on my part any personal considerations.

I believe Governor Brown has a heart, even though he believes I do not.

I believe he is a good American, even though he feels I am not.

And therefore, I wish him well because he is the Governor of the first state. He won and I want this state to be led with courage. I want it to be led decisively and I want it to be led, certainly, with the assurance that the man who lost the campaign never during the course of the campaign raised a personal consideration against his opponent — never allowed any words indicating that his opponent was motivated by lack of heart or lack of patriotism to pass his lips.

I am proud of the fact that I defended my opponent's patriotism.

You gentlemen didn't report it, but I am proud that I did that. I am proud also that I defended the fact that he was a man of good motive, a man that I disagreed with very strongly, but a man of good motives.

want that—for once, gentlemen—I would appreci-ate if you would write what I say, in that respect. I think it's very important that you write it—in the lead—in the lead.

Thanks Volunteer Aides

Now, I don't mean by that, incidentally, all of you. There's one reporter here who has religiously, when he was covering me—and incidentally, this is no reflection on the others, because some of you, you know, weren't bothered. One reporter, Carl Greenberg—he's the only reporter on The [Los Angeles] Times that fits this thing, who wrote every word that I said. He wrote it fairly. He wrote it objectively.

I don't mean that others didn't have a right to do it differently. But Carl, despite whatever feelings he had, felt that he had an obligation to report the facts as he saw them

I am saying these things about the press because I understood that that was one of the things you were particularly interested in. There'll be no questions at this point on that score. I'll be glad to answer other questions.

Now, above everything else I want to express my appreciation to our volunteer workers.

It was a magnificent group. Five hundred thousand dollars was spent, according to Newsweek Magazine, to get out the vote on Election Day. They had a right to do that if they could get the money. We didn't have that kind of money. But, believe me, we had wonderful spirit.

And our 100,000 volunteer workers I was proud of. I think they did a magnificent job, I only wish they could have gotten out a few more votes in the key precincts, but becauset hey didn't Mr. Brown has won and I have lost the election.

I'd like to say a word nationally. I know that some of you are interested in that. I have not been able to appraise the results for the Congress because not enough of them are in.

I only understand that we approximately broke even. Is that correct — in the Congress?

Well, at least that's what I have. Do you have a report on the Congress—any of you It's about even?

Q.—The Democrats picked up some. A.—They picked up some

Q.—Some in the Senate and —A.—Oh, I know in the Senate they did. Yeah, Bob, I understood that, but in the House, I understand we picke up five in the House. We can't tell, because California isn't in on that yet.

Notes Rockefeller Victory

Well, the most significant result of this election was what happened in four major states: Rockefeller's victory in New York, Scranton's victory in Pennsylvania, Rhodes victory in Ohio, Romney's victory in Michigan—means that in 1964 the Republican party will eb revitalized.

Now, it will be revitalized, of course, provided the Republicans in California also can under new leadership — not mine—because I have fought the fight and now it's up to others to take this responsibility of leadership, and I don't say this with any bitterness, because I just feel that that's the way it should be.

But the Republican party under new leadership in California needs a new birth of spirit, a new birth of unity, because we must carry California in '64, if we are to carry the nation.

But when you look at New York and Pennsylvania, Ohio and Michigan and the solid Republican Midwest, 1964 is a horse race.

I say this with no indication that I don't think that President Kennedy has immense popularity at the moment—popularity which came out as a result of his handling of the Cuban situation.

But, on the other hand, now the problem s arise: what will happen in Cuba? Can we allow this cancer of Communism to stay there? Is there a deal with regard to NATO? Is there going to be with regard to NATO and the Warsaw pact? Are we going to continue any kind of an agreement in Cuba, which means that Khrushchev got what we said we would never agree to before he made his threat with regard to his missiles and that is, in effect, ringing down an Iron Curtain around Cuba?

These are the things that Mr. Kennedy, of course, will have to face up to, and I just hope — and I'm confident that if he has his own way he will face up to them, if he can only get those who opposed atomic tests, who want him to admit Red China to the U. N., all of the woolly heads around him — if he can just keep them away from him and stand strong and firm with that good Irish fight of his, America will be in good shape in foreign policy.

'America Has Got to Move'

Domestically — I'm answering these questions because I know that some of you will ask them — Domestically, the economy needs to get going again. The Cuban thing, of course, has had a tendency to obscure that. A lot of defense contracts have come into California and

other areas. 'Im not complaining about it. That's the way the political game is played.

But I do feel that it is important that the economy get going again and I trust that through tax reform or some other device, relying on individual enterprise and individual opportunity, that the economy will get going again.

To me, more important than anything else, America has got to move now. It's got to move forward economically, with productivity. It's got to move forward — I'll say it in the presence of my good friend from Britain here—Ed Tetlow [of The London Telegraph]—it's got to move forward relying on individual enterprise and individual opportunity.

One last thing: What are my plans? Well, my plans are to go home. I' mgoing to get acquainted with my family again. And my plans, incidentally, are, from a political standpoint, of course, fo take a holiday. It will be a long holiday. I don't say this with any sadness. I couldn't feel, frankly, more —well, frankly, proud of my staff for the campaign they helped me to put on. We campaigned against great odds. We fought a good fight. We didn't win. And I take the responsibility for any mistakes. As far as they're concerned, they're magnificent people, and I hope whoever next runs in California will look at my staff and take some of these people—use them — because they are — they're great political properties, shall we say, putting it in the — in a very materialistic way.

Has No Hard Feelings

One last thing: People say, What about the past? What about losing in '60 and losing IN '64? I remember somebody on my last television program said, "Mr. Nixon, isn't it a comedown, having run for President, and almost made it, to run for Governor?" And the answer is I'm proud to have run for Governor. Now, I would have liked to have won. But, not having won, the main thing was that I battled — battled for the things I believed in.

I did not win. I have no hard feelings against anybody, against my opponent, and least of all the people of California. We got our message through as well as we could. The Cuban thing did not enable us to get it through in the two critical weeks that we wanted to, but nevertheless we got it through, and it is the people's choice.

They have chosen Mr. Brown. They have chosen his leadership, and I can only hope that that leadership will

now become more decisive, that it will move California ahead and, so that America can move ahead — economically, morally and spiritually —so that we can have character and self-reliance in this we need. This is what we need to move forward.

One last thing. At the outset, I said a couple of things with regard to the press that I noticed some of you looked a little irritated about. And my philosophy with regard to the press has really never gotten through. And I want to get it through.

This cannot be said for any other American political figure today, I guess. Never in my 16 years of campaigning have I complained to a publisher, to an editor, about the coverage of a reporter. I believe a reporter has got a right to write it as he feels it. I believe if a reporter believes that one man ought to win rather than the other, whether it's on television or radio or the like, he ought to say so. I will say to the reporter, sometimes that I think well, look, I wish you'd give my opponent the same going over that you give me.

Gives Views on Press

And as I leave the press, all I can say is this: For 16 years, ever since the Hiss case, you've had a lot of fun — a lot of fun — tnat youzve had an opportunity too attack me and I think I've given as good as I've taken. It was carried right up to the last day.

I made a talk on television, a talk in which I made a flub — one of the few that I make, not because I'm so good on television but because I've done it a long time. I made a flub in which I said I was running for Governor of the United States. The Los Angeles Times dutifully reported that.

Mr. Brown the last day made a flub — a flub, incidentally, to the great credit of television that ws reported —I don't say this bitterly—in which he said, "I hope everybody wins. You vote the straight Democratic ticket, including Senator Kuchel." I was glad to hear him say it, because I was for Kuchel all the way. The Los Angeles Times did not report it.

I think that it's time that our great newspapers have at least the same objectivity, the same fullness of coverage, that television has. And I can only say thank God for television and radio for keeping the newspapers a little more honest.

Now, some newspapers don't fall in the category to which I have spoken, but I can only say that the great metropolitan newspapers in this field, they have a right

to take every position they want on the editorial page, but on the news page they also have a right to have reporters cover men who have strong feelings whether they're for or against a candidate. But the responsibility also is to put a few Greenbergs on, on the candidate they happen to be against, whether they're against him on the editorial page or just philosophically deep down, a fellow who at least will report what the man says.

That's all anybody can ask. But apart from that I just want to say this:

Among the great papers in this country that the people say that I should be concerned about—The Lousiville Courier, The New York Post, The Milwaukee Journal, The Fresno and The Sacramento Bee—I couldn't be—disagree with that more. I want newspapers. If they're against a candidate I want them to say it.

I believe they should say it. I don't mind reporters saying it. I would hope that in the future, as a result of this campaign, that perhaps they would try at least simply to see that what both candidates say is reported, that if they have questions to ask of one candidate they ask the same questions of the other candidate.

The last play. I leave you gentlemen now and you will now write it. You will interpret it. That's your right. But as I leave you I want you to know — just think how much you're going to be missing.

You won't nave Nixon to kick around any more, because, gentlemen, this is my last press conference and it will be one in which I have welcomed the opportunity to test wits with you9I have always respected you. I have sometimes disagreed with you.

But, unlike some people, I've never canceled a subscription to a paper and also I never will.

I believe in reading what my opponents say and I hope that what I have said today will at least make television, radiop the press first recognize the great responsibility they have to report all the news and, second, recognize that they have a right and a responsibility, if they're against a candidate, give him the shaft, but also recognize if they give him the shaft put one lonely reporter on the campaign who will report what the candidate says now and then.

Washington

Richard Nixon's Farewell A Tragic Story

By JAMES RESTON

WASHINGTON, Nov. 8 — There is an element of tragedy in Richard Nixon's farewell. Two years ago he was within 100,000 votes of the American Presidency and today, unelected and unmourned, he is an unemployed lawyer in Los Angeles. No wonder he slammed the door as he went out.

The British do it better. They find a "safe seat" in Parliament for the defeated leader of a party, and, being sensitive to human frailty, pass him along in later years to the dignity of the House of Lords.

Our politics are more savage. The gap between victory and defeat is almost too wide. The winner gets more than he can handle and the loser more than he can bear. We put them in the White House before they are ready and retire them before they are ripe.

It was this system that produced Nixon in the beginning and destroyed him in the end. He came to power too early and retired too soon. He mastered the techniques of politics before he mastered the principles, and ironically it was this preoccupation with techniques that both brought him forward and cast him down.

Dick Nixon got into national politics by using his bad qualities rather than his good qualities—of which he has many—against Jerry Voorhees and Helen Gahagan Douglas, and he reached almost to the pinnacle of our national life at least partly by accident.

For he came along at a time when the Republicans happened to be looking for a Vice-Presidential candidate who could symbolize "youth," the growth of the West, and anti-Communism. This was what the system required in 1952 as a running mate for Eisenhower—this and Nixon's political skill to back up Ike's lack of political experience. So he was nominated and elected, and then another ironical thing happened.

Like most Americans who reach the top councils of their Government, he grew up with the job and used his good qualities in the performance of it, but the job itself dragged him back into the political arena. To Eisenhower, who didn't like political rallies until he retired, Nixon was the Vice President in charge of the party. He was the point of the Republican spear, always tilting with the opposition in the exaggerated rhetoric of the political wars, and inevitably this pugnacious and aggressive role perpetuated his reputation as the symbol of everything that is harsh and devious in American political life.

Maybe this had something to do with his defeat in 1962. Maybe it was merely his appearance. Yet there was something else: the American people will put an aggressive district attorney type into almost any office. But the Presidency, they seem to feel, requires that power be tempered by wisdom and even by mercy, and these were certainly not his most obvious qualities. See, also, Tom Dewey.

What was most obvious about Nixon particularly to the press, those recorders of the obvious, was his preoccupation with the machinery of politics. Everything seemed to be contrived, even the appearance of naturalness. He attacked planning but planned everything. He seemed bold and elaborately objective in public, but in private seemed less composed, even uneasy and disturbingly introspective.

This was the root of his trouble with the reporters: not that they were refusing to report what he said but that they were insisting on reporting all the rest of the picture—not only the words but the techniques, not only the public posture but the private posture, not only the lines of the play but the elaborate stage directions.

Always here in Washington there was this terrible feeling among reporters that seemed to come out only in flashes in private or under pressure in public—that there was a vast difference between appearance and reality and that it was important, maybe even important to the nation, to try to define which was which.

Even in his farewell address, he insisted on taking responsibility for "any mistakes" in the campaign, and then blamed his "magnificent" staff for blowing the election. Similarly, he said he "respected" the reporters while accusing them of betraying their responsibility.

News and Truth

No public figure of our time has ever studied the reporters so much or understood them so little. He thought the reporter should merely be a transmission belt for what he said, not of why he said it. Like the cigarette man, he insisted that "It's what's up front that counts," while the reporter, constantly haunted by the feeling that he might deceive the reader merely by reporting the carefully rehearsed lines in the play, insisted on recording what was going on back stage.

Nixon always resented this. He never seemed to understand the difference between news and truth. To him what he said was "news" and should be left there.

Maybe he was right. It could be that the "real Nixon" was the one on stage, but that is beyond journalism now and will have to be left to the historians and the psychological novelists.

November 9, 1962

ROCKEFELLER SEES THREATS TO NEWS

Administration Intimidates 2 Reporters, He Says

By JOSEPH A. LOFTUS
Special to The New York Times

FRENCH LICK, Ind., Oct. 11 —Governor Rockefeller implied today that the Kennedy Administration had not only manipulated the news but also had tried to intimidate newsmen.

He cited two instances to support his contention.

The New York Governor, on his way to a Republican conference in Eugene, Ore., where he and Senator Barry Goldwater of Arizona are to speak on the same day, stopped for a luncheon talk to the Indiana Bar Association.

His speech carried a strong political flavor.

Mr. Rockefeller told of "a national news correspondent of long experience who was importantly responsible for making the Billie Sol Estes scandal into national news."

"He reports the following," the Governor declared, "that he had gone to the Attorney General's office to ask several questions in relation to the case; that the Attorney General, with the chief of the Criminal Division present, berated and quizzed the reporter for most of one hour about incidents in his own career; and that during the interrogation, the Attorney General leafed through pages of what appeared to be a lengthy investigation report about the newsman, which he had on his desk in front of him."

"The correspondent construed this as a calculated effort at intimidation," Mr. Rockefeller said.

The newsman in question is reported to be Earl Mazo, national political correspondent of The New York Herald Tribune, who is now on leave.

As a second example, the Governor spoke of another newsman — presumably Victor Lasky—who, he said, "has publicly stated that he received information that a Justice Department official made inquiry of the Senate Internal Security subcommittee to see what information about the author the subcommittee had in its files."

Mr. Lasky, a freelance writer, is author of the recently published "J. F. K.: The Man and the Myth."

Mr. Rockefeller's speech was built on the theme that administrative agencies in Government today have such vast power that great restraint and discretion are needed. He said:

"The awesome array of powers in the hands of our Federal Government, indeed, by its very presence, may produce intimidation, and, in unthinking or unscrupulous hands, it can result in retaliation or manipulation."

Mazo Recalls Incident
Special to The New York Times

ISLE OF PALMS, S. C., Oct. 11—Earl Mazo, national political correspondent of The New York Herald Tribune, recalled today the incident that Governor Rockefeller cited as an example of attempted intimidation of reporters by Attorney General Robert F. Kennedy.

Mr. Mazo is on leave from his newspaper to write a book on political polling.

He said that in July, 1962, after returning to Washington from Texas, where he had written about the Billie Sol Estes scandal, he obtained an interview with the Attorney General.

Mr. Mazo said that after Mr. Kennedy answered his few questions the Attorney General berated him for about an hour over his handling of the story.

"The Attorney General called me names and I called him names," Mr. Mazo declared.

"It seemed funny at first," he continued. "But there was something frightening about it. It was a clear attempt at intimidation. He introduced the man sitting with him as head of the department's Criminal Division and they kept referring to a big report they had and asking me questions."

Mr. Mazo said his experience was only one of several in which Washington correspondents felt that attempts were made to influence their reporting through intimidation by the Attorney General.

October 12, 1963

PRESIDENT IS HOST ON TOUR AT RANCH

Johnson Phones Christmas Greetings to Eisenhower, Truman and Hoover

By TOM WICKER
Special to The New York Times

AUSTIN, Tex., Dec. 25 — President Johnson delayed Christmas dinner for 23 guests today while he gave reporters a fast tour of the LBJ Ranch house, distributed souvenir ashtrays, and announced a new executive order to reduce Government employment.

He also found time in a busy day to put in Christmas calls to former Presidents Dwight D. Eisenhower, Harry S. Truman and Herbert Hoover. General Eisenhower is in Palm Springs, Calif., and Mr. Truman and Mr. Hoover are in New York.

What started as a brief picture-taking session on the President's front lawn turned into an hour-long scramble. It was partly a news conference, partly a tour of the 100-year-old main house at the ranch and partly a monologue by Mr. Johnson.

The turkey cooled, the guests waited and Mrs. Johnson made the best of it.

The President showed his art collection, discussed Government business, handed out ashtrays, introduced his relatives, talked about the cattle business and his land holdings, posed for photographers and turned on the outdoor sound system.

President Is Undeterred

Mrs. Johnson had planned to open her house to reporters on Friday. Today it was full of family and friends.

That did not deter Mr. Johnson as he invited in the large group of reporters.

"It won't take but a minute," he told his wife.

Mrs. Johnson replied, somewhat ominously, "Whatever you say, darling."

A few minutes later, Mr. Johnson led the news group to the bedroom door. It wouldn't open.

"Mrs. Johnson's locked the bedroom on me," the President said. Then he knocked harder.

Mrs. Johnson was smiling gamely when she opened the door.

Mr. Johnson identified a portrait of Senator Stuart Symington, Democrat of Missouri, as "Lady Bird's boy friend."

The President seized a somewhat hectic occasion to announce unofficially that he was sending an order to the heads of all agencies and departments. It contained the information that Government employment would be reduced in the next fiscal year, beginning July 1.

There has not been a decline in a decade, Mr. Johnson said, noting that in the last three years Federal employment rose by 131,000 jobs.

The order told the agency heads, however, that even the reductions that had been made were not good enough. Further efforts were asked and each agency and department head was instructed to make quarterly progress reports beginning next April.

Some agencies, Mr. Johnson said, have eliminated thousands of jobs. But he gave no total for the reduction in prospect.

The text of the order was issued later by the White House.

Confers on Cyprus

Mr. Johnson also said he had conferred "two or three times" by telephone with Secretary of State Dean Rusk on the situation in Cyprus. Fighting has broken out there between the Greek and Turkish populations.

Noting that there were about 1,700 American citizens in Cyprus, the President said that the Government was "watching very carefully" the developments there. He recalled that he had visited the island last year, at the request of President Kennedy, and said he was keeping "in constant touch" with the situation.

It was a busy Christmas Day for the President, who was relaxed, informal and obviously happy to be back on his home grounds.

He arose at 6 A.M. and went with a friend and fellow rancher, Judge A. W. Moursund, to inspect and feed the LBJ Ranch herd of about 100 thoroughbred Herefords. Mr. Johnson had not previously seen some of his newest stock.

See Many Deer on Trip

Later, he and Mrs. Johnson rode with Judge Moursund around some other Johnson land holdings to look at beef cattle and other livestock. They also saw lots of the deer that abound here, the President said.

"We've seen a lot of deer but we haven't killed one yet," Mr. Johnson said.

The morning was so busy that the traditional breakfast of deer-meat sausage and hominy grits was skipped. "We'll have that when Mr. Erhard's here," Mrs. Johnson said, referring to the two-day visit this weekend of Chancellor Ludwig Erhard of West Germany.

The Johnsons also took flowers to a Lutheran church nearby, and their two daughters attended services there.

The President and his wife visited several neighbors and found time for a traditional Texas rite, a land deal.

Takes Rolls to Sorensen

Mr. Johnson concluded a lease this morning for several acres of what he called "stomping ground" across the state highway that runs along the front of his ranch. The purpose was apparently to make room for some of the extra security and tourist-handling arrangements that will be necessary now that Mr. Johnson has become President.

The President also visited Clear Lake Ranch, a nearby property where Theodore C. Sorensen, a White House aide, and his sons will be quartered for a few days during the Christmas holidays. He took over stocks of tomato juice, sweet rolls and hot rolls, Mr. Johnson said.

Mr. Sorensen will be here to work with the President on the State of the Union Message that Mr. Johnson is scheduled to deliver to a joint session of Congress next Jan. 8.

Mr. Johnson said he had "got off a few memos" on that speech in his spare time today. He wanted to include in it, he said, some "factual and specific" material on the budget and other economic matters, the sort of material that might ordinarily go into the Economic Message later.

The budget and Government spending were still apparently occupying him more than any other issue. The President said he had been up last night until after midnight, when he "finalized" the order on Government employment that was issued today.

Mrs. Johnson Wears Red

It was a beautiful, clear day, with temperatures in the 60s and 70s, when two busloads of reporters and photographers arrived at the LBJ Ranch.

At 2:20 P.M., Mr. and Mrs. Johnson and their daughters came out of the house for a picture-taking session on the front lawn.

Mrs. Johnson wore a red suit and jacket with a pearl necklace. Lynda Bird Johnson wore a red dress—a Finnish version of the shift, the President explained. Lucy Baines Johnson was in a white suit with red trim.

Mr. Johnson wore a green checked jacket, khaki trousers and yellow, tooled-leather Western boots with low heels.

Four peahens strutted on the lawn around the first family as the cameras began to click. Perched on a large air-conditioned jutting from a window of the house was a spectacular peacock, with blue breast and crest.

Mrs. Johnson said she hoped the reporters were enjoying the warm Texas weather and the President added: "I hope we can have this kind of weather for Mr. Erhard."

Menu Is Described

This started a running conversation that was to go on for more than 50 minutes. Mrs.

Johnson told of the turkey and cornbread, dressing on the Christmas menu. Mr. Johnson recounted the day's activities and talked about the budget, and both tossed off historical lore about the ranch and the Johnson family.

Then Mr. Johnson sent an aide running into the house for the text of his order on Government employment, and discussed it for a few minutes.

"How big is the total reduction in Federal employment?" asked Garrett D. Horner of The Washington Star.

"Isn't it just enough that we cut it, Mr. Horner?" the President asked, smiling. "You don't know how hard that was."

He was asked what he would do tomorrow.

"I hope Jack Valenti [an aide] gets back here and gets me up at 6:30," Mr. Johnson said.

"I hope not," Mrs. Johnson broke in.

The President said that his old friend, former Gov. Buford Ellington of Tennessee, would arrive at the ranch so he, the President, could "get his counsel on a good many national problems."

Family Is Introduced

Some of those problems, he said, grinning broadly, might be discussed with Governor Ellington "over the carcass of a deer."

Then Mr. Johnson called members of his family and friends from the house to pose for photographs and introduced them individually.

"Uncle Huffman," he said to Huffman Baines, "how old are you?"

"I don't know," Uncle Huffman replied forthrightly.

"He's 79 and looks 59," the President said.

When he introduced his aunt, Mrs. Jessie Hatcher, he recalled that "I was in her dining room when I announced I was going to run for Congress in 1937."

Then it was the turn of his cousin, Mrs. Oriole Bailey, who lives "just down the road." Cousin Oriole, Mr. Johnson said, kept the family "physically fit," because they frequently walked down to visit her.

When the President introduced Bernard Rosenbach, Lynda Bird Johnson's fiancé, as a Navy ensign, Lynda Bird interrupted to say that Mr. Rosenbach had just been made a lieutenant junior grade.

"Can I say where he's going?" the President asked.

"If you can't, who can?" Lynda replied.

"He's going back to his destroyer and going to Cuba—Guantanamo," the President said.

Then he turned his attention to Lucy Baines Johnson.

"Lucy's boy friend hasn't arrived yet," he said, "but he's on the way from Wisconsin. I mean, one of her boy friends."

Shows Pride in Ranch

Throughout the introductions and picture-taking, Mr. Johnson displayed his obvious pride in the ranch that has been in his family for a century and that he and Mrs. Johnson bought from an aunt in 1951. He pointed out the 300-year-old live oaks on the front lawn and lamented the disappearance of a grove of pecan trees, washed away in a flood of the Pedernales River.

The river runs between the ranch house and the highway about 100 yards from Mr. Johnson's front porch.

Of the old house itself, originally a stone fort but since converted into a spacious two-story house primarily of white clapboard, the President commented:

"There's a big fireplace in there that they [his ancestors] cooked in. Every time they made some calves and sold some cotton crop, they added on to the house."

Notes Houston Letter

Despite Mrs. Johnson's anxiety to get on with her Christmas dinner, the President then led the reporters and photographers through the House. He pointed out a framed copy of a letter from Sam Houston to his great-grandfather; a desk that may have been used by Thomas Jefferson and formerly belonged to the late Senator Arthur H. Vandernberg, Republican of Michigan; an ornate saddle given him by President Adolfo Lopez Mateos of Mexico, and breeding certificates for two prize Tennessee walking horses.

When photographers started to take pictures of the Jefferson-Vandenberg desk, Mr. Johnson stopped them.

"Don't take pictures of the desk," he said. "There's some Secret Secret documents on there."

He seemed particularly proud of the many oil paintings he has collected and that hang in the ranch house. Two of them were by Porfirio Salinas, the well-known landscapist from San Antonio. One, showing a cactus in bloom, led Mr. Johnson into a discourse on how cactus can be converted into low-protein food for cattle.

Over the stone fireplace in his office, where the family Christmas tree was surrounded

with piles of gifts, there hangs a portrait of Mr. Johnson by Gilbert Palmie. Mr. Johnson described Mr. Palmie as a friend of "Senator [Richard B.] Russell and Senator [Herman] Talmadage," both Democrats of Georgia.

In the attractive dining room, from which a large picture window looks out over the rangeland, places were laid for 28 persons. A large armchair marked the President's place.

After the house tour, Mr. Johnson showed the reporters his "friendship walk," leading to a swimming pool that he said he designed while recovering from a heart attack in 1955. On each stone of the friendship walk, some famous visitor had scratched his name, including 'John F. Kennedy, 1960.'

The President also made it plain that the LBJ Ranch had 400 acres, not the 5,000 sometimes reported, although he conceded that he and Mrs. Johnson together owned or leased more than 4,000 acres.

The late Speaker Sam Rayburn once visited the LBJ Ranch, Mr. Johnson said, and delivered the following judgment: "I thought it was a big ranch and it's just a little old farm." Mr. Johnson dispatched an aide to bring him several boxes of souvenir ashtrays, inscribed with his signature, that he purchased in Norway last fall. He passed out one to each of the news group.

Then he asked Lynda Bird: "You know where to turn on the Muzak over there?"

Lynda Bird did, and swing music suddenly boomed from a huge live oak, wired for sound.

As the reporters were returning to their buses, Mr. Johnson began picking up several paper wrappers that had fallen to his lawn. The ashtrays had been wrapped in them.

Then, from his porch, he called out one last piece of information.

"If any of you are the faintest bit interested," he shouted, pointing, "you can go over there and see the loading pens. That's where the cattle go out and the money comes in."

Advertising: The Political Campaign Trail

By PETER BART

The politicians have put in a busy week marshaling support on Madison Avenue.

The Democratic National Committee held discussions with two agencies — Kenyon & Eckhardt, Inc., and Doyle Dane Bernbach, Inc. — and is expected to announce its choice within a few days. Kenyon & Eckhardt, incidentally, held discussions with the Republicans prior to the 1960 campaign but did not become their agency.

The Democratic party may channel between $2 million and $3 million through its agency during the forthcoming Presidential election.

While the Democrats were making up their minds, Senator Barry M. Goldwater decided to appoint Fuller & Smith & Ross, Inc., to handle his advertising during the campaign for the Republican nomination.

The Arizonan's campaign will involve a "substantial" amount of money, according to one source.

Rockefeller's Plans

Governor Rockefeller has not as yet named an agency to handle his campaign, but is expected to do so a short time after the New Hampshire primary.

The official agency of the Republican National Committee is the Leo Burnett Company of Chicago. The Republicans traditionally used Batten, Barton, Durstine & Osborne, Inc., during Presidential campaigns, but they retained the Burnett agency a year ago because of its "grass-roots approach."

The Democratic National Committee used Guild, Bascom & Bonfigli, Inc., in 1960 and Norman, Craig & Kummel, Inc., in 1956. On both occassions the account supervisor was Miss Reggie Scheubel.

Miss Scheubel, now a vice president at Gumbinner-North, Inc., plans to sit this campaign out.

More Style, Less News at Johnson's Conference

By HENRY RAYMONT
Special to The New York Times

WASHINGTON, March 7—A friendlier and more relaxed atmosphere prevailed today at President Johnson's second news conference to be televised and broadcast live to the nation.

The President decided to have it this way after his first such effort, a week ago today, was criticized both for its setting and for his constrained performance.

Mr. Johnson's mood, the sunfilled, elegant East Room of the White House and a glorious spring day combined to make it his best news conference thus far. From a stylistic point of view, that is.

For as far as news is concerned, it was less productive than last week's meeting in the impersonal, airless International Conference Room of the State Department.

The East Room is the ballroom of the White House. Today's Presidential news conference was believed to be the first ever held there.

3 Hours' Notice

It was Mr. Johnson's seventh news conference. As with most of the others, there was little advance notice. Pierre Salinger, White House press secretary, made known at 12:15 P.M. that it would be held at 3:30.

Mr. Johnson walked into the East Room at a brisk pace, smiling at some 120 assembled newsmen and looking at ease. His daughter Lynda Bird, wearing a bright red cotton dress, followed him and sat down in the back row of chairs among the newsmen.

The conference began promptly at 3:30 and lasted 29 minutes.

The President stood behind a lectern. He spoke far more rapidly than usual in clipped sentences that curbed his Texas drawl and made for a livelier meeting.

At the State Department last week, Mr. Johnson remained seated and looked uncomfortable. His answers were generally long and sounded apathetic.

Today, flanked by life-sized paintings of President and Mrs.

December 26, 1963

February 21, 1964

Washington, Mr. Johnson concentrated on improving his news conference style.

The President spent the first nine minutes announcing 43 appointments and reading a buoyant account of the state of the economy following the enactment of the tax cut. With obvious satisfaction, he also read a report of his efforts to give women a more prominent role in the Government.

Fittingly, it fell to Helen Thomas of United Press International to open and close the question period. The President also recognized four other women reporters.

To forestall any criticism that the President might be deliberately taking up time with prepared statements, Mr. Salinger had previously announced that the conference could go on well beyond the usual half hour.

But Miss Thomas, after taking note of the diminishing number of raised arms, decided to call out "Thank you, Mr. President" a minute before 4.

Of 25 questions, 9 dealt with international issues and 16 with domestic politics and economic matters.

Eye On November

The President's replies reinforced the belief that as a natural politician his main enthusiasm and energies are dedicated to the national scene and to a Democratic victory next November.

In his longest and most detailed answer he gave an exposition of how he hopes to reduce the budget deficit by more than 50 per cent and still ask for $500 million for his fight against poverty.

Without referring to notes he ticked off budget figures for his programs for education, urban renewal and Appalachia.

His replies on such foreign policy issues as the war in South Vietnam and relations with France and the Soviet Union were generally repetitions of statements made yesterday by Secretary of State Dean Rusk.

When the conference ended, the President looked as relaxed and friendly as when he walked in. There was none of the self-conscious quality of a screen test that many observers detected in his first televised news meeting.

Before he left the East Room, Mr. Johnson shook hands with several reporters. He then went to the White House swimming pool for a dip.

White House aides said that Mr. Johnson's news conferences were still in an experimental stage and that the President might test other rooms before he settles on a permanent home for the meetings.

March 8, 1964

Democrats Choose Doyle Dane

By PETER BART

Doyle Dane Bernbach, Inc., will be the official advertising agency for the Democratic National Committee during the 1964 Presidential campaign, reliable sources said yesterday. Neither the committee nor the agency would comment on the report.

Selection of Doyle Dane Bernbach followed several weeks of intensive negotiations with several agencies — negotiations that took some unexpected twists and turns.

At one point, Kenyon & Eckhardt, Inc., expressed interest in the $2.5 million account, only to withdraw amid rumors of client pressure. Doyle Dane Bernbach entered the picture, but then reportedly withdrew after a difference of opinion with certain Democratic negotiators.

The Democrats then started negotiating with Grant Advertising, Inc., but those negotiations broke off last week.

Doyle Dane Bernbach is widely regarded as a leading creative agency on Madison Avenue. Its billings have soared from $5 million to $76 million over the last decade, and its leading clients include Volkswagen, Avis, Inc., the H. J. Heinz Company and the French Government Tourist Office.

The Republicans already have appointed an agency for the coming elections — Leo Burnett Company of Chicago. Senator Barry Goldwater recently chose Fuller & Smith & Ross, Inc., as his agency. Governor Nelson Rockefeller has not yet officially named an agency. McCann-Marschalk, Inc., has represented him in the past and is thought to be the leading contender.

March 20, 1964

PERSONAL POLITICAL PANACEAS HIT TV

By ARNOLD H. LUBASCH

NEWS interview programs are a necessity for politicians seeking national office, political candidates are a necessity for interview programs in a Presidential election year, and the logical result is a profusion of candidates broadcasting their personal prescriptions to cure the nation's infinite ills.

Each of the three major television networks has a regular Sunday interview show, with "Meet the Press" on the National Broadcasting Company, "Face the Nation" on the Columbia Broadcasting System and "Issues and Answers" on the American Broadcasting Company.

They are now featuring interviews with announced candidates, unannounced candidates, potential candidates, perennial candidates, hopeful candidates, hopeless candidates and the bountiful breed known as dark-horse candidates.

Drag Race

American political lore demands that a candidate for the White House must be a humble, unpretentious, reluctant champion of the people who has to be dragged into the Presidential race against his own will and wishes.

As a result, reluctant candidates with well-cultivated humility complexes are being dragged into broadcasting studios each Sunday to proclaim their lack of candidacy, if not their lack of candor, to prospective voters from coast to coast.

Prominent Republican contenders who have already appeared on all three interview programs, or are scheduled to complete the circle soon, include Gov. William W. Scranton of Pennsylvania, Gov. George Romney of Michigan, Senator Margaret Chase Smith of Maine, Senator Barry Goldwater of Arizona and Gov. Nelson A. Rockefeller of New York.

Former Vice President Richard M. Nixon and Ambassador Henry Cabot Lodge, the 1960 Republican candidates, have not made themselves available lately for quizzing by the network interviewers, but they are likely to do so when they feel this will most enhance their 1964 Presidential prospects.

On the Democratic side of the television screen, with President Johnson assured of the top nomination, the Vice Presidential hopefuls appearing on the interview shows include Senator Hubert H. Humphrey of Minnesota, Sargent Shriver, the Peace Corps director, and Adlai E. Stevenson, the chief United States representative to the United Nations.

Stevenson announced his readiness to accept the Vice Presidential nomination when he replied to a question by Lawrence E. Spivak on "Meet the Press" last December.

The impact and importance of the interview programs were stressed by Spivak, the "Meet the Press" producer and permanent panelist, who is noted for his persistent and probing questions. Asserting that his program strives to dig deeply, not to put anyone on the spot, Spivak observed that a show of this kind would destroy itself quickly if it were not fair and responsible.

The late President Kennedy, who appeared on "Meet the Press" eight times from young Congressman to Presidential candidate, is regarded by Spivak as the most effective and responsive guest ever interviewed on the program.

In a 1960 speech, while campaigning across the country for the Presidency, Kennedy indicated his regard for "Meet the Press" by referring to it as "the 51st state."

Statements made on the program are credited with launching the boom for Gen. Dwight D. Eisenhower and the draft for the then Governor Stevenson of Illinois that resulted in their selection as the Republican and Democratic candidates for President in 1952.

After his defeat by General Eisenhower, Governor Stevenson encountered Spivak at a dinner, pointed an accusing finger at the producer-panelist and said, "You got me into all that trouble."

The co-producers of "Face the Nation" said recently, "Our aim is to figure out where the most news lies and to pursue that path as directly as we can, so we can be lively and fast-moving without trying to provoke a guest." According to the "Issues and Answer" producer, Peggy Whedon, timing is especially important because a successful interview depends on presenting the right guest at the appropriate time to make the most news.

"Issues and Answers" is now in its fourth year with Howard K. Smith and a pair of A.B.C. correspondents taking turns on alternating Sundays in a format that strives for an atmosphere of intimate and dramatic discussion.

"A producer has to live cuddled up to the wire services and employ network spies," says Mrs. Whedon.

April 12, 1964

Washington

How to Pick Up Votes Without Politics

By JAMES RESTON

WASHINGTON, April 16—The best politics for a President in the early stages of an election campaign are no politics, and President Johnson has clearly mastered the art of the non-political appeal.

He spent two minutes of his press conference today explaining that he thought he should avoid politics until the nominating conventions, and the other 28 minutes politicking all over national television.

Is prosperity a good campaign theme? He made the country sound rich beyond the dreams of avarice. Isn't everybody against unemployment and inflation? He denounced them as the enemies of mankind and rattled off figures to prove they were in retreat.

Work for the working man, profits for the investor, stable prices for the consumer, help for the aged and the needy, equality at long, long last for the Negro, higher wages for the embattled bureaucrat—this was his highly political non-political catalogue of promises and hopes.

Probably the President didn't think he was playing politics today. He doesn't have to think about it: He just does it naturally, as a bird flies or a fish swims.

Jokes From Johnson?

Knowing the American Society of Newspaper Editors was in town, he invited the whole gang to a press conference. Knowing, too, that some of them had been saying he could never play the question and answer game as well as President Kennedy, he staged the show in Kennedy's State Department Auditorium, and even started off with a couple of typical Kennedy jokes.

This was something new. Lyndon Johnson off-screen is a storyteller and an accomplished mimic with a remarkably expressive face and hands, but off-screen or on, he has never been known before to laugh at himself.

Not, at least, until today. Last week he was in a sputtering rage about stories that he was driving too fast, but he opened his press conference by assuring the editors that he had not driven over from the White House.

Later when he was asked whether the Presidency was harder than he had anticipated, he remarked that he hadn't had much time to anticipate it, and—in what was clearly the understatement of the day— added that he enjoyed the job and was prepared to continue in it.

The advantages of a President seeking election are impressive. He can command a national television audience almost at will. He is surrounded by the trappings and influence of his office. He is the center of the largest collection of private information in the nation and he can use it at will.

When he moves out of the White House, he is surrounded by the law, flanked by the experts, and assured an attentive audience. When he evades tough questions, he cannot be pursued even by the most determined reporter, for there is always the danger, especially on television, of seeming to be disrespectful to the highest official in the land.

His opponents for the Presidency, in contrast, usually have to buy their way on to the television screen, spend a good deal of time in airports waiting for tardy commercial planes, and are often questioned by accusatively belligerent reporters as if they had just robbed the United States Treasury.

President Johnson is clearly determined to exploit these advantages. Even hostile editors are always pleased to be invited to the White House, and they have been going in and out of there this week as if they were Prime Ministers.

Also, he is learning that a President can use these conferences to answer more questions than he is asked. For example, one of President Johnson's major problems is to reach out to many young people of this country, who are still grieving for President Kennedy, and to many educated people who feel that President Johnson is not so concerned as his predecessor about education.

Accordingly, he arrived at his press conference with an announcement that he had established a program of "Presidential Scholars". This title, he explained, would be given to outstanding students from secondary schools, private and public, and he announced a selection committee composed of distinguished educators from all faiths and sections of the nation.

It would, of course, be churlish to suggest that he had anything in mind except the elevation of the mind and the dramatization of excellence, and yet, again, it would be difficult to say that this announcement hurt him politically.

With this conference, the Johnson experiment with the news industry is now complete. He has seen the reporters and editors singly and in groups, on and off the record, at the ranch and in his swimming pool, on television (tape and live), over coffee and other beverages, on the ground and in the air. Next to the Royal Shakespeare Company, which is playing here at the National Theater, it is the best repertory performance in town.

April 17, 1964

PRESIDENT CHIDES PRESS ON 'ADVICE'

Johnson, Ex-Editor, Jokes About News Coverage

Special to The New York Times

WASHINGTON, May 11 — President Johnson praised and poked fun at the press today. He emphasized the role of the press in helping preserve freedom, but jokingly chided newsmen for offering him so much free advice.

"William Allen White once said that the newspaper is the embodiment of democracy," the President remarked. "I guess this explains why newspapermen are so free in their advice about how to run the country."

The President was commenting on the role of the press during the presentation of the awards to winners of the intercollegiate journalism competition sponsored by the William Randolph Hearst Foundation.

Mr. Johnson presented the gold medallion first prize to Hal David Hall, a junior at the University of Tennessee, and the silver medallion second prize to Jean Heller, a junior at Ohio State University. Dean Norval Neil Luxon of the University of North Carolina journalism department received a gold medallion in recognition of first place among the country's 47 accredited journalism schools.

"As long as the press is free and young Americans like you pursue journalism as a profession, democracy will be free," the President told the winners.

"You have chosen a career in the national interest," he said. "No calling is more important and no task more influential, and no work more inspiring than that of a steward of truth."

But most of the President's comments about the press were in a lighter vein. He said that he had once been editor of The Southwest Texas State Teachers College Star, his college newspaper.

"But as you can see, I did not do as well as you have done, so I did the next best thing and went into politics," he said.

Mr. Johnson told the audience, gathered in the White House Flower Garden for the award ceremony, that he enjoyed meeting with newsmen and that he learned a great deal from them.

"In the White House press corps alone there are at least half a dozen experts already on animal husbandry," he said with a smile, referring to news reports on his picking up of the family beagles by their ears.

Present for the ceremony at the White House were William Randolph Hearst Jr., editor in chief of the Hearst newspapers; Frank Conniff, national editor of Hearst newspapers; and R. Robert L. Johnes, director of the University of Minnesota School of Journalism and president of the American Association of Schools and Departments of Journalism.

May 12, 1964

Advertising: Race for White House Costly

Primary Campaigns Need Expert Aid And Stamina

By SAL NUCCIO

Some people still question the use of Madison Avenue talent in political campaigns, and others continue to deplore the amount of time and cash expended on Presidential primaries. But both practices have been etched even more deeply this year on the tintype of American life.

Republican aspirants to the Presidency have accounted for most of the campaigning, for they are scrambling for the chance to unseat a Democrat. With President Johnson slated to head his party's ticket, only peripheral Democratic contestants have been in primary forays.

Governor Rockefeller and Senator Barry Goldwater are the only Republican contenders who have national organizations, extensive advertising and public relations staffs and sizable treasuries.

A fragmentary organization has been formed by supporters of Henry Cabot Lodge, Ambassador to South Vietnam, who has remained silent about his political intentions. There also is no apparent national organization working for former Vice President Richard M. Nixon.

The organizations of other Republicans appear to be nominal. Among them are those of Gov. William Scranton of Pennsylvania, Senator Margaret Chase Smith of New Hampshire and Harold Stassen.

Most campaigners appear eager to engage expert communicators, and do so, if they have the money. But the talent, unless donated, is expensive. Further, purchase of advertising space or broadcasting time for political messages generally is on a cash-in-advance basis.

Such dependence on cash resources in political campaigns has caused distress in many quarters. There have been recommendations that a bipartisan committee lay ground rules for campaigns, limiting their length and cost. Others advocate that broadcasters equitably provide free radio and TV time to candidates.

Pre-convention political aspirants have an especially difficult time raising money, relying mainly on personal appeals. Thus, their use of advertising experts usually is limited.

Messrs. Rockefeller and Goldwater, however, can

The New York Times
Campaign material used by Governor Rockefeller and Senator Barry Goldwater of Arizona

raise sizable sums through their organized political followings. The Senator apparently has a more difficult time, because he cannot match the Governor's personal wealth. It has been rumored that Mr. Rockefeller is prepared personally to spend up to $6 million on his campaign.

Perhaps because of this difference, the two prime contenders for the Republican nomination have distinctively different organizations. The Goldwater national campaign committee hired an ad agency, Fuller & Smith & Ross, Inc., to help plan and coordinate programs for the national and quasi-independent state committees. The agency's participation and planning are regulated by the flow of contributions to the campaign.

On the other hand, Governor Rockefeller has more than 70 paid and 40 volunteer workers at his national headquarters here. They include advertising and public relations experts, researchers and writers. Certain gubernatorial staffers also help.

Local ad agencies are used to buy time and space for ads prepared by the headquarters staff. State committees also conduct cooperative programs with national headquarters.

The Goldwater account was likened to "working with a decentralized company," by George R. Lyon, vice president and manager of New

York operations at Fuller & Smith. "Working under incredible deadlines can be challenging," he said. "We had only five days to prepare the network TV show on May 13."

Carl R. Giegerich, account supervisor, noted that Fuller & Smith accepted the Goldwater account Feb. 10, just a month before the New Hampshire primary. The first ad ran in that state Feb. 24. An immediate decision was to shoot extensive newsreel-type film, from which telecasts could be made.

Among those were 26 15-minute programs on three New Hampshire TV stations. Governor Rockefeller's staff also scheduled telecasts in that state. Both efforts were supplemented by print ads, posters and personal appearances. However, the absent Mr. Lodge easily won the contest on write-in votes.

Extensive television promotion and personal campaigning appeared helpful to the Governor in Oregon. The Senator supplemented TV promotion with personal appearances in Illinois, but his victory was not considered as resounding as it might have been.

Indicative of the high cost of television, the Goldwater committee's greatest single expense was the more than $100,000 spent on the May 13 program on the C.B.S. network.

Expenditures have generally

been more lavish at Rockefeller headquarters. Among other things, a special biographical film was made for TV, books have been written, a tabloid-size newspaper is being published, and other campaign material is being produced in profusion.

Among Mr. Rockefeller's specialists are Charles F. Moore Jr., retired public-relations vice president of the Ford Motor Company, and Jerry Danzig, former producer of Dave Garroway's "Today" show on N.B.C.-TV.

Local Goldwater committees may engage their own ad agencies, indicating the complexity of the Senator's organization. In California, for example, the Baus & Ross Company is working on the June 2 primary, with the cooperation of Fuller & Smith's Los Angeles office. The state committee pays B. & R.

As complex as the Goldwater and Rockefeller organizations are, they are only adequate for concentrated local actions, not broad national efforts. The convention victor will be reinforced by the Leo Burnett Company, Inc., the agency designated by the Republican National Committee. Its Democratic counterpart will be Doyle Dane Bernbach, Inc.

It remains to be seen how these agencies will do. One thing is certain: they have the advantage of time in which to research and plan their campaigns.

24 Pages of Praise for Johnson Appear Today in 14 Newspapers

Special to The New York Times

WASHINGTON, June 13— President Johnson's as yet unannounced candidacy will receive a big push tomorrow with the appearance of a 24-page supplement in 14 newspapers with a combined circulation of about 10 million.

Although described by its creator as "not a political document," the Sunday supplement is a frankly adulatory publicity release for Mr. Johnson.

It was paid for by the President's Club, established by President Kennedy about two and a half years ago as his personal political fund-raising vehicle and continued by President Johnson.

Neither the club nor the public relations concern that worked on the supplement would disclose its cost. Informed sources estimated that it would take more than $350,000 to produce and circulate such a supplement at the standard advertising rates for pre-printed material in the 14 newspapers.

The idea for the supplement was proposed to the Democratic National Committee by Robert S. Maurer of the Washington public relations concern of Maurer, Fleisher, Zon & Associates, after Mr. Maurer saw a supplement on Mr. Johnson published by The Dallas Times-Herald.

Mr. Maurer is a Democrat. His concern principally represents labor unions.

When it appeared that it would take some time to line up commercial advertisers to finance the supplement; the committee asked the President's Club to take on the sponsorship.

The club has about 2,000 members, most of whom are Democrats. About 200 are Republicans who supported President Kennedy and now want to support Mr. Johnson on the national level but Republican candidates in their home communities, according to Arthur B. Krim, club chairman, who is president of the United Artists Corporation.

As it is, the supplement carries the word "advertisement" in small type on the front cover and every other page except the inside of its front page and the back.

It is dedicated "To the Office of the President of the United States of America and to the 36 men in the history of our country who have borne the title, Mr. President."

Its contents, however, consist almost entirely of pictures featuring Mr. Johnson, flattering captions and quotations from his public utterances.

The supplement, it is also written, "is presented in the public interest by the President's Club."

Mr. Maurer said that the newspapers in which the supplement would appear are The Boston Globe, The New York Times, The Philadelphia Inquirer, The Pittsburgh Press, The Cleveland Plain Dealer, The Detroit News, The Chicago Sun-Times, Chicago's American, The Milwaukee Journal, The Minneapolis Tribune, The Seattle Times, The San Francisco Examiner, The Los Angeles Times and The Buffalo Courier-Express.

SENATOR CHARGES LIES TO THE PRESS

Accuses Some News Media of 'Utter Dishonesty'

SAN FRANCISCO, July 17 (UPI) — The Republican Presidential nominee, Senator Barry Goldwater, has charged in an interview that some of the news media have resorted to "utter dishonesty" and "out-and-out lies" in reporting his campaign activities.

The Arizonan made the comments in a copyright filmed interview last night with Ralph Painter of KOOL-TV in Phoenix. Mr. Painter and his wife, Sara, covered the Republican National Convention for the station.

Mr. Painter asked Mr. Goldwater whether he was satisfied with the press coverage he had received during the campaign.

"I don't use the black brush on newspapers or the radio or the TV," Mr. Goldwater replied. "Newspapers like The New York Times have to stoop to utter dishonesty in reflecting my views. Some of the newspapers here in San Francisco like The Chronicle—that are nothing but out-and-out lies. Now if they disagree with me, fine, that's their right."

He was also critical of the Columbia Broadcasting System, claiming the network had "pulled three sneakers on me that I'll never forgive them for."

Cites Network Reporting

He said the network, in one example, had reported he was going to Germany after the convention to "return to the site of the Fuehrer's point of starting and start my campaign there, that I had an invitation to speak in Germany to a right-wing group, [and] that my effort would be to cement the relations between the extremist groups in America and Germany."

"This is nothing but—and I won't swear but you know what I'm thinking — a dad-burned dirty lie," he said.

Mr. Goldwater said members of his staff had contacted the president of the network, Dr. Frank Stanton, and told him the program was in error but "they haven't had the decency to apologize."

He said, "The other networks were very, very accurate, and very kind."

"I know some of the men personally. dislike my position but it was hard to discern," he declared.

Mr. Goldwater also said he was thinking of kicking off his campaign for the Presidency in Prescott, Ariz. He said he would take a vacation but has not decided where he will go.

C.B.S. Denies Charge

C.B.S. issued the following statement last night:

"C.B.S. cannot understand why the story Senator Goldwater refers to caused him to cancel his trip to Germany. Senator Goldwater denied the story and his denial was carried widely by newspapers, radio and television.

"The president of C.B.S. was not contacted by any member of Senator Goldwater's staff. The C.B.S. News correspondent on the story in question, Daniel Schorr, broadcast the following clarifying statements from Germany on the C.B.S. World News Roundup Thursday morning:

" 'In speaking the other day of a move by Senator Goldwater to link up with these forces (Schorr refers to German right-, wing forces) I did not mean to suggest a conscious effort on his part, of which there is no proof here, but meant more a process of gravitation which is visible here.'

"The balance of Senator Goldwater's interview speaks for itself."

Advertising: Democrats, G.O.P. Woo Voters

Drives to Continue Through Nov. 2, Election Eve

By LEONARD SLOANE

Over the next five weeks, television viewers will find that increasingly the "message from our sponsor" will be from the Democratic and Republican parties.

TV spots and sponsored programing will appear on all three networks through Nov. 2, Election Eve. On that night the campaigns of both parties will culminate with programs designed to offer final convincing arguments why citizens should vote for President Johnson or Senator Barry Goldwater.

Ads for the two major parties' national campaigns will also appear on radio and in newspapers and magazines. But the overwhelming bulk of the close to $9 million that will be spent on media advertising will go to television in order to "sell" the candidates to the public.

Television advertisements will seek to convince voters of the merits of the views of the Presidential candidates. Print ads will follow a similar theme, with the Democrats also attempting to capitalize on the Republican split during their national convention.

Handling the account for the Democratic National Committee is Doyle Dane Bernbach, Inc. The Republican National Committee has hired Erwin Wasey, Ruthrauff & Ryan, Inc., a subsidiary of the Interpublic Group of Companies, Inc. Both agencies have 30 to 40 persons working on the accounts in Washington and New York.

●

On the Democratic side, advertising will seek to pound home the theme that "the stakes are too high for you to stay home." Lloyd Wright, the party's media coordinator, says that Democratic ads will "take the record of this Administration to the American people."

The national committee's advertising budget of about $4 million is almost all committed to television, although it is preparing some newspaper ads that are being offered to state committees and citizens groups for local sponsorship.

Network television will account for $1.7 million of the budget, with the rest of the broadcasting allocation earmarked for spot TV and radio. Twenty-second and one and five-minute television spots have been prepared by Doyle Dane.

Two of these spots have already stirred up a brouhaha

What they really think about their candidate.

In your heart you know he's right about
MORAL CRISIS

Barry Goldwater says: "Americans everywhere are indignant about the moral decay in Washington and nobody should accept corruption in positions of public trust as a way of life. All it takes to clean it up is an administration that really wants it cleaned up—an administration with the moral courage to fire the influence peddlers and graft takers no matter whose friends they may be."

VOTE FOR BARRY GOLDWATER

Democratic advertisement, left, emphasizes division within Republican party with quotations from other G.O.P. leaders. Republican National Committee is countering with appeals directed to a variety of sentiments on such issues as peace, morals and rights.

amid charges of unfair practices. One shows a girl pulling petals off a daisy followed by a countdown that is ended with a nuclear explosion. A voice is then heard urging support for President Johnson.

The other commercial shows a girl licking an ice cream cone and contrasts vitamins A and D with radioactive poisoning. It then says that Senator Goldwater wants to continue exploding test bombs.

Both Dean Burch, chairman of the Republican National Committee, and Senator Everett M. Dirksen, Republican of Illinois, the Senate minority leader, have made formal complaints about the daisy commercial. And the Democrats say that the ice cream spot — whose text was deplored and then entered in the Congressional Record by Senator Thruston B. Morton, Republican of Kentucky — has not been rescheduled.

The Democrats have purchased the 10 to 11 P.M. time slot on Nov. 2 over the National Broadcasting Company network, when President Johnson and his running mate, Senator Hubert H. Humphrey, will probably summarize the campaign issues as they see them. A similar 30-minute program next month is also being contemplated by the committee.

The Republicans are spending about $4.8 million to advertise their national candidates, of which all but $200,-000 will be spent on national and spot television and radio. The rest will be used for outdoor, newspaper and magazine advertising and collateral material.

Albert Tilt, vice president of Erwin Wasey, says the Republican ads will cover such issues as foreign policy, morality and peace. A slogan already used frequently is "In your heart, you know he's right."

"The vast majority of the viewing audience has never seen Senator Goldwater until our first half-hour program," Mr. Tilt says. "He's an extremely strong TV personality and we hope to have one such program a week."

The Republican National Committee pre-empted a half-hour time slot on N.B.C. last Tuesday that had been slated for the initial broadcast this season of "That Was the Week That Was." It has also purchased that period on Oct. 6 and 13.

The Republicans, in fact, placed a time order for the same 9:30 to 10 P.M. slot next Tuesday. However, the Democratic National Committee had already bought a one-minute spot during the revue that evening, so the program will have its première on Sept. 29.

"T.W. 3" is one of N.B.C.'s three half-hour weekday evening shows and, as such, is highly susceptible to pre-emption by the political parties that want to purchase its time period to present 30-minute programs.

The Republican Election Eve television program has not been formulated yet, declares Mr. Tilt. But he notes that it will be presented over the Columbia Broadcasting System network and both Senator Goldwater and his running mate, Representative William E. Miller of New York, will appear.

One highlight of the Republican print campaign will be an eight-page advertisement in the October issue of the Reader's Digest. This ad, which cost more than $300,-000, was placed by the Leo Burnett Company, which had been the Republican agency until it was replaced by Erwin Wasey in August following Senator Goldwater's nomination.

The Reader's Digest ad, sponsored by Citizens for Goldwater-Miller, contains a photograph of the Republican Presidential candidate and copy outlining his positions on issues like the United Nations, Southeast Asia, civil rights and social security. Reprints will be offered by the Republican National Committee.

When the tumult and the shouting die, however, the voters will go into the polling booths on Nov. 3 and make their decisions based on what they've seen, heard and read in the ads—or felt right from the outset of the campaign.

Advertising:
Post-Mortem on G.O.P. Drive

By SAL NUCCIO

"More than half the voters didn't know Barry Goldwater at the outset of his Presidential campaign. That was but one of several problems that had to be solved in 'merchandising' him."

That was the observation yesterday of an official at Wasey, Ruthrauff & Ryan, Inc., the Republican National Committee's advertising agency. However, he was quick to add:

"The landslide victory by President Johnson indicated that the gap was too great, even at the start of the campaign, to be closed by any magic political or advertising formula. Thus, if the problems in advertising had not existed, its effectiveness may have reduced the margin of defeat, but it would not have eliminated it."

Wooing the Undecided

Surveys suggested at the outset of the campaign, the agency official said, that there was a large number of undecided voters who "could turn the tide, if won over to the Goldwater camp. They were the campaign target—or should have been."

The vastness of both the Republican and Democratic ad programs was underscored by the Erwin Wasey official's observation that a corporation would have to budget $25 million to $30 million to conduct a comparable year-round program.

Each political party reportedly spent $4 million to $5 million on advertising—mostly on television—in the eight weeks of campaigning. The total cost of each major party's campaign was estimated at $12 million.

Erwin Wasey's spokesman asserted that the brevity of the campaign made it essential, "from an advertising point of view," to have pre-selected issues on which the ad program could be based.

'Product Claims' in Conflict

However, he noted, Senator Goldwater first had to be introduced to the voters. Then they had to be told of his philosophy—"what he stood for." The result, the ad man indicated, often was a confusion of "product claims."

"There was not time, in the eight weeks, to pinpoint the basic issues and then capitalize on them," he asserted.

On the other hand, James H. Graham, supervisor of the Democratic National Committee account at Doyle Dane Bernbach, Inc., said his agency brought the campaign "to the basic issues—life or death, nuclear responsibility or irresponsibility."

Conceding that nuclear responsibility became a major issue, the Erwin Wasey man said a major limitation was the inability of an agency to do extensive research in preparing for the Presidential race. He added:

"A party's national committee after nomination of the candidate—other than the incumbent—is like a completely reorganized corporation. The top man—the candidate—brings in his own people and decides how money will be spent. He may not agree to pay for research that had been completed before his nomination."

It was noted by other observers — on Madison Avenue and elsewhere—that political judgment of the weight of issues was quite different from the public's judgment. In illustration, the emphasis on honesty in politics and on morality was "wasted on the voters," according to one observer.

'Lack of Central Voice'

"Aggravating the compound problem of being unable to choose effectively and then capitalize on campaign issues," an ad man experienced in political campaigns noted, "is the lack of a central voice in a campaign organization. Further, members of a party's national committee generally do not understand or appreciate the purpose or nature of advertising."

In the Goldwater campaign, one observer noted, agreement had to be reached by three national headquarters groups — "the Senator's personal group," the financial backers and the professional political group. One ad man involved in the campaign said:

"You couldn't convince them that the voters' favorite entertainment shows — like 'Petticoat Junction' — shouldn't be pre-empted."

The Erwin Wasey spokesman, noting that his agency won the G.O.P. account from the Leo Burnett Company only last August, said, "We initially recommended that major stress should be on TV spot announcements—not on half-hour shows."

Studies have shown, he said, that a political program generally loses much of its TV audience.

For example, he said, a political program that pre-empted an entertainment show with a 24.7 rating would drop to a 14 rating within the first minute, and end with a 12 rating. The rating indicates the percentage of TV homes tuned to the particular show.

Argument for Brevity

The argument in favor of low-cost TV spots, the ad executive asserted, was that "people didn't tune them out. They maintained the same large audience of the regularly scheduled programs preceding and following them."

Spots also reduce waste, he said, "concentrating your dollars where they will do the most good. This is segmented marketing, in which you divided the nation into some 190 TV markets, and place your announcements where they will do the most good."

Closing on a positive note, the Erwin Wasey executive said: "For an ad agency, a political campaign is exciting and stimulating. It's hard to imagine finding businessmen as devoted to a cause as are members of a political campaign team."

Goldwater
Rejoins Critics
as a Columnist

By GLADWIN HILL

Special to The New York Times

LOS ANGELES, Jan. 4 — Barry Goldwater has changed jobs from Senator to syndicated newspaper columnist with a comradely bow to the "pundits" with whom he recently was unhappy.

Observing that he was now a "stable-mate" of such recent critics as Walter Lippmann and Joseph Alsop, the defeated Republican Presidential candidate remarked:

"I join them and the rest of the newspaper fraternity gladly without the slightest trace of prejudice or rancor."

The Arizonan, whose Senate term expired today, resumed yesterday the thrice-weekly commentary of public affairs he started four years ago and suspended during the Presidential campaign.

He said he would not criticize actions of the Johnson Administration "merely because the event involved was participated in by people who once opposed me," but that he would adhere to his "conservative principles."

Carried by 75 Papers

The Los Angeles Times Syndicate said the column was going to 75 newspapers with an aggregate circulation of 10 million — "more than at his previous peak," although this had involved 125 papers.

Mr. Goldwater is writing from his home in Phoenix and keeping his eye on Washington through what he called "a personal research operation" there. One of Mr. Goldwater's former assistants, Tony Smith, is understood to have established a research service, but there was no confirmation that this was the one in question.

Before the campaign, the earnings from Senator Goldwater's columns were earmarked for charities. No such arrangement has been specified this time, the syndicate manager, Rex Barley, said.

In his first new column, Mr. Goldwater sprinkled some verbal oil on the troubled waters of his campaign relations with the press. He said that the newspaper reporters "who followed me around week after week did a fair and impartial job."

"There have been charges that I was unfair to some of the press and that I in turn was victimized by a hostile press," he continued.

A 'Natural Offshoot'

"This is a natural offshoot of almost every political campaign," he said. "I recognize that many individual newsmen disagreed with me and that some of them let their differences enter into their writings."

However, he added, he was sure some of the misunderstanding grew out of public confusion between news stories and the quite proper expression of opinions by commentators.

In a prior announcement of his journalistic resumption, Mr. Goldwater remarked that "I shall be writing without the restrictions which as a U.S. Senator imposed limitations on what I could say in print. A lot of my earlier columns were devoted almost entirely to political philosophy. Now all restrictions, except those dictated by judgment and good taste, have been lifted. I am free to speak my mind after the fashion of other newspaper columnists."

Among the new publishers of the column, the syndicate reported, were newspapers in Boston, Houston, Miami and Minneapolis.

Johnson and News 'Leaks'

By ARTHUR KROCK

WASHINGTON, Jan. 23—President Johnson, who ponders deeply on what is fitting to the occasion, chose the quiet approach to important pronouncements on his Inaugural Day. He can make the rafters ring when he wants to. But on Wednesday he summoned the American people to the creation of the Great Society in low tones and with impassive facial expression.

"If you were to make little fishes talk," said Oliver Goldsmith to Samuel Johnson, "they would talk like whales." The President made his whales talk like little fishes Wednesday.

This was, of course, but another way of trying for the dramatic effect which is indispensable to the attainment of the aims of statesmen. It is a subtle way, but the President is a subtle man. That characteristic has already invested his Administration with a style which may be described as "Texas Florentine." And one of its manifestations is resentment by the President of news disclosures, before he is ready to make them himself, that is reputed to have taken form in long postponements of action on decisions he has already made, and even reversals of some decisions.

'Leaks' a Problem

News "leaks" have always vexed a President, unless they have been contrived at his instance or with his knowledge and approval. But, on the authority of members of his official household, Mr. Johnson's annoyance is of historic proportions. These persons also are the sources of reports, widely credited in Washington, that press forecasts impelled him to cancel at least one non-urgent appointment he had decided to make, at least one major policy he had decided to invoke; and to defer two other appointments at the expense of the anguish of the expectants.

The credence given these reports, in combination with the subtlety of some of the President's techniques, account for a half-formed conjecture that on the night of the Inaugural he announced a new Cabinet appointment in a manner without precedent. Speaking from his box in the ballroom of the Sheraton-Park Hotel, Mr. Johnson twice referred to the presence of "the Attorney General." The reference was to Nicholas deB. Katzenbach, who has only been acting in this capacity. But there has been no announcement of a choice by the President of an Attorney General in fact. And Mr. Johnson is usually scrupulous in his public use of official titles.

Hidden Meanings

If the President were not a complicated man the reference to Katzenbach as "the Attorney General" would have passed as a mere courtesy befitting the occasion, and most probably that is all it was, even if the courtesy materializes ultimately into the fact. But when the complication is one of subtleties which in open practice are not too fancifully described as "Texas Florentine," a political community in particular is likely to look for hidden meanings where there aren't any.

As for Katzenbach, the press has reported with sufficient authority that his name heads the list of those submitted to the President by Director John A. McCone of the C.I.A. as qualified to replace McCone. It is to be hoped that the publication will not close the White House door on that preferment to an outstanding public servant if Katzenbach is not to be promoted to Attorney General.

The high degree of the President's annoyance over published forecasts of his acts before he can announce them himself has compounded a normal problem of the press. This can be expressed in two questions. If prior publication will deprive Government of the service of the person determined to be best-qualified, or cause the deferment or abandonment of policy, is the publication a disservice to the national interest? But if publication is withheld for this reason, does not that effect an indirect censorship and news management which is an even greater disservice to the national interest?

A responsible press is bound to answer the second question in the affirmative, and proceed accordingly. And, though the history of the Presidency suggests that no incumbent has changed plans because of

their prior publication to a greater extent than Mr. Johnson is reported to have done, this history also shows that such an attitude cannot be long maintained. The qualification "reported to have done" is necessary in fairness and in fact, because the President's reaction has doubtless been exaggerated, though the sources are within his own Administration.

Protection

There is, however, substantial evidence that he is determined his ship of state shall be caulked with unexampled tightness against news leaks, large or small, harmless or troublesome. His assistants will not venture to disclose the merest informative detail without his explicit authority, if the information can possibly be traced to them. This has made a farce of a legitimate and essential channel of information, the so-called briefings of reporters by his press secretary, George Reedy. And in the President's sparse recorded news conferences his answers to questions about matters he is known to be considering have been largely unresponsive.

Superficially, Mr. Johnson is more accessible to mass reporting than any of his predecessors. But this access often is that of a winded band of newsmen, trying to keep up with the long-legged canter which is his stride, trying to hear his low-keyed remarks or replies to questions at an impossible distance, and write down their notes as they run. The most solid information of his plans and attitudes he prefers to convey to the public in private talks with individual reporters where he can prescribe, and properly, what can be published, and in what person his discourse shall be cast.

Arbitrary Choices

The President has been extremely generous and helpful in the employment of this convenient and safe medium, not only having already given more private interviews for publication than any predecessor over a comparable period of time, but reserving his communication largely to the domestic press. Necessarily, however, the selection of the beneficiaries is arbitrary, and the method is not an acceptable substitute for the recorded mass news conference.

But, most important of all, it does not compensate for his rigid channeling in himself of the news of his Administration.

President Envies Freedom of Press To Come and Go

Special to The New York Times

WASHINGTON, May 14— President Johnson joked today about the trouble he had getting outside the White House and the trouble he had keeping newsmen inside it.

In a rambling talk to a group of school administrators, Mr. Johnson also made gentle gibes at a Senator, journalism, Presidential critics and, it seemed, himself.

It was a pleasant evening when the President walked out of his office to the steps of the White House Rose Garden to talk to the educators and reporters.

He apologized to the educators because they had had to take a long route to the garden through the Northwest Gate rather than the shorter way through the Southwest Gate.

"Your difficulty in getting in, however, is nothing compared with what I have getting out," the President said amid laughter.

In contrast, he said, newsmen seem to be the only really free group in town.

This may have been an allusion to the fact that the President has sometimes wanted to make announcements when the White House reporters were out or gone for the day.

It may also have been an allusion to the fact that Mr. Johnson has recently, in effect, been giving the reporters a one-hour lunch period, a limit that many newsmen have been stubbornly ignoring.

"We have a freedom of information policy and they are utilizing it," Mr. Johnson said.

He said that at a school he had been planning to take the reporters with him to the National Education Association headquarters to look in on the meeting of the school administrators. But Mr. Johnson said, his special assistant, Horace Busby, "said there had been complaints that I was walking too much."

The President joked that he did not think it was necessary for him to say much to the administrators because "I understand you already heard from my old friend Wayne Morse," Democratic Senator from Oregon.

The President said that America was anxious to help other peoples, then remarked that he had said that before—in fact, in some people's opinion "so often."

He said, "Americans do not want to live in a world where force is supreme."

He remarked that there was much to be done in the United States but that these were essentially good times.

"All of us have a little martyr in us and develop a martyr complex mighty easily," he said.

One newsman was heard to say, "Hear, hear."

May 15, 1965

In The Nation: Silence in the White House

By ARTHUR KROCK

WASHINGTON, May 24— For almost a fortnight now President Johnson has retreated into what, for him, is comparative silence. Instead of constantly appearing in person on the first pages of newspapers and video screens, he has been absent from both on most of the days and nights in this period, in sharp contrast with the weeks previous when its exposure was almost total and incessant.

By this ubiquity Mr. Johnson seemed to be in danger of overexposure—a condition which weakens the impact on public opinion that is the design of every occasion of direct communication between the President and the people.

During the first two weeks in May, television viewers were virtually certain to behold and hear the President on their sets at any hour and on any channel. Of the daily major headlines, one or more invariably introduced an item of news he had made and announced in person. A steady outflow of other Washington dispatches bore those marks which make it unmistakable their content was acquired from Mr. Johnson at firsthand and authorized for publication.

Reporters at the White House were virtually on continuous alert for summoning to informal news conferences with the President. These included the most informal of all—Mr. Johnson's striding walkabouts in his big backyard, talking about everything, with the press trying to keep his pace, and at the same time hear and make notes of what he was saying.

But since May 13, when television and the front newspaper pages recorded his speech to the American Association of Cartoonists, in which he charged Communist China with obstructing a political solution of the war in Southeast Asia that would be of beneficial interest to the North Vietnamese, the President has mostly been an absentee from the major headlines and the video screens. In the issues of this newspaper of May 17, 20, 21, 22 and 24 nothing he said or did was recorded on page one, and there was no Presidential interruption of TV programs.

Page One News

On May 16 there were first-page reports of his announced intention to ask Congress to cut or remove certain excise taxes and his call for a coalition government in the Dominican Republic. On May 18 the same display was given to the actual dispatch of his excise cuts message to Congress. The next day the President's request to Congress to repeal Section 14-B of the Taft-Hartley Act, his assurance of a "blank cheque" for whatever weapons American military forces in Vietnam might require, were similarly featured. But only once in this period—on May 18—did he call in the reporters and newscameramen, to personalize an announcement on preschool guidance centers.

The President's sole appearance on page one of this newspaper, May 23, was in an account of a $1,000 per plate dinner he attended in New York City. Compared with his personal public exposures in the preceding weeks, he has been a recluse for the last fortnight.

But privately he has even intensified the missionary labors for understanding and support of his acts and policies that he had conducted so constantly in the open as to invite the diminishing returns of overexposure. The President had a long meeting with editors of the Cowles Publications; another with hierarchs of The Associated Press. He devoted a whole evening last week to exhortation of a group of newspaper editors. For almost five hours in the same week the President, according to some who were there, talked steadily to members of the staffs of several weekly news magazines, devoting part of the time to criticism of certain editorial comment on and reporting from the Dominican Republic. Mr. Johnson took one of his walkabouts — with President Park of South Korea. But the usual drove of reporters was permitted to tag along only briefly. And there was published but one of the normally large quota of those authorized newspaper articles which make it clear the author has had a private interview with the President.

Thus, whether or not because Mr. Johnson realized his previous overexposure and its perils, for two weeks he has at least created the effect of agreeing with Oliver Wendell Holmes père that "silence, like a poultice, comes/To heal the blows of sound." Considering the President's host of troubles, old Dr. Holmes's prescription is good for what ailed him.

May 25, 1965

Washington: Mr. Moyers to the Rescue

By TOM WICKER

WASHINGTON, July 8 — President Johnson has been getting a bad press lately. George Reedy is leaving his job as White House press secretary. Not many reporters in Washington thought Mr. Reedy was effective in that job.

Those are facts and the inevitable conclusion of all too many people probably will be that a petulant President has fired his press secretary because he couldn't persuade the newspapers not to be beastly. It is a wrong conclusion — for any tempted to draw it — and it is unfair both to George Reedy, a decent, hard-working man, and to Lyndon Johnson, whose interests have claimed fourteen of Mr. Reedy's prime years.

Medical Reasons

Mr. Reedy's reason for leaving his excruciating job is exactly what he said it was; he has been living in increasing agony with a foot ailment that will require extensive surgery and treatment and he is not physically up to the demands of the press office.

Mr. Johnson did not fire Mr. Reedy, nor was he planning to. The medical reasons for the latter's "leave of absence" are entirely valid and cloak no other motives on the part of either man.

Nevertheless, there are few in Washington today who believe big George Reedy with his ever-present pipe and maddeningly slow drawl ever will meet the reporters again in the press office off the west lobby of the White House.

There are indications, moreover, that the President now may pause to reassess the vital questions of his press policies, his press officer and the relationship that ought to exist between President and official spokesman.

The Big News

For instance, it was Bill Moyers—Mr. Reedy's temporary replacement—who announced late today that Ambassador Maxwell D. Taylor had resigned and that Henry Cabot Lodge would again go out to Saigon. During Mr. Reedy's tenure, news of that magnitude invariably was made by the President himself, often in hasty television appearances.

A year ago, for instance, it was Mr. Johnson who announced that General Taylor was to be the Ambassador to South Vietnam. Thus the prominence granted Mr. Moyers as spokesman today was in itself a creeping step toward upgrading the press office.

The real upgrading, however, is in the mere appointment of this remarkable young man who already had become the Ted Sorensen, the Sherman Adams (minus any shreds of vicuna), of the Johnson Administration. When the tragic Walter Jenkins resigned, it was Bill Moyers who was named to replace him. Now, still another White House Now still another White House and the record is clear that Mr. Moyers has enhanced every office he has filled.

There has never been a suggestion here that Bill Moyers is a patsy for the demanding Lyndon Johnson, a yes-man, or a Texas provincial. Except for the President himself, he has become the most important cog in the White House machine and the most esteemed of the Johnson staff.

Johnson's Selection

Mr. Johnson knows that better than anyone and it can only be concluded that his selection was intended to put his best man to work on what had become one of his most difficult problems.

It is difficult, to a great extent, because of Lyndon Johnson himself. His own press secretary to an extent never before known, Mr. Johnson never gave George Reedy the free rein, the full range of information, the power to make decisions, the full authority of an official voice.

Lost Privilege

Pierre Salinger decided to leave the job when he realized —or at least came to believe— that he no longer had the privilege accorded him by John Kennedy of walking into the President's office unannounced at any time to put a question or get a fill-in. All these things are essential to a successful official spokesman trusted on all sides.

If any man commands the President's confidence enough to be given that kind of autonomy, it is Bill Moyers. If any White House aide has the full respect of the press, it also is Bill Moyers.

This is no small gain. A President's most direct link to the people is the press, and his most direct link to the press ought to be his press secretary. There need not be sweetness and light between the two sides, but there has to be mutual respect if both press and President are to get their work done.

July 9, 1965

Moyers' First Day in New Job Brings Twin News Conferences

By ROBERT B. SEMPLE, Jr.
Special to The New York Times

WASHINGTON, July 9 — On his first full day as White House press secretary, Bill D. Moyers held a full-scale press briefing and then produced the President for a news conference.

He also named and introduced a new staff member, an assistant to himself.

The form, content, and unusual aftermath of the briefing —the "quickie" news conference with the President—suggested that a new era in press relations may have begun at the White House.

Mr. Moyers, one of Mr. Johnson's most trusted assistants, succeeded George E. Reedy Jr. as Presidential press secretary yesterday. Mr. Reedy began an extended leave of absence for medical reasons.

The new staff member is Harold C. Pachios, a 28-year-old native of Maine, whose appointment was announced at the morning White House briefing.

Mr. Pachios is not on the White House payroll yet, but hopes to be shortly. His official title will be assistant to the press secretary. Joseph Laitin is remaining in the press office as assistant press secretary—the No. 2 job.

Mr. Pachios was educated at the Kent School in Connecticut and at Princeton, from which he was graduated in 1959. He served as Mr. Moyers' assistant when he was deputy director of the Peace Corps and then served as an advance man in President Johnson's 1964 campaign.

He also worked briefly with the Vista program in the Office of Economic Opportunity, and for the last few months has been assisting Mr. Moyers on research for the President's legislative program.

He hopes to obtain a law degree from Georgetown University later this month.

At the briefing, Mr. Moyers, 31, balanced a long, thin black cigar lightly between his fingers and radiated the crisp confidence of one who has the ear of his boss, the confidence of his boss and a reasonably sure knowledge of what the boss plans to do next.

For example, he revealed that over the weekend the President would have no official visitors of prominence and no news conference, but that he would do some boating and attend church on Sunday.

This was an unusually large amount of advance information on a Presidential weekend and the fact that it was given was surprising.

Mr. Reedy, who wore rumpled suits and smoked a bulky, professorial pipe, was leery of Mr. Johnson's unpredictable habits. Accordingly, he provided little specific information on the President's plans and customarily advised the press to remain prudently prepared for any eventuality.

Mr. Moyers also announced that Mr. Johnson would carry with him, for weekend scrutiny, a recent report on the supersonic transport program, preliminary studies of the budget for the 1967 fiscal year and preliminary staff reports on "Project 66," the White House name for the Administration's legislatiive program for next year.

Mr. Moyers seemed more inclined than his predecessor to debate matters of policy, and this may be the most significant difference of all.

For example, Mr. Moyers was asked whether a speech by Senator Robert F. Kennedy this morning constituted a challenge to Administration thinking on Vietnam.

This elicited a review of Mr. Johnson's policy, a quick recapitulation of his proposals for unconditional discussions and the terse, confident conclusion that the Senator's speech was not substantively different "from what we have said."

After the briefing, the President answered questions in his office for about 25 minutes, dealing mainly with the Vietnam war and the domestic economy. Mr. Moyers stood slightly behind him, ready with information and occasionally providing it.

He gave the reporters about an hour to file their articles. Then, in his new role as press secretary, he joined them on the flight to Texas—there to discover whether his confident estimates of the President's weekend plans were accurate or whether, as Mr. Reedy might have put it, "imprudent."

July 10, 1965

In The Nation: The Day LBJ Didn't Broadcast

By ARTHUR KROCK

WASHINGTON, Sept. 15— There was something very big missing yesterday on the television screens of the nation and on the local TV news broadcasts. For the first time in recent memory the President of the United States failed to make even one of his familiar appearances, standing tall behind the lectern in the White House television room that bears the President's seal and making announcements which ranged from matters of grave import to those his predecessors left for subordinates to disclose, frequently in the form of mimeographed handouts.

So constant have been these electronic projections of the President to the people that his footage on national news broadcasts may recently have been exceeded only by Huntley-Brinkley, Cronkite or Jennings. And Mr. Johnson has a special advantage over these professionals on the screens they share. The news they broadcast must have some inherent claim to importance and public interest. The President is not bound by this standard of selection because whatever he chooses to broadcast, however trivial or routine, is an undeniable claimant for TV time by reason of the fact that he announces it in person.

But yesterday even the President's reception of the astronauts was conveyed to the public in the form of a silent motion picture. The lectern with the Presidential seal was absent from the screen, although the occasion was typical of many in which this impressive symbol of power was moved into the foreground, Mr. Johnson along with it, and the inevitable speech to the immediate and to the distant audience began.

As night came on, and the clock struck eleven, millions of Americans must have settled down for the late news reports with a confidence born of experience that they would see Mr. Johnson in action, and at least hear him talk about something. Perhaps an announcement that the gross national product, reacting to the pound and the penny as anticipated by the New Economists, would now reach $1,000 billion instead of $999 billion in the calendar year. Perhaps a talkative post-prandial stroll with Him and the overworked White House reporters in the Rose Garden. If not these, surely a revelation that, after intense persuasion, one of the greatest sociologists in the country had been induced to join the Administration as Executive Assistant to the Deputy Assistant Secretary of a Secretary of the new Department of Urban Affairs yet to be chosen.

But no. Except for a brief repetition of the glimpse of him at the ceremony for the astronauts, the foremost personality of news television was missing from the screen for the first time in ready memory. What could the reason be? Was it a planned abstention? Or was the President temporarily bored with the job of getting fixed up with those gadgets required by the TV technicians?

This reason could be most sympathetically understood by any who have been obliged to meet the requirements. But it is possible that the President has heard and heeded the counsels of some that his steady resort to television has exposed him to the danger of "overexposure." Certain warnings have come from the country that Mr. Johnson, like Wordsworth's world, has been "too much with us." Some feelers of the public pulse are now reporting that such an attitude is forming.

If so, despite the belief credited to his gifted press secretary, Bill Moyers, that there is no such thing as Presidential "overexposure," there are suggestions in American political history that there is. And in Mr. Johnson's case it could be attributed in part to his use of television for numerous broadcasts in person of matters which did not rate the eminence of their source; and for reading lengthy statistical statements at televised news conferences that limit the time for questioning by the reporters.

But overexposure on television could also be the product of a forming situation which public pulse-feelers have detected. That is, that the President has demanded of Congress, and Congress has granted, too much major legislation too fast; that the American people generally want him to call a halt during which the effectiveness of these Great Society programs can be tested and some calculation of their ultimate costs can be made. If this national mood is materializing—and public sentiment often has been ahead of Congress in the past—then the constant appearances on television of a President who was associated with the drive for more "full speed ahead," as Mr. Johnson is, could "overexpose" him.

But this cannot be assumed from just one day of Presidential silence.

September 16, 1965

Washington: Hocus-Pocus at the White House

By JAMES RESTON

WASHINGTON, Jan. 6—When Bill Moyers took over as White House press secretary, he had a single aim. This was to establish confidence in the integrity of the public and private statements made in the name of the President.

Nobody ever worked harder than Moyers to avoid this assignment or to achieve this objective after the job was forced on him, but the sad fact is that the thing has not been done. The "crisis of confidence" he vowed to end is still with us, and the events of the last few days and weeks here have actually made it worse.

In explaining the recent dramatic diplomatic offensive to bring about peace talks in Vietnam, Ambassador Arthur Goldberg told the press: "There has been great concern as to whether we really are pursuing what has been said is a path to peace. . . . We have a great problem here maintaining our credibility with our own people. . . ."

In explaining today why the President had not intervened in the New York transit strike, the White House said that Mr. Johnson had not been invited to do so. Technically, this was quite true at the time, if "intervention" means putting the President personally into the negotiating chamber; but practically, the President needs no invitation to say publicly what he thinks about that fiasco, and as a matter of fact, he actually intervened through his Secretary of Labor to try to bring about a settlement even before Secretary Wirtz went to New York at Mayor Lindsay's request.

Fact and Fiction

The White House statements about the steel negotiations have been even less candid. For some unexplained reason, Mr. Moyers took the position that the whole settlement with United States Steel came as a sort of pleasant surprise to the President over the news tickers.

As a matter of fact, Roger Blough, board chairman of U.S. Steel, was down here talking to a member of the Cabinet—apparently Secretary of Defense McNamara—about the problem,

and if the settlement was a surprise to the President, it certainly was no surprise to several of his principal associates.

Nevertheless, even after the settlement was reached, the White House kept playing games with the reporters. "I don't know," Mr. Moyers told them this afternoon, "with whom any of the steel company officials might have met. I do know there were no meetings at the White House and no meetings involving White House officials."

All this may be true, but it differs widely from the private accounts of men actually engaged in the whole steel controversy, and the point is that there is now such doubt about these White House statements that many people here simply do not believe that it is true.

Heavy Pressure

What is generally believed is that the Administration put severe pressure on the steel companies not to go along with Bethlehem's $5-a-ton price rise; that at least one member of the Cabinet discussed what would be acceptable to the Administration, and that all this was done with the knowledge of the President.

The Paradox

The pressures on the White House now both at home and abroad are severe. Nobody questions it. The war in Vietnam is heating up the economy, and the strike in New York is tearing it down. All the dreams of a year ago about peace in the world and a war on poverty and a Great Society at home have been affected.

But the public relations techniques of the Administration are merely making things worse. The President is trying desperately to start peace negotiations over Vietnam. He is trying to hold back prices, and he is doing far more than is generally realized to end the paralysis in New York.

In the process, however, and not for the first time, his maneuvers are getting in the way of his purposes, and the paradox of it is that Moyers, who is actually the conscience of the White House, is caught in the middle.

By ROBERT P. SEMPLE Jr.
Special to The New York Times

WASHINGTON, Jan. 10 — Bill D. Moyers, the Presidential press secretary, says that news conferences are designed to serve the "convenience of the President, not the convenience of the press."

He also said that the news conference is primarily a device to let the President "say what is on his mind," and that the practice of "planting" questions with reporters beforehand is designed to make certain that someone asks the President questions he is prepared for and wants to talk about.

Mr. Moyers acknowledges that he planted a number of questions before a news conference on Aug. 25, but he denies that this practice tends to inhibit or prevent reporters from asking questions on other matters of public concern.

Mr. Moyers, generally considered the President's top aide, expressed these views in an interview with Paul Niven, a commentator for the National Educational Television Network. The interview, taped on Dec. 24, was shown to Washington viewers tonight and will be televised on Channel 13 in New York City at 7:30 P.M. Wednesday.

The press secretary dealt with a variety of matters in general terms—next year's legislative program, the role of a Presidential assistant, and Mr. Johnson's sense of humor. But much of the interview involved his feelings about the press with whom he deals every day. He expressed some of these feelings rather sharply, among them these:

¶The Washington Press, he declared, "tends to write its opinions of a matter, and then to seek out facts for it."

¶Many of the articles he reads show "very poor judgment," and are "very poorly informed." He gave the example of a reporter who wrote that the President had ordered Vice President Humphrey to visit Vietnam and then, when the White House denied that the President had issued the order, wrote another story suggesting that Mr. Moyers was not telling the truth. Mr. Moyers insisted the original article was wrong in the first place and that the second had been written to cover the reporter's earlier error.

He said that both he and the President preferred to communicate with the American people through radio and television.

"The President feels that he is better served, and I share this very strongly." Mr. Moyers went on, "if he can talk directly to the people through radio and television, than if the people have to decide upon what some other human being

January 7, 1966

—subject to all the frailties of human nature—interprets as his intentions, or as his policy."

He remarked that "interpretation" by the writing press was unquestionably useful, but said that "so often the interpretation is off base."

The gist of Mr. Moyers's argument seemed to be that the average citizen had a better chance to judge the President's policies when they were beamed at him over the airwaves instead of being filtered through a newspaperman's typewriter.

On the subject of news conferences generally, Mr. Moyers said that he preferred "informal conversations" between reporters and the President to what he called "televised extravaganzas," but he acknowledged that "they're part of the scene, "they've become sacred, and I'm sure they will continue."

The President's last televised news conference was held in the White House on Aug. 29. He has had several long "background" sessions with reporters since then, but the scarcity of news conferences has provoked considerable discussion here.

Mr. Moyers said he believed that there were more desirable ways of getting the news out than "the circus of a press conference."

However, he did say that before one such "circus" — the news conference on Aug. 25— he had acted in part as ringmaster.

Dislikes Press 'Circus'

"I did suggest to some reporters," he said "that the President had on his mind certain problems, and that I was certain that he was prepared

to deal with those questions" if the reporters asked about them.

Mr. Niven asked whether this practice did not raise a serious threat to "the traditional function of a news conference."

This function, Mr. Niven said, is to allow the press, representing the public, to question the President about matters of public concern—in short, to let the President know what was on their minds and their readers' minds.

"In the first place," Mr. Moyers replied, "many questions weren't planted. There were two or three subjects that we wanted to be certain were touched upon in that press conference because the President had been giving a good of time to them.

"I don't think the press has ever justifiably felt that the press conference was any other device than one for the President to say what is on his mind," he went on. "It is the prerogative of the President to decide how he's going to make himself available to the press and how and when he makes certain information available to the press.

"It's to serve the convenience of the President, not the convenience of the press that Presidential press conferences are held. There is no right—I mean the President has no statutory obligation to hold press conferences.

"His job is to make information known to the public. The press conference is a convenient device for doing that—for achieving that purpose. But there is no law, and in fact there's no inherent procedure that says he must do it in this way or that way."

January 11, 1966

PRESIDENT WEIGHS TV 'FIRESIDE CHAT'

WASHINGTON, Feb. 14 (UPI) — President Johnson is considering another one-hour televised "fireside chat" with newsmen to explain his views on problems confronting the nation.

The program would be similar to the informal television conversations with newsmen that President Kennedy introduced. Mr. Johnson appeared on a similar program in March, 1964.

The White House said today that a proposal for a television chat in the near future had been submitted to the President by the American Broadcasting Company, the Columbia Broadcasting System and the National Broadcasting Company.

Bill D. Moyers, White House press secretary, said no date had been set and no final decision made. But he said Mr. Johnson was considering the proposal.

February 15, 1966

Democrats Want TV to Bid on '68 Tilt

The Democrats are thinking of a plan that would put politics in the same league with big-time athletics.

The party would like television networks to bid for the privilege of televising their national conventions. This could yield as much as $2-million toward defraying expenses, a spokesman said yesterday.

"They do it on major sports events," Wayne Phillips, director of public information for the Democratic National Committee, told The Associated Press in Washington.

"Instead of having all three networks cover the convention, which has gotten to be a madhouse, we'd try to sell the time to them," he explained.

The television networks were less than enthusiastic about the suggestion.

"An astounding proposal," said Elmer Lower, president of the American Broadcasting Company's news department.

The Columbia Broadcasting System was astounded in more words.

"We can't believe this is a serious proposal for handling something as important as the selection of the potential President and Vice President of the United States," observed Richard S. Salant, acting president of C.B.S. News. "If they want to treat themselves as if they were a commercial spectator sport, that's their business. As a news organization, we intend to cover their convention as news."

William R. McAndrews, executive vice president in charge of National Broadcasting Company news, said that he would have nothing to say until the plan was proposed officially.

Mr. Phillips said that he had not discussed the subject with the networks. In Washington, the Republican National Committee said only that it had no similar plan.

Mr. Phillips said that he had been assigned to look into this method of raising money that could substitute for funds that might be lost to the party if an amendment to the $6-billion tax bill is passed by Congress.

The amendment, proposed by Senator John J. Williams, a Delaware Republican, would outlaw income-tax deductions for "indirect political contributions." Some corporations de-

duct as business expenses the cost of advertisements in political publications and of other party fund-raising projects. The amendment would bar these deductions if profits from such publications and functions benefited a political party.

Mr. Phillips said that advertising had raised $2-million at his party's 1964 convention. He said that this is the sort of money that must be replaced if the amendment becomes law.

The suggestion raises a number of questions for which nobody seemed to have an immediate answer. Could other networks be barred from a public place such as a convention hall? How would this affect sponsorship of conventions?

Such sponsorship partly defrays network expenses for coverage. Sponsorship of sports events covers the high prices networks bid for them, such as the $37.6-million C.B.S. is paying to televise National Football League games this year and next, plus $2-million for the 1966 title game. N.B.C. pays $34-million to televise regular American Football League games.

Also convention delegates have always welcomed the opportunity to play to a three-network audience. There have been shorts from politicians when broadcasters have even hinted at one-network coverage.

After the national conventions of 1964, many television stations questioned whether it was necessary to have them blanketed by all three networks. The public, in many areas, they said, had been deprived of other entertainment for eight days.

Their concern reflected protests from viewers who lived where only network programing was available. Where there were other stations, the independent stations carrying sports or entertainment noted a sharp rise in ratings, drawing far more viewers than the conventions.

Mr. Phillips's equation of the conventions with sports programing drew some unofficial comment from network executives.

"We've referred the plan to our sports department," equipped one programmer.

"What will we do?" asked another. "Would we have to pay more for the Democrats, who have the President, than for the Republicans?"

March 12, 1966

169

MAYOR PLANNING TELETHON SERIES

Calls It Equivalent of New England Town Meeting

By THOMAS P. RONAN

Mayor Lindsay announced yesterday that he would conduct telethons so that New Yorkers could phone him directly "with their suggestions, complaints and other comments."

"This will be the metropolitan equivalent of the New England town meeting," he said at a luncheon of the International Radio and TV Society at the Waldorf-Astoria Hotel.

He said plans for the telethons, which would be part of his over-all effort to use television and radio more extensively, would be in final form within a month or so.

An aide said later that the length and frequency of the telethons had not been decided but that they might run "an hour or so on an experimental basis and then be extended if they work out."

The word telethon is normally applied to lengthy television shows running considerably more than an hour during which questions are telephoned in or persons on the show solicit contributions by telephone for some charitable cause.

On last election eve, Mr. Lindsay held a two-hour telecast during which he answered telephoned questions. He considered this so successful that he tried to buy additional time. When he was unable to do so, he moved to a radio station where he answered questions from 2 A.M. to 3 A.M.

Show Called Valuable

Mr. Lindsay told the luncheon guests that television and radio had been "very valuable" to him during his election campaign and since he had become Mayor.

"In New York City, it almost goes without saying, there are no less than two sides to every public question and very often a half-dozen or more," he declared. "It is essential to the demands of leadership that the Mayor strive to communicate his plans and explain his deci-

sions directly to the people who elected him."

Representatives of three of the major television stations here said yesterday they had heard nothing of the telethon plan until the luncheon.

Mr. Lindsay devoted most of his speech to a discussion of the exodus of television production from this city to Hollywood and his plans to reverse the trend.

He said that last autumn only 10 of the 96 entertainment shows on the three national networks were produced here. Most, he said were music, game and variety programs and only two were drama series.

"Thus an industry contributing billions of dollars yearly to tis city's economy — in salaries, in facilities, in billings, in purchases — moved most of its operations away," he said.

He cited as probably the basic reason for the move the industry's accelerated use of film and tapes and Hollywood's ability to shift from motion picture to television production.

He said other reasons that had been mentioned were that Hollywood had more studios, more cooperative unions, a larger pool of actors and better weather.

He said he was considering a proposal to issue one permit for all the shooting done by one production unit. Another proposal under study, he said was the assignment of an assistant to the Mayor to improve and speed cooperation between the industry and city officials.

Advance Notice Required

He noted that the present law required that an application for a shooting permit be filed at least 72 hours in advance of the shooting. He said that this in effect required a producer who wanted to shoot a scene in the rain "to predict precipitation three days in advance" and that he was considering reducing the time period.

He described as a promising development the announcement by the Madison Square Garden Corporation that it planned to build a television and motion picture center on Manhattan's West Side. This, he said, might give the city a badly needed "unified film production complex in which every step from start to finish, can take place under a single roof."

Johnson Aide Scores Capital Newsmen

Special to The New York Times

WASHINGTON, April 20— Robert H. Fleming, the new deputy press secretary at the White House, has complained that some Washington reporters are not doing their jobs "very well."

Mr. Fleming said he was not "indicting all reporters, or even all those covering the White House." But he complained that there was too much "poor reporting" by the Washington press corps.

Mr. Fleming made his unusually frank charges against the Washington press corps in a speech Monday before the local chapter of Sigma Delta Chi, a journalism fraternity. In response to inquiries, the White House press office today made available a transcript of the Fleming comments.

What was unusual about the indictment was that it came from a man who only recently was a member of the Washington press corps and that Mr. Fleming named specific articles and reporters in his criticism. Until two months ago Mr. Fleming was news director of the Washington news bureau of the American Broadcasting Company. He said his criticism was based on his experiences since taking over as a deputy to the White House press secretary, Bill D. Moyers.

'Irritated and Angry'

As one specific of why he has become "irritated, angry and not yet furious" with the Washington press corps, Mr. Fleming cited a statement by Stewart Alsop, a columnist, that the "bleeding ulcer" of Mr. Moyers can be attributed in part to the fact that President Johnson is "an immensely difficult man to work for." The fact, which the columnist could easily have established, Mr. Fleming said, is that the doctors have pronounced Mr. Moyers's ulcer "cured."

Another example cited by Mr. Fleming was how another columnist, Andrew Tully, had complained in a letter to the editor of The Washington Evening Star that Mr. Moyers "seems to be spending most of his time" telling Washington reporters "how stupid and even corrupt they are." With just a little checking, Mr. Fleming said, any reporter could find out that "nobody who is important to the President spends 'most of his time' making speeches."

Mr. Fleming also cited a newspaper article in which a

reporter, Douglas Kiker of The New York Herald Tribune, proposed to "project himself into something" by writing that "President Johnson is in a foul mood this Easter Sunday, apparent for all to see." The article, Mr. Fleming pointed out, was written on Saturday by a reporter who was 78 miles away from the President's ranch.

'Offended' by Reporter

Mr. Fleming also took to task an Associated Press reporter, Frank Cormier, who, he complained, showed no interest when Mr. Fleming asked for a copy of an Associated Press dispatch from Saigon that the President had sent orders to American officials in Saigon to "win the war in '67 or else." Mr. Fleming said he was so "offended" that the reporter had not inquired whether the dispatch was accurate that he took the initiative in denying the Saigon report.

As another "extreme," Mr. Fleming cited the case of a reporter not identified, who suggested he was "withholding news" when he refused to provide quotes on what the President said to George Hamilton when the actor arrived at the ranch to call on Lynda Bird Johnson.

Since taking over the White House press post, Mr. Fleming said he had spent "some private moments being annoyed with my friends in the press corps.

"They want comfort; they want reliable lids [a journalistic term that no more news is expected]; they want transcripts; they want advance travel plans; they want jet-speed airplanes to jet-age hotels where they hope to have a leisurely, horse-and-buggy schedule."

Criticism Tempered

In making such demands, he said, the reporters "believe their own importance as channels of communication—at least around the White House where the channels can sometimes face flash floods on little or no notice."

But he tempered his criticism by saying that "about the time I get bitter toward White House correspondents, I get awestruck at their stamina, their energy, their devotion to the jobs."

Mr. Fleming said the purpose of his criticism, as well as that recently expressed by Mr. Moyers, was to "generate some self-examination on reporting" within the journalistic profession.

SALINGER SUGGESTS A U.S. PRESS PANEL

Special to The New York Times

WASHINGTON, Sept. 7 — Pierre Salinger proposed today that President Johnson appoint a commission to make a "study of the relationships between the Government and the press in the cold war era."

Mr. Salinger, former press secretary to Presidents Johnson and Kennedy, told a luncheon at the National Press Club that "the central issue is how the press, with its great freedoms embodied in the American Constitution, can operate as freely as possible in a democratic society locked in a struggle with some of the great secret societies of all time."

He said he did not "favor censorship in any form." But he said that he had "suggested restraint in the past, and suggest restraint today, in the area of national security news."

Mr. Salinger proposed that the commission be made up of representatives of the press media and that it include persons who have served in Government and a small group of persons who represent neither the press nor the Government.

Mr. Salinger, 41 years old, is vice president for international affairs for Continental Airlines. He remained as President Johnson's press secretary for four months after President Kennedy's assassination in 1963 and later served briefly as a Senator from California. He is the author of a new book, "With Kennedy," published by Doubleday & Co.

TV: Questions on Campaign-Aid Tax

By JACK GOULD

THE use of Federal income taxes to finance Presidential campaigns is a numbing prospect for the television viewer. Apparently it is not enough that the taxpayer should have to look at the wretched political spot announcements that make a farce of civilized governmental processes; now he is being invited to pay for them.

Senate passage on Saturday of the campaign financing amendment to the tax bill, under which the taxpayer could voluntarily assign $1 of his tax payment to a Presidential campaign kitty, potentially represents a whopping windfall for the TV industry. The dominant item of campaign expense is the purchase of time on the home screen.

If enough taxpayers agree to become participating sponsors, the Democrats and Republicans might have $70-million to divide in 1968, according to Washington dispatches. What is still far from fair, however, is whether such a sum would be a floor or ceiling on campaign expenditures. The likelihood of the two major parties agreeing that the extent of their TV exposure before the viewers should be the same runs counter to all experience. The $70-million may just put added economic steam under the TV political pot, not cool it off.

Senator Russell B. Long, Democrat of Louisiana, in introducing the campaign-financing amendment to the tax bill, said it would help curb improper influences by large campaign contributors. But that argument puts the cart before the horse. Why are campaign costs so high? And why is so much unfairness built into the present use of television?

Instead of trying to use public funds to cover the costs of present abuses, attention should be directed to the cause of those abuses.

One of the basic causes is the political manipulation of television for partisan advantage. This opportunity is built into the communications law and has been skillfully exploited by those familiar with the nuances of the preposterous application of the equal-air-time provision.

The networks and individual broadcasting stations have offered hours of free time without charge to political candidates. But the campaign strategists have often turned such tenders down and knowingly driven up campaign expenditures.

In the last Presidential race, for example, established TV news programs sought appearances by President Johnson and Senator Barry Goldwater. Virtually all the overtures were rejected by the White House, allegedly because the Democratic party saw no point in giving free exposure to the Republican aspirant. Unless both candidates agreed to appear, the networks were open to violation of the principle of equal time.

In effect, therefore, if one candidate feels he is better known than his rival he can exert a veto power over his opponent's free appearances and force him to buy time. This strategic attitude also accounts for the invariable nonsense over challenges and counter challenges on the subject of TV debates, which do not involve any campaign costs. One candidate, usually the one enjoying the publicity advantage of being an incumbent, sees no purpose in putting a rival on an equal stature in the public eye.

Much of the large costs of politics on television is by design and lies in the weakness of the Communications Act, which exempts paid political broadcasts from the criterion of equal time. Upon selling hours of time to one candidate, all a broadcaster must do is agree to make similar time available to other contenders. But if the other contenders cannot come up with the money, they are for practical purposes kept off the air. The social importance of this situation is the universal belief by all politicians that television is now essential to elections.

The disadvantages of the procedure, moreover, are abundantly evident in the present gubernatorial race in New York. Governor Rockefeller started a series of spot announcements long before he and Frank D. O'Connor, the Democratic candidate, were nominated. Mr. O'Connor has been snowed under with Rockefeller spots and Franklin D. Roosevelt Jr., the Liberal party's designee, is barely heard at all. Obviously they do not have the economic resources of the "Friends of the Rockefeller Team," nominal sponsor of the Governor's messages.

Governor Rockefeller's spots are thoroughly typical of the emotional oversimplification of government inherent in trying to convert politics to the level of washing-machine detergents. The nonsense about fish being delighted by the Governor's efforts to halt water pollution, and about the Governor paving enough roads to extend to Hawaii and back are symptomatic of how spot announcements have reduced serious issues to handy slogans designed to stress the element of a candidate's personality.

Senator Long's hastily conceived measure, which applies only to Presidential campaigns, may ultimately serve a useful purpose if it results in a larger re-examination of politics on television.

Thought might well be given, for instance, to the question of whether a medium that exists through free use of the air waves belonging to the public should not be expected to donate a certain percentage of hours to the task of choosing a President. A generous amount of such time might not actually exceed what the networks already have been prepared to offer if they had not been hobbled by restrictive legislation.

The British system of handling politics in broadcasting may warrant scrutiny. A limitation on the number of TV hours under the control of the parties carries an automatic safeguard against one party outscoring the other and allows for proportional representation of minority parties, something the Long amendment does not.

For many years Dr. Frank Stanton, president of the Columbia Broadcasting System, repeatedly, if futilely, has urged a thorough re-examination of the problems of TV in politics. In particular he has appealed for studies to be started well in advance of the deadline pressures of an imminent Presidential campaign. His words deserve heeding now because raising more money to finance the soaring costs of political advertising on TV is not the answer. Presidential campaigns, not to mention the contests for lesser offices, need to be directed away from Madison Avenue's philosophy and back to the lucid and earnest concern for serious issues. Such concern would better serve the electorate and also significantly curb the assorted perils of spiraling expenditures to win public office.

Advertising: Campaigning for Campaigners

By PHILIP DOUGHERTY

Over at Jack Tinker & Partners, the clients include beer, pharmaceuticals and Governor Rockefeller; at Richard K. Manoff, Inc., it's beer, liquor, canned goods and Frank D. O'Connor, and at Furman, Feiner & Co., it's the A.F.L.-C.I.O., I.L.G.W.U. and F.D.R. Jr.

People selling is very big these days.

With less than two weeks remaining before the big day in the race for the governor's chair, the agencies are planning their last-minute thrusts. Sorry, can't tell you what they are exactly. They're either being kept secret because of the competition or the planners are not sure because of money.

But it can be reported, thanks to highly placed, reliable and well-informed sources (Jack Conroy at Tinker and William F. Haddad at O'Connor headquarters) that the Republican candidate will soon have ads in every weekly and daily newspaper in the state and the Democratic standard-bearer's ads will continue to be reminders of television appearances.

So far in the television campaigning, there has been a vast difference between the length and types of advertising used for the candidates. Governor Rockefeller's started in July, with, as Mr. Conroy put it, "a light schedule, now it's peaking, naturally."

Tinker, which is part of the Interpublic Group of Companies, has prepared "a dozen or 14" commercials.

"We tried to show what the Governor has done on the more important issues in a very positive way," explained Mr. Conroy. "None of us here are politicians, just professional ad men," he continued. "They (the Republicans) provided us with the basic information on which issues were considered important."

There had been comment in some circles that the well-made TV messages were not making their point. Mr. Conroy, however, said that his people had checked early in the campaign and found that they were. So there. He called them "soft sell."

Mr. Conroy indicated that the amount of billings was, for the moment, classified.

Mr. Haddad, whose United States Research and Development Company has been retained by Mr. O'Connor, wasn't shy about estimating Republican expenditures.

"Two million and that's a minimum, minimum, minimum," he said repetitively.

He put the Democrat spending at "less than $50,000."

Of their presentation of the candidate, he said, "We're not using any gimmicks, just have him talking to the camera. Frank O'Connor is not the kind you have to hide. The best thing we have is O'Connor."

Neither the Manoff nor Tinker agencies have had candidates as clients before. Little Furman, Feiner, with $1.25-million in annual billings, however, has done its best in days gone by for both Liberals and Democrats. Their John Morgan headed the national television spot campaign for President Kennedy in the "ethnic market."

For Mr. Roosevelt's TV spots, which are usually live telephone-answering sessions, the agency is only arranging the time spots and telephone installations, Mr. Morgan said.

Leeds Advertising, Inc., is handling the print media for the Liberal Party candidate, with "mostly small space ads to tie in with TV appearances."

While these four agencies are working locally for their candidates, de Garmo, Inc., is going national and nonpartisan.

In behalf of their client, the A.B.C.-Owned Television Stations in New York, Chicago, Detroit and San Francisco, they have prepared ads, to run on Nov. 2 in those cities explaining the propositions and amendments to the voters. The ads will say "You'd swear they were written by some Philadelphia lawyer," and "Watch out. Sometimes 'No' means 'Yes!'"

And one more thing, before anyone lifts an angry pen to protest unfairness. Paul L. Adams, the Conservative candidate, doesn't have an agency.

Will the Real Candidate Stand Up?

By VAL ADAMS

THE television networks are turned on for Tuesday night's off-year election. Don't plan to watch "The Girl From U.N.C.L.E.," "Petticoat Junction," "The Pruitts of Southampton" and other regularly scheduled shows. All are pre-empted. Watch instead the up-to-the-minute voting tabulations on your favorite candidate. And long before all the votes are in, the networks will be making forecasts of probable winners.

The National Broadcasting Company has Electronic Vote Analysis, a computer system that projects and analyzes election results. The Columbia Broadcasting System refers to its computation arrangement as Vote Profile Analysis. The American Broadcasting Company has not named its system, but it alleges it has a $2-million computer just as big as anyone else's.

The reporting of election returns, and who voted which way and why, is a pretty serious business with the networks. The commentators on the air ad lib, for the most part. Each network, however, does have an election night rehearsal some days before election day. It is done so all those involved can go through a routine that helps them to familiarize themselves with their jobs on election night.

Last week A.B.C. had a rehearsal in which William H. Lawrence, political editor, and John Kraft, political analyst, participated. Mr. Kraft makes all sorts of surveys in advance to determine political thinking.

During the A.B.C. rehearsal, there was a segment in which Mr. Lawrence was to question Mr. Kraft about election happenings. Normally, the two would have faked the whole thing, but Mr. Lawrence decided to prepare a script that would satirize the the situation. With Mr. Lawrence asking the questions, excerpts from the script went like this:

Q. Mr. Kraft, what is the major finding of your political surveys?

A. Political sands are shifting.

Q. How can you tell?

A. Our interviewers met voters face-to-face, head-to-head and eyeball-to-eyeball. We fielded the questionnaires, tabulated the results and made our findings.

Q. But this is election night —not a poll. What happens now?

A. When our battalions have massaged the vote we'll noodle the figures and chew the strands.

Q. What is the most significant feature of the 1966 elections?

A. Interface.

Q. Excuse me, I'm not sure what Interface is.

A. Neither am I.

Q. Some of the races seem terribly close. Why is that?

A. The situation is murky.

Q. Are all our [vote reporting] troops in place?

A. We're touching base everywhere.

Q. Are you really confident?

A. It's now one minute to midnight and it's a walking-on-eggs situation.

Q. Have we taken out insurance?

A. The entire program has been fail-safed.

Q. In what way?

A. The team has been suited up, phased in and made ready for a stiff final round. We will re-trigger where re-triggering is necessary.

Q. What is our status now?

A. I'd say we are hell bent for election.

MOYERS RESIGNING AS JOHNSON'S AIDE TO HEAD NEWSDAY

By MAX FRANKEL
Special to The New York Times

WASHINGTON, Dec. 14—Bill D. Moyers, President Johnson's intimate friend, adviser and press secretary, is resigning from the White House staff to become publisher of Newsday, the prosperous Long Island afternoon newspaper.

Mr. Moyers, 32 years old, is the last of the team of assistants assembled by Mr. Johnson when he became President three years ago.

He will leave on Jan. 31 and be replaced as press secretary by George C. Christian, 39, an old family friend of the Johnsons, who came to the White House last May from the staff of Gov. John B. Connally Jr. of Texas.

The indications are that Mr. Moyers will depart with the President's blessings to accept an extraordinary offer that promises him financial independence within a few years despite heavy obligations to a number of relatives.

As publisher of Newsday he will succeed Harry F. Guggenheim, the 76-year-old president of the company who has run the paper since the death in 1963 of its founder, his wife, Alicia Patterson.

Another Aide Also Resigning

Mr. Moyers coupled the announcement of his resignation with the disclosure that Jake Jacobsen, another close friend of the President, planned to resign as legislative counsel early next year. He will return to private law practice in Austin, Tex., after serving for nearly two years as the President's constant aide and companion, both here and at his Texas ranch.

No replacement for Mr. Jacobsen has been named.

The departures are expected to increase still further the load borne at the White House by four special assistants.

Many of Mr. Moyers's duties in planning Administration tactics, evolving domestic programs and writing speeches will fall to Harry C. McPherson Jr., Joseph A. Califano Jr. and Douglass Cater Jr., all liberals whom Mr. Moyers helped to recruit and guide toward ever greater responsibility.

Associated Press Wirephoto

MOYERS AND THE MAN FOLLOWING HIM: Bill D. Moyers, right, as he announced his resignation yesterday as the White House press secretary. Behind him is George C. Christian, who will take over the position on Jan. 31.

Mr. Jacobsen's more personal services for the President will probably devolve on W. Marvin Watson, a conservative Texas businessman who is usually at Mr. Johnson's side and who has handled his appointments schedule.

But none of the men now in the White House is likely to achieve the almost filial bonds that linked the President and Mr. Moyers. The younger man, an ordained Baptist minister, has been close to Mr. Johnson all of his adult life, and worked directly for him for most of those years.

Yet he also preserved a sense of detachment from which he derived a strong ambition to establish his own identity some day and to find his own career in public service.

Mr. Moyers showed some interest earlier this year in the position of Under Secretary of State. Later, when the President made known his intention to keep him at the White House indefinitely, he tentatively decided to set out on his own after the 1968 election.

That apparently was Mr. Moyers's reply when Mr. Guggenheim first solicited his interest in Newsday last August. But the death of his brother, James H. Moyers, also an assistant to the President, from an overdose of prescribed drugs in September suddenly added to the press secretary's already considerable financial obligations. His brother left a wife and two young children.

At that point, Mr. Moyers gave stronger consideration to the offer and discussed it at great length with the President.

"The President has told me

that he fully understands the reasons for the considerations which have led to this decision," Mr. Moyers said.

"I spent considerable time with the President discussing this," he added. "I would say, and I will say, that if the President had felt that this was anything but the excellent opportunity that it is, I would likely not have been interested. I value his judgment."

Mr. Moyers said he was reluctant to go, but felt strongly "that because of my family's interest I should go." He is married to the former Judith Suzanne Davidson of Dallas. They have three children aged 7, 3 and 2.

Cites Paper's Independence

The Moyerses will probably settle in Port Washington, L. I. His full title at Newsday will be publisher and chief operating officer, giving him active charge of both editorial and business operations.

Beyond the financial attractions of the job, he said, he was drawn to it by the independence of the paper "politically and philosophically."

He told newsmen that he did not regard the change as a diversion from his interest in public service because "you in 'our profession' have a great public trust, hold a great public trust, not unlike that of public officials who are actually in office."

"I do not consider the line between publishing and politics or public life to be a very visible line," he added.

Mr. Moyers does not plan to write in the foreseeable future, either for the newspaper or about his experiences in the Johnson Administration.

He denied that he had any conflicts or quarrels with any one at the White House. Of the President, he said:

"My personal devotion to him to what I consider to be his philosophy of public service and of Government is undiminished in any extent. This decision to leave the President has, in frankness, been the most difficult decision I have made."

Mr. Moyers came out of virtual seclusion to announce his resignation, after rumors of it had spread through Washington and New York and one report had reached print in The New York Daily News.

He retired to a back room after about 10 days ago to help work out next year's legislative program and to draft the State of the Union message for the President. After its delivery Jan. 10, he plans to take two weeks off before moving north.

To Mr. Christian, whose promotion he had recommended, Mr. Moyers gave only one line of public advice: "Work hard and maintain a sense of humor."

Mr. Christian was born and raised in Austin, Tex., near Mr. Johnson's native hill country, where George Christian Sr. had been a well-known district attorney. The families have known each other for 30 years. The future press secretary studied English and journalism at the University of Texas before and after service in the marines in World War II. After a brief stint as sports editor for the Temple (Tex.) Daily Telegram, he worked for seven years for the International News Service, as sports writer and later political correspondent.

In 1957 he became press secretary and executive assistant to former Gov. Price Daniel, jobs that he retained under Mr. Daniels's successor, Governor Connally. He came to the White House as an administrative assistant in Mr. Moyers's office last May.

After the death of his first wife, Mr. Christian was married in 1959 to the former Jo Anne Martin, a lawyer here and in Texas. They have five children.

Mr. Jacobsen, 47 years old, also came to Mr. Johnson from the staff of Governor Daniel. He is a native of Atlantic City, N. J., who moved to Texas while serving with the Army Air Corps and remained to get his law degree. He went on to serve as an assistant attorney general there and develop a private practice, with prominent sideline duties in the state's Democratic party.

He has a reputation as an astute legislative tactician. In Washington he is known as a personable and gracious man who has preferred to stay out of the limelight.

Over the last year, when the White House moved to a paneled ground floor room at the LBJ Ranch, Mr. Jacobsen and a secretary worked in the same room with the President.

He is married to the former Florene Jones of Nacogdoches, Texas.

173

Man With Many Hats
Billy Don Moyers

Special to The New York Times

United Press International Telephoto

*"I'm here if you
need me."*
(Bill D. Moyers at the White
House yesterday.)

WASHINGTON, Dec. 14—
In the summer of 1954, a young North Texas State College student wrote Senator Lyndon B. Johnson a letter, advising him how to win the young people's vote in a re-election campaign. It was such an impressive letter that the young man wound up as an interne on the Senate majority leader's staff. Five years later, after studies at the Universities of Texas and Edinburgh and acquiring a Bachelor of Divinity degree from the Southwestern Baptist Theological Seminary, the youth joined Mr. Johnson's Senate staff more permanently.

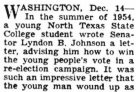

By the time the Senator became Vice President of the United States in 1961, Billy Don Moyers, at age 27, was one of his principal assistants.

Later, when he was deputy director of the Peace Corps, his connection with Mr. Johnson was so strong that when trouble broke out between warring Texas political factions over a forthcoming visit by President Kennedy and the Vice President, Mr. Moyers was sent to Austin to put the matter right.

He was in that city on Nov. 22, 1963, when the word came that John F. Kennedy had been assassinated in Dallas and that Lyndon B. Johnson would be sworn as President.

'I'm Here If You Need Me'

Mr. Moyers chartered a plane to Dallas. When he reached the airport there, he was barred by the Secret Service from entering the Presidential plane. He scribbled a note and sent it in to Mr. Johnson: "I'm here if you need me," it said.

The new President did. He took Bill D. Moyers aboard, and he has been aboard through all the remarkable highs and lows of the Johnson Administration until today, when he resigned to become publisher of the prosperous Long Island daily tabloid, Newsday.

It will not be Bill Moyers's first newspaper experience. As a schoolboy in Marshall, Tex., where he was born to a struggling family on June 5 in the Depression year of 1934, he served as the ace reporter for The Marshall News-Messenger and later for The East Texas Daily.

And since July 8, 1965, as one of the most remarkable collector of hats ever worn by a White House staff member, he has been wearing that of President Johnson's press secretary.

Mr. Moyers's departure to a lucrative executive position leaves no one on the Johnson staff who has been there since the day the President took office. During that time, despite his youth, Mr. Moyers became one of the most influential and active staff aides in Presidential history.

Close Advisor to Johnson

He was the major figure in putting together the Great Society program of social and welfare legislation in early 1965. He has been one of the President's chief advisors on foreign affairs — and many Administration figures, including David K. E. Bruce, the Ambassador to Britain, advised Mr. Johnson to make him Under Secretary of State when George W. Ball resigned last summer.

The President decided, instead, to keep Mr. Moyers as his press secretary, closest personal advisor, and political and diplomatic trouble-shooter.

It was Bill Moyers, for instance, who negotiated in advance practically everything that Mr. Johnson put his official stamp upon during his Asian tour this fall, just as two years ago it was Bill Moyers who was the primary planner and strategist in Mr. Johnson's triumphant political campaign against Barry Goldwater in the Presidential election.

When Walter Jenkins, then Mr. Johnson's top assistant, resigned in personal difficulties at the height of that campaign, Bill Moyers was upgraded to his place on the staff. And when the President first began to get a bad press and to suffer slipping popularity in the summer of 1965, it was to the former Marshall News-Messenger reporter that he turned for a new press secretary—without, of course, relieving Mr. Moyers from any of his other duties.

Much of the Presidential prose in the Johnson years, moreover, has come straight from the Moyers typewriter, on which he pecks more or less efficiently.

Despite all this, at 32, Bill Moyers is a mild-mannered, bespectacled, pleasant chap, who smokes long, thin cigars, discloses very little of the fact that he is an ordained Baptist minister, displays lingering traces of a Texas accent, and occasionally throws into his conversation a lofty quotation or a reference to the ancient Greeks.

Even in the White House, he is addicted to practical jokes—one of which involved a fake resignation by a former White House assistant, Richard D. Goodwin. It got so far out of hand that Mr. Moyer himself had to rescue the spurious document from President Johnson's desk.

The youthful Texan somewhat dignified himself when he came to the White House by insisting on "Bill D." instead of the Southern "Billy Don." He lives simply in the Virginia suburbs of the capital with his wife, Judith, and their three children, and although he once suffered from an ulcer, he has subdued it with enough milkshakes to permit him occasionally to indulge his passion for barbecue and Mexican food.

For the last three years, however, his life has been centered in the White House, from which disgruntled reports have sometimes been heard that he is a tough empire builder who lets little stand in his path.

On the other hand, he is regarded by many associates as the personification of Mr. Johnson's best instincts, the most liberal influence in the White House. He will have none of that.

"I haven't made Lyndon Johnson," he once said, in his modest manner. "It's quite the opposite."

What makes him run so hard? His old boss at the Peace Corps, Sargent Shriver, thinks it is a lingering "religious motive." A colleague at the White House, Harry C. McPherson Jr., a special assistant to the President, calls him a "liberal believer—a Methodist instead of a Baptist in his sense of service. You give yourself utterly, you don't just preach."

But no one who knows him doubts that Bill Moyers has as strong an urge to power as his boss in the White House. He has made it plain to friends that he wants to make a life in the public service and therefore the betting in this city today was that Newsday had hired itself a first-class executive and publisher—so good, in fact, that some President, some time in the future, would call him right back to Washington.

Washington: On Disposable Press Secretaries

By JAMES RESTON

WASHINGTON, Dec. 15—President Johnson seems to have invented the disposable press secretary. He uses them up and tosses them away like paper napkins: four in three years, not to mention Bob Fleming, an indestructible character who stays around as a spare.

Bill D. Moyers, the last to resign, could probably have been saved, but not as Johnson's Boswell. He wanted to go to the State Department as a roving ambassador, as he had earlier hoped to replace George Ball as Under Secretary of State, but it didn't work.

An Indeterminate Sentence

Both Ambassador David Bruce and Associate Justice Abe Fortas urged the President to appoint Moyers to Ball's job, but he refused. At that time the President apparently told Moyers he wanted him to stay at the White House. This confronted Moyers with an indeterminate sentence as the President's personal spokesman and threatened his health, his reputation as a meticulously truthful man and his solvency. So he resigned after hearing about notoriously high salaries in the newspaper business.

Mr. Moyers is really a casualty of the Vietnam war. He was badly wounded at Credibility Gap and has been limping ever since. Either he had to restore confidence in the good faith of the White House or in the end become a symbol of the lack of confidence. He chose not to go broke in a hopeless cause.

Wear Out or Get Out

Nevertheless, there is a great deal to be said for the disposable public servant in Washington. The physical and mental pressures on the men at the top of this Government are too intense and relentless to be endured indefinitely. They either get out or wear out, except for the stubborn martyrs who make things worse by wearing out and staying on.

The law of diminishing returns has been depleting Moyers for some time. He really fought to restore confidence between the President and the press, but between decontaminating the reporters' questions and sanitizing the President's answers, his energy and authority inevitably suffered. A man can say "no" to Lyndon Johnson for a while, but it is not a progressively successful formula.

Then, too, the frustrations of fighting these two devilish wars in Vietnam and the cities are even harder on officials these days than the physical labor. Some of them do not agree with the President's priorities. Some want the poverty program to have more funds, some less; some want the bombing stopped, some want it extended; the Joint Chiefs, not satisfied with a $70- or $75-billion defense budget next year, want to add an antiballistic missile-defense system and build shelters before houses. These are important issues, but they do not make the Johnson Administration a very happy ship.

It has many good qualities. It works hard, but it is a desperate grind, without much inspiring leadership or intellectual excitement, and this is probably the real meaning of the Moyers resignation. For the young men are not yearning to come to Washington as they were under Kennedy. The mortality rate is high and the flow of outstanding replacements is low.

This is not because the President has put his cronies in top jobs. He has been remarkably objective and non-political in his appointments. John Macy of the Civil Service Commission, an able and imaginative public servant, has been stockpiling fresh talent as fast as he can, but the atmosphere of this Administration simply does not attract as many brilliant volunteers as the pressures and the Johnson system devour.

Accordingly, Moyers is not the only official here who dreams of taking refuge on Long Island. Sargent Shriver, director of the Skirmish on Poverty, is not very happy. He is being shortchanged by the Congress and ignored by the President, and if his agency is cut up and scattered to Labor, H.E.W. and other departments, he may very well join the Kennedy Government in Exile.

Secretary of Commerce Connor is not deliriously joyful either, though Secretaries of Commerce rarely ever are. Like a lot of other officials here, he has been arguing for a tax increase ever since the spring, but in the struggle between taxes and votes, he lost.

So there will probably be a lot of changes here in the next few months, and this in itself is not bad. A government, like a pro football team, needs reserves. The problem is how the President is going to find and hold them if he cannot hold as able, loyal and valuable an aide as Bill Moyers.

December 16, 1966

'Credibility' of Press

SAN FRANCISCO, Dec. 28 (UPI)—Labor Secretary W. Willard Wirtz questioned today the "credibility" of news media in covering Government affairs.

In an address before the Industrial Relations Research Association here, the Secretary observed that in the last year "the press has been full of reports about 'the credibility gap,'" a phrase that has emerged to describe lack of candor by Government officials.

The Government is obligated to provide accurate information to the press, he said, but the press is equally obligated to report the news in perspective.

"Would the media accept a share of responsibility for promoting a standard of not just a right to know, but an obligation to know?" he asked.

Includes Trust Funds

"It is worth asking," Mr. Wirtz went on, "what standard of 'credibility' it is that inspires or permits an editor to persist in protesting the alleged inflationary effects of the paper imbalance of the Government's 'administrative budget' when he knows (and knows most of his readers don't know) that only the much more nearly balanced 'national income accounts budget' bears any relationship to national economic stability?"

The national income accounts budget, unlike the administrative budget, includes all Federal trust funds such as those for social security and highway construction.

Because most of the funds are derived from taxes, they would reflect any changes in purchasing power and therefore would be a more accurate economic indicator.

Until recently, however, most Presidents have talked of their spending plans in terms of the administrative rather than the national income accounts budget.

Mr. Wirtz said the Government was basing its policy increasingly on statisticians' measurements of the national condition and on reports of those measurements in the news media.

The validity of such actions depends on whether the measurements and the reports are accurately made and understood, he said. He went on:

"There is no communication of truth unless it is heard as well as understood. If it is hidden in a haystack of tabular exhibits or back of the obituaries on page 37, it isn't part of the significant truth.

"Statistics are dull news—except for the bbox scores of doom and disaster, casaulty lists or holiday deaths on the highways.

"But is it too much to ask that when national policy is put at stake, there be a higher standard of communication ethics than readers' or listeners' obsessions?"

December 29, 1966

ROMNEY IS CRITICAL OF NEWS COVERAGE

LANSING, Mich., Jan. 9 (UPI) — Gov. George Romney said today that news coverage of some of his activities had been "rather superficial" and implied that reporters were too preoccupied with his possible Presidential candidacy.

At a news conference, Mr. Romney said he was "not complaining, just commenting."

The subject came up when Mr. Romney was asked why he had not announced his trip to New York City Friday, ostensibly to visit friends. Mr. Romney replied:

"I told you fellows straight out several weeks ago that I'm not going to tell you about every appointment or every trip I make. And I'll tell you why: There are too many political anthropologists who proceed to place a political interpretation on things they don't justify."

A "political anthropologist," Mr. Romney said, is one who takes a phrase and builds an article "just as an anthropologist can take a jaw bone and build a skeleton."

Mr. Romney cited news coverage of his activities at the Republican Governors Conference at Colorado Springs and at the National Governors Conference at White Sulphur Springs, W. Va., both held in November.

January 10, 1967

WIRTZ CRITICIZES NEWS COVERAGE

By DAMON STETSON

Labor Secretary W. Williard Wirtz criticized news media yesterday for "selective coverage" and for emphasizing negative rather than positive aspects of the news.

In a luncheon address at the Overseas Press Club, he suggested that a considerable part of what the public read and saw and heard about the conduct of its public affairs was "a diluted and artificially colored version of fact and truth."

He attrbiuted this to the separate misdemeanors" of public "sometimes equal sometimes lic officials and the news media.

Mr. Wirtz said that it wasn't a matter of truths and lies but that the problem was "with the truth that lies — when it is turned against itself by someone's passing off part of it as the whole; by putting in words that deliberately mislead the reader but leave the writer ample alibi; by adding an adverg; by some trick juxtaposition of words and facts; by leading a story with some little sick fact that infects everything that follows."

Invited by Riesel

Secretary Wirtz said that Victor Riesel, labor columnist and president of the Overseas Press Club, had invited him to address the club's members and to expand on remarks he made last December in San Francisco in criticism of the press.

The Cabinet officer questioned a story about an address by a public official, discussing how to achieve peace, that began with an account of 50 student hecklers. He decried emphasis on draft card burners, narcotics addicts and lovers of four-letter words when the present generation of youth, he said, was working harder at its books than any before it and announc-

ing its ideals of service by oversubscribing the Peace Corps.

He asked whether truth or Mammon was being served in reporting every incident of isolated indecency or immorality at a Job Corps camp" without putting it in the context of tens of thousands of inherently decent but previously dead-end kids being pulled back at those camps from what would otherwise have been lifetime commitments to indecency and immorality."

Mr. Wirtz said that nobody wanted the press to play Pollyanna. But he asked why the causes of race riots should not be covered as fully as their consequences.

Reference to Powell

"I wish there were front-page pictures every day in every New York paper of the alleys and the hallways and the schools in Harlem and Bedford-Stuyvesant —instead of stories about breaking the faith in Bimini," he said, in an apparent reference to Representative Adam Clayton Powell.

Mr. Wirtz said that last week he had written his second or third letter to the editor in 50 years "only to see it put by The New York Times herself to the petty little editing deceits of a misleading sub-head added and the punch-lines tucked more inconspicuously into the end of the preceding paragraph."

The letter, dealing with the Secretary's stand on wage and price guideposts, was printed in The Times on Feb. 13.

A. H. Raskin, acting editor of the editorial page in the absence of Editor John B. Oakes, who is on a tour of the Far East commented on the criticism as follows:

"Secretary Wirtz's letter was run as the lead item in The Times letter column without the deletion or change of a single word. If there is a fairer way to handle such matters, I don't know what it is."

February 28, 1967

Editors Criticize Johnson News Policy
but Back War Decisions

Report Says He Hurts Image and Credibility

Special to The New York Times

WASHINGTON, April 20—President Johnson was chided today by a committee of top editors for "consistently trying to make the news sound or seem better than it is."

Pointing particularly to Vietnam, a committee of the American Society of Newspaper Editors said: "The war has escalated to the accompaniment of almost unbroken succession of pronouncements that it was going in the opposite direction, or at least that something else was happening."

Although conceding "some slight improvement" in recent months, the committee said in a report to the annual convention that "President Johnson continues to hurt his image and his credibility." The society is meeting in the Shoreham Hotel here.

The editors also criticized the National Aeronautics and Space Administration for its handling of public information about the Jan. 27 Apollo 1 moon capsule fire in which three astronauts lost their lives.

'Misleading Information'

"NASA information not only was late and sparse," the report said, "but some of it was deliberately misleading, some of it inaccurate."

The committee complained that it took two hours for news media to learn that all three astronauts were dead, although the agency knew within five minutes.

The editors were generally satisfied with the Pentagon's ground rules for news coverage of the war in Vietnam, although the report noted some reservations and added that the Pentagon tried "constantly" to manage the news in favor of the military.

In a related report on newspaper coverage of crime, the committee charged that "almost daily attempts" were being made by police officers, prosecutors and judges "to muzzle the press so law enforcement can operate behind closed doors."

The committee, which studied the question for a year, attributed this to the United States Supreme Court's ruling last June in the Sheppard murder case and to a tentative proposal to restrict crime news coverage made in September by a committee of the American Bar Association.

The Court threw out the conviction of Dr. Samuel H. Sheppard for the murder of his wife on the grounds that publicity surrounding the trial amounted to a "circus" atmosphere.

The bar association report suggested sharp curbs on crime accounts, mostly through the use of the contempt power against police officers, prosecutors, court attachés and defense lawyers.

'Middle Course'

"A succession of judges, lawyers and policemen have misinterpreted and over-reacted to both events," the committee said, "demonstrating ever more clearly that news sources in criminal proceedings will be dried up almost completely unless members of the press are ready to fight every time the occasion arises."

In order to avoid "nationwide guerrilla warfare," the committee, despite some dissent within its own ranks, suggested the following "middle course":

¶Increased contacts between newsmen and lawyers at the local level to improve understanding on both sides and to evolve practical, working agreements that minimize the problem.

¶Continued efforts by the editors' society, in cooperation with other professional media groups, to modify the bar association proposals before they become final.

¶A vigorous educational campaign by editors to take the case for newspapers to the public.

¶Specific, all-out opposition by individual newspapers to any effort to restrict the responsible editor's prerogative to print what he thinks the public needs to know about law enforcement.

The report of the Freedom of Information and Press-Bar Committee was presented to over 500 editors attending the three-day session.

Most in Poll Endorse Actions in Vietnam

WASHINGTON, April 20 (AP)—A check of newspaper editors indicated strong support today for President Johnson's handling of the Vietnam problem although many editors believe the Administration has bungled in telling people about it.

Seventy-nine of 103 editors polled at random during the convention of the American Society of Newspaper Editors here voiced generally enthusiastic support for the Administration's policies in Vietnam.

The 24 who objected were divided between hawks and doves. Nine urged a step-up in the pace of the war and 15 called for more intensive peace efforts and an end to bombings of North Vietnam.

"I think what's being done is the right thing," said William W. Baker, editor of The Kansas City, Mo., Star, "but Johnson's unable to tell people exactly what we are doing."

"It's more than just a credibility gap," Mr. Baker added. "It's an understanding gap."

The editors—polled from among the 530 attending the convention—were asked for their personal views; not those of their papers. Some of the President's harshest critics asked that their names not be used because they said their views conflicted with the views of their publishers.

Many Johnson supporters — and some of his critics — expressed regret that the war had been permitted to get to its currently unresolved stage, but said they thought Mr. Johnson was doing a good job now.

Warren Phillips, executive editor of The Wall Street Journal, described himself as a "regrettable" supporter of Mr. Johnson, and added: "Johnson is really the one who got us in as deep as we are. He mishandled that but now that we are in so deep, he's doing as well as anybody could to get it resolved."

Eugene F. Hampson, managing editor of The Plainfield, N.J., Courier-News, saw it a little differently. "I think Johnson inherited something he can't do much about," Mr. Hampson said. "I don't blame him at all."

Alternatives to present Administration policy in Vietnam were forthcoming from the Johnson critics, especially those with more hawkish views.

Robert C. Herrick, editor of The Muskegon, Mich., Chronicle, said, "If we have to fight, let's go all the way. Let's knock 'em out in China."

Most of the Johnson critics with more dovish views emphasized that they thought the best road to peace was through increased negotiations.

"We ought to get any kind of honorable settlement we can," said Mark Ethridge Jr., editorial director of The Detroit Free Press.

April 21, 1967

M'NAMARA SCORES NEWS CENSORSHIP

Criticism Follows Incident Involving Service Paper

By BENJAMIN WELLES
Special to The New York Times

WASHINGTON, May 1 — Robert S. McNamara, the Defense Secretary, said today that "news management and meddling" with news would not be tolerated in the Defense Department.

In a memorandum he ordered his civilian and military subordinates to observe a policy of "maximum disclosure" of news, except information judged to be of "material assistance to potential enemies."

The memorandum was made public through the Pentagon's Office of Public Affairs.

Representative John E. Moss, Democrat of California, who is chairman of the House Subcommittee on Foreign Operations and Government Information, praised Mr. McNamara's action, which he said would "help deter the nonsensical military meddling with the free flow of news to the general public and to the armed forces."

Mr. Moss's subcommittee is investigating charges of military censorship in the European edition of Stars and Stripes. He said his inquiry would continue to "assure that the secretary's stated policy achieves its objectives."

Mr. McNamara's instructions appeared to be directed at Thomas D. Morris, Assistant Secretary for Manpower, and Phil G. Goulding, Assistant Secretary for Public Affairs.

Mr. Morris' responsibilities include the supervision of the armed forces radio and television service and periodicals, such as Stars and Stripes, intended for servicemen. Mr. Goulding's jurisdiction covers the release of Defense Department information for the general public.

Vigorously Worded

In his vigorously worded memorandum Mr. McNamara made clear that managed news or meddling would not be tolerated "either in external public information or internal troop information."

Well informed sources said the order was intended to halt attempts by military commanders to censor newspapers and radio and television programs serving military personnel.

The sources recalled an incident in March when Col. George E. Moranda was relieved of his duty as public affairs officer of the United States Army's European headquarters at Heidelberg at the order of Gen. Andrew P. O'Meara, the army commander in Europe.

Although Colonel Moranda's transfer was officially laid to a "loss of confidence in his suitability" it was generally attributed to his refusal to suppress an article in Stars and Stripes, reporting the arrest of Michael A. McGhee, son of George McGhee, United States Ambassador to West Germany, on charges of driving while under the influence of drugs.

The Pentagon later acknowledged that Army headquarters in Europe had instructed the service paper to drop the article after it had appeared in two editions. At the same time it denied that Colonel Moranda's relief from his post had resulted from the incident.

The Defense Department announced on March 30 that General O'Meara would retire June 1 after 37 years of active service and would be replaced by his deputy, Leut. Gen. James H. Polk.

The wording of Mr. McNamara's memorandum left no doubt that this incident had been an important factor in the Pentagon's determination to crack down on censorship efforts by military commanders and by ranking Defense Department civilians.

In directing Mr. Goulding to assure that "nothing inhibits the flow of unclassified military information to the American public," Mr. McNamara emphasized that members of the armed forces constituted "an important segment" of this public.

"They are entitled to the same unrestricted access to news as are all other citizens," he declared. "Interference with this access to news will not be permitted."

"The calculated withholding of unfavorable news stories and wire-service reports from troop information publications such as Stars and Stripes or the censorship of news stories or broadcasts over such outlets as Armed Forces Radio and Television Service is prohibited," the Secretary added.

Mr. McNamara directed Mr. Morris to take "all" actions necessary to assure a "free flow of information to our troops."

News Media Scored on Race Coverage

By PETER KIHSS

A Justice Department community relations official declared yesterday, "I don't think there will be law and order in this country until there is justice for black people."

Whites believe Negroes are "better off than they really are" and this is in part "because the news media are not doing their job," the official, Benjamin Holman, assistant director of media relations for the Community Relations Service, said.

Mr. Holman spoke at the opening of a two-day Conference on Mass Media and Race Relations arranged by his agency under an $8,500 contract with the American Jewish Committee. The sessions, co-sponsored by the American Civil Liberties Union and the Columbia University Graduate School of Journalism, were held at the school and attended by 100 communications media participants.

The participants received a 2,300-word preliminary report" by the Federal agency on news coverage of racial disturbances this summer in Buffalo, Newark, Detroit and Houston. This found "much improvement" compared with reporting of 1964 and 1965 disorders.

Racial Polarization

"If this nation is to veer from a course toward increasing racial polarization, the media will have to view racial disorders as much more than a Memorial Day casualty toll," the report said. "The phrase, 'the white press' must cease to come so easily to the lips of the Negroes.

"The challenge to the news media is whether it can do more than chronicle the fears and discomforts of whites caused by Negroes. The media should attempt to convey, to both black and white, the underlying causes of the dilemma and what must be done to resolve it."

The report said that, "with the knowledge that the challenge of civil disorders will continue," each news media should designate specific manpower and make advance plans for handling such situations.

In Chicago, the report said, "for several years some minor incidents with racial overtones have been contained through restraint or delay on the part of the news media" in "temporary withholding of initial news reports."

"A news moratorium in the early stages cannot bring a halt to major racial disturbances," the report said. But it asserted that "voluntary restraint in the early stages, when there is some doubt as to the extent of the violence, can be of benefit to the community and certainly does no harm."

The report criticized law enforcement officials in Newark for hostility to news coverage, while also charging the coverage in Newark "generally would give the impression that it was simply a battle of 'good guys' in blues and fatigues against hordes of black snipers, bombers and looters."

Wirtz Chides Press, Saying It Stresses Only the Bad News

WASHINGTON, Nov. 13 (AP)—Secretary of Labor W. Willard Wirtz said today the nation's news media has ignored the progress made by the Democratic administrations during the last six years and had concentrated, instead, on bad news.

"I'm tired of it," said Mr. Wirtz, complaining there was too much emphasis on the Vietnam war, worry about inflation, Negro riots and slum problems.

He said not enough had been written about the accomplishments of the administrations of Presidents Johnson and Kennedy.

He made these points while speaking at an awards ceremony of the United States Information Agency. In particular, he attacked a recent article in the Wall Street Journal that reported Government employes were suffering "disenchantment, exhaustion, resentment, listlessness, terror, disorientation, suspicion, joylessness, and hate."

"The more basic story, which would be newsworthy, is that these people find today beneath the bramble bush of all that is irritating an achievement in these past six years under the leadership of two magnificent Presidents unparalleled in the history of this or any other nation," he said.

In New York Edward R. Cony, managing editor of the Journal, said he disagreed with the basic premise of Mr. Wirtz that the press concentrates on bad news.

"I think it's natural to provoke a reaction such as Mr. Wirtz's when you're attacked," Mr. Cony said.

"But only two days before the story he cites, we ran a story of almost equal length which in effect gave the Administration credit for acting now to avert riots next summer.

"That's the kind of story the politicians tend to overlook. But it's not only politicians who are that way."

The Treat — and the Treatment — of News

By JACK GOULD

THE coverage of news on television, particularly complex international affairs, has rather suddenly attracted the interest of many prestigious organizations not usually identified with the vagaries of the home screen. Their involvement with what is shown on the tube cannot be ignored by thoughtful people. The World Peace Foundation, the Carnegie Endowment for International Peace and the Foreign Policy Association will open on Jan. 17 a four-day closed seminar at Dedham, Mass., on how TV's treatment of news from underdeveloped countries might be improved. Working practitioners in broadcasting — including key network news officials — academicians specializing in communications and authorities on the less-developed countries are scheduled to participate.

Freedom House, under the leadership of Dr. Harry D. Gideonse, president, and Leo Cherne, chairman of the executive committee, have taken preliminary steps toward weighing the idea of whether the flow of TV news —and perhaps that of the printed press — might be periodically reviewed by a private commission.

In addition, International Broadcast Institute, embracing journalists, broadcasters and academicians both here and abroad, is setting up the nucleus of a global organization that would open up a new channel of communications for the exchange of views on outstanding problems and opportunities in an era of rapidly expanding technological advance. The trustees of the Rockefeller Brothers Fund have promised the Institute substantial financial help on the condition that other philanthropies also provide matching aid. Further word from the Ford Foundation, which helped finance the organizational meetings of the Institute, is expected in due course.

Under the leadership of the American Newspaper Publishers Association, a new group called the International Press Telecommunications Committee, with an office in London, also has been established. It is one of the few such organizations enjoying participation by journalists from Eastern Europe. The interest of the ANPA marks an important forward step because it tacitly recognizes that in a matter of news it is not feasible to isolate one medium from another.

The significance of the proliferation of distinguished groups sponsoring an international dialogue on what TV is doing — or could do—is manifold. And the new trend, it might be added, has enjoyed discreet encouragement from the White House as potentially helpful in determining the United States' future role in communications.

One little noticed factor in the developing global concern over the uses of TV is the expansion of set ownership in many countries overseas. The United States was the first country to achieve a set saturation of better than 90 per cent of the population with access to many stations. Overseas, because of different economic problems, the TV boom was 10 to 15 years later in coming and only now is the awesome power of the tube being increasingly felt. The International Broadcast Institute was possibly the first to sense this belated explosion and to create machinery for turning it to global good rather than narrow nationalistic concerns.

The emerging nations, in fact, have one advantage in starting from scratch in applying developed technology to their own needs; conceivably, they could avoid the wastes and haphazard planning that have attended TV's growth in industrialized countries.

*

But domestically, the participation of many individuals and groups who, previously, have remained detached from the rough and tumble of TV is especially noteworthy. Many intellectuals who could contribute substantially to the evolution of the medium remained aloof. Moreover, a great number has not watched much TV, which is a recurring burden for enlightened broadcasters who so often must patiently explain that they have already done the program that well-meaning reformers said should be done.

Thus far, the assorted groups interesting themselves in the TV news output have scrupulously avoided any hints of censorship or dictation. Actually, the seminars and international meetings have run more to the nature of mutual educational experiences with the broadcasters explaining the realities of their medium and the academicians stressing the increasing social implications of the visual tool.

Such constructive confrontations may be a vital prelude to the harnessing of electronics for the international public weal. The scientists have done their share in opening the skies to international satellite communications, but on the ground there has been an appalling lag in putting the innovations to work, both for viewers in the highly industrialized and more sophisticated nations and in the newer countries still finding their way.

The heightened involvement of many individuals in television's contribution to the informational process is, in part, one of those illusive and intangible benefits attended to the debates, discussions and controversies over noncommercial television in the United States. McGeorge Bundy, Ford Fund president, and Dr. James R. Killian, chairman of the now dissolved Carnegie Commission for Educational Television, did light a spark of concern over the home screen that is now spreading beyond their direct interest in the Corporation for Public Broadcasting.

Previously, there were fitful TV dialogues involving the broadcast industry, Congress and the Federal Communications Commission, but the leadership of the private community was barely heard at all. Now the cast of participants is expanding with phenomenal rapidity, as exemplified in the enlargement of Thomas Hoving's National Citizens Committee for Public Broadcasting.

Progress will take time but, since so much popular TV is beyond the proverbial pale, it is reassuring to see able minds representing a true cross-section of the community dig in and make their thoughts known. In the long-run, the gains to be derived could be of far more lasting importance for all kinds of television — commercial and noncommercial — than tabulating the transitory hits and flops of the moment. The momentum of the broadened dialogue needs to be preserved and hastened at all costs.

December 10, 1967

Publisher Lays Distortions To Johnson Administration

PHOENIX, Ariz., Jan. 13 (AP)—The Johnson Administration "has resorted to distortions of fact and half-truths of history" in trying to put itself in the best possible light, John S. Knight, the publisher, said today.

Accepting the John Peter Zenger Award at the Arizona Newspapers Association convention, Mr. Knight, editorial chairman of newspapers in Miami, Detroit, Charlotte, Akron, Miami Beach and Tallahassee, called on all newspapers to join in a crusade for truth.

"If there are those among us who have never joined the crusade for truth nor tasted the blood of the bureaucrat, I counsel you to begin exposing and opposing the exercise of arbitrary power, now at its zenith in this nation," he said.

The award is made annually by the University of Arizona in recognition of outstanding service in freedom of the press and of the people's right to know.

January 14, 1968

Ross Asserts Democrats Get Unfair Press Handling

The Democratic opposition to Mayor Lindsay "cannot crack certain major newspapers in this town," the majority leader of the City Council said yesterday.

"The New York Times has decided that Mayor Lindsay is Page 1 and that criticism of him is Page 33," said the leader, David Ross.

He said his criticism applied to "two of the three newspapers" and "a couple of the television stations." He said that one TV station, which he did not identify, had demanded editorially that the Council pass promptly a governmental reorganization plan that the Mayor had not yet submitted.

Mr. Ross spoke on the WNBC-TV "Searchlight" program. Other than to mention The Times on the program, in answer to a question that mentioned the newspaper, he declined to identify the targets of his criticism.

January 29, 1968

CALLS FOR NATION TO HEAL ITS RIFTS

Special to The New York Times

CHICAGO, April 1—President Johnson described today his refusal to run again as an effort to save the integrity of his office. He urged candidates for the job, the press and the nation at large to guard "against the works of divisiveness, against bigotry, against the corrupting evils of partisanship in any guise."

"At no time and in no way and for no reason can a President allow the integrity of the responsibility of the freedom of the office ever to be compromised or diluted or destroyed because when you destroy it, you destroy yourselves," Mr. Johnson said.

"And I hope and pray," he went on, "by not allowing the Presidency to be involved in division and deep partisanship I shall be able to pass on to my successor a stronger office, strong enough to guard and defend all the people against all the storms that the future may bring us."

His conduct in office, Mr. Johnson said, had involved the conscious sacrifice of public popularity to his "better judgment" on the issues.

But even after his decision not to seek another term, he said, there remained the problems of fair and honest presentation of the issues and reasonable debate during elections.

"Reason must prevail if democracy itself is to survive," the President declared in a speech to a convention of the National Association of Broadcasters here.

The President flew to Chicago on short notice this morning — his first appearance before the public since his surprise disclosure last night that he would not run again.

He was given a warm greeting by the broadcasters, but they interrupted his speech with applause only once — when he promised that Government would never interfere with the free management of information.

At the same time, Mr. Johnson implored the communications media not to yield to "the popular, the fashionable, the 'in'" when presenting complex issues to the nation.

"Being faithful to our trust ought to be the prime test of any trustee—in office or on the airwaves," he said.

Acknowledging his own "shortcomings as a communicator," the President dealt at length with what he portrayed as a lack of balance in press and television coverage of the news.

In the process he implied that positive aspects of the nation's development — and achieve-

ments of his administration—were at times deprived of public attention.

It occurred to him last night while waiting to broadcast his peace appeal to Hanoi, Mr. Johnson said, that television might be better suited to the coverage of conflict than the words that public leaders use to try to end it.

"It is more 'dramatic' to show policemen and rioters locked in combat than to show men trying to cooperate with one another," he said.

"The face of hatred, of bigotry, comes through much more clearly no matter what its color," he said. "The face of tolerance I seem to find is rarely 'newsworthy'."

And so, too, he added, with a man being trained for a job, or a child learning in his Head Start program or an older person receiving Medicare benefits.

"Peace, in the news sense, is a 'condition'," he said. "War is an 'event.' Part of your responsibility is simply to understand the consequence of that fact— and to try as best you can to draw the attention of the people to the real business of society: finding and securing peace at home and abroad."

The President reiterated his hope and prayer of last night that North Vietnam would cooperate with him in ending the war. For the time that remains to him in office, he said, he would do all he could to hasten the day of peace and harmony in America.

But Mr. Johnson also reiterated his sense of "very deep and very emotional" divisions in the land.

"With all my heart I just wish this were not so," he said. "My career in public life —my whole life in fact—has been devoted to the art of finding an area of agreement. I have been called a seeker of 'consensus', more often in criticism than in praise. And I have never denied it."

"Yet along the way I also learned that no leader can pursue public tranquility as his first and only goal," Mr. Johnson added. "Because for a President to buy public popularity at the sacrifice of his better judgment is too dear a price to pay. The nation cannot afford such a price and this nation cannot long afford such a leader."

He did not come to Chicago to preach or sermonize, the President said, but only to remind the broadcasters that great power requires great responsibility.

"This is true for broadcasters just as it is true for Presidents — and seekers for the Presidency."

April 2, 1968

179

Transcript of President's Speech to Broadcasters

Following is the text of President Johnson's speech to the National Association of Broadcasters in Chicago yesterday, as recorded by The New York Times through the facilities of A.B.C. News:

Mayor Daley, Mr. Ragalewski, ladies and gentlemen.

Some of you might have thought from what I said last night that I'd been taking elocution lessons from Lowell Thomas. One of my aides said this morning—said things are really getting confused around Washington, Mr. President. And I said how's that? He said it looks to me like that you're going to the wrong convention in Chicago. And I said, well, what you overlooked was yesterday was April Fool's.

Once again we are entering the period of national festivity which Henry Adams called the dance of democracy. At its best, that can be a time of debate and enlightenment. At its worst, it can be a period of frenzy. But always it is a time when emotion threatens to substitute for reason. Yet the basic hope of a democracy is that somehow amid all the frenzy and all the emotion that in the end reason will prevail.

Reason just must prevail if democracy itself is to survive.

As I said last evening there are very deep and very emotional divisions in this land that we love today, domestic divisions, divisions over the war in Vietnam. With all of my heart I just wish this weren't so. My entire career in public life —some 37 years of it—has been devoted to the art of finding an area of agreement because generally speaking I have observed that there's so many more things to unite us Americans than there are to divide us.

Emphasizing Divisions

But somehow or other we have a faculty sometimes of emphasizing the divisions and the things that divide us instead of discussing the things that unite us.

Sometimes I have been called a seeker of consensus —seeker of consensus. More often that has been criticism of my actions instead of praise of them. But I have never denied it because to heal and to build support, to hold people together, is

something I think that is worthy and I believe it is a noble task and it's certainly a challenge for all of us in this land and this world where there is restlessness and uncertainty and danger.

In my region of the country, where I have spent my life, where brother was once divided against brother, my heritage has burned this lesson and it's burned it deep in my memory. Yet along the way I learned somewhere that no leader can pursue public tranquility as his first and only goal.

Because, for a President to buy public popularity at the sacrifice of his better judgment is too dear a price to pay.

This nation cannot afford such a price and this nation cannot long afford such a leader. So the things that divide our country this morning will be discussed throughout the land and I'm certain that the very great majority of informed Americans will act as they have always acted to do what is best for their country and what serves the national interest.

But the real problem of informing the people is still with us and I think I can speak with some authority about the problem of communication. I understand far better than some of my severe and perhaps intolerant critics would admit my own shortcomings as a communicator.

'Just The Right Word'

How does a public leader find just the right word or the right way to say no more or no less than he means to say, bearing in mind that anything he says may topple governments and may involve the lives of innocent men.

How does that leader speak the right phrase in the right way under the right conditions to suit the accuracies and contingencies of the moment when he's discussing questions of policy so that he does not stir a thousand misinterpretations and leave the wrong connotation or impression?

How does he reach the immediate audience and how does he communicate with the millions of others who are out there listening from afar?

The President, who must call his people and summon them to meet their responsibilities as citizens in a hard and an enduring war often ponders these questions and searches for the right course.

You men and women who are masters of the broadcast media I think surely must know what I am talking about. It was a long time ago a President once said "the printing press is the most powerful weapon with which man has ever armed himself." And in our age the electronic media have added immeasurably to man's power.

You have within your hands the means to make our nation as intimate and as informed as a New England town meeting. Yet the use of broadcasting has not cleared away all the problems that we still have of communication.

Leader in 'Time Capsule'

In some ways, I think, sometimes it has complicated them. Because it tends to put the leader in a time capsule. It requires him often to abbreviate what he has to say. Too often it may catch a random phrase from his rather lengthy discourse and project it as the whole story.

How many men, I wonder, Mayor Daley, in public life have watched themselves on a TV newscast and then been tempted to exclaim: "Can that really be me?"

Well, there is no denying it. You, the broadcast industry, have enormous power in your hands. You have the power to clarify. And you have the power to confuse.

Men in public life cannot remotely rival your opportunities, because day after day, night after night, hour after hour, on the hour, you shape —and the half-hour sometimes—you shape the nation's dialogue. The words that you choose, hopefully always accurate, hopefully always just, are the words that are carried out for all the people to hear.

The commentary that you provide can give the real meaning to the issues of the day or it can distort them beyond all meaning.

By your standards of what is news you can cultivate with them or you could nurture misguided passions. Your commentary carries an element of uncertainty.

Lack of Record Cited

Unlike the print media, television writes on the wind. There is no accumulated record which the historian can examine later with the 20-20 vision of hindsight, asking this question: How fair was he tonight? How impartial was he today? How honest was he all along?

Well, I hope the National

Association of Broadcasters, with whom I have had a pleasant association for many years, will point the way to all of us in developing this kind of a record, because history is going to be asking very hard questions about our times and the period through which we are passing. And I think that we all owe it to history to complete the record.

But I did not come here this morning to sermonize in matters of fairness and judgment. No law and no set of regulations and no words of mine can improve you or dictate your daily responsibility. All I mean to do—what I'm trying to do—is to remind you where there's great power there must also be great responsibility.

This is true for broadcasters just as it's true for Presidents, and seekers for the Presidency.

What we say and what we do now will shape the kind of a world that we pass along to our children and our grandchildren. And I keep this thought constantly in my mind during the long days and the somewhat longer nights when crisis comes at home and abroad.

I took a little of your prime time last night. I wouldn't have done that except for a very prime purpose. I reported on the prospects for peace in Vietnam. I announced that the United States is taking a very important unilateral act of de-escalation which could —and I fervently pray, will— lead to mutual moves to reduce the level of violence and to de-escalate the war.

As I sat in my office last evening waiting to speak I thought of the many times each week when television brings the war into the American home. No one can say exactly what effect those vivid scenes have on American opinion.

Historians must only guess at the effect that television would have had during earlier conflicts on the future of this nation. During the Korean War, for example, at that time when our forces were pushed back there to Pusan. Or World War II, the Battle of the Bulge, or when our men were slugging it out in Europe, or when most of our Air Force was shot down that day in June, 1942, off Australia.

But last night television was being used to carry a different message. It was a message of peace and it occurred

to me that the medium may be somewhat better suited to conveying the actions of conflict than to dramatizing the words that the leaders use in trying and hoping to end the conflict.

Certainly it is more dramatic to show policemen and rioters locked in combat than to show men trying to cooperate with one another.

The face of hatred and of bigotry comes through much more clearly, no matter what its color, and the face of tolerance I seem to find is rarely newsworthy.

What Makes News

Progress, whether it's a man being trained for a job or million being trained, or whether it's a child in Head Start learning to read or an older person, 72, in adult education, or being cared for in Medicare, rarely makes the news, although more than 20 million of them are affected by it.

Perhaps this is because tolerance and progress are not dynamic events such as riots and conflict are events.

So peace in the new sense is a condition. War is an end. Part of your responsibility is simply to understand the consequences of that fact, the consequences of your own acts. And part of that responsibility, I think, is to try as very best we all can to draw the attention of our people to the real business of society in our system, finding and securing peace in the world, at home and abroad and for all that you have done. And that you are doing and that you will do to this end. I thank you and I commend you.

I pray that the message of peace that I tried so hard to convey last night will be accepted in good faith by the leaders of North Vietnam. I pray that one time soon the evening news show will have not another battle in the scarred hills of Vietnam, but will show men entering a room to talk about peace. That is the event that I think the American people are yearning and longing to see.

President Thieu of Vietnam and his Government are now engaged in very urgent political and economic tasks which I referred to last night and which we regard as very constructive and hopeful. And we hope the Government of South Vietnam makes great progress in the days ahead.

But sometime in the weeks ahead immediately, I hope

President Thieu will be in a position to accept my invitation to visit the United States so he can come here and see our people, too, and together we can strengthen and improve our plans to advance the day of peace.

Plea for Unity

I pray that you and that every American will take to heart my plea that they guard against divisiveness.

We have won too much and we have come too far and we have opened too many doors of opportunity for these things now to be lost in a divided country where brother is separated from brother.

And for the time that is allotted me, I shall do everything in one man's power to hasten the day when the world is at peace and Americans of all races and all creeds and of all convictions can live together without fear or without suspicion, without distrust in unity and in common purpose, because united we're strong, divided we're in great danger.

Speaking as I did to the nation last night, I was moved by the very deep convictions that I entertain about the nature of the office that it's my present privilege to hold.

The office of the Presidency is the only office in this land of all the people.

Whatever may be the personal wishes or the preferences of any man who holds it, a President of all the people can afford no thought of self. At no time and in no way and for no reason can a President allow the integrity of the responsibility of the freedom of the office ever to be compromised or diluted or destroyed because when you destroy it, you destroy yourselves. And I hope and I pray by not allowing the Presidency to be involved in division and deep partisanship I shall be able to pass on to my successor a stronger office, strong enough to guard and defend all the people against all the storms that the future may bring us.

You men and women who have come here to this great progressive city of Chicago led by this dynamic great public servant, Dick Daley, are yourselves charged with a peculiar responsibility.

You are yourselves the trustees — legally accepted trustees, legally selected trustees—of a great institution on which the freedom of our land utterly depends.

A Key to Security

The security, the success of our country, what happens to us tomorrow rests squarely upon the media which disseminates the truth on which the decisions of democracy are made. We get a great deal of our information from you, and an informed mind is the guardian genius of democracy.

So you are the keepers of a trust and you must be just. You must guard and you must defend your media against a spirit of action, against the works of divisiveness, against bigotry, against the corrupting evils of partisanship in any guise.

For America's press as for the American Presidency, the integrity and the responsibility and the freedom—the freedom to know the truth and let the truth make us free —must never be compromised or diluted or destroyed.

The defense of our media is your responsibility. Government cannot and must not and never will, as long as I have anything to do about it, intervene in that role.

But I do want to leave this thought with you as I leave you this morning. I hope that you will give this trust your closest care. Acting as I know you can to guard not only against the obvious but to watch for the hidden, the sometimes unintentional, the often petty intrusion upon the integrity of the information by which Americans decide.

Men and women of the airways fully as much as men and women of public service have a public trust, and if liberty is to survive and to succeed that solemn trust must be faithfully kept.

I do not want and I don't think you want to wake up some morning and find America changed because we slept when we should have been awake, because we remained silent when we should have spoken up, because we went along with what was popular and fashionable and "in," rather than what was necessary and what was right.

Being faithful to our trust ought to be the prime test of any public trustee in office or on the airways and in any society all you students of history know that a time of division is a time of danger, and in these times now we must never forget that eternal vigilance is the price of liberty.

Thank you for wanting me to come. I've enjoyed it.

Editors Assert Administration Practices Deceit for Its Own Sake

WASHINGTON, April 17 (AP) — A committee of the American Society of Newspaper Editors said today that "the credibility gap yawns wider in the Johnson Administration than it did in preceding regimes largely because this Administration follows a policy of obscurantism for its own sake."

At the same time, however, editors attending the society's annual convention here indicated in a random sampling of opinion that they thought history would judge President Johnson as a good President and, if he succeeded in settling the Vietnam war, perhaps even a great one.

In a report dealing with the "credibility gap," the society's Freedom of Information and Press-Bar Committee said:

"The Pueblo incident, the surprise and success of the Tet offensive, and the shocking post-mortem of the 1964 Tonkin Gulf incident all combined to damage further whatever credibility the Administration had left.

"All administrations manipulate the news to a greater or less extent, all have been known to conceal . . . and even lie about important information when it served their interests to do so.

"Coping with this is the task of every Washington reporter and the ability to cope with it is what separates the men from the boys. But under LBJ the coping is immeasurably more difficult because official deceit is practised both when there is reason for it and when there is not."

The committee said that blaming the press for bad news had become more widespread partly because of "the sheer volume of bad news."

The report said the press blamed for building up black power leaders, for failing to report the plight of Negroes, for "too horrible" television war coverage, for showing "only our side being beastly in wartime," for over-reporting hippies and the use of drugs, and for being the "spokesman of the establishment."

"The educated citizen blames the press because it only reflects accurately how confused and troubled the world is instead of producing panaceas," said the report.

"As the press is generally blamed," it continued, "the danger is that more and more people will begin to feel that what they want is less freedom of information. This threat to free press is real, and it is not lessened by the fact that it is all of a piece with the rest of the confusion of the times."

Sixty editors at the conference, asked about Mr. Johnson's place in history, said it would hinge largely on what happened in the coming final months of his Administration.

"Inevitably he'll be a good President," said Frank Angelo, managing editor of The Detroit Free Press. "The measure of greatness will be the perspective of history on Vietnam."

"If he settled the Vietnam war, it will judge him extremely well. If not, mediocre," said J. Edward Murray, managing editor of The Arizona Republic.

One-third of the editors polled said it was too early to answer, particularly while Mr. Johnson was probing for peace in Vietnam.

Of the 40 who expressed opinions, 24 predicted history would look quite favorably upon Mr. Johnson. Eleven foresaw mixed or average ratings. Five listed the President as below average.

"I think he's been a good President," said Cy King, executive editor of The Buffalo Courier-Express. "I think he's had a rather incredible string of untoward events, including the Vietnam war which he inherited."

"In the domestic field he's done many things that will become part of our permanent social setup," said Vermont Royster, editor of The Wall Street Journal. "Only history will prove whether he's been right in Vietnam, but he's been resolute, and I think that required courage on his part."

"His defense of our commitments in Vietnam, although politically unpopular, is really in the tradition of strong Presidents," said Sylvan H. Meyer, editor of The Gainesville, Ga., Times.

William B. Smart, editor of the editorial page of Salt Lake City's Desert News, said history would find Mr. Johnson a poor President because of "lack of control of domestic matters, particularly the economy, and obvious failures in foreign policy."

Robert J. Leeney, executive editor of The New Haven Register, said: "I think he'll turn out to be a middle-ground President who had integrity enough to step back when circumstances closed in on him."

April 2, 1968

April 18, 1968

A.B.C. Charges Wallace Aide
Seized Film of Shelton Greeting

By VAL ADAMS

The American Broadcasting Company news division charged yesterday that a "personal bodyguard" of former Gov. George C. Wallace of Alabama had seized and destroyed television film showing Mr. Wallace shaking hands with Robert M. Shelton, Imperial Wizard of the United Klans of America.

Elmer W. Lower, president of A.B.C. News, said that Mr. Wallace, a third-party Presidential candidate, had ordered the bodyguard to seize the film at a $25-a-person fund-raising dinner Wednesday night in Eutaw, Ala., about 50 miles southwest of Birmingham.

[Mr. Wallace denied the charge yesterday, United Press International reported. After he had arrived at Friendship International Airport near Baltimore, Mr. Wallace was quoted as having said: "I haven't ordered anybody by force to seize anything."]

Mr. Lower said the seizure had taken place after Mr. Wallace, who had been shaking hands with numerous persons in a receiving line, realized that an A.B.C. cameraman had made pictures of him shaking hands with the Ku Klux Klan leader.

Sam Donaldson, an A.B.C. news correspondent who covered the fund-raising dinner, said:

"I think Governor Wallace was surprised when he found Shelton was there."

Right after the filming occurred, Mr. Donaldson said, Mr. Wallace said to him:

"The whole conclusion in your mind and that of your network was to contrive the picture like some of you have contrived marches to be held to get TV coverage."

Mr. Donaldson denied that filming of the Wallace-Shelton handshaking had been contrived. The camera crew had taken about 300 feet of film of the receiving line before Shelton came into view, Mr. Donaldson said, and there had been no attempt to single out the Klan leader.

Mr. Lower protested the incident in a telegram to Mr. Wallace that said, in part:

"This violates the very basic rights of the news media to report your Presidential campaign. May I have your personal assurance that there will be no repetition and that A.B.C. news personnel will be free to cover your campaign unhindered by members of your entourage."

Last night, Mr. Lower received this reply from Mr. Wallace:

"I regret the incident and the events surrounding the occurrence of the incident referred to in your telegram. We are happy to have A.B.C. with us."

Reached by The Associated Press in Tuscaloosa, Ala., Shelton said he had attended the rally, but refused to say whether he had joined the file of people who shook Mr. Wallace's hand.

"I don't see that there's any issue involved," Shelton said. "I was there and paid my money to support him just like everybody else."

June 28, 1968

Wallace Asks TV Coverage

GREENSBORO, N.C., Aug. 11 (AP)—George C. Wallace said tonight that he would ask the three major television networks for coverage of the national convention of his American Independent party equal to that given the major party conventions. Appearing on a television program, the former Alabama Governor said he believed the networks would grant his request.

August 12, 1968

Government and Press
It's Still an Uneasy Alliance

WASHINGTON—Does a President, or even a President-elect, have a need and right to meet secretly sometimes with an aide, a Senator or even the Governor of New York? Obviously he does. Will the news eventually leak out and produce gossip, speculation and interpretation of varying degrees of accuracy? Usually, it will.

That is what happened last week after Governor Rockefeller called privately on President-elect Nixon in New York. At first, Nixon's spokesman knew nothing of the encounter and pleaded ignorance. After he found out, he didn't bother to confirm reporters' independent information. The next day he appeared embarrassed and looked silly, all the more so since the headlines were full of the news that Herbert G. Klein had been appointed Director of Communications in the next Administration with the job of preventing a "credibility gap."

The incident belongs in the files of tremendous trifles, but the problem of the Presidency versus the press is a chronic feature of Washington life.

Tension dominates the relationship between the information brokers and their Government sources. And it must. They need each other, but they are formally accountable only to others. They deal with each another without established rules or procedures for settling grievances.

There are more than 2,000 reporters loose in Washington and the Government employs hundreds of persons to service them—thousands if you count officialdom's dealings with the public through supplementary channels, such as the lecture platform and the United States Mail.

At their worst, the official spokesmen choke the channels of information with poor advice to both the policy-makers and the press.

At their best, they offer not only formal briefings on announcements but also guide reporters to an understanding of the motives and pressures felt in government, bring reporters and officials together and advise their superiors on the care and feeding of the hungry scribes.

Unchecked Powers

Only a few succeed, however, in gaining full access to the information that the press seeks and even the best are still searching for effective ways to bring television into the daily information process.

Depending on his skill, a President and his official family have almost unchecked powers of communication. They can command the air waves with the slightest hint of crisis, and they can seal their files with the slightest pretext of national security. They can take the world to the brink of nuclear war, as in the Cuban missile crisis, or into a long and costly conventional war, as in Vietnam, before anyone in the press or public fully realizes what is happening.

Depending on its skill, however, the press can persist and persuade even a skeptical public that there is fire in those smoky files. It can report rumor along with facts and speculation along with interpretation, raising questions where it has no answers and raising even wrong questions where it lacks information. It can sharpen the public's memory and place today's truth beside yesterday's. It can dramatize its own frustrations on the prowl for news and give voice to inquisitors and dissenters in Congress and elsewhere. It does.

Over the long pull, it is probably a fair contest. Bruised reputations, like Harry Truman's, are repaired and healed over time. Excesses of power, like John Kennedy's or Lyndon Johnson's in the Caribbean, are gradually exposed and restrained. At any given moment, the President or the press tend to be up or down on the see-saw, vying for credibility and balancing their rival ambitions and responsibilities.

Klein's predecessors, even with the more modest titles of White House press secretary, have succeeded or failed in direct proportion to their ability to serve these rival masters. They and their agents throughout the executive branch—usually called Assistant Secretaries of Public Affairs—have been able to inform only to the extent that they know the thoughts and facts of their policy superiors. They have been able to influence, manage or even manipulate the news only to the extent that they have been trusted as the conveyors of information.

The new Director of Communications will be directing a bloody brawl if he cannot persuade his President to operate in a general climate of candor. Even then, because information is power here, it will be hoarded and guarded and therefore also stolen and misused.

But public policy in these matters must precede the details: How many news conferences, and what kind? How much discipline over the public and private talk of officials, and what kind? How much pretense of unity and how much damaging confession of conflict? How much favoritism for the friendly press and how much courting of the opposition?

The very appointment of Klein raised fears in Congress and in the press that Nixon was creating an information "czar." But the mild-mannered former editor of The San Diego Union is not a likely candidate for any imperial assignment, and the complaining members of Congress and newsmen are not fit subjects for any czar.

The grand tension will persist and the mechanical problems of daily communication will vary in form with the seasons. The crucial question for a President in this realm is how he will balance the obvious need for private deliberation, consultation and maneuver against his sense of obligation to a clamoring and even critical public and press. The crucial answer is nothing less than an aspect of statesmanship. The Director of Communications in the next Administration will be Richard Milhous Nixon. —MAX FRANKEL

NIXON REPORTED WOOING DEMOCRAT

Offer to Clifford Is Hinted— Herbert Klein Is Named Communications Chief

By ROBERT B. SEMPLE Jr.

Richard M. Nixon is said to have begun active negotiations with one and possibly more prominent Democrats for Cabinet-level posts in his Administration. He is also said to believe that he should select the Democratic members of his Cabinet before proceeding with other high-level appointments.

In a busy day yesterday, however, the President-elect did announce one key appointment. He named Herbert G. Klein, a California newsman, as his director of communications for the executive branch of government, with what appeared to be unusual supervisory powers over all Government information services.

Mr. Nixon pledged on Sept. 19 to include Democrats in his Administration. Conversations here and in Washington yesterday suggested strongly that he had already made overtures to one or more members of the opposition party.

According to these conversations, he has yet to win the acquiescence of any of those to whom overtures have been made. Until he does, however, he is not likely to make other major appointments.

The President-elect was said to be convinced that the appointment of "real" Democrats — that is, men visibly identified ideologically and politically with the opposition — would be a necessary component of his efforts to re-unite the country and establish a firm bi-partisan approach to pressing international problems, including Vietnam.

Among those with whom Mr. Nixon was believed to have begun discussions — at least through intermediaries — was Clark M. Clifford, the Secretary of Defense. Nixon sources would not confirm that a firm offer had been made, but they acknowledged that Mr. Clifford was under "serious consideration."

Mr. Nixon expressed "interest" yesterday in a proposal offered by Senator Jacob K. Javits, Republican of New York, to retain at least one member of the two-man Paris negotiating team to insure "continuity" in the peace talks.

Mr. Nixon had one-hour conferences with Mr. Javits and with Prof. Henry Kissinger of Harvard, Gov. James A. Rhodes of Ohio, a Republican, and Senator John G. Tower, Republican of Texas.

Humphrey Bars Post

Meanwhile, it was learned that Vice President Humphrey would not take a job in a Nixon Administration. Mr. Humphrey was quoted as saying this in an interview in the Miami News. Nixon aides here confirmed that the probabilities that Mr. Humphrey would join Mr. Nixon were now "zero."

They were less unequivocal, however, when asked whether Mr. Humphrey had been offered a job, and there were some indications that he had. His name, along with Mr. Clifford's has figured heavily in the incessant speculation over Mr. Nixon's high-level choices for his Administration.

What appeared to be Mr. Nixon's quickening interest in including Democrats in his Cabinet came to light when newsmen sought to discover the reasons for the strikingly deliberate manner in which the President-elect has gone about choosing his top associates.

In the three weeks since the election, he has named only a handful of White House aides, and most of these were predictable appointments.

According to the standard public explanations, Mr. Nixon is taking his time to make certain that he gets "the best possible men." He is also besieged daily with recommendations from men like Mr. Javits, whose counsel he respects, and he must spend much of his time considering these suggestions.

However, it appears now that one major reason for the delay is Mr. Nixon's anxiety to find and place prominent Democrats in high posts as an early gesture of national unity. He is said to believe that at least one of the three big posts— Secretary of State, Treasury or Defense—might well go to a Democrat, and it is his search for the right man, that in the words of intimate associates, is "causing the logjam."

Mr. Klein's appointment was announced on Mr. Nixon's behalf by Ronald Ziegler, who worked under Mr. Klein during the campaign and who will serve as White House press spokesman.

Mr. Klein's post as director of communications is a new one in the executive branch. Mr. Ziegler, in his formal announcement, described Mr. Klein's duties, and the philosophy behind them, in these terms:

"President-elect Nixon intends to emphasize in his Administration the need for free access to information in all departments of Government, to the extent that it does not endanger national security.

"The execution of this philosophy will be one of Mr. Klein's primary responsibilities. In this position Mr. Klein will serve as a spokesman for the executive branch as a whole. He will coordinate the activities of public information officers in every branch of government."

No Government information officer has ever been given such a broad mandate, and Mr. Klein, former editor of The San Diego Union, was questioned closely about the exact nature of his duties when he appeared before newsmen later.

Although he stressed that his principal role would be to "coordinate" the flow of news from the Government, he said that Cabinet officers would be able to speak freely without first consulting with him.

In his public remarks and in conversation later, he said he would maintain offices outside the White House, in the Executive Office Building, would require a staff of four to six "top" people, and would play a leading role in recruiting the information officers for the various executive departments and agencies.

Will Encourage the Flow

He said he conceived his task to be one of encouraging the flow of news and information, rather than suppressing it, adding:

"Truth will become the hallmark of the Nixon Administration. I'm charged directly by the President to emphasize [to] every department of Government that more facts should be made available. With this kind of emphasis, we feel that we will be able to eliminate any possibility of a credibility gap in this Administration."

However, Mr. Klein's broad powers immediately raised questions about the possibility of restraint on the information activities of specific agencies and departments — and the possibility, as well, that Mr. Nixon might seek to exercise tight control of news through Mr. Klein.

In an interview later, however, the 50-year-old editor, who served as Mr. Nixon's communications manager during the campaign, said he abhorred "censorship" and had opposed it in his capacity as a professional newspaperman.

Asked whether he would seek to practice "news management," he said that the phrase as generally used carried a "negative connotation" but added:

"If you want to take it literally — yes — it has some validity."

By these and other remarks, Mr. Klein seemed to be drawing a distinction between an official who manages news to suppress it and an official who manages it to insure its widest possible distribution.

Mr. Javits appeared before newsmen after conferring with

the President-elect in Mr. Nixon's suite of offices on the 39th floor of the Hotel Pierre. He said that he had told Mr. Nixon of his deep interest in "the continuity of the negotiations" in Paris. He said he had suggested that at least one of the two negotiators now there—Cyrus R. Vance and W. Averell Harriman—be left in Paris after inauguration day, Jan. 20.

"Mr. Nixon showed interest in the question of continuity," Mr. Javits reported.

Mr. Javits said he and the President-elect had discussed urban problems. He reported that Mr. Nixon seemed prepared to retain and to fund existing Federal programs that appeared to be working while at the same time encouraging the private sector to take a greater role in antipoverty efforts.

November 26, 1968

Minister of Information

The responsibility which President-elect Nixon has assigned Herbert G. Klein is spectacularly comprehensive. Mr. Klein is to be nothing less than Director of Communications for the whole executive branch of the Federal Government. He is to serve as a kind of Minister of Information.

Some European democracies have officials with comparable assignments. But in those countries the Government usually controls all or part of the radio and television industries, and the newspapers do not have the constitutional protection afforded in the United States by the First Amendment.

The Washington press corps performs a quasi-parliamentary function because its members can question the President and senior officials who are not answerable to Congress, as they would be in a parliamentary country. This inquisitorial function is ill-defined and anomalous, but the press corps guards it jealously. Let a President or Cabinet member go long periods without holding a news conference, and the press is sure to set up a clamor of protest. No European Minister of Information has to contend with such a tradition of stiff-necked independence and assertiveness.

Used to foraging for news among their own sources, newsmen are not likely to take kindly to having Mr. Klein centralize the flow of information. They may see his office as yet one more layer of officialdom between the press and the actual decision makers.

Much will depend upon how Mr. Klein envisages his new duties. Former Senator William Benton of Connecticut years ago urged the appointment of an official who would work in behalf of the press, forcing Government to make more information available. In some of his remarks the other day, Mr. Klein sounded as if he saw himself as an ombudsman for the Fourth Estate, "eliminating any possibility of a credibility gap." And—all to the good—he specifically rejected any idea of "censorship" or trying to make everyone in the Administration "speak with one voice." He added that "the hallmark of the Nixon Administration will be truth."

But every Administration tends to clamp down on news if the news is bad. Mr. Klein made it plain he intends to work closely with the Republican National Committee, whose sole excuse for existence is to make the Nixon Administration look good at all times. Everyone can agree that both the nation and the new Administration will best be served in the long run by a consistent policy of candor, but the new director of communications will have no easy time in executing it when public and political obligations conflict as they inevitably will during the next four years.

Nixon and His Press Relations

By MAX FRANKEL
Special to The New York Times

WASHINGTON, Nov. 26 — Now that, after all, the press does have Richard M. Nixon to kick around some more, the President-elect has designated his soft-spoken friend, Herbert G. Klein, to run interference for his Administration. Mr. Klein will have the grandiose title of Director of Communications and the simple assignment "to eliminate any possibility of a credibility gap." At the Johnson White House, astride the gap, they chuckled at the news, taking a certain grim delight in the expectation that the director and the director of the director would soon be facing "reality."

News Analysis

For reality, in official Washington circles, often pictures the operatives of press, radio and television as hungry wolves who will devour human flesh unless regularly fed some bloody pap.

And when the newsmen strike where it hurts, they are usually judged to be in league with ignorant or spiteful bureaucrats who disloyally peddle their frustrations, dissents and even secrets to the public.

It would be novel indeed if the Nixon Administration did not reach the same conclusion about the press from time to time, when either the national security or its political purity is compromised.

Government and press need one another and manipulate one another, yet an immutable conflict of interest colors the relationship. For every charge of secrecy there is a reply of ignorance, and for every complaint about the misuse of information there is a reply of prejudice in its handling.

Previous Coordinators

The mistrust is mutual and as old as the Presidency itself. Thus despite the novelty of the title, Mr. Klein's assignment and function will not be new to Government.

Pierre Salinger under President Kennedy and George Reedy, Bill D. Moyers and George Christian under Presi-

dent Johnson have long tried to "coordinate" the activities of information officers, as Mr. Klein intends to do.

By removing himself from the daily, often trivial press briefings that these men endured, Mr. Klein may gain more time and perspective for his job, but there is no escape from the essential conflict.

President Johnson's damaging reputation for incredibility rests fundamentally not on his excessive secrecy, secretive though he is, or on his petty evasions, evasive though he is.

His style of personal political maneuver has made him hostile to speculation and premature disclosure just as other Presidents have been about their more obviously sensitive international diplomacy.

Surely Mr. Nixon would not wish to be called secretive simply because he is protecting his thoughts about Cabinet appointments until he has completed negotiations and preparations for their announcement.

What magnified Mr. Johnson's problems was the widespread impression among the people and in the Congress that he had taken the country secretly to war in Vietnam and that on this issue, and others, he was wielding enormous powers of commitment with inadequate or even misleading accounts to the public.

President Eisenhower authorized lies in the U2 spy plane-crisis with the Soviet Union in 1960. President Kennedy authorized great lies about American involvement in the invasion of Cuba in 1961 and white lies about a cold that brought him hurrying to Washington for the missile crisis in 1962.

President Johnson authorized a medium-weight lie about how he intervened in the Dominican Republic merely to save lives in 1965. Mr. Nixon will probably find his reasons for bending the truth.

The tolerance of the public for official prevarication has been considerable on cold war issues. And recent experience suggests that resentment of "news management" injures

November 27, 1968

Government most when it grows into resentment of policy.

Mr. Nixon proved in this year's election campaign that he could successfully "manage" news and newsmen where he had conspicuously failed in 1960 and 1962, even though the reporters closest to him still feel deprived of facts and revelations about his basic views and character.

Through the campaign, Mr. Klein could indeed direct the flow of communication and the candidate could yield to much of his direction. But a President bearing extraordinary responsibilities, and balancing his credibility with the public and Congress against his credibility in nuclear diplomacy, usually winds up as his own director.

Mr. Klein will fail if he tries to eliminate the inevitable tensions, the quarrels over access, timing of announcements, and anonymous briefings, or if he tries to prevent every exaggeration, false report or hostile interpretation, through excessive control.

HE will succeed if he does nothing more than tutor President and public alike in the thesis that President Kennedy enunciated when he quipped that he was reading more and enjoying it less in the White House.

"I think that they are doing their task, as a critical branch, the fourth estate," he said of the press. "And I am attempting to do mine. And we are going to live together for a period and then go our separate ways."

And it was Mr. Reedy who best defined the separate jobs and separate ways after he failed to rescue President Johnson from that much celebrated gap.

"A political leader," he said, "is essentially an advocate — a man who is seeking to shape the world toward ends he considers worthy — a newspaperman, on the other hand, is one whose job it is to chronicle daily events and to place the facts before the public in some reasonable perspective. Events and facts have a life of their own . . . .

"A democratic society is inconceivable without tension, and the objective reporting that democracy requires will always produce tension."

November 27, 1968

JOHNSON TO LEAVE WITHOUT GRUDGES

By BERNARD GWERTZMAN
Special to The New York Times

WASHINGTON, Jan. 17— President Johnson made peace with the press today, teased his family, lamented that he had not been able to end the Vietnam war and philosophized on problems of race, youth, housing and population.

In one of his longest and most free-wheeling news conferences, Mr. Johnson said he was leaving Washington on Monday full of gratitude and without any grudges.

He seemed completely at ease in what was probably his final session with the press. Like many of his previous news conferences, this one was held under somewhat unusual circumstances.

The President, accompanied by his wife, dropped in on the annual business meeting of the National Press Club because he said he could not depart without visiting his "fellow clubmates and fellow travelers."

He was alluding to his honorary membership in the club and his frequent trips on which he was always accompanied by members of the press.

Following the 56-minute session, the Press Club members and other newsmen present gave Mr. Johnson a long, standing ovation, and several shook his hand as he left the club's ballroom.

Mr. Johnson's mood was his informal best—sarcastic, earthy and humane, a mixture that has confounded friends and critics throughout his five years and two months in the White House.

Few Presidents have had closer relations with the press, and few have suffered and complained more about attacks on his personality and behavior.

Noting that John W. Heffernan, chief of the Reuters Bureau in Washington and the new president of the Press Club, would be sworn in shortly, Mr. Johnson said:

"Since I was sworn in I have been known to utter a few oaths myself. Many of them weer at times directed at members of the press."

He said that he would be "less than candid" if he did not acknowledge difficulties in communication with the press, but now that he was leaving, "all is forgotten." [Opening statement, this page.]

He made fun of some of the "flaps" of his Administration and even laughed at himself, a rare act by him in public.

He said that among his "complaints" was that he had been misquoted in saying a Peter Hurd portrait of him was ugly.

"I thought it was a pretty good likeness," he said, "except for one little detail: It left off the halo."

On his Far Eastern trip in 1966, Mr. Johnson said that an ancestor had fought at the Alamo, and reporters wrote that their research had turned up no such ancestor. Mr. Johnson said today that the Alamo quote had been true, but "what I was trying to say was that my ancestor was in a fight at the Alamo—Alamo Hotel in Eagle Pass, Texas."

He said he had opened his shirt to show his gall bladder operation scar in 1965 only because Sarah McClendon, a Texas newswoman with a strident voice, had demanded:

"Mr. President, you have been in office almost two years and what do you have to show for it?"

Mr. Johnson has been making the rounds in Washington this final week in office, jesting with Senators, waxing sentimental about Secretary of State Dean Rusk and showing off his 18-month-old grandson, Lyn, the child of his younger daughter and Airman 1st Cl. Patrick J. Nugent.

Teases His Wife

He teased his wife and younger daughter by saying that Mrs. Johnson was opposed to taking the child everywhere. Mr. Johnson said that he and Mrs. Nugent had outvoted his wife. [Question 9.]

He said that he had asked Mrs. Nugent to bring Lyn to the Capitol for the State of the Union Message because even if the child did not remember the occasion, "I would."

Mrs. Johnson cried that night, not because of emotion, the President said, but because of the fear that Lyn would drop his baby bottle on the head of Representative H. R. Gross, Republican of Iowa.

Mr. Gross is a Congressional watchdog who has annoyed many Presidents.

The Presidetn said that Lyn was not with him today because he was "confined to quarters" at the White House for playing with Senator Everett McKinley Dirksen's eyeglasses last night at a Senate reception for Mr. Johnson.

In a serious vein, Mr. Johnson said that he had considered nominating Arthur J. Goldberg to be Chief Justice of the United States both before and after the Senate balked at confirming Associate Justice Abe Fortas for the post. Mr. Goldberg had been an Associate Justice before becoming Chief United States Representative to the United Nations. [Question 4.]

The President was rather philosophic about some of the major issues. He said that there was a great deal of unfinished busines he was turning over to Richard M. Nixon, paramount of which was the Vietnam war.

He said that if he could have one thing it would be the ability to bring back all the men from Vietnam that he had sent there. But he observed that there still was no peace. [Question 10.]

Asked if he regretted his decision either to intervene in Vietnam or not to seek re-election, Mr. Johnson said "No." [Question 3.]

His answer to why the Democratic party lost the election was, "They didn't get enough votes."

On his achievements as President, he cited the open housing bill, the voting rights legislation and the breakthroughs in space. He said that many of the problems in the nineteen-sixties could have been dealt with more satisfactorily if action were taken in the nineteen-fifties when they first became apparent [Question 6.]

It was clear that he viewed the Voting Rights Act of 1965 as the most dramatic bill passed in his Administration, saying that it was "almost like Lincoln's Emancipation Proclamation, except it did not just extend to the states in rebellion."

Asked if he would undertake any missions for Mr. Nixon, Mr. Johnson said he could not foresee any at this moment, but "as long as I live I want to be at the service of whoever happens to be President."

He said he would not "withdraw my options" on running someday for the Senate again, but said he did not leave public life with the intention of entering it again.

Earlier in the day, Mr. Jonnson met for the last time with his cabinet and received as a farewell gift, his high-backed leather arm chair that he used at Cabinet meetings.

The Senate set aside time to praise Mr. Johnson's record.

Senator Edward M. Kennedy, Democrat of Massachusetts, said that the circumstances that had brought Mr. Johnson to the Presidency had made inevitable speculation that strained relations between him and the Kennedy family.

"President Johnson was a loyal lieutenant of John F. Kennedy," the Senator said. "He campaigned hard and effectively for the election of Senator Robert Kennedy and myself to the United States Senate. He was extremely gracious to all of us after the events of November, 1963.

"The differences that developed later on came not from personal grievances but from the obligation of men in public life to discharge their responsibilities to the people of the United States as they saw them and from what at the time were fundamental differences over important public policies."

January 18, 1969

CHRISTIAN DENIES HE LIED TO PRESS

But White House Aide Says He Withheld Some Data

WASHINGTON, Jan. 19 (UPI) — George Christian, outgoing White House press secretary, said today that he had never deliberately lied in behalf of the Johnson Administration but had withheld some information from the press in the national interest.

"In serving the people, the Government has the right not to tell the full story," he said.

Appearing on the National Broadcasting Company's television program, "Meet the Press," he said "there were instances in this Administration where the full story was not told immediately," such as during sensitive negotiations.

Asked for an example, Mr. Christian, who has served as the top press officer to President Johnson for the last three years, cited the recent negotiations with North Vietnam.

He said that the talks with North Vietnam to end the United States bombing and set up the Paris talks, had been withheld from the public for about two weeks.

He was then asked if he had ever lied, and he answered, "I have not deliberately lied."

On other subjects Mr. Christian said:

¶"In all candor," the press sometimes distorted the news and this "was a factor" in the often cool relationship between Mr. Johnson and the press.

¶In the long run, historians will prove Mr. Johnson's Vietnam policy was correct. "He has not a single regret" regarding his Southeast Asia policy.

Mr. Christian described the Johnson Administration as an "action Administration" and described the President's tenure as "one of the most productive periods" in American history.

January 20, 1969

WHITE HOUSE AIDES HELD FREE TO SPEAK

WASHINGTON, Oct. 24 (AP) —Ronald L. Ziegler, the White House press secretary, repeated today that Administration officials were not leashed when they made speeches and added the American people would be ill-served by any advance censorship.

Mr. Ziegler said the Administration had stressed its openness and that this fitted in with free discussion.

What brought this out was a question if there were any plans to review a speech Vice President Agnew is slated to deliver at Harrisburg, Pa. The Vice President encountered some censure after a New Orleans speech that was widely viewed as criticism of leaders on Oct. 15.

"The President does not put a leash on members of the Administration, the Cabinet," Mr. Ziegler told reporters.

The press secretary was told at one point he seemed to be suggesting the Vice President appeared to have almost a total autonomy in what he said. Mr. Ziegler replied he thought the Vice President and all other officials should be and were free to discuss matters of national importance, but before any official made a statement involving national security it of course is a matter of discussion.

October 25, 1969

Isn't Choosing a President as Important as a Moon Shot?

By NEWTON N. MINOW,

In a recent Sunday column, Jack Gould criticized a proposal that, before Presidential elections, all TV and radio stations across the country simultaneously carry talks by the candidates. At given times, the public would have the option of tuning in to those talks—or turning their sets off. This proposal for "Voters' Time," advanced by the Twentieth Century Fund's Commission on Campaign Costs in the Electronic Era, was termed by Gould "Big Brotherism." Here the chairman of the commission, a former head of the FCC, replies.

JACK GOULD'S column of October 12, "Will We All Have to Listen to Big Brother?," is a valuable addition to public debate on the issue of escalating costs of radio and television time for political candidates. His criticism of the Report of the Twentieth Century Fund Commission on Campaign Costs in the Electronic Era represents a point of view which our Commission anticipated—but I regret that he did not give any attention to our arguments on the other side.

Our Commission was composed of five men with widely different political views and backgrounds. Dean Burch, former Chairman of the Republican National Committee, was long identified with the campaigns of Senator Goldwater. Robert Price, former Deputy Mayor of New York City, managed the Mayoral campaign of John Lindsay in 1965. Thomas Corcoran, a key adviser of President Franklin D. Roosevelt, has been active in Democratic politics for four decades. Alexander Heard, Chancellor of Vanderbilt University, is a leading scholar and headed the bipartisan commission on the question of campaign finance appointed by President John F. Kennedy. I have been involved in four Presidential campaigns, most intimately in the 1952 and 1956 campaigns of Gov. Adlai E. Stevenson.

Nevertheless, the five of us came up with unanimous recommendations arrived at only after deliberate study, extensive debate, and subordination of our own partisan positions. We recognize that Voters' Time—our proposal that all radio and television stations in the country be required to carry some prime time one-half hour broadcasts simultaneously in each time zone — is a fundamental change in the way campaigns are now carried on. But we believe such fundamental change is essential unless we accept the idea that a candidate's access to the electorate should depend upon his access to big money.

The democratic process requires open forums for political ideas and the widest possible dissemination of information. As Gould points out, this can perhaps best be achieved by debates between the candidates. We agree, and said so in our report. But no unwilling candidate can be forced to debate. President Johnson in 1964 and Mr. Nixon in 1968 both thought they were ahead—and declined to debate. It still takes two to tango—or debate. Wishing it otherwise, as Gould does, simply won't produce a debate.

There are now two kinds of political broadcasting. One is the kind the candidate purchases; the United States is the only country in the world where this kind of broadcasting exists. The other kind is the program which the broadcaster provides as a public service, e.g., "Face the Nation," "Meet the Press," the Great Debates of 1960. We applaud the latter enthusiastically — and indeed we recommend that the equal time law be suspended in 1972 as it was in 1960 to permit such debates to occur again.

But our Commission's main concern was with the other kind — and the more than $40-million spent by the parties and candidates for radio and television time in the 1968 general election campaigns. The Presidential candidates alone spent more than $20-million in the general election campaign of 1968 for broadcasting time —which was four times the amount spent in 1956. Around three-quarters of this was spent on "spots" — short, commercial-like announcements which contributed little to a serious discussion of the issues.

Our Commission concluded that the voter has much to lose from present arrangements. We concluded: "Letting ability to pay determine access to the great audience and fostering the development of commercial-like campaign spots rather than rational political discussions may in time subvert the democratic process."

Therefore, we propose a new kind of political broadcasting: one which does not belong to the candidate and which does not belong to the broadcaster. Instead, it will belong to the voter. Thus Voters' Time would be purchased with public funds by the Federal government from the broadcaster — at half rates—and would be carried simultaneously by every radio and television station for at least six half-hour periods in prime time in the five weeks preceding a Presidential election. The cost? Less than mailing a 5-cent postcard to every voter.

The broadcasting industry has objected to this proposal on the ground that the public would give up its freedom of choice during those half-hours. Gould argues that this would be a terrible precedent "save in a moment of genuine national emergency."

We believe a Presidential election is as crucial as a genuine national emergency. For on the decision of the American electorate hangs the fate of millions at home and abroad, war and peace, survival itself.

Of course, there will be some people who will object to their favorite program being pre-empted for a half-hour every four years. We suggest that they are under no obligation to turn on their radio or television sets during this imposition, or they can turn them off, and thus tune out their responsibilities as citizens of a republic which depends upon its citizens to cast informed votes.

*

We think that if Voters' Time were in effect, a great new American tradition would quickly develop in which Americans would sit down together to watch, listen, and make judgments about the men who would lead them. We also believe that to compare Voters' Time with conventional programming is to lose sight of the unique importance of Presidential elections and would compromise the seriousness of the Presidential race. We also believe that as the institution of Voters' Time developed, this direct and regular confrontation with the candidates would give voters a sense of direct participation in Presidential politics heretofore unknown.

Broadcasters pre-empt regular program schedules periodically for events of great importance. A Presidential speech, a moon shot, a Presidential funeral. Is a Presidential selection less important?

Burch, New F.C.C. Chief, Defends News on TV

Makes Speech Before Group That Criticized Medium

By FRED FERRETTI

Dean Burch, new chairman of the Federal Communications Commission, defended commercial television broadcasters yesterday against a charge that their day-to-day news efforts failed the public interest.

Speaking at the awards ceremony of the Alfred I. du Pont Columbia University Broadcast Journalism Awards in Columbia's Low Memorial Library, Mr. Burch took issue with a survey of broadcasting issued in conjunction with the awards. The report, which studied television and radio news for the broadcast year 1968-69, contended that television performed with grace and power when it was broadcasting major news events live, but that its daily efforts were poor.

United Press International
Dean Burch

First Speech in Role

Mr. Burch was introduced by Richard T. Baker, acting dean of the Columbia Graduate School of Journalism as the "new, new, I mean shiny new," chairman of the F.C.C.," and Mr. Burch went right to work.

"I think," he said, "that we would all agree that for all the criticism of broadcast journalism there is not much in the way of thanks for the service it performs.

"We have all noticed that we are in an era of tearing down, and of restructuring. Lots of people want to destroy broadcasting as we know it."

Those who deliver what Mr. Burch called "unthinking criticism" are guilty of "copping out," he said, just as those in the networks who are quoted as saying that "the public gets only what it deserves . . . I suggest that no one in this room has the one answer to what is the public interest and how it is to be protected."

He said there were many "existing things to be done. We must improve but we must have a starting point. Criticize, yes. Tearing down, no."

Deplores Taking Sides

He said he hoped that all connected with the television industry on whichever side would stop generalizing about each other as "good guys and bad guys." He hoped further, he said, that "all of us will be receptive to an idea, whatever its source."

Speaking for himself, he said: "I am not going to stand here and tell you that I've been lying awake for five years thinking of all the answers to what's wrong with television." He said he thought that some might feel it appropriate for his first speech to include a slogan or phrase that would become memorable:

"I thought of vast wastland and rejected that. I thought of effete snobs and rejected that. I thought of extremism in defense of liberty is no sin and rejected that."

Laughter followed Mr. Burch's references to Newton Minow, a former F.C.C. chairman, Vice President Spiro T. Agnew and Senator Barry Goldwater, for whom Mr. Burch was campaign chairman when the Senator sought the Presidency.

Critical of Criticism

Before he spoke Mr. Burch talked with reporters about some of the questions facing broadcasters and the Federal Communications Commission. Of the awards survey he said it was "quick to indict but not so quick to offer solutions."

Asked if he favored governmental subsidization of political campaign broadcasts he said: "Commercial broadcasting should not be asked to pay the whole freight."

Refuses to Go On Record for or Against Pastore Bill

He refused to put himself on record on either side of the bill offered by Senator John O. Pastore, Democrat of Rhode Island, on which he will testify publicly next week.

The Pastore bill would make it virtually impossible for groups to challenge existing broadcast licenses. It has been criticized by citizens' groups as granting broadcasters licenses in perpetuity. Mr. Burch said he had studied the bill. "I'm not for or against it. I guess you could say I'm somewhere in between."

Blacks Might Be Losers

It was suggested to Mr. Burch that passage of the bill might effectively shut blacks out of station ownership. He agreed that it was a possibility, "because it would perpetuate the status quo. That interpretation has been made."

He added that "there seems to be a good deal of legislative support" for the Pastore bill.

His predecessor, Rosel H. Hyde, said some time ago that President Nixon might be moving toward establishment of a Cabinet-level Secretary of Communications, who would effectively control the F.C.C. and the entire governmental communications spectrum. Mr. Burch said he was aware of "several proposals along these lines. I think I'll have to address myself to that question in time."

The awards of silver scrolls, designed by Louis Kahn, went to:

Dr. Everett C. Parker of the United Church of Christ for persistent efforts to serve the public's interest in broadcasting.

The National Broadcasting Company for a documentary study of chemical biological warfare.

Public Broadcast Laboratory of National Educational Television for a report on the military industrial complex.

Local stations KNBC-TV in Los Angeles and WSB-TV in Atlanta for investigative reporting.

Station KQED-TV of San Francisco and radio station WRKL in Mount Ivy, N. Y., for coverage of local elections.

Eastland Assails
'Liberal Press'

By WARREN WEAVER Jr.
Special to The New York Times

WASHINGTON, Nov. 13 — The Senate opened debate today on the nomination of Clement F. Haynsworth Jr. for the Supreme Court with a charge by one of his supporters that he was being victimized by the "liberal establishment" and the "liberal press."

James O. Eastland, the Mississippi Democrat who heads the Senate Judiciary Committee, contended that the facts of the case had been distorted and misrepresented in news coverage.

"The studied purpose of these [press] methods and the desired result of their authors is to discredit ideas and destroy men who cannot be counted on to dance to the tune of the liberal press," he said.

As debate opened on the nominee of President Nixon, the confirmation vote expected next Tuesday or Wednesday appeared likely to most observers to be very close. For the first time today, a Republican who had planned to vote against Judge Haynsworth switched and announced his support.

Senator James B. Pearson of Kansas, who had first been listed as against the nominee and then as undecided, told the Senate that he had "sought a decision which would be representative of the will of the people of Kansas" and had found that sentiment "overwhelmingly in favor" of confirmation.

Privately, Mr. Pearson told friends that his decision had become the price for his continued participation in the Republican party in Kansas. His colleague, Senator Robert J. Dole, came out for Judge Haynsworth on Monday, but-

tressing his case with endorsements from a number of Kansas judges.

Senator Stuart Symington, Democrat of Missouri, announced on the floor that he would vote against confirmation, but most tallies had already listed him in that camp so his statement did not have the impact of Senator Pearson's.

A head count by The New York Times showed 39 Senators committed to Judge Haynsworth or leaning toward him, 51 opposed to confirmation or leaning that way and 10 undecided.

The pro-Haynsworth forces maintained, however, that they had as many as 47 Senators ready or inclined to vote for confirmation with eight still uncommitted. Their theory was that President Nixon ought to be able to win over three of those eight votes, to create a 50-to-50 tie and permit Vice President Agnew to break it and obtain confirmation.

Stress on Individualism

If Mr. Nixon is lobbying personally for Judge Haynsworth, there was little evidence of it in his visit to the Senate today. In a brief speech from the rostrum, he stressed his respect for the Senate tradition of individualism, with each member making up his own mind.

The President said he understood why there was sometimes criticism of the Administration in Congress, and he called it "one of the strengths of the system instead of one of its weaknesses." He made no direct reference to the Supreme Court nomination.

The first such criticism in the formal Haynsworth debate came from Senator Birch Bayh, Democrat of Indiana, who has been one of the major critics of the nomination. He said that "to restore public confidence in the Court, we in the Senate

should consent to a nomination only if the nominee has established those ethical standards which inspire confidence."

"In nominating Judge Haynsworth to the Supreme Court," Mr. Bayh continued, "President Nixon has not presented the Senate with such a man. Though I believe Haynsworth to be honest, he has not shown the proper sensitivity to ethical problems which have arisen during his career. Indeed, that career has been blemished by a pattern of insensitivity to the judicial precept's concerning the appearance of impropriety."

The long-awaited debate opened on a low key. It was just before 5 P.M., after a long day of Senate business, and only seven or eight members were in the chamber as Senator Eastland began reading his 60-page text.

"It is not the Judge Haynsworths who are out of touch with America and with the values and aspirations of the American people," he declared. "Perhaps it is the so-called liberal establishment that does not understand what is in the minds and hearts of the American people and does not fully comprehend the issues, the ideas and the forces that are sweeping and changing this land of ours."

Senator Roman L. Hruska of Nebraska, the ranking Republican on the Judiciary Committee, said the real issue was "President Nixon's attempt to restore some balance to the Supreme Court of the United States."

"Much of the energy of the anti-Haynsworth campaign has come from labor and civil rights groups that simply disagree with his decision," Senator Hruska said. "This is the genesis of the attack on his ethics. Philosophy, not ethics, is the real controversy here."

Press and TV Rules for Covering News Differ

By JACK GOULD

The heart of the difference in covering news on television and news in print, as illustrated last week by the controversy stirred up by Vice President Agnew's speech criticizing the TV networks, lies in the ground rules covering the two media.

Television operates under a Federal license because there is not enough room in the air for everyone who might like to own a station. Newspapers do not operate under a Federal license and, if a person has enough money, he is free to publish anything from a pamphlet to a daily journal.

To the layman perhaps the foremost question involves the First Amendment guarantee of freedom of speech. If television is a dominant medium reaching the most people every day, why should it be denied such constitutional protection? If a newspaper caters to a much smaller circulation on a local area, why is it guaranteed the protection?

Some Must Be Rejected

The Supreme Court has repeatedly supplied the answer. Access to broadcasting is not available to everyone who might wish to use it, and because it cannot be used by all, some who wish to use it must be denied. Only recently this philosophy was again upheld in the Red Lion case before the Court, and from this finding stems the multiplicity of complex rules and regulations that govern radio and TV.

In this case Fred J. Cook, a liberal writer, won time to answer the Rev. Billy James Hargis, a rightwing preacher, as a result of the latter's attacks on him over station WGCB, the only outlet in Red Lion, Pa.

It does not matter that in some areas of the country there might be room on the air for all those economically capable of broadcasting. It only takes a single case to establish the principle of law.

Even if a huge conglomerate wanted to start a new television station in New York City on a choice channel, it would be blocked. All the available channels have been spoken for and are in use. To add another select channel would mean intolerable interference in such cities as Philadelphia or New Haven.

Must Pick and Choose

In short, the scarcity of channels forces the Federal Communications Commission to pick and choose among operators and applicants who best promise to meet the time-worn phrase of the "public interest, convenience or necessity."

Printed material is not subject to any such strictures: The Atlantic and Harper's can go their merry way and so can trash in print. It is the difference between a scientifically closed market place and a free-for-all in competition.

For years the broadcasting industry has fought for all the guarantees of the First Amendment but to no avail. If the First Amendment cannot guarantee everyone's freedom of expression, then there is no longer the First Amendment, the Supreme Court has ruled in effect.

'Fairness Doctrine'

The inevitable consequence is that the Federal Government, through the Federal Communications Commission, must be guided by a rule making the limited number of channels available to the maximum number of persons. This policy has led to a host of rules, almost all of which have the ingredients of protracted litigation.

Topping the list is what the commission calls its "fairness doctrine." This is a broad guideline stipulating that a broadcasting station must bend every effort to seeing that all the people, not just some, have a chance to be heard. If Joe Doe criticizes John Doakes, then under the fairness doctrine Doakes is deserving of a hearing. The measure's intent is to achieve maximum democracy under unavoidable restraints.

The basic concept of the fairness doctrine applies to the celebrated section 315 of the Communications Act, only under more ironclad and specific conditions. If a broadcaster donates time to one duly designated candidate for political office, then it is his requirement to offer the same opportunity to all other candidates in the field.

Basis of Newsworthiness

The rule is waived in the case of regularly scheduled newscasts but in effect is bypassed by rich candidates' buying more time than poorer ones. This in itself has aroused heated controversy. In a Presidential contest there may be as many as 20 candidates qualified on the ballot of one state or another.

Whereas newspapers enjoy the privilege of concentrating on candidates of prime newsworthiness and can give them free space, TV is not so privileged. The home screen would have to allot equal time to all and the result could occupy much of the broadcast day.

Unlike newspapers, which can elect how to divide their space among human interests, broadcasting cannot do so without documentation. In applying for a new license or a renewal, a station must stipulate the number of hours in a random week that will show in percentage figures how much time will be devoted to news, public affairs, religious programing, entertainment and sports.

In a recent sample week, WNBC-TV in New York allotted 14 hours a week to news, WCBS-TV, 15 hours, and WPIX, 2 hours 17 minutes. In public affairs the figures ranged from 16 hours for WNEW-TV; 5 hours for WNBC-TV; 3.6 hours for WABC and 3 hours 30 minutes for WCBS-TV. To the vexation of some F.C.C. commissioners there is no minimum set on how much public service adequately serves the public.

Rebuttals Allowed

Most stations classify the late evening talk shows under the category of entertainment, for which a lump percentage figure can be filed without a specific breakdown of details. But in practice under the fairness doctrine, if one grossly abuses an absent celebrity the usual practice is to invite the offended individual to submit a rebuttal at an early date.

The irony of television is that the set in the home is probably one of the most wasted instruments devised by man. There are two channel bands, 2 through 13 and 14 through 83. But in many communities perhaps only three stations can be seen.

This is one of the arguments in the controversial issue of cable television. In one cable connected between an essential control point and the individual home the number of channels conceivably could be expanded to 50 or more, but still not enough to satisfy virtually every cultural, educational or entertainment need.

But rewiring the United States and asking the individual to pay $5 a month for the privilege ranks as one of the future's uncertainties.

Rallies Called Peaceful

By JAMES M. NAUGHTON
Special to The New York Times

WASHINGTON, Nov. 17 — The White House reaffirmed today President Nixon's intention to seek peace in accordance with his own plan, but took a more conciliatory attitude than some Administration officials have taken toward protesters and the press.

Ronald L. Ziegler, the White House press secretary, said it was "generally the White House view" that mass demonstrations by Vietnam policy critics last week were "generally peaceful"—a view that clashed with the opinion of Attorney General John N. Mitchell.

Mr. Ziegler also declared that the Administration has "absolutely no desire" to censor the news. At the same time, he defended Vice President Agnew's speech criticizing the television networks and remarks by Herbert G. Klein, Mr. Nixon's Director of Communications, broadening the criticism to include all news media.

Mr. Agnew, in a speech Thursday in Des Moints, Iowa, accused the networks of a selective and biased presentation of news, and yesterday Mr. Klein said all news media needed to re-examine their coverage.

The point both Mr. Agnew and Mr. Klein sought to make, said Mr. Ziegler, was that the media should "examine themselves."

The Question Remains

As the Administration settled back into its normal routine following the march by some 250,000 protesters on Saturday, the question remained, as Mr. Zeigler stated it, "how to achieve peace."

He said Mr. Nixon would follow the plan he outlined Nov. 3 in a nationwide television address. In that address the President rejected a "precipitate withdrawal" from Vietnam and spoke of seeking a measured pace of disengagement.

"With the belief that the American people support him, the President is determined to seek a just and lasting peace," said Mr. Ziegler. "He could not be more totally committed to achieving it."

Nevertheless, the debate continued in the capital about both the technique of the demonstrators in seeking to alter the President's view and the criticism of the news media being issued by Administration leaders.

Mr. Mitchell issued a statement yesterday, contending that "the planned demonstra-

tions were marred by such extensive physical injury, property damage and street confrontations that I do not believe that—over-all—the gathering here can be characterized as peaceful."

Mr. Ziegler's comments today — that there were some "glaring examples" of violence but that the two major events sponsored by the committee were "generally peaceful"—ran counter to the tone of the Attorney General's statement. The two events were the 40-hour candlelight march past the White House and the mass march and rally here Saturday.

The President's press spokesman declined to say whether Mr. Nixon agreed with Mr. Mitchell, but he said that his own comments reflected "the White House view."

Similarly, Mr. Ziegler's approach toward the mushrooming controversy over the Vice President's attack on television news commentators reflected a more moderate stance.

"There is absolutely no intention on the part of Herb or the Vice President to suggest there should be censorship or there should be Government intervention in this," said Mr. Ziegler.

Former Vice President Humphrey, however, saw in Mr. Agnew's speech last Thursday and in the complaints later voiced by Mr. Klein and Mr. Mitchell "a deliberate and calculated" attempt to suppress dissent.

Commissioner Nicholas Johnson of the Federal Communications Commission, who has voiced concern in the past about what he views as growing political power of TV network executives, criticized Mr. Agnew today for having "frightened network executives and newsmen in ways that may cause serious and permanent harm to independent journalism and free speech in America."

Mr. Ziegler denied reports published in Time magazine that the President had ordered the Vice President to make the speech last week, although he confirmed that one of the Presidetn's speech writers. Patrick J. Buchanan, "could have contributed some thoughts and ideas" to the speech.

In the speech, Mr. Agnew criticized television commentators for their analyses of the President's Nov. 3 address.

Mr. Ziegler said that Mr. Buchanan, a conservative who wrote some of Mr. Nixon's most outspoken "law and order" speeches during the 1968 campaign, "may have had, and I think did have, some thoughts regarding this" and could have passed them on the Vice President's staff.

Questions from reporters about Mr. Nixon's own views on the Vice President's speech were brushed aside by Mr. Ziegler. At one point he flatly refused to ask Mr. Nixon for his comments.

Commissioner Johnson said, in a speech at the University of Iowa, that Americans were in Mr. Agnew's debt for bringing the issues and tactics of television news coverage into the open.

He expressed concern, however, that Mr. Agnew and other Administration officials were "demanding more favorable coverage."

The impression that the Government, which controls issuance of television licenses, is threatening the networks "at least appears worse," said Mr. Johnson, "when President Nixon selects as F.C.C. chairman the former head of the Republican National Comitee, who is scarcely on the job before obtaining transcripts of televised comments of which the President disapproves."

Dean Burch, sworn in Oct. 31 as Mr. Nixon's appointee to head the commission, telephoned the three networks Nov. 5 to ask for transcripts of commentaries on the President's Vietnam policy speech.

The Senate Republican whip, Robert P. Griffin of Michigan said in Detroit today that television news coverage gives "a distorted picture of what's going on in Washington."

Klein Gives Elaboration On Calls to TV Stations

By FRED FERRETTI

Herbert G. Klein, Director of Communications for the Nixon Administration, said yesterday that on occasion the White House had phoned television stations to ask what their editorial treatment of the President would be.

However, he said, it was only "Which side are you on, or something like that."

On Tuesday Mr. Klein reported that he had never asked a broadcaster what the tone of an editorial on President Nixon was likely to be, but he added that he could not say that such inquiries had never been made from his office.

Mr. Klein said yesterday the stations called had "seemed pleased" that the White House was interested.

He termed the calls "proper." He said some of them had been made before appearances by President Nixon and "in many cases they came after the fact."

Mr. Klein made his remarks at a news conference before addressing 750 executives of networks and local stations at the Plaza Hotel.

Last Sunday, Mr. Klein said that all news media should re-examine themselves.

Criticism and Conciliation

Yesterday Mr. Klein addressed a luncheon meeting of the International Radio and Television Society.

With the three network news presidents sharing a dais with him, he renewed his criticism of the nation's media, yet took pains to be conciliatory.

Vice President Agnew, in a speech last Thursday in Des Moines, Iowa, had severely crit-icized the American Broadcasting Company, though not by name, for employing former Ambassador W. Averell Harriman as an analyst following the broadcast of President Nixon's Nov. 3 address on Vietnam.

Yesterday Mr. Klein, who sat next to A.B.C.'s vice president for corporate relations, James Haggerty, said that Mr. Haggerty was a fine man and a fine press secretary (to President Eisenhower) and that he had been somewhat of an inspiration to him.

Mr. Klein suggested that Mr. Agnew had raised questions that the broadcasting industry had given "not enough thought to," and he expressed the hope that when the "passion" died down, the questions raised would be "looked at coolly."

Censorship 'Not an Issue'

He then posed several rhetorical questions and answered them. He said it had been asked if the Nixon Administration was proposing censorship or attempting intimidation.

"No," said Mr. Klein, nobody in the Administration "has any desire for censorship."

"You can't have a free country under censorship," he said. "That's not an issue."

Mr. Klein asked if the Government was attempting to stifle news analysis and commentary, and answered, "There is a growing need for interpretation, but there is also need for an examination of how it takes place."

He said the age of complexity in which we live "increases the need for proper interpretation."

He asked if the Government was threatening the broadcasting industry with controls through the Federal Communications Commission, and answered:

"There is no threat but lots of Americans have doubts of the believability of the industry."

He urged the press to "continue to watch the activities of my office" and to criticize, but said that "they should not resist criticism back."

Mr. Klein said the Nixon Administration implied "no threats" and that there was "no intent to interfere with the rights of radio and TV."

C.B.S. Executive Quoted

On Tuesday, Richard Salant, president of news for the Columbia Broadcasting System, was quoted as saying that the White House had asked C.B.S. affiliates in Minneapolis and Los Angeles whether they planned editorials and what they intended to say. A call from Mr. Klein's deputy, Al Snyder, was made to WCBS-TV here, asking simply whether an editorial on Vietnam was planned. According to a source at WCBS-TV, Mr. Snyder did not ask what the content was to be.

It was reported yesterday that President Nixon had personally congratulated, by letter, station WNHC-TV in New Haven for editorially noting that there was a large segment of the population that did not favor total immediate troop withdrawal.

WNHC-TV is owned by Triangle Publications Inc., and is headed by Walter H. Annenberg, the President's appointee as Ambassador to Britain.

The Taft Broadcasting Company, with stations in Ohio, Pennsylvania, Missouri and upstate New York, said it had editorialized on national issues and on the President but had never received any inquiries from the White House. Reven Frank, president of news for the National Broadcasting Company, also said that he had received no inquiries on any commentaries. N.B.C. stations do not editorialize.

Washington: The Power of the Presidency and Television

By JAMES RESTON

WASHINGTON, Jan. 27 — President Nixon has clearly decided to use the power of the Presidency, plus the power of network television, to combat his opponents in the Democrat - controlled Congress and presumably to establish a Republican Congress in November.

This is quite a combination and quite a gamble. Thoughtful observers here have wondered, ever since the inception of nation - wide television, what would happen if a determined President, who had both the will and the ability to use the networks effectively, really set out to exploit television for his political advantage.

President Eisenhower had the personality, the popularity, and the ability to use television in this way, but not the will. President Kennedy had the ability and the will to use it, but for some unexplained reason, was afraid of what he called over-exposure. President Johnson had the will, but neither the personality nor the ability to use it effectively. But President Nixon, by going to the networks to veto the money bill for health, education and welfare, has indicated both a determination and an ability to use it to appeal to the

people over the head of the Congress to achieve his political objectives.

The possibilities and implications of this are worth a little reflection. The President has available in the White House a television studio hooked into the networks. This is necessary for great occasions of state or for emergencies, but it is also available to him whenever he has a major controversy with the Congress: for example, when he wants to explain his veto of the H.E.W. bill to the American people. After all, it would be rather awkward, even for Frank Stanton at C.B.S., to say no.

This, of course, is precisely what the President did in his H.E.W. controversy. He vetoed the bill on television with a flourish. He did not deliver a balanced Presidential presentation of the problem, but a one-sided, self-serving and even self-righteous argument for his veto. It was very effective and very misleading, and it raises questions far more important than the H.E.W. bill.

The Doctrine of 'Fairness'

What about the doctrine of "fairness," which Vice President Agnew was so concerned about not so long ago? How can Senators who oppose the President

get "equal time" when they are talking to a half-empty chamber, while the President is arguing his case, from the majesty of the White House, before an audience of millions?

Beyond this, there is a more immediate problem. This is that the President is now by-passing or reaching beyond the Congress to the people, and this is his gamble. He is just going into his second year in the Presidency. He has indicated the outlines of his policy—welfare, taxes, crime, conservation, and all the rest—but his major proposals have not been voted into law.

The Power of Congress

They have to go through the Congress. The Congress is controlled by the Democrats. The Democrats are divided, with a cooperative saint as their leader in the Senate, and a weak and tired octogenarian, or thereabouts, as their leader in the House, and a liberal Senator from a conservative state as chairman of the Democratic National Committee.

In short, the Democrats are in deep trouble. But nothing will unify them more, or arouse their partisan dander, than a President who tries to ride over their majority by partisan television appeals to the people.

This is a provocation to a partisan battle at a time when the country needs a little time and unity to put through many of the sensible programs the President has suggested.

The Partisan Furies

After the President's televised veto message, the partisan furies are rising. After proclaiming in his State of the Union Message that "what this nation needs is an example ...; of spiritual and moral leadership . . . which would inspire young Americans with a sense of excitement. . ." Mr. Nixon, who has been talking about an era of quiet understanding at home, and of negotiation rather than confrontation abroad, has now gone to the television with a narrow political argument which is building up a real confrontation in a Democratic Congress, whose support he needs for the programs he says are essential to the nation.

It is very odd: a noble generous State of the Union Message one day, and a narrow party speech on television a few days later. All this is a fairly good illustration of why there is so much distrust and cynicism in the country, particularly among the young, about American politics and politicians.

January 28, 1970

Washington: Making Things Worse Than They Are

By JAMES RESTON

WASHINGTON, Aug. 4—Ever since President Jefferson announced that Aaron Burr was guilty of treason in the Gen. James Wilkinson conspiracy case (he was later acquitted), Presidents of the United States have been in trouble over careless or ill-considered public remarks.

Accordingly, there is nothing particularly new about President Nixon's recent statement that Charles Manson, the hippie cultist now on trial in California, "was guilty, directly or indirectly, of eight murders without reason."

Like former Attorney General Herbert Brownell, who got in trouble during the Eisenhower Administration for passing judgment in the Harry Dexter White case, Mr. Nixon merely talked before thinking, and is entitled to a presumption of innocence, which he later granted to Mr. Manson.

The News Conference

The incident raises, however, the old question of how to protect the President of the United States in these days of instant news from unintended and potentially damaging blunders during extemporaneous news conferences.

Every President since Herbert

Hoover has become increasingly casual or bold about talking to reporters. Mr. Hoover insisted on written questions at his news conferences; Franklin Roosevelt banned them at his first press conference, but insisted that his answers be reported in the third person. With the advent of television, news conferences were first taped in advance for release later, but Mr. Nixon has insisted on addressing the reporters "live" on TV and without notes.

He is a master of the art and the political advantages are obvious. He conveys the impression of controlling a wide range of complicated subjects and of facing his critics manfully under difficult and often dangerous conditions.

The President's Staff

But Presidents, like baseball pitchers, don't always hit the mark. Unlike Jefferson, who assured the Congress in writing that Aaron Burr's "guilt is placed beyond question," Mr. Nixon merely stumbled into the guilty charge against Manson and then hesitated about setting the record straight.

It is odd that a President, trained in the law, should have violated the elemental presumption of innocence, particularly during a lecture on the majesty of the legal process, but what

is even more surprising is why his staff did not protect him in time to keep the blunder from going out on the national television.

Attorney General Mitchell was at his side. He and other members of the President's official family realized what had happened, but either they hesitated to make it clear to the President in time or the President's instructions were not carried out accurately by Ronald L. Ziegler, the White House press secretary.

Accordingly, the correction was not made until four hours later when the Presidential plane got to Washington, and even then the big jet was circling Andrews Air Force Base to get the correction in order.

The interesting thing here is that the President's original charge of guilt was not going out on live network television. It was being taped for release later. Thus, the blunder could easily have been corrected before the damage was done. The question, therefore, is whether the staff was alert and confident enough to tell the President what had happened, and if so, why Ziegler came back with a mystifying "clarification."

The relations between a President and his staff are private,

and nobody can be quite sure whether Mr. Nixon's staff is timid or intimidated. It is certainly intelligent, but in this case something obviously slipped.

Why Not Later?

Beyond this, it is not quite clear why these Presidential news conferences cannot always be taped and checked for bloopers before they are released. After all, even the football games have instant replay, and even Congressmen have the right to revise and extend their remarks in the Congressional Record.

The trouble is in catching up with charges after they are made, even when corrected. Albert J. Beveridge, writing in *The Life of John Marshall*, says of Mr. Jefferson's charge against Burr:

"The awful charge of treason had now been formally made against Burr by the President of the United States. This . . . at once caught and held the attention of the public, which took for granted the truth of it . . . ."

Mr. Nixon's slip, of course, is not comparable, but it was recoverable, and the odd thing was that the President and his staff were still trifling with it four hours after the accident.

August 5, 1970

191

Nixon's Strategy for Reaching the Public Largely Bypasses Washington Press Corps

By RICHARD HALLORAN
Special to The New York Times

WASHINGTON, Aug. 23—The Nixon administration has come up with a new strategy for getting its policies across to the American public: reaching out to metropolitan newspaper editors and regional television executives throughout the land.

In football parlance, the Nixon Administration has made an end run around the Washington press corps.

The strategy, devised by Herbert G. Klein, the President's Director of Communications, includes the following:

¶Top-level briefings for news executives. The briefings are led by the President himself, and the participants include senior members of the Administration such as Henry A. Kissinger, the President's assistant for national security affairs.

¶Briefings on legislative proposals for reporters around the country by Administration teams.

¶Special mailings to editorial writers, radio and television station news directors, and writers who focus on particular fields such as pollution.

¶Direct appeals to the public through Presidential television addresses or televised news conferences that the President can control.

¶A minimum of Presidential contacts with the White House press corps, with those contacts almost always in formal meetings.

Mr. Klein said that his plan intended "no reflection on the Washington press corps, which has to follow things minute by minute."

"We're looking at the long range and trying to provide a full range of facts to those who are editing or writing editorials," he added.

"The more resources they have to decide on an issue, the better," Mr. Klein said. "It's difficult for people out there to get all of the background on all of the issues. We've made a major effort to give them a factual presentation."

A former aide to the President said Mr. Nixon believed he had a better chance of getting through by direct means than by having his views filtered by Washington reporters. "The President feels that the White House press corps has not been giving a faithful representation of his Administration," he said.

George Christian, one of President Johnson's press secretaries, admires the "finesse" of Mr. Klein's tactics. Having had his own battles with the Washington press corps, Mr. Christian said, "I can understand why they would want to go directly to opinion makers."

"I sit back in some admiration for having some sort of plan to get the word out," Mr. Christian said. "It is a lot more of a concerted effort than anything we tried to do. They work overtime to get their ideas across."

The Administration evolved the plan over the two years since the 1968 election campaign. The latest moves have been private briefings at the summer White House in San Clemente, Calif., and in New Orleans for regional news executives.

40 in San Clemente

About 40 news executives from all over the country were invited to the San Clemente briefing last June. The President spoke briefly, then Mr. Kissinger delivered a long exposition of the Administration's foreign policy

Lieut. Gen. John W. Vogt Jr., director of operations for the Joint Chiefs of Staff, and William H Sullivan, Deputy Assistant Secretary of State for East Asian and Pacific Affairs, also sopke, to defend the Administration's policy on Cambodia.

In New Orleans last week Mr? Kissinger again spoke on foreign policy, to Southern editors. Assistant Secretary of State Joseph Sisco, who is the key American negotiator on the Middle East question, outlined the Administration's efforts to stimulate Arab-Israeli peace talks

Similar briefings are being planned in San Clemente this month for Western editors and in Chicago next month for Midwestern editors. A third may be held later in the East.

Robert Healy, executive editor of The Boston Globe, said he found Mr. Kissinger "very effective" in San Clemente. "He has a faculty for taking you inside," Mr. Healy said. "That was particularly useful for The Globe, which has been critical of the Administration and the war in Vietnam."

The briefing resulted in several editorial columns in The Globe setting out the Administration's position in general, and on Indochina and the Middle East in particular. Mr. Healy said that the briefing had not changed his paper's opinion on Indochina "but the Administration came out well in editorials on the Middle East question."

Emmett Dedmon, editorial director of The Chicago Sun-Times, also praised Mr. Kissinger's explanation of the Administration's basic philosophy on foreign policy, but Mr. Dedmon said his paper still believed that "the push into Cambodia was not worth the price the Administration paid domestically."

"The briefing didn't change our position," he said, "but better-informed editorials were written."

A Southern editor, who asked not to be named, said the briefing in New Orleans was "useful to people out here in the boondocks." He said, "It was good to hear the Administration's view first hand and not have to rely on the wire services, or a correspondent, or television."

An Eastern editor, who also asked not to be named, took the opposite view. "It wasn't worth the money to go out there just to hear the Administration say the same old thing." He also said, "We're trying to make evident to Mr. Klein that we're not in his pocket."

Besides the briefings, Mr. Nixon has made personal visits to two newspapers recently. He had lunch with editors of The Washington Star last month and of The New York Daily News last week. Both have generally supported the Administration.

A year ago last spring, the Administration began sending teams out to brief editors and reporters of influential regional papers on legislative proposals. Three representatives, one an Assistant Secretary, explained postal reform. Another team—from the Department of Health, Education, and Welfare; the Department of Labor, and the White House — discussed welfare reforms. A third took up draft reform.

Mood of the Country

White House sources said the briefing teams also took soundings on the mood of the country. "We can tell quite a bit from the lines of questioning," said one official. "We had a resident hippie in one city give us some insights into the youth movement."

Even before such briefings were started, Mr. Klein's office started sending transcripts of Presidential speeches and remarks to about 1,200 editorial writers and radio and television news directors.

"Editorial writers don't ordinarily see the source material," said an official, "because the reporter in Washington may be sending out only a 700 to 1,000-word story." Seeing the original gives the writer the context in which the President intended his statement to be taken.

In addition, the White House sends printed copies of major Presidential messages to publishers and editors. Messages on specific subjects go to writers who specialize in that field. The environmental message, for instance, went to outdoor writers.

Today, the Nixon Administration's approach to the Washington press corps is in marked contrast to the Johnson Administration's.

Mr. Nixon has held only two informal meetings with the White House press this year. Mr. Johnson averaged about 18 meetings a week with reporters, either alone or in small and large groups. Cabinet officers hold backgrounders rarely. Secretary of State William P. Rogers has discontinued the practice of his predecessor, Dean Rusk, who met with State Department correspondents almost every Friday evening.

Although Administration officials contend that Vice President Agnew's criticism of the press is not part of the over-all strategy, his attacks have diverted the attention of many Washington correspondents while other spokesmen are spreading the word.

Mr. Nixon will continue to use television as a major means of reaching the public, White House sources said. Perhaps the best measure of his effectiveness has been the outcry from Democrats in Congress for equal time.

White House sources said the President would stick with televised news conferences rather than alternate them with those for the pad-and-pencil press. The President is much more the master on television.

He selects the reporters who will ask the questions. As every President has, Mr. Nixon has questions he wants to answer. Moreover, few reporters, knowing the camera is on them, have shown themselves adept at asking sharp questions

But the biggest thing going for the President is the clock. The usual 30-minute time limit imposed by television precludes follow-up questions from a reporter who does not want to look as if he is hogging the show. And the President can filibuster a bit to run out the clock if he thinks he is in trouble.

August 24, 1970

Nixon Tries Some New Approaches To the Press

SAN CLEMENTE — The relationship between the press and any President usually turns more on the personality of the Chief Executive than the collective personality of the reporters, which changes little from Administration to Administration. All Presidents have the same objective — mainly, to win maximum exposure of their views in the best possible light — but the techniques they employ are as different as the men themselves.

Mr. Kennedy, for example, exercised great charm, encouraged camaraderie, and in the end gave some members of the press the sense (always illusory, and sometimes fatal) that they, too, were participants in the great decisions of government. Mr. Johnson, meanwhile, depended upon sheer force. Alternately massaging and berating those who covered him, he tried to *command* a favorable press. The fact that he failed did not diminish the virtuosity of his effort.

Mr. Nixon is a different breed altogether. He is a shy man, and his relations with the press are distant. He is also a wary man, and his attitude toward working reporters still seems to be marked by the scars of earlier campaigns. Thus, where his predecessors were personal, Mr. Nixon is reserved. He seeks maximum exposure of his views with minimum personal risk, and, therefore, has come to rely not on himself but on intermediaries.

For one thing, he has virtually abolished the personal, individual interview. Many of the press welcome this, and there is much

that is good in it. He does not play favorites; his inaccessibility applies impartially to all reporters, with the exception of a few favored columnists.

Meanwhile, he has installed a communications director, Herb Klein, to spread the gospel to the provinces. When he does not speak through Mr. Klein he speaks through his aides or his press secretary, Ronald L. Ziegler, who is as honest as any press secretary has ever been and is sufficiently charming to anesthetize the nastiest newsman. When Mr. Nixon wishes to disarm or pummel the press, he sends Vice President Agnew sallying forth to combat.

When Mr. Nixon appears in a public forum, it is usually at an evening news conference in the East Room of the White House, or in a direct television appearance before the American people, or in some similarly highly controlled format.

Midway into the second year of his Presidency, Mr. Nixon has now devised yet another tactic in his continuing effort to get his views across to the American public without directly exposing himself: namely, "regional" briefings on foreign policies for editors, publishers and broadcasters who work in cities distant from the Eastern Seaboard. He held a "national" assemblage of top publishers and editors chosen by Mr. Klein in San Clemente in July; conferred with Southern news executives in New Orleans two weeks ago; and last Monday, a briefing was arranged here for 39 editors and executives from 13 Western states.

The impresario of these events is the indefatigable Mr. Klein, and the format for each session is much the same. Last Monday, for instance, the Western executives arrived at the Los Angeles airport by separate means and were flown to the San Clemente compound by helicopter. Mr. Nixon appeared and made a few brief and undramatic introductory remarks, then turned the show over to two high-ranking briefers from the White House

and the State Department.

The identity of these briefers, under the ground rules governing "background" sessions, is supposed to be a secret, and the White House does not look kindly on those who employ subterfuge to identify them. But the Russians know who they are. The Pravda man who covers the White House does not attend the briefings but probably has a decent idea of what's going on, so does most of official Washington, and so does the Columbia Broadcasting System, which sent a camera crew into Monday's briefing to get some footage for a show on Henry A. Kissinger, the President's chief adviser on national security affairs.

This is not to say that Dr. Kissinger, who was identified by a New Orleans newspaper as the briefer at a similar backgrounder there two weeks ago, is wholly responsible for everything that emerges from these sessions. But the White House could do worse than to put him in front of a group of news executives. He is an exceptionally articulate man, who seems to speak in full paragraphs (with transitional phrases, no less), an intellectually impressive man with a good understanding of where he and the President want the country to go in foreign policy. He is funny, charming, a combination of McGeorge Bundy, Walt Rostow and the oracle of Delphi. Seasoned reporters who were devastated by him in the beginning are used to his presentations by now. But his presence still has enormous impact on the managers of radio stations from, say, Arizona, who are hearing him for the first time.

There are numerous pluses in Mr. Nixon's impersonal system of disseminating the news. Mr. Ziegler is a superb buffer. Mr. Kissinger and his confederates are masters at fitting discrete international occurrences into a general framework of foreign policy. Through the medium of "backgrounders" for editors and publishers, the White House point of view is made available to hundreds of people (and mil-

lions of readers) who do not have the funds to employ a regular White House correspondent or staff a Washington bureau.

It is equally true, moreover, that Mr. Nixon is probably assisted politically when he furnishes regional newsmen with helicopters, and exposes them to his highest officials. Indeed, there have been many complaints that these "backgrounders" are designed mainly to help the President in the public opinion polls, but an equally good case can be made that the country is well served when the President shows not only his face but his hospitality to opinionmakers in areas other than the Eastern Seaboard.

But there are disadvantages to Mr. Nixon's procedure, too. There have been complaints, for instance, that in speaking to the publishers and executives, Mr. Nixon is deliberately going over the heads of the working press and running around their ends. This may not be a really valid complaint, however, because the working White House reporters are admitted to the briefings.

The real weakness in the Nixon technique arises from the fact that there is no real substitute for direct exposure to the President on a fairly regular basis. Few reporters wish to return to the backrubbing days of Lyndon Johnson. Moreover, there is nothing in the Constitution requiring the President even to show his face to newsmen. But it is equally true that no one is better equipped to explain policy, clarify ambiguities and lend color, tone and nuance to an Administration than the President himself.

As a rule, six or seven weeks go by between Mr. Nixon's news conferences, leading to periods of national uncertainty that even the most energetic and articulate of his associates cannot fully dispel. As a modest beginning toward a somewhat more personal diplomacy toward the press, therefore, Mr. Nixon might wish to increase the frequency of these appearances.

—ROBERT B. SEMPLE Jr.

Benefits of Campaign TV Vary

By CHRISTOPHER LYDON
Special to The New York Times

WASHINGTON, Oct. 30—The blessings of campaign television, the politician's favorite medium, are unevenly distributed around the country. For all its magic, television is disproportionately expensive in many areas and virtually unusable in a few.

Uneven choices faced different candidates as they shopped for 30-second spots at the end of the evening news last night on their local Columbia Broadcasting System affiliated stations. For example:

¶At KPIX-TV in San Francisco, Senator George Murphy could get the attention of about 265,000 homes, all of them in California, at the political discount rate of $881. That amounts to about $3.30 for every thousand homes watching, a price that politicians elsewhere view as an enviable bargain.

¶Senator Harrison A. Williams, Jr., Democrat of New Jersey, must go to Philadelphia to reach the southern half of his state. Because most of the audience tuned to Philadelphia stations lives in Pennsylvania, Maryland and Delaware, 75 cents out of every dollar that Senator Williams spends there is wasted on people who cannot vote for him. For delivery to New Jersey homes, the real price of a half-minute spot on WCAU-TV last night was $14.50 a thousand, more than four times the California price, and Senator Williams turned it down. He has reluctantly decided that he cannot afford any Philadelphia television, even though his Republican opponent, Nelson G. Gross, is buying $100,000 worth of television time.

In Connecticut, the Rev. Joseph D. Duffey, the Democratic candidate for the Senate, is particularly eager to reach Fairfield County — the home of 26 per cent of the state's voters, the base of his Republican opponent, Representative Lowell P. Weicker Jr., and an area where Mr. Duffey's recognition factor is relatively unknown.

But Fairfield County gets most of its television signals from New York City, the largest and most expensive television market in the country. To buy 30 seconds at the end of the Walter Cronkite show on WCBS-TV, Mr. Duffey would have had to pay the full $1,500, even though he was interested in only 4 per cent of the station's audience.

Variations Seen

The effective rate for reaching Connecticut homes would have been $62.50 a thousand, or 20 times Senator Murphy's rate in San Francisco. Over the years, only a very few Connecticut candidates have been able to afford New York television. Mr. Duffey cannot, and his Fairfield County campaign is suffering accordingly.

Connecticut and New Jersey offer extreme but not isolated examples of television's disproportionately high cost in places that are served substantially by out-of-state stations.

The variation from state to state in the efficiency, or real cost, of television advertising directly affects the campaign planning of candidates.

More significantly, it is contended that this variation will tend to make unfair any general limit on broadcast spending, such as the 7-cents-a-voter ceiling that President Nixon recently vetoed.

In all but a few Congressional races, where the borders of the district and the boundaries of the local television market happen roughly to coincide, television remains an uneconomical medium of political battle.

Old Campaign Styles

But even in statewide races, there are a few places where it would be prohibitively expensive to campaign on television and where older styles may yet survive.

Delaware, for example, like New Jersey, has no commercial television stations of consequence. Politicians have the choice of buying Philadelphia stations or nothing. A few wealthy candidates make token television campaigns.

Most of the others, including both contestants in the Senate race this year, go without, and Delaware seems destined to become a refuge for pretelevision campaign styles, a place where billboards, newspapers and radio remain the dominant advertising media.

But such accidents of geography in the configuration of television markets constitute one of the few remaining obstacles to the further expansion of television campaigning.

Media Experts Doubt Value of TV Ads

By CHRISTOPHER LYDON
Special to The New York Times

WASHINGTON, Nov. 4.—Television proved to be less than a magic medium in yesterday's elections.

In both parties and in a wide variety of races around the country, candidates who made TV advertising the main support of their campaigns were disappointed.

And in the aftermath today, the widely consulted media specialists—many of them embarrassed by their won-and-lost records—seemed to agree that, while television can clearly turn unknowns into serious contenders, its value in final elections is far from decisive.

Governor Rockefeller of New York, whose $1.5-million television budget was the largest in the country this year, re-established his reputation as the lavish master of the medium.

But most of the men who became known as "TV candidates," including Mr. Rockefeller's brother, Winthrop—who was defeated yesterday in his bid for a third term as Governor of Arkansas were losers in the election.

There were at least three Senate candidates—all Democrats—who, it is generally agreed, could not have been nominated without the benefit of expensive "blitz" promotions early in the campaign. They are Representative Richard L. Ottinger in New York, Howard M. Metzenbaum in Ohio and Sam Grossman in Arizona. All of them lost.

At the same time, three men who defied the new fashions governing television spending and style were winners.

In Florida, State Senator Lawton Chiles, who got TV news coverage for his 1,003-mile campaign walk through the state but bought only $30,000 worth of commercial time, won handily over Representative William C. Cramer, who had more funds and access to the White House's highly regarded television advisers.

In Pennsylvania, Milton J. Shapp won the governorship with a purposefully amateurish-looking handful of television spots and about $300,000 worth of advertising time—a quarter of the amount he spent four years ago on a campaign that brought him from obscurity but could not elect him in the final race.

And in Texas, Gov. Preston Smith was re-elected with the help of distinctly plain commercials—60-second spots that pictured him working silently at his desk as an announcer's voice commended him for his diligence.

"Preston Smith's commercials were the worst I've ever seen, but they won," said Harry Treleaven, bitter and incredulous at the failure of the commercials he designed to elect Representative George Bush in the Texas Senate race.

Mr. Treleaven directed President Nixon's advertising effort in 1968, and had been assigned to five Senate races in which the President was especially interested this year. Four of his five candidates were defeated.

"I've got to go back and figure out what really does elect candidates," he said today. "Yesterday's record doesn't say that the medium wasn't effective, but I may say something about the way we used it."

A number of Mr. Treleaven's competitors in the television consulting business did not fare much better. The Washington firm of Bailey, Deardourff and Bowen did not have a single winner in its several statewide races although it had massive spending advantages in its campaigns for Nelson C. Gross, the Republican senatorial candidate in New Jersey, and Lieut. Gov. Raymond Broderick, who ran for Governor against Mr. Shapp in Pennsylvania.

Charles Guggenheim of Washington, often credited with creating the slice-of-life, documentary style in political advertising, had five losers yesterday and four winners — including Senator Edward M Kennedy, Democrat of Massachusetts, and Senator Philip A Hart, Democrat of Michigan, who appeared unbeatable with or without their TV campaigns.

David L. Garth of New York, made famous by his television campaigns with Mayor Lindsay, won yesterday with two Democratic candidates for the Senate—John V. Tunney in California and Adlai E. Stevenson 3d in Illinois. Mr. Garth also managed the successful TV campaign of John J. Gilligan in the Ohio gubernatorial race, but was unsuccessful in the Ottinger campaign, his favorite, which most sharply tested television's ability to elevate a regional politician to big-state power in one swift effort.

Joseph Napolitan, a strictly Democratic consultant who directed winning gubernatorial campaigns in Hawaii and Maryland but lost in Massachusetts with Mayor Kevin H. White of Boston, said today that he could already see next year's styles emerging. "We'll get away from slick spots now," he said, "and go back to homey, face-to-the-camera stuff, because it will seem new."

Over-all, he said, television's importance in politics has been confirmed and will grow further. Mr. Napolitan, who directed Mr. Shapp's 1966 campaign but was not invited back this year, scoffs at the suggestion that Mr. Shapp's victory this year owes little to television.

"Nobody would ever have heard of Milton Shapp if he hadn't conducted the biggest blitz ever seen in Pennsylvania," Mr. Napolitan commented. "If he hadn't won the Democratic primary with television in 1966, he would not have been elected yesterday."

There was no consensus today on the wisdom of the bluntly accusatory commercials —variously described as "dirty" and "hard-hitting" — in which Republican candidates used isolated votes or quotes from their opponents' records to suggest their alliance with Yippies at home and the nation's military enemies abroad.

"It didn't work the way we planned in North Dakota," Mr. Treleaven said of the attack on what was called "the curious record of Senator Quentin Burdick." He added: "The same approach did work in Tennessee." Representative William E. Brock's victory over Senator Albert Gore, Democrat of Tennessee, was Mr. Treleaven's only triumph.

Outside Consultants

Regardless of the results, many of the specialists in political media felt they had consolidated a major role for themselves in the 1970 campaign. One measure of their expanding influence is that substantially more than half the candidates for the Senate and Governors' offices this year felt they had to retain out-of-state consultants on the use of television.

In many of these campaigns the media men were recognized as figures that ranked with or above the "campaign managers" of record. Many TV specialists now speak casually of their wins and losses as if their work were the central campaign.

Yesterday's results may require a new humility, however, and could lead to some retrenchment.

At the Republican National Committee headquarters early today, one of the key operatives in the 1968 Nixon campaign saw a significant change coming as he reviewed the spotty record of the TV campaigns:

"Coca-Cola spends millions of dollars on advertising every year just to hold its share of the market," he said. "Hershey had the chocolate market knocked without spending a dime on advertising.

"We're entering the Hershey phase in politics now. Television, after all, is just one of several means of people-to-people contact. There will be a healthier mix from here on out, and it's going to be a good thing."

Mr. Nixon and the Press: A Few Questions

By MAX FRANKEL

Special to The New York Times

WASHINGTON, Dec. 9— President Nixon will hold his first news conference in 19 weeks tomorrow evening, and the event has raised many more questions here than he can possibly handle in the allotted 29-minute television slot. When the President last submitted to public questioning, there was still official hope of negotiating an end of the war in Vietnam. There were plans to submit a balanced budget next year in expectation of full economic recovery. There was no quarrel over Soviet cheating in the Suez ceasefire zone. There was hope of enacting a major welfare reform. There had been no acknowledged bombing and landing in North Vietnam. There was no dispute about the President's campaign tactics or claims of victory at the polls. There was no Marxist government in Chile and no threat of another missile crisis in Cuba. There was a Walter Hickel in the Cabinet.

News Analysis

Now, in what seems like a wholly new phase in the life of the Nixon Administration, these subjects and many others cry out for clarification. Some citizens have written to Washington reporters suggesting questions and asking why the President is not facing them more often.

Ironically, Mr. Nixon's announcement of tomorrow's news conference has provoked not only the usual compilation of possible inquiries but also a great deal of discussion among reporters and with White House officials about the value and format of the whole proceeding.

18th Session in 2 Years

This will be Mr. Nixon's 18th news conference in two years, the 12th on television. His three immediate predecessors held an average of 22 to 27 a year, including many impromptu gatherings in his office by President Johnson, mostly televised meetings by President Kennedy and mostly formal but untelevised sessions by President Eisenhower.

President Nixon has steadfastly refused to commit himself to any fixed schedule of meetings with the press, reserving the right to decide when they served the public (and the Administration's) interest and suggesting that he often preferred other forms of communication such as formal speeches and background briefings with editors and publishers around the country.

His policy has evoked complaints not only from Washington newsmen but also from students of the political scene. Some have deplored the infrequency and irregularity of the news conferences. Some have blamed the presence of television cameras for the allegedly excessive "politeness" of reporters' questions. Others have criticized the random selection of questioners, the lack of follow-up inquiries to incomplete answers and the absence of the sharp give-and-take heard at question time in the British Parliament.

Mr. Nixon has tried on a few occasions to limit the subject matter of the questions but most other suggestions for change have been ignored. So the news conference remains, as in other recent administrations, primarily as a vehicle for the President with relatively little risk that he can be forced to deal with a point he prefers to ignore.

A List of Questions

Nonetheless, even some Administration officials have hoped for more regular appearances to convey their purposes and programs to the country. Some have also recalled that President Kennedy had a strong private motive for regular sessions because the preparation for them forced the huge Federal bureaucracy to brief him on every potentially embarrassing matter.

Probably more important than these procedural questions, however, are the many inquiries that have been piling up in recent months for tomorrow's news conference. Here is a random list from one newspaper office:

The economy—Now that recovery has been delayed, what is your new target for unemployment in 1972? Do you share the view of your principal advisers that further inflation will be due almost entirely to excessive wage increases? Precisely how much growth in the money supply have you been promised in the "commitment" of the Federal Reserve Board? What have you done to ease the conversion from military to civilian production and what special efforts are planned to help job-seeking Vietnam veterans? Have you changed your mind about vetoing the trade bill if it limits imports other than textiles?

The war—Did the raids and landing in North Vietnam violate the 1968 "understanding" on a bombing halt and do you plan other new forms of attack? With negotiations going nowhere, is "Vietnamization" the only remaining path out of the war? If that is going well,

can you announce another annual target for troop withdrawal or a deadline for total disengagement? How long will Americans have to fight or fly in combat in Asia? How will "Vietnamization" win the release of American prisoners?

The campaign—What limitations do you think should be applied to the financing and conduct of political campaigns? Why did you risk injury before a hostile crowd in San Jose? In what ways are Republicans less "permissive" than Democrats toward radicals? What is your answer to Administration officials who believe your party suffered a setback last month, partly because you and the Vice President preferred attack on the Democrats to emphasis on your record? Will you debate your opponent in 1972?

Law and order—Why have you waited six months without appointing a director of the Law Enforcement Assistance Administration? Do you approve of J. Edgar Hoover's making undocumented public charges about a kidnapping plot or his public rating of his superiors in the Justice Department? Will you seek new internal security legislation? Why have you not commented for 10 weeks on the Scranton commission's analysis of campus unrest? Having found the pornography commission's report to be morally bankrupt, how will you deal with the subject? Do Government-paid attorneys have different responsibilities in representing the poor than private attorneys for paying clients? Will you permit Secretary Romney to promote racially integrated housing in the suburbs? Do you favor the amendment on equal rights for women?

Domestic programs — What have you personally done to win over Republican Senators to support of the welfare reform? Are you having trouble filling long-vacant positions in the fields of health and education? What kind of new health programs can the country afford? When will you reveal an urban policy for new communities and to guide pattern of city growth? Should the Federal Government help rescue struggling parochial schools? What has happened to your first-five-year-of-life program for children? How did Secretary Hickel lose your confidence and which of his policies at the Interior Department will you change?

Foreign affairs — What can we do to protect democracy and American assets in Chile? What was the Soviet threat that evoked warnings of another crisis in Cuba and what are the terms of your new understanding with Moscow? What new arms are being sent to Israel and what can the United States do to offset Soviet involvement if the fighting at Suez is resumed? Has the Soviet Union surpassed the United States in strategic strength? Do you favor the seating of both Communist China and Taiwan in the United Nations? What explains the deterioration in relations with Japan?

Finally: Would you give more news conferences if you could always read the questions in advance?

'Government by TV' Charged by Johnson of F.C.C.

By CHRISTOPHER LYDON
Special to The New York Times

WASHINGTON, Dec. 13 — Nicholas Johnson, a member of the Federal Communications Commission, described the Nixon Administration today as a case study in "government by television."

As he outlined it to an international convention of political consultants in London, the new style of government is a threat to constitutional democracy. It is marked, he said, by the force feeding of ideology, the manipulation of news events and the suppression of dissent — all abetted by the intimidation of broadcasters.

Mr. Johnson's speech — 40 pages of text and 10 pages of footnotes — also indicated that virtually no episode in President Nixon's relations with the media goes unnoticed and uncatalogued by Mr. Johnson's staff.

Mr. Johnson's speech, the most detailed expressions of themes he has emphasized many times before, was prepared for delivery tomorrow and released here today.

No Conspiracy Seen

Mr. Johnson's attack cites scores of familiar items—from Vice President Agnew's attack on TV commentators in November, 1969, to the assertedly "nonpolitical" broadcast of a program honoring the Sontay prison camp raiders between halves of the Army-Navy football game two weeks ago—to illustrate his general contention that the television networks have been made more and more responsive to the national Government's wishes.

Government by television, Mr. Johnson said, is not the result of a "conspiracy," nor does it involve "a single man or industry." At the same time, he said, it is not entirely ac-

Associated Press
Nicholas Johnson

cidental. President Nixon, he said, has used television "more, more consciously, and in a more wide-ranging way, than any prior President."

The fact that government by television is not based on a single conspiracy, he suggested, is no reason to be less concerned about its consequences.

"The press bears a special opportunity and responsibility in this regard," he said. "It must investigate and expose the charades and facades. And it must develop its own traditions, including firm positions on pressure it will not tolerate —such as subpoenas and calls from Directors of Communication. The public must be educated about the uses of, and pressures upon, the media."

Mr. Johnson, 36 years old, was appointed to the seven-member F.C.C. by President Johnson in 1966 and has said that he will serve until his term expires in mid-1973. He is a Democrat.

Many of the Nixon Administration's approaches to the media are unprecedented, Mr. Johnson argued, starting with

the appointment of Herbert G. Klein to the new post of Director of Communications—a title, Mr. Johnson said, "which has a strongly authoritarian ring to it" and was "formerly unknown outside Fascist and Communist countries."

Censorship Charged

Until Mr. Agnew's speech in Des Moines last year, Mr. Johnson said, no Administration had combined an attack on broadcasters with such a pointed reminder that television facilities are licensed by the Federal Government. Despite the Administration's denial of an intent to censor, he said, the result of Mr. Agnew's speech and other Government actions has been censorship.

Mr. Johnson argued that Dean Burch, the chairman of the commission, had contributed to the same result when he called the three network presidents for transcripts of their commentators' remarks on a Presidential address.

As a result of the calls, Mr. Johnson said, "the broadcasting industry had received the message, whether or not Burch intended it, the F.C.C. was going to be run as a branch office of the White House, and that its powers might very well be used to punish those who failed to provide the propaganda support the Administration desired."

Mr. Johnson also objected to the White House conference with broadcasters and executives of the record industry that contributed to the inclusion of antidrug messages in a number of popular entertainment programs.

"The Administration has made it clear that, at least for certain purposes, it considers private television programing as an arm of the Government's public information efforts," he said.

The New York Times   Associated Press

No Thank You, Mr. President

By HERBERT G. KLEIN

WASHINGTON — Right after the President's most recent news conference, one of the reporters was heard to say, with grudging admiration, "We never laid a glove on him."

Perhaps so. But the comment raises the question of what direction press conferences are moving today — whether they be Presidential or otherwise.

Have the Sunday televised press programs influenced reporters more to a format of showmanship than to inquiry into news subjects? Is the effort to throw the tricky question interfering with the legitimate pursuit of information?

These questions and others are accentuated as we see the media debating the frequency, style and effect of the Presidential news conference.

And this brings up the basic question of what the President's news conference is—and what it is not.

The essential purpose of the news conference is to transmit information from the President to the people. It was never intended to be a debate, or a show, or an arena for either the President—or the reporters—to show off skills or throw off animosities.

Our informational process has been evolving for many years. The press conference is a sound and necessary institution.

Regardless of format or frequency, there have been press complaints about each President. Now there is considerable complaint — stemming originally from the White House news corps, but going beyond it—that the President does not hold enough press conferences. He has had nineteen meetings with the press in twenty-three months.

What is too often overlooked is the fact that these conferences are only one of many ways in which the President communicates with the people. There are, of course, many off-camera

How the Press Looks From the Other Side Of the Conferences

methods of communication—messages, statements, speeches, remarks, letters —and President Nixon constantly uses these. The President's key appointees also articulate the President's views, including his press secretary, Ron Ziegler, who fields all types of questions in twice-daily briefings. He often has gone directly to the nation on television to discuss key issues. In fact, his televised appearances have reaped partisan complaint that he may be taking unfair advantage of his adversaries by communicating too often through TV.

The televised press conference is effective, but admittedly it has definite limitations for both the reports and the President. Some members of the Gutenberg set complain privately and even publicly that the televised session has become too much of a show. Television reporters complain when cameras are not present. It's hard to win.

Many cite statistics of one President versus another. But basically they ignore the type of press conference. They also do not recognize the delicacy and complexity of the age in which we live.

On critical areas of foreign policy — often the principal subject of a major news conference — every word has an effect. A misinterpretation by the British on a Truman statement on atom bombing was world-shaking; a misstatement today would be far more momentous.

President Nixon has touched every area of foreign policy and without a misstep. But the point is that there are times when it is better to be silent than to speak or to speak and dodge

or lie. The President refuses to do the latter.

If the President plays it safe and merely reviews existing policy, the media criticizes the fact that there is "nothing new."

Let's face it: A Presidential news conference—with 300 reporters clamoring for their moment on camera and with 50 million viewers watching — is not the ideal format to reveal policy to world powers or to explain it in depth to the nation.

The national media in recent weeks has made a considerable argument that the news conference is the basic factor in the people's right to know. It does fill an important function.

But the conference is the President's. This is undisputed.

The press argues that the President today just delegates responsibilities. This also is correct if he is to have time for the big decisions. But in preparing for a press conference, a President in effect must turn away from delegation and assume all responsibilities if he is to answer questions on every detail in government.

In a Washington hotel, three days before the President's December 10 conference 25 members of the national news corps met to discuss the coming confrontation. Following that meeting, some participants returned to their news rooms and studios and spun out "news" stories about what had occurred at the meeting, and in those stories they voiced their own professional grievances about the infrequency of their meetings with the President.

This raises an interesting question of ethics and public practice: Should the newsmen be using their positions in the communications media to advance their personal complaints that they are not getting enough shots at the President?

Following that pre-conference, some of the reporters who were there took pains to say they were not part of a

cabal or conspiracy and that in no way did they discuss either the order or the subject matter of the questions that would be asked at the forthcoming conference. Whether or not they did, the timing of the meeting did nothing to enhance press credibility.

In all the criticism of Presidential news conferences, the media seems to have forgotten a few of the basic and balanced arguments the other way. All of the President's press conferences have been live, with no attempt to tone them down or edit them. Even in his one-hour conversation on foreign policy with the networks, the program was live.

This also is a President who does not berate publishers or reporters. A minor point, maybe. But one the press has complained about before. It also can be said that Government over-all is more open and creditable than two years ago.

A legitimate point is the need for follow-up questions to clarify earlier statements. The President and his staff are considering a variety of formats which would help this. But the fact is that even under the present format, there is ample opportunity for follow-up by other reporters. Too often reporters are locked into their own previously worked out question or subject and stay with this no matter what else happens.

I would agree fully with the media that there is a need for press conferences, not only Presidential but throughout government. The President would hope that circumstances would make them more frequent in the coming year. It also is accepted that an adversary relationship between press and government is healthy. The case to be made is that the need for improvement in communications has two sides—press as well as government.

Herbert G. Klein is President Nixon's director of communications.

One-Sided 'Conversation'

By TOM WICKER

WASHINGTON, Jan. 6—At the close of his latest "conversation" with four television reporters, President Nixon recalled that they had had the first such talk about six months ago and said that "we'll give you another shot" about six months hence.

That's fine, and no doubt the public as well as the networks and the writing press will take all they can get; but these occasions are no substitute for nonbroadcast Presidential news conferences, or for some other form of close-in, direct questioning of the President by persons not beholden to him.

Some of the trouble is to be found in the idea of a "conversation." This rather suggests a polite exchange among equals, not an adversary situation; but since in practice the participants are not equals at all, the form of polite exchange works splendidly to relieve the President of any real challenge, dispute or searching inquiry.

This effect is enormously magnified by having the "conversation" take place on television. Those who have talked with Presidents in private circumstances will testify that it is difficult enough, even then, to speak to the great man with anything but deference and—when disagreement is unavoidable—apologetic circumlocution. It is much harder before the cameras.

The point is not that the interrogators were timid or under instructions to go easy on Mr. Nixon. The point is that in a conversational setting, with all its pleasantries, and with the nation watching via television, it is all but impossible to be hard on the President of the United States.

Those who have asked tough questions at televised news conferences know they will probably get mail denouncing them for having "insulted our President." Really disputatious questions from anyone during the "conversation" would quickly have lit up network switchboards with outraged calls. Perhaps more important, reporters do not themselves wish to appear rude to the President, or to show disrespect for his office; nor do they wish to divert something like the "conversation" into a sharp argument or a press-President confrontation.

This has little to do with the personalities involved—neither the President nor the reporters. As to the former, it is rather a commentary on what George Reedy has rightly called the "monarchy" we have created in the White House, no matter who occupies it.

As to the latter, most newspapermen would be just as restrained by the circumstances as their television colleagues have been, and probably would be less at ease in the medium; and while some suggest the regular White House reporters would be sharper questioners, that is a dubious proposition. The White House reporters have to live with Mr. Nixon and his staff every day, and in any case do not have the public prestige of the network anchor men and commentators. They would be even less evenly matched with the President.

In fact, television news conferences open to all reporters have most of the drawbacks of the "conversations," plus some of their own—although the questioners are more anonymous, hence somewhat less inhibited. The ironic truth seems to be that television actually results in there being less check on Presidential policies than was the case before news conferences were televised; rather than providing reporters a more public forum in which to question a President, television provides a President a better opportunity to make his case directly to the public.

As only one example, Mr. Nixon said again the other night that he would enforce the law against communities with a discriminatory housing policy, but that he would not "go further than the law to force integration in the suburbs."

No one challenged this, followed up, or in any way tried to develop what, that very day, a Federal Circuit Court in Philadelphia had ruled. The court said the Federal Government had a positive duty to consider whether the impact of federally supported housing projects would be to increase or to maintain segregation. That is not to "force" integration; it is rather to make certain that public decisions on housing, zoning and the like, which may be nondiscriminatory by legal definition, do not have the net effect of increasing or maintaining segregated housing.

But those who relied on the "conversation" for their information on this matter received no hint that such complexities might be involved. Since the vast majority undoubtedly opposed "forced integration" too, Mr. Nixon was allowed to turn himself a quick political profit, tax-free.

January 7, 1971

Somebody Else Decided To Televise Nixon Talk

By JAMES M. NAUGHTON
Special to The New York Times

WASHINGTON, Jan. 7 — President Nixon told the nation, in his "Conversation" with four television newsmen Monday night, that he had not been in charge of the campaign to elect Republicans to Congress last November. Neither, it would seem, was anyone else. The President told the newsmen that the

Washington Notes tactical error of rebroadcasting, on election eve, his denunciation of the demonstrators who stoned his limousine a few days earlier in San Jose, Calif., would not have occurred "had I been, shall we say, running the campaign."

Who was in charge of the decision to rebroadcast the speech? "I'm frank to tell you I don't know," said Harry S. Dent, the chief White House political operative.

"I know I didn't do it," said Murray M. Chotiner, another White House political aide.

Mr. Dent said he did not believe Charles W. Colson, their associate, had been responsible, either.

Attorney General John N. Mitchell, who was the manager of Mr. Nixon's 1968 campaign, was not responsible because "he didn't play a significant role" in the 1970 effort, Mr. Dent said.

A spokesman for the Republican National Committee said that the party chairman did not even see the film before it was telecast nationally.

"You could say it was a decision by a committee," another White House aide said. He would not indicate, however, who had been on such a committee.

Still another Administration official who was involved in the campaign said that he wondered about Mr. Nixon's remark, adding, "I suppose he was engaging in legalistic evasion."

•

In the television interview, Mr. Nixon, referring to an opinion poll commissioned by Life magazine, commented that he did not quote polls "if I've taken them." Four days earlier, over New Year's Eve cocktails in his office, he told a small group of correspondents that the White House did not conduct such polls.

Mr. Nixon does, however, have access to opinion samples of the Republican National Committee.

The opinion sampling on the President's latest television performance was mixed within the White House. The morning after the telecast, Mr. Nixon received high praise and a standing ovation from his Cabinet.

He told the Cabinet members, though, that his daughters, Tricia and Julie Nixon Eisenhower, had informed him his comments on the economy had been the "dullest" part of the program.

But Mr. Nixon said he had received a telephone call from "a friend of Tricia's at Harvard"—Edward Finch Cox, a law student who is rumored to be seeking Miss Nixon's hand in marriage—who reported that the economic discussion had been "the most interesting."

•

The telecast caused some consternation among public affairs officers in various Federal agencies. They are required to submit, in advance of each Presidential press interview, likely questions (and answers) within their fields of expertise.

Mr. Nixon's second conversation with newsmen was announced only two working days before it occurred, putting the public affairs representatives under an unusual deadline.

"I'm not coming up with any new questions," said one of them. "This time I'm just rewriting the questions and answers I sent in before."

•

One of the first questions to be decided by Senator Edmund S. Muskie, when he returns from his current tour of the Middle East and the Soviet Union and completes the hiring of a staff to help him seek the Democratic Presidential nomination, will be whether to undertake a national voter registration drive on college campuses.

Most experts believe that the Supreme Court decision approving the 18-year-old vote in Federal elections is unlikely to favor one political party over another.

But the Maine Senator's aides recognize that one young segment of the electorate that might tend to vote as a liberal bloc is college students. Since many of them attend school out of their home states, though, it could take a concerted effort to get them registered to vote in large numbers.

Such an effort, funded by supporters of Mr. Muskie, could serve a dual purpose of identifying the Senator with the new voters, it is thought.

January 8, 1971

President and the Press

By WILLIAM H. LAWRENCE

Good Give-and-Take Is a Responsibility That Goes Two Ways

WASHINGTON—From what I have been hearing and reading recently, it appears to me that the Presidential news conference is in deep trouble, endangered both by its *alleged* friends and its *known* enemies.

It is, I think, an important forum for informing the citizens not only of the United States but of the world as well, and we must not let it fall into disrepute from disuse, neglect, perversion or controversy.

Nobody I know who has ever been to one or conducted one of them holds it to be perfect; indeed, it may be, to paraphrase Winston Churchill's celebrated remark about democracy, "the worst form . . . except all those other forms that have been tried from time to time."

As a long questioner of Presidents dating back to Franklin D. Roosevelt's second term at the beginning of 1938, I think the success of the news conference depends entirely upon the *quality* both of the President then in office, and the *qualifications* of the reporters assembled to question him.

Some critics have acted as if the only reason for the decline and imminent fall of the news conference as an informative institution has been the bright lights and the gleaming red eye of the television cameras taking it to the nation live as it is being held. Others have placed the blame squarely on the President exclusively. No one of these reasons tells the truth, the whole truth and nothing but the truth.

As the White House correspondent at that time for The New York Times, I opposed, in 1961, the intention of President Kennedy to inaugurate live television broadcasting of the news conference. It would, I felt, open the door for the press corps "hams" to make a show of themselves and it to please their employers or to seek an even larger audience. There was also, and more importantly, the danger that a President, speaking informally and in response to a tough question on foreign affairs that had not been anticipated, might inadvertently reply incorrectly with damaging consequences for at least amity among nations if not the graver cause of peace on earth.

I enjoyed the easy informality, the breeziness of FDR's days with an occasional and genuine off-the-record confidence, but as the press corps grew and became more international in character those days passed and live broadcasting did not create all the problems I feared in advance. Indeed, not all news conferences are broadcast live now, and I do not see any great difference in their generally poor quality whether on camera or off.

Both the President and the reporters are to blame, in my opinion.

President Nixon, who perspires heavily under questioning even by a friendly hand-picked panel, simply doesn't like the news conference, on or off camera, and no amount of protestation that he does can change the fact. In the twelve months of 1970, Mr. Nixon held four news conferences, on and off camera. Compare that, if you will, with Franklin Roosevelt's record of more than 80 per year for the 12 long years he occupied the White House in peace and war.

Mr. Nixon simply doesn't like to level. He prefers to dance around a question. Occasionally you get a direct, to the point answer to a direct question; but it is news when you do. And if a President has decided, in advance, to evade nearly all the questions he may be asked, the news conference is not worth his time or that of the reporters attending it.

If Mr. Nixon doesn't like to answer direct questions, many reporters apparently lack the ability to ask a direct question. Some feel the need for a long preface not necessarily of facts but often including the reporter's opinion before he gets around to posing the question itself. I have felt not infrequently that any President might respond by asking a long-winded questioner whether he wanted an answer to his *opinion* or to his *question*.

Too many reporters arrive with their question already prepared—some even written out—and they stick to this one question with single-minded devotion, paying no attention to other questions that are asked—the answers to which deserve, indeed often cry out for follow-up questions that might clarify the issue. Beyond doubt there is far too little pursuit. This often is blamed on the large number of reporters at a regular White House news conference, but this gap was not filled noticeably when the President talked for an hour just to four network correspondents recently. Sometimes I feel as if the art of questioning and the art of listening both have disappeared.

In brief, this President and the reporters need a drastic change in course. The news conference is far from perfect, but right now it is not only the *best* but it is the *only* direct approach to finding out what a President may be thinking.

January 12, 1971

Candor Toward Press

By ERIC SEVAREID

WASHINGTON — Tension between the Washington press corps and the President of the United States is chronic though it varies in degree from time to time and President to President. It is as necessary and creative a tension as that between President and Congress or Congress and Supreme Court. We are constantly told that a President has no obligation to hold news conferences. He has an inescapable obligation to do so since he cannot be summoned by either Congress or the Court, and can, in this age of electronics, argue his own case uninterrupted to the whole nation directly, and at times and under circumstances of his own choosing.

The Agnew imputations notwithstanding, it is the power of government that has grown in this last generation, more than the power of the press, and within government, the power of the Presidency.

So that "press corps"—swollen in size, anarchic in form, containing in about Congressional proportions its share of modest scholars and noisy amateurs—must do what it can to put questions to the President and—this is the hard part — get candid and illuminating replies within the limits of national security. The news conference transaction rarely works to anybody's full satisfaction. It has been working badly under Mr. Nixon for a lot of reasons.

In the first place, his is a thin-ice Administration. It came into power by a popular vote of only 42 per cent.

The matter is worsened further by the fact that while most White House crowds develop a degree of paranoia about the press in time, this crowd began that way. The reasons for Mr. Nixon's dislike and distrust of so much of the press go back twenty years and already fill volumes. It is also unfortunately true that a few writers in the press will give this President no benefit of any doubt.

But it was not out of spite that Mr. Nixon loosed the Vice President upon the press in the autumn of 1969, a time, incidentally, when the Administration was faring well in the press. He had carefully studied the Johnson "credibility gap," knew how fatal such a gap might prove for himself as he tried the exceedingly delicate operations of quitting a war without defeat and checking inflation without a depression. Dangers and setbacks were inevitable. What better way to avoid or postpone your own credibility gap than to impugn in advance the credibility of those who report and interpret your actions?

The over-all strategy was threefold: Create public doubt that the reporters are treating you fairly; avoid direct meetings with them as far as possible; use television prime time as often as possible for unimpeded presentation of your case to the people. This couldn't last. The Washington press as well as the Democratic National Committee blew up, and with the President's sudden loss of statesmanlike dignity in the election campaign, everything has now reverted to square one.

The President and his staff are making a real college try at devising formats that will satisfy the press reasonably well and protect the President's interests reasonably well. He has promised more frequent general news conferences.

In the meantime, the President has tried the second of what is apparently to be a well-spaced series of "conversations" with three of four network reporters. These affairs are lengthier, more revealing of the man's mind, both in what he says and avoids saying, but they are certainly not "conversations," because the audience wants the President's views, not those of the reporters, and for the same reason they cannot be debates, which various critics in the press seem to think they should be. The anti-Nixon critics suffer the nonsensical notion

---

that there is some secret question or line of questions that will crumble Mr. Nixon to dust in full view of the nation.

What is necessary is that the questions be substantive, concerning matters on the public mind, and not whether they are "hard" or "soft." Most of them were very substantive, therefore rather easily anticipated by the President's briefers. The trouble is that too many answers were soft—diffuse, deliberately time consuming, and sometimes off the point.

One change in format might be tried. It was, in fact, suggested by someone in the White House in advance of the Jan. 4 "conversation." That was to let each of the four reporters engage the President directly and exclusively on one area of special interest for ten minutes, with the last twenty minutes

a free for all.

Providing that the President did not resort to lengthy replies, this might have made for closer follow-up interrogation. I was quite willing to try this and my impression was that at least two of the other three reporters were equally willing. But Mr. Nixon was not.

With all of its imperfections, this miniature news conference did make news—on taxes, controls, etc.—and it did provide insights into the President's mind, method and purposes on a variety of issues. Were this not so, the most serious of our newspapers would not have spent a full week repeating and analyzing the President's responses.

I have taken part in Presidential news conferences since the days of·

Roosevelt. Whatever the format, whatever the cast of characters, they are generally productive of ιinformation and understanding in one degree or another. The precise degree depends almost entirely upon the temperament and self-confidence of the man in the White House. The more confidence he has, the more often he will schedule these transactions. After two years in office, said Mr. Nixon on Jan. 4, "I know more. I am more experienced." It would be good to think this is one reason he plans on additional news conferences this year. ·A bearing of friendliness and candor toward the press will not endanger him or his policies. In the long run it will reinsure both.

Eric Sevareid is a news analyst for C.B.S. in Washington.

January 21, 19?

Letters to the Editor

Candor, the Press and the President

To the Editor:

In his Jan. 21 Op-Ed article, "Candor Toward the Press," Eric Sevareid asserts that a President has "an inescapable obligation" to hold news conferences "since he cannot be summoned by either Congress or the Court and can, in this age of electronics, argue his case uninterrupted to the whole nation directly, and at times and under circumstances of his own choosing."

Apart from the matter of Presidential news conferences, Mr. Sevareid's concern bears directly on certain well-publicized differences of opinion I have had with these news commentators who share his rather insular view that, save for their expert guidance and interpretation, the American public would be beguiled or misled by the President and other elected officials.

To begin, it should come as something of a surprise to anyone familiar with the U.S. Constitution that an American President cannot be called to accountability by the Congress, the courts or the nation. Indeed, in lieu of the Nielsen or Arbitron ratings to which Mr. Sevareid and his fellow commentators are solely answerable,

a President's accountability for daily decisions and actions to "either Congress . . . the Court" or "the whole nation" is implicit in our constitutional system of checks-and-balances, not to mention the American electoral process.

Plainly, what disturbs Mr. Sevareid then is that a President, on occasion, is able to "argue his own case uninterrupted." This is simply to say that our elected national leader at times exercises the same right in speaking to the people of the country that network commentators enjoy each day.

In this regard, I suggested several months ago that it might make for better public understanding of "the news of the day" if those commentators who interpret events for "the whole nation" were to be interviewed, on a voluntary basis, by knowledgeable persons outside their professional discipline. As I recall, Mr. Sevareid's response to this suggestion was that he has been on-the-air for thirty years and his views are known.

Conceded, unlike the public official, the commentator has the privilege of shunning television interview formats in which he is called to answer rather

than ask questions. Yet it is difficult to forgo an observation that Mr. Sevareid would not for an instant tolerate an evasion such as "my views are known," were a public official to offer this rationale in refusing to appear on C.B.S.'s "Face the Nation."

To be sure, I have never suggested that any member of the news media submit to any form of Government inquisition — though that interpretation was given my remarks by those in the media who suffer the "degree of paranoia" which Mr. Sevareid ascribes to members of the Administration. All I have asked, "in this age of electronics," is that those empowered solely by authority of network-and-sponsor to "argue" their case "uninterrupted to the whole nation directly" perform the valuable public service they demand of all other public spokesmen.

I would hope, therefore, that Mr. Sevareid, as a dean of news commentary, might agree to such a television interview format. He might find, to paraphrase his own conclusion, that a bearing of candor toward those who question his daily expertise will not endanger him or the principle of freedom of the press which we all cherish. In the long run it will reinsure both.

SPIRO T. AGNEW
Washington, Feb. 3, 1971

February 9, 19?

The President's Image

Increase in His Public Appearances Called Attempt to Improve Ratings

By ROBERT B. SEMPLE Jr.
Special to The New York Times

WASHINGTON, March 21—There is no real dispute here anymore that the quantum jump in President Nixon's public exposure, including tomorrow night's scheduled interview with Howard K. Smith, is designed in large part to smooth the edges of the Nixon image, to present to the public the appealing Presidential personality that his staff says it sees in private, to provide a variety of settings in which to explain his policies, and to lift his ratings in the public opinion polls.

News Analysis

But the effort, now entering its third month, raises two related questions: Has this forceful public display of personality been matched by a similar assertiveness in his private deliberations within the Government? And does it presage any change in fundamental policy? The answer to the first would seem to be yes. The answer to the second, no.

Reporters who try to inquire behind the President's public appearances are invariably told by his senior assistants nowadays that they have never seen him in better shape. He is said to be optimistic and confident and he is "tracking well," which means, in the parlance of the Nixon White House, that he is less easily distracted by small annoyances and is thereby able to devote full attention to major decisions and make them quickly, even if it means overriding the views of some of his most powerful advisers.

An Example Offered

The favorite example offered by his staff is Mr. Nixon's recent decision to try to control wages in the construction industry by suspending provisions of the Davis-Bacon Act, in effect allowing nonunion workers to compete for jobs with higher-paid union workers, and allowing contractors to play one off against the other to negotiate less costly wage settlements.

The overwhelming advice of his aides was that a better route would have been to impose a selective wage-price freeze on the construction industry. But Mr. Nixon warned that this would involve the Government as a third party in literally hundreds of wage-price settlements, create a precedent for similar action against other high-wage industries, and lead, in time, to an unofficial set of national wage-price controls.

It is also pointed out, for the benefit of newsmen wanting to know whether the President is as much in command of his official family as he is of his public appearances, that he had no difficulty countering a weak and indecisive effort by his Budget Bureau to cut seriously into military spending, and that he again overrode the advice of a majority of the senior advisers who urged him to accept the bargain on textile imports worked out by Representative Wilbur D. Mills, chairman of the House Ways and Means Committee, and the Japanese textile industry.

Mr. Nixon argued that the Arkansas Democrat's maneuvers had challenged the President's authority to conduct foreign affairs, and vowed to pursue his own efforts to work out a broader agreement directly with the Japanese Government.

Heading Off Embarrassments

Mr. Nixon's aides also insist that he is moving more quickly and authoritatively to head off potential political embarrassments of the sort that bedeviled him during his first 24 months in office. He decided quickly, for example, against the appointment of Alain Enthoven to a prestigious environmental post when his political aides decided that Mr. Enthoven's long association with the Kennedy Administration (he was one of former Defense Secretary Robert S. McNamara's original whiz kids) could, for reasons yet unexplained, prove embarrassing.

The fact that his two top domestic policy advisers—John Ehrlichman and George P. Shultz—had recommended Mr. Enthoven and even told him he would get the job had little weight with a President who spent part of his first two years in office making, and then withdrawing, appointments of people who offended his political allies.

Taken singly or collectively, none of these actions would seem to provide much reassurance to Administration critics who hoped that Mr. Nixon's efforts to alter and soften his public image might reflect a new responsiveness to public complaints, and a readiness to make adjustment in his underlying policy. His decisions against a wage-price freeze, for military spending, and against Mr. Mills are all fully consistent responses from a man who has long believed, and still believes, in the capacity of the free market to adjust wages, in the importance of a strong national defense, and in the prerogatives of the Presidency.

The internal evidence that Mr. Nixon is now more determined than ever to stick by his basic policies in Vietnam, the economy and elsewhere has, if anything, been reinforced by what he has been saying publicly during his recent spate of interviews. While some of his aides plainly hope that these appearances will persuade people that there is a "new" Nixon, the President has regularly made it clear that his main purpose is to make sure the public understands the "real" Nixon.

Two Interviews

The firm impression one gets after reading his interviews with the National Broadcasting Company's Barbara Walters and The New York Times's C. L. Sulzberger—to take only two examples—is that of a man who is prepared to live with himself and his policies.

He told Miss Walters that he would not wear sport shirts as long as he felt more comfortable in business suits, and he told Mr. Sulzberger that he would stick by his policies in Vietnam because they provided the surest way to end the war without being defeated by it.

"I am certain a Gallup Poll would show," Mr. Nixon told Mr. Sulzberger, "that a great majority of the people would want to pull out of Vietnam. But a Gallup Poll would also show that a great majority of the people would want to pull three or more divisions out of Europe. And it would also show that a great majority of the people would cut our defense budget. Polls are not the answer. You must look at the facts."

In short, Mr. Nixon is taking to the air waves these days to explain his policies and, he hopes, win support for them. He may be trying to improve his image, but this does not mean that he is seeking to change his fundamental convictions. Any other view of the present public relations blitz involves wishful thinking.

4 THE FIGHT FOR FAIRNESS

As every candidate knows,
it's money that makes the
political world go 'round

POLITICS ON THE AIR A CAMPAIGN PROBLEM

G. O. P. Charges of 'Influence' by the Administration Denied by Radio Chiefs, Who Insist on Control

By ORRIN E. DUNLAP JR.

When President Roosevelt decided to use radio to transmit his Congressional message to the people, he stirred up a hornet's nest which not only indicated how bitter the coming campaign may be, but also revealed the difficult position in which radio broadcasting companies find themselves when the political pot begins to boil. There were outcries in Congress of unfairness, talk of an investigation of the Federal Communications Commission—which is already investigating itself—and charges of an air monopoly.

But even more interesting has been the correspondence between Chairman Henry P. Fletcher of the Republican campaign committee and broadcasting officials, in which an effort has been made to determine not only some basis for fairly equal time allotments, but also some means for controlling the content of speeches and other broadcast material in a year which Postmaster General Farley has said will be marked by "dirty politics."

The broadcasters assert that they have always afforded equal opportunity on any important political issue, but they take the position that broadcasting is something like publishing a newspaper and that editorial decision rests with the companies.

William S. Paley, president of the Columbia Broadcasting System, told Mr. Fletcher that "it is not possible or wise for broadcasting to adopt a mathematical formula for fairness."

The N. B. C. Position.

M. H. Aylesworth, vice chairman of the National Broadcasting Company, said: "We are glad to afford the representative or representatives of the Republican party whom you may select the facilities of the NBC for such discussion from time to time."

The charge was then made by Mr. Fletcher that the broadcasting companies were unduly swayed by political influence and that the Federal Communications Commission had been derelict in not taking action against the broadcasting systems. Mr. Paley replied that the commission had no power to influence his company politically and that if it attempted to do so it would quickly be checked in the courts. His company, he said, had never sold time for political pur-

poses before a convention, but had offered it free to both parties.

"You have never asked us for free facilities and been refused," he wrote. "What you did ask us was to assume in advance that an address by the President of the United States to the people of America and their Congress was a political speech and to set aside in advance of the delivery of that speech comparable time for a Republican answer.

"We refuse to treat the President of the United States other than as the President of the United States and shall continue so to refuse. * * * We shall distinguish between the President as President and Franklin D. Roosevelt as a candidate for office."

Skits Barred From Air.

That this left Mr. Fletcher still unsatisfied was evident from his answer, and from the fact that no Republican speakers were immediately offered. Then another factor was injected into the dispute which again brought to the fore the editorial point of view stressed by Mr. Paley. The Republicans, having claimed that Mr. Roosevelt had unduly dramatized his message to Congress by reading it over the microphone to the entire country, with Congressional applause as stage effects, demanded the opportunity of also becoming dramatic by offering political "skits" of national issues.

This both the major broadcasting companies refused, after listening to recordings of a skit entitled "Liberty at the Cross Roads." Lenox R. Lohr, president of NBC, said that his company tried to present both sides of political issues on the basis of "straightforward statement of fact and opinion openly and directly made by responsible spokesmen," and that to dramatize politics would open such discussions to dramatic license. And Mr. Paley said:

"Appeals to the electorate should be intellectual and not based on emotion, passion or prejudice. We are convinced that dramatization would throw the radio campaign almost wholly over to the emotional side.

"Then, too, we believe that the dramatic method, by its very nature, would tend to over-emphasize incidents of minor importance and significance, simply because of the dramatic value."

Danger of "Ghost" Voices.

The broadcasters believe that, no matter how dramatic the show, such fictionized presentation of facts is not always fair, because actual happenings and conditions are too easily distorted in the listener's mind when the imagination fed by sound is stirred by the phantom voices of radio mimics, which in themselves are not true.

Radio listeners may also believe that the speakers are on the air in person, while in fact they are being "ghosted" by actors. With the out-and-out speech, however, the spellbinder himself is more likely to be held responsible by the listener for what he says. The radio officials describe the dramatization as an ethereal editorial; the speech they liken to a signed article. The talk is more easily answered by the opponent than is a fictionized presentation; so the broadcasters are urging the politicians who are formulating the radio battle lines to play fair and let words be their bullets rather than drama whooped up by music, screams and all sorts of sound effects which might toy with the imagination and emotions.

The law governing political broadcasting is very plain. It is in Section 18 of the Radio Act of 1927 and reads:

If any licensee shall permit any person who is a legally qualified candidate for any public office to use a broadcasting station he shall afford equal opportunities to all other such candidates for that office in the use of such broadcasting station, and the commission shall make rules and regulations to carry this provision into effect: Provided, that such licensee shall have no power of censorship over the material broadcast under the provisions of this section. No obligation is hereby imposed upon any licensee to allow the use of its station by any such candidate.

The broadcasting station also, like the publisher of a newspaper, can be held liable for libel or slander.

British System Differs.

The controversy brings up again the differences between the British and American broadcasting systems and policies.

The British system is a monopoly, functioning under royal charter, and is supported by a fee collected from listeners instead of by advertising revenue. It is not directly controlled by the government, although the government appoints the director general and governors.

The BBC, to use the words of an Englishman, "has put upon the shoulders of the politicians themselves the responsibility of dividing the time devoted to political talks, prior to a general election. A Parliamentary committee distributes the radio time for party issues."

What the outcome of the present controversy here will be is as yet uncertain. But Mr. Roosevelt's dramatic use of the radio has made it a foregone conclusion that radio time and its uses in politics will be closely watched.

January 19, 1936

TALK WILL NOT BE CHEAP

By ORRIN E. DUNLAP Jr.

TALK will not be cheap this year, the politicians are discovering as they seek time on the air for the national political campaign. Radio costs have risen since the New Deal staged its triumphant verbal bombardment in 1932. Size of the networks has increased, too.

An hour rally after sunset on the Columbia hook-up four years ago cost $17,000. This year the charge for a ninety-six-station network is approximately $18,395. The WEAF sixty-five-station "web" has increased from $12,880 an hour to $16,040; and WJZ's sixty-three-station rate is currently $14,640, while in 1932 the charge was $11,740. And in addition, there is now the Mutual network with four main transmitters priced at $3,025 for sixty minutes after supper time. So if the political warriors want an hour slice of radio's time at night it will cost about $52,000 for coast-to-coast coverage by a hook-up comprised of more than 200 stations.

* * *

THE drop of the gavel at national political conclaves will be the signal for the barrage to begin. The Republicans will rally 'round the microphone on June 9 at Cleveland's Municipal Auditorium, and the Democratic horde on June 23 will sweep down on Philadelphia's Auditorium. The broadcasters are making elaborate plans to be on the scene with their latest paraphernalia and microphones will be everywhere so as not to miss a single trick.

Numerous technical innovations are planned for this quadrennial event, which the broadcasters always look forward to as "the biggest show on the air." Regular programs in numerous instances will be brushed aside to make way for the orators; politics is considered well within the formula of "public interest, convenience and necessity." Soon the floodgates of oratory will open, further justified by the radio people as "a short course in civil government."

A "pause interpreter" will be introduced by the National Broadcasting Company. He will be an expert on convention tactics, assigned to a microphone on the speaker's platform. His job will be to explain what is going on during "time out," if ever there is such a gap of silence during the bedlam of a political convention. The broadcasters say that even while the delegates in the hall are wondering what question of procedure has halted action temporarily, the unseen audience will know exactly what is "in the air," because the interpreter will whisper secrets to the "mike."

Then, too, for the first time in history, there will be a microphone on the floor of the hall for each delegation. These pick-ups will be under the direct control of the permanent chairman through an engineer at his elbow, who will juggle the "mikes" by electric buttons on a panel board on the speaker's rostrum. This is expected to make broadcasting more flexible, and there will be no necessity for the chairman bellowing above the clamor for a delegate in some far corner of the hall to speak louder. The microphone will pick up the voice and the public address horns, as well as the entire radio system, will hear what a delegate has to report.

A corps of regular announcers will be supplemented by political specialists and commentators. The National Broadcasting Company announces it will send Walter Lippmann and Dorothy Thompson, authors and political writers, into the arena along with William Hard, veteran political analyst, Lowell Thomas and Edwin C. Hill, commentators. H. V. Kaltenborn and Mabelle Jennings will be Columbia's main "air columnists" on the scene, but it is expected that prominent newsmen will be invited from time to time to step up from the press section to broadcast. Gabriel Heatter, commentator, and several Chicago Tribune men will be the "voice" of the Mutual network, with WOR as the New York outlet.

Radio technicians describe the equipment to be used at the conventions as "the most comprehensive ever devised." The microphone, however, will be inconspicuous compared to the way it has been flaunted at past conventions. The great battery of "mikes" on the speaker's rostrum will be missing because the eight microphones feeding all stations are to be concealed.

All in all, there will be five radio pick-up points: the floor, the speaker's stand, the "pause interpreter," the announcer's booth in the proscenium arch and a special studio on the balcony floor, chiefly for interviews. The same arrangement will be followed at both conventions. So intricate is the radio

plan compared to the eighteen-station, East-Middle West hook-up, that handled the 1924 convention, the first to be radioed, that the broadcasters contend each listener will have "a seat by proxy" no matter in what part of the country he may eavesdrop.

* * *

RADIO will rule politics more than ever this year. It is expected night sessions will be featured so that the folks back home will all be at the fireside listening when the favorite sons swing out to bask in a moment or two of glory on the national stage. The keynote speeches will be night affairs, too. The Republicans have selected June 9 at 9 P. M., for this event, for that is generally considered one of radio's most witching hours.

June on the air will hum with politics; so will July, August, September and October. Already the showmen are wondering what is going to happen to their regular programs. They are not anxious to see too many "commercials" sidetracked because that generally means loss of revenue. But the politician has his big inning only once in four years; he says the electorate must hear what he has to say in "public interest, convenience and necessity." It is difficult to convince him that a bedtime story is more important, at least to one element in the nation, than his speech on platform planks and promises.

The broadcasters are aware from past performances that they must wear diplomatic gloves this Summer. It is no easy task during a national political campaign not to tread on toes of politicians, sponsors and listeners.

If a politician's allotted time is up and his speech is abruptly ended to avoid overlapping a scheduled performance, he has on occasions cried censorship and his constituents condemn radio as unfair. At the same time there are others anxious to be entertained by radio's regular bill of fare; they are irked when the politician overlaps the show. The broadcasters already see evidence that they will be confronted with a big cross-word puzzle that will be with them throughout the good old Summer-time

MONEY VALUE OF SPEECHES

From the Republican National Committee at Chicago comes another report of financial worry. Not half the planned budget of $8,000,000 has come in, and the sorrowful explanation is added that few "large gifts" to the campaign fund are at present being made. The committee now expects to finance by itself something like two millions of dollars in order to face the absolutely necessary expenses before the election. Among the items to be covered is one that will answer a question already asked by many curious people. What does it cost to put speeches on the air? The Republican National Committee figures its radio expense at between $50,000 and $75,000 a week, and plans to spend at least $100,000 for national hook-ups during the last week of the campaign. This gives ample notice to listeners-in. From Oct. 26 to Oct. 30 they will know what to avoid. With the Democratic orators also competing, one could hardly miss a speech if he risked turning on any station whatever.

Both parties seem to be spending a large amount for a doubtful return. The wonder of radio has long since departed. It is now reckoned among the commonplaces of life. People turn it on automatically, but discount or ignore a great deal that is poured into their ears. Political speeches, in particular, have a way of rapidly becoming tiresome. After a short time, nothing new can be said. Speakers absolutely appear to become bored with the sound of their own voices, and with the routine which they are expected to follow. Too often, like the speaker of whom LOWELL wrote, they stop every few minutes to "state their case," and finally end up in desperation by misstating it.

Despite all that can be said, it remains true that many politicians believe that they shall be heard for their much speaking. The radio enables them to speak oftener and to more people than ever before. But there is danger that the public, in the glut of political oratory during the next two weeks, will be inclined to say, "Something too much of this."

October 21, 1936

POLITICAL AIR TIME TO COST $2,000,000

National Broadcasting System Alone Expects to Receive $800,000 From Parties.

OTHER CHAINS VERY BUSY

Radio Listeners Will Be 'Bombarded' From Now Until Election Day, Say Officials.

A bill of about $800,000 will be presented to the various political parties by the National Broadcasting Company for time on the air during the 1936 campaign, it was revealed yesterday. In radio circles it is believed the total expenditure for political broadcasts throughout the nation this year will exceed $2,000,000.

Up to Oct. 17 the Republican National Committee spent $265,000 for broadcasting over the WEAF and WJZ networks, according to the NBC statisticians. The Democratic National Committee, up to the same date, spent $165,000 and the Com-

munists $20,000. In addition $75,000 has been spent by all parties to date for local and State broadcasts.

With less than two weeks of the campaign remaining, the radio listeners are to be "bombarded" with a political barrage, according to the number of political speeches scheduled on the books of the NBC.

From now until election the Republicans have contracted for more than $90,000 worth of radio facilities through NBC outlets; the Democrats, $65,000; Communists, $15,000; Socialists, $7,000, and the Union Party, $9,000.

For local broadcasts an additional $15,000 worth of time has been booked. It is expected that at least another $50,000 may be added for rallies now being planned but as yet not definitely booked for broadcasting.

Inquiry at at the Columbia Broadcasting System for the amount netted from politics since the campaign opened did not yield information.

"We are not at liberty to disclose such figures," said a representative of the Columbia System. "It is up to the national committees to release that information. As far as we are concerned, we, of course, have the figures and have no reason to keep them secret, but it is their business to report on their expenditures."

The campaign costs over the Mutual Broadcasting System will not be released until after election day, according to a representative of WOR, the New York outlet for the hook-up.

May 10, 1936

October 23, 1936

205

THE FINAL 'WORDS'

Politicians to Invade the Air This Week —Roosevelt and Landon at Big Rallies

RADIO listeners are warned that the air this week will be saturated with politics. President Roosevelt is scheduled for two broadcasts and Governor Landon for four, between now and next Sunday.

The President will be heard on Wednesday at the fiftieth anniversary celebration of the unveiling of the Statue of Liberty. On Saturday night he will speak at a rally in Madison Square Garden.

Governor Landon is listed for Monday at Philadelphia; Tuesday, at Pittsburgh; Thursday, New York, and Saturday, St. Louis. (Time schedules and stations are listed in the radio program on another page in this section.)

The broadcasters report that the night of Nov. 2 will be one of political "fireworks." The Democrats, who in 1932 "sewed up" the hour from 11 o'clock to midnight on election eve, have done likewise for Nov. 2, 1936, for a nation-wide rally during which President Roosevelt will have the "last word" over a vast network before the voting begins.

The G. O. P., following the same last-minute tactics as in 1932, has arranged for Governor Landon to be on the air between 10 and 11 o'clock, election eve, but he will speak over a smaller hook-up than Mr. Roosevelt. While Mr. Landon is on the WEAF network the Communist party will be holding a final rally over WJZ's chain. William Lemke of the Union party is scheduled for WJZ's network that evening from 9:30 to 10 o'clock.

It is reported that the Republican National Committee plans to spend at least $100,000 on the national hook-ups between now and election day, and a representative of the Democratic committee reports it will "spend plenty too."

Radio will "eat" that amount quickly. In fact, two nation-wide broadcasts of an hour each over the combined networks would call for more than $100,000, so that in two hours after sunset the fortune would be gone to the winds. The combined hook-ups, involving about 250 stations, cost approximately $52,000 for sixty minutes.

The general fund is not expected to go for such big broadcasts, but will be spread across the hours and scattered among many stations, disrupting quite generally the regularly scheduled shows.

The politicians during this campaign have, in the words of a broadcaster, "been smart enough to stay off the Sunday air." Past experience has taught that listeners resent too much politics and complain bitterly when politicians become oratorical on the Sabbath.

October 25, 1936

JERSEY DEMOCRATS GOT REYNOLDS LOAN

$100,000 Was Used to Pay for National Committee Radio Time; Inquiry Is Told

Special to THE NEW YORK TIMES.

WASHINGTON, Jan. 8 — R. J. Reynolds, of the North Carolina Tobacco family, lent $100,000 to the New Jersey Democratic State Committee in the recent Presidential campaign at the suggestion of Oliver Quayle, then treasurer of the Democratic National Committee, Charles Quinn, secretary of the New Jersey Committee, testified today before the Senate Committee Investigating Campaign Expenditures. He said some of this money was used to pay for radio speeches of President Roosevelt and Senator Norris, and $39,000 was turned over to the New York Democratic State Committee and used for radio time, he was told.

Mr. Reynolds will take up the duties of treasurer of the Democratic National Committee on Friday, succeeding Mr. Quayle, who will become assistant to Chairman Flynn.

Senator Tobey charged that the loan was only a scheme to avoid the law which limits individual campaign contributions to $5,000, and intimated that the contracting parties had no idea of repayment.

No money has been collected by the New Jersey Democrats to pay the loan, Mr. Quinn said, and undoubtedly it will be necessary to renew the note, which was made Oct. 31 for ninety days.

The committee adopted a motion by Senator Tobey to subpoena Mr. Reynolds and Mr. Quayle to explain what he characterized as "an unusual transaction."

Mr. Quinn told the committee that he did not consider the making of the note an attempt to avoid the technicalities of the law.

"It happened this way," he added. "Mr. Quayle called me up from New York and said 'we will go over our $3,000,000 limit of expenditures fixed in the Hatch act, I am afraid, and we need money for last-day radio broadcasts.' I told him that these broadcasts should be made but did not know how to help. He suggested that Reynolds would give it through a loan. And that was just what happened and the whole story."

"You did not think this unusual," Senator Tobey asked.

"No, it seemed natural and proper to us and it is," the witness replied.

When the New York committee came to the rescue it signed a note for $39,000. This note was turned over to Mr. Reynolds with one of $61,000 issued by the New Jersey committee and signed by its treasurer, James Baker, but with no endorsers.

Senator Tobey asked how the committee expected to pay the Reynolds $100,000 note in ninety days if it was able to raise only $29,000.

"If we really started out to pay the note Mr. Baker could raise the amount," Mr. Quinn replied.

"I believe, and most people who read this will believe, that the loan was made as a contribution," Senator Tobey said. "The sky is the limit in a loan but a rich man can only make a contribution of $5,000."

Mr. Quinn denied that New Jersey had an organized assessment of officeholders. Senator Tobey said several witnesses had told the committee an assessment was 3 per cent of their salaries was levied.

The Senator charged that the committee's failure to subpoena Jersey City pay-rolls made "a farce of the investigation."

"Something is being covered up that should not be covered up and I am not the kind of fellow that can stand for that," he added.

'52 CAMPAIGN COSTS BIGGEST IN HISTORY

Special to THE NEW YORK TIMES.

WASHINGTON, June 28—One thing is certain amid all the uncertainty about whom the great political parties will nominate and who will be elected President. That is that the 1952 campaign will be the most expensive in history, topping the record of $40 million spent by the two parties in 1940.

It would be true even without the extraordinary pre-convention campaigns in both parties and the unusually fierce interparty struggle that is expected to follow. Record expenditures became a certainty with the advent of television, at once a most persuasive and most costly political asset.

The Republican party spent $650,000 for radio and some slight use of television in 1948. In that campaign, the Democrats put up $750,000 for use of the same media in about the same proportion.

Both parties, planning ahead for the fall campaign, are talking in terms of radio-TV budgets double the size of those of 1948.

And plan ahead they must, because if they fail to do so and pre-empt time already assigned, they have to pay the full cost of all the non-cancellable talent expenses. More than $250,000 of the $750,000 the Democrats paid for radio-TV time in 1948 went to pay for such unused talent.

Cost of Best TV Time

Some idea of the fabulous cost of TV time is illustrated by the National Broadcasting Company's network rate. A half-hour of Class A time—that is between 6 and 11 P. M. and Saturday and Sunday afternoons—costs $30,365.

Actually both parties will be using far more radio time than they will TV time, but the television budget will be substantially the larger.

But radio and television, while a major item, are only one costly item in campaigning. The cost of politicking in times of inflation has risen with the cost of living, and such essentials as campaign buttons, literature and campaign trains daily become more expensive.

It is estimated that just the cost of running a campaign train today is twice what it was in 1940.

Guy George Gabrielson, Republican National Chairman, told the Senate Elections subcommittee last fall that it would cost at least $450,000 to distribute just one piece of campaign literature to 10,000,000 homes.

F. C. C. MEASURE GAINS

Congress Backs Bill Setting TV, Radio Rates for Politicians

WASHINGTON, July 2 (UP)—Congress approved and sent to the White House today a compromise bill to streamline the Federal Communications Commission and bar radio and television stations from charging premium rates for political candidates.

The House and Senate both gave final approval to the bill as modified by Senate-House conferees.

The bill, designed to speed up agency procedures, specifies radio and TV stations must charge politicians no more than rates charged for comparable time used for commercial purposes.

The House also passed a bill to increase the retirement pay of some 166,000 Civil Service workers by $324 a year or 25 per cent, whichever is less.

The House also voted $180,000 for new Congressional investigations into obscene literature, election frauds, tax scandals and tax-exempt foundations. It already has spent a record $3,215,000 this session for investigations.

NETWORKS FACING LOSS ON CAMPAIGNS

Conventions Alone Cost Three Chains $3,000,000 Above Fixed-Fee Package Plan

The high cost of covering political conventions by television and radio, particularly until 4 o'clock in the morning with hundreds of engineers and commentators standing by, may cost the networks several million dollars this year for gambling on politics.

Preliminary and unofficial estimates indicate that coverage of the recent Republican and Democratic National conventions has cost three broadcasting companies $3,000,000 beyond what the sponsors paid.

The National Broadcasting Company is said to have lost at least $1,500,000 on its television and radio coverage, the Columbia Broadcasting System $1,000,000 and the American Broadcasting Company $500,000.

Blanket coverage was sold to sponsors last winter at a fixed fee under a package plan, which also included sponsorship of election returns on Nov. 4, and, in the case of one network, a thirteen-week "Get Out the Vote" campaign.

For the amount paid by sponsors the networks had agreed to furnish a minimum of twenty hours of coverage at each convention, but many additional hours of air time were incurred because of the lengthy sessions.

The networks also had to make many rebates to sponsors of regular programs, which were canceled at the last minute. No rebates are necessary if a sponsor is given sufficient advance notice.

The political packages sold to sponsors will bring the three broadcasting companies a total of $8,200,000 over a period of four months, an amount that probably will be considerably behind the industry's total costs.

CAMPAIGN OUTLAYS PUT AT $40,000,000

Weeks, G. O. P. Finance Chief, Favors Revisions to Make Hatch Act 'Realistic'

Sinclair Weeks, finance chairman of the Republican National Committee, estimated yesterday on a visit to Gen. Dwight D. Eisenhower's headquarters at the Commodore Hotel that between $40,000,000 and $50,000,000 was spent in the recent campaign by the two major political parties.

This figure, he emphasized, includes spending by volunteer organizations, state, county, city and other local committees backing candidates of either of the two major parties, along with the expenditures in the Presidential, Senatorial and House campaigns.

Mr. Weeks voiced the opinion that present limitations on campaign spending by national committees embodied in the Hatch Act, adopted in 1940, should be revised by Congress. The limitations are not only unrealistic, but full of loopholes, he said.

The limitation of $3,000,000 on expenditures by a national committee is unrealistic, he explained, because it is based on 1940 prices and 1940 practices. It is meaningless, he went on, because it can be circumvented so easily by the device of forming several separate national committees and by assigning part of the usual national committee expenses to state or local organizations.

Cites Broadcast Costs

As an example of the increase in campaign costs since the law was adopted in 1940, Mr. Weeks cited General Eisenhower's combined radio and television program on election eve. This program alone, he reported, cost about $285,000 and was, in his judgment, worth the money because, he said, it decided a number of

still undecided voters to cast their ballots for General Eisenhower.

At the time the law was adopted, he pointed out, there was no television network and Congress had no idea of the costliness of this campaign medium.

Mr. Weeks declined to apportion his estimate of total expenditures between the Republican and Democratic parties, but he expressed the opinion that Republican outlays did not exceed those made on behalf of Democratic candidates. In the latter category he included such items as the expenditures made by the Liberal party in New York by the various labor unions through organizations set up for influencing political action.

The Republican finance chairman said he reported to General Eisenhower yesterday that Republicans had wound up the campaign with enough money to pay outstanding bills and still have a little left over for regular activities next year.

Although he has not yet "thought out" a full program for revising the Hatch Act, Mr. Weeks said he expected to submit suggestions for changes to Congress.

Urges 'Realistic Limits'

"If the people, through their representatives, want to control campaign expenditures they should have a law with realistic limits that will allow a party to adequately sell its bill of goods and then put teeth into the law to hold to those limits," he continued.

As part of the revision, Mr. Weeks said it would be a good idea, in his opinion, if contributors to political campaigns were permitted to deduct their donations, "up to a modest limit," from their taxable income. Contributions to a political campaign are not now deductible.

The limit Mr. Weeks had in mind apparently was somewhat less than the $5,000 limit now imposed on gifts by a single contributor to a single committee, but he declined to specify the amount.

The theory in allowing such deductions, he explained, was that a citizen was making his contribution as a means of insuring that the country got what the citizen believed was good government

CONTROLLING CAMPAIGN FUNDS

Even without the advent of television, the federal laws governing campaign expenditures have long been unrealistic and ineffective. And now that television has developed into a major medium for the waging of electoral battles, the cost of campaigning has skyrocketed and the necessity of modernizing the law has become imperative. This week a special committee of the House of Representatives will begin hearings on this subject.

Under existing federal statutes no national campaign committee may spend more than $3,000,000 in any one year, no Senatorial nominee more than $25,-000 or House nominee more than $5,000 per campaign, and no individual may contribute more than $5,000 to any single nominee or committee in a federal election. Yet reasoned estimates of the sum poured out in the recent campaign range up to as much as $100 millions, spent by literally thousands of political committees. The limitations of existing law contain so many loopholes that evasion of their intent is the rule rather than the exception.

There are many possible ways of tackling the problem. Some day important speeches in major political battles may be broadcast gratis over radio and television as a matter of course. But until that day comes it is obvious that national campaign expenditures are going to demand enormous sums; and if the sums come mainly from relatively few private sources—as now they must—there will always be the danger of both parties selling out to the highest bidder, no matter how impeccable the character of every individual on the ticket. Therefore, such careful thinkers as Senator Douglas have suggested that the solution might be for public funds to pay for strictly limited campaign costs. In this event satisfactory safeguards would have to be set up for third parties, and provision would somehow have to be made for primaries, for in a substantial number of states the primary is more important than the general election.

But even in the absence of so drastic a reform there are many improvements that could and should be made in existing law. Senator-elect Mansfield of Montana has proposed a number of them, including provisions for fuller publicity. With good reason, public interest in this matter is now high; and Congress should lose no time in bringing the law governing political campaigns into closer touch with reality.

November 30, 1952

House Opens Inquiry Today —Party Chiefs Feel TV Makes Limits Obsolete

By CLAYTON KNOWLES

Special to THE NEW YORK TIMES.

WASHINGTON, Nov. 30—The House of Representatives will open an investigation into campaign spending tomorrow that is widely expected to document the case for raising the $3,000,000 limitation now imposed on spending in a national campaign by any one political committee.

Leaders of both major parties, many of whom will testify during the first week of the hearings, agree that the advent of television has made it impossible for the parties to maintain even a pretense of financing a national campaign through their regular organizations.

Television time costs in the neighborhood of $33,000 for a choice half hour. The Republican and Democratic National Committees each earmarked at least half of their respective $3,000,000 funds this year for television and radio expenses, and, because the final bill was much larger, the difference had to be covered by volunteer organizations.

Representative Hale Boggs of Louisiana, who heads the inquiry as chairman of the Special House Committee to Investigate Campaign Expenditures, declared today that his group wanted expert opinion on "problems that arise in a video-era campaign."

"The recent campaign added 'jet stops' to the 'whistle stops' and expensive TV rhetoric to the fireside chats," he said. "The enactors of laws which were passed in 1925 and 1939, as were the ones under which we are presently operating, could not possibly have foreseen these drastic changes in campaign techniques and the alarming costs of these techniques."

Mr. Boggs placed the cost of the recent campaign somewhere between $50,000,000 and $100,000,000.

He emphasized that the hearings should not be considered "a partisan political proceeding." The witnesses will include national and state political leaders of both major parties, as well as experts in particular fields.

"These witnesses," he said, "are all experienced in their fields and should be able to assist us materially in accomplishing the duty imposed upon us—that of making sound and constructive recommendations for remedial legislation to the Eighty-third Congress."

Because the parties' national committees cannot foot the whole bill under existing limitations many auxiliary "citizens" and "volunteer" groups, as well as political subsidiaries of labor unions and other organizations, are play-

Election Expenditures by States

The following table was compiled from reports submitted by correspondents of THE NEW YORK TIMES on campaign expenditures in 1952. The total figure for the states does not purport to be the total actually spent, but wherever possible it represents the total according to official reports or the statements of competent party officials.

Where outlays of labor groups went to Democratic candidates they have been added to the column of Democratic spending.

Differences between the total given and the sum of the Republican and Democratic spending arise because a breakdown of spending by the parties was not always available, as authoritative estimates could not always be balanced with known itemized spending and because in some instances money spent to get out the vote has been included in the total.

Duplications have been eliminated wherever possible and, where there was a variance in estimates, the more conservative figure was used.

An (R) after the state's name means the state went Republican in the Presidential election. A (D) means it went Democratic.

State.	Total.	Republicans.	Democrats.
Alabama (D.)	$150,000	$100,000	$50,000
Arizona (R.)	55,538	37,680	17,858
Arkansas (D.)	112,119	87,119	25,000
California (R.)	1,950,000	1,200,000	750,000
Colorado (R.)	169,229	138,000	31,229
Connecticut (R.)	1,300,000	809,130	431,200
Delaware (R.)	185,000	110,000	75,000
Florida (R.)	203,700	138,700	65,000
Georgia (D.)	189,800	111,000	78,800
Idaho (R.)	142,000	123,200	18,800
Illinois (R.)	2,500,000	870,000	Unavailable
Indiana (R.)	920,582	636,564	284,018
Iowa (R.)	437,000	250,000	187,000
Kansas (R.)	545,050	339,600	202,450
Kentucky (D.)	402,000	255,000	135,000
Louisiana (D.)	275,000	175,000	100,000
Maine (R.)	146,683	92,588	54,095
Maryland (R.)	270,000	45,138	118,158
Massachusetts (R.)	2,000,000	935,413	233,861
Michigan (R.)	1,745,939	1,456,835	289,104
Minnesota (R.)	415,000	240,000	175,000
Mississippi (D.)	236,500	36,500	200,000
Missouri (R.)	740,922	448,648	292,274
Montana (R.)	273,849	37,014	8,608
Nebraska (R.)	135,226	99,578	35,648
Nevada (R.)	49,980	43,680	6,300
New Hampshire (R.)	64,000	51,000	9,000
New Jersey (R.)	1,467,766	842,010	574,765
New Mexico (R.)	164,000	60,000	104,500
New York (R.)	1,977,188	1,061,251	796,112
North Carolina (D.)	237,908	104,346	130,062
North Dakota (R.)	79,716	63,216	16,500
Ohio (R.)	2,691,598	2,050,651	52,152
Oklahoma (R.)	448,145	281,677	166,468
Oregon (R.)	1,008,832	257,414	56,058
Pennsylvania (R.)	4,000,000	2,334,023	428,270
Rhode Island (R.)	125,000	Unavailable	125,000
South Carolina (D.)	200,000	92,320	24,500
South Dakota (R.)	80,033	80,033	Unavailable
Tennessee (R.)	100,000	11,382	23,749
Texas (R.)	1,220,000	770,107	220,000
Utah (R.)	250,000	150,000	100,000
Virginia (R.)	213,736	160,628	32,100
Vermont (R.)	43,249	37,749	5,500
Washington (R.)	1,024,500	528,000	446,500
West Virginia (D.)	248,494	197,901	50,593
Wisconsin (R.)	916,696	792,919	122,060
Wyoming (R.)	43,273	26,834	16,439
Totals	$32,155,251	$18,769,848	$6,847,725

ing an increasingly important role in financing national election drives.

Prominent among the witnesses during the first week will be representatives of such organizations.

Following is the schedule of the witnesses:

Tomorrow—Representative Clarence J. Brown of Ohio, Republican National Committeeman; Hermon Dunlap Smith and John Paulding Brown, chairman and counsel, respectively, of Volunteers for Stevenson.

Tuesday—Arthur E. Summerfield, the chairman of the Republican National Committee; James P. McGranery, the Attorney General, and Neil Staebler, Michigan Democratic chairman.

Wednesday—Stephen A. Mitchell, Democratic National Chairman;

Walter Williams, chairman of Citizens for Eisenhower; Dr. James K. Pollock, professor at the University of Michigan, and Ralph W. Hardy, director of Government relations for the National Association of Radio and Television Broadcasters.

Thursday — Paul A. Walker, chairman of the Federal Communications Commission; James L. McDevitt, director of Labor's League for Political Education (American Federation of Labor), and Sheriff Thomas E. Whitten, chairman of the Allegheny County Republican Committee of Pennsylvania.

Friday—Robert A. Gray, Florida's Secretary of State; Sinclair Weeks, chairman of the Republican Finance Committee, and Norman A. Sugarman, Assistant Commissioner of the Bureau of Internal Revenue.

At Least $32,155,251 Spent On Election, Survey Indicates

New York Among 12 States That Hit Million Mark— G. O. P. Tops Democrats

By DOUGLAS DALES

A forty-eight state survey by correspondents of THE NEW YORK TIMES to determine expenditures in the 1952 political campaign indicated that at least $32,155,251 had been spent by political organizations, independent groups and candidates.

This is a rock-bottom figure. It is by no means the total that was spent. That total probably never will be ascertained.

Going into the $32,155,251 figure were only those costs that could be gleaned from officially filed reports or, in their absence, which was common, from the estimates of competent political fiscal officers or election officials.

In a few cases nothing could be obtained from these sources. And much local spending simply could not be ascertained.

A dozen states were clearly in the million-dollar spending class— New York, New Jersey, Connecticut, Massachusetts, Pennsylvania, Illinois, Ohio, Michigan, Oregon, Texas, California and Washington. Two others, Indiana and Wisconsin, were so near the million-dollar mark that final reports will probably put them there.

One thing seemed clear from the survey: The estimate of $40,000,-000 to $50,000,000 as the cost of the 1952 campaign to both parties, recently made by Sinclair Weeks, finance chairman of the Republican National Committee, was no exaggeration and might turn out to have been on the conservative side.

The high cost of campaigning in this era of television, radio and airplanes has been focusing attention in recent weeks on proposals for reforms in expenditures and the reporting of them.

Loopholes in State and Federal corrupt practices laws relating to limits on campaign spending are widely criticized as vitiating the laws. With a view to rewriting the Federal law, a special committee of the House of Representatives will begin hearings in Washington today. Top officials of the major parties, television officials and others with pertinent information have been subpoenaed.

Amounts for Television

The estimated total spent by the two major parties and their various committees for network radio and television campaigning was $3,511,-800. The Republicans spent $2,083,-400 and the Democrats $1,428,400.

These figures, however, do not include thousands spent on regional networks and on individual station programs throughout the country, an additional amount that easily could bring the total broadcasting bill to more than $5,000,000.

The amount of $3,511,800 was tallied from estimated figures supplied by the various networks.

Campaign reports showed that television, radio and newspaper advertising accounted for the bulk of spending. The extensive use of television has been an important factor in increasing campaign spending.

On the other hand the use of air waves has been cited as one of the reasons to postpone the dates of the national nominating conventions, traditionally held in June or July.

It is commonly suggested that the conventions be held after Labor Day to cut the period of campaigning. With the medium of television it is argued that there is no need for the present long period.

It was impossible for correspondents working on the survey to break down the spending by parties, but what could be allocated indicated that the Republicans had spent much more than the Democrats. Assignable to Republicans was $18,769,843 and to the Democrats $6,847,725.

On the basis of an indicated spending of $1,977,188 in New York State, the cost for each of the nearly 7,000,000 voters was 28 cents. This was the same as the cost in Vermont, where a vote of 152,400 was cast and $43,249 was spent. The cost per voter was 43 cents in Wyoming, 88 cents in Pennsylvania, 41 cents in California, and $1.19 in Connecticut.

Two Barred by Senate

Probably the most expensive campaign for the United States Senate was that of Senator-elect John F. Kennedy, Democrat, in Massachusetts. Mr. Kennedy reported spending $15,866, but committees on his behalf for the improvement of the shoe, fishing and other industries of the state, spent $217,995. An official report from the Kennedy Campaign Committee is yet to come.

Mr. Kennedy's opponent, Senator Henry Cabot Lodge Jr., who was named Saturday as the next head of the United States delegation to the United Nations, reported spending $11,000. A committee working for him spent $58,413. The campaign of Senator William Benton, Democrat, defeated in Connecticut, cost about $147,000.

On some occasions the United States Senate, which is the sole judge of the fitness of its members, has questioned high campaign spending. A Senator's salary is $12,500 a year.

The Senate denied a seat in 1926 to Frank L. Smith, elected from Illinois, because of his campaign financing. He reputedly spent $458,782, of which $203,000 came from officers of public utilities. He was at the time a member of the Illinois Commerce Commission, a utility regulatory body. In the same year the Senate refused to seat William S. Vare of Pennsylvania, who reportedly spent $785,-000 in the Republican primary.

One defect pointed out in the present laws is that limits are placed on a candidate's spending, and on that of the national committees, but there is no limit on the number of committees that can be set up independently.

Committees Allowed 3 Million

A final filing of campaign receipts and expenses by the national political committees with the clerk of the House of Representatives is not due until Jan. 1. Both committees concede they spent close to the $3,000,000 allowed. The Republican budget called for putting $1,800,000 in television and radio while the Democrats planned to spend $1,500,000 in this area.

The national committees get their money largely from quotas assigned to state committees but also receive contributions directly from individuals.

The Republican Senatorial and Congressional Committees jointly had a budget of $1,800,000, of which $1,200,000 was earmarked for House contests. The Democrats were less fortunate. Their Senate and House Campaign Committees raised about $82,000, which was parceled out where most needed.

The Democratic deficiency was offset in part by aid from organized labor. The American Federation of Labor spent $245,000, mostly to help Congressional candidates. The Congress of Industrial Organizations similarly put up $600,000.

An obstacle to the obtaining of information on campaign spending is the absence in several states of laws requiring the filing of campaign statements and the weakness of the laws in some other states. Illinois, Florida, Arkansas, Louisiana and Nevada are among states in which no filing is required.

In Tennessee the law is so vague that the state courts held a few years ago that a candidate could not be barred from office for failing to file. South Carolina requires filing only by candidates. In Vermont, candidates are required to report primary election expenditures, but not what they spent in the general election.

The following is a summary of the campaign spending by states as reported by correspondents of THE TIMES:

ALABAMA

While details are lacking, indications are that the recent campaign was the most costly in Alabama's history. Informed sources, who requested anonymity, estimated that the Democrats spent about $50,000 and General Eisenhower's supporters twice that figure.

These totals do not include an undetermined amount sent by the state political committees to their national organizations or the amounts that were spent by the national committees in the state. Heads of regular and volunteer organizations were unwilling to be quoted on any figures.

ARIZONA

The State Republican Committee spent $13,680 and donated $23,000 to the National Republican Committee. The Democratic state organization spent $17,858. Filing of election expenses is not required until next Thursday and it was not known what contribution, if any, was made to the Democratic National Committee or what was spent in the state by the national committee. The Republican National Committee sent $1,000 to Arizona for use among Indian voters.

The total known expenditures of $55,538 do not take into account money spent by local political organizations, labor and volunteer organizations.

ARKANSAS

Arkansas does not require the filing of campaign expenditures or contributions, so it is virtually impossible to obtain anything like an accurate picture of election spending.

The Republican state organization raised $87,119, twice the amount raised in 1948. It spent $16,960 in the state. Part of this went to candidates in state and district contests. The balance of $71,159 was sent to Republican national headquarters and to the National Citizens for Eisenhower Committee.

The Democrats had a state fund goal of $100,000, but the amount raised has not been disclosed. The state committee sent $25,000 to the national party treasury. Observations indicated that the Democrats had spent far less in the campaign than the Republicans.

CALIFORNIA

The campaign was in the million-dollar category in California. What the total figure may be awaits the untangling of collection and expense figures among a maze of overlapping professional and volunteer groups.

A survey of the principal organizations indicates that the Republicans spent roughly $1,200,000 and the Democrats $750,000, but little allowance is made in these figures for spending in legislative contests.

Some campaign spokesmen put as high as 50 per cent the amount that went for radio and television, with 25 per cent for literature and the rest for billboards and other items. Republican sources said $500,000 was sent to the national committee while the Democrats sent about $100,000 to their national committee.

In Southern California, Republicans raised and spent $210,000 on the Presidential race alone. Financial experts put the Northern California figure at more than $200,000 for San Francisco County, although this included some funds spent on legislative contests.

Democratic fiscal spokesmen said their party had spent $150,-000 in the Presidential fight in Northern California and twice that in the southern counties. They asserted Republican spending must have reached $2,000,000. They put their own, for all purposes, at $500,000.

Reports filed with the Secretary of State on Congressional fights showed the Republicans had spent at least $200,000 and the Democrats about $100,000, but persons on both sides conceded these figures were too low.

Labor leaders reported the A. F. L. spent about $82,000 and the C. I. O. about $50,000.

COLORADO

The deadline for filing campaign expenditure reports in Colorado is next Thursday and data on total expenditures are meager. Allan Phipps, Republican finance chairman, said the state committee spent $75,000. The committee sent $55,000 to the national committee and received no aid in return. The Citizens for Eisenhower spent $8,000 at the state level, with the amounts spent by local units unavailable.

Joseph F. Little, Democratic state chairman, put the state committee's expenditures at $31,229, including $15,000 distributed among county organization. No aid was received from the Democratic National Committee.

CONNECTICUT

It is the opinion of the Connecticut correspondent that final reports will show a record spending of at least $1,300,000 and probably closer to $1,500,000. The state law requires candidates and their committees to file on Nov. 19, but gives party organizations until Dec. 20 to submit reports.

Top party leaders are reluctant to talk freely on campaign costs. The Republican practice is to pay bills out of one fund, while the Democrats let their candidates operate on their own.

The correspondent's estimate takes into consideration the Dec. 20 filings, which he estimates will show $500,000 spent by the Republican state organization and $75,000 by the Democratic.

Reports of Nov. 19 showed $412,000 spent on the two Senate contests, with the Republican total incomplete. The later Republican reports are expected to bring the Senate campaigns costs to $500,000. Senator William Benton, Democrat defeated for re-election, and committees for him, spent the top amount, $147,000.

Nominees for the House of Representatives spent about $75,000. The Eisenhower committee reported expenses of $113,000; the Stevenson-Sparkman fund, $6,200; the state C. I. O., more than $50,000; the Committee for Democratic State Legislators, $51,000; the Volunteers for Stevenson, $26,000; the Fairfield County Republican Organization, $58,000.

DELAWARE

Delaware law does not require the filing of reports until Dec. 15, but high party officials said Republican spending at the state level was about $110,000 and Democratic spending about $75,000. These figures do not include the spending of candidates or their committees or the spending of independent groups for the national tickets.

FLORIDA

Kirk A. Landon, state chairman of the Florida for Eisenhower group, estimated that $90,000 had been spent by the State Republican Executive Committee and various independent groups. Florida law does not require state political committees to file campaign expense reports. The $90,000 does not include $48,700 sent to the Republican National Committee.

J. Irvin Walden, secretary-treasurer of the Democratic State Committee, said the state organization had spent $15,000 and had sent nothing to the national committee. Independent Democratic groups and county organizations spent $50,000, according to a state com-

mittee official who asked not to be identified.

GEORGIA

In Georgia, the Republican organization made the greatest effort in financial activity, with the state central committee reporting collections of $126,000. In contrast to this, state Democrats raised only $78,000.

The Republican organization sent $62,000 to the national party, spent $49,000 in the state, and retained $15,000 to continue its activities.

The Democrats sent a total of $55,000 to their national committee and spent about $23,800 for state and local contests.

IDAHO

The campaign cost a minimum of $142,000 in Idaho. On the Republican side $78,000 was expended in the state, $22,200 was sent to the national committee, about $12,000 was spent on visits of Senator Robert A. Taft and General Eisenhower, and $6,000 by the Eisenhower-Nixon Committees. Republican battalions to get-out-the-vote spent $5,000. Democrats put spending at the state level at $10,000 and estimated $8,800 more had been spent by county organizations.

ILLINOIS

Governor Stevenson's home state has no law requiring candidates and committees generally to file reports with the Secretary of State. It is the opinion of the correspondent that $1,250,000 was spent by both parties. Because of the absence of a filing law, it is probable that no one ever knows for certainty what is spent by the 102 county organizations, the state committees and the hundreds of independent and voluntary groups at the various levels of government.

Attempts to get any sort of a figure on Democratic spending were rebuffed by party officials. Edward Ryerson, chairman of the Republican Citizens Finance Committee, said that $870,000 had been spent by the committee in Illinois and declined to say what, if any, contribution above that had been made to the national committee. His committee collected $970,000 and had a balance of $250,000 from last year, which made $1,220,000 available for the campaign.

Offices of the Citizens for Eisenhower and Volunteers for Stevenson have been disbanded. Balances in their accounts, if they existed, were turned over to state party organizations, which are said to be working on an audit of these independent groups.

INDIANA

Campaign spending appeared to have reached a new high in Indiana with the Republicans reporting total expenditures of $636,364 and the Democrats $284,018.

Fund raising by both parties was vigorous and successful and one veteran Republican said the number of contributors had been the greatest in his memory.

The United Republican Finance Committee raised $441,897, the bulk from a door-to-door canvassing drive. It distributed this as follows: $217,363 to county committees, $195,210 to the state committee, and $16,833 to district committees.

The Republican State Committee

received $356,216 and spent $319,082. A committee for Senator William Jenner raised $111,938, of which $59,615 went to the state committee.

Two independent committees for Eisenhower raised and spent $34,383.

The Democratic State Committee took in $220,444 and spent $262,887. The party's women's division collected $2,795 and a club supporting

---

Campaign Funds Include Bad Check and Feathers

Most campaign spending goes for advertising in one form or another. Here is how some other money was spent:

In South Carolina, $1,000 was spent to build a platform for a rally for Gen. Dwight D. Eisenhower and $50 went to cover a bad check given to the Eisenhower campaign.

Democrats for Eisenhower in Texas listed as one of their expenses the printing of 4,000,000 sample ballots to show life-long Democrats how to split their votes.

In Philadelphia, Democrats spent $141,700 to "man" the polls.

In Richmond, Va., a get-out-the-vote group spent $1,200 on gold feathers to be used to signify that the wearer had paid his poll tax and was therefore eligible to vote.

Gov. Henry F. Schricker produced $31,874, spending $18,665.

IOWA

This year's political campaign was the costliest in Iowa's history. Parties have until Dec. 4 to file formal statements, and full figures have not been posted. Democratic officials estimated their state committee and independent fund-raising groups had spent $97,000 and their county committees an additional $90,000, a total of $187,000. A Republican spokesman estimated his party had spent $250,000.

KANSAS

On the basis of rough estimates, politicians and their parties spent $545,000 on the 1952 election. This was divided as follows: $202,450 by the Democrats, $339,600 by Republicans and the remainder by independent groups. State law requires full filings by Dec. 4, but only scattered official reports were obtainable yesterday.

KENTUCKY

Preliminary figures indicate that the bill for Kentucky's elections has reached a total of $402,000. Reports do not have to be filed until Dec. 6, but on the basis of those already in, and estimates of party officials, the Republicans spent about $255,000 and the Democrats about $135,000.

Neither major parties received aid from their national committees but each sent part of its collected funds to the higher groups. The Republicans passed on $20,000 and the Democrats $32,000. The latter was raised by $5 gifts.

The Citizens for Eisenhower spent $12,500 in Louisville.

LOUISIANA

Louisiana has no campaign filing law. Reliable party sources

estimated Republican expenditures had been about $175,000 and Democratic spending about $100,000, but it is the opinion of the correspondent that these figures are conservative.

MAINE

For the Presidential election, less than $3,000 was spent in Maine. The Republicans spent $150 for spot radio announcements, the Democrats $1,980, mostly for direct mail and radio advertising, and the Progressives $643, a total of $2,773.

The important Maine campaigning, however, was for the Sept. 8 election, when the Republicans elected a Governor, a Senator and three Representatives. In this election Republicans spent $51,125 and Democrats $32,108.

Neither major party received money from national committees, but the Republican Congressional candidates received $11,000 from National funds. The Republicans sent to their national committee $43,500 and the Democrats $2,820. An Eisenhower committee spent $4,000 in pre-convention activities, nothing in the campaign.

Both parties ignored a state law requiring reports on campaign expenditures within fifteen days after an election.

MARYLAND

Reports filed by Maryland political groups indicate that about $270,000 was spent in the political campaign. Reports were due Nov. 24, but no accurate totals were available yet. The Democratic State Committee indicated that its expenditures totaled $118,158, while the Republican State Central Committee reported expenses of $45,138, exclusive of independent committees and Congressional races. Volunteers for Stevenson and Citizens for Eisenhower each spent $10,000. In addition to the latter the Citizens for Eisenhower and Nixon spent $10,400.

MASSACHUSETTS

The generally accepted figure on the cost of the campaign is $2,000,000, an estimate first made by Charles Gibbons, Republican, who is slated to be the next Speaker of the Massachusetts House. Attempts to break this figure down have met with stalling tactics, including outright refusal to divulge figures.

Candidates are required to file expense reports by Nov. 18, while committees have until next Thursday. As the latter deadline approaches the existence of a number of industry committees for the election of Representative John F. Kennedy to the Senate is being disclosed.

Mr. Kennedy reported spending $15,866 to defeat his opponent, Senator Henry Cabot Lodge Jr., who reported spending $11,000, both well within the $20,000 limit imposed by state law.

A Committee for Improvement of the Textile Industry spent $62,487 for Mr. Kennedy. A committee for Improvement of the Massachusetts Shoe Industry similarly spent $44,500. A Committee to Improve the Fishing Industry spent $45,587. A Build Massachusetts Committee spent $61,421 for Mr. Kennedy.

Contributions of $1,000 to each of these committees were attributed to the parents and to each of five brothers and sisters of the candidate. An Independents for Kennedy Committee spent between $3,000 and $4,000. John Ford, treasurer of the official Kennedy Committee, refused to disclose any expenditures before filing his report. Without this, known spending for the Senator-elect was $233,861.

Senator Lodge was aided by a Committee for the Elimination of Waste in Government, which spent $58,413.

The Republican State Committee acknowledged having spent about $750,000 on the campaign, and reported a deficit of $76,000. State Democratic officials pleaded they had "no idea" on expenses and said auditors were working to meet the Thursday deadline. Citizens for Eisenhower spent about $40,000. Stevenson Volunteers could make no estimate.

MICHIGAN

Reports filed by major party organizations indicate campaign spending might have hit the $2,000,000 mark in Michigan. The Republicans are known to have spent $1,256,835 and the Democrats $289,104. While these figures include some spending by Wayne County (Detroit) organizations, they do not include spending in the eighty-two other counties, nor a full accounting of the sale of $5 Stevenson certificates. The correspondent reported there was ample evidence that the amounts reported accounted for no more than a fraction of the totals actually spent.

The Republican State Committee spent $358,000, sent $69,550 to the national committee, $66,500 to the National Republican Congressional Committee and $17,000 to the National Senatorial Committee. It contributed $40,400 directly to Congressional candidates.

Wayne County Republicans collected $261,213 before the primary and $697,467 after, a total of $958,680. The contributor list reads like a Who's Who in industry and finance, with ninety individual contributions of $1,000 or more listed in a five-pound report. One item shows $37,500 spent on one Eisenhower rally.

The Wayne County Democratic organization reported spending $8,253. The Democratic State Committee spent $157,551 and has unpaid bills of $21,360. Volunteers for Stevenson spent $23,000 in Detroit. Senator Blair Moody and several committees working for him reported having raised $98,940. The Senator's personal report listed expenses of $37,224, while the Wayne County Committee for his campaign spent $36,224.

MINNESOTA

Minnesota's major political parties spent $415,000, based on incomplete returns and the estimates of party leaders.

Republican finance officials said $240,000 had been used in state, national and local races. Because of a smaller spending for the gubernatorial and United States Senatorial campaigns, this was less than in 1948.

The coalition of Democratic and Farmer-Labor parties spent about $175,000 on all races.

Neither side reported contributions to its national party, but the Republicans received $8,000 from their national headquarters for Congressional races.

MISSISSIPPI

W. G. Johnson Jr., chairman of Democrats for Eisenhower, said his organization's spending totaled $36,500. Gov. Hugh White, who headed the Democratic campaign organization, said expenditures for the Stevenson ticket were under $200,000.

MISSOURI

Republicans in Missouri spent at least $448,648 in the national campaign while the Democrats paid out a minimum of $292,274, it was indicated by the best figures currently available. Leaders of both parties said they could have spent much more if they could have collected it.

Actual expenditures of both parties may safely be presumed to have been considerably higher than those indicated above. It is generally agreed that campaign costs in Missouri were about the same as in previous elections. Democrats had a harder than usual time in getting funds from their usual sources, particularly in Kansas City. Indecisive leadership in one key Republican post resulted in much Eisenhower money going to the national rather than to the state group.

Party officials reported the Republican State Committee had spent around $250,000, the Democratic committee $78,124. Because of a thirty-day deadline, few reports have been filed. In St. Louis City and County Republican groups spent at least $141,048 and Democratic groups $164,450. In Jackson County (Kansas City) Republican spending was $99,000 and Democratic $60,000.

An aide to Senator-elect Stuart Symington said $4,000 had been spent in the election and $15,000 in the primary contest, for which friends had raised between $60,000 and $70,000. His opponent, Senator James P. Kem, Republican, spent about $16,000 on the November election aside from traveling costs, an aide said.

MONTANA

Finance chairmen for Montana political parties reported $45,622 had been spent in the recent campaign. Added to this is $256,501 spent by individual candidates from both parties, $14,598 by independent organizations, and $2,750 by twenty-two candidates for district judicial offices, a total of $273,849.

The only available breakdown of these funds revealed that the Republican State organization spent $37,014 and the Democrats $8,608.

NEBRASKA

Republicans in Nebraska outcollected their Democratic rivals five to one and outspent them by about three to one.

Reports filed with the Secretary of State revealed that a total of $135,226 had been spent. Of this, the Republicans spent $99,578 on national, state and local races and the Democrats $35,648.

Republicans also contributed $57,600 to the National Republican Finance Committee.

Democrats, on the other hand, received $7,324 from their national committee but, despite this, had a deficit of $10,000, now secured by a loan from a Lincoln bank. Two thousand dollars of it has since been repaid.

A One-Minute TV 'Spot' Costs More Than a Five

Special to THE NEW YORK TIMES.

SEATTLE, Wash., Nov. 30—The survey of campaign costs in Washington turned up an odd arrangement on television advertising rates under which it cost political parties more for a one-minute spot announcement than for a five-minute show.

Campaign officials, who said television advertising was among its biggest outlays, reported a rate of $135 for a twenty-second spot announcement and $170 for a one-minute "spot."

They said they had a special rate of $160 for a five-minute show.

NEVADA

Spending at the state level was about $50,000. The heaviest candidate spending was by Senator George W. Malone, Republican, whose campaign cost about $32,000. His defeated Democratic opponent, Thomas Melching, said he had spent $4,000. Representative-elect Cliff Young, Republican, also reported spending $4,000. The Republican State Committee collected $13,480. William J. Crowell, state Democratic chairman, said he had spent $700, Volunteers for Stevenson about $1,600.

NEW HAMPSHIRE

The Republican State Committee reported spending $51,000, of which $20,000 was sent to national party headquarters. The Democratic State Committee reported it spent $9,000. Two candidates for the House spent jointly $4,000. Aside from this the preferential primary in February is understood to have cost the Eisenhower forces $65,000 and the Taft forces $50,000. Spending was the highest ever reported.

The State Legislative Council is recommending to the new Legislature a $100,000 ceiling biennially for state political committees. The present ceiling is $25,000, but there are many categories of exemptions. The council also would require reports of spending in Presidential primaries.

NEW JERSEY

Reports and informed estimates of spending down to the local level indicate the New Jersey campaign cost about $1,500,000, but this figure is probably low.

The State Republican Committee had a fund of $594,000, from which it disbursed $210,000 to the national committee and $237,600 to counties, with $40,000 remaining for office expenses. At $100 a district, county spending by Republicans was $385,000, or $147,400 above the state committee allocation. Eisenhower clubs sent about $39,000 to the national organization, spent $9,000 on headquarters, and 150 local clubs raised and spent about $200 each.

The Democrat campaign was run by the National Democratic Club, which had about $150,000, but spent part of this on preliminary expenses only indirectly related to the campaign. The inactive State Democratic Committee spent about $3,000, an official reported, and at $75 a district, Democrats spent about $290,000 on the

local level. The A. F. L. spent $10,000 and the C. I. O., $67,000, to help the Democratic cause. Stevenson Volunteers raised $20,000.

Senator H. Alexander Smith, Republican, reported spending $23,000 aside from state and national committee help. His defeated opponent, Archibald S. Alexander, reported spending $23,310. Republican House candidates spent $57,610 and their Democratic opponents $11,455. County officer campaigns' costs were about $50,000.

NEW MEXICO

Official filings in New Mexico will be made next Thursday. Joseph B. Grant, Democratic state treasurer, estimated the state committee's outlay was about $100,000 and said there was a deficit of $4,500. Fred W. Moxey, State Republican chairman, said his committee's spending had been upward of $60,000 and that there was a balance on hand of $230. Neither party received any aid from their national committees.

NEW YORK

The nation's largest state continued to rank near the top when it came to political expenditures.

The two major parties, with only their state committees and major campaign committees reporting, listed expenditures totaling $1,799,171. Added to these were outlays of $39,696 by the Liberals, $60,327 by the American Labor party, $58,192 by the C. I. O., $6,300 by the state Communist party, and other smaller contributions by nonpartisan groups, bringing the total reported expenditures to $1,977,183.

These figures do not include expenditures by individual candidates for the state's forty-five Congressional and two Senatorial seats. Nor do they include those for the 206 seats in the Legislature and the scores of state judicial posts. These accounts, due Nov. 24, are still straggling in to local election boards. When totaled, they should reach another $1,000,000 or more.

The State Republican Committee and the United Republican Finance Committee listed total outlays of $875,613. Added to these were $64,882 by the Kings County Republicans, $95,105 by the New York County Republicans, and $25,351 by individual campaign committees. Together these totaled $1,061,251.

The Democratic State Committee and the Volunteers for Stevenson spent $648,601. In addition Bronx Democrats listed costs of $41,470 and the Queens Democrats of $34,719. These, plus the C. I. O. and individual groups, gave a total of $796,112.

Both major parties listed debts. The Republicans showed $50,000 owed to the Manufacturers Trust Company and the Democrats $16,345 owed to the Bronx Democrats.

Most of each party's expenditures, excluding normal costs for campaign workers and headquarters, were for television and radio time. The Republicans listed $227,290 to the firm of Batten, Barton, Durstine & Osborne plus $20,844 to other agencies. The Volunteers for Stevenson listed $122,457 for radio and television, and $16,494 in similar expenses by the state committee.

NORTH CAROLINA

In the costliest election in North Carolina's history, the Democratic State Executive Committee reported it had spent $100,062, while the State Republican Committee reported spending $32,005. The State Citizens for Eisenhower set its expenditures officially at $17,341.

Informed estimates of spending at the local level indicated the Democrats had spent $30,000, the Republicans $30,000 and the Citizens for Eisenhower $25,000. These are regarded as conservative. The League of Women Voters estimated it had spent $3,500 to get out the vote and that the value of donated radio and television time had been many times that amount.

NORTH DAKOTA

Campaign spending in traditionally Republican North Dakota amounted to about $52,500, with Republicans spending $36,000 and the Democrats $16,500. In addition, Republicans sent $27,216 to their national committee. Practically nothing was spent in the Senatorial race because Senator William Langer was looked on with favor by the Democrats, who gave little support to their own candidate. The figures above, estimated by party officials, are regarded by them as liberal.

OHIO

Expense accounts filed with the Secretary of State showed about $2,691,598 spent by both parties and other organizations in the Ohio campaign. Except for $967,189 given to Republican County organizations and $175,000 sent to the Republican National Committee, this spending was at the state level and the total figure does not purport to include what was spent locally.

Expense accounts for candidates and committees on the local level are filed with the eighty-eight county election boards and were not obtainable for the survey. In one county Franklin (Columbus) Republican spending was estimated at $50,000, including $16,362 raised locally.

In compiling the state totals, the correspondent made every effort to eliminate duplications, but some probably remain.

The State Republican Finance Committee received $2,031,494 and has a balance of $10,105. It used $120,000 for its operating expenses. Among disbursements was $657,400 to the State Executive Committee for the state campaign.

Three Democratic state organizations reported expenses of $48,831, including a $773 deficit. Labor and independent political groups reported total spending of $165,083.

OKLAHOMA

The Republican State Committee spent $123,325 on its own, sent $68,527 to the national committee and gave county organizations $54,825, a total of $246,677. Citizens for Eisenhower spent $35,000 more. The Democratic State Committee spent $98,776 and sent $55,629 to the national committee, a total of $154,405. Citizens for Stevenson spent $11,863.

County organizations raised funds spent primarily in support of county tickets and there is no estimate available on which this would add to the total.

The campaign costs were regard-

ed as light in comparison with what is usually spent for a statewide Democratic primary. The bulk of spending went for radio and television time.

OREGON

Oregon campaign costs, excluding all county and city races except those for mayor and city councilmen in Portland, exceeded $1,000,000.

Statements filed with the State Election Bureau revealed that the Republicans had spent $221,728 for General Eisenhower and $35,686 for state candidates. The Democrats spent $23,988 for Governor Stevenson and $32,070 for state candidates.

Nonpartisan campaigns, principally in Portland, cost $56,690, and $637,669 was spent supporting or opposing measures on the ballot. Independent groups for either candidate accounted for the remainder.

PENNSYLVANIA

Pennsylvania is near the top of the list in campaign spending. The filing deadline is next Thursday. A State Election Bureau official estimated 1952 reports would show spending of $4,000,000. He based this on the wider use of television and cost increases since 1948, when $3,000,000 was spent.

Republican spending of $2,334,023 and $428,270 by the Democrats at the state level is known. This includes some local spending from state Republican contributions and Democratic spending in Philadelphia. In Pittsburgh and Harrisburg neither political parties nor independent groups were willing to give even rough estimates and the same resistance was encountered from the Republican Central Campaign Committee in Philadelphia.

Frank C. P. McGlinn, executive secretary of the Republican State Finance Committee, said "roughly" $2,000,000 had been spent in the state by Republicans exclusive of national radio and television programs paid for by the national committee or others.

Major expenditures listed by Mr. McGlinn included $315,389 to the Central Campaign Committee of Philadelphia, $93,987 to the Southeastern Pennsylvania Citizens for Eisenhower, $130,000 to the Republican State Committee; $10,000 to the National Citizens for Eisenhower, $22,000 to the Pennsylvania Citizens for Eisenhower, $47,000 for Congressional campaigns, $420,000 to the National Congressional and Senatorial Committees and $100,000 for administration. He said the State Committee had spent about $250,000 more and that the various Eisenhower committees also had spent beyond the contributions he listed.

Joseph McLaughlin, publicity director for the Philadelphia Democratic City Committee, estimated that the committee spent $305,000, including $141,700 for precinct workers at $100 a precinct. He thought the State Committee itself had spent little, possibly no more than $30,000. Labor helped the Democrats out at least to the extent of $93,270.

RHODE ISLAND

The only major campaign cost figure comes from Frank Rao, Democratic state chairman, who said his office had disbursed funds between $90,000 and $125,000. He

declined to estimate what had been spent locally, but observers in Providence said the major Democratic spending had been handled through the state fund and that the higher figure cited by the state chairman would nearly cover Democratic costs.

No Republican figures were available because of the absence from the state of Charles H. Eden, state chairman. Newspaper advertising indicated the Republicans outspending the Democrats two-to-one. Mr. Rao estimated that the Republicans had spent twice as much as his party, but impartial observers believed the spread between the parties was not great. Citizens committees for various candidates spent substantial sums, but their disbursements are not available.

SOUTH CAROLINA

Expense reports are required only from candidates in South Carolina. Best estimates are that at least $200,000 was spent by the major parties. A Democratic official said the party had spent $24,500. South Carolinians for Eisenhower released a report showing $65,770 had been spent. One item was $1,000 for a platform for an Eisenhower rally at Columbia. Another was $50 for a bad check. A study by a University of South Carolina faculty member indicates Republican spending totaled $203,000 and Democratic $38,200.

SOUTH DAKOTA

The Republican State Committee raised $89,713 and spent $76,927, W. R. Wilder, treasurer, reported. Bills of $500 to $1,000 are outstanding. It gave the national committee $20,990 and spent $20,297 on radio, television and newspaper advertising. Ford dealers sent an estimated $2,500 to the national Eisenhower fund and an organization of professional men for Eisenhower spent small amounts locally. Filing of reports is required by Thursday. Democratic books are in the hands of Ward Clark, state chairman who was out of the state last week.

TENNESSEE

Unofficial estimates put campaign costs at $1,000,000, but official statements due Thursday probably will show spending of around $100,000. Tennessee's filing law is vague. Technically first reports are due from candidates and their managers five days before election and final reports thirty days after the election. Few candidates and no managers filed preliminary reports.

Final reports filed by Senator-elect Albert Gore, Democrat, and Representative Howard Baker, Republican, show they spent $2,803 and $4,444, respectively. A later report by the Democratic state chairman, Buford Ellington, showing $7,188 expenses for three candidates, listed $3,080 as having been given to Mr. Gore, a discrepancy Democratic headquarters did not explain. An accountant preparing a Democratic State Committee report estimated earlier that the committee's spending would be $20,000. No estimate of spending by Volunteers for Stevenson was available.

Guy L. Smith, State Republican chairman, said "I don't know how much we spent and could not give

an estimate now. It was only a nominal amount."

Citizens for Eisenhower raised $1,600 at the state level. No figure was available on amounts raised by local units.

TEXAS

Reliable sources indicated that about $1,000,000 had been spent to carry Texas for General Eisenhower, most of it furnished by Democrats following the lead of Gov. Allan Shivers. The Democratic State Committee was practically idle for the campaign, with the Stevenson-Sparkman organization, run by Speaker Sam Rayburn, campaigning for the Democratic national ticket.

A person high in the Democrats-for-Eisenhower movement said $250,000 had been spent through the state headquarters, but this did not include what had been spent by units in most of the 254 counties. The State Republican Committee disbursed about $500,000, including $263,616 sent to the national committee. In addition a lot of money is reported to have been sent directly by wealthy individuals to the national committees of both parties.

James Sewell, campaign manager of the State Stevenson-Sparkman Club, said the final audit would show that about $110,000 had been spent, and that at least that much more had been expended on the local units.

UTAH

Campaign costs officially entered Nov. 8 with the Secretary of State showed outlays of $80,466. Privately, Democratic officials estimate their campaign cost $100,000 at all levels. Similar Republican estimates put the party's spending at $150,000. Only two things can be said with certainty about the campaign. It was the most costly in the state's history and the Democrats are in the red. State committees are limited to spending $34,383, or 12½ cents per voter. The official report showed the Democratic outlay at $30,772, the Republican $26,069.

VERMONT

With Vermont's three electoral votes conceded to the Republicans in advance, the main election spending was for state candidates. Negligible amounts were spent on the national races. A Citizens for Eisenhower Committee was the only independent organization in the campaign. It raised and spent $2,197. The Republican State Committee raised $26,000 for the national committee and $9,552 to re-elect Gov. Lee E. Emerson. Democratic sources raised $2,500 for the national committee and the state organization spent $3,000 for Governor Emerson's opponent, Robert W. Larrow.

VIRGINIA

Republicans and Democrats for Eisenhower spent $6 for every dollar spent for Democratic candidates. At least $160,628 was raised and spent for the Eisenhower-Nixon slate, while outlays for Democratic candidates are known to have been $52,100. Congressional contests, not broken down by parties, cost about $21,018. Three Republican House candidates were elected, the first in twenty years, and General Eisenhower carried the state by 80,000.

Democrats reported they had a

difficult time raising funds and could have made a better showing with more money. Eisenhower groups conceded their liberal support came from persons usually contributing to the Democratic cause.

A leader of the Democrats for Eisenhower said $80,000 had been raised by the organization. The State Republican Committee raised $66,000 and sent about half to the national committee. The Democratic State Committee reported its spending between $20,000 and $21,000. In Richmond, Democrats for Eisenhower spent $20,000, a leader of the group said.

WASHINGTON

Washington had its first million-dollar election. The looseness of the state's filing law makes reports largely meaningless and there is no penalty for failure to file. Top Democrats estimated their costs at $450,000 and $150,-000 more was spent on the September primary. A competent estimate of Republican spending put the party's bill at about $528,000, but no figure for the primary was available.

Democrats put Republican spending nearer to $900,000 and the Republicans asserted their opponents had spent about $600,000.

Republicans gave the national committee $83,000 and the Democrats sent $8,000 to $10,000 to their national committee. Each party spent something more than $400,000 for individual candidate races.

WEST VIRGINIA

An incomplete tabulation shows campaign spending in West Virginia of $248,494. A Democratic State Committee report listed $55,-285 in contributions and expenses of $26,212. The committee for Senator Harley M. Kilgore, Democrat, spent $24,381.

The Republican State Committee has not filed its after-election report. It is known to have sent $25,000 to the national committee. Pre-election statements show the Republican State Executive Com-

mittee through Oct. 21 had received $78,600 and spent $78,349. The Republican Finance Committee reported receipts through Oct. 23 at $98,935 and expenses of $87,-597. Citizens for Eisenhower received $6,665 and spent $3,370 through Oct. 31, while the committee for Chapman Revercomb, Republican candidate for the Senate, raised $9,175 and spent $3,585 through Oct. 21.

WISCONSIN

Known campaign spending in Wisconsin by political parties at the state and local level and by candidates totaled $916,696. This was exclusive of $206,029 spent by the Republicans in the primary campaign and $9,165 by the Democrats.

The state Republican organization reported expenditures of $577,-437 and receipts of $465,914. Democratic state spending amounted to $53,946. Spending by various Republican candidates, their committees and by independent groups brought Republican spending to at least $792,919. Similarly, the Democratic total was $122,060. Minor parties spent $1,717.

The McCarthy Club for the re-election of Senator Joseph R. McCarthy, Republican, reported receipts of $60,546 and spending of $34,489. The Senator personally collected $24,087 and spent $18,869, his report shows. Farmers for McCarthy spent $1,875.

WYOMING

Incomplete reports indicate Republican spending amounted to $26,834 and that the Democrats spent $16,439. A preliminary report of the organization for the re-election of Senator Joseph C. O'Mahoney, Democrat, listed among its receipts $1,000 from the C. I. O., $500 from Averell Harriman of New York and $500 from a New York group called the National Committee for an Effective Congress. The Wyoming Lincoln League, supporting the Republican ticket, spent $14,750.

FULL DETAIL URGED ON ELECTION FUNDS

Representative Brown Would End All Limits on Costs, Substituting Disclosure

By CLAYTON KNOWLES
Special to THE NEW YORK TIMES.

WASHINGTON, Dec. 1—Representative Clarence J. Brown of Ohio, prominent both in the Republican party and in Congress, recommended today the scrapping of all limitations on spending in a national political campaign and the substituting of a system of full disclosure of all expenditures.

The present $3,000,000 limitation imposed on each of the national political committees, he asserted, "just doesn't mean anything at all and we might as well be honest and frank with the American people and, as the Congress, say so."

The first witness in the House of Representatives investigation of spending in the 1952 campaign, Mr. Brown expressed confidence that full disclosure would be enough to keep expenditures within bounds.

This view was challenged directly by another witness, Herman D. Smith of Lake Forest, Ill., who headed Volunteers for Stevenson, which supported the Presidential candidacy of Gov. Adlai E. Stevenson of Illinois. Mr. Smith urged a more liberal but all-embracing limitation be set for Presidential campaigns.

Asked for his estimate of what political spending in the recent national campaign had been, Representative Brown, a member of the Republican National Committee, said:

"It will be a wild guess, but I would hate to have to pay out of my own pocket all that was spent over $80,000,000 or $100,000,000 in the last campaign."

Calls Laws Unrealistic

He said that during the course of the campaign he had made a rough count of the number of auxiliary committees that were helping to foot the radio-television bills of the two national committees and "got up to twenty or thirty of these organizations." Each would be entitled to raise and spend $3,000,000 if it operated in two or more states.

Mr. Brown told the special investigating committee, headed by Representative Hale Boggs, Democrat of Louisiana, that both the Federal and state laws were unrealistic, too, in the limitations they imposed on spending in Senatorial and Congressional campaigns. Under Federal law, the

maximum permissible in a Senatorial campaign is $25,000, while no more than $5,000 can be spent in a House race. Limitations by many states are even tighter.

In addition to revising Federal law on this score, the Ohio Representative suggested that the committee, which will seek to draft an improved election law, look into the idea of having Congress require the reporting of funds in primary election and pre-convention campaigns involving Federal offices.

Mr. Brown was somewhat skeptical whether selection of Presidential nominees in a national primary would reduce spending. He also expressed doubt about the practicality of imposing a limitation on the duration of political campaigns.

An 'Amateur's' View

In challenging Mr. Brown's recommendation for the lifting of all limitations on spending in Presidential campaigns, Mr. Smith said he did not think the publicity given to full disclosure of expenditures would be sufficient "as a deterrent" to big spending. He conceded, however, that he was a political novice, declaring that nothing in the outcome of the election had "changed my amateur status."

He recommended that, in addition to a strict limitation on over-all spending in a national campaign, a further specific limitation should be placed on the amount that could be spent for radio and television time.

Of the $740,000 spent by Volunteers for Stevenson in the recent campaign, $421,000 went for radio-TV time.

Mr. Smith's views were strongly supported by John P. Brown, a Washington attorney who served as counsel to the Volunteers for Stevenson. Both agreed that a Presidential candidate, confronted with a realistic limit on over-all spending, should have authority to say what organizations should work for him during the campaign.

Asked where the over-all limitation should be placed, Mr. Smith confessed that the best he could suggest would be "determining the amount spent in this campaign, taking 25 per cent of it and there is your figure."

He said that he had no idea how much had been spent, except that it had been too much, and referred the committee to a survey made by THE NEW YORK TIMES, which fixed $32,155,251 as a minimum figure. The survey was published today.

Mr. Smith suggested also that the duration of the campaign might be properly curtailed and that a limit might be put even on such spending as is involved in newspaper advertising.

Much of the opening day's testimony was interspersed with laughs as the witnesses, while making serious recommendations, tackled the subject in good humor. Attorney General James P. McGranery and Arthur E. Summerfield, Republican National Chairman, will be among tomorrow's witnesses.

ELECTION 'PROBLEM' CITED BY MITCHELL

Need of a 'Fair Presentation' of Both Sides to People Stressed by Chairman

WASHINGTON, Dec. 4 (AP)—The chairman of the Democratic National Committee told election law investigators today that the key to their problem was "a fair presentation of the opposite sides to the people."

Stephen A. Mitchell, who became committee chairman when Gov. Adlai E. Stevenson of Illinois, won the Democratic Presidential nomination, said that "you do have a problem" when "the money and the press are on one side."

Mr. Mitchell told a special House of Representatives investigating committee that such a situation had existed in the 1952 national campaign.

Mr. Mitchell added that the Republicans had three dollars to spend for every dollar the Democrats had. He also said many newspapers had given much more space to Gen. Dwight D. Eisenhower than they had to Governor Stevenson.

"When the money and the press are on one side you do have a problem," he said. "So long as you can get a fair presentation of the opposite sides to the people you don't have too much of a problem."

Mr. Mitchell estimated the Republicans had spent "well over twice as much" as the Democrats on radio and television. He said the Democratic National Committee had spent about $400,000 on those media, while other committees supporting the Democratic ticket had spent an estimated $1,200,000.

Calls Limitation Too Small

Mr. Mitchell said there ought to be some way to prevent people of large financial means from controlling a nomination or an election. While asserting that observation was not directed at the 1952 campaign, he added "that has happened."

Discussing present election laws, he said the $3,000,000 limitation on expenditures by a political committee in any one year was too small, and the limits of $25,000 and $5,000 for Senatorial and House candidates, respectively, "are simply ridiculous."

In this year's campaign, he said, the Democratic National Committee received $5,000-contributions from only forty-eight of the 126,-000 contributors. About ninety-five out of every 100 contributions, he added, were for less than $500.

From the Federal Communications Commission, the committee received a request that Congress expressly exempt broadcasting stations from libel suits over political speeches that they were not allowed to censor or reject.

Walker Explains His Stand

Paul A. Walker, F. C. C. chairman, declared the effect of the present law was to make radio and TV liable for actions over which they had no control.

Existing law, he said, prohibits the stations from censoring speeches made by political candidates if an opposing candidate has already spoken over the same facility, but it does not relieve the station from liability for libelous remarks. Furthermore, the law requires a station to give equal broadcasting opportunities to all candidates.

A station may exclude all candidates if it wants to but once it has permitted one candidate to speak it may not turn down the others or censor their speeches.

Hale Boggs, Democrat of Louisiana, and committee chairman, asked whether a radio station would be required to permit "a crackpot or an insane person" to make an uncensored speech if he was a qualified candidate and an opponent had used the same facilities.

Mr. Walker's answer was yes, with the observation that state laws should not permit such a person to qualify as a candidate.

Mr. Walker said he felt the record of the broadcasting industry in this year's political campaign was "on the whole one of which we can be proud."

Senate Chiefs Ask Reform In Election Law This Year

Johnson Receives Knowland's Support for Campaign Spending and Gift Curbs —Primaries Would Be Exempt

By RUSSELL BAKER
Special to The New York Times.

WASHINGTON, Feb. 24—The Senate leaders of both parties came out today for limited reform of the election laws before the 1956 campaign.

Lyndon B. Johnson of Texas, the Democratic leader, said that "realistic" bipartisanship could guarantee early passage of a bill that would put all campaign contributions "in a goldfish bowl" for public scrutiny.

William F. Knowland of California, the Republican leader, endorsed Senator Johnson's proposal in principle and agreed that some reform should be enacted before the 1956 elections.

The two men represent a powerful coalition of Senate forces that would normally assure passage of any measure. Their decision to combine strength on this issue stems from the furor over lobbying and campaign contributions connected with passage of the natural gas bill.

Mr. Johnson had three proposals for tightening up existing law. They were:

1. To encourage more small contributions by allowing tax deduction on gifts up to $100 a person.

2. To permit television and radio networks to give free and equal time to major parties, without being bound to accommodate fringe parties in the same way.

3. To require "stringent reporting" of all contributions to a general-election campaign and to impose "realistic limits" on campaign spending.

In vetoing the gas bill President Eisenhower complained of "arrogant" lobbying practices by some of its backers. Behind this complaint was the gas lobby's use of campaign contributions.

Senator Johnson's proposal would not cover primary campaigns. In about twenty states either the Democratic or Republican party is overwhelmingly dominant. Most political spending in these states is for primary elections where victory is tantamount to election.

Thus, under his proposal most of the Democratic South and the predominantly Republican New England and Midwest would not be covered in so far as the heaviest political spending is concerned.

The important goal, Senator Johnson said, is to get "a good strong election bill that can give us honest elections" and to get it this year.

Senator Knowland agreed that the present law needed changing before the Presidential election.

Details Not Worked Out

Mr. Johnson had only a general outline of his proposal today. None of the details have been worked out. There is still, for example, no informed guess as to what "realistic limits" for spending in each state might be.

It is understood, however, that these limits would probably be based on the size of each state's electorate.

The leaders' sudden proposal to write a new law came just one day after a select eight-man Senate committee had been named to investigate the whole broad field of campaign spending and lobbying pressure.

The special committee is not required to report until after the next election. Mr. Johnson said that his proposal was not designed to cut the ground out from under the select committee. The need, he said, is for action before the election.

Other Senators who strongly endorse the special investigation agreed that the Johnson plan for early action on electoral reform was sound because it represented an attempt to "strike while the iron is hot."

Some degree of reform this year when the issue is ripe would be preferable to waiting for wider changes next year when all might fail because of public apathy, one influential Democrat argued.

Mr. Johnson's choice of a limited reform bill ignored a comprehensive measure worked out last year by Senator Thomas C. Hennings, Democrat of Missouri, who is chairman of the Elections Subcommittee.

The most important difference between the Hennings bill and the Johnson proposal is that the former would cover primaries while the latter would not.

A sampling of liberal Democratic opinion indicated that this wing of the party would favor the more comprehensive law. The idea of covering state primaries with Federal law impinges on the always inflammatory issue of state's rights. Thus it could expect to arouse bitter opposition from southern Democrats and Old Guard Republicans.

Floor Fight in Prospect

Supporters of the Hennings bill, nevertheless, are talking of making a floor fight for primary coverage. It is understood that Mr. Hennings is also prepared to take a strong stand in that regard.

Organization of the select investigating committee will probably not begin until next Tuesday or Wednesday. Senator Albert Gore, Democrat of Tennessee, is the probable choice for chairman. But he is maintaining a discreet silence about his plans in the absence of a formal grant of authority.

Senator Barry Goldwater, Republican of Arizona, who is a member of the committee, explained why he had resigned as chairman of the Republican Senatorial Campaign Committee.

He said that his campaign activities "would be incompatible" with membership on the select committee.

A long-time critic of labor union political activities, Mr. Goldwater said that he was disturbed by "the pressure tactics of certain people who claim to represent large groups of voters and, thereby, make their demands felt" in Congress.

"The clear light of investigation," he said, "could now be thrown on Americans for Democratic Action, the Committee for an Effective Congress and the labor unions, as well as the National Association of Manufacturers and the oil lobbies."

On the Democratic side Mr. Gore, and Senator John F. Kennedy of Massachusetts, resigned from that party's Senatorial Campaign Committee because of their membership on the investigating committee.

ELECTION BUDGET OF G.O.P. $7,000,000

The Republican National Committee will spend $7,000,000 on its 1956 political campaign, its chairman, Leonard W. Hall, said yesterday.

Mr. Hall, who will be a delegate-at-large from New York to the Republican National Convention opening Aug. 20 in San Francisco, spoke at an organization meeting of the Queens County Republican executive committee at the Oakland Country Club in Bayside, Queens.

The $7,000,000 called for by the budget will include $2,200,000 for television time for which he already has contracted, Mr. Hall said.

The national chairman also announced that he had certified 4,314 correspondents, representing newspapers, magazines, television and radio, to cover the convention. This, he said, was the largest group of its kind ever to ask to attend such a convention.

The correspondents will require 936 desks around the podium in San Francisco's Cow Palace, he said. The auditorium has a capacity of 15,000. After the correspondents and delegates are provided for, Mr. Hall said he would have only 4,000 tickets left for general distribution. He said he had ten men working on pre-convention arrangements in San Francisco.

Mr. Hall called himself a firm believer in the effectiveness of television for campaigning.

"On television you can get practically the same impact as from a personal appearance," he added.

He cited the influence on the public of speeches broadcast over closed-circuit television from scores of "Salute to Eisenhower" dinners across the country last winter on the third anniversary of the President's inauguration.

These dinners, most of them $100-a-plate affairs, netted about $5,000,000. Half the profit went to local organizations, the other half to the national committee and separate committees to elect Republicans to the House and Senate.

Mr. Hall appealed for a gain in Republican representation in Congress. He predicted that organizational work being done in the South would increase the number of Republicans sent to Congress from that section.

Stressing the importance of gaining Congressional strength, he asserted that the Democratic Congress had not given the President the help it promised to him in 1954.

Mr. Hall said there was no doubt in his mind "that our ticket is going to be Eisenhower and Nixon, and that we are going to give them a better vote than we did four years ago."

"This is going to be one of the toughest campaigns we have ever had," he added, "and I believe you should look at it that way."

Topics

Democracy's Unsolved Problem

Once every four years at this time of year we begin to concern ourselves with what has been called the great unsolved problem of democracy: campaign financing. And each quadrennial concentration on the problem finds it more severe, since the demand for political funds, like so much else in our country, continues to grow at an astounding pace. A half-hour nationwide television hook-up for a political talk can cost $100,000—more than Lincoln spent in his entire campaign 100 years ago. The first million-dollar campaign, on behalf of James A. Garfield in 1880, was regarded as staggering, and when Mark Hanna raised $3,500,000 to help put William McKinley in the White House in 1896, the absolute peak was thought to have been reached. In 1922 the Senate condemned the expenditure of $195,000 in a Senatorial campaign as "dangerous to the perpetuity of free government," yet today it is common for a Senator's campaign to cost more than his total salary of $135,000 for a six-year term of office, and the late Robert A. Taft placed the cost of his 1950 campaign at $513,000.

A Miserable Failure

An inquiry into campaign spending in the 1956 Presidential and Congressional races was conducted by a Senate subcommittee. Its report accounted for expenditures of $33,100,000—$20,700,000 for Republican candidates, $11,900,000 for the Democrats and about half a million for minor-party hopefuls. The subcommittee added, though, that actual expenditures could not even be estimated, and some political scientists put the sum at close to $200,000,000, compared to an estimated $140,000,000 in 1952. The laws designed to control campaign spending, in the unanimous voice of the Senate subcommittee, "fail miserably to do so." It lamented the "unhealthy state of political affairs" in which Republican candidates were supported by so-called big business while the contributions of organized labor went almost entirely to Democrats. It has been estimated that 90 per cent of the money raised in Federal election campaigns is contributed by less than 1 per cent of the population.

Closed-Circuit Television

In the face of all this we welcome one new instrument that could provide mass participation in political fund-raising: closed-circuit television. The Democrats made a closed-circuit splurge during the second-term Presidential campaign of Franklin D. Roosevelt at the $100-a plate level of the Jackson Day dinners. On two occasions more recently the Republicans have used closed-circuit TV in a way that suggests wider application in the future. A "Salute to Eisenhower" in 1956 linked 63,000 Republicans gathered at fifty-six dinners across the country, netting $5,000,000 in one night. This sum was topped a few weeks ago when more than 100,000 Republican diners in eighty-three cities joined in a national "Dinner With Ike."

Cross-Country Network

It is no mere fantasy to picture these cities linked by closed circuit in vast fund-raising rallies of the future attended by hundreds of thousands of ordinary voters, each contributing a nominal sum to party coffers. By this dramatic means of mass participation party reliance on big business or big unions for funds could conceivably be eliminated, while a truly democratic sense of taking part would be spread across the country. There is little doubt about the need for large funds in these days of an expanding electorate and increasingly expensive media of mass communication. In the last Presidential election more than 63,000,000 Americans went to the polls, and just to reach them by a single 2-cent mail communication today would cost more than $1,250,000. "Politics," as Will Rogers used to say, "has got so expensive that it takes a lot of money even to get beat with." Maybe the little black box now in the living room can be the answer to democracy's unsolved problem.

TV FINALES' COST
PUT AT $500,000

Nixon's Outlay Is Estimated About Double Kennedy's —Coverage Is Wide

Hurried all-out television efforts marked the last day of the 1960 Presidential campaign yesterday and last night, with unofficial estimates that the Republicans had spent $350,000 to $400,000 and the Democrats $200,000.

A four-hour telethon by Vice President Nixon, in which the Republican Presidential candidate answered telephoned questions over an American Broadcasting Company network of 157 stations from 2 P. M. to 6 P. M., was reported to have cost about $200,000.

A rebuttal by Senator John F. Kennedy, the Democratic Presidential nominee, on 148 stations of the same network from 6 P. M. to 6:30 P. M. was estimated in television quarters to have cost about $50,000.

A rebuttal to Senator Kennedy by Thomas E. Dewey, 1944 and 1948 Republican Presidential candidate, then followed on eighty stations of the A. B. C. network from 6:30 P. M. to 6:45 P. M. This was estimated to have cost a total of $35,000 to $40,000—time being more expensive in quarter-hour segments than in the half-hour or longer periods, for which discounts are provided.

Nixon Spending Estimated

Both sides then had other telecasts during the night, some of it only booked late yesterday.

Pierre Salinger, Senator Kennedy's press secretary, asserted the Republicans were spending $600,000 for their day's television efforts. He said this was an estimate by Guild, Bascom & Bonfigli, a San Francisco advertising agency.

"This is the largest expenditure for television or radio time on the day before election in history," Mr. Salinger said. "We are demanding to know from the Vice President sometime during his telecast what is the origin of these funds and what commitments were made to get them."

Mr. Salinger said the Kennedy camp had sent appeals to Democratic state chairmen in twenty-five states asking them to chip in for the A. B. C. rebuttal and two fifteen-minute spots on the National Broadcasting Company and Columbia Broadcasting System networks. Basic time costs, he said, might be $125,000, beyond which would be production costs required for canceled programs.

In Washington, Leonard W. Hall, Mr. Nixon's campaign manager, said the television time for the Vice President's telethon cost $164,000 for the four hours. He noted there would be additional expenses for telephone charges and preempted programs, but the time cost was "considerably less than prime evening time."

Telethon Sponsors Listed

Mr. Hall said the telethon was sponsored by five groups—the Republican Committee, the Independent Television Committee for Nixon-Lodge, the Volunteers for Nixon and Lodge, the National Republican Senatorial Committee and the National Republican Congressional Committee.

L. Richard Guylay, public relations director for the Republican National Committee, said the Independent Television Committee had been set up because the law limits the national committee's spending for radio and television programs to $3,000,000. Both parties, Mr. Guylay said, set up independent committees because they expected to spend more than $7,000,000 each on such programs.

Mr. Guylay said evening television time costs anywhere from $80,000 to $125,000 a half hour.

The Kennedy rebuttal was sponsored by Citizens for Kennedy and Johnson, and the Dewey sur-rebuttal by the Republican Senatorial Committee.

President in Appeal

President Eisenhower, Vice President Nixon and Henry Cabot Lodge, Republican Vice President candidate, appeared on the C. B. S. network from 10:30 to 11 P. M. at a cost esimated at $50,000 to $70,000. They also appeared from 11 P. M. to 11:30 P. M. on the N. B. C. and A. B. C. networks at costs guessed a perhaps $40,000 to $45,000 each.

Senator Kennedy had last-minute bookings on the C.B.S. network from 6:30 P. M. to 6:45 P. M. and 7 P. M. to 7:15 P. M., as well as WCBS, in New York in between, for a cost of perhaps $60,000. He also appeared on the N.B.C. network from 7 P. M. to 7:15 P. M. at a cost that might have exceeded $35,000.

Senator Kennedy also took part in a half-day CBS network telecast with his Vice Presidential nominee, Senator Lyndon B. Johnson, from 11 P. M. to 11:30 P. M. that may have cost $50,000 to $70,000.

Response for Both Sides

WASHINGTON, Nov. 7 (UPI) —The Republican National Committee said tonight it was getting "loads" of money orders as a result of the plea for funds made during Mr. Nixon's telethon.

On the other side, Henry M. Jackson, Democratic National Chairman, said in a statement that financial contributions "by the hundreds" have been pouring into Democratic headquarters as a result of the Nixon telethon.

Money and Methods
Dominating Pennsylvania
Race for Governor

By BEN A. FRANKLIN
Special to The New York Times

PITTSBURGH, Sept. 10—One of the toughest and perhaps costliest governorship campaigns in the country is taking shape in Pennsylvania under unorthodox ground rules forced on both parties by a candidate who is the choice of professionals of neither.

Milton J. Shapp, a millionaire, has used sophisticated polling, demographic research, data processing, wholesale advertising and money on a scale never seen in Pennsylvania before.

Mr. Shapp is the antiorganization nominee who won the Democratic primary in an upset last May.

His methods and money, rather than his or the Republicans' program, may turn out to be the big issue in Pennsylvania. And, according to Mr. Shapp's advisers, that is not necessarily to his disadvantage As a self-made millionaire, Mr. Shapp frequently points out that he is "beholden to no powerful vested interests."

Better Known Than Rival

The 53-year-old electronics manufacturer is already slightly better known in Pennsylvania, according to an independent poll published this week, than is his Republican opponent, Lieut. Gov. Raymond P. Shafer, 48. Mr. Shafer has been in public life for years. Mr. Shapp was almost unknown until this year.

Across the state this week and at a Republican meeting in Pittsburgh today, evidence of the uncertainty injected by the Shapp campaign loomed larger than what normally passes as "the issues."

The Republicans were here today to approve the strategy and platform in Mr. Shafer's campaign to succeed Gov. William W. Scranton. The platform is regarded as unusually liberal for a Republican campaign document in Pennsylvania. It includes an unqualified pledge of state legislation forbidding disdeployment of hecklers and the crimination in the sale or rental of all private housing, a call for state aid to cities, "the abolition of ghetto neighborhoods," and major pledges to organized education and labor, including unequivocal opposition to a right-to-work law.

But its publication has been overshadowed in news reports by Republican distraction — Shapp forces label it "desperation" — over Mr. Shapp.

Personal Battle Feared

Governor Scranton is known to believe that the Republican reaction to Mr. Shapp's hard-driving and unorthodox campaign may tend to submerge profitable G.O.P. exploitation of the four-year Scranton record in Harrisburg and thus set the stage for a bruising battle of "personalities."

For reasons both of personal taste and party strategy, some top Republicans said they deplored the prospect of that kind of battle with Mr. Shapp, the first Jew to run for Governor in Pennsylvania.

However, at the first big Republican rally of the campaign Thursday night, televised on a paid statewide network from the Syria Mosque here, Governor Scranton, Mr. Shafer and Senator Hugh Scott, Republican of Pennsylvania, all attacked Mr. Shapp with a gusto that seemed to betray few regrets.

Senator Scott, who is noted as an outspokenly tough campaigner, said that all Republicans were, "against the merger of Milton Shapp's money and Pennsylvania's future."

Mr. Scranton joined in by saying that "Ray Shafer doesn't believe in buying elections."

Mr. Shafer himself gave his most pointed delivery, in a speech impaired by the unscheduled expenditure of his television time by others, to what already appears to be the major theme of the Republican campaign — the cry that "the governorship of Pennsylvania is not for sale!"

Shafer campaign buttons bearing a photograph of the state house with a "not for sale sign on it were being distributed here at the Republican State Committee meeting in the Pittsburgh Hilton Hotel.

Scores Rival's 'Obsession'

In his television address, Mr. Shafer said "there is not enough money in the whole world to trick Pennsylvanians into four years of paying so dearly for one man's obsession with personal power and wild-eyed schemes that have hidden price tags."

He described as "the common enemy of all Pennsylvanians" Mr. Shapp's "voice of gloom broadcasting in a bustling Pennsylvania." This was a reference to Mr. Shapp's extrordinary use of radio and television time, apparently unmatched in any Pennsylvania campaign.

The "common enemy," Mr. Shafer continued, also included Mr. Shapp's "collection of half-baked schemes that guarantee only one thing, and that is to bankrupt Pennsylvania and tax her people to the wall."

And, he continued, the "common enemy" also was "the hidden camera and microphone, hard at work this very hour, grinding out rigged television commercials that twist the truth."

By that, Mr. Shafer made clear he meant the motion picture film crew that Mr. Shapp's Philadelphia strategists have assigned to photograph the Republican candidate while he is campaigning. Republicans charge that the Shapp camera crew "passed itself off as from the Canadian Broadcasting Company," while "trying to photograph our candidate picking his nose, or something."

There was also an angry charge that the Shapp forces had planted hecklers in Mr. Shafer's audiences with the hope of filming him in public distress.

Mr. Shapp's aides denied the deployment of hecklers and the alleged Canadian or other false identification of the film crew. But the existence of the film crew and its assignment to Mr. Shafer were acknowledged and defended as entirely proper.

While there remains the possibility that Democratic regulars may "cut" Mr. Shapp in the wards and precincts, several Democratic professionals admitted in interviews this week that their uneasy feeling of contempt for the unconventional candidate may have been hasty.

Mr. Shapp is spending freely from his own fortune — estimated at from $8-million to $15-million. It helps to create the image of a "winner" that he badly needs in his own party.

He reported spending $1.4-million on the primary campaign, alone. The figure was not regarded as notably out of bounds for an aggressive race in a difficult primary in a large state. But it was grossly larger than any total ever publicly acknowledged by any other Pennsylvania candidate. Partisans of each candidate have sued the other, demanding an audit of primary expenditures.

As the general election campaign began, Mr. Shapp also announced that he had sold his interest in the Jerrold Corporation, the electronics manufacturing concern that he founded and that bears his middle name. The price, he said, was $10-million.

Much of this sum presumably is now available to advance the Shapp cause, for Mr. Shapp is described by associates as having another "comfortable fortune" in trust for his family and for retirement.

A polltaker himself, Mr. Napolitan scoffed at a private survey by Governor Scranton's polltaker, E. John Bucci, that gave Mr. Shafer 53 per cent of the vote and Mr. Shapp 47 per cent, and forecast the defeat of Mr. Shapp by 240,000 votes.

Public Opinion Surveys, Inc., of Princeton, N. J., which conducted the poll showing Mr. Shapp to be better known than Mr. Shafer, had another poll this week on the preference for candidates.

The results, published in a number of Pennsylvania newspapers, indicated that 47 per cent now favor Mr. Shafer and 34 per cent support Mr. Shapp, with 19 per cent undecided and a slight tendency of the "undecideds" toward Mr. Shapp.

Mr. Napolitan's polls reportedly showed a much closer race.

COST OF CAMPAIGN BECOMES AN ISSUE

Democrats Say Rockefeller Tries to Buy Re-Election

By ROBERT E. DALLOS

A nervous little man with both his hands and his mouth stuffed with cigarettes has become an issue in the campaign for Governor.

He is the star of a television commercial that says that Governor Rockefeller is opposed to air pollution.

"Just breathe for 24 hours and you get what you'd get from two packs of cigarettes every day," a voice in the commercial says. "The Governor of New York doesn't want you breathing that kind of air."

The issue is not so much what the commercial says as what it and seven others being shown across the state cost.

Mr. Rockefeller's opponents who have yet to air a commercial themselves, have charged that the commercials show that he is spending too much on radio and television as well as on such items as the campaign headquarters—a floor and a half at the New York Hilton Hotel.

"This is an attempt on Governor Rockefeller's part to buy the election whatever it might cost," John J. Burns, State Democratic Chairman, charged in an interview last week. "This Madison Avenue brainwashing is hard to combat.

"Our candidate, Frank D. O'Connor, doesn't have the enormous wealth that Governor Rockefeller brings into this campaign. It raises the question: 'Can a man of modest means be elected governor?'"

A spokesman for Franklin D. Roosevelt Jr., the Liberal party's gubernatorial candidate, said:

"We cannot and do not expect to spend anywhere near the amount that Rockefeller has budgeted for TV. We think it is essential that some kind of a ceiling be placed on this sort of thing."

The Republicans won't say how much television time they have been buying or what their total advertising outlay will be. They contend their opponents are greatly exaggerating such expenditures.

"Whatever may be Governor Rockefeller's personal means," says Senator Jacob K. Javits, his campaign chairman, "he certainly will not use them in any way to buy an election. Experience has demonstrated that both parties raise and spend about the same amount of money in a state campaign."

The Federal Communications Commission, however, found Republicans spent twice as much as Democrats on television in 1962, when Mr. Rockefeller was elected to a second term.

The Republicans spent $663,-251 on radio and television for all candidates while the Democrats laid out a total of $328,-764.

See $5-Million Cost

The Democrats say Mr. Rockefeller has already spent $1-million for air time and that total spending will reach $5-million by election time on Nov. 8.

The Democrats, who only last week chose an agency to produce their advertising and expect to air their first spot next Saturday, say they will spend no more than $750,000 for air time during the entire campaign.

Mr. Burns admits that the spot ads, produced by the Jack Tinker & Partners Advertising Agency, are "clever."

One, for example, shows a man in his 40's looking cheerful despite the work that he's doing, pushing a broom down a long hallway.

The voice accompanying the film meanwhile is praising what the Governor has done to raise the State's minimum wage.

When the man finally hears that "next New Year's Day it [the minimum wage] will become $1.50," he looks squarely into the camera, pulls a New Year's Eve party squeaker from his pocket and blows it.

The agency hired by the Democrats, Richard K. Manoff, Inc., is currently filming Mr. O'Connor as he campaigns to make spot commercials. A party official says "the issues and the man will be shown in our ads—and we won"t resort to gimmicks."

A Democratic spokesman said Mr. Rockefeller had been able to get a head start because "we did not have a candidate until the convention just a couple of weeks ago."

Mr. Rockefeller has been advertising on television since early July. A check with a few of the major stations shows he has greatly stepped up his buying in the past week.

Last week, the Rockefeller camp purchased another $50,000 in prime evening time on radio station WABC to add to the $50,000 he had booked earlier. Radio station WNBC has already booked 75 spot announcements for the Rockefeller forces, making the total booked to date about $125,000.

PRESIDENT URGES TREASURY FINANCE CAMPAIGN COSTS

In Message to Congress, He Seeks Sweeping Reform in Races for Presidency

FULL DISCLOSURE ASKED

Johnson Requests a $5,000 Ceiling on Contributions to Any One Candidate

By TOM WICKER
Special to The New York Times

WASHINGTON, May 25 — President Johnson urged Congress today to pay for most of the costs of Presidential campaigns directly from the Federal Treasury and to begin a study of better ways to finance lower level elections.

The proposed Presidential campaign financing plan would differ sharply from the one sponsored by Senator Russell B. Long of Louisiana, which Congress approved last year but suspended for improvements this year.

In a long message to Congress, Mr. Johnson said that since "the costs of campaigning are skyrocketing" the heavy financial burdens imposed on parties and candidates had created "a potential for danger —the possibility that men of great wealth could achieve undue political influence through large contributions."

Other Major Proposals

In addition to the financing plan, the President proposed the following:

¶Restrictions on political contributions, with no individual, family or organization to be permitted to give more than $5,000 to any candidate.

¶Fuller disclosure of all contributions to and expenditures by any candidate for Federal office, and the removal of "totally unrealistic and inadequate" ceilings on campaign expenditures.

¶Stricter regulation of lobbying and contributions by Federal contractors.

¶An act to make citizens who move just before a Presidential election eligible to vote for President in a new state if they establish residence there before Sept. 1.

Sweeping Changes

The heart of the President's message, and the most sweeping changes he proposed, had to do with financing Presidential campaigns. His proposals will be referred, in the Senate, to the Finance Committee, of which Mr. Long is chairman.

That committee has a mandate from the full Senate to propose an elections reform bill as a replacement for the suspended Long act, which would have permitted all payers of income tax to check off volunteer dollar contributions.

The plan proposed by Mr. Johnson would work this way:

In each Presidential election year, Congress would appropriate a fund to pay for major elements of the campaign. There would be no formula to govern the size of this fund, but the amount would be calculated in consultation with an advisory board to the Controller General, who would disburse and audit the money.

In his book, "Financing the 1964 Election," Herbert E. Alexander of the Citizens Research Foundation of Princeton, N. J., reported that the two major parties' campaign costs at the national level totaled $29-million—$17.1-million for the Republicans and $11.9-million for the Democrats.

The Federal fund would be divided evenly between the major parties—defined as those that had polled 25 per cent or more of the popular vote in the previous Presidential election. A minor party—defined as one that polled between 5 and 25 per cent of the vote in the current election could be reimbursed "at its expenditures immediately after the election.

Minor-party reimbursement would be according to the per-vote expenditures of the major parties. If, say, the major parties had spent $40-million and 80 million votes had been cast, a minor party would be reimbursed at the rate of 50 cents for each vote it had received.

The major parties, however, could draw funds during the course of the campaign, against the total permitted them, by presenting certified vouchers for expenditures to the Controller General. Minor parties would have to raise operating money privately while a campaign was in progress.

The Federal money could be spent only "to bring the issues before the public"—that is, for radio and television, newspaper and periodical advertising, preparation and distribution of literature and travel costs.

These are considered by political professionals to be the major elements of campaign expense. Mr. Alexander reported in his book that the two major parties had spent $11-million in 1964 on Presidential and Vice-Presidential campaigning on radio and television alone.

For other expenses — staff salaries, telephones, administra-tion and the like — no Federal money could be spent. Thus, the money for these expenditures would still have to be raised through private contributions, as would the operating funds of the national party committees in the years between elections.

No primary or convention expenditures could be charged by any candidate or party to the Federal funds. Only official party nominees could benefit from the subsidy.

Parties spending Federal money would be limited in the amount they could spend in any one state. The percentage of the total that could be devoted to a state could not be more than 140 per cent of the relation of that state's population to the national population. Thus, in a state with 10 per cent of the national population, no more than 14 per cent of a party's share of the Federal subsidy could be spent.

There would be no minimum amount that a party would be required to spend in each state, however. Thus, candidates and parties would retain considerable flexibility in allocating their funds on the basis of political necessity or expedience, or any other ground.

At the close of a Presidential campaign, the Controller General would audit the fund, report the totals paid to all parties participating and disclose the campaign expenses of these parties as well as any misuse of the funds. This would include expenditures from private contributions.

In case of misuse of Federal money, the party responsible would have to refund the amount involved to the Treasury, with a penalty of up to 50 per cent additional imposed on any willful misuse. Criminal penalties would also be provided.

At a White House briefing Joseph A. Califano Jr., special assistant to the President, said the plan had been developed in consultation with many members of Congress and with numerous experts in the field, including Richard E. Neustadt of Harvard University, the chairman of a group that made an undisclosed study of the subject for the President.

Mr. Califano said the proposal was intended as a general guideline for the deliberations of the Senate Finance Committee, and that Mr. Johnson would not insist on every detail of his proposals. He would not, for instance, object to the inclusion of a formula that would make automatic the amount of a Congressional appropriation for campaign expenditures; such a formula might be based on the size of the vote in the previous election.

Stanley Surrey, an Assistant Secretary of the Treasury, said at the White House briefing that he had "a feeling that there's general agreement on public financing."

"The search is for mechanics" to make the program equitable and effective, he said.

In his message, the President called on Congress to "consider promptly the problem of campaign financing and enact appropriate legislation." He added:

"I have no desire to ask that the provisions be made applicable to any campaign in which I may be involved. On the other hand, I have no desire to request that any such campaign be exempted from modernizing legislation which Congress might enact."

In the Senate fight over the Long act, which would have provided Federal funds for the 1968 campaign, the Johnson Administration gave strong support to Senator Long's efforts to keep the act on the law books.

Other major aspects of the President's message had to do with full disclosure of expenditures of candidates for Federal office and the $5,000 limitation on individual campaign contributions.

The latter would permit any person, or any family, or any organization, to contribute up to $5,000 to as many different candidates as desired; but it would prevent the relatively common practice of contributing more than $5,000 to a single candidate by making separate contributions to numerous committees organized on the candidate's behalf.

The full disclosure provisions would require from "every candidate" for Federal office, "including for the Presidency and the Vice-Presidency, and every committee, state, interstate and national, that supports a candidate for Federal office" a report on "every contribution, loan and expense item over $100."

These reports would be required, for the first time at the Federal level, for primaries and convention nomination contests. It would also be a new development for such reports to be required of state committees formed on behalf of a candidate.

Authorities in the field criticized the fact, however, that under the Johnson proposals the reports would be made to the clerk of the House of Representatives and the secretary of the Senate. They said the key to full disclosure was whether those to whom the reports had to be made would prosecute candidates and committees who did not report, or who reported incompletely.

Mr. Johnson endorsed a Senate-passed bill that would require registration of those whose "substantial purpose" is to influence legislation rather than those whose "principal purpose" is to do so, as the law now requires. And he urged the repeal of present campaign ceilings—$3-million for national committees, $25,000 for senatorial candidates, and $5,000 for House candidates.

Excerpts From President's Message

Special to The New York Times
WASHINGTON, May 25—Following are excerpts from a message President Johnson sent to Congress today on "The Political Process in America":

III
CAMPAIGN FINANCING

The proposed Election Reform Act of 1967 is corrective, remedying present inadequacies in the law. It goes hand in hand with the pursuit of another goal—to provide public support for election campaigns.

The Background

Democracy rests on the voice of the people. Whatever blunts the clear expression of that voice is a threat to democratic government.

In this century one phenomenon in particular poses such a threat—the soaring costs of political campaigns.

Historically, candidates for public office in this country have always relied upon private contributions to finance their campaigns.

But in the last few decades, technology—which has changed so much of our national life—has modified the nature of political campaigning as well. Radio, television, and the airplane have brought sweeping new dimensions and costs to the concept of political candidacy.

In many ways these changes have worked to the decided advantage of the American people. They have served to bring the candidates and the issues before virtually every voting citizen. They have contributed immeasurably to the political education of the nation.

In another way, however, they have worked to the opposite effect by increasing the costs of campaigning to spectacular proportions. Costs of such magnitude can have serious consequences for our democracy:

¶More and more, men and women of limited means may refrain from running for public office. Private wealth increasingly becomes an artificial and unrealistic arbiter of qualifications, and the source of public leadership is thus severely narrowed.

¶Increases in the size of individual contributions create uneasiness in the minds of the public. Actually, the exercise of undue influence occurs infrequently. Nonetheless, the circumstances in which a candidate is obligated to rely on sizable contributions easily creates the impression that influence is at work. This impression — however unfounded it might be — is itself intolerable, for it erodes public confidence in the democratic order.

¶The necessity of acquiring substantial funds to finance campaigns diverts a candidate's attention from his public obligations and detracts from his energetic exposition of the issues.

¶The growing importance of large contributions serves to deter the search for small ones, and thus effectively narrows the base of financial support. This is exactly the opposite of what a democratic society should strive to achieve.

It is extremely difficult to devise a program which completely eliminates these undesirable consequences without inhibiting robust campaigning and the freedom of every American fully to participate in the elective process. I believe that our ultimate goal should be to finance the total expense for this vital function of our democracy with public funds, and to prohibit the use or acceptance of money from private sources. We have virtually no experience upon which to base such a program. Its risks and uncertainties are formidable. I believe, however, that we are ready to make a beginning. We should proceed with all prudent speed to enact those parts of such a program which appear to be feasible at this time.

Presidential Campaigns

THE PROBLEM

The election of a President is the highest expression of the free choice of the American people. It is the most visible level of politics—and also the most expensive.

For their free choice to be exercised wisely, the people must be fully informed about the opposing candidates and issues. To achieve this, candidates and parties must have the funds to bring their platforms and programs to the people.

Yet, as we have seen, the costs of campaigning are skyrocketing. This imposes extreme and heavy financial burdens on party and candidate alike, creating a potential for danger—the possibility that men of great wealth could achieve undue political influence through large contributions.

In recognition of this problem, the Congress last year enacted the Presidential Election Campaign Fund Act. By so doing, it adopted the central concept that some form of public financing of Presidential campaigns would serve the public interest.

I did not submit or recommend this legislation. It was the creation and the product of the Congress in 1966. As you will recall, it was added as an amendment to other essential legislation. When I signed that act into law last November, I observed that "it breaks new ground in the financing of Presidential election campaigns" and that the "new law is only a beginning." It was my belief then, as it is now, that the complex issues involved in this new concept required extensive discussion and penetrating analysis.

Over the past six weeks, we have heard men of deep principle and firm conviction engage in a spirited and searching debate on the law. While there were honest and vigorous disagreements, they were voiced by those who share a common faith in the free ideals which are the bedrock of our democracy.

THE ISSUES

The course of the debate has illuminated many of the issues which underlie the matter of Presidential campaign financing. For example:

¶In what amount should Federal funds be provided for these campaigns?

¶What limitations should be placed on the use of these funds?

¶Should there be a complete bar on the use of private contributions for those aspects of campaign financing which would be regularly provided through appropriations?

¶Can the availability of public funds result in an undue concentration of power in national political committees? If so, what steps can be taken to prevent it?

¶Is the tax check-off method a sound approach or is a direct appropriation to be preferred?

¶How can equitable treatment of minor parties be assured?

¶What sanctions would be most effective to insure compliance with the law?

¶Whatever the ultimate formula, how can we preserve the independence, spirit and spontaneity that has hallmarked American political enterprise through the years?

THE RECOMMENDATIONS

Against this backdrop of concern for the political process, the protection of the public interest, and the issues that have been raised, I make these 11 recommendations to improve and strengthen the Presidential Election Campaign Fund Act:

[1]

Funds to finance Presidential campaigns should be **provided by direct Congressional appropriation,** rather than determined by individual tax check-offs.

This approach would:

¶Provide the opportunity for Congress to make a realistic assessment, and express its judgment, of what it would cost Presidential candidates or parties to carry their views to the voters. This assessment should consider the recommendations of the special advisory board to the Controller General, created under the Presidential Election Campaign Fund Act.. The board consists of representatives of both major political parties. Based on this review and recommendation, Congress could then appropriate the necessary funds.

¶Make the amount appropriated for the campaign fund more stable, by removing its uncertain reliance on tax check-offs, whose numbers might bear no reasonable relationship to the amount required to bring the issues before the public.

[2]

The funds should be used only for expenses which are needed to bring the issues before the public.

Under the procedure I recommend:

¶The funds so appropriated would be used to reimburse specified expenditures incurred during the Presidential election campaign itself, after the parties have selected their candidates.

¶The amount appropriated should be adequate to defray key items of expense to carry a campaign to the public and thus be limited to the following items: radio and television, newspaper and periodical advertising, the preparation and distribution of campaign literature, and travel.

¶The amount of the fund for the major parties as finally determined by the Congress would be divided equally between them.

[3]

Private contributions for major parties could not be used for those items of expense to which public funds could be applied.

Private contributions, however, could be used to defray the costs of other campaign expenses. These would include the salaries of campaign workers, overhead, research and polls, telegraph and telephone, postage and administrative expenses.

Citizens who want to make contributions to the party or candidate of their choice will be free to do so. Party workers at the grass roots will be able to pursue their neighborhood activities, a responsibility which is deeply woven into the fabric of American political tradition.

But under the measures I have proposed, the major burden of raising money for soaring campaign costs will be lifted from a Presidential candidate's shoulders. No longer will we have to rely on the large contributions of wealthy and powerful interests.

[4]

A "major party" should be defined as one which received 25 per cent or more of the popular votes cast in the last election.

A percentage-of-votes test is more realistic than the fixed number of votes (15 million) now in the present law. It recognizes our growing population with more Americans entering the voting ranks each year.

[5]

A "minor party" should be defined as one which received between 5 per cent and 25 per cent of the popular votes cast in the current election.

For the same reasons I described above, the eligibility test for Federal support should not be based on a fixed number of votes (5 million) for "minor parties" in the current law, but rather on the percentage of votes received.

Third-party movements can support the rich diversity of American political life. At the same time some reasonable limitations should be developed so that Federal financial incentives are not made available to parties lacking a modicum of public support—or created solely to receive Government funds.

Under this proposal, "minor parties" would receive payments based on the number of votes they receive in the current election. The payment for each vote received by a minor party would then be determined so as to be the equivalent of that made to the major parties.

For example, assume that two major parties received a total of 80 million votes in a prior election, and Congress had appropriated a $40-million campaign fund for those two parties. Although the major parties would share equally in that fund ($20-million each), the allocation would amount to 50 cents per vote cast for those parties. Using the 50 cents per vote as the guideline, a minor party receiving 5 million votes in the current election would be entitled to $2.5-million for its recognized campaign expenses.

[6]

A "minor party" should be eligible for reimbursement promptly following an election.

A "minor party" should be able to qualify promptly for Federal funds based on its showing in the current election, rather than wait four years until the next election. This added source of funds should enhance a minor party's opportunity to bring its programs and platforms into the public arena.

[7]

The percentage of Federal funds received by a major or minor party which could be used in any one state should be limited to 140 per cent of the percentage the population of that bears to the population of the country.

This would prevent the concentration of funds in any particular state and would minimize the ability of national party officials to reduce the role and effectiveness of local political

organizations. At the same time, it would retain the flexibility necessary to carry a party's programs to the public. The Controller General should be empowered to issue rules for the equitable allocation, on a geographic basis, for national campaign expenses, such as network television.

[8]

The Controller General should be required to make a full report to the Congress as soon as practicable after each Presidential election.

This report should include:

¶Payments made to each party from the fund.

¶Expenses incurred by each party.

¶Any misuse of the funds.

[9]

The Controller General, should be given clear authority to audit the expenses of Presidential campaigns.

It is imperative that the strictest controls be exercised to safeguard the public interest. The General Accounting Office is the arm of the Government which I believe is best suited to monitor the expenditures of the fund.

Payments from the fund would be made only upon the submission of certified vouchers to the Controller General.

If the Controller General's audit reveals any improper use of funds, the following sanctions would be applied:

¶The amounts involved would have to be repaid to the Treasury.

¶If the misuse is willful, a penalty of up to 50 per cent of the amount involved would be imposed.

[10]

To bring greater wisdom and experience to the administration of the act, the Controller General's special advisory board on the Presidential election campaign fund should be expanded from 7 to 11 members.

This advisory board is faced with a heavy and demanding task. It must "counsel and assist" the Controller General in the performance of his duties under the act.

The membership of the board now consists of two members from each major political party and three additional members. I recommend that the board be enlarged to encompass the wisdom and experience of four distinguished Americans:

¶The majority leader of the Senate.

¶The minority leader of the Senate.

¶The Speaker of the House of Representatives.

¶The minority leader of the House.

[11]

Criminal penalties should be applied for the willful misuse of payments received under the act by any person with custody of the funds.

The penalties should be a fine of not more than $10,000, or five years' imprisonment, or both. Criminal penalties would also be applied against

any person who makes a false claim or statement for the purpose of obtaining funds under the act.

Other Campaign Financing

We should also seek ways to provide some form of public support for Congressional, state and local political primaries and campaigns.

Here, the need is no less acute than at the Presidential level. But the problems involved are as complex as the elections themselves, which vary from district to district and contest to contest.

Because the uncertainties in this area are so very great, and because the issues have not received the benefit of the extensive debate that has characterized Presidential campaign financing, I pose for your consideration and exploration a series of alternatives.

In 1961, President Kennedy appointed a distinguished, bipartisan commission on campaign costs to take a fresh look at the problems of financing election campaigns. Although the commission devoted its attention to the problems of campaign costs for Presidential and Vice-Presidential candidates, it pointed out that the measures proposed "would have a desirable effect on all political fund raising."

The commission's 1962 report and recommendations were endorsed by Presidents Dwight D. Eisenhower and Harry S. Truman as well as leading Presidential candidates in recent elections.

Based on the commission's recommendations and the later reviews and studies of campaign financing, there are several alternatives which should be considered. These alternatives all involve public financing of campaigns to a greater or lesser extent. Among them are:

¶A system of direct appropriations, patterned after the recommendations made herein for Presidential campaigns, or modeled after recommendations pending in the Congress.

¶Tax credit against Federal income tax for 50 per cent of contributions, up to a maximum credit of $10 per year.

¶A matching incentive plan in which the Government would contribute an amount up to $10 for an equal amount contributed by a citizen, whether or not a taxpayer, to a candidate or committee.

¶A "voucher plan" in which Treasury certificates for small amounts could be mailed to citizens who, in turn, would send them to candidates or committees of their choice. These vouchers could then be redeemed from public funds, and the funds used to defray specified campaign expenditures.

I believe these deserve serious attention along with other proposals previously recommended and suggested to the Congress. Each alter-

native offers particular advantages. Thorough review may reveal that one is to be clearly preferred over the others, or that still other courses of action are appropriate. Whatever the outcome, any such review should reflect a realistic assessment of the amount of funds needed in these campaigns and the extent to which the funds should be provided by public means.

I recommend that Congress undertake such a review.

I have asked the Secretary of the Treasury and the Attorney General to cooperate fully with the Congress in its exploration of these alternatives in order to give all the help the executive branch can to the Congress as it seeks the best Congressional election campaign financing program.

Campaign Spending: New Start

Now that the Senate has fought its way out of the parliamentary shambles of the campaign finance debate, it can get properly started on seeking viable solutions to this difficult, many-sided problem.

The principal antagonists in the acrimonious struggle of the past several weeks each had hold of a different piece of the truth. Senator Gore of Tennessee, whose viewpoint ultimately prevailed, was right in seeing the dangers that might develop if the two national party committees gained possession of up to $60 million in public funds. The factions in control of the respective committees could use this public subsidy as a slush fund to manipulate party conventions and influence local and state, as well as Federal, candidates.

Senator Long of Louisiana, who suffered an interim defeat, was right in seeing that an infusion of public funds into the political system is necessary if candidates of ordinary means are not to be priced out of politics altogether. The question is how best to bring that about.

* * *

In the past, both tax credits and tax deductions for individual contributors to political campaigns have been proposed, but have not found majority support in Congress. Many politicians are convinced that these devices would not substantially increase the number of contributors and would only constitute an unnecessary, indirect subsidy to those who already contribute. However, direct underwriting of all campaign costs by the Treasury would undermine citizen participation in politics and lead the Government into the dangerous business of structuring the political behavior of the American people.

An older school of thought believed that establishing ceilings on the amount of money that could be spent in politics would have a purifying effect, but rising costs and the ingenuity of candidates have defeated that idea. A more popular viewpoint today favors abolishing all ceilings and relying exclusively upon the policing power of publicity. But whether the Government tries to control the total amount of money spent in politics by rigid ceilings or by full disclosure, neither approach helps the candidate who lacks sufficient funds to wage an adequate campaign. His problem is not the corrupting presence of money from dubious sources, but the dreadful absence of it from any source.

The Senate Finance Committee hearings can usefully be aimed at isolating those costs that the public could defray and those that could best be met by private fund raising. There is also need for better reporting and fuller disclosure of contributions and more timely, effective enforcement of the laws governing campaign spending. The objective should be to evolve some mixed public-and-private system of financing political campaigns which would liberate candidates at all levels from unhealthy pressures but not subvert the variety and spontaneity of the nation's politics.

May 14, 1967

Toward Campaign Reform

President Johnson's message to Congress on political campaign expenditures substantially advances the effort to devise a mixed public-and-private system of financing election contests.

We do not agree with the President that the "ultimate goal" should be to pay for all campaigns, local, state and Federal, out of public funds. The prohibition of private contributions would, we believe, undercut citizen participation in campaigns and tend to create apathy. The President himself recognizes that the "risks and uncertainties are formidable."

But we have no difficulty in agreeing with Mr. Johnson's proposal for a limited experiment in Government-financed campaigns at the Presidential level. Under his plan, Congress would appropriate funds to pay for specific expenses such as radio and television costs, newspaper advertising, distribution of campaign literature and travel. Other costs would be defrayed as they are now by private contributions. The tax return checkoff plan incorporated in last year's law, now in limbo, would be abolished.

This plan is worth a trial, although it is unquestionably open to criticism. During the recent Senate debate, Senator Kennedy of New York argued that it would not be possible, as a practical matter, to limit the spending of public funds for some campaign purposes and not for others. Senator Clark of Pennsylvania has suggested that radio and television stations be required to provide free time to candidates. But it is better to go ahead with the President's plan and gain some practical experience. If abuses develop, they can be remedied by future legislation.

President Johnson makes several excellent recommendations to achieve full disclosure and more effective enforcement of limits on private contributions. Every candidate and every committee supporting a candidate for Federal office should be required to report contributions and expense items exceeding $100. It is highly desirable to extend coverage of the disclosure laws to include conventions and primaries. Transfer of enforcement to the Controller General would enhance the law's effectiveness.

The President is right to call for the abolition of the unrealistic ceilings on total expenditures. We are not quite so sure about his proposal for a $5,000 limit to individual contributions. As long as there is full disclosure and uas long as some form of Federal assistance to all candidates tends to redress the balance of financial power, it might be simpler to have done with ceilings altogether.

The rights of minor-party candidates seem generously safeguarded under the President's plan. The danger of excessive control by national party chairmen is not wholly avoided, but any experiment involves some risks and unknowns. With campaign costs steadily rising, the time for an experiment in publicly financed campaigning has surely arrived.

May 26, 1967

Campaign Financing

Questions Raised by Johnson's Plan For Subsidies in Presidential Votes

By TOM WICKER
Special to The New York Times

WASHINGTON, May 26—A long debate in the Senate and extensive investigations by the President's advisers have produced a new White House plan for public financing of Presidential campaigns. But they also have demonstrated that no one knows much about the White House plan will work.

Among the questions for which there are no sure answers are the following:

News Analysis

¶What effect will Federal subsidies to national political parties have on state parties and on the structure of American politics?

¶Should public financing ultimately cover all Federal elections? Presidential primaries? State elections and primaries?

¶What about voluntarism? Tax deductions and credits, for instance, while a limited form of public financing, would retain for the citizen the element of choosing to whom his money would go and deciding if he wants to contribute at all.

The Right to Choose

At some point, moreover, is there not a constitutional question, as well as a problem of democratic procedure, about a citizen's right to contribute to parties and candidates he supports?

There are some immediately practical questions, too. For instance, the Republicans traditionally raise and spend more than the Democrats in Presidential campaigns—$17-million to $11-million in 1964, at the national level. But the Johnson plan would provide a single Federal subsidy, to be split evenly between the two major parties (qualified minor parties would be reimbursed out of additional funds).

Will the Republicans, therefore, support a plan that would give the Democrats guaranteed parity in fund-raising and spending?

Some observers believe that this situation motivated Senator Russell B. Long's extended fight in the Senate for his own public financing plan — a fight in which the full weight of the Johnson Administration was on his side.

Traditionally at a fund-raising disadvantage, the Democrats might be even worse off than usual next year, since President Johnson's popularity has fallen far below the peaks of two years ago and there is widespread uneasiness about the war in Vietnam.

Republicans in the Senate, obviously not coincidentally, lined up almost unanimously against the Long proposals, which would have financed the Johnson campaign with as many as 30 million Federal dollars.

Right now, moreover, no one really knows how much a Presidential campaign, from convention nominations to Election Day, ought to cost—much less how much they actually do cost.

National Level Costs

The $29-million total for the two major parties in 1964 covered only national level expenditures; it did not include state party expenditures, those of nonparty committees and individuals, free television time, expenditures by other candidates that affected Presidential campaigning, the costs of the primary campaigns of various Republicans, and inumerable other relevant expenses.

Herbert E. Alexander, former executive secretary of the President's Commission on Campaign costs, has estimated that perhaps $200-million was spent in the 1964 elections for all offices; some large part of this would be chargeable directly to the Presidential contest.

Should Congress, therefore, appropriate something in the neighborhood of $29-million, plus an estimated sum for the potentially bigger electorate of 1968, thus covering only national-level Presidential campaign costs? Or should it provide far more, so that the national party committees could "farm out" funds to state and local parties and committees? No one is sure.

One major question is whether there is not in all this the likelihood of a much tighter grip by the national party committees on their state and local parties, and on the choice and preferment of candidates for other offices.

If national party committees had control of vast Federal subsidy funds, and particularly if this inhibited private contributions, state and local political organizations could become dependent on national committee decisions about campaign spending. Although the money is intended at present only for Presidential campaigning, it could still have considerable effect on the campaigns of lesser candidates on the same party ticket; thus, candidates themselves might become chary of offending or differing from a national committee—particularly one dominated by a President in office—that controlled the campaign cash register.

Whether this effect would develop, and whther if it did the result would be a beneficial party discipline or a stifling party conformity, cannot be answered until there has been some experience with the system.

The question might be avoided if all, or even most, elections for Federal and state offices were financed publicly, and if some of the subsidy money could be controlled at the state level. But, as Mr. Johnson pointed out in his message to Congress yesterday, "the problems involved are as complex as the elections themselves, which vary from district to district and contest to contest."

Constitutional Question

The President nevertheless expressed himself in favor of financing all elections publicly, at some time in the future, with all private contributions barred by law. But this might raise the constitutional question whether a citizen is not as entitled to spend his money in support of a candidate as he is to vote for him.

Nor is partial public financing, as provided for in Mr. Johnson's plan for Presidential campaigns, necessarily workable. He would limit subsidy money to expenditures for radio and television, advertising, literature and travel; private funds would have to be raised for all other purposes.

This could cause bookkeeping and auditing difficulties, and it still leaves opportunity for the "big money" contributor to exert his influence—particularly since the parties also would have to raise operating funds from private sources in the three years between Presidential elections.

If the public financing remained limited only to Presidential contests, the "big money" might simply be redirected — to Congressional, state and local elections where, in many ways, it could have more ill effects than in the relatively exposed Presidential campaigns.

Technological Society

But it is undeniably true that in a modern technological society, as Mr. Johnson pointed out, "the costs of campaigning are skyrocketing. This imposes extreme and heavy financial burdens on party and candidate alike, creating a potential for danger — the possibility that men of great wealth could achieve undue political influence through large contributions."

It is basically for that reason that a climate now exists in Congress in which a public financing plan on the limited basis proposed by the President might win acceptance. Little is known about the possible effects and ramifications, but a number of politicians and academic experts believe the experiment is worth trying just to find out if it really is the right alternative to the present system.

May 27, 1967

SHORTER CAMPAIGNS TO CUT COSTS URGED

WASHINGTON, May 28 (AP)—Senator John J. Williams said today that the best way to reduce the cost of presidential election campaigns would be to shorten the campaign period.

He said he had written to the Republican and Democratic national chairmen and asked them to consider campaigns of about five weeks, rather than two months or more.

Both chairmen presumably will testify in public hearings in the Senate Finance Committee on the question of Government financing of election costs.

The Delaware Senator, senior Republican on this committee, said he hoped the chairmen would comment on his letter.

Paul H. Douglas, the former Democratic Senator from Illinois, yesterday urged tax-paid national election campaign.

In an interview in the current issue of Look magazine, he said that campaign obligations now were generally paid for by offering wealthy donors special Government considerations.

"The public is paying for the elections right now by having to absorb these extra costs," he declared.

May 29, 1967

BROADCAST COSTS IN POLITICS SPURT

'66 Off-Year Outlay Close to '64 Presidential Year

By EILEEN SHANAHAN
Special to The New York Times

WASHINGTON, July 10— Political candidates spent almost as much for radio and television advertising in 1966, a year without a Presidential campaign, as they did in 1964, a Presidential election year.

The Federal Communications Commission reported today that candidates of all parties spent a total of $32-million for spot announcements and political programs last year. The figure represents a jump of 60 per cent from the total spent in 1962, the last non-Presidential election year.

Last year's total almost equaled the $34.6-million spent in 1964, for Presidential and non-Presidential campaigns combined. The non-Presidential portion of the outlays in 1964 was $21.8-million.

Democratic candidates spent more than half as much again than did Republican candidates in 1966 — $18.5-million, compared with $12.2-million.

The larger Democratic outlays for radio and TV advertising were accounted for, however, by their heavier expenses in primary elections— mainly in the South.

For the November general elections, the Republicans outspent the Democrats, $10.4-million to $8.5-million.

The commission's report on paid campaign advertising showed that all of the increased spending, compared with 1962, came from an increase in spot announcements and that the increase was greater for radio than for television.

Paid political ads on standard A.M. radio accounted for 41 per cent of the money spent on political broadcasts in 1966 —a total of $13.1-million. That was an increase of 70 per cent in the dollar charges for radio advertising, compared with an increase of 50 per cent for television.

Radio and TV station billings for spot announcements, totaling $27.5-million, were 85 per cent higher than in 1962. Outlays for sponsorship of entire programs, however, declined from $5.2-million to $4.5-million.

Although the Democrats have consistently outspent the Republicans since 1962 for broadcast advertising, the margin widened considerably last year. In 1964, the Democrats spent $17.8-million, compared with the Republicans' $15-million. In 1962, the figures were Democrats, $12-million, Republicans $7.5-million. In 1960, the Republicans outspent the Democrats, $7.6-million to $6.2-million.

Campaign Finances

How to Audit—and Foot—the Big Bill

By EILEEN SHANAHAN

WASHINGTON — "It used to be, in the old days when I went around the state with my grandfather, that what you needed to get elected to office was a big cigar, a shadbelly vest, and a constitution that permitted you to stand out in the hot July sun and talk for two and a half or three hours. Well, that day is gone. There is a new way of communicating with people and that is television. You are not out making a speech in the July sun before a couple of hundred or a couple of thousand people. You are getting into the living room, talking directly to families in literally millions of homes. The costs are colossal."

Thus did Senator Thruston B. Morton, Republican of Kentucky, recently describe one of the greatest changes that has come about in political campaigning in the past 20 years. Some reliable figures showing just how colossal the cost of broadcast political advertising has become were published last week by the Federal Communications Commission.

A commission survey of the nation's radio and television stations showed that the total charges for political "spots" and broadcasts reached $32-million in last year's election. About two-thirds of it financed broadcast advertising for the major political jobs that were at stake in 1966— Governors, U. S. Senators and U. S. Representatives.

Rising Outlays

The figure is just $2.5-million less than the total spent on broadcast political advertisements in 1964 — a year in which there was also a Presidential election. Compared with the outlays in 1962, the last non-Presidential year, the 1966 costs were up 60 per cent.

How much higher they will go, no one can predict. But the nation's leading nonpartisan expert on the costs of campaigning, Herbert E. Alexander of the Citizens Research Foundation in Princeton, N. J., says that the 1966 figures indicate that the 1968 bills for broadcast political advertising "will approach $50-million."

The question is how these enormous and rapidly increasing political campaign expenses ought to be financed and what restrictions should be placed on the sources of campaign money. Congress this year seems more in a mood to do something about these problems than it has been at any time in recent memory.

In the House of Representatives it is control of potential corrupt practices that has taken priority. The House Elections Subcommittee, just two weeks ago, approved legislation that would impose a few new limits on campaign contributions and vastly expand the amount of information that must be made available to the public on the sources and uses of campaign funds.

The bill follows, in general, proposals made by President Johnson a year ago, though it is stronger in some respects and weaker in others. It would close what are perhaps the two most important loopholes in the present Corrupt Practices Act by requiring reports from all campaign committees that raise or spend as much as $1,000, and extending the coverage of the act to primaries.

In the Senate it is the issue of how to raise more political money that is receiving the most attention. Hearings have been held by the Finance Committee on a proposal by President Johnson to finance Presidential campaigns out of the Government's treasury —in amounts yet to be specified. The use of Federal funds rather than contributions for Presidential campaigns would presumably make it easier to find contributors to campaigns for lesser offices.

Under the President's proposal, whatever money was appropriated by Congress to finance Presidential campaigns would be evenly divided between the major parties, which would get their money as the campaign progressed. Minor parties would be reimbursed after the election, in proportion to the number of votes they polled.

The Senate hearings have turned up relatively little support for the President's idea, however, and most committee members seem to be leaning toward some limited tax incentive—a deduction or a credit—for the first $20 or so of any campaign contribution. The law currently on the books was sponsored by Senator Russell B. Long. It was passed last year but never used and seems certain to be dropped. It would permit each taxpayer to earmark $1 of his taxes to finance Presidential campaigns.

Mr. Johnson's proposal for Presidential campaign financing came with a renewed plea to tighten reporting requirements and place some new restrictions on contributions. But this matter

July 11, 1967

falls under the jurisdiction of another Senate committee, Rules and Administration, which has done nothing about it yet.

Those who are concerned about the costs of campaigning and the influence with elected officials that at least some campaign contributors clearly expect to buy, are trying to find a means of tying the two halves together in the Senate, so that the funding bill is not considered before the Congressional reorganization bill. As one Senator said in another connection last week, "If you give them the ice cream first, they won't eat their spinach."

HAGERTY SEES RISE IN CAMPAIGN COSTS

Says Networks May Have to Give Time to Candidates

By WILL LISSNER

James C. Hagerty, press secretary for President Dwight D. Eisenhower, said here yesterday that the cost of Presidential campaigning was "getting out of hand."

"I think we will have to go eventually to the British system under which time would have to be given by the networks to the major candidates for President and Vice President," he added.

Mr. Hagerty, who is now international vice president of American Broadcasting Companies, spoke at a symposium on the influence of the mass media on opinion-making in American society held at Columbia College by the college's Board of Managers, an undergraduate student group. About 400 people attended, most of whom were from eastern colleges and universities.

Mr. Hagerty, who began his career as a reporter for The New York Times, recalled the days when he was assigned to accompany candidates on whistle-stop campaigns on which they reached only small sections of the public, and remarked that television and radio had revolutionized political campaigning.

Independents Gain

He said that by giving candidates access to tens of millions of people in their living rooms, the broadcast media had given the balance of political power to the independent voter.

"But all this is getting too darn expensive for any party," Mr. Hagerty declared.

David Schoenbrun of Columbia's School of International Affairs, a writer and former news correspondent, argued that a great weakness in reporting in America resulted from "worship of a false-god— objectivity."

Mr. Schoenbrun pleaded for more analysis, particularly in connection with the Vietnam war, so that apologists for governments who interpret the record controversially would be confronted with other interpretations.

Four newspaper executives commended the report of the President's Advisory Commission on Civil Disorders for making clear the areas in which newspapers could improve their reporting on the racial crisis as well as in acknowledging the press, by and large, had adequately covered civil disorders.

They were Ben W. Gilbert, deputy managing editor of The Washington Post; Ralph McGill, publisher of The Atlanta Constitution; James A. Wechsler, editorial page editor and columnist of The New York Post, and A. M. Rosenthal, an assistant managing editor of The New York Times.

Mr. Gilbert said the report had made clear that the American press, except for the Negro press, had been reporting on the situation of the Negro through white eyes, instead of from a color-blind viewpoint.

Mr. Rosenthal said the effort to publicize the sociological causes of civil disorders was one aspect of "a whole new phase of newspapering," one that promised "an exciting future."

He said that the press was now trying to report what people think and why they think the way they do, and that the effort added a new dimension to the reporting and interpretation of news.

CONVENTION ADS NOW DEDUCTIBLE

Business Regains Tax Break on Booklets of Parties

Special to The New York Times
WASHINGTON, June 12— Hotels, restaurants and other local business in the Chicago and Miami areas will be able to take the normal tax deduction of the cost of advertisements placed in programs of the national political party conventions.

This is the effect of a bill passed quietly yesterday by the House and Senate and sent to the White House, where President Johnson's signature is expected.

The new legislation is designed to undo one small and specific aspect of legislation banning tax deductions for any type of advertising in political programs that was passed in 1966, after widespread criticism of such advertising in programs of both major political parties.

The Democratic party made a reported $1.5-million from selling advertising at $15,000 a page, mainly to large corporations, in its program for its convention in Atlantic City in 1964. The Republican party subsequently and successfully solicited the same corporate advertisers, many of them holders of government contracts, to place ads in a Republican handbook published in 1966.

July 16, 1967

March 10, 1968

Terminated by Congress

The advertising was seen by many as an evasion of the intent of the Corrupt Practices Act, which bars direct contributions to political campaigns by corporations, and Congress, therefore, terminated the tax deductibility of corporate expenditures on advertising in any type of political publication.

The bill that was passed yesterday was designed to restore tax deductibility only to the costs of advertising that represent real advertising and not indirect campaign contributions.

Under the bill, the costs of the ads, to be tax-deductible, will have to be "reasonable," when compared with the business the advertiser expects to gain from them.

The charges in the 1964 programs were excessive, when viewed in the light of the number of people reached and the rates charged by regular commercial publications for audiences of similar size.

The legislation, sponsored by Senator Everett McKinley Dirksen, Republican of Illinois, was originally attached to the pending tax increase bill when it was passed by the Senate earlier this year.

It was detached from that long-stalled measure, and passed separately yesterday, so that the political parties can begin trying to sell ads in their convention programs right away.

The Treasury Department, which has jurisdiction over all tax matters, informed Congress that it had no objection to the Dirksen bill, and President Johnson is, therefore, expected to sign it.

June 13, 1968

Sweetener for the Parties

Congress has come to the aid of the parties in this election year by opening a crack in the door it supposedly closed two years ago against evasions of the Corrupt Practices Act. Both Senate and House have quietly passed a bill to repeal the present ban on tax deductions for advertising in the programs at national political conventions.

To be sure, the bill seeks to bar the flagrant abuses that finally moved Congress to enact the prohibition in 1966. It specifies that the advertising be genuine, not disguised campaign contributions, and that its costs be "reasonable," rather than the $15,000 a page the Democrats exacted for their 1964 convention program.

But who can really determine whether advertising is genuine or its costs "reasonable" in relation to the expected return? And why the haste to repeal a ban for which Congress saw a need only two years ago? There are less compromising ways for the parties to build their campaign war chests and there are emphatically more urgent issues before this Congress.

June 15, 1968

Bill Aims to Cut TV Campaign Costs

By FRED FERRETTI

A bill that would drastically reduce the cost of televised political commercials for Senate and House candidates will be introduced in both houses of Congress next week.

The legislation, drafted by the National Committee for an Effective Congress, would limit political candidates' television exposure to a period beginning five weeks before Election Day in November, and would set limits on what stations could charge candidates for commercial time.

The bill will be co-sponsored in the Senate by Senator Philip A. Hart, Democrat of Michigan, and Senator Robert B. Pearson, Republican of Kansas. Representative Torbert H. MacDonald, Democrat of Massachusetts and chairman of the House Communications sub-committee, will introduce it in the lower House.

Stipulations of Bill

The bill provides that each legally-qualified Senate candidate would be entitled in a general election to buy 120 one-minute commercial spots or their equivalent and one 30-minute program-length broadcast, or its equivalent, on each station serving the area in which he is a candidate. "Area" is defined not only as the district in which the station is located but also as a station whose broadcast-area population contains at least one-third of the population of the Congressional district. The broadcast area is the contoured region of the station's signal as prescribed by the Federal Communications Commission.

The proposed legislation stipulates that each legally-qualified candidate for the House shall be permitted to buy 60 one-minute commercials and one 30-minute program, or their equivalents.

The rates for one-minute spots would be about 30 per cent of what they are now. The half-hour program rates would be 20 per cent of current rates.

Allowances would be made for different rates in prime time and non-prime time hours. In New York, the cost of a one-minute commercial in prime time is as high as $7,800.

The bill specifies that candidates must make requests to buy time 60 days before the general election; or 42 days prior if a special primary had been called within that 60-day period. Forty days before the election, the station would be required to submit a list of available time slots to candidates.

Under the bill, the F.C.C. would have the authority to require commercial stations to keep financial records for four months prior to the election, so that rates could be established for the political commercials.

Russell D. Hemenway, national director of the National Committee, called the bill "professional" and "moderate."

He said the committee considered, then rejected, an addition to the bill that would have covered primary elections and included radio in the provisions. Mr. Hemenway said "television is the logical area in which first to concentrate such effort because it is the one factor most responsible for the upward spiral of campaign costs and because, as the recent F.C.C. Survey of Political Broadcasting in 1968 so accurately shows, broadcasters tend increasingly to regard campaigns as a commercial rather than public service opportunity."

Mr. Hemenway said his organization has lobbied for the bill, which has taken a year to draft. There has been some resistance, he said, because "some incumbents don't want to do anything for challengers," but the bill's moderate tone has been "persuasive," he said.

The committee is a 21-year-old bipartisan citizens' action group. Among its members are George Biddle, Thomas K. Finletter, Orin Lehman, Hans Morgenthau, Stewart Mott, Telford Taylor and Barbara Tuchman. Henry Steele Commager, the historian, is a vice chairman.

September 4, 1969

225

Free Election Air Time

The cost of running for high public office—anything from President of the United States to Mayor of New York—has gone through the ceiling. The main reason is the cost of TV time.

The Federal Communications Commission report on 1968 political broadcasting costs shows that $58.9 million was spent—a 70 per cent increase over the previous Presidential election year. In New York's race for Mayor, specials and spot commercials on radio and television will cost the candidates just about as much money as they can raise to buy time. A million dollars or more is expected to be spent before Election Day.

There are two intertwined problems: the regulation of campaign spending and equitable access to network and station time by legitimate candidates.

The Federal and state laws purporting to regulate campaign expenditures are lamentably feeble. Thirty-nine states and the Federal Government have statutes controlling campaign spending but they are full of loopholes. The need is for a Federal Elections Commission which could audit and supervise collection and spending—covering not only general elections but also primaries and conventions. At the state level, reform is needed to put teeth into present laws.

In an effort to reduce TV campaigning costs, the National Committee for an Effective Congress, a bipartisan organization, has drafted a measure that would permit Senate and House candidates to buy time at 20 to 30 per cent of the normal commercial rate. With a similar goal of access, a Twentieth Century Fund plan would provide for a 50 per cent discount off the normal commercial rate. It would apply to both Presidential and Congressional candidates. In the case of Presidential candidates, every station in the United States would have to carry certain programs simultaneously without exception 35 days before an election. This might be more burdensome on viewers than stations.

Under the plan advanced by the Twentieth Century Fund, the cost of this discounted time would be shifted to the Federal Government. The candidates would pay nothing and the stations would be reimbursed, in effect by the viewer-taxpayer. This proposal has been questioned by Commissioner Nicholas Johnson of the F.C.C., who maintains that "an industry that is using public property, the airwaves," should not "hold up the elected public officials and make them pay to get time from public property."

In our opinion, a certain amount of time should be provided by the networks and stations to Presidential and Congressional candidates, without cost, for a limited period before Election Day. Candidates could still be allowed to purchase time but free time would insure that all candidates would be heard.

NETWORKS FAVOR CAMPAIGN AD CUTS

N.B.C. Would Reduce Rate for Candidates by Half

By FRED FERRETTI

The presidents of the nation's three commercial television networks told a Senate subcommittee yesterday that they favored discounts for commercials by political candidates. Their unanimity was seen as an attempt to head off legislation to make such rate reductions mandatory.

The suggestions for discounts ranged from a proposal by Julian Goodman of the National Broadcasting Company for a network-wide 50 per cent reduction to espousal of the general concept of discounts, without a specific figure, by Dr. Frank Stanton of the Columbia Broadcasting System. Leonard Goldenson, president of the American Broadcasting Company, proposed a one-third reduction in political commercial costs.

The network executives testified before the Senate Sub-committee on Communications, headed by Senator John O. Pastore, Democrat of Rhode Island, which is considering two proposals for reducing time costs. The executives' statements were released in New York.

Congress Races Affected

The first rate discount plan, proposed by the National Committee for an Effective Congress, would require networks by law to reduce rates for candidates for the House and Senate. The second, proposed by the Twentieth Century Fund's Commission on Campaign Costs in the Electronic Era, would provide governmental subsidies to pay for political time.

Mr. Goodman's plan called for one-minute commercial spots at 50 per cent of the prevailing commercial rate; and the offer of five-minute positions after the "Today" show and the N.B.C. movies, whenever those run short. Those would be available for the 1972 election year, said Mr. Goodman. He made a similar proposal for reduced rates for the 1968 elections. Recently N.B.C. announced that its five owned and operated stations were offering 25 per cent discounts for the elections this fall.

Mr. Goldenson said A.B.C.'s offer of a 33 1/3 per cent political discount would pertain to the 1972 elections. He told the subcommittee: "It would indeed be unfortunate and would undermine the very basic structure of our form of government if candidacy for public office were to become the exclusive preserve of the wealthy or those with ready access to private wealth."

A.B.C. recently initiated a one-third discount for the upcoming elections at its five owned and operated stations.

Dr. Stanton agreed that candidates should get cut rates, but he did not suggest any particular percentage. C.B.S. currently gives political candidates what it calls an "end rate," which is the rate charged long-range advertisers. In effect it is a reduction.

Time Set-Aside Opposed

All the network presidents opposed that portion of the Twentieth Century Fund proposal that would dictate that on a certain night all television stations would have to carry simultaneously candidates' appearances. Mr. Stanton called it "forced feeding." Mr. Goldenson said that it created a "captive audience." Mr. Goodman called it "commandeering" and "wholly wrong."

Rosel M. Hyde, the outgoing Federal Communications Commission chairman, told the subcommittee he favored the concept of reduced time charges for political candidates, but opposed the effective Congress group's bill because it didn't go far enough. It would legislate discounts only for candidates for the Senate and the House.

Congress Takes Up High Cost of TV Politicking

By WARREN WEAVER Jr.
Special to The New York Times

WASHINGTON, Oct. 26 — Twenty years after television began to have an impact on national politics, Congress has finally begun to grapple with the complex problems raised by this very expensive, very effective medium.

For the first time, a Senate subcommittee is giving serious consideration to a bill that would guarantee political candidates a minimum amount of television exposure during a campaign at greatly reduced rates.

The reform act is deliberately a very modest proposal. It only affects Senators and Representatives. It does not mandate any free television time. It does not restrict in any way what a candidate spends for television over and above the guaranteed cut-rate minimum.

But if it can be passed, even in still more modest form, it will establish the principle that Congress has a responsibility to regulate use of the most powerful political instrument now available, and that will be a very important principle indeed.

It has already won the opposition of the three major television networks, whose presidents told the Senate Commerce Subcommittee on Communications last Wednesday that they would gladly give discount rates to political candidates, but did not want to be forced into it by law.

As drafted by the National Committee for an Effective Congress, the bill would entitle every Senate candidate, incumbent and challenger alike, to 120 one-minute prime time television spots or the equivalent, and one 30-minute continuous program or the equivalent, in segments of five minutes or more.

House candidates, except those who run statewide, would get 60 one-minute spots, but the same 30 minutes of program time. No one would have to buy the time, but those who did would pay only 30 per cent of the commercial rate for spots and 20 per cent for program time.

The underlying purpose of the legislation is to insure to some extent that Congressional office does not become restricted to the very rich.

Some Members Hold Back

In addition to the broadcasters, there are opponents among the members of Congress themselves, although the measure has nearly 40 sponsors in each branch. There are two sources of reluctance: The fear that the Senators and Representatives will appear to be voting themselves a bonus and the fact that the resulting program would give a substantial assist to non-incumbents.

Senator John O. Pastore, the Rhode Island Democrat who heads the communications subcommittee, will probably exercise the single most important influence over the fate of the legislation. Its sponsors believe they have a majority in his subcommittee and the full commerce committee, if he will move the bill forward.

There is some disposition on the subcommittee to believe that television rate reductions for political candidates is a sound proposal, but that the amounts of time set in the bill may be excessive.

It seems unlikely that the bill can get to the Senate floor until early next year. The goal of its backers is to have it enacted in time to assist candidates in the 1970 Congressional elections.

The network presidents were the only opposition witnesses in three days of hearing before the Pastore subcommittee. Members of Congress, advertising executives and professional campaign consultants supported the bill.

October 27, 1969

Congressional Air Equality

The Campaign Broadcast Reform Act now under Congressional scrutiny offers political candidates a realistic opportunity of access to radio and TV stations regardless of their personal wealth or the amount of their campaign contributions.

As drafted by the National Committee for an Effective Congress, the proposed law would give Congressional candidates not free time but bargain-rate time. The legislation would provide candidates for Congress minimal amounts of television spot and program time at discounts of 70 or 80 per cent in the five weeks preceding each general election. A candidate would not be prohibited from buying additional time at regular rates. That would leave a rich candidate still able to saturate the airwaves.

Nevertheless, the proposed act is at least a start toward reducing the great advantage money now gives a well-financed candidate over one with meager funds. Fairer access to the airwaves will help turn the quest for Senate and House seats into something other than the sale of a product.

November 19, 1969

BILL WOULD CURB CAMPAIGN TV COST

Senate Panel to Vote This Week on Pastore's Plan— Some Free Time Sought

---

By CHRISTOPHER LYDON
Special to The New York Times

WASHINGTON, March 15— The Senate Commerce Committe is expected to vote this week to adjust the basic rules of political advertising to deal with the central role—and devastating cost — of television campaigning.

Legislation conceived by Senator John O. Pastore, who is considered Congress's most influential specialist in broadcast matters, has provisions that would do the following:

¶Suspend permanently the "equal time" rules for Presidential and Vice-Presidential candidates, making unsponsored TV debates between Democratic and Republican candidates a regular part of national campaigns. The bill would encourage broadcasters to offer free time, though not necessarily equivalent time, to "significant" third and fourth-party candidates.

¶Establish a candidate's discount, 25 per cent off commercial rates, in the last four weeks before certain elections —including Senate, House and gubernatorial campaigns.

¶Clamp a relatively low limit on the amount of money a candidate could spend on broadcast advertising: no more than 5 cents for every popular vote cast in the last election for that office.

Senator Pastore, a Rhode Island Democrat, is confident of Senate support for his proposal. But House approval and the President's signature are uncertain, especially in an election year when the affluent Republican party is not conspicuously concerned about the high cost of campaigning.

The nickel-a-vote formula would drastically diminish political spending on radio and television, though the provision of free time in national campaigns might increase the exposure of Presidential and Vice-Presidential candidates.

On the basis of the turnout of more than 73 million voters in the Presidential election of 1968, national tickets (treating Presidential and Vice-Presidential pairs as a unit) could spend about $3.6-million apiece on broadcast advertising.

In the campaign of 1968, by comparison, the Democrats spent $6.1-million on radio and

TV in their final drive for the Presidency. The Republican effort that elected Richard M. Nixon and Spiro T. Agnew cost more than double that—$12.6 million — for broadcast advertising alone.

The same nickel-a-voter rule would mean even deeper cuts, relatively speaking, in the spending on state campaigns. In the State of New York, for example, where 6 million votes were cast in the Governor's election in 1966, candidates could spend only $300,000. — much less than candidates are currently budgeting for TV and a small fraction of what Governor Rockefeller spent on his last, heavily televised campaign.

In campaigns for the House of Representatives, candidates could spend $20,000 on broadcast advertising, whether or not that figure could be justified by the nickel-a-voter formula.

Vote Expected Thursday

Senator Pastore's bill, which will be voted on by the Commerce Committee in a closed session on Thursday, is significantly different from the proposal that attracted wide Congressional support last fall.

The earlier bill, drafted by the National Committee for an Effective Congress, guaranteed a minimum of TV exposure for all candidates and mandated much larger discounts in the cost of advertising time.

It set no limits on spending, however. Also, it did not treat with Section 315 of the Federal Communications Act, which, by requiring equal access for major and minor candidates, has effectively barred free confrontations between the main rivals for political office.

In 1960, the suspension of Section 315 made possible the TV debates between John F. Kennedy and Mr. Nixon. But in the campaigns of 1964 and 1968, Congress declined to waive the "equal time" rule.

The emergence of George C. Wallace as a third-party candidate in 1968 compounded the difficulties of defining fair treatment of all candidates.

Under Senator Pastore's bill, the private broadcast networks would have the ultimate responsibility for deciding which candidates, in addition to the Republican and Democratic contenders, were "significant" and how much free time would be "fair."

Years of Debate

Once Section 315 was suspended, a third-party candidate would have no appeal beyond the networks concerning the treatment he receives. He can now appeal to the Federal Communications Commission.

The vagueness of Senator Pastore's bill on the issue of fairness reflects years of inconclusive debate about the rights of minority parties. According to a key aide to the Commerce Committee:

"Our argument is that the moment you start drawing up a formula, you run into difficulties. The networks have said, 'Try us.' They've said they would have treated George Wallace as a significant candidate if we had suspended Section 315 in 1968. We would let them use their judgment."

The same staff aide argued that advertising discounts for candidates were valueless unless accompanied by spending limits.

"A simple discount gives the rich candidate a chance to buy more time than ever," he said. "If you're really concerned about the candidate of modest means, there has to be a ceiling on what every candidate can spend."

At Senate hearings last fall, the presidents of the three national television networks offered to make candidate discounts available on a voluntary basis, but they opposed any statutory discount. All three networks have traditionally favored suspension of Section 315 for major campaigns.

Crisis in TV Campaigning...

The Senate Commerce Committee is scheduled to vote this week on a bill ostensibly drawn up to give candidates of modest means a fair chance to do some television campaigning.

The importance of such an objective cannot be overestimated if the electoral system is to remain democratic. But the measure, introduced by Senator Pastore of Rhode Island, is not the way to achieve it. Unlikely to pass, it would be even less likely to accomplish its essential purpose if it did. The rival bill, brought in by Senators Hart of Michigan and Pearson of Kansas, impresses us as more realistic.

The Pastore proposal would guarantee candidates television time in the last month of a campaign at a 25 per cent discount from commercial rates; it would also limit the amount of money any candidate could spend on such broadcasts. But since the discount would be based on the highest price the network could command, the cost to a hard-pressed campaigner would still be extremely heavy.

The limit on broadcast spending would permit the Democrats to lay out only half of what they spent for television in their unsuccessful campaign of 1968 and would restrict the Republicans to a mere 25 per cent of what it took them to win. The chances of Congress approving such a reduction seem microscopic.

The Hart-Pearson bill, long nurtured by the National Committee for an Effective Congress, would impose no TV spending limits at all. Such ceilings have been totally unsuccessful in other aspects of campaign financing, as suggested below; in the case of TV, they would also be of doubtful constitutionality. But the measure would compel a much more drastic reduction in price for a fixed minimum of television exposure. The purpose would be to assure the underprivileged candidate a reasonable time on TV for a reasonable outlay of cash.

So modest a proposal should evoke a minimum outcry even from Congressional incumbents, who traditionally frown on any plan that might be helpful to a challenger. But, in the larger framework of campaign financing, far more must be done—and soon.

...and a Need for Action

Such is the legerdemain of political fund-raising that two West Coast businessmen (one of them an ex-convict) advanced some $240,000 apiece to the Humphrey Presidential campaign of 1968 without in the least violating a law limiting such contributions to $5,000. The explanation is that while the two contributors were prohibited from giving more than that modest sum to the candidate himself or to any campaign committee, they were perfectly free to give it to each and every such committee his managers cared to set up. In this case they gave to 48 of the 97 such agencies, including Doctors for Humphrey-Muskie, Dentists for Humphrey-Muskie, and Economists, Conservationists, Advertising Executives, Sports Stars, etc.—all for Humphrey-Muskie.

The practice is universal, and by no means confined to occupations. The Nixon-Agnew ticket enjoyed the fund-channeling support of temporary organizations like Victory '68, Tennessee for Nixon and one called Thurmond Speaks. But there are countless loopholes like this that make of present corrupt practices legislation one huge escape hatch. Primaries, for a starter, are exempt from such regulation altogether, although they may involve sums as high as the $2 million spent by Max Rafferty and Thomas Kuchel in pursuit of the Republican Senatorial nomination in 1968.

Congressional candidates, obliged to report all spending made with their "knowledge or consent," find the law no problem; they have only to blind themselves to what others spend for them. One Senator's executive assistant was only more candid than most when he explained: "We are very careful to make sure that the Senator never sees the campaign receipts; they go right to the committee." The Pennsylvania Senatorial campaign of 1968 cost about a million dollars; the total expenditure as legally reported to the Senate was $6,236.

* * *

What keeps these and other absurd loopholes from being closed is not so much hypocrisy as it is the great unsolved problem of staggering campaign costs. If the laws were made effective enough to do what they are ostensibly intended to do, only the richest could afford to run for office, and even they would be in trouble. Governor Rockefeller spent something like $5 million of his own to be re-elected in 1966. Total campaign costs, Presidential and Congressional but excluding primaries, rose from almost $30 million in 1956 to more than $70 million in 1968.

Even now, says Senator Inouye of Hawaii, "I am afraid that realities and practicalities of the election process have, to some extent, developed a new aristocracy of wealth and power." True, a man rich enough to finance his own campaign may be rich enough to be independent in office as well — the Roosevelts, Rockefellers, Harrimans and Kennedys have not governed like plutocrats — but Americans are not ready for government by an aristocracy of money, however enlightened. Yet an even greater problem is posed by the candidate of moderate or low income who has had to mortgage his independence in order to be elected. To what extent can he regard his public office as a public trust?

To ask a Congress as far behind schedule as the 91st to address itself to the vast and politically sensitive question of overhauling campaign finances may well be an exercise in futility. But the situation is fast becoming critical, especially in view of the skyrocketing costs of television. If the 91st cannot produce legislation to deal with the complexities of reporting or of tax credits for political contributions, it could at least decide on some of the simpler reforms that have been proposed. Specifically, it can spread the advantages of television, as the Hart-Pearson bill provides. It should, in simple fairness, make the franking privilege, a major boon to Congressional incumbents, available to their challengers as well. And it could, with even less pain to itself, vote to require the states to take on the financial burden of registering all their voters—a burden now assumed without logic or fairness by the parties and often by the candidates themselves.

TV DEBATE BILL GAINS IN SENATE

Measure Would Cut Costs for Future Candidates

Special to The New York Times

WASHINGTON, March 19—The Senate Commerce Committee unanimously approved today a bill to encourage free television debates between Presidential and Vice-Presidential candidates and to reduce the cost of television time for all political candidates.

The measure, however, is not supported in its present form by a majority of the committee. Two opposing groups within the committee agreed to send the bill to the Senate floor, where their differences could be fought out through the amending process.

The bill, as approved in today's vote, would repeal "equal time" rules applicable to candidates for the nation's two highest offices and encourage but not require that time be provided for significant third- and fourth-party candidates.

It is generally assumed that this would result in the networks' granting free time for debates to Democratic and Republican candidates, while providing some time to other candidates in consultation with the Federal Communications Commission.

Time was granted in 1960 for the Kennedy-Nixon debates when the "equal time" rule was temporarily suspended.

Doubts on Debate

However, knowledgeable sources question whether President Nixon would be willing to debate a candidate in 1972. They point out that President Johnson was unwilling to debate Barry Goldwater in 1964 and that Mr. Nixon shied away from a debate with Hubert H. Humphrey in 1968.

The approved bill would also require that television networks and individual stations charge candidates — local, state, and national—their lowest unit rate.

This would presumably mean that the stations would charge the discount rate that they give to major sponsors who advertise on season-long shows or those rates given shows presented at hours when few viewers are presumed to be watching.

This provision was voted as a compromise between two proposals for requiring the stations to grant candidates a discount from commercial rates.

One proposed discount, favored by Senator John O. Pastore, Democrat of Rhode Island, would grant the candidate 25 per cent off the commercial rate during the last four or five weeks of certain campaigns—including Senate, House and Gubernatorial.

Senator Philip A. Hart, Democrat of Michigan, and Senator James B. Pearson, Republican of Kansas, argued in committee for a discount rate similar to Senator Pastore's but with limits on the number of spot promotions.

Amendments Expected

Both proposals are expected to be presented in the form of amendments to the bill when it reaches the Senate floor in late April or early May.

Opponents of Senator Pastore's discount provision argued in committee that without a limit the richest candidate can buy more time slots on a station. They favor the limit on short 30-second and one-minute spot promotions because many experts have stated that these were the most effective.

Senator Pastore has a formula for limiting the amount candidates could spend on broadcast advertising and is expected to propose in an amendment that candidates be limited to 5 cents for every popular vote cast in the last election for that office.

Critics believe this is too limiting. They note that on the basis of 1968 Presidential turnout of 73 million voters future candidates for that office would be limited to about $3.6-million each.

During the 1968 campaign, by comparison, the Democrats spent $6.1-million on broadcast advertising and the Republicans spent $12.6-million on TV and radio to elect Richard M. Nixon and Spiro T. Agnew.

The Senate is expected to have a full debate on these questions as well as others, including where the responsibility for enforcing spending limits would be placed.

The networks have traditionally opposed any statutory discount while always expressing support for suspension of the "equal time" rule in major contests—and Senate sources implied that the emergence of George C. Wallace as a third national candidate in 1972 could raise legal questions if any legislation were passed.

Campaign TV Costs

To the Editor:

In criticizing Senator Pastore's proposal which reportedly would give political candidates 25 per cent discounts from commercial television rates, your March 17 editorial inaccurately states ". . . since the discount would be based on the highest price the network could command, the cost to a hard-pressed campaigner would still be extremely heavy."

Out of hundreds of races which would be affected by the bill, only those for two offices —President and Vice President— ever involve the purchase of time on any of the nationwide networks.

While some individual stations may benefit financially from election-year activities, sale of network time to candidates involves pre-emption of better paying advertisers, entirely apart from the tremendous, unrecouped costs of convention and campaign coverage, and the extensive free time contributed by the networks.

Central Problem

By misapprehending the problem as one related to networks, your editorial misses the central problem: In a fiercely competitive Congressional race, will a reduction in the price of television time reduce campaign expenditures or merely escalate the use of television?

Television is not presently an important element of campaign costs for most Congressional candidates in the nation's large metropolitan areas. Paid political announcements are not an efficient use of the medium, because each constituency represents only a small part of a station's total audience. For a New York City station serving 38 Congressional districts, approximately 97 per cent of the audience would not be in a given candidate's district.

Looking at national campaigns only, the cornerstone of the Pastore bill, I would submit, is the repeal of the "equal-time" provision of the Communications Act. Its temporary suspension in 1960 enabled the Columbia Broadcasting System to devote 32¼ hours to personal appearances of the Democratic and Republican Presidential and Vice-Presidential candidates and their supporters, with no charge to them —at a value, not including regularly scheduled news broadcasts and convention coverage, exceeding $2 million. Additional free time offered, but not accepted, exceeded $700,000.

NBC and ABC likewise donated generous amounts of time.

Finally, like C.B.S., many broadcasters throughout the nation, as a matter of long-standing policy, extend preferential treatment to candidates — that is, substantially reduced rates, optimum time, and opportunity to pre-empt commercial availabilities.

FRANK STANTON
President, C.B.S.
New York, March 19, 1970

HOUSE SETS LIMIT FOR TV SPENDING IN ELECTION RACES

Broadens Senate's Version to Include Primaries and Some State Contests

By CHRISTOPHER LYDON

Special to The New York Times

WASHINGTON, Aug. 11—The House moved today to cut campaign costs and control television's impact on politics by limiting the expenditures that candidates may make on broadcast advertising.

The House bill, approved by a vote of 272 to 97, broadened the spending limits that the Senate enacted earlier to cover not only Presidential and Congressional elections, but also primaries and state races for Governor and Lieutenant Governor.

The House also postponed the effective date of the legislation until next year. The Senate wrote the original bill to cover this year's elections, and is expected to press for immediate effectiveness when the bill goes to a Senate-House conference committee.

Equal Time Rule

Like the Senate bill, the House version repeals — for Presidential and Vice-Presidential campaigns — the rule that broadcasters must give equal time to all candidates. Thus, if the bill becomes law, the presence of fringe candidates on the ballot will no longer block debates or other free network time for the principal contenders.

The House also concurred with the Senate in requiring that broadcasters charge candidates the lowest time rate available to bulk commercial buyers, a change that would cut political costs by as much as 40 per cent.

Thus, while candidates would not be free to spend as much as they do now, their money would stretch further. Broadcast budgets could not exceed 7 cents for every person that voted in the last election for the office being contested.

$5.1-Million Ceiling

On the basis of the 1968 election returns, that formula would limit the spending of Presidential and Vice-Presidential candidates in 1972 to $5.1-million—or about 40 per cent of what the Nixon-Agnew ticket spent on radio and television two years ago.

The ceiling for individual states would vary with population and political participation. In New York, where slightly more than 6 million people voted in the last state elections, a candidate for Governor or Senator could spend about $430,000 in the final race—a small fraction of Governor Rockefeller's broadcast budget four years ago.

In primaries, candidates could spend half of the amount allowed for elections. Thus, the limit in New York primaries would be approximately $215,000—or about a quarter of what Representative Richard L. Ottinger has acknowledged spending on television in his successful race for the Democratic Senatorial nomination last June.

The National Committee for an Effective Congress, a bipartisan reform organization that drafted and lobbied for the political broadcasting bill, had stressed that the limitation of expenses—and of the political obligations that are tied to contributions—was its most important virtue.

Defense Against Rich

But many members of Congress have reportedly embraced the bill as a defense against rich opponents who might otherwise "buy political office," it was charged today, through saturation TV campaigns.

There were indications in the House discussion of the bill today that the victory in Ohio's Democratic primary last spring of Howard M. Metzenbaum, a wealthy but obscure candidate for the Senate nomination, over John Glenn, the former astronaut, had been a profound shock.

The lesson that was repeatedly drawn was that if so revered a figure as Mr. Glenn could be undone by a heavy television campaign, no incumbent was secure against a well-financed "blitz." Thus, the notion of a limit on broadcast expenditures has had strong support in both houses of Congress and among both Democrats and Republicans.

Presidential Debates

Democratic proponents of the bill spoke enthusiastically today of the prospect of Presidential debates in 1972 similar to those in 1960. There was no consideration, however, of repealing the "equal time" rule for all elections, so as to expose incumbent Senators and Representatives to TV debates in their home districts.

Russel D. Hemenway, director of the National Committee for an Effective Congress, acknowledged these and other inconsistencies in his general defense of the bill today. The bill, he said, "has been attacked as a protector of incumbents and a boon to Democrats, an unfair discrimination against broadcasters as opposed to other campaign suppliers." He added: "But to let the relative and usually temporary advantage of one party or category of candidates distort the issue is forever to evade the problem. The fact is that this bill is the first real step toward badly needed reform."

Representative Torbert H. Macdonald, the Massachusetts Democrat who managed the bill, said that broadcasting had been singled out for control because it was the most effective medium of political advertising, because it was the general area where "runaway" spending has been concentrated and because broadcast expenditures could be easily and precisely monitored.

Senate Approves Curbs On Political TV Spending

By JOHN W. FINNEY
Special to The New York Times

WASHINGTON, Sept. 23—The Senate, over token Republican opposition, completed Congressional action today on legislation designed to restrict the growing political costs of campaign advertising on television and radio.

The legislation, regarded by many in Congress as the most significant campaign finance reform since the Corrupt Practices Act was passed 45 years ago, was approved by a 60-to-19 vote. Eighteen of the dissenting votes were cast by Republicans.

The bill, a compromise between earlier Senate and House versions, was approved last week by the House by a vote of 247 to 112 and now goes to President Nixon for his approval.

Within Republican circles, there were hints that the President might veto the bill, which has been generally opposed by Republicans since it was introduced a year ago at the urging of the National Committee for an Effective Congress, a bipartisan group that supports moderate and liberal political candidates.

Senator Hugh Scott of Pennsylvania, the Senate minority leader, raised the possibility of a Presidential veto when he told the Senate that, while he supported the objectives of the bill, it was "loosely drawn" and that, "if the bill were to be vetoed, I would have to support the veto."

Privately, however, a White House aide told one of the drafters of the bill that the talk of a veto was "exaggerated."

Political Problem

While the White House attitude remained unclear, the bill's sponsors hoped that political pressures would not permit the President to veto a measure designed to deal with what is widely regarded as one of the most pressing political problems: the rising costs of campaigning brought about by the increasing use of television.

Even if the President does sign the legislation, it probably will not go into effect until after the Nov. 3 elections.

One of the most controversial features of the legislation was its effective date. As finally worked out, the legislation provides that it will go into effect 30 days after being signed into law by the President. Because of Congressional delays — mostly by Republicans—in passing the compromise bill, the legislation is not expected to be signed by Mr. Nixon in time to go into effect this year.

One possible Presidential objection to the bill is its repeal of the "equal time" provision in the Federal Communications Act. This provision, which has always been an impediment to television debates between Republican and Democratic Presidential candidates, requires the networks to provide equal air time to minority party candidates. With the repeal of this provision, President Nixon will find it more difficult to resist challenges to television debates in the 1972 Presidential campaign.

Spending Limitations

Although never publicly stated, an underlying Republican objection to the bill was the spending limitations it would impose on political broadcasting — limitations that many Republicans felt could work to the advantage of the relatively indigent Democratic party as well as the Democratic incumbents who control Congress.

It was expected that the bill would significantly curtail in most states the amount being spent on political broadcasting, which has risen drastically in recent years and now probably amounts to more than $50-million in an election year.

The spending limitation would apply to candidates for President, Vice President, Congress, Governor and Lieutenant Governor.

In general elections, the candidates would be required to limit their spending for radio and television time to the equivalent of 7 cents for each vote cast in the last election for the office for which they are running, or $20,000—whichever is higher. In primaries, the candidates would be limited to half the amount permitted for general elections.

Presidential and Vice-Presidential candidates would be exempt from the spending limitation in primaries, but not from the over-all limitation.

Based on the number of votes cast in the 1968 Presidential election, it was believed that the bill would limit each major party to less than $6-million in broadcast spending for its Presidential ticket in 1972.

$19-Million in 1968

Two years ago, the Republicans spent more than $12-million for radio and TV advertising to elect Mr. Nixon, while the Democrats spent $7.1-million in their unsuccessful effort to elect former Vice President Hubert H. Humphrey.

In New York State, for example, the legislation would result in a sharp curtailment in the amount being spent on television and radio campaigning. A senatorial candidate under the limitations would be permitted to spend $460,700 in this year's election in New York.

In comparison, Representative Richard L. Ottinger of Westchester, the Democratic-Liberal senatorial candidate, reportedly has budgeted $1.5-million for radio and television time in his campaign.

To a certain extent, these spending limitations are offset by reduced costs for politicians purchasing air time. The bill provides that broadcasters must sell political candidates air time at the lowest price charged commercial advertisers. The effect is to give political candidates the same discount granted major advertisers, and the result is expected to be a 25 to 50 per cent reduction in the price charged political candidates for broadcast time.

Nixon Said to Plan Veto of Cost Limit In TV Campaigning

By WARREN WEAVER Jr.
Special to The New York Times

WASHINGTON, Sept. 30—President Nixon was reported by key political advisers today to be preparing to veto the bill limiting campaign expenditures for radio and television.

The measure, which cleared Congress in final form a week ago, can not have any impact on the 1970 elections in any event. With the President out of the country and a 30-day delay written into the bill, it could not become effective until Nov. 4 at the earliest—the day after the election.

But if it were signed by Mr. Nixon, it would impose a ceiling of about $5.1-million on the amount that any political party could spend on radio and television promotion for its national ticket in 1972.

On the basis of 1968 figures, this would prove more of a limitation to the Republicans, who spent more than $12-million for the Nixon-Agnew campaign, than the Democrats, whose radio-television investment in the Humphrey-Muskie ticket was about $7.1-million.

The Republican National Chairman, Representative Rogers C. B. Morton of Maryland, has strongly urged the President to disapprove the campaign spending bill on the general theory that it represents only a partial attack on the overall problem of holding down the cost of politics.

Mr. Morton also believes that the measure would discriminate against candidates who do not already hold public office, since they would suffer more from the media limits than incumbents who get a certain amount of free air time in the course of normal news coverage.

Under the campaign spending bill, every candidate for President, Vice President, Senator, Representative, Governor or Lieutenant Governor would be limited to buying an amount of television and radio time equivalent to 7 cents for every person who voted in the last election for the office for which he is running.

It is regarded by its sponsors, among them the National Committee for an Effective Congress, as a first step toward countering the trend toward limiting political competition to candidates who are personally wealthy or are subsidized by wealthy organizations.

Some Democrats believe that a veto of the legislation by President Nixon would raise a potent issue for the current Congressional campaign, opening Republicans to the charge that their Administration was favoring not only the rich over the poor but also itself.

If Mr. Nixon does veto the measure, an effort will be organized to override the veto, which requires two-thirds majorities in both houses. The final version of the bill passed the Senate, 60 to 19, and the House, 247 to 112. Presidential disapproval would probably erode Republican support, however.

Access to the Village Green

Those who favor unlimited television spending in political campaigns are not giving up just because Congress has finally passed a bill to impose some restraints. There is increasing pressure on President Nixon to veto the measure, much of it on plainly spurious grounds.

Time now makes pointless the still-expressed fears that the law would unfairly affect commitments already made in the current campaign or that it would upset tactical plans for the homestretch. The earliest date the President could sign the measure, on his return from Europe, would be next Monday. Since by its own terms the law can go into effect only thirty days after signing, it would miss this year's campaign by two days.

The continuing opposition, then, has nothing to do with the unfairness of changing the rules in the middle of the game, which was in fact an issue early in the Congressional debate. It is, rather, a desperate effort to stave off a permanent reform not generally favored by candidates with money to spare or broadcasters ready to relieve them of it. For the most part it is so partisan in origin that the President cannot yield to it without invoking the charge of having put party above a nationally needed reform.

It is Democrats—usually less soundly financed than their opponents—who are even now proposing immediate voluntary curbs and Republicans who are ignoring their overtures. For every exception, like Mrs. Romney in Michigan or Senator Prouty in Vermont, there are four or five Republicans who will have no part of such an agreement. Not least among them, either in wealth or in subtlety, is Gov. Nelson A. Rockefeller. Planning to carry his case to "the maximum number of people," he describes the mass media as today's equivalent of "the town meeting and the village green." They are—which is precisely why it should not take the Rockefeller green to win access to them.

PRESIDENT VETOES TV SPENDING CURB FOR '72 ELECTIONS

Says It Limits Candidates in Presenting Message and Hurts Urban Aspirants

HE FACES 2 CHALLENGES

Democrats Likely to Press Issue in Campaign and to Seek to Override

By WARREN WEAVER Jr.
Special to The New York Times

WASHINGTON, Oct. 12 —President Nixon vetoed today the bill that would have limited television and radio spending in political campaigns, beginning with the 1972 Presidential election.

The President said the bill, which had cleared Congress with substantial bipartisan support, had "highly laudable and widely supported goals" but was "worse than no answer to the problem—it is a wrong answer."

Mr. Nixon's veto faces two immediate challenges: Sharp criticism by Democratic Congressional candidates in the remaining three weeks of the campaign and an effort to override his veto, probably during the post-election session of Congress that will begin Nov. 16.

O'Brien Begins Attack

The Democratic national chairman, Lawrence F. O'Brien, led off the political attack by charging that the President vetoed the bill because it would have "stopped the Republican party's campaign to saturate the public airways with paid spot commercials."

Russell D. Hemenway, director of the National Committee for an Effective Congress, which sponsored the legislation, suggested that the veto also represented "a Presidential effort to avoid the possibility of meeting his 1972 opponent in open debate."

The bill would have limited radio and TV campaign spend-ing by Presidential, Congressional and gubernatorial candidates and repealed the "equal time" provisions for Presidential elections in the Federal Communications Act.

In his veto message, President Nixon gave the following reasons for disapproving the bill:

¶It would limit only radio and television spending, and candidates would simply use the same money — perhaps even more — on newspaper ads, billboards, pamphlets and direct mail.

¶By limiting television and radio appearances, it would "severely limit the ability of many candidates to get their message to the greatest number of the electorate."

¶By setting a dollar limit rather than a time limit on broadcast campaigning, it would discriminate against urban candidates who must pay much higher rates for air time.

¶By requiring broadcasters to charge candidates a minimum rate, it would put Congress in the business of setting rates for private industry, "a radical departure."

¶It would not deal with radio and television spending by committees or individuals not directly connected with candidates, directed at an election in which the candidates' own spending was limited.

¶It would raise the possibility that an election result might be challenged and determination of a winner might be delayed if there were charges of violating the spending limits.

¶It would not affect the incumbent's built-in advantage of getting free media coverage but would place a limit on the challenger's ability to counter this advantage, endangering "an honored part of the American political tradition."

Prospects Are Uncertain

The prospects for overriding the President's veto are uncertain. All four Congressional votes — one in each house on separate versions and on the final compromise — were by more than two-thirds majorities, the required percentage for enacting a measure over White House disapproval.

However, on those occasions no firm party lines had been drawn, and a number of Republicans supported the measure. If the President's action solidifies Republican opposition, the effort to override will fail, as the Democrats do not enjoy two-thirds majorities in either house.

A White House official said the Administration had "reasonable expectations" that the veto would be sustained. Senator Warren G. Magnuson, Democrat of Washington, chairman of the Senate Commerce Committee, predicted it would be "very, very close."

Senator Philip A. Hart, Democrat of Michigan, one of the measure's original backers, said it would be "tough . . . now that he has made it a President-against-us issue." He said Mr. Nixon had some valid criticisms, but complained that "we didn't hear a damn word from him when we were trying to get this bill through."

Senator Daniel K. Inouye, Democrat of Hawaii, chairman of the Democratic Senate campaign committee, predicted that the veto would be overridden, "at least in the Senate."

The effect of the bill would be to limit television and radio spending, for time but not production costs, to $5.1-million for each party's national ticket in 1972. In 1968, the Republicans spent $12.7-million and the Democrats $6.1-million.

The measure would affect candidates for President, Vice President, Senator, Representatives, Governor and Lieutenant Governor.

The bill also would suspend the "equal time" provisions in order to permit televised debates between the major party candidates for President without having to include token candidates from insignificant parties.

No Alternative Planned

The White House official who briefed reporters on the veto said Mr. Nixon had not based his disapproval on the equal time question. He declined to predict whether the President intended to debate his Democratic opponent in 1972, as he did in 1960 but not in 1968.

The White House official said the Administration had no plans "at this time" to submit legislation of its own in the area of campaign spending.

"We don't have any legislation in mind, but we recognize this as being inequitable," he said.

As for Democratic criticism of the veto, the White House official said that "there shouldn't be any campaign issue raised" if the President's action were "correctly understood."

Mr. O'Brien disagreed. As a result of Mr. Nixon's action, he said, "the American people must stand up and be counted on Nov. 3—they must deliver a resounding rebuff to the Republican party and to the Nixon-Agnew Administration."

"The votes of the American people are not for sale," the Democratic chairman added, "not even at the price that the Republicans are willing to pay."

Speaking for the National Committee for an Effective Congress, Mr. Hemenway, said: "President Nixon's veto of the first significant reform of campaign finance laws in 50 years is the most flagrant example of partisan interest we have witnessed in [the organization's] 22-year history."

Text of the Veto

Special to The New York Times
WASHINGTON, Oct. 12— Following is the text of President Nixon's message to the Senate accompanying his disapproval of the bill that would have limited campaign spending for television and radio:

I return herewith, without my approval, S. 3637, a bill to revise the provisions of the Communications Act which relate to political broadcasting.

This legislation is aimed at the highly laudable and widely supported goals of controlling political campaign expenditures and preventing one candidate from having an unfair advantage over another. Its fatal deficiency is that it not only falls far short of achieving these goals but also threatens to make matters worse.

S. 3637 does not limit the over-all cost of campaigning. It merely limits the amount that candidates can spend on radio and television. In doing so, it unfairly endangers freedom of discussion, discriminates against the broadcast media, favors the incumbent officeholder over the officeseeker and gives an unfair advantage to the famous. It raises the prospect of more—rather than less— campaign spending. It would be difficult, in many instances impossible, to enforce and would tend to penalize most those who conscientiously attempt to abide by the law.

The problem with campaign spending is not radio and television; the problem is spending. This bill plugs one hole in a sieve.

Candidates who had and wanted to spend large sums of money, could and would simply shift their advertising out of radio and television into other media—magazines, newspapers, billboards, pamphlets, and direct mail. There would be no restriction on the amount they could spend in these media.

Hence, nothing in this bill would mean less campaign spending.

Might Increase Spending

In fact, the bill might tend to increase rather than decrease the total amount that candidates spend in their campaigns. It is a fact of political life that in many Congressional districts and states a candidate can reach more voters per dollar

233

through radio and TV than any other means of communication. Severely limiting the use of TV and radio in these areas would only force the candidate to spend more by requiring him to use more expensive techniques.

By restricting the amount of time a candidate can obtain on television and radio, this legislation would severely limit the ability of many candidates to get their message to the greatest number of the electorate. The people deserve to know more, not less, about the candidates and where they stand.

There are other discriminatory features in this legislation. It limits the amount of money candidates for a major elective office many spend for broadcasting in general elections to 7 cents per vote cast for the office in question in the last election, or $20,000, whichever is greater. This formula was arrived at through legislative compromise and is not based on any scientific analysis of broadcast markets. It fails to take into account the differing campaign expenditure requirements of candidates in various broadcast areas.

In many urban centers, the $20,000 limitation would permit a Congressional candidate to purchase only a few minutes of broadcast time, thus precluding the use of radio or television as an effective instrument of communication. On the other hand, $20,000 spent on television broadcasting in another district would enable a candidate to virtually blanket a large area with campaign advertising spots. For example, 30 seconds of prime television time in New York City costs $3,500; in in the Wichita - Hutchinson, Kan., area it costs $145.

Questions Are Raised

S. 3637 raises a host of other questions of both principle and practice. It would require that broadcasters charge candidates no more than the lowest unit charge of the station for comparable time. This is tantamount to rate - setting by statute and represents a radical departure for the Congress which has traditionally abhorred any attempt to establish rates by legislation.

Among the other questions raised and left unanswered are these: How would expenditures of various individuals and organizations not directly connected with the candidate be charged? Would they be considered part of a candidate's allowed total expenditure, even if they were beyond the candidate's control? And how would money spent by a committee opposing a candidate be accounted?

Would it be included in the total for that candidate's opponent, even though spent without his consent or control? This bill does not effectively limit the purchase of television time to oppose a candidate.

In the end, enforcement of the expenditure limitation would in most cases occur after the election. This raises the possibility of confusion and chaos as elections come to be challenged for violation of S.3637 and the cases are still unresolved when the day arrives on which the winning candidate should take office.

Advantage to Incumbents

There is another issue here which is perhaps the most important of all. An honored part of the American political tradition is that any little known but highly qualified citizen has the opportunity to seek and ultimately win elective office. This bill would strike a serious blow at that tradition. The incumbent—because he has a natural avenue of public attention through the news media in the conduct of his office—would have an immeasurable advantage over the "out" who was trying to get in. The only others who would share part of this advantage would be those whose names were well-known for some other reason.

What we have in S.3637 is a good aim, gone amiss. Nearly everyone who is active or interested in the political process wants to find some way to limit the crushing and growing cost of political campaigning. But this legislation is worse than no answer to the problem—it is a wrong answer.

I urge that the Congress continue to analyze and consider ways to reach this goal through legislation which will not restrict freedom of discussion, will not discriminate against any communications medium, will not tend to freeze incumbents in office, will not favor the famed over the worthy but little-known, will not risk confusion and chaos in our election process and will not promote more rather than less campaign spending. Such legislation will have to be far better than S.3637.

I am as opposed to big spending in campaigns as I am to big spending in government. But before we tamper with something as fundamental as the electoral process, we must be certain that we never give the celebrity an advantage over an unknown, or the officeholder an extra advantage over the challenger.

Let the Buyer Beware

By JAMES RESTON

Ever since President Nixon vetoed the bill to limit the amount of money candidates can spend on television advertising, the public prints have been full of gloomy predictions that the fat cats were about to take over the television screens, brainwash the voters and buy up all the seats of power in the Great Republic.

Well, it's no joke. Madison Avenue is now the road to the White House. A pleasant smile, a big bankroll and twenty commercials a day look good like a candidate should (what do you want—bad grammar or bad taste?), but there must be some way to protect the public from this political huckstering.

If we are forced by the President to put TV political advertising on the same footing as commercial advertising, we could at least adopt some of Senator Hart's "truth in advertising" devices.

As in the cigarette ads, for example, there is no reason why the grinning picture of your favorite political scoundrel should not carry the warning "this candidate may be hazardous to your health." Or perhaps it might be possible to print the dirt or falsehood content in each of his speeches.

The "truth in packaging" bills forbid the seller to deceive the buyer by putting a cupful of corn flakes in the big, big jumbo giant family size package, and they don't allow your corner whisky peddler to water the booze.

Under the present non-rules of political advertising, however, any political pygmy can be packaged to look like the Chief Justice of the United States. With pancake make-up, hair dye, a good wig and a Teleprompter, all a candidate needs, other than money, is an eighth-grade capacity to read somebody else's ideas and he has a pretty good chance of winning.

This depends, however, on the assumption that the voters are boobs who can do nothing to combat this political pollution, and this is not precisely true. The present system rests on the conviction that the more a voter sees a politician the more likely he is to vote for him.

There is no reason, however, why the voter should not take precisely the opposite position. Tom Dewey lost the 1948 Presidential election partly because somebody said you had to know him well to dislike him. It is a rough rule of thumb, and might lose us a few good well-heeled candidates, but things wouldn't be much worse if you resolved any doubts by voting for the candidate who advertised the least.

This is not quite as silly as it sounds. Even the officials of the big television networks, who are not indifferent to making money, favored the TV advertising bill the President vetoed; and so did a majority of the members of the House and Senate, even many of them who stood to gain by unlimited television advertising.

The reason for this is perfectly clear. Increasingly over the last 25 years, the cost of television campaigning has got beyond the financial means of all but the very richest of men and forced candidates to solicit funds vastly beyond the legal limits. Thus, for example, a Republican Administration now engaged in a campaign emphasizing the importance of "law and order" is financing that campaign in ways it knows to be unlawful and then vetoes the first orderly bill on limiting campaign expenditures.

The Democrats, of course, are doing the same thing, only not so effectively, but everybody is trapped in the corruption of the TV financing problem, and this was why not only the networks but also the politicians voted to control it.

Still, the remedy lies not with the President but with the voters. He can fly around the country and give men like Senator Smith of Illinois and Senator George Murphy of California some "visibility," but he can't give them anything else.

The problem therefore is to prove that spectacular political advertising that distorts the political process doesn't pay. They can "sell" their candidates, but the voters don't have to buy.

Maybe there will be a new TV campaign bill by the time of the Presidential election of 1972, for the Congress is for it, but meanwhile the rule of thumb is worth trying in November: "Let the voter beware: The candidate you see the most may be hazardous to your health."

Senate Democrats Woo G.O.P. Votes to Override Nixon's TV Spending Veto

By **WARREN WEAVER** Jr.
Special to The New York Times

WASHINGTON, Nov. 17—The attempt to override President Nixon's veto of the bill to limit television and radio spending in political campaigns will open in the Senate early next week.

Senator Mike Mansfield of Montana, the majority leader, announced today on the floor that the vote, which will require a two-thirds majority, would be taken on Monday. Other strategists indicated that it might be postponed until Tuesday if a Monday nosecount of support fell short.

The Senate vote, which now appears likely to be very close, has precipitated a bitter political struggle between the White House and a relatively unified Democratic delegation over the support of a dozen or more Republicans.

President Nixon, through his agents on Capitol Hill, is reminding Republican Senators daily that the television bill represents a clear-cut issue of party loyalty, that a vote to override is a vote against their President and their national political leader.

The Democrats and their allies in the labor unions and nonpartisan groups are making the nonpolitical argument to the Republican Senators, maintaining that the overriding issue is controlling soaring campaign costs for both parties rather than supporting or opposing Mr. Nixon.

The Senate approved the measure vetoed by the President by a 60-to-19 vote, with 17 Republicans among the supporters. Backers of the bill believe that if they can retain the votes of a dozen of these Senators the motion to override will succeed; as of today, they had about half that number.

Absenteeism creates major questions. If all the Senators except Karl E. Mundt of South Dakota, who is recovering from a stroke, were present on Monday, it would take 66 votes to override—say, 12 Republicans and 54 of the 58 Democrats now serving in the Senate.

Supporters of the television spending limitation believe they will get the votes of all but one or two Democrats, but they cannot be sure all their backers will be present.

Some indication of how close the vote may be can be obtained from the fact that the would-be overriders were considerably encouraged by the presence of Senator Adlai E. Stevenson 2d of Illinois, sworn in today to replace Ralph T. Smith, a Republican. The switch gave them one vote.

Among the organizations working to override the President's veto are the National Committee for an Effective Congress, which helped draft the bill; the American Federation of Labor and Congress of Industrial Organizations; the United Automobile Workers and Common Cause, the new citizens' lobby headed by John W. Gardner.

The vetoed measure, which would not become effective until the 1972 Presidential campaign, would limit each party to about $5.1-million for television and radio time. In 1968, the Republicans spent $12.7-million and the Democrats $6.1-million.

Critics of the veto have argued that Mr. Nixon was attempting to preserve the financial advantage traditionally enjoyed by the Republican party and also to eliminate the possibility of debates between the two major party candidates in 1972.

Among the Republican Senators understood to be recruiting support for the bill among their colleagues are Charles E. Goodell of New York, whose reelection campaign was not supported by the White House; James Pearson of Kansas, a co-sponsor of the measure; and Mark O. Hatfield, an increasingly active political critic of the Administration.

The Post-Newsweek stations argued today that campaign spending should not be controlled by restricting investment in broadcasting. The group includes three television and three radio stations owned by The Washington Post and Newsweek magazine.

If the Senate should vote to override, the final decision will not be taken in the House until after Thanksgiving. There was a good deal of uncertainty today as to the outcome. Some observers thought it would be harder to get a two-thirds majority there while others believed that the eSnate's overriding would assure similar action in the House.

CAMPAIGN LIMITS FAVORED IN POLL

Expense, Tone and Length All Found Objectionable

Special to The New York Times

PRINCETON, N. J., Nov. 21 —The public is upset over the conduct of political campaigns and one of its chief complaints is soaring campaign spending, according to the Gallup Poll.

"If you don't have a million bucks, you might as well forget about running for political office these days," said a Norfolk, Va., barber when interviewed in a nationwide poll now being completed.

Based on early returns for the survey, eight in 10 Americans now favor a law that would put a limit on the total amount of money that can be spent for or by a candidate in his campaign for public office.

The Senate is scheduled to vote Monday on President Nixon's veto of a bill to limit television and radio spending in political campaigns. The vetoed measure, which could not become effective until the 1972 Presidential campaign, would limit each party to about $5.1-million for television and radio time. In 1968, the Republicans spent $12.7-million and the Democrats $6.1-million.

A Wide Range

The complaints of Americans cover a wide range. In addition to favoring a reduction in campaign spending, many would like to see campaigns "cleaned up," with less name calling and distortion of issues.

The change called for next most often was to shorten the campaigning period, which now normally runs from Labor Day to early November.

Another criticism on the public's list is that political candidates fail to discuss issues a well-defined and meaningful manner.

All persons in the survey were asked this question:

Would you like to see any changes in the way political campaigns are conducted?

Seven in 10 Americans, or a projected 84 million adults, proposed changes. This is a higher proportion than recorded following any previous Presidential and Congressional campaign when similar questions were asked.

One person in seven (14 per cent) does not favor any change in the way campaigns are currently conducted.

The results reported today are based on personal interviews with 1,481 adults out of a total of more than 1,550 who were reached in the survey. Interviewing was begun Nov. 13 with the bulk of the interviewing completed by Nov. 15.

The question dealing with a limit to campaign spending is as follows:

Would you favor or oppose a law which would put a limit on the total amount of money which can be spent for or by a candidate in his campaign for public office?

The national results were:
Favor 78%
Oppose 15%
No opinion 7%

Ingrained in the thinking of many Americans, it was found, is the belief that every person should have an equal chance to run for office and that money should not be a controlling factor.

November 22, 1970

Money vs. Men

Will Rogers once observed that the United States Senate was the best that money could buy. That witticism may soon be a somber description of reality if the cost of campaigning for political office in this country continues to spiral out of control.

The bill to regulate political advertising on radio and television which President Nixon vetoed and which the Senate reconsiders tomorrow is an attempt to control this spiral. It limits spending by candidates for radio and television time in general elections to seven cents per voter and to half that much in primaries. It covers campaigns for the Presidency, Congress, and state governorships. Broadcasters would be required to sell time to candidates at the lowest rate which they offer their commercial customers.

This formula means that in 1972, each party could spend $5.1 million for radio and television time for its Presidential ticket. In 1968, the Nixon-Agnew ticket actually spent $12,687,953 and the Humphrey-Muskie ticket spent $6,143,277. In New York, a candidate for Senator or Governor could only spend approximately $500,000 instead of the undetermined millions which candidates poured forth this year.

President Nixon offered some curious reasons for vetoing the bill. He said it might "favor the incumbent over the officeseeker." That is on the theory that a challenger needs to spend more to make himself as well known as an incumbent. But as matters now stand, an incumbent can usually use the advantage of being in office to raise more campaign money than his opponent. The only exceptions are when the challenger is a millionaire spending his own money or is the protégé of special interests who hope to gain by his election.

Mr. Nixon's veto message also asserted that the bill "unfairly endangers freedom of discussion." Whatever else it might be called, a television blitz of thirty-second and sixty-second "spots" is not a "discussion" of the issues.

The bill, according to Mr. Nixon, would "severely limit the ability of many candidates to get their message to the greatest number of the electorate." But the existing dollar-take-all arrangement cruelly deprives candidates of moderate means from getting their message across while rich candidates are free to saturate the airwaves.

It may be that President Nixon vetoed the bill because his party is well financed and the Democrats are deep in debt. Or it may be that what he really dislikes is the provision in the bill repealing Section 315(a) of the Communications Act of 1934 and thus opening up the possibility of televised debates between major candidates for President without having to include every minor party candidate. Mr. Nixon has no reason to recall happily the television debates of the 1960 campaign.

Whatever his reasons, President Nixon has made an intense effort to line up Republican Senators to support his veto. Yet this bill was not originally a partisan matter. It was passed by the Senate by 60 to 19 and by the House 247 to 112 and has had substantial support in both parties. Republican members who are under pressure to change their vote face an agonizing choice between party loyalty and what they know is right.

One Republican Senator who still supports the bill— Clifford Case of New Jersey—observed the other day: "To an unusual degree much of the political comment during this year's elections focused on money: How much Candidate A had versus Candidate B, where each got it, what each did with it, and—after the elections were over—how relatively little of either contributions or expenditures showed up in the reports required of candidates by Federal and state laws."

The pending bill would not solve all campaign expenditure problems, but it would do much to lighten the miasma of money which now pervades politics, smothering and deforming the competition of men and ideas.

236

To Control Campaign Costs

Ewert·Karlsson

By JOHN W. GARDNER

WASHINGTON—One thing is agreed on by virtually all candidates—winners or losers—in the recent election: Campaign spending has gotten wildly out of hand. Historically speaking, that is the most notable fact about the whole election.

The disastrous rise in expenses is due to the cost of television time. Excessive, inordinate, almost unlimited amounts were spent for that purpose.

Such costs not only introduce an element of unfairness into the system, they greatly increase the possibility of corruption. Congress can take an important step in that direction by repassing, over a Presidential veto, a bill that would prevent repetition of the insane expenditures of the 1970 campaign.

No one will ever know how much was actually spent. The law governing disclosure of campaign contributions is so full of loopholes that we can only guess. But is has been estimated that in this off-year election spending may have exceeded the Presidential election two years ago, when (according to guesstimates) more than $200 million was expended.

One can, of course, identify big spenders who lost, and small spenders who won, but no political practitioner seriously doubts that, lacking controls, the era of astronomical spending for TV campaigning is here to stay. Exceptions to the rule make good conversation, but there are few candidates or political managers in the country who would choose not to plunge heavily on TV spots if they could afford it.

What does it mean for our system? It means final disintegration of the American folk belief that any poor boy can run for office. In most areas today a more correct statement would be that anyone can run for office provided he is wealthy or willing to put himself under obligation to sources of wealth. Could there be a more complete denial of what America stands for?

Most candidates are not wealthy, and too many must choose the second course—being beholden to powerful individuals or special interests. No matter how ethical a public official is, how can he fail to feel indebted to

Congress Should Repass Bill President Vetoed Limiting TV Spending

the sources of wealth that made his campaign possible? Many maintain high standards despite such pressures, but many do not. Venality is a harsh word, but in the simplest terms, a good many of our public officials are being bought and paid for.

The process feeds on itself, since general public knowledge of huge costs and wealthy donors must surely discourage modest contributors. Thus an army of small givers is replaced by a platoon of powerful backers. And democracy is the loser.

Coming at a time when Americans of all ages and from all segments of our national life are questioning our political institutions, this new invitation to public cynicism could have a devastating impact. If something is not done, quickly, to restore fairness and remove the hazards of venality our system will have sustained serious injury.

The present Congress did try to do something. Last September it passed a bill limiting a candidate's spending in

a general election to seven cents for every voter who cast a ballot in the previous election for the same office. The limit was set at three and a half cents for primary elections. The bill provided that stations had to give a political candidate the lowest rate charged to any advertiser—that is, at a discount.

Finally, the bill repealed the "equal time" provision under which Presidential candidates of splinter groups were entitled to as much free TV or radio time as those of the major parties. Repeal of this provision would encourage face-to-face debates instead of commercial spots and do much to enlighten the public.

The bill was a significant beginning. Unfortunately, President Nixon vetoed it. He argued that it would shift political spending from broadcast to other media. He said it would give the incumbent an unfair advantage over the challenger. But many believe he vetoed it because the Democrats suffer more than the Republicans under existing financial pressures.

Rightly judged, it isn't a question of which party suffers more. The nation suffers. Our political system suffers.

Those who supported the bill now face a choice familiar to all who seek practical changes in any field. The bill is only a beginning. Should it be allowed to die, so that a new Congress can work out a broader and stronger bill? Or should Congress seize this opportunity to correct a situation that is a national scandal?

Congress should move at once, overriding the President's veto. Eventually controls must be extended beyond broadcast time to include newspaper, magazine, billboard and mail advertising. But that can be done later. All of the great reforms in our national life have been made piecemeal.

If Congress overrides the President's veto it will have taken a long step toward fair political contests, a long step away from the pitfalls of venality, and a necessary step toward restoring our faith in the workability of the elective system.

John W. Gardner, former Secretary of H.E.W., heads the Urban Coalition and Common Cause, a new national citizens organization.

SENATE SUSTAINS VETO OF FUND CURB ON TV CAMPAIGNS

Bid to Override Nixon Fails by Four Votes as Five in G.O.P. Change Position

PRESIDENT IS PLEASED

O'Brien Calls Result 'Tragic' —Scott Pledges to Seek Wider Bill Next Year

By WARREN WEAVER Jr.
Special to The New York Times

WASHINGTON, Nov. 23 — The bill to limit spending for television and radio time in political campaigns died today when the Senate failed to muster enough votes to override President Nixon's veto.

The vote was 58 to 34 in favor of overriding, four votes short of the required two-thirds majority.

Six Democrats sided with 28 of the 37 Republicans in support of Mr. Nixon. Had they voted with their party colleagues, the veto would have been overridden. Five Republicans who supported the measure earlier this fall voted today to sustain the veto.

"The President is always pleased when decisions he makes are upheld," said Ronald L. Ziegler, the White House press secretary. "We felt we had clearly stated the reasoning behind the veto, and we're pleased that this was agreed to." Mr. Nixon vetoed the bill six weeks ago.

Scott Plans Effort

Senator Hugh Scott of Pennsylvania, the Republican minority leader, who voted against overriding, promised to help draft a more comprehensive substitute bill next year.

The Senate vote came after three hours of debate, in which supporters of the television spending measure conceded that it was an imperfect solution to the problem and critics of the bill almost uniformly conceded that something similar had to be passed soon.

The bill would have limited spending for radio and television time in the 1972 election to $5.1-million for each national ticket, based on 7 cents for each vote cast in the last Presidential contest. In 1968, the Republicans spent about $12.7-million and the Democrats about $6.1-million for this purpose.

It would also have limited spending by candidates for Senator, Representative, Governor and Lieutenant Governor, based on the most recent vote for each office.

The Democratic national chairman, Lawrence F. O'Brien called the Senate vote "tragic" and predicted that it would deal "a severe blow" to efforts to reform political campaigning at all levels.

"In hewing abjectly to the Republican party line as laid down by the White House," Mr. O'Brien declared, "those Republican Senators who changed their original positions in favor of the bill to a vote for Mr. Nixon's veto have only increased our suspicions that the veto had but two purposes: To protect the traditional Republican advantage in campaign finances and to protect Mr. Nixon from the possiblity of having to debate the issues with his Democratic opponent in 1972."

The Democrats who chose to back Mr. Nixon were Senators James B. Allen of Alabama, John L. McClellan of Arkansas, Thomas J. Dodd of Connecticut, James O. Eastland of Mississippi, Allen J. Ellender of Louisiana and John C. Stennis of Mississippi.

The Republican Senators who supported the measure on final passage Sept. 23 but voted to sustain the veto today were: George D. Aiken and Winston L. Prouty of Vermont, Margaret Chase Smith of Maine, John J. Williams of Delaware and Milton R. Young of North Dakota.

Two Republicans who voted for the bill in September, Senators Jack Miller of Iowa and William B. Saxbe of Ohio, reported today that they would have voted to override but instead took a "pair" with an absentee, Senator Karl E. Mundt of South Dakota, who would have voted to sustain.

The practical effect of such a pair is to cancel out two votes to compensate for one that could never have been cast. Senator Mundt has been out of the Senate for the last year, recovering from a stoke.

In ordinary votes, a pair involves only two Senators—one giving up his vote as a courtesy to an absentee who would have voted the opposite way. But on a motion to override a veto, requiring a two-thirds majority, two Senators who would have voted to override must give up their votes to form a pair with one absentee who favors sustaining.

On a second pair, two Democrats, Senators Gale W. McGee of Wyoming and John J. Sparkman of Alabama, declined to vote to override because Senator Peter H. Dominick, Republican of Colorado, could not be on hand to cast his vote for the President.

If all four paired Senators had cast their votes to override, the motion would still have failed. The vote then would have been 62 to 34, two short of a two-thirds majority of 64.

Opponents of the measure argued that the dollar limits were unfair to candidates in states where the cost of television was higher because the market was more competitive or the stations could reach only a small part of the candidate's electorate.

Senator Scott, who said after the vote that this was the first time the Senate had sustained a veto since 1965, promised to work next year for a bipartisan bill that would limit spending for all media, base its television allocations on time instead of money and include requirements for much more extensive disclosure of campaign income and spending.

Gentlemen, Please, No More Crocodile Tears

By JACK GOULD

THE Senate's refusal to override President Nixon's veto of a measure calling for reform in political campaign expenditures suggests that the new Congress should separate two issues which regularly lead to a stalemate in politics and television.

In the vetoed measure, the issue of the use of money by a rich candidate to overwhelm an unknown with costly spot announcements was linked with suspension of Section 315 of the Federal Communications Act. Suspension of the section would allow the networks to cover major candidates for the Presidency without giving equal time to fringe aspirants who might qualify for a place on the ballot in any one of the 50 states.

Both in reports on TV and in newspapers, suspension of Section 315 has become synonymous with debate in the manner of the late President Kennedy's celebrated confrontation with the then Vice President Nixon. Ever since Mr. Nixon lost out in the studio bout in 1960, debates themselves have become a matter of political controversy.

Since no office holder in his right mind is going to invite a political risk if it can be avoided, debates have been a hangup for both President Nixon and former President Johnson. Both have exerted pressure to stay out of the TV ring and both have succeeded, albeit President Nixon had to hold out the olive branch of some more comprehensive measure to induce four Senators to kill the latest reform attempt.

The issue of excessive campaign expenditures is inordinately complex and a provision that TV campaign outlays bear some percentage relationship to the number of qualified voters sounds like some ideal type of input for a computer. To lower the boom on TV advertising and not on other media is discriminatory. But what Congress could hope to regulate stickers on car bumpers or curb a wealthy candidate from phoning every voter in his state? There are many dodges for circumventing a TV expense limitation but nonetheless any interim step to reduce the volume of cynical spot announcements would be thoroughly welcome.

*

But if the new Congress does indeed propose to entertain some reform—and it is not hard to get a favorable bet that the issue will be dragged out in interminable hearings so that nothing changes for the 1972 election—it would seem time to remove the bugaboo of "debates" with their inevitable connotation that the public will pick a winner or loser far in advance of Election Day.

Section 315 does not contain even one word about debates. All the suspension of the measure will do is take the handcuffs off TV and let electronic journalism do some political reporting in depth, instead of being a patsy for the image makers in control of paid spot announcements.

As a practical matter, it is ludicrous to expect TV to do a decent job of covering the major challengers to the nation's highest office and also be required to devote equal hour upon equal hour to relative unknowns of scant or non-existent news value. The noble goal of fair play for all has reduced itself to a veritable blackout of everyone—a happy situation for the dominant figure of the moment who wants to keep TV under his thumb.

The new Congress and the broadcasters themselves should forget about debates and recognize the potential of the suspension of Section 315. An infinite variety of formats avoiding the combative nature of debates can be utilized and the viewer would be the gainer. In the last Presidential election, no TV network offered a documentary on the strategies and problems in the rivalry between Mr. Nixon and Hubert H. Humphrey. TV was better equipped than the printed page of a best-seller to show the electronic technique of the selling of a President, with its recourse to a traveling road show in which members of the balanced TV studio audience ask the same questions in region after region. There was also no independent reportorial insight into Mr. Humphrey's predicament—linked to the Johnson Administration and yet endeavoring to assert that he was his own man.

Under Section 315, any program outside of regularly scheduled newscasts or interviews is verboten unless another dozen or so hours are accorded to rich candidates. Thus, while no newspaper is asked to abandon its rudimentary judgment of what interests the country, TV, operating under a Federal license, is quarantined for the duration. The smidgens of independent reporting and regular newscasts are overwhelmed by political advertising, and if candidate X disdains to appear on "Meet the Press," "Face the Nation" or "Issues and Answers," the networks know they will be clobbered for partisanship if they give time to candidate Y.

*

Section 315 deserves to be unceremoniously junked and the tiresome quarrels over debates thrown out. Under circumstances agreeable to candidate X, he can be interviewed by network reporters in a calm atmosphere on such matters as the economy, foreign policy and the war. And then, in due course, the same courtesy can be extended to candidate Y. Decorum is preserved, the tension of confrontation avoided, and the viewer afforded an opportunity to decide which candidate's approach he prefers.

If, for expedient reasons, either the Democratic or Republican candidate wants to cop out and reiterate his canned speeches, the privilege still remains his. But TV will be free to document the fact, show how and why the practice works, and still be free and clear to cover his opponent, who might prefer different campaigning methods.

A standard argument against suspension of Section 315 is that minority parties would be cut out of the scene and denied what little time on the air they now can find. For the record, this certainly wasn't the case in 1968 when George Wallace was a major factor of hot news value and, without any governmental prodding, was accorded generous time.

But it should be appreciated that suspension of Section 315 does not involve dissolution of the over-all "Fairness Doctrine" of the FCC, governing equitable access to the airwaves. Moreover, matters have greatly changed since Supreme Court Justice Byron L. White, writing for the majority in the so-called "Red Lion" case, unequivocally asserted the primacy of the viewer over the broadcaster. In short, TV can and should have far more independence in political reporting but under the law it cannot shrug off obligations to minorities. In campaigns, the FCC traditionally and admirably acts with surprising dispatch on such issues.

In sum, the politicians of all persuasions have expediently made a self-serving jungle of the problems of campaigns on TV and thus far have displayed a lamentable, if convenient, approach to sensible solutions. Clearly, their last concern is that of the viewers who, for just one election campaign, would like some answers to the problems on their minds. If the costs of campaigning have risen outrageously and dangerously, one part of the answer is that many politicians do not mind the cost. If TV were set free from the hobbles imposed by the politicians, the set owners might gain immeasurably, gaining the opportunity to contrast facts with the hogwash of spot announcements. The White House and Congress are the prime abusers of the principle that the airwaves belong to the people—not to them.

Whether President Nixon and members of the new Congress are genuinely in favor of independent access to the home screen—not forced access amid crocodile tears—will be an interesting question in 1971. But as long as Section 315 is on the books their partisan yelps are phony.

*

Forget the debates and let the best documentarians have their heads to show events as they are, with TV footing the bills. If the politicians want accessibility to the screen only on their own terms, they are the ones who must take the blame for jacking up the price of politics. Their professions of alarm fail to be convincing; they are, in the last analysis, TV sponsors, not candidates willing to take the rough and tumble of free reportage.

To talk about the freedom of speech inherent in spot commercials is a very cute trick. The more apt definition is "controlled propaganda" and nobody is being kidded. The cost of spots is secondary to the debasement of genuine free speech.

Campaign Expenditures...

Common Cause, the citizens' lobby organized by John W. Gardner, is leading the attack on two serious abuses in the nation's political life—the seniority stranglehold on Congress and the debasing power of money in political campaigns. In an effort to correct the latter abuse, the organization has filed suit in the Federal District Court in Washington to have present political spending practices declared illegal and the behavior of the parties brought under court supervision.

The suit seeks to revive the moribund Corrupt Practices Act of 1925, which established a limit of $5,000 on individual contributions to a candidate for Congress or the Presidency. It also set spending limits, such as $3 million for a Presidential campaign.

The politicians long ago learned to leap those fences. During every campaign they create—in Mr. Gardner's words—a "multiplicity of dummy committees" in behalf of each candidate. A contributor can give $5,000 to each of these paper outfits. He can also contribute in the names of his wife, his infant children and other relatives.

This flagrant cynicism makes a mockery of regulation and brings law into contempt. The Common Cause suit,

if successful, would result in the court's declaring these dummy committees and these multiple contributions illegal. Such a decision could bring the campaign spending issue to a climax and force Congressional action since no modern campaign could be waged within the old limits set by the 1925 law. Reconsideration by Congress, rather than a court victory, is the ultimate objective of the suit.

An effective, up-to-date law should start from a more constructive premise than the setting of limits. Any dollar limitation is inherently difficult to enforce and tends to encourage under-the-table transactions. What is important is to encourage more equal access to the political arena. Television costs should be reduced and some free time made available to every candidate. Candidates could be granted one or two postage-free-mailings. A candidate for President could be allowed free airplane transportation from the time of his nomination to the election.

By such direct and indirect subsidies, the soaring cost of campaigning could be brought down and men of moderate means enabled to compete more effectively with rivals who are rich or are the chosen instruments of the rich.

January 18, 1971

Congress Braces for a Battle Over Campaign Spending Curbs

By WARREN WEAVER Jr.
Special to The New York Times

WASHINGTON, Feb. 14 — Congress is bracing for what is likely to be the first major political battle of the new session, the issue of regulating campaign spending.

The outcome is almost certain to affect the 1972 Presidential election, either by establishing stringent new ground rules for the candidates or by enabling one of them to blame the other for the absence of any limitation on the skyrocketing costs of campaigning for political office.

Unlike most of the major questions before the 92d Congress, which are likely to simmer along with little action for a year or more, campaign financing legislation will probably be considered within the next six or eight months, a relatively short time by Capitol Hill standards.

This is true because any new law affecting election spending for 1972 must be on the books by the end of this year to apply to the Presidential primary campaigns, which traditionally get under way in New Hampshire in January.

Vetoed by Nixon

Four months ago, President Nixon vetoed a bill that would have limited television and radio spending in political campaigns, in part on the ground that it should have restricted other types of spend-

ing as well.

Democratic leaders were highly critical of the President's veto, contending that he had acted to perpetuate the traditional Republican advantage in fund raising. They were unable, however, to override the veto despite Democratic majorities in Congress. In any event, the bill was too late to have affected the 1970 campaign.

The major question in the renewal of the controversy this year is the attitude of the White House. At the time of the veto, the Administration had no plans to draft any alternative legislation, although Mr. Nixon acknowledged in his disapproval message that the problem was serious and the effort to meet it laudable.

Senator Hugh Scott of Pennsylvania, the minority floor leader, is drafting a bill that will be submitted to the White House before it is made public. That could either become the official Republican proposal or wind up as the Scott bill.

Anderson Bill

Representative John B. Anderson of Illinois, chairman of the House Republican Policy Committee, introduced a tough bill late last year for which he tried to obtain White House endorsement and failed. It would have imposed dollar spending limits on national and Congressional candidates, about $7-million for those running for

President.

Although it can arouse strong partisan responses, campaign spending is by no means an issue that the Democrats uniformly promote and the Republicans similarly oppose. If all the Democratic Senators had voted to override the Nixon veto last November, the move would have succeeded.

In addition, one of the principal campaign bills before the new Congress is cosponsored by Senators Mike Gravel, Democrat of Alaska, and James B. Pearson, Republican of Kansas. The bill includes three more Republicans among its 11 other sponsors.

The other major measure dealing with campaign spending is sponsored by Senator John O. Pastore, Democrat of Rhode Island, whose Senate Subcommittee on Communications will open hearings on the problem in about two weeks.

New Features

The Pastore bill includes the measure that President Nixon vetoed and has two new features: tax incentives of a $20 credit or a $100 deduction to encourage political contributions, and an extension of the limits on candidate spending to cover printed matter, as well as radio and television.

The Gravel-Pearson bill approaches the television problem by guaranteeing all candidates free time, in addition to limiting the amount any one of them can spend for commercial telecasts. It would provide six half-hours to each major party candidate for President and two to his running mate, and

would authorize a study of similar treatment for Senate and House candidates.

Senator Gravel is also sponsoring a bill that goes considerably further by providing for public underwriting of campaigns, with national funds from which Presidential and Congressional candidates would receive 20 cents for every vote cast for the office they seek in the last election. To qualify, the candidates would have to open their financial records to a Federal commission.

Technical Problem

Lumping these various political provisions into a single bill raises a technical problem for Congress. The Pastore bill, for example, must be cleared by three Senate committees — Commerce, Rules and Finance — because it includes tax changes and disclosure requirements as well as new limits on communications media.

Some members of Congress want to go beyond these proposals. They would enact relatively low dollar ceilings for all Senate and House races, prohibit the use of television "spots" as misleading and finance mailings and television time for all candidates.

In political terms, the Democrats are anxious to put some limitation on the amount Mr. Nixon can spend on his re-election campaign by presenting him with a bill he will have difficulty vetoing. The Administration is expected to seek a considerably less restrictive bill that would also be more acceptable to members of Congress reluctant to accept curbs on their own campaign spending.

February 15, 1971

Campaign Finance Bill

By WARREN WEAVER Jr.
Special to The New York Times

WASHINGTON, Feb. 21—The campaign finance legislation that Republicans are preparing to introduce this week sets no limits on the amount candidates may spend to get themselves elected.

Unless Senator Hugh Scott, the Senate minority leader, has a last-minute change of heart, his bill will not attempt to deal directly with a problem that many other politicians regard as critical: the soaring cost of campaigning, particularly on television.

As a result, for many members of Congress, including most Democrats, the Scott proposal is not likely to represent an acceptable alternative to the bill that President Nixon vetoed last October. That measure would have put a ceiling on candidates' spending for television and radio.

Imposing a Ceiling

Some backers of limits on campaign spending are encouraged, however, by the fact that Republican leaders are getting involved in the general issue, even if somewhat tentatively. The Scott bill was prepared in consultation with the White House, but it is not an Administration measure and may attract some Democratic co-sponsors.

An earlier version of the Republican measure would have imposed a ceiling on the amount Presidential and Congressional candidates could spend for postage, telephone and telegraph, and television, radio and newspaper advertising, this responding to President Nixon's objection that the 1970 bill was unfair in curbing only broadcast activity.

The proposed limits were deliberately set high. In 1972, they would have been about $18-million for each national ticket, up to $2.5-million for a Senate candidate in a large state and between $45,000 and $75,000 for House races depending on the size of the district. But in drafts of the Scott bill circulating this weekend, the limits had been dropped.

Among the provisions of the Republican measure, which will be co-sponsored by Senator Charles McC. Mathias Jr. of Maryland, are:

¶Strict requirements for public reporting of all campaign contributions and expenditures, with the system monitored by a new Federal commission.

¶Limits on the amount of money that an individual or committee can contribute to a single campaign. The tentative figures are $15,000 for the national ticket, $10,000 for the Senate and $5,000 for the House.

¶Repeal of the Federal statute that discourages televised debates between the major-party Presidential candidates by guaranteeing similar exposure to all minor-party nominees.

¶A requirement that all communications media — newspapers, magazines and billboards, as well as radio and television —must charge political candidates their lowest rates.

¶Authorization for each candidate to make one or two mailings of literature to his constituents in the last month of the campaign at an artificially low postage rate — about one and a half cents for each piece.

¶A tax credit of up to $25 or a deduction of up to $100 for contributions to political parties to encourage more broad-based financing of campaigns.

Although the package does not go as far as some members of the Congress would like, advocates of more stringent campaign limits believe that the Scott proposal could lay the foundation for more extensive Republican support when the controversial issue reaches the floor later this year.

A Composite Measure

In the Senate, where the first action is expected, the final bill will almost certainly be a composite of several campaign financing measures, including one with bipartisan backing and one co-sponsored by Senator Mike Mansfield of Montana, the majority leader, and Senator John O. Pastore of Rhode Island, chairman of the Senate Communications Subcommittee.

The most serious opposition to all such legislation is in the House. It centers on the issue of mandatory disclosure of political contributions and spending. Many Representatives are reluctant to authorize a listing of their financial sponsors, making wealthy contributors vulnerable to pressure from competitive fund-raising and providing them with a political identification that some would just as soon avoid.

The 1970 bill that President Nixon vetoed won approval by large margins in both houses, but it did not contain any disclosure provisions. Observers believe that any attempt to regulate campaign spending can be effective only if a strictly enforced national reporting system of income is included as part of the reform.

The White House reportedly favors the disclosure provisions of the Scott bill on the theory that they would flush out major contributors to Democratic campaigns who might prefer to remain in the background.

February 22, 1971

Controlling the Cost of '72

By TOM WICKER

WASHINGTON, Feb. 22 — Senator Hugh Scott of Pennsylvania, the minority leader, is circulating a campaign finance bill that is apparently not an official Nixon Administration proposal, and which does not provide for limitations on what candidates may spend to win election.

This suggests that Mr. Nixon, despite having vetoed a campaign spending bill passed last year by the Democratic Congress, does not plan to put forward an Administration alternative this year. Since Mr. Scott and his co-sponsor, Senator Charles Mathias of Maryland, prepared their bill in cooperation with the White House, it also suggests that Mr. Nixon will not support a limitation on spending.

Because the measure Mr. Nixon vetoed would have put stiff and self-enforcing limits on the biggest item of campaign spending—television—it may seem that the Scott-Mathias bill is little more than a pale imitation, designed to perpetuate the Republican financial advantages.

But Democratic leaders ought to think twice before they insist on a measure that limits spending. In the first place, Mr. Nixon possesses not only the veto power but the political muscle to drum up needed Republican support for a campaign finance bill. It seems reasonably clear that he is likely to use the former, as he did last year, and forget the latter if the Democrats insist on a ceiling on political spending.

In the second place, if the Scott-Mathias bill represents a package Mr. Nixon would accept, there is much to be said for getting it into the law before 1972, rather than suffering another veto of a more stringent measure. The draft was developed with the aid of the National Committee for an Effective Congress, a main sponsor of last year's bill, and contains these useful provisions:

A new Federal commission to enforce strict reporting of all campaign contributions and expenditures; feasible limits on individual and committee contributions; subsidization of some campaign postage costs; tax credits and deductions to encourage small contributions; permanent repeal of Federal laws that now bar televised Presidential debates, and a rule that all advertising media must extend their lowest rates to political candidates.

One important provision in the section on contributions would prevent candidates from contributing to their own campaigns more than $50,000 (if running for President or Vice President), $35,000 (if running for the Senate) or $25,000 (if running for the House). Contributions from members of their families would also be limited, thus largely preventing wealthy persons from overwhelming less wealthy opponents.

Finally, there is a substantial case to be made *against* imposing limits on campaign spending. The most important point against such a ceiling is that it would limit a challenger to the same amount an entrenched incumbent could spend.

A non-incumbent in many cases needs to spend more money just to "start even" either in a primary against an incumbent with strong organization support or in an election against a well-known incumbent. Thus, a spending limit would often work to the advantage of the "ins" of both parties and the political status quo.

There may also be a constitutional problem, since some authorities believe that an expenditure for speech is essentially the same thing under the First Amendment as speech itself. If a candidate already had spent whatever amount the law permitted, would it be constitutional to prevent some individual or group from spending their own money to express support for him, or opposition to his opponent?

Again, it would be difficult to enforce over-all spending ceilings if a candidate himself was not responsible for controlling all expenditures in his behalf. Yet it seems a dubious proposition indeed that a citizen may not, if he wishes, take out an ad to express his personal political convictions. Effective enforcement would appear to limit constitutional rights; but protecting constitutional rights would make enforcement of over-all spending ceilings next to impossible.

If some way could be found to limit television spending, particularly for advertising, without limiting over-all expenditures, that might answer the constitutional problem as well as bring the cost of campaigning down to a level more accessible to all potential candidates. For the moment, and taking Mr. Nixon's veto powers into account, the Scott-Mathias bill looks like the best bet to apply some practical regulation to the cost of politicking in 1972.

February 23, 1971

Campaign Spending Reform

The Nixon Administration is either inefficient or obstructive in its approach to the important problem of excessive spending in political campaigns.

With commendable speed, a Senate subcommittee chaired by Senator Pastore of Rhode Island announced on Feb. 3 that it would hold hearings on a bill to replace the measure which President Nixon vetoed last year. The hearings were held March 2 through 5. As is customary, the record was held open an additional week to permit any interested person to file a written statement.

Throughout this period the White House and the Justice Department remained inscrutably silent despite repeated requests for their views. But last week, when the committee started to draft a bill, the Justice Department suddenly announced that it wanted to testify after all. Senator Scott of Pennsylvania, the minority leader, began busily to recruit additional witnesses. G.O.P. members of the subcommittee objected to drafting sessions on the bill while the Senate was in session, a routine move to delay action.

Senator Pastore has now held up the bill and agreed to further hearings starting today. These few lost weeks will make no difference, but reasonably prompt action is necessary if any law is to take effect before the Presidential primaries begin early next year. Since it has been more than five months since Mr. Nixon vetoed the last bill on this subject, there are reasons to fear that the Administration's dilatory behavior is no accident.

The bill killed by Mr. Nixon would have limited candidates to an expenditure of seven cents per voter for television advertising. This was a limited reform but highly desirable because it would be easily enforceable and because television advertising is the most expensive item in most political campaigns. The President advanced the unconvincing argument that, if one item was controlled, all should be.

The bill introduced with tacit White House backing by Senator Scott sets no over-all limits but would restrict what a candidate could spend from his own fortune and also individual contributions by other persons. Such limits have proved almost impossible to enforce. If any limits are written into law, they would better be designed to control expenditures by the candidate for specific purposes such as television or newspaper advertising.

Aside from the vexed problem of setting limits, there are several other proposals contained in the various bills now being studied by the Pastore subcommittee. These include creation of a Federal commission to enforce strict reporting of all contributions and expenditures. Complete and timely disclosure would in itself be a major safeguard. All advertising media should extend their lowest rates to political candidates. The Federal Government should subsidize candidates to meet some of their campaign costs such as mailings at free or reduced postage. Candidates nominated for President could be provided with free aircraft for campaign travel.

Political campaign costs are a necessary investment in democratic self-government. They could be drastically reduced by stringent and effective government controls as they have been in Britain and most other democracies. But, if President Nixon and many members of Congress refuse to accept this kind of purifying discipline, full disclosure can still do something to reduce the corrupting power of money in politics. And much can be done by Federal subsidies to make access to political power more nearly equal for all citizens.

March 31, 1971

Money In Politics

The bill to regulate the spending of money in Federal elections continues its tortuous progress through the Senate. The Rules Committee has significantly weakened the bill in one respect and strengthened it in two others. The weakening provision would have the effect of doubling the amounts which candidates could spend on radio and television, permitting an expenditure of $13.9-million next year for electronic advertising, more than was spent for this purpose by the Nixon-Agnew ticket in 1968. A low ceiling is desirable to keep voters from being swamped by saturation campaign advertising on television.

Two other Republican-sponsored changes improve the bill. One strikes the limit of $5,000 on individual contributions, a limit that has proved unenforceable and would only invite more subterfuge and collusion if preserved in the new law. It is better to rely upon complete and timely publicity to regulate the relationship between a candidate and large donors.

Another amendment shifts receipt of candidates' reports from the notoriously uncommunicative Secretary of the Senate and Clerk of the House to the Comptroller General. Republicans like this change because they do not want the officials of a Democratic Congress to control disposal of the patronage jobs which the law would create. By contrast, the General Accounting Office under the Comptroller General is staffed by civil service employes.

But an independent electoral commission is still the best solution. Only a new agency with its own leadership can make the fresh start urgently needed in the campaign financing field, so long obscured by a smog of cynicism and evasion of the law.

June 10, 1971

The Politics of Money

By PHILIP M. STERN

WASHINGTON—Almost every major domestic problem in America has its roots, in my view, in a deeper, more basic malady: the manner in which we finance political campaigns, with candidates heavily dependent on "interested" givers who expect a return on their investment, usually in the form of some governmental favor or largesse.

For example, the skewing of national priorities is largely traceable to political financing. With candidates so reliant on large contributors, mostly from industry, it is not surprising that the political system produces billions for an oil depletion allowance or corporate tax write-offs and pittances to combat hunger, pollution, housing shortages, etc.—problems mainly of concern to political noncontributors.

The anachronistic Congressional attitudes that flow from long tenure, old age and the seniority system stem largely from current fund-raising practices, which are heavily biased in favor of the power-dispensing incumbent office-holder and against the newcomer (last year 359 out of 379 incumbent House candidates were re-elected). Many would-be challengers, in fact, are frozen out before they begin, sheerly for lack of financing.

With a constricted political system, and, with the makeup of Congress largely static, no wonder the pace of change is so maddeningly slow.

The only effective way to open up politics, give newcomers and new ideas a chance and dilute the power of the big giver, is through public financing of election campaigns. That would not really be a radical change. The public already pays—and pays dearly—for the manner in which we now finance campaigns.

To take one dramatic example, the public now must lay out $5 billion a year in added oil and gas prices because the President declined to abolish oil import quotas as recommended, in the national interest, by his own Cabinet committee. When a President rejects a $5-billion saving for tens of millions of consumers in favor of higher prices and profits for a few oil companies, just four of whose executives contributed $300,000 to the 1968 Republican cause, the concept of "one-man, one-vote" is a joke.

The remedy does not lie in curbing political spending (via expenditure ceilings or free TV time). It's not the spending that's publicly harmful; it's how and from whom the money is *raised*, and in the disproportionate influence that large contributors (unions as well as corporations) are bound to wield.

Public financing of campaigns would be the best investment the American taxpayers could make. Even a generous program of Federal assistance, covering all primary as well as general elections for House, Senate and President, would only cost about $93 million a year (or just 69 cents per citizen of voting age)—just one-fiftieth of what the public is now paying for oil import quotas alone. Thus, if public financing could reverse that one Government policy, the taxpayers would have a 5,000 per cent return on their investment!

Use of the public subsidies for candidates' personal enrichment could be avoided by having the U.S. Treasury make payments directly to the purveyors of political services (i.e., to the broadcasters, newspapers, printers, etc.) so that the candidates themselves would not receive or handle any of the Federal money.

To encourage small-scale private gifts, there should also be tax-credit incentives but, to assure that no citizen wields undue influence, no gift of more than, say, $25 should be allowed.

The conventional wisdom insists that public financing of campaigns is inherently unpalatable to the voters. Yet TV viewers of "The Advocates," after hearing the pros and cons last October, voted 76 per cent in favor of Federal campaign assistance with just 21 per cent against—one of the most one-sided votes in the program's history.

Moreover, public funding of campaigns, already successfully in effect in Puerto Rico and Quebec, has just been officially embraced by the Democratic National Committee and is embodied in at least two Senate bills (by Senators McGovern and Gravel).

So this is far from a blue-sky political idea. It is gaining acceptability, perhaps because members of the nonaffluent, noncontributing public are catching on to the fact that they are already picking up the tab for a political system that answers much more to the big givers than it does to them.

—————————

Philip M. Stern, journalist and former Government official, is author of "The Shame of a Nation."

NETWORK OFFICIALS ASK HIGHER CEILING

Special to The New York Times

WASHINGTON, June 10—Officials of the three major networks agreed today that campaign spending limits for radio and television should be twice as high as those on which Senate Democratic leaders have agreed.

Executives of the Columbia Broadcasting System, the National Broadcasting Company and the American Broadcasting Company called separately for a single, over-all ceiling on media spending, all of which could go for television if the candidate wished.

The network officials testified before the House Communications Subcommittee, headed by Representative Torbert H. Macdonald, Democrat of Massachusetts. He has sponsored a bill limiting media spending to 10 cents for each eligible voter, no more than half to go for radio and television.

The Senate Democratic Policy Committee has agreed on a similar ceiling, to be written into a pending campaign bill when it reaches the floor next month. As cleared by the Rules Committee, the measure has a 10-cent ceiling, all of which can be used for radio and television.

June 11, 1971

June 11, 1971

1968 Political Campaigns
Set $300-Million Record

By R. W. APPLE Jr.
Special to The New York Times

WASHINGTON, June 19 — The campaigns of 1968 cost $300-million, more than ever before, and represented a 50 per cent increase in only four years. The Republicans outspent the Democrats almost 2 to 1.

By comparison, the increase in the 12 years between 1952 and 1964 was only 43 per cent. The jump in the cost of getting elected reflected the enormous cost of television, the fact that both major parties had Presidential primary contests and the candidacies of two multimillionaires—the late Robert F. Kennedy and Governor Rockefeller.

The cost per vote was 60 cents, also a record.

Those are the conclusions of the most extensive survey of campaign spending ever undertaken. It was carried out by the Citizens' Research Foundation of Princeton, N. J., and is detailed in "Financing the 1968 Election," a book by the foundation's director, Herbert E. Alexander. The book will be published Thursday.

Because of the looseness of the reporting laws, the tabulation is incomplete, but it contains much fresh information.

Perhaps the most surprising finding in Dr. Alexander's study is the report that former Senator Eugene J. McCarthy of Minnesota, the unsuccessful antiwar candidate for the Democratic nomination, spent $11-million. At the time, his effort was pictured as poorly financed.

Five contributions of more than $100,000 to Senator McCarthy are listed. They are: Stewart Mott, the philanthropist, son of a founder of the General Motors Corporation, $210,000; Mr. and Mrs. Jack Dreyfus Jr. of the Dreyfus Fund, at least $100,000; Ellsworth T. Carrington, a 46-year-old Wall Street account executive (customer's man), who said he made his money "in the market," $100,000; Mr. and Mrs. Martin Peretz of Cambridge, Mass. — a Harvard professor who is married to a Singer Sewing Machine heiress—$100,000, and Alan Miller of Boca Raton, Fla., $108,000.

Mr. Miller, a retired industrialist from Pennsylvania, is one of the shadowy figures on the list. Not much is known about him except that he is an elderly former Republican who came forward voluntarily because of his opposition to the Vietnam war and sent two unsolicited $50,000 checks.

At one point, he came to New York in an ambulance to meet with Howard Stein, one of the principal McCarthy fund raisers. He was unable at the time to sit up because of a back ailment. Mr. Stein visited him at the St. Regis Hotel and came away with another contribution.

The campaign of 1968, Mr. Alexander writes, "brought more left-of-center or moderate money onto the political scene than at any time" in history.

Yet the third-party candidacy of George C. Wallace of Alabama was also well financed. It cost at least $9-million, most of which was raised in small sums in the most successful grass-roots fund-raising campaign ever seen in American presidential politics.

The huge McCarty expenditures in the pre-convention period helped to account for the fact that 11 of the 14 biggest contributors made most of their contributions before the parties named their candidates.

Dr. Alexander itemized pre-convention spending as follows: Lyndon B. Johnson, $1-million; Hubert H. Humphrey, $4-million; Mr. McCarthy, $11-million; Mr. Kennedy, $9-million; George McGovern, $75,-000; Lester G. Maddox, $50,000; President Nixon, $10-million to $12-million; Governor Rockefeller, $8-million; George Romney, $1.5-million; Ronald Reagan, $650,000, and Harold E. Stassen, $90,000.

Mr. Nixon's general election expenses were $24.9-million, Mr. Humphrey's $10.3-million.

The Rockefeller effort, like that of Senator Kennedy, was largely family financed. The largest single contributor in 1968 was Mrs. John D. Rockefeller Jr., the Governor's stepmother, who gave him $1,482,-625. According to Mr. Alexander's estimate, she also paid almost $850,000 in Federal gift taxes.

A total of 14 contributions of $100,000 or more are listed.

The list is full of names famous in the annals of American finance and industry—du Ponts, Fords, Pews, Mellons, Olins, Whitneys, Lehmans.

But there are others that are surprising. For example, Mrs. Margery F. Russell of Portland, Ore., an heiress to the fortune generated by Oregon's Meier and Frank department stores, contributed $94,613 to the unsuccessful campaign of Walter Blake, a right-winger on the model of Dr. Max Rafferty of California, for Superintendent of Public Instruction in Oregon.

Dr. Manfred Clynes, director of the Biocybernetics Laboratories at Rockland State Hospital, Orangeburg, N. Y., donated $30,000 to Senator McCarthy, according to Dr. Alexander. He said in a telephone interview that he had made his money through the invention of medical computers and gave his "first and only political contribution for peace."

Bob Hope, the comedian, gave $16,000 to the Republicans; Gene Autrey, the cowboy singer, gave $15,000 to the Republicans, and Barbara Tuchman, the historian, gave $20,-500 to the Democrats, along with her husband, Lester, a New York physician.

Fourteen persons who were named ambassadors by President Nixon contributed to his campaign. The largest sum was $51,000, given by Guilford Dudley Jr., a Nashville insurance man, now Ambassador to Denmark.

Democratic fund-raising for the general election campaign went so badly that the party was obliged to borrow heavily. John Factor, a real estate man once known in the Chicago underworld as Jake the Barber, lent $240,000, as did Lou Wasserman, the head of MCA, Inc. Nineteen other persons lent $100,000 each, including several New Yorkers.

They were the following:

Herbert A. Allen, New York investment banker.

The late Lester Avnet, New York electronics executive.

Jacob Blaustein, Baltimore oil executive.

Arthur G. Cohen, New York real estate man.

Robert W. Dowling, New York real estate man.

Milton Gilbert, New York trucking executive.

Milton Gordon, New York investment banker.

H. E. Gould, New York manufacturing executive.

Leon Hess, New York oil executive.

Francis S. Levien, New York manufacturing executive.

John Loeb, New York investment banker.

Arthur S. Murphy, New York distilling company executive.

Patrick O'Connor, Minneapolis attorney and former Democratic national finance chairman.

Jeno Paulucci, Duluth, Minn., food company executive.

Arnold M. Picker, New York motion picture executive.

Robert E. Short, Minneapolis trucking executive and former Democratic National Finance chairman.

Edwin L. Weisl, New York attorney and former Democratic National Committeeman from New York.

Few of the loans have been repaid, and they will probably be settled, if at all, for a few cents on the dollar. The party is still $9.3-million in debt with 1972 approaching.

You Are Being Had

By JOHN W. GARDNER

WASHINGTON—It isn't a pleasant thing to admit that in this great nation elective offices can be purchased; that votes of Federal, state and local officials are bought and sold every day; that access of the people to their government is blocked by a Chinese Wall of money.

It isn't pleasant but it's a fact—and, today, a dangerous fact.

Americans in every walk of life are increasingly skeptical about their political and governmental institutions. They doubt that these institutions, which are supposed to serve them, are in fact doing so. And that withdrawal of confidence bodes ill for the Republic.

People need to feel they have access to their government. They need to believe their government is responsive. They need to feel it can be called to account. But wherever they look they find that "the access of money to power" is blocking the access of people to power.

There are honest politicians and we owe them respect. But the pervasive and degrading influence of money in politics is making it harder for them to be effective.

The people are not helpless. They could act decisively in their own behalf. The difficulty is that the American people can't be bothered with the grimy details of how the political system works. So they end up being had.

Three basic measures are needed at once: (1) control of campaign financing (2) lobbying controls and (3) full disclosure of conflict of interest on the part of legislators. Those three measures, put into effect in the fifty state legislatures and the Congress of the United States would change the political and economic landscape of this country.

The urgent item at this moment is control of campaign financing, currently under consideration by Congress.

The election campaign of 1970 was a rude awakening to millions of Americans. It finally hit them that we are no longer a nation in which any man can run for office and hope to win. In most states and districts he has to be wealthy or put himself under obligation to sources of wealth.

For perhaps sixty days after the election the newspapers were filled with shocking stories of excessive spending. Then, as often happens, the wave of indignation passed. Now serious control measures are under debate, but the attention of the people has been diverted to other issues. And when the people are looking the other way the public interest is all too often butchered.

An example is to be found in the enforcement provision of the bill now moving through the Senate. All responsible experts on campaign financing control have recommended that enforcement be in the hands of an independent elections commission. Yet many members of Congress still urge that enforcement be lodged with the clerk of the House and the secretary of the Senate. And these are the gentlemen who have made the enforcement of present campaign financing laws a national joke.

They have no appetite for enforcement. They never will have. They are political appointees of the majority party. It is no coincidence that the split on this issue tends to be along party lines.

Another defect of the Senate bill as well as the bill before the House Commerce Committee is failure to provide subsidy of broadcast time as recommended by the Twentieth Century Fund in its "Voters' Time" proposal and by others. Skyrocketing campaign costs are due chiefly to television. A return to sanity requires that the cost to the candidate be somehow reduced. The stations might be required to provide time free, or at reduced rates. Or they might provide free time that would be tax deductible. Or the Federal Government might subsidize the time.

Another way to reduce the influence of money in campaigns is to legislate a ceiling on expenditures—particularly media expenditures, which can be monitored most easily. Proposals have been made to the Congress to establish limits on both expenditures and contributions. Some experts believe that contribution ceilings are not enforceable, but that is no more than a guess. The combination of contribution ceilings, expenditure ceilings, full disclosure and an independent enforcement mechanism has never been tested. The concept of limiting individual financial influence is so basic that we should give it a try. There is some debate on the constitutional issue, but the appropriate place to test that is in the courts.

It is reasonably certain that the Senate will pass this summer a campaign financing control bill that is close to adequate. But the House of Representatives poses a real obstacle. As of this writing it would appear that the House intends to let the issue die. If it does, the sordid interplay of money and politics will go on and on.

John W. Gardner, a former Secretary of Health, Education and Welfare, now heads Common Cause.

July 4, 1971

Giving It a Jolt

By TOM WICKER

IN THE NATION

WASHINGTON, Aug. 30—The law now provides that no one may contribute more than $5,000 in any one year to a candidate for Federal office, and that no political committee shall collect or spend more than $3 million in any one year. But everyone who engages in, writes about or has anything else to do with politics knows that these statutes are as violated as the Ten Commandments, and far more systematically.

Yet, there never has been a prosecution, much less a conviction. The reason is not really that the national political parties cleverly get around the limitations by setting up multifarious committees, supposedly independent, which then receive and expend $3 million each, and to each of which any fat cat may throw $5,000 with impunity.

These are transparent subterfuges. The real reason no one has ever been prosecuted or jailed for violating the campaign spending statutes is that, particularly in the age of television, these restrictions are simply not practical; therefore all political parties have a common necessity to violate them. As a result, no Attorney General has or will prosecute, because he would either be biting the hand that fed the President who appointed him, or hitting an opposing party that sooner or later would be in position to hit back. This is not exactly a conspiracy; it is just a common understanding to do nothing, arising from common interest.

In these circumstances, the general public, or any individual voter, has three remedies for the wrong that may be done by this system of living above the law. The first remedy is for the Attorney General to prosecute; but none ever has. The second remedy is for an aggrieved individual or organization to collect the evidence of lawbreaking and force a prosecution; on the face of it, that is not easy, and is somewhat above and beyond the call of even the good citizen's duty.

The third remedy is to seek new and better legislation from Congress, which citizens in one form or another —from private personages to big organizations — have been doing for years with notable lack of success. A bill restricting television spending did get through Congress last year, only to be vetoed by President Nixon; and a broader-gauged bill has passed the Senate this year, but only to dubious prospects in the House and to the ultimate possibility of another veto.

That is why it is important that Federal Judge Barrington D. Parker refused here last week to dismiss a suit by Common Cause, the big citizens' lobby, against the major political parties. The suit seeks declaratory and injunctive relief from what it contends are persistent circumventions of the present campaign-fund statutes by both Republicans and Democrats as well as the Conservative party of New York State.

The immediate meaning of Judge Parker's ruling is that attorneys for Common Cause can now proceed to what lawyers call "discovery" of the financial records of the major parties. The principal fund-raisers can be brought into court as sworn witnesses and made to testify about their records and procedures, an extraordinary opportunity for public disclosure of who has been financing politics in America, through what means, and to what extent.

Unless the major parties are able to fend off this dread prospect with legal maneuvers, which appears unlikely, the only way to avoid such disclosure appears to be the passage of the legislation now pending in the House. It would abolish present unrealistic limitations on contributions and expenditures in favor of a system of spending on a cents-per-vote basis, remove the limitations on individual contributions, and impose improved reporting procedures of both contributions and expenditures.

The alternative to passage is the almost certain exposure in Federal court of Republican, Democratic and Conservative financial records. At least, that's the way Common Cause and its attorneys see the situation, and that is in large part the reason the suit was brought—to put on the pressure for reform.

Some attorneys wonder if Judge Parker's ruling might not open the door to frivolous or malicious suits to expose the financial records of various organizations or individuals. To others, the suit provides one more example of the lengths to which it is often necessary to go to get redress and reform in America. As John Gardner of that organization once observed, you have to give the system "a real jolt."

August 31, 1971

The Equal Time Debate

FLETCHER AGAIN ASKS TIME.

He Calls on CBS for Equality With the 'Party in Power.'

WASHINGTON, Jan. 14 (AP).—Protesting that President Roosevelt's "Congressional broadcast" opened the 1936 campaign, Chairman Fletcher of the Republican National Committee renewed today his request to the Columbia Broadcasting System for facilities equal to those granted to "the party in power."

In a letter to William S. Paley, president, he denied refusing time offered by the chain.

The offer was "so unsatisfactory and hedged about" that he did not take it up immediately, Mr. Fletcher said, adding:

"However, in the course of the political campaign, which was opened by the President's Congressional broadcast, I shall hope that Republican speakers will receive comparable time at equally desirable hours over comparable stations, as may be granted to the spokesmen of the party in power. You will receive requests to this effect from time to time."

Topics of The Times

Voices in the Air. By now it seems clear that Chairman Fletcher of the Republican National Committee has thought better of it. He will not ask the courts for a writ of mandamus against the broadcasting companies, compelling them to give the Republicans as much time as they give the Roosevelt Administration. And one reason why Mr. Fletcher has thought better of it is that no court can give him a mandamus compelling the radio audience to listen to Republicans as much as they do to Democrats; or the other way about.

Under our system of government the Administration is bigger news than the Opposition—at least, until such a time as it begins to look that the Opposition might be the next Administration. The President of the United States is always news. If he chooses in his speeches to give to the party what was meant for the State, it is the Opposition's hard luck. The newspaper editors are helpless in the matter, as news.

So are the broadcasting companies, when the President of the United States speaks. But these "must" subjects are rare; and in the normal run of business the broadcaster, like the news editor, must be allowed to allocate his space—or time—by his own judgment of news values. This is particularly important for the radio because its display is all "front-page," in the nature of things.

Drama Makes News. There are ways in which an opponent of the President of the United States may get himself more news space and news time than the President. The secret is to put on a show so much superior as to overcome the big advantage which the Chief Executive enjoys by prescription. One such test is sure to come off early next Summer with the two national conventions.

Today it seems plain that the Republican convention will get more newspaper space and more radio time than the Democratic convention. The meeting of the Democrats in Philadelphia will be a cut-and-dried affair. Mr. Roosevelt in his Jackson Day speech speculated mildly as to who the Democratic candidate will be, but the public and the newspaper editors do not share his doubts on the subject. On the other hand, the Republican meeting in Cleveland will be full of uncertainty and drama. People will scarcely hang over the radio to find out who has been nominated at Philadelphia. They will be tuning in on Cleveland all the time.

Radio Potency Exaggerated. Radio is new, and in this business of politics and parties it enjoys a prestige that, in this country especially, attaches to novelty. Actually there is good reason for thinking that people have been greatly exaggerating the potency of this new engine of public opinion. It is too easily taken for granted that any speaker who goes on the air has a vast number of his countrymen hanging on his words. If they do listen to him it is too easily taken for granted that the radio orator holds the fortunes of his country in the palm of his hands.

It is not so simple as all that. In the first place there seems to be no very convincing way of measuring the size of a radio audience. People largely guess about the "millions" of radio listeners who rally to this or that orator. It is still harder to measure the spell which the orator casts over his audience. There are telegrams and post-cards, to be sure, but they do not say how long the spell under which they have been written will endure.

Not very long ago Father Coughlin was supposed to speak to 5,000,000 radio listeners and therefore to "control" 5,000,000 votes; the transition from listener to voter in such cases is always automatic. But the prestige of Father Coughlin today scarcely reflects such a mighty armament of voters.

Other Public Vehicles. Mr. Roosevelt's own case is still more instructive. Chairman Fletcher of the Republican National Committee will be the last man to deny that Mr. Roosevelt's popularity is not what it used to be. Yet this decline in the President's fortunes, if it is a fact, has taken place at a time when Mr. Roosevelt has had more than his proper share of free access to the radio, as Mr. Fletcher so strongly feels. Say that the Literary Digest poll has meaning only for the odd 2,000,000 voters who participated. Yet within that fair-sized body of voters a change has taken place from 3 to 2 for Mr. Roosevelt to 3 to 2 against him. As our best radio speaker the President certainly should have been able to prevent such an overturn.

The fate of the American Republic and of our civic liberties will not be decided solely by radio. We also have newspapers, meeting halls, and free speech in the public squares and on the soap-boxes. They are older institutions than radio, but still count for something.

Any one who wants to know how easy it is to maintain neutrality need only observe how neutral the chairman of a neutrality inquiry committee can be.

FREEDOM OF THE AIR.

In view of the fact that the political use of the radio will be greater than ever this year, discussion of its possible limitations has become active. Of course there can be no such thing as absolute "freedom of the air." There must be a certain degree of control. The authorities and the broadcasting companies have, for example, the right and the duty to keep indecent or libelous matter off the air. And nobody disputes that some Government agency must pass upon applications for new stations. and must equitably allot wave lengths. Otherwise the air would be filled with conflicting and unintelligible sounds, making the radio a nightmare. But while this is granted by all, there remain questions about the apportionment of time between political parties, and about the terms upon which debaters of current issues should be allowed access to the radio.

Everybody remembers how a controversy was started when President ROOSEVELT'S message to Congress was sent out on a nation-wide hook-up. Chairman FLETCHER of the Republican National Committee at once demanded that equal facilities be accorded to Republican speakers who wished to reply to the President. Perhaps Mr. FLETCHER was not entirely sincere and did not expect his request to be granted. as it was not at the moment. But an exchange of correspondence followed which made it clear that the leading broadcasting companies intend to be impartial in this matter. They even promise to "give" time to selected political speakers, instead of ruling that it must be paid for. This is important. The real question being not whether there can be an unqualified freedom of the air, but whether there should not be equality in the use of the air, it is evident that no discrimination should be made in behalf of the party committee having the larger funds at command. It might buy up most of the time, or the most eligible time. at the disposal of the radio, and thus shut out its rivals from an equal opportunity to reach the public. Nothing of that kind is likely to happen.

The real difficulty will arise over the choice of political speakers over the radio. There will naturally be some privileged characters. The President should have as much time, and as frequently, as he thinks necessary. Nor ought his rival nominee for the Presidency to be limited in any way. But below that high rank, who shall decide? The suggestion has been made that the selection of competent speakers on either side should be left to the respective national committees. But they could not properly have unlimited power in that way, or in the apportionment of time. In some way, either by common consent, or by the action of the broadcasting companies, equality of treatment, as between parties, and limitation of time. as regards individual speakers, should be equitably fixed.

We have not yet fully measured the effect of the radio on political speaking. One obvious result of the shortness of the time permitted is to make speeches and joint debates more direct, simple and compact. A United States Senator who has been accustomed to address empty desks for three or four hours, speaking as he does "for Buncombe" or the Congressional Record, would profit greatly in effectiveness and in style by being held down to, half an hour on the radio or, better still, to fifteen minutes. And the rule should be absolute that when a speaker —except the President or the rival candidate for the Presidency — runs over his time by as much as ten seconds he should be instantly cut off. If he protests against this he might be reminded of the saying of Mr. EVARTS when asked how long a sermon ought to be. His reply was: "Twenty minutes, with a leaning to the side of mercy."

One hesitates to predict what influence on the election the radio may have. It should surely lead to wider discussion of the political issues of the day. It will place millions of Americans in the position of being present at joint debates between public leaders. We have been recalling the famous and epoch-making Lincoln-Douglas debates of 1858. They were heard by audiences large for that time and occasion, but which were a mere handful compared with the great multitude of listeners-in today. It is a wonderful experiment. the outcome of which cannot be measured as yet. One consequence will plainly be to discredit monotony of theme and treatment. When Mr. BRYAN ran for the Presidency in 1896, he traversed the country making virtually the same speech in city after city. He could not do that over the radio today. People would not tolerate a literal repetition of what they had already heard. This fact should make for greater variety as well as for more restraint in our political speaking over the radio during the campaign. That would be of benefit to all concerned, no matter whether great masses of voters are swayed or not by the voices that come out of the air.

LIMIT ROOSEVELT TALKS

Two Coast Radio Stations Bar Free 'Campaign Speeches.'

LOS ANGELES, Sept. 10 (Æ).— President Roosevelt's "fireside chats" cannot be handled by radio stations KFI and KECA here unless the talks are paid for, according to Harrison Holloway, general manager of the stations. Mr. Holloway described the talks as "nothing more than campaign speeches, in our opinion, and cannot be released unless paid for by the Democratic National Committee."

This is the reason, he said, why the stations canceled their scheduled participation in the network broadcast of the President's talk last Sunday night.

"If the President speaks at dedications or public events of national interests, at any time when he is officiating as President rather than a candidate for office, we shall be happy to broadcast his remarks as a matter of civic interest. But if he seeks to use the facilities of KFI or KECA in the interest of re-election, we must necessarily answer negatively any request or demand for free time.

"The talks by Governor Landon are being paid for by the Republican party and we see no reason why the Democrats should not reimburse us similarly."

February 16, 1936   September 11, 1936

SENATOR DROPS A 'BOMB'

Mr. King's Hint of Favoritism on the Air Revives An Old Idea for New Legislation

THE bombshell that dropped into the bailiwicks of broadcasting during the past week was tossed by Senator King of Utah. He hinted that the broadcasters were favoring the administration in allotting radio time to speakers discussing the pros and cons of President Roosevelt's proposal for reorganization of the judiciary and the Supreme Court.

Spokesmen for the broadcasters had little comment except to reveal by program statistics that they had showed no bias and had quite evenly distributed their time, watts and waves to both sides of the controversy.

Senator King's Purpose

Senator King, a member of the Senate Judiciary Committee, stated he will introduce a resolution calling for an inquiry as to whether or not charges that the networks are favoring administration spokesmen in the current Supreme Court debate are true, unless he is convinced meanwhile that there is no basis for the allegations.

The threat comes as an aftermath to complaints from Senator Wheeler, Democrat, of Montana, chief spokesman of the Senate bloc opposing the President's court reorganization plan.

Senator King explained that his purpose is to determine whether the broadcasting companies are being dominated or influenced by the Federal Communications Commission or the administration in granting greater facilities to administration spokesmen.

"If they are exercising this brutal power—if they really have this brutal power—in this fight, then it is time for some such investigation," Senator King said. "In my own opinion they are discriminating against the opposition. Complaints are coming in to indicate this, and if I can obtain some additional facts, I shall introduce such a resolution."

Actually, there is no law that would require the networks to give equal time to spokesmen for and against the President's court plan, but it is obvious that the broadcasters would not engage in any policy knowingly that would antagonize a number of influential Senators, according to observers in Washington.

While a Senate inquiry might not penalize the broadcasters directly, it might well result in the passage of legislation that would require all stations to give equal time to both parties in public debate as is now required for political candidates.

A bill, introduced by Representative Scott, Democrat, of California, seeking such a requirement, is now pending in the House. Radio men are no doubt aware that complaints such as those of Senators King and Wheeler might well be the lever that would dislodge it and turn it into law.

Radio and the Candidates

It is pointed out in the radio law that any violation of section 315 of the Communication Act of 1934 shall be sufficient ground for the revocation or denial of a broadcast license. Section 315 reads:

If any licensee shall permit any person who is a legally qualified candidate for any public office to use a broadcasting station, he shall afford equal opportunities to all other such candidates for that office in the use of such broadcasting station, and the commission shall make rules and regulations to carry this provision into effect: Provided, that such licensee shall have no power of censorship over the material broadcast under the provisions of this paragraph. No obligation is hereby imposed upon any licensee to allow the use of its station by any such candidate.

The accusations of bias in the current controversy happened when the broadcasters were still congratulating themselves that they had survived the 1936 national elections without being accused of partiality, although there were listeners here and there who on several occasions thought they sensed censorship on the part of the radio stations. Nevertheless, considering the campaign on a national scale and the vastness of the audience coupled with its varied political beliefs, the broadcasters felt that they navigated the chaotic ethereal sea of politics on a course that veered neither right nor left.

In The Nation

A Proposed Limit on Opposition's Function

By ARTHUR KROCK

Throughout this country there has seemed to be of late a growing thirst for information. The wide spread of forums attests it; so do the increased numbers of newspaper and radio commentators, and the greater concentration on Washington of the spotlight of inquiry. While the sum of all this includes a disproportionate amount of interested propaganda, its source is the public wish to be informed.

Those who have participated in forum and institute discussions lately have found that the American people, as represented in such cross-sections, reveal another intense desire. Noting the disappearance of the Republicans in Congress as opposing effectives, and observing further that Democrats in any numbers have not resisted the administration save on a few special items in the New Deal program, the forum audiences continually are asking how an Opposition in Washington can be assured in times like these when a President and his party are so overwhelmingly in power.

If these audiences reflect the popular view, then the American people want opinion and formal opposition, and they want facts as they have never wanted them before. Is it conceivable that they do not want facts except from two sources—the party in power and its outside supporters? That is wholly unlikely. Yet such a rule of public reasoning appears to be the prevailing thought of the New Deal Liberals, a thought they would enforce upon the consciousness of the country.

On every side, since the professional advocates of the administration got back their wind after the Justice Black revelations, they have united in one attack on those publications which made them. They have disparaged them, not on the ground of falsity but on the point of their source. Because the articles originated with a newspaper whose publisher is opposed to the New Deal and the President, they are held not worthy of serious attention. Because the source from which they sprang would like very much to see another personnel in control of the government, it is urged that the publications be viewed solely from that aspect. Whether guilty or innocent, it is contended by the New Deal Liberals, the Justice should be upheld because information about him came from the enemies of his regime.

Politically Managed News

If that viewpoint should be sustained by the country, then it will be useless to give to the people essential information about their government unless the giver is selfishly committed to the maintenance and success of that government—a paradox. The people would have to depend for the real news of what their governors are doing on the governors themselves or their spokesmen. Unless a fact bore the Federal brand it should be ignored or resented, despite its truth or implication, say the New Deal Liberals.

That absurd and destructive thesis, if sustained, would end the usefulness of independence and objectivity in the press, in Congress or among the citizenry. Public opinion—if it supported such a thesis—would, by closing its ears and eyes to truth from certain sources, effectively set up a system of politically managed news. Americans would be no better off than Germans, Italians or Russians under their present dispensations. And there would be no chance of the development and continuance of an Opposition unless the New Deal Liberals fell out among themselves and risked their own jobs.

Need for Information

This is the logical destination of the argument that, because certain publications come from persons unfriendly to, or independent of, the administration, they should be disregarded by all true liberals, and those affected by the publications should be absolved.

Even at the present time, when getting away with anything seems to be the administration's fairy gift, that argument will probably not win a majority sufficient to put it in control of the national mind. The most it does is to reflect seriously upon the good faith, good sense or patriotism of those who have lately banded together to make it. Its end would be the selfish and corrupt canalization of news and the complete suppression of that Opposition for which there is an increasing demand in the United States. And the demand comes—as in this space—from many who steadily make public acknowledgment of the President's achievements for the general welfare.

Of the vital necessity for information about public affairs and public men, whatever the source and whatever the motive, there is no need to write. Such information marks one of the fundamental differences between a democracy and other forms of government. And democracies have so instinctively and always recognized the health that comes from the existence of rivals to those in power that the British solemnly stand by what they call His Majesty's Opposition. That may be a comic phrase, taken literally. But it denotes something vital in democratic processes.

In days like these, when the national Republican party is so weak that its representatives in Congress dare not speak out on acute issues, the need to foster opposition by fair facts is greater than ever.

October 1, 1937

KNOX URGES RADIO FREE AT ELECTIONS

To Put Issues to People, He Proposes Equal Time for Parties in Campaigns

REPUBLICAN FUND PROJECT

Special to THE NEW YORK TIMES.

DES MOINES, Iowa, Feb. 22.—Asserting that the Republican party must change its method of raising campaign funds if it would "become again the party of the plain folks of America," Frank Knox, the party's 1936 Vice Presidential nominee, proposed tonight that national campaign contributions be limited to $1,000. He suggested a plan whereby $3,000,000 would be available to the party for a Presidential campaign.

Mr. Knox proposed also free broadcasts for political parties "near election time" in a national campaign.

In a speech at a Washington's Birthday banquet of the Polk County Republican organization, Mr. Knox accused the New Deal Administration of "open contempt of the law in its flagrant abuse of executive power over the channels of publicity."

Holding that "all is confusion," nowhere greater than in the White House, he said that the situation offered the Republican party a magnificent opportunity.

He enlarged on views he expressed in a speech at Cleveland Jan. 11 on lowering excessive tariff schedules, and asserted:

"We should lead the way back to a sane interchange of goods and services. That way lies peace. On the other hand, continuation of the world on its present course leads inevitably to war."

Campaign Funds Proposal

Outlining his plan for raising campaign funds, Mr. Knox, publisher of The Chicago Daily News, said that out of the 600,000 individuals who contributed to the 1936 Republican campaign, it would not be difficult to find 10,000 who would give $100 a year to support the party, thus providing an annual income of $1,000,000. He dubbed these supporters the "Ten Thousand Club."

"Then," he continued, "once in four years let the party undertake to find a paltry 2,000 individuals who would be able and willing to contribute $1,000 to the campaign fund to promote the election of a Republican President and Congress. That would mean a total campaign fund of $2,000,000.

"This, with $1,000,000 from that year's receipts from the Ten Thousand Club would give the national chairman a total of $3,000,000 for the Presidential campaign, enough for all legitimate purposes if one additional step is taken.

"What I have in mind is the cost of radio broadcasting. It has already become very nearly the largest

single item in the expense of a campaign. Radio, in a sense, is a natural monopoly. Each station uses a certain wave frequency. It is granted the right to this frequency, and is protected in its enjoyment of it, by the Federal Government, representing all the people.

"Why not, as a partial compensation for this privilege, require that, near election time, both great parties be allowed, without expense, an equal amount of time on the air, to the end that both sides of all issues be fairly and adequately presented to the people? Minor parties should, of course, be treated with proportionate consideration."

Hits Roosevelt Publicity Spending

Turning to New Deal publicity, Mr. Knox said the law provided that no money appropriated by Congress could be used "to compensate any publicity expert," unless specifically appropriated for that purpose. No such appropriations had been made, he continued, but, in defiance of the law, there were about 300 men and women in Washington employed as publicity experts, their payroll being in excess of $1,000,000 a year.

He said a careful estimate of the total expenditures of the Roosevelt Administration during the campaign year of 1936 showed more than $5,000,000 of public funds spent in violation of the law. A pledge to "stop this form of unfair and illegal use of executive power should be a part of a constructive Republican program," he added.

Mr. Knox declared a farm-aid program to be "a proper concern of government, just exactly as is the protection of the wage standard of the industrial workers in the cities."

"We should also pursue, along sound economic lines, the subject of farm credit," he said. "The farmer, like other business men, should have made available to him abundant credit at low interest rates. I am sure that there can be developed a system of agriculture credit that will satisfy legitimate needs in the farm-mortgage field and will also provide for loans on farm products which can be stored on the farm.

"Government participation in such a farm credit system could and should be limited to some form of guarantee comparable to that which is provided for bank deposits under our present banking laws."

Would Restore Competition

He asserted that democracy and a planned economy "will not team together" and that "the only way to regain our prosperity is to insist upon competition in business."

"Let us then, as a party, declare militantly for the intelligent revision of our anti-monopoly laws, to the end that real competition be restored in all forms of business save those which are natural monopolies and which, accordingly, must be regulated by government in the public interest," Mr. Knox said.

He recalled President Roosevelt's Jackson Day speech, in which the President declared he was fighting "for the integrity of the morals of democracy."

In this connection, he accused Mr. Roosevelt of breaking his word and repudiating his pledges by increasing, instead of decreasing, the costs of government, going off the gold standard, permitting relief funds to be used "by unscrupulous machine politicians," replacing pension funds "with government I O U's."

February 23, 1938

PLANS RADIO RULES ON POLITICAL TALKS

Special to THE NEW YORK TIMES.

WASHINGTON, June 23.—Frank R. McNinch, chairman of the Federal Communications Commission, said today he would lay before the commission soon the question of promulgating rules for distributing time to political candidates by licensed stations, an action directed by law, but never taken by the FCC.

His statement came as Representative Cox, Democrat, of Georgia, suggested in remarks in the Congressional Record issued today that George H. Payne of New York, a member of the FCC, should resign from the commission, charging that he is "entirely irresponsible" and a "trouble-maker."

The chairman's announcement came after a newspaper man cited a complaint of a Virginia candidate for the National House that he found all available time on his local station bought up by his primary opponent.

Drawing of rules would be a delicate matter, Mr. McNinch said. The statute provides that, if a station sells or grants time to any legally qualified candidate, it must afford equal opportunity to all other candidates for the same office. It sets forth, however, that stations are not obligated to sell or grant time to any candidates.

Mr. Cox, in his attack on Mr. Payne, said he reached his conclusion as a result of the FCC member's failure, in testifying before the House Rules Committee on a proposed investigation of the commission, to substantiate his charges that commission members are unduly influenced by lobbyists.

"It is my opinion," he stated, "that the restoration of confidence in the commission would be aided if Commissioner Payne were separated from it. With the chairman given associates who will cooperate with him, there can be no question but that the commission will quickly overcome the injury done it in the public mind by Mr. Payne."

The Georgian asserted that, in supporting his demand before the Rules Committee for an investigation of the commission, which the House later rejected, Mr. Payne charged other Commissioners with being amenable to lobbyists, but refused to say which members he referred to.

Then after "reluctantly agreeing" to be more specific in an executive session, Mr. Cox charged, Mr. Payne denied he had made such an agreement.

Mr. Cox then asserted that Mr. Payne, after giving his original charges to the press, also apparently failed to "make any attempt to publicly retract the charges which he admitted to the committee were without foundation."

Mr. Payne, in a reply today to Mr. Cox, declared that the latter "is trying to make a case for monopoly and abuse on the radio."

Asks Broadcasts for Senate

WASHINGTON, March 16 (AP)—Senator Downey of California suggested today that the Senate set aside two hours each day for speechmaking on "extraneous matters" and that these speeches be broadcast. For this purpose Mr. Downey told a joint committee studying Congressional reorganization, the Senate should meet two hours earlier than its traditional noon opening time.

REPORT HITS FCC ON ATHEISM RULING

Chairman of Agency Attacked Asserts It Does Not Say Radio Must Give Time for Views

WASHINGTON, Sept. 18 (AP)—A Congressional committee today assailed two rulings of the Federal Communications Commission dealing with atheism and with political broadcasts as "dangerous and mischievous." The one touching on atheism was described as "a dangerous and unwarranted policy of 'thought policing' that has no basis in law."

The decisions criticized by the committee headed by Representative Forest A. Harness of Indiana, are known in the broadcasting industry as the Scott decision and the Port Huron decision. The former has been interpreted widely as a ruling that time on the air must be given to atheists to reply to religious broadcasts.

The Port Hurron decision held in effect that radio stations have no right to censor libelous or slanderous statements in political broadcasts. This ruling, the committee said, left broadcasters in "a dilemma of self-destruction, inasmuch as they would be required to answer to the commission if they eliminated defamatory remarks, and yet might face criminal and civil prosecution under state laws if they permitted such material to go on the air."

The committee said the problem had been "substantially resolved" by FCC assurance that for the time being, at least, "the honest and conscientious broadcaster who uses ordinary common sense in trying to prevent obscene and slanderous statements from going out over the air need not fear any capricious action."

The house committee said of the Scott decision that the FCC "clearly invades the field of legislation and indulges in quasi-judical legislation on a subject which Congress clearly decided to be outside the Communications Act."

If applied literally, the committee said, the Scott decision "would have the effect of either driving religious programs from the air, or flooding the homes of listeners with a barrage of unwelcome attacks on religion."

"If the dictum contained in the Scott decision were literally applied, atheists would be entitled to answer each Protestant, Catholic, or Jewish program," said the report, and "the apostles of unbelief would have as many programs as were given to all the religious groups combined."

The alternative left to broadcasters, it commented, would be to refuse to accept any religious programs, a course that would be "advantageous only to the atheists and to the Communists." But unless the FCC actually and unequivocally expunges the "language of its opinions," the committee said, it will propose remedial legislation when Congress meets again.

The chairman of the commission, Wayne Coy, made this comment: "The Scott decision does not say that when a radio station carries religious broadcasts, atheists or persons or groups with similar views are entitled to radio time for the expression of their views. I say this with full knowledge that some persons have misinterpreted the Scott decision to hold opposite views.

"What the Scott decision has emphasized is the principle that a radio broadcast licensee in exercising his judgment as to what is a controversial issue should not deny time over his broadcast facilities for the expression of a particular point of view solely because he does not agree with that point of view."

June 24, 1938

March 17, 1945

September 19, 1948

OPEN AIR TIME ASKED FOR POLITICAL DRIVES

WASHINGTON, April 17 (Æ)— Senators are apprehensive that television and radio fans will get angry if their favorite programs are blacked out this fall for election campaign speeches. They asked the radio and television industry today to leave some open program spaces in the months ahead for political campaigning.

Senator A. S. Mike Monroney, Democrat of Oklahoma, said that otherwise, if programs were scheduled and then had to be blacked out, the fan likely would say:

"Why the dirty so-and-so (meaning the politician) has canceled out my favorite program."

This came up at a Senate Elections subcommittee hearing on election law reforms.

Officials of the National Broadcasting Company and the Columbia Broadcasting System said the program scheduling suggestion was a constructive one.

Joseph Y. Heffernan, financial vice president of N. B. C., said the cost of time for television broadcasts on the system's interconnected network of fifty-two stations is $27,920 for thirty minutes. This is for choice night time hours and Saturday and Sunday afternoon.

Adrian Murphy, president of C. B. S. radio, told the Senators the night time cost for political broadcasts on the C. B. S. radio network is $14,100 for half an hour.

But if candidates take over time of a regularly sponsored and scheduled program they also pay for the non-cancelable out-of-pocket expenses for talent and for advertising commissions.

So the idea of leaving blank spaces in program schedules for the months ahead not only might save politicians from losing friends among program fans, but also might save them money, Mr. Monroney explained.

April 18, 1952

TEXAS 'STEAL' LAID TO TAFT MANAGERS

Lodge Denounces 'Cheating'— Ohio Senator Seeks Network Time to Match General's

By JAMES RESTON
Special to The New York Times.

WASHINGTON, May 27—The Taft and Eisenhower forces really got down to brass knuckles today in their pre-convention maneuvers for the Republican Presidential nomination.

Senator Henry Cabot Lodge Jr., of Massachusetts, campaign manager for General of the Army Dwight D. Eisenhower, who announced when he took the job that he never would attack any other Republican candidate, openly accused Senator Robert A. Taft's managers in Texas of "stealing" the general's Texas delegates and of "political cheating."

This was a reference to the action of the Texas Republican State Executive Committee, which refused to recognize the Eisenhower delegates elected in county and district conventions.

Coincidentally, Senator Taft protested publicly that the broadcasting companies of the nation were giving undue advantage and "unprecedented coverage" to General Eisenhower's June 4 speech in Abilene, Kan. The Ohio Senator demanded that he be given equal facilities two days later.

Senator Lodge declared in a written statement that the "high-handed" action of the Taft forces in Texas was a "shocking display of poor sportsmanship" that would appear "scandalous and shameful" to the public.

Text of the Statement

The text of the statement, which was regarded as the sharpest intra-party statement of the campaign, follows:

Stealing a man's vote is just as wrong as burglarizing his home. But it happened wholesale in Texas yesterday, when the huge majority of Texas who had voted in good faith for Eisenhower in almost every district were told their votes did not count.

This threatened loss of convention strength can easily be absorbed. But the public scorn for political cheating will never be absorbed. Nomination by trickery is a useless nomination. No one whose power is built on the shifting and malorodous sands of corruption can effectively raise his voice against corruption by the present Democratic Administration.

Representative Carroll Reece, Southern manager for Senator Taft, let the cat out of the bag last Friday when he announced that he believes his forces "will control the convention Credentials Committee" and thus may be able to say which contesting delegates are recognized."

This is a brazen statement which totally disregards the merits and justice of each case. In the last analysis, it is the rank and file of Republican delegates on the floor of the convention at Chicago who will have to decide between right and wrong.

The high-handed action in Texas added to the disregard of the majority in Louisiana is a shocking display of poor sportsmanship. It will appear scandalous and shameful to the public. It critically weakens the Republican party with fateful consequences at election time which no one can now foresee. There can be no good future for men whose drive for power depends on political zombies—those who, though politically dead, still try to walk.

In a letter to the American Broadcasting Company, the Columbia Broadcasting System and the National Broadcasting Company, Senator Taft characterized General Eisenhower's forthcoming address in Abilene as a "political speech" and observed that the arrangements that were being made for that address were even more elaborate and expensive than those usually accorded to the President of the United States.

Reflector Towers Built

In order to provide television coverage of the Abilene speech, large reflector towers had to be built every thirty miles in the 140 miles between Abilene and Kansas City, Mo.

Eisenhower managers here stated this evening that the Abilene talk was not a political address in the sense implied by Senator Taft. Everything the general did, they added, undoubtedly would have "political implications," but the address in his home town was primarily his response to a "homecoming celebration."

[In New York, N. B. C., A. B. C. and C. B. S. said that they planned to carry the Eisenhower address on both television and radio network hook-ups. Because of previous programming, N. B. C. has arranged to record the broadcast and transmit it later, but it was explained that this was only a temporary scheduling, subject to later revision. All other transmission will be simultaneous with the general's talk.]

Mr. Taft wrote the broadcasting companies that he felt this constituted "quite unprecedented coverage of a political speech, involving as it does the blacking out of the rest of the country from other viewing or listening except for this single event."

Cost of Facilities

The Ohio Senator added that according to his information the installation of facilities for the transmission of the Eisenhower speech would cost about $100,000.

"It is the type of facility," he said in his letter to the broadcasting companies, "usually arranged only for the President of the United States and I doubt if ever has the President spoken where extreme measures were needed to provide facilities which involved the expenditure of large sums of money."

Accordingly, Mr. Taft requested that equal facilities be provided to him at the same time on the evening of June 6.

Senator Estes Kefauver of Tennessee, candidate for the Democratic Presidential nomination, also demanded radio and television time equal that given Eisenhower for his Abilene speech. He left open the question of date.

Section 315 of the Communications Act of 1934, under the heading, "Facilities for Candidates for Public Office," deals with this question in these terms:

"If any licensee shall permit any person who is a legally qualified candidate for any public office to use a broadcasting station, he shall afford equal opportunities to all other such candidates for that office in the use of such broadcasting station, and the commission [Federal Communications Commission] shall make rules and regulations to carry this provision into effect, provided that such licensee shall have no power of censorship over the material broadcast under the provisions of this section.

"No obligation is hereby imposed upon any licensee to allow the use of its station by any such candidate."

Mr. Taft did not refer to this law. He merely based his request on the ground that his principal opponent for the Republican Presidential nomination was receiving facilities to reach the people of the country not heretofore granted to anyone else.

The networks had no official comment immediately on the two Senators' request. However, one network source remarked that Senators Taft and Kefauver had had abundant radio and television time on various programs while General Eisenhower had been making no appearances.

May 28, 1952

251

'EQUAL-TIME' IDEA SCORED BY A.C.L.U.

Group Tells F. C. C. Practice Could Lead to Endless Attacks and Replies

The American Civil Liberties Union yesterday urged that the concept of "equal time" to answer radio and television political attacks be abandoned.

In a letter to the Federal Communications Commission the union declared that the practice was one that could lead to an endless chain of attacks and counterattacks.

Instead, it said, broadcasters should voluntarily schedule programs to give a "fair representation" of a public figure's views. Private persons attacked individually, it said, should get an "equitable opportunity" to make a specific reply, but not necessarily equal time.

The union urged that the F. C. C. promote the voluntary application of the proposals among radio and television stations. Strict rules, it said, would cause confusion and smack of censorship.

The commission now requires that a radio or television station that grants time to the representative of any political party make equal time available on the same basis to the representatives of other parties.

This grows out of a provision of the Communications Act of 1934 providing that a station granting time to any candidate for public office must give equal opportunity to all other candidates.

The requirement does not apply to attacks made on individuals. But it is the practice of radio and television broadcasters to allow equal time for a reply by an individual who has been seriously and specifically attacked.

The distinction came up in March 1954 when Adlai E. Stevenson, during the Congressional campaign, called the Republican party half Eisenhower and half McCarthy.

The major networks granted equal time to Vice President Richard M. Nixon to reply on behalf of the Republican party. But they demurred at granting equal time to Senator Joseph R. McCarthy, Republican of Wisconsin, to answer what he considered a personal attack.

January 4, 1956

"Equal Time"

The American Civil Liberties Union last week urged the abolition of the legislative concept of "equal time" to answer political attacks made on the air. Instead it urged that the broadcasters take it upon themselves to provide equitable opportunity for balanced presentation of conflicting opinions.

Some such course is the only practical one for the forthcoming political campaign. Under the existing rules of the Federal Communications Commission, a broadcaster cannot give one candidate time on the air without assuring equal time for all others seeking the same office.

Often there may be an army of candidates from small parties who loudly demand time if it is accorded the nominee of major parties. As a result, instead of covering the candidates who are genuinely newsworthy figures, a broadcaster may just throw up his hands and do nothing, rather than allot valuable time to unknowns who do not have a ghost of a chance of election.

Common sense rather than legislation is the better guarantee of fairness. Competent newsmen—and the stations have many of them—intuitively know those candidates, be they representatives of two, three or whatever number of parties, who have a valid claim to a platform. In the long run sound news discretion will assure both a fairer and more ample use of the airwaves than an impractical bureaucratic fiat.

January 8, 1956

F. C. C. CHIEF OPPOSES 'EQUAL TIME' CHANGE

WASHINGTON, Jan. 31 (UP)—The Federal Communications Commission warned today that proposed changes in the "equal time" broadcast law could lead to political "censorship."

George C. McConnaughey, commission chairman, testified before a House Commerce subcommittee he objected to a measure under which radio stations could give less free time to minority party candidates than to candidates of the two major parties.

Supporters contend the bill would allow stations to provide broader coverage of major campaigns. At present they must make any free air time equally available to all political opponents.

In the 1952 Presidential campaign, for instance, they had a legal obligation to give as much free time to the sixteen minority party candidates as to General Eisenhower and Adlai E. Stevenson.

Critics of the law have said it encourages publicity seekers to enter campaigns merely to take advantage of free broadcast opportunities.

"The commission firmly believes that it is in the public interest for broadcast stations to provide the widest possible coverage for election campaigns," Mr. McConnaughey said.

February 1, 1956

FREE RADIO-TV TIME URGED IN CAMPAIGN

WASHINGTON, Feb. 3 (UP)—The Columbia Broadcasting System asked Congress today to permit it to offer major Presidential candidates free radio and television time to debate the 1956 campaign issues.

Richard S. Salant, vice president chairman, Representative Oren subcommittee this was impossible now because the law required that equal time be given to all legally qualified candidates, regardless of their obscurity. He said eighteen political parties put up Presidential candidates in the 1952 election.

The subcommittee is considering proposed legislation to give the broadcasters some discretion in exercising news judgment in political campaigns. The bill was introduced by the subcommittee chairman, Representative Oren Harris, Democrat of Arkansas, at the request of C. B. S. It is opposed by a majority of the Federal Communications Commission.

Mr. Salant said the proposed change in the law "could make it possible for some 115,000,000 people simultaneously to see and hear the Presidential candidates debate."

February 4, 1956

BUTLER ASKS CURB ON FREE AIR TIME

Urges at Hearing That Only Responsible Candidates Be Allowed Radio, TV Replies

Special to The New York Times.

WASHINGTON, Feb. 7—Law giving equal free radio and television time to opposing political candidates is defeating its own fair play objective, a House of Representatives subcommittee was told today.

Paul M. Butler, chairman of the Democratic National Committee, sounded the warning. He urged amendments to current statutes that would confine the free-time debates to responsible candidates of responsible parties. He did not limit his arguments to the Democratic and Republican parties. If a strongly backed third party came along, he suggested that it be let in.

The right of free time to answer political statements only applies when those first statements are made on free time. If a political candidate wishes to answer a broadcast that is paid for by a political organization he must pay or get someone to pay for his time.

In 1952 there were eighteen Presidential candidates. Each, under existing statutes, had the right to demand equal free air-time to answer questions raised by any other contender who also had spoken on free air-time.

Had all of them responded, Mr. Butler said, radio and television might have been choked to a point where they would have completely lost their entertainment appeal and be put out of joint economically.

Mr. Butler seemed to have lost none of his faith, however, in the equal distribution of free-air time between Democrats and Republicans—or with serious and well-sponsored third parties. He suggested, though, that the candidates of groups getting free air time prove material public support, something like the receipt of 1,000,000 ballots in previous elections, or a petition support of around 500,000.

February 8, 1956

SPUR TO USE OF TV IN POLITICS URGED

Brookings Report Proposes That Equal Free Time Apply Only to Key Candidates

Special to The New York Times.

WASHINGTON, Feb. 26—The Brookings Institution proposed today a law revision to promote wider use of television in political campaigns.

It declared that the requirements of Section 315 of the Federal Communications Act should be relaxed. The requirement that television stations grant free time to all candidates for a political office if it grants free time to one restricts the campaign use of the medium, it added. It urged that the section be amended to apply only to leading candidates of major parties.

The Brookings Institution is a private research organization. Its recommendation was in the report on a study, "Television and Presidential Politics," made by an institution staff member, Charles A. H. Thompson. He was staff director of the President's Communication Policy Board in 1950 and 1951.

Appraisal of Amendment

Section 315, Mr. Thompson contends, does not work out in practice. The proposed amendment, he asserts, would not only help major candidates but others as well.

Networks or stations, he adds, would be able to choose the most newsworthy and important among third or other party candidates without incurring the obligation of free time for all that candidate's rivals.

Earlier attempts to accomplish the purpose stated in today's report have met with differences of opinion. Commenting on one of them George C. McConnaughey, chairman of the Federal Communications Commission, cautioned against discriminating between candidates and parties.

Spokesmen for the television industry have said that the equal-time section has tended to cut down the amount of time networks were willing to give to major candidates. In view of this, Congress is considering legislation that would eliminate trivial candidacies and parties from the section's guarantee.

Today's study also considers other questions of public policy presented by television's role in the political scene.

It says that recent assertions by television networks of their right to editorialize raises the question whether they should state their editorial preferences among parties and candidates. It concludes that this issue is not serious in view of the industry's relationships to its audience and its sponsors.

Warning on Exerting Right

Attempts to exert the editorial right without previous announcement giving viewers a choice of whether or not to watch a program could bring harmful reaction to a station and to the sponsors of a program, it declares.

It adds, however, that a statement of political preference, along with continued full and objective news services, might be a welcome step toward increased political responsibility and maturity for television.

The study finds only slight danger that sponsors for the televising of political conventions might try to interfere with the convention as a nominating process. This danger is offset, according to the study, by the vigilance of both parties and of the networks and by the economic position of the sponsors.

Television has the right, the study holds, to equal access with other media to the proceedings of the national committees and of the conventions.

The report suggests that television coverage of political conventions can make for better-organized procedures. It adds that both major parties, with perhaps an eye to the viewer, are taking steps to eliminate or reduce some time-consuming activities.

February 27, 1956

'EQUAL' AIR TIME POLITICAL THORN

Some Queries and Answers on Recurring Controversy Over F. C. C. Rules

By JACK GOULD

What are the rules for giving equal time on radio and television to political candidates?

The question arose immediately after President Eisenhower's explanation Wednesday of his willingness to seek a second term. It will come up repeatedly from now until November.

In theory the rules are simple; in practice they are difficult to administer. In either case they are controversial. Herewith the A B C's of the rules together with major points of disagreement:

Who makes the rules on political broadcasts?

The Federal Communications Commission, the agency established by Congress to license radio and TV stations. It functions under the Communications Act of 1934, as amended.

What is the commission's basic position?

A broadcaster must use public property—the airwaves—to be in business. As a condition of his license, he has an obligation to serve all the people, not just some. This dictates that in all controversial programs, including discussions and political broadcasts, there must be a "fair and balanced presentation" of different opinions.

What is the specific provision applying to political candidates?

Section 315 of the Communications Act, the pertinent part of which reads as follows:

"If any licensee shall permit any person who is a legally qualified candidate for any public office to use a broadcasting station, he shall afford equal opportunity to all other such candidates for that office in the use of such broadcasting station."

What is a "legally qualified candidate?"

As construed by the F. C. C., the phrase means "any person who has publicly announced that he is a candidate for nomination by a convention of a political party, or for nomination for election in a primary, special or general election, municipal, county, state or national, and who meets the qualifications prescribed by the applicable laws to hold the office for which he is a candidate."

What is the test of a candidate's being "legally qualified?"

This is determined mainly by the law of the state in which he is a candidate. In some states he becomes qualified merely by announcing his candidacy; in others, he must follow the required procedure for obtaining a place on a ballot.

May a station deny a candidate "equal opportunity" because it believes he has no possibility of being elected or nominated?

No. The F. C. C. says a station cannot make a subjective determination of a candidate's chances of success.

What is the major criticism of the equal time rule?

The Columbia Broadcasting System and the National Broadcasting Company have noted that if they give time to major candidates they are compelled to accord equal treatment to many minor parties. Farrell Dobbs, perennial Socialist Workers' candidate, wanted time to answer General Eisenhower yesterday.

In the last Presidential election there were fourteen candidates. To give so many proportionate time, it is held, is economically impossible and not warranted by public interest. The effect of the provision, it is maintained is merely to curtail political discussion on the air.

Opponents of the provision argue that they should be allowed the same discretion as a newspaper editor in covering politics.

What is the major argument for the equal time provision?

To permit discrimination between candidates, it is contended, can lead to abuses worse than those that may now exist. The candidate who runs independently of the major parties must be assured an opportunity to be heard over publicly owned airwaves. Many reform movements on the local level have been started outside the existing parties; they might be thwarted in advance if not assured equal time on the air.

Some stations, it is noted, also are not eager to have to make their own decisions on political broadcasts.

May a radio or TV station editorialize in favor against a candidate?

Under F. C. C. rules, yes. However, the editorial must be labeled as such and the station must be prepared to give equal time to those opposing its point of view.

What is a recurring problem in interpreting the equal time provision?

The dual role held by the man who is President. When he gives a speech or participates in a press conference, the question arises whether he is speaking in his capacity as the elected leader of the country or the head of his political party.

Broadcasters hold that what a President may do or say is often a matter of national importance transcending political considerations. On the other hand, they recognize that by reason of his office, he has an automatic advantage in public relations over a rival nominee. Drawing a line is a perennially ticklish matter.

How Is Equal Time Apportioned?

In many ways. Yesterday, for instance, the networks maintained they did not have to give time for Democrats to answer President Eisenhower because they had previously reported the candidacy announcements of Adlai E. Stevenson and Senator Estes Kefauver of Tennessee. This is one criterion. Another is matching a specific broadcast by others of equal length over the same stations and at the same hour.

Equal time occasionally is hard to apportion. A party may have a state convention contest, for instance, that takes a long time to resolve; another may pick a nominee by acclamation. Yet the latter may insist on equal time on the air. This happened two years ago and, as a consequence, one network decided not to do any coverage.

When does the equal time issue partly resolve itself?

Once nominations have been made at conventions. Then time is sold for speeches and rallies. The party with the most money can buy their own time; the broadcaster is only obligated to make time available if the other party wants to buy it.

But the equal time dispute may arise in connection with other programs, such as panel shows or news. Broadcasting realizes it is in the political hotseat until Nov. 7, the morning after the returns are in.

March 2, 1956

Major Party Spokesmen Oppose Equal Air Time for Minor Groups

By VAL ADAMS
Special to The New York Times.

CHICAGO, April 18—James C. Hagerty, press secretary to President Eisenhower, said today he saw no reason why all political parties should be granted equal radio and television time with the two major parties in an election year.

The same opinion was expressed by J. Leonard Reinsch, radio and television consultant of the Democratic National Committee.

Both addressed the convention here of the National Association of Radio and Television Broadcasters. They spoke at a forum on political telecasts.

Mr. Hagerty suggested the elimination from the air of what he called "splinter parties."

Section 315 of the Communications Act states that any station or network that provides time for a legally qualified candidate must also make time available for all other candidates. Some broadcasters have told Congress they believe the rule is a disservice to the public and should be changed.

Mr. Reinsch, who is also executive director of radio and television stations in Atlanta, Ga., Dayton, Ohio, and Miami, Fla., touched on the subject in this manner:

"With the present Section 315 we are not in position to completely fulfill our public service obligations. For if we give time to candidate number one, we must give equal facilities to candidates 2, 3, 4, 5, etc. With modern means of communication the American people are entitled to see and hear the national candidates, but that obligation should not carry to a dozen other splinter candidates representing the Vegetarians or the Greenbacks or any other special party."

Mr. Reinsch said he was sorry to report that only a few broadcasters had expressed reaction to proposed changes in Section 315. Frank Stanton, president of the Columbia Broadcasting System, some months ago was the first to ask Congress to make a change.

"More stations," Mr. Reinsch said, "will have to take a stand on legislative proposals of this type if our industry is to assume its rightful position as a leader among news media."

Before the forum, Mr. Hagerty was asked if he thought networks were obligated to grant equal time to the Democrats after President Eisenhower's broadcast on the farm bill veto last Monday. He answered:

"I don't look upon that as a particularly political talk. Whatever the network wants to do is up to them."

The Democratic National Committee asked for and received equal time to present a spokesman in answer to the President's address.

Equal Time Defended

The American Civil Liberties Union announced yesterday that it opposed any change in the present Federal Communications Commission regulation that equal radio and television time must be offered to all qualified political candidates. Recently there had been various proposals that Section 315 of the Communications Act be amended to permit networks and stations to give time to the two major political parties without having to make time available to all.

The organization said that Section 215 had made a contribution toward giving smaller parties some time on the air at national, state and local levels. The proposed amendments would keep these parties off the air, the organization stated, "a result which is contrary to the democratic and civil liberties concept of discussion for all."

August 1, 1956

INDUSTRY ASSAILS 'FREE TIME' ON AIR

Broadcasters Urge at House Hearing Ban on Law Edict Covering Political Pleas

By C. P. TRUSSELL
Special to The New York Times.

WASHINGTON, Dec. 18—The broadcasting industrdy urged Congress today to repeal the law requiring "free time" for clashing political candidates.

Harold E. Fellows, president of the National Association of Radio and Television Broadcasters, representing almost all licenses, told a special House investigating committee that repeal would be in the interest of the public and of the candidates as well.

He said that the "free time" phase of the law was threatening to disgust those in the public who found political rivalries taking the place of the programs they tuned in. This, he held, would hurt radio and television as an enterprise and deprive the public of crucial arguments it should hear in the course of a campaign.

Requirement of Law

At issue is Section 315 of the Communications Act of 1934, as amended. This requires that when a candidate makes an appeal over a radio or television station the station must grant free time for a reply by rival candidates.

Mr. Fellows pointed out today that in 1952 there were eighteen candidates for the Presidency and said that under the law as it now stood all the minor candidates could demand free time on radio or television equal to that granted the candidates of the major parties.

Proposals that have been made in congress, he said, might lead to discriminations between parties and condidates. He indicated a view that the F.C.C. opposed repeal of the section but might endorse amendment it regarded as a means to improvement.

A member of the committee, Representative Patrick J. Hillings, Republican of California, commented that the plea of the broadcasters seemed to be a "self-serving" approach to the many problems involved. He suggested that the broadcasters, instead of seeking repeal, initiate a positive approach designed to improve the provisions of the law rather than eliminate them.

Mr. Fellows countered that, even with repeal of the "equal time" the broadcasters would be under controls perhaps stranger than those of the law.

He said that the mere granting of a license to a broadcasting unit was proof of its genuine concern for the public interest. He remkinded that broadcasting stations must have their lincses renewed periodically.

In the matter of fair play to all candidates through "free time," he emphasized, the F. C. C., if it found unfairness, could refuse to grant a renewal of the license.

Archibald S. Alexander, who directed the Volunteers for Stevenson and Kefauver in this year's Presidential campaign, recommended a limit on the gross contributions an individual could make in a campaign. The law now limits a contribution to $5,000 to any campaign committee, but there is no ceiling on the number of committees that can be organized.

Mr. Alexander suggested a limit of $10,000 to $15,000 gross for an individual contributor.

December 19, 1956

Easing of Equal-Time Urged

MILWAUKEE, Nov. 18 (P)—The Radio-Television News Directors Association has called for modification of Section 315 of the Federal Communications Act, which requires that radio and television stations grant equal time to all candidates for public office. The resolution was passed at a closing session of the group's annual convention.

November 19, 1956

NEWS OF TELEVISION AND RADIO

By VAL ADAMS

POLITICAL candidates in this year's races need not expect invitations to appear as guests on radio and television programs until after election day in November. No matter how great his fame or popularity, an office seeker has virtually no chance of being a mystery guest on "What's My Line?" and probably would not be allowed even to take a bow on the Ed Sullivan show.

It's the old inflammable question of "equal time" or "equal opportunity," which is recorded in Section 315 of the Communications Act and subject to various interpretations. One part of the section states:

"If any licensee shall permit any person who is a legally qualified candidate for public office to use a broadcasting station, he shall afford equal opportunity to all other such candidates for that office in the use of such broadcasting station."

Canceled

This rule, or the interpretation of it by the Columbia Broadcasting System, caused a Jack Benny radio show to be canceled last Sunday and another substituted. The incident was equally as funny as Mr. Benny, one of our top comedians.

Recently the network sent out advance program information saying that Gov. Goodwin

J. Knight of California would be a guest on the Benny show May 25. Governor Knight is a candidate for the Republican nomination for United States Senator.

After the Benny radio schedule was published in California newspapers, the C. B. S. office

Election Year Changes Program Policy— Other Items

in Hollywood was notified that Mr. Knight's "opposition" in the primary election demanded "equal time." The ironic twist is that the Benny show currently on the air uses recordings of programs that were broadcast live several years ago. Governor Knight had appeared in person on the show about 1952 or 1953.

The C. B. S. answer to the "equal time" demand was to cancel the program featuring Governor Knight and substitute another of Mr. Benny's recordings.

C. B. S., which asked Congress more than two years ago to make change: in Section 315, is extremely sensitive about the rule as it now reads. Yesterday, WCBS-TV, the Columbia station here, discontinued a program series titled "Congressional Close-Up." Each week the program had presented a discussion of public issues by Congressmen from New York, New Jersey and Connecticut. Sam Cook Digges, station manager, commented:

"We couldn't continue the program because many Congressmen are running for re-election. By law we would have to give equal time to all their opponents. Why, even if a candidate just went on the Ed Sullivan show to accept an award, all his opponents could demand that they be put on the show, too."

Incident

Such an incident involving the Sullivan show already has hap-

pened, according to C. B. S. Several weeks ago Gov. Joe Foss of South Dakota sat in the studio audience and was identified on camera. Since the Governor seeks the nomination for the House of Representatives in a Republican primary, his opponent has asked C. B. S. for equal time.

Although C. B. S. seems inclined to avoid all political candidates, the National Broadcasting Company's policy is a bit different. When a producer at N. B. C. wants to use on his program a person who, by coincidence, is running for office, the producer must notify Edward Stanley, director of public affairs, two weeks in advance.

Mr. Stanley then determines whether opposing candidates can be given "equal opportunity" at a later date by N. B. C. If they can, the producer is told to go ahead with his plans. If it is not practicable to give equal time to all candidates, in Mr. Stanley's judgment, the producer is told to find another guest—one who is not seeking office.

It remains to be seen how Section 315 will be interpreted in specific cases this year by the American Broadcasting Company. John Daly, vice president in charge of news, special events and public affairs, commented:

"We will take a look at the various situations in a practical sense."

One station here that has not yet invoked Section 315 is WINS radio. Each week it continues to grant free time for talks by Governor Harriman and Representative Emanuel Celler, Democrat of Brooklyn. Both are running for re-election. Jock Fernhead, WINS manager, said last week he had not thought about dropping either program.

RULING ON POLITICS BY F. C. C. ASSAILED

WASHINGTON, Sept. 13 (AP) — The National Association of Broadcasters protested yesterday that chaos would result from a new ruling of the Federal Communications Commission on political broadcasts. It asked the F. C. C. to reconsider its ruling extending equal-time provisions for political candidates to their spokesmen and supporters.

The ruling "is so fraught with endless problems, not susceptible of equitable solutions," the association said, "that sheer chaos in the field of political broadcasting must inevitably ensue."

An association spokesman said the problem applied to purchased broadcast time as well as to free time given to candidates. Under F. C. C. regulations, when a broadcaster sells time to a candidate he must at the same time make an equal amount of time available to any opposing candidate who may wish to buy it.

In a letter to D. L. Grace of Fort Smith, Ark., on July 3, the association said, the F. C. C. stated a candidate offered equal time to reply to an opponent "may use the facilities in any manner he sees fit," including having a spokesman appear for him.

June 1, 1958

September 14, 1958

F.C.C. ISSUES GUIDE ON EQUAL AIR TIME

WASHINGTON; Oct. YY (UPI) — The Federal Communications Commission said today that even a Communist candidate was entitled to radio and television time equal to that given other office-seekers.

The commission issued a new guide for broadcasters on use of their facilities by candidates for public office.

Generally speaking, the guide said that if a radio or TV station owner grants air time to any legally qualified political candidate, he must do the same for rival contenders.

The document contains the latest interpretations of Section 315 of the 1934 Federal Communications Act, widely known as the "equal-time" provision of the law. This rule applies only to candidates and not political parties, the commission emphasized.

Even if a candidate merely takes a bow or makes a brief statement on a show, his opponent is entitled to make a similar appearance "no matter how perfunctory," the F.C.C. said.

The rules do not permit substitutes to appear in place of the candidate who is granted equal time, the document said.

TELEVISION NOTEBOOK

Equal Time Headaches —Godfrey's Format

By JACK GOULD

WITH the election now over it is time that the television industry seriously renews efforts to obtain a modification of Section 315 of the Federal Communications Act. This is a silly proviso that no station can give free time for the presentation of major candidates for public office without giving equal time to all and sundry minority aspirants.

The effect of Section 315 is simply to quash virtually all political programs presented by networks or stations themselves and to leave it up to the candidates with the most money to dominate the airways during the campaigning period.

Under Section 315 a station cannot allot more free time to the Republican and Democratic parties, which are known to command millions of votes, than to splinter parties that enjoy only a picayune following. If any candidate has legally won a place on the ballot, a broadcaster in the past has been dutybound to give the anonymous Mr. X just as much time as, say, President Eisenhower or Adlai E. Stevenson.

Hesitant

When it is appreciated that in a Presidential election the number of such candidates literally may run to the proverbial dozens, it can be better understood why broadcasters hesitate to take the initiative. The problem is not merely assigning a half-hour each to the Republicans and Democrats, for example. It may also mean the reservation of six free hours, of which four would be a virtual waste of time from the standpoint of legitimate news interest.

Section 315, in other words, stands as almost an insuperable barrier to what could be TV's most useful role in politics: face-to-face debate between the really important candidates. So long as the studio must be cluttered by political nonentities, the chances for a meaningful exchange of views are held to a minimum. The political forum is reduced to a game of "Ring-Around-the-Rosie," which affords ample opportunity for participants to avoid direct answers.

Outright repeal of Section 315, however, would be most unwise without the substitution of other safeguards to assure a reasonable representation for minority parties. But it should not be too difficult to devise a schedule whereby the amounts of time assigned to a party could bear some relationship to its strength as previously registered at the polls.

The intent of Section 315— to afford all candidates equal access to publicly owned airways—unquestionably is commendable. But in practice it has simply led to a political vacuum and prevented the broadcasting industry from doing an adequate journalistic job in politics.

One can readily imagine the chaos in newspapers if every word accorded to the Republicans and Democrats had to be matched with equal space for anyone and everyone who got on the ballot. Yet that is the dilemma confronting television and radio and it is one of the primary reasons why the costs of campaigning on the air steadily rise. Section 315 needs reconsideration in the light of reality, not theory.

* * *

Change

Arthur Godfrey's decision to do away with a studio audience and concentrate on informal banter appears to be working out happily for a number of people.

Mr. Godfrey himself is more relaxed than he has been in several years. But the story of his first week under the revised format, of course, was primarily the emergence of Jackie Gleason as an extemporaneous wit and an interesting observer of the passing scene.

Unfortunately, the excerpts from the conversations between Godfrey and Mr. Gleason, shown last Tuesday on the former's evening program, did not do them both full justice. The flavor of their badinage was somewhat lost in the cutting. In his original appearances Mr. Gleason was warm and provocative as well as amusing. It was a refreshing change from the image of Reggie Van Gleason that had been firmly implanted in the minds of many viewers.

Success

The Godfrey conversational gambits also helped another individual who a season ago had known the anguish of being caught out of character, John Crosby, critic of The New York Herald Tribune. As the host of "Seven Lively Arts," he more than lived up to Faye Emerson's amiable description: "Mumbles Crosby." He seemed to be fighting a Teleprompter, looked frightened to death and appeared to wish he had never momentarily forsaken his typewriter.

With Mr. Godfrey, however, Mr. Crosby was assured, amiable and good-humored, practically a completely different individual on the screen.

Miss Emerson herself demonstrated on Mr. Godfrey's program that while television constantly wonders what it could do next it might find the answer by asking TV people. She suggested that more women should be put to work in television as reporters on major national news events. Why must only men be experts on politics? Might not the fairer sex also provide a different perspective on the day's happenings and add to a viewer's interest in information? Pauline Frederick of the National Broadcasting Company has shown that the girls can hold their own with the best of the gentlemen. Miss Emerson's proposal makes exceedingly good sense.

ABOUT 'EQUAL TIME'

To the Radio-Television Editor:

MY associates and I are most heartened by Jack Gould's perceptive article last Sunday on Section 315 of the Federal Communications Act. We agree that the equal-time provisions of the law, however well-intentioned, have resulted in harmful sterility.

Radio and television can make a significant contribution to greater public participation in election campaigns and to a more informed electorate by providing opportunity for face-to-face candidates' meetings, debates and interviews through which the voters could get a more accurate firsthand evaluation of the candidates than is now possible. As Mr. Gould noted, Section 315, by its rigid insistence of equal time to the most obscure candidates, makes this impractical.

I would note, however, that the situation is even worse and more rigid than the article indicates. Section 315 requires us to give equal time not only to "any candidate [who] has legally won a place on the ballot," as Mr. Gould pointed out; it also requires us to give equal time to any candidate who is not eligible for the ballot and indeed has not even been nominated by any party. Many states permit write-ins, so that under Section 315 we are obliged to give equal time to any individual whose name can be written in on the ballot.

Solution

Further, Mr. Gould suggests that a possible solution would be to devise a schedule whereby the amounts of time assigned to a party could bear some relationship to its strength as previously registered at the polls. This would in no way alleviate one of the most acute problems which face broadcasters: the problem of candidates for nomination. Section 315 requires us to give equal time to all competing candidates for a nomination, no matter how obscure the asserted candidate for nomination is or how hopeless his chance.

The reach of this requirement is indicated by our experience in 1952 when, after we had given time to General Eisenhower and Senator Taft as candidates for the Republican Presidential nomination, we were required to give equal time on the full network to an obscure bookseller in St. Louis who, a few weeks later, could not even get his credentials accepted to get into the Republican National Convention.

Mr. Gould's suggestion that there be some sort of proportional representation, rather than repeal of Section 315, has a surface attraction, but it gives rise to many mechanical and practical problems. It does not take into account new political movements such as the Bull Moose party in 1912, or the Fusion party in New York.

And in any event, if a broadcaster should provide six half hours for debate between Republican and Democratic parties, on what equitable basis can time be proportionately assigned to a splinter party, which, as in the case of New York State, polled less than one-half of one per cent of the total vote. Is it practical to grant such a splinter party a total of one minute?

In the last analysis, we are persuaded that the most comprehensive and practicable solution is the repeal of Section 315. The requirements that a broadcaster maintain fairness and balance would still remain and, together with public opinion and public reaction against unfairness, would provide sure bulwarks in the public interest.

As Mr. Gould wrote a few years ago when dealing with the same subject, if a broadcaster is not deemed qualified to make his own journalistic decisions in this area, then one can only ask by what standard the broadcaster is qualified to have a license at all.

RICHARD S. SALANT,
Vice President, Columbia
Broadcasting System.
New York.

REBUTTAL

To the Radio-Television Editor:

Mr. Jack Gould's concern for the obstacles that Section 315 of the Federal Communications Act places before Republican and Democratic Party monopoly of the TV and radio networks is touching. It would be nice if these two Siamese twins of capitalism could be left alone to "debate" contrived issues with one another, with the bill being footed by their adoring networks (although nothing prevents them from doing so now at a price they can well afford, hence, it may be that they have no real desire to do so). But even more touching is his concern for a "reasonable representation for minorities," and I am sure that if he has any question of what is reasonable he can get the advice of Carmine DeSapio, who recently made similar suggestions regarding Section 315.

Mr. Gould must be patient, for the spirit of democracy has taken deep root in this country, and it takes time to effectively bridle it. But his approach is right: do not ban the minority parties outright, but make them hurdle obstacles which in all fairness one couldn't make the major parties hurdle. This would insure democracy without letting it go too far. It is the same approach which did away with the many minority parties that used to get on the ballot with ease * * *.

BRUCE CAMERON,
Member, Socialist Labor Party.
New York.

November 23, 1958

F.C.C. Applies Equal-Time Rule To TV Newscasts of Candidates

By RICHARD F. SHEPARD

Brief glimpses of the Mayor of Chicago on television newscasts entitle his rival in next week's mayoralty primaries to equal time on camera, according to a Federal Communications Commission ruling announced here yesterday.

The newscasts included a twenty-second shot of the Mayor as he greeted the President of Argentina, a one-minute shot of him opening a March of Dimes drive and other short appearances.

The Columbia Broadcasting System immediately charged that "the F. C. C. decision will virtually black out election coverage on radio and television— both network and local."

C. B. S. owns WBBM-TV, which was one of the stations that carried the disputed news films.

The network petitioned the commission yesterday to reverse its ruling. This was the first step in a move that might take the matter to a Federal court should the F. C. C. maintain its position.

The question involves interpretation of Section 315 of the Federal Communications Act. This requires any broadcaster to provide any bona fide candidate with equal opportunity to use its facilities if they are used by a rival candidate.

Section 315 is entitled "Candidates for public office; facilities" and refers only to "legally qualified candidates." Broadcasters, in addition, are allowed to editorialize, but must maintain balanced programming.

However, a ruling reported by the F. C. C. last October held that this section did not apply in cases where the candidate "in no way initiated either the filming or the presentation of the event and that the broadcast was nothing more than a routine newscast by the station in the exercise of its judgment as to newsworthy events."

The latest ruling resulted from a complaint by Lar Daly, candidate for both the Republican and Democratic nominations in next Tuesday's primaries. He demanded time equal to that given on newscasts to Mayor Richard J. Daley, the Democratic incumbent, and to Representative Timothy P. Sheehan, who is seeking the Republican nomination.

The news films also included sequences showing the Mayor and Representative Sheehan filing petitions as candidates. Mr. Daly's lawyer, Howard Newcomb Morse, protested to the commission that none of these scenes constituted "official ceremonies," and that his client was entitled to equal time.

The commission's decision was sent in a telegram to the stations, saying that the film clips "constituted 314 'use' entitling Lar Daly to equal opportunity." There was no further explanation of the decision.

Decision Is 'Informal'

However, an F. C. C. spokesman in Washington said yesterday that this was a common practice in political equal-time cases where there was no time for formal opinions. It was an "informal verbal ruling," he said, with no documents or arguments beyond the communications sent by the parties.

The seven F. C. C. commissioners voted 4 to 3 to grant time to Mr. Daly to equal the appearances of Mayor Daley on the March of Dimes kick-off and the welcome to Argentina's President. The dissenters appeared to regard these as in the nature of official duties. However, the commissioners were unanimous on the other cases.

"If even regularly scheduled news programs must turn their microphones and cameras away from any news event which involves a person who happens to be a candidate for office, the free press and the right of people to be informed has suffered a shattering blow," said Sig Mickelson, vice president and general manager in charge of C. B. S. News.

"C. B. S. has filed a petition to reverse its decision and contending that the ruling is erroneous and unconstitutional," he added. "C. B. S. will take all possible steps before the F. C. C., the courts and the Congress to avoid this grave injury to the press and the people."

Easing of Equal Time Urged

WASHINGTON, March 9 (UPI) — Representative Glenn Cunningham, Republican of Nebraska, introduced a bill today to exempt regular news programs and commentaries from the law requiring radio and television stations to give political candidates equal broadcast time. The bill would waive the provision in cases in which candidates appeared on news programs "in no way initiated" by them.

STANTON SCORES EQUAL TIME RULE

C.B.S. Chief Says Network May Present Editorials on Air Protesting F.C.C. Act

By VAL ADAMS
Special to The New York Times.

CHICAGO, March 14—Frank Stanton, president of the Columbia Broadcasting System, said today that the C. B. S. television network may present on-the-air editorials opposing a recent ruling by the Federal Communications Commission. It is believed that such a development probably would be without precedent in broadcasting.

Although the network is not licensed by the F. C. C., the parent company owns six television stations that operate by authority of the Federal agency. If C. B. S. goes ahead with its editorials it would be voicing opposition to the F. C. C. on the very channels granted to it by the governmental body.

In a speech to more than 350 executives from C. B. S.-affiliated stations, Mr. Stanton attacked an F. C. C. decision stipulating that the "equal time" rule applies where a political candidate happens to be seen in regular newscasts. He said the decision denied to broadcasters "the right to assume and exercise the responsibility for editorial control of our own news programs."

After pointing out that C. B. S. had asked the F. C. C. to reconsider and reverse itself, Mr. Stanton added:

"If it does not, we are going to appeal to the courts; we are going to appeal to the Congress, and we are going to appeal to the people."

After his formal speech, Mr. Stanton was asked if appeals to the people might include on-the-air editorials. He replied:

"That's just what we are thinking about."

When asked if he, himself, might go on the air to deliver the editorials, he declared:

"I'm not sure, although it is possible. We just haven't planned that far yet. We will not present any editorials until the F. C. C. has answered our petition requesting it to reverse itself."

The ruling opposed by Mr. Stanton was made by the F. C. C. last month. It involves an interpretation of Section 315 of the Federal Communications Act, which says that a broadcaster who makes his facilities available to one bona fide political candidate must make them available to all rival candidates.

The commission issued the ruling after it had received a complaint from Lar Daly of Chicago, who was candidate for nomination in the mayoralty primaries. He demanded time equal to that given on television newscasts to Mayor Richard J. Daley, Democratic incumbent, and Representative Timothy P. Sheehan, who sought the Republican nomination.

In regular newscasts on several Chicago stations, Mayor Daley had been shown, by means of film clips, greeting the President of Argentina and opening a March of Dimes drive. The mayor and Mr. Sheehan also were shown filing petitions as candidates.

Mr. Stanton said that the Daly decision "for all practical purposes makes it a mathematical impossibility for broadcasting to report any political campaign in its own way and take advantage of its own technical capabilities." In declaring that "there is a danger to all our journalism—printed as well as electronic," he added:

"Look for a moment at the situation of printed journalism. Because of special mailing privileges, vital to the economic health of most periodicals and many newspapers, there is an avenue of approach for attempts to apply mathematical formulae to the editorial contents. A case —utterly outrageous yet no more outrageous than the Daly ruling —could be made for the notion that if a magazine or a newspaper has a partially subsidized circulation through mailing rates and records the words of a political candidate, then the other candidates should be entitled to equal space."

February 21, 1959

March 10, 1959

March 15, 1959

TV STATIONS ASK EDITORIAL RULES

Broadcaster Unit Head, in Chicago, Cites Need for F. C. C. Clarification

By VAL ADAMS
Special to The New York Times.

CHICAGO, March 15—Radio and television stations would like to editorialize just as newspapers do but they are hindered by a lack of governmental clarification of the thorny "equal time" issue.

This statement was made today by Harold E. Fellows, president of the National Association of Broadcasters, as more than 2,000 broadcasting executives assembled here for their annual convention. Mr. Fellows said the Federal Communications Commission on some occasions had urged broadcasters to editorialize but had not drawn up any clear ground rules for such a practice.

Generally, the Federal Communications Act says that a station must maintain a balance in programming. Where one point of view is put forth, efforts must be made to assure that any opposing points of view also are presented.

Despite the handicaps the stations feel they face in editorializing, the N. A. B. soon will issue a study it has prepared that will guide stations in offering some form of editorials. Mr. Fellows said that more and more radio stations were beginning to experiment with editorials in a limited way.

Financial Loss Cited

So-called editorials on some stations, however, are hardly more than public service announcements. There is a tendency in some cases to "editorialize" on matters that are virtually free of controversy.

Mr. Fellows was asked what he thought of the future of radio networks, which have suffered great financial losses since the advent of television. He replied:

"I don't think there ever will be less than two radio networks operating from coast to coast."

When asked if that meant he thought two of the existing four radio networks would eventually go out of business, he said he would not make that prediction. He added that it was possible there might always be three networks in operation.

The N. A. B. convention will run through Wednesday. All seven commissioners of the F. C. C. will attend as part of the official agenda and John C. Doerfer, the chairman, will make a luncheon address Tuesday.

Today the Columbia Broadcasting System completed a pre-convention meeting of its television affiliates here.

Two Shows Scheduled

Hubbell Robinson Jr., executive vice president of C. B. S.-TV programs, said two one-hour shows would be scheduled on Tuesday and Wednesday evenings from 7:30 to 8:30 o'clock. He admitted that C. B. S. had "not been able to get off the ground" this season in those hours because of strong competition on other networks.

Mr. Robinson said the Tuesday show would be a space adventure series titled "Out There." It will be produced in association with Paramount Pictures. Mr. Robinson declined to identify the Wednesday program, but told the affiliates it "involves a property you all know well."

Sig Mickelson, vice president of news for C. B. S., said that in the latter part of May, the TV network would present a one-hour documentary on James R. Hoffa, head of the International Brotherhood of Teamsters.

The American Broadcasting Company also held an affiliates meeting here today. Tom Moore, vice president of television programs, said that Dodge had renewed Lawrence Welk's Saturday night show for next season. He declared that the band leader also would star on a Thursday show next season from 10 to 11 P. M. Plymouth, which currently sponsors Mr. Welk on Wednesday evenings, will drop the program at the end of this season.

March 16, 1959

F.C.C. HEAD ASKS 'EQUAL TIME' END

Doerfer Favors Repeal of Law, Leaving Matter in Broadcasters' Hands

BY VAL ADAMS
Special to The New York Times.

CHICAGO, March 17 — John C. Doerfer, chairman of the Federal Communications Commission, said today that he favored repeal of Section 315 of the Federal Communications Act.

The section is a source of great controversy and has been a troublesome issue for broadcasters. It says a station that permits a legally qualified candidate to use its facilities "shall afford equal opportunities to all other such candidates for that office in the use of such broadcasting station."

During a press conference at the annual convention of the National Association of Broadcasters, Mr. Doerfer discussed his views on Section 315, which he suggested might need changes. When asked what changes, Mr. Doerfer replied: "I would repeal it."

His statement came at a time when broadcasters are extremely concerned about a recent F. C. C. ruling that upheld a complaint based on Section 315.

Lar Daly, who was a candidate for the mayoralty nomination in a primary election here, demanded equal time from television stations after Mayor Richard J. Daley, a candidate for re-election, had been seen in regularly scheduled news programs. One portion of the complaint pertained to news film clips in which Mayor Daley was shown welcoming the President of Argentina and opening a March of Dimes campaign.

Networks Asked Reversal

By a vote of 4 to 3, the F. C. C. ruled that Lar Daly must be granted equal time. In effect, the commission said that Section 315 applied not only to programs of political speeches but also to news programs, even where a candidate for re-election is performing an official function of his office.

Mr. Doerfer voted with the minority. After the F. C. C.'s decision last month, all three television networks filed petitions asking the commission to reconsider and reverse itself.

Mr. Doerfer said today that it was possible for the F. C. C. to reverse its decision, but he would make no predictions. He declared that he would like to see a policy evolved whereby the commission could distinguish between news and a "political presentation."

In a luncheon speech at the Broadcasters Association convention, Mr. Doerfer declared:

"An informed public is indispensable for the continuance of a democratic society. If every presentation of a duly elected public official, who happens to be, at a given time, a qualified candidate for an office must be matched by an equal amount of free time by all other such candidates, then the essence of Governmental news will be emasculated during campaign periods. The broadcaster will be shorn of any journalistic judgment during this critical period."

Safeguards Listed

The F. C. C. chairman said broadcasters "should be given the right to make the judgment as to what constitutes news or what programing fills the needs of the public and not the candidates." As for what he considered safeguards to protect the public interest, Mr. Doerfer added:

"This would not mean that a broadcaster could indulge in his biases or prejudices with impunity—even in respect of crackpots or rank opportunists. * * * I sincerely doubt that a broadcaster who must stake his license every three years against his record would take a chance of resorting to chicanery or unduly promote a favorite candidate under the guise of legitimate newscasting or a public interest panel discussion."

Changes or repeal of Section 315 would have to be made by Congress.

In another convention development today, television members of the N. A. B. voted approval of a proposed information campaign on a national basis. In the convention's keynote address yesterday, Robert W. Sarnoff, chairman of the National Broadcasting Company, had urged the industry to unite in a campaign to combat charges that TV is mediocre, unworthy and time-wasting.

Harold E. Fellows, president of the N. A. B., will appoint a committee of broadcasters "to develop specific plans for the design, financing and implementation" of the campaign.

March 18, 1959

EISENHOWER ASKS EQUAL-TIME CURB

Would Exempt Radio and TV News Shows From Rule

By FELIX BELAIR Jr.

Special to The New York Times.

WASHINGTON, March 18—President Eisenhower started a move today to exempt news programs on radio and television from a Federal requirement that equal opportunities be afforded all candidates for a public office.

The President denounced as "ridiculous" the effect of a recent decision by the Federal Communications Commission. This held that news presentations fall within the meaning of Section 315, or "equal time" provision, of the Federal Communications Act. He instructed Attorney General William P. Rogers to determine whether remedial legislation could be drafted or other appropriate action taken.

In making known the President's action, James C. Hagerty, White House press secretary, said President Eisenhower had no quarrel with the F. C. C. The agency was acting under the present law, which it has, itself, asked to be changed, Mr. Hagerty explained. He said the President had in mind the effect of the decision in saying it was "ridiculous."

"The F. C. C. said that even on news shows equal time had to be given opposition candidates," Mr. Hagerty said. "The President thinks this is ridiculous. He has asked the Attorney General to consider whether any remedial legislation can be drafted or whether any other appropriate action can be taken in this connection."

Complaint Sparked Ruling

A complaint of Lar Daly, candidate for the Chicago mayoralty nomination on both Republican and Democratic tickets, sparked the recent F. C. C. ruling. He demanded equal time from television stations in the area after Mayor Richard J. Daley, candidate for re-election, had been seen on regularly scheduled news programs.

The commission divided, 4 to 3, in ruling for the first time that Section 315 applied to news programs as well as to partisan speeches of political candidates.

John C. Doerfer, F. C. C. chairman, called for repeal of the controversial section yesterday at the annual convention in Chicago of the National Association of Broadcasters. He had voted with the minority on the Lar Daly case.

Mr. Doerfer said he would like to see a policy evolved whereby the F. C. C. could distinguish between news and a "political presentation" in adjudicating demands for equal time. Whether Congress should be asked to give the agency this discretionary authority was one of the questions the Attorney General was asked by the President to consider.

Explanation of Action

Mr. Hagerty, in explanation of the President's action, said it was "ridiculous" to attempt to say by law how the news was to be presented by radio or television.

There had been no discussion between the President and the Attorney General on the controversial question of whether equal time had to be extended "even to crackpot candidates" under the recent F. C. C. ruling.

In arguing yesterday for authority in the F. C. C. to determine whether a program served primarily the need of the public or of a political candidate, Mr. Doerfer said:

"This does not mean that a broadcaster could indulge in his biases or prejudices with impunity—even in respect of crackpots or rank opportunists.

"I sincerely doubt that a broadcaster who must stake his license every three years against his record would take a chance of resorting to chicanery or unduly promote a favorite candidate under the guise of legitimate newscasting or a public interest panel discussion."

Mr. Hagerty said the "ridiculous" aspect of the present communications law had come to the President's attention through discussion of it in the newspapers and that the President wanted him to express his thanks for this service.

March 19, 1959

'Equal' Time on the Air

It is a good thing that the recent Chicago case has brought out into the open the question of "equal" time on the air for opposing political parties or candidates. If it is applied rigidly its results can be just what the President called them—"ridiculous." This is a clear instance of a situation in which "the letter of the law killeth."

Theoretically, a man or a party seeking public office should have no unusual advantage in air time that is denied to the opposition. This is all to the good and few persons would quarrel with this thesis. We believe in fair play. If a candidate employs air time for the direct purpose of getting votes his opponents should not suffer because commensurate time is denied. They, also, are entitled to try to get votes.

But when this presumptive principle of fair play is broadened out to the point that it covers the presentation of news that is news for its own sake, and not for the sake of a party or a man, and the result is a partisan demand for "equal" time, the end product can be really "ridiculous." If an eminent Democrat appeals for the Red Cross or greets a foreign visitor, presumably an equally eminent Republican should have the same opportunity to be seen and heard on the air. This is nonsense, on the face of it.

Many persons in public life are "news" because of the offices that they hold or because of traits in personality. To suggest that a counterweight air time should be set up in each case is absurd. The political affiliation of the individual may have nothing whatever to do with the element of "news" in his appearance.

What is obviously needed here is flexibility in the law and common sense in its application.

March 22, 1959

TV EDITORIALS URGED

Kaltenborn Tells Analysts to Use New Privilege

MILWAUKEE, May 20 (AP) —H. V. Kaltenborn, news analyst of radio and TV, told members of the Wisconsin Broadcasters Association last night to start editorializing. He also urged them to defy a Federal Communications Commission ruling that equal time be given to opposing political candidates in news programs.

"It is an essential part of the democratic process to give your opinion and what it stands for," Mr. Kaltenborn, a native of Milwaukee, said. "Broadcasting has not taken advantage of the recent decision by the F. C. C. to broadcast editorial opinion. I urge each of you to go back to your stations and deliver at least one editorial each week."

Mr. Kaltenborn added that the F. C. C.'s ruling governing equal attention to political candidates in news programs was "foolish." He advised broadcasters to ignore the ruling and "take it to court if the F. C. C. tries to enforce it."

May 21, 1959

'EQUAL TIME' SCORED

Broadcasters Want News Programs to Be Exempt

WASHINGTON, June 13 (UPI)—A committee of the National Association of Broadcasters urged today that news programs be exempted from "equal time" provisions of the Federal Communications Act.

The association's Freedom of Information Committee adopted a resolution protesting a ruling by the Federal Communications Commission in the Lar Daly case in Chicago.

The F. C. C. decreed in that case that if one candidate's activities were covered in news broadcasts or telecasts, other candidates must be given equal time. Attorney General William P. Rogers has protested the ruling on the ground that it interferes with freedom to report the news.

The controversial ruling was entered in behalf of Lar Daly, a candidate for Mayor of Chicago. The F. C. C. granted Mr. Daly air time equal to that of Mayor Richard J. Daley, whose activities had been covered on news programs.

June 14, 1959

F. C. C. Reaffirms Equal-Time Ruling

Special to The New York Times.

WASHINGTON, June 16
The Federal Communications Commission refused today to change its ruling that the "equal time" edict for political rivals applied to news programs as well as other broadcasts.

The White House repeated that President Eisenhower still believed that the situation presented by the ruling was "ridiculous."

Comment from the broadcasting networks indicated renewed calls on Congress to change the law.

The Department of Justice, normally the defender of Federal agencies in court, also said it would argue against the F. C. C. interpretation of the law if the case went to court.

The Communications Commission takes the position that it is simply following the law. A formal opinion on its decision today is expected to be made available tomorrow.

The seven-man commission was split today. In the majority were Rosel H. Hyde, Robert T. Bartley, Robert E. Lee and Frederick W. Ford. John S. Cross dissented in part and concurred in part. The dissenters were the chairman, John C. Doerfer, and T. A. M. Craven.

The law provides that when a radio or television station gives or sells broadcast time to a candidate, his rivals are entitled to the same consideration. Not until last February were newscasts considered subject to this "equal-time" requirement.

At that time, the Communications Commission acted on a complaint against a Chicago station, which had shown on a newscast brief clips of Mayor Richard J. Daley welcoming the President of Argentina to Chicago and in two other short episodes. Mayor Daley was a candidate for renomination at the time. Lar Daly, running for the Republican and Democratic nominations for mayor, demanded equal time.

Section 315 of the Communications Act of 1934 says that if a station permits any candidate to "use" the station, it shall "afford equal opportunities" to rival candidates.

The commission held, by a vote of 4 to 3, that the station had let Mayor Daley "use" the station when it showed him greeting the Argentine President and appealing for contributions to the March of Dimes campaign.

The commission, however, was unanimous in deciding that another phase of the telecasts had come under the provisions of Section 315, thus entitling Mr. Daley to equal time. The telecast showed Mayor Daley and another candidate filing their political petitions, accepting formal political endorsements, and certain political interviews.

A review was sought by several broadcasting networks and stations with support from the Attorney General, William P. Rogers.

Networks Urge Law Change

The four major networks responded yesterday to the affirmation of the stand of the Federal Communications Commission by urging Congressional action to change the law.

John Daly, vice president in charge of news, special events and public affairs for the American Broadcasting Company, said that in the absence of legislation, "it would be patently impossible for these media to fully represent the primaries, conventions and election campaigns of 1960 to the American people."

A statement from the Columbia Broadcasting System said that "we feel that this underscores the need for remedial legislation."

Malcolm E. Smith Jr., chairman of the Mutual Broadcasting System radio network, called for a "breaking down of the various Jericho walls still standing in broadcasters' ways" so that full news coverage could be guaranteed on the air.

The National Broadcasting Company said that its view would be expressed Friday by its chairman, Robert W. Sarnoff. Mr. Sarnoff will testify then before the Communications subcommittee of the Senate Interstate and Foreign Commerce Committee in Washington.

TV: Equal Time Issue

Senate Commerce Unit Is Urged to Act Quickly on F. C. C.'s Candidate Rule

By JACK GOULD

IN light of the Federal Communication Commission's refusal yesterday to reverse itself on the issue of equal time for political candidates appearing in television newscasts, tomorrow's hearings of the Senate Committee on Interstate and Foreign Commerce in Washington become vitally important.

Only new legislation amending the communications act will suffice to terminate the ludicrous situation in which a broadcaster must give equal time to dozens of splinter candidates if, in the course of normal journalistic routine, it shows the face of one national figure running for office.

Both the Senate committee and Congress as a whole must act with dispatch; time is running out. Preliminary campaigning in the Presidential election undoubtedly will be starting by early next winter and, unless the equal-time problem is clarified promptly, a broadcaster will have grounds for abandoning an important phase of his informational function. The viewer who wants to follow politics on TV stands to lose the most.

There is also a further reason why Congress should step in and take command. The tactics employed by the Administration, unfortunately, have had certain drawbacks.

●

President Eisenhower's repeated condemnation of the F. C. C. original ruling has been instrumental in bringing the matter to wide public attention. But in some quarters the move of Attorney General William P. Rogers in urging the F. C. C. to reconsider has been construed as an Administration incursion on the prerogatives of the F. C. C.

The F. C. C. may be dead wrong in its decision, as it is widely believed to be in this instance. But there is something to be said for maintenance of the regulatory agency's independence against the pressure of administrative appointees who may think broadcasting should be run differently. As a creature of Congress, the F. C. C. must be primarily responsible to the legislative body, which, in turn, should get on with the task of clarifying an item of law that has provoked honest confusion. Since the F. C. C. at different times has interpreted the law in different ways, obviously it is time the matter were cleared up.

The dilemma of the broadcaster with respect to the equal time provision, known as Section 315 of the Communications Act, is genuine.

Under the F. C. C. interpretation a broadcaster cannot devote one minute to a candidate's opening a new bridge or dedicating a monument without giving a minute to every other declared candidate to the same office. In national elections the number of Presidential candidates may run to a dozen or more. Without revision of Section 315, each of these gentlemen can insist upon being seen every time any one of them gets before the TV public for any reason whatsoever.

The inevitable consequence is that a broadcaster is going to think twice before showing one political candidate in a news program lest he assume the burden of presenting a whole parade of aspirants.

In its journalistic function television must be allowed leeway to exercise its own judgment, which thus far it certainly has not abused. If the video medium is to be reduced to reporting by slide rule, without regard to the importance of news or its value to the public, then sooner or later it will either desert the journalistic field or become a happy hunting grounds for an endless parade of splinter candidates and eccentrics.

●

Because the air waves are licensed to serve all the public, which means the important minorities as well as the obvious majority political groups, broadcasting always must live with some restrictions not common to the press. But these conditions are adequately met in the provision that if a broadcasting station either sells or donates time to one candidate in order to solicit votes it must do the same for all others.

Actually, Congress should not find it inordinately difficult to put into law a distinction that readily solves the problem. The equal time provision should apply to those programs where the political candidates or their parties control the content of the presentation. It should not apply to programs where the networks and stations, as part of their reportorial duty, determine the content.

NBC SEES NEWS 'GAG' IN EQUAL-TIME RULE

WASHINGTON, June 29 (AP)—Unless Congress modifies the controversial equal-time ruling "a major curtailment of television and radio political coverage in 1960 is inevitable," the board chairman of the National Broadcasting Company said today.

Robert W. Sarnoff, the chairman, testified that the rule applying the equal-time doctrine to newscasts was a "gag" that "curtails the freedom of journalists to report and edit the news."

Mr. Sarnoff appeared at the opening of a three-day hearing by a house subcommittee on various bills aimed at exempting television and radio news programs from the equal-time law.

The bills were inspired by a ruling of the Federal Communications Commission last February that when a radio or television station covers a political candidate in a newscast it must give equal time to opposing candidates.

Previously, the Commission had interpreted the equal-time law to apply only when a station had granted a candidate broadcasting time for political campaigning.

Mr. Sarnoff called the new ruling "unsound in principle, unrealistic in practice and harmful in effect." Then he said:

"Its clear and immediate result is to clamp a political gag on the special techniques of television and radio journalism virtually on the eve of a national political campaign."

C.B.S. Show Bars Humphrey To Avoid Equal-Time Demands

By W. H. LAWRENCE
Special to The New York Times.

WASHINGTON, July 16 — Senator Hubert H. Humphrey of Minnesota was adjudged today, against his will, to be an avowed Democratic Presidential aspirant.

The ruling authority was the Columbia Broadcasting System. It notified the Senator today that it was withdrawing its invitation for him to appear on "Face the Nation," which was to have been televised and broadcast from Minneapolis next Sunday afternoon.

The penalty was one that would give nightmares to any politician if universally applied —no free national radio or television time for about a year.

In his effort to stay on the C. B. S. show, Senator Humphrey had given the network a written declaration that "I am not a candidate for the Presidency."

But the company's lawyers ruled otherwise. They feared that if Senator Humphrey was allowed to appear, "Face the Nation" would be required to give equal time to "insignificant or obscure or now unknown aspirants for the Democratic Presidential nomination."

Senator Humphrey, however, was apparently still not completely cut off from the television audience. Later today he announced that he had accepted an invitation to appear tomorrow on the National Broadcasting Company's morning show, "Today."

The Senator said the N. B. C. invitation had been extended about two hours after C. B. S. had withdrawn its bid.

The C. B. S. lawyers decided that the action of Senator Humphrey's friends in proclaiming his Presidential candidacy this week spoke louder and with more clarity than the Senator's own demurrer.

The reference was to a well-publicized news conference Tuesday, conducted in part by telephone hook-up between St. Paul, Minn., and Washington, in which Senator Eugene J. McCarthy, Minnesota Democrat, and Gov. Orville L. Freeman of Minnesota announced the formation of a "Humphrey for President Committee."

The C. B. S. lawyers said it was their opinion that this announcement "and the general news treatment thereof" would be construed to make Senator Humphrey a candidate within the meaning of the Federal Communications Act. And this would mean, the network went on, that any other candidate could demand equal time to the detriment of "Face the Nation" as an "important informational program."

Senator Humphrey called the decision "unnecessary and unfounded." He indicated that he thought the ruling would apply against the other "potential" candidates.

"There have been hundreds of such announcements by other people in behalf of senators, governors and others who are often described as potential candidates for President or Vice President," he said. "When I get ready to be a candidate I'll personally make the announcement."

Although C. B. S. said it had acted regretfully with relation to Senator Humphrey, there was a feeling in Washington that politics had not been totally absent from the decision.

Columbia and the other networks are now seeking from Congress a general revision of the "equal-time" rule, with reference both to news broadcasts and to television panel shows such as "Meet the Press" and "Face the Nation."

The equal-time requirement was recently made much more stringent by a ruling of the Federal Communications Commission, which the F. C. C. reaffirmed even after President Eisenhower had called it "ridiculous."

This ruling concerned Lar Daly of Chicago, a perennial candidate who runs for many offices but gets few votes.

In this year's Democratic primary for Mayor of Chicago, the F. C. C. upheld Mr. Daly's demand that he was entitled to equal time with Mayor Richard Daley of Chicago even when the Mayor was shown on television news programs performing official functions.

Senator Humphrey was singled out for the C. B. S. ban because his backers went further, by forming their "Humphrey for President Committee," than had the supporters of other unannounced candidates for the Presidency, such as Senators John F. Kennedy of Massachusetss, Stuart Symington of Missouri and Lyndon B. Johnson of Texas.

All of these men are running, of course, but they have refrained from saying so, in part, perhaps, because of the possible loss of free radio and television time.

One thing is certain. None of the announced or unannounced Presidential aspirants will vote against the revision of the communications law that is sought by the broadcasters.

HUMPHREY SCORES EQUAL-TIME CURBS

On N.B.C. Show, He Says Law Could Silence Anyone Mentioned for an Office

By RICHARD F. SHEPARD

Senator Hubert H. Humphrey, Democrat of Minnesota, said yesterday that equal-time restrictions could make a "shambles" of public service programing on radio and television.

The Senator also told a television audience that " I couldn't help but feel that maybe I was getting a little high-pressure lobbying here yesterday," when the Columbia Broadcasting System canceled his scheduled appearance next Sunday on its "Face the Nation" program.

The reference to "lobbying" concerned a bill now pending in Congress that would exempt news and related programs from the requirement to give equal time to all candidates if one candidate appears on any of them. The broadcasters are in favor of such a change in the law.

Mr. Humphrey's comments were made on the National Broadcasting Company's "Today" show. His appearance on the network underscored differences within the industry on how to handle prominent political figures under the present Federal Communications Act, which provides that equal time be guaranteed to all candidates.

Sees Blanket Ban

Senator Humphrey said that if the C. B. S. action was "followed up in meticulous detail it will mean. literally, throwing off the air and television every person that is mentioned for public office."

C.B.S. based its decision on the premise that the Senator was a candidate for the Democratic Presidential nomination, despite his written declaration that he was not. The network feared that it would have to give equal time to "insignificant or obscure or now unknown aspirants" for the nomination.

N. B. C., meanwhile, said it had invited Senator Humphrey to appear on "Today" before it knew that C. B. S. had canceled the Senator's appearance on its Sunday program.

"In the opinion of N. B. C.'s legal counsel, Senator Humphrey was not then a candidate for nomination within the meaning of Section 315 of the Communications Act," a statement declared.

Hopes for Quick Passage

It noted that, in any event, it hoped for swift passage of the amendment that would eliminate the situation.

N. B. C. has scheduled Governor Rockefeller as a guest on "Meet the Press" Sunday, although some broadcasters believe that Mr. Rockefeller is a candidate for the Republican Presidential nomination because he has not yet asked that his name be withdrawn from the New Hampshire primaries.

Although Senator Humphrey was ruled off "Face the Nation," a public affairs show of C. B. S., he has been seen on news film this week on the station owned by that network in Los Angeles.

Representative F. Edward Hébert, Democrat of Louisiana, will replace Senator Humphrey on "Face the Nation" Sunday, C. B. S. announced yesterday.

A. B. C. Orders Clearance

The American Broadcasting Company said it had ordered consultation with high officials before the broadcasting of material about Senator Humphrey, Governor Rockefeller, Gov. Earl K. Long of Louisiana, Henry Krajewski and Lar Daly. Mr. Krajewski and Mr. Daly are perennial candidates who run for many offices. Governor Long is seeking re-election.

An official of the Mutual Broadcasting System radio network said news would be covered as it happened, regardless of the equal-time provision. Senator Humphrey will be heard on that network's "Reporters Round-Up" on Sunday, July 26.

July 18, 1959

Stanton Appears on TV to Plead For Curb on Equal-Time Rule

Frank Stanton, president of the Columbia Broadcasting System, went on the air yesterday to plead for prompt Congressional action to relieve radio and television news broadcasts from equal-time restrictions.

If such action is not taken, he said, "we will have no choice but to turn our microphones and television cameras away from all candidates during campaign periods."

Mr. Stanton stated his network's stand on the equal-time issue at the end of a C. B. S. "Behind the News" television program devoted to a discussion of Section 315 of the Federal Communications Act of 1934. This is the so-called equal-time section, dealing with political candidates.

The effect of a recent ruling of the Federal Communications Commission is that the networks must, in their news coverage during a political campaign, give equal time not only to substantial candidates but to every fringe candidate who throws his hat into the ring.

This, according to Mr. Stanton, is impossible. Referring to the 1960 Presidential campaign as the "most important story in our national life," he said television coverage had been virtually "blacked out" by the ruling.

"Television has been told," he continued, "that it can do either the impossible or nothing in bringing you first-hand the candidates for major offices."

Mr. Stanton reminded his listeners that remedial legislation was pending in Congress. A Senate bill stipulates that newscasts, news interviews, news documentaries, on-the-spot coverage of news events and panel discussions will be exempt from Section 315.

A House bill stipulates that newscasts, news interviews or any on-the-spot coverage of news events in which the appearance of the candidates is incidental to the presentation of the news will be exempt from Section 315.

Mr. Stanton described the Senate bill as a "minimum essential" of the freedom of television to help all of us know the candidates and issues in the critical election campaigns of 1960 and the years beyond."

He promised that, if remedial legislation was passed, the broadcasters would not discriminate among the major parties or among the substantial candidates.

"All we ask," he said, "is the right to distinguish, as any sensible citizen would do, between the major parties and the splinter parties, between the significant candidates and the fringe or obscure candidates. We do not ask for the right to discriminate—only to distinguish."

July 27, 1959

Use of 'Equal Time' on Air

TO THE EDITOR OF THE NEW YORK TIMES:

Senator Humphrey was not a victim of the "equal time" provisions of Section 315. The Senator is not yet a candidate for office but merely a candidate for a candidacy. And as such he was not entitled to "equal time."

The Federal Communications Commission's "Public Notice" dated Oct. 1, 1958, makes this crystal clear. Under Section 5, Subsection 25, the question is asked: "If the station makes time available to candidates seeking the nomination of one party for a particular office, does Section 315 require that it make equal time available to the candidates seeking the nomination of other parties for the same office?" The FCC ruled: "No * * * 'equal opportunities' need only be afforded legally qualified candidates for nomination for the same office. * * *"

And in Subsection 26 the question is asked: "If the station makes time available to all candidates of one party for nomination for a particular office, including the successful candidate, may candidates of other parties in the general election demand an equal amount of time under Section 315?" and the FCC ruled: "No."

Then why the clamor? Unquestionably it is based on a desire to reduce, or eliminate entirely, the participation of minority-party candidates in "equal opportunities" and confer a monopoly on the use of the air waves (which are the private property of no man or group) upon the two major political parties. Minority parties will be "muzzled" and radio and TV will be "so devoid of opinion content" because of the unity of thinking of major party candidates that these media will "stay at the moron level."

AARON M. ORANGE.
New York, July 21, 1959.

July 28, 1959

'EQUAL-TIME' CURB ADOPTED BY HOUSE

Bill Exempts News Shows From F. C. C. Requirement —Senate Must Act Again

Special to The New York Times.

WASHINGTON, Aug. 18 — The House of Representatives passed a bill today to exempt news programs from "equal-time" provisions of the Federal Communications Act.

The measure, approved by voice vote, would nullify a ruling by the Federal Communications Commission that President Eisenhower and others have called "ridiculous."

The 1934 Communications Act says that if a radio or television station allows a political candidate to "use" its facilities, it shall afford "equal opportunities" to all other candidates for the same office.

In the disputed ruling, the F. C. C. held last February that the requirement applied to news programs as well as to other appearances by candidates.

Chicago Program at Issue

At issue was a Chicago television news program that showed Mayor Richard J. Daley welcoming President Arturo Frondizi of Argentina and in two other short episodes. Lar Daly, a third-party candidate for Mayor, demanded equal time. The F. C. C. held that he was entitled to it.

The House bill now goes back to the Senate, which passed a similar measure July 28.

Both bills would clearly exempt newscasts, including news interviews and on-the-spot coverage of news events, from equal-time requirements.

The Senate version lists various types of programs to which the exemption would apply. Panel discussions were removed from the list just before passage.

The language of the House bill is broader and less specific. Representative Oren Harris, Democrat of Arkansas and floor manager of the measure, said during today's debate that the exemption was intended to include such news-type panel discussions as "Meet the Press" and "Face the Nation" "as long as they continue to be a regular bona fide news program."

Mr. Harris said the F. C. C. ruling, if permitted to stand, would prevent television coverage of the 1960 Democratic and Republican National Conventions.

CONFERENCE AGREES ON EQUAL-TIME BILL

WASHINGTON, Aug. 26 (UPI)—A Senate-House conference committee agreed today on a compromise bill to allow radio and television stations to feature political figures on news, interview or documentary programs without granting equal time to opponents.

The conferees said the exemption would apply to "bona-fide newscasts and bona-fide news interviews." It would also apply to "bona-fide documentaries" where the candidate's appearance was incidental to the program.

It would likewise apply to on-the-spot news coverage of political candidates.

The conferees, who will meet again tomorrow to draft the final language, agreed on a report that would make clear that regularly scheduled interview and panel programs would be exempt.

CONFEREES CLEAR EQUAL-TIME PLAN

Moss Alone Balks as Bill Is Sent to House—Panel News Shows Exempt

WASHINGTON, Aug. 27 (AP) —A Senate-House committee completed today a compromise bill that would exempt television and radio stations from having to give equal time to political candidates on news programs.

The conference committee sent the compromise to the House, which would act first. Senate action will come later.

Representative John E. Moss, Democrat of California, was the only conferee who refused to sign the agreement. He said it "opens the way to almost certain abuse by some individual stations in political situations."

Mr. Moss said he would fight the compromise in the House. He contended in an interview that the bill would remove practically all restrictions from panel discussions and similar shows.

Exempts Panel Shows

The conference report contains language intended to make clear that the exemption from the equal time requirement applies to regularly scheduled panel shows. Backers have said this exemption would cover such programs as "Meet the Press" and "Face the Nation."

As finally approved by the conferees today, the compromise provides that the equal time requirement under the Federal Communications Act shall not apply to the appearance by a legally qualified candidate for public office on any bona fide newscast, news interview, or news documentary if the appearance of the candidate is incidental to presentation of the subject.

Also exempted would be on-the-spot coverage of bona fide news events, such as political conventions.

The legislation is an outgrowth of an action by the Federal Communications Commission earlier this year. The F. C. C. reaffirmed then that the law required equal time to be given to other candidates if one was shown on a newscast.

Spokesman for the television and radio industry said they would not be able to cover political campaigns if they had to give equal time to anyone running for office, including splinter party candidates.

HOUSE VOTES TO EASE EQUAL-TIME RULES

WASHINGTON, Sept. 2 (AP) —The House passed today a compromise bill to protect television and radio stations from demands for equal time on news programs by candidates for office.

The standing vote of 142-70 sent the bill, worked out in conference with the Senate, to that body for final legislative action.

The bill exempts four categories of broadcasts from the requirement that a candidate must be allowed time equivalent to an opponent's appearance.

The exempted categories are bona fide newscasts, news interviews, news documentary presentations and on-the-spot coverage of bona fide news events.

The legislation is aimed at the Lar Daly ruling of the Federal Communications Commission. The commission upheld a complaint by Mr. Daly, a frequent office-seeker, that he had been denied equal time with opponents on news programs when he was running for Mayor of Chicago.

The compromise bill emphasizes that Congress did not mean to relieve stations of their obligations to balance genuinely political broadcasts.

EQUAL-TIME RELIEF GOES TO PRESIDENT

WASHINGTON, Sept. 3 (UPI) — Final Congressional approval was given today to a bill exempting "bona fide" news programs from the law requiring radio and television stations to give equal time to political candidates.

The Senate acted by voice vote without dissent after a brief but sharp debate as to whether the exemption should apply to panel shows like "Meet the Press," "Face the Nation" and "College News Conference."

Senator Clair Engle, Democrat of California, asserted that newspapers had given Democratic candidates "the business." He called radio and TV "the last refuge" for Democratic campaigners and said he did not want such outlets for the party destroyed.

Senator John O. Pastore, Democrat of Rhode Island, chief spokesman for the measure, said it required that panel shows be regularly scheduled to meet the "bona fide" test and be controlled by the station or network.

Mr. Engle said that he was not worried about network panels but about local shows because "they can be rigged."

EISENHOWER SIGNS 'EQUAL TIME' CURB

WASHINGTON, Sept. 14 (UPI)—President Eisenhower signed today the bill to exempt radio and television newscasts from "equal time" demands of political candidates.

In a statement he said that the new law would make possible "the continued full participation of radio and television in the news coverage of political campaigns which is so essential to a well-informed America."

He had no doubt, he declared, that stations can be relied upon to carry out the provisions of the act "fairly and honestly * * * without abuse or partiality to any individual, group or party."

The law was prompted by a Federal Communications Commission ruling that Lar Daly, a candidate for Mayor of Chicago, was entitled to time equal to that in a newscast showing Mayor Richard A. Daley at a ceremonial function during the campaign.

September 15, 1959

EQUAL-TIME REJECTED

F.C.C. Bars Plea Based on Candidate's Weather Show

WASHINGTON, March 17 (AP)—The Federal Communications Commission turned down today a demand for equal air time based on a candidate's handling of weather programs.

The question was referred to the F. C. C. by Waco, Texas, stations KWTX-AM-TV, where Jack Woods is employed to broadcast weather reports several times a day on both the radio and TV outlets.

Mr. Woods recently announced his candidacy for the Texas legislature. An opponent, William H. Brigham, also of Waco, asked for matching time on the KWTX microphones and TV cameras.

KWTX Broadcasting Company told the F. C. C. that the programs were restricted to the weather and that Mr. Woods "is now identified on these programs not by name, but as the TX Weatherman."

The commission agreed unanimously that his broadcasts did not bring the equal time provision into play.

March 18, 1960

TV: Battle of Unequals

Kennedy Held Not Entitled to Rebuttal Because Truman Is Not a Candidate

By JACK GOULD

BY the end of the current political campaign it is possible that the television viewer will demand equal time to protest further controversies over equal time.

The latest episode, involving Senator John F. Kennedy's desire for a half hour to answer former President Harry S. Truman, is all too typical of the silly confusion surrounding the ground rules for electronic campaigning.

In a matter of hours after Mr. Truman had cast aspersions on his maturity, Senator Kennedy dispatched telegrams to the Columbia Broadcasting System and the National Broadcasting Company. Under Section 315 of the Federal Communications Act, he said, he was entitled to equal opportunity for rebuttal.

The singularly efficient Kennedy camp was not up on its video facts of life. Section 315 guarantees equal time only to bona fide candidates for the same office. Since Mr. Truman is not a candidate for the Presidential office, which Mr. Kennedy seeks, the networks pointed out that Section 315 did not apply.

Once having set aside Section 315, however, N. B. C. agreed to devote a half hour for live coverage at 4:30 P. M. today of Senator Kennedy's news conference in the Roosevelt Hotel. Robert E. Kintner, N. B. C. president, noted that it was "a good story" that should be covered regardless of legalisms.

Technically, under Section 315, the presentation of Senator Kennedy now could involve N. B. C. in setting aside thirty minutes each for Senators Stuart Symington and Lyndon B. Johnson. From a practical standpoint, it is not expected that Senator Symington would want to add a postscript to Mr. Truman's remarks. For Senator Johnson a plea for equal time would constitute public announcement of his candidacy.

Dr. Frank Stanton, C. B. S. president, upon receiving Senator Kennedy's wire, also argued that Section 315 did not apply and offered a half hour to a representative of the Democratic candidate. By presenting a representative rather than the candidate himself, the future complications under Section 315 presumably could be avoided by the network.

Yesterday, after Senator Kennedy's decision to appear at his own news conference, C. B. S. confirmed that it would not cover the candidate on a live basis. Rather it will tape the proceedings and then later use them in such manner as news judgment dictates.

The conflicting positions adopted by N. B. C. and C. B. S.—the American Broadcasting Company stayed out of the rumpus by not carrying Mr. Truman in the first place—both have merit.

The clear-cut policy of N. B. C. to cover the news and worry about the consequences later is imminently appealing. If every political flurry on the airwaves must lead to an emergency session of the American Bar Association, the net effect will be only to reduce the scope and depth of TV's news coverage. By this time the defects of Section 315 have been amply dramatized and the public interest properly should take precedence over the TV industry's legislative problems.

Yet the C. B. S. network's implied position that it alone, not the candidates, should decide how political news will be covered has validity. Prominent figures in both parties do have a tendency to try to boss around TV in a manner that they would not think of applying to the press.

Instead of tirelessly crying for equal time on TV, it would be refreshing if some candidate announced when and where he would make a rebuttal and then credit TV with the good sense to cover the story. If TV didn't measure up, then the medium would really invite a lively Donnybrook.

●

At all events it must be hoped that Congress, when it reconvenes, will act promptly to suspend certain provisions of Section 315 for a trial period. The chief advantage of the suspension would be to relieve the networks of the ludicrous obligation to give every Tom, Dick and Harry who wanted to be President as much air time as the nominees of the Republican and Democratic parties.

But, more realistically, the suspension of this odious feature of Section 315 would remove the underlying cause of contention over equal time. It has become hard to tell whether some broadcasters are interested in covering the news or using Section 315 as an excuse not to do so.

One wry soul observed yesterday that actually both N. B. C. and C. B. S. should be grateful to Mr. Truman. It is not every political figure who is thoughtful enough to stir up a controversy during the inexpensive daytime hours of TV—let alone do it over a holiday week-end when interest in the home screen normally lags.

July 4, 1960

TV: Minorities' Position

Stand of A. C. L. U. on Issue of Equal Air Time Regarded as of 'Dubious Validity'

By JACK GOULD

THE present plan to suspend the equal-time provisions of Section 315 of the Federal Communications Act to permit television debates between Vice President Nixon and Senator John F. Kennedy has drawn the disapproval of the American Civil Liberties Union.

Patrick Murphy Malin, executive director of the group, applauds the idea of the debates as "a healthy and politically educational event." But he suggests that they should not be authorized without a guarantee that anyone legally qualified to run for the Presidency, no matter how small his followng, receive "some little time on the air."

A resolution suspending the equal-time provision was approved by the Senate on June 27 and, according to Mr. Malin, "is reportedly to be rushed through the House by a voice vote under suspension of the rules, as soon as that body reconvenes on Aug. 15."

However, there also have been hints in Washington that some Southern members of the House may try to block the suspension lest it jeopardize opportunities for a future minority Southern movement to gain TV time.

Last week Mr. Nixon and Mr. Kennedy indicated a willingness to debate, and the three major networks—the National Broadcasting Company, the Columbia Broadcasting System and the American Broadcasting Company—made offers of free time if Section 315 were suitably modified.

Under the existing law the networks cannot grant free time to the Republican and Democratic Presidential candidates without offering the same privilege to perhaps a dozen or more minority candidates. The effect of the law has been to preclude both debate and considerable independent political reporting on TV because of the prohibitive cost of including every small party.

On Saturday the Constitution party, meeting in Dallas, Tex., demanded equal time to answer Vice President Nixon and Senator Kennedy in the event that they have a debate. The party has not yet chosen its candidates.

The Civil Liberties Union noted that the proposed repeal of the equal-time provision was supposed to be a temporary step, subject to review by the Federal Communications Commission, but it feared that in all probability the measure would become a permanent fixture.

"Were the repealer to be made permanent, Congress would, in effect, have granted a monopoly in perpetuity for the Republican and Democratic parties and would decree the defeat of any new third party as well as the effective elimination of all present minor parties," Mr. Malin said.

He added that the A. C. L. U. had serious doubts as to the constituionality of any Congressional act, that bestowed on some nominees, representing the two major parties, a "monopoly of the airwaves."

The organization proposed that instead of eliminating the provision for equal time the clause be supplanted by a phrase calling for "equitable time" for all candidates.

Under such a concept, Mr. Malin noted, there should be a statutory requirement that "some free time" be accorded by the TV networks to all legally qualified candidates. This system would be flexible enough to enable broadcasters to "use their judgment in allotting relative amounts of time," he said. The major Presidential candidates could be seen, but there would be protection for the minority figure with a serious, if unpopular, cause to present.

Actually, the core of the Civil Liberties Union proposal does not differ too materially from the position of the networks themselves. They contend that in the long run sensible and practical apportionment of free time must depend on the judgment of the broadcasters and not on any rigid legislative formula.

It should be noted that suspension of the equal-time provision will not relieve a station of the basic responsibility under its license to report controversial issues fairly. As Dr. Frank Stanton, C. B. S. president, has testified, the emergence of a Southern political group, for example, would be covered as a matter of straight news interest. So also would other minorities of obvious importance. What the networks do wish to avoid is the dissipation of costly time for an eccentric dressed up in an Uncle Sam suit.

The discerning viewer will endorse the A. C. L. U.'s concern over the smallest parties, but its suggestion that the medium of television should be compelled to give "some free time" on a coast-to-coast basis to all persons who qualify as a Presidential or Vice-Presidential candidate in any of the fifty states seems of dubious validity. Legal determination of the word "some" could be highly controversial, and extension of the law to local candidates soon would follow.

To dictate to broadcasters that persons must receive free time on television would not seem to be the happiest of solutions to the problem of equal time. A trial period, in which the broadcasters could show how they would behave if allowed the same freedom as other journalistic media, would seem a wise first step.

EQUAL SPACE LAW FOR PRESS URGED

Head of Young Democrats Asks Industry to Follow Lead of Broadcasters

WASHINGTON, June 13 (AP)—The Young Democratic Clubs called on the nation's newspaper publishers today "to follow the lead of the broadcasting industry's equal-time pledge by offering equal space" for Democratic and Republican Presidential candidates.

"But, if they refuse, it should be made mandatory by law for all newspapers with interstate distribution or which use the Post Office for distribution," said Roy A. Schafer, national president of the Young Democratic Clubs of America.

Mr. Schafer wired Senator John O. Pastore, Democrat of Rhode Island, asking that the Senate Commerce subcommittee that he heads include newspapers in its study of equal TV-radio broadcast time provisions for the major Presidential candidates. Aides said Senator Pastore had not yet seen the telegram.

"Ninety per cent of American newspapers either fly the G. O. P. symbol on their masthead or otherwise toady to the Republican party," Mr. Schafer said.

"Slanting and play of news stories and editorials are not worthy or in keeping with the American tradition of a free press," he continued.

"Monopoly newspapers, otherwise known as one-paper towns, have the same obligation to the general public as institutions and public utilities. This is especially true in communities whose newspaper owner also owns the television and radio stations.

"This pattern of gobbling up opposing voices in the form of competing newspapers and ownership of television stations by press lords is again making itself evident by the merger talks between the only two wire services."

Frank J. Starzel, general manager of The Associated Press, said "there have been no merger talks between the two news services and none is contemplated."

A spokesman for United Press International said UPI "had never discussed a merger with its rival, The Associated Press."

"Competition between the two news services is a mainstay of press freedom," he said.

U. S. PRESS IS UPHELD

Young G. O. P. Leader Calls Political Coverage Honest

WASHINGTON, June 16 (UPI)—Young Republicans took issue with Young Democrats today and said the American press was doing an honest job of covering political news and should not be made subject to Federal laws.

Ned Cushing, chairman of the Young Republican National Federation, issued a statement replying to Roy Schafer, national president of the Young Democratic Clubs. Mr. Schafer said earlier this week that newspapers should be made subject to new Federal laws requiring equal space for both parties unless they gave such space voluntarily. He charged that newspapers were biased in their handling of political news.

In reply, Mr. Cushing said:

"The American press is rigidly fair in its reporting of political news and if the newspapers have partisan opinions they appear only on the editorial page and are labeled as opinion."

Salinger and Klein Praise Press On Effort to Be Fair in Campaign

But Aides to Candidates Cite Exceptions at Sigma Delta Chi Parley—Study of Interpretive Reporting Asked

By RUSSELL PORTER

Pierre E. Salinger and Herbert G. Klein, press secretaries to President-elect John F. Kennedy and Vice President Nixon, respectively, agreed yesterday that the press as a whole had tried to report the Presidential campaign fairly.

Mr. Klein did not go so far as Mr. Salinger, who said the great majority of newspapers had been fair and only a small number unfair.

Mr. Klein said he had not studied the evidence closely enough to say whether political reporters had been unfair to Mr. Nixon, but he suggested that newspaper editors investigate charges to this effect. He said Mr. Nixon had received many letters saying that some newspaper, radio and television coverage had been biased against him.

The two press secretaries spoke at a panel session of the fifty-first national convention of Sigma Delta Chi, professional journalistic society, at the Biltmore Hotel. More than 550 delegates representing more than 16,300 members of the society are attending the four-day convention, which ends today.

Praise Each Other's Work

Both speakers, on first-name terms, praised each other's work in the campaign. Mr. Salinger, speaking first, said a great majority of the papers reported the campaign fairly and, in his opinion, Mr. Kennedy received the fairest press coverage of any Democratic Presidential candidate in recent years.

"The press as a whole is to be commended for the manner in which it covered the campaign," he said.

However, he charged that a small number of papers had acted like adjuncts of the Republican National Committee, especially in their selection and display of news on their front pages during the campaign.

Mr. Salinger named only two papers among those he accused of unfair treatment. They were The Indianapolis Star and The Manchester (N. H.) Union Leader.

Holding up photo copies of several early November issues of The Indianapolis Star, he read off front-page headlines that he said showed a concentration of stories favoring the Republicans. Top stories dealt with a welcome given Mr. Nixon at Spokane and with President Eisenhower's activities, Mr. Salinger noted, while a headline at the bottom read: "Gunwielder at Kennedy Rally Seized."

Peace Corps Talk Cited

Mr. Salinger said one issue of The Star gave its lead story to an attack on Mr. Kennedy by President Eisenhower, and a smaller display at the bottom of the page to Mr. Kennedy's "peace corps" proposal.

According to Mr. Salinger, this proposal for a peace corps of young men to carry the message of this country's desire for peace throughout the world was one of Mr. Kennedy's major campaign speeches.

Mr. Salinger suggested that a committee of leading citizens be set up to study press coverage in Presidential elections. The mere publication of reports by such a committee, he went on, should help curb partisan bias in some papers.

Mr. Salinger emphasized that only 16 per cent of the nation's newspapers, with 15.8 per cent of the circulation, supported the Democratic candidate.

Mr. Klein said in reply that many papers supporting Vice President Nixon editorially carried columnists who supported both sides.

"I saw a study yesterday of seventeen papers, of which four supported Kennedy, eleven or twelve supported us, and one or two were neutral," Mr. Klein said. "Kennedy received a total of 11,810 inches of space and Nixon, 8,897 inches. Kennedy and Johnson together got 13,407 inches; Nixon and Lodge, 9,569 inches."

According to Mr. Klein, these figures showed how the newspapers "tried hard to balance the news."

"Papers supporting us leaned over backward to be fair," he added. "Most papers supported Nixon editorially, but most columnists supported Kennedy, and their editorial pages were pretty well balanced."

Stresses News Coverage

Mr. Klein centered his attention on news coverage, saying things had happened that should cause editors to take a second look at interpretative reporting. He quoted an editorial in The New York Daily News charging that some reporters had written biased stories against Mr. Nixon.

He suggested that Sigma Delta Chi appoint a committee to consider whether interpretative reporting in the campaign had gone beyond a proper assessment of the situation, and had strayed into the realm of editorial writing or personal emotion and bias.

Such a committee, he went on, might study ten or fifteen big stories of the campaign, comparing texts of statements by both candidates with what was reported.

Mr. Klein cited some stories severely critical of Mr. Nixon without identifying the newspapers in which they had appeared, and added: "Are these isolated examples, or do they represent something far greater? I don't know the answer."

Mr. Klein said most of the reporters who covered the Presidential candidates appeared to favor Mr. Kennedy, but he did not accuse them of biased reporting. He agreed that most reporters covering the campaign had been fair and impartial.

Bright Future Seen

Turner Catledge, managing editor of The New York Times, told another session of the convention that the future of newspapers was never brighter than it is today.

He said newspapers that have appealed to the readers' need for news and have been wisely managed have made great progress. On the other hand, he went on, those that have shown less respect for news have not progressed.

The convention voted in favor of changing the official designation of Sigma Delta Chi from "fraternity" to "society." It also raised the annual dues from $5 to $10 a year.

Governor Rockefeller addressed a dinner session of the convention last night and answered questions from the audience.

In a question referring to Vice President Nixon's loss of New York State in the election, the Governor was asked:

"Is is true that you threw New York?"

"I never worked so hard at anything in New York as I did in this campaign," he replied.

Mr. Rockefeller pledged himself to support Sigma Delta Chi's campaign to make more government information available to the public.

Indianapolis Editor Replies

INDIANAPOLIS, Dec. 2 (UPI)—Robert Early, managing editor of The Indianapolis Star, said, "We plan our news stories according to their news values," in replying tonight to criticism of the newspaper's coverage of the Presidential campaign.

"In the recent campaign," Mr. Early said, "we editorially backed Mr. Nixon. We gave both sides equal space on the

267

news side. We always used news value judgment in determining the play."

Publisher Denies Charge

MANCHESTER, N. H., Dec. 2 (UPI)—William Loeb, publisher of The Manchester Union Leader, said tonight it was "hard to understand" a charge that his newspaper's coverage was biased during the Presidential campaign.

Mr. Loeb said his paper, which was criticized by Senator Kennedy during an election eve speech here, gave banner headline treatment to what he called the Democrat's "vicious attack against the paper and its publisher."

On the other hand, he said, "We challenge Mr. Salinger to show us any other newspaper which gave the Democrats a better break in its news columns and in its letters to the editor page than did The Union Leader."

Chairman of House Unit Urges Briefer Campaigns

Davis Suggests the Parties Hold Conventions Later

Special to The New York Times.

WASHINGTON, Dec. 15 — Representative Clifford Davis of Tennessee, the chairman of a special House Elections Committee, said today he would recommend that future Presidential campaigns be limited to a month or six weeks.

He said he believed this could be accomplished without legislation. He suggested an agreement between the two major parties to hold their nominating conventions in September instead of July.

The chairman gave reporters these views after his committee held hearings on the matter and on other questions growing out of this year's Presidential campaign.

The opinions Representative Davis expressed coincided largely with those offered by several witnesses, including Dr. Frank Stanton, president of the Columbia Broadcasting System, and Robert W. Sarnoff, chairman of the National Broadcasting Company.

Equal Time Attack

Dr. Stanton and Mr. Sarnoff also urged repeal of the provision requiring radio and television outlets to give all candidates for an office equal broadcast time.

Congress suspended this provision last year, but only for the campaign of 1960 and only for Presidential and Vice-Presidential candidates. This made possible the series of debates between Senator John F. Kennedy and Vice President Nixon. Both television executives said wide coverage by the networks made shorter national campaigns feasible and desirable.

Representative Davis said after the hearings that repeal of the equal-time provision would be given serious study.

A Republican member, Representative William C. Cramer of Florida, said he, too, favored a four-to-six-week campaign.

Future Debates Urged

WASHINGTON, Dec. 15 (AP)—A political scientist said today the public should insist that the Presidential candidates of 1964 contest with each other in television appearances, whether they want to or not.

Generally, the feeling has been that a President running

Witnesses Seek End of Rule on Equal Broadcast Time

for re-election would not be willing to give an opponent the benefit of increased television exposure.

But Col. Charles A. H. Thomson, specialist in communications for the Rand Corporation of California, said in a lecture at the Brookings Institution:

"Debates are so clearly superior as a means of getting the candidates to talk about the same thing, to be able to correct distortions and misstatements on the spot, and to present themselves to the same huge audiences, that the preferences of the candidates should not be the primary consideration."

G. O. P. ASKS REPLY TO KENNEDY ON TV

Will Seek a Similar Forum Over 3 Major Networks

WASHINGTON, Dec. 18 (AP) — The Republican National Committee served notice today that it would ask all three networks for a forum comparable to that accorded President Kennedy in his televised interview last night.

The committee said this would only be fair because last night's show "resulted in substantial benefits to the Democrats and their probable 1964 candidate".

A statement issued through William B. Sprague Jr., public relations director of the committee, said: "Republican National Committee officials have decided to seek from the three major television networks facilities at some future date comparable to those accorded President Kennedy last night."

"While we do not at this time contemplate a flat demand for equal time, we feel that the program resulted in substantial benefits to the Democrats and their probable 1964 candidate.

"Thus, in all fairness, we would hope to be granted facilities for favorable and full exposure of the Republican viewpoint.

"A format which will best serve the interests of the Republican party and the networks by ensuring a maximum degree of audience interest will be worked out through careful planning."

Federal communications law provides that equal time must be granted political candidates. Officially, Mr. Kennedy was speaking as the President, although, of course, any President's words can have an effect on his political future.

Aside from this provision of law, a policy of the Federal Communications' Commission calls on TV-radio stations to give well-rounded presentations of controversies.

What sort of program to put on is something of a problem for the Republicans.

About the only single individual the Republicans could produce for such a program would be former President Dwight D. Eisenhower. There is reluctance in party quarters to call again on the former President for such a task at this time.

Unless Republicans agreed on General Eisenhower to reply to President Kennedy's statement they would face the necessity of producing a panel.

HOUSE UNIT SHIES AT SESSIONS ON TV

Rules Panel Fails to Act on Broadcast of Hearings

By C. P. TRUSSELL
Special to The New York Times.

WASHINGTON, March 5 — House promoters of televised committee hearings appeared today to face more disappointments.

After a long public hearing the Rules Committee postponed, apparently indefinitely, even considering permitting the question to go to the House floor.

The chief sponsor of legislation to permit televising and other broadcasting of committee proceedings was Representative Oren Harris, the Arkansas Democrat who heads the Committee on Interstate and Foreign Commerce.

Mr. Harris had decide to back the idea after years of apparent indecision. He emphasized that his conversion should in no way reflect on the memory of the late Speaker Sam Rayburn, who for many years prohibited television presentation of proceedings.

Representative Harris said he had discussed the matter with the incumbent peaker, John W. McCormack. Mr. McCormack, he reported, declined to take an official position, but left the decision to the rules panel. Mr. Harris argued that the people had a right to observe their representatives in action.

Proposal Is Questioned

Members of the Rules Committee raised a number of questions about the proposal, that included the following:

¶Did the House leadership really want House hearings televised?

¶If committees put on TV shows, would the movement spread to the House floor, where the picture might not always be an inspiring one?

¶Could rules be drafted to prevent an individual member of the House—or a group of them—from scene-stealing and general demagoguery?

¶Could a hearing be made partisan by a manipulation of questions and shutting off of rebuttals?

¶Could both sides of an issue be presented in a single, necessarily limited telecast?

The usual Rules Committee procedure at the end of a hearing is to go into executive session to make a decision. Today the rules members went to lunch instead.

Representative Howard W. Smith, Democrat of Virginia, the chairman, made only one observation: "The idea doesn't seem to have much support, does it?" He said he did not know when the committee would meet again.

March 6, 1963

HOUSE WOULD LIFT EQUAL TIME IN '64

Votes to Suspend TV Rule on Presidential Candidates

By C. P. TRUSSELL
Special to The New York Times

WASHINGTON, June 19— The House of Representatives approved today a suspension, for the 1964 campaign, of the law that gives equal broadcasting time to candidates for the Presidency and the Vice Presidency. The vote was 263-126.

Such a suspension had been sanctioned in the 1960 campaign. It made possible the television and radio debates between John F. Kennedy and Richard M. Nixon.

Similar confrontations of the 1964 nominees appeared to be in the minds of the sponsors of the bill, which now goes to the Senate. Early action is expected there.

Under the equal-time law, a broadcasting station providing time to a political candidate must offer equal time to all other candidates for the same office. Under a suspension, a station or network would be allowed to put on the air only the two major candidates, as in the 1960 debates.

Republicans in the House were most vocal in opposition to the new suspension. Yet their ranks split sharply, and some of the strongest arguments for the bill came from their side.

Some Southern Democrats denounced it, saying it could stifle minorities and give manipulation powers to the broadcasting companies in programing debates and speeches.

Some opponents voiced the suspicion that the broadcasting companies were using this proposed suspension as an avenue toward repeal of the equal-time law.

The bill assumes that the Presidential campaign will begin Aug. 20, 1964. Its scope covers "the 75-day period immediately preceding Nov. 3," Election Day.

June 20, 1963

F. C. C. HEAD ASKS EQUAL-TIME CURB

Would Suspend Requirement Again for '64 Campaign

WASHINGTON, June 26 (AP)—The chairman of the Federal Communications Commission advocated today another suspension of the requirement for equal free time for political broadcasts by major Presidential and Vice Presidential candidates.

The idea is to encourage more radio - television appearances by the candidates, such as the debates of 1960 between President Kennedy and Richard M. Nixon, his Republican opponent.

Those debates were carried on under a suspension of the requirement that radio and television stations must allow time for all candidates for political office.

E. William Henry, the commission chairman, appeared before the Senate Commerce subcommittee on communications. He said he agreed that a requirement that Presidential candidates of minor parties have equal free time would limit the public's opportunity to see the major aspirants.

Under peppery questioning, he refused to endorse legislation that would widen the suspension to cover broadcasts by candidates for the Senate, House of Representatives and for Governor. He also refused to approve a proposed repeal of the equal-time statute.

The hearing was marked by Senator Strom Thurmond's charge that the major networks were giving one-sided coverage to civil rights controversies.

The South Carolina Democrat, saying "I am speaking for the South," urged the F.C.C. to note that networks were engaged in "if not a conspiracy, a determined effort" to give only one side of the issue.

Senator John O. Pastore, Rhode Island Democrat, who heads the subcommittee, said he could not understand why Mr. Henry would not approve legislation introduced by him to extend the equal-time suspension to Congressional and gubernatorial candidates.

"We are giving you our best collective judgment," Mr. Henry replied.

Mr. Henry endorsed a Senate bill to suspend the equal-time provision for major candidates only in 1964. The bill was introduced by Mr. Pastore in behalf of a Presidential study commission and is similar to one passed by the House.

The commission chief suggested that clarifying language be written into it.

June 27, 1963

RADIO-TV SCORED ON EDITORIALIZING

House Committee Is Told of Abuses as Hearings Open

WASHINGTON, July 15 (AP)—A Democratic Representative from South Carolina urged Congress today to halt what he called "abusive editorializing over the air waves."

The Representative, Robert W. Hemphill, spoke as a witness at the opening of fact-finding hearings conducted by a House Commerce subcommittee.

He said a government policy that permitted broadcast editorializing "cannot but work a hardship on the broadcaster, the Federal Communications Commission, the [political] candidate and the public."

"It affronts my sense of justice and fair play to have one of these monkeys get on the radio station," because the commentators who broadcast editorials sometimes do not know what they are talking about, he continued.

Mr. Hemphill complained that persons who are the subjects of broadcast editorials were not notified in advance and did not have a chance to rebut.

He also charged that newspapers were sometimes abusive and inaccurate, but he said, "I still want to give them their freedom. I wish I could give them some integrity."

Californian Opposes Controls

Representative Lionel Van Deerlin, Democrat, from California, who is a former radio-television commentator, spoke out against any controls over broadcast editorials. He said the hearings themselves "may tend to discourage, if not to intimidate," stations that broadcast editorials.

"Rather than seek to hobble our editorialists of the air, it seems to me that we should join F. C. C. commissioners and the National Association of Broadcasters in seeking to stimulate the full and free discussion of public issues," he said.

Another South Carolina Democrat, Representative William Dorn, joined Mr. Van Deerlin in advocating freedom for broadcasters to voice editorial opinions.

Representative Durwood G. Hall, Republican from Missouri, said Congress should give "urgent consideration" to what he called one-sided presentations on major national issues by the television networks. Asked whether he wanted the Government to regulate networks, Mr. Hall told the subcommittee, "if that's where the axle is squeaking, that's where the grease ought to be."

'Liberal' Orientation Scored

He said the networks were editorializing under the guise of public affairs programs that were "liberal-oriented" and misleading to the public. However, he said he favored self-policing by the industry rather than any attempted remedy through legislation.

A broadcaster said that if Congress halted broadcast editorials, "you will have succeeded in transforming the wasteland into a waste-of-time land."

Sherwood R. Gordon, president and general manager of radio stations KSCO, San Diego, and KBUZ, Phoenix, Ariz., asserted that most Americans lived behind "the paper curtain of a single editorial voice" because they had only one local newspaper. The tremendous power vested in newspaper publishers, he said, can only be counterbalanced by those broadcasters who have the courage of their convictions to contribute a diffusion of editorial thought."

F.C.C. COOL TO BILL ON EDITORIALIZING

Asks Congress Not to Pass Any New Radio-TV Law

WASHINGTON, July 16 (AP)—The chairman of the Federal Communications Commission asked Congress today to avoid legislation dealing with radio and television editorials. But members of the House Commerce Committee indicated they will not go along with the suggestion of E. William Henry, the new chairman, that rules governing broadcast editorializing be left to the F.C.C.

Mr. Henry told a subcommittee fact-finding hearing that the Commission plans to draft more specific rules on broadcast editorials in time for the 1964 election campaign.

He said the F.C.C. agrees with the essential principles of a broadcast editorial bill sponsored by Representative John E. Moss, Democrat of California. "Nevertheless," Mr. Henry declared, "We respectfully suggest that legislation is not as appropriate in this area as commission rulemaking or policy declarations derived from ever-increasing knowledge in this evolving field."

Impatience Expressed

Mr. Moss and other committee members said the F.C.C. has not done much about problems of radio and television editorializing. They feel that it is time for Congress to act. "I think the tools were given to the Commission, but I don't think they have been used as we had hoped they would be used," Mr. Moss said.

"If anything is in a state of confusion today in radio and television," said Representative John B. Bennett, Republican of Michigan, "it is the right of broadcasters to editorialize and of people to reply."

The F.C.C. chairman said the commission encouraged broadcast editorials within the bounds of fairness. He feels, he explained, that fairness requires the station to offer comparable reply time to the people identified with an issue attacked in a broadcast editorial. He said a broadcaster "has no right to express his own opinion and let all other opinions go by the board."

Mr. Henry suggested that the right to reply to a broadcast editorial should provide for appearances by spokesmen for the defensive candidate—not by the candidate himself.

Equal Time a Factor

Otherwise, he said, the equal-time requirement might lead to a "merry-go-round" of appearances by all candidates for the office involved, a situation that would tend to discourage station editorializing.

Mr. Moss said that if he were a candidate under editorial attack he would object to being restricted to having a spokesman reply for him. "I think I, as a candidate, am really the only spokesman for myself," he said. "I think we should make clear the right of the candidate to respond."

The Moss bill covers political editorials broadcast by radio and television stations. It would require a station that endorses a candidate for office to offer equal opportunity to other candidates to reply to a campaign editorial.

The bill also would require the station to send other candidates transcripts of the editorial within five days of the broadcast. It would bar editorializing for or against a candidate during the last two days before the election.

TV PRESIDENTS URGE MORE EDITORIALIZING

WASHINGTON, July 18 (AP) The presidents of the Columbia Broadcasting System and the Westinghouse Broadcasting Company said today that Congress should seek to encourage, not hamper, radio and television editorializing.

Dr. Frank Stanton of C.B.S. said that he would like to see Congress exempt broadcast editorials from the law requiring equal air time for political candidates.

"By trying to legislate fairness," he said, "I think you make it more difficult for the broadcaster to do a decent and responsible job of serving the people."

Donald H. McGannon, president of Westinghouse Broadcasting, urged a House Commerce subcommittee "to oppose any legislation, rules, restrictions or policies that will hamper editorialization as we now know it.

"To the contrary," he said, "I urge you to state yourselves in a manner that will encourage an even greater number of broadcasters to undertake this task in a serious, systematic and responsible way."

Dr. Stanton said he would favor a situation in which stations editorializing in favor of a political candidate could offer the opposition candidate equal time for a personal response.

At present, the station can comply with F.C.C. fairness requirements by letting a spokesman do the replying.

Editorializing on the Air

The right of broadcasters to editorialize is permitted by the Federal laws regulating radio and television.

In recent times it has been more than allowed; it has been encouraged by Federal Communications Commissioners trying to persuade the stations to improve their programing. This is as it should be if Americans are willing to trust themselves to read, see and hear fact and opinion and then make up their own minds. The American public, getting its information from a multitude of sources, does not hold any one sacrosanct.

To regulate editorializing on the air waves—a question that a House subcommittee is now considering—would be even more difficult than the provision of law requiring equal time for political candidates. This regulation, a highly unsatisfactory one, was suspended in 1960 and probably will be again in 1964. It certainly should be.

As a practical matter, a station can no more give exact equal time in minutes to candidates than can a newspaper give exact equal space in inches. News cannot be measured with either a pica rule or a stopwatch. Indeed, the F.C.C. has found that 96 per cent of the 148 stations taking an editorial stand on candidates carried programs giving an opposite viewpoint from their own. They have shown a sense of responsibility.

At license-renewal time the F.C.C. can and should look closely at the promised scheduling and performance of stations. License renewal need not be automatic. But neither should it be political, which is what it would be in danger of becoming if Congress got into the act of telling the stations how to deliver their editorials.

July 20, 1963

SPEAKING OUT

Broadcasters Must Be Free to Develop Editorials, Unhampered by Laws

By JACK GOULD

THE day when a national television network editorially endorses one Presidential candidate and opposes another, which could add a fillip to campaign festivities, does not appear to be one of the imminent occurrences of the 1960's.

But intensification of interest by local broadcasters in sagely kibitzing on assorted issues and, to a lesser extent, proclaiming their choice of a preferred regional candidate does appear to be steadily growing. And concurrent with broadcasting's discovery of its editorial voice there has been a flurry of alarums in official Washington.

The House Communications and Power Subcommittee is holding hearings on whether radio and TV editorializing may do grievous harm to the public figure who is scorned. The Federal Communications Commission is contemplating the issuance of a helpful directive to guide station owners in the expression of their personal opinions.

Editorializing by broadcasters has had a long and an involuted history. Back in 1941 the F.C.C. banned outright all editorial expressions in what was known as the "Mayflower decision," which had nothing to do with a maritime facility but was part of the trade name of a Massachusetts broadcasting company brought to book. In 1949 the commission changed its stand and endorsed editorial activity conducted within an over-all doctrine of fairness.

Coincidental with the policy reversal, a new generation of spirited station owners has undertaken much more editorializing, though it is still far from a universal practice on the air. Individual broadcasters believe they can trace substantial civic progress to judicious application of the electronic needle, often in contradiction to the position of some newspapers that have allowed their editorial pages to slip into innocuity.

Their Goal

In the background of the campaign for editorializing there has been the matter of overcoming broadcasting's inferiority complex in journalism. Station owners yearn for the greater respect and freedom enjoyed by newspaper publishers and are convinced that such equality cannot be attained until they are a directing force in a community rather than merely a glamorous mirror.

If the theory of such a parallel is simply suggested, the disparity of conditions applying to broadcasting and the press hardly could be more marked. For one thing, under the station licensing authority vested by Congress in the F.C.C., the House and Senate enjoy a ready made handle with which to lift open the Pandora's box of investigating a medium's rights and powers to editorialize.

In calling the House subcommittee hearing the group's chairman, Representative Walter E. Rogers, Democrat of Texas, indicated misgivings that politicians might be receiving an ethereal comeuppance without opportunity for suitable redress.

The broad fairness doctrine calls upon a station management that expresses its own opinion to make an effort to obtain views in opposition. In the hearing there were indications that this procedure had not always been pursued and the TV screen might be turned into a shrill soapbox.

Similarly, there appears to have been a sticky issue in the matter of responding to editorials taking a position on candidacies. The right of decision on who should do the answering has been entrusted to the station licensee. There was a feeling in the hearing that the aggrieved party at least should have an express opportunity to defend himself. Representative John E. Moss, Democrat of California, favors legislation to guarantee the point, while the F.C.C. believes it already has adequate powers to cover such a contingency.

One complicating element is that if a station applauds Candidate A for dogcatcher, must it give rebuttal time to Candidates B, C, D and E, who might covet the post? The numbers game goes on and on.

Many broadcasters would be delighted if the editorializing issue went away, because to render one endorsement can invite a host of complaints. They also believe that broadcasting's reputation for impartiality would be compromised if a station

271

owner beat the drums for a favorite or took a position in a controversy.

Essential Need

But Dr. Frank Stanton, president of the Columbia Broadcasting System, was much more attuned to the 20th century when, in his testimony before the House subcommittee, he said editorials were essential to the stimulus of constructive discussion and criticism. Television today reports, interprets and analyzes the news; to abandon the companion function of reaching some conclusion on issues and recommending solutions is to take less than full advantage of journalism's resources for constructive citizenship.

Broadcasting purposely has started slowly and hesitantly in editorializing, perhaps, in part, for fear of arousing Congressional feelings, but it may be time for the adoption of some definitive pattern. On many stations editorials are introduced at odd hours and intervals. Some on radio are done so briefly as to border on partisan sloganeering amid interludes of rock 'n' roll.

Stations anxious to give stature to their editorial pages of the air would be well advised to adhere to a fixed schedule, to speak out with consistency. And then as an integral part of the program there could be visual letters to the editor, which not only would be scrupulously fair but also potentially good viewing.

Legislative efforts to assure fairness and balance are doomed in the long run to failure, if only because no matter how sincerely motivated, they invite suspicions of censorship or outright suppression. Editorializing is bound to come; the job of mature and discriminating broadcasters is to demonstrate by example that the practice will benefit both television and the viewer, that no new law is needed.

SENATORS ADVANCE EQUAL TIME BILL

WASHINGTON, Sept. 10 (AP)—The Senate Commerce Committee approved today a resolution to suspend the equal-time requirement for political broadcasts by major party Presidential and Vice-Presidential candidates in 1964.

The measure, already passed by the House, is similar to legislation enacted in the 86th Congress to make possible the Kennedy-Nixon debates on radio and television in 1960.

A section of the Federal Communications Act requires that if a radio or television station provides time for one candidate for a political office, it must provide equal time for all other candidates for the office.

The resolution as approved by the Commerce Committee would suspend this section with respect to major party candidates for 60 days immediately preceding the election on Nov. 3, 1964.

As passed by the House, the measure provided for a 75-day suspension. The Commerce Committee explained that it had reduced the period to 60 days since this appeared to be ample.

SENATE APPROVES EQUAL-TIME CURB

Acts to Allow TV Debate by 2 Presidential Nominees

WASHINGTON, Oct. 2 (AP) —The Senate passed by voice vote today a bill to clear the way for radio and television debates by the Democratic and Republican Presidential candidates next year.

The measure would suspend for the 60 days immediately preceding the election on Nov. 3, 1964, a requirement of the Federal Communications Act. The act requires that broadcasting stations provide equal time for all candidates for a public office if time is provided for any of them.

The practical effect is to permit broadcasters to give or sell time to the major party candidates without obligating themselves to provide it also for a possible host of minor candidates.

Senator John O. Pastore, Democrat of Rhode Island, floor manager for the bill, said the measure would do "what we did in 1960 that made possible the famous debates between President Kennedy and former Vice President Nixon."

The House passed a bill last June 19 providing for a 75-day rather than a 60-day suspension of the equal time requirement. The shorter period was inserted by the Senate after the Democrats decided to put off their national convention until late August.

The measure, which applies to candidates for Vice President as well as President, now goes back to the House for action on the Senate amendment.

Although the Senate passed the bill without any discussion, Senator Norris Cotton, Republican of New Hampshire, said in a statement that he supported the measure but should perhaps be chary of it from a strictly political point of view. Senator Cotton said "there is substantial evidence to indicate that Vice President Nixon may have lost the 1960 election" as a result of the debates that year.

EQUAL TIME DEBATE

By JACK GOULD

THE controversy over televised debates in the forthcoming campaign between President Johnson and Senator Barry Goldwater is obscuring a point of greater importance than the possibility of dramatic face-to-face confrontation.

If the existing law is not suspended so that networks and stations can give time to the major parties without making the same provisions for minor parties, the broadcast media are going to be seriously handicapped in reporting basic developments in the campaign.

Section 315 of the Federal Communications Act provides that if the network grants time to a single candidate, then it must give an equal amount of time to every other person who is a certified candidate for that office. The thought behind the position is admirable on the surface—that is, to assure that minority aspirants to office will not be denied access to the publicly owned airways.

Inviting Chaos

Application of the principle, however, only invites chaos or indifference in reporting politics. If a network were to decide to do a special program, for example, on the background and career of the two men with a reasonable chance of election, then under Section 315, the network also must set aside perhaps as much as 10 more hours for all other entrants in the Presidential race. In most recent campaigns, there have been at least a dozen candidates.

As a consequence, the network or station is naturally bound to be hesitant about granting an hour or two of newsworthy material if it must add on another five to 10 hours that are not. A situation wherein a newspaper could not carry the text of President Johnson and Senator Goldwater without also regularly carrying all the texts of 10 minor candidates is too ludicrous to contemplate. Yet that is essentially the potential dilemma of the broadcast media in a campaign if the equal time law is not relaxed.

In the 1962 gubernatorial campaign in California, the United Press International news service sponsored a luncheon appearance of the two candidates, former Vice-President Richard M. Nixon and Gov. Edmond G. Brown.

Third Candidate

The TV industry covered the meeting as a normal news event taking place outside of any video studio and arranged by an outside group. Yet the commission ruled that TV nonetheless had to accord equal time to a third candidate who was not a participant in the original news happening.

The implications of this precedent are far-reaching for the forthcoming presidential campaign if Section 315 is not suspended. In effect, it would appear to mean that TV can only function within the framework of existing TV news programs, and that if the medium undertakes any reporting of a special nature, it could be liable to severe consequences in terms of costly air time.

So far there has not been a test before the F.C.C. of whether highly political press conferences held by major Presidential candidates during a campaign might not invite legitimate demands for equal time from minority candidates. The commission could face some knotty questions this fall from minority candidates who have become highly sophisticated in exploiting the equal time controversy. Last week there were rumors that a showdown on the intriguing question might be in the offing.

In 1960, the equal time provision was suspended by Congress in regard to the candidates for President and Vice President. Such action was necessary before there could be the debates between the late President Kennedy

and Mr. Nixon. But not so apparent at the time was a companion gain: the same act of suspension enabled the networks and stations to do a vast amount of reporting of the campaign on their own initiative and at their own expense.

For years, the equal time provision has been a political football and in many ways it is a pity that the spectacular debates were instituted before the problem was resolved. Dr. Frank Stanton, C. B. S. president, long has appealed for clarification free from the pressures of the campaign year; it is time his advice was heeded.

Surely, some long-range policy could be developed to protect the interests of serious minority candidates without automatically guaranteeing to them the same attention granted the two men certain to divide the overwhelming majority of votes.

But, meanwhile, with the start of the campaign only days away, it is time that the onus of Section 315 was lifted so that the networks could go ahead with confidence on their plans for political coverage to supplement the paid political broadcast. The independence and scope of the news medium is not a matter to be left to campaign managers and candidates acting through responsive members of House and Senate committees. Yet, in effect, this is what is happening in Washington through the erroneous assumption that only the fate of the debates hinges on Section 315. Much more does.

EQUAL-TIME RULE AFFECTS JOHNSON

F.C.C., in a 4-3 Vote, Says Regulations on Campaign Cover News Meetings

---

By ANTHONY LEWIS
Special to The New York Times

WASHINGTON, Oct. 1— The Federal Communications Commission ruled today that any radio or television station carrying one of President Johnson's news conferences in full must grant equal time to other Presidential candidates.

The vote was 4 to 3 for this new and striking interpretation of the equal-time law.

The ruling will not affect any station's right to carry excerpts from a Presidential news conference as part of a regular news program. The F.C.C. said stations could do so in the exercise of their "bona fide news judgment."

The effect will be, however, to prevent virtually any broadcasting of the President's news conferences in full. Any station that did so would have to grant equal air time not only to Senator Barry Goldwater of Arizona, the Republican nominee, but also to the nominees—perhaps up to 10 in number—of minor parties.

Because there is no practical way of editing a news conference as it occurs, live broadcasts will be most unlikely for the remainder of the campaign. In practice, the networks have seldom broadcast the President's news conferences in full as they happened.

In the majority today were the commission's chairman, E. William Henry, and Robert T. Bartley, Robert E. Lee and Kenneth A. Cox. The dissenters were Rosel H. Hyde, Frederick W. Ford and Lee Loevinger.

None of the seven was put on the commission by President Johnson. Three were named by President Kennedy, two by President Eisenhower and two by President Truman.

The issue before the commission was the meaning of 1959 amendments to the 1927 law requiring stations to grant equal time to other candidates for office when time has been given to one candidate.

In an effort to make the law less rigid, the statute of 1959 exempted from the equal-time rule — among other things — "bona fide news interviews" or

"on-the-spot coverage of bona fide news events." The question was whether Presidential news conferences came within either of those categories.

The majority found that the conferences were not "interviews" within the statute because they were not "regularly scheduled" and were not controlled by the broadcaster. Those elements were mentioned in a Congressional report on the 1959 law.

The majority also rejected any exemption of news-conference coverage as bona fide news events. If that were done, it said, the equal-time rule would be a sham because stations could cover any candidate's activities as "news events" and be exempt.

Two of the dissenters—Mr. Ford and Mr. Loevinger—disagreed on this second point. They said in sharp language that a President's news conference was undeniably a genuine news event.

"The majority," Mr. Ford said, "in effect is denying a physical fact recognized by representatives of all news media throughout the world, otherwise those representatives would not be present."

Mr. Loevinger said that the majority ruling on this point defied "common sense." He said it was "a fact known to all that the press conference of the President of the United States is the source of some of the most important news in the world today."

He scoffed at the majority because, he said, it did not "distinguish between the President of the United States and a candidate for that office, or for that matter a candidate for the office of county sheriff."

"The President is the chief of state of this sovereign nation," Mr. Loevinger said. "The position is wholly unique.

"The ruling on the commission is not merely wrong but is unfair to the President, the candidates for President, the broadcasters and, most of all, to the American electorate, which is entitled to all the news it can get in aid of its judgment in selecting the President."

This general ruling was sought by the Columbia Broadcasting System. In a letter of Aug. 27, it asked the F.C.C. whether broadcasts of news conferences would come within the equal-time requirement.

One result of the decision could be to spur future efforts for further modification of the equal-time law. Commissioner Ford said that he would urge its repeal and replacement by a flexible authorization for the F.C.C. to make rules for campaigns.

In 1960, to avoid the burden of minor-party candidates' demanding equal time, Congress waived the rule to allow debates between the Democratic and Republican candidates for President. This year a similar effort failed when President Johnson did not endorse it.

C.B.S. 'Disappointed'

The Columbia Broadcasting System was the only network to make formal comment yesterday on the F. C. C.'s ruling. Dr. Frank Stanton, president, said:

"We are disappointed but not at all surprised. Our fear that the Presidential press conferences were not exempt from the equal-time requirements has been one of the reasons we have pressed so vigorously for the suspension of Section 315 of the Communications Act.

William R. McAndrew, executive vice president of news for the National Broadcasting Company, said that whenever news conferences were open for radio-television coverage during the election campaign, N. B. C. would tape or film them and use excerpts on regularly scheduled news programs.

The American Broadcasting Company said that it had no comment on the F. C. C. ruling.

The National Association of Broadcasters said the F. C. C. decision demonstrated the "absurdity" of the equal-time section of the Communications Act.

The Equal-Time Barrier

F.C.C.'s Ruling Is Viewed as a Clash Between a Concept and Public Good

By JACK GOULD

The ruling of the Federal Communications Commission that a Presidential news conference becomes a political broadcast during a campaign year is the latest chapter in the tortuous controversy over equal time on the air. The controversy stems from a noble concept of law that has run afoul of mathematical practicality. The premise underlying Federal regulation of broadcasting holds that the airways, the unseen carriers of a program from a transmitter to a person's receiver, are the property of the public. And a key phrase says that the airways must be used to serve "all the people of the United States."

News Analysis

If the interests of all, not just some, are to be served, according to long-standing policy of the F.C.C., then every properly qualified candidate for political office is entitled to equal opportunity in presenting his views to those who may wish to tune them in. If a station grants a half-hour to one candidate, it must give a half-hour to every other contender in the field.

Electronic Equality

Any other course, it is reasoned, would deprive a minority candidate of an access to the airways to which he has as much legal right as the majority-party figure. The sense of the philosophy is embodied in Section 315 of the Communications Act.

The only trouble with Section 315 is that it does not work as intended. In a Presidential year many people want to be President. In addition to the nominees of the Republican and Democratic parties, there may be as many as 10 minority candidates legally entitled to ask for the same treatment accorded majority candidates.

Accordingly, the problem of the broadcaster under Section 315 is that if he gives an hour each to the Republican and Democratic nominees, he may be obligated to give 10 hours of cumulative free time to candidates in whom most of the public has scant interest. The total time accorded to minority candidates would drastically exceed the total given to majority candidates. The cost of underwriting 10 hours of coast-to-coast network time to obtain two hours of material of dominant interest would be prohibitive.

In 1959 the F.C.C. tried to find a partial solution. It ruled that a broadcaster could give time to Republican and Democratic nominees and largely forget about the minority candidates if it was done within the framework of bona-fide newscasts, such as the Huntley-Brinkley, Walter Cronkite and Ron Cochran news shows, and bona-fide news interviews, such as "Face the Nation," "Meet the Press," and "Issues and Answers."

The ruling was intended to sustain the viability of electronic journalism where it was recognized that normal editorial judgment had to play a part in deciding news content.

In 1960 the provisions of Section 315 were completely suspended with respect to Presidential and Vice-Presidential appearances. The experiment made possible the debates between John F. Kennedy and Richard M. Nixon.

But late this summer an effort to suspend Section 315 again was tabled by the Democratic majority in the Senate, acting, it was generally believed, at the behest of President Johnson.

The Columbia Broadcasting System felt it necessary then to ask the F.C.C. to stipulate the character of a news conference of a President running for re-election. Was it a news presentation or a political broadcast?

Actually the question was largely academic, since there have been no telecasts of Presidential news conferences since Mr. Johnson's nomination. It was, however, an effective means of dramatizing Section 315 and perhaps enlisting public support for its modification or suspension.

But the larger issue behind Section 315 is the realization by some broadcasters that they have lost substantial control over their own medium during a campaign year. The politicians are calling virtually all the shots.

President Holds Back

So far President Johnson has turned down all offers of free TV time, running into the millions of dollars, within regularly scheduled news-interview programs. If he does not accept, then free time cannot be given to Senator Goldwater without violating the basic-fairness policy of broadcasting.

Yesterday's F.C.C. ruling is not apt to disturb President Johnson unduly. So long as he appears in the nightly newscasts, surrounded by huge crowds, it could be more practical politics than becoming involved in the questions and answers of a news conference.

It is the viewer who has been the chief loser under Section 315. The remedy lies with Congress, not the F.C.C., but the sheer power of TV precludes the likelihood of early action. The political influence of the medium is simply too great for its control in a campaign year to be kept out of partisan strategic considerations. Section 315 is but a symptom of a problem of growing seriousness, a problem that deserves the public concern for which responsible broadcasters have been asking.

F.C.C. Chief Backs Equal Time With Some Minor Modifications

Henry Call for Amendments for More Free Broadcasts

By LAWRENCE E. DAVIES

Special to The New York Times

SAN FRANCISCO, Jan. 15—The chairman of the Federal Communications Commission opposed here today the repeal of the equal-time requirement for political campaign broadcasts.

However, the chairman, E. William Henry, proposed changes in the controversial Section 315 of the Communications Act.

He called attention to recent denunciations of the section by the executives of the broadcasting networks and then declared:

"Well, at the risk of being run over by this bandwagon, I would like to enlist today as an advocate of equality. For my fundamental response to them is rather like Andrew Jackson's instruction to his troops at the Battle of New Orleans: 'Boys, elevate them guns a little lower'."

Mr. Henry made his proposals and covered other problems of the broadcasting business in a speech to the Commonwealth Club of California, in a news conference that preceded it and in a question-and-answer period following the talk at the Sheraton-Palace Hotel.

Cites $40 Million Estimate

The chairman painted a backdrop that included an estimate of expenditures of $40 million by political television and radio broadcasts during the 1964 campaign, half at the national level.

Asserting that repeal of Section 315 would "profoundly alter the condition of political debate in this country," he advocated:

¶That broadcasters be required to grant free time equal to that bought by a major candidate — to be divided between that candidate and his rival.

¶That with respect to free time, broadcasters provide equal time only for candidates of parties that polled a specified percentage of the vote in the last election or who qualified through a petition procedure. The percentage he suggested was 4 or 5.

¶That broadcasters insure some free time for minority candidates.

Repealing Section 315, Mr. Henry asserted, would enable broadcasters to censor political campaigns. Repeal also would make broadcasters subject to libel suits, he said, and they should not have this "burden."

Mr. Henry said that 171 television stations with 75 owners served the nation's 50 top markets with nearly three-fourths of the homes having television sets. Nine organizations, he siad, controlled three-quarters of the stations reaching 40 per cent of the homes with television.

"Do we really want to put broadcasters in a position," Mr. Henry asked, "to say to candidates, 'If you want to reach the people through this medium, you must do so on our terms and in the way we think best?' I think not."

He said his "doubts about the wisdom of the repeal of Section 315 do not stem from a low estimate of the fairness and objectivity of broadcasters; they arise much more out of questions concerning the wisdom of placing that power in the hands of any single group of men."

January 16, 1965

Roosevelt Asks TV Networks to Allot Time Fairly

By DOUGLAS ROBINSON

Special to The New York Times

SYRACUSE, Sept. 17—Franklin D. Roosevelt Jr., the Liberal party's candidate for Governor, called on the television networks tonight to work cut a "fair allocation" of paid television time during the campaign.

In the first major speech of his campaign, Mr. Roosevelt complained that the personal wealth of Governor Rockefeller and the coffers of the Democratic party behind its nominee, City Council President Frank D. O'Connor, was "giving them a monopoly."

News Coverage is 'Fair'

"I hope shortly to raise a little money in order to buy some time, but my opponents meanwhile are buying up all of the available time," Mr. Roosevelt told 500 delegates at the regional convention of the United States Junior Chamber of Commerce.

The candidate made it clear that he was not raising an issue about television news coverage, which he said had been "eminently fair."

"I am contending that there is something fundamentally wrong with a system that places a candidate who cannot pour millions into television at a fundamental disadvantage," he said.

Mr. Roosevelt asserted that he had been unsuccessful in persuading Governor Rockefeller and Mr. O'Connor to meet with him on the matter "for the purpose of limiting expenditures."

"But they are not the only ones who have a responsibility in this matter," he said. "Do not the television networks themselves have a responsibility to our democratic system which can only be fulfilled if there is an equitable allocation of television time?"

Mr. Roosevelt, who hopes to raise $600,000 for his campaign, said he suspected that if he did get the funds. "I may have to get down on bended knee to plead with the television networks to sell me time."

In his speech, which was liberally sprinkled with references to "my father" and "my mother," Mr. Roosevelt attacked political bossism.

Reiterates Primary Call

He repeated his call for statewide primaries and urged a program of judicial reform that would include a statute barring court employes from participating in politics.

He also advocated the placing of Boards of Election commissioners under civil service to "enormously reduce the power of the old-line machines to harass by technicality and legalism the insurgent and independent candidate."

In New York City, the commissioners are appointed by the City Council upon the recommendation of the two major parties.

Mr. Roosevelt also recommended a state code of ethics that would bar party officials, as well as legislators and their employees, from practicing law before state agencies.

The candidate made two references to Martin Tananbaum, president of Yonkers Raceway, whom Mr. O'Connor is reported to have ruled out of an active role in the Democratic campaign.

Mr. Roosevelt referred to Mr. Tananbaum as the "czar of the Yonkers Race Track" and said he was among a handful of bosses who got together in secret "to divide up the spoils." He also said that Mr. Tananbaum was "leading the fundraising pack" for the Democrats.

Earlier in the day, Mr. Roosevelt marched a short way up Fifth Avenue in the annual Steuben Day Parade. He got a warm response from the crowd, who recognized him easily since, at 6 feet 4 inches, he towered over other politicians and officials, including Mr. O'Connor.

The cry of "There's Roosevelt!" ran through the spectators.

Although they marched in the same rank, Mr. Roosevelt and Mr. O'Connor ignored each other. Governor Rockefeller however, gave Mr. Roosevelt a warm handshake in the grandstand.

Before leaving for Syracuse, the Liberal candidate issued a statement saying that the O'Connor strategy to hide Mr. Tananbaum for the duration of the campaign wil fool no one."

Mr. Roosevelt repeated previous charges that Mr. Tananbaum had participated in the selection of the Beame-O'Connor mayoral ticket last year and in the selection of this year's Democratic slate. He also renewed his challenge to debate Mr. O'Connor on the issue. Yonkers Raceway is one of three tracks that are under investigation for the alleged fixing of races.

September 18, 1966

Stanton Tells Senate Committee Equal Time Rule Is Unworkable

President of C.B.S. Declares Curbs on Broadcasters Hurt Election Coverage

WASHINGTON, July 20 (AP) — The equal time requirement of the Federal Communications Act is wrong and unworkable, Dr. Frank Stanton, president of the Columbia Broadcasting System, said today.

He told the Senate Communications subcommittee that the provision "prevents the broadcast media from realizing their full potential as effective tools of Democracy during the critical period of election campaigns."

The subcommittee is considering bills on radio-television coverage of political campaigns and elections.

Dr. Stanton opposed proposals that would require stations to give free time to candidates. He opposed, too, any efforts to curb the practice under which broadcasters project the outcome of elections on the basis of returns from key areas.

Bruce Dennis, president of the Radio Television News Directors Association, also opposed the free time proposal and urged that the equal time rule be repealed or limited.

Under the equal time requirement, stations must make the same amount of time available to all candidates for a given office.

A station that staged a debate as a public service between the two major candidates for an office would be subject to demands for equal time from minor parties.

The equal time requirement was suspended for the 1960 Presidential race, allowing debates between the Democratic and Republican candidates.

Mr. Stanton proposed that the equal time requirement be eliminated for Federal, state and local elections.

"Broadcasters ought to be free to cover all significant elections and all significant candidates," he commented.

The president of C.B.S. told the subcommittee that a bill to require free time for Federal, state and, where feasible, local, offices made no distinction between elections and primaries or between party nominees and self-declared candidates.

The legislation, he said, would create critical time problems for broadcasters "from the sheer volume of political broadcasts, accomplishing nothing except the alienation of audiences from candidates and stations alike."

Dr. Stanton also told the Senators that studies had shown there was no foundation to criticism that the projection of election results had influenced voters in areas where the polls had not yet closed.

"There is too much interest in elections for the national temperament to endure an information blackout," he added.

Associated Press Wirephoto

Dr. Frank Stanton, president of Columbia Broadcasting System, appearing before the Senate panel.

McCarthy Complains to F.C.C. On Denial of Equal TV Time

By E. W. KENWORTHY
Special to The New York Times

WASHINGTON, Dec. 22 — Senator Eugene J. McCarthy filed with the Federal Communications Commission today a formal complaint against the Columbia Broadcasting System for refusing to provide him equal time to respond to President Johnson's television and radio broadcast last Tuesday.

Meanwhile, the National Broadcasting Company and the American Broadcasting Company announced that they, too, were rejecting the Minnesota Senator's request for time to answer the President's statements linking Mr. McCarthy's bid for the Democratic Presidential nomination to Senator Robert F. Kennedy of New York.

Senator McCarthy's office said that it had discovered the rejections by N.B.C. and A.B.C. after it drafted the text of its telegram to the F.C.C. and had amended the telegram to request that its complaint against C.B.S. be treated as a complaint against all three networks.

Choice Is Favored

Senator Kennedy said before Senator McCarthy's formal announcement of his entrance into five Presidential primaries that he favored giving the voters a choice but that he expected Mr. Johnson to get the nomination.

The basis of Mr. McCarthy's request for equal time was President Johnson's reply when he was asked what effect "the candidacy of Senator McCarthy and the position of Senator Robert Kennedy will have on the Democratic party."

The President said:

"I just don't know—I don't know what the effect of the Kennedy-McCarthy movement is having in the country."

He went on to say that he was "not privileged to all the conversations that may have taken place" between the two Senators, adding:

"I just observe they have had some meetings and some discussions. I do know the interest of both of them in the Presidency and the ambition of both of them. I see that reflected from time to time."

In using the phrase "the Kennedy - McCarthy movement," President Johnson appeared to indicate that he gave credence to suggestions that Senator McCarthy was a "stalking-horse" for Senator Kennedy.

According to this view, if Senator McCarthy wins two or three primaries, or even does well in them, he will step aside to make way for a full-scale challenge at the convention by the late President's brother, who is more of a national figure than he is.

Senator McCarthy and Senator Kennedy have both criticized the President's Vietnam policy.

Reasons for Request

In requesting the networks for equal time on Dec. 20, Senator McCarthy contended the following:

¶Under section 315 of the Communications Act, broadcast stations must grant all candidates for the same office equal opportunity to present their views. Mr. Johnson is obviously a candidate even though he has not announced.

¶The phrase "Kennedy-McCarthy movement" was "inaccurate" and constituted "a personal attack" upon him, which he was entitled to answer.

¶Under the F.C.C. "general fairness" doctrine, he should have opportunity to reply to President Johnson's statement on the Vietnam war.

In his formal complaint today, Mr. McCarthy stressed that the networks and the agency would be unfair if they allowed the President to use his office for campaigning while maintaining the fiction that he was not a candidate because he had not announced his candidacy.

F.C.C. Issues Statement

For the networks to pretend that President Johnson is not a candidate for re-election, Mr. McCarthy said, "is to deny a fact which every American child knows."

Therefore, he went on, "what is at stake here is the integrity of the American communications system."

"An incumbent President has built-in advantages enough," he said, "in communicating with the people. To give him this added advantage is to turn a communications system of America into a political engine for the re-election of incumbent Presidents."

The complaint was filed for Senator McCarthy by Blair Clark, his campaign manager.

Meanwhile, the F.C.C. challenged a contention by James Reston of The New York Times that the agency's regulations covering broadcast political attacks were "impracticable if not unworkable and unconstitutional."

The commission issued the following statement concerning a column by Mr. Reston in today's issue of The Times:

"Mr. Reston's column today has a number of errors and misconceptions that should be corrected.

"The main error in the column is the assertion that the F.C.C. rule on personal attack enables any politician to demand free time to reply to anything he considers an attack by another politician or even a news commentator.

"The F.C.C. rule explicitly states that it is inapplicable where personal attacks are made by candidates, their authorized spokesmen or those associated with them in the campaign on other such candidates, their authorized spokesmen or persons associated with the candidates in the campaigns.

"The rule does take into account 'the practical operations' of politicians.

"The rule also takes into account the 'practical operations' of broadcasters. Bona fide newscasts and on the spot coverage of a bona fide news event are exempted from the personal attack rule. An attack made in an editorial or similar commentary, however, would come under the rule.

"In other words, if a station or network makes a personal attack on a politician in an editorial or similar commentary, it does have to notify him and give him an opportunity to respond.

"The commission has also made clear that a personal attack does not occur just because someone is mentioned or his views on some subject are vigorously disputed.

"The commission has stressed that the attack must be one involving such matters as a person's honesty or integrity—calling an official an embezzler or

a crook for example. Licensees have operated under these policies for over five years without any indication that debate has been inhibited or rendered less wide open or robust.

"Finally, it should be noted, that in the case specified by Mr. Reston, networks appear to have had no difficulty making a judgment on the complaint just as they have been able to handle fairness complaints in the past."

N.B.C. and A.B.C. Reply

The latest rejections of Mr. McCarthy's request for equal time were made in telegrams to Blair Clark in Washington from William R. McAndrew, president of N.B.C. News, and Everett H. Erlick, vice president and general counsel of the American Broadcasting Companies, Inc.

Both wires said that Mr. Johnson was not an announced candidate for the Presidential nomination and therefore the equal time requirement of Section 315 of the Communications Act did not apply.

The networks also rejected the contention that President Johnson's remarks constituted "a personal attack" on Mr. McCarthy.

A.B.C. said that Mr. McCarthy had been afforded an opportunity to respond to the President's remarks on the network's radio and television facilities last Wednesday.

It said that the Senator is scheduled to appear on A.B.C.'s "Issues and Answers" Jan. 7.

C.B.S. refused Senator McCarthy's request Thursday.

'EQUAL TIME' RULE CRITICIZED HERE

Theodore C. Sorensen has suggested that Congress should suspend the "equal time" requirement of the Communications Act as it applies to Presidential and Vice Presidential candidates for the duration of this year's national election campaign.

Such a step, he declared yesterday, would permit substantial amounts of free television and radio time to be allocated to Presidential candidates of the two major parties without requiring equal time for each of the dozen or so minor party candidates.

The suggestion was one of several about the role of broadcasting in the forthcoming election campaign. Mr. Sorensen, a former Presidential assistant, spoke at a monthly luncheon of the New York Chapter of American Women in Radio and Television held at the Plaza Hotel.

In urging temporary suspension of Section 315 of the Communications Act (the "equal time" provision), Mr. Sorensen said Congress should take such action "at the earliest opportunity" to free broadcasters from the restriction during the primaries and the preconvention campaign.

Other Suggestions Noted

Among other steps to help the American people choose their President in 1968, Mr. Sorensen suggested the major

TV and radio networks give the two major Presidential candidates, free of charge, an hour a week of prime time to be scheduled at the same time for the eight weeks before the election.

Four of these hour-long broadcasts, he said, could be used for joint appearances or debates between the two Presidential candidates as a means of dramatizing their differences, and the other four could be divided into half-hour segments to be used as the candidates please.

He also said Congress should prohibit purchase of network announcements more than five minutes long by or in behalf of Presidential or Vice Presidential candidates. Such a limit, he said, might persuade the parties "to make corresponding reductions in their broadcast budgets." These ran to almost $25-million dollars in 1964, when nearly half went for the Presidential campaign.

He also endorsed a proposal made earlier by Dr. Frank Stanton, president of the Columbia Broadcasting System, for a national voting holiday. If the polls all over the country were open during the same 24-hour period, he pointed out, computer projections based on returns from the Eastern states would be unable to influence the voting in Western states.

Mr. Sorensen, the author of "Kennedy," a biography of the late President, is currently a partner in the law firm of Paul, Weiss, Rifkind, Wharton & Garrison.

EDITORIAL RULES OF F.C.C. VOIDED

CHICAGO, Sept. 11 (UPI)—A Federal appeals court set aside today Federal Communications Commission rules requiring broadcasters to give equal time to persons subjected to criticism in editorials aired by radio and television stations.

The decision of the United States Court of Appeals for the Seventh Circuit was unanimous. It was contained in a 30-page opinion drafted by Judge Luther M. Swygert, with Judges Roger J. Kiley and Latham Castle concurring.

The opinion said: "In view of the vagueness of the commission's rules, the burden they impose on licensees, and the possibility they raise of both commission censorship and licensee self-censorship, we conclude that the personal attack and political editorial rules would contravene the First Amendment."

The petition for review of

the rules, adopted in July, 1967, was filed by the Radio and Television News Directors Association and was joined by eight broadcasting companies.

Separate petitions filed by Columbia Broadcasting System and the National Broadcasting Company were consolidated with that of the news directors.

The decision nullified two F.C.C. rules—one requiring a station to offer the subject of editorial criticism a reasonable opportunity to respond, and one requiring a station making a political endorsement to offer other candidates time to respond.

The opinion said, "Allowing the [F.C.C.] to selectively enforce the rules so as to prevent the expression of views it believes to be contrary to the best interests of the American public would cast the commission in the role of a censor, contrary to the express provisions of the Federal Communications Act."

The court said the rules were "unclear" and the F.C.C. had failed to clarify them.

TV: 'Equal Time' Masks Extent of Curb on Reporting

Broadcasters Escape Public Obligation

By JACK GOULD

THE controversy over tele-vised Presidential debates has obscured a more important issue regarding the home screen in an election year. Last week's failure of the Senate to suspend Section 315 of the Federal Communications Act not only thwarted the remote chance of face-to-face confrontations of the candidates; it also further cemented a stringent curb on the volume of badly needed independent political reporting by television.

The most widely publicized provision of Section 315 is the stipulation that if one qualified candidate receives free time, all candidates must receive time. Had the law not been suspended in 1960 for the four hours of debate between John F. Kennedy and Richard M. Nixon, 44 hours of free time would have been due the other 22 qualified candidates. One eligible party for coast-to-coast exposure in 1964 was the Universal party: it received 19 votes in California.

In the absence of any definition of what is a qualified candidate, the broadcasters are not going to volunteer unlimited free time, so it is left to the politicians to decide the matter every four years.

●

President Johnson did not want debates four years ago and Mr. Nixon does not now. But once again the smoke-screen of debating debates serves a dual purpose: Selfish broadcasters are spared any economic sacrifice, and the politicians retain control over the television medium.

The unpublicized sleeper in Section 315 is paragraph 3, which exempts "the bona fide news documentary" from the equal time obligation. But in parenthesis the law pointedly notes that such a documentary can only be done "if the appearance of the candidate is incidental to the presentation of the subjects covered by the news documentary."

The effect is obvious. No network can do a documentary on a Presidential contest and still keep a candidate incidental to the content. It would be like doing a special on the invasion of Czechoslovakia and treating the Soviet soldiers as an incidental contribution to the event.

The Columbia Broadcasting System, for example, prepared an hour on George C. Wallace but has not been able to use it as a separate entity. Since regularly scheduled newscasts are exempt both from equal time restrictions and the incidental nonsense, a short sequence on the former Governor's regime in Alabama was slipped into Roger Mudd's telecast on Saturday evening.

Included in the C.B.S. sequence was the testimony of several local politicians who said the power of the Wallace machine was absolute and extended from the courthouse to the Governor's mansion.

One of those interviewed was a young Alabama delegate who had favored Senator Edward M. Kennedy at the Democratic National Convention in Chicago. Upon his return, he said, he and his family had been subjected to so much harassment by Wallace supporters that he had felt it wise to retire from politics and had done so.

Paragraph 3 seemingly also prevents television from matching issue by issue the positions of Mr. Nixon, Vice President Humphrey and Mr. Wallace. Only the format of a documentary has the elasticity in time and movement to catch up with candidates talking at different times and different places on a common issue. It would be no substitute for the drama of debates, to be sure, but it could pinpoint the numbing ambivalance that makes this campaign so monotonous and uninspiring.

●

Paragraph 4 of Section 315 theoretically exempts "on-the-spot coverage of bona fide news events." But when United Press International agreed in 1962 to sponsor a gubernatorial debate in California, and the C.B.S. stations in Los Angeles and San Francisco planned to cover the full proceedings, the Federal Communications Commission ruled the idea an evasion.

Under that ruling, which no one had the gumption to appeal to the United States Supreme Court, it clearly appears that TV can only pick up snippets from any

Better News Programs an Obvious Remedy

debate, whether arranged by a group of newspapers, the League of Women Voters or the Boy Scouts of America. Section 315, it will be realized some day, affects political life not only on the screen but off, simply because television does.

By effectively barring expanded documentary coverage of political news in a political year, the act of Congress has the practical consequence of ridding all prime evening time of tough and impartial reporting. The law lets the parties take over the peak viewing hours with paid political broadcasts and obnoxious spot announcements. Advertising is exempt from equal time; journalism, is not.

●

One drastic remedy that could be instituted by the networks before 1972 is a regular prime time hour-long newscast that presumably would be exempt from all restrictions of Section 315, such as the deserving "News Front" on Channel 13 and the Eastern Educational Network. Congress never will end the quadrennial farce about debates and equal time. Responsible broadcasting alone can force a change by rescheduling and enlarging its evening news fare to make Section 315 academic. It could even give a break to fringe candidates, the men and women first ruled off the public airways by the law designed to prevent their disfranchisement.

October 14, 1968

Why Should Mr. Nixon Have The Show All to Himself?

By JACK GOULD

DEMOCRACY's traditional basis of checks and balances between the administrative, legislative and judicial branches of Government has been knocked askew by the television age. As matters stand, the White House has all the advantages of gaining access to the minds of the voting viewer while, for practical purposes, Congress and the Supreme Court are blacked out. The picture of Government on the home screen is badly distorted precisely at a moment when the country faces a multitude of grave issues.

If the public primarily relies on TV for essential information on public affairs—and on a national level the point hardly is open to serious dispute—the mass audience only hears the full text of remarks by the President. Otherwise there are corridor interviews or superficial talks with Congressmen on weekends and usually nothing more than a few excerpts from what may be landmark decisions by the Supreme Court. Noble statements about true balance notwithstanding, the set-owner remote from the capital is not a genuine party to his full Government in action.

If, as James Reston recently observed, President Nixon is going over the heads of Congress to reach the people via TV, while rebuttals or elaborations by members of Congress are heard only in the often-deserted chambers of the House and Senate, perhaps the fault lies less with TV than with the legislators and jurists themselves.

*

The President, with nothing more than a telephone call from his office, can order up network coverage whenever he wants to. Mr. Nixon's adroit choice of times—in the middle of newscasts or movies—suggests that he knows how ratings can serve his purposes.

However, except for the occasional Senate committee that welcomes TV's presence at a hearing, the video medium is barred from the floor of Congress, largely at the instigation of senior members. To be sure, much of the most important business of Congress is done in committee sessions, but if the Senators and Representatives knew that TV would record their open deliberations—or let pictures of the barren chambers speak for themselves—isn't it conceivable that Congressional attendance would increase? Might this not be, as well, a step toward reacquainting the mass audience with the separation of powers? If the power of Congress has waned in recent years, is it altogether coincidental that it has been a TV absentee?

Years ago there was the argument that with TV's presence Congressmen would become "hams" playing to the camera, with the result that many speeches would become dull, interminable filibusters. In the televising of many state legislatures, however, this has not proved to be the case. With the presence of the medium taken for granted, as at the United Nations, the legislators address themselves to the business at hand. And if they are persistently absent or taking a snooze, the reaction among their own constituencies back home might be interesting.

By barring TV, Congress—consciously or not—is giving the President ever-increasing power and diminishing its own collective influence with the electorate. Many other factors, of course, are responsible for this trend but there is something amiss in a democracy in the electronic era when the public never sees its chosen parliament actually at work.

*

The Supreme Court has been even stricter with respect to TV's presence. Why? All the preliminaries, where a defendant might be ill at ease or a cheap sideshow might develop, have been completed. The court is entertaining a final legal appeal restricted to attorneys for the competing parties and the news media are legitimately interested not in minor matters but the landmark decisions which can and have affected the country's future course.

The dignity of the Court could readily be maintained by instant ouster of any TV representative who violated prescribed conditions. One can only speculate on how much better the country might have understood the Court's rulings on desegregation of schools and many other issues of social significance had the proceedings been televised nationwide. The average soul does not have the time to pore over yards of printed text but there is something immensely absorbing in seeing for one's self the personalities and demeanor of the lawyers and justices, and listening first-hand to the arguments and questions that develop during the proceedings.

It has been contended, and reasonably so, that the commercial networks would not devote the hours of time necessary for total coverage of either Congressional or Supreme Court deliberations. But between total coverage and no coverage at all there are many compromises that could serve the public interest. There would be occasions when pre-emptions would be as warranted as in the case of a Presidential address; the hour-long documentary format could embrace a great deal of information about the currently unrepresented branches of Government. Or such programing would be made to order for noncommercial TV and might materially strengthen public TV's appeal for Federal funds.

*

When the founding fathers established the separation of powers they had no way of anticipating that electronics might bypass their intentions insofar as the public's involvement is concerned. But in the 1970's television undoubtedly has the greatest influence on polls—and polls, in turn, have shaped political action. Government and television are prone to constant bickering on matters of either scant or distant interest to the viewer. They should seriously reconsider whether their relationship with one another, and also their relationship with the viewing public, do not demand review in light of today's technology. Too many doors are still closed in Washington for the country's good.

DEMOCRATS WEIGH PLEA ON C.B.S. BAN

Party, Refused Time, May Take Case to the F.C.C.

By R. W. APPLE JR.
Special to The New York Times

WASHINGTON, March 21— The Democratic National Committee has asked lawyers to evaluate the legal situation arising from the Columbia Broadcasting System's refusal to sell the party television time for a documentary and fund-raising appeal.

If they conclude that the party has a case, committee sources said today, a new approach will probably be made to the network. If that fails, the sources indicated, the party is likely to appeal to the Federal Communications Commission or instigate legal action.

The background to the dispute—another chapter in the complex, politically significant relationship between parties and broadcasters—was outlined as follows by leading Democrats:

Early in January, two New Yorkers, who have been substantial contributors to the party in the past, offered to raise money for a prime-time Democratic televison show, including a 25-minute documentary followed by a five-minute appeal for contributions.

At first, the plan was to use stock footage and to broadcast the program on only one network. The cost would have been about $130,000. Later it was decided to shoot new film and try for all three networks. The cost was increased to about $300,000.

April 22 Was Date

The National Committee chose Wednesday, April 22, at 8:30 P.M. as the air time.

The National Broadcasting Company agreed to the plan, although it suggested another time. C.B.S., after negotiations conducted primarily by telephone, said no. When C.B.S. turned it down, the committee decided not to approach the third network—the American Broadcasting Company.

In a farewell speech to the National Committee on March 5, the outgoing chairman, Senator Fred R. Harris of Oklahoma, said that he was "very disturbed" by the C.B.S. refusal. His successor as party chairman, Lawrence F. O'Brien, has decided to press the matter if possible.

The committee sources declined to identify the lawyers working on the problem, but one of them is presumably Joseph A. Califano Jr., who served under President Johnson as a domestic adviser. Mr. Califano was named general counsel of the committee today, succeeding David Ginsburg.

Richard W. Jencks, president of the C.B.S. Broadcast Group, said in a telephone interview that the network's policies "do not permit the sale of time for presenting currently controversial points of view except during electoral campaigns."

Long-Standing Rule

Mr. Jencks said that this was a long-standing rule at C.B.S. A year ago, he recalled, the network turned down a proposal for a broadcast of a rally by opponents of the antiballistic missile. It has also refused to sell time for a drama program assembled by United Nations supporters.

"The policy has its roots," Mr. Jencks added, "in our obligation to give fair, objective over-all coverage to the issues of the day. To a lesser degree, it has its roots in our belief that our own news organization can give a fairer presentation."

If Representatives or Senators up for re-election in 1970 were to appear on the program, he said, the network might be obligated under Federal Communications Commission regulations to sell their opponents equal time—or even give it to them. Democratic officials take the view that the 1970 election year has already begun—the first primary elections were held Tuesday in Illinois—and that their request to buy time is no different from a request made in a Presidential year.

Fulbright Calls Full Access to TV For Congressmen Vital to U.S.

By CHRISTOPHER LYDON
Special to The New York Times

WASHINGTON, Aug. 4 — Senator J. W. Fulbright said today that the balance in American Government would be effectively destroyed unless Congress could command automatic access to network television—the same access that the President now enjoys by informal courtesy of the broadcasting industry.

The Arkansas Democrat's proposal to legislate Congress's right of access was immediately challenged by the commercial networks as an invasion of journalistic freedom.

Senator John O. Pastore, chairman of the Senate Communications Subcommittee, which opened hearings on the Fulbright resolution this morning, indicated that he opposed the legislation but hoped to achieve the same goal — a wider airing of Congressional views — through negotiations with network officials.

Though Senator Fulbright's solution was controversial, his statement of the problem seemed likely to dominate the hearings that will continue through the week.

"Communication is power," he said, "and exclusive access to it is a dangerous, unchecked power."

Senator Pastore pledged a fundamental review of the power of communications, studying the traditional doctrine of "fairness" in broadcasting and the emerging question of "access" that asks, in effect: what people, and what kind of ideas, will get to use the medium that is increasingly recognized as an indispensable device for getting the nation's attention?

The Federal Communications Commission is grappling this week with many of the same issues—including the right of a meatcutters union in Florida to use radio ads to promote a boycott, the Democratic National Committee's demand that their fund-raising TV commercials not be rejected simply because they are "controversial" and the right of different coalitions of Senators to answer President Nixon, and each other, on the subject of the war in Southeast Asia.

The F.C.C. members will be the last witnesses to testify before Senator Pastore's subcommittee. Whether the commission will vote on its pending cases in time to seize the initiative in resolving the broader issues is not clear.

Senator Fulbright emphasized this morning that the focus of his bill was "institutional, not partisan," and that he was more concerned about the balance among Government's branches, than the balance of Democratic and Republican parties.

His proposal, which would give voice to policy dissenters within the President's party, clearly reflected his own bitter experience as an opponent of former President Johnson's policy in Vietnam. Further, in the current situation, where a Republican President faces a predominantly Democratic Congress, his proposal would have the effect of designating Congressional leaders over the Democratic National Committee as the primary spokesmen of the opposition.

Senator Pastore and other members of the communications subcommittee doubted that Congress could ever state its composite view on important controversies in a clear and forceful voice. They also questioned whether Congress had any peculiar right to answer the President's TV appearances.

"If you give Congress the right to reply to the President," said Mr. Pastore, a Democrat from Rhode Island, "you may have to give everybody else the right to rely to the President—and to reply to the Congress, too."

Wrangling Foreseen

Senator Fulbright suggested that the House and Senate should divide Congress's TV time evenly and that, within the respective branches, spokesmen for different issues would emerge naturally and time would be allotted fairly—without squabbling.

Other Senators suspected that the rivalry to become TV advocates would become a bone of endless contention and that on the most important issues, Congress would be unable to agree on a spokesman and thereby default its time. In the Senate, Mr. Pastore said, "I can give you the names of five guys that would never give the rest of us a chance."

The spectacle of endless debate within Congress would actually undermine significant confrontations with the President on issues, Senator Charles E. Goodell, Republican of New York, argued.

March 22, 1970

"Flesh out the fairness doctrine," Senator Goodell proposed instead. "See to it that the great public issues are debated on television, but delegate the supervision of the debates to the F.C.C. and the networks."

Insisting that Congress must set the rules, Senator Fulbright stated explicitly that his proposal was a conscious indictment of television journalism. TV news is obsessed with trivia, he said, and even the interview programs are too full of artificial conflict to permit the development of ideas. Left to its own devices, Senator Fulbright charged, television will never find it in its business interest to give Congress the attention it deserves.

Network officials charged in written statements today that Senator Fulbright's proposal would undermine TV's independent role as "auditor" of the news and make the medium a simple "conduit" of Government policy. The Presidents of the three commercial networks will have the opportunity for a fuller, direct response before the communications subcommittee tomorrow morning.

Before the F.C.C. and the Senate, the real heart of the continuing controversy is the commission's "fairness doctrine," which insists on balanced treatment of controversial isues but makes individual stations the arbiters of what is controversial and what is balanced.

With respect to access, traditional policy makes license holders accountable for everything they broadcast, and gives them a corresponding freedom to pick and choose their programming — not only in news and entertainment but among commercials, too.

In The Nation: Putting Congress on the Tube

By TOM WICKER

Any number of objections can and will be raised to Senator J. W. Fulbright's demand that Congress get automatic access to network television, just as the President does. But this demand nevertheless recognizes two fundamental facts of political life today.

The first, of course, is the power of the medium, which obviously is altering the nature of government and politics. The second is not so obvious; it is the fact that in the late twentieth century the United States has developed a Presidential form of government in which Congress, no matter which party controls it, plays the role of loyal opposition.

White House-Senate Clash

This has been most apparent in recent years in the developing conflict between the White House and Congress, particularly the Senate, over control of foreign policy and the war-making power. To the extent that opposition to the war in Vietnam, for instance, has had an institutional base, it has not been so much in either party as in the Senate.

This struggle began against President Johnson, and it is not fundamentally different now that President Nixon is at the other end of Pennsylvania Avenue (except that more Democratic Senators now can be counted upon). Nor is the clash limited to foreign policy matters; Congressional resistance to development of the ABM system, for example, is centered almost as much on the question of domestic spending priorities and technical feasibility as on the international implications of the system.

Congress still is organized on the outmoded thesis that the party of the President supports him and that the other party opposes him. In fact, that distinction has little meaning any more; the Republicans on the Senate Finance Committee are just as strong in opposition to Mr. Nixon's welfare reform as is Senator Russell Long, the Democratic chairman. Senator Everett Dirksen used to seem less the opposition leader and more nearly Lyndon Johnson's spokesman, and there have been times in this Congress when the opposite has appeared to be the case between Hugh Scott, the Republican leader, and Mr. Nixon.

The major reason for this state of affairs is suggested by the basic difficulty with Senator Fulbright's proposal: Who will speak for Congress? This branch of government represents a huge collection of constituencies, it is divided into two houses, numerous committees and unofficial principalities, and hundreds of personalities. It cannot in the nature of the case speak with a single voice.

It cannot, either on television or in government itself; that is why, in the face of the massive and complex tasks of the twentieth century, the power of the relatively unified and coherent executive branch has so far overshadowed that of Congress. The executive branch, of course, has its own warring constituencies and conflicting interests, but in the Presidency it has a powerfully consolidating office at the top. And if there has been a discernible trend within the executive branch in recent years, it has been the steady centralization of even more power in the hands of the President and his staff.

The net effect has been that an executive branch of increasing power has been speaking for something it defines and then labels "the national interest," while Congress, in its Balkanized fashion, usually represents less-than-national interests. Sometimes, as in the case of various predatory lobbies, or cities like Charleston, S. C., or powerful interest groups, it does this all too well.

More often, in trying to represent some other view against the "national interest" as defined by the executive branch — for instance, in questioning the secret war in Laos or in increasing funds for some domestic social program over the President's budget — Congress finds itself at a disadvantage.

How much more will that be the case in the years to come as the nation gets its information more and more completely from television, and if—as now threatens to be the case—access to television is limited primarily to a single powerful man at the head of an executive branch that is more and more under the dominance of his personal staff.

That is what concerns Senator Fulbright, what ought to concern even Republican leaders in Congress, what must surely perplex television officials, who are already besieged by the claims of the two major political parties to network access. Perhaps, in the case of Congress, the answer lies in greatly increased television showings of the two houses and their committees at work; and that could have the useful side effect of forcing Congress at last to adopt an organization and procedures that could stand the harsh exposure of the tube.

August 5, 1970

August 6, 1970

TV Heads to Consider More Time for Congress

By CHRISTOPHER LYDON
Special to The New York Times

WASHINGTON, Aug. 5—The presidents of the three commercial television networks said today they would consider new, voluntary means of balancing their coverage of Congress and the President — possibly including grants of prime evening time in which Congress could pick its spokesmen, issues and format.

But all three executives, testifying before a continuing Senate study of fairness and access problems in the regulation of TV, said that legislation that made the airing of Congressional views mandatory would interfere with their freedom as journalists.

The Repubican National Committee proposed today that Congress open its doors to expanded coverage by a simple change in its working rules.

"It is inconceivable to us," said W. Theodore Person, a special counsel to the Republican party on communications, "that if the Senate had called a 2- or 3-hour session in prime time to debate the Cambodian action, the networks could have been kept away — except by barring the doors as you now do."

'Intriguing' Thought

Senator John O. Pastore, the subcommittee chairman, pressing for a negotiated settlement of the dispute over time to match the President's use of TV, said the thought of televising House and Senate proceedings was "intriguing." Others suggested that the Senate, which continues to ban still photographs in its chamber and is only now installing an electric sound system, would never approve the change.

At the same time the networks were pledging to think of new ways to give Congress more voice, Dr. Frank Stanton, president of the Columbia Broadcasting System, indicated he was considering some retrenchment of the newly inaugurated "loyal opposition" series.

Senator Robert P. Griffin of Michigan, the Republican whip, told Dr. Stanton angrily, "you've given equal time to the

The New York Times (by Mike Lien)

Television network presidents appearing before Senate panel on fairness are, from left, Julian Goodman of N.B.C., Leonard H. Goldenson of A.B.C. and Dr. Frank Stanton of C.B.S.

was unduly harsh and said, "If this is the way the 'loyal opposition' continues, we would have to reconsider our policy."

In his original announcement of the "loyal opposition" idea, he said he referred to the performance by Lawrence F. O'Brien, chairman of the Democratic National Committee, in the first program in the series early last month.

Who's going to answer that?" Senator Griffin asked.

Dr. Stanton first insisted that "unless we're forced by the Federal Communications Commission, we won't offer any time for an answer"—such as the Republican National Committee has demanded.

Senator Griffin argued that the prospect of partisan rebuttals would force President Nixon to avoid television or to take an equally aggressive, partisan tone himself. When he asked Dr. Stanton a second time whether "you'll allow these hatchet political attacks to continue," the C.B.S. head seemed to agree that Mr. O'Brien's style

in June, Mr. Stanton said C.B.S. contemplated giving the out-of-power party four or five 25-minute time segments each year. Today, however, he said he had made no comment to the Democrats for any specific number of programs, and had no plans now for showing a second installment.

"This is some improvement," Senator Griffin commented.

Joseph A. Califano, general counsel to the Democratic National Committee, said that until today the party had been expecting that the next round in the "loyal opposition" series would come "soon."

Network Heads Disapprove

Each of the network presidents disapproved the specific resolution that prompted the hearings, a proposal by Senator J. W. Fulbright, Democrat of Arkansas, to give Congress the right to pre-empt network time for the expression of its views.

"It is the public's right to be informed which is paramount," said Leonard H. Goldenson, president of the Ameri-

can Broadcasting Company, rather than the right of a particular Senator, Representative, political party or group to broadcast its views on a given subject.

"The freedom and flexibility afforded the broadcaster under the 'fairness doctrine' to select in good faith the spokesmen for the representative viewpoints seems the best means yet devised for insuring that the public is exposed to all significant points of view on important public issues."

Broadcasting must use "independent news judgment to deal with political events as they occur," said Julian Goodman, president of the National Broadcasting Company.

Senator Edmund S. Muskie of Maine, who has been working separately on behalf of the Senate Democratic Policy Committee to get broader access to television for Congressional leadership, testified this morning in support of Senator Fulbright's resolution but said he thought the same objective could be won by negotiation.

August 6, 1970

282

F.C.C. Backs TV Industry Over Right to Refuse Time

By CHRISTOPHER LYDON
Special to The New York Times

WASHINGTON, Aug. 6—As Senate hearings continued on whether Congress had the right to free television time to explain its views, the Federal Communications Commission reasserted today the pre-eminent right of the broadcasting industry to decide which spokesmen and which ideas could use its facilities.

In the first of two decisions on the question of access to the airwaves, the commission upheld the right of WTOP, the Post-Newsweek radio station here, to reject the antiwar spot ads of Business Executives Move for Vietnam Peace.

In the second case, the commission declared that broadcasters must accept the Democratic National Committee's fund-raising commercials but might refuse to let those commercials be used for the discussion of policy issues.

The commission chairman, Dean Burch, appeared this afternoon before the Senate Communications Subcommittee. He explained that both actions rested on the doctrine that broadcasters, though they must give exposure to public controversies and treat them fairly, may pick and choose among different means of doing so.

"It is this right of the public to be informed," he said, restating the commission's 20-year-old Fairness Doctrine, "rather than any right on the part of the Government, any broadcast licensee or any individual member of the public to broadcast his own particular views on any matter, which is the foundation stone of the American system of broadcasting."

Nicholas Johnson, the one dissenter against the six-man commission majorities on both decisions today, said that the Constitution's guarantee of free speech supported a broad claim of access to television, which he said is now the principal medium of political communication.

He forecast a court test of the issue that would vindicate his position.

Judicial precedent, though not specifically addressed to broadcasting issues, "guarantees to individuals a right of access to forums generally open to the public for expression of views," he wrote in his dissent to the ruling on antiwar spot ads.

"The commission and the courts," he said, "must begin to draw guidelines for access to the broadcast frequencies, seeking to insure that the electronic media of 20th century communication are as open to the public as the soap boxes, public parks and town hall meetings of the last century."

Concessions Approved

The commission's decision on the Democratic National Committee's complaint expressed official approval of concessions that the commercial networks had already granted in the last three weeks.

The Democrats filed their complaint last May after the Columbia Broadcasting System had refused to sell them time for the solicitation of contributions and the discussion of public issues. The complaint sought a general ruling that broadcasters could not refuse paid time to "responsible entities, like the Democratic National Committee."

While the complaint was pending, C.B.S. announced a new series of free "loyal opposition" programs in which the Democratic party could respond to President Nixon, and it also declared it would sell one-minute spots for fund-raising.

At the same time, the American Broadcasting Company, which had formerly refused ads taking one side of a public issue, modified its policy but only for the benefit of national political parties.

The commission's decision today indicated that broadcasters need not go further. For example, they do not have to sell fund-raising ads to groups other than political parties, nor do they have to offer political parties more than one-minute spots for their commercials.

In dismissing the "right" to discuss issues, the commission said that the Democrats' request would have undermined the broadcasters' control over "the manner in which the public is to be informed."

Mr. Johnson, in his dissent, said that the commission should require broadcasters to accept all paid ads, commercial or political, on a two-year trial basis.

"If ghetto residents of our major cities wish to purchase announcements decrying the rat-infested, disease-ridden slums in which they are forced to live, they must be given their say," he said. "If the Daughters of the American Revolution wish to announce their support for the Vietnam war, they must be given their say.

"There will be time later to assess and evaluate—to consider, for example, whether the views of the rich predominate —at least, to a greater extent than they now predominate in mass media advertising."

Joseph A. Califano Jr., the general counsel to the Democratic National Committee, who had earlier pledged to appeal the case to the Supreme Court if necessary, said this evening that he could not comment in detail on the ruling until the commission's full text was released tomorrow.

Meanwhile, before the Senate Communications Subcommittee, the Westinghouse Broadcasting Company, the National Association of Broadcasters and the Corporation for Public Broadcasting all stated that it was both unnecessary and improper to give Congress a statutory authority to pre-empt TV time for the expression of its views.

Senator J. W. Fulbright, Democrat of Arkansas, has proposed such legislation, and Senator George S. McGovern, Democrat of South Dakota, endorsed it today.

Growing Fight for Access to The TV 'Soap Box'

WASHINGTON—Who gets to use television? Almost everybody would like to, but only one man, the President, is assured of the chance and even that is by courtesy, not right.

In three days of hearings last week, the Senate probed some of the emerging questions about access to TV: Should Congress, for example, be able to commandeer the nation's attention, via the networks, as the President so often does? Or does the "right of reply," if there is such a thing, fall rather to the party out of power—in this case the Democratic National Committee?

Does any general right of access rub off on individual citizens or representative groups? May policy advocates who can't get free time buy their way onto the air and hustle their ideas like any other commercial product? Or would rich corporations use such a license to tighten their grip on popular opinion?

Just how—come to think of it — has broadcasting managed all these years to avoid (except during political campaigns) controversial ads for public causes, the send - money - for - this and write - your - Congressman-about-that campaigns that have always been a staple of American newspapers?

Old Orthodoxies

But even as the hearings were raising these questions, the Federal Communications Commission, acting on petitions for air time, issued a dogged restatement of old orthodoxies that injected new fuel into the controversy.

The Business Executives Move for Vietnam Peace had appealed the refusal of WTOP, the Post-

Newsweek radio station here, to sell time for their antiwar spot ads. And the Democratic party, having been turned away from the Columbia Broadcasting System when it tried to buy a half-hour, asked for a general ruling that broadcasters could not make a policy of excluding fund solicitations or "controversy" when "responsible entities" offered to pay for the time.

Rejecting both petitions, the F.C.C. reasserted the doctrine that though listeners have a right to hear balanced treatment of public issues, no individual or group has a right to be heard. Thus, there is no right of access, the commission said, confirming the broadcaster's role as powerful "trustee" and gatekeeper of the public airwaves. Both decisions were supported by solid 6-to-1 majorities (with Nicholas Johnson in dissent) and substantial precedent at the F.C.C.

Yet no one expects the broader question to be dropped there. In the Senate, J. W. Fulbright, whose Foreign Relations Committee has suffered White House neglect under Democratic and Republican Presidents, is arguing that the vital balance of executive and legislative branches will be destroyed unless Congress wins automatic access to the networks, such as the President now enjoys. Further, the Democratic party, which fears bankruptcy and maybe oblivion if it can't reach potential donors through television, will surely appeal the F.C.C.'s new decision — to the Supreme Court if necessary.

Continuing Problem

The more these cases are studied, the more they will seem little fragments of a broad, continuing problem. At the F.C.C., the Amalgamated Meatcutters of Quincy, Fla., are still pressing their appeal against the local radio station that rejected their ads for a packing-house boycott. And before the Senate's communications subcommittee last week, Absalom Jordan, speaking for Black Efforts for Soul in Television, told Senator John O. Pastore that if it seems difficult for Congress to get a hearing, he should imagine the frustration of black Americans watching the white-owned media.

"Black people have a great deal of sympathy," Mr. Jordan said, "for the Democratic party and antiwar Senators who are just beginning to understand what it means to be denied access to the most powerful and persuasive means of communication. But we hope you continue to fight so that not only 535 Senators and Congressmen can have access to the public airwaves but also 22 million black people and, in fact, 180 million other Americans."

The new struggle over television is less a matter of "fairness" than "access"; and it springs less from President Nixon's record rate of prime-time appearances than from a lesson Mr. Nixon applied in his successful 1968 campaign: Don't submit to the interview shows and don't rely on the news; buy the time outright and deliver the message your own way.

Implicit in that theory and in the campaign for broader access to TV is a harsh critique of TV journalism. Senator Fulbright complained last week that TV news is mostly trivia and, in his demand for blocks of network time under strictly Congressional control, made a blunt claim for politicians that seemed to echo Vice President Agnew: "I think we should have something to say about what's news."

Others are saying that the networks as "trustees" of the public dialogue can't supply the necessary diversity or subjectivity on their own. C.B.S., in its recent offer to turn over four or five half-hours of prime time a year to the political party out of power, seems to have conceded the point indirectly.

Broadcasters, of course, see the demand for access as an infringement on their First Amendment freedom as newsmen. But increasingly, the case against them will be waged in terms of the same First Amendment's guarantee of free speech. "The electronic media of the 20th century," Commissioner Johnson said in his F.C.C. dissent last week, must be "as open to the public as the soapboxes, public parks and town hall meetings of the last century."

—CHRISTOPHER LYDON

Here They Come, Equal or Not

By JACK GOULD

IT is not often that viewers, lawyers, government officials, academic study groups and politicians find themselves chasing the same electronic butterflies. But every two or four years the same old dance recurs.

Between now and Election Day the mixed cast is certain to be bewitched or bewildered by assorted hassles over access to the airwaves by incumbent office holders and their challengers, and over the knotty question of whether both sides of controversial issues are being fairly presented.

Much of the confusion arises from assorted provisions of the Federal Communications Act, periodically interpreted and reinterpreted by the F.C.C. commissioners themselves; from decisions by the Supreme Court, and from the multitudinous bills before Congress that are always conveniently raised too late to disturb the knowing politicians.

A glossary of terms might be helpful. Public interest, convenience or necessity: these five words, taken from the Federal Communications Act, have generated argument and litigation for years. They define the ideal which a broadcaster commits himself to serve by reason of his license. But determining what kind of radio or TV is in the public interest can be as far-ranging and difficult as trying to persuade more than 200 million Americans to agree on anything.

There never will be complete agreement and probably there shouldn't be. But the oft-disputed phrase lies at the heart of assorted citizen complaints that a broadcaster's interpretation of the "public interest" may take the form of not getting too involved in the community, or of disenfranchising blacks, for instance, where an outlet may reflect the dominance of community white power.

*

FAIRNESS DOCTRINE: The "fairness doctrine," originally announced in 1949 and redefined since then, is designed to cover the problem of reporting controversial issues and presenting opposing viewpoints on each issue. The doctrine applies at all times in broadcasting, not merely in political years.

It was under the fairness doctrine, for instance, that the F.C.C. recently directed the networks to give time to opponents of President Nixon on the Indochina issue. As originally construed, the fairness doctrine affords wide latitude to the broadcaster himself in coping with the problem. Its essential philosophy is designed to judge whether the record of the broadcaster over a reasonable period of time was adequately balanced.

One weakness of the fairness doctrine is that under past F.C.C. laxity a broadcaster could be fair by giving *neither* side to a dispute any time on the air, a practice, incidentally, which didn't hurt his income from reruns of old movies, either.

It was in December, 1966, that the imaginative John C. Banzhaf 3d, a private citizen in New York, extended the fairness doctrine to broadcasting's most tender nerve —advertising.

Because other branches of the Federal Government had deemed cigarettes as possibly hazardous to health, Mr. Banzhaf successfully succeeded in persuading the F.C.C. to order anti-cigarette commercials. All cigarette advertising will leave the air after the first of the year.

No one can say where this trend among aroused consumers may end. If detergents are harmful to water supplies, do ecologists and environmentalists have the right to reply? If automobile manufacturers and oil concerns contaminate the air, should they not be answered over airwaves owned by the public, something the City of New York's Environmental Protection Administration has already asked?

And if possible harm to the body merits rebuttal, what about possible harm to the mind, particularly of the young? Does fairness stop with products or does it extend to ideas embodied in programs intended for those still too young to sort the wheat from the chaff? Hence Dean Burch, F.C.C. chairman, is not dismissing out of hand the contention of Boston mothers that hard-sell advertising, notably of cereals and toys, should be removed from Saturday morning video.

EQUAL TIME: This is perhaps the thorniest issue of all because it is so often confused with the fairness doctrine and can so easily get out of hand. The equal time provision, technically known as Section 315, applies specifically to legally qualified candidates for office. If a broadcaster gives or sells one candidate air time, then he must give all of that candidate's opponents the same break. Exempt from the provision are regularly scheduled newscasts or interviews.

But the confusion over equal time stems from the fact it is a phrase easily misunderstood by laymen and politicians who think in fundamental terms. When the Columbia Broadcasting System presented "The Loyal Opposition," Lawrence F. O'Brien, chairman of the Democratic National Committee, roamed all over the partisan political lot, not merely disagreeing with President Nixon on Cambodia. So that raised a new set of issues which the Republicans now want to answer.

Yet no "equal time" regulation is at stake, only the broad concept of fairness because no certified political candidates are involved. What remains to be seen is whether "the fairness doctrine" becomes an interminable game of tit for tat.

*

But nowhere does the equal time concept become more confusing than in the case of the President of the United States. To mark a dividing line between a President speaking as the nation's leader and Commander-in-Chief, and speaking as a politician, is practically impossible save in instances of critical national security.

PERSONAL ATTACK: This is essentially an extension of the fairness doctrine. The Supreme Court sustained the contention of the F.C.C. that if Mr. A attacks the honesty or character of Mr. B, then Mr. B must be duly notified of the nature of the attack and invited to respond.

CAMPAIGN EXPENDITURES: It is amusing to see straight faces in Washington pretending that there might be a chance this fall to curtail political spot announcements and whopping campaign expenditures. The Madison Avenue boys knew better: contracts for good spots had been consummated by the rich candidates many days earlier.

In this respect the whole business of politics on TV is something of a charade. Invariably, the breast-beating comes too late to affect the next immediate election. To stay in power or to increase one party's control in Congress always is a tidy escape hatch for doing absolutely nothing. The only workable solution is to cut down on the length of campaigns and remove the process of government from the marketplace. In the long run broadcasting might find it cheaper, assuming the medium played it square and assigned good prime time. All the gibberish about reducing the costs of spots misses the point: they should be abolished for the *public interest, convenience* and *necessity.*

Equal Time Urged for Strong 3d Party

By WARREN WEAVER Jr.
Special to The New York Times

WASHINGTON, March 2—Dean Burch, chairman of the Federal Communications Commission, proposed today a revision of the campaign television laws that would guarantee equal exposure to a "significant" third-party candidate like George C. Wallace.

The Nixon Administration official said that the present "equal time" provision insured that no candidate got free television time by requiring that it go to all of them, including such "fringe" competitors as the Socialist Labor and Vegetarian nominees.

The change he advocated at a hearing of the Senate Communications Subcommittee could result in three-way televised debates in 1972 between President Nixon, his Democratic opponent and Mr. Wallace, if the Alabama Governor should decide to repeat his 1968 candidacy.

Evasive on Fund Limit

Mr. Burch testified as the Senate panel began considering proposals to limit campaign spending, but he did not shed much light on whether President Nixon might sign a bill with a ceiling on political expenditures.

The commissioner declined to take a position on whether there should be a dollar limit for all political advertising by a candidate, saying this was up to Congress.

Last June, in testimony before a House committee, Mr. Burch endorsed the concept of a statutory ceiling for campaign spending for radio and television. Last fall, Congress approved a bill with such a ceiling, but President Nixon disapproved it on the grounds that it discriminated against the electronic media.

The disapproved measure would have repealed the equal time provision to make it possible for the networks to hold such debates and restrict them to the two major-party candidates.

Commissioner Burch said today, however, that if Congress would not accept his proposal to include serious third-party contenders in free campaign television, the commission would then support a permanent repeal of the equal time guarantee, such as the President disapproved.

Senator John O. Pastore, who heads the Communications Subcommittee, left no doubt that he wanted a campaign bill with spending limits. He said the cost of running had "reached the point of being scandalous," putting "high public office up for sale to the highest bidder."

The Rhode Island Democrat is sponsoring a bill that would limit broadcast spending for national candidates to about $5-million and other media spending to $10-million. The National Committee for an Effective Congress endorsed a limit of about $13.5-million for all advertising and telephone expense. The committee has participated in drafting several of the campaign measures.

Although Commissioner Burch did not endorse any ceiling, he said in response to a question from Senator Pastore that the proposal to limit radio and television spending could be enforced.

Some politicians believe that President Nixon could benefit in 1972 from a public position in the center of the spectrum, widely publicized on television, between the Democratic nominee on the left and Mr. Wallace on the right. The Alabama Governor, they believe, could use such national recognition to cut back Democratic gains in the South, to Mr. Nixon's profit.

Senator Pastore said he hoped the subcommittee would have a campaign bill ready "within weeks." To be effective for the 1972 election, any new law must be enacted by late this year, in time to affect the primary elections.

Broadcasters Ask Repeal
Of Equal Time Provision

WASHINGTON, March 5 (AP)
—The National Association of
Broadcasters urged today the
repeal of the so-called equal
time law so as to permit major
party candidates for President
and Vice President to debate on
television next year.

"Broadcasters stand ready
and willing to provide free
time," said the association's
president, Vincent Wasilewski.

"The capricious operation of
Section 315 [of the Federal
Communications Act], however,
makes it impossible for broadcasters to perform this public service responsibility," he
added.

Mr. Wasilewski testified before the Senate Communications Subcommittee. The present law provides that, if any
candidate is given free television time, all his opponents
including those of minor parties, must receive equal time.

The Unfairness Doctrine

*'Never has the subpoena been used as viciously, as
irresponsibly and as often against freedom of the press
as it has this year.'*
—Freedom of Information Committee,
American Society of Newspaper Editors.

By JAMES RESTON

WASHINGTON, April 13—The American Society of Newspaper Editors is in
Washington again for its annual skull
practice, and this year it has some
serious questions to discuss, for all
news reporters and editors—radio and
television even more than newspaper—
are under mounting pressure from all
branches of the Government and from
the public as well.

In the last year the Defense Department has gone beyond the normal regulations on battlefield reporting to
censor the news on the war in Laos
and limit access to the primary areas
of combat. Also, as the editors' Freedom of Information Committee charged
in its annual report: "Never has the
subpoena been used as viciously, as
irresponsibly and as often against freedom of the press as it has this [past]
year."

Reporters and editors in radio and
television have had even more difficult
problems, for while the newspapers
usually have the protection of the freedom of the press amendment to the
constitution in the courts, the networks and their affiliated stations are
licensed by a Government which has
the power to impose its notion of
"fair reporting" by threatening to
withdraw a station's license.

The threats, of course, are always
oblique. Thus, in recent weeks, Vice
President Agnew has not only been
running a campaign against the Columbia Broadcasting System's program on
the Defense Department's propaganda
apparatus ("The Selling of the Pentagon") and demanding the right to edit
his own copy on the subject over the
C.B.S. network, but the Investigations
subcommittee of the House Interstate
and Foreign Commerce Committee has
subpoenaed C.B.S. to produce all its
notes and unused film and disbursements of money on the Pentagon program.

These are issues—the radio and television as well as the newspaper subpoenas—that deserve more attention
from the newspaper editors than they
have been getting. Newspaper editors
howl like a scalded dog whenever any
Government official asks to see their
reporters' notes or questions their
news judgment—and quite right, too—
but they are comparatively quiet when
the Vice President or committees of
the Congress demand the same thing
of the radio and television reporters.

This double standard could use a
little more examination from the newspaper editors here this week. The basic
assumption of the First Amendment
was that the people in a democratic
society had a better chance to get a
fair presentation of the news from a
multitude of free reporters than from
reporters regulated by the Government.

The Founding Fathers had no illusions about the infallibility of the
press. Their comments about our stupidity, inaccuracy and bias make Spiro
Agnew's sound almost genial. But they
were persuaded that the risks of freedom were less than the risks of legal
strictures or Government control, and
it is hard to argue that this protection
for the newspaper reporters should not
now be guaranteed to the radio and
television stations, which now supply
a majority of the American people
with their first reports of the news.

There is, of course, nothing wrong
with the Vice President complaining
publicly about bias in the press and
the radio and television. As he is constantly pointing out, he has his freedom of speech too, and since major
newspapers select about 100,000

words a day out of almost two million, it would be remarkable if there was not an argument about whether the selection and front-page presentation were "fair."

The difference is that newspaper editors can tell the complaining Vice President or the members of the House Investigations subcommittee to go climb the Washington Monument and the radio and TV editors are not quite so free. They are under Government license. They use "the people's airwaves" (as if the newspapers didn't use the people's streets and interstate highways), and they operate under different rules.

They must submit to an official "fairness doctrine," which is a Government and not a professional journalist's standard. It is enforced, or is at least under threat of being enforced, by a Government licensing agency. The radio and TV people must answer when the F.C.C. inquiries are made, and truth is not necessarily a defense.

It is ironic that the F.C.C.'s "fairness doctrine" was intended to assure precisely that, but everything depends on who is deciding what is "fair," and the guess here is that the Founding Fathers would still bet on Walter Cronkite rather than on Mr. Agnew.

Nevertheless, the public reaction to all this is clearly divided. The people have heard all the arguments between Government and press, and it is fairly obvious that their confidence is not unbounded in either institution.

Part of this is due to the fact that the newspaper, radio and television editors have not been very good at self-criticism, or in establishing an effective "fairness doctrine" of their own, which is why there is so much public criticism of reporting, and why there is now so much talk of establishing some kind of local and national news council machinery to review the record of the papers and stations.

No doubt there will be much discussion of these issues in Washington this week, particularly the newspaper side of the question, but the immediate threat of Government pressure and influence is on radio and television, and if their freedom is impaired, even the freedom of the printed press is not likely to be unaffected.

White House Aide Urges
Major Changes for TV

By JACK GOULD

The White House Office of Telecommunications called yesterday for elimination of the fairness doctrine in radio and television, alteration of the station license renewal process to get the Government out of programing and the beginning of the de-regulation of radio.

Clay T. Whitehead, director of the office, said that he believed television needed a major revision of the Communications Act of 1934. At present, he said, the Federal Communications Commission and the courts are making the broadcaster a government agent.

Mr. Whitehead spoke at a luncheon meeting of the International Radio and Television Society at the Waldorf-Astoria.

Substitute Act Urged

In place of the fairness doctrine, Mr. Whitehead said, Congress should substitute an act providing for individuals to use the airwaves and assurances that the public at large will have adequate coverage of public issues.

Such an act should allow for time to be sold on a first-come, first-served basis with no rate regulation, Mr. Whitehead said. The individual would have the right to speak on any matter, whether it be to sell razor blades or urge an end to the Vietnamese war, he added.

The right of such access should be enforced through the courts and not through the Federal Communications Commission, Mr. Whitehead proposed. He said that the renewal of a station's license should be based on the totality of an outlet's service to the community and not judged on a case-by-case complaint standard.

Mr. Whitehead urged extension of the duration of a license beyond the present three-year

Whitehead Suggests Shift From Fairness Doctrine and License Revisions

period and said that the F.C.C. should entertain competing applications for a channel only when a license was not renewed or revoked. Challenges to existing licensees are at present a highly controversial matter.

Mr. Whitehead said that he had proposed this week to Dean Burch, F.C.C. chairman, the selection of one or more large cities in which radio assignments and transfers would not be subject to the present regulatory inquiries on the ground that in the vast majority of cases the procedure is superfluous.

The head of the White House office said he had no legislation "tucked in my back pocket" and merely wanted to start a dialogue in the belief that the present mode of regulation had not worked. Asked by a broadcaster after lunch if President Nixon concurred in his recommendations, Mr. Whitehead said: "He believes in the general tone of it."

The National Broadcasting Company characterized Mr. Whitehead's speech as "like a breath of fresh air" but noted that some points needed clarification. The American Broadcasting Company approved minimizing government controls and said it would study the proposals. The Columbia Broadcasting System declined to comment.

he sense that po
significantly, at
again to have des
decline in report
of Diem's leaders
with inefficiency
declined signific
coup plotting.   S
and the military
improved capabili
operations agains
are now seeking t
positively to the

5 REGULATING THE MEDIA

n a State Department memo in the Pentagon papers
ssified material, but should it have been?

NEED FOR VIGILANCE SEEN BY PUBLISHERS

Restrictions on the Press Constitute Ever-Present Menace, It Is Held.

'ODIOUS,' SAYS BARNUM

Davis, Bryan and Sulzberger Are Others Who Call for Alertness to Danger.

Jerome D. Barnum, publisher of The Syracuse (N. Y.) Post-Standard, opened the discussion of freedom of the press yesterday morning at the annual convention of the American Newspaper Publishers Association in the Waldorf-Astoria.

Denouncing "the whole odious business" of the seizure of telegraph messages of citizens, including publishers, by the Black Committee of Congress in conjunction with the Federal Communications Commission, Mr. Barnum declared that action taken by the association, in aid of members whose rights were invaded, "has served to put an end to these illegal efforts to obtain the private papers of citizens of the United States, at least for the present."

"I think it is safe to say," he added, "that there will be no more of it by the Federal Communications Commission. This association owes a debt of gratitude to the publishers who had courage enough to institute proceedings in the court which for all time should settle the question."

Benefits All the People

He said that the right of freedom of press was not inserted in the Constitution for the benefit of publishers as a class, but for the benefit of the people as a whole.

"Publishers," he continued, "are merely the trustees of the right of the people to have information on which to base their opinions. Whether that information may be in the nature of news, editorial comment, or advertising, it is imperative in this day and age, if that valuable heritage is to be preserved, that all publishers should be vigilant not only in its defense, but alert to prevent any insidious attacks from whatever source they may come."

Mr. Barnum then introduced Howard Davis, business manager of The New York Herald Tribune, former president of the association and former chairman of the newspaper code committee under the NRA. Mr. Davis said that early in the code negotiations he became convinced that "certain influential groups in Washington desired to have the press overhung with threats that at least would temper criticism of the more courageous newspapers and possibly silence entirely all criticism from those not so courageous."

Sees "European Methods"

The recent actions of the Black committee, he went on, constituted a "shocking attempt to impair or abridge the freedom of the press and the rights of the individual." He charged that the situation "smacks pretty much of European methods under dictatorship." The most "amazing" thing about "this bold threat to our constitutional liberties," he went on, was that there had not been more vigorous protest from those whose telegrams were seized. The majority of newspapers, he feared, "do not seem to be aware of the seriousness of this and similar threats to constitutional freedom."

He attributed to the proponents of certain legislation the motive of seeking to hold "these threats over newspaper editors" and to "intimidate them and thus prevent frank and pointed criticism of their acts."

"The freedom of the press granted in the First Amendment to the Constitution," he went on, "was not placed there for the benefit of publishers, but solely for the protection of the people. Therefore you as publishers are the trustees of this priceless privilege and it is your duty to defend and preserve it for the welfare of the people."

The next speaker was Dr. John Stewart Bryan, publisher of The Richmond (Va.) News-Leader, president of William and Mary College and former president of the association.

Struggle an Ancient One

"The attacks we have on freedom of the press are not new," he said. "Civilization isn't new. Our struggle isn't new. The world isn't new. Everything has come back here again in the same old circle. We find ourselves today under electric lights in air-conditioned buildings, meeting the same kind of problem under a different guise that mankind has met all the way up in its struggle from the beginning. If there was no struggle there would be no life."

He said that the freedom of the press meant freedom for all.

"Whether we like it or not," he went on, "we are responsible for the press, because we have got to be wise enough and courageous enough and patriotic enough and generous enough to admit freedom for people that we do not like. We have got to permit freedom of speech, freedom to teach, freedom to write, freedom to approach. We have got to know that if we are doing this thing we are pursuing a course that is infinitely difficult."

Dr. Bryan said that freedom of the press was just one aspect of life. He thought it had come up at this time because of conditions brought about by the World War, which, he said, had "wrung us spiritually dry." "It took out of us our emotion and courage and will to fight," he added, "and the only reason on earth that people stand for dictatorships is because they have lost the courage and the will to stand for themselves."

Demands an Upright Press

Arthur Hays Sulzberger, president and publisher of THE NEW YORK TIMES and member of the original code committee of the association, said that he was not convinced that the Roosevelt administration had designs upon the freedom of the press or any fundamental rights of citizens, but that he believed those rights had been "placed in serious jeopardy."

He emphasized that the constitutional guaranty against abridging the freedom of the press was "the statement of an essential liberty of a free people and not a grant of immunity extended to a particular trade or profession."

Posing the question whether the newspapers were measuring up to their responsibility, he pointed out that a growing disposition exists on the part of the public to be skeptical of what it reads in the press and to distrust newspaper motives. The public is making three indictments of the press, he declared. First, he said, were doubts as to the accuracy of reporting; second, a feeling that the personal interests of publishers are often put ahead of public service; and, finally, a failure to keep editorial opinion out of the news columns and a failure to present both sides of controversial questions adequately.

"We have called insistently and justly," he added, "for the full maintenance of the freedom of the press. The people, in supporting this call, have emphasized the mutuality involved therein. It is their right, this freedom of the press; their right to have accurate news, fairly presented; their right to have the news 'without fear or favor, without regard to any party, sect or interest involved.' That is the other, and equally important, aspect of freedom of the press."

RADIO MEN WARNED TO 'WATCH STEP'

WITH several warnings ringing in their ears, broadcasters from all parts of the country have returned home from the National Association of Broadcasters' sixteenth annual convention held during the past week in Washington.

They met to reorganize the NAB; they heard Frank R. McNinch, chairman of the FCC, caution on monopoly in broadcasting, warn them not to become profiteers and to "police" the programs.

Mr. McNinch pointed to that vital phrase in the law which specifies that American broadcasting stations must serve in "public interest, convenience and necessity." He denied that the FCC wants the power of censorship, which the Communications Act of 1934 does not give it.

President Roosevelt in a message to the broadcasters said in part:

"The broadcasting industry has, indeed, a very great opportunity to serve the public, but along with this opportunity goes an important responsibility to see that this means of communication is made to serve the high purposes of a democracy. I have the high hope that the industry, under the guidance of and in cooperation with the Federal Communications Commission, will prove itself to be worthy of the great public trust reposed in it."

Wheeler Urges Freedom

Senator Burton K. Wheeler, chairman of the Interstate Commerce Committee, urged the broadcasters to protect radio as a powerful instrument of mass communication, because, as he said, "Free speech, as exemplified by a free radio and a free press, has made its contribution to the survival of our political system in which democracy has survived."

"Neither you nor I want to see government ownership in American radio," said Senator Wheeler in advising the radio industry to guard against monopoly.

"There are several species of monopoly that might get a stranglehold on radio," he continued. "All deal with power. One is power in

watts, high power protected over unlimited areas. A second is power in numbers of stations concentrated in identical ownership. The third relates to the power and the status of the networks. Each deals with the extent of influence, of coverage, in the hands of a single person or group.

"We cannot ignore the signs or the tempo of the times," Senator Wheeler admonished. "Only broadcasting's own folly would make the threat real. And that would evolve if we allowed any entities in the industry to become too large, too potent, to permit them to reach the point where the influence they exert is so great as to create political animosities and internecine strife that could only result in its destruction."

Referring to the requirement that rival political candidates be treated equally as the "doctrine of fair play," the Montana Senator asserted:

"Congress did not write into the law all the specifications which would require licensees to adhere to this doctrine of fair play. To undertake such a task would lead into immense difficulties, and when the job was finished such legal specifications might abridge the right of free speech itself. However, Congress did say that you, as a licensee of a broadcasting facility, cannot take sides in a political controversy by denying the use of your station to one candidate and granting it to another. And I think you will all agree that this is a sound principle."

McNinch Expects Investigation

Commenting on the address of Senator Wheeler, in which he cited the danger of monopoly within the broadcasting industry, Mr. McNinch said:

"My word to you on this subject is that it is the duty of the Communications Commission to prevent the development of a monopoly or to set about to destroy it if one exists. I have no less determination than that I shall contribute all that I can toward these ends.

"I am not particularly interested

in whether there may be a technical or legal monopoly, for my concern runs quite ahead of that consideration to discover whether there is such a concentration of control as to amount to a practical monopoly. If there is a monopoly, it exists in direct violation of the law; if there is no monopoly, may I suggest that you yourselves re-examine to what extent there is centralization of control and whither it is tending?

"I have in mind suggesting to the commission that it proceed soon to investigate this question as to whether there is a monopoly and whether there is any undue or anti-social centralization of power and control," said Mr. McNinch. "This would mean also an investigation of the chain broadcasting systems.

"So much has been said in the Congress and by the press generally about monopoly and the control of the industry by chains that the time is here when we must deal with these problems by fully exploring these matters so we may have exact information upon which to predicate judgments and policies."

Mr. McNinch in reference to programs said that his comments were made in a "cooperative and purely advisory spirit."

"I do not believe in nor want the power of censorship," he asserted. "I read many, many complaints against program features that do not seem to warrant active consideration. However, I am pursuing the practice of forwarding to the stations complained against those protests which appear to have sufficient merit to justify bringing them informally to the attention of the station to the end that it may know something of the complaints forwarded to the commission. This is done in the hope that it may be of some service and not with any thought whatever that the reference of any such protest or complaint to you carries with it any implication that the commission has formed any conclusion or judgment upon the matter.

No Place for Fortune Hunters

"You know as well as the members of the commission what is fair play, what is vulgar, or indecent, or profane, or what may reasonably be expected to give offense. In such situations the commission has a duty to the listening public to discharge, for your license is dependent upon your serving the public interest, convenience and necessity."

Referring by implication to the NAB reorganization plan, Chairman McNinch said that broadcasting calls for a high type of leadership and yet warned the broadcasters against "autocratic power within the industry.

"Of all industries, it seems to me that radio—because it is so essentially social in its implications and effects—calls clearly for leadership that has social vision and a mature wisdom which understands that the only safe and sure way to win and hold the public favor is through an enlightened, genuine and unselfish purpose to serve the best interests of the public.

"Beware of reliance upon propaganda and political pull and influence. These are broken reeds upon which you dare not lean.

"The leaders of this industry must be able to take the long view and not look too closely and immediately at profit, for a just public is always willing to pay a fair return for a valuable service rendered but is quick to discern the devices of the profiteer. You are in a high sense trustees of a public resource, and the public neither expects nor will it tolerate that this resource shall become primarily the plaything of fortune hunters."

Craven Opposed to Censorship

Commissioner T. A. M. Craven, in an address to the convention, declared it is proper that radio broadcasting in this country be operated by private industry and it is equally proper and necessary that this industry be encouraged to earn reasonable profits when it renders good service to the public. The Commissioner said that he was personally opposed to any form of censorship, either direct or indirect.

By unanimous vote the NAB adopted the reorganization plan and named seventeen regional directors, who selected six directors at large: Edward A. Allen of Lynchburg, Va.; John Elmer, Baltimore; Harold Hough and Elliott Roosevelt, Fort Worth; Lambdin Kay, Atlanta, and Frank M. Russell of Washington.

The reorganization plan calls for a paid president and a paid secretary-treasurer and a broad administrative set-up, which, however, must be passed upon by the new board of directors.

Roosevelt Admits Radio Men

Special to THE NEW YORK TIMES.

WASHINGTON, May 1.—The White House granted to radio-news commentators today the same privileges of attending and reporting President Roosevelt's press conferences as those accorded to newspaper correspondents. The action followed the opening of sections of the Senate and House galleries to the radio commentators.

RADIO GALLERIES OPENED

Congress News Broadcasters Are Congratulated by President

WASHINGTON, July 24 (AP).— President Roosevelt sent his congratulations today to radio newsmen in connection with the formal opening of radio galleries in the Senate and House.

Speaker Bankhead presented a key to the House gallery to Fulton Lewis Jr., president of the Radio Correspondents Association, at a ceremony in the House chamber.

Mr. Roosevelt said in a letter to Mr. Lewis that the event "marks a decided step forward in the dissemination of news concerning the deliberations of our national Legislature."

The President said he wanted to point out that in broadcasting news of debate in Congress "ultimate public opinion will be based on the impartiality and fairness of the reporting."

ARTHUR KROCK SEES THREAT TO PRESS

Says New Deal Preachment of 'Class War' Against Papers May Lead to Curbs

SULLIVAN WARNS OF TREND

NLRB and AAA Encroach on Property Rights, He Holds— Eliot Discounts Axis 'Words'

Special to THE NEW YORK TIMES.

SYRACUSE, N. Y., Oct. 7—Arthur Krock, Mark Sullivan and Major George Fielding Eliot, speaking at a meeting of the New York State Society of Newspaper Editors today, warned against dangers of the day affecting the free press and the rights of all United States citizens.

Mr. Krock, Washington correspondent for THE NEW YORK TIMES, stated that the American newspapers may soon face efforts to restrict them. The press, he said, must prepare to "preserve its freedom" against such efforts.

The Administration, he said, holds the American press "untruthful and unfair."

"Like any statute," he continued, "the Bill of Rights can be made to conform to a new prevailing philosophy and political purposes. From my personal observations and experiences during these last seven years, I do not trust the current philosophy when applied to the ancient freedom of the press."

"Ingenious efforts" at restriction he asserted, "have begun with a constant attempt to extol the radio and the news reels, to preach a class war against the press."

Mr. Krock said that the Administration had perfected a formula for government propaganda.

"Its basis is the President's press conference," he said. "The first layer imposed on the basis of the press conference consists of official favors surreptitiously extended to syndicated columnists who are 'sympathetic.'"

Press Agents Are Cited

The next layer in the structure is composed of government press agents. They describe Federal acts in favorable terms and gloss over errors, he asserted.

"The capstone was set in place by the President himself," he added. "It is composed of technical denials of substantially true news stories, and steady implications that the press is unreliable and often venal."

Mr. Sullivan, New York Herald-Tribune writer, said that unless a current trend in government was reversed, a fundamental change was ahead. He asserted that the National Labor Relations Board and the Agricultural Adjustment Administration were encroaching on property rights, which he declared were the keystone of American liberties.

He said that the trend could be stopped only by a complete reversal.

"Unless reversed," he added, "the process is automatic and inevitable. Election of Willkie would reverse it and election of a Congress opposed to the New Deal would do likewise.

"Our attention is being drawn basically away from this process by the war. If we were attending to domestic issues we would see this clearly."

Major Eliot, writer and commentator on military subjects, told the society that the first duty of the American press in the light of the European situation was to overcome the campaign of the Axis powers to arouse fear in America.

"Some things in the press would have you believe that if anything happens to England Hitler in a few days will bound out of a Forty-second Street subway followed by a band of Storm Troopers," he said.

Mere words, most of them empty and meaningless, were being employed by the Axis to frighten Americans, he asserted.

Mr. Krock's address, in part, follows:

Tells of Special Favors

"Many, if not all, American governments have gone to war with at least a section of the press. In one way or another, all of them have circulated favorable propaganda about their activities, and have sought to check factual publication which brought their acts under criticism.

"But they were amateurs by present comparison.

"The New Deal has perfected a formula. Its basis is the President's press conference where Mr. Roosevelt calls almost all the reporters by their first names. And when he lectures the press, as he does very often, he ascribes its sins to editors and publishers, implying that the reporters are fine fellows in economic bondage to a bad lot of masters.

"The first layer imposed on the basis of the press conference consists of official favors surreptitiously extended to syndicated columnists who are 'sympathetic.' They are given special material for books and 'inside' stories of this and that— material withheld by them from the publishers who pay for their columns. The material always celebrates the sources. And the sources are always concealed.

"This has resulted in a rash of syndicated writings and propaganda volumes. The new data in them are furnished at the expense of the daily news reporters.

Sees Manipulation of News

"The next layer in the structure is composed of the battalion of government press agents. They work day and night, at public expense, to circulate every Federal act in favorable terms, to gloss over errors and to conceal what for any reason is not desired to be known. They attend the White House press conferences for the first time in history.

"The capstone, like the cornerstone, was set in place by the President himself. It is composed of technical denials of substantially true news stories and steady implications that the press is unreliable and often venal.

"The persistence of this viewpoint which suffuses the New Deal —and which countless disproofs have not altered—is important. It emerged in the days of NRA when the Administration sought to license the press. It will be of even greater importance if the Administration and its Congress majority are retained in office. Through certain animations of existing laws an official group in Washington, embedded in power, could circumvent the Bill of Rights and move toward control of the press.

"It was under Wilson that the government, as an institution, learned how to formulate and use propaganda. Until that time propaganda had been personal. In the time of President Hoover government propaganda, through the gradual and growing employment of press agents for the departments, began to attain the status of a major official industry, to come to full flower under Roosevelt and the New Deal.

"The Franklin Roosevelt administration has devised the channel publicity system. This is an arrangement whereby an official—usually a former newspaper man—is the only direct contact point between the press and the department. He decides what departmental people shall be interviewed, and on what subjects. He obtains, prepares and issues information on matters for which the department desires publicity and passes on newspaper requests on other subjects.

"Several of these press representatives of the government, notably those in the Treasury, Justice and Commerce Departments, and the news agents of some of the administrators—have greatly improved the quality of public information in their fields.

"But the system has major faults. It is an incentive to laziness on the part of the press. It conceals many leads to official acts of which the public is not apprised, because the official does not wish it to be apprised.

"The channel system would completely substitute the dead printed leaflet—what we call the hand-out—for the warm and living speech of public men. It has been rigidly applied to the non-partisan group of private citizens summoned to Washington as the Advisory Committee on National Defense.

"All responsible officers of the government in Washington today

pattern their press conferences after those in the White House. But though he has many imitators, the President has no rivals in this particular. Genial, charming, shrewd and daring, he meets the press on his own ground and wins most of the battles. The newspaper men are his guests. They may not press a question beyond a certain point, and if the President chooses to evade, for instance (an art in which he is most skillful), they cannot venture to try to corner him. He has utilized his press conferences not only to such information as he wishes to supply, which is his prerogative, but also to disseminate information valuable to his purposes, which is his privilege, and sometimes, with the preface of 'off-the-record,' putting a lid on news he wishes had not come to the boiling point.

"In repayment of liberties without parallel, the American newspaper and its makers must seek and deserve the friendship of the public alone, to whom the government belongs. They must know no enemy except those they deem enemies to the general welfare, and be prepared to prove their estimate. They must forego rewards open to other industries and citizens; respect private rights and inclinations; publish both sides of questions, and follow the practices of gentility.

"By so doing the press may be able to preserve its freedom against efforts to restrict it which may soon be made, efforts more definite and more ingenious than have ever been made before. These have begun with a constant attempt to extol the radio and the newsreels, to preach a class war against the press. But it will not succeed unless the

checks and balances of the two-party system and the interplay of three coordinate governing branches are swept away."

In a general off-the-record discussion the editors considered wartime censorship and the desirability of adopting resolutions in favor of adequate national defense and denouncing subversive activities.

Wilbur Forrest, assitant editor of **The New York Herald-Tribune,** president of the society, appointed a committee to draft the contemplated resolutions.

FCC DECREE BARS BIAS ON THE RADIO

WAAB, Boston, Reprimanded for the Broadcasting of Political Editorials

MUST 'PRESENT ALL SIDES'

Head of Yankee Network Gives Pledge of Future Fairness and Retains License

WASHINGTON, Jan. 17 (P)—A declaration that a radio station could not be "an advocate," but must present "all sides of important public questions fairly, objectively and without bias," came today from the Federal Communications Commission.

The commission reprimanded Station WAAB of Boston "for past practices," but renewed its license because, it said, John Shepard 3d, president of the Yankee Network, Inc., the licensee, had given a pledge that the station would not "color or editorialize" news in the future.

Beginning early in 1937 and continuing through September, 1938, the commission asserted, it was the policy of WAAB "to broadcast so-called editorials from time to time urging the election of various candidates for political office or supporting one side or another in various questions in public controversy."

In these editorials, the commission added, "no pretense was made at objective, impartial reporting."

Showed "Misconcept" of Duties

Declaring that the station "revealed a serious misconcept of its duties and functions under the law," the commission said:

"Radio can serve as an instrument of democracy only when devoted to the communication of information and the exchange of ideas fairly and objectively presented. A truly free radio cannot be used to advocate the causes of the licensee. It cannot be used to support the candidacies of his friends. It cannot be devoted to the support of principles he happens to regard most favorably. In brief, the broadcaster cannot be an advocate.

"The public interest—not the private—is paramount."

In renewing WAAB's license, the commission asserted that it was relying upon "comprehensive and unequivocal representations as to the future conduct of the station." It added:

"Should any future occasion arise to examine into the conduct of this licensee, however, the commission will consider the facts developed in this record in its review of the activities as a whole."

The commission denied an application by the Mayflower Broadcasting Corporation to replace WAAB on the air.

The Communications Act provides

that the commission, before licensing a broadcast station, must find that "public interest, convenience and necessity" will be served. In its recent annual report the commission said that it had "the duty of determining whether the past conduct of stations has been consistent with their obligations under the law."

License Period Is Year

Broadcast stations are licensed for a one-year period, although the Communications Act authorizes a maximum of three years. Officials said that the commission used the one-year period instead of the maximum to "keep a better check" on station operations.

In discussing the "editorials" broadcast by WAAB, the commission declared:

"It is clear—indeed the station seems to have taken pride in the fact—that the purpose of these editorials was to win support for some person or view favored by those in control of the station.

"Under the American system of broadcasting it is clear that responsibility for the conduct of a broadcast station must rest initially with the broadcaster. It is equally clear that with the limitations in frequencies inherent in the nature of radio, the public interest can never be served by a dedication of any broadcast facility to the support of his own partisan ends.

"Freedom of speech on the radio must be broad enough to provide full and equal opportunity for the presentation to the public of all sides of public issues. Indeed, as one licensed to operate in the public domain, the licensee has assumed the obligation of presenting all sides of important public questions fairly, objectively and without bias."

Affidavits Summarized

The commission said that Mr. Shepard, replying to a request for details as to the conduct of WAAB since September, 1938, had filed two affidavits.

"Apparently conceding the departures from the requirements of public interest by the earlier conduct of the station," the commission said, "these affidavits state, and they are uncontradicted, that no editorials have been broadcast over Station WAAB since September, 1938, and that it is not intended to depart from this uninterrupted policy. The station has no editorial policies.

"In the affidavits there is further a description of the station's procedure for handling news items and the statement is made that since September, 1938, 'no attempt has ever been or will be made to color or editorialize the news received' through usual sources.

"In response to a question from the bench inquiring whether the commission should rely upon these affidavits in determining whether to renew the licenses (WAAB's main and auxiliary transmitters), counsel for the Yankee Network, Inc., stated at the second argument, 'there is absolutely no reservations whatsoever, or mental reservations of any sort, character or kind with reference to those affidavits.' They mean exactly what they say in the fullest possible amplification that the commission wants to give them.'"

October 8, 1940

January 18, 1941

ROOSEVELT DENIES CENSORSHIP PLANS

But He Condemns Publishing of Arrival Here of British Battleship for Repairs

---

HAILS BULK OF THE PRESS

Knox Declares Here That His Plea to Newspapers Was Only Courtesy to Britain

---

Special to The New York Times.

WASHINGTON, April 8—President Roosevelt reiterated today his determination not to impose a mandatory censorship on the press, but condemned those newspapers which published news of the arrival of the British battleship Malaya in New York for repairs.

A correspondent of The New York Daily News, which published the report and later an editorial advocating compulsory censorship of military news on the ground that newspapers could not decide what they should censor, recalled to the President that Secretary Knox had praised those newspapers which did not publish the news of the arrival. The reporter suggested that this might be a reflection on newspapers which did publish the story.

The President interrupted and said that it was and that he thought the editorials in papers which did print the arrival report and carried pictures of the war vessel were the lamest excuses to get square with their reading publics that he had ever read.

Permits Direct Quotation

Asked by the same correspondent if he favored censorship, the President replied that he had noticed the same papers which told of the ar-

rival of the ship advocated legal clamping down of censorship. He, in turn, asked what other newspapers would think of this, indicating the strong belief that they did not want mandatory censorship now.

"I much prefer to go along with the overwhelming majority of the newspapers at this time," the President stated, remarking that he could be quoted directly upon that point.

A reporter immediately asked whether the phrase "at this time" meant that a censorship was contemplated later. President Roosevelt said no, because nothing else is in sight at this time.

The Navy Department had requested newspapers not to print news of the arrival of British or other foreign warships in American harbors for repairs or other purposes because such information might be valuable to enemies of the nations to which the ships belonged. Secretary Knox had requested voluntary cooperation in suppressing such news. Some New York newspapers, however, published the news of the Malaya's arrival, together with pictures.

Knox Denies Censorship Aim

Noting that there was a vast difference between a request not to print certain information and a censorship, Secretary Knox declared here last night that no thought of censorship of the press was in his mind when he recently requested newspapers not to print the news of the arrival of British warships in American waters.

His statement was made when, accompanied by his aide, Captain Frank Beatty, and his secretary, John O'Keefe, he arrived at La Guardia Field in a Navy transport plane to attend the ceremonies at the Brooklyn Navy Yard this morning at which the battleship North Carolina will be commissioned.

Concerning a recent newspaper editorial suggesting that an official censorship might be the solution of what should or should not be published by the daily press, Mr. Knox replied that he had already made a statement in Washington about such matters.

REITERATES DESIRE TO BAR CENSORSHIP

But Stephen Early Says That Restriction on Messages Abroad Is Under Study

---

VOLUNTARY CURB PRAISED

Asserts It 'Has Got to Work' Because None Here Want Alternative to It

---

Special to The New York Times.

WASHINGTON, April 9—Stephen Early, White House secretary, reiterated today that the government had no intention of establishing a domestic press censorship, but emphasized the fact that James L. Fly, chairman of the Federal Communications Commission, was chairman of a committee studying means of controlling international cable and radio messages so that defense secrets would not be transmitted abroad.

The matter came up when a reporter asked what value there was in a voluntary suppression by newspapers of news of the movement of foreign and domestic war vessels if news about them could be sent abroad by foreign agents legitimately in this country. Outright censorship of cablegrams, radiograms and mail going abroad is widely expected in case this country becomes involved in war.

Mr. Early remarked that there was one point he wished that President Roosevelt had mentioned yesterday. Some newspapers, Mr. Early said, called the present voluntary system an imposed censorship, whereas "it is an attempt to avoid a censorship."

"Doesn't that imply that if the voluntary system is not followed a formal censorship will be imposed?" a reporter asked.

"This will work out on voluntary grounds," Mr. Early answered. "It has got to work out on voluntary grounds. We don't want censorship; the newspapers don't want censorship; the President doesn't want it, I don't want it and Lowell Mellett [director of the Office of Government Reports] doesn't want it."

Mr. Early said that the situation which grew out of the publication by some newspapers of the recent arrival in New York of a British battleship had a certain "educational" value. Newspapers would suppress such news voluntarily, he felt sure.

"Ships are not going inland," he remarked. "All you have to do is educate the newspapers along the coast and the press associations. If you do that, and I think it can be done on a voluntary basis, you have no problem."

JONES SEES DEFENSE 'BETTER THAN GOOD'

But Commerce Head Fears That the People Do Not Realize Its 'Imperativeness'

COMPLACENCY IS SCORED

No Censorship Expected Unless Forced by Short-Sighted Few, He Tells Associated Press

---

The progress of national defense is "better than good," it was reported by Jesse H. Jones, Secretary of Commerce, in an address before several hundred members of The Associated Press at their forty-first annual luncheon yesterday at the Hotel Waldorf-Astoria.

Mr. Jones, who is also Federal Loan Administrator, explained that he was "fairly close to defense activity" and that he feared the people of the country generally have not realized the "imperativeness" of the situation.

As publisher of The Houston (Texas) Chronicle, Mr. Jones is a member of The Associated Press, but he confessed that official duties in Washington had left him "little time" for his publication.

After warning that there was no place in the present defense effort for any "complacency," "indifference," or "obstruction," Mr. Jones asserted that the people of the country would be fortunate if the personal sacrifices they are asked to make proved to be only temporary.

Opportunity for Press

He declared that the press had never had a greater opportunity for service and cautioned that "if there is any censorship of the American press, it will be brought on by those short-sighted few who blindly and stubbornly refuse to recognize the responsibility that inevitably goes with freedom."

Robert McLean, president of The Associated Press, and publisher of The Philadelphia Evening Bulletin, presided at the luncheon. Before presenting Mr. Jones, Mr. McLean said:

"It has been our custom at these annual gatherings to drink the one and only toast to the President of the United States."

The members stood and drank the Presidential toast.

Citing Mr. Jones's official titles and noting that he formerly headed the Reconstruction Finance Corporation, Mr. McLean added:

"The American people owe him more than he will ever realize."

As administrator of the Federal Loan organization, Mr. McLean suggested that Mr. Jones "runs the biggest loan shop in the history of the world," adding that "he has got most of his money back and with faith sublime he expects to get the rest of it. He is a man among billions."

With freedom of the press suppressed nearly everywhere else in the world, Mr. Jones declared that "fortunately, in America, the people have the services of such agencies as The Associated Press, which strives to search out the news and report it impartially and completely."

Free Press Not To Be Abandoned

"As for freedom of the press," he said, "in my view, and as President Roosevelt told the newspaper editors last week, we will never abandon the high ideal that the press should be free to seek out and to print the news and the truth, unless temporarily certain items having a military bearing might better go unpublished.

"If the aggressor nations are successful, our generation is apt to see little of tranquillity. We will probably not be able to maintain our way of life. We will certainly not be able to maintain our high standard of living.

"Maybe, we can't be invaded, but we might become isolated economically, and that would inevitably lead to war. Trade outlets are the cause of most wars.

"If we are to get ready to defend ourselves, let's be sure that we do a good job of it. That means that we must give up some of the things we have been used to. We may have to submit to price controls—and that will be difficult—to make sure that the defense effort is not impeded. A government agency has been set up to guard against runaway prices. We should support that effort and we should adopt a program of taxation which will pay a large part of the defense cost currently. That's where the shoe will pinch, but I'm sure the American people are willing to be taxed as never before."

Mr. Jones cited more than 14,000 separate prime contracts and probably more than 100,000 sub-contracts for national defense that have been let in recent months. He said they called for the expenditure of more than $12,500,000,000. After breaking down that figure, Mr. Jones asserted:

"Any one who thinks that this is not progress doesn't know what he is talking about."

Following is the text of Secretary Jones's address before the annual meeting of The Associated Press:

As much as I appreciate the invitation to address The Associated Press, I am sure Mr. McLean and my other friends among your directors did not invite me to speak solely as a fellow-publisher. Possibly your invitation came because today is Texas's birthday, the 105th anniversary of the Battle of San Jacinto, where Sam Houston won independence for Texas.

Whatever the reason, I am honored by the invitation. It is a privilege to meet with you and discuss informally some of our current problems.

Publishers everywhere in America are probably asking themselves two fundamental questions: First, like all patriotic citizens, they want to know about the defense program and how well it is getting along. Second, they want some one to essay the role of prophet and give them a glimpse into the future after the war.

They would like answers to many perplexing questions. We all would. Some are concerned about the freedom of the press. When they contemplate the disasters which have befallen the press in some other countries, the more pessimistic are afraid that the same fate might be in store for them here. I have no such fear.

I am not so naïve as to assume that I can come before you and speak with authority as a publisher. I have not given a great deal of time to The Houston Chronicle, although I would regard it a high privilege to be primarily a publisher and an editor. It is a role worthy of the ambitions of any one. It affords an opportunity to be of service to one's community, and to one's country.

Privilege Sometimes Misused

That this privilege is sometimes misused, or carelessly and thoughtlessly exercised, does not warrant condemning the entire press. Fortunately, most publishers and editors of American newspapers can be depended upon for a high order of integrity and patriotism. Fortunately, in America the people have the services of such agencies as The Associated Press, which strives to search out the news and report it impartially and completely.

As for the freedom of the press, in my view, and as President Roosevelt told the newspaper editors last week, we will never abandon the high ideal that the press should be free to seek out and to print the news and the truth, unless temporarily certain items having a military bearing might better go unpublished.

Despite any of our shortcomings, it is safe to say that in no other part of the world is so much information so well presented. I might add, parenthetically, that over the years The Associated Press had made a great contribution toward this achievement.

Here in the United States the press has reached its greatest height. To realize that, one need only compare American newspapers with those of any other country. In their news coverage, in the wide variety of it, in the character of its presentation, the newspapers of this country are unequaled. The very freedom of our press and the place it occupies in our lives gives it vast power.

But we should not forget that with that power goes responsibility. The greater the freedom, the greater the necessity that it always be exercised wisely and in the public interest.

It is by recognition of that responsibility that the American press will best serve its own future, and the cause of a free press everywhere in the world.

The careless or unreliable publisher or writer or news agency not only performs a disservice to his country, and its defense in times like these, but he performs a direct disservice to the newspapers of America.

The Short-Sighted Few

If there should ever be censorship of the American press, it would be brought on by those short-sighted few who blindly and stubbornly refuse to recognize the responsibility that inevitably goes with freedom. But as a government official I am glad to be able to say that I have never seen any indication that any one in government wanted to do any censoring, unless it be information which might aid those who are not America's friends.

Freedom of the press is a part of the heritage of every free-born son of this democracy. It is a vital fundamental of our way of life. It is through the press, the dailies, the weeklies, and the magazines, that America speaks.

When editorial opinion strays widely from American thought, publishers might well afford to take stock of themselves and try to ascertain why.

We should not bring about any lessening of our freedom or our influence through our own failings. Let's keep our standards high.

May I suggest that you check and double check the more sensational angles of stories which involve relations between this nation and other countries. Resolve any doubts in favor of the non-sensational approach. To do so may be helpful to the men who are wrestling with our foreign relations.

Our press has never had a greater opportunity to serve our country than it has today. First, in printing impartially all the news that should be printed, and second, in arousing the people to the realization that our safety and our way of living are growing less secure by the hour; that hundreds of millions of people are at war destroying life and property and fine things inherited from many generations; that civilization is having a severe test and will be fortunate to survive.

I shall not embark upon any path of prophecy. Only a year ago at your meeting here, you had several war correspondents who talked like people from a strange world. Little did any of us realize then the situation we would face today. How then, can we foretell tomorrow?

But without getting into the realm of speculation, if the aggressor nations are successful, our generation is apt to see little of tranquility. We will probably not be able to maintain our high standard of living. Our economy cannot compete with slave labor—and the great mass of the people of the Axis powers and their captives are little more than slaves. They must live and work as they are told. They must accept such reward for their services as an all-powerful and ruthless state sees fit to give them. They may have butter only when guns are not needed.

And that brings me to the progress of our defense program. One need only recall our lack of preparedness when you met here a year ago to see how far we have come. We did not even visualize the possibility of defense activity on anything approaching the scale on which it is now organized. It is not easy for a peace-loving people like ours to change overnight from purely peacetime pursuits to complete all-out effort at arming, even for defense.

This is particularly true because we have always had faith in the protection of the oceans, and have always believed that no power could invade us.

Maybe we can't be invaded, but we might become isolated economically, and that would inevitably lead to war. Trade outlets are the cause of most wars.

Defense Work In Progress

In the period of these few months, more than 14,000 separate prime contracts, and probably more than 100,000 subcontracts, have been let for the manufacture of everything from a corporal's chevrons to bombers and battleships. These contracts call for the expenditure of more than $12,500,000,000. Seven hundred and eighty-four new defense plants costing more than $2,100,000,000 have been built or are under construction by the War and Navy Departments.

In addition to these, the RFC is building or financing more than 100 defense plants at a cost of $650,000,000. All of these plants are for the manufacture of war supplies.

The RFC is accumulating reserve supplies of copper, tin, antimony, chrome, asbestos, zinc, graphite, manganese, tungsten, rubber, wool and a few other items of strategic materials. Most of these materials come from foreign countries.

RFC has made commitments for the expenditure of more than $1,500,000,000 for defense, all in cooperation with the War and Navy Departments, OPM, and other defense agencies. This is in addition to war and navy contracts. No day is dull in defense activity.

Any one who thinks that this is not progress doesn't know what he is talking about. Negotiating this many contracts involving in round numbers $16,000,000,000 is progress, and production is getting well under way. No doubt some mistakes have been made and some delays occasioned. It could not be otherwise. But we have capable men from industry and government in charge of defense work, in addition to the regular staffs of the Army and Navy.

And don't think these service men are not capable. They have spent years in studying our military needs and know how to meet them. General Marshall told me only two days ago, after visiting camps and cantonments throughout the country, that we have 1,250,000 as fine men in training as he has ever seen, and that he had never seen higher morale in any army.

I am fairly close to defense activity. I have seen it in the sprouting stage and now I see it bearing fruit. Its progress is not satisfactory in all respects, but under the circumstances I think it is better than good.

No Room for Complacency

I am afraid, however, that as a people we have not yet realized the imperativeness of our defense necessities, that we have not yet been shocked. There is no room in America today for complacency. There is no place for indifference. Certainly there is no place for obstruction and it should not be tolerated. No matter how fast defense production climbs, it will not be fast enough to meet the need nor to satisfy our state of mind—our anxiety. There is no place in the crucial world of 1941 for any delay or any excuses.

There is no room for selfishness, whether it be the selfishness of industry seeking undue profits, or of labor seeking unjustifiable wage increases and endeavoring to utilize the emergency to fight jurisdictional and internal battles. There is no place for profiteering of any kind. And there is no time for any stoppage of vital work to argue about the terms on which it is done. There must be but one selfishness, the selfishness of all of us for the protection of American democracy. It must not be sacrificed.

The time is rapidly approaching when each of us will be called upon to measure our patriotism, our love of freedom, and our devotion to the democratic way of life in terms of individual sacrifice. We will be fortunate if this sacrifice represents only a temporary doing without some of the things to which we have become accustomed—a little personal inconvenience.

We are too inclined to take it for granted that aid to Britain and the other democracies, and even our own defense, mean only the training of a few soldiers and sailors, and the appropriation of a few billions of dollars, followed by orders for airplanes, guns, ships and tanks.

Spending Billions a Real Job

Our defense expenditures are now running at the rate of $9,000,-000,000 to $10,000,000,000 a year. The end of the year will undoubtedly see this rate stepped up to as much as $15,000,000,000 yearly, possibly more. To most of us, the difference between $1,000,000 and $1,000,000,000 is whether you spell the word with a "b" or an "m," but spending $1,000,000,000 or $10,000,000,000 is a real undertaking.

It is impossible to understand fully the meaning of these huge appropriations of money until we translate them into labor and materials.

Fifteen billion dollars is more than all the wages and salaries paid by all the manufacturing plants in the United States in any one year. It is twice the value of all the agricultural products produced in the United States in any recent year by our 6,000,000 farm families.

Some people seem to think that this colossal effort at defense need not interfere with business as usual. The European war might now be over if some of the democracies involved had not taken just that view in the beginning. And experience should teach us that anything short of a maximum effort—maximum aid to

Britain and the other democracies, and maximum preparation for the defense of the Western Hemisphere—may be worse than no effort at all.

If we are to get ready to defend ourselves, let's be sure that we do a good job of it. That means we must give up some of the things we have been used to, when actually we will have more money in circulation from the government spending all these billions for defense.

Price Control Possible

With the expenditure of these billions we must guard against inflation and runaway prices. We may have to submit to price controls to make sure that the defense effort is not impeded. A government agency has been set up to guard against runaway prices. We should support that effort, and we should adopt a program of taxation which will pay a large part of the defense cost currently.

We are in the most momentous period in modern history. Whether it will be a grim, tragic tale of long and arduous struggle, or will lead to a peaceful and better world, depends upon the military outcome.

Putting first things first, the war must first be won. We are helping the democracies because we believe the survival of democracy is essential to our civilization. We should not underestimate the task. We will be called upon to pay dearly for something we would like to have avoided, something unnecessary and inexcusable. But when outlaws are at large and our future is at stake, we have no choice but to prepare to defend ourselves against aggression from any source.

If we would preserve the kind of life we have been accustomed to, and want to continue to enjoy, we must lay gun on gun until every threat to our security has been met.

ARMY, NAVY GET CONTROL OF RADIO

Use or Closure of Private Facilities Is Covered in Order Signed by the President

'BATTLE ROOM' IS READY

Army - Navy Communication Center Is Put Into Operation in the White House

By FRANK L. KLUCKHOHN
Special to THE NEW YORK TIMES.

WASHINGTON, Dec. 10—In his capacity as Commander in Chief, President Roosevelt today authorized military control or closure of as many private radio facilities as the government deemed necessary. Action would be taken immmediately, the Defense Communications Board stated.

The President also instructed the War and Navy Departments to release news on the American repulse of Japanese forces at Luzon, the Philippines, and on the battle for control of Cavite near Manila, and on naval actions involving the Asiatic Fleet in near-by waters. He also approved the establishment of martial law in Manila.

He sent a message to Generalissimo Chiang Kai-shek of China, welcoming American-Chinese association in this war against Japan, and assured General John J. Pershing, who offered his services, that these "will be of great value."

Intensifying his activities as Commander in Chief of the Army and Navy, Mr. Roosevelt held a staff conference to discuss war developments and plot new moves meeting with technical and political leaders of the armed and diplomatic services. Meanwhile the installation of a unique Army-Navy communications center across the hall from his office at the White House was completed.

Meets His "Inner Cabinet"

At midday, the President conferred for an hour and a half with his "inner war cabinet" before going to his office to receive reports from the new "battle" room on what had developed while the conference was in progress.

Those present at the meeting of the "inner war cabinet" included Secretaries Hull and Stimson; the acting Secretary of the Navy, James V. Forrestal, Admiral Harold B. Stark, Chief of Naval Operations; General George C. Marshall, Army Chief of Staff, and Sumner Welles, Under-Secretary of State. In keeping with the policy enun-

ciated by the President in his speech last night, no news was made public about this conference.

President McKinley had what was known as a "war room" on the second floor of the White House during the Spanish-American War, but this merely contained maps, and communications facilities were absent. President Wilson had no such facility during the World War.

In President Roosevelt's "battle" room, established today, telephones and other modern instruments of communication were set up. As soon as the War and Navy Departments received information this was carried into this new White House nerve center, where Army and Navy officers plotted movements on maps, according to one of those who was in the room.

Thus the Commander in Chief was in a position to get a quick minute-to-minute picture of the war and to issue orders if the situation warranted. The room employed was large and formerly served as an official "inner" waiting room.

The move to give the government control of the radio was announced in the following statement:

"The President has just signed an Executive order recommended by the Defense Communications Board, which order gives the board authority to designate radio facilities for use, control, inspection, or closure by the War or Navy Departments, or other agencies of the government.

"The order has unanimous approval of the Army, Navy, State and Treasury Departments and of the Federal Communications Commission.

"The purpose of the order is to insure the national defense and the successful conduct of the war.' "

Subsequently, the FCC announced that the Army and Navy, "by agreement," would take over some facilities and close others. It was officially denied that this constituted "censorship."

The statement, issued by James Branch Fly, chairman of the FCC and DCB, said that the Executive Order signed by the President meant simply that the Executive was delegating to the DCB authority which was given to him under Section 606 of the Federal Communications Act.

"It does not mean any general taking over of radio by the government is contemplated," it was stated. "There is no change in policy or plans. The step is a procedural one. It long has been known the military may require certain communications facilities; many of these already have been arranged for by agreement.

Censorship Is Denied

"Under today's Executive Order, the Army and Navy will now, when necessary, arrange to take over or close radio facilities. The DCB thus relieves the President of extra duties."

The statement added that the DCB "is not undertaking censorship."

The DCB, appointed some time

ago, consists of Mr. Fly, Herbert Gaston of the Treasury, Major Gen. Dawson Olmstead, Army Chief Signal Officer; Rear Admiral Leigh Noyes, Director of Naval Communications; Breckenridge Long, Assistant Secretary of State, and representatives of the radio, telegraph and telephone industries.

On the heels of this action Neville Miller, president of the National Association of Broadcasters, urged all broadcasting stations "to exercise unusually careful editorial judgment in selecting news." The statement also endorsed the War Department "recommendation" that ordinary periods for a program should not be interrupted for war bulletins and that such bulletins should be released only at "definite periods."

The 90,000,000 people, or 92.4 per cent of the adults of every family in the nation, who, according to radio check-ups, listened to the President's address last night, seemed favorable to the address, Stephen Early, Presidential secretary, asserted.

The Executive received about 600 telephone calls and telegrams before he retired last night, Mr. Early said, adding that "without exception, they show a complete unanimity."

RADIO TO BE SILENCED ON THREAT OF AIR RAID

Control in All Areas Given to Army Interceptor Command

WASHINGTON, Dec. 12 (U.P)— The War Department announced today a plan for prompt suspension of radio broadcasting operations when enemy air raids are threatened anywhere in Continental United States.

The plan was drafted by the Federal Communications Commission, the radio branch of the War Department's Bureau of Public Relations, telephone services and the Army Air Force's interceptor command. It goes into effect immediately.

Stations will be grouped by radio control areas within the regions of the interceptor commands. In case of an alarm, the interceptor command will order stations in given areas to shut down.

The orders apply to standard broadcast, high frequency, television and relay broadcast stations.

Officials said the plan should assure "speedy and accurate transmission" of orders to cease broadcasting and also should eliminate "unnecessarily imposed silences."

When all-clear conditions exist, the interceptor command will advise stations in the control area to resume operations.

The department said that this or a similar announcement would be made when service must be temporarily suspended:

"At this time, ladies and gentlemen, radio station —— is temporarily leaving the air in conformity with the national defense program. Keep your radio on so that upon resumption of our service we may bring you the latest information."

BRICKER SEES PERIL TO PRESS FREEDOM

Ohioan Says New Deal Tries to Undermine Newspapers

COLUMBUS, Ohio, Feb. 4 (AP)— Gov. John W. Bricker declared tonight that the Roosevelt Administration had made "a studied attempt to undermine the newspapers and radio" and called for lifting of governmental restrictions which he contended endangered the freedoms of press and speech.

Governor Bricker, a candidate for the Republican Presidential nomination, said that all sources of information must be kept open and proposed, though "it may be millennial," a free press throughout the world.

Administration literature, Mr. Bricker told the Ohio Newspaper Association, has become full of expressions which "are evidence of a calculated purpose to discredit the press."

The spirit of freedom, the Governor declared, cries out for intelligent leadership from the press.

"If that leadership fails," he said, "American liberty is in danger. Political propaganda must be destroyed as an instrumentality of government. We must insist that appropriate sources of information be kept open to the press of the country. Public information should never be restricted to the handout, off-the-record and not-for-attribution methods. News must be available and free to all alike, as well as the right to print the news.

February 5, 1944

Political Censoring Refused

WASHINGTON, Oct. 30 — The Federal Communications Commission emphasized today that it had no power of censorship over political broadcasts when it denied a petition by William B. Rubin of Milwaukee to order CBS, Mutual, NBC, the Blue Network, and affiliated stations to show cause why their licenses should not be revoked because of certain statements about President Roosevelt in speeches on the radio by Governors Dewey and Bricker, and Representative Clare Boothe Luce.

FUND GROUP SCANS INSURANCE FIRMS

Also Acts on Complaints of Partisanship by Sponsored Radio Commentators

WASHINGTON, Nov. 4 (AP)— The Senate Campaign Expenditures Committee disclosed today that it was making preliminary charges of partisan political activity by insurance companies and by radio commentators on sponsored broadcasts. It reported also that it was gathering newspaper clippings with a view to studying the objectivity of the campaign news coverage.

Robert T. Murphy, committee counsel, said in a statement:

"Inquiries are being made at the present time into a complaint that insurance companies have been actively engaged in political activity, to determine whether or not the facts warrant a full scale investigation.

"Similar inquiries are being made on a tentative basis to determine whether or not the committee would be justified in studying sponsored radio broadcasts purporting to be impartial news commentaries and which are alleged to be, in fact, highly partisan.

The committee has accumulated thousands of newspaper clippings which may later form a basis for an effort on the part of the committee to evaluate newspaper coverage of the campaign in terms of relative objectivity.

"This particular project has not yet been presented to the full committee and may not materialize because of the obvious difficulties, both in time and judgment."

Mr. Murphy declined to identify the radio broadcasters under committee scrutiny, but named several insurance companies and insurance company officials against whose activities, he said, complaints had been filed.

Among those named and the charges concerning them were the following:

The Pennsylvania Manufacturers' Casualty Insurance Company of Philadelphia, asserted by a complainant to have distributed literature supporting Governor Dewey, Republican Presidential nominee.

H. K. Dent, Seattle, president of the General Insurance Company of America and two associated companies, said to have distributed to stockholders and employes of the companies a letter declaring that a Communist-sponsored "revolution by ballot" was under way. The letter mentioned no candidate or party and bore a notation by Mr. Dent that he had written the letter as a private citizen.

The People's Committee to Defend Life Insurance and Savings, with headquarters in New York, said to have sponsored Dewey-Bricker rallies in various States.

December 11, 1941 · December 13, 1941 · October 31, 1944 · November 5, 1944

297

PUBLIC SERVICE

FCC Head Urges Broadcasters to Remedy Ills of Excessive Commercialism

By PAUL A. PORTER
Chairman, Federal Communications Commission

(The following is an extract from Mr. Porter's speech last week before a meeting of the National Association of Broadcasters in Washington.)

TODAY many influential broadcasters have expressed to me deep concern over what they themselves describe as an alarming trend toward "excessive commercialism." They see, as do many of us who have studied the great progress of this industry, developments which unless checked may lead to real difficulty in the future. I have been told, as I am sure many of you have, that somehow there must be a determination as to whether broadcasting is simply going to operate as an advertising and entertainment media or whether it will continue to perform, in increasing measure, public-service functions in addition. I want broadcasters themselves to provide the answer to that question. The cloud on the horizon is bigger than a man's hand and I know that responsible broadcasters see it and are concerned about it.

Naturally you are asking yourselves the question as to what extent the commission may propose to inject itself into this particular field. I wish I could tell you the answer to that one but I can't because I don't know. I am familiar with all the arguments about the Government keeping its rude, bureaucratic hands off of anything that smacks of program control and I am in agreement with most of those arguments. I am likewise conscious of the limitations imposed by Congress in the statute with respect to matters involving censorship and am fully aware of the dangers of any Government agency, legislative or administrative, toying with standards of program content.

But under present circumstances one of the issues involved has taken a different form and it has been laid right on the commission's doorstep. Briefly, the facts are these: An applicant seeks a construction permit for a new station and in his application makes the usual representations as to the type of service he proposes. These representations include specific pledges that time will be made available for civic, educational, agricultural and other public-service programs. The station is constructed and begins operations. Subsequently, the licensee asks for a three-year renewal and the record clearly shows that he has not fulfilled the promises made to the commission when he received the original grant. The commission in the past has, for a variety of reasons, including limitations of staff, automatically renewed these licenses even in cases where there is a vast disparity between promises and performance.

License Renewal

We have under consideration at the present time, however, a procedure whereby promises will be compared with performances. I think the industry is entitled to know of our concern in this matter and should be informed that there is pending before the commission staff proposals which are designed to strengthen renewal procedures and give the commission a more definite picture of the station's over-all operation when licenses come up for renewal.

I have no present views as to what further steps should be taken when it appears from the record in a specific case that an applicant has completely disregarded the representations upon which he obtained his original grant. Obviously no one would advocate that the representations made in the original application constitute a rigid blueprint for the future. Experience will dictate new and superior methods of performing public service. But in cases where commercial opportunities cause a complete abandonment of other services which he has agreed to perform, a different question is raised. I am not charging that broadcasting generally has tossed public service out the window. We all know that is not true. What I am saying is that there seems to be a growing body of responsible opinion that believes that the public functions of broadcasting are becoming submerged by commercialism.

Under these conditions the commission is confronted with a real problem. Are we of the commission to assume that the statutory standard of public interest becomes a mere negative presumption, and that so long as the license violates none of the specific prohibitions against obscenity, lotteries and the like, the regularatory authority is not to inquire further into the licensee's general performance? I do not believe Congress so intended—or at least some individual members of the present Congress are looking to the commission for some clarification of policy in this respect.

Believing as I do in the great potentials of this industry, it is my personal view that broadcasting can never be content to become merely adequate. It can and must continue to seek new and more engaging methods to win and maintain public approval. And in evaluating public approval, it seems to me, the tastes and interests of minorities must be taken into account. Above all, it seems to me, that it does no good to merely resent criticism: The nature of broadcasting is such that most listeners feel a proprietary interest in its operations and, I recognize too, that it is often true that the sins of a few are charged against the industry as a whole. But the obvious course is to seek to remove the cause of justifiable criticism.

It is my personal position, as I have indicated, that it is far better for broadcasters themselves to take whatever actions may be necessary to eliminate the causes of general public dissatisfaction. I would view with great reluctance attempts to legislate more detailed standards in the field of the public-service obligations of broadcasting. I have grave doubts not only as to the propriety but as to the practicability of spelling out by mathematical formula or some other device the general methods which broadcasters should follow in discharging their public-service functions.

The question of freedom of broadcasting is involved, and those of us who feel deeply about this subject want broadcasting to remain free because it deserves to and not simply because it may under our system be entitled to claim some kind of immunity from enforced standards of conduct.

What I have said lacks specificity. And I have been general on purpose. But I think responsible broadcasters are aware of the nature of the problems to which I have alluded. I have attempted to call attention to considerations which I know are of concern to you, to increasing segments of public opinion, to the Congress and the commission. I have no suggestions as to any general remedy for the problem. I think the answer rests primarily with the broadcasting industry, and it is my hope that there will be honest public discussion on the basic questions of policies and procedures and that action will follow which will make it apparent to all that broadcasting can and will perform those functions which Congress intended it to perform and which its licenses require of it.

March 18, 1945

NEW BILLS REVISE RADIO ACT SHARPLY

WASHINGTON, May 23 (AP)—Bills to bar political broadcasts on election day and the day before and to make other sweeping changes in radio regulations were introduced today by the Republican chairmen of the Senate and House Commerce Committees.

The identical measures by Senator Wallace H. White Jr. of Maine and Representative Charles A. Wolverton of New Jersey, also would require radio stations to grant "equal opportunities" for broadcasting to both sides in political controversies and to speakers on non-political public issues. At present, stations which give free time to one political speaker must give the same amount of free time to the opposing side.

Mr. White said that the proposed measure defined "equal opportunities" to cover "not only the time and number of stations used, but also the cost, if any, for use of the facilities."

Other major provisions would deny the right of radio stations to censor political broadcasts but exempt them from libel or slander suits in such cases; forbid a single person or company to own radio stations serving more than one-fourth of the country's population; require radio stations to make known to listeners "all pertinent details about those who speak over the radio" and "plainly label editorial opinion or comment as distinguished from straight news," and require news broadcasters to specify the source of their news.

Senator White said that there was no desire to prevent the broadcasting of opinion or comment but only to label it as such.

Another provision in the measure, which is the result of seven years of congressional study, would make it clear that the Federal Communications Commission "does not have the authority to tell a licensee, directly or indirectly, what he can broadcast or cannot broadcast, or how he should run his day-to-day business."

Representative Wolverton said that during the last ten years the commission under the regimes of James L. Fly, Paul Porter and Charles M. Denny had been "in constant difficulty both in and out of congress over its policies."

The present radio act basically is more than 20 years old, he added, "and the industry, which has made tremendous strides in a quarter of a century, is handicapped by antiquated legislation."

A section of the Bill prohibiting discrimination between licensees, said Senator White, would "prevent the commission from adopting any rule, regulation or policy which denies radio broadcasting licenses to newspapers."

May 24, 1947

CIO ASKS FCC FORBID 'CENSORING' BY RADIO

Special to THE NEW YORK TIMES.

WASHINGTON, May 10 — The Congress of Industrial Organizations asked the Federal Communications Commission today to confirm its tentative decision in the "Port Huron case." This decision was to the effect that a radio station licensee may not—state libel laws to the contrary notwithstanding—"censor" the content of a political broadcast, by amendment or elimination or by denial of its facilities for discussions in which the arguments of the candidates are punctuated with personal references, either defamatory or libelous or both

The CIO, and its Political Action Committee, in a statement issued today declared:

"We feel that the principles set forth in the Port Huron case not only pave the way for greater freedom of political discussion in radio but also represent an important step toward giving workers' organizations more equitable access to the country's broadcasting facilities.

"Official representatives of the CIO, and in particular candidates for political office within its ranks, are willing to accept the responsibility for allegedly libelous statements which may result in court action."

Radio station operators in several states, however, have protested the proposed decision on the ground that if maintained they would be confronted with a choice between risking loss of their licenses by FCC action for refusal to broadcast the material in question, and the loss of their stations through the operation of state laws by which, for the broadcasting of libelous matter, they would become subject to damages in amount sufficient to put them out of business.

May 11, 1948

Factual Political News, but No Comment, Permitted for Army's Papers and Radio

Special to THE NEW YORK TIMES

WASHINGTON, May 13—Army newspapers and broadcasting stations must refrain from support or criticism of special political candidates or issues, the Department of the Army ordered today in a circular distributed to all commands.

The circular was designed to clarify standing orders, required by law, under which all service personnel must be informed about candidates for office, voting dates and other details of election news. It said:

"It is appropriate for the Army to make available to its personnel stationed outside the continental United States sufficient current political information to enable them to vote intelligently."

Nevertheless, the circular stated, "any material which is paid for in whole or in part with Federal funds (such as newspapers or radio stations) * * * must not contain political propaganda obviously designed to affect the result of any election."

Rules for Army-published newspapers are:

"(1) Army newspapers will not contain political editorials nor * * * comment, criticism, analysis, or interpretation of news of a political nature.

"(2) Theater-wide newspapers published by the Army * * * such as the 'Stars and Stripes,' which normally carries world news, will * * * be a faithful reflection of political news of a factual nature procured from nationally recognized United States news services.

"(3) Local newspapers (those other than theater-wide newspapers) will contain no political news."

Radio regulations are:

"(1) Oversea radio stations controlled by the Army are authorized to broadcast political news of a factual nature furnished by nationally recognized United States news services. Political news broadcasts will not include comment, criticism, analysis or interpretation.

"(2) Army short-wave stations are authorized to broadcast political news of a factual nature released by the State Department or by nationally recognized United States news services.

"(3) Political addresses * * * will be restricted to transcriptions distributed by Armed Forces Radio Service. Addresses of Presidential candidates should be scheduled during the most advantageous listening hours of the day. Adequate advance notice should be broadcast, giving the date and hour of address."

May 14, 1948

FCC UPHOLDS RULE ON POLITICAL LIBEL

Decision Forbids Censorship by Radio Station, Contending Speaker Is Responsible

By WINIFRED MALLON
Special to THE NEW YORK TIMES.

WASHINGTON, June 30—In a final decision reaffirming a previous ruling, the Federal Communications Commission announced today that the licensee of a radio station while at liberty to deny the use of his facilities to candidates for political office may neither censor for libelous content any of their broadcasts, nor be sued for damages.

The speakers, said FCC, and not the station, are "completely liable" for statements made by them.

Issuance in finality of this policy declaration by the FCC has been opposed by the National Association of Broadcasters and individual owners of radio stations, especially those who under the laws of the state in which they are operating are held responsible for the libellous content, if any, of material, political or otherwise, broadcast over their facilities.

Interpretation Based on Intent

Nevertheless, under the 1934 Communications Act, as amended, no other interpretation of the intent of Congress is possible, according to the Commission. Section 315 of that Act on which its ruling is based, states specifically:

"If any licensee shall permit any person who is a legally qualified candidate for any public office to use a broadcasting station, he shall afford equal opportunities to all other such candidates for that office in the use of such broadcasting station, and the Commission shall make rules and regulations to carry this provision into effect. Provided, that such licensee shall have no power of censorship over the material broadcast under the provisions of this section. No obligation is hereby imposed upon any licensee to allow the use of its station by any such candidate."

The law having thus tied the hands of the licensee, the commission argues that liability is clearly intended to attach to the speaker who, whether talking on free or paid time, is responsible, as the station is not, for what he says, and who is "completely liable for the contents of his remarks."

Censorship Is Defined

Neither the licensee, nor the commission itself, it is stated, has power of "censorship" to limit or interfere with the "right of free speech" other than to prevent, as provided by law, the broadcasting of "obscene, indecent, or profane language."

Today's ruling represents the last act in the so-called Port Huron case, occasioned by the refusal of Station WHLS at Port Huron, Mich., to broadcast more than one of a series of broadcasts on a local election issue, the first having been complained of as libelous. The licensee, after examination of the other scripts, conclude that they did contain possibly libelous material and canceled all broadcast schedules in that connection.

As a result, Station WHLS has been operating on temporary authority since 1945, pending final decision by the Commission on its application for renewal of license, which as announced today is that the action taken by the licensee constituted censorship but was not willful, there having been no prior clarification of the rule, and that renewal therefore should be approved.

July 1, 1948

LIBEL ON RADIO HELD NOT STATION'S FAULT

WASHINGTON, Aug. 5 (P)—Wayne Coy, chairman of the Federal Communications Commission, told a special House investigating committee today that he does not think radio stations should be held responsible for libelous or slanderous statements in broadcast of political speeches because Federal law prohibits stations from censoring such speeches.

Two other witnesses, W. Theodore Pierson, Washington lawyer, C. K. Richards, assistant attorney general of Texas, disagreed. They said radio stations can't count on any such immunity unless Congress specifically says so.

Mr. Coy recommended that Congress act to give radio stations immunity from libel suits arising out of political broadcasts

The House committee is starting what Chairman Forest A. Harness, Republican, of Indiana, said will be a "searching investigation" of all the activities of the commission.

At present, the inquiry is limited to the effect of the commission's decision on June 28 in the so-called Port Huron case in which a majority of the commission held radio stations may not censor political broadcasts even though they might be sued for libel under state laws.

Mr. Coy said that while stations censoring political speeches jeopardize their chances for license renewal, the commission is aware of the difficulties and judges each case on the facts.

Mr. Pierson and Mr. Richards said that present laws give radio stations no immunity from libel.

Mr. Coy agreed that the commission's opinion does not provide radio stations without any immunity from libel and said "quite a number of states" have been holding that stations are liable under state law.

August 6, 1948

Coy Backs Broadcasters on Libel

WASHINGTON, Aug. 6 (UP)—The special Congressional committee investigating the Federal Communications Commission tonight wound up its radio censorship hearings on a cheerful note for broadcasters. Chairman Forest Harness said the committee had received assurances from Wayne Coy, chairman of the Commission, that no broadcasters' license would be revoked if he continued to forbid libelous statements in political broadcasts.

August 7, 1948

FCC HINTS IT WANTS MORE RULE OF RADIO

WASHINGTON, Feb. 25 (UP)—The Federal Communications Commission hinted today that it would like more power to regulate chain broadcasting. The agency said it believed it was time for a new investigation of radio and television network practices.

The commission's views were set forth in a letter to Chairman Edwin C. Johnson, Democrat, of Colorado, of the Senate Interstate Commerce Committee, who recently submitted a series of questions dealing with FCC policy on television.

Replying for the commission, Chairman Wayne Coy touched on network broadcasting in connection with a question about prevention of monopolistic control in the manufacture of television equipment and in television programs.

Mr. Coy replied that the commission had no control over manufacturers as such but that it did consider activity which might be deemed monopolistic in connection with manufacturers who have transmitting licenses or are applying for licenses.

He also replied that the agency was making a study of the patent situation to see whether any practices were inconsistent with the anti-trust laws.

On the question of program monopoly, Mr. Coy said the commission had made no investigation of chain broadcasting since 1941 and that it dealt at that time with standard broadcasting.

He said most of the chain broadcasting regulations had been carried over into the television and frequency modulation fields and that separate investigations might be needed.

February 26, 1949

White House Censors Air Pictures Of President on Vacation Beach

By ANTHONY LEVIERO
Special to THE NEW YORK TIMES

KEY WEST, Fla., March 14 — The White House today imposed a firm censorship on news photographers after they had taken still and newsreel pictures of President Truman, Chief Justice Fred Vinson and others disporting on a beach here.

The veteran White House camera men, who are well known to the President, were aloft in a Navy blimp on an authorized flight. As they flew off the beach at 200 feet, their cameras clicking, the Chief Executive doffed his cap and waved to them.

Later, however, Charles G. Ross, Mr. Truman's press secretary, ordered their films confiscated. He ordered the airship to stay aloft until he, with James Rowley, head of the White House Secret Service detail, and Rear Admiral Robert L. Dennison, Mr. Truman's Naval aide, made a fast eight-mile automobile trip to Boca Chica Naval Air Station.

In a confused situation, left unclear even after Mr. Ross' customary news conference this afternoon, the only certain fact was that the White House appeared to have a policy relating to Presidential security and privacy, but had not notified either news men or Navy officials.

President Truman became aware of the censorship incident in the afternoon, as Mr. Ross explained, only after word of it was flashed by news tickers and Mr. Ross began to get reverberations from Washington.

The five photographers said they had received clearance for the flight last week after taking it up first with Lieut. Comdr. William Rigdon of the White House staff and later with Admiral Dennison. Then the Navy arranged to take them up. They started these arrangements with Commander Rigdon before the arrival of Mr. Ross last week.

The photographers assumed there would be no objection by Mr. Ross and neither they nor, apparently, Admiral Dennison nor Commander Rigdon, notified him of the planned flight.

Mr. Ross said he banned the photographers on the ground of the President's personal security and privacy. The Navy cleared the flight, requesting only that no close-up photographs be made of Navy installations, which include the most advanced submarine and anti-submarine research projects.

The photographers are Byron Rollins of Associated Press Photos, who has covered the White House for thirteen years and is president of the White House News Photographers Association; Thomas Craven of Paramount News, acting as pool photographer also for Metro-Goldwyn-Mayer, Fox, Universal and Pathé Newsreels; Alfonso Muto of International News Photos; Milton Freier of Acme Newsphotos and Joseph Vadala of National Broadcasting Company Television.

The photographers reported that Mr. Ross took their films and turned them over to Mr. Rowley, saying they would be developed by the Navy. The camera men protested, asserting that the Navy laboratory men would not do a competent job by newspaper standards. The photographers added that Mr. Ross then declared their pictures never would be published.

Thereupon the three still men—Messrs. Rollins, Muto and Freier—took back their films from the Secret Service agent and destroyed them on the spot.

The movie men—Messrs. Craven and Vadala—because they had other noncontroversial matter on the same reel with the 200 feet they had exposed on the flight, agreed to confiscation and to Government developing of the film in Washington.

Hint of Approval Is Disputed

At his regular news conference at 4 P. M., Mr. Ross, appearing perplexed and unhappy about the incident, implied that he might have cleared some of the pictures after they had been developed.

He was challenged immediately, however, by Mr. Muto, who interposed:

"You said these pictures would never see publication, so rather than give you the pleasure of censorship we destroyed them."

"This morning." said Mr. Ross, in opening his conference, "while the President was at the beach [within the naval station], a Navy blimp came by, flying quite low. I was surprised to see it there. I thought the Navy had sent it over with Navy photographers to take pictures. I looked up and saw the White House photographers."

Mr. Ross said he returned to the winter White House, gave orders to keep the airship aloft, then went to the airport. He explained his action "on the ground of security and I might have said but did not say [at the airport] a completely unauthorized invasion of his [the President's] privacy."

"I made a request that the pictures be not used," said Mr. Ross. "I suggested that they might be developed on the Naval base and select those that could be used. The consensus was that if the Navy developed them they would spoil them. I also said that any pictures not cleared wouldn't be used in any case. The men themselves preferred to have them destroyed."

Repeatedly Mr. Ross was asked to explain what he meant by "security." Once he said, "I know the Secret Service men have a difficult job because of the increased news interest in the President makes more difficult the work of the Secret Service."

Unrestricted Maps Cited

One reporter pointed to an unrestricted map on the wall of the Bachelor Officers' Quarters, where the conference was held, showing the location of the winter White House and the restricted beach.

Each correspondent, upon his arrival, received from the Key West Chamber of Commerce a map of the island, pin-pointing ten places of interest, including: "10. Naval Station: location of 'Winter White House'." It also shows the Fort Taylor area where the beach is situated, but does not specifically identify it. A similar map was put out by the Key West Newcomer Welcome Service.

Mr. Ross said that if a request for the pictures, which included aerial pictures of the President's cottage, had been made to him "we could have worked out something mutually satisfactory."

Mr. Craven told Mr. Ross that he had specifically requested permission from Commander Rigdon and Admiral Dennison to take pictures of the winter White House and of the beach. In reply to a question from Mr. Ross, however, he conceded that he had not specified a picture of the beach with the President there.

A reporter asked if the matter could not have been handled on a basis of trust—have the photographers develop their own film and submit them for clearance. One pointed out that during the war tremendously important pictures involving security were handled this way. Mr. Ross said the matter "could have been handled in a number of ways," but that this method had not been thought of at the airfield.

"The decision is mine and I assume full responsibility for it," Mr. Ross said.

President To Be Their Guest

The photographers are embarrassed by the incident, for Mr. Truman is to be guest of honor at their association's dinner in Washington Saturday night.

The cameramen were in the blimp from 11:08 A. M. to 12:36 P. M. The official records show that the beach photos were taken at an altitude of 200 feet, with only Mr. Vadala using a telephoto lens to somewhat enlarge the tiny figures. Navy authorities said they knew pictures would be taken of the area including the President's cottage, but did not know the White House would object.

Last week Frank Bourgholtzer, correspondent of the National Broadcasting Company, innocently walked up to the fence of the President's cottage and took snapshots of it for his souvenir album. He took pictures on parts of two films; the Secret Service confiscated both.

A few days later Mr. Bourgholtzer and another reporter were at Naval headquarters, just in front of the cottage, and the public relations officer freely gave them eight-by-ten-inch prints of the cottage without any restrictions on its use.

Tourists are allowed to drive by the cottage and snap it with their cameras when the President is not here, but are barred when he is.

Marshall to Pay a Visit

The furore overshadowed the incidental news of another routine day of the President's vacation. One item is that Gen. George C. Marshall, former Secretary of State, and William D. Pawley, former Ambassador to Brazil, who are in Florida, will have lunch with the President tomorrow. It will be a purely social call, Mr. Ross said.

Another fragment of news was that Mr. Truman was studying various phases of his program to reorganize the Government along the general lines recommended by the Hoover Commission. Dr. John R. Steelman, the assistant to the President, has been in communication with Frank Pace, Budget Director, on this subject.

Justice Vinson will end his stay here on Wednesday. Mr. Ross said the Chief Justice and the President had had some private talks but he did not know the topics. Before Mr. Vinson's arrival on Saturday, his visit had been termed "purely social."

World's Worst Censorship in U.S., Asserts Lomakin, Ousted Consul

By HARRISON E. SALISBURY
Special to The New York Times

MOSCOW, March 15—Jacob M. Lomakin, former Soviet Consul General in New York, who is the new acting chief of the Foreign Office Press Department, said today that the United States maintained the world's worst news censorship.

The occasion was a reception given by Andrei Y. Vishinsky to the North Korean delegation headed by Premier Kim Il Sung. It was Mr. Vishinsky's first social appearance since he was elevated to the post of Foreign Minister, succeeding Vyacheslav M. Molotov.

[Mr. Lomakin was ordered to leave the United States last August after Mrs. Oksana S. Kasenkina, a Russian teacher, had leaped from a window of the Consulate, where she charged she had been held a prisoner. The State Department said that Mr. Lomakin had abused his office and had made false statements to the American people as well as to his own Government.]

Mr. Lomakin expansively criticized the United States press, which he said was controlled by at least three "glavlits." "Glavlit" is an abbreviation for the Soviet agency that censors foreign dispatches. Mr. Lomakin said the American glavlits included the Post Office Department, advertisers, business men and the State Department as well as others. He quoted Professor Zechariah H Chafee of Harvard as "admitting to me personally that the United States has the worst censorship."

[Prof. Chafee and Mr. Lomakin represented the United States and Russia, respectively, on the United Nations subcommission on the Freedom of the Press. They were frequently at odds in discussions at Lake Success.

Mr. Lomakin recalled that he was once a Tass correspondent in New York. He said he never was invited to interview any American officials or to visit the White House, whereas "in Moscow correspondents are invited everywhere. Mr. Lomakin said United States officials made it a point of not talking to Tass correspondents but he agreed that Laurence Todd, Washington correspondent of Tass, attended White House press conferences.

Mr. Lomakin described White House press conferences as "entirely propaganda." He said: "In New York Tass sends to Moscow reports of THE NEW YORK TIMES, the United Press and the Associated Press. In Moscow you send to New York reports from Tass, Izvestia, and Pravda. It's the same thing."

Mr. Vishinsky reminded the foreign newspaper men that he had started his career on a Baku newspaper forty-five years ago. Asked if he had seen any change in journalism during that time, Mr. Vishinsky said "no." He added that the revolution had changed newsmen in Russia, but that in the West "you haven't had a revolution."

WHITE HOUSE CUTS NEWSREEL FILMS

21 Feet of Pictures Taken From Blimp Censored—Security Is Given as Reason

By ANTHONY LEVIERO
Special to The New York Times

KEY WEST, Fla., March 17—Two newsreels of President Truman's vacation activities, made from a Navy blimp and confiscated on Monday, were released today after the White House censored twenty-one of a total of 400 feet of film.

Acting on grounds of security, a group consisting of White House aides, Naval Intelligence agents and Navy line officers cut out scenes showing the winter White House in relation to neighboring naval installations.

The White House released beach scenes of the Presidential party, including the President and Chief Justice Fred Vinson, but made it clear that this was an exception. Eben Ayers, assistant White House press secretary, said that White House policy prohibited beach scenes as an invasion of Mr. Truman's privacy and that this policy would be maintained in the future.

The two reels were projected on a screen this afternoon in the winter White House. Mr. Truman himself was not present as the films were censored.

Still Photos to Be Extracted

One 200-foot film had been made by Thomas Craven of Paramount News, who is also acting as pool photographer for Metro-Goldwyn-Mayer, Fox, Universal and Pathé Newsreels. Eleven feet were cut out of his reel. Ten feet were sliced out of the 200-foot film taken by Joseph Vadala of National Broadcasting Company television.

Under the release arrangement announced by Mr. Ayers, still men will be permitted to extract still pictures from the films for publication in newspapers.

The official review party consisted of Dr. John R. Steelman, assistant to the President; Rear Adm. Robert L. Dennison, naval aide to Mr. Truman; James Rowley, chief of the White House Secret Service detail; Capt. Cecil C. Adell, commandant of the Key West Naval Base; Comdr. Eli Vinock, base operations officer; Mr. Ayers, and two naval intelligence agents, Frank Jackson and Cecil Sewall.

"The Secret Service was not concerned with today but with what the future might bring," said Mr. Ayers. He would not elaborate on this rather cryptic statement, but it was understood that the cut portions of the film showed the Presidential cottage as a conspicuous landmark among important naval installations.

Declines to Call It Censorship

The films were seized on orders of Charles G. Ross, Mr. Truman's press secretary. He charged that the pictures were taken without his knowledge, although the camera men had cleared the trip a few days before his arrival in Key West. Three still photographers destroyed pictures they had taken from the blimp rather than permit confiscation.

Mr. Ayers declined to call the action censorship. Asked to define it by reporters, he replied:

"I would say simply that it is following out a policy in which newspapers and photo people have cooperated right along."

Mr. Ayers conceded, however, that a similar case had not arisen in peacetime. He said the final decision was made by himself, Admiral Dennison and Mr. Rowley.

A reporter showed a Chamber of Commerce map pointing out the location of the naval station and mentioning the cottage. Mr. Ayers said it was not nearly so telltale as the film, which showed the streets leading to the building as well as other important naval landmarks.

SOVIET BLOC IN U. N. FAILS ON PRESS CURB

Social Group Rejects Proposal for Suppression of News Deemed False, Warlike

By KATHLEEN TELTSCH
Special to THE NEW YORK TIMES.

LAKE SUCCESS, April 13—The Social Committee of the United Nations General Assembly today rejected a proposal to insert in a proposed convention on news gathering a section that would, in effect, allow governments to suppress material that they deemed false, distorted or likely to provoke war.

Thirty-four nations voted against the proposal, introduced by Poland and supported only by the Soviet Union, Byelorussia, the Ukraine, Czechoslovakia and Yugoslavia.

The Polish proposal was offered as an amendment to the definition of "news material" in the proposed convention.

Poland sought to add the statement that such material must be "neither designed nor likely to provoke or encourage any threat to the peace, breach of the peace or act of aggression, and that is not intended as a dissemination of false or distorted reports likely to injure friendly relations between states."

Rejection of the Polish measure was voted at the end of six hours of debate, during which the United States, Britain, France and others protested that it would open the way to unlimited government control. On similar grounds the committee members also turned down a Peruvian amendment that would have restricted news material to mean "authentic" news material.

The major part of the session, however, was devoted to new criticisms leveled by the Slav states at the Western press, particularly newspaper and radio operations in the United States, and to replies to these charges.

Jan Drohojowski, Polish delegate, touched off the debate by referring to a press conference held yesterday by Erwin D. Canham, United States representative on the Social Committee, at which Mr. Canham criticized Polish and Mexican amendments to the proposed convention. The Polish delegate maintained that advance discussion of prospective amendments "could be construed" as meant "to intimidate certain delegates."

Mr. Drohojowski went on to cite criticisms of the American press by American spokesmen. He quoted Benjamin Franklin, Thomas Jefferson, Harold L. Ickes, former Secretary of the Interior, and Archibald MacLeish, former Assistant Secretary of State.

While the United States has postal laws against lewd and obscene material being carried in the mails, the Polish delegate concluded, there are none against "war mongering."

In reply, Mr. Canham contended that since the Polish amendment sought to limit freedom of the press, it was "logical" that the Polish delegate should try to deprive delegates of their right to attend press conferences or reply to questions of reporters. "That is entirely in the spirit of his amendment," he added.

The United States representative also denied emphatically that he had attempted to "intimidate" other delegations.

CENSORING OF NEWS CURBED BY U.N. UNIT

Social Committee of Assembly Votes Down Soviet Bloc in Adding New Proviso

By KATHLEEN TELTSCH
Special to THE NEW YORK TIMES.

LAKE SUCCESS, April 18—Over vigorous Soviet objections, the Social Committee of the United Nations General Assembly tonight approved the first part of an article on censorship for incorporation into an international convention on news-gathering.

By a vote of 23 to 8 the committee decided to include in the convention a proviso that outgoing news dispatches shall not be censored, edited or delayed except in situations relating directly to the protection of national defense of a country.

The delegates from the Soviet Union, Byelorussia, Yugoslavia and the Ukraine sought unsuccessfully to defeat this part of the article. They insisted that it would mean a violation of the sovereign rights of states. It would, moreover, they held, transform the United Nations press convention into a document that protected only the rights of "monopolists" of the press, radio and cinema.

On the other hand, delegates from the United States, Britain and other countries argued that if peacetime censorship was unavoidable, it should be restricted rigidly to situations "directly relating" to the protection of national security or defense. By a vote of 33 to 6, the committee turned down a Polish amendment to this article that would have deleted the words "directly relating."

Meets Linguistic Difficulties

As finally approved, the first part of the censorship article uses the phrase "national defense." The Australian delegation proposed this to meet linguistic and interpretive difficulties encountered in using the words "national security." This part reads:

"The contracting states [to the convention] shall permit egress from their territories of all news material of correspondents and information agencies of other contracting states without censorship, editing or delay; provided that each of the contracting states may make and enforce regulations relating directly to the maintenance of national defense. Such of these regulations as relate to the transmission of news material shall be communicated by the state to correspondents and information agencies of other contracting states in its territory and shall apply equally to all correspondents and information agencies of other contracting states."

Supported by the Slavic members on the committee, Semyon K. Tsarapkin, Soviet delegate, charged that the United States and British press was in the hands of a small number of "monopolists, press barons."

Attacks Press in U. S.

In the United States, he asserted, the State Department has a voice in the space given to foreign news, advertisers regulate the contents of the newspapers and bank corporations give basic directives to the news agencies. Mr. Tsarapkin added:

"Take THE NEW YORK TIMES, the most responsible organ of the United States press—just see how it kowtows before the House of Morgan and how it is connected with the Morgan household and how this household controls this corporation headed by Sulzberger."

In reply to the Soviet attack, Ernest Davies of Great Britain upheld the freedom of both the British and United States press in contrast to Soviet restrictions that, he contended, censored every item going overseas.

Erwin D. Canham, United States delegate also retorted to the Russian criticisms. If there were really press monopolies in this country, he held, there would have to be 1,700 of them.

RADIO BAN LIFTED ON EDITORIALIZING

FCC Lets Stations Express Own Views if the Opposing Attitudes Are Presented

By LEWIS WOOD

Special to THE NEW YORK TIMES.

WASHINGTON, June 2—The eight-year-old barrier against radio broadcasting stations expressing their personal views on public questions over the air was relaxed by the Federal Communications Commission today.

Henceforth, these individual viewpoints may be expressed, but only as part of "a reasonably balanced presentation" of all the attitudes on a particular issue. To put it colloquially, the individual broadcaster may project his own views on a controversial subject, but not in such a "partisan" way as to give the listeners only one side of the discussion. The "format" in each instance would be left to the station itself.

Relaxation of the 1941 rule came in a policy statement by four members of the seven-member FCC. These were Commissioners Rosel H. Hyde, Edward M. Webster, Robert F. Jones and George E. Sterling. Commissioner Frieda Hennock, the only woman member, dissented. She held that the command against radio editorializing should continue "in the absence of some method of policing and enforcing the requirement that the public trust granted a licensee be exercised in an impartial manner."

Wayne Coy, chairman, and Commissioner Paul A. Walker, now absent from the country, did not participate.

Webster Asks Clearer Edict

While Mr. Webster concurred in the principle of allowing the radio stations to editorialize, he criticized the policy statement as unclear and leaving a licensee "in quandary and a state of confusion." He thought the broadcaster was entitled to know what he could, or could not, do, in "as concise and unequivocal language" as possible.

The action of the commission follows exhaustive hearings in March and April, 1948, when about seventy witnesses from the broadcasting industry and related fields testified. The hearings were held chiefly because of demands for relaxation of the rule against editorializing. The 1941 rule had stated that the broadcaster "cannot be an advocate" and cannot "support principles he happens to regard most favorably."

Announcing the new policy, the FCC said that the public should continue to have "a reasonable opportunity to hear different opposing positions on the public issues of interest and importance" in the community. The commission believed also that, under the American system of broadcasting, the individual licensees of radio stations "have the responsibility for determining the specific program material" to be sent out over the air.

"This choice, however," the statement continued, "must be exercised in a manner consistent with the basic policy of the Congress that radio be maintained as a medium of free speech for the general public as a whole rather than as an outlet for the purely personal or private interests of the licensee.

"The particular format best suited for the presentation of such programs in a manner consistent with the public interest must be determined by the licensee in the light of the facts of each individual situation. Such presentation may include the identified expression of the licensee's personal viewpoint as part of the more general presentation of views or comments on the various issues, but the opportunity to present such views may not be utilized to achieve a partisan or one-sided presentation of issues.

"Licensee editorialization is but one aspect of freedom of expression by means of radio. Only in so far as it is exercised in conformity with the paramount right of the public to hear a reasonably balanced presentation of all responsible viewpoints on particular issues can such editorialization be considered to be consistent with the licensee's duty to operate in the public interest. For the licensee is a trustee impressed with the duty of preserving radio for the public as a medium of free expression and fair presentation."

Paley Sees "Great Step Forward"

William S. Paley, chairman of the board of the Columbia Broadcasting System, said in New York last night that the FCC's action was "a great step forward for broadcasting."

As a result of the decision, he added, "CBS intends from time to time to broadcast radio editorials in its own name."

The other networks—NBC, ABC and Mutual—had no immediate comment.

APPEAL UPSETS RULING ON RADIO CENSORSHIP

Special to THE NEW YORK TIMES.

PHILADELPHIA, Dec. 20—The Third United States Circuit Court of Appeals ruled today that the Federal Communications Act does not prohibit radio stations from censoring political speeches of supporters of candidates, but only the speeches of the candidates themselves.

The eleven-page decision, written by Judge Albert B. Maris and concurred in by Judges Gerald McLaughlin and Austin L. Staley, reversed an opinion handed down last March by District Judge William H. Kirkpatrick.

The Appellate Court held that Judge Kirkpatrick erred in dismissing a libel suit filed by David H. H. Feliz, an attorney, against three Philadelphia radio stations, and ordered the case reheard.

In November, 1949, Mr. Feliz sued Westinghouse Radio Stations, Inc., operators of KYW; Triangle Publications, Inc., operators of WFIL, and WCAU, Inc., for $50,000 each. He charged that William F. Meade, then chairman of the Republican Central Campaign Committee, had defamed his character in two speeches.

Mr. Feliz contended that the radio stations were liable for not censoring the remarks of Mr. Meade, who was not a candidate for an elective office himself, in dismissing the suit, Judge Kirkpatrick ruled that the radio stations are not permitted to censor political addresses.

The Appellate Court's opinion stated that the Federal law applied "only to the personal use of radio facilities by the candidates themselves, the House of Representatives having definitely rejected the attempt on the part of the Senate to extend those provisions to include supporters and opponents of candidates as well as candidates themselves."

OLD ARGUMENTS REVIVED ON ANTI-GAMBLING BILL

Senate Measure Is Like Others Which Have Attempted to Impose a Kind Of Censorship on the Press

THE CONSTITUTIONAL QUESTION

By ARTHUR KROCK

WASHINGTON, May 27—The Senate Committee on Commerce, by approving a bill designed to obstruct big book-making on horse races, dog races, etc., once more has raised the fundamental issue of government censorship of legitimate news. The attempt to pass a censorship law occurs about once in every session of Congress, and thus far it has failed. This bill, though such is not its proclaimed purpose, or possibly its intent, falls into the same category.

It fixes criminal penalties for any person or organization receiving or transmitting information about specified sporting events, before they take place, which could serve as a guide to "gamblers" on the outcome of these events. This information, now regularly published in the press, and also broadcast, between the time such an event is scheduled and its occurrence, includes odds, shifts in odds, wagers made, entries withdrawn, jockeys changed, weights and similar details. Because this information can be and is used by bettors, and by professional gamblers in the conduct of their business, the Commerce Committee would prevent its publication and other forms of transmission across state lines on penalty of a $1,000 fine, or a year in prison, or both.

The pattern of legislative thinking is familiar:

(1) All gambling is morally bad. Professional gamblers are a corrupting influence among the people. Wagering on horse and dog races is gambling and hence it, too, is morally bad. News which can lead to decisions affecting wagering must therefore be excluded by government censorship in the interest of public and individual morals. This will discourage wagering by persons across state lines from the scene of action; that in turn will make the professional taking of wagers an unprofitable business; and "a clear and present danger" (Justice Holmes in *Schenk v. the United States*, 1919) will thus be reduced or even dissipated.

States May Follow

(2) While Congress has the power to apply this censorship to interstate communications only, that will encourage the states to follow suit. And perhaps even the Supreme Court in upholding the law will somehow extend it to intrastate transmission as well.

As drawn, the bill would make a newspaper criminally liable for publishing a dispatch on the morning before the Kentucky Derby or the Preakness is run which gave any of the proscribed information, if that newspaper were situated outside Kentucky or Maryland. If a jockey, for example, were murdered, or committed suicide, or were kidnapped, or otherwise eliminated, or the favorite dropped dead, to publish this would violate the law because it would convey the fact of a change in the prospect. The bill's sponsors disavow any such purpose but it could be so interpreted. And censorship is conceded in the statement of one sponsor that the newspapers could continue to print "most" of what they do now.

The information at issue is, of course, only a by-product of racing itself. Were there no racing on horse and dog tracks it would not exist. But racing is conducted under the permission of the several states, exercising an authority which Congress has no warrant to supersede because that is not among its "enumerated powers" which are listed in the Constitution. Therefore, the partisans of the movement were obliged to choose this indirect way to attack what they conceive to be a national evil. Yet as a measure of censorship it is, as noted above, as direct as any which has ever been attempted.

Freedom of the Press

The freedom of the press, guaranteed in the First Amendment, has often been proclaimed to be in danger from government when it was not. Like other vital institutions of the republic its name has been taken in vain to shield something unworthy—obscenity, malicious or irresponsible libel or incitation to public disorder or group persecution. But what the Supreme Court said in *Robertson v. Baldwin* 1897 made especially clear the distinction between press freedom and license:

The freedom of speech and of the press does not permit the publication of libels, blasphemous or indecent articles, or other publications injurious to public morals or private reputation.

Pari-Mutuels in States

Before and since the responsible press has accepted that demarcation and the courts have upheld it. But the press has steadfastly maintained that the right to print outside these banned categories is asserted in the Constitution. And, since racing is legalized in many states, most of which also legalize the system of wagering known as pari-mutuel, the burden of proof is heavy on those who contend that it is "injurious to public morals" to carry informatory details of these legalized operations.

That argument is destroyed by the plain fact that, if wagering or betting on races is "injurious to public morals," the existence of racing and not the news of it is the root cause of the "injury" they profess to behold. By the same reasoning all news of crime should be suppressed by Government censorship because all crime is bad, some is organized, and news of it may prompt emulation.

That, too, has been urged by some citizens, including legislators. For censorship commends itself as a favorite weapon to many of good intent who have a particular social objective in view and do not realize that, if they are permitted to possess it, others with other objectives are equally eligible. That would wipe out the First Amendment and with it one of the greatest protections to the public against official tyranny and the fatal state of being uninformed.

Jefferson's Views

Jefferson, who led the fight to add the Bill of Rights to the Constitution, was acutely aware of the evils of Government censorship among a free people. Of the First Amendment, which the Senate bill, however unintentionally, would undermine, he wrote on numerous occasions. In his day the large issue was whether a press which he justly termed "licentious" should be shackled or free; whether, for what was distorted in the guise of "news" as well as in its expressions of opinion, it should be under official censorship or subject only to "liableness to legal prosecution for false facts printed and published." Powerfully and often he chose press freedom, and it has been embedded in the laws and customs of the United States ever since.

Jefferson, though the "news" of his era was more often than not a perversion of the reputed article, construed his First Amendment as a guarantee of the right to print it, believing that this guarantee, and not its abuse, was the chief concern of a democracy. That is not even the issue raised by the bill which the Senate committee has approved. Here is no question of distortion, slander or malice. What the measure could be used to restrict is reporting of actual facts about an activity sanctioned by law.

HEMISPHERE PRESS FOUND A BIT FREER

Curbs Exist in Some Nations but Situation Has Improved, Editors' Committee Says

Restrictions on freedom of the press still exist in many of the twenty-four nations of the Americas, although in the last year the situation "has experienced an encouraging change," a committee on press freedom reported yesterday.

The four-man group made its report before the sixth Inter-American Press Conference, made up of newspaper publishers and editors of the Western Hemisphere, at the Waldorf-Astoria Hotel. The report will not be acted upon until tomorrow, when sharp discussion is expected.

The committee was made up of Tom Wallace, editor emeritus of The Louisville Times and conference chairman: Carlos Mantilla Ortega, director of El Comercio of Quito, Ecuador; Guillermo Martinez Marquez, director of El Pais, Havana, and Julio Gerzon, editor of La Prensa, New York.

The report criticized Argentina most sharply. Listing the decrees by which the Government there expropriated newsprint, the report also told of laws by which newspaper men became subject to imprisonment for criticizing the Government. It said that one paper had been closed for "defects in its sanitary installations," but remained closed after the situation was corrected.

Fifty Argentine newspapers were closed in a single day early this year, the report said, while six others and three magazines had been closed since. It added that at present three newspapers remain shut.

Freedom of the press was suppressed in Colombia with the declaration of a state of siege last November, the report declared. It said that since then censorship had been in effect for newspapers and press dispatches to foreign countries and listed three instances when editions were not permitted to appear.

In the cases of Peru and Venezuela, the committee said that restrictions on freedom of the press contained in the conferences report last year still existed. In the Dominican Republic, as last year, the "situation is not propitious for freedom of expression." It added that in Paraguay "the atmosphere in which the press operated during the last year has improved."

Guatemala restricted freedom of the press when a state of siege was declared last July, the report noted. Restrictions also existed for a time this year, it said, in Bolivia, Haiti, Honduras and Nicaragua, but have been lifted. However, it said that in Nicaragua, while de facto freedom of the press exists, legislation permits the President to impose "previous censorship" on any paper.

The report added that Chile, Brazil and Cuba had freedom of the press, except for some restrictions on Communist newspapers.

The United States also was described as having full freedom of the press. However, the report noted that President Truman said the Communist-control bill gave the Government the power of thought-control. It said that "if this faculty were exercised, liberty of the press would be at least threatened, if not directly affected."

TIGHT LID ON NEWS AIM OF NEW ORDER

Draft Fought by Editors Will Be Signed Soon by Truman for Security, Capital Hears

WASHINGTON, Sept. 22 (AP)—The Administration soon will impose military security more tightly around information in the civilian end of the Government. An Executive Order, said by White House spokesmen to be "in the final drafting stage," awaits the signature of President Truman.

The proposed order has been shown in confidence to a small group of editors who, officials concede, did not like it. They have not condemned it publicly, however.

There is virtually no question, it was said today, but that Mr. Truman will issue the order within days or weeks. It is aimed particularly at the non-defense agencies and is supported by pressure from the Pentagon as a safeguard on information concerning mobilization activity in which the military and civilian agencies must cooperate closely.

Some Elements in Order

The contents still are an official secret. These elements, however, are known:

1. It will instruct every department and agency to "classify" as secret, confidential or otherwise restricted — information vital to the national security.

It will spell out uniform safeguards for the handling of classified matter—specifying which papers should be locked in safes, which may not be discussed by telephone, etc.

It will make it "painfully clear," according to a Government source, that such hushed information must truly involve national security — meaning, that the order must not be used to suppress news which it might be more convenient to withhold.

4. But it will not attempt to define what information should be classified, and will leave it to each of the sixty-odd department and agency heads, and their designated subordinates, to use their own judgment.

Such discretionary powers always have been a target of opposition from newspaper men. In this case an official familiar with the pending order acknowledges that "it isn't foolproof."

By this he meant that it is subject to abuse, possibly to hide blunders or errors, perhaps to save administrators from being bothered by reporters and information-seekers, perhaps through a well-intentioned desire to play it safe.

On the other hand, Government men believe, only a handful of the civilian agencies may set up security systems. They will not be obliged to do so unless they feel there is need.

"Secret" Stamp Often Used

Outwardly, at least, few if any agencies seem to be lax in hedging their operations with precaution. It is a frequent tendency of civilian officials, as some will admit, to resolve any doubts about security by just reaching for the rubber stamp marked "secret."

Besides the four familiar grades of restraint—"restricted," "confidential," "secret" and "top secret" —some ultra-hush rubber stamps appeared now and then. "Cosmic" showed on some documents concerning foreign military aid. Other top-top-secret papers are marked "Eyes only," which means for the eyes of the addressee alone.

Papers are transmitted in double-opaque envelopes. Documents from the Pentagon arrive at civilian agencies escorted by troopers with guns on hips. Only classified janitors can dispose of classified trash.

The White House is aware that editors generally oppose the whole idea of the order. It hopes, however, that operations under the system can be kept so clean and free from abuse that newspaper men will learn to live with it.

U. S. ADDS CONTROLS ON SECURITY DATA

Truman Says Order Is Aimed at 'Potential Enemies,' Must Not Bar Legitimate News

EDITORS GROUP CONSULTED

But Committee Opposed Rule in Original Draft, Fearing Suppression of Information

Special to THE NEW YORK TIMES.

WASHINGTON, Sept. 25—President Truman signed today an executive order tightening and standardizing the handling of security information by all Government departments, agencies and employes.

Taking into account protests by some newspaper editors that the order might restrict the flow of legitimate news, Mr. Truman, in a letter to all agency heads affected by the new regulations, said:

"To put the matter bluntly, these regulations are designed to keep security information away from potential enemies and must not be used to withhold nonsecurity information or to cover up mistakes made by any official or employe of the Government."

In a single-page executive order accompanied by eleven pages of detailed regulations, Mr. Truman directed all governmental offices to put in effect the classification system now used by the State and Defense Departments.

Four Grades Established

Four grades of classified information are established, ranging from restricted, through confidential to secret and top secret. The order said use of the highest classification should be held at an absolute minimum by the designated security officer of each department or agency and that the major test for stamping "Top Secret" on any document should be "recognition of the fact that unauthorized disclosure of information so classified would or could cause exceptionally grave danger to the national security."

Mr. Truman declared that there was "no element of censorship, either direct or implied," in the order and that it was his hope that by clearly segregating security from nonsecurity information, "the American people will receive more, rather than less, information about their Government."

The order was issued after a study by a subcommittee of the National Security Council. A committee of the American Society of Newspaper Editors, headed by Alexander F. Jones, A. S. N. E.

president, had been consulted about it.

The editors' society disclosed tonight that it had protested to the White House in July, when the order was originally drafted, that it would tend to suppress "much news to which the public is entitled."

Reporters were given a preview and explanation of the order at a news conference yesterday by Joseph Short, White House press secretary.

Short Offers Aid

Many of the correspondents expressed to Mr. Short the fear that a standardized security system introduced into departments that had not dealt with such problems in the past would create an atmosphere in which legitimate news would be withheld.

One of the reporters suggested that officials vested with new classification powers would get "buck fever" and would tend to "play it safe" by classifying material that should not be classified.

Observing that he might be "sticking my neck out," Mr. Short promised his office would help out whenever a reporter ran into a situation where he thought legitimate news was being withheld and found himself unable to persuade the department head to release it.

Mr. Truman emphasized that the order governing the handling of state secrets applied only to officials and employes of the Federal Government, and added that "the public is requested to cooperate, but is under no compulsion or threat of penalty to do so."

Cautions Agency Heads

"I wish to urge upon every department and agency head conscientious adherence to the spirit and letter of these regulations in the interest of safeguarding the national security on the one hand, and the protection of the public's right to information on the other hand," Mr. Truman said.

"In the latter connection, I expect each department head or his designated subordinate to investigate promptly and carefully any alleged instance of unjustified use of security classifications.

"In considering such instances and indeed in original determinations on classification, it should be borne in mind that improper application of the classification powers is repulsive to our democratic form of government and burdens Government procedures with unnecessary and expensive restrictions."

The regulations, largely technical in nature and spelling out in detail the manner in which Federal employes shall handle classified information, become effective thirty days after their publication in the Federal Register.

The President said the new order was made necessary by the fact that "security information occasionally involves, and must be handled by, agencies which normally do not handle security information." Asked if the order were temporary or more or less permanent, Mr. Short told reporters that the order would remain in effect as long as the world situation remained so disturbed.

AP EDITORS ATTACK CURB ON U. S. DATA

Vote to Protest Truman Order —Convention Also Asks Move to Win Oatis' Freedom

SAN FRANCISCO, Sept. 26 (AP)

Leading American editors voted unanimously today to prepare resolutions formally protesting President Truman's new executive order classifying information.

By a show of hands, some 250 editors also urged the strongest steps possible to win the release by Czechoslovakia of William N. Oatis, imprisoned Associated Press correspondent.

The actions were taken at the opening of the annual meeting of the Associated Press Managing Editors association.

President Truman's order, announced in Washington yesterday, extends authority to classify information to all civilian government agencies. The order was described by J. R. Wiggins of The Washington Post as the most important censorship problem of the coming year.

James S. Pope, managing editor of The Louisville Courier-Journal, told the editors, "It seems we have been kicked back over our own goal line" in the fight for press freedom.

Mr. Pope said the American Society of Newspaper Editors' Committee on Freedom of Information had done its best to stop the order. The committee, of which Mr. Pope is chairman, protested to Joseph Short, presidential secretary.

Mr. Pope said the order gave each Government department head additional authority to classify information. He pointed out that this authority also could be

delegated to anyone the Government official chose to designate.

Mr. Wiggins expressed hope that 'courageous editors can find means of circumventing the order." He pointed out that the document failed to provide penalties for violations.

The editors also heard a proposal by a committee of their members that the United States sever diplomatic relations with Czechoslovakia if Mr. Oatis could not be freed by other methods.

After the chairman announced that resolutions would be drafted on the classification of information and on the Oatis case, Kent Cooper, executive director of The Associated Press, recommended: "Invite anyone who has suggestions on these two transcendently important questions to come and sit with the committee."

Mr. Wiggins read a report from Turner Catledge, executive managing editor of THE NEW YORK TIMES, on the coverage of news behind the Iron Curtain. Mr. Catledge was unable to attend the meeting.

The report said censorship, intimidation, threats of arrest and harassment of families had made it impossible for Associated Press and other American correspondents to obtain spot news through the Iron Curtain.

The report suggested that a "flanking attack" aimed at getting out news around the Iron Curtain, rather than through it, should be stepped up.

Mr. Catledge wrote: "In this flanking attack the best sources are not directly within the Iron Curtain. They have to be tapped in Washington, Rome, Paris, Hong Kong, New Delhi — among emigré groups and elsewhere."

He warned that in carrying out this sort of coverage, the news must be carefully screened.

The report said, "We will simply have to accept news from the Iron Curtain for what it is. We should not, however, present it as anything less than highly censored, and often purposely doped stories."

CLASSIFYING INFORMATION

The sweeping Presidential order providing for the classification of information throughout all the executive branch of the Government raises serious questions. It goes without saying that there are some matters essential to the national defense that need to be kept secret. It is also apparent that we would profit by some uniform system of classification and release. But after those things are taken into account there is still reason to question the wisdom of the form in which action has been taken.

The Presidential order is broad in its powers but vague in its definitions. A striking weakness is the failure to make any provision for systematic and periodic review of how it is being put into use. Vast discretion is placed in the hands of a large number of officials with no adequate check upon how that discretion is exercised. The result is that the effect of this order will depend on a considerable number of very fallible human judgments. If those judgments are uniformly good the procedure may do little harm. If the judgments are bad the machinery that the President has authorized can be used primarily not to protect national security but to cover up the mistakes of office-holders that ought to be exposed.

Unfortunately, the tendency in the classifying of information is almost invariably to over-classify rather than to under-classify it. It is much safer for an uneasy security officer to stamp a document "secret" than to authorize its release. Some of the abuses of this tendency in the past have been positively fantastic, and there is reason to be apprehensive over their possible repetition under a system without adequate safeguards.

Thomas Jefferson several times pointed out that the success of real government by consent depended primarily upon the enlightenment of the electorate. A policy that tends to dry up information at the source through the device of classification will work against that enlightenment. We do not want security information to come into the hands of our adversaries if it can be avoided. But we do want all sorts of information in the hands of our public all the time.

The President's order will be justified only if it is carried out with supreme skill and intelligence. That puts a heavy burden on a very large number of persons.

September 28, 1951

SECURITY ORDER ATTACKED

Bricker Offers Bill to End Curb on Civilian Agencies' Data

WASHINGTON, Sept, 28 (UP)—Senator John W. Bricker, Republican of Ohio, introduced a bill today to scrap President Truman's order extending to civilian government agencies the security restrictions imposed by the State and Defense Departments.

The move came only a few hours after Mr. Truman forced the Office of Price Stabilization to withdraw a censorship order that had forbidden its employes to disclose any information that might "cause embarrassment to O. P. S."

September 29, 1951

RULES ON INFORMATION RAISE CENSORSHIP ISSUE

Security Test of State and Defense Departments Is Applied to Others

By ANTHONY LEVIERO
Special to THE NEW YORK TIMES.

WASHINGTON, Sept. 29 — Renewed concern over the possibilities of covert censorship arose this week as a result of President Truman's Executive Order concerning the control of national security information.

What he did, in brief, was to apply to all Government departments the security regulations that have been in force for years in the Defense and State Departments.

The vital aim of our security classification system is to protect our national defenses from an enemy or a potential enemy. Information of this nature is classified in four categories, depending on its importance.

Any person who turns over a classified document to an enemy agent would be subject to the severe penalties of the espionage laws. Any Federal employe who endangers such a document through neglect or otherwise, without placing it in hostile hands, would be subject to lesser legal penalties or administrative discipline.

Mr. Truman's action requires close but dispassionate study by the public, and particularly the press. Censorship has been repugnant to the American people ever since the founding of the republic.

The President's action, however, had nothing to do with censorship as such. What it did involve though, was an increased potential for something worse than open censorship, and that is why the press was concerned by his edict and some editors condemned it out of hand.

This was the potential of hidden censorship, of locking up information that the public is entitled to have. The danger here would be that the public would not know how much, why or what categories of data were being withheld.

Points in Truman Plan

Salient features of the President's action, scrutinized against the background of the established system, are these:

(1) The regulations were not made more stringent. In force for many years and used principally in the Defense and State Departments, they were extended to all other departments, which, because of the Korean war and the threat of Soviet communism, are handling national security data in considerable volume. The use of economic forces as part of our grand strategy, and the stockpiling of critical materials, for instance, have given an important national defense role to the Commerce Department.

A CRITICAL VIEW

White in The Akron Beacon-Journal
"Look, boss, they're stealing our stuff!"

(2) The action was not directed against the press but against spies who have already demonstrated that they could obtain our most vital wartime atomic secrets.

(3) The regulations themselves were not changed or made less stringent, but President Truman introduced a general liberalizing factor into the whole system. He did this by requiring that all documents affecting national defense, apart from being labeled "top secret," "secret," "confidential," or "restricted," would also be labeled "security information."

Some objections raised against the President's order are:

(1) It would allow officials to cover up administrative blunders and politically motivated projects under the guise of national security.

(2) It would permit an official to leak out only that part of a confidential policy which suited his ends and to suppress adverse aspects of it.

(3) The order, as the American Society of Newspaper Editors pointed out, does not contain adequate provisions for declassifying, or removing the wraps from, confidential information after the need for secrecy has passed; and there is no regularized channel to appeal for the declassification of material.

Affirmative Declaration

The first of these objections is a serious one. It recognizes a danger that has always existed, with or without security regulations, and only an alert press, digging tenaciously at news sources in Washington, can minimize it.

But the new regulations impose on an official who classifies a document the requirement to make in fect an affirmative declaration at the document in fact is being classified to protect a military secret and not some administrative blunder or political motive.

This new rule, coupled with President Truman's dictum that the practical effect of the regulations should be to make more rather than less information available to the people, is novel and should have a salutary effect if it is not abused.

As to the second objection, the "leak" has an opprobrious connotation because it has been used to give out partial facts for ulterior purposes to newsmen. The wise newspaper man often rejects a "leak" when he recognizes that he is not getting the full picture. Here again, however, Government policies are often kept from the public even though they are not classified and it is up to the corps of correspondents to ferret them out.

How "Leak" Is Used

In a good sense the "leak" is used to give the press guarded news or guidance about plans or actions whose full disclosure would be useful to the enemy. Responsible officials often give classified data to individual newspaper men or to press conferences to use without direct attribution to the source or on an off-the-record basis for guidance.

The third objection, the lack of regularized declassification machinery, has long been recognized in the Federal service itself and no satisfactory solution of the problem has yet been proposed. Under the regulations the agency classifying the material is the only one authorized to declassify it, one major reason for this being the necessity to protect sources that furnish enemy intelligence.

Officials dispute the contention made at the meeting of the Associated Press Managing Editors Association in San Francisco that the President's order grants each department additional authority to classify information. They point out that the authority to classify national security data has always existed for any Government official and that the new order was designed to make the procedures uniform throughout the Federal establishment.

Observers who have studied the President's action carefully find nothing sinister in it, though they urge the caution that it must be watched for violations by officials at lower levels.

Lack of Machinery

Those who had inside wartime experience with it found that ineptness and administrative cowardice were to blame far more often than unethical motives when faults were uncovered.

The biggest weakness recognized in the document security system is the lack of established machinery to survey material continually and declassify it when the passage of time or circumstances justify it. President Truman has directed the Interdepartmental Committee on Internal Security to conduct periodic surveys to encourage declassification.

Out of the war was derived a vital guiding principle in dealing with secrets and it was one that wise officials learned should be applied day to day if it was to be effective in a time of censorship. It may be stated thus: Does the importance of keeping the people adequately informed outweigh the probable harm that may result from the disclosure of this information?

September 30, 1951

Truman on Security

When an Army officer makes a report to the Pentagon—for example, on the performance of a new weapon—he must mark it to show whether or not it is to be made public. If he thinks the document should not be made public he "classifies" it in one of four grades: Restricted, Confidential, Secret or Top Secret. Restricted documents, including such things as training manuals, are available to anyone in the Army. Confidential and Secret information must be kept in a safe, under Army rules, and is open only to men working in the particular field. Top Secret papers are limited to persons whose names are on a list attached to the documents. Theoretically, all types of classifed material are barred to the public. Actually, reporters have fairly ready access to Restricted papers and sometimes see even Top Secret documents.

The Defense and State Departments use this four-grade classification scheme, while the Atomic Energy Commission and Federal Bureau of Investigation have security methods of their own. But Tuesday, on the advice of the National Security Council, the President issued an executive order directing all other Government departments to adopt the Defense-State classification plan. He said the step was necessary to prevent leakage of Defense or State classified information through other departments which have become increasingly involved in defense planning.

The President directed department heads to classify nothing but genuine security material and to beware of putting security information in too high a classification.

Protests by Press

Nevertheless, the security order drew sharp protests. The American Society of Newspaper Editors made formal complaint, and there were critical editorials around the country. These were the main objections:

- The order was too vague about what was to be classified and in which classifications, gave too much discretion to department heads and allowed no appeal from their decisions.
- The order might be abused by some officials to cover up mistakes by classifying evidence against them.
- As a result of the order there might be a general "news fear" in the Government; officials might classify almost everything to be on the safe side.

The day after the order was issued there was an episode which incited comment on the President's decision. A subordinate official of the Office of Price Stabilization put out a staff notice—not connected in any way with the Presidential security directive—which ordered employes not to give out information that might be "embarrassing to the O. P. S." There was an uproar in Congress. A few hours later President Truman directed the O. P. S. to rescind the notice.

September 30, 1951

Suspicion of News Tinkering Overcasts Edict on Secrecy

Approach of the Administration to Public Information Likened to a Press Agent's

By JAMES RESTON
Special to THE NEW YORK TIMES.

WASHINGTON, Oct. 2—Several events of the last few weeks indicate why the press and radio have been slightly skeptical of President Truman's recent order authorizing Federal civilian agencies to withhold information from the public for security reasons.

Among these events were the following:

1. At the recent meeting of the North Atlantic Council in Ottawa, Secretary of State Dean Acheson not only opposed publication of limited and officially edited summaries of the general debate on the world situation, as proposed by public relations officers of the North Atlantic Treaty Organization, but also opposed publication of the agenda of the meeting. Incidentally, the official agenda had already been published when he opposed publication of it.
2. The State Department placed a "restricted" stamp on a catalogue of the names and hotel addresses of the delegates at the recent Japanese Peace Treaty Conference in San Francisco. This prevented reporters from getting the list until other delegations, objecting to the ruling, made the list public.
3. The White House recently blocked publication of a report by one of its own top officials because the report was critical of some aspects of the Administration's rearmament effort, and presumably because it co-

incided with the dismissal of General of the Army Douglas MacArthur.

4. The Treasury Department recently held back news of irregularities in the Internal Revenue Bureau in St. Louis until compelled to acknowledge the problem by disclosures on Capitol Hill.

5. After many weeks of negotiation with the N. A. T. O. countries on sharing the cost of certain bases in Europe, an agreement was signed at Ottawa last month. Not even the principles of this agreement or the percentages of the cost have been made public.

6. State and Defense Departments repeatedly denied reports of differences with General MacArthur over the conduct of policy in the Far East though these eventually led to a dismissal for which the public was entirely unprepared.

7. The Department of Defense sat on the recent disclosures of the death of two officers of the Office of Strategic Services in the famous Holohan case until forced to release the information by an article in True magazine.

These are all run - of - the - mine cases. They do not compare with the Administration's secret deal to bring the Ukraine and Byelo-Russia into the United Nations. Nor do they raise security questions, as did the Kuriles-South Sakhalin-China Railroad deal, which was designed to bring the Soviet Union into the war with Japan.

Suppressions of Convenience

Most of them were suppressions of convenience, designed to ease the process of negotiation, as in the cost-of-bases deal, or to save the Administration embarrassment, as in Numbers 3, 4, 6 and 7 above. President Truman's new order on handling security information was not intended to protect or encourage suppressions of convenience. On the contrary, it specifically condemned such suppression.

Nevertheless, the order created some apprehension here because the Administration's approach to public information is very much like a press agent's approach.

That is to say, the Administration's tendency is to turn the flow of information on or off in accordance with the tactic of the moment, flooding the wires with "news" when it wants to put something over, and closing down on information if disclosure might prove embarrassing.

There were some security angles to the Ottawa conference that had to be handled carefully—although it is doubtful if any N. A. T. O.

military scheme can be put into effect in Europe without the Communists, who are part of almost every continental army, knowing all about it—but in the main that conference dealt with several basic criticisms of United States policy, which our officials did not particularly want publicized.

Therefore, at Ottawa, a strict security policy was invoked. The following week, however, Premier Alcide De Gasperi of Italy came to Washington, and the Government wanted publicity. So the big information machine was put to work. Background press conferences were held all over the place; communiqués, speeches, statements of approval were issued galore. Officials who wouldn't look at a reporter in Ottawa were suddenly amiable and even loquacious on those aspects of the visit they thought would impress opinion in Italy.

Matter of News Values

Just why this visit was more newsworthy than the visit of the Canadian Prime Minister Louis S. St. Laurent a few days later was not clear, but in the De Gasperi case the Administration decided to "make news" while on the other visit—during which Mr. St. Laurent made the decidedly newsworthy suggestion that Canada build the St. Lawrence Seaway herself if necessary—the Administration gave him short shrift and even sent Maj. Gen. Harry Vaughan to the airport to meet him.

In short, there is a widespread suspicion here that the Administration tinkers with the news over and above the requirements of security, and partly as a result of the rearmament program, partly in response to Congress' emphasis on security regulations, is now more security-minded than anybody except the Russians.

At Ottawa, the United States Embassy was protected by the Marines, who went to elaborate security checks before allowing reporters to enter the building, even in the company of high United States officials. At the Japanese Peace Treaty Conference in San Francisco, the State Department placed steel-helmeted soldiers of the Sixth Army on the stage until the Australians pointed out that, after all, this was a "peace" conference.

Thus, the new Administration security-information order has received the raised-eyebrows treatment, because, regardless of its intent, it must be implemented by many men who have been playing heroes and villains with the news over last few years.

OFFICIAL TO FREE U. S. NEWS URGED

'People's Advocate' Proposed by Benton — He Denounces 'Restricted' Classification

WASHINGTON, Oct. 3 (UP)— Senator William Benton, Democrat of Connecticut, proposed today the appointment of a "people's advocate" to "fight" for the release of information to the public.

His proposal, Mr. Benton said in a Senate speech, was prompted by President Truman's order directing civilian agencies to withhold information deemed necessary to protect defense secrets.

"We need appointment of a top-ranking Government official to fight as hard to release information as some have been known to fight to suppress it," he said.

Senator Benton proposed that the "people's advocate" be a civilian member of the National Security Council. The Senator said he should have counterparts in all key Government agencies working under his direction.

Mr. Benton described as "an absurdity" the Government's classification of "restricted" information—the least restrictive of four categories of information that must be withheld.

He said the classification often was "carelessly handled" by officials and employes and "invites sloppy decisions in marginal cases."

Senator Benton recalled that the Committee for Economic Development, a private group, had recommended two years ago the appointment of an additional civilian member of the National Security Council. His job would be to "argue the case" for disclosure on important matters.

Wants Aid of Press

Senator Blair Moody, Democrat of Michigan and former Washington correspondent, suggested selecting a group of Washington newspaper men to help the Administration draft its security regulations. Senator Benton said that perhaps the American Society of Newspaper Editors should set up a committee for that purpose.

He said the President's order should be supplemented, not repealed since there is no good argument against having "uniform" security rules for all agencies. The order extends security regulations used by the Defense and State departments to other agencies handling security information.

Senator Benton said the regulations could be improved by reducing classifications to "top-secret," "secret" and "classified," thereby knocking out "restricted" classification, and by setting a drastic limit on the number of officials who could classify material "top-secret" and "secret."

October 3, 1951

October 4, 1951

TRUMAN'S PRESS VIEWS MYSTIFY THE CAPITAL

He Criticizes Publishers of Military Information Even Though Facts Are Obtained From Federal Sources

MAYBE HE GOT 'BUM STEER'

By ARTHUR KROCK

WASHINGTON, Oct. 6—The President's comments on what should and should not be published in the interest of national security, uttered at his Thursday press conference and promptly denatured by his Press Secretary an hour later "at the President's direction," have created a mystery because:

(1) In saying that due consideration of the "welfare of the United States" should have counseled publishers not to print certain maps and details of new weapons which were furnished them by responsible Government authorities, Mr. Truman assailed the wisdom and efficiency of his own chosen administrators.

(2) In his blanket criticism of the press and radio for making public what he said are "95 per cent of our military secrets," Mr. Truman attacked by inference the judgment and patriotism of both, not excluding newspapers which recently he has praised for maintaining the highest standards of journalism. He added that much of what they have published gave potential enemies the same service that spies seek to give.

Voluntary Censorship

(3) Though he repudiated the wish to impose censorship in any form, including the "voluntary" kind, the burden of his remarks was that the press and radio should act as voluntary censors of his own Administration.

(4) When the President issued his recent executive order, extending to every Government agency the power of the State and Defense Departments to withhold from publication documents deemed pertinent to national security by any agency's designated censor, his Press Secretary, Mr. Joseph Short, said the act was not related to increasing publicity of confidential information. But at Thursday's press conference the President based the order on a Yale University survey which, he said, disclosed the "95 per cent." adding that he had not signed the order until he read the survey.

(5) Mr. Truman, in the question-and-answer period, went so far as to say that the primary responsibility for keeping "military secrets" rests on "publishers."

(6) As "clarified" by Mr. Short after the press conference, the President's meaning was simply that no "military" information should be made public by "citizens," including publishers, unless it comes from "responsible officials qualified to judge the relationship of such information to the national security." But this restriction is self-imposed by the overwhelming majority of reporters and publishers; Mr. Short's "clarification" quite reversed the trend and much of the text of Mr. Truman's stern lecture to his Thursday auditors; and it supplied no rule of thumb whereby in every instance responsible and qualified officials can be distinguished from those who are not.

The Take-Off Was Calm

For these reasons Mr. Truman's tongue-lashing of the press and radio is very difficult to explain or even understand. He began the meeting with a very dispassionate and, from his standpoint, very sensible account of why he issued the executive order expanding the right to "classify" Government papers. It surely made no sense, he remarked, to lock up a secret military document in the Pentagon and permit a copy to lie on the desk of some lawyer in the Department of Justice. He clearly and tolerantly described how easy it is to agree that national security and the Bill of Rights must simultaneously be maintained and how hard it is to find the means of doing that, especially in a time of national peril.

The President, correctly assuming that no reasonable person could contend that military secrets should be made public, said his executive order was the best means he had discovered to attain the two objectives and that he will change it to repair any deficiencies of which he may become persuaded. Among these, he repeated, were abuses by any agency of the new authority he has given, such as suppression because of over-zealousness or because some official wants to conceal a blunder or some other embarrassing revelation. Mr. Truman told the group that he hates censorship; and, if by this term is meant Government power, with penalties, to prescribe what a newspaper may and may not publish, there is no doubt of his sincerity.

The Second Becomes First

But all this was so greatly at variance with his subsequent remarks, and the indignation which seemed to prompt them, that the whole record presents a mystery. The "clarification," canceling the President's new and bizarre concept of the duty of the press, made it plain that on second thought Mr. Truman realized it was unsound and that his lecture had been unfair. Throughout the dissertation Mr. Short revealed with gestures and by a couple of agonizing whispers to his chief, who received them impatiently, that the President's second thought was his secretary's first. Undoubtedly Mr. Short was chiefly responsible for the later statement in which the President was represented as meaning the opposite of what he previously had said.

The unanswered question remains: Why did Mr. Truman say these things? Possibly the explanation is that he was irritated over criticisms of his executive order, viewing them as uninformed and unfair. The problem to which the order is addressed has stumped some of the most enlightened of our public servants, among them a man with passionate devotion to the Bill of Rights, James Forrestal, and the President had spent weeks in considering how to deal with it. Many of the criticisms have come from the auditors at his press conference, and perhaps the sight of them as he read his defense of the executive order brought all this to mind and temporarily routed clear thinking and discretion.

But a better explanation has been suggested to this correspondent by a person in a position to know the background of the President's lecture. "The boss just got a bum steer," he said. He did not elucidate. But, since Mr. Truman was attacking the press for printing material which was furnished by those very "responsible and qualified" officials whose releases, his "clarification" conceded, could be accepted by any "citizen" as "safe" to make public, the meaning of the "bum steer" comment seems clear.

Possible Explanation

The person who made it evidently has been informed that the President did not know, when he attacked certain publications, that they had been furnished to the press by fully responsible officials; and had gathered from informants that the "newspapers and slick magazines" obtained and published them without authority. Believing, as he told the press conference, that the publications were harmful to security, the President saw in them total disregard for the nation's welfare on the part of the press. And by the time the truth dawned on him, Mr. Truman was too far afield to get back.

This could explain an otherwise inexplicable outburst. But if true, it suggests that no administrator will be reprimanded by the President for super-censorship.

EDITOR CALLS ON ALL TO GUARD FREE PRESS

Special to The New York Times.

EVANSTON, Ill., Oct. 12—Discussing the current agitation over he Presidential order on classification of vital information, Turner Catledge, executive managing editor of THE NEW YORK TIMES, declared here today such regulations must be justified in the light of the larger purposes to be served.

Speaking at the Centennial Conference on Communications at Northwestern University, Mr. Catledge said that while it was up to practical professional people to man the barriers against encroachments, the duty to keep the press free devolved upon all.

"Our primary task right now," he said, "is to make the administrators of government and the general public equally aware of their indivisible stake in the matter."

He asserted that basic decisions on withholding information should be made only by competent authorities who would take full responsibility before the electorate for their acts.

"Also, whatever restrictions that may then be imposed should be made subject to some sort of review by persons not directly concerned with the Administration," he said.

Edward W. Barrett, Assistant Secretary of State for Public Affairs, told the conference that the Voice of America had overcome Russian radio jamming "at least 100 per cent more effectively than eighteen months ago" and that the output of the Voice had been increased 50 per cent.

He said Russia was spending $228,000,000 for propaganda and that the "big lie" cost the satellites $481,000,000. He held that 70 to 90 per cent of the people in the satellite states were opposed to their Communist regimes.

FIGHT OVER CENSORSHIP GOES ON IN WASHINGTON

Whether the President's Order Will Slow or Speed News Is Uncertain

By ANTHONY LEVIERO

Special to The New York Times.

WASHINGTON, Oct. 13—Washington correspondents are priming their squirrel guns for the open season on self-appointed censors. The slaughter promises to be awful if any bureaucrats are caught abusing President Truman's security order by withholding information that should be made public.

The open season begins in about a week, when the controversial order becomes effective. While the press is preparing to do some sharpshooting, the Executive Department is already reacting to the furor caused by the order.

Although the security order had been in preparation for many months, President Truman said he had not signed the order until he was told of a Yale University survey made at the request of the Central Intelligence Agency. The President said the survey showed that 95 per cent of our military secrets had appeared in the press.

This percentage figure was received with skepticism. New information not only indicates that the skepticism was justified but dispels the impression that the secrets referred to were leaks from unauthorized or irresponsible sources. Much of the data came from quite legitimate, formal news releases.

Was a Rough Estimate

It is learned now that the President was given the 95 per cent figure as a preliminary, rough estimate subject to later revision, to indicate broadly that a great proportion of our security projects are released to the public.

Briefly stated, the problem of security and the reasons for the order are these: The Korean war and the menace of Communist subversion have increased the need for safeguarding information concerning the national defense program. The Defense and State Departments have long had a system for "classifying" or labeling such data so that it would be properly safeguarded by the users of that material.

Since most other Federal departments have received increasingly important roles in the mobilization program, they have been handling military secrets. The purpose of the order was to extend the Defense and State Departments' security system to all other departments.

Actually the other departments have not been exempt from the security regulations. Whenever they handled a national security project they were required to classify it and handle it in exactly the same way as the State and Defense Departments. Therefore the President's order in a large sense was pro forma, making explicit and applying uniformly a system that only two departments previously had a real need to maintain.

Covering Up Information

It is clear, then, that the order was not addressed to the press but to the Government service to solidify the safeguards against espionage. It should be borne in mind, however, as the press knows from long experience, that the order can be used to cover up information having nothing to do with national security. An official can slap his rubber security stamp on the documents that might betray his blunders or embarrass the Administration. He is the man that the press will try to flush out.

Here is the effect of the security order, as it will operate within a Government department: Assume that even certain experts in the Fish and Wildlife Service of the Interior Department might be assigned to carry out a vital security project, say in conjunction with the Defense Department.

How the System Works

A unit chief in the Fish and Wildlife Service completes the project and prepares the documents. Assume that fairly important security operations are involved, or that the papers discuss the hostile activities of a potential enemy.

Assume the decision is to grade the data "confidential." That is the extent of the classification procedure as of now, and the confidential paper would be made available only to those other persons in the Federal service who are concerned with its use.

After the order goes into effect, however, and this is a new requirement such a document will also have to be stamped "security information." Therefore the classifying official is required to make an affirmative declaration that the document deals with national security and not the security of

the Democratic party or his personal job security.

Editors and publishers feared that many officials would interpret the order, despite Mr. Truman's admonitions to the contrary, as a license to withhold all kinds of information. Therefore, they sought vainly to prevent its issuance.

B. M. McKelway, editor of The Washington Evening Star and a member of a committee of the American Society of Newspaper Editors that wrestled with the problem in meetings with the White House staff, said the chief objections raised were these:

The authority to classify information should not be granted so widely to every agency head; the order was vague as to definitions of what was security information, and it failed to make specific provisions for review of such information and for appeals from improperly classified data.

The committee suggested that if the order were issued, a central appeal board should be established to pass on the rulings of Government officials. It questioned the advisability of granting to an agency head "the discretion to determine how much and what of the public's business should be disclosed to the public."

Administration's Answer

The answer of Administration officials to these criticisms are these: Definitions were sought and the Army's ground rules were studied. But in them they found such words as "embarrassment" and "prestige"—embarrassment of, or damage to the prestige of the United States—as reasons for classifying data in the less important categories.

The Interdepartmental Government Committee coping with the problem decided that to include such terms in the order applying to purely civilian agencies might be taken as a virtual license to withhold information on grounds of embarrassment or prestige.

There was less leeway for abuse by merely laying down the broad requirement that classification would be used only for "national security information," the group held.

The Administration is now considering the establishment in each agency of a committee of three, consisting of one security officer, one information officer and one operations officer who would keep classified material under study with the aim of down-grading or declassifying it altogether as the need to keep it secure diminishes. It is believed that committees on this pattern will be authorized in about two weeks.

The Interdepartmental Committee on Internal Security of the Administration is also planning to hire one or two persons familiar with classified material who would make spot checks in the various departments to determine if the spirit of the President's order was

WASHINGTON CENSORSHIP

FREEDOM OF INFORMATION

The Nashville Tennessean

being observed. These roving agents would also serve as advisers to agencies having little experience in handling defense secrets.

Whether the President's order will serve to slow up or speed the release of news remains to be see The airing of the issue makes either result possible. The public is waiting to see whether it will be applied with good faith and good sense.

M'LEAN DENOUNCES TRUMAN NEWS CURB

'Creeping Censorship' of Kind Never Before Set Up in U. S. Could Result, A.P. Head Says

By WILLIAM G. WEART
Special to THE NEW YORK TIMES.

PHILADELPHIA, Oct. 15—The recent executive order in which President Truman authorized heads of Government agencies to classify news to be withheld from publication was denounced today by Robert McLean, president of The Associated Press and The Philadelphia Bulletin Company.

Mr. McLean warned that a "creeping censorship of a kind never before established in this country" could result from the order empowering heads of Government departments to withhold information on the basis of what they themselves decided was vital to national security.

Emphasizing the positive value of an informed citizenry, the publisher told 600 financial, industrial and business leaders at a Pennsylvania Week luncheon of the Chamber of Commerce that newspaper men "view with concern the growing tendency in this country to foreclosure of information at the source whether that source be local, state or Federal Government."

This concern runs so deep, he said, "that the American Society of Newspaper Editors has established a standing committee to analyze and assist in opposing the tendency."

"This committee," he continued, "was asked last July to study the recently issued executive order on security. Its advices were not heeded."

Mr. McLean spoke after receiving the Commerce and Industry

Award given annually by the Philadelphia Chamber of Commerce to the Pennsylvanian adjudged to have contributed most to his industry.

In making the presentation, Albert M. Greenfield, president of the chamber, said that "as president of The Associated Press, Robert McLean has safeguarded a free press for our people: he has emphasized our original concepts of liberty and justice, and he has aided in fighting all of the foreign 'isms' that endangered the very lives of our people."

Declaring that nations that recognized and preserved basic human rights were bound to survive, Mr. McLean said:

"We as a people," are dedicated to the principle of self-government; that given the facts the public judgment is sound. This requires that the widest possible information be available to all—consonant with the national safety."

Mr. McLean said that in searching for means to preserve liberty and strength in this nation "we must keep before us always the thought that between more and less censorship the greater danger lies in more censorship than any particular situation may warrant, just as the danger to our liberties lies in more and more government until in the last analysis we let government do all things for us and we have the colletivist state."

Earlier, the publisher said, that governments everywhere were seeking to control the avenues of news.

"They seize," he added, "the lines of communication, set up agencies of information, suppress in one nation after another the free press.

"Nor is this limited to the totalitarian states. There are presently bills in parliaments of India and Iran for greater control of what is printed. Those professing belief in freedom of expression move in the United Nations for broader powers of censorship."

October 14, 1951

October 16, 1951

CLEAR RULES ASKED ON CENSORING NEWS

Special to The New York Times.

WASHINGTON, Oct. 17 — A group of newspaper editors urged President Truman today to issue clearer definitions of security information that Government agencies should withhold. They also called for the establishment of a better appeals machinery for deciding when disputed classified information might be made public.

Mr. Truman told the group, representing the Associated Press Managing Editors Association, Inc., that he would consider specific changes if they would give him their ideas of "clearer definitions" and a more satisfactory method of ironing out controversies over whether certain information should be released to the press.

Headed by Herbert Corn of The Washington Star, president of the organization, the delegation spent forty minutes with President Truman and another hour with his press secretary, Joseph Short. Other conferees were J. Russell Wiggins of The Washington Post, John Colburn of The Richmond Times-Dispatch, and MacLean Patterson of The Baltimore Sun.

Their objections grew out of a recent Presidential order extending to all Government agencies and departments a uniform system of handling classified security information, designed to keep vital secrets from enemy knowledge.

Editors Issue Statement

Emerging from the White House, the editors gave out this statement:

"We presented our resolution of the Associated Press Managing Editors' Association to the President and went over with him some of the specific objections set forth in the resolution.

"We discussed particularly the definition of 'top-secret, secret, confidential and restricted' [information] and the President urged that the Associated Press managing editors suggest clear definition.

"Lack of appeals machinery was discussed and the President suggested Mr. Short is the proper tribunal for appeals, but he invited suggestions for clarifying this.

"The President said he would not hesitate to modify the order on the basis of constructive suggestions as long as the basic safeguards to security were maintained."

The editors presented a resolution adopted at the San Francisco conference of Associated Press managing editors that declared the order was "a dangerous instrument of news suppression" that extended the "cloak of military security" to civilian agencies.

Mr. Corn told reporters that the editors would attempt to draw up their own set of clearer definitions regarding classified information, and would make suggestions for improved machinery to handle appeals.

October 18, 1951

CURB ON NEWS DECRIED

Editorial Group Exhorts Truman to Modify 'Security' Order

CHICAGO, Oct. 18 (AP) — The National Editorial Association, which includes some 5,400 weekly and small daily newspapers, called on President Truman today to modify his "security" order permitting civilian agencies to withhold certain news.

In a unanimous resolution at the opening of its fall meeting, the group said it viewed "with the gravest apprehension the encroachment by the President's 'security' order on the American people's right to know."

"The editors feel that the restriction constitutes a most serious threat to the traditional accessibility to information which is inherent in the Bill of Rights," the resolution declared. It continued:

"The members of the National Editorial Association reaffirm their adherence to their traditional responsibilities which safeguard and protect at all times the security of the nation.

"Be it resolved, therefore, that the National Editorial Association strongly urge President Truman to consider and adopt necessary modifications of his security order which would maintain the American public's Constitutional right of information."

October 19, 1951

SECURITY RULES SET ON DEFENSE OUTPUT

Fleischmann Acts to Comply With Presidential Order — Press Criticism Invited

Special to The New York Times.

WASHINGTON, Oct. 26 — New security rules governing production data were announced today by Manly Fleischmann, head of the Defense Production Administration and the National Production Authority.

The regulations were designed to comply with President Truman's Sept. 25 Executive Order, which is effective next Monday, that directs all Federal departments and agencies to put in effect a four-grade classification system for information.

Mr. Fleischmann issued a directive providing for the following:

1. Enforcement of classification, transmission and handling regulations for classified information to remain the responsibility of security officers of the two defense agencies.
2. Formation of a four-man review committee, consisting of James F. King, deputy D. P. A. administrator; Edward K. Moss, assistant administrator for public administration of D. P. A. and N. P. A.; C. H. Kendall, D. P. A. general counsel, and R. W. Lawrence, D. P. A. director of security.
3. Authorization for Mr. Moss to declassify information for public distribution whenever in his judgment it is necessary for conformance to the basic information policy of the agencies.

Basic Policy Described

This basic policy, which was formulated in October, 1950, provides:

"Full information on activities will be available in all cases except when its release would affect the national security. This policy includes information matters under consideration by N. P. A. unless premature disclosures would adversely affect proposed actions.

"Proposals, recommendations and statements resulting from discussions with industry advisory committees, as well as similar matters from other non-Government sources to N. P. A., will be regarded as public information."

A spokesman for the two agencies emphasized that the new order, with the exception of the four-man committee and new authorization for the assistant administrator, would make little change in the established security arrangement.

Mr. Fleischmann said that the public had a fundamental right to information on the activities of Federal agencies, then added:

"If at any time representatives of the press, other news media, or outside groups believe that D. P. A. or N. P. A. material is not being properly handled, they are invited to contact the assistant administrator of public information directly.

"Because of their vital role to public understanding of government operations, their advice and recommendations will be particularly welcome."

Few Changes Held Needed

Mr. Fleischmann's two agencies were the first to announce plans for implementing the President's order. At the White House, a spokesman said that relatively few departments and agencies would be materially affected by observing the order, since many of them already were carrying it out, while others had such elaborate security set-ups that only minor changes were necessary.

"One will be able to look into the agencies Monday morning and see nothing different than today so far as this order is concerned," he added.

Four grades of classified information were established, ranging from restricted, through confidential to secret and top secret. The Presidential order specified that use of the top secret classification should be held at an absolute minimum with the major test being whether the material "would or could cause exceptionally grave danger to national security."

October 27, 1951

NEW METHOD URGED TO FIGHT NEWS BAN

Senators Seeking to 'Repeal' Truman Order Are Advised to Draft a Substitute

Special to The New York Times.

WASHINGTON, Nov. 29 — The Republican authors of a Senate bill seeking to "repeal" a Presidential order restricting so-called security information from the Federal agencies got legal advice today to withdraw and start afresh.

The professional staff of the Senate Committee on Expenditures in Executive Departments, which has the bill in charge, recommended that if Congress was to do anything it should proceed not by trying to knock out the President's directive but by preparing one of its own with the force of law.

In a paper prepared by a legal member of the staff, Eli E. Nobleman, it was "suggested" that the pending measure, by Senator John W. Bricker of Ohio and others, could not be effective and might be attacked as an intrusion upon the President's constitutional powers. Senator Bricker was not available for comment.

Mr. Nobleman said in effect that while Congress had the right to make such affirmative directions as it wished governing the Federal agencies it might find it impossible simply to nullify the directions the President himself had given.

The Presidential order was issued in December. It authorized all Government departments, and not simply the State and Defense Departments as heretofore, to "classify" or withhold from the public any official information "the safeguarding of which is necessary in the interest of the national security."

It has been attacked by many Senators as well as bodies of editors as an act of censorship raising a threat to a free press.

Mr. Truman, in a news conference Oct. 4, defended his action. He was not trying to suppress information, he said, but was "trying to prevent us from being wiped out." The purpose of the order, he asserted, simply was to try to keep valuable information from our enemies.

November 30, 1951

In The Nation

The Powers of Congress Over Executive Orders

By ARTHUR KROCK

WASHINGTON, Dec. 6—Two methods by which Congress next year might greatly modify or supplant the President's recent rules for withholding official information from the public are now being debated, and they will be closely examined in the scheduled hearings on the problem by the Senate Expenditures Committee. One proposal is outright repeal of Executive Order No. 10,290, in which Mr. Truman prescribed for his subordinates rules to govern the release of public documents. The other is that Congress substitute for the order detailed regulations of its own.

These alternatives were examined in a memorandum to the Senate committee by Eli E. Nobleman, a member of its professional staff, who is also a member of the New York bar. They were accepted as the basis for a decision either way by Senator Bricker of Ohio, who introduced the bill for outright repeal.

The President's order has been widely protested by the press and by other institutions and citizens as providing legal sanction for public officials to exercise a tendency, inherent in many of them, to withhold and suppress information that might embarrass individuals in the Government or the political party in power. Press committees have made the same penetrating and unfavorable analysis of the order. And there has been much criticism of the regulations in Congress.

Mr. Truman has said his mind is open to proof that the order opens the way to abuses of the duty of officials to keep the people informed of their acts and hence should be modified. But he also said he has not yet received this proof and remains convinced that the order will accomplish the stated purpose for which he had it drafted. This purpose, he said, was to increase the flow of legitimate public information and at the same time guard the national security against publications that would imperil it.

Among those who concede the President's sincerity in these statements, and who also agree that there have been irresponsible and dangerous publications from the standpoint of national security, there are many, however, who think the regulations go too far. And these critics share the opinion that they provide bureaucrats and officials who want to conceal their blunders with a powerful means to suppress what belongs in the public domain. Unless, therefore, the President modifies the order in a way to prevent such abuses before the Senate committee is ready with a corrected plan, these persons support the proposal of a legislative remedy.

The Salient Points

In his memorandum for the Senate committee Mr. Nobleman made several points:

1. No question exists of the power of the President to have issued the order. Under his constitutional obligation to "take care that the laws be faithfully executed," and his powers to appoint and remove certain executive officers at his pleasure, he has general authority to direct the manner in which his subordinates shall exercise his responsibility.

2. In this executive order the laws of which he was "taking care" * * * "would seem to be those sections of the Federal Criminal Code which are concerned with internal security and the safeguarding of classified and security information in particular and espionage in general."

3. But it is a well-settled rule that an order or any other executive action "cannot contravene an act of Congress which is constitutional." When it collides with a statute the statute will prevail, and the President cannot legally direct his subordinates to disobey it.

4. But the precise question whether Congress has the power to repeal an executive order, "issued pursuant to a constitutional power of the President which is neither specifically conferred nor is exclusive, has never raised a justifiable controversy and has never been decided by the courts." The President might treat repeal of his order as an invasion of his powers.

5. If, however, Congress should affirmatively legislate "in clear and unmistakable terms" its policy with respect to the matters covered by this executive order, the President in disregarding it would "clearly defy the law, since it is well settled that the first duty of a subordinate of the President is to the law."

The Senator's Objections

Senator Bricker, on reading this memorandum, issued a statement in which he said he was in general agreement with Mr. Nobleman, and that his repeal bill had already achieved one of its purposes by assuring that hearings on the order would be held by the Senate committee. Pending these, he said, "I urge everyone concerned with the maintenance of a free press to consider the alternatives."

The objections Mr. Bricker raised to affirmative legislation were that it would be difficult (a) "to avoid unduly rigid and extremely detailed legislation"; (b) not "to create a system of censorship which would be regretted in more normal times"; and (c) to keep within the scope of the order so that no question of challenging the President's exclusive jurisdiction could soundly arise. But, said Mr. Bricker, he is all for examining both methods to discover the better one.

This will be the next step unless Mr. Truman previously satisfies the critics of the order.

TRUMAN CRITICIZES A. P. EDITORS' GROUP

Special to THE NEW YORK TIMES.

WASHINGTON, Dec. 18—President Truman sharply criticized today a committee of The Associated Press Managing Editors Association that withdrew an offer to submit proposed clarifying improvements and changes in his executive order establishing uniform security standards for safeguarding governmental information.

The White House made public a letter from Mr. Truman to Herbert F. Corn, managing editor of The Washington Star and president of the association, in which the President said that he could not understand "why you editors reversed yourselves and passed up this opportunity to serve the cause of freedom of information in the dangerous days ahead when the safety of our country and the freedoms for which it stands are in peril."

Mr. Corn and three other news executives conferred with the President on Oct. 17 to acquaint him with the Managing Editors Association's resolution denouncing the executive order. Mr. Truman invited the committee to submit any proposals it might have to improve the order, which was issued last Sept. 25.

Dangerous Barrier Seen

On Dec. 4, Mr. Corn wrote the President that the committee had discussed with the association's executive group "your suggestion that the A. P. M. E. try to write better definitions as to which Government records shall be classified as top secret, secret, confidential and restricted."

"The executive committee of the A. P. M. E. cannot accept this invitation because it feels that the order itself erects dangerous barriers between the people and their Government," Mr. Corn said.

Mr. Truman in his reply said the Corn letter indicated that the Managing Editors Association "intends to stand on the outside and carp and criticize without being at all helpful."

"I also want to refer again to the matter of protecting secrets from the enemy and to say: This is your country as well as mine." Mr. Truman asserted. "We can only win in the present struggle if we all work together."

He added a hand-written postscript that said he had not "given up the idea of advice from practical newsmen."

Joseph Short, White House press secretary, said that Mr. Truman did not regard any order as necessarily perfect and would like to improve on it "if anybody has a better idea to suggest."

TRUMAN AND CORN LETTERS

WASHINGTON, Dec. 18 (AP)—Following are the texts of letters exchanged between President Truman and Mr. Corn:

Letter From Mr. Corn

Dec. 4, 1951.

Dear Mr. President:

The committee of the Associated Press Managing Editors Association, which was given a courteous hearing by you and Mr. Joseph Short on Oct. 17, has reported that conversation to the executive committee of A. P. M. E.

As you know, the A. P. M. E. is an association of newspaper editors from the 1,700 American newspapers which are members of the Associated Press. It was these editors, in convention in San Francisco, who unanimously condemned the executive order extending the right of Government departments to classify information.

The committee delivered your suggestion that A. P. M. E. try to write better definitions as to which Government records shall be classified as top secret, secret, confidential and restricted.

The executive committee of the A. P. M. E. can not accept this invitation because it feels that the order, itself, erects dangerous barriers between the people and their Government.

Sincerely yours,
HERBERT F. CORN,
President,
Associated Press Managing
Editors Association.

Reply by Mr. Truman

Dec. 17, 1951.

Dear Mr. Corn:

I am unable to reconcile your letter of Dec. 4 with statements made to me by members of the special committee off the Associated Press Managing Editors Association on Oct. 17.

That committee, which included you, made the following statements to me:

(1) The Associated Press managing editors were as interested as I am in protecting secrets from the enemy.

(2) That you were sure I had acted in good faith in signing the order and that I was sincere in the letter of transmittal to departments and agencies in admonishing all officials of the Executive Branch to guard against abuse of the order.

(3) You (the committee) told me that the order was imperfectly drawn and, at the conclusion of our conversation, you as a group informed me that you would suggest changes therein.

You may recall that, as we sat down together, Mr. [J. Russell] Wiggins, chairman of the committee, assured me that the committee had constructive criticisms to make and I replied that I wished to hear them. The burden of your criticism, as I recall it, was against "definitions" and you went out of my office promising to write better ones.

Your concern over definitions seemed to arise from a fear that some agencies, particularly civilian agencies, might classify nonsecurity information, something I had explicity prohibited in my memorandum to all department and agency heads.

I said, "to put the matter bluntly, these regulations are designed to keep security information away from potential enemies and must not be used to cover up mistakes made by any official or employe of the Government."

Although I thought your fears were groundless, nevertheless I was glad to have you offer suggestions so that every effort could be made to reinforce my policy of confining the order to matters genuinely involving the safety of our country.

I hope I was not naïve in accepting in good faith the statements made by Mr. Wiggins and other members of the committee. The atmosphere of our meeting was one in which all agreed that working together we could bring forth changes that would be satisfactory to all.

My attitude has not changed. I still feel that way. But your letter would indicate that The Associated Press managing editors, after indicating otherwise, intend to stand on the outside and carp and criticize without being at all helpful.

Sees Opportunity Passed Up

I would like to remind you that I received your committee at the request of Mr. Wiggins. I did not single out your association for the role of re-drafting the order. At their meeting with me, members of the committee suggested that improvements could be made in the order. Then when I countered that I would be glad to improve the order, you said that your committee would make a try.

I thought that, because your group espoused freedom of information, it might be willing to join me in reinforcing that principle. I still can not understand why you editors reversed yourselves and passed up this opportunity to serve the cause of freedom of information in the dangerous days ahead when the safety of our country and the freedoms for which it stands are in peril.

I also want to refer again to the matter of protecting secrets from the enemy and to say: This is your country as well as mine. We can only win in the present world struggle if we all work together.

Very sincerely yours,
HARRY S. TRUMAN
(The following postscript was hand-written by the President.)
I have not given up the idea of advice from practical newsmen.

COULD SEIZE PRESS, PRESIDENT IMPLIES

WASHINGTON, April 17 (UP)—President Truman indicated today that he believed he or any United States President had the theoretical power to seize newspapers and radio stations to protect the national welfare in war or great emergency.

But a White House spokesman quickly added that it was "absolutely unlikely" anything of that nature ever would have to be done.

Mr. Truman's view, given at a news conference, startled some of the editors here for the annual meeting of the American Society of Newspaper Editors.

Controversy has boiled over the President's seizure of the steel mills.

One of the visiting editors asked the President:

"If it is proper under your inherent powers to seize the steel mills, can you in your opinion seize the newspapers and the radio stations?"

Mr. Truman replied that under similar circumstances the President had to do whatever he believed was best for the country.

The President refused to elaborate. But White House sources said the President's point was that he had power, in an emergency, to take over "any portion of the business community acting to jeopardize all the people."

These sources said the President could take over anything from a corner drug store, up to and including an entire industry, under certain circumstances.

They noted that President Abraham Lincoln had taken over the railroads and several newspapers during the Civil War and the late President Roosevelt had seized an aircraft plant in California during World War II.

They emphasized, however, that the President was giving a hypothetical answer to a purely hypothetical question. It is "absolutely unlikely" that radio stations and newspapers ever will be seized in this country, the White House sources added.

Several of the editors, many of whom attended the press conference, did not believe the President actually meant he had power to take over radio stations and newspapers.

Alexander F. Jones, president of the Society of Newspaper Editors and editor of The Syracuse (N. Y.) Herald-Journal, said: "What I thought the President meant was that he has the power to take over steel. It would be putting words in his mouth to say anything else."

But Walter M. Harrison of Oklahoma City, former president of the society, said: "I think he meant he could take over the papers, radio and everything else. If that isn't on the edge of totalitarianism, I don't know what is."

Mr. Truman contends he seized the steel industry under his powers to protect the safety and welfare of the people.

SEIZURE OF PRESS CALLED DOUBTFUL

White House Says Right Exists Only for Remote Crisis—Law Permits Radio Shutdown

Special to THE NEW YORK TIMES.

WASHINGTON, April 18 — The White House minimized today President Truman's remark yesterday implying that he had the power to seize newspapers and radio stations in an emergency.

Joseph Short, White House press secretary, was asked for clarification or amplification of Mr. Truman's answer to a question at his news conference.

"It was a purely academic and hypothetical question and there is no amplification or comment on it," Mr. Short said.

A reporter then said that some editors, members of the American Society of Newspaper Editors, seemed to interpret Mr. Truman's reply as affirmative.

"You can quote them on it," Mr. Short retorted.

The society is having its annual meeting here. Several hundred members attended the conference in the unfamiliar setting of the auditorium of the Natural History Building of the Smithsonian Institution. Some reporters covering the conference as well as some editors had not heard either the question or Mr. Truman's reply clearly in the big hall.

The official White House transcript today showed the exchange as follows:

"Mr. President, if you can seize the steel mills under your inherent powers, can you in your opinion also seize the newspapers or and (sic) the radio stations?"

The President replied that under similar circumstances the President of the United States had to act for whatever is for the best of the country. That was the answer to the question, the President said to the questioning editor.

Under White House rules, the President's press conference remarks may not be quoted directly.

Members of the White House staff said they saw no likelihood of a situation that would bring about such seizures. They expressed the belief that Mr. Truman, replying to a hypothetical question, was thinking of remote possibilities of great peril.

Nevertheless Mr. Truman's remark plainly suggested that he believed he had implied powers under the Constitution that conceivably might allow him latitude to include the press and radio. In his recent controversial seizure of the steel mills he relied on these implied powers, which the steel industry is seeking to test in the courts.

In his reply, he said that is the answer to the question.

Radio Seizure Authorized

A law passed last year authorizes the President, upon the proclamation "that there exists war or a threat of war, or a state of public peril or disaster or other national emergency, or in order to preserve the neutrality of the United States," to close down any radio station.

This was an amendment to the Federal Communications Act of 1934. A parallel section in the Civil Defense Act permits the President, after a warning of an air attack, to close radio stations whose broadcasts would provide an enemy a guiding beam.

It was learned that Mr. Truman has been strongly influenced by his predecessors, particularly by President Lincoln, who in time of rebellion seized persons and newspapers by force.

Press Group Asks Safeguard

BALTIMORE, April 18 (AP)—The directors of the Maryland Press Association approved today a resolution calling for a "new amendment to the Constitution providing safeguard against the exercise of dictatorial power by the President of the United States."

The action was taken, the resolution stated, because the President "has intimated publicly that he believes he has the inherent power to seize property, whether it be a public utility, an industry or the press."

AIR LIBEL SUIT CURB OMITTED FROM BILL

Conferees Also Kill Clause to Protect Publishers on TV and Radio Station Permits

WASHINGTON, July 1 (UP)—A joint Senate-House conference committee threw out today a proposal to exempt radio and television stations from libel suits stemming from slanderous or defamatory remarks by political candidates.

The conferees also killed a provision barring the Federal Communications Commission from discriminating against newspaper publishers in granting radio or television station licenses. They felt that there was no need for such a prohibition.

After omitting the two provisions, the conferees approved a compromise bill designed to modernize the commission's procedures. The measure now goes back to the House and Senate, which forced the conference by approving conflicting bills.

Senator Ernest W. McFarland, Democrat of Arizona, said that the House-approved libel provision was dropped because no hearings had been held on it and because the conferees believed that it deserved more study.

Supporters of the proposal argued that radio and television stations were caught in a squeeze because they were not allowed to censor statements made by political candidates, but were held responsible for what went out over the air.

Mr. McFarland said that the anti-discrimination provision was killed because newspaper publishers were not being discriminated against, and that "we felt that if you put one industry in, you would have to put them all in."

The clause would have subjected the commission to suits seeking to compel it to issue radio and television station licenses to newspaper owners, he added.

The conferees approved a provision permitting stations to charge political candidates only the amount charged for comparable time for other users. The House version said that political rates could not exceed "minimum" charges for comparable use of the air. Some candidates have said that they were charged more than regular advertising rates.

The libel provision knocked out by the conferees would have exempted stations from responsibility for remarks made by candidates using their facilities, unless the station "wilfully" aided the slander.

Mr. McFarland, Senate Majority Leader, said that he hoped to take the conference report to the Senate floor tomorrow or Thursday.

July 2, 1952

NEWS RELEASES CRITICIZED

Editorial Writer Calls U. S. Copy Handouts Form of Censorship

DENVER, Nov. 17 (AP)—Government handouts to reporters were listed today as one form of censorship of the news by Charles C. Clayton, St. Louis newspaper man and president of Sigma Delta Chi, the national professional journalistic fraternity.

The organization will hold its national convention here Wednesday through Saturday.

"Censorship takes many forms—withholding of news, secret meetings of public groups and information by handout among them," Mr. Clayton said in an interview. He is an editorial writer for The St. Louis Globe-Democrat.

Referring to Government press releases, he added: "It's censorship if you print only what they hand out."

November 18, 1952

SHIELDING OF DATA DECRIED BY EDITOR

CLEVELAND, Dec. 2 (UP)—Louis B. Seltzer, editor of The Cleveland Press, a Scripps-Howard newspaper, today proposed that radio, television and newspapers set up a "board of objective inquiry" to examine threats to freedom of information.

Mr. Seltzer made his proposal in an address before the seventh annual convention of the National Association of Radio News Directors here.

"Government has become so intricate," he said, "that it has set up a series of protective shields—such as the press conference and the handout—between itself and the public."

As a result, radio, television and the newspapers were rarely going to the source of news, Mr. Seltzer said. "Instead, they are getting from somebody else that information which is tailored to fit the needs of the Federal agency involved," he said.

"Democracy and the free press are indispensable one to the other," Mr. Seltzer added. "If we don't do something real about the problem of shrinking information —against barriers to free information—we are going to regret it some day."

He said it was "a disgrace" that there was not more investigative reporting by the press associations in Washington and in state capitals.

However, he declared, the press associations, radio, television and newspapers were not alone to blame. "I don't recall any time in our history when there has been so much indifference and negligence on the part of our citizens," he said.

December 3, 1952

'56 ADVICE FOR RADIO, TV

Bartley of F.C.C. Advises on Early Campaign Policy

SARANAC INN, N. Y., Sept. 23 (AP)—A Federal Communications Commissioner advised broadcasters tonight to develop station policy on political talks well in advance of the 1956 Presidential campaign.

Robert T. Bartley told the National Association of Radio and Television Broadcasters:

"Don't wait until after the first candidate is permitted to make an hour-long speech, for then it is too late. The first request the broadcaster honors starts the chain reaction, and he may find his entire program schedule disrupted."

At today's luncheon session, Harold E. Bellows, president of the association, reported that the organization had grown rapidly in the last ten years. He attributed this to "the need among broadcasters to pool resources, efforts and talents to deal with the numerous and complex federal-state legislative problems."

The three-day meeting ends tomorrow.

September 24, 1955

S. E. C. AIDES FAVOR WITHHOLDING DATA

WASHINGTON, Jan. 31 (AP)—Officials of the Securities and Exchange Commission said today that it was often in the best public interest to withhold information handled by the S. E. C.

J. Sinclair Armstrong, commission chairman, and other officials appeared before the House Government Information subcommittee studying the information policies of Federal departments and agencies.

Byron D. Woodside, director of the Division of Corporation Finance in the S. E. C., said: "It's been the commission's view over the years it's in the best public interest not to make certain information public."

Representative John E. Moss, Democrat of California, subcommittee chairman, criticized this as the wrong attitude.

"In other words, you would not release information unless it was justified," Mr. Moss said. "We have hopes the emphasis will change to where you would have to justify withholding."

A newspaper man testified at the hearing that S. E. C. and many of the other agencies were "little principalities of their own, with their own types of censorship."

Leslie Gould, financial editor of The New York Journal-American, also said too much of the information that should be getting out to the public was considered "top sacred."

February 1, 1956

EDITORS DEBATE PRESS RED HUNT

One Says Eastland Inquiry Perils Liberty, 2d Backs Right to Call Newsmen

By RUSSELL BAKER
Special to The New York Times.

WASHINGTON, April 19—The Congressional search for Communist infiltration of the press was both assailed and defended today before the convention of the American Society of Newspaper Editors.

Irving Dilliard of The St. Louis Post-Dispatch, told his colleagues that the Senate Internal Security subcommittee's investigation of several employes of The New York Times last winter had been an invasion of freedom of the press.

Vermont Royster, of The Wall Street Journal, replied that the Constitution guaranteed newsmen no more immunity from Congressional investigation than it accorded "college professors, bricklayers or strip-teasers."

The debate occurred in one of three discussion groups that grappled with major problems confronting newspapers in 1956. The other two groups discussed television's impact on newspaper political coverage and editorial attitudes toward integration.

Mr. Dilliard's argument was that liberty is lost, not abruptly, but by erosion, and that the Senate investigation of Times employes might have started the eroding process by intimidating other papers into silence.

112 Papers Silent

Of 193 papers in the nation's hundred largest cities, he said, 112 took no editorial stand on the inquiry headed by Senator James O. Eastland, Democrat of Mississippi.

Thirty-five were critical of some phase of the committee's activity and only a "considerably smaller" number voiced strong support for The Times' position, he said.

In an editorial printed last Jan. 5, The Times commented on the hearings of the Eastland subcommittee, taking the position that it had been singled out for attack by the subcommittee because of its stand on several civil rights issues, including opposition to school segregation.

The editorial said that neither the subcommittee or any other agency "outside this office" would determine policies of The Times.

The Times, it said, "will continue to determine its own policies. It will continue to condemn segregation * * * it will continue to defend civil rights."

Thirty-three papers supported the investigation and ten took "inconclusive" positions, Mr. Dillard said.

The high percentage of papers that had no editorial comment was "an impressive finding," he said. "Did Senator Eastland's boldness in concentrating on The New York Times so impress the press that many editors found it desirable to avoid commenting?" he asked.

Mr. Dilliard questioned what the effect on freedom might be if many editors "chose to keep silent * * * to accommodate themselves to the investigators" in a series of press investigations.

Mr. Royster thought that Mr. Dilliard was unduly alarmed by "nonexistent specters on the landscape." Freedom of the press, he argued, was "essentially protection of the people's right to know."

It was "strange," he added, that this should be interpreted to mean that Congress should be barred from asking questions of newspaper men.

Intimidation Denied

The New York Times, Mr. Royster said, was not intimidated by the Eastland investigation. If other papers should be intimidated by similar inquiries, he added, "the fault would lie not so much with Senator Eastland, but with ourselves."

The Constitution guaranteed the press neither public esteem nor immunity from the threat of intimidation, he said. Esteem had to be earned and threats of intimidation had to be resisted with courage, he added.

In the panel discussion of integration, the editors heard Lenoir Chambers of The Norfolk Virginian-Pilot criticize many Southern papers for what he called their failure to give serious study to the constitutional basis for the Supreme Court decision outlawing segregation in public schools.

Mr. Chambers implied that many southern editors had accepted too readily the general thesis that the Supreme Court's ruling was an unconstitutional invasion of state's rights.

He urged the creation of a Presidential commission that would develop suggestions for solutions and thus give opportunity for "the moderate mind of the South" to regain a voice in the turmoil.

John Q. Mahaffey of The Texarkana (Tex.) Gazette and Daily News pleaded with northern editors to be "a little bit more moderate on this matter." The South, he said, was "just not ready for it."

Harry M. Ayers of The Anniston (Ala.) Star painted a picture of resistance so strong in Alabama that integration could never be achieved.

The panel on political coverage heard five veteran newsmen agree that television had not made the political reporter obsolete.

It would still be the newspapers' job to get the story the cameras could not catch and to give meaning to the bewildering bits and pieces of politics seen on the home screen, they agreed.

The panelists were A. H. Kirchhofer of The Buffalo Evening News; George Cornish of The New York Herald Tribune, Gould Lincoln of The Washington Star, Charles Lucey of Scripps-Howard Newspapers and Roy A. Roberts of The Kansas City Star.

April 20, 1956

Officials Try to Conceal News, Head of Publishers' Group Says

By RUSSELL PORTER

Richard W. Slocum, president of the American Newspaper Publishers Association, charged yesterday that Federal, state and local government officials were interfering with freedom of the press. He said they did so by withholding information that the public was entitled to have.

Mr. Slocum, who is executive vice president of The Philadelphia Bulletin, spoke at the seventieth annual convention of the association at the Waldorf-Astoria Hotel.

Mr. Slocum said free access to public information was essential to a free press and was one of the basic rights of a free people.

"We are the active trustees of that right and we intend to continue vigilant and vigorous in its assertion, for Government agencies tend to act like clams," he told his fellow publishers. "There are mollusks of this variety in Government from the high echelons in the Federal establishment to the lower levels of local authority."

Mr. Slocum charged that officials were stamping "top secret" on matters about which the public had a right to know. Officials, he said, are finding "a hundred excuses" for refusing to discuss their activities.

"No one connected with newspapers wants to publish the slightest thing that may truly harm national security," he went on. "The trouble arises and the public gets short-changed on information because many public officials have an out-sized sense of what is important to national security."

He praised Representative John E. Moss, Democrat of California and chairman of a House subcommittee on Government information, for conducting "a wholesome study of the withholding of information within Government."

He urged editors and publishers to back the subcommittee, saying:

"Strangely, newspapers have not been acting to support the purpose of this subcommittee. The Washington press corps has largely ignored its activities."

Mr. Slocum asserted that the entire relationship of the Government and the press called for "constant vigilance and an outspoken voice."

"Hearings like those of the Senate Eastland committee, which called a number of New York City newspaper men be-fore it, must be looked at to determine whether the motive was as stated or directed at certain newspapers with the thought of reprisal or intimidation."

Senator James O. Eastland, Democrat of Mississippi, is chairman of the Senate Internal Security subcommittee. It has held public hearings for the stated purpose of investigating Communist attempts to infiltrate the press. The New York Times last January published an editorial charging that it had been singled out for attack because of its stand for civil rights and against racial segregation in the public schools, in opposition to Senator Eastland.

Daily Worker Case Discussed

Mr. Slocum also referred to the recent seizure of The Daily Worker, the Communist publication, by Federal agents in a tax case. He said:

"Procedure of the Treasury Department in seizure and padlocking of any newspaper demands critical scrutiny. It is easy for some to pass over an incident like the recent seizure and padlocking of The New York Daily Worker with the thought that this was a Communist newspaper and Communists deserve nothing better. But an act looked at lightly which violates a safeguard can well be used as a precedent.

"Normally the government seizes property only when there is danger that assets of a delinquent taxpayer may disappear pending final determination of the liability. The possibility of disappearance of assets in this case must be considered in deciding whether harassment was the objective rather than normal considerations of jeopardy assessment.

"The press should let it be known that it will fight any singling out intended as harassment or interference with the public right to a free press."

Election Charges Forecast

Mr. Slocum predicted that this year's Presidential election campaign would bring a repetition of 1952 charges that the newspaper publishers operated a "one party press" in favor of the Republicans. On the other hand, he said, accusations of Democratic leanings among the national press corps and political reporters may be expected.

"Undoubtedly there will be criticism from persons in both parties," he went on. "But we urge that in any criticism they name specific newspapers for a specific performance or lack of it, not cast an accusation against the whole press or any special part of it."

Mr. Slocum expressed confidence that the press would meet its obligation of "full, fair, objective and unbiased reporting of the campaign."

"The editorial columns are the proper place for the recognized right of the editor to express his opinion," he said, "and the press is not erring in its responsibility when it shows a preference in the editorial columns so long as it is accurate, adequate and objective in reporting in its news columns."

Gainza Paz Urges Free Press

Dr. Alberto Gainza Paz, publisher of La Prensa of Buenos Aires, spoke out of his own experience in urging the publishers never to give up the fight for a free press.

His newspaper was confiscated by the Juan D. Perón regime in 1951. He himself was exiled until last year, when the Government was overthrown and he regained control of the paper.

He thanked the A. N. P. A. for a resolution adopted at its 1952 convention, which he attended, supporting him and condemning the Perón regime.

"We must never withhold our support and stimulus to whomever is fighting for a cause we believe worthy and just," he went on. "It is not enough to recognize, in an undertone, the justice of a cause. The right and practical thing to do is to fight those people who thrive on injustice.

"Never let us lose faith in the great human causes, and never let us deny them our help.

"Many times while the dictator ruled in Argentina, I said it was necessary to raise the cry of alarm and show how the suppression of a free press had eased the way for the police state, how the destruction of independent newspapers had opened the way to destroy all other liberties.

"Without a free press, the people were deaf, dumb and blind. Argentina's oppression was thus a tragic example for some other American nations, where liberty is under a creeping siege."

Stresses Need for Resistance

Dr. Gainza Paz decried pessimism in the face of attacks on freedom, saying:

"We need not say, 'nothing can be done.' That weak statement ought never to be heard in the Americas, the continent of liberty, hope and human miracles.

"Every people battling for their rights is a new denial of what has come to be called a 'realistic policy' in dealing with tyrants. That policy is more cynical than realistic, too cool and calm about injustice.

"It is a short-sighted policy, without faith, but unhappily it sometimes gains credence in the foreign offices of our governments."

Mr. Slocum, replying to the speaker, assured him that the press of the United States would not forget its duty but would always take up the right for the oppressed.

Turning to the purely business affairs of the convention, Mr. Slocum warned that no relief was in sight for the newsprint shortage. He urged publishers to "look ahead, anticipate growth, measure daily allowable newsprint use against sure supply, and arrange for stepped-up newsprint contracts for the years to come."

"The shortage is due," he said, "to the tremendous use of newspaper space in response to reader and advertising needs, particularly the suddenness of the increase."

He expressed the opinion that newsprint manufacturers should keep current prices stable. He said their financial statements and their plans to invest many millions in new production showed that today's prices provided an adequate return to them.

April 26, 1956

Report on 'Leaks' Blames Armed Services For Keeping Too Much Information Secret

WASHINGTON, Nov. 9 (UP)— A special Defense Department committee told Charles E. Wilson, Secretary of Defense, today that the armed services tried to keep too much information secret.

The committee said this was one reason the Defense Department had been plagued with "leaks" of classified material to the press and other "unauthorized persons."

The committee, headed by Charles A. Coolidge, Boston attorney and former Assistant Secretary of Defense, was set up by Mr. Wilson last summer. It was asked to find out why so much information the department tried to keep secret found its way into public channels.

The Defense Department said the report, sent to Mr. Wilson today, would not be made public until next week.

However, Defense Department and Congressional sources disclosed that it had criticized the department's "over-classification" of information.

The committee, it was reported, also told Secretary Wilson the department's security set-up was so large and complex that it could not function effectively and efficiently.

Mr. Wilson appointed the special Coolidge committee last Aug. 13 with instructions to plug the leaks of defense information to "unauthorized persons."

"In the interests of national security this must stop," he said.

The Secretary declared that unauthorized disclosures could cause "serious damage to the nation." He asked the five-man committee for recommendations to provide greater protection and safeguards for security information.

The committee, it was indicated, in effect backed the recent criticism of Trevor Gardner, former Assistant Secretary of Air, that too many persons had authority to stamp information secret and that too much information was classified secret as a result.

November 10, 1956

DEFENSE 'SECRECY' TOPIC OF INQUIRY

House Unit Slates Hearing Tuesday on Restricting of Information by U. S.

Special to The New York Times.
WASHINGTON, Nov. 10—A special House investigating subcommittee will set out Tuesday to determine whether the Defense Department has been suppressing information that the public should have.

The issue, it appeared, would be whether the armed services, dedicated to the preservation of the national security, had gone too far in withholding information that could have been released without danger.

The panel is headed by Representative John E. Moss, Democrat of California, who was re-elected Tuesday. It began its inquiry last summer. In October it expressed suspicion that many government agencies had withheld information from the public in instances where they had no legal authority to do so.

Resumption of the investigation will focus upon the Department of Defense, with public hearings continuing through Nov. 16. Under particular scrutiny will be a report made by a special civilian committee created in August by Charles E. Wilson, Secretary of Defense.

The committee, headed by Charles A. Coolidge, a former Assistant Secretary of Defense, was assigned to discover how information held under cover by the department had "leaked" to publication.

Report Completed
The report of the Coolidge committee has been completed and is now before Secretary Wilson for his study. Wilbur A. Brucker, Secretary of the Army; Charles S. Thomas, Secretary of the Navy; Donald A. Quarles, Secretary of the Air Force, and Robert Tripp Ross, Assistant Secretary of Defense, have been called for Nov. 16 to discuss this report.

Heads of research and development units of the Defense Department will appear before the House subcommittee next Tuesday. They will be questioned on restrictions placed on scientific information. Improvements in the security classification system also will be sought.

On Wednesday, the panel will question counsels of the Defense Department, spokesmen for the three armed services and judges advocate general as to legal right to restrict information, including information from courts-martial.

Two Sessions on Thursday
Two sessions were planned for Thursday. In the morning the subcommittee will examine the Defense Department units that review Pentagon speeches and news releases to see whether they have gone too far in denying information in the name of national security.

The afternoon will be devoted to questioning public information experts about the operation of that section, and on allegations that they have restricted information unduly.

Friday sessions will be given to the questioning of the Secretaries of the armed services and others. It was indicated that emphasis would be put upon the "editing" of speeches by Pentagon officials, which has provoked criticism from numerous points.

November 11, 1956

CENSORSHIP ASSAILED

Editor Sees Danger of U. S. Dictatorship in News Ban

Special to The New York Times.
CINCINNATI, Jan. 19 — The path followed by President Truman during his Administration and now by President Eisenhower in the censorship of news "is a road that can be used toward dictatorship," Norman E. Isaacs, managing editor of The Louisville Courier-Journal and Times, said here tonight.

He spoke on "America's Iron Curtain" before 500 persons at the Rockdale Avenue Temple's 133d annual dinner. Mr. Isaacs said that neither Mr. Truman nor General Eisenhower were "dictatorial types" but that under their Administrations there had been forged "the ideal tools for the use of an unscrupulous man or group of men."

Mr. Isaacs is a former president of The Associated Press Managing Editors Association and served as national chairman of that organization's Freedom of Information Committee.

On the Federal, state and local levels, governmental executives are taking the people toward abandonment of free institutions and the acceptance of secret institutions, Mr. Isaacs said.

January 20, 1957

POLITICAL SECRECY ASSAILED BY EDITOR

ROCHESTER, N. Y., Jan. 29 (AP)—A newspaper editor accused politicians today of developing a philosophy that asserts decisions of government should be made without "the prior restraint of an informed public opinion."

The statement, by V. M. Newton of The Tampa (Fla.) Tribune, chairman of the Sigma Delta Chi committee on freedom of information, was read before members of the New York State Society of Newspaper Editors.

Mr. Newton's statement was followed by an explanation by Victor E. Bluedorn of Chicago, executive director of Sigma Delta Chi, national journalism fraternity. Mr. Bluedorn warned against "the dangers" of suppression of "the right of people to know."

Mr. Newton's statement said:
"The politician has managed to drape a 'paper curtain' of secrecy around large segments of free American government.

"This 'paper curtain' of secrecy has been securely pulled over virtually all of Federal executive government, and over at least half of Federal legislative government, and it now is being extended into Federal judicial government and into all lower levels of American government."

Mr. Newton and Mr. Bluedorn urged the New York editors to press for a state law requiring all governing bodies to transact business in public sessions.

January 30, 1957

SECRECY UPHELD BY WHITE HOUSE

President's Counsel Tells Protesting Editors That Policy Will Continue

WASHINGTON, April 4 (Æ)—The White House has refused to withdraw an order by President Eisenhower fixing secrecy standards for Government information.

Gerald D. Morgan, special counsel to the President, said in letters to two editors, made public today, that the 1953 directive gave "the minimum protection necessary to the defense interests of the nation."

Mr. Morgan was replying to a resolution adopted by The Associated Press Managing Editors Association. It urged rescinding of the order on the ground it was being invoked increasingly to withhold information. The resolution contended that the public was entitled to the information.

The Eisenhower order authorizes certain officials to classify information as top secret or confidential, depending on the degree to which they believe its disclosure would hurt national security. Another security classification, restricted, was eliminated by the 1953 order.

Frank Eyerly, managing editor of The Des Moines Register and Tribune and president of the association, voiced disappointment that Mr. Morgan made no mention of an association proposal that the President at least take steps to prevent misuse of his order.

Mr. Eyerly said in a letter to Mr. Morgan that the Administration apparently "is unwilling to issue a clarifying directive." The A. P. M. E. head added that the editors therefore would make the matter "a continuing topic of discussion, editorialization and public debate."

In addition, V. M. Newton Jr., managing editor of The Tampa Tribune, wrote Mr. Morgan that he doubted if General Eisenhower had been told "all the facts in this very grave matter concerning the vital interests of the American people."

Mr. Newton, who was president of the association when the resolution was adopted last November, said General Eisenhower undoubtedly intended his order to give "some relief from the blanket censorship order" issued by President Truman. But instead, Mr. Newton said, officials are using the Eisenhower order to bring about an opposite result.

April 5, 1957

INFORMATION POLICY OF U. S. SCRUTINIZED

Special to The New York Times.

PRINCETON, N. J., May 15—Three veterans of the interplay between the Federal Government and the press over security matters spoke here today at a Princeton University symposium. They agreed that the people and press must constantly guard against unnecessary classification of Government information.

The speakers were Edward W. Barrett, a former Washington correspondent and editor and Assistant Secretary of State for public affairs under President Truman; William H. Jackson, former special assistant to President Eisenhower, and John B. Oakes, editorial writer for The New York Times.

Mr. Barrett, who is dean of the Graduate School of Journalism at Columbia University, proposed "a periodic review of classification policies by legislative committees, both Federal and state."

Mr. Jackson, a lawyer, declared that "we managed to tell the Russians just the things they want to know while keeping the American people from vital facts they need to know as members of a democracy."

Mr. Oakes contended that "a more pressing matter is the failure of newspaper publishers to take security seriously." He remarked that "we never see a press association criticize one of its members for indiscreet reporting which threatens the nation's security and well-being."

May 16, 1957

OFFICIAL SECRECY HIT

All Levels of Government Said to Withhold Data

LENOX, Mass. June 1 (Æ)—William Dwight, president of the American Newspaper Publishers Association, said here tonight that the people's right to know how their money was being spent "is being abridged at every level of Government."

"Too many in Government, whether local, county, state or Federal, subscribe to this attitude that the people should only know what they think is good for them to know," Mr. Dwight said in a speech at a convention dinner at the Massachusetts Association of School Committees.

Mr. Dwight is president of The Holyoke (Mass.) Transcript-Telegram.

June 2, 1957

2 IN HOUSE SCORE LEAK PROPOSALS

Celler and Moss Criticize Security Group's Plan to Penalize Newsmen

WASHINGTON, June 23 (Æ)—Two members of Congress studying the report of the Commission on Government Security, criticized today a recommendation aimed at halting leaks of secret information.

Representative Emanuel Celler, the Brooklyn Democrat who heads the House Judiciary Committee, said that "at first blush" this and some other commission proposals appeared to be unconstitutional.

The twelve-member study group recommended that Congress make it a crime for newsmen and other private citizens to disclose secret information, even if they did not intend to harm the national interest. Such strictures now apply only to Government employes. The commission proposed a maximum penalty of five years in prison and a $10,000 fine.

Representative John E. Moss, Democrat of California and head of the Government Information subcommittee in the House, demanded that the commission, set up by Congress, produce "whatever evidence you have to support your implication that reporters have been stealing secret information."

Representative Celler also said that he could not accept, in the form submitted, the commission's proposal to legalize the use of wiretap evidence in court cases involving national security.

These are only two of the suggestions made by the commission for sweeping changes in the loyalty-security program. The group was named by President Eisenhower and Congress.

Some Reforms Praised

The American Civil Liberties Union applauded yesterday several reforms that had been proposed by the commission. But in a preliminary analysis, it deplored continuing passport denials and wiretapping.

Patrick Murphy Malin, the union's executive director, said the report by the commission set up by Congress in 1955 "points the way toward correction of many abuses of civil liberties."

He hailed particularly proposals to reform the Federal employe program. One would grant hearings to all applicants for Government jobs and to employes whose loyalty is questioned. Another would improve confrontation and cross-examination by revealing sources of information except for official counter-intelligence agents. A third would provide for the subpoenaing of witnesses at hearings.

The commission rejected proposals to extend the industrial security program to cover all persons with access to defense plants. Mr. Malin said this "can help prevent investigations of millions of persons having no real contact" with secret data.

The proposed creation of a Central Security Office, he said, requires further study. But such a move, he declared, "could ease pressure on civil liberties" by stressing uniform regulations and better training for security officers.

On the other hand, Mr. Malin saw "a serious curb on individual freedom" in proposals to continue the State Department's power to deny passports and to prevent people from traveling to places it did not authorize. He also regretted that the commission had failed to urge an end to wiretapping by the Department of Justice.

June 24, 1957

319

Security vs. Freedom

An Analysis of the Controversy Stirred By Recommendation to Curb Information

By JAMES RESTON
Special to The New York Times.

WASHINGTON, June 24—According to James C. Hagerty, who should know, President Eisenhower thinks the Commission on Government Security has turned in a "good report."

The report, however, contains a recommendation that produced a stir in Washington today and foreshadowed another battle over Government censorship, if it is finally supported by the White House.

The point in controversy, sent to the President last Saturday, is as follows:

"The commission recommends that Congress enact legislation making it a crime for any person willfully to disclose without proper authorization, for any purpose whatsoever, information classified 'secret' or 'top secret,' knowing, or having reasonable grounds to believe, such information to have been so classified."

In a commentary on this recommendation, the commission said it believed "that such legislative enactment would act as a genuine deterrent to those who, without giving serious thought to the over-all security picture, but without pernicious or subversive intent, deliberately compromise vital defense information for the sake of publicity or for any commercial or other purpose."

Same Fate Met

This has met the same fate as almost every other attempt to limit the freedom of the press in the name of national security. It has been bitterly condemned, not because its objectives are bad, but because it is so broadly defined as to discourage all premature disclosures, those in the public interest as well as those not in the public interest.

The history of recent years is full of illustrations of the dangers of such broad legislative proposals.

Franklin D. Roosevelt's deal with Joseph Stalin at Yalta to bring the Ukraine and Bylo-Russia into the United Nations was classified "top secret." Elaborate efforts were made to conceal the arrangement. The late Bert Andrews, Washington correspondent of The New York Herald Tribune, found out about it.

He "willfully," even gleefully reported it, knowing full well that it was classified "top secret." Under the proposals of the Commission on Government Security, if law at the time, he would have been subject to a fine of $10,000 and five years in jail.

The late Paul Adnerson of The St. Louis Post Dispatch broke the Teapot Dome scandal in the Twenties. Again "secret" documents were "willfully" published without Government authorization. Nobody suggested sending him to the pokey.

Arthur Krock of this newspaper discovered and "willfully" published the "secret" Government plans to introduce the National Recovery Act and to go off the gold standard in the early days of the New Deal.

This newspaper also published the original plans of the United States, Britain, France and the Soviet Union on the formation of the United Nations. Again they were marked "top secret" and the Federal Bureau of Investigation was called in to make an official investigation of the disclosure.

In this case, though the Government maintained that publication would block formation of the United Nations, the main result was a long debate on the Big Five veto power and the assumption that the five major powers could agree on a postwar settlement. This, in turn, helped clarify the issue and contributed to some modifications of the Charter, but under the legislation now proposed by the Commission on Government Security, it would have been a clear case for criminal action.

Numerous Cases

More recent cases are almost too numerous to catalogue. Certainly some of the "secret" papers disclosed by newspapers in the Dixon-Yates deal would come under the purview of the proposed law. Similarly, some of the information indicating the possibility of an outbreak of war last year in Egypt would have been subject to legal scrutiny.

These are only a few illustrations of why the Administration is being urged to take a close look at the whole report before pronouncing judgment on it.

The commission apparently had no intention to cover questions of this kind. Its recommendation for punitive legislation came at the end of a long section dealing with the dangers of passing information to spies, but it goes on from this question to make the following observation:

"The commission found to its dismay that one frustrating aspect of this over-all security problem is the frequent unauthorized disclosure without subversive intent of classified information affecting national security. Several instances were noted where information emanating from the Department of Defense, and subsequently determined to have been classified, has found its way through various media into the public domain, when in deference to the interests of national security more restraint should have been exercised before dissemination.

"Airplane journals, scientific periodicals and even the daily newspapers have featured articles containing information and other data which should have been deleted in whole or in part for security reasons.

"In many instances the chief culprits responsible for any unauthorized publication of classified material are persons quite removed from Government service, and therefore not amenable to applicable criminal statutes or other civil penalties.

"Congressional inaction in this particular area can be traced to the genuine fear of imposing undue censorship upon the bulk of information flowing from the various governmental agencies, and which the American people, for the most part, have the right to know.

"Any statute designed to correct this difficulty must necessarily minimize constitutional objections by maintaining the proper balance between the guarantee of the First Amendment, on one hand, and required measures to establish a needed safeguard against any real danger to our national security."

This task of finding the "proper balance" between freedom and security is precisely the problem that has divided opinion in America from the days of the constitutional convention to last week's rulings of the Supreme Court.

Many men have proposed laws to deal with it, but most of them have found that the question was more intricate than they originally imagined.

'BETRAYAL' OF U.S. LAID TO NEWSMEN

Security Aide Says Defense Secrets Were Disclosed

By E. W. KENWORTHY
Special to The New York Times.

WASHINGTON, June 30 — Loyd Wright, chairman of the Commission on Government Security, said today he knew of many instances in which American journalists had written "dark chapters of betrayal" of the nation's defense secrets.

Mr. Wright said the people had a right to know of these betrayals, but that "the responsible official" in the Defense Department had refused to declassify the secrets that had been disclosed.

Despite the commission's duty not to reveal these violations of security by the press, Mr. Wright said, there are enough examples "freely available to anyone who reads the daily papers" to demonstrate "that the danger is real."

The instances, he said, give support to the commission's proposal for broadening the laws making it a crime to disclose secret information.

Mr. Wright listed twenty-six newspaper and magazine articles over the last sixteen years that, he said, had been supplied to the commission by the Department of Defense as "examples of publication prejudicial to the national security."

The commission, composed of two Senators, two Representatives and eight public members, was created by Congress in November, 1955, to study the whole security program.

The commission's final report included draft legislation to penalize the unlawful disclosure of information affecting the national defense by persons inside and outside the Government.

At present only Government employes can be punished for simple disclosure of classified information. A newspaper man, for example, can be prosecuted only under two circumstances—under the conspiracy law if he connives with a Government employe to obtain the information, or under the espionage laws if he purloins the information and discloses it with reason to believe he may thereby injure the United States or aid a foreign nation.

The proposed law would make disclosure by anyone punishable by a fine up to $10,000, imprisonment up to five years, or both.

In a personal appendix to the report, Mr. Wright said "no citizen is entitled to take the law, and the safety of the nation, into his own hands."

"The purveyor of information vital to national security, purloined by devious means, gives aid to our enemies as effectively as the foreign agent," Mr. Wright asserted.

The proposed law and Mr. Wright's statement brought protests from members of Congress, publishers and editors. They have complained that Government officials too often put the "secret" stamp on information that should be made public.

On the day the commission issued its report, Representative John E. Moss, California Democrat who heads the House Government Information subcommittee, wrote to Mr. Wright, challenging him to cite "evidence you have to support your implication that reporters have been stealing secret information."

Mr. Wright replied that he would be happy to comply, and his statement today is his response to Mr. Moss' challenge.

Mr. Wright's examples are not likely to still the clamor, it was agreed here. These are some samples:

¶ "A metropolitan daily in December of 1953 published quite accurately the then highly classified information relative to the so-called 'New Look.' "

¶ "A national weekly in January, 1956, carried an article on missiles. The article contained many general statements, some of which were in error; however, in other respects the information was essentially correct and disclosed characteristics of missiles which were still in a highly classified status."

Senators John Stennis, Democrat of Mississippi, and Norris Cotton, Republican of New Hampshire, members of the commission, did not seem happy about Mr. Wright's statement. Both Senators emphasized that it was the chairman's "own personal statement."

Senator Cotton said that, so far as he could recall, "no horrible examples reflecting on newspapers and magazines were presented and discussed in the meetings of the commission."

Indeed, Mr. Cotton said, most of the emphasis was "on a lot of stuff classified that shouldn't be."

Mr. Wright himself was on his way home to Los Angeles, where he heads a prominent law firm.

Reporting his difficulties in getting declassification, Mr. Wright said:

"Many instances [of disclosure of secrets] were revealed in the course of the commission's study. During the past week I requested the responsible official to release a part of this information which, in my opinion, no longer required secrecy. * * *

"I regret to report that this request for declassification was denied, and that the information is apparently entombed forever, with the final rites of classified burial, in the bureaucratic graveyard of a maze of files, never to be disseminated to the American people who are entitled to know the full details of these dark chapters of betrayal."

The armed services, officials pointed out, seldom confirm security breaches because to do so would inform potential enemies of the accuracy of the information.

In The Nation

The Guarding of Essential Secrets of Defense

By ARTHUR KROCK

WASHINGTON, July 1—The proposal by the Commission on Government Security, that criminal penalties be visited on those who publish any information contained in documents marked "top secret" or "secret" by officials authorized to make these classifications, revives but only further confuses a problem of great perplexity for a nation operating under the First Amendment. And about the same thing can be said of most of the discussion that has followed this proposal.

Under existing law those who publish such information can be criminally prosecuted only if they "conspire" with a Government employe to obtain the information; or "purloin" (steal) and publish it in "reasonable" awareness that this will impair the security of the United States and aid another nation. But under the commission's proposal, of which Chairman Wright has become the special champion, this could happen:

1. A responsible military or civilian official decides the public should know the contents of a document classified as "top secret" or "secret" that, in his opinion, has been so marked to shield another official from the adverse consequences of grave error or misdoing that would follow publication. Or this responsible official believes that national security requires the publication to demolish a disastrous policy in the making—"disaster" in many instances being implicit in the choice of the program of another service branch.

2. Professing, however, and believing, that he is moved only by considerations of national security, this responsible official arranges that the document shall come into possession of the public press. And it is published on the judgment of the publication that it is within the domain of legitimate information and neither damages national security nor aids another nation.

3. The Department of Justice prosecutes those responsible for the publication and they are subject on conviction to a maximum fine of $10,000 and/or a maximum prison term of five years.

4. The Government will merely have to prove that the document involved was marked "top secret" or "secret" by officials authorized to make these classifications.

This is a very different concept from that of criminal punishment for thievery or conspiracy with respect to such publications. And in the above circumstances it would violate the established guarantees of the First Amendment. Also the proposal protects public officials who use their classifying power to cover up errors and wrongdoing.

Forrestal's Study

Yet it is perfectly true, as Chairman Wright asserted in a statement today, that publications in this official documentary area have endangered national security, and have appeared even in time of war. It is also perfectly true that some means consonant with the First Amendment should be found to prevent such publications. But until military and civilian officials cease furnishing them voluntarily (and they have been the source of most of these publications) the problem will remain that Wright and his commission would meet by deeply infringing the right of the press to furnish the public with information that, in its judgment and on its responsibility, the public is entitled to have and inflicts no damage to security. Such information, under the Wright proposal, would be subject to the same criminal penalties as that which, by prevailing journalistic standards and in the plain interest of national security, should not be published at all.

One of the great public servants of this generation, the late James V. Forrestal, grappled with this problem as our first Secretary of Defense. He could not solve it—and never would have tried the Wright Commission method. But he came to two tentative conclusions. One was that the root of the trouble was in governmental personnel. The other was that, if and when a Government advisory committee could be established which the press and the people would accept as above self-serving, information originating in classified documents could be regularly referred to this committee by the press and its advice as to publication would be followed. But Forrestal never could envisage a committee with that acceptance in peacetime.

In this correspondent's files is a memorandum of a meeting on this complex subject, Dec. 20, 1948. Those present, in addition to the oversigned, were Forrestal, Generals Eisenhower, Bradley, Vandenberg, Cates and Mark Clark and Admiral Denfeld. The subject was a magazine article that was presented as the official plan for fighting a war with the Soviet Union.

Only two suggestions came from this distinguished group. General Bradley said the material should have been referred to the top Pentagon tier—for guidance, but with no obligation to abide by it; and that the article should have been preceded by an editorial disclaimer of presenting the official "master plan." General Eisenhower said that, if it was the "master plan," the Russians should not have been informed of it through any channel; if it was not, and the idea was to confuse the Russians, that was equally bad because our people would also be confused.

SECURITY AND THE PRESS

Chairman Loyd Wright of the Commission on Government Security must have realized that he would be stepping into a hornets' nest when he personally asked Congress to give "special consideration" to the Commission's proposal to extend to everyone the penalties against unauthorized disclosure of classified information. He must have enjoyed stirring up the hornets' nest even more when he re-emphasized this recommendation by describing a number of alleged security breaches on the part of the press during the past two decades as "dark chapters of betrayal."

Whatever else he may be doing by thus stressing this one small part of the Commission's many recommendations, Mr. Wright is not making friends or influencing people. In some ways this is too bad, because the Commission made a large number of important proposals covering the Federal Government's entire security program, and many of these recommendations were good ones. Some, as we have previously noted on this page, were not so good; but there were enough valuable and progressive changes proposed in the report to warrant careful consideration of the whole. It would be unfortunate if the entire report, including its good features, were lost in the developing controversy over Mr. Wright's—and presumably the Commission's—exaggerated fears over disclosure of any classified information at all to persons unauthorized to receive it.

Apparently goaded by Representative John Moss to produce "whatever evidence you have to support your implication that reporters have been 'stealing secret information,'" Mr. Wright has now issued a list of such alleged instances. Many of the stories and articles cited could hardly have damaged the security of the United States or led to the "disastrous" consequences that Mr. Wright so acutely fears. But one or two of them could have, most particularly the famous examples from the second World War when just before Pearl Harbor one newspaper published a detailed war plan, including figures, and later when it published the fact that the United States had broken the Japanese code. We do not believe it is doing the newspaper profession any good to try to gloss over the fact that disclosures of this sort are indeed breaches of security of tremendous potential or actual damage; and they deserve prosecution.

However, it is a long jump from such patently dangerous publication to the disclosure of any piece of information that happens to be classified. The security of the United States is of prime importance; but so is the First Amendment. Automatically to make it a crime, as the Commission would do, to publish anything that a Government official (military or civilian) had marked secret could and unquestionably would seriously interfere with the public's right to know what is going on in this increasingly complex and diffuse Government of ours. Many of the most vital news stories of recent years could never have been published under such rules. Failure to publish them would actually have resulted not in an increase in the security of this Government but rather in positive harm to the American public, whether we refer to Teapot Dome, the U. N., Dixon-Yates—or many, many others.

A sensible balance, as usual, has to be reached on this matter. No responsible newspaper wants to damage the security of our country; yet occasionally there are cases of irresponsibility. No Government official would admit that he didn't believe in the fullest freedom of the press consistent with national security; yet there are frequent cases of official concealment for entirely ulterior reasons. It is possible that some tightening of existing legislation may be desirable, but with it should go—as indeed the Commission also recommends—a loosening of some of the official chains. In any case, it is certain that a law as stringent as the one proposed is not the answer to this always-difficult and always-present problem.

Air Force Appeals to Wilson to Remove The News Blackout on Its Missile Tests

WASHINGTON, July 8 (UP)—The Air Force is protesting the news blackout on guided missile tests to Charles E. Wilson, Secretary of Defense.

The action was disclosed by Brig. Gen. Arno H. Leuhman, information chief of the Air Force, in testimony today before a House of Representatives subcommittee that is investigating defense information policies.

General Leuhman said that he and other officers had asked James H. Douglas, Secretary of the Air Force, to appeal to Mr. Wilson to reverse a memorandum issued April 25 by Murray Snyder, Assistant Secretary of Defense.

Mr. Snyder's directive allows the Air Force to admit that a missile has been fired and to say whether any casualties resulted. But it forbids any disclosure of the type of missile or any other details.

General Leuhman told the subcommittee that the Air Force had been wrongfully criticized for lack of progress on missiles. He said Mr. Snyder's directive should be modified so that the Air Force could "give the public an idea of how we have progressed."

General Leuhman and Brig. Gen. A. J. Kinney, former information chief of the Air Force, were questioned about leaks of classified information. The questions were posed by Representative John E. Moss, Democrat of California and chairman of the subcommittee.

Both officers said that they knew of no instances in which documents had been stolen by newsmen. Rear Admiral E. B. Taylor, the Navy's information chief, said he, too, was not aware of any such cases.

A commission that studied Government security programs recommended recently that it be made a crime to publish Government secrets. Loyd Wright, chairman of the commission, referred to instances in which he said newsmen had "purloined" data.

A Freedom Is Ignored

By JAMES RESTON
Special to The New York Times.

WASHINGTON, Aug. 8—The Senate has taken much pride recently in its efforts to defend both the right to vote and the right to a jury trial.

But in its concentration on these issues it has almost wholly ignored the Constitutional prohibition against Congressional infringement of the freedom of the press.

Indeed, while the civil rights bill, as passed by the House and Senate, clearly attempts to strengthen the Fourteenth and Fifteenth Amendments to the Constitution, it has almost certainly violated the First Amendment's protection against Congressional censorship.

This was done when the House Judiciary Committee, on the motion of Representative Francis E. Walter, Democrat of Pennsylvania, inserted a clause in the Administration's bill subjecting reporters to a $1,000 fine or a year in jail if they published testimony taken in private by the proposed Civil Rights Commission without the consent of the commission.

This amendment went through both the House and Senate almost by accident. The purpose of it was never explained. The need for it was never debated. And while one or two Senators mentioned it after it had been spotted by the press, this was done only after the time had passed for deletion.

Consent Is Required

Thus, though the First Amendment to the Constitution expressly forbids the Congress to pass any law "abridging the freedom of speech or of the press," subsection G of section 102 of the bill as passed by both Houses now states:

"No evidence or testimony taken in executive session may be released or used in public sessions without the consent of the commission.

"Whoever releases or uses in public without the consent of the commission evidence or testimony taken in executive session shall be fined not more than $1,000, or imprisoned for not more than one year."

In an effort to avoid the embarrassment of passing such a clause without even debating it, the Senate has acquiesced in an argument by Senator Jacob K. Javits, Republican of New York, that the Congress intended this to apply, not to reporters but only to officials of the Civil Rights Commission.

It is true that the rules governing committees of the two

houses of Congress often use precisely this language in prohibiting committee officials to "release or use" secret testimony, and this may very well have been the intent of Representative Walter.

Nevertheless, the language is generally regarded here as being ambiguous in the extreme, for if a reporter publishes information taken in executive session by the Civil Rights Commission without the commission's "consent," he clearly "uses in public" this information, and thus can be consigned to the pokey for a year.

What happens after almost all secret sessions of Presidential or legislative commissions is well known. Reporters hang around the closed doors. They spot friends and relatives of witnesses inside. They button hole the witnesses when they come out, and by a variety of methods, including appeals to man's weakness for getting his name in the papers, wrangle out of said witnesses what went on inside.

This process has gone on ever since the first corridor was erected in these parts, usually with the cooperation of the distinguished gentlemen who sit in the Congress, and often to the enlightenment of the public at large. But now the Congressmen, in a moment of inattention, are saying that, if practiced outside the Civil Rights Commission door, it may cost the reporters $1,000.

Entirely aside from the fact that few reporters in Washington have $1,000, the general feeling here is that this is a curious thing to do in the name of civil rights, and that some way ought to be found to strike it out.

No Cure Figured Out

The difficulty, however, is that nobody has yet figured out how to do it, even though most Senators and Congressmen concede when it is pointed out to them, that they did not know it was in the bill.

What those two strategists from Texas, Lyndon B. Johnson, majority Senate leader, and Sam Rayburn, House Speaker, are trying to arrange is for the House Rules Committee to agree to the Senate bill as passed, warts and all.

They do not like warts any more than a lot of others, but they fear that once any effort is made to amend the Senate bill, a whole flood of amendments will follow, opening the entire wrangle once more.

Nevertheless, an effort will be made to get an exception in this case. Senators and Congressmen are constantly charging the executive branch with a tendency toward censorship. Consequently, they are embarrassed to find that in this instance they have, in a fit of absentmindedness, almost done it themselves.

August 9, 1957

PENTAGON REVISES INFORMATION RULES

WASHINGTON, Aug. 20 (AP)—Charles E. Wilson, Secretary of Defense, deleted today from regulations on the release of military information a requirement that such news must make a "constructive contribution" to national security.

The change was one of several included in a revision of military information directives.

Murray Snyder, Assistant Secretary of Defense for Public Affairs, said the "irritating phrase" about a constructive contribution had been misconstrued by such critics as Representative John E. Moss, Democrat of California, and chairman of the House Government Information subcommittee.

Mr. Snyder said Mr. Moss had expressed fear that the requirement might be used by defense officials to flatter the department or to cover up mistakes.

Mr. Moss said the changes appeared to be improvements.

Mr. Snyder said the new directive left unchanged the basic meaning and intent of the Pentagon's attitude toward release of information.

The rewritten directive states specifically that information originating within the defense establishment must be reviewed for "conflict with established policies or programs" as well as for violations of security.

August 21, 1957

FINES FOR NEWSMEN IN LEAKS PROPOSED

WASHINGTON, Oct. 30 (AP)—Enactment of a bill under which newsmen and others could incur stiff fines and imprisonment for disseminating Government "secrets" was urged today by Loyd Wright, who headed the Commission on Government Security.

Mr. Wright told the American Society for Industrial Security, at its annual meeting here, that he had been assured the legislation "will be taken up as one of the first orders of business when Congress reconvenes next January."

He also told reporters he "regretted" the publication by Aviation Week magazine of a story now stirring a Government furor—disclosure that the United States long had had radar equipment in Turkey keeping watch on Soviet missile firings.

Mr. Wright, whose twelve-member commission in June had recommended a 106-section bill tightening security rules in some circumstances and easing them in others, said:

"Mind you, I think a lot of the Government's security classification is nonsense. On the other hand, no private citizen has the right to usurp the powers of duly constituted authorities."

October 31, 1957

U. S. EASES CAMERA BAN

Allows News Photos in Public Areas of Federal Buildings

WASHINGTON, Nov. 14 (UP)—Representative John E. Moss, chairman of the House Government Information subcommittee, said today that some restrictions against news photographers in Government buildings had been dropped.

The California Democrat said photographers would no longer need prior permission to take pictures in such public areas as corridors, lobbies, foyers and auditoriums of Federal buildings.

Mr. Moss also said that Federal judges would continue to have authority to bar photographers in areas of Federal buildings directly under their control, such as courtrooms.

Similarly, he said, other tenant agencies will continue to make their own decisions on photographs in the office space they control.

Mr. Moss said the new rules had been put into effect on Oct. 30 by the General Services Administration, which operates the Government's buildings.

November 15, 1957

AGENCY PROPOSED TO INFORM PUBLIC

Physicist Calls for Institute of Enlightenment Aimed to End 'Confusion'

By LAWRENCE E. DAVIES
Special to The New York Times.

PALTO ALTO, Calif., Dec. 20—The creation of an Institute of Public Enlightenment to serve as a "management consultant firm" for the American public was proposed tonight.

Dr. William Shockley, a 1956 Nobel Prize winner in physics, issued the call as a result of the orbiting of two satellites by the Soviet Union this year, with ensuing "confusion" in this country.

Dr. Shockley said in a paper delivered at a dinner meeting of the American Physical Society that the institute he proposed should protect the people from "surprises from events like sputnik."

Just as the non-partisan National Bureau of Standards shoulders responsibility for "furnishing impartial appraisals in the field of things," he asserted, the institute would furnish "impartial appraisals in the field of thoughts."

Likened to a Doctor

"At the present time," he went on, "no agency exists to inform and motivate the people in their own national interest. Motivation research in product advertising has the objective of interesting people in things which they may not have realized they need.

"The public press exists by being popular with its readers and, with the exception of some courageous editors and columnists, does not dare to force unpalatable but important ideas on the people. The Institute of Public Enlightenment, if Government - supported, would be like a doctor who the patient pays to give him treatments, pleasant or not, which are necessary for his health."

Dr. Shockley likened the nation to a giant automation machine having a feed-back path that tells its control mechanism when an error has been made in trying to solve a problem.

Dr. Shockley, the co-developer of the transistor, proposed an institute supported preferably by privately granted funds and having a Board of Governors from a wide base.

As for its budget, "our national problems," he said "deserve and could use an advertising effort comparable to that for cigarettes or for automobiles or for underarm deodorants."

"Old Science" Used

Dr. Shockley, formerly of the Bell Laboratories, who now operates his own laboratory in this area, said that actually the Soviet Union had used "old science" and had applied it in the successful orbiting of its satellites.

The banquet followed a day of reports from an international collection of scientists in the Hall of Physics at Stanford University. It was the second day of a three-day meeting of the American Physical Society.

American and Russian physicists reported on research results confirming theoretical findings that won the 1957 Nobel Prize in physics for two Chinese-born scientists in this country.

The award had gone to Dr. Chen Ning Yang of the Institute for Advanced Study at Princeton and Dr. Tsung Dao Lee of Columbia University for overthrowing the law of parity. This idea was that particles in nature were evenly matched according to direction of spin, rotation, division of magnetic radiation, etc.

Dr. Maurice Goldhaber of the Brookhaven National Laboratory and Dr. S. J. Mikitin of the Moscow Institute for Thermal Research reported on studies confirming the findings.

TV STATION UPHELD

North Dakota Court Backs Ruling in Libel Suit

BISMARCK, N. D., April 3 (AP)—North Dakota's Supreme Court ruled today television station WDAY of Fargo was not liable for statements made over its facilities by a candidate in the 1956 general election campaign.

In a 4 to 1 decision, the court affirmed the action of District Judge John C. Pollock, who dismissed a $100,000 libel suit brought by the North Dakota Farmers Union against WDAY and A. C. Townley.

It was believed here to be the first time an appellate court has ruled on the question revolving around Section 315 of the 1934 Federal Communications Act—commonly known as the "equal time" law.

The law requires broadcasters who permit speeches by one or more candidates for an office to give equal time to other candidates for the same office. It also states that the broadcaster may not censor the speeches granted on this equal time basis.

HOUSE VOTES CURB ON USE OF SECRECY

Amends 1789 Law to Prevent Executive From Citing It to Withhold Information

By C. P. TRUSSELL
Special to The New York Times.

WASHINGTON, April 16—The House of Representatives passed by a voice vote today a bill to stop the Government from withholding information under a vague law enacted in 1789. The bill was sent to the Senate.

The 1789 law, it was held in debate, was enacted only to give George Washington a hand in establishing his new Government, but now is used to withhold information from Congress and the public.

Today's action gave Congress the first round in a year-long contest with the executive branch, in which th elegislators have contended they have had trouble getting information they needed for investigations and floor debates.

The Senate already is working on the problem. At a hearing today, the Senate Subcommittee on Constitutional Rights heard testimony from spokesmen for the press, radio and television urging Congress to break down barriers set up against the release of information.

There has been no attempt in this fight, the testimony emphasized, to force making public information and records that would operate to the advantage of a potential enemy.

The bill passed by the House was one of the briefest measures ever handled in Congress. It consisted of an amendment to the 1789 law, couched in a single sentence:

"This section does not authorize withholding information from the public or limiting the availability of records to the public."

It applied only to what is now known as the "housekeeping" law of the George Washington Administration.

The bill containing this amendment was accompanied by a report expressing present Congressional intent. The report said this curb on use of the 1789 law to withhold information would have no effect upon the withholding of information vital to national defense.

Representative John E. Moss, Democrat of California, who is heading a continuing investigation into the withholding of information, called this just a first step in opening to the public records that could be released without danger to national security.

He emphasized that the measure passed today would not affect existing law that gives secrecy to the following information:

¶Military and diplomatic secrets.

¶Income tax returns and trade secrets received by the Government in confidence.

¶Federal Bureau of Investigation reports.

¶Information that can be withheld legitimately under other laws enacted by Congress.

It was brought out that more than seventy specific laws had been enacted to give protection to Government information that might be helpful to a potential enemy.

So, Representative Moss said, the only curb in this "first step" would be to keep department and agency officials from suppressing facts about their own operations by taking refuge to the 169-year-old law, in cases not covered by specific statutes.

Representative Clare E. Hoffman, Michigan Republican, led the fight against the bill. He and other Republicans tried to change the measure with amendments which they held would "bring clarification out of confusion."

December 21, 1957

April 4, 1958

April 17, 1958

324

Pentagon Censorship Assailed By Moss at Editors' Convention

It Has Reached an Alarming Degree, Coast Democrat Tells Opening Session

WASHINGTON, April 17 (UP) —Representative John E. Moss, fresh from a House vote against Government secrecy, told newspaper editors today censorship of Defense Department information "has reached an alarming degree."

The California Democrat told the opening session of the annual convention of the American Society of Newspaper Editors that the fight against Government censorship was far from over.

He said "recent instructions" from President Eisenhower to Neil H. McElroy, Defense Secretary, to centralize military information "have increased the dangers of management of news about the nation's defenses."

Associated Press
Representative John E. Moss

However, the editors loudly applauded President Eisenhower when he told them he hoped his reorganization plan would mean "that the number of individuals assigned to rival publicity campaigns in the Defense Department will be drastically reduced."

Mr. Moss heads the House subcommittee on Government information that spearheaded a successful House fight yesterday for a bill to halt use of a 159-year-old "housekeeping" law as an excuse for withholding Government information.

Veto Held Possible

All ten Cabinet departments opposed the measure, raising the possibility of a veto if it reaches the President's desk in its present form. It still must clear the Senate.

Senator Thomas C. Hennings Jr., Democrat of Missouri, chairman of the Senate Constitutional Rights subcommittee, said in a statement read to the editors that his group already had begun consideration of the bill.

He said editors and others had given "convincing testimony" in favor of the bill. But he added that it would be "helpful if we could clear away some of the misunderstanding" about the Administration's attitude.

Mr. Hennings said William P. Rogers, the Attorney General, first said he would not oppose the measure under certain con-

ditions and later "flatly opposed the bill."

Virginius Dabney, editor of The Richmond (Va.) Times Dispatch, who is association president, said House passage was "a great victory for the people of the United States."

But Mr. Moss, in declaring the fight was not over, said the President's military reorganization plan instructed Mr. McElroy to tighten controls over distribution of military information to curb interservice rivalry.

"The President's move is a dangerous one," Mr. Moss said. "Censorship of opinions or facts which fail to fit 'policy' already has reached an alarming degree under Assistant Secretary of Defense Murray Snyder."

Mr. Moss said Mr. Snyder "apparently" had been "set up as the undisputed censor of what the public shall know about the vast military establishment."

Herbert Brucker of The Hartford (Conn.) Courant, chairman of the association's Freedom of Information Committee, called House approval of the anti-secrecy bill "one of the most significant victories in the battle for the people's right to know."

Dr. Harold Cross, the society's freedom of information counsel, reported both "gains and losses" during the last year in the fight against censorship.

April 18, 1958

U. S. SECRECY IS SCORED

Upstate Editor Says People Are Kept in 'Ignorance'

SARANAC LAKE, N. Y., July 19, (AP)—An upstate editor charged today that the Federal Government had been keeping the people in "ignorance of the true state of our affairs."

Roger Tubby, co-publisher of The Saranac Lake Adirondack Enterprise, who was press secretary to President Harry S. Truman, made the statement in yers section of the State Bar Association.

"If we are effectively to support the Government in this time of crisis," he said, "we should understand clearly what our situation is, the good and the bad of it. The stamp of secrecy has covered up not only our own weaknesses but also Russia's strength."

July 20, 1958

SECRECY NOT IMPOSED

Defense Department Denies Tightening Over Crisis

WASHINGTON, July 27 (AP) —The Defense Department has assured a House committee it is not tightening secrecy screws on news because of the Mideast crisis.

"We will continue to keep the public promptly and fully informed as to our activities, within the bounds of national security," Murray Snyder assistant secretary, wrote Representative John E. Moss, Democrat of California and chairman of the Government Information subcommittee.

He added in reply to an inquiry from Mr. Moss:

"There has been no change in the information policy of the Department of Defense in connection with the current Middle East situation.

"Our policy remains that of making the maximum information available to the public, consistent with military security and the over-all national interest."

July 28, 1958

PENTAGON ACCUSED

Moss Charges It Censors News of Its Failures

TUCSON, Ariz., Jan. 10 (AP) —Representative John E. Moss, Democrat of California, accused the Pentagon today of trying Soviet-style control of the news —giving out the good news and hiding the failures.

He denounced this as dangerous in a democracy.

Representative Moss, chairman of the House Government Information Subcommittee, referred especially to news about the launching of nonmilitary missiles and satellites.

January 11, 1959

PENTAGON ACCUSED OF 'NEWS CONTROL'

WASHINGTON, Jan. 22 (UPI)—House investigators accused the Defense Department today of stepping up efforts to "manage the news" and make political propaganda out of missile firings.

The House Government Information subcommittee recalled that it had warned in the last session of Congress that defense officials were trying to "govern and control" missile and satellite news.

These efforts on the part of the department have been "intensified," the subcommittee said in a report on the results of its activities in the last session.

"As additional missile and satellite shots have been attempted," it said, "there have been indications of perversion of the military security system to cover embarrassment, inefficiency and possible mismanagement."

The report also said nothing had been done by the Eisenhower Administration on the subcommittee's recommendation for a uniform system of security clearance for scientists employed by the government and defense contractors, except to make a number of studies.

January 23, 1959

TV SAFEGUARDED IN POLITICAL LIBEL

High Court Holds Stations Immune Under Equal-Time Law and Censoring Ban

By ALLEN DRURY
Special to The New York Times.

WASHINGTON, June 29 — The Supreme Court ruled today that broadcasting stations could not be sued for libelous statements made by political candidates to whom they were forced to give equal broadcasting time.

The Court, in a 5 to 4 decision, held that immunity from suit had been granted to radio and television stations by law. The grant was made, the Court said, when Congress passed a law requiring the stations to give equal time to opposing candidates but barring them from censoring the candidates' speeches.

The majority opinion upheld a similar ruling by the North Dakota Supreme Court. The case involved a broadcast in 1956 by station WDAY of Fargo of a speech by A. C. Townley, candidate for United States Senator.

Mr. Townley charged that his opponents were conspiring with the Farmer Educational and Cooperative Union of America, North Dakota Division,"to establish a Communist Farmers Union Soviet right here in North Dakota." His opponents were Quentin Burdick, Democrat, and Senator Milton R. Young, Republican.

Immunity Is Claimed

The Farmers Union sued WDAY for $100,000. The station conceded that the union had been defamed. It argued, however, that it should not be held liable because it had been compelled to accept the broadcast under a provision of the Federal Communications Act that also banned censorship of the candidate's remarks.

Justice Department attorneys said today that newspapers reprinting libelous matter broadcast under the terms of the court's WDAY decision would be protected by the so-called rule of "fair comment" from being sued for libel.

Thus, if the papers reprinted the broadcast libelous matter verbatim with clear identification of source, they would not be subject to suit. But if they distorted the statements or added further comments of their own of a libelous nature, they might be.

The Supreme Court majority that upheld today the argument of WDAY was composed of Justice Hugo L. Black, who read the opinion; Chief Justice Earl War   and Justices William O. Douglass, Tom C. Clark and William J. Brennan Jr.

Justice Felix Frankfurter read the minority opinion for himself and Justices John M. Harlan, Charles E. Whittaker and Potter Stewart.

The majority said that the pertinent section of the Communications Act, Section 315, superseded state laws against libel.

The majority further said that "whatever adverse inference may be drawn from the failure of Congress to legislate an express immunity [from libel], is offset by its refusal to permit stations to avoid liability by censoring broadcasts."

'Far From Easy' Matter

The decision that a broadcasting station would have to make if it attempted to remove libelous matter "is far from easy," the opinion went on. If the Farmers Union argument were upheld, the majority said, the question would have to be resolved during the heat of a political campaign and often without adequate consideration or basis for decision.

"Quite possibly," the majority continued, "if a station were held responsible for the broadcast of libelous material, all remarks even faintly objectionable would be excluded out of an excess of caution. Moreover, if any censorship were permissible, a station so inclined could intentionally inhibit a candidate's legitimate presentation under the guise of lawful censorship of libelous matter."

Hardship Held Secondary

Justice Frankfurter argued for the minority that "due regard for the principle of separation of powers limiting this court's functions and respect for the binding principle of federalism, leaving to the states authority not withdrawn by the Constitution or absorbed by the Congress, are more compelling considerations than avoidance of a hardship legally imposed."

The minority asserted that the argument that Congress had acquiesced in giving immunity from state libel laws to broadcasters because it had repeatedly refused to legislate on the matter, "raises political stalemate and legislative indecision to the level of constitutional declaration."

Lawyers in the case were Edward S. Greenbaum and Mrs. Harriet F. Pilpel of New York, for the Farmers Union; Harold W. Bancroft of Fargo, N. D., for WDAY.

For the National Association of Broadcasters, Douglas A. Annello of Washington filed an amicus curiae brief supporting WDAY's position.

PENTAGON ISSUES CENSORSHIP PLAN

Hitherto Secret Guide Gives Basic Policy for Military in the Event of War

Special to The New York Times.

WASHINGTON, July 18— The Department of Defense has issued new guidelines for the military in planning censorship in the event of war.

The guidelines, which establish the general objectives, policies and responsibilities for wartime censorship, were contained in a Defense Department directive entitled "Censorship Planning."

Until recently this basic policy directive on censorship was handled as secret information by the Defense Department.

The Directive had been listed "for official use only"— a security classification that has evolved within the Government to replace the "restricted" security category abolished by President Eisenhower.

The directive makes no basic changes in the emergency censorship planning that has been under way for several years within the Defense Department and the Office of Civil and Defense Mobilization.

Rather, it restates past policy on censorship planning and incorporates in one document past directives on the subject.

Censoring Held Vital

In its statement of basic policies, the directive notes that "censorship is an indispensable part of war and planning for it should keep pace with other war plans."

Censorship, the directive states, will be used only for these objectives:

¶"To keep from the enemy information which would aid his war effort or would hinder our own or that of our allies."

¶"To collect information of value in prosecuting the war and to make that information available to the proper agencies."

"Censorship," the directive continues, "will not conceal Government errors, will not suppress criticism of censorship itself, will not assist in the enforcement of peacetime statutes unconnected with the war effort and will not become a guardian of public morals."

Responsibility Fixed

Over-all responsibility for coordinating plans for censorship in the event of a national emergency or war rests with the Office of Civil and Defense Mobilization.

The Defense Department, in turn, has been given responsibility for drafting censorship plans covering telecommunications traffic, mails entering and leaving the United States, news material originating in combat zones, personal communications of military personnel and communications in areas under military control.

The directive assigns responsibility among the individual services for these specific areas of censorship. It also establishes an interservice committee to coordinate censorship planning within the Defense Department.

The directive gives two basic objectives in exercising "field censorship" over the press in military zones.

They are "to insure the prompt release to the public of the maximum information consistent with security [and] to prevent the disclosure of information which would assist the enemy."

EXECUTIVE SECRECY IN U. S. DENOUNCED

Special to The New York Times.

SAN FRANCISCO, Oct. 7—Executive secrecy in Washington was denounced before the Inter-American Press Association here today as a clear and present danger to freedom of the press.

A committee headed by Jules Dubois of The Chicago Tribune also reported that freedom of the press did not exist in Bolivia, the Dominican Republic, Nicaragua and Paraguay, and was threatened in other Latin-American countries, including Cuba.

Criticism of the United States centered on the Eisenhower Administration's interpretation of executive privilege, under which department heads may withhold information they believe to be confidential executive business.

October 8, 1959

BILL SEEKS FREE TV IN PRESIDENCY RACE

WASHINGTON, March 10 (UPI)—Two Senators urged Congress today to provide free television time to Presidential nominees.

They offered a bill designed to provide free time at "prime" viewing hours to major-party nominees. Each candidate would get two half-hour periods a week from each network and local station.

The bill was offered by Senators Warren G. Magnuson. Democrat of Washington, and A. S. Mike Monroney, Democrat of Oklahoma. Before they completed their discussion, three other Democratic Senators, Estes Kefauver of Tennessee, John O. Pastore of Rhode Island and Frank Church of Idaho, became co-sponsors.

Mr. Pastore. chairman of a broadcast subcommittee for the Interstate Commerce Committee, promised to hold hearings as soon as possible after the Senate's civil rights debate was over.

Mr. Magnuson is chairman of the parent committee.

Mr. Magnuson said the bill, as now drafted, would provide time only for Presiential candidates, except that the Vice Presidential aspirant for each party could substitute on two of the free programs. The programs would be held every week during the eight weeks preceding Election Day. No other substitutions would be permitted.

March 11, 1960

C.B.S. UPHELD BY F.C.C.

Butler's Protest Against Rule on Broadcast Turned Down

WASHINGTON, March 11 (AP)—The Federal Communications Commission has turned down a protest against a Columbia Broadcasting System policy of not accepting paid political broadcasts to be carried at the same time on other networks.

The protest had been registered by Paul M. Butler, Democratic national chairman.

The commission said in a letter to Mr. Butler it would be arbitrary for it to direct C. B. S. to change its policy and to broadcast a particular program at a specified time.

Mr. Butler had protested that under the C. B. S. policy, a White House message that might include political overtones could be presented on a multiple network telecast. But he said that if a major political party wanted to buy time to answer a Presidential address during a campaign, it would be denied equal opportunity to present its views over C. B. S. if the party also took time on another network.

March 12, 1960

A.B.C. Offers Time For the Nominees; Fights Compulsion

Special to The New York Times.

WASHINGTON, May 19—A third major network offered today to make free television time available this fall to the major parties' candidates for President and Vice President.

Oliver Treyz, president of the American Broadcasting Company, put his network on record before a Senate subcommittee. His proposal differed from, but did not appear to be incompatible with, ideas advanced by the Columbia Broadcasting System and the National Broadcasting Company.

In a related development today, the Federal Communications Commission began to seek data from all licensed television stations to determine what their policies on political broadcasts had been and what they planned for this year's election campaign.

The commission's announcement said the information was being sought for the Communications subcommittee of the Senate Interstate and Foreign Commerce Committee. The panel is holding hearings, on legislation that would compel the networks to make time available to major Presidential candidates.

The announcement also said the data would "assist the commission in the discharge of its statutory responsibilities" to require that broadcasters operate in the public interest.

Passage of the Communications subcommittee's "compulsory" bill is considered unlikely. It is modeled on a proposal of Adlai E. Stevenson.

Mr. Treyz denounced the bill today, as Dr. Frank Stanton, president of C. B. S., and David Adams, the senior vice president of N. B. C., had done.

The A. B. C. executive proposed that each of the networks offer a free hour in prime viewing time in three of the nine weeks preceding the election. By rotation, the networks thus would provide the candidates one hour a week for nine weeks.

To make this possible, Mr. Treyz said, Congress would have to provide a temporary waiver of the "equal-time" provision for Presidential and Vice-Presidential candidates. Otherwise, he said, the candidates of splinter parties would demand to share the free time.

Dr. Stanton, for C. B. S., offered one free hour a week for eight weeks, to be used jointly or half-and-half by the two candidates. He offered also to include any significant third party candidate, but said his network would not join other networks for simultaneous broadcasts.

N. B. C. proposes eight hour-long programs in the format of "Meet the Press," with newsmen questioning the candidates on alternate broadcasts.

May 20, 1960

PRESIDENT URGES PRESS LIMIT NEWS THAT HELPS REDS

He Tells Publishers Threat to Security Justifies Use of Wartime Measures

By RUSSELL PORTER

President Kennedy urged the press last night to cooperate voluntarily with the Government, as it does in wartime, to prevent the unauthorized disclosure of news helpful to enemies of the United States.

He solemnly asserted that such an appeal was justified by the unprecedented nature of Communist "cold-war" tactics and their threat to national security.

The President extended his appeal to all other groups—especially business, labor and Government officials — asking them to exercise similar self-restraint and self-discipline. All should subordinate their own rights and comforts to the national good, he declared.

He warned that the danger from Communist secret methods, infiltration, subversion, intimidation and guerrilla tactics all over the world posed a threat to this country that had never been exceeded even in actual war.

Speaks to Publishers

Mr. Kennedy spoke at the annual dinner of the Bureau of Advertising of the American Newspaper Publishers Association at the Waldorf-Astoria Hotel. The dinner closed New York's annual Press Week, which included annual meetings of The Associated Press and United Press International.

Mr. Kennedy's visit to New York was his first since he became President. He arrived at La Guardia Airport's marine terminal at 4:22 P. M., by plane from Washington.

A small group met him at the airport and sparse crowds watched as he drove to Manhattan in a closed black limousine. About 1,500 persons gathered to greet him when he arrived at his local headquarters at the Carlyle Hotel, Madison Avenue and East Seventy-sixth Street. He waved and smiled to the crowd, which cheered and applauded him.

Anti-Communists Picket

More than 2,000 anti-Castro Cubans and anti-Communist

Hungarians gathered near the Waldorf-Astoria last night. They sang, chanted, waved banners and held aloft signs urging the President to continue his opposition to communism.

"Cuba Si, Russia No," and "Fidel—Traitor" were chanted. Signs read: "Kennedy, Make Good on Your Promise—Do Not Abandon Us Cubans."

In his speech the President repeatedly emphasized his belief that Communist "cold war" tactics constituted a threat that ranks with war itself.

"This is a time of peace and peril which knows no precedent in history," he said at one point.

"Our way of life is under attack," he declared again. "Those who make themselves our enemy are advancing around the globe. The survival of our friends is in danger."

Again he asserted:

"The danger has never been more clear and its presence has never been more imminent. It requires a change in outlook, a change in tactics, a change in missions—by the Government, by the people, by every business man, union leader and newspaper."

"No war ever posed a greater threat to our security," he said.

Communism, he said, is a "monolithic and ruthless conspiracy" that is attacking all around the world with tactics conducted with wartime discipline.

Even if no war is ever declared in the traditional way, he went on, the security and survival of the nation and its freedoms are endangered.

He recalled that enemy leaders had boasted that American newspapers had supplied them with valuable facts they could not have obtained elsewhere except by espionage.

Details of secret preparations to counter secret enemy moves have been published, he went on. He cited stories that had "pinpointed" the size, strength, location and nature of forces and weapons and plans and strategy for their use.

In one case, he went on, details were printed about a secret mechanism, forcing its alteration at considerable expense in time and money.

He identified the device as one used to track satellites.

Voluntary Curb Sought

The President said such stories were published by loyal and patriotic papers that would not have run them in time of open war. They had subjected the stories only to the test of journalism and not to the test of national security as they would have done in wartime, he said.

In the present world situation, he held, newspapers should voluntarily apply the test of national security and accept the need for greater governmental secrecy on all matters affecting national security. He suggested that they recommend machinery for resuming wartime precautions, and promised to cooperate

to make such a system work.

In time of war, he noted, the press joins with the Government in an effort, based largely on self-restraint and self-discipline, to prevent unauthorized disclosures of facts to the enemy.

The President explained he was proposing only that the press exercise the same self-restraint and self-discipline now. He asked it to re-examine its obligations, and recognize the nature of the country's peril.

"Every newspaper now asks itself, with respect to every story: 'Is it news?' All I suggest is that you add the question: 'Is it in the interest of national security?' And I hope that every group in America—unions and business men and public officials at every level—will ask the same questions of their endeavors, and subject their actions to this same exacting test."

President Kennedy reminded the publishers that the courts have held that in time of "clear and present danger" the constitutional rights of free press and free speech must bow to the requirements of national security.

"If you are awaiting a finding of clear and present danger," he said, "I can only say that the danger has never been more clear and its presence has never been more imminent."

Full Data Promised

The President emphasized that he was not proposing official censorship or new security classification of Government news. He promised not to allow his speech to be used as a pretext by officials in his administration to censor news, stifle dissent, cover mistakes or withhold facts the public had a right to know.

At this point, he was interrupted with applause from the audience of 1,700. The publishers applauded again a few minutes later when he assured them:

"I am not asking your newspapers to support me at all times on the editorial page—this is not utopia yet. But I am asking your help in the tremendous task of informing and alerting the American people."

These were the only interruptions in his twenty-minute speech.

The President, who was accompanied here by Representatives Eugene J. Keogh and Emanuel Celler, New York Democrats, stayed in New York overnight. Today he will resume here a series of talks that he has been having with national leaders on developments on the world scene. He will visit former President Herbert C. Hoover, General of the Army Douglas MacArthur, Dag Hammarskjold, Secretary General of the United Nations, and Adlai E. Stevenson, United States Representative at the United Nations.

Political Meeting Set

A 10:15 A.M. meeting has been set up at the Carlyle with Representative Charles A. Buckley and City Council Majority Leader Joseph T. Sharkey, the Democratic leaders in the Bronx and Brooklyn, respectively.

This meeting, set for a half-hour, is charged with obvious political overtones in view of the confused state and local situation here in a Mayoralty election year. Channels for the distribution of Federal patronage still remain to be cleared here.

The President will leave the Waldorf-Astoria Hotel at 2:15 P.M., after lunching there with Mr. Stevenson, for the heliport at Thirtieth Street and the Hudson River. There he will board a helicopter that will take him to International Airport. He then will fly to Chicago to address a $100-a-plate Democratic fund-raising dinner tonight.

He will return to Washington by plane after the speech.

Text of Kennedy's Speech to Publishers

Following is the text of President Kennedy's address last night to the Bureau of Advertising of the American Newspaper Publishers Association at the Waldorf-Astoria Hotel, as recorded by The New York Times:

I appreciate very much your generous invitation to be here tonight.

You bear heavy responsibilities these days and an article I read some time ago reminded me of how particularly heavily the burdens of present day events bear upon your profession.

You may remember that in 1851 The New York Herald Tribune, under the sponsorship and publishing of Horace Greeley, included as its London correspondent an obscure journalist by the name of Karl Marx.

We are told that foreign correspondent Marx, stone broke, and with a family ill and undernourished, constantly appealed to Greeley and Managing Editor Charles Dana for an increase in his munificent salary of $5 per installment, a salary which he and Engels ungratefully labeled as the "lousiest petty bourgeois cheating."

But when all his financial appeals were refused, Marx looked around for other means of livelihood and fame, eventually terminating his relationship with The Tribune

and devoting his talents full time to the cause that would bequeath to the world the seeds of Leninism, Stalinism, revolution and the cold war.

If only this capitalistic New York newspaper had treated him more kindly; if only Marx had remained a foreign correspondent, history might have been different and I hope all publishers will bear this lesson in mind the next time they receive a poverty-stricken appeal for a small increase in the expense account from an obscure newspaper man.

President and Press

I have selected as the title of my remarks tonight "The President and the Press." Some may suggest that this would be more naturally worded "The President versus the Press." But those are not my sentiments tonight.

It is true, however, that when a well-known diplomat from another country demanded recently that our State Department repudiate certain newspaper attacks on his colleague it was unnecessary for us to reply that this Administration was not responsible for the press, for the press had already made it clear that it was not responsible for this Administration.

Nevertheless, my purpose here tonight is not to deliver the usual assault on the so-called one-party press. On the contrary, in recent months I have rarely heard any complaints about political bias in the press except from a few Republicans. Nor is it my purpose tonight to discuss or defend the televising of Presidential press conferences. I think it is highly beneficial to have some 20,000,000 Americans regularly sit in on these conferences to observe, if I may say so, the incisive, the intelligent and the courteous qualities displayed by your Washington correspondents.

Nor, finally, are these remarks intended to examine the proper degree of privacy which the press should allow to any President and his family.

If in the last few months your White House reporters and photographers had been attending church services with regularity that has surely done them no harm.

On the other hand, I realize that your staff and wire service photographers may be complaining that they do not enjoy the same green privileges at the local golf courses which they once did.

It is true that my predecessor did not object as I do to pictures of one's golfing skill in action. But neither on the other hand did he ever bean a Secret Service man.

Discusses Responsibility

My topic tonight is a more sober one of concern to publishers as well as editors.

I want to talk about our common responsibilities in the face of a common danger. The events of recent weeks may have helped to illuminate that challenge for some; but the dimensions of its threat have loomed large on the horizon for many years. Whatever our hopes may be for the future—for reducing this threat or living with it—there is no escaping either the gravity or the totality of its challenge to our survival and to our security—a challenge that confronts us in unaccustomed ways in every sphere of human activity.

This deadly challenge imposes upon our society two requirements of direct concern both to the press and to the President — two requirements that may seem almost contradictory in tone, but which must be reconciled and fulfilled if we are to meet this national peril. I refer, first, to the need for far greater public information; and, second, to the need for far greater official secrecy.

The very word "secrecy" is repugnant in a free and open society and we are as a people inherently and historically opposed to secret societies, to secret oaths and to secret proceedings. We decided long ago that the dangers of excessive and unwarranted concealment of pertinent facts far outweighed the dangers which are cited to justify it.

Even today, there is little value in opposing the threat of a closed society by imitating its arbitrary restrictions. Even today, there is little value in insuring the survival of our nation if our traditions do not survive with it. And there is a very grave danger that an announced need for increased security will be seized upon by those anxious to expand its meaning to the very limits of official censorship and concealment.

That I do not intend to permit to the extent that it's in my control. And no official of my Administration, whether his rank is high or low, civilian or military, should interpret my words here tonight as an excuse to censor the news, to stifle dissent, to cover up our mistakes or to withhold from the press and the public the facts they deserve to know.

Discipline Asked

But I do ask every publisher, every editor and every newsman in the nation to reexamine his own standards, and to recognize the nature of our country's peril. In time of war, the Government and the press have customarily joined in an effort, based largely on self-discipline, to prevent unauthorized disclosures to the enemy. In times of clear and present danger, the courts have held that even the privileged rights of the First Amendment must yield to the public's need for national security.

Today no war has been declared—and however fierce the struggle may be, it may never be declared in the traditional fashion. Our way of life is under attack. Those who make themselves our enemy are advancing around the globe. The survival of our friends is in danger. And yet no war has been declared, no borders have been crossed by marching troops, no missiles have been fired.

If the press is awaiting a declaration of war before it imposes the self-discipline of combat conditions, then I can only say that no war ever posed a greater threat to our security. If you are awaiting a finding of "clear and present danger," then I can only say that the danger has never been more clear and its presence has never been more imminent.

Danger Cited

It requires a change in outlook, a change in tactics, a change in mission by the Government, by the people, by every business man or labor leader and by every newspaper. For we are opposed around the world by a monolithic and ruthless conspiracy that relies primarily on covert means for expanding its sphere of influence—on infiltration instead of invasion, on subversion instead of elections, on intimidation instead of free choice, on guerrillas by night instead of armies by day.

It is a system which has conscripted vast human and material resources into the building of a tightly knit, highly efficient machine that combines military, diplomatic, intelligence, economic, scientific and political operations.

Its preparations are concealed, not published. Its mistakes are buried, not headlined. Its dissenters are silenced, not praised. No expenditure is questioned, no rumor is printed, no secret is revealed. It conducts the cold war, in short, with a wartime discipline no democracy would ever hope or wish to match.

Nevertheless, every democracy recognizes the necessary restraints of national security —and the question remains whether those restraints need to be more strictly observed if we are to oppose this kind of attack as well as outright invasion.

For the facts of the matter are that this nation's foes have openly boasted of acquiring through our newspapers information they would otherwise hire agents to acquire through theft, bribery or espionage; that details of this nation's covert preparations to counter the enemy's covert operations have been available to every newspaper reader, friend and foe alike; that the size, the strength, the location and the nature of our forces and weapons, and our plans and strategy for their use, have all been pinpointed in the press and other news media to a degree sufficient to satisfy any foreign power; and that, in at least one case, the publication of details concerning a secret mechanism whereby satellites were followed required its alteration at the expense of considerable time and money.

The newspapers which printed these stories were loyal, patriotic, responsible and well-meaning. Had we been engaged in open warfare, they undoubtedly would not have published such items. But in the absence of open warfare, they recognized only the tests of journalism and not the tests of national security. And my question tonight is whether additional tests should not now be adopted.

Voluntary Plan Sought

That question is for you alone to answer. No public official should answer it for you. No governmental plan should impose its restraints against your will. But I would be failing in my duty to the nation in considering all of the responsibilities that we now bear and all of the means at hand to meet those responsibilities if I did not commend this problem to your attention, and urge its thoughtful consideration.

On many earlier occasions, I have said—and your newspapers have constantly said - that these are times that appeal to every citizen's sense of sacrifice and self-discipline. They call out to every citizen to weigh his rights and comforts against his obligation to the common good. I cannot now believe that those citizens who serve in the newspaper business consider themselves exempt from that appeal.

I have no intention of establishing a new Office of War Information to govern the flow of news. I am not suggesting any new forms of censorship or new types security classifications I have no easy answer to the dilemma I have posed, and would not seek to impose it if I had one. But I am asking the members of the newspaper profession and the industry in this country to reexamine their own responsibilities - to consider the degree and the nature of the present danger—and to heed the duty of self-restraint which that danger imposes upon us all.

Every newspaper now asks itself, with respect to every story: "Is it news?" All I suggest is that you add the question: "Is it in the interest of national security?" And I hope that every group in America—unions and business men and public officials at every level—will ask the same question of their endeavors, and subject their actions to this same exacting test.

And should the press of America consider and recommend the voluntary assumption of specific new steps or machinery, I can assure you that we will cooperate wholeheartedly with those recommendations.

Perhaps there will be no recommendations. Perhaps there is no answer to the dilemma faced by a free and open society in a cold and secret war. In times of peace, any discussion of this subject, and any action that results, are both painful and without precedent. But this is a time of peace and peril which knows no precedent in history.

Obligation to Inform

It is the unprecedented nature of this challenge that also gives rise to your second obligation — an obligation which I share. And that is our obligation to inform and alert the American people—to make certain that they possess all the facts they need, and understand them as well — the perils, the prospects, the purposes of our program and the choices that we face.

No President should fear public scrutiny of his program. For from that scrutiny comes understanding; and from that understanding comes support or opposition, and both are necessary. I am not asking your newspapers to support an Administration. But I am asking your help in the tremendous task of informing and alerting the American people. For I have complete confidence in the response and dedication of our citizens whenever they are fully informed.

I not only could not stifle controversy among your readers—I welcome it. This Administration intends to be candid about its errors; for, as a wise man once said: "An error doesn't become a mistake until you refuse to correct it." We intend to accept full responsibility for our errors; and we expect you to point them out when we miss them.

Without debate, without criticism, no Administration and no country can succeed — and no republic can survive. That is why the Athenian lawmaker Solon decreed it a crime for any citizen to shrink from controversy. And that is why our press was protected by the First Amendment—the only business in America specifically protected by the Constitution —not primarily to amuse and entertain, not to emphasize the trivial and the sentimental, not to simply "give the public what it wants"—but to inform, to arouse, to reflect, to state our dangers and our opportunities, to indicate our crises and our choices, to lead, mold, educate and sometimes even anger public opinion.

Wider Coverage Urged

This means greater coverage and analysis of international news—for it is no longer far away and foreign but close at hand and local. It means greater attention to improved understanding of the news as well as improved transmission. And it means, finally, that government at all levels, must meet its obligation to provide you with the fullest possible information outside the narrowest limits of national security and in intent to do it.

It was early in the seventeenth century that Francis Bacon remarked on three recent inventions already transforming the world; the compass, gunpowder and the printing press. Now the links between the nations first forged by the compass have made us all citizens of the world, the hopes and threats of one becoming the hopes and threats of us all. In that one world's effort to live together, the evolution of gunpowder to its ultimate limit has warned mankind of the terrible consequences of failure.

And so it is to the printing press — to the recorder of man's deeds, the keeper of his conscience, the courier of his news—that we look for strength and assistance, confident that with your help man will be what he was born to be: free and independent.

PRESS IS CAUTIOUS ON KENNEDY PLEA

Voluntary News Curbs Are Stressed by Ferree

Newspaper publishers and executives reacted cautiously last night to President Kennedy's appeal for self-regulation by the press on stories affecting national security.

Mark Ferree, executive vice president and general business manager of the Scripps-Howard Newspapers and president of the American Newspaper Publishers Association, before which Mr. Kennedy spoke, said:

"The publishers will respond patriotically to any appeal by the President, but I am sure that voluntary censorship will be the only kind that will be workable and acceptable to them."

Benjamin M. McKelway, editor of The Washington Star and president of The Associated Press, said:

"I know of no responsible newspaper which would print material damaging to the interests of the country. The old problem is: What is it that is damaging to the interests of the country?

"I think that the job of protecting security is one that lies with the Government by policing its own sources of information. A specific proposal will be received with great interest."

John Cowles, publisher and editor of The Minneapolis Star and Tribune, said:

"I fully agree with President Kennedy as to the gravity of the international situation and the need for self-discipline on the part of the press * * *.

"If even a few newspapers or radio stations publish or broadcast news that may be helpful to the enemy, that information is available to the enemy, and it is difficult to say that other publications or broadcasters should then deprive their readers or listeners of that news.

"I would suggest the President appoint a committee from the press to propose a possible plan."

William Randolph Hearst Jr., editor in chief of the Hearst Newspapers, said:

"He [President Kennedy] makes it clear that we are in a war. Having been a war correspondent, I can well understand the need for security."

Palmer Hoyt, publisher and editor of The Denver Post, declared:

"I think the free press will consider the seriousness of the situation as outlined by the President, and that most newspapers will go along. The difficulties in a free country lie in who is going to set up the ground rules."

ETHICS CODE GIVEN TO FEDERAL AIDES

Directive Bars Disclosure of 'Official Information' —Job Conduct Outlined

Special to The New York Times.

WASHINGTON, July 26—The White House has issued a new code of conduct for Federal employes that prohibits them from disclosing "official information."

The document also prohibits Government workers from making use of, or permitting others to make use of, "official information not made available to the general public, for the purpose of furthering a private interest."

No definition of "official information" was provided.

Pierre Salinger, White House press secretary, said he believed the term was intended to cover the sort of information that might, for instance, have an effect upon the stock market, or the possession of which might enable someone to anticipate market fluctuations.

To Seek Clarification

He said he would seek a clarification of the term. It is not among those used to cover information essential to the national security, such as "restricted," "secret," "classified" or "top secret."

Mr. Salinger indicated, however, that he did not believe it was intended to create a new information classification.

The code, prepared by the Civil Service Commission, is being circulated with a covering memorandum from Frederick G. Dutton, a special assistant to President Kennedy.

The memorandum calls the code a "statement of minimum standards of conduct for civilian employes."

Mr. Dutton's memo said that "each department and agency head will be responsible to bring the proper minimum standards of conduct to the attention of all its employes." Another provision of the code prohibits Government workers from outside employment, including teaching, lecturing or writing, that "might reasonably result in a conflict of interest or an apparent conflict of interest."

Outside employment that would interfere with a worker's performance, or reflect discredit on the Government, was ruled out, too, although there was no general prohibition of outside jobs.

Employes were also warned not to accept gifts, gratuities or favors "which might reasonably be interpreted by others" as affecting their impartiality in dealing with the donor.

Financial interests in conflict with the duties of an employe, or growing out of information obtained through his duties, were also ruled out.

Another section banned the use of Federal property "of any kind" for other than "officially approved activities."

More general provisions adjured Government workers to conserve Federal property and "conduct themselves in such a manner that the work of the agency is effectively accomplished."

The code suggested, however, that workers "must also observe the requirements of courtesy, consideration and promptness in dealing with or serving the public or the clientele of their agency."

The code's most brusque enjoinder was its last:

"Employes are expected to meet all just financial obligations."

April 28, 1961   April 28, 1961   July 27, 1961

MAHONEY TO PUSH FOR SECRECY BAN

Moses Likely to Fight Move to Curb State Authorities

By DOUGLAS DALES
Special to The New York Times.

ALBANY, Jan. 19—Senator Walter J. Mahoney said today that he would sponsor legislation requiring state-created authorities to open their records for scrutiny by the press and public.

The majority leader's announcement foreshadowed probable renewal of sparring between the Legislature and Robert Moses in his capacity as chairman of several public authorities.

Last July, in the Court of Appeals, Mr. Moses' Triborough Bridge and Tunnel Authority blocked efforts of The New York Post to inspect the agency's records.

In a 5-to-2 decision the court, the state's highest tribunal, said that while it was "strongly in favor of enforcing the Government's duty to disclose to its citizens the course of conduct of its various departments, in the case of a public authority it is for the Legislature, rather than the courts, to decide to what extent its operations may be subjected to public scrutiny."

Other Measures Blocked

Mr. Moses, who also heads the State Power Authority and the Jones Beach State Parkway Authority, has succeeded in recent years in preventing passage of legislation that would have curtailed the powers of public authorities.

The drive to give the Legislature a greater measure of control over the semi-autonomous agencies it has created was given impetus in 1956 by a report of the Temporary State Commission on Coordination of State Activities. Mr. Moses was credited with blocking passage of all but a few of the forty-eight bills recommended by the commission.

The new proposal by Mr. Mahoney, a Republican of Buffalo, would bring the Public Authorities Law into line with the General Municipal Law, which requires municipalities to make their records public at all times.

Authorities have been required since 1939 to submit annual reports to the Governor and to the Legislature, and since 1951 to the State Controller, but the adequacy and value of these reports have been challenged by the Legislature.

PRESIDENT SEES NO TV CONTROLS

Says Aim Is to 'Encourage' Use of Better Programs

By JOHN P. SHANLEY
Special to The New York Times

WASHINGTON, Jan. 31—President Kennedy said today he did not foresee new controls over television programs by the Government.

The question was raised at his news conference in the wake of testimony by the heads of two networks before the Federal Communications Commission here.

Mr. Kennedy was asked if he could foresee circumstances under which Federal supervision of television shows might become necessary or useful. [Question 13, Page 10.]

Describes Minow's Aim

He said "no," then asked if the questioner meant a different kind of supervision or "a different relationship than that which now exists."

When the questioner said that he was referring to supervision of program content, the President replied:

"No, I don't."

He noted that the F. C. C. had regulations pertaining to the percentage of public service programs to be shown.

Referring to Newton N. Minow, F. C. C. chairman, Mr. Kennedy commented:

"Mr. Minow has attempted not to use force, but to use encouragement, in persuading the networks to put on better children's programs, more public service programs."

The President said he did not know anyone who was considering a change in the "basic relationship which now exists" between the Government and broadcasters. He recalled that Mr. Minow had also denied any contemplated change.

Robert W. Sarnoff, board chairman of the National Broadcasting Company, testified Monday that the F. C. C. "had already reached the view that it should be empowered to regulate networks."

He maintained that the commission was not empowered to say what the public should get.

Speaking of the importance of freedom for the public to choose the programs it wanted, Mr. Sarnoff said:

"Against this remarkably effective system of free choice, some would impose the centralized authority of the Government to determine what is good for the public to see and hear."

Mr. Minow, taking issue with Mr. Sarnoff that day, said the commission regarded freedom of expression as "the most important thing in this country."

On Jan. 24 Dr. Frank Stanton, head of the Columbia Broadcasting System, expressed concern over "a drift toward indirect, but nevertheless effective, program control by the Government."

In an opening statement that day Mr. Minow said the F. C. C. did not intend to invade the program function of broadcasters. He emphasized that censorship was forbidden by the Communications Act, under which the agency operates.

The F. C. C. hearing resumes tomorrow with other representatives of N. B. C. expected to testify.

'Official Weight' of Minow's Comments Disturbs TV Networks

F. C. C. Chairman Has Often Given Views

By JACK GOULD

CAN remarks of the chairman of the Federal Communications Commission be construed as dictation of television program content, or do they fall suitably within President Kennedy's endorsement of the use of "encouragement" to improve network scheduling?

In some ways the question is the most intriguing phase of the current inquiry of the F. C. C. into the practices of the networks. Yet it has been neatly side-stepped by officials of the Columbia Broadcasting System and National Broadcasting Company and by members of the commission.

William R. McAndrew, executive vice president of N. B. C., in charge of news, came closest yesterday morning to meet the issue that lies at the heart of much of the network apprehension over the intentions of Newton N. Minow, chairman of the Federal Communications Commission.

In his testimony in Washington, carried in full over the Municipal Broadcasting System's radio station, WNYC, Mr. McAndrew challenged directly Mr. Minow's complaint of some weeks ago that there was no news programing in the middle of the evening TV schedule.

Without mentioning the F. C. C. chairman by name, Mr. McAndrew said that such a particular matter of programing would appear best left to the "skills and judgments of the broadcaster."

"The question of how long a news program should be and when it should be scheduled would seem similar to questions as to whether a newspaper should run a particular story on Page 1 or Page 3; whether the story should occupy a half column or two columns; how many editions of the paper should be published; and when they should be delivered to the newsstands," Mr. McAndrew said.

Mr. Minow, the only commissioner to raise the news problem, did not attend yesterday's hearing and his fellow commissioners avoided pressing the point. But, earlier in the week, Mr. Minow did not rise to similar bait offered by Robert W. Sarnoff, chairman of N.B.C., who asked whether the commission should "indicate" the program or type of scheduling it favors.

Such an expression of opinion from a licensing authority, Mr. Sarnoff said, carries an "official weight" that is absent from similar expressions by private individuals.

The concern of C.B.S. and N.B.C. is whether Mr. Minow, by use of such public relations devices as speeches, interviews, signed magazine articles and letters, is indirectly influencing the composition of programing while at the same time denying that the full commission, either on its own initiative or through proposed legislation, would entertain such a move.

For his part, Mr. Minow categorically has rejected insinuations that he has been overstepping the bounds of his authority. He has stated that his only intent has been to stimulate network thinking in areas that a substantial body of public opinion has said needs improvement. He has added that he does not intend to be silenced by network cries of "censorship."

Since his speech of last May characterizing much of video as a "wasteland," however, Mr. Minow admittedly has gone further than any previous chairman. In addition to complaining that there was no mid-evening news broadcasting — early evening network newscasts end at 7:30 and final local newscasts do not come on the air until 11 P.M.—Mr. Minow has recommended that there be children's programing at the specific hour of 5 P.M.

The F. C. C. chairman also has championed the concept of an unproduced program entitled "Discovery;" applauded such programs as "Victoria Regina," "C. B. S. Reports" and the Yves Montand variety hour; endorsed a specific public affairs program service of Ted Cott, independent producer, and looked with favor on network initiative in not scheduling special programs at the same hour.

The networks feel that such suggestions are symptomatic of rule by the raised eyebrow or regulation by press release. They say that in urging a specific type of programing at 5 P. M., for example, Mr. Minow by inference is recommending that the chains drop the shows now carried at that hour. The philosophical argument of the networks is that the F. C. C. chairman is keenly aware that in a sensitive industry such as broadcasting, always nervous at license renewal time, his smallest hint may be obeyed.

They feel that this view has been confirmed at the hearings by Mr. Minow's inquiries as to whether the current TV controversy, which he had admittedly engendered in large measure, has had some beneficial consequences in network behavior.

But Mr. Minow unquestionably picked up important support for his tactics last week. In his press conference President Kennedy said that Mr. Minow was using encouragement, not force, in persuading the networks to carry better children's shows and more public service programs. The White House endorsement of Mr. Minow's application of persuasion to the TV network undoubtedly will have the effect of increasing broadcasting's attentiveness to the chairman's every word.

The response of Mr. Minow to this reaction is that if broadcasters lived up to their promise of balance in programing their fears of Washington could be put at rest. But the networks, in turn, note the ambiguity of President Kennedy's remarks on F. C. C. regulation in regard to the percentage of time devoted to public service. Legally, the F. C. C. does not fix the percentage but rather is empowered to enforce whatever percentage is volunteered by the broadcaster.

The nub of the debate is whether Mr. Minow is seeking to use the forum of public opinion to achieve an end—an increase in the public service percentage—that might not be readily attained through the machinery of the Federal Communication Commission or Congress.

MR. MINOW'S FIRST YEAR

F.C.C. Chairman's Work Will Cause Talk at Industry Meeting

By JACK GOULD

HOW has Newton N. Minow done in his first year as chairman of the Federal Communications Commission? The question will be on the lips of the nation's broadcasters this week as they again play host to the vigorous young New Frontiersman who last spring said they were presiding over a television wasteland.

So far, Mr. Minow has not done badly at all. His celebrated nudge to the conscience of the broadcasting industry has not resulted in a flowering garden on the home screen, to be sure. But in many intangible ways he has had a beneficial influence, which, taken in conjunction with other forces, has served the general good of the viewer.

It was last May that Mr. Minow jolted the convention of the National Association of Broadcasters with his colorful charge that much of TV's programing was beyond the pale. This week he returns to the fortieth annual meeting of the trade organization, and on Tuesday will deliver the principal address, this time on the subject of radio. But in the cocktail breaks in Chicago, the principal talk of the delegates is certain to revolve around the deeper implications of Minowism.

Speech

In many respects the "wasteland" address in and of itself stands as Mr. Minow's most formidable accomplishment. At the time of its delivery some broadcasters muttered that the chairman was a brash young critic who had gone off the deep end and was intoxicated with the heady wine of his press notices.

No one would wish to dispute the enormous facility of the New Frontier in matters of publicity, but in the case of the F. C. C. such a narrow view of Mr. Minow's regulatory choreography is to miss the main point. Frederick W. Ford, former chairman and still a commissioner, had accomplished some small wonders in rehabilitating the F. C. C. image after it had been tainted by scandal. But the commission's prestige still was in need of a fundamental overhaul.

Awareness

In a single luncheon speech, Mr. Minow practically achieved that end. He may have been guilty of exaggeration in his TV diagnosis, but there is no doubt the video audience now is more aware of the existence of the F. C. C. than ever before. Into the arena of public opinion he has projected a second contender — the agency established by Congress to protect the public interest in broadcasting—as a factor to be reckoned with in charting the home medium's future course.

It was the shock of the F. C. C.'s overdue assumption of its responsibilities that left the assembled broadcasters in a state of anxiety that continues to prevail beneath the surface. Mr. Minow's firm declaration that a broadcaster had better perform on the air as he promised he would was not a revolutionary principle; in regulatory circles it was old hat. The novelty of the Minow approach was the suggestion that the principle should be enforced.

Now and again Mr. Minow admittedly has skated on fairly thin ice. In trying to deal in concrete terms with the matter of the public interest, he has veered from generalizations on programing to specifics. But he subsequently has backed off and no one in the industry has been able to show where the F. C. C. has been either a censor or a dictator. No governmental threat to TV's freedom, in any case, holds a candle to the limitations imposed by some advertisers.

Response

Probably the most surprising aspect of Mr. Minow's administration has been the lack of articulate rejoinders from the industry. The National Broadcasting Company and the Columbia Broadcasting System have voiced fears over what the commission may do in some unspecified way at some unspecified time, but their arguments have not caught much of the public fancy. They have been on the defensive.

But if Mr. Minow's public-relations stroke was a formidable device, it may have been answered by one reflecting a high degree of vision. LeRoy Collins, president of the N. A. B. and former Governor of Florida, almost single handedly prevailed upon the broadcasting industry not to reply with a burst of heated press agentry. He quickly recognized that debating a "wasteland" was a negative pastime and might well only compound the industry's difficulties.

Instead, Mr. Collins, over the past year, has been something of an unsung missionary in the field, trying to bring the broadcasters around to the view that the best answer to Mr. Minow lies in performance on the air and not in protest. He has avoided the type of knockdown battle between Government and industry that in the past never did help the N. A. B. In trade-organization operation it has been something of a lesson to watch Mr. Collins strive to turn an industry around to an affirmative viewpoint.

In some quarters, Mr. Minow's influence in the past year undoubtedly has been oversimplified. In the area of public-service programing, where the improvement has been most marked, the momentum of world events has played a large part. The recalcitrance of the Soviet Union and the energy of the Kennedy Administration have been reflected on the TV screen as in other phases of the national life.

Shake-Up

Similarly, the recent shake-up in the executive echelons of the American Broadcasting Company is much more due to competitive business factors than the F. C. C. Oliver Treyz, who resigned as TV president, fundamentally was a victim of the ratings that he lived by. Hubbell Robinson, perhaps the most genuinely theatrically minded key executive in TV, is also returning to the top programing post at C. B. S., a move stemming in part from the renewed health of N. B. C.

But not the least interesting aspect of Mr. Minow's first year in office is the revelation of what he cannot do; in fact, the chairman's big problem may be how to sustain his own momentum. With respect to the quality of entertainment programing, still video's primary problem, his hands are tied by the law. Contrary to the view of some overzealous academicians, it is anything but a simple matter to revoke a TV license and make an object les-

son of a stray sinner. To move precipitously in such an area and be reversed in the courts could leave the commission with drastically reduced influence.

View

In fact, it is from television's long-range standpoint that Mr. Minow's position may be the most precarious. The commission has suffered a severe blow with respect to trying to solve the problem of finding more room on the air for TV stations. In effect, it has promised Congress not to try to convert some areas of the country to Channels 14 through 83, so-called ultra-high-frequency television. Political opposition to loss of any existing service on Channels 2 through 13 has been overwhelming.

What this means is that the F. C. C. has virtually abandoned hope of ever shifting all of television to the U. H. F. channels. From a practical standpoint, such a step may have been unavoidable, but it has been taken much too casually.

In exchange for its compromise of the immediate allocations controversy — some innocuous wording will try to ease the F. C. C. pain—Mr. Minow and his colleagues are going all-out on another route they hope will lead to the same end. This is the measure that would require all future television receivers to be equipped to receive Channels 14 through 83 as well as 2 through 13. The social aim is admirable, but whether the idea will work out in practice in the next decade or so remains to be seen.

Present TV broadcasters, meanwhile, are assured of no more significant competition for years to come. At the very least, this would seem to dictate a reasonable industry attitude toward the Government's justified concern that such stations not abuse their preferred status.

Future

Whatever the uncertainties of the future, however, there can be no question that Mr. Minow, over-all, has stimulated a far broader discussion of the perplexities of television than existed before he took office. In the world of television, he has introduced what could be likened to a more realistic system of checks and balances between industry and Government. If the method has the net effect of keeping both the broadcasters and the F. C. C. commissioners on their toes in the days to come, the ever-patient viewer will gain.

SENATORS REBUKE FULTON LEWIS JR.

Say Newscasts Editorialized During 1960 Campaign

By BEN A. FRANKLIN
Special to The New York Times.

WASHINGTON, April 17—A Senate subcommittee asserted today that Fulton Lewis Jr., the Mutual Broadcasting System commentator, was guilty of "a clear abuse of newscast time" during the Presidential campaign of 1960.

A report said Mr. Lewis had "openly endorsed and editorialized in favor of one of the major candidates" in violation of the Federal Communication Commission's "fairness doctrine." It suggested that he "should probably be barred from use of the medium."

Mr. Lewis, a veteran broadcaster, could not be reached for comment. But the subcommittee's excursion into the hitherto sacrosanct realm of broadcast news was viewed as a "hugely controversial" step by other radio and telephone spokesmen.

The report said the subcommittee's study of political reporting on the air had found that "in most cases" the networks' handling of campaign news had been "balanced quantitatively."

It made only one qualitative

judgment the one involving Mr. Lewis—and there were indications that the three subcommittee members were divided on the propriety of drawing such conclusions. They are Ralph W. Yarborough, Democrat of Texas, the chairman; Gale W. McGee, Democrat of Wyoming, and Hugh Scott, Republican of Pennsylvania.

The report objected specifically to a newscast by Mr. Lewis on Nov. 7, 1960, Election Eve, in which he announced that "I shall cast my vote for Richard M. Nixon."

According to a published collection of the scripts of all the networks' fifteen-minute radio and television newscasts during the 1960 campaign, compiled by the committee as part of its study, Mr. Lewis told his Election Eve listeners:

"I shall do so for a wide combination of reasons, not the least of which results from a careful day-by-day study of the two candidates and their capabilities and their campaigns, and the resultant conviction that Mr. Nixon is more sound, more stable and a less emotional individual than his opponent, Senator Kennedy."

Mr. Lewis said that he had been "influenced, also, by the advice of the President of the United States, whom I admire intensely and whom I believe to be one of the greatest and most sincere Americans of all time."

Referring to Mr. Lewis' broadcast of Nov. 7, the report said that "so-called newscasters who abuse the public franchise in such a manner should probably be barred from use of the medium."

FULTON LEWIS JR. HITS SENATE CHARGE

Special to The New York Times.

WASHINGTON, April 18 —Fulton Lewis Jr. today described as "a totally unwarranted political charge" the complaint of a Senate subcommittee that he had "abused newscast time" by editorializing in favor of Richard M. Nixon during the 1960 Presidential campaign.

The Senate Subcommittee on Freedom of Communications asserted yesterday that Mr. Lewis' election eve broadcast, Nov. 7, 1960, had been such a flagrant violation of the "fairness doctrine" of the Federal Communications Act that Mr. Lewis "should probably be barred" from the air.

The subcommittee said this could be done by the Federal Communications Commission.

Mr. Lewis said today, "I am not a newscaster, I am a commentator." However, he acknowledged that his program, "The Top of the News With Fulton Lewis Jr.," was not identified on the air as "commentary." It is billed as a "news" broadcast.

The subcommittee's suggestion that he be barred from the air he described as "a clear violation on their part of the prohibition against censorship" contained in the Federal Communications Act.

In the disputed broadcast Mr. Lewis announced that "I shall cast my vote for Richard M. Nixon." He gave as one of several reasons a contention that some of Senator John F. Kennedy's campaign advisers had urged an economic policy that "to my mind is just a slightly masqueraded form of the philosophy under which the Communist governments of the world are operating."

Minow Given Peabody Award For Service to TV and Radio

Chairman of F.C.C. Is First Government Official Cited— Twelve Others Honored

By VAL ADAMS

Newton N. Minow, chairman of the Federal Communications Commission, won a George Foster Peabody award yesterday for his efforts "to rescue the [television] wasteland from the cowboys and private eyes."

He became the first Government official to be cited by the Peabody committee, which issues awards for "distinguished achievement by television and radio." A telegram from President Kennedy was read at a luncheon in the Pierre Hotel, where the awards ceremonies were held. It said:

"I note with pride that Newton N. Minow is to receive a Peabody special award—and as President, I am glad one of our boys made it."

President Kennedy appointed Mr. Minow to the F. C. C. chairmanship early last year.

Mr. Minow, one of thirteen award winners for 1961, told an audience of 600 that he considered the award was not for him personally but in recognition of the Government's role in broadcasting.

"Whether we like it or not," he added, "the Government has a role to play." Then he assured the broadcasters that with their cooperation, "your Government will maintain a climate in which you are free to create."

Television awards for news and entertainment went, respectively, to "David Brinkley's Journal" and "The Bob Newhart Show" on the National Broadcasting Company network.

Lippmann Gets Award

Walter Lippmann, the columnist of The New York Herald Tribune who appears once or twice a year on "C. B. S. Reports," received an award for "television contribution to international understanding." The program is televised by the Columbia Broadcasting System.

Fred W. Friendly, executive producer of "C. B. S. Reports," received a special award.

Other Peabody awards were: Television Education: "An Age of Kings," produced by the British Broadcasting Corporation and presented here by WNEW-TV and the National Educational Television network, and "Vincent Van Gogh: A Self-Portrait," N. B. C.

Television Youth and Children's Programs: "Expedition," American Broadcasting Company.

Television Public Service: "Let Freedom Ring," KSL-TV, Salt Lake City, Utah.

Radio Education: WNYC, New York, for "The Reader's Almanac" and "Teen Age Book Talk."

Newton N. Minow, Federal Communications Commission chairman, with award.

Radio Entertainment: WFMT, Chicago, for its "Fine Arts Entertainment."

Radio Contribution to International Understanding: WRUL, Worldwide Broadcasting's short-wave station, for United Nations General Assembly broadcasts in English and Spanish.

Special award: Capital Cities Broadcasting Corporation for "Verdict for Tomorrow: The Eichmann Trial on Television."

Bennett Cerf, chairman of the Peabody committee, announced the awards at a luncheon sponsored by the New York chapter of the Broadcast Pioneers. The awards were presented by Dean John E. Drewry of the University of Georgia's Henry W. Grady School of Journalism, which administers the awards with the Peabody board.

Entries are submitted by stations, networks, radio-tv editors or any organization or individual. The thirteen-man board consists of critics, educators, lawyers and others.

The awards were established to perpetuate the memory of the late George Foster Peabody, a native of Columbus, Ga., who became a New York banker.

Radio Broadcaster's Right to Endorse Political Candidates Is Discussed

By JACK GOULD

FULTON LEWIS JR., the commentator for the Mutual Broadcasting System, has all the luck. No sooner do his nightly yearnings for a gentle life around a McKinley tea cozy begin to pale than a liberal group rushes to his rescue by complaining over the way he pours.

The Senate Subcommittee on Freedom of Communications is the latest addition to the lengthy list of awkward antagonists who persist in nurturing the Lewis rating. The group had suggested that broadcasting's freedom of political discussion would be enhanced by sealing the lips of the man from Mutual if he did not mend his ways.

The committee's anguish was occasioned by Mr. Lewis' declaration on election eve in 1960 that he would vote for Richard M. Nixon for the Presidency. By the commentator's open advocacy of one candidate over the other, the committee reasoned, the doctrine of fairness in broadcasting was jeopardized and Mr. Lewis should be placed in the durance vile of dead air.

Within the recent past, of course, Mr. Lewis' pretenses to being only a "newscaster" are about as plausible as arguing that David Lawrence writes without a point of view. For some time the radio commentator has openly disappointed by the failure of both Republicans and Democrats to recognize that their search for helpful leadership could come to a perfectly logical conclusion.

That the committee was disturbed by Mr. Lewis' election eve enthusiasm for President Kennedy's rival merely suggests that its members had not listened to him very faithfully. The specific announcement of his contemplated behavior in the polling booth had roughly the same element of surprise as an alcoholic's agreeing to take another nip from the working bottle.

Mr. Lewis undoubtedly did err in endorsing Mr. Nixon by name. The more accepted ploy in broadcasting is to admire or deprecate a candidate's policies without making a final commitment as to whether he would be any good in the job. This procedure preserves the nicety of leading the listener to the end of the diving board without pushing him off.

But the Senate subcommittee's ambitions to require Mr.

April 19, 1962

April 19, 1962

Lewis to conform in perpetuity are as extreme as they are futile. The remedy for preserving political equilibrium in broadcasting does not lie in coast - to - coast shushing of a journalistic organizer who by and large talks only to his own paid-up membership. Rather it rests in more vigorous steps to sustain the diversity of opinion among commentators, to make sure that there is a civilized balance among the various hues comprising the political spectrum.

In a way the impulse of Mr. Lewis to don the editorial mantle may be symptomatic of a reaction to a vacuum in broadcasting. After years of pious pleading for the right to editorialize most stations have only tiptoed through the demanding rigors of exercising the privilege.

The lively local radio station WMCA knows how to talk to a point and there are a few other broadcasters who do not hesitate to name names. But many outlets equate the function of editorializing with wholehearted endorsement of strikes that do not inconvenience the public and rush hours that are free of traffic congestion.

Caution

These feeble balms to the conscience may appear impressive in logs designed to suggest that a community voice has bravely cleared its throat. But sooner or later the broadcasters will have to come to grips with the stickier proposition of recommending Mr. Doe for a given post and incurring the displeasure of the political contestant who is proposed for privacy.

To ask such specific forthrightness of stations that survive through the grace of Federal franchises may be expecting a lot. The reluctance to test the wrath of a party that in due course may repopulate the Federal Communications Commission is strong indeed. But the continued anticipation of possible reprisals in the long run can be far more paralyzing than facing such problems if they ever occur.

Individuals and committees of the Senate at the moment seem to be involving themselves much too deeply in program content, casually urging that one figure be thrown off the air, using an isolated show as an excuse for invoking more dangerous curbs on program independence and conducting assorted other inquiries of vague purposes.

Mr. Lewis may have spoken up in the wrong way at the wrong time. But such an excess is of minor consequence in comparison to the spectacle of a Senate subcommittee presuming to judge who should or should not be on the air or a supine industry condoning the serious implications of the affair merely because the victim can be an enormously trying individual.

April 29, 1962

HOUSE PREPARES INQUIRY ON PRESS

Groundwork Is Being Laid to Cover Broad Field

By C. P. TRUSSELL
Special to The New York Times.

WASHINGTON, July 14—An antitrust panel of the House Judiciary Committee is preparing a broad inquiry on the press and other news media. Public hearings are scheduled to begin soon after the adjournment of Congress.

Representative Emanuel Celler, Democrat of Brooklyn, will head the inquiry. Mr. Celler, dean of the New York congressional delegation, is chairman of the committee.

"We shall avoid like the plague any censorship," Mr. Celler said. "We are not gunning for any newspaper or individual. We just want the facts."

The facts, Mr. Celler explained, concern consolidations and the disappearance of newspapers, the organization and operations of newspaper chains and wire services, non-journalistic ownership of news media through bank trusts, and the effects of concentrated ownership in mass communications in any city.

Suburban Areas a Target

The inquiry, he said, will reach into costs of production, handling of news and the impact of syndicated columns on the gathering and presentation of local news.

Further, Mr. Celler said, an examination will be made of the fast-growing suburban press; radio and television reporting; the effects of TV-radio competition in the gathering and presentation of news, and the depth of coverage.

tion with newspapers, instances of fading competition in the gathering and presentation of news, and the depth of coverage.

"Is it healthy to have one entity owning the morning and afternoon newspaper?" he asked In a number of instances, also, the same ownership that controls the morning and evening papers in a given city also controls the sole radio or television station.

"We shall endeavor to find out whether, in those cities, the news is slanted according to the prejudice or idiosyncrasies of these common owners; whether the editorial policy is consistently politically slanted."

In its preliminary work the

July 15, 1962

inquiry staff, headed by Stuart H. Johnson Jr., is undertaking "a newspaper content" study at the Library of Congress.

Merged newspapers are under examination as to what and how much they published before and after consolidations in the way of self-produced news, the retention or dropping of columnists, or other changes.

Mr. Johnson said that news media mergers, particularly those that occurred recently in New Orleans and San Francisco, would be studied.

He cited the purchase of The New Orleans Times-Picayune and Item by S. I. Newhouse, and the Hearst Publishing Company's acquisition of sole ownership of The San Francisco News-Call Bulletin from Scripps-Howard.

"We are interested, too," he said, "in the suburban press, with its advantages of lower production costs, and the steadily rising costs of production in the metropolitan areas.

"We want to see how the wire services operate and, at great cost, how they 'homogenize' the news for local and widely spread presentation.

"Also, we are interested in seeing whether or to what extent the columnists might be drying up local talent in assaying the news of the day."

Mr. Johnson said he did not want the inquiry to be viewed as an "investigation" or "inquisition."

"We are very much aware of the First Amendment [which includes freedom of the press]," he said. "We are also aware that the courts have said you can distinguish between the business practices and the editorial operations of newspapers.

"If anyone doesn't choose to testify on editorial content, that is up to him. We will not subpoena witnesses. The people we have talked to so far have been very cooperative."

The witnesses, he said, will include owners of news media and syndicates, broadcasting officials, representatives of the Justice Department and the Federal Trade Commission, and members of Congress.

Mr. Johnson, a graduate of the Yale Law School, has been a practicing attorney in New York for ten years. His legal staff of seven includes a former attorney for the Federal Communications Commission, a former Justice Department attorney with experience in handling cases involving the press, and a former newspaper reporter.

U. S. CURB PROPOSED ON TV SENT ABROAD

WASHINGTON, Aug. 23 (UPI)—A Federal Communications Commission official has told the White House that the rising star of international television means that the Government must consider some type of control over programs shown in foreign countries.

The suggestion was made in a memorandum by Tedson J. Meyers, administrative assistant to Newton N. Minow, chairman of the F. C. C.

The central recommendation of the Meyers study was the establishment of an Office of International Television to make sure that the broadcasting resources of the United States developed "along lines most beneficial to the foreign policy of the United States."

Mr. Meyers said that the office would have to decide "whether it is desirable to establish criteria for the content of American programming displayed overseas—and if so, how such criteria should be determined and applied."

August 24, 1962

U. S. Urges Editors to Use Care On Information Vital to Security

Advisory Memorandum Asks Discretion on Data About Deployment, Weapons and Vulnerability of Targets

Special to The New York Times

WASHINGTON, Oct. 24—The White House asked newspapers, news magazines, radio and television stations today to use "caution and discretion" in handling certain kinds of information regarded by the Defense Department as "vital" to national security during the Cuban crisis.

In announcing the categories of military information, the White House said that the Department of Defense had already ordered all military commands not to make public such information.

However, the White House statement added, it is possible that "such information may come into the possession of news media."

Since the publication of such information would be "contrary to the public interest," the White House said that it was asking editors and radio and television news directors to be discreet and cautious in their use of it.

A White House official stressed that the memorandum being sent to editors and radio-television news directors was not binding on them, and simply provided them with guidance.

A White House official insisted that the White House request did not amount to the "voluntary censorship" by which the press and radio were guided in World War II and the Korean War.

However, newspapermen who were in Washington during those two wars found it difficult to see where the difference lay.

For example, in World War II, Byron Price, who was called the director of censorship, operated "voluntary censorship" in the manner proposed today in the White House memorandum.

Mr. Price issued categories of information, the publication of which the Government regarded as detrimental to the national interest. There were no penalties for not following this guidance. Editors who were in doubt whether to publish information called Mr. Price and got his instant advice.

TEXT OF MEMORANDUM

WASHINGTON, Oct. 24 (UPI)—Following is the text of the White House memorandum today regarding information involving national security:

Memorandum to editors, and radio and television news directors:

The following information is considered vital to our national security and therefore will not be released by the Department of Defense. De-

spite this fact, it is possible that such information may come into the possession of news media. During the current tense international situation, the White House feels that the publication of such information is contrary to the public interest. We ask public information media of all types to exercise caution and discretion in the publication fo such information.

1. Any discussion of plans for employment of strategic or tactical forces of the United States including types of equipment and new or planned location of command or control centers or detection systems.

2. Estimates of United States capability of destroying targets, including numbers of weapons required, size and character of forces required, ability of these forces to penetrate defenses, and accuracy or reliability of our forces or weapons systems.

3. Intelligence estimates concerning targets or target systems, such as numbers, types and locations of aiming points in the target system, enemy missile and bomber forces, etc.

4. Intelligence estimates of enemy plans or capabilities, or information which would reveal the level of success of United States intelligence efforts or operations with respect to Cuba or the Communist bloc.

5. Details as to numbers or movements of United States forces, including naval units and vessels, aircraft, missile forces or ground forces, ammunition, equipment, etc. Announcement may be made of such unit movements after the movement has been completed.

6. Degree of alert of military forces.

7. Location of aircraft or supporting equipment. Presence of aircraft observable in the public domain may be confirmed.

8. Emergency dispersal plans of aircraft and units including dispersal capabilities, times, schedules or logistical support.

9. Official estimates of vulnerability to various forms of enemy action, including sabotage, of United States armed forces and installations.

10. New data concerning operational missile distribution, numbers, operational readiness. Estimates of effectiveness of strike capability of missile forces.

11. Details of command and control systems, including

new or planned command posts and facilities, estimates of ability to survive enemy attack, security measures, etc., including sea or airborne command posts.

12. Details of airlift or sea-

lift capabilities, including size and nature of forces to be lifted, time limits for such lifts, and supply capabilities, with respect to possible specific areas of operation.

October 25, 1962

Managing the News

The old problem of whether or not the ends justify the means cropped up in a form relatively new to the United States yesterday.

Arthur Sylvester, Assistant Secretary of Defense for Public Affairs in the Pentagon, frankly admitted the Government had managed, controlled and dammed up the flow of news about the Cuban crisis, and he indicates it expected to continue to do so. He envisaged news as "part of . . . weaponry," and declared flatly that "the results . . . justify the methods we use."

There is no doubt that "management" or "control" of the news is censorship described by a sweeter term. There is no doubt that it restricts the people's right to know. There is no doubt that public positions upon great national issues cannot be intelligently formed unless the facts are available. There is no doubt that a democratic government cannot work if news of and about that government is long suppressed or managed or manipulated or controlled.

There is also no doubt that in time of crisis a sense of responsibility and restraint on the part of all public information media is imperative. The withholding by voluntary restrictions or, in time of war by censorship, of certain types of military and security information is imperative. But to attempt to manage the news so that a free press should speak (in Sylvester's words) in "one voice to your adversary" could be far more dangerous to the cause of freedom than the free play of dissent, than the fullest possible publication of the facts.

October 31, 1962

In The Nation

National Security and the 'Flow' of Information

By ARTHUR KROCK

WASHINGTON, Nov. 21—It required a second round of questioning at the President's news conference yesterday to define the issue the press has made over the information-dispensing policy of the Administration. President Kennedy's answer to the first inquiry could have created the public impression that the recent protests of the press were against official restriction of publications of activities in the military and intelligence areas at the height of the Cuban crisis. These, as he said, would have been "extremely inimical to the interest of the United States."

But in Mr. Kennedy's exchange with his second questioner, Raymond P. Brandt of the St. Louis Post-Dispatch, the actual issue was made clear. It is, that the regulations of specific relations between newsmen and officials that were recently promulgated in the Departments of Defense and State are inherently restrictive of the flow of information which it is the legitimate province of the press to publish and the right of the American people to know. In announcing that he had already ordered the modification of some of these procedures, the President said he would modify them further on evidence they were still inhibitive of publications that would not weaken national security.

This narrows the real issue raised by the press. But it does not dispose of it. There is a basic functional conflict involved. The responsible press is trained to recognize, and will not publish, news inimical to national security. The press knows that international crises do and must enlarge this category.

But if and when Government has shown a tendency to inflate the category, and also virtually polices the contacts of officials with news reporters, both press and public are denied the legitimate information which, as the President himself acknowledged yesterday, "any Administration really must depend on as a check on its own actions." This current tendency was reflected in Brandt's query after the President's promise to assure that regulations on information do not deny to the public news to which it is entitled: "How are you going to find out."

This is the very heart of the public information problem. To the military mind all news of service activities involves possible damage to national security in any period. The State Department shares this estimate in considerable degree. And it is difficult for any President to distinguish between information restricted because it may embarrass an official or because it may injure the project in hand.

Mr. Kennedy was not challenging any view of the responsible press, or discussing the real issue, when he said "I have no apologies" for the total secrecy in which the Administration enveloped its finding that the Soviet weapons installations on Cuba were offensive, endangering our security and that of the Western Hemisphere, and decided on the military and diplomatic measures for the removal of these weapons. It was only after the Defense and State Department regulations were imposed that legitimate public information came under the ban on which the protest was based.

Prior to the Directive

For example, inquiries in the public interest for clarification of policy, not the necessarily secret steps taken to effect it, went unanswered. And, though the precedent of international law is to announce the area covered by a naval blockade, this information also was denied. Yet the press had proved its responsibility in protecting national security before the regulations were issued that require officials to write reports of any contacts they have with reporters unless another official is present—either procedure inhibiting the "flow" of legitimate news.

This proof was given not only by the fact that, as the President said, one newspaper learned, on Oct. 21, but "in the public interest" did not print, "some of the details" of the Cuban program he would announce on Oct. 22. The proof is furnished also by prior dispatches in which other alert Washington reporters refrained from making the deductions which logically arose from the identities of certain Government personnel they saw hurrying to continuous conferences; from the President's sudden break-off of political campaigning because of a "cold" they knew he didn't have; and from the explanation by an unusually vociferous chorus of conferees that the secrecy imposed on them was the most ever.

KENNEDY ACCUSED OF NEWS CONTROL

Rep. Moss Urges Press to Lead Discussion of Issue

SAN FRANCISCO, Nov. 30 (AP)—A Democratic Congressman said tonight that President Kennedy had taken firm control of the management of Government news in a manner that was "unique in peacetime."

This point was made by Representative John E. Moss of California, chairman of a special House subcommittee of government information.

He called for a broad public discussion of the situation "to make sure the people's need to know the facts of Government is fulfilled."

The nation's press, he said, should lead the discussion.

Mr. Moss criticized the news-handling policy of his own party's Administration, in a speech prepared for the California Press Association conference.

He attacked restrictions imposed on covering underground nuclear tests in Nevada, secrecy about all military space activities, a recent "blackout" in information about Soviet satellite efforts, and the manner of applying the news guidelines laid down by the Government during the Cuban crisis.

A 'Disturbing Period'

"We have in the past few weeks experienced a degree of Government news management which is unique in peacetime," he said, "a disturbing period of unplanned and unprecedented news management."

Mr. Moss conceded that the problem was not new and because of the need to safeguard sensitive and classified information he went on, the Government moves are "not all bad, nor all good."

But now, Mr. Moss said, "important news-making events are under firm Presidential control."

He reviewed Mr. Kennedy's actions in this field. Three months after office, Mr. Moss said, the President asked the press, in a speech before the American Newspaper Publisher's Association, to exercise special restraint in printing news about Government actions.

"Even though no Government guidance was provided," Mr. Moss said, "there were restraints imposed by the Government."

At this point he cited the secrecy about Nevada's underground nuclear tests, "which previously had been ooen to reporters and photographers."

"Instead of first-hand information about testing activities, the press got handouts," he said.

Mr. Moss also objected to restrictions on news about military space activities.

"All information about the billions od dollars spent by the military in space research is channeled through the Pentagon's single public information voice." he said.

Calls 'Blackout Complete'

He then recalled that last September the National Aeronautics and Space Administration said six Soviet attempts to send space probes to Venus and Mars had failed.

Since then, he said, "there had been a complete blackout on information about Russian satellite efforts."

"This is the kind of news management that causes grave concern . . ." he said. "If we cover up Russian successes, we can certainly cover up our failures. This leads to a dangerous delusion of the American people."

Mr. Moss said he had not been perturbed about the 12-point White House memorandum listing sensitive information that the press was asked to withhold during the Cuban crisis.

"The memorandum was nothing new," he said. "But the unplanned method by which it was issued certainly is a new approach to censorship of government news."

He said wire service and broadcasting representatives hastily summoned to the White House should not have been put "in the difficult position of accepting or rejecting guidelines for self-censorship after one hurried conference."

November 22, 1962

December 1, 1962

In The Nation

More Complications Trying to 'Manage the News'

By ARTHUR KROCK

WASHINGTON, Dec. 3—With every new publication of events in the internal Administration debate which preceded President Kennedy's Oct. 22 announcement that offensive Soviet weapons installations in Cuba must be dismantled, more evidence appears of the hazards incurred by the decision of a Government of this democracy to manage the news as an instrument of national security policy. The latest evidence shows that once the critical situation is eased for which the program was invoked, some of its operators have acquired the habit, and logically progress to management of the news for other purposes.

Among these purposes are certain to be the desire of A to let the people know, though favored publication outlets, how right A was all along and how wrong was B. And many A's and B's necessarily participate in the inner Government councils on how to deal with a problem as grave as the Soviet installations of offensive weaponry in Cuba. Therefore, if A gets, or thinks he gets, the nod of high authority for showing up B, or even decides on his own that high authority will be served by this, management of the news becomes the personal instrument that is its evil potential.

A Source of Rancor

Then also the policy becomes common property as a personal instrument of the B's and all the other A's. And among the consequences are rancor in Government and politics; White House embarrassment for an event in which it may or may not have culpability; and official denials which materialize the always latent public doubt of whom and what to believe. But in this instance some of these could have been avoided if in the first place there had not been control and manipulation of news far beyond the requirements of national security.

The article which stimulated the above consequences had that effect today for three reasons in particular. Both the authors, Stewart Alsop and Charles Leffingwell Bartlett, have favored access to several of the principal participants in the formulation of the President's Cuban

decision that was conducted in the most dramatic setting of secrecy ever imparted to such highly visible official conferences. Both are keen in discerning and discounting personal motives. And Bartlett is in the President's confidence as much as any of his most trusted counselors—a confidence, moreover, which he has respected with the utmost scruple, personally and professionally, to any limit imposed. Hence, when an article of his co-authorship attributed to certain conferees positions on how the Cuban crisis should be dealt with, it was naturally invested with the ring of authority.

So far as this reporter is concerned, he has no doubt that Bartlett and Alsop had excellent professional reasons to credit their sources. But other sources in whom this department has equal confidence gave a markedly different version today of some of the fundamental details in the article. For examples:

Another Version

1. Adlai E. Stevenson did, in this version as in the other, favor a "softer line" in dealing with the Cuban crisis. He first proposed that the naval blockade be limited to ships bringing "offensive weapons" to Cuba. But as the President's decision evolved, to prescribe a broader and more rigid program, Stevenson went along "without any objections."

2. Neither Secretary of the Treasury Dillon nor Director McCone of the Central Intelligence Agency urged an immediate air strike on the Soviet installations, irrespective of a blockade, with "negotiations" to come afterward. Secretary of Defense McNamara originally favored a gradually tightening naval blockade, to be followed by whatever military measures were later determined to be needed for the full satisfaction of Mr. Kennedy's ultimatum. The program finally adopted, which the co-authors of the article celebrated as the "McNamara plan," varied at least in this respect from the Secretary's first concept.

These differences—whether of recollection or in notes made of the meetings—are not unusual. Washington is very accustomed to them. But the tumult here today over the Bartlett-Alsop article is because Washington is not accustomed to such flat contradictions of flat statements among the intimates of high authority. However, if management of the news continues its growth in practice, the situation may become more familiar.

'Managed News' Hearings Due to Start on March 18

WASHINGTON, Feb. 15 (UPI) — A House subcommittee hopes to start hearings March 18 on the Administration's "managed news" policy.

The sessions will cover the broad area of Government information but will not deal with specific complaints.

The hearings stem from complaints of newsmen during the Cuban crisis that the Government on occasion withheld non-security information and that it attempted to "manage" the news with some pieces of information it did give out.

The Government Information and Foreign Operations subcommittee, headed by Representative John Moss, Democrat of California, will conduct the inquiry.

As envisioned now, the hearings will be more in the form of seminars than an investigation. Witnesses will not be placed under oath and will talk freely with subcommittee members. A witness list has not been drawn up but those appearing will fall into two categories — high level Government information officers and representatives of press groups.

February 16, 1963

Federal Aide Defends Some Control of News

WASHINGTON, March 10 (AP) — An Assistant Secretary of State said tonight that there would be "chaos and a great dangerous state of affairs" without some "management" of the news by both United States Government and the press.

The official, Robert J. Manning, defined the term "management" in the sense of bringing coherence out of a welter of facts. He denied that the Kennedy Administration managed news with the aim of distortion.

The assistant secretary who directs public affairs and press relations for the State Department, gave his views in a taped television interview for the American Broadcasting Company.

Criticism of asserted news management by the Kennedy Administration has grown to some prominence since the original news blackout early in last October's Cuban crisis.

Washington

How Adam, Miss Eve 'Managed the News'

By JAMES RESTON

WASHINGTON, March 19—The Congress is now investigating charges that the Kennedy Administration is "managing the news," and this investigation may help put the problem in better perspective.

The problem has increased in the last generation partly because the nation is in a state of half-war and half-peace, partly because television tends to give the party in power a publicity advantage over the opposition, and partly because the U.S. is now involved with over 40 allies, whose interests have to be consulted before official moves are publicized.

For the first time in the peacetime history of the U.S. we now have a secret service, whose activities are concealed. The Central Intelligence Agency, for example, was flying its U-2 planes over the Soviet Union for four years before one of them was finally shot down in 1960. Nothing was said about this until it was announced by the Soviet Union, and even then, the official announcements in Washington distorted the facts.

This was a clear case of "managing the news" for security reasons. Under Kennedy the same thing was done to cover the C.I.A.'s operations in the Bay of Pigs invasion, and of course the naval and military moves prior to the Cuban blockade were also "managed" to mislead the enemy.

Reporters' Fault

Diplomatic information, not necessarily involving military security, is also often controlled. For example, if the U.S. wishes to explore the possibility of a new legal statute for Berlin, which it doesn't, it obviously has to discuss this in private with the North Atlantic allies before starting a public controversy which could only benefit the Soviets.

Accordingly, a nation involved with allies in a cold war, which is partly secret, partly economic and diplomatic, does control the news more than in the days when Washington had no secret service, no allies and no responsibilities for leading a worldwide coalition.

There are, however, dangers involved here, and Congress is right to look into the problem. The key questions are whether this Administration is more or less available for questioning than past Administrations operating under similar circumstances and whether the reporters are exploiting every opportunity to question.

My impression is that the top officials of this Administration are more available than any other set of officials here in the last 20 years. The basic problem for the resourceful reporter here under Eisenhower and Truman was that, when big news was breaking, the officials available to the reporter were not informed about what was happening, and the officials who were informed were not available because they were dealing with the crisis.

This is still true to some extent now, but it is less true than at any other time in my Washington experience. By far the easiest way for officials to 'manage the news' is to announce what they want to announce, and then make themselves scarce. Even during the height of both Cuban crises, however, the officials who knew what was happening were taking urgent calls from reporters at all hours of the day and night.

Foreign Aspects

It is true that this Administration reads more and complains more about criticism than any other in the last generation, and because they are more available, it may be that they have conned a few reporters into being more sympathetic than good skeptical reporters should. But that, if true, is the fault of the reporters.

What President Kennedy does that troubles his politic·l opposition is that he "dominates the news" more than he "manages the news." He is the central figure in the capital, the presiding officer over a rather drab Cabinet, the main source of big news, and the master of all the techniques of television and news distribution.

It is a matter of opinion whether the Kennedy Administration is more or less guilty of "managing the news" than the Eisenhower, and after watching the way the news was handled to create the "Spirit of Geneva" at the summit conference of 1955 and how it was handled during Eisenhower's second illness, I would say things are getting better rather than worse.

The problem, however, exists and has to be watched. It really all started in the Garden of Eden. Miss Eve, the original well-informed circle, did not, according to our information, tempt Adam with that apple at all. She tempted him with something else. But she "managed the news" and got away with it fairly well.

Salinger Disavows Managing the News But Accuses Editors

By United Press International.

WASHINGTON, March. 22 —Pierre Salinger, White House press secretary, threw the charge of "news management" back at the nation's editors and broadcasters today. He called for a study to determine whether they were handling news in the public interest.

Mr. Salinger advanced the proposal at a luncheon of the Women's National Press Club here. The White House released excerpts from his remarks.

He vehemently denied that news management was a policy of the Kennedy Administration. He cited examples of news stories that he said were either slanted or untrue. He said this was "news management in its purest form."

"The Government cannot and could not present a false image to the public," Mr. Salinger said. "The activities in Washington and around the world are too closely covered by the press to make this possible, even should an Administration have such a desire—and I assure that has not been and never will be the policy of this Administration."

He said it was not even true that the term "news management" originated with the Kennedy Administration. He said the phrase was coined in 1955 by James Reston of The New York Times in discussing information activities of the Eisenhower Administration.

Suggests a Survey

After pleading not guilty of news management, even during the worst of the Cuban crisis, Mr. Salinger said he thought there was only "one legitimate place where news can be managed — at the desks of our newspapers' city editors and managing editors and at the desks of our radio and television station news directors."

"And it is here, I believe," he said, "that the really fundamental study should be made to determine whether news is being managed in the public interest.

"I believe by and large that the news is being managed fairly by the news organizations. But there are so many glaring examples lately of where it is not, that such a fundamental study would be useful."

The examples of what Mr. Salinger considered news management all involved newspapers or magazines. He did not cite any examples of so-called news management by radio or television. His examples involved:

¶Much heavier devotion of coverage by one unidentified Eastern daily of the Billie Sol Estes case —- involving actions of a Democratic Administration than was devoted by the paper to the stockpiling probe involving a Republican Administration.

¶The manner in which a Midwest newspaper and a national magazine phrased questions in a public opinion poll. Because the questions were posed negatively, Mr. Sallinger said, it was no surprise that the Administration came off loser.

¶The case of "the great newspaper chain" that printed stories that Russian planes had overflown the southeastern United States. Mr. Salinger called these stories absolutely and completely untrue" and said the editor refused to back down on his story.

Mr. Salinger said he had offered in the latter case to have any top officials of the Government, including President Kennedy, call the editor personally and tell him the facts if the editor would admit that his newspapers were wrong. The editor thus far has not answered this proposal, he said.

"Let me say we in Government are neither stupid enough to believe we can fool you nor clever enough to do it if we wanted to," Mr. Salinger said. "We believe that the Government is peopled with men and women of integrity and good intentions.

"We do not want to nor will we deceive the American people. We hope that you, as journalists, will uphold your vital function in the role of telling the American people the facts."

Mr. Salinger prepared for his appearance by reading the transcript of a House hearing Tuesday in which 10 spokesmen for publishers, editors, broadcasters and other news media groups strongly assailed Federal news policies.

The charges, ranging from "lies" in the Cuban crisis to "a bad attitude" on the part of Arthur Sylvester, Pentagon information chief, were raised before the House Government Information subcommittee headed by Representative John E. Moss, Democrat of California.

Mr. Sylvester, a prime target in the testimony, is scheduled to appear before the Moss group Monday. So is Mr. Sylvester's State Department counterpart, Robert Manning.

Mr. Salinger said yesterday he had not been invited to testify before the Moss subcommittee and he did not plan to do so. In a recent television interview, he was asked about earlier news management changes and described the accusations as "greatly overworked."

He said in the Feb. 27 appearance that he always had "held to the theory that the news should go out as it happens" but that when national security is at stake there may be restrictions.

2 U.S. AIDES BACK SECRECY IN CRISIS

Sylvester and Manning Tell House Group That Security Forced Cuban Silence

By CABELL PHILLIPS
Special to The New York Times.

WASHINGTON, March 25 — Two Government information officers told Congress today that the flow of official news sometimes has to be slowed in the interest of national security.

This was the burden of testimony given the House subcommittee on Government information today by Arthur Sylvester, Assistant Secretary of Defense for Public Affairs; and Robert J. Manning, his opposite number in the Department of State. Both officials have figured recently as targets in the current controversy over charges of news management by the Kennedy Administration.

In his testimony before a crowded hearing room this afternoon, Mr. Sylvester asserted that "in times of crisis information which ordinarily would be made available to our citizens must temporarily be withheld in in order to deny it to our enemies."

Under Recent Criticism

The defense official has been under attack recently for his news policies at the Pentagon. This has grown principally out of his admission that certain information was denied reporters during the height of the Cuban crisis last October. He was quoted later as saying that under certain circumstances, the Government is justified in "lying" if the alternative would be nuclear destruction.

He told the committee today that as a newsman for more than 35 years "I am sensitive to the people's right and access to factual information about their Government."

But as a public official, he said, "I am also aware that in time of extreme national peril there are other considerations in addition to news dissemination."

The Government's controlled news policy during the Cuban crisis last year fell into two phases, Mr. Sylvester said, and was determined by the President and the National Security Council.

Blackout Called Vital

The first phase covered the period between the discovery of offensive missiles in Cuba and the President's "quarantine"

United Press International Telephoto

DEFEND WITHHOLDING OF NEWS: Arthur Sylvester, left, Assistant Secretary of Defense for Public Affairs, huddles with Robert J. Manning, his counterpart in the State Department, prior to their appearance at House hearing on news "management."

speech on Oct. 22. It was necessary to conceal from the Russians, and thus from the American public, he explained, the extent of our intelligence until a plan of action could be completed and cleared with other interested governments.

The second phase occurred during the period when the Russians actually began the dismantling and removal of the offensive weapons. Mr. Sylvester said it was necessary to issue "guidelines" to military commands at that time to protect the movement of ships and aircraft, and to avoid any public comment on the Cuban situation beyond what was being officially said in Washington.

This was the subcommittee's second public airing of the news management controversy. Last week a panel of newspaper publishers E. Moss, Democrat of California, said that a hearing would be held on present preparations for war time censorship.

State Office 'Wide Open'

At the morning session Mr. Manning said "the State Department is as wide open as Yankee Stadium, and the ad-

mission is free."

Mr. Manning defined the philosophy of a Government information director as being "to find out the facts, get them into perspective, and, within the limitations of national security, put them out truthfully and quickly."

But conflicts inevitably arise, he said, because of the different concepts that the Government and the press have as to their obligations.

Under certain circumstances, he said, the Government relishers and radio and television executives was invited by the committee to suggest ways in which the Government's news policies could be improved. The chairman, Representative John quired an interlude of secrecy in which to conduct certain delicate negotiations or to perfect certain policies. Premature disclosure would have the same effect, he added, "as it does on photographic film."

Opposing this, he said, is the need and the right of the public in a democratic society to be fully informed about the policies of its Government.

"There are moments when the interests of the Government serving the people and a press informing the people do not coincide," he added.

Mr. Manning was questioned at some length concerning a directive issued by his office last October instructing officials in the department giving interviews to newsmen either to have a representative of the Public Affairs Office sit in on such interviews or to report the substance of such interviews to him. This directive, rescinded after a month, has often been cited as an instance of news management by the Administration.

Today Mr. Manning said the purpose of the directive was not to "monitor" or "inhibit" the free flow of news out of the department. Instead, he said, it was "a sociological experiment" to find out how much direct communication there was between reporters and officials, and to learn whether this intercourse could be increased or improved.

This explanation did not seem convincing to Representative Henry Reuss, Democrat of Wisconsin. Since the directives came at about the time the Cuban crisis was developing, he suggested that it was a device to control the disclosure of information about it.

ENGLE SUGGESTS SYLVESTER RESIGN

Special to The New York Times.

LOS ANGELES, March 28 — Senator Clair Engle, California Democrat, today called for the resignation of Arthur Sylvester, Assistant Secretary of Defense for Public Affairs.

Mr. Engle told a news conference that he thought "it would be to the advantage of the Department [of Defense] for Mr. Sylvester to resign."

Mr. Sylvester, Defense Department information officer, has been under attack during charges of news management by the Kennedy Administration.

Senator Engle, a member of the Senate Armed Services Committee, said some of Mr. Sylvester's policies do not "make much sense." He said Mr. Sylvester had succeeded in putting both feet in his mouth at the same time.

He accused the information officer of leaking stories critical of the Senate Investigations Subcommittee looking into the controversial TFX warplane.

The Senator also criticized Secretary of Defense Robert S. McNamara for relying on "whiz kids" rather than experienced combat officers in the Pentagon and for over-emphasis on missiles at the expense of the RS-70 and Skybolt programs.

CENSORSHIP CODE EXPECTED IN FALL

WASHINGTON, July 1 (AP) —A "standby code for voluntary censorship" will be sent to every newspaper and broadcasting office in the country about Sept. 1, if President Kennedy gives his approval.

The code would be a modern version of the guidelines used in World War II for handling military information.

The Office of Emergency Planning said today a proposed final draft is being written by Byron Price, a former executive news editor of the Associated Press. Mr. Price directed the World War II Office of Censorship.

Mr. Price would be the head of any new censorship agency in the event of war, a spokesman said. The office would be independent, civilian-controlled, and responsible only to the President.

Broadcast Executives Tell Kennedy of 'Encroachment'

WASHINGTON, Aug. 22 (UPI) — A group of broadcasters discussed with President Kennedy today what they felt was federal encroachment on broadcast content and radio-television editorials.

The President met with 19 radio and television executives at the White House. Over the last two years, 21 similar conferences for editors and publishers of newspapers have been held on a state by state basis.

Lawrence H. Rogers 2d, executive vice president of the Taft Broadcasting Company, Cincinnati, said editorializing on the air had been discussed in "some detail." He declined to say specifically how the President felt about the matter.

Asked if the radio and television executives had any particular complaints for the President, Mr. Rogers said "they generally aired their views on what they feel is encroachment of federal authority on broadcast content beyond provisions of the federal law."

Stanton Terms Prospects Good For Analysis of Code on Trials

By VAL ADAMS

Dr. Frank Stanton, president of the Columbia Broadcasting System, said yesterday that the "outlook is most promising" for the Brookings Institution to make a study of the issues involved in news coverage of judicial proceedings by television and print media. Such a study would analyze the degree to which individual rights of defendants are compromised by the rights of news media to report and the public to know.

Dr. Stanton spoke at a conference of C.B.S. television affiliates at the Hilton Hotel. He also said a recent poll showed that 71 per cent of the United States population would like to see televised debates this year between the major Presidential nominees.

On March 26, Dr. Stanton had voiced sharp criticism of the behavior of television and the press in covering the trial of Jack Ruby in Dallas. Ruby murdered Lee H. Oswald, accused assassin of President Kennedy. The C.B.S. official urged the establishment of a code of conduct applicable to television and the press, members of the legal profession and police officials in judicial proceedings.

Dr. Stanton said yesterday that the Brookings Institution had "consulted with the president of the American Bar Association and a number of others and will be making recommendations to its own board this Friday."

Robert D. Calkins, president of Brookings, said in Washington that officers of the institution would inform the board of trustees of the proposed study in a meeting Friday. The chairman of the board is Eugene R. Black, retired president of the International Bank for Reconstruction and Development.

"But we are not putting forth a finished proposal for their consideration," Mr. Calkins added, "so far the institution is uncommitted. The trustees will be asked if we should undertake the study."

The institution is a nonpartisan, nonprofit organization engaged in research and education in the social sciences.

Mr. Calkins said that any study by Brookings would result in a "background paper that would analyze issues" pertaining to conflicting rights in television and press coverage of judicial proceedings.

Referring to a Gallup poll taken last week, Dr. Stanton said that 71 per cent of those interviewed said they wanted to have Presidential campaign debates this year just as in 1960. Last year the House of Representatives and the Senate passed separate and slightly different bills calling for a temporary waiver of the equal-time law in order to accommodate televised debates between the two major candidates.

James T. Aubrey Jr., president of the C.B.S. television network, told affiliate representatives that they would be paid for carrying the National Football League games during the regular season in 1964 and 1965. When C.B.S. bought rights for the huge fee of $28.2 million, it had informed affiliates that station payments would be eliminated.

SENATE PANEL VOTES TO EASE NEWS FLOW

WASHINGTON, July 21 (UPI) — The Senate Judiciary Committee approved today a bill to give news media more access to Government information.

A committee spokesman said the legislation would amend the present public information law to make it "a disclousure rather than a withholding statute."

He said that, for the first time, the law would grant news media the right to go to court and force a Government agency to reveal information if it could not justify withholding it.

The legislation is part of a freedom-of-information bill that also was discussed today at a Senate Judiciary subcommittee hearing.

The subcommittee conducted hearings on the possibility of combining the over-all bill and another measure relating to the qualifications of attorneys who practice before administrative agencies.

PHILADELPHIA BAR TO VOTE ON PRESS

Special to The New York Times

PHILADELPHIA, Oct. 23—The 3,700-member Philadelphia Bar Association will vote at a special meeting Nov. 9 on a new statement dealing with "recommendations concerning fair trial and free press."

The statement was adopted unanimously by a joint committee of the Bar Association and some sections of the news media. Representatives of the city's three major daily newspapers—The Bulletin, Inquirer and Daily News—did not participate.

After noting that it was the mutual obligation of both the bar and the news media to safeguard "the socially necessary function of a free press in its obligation to inform the public and the rights of individuals to fair trial," the statement declares:

"It is desirable, therefore, for both the bar and the news media to establish standards of self-restraint which provide reasonable guidelines in reporting pre-trial and trial procedures.

"The following specific areas are especially susceptible to prejudicing the rights of the accused and, therefore, it is agreed when a suspect is arrested, every member of the community is equally concerned that the suspect be freed if innocent of the charge against him and convicted if guilty.

"This demands that the suspect's jury decide his cases only upon the law and the evidence submitted at the trial.

"Unless there are overriding public policy considerations, it is suggested that the news media do not publish the prior criminal history of the accused, purported admissions or confessions made by the accused in the absence of his council, or expressions of the guilt or innocence of the accused."

The statement also suggested that joint discussions be continued through permanent committees "in order to obtain and maintain agreement on fundamental principles dealing with free press and fair trial."

"Our constitutional right to the unfettered dissemination of news, and our constitutional right to fair trial on the merits, unaffected by prejudgement or passions," the statement continued, "are equally essential to our liberty and well-being."

"All who have considered the problem involved in the simultaneous application of both these principles share the desire to protect and cherish both of them," it goes on.

"It is obviously more desirable to solve the above problems by standards of self-restraint than by rules of court or legislation," it concludes.

INFORMATION BILL SENT TO JOHNSON

House Votes, 307-0, to Open Federal Records to Public

By WILLIAM M. BLAIR

Special to The New York Times

WASHINGTON, June 20 — A bill to grant Americans the right of access to Federal records cleared Congress today and was sent to President Johnson.

The House passed the measure by a vote of 307 to 0. The bill, designed to insure the public's right to know about Government affairs, also specifies categories of information that could be kept secret. The Senate passed the bill last Oct. 13.

President Johnson is expected to sign the bill, although some Government officials believe that freedom of information is the concern of the Executive department, not Congress.

Nevertheless, Representative John E. Moss told the House today that the measure had been "worked out carefully with the cooperation of White House officials and representatives of major government agencies."

House passage was a personal victory for Mr. Moss, who spent 10 years fighting to remove barriers to information on Government activities and action. The California Democrat is chairman of the Foreign Operations and Government Information subcommittee of the House Committee on Government Operations.

Mr. Moss said that "most important" was the provision of the bill that calls for court review of a refusal to make information available.

"It is this device which expands the rights of the citizens and which protects them against arbitrary and capricious denials," he told the House.

The bill provides that a person may seek recourse in Federal District courts in cases where information has been withheld. The courts shall have jurisdiction to enjoin an agency from the withholding of records and to order the production of records improperly withheld from a complainant.

In the event of noncompliance with the court's order, the District Court may punish the responsible officers for contempt. The bill proscribes no penalties.

This is "the first time in our Government's history," Mr. Moss said, "that there will be proper arbitration of conflicts over access to Government documents."

The bill applies only to agencies of the Executive branch of the Federal Government. It would not affect the public's right to get more information from Congress, and it does not deal with Executive privilege—the power Presidents have used to keep some information from Congress.

Thirty-seven states have "open records" laws similar to the one approved today, according to the Freedom of Information Committee of Sigma Delta Chi, the honorary journalism fraternity, which supported the measure. Twenty-nine states also have "open meeting" statutes.

House passage came in little over an hour. No voice was raised against the bill after Mr. Moss asserted that the problem was not political but was one that would exist "as long as we have representative government."

Senator Edward V. Long, Democrat of Missouri, who sponsored the bill in the Senate, called final passage a "historic victory for the public's constitutional right to know what their government is doing."

The bill amends the "public information" section of the 20-year-old Administrative Procedure Act. This permits the withholding of any Federal records if secrecy is required "in the public interest" or if the records relate "solely to the internal management of an agency."

Text of Johnson's Statement on the Information Bill

SAN ANTONIO, Tex., July 4 (AP)—Following is the text of a statement issued by President Johnson on the signing of the freedom of information bill:

The measure I sign today, S. 1160, revises Section 3 of the Administrative Procedure Act to provide guidelines for the public availability of the records of Federal departments and agencies.

This legislation springs from one of our most essential principles: A democracy works best when the people have all the information that the security of the nation permits. No one should be able to pull curtains of secrecy around decisions which can be revealed without injury to the public interest.

At the same time, the welfare of the nation or the rights of individuals may require that some documents not be made available. As long as threats to peace exist, for example, there must be military secrets. A citizen must be able in confidence to complain to his Government and to provide information, just as he is—and should be—free to confide in the press without fear of reprisal or of being required to reveal or discuss his source.

Protection a Right

Fairness to individuals also requires that information accumulated in personnel files be protected from disclosure. Officials within Government must be able to communicate with one another fully and frankly without publicity. They cannot operate effectively if required to disclose information prematurely or to make public investigative files and internal instructions that guide them in arriving at their decisions.

I know that the sponsors of this bill recognize these important interests and intend to provide for both the need of the public for access to information and the need of Government to protect certain categories of information. Both are vital to the welfare of our people.

Moreover, this bill in no way impairs the President's power under our Constitution to provide for confidentiality when the national interest so requires. There are some who have expressed concern that the language of this bill will be construed in such a way as to impair Government operations. I do not share this concern.

I have always believed that freedom of information is so vital that only the national security, not the desire of public officials or private citizens, should determine when it must be restricted.

I am hopeful that the needs I have mentioned can be served by a constructive approach to the wording and spirit and legislative history of this measure. I am instructing every official in this Administration to cooperate to this end and to make information available to the full extent consistent with individual privacy and with the national interest.

I signed this measure with a deep sense of pride that the United States is an open society in which the people's right to know is cherished and guarded.

July 5, 1966

NEWS MANIPULATION BY U.S. IS CHARGED

MEXICO CITY, Sept. 27 (UPI) News management and the apathy of the press in fighting it are today's greatest and growing danger to the United States Government and a free press, Frank R. Ahlgren, editor of the Memphis (Tenn.) Commercial Appeal, said today.

Speaking at the third work session of the seventh annual United Press International editors' conference, Mr. Ahlgren attacked "cynical news manipulators in Washington" to whom he attributed "the stream of lies and calculated misinformation coming from Government sources."

He spoke after Phil Newsom, foreign news analyst of United Press International, in a report on Vietnam, said the American people might not be getting the full story behind the war. Mr. Newsom, just back from Saigon, said "the fault lies in Washington."

The conference is attended by 300 United States editors and publishers.

September 28, 1966

Broadcasters Face Inquiry

WASHINGTON, Oct. 22 (UPI) — The chairman of the House Commerce Committee served notice on broadcasters today that he would investigate the practice of radio and television stations endorsing political candidates next year. Representative Harley O. Staggers, Democrat of West Virginia, said Congress never intended that broadcasters should have this right when they receive an operating license from the Government.

October 23, 1966

Aides Reporting to Johnson About Talks With Newsmen

WASHINGTON, Feb. 21 (AP) —President Johnson is getting periodic reports on conversations between top Federal officials and newsmen.

The White House press secretary, George Christian, said today that all of Mr. Johnson's special assistants at the White House advised him daily of "such press contacts as have any significance."

In addition, he said, some officials outside the White House "send in such information as they think I may need."

Asked if these accounts of interviews were relayed to Mr. Johnson, Mr. Christian said, "When some of it is pertinent or informative, I do send him a memo on it."

The press secretary said the main purpose of the system was to help him coordinate information activities and keep informed about questions being raised by reporters.

February 22, 1967

Johnson Threat to Cabinet On News Releases Reported

President Johnson is reported to have warned the members of his Cabinet once that if they did not stop issuing premature news releases he would "put a couple of professional politicians in your offices to show you fellows how to do it."

"Now I've told you before to stop this practice," Mr. Johnson is quoted in the current issue of McCall's as having told his Cabinet. "I don't like to see publicity on matters that haven't been reported out of committee."

The President is quoted as having said later in the same Cabinet meeting: "If you don't get your legislation passed, all the announcements will do no good at all."

The McCall's article is based on a forthcoming book by Jim Bishop, "A Day in the Life of a President."

March 22, 1967

PENTAGON AIDE FINDS NEWS BAR EXCESSIVE

WASHINGTON, April 20 (AP)—The Defense Department's new public affairs chief agreed today with members of the House Government Information Subcommittee that too much Pentagon information was classified.

"Not only is this information denied to the people, but over-classification tends to downgrade the security system and is apt to result in inadequate protection being given that information which truly must be kept secure." the public affairs official, Assistant Secretary of Defense Phil G. Goulding testified.

Mr. Goulding outlined a number of areas, including troop movements and access to Kwajelein atoll in the Marshall Islands and crash scenes in which his office was seeking declassification or greater access for newsmen.

Representative John E. Moss, Democrat of California, chairman of the committee, called Mr. Goulding's testimony refreshing because of his emphasis on "the importance of disclosure."

The only disagreement between members of the subcommittee and Mr. Goulding came over the Pentagon policy requiring officers to report to their superiors on any conversations with reporters when public affairs officials were not present.

"I am most hopeful." Mr. Moss said, "that the directive will be rescinded."

April 21, 1967

McNamara Drops Curb On News Interviews

WASHINGTON, June 30 (UPI) — Defense Secretary Robert S. McNamara today rescinded an order that required Pentagon officials to report conversations with newsmen to the public information office.

The memorandum was issued Oct. 27, 1962, by Arthur Sylvester, then Assistant Secretary of Defense for Public Affairs. It provided that no report need be made if a public information official sat in on the interview.

Mr. McNamara said the memorandum had been issued to discourage individual armed services and defense bureaus from voicing their own view and ignoring the broader national interests.

He said that "special pleading by narrow special interests has largely been ended within the department."

July 1, 1967

343

RESTRAINT URGED IN RACE RIOT NEWS

U.S. Officials Seek Delays Pending Police Action

By FRED P. GRAHAM
Special to The New York Times

WASHINGTON, July 7 — Officials of the Justice Department have been quietly meeting with news media representatives in racially tense cities to urge restraint in reporting racial outbursts, a department spokesman said today.

The efforts are aimed at persuading local radio and television stations not to broadcast news of incipient riots until the police have had time to reach the scene and bring the incidents under control.

A spokesman for the Community Relations Service, the racial conciliation arm of the Justice Department, said today that meetings had been held since April with city officials and news media representatives in a dozen cities. Among them were New York, Indianapolis, Milwaukee, New Orleans, Chicago, Houston, St. Louis, Omaha and Buffalo.

The meeting in Buffalo was held during the first week in June, three weeks before a four-day rampage by Negro youths broke out. The spokesman said the media there had not prepared new procedures by the time the rioting occurred. But he said that one radio station had immediately issued guidelines to its newscasters in an attempt to avoid inflammatory reporting.

More Meetings Planned

The Community Relations Service is planning similar meetings in four or five other cities, including Washington. Government officials would not identify the other cities for fear of stirring up racial troubles there.

The spokesman said that leaders in a few cities had turned thumbs down on the meetings. These cities were not identified. News media representatives also balked in a few cases, not wanting to be bound by news reporting guidelines,

the spokesman said.

According to the spokesman, the Community Relations Service invited police officials and newsmen to meet together in each city. They were given papers outlining a system that had been worked out in Chicago for handling disaster news by the broadcast media.

The "Chicago plan" was worked out in 1955 after radio reports of an airplane crash brought thousands of spectators to the scene before ambulances arrived. This delayed the hospitalization of the crash victims.

Under the plan, broadcasters in Chicago agreed not to report disturbances that had been broadcast on the police radio until they received clearance from the police. The police, in turn, broadcast information as soon as possible on whether the incident had been brought under control, or on whether it was so far out of control that disclosure would not affect it.

According to the Community Relations Service, the radio stations and the police in Omaha adopted a version of this plan last month for use in racial flare-ups.

Meeting Held Here

The Community Relations Service sponsored a meeting between representatives of the news media and human rights groups and policemen on May 6 at the Brotherhood in Action Building in Manhattan.

Roger W. Wilkins, the service's director, asked then that discretion be used in handling racial flare-ups for fear of distorting the incidents and possibly making them seem larger than they were.

The meeting was attended by about 75 persons, including representatives from the Mayor's office, the police, the Human Rights Commissions of New York City, New York State, New Jersey, and Connecticut and the news media.

Jacques Nevard, deputy commissioner for press relations for the New York Police Department, said that no specific agreements had been sought from broadcasters in the city.

He said: "All we did was ask the news media to do such things as check rumors with us, and we, for our part, agreed to answer their questions and provide the news as quickly as possible." The situation has "never been a problem here," he added.

July 8, 1967

F.C.C. Exempts Newcasts From 'Personal Attack' Rule

WASHINGTON, Aug. 3 (UPI) —The Federal Communications Commission exempted news broadcasts and on-the-spot news coverage today from the "personal attack" provisions of its fairness doctrine.

Under the doctrine, a station airing such an attack is obliged to notify the person under attack and to provide him with a transcript. Under the new order, this will no longer be required for newscasts or for coverage of news stories as they are breaking.

The F.C.C. made it clear, however, that news interview shows and news documentaries must continue to meet all specifications of the fairness doctrine.

August 4, 1967

A Lively Impatience with the Status Quo

By JACK GOULD

A YOUNG, lithe maverick with a knack for phrase-making and a restless impatience with the status quo has burst upon the Washington broadcasting scene. He is Nicholas Johnson, and, in nine months as a member of the Federal Communications Commission, he has already established a record for yeasty dissent that clearly makes him the most controversial figure in the regulatory agency.

Two weeks ago, in condemning the wholesale renewal of hundreds of station licenses without fuller study of how the outlets had actually performed on the air, Commissioner Johnson accused the FCC majority of adopting a "complacent and comfortable hear-no-evil, see-no-evil slouch in front of the radio and television sets of America." He likened the FCC to a sturdy tower of ambivalence that was born of the conflict between authority and inaction and suggested that the public had been massively hoodwinked into believing that the commission was a guardian of standards in broadcasting.

In an even more publicized case, that of the proposed mergers of the American Broadcasting Company and the International Telephone and Telegraph Corporation, Commissioner Johnson not only condemned the deal itself as contrary to the public interest, but also roasted his colleagues for giving it the once-over-lightly treatment. Within the commission, he had support from Commissioner Kenneth A. Cox and particularly veteran Commissioner Robert T. Bartley, who actually was first to speak out against the merger. After the belated intervention from the Department of Justice, the agency now has set down the merger for a further hearing.

Typically, however, it was one of Commissioner Johnson's reservations that attracted attention: Because of IT&T's vast overseas interests he wondered if a merger would hobble the independence of ABC News. That Nicholas Johnson should spawn an instant storm

within the FCC was not altogether a surprise since in his previous governmental post (Maritime Commissioner), he had the shipping industry in a furor. At that time opinions of Johnson varied, depending on with whom—and where—one took refreshments in Washington. Some found him a stimulating new spirit in the Maritime Administration; others found him a regulatory batsman who was better at wild swinging than hitting the ball.

*

When President Johnson appointed Nicholas Johnson to the FCC last June it was no secret that the White House hoped the new commissioner would not immediately don the mantle of a rugged crusader. There were even hints that after several years Commissioner Johnson might be in line for the chairmanship.

Neither hope nor hint apparently affected Commissioner Johnson's zeal to travel his own road; he's been a man on the move for

Nicholas Johnson of the FCC
A rugged crusader!

The New York Times (George Tames)

quite a while. A 32-year-old Unitarian and a Democrat who received his law degree and a Phi Beta Kappa key from the University of Texas, he served as clerk to Associate Justice Hugo L. Black, taught at the University of California Law School, practiced law in Washington and then was tapped for the Maritime Administrator's job.

His legal forte has always been the bewildering intricacies of the regulatory agencies; in crossing the FCC threshold he immediately made clear that he was not interested in the minutiae of radio and television but rather in what he deemed to be the big issues slighted in the FCC's preoccupation with its mammoth workload of a routine character.

In speeches and dissents, Commissioner Johnson quickly observed that almost all important social and technical research in communications is done *outside* the government—yet the FCC is charged by Congress with taking the initiative in developing communications. He believes government could profitably invest in planning and research of a magnitude no less than that supported by the American Telephone and Telegraph Company.

The canvas upon which the Commissioner is placing his first independent strokes covers, in effect, the panoramic scene of communications. In a nutshell, he argues that standards of program performance, UHF television, pay television, separation of AM and FM radio stations, constantly escalating profits of commercial TV, satellites, educational TV, channel and trafficking in station ownerships cannot be judged in isolation, but must be taken as part of a whole requiring coherent direction and focus.

Droll broadcasters cynically observe that eager new FCC commissioners and the Russians usually have much in common: they always think they were the first to discover broadcasting. And, admittedly, Johnson is a good deal more persuasive in posing some of

the problems that lie ahead than in working out the pragmatic solutions. The fate of many of his ideas really turns on doubling or tripling the FCC budget. Congress, meanwhile, has made it clear that it doesn't want too strong a regulatory agency and has shown scant willingness to go along. This was the roadblock that ultimately disillusioned Newton N. Minow and E. William Henry. Congress sets up a body supposedly strong in expertise and then never trusts it to resolve big problems.

*

Nonetheless, Johnson obviously is going to be a commissioner to watch. His tart criticism and pursuit of publicity have not endeared him to all his colleagues who have worried for many years over the causes he espouses. His is the thrill of a new romance to be expected of an active mind suddenly immersed in the unending ramifications of communications. When he finds himself out-voted for a few more months, the virus of frustration may set in, as it did with most of his provocative predecessors. And the route from an FCC chair to an industry job is a well-trod path.

But conceivably Johnson may have luck and historical timing on his side. The debate over educational TV, satellites, the proposed ABC-ITT merger, the explosive entry of the commercial networks into publishing and ever-soaring profits of video are creating a climate for a basic social and economic re-examination of the broadcasting media. A lively scrapper who is determined to ask questions as if they had never been asked before could have a valuable role as a progressive catalyst. The broadcasters who thought the Washington scene was likely to quiet down may have been stronger on wish-fulfillment than realism. At least in Nicholas Johnson there is a twist: so far he has been rougher on the FCC and, inferentially, on Congress than on the industry. Coping with *that* ploy could be something pretty different.

F.C.C. Sets Rules Clarifying Doctrine On Right of Reply

WASHINGTON, July 6 (AP) —The Federal Communications Commission made public today new rules under which a broadcasting station that criticizes an individual over the air must supply him with a transcript of the broadcast and offer an opportunity to reply.

The new rules also require that if a station is to broadcast an editorial within 72 hours of an election day, the individual or group criticized in the editorial must be notified before it is broadcast.

The commission adopted the new regulations unanimously at its meeting yesterday. The regulations were issued under the commission's fairness doctrine, which requires that all sides of controversial issues be given a chance to be heard on broadcasting stations.

This doctrine was recently upheld by the United States Court of Appeals for the District of Columbia.

The new rules require notification and an offer of time within one week in cases of a personal attack over the air and within 24 hours in the case of a broadcast editorial.

An F.C.C. statement said the rules were issued to clarify the obligations of broadcasters "where they have aired personal attacks and editorials regarding political candidates." The commission's action also permits it to impose fines in case of violations.

The F.C.C. said the new regulations, in its view, neither alter nor add to the substance of the fairness doctrine, but simply clarify it and make it more precise.

INFORMATION LAW EFFECTIVE TODAY

But Agencies Expect Little Change in Disclosing Data

WASHINGTON, July 3 (AP) —Federal agencies will begin working tomorrow under a new Freedom of Information Act, but few of them expect important changes in the way they disclose public records.

Despite this consensus among administrators, Congressional supporters of the law say they will make sure it is observed.

Senator Edward V. Long, Democrat, the Senate sponsor of the bill, said he was "sure that there are bureaucrats who are going to hang on to their secrecy until the bitter end."

But, he added, "we've worked far too long and hard on this law to see it mangled by Federal red tape."

One agency official, questioned in a survey conducted to see how the new law will change procedures, replied: "I don't see three cents worth of difference."

Several other administrators said they thought the law was confusing and open to different interpretations. And Attorney General Ramsey Clark said "definitive answers may have to await court rulings."

The law provides that any citizen may see any government document in the files—but lists nine categories of material that are exempt from this stipulation. These range from defense secrets to interagency memos to files that, if made public, would invade an individual's privacy.

As for files not exempt, many agencies said in the survey that they had been making them available to the public all along.

A typical comment in this regard came from George Christian, the White House press secretary, who said: "We give you everything that isn't classified."

Mr. Christian noted that routine working papers were stamped "for administrative use only," which in effect makes them secret.

March 26, 1967   July 7, 1967   July 4, 1967

Spirit of Information

The significance of the Freedom of Information Law which symbolically took effect July 4 cannot be measured in statutory words alone. Government bureaucrats can take comfort in both the rules and the exceptions. What is more important is that such a law is on the books at all. How it will work will depend primarily on the tone and style set by the Administration and Congress.

The new law's most important provision establishes the right of judicial review of administrative decisions to withhold records, with the burden on the Government to justify any censorship. The new law is expected to make it easier to ascertain contents of Government contracts, the procedures of Federal agencies, and how members of regulatory bodies vote.

But this does not mean that the Government's confidential or commercial records will be thrown open to the public. Restrictions on security matters—if not managed to deceive press and public — have long been accepted. So, too, personal facts about both Government employes and private citizens whose names are in Government files should be safeguarded. Difficulties may arise in the in-between area where powerful agencies are asked to disclose records on their regulations and decisions. Here is where the public's right to know can become a reality if not blocked by bureaucratic subterfuge.

CONGRESS POLLED ON NEWS ETHICS

Many Favor Code to Cover Capitol Correspondents

By JOHN HERBERS
Special to The New York Times

WASHINGTON, Nov. 6 — A poll of Representatives and Senators indicates that many favor the adoption of a code of ethics for news-gathering personnel accredited to cover Congress.

The poll, conducted by Representative William L. Hungate, Democrat of Missouri, further indicates:

¶Members of Congress believe that radio does a better job of covering national issues than newspapers and television do and is more accurate in reporting Congressional activities.

¶U.S. News & World Report is the news magazine preferred by most members of Congress, and the most frequently read newspaper column is that by Rowland Evans and Robert Novak.

These findings were based on 150 replies that Mr. Hungate received in response to questionnaires sent to all 433 Representatives and 100 Senators.

Most Replies Unsigned

This, he said, was not a scientific sample because most of the replies were unsigned, and he did not know the party affiliation or regional breakdown of those replying.

He said, however, that he thought the replies had been sufficient to convey in general what members thought about the performance of journalists and broadcasters who report on Congress.

Mr. Hungate announced the results at a news conference in the Rayburn House Office Building this morning. Because "the conduct, qualifications, efficiency and ethics of Congressmen are frequently a matter of journalistic interest," Mr. Hungate said, he thought "a reverse appraisal might prove interesting."

Congress has been criticized this year in the area of ethics.

Also this year the House refused to seat Adam Clayton Powell, Democrat of Harlem, on a charge of misuse of public funds, and the Senate censured Thomas J. Dodd, Democrat of Connecticut on a charge of misuse of campaign funds.

The Senate ethics committee investigated a charge by Life magazine that Edward V. Long, Democrat of Missouri, had used his office in an unsuccessful attempt to help James Hoffa, the Teamsters president, evade conviction for jury tampering. The committee found no basis for the charge.

Ethics Code Sought

Representatives appointed to a permanent committee to deal with the problem of ethics have been attempting to draft a code of conduct that would be accepted by the full House. The Senate ethics committee has been doing the same.

Mr. Hungate is a 44-year-old Harvard-educated lawyer whose district, along the Mississippi River north of St. Louis, includes Clarksville, the home town of Senator Long. He has been in Congress since 1964.

One of the questions sent to members asked: "Would you favor a code of ethics to be adopted for application to all radio, TV and newspaper personnel accredited to House and Senate galleries?"

Of the replies, 91 said they would, 43 said they would not and 11 had no opinion.

Reporters accredited to the Congressional galleries are now subject to admissions tests approved by Congress and administered by an elected committee of correspondents.

Under the rules, they must be bona fide correspondents of good repute, with news work their principal source of income; they may not be engaged in publicity work, may not be lobbyists and may not be on the Government payroll.

Press Group Hails Easing of Secrecy During 1967

By DONALD JANSON
Special to The New York Times

CHICAGO, Nov. 12 — Sigma Delta Chi, the professional journalism society, issued a report today calling 1967 "a historic turning point" for efforts to limit secrecy in Government.

But the report, by the organization's freedom of information committee, also accused the Johnson Administration of impeding even greater progress.

The report was issued by Sigma Delta Chi headquarters here in advance of the society's annual convention in Minneapolis, beginning Wednesday.

It called the Freedom of Information Act, which went into effect July 4, a major "breakthrough" in journalism's drive for greater access to public information.

The act makes all Government documents and records available to the press unless national security, invasion of personal privacy or other overriding reasons exempt them.

The report cited many instances in which reporters had used the law to penetrate bureaucratic secrecy in Federal agencies.

But the committee questioned whether President Johnson himself was making an effort to comply with the spirit of his own pronouncement in signing the act.

"A democracy works best when the people have all the information that the security of the nation permits," he said then. "No one should be able to pull curtains of secrecy around decisions which can be revealed without injury to the public interest . . . I signed this measure with a deep sense of pride that the United States is an open society in which the people's right to know is cherished and guarded."

McNamara Move Hailed

The President has belied these "fine words," the report said, by continuing to organize impromptu Presidential press conferences to exclude many media representatives and to employ them for "a White House snow job."

It was equally critical of the State and Defense departments.

The committee applauded Defense Secretary Robert S. McNamara for abolishing his five-year-old department rule that all Pentagon officials, who talked to newsmen must make a report on those contacts before the end of the working day.

But it criticized the department for continuing to "pour out inaccurate information on everything from the controversial TFX [multi-service fighter-bomber] matter to the question of whether there was Joint Chiefs disagreement over the conduct of the Vietnam war."

The committee called the White House and Pentagon "the two most difficult" news sources to budge in seeking compliance with the new law.

It also accused the State Department of misusing the claim of national security to withhold information, but it said the new law had been effective in an indirect way.

"Perhaps the most salutary effect," the committee said, "is the one hardest to measure—the influence it has had on the attitude of Government officials. Many public information officers have commented that the law gives them an effective weapon to use internally against the policy makers whose inclination is to hide facts."

On another issue, the report of the American Bar Association Committee on Fair Trial and Free Press, which will be acted on by the bar group next February, is "an open invitation for arbitrary actions by courts that are corrupt or blind to the necessity of avoiding undue restraint upon the information available on crime, criminal law enforcement and the courts."

If adopted, the report would severely restrict members in disclosing information on arrests, trials and other aspects of pending cases.

The report said that there was a "continuing need" to expose "untruths and misleading statements that are the credibility gap" in the Johnson Administration.

November 13, 1967

Washington: The Politicians and the Broadcasters

By JAMES RESTON

WASHINGTON, Dec. 21 — The television networks and stations of this country are obviously going to have a rough time during the Presidential election campaign, for they are stuck with a set of Federal Communications Commission regulations that are impractical if not unworkable and unconstitutional.

For example, when President Johnson said on his latest national TV broadcast that he "didn't know what the effect of the Kennedy - McCarthy movement is having in the country" but that he did "know of the interest of both of them in the Presidency and the ambition of both of them," Senator Eugene McCarthy's campaign manager demanded that the three major TV networks give the Senator a half hour of free time on the ground that this was a "personal attack" on the Senator. C.B.S. is saying no, and for good reasons.

The Back Stairs Tricks

The background of this broadcast clearly indicates the President's political interest in his performance. First, the interview with the C.B.S., N.B.C. and A.B.C. White House correspondents was recorded on tape the day before it was shown. It ran more than fifteen minutes beyond the hour show and the White House requested the right to suggest what should go in and what should come out if "national security" considerations were involved.

The networks agreed to this in principle, but the cuts proposed by the White House involved several that had nothing to do with "national security," and the President was so concerned to get the cuts he wanted that he took a copy of the tape along on Air Force One when he flew off to Australia and kept radioing back more "suggestions" on the way.

In the case of this broadcast, the White House not only tried to manage the news but tried to manage the advertisements about the news as well. On the morning of the broadcast a half-page ad was offered to The New York Times, The Washington Post and The Los Angeles Times which looked as if it had been sponsored by the networks themselves. Actually, it was paid for by a friend of the President and arranged through the Washington ad agency that usually represents the Democratic National Committee.

Finally, the President did take a dig at both McCarthy and Kennedy by implying that there was collusion between them in what he called "the Kennedy-McCarthy movement," but if this is the worst "personal attack" Senator McCarthy has to endure in the coming months, he will set a record for political immunity.

Nevertheless, the F.C.C. rules on "personal attack" enable any politician to demand free time to reply to anything he considers an attack by another politician or even a news commentator, regardless of whether the offending remark is true or not.

"When," says Section 73.123 of the F.C.C. regulations, "during the presentation of views on a controversial question of public importance, an attack is made upon the honesty, character, integrity or like personal qualities of an identified person or group, the licensee [station or network] shall, within a reasonable time and in no event later than one week after the attack . . . offer a reasonable opportunity to respond over the licensee's facilities."

The Loose Regulations

What is "an attack"? How do you define "honesty, character, integrity or like personal qualities? Suppose Eric Sevareid, in a moment of reckless impetuosity, were to suggest one night that Jimmy Hoffa and Bobby Baker are men of dubious character, and Jimmy objects—is C.B.S. to set up a color camera in jail and let Mr. Hoffa proclaim his integrity to the nation?

Time for Review

This whole field of television and politics could stand a review before the oratorical avalanche hits us at the end of the winter. It should not be impossible for the public to know who sponsored political advertisements, or whether a Presidential "conversation" is being shown as it was or as it came out after being edited by the President and his staff.

And if a newspaper can suggest that a politician is not necessarily of saintly character without having to print his assertions that he is a saint, why should a television station be expected to follow totally different rules?

Fortunately, this F.C.C. regulation is now being tested in the courts, not because the principle of the personal attack doctrine is wrong, but because the rule was obviously written by some lawyer who didn't understand the meaning of words or the practical operations of either broadcasters or politicians. The hope here is that next year the rule will be changed, but there is no guarantee that the courts will take note of the election calendar.

December 22, 1967

EDITORS SEEK RIGHT TO INSPECT RECORDS

ALBANY, Feb. 6 (AP)—The New York State Society of Newspaper Editors today urged enactment of a broad state law that would permit newsmen to inspect the records of public agencies.

Millard Browne of The Buffalo News said that 37 states had adopted such laws and that the New York State Legislature should follow suit.

A resolution calling for adoption of such legislation was approved unanimously by members attending the society's three-day winter meeting, which concluded today.

The editors recommended that the records of all agencies, corporations and authorities of government be open for inspection, unless otherwise specified for such records as welfare rolls.

New Freedom of Information Law: Fact-Seekers Testing Its Effectiveness

By JOSEPH A. LOFTUS
Special to The New York Times

WASHINGTON, Feb. 17 — The Veterans Administration, using public funds, tested for its own purposes several brands of hearing aids. Consumers Union asked for the results and was refused. It has appealed to the V.A.'s chief medical director, possibly as a preliminary move to court action.

An officer at Fort Myer, Va., using postage-free stationery, solicited Washington liquor lobbyists and wholesalers to provide 372 fifths of liquor for a Valentine's Day Army ball.

Requests for a copy of that letter, and another letter apparently withdrawing the solicitation, were refused at first on the ground that disclosure "would serve no useful purpose." An appeal to a higher level in the Army brought a reversal of that decision. The appeal was based on the freedom of information law of 1967.

The Interior Department refused to give the Shell Oil Company access to records of mining claims in Colorado. The company went to court and a district judge there ruled that the records were not protected by the "internal memorandums" or "investigatory files" exceptions of the new law. The Government released the requested data.

Request Was Rejected

The Barceloneta Shoe Corporation of San Juan, P.R., which was accused of unfair labor practices, sued for access to all the evidence of the case in the files of the National Labor Relations Board. A Federal court rejected the company's request.

At least 12 of these suits have been filed since the new law took effect last July 4. Only two cases have been decided. None was filed by a publication.

The fact-seekers win some and lose some. The testing process probably will go on for several years before the real effect of the law is clear.

"Only a novice in governmental affairs," said the American Bar Association's utility section newsletter of Jan. 1, "would anticipate that passage of the Freedom of Information Act last July portends any universal voluntary change in the traditional determination of Government agencies to conduct their business in secrecy.

"Interagency and intraagency reports will not be released except under compulsion and under the policy of Congress. Compulsion can only be supplied by Federal district courts."

Kennedy Pact Released

The effect of the law cannot be measured in court decisions alone. The National Archives has an agreement with the Kennedy family that the pictures and X-rays of President John F. Kennedy's body will not be made available to serious scholars and experts until 1971. The New York Times asked to see the agreement.

The Archivist, Dr. Robert H. Bahmer, called back the next day and said that after checking the Freedom of Information Act, he felt the terms of the agreement could not be kept confidential. He released the agreement for publication after notifying the Kennedy family.

The Washington Post asked the Health, Education and Welfare Department for investigators' reports of racial discrimination in the Mississippi welfare program. The request was refused until The Post invoked the new law and filed with the department a written challenge of the decision to withhold.

Business Week, a McGraw-Hill publication, used the threat of the law to get from the Defense Department the amounts bid by unsuccessful competitors on contracts to supply drugs to the military services.

The Union Carbide Corporation obtained from the Public Health Service the details of medical examinations of miners suffering from uranium poisoning. The company first obtained authorizations from each miner.

The Federal Reserve Board, largely because of the law, is now publishing, three months after the event, a summary of the decisions of the key Federal Open Market Committee, which meets every three weeks. Before, this information had been published only once a year.

Samuel J. Archibald, director of the Washington office of the University of Washington's Freedom of Information Center, in a discussion of the law, said:

"The value of the law depends not only upon court enforcement but, even more important, upon intelligent administration and upon continued public pressure.

"Some of the regulations issued by Federal agencies to administer the law are good. Others show that some Federal officials still have a minimum regard for the people's right to know the facts of government."

Second Look Succeeds

"The mere threat of a suit, in some cases, has influenced the Government agencies to take a second look at their information practices, and the second look often resulted in disclosure.

"By granting any person the right of access to Government records and by permitting court enforcement of that right, the law removed decisions on disclosure of public information from the lower levels of bureaucracy. The top officials who now make the decisions are much more responsive to the democratic pressures implicit in the people's right to know.

Arbitrary refusals to disclose information — the hallmark of the petty bureaucrat — are becoming fewer and fewer."

Still, many requests are rejected and, so far as could be learned, the agencies are standing their ground.

John Herling of the National Newspaper Syndicate learned that the Kennecott Copper Corporation and the Peabody Coal Company has asked the Federal Trade Commission for a premerger clearance. The clearance was denied but the commission made no announcement and would not admit it had made a decision. Mr. Herling asked for the vote and how each commissioner voted. The request was refused. He is preparing a formal challenge.

Clearance Data Refused

The Justice Department, which also considers premerger clearance requests, has refused to say whether it has given clearance in particular cases.

The Securities and Exchange Commission regards its correspondence with the New York Stock Exchange, for example, as "internal papers."

Futile requests for access to this correspondence have been made by The New York Times and presumably by other newspapers.

News hunters are often frustrated by means other than a flat refusal of disclosure. Delay is often the equal of denial. What is news today may be worthless tomorrow.

Many agencies want requests for information channeled through their public information offices, a system that often denies a reporter access to the Government source best qualified to answer the questions.

Many office holders have been geared over the years to that system, so they buck even the routine questions to the public information office. The effect often is delay and professionally shaped and filtered information.

The idea of freedom of information, and the action that translated that idea into a statute, were based on the public's right to know and were not particularly for the benefit of the press. The press serves as a channel for the transmission of Government information, but there is much information in which the press is not interested.

An insurance company, for example, wanted from the Defense Department the names of discharged service men. The request was refused on the ground that it would be an invasion of privacy.

This raises the question whether it is the business of the Pentagon to police the users of information that may otherwise be in the public domain, or whether a citizen's service and discharge is a private matter.

Center to Be Set Up

A Citizen's Advocate Center is about to make its appearance on the Washington scene. The Field Foundation and the Rockefeller Foundation have given it interim grants of $15,-000 each. The Ford Foundation is considering a request for more substantial funds.

Two lawyers, Edgar S. Cahn and Stephen Rosenfeld, are shaping the new center, which will try to extend the rule of law to the grant-making process in Government. Administrators, said Mr. Cahn, every day make cash grants that affect people's lives without their knowing what those determinations are or what they are based on.

Mr. Cahn and Jean Camper Cahn, his wife, who also is a lawyer, deal with the problem in an article that will be published next month by The Harvard Law Review.

They question some exemptions under the Freedom of Information Act, contending that they are "worded so ambiguously that they may undo all that the act sets out to accomplish."

Hinges on 2 Factors

Two factors, other than litigation and court decisions, they wrote, "will ultimately determine the import of this act."

"First," they said, "Congress must monitor implementation of this act carefully; there are already clear signs that at least certain Congressmen and Senators are prepared to do so.

"Second, and possibly more important, compliance will rest upon the extent to which the act is used by the general public, by the press and media, by grantees and citizen groups."

Congress itself is less than a model for open decisions openly arrived at. Congressional Quarterly, a private publication, reported that Congressional committees in 1967 held 39 per cent of their meetings in private. That is, 2,696 meetings were open and 1,716 meetings were closed. All 383 House Appropriations Committee meetings were closed.

"The reason usually is," said a long-time Capitol reporter, "that members don't want their constituents to find out and flood them with mail, phone calls and telegrams protesting this or that committee decision and demanding reversal of decisions. By the time the decisions become public knowledge it is often, if not always, too late to protest, as the bill has already been reported out."

CLIFFORD ORDERS INQUIRY ON LEAKS

Special to The New York Times

WASHINGTON, March 23—Secretary of Defense Clark Clifford has ordered a security investigation throughout the Defense Department after the publication of recent news articles allegedly based on classified information.

Government officials, who confirmed today that the inquiry was under way, said that since taking office Mr. Clifford had been unpleasantly surprised to read in several newspapers and journals information still considered to be top secret by his office. Mr. Clifford succeeded Robert S. McNamara as Secretary on March 1.

Among the newspapers privately cited by official sources were The New York Times, The Washington Star, The Washington Post and several trade journals specializing in technical military information.

These sources could not confirm that President Johnson had ordered the investigation, but they noted the President's known aversion to news leaks of any kind.

Reporters with long experience covering the Pentagon and other military headquarters noted that security investigations of alleged news leaks came in cycles and could generally be expected when a new Defense Secretary takes over.

In 1961, they recalled, premature publication of a top-secret Kennedy Administration memorandum, proposing the withdrawal of all nuclear weapons from the North Atlantic Treaty Organization, set off a wide hunt for the sources of the leak.

Report on F-111 Plane

The recent articles that appear to have especially attracted the attention of President Johnson, Secretary Clifford and senior Pentagon officials included the following from The New York Times.

¶March 8, reporting the imminent dispatch of the controversial F-111 swing-wing bombers for combat duty in Vietnam.

¶March 9, reporting that Gen. William C. Westmoreland had asked for 206,000 more troops for Vietnam. This request was said to have touched off a "divisive" internal debate high in the Johnson Administration.

¶March 12, reporting that Gen. Earle G. Wheeler, chairman of the Joint Chiefs of Staff, had discussed at the White House a plan for calling up about 30,000 reservists to permit the deployment of at least one combat division to Vietnam in the next several months.

¶March 20, quoting excerpts from General Westmoreland's year-end report to Washington, submitted 29 days before the recent enemy offensive. In it the United States military commander in South Vietnam predicted that the allied war gains of last year would be increased manyfold in 1968.

"The [Westmoreland] document was classified secret," one Government source said. "Obviously, when the Secretary or his security people see it in the newspapers, it's a direct challenge. Under the law it's their responsibility to stop publication of classified material and that's just what they're trying to do."

Other articles said to have aroused Pentagon ire included recent reports in The Washington Star of alleged deficiencies in the naval version of the F-111 bomber; and in The Washington Post and in several technical trade journals describing new combat materiel and techniques being used in Vietnam.

Informed sources denied that the word had gone out to civilian officials or to military officers throughout the Pentagon to avoid meeting newsmen.

Could Involve 5 Agencies

Officials were reluctant to discuss details of the inquiry. They confirmed, however, that at least five security services could be participating—the Defense Department's own security organization, under Solis Horwitz, Assistant Defense Secretary for Administration; the individual security services of the three armed services, and the F.B.I.

An F.B.I. spokesman declined comment on a report in The Washington Star last night that the bureau's agents were participating in the investigation.

At least one reporter, William Beecher of The Times, has already been questioned by Pentagon security agents about the sources of recent articles. Mr. Beecher declined to divulge the names of his sources.

"There's no law prohibiting newsmen from publishing anything they can get," one source said, "but there very definitely is a law prohibiting Government personnel from revealing classified information. It's not just a question of embarrassing the Administration — published quotes from a cabled document could jeopardize our codes."

There were private indications that the March 9 article in The Times reporting General Westmoreland's request for 206,000 more troops was being blamed in high Administration circles for contributing to the recent gold crisis by exacerbating international uncertainty about American military and fiscal escalation in the Vietnam war.

WATCHDOG PANEL IN HOUSE DISPUTE

By FELIX BELAIR Jr.
Special to The New York Times

WASHINGTON, April 17—An order abolishing the House watchdog Subcommittee on Freedom of Information and Government Operations has raised a storm of bipartisan protest in that body and threatens a split in the Democratic leadership.

The order, issued by Representative William L. Dawson, Democrat of Illinois, chairman of the parent Committee on Government Operations, would eliminate the only Congressional group with jurisdiction over compliance with the freedom of information law. Under the law, the only other recourse for appeals by the press would be the judicial process.

The chairman's order would also eliminate the group whose investigative work on foreign aid expenditures has been regarded as the most effective in Congress. Its continuing inquiries into black marketing and corruption, as well as failure of land reform in Vietnam and of self-help programs under the Alliance for Progress with Latin American countries, would be turned over to a subcommittee on special studies.

Mr. Dawson's order eliminating the subcommittee has been challenged by its chairman, John Moss of California, and the ranking Republican member, Ogden R. Reid of Westchester. Mr. Moss is the fourth ranking member of the House Democratic leadership, serving as assistant majority whip.

Mr. Moss has told friends that he will fight Mr. Dawson's order in the Government Operations Committee or on the floor of the House "if necessary." Observers believe that if the contest reaches the House floor it will result in an overwhelming victory for Mr. Moss.

Mr. Dawson's decision to abolish the Moss subcommittee was made known in a letter to Representative Florence P. Dwyer, Republican of Elizabeth, N. J., on April 11. In it, he mentioned a cut of $300,000 in subcommittee funds by the House Administration Committee from $850,000 to $550,000.

The letter did not mention that Democrats and Republicans on the subcommittee suggested at the time that a supplental appropriation might be submitted later in the year.

Mr. Dawson said, "The record is clear, however, that we must tighten up our operation and make some reduction in staff before we request such funds."

Reorganization Planned

"I have therefore decided," Mr. Dawson added, "to reorganize the committee on a seven subcommittee basis in accordance with jurisdictions. We would appreciate having your designation of an additional minority member for the special study committee, and any other changes in subcommittee membership."

Mr. Moss withheld comment on the Dawson plan and did not make public his letter to Mr. Dawson challenging it. However, the letter was understood to coincide with the following letter from Mr. Reid to Mr. Dawson:

"An attempt to muzzle the Subcommittee on Government Operations and Freedom of Information is a disservice to the nation at a time when the Congress bears an especial responsibility to the American people to provide independent information and evaluation.

"This is not an hour for politics, petty jurisdictional niceties nor for an arbitrary resurgence of the seniority system at the expense of the majority democratic process.

"Our system of Government works well only when decisions are reached on the basis of facts, clear principles and thoughtful advance consideration of alternatives.

"At a critical juncture in our affairs—when dissent is not always encouraged—the abolition of the watchdog subcommittee on foreign operations and freedom of information in the Congress should not be permitted."

Some members—Democratic and Republican—professed to be at a loss to understand the reasons for Mr. Dawson's order. There was general disbelief that it was for purposes of economy, and some suggested that the order was not his own but had been suggested by the executive branch.

The watchdog group has been critical of the Administration for the last two years, particularly in the matter of maladministration of foreign aid to South Vietnam. Its report on widespread corruption among Vietnamese officials was labeled by the General Accounting Office as a "milestone" in Congressional committee reporting.

More recently the watchdog group reported that the failure of land tenure reforms in South Vietnam threatened the stability of the Saigon Government. The panel suggested that even with a military victory against the North, the South Vietnamese still could lose the war in the absence of meaningful land reform.

The subcommittee is now reviewing the efficacy of the Alliance for Progress, for which the Administration has asked an appropriation of $625-million in the fiscal year beginning July 1.

April 18, 1968

DAWSON MAY RETAIN INFORMATION PANEL

WASHINGTON, May 7 (AP)—Representative William L. Dawson, apparently abandoning plans to abolish the Subcommittee on Foreign Operations and Government Information, has asked more money to let it continue.

The subcommittee, headed by Representative John E. Moss, Democrat of California, has championed access to Government information. It initiated an investigation of corruption in the aid program in Vietnam. Mr. Moss has also criticized Lieut. Gen. Lewis B. Hershey, the Selective Service director.

Mr. Dawson, an Illinois Democrat, is chairman of the House Committee on Government Operations. He had cited economy in proposing a committee reorganization under which the Moss subcommittee would have been abolished. But Republicans and some Democrats opposed the action, which Mr. Dawson never formally announced.

Mr. Dawson announced no plan to continue the subcommittee, but he did ask an additional $250,000, which he said "is the amount we need to continue without substantial changes in our structure."

The request was inserted as a statement in yesterday's Congressional Record.

Mr. Dawson had originally requested $875,000 to run the committee this year. His reorganization plan was developed after the House Administration Committee cut that to $555,000. The added $250,000 he asked, if granted, would restore most of the cut.

May 8, 1968

U.S. Agencies Urged To Free Information Under Act of 1967

WASHINGTON, June 8 (AP)—Senator Edward V. Long, Democrat of Missouri, urged all Federal agencies to implement the letter and the spirit of the Freedom-of-Information Act, which became effective last July 4.

The act is designed to prevent the withholding of information from the public except in specifically listed areas, such as records involving national security and invasions of privacy.

Individuals denied access to documents have a right to seek injunctive relief in the courts.

Senator Long, chairman of the Senate Administrative Practice and Procedure subcommittee, said in a statement he was surprised that the news media had not taken greater advantage of the remedies provided by the act.

"I feel certain that if more people were aware of the act, especially newsmen, we would see more demands for information being made on the agencies," he said.

Mr. Long said that a report prepared by the subcommittee was compiled to determine whether Government agencies "were cooperating fully in achieving the public's right to know."

Questionnaires were submitted to a number of agencies on what steps they have taken to carry out the intent of the act.

The report said that the success or failure of the act greatly depended on its faithful execution by government officials and that "the record of the agencies in this regard is far from clear."

June 10, 1968

Information Bill Introduced

WASHINGTON, June 25 (AP) — Representative William V. Roth, Republican of Delaware, said today that there was a need for a central, comprehensive repository where meaningful information on all operating Federal programs could be found. Mr. Roth, along with 45 other Republicans and 14 Democrats, introduced a bill that would require the President to publish each year a comprehensive compendium of Federal assistance programs and to update it monthly.

INFORMATION LAW ASSAYED IN HOUSE

Report Finds Some Flaws but General Obedience

WASHINGTON, Nov. 27 (AP) — A House Government Operations subcommittee reported today that some "arrogant public information policies" still existed in Federal agencies but that a new law aimed to stop them was generally being observed.

The subcommittee, headed by Representative John E. Moss, Democrat of California, made public a compilation and analysis of the Freedom of Information Act that became effective July 4, 1967.

The law was designed to restrict the authority of agencies and bureaus to withhold information about their activities from the public. It provided for exemptions in limited cases, chiefly involving national defense or foreign policy.

The philosophy behind the law, the report said, was that any person should have clear access to agency records without having to state a reason for wanting the information.

A preliminary examination, the report added, discloses that most regulations dealing with the release of information "meet the letter and spirit of the law."

Military Rule Cited

As an example of what it called "arrogant" policies, the subcommittee said that the Department of Defense and the Army, Air Force and Navy had issued almost identical regulations exempting some records from disclosure through qualifications "clearly outside the scope and intent of the act."

The Federal Trade Commission, it added, also "flouts the law" in some cases by requiring information seekers to state reasons for their requests.

The subcommittee suggested that there be more uniformity in regulations dealing with the mechanics of obtaining access to information and in fees charged to cover the clerical expenses involved.

Wrong Men for the F.C.C.

The expected Presidential nomination of Dean Burch as chairman of the Federal Communications Commission could affect radio and television management and programing for years—adversely. There is nothing in the former G.O.P. chairman's record or experience to show that his appointment would encourage the stations and networks to improve the quality of broadcasting, an industry operating under Federal license.

The F.C.C. chairmanship is one of the most powerful and politically influential posts in the United States. The commissioners and especially the chairman set the compass of station behavior. They can be rubber-stamps, as most have been in the past, renewing franchises without blinking every three years. Or they can look closely at promise, performance and public challenges as the law requires.

Through its decisions and rule-making powers, the F.C.C. can play a crucial role in determining what is "equal time" in political campaigns—including the next Presidential election. If reforms are to be made in providing greater opportunities for candidates out of office and inducing the networks to offer more free and debate time, the next F.C.C. chairman will have to be a person respected for his impartiality by members of both parties in Congress.

Mr. Burch, called by Barry Goldwater "the best national chairman the Republicans ever had," was forced out in the spring of 1965 after holding that position for less than a year. The Arizona lawyer was totally identified with the party's conservative wing.

* * *

President Nixon's expected nomination of Robert Wells for a second vacancy on the F.C.C. bodes no better for improvement in TV and radio. Mr. Wells is a broadcaster with interests in radio stations in the Middle West. Of greater significance is the fact that he is a member of the National Association of Broadcasters' radio code review board, meaning that he is very much a part of the system that F.C.C. reformers desire to change by raising standards of public performance. Mr. Wells is already on record against competitive challenges for broadcast licenses.

This is a time of vast communications changes over the entire spectrum of broadcasting. It is a time when decisions will have to be made to advance or stop the growth of the Corporation for Public Broadcasting and the educational stations. The need in new F.C.C. appointments is for men who can match the commission's mandate of public interest and necessity.

June 26, 1968

November 28, 1968

September 2, 1969

Hyde Wants Cabinet-Level Rule of Broadcasting

By FRED FERRETTI

Rosel H. Hyde, outgoing chairman of the Federal Communications Commission, said yesterday that creation of a Cabinet-level Secretary of Telecommunications, with centralization of all governmental and non-governmental commuications functions, was "a suggestion which deserves consideration."

Mr. Hyde, who will soon be replaced as F.C.C. chairman by Dean Burch, addressed 1,000 executives in broadcasting at a luncheon meeting of the International Radio and Television Society at the Waldorf-Astoria Hotel.

He said that such an appointment as he described would be beneficial in two ways. First, he said, a single Cabinet department "might fare better in obtaining the needed funds," for administering the expanding communications facilities of the country. Second, it would thwart suggestions currently making the rounds, which would fragmentize the powers and functions of the F.C.C.

Rostow Report Countered

At a news conference later, Mr. Hyde was asked if his warning against dilution of F.C.C. powers was based on any information he might have from the Nixon Administration.

He said, no, but that he was aware of discussions along those lines, as well as the report, made to former President Johnson by Eugene Rostow, which advocated that the frequency allocation function of the F.C.C. be taken away from that agency and given to another arm of government, "perhaps the Commerce Department."

Mr. Hyde urged the broadcasters to give "a dramatic response" to his call for more free and reduced-rate political broadcasting time.

Fears Detailed Censorship

He also said that he hoped the F.C.C. would not in the future see itself as the censor of broadcast journalistic freedom, but rather that the agency would oversee broadly the broadcasters' efforts at honest handling of the news.

To pick at individual day-to-day cases, said Mr. Hyde, was to become a censor. The general supervision approach by the F.C.C. would carry, he said, greater reliance on the integrity of the broadcasters.

Mr. Hyde also ridiculed the opponents of pay television, who "claim that pay TV will kill commercial television." The F.C.C. announced two weeks ago that it would begin accepting applications for pay TV franchises, subject to Congressional approval.

Appeals Court Says F.C.C. May License Pay TV Broadcasts

WASHINGTON, Sept. 30 (AP) —The United States Court of Appeals today supported the Federal Communications Commission's plan for licensing pay television throughout the nation.

The F.C.C. policy stand, announced last December, had been challenged by the National Association of Theater Owners and the Joint Committee Against Toll TV.

The court here rejected each of the objections raised. It declared that the F.C.C. was within its legal rights in approving pay television, had not infringed on freedom of speech, and was not creating any financial discrimination against the poor.

Congress May Act Now

The decision leaves any actual start of pay television in the hands of Congress. The F.C.C. declared its pay TV rules in effect last June, but promised not to authorize any actual operations for 60 days after the appeals court decision. That gives Congress until Nov. 30 to take action before the F.C.C. would feel free to begin issuing pay-TV broadcast licenses.

More than 20 bills have been introduced in the House to block the new licenses, but the House Commerce Committee has not yet scheduled hearing on any of them. Hearings had been scheduled to begin in September but were postponed twice.

Under the system approved by the F.C.C., one pay television station could operate in any area that has four other stations whose commercial broadcasts can be received free.

TV Station Drops Bid to Oust Johnson

By JACK GOULD

Don Elliott Heald, general manager of WSB-TV in Atlanta, disassociated his station yesterday from last week's action of four Southeastern broadcasting organizations in asking for the removal of Nicholas Johnson as a member of the Federal Communications Commission.

In a telegram, Mr. Heald, whose outlet is owned by The Atlanta Constitution and Journal, said he thought such a step was an "improper approach." He said he had left the meeting prior to the dismissal demand by the heads of the trade groups in Florida, Georgia and South Carolina and North Carolina. He was unavailable for further comment throughout the day at his office in Atlanta.

At Mr. Johnson's office in Washington it was said the commissioner has received over 700 letters following his appearance on "Face the Nation," virtually all of them favorable. On the program, the commissioner was sharply critical of TV as a whole, urged free air time for political candidates and cited what he felt were other shortcomings in television's performance, including corporate links to other media.

In Washington there were reports that Mr. Heald was not the only broadcaster who might disapprove of the tactic of trying to oust an F.C.C.

commissioner before the expiration of his term because of resentment over criticism of the medium.

Some broadcasters, pleading anonymity for the moment, said that while they disagreed with Mr. Johnson they did not see the wisdom of bestowing a degree of martyrdom on the commissioner. They suggested that he thrived on controversy, which might only encourage criticism of TV, and that it was better strategy not to overreact, particularly since Mr. Johnson was usually a minority voice in F.C.C. affairs. They predicted nothing would come of the demand.

One broadcaster recalled that the late James Lawrence Fly, while F.C.C. chairman, had characterized radio as "a dead mackerel in the moonlight—it both shines and stinks," and that Newton N. Minow, also a former chairman, had called television a "vast wasteland." Time passed, the broadcaster wryly noted, and both former chairmen later included commercial broadcasters among their legal clients.

Meanwhile, Harry Belafonte, the performer, announced that he would throw his full support behind Mr. Johnson's retention in office. His office said that he and Chiz Schultz, vice president and executive producer of Belafonte Enterprises, planned to write Vincent T. Wasilewski, president of the National Association of Broadcasters, not to entertain the demand of the affiliated trade organizations in the Southeast.

Mr. Schultz said that Mr. Johnson was the only F.C.C. commissioner who always made himself readily accessible to Belafonte Enterprises. Mr. Belafonte is associated with the group seeking the license of Channel 11 in New York.

Moscow Journalism Dean Says Press in U.S. Is Restricted, Too

Special to The New York Times

PALO ALTO, Calif., Oct. 18 — The inability of the mass media to criticize values and the ills inherent in a society is a problem for both the Communist and capitalist press, the dean of the department of journalism at the University of Moscow said this week.

Dean Yessen N. Zassoursky, addressing a graduate class in the department of communications at Stanford University, said yesterday that the Soviet press would not question the basic assumptions of Communism and that the United States press was not free to question capitalist values.

"We believe in certain values of Marxism-Leninism," he said. "Ideas alien to Communism are not expressed in our press."

And he said that American reporters were inhibited by advertisers and were not free to criticize capitalism.

"Not every advertiser tells every paper what to write, but still I think those advertisers determine the frontiers of criticism and the fundamental problems which should or should not be touched upon," he said.

"Therefore they have as much freedom as advertisers give them," he said. "Would advertisers let a paper advocate social revolution or the overthrow of the Government by working classes or students?"

But he praised the American journalists of the early 20th century who were famous for their muckraking efforts. He said that publishers had "stopped them" when their interests conflicted.

He said that American newspapers were "the mouthpieces of those who own them."

The dean said the Soviet press was free to criticize an operation of a factory or farm because the plant was run "in the name of the people," but he said that no American newspaper would be able to criticize sharply the operations of "Ford or Rand."

"It is not to you they belong," he said.

But Mr. Zassoursky, who spoke in an almost flawless English with only a slight accent, said that both American and Russian journalists worked well at criticizing Government problems and inefficiencies.

"It is a Soviet journalist's duty to ask a Government official a question on unsolved problems," he said.

He praised the efforts of American journalists writing about Government, and singled out James Reston of The New York Times. "We agree a lot with James Reston," he said. "He's a perceptive man."

Mr. Zassoursky, whose department includes 2,600 students and 90 faculty members, is touring the United States this month to visit with journalism students and to study American newspapers.

He arrived in New York on Oct. 8, and has visited Ann Arbor, Mich., and Minneapolis. He will return to Moscow on Oct. 23, after stopping in Washington and Philadelphia.

RADIO-TV CENSORING DENIED BY PENTAGON

WASHINGTON, Jan. 16—The director of information for the armed forces denied today that military officials censor the radio and television stations that broadcast news to United States servicemen overseas.

The director, John C. Broger, said that the stations—some of which have been criticized by military personnel in Vietnam—operate under a policy of "no censorship or news management." But, he explained, the policy is subject to the wishes of the host country and the discretion of local military commanders.

In Vietnam, several servicemen who are announcers on the American Forces Vietnam Network have charged the network with censorship.

In one case, a broadcaster, specialist 5 Robert Lawrence of Atlanta, who made his accusation on the air, was told afterward that he was being charged with disrespect to a superior and being absent without leave, because he refused to drive a truck as ordered.

Mr. Broger said today that the incident that led to the charges had occurred on Dec. 28, and that the court-martial action against specialist Lawrence had been begun before the broadcast in question.

Mr. Broger, who appeared at a briefing for Pentagon correspondents, said the policy of observing the wishes of the host government means that "we will be careful" about the items that are broadcast.

News Media Heads Cite Their Concern On U.S. Subpoenas

Executives of major news-gathering organizations expressed criticism and concern here yesterday in response to recent Government subpoenas of reporters' notes, tape recordings, news film and unedited files of news media.

There were statements by The New York Times, the Columbia Broadcasting System, Time Inc. and Newsweek.

They came only a day after the most recent Government action, a subpoena directing Earl Caldwell, a correspondent for The Times in the newspaper's San Francisco bureau, to appear before a Federal grand jury investigating the Black Panther party.

Arthur Ochs Sulzberger, president and publisher of The Times, said:

"All citizens, including newspapermen, have a duty to respect proper judicial processes, but The Times intends to use all its resources to make sure that no judicial action violates the constitutional guarantees of a free press and the rights of newspapermen to carry on their work freely and without coercion.

"Toward this end, Harding F. Bancroft, executive vice president of The New York Times, is in San Francisco at my request to give every possible assistance to Mr. Caldwell and to the attorneys we have engaged for him."

"The Times is concerned with what action might be taken in regard to Mr. Caldwell, and also the possibility that the increasing use of the subpoena to elicit information from newspapermen might hinder them in their pursuit of the news. It could well set up a barrier between reporters and their sources of information. The use of the subpoena power must be balanced against the right of the press to operate freely and the right of Americans to a free and unhampered flow of information."

In San Francisco last night, sources said that the Federal grand jury before which Mr.

Caldwell was directed to appear today would not meet. The sources said the next grand jury meeting scheduled was Feb. 11.

The United States Attorney's office is caught up in a change of administration from that of Cecil Poole, the Democratic appointee who ended nine years' of service on Monday, and James Browning, the new Republican appointee.

Other Statements Issued

Other statements were issued yesterday by Dr. Frank Stanton, president of the Columbia Broadcasting System, and by Hedley Donovan, editor in chief of Time Inc.

At The Wall Street Journal, a group of reporters signed a petition asking "for the assurance of our editors that this newspaper will not allow itself to be put into the role of government investigator or lend unintentional support to political organization as these other news organizations have done."

The reference to other news organizations concerned C.B.S., Time, Life and Newsweek.

C.B.S. has received Government subpoenas demanding a complete record of correspondence, memorandums, notes and telephone calls and for news film in connection with a program on the Black Panther party.

Federal courts have subpoenaed the unedited files and unused pictures of Time, Life and Newsweek magazines dealing with the Weatherman faction of the Students for a Democratic Society. The group is composed of militant revolutionaries.

C.B.S. announced last week that it would comply with the Government's demands, but in his statement yesterday, Dr. Stanton observed:

"The question of the extent to which news gathering organizations and reporters can be required in certain criminal proceedings to provide material gathered in the course of news functions but not published or broadcast is an immensely important one.

"Broad unrestricted access to reporters' notes, notebooks and other materials not published or broadcast can have a direct and seriously adverse effect on the free flow of information, and access to news sources.

"It is, therefore, the intention of C.B.S. to contest demands of this nature as soon as appropriate cases are presented. We have instructed our attorneys to proceed accordingly."

The subpoenas were issued to

C.B.S. and to Mr. Caldwell in connection with a charge by the Government that David Hilliard, a Black Panther, had made a threat against the life of President Nixon during a speech on Nov. 15.

Subpoena Deplored

Mr. Donovan, in his statement, deplored the increase in the number of subpoenas being issued to the press and said that such action "appears to make the press an arm of law-enforcement agencies, which is not its role."

"In some cases, indeed, we believe that law enforcement agencies have found it convenient to force the press to supply them with information that the should have obtained themselves," he said.

Mr. Donovan added:

"We clearly understand that our obligation to cooperate with judicial procedure is the same as that of any other organization or citizen.

"It is our opinion, however, that the press has served the public interest on many occasions by publishing material that could not have been obtained without interviews conducted on a confidential basis between the report erand his subject. The threat of frequent and indiscriminate subpoenas endangers that confidential relationship and could seriously undermine the ability of the press to search out and report the news.

Legal Action Considered

"It will be this company's policy," Mr. Donovan stated, "to analyze each subpoena carefully and weigh its relevance to trial proceedings or criminal actions. Should we believe that there is no immediate relevance and that a law enforcement body is on a 'fishing expedition' for information, we will take appropriate legal action to contest the subpoena."

Osborn Elliott, editor in chief of Newsweek, issued a statement on subpoenas last night, and Sterling Soderlind, the managing editor of The Wall Street Journal, said he planned to issue such a statement shortly.

In his statement, Mr. Elliott characterized the "indiscriminate use of subpoenas," either by the Government or by defense attorneys as a threat to the role of the press in a free society.

Mr. Elliott said, in part: "Under pressure of subpoena we may be legally compelled to submit our files, but we believe that all confidential sources must and will be protected. We have been subpoenaed at various times by both the Govern-

ment and the defense, and our position has been consistent.

"We have not revealed the identity of confidential sources to anyone, and we intend to resist by all the means at our disposal any unwarranted uses of the subpoena power."

At The Wall Street Journal, 23 of 33 general reporters signed the petition, which said:

"The subpoenas are a dangerous device which could be used to make us betray virtually any source in the future. We urge the entire profession to join us in defending press freedom against this destructive practice."

Another statement of protest to the subpoena served upon Mr. Caldwell was issued by Ernest Dunbar, senior editor of Look magazine and chairman of the New York Chapter of Black Perspective, an organization of black professional journalists.

Mr. Dunbar said, "We feel this action not only violates the reporter's confidentiality but equally transforms him involuntarily into a Government agent. Such an action is especially onerous in the case of a black reporter whose credibility, reputation and ability to function in the black community would be destroyed by such forced testimony."

Position Disputed
Special to The New York Times

WASHINGTON, Feb. 3 — A Justice Department official's contention that it was policy to subpoena newsmen was disputed by three former high officials of the department today.

The official said yesterday that the department had for years obtained information from newsmen, either voluntarily or through subpoenas.

Asked today for examples, he said the indictment of several Chicago policemen in connection with riots at the 1968 Democratic National Convention was such a case. However, he could not cite other examples, particularly in the South where the department reported most of the information was obtained.

The three former officials, who worked under the previous Administration, said they could recall no case in which the department subpoenaed notes and tape recordings of newsmen.

The three were Herbert J. Miller Jr., Assistant Attorney General in the Criminal Division; John W. Douglas, Assistant Attorney General in the Civil Division, and Harold F. Reis, executive assistant to the Attorney General.

U.S. JUDGE CAUTIONS ON CURBING MEDIA

Judge Irving R. Kaufman of the United States Court of Appeals for the Second Circuit, said last night that the First Amendment guarantees not only the right to advocate ideas but also the right to advocate them effectively through mass media.

Some groups have less access to certain media than others, he noted, and if governmental restraints on media are applied indiscriminately, these groups will lose their ability to reach the public.

In a speech prepared for delivery last night as the 11th annual James Madison Lecture at the New York University School of Law, Judge Kaufman said:

"Some members of our society have plentiful access to radio, television, newspapers and other means of mass communication to convey their messages. Others have almost none."

Therefore, he continued, "if all means of dissemination of ideas in public places were prohibited, the former would be little affected, while the latter would be effectively silenced, giving the views of those with access to the legally favored media overpowering influence."

March 19, 1970

Wider Press Bills Urged

WASHINGTON, Aug. 12 (UPI) —Legislation designed to put daily newspapers under the Federal Communication Commission's "fairness doctrine" was introduced today in the House by Representative Leonard Farbstein, Democrat of Manhattan. He said companion bills would extend the F.C.C. doctrine, which requires the presentation of conflicting views on radio and television, to newspapers in communities of 25,000 or over that do not have two separately owned papers.

August 13, 1970

F.C.C. ORDERS TV TO SET PRIME TIME FOR WAR CRITICS

President's Extensive Use of Medium to Defend His Policy Cited as Reason

STAND CALLED FLEXIBLE

Automatic Replies to Nixon Appearances Ruled Out —Format Undefined

By CHRISTOPHER LYDON
Special to The New York Times

WASHINGTON, Aug. 14—The Federal Communications Commission said today that President Nixon had made such extensive use of television to defend his conduct of the war in Indochina that the networks must now give opponents a chance to present critical replies on prime time.

The requirement that broadcasters not simply cover the other side but give uninterrupted, premium exposure to the President's opponents was the first of its kind and appeared likely to alter Mr. Nixon's use of the medium.

At the same time, the F.C.C. declared that it was not creating an automatic right of reply to any Presidential broadcast and was leaving substantial flexibility of judgment in the hands of broadcasters—including the selection of opposing spokesmen and the format of their programs.

Special Claim Denied

In related rulings on broadcast "fairness," the commission denied that the coalition of United States Senators who have backed a legislative amendment to end the war" had any special claim to be recognized on TV as the President's official critics.

Further, it declared that the Columbia Broadcasting System, which designed a "loyal opposition" series to let the Democratic National Committee balance Mr. Nixon's use of TV, must now let the Republican National Committee respond to the Democrats' response.

And finally, the commission ruled that Senator Robert J. Dole of Kansas and other Republican supporters of President Nixon's Vietnam policies had no right to free reply time in which to answer a paid broadcast by a panel of antiwar Senators last May.

'Fairness Doctrine'

In an opinion that sought to relate each of the specific decisions to a general doctrine, the commission emphasized that none of the cases before it had fallen under the so-called "equal time" rule governing broadcast treatment of political candidates.

Rather, the F.C.C. stated, the questions pertain to the "fairness doctrine," a much less precise rule that gives broadcasters wide discretion in deciding what issues are controversial and how they shall be treated.

Nonetheless, the commission ruled, President Nixon's use of evening network television for five direct speeches to the nation in the seven months between his exposition of the policy of Vietnamization last November and his defense of the Cambodian incursion in June was an exceptional matter.

The commission declared that the balance of network coverage—in their news and discussion programs—slightly favored the Administration view of the war. Yet the five appearances by Mr. Nixon, whom the commission pointedly described neither as Commander in Chief nor as the nation's Chief Executive but as "the leading spokesman of one side," created a significant imbalance, the F.C.C. said.

The commission majority declared, "We believe that in such circumstances there must also be a reasonable opportunity for the other side geared specifically to the five addresses," and then delivered the core of its decision in the following parenthesis, "(ie., the selection of some suitable spokesman or spokesmen by the networks to broadcast an address giving the contrasting viewpoint).

"We wish to stress," the commission continued, "that we are not holding that such obligation arises from a single speech—that where an uninterrupted address is afforded one side, the fairness doctrine demands that the other side be presented in the same format. Rather, our holding here is based upon the unusual facts of this case—five addresses by the outstanding spokesman by one side of an issue."

Thus, the commission gave Mr. Nixon no precise guidance as to how often or how long he could speak without justifying a reply. It did specify that "in the case of a single Presidential address, there is no requirement that it be met by a countering single statement," yet it did not say whether three Presidential addresses— or four—would warrant the same response as five.

Broadly, the commission's ruling appeared to serve notice on the President that he could not consider himself or his TV statements — even on foreign policy and especially on Vietnam — "above the battle" and noncontrovesial.

Similarly, the commission appeared to have warned the networks that they must monitor the President's addresses more carefully for contents that can be challenged.

The F.C.C. vote on the collected "fairness" decisions was 5 to 2, and was the first in the general fairness area that united Dean Burch, the Republican chairman of the commission, and Nicholas Johnson, a frequently dissenting Democrat, in the majority.

Others in the majority were Robert E. Lee and Robert Wells, both Republicans, and Kenneth A. Cox, a Democrat. The two dissenters were Robert T. Bartley and H. Rex Lee, both Democrats.

In separate action on Capitol Hill today, the Democratic leaders of the House decided unexpectedly not to call for a vote on amended legislation to limit the political use of television advertising in this year's election campaign.

Since the House adjourned today until Sept. 9, and the political broadcasting bill is now written to take effect 30 days after final enactment, it appeared unlikely that it would have its intended impact in 1970.

The Democrats, suffering from a relative shortage of campaign funds, had hoped to impose the spending limit over Republican opposition. But at the opening of the House session today, the leadership discovered that 100 Democrats were absent, and accordingly postponed consideration of the bill.

BURCH CLARIFIES TV REPLY RULING

By CHRISTOPHER LYDON
Special to The New York Times

WASHINGTON, Aug. 18— Dean Burch, chairman of the Federal Communications Commission, emphasized today that the agency's order requiring the television networks to give prime-time exposure to critics of the Administration's policy in Vietnam was not a grant of "equal time" to match President Nixon's appearances.

Mr. Burch said that at least six newspapers and The Associated Press had reported the decision incorrectly as being "anti-Nixon" or involving "equal time." He said The New York Times, Newsweek and Time magazine had misconstrued the ruling in other respects.

White House officials, distressed at the suggestion in first reports that the F.C.C. decision would inhibit the President's use of television, worked over the weekend with Mr. Burch's personal staff in follow-up briefings with reporters.

The White House expects that the President will still enjoy a favorable balance of TV time, these officials said, and the grant of limited reply time will not discourage Mr. Nixon from using the medium as heavily in the future as he has in the past.

Mr. Burch, whom President Nixon appointed nearly a year ago to head the seven-member F.C.C., issued a statement this afternoon to "clear up" the decision, which was first announced in an agency press release last Friday.

While the mandatory exposure of opposition spokesman was designed to balance Mr. Nixon's five addresses on Vietnam and Cambodia, Mr. Burch said, the F.C.C. had not specified equal time or, in fact, any amount of time that the other side should get.

Further, he said, "we have expressly rejected any principle embodying right of reply or rebuttal to the President."

The decision did not relate essentially to Mr. Nixon or the Presidency, Mr. Burch said, but to the "issue" of Indochina. Television's coverage of that issue was "roughly balanced," the commission found, except for "the five opportunities in prime time for the leading spokesman (the President) of one side to address the nation on this issue."

Mr. Burch's statement continued, "In such circumstances, time should be afforded for at least one more uninterrupted opportunity by an appropriate spokesman for the other viewpoint."

"Our ruling," he emphasized, "was not intended to discourage in any way the networks' presentation of Presidential reports to the nation. We recognize their importance to an informed public opinion as do the networks."

In reporting the ruling in its issue of Saturday, Aug. 15, The New York Times stated:

"The Federal Communications Commission said today that President Nixon had made such extensive use of television to defend his conduct of the war in Indochina that the networks must now give opponents a chance to present critical replies on prime time."

"The requirement that broadcasters not simply cover the other side but give uninterrupted, premium exposure to the President's opponents was the first of its kind and appeared likely to alter Mr. Nixon's use of the medium."

Mr. Burch quoted those two paragraphs in his statement today and commented:

"First of all, the F.C.C. did not say what The Times states it said. Secondly, the commission was at pains to point out, in its press release, that it was not engrafting an equal opportunities requirement in a fairness area and as pointed out above, the commission carefully avoided any suggestion that the Presidential reports to the nation be discouraged."

The Times's report had specified that "the F.C.C. declared that it was not creating an automatic right of reply to any Presidential broadcast." The report also noted that the decision was drawn under the general "fairness" doctrine rather than under the "equal opportunities" or "equal time" rule that applies strictly to political candidates.

Mr. Burch said that a number of papers had wrongly reported the ruling as involving "equal time" and being "anti-Nixon." He mentioned, in those categories The Christian Science Monitor, Chicago Today, The Washington Star, The Chicago Sun-Times, The Boston Globe, The St. Paul Pioneer Press, The Associated Press and The National Observer.

Newsweek's conclusion that the decision established "a new fairness doctrine" and Time's speculation on "radically changed Presidential broadcast habits" were both unjustified, he said.

Johnson of F.C.C. Advocates Right of TV Reply to President

By CHRISTOPHER LYDON
Special to The New York Times

WASHINGTON, Aug. 30 — Nicholas Johnson, a member of the Federal Communications Commission, said today that every time the President spoke to the nation on television, the networks should give comparable treatment to opposite views.

"Whenever a President speaks," Mr. Johnson wrote, "one could almost say that, by definition, he has spoken on what the Fairness Doctrine characterizes as a 'controversial issue of public importance' —if it wasn't such an issue before he expresses his views, it is after he speaks.

"I think it is imperative that leaders of opposing parties, and opposing viewpoints in Congress, be given the opportunity to rebut his unilateral statements. This rebuttal is necessary to present different views on issues, to represent opposing political parties and to the very perpetuation of a system of coequal branches of national Government in a television age."

Mr. Johnson's views were expressed in a concurring statement on the commission's decision two weeks ago that required the networks to give prime time exposure to critical spokesmen answering President Nixon's five addresses on the subject of the Indochina war.

Mr. Johnson, a Democrat, was allied in the commission majority on that decision with Dean Burch, the commission's Republican Chairman. But individual "clarifications" by the two men have now disclosed pointed differences of approach.

After White House officials had sought to dispel the impression that the decision would inhibit Mr. Nixon's use of TV, Mr. Burch declared that the commission had "expressly rejected any principle embodying right of reply or rebuttal to the President."

Mr. Johnson said today that the commission should properly move toward establishing such a right of reply.

"If one branch of the Government increasingly gains effective access to the media of communications, while the other branch is systematically excluded, then the power balance, presumably designed to safeguard our citizenry from the tyrannies and abuses of executive power, will be upset," Mr. Johnson said.

Replies to the President are all the more important, he said, since the commission denied antiwar groups and the Democratic National Committee any "right of access" to the media.

"It is ironic," he said, "that the only persons in the country with direct access to millions of television homes are the hawkers of commercial goods and services — deodorants and mouthwashes — and the President. If the President, by merely snapping his fingers, can acquire instant simultaneous access to all four television networks, then how can we in good conscience refuse to grant rebuttal time to opposing spokesmen and leaders from the Congress?

'Extraordinary Haste'

Mr. Johnson also chided Mr. Burch for criticizing press accounts of the commission's original decision and questioned the "extraordinary force and haste" with which Mr. Burch insisted that the ruling would not hurt President Nixon.

By expressing the hope that Mr. Burch's "clarification" had not been dictated by the White House, Mr. Johnson stirred up old reports that Mr. Burch's attack on the press had had high-level encouragement.

"One cannot help but wonder," Mr. Johnson wrote, "where else one could so rapidly obtain such a thorough analysis of the nation's newspaper coverage of the President —including accounts in The St. Paul Pioneer-Press, Chicago Today and Chicago Sun-Times— none of which appeared in the F.C.C.'s internal newspaper reporting service or are from papers prominently displayed on the chairman's coffee table."

August 31, 1970

F.C.C. Stands By Its Ruling Ordering G.O.P. Broadcast

Special to The New York Times

WASHINGTON, Sept. 24— The Federal Communications Commission declined today to reconsider its ruling that the Columbia Broadcasting System must let the Republican National Committee respond to the "loyal opposition" broadcast last July by Lawrence F. O'Brien, the Democratic chairman.

The company immediately announced that it would file suit to block the ruling. Mr. O'Brien said that any Republican use of free TV time between now and Nov. 3 "could unfairly influence the outcome of the elections."

The "loyal opposition" telecast was originally conceived as the first of four a year in which the party out of power could respond to the President.

The Commission reiterated today, however, that the network's effort to balance Presidential appearances should be organized on issues that the President had discussed. By making their broadcast "party oriented," rather than "issue-oriented," the commission said, the Democrats triggered the right of further response by the Republican party chairman.

September 25, 1970

TV as a Free Medium

Julian Goodman Defies Pressure; Licenses Provide Political Leverage

By JACK GOULD

Major elements of television are bracing for a tilt with Congress and the Nixon Administration on the exercise of reportorial independence by a journalistic medium that operates under a Federal Government license. The issue, one of the oldest in the evolution of broadcasting, is coming to a climax over the coverage of fighting in Laos.

News Analysis In a step believed to be without parallel in radio or television, Julian Goodman, president of the National Broadcasting Company, a former journalist himself, is sending a personal letter to every member of the Senate and the House, objecting to a recent Congressional review of film footage from Laos.

Senator Clifford P. Hansen, Republican of Wyoming, arranged to show a compilation of reports on Southeast Asia by N.B.C. and the Columbia Broadcasting System. The summaries were made by Vanderbilt University and shown on March 12, on Capitol Hill.

After the presentation Senator Hansen charged bias and distortion, a theme picked up by a number of other members of Congress who support President Nixon's policies in Laos. The President and Vice President similarly have disputed TV coverage in Laos as incomplete or too negative.

Mr. Goodman, whose views also reflected those of Richard S. Salant, president of C.B.S. News, denounced the Congressional review of news reports as unsupportable and dangerous to the free flow of facts to a people of a democracy. He

said N.B.C. had engaged in straightforward presentation of actuality, reporting the good and the bad on the military scene. He came as close as any important prominent broadcaster in recent years has to condemning partisan Congressional second-guessing on the issue of TV accuracy and fairness.

Restrictions Are Resented

What Mr. Goodman did not spell out in precise language— though the implication was unmistakable—is that because TV must operate under licenses, politicians championing one view on an issue of crucial national concern are exerting covert pressure either to impugn the integrity of the home screen or frighten the medium into taking a softer and more pliant line. Mr. Goodman made it clear that N.B.C. would not surrender its judgment, and defended his network's coverage as fair.

Ground rules covering TV journalism have always rankled radio and TV reporters. Yesterday many questioned whether the Senator would paste together all the reports of newspapers, which do not need a Federal license to function, for a public assault on the Fourth Estate. The licensing requirement of broadcasting has afforded Congress, the White House and the Federal Communications Commission a disciplinary wedge from which the print media are immune. This is the question that's being asked: Can the networks, which admittedly have far larger national audiences than any single newspaper, fully discharge their responsibilities under the implied threat of a possible loss

357

of franchise?

The United States Supreme Court has ruled against individual broadcasters who have displayed manifest unfairness in the presentation of opinion. And necessarily a finding decided in the case of one delinquent becomes the law of the land applicable to all broadcasters.

New Urgency Arises

But with the White House understandably anxious that its view should prevail, and a Pentagon upset by even the slightest aspersion on its activities, the principle of the Federal Government exerting real or implied control over TV journalism, in the opinion of many major broadcasters, acquires new significance because of events in Laos. If the findings of reporters in the field, to the extent the Pentagon accords them mobility, do not jibe with official Washington statements, where does the acid test of public service lie?·

Even Walter Cronkite, one of the anchormen most careful in keeping himself out of the news personally, on Tuesday night reported the involved convoluted language used by the military to explain American air strikes in Indochina. "Oh," he said, after a pregnant pause.

The growth of TV's power in journalism raises a fundamental question, according to many broadcasters: If TV is the dominant means, numerically at least, of informing the public, has the United States walked into the trap of having the Government attempt to influence that medium's output through the licensing requirement?

The answer contains arguments without end, but in the minds of many TV journalists the issue has suddenly been sharpened: Has the legalistic credo of Government-regulated fairness hobbled journalistic dedication to inquiry?

March 25, 1971

News Groups Appeal to High Court Against Subpoenaing of Reporters

Special to The New York Times

WASHINGTON, Sept. 20 — Widely differing elements of the news industry have filed friend-of-court briefs with the Supreme Court in the past few days, warning that the increasing issuance of subpoenae to the news media is threatening press freedom but disagreeing as to what the courts should do about it.

Today was the deadline for amicus briefs in three press subpoena cases that will be heard early in the high court term that begins on Oct. 4.

Briefs flowed into the clerk's office over the weekend, filed by such diverse journal elements as the reporters' and photographers' organizations, the American Society of Newspaper Editors, The New York Times and all three major television networks.

They presented data showing that the practice of subpoenaing journalists increased markedly as prosecutors' investigations of political radicals grew in the last two or three years. Unless journalists are shielded from having to testify, they argued, sources will stop talking to them and the flow of information to the public will dry up.

But a long-standing division between journalists was reflected in the solutions that were urged on the Court. Some of the news media organizations said that it would be sufficient to shield newsmen from testifying except in certain unusual circumstances, while others insisted that newsmen must have an absolute privilege not to testify.

The former position was taken in a brief filed by Prof. Alexander M. Bickel of the Yale Law School, who took a similar non-absolutist position last June in representing The New York Times in its successful litigation against the Government's efforts to suppress the Pentagon papers.

Professor Bickel said that the volume of press subpoenas had risen tremendously recently as prosecutors sought to use newsmen as "a springboard for investigation" or as "an investigative arm of the Government."

The brief contained an appendix listing 124 subpoenas that were served in the last two and a half years on the National Broadcasting Company, the Columbia Broadcasting System and their wholly owned subsidiary companies. Some of the subpoenas were sought by defense lawyers.

The Bickel brief asserted that newsmen should not be required to respond to grand jury subpoenas unless there was first a showing that they probably had knowledge of a specific crime, that the information could not be obtained from other sources and that the Government had a compelling need for the information.

Such a compelling need, according to Professor Bickel, could only be justified in an investigation of a major crime — not an inquiry of such victimless activity as prostitution, narcotics and gambling offenses.

The cases before the Supreme Court concern Earl Caldwell, a New York Times reporter, who refused to enter a grand jury room to testify about Black Panther activities; Paul Pappas of WTEV-TV in New Bedford, Mass., and Paul M. Branzburg, a reporter for The Louisville Courier-Journal. The latter refused to testify about black militant and narcotics activity, respectively.

Professor Bickel argued that none of the subpoenas against the three were justified. The brief was filed for the New York Times. N.B.C., C.B.S., The American Broadcasting Company. The Chicago Sun-Times, the Chicago Daily News, the Associated Press Managing Editors Association, the Associated Press Broadcast Association and the Association of American Publishers.

Briefs filed by The Newspaper Guild and the Authors League of America took a similar nonabsolutist position.

However, three amicus briefs filed by other news media groups insisted that the First Amendment creates an absolute and unqualified "newsmen's privilege." These groups were the American Society of Newspaper Editors, Sigma Delta Chi journalism fraternity, the Dow Jones Publishing Company, The Washington Post, Newsweek magazine and the National Press Photographers Association.

Publishers Warned of Threats to U.S. Freedoms

By HENRY RAYMONT

The Association of American Publishers held its fall meeting yesterday amid warnings that Government censorship and radical pressure groups are increasingly threatening the nation's First Amendment freedoms.

A report by the association's Freedom to Read Committee likened the situation to the McCarthy era of the early nineteen-fifties, "when attacks on intellectual freedom by the Government and various pressure groups were at their peak."

Senator Sam J. Ervin Jr., chairman of the Senate Subcommittee on Constitutional Rights, in a speech delivered to the closing dinner at the end of the day-long meeting at the Biltmore Hotel, said:

"If America is to be free, her Government must permit her people to think their own thoughts and determine their own associations without official instruction or intimidation."

Moralists Assailed

At a luncheon session the association heard Homer D. Babbridge Jr., president of the University of Connecticut, assail what he called "a virulent new version" of American moralists, who he said were interfering with free cultural exchanges among nations.

He cited the Jewish Defense League's disruption of concerts by Soviet artists, groups on campuses who thwarted speakers from Greece and Portugal and critics who urged a pullout from Olympic competitions in South Africa because of that country's racial policies.

Senator Ervin's speech was

September 21, 1971

358

the high point of a day in which more than 300 chief executives from literary and educational publishing houses and university presses discussed such diverse subjects as international copyright problems, dwindling funds for libraries and Government pressures against the publication of controversial materials.

In an extensive analysis of the First Amendment, Senator Ervin, a North Carolina Democrat, developed arguments he has been using against the Nixon Administration on such issues as the use of lie detectors on Federal employes, Army surveillance of private citizens and President Nixon's Executive order expanding the mandate of the Subversive Activities Control Board.

Concern Is expressed

The Senator's speech reflected a concern that leading members of the publishing community have frequently expressed and that was often a factor in yesterday's panel meetings and general discussions — namely, that Government attempts to interfere with such publishing ventures as the Pentagon study of the Vietnam war or the dissemination of radical books in libraries represented a threat to freedom of speech and press.

"It is a critical fact that we are now faced with the necessity of defending the First Amendment," W. Bradford Wiley, chairman of the association, said at a morning meeting. "Nothing like this had happened since the days of Senator Joseph R. McCarthy."

Kenneth D. McCormick, vice president of Doubleday and chairman of the association's Freedom to Read Committee, reported that, among other activities this year, the committee had protested a contempt citation against the Columbia Broadcasting System for refusing to supply out takes, or unused film, from its documentary "The Selling of the Pentagon" and had filed a brief opposing the Government action against The New York Times and other newspapers for publishing the Pentagon Papers.

Mr. McCormick said the association would also file a brief in behalf of the Rev. Phillip F. and the Rev. Daniel J. Berrigan, supporting the rights of Federal prisoners to disseminate their writings and recordings to publishers and the public.

Declaring that pressures from private groups to have certain titles removed from public and school libraries were no longer confined to pornography and sex education, he said:

"It is more and more the book that really talks about the war and gives two sides of it, that presents the race problem as more than an unfortunate spat between two regions, that presents the United States as a country that's been right sometimes and wrong at others."

Other speakers who expressed concern that the political acrimony was interfering with the free exchange of ideas were John C. Frantz, executive chairman of the National Book Committee; Whitney North Seymour, a former president of the American Bar Association, and Harrison E. Salisbury, editor of the Op-Ed page of The New York Times.

In introducing Senator Ervin, Robert L. Bernstein, president of Random House, who is vice chairman of the association, noted that the Senator's subcommittee planned to start hearings on Sept. 28 on "the meaning of the First Amendment's prohibition against abridgement of freedom of the press" and that publishers, newspaper editors and government officials had been invited to testify.

Pounding away at a favorite theme, Senator Ervin said that the First Amendment "is based upon an abiding faith that our country has nothing to fear from the exercise of its freedom as long as it leaves truth free to combat error."

If the right to express dissent is respected, he declared, "violent revolution has no rational or rightful place in our system."

Mr. Ervin, a political conservative who is considered the leading constitutional law expert in the Senate, said President Nixon's order strengthening the mandate of the Subversive Activities Control Board was "beyond the constitutional power of the President," too broad to have any legal value and in violation of the First Amendment.

Mr. Nixon's order, issued July 2, gave the board the power to hold hearings to help determine which organizations should be classified as subversive by the Attorney General.

Before the order, the board, an independent, semijudicial agency created in 1950, had had little work to do for several years.

CASES
IN POINT

*Seven historic examples of the
sometimes astonishing ways
the media and politics interact,
ranging from a master politician
who invented a second use
for early-morning walks to the
role of the press in foreign policy*

Cases in Point — 1: The Walking President

First Stroll in 7 Years Without a Bodyguard

Former President Truman walking along West Walnut Street in Independence yesterday

Associated Press Wirephoto

By RICHARD J. H. JOHNSTON
Special to THE NEW YORK TIMES.

INDEPENDENCE. Mo., Jan. 25—Harry S. Truman marked the first Sunday since he left the White House and became a private citizen with a brisk morning walk through the familiar streets of his home town. He spent the afternoon reading newspapers and helping Mrs. Truman straighten out their home.

At about 9:20 A. M., as churchgoers began to appear on the streets of Independence, the former President emerged from his home for his first stroll without a bodyguard since his succession to the Presidency in April, 1945. He strode briskly for forty minutes, pointing out historical sights of the town to the small group of reporters accompanying him. Dressed in a plaid suit and the double-breasted blue overcoat he wore last Tuesday at the inauguration ceremonies in Washington, and swinging one of his American Legion convention canes, Mr. Truman joked with reporters about their cold, dawn ride from Kansas City to their vigil outside his home here.

With the former President leading the way, the group paced steadily along toward the Jackson County Courthouse in the town square.

As Mr. Truman paused to point out historical sites along the way, he waved now and then to old acquaintances en route to church.

Mr. and Mrs. Truman did not attend church today because they felt they should wait till the townfolk became accustomed again to seeing them. They were particularly anxious, it was known, to avoid curious stares, which they felt would not be in keeping with the Sabbath.

Mr. Truman let it be known that he and his wife were most pleased that the majority of their fellow citizens of Independence were accepting their return home and presence in the community as a matter of course.

The Trumans want to get their home in order as quickly as possible. The former President observed when asked whether his residence had yet been opened to visitors:

"Things are still quite upset in the house."

Mr. Truman on his walk dwelt on the significance of Independence in the opening of the West, recalling that it was a jumping-off point for pioneers heading for the California, Oregon and Santa Fe trails.

Stopping before a log structure, now in the process of reconstruction, Mr. Truman explained that it was the original Jackson County Courthouse.

He said that old county ledgers showed that the cost of the original construction was $750.

"I remember," he related, "it cost $750 to build, but the funny thing is they had to have fifteen gallons of whisky and ten tin cups to drink it from to complete the job."

At one point in his recollections Mr. Truman chuckled and said to the reporters:

"I could rattle my head all day about this town and I would probably bore the hell out of you."

Standing before a marker commemorating the spot at the eastern terminus of the California Trail, the former President told his listeners that it was Sam Weston, a blacksmith in Independence, who wrought iron tires, repaired guns and bound ox carts with stout bands for the pioneers' journeys into the wilderness.

Near the First Baptist Church, J. R. Hickman of Independence, holding his 2-year-old daughter Gail Sue in his arms, stopped and said: "Good morning, Mr. President."

Little Gail Sue, clad in a red snowsuit, smiled shyly at Mr. Truman. He shook hands with Mr. Hickman and, patting Gail Sue on the head, declared: "This is a mighty fine little girl you have here."

From time to time during the walk people passing both on foot and in cars cried: "Good morning, Mr. President, nice to have you home."

"Good morning, mighty nice to be home," Mr. Truman called back.

Various buildings and locations in town reminded Mr. Truman of their part in the history of Independence and of Missouri.

"There are more rebels here," he said, "than in any other part of the country."

He talked briefly about Missouri's role in the bitter border fights with Kansas during and after the Civil War.

At this point an Independence police radio car drew away from the curb at the City Hall a short distance behind the walking group. It followed slowly behind Mr. Truman and the reporters for several blocks. It then resumed routine rounds. It was an impromptu, temporary guard for Mr. Truman that had not been arranged, local authorities said.

As he passed the Independence public school he was asked if that was the school he attended.

He said it was the same school in a new building.

"The old building burned down," he added. "All the records were destroyed. As a matter of fact, my records were burned up too. There's no evidence I ever went to school there."

As the small party turned back toward the Truman home, the former President said that his plans for the day would keep him indoors.

He said that he was still assisting Mrs. Truman with the unpacking but that she would rather he did not. "But I want to do it," he declared.

He went on to say that it was his impression that Mrs. Truman would rather have him out from under foot while she was getting the house in order. However, he added, he intended to spend a part of the afternoon helping with the unpacking and putting things away.

"I ought to get out and see my sister [Miss Mary Jane Truman of Grandview]," he remarked. "She has been raising thunder with me for not getting out to see her since we've been back."

Before re-entering his home, the former President stood chatting with the reporters. Someone observed that it was good to get away from questions and answers concerning politics. Mr. Truman agreed.

"What do you think of the abolition of the two-platoon system in collegiate football?" he was asked.

"That should have been done a long time ago," he replied. "It's just too expensive for the small schools and I am glad to see them get rid of it."

He then wished those accompanying him a pleasant day and strode into the house.

By 10 A. M. North Delaware Street, on which the Truman home stands, was well filled with parked cars whose owners and their families were at worship in near-by churches. None had given more than a passing glance to the Truman house.

January 26, 1953

TRUMAN ENDORSES STEVENSON'S TALK

It 'Covered the Ground,' He Says of Miami Attack on G. O. P.-McCarthyism

Former President Harry S. Truman endorses "entirely" the speech in which Adlai Stevenson declared that President Eisenhower had accepted "McCarthyism" as the Republican party's "best formula for political success."

The speech delivered by Mr. Stevenson, 1952 Democratic candidate for the Presidency, at Miami Beach Saturday, "covered the ground very well, and stated the Democratic attitude as clearly as could be done," Mr. Truman declared here yesterday.

"He has a way of expressing things that's in a class by itself," the former President said. "I endorse the speech entirely."

Apparently Mr. Stevenson, whose 1952 nomination was due largely to Mr. Truman's sponsorship, had not consulted with the former President in the preparation of the address. Earlier in the day, Mr. Truman declined to comment on it, saying he had not yet read it.

Mr. Truman also refused to discuss the current controversy between Senator Joseph R. McCarthy and the Army, terming it a private fight within the Republican party.

Evocations of Smiles

Most of Mr. Truman's comments were made on the run as reporters trailed him on his usual early morning walk and on a hike to Rockefeller Center and back to his suite at the Waldorf Astoria Hotel.

While at Rockefeller Center, used the introduc—

March 8, 1954

TRUMAN, M'CARTHY DUEL WITH QUIPS

Weapons in Exchange Here Are Barbed Remarks at a Distance of Few Blocks

Former President Truman and Senator Joseph R. McCarthy engaged in a duel of quips here yesterday at a distance of several blocks.

Reporters informed Mr. Truman on his customary early morning stroll that the Wisconsin Republican Senator's hotel had received a phone call warning that "something terrible" was going to happen to Mr. McCarthy.

Mr. Truman smiled.

"Oh, pshaw," he said. "I don't see why anyone would want to kill him. We'd have no entertainment at all if they killed him."

Then Mr. Truman added soberly:

"I don't believe in government by assassination. The best assassination a politician can get is a vote assassination."

Mr. Truman was walking near the Waldorf-Astoria Towers, where he was staying, when he made his quip.

At a press conference later at the Park Lane Hotel, Forty-eighth Street and Park Avenue, Mr. McCarthy was told of Mr. Truman's remark.

"It's a waste of time to answer dead politicians," the Senator retorted.

In response to another question about Mr. Truman's remark, Mr. McCarthy said: "Harry still has his sense of humor."

The phone call threatening Mr. McCarthy was received by the Waldorf-Astoria, at Park Avenue and Fiftieth Street, early yesterday morning, a spokesman at the hotel said.

During his stroll, Mr. Truman also was asked if he would predict the political defeat of Senator McCarthy. Mr. Truman, whose 1948 victory upset the political pollsters, said he was making no prediction. He then added:

"Most political prophets make more mistakes than anyone else."

The former President left for his home in Independence, Mo., at 2:15 P. M. when he boarded the Knickerbocker at Grand Central Terminal for St. Louis. He was accompanied by Mrs. Truman, with whom he arrived here last Friday.

Mr. and Mrs. Truman were accompanied to the station by their daughter, Miss Margaret Truman, Harold K. Hastings, resident manager of the Waldorf-Astoria, and William Hillman, Mr. Truman's biographer.

As the former President walked down the ramp to board the train, he was greeted by a number of women with such friendly expressions as "Hello, Mr. President" and "You're still my President."

Some persons already seated in the train tapped on the windows and waved to him.

March 10, 1954

TRUMAN HEALTHY, VIGOROUS, JAUNTY

Ex-President Takes Morning Walk, Sees Old Friends, Visits Senate Pages

Special to The New York Times.

WASHINGTON, April 16 — Former President Truman maintained his usual pace on his usual early morning walk today. But, he revealed to reporters, he has cut down the mileage.

Instead of two miles he now does one and one-quarter miles.

"But I keep up the same pace and churn up the same heat," he said as he clipped off the 130 paces a minute he learned in World War I.

"I'm all right physically," he said. "It's mentally and financially I have trouble."

His big news announcement was that ground-breaking ceremonies for the Memorial Library that will house his state papers and mementos of his White House days will be held on May 8, his seventy-first birthday.

The date was set by the building committee of the Harry S. Truman Library, Inc. The committee met this morning with Mr. Truman. Others at the meeting were Basil O'Connor, president of the library corporation; former Secretary of State Dean Acheson, vice president; Wilmer J. Waller, treasurer, and David Lloyd, executive secretary.

The library is estimated to cost $1,750,000 of which the committee reported more than $1,000,000 had been raised. The library site in Slover Park in Mr. Truman's home of Independence, Mo. is six blocks north of the Truman home.

Sees Louis Johnson

After his walk Mr. Truman had breakfast with Louis Johnson, an old friend whom he dismissed in 1950 as Secretary of Defense.

Mr. Johnson once described Mr. Truman as "the greatest living American" and was the force behind raising money for Mr. Truman's successful 1948 campaign. But two years later he turned in his resignation after critics attacked him for economies which they charged left the country unprepared when the Korean war broke out.

After breakfast Mr. Truman met with a group of eight Senate page boys, who brought photographs of the former President to be autographed. One boy told him the pictures were trading material on Capitol Hill among page boys and other employes.

Mr. Truman replied with a grin that he had found that out when he was a Senator. He said a page boy once had told him that the autographs of four Senators were worth one movie star autograph in a trade.

"I wonder what a former President's autograph is worth," mused Mr. Truman, who took office ten years ago this week on the death of President Franklin D. Roosevelt. "It ought to be worth more than one movie star's," he added.

April 17, 1955

TRUMAN STRESSES PRESIDENT'S LOAD

The Man Should Be Able to Do Work of 6, or Not Take Job, He Asserts Here

By WAYNE PHILLIPS

Former President Harry S. Truman said yesterday that a President should be able to do the work of six men, or he should not be in the White House.

This was one of a series of comments on the physical demands of the Presidency that he tossed off to reporters during a busy day in New York.

They were in response to questions about the possibility of his accepting a draft to run for President again. That they also applied to President Eisenhower was not made specific.

Mr. Truman refused to discuss whether General Eisenhower should run for re-election. To do so, he said, "wouldn't be proper."

But he firmly closed the door on any possibility that he would again seek the Presidency. Describing himself as "just a retired has-been," he said his position was the same as that once taken by the Civil War general William Techumseh Sherman.

The general said, and Mr. Truman quoted him correctly, "If nominated, I will not accept. If elected, I will not serve." The statement was in a telegram to the 1884 Republican National Convention, which was about to draft him as a candidate.

Disavows Candidacy

"I'm not a candidate for anything," Mr. Truman said. "If I were 46 or 50 it might be different. But I believe I have served my country, and after thirty years in public office I do not care for it again at this age and time."

Mr. Truman will be 72 years old on May 8. He was 67 on March 29. 1952. when he an-

nounced he would not again be a candidate for President. President Eisenhower, who is recovering from a heart attack, will be 66 next Oct. 14.

The former President's vigorous appearance yesterday contrasted with his plea of age. He was up at 6:30 A. M. after having gone to bed at 11 P. M. Tuesday.

At 7:26 he left the Carlyle Hotel at Madison Avenue and East Seventy-sixth Street for a brisk twenty-five-minute, sixteen-block walk before breakfast.

A force of twenty-five newsmen, including a newsreel photographer on roller skates, dogged his steps throughout the walk in a spectacle that has become a fixture of Mr. Truman's visits here.

"The Presidency is a killing job and a man must be young enough and vigorous enough to meet the situation," he said later. "The job has killed many a man—and I could name half a dozen."

Breakfast at the Hotel

Mr. Truman met the press again at 10 A. M. at the hotel, after breakfasting there with Mrs. Truman and their daughter, Margaret, who resides there.

He told questioners, who again inquired if he might run again, that people had been urging him to become a candidate ever since he announced his withdrawal four years ago.

"But they are barking up the wrong tree," he said. And again he quoted the position of General Sherman.

Mr. Truman had luncheon at the hotel, and in the afternoon sat for a sculptor who was putting the finishing touches on a bust for the Ben-Yehuda National Musuem in Jerusalem.

René Shapshak is executing the bust on commission for the Government of Israel. Most of the work was done last week at Independence, Mo., where Mr. Truman lives.

Mr. Truman had dinner last night at the home of a friend. This morning he will breakfast with Governor Harriman at the Governor's home. And this evening he speaks at the fund-raising dinner of the Democratic State Committee at the Sheraton-Astor Hotel.

TRUMAN LAUDS HERTER

He Says New Secretary Did 'a Good Job' at Paris

WASHINGTON, May 1 (AP) —Harry S. Truman today praised Secretary of State Christian A. Herter for "a good job" at Paris. The former President also put in a good word for Mr. Herter's two top aides.

Mr. Truman said he hoped very much that Mr. Herter and the Western foreign ministers could get an agreement with the Soviet Union at Geneva this month that would ease tension over Berlin.

And, as if to explain his benign before-breakfast mood, Mr. Truman commented in a walking-talking exchange with reporters:

"I never throw bricks at American foreign policy."

The former President lauded the promotion of Douglas Dillon to the No. 2 spot at the State Department, and the plan to elevate Robert Murphy from deputy to Under Secretary of State as No. 3 man.

TRUMAN TERMS END OF TRUJILLO FITTING

Former President Harry S. Truman said yesterday that he did "not like government by assassination," but that Generalissimo Rafael Leonidas Trujillo Molina of the Dominican Republic had met "the end of all dictators from Julius Caesar on down."

Mr. Truman. interviewed on his early morning walk, did not back away from his criticism of former President Dwight D. Eisenhower on Saturday at a political dinner in Washington. He then described General Eisenhower as a "do-nothing" President who had had a "do-nothing Administration."

"He and his boy [Richard M. Nixon] have been making remarks about Democrats and I was just answering them back," Mr. Truman said.

"I see no reason why I should pat him on the back or pinch him on the cheeks," Mr. Truman said. "I gave him the most orderly turnover of Government that any President has ever had and he never appreciated it."

Mr. Truman, who is staying at the Carlyle Hotel, later lunched with Premier David Ben-Gurion of Israel. Mr. and Mrs. Truman, who came to New York by train Wednesday, are visiting their daughter, Mrs. Clifton Daniel, and her family.

Their two grandchildren will have a birthday party over the week-end. Clifton Truman Daniel will be 4 years old Monday; William Wallace Daniel was 2 May 19.

February 2, 1956   May 2, 1959   June 2, 1961

TRUMAN RIDICULES STAND BY WALLACE

Former President Harry S. Truman said yesterday that Gov. George C. Wallace of Alabama was "making an ass of himself" in using state troopers to prevent public school desegregation in his state.

"The Governor," Mr. Truman said, "should be enforcing the laws, rather than using his office to break them."

Mr. Truman gave his views in an informal interview during his usual morning stroll from the Carlyle Hotel, where he is staying during a visit to the city. The 79-year-old former President, wearing a gray suit, kept up his customary brisk pace.

He said that the actions of Governor Wallace as well as those of other stanch segregationists "have been most injurious to our image abroad."

Asked whether the United States should continue giving aid to the South Vietnam Government of President Ngo Dinh Diem in view of its defiance of demands for reform, Mr. Truman replied: "A country which does not comply with the United Nations Charter does not deserve aid from any source."

He predicted that the nuclear test ban treaty, which will be debated in the Senate today, would be approved.

VIOLATIONS OF TRUCE SCORED BY TRUMAN

Former President Truman strode briskly in numbing cold yesterday on his accustomed morning constitutional walk, offering the following comment:

¶Texas cooking is "better than French."

¶Vietcong violations of the Christmas truce were "a dirty trick."

¶The joys of Christmas: Best when you "spend it with your grandchildren."

¶Peace marchers "don't know what's going on."

¶Missouri weather is "absolutely the same as New York's."

The former President, accompanied by a hard-pressed escort of reporters, left the Carlyle Hotel, 76th Street near Madison Avenue, at 7:30 A.M. The walk took him up Madison Avenue to 82d Street and back.

His cheeks glowing, the 81-year-old former Chief Executive remarked to his escorts:

"I don't know if it does you any good, but it does me a lot of good."

Mr. Truman and his wife, Bess, are here for a holiday visit with their daughter, Mrs. Clifton Daniel, her husband, and their three sons. Mr. Truman said he and Mrs. Truman would return to Independence, Mo., by plane tomorrow.

Nixon Affirms Getting Fund Of $16,000 From Backers

By GLADWIN HILL
Special to The New York Times.

ABOARD NIXON CAMPAIGN TRAIN, in California, Sept. 18—Senator Richard M. Nixon, Republican nominee for Vice President, today confirmed published reports that since his election to the Senate he had accepted about $16,000 in contributions from supporters. He said the money had been used for mailing and other political expenses for which some members of Congress drew official allowances, but which he felt "should not be charged to the Federal Government."

In a special statement issued on his campaign train, running from Los Angeles to Sacramento on the first leg of a ten-day tour of the West, the Californian said he had taken this course as a means of "playing completely square with the taxpayers."

The published reports quoted Dana C. Smith of Pasadena, Calif., leader of the Southern California Citizens for Eisenhower and Nixon Campaign, as stating that a group of Nixon supporters—whose identities were not disclosed but who were labeled in some reports as "the Millionaires' Club"—had contributed the money "to enable Dick to do a selling job for the American people in behalf of private enterprise and integrity in government."

Senator Nixon's statement follows:

"I have been informed that a New York newspaper today published an account of a fund collected by some of my supporters in the 1950 Senatorial campaign to take care of political expenses which I believe should not be charged to the Federal Government.

"The facts concerning this fund, which approximated $16,000 in the past two years, are as follows:

"It handles postage for mail on which I do not choose to use the much-abused Senatorial franking privilege. It defrays necessary travel expenses. It pays the cost of printing speeches and documents which otherwise might have been printed at the taxpayers' expense. It pays for extra clerical help needed to answer mail from my home State of California, which has 11,000,000 population.

"As an alternative I might have resorted to the use of tax-paid facilities, free government transportation, or I might have put my wife on the Federal payroll as did the Democratic nominee for Vice President [Senator John J. Sparkman of Alabama].

"I did none of these, nor have I been accepting law fees on the side while serving as a member of the Congress. I prefer to play completely square with the taxpayers."

The Senator did not elaborate on this statement. Aides indicated informally that the money had been contributed only as needed, and that, since Senator Nixon considered it perfectly proper, presumably the practice might continue.

The Senator declared he had not listed the $16,000 fund on his income tax because he had never handled the fund.

Its disbursement, he added, had always been in the hands of the committee of supporters headed by Mr. Smith.

His statement was made in response to a reporter's specific question, in amplification of his previous statement on the fund.

An aide said that Senator Nixon's only personal contact with the moneys might have been in instances in which he advanced personal funds for the special purposes designated, and later received reimbursement from the fund for the outlays.

Peter Edson, columnist for the Newspaper Enterprise Association Syndicate, quoted Mr. Smith as saying, as principal trustee of the fund, that contributions had been accepted only from individuals, and not from any corporations, and that he knew of no efforts by contributors to seek any favors in return.

Senator Nixon started off his first major campaign swing on a thirteen-car special train, with a 400-mile run through California's rich Central Valley punctuated by a series of aggressive rear-platform "whistle-stop" attacks on the National Administration and its chosen successor.

Asks Nixon Be Told to Quit
Special to The New York Times.

WASHINGTON, Sept. 18—Stephen A. Mitchell, chairman of the Democratic National Committee, called on Gen. Dwight D. Eisenhower today to demand the resignation of Senator Nixon as Republican candidate for Vice President.

The challenge was based on published reports that Mr. Nixon, since his election to the Senate in 1951, had accepted what Mr. Mitchell called, "large gifts from wealthy Californians." The published stories said the money was donated to Mr. Nixon to meet extra office expenses, such as radio and television fees, extra secretarial help, and similar items not covered by his Senate allowances, and which he, personally, was financially unable to bear.

Glen Lipscomb, executive secretary of Mr. Nixon's Washington campaign headquarters, described the money as "a private fund to be used to cover expenses of running Nixon's office that are not covered by his Government allowances."

"The challenge to General Eisenhower is simple," Mr. Mitchell said in a prepared statement issued by the Democratic National Committee.

"Either he will ask Senator Nixon to resign as the Republican nominee for Vice President, so that he can be replaced on the ticket by someone who has not lost his sense of public morals, or he will change his earlier statement to read, 'I would rather be elected President than to do without the help of those who have lost their sense of public morals.'"

This was a reference to a statement by General Eisenhower early in his campaign, in an attack on the alleged corruption of the Truman Administration. At that time the Republican Presidential candidate said that he would "rather not be elected President than be elected by the help of those who have lost their sense of public morals."

"General Eisenhower has been making a great show of indignation over corruption," Mr. Mitchell went on. "In demagogic speeches he has sought to give the impression that honesty among Government employes is the exception rather than the rule.

"He has followed up this loose talk with pious protestations of what he would do about corruption.

"Yet when one of his first political backers, Governor Payne of Maine, became enmeshed in a nasty liquor scandal on the eve of the Maine election, General Eisenhower met this scandal in his own family with deafening silence. The result was that Governor Payne is now a Senator-elect.

"This was a comparatively small test of General Eisenhower's sincerity as compared with today's revelation that Senator Nixon has been accepting donations from wealthy California businessmen to supplement his salary as a Senator.

"Senator Nixon knows that this is morally wrong. General Eisenhower knows that this is morally wrong. The American people know that this is morally wrong. By no standard of public morals or of private morals can such conduct be condoned or explained away."

Nixon Retorts to Mitchell

SACRAMENTO, Calif., Sept. 18 (AP)—Senator Nixon tonight hotly rejected as "a political smear" a suggestion by the Democratic National Chairman that he (Nixon) resign as Republican Vice-Presidential nominee. The suggestion was based on a charge that Mr. Nixon was "morally wrong" in defraying Senatorial expenses from $16,000 donated by wealthy backers.

"It's an attempt to pull a political smear," Mr. Nixon said here as he changed from train to plane on a campaign tour.

Then he shot back a question for the Democratic National Chairman, Mr. Mitchell:

"Why doesn't he ask Sparkman (United States Senator John Sparkman of Alabama, the Democratic Vice-Presidential nominee) to resign because his wife is on the (government) payroll?"

General's Aides Learn of Fund
Special to The New York Times.

OMAHA, Sept. 18—Officials on the Eisenhower train were informed of the charges that Senator Nixon had accepted more than $16,000 from California supporters, when newspapers were put aboard at Des Moines.

They refused to comment, however, pending a detailed check of the facts. Efforts were being made by the Eisenhower managers to talk directly with Senator Nixon.

Tells How Fund Was Spent

PASADENA, Calif., Sept. 18 (AP)—Mr. Smith, a lawyer, of this city, said that between $16,000 and $17,000 has been spent to pay bills incurred by Mr. Nixon in representing California. Mr. Smith, who said he disbursed the fund, said none of the money was for personal expenses.

He added that a group of from fifty to 100 southern Californians had paid into the fund and that the Senator would present expense bills for payment.

Mr. Smith declared that the $2,500 annual expense money allowed to Senators by the Federal Government was "nothing approaching enough for a Senator representing a state as large as California."

He said that payments had been made on bills incurred before Mr. Nixon was nominated for Vice President. It was planned to continue payment of expenses Senator Nixon incurred while representing the state, he added. The lawyer was finance chairman for Mr. Nixon when he successfully ran for the Senate two years ago, and is the Southern California chairman of the Eisenhower Volunteers.

"No member of the group has ever asked Senator Nixon for any special favors of any description," Mr. Smith said. "If any of them had, we would not have accepted any further contributions."

Although the financing group was believed to be predominantly Republican, Mr. Smith said he had not asked their political affiliation. The fund was set up after Mr. Nixon's election as Senator.

September 19, 1952

BACKED AS HONEST

Possibility of Getting Him to Quit Race Weighed but Is Not Pushed

GENERAL ATTACKS RIVAL

Asserts in Kansas City That 'Bosses' Blocked Kefauver to Boost Stevenson

By JAMES RESTON
Special to The New York Times.

KANSAS CITY, Mo., Sept. 19—Gen. Dwight D. Eisenhower announced tonight that a complete accounting would be made of the $16,000 given to his running mate, Senator Richard M. Nixon of California, by some of the Senator's political supporters.

The general preceded his speech here—a sharp attack on Gov. Adlai E. Stevenson of Illinois as a front man for the nation's big-city political bosses—by announcing that he had complete confidence in Senator Nixon.

The accounting on where the funds came from and how they were spent, the general said, will be made by Dana C. Smith of Pasadena, Calif., trustee of the fund, which Senator Nixon said had been originated "to support my fight against communism and corruption in Government."

This was the most hectic day in the Presidential campaign for General Eisenhower. He spent most of the day, as his campaign train rolled south through Nebraska to Kansas City, in a series of conferences on the Nixon problem with his principal advisers.

Withdrawal Considered

It is known that the possibility that Senator Nixon might have to be asked to withdraw from the race was discussed in these conferences.

It also is known that at one point during the day it was proposed to the general that he should try to have the facts in Senator Nixon's case placed before the Senate Committee on Ethics in Government, which is headed by Gov. Adlai E. Stevenson's own senior Senator from Illinois, Paul H. Douglas. This idea apparently was abandoned, however, somewhere along the Missouri-Nebraska border.

When the general's campaign train reached this city, however, there was another long conference between the candidate and his advisers and then a new beginning for this evening's speech was released to the press. This contained two things:

First, a long statement by Senator Nixon that had been given to one of the general's associates this afternoon and, second, a statement of the general's confidence in the California Senator.

The general stated: "Before I begin my formal remarks tonight, I want to say a few words regarding statements appearing in the press relative to Senator Nixon.

"Because he and I have been campaigning all day in different parts of the country I have not been able to talk directly with him about the fund which was provided by some of his constituents to meet certain political expenses. One of my associates had a talk with him by telephone and through this associate Senator Nixon gave me the following message:

"'Because of continued misrepresentation concerning disbursement of a fund which was collected and expended for legitimate, political, purposes, I have asked the trustee of this fund, Dana Smith of Pasadena, Calif., to make a full report to the public of this matter.

"'He will issue a complete accounting of the fund and its uses. It is my firm intention to prevent any misunderstanding about this fund.

"'This whole issue developed as a deliberate smear attempt by persons intent on perpetuating the present Administration in power. The only way to answer a smear is with the truth. This we shall do.

"'The facts will show that public spirited citizens who contributed to this fund asked nothing of me nor did they receive anything from me in any way of special favors, consideration or treatment. The facts will show that not one red cent was spent by me for my personal use.

"'The facts will make it crystal clear that such a legitimate political fund originated in an earnest and unselfish desire on the part of contributors to support my fight against communism and corruption in Government.'

"I have worked with and have confidence in Senator Nixon. I have read this statement to you because I believe it is an honest statement.

"Knowing Dick Nixon as I do, I believe that when the facts are known to all of us they will show that Dick Nixon would not compromise with what is right. Both he and I believe in a single standard of morality in public life."

The crowd of 9,500 in the auditorium cheered twice during the reading of Senator Nixon's statement, once when it promised a "full report" of the facts, again when it stated that the intent of the fund was to fight communism and corruption, and then cheered when the general said that he had confidence in Senator Nixon.

After reading this statement to his audience in a city noted for its Democratic political organization, General Eisenhower then opened his attack upon corruption in the Administration, and for the first time he really made a frontal assault upon his opponent for the Presidency, Governor Stevenson.

He said that Senator Estes Kefauver of Tennessee had demonstrated last spring that he was the popular choice among Democrats for that party's Presidential nomination.

"But who was this Senator?" the general asked. "He was the man who had been going up and down and across this country, courageously exposing to the view of the American people the trail of boss politicians. He exposed their coast-to-coast use of politics as a means to promote crime, corruption and organized immorality."

'Heirs' of the Machines

However, the Republican nominee asserted, Senator Kefauver's candidacy ran head-on into the Democratic city bosses. He asked: "Could it be that they blocked him because he had exposed them?"

General Eisenhower then asked another question:

"And who gave the final conclusive nod—who delivered the votes—that sewed up the nomination for the present Democratic candidate? The bosses. The heirs and joint heirs of the Kelly machine in Chicago, the Tammany machine in New York, the Hague machine in New Jersey, and the Pendergast machine in Kansas City—to name a few of them."

Just as Governor Stevenson had taunted the general for supporting such Republican Senatorial candidates as Senator Joseph R. McCarthy of Wisconsin and William E. Jenner of Indiana, so the general remarked: "I sympathize with the nominee of the Democratic party because of the company he is obliged to keep."

The general tried several new things tonight. He not only made a stronger personal attack on Governor Stevenson than ever before, but he also tried to split the Democratic party, as the Democrats have tried to split the conservative and liberal wings of the Republican party, by emphasizing Senator Kefauver's victories in the primary elections and his loss of the nomination to Governor Stevenson.

Also, while the General emphasized that he was going to be "serious" in this campaign, his own script had a little more zip in it tonight than usual. Finally, he took part in a question-and-answer political broadcast on television in which selected citizens outside the studio asked him questions and he answered them from the TV studio. His advisers were pleased with the results of this experiment and plan to repeat it.

In view of the fact that he was going to make so sharp an attack on his opponent and the Democratic party on the corruption issue in the Municipal Auditorium this evening, General Eisenhower was known to have been somewhat alarmed earlier that some of the Democrats in the audience might heckle him on the Nixon issue. This was one of the primary considerations that led him and his advisers to decide to open his speech with his statement on Senator Nixon.

It would be difficult to underestimate the impact of the Nixon incident on the general and his advisers today. They were optimistic when they started out on this twelve-state journey into the Middle West and the border states. They felt that their recent southern journey had ended the lassitude and pessimism that had been so prevalent in the Republican camp during the month of August. Moreover, the first three days of this tour went even better than they had anticipated. They expected that they would be well received in Indiana and Illinois, which are normally Republican strongholds, but their receptions, particularly in South Bend, Ind., and Aurora, Ill., were spectacular by any standards, and when more than 300,000 persons turned out in St. Paul and Minneapolis, a liberal community that has been with the winning President ever since the election of 1920, they were convinced that they were running with a strong political current in favor of a change in the National Administration.

Slow to Recognize Problem

It was not until the Nixon story broke, however, that the optimism began to subside and even then the general's advisers were slow to recognize that they had a major problem on their hands.

Yesterday afternoon at Des Moines, Iowa, a bundle of copies of a newspaper—The Des Moines Register—was thrown aboard the train, but this carried merely a newspaper report of the charge that said Senator Nixon had benifited by an expense fund amounting to more than $16,000. Besides, the general went to bed for a nap right after his Des Moines speech and did not hear about the report until late last night.

Even then, comparatively little attention was paid to it by the general's advisers because The Omaha World-Herald, which was circulated through the train last night, put the story of the Democratic party's demand that Mr. Nixon resign on page 57.

By this morning, however, the general himself was concerned. He called a meeting before 8 o'clock in the rear car of the campaign train. This was attended by Gov. Sherman Adams of New Hampshire, his principal assistant; Arthur E. Summerfield, chairman of the Republican National Committee; Senators Frank Carlson of Kansas and Fred Seaton of Nebraska, and Dr. Milton Eisenhower, the general's brother.

Previously, Mr. Summerfield had read a news agency account of Senator Nixon's explanation of why he had used the expense fund. Dissatisfied, Mr. Summerfield called the Senator in California and took down the text of the Vice Presidential nominee's statement, as dictated by one of Senator Nixon's aides.

What went on in this first meeting was not disclosed but it can be said that there was agreement that Senator Nixon's explanation could not be allowed to end the matter; that in fairness to Senator Nixon, whatever was done should be done on the basis of facts and not of charges; and that the incident must be treated with the utmost seriousness.

It was agreed in that meeting that a statement should be issued making clear that the general was dealing with the situation. After the train started south through the Nebraska farmlands, James C. Hagerty, the general's press secretary, issued this statement in the general's name:

"I have long admired and applauded Senator Nixon's American faith and determination to drive Communist sympathizers from offices of public trust.

"There has recently been leveled against him a charge of unethical practices. I believe Dick Nixon to be an honest man. I am confident that he will place all the facts before the American people fairly and squarely.

"I intend to talk with him at the earliest time we can reach each other by telephone."

Meanwhile, the general had a busy morning. He made back-platform speeches to crowds varying between 1,000 and 3,000 in four Nebraska towns, Plattsmouth, Nebraska City, Auburn and Falls City. And this was what was going on in the rest of the train:

In the private quarters of the end car, his wife was not feeling well early in the morning and had to miss the first two stops for the first time on the tour. In the same car his aides were still discussing whether it would be best to have Senator Nixon come to St. Louis to meet him; whether to contact other leaders of the party for their opinions of the Nixon incident; whether to bring a Congressional committee of inquiry into the Nixon case; how to get all the facts in the case together; and, last but not least, what to say in Kansas City tonight.

At the same time the general had to keep going into the next car to greet the Nebraska politicians who were coming aboard at every stop, and to visit with them and urge the party workers to get

out and ring door bells for the ticket in November. Consequently it would be something of an over-statement to say that his back-platform speeches were as effective today as they had been earlier in the week.

In his first stop, at Plattsmouth, he spoke for barely a minute then introduced his wife, only to remember that she wasn't available.

At Nebraska City, he referred, directly to the issue of corruption in the Democratic Administration.

"We have to get rid of people," he said, "who regard public office as an opportunity to enrich or aggrandize themselves. We have to get a government that believes itself the servant of the people, that is cognizant of, and wants to know, your opinions as a segment of the United States in order to decide what policies we shall adopt. That is the simple faith that I am trying to spread over this United States.

"I have come to you so that you may have your own opportunity to decide in these few brief moments whether I am sincere or whether I am not. That is for you to decide. * * *"

At the other stops in Nebraska he introduced the same themes he had discussed in Indiana, Illinois and southern Minnesota, only more briefly.

At Auburn, he said, "We have evidence of venal practices in Gov-

ernment, in the Internal Revenue Department, the Justice Department, the Agriculture Department; people using their office either for political purposes or for their own enrichment. That kind of thing comes because the Government has grown too far from the people. Along with it they have been absorbing the proper responsibilities of states and communities and taking them into the Federal Government so as to extend their power over us."

By the time the train reached St. Joseph, Mo., however, the repercussions of the Nixon affair had begun to become apparent. Here the general had a large crowd of about 8,000 spread over the railroad yards and upon the tops of houses and signal poles. He told them that he felt it would not be possible to get peace or honest government unless the Republicans were put in charge in Washington, and then he gave them his usual pledge, that if elected he would work for all the American people and not just some segment of them.

As the train left, however, somebody threw aboard a lot of copies of the St. Joseph News-Press, which carried at the top of its front page the following item:

"The News-Press editorial policy supports the Eisenhower-Nixon ticket. Yesterday it developed that some rich men set up a trust fund for Vice-Presidential Repub-

lican nominee Richard Nixon, Senator from California.

"This morning some one in the composing room displayed his poetic talent and indited the following, which may get no little circulation:

THEY'RE FIXIN' MR. NIXON
We have often heard the shout
"We must turn the rascals out.
    The rate they're leading us to
        ruin isn't slow."
But cleaning up their own backyard
    May be just a wee bit hard
        When millionaires are slipping
            them the dough.

While the train was moving on south in Missouri to Kansas City one of General Eisenhower's aides let it be known in the press room that a statement would be issued in Kansas City before the general made his evening speech.

Thereafter the Republican nominee arrived at the depot, was met by a crowd of about 1,000 and paraded to his hotel. For the next hour, while he was trying to get a little rest, he was treated to the sound of a noise truck outside, blaring away, "If you're tired of the red herrings in Washington, of Dean Acheson, of corruption and of crooked officials, elect Gen. Dwight D. Eisenhower."

The general's party will leave here tomorrow morning and continue his whistle-stop tour until he reaches St. Louis tomorrow night.

Text of General Eisenhower's Speech at Kansas City

KANSAS CITY, Sept. 19 (AP)—Following is the text of Gen. Dwight D. Eisenhower's speech tonight at the Municipal Auditorium in Kansas City:

Before I begin my formal remarks tonight, I want to say a few words regarding statements appearing in the press relative to Senator Nixon.

Because he and I have been campaigning all day in different parts of the country I have not been able to talk directly with him about the fund which was provided by some of his constituents to meet certain political expenses. One of my associates had a talk with him by telephone and through this associate Senator Nixon gave me the following message:

"Because of continued misrepresentation concerning disbursement of a fund which was collected and expended for legitimate, political, purposes, I have asked the trustee of this fund, Dana Smith of Pasadena, Calif., to make a full report to the public of this matter.

"He will issue a complete accounting of the fund and its uses. It is my firm intention to prevent any misunderstanding about this fund.

"This whole issue developed as a deliberate smear attempt by persons intent on perpetuating the present Administration in power. The only way to answer a smear is with the truth. This we shall do.

"The facts will show that public spirited citizens who contrib-

uted to this fund asked nothing of me nor did they receive anything from me in any way of special favors, consideration or treatment. The facts will show that not one red cent was spent by me for my personal use.

"The facts will make it crystal clear that such a legitimate political fund originated in an earnest and unselfish desire on he part of contributors to support my fight against communism and corruption in government."

Confidence in Senator

I have worked with and have confidence in Senator Nixon. I have read this statement to you because I believe it is an honest statement.

Knowing Dick Nixon as I do, I believe that when the facts are known to all of us they will show that Dick Nixon would not compromise with what is right. Both he and I believe in a single standard of morality in public life.

I am told that if I tried to describe bad government to the average Kansas Citian, he wouldn't say in the old Missouri phrase "Show me." He'd probably say instead that right here in Kansas City, he had already been shown! He never wants to be shown again.

I take it for granted that most Kansas Citians know exactly what a boss politician looks like. They know exactly what boss politics smell like, and the cost to them of bad public management and low public morals. They know exactly what boss rule feels like.

Here you have conclusively proved that you don't like boss government. I have a feeling as I go around the country that on Nov. 4 the people of America are going to prove that they don't like it either.

Without minimizing the effective work done here by others, I want to pay tribute to the women of Kansas City, who, when they were faced with bad government, made clean government a crusade. All over this country women in a like crusade are taking their political brooms in hand. I have yet to hear of a more powerful political weapon than a broom in the hands of a morally indignant woman.

Women will understand what I mean when I say that what Government is in need of is not a "lick and a promise" kind of cleaning. It is not in need of merely a fall housecleaning to be followed maybe by a spring house-cleaning. What our Government is in need of is an all-out and all-through cleaning by an administration which thereafter will keep it clean.

Republican Persistence Hailed

Now when it comes to outright corruption of any kind I know the first thing to do about it. We believe in jailing the guilty parties and in firing those who have condoned guilt.

Thanks largely to Republican persistence, there has been a widespread exposing of scandals in our Federal Government. A good many people in public life or holding public office have been

jailed or fired or allowed to resign because of "ill health."

I think I know what you want in dealing with this situation. You want an administration that does not leave the discovery and uprooting of corruption to mere chance. You want an administration which does not wait around until Congressional committees are obliged to dig it out.

You are looking forward to an Administration which will put every investigative agency of our Government on the job and keep those agencies on the job until the last crook and near crook have been run down and run out. Then I am for going on from there to see to it that we have an incorruptible Government because political appointments are given only to incorruptible men and women.

What is the source of these unprecedented misdoings in our national Government? The answer is not hard to find. This Administration has allowed and helped the machine bosses in our cities to move their kind into Federal posts and to practice on the national level the vicious morals of boss politics.

I need not recite to you the long list of those who have had and still have a pass to inner offices on the highest level of Government.

One thing the bosses have not done: They have not quit the party too long in power. One thing has not happened to them: The party too long in power has not thrown them out—not one of them. Who, if that party 'tried to throw them, would do the throwing?

Can we trust the party that elevated them, that desperately needs their bought and delivered votes? You and I know better than that—and so do the American people.

The American people know the whole sorry record. Let us look at that record—a recent part of it. At the Democrat National Convention one candidate for the nomination, a distinguished United States Senator, was far out in front with the rank and file of his party. In every poll, in every primary vote, he led all others among the rank and file of party members. But who was the Senator? He was the man who had been going up and down across this country, courageously exposing to the view of the American people the traits of boss politicians. He exposed their coast to coast use of politics as a means to promote crime, corruption and organized immorality.

What happened to the candidacy of the Senator who had done these things? You know what happened to it: It ran head-on into the city bosses.

Could it be that they blocked him because he had exposed them? And who gave the final conclusive nod—who delivered the votes—that sewed up the nomination for the present Democrat candidate? The bosses. The heirs and joint heirs of the Kelly machine in Chicago, the Tammany machine in New York, the Hague machine in New Jersey, and the Pendergast machine in Kansas City—to name a few of them.

I sympathize with the nominee of the Democrat party because of the company he is obliged to keep.

Perhaps he may disown that company altogether. But this is the pay-off question: Will the bosses disown him? Have you detected any signs of alarm from them? Have you heard any reports that they are dismantling their machines in fear lest their party and their candidate win? Have you heard that any of them in death-bed conversions have turned Republican?

Of course you haven't, and you won't. Every one of these bosses will go all out and down the line, to deliver by whatever means, on Nov. 4. They will do that, not because they believe their candidate is one of their own kind.

They are smart enough to know that if he were one of their kind neither they nor their party would have a chance to win.

They are smart enough to know what they need this year. They need it this year more acutely than in many, many years. They know above everything else that they need an honest man out in front. Well, they've got one.

What they really fear is a Republican victory on Nov. 4. That will mean honesty, not only out in front, but honesty both front and back.

What People Are 'Due to Get'

That I can assure you is the kind of government the American people are looking for. It is exactly what they are due to get.

You probably get the idea from the press that on these campaign trips across the country I do all the talking. I am happy to report to you that I don't. The people also talk.

Associated Press Wirephoto

A PAT FOR LUCK: Gen. Dwight D. Eisenhower gives an emblematic G. O. P. elephant a pat before making a speech in Omaha Thursday.

They talk back and they talk up and don't think they ever hesitate. They talk by the letters they write me and the notes they leave on the train. They talk by telegrams. They talk by the way they shout in strictly non-radio language, "Give 'em this, Ike," or "Give 'em that."

And nothing I could say to the people could be one-tenth as important as what the people have been saying to me. North, south, east and west, they have been saying, "we've had too much for much too long."

Part of the job ahead is ferreting out and punishing individual offenders; but that is only a small part.

These disclosures of graft, dishonesty and inefficiency in high and low offices are merely the symptoms of a morbid disease within. The remedy for such an illness lies far deeper than dealing with external symptoms.

Before there can be any cure, there must be a probing for the cause. The doctor cannot write a sound prescription before he has made his diagnosis.

So here, no true cleaning of our governmental house can be effected until we are able surely to find out how the guilty ones obtained their positions of trust and authority in our national Government.

We must ask, and get the answers to these questions. How was it possible that such men as these were given high offices of public trust? What tests were used to ascertain their fitness and their qualifications?

What were their records before they were appointed? What and whose influence was used? What debts were being discharged? What obligations were being incurred? And lastly, what services were these men to render to those who sponsored their appointment?

You cannot cure a disease so long as its roots remain untouched. We will get at its roots.

Then we will have in Washington an Administration which measures up to the standard set more than a hundred years ago by Henry Clay. He said: "Government is a trust, and the officers of Government are trustees, and both the trust and the trustees are created for the benefit of the people."

Running On the Record

Now the whole country has it on the highest authority that the candidate of the Democrat party must run on the record of the present Administration. That seems perfectly obvious. That is what the Democrat candidate seems to be trying to do.

But his efforts to run on the record of his party too long in power seems like the story of Little Liza trying to cross the river on the ice—carefully, fearfully, picking her way, jumping from ice cake to ice cake. She made it —but I don't believe the Democrat candidate will.

In the record of this Administration there simply aren't enough ice cakes that are big enough or safe enough!

Let us look at some of the other things which the candidate of the party too long in power must try to run on. Let us look at that record in terms of your own family, in terms of family affairs and household management.

Most families have to plan their spending and within reasonable limits, they have to make sure that they do not spend more than they plan. So do most business men. Have you heard of a single, sizable Administration project that did not cost more—multiplied millions more—than the plans called for? No, the record of this Administration in extravagance and waste is a mighty poor record to have to run on.

If in your family affairs you find that your plan to build an addition on the house is going to cost a lot more than you figured on, what do you do? You don't go ahead, regardless. You call up the carpenter, the painter and the brick mason—and you call off the project. Have you ever heard of an Administration project being called off because it cost too much?

No—I don't believe the American people get any satisfaction from the record of this Adminis-

tration in its irresponsible spending of your money.

Or take another problem—one that you meet up with every day. Let's suppose that tomorrow morning you go to the grocery store to do the family shopping. The grocer has all the things you want to buy. You have what looks like $20 to buy them with. But long before you have shopped your way from the vegetable counter to the meat counter, you discover that what looks like $20 isn't $20 at all. In terms of what that much money would have bought in 1940, your $20 is worth exactly $10.40.

Now don't blame the grocer or the wholesaler or the farmer for cutting your dollar almost in half. They are not the cause. Like you, they are the victims. The cause is inflation. And what is the cause of inflation?

Calls It 'Calculated Policy'

Let me quote an answer to that question from a recent editorial in a great newspaper: "Inflation has been the calculated policy of the White House on the labor front, the fiscal front, and the agricultural front."

Inflation, folks, is another very shaky part of the record of this administration.

Now the chances are that in your family, your husband today gets more pay in dollars than he got two years ago, in 1950. Two years ago the average factory worker got about $3,000 a year. Today he is making about $3,500. But are he and his family $500 better off?

Let's look at that record. In those two years the income tax this working man has to pay to the Federal Government has more than tripled. The purchasing power of his remaining dollars has nosedived.

The result is that this worker and his family are on an economic treadmill. And tread as hard as they will, they are not even staying where they were. They are slipping back. Their $500 gain in wages has been wiped out by inflation and by taxes. Today, in what they can buy, they are actually worse off.

I do not believe that the candidate of the Democrat party will get very far on that record of treadmill prosperity.

That is the record—but it is only part of the record. I can assure you that the whole record will be laid out for the American people to take a good look at between now and next November 4th. I can also assure you that the Democrat candidate will run on that record because he will not be allowed to run away from it!

Between the Democrat and the Republican parties, there are deep differences. They are irreconcilable differences. And these differences add up to determine not only the way our present problems will be solved, but the direction in which America for the indefinite future will be headed.

The Democrat party has little faith in the people: in their capacities to do for themselves. The Republican party puts its faith in the people and points to America as proof of what the people can do for themselves.

Out of its lack of faith in the people, the Democrat party offers as the answer to every problem more government, at more public cost. Out of its faith in the people, the Republican party offers better government at less cost.

The Democrat party proposes more and more government in Washington — remote from the people. The Republican party wants to strengthen government on the state and local level—close to the people.

The Democrat party offers waste as a way of life and higher taxes as a virtue. The Republican party believes with Jefferson that "frugality" is the first among government virtues, and proposes to get 100 cents worth of good government out of every tax dollar.

Blieves Peace Is Possible

For the most serious of all problems—the problem of war and peace in our world—the Democratic party offers no long time policy at all—but only improvised policies of stop and go, zig, zag and zig. The Republican party believes that we can have lasting peace in our world. It proposes that we work out and adhere to an immediate and long-range program for peace that will be clear and positive and to which all Americans and all peave-loving peoples will rally.

These differences, ladies and gentlemen, are the issues of this campaign. They are not issues to be taken lightly, or lightly treated. They are serious for every American. That is the way I shall continue to treat them.

Especially are those problems serious for what we oldsters call the younger generation. Young people with their idealism, their faith and their hopes must have a fair chance to shape the nation which will be theirs.

My closing words tonight are directed to the young people of America.

After November Fourth, I believe America can once more look with confidence to the future. That future can be—will be—greater, far greater, than our past has been. It is my deep conviction that in the years ahead we will realize to the full the promise of America. That is youth's immediate challenge. That is youth's long-time opportunity. That is its lifetime task.

Vice Presidential Nominee Says 'Crooks' Attack Him

He Also Delays His Train on Coast to Reply to Query on $16,000 Aid

By LAWRENCE E. DAVIES
Special to The New York Times.

ON THE NIXON TRAIN, at Red Bluff, Calif., Sept. 19—Senator Richard M. Nixon, Republican Vice Presidential nominee, took the offensive today and drew cheers from station platform crowds by denouncing "smears" from "Communists and crooks" as he carried his first whistle-stop campaign tour through northern California and into Oregon.

He established a pattern early in the day for dealing with the disclosure that, during the last two years, $16,000 of his expenses as a Senator had been paid from a fund raised by supporters who saw eye to eye with him on the free enterprise and governmental integrity issues.

The disclosure was made yesterday by Dana C. Smith, a Pasadena, Calif., lawyer and leader of the Southern California Citizens for Eisenhower and Nixon.

Developments indicated it came as a complete surprise to Gen. Dwight D. Eisenhower, Republican Presidential nominee, but a spokesman on the Nixon train said that as the result of telephone conversations between the campaign trains of the two running mates, there was to be expected no change in the pattern set by Mr. Nixon in meeting the unexpected issue.

From a crowd of about 500 that met the train at Marysville, first stop of the day, a voice cut into one of the nominee's sentences to demand:

"Tell them about the $16,000."

Train Delayed for a Reply

Senator Nixon asked that the train's departure be held up while he charged that after he had received the nomination for Vice President at the Republican convention at Chicago in July, he received this warning:

"That if I continue to attack the Communists and the crooks in this government they would continue to smear me."

He added:

"And, believe me, you can expect that they will continue to do so." Senator Nixon began by reminding his hearers of his investigative work as a member of the House Committee on Un-American Activities, in which he is credited with a major role in obtaining the indictment and conviction of Alger Hiss, a State Department official,

Associated Press

Senator Richard M. Nixon

on a perjury charge in connection with alleged pro-Communist activities.

"Ever since I have done that work," Mr. Nixon went on as the crowd applauded, "the Communists the left-wingers, have been fighting me with every smear that they have been able to do.

"They started it yesterday—you saw it in your morning papers. They tried to say that I had taken money, $16,000. What they did not point out is this: That what I was doing was saving you money, rather than charging the expenses of my office, which were in excess of the amounts which were allowed by the taxpayers and allowed under the law; rather than taking that money and rather than using the money, the taxpayers' money for those purposes, what did I do?

"What I did was to have those expenses paid by people back at home who were interested in seeing that the information concerning what was going on in Washington was spread among the people of their state.

"Let me go on and say this: What else, what would you rather have me do."

A Reference to Sparkman

Applause and cheers greeted this question and he continued:

"I'll tell you what some of them do. They put their wives on the payroll. That's what Mr. Sparkman did."

This was a reference to Senator John J. Sparkman of Alabama, the Democratic Vice Presidential nominee.

"I don't believe in putting my wife on the payroll and taking your money and using it for that

purpose," Senator Nixon declared. "I think most of you will agree with me on that.

"And Pat Nixon (Patricia Ryan Nixon, his wife) has worked in my office night after night after night, and I can say this, and I say t proudly, she has never been on the Government payroll since I have been in Washington, D. C."

More applause and some shouts interrupted him here, and the nominee then took up "Point 2," asking:

"What else would you do? Do you want me to go on and do what some of those people are doing? Take fat legal fees on the side?"

Says He Eschewed Legal Fees

Senator Nixon continued:

"Perhaps you ought to know this: During the time I have been in Washington—I am proud of this —I've never taken a legal fee, although as a lawyer I could legally but not ethically have done so. And I am never going to in the future, because I think that's a violation of a trust which my office has.

"Just let me say this before I leave, let me say this: They have told you, and you can be sure that the smears will continue to come and the purpose of those smears is to make me, if possible, relent and let up on my attack on the Communists and the crooks in the present Administration.

"I'm going to tell you this: As far as I'm concerned, they've got another guess coming, because what I intend to do is to go up and down this land, and the more they smear me the more I'm going to expose the Communists and the crooks and those that defend them until they throw them all out of Washington."

At the next stop, Chico, also in the rich agricultural Sacramento Valley, where police estimated the crowd at 700 to 800, Senator Nixon did not wait for a question about the $16,000.

Toward the end of his talk in which, as at Marysville, he dealt largely with farm themes and asked for control of power and water resources locally instead of "by bureaucrats in Washington," he called attention himself to the fund disclosure and again called it a "smear."

He said that attempts to "smear me personally" could be expected "from now to election day," but he asserted he was "proud of my record" and shouted that he was not going to let up on my attacks on those responsible for selling this country down the river."

It seemed evident that General Eisenhower had been unaware of the payment of some of Mr. Nixon's expenses for stamps, printing costs, extra clerical help and travel since the latter's election to the Senate.

A spokesman on the Nixon thirteen-car campaign special said:

"It may be assumed that General Eisenhower was not aware of the existence of the trust fund."

This informant added there was "no point in bringing it to his attention, since its existence was no secret, no attempt had been made to hide it" and the nominee did not consider he was doing anything unethical by having some of his expenses met from the fund.

'Left-Wing Elements' Cited

Mr. Nixon, himself, in a statement last midnight had charged that "left wing elements" had "tried to manufacture and create an air of suspicion over a matter which is completely open and above board in every respect." •

Following the Chico speech the train was delayed more than half an hour by a series of telephone conversations. Eisenhower strategists had telephoned to the Nixon train, it was stated, to engage in "liaison conversations" that had been planned to take place from time to time between the advisers of the team mates "to coordinate campaign problems."

The matter of the $16,000 "came up," a spokesman related, and added:

"The Eisenhower people were told about the crowd reaction at Marysville and were very pleased."

General Eisenhower, he said, did not get on the phone but Senator Nixon had a "very brief" conversation with Senator Fred Seaton of Nebraska, one of the Eisenhower's advisers.

Asked if the Eisenhower aide was seeking an explanation of the $16,000 matter, the spokesman replied he was "sure that was not the program." He said that Murray Chotiner, campaign manager for Senator Nixon, had talked with the Eisenhower train and with Washington headquarters, but the trends of the conversations were not disclosed.

As his train sped northward Senator Nixon made speeches from the rear platform at Red Bluff, Redding and Dunsmuir before crossing from his home State for Oregon, where his schedule called for evening stops at Ashland, Medford and Grants Pass.

Praise for the Valley Growers

All up through the Sacramento Valley he sought votes on the theme that the farmers who raised peaches, pears, almonds and other specialty crops for which California is noted, should have the same price support protection that the big wheat and corn growers of other states get.

Referring to the great Federal dams built or under construction in the Valley he drew applause by declaring that it was "time we had engineers rather than propaganda agents in the Bureau of Reclamation."

"I think you know what I mean by that," he added.

Private power interests of California have engaged in a running fight with the Federal Bureau of Reclamation in connection with some aspects of the Central Valley Power and Water project.

At Chico, Senator Nixon caused some disappointment among local folk by praising a former fellow student at Whittier College, Mark Jacobs, as vice principal of the Chico High School. Mayor Theodore Meriam of Chico said Mr. Jacobs had that position not at Chico but at Marysville, a previous stop.

Senator Nixon at Red Bluff drew a crowd, that after an hour-and-a-half wait in the heat, numbered around 300 when the train pulled in.

At several places he called for development of a program that would "stop the dumping products in the United States," that otherwise American farmers "are going to be right behind the eight ball."

To the younger members of his audience he said that "boys 14, 15 and 16 will be over in Korea fighting or in the Army if we don't have a change in our foreign policy."

At Redding late, not far from the Shasta Dam, where about 700 persons were assembled, Mr. Nixon told them the "opposition" had engaged in a "frantic attempt to smear me," and he again denied any wrongdoing in relation to the fund.

"Do you think when I come out to California to make a political speech the taxpayers ought to pay the bill? No."

That, he said, was the type of thing paid for out of the fund supplied by California supporters.

Almost everywhere he asked whether the people were satisfied with the Administration, whether they thought they were getting their money's worth, and got back in reply vociferous "No's!"

Paper Demands Withdrawal
By PAUL P. KENNEDY
Special to THE NEW YORK TIMES.

WASHINGTON, Sept. 19—Senator Nixon came in for further attack today over his acceptance of about $16,000 in contributions from supporters since his election to the Senate.

The Washington Post, editorially supporting the Republican ticket, published an editorial tonight asking that Senator Nixon withdraw his candidacy. Such a withdrawal, the editorial said, "would provide the Republican party an unparalleled opportunity to demonstrate the sincerity of its campaign against loose conduct and corruption in Government."

A spokesman at the newspaper said, after Gen. Dwight D. Eisenhower's second statement in support of Senator Nixon, "we will stand on our editorial."

Senator Karl E. Mundt of South Dakota, co-chairman of the Republican Speakers Bureau, defended Senator Nixon, declaring the attack on him a "filthy" maneuver by "left-wingers, fellow-travelers" and a "self-admitted three-year member of the Young Communist League."

Called 'Smear' Tactics

He identified the former member of the Young Communist League as James Wechsler, editor of The New York Post, which published the first report on the Nixon fund.

Referring to the report, Senator Mundt said:

"This is the type of smear tactics Wechsler and the other left-wingers and fellow-travelers have learned so well to use.

"Both the origin of this matter and the collaborationist method by which it is sought to make an issue of it are filthy and beneath contempt."

In New York Mr. Wechsler said:

"When a pro-Eisenhower newspaper exposes unethical practices in Government the Republicans call it a public service; when a pro-Stevenson newspaper uncovers similar conduct on the Republican side it's called subversion.

"Senator Nixon has not challenged a single fact in The Post story.

"What facts were 'twisted,' Senator Mundt?"

The Washington Post said at the outset of its editorial that it did "not doubt that Senator Nixon was free of any improper motives or immoral intentions" in accepting the contributions.

The editorial stated later, however, that "this newspaper is especially disturbed by the Nixon episode because our original endorsement of General Eisenhower was based on the assumption that he, more than any other candidate, could clear the air in Washington of the poison of scandal and corruption."

"We expressed a belief," the editorial continued, "that Ike 'would be the dynamic force to rejuvenate our politics.' We still harbor that hope, but it is obvious that his efforts will be gravely handicapped if his running mate exemplifies the unethical conduct that he is denouncing."

No Comment by Tax Office

A spokesman for the Bureau of Internal Revenue said that it had "no comment" on the report of gifts to Senator Nixon and how they had been handled for tax purposes.

A Bureau official who is a technician on the intricacies of income taxes stated, however, that in general these things were true:

1. A gift "in fact" is not taxable in the income of the person who receives the gift. The person who gives it may have to pay a tax, particularly if the gift is made out of income, not out of capital.

2. The "ordinary and necessary expenses" of a business may be deducted from a person's income in tax returns and holding a public office is considered a business.

3. Campaign expenses are not deductible.

Allan S. Haywood, executive vice president of the C. I. O., declared tonight that "California business men who have made contributions to Senator Nixon's 'mutual fund' earned handsome dividends on their investment every time the Senator cast a vote on the floor of the United States Senate."

Calls for the 'Full List'

Challenging the Republican Vice Presidential nominee to reveal the full list of contributors to the "Poor Richard Fund," Mr. Haywood said in a statement:

"The administrator of the trust fund for 'Poor Richard' is Dana C. Smith, a Pasadena corporation lawyer who specializes in tax cases. Just one year ago, in September, 1951, Nixon repaid, with considerable interest, the investment Smith had made in him.

"Nixon voted against plugging excess profits tax loopholes, against the depletion loophole which gives the oil industry tremendous tax benefits, against increasing the capital gains tax from 25 to 28 per cent, against repealing the split income tax provisions, which benefit only those who make more than $10,000 a year, and against the withholding tax on dividends.

"Nixon also has proved to be a sound investment for the three California real estate men who each bought a 'piece' of the Republican Vice Presidential nominee—Robert and George Rowan and Morgan Adams Jr.

"Nixon's voting record on housing and rent control bills shows that the California real estate men knew a good investment when they saw one. Last June Nixon voted to cut the public housing program from 75,000 units a year to 5,000. In the same month he also voted for an amendment permitting rents on housing around military installations and defense plants to be increased.

"The people who paid the money to Nixon seem to be satisfied that they got their money's worth, or they would have discontinued the fund long before now. In fact, they are so satisfied that they openly say that they plan to subsidize some one else in the event Nixon becomes Vice President."

Counts Calls for Inquiry

Dr. George S. Counts, Liberal party candidate for Senator, called last night for a full investigation of the Nixon fund.

"Corruption assumes many guises," he said. "We have seen the Joseph McCarthys [Senator Joseph R. McCarthy, Republican of Wisconsin] and the Bill O'Dwyers [Ambassador William O'Dwyer] in action and we have seen the trail of the mink coats.

"It is conceivable that the Nixon fund of $16,000, created by the California Volunteers for Eisenhower, was not designed to influence the opinions and actions of Senator Nixon? This is a question that General Eisenhower should answer.

"Obviously, this entire matter must be probed to the bottom before Nov. 4."

September 20, 1952

THE NIXON FUND

The "fifty to 100" private citizens who during the past two years have contributed some $16,000 to Senator Nixon to help him meet the expenses of his office showed poor judgment in making such a gift, and Senator Nixon has shown poor judgment in accepting it. There is no evidence that any graft or corruption is involved, and we do not think that any fair-minded person, uninfluenced by partisan considerations, would say that there was. With the facts we have before us there is also no evidence that any favors were sought by contributors to the fund. But there is no doubt that both the Senator and his benefactors have indulged in a bad practice that could lead to vicious abuses. Mr. Nixon must realize that this practice is not to be condoned, particularly on the part of a Republican Vice-Presidential nominee whose campaign is based in large part on raising the moral level of government.

Admittedly it is not easy to draw a clear distinction in principle between the accepted practice of giving campaign-contributions to candidates for office and the unusual practice, followed in this instance, of giving a sort of sustaining fund to a man who has already achieved office. But there is a difference, if for no other reason than that the one is accepted, and specifically recognized and circumscribed by law, while the other is not. Mr. Nixon says that the funds were used for postage, travel, printing and clerical expenses in the course of his duties as Senator from California. We see no reason to question the statement; but we think it far better for such expenditures to be paid from public than from private sources, no matter how disinterested the latter may be.

The question which the Republican leaders must now face, and decide without loss of time, is whether Mr. Nixon's record in this matter has not impaired fatally his usefulness as a candidate for the office of Vice President.

September 20, 1952

Nation's Press Divided on Nixon; Disapproval Expressed by 2 to 1

The nation's press was divided yesterday in its editorial comments on the disclosure that Senator Richard M. Nixon had received an $18,235 "expense fund" from a group of his California supporters.

A study of almost 100 representative papers, the majority of them supporters of the Eisenhower-Nixon ticket, showed disapproval of the Vice-Presidential candidate's action by a ratio of almost 2 to 1.

A few papers demanded Senator Nixon's immediate withdrawal from the race; others envisioned this as a possibility later, if proof were forthcoming that the Senator had violated the law.

Newspapers supporting the Senator argued that the contributions were made necessary by today's high living costs and the amount needed to meet the demands of public office. Many of these papers also attributed the disclosure of the "expense fund" to left-wingers and others anxious to damage the Republican cause.

Many of the editorials absolved Gen. Dwight D. Eisenhower, Senator Nixon's running mate, of knowledge of the fund and there were numerous expressions of regret that the general had been placed in an embarrassing position. Several papers referred to the disclosure as a "stigma" cast upon General Eisenhower as his campaign was reaching its fullest power.

Among the papers that followed the lead of The Washington Post in urging Senator Nixon's withdrawal were two Richmond, Va., papers, The News Leader and The Times-Dispatch. Both are supporters of the Eisenhower ticket. The News Leader said it was asking for the Senator's "resignation"

with the "deepest sense of disappointment." The Times-Dispatch declared that exposure of Senator Nixon's "clandestine arrangement" might spell the defeat of General Eisenhower.

The Denver Post, also an Eisenhower supporter, said the failure of Mr. Nixon to resign might lend color to the charge that the Republican party "has lost the capacity for decisive action."

Among the papers supporting Mr. Nixon was The Minneapolis Star, which said that the Republican Senator had chosen the "most open and straightforward of all legal ways" to augment his official income.

Another supporting newspaper, The Detroit Free Press, observed that "it looks to us as if the Truman-Stevenson board of strategy is attacking Nixon as a 'red herring' to distract attention from the ever-growing exposures of corruption that seems to lead directly to the White House and the cronies that infest it."

The Dallas, Tex., News, an Eisenhower supporter, said that neither Senator Nixon nor Senator John Sparkman of Alabama, the Democratic Vice Presidential nominee, had "committed an illegal act." The reference to Senator Sparkman was to the fact that he has employed his wife as his secretary. The paper said it was doubtful if almost 100 per cent of the members of the House and Senate did not receive "extra-curricular stipends without violating the law."

The roll of papers criticizing Senator Nixon included The St. Louis Post-Dispatch, which has not yet committed itself to either candidate. The paper said that even if an "audit" of the "expense fund" indicated that "every cent went for postage stamps," it would not effect the "basic moral principle here involved." The paper declared that the Nixon incident had forced upon General Eisen-

hower "one of the most critical decisions" of the campaign.

The Illinois State Register of Springfield, which is supporting Governor Stevenson, remarked that Senator Nixon "will have to do a lot of explaining."

The Louisville Times, uncommitted, said it joined with General Eisenhower in hoping that Senator Nixon "will place all the facts before the people fairly and squarely."

The Chicago Sun-Times, supporting Eisenhower and Nixon, said that unless Senator Nixon "comes completely clean on the identity of his patrons, and unless he accounts for the expenditures from the secret fund in the most minute detail, many Americans will feel that he has repaid honor with dishonor."

A similar call for "complete facts" came from The Hartford, Conn., Courant, an Eisenhower ticket supporter, which said that "the nearer Senator Nixon comes to that, the better off he and his party will be."

The Milwaukee Journal, uncommitted, observed that Senator Nixon may not have violated the law but that the "expense fund" was a violation of "good sense and creates the occasion for corruption whether corruption exists or not." The paper declared that Mr. Nixon had been campaigning against corruption and "captive candidates," and added: "But he is open to both charges."

The New York Post, which is supporting Governor Stevenson and carried the original story of the Nixon affair, said that the Senator's "presence on the Republican ticket will haunt and harass General Eisenhower until Election Day."

The Baltimore Sun, which has endorsed General Eisenhower, said that even if Senator Nixon had acted in all innocence and made no unethical use of the money, "he still stands disclosed as lacking in discernment and sensitivity."

A paper supporting Governor Stevenson, The Daytona Beach, Fla., News, remarked that if Senator Nixon "wasn't corrupt when he accepted money from selected constituents, then just where does corruption end and merely questionable practice begin?"

September 21, 1952

Excerpts From Editorial Comment on Nixon Special Expense Fund

Following are excerpts from editorial comment in newspapers gathered by THE NEW YORK TIMES on Senator Richard M. Nixon's special expense fund:

Northeast

NEW YORK CITY

Should Offer to Withdraw

The Herald Tribune (Ind. Rep. For Eisenhower)

There is no question but that the financial arrangements by which the Republican Vice Presidential nominee furthered his work were ill-advised. On the basis of the revealed facts, Senator Nixon's personal honesty should not be impeached. We share with General Eisenhower a conviction of the Senator's integrity. General Eisenhower has correctly withheld judgment until he could talk with Senator Nixon. Others can afford to wait as long. Eisenhower has handled difficult personal situations before, in which men of good intent have through some misstep or excess of zeal jeopardized the cause they support. He has combined absolute justice to the individual with clear determination to keep the big objective in view. The proper course of Senator Nixon in the circumstances is to make a formal offer of withdrawal from the ticket. How this offer is acted on will be determined by an appraisal of all the facts in the light of General Eisenhower's unsurpassed fairness of mind.

'A Belly Punch'

The Daily News (Ind. For Eisenhower)

A belly punch has just been thrown at Senator Richard M. Nixon of California, Republican candidate for Vice President, by a small, semi-busted New York leftist publication. This punch concerns a fund of $16,000 set up for Nixon (who is not wealthy). The money, according to the Fair Deal smearers, is a big slush fund. Nixon replies that the fund is not managed or touched by him, and is used "to take care of political expenses which I believe should not be charged to the Federal Government." There the matter stands. We think Nixon has made a good start at returning this belly punch. His next logical move would be to have the fund produce its books and records for all the inspection anybody wants to make of them. We hope he'll do that soon. Isn't politics a honey of a game, though?

'It Is Not Sound Policy'

The World-Telegram and Sun (Ind. For Eisenhower)

It is not sound policy for any public official to accept a subsidy of any kind from any source other than the income he is provided by law. Strict adherence to this principle is essential if the integrity of representative government is to be maintained. "As an alternative," he (Senator Nixon) has explained, "I might have resorted to the use of tax-paid facilities, free Government transportation,' or I might have put my wife on the payroll as did the Democratic nominee for Vice President (Senator John J. Sparkman of Alabama)." The alternatives Senator Nixon has cited cannot be condoned, although in practice they are all too commonplace. But the fact that he does not indulge in such practices does not make his own position right.

'Devastating Indictment'

The Post (Ind. For Stevenson)

After many anguished hours, General Eisenhower has reaffirmed his wistful hope that Senator Nixon can explain everything. In violation of all the McCarthy rules of jurisprudence, Governor Stevenson has simultaneously suggested that judgment on Nixon be suspended until he makes a full accounting of the special fund set up by California's 'millionaires' club" in his behalf. So Nixon is assured his day—or week end—in court. But nothing that Nixon and his desperate apologists have said or done indicates that he will be able to alter the devastating indictment against him. Who were the men who subsidized the Nixon fund? What were their stakes in legislation pending before the Senate? What, in short, did they expect to get for their money? These are the questions Nixon must answer—and which he has so far totally failed to meet.

First Move Np to Nixon

The Brooklyn Eagle (Ind.)

The revelation poses a serious problem for the Republicans. There is no question that this arrangement was extremely unwise. Furthermore, it may be regarded by General Eisenhower as so harmful to the Republican campaign as to require that the Senator withdraw from the ticket. The general has already expressed his faith in the integrity of Senator Nixon, which we share, but he had proceeded to get all the facts in the case. If it is deemed necessary that some action be taken, it is our feeling that the first move will come from Mr. Nixon himself.

NEWARK

Crusade Hampered

The Evening News (Ind. for Eisenhower)

For Mr. Eisenhower to request Senator Nixon to retire as his running-mate and to seek a new Vice-Presidential nominee from the Republican national committee would be a drastic, unprecedented step. But unless Mr. Nixon gets out, it is clear that Mr. Eisenhower's effective use of their activities in Washington" issue will be narrowed; that Governor Stevenson and President Truman, in his forthcoming whistle-stop tour will taunt the Republican candidates with setting up a dual moral standard.

PHILADELPHIA

Explanation Demanded

The Inquirer (Ind. for Eisenhower)

The disclosure is a serious matter that demands explanation. Attempts made by some of Nixon's friends to fasten the label of "Communist smear" upon reports of the fund miss the point entirely. The question is this: Was it right or wrong for him to accept these contributions? Senator Nixon may have a wholly acceptable explanation—with details, not generalities—showing that there was nothing improper or unethical about any part of the transaction. He should produce it at once.

HARTFORD

Lay Facts on the Line

The Courant (I. I. Rep. For Eisenhower)

General Eisenhower has had great success in standing as the symbol of a deep national resentment at motheaten morals and downright crookedness in public office. It will hurt his cause if it turns out that there has been anything remotely like that on his own team. All in all, there is no substitute for laying the facts on the line, and examining them with calmness and candor. The nearer Senator Nixon comes to that, the better off he and his party will be.

PITTSBURGH

Eisenhower Campaign Hurt

The Post-Gazette (Ind. For Eisenhower)

People begin wondering whether a man who kicks in a few hundred bucks to help a lawmaker make clerical ends meet, might not ask a favor in return. And even if the favor is never asked, the lawmaker has no business accepting such money, however noble the ends he seeks. He (Nixon) has hurt the campaign of his thoroughly honorable superior, General Eisenhower.

The South

WASHINGTON

Nixon's Fitness Questioned

The Star (Independent)

The cry of "smear" is no answer to the charge that has been brought against Senator Nixon. For this charge is not a smear. The admitted facts alone raise a serious ethical question a question which bears on both the usefulness and fitness of Senator Nixon as Republican Vice Presidential nominee. The point is that Senator Nixon is the second man on the G. O. P. team dedicated to a "crusade to clean up the mess and the corruption in Washington." Suppose it could be shown that the C. I. O. or members of the board of the National Association of Manufacturers were making regular contributions to defray the office expenses of a Senator. What would Senator Nixon say about that? It requires no gift of clairvoyance to see that this disclosure will acutely embarrass the Republican campaign. Had the facts been known in advance, it is virtually certain that Mr. Nixon would not have received the G. O. P. nomination.

Nixon Quoted on Boyle

The Post (Ind. For Eisenhower)

Senator Nixon saw the proprieties very clearly in another case almost a year ago. In October, 1951, he demanded that William M. Boyle and Guy Gabrielson resign as National Chairmen of their parties because of their activities in connection with R. F. C. loans. He stated then that, although he could find "no evidence of moral turpitude in the actions" of either chairman, nevertheless their resignations would help achieve the "paramount need" of restoring public confidence in the Federal Government. Senator Nixon was right then and his advice is even more applicable to his own case today.

LOUISVILLE

Tries to Change Subject

The Courier-Journal (Ind. Dem.)

Senator Richard Nixon makes a quick try at changing the subject as news of his secret expense account, the gift of wealthy constituents, gets out and around. It is, he says, "a typical left-wing smear." It is not going to slow up his "attack on communism and corruption." This, however, does not hide the point that the gifts were made and taken. The facts as first laid out by The New York Post, are not denied.

BALTIMORE

'Lacking in Discernment'

The Sun (Ind. Dem. For Eisenhower)

Just wherein and to what extent Senator Nixon's outside fund departs from the dubious but accepted practices of other political professionals we do not pretend to say. There has been no charge that the money his misguided friends have given him was used for any purely personal purpose. But many people, we are afraid, will bear in mind the old saying that the man who pays the piper calls the tune. * * * Senator Nixon ? * * stands disclosed as lacking in both discernment and sensitivity. There are millions of Americans who believe that the most urgent need of this country is to get rid of an Administration which has grown arrogant and corrupt after twenty years. They will resent Senator Nixon's failure to disclose in advance this undoubted weakness in his record because it makes the task of electing General Eisenhower more difficult.

ATLANTA

Nixon Called Liability

The Constitution (Dem. For Stevenson)

Senator Nixon has shown extremely poor judgment. His admitted indiscretions have turned him into a distinct liability as the Republican Vice Presidential candidate.

RICHMOND

Resignation Asked

The News Leader (Ind. For Eisenhower)

It is with the deepest sense of disappointment that this newspaper * * * asks Senator Nixon to resign his candidacy. It seems unimportant the gifts were made to some sort of special fund. The money was constructively available to Senator Nixon, to be spent on his say so, and the damning point is that it was given to him after his election, and not before his election, when he faced an expensive political campaign. * * * But post-campaign gifts, no matter how honorably they are received and how properly they are spent, inevitably must smack of the greased palm, the bought politician. His Senator Nixon's record, so far as we are advised, is one of unimpeachable devotion to the public interest. But his acceptance of these post-election gifts cannot be explained away.

Eisenhower Defeat Feared

The Times-Dispatch (Ind. Dem. For Eisenhower)

Senator Nixon's secret acceptance of a $16,000 "supplementary expense fund" from a group of private subsidizers was an unforgivable breach of Senatorial ethics. Exposure of this clandestine arrangement by a New York newspaper may spell the defeat of General Eisenhower unless Nixon has the decency to resign at once as the Vice Presidential nominee.

CHATTANOOGA

Public Should Get Facts

The Times (Ind. for Eisenhower)

It is certain that special funds for Senators provided by special interests cannot be permitted to become an accepted practice. If Senator Nixon's acceptance of this assistance was unethical, it does not become ethical merely because "Leftists" disclosed the facts. Nor does it become ethical merely because other Senators use unethical means to supplement their incomes. It is clear that General Eisenhower does not accept Mr. Nixon's charge that he is the victim of a "Communist smear" as a satisfactory explanation. The best basis on which the people could arrive at a fair judgment would be for Senator Nixon to follow General Eisenhower's advice and place all the facts before the public fairly and squarely.

Midwest

CHICAGO

Full Disclosure Urged

The Tribune (Ind., Uncommitted)

There is no question about the fact that Mr. Nixon has received the money or that it was contributed by private individuals. Now that some of the names of the contributors have been revealed, it should not be difficult to determine whether the motives in giving and receiving were honorable. Mr. Nixon has borne a good reputation and received his nomination largely in recognition of his notable services in the uncovering of the Hiss treason. He owes it to himself and his party to disclose every facet of the questioned transaction.

'Total Truth' Demanded

The Sun-Times (For Eisenhower)

When he agreed to accept the Vice Presidential nomination, Nixon assumed grave obligations as well as honors. Unless he comes completely clean on the identity of his patrons, and unless he accounts for the expenditures from the secret fund in the most minute detail, many Americans will feel that he has repaid honor with dishonor. The least that the American people and Eisenhower expect is that Nixon will come forward with the total truth. If he does less, the inescapable conclusion is that the implications of the secret expense account are even more serious than they appear to be on the surface.

DETROIT

Detailed Statement Sought

The Free Press (Rep. For Eisenhower)

This paper believes that Chairman Smith should reveal the names of those who contributed to this fund along with a detailed statement of just how the money was used. It would clear the air. If there is no charge of graft or personal aggrandizement then the problem comes under the heading of ethics.

MINNEAPOLIS

Nixon Defended

The Star (Ind. For Eisenhower)

There are legal ways and customary ways by which members of Congress augment their official income, and there are illegal ways. Senator Nixon has chosen the most open and straightforward of all legal ways to do so, and stands entirely ready to make any accounting his accusers want. One additional remark should be made about the attack on Senator Nixon. It came from James Wechsler and The New York Post. Mr. Wechsler was a Washington correspondent before he became managing editor of The Post. He knows quite well there is nothing unusual or questionable about what Senator Nixon has done.

ST. LOUIS

Nation Awaits Showdown

The Post-Dispatch (Ind. Dem.)

It would be a mistake to suppose that the crucial issue of the case is what Senator Nixon did with the $16,000. Even if every cent went for postage stamps, that will not affect the basic moral principle involved. That principle is the old and simple one: Is it right for a United States Senator to work for two paymasters * * *? It is clear that Senator Nixon has been guilty of precisely the same practices against which he and General Eisenhower inveigh with such high moral fervor when accusing Democrats of corruption * * *. General Eisenhower now faces one of the most critical decisions of his campaign. Will he rise above the muck of partisanship to give the daring demonstration of fearless independence which is expected of him? The stakes are incalculable and the whole nation awaits a showdown.

KANSAS CITY

Accounting Will Decide

The Star (Ind. Rep. For Eisenhower)

General Eisenhower has expressed complete faith in Senator Nixon. That confidence is based on Eisenhower's knowledge of the man and his record and, on the pledge of Nixon that he would give a full accounting of all funds contributed in his behalf. The Star awaits that accounting and its opinion on the Nixon development will be governed absolutely by the evidence, by all the facts and circumstances that have a bearing on the case. Only so can justice be served both with respect to Nixon and the public demands. No form of dishonesty or corruption can be condoned.

OMAHA

A Shadow Cast

The World-Herald (Ind. Pro-Eisenhower)

Mr. Nixon had accepted an arrangement which morally was difficult to defend. Call it indiscretion or the result of political inexperience. Point out that there never has been a breath of scandal directed at Mr. Nixon, and that he is known everywhere as a forthright, exceptionally able and honest man. All these things are true. Nevertheless General Eisenhower has been placed in an embarrassing position. He is campaigning vigorously against the dishonesty of the Administration officials, and a shadow has been cast upon his own running mate.

ST. PAUL

Senator Gets Clean Bill

The Pioneer Press (Ind., for Eisenhower)

With the audit made public Saturday of the supplemental campaign fund for Senator Nixon, the two-day sensation will subside and those who jumped to excited conclusions can jump back again. There is not one scintilla of corrupt purpose or corrupt effect in the whole affair, and it leaves Senator Nixon with a clean bill of political health.

MILWAUKEE

Good Sense Violated

The Journal (Ind. Uncommitted)

It may not violate the law. But it violates good sense and creates the occasion for corruption whether corruption exists or not. Mr. Nixon has been campaigning heatedly against corruption and "captive candidates." His own case may be, as he says, different—but he is open to both charges. Here is another argument for opening Federal tax returns to public inspection, to find out how many other Congressmen get "second salaries" and who is paying them and so is in a position to 'call the tune.'"

Southwest

DALLAS

Fund Called 'Above Board'

The News (Ind. Dem.)

Senator Nixon's California-supplied expense fund is political ammunition for the Democrats. Senator John Sparkman's nepotism in keeping his wife on the Federal payroll is political ammunition for the Republicans. Both have been above board about the arrangement. Neither has committed an illegal act. Nor has Vice President Alben Barkley in getting $1,000 a night for $50 speeches on V-P time. It is doubtful if you could call the roll of either Senate or House without finding that close to 100 per cent of the members received extra-curricular stipends without technically violating a law. As to whether it is morally wrong, that is another matter. But with either party's politicians, it is only morally wrong if done by a member of the other party.

SANTA FE

'The Mess in California'

The New Mexican (Ind. Dem.)

As long as Nixon voted "right," according to the lights of these wealthy operators, he could count on "expense money." Presumably, then, if Nixon at any time incurred their displeasure the funds would be cut off. It becomes increasingly obvious that morality or lack of morality is not a party matter, and the Republican effort to ride into power on a program of damning corruption simply is a subterfuge to cover up the lack of real issue. "The mess in Washington" slogan used so often in the campaign now becomes "the mess in California."

Mountain States

DENVER

'A Regrettable Stigma'

The Post (Ind., for Eisenhower)

The failure of Richard Nixon to resign as Vice Presidential candidate of the Republican party, or be asked to quit by General Eisenhower, gives color as of this moment to the charge that the G. O. P. has lost the capacity for decisive action. It is a regrettable stigma to impose upon Mr. Eisenhower at the dawning of his power and influence for the betterment of the Republican party. The general is confronted with a decision that will make or break his bid for national leadership.

Far West

SAN DIEGO

Smear Should Boomerang

The Union (For Eisenhower)

The left-wing attempt to smear an honest young crusader, Senator Richard Nixon, should prove to be a boomerang. Californians, especially, may resent this cleverly planned attempt to undermine this state's hard-hitting Senator with a distortion of facts regarding political contributions * * * Senator Nixon did not handle the money but bills for printing, mailing, answering letters and similar services were handled by a committee of well-known public leaders, men of good reputation. This is an honest and forthright way to serve his constituents.

SACRAMENTO

'Pet of Millionaires'

The Bee (Uncommitted)

The man who the people of the sovereign state of California believed was representing them actually is the pet and protégé of a special-interest group of rich Southern Californians. To put it more bluntly, Nixon is their subsidized front man, if not, indeed, their lobbyist. The solicitude of this group of millionaires for Nixon's welfare is touching indeed. It certainly will overwhelm them and perplex the man on the street who has come to believe members of the United States Senate could keep themselves free from pressure without the need of a subsidy from Republican millionaires. And that, Mr. and Mrs. America, isn't funny either.

TWIN WORRIES VEX EISENHOWER CAMP

Aides Gloomy Over the Public's Reaction to Nixon Incident and Accord With Taft

By JAMES RESTON
Special to THE NEW YORK TIMES.

ABOARD THE EISENHOWER SPECIAL, Jefferson City, Mo., Sept. 20—This was a gloomy day in Missouri, but it was no gloomier than the Republican gentlemen in the rear of Gen. Dwight D. Eisenhower's campaign train.

The reasons for the gloom, other than a steady drizzle, were:

¶The telegrams on the so-called "Nixon incident" were something less than complimentary. They seemed to be saying that in an ordinary political campaign against an ordinary political opponent, taking $18,235 above salary and normal expenses might be all right, but that in a "crusade" for moral principles it was a major embarrassment.

¶The editorial comment that was wired in here on the special fund contributed to Senator Richard M. Nixon, Republican Vice Presidential nominee, especially from many prominent papers that have supported the Eisenhower-Nixon ticket, was even worse.

¶Both the letters and the telegrams arriving on General Eisenhower's "recent reconciliation" with Senator Robert A. Taft of Ohio show that the Middle West was pleased but that the independent voters and the newspapers everywhere were at least slightly puzzled.

¶Finally, at least some of the general's advisers feel that he was "let down," first by Senator Nixon and secondly by his own personal staff in the handling of both the Nixon incident and the meetings with Senator Taft.

The Independents Upset

The problem created by the Nixon incident and the results of the Taft meeting was primarily that of the independent vote. The reports from the Republican professional politicians were not bad on either the Nixon incident or the Taft meeting but the independents were obviously upset and General Eisenhower has at least a tentative plan for dealing with both problems.

First, he does not regard the Nixon incident as closed. His attitude as of 4 o'clock this afternoon was that the report on the expense account raised by Senator Nixon's constituents in California must be as clean as a hound's tooth—"or else." Just what the "or else" means, however, is still doubtful in General Eisenhower's mind.

In dealing with the case, he is resolved first to get at the facts, and he is also clear as to what his basis of judgment should be on those facts. It should, he feels, be not whether what was done was "illegal" but whether it was in any way immoral.

His attitude is that he is engaged in a crusade for better government and that he would be in an untenable position if this crusade were compromised in any way.

The general still has confidence in Senator Nixon's honesty. He recognizes that even a great man could make a mistake but he finds it extremely difficult to believe that a young man of 39, with a promising political future, could be guilty of wrongdoing.

Disturbed on Two Scores

On two accounts, the general is somewhat disturbed: first that Senator Nixon did not confer with him or with any one else in his organization before issuing statements about the charges, and secondly, that his staff did not inform him about the charges until very early yesterday morning—which was almost eighteen hours after they heard about them.

This is generally regarded on the Republican nominee's campaign train as one of two rather important staff failures in the last fortnight. The other staff failure took place on the evening before Senator Taft's famous "reconciliation" breakfast with the general in New York last week.

When Senator Taft arrived in New York, Senator Frank Carlson of Kansas, one of the general's most dependable personal friends and advisers, went to the airport to meet him.

At that time Senator Taft gave Senator Carlson a copy of the memorandum of his views on the Taft-Hartley Act, the Federal Budget, the "primary" threat of "creeping socialism," etc., and told Mr. Carlson that he wished the general to have this paper that night so that he could study it and so that it could be used as a basis for the discussion at the following day's breakfast.

No Staff Work Possible

Senator Taft also was understood to have told Senator Carlson that if there were agreement on the memorandum, he hoped it could then be made public.

When he got to Manhattan, however, Senator Carlson decided that he would not show the memorandum to the general that night. He has said since that he did not do so because he did not want to "bother" the general with it.

If he had, Senator Carlson said, the general would have been working on it until late that night and probably would have lost some sleep over it. With this in mind Senator Carlson kept the extremely important memorandum to himself.

Accordingly, General Eisenhower did not see the memorandum until the following day, when Senator Taft himself produced it at the breakfast meeting. No staff work was done on it ahead of time; the general did not ask for time to discuss it with his advisers when he saw Senator Taft; he merely went over it and made a few suggestions to the Ohio Senator.

Moreover—and this is now recognized in Eisenhower headquarters as a mistake—he allowed the memorandum to be put out by Senator Taft as representing their agreed views, and was astonished later when this was interpreted as a major policy statement that Senator Taft had persuaded him to adopted as his own.

It is now realized in the Eisenhower camp that the Taft memorandum was a much more important document than either Senator Carlson or the general thought at the time; that it should have been carefully discussed before the Taft meeting; and that, even during the meeting the general should have foreseen the possibility that the memorandum would be interpreted as a capitulation to the Senator, and as the price of Senator Taft's support.

No Blame for Senator

In fact, Senator Taft never put the memorandum forward as a set of conditions. He made no demands at all for his support, and General Eisenhower does not in any way blame Senator Taft for the interpretations put on their reconciliation meeting.

The general's advisers—and presumably the general himself—now recognize, however, that they did not make clear to the country what did happen in that meeting, that he did not articulate his position so that even his friends and supporters understood what he was trying to do.

As a result, what started out as an extremely successful political tour of the Middle West and the border states finds the general and his advisers this afternoon rolling 'along by the Mississippi River both out of sorts and out out of position.

They have seen on this trip the advantages of winning the enthusiastic support of Senator Taft (as this is being written Senator James P. Kem, Republican of Missouri, an avowed Taft supporter and opponent of General Eisenhower's candidacy at Chicago, is out on the back platform extolling him as one of the great Americans of our time).

Even now, the machinery of the party is largely in the hands of men and women who still express a fierce loyalty for the Ohio Senator, but the problem before the general now is to regain first the understanding and then the votes of the independents who were so enthusiastic about his candidacy in the spring and early summer.

Plans to Clarify Views

The general's advisers feel this job could be done better in other sections than in rolling slowly through the border states and making eight or ten speeches a day.

Nevertheless, they are going to try to work on it in the forthcoming five days. Specifically it is understood that General Eisenhower will make clear soon in one or two major addresses on foreign affairs that, despite his meeting with Senator Taft last week, he has not changed his approach or his policy in this field. And secondly, he is planning in Baltimore on Thursday night to explain precisely what he has been trying to do in his meetings with Senator Taft and other Republican leaders.

In this speech he is expected to make these points:

¶He did not seek or accept the nomination to "preside over the liquidation of the Republican party." His mission was and is not to divide the party, but to unite it.

¶The curse of political life in Europe, where he has been serving in the last few years, is the failure of politicians to compose their differences within the major political parties—the tendency for the minority group in a political party to reject conciliation and to break away and form a multitude of splinter parties, none of which can provide stable government.

¶Accordingly, the general intends to explain that he is seeking to bring his party as close together as possible, always remembering that it is not possible and probably not even desirable for everybody in a political party to feel the same way about everything.

¶Gov. Adlai E. Stevenson of Illinois has opposed the idea of "guilt by association" in his criticism of Senator Joseph R. McCarthy of Wisconsin and others. But he has come very close to adopting this same technique in his attacks on General Eisenhower. General Eisenhower expects to emphasize that his support of other members of his party who are running for Congress does not mean that he has adopted their views or approved their tactics. He does not intend to allow his opponent to use the tactic of "guilt by association" against him. And he intends to make clear to the satisfaction of the independents that he seeks unity based on principle and is not capitulating to anyone or asking anyone to capitulate to him.

¶The late Senator Arthur H. Vandenberg, Republican of Michigan, is one illustration of the idea he has in mind. Every party and most of its members, he hopes to point out, are changed by events, particularly if the party has responsibility for trying to control and guide those events. Accordingly, as the development of Senator Vandenberg's philosophy showed, it is not wise for the leader of a party to assume that either change or honorable reconciliation is impossible.

In short, the Republican nominee has reached a new and critical phase in his campaign. His capacity for leadership, so largely responsible for his being nominated, is now being tested in his handling of the Nixon and Taft incidents.

For the last two weeks he has been trying to unite his party. His hope now is that he can hold the party together and regain some of the independent support he has lost.

September 21, 1952

FUND RAISED FOR NIXON HAS BOOMERANG EFFECT

First Result of the Disclosure Is to Weaken the Republican Case for Complete Change at Washington

STEVENSON'S MAJOR CONCERNS

By ARTHUR KROCK

WASHINGTON, Sept. 20—The revelation that Senator Nixon, the Republican candidate for Vice President, is endowed by private persons out of a continuing fund, unreported to the income tax authorities either by the contributors or the Senator, is a bombshell and a boomerang.

It is a bombshell because, regardless of the excellence of the motives of all concerned and the use to which the fund has been put, the arrangement reflects a dull sense of ethics on Nixon's part. It is a boomerang because General Eisenhower and his running mate have been concentrating on the low ethical and moral climate of the Truman Administration as a principal reason why there must be a "change" and why only they and the Republican party can sweep away "the mess in Washington."

The fact that Nixon called for the resignations of both the national party chairmen—Guy Gabrielson and William Boyle—last spring when it was disclosed that each had represented claimants before the Reconstruction Finance Corporation accentuates the boomerang nature of the disclosure. This reverse effect is accentuated by the circumstance that Nixon apparently never told the Republican leaders who chose him to run with Eisenhower about an arrangement that, if known to them, would certainly have caused them to look elsewhere.

Eisenhower's Chances Hurt

Whether the damage to Eisenhower's major campaign strategy is temporary or permanent, small or irreparable, cannot be estimated until the itemized accounting of the fund has been thoroughly inspected, the pressure on Nixon to withdraw has ended one way or the other, and all the attacks and defenses are in the record. But the exposure has hurt Eisenhower and his chances of election.

The instant attack of the Democrats, led by National Chairman Stephen A. Mitchell, is the classic political tactic in the circumstances. But Stevenson never showed his political acumen more clearly than when he called for all the facts before the passing of final judgment by anyone. The campaign had reached the point where each Presidential candidate was maneuvering to reverse the issues posed by his rival and hoist him on his own petard. To this strategy by the Democrats the Nixon incident is made to order.

When Senator Fulbright was conducting his investigation into official irregularities in the Reconstruction Finance Corporation—a model for all Congressional inquiries in the dignity, fairness and responsibility of its procedures—he made, over and over again, a certain point. To the plea that an act was not "illegal," the Senator replied that to him, however, it seemed "improper," and that impropriety also was a breach of public trust.

Stevenson Strategy

If it develops that the failure of Nixon and the contributors to his fund to make an accounting to the Income Tax Bureau was legal, that will not remove the opportunity of the Democrats to stress it as improper. And, having a Presidential candidate of integrity as unimpeachable as that of Eisenhower, some Stevenson strategists see an advantage for him even if the only consequence of the Nixon story is to produce a public psychology of "a plague on both your houses." For Nixon is Eisenhower's running-mate, not Stevenson's. And the following remarks the General made in the Farm Belt Thursday are typical:

We will restore and keep the public service at the high level of honor and distinction to which it is entitled * * *. I can promise you that we won't wait for Congressional prodding and investigations. The prodding this time will start from the top. And when we are through the experts in shady and shoddy Government operations will be on the way back to the shadowy haunts, the subcellars of American politics from whence they came.

To the Democrats the news about Nixon that broke while Eisenhower was speaking provided an instance of the biter bit, a development highly rated in professional politics. And on other issues both candidates and their advisers were busy trying to turn the attack of the opposition in their favor, for example:

(1) Stevenson has been going through the country, needling the Republicans with deft wit, irony and humor. After a couple of weeks of this, the Eisenhower strategists concluded the time was ripe for an effective counterplay. This was, to represent Stevenson as a light jester on grave matter, and therefore unfit for the Presidency. Whereupon Eisenhower began sternly to rebuke his opponent for levity, for finding funny such things as the Korean war. And, pursuing the tactic of turning the enemy's flank, Eisenhower constantly described some perilous condition in the world and the country, blamed it on the Administration and asked: "What's funny about that?"

(2) Stevenson immediately adopted the counter-tactic of accusing the Republicans of being solemn in

an effort to make the trivial seem portentous. Having no issue, he said, they had to resort to trying to make one of his humor. "If I were imperishably wedded to some of the folks they are," he commented, "I couldn't be very humorous, either." And he called the Republicans the "backward - looking party," "the party of the past," and remarked that G. O. P. stands for "grouchy old pessimists."

Who's the "Captive" Now?

(3) In his speeches Eisenhower has been calling Stevenson a "captive" candidate of President Truman, stuck with the Truman record of "fumbles and blunders" and corruption. Because of this, said the General, Stevenson could not bring about a "change" in Washington or clean up the "mess" made by those to whom he is bound by party ties.

(4) Stevenson's maneuver in reverse was to taunt Eisenhower with his promise to "support" all Republican candidates, including Senators McCarthy and Jenner, and he said it was the first time in his experience that a party went to the people with the battle-cry "Turn the rascals in." Moreover, when it came to discussing "captives," replied Stevenson, Taft had captured Eisenhower. The victorious convention candidate had "surrendered" to the defeated one. The General was now "merely an assistant professor on the staff of Dr. Taft, and I suspect it is no laughing matter to him." Refusing to endorse all Democrat candidates, Stevenson asked: "What kind of control do you get anyway from men who oppose everything you stand for?"

But the Nixon revelation did not dispose of three of the principal concerns of Stevenson and his managers: (a) what President Truman will say in his whistle-stop tour; (b) how deep runs the popular wish for a change; and (c) how much disclosures of official corruption have contributed to this wish. And they can only intimate delicately to the President what they wish he would not say on points in the record where the Administration has been on the very unpopular side.

Thus the campaign has reached the traditional stage of thrust and parry on each side, with the latest and sharpest thrusts Stevenson's.

New Turn

Questions Over Nixon

The Republicans have pegged their campaign largely on one theme—that it's time for a change because of the "top to bottom mess in Washington." In developing this theme they have pounded relentlessly on two charges— that the Administration has been "riddled" with corruption, and that it has been "slow" in weeding Communists out of Government.

Last week the corruption issue was clouded by a dramatic development that distressed the Republicans and gladdened the Democrats. It was disclosed that the Republican Vice Presidential nominee, Senator Richard M. Nixon, had received over $18,000 from a group of supporters in the past two years. Nixon said the money had been used to defray Senatorial and not personal expenses and that the injection of the story into the campaign was a "typical left-wing smear." Eisenhower, after hearing Nixon's explanation, said he had "confidence in Senator Nixon." However, he was said to be determined that Nixon must come out of the affair clean as a hound's tooth—or else. The question was raised—in both political camps and in several newspapers— of the possibility of Nixon's resignation from the G. O. P. ticket.

The issue of "communism in government" was overshadowed during the week by the Nixon affair. Nevertheless, both parties showed awareness of the political importance of the issue indicated in Senator Joseph R. McCarthy's smashing primary victory in Wisconsin two weeks ago. There was talk of bringing McCarthy into the national campaign for Eisenhower. Adlai Stevenson and President Truman, for their part, kept up a drumfire against Eisenhower for his implicit endorsement of McCarthy.

Truman and Taft

Before the Nixon affair broke, political observers were preoccupied with the possible effects on the campaign of the expanded roles assigned to President Truman and Senator Taft. They were convinced that the campaign might well turn on the twin questions of whether Eisenhower is "the captive" of Taft and whether Stevenson is "the captive" of Truman, and on how the voters felt about the answers. The questions were im-

NIXON: "This whole issue [is] a deliberate smear attempt by persons intent on perpetuating the present Administration in power."

plicit in the week's events in both campaigns.

On the Republican side Senator Taft, following his "peace meeting" with Eisenhower two weeks ago, leapt into the campaign with both feet and was lambasting the Administration's policies at home and abroad. Senators who had bitterly fought the Marshall Plan and NATO were trying to snuggle up to Eisenhower. In New York the convention of the American Federation of Labor, plainly reacting to the Taft-Eisenhower "pact," listened politely to an Eisenhower speech and prepared to endorse Stevenson. And all week long Stevenson commiserated Eisenhower supporters for the "abject surrender" of the general to Taft.

On the Democratic side, President Truman was also in the thick of the fray, charging the Republicans with whetting their knives against labor, and devising plots for a return to horse and buggy days. In South Carolina Gov. James F. Byrnes walked off the reservation—as Texas and Louisiana Democrats did earlier—with a 2,500-word blast against Stevenson for not dissociating himself from President Truman. And all week long Republicans kept hammering away at the theme that Stevenson could not possibly rid Washington of the "mess" of "cronies, crooks and the disloyal" whom he would inherit from Truman.

For the Presidential candidates themselves it was a tough week of oratory. Eisenhower rolled from New York through the Midwest to Minnesota and then down to Missouri. Stevenson swung through New England and down to Richmond.

The journeys ahead are long and only partly charted. This week Eisenhower will loop back through the Midwest to North Carolina, and Stevenson will follow a jagged course from New York (where he addresses the A. F. L. tomorrow) to Maryland, Indiana and Kentucky.

The Corruption Issue

The corruption issue that has played so large a part in the campaign has been in the headlines for three years. It has ranged through politically sensitive offices of Government — the Reconstruction Finance Corporation, the Internal Revenue (tax-collecting) Bureau, the Department of Justice's Tax Division—and has even washed up to the doors of the White House itself. There have also been charges that some Congressmen have overstepped the bounds of legitimate concern for the interests of their constituents.

The forms of corruption have been many—dubious Government loans to businessmen, tax-fraud cases "fixed," "favors" done, the "right doors" opened, influence "peddled." The price paid has also varied widely — from large sums in outright bribes to mink coats and free vacation trips. The scandals have been followed by shake-ups and many scores of indictments and dismissals.

From the outset there has been controversy over where the major share of credit for exposing corruption lies—in the Administration or in

the Republican opposition. The Administration claims that it took the initiative and that the investigations were carried forward by Democratic-controlled committees of Congress. The Republicans claim that the Administration moved sluggishly and under persistent Republican prodding. At all events the G. O. P. has made plain from the beginning of the campaign that it was staking much on the corruption issue — and the response of the crowds to Republican cries against the "mess in Washington" have convinced observers that the issue is potent.

In the Republican campaign Nixon has had the task of day-in, day-out slugging on corruption as well as on communism in government. Nixon, in fact, had been selected as Eisenhower's running mate largely because he was believed the best suited to this role. Eisenhower's managers wanted someone for the second spot who was young, vigorous and who had made a name for himself as an investigator. Nixon seemed to fit the bill. He was only 39. He had been responsible for unearthing enough evidence against Hiss to put the case in the courts.

Story Breaks

Last Thursday morning in Los Angeles, Nixon boarded his thirteen-car special train for his first major whistle-stop campaign—a 400-mile trip up the Central Valley. He was covering his home ground and hitting the same spots that Stevenson visited two weeks ago. At town after town, Nixon struck out—at the "scandal-a-day Administration."

Then, on Thursday afternoon three thousand miles away, The New York Post, a paper supporting Stevenson, hit the streets with the headline: "SECRET NIXON FUND!" The story said that in the past two years Nixon has received between $16,000 and $17,000 from a fund set up by some of his supporters in his '50 Senatorial campaign. The story was based on an interview with Dana C. Smith, attorney, who was trustee of the fund. This is how The Post got the story:

Some weeks ago The Post assigned reporter Leo Katcher to do a series on Nixon. In the course of doing research he met up with a correspondent of the Reporter Magazine and a reporter from The Los Angeles Daily News, who were also working on a Nixon story. The three men pooled their efforts. In interviewing people they heard mention of a fund that had been set up to help Nixon, and they were referred to Mr. Smith. Last Monday they called on Smith and talked with him for two hours. He talked freely about the fund, apparently not realizing it would make big news. He said that the fund was raised "because Dick Nixon is the best salesman against socialism * * * and government control of everything in the country" and that "we limited contributions from any one source or any one family to $500 a year so that no one could say we were buying a Senator."

A few minutes after The Post broke the story, it was moving across the country on news agency wires. It reached Nixon's train, and at Merced he called in reporters. He

said the story was true, but the money had been used for postage on mail he did not wish to frank, reprinting speeches, travel and extra clerical help—"political expenses which I believed should not be charged to the Federal Government."

Late in the afternoon the story reached the Eisenhower train at Des Moines, when a bundle of papers were tossed aboard. Eisenhower aides paid scant attention to it. However, National Committee Chairman Arthur E. Summerfield was not entirely satisfied with the statement Nixon had made and put through a call to him.

Eisenhower Acts

By Friday morning the story was red hot. Before eight o'clock, as the train rolled through the fields of northern Nebraska toward Kansas City, Eisenhower took the initiative and called a meeting in the rear car. It was decided that nothing should be done until Eisenhower had more facts. Thereupon, the general issued a statement, saying he would talk with Nixon as soon as he could reach him by telephone. He said: "I believe Dick Nixon to be an honest man."

The story continued to boil. Through most of the day Eisenhower conferred with his advisers between platform appearances. The possibility that Nixon might have to be asked to withdraw was discussed. A proposal to have the facts laid before a Senate committee was advanced and discarded. Eisenhower aides had been unable to contact Nixon. Time was pressing, because the general was scheduled to deliver a blast against "bossism" and corruption in Kansas City—former stronghold of Boss Tom Pendergast who had set President Truman on the political ladder and who had later been sent to prison for income tax evasion. In California, Nixon was drawing cheers when he told his audience "that what I was doing [by accepting the fund] was saving you money."

Nixon's Explanation

In the late afternoon, Senator Fred Seaton of Nebraska, on Eisenhower's staff, got through to Nixon's train. Nixon read him a statement. At Kansas City that night, Eisenhower began by saying he had a message to read from his running-mate. The Nixon statement said Smith would make "a full accounting of the fund." He added: "This whole issue developed as a deliberate smear * * * by persons intent on perpetuating the present Administration."

By midnight the morning papers were out. THE NEW YORK TIMES said there was no reason to doubt Nixon's explanation, but "the question which the Republican leaders must now face, and decide without loss of time, is whether Mr. Nixon's record in this matter has not fatally impaired his usefulness as a candidate * * *." The New York Herald Tribune said Nixon should make "a formal offer of withdrawal."

Arriving in New York from his New England trip, Stevenson said there were three questions: "Who gave the money, was it given to influence the Senator's position on public questions and have any laws been

violated?" Stevenson said he was sure "the great Republican party will ascertain these facts and act in accordance with our best traditions * * *." He warned against "condemnation without all the evidence, a practice all too familiar."

Yesterday Mr. Smith, the Nixon fund trustee, released a preliminary accounting. On the receipts side he listed seventy-five contributors, many of them well known California Republicans, one of them Herbert Hoover Jr. The contributions totaled $18,235. On the disbursement side there was a general accounting that included $3,430 for travel and hotel expenses, $2,017 for radio and TV and lesser amounts for postage, telephone calls and extra office help.

These sums, of course, were apart from Nixon's Government salary of $12,500 as a Senator and his tax-free expense allowance of $2,500. He gets over $60,000 for clerical help and other expenditures, plus special cash funds for airmail stamps, telegrams and long-distance calls. Altogether these Government payments come to more than $75,000.

The Effect

Late yesterday Eisenhower had not yet given his final answer on the Nixon affair. The feeling among neutral observers was that regardless of what happens next the Republican ticket has suffered some damage and that the Democrats have been given a counter to the Republicans on the corruption issue.

Eisenhower, it is agreed, now faces difficult alternatives. The feeling is that if Nixon remains on the ticket he will be a target for continual Democratic attack, regardless of what the full story of the Nixon fund turns out to be. Moreover, it is argued that the question is not simply one of legality but of ethics, since Eisenhower has declared that he is leading a "moral crusade." It was authoritatively reported yesterday that Eisenhower himself takes this view of the affair and will insist that his crusade must not in any way be compromised.

On the other hand, Nixon's departure from the G. O. P. ticket would, it is believed, confront the G. O. P. with a serious situation. It is late in the campaign to be splitting tickets and putting new ones together. Nixon's resignation from the ticket, so the theory goes, would not remove his name from the campaign. Nevertheless, some observers feel that in dropping Nixon, Eisenhower might convince many voters of the depth of his sincerity as a champion of integrity and ethics in Government.

There was no indication that Nixon would offer to withdraw, or that if he did, Eisenhower would accept. But, should Nixon retire, the National Committee could fill the vacancy either by choosing a new nominee or calling another convention.

EISENHOWER TALKS TO NIXON ON ISSUE OF EXPENSE FUNDS

Phones Running Mate From Train in St. Louis After Day of Deliberating Issue

RESULT IS NOT DISCLOSED

General Had Asked Aides for More Facts on $18,235— Advisers Are Divided

By JAMES RESTON
Special to THE NEW YORK TIMES.

ST. LOUIS, Sept. 21—Gen. Dwight D. Eisenhower talked to his running mate, Senator Richard M. Nixon of California, by telephone just before midnight tonight after spending most of the day meditating about whether to recommend the Senator's withdrawal from the Republican ticket.

This was the first time the two men had talked to each other since the controversy had arisen over Senator Nixon's acceptance of an $18,235 expense fund from some of his California supporters. Nothing was disclosed, however, on the nature or the result of the conversation, which the general initiated from his campaign train here. Senator Nixon is campaigning in Portland, Ore.

[In Portland, Senator Nixon's camp announced that the two candidates had talked for twenty minutes but did not disclose any result of their conversation.]

Earlier it had been indicated that the Presidential nominee was not satisfied with preliminary reports issued in California about the source of the fund and the purposes to which it had been put.

Studied Their Affiliations

During the day the general had gone over the names of the men who had contributed the $18,235 to the unofficial expense fund. He studied their affiliations and the itemized accounting of where the money had gone. Then he asked his aides to get him more facts.

One item listed $6,166 for stationery. What, asked the general, was the stationery used for?

Another item was $3,430 for travel expenses. Who, the general wanted to know, did the traveling, and where and for what purpose?

Also, he asked: Who raised the money? What was the appeal? Who were the donors and did they stand to benefit by any actions of Senator Nixon? In short, he apparently was not satisfied either with Senator Nixon's public statements or with the accounting made public yesterday.

The general got little help in reaching a decision from his advisers, for the men whom he has disciplined himself to consult for the last ninety days were about as divided as they could be.

One group was for keeping Senator Nixon on the ticket unless further investigation proved that there had actually been a violation of the law or concrete evidence that the money was used for Mr. Nixon's personal gain. The arguments of those who took this position were as follows:

¶The Senator did nothing that many other Senators were not doing.

¶The public made a distinction between taking private funds and benefiting from public funds.

¶The funds were used for a good purpose—fighting communism and corruption in the Federal Government. Therefore the incident might actually do the Republican campaign some good if the Democrats did make an issue of it. On this point, the advisers in this group, most of whom are professional politicians, observed that Mr. Nixon's crowds had greatly increased since the fund disclosure and were now larger and more responsive to the Senator than Governor Dewey's crowds were in the same area in 1948.

¶ If Senator Nixon were "dumped," the Democrats would not drop the issue but take his dismissal as evidence of guilt, and the Republicans would be left with the problem of picking a successor —an exercise that might split the Left and Right wings of the party all over again.

Arguments on Other Side

The group that favors his dismissal was even more determined in its arguments, which included the following:

¶ By raising and using a secret fund, Senator Nixon violated the moral code on which General Eisenhower has based his campaign for election to the Presidency.

¶ By keeping him on the ticket, General Eisenhower would condone the practice of raising secret funds to be used by Senators for purposes that the Senators themselves approve.

¶The objective might have been all right in Senator Nixon's case, but it was bad practice. Good ends did not justify improper means.

¶The press reaction suggested that Senator Nixon now was a political liability, but even if he were not, that was not the point. The point was that what he did was wrong, even if many others in the Senate did it, and therefore could not be tolerated by a candidate running a crusade for moral principles.

¶If Senator Nixon did remain, the voters who supported the Eisenhower candidacy because they believed it was a moral crusade would be disillusioned, and the Democrats would cry "hypocrisy" every time the corruption issue was raised.

The full story on certain important factors in today's developments has not been disclosed. Senator Fred Seaton, Republican of Nebraska, one of the general's aides, spoke to Senator Nixon during the day, but what was said was not discussed.

Similarly, though it was generally assumed that the general or his aides had talked with Gov. Thomas E. Dewey of New York, Senator Robert A. Taft of Ohio and other leaders of the party about the Nixon incident, everybody around the general was being very secretive about who did what.

It also was not at all clear to those riding on the train whether anybody in the general's so-called inner-circle really was talking frankly to the nominee about the campaign. What evidence is available on this point, indeed, is that at least some men who were very close to the general before the nomination now indicate that in the last sixty days the tendency to sound off on what they think about fundamental issues in the campaign has declined noticeably.

Two examples will illustrate the point:

First, several of the men close to the general are disturbed about his formal speeches. In private conversation, they say that the speeches lack distinction and imagination—especially when compared with the speeches made by the general's opponent, Gov. Adlai E. Stevenson of Illinois—but when they are asked whether they have ventured to mention this conviction to the general they say well, no, they have not.

"The general has said," one of them asserted today, "that if elected he will enlist the support of the best brains of the country to help him in his enormous tasks, but I've got to admit that in his present campaign he has not mobilized the best brains in the Republican party—nothing like it."

But when the author of the above was asked whether he had said this to the general, his answer was that he had not.

Second, and more seriously, some of the general's aides concede that, in addition to withholding their honest opinions about the general's speeches, they are not blurting out to him what they really think about the broad strategy of the campaign.

For example, some of them feel that ever since he won the nomination, he has blurred the original idea of a strong liberal leader, and, especially since his meeting with Senator Taft in New York last week, actually encouraged the belief that the leader was not leading.

Now these same aides believe that the Nixon case has dramatized the question as to whether the general is going to take command and make decisions in accordance with the principles he has emphasized in his campaign.

James C. Hagerty, the general's press secretary, announced today that the Republican nominee would make a long trip west, starting in New York Sept. 30.

From there he will go to Michigan, Oct. 1; Illinois, Oct. 2; Wisconsin, Oct. 3; Minnesota and North Dakota, Oct. 4; Washington, Oct 6; Oregon, Oct. 7; California, Oct. 8-9; Arizona, New Mexico and Utah, Oct. 10; Salt Lake City, Oct. 11-12. Thereafter, he is expected to go to Texas, and Louisiana.

He will leave here tomorrow morning at 4:30 o'clock and speak tomorrow in Indiana, Kentucky and Ohio.

One aide said today that more than 400 telegrams had been received on the Nixon matter.

"How many were for keeping him," a reporter asked, "and how many for casting him away."

This was a reference to a Biblical quotation from Ecclesiastes that the general had used as a theme of his speech in Des Moines: "A time for keeping and a time for casting away" (Ecclesiastes 3:6).

The aide said that the telegrams were running about 50—50.

NIXON TO GIVE DATA ON FINANCES TODAY

Senator Is Fighting to Remain on the Ticket—Decision Expected by Tomorrow

By LAWRENCE E. DAVIES
Special to THE NEW YORK TIMES.

PORTLAND, Ore., Sept. 21—Senator Richard M. Nixon talked for twenty minutes late tonight with Gen. Dwight D. Eisenhower, the Republican Presidential nominee, presumably on the question of whether the Senator, under fire for using contributions from supporters to help pay his expenses in office, should withdraw as the general's running mate.

James Bassett, the Senator's press secretary, after a long conference with Mr. Nixon, said that he could "not tell you any more about the phone call," which was made in St. Louis by the general.

Asked whether Senator Nixon planned to go on with his campaign schedule, the secretary replied: "That is the plan now."

Earlier, the Senator had announced that he was preparing "a complete statement of my entire financial history." One of his aides said the report would be released tomorrow.

"I realize," the Senator said, "that it [the statement] will be misrepresented, but I feel that when any question is raised about any public official, he should make this information available to the public."

A complete clarification of the Vice Presidential nominee's status may be expected within forty-eight hours.

This was made known here today as advisers of the Senator, who was described as "fighting mad," conferred by telephone with aides of General Eisenhower, and with Republican National Committee officials in Washington.

Mr. Nixon's anger was attributed to the attacks against him because he permitted the payment of $18,235 of his political expenses during the last two years from a trust fund set up by California supporters.

Now that an accounting of the trust fund, with a list of contributors, has been made public by the trustee, Dana C. Smith, a Pasadena attorney, and now that conversations have been held between Eisenhower and Nixon advisers on what has become the paramount issue of the campaign for the moment, Mr. Bassett was asked today whether some sort of statement from a high level was in sight giving a "final conclusion."

Such a statement was promised within forty-eight hours. The ac-

cepted implication was that the statement, or whatever form the final conclusion might take, would end once and for all the speculation as to whether Senator Nixon would be retained on the ticket or be asked to withdraw as General Eisenhower's running mate.

So far every statement by Mr. Nixon and his advisers has carried either the clearly uttered or implied word that the Vice Presidential nominee has absolutely no thought of quitting the race. He believes he has done no wrong, legally or morally.

To bulwark his own beliefs, his press secretary made public about 500 telegrams received by mid-afternoon dealing with the subject of the trust fund and its uses.

Those who perused these telegrams could find not a single condemnatory message. All of the telegrams in one way or another expressed faith in Senator Nixon and exhorted him to "stand pat" or "keep up the fight against the 'smear gang'" or "carry on to victory."

Some came from personal friends of the Senator, many from persons unknown to him. Most of them were assumed by his aides to have been sent by Republicans.

One signed "The Aroused Citizens of Whittier," residents of Mr. Nixon's town in California, told the Senator that the townspeople were solidly behind him and continued:

"We know you are honest and forthright. We sent you to Washington to fight corruption and Communists in Government and to protect and represent the citizens of California.

"We have never regretted backing you with our resources and energies and we again reaffirm our faith in you and pledge to you our full support in your crusade against such evils."

At any rate, Senator Nixon intended as of tonight to resume his campaign tour tomorrow on schedule. The trip will take him during the day to Seattle, with a number of whistle stops along the way.

Most of the telephone conversations last night and today, as had been the case previously, were between Murray Chotiner, the Senator's national campaign manager, and Senator Fred Seaton of Nebraska, one of General Eisenhower's advisers.

Mr. Chotiner also talked with Arthur E. Summerfield, the Republican National Chairman. Senator Nixon, too, has talked with Senator William Rogers, a Washington attorney who is on the present tour as Mr. Nixon's personal representative, has joined in some of the telephone talks.

There was no doubt among some of the Nixon associates that even if the Senator remained as the Vice-Presidential nominee — and any other course was seemingly regarded by them as unthinkable—the trust fund and its uses would be a continuing campaign issue, if the Democrats could keep it going.

Newspaper men accompanying the Nixon campaign train during the last three days since the trust fund matter arose with startling suddenness have noted these things:

¶The whole uproar seems to have surprised Senator Nixon more than anyone else.

¶There is at least an implied feeling among some of the Senator's associates that persons around

Associated Press Wirephoto

ACKNOWLEDGES CHEERS: Senator Richard M. Nixon, Republican Vice Presidential nominee, waving to audience in Portland, Ore., on Saturday night.

General Eisenhower have got a bit "hysterical" over the developments.

These conclusions have been reached in the knowledge that Senator Nixon and his staff are aware of many editorial demands for his withdrawal as the nominee and that they have been apprised of an announcement by James C. Hagerty, General Eisenhower's press secretary, that of hundreds of telegrams on the subject reaching the general, about half favor his asking Mr. Nixon to quit.

What Senator Nixon and his advisers have seen themselves, however, is not merely a batch of 500 or so telegrams supporting his own stand, but the reaction of audiences to which the nominee has explained his position.

At nearly every station stop and before a crowd of 1,800 that jammed Grant High School auditorium here last night, the Senator has drawn applause and in many cases cheers for his allusion to the condemnation of the trust fund as a "smear" by "left-wingers and Communists."

He has taken the position that he was saving the taxpayers money by letting political supporters help pay for his political trips, his political printing and mailing bills, and that the taxpayers ought to be grateful for this saving.

This is true, his associates insist, despite the fact that he collects the amounts allowed him for office and personal expenses.

Take first the matter of printing political statements.

Mr. Nixon's aides assert that many members of Congress get this job done at the taxpayers' expense by having their political grist printed in The Congressional Record, then having reprints made with the taxpayer footing the bill.

Then, it is said, these reprints are mailed out by the thousands through an abuse of the franking privilege. In this way, they avoid paying postage. What materials may be mailed under the privilege

of Government officials to use the "frank" instead of stamps depends, in practice, upon individual attitudes and the abuse of the privilege is a costly item for the taxpayer, according to the Nixon supporters. They assert that Senator Nixon never has used the frank on strictly political mail.

Regarding the matter of political trips, Mr. Nixon's associates say that it is not uncommon for a member of Congress to get himself made a one-man subcommittee and be sent on a trip to his home area ostensibly to conduct an investigation, but actually to permit him to build his political fences.

The cost is borne by the taxpayers.

There are various other subterfuges, according to them, through which men who otherwise would be financially unable to maintain their places in the House and Senate obtain funds to supplement their salaries and expense allowances.

Senator Nixon, they declare, never has indulged in these practices, one of his associates added vehemently:

"The trouble with Nixon is he's too damned honest."

Today Senator Nixon interrupted his strategy planning long enough in the late morning to attend a service at the First Friends Church of Portland with Mrs. Nixon. This part of his schedule was not announced in advance. A spokesman explained that the church visit was purposely not made known because "Dick doesn't believe in political religion."

There was nothing on his formal schedule for the day except attendance at a supper given by the men's Temple Club at Temple Beth Israel. Mr. Nixon was billed for a twenty-minute talk, for which he prepared no manuscript.

Tomorrow's schedule includes train stops for talks at Kelso, Centralia and Olympia before arrival at Seattle for the main address of the day in Norway Hall.

September 22, 1952

M'CARTHY BACKS NIXON

Says Californian Has Given 'Complete Answer to Smear'

MILWAUKEE, Sept. 21 (*P*)—Senator Joseph R. McCarthy, who is seeking re-election in Wisconsin, issued this statement today on behalf of Senator Richard M. Nixon, Republican Vice Presidential candidate:

"Nixon's frank accounting of his additional expenses paid by friends shows that he did not personally profit by one cent.

"The money was spent to render better service to his California constituents.

"The Left-wing crowd hates Nixon because of his conviction of Alger Hiss, the man for whom Adlai Stevenson testified.

"The Communists know that Nixon's election will be a body blow to the Communist conspiracy.

"Dick Nixon has given a complete answer to this new smear invented by The New York Post, whose editor admits he once was a member of the Young Communist League."

In New York, James A. Wechsler, editor of The Post, commented:

"No one has challenged a single fact contained in The Post's story about Senator Nixon.

"Senator McCarthy is fully aware of my anti-Communist record over the last fifteen years.

"In his defense of Senator Nixon's financial arrangements, McCarthy sounds like a man with a guilty conscience."

SENATOR CUTS TRIP

Interrupts His Campaign in Portland, Ore., and Flies to Los Angeles

WILL GIVE AN 'ACCOUNTING'

Summerfield Says Republican Committees Will Pay $75,000 for Radio-TV Broadcast

By GLADWIN HILL
Special to THE NEW YORK TIMES.

LOS ANGELES, Sept. 22 — A cheering crowd of several hundred persons greeted Senator Richard M. Nixon this afternoon on his arrival here in his home district from Portland, Ore., to make a nationwide talk, over television and radio, about the controversial $18,235 special-expense fund given to him over a two-year period by a group of wealthy Southern California supporters.

The Republican Vice Presidential candidate, under severe criticism from both the opposition and elements in his own party for his acceptance of this money, clambered onto the hood of a sedan parked by the edge of the Los Angeles International Airport, and, with his wife Patricia beside him, smiled and waved and briefly thanked the crowd for its support.

[The United Press quoted a member of the Nixon party as saying that the Senator would withdraw "within the next seven days," adding that "Nixon has been thrown to the wolves."

[The source, who refused to be identified by name, said the announcement would come from Gen. Dwight D. Eisenhower's headquarters or the general himself, rather than from the Senator. The source said: "Nixon will never go to Missoula." He is scheduled to resume his whistle-stop tour in Missoula, Mont.

[Later, Senator Nixon denied the report and said he would continue his tour after the speech.]

Senator Nixon and his wife went directly from the airport in a police-escorted limousine to the downtown Ambassador Hotel. There he planned to remain, in 'he words of an aide, "in seclusion," and work on his talk until delivery time.

To Give Accounting

Mr. Nixon has promised to give a complete accounting of his per-

LOS ANGELES BOUND: Senator and Mrs. Richard M. Nixon aboard a chartered plane that left Portland, Ore., yesterday. The Republican Vice Presidential nominee will make a nationwide radio and television broadcast in defense of his use of the funds received from friends.

Associated Press Wirephoto

sonal and political finances in his broadcast over the television network of the National Broadcasting Company and the radio networks of the Columbia Broadcasting System and the Mutual Broadcasting System between 6:30 and 7 P. M. Pacific daylight time (9:30 and 10 P. M. Eastern daylight time) tomorrow.

[General Eisenhower, campaigning in the Midwest, said he would await Mr. Nixon's report on the expense fund before passing judgment on his running mate.]

Arthur E. Summerfield, Republican National Chairman, announced in Washington, that the radio-TV time would cost more than $75,000. He said the bill would be paid by the National Committee and the Republican Senatorial and Congressional Campaign Committees.

In making the announcement, Mr. Summerfield said:

"Senator Nixon has devoted a great part of his life to fighting communism and exposing traitors. In World War II, like millions of other fine young American men, he served his country gloriously.

"Now a smear of him has been initiated by men who have promoted communism, supported traitors, and never fought so much as one day for their country.

"I think every man and woman in America who has read even so

little as one word of this attempt to besmirch the reputation of a great American, owes it to themselves and their country to see and hear Senator Nixon tomorrow night."

At the airport Senator Nixon expressed appreciation for the "thousands of wires" of support received from all parts of the country.

"This is the time you find out who your friends are * * * We won't let you down," he declared.

His eyes were slightly red. Mrs. Nixon likewise smiled and waved, manifesting no · emotion except pleased appreciation.

Among a small group of Republican leaders at the airport to meet him was Representative Donald Jackson of Santa Monica.

After calling Senator Nixon, in an informal statement to reporters, "a thoroughly honest sincere fellow," Representative Jackson added:

"The existence of such a supplementary fund as Senator Nixon's is not unusual."

He did not elaborate on the remark.

It was expected that in the interval from now until his speech Mr. Nixon might talk with some regional Republican leaders in person, and very likely with national party leaders by telephone, but no specific arrangements were disclosed. His press secretary, James E. Bassett Jr., said he would make no public statements until his speech.

In conformance with Senator Nixon's previous statement that he would finish out his scheduled ten-day tour of the West—which he interrupted after four days for his dash back to Los Angeles—it was tentatively planned that after the radio-television talk, the candidate would fly to Missoula, Mont., to pick up the tour's original chronological schedule. Several talks in the state of Washington were canceled for his trip here.

A "complete statement of my financial history," which the Senator previously had said he would make public today, would, Mr. Bassett said, in view of the sudden change in itinerary, probably be partly covered in tomorrow's talk, with a simultaneous statement being released giving full details.

For an hour before the plane's arrival, the airport terminal building and outside concourses had been teeming with enthusiastic and seemingly undaunted partisans, wearing luminiscent "Ike and Dick" stickers and placards with such legends as "Nixon will fight and win," "Dick—we're with you" and "We trust in Nixon."

Other placards identified many of the boosters as members of the suburban Los Angeles and Young Republican organizations.

Mr. Bassett said that, although the Senator would work his talk out with great care, he would not use a prepared text or even notes when he spoke.

CONTROVERSY IN OREGON
Evidence Seems to Be That Nixon Will Remain on Ticket

By LAWRENCE E. DAVIES
Special to The New York Times.

PORTLAND, Ore., Sept. 22—Senator Nixon left Portland in the midst of a controversy without disclosing whether he was staying or quitting as the running mate of General Eisenhower, the party's Presidential standard bearer.

The evidence was substantial, however, that as of this time the 39-year-old Senator from California was still General Eisenhower's partner on the national Republican ticket.

Following is an outline, with some of the times only approximate, of what took place in the Benson Hotel, headquarters of the Nixon campaign party, from the time the Senator returned there at about 10 o'clock last night from a supper meeting of the Temple Men's Club of Temple Beth Israel that he addressed.

10:05 P. M.—Senator Nixon went to the telephone in response to a call from General Eisenhower in St. Louis. They talked until 10:25 or a little later.

11 P. M.—Newspaper men covering the Nixon tour were notified to stand by in the press room for an announcement.

11:30 P. M.—Mr. Bassett, the Senator's press secretary, came into the room after reports already had come from St. Louis about the Eisenhower - Nixon conversation. Mr. Bassett made a similar announcement but parried questions whether Senator Nixon would resign.

11:50 P. M.—Word was passed to reporters to stand by again for an important announcement.

1:05 A. M., Monday — After reporters had telephoned or wired their offices about the long wait and its possible implications Mr. Bassett reappeared, this time with several companions.

"You all know the guest of honor," Mr. Bassett said.

Senator Nixon took over and began:

"I've come down to announce that I am breaking off——"

The words had an electrical effect on his hearers. The nominee paused to enjoy the startled looks. Then, deliberately, he started over and this time slowly dictated this statement:

"I've come down to announce that I am breaking off my campaign trip tomorrow for the purpose of going to Los Angeles to make a nation-wide television and radio broadcast. The time for the broadcast has not yet been set. It will either be Tuesday or Wednesday night and we will be using both the N. B. C. and C. B. S. networks.

"The broadcast incidentally will be a half hour. In line with my conviction that the truth is the best answer, both to a smear and to honest misunderstanding, I intend to lay before the American people all the facts concerning the fund which was used for political purposes and in an unprecented action I am going to present to the American people my entire personal financial history from the time that I entered political life.

"I informed General Eisenhower tonight in a telephone conversation of my decision and he agreed that that was the proper way to handle the situation. I have just talked to Senator [Harry P.] Cain of Washington, who was going to accompany me on my trip through Washington and he is taking over my speaking schedule during the time that I will be in Los Angeles preparing and delivering this television-radio broadcast. [Since the announcement, the Washington campaign trip has been postponed until Mr. Nixon may return to the region sometime before election day.]

"I shall resume the tour the day after the broadcast is made."

As the nominee hesitated before leaving the room, he was asked:

"That means you're staying on the ticket?"

"That means," Mr. Nixon retorted, "that I intend to continue the tour."

Someone demanded, "Let's get this straight," and the question was asked again. The newspaper men were informed by an aide of the Senator that this was not a press conference, but they insisted on an answer.

Mr. Nixon took Mr. Bassett and Murray Chotiner, his campaign manager, into an adjoining room for consultation. Back again the nominee repeated the question, "That means you're staying on the ticket?" and gave this response:

"My answer to that is that I have no further comment than to continue the tour. We are going to take a chartered DC-6 to Los Angeles."

'I'M NOT A QUITTER'

Senator Says He'll Let Republican National Committee Decide

HE REVIEWS HIS FINANCES

Accepts Bid to Meet General— Cites Legal Opinions on Use of $18,235 Fund

By GLADWIN HILL
Special to The New York Times.

LOS ANGELES, Sept. 23—Senator Richard M. Nixon, in a nation-wide television and radio broadcast tonight, defended his $18,235 "supplementary expenditures" fund as legally and morally beyond reproach.

He laid before the Republican National Committee and the American people the question of whether he should remain on the Republican party's November election ticket as the candidate for Vice President.

Rising, near the end of his talk, from the desk at which he had sat, Senator Nixon urged his auditors to "wire and write" the Republican National Committee whether they thought his explanation of the circumstances surrounding the fund was adequate.

"I know that you wonder whether or not I am going to stay on the Republican ticket or resign," he said. "I don't believe that I ought to quit, because I'm not a quitter * * *

Decision 'Not Mine'

"But the decision, my friends, is not mine. I would do nothing that would harm the possibilities of Dwight Eisenhower to become President of the United States; and for that reason I am submitting to the Republican National Committee tonight, through this television broadcast, the decision which it is theirs to make. * * *.

"Wire and write the Republican National Committee whether you think I should stay or whether I should get off; and whatever their decision is, I will abide by it."

Later he accepted an invitation from General Eisenhower for a conference.

In a half-hour talk that was partly personal, including a frank exposition of his finances, and partly an appeal for support of the Republican ticket such as he has been making in his current whistle-stop tour, the Senator declared of the Southern California supporters' fund disclosed last week:

"I say that it was morally wrong if any of that $18,000 went to Senator Nixon for my personal use.

"I say that it was morally wrong if it was secretly given and secretly handled.

"And I say that it was morally wrong if any of the contributors got special favors for the contributions that they made."

But he declared that, on all three points, the factual answer was negative.

Speaks With Assurance

The candidate, clad in a gray suit and a dark tie, delivered his address in a Hollywood radio-television studio—from which the public was excluded—with composure and assurance. His wife, Patricia, was seated close to him, and he made frequent references to her in detailing his career.

His talk also was peppered with barbed references to the Democratic opposition.

Referring to an Illinois political fund with which Gov. Adlai E. Stevenson, Democratic Presidential nominee, has been linked, Senator Nixon, while stipulating that he did not "condemn" this, suggested that both Mr. Stevenson and his running mate, Senator John J. Sparkman of Alabama, should "come before the American people" and report on their incomes.

"If they don't," he said, "it will be an admission that they have something to hide."

In support of his position, he cited two independent reports he had prepared, one on his finances and one on the legal aspects of the "supplementary expenditures" fund, for the information of Gov. Sherman Adams of New Hampshire, campaign executive of General Eisenhower, the Senator's running-mate.

The full texts of the two reports, one by Price, Waterhouse & Company, national accounting firm, and the other by Gibson, Dunn & Crutcher, Los Angeles law firm, in the form of letters to Governor Adams, were distributed by his press staff simultaneously with the broadcast.

The Senator read verbatim the conclusion of the law firm's report, which followed a half-dozen closely typed pages of legal references and citations. It said:

"It is our conclusion that Senator Nixon did not obtain any financial gain from the collection and disbursement of the fund * * * that Senator Nixon did not violate any Federal or state law by reason of the operation of the fund, and that neither the portion paid * * * directly to third persons nor the portion to Senator Nixon to reimburse him for designated office expenses constituted income to the Senator which was either reportable or taxable as income under applicable tax laws."

The Legal Report

The legal report said that in the correspondence files of the fund "we have found nothing which indicated, either expressly or by implication, that the contributors expected or received any services or assistance from Senator Nixon."

Citing Title 18 of the United States Code, 1914, making it an offense to give or for a Federal official or employe to receive, "any salary" other than governmental salary, the report commented:

"Even if it be assumed that a United States Senator is a Government official or employe under this section, the section is inapplicable to the payments made to or from the D. and C. Smith fund because none of such payments constituted a salary received by Senator Nixon."

The report then cited a 1922 ruling by the Attorney General of the United States that acceptance of travel expenses from "third parties" by Government officials did not constitute "salary" under the prohibition.

The report cited several statutes against Federal legislators receiving gratuities to influence legislation, and added "there is no evidence that Senator Nixon assisted any contributors in the prosecution of any claim."

On the tax question, the report cited several court decisions to the effect that since the Senator had not performed nor was expected to perform services for the contributions, "it is our conclusion that the amounts contributed do not constitute income to the Senator under applicable Federal or state income tax laws."

In his resumé of personal finances, the candidate said that at the time of his first Congressional campaign in 1946, after his discharge from war service in the Navy, the lifetime savings of both him and his wife totaled less than $10,000, in government bonds.

He said that, aside from his Federal salaries and allowances, his only income since had been $1,600 in back payments from his suburban Whittier law firm, with which he had severed connections, $4,500 in family inheritances, and $1,600 a year from paid nonpolitical talks.

The family's current assets, he continued, consisted of a $41,000 house in Washington—on which he owed $20,000—a $13,000 house in Whittier—on which he owed $3,000; $4,000 in life insurance, his expiring G. I. insurance policy; furniture and a 1950 Oldsmobile.

Their debts, he continued, in addition to the mortgages, were a $4,500 loan from the Riggs National Bank in Washington and a $3,500 loan from his parents.

Before the broadcast, Representative Joseph W. Martin Jr. of Massachusetts, Republican floor leader on a speech-making tour in Southern California, telegraphed Senator Nixon:

"Keep your chin up. I and all my associates are standing by you to the limit. We know that when you go on the air tonight you will win the election in a single broadcast."

The speech was delivered in the National Broadcasting Company's televison studio in the El Capitan Theatre in Hollywood.

Original plans were for the Senator to speak from the main studios of the National Broadcasting Company a few blocks away, but the change was made, a campaign aide said, because of better lighting facilities in the theatre, where many large television shows have been staged.

The broadcast was carried on N. B. C.'s national television network and on the Columbia and Mutual Broadcasting Systems' radio networks. The cost, about $75,000, was paid by the Republican National Committee and the Republican Senate and House Campaign Committees.

The preparation of the speech occupied most of the Senator's waking hours during the twenty-seven-hour period from his arrival at the Ambassador Hotel yesterday until his television appearance.

He flew to Los Angeles in his chartered DC-6 from Portland, Ore., interrupting midway a ten-day campaign tour by train and plane of eleven Western and Southern states.

At dinner time yesterday, the candidate took about an hour out for a swim in the hotel's pool with his campaign assistant, William Rogers, Washington lawyer, and immediately afterward returned to his and Mrs. Nixon's three-room suite on the hotel's fifth floor.

They had their meals in the suite.

Aides Help Preparation

Senator Nixon had prepared his remarks in detail. In this, he was assisted by his campaign manager, Murray Chotiner, Los Angeles lawyer; James E. Bassett Jr., his press secretary; Mr. Rogers; and his confidant, Representative Patrick J. Hillings, his successor in the House from his home district of Whittier, a Los Angeles suburb.

His preoccupation with the talk precluded his taking personal cognizance, at least publicly, of a published report that his office facilities in Washington had been used by Mr. Smith in connection with litigation of a $500,000 tax case. The case involved a Smith family property, the Red River Lumber Company, in Northern California.

Asked about the report, Mr. Bassett already issued a statement: "The Senator himself is unavailable for comment, since he is engaged in preparing his important talk for tonight. However, we can reiterate what the Senator already made abundantly clear — he has never given any special favors either as Congressman or as Senator for special consideration."

Mr. Nixon was first elected to the House of Representatives in 1946, and to the Senate in 1950. He defeated Representative Helen Gahagan Douglas for the seat previously held by Senator Sheridan Downey.

Speech Is Transcribed

In the absence of an advance text of Senator Nixon's talk, his staff arranged for a battery of stenographers to transcribe his words from a television screen in an improvised press room off the Ambassador's ground-floor concourse, so that an "official" text could be distributed.

The Senator's party occupied thirty-two rooms on the Ambassador's fifth floor. Robert Hamilton, tour "security" officer, stood guard outside the Senator's suite.

While most of the Senator's staff were closeted with him throughout the day, virtually precluding communication between the candidate and the press, a definitely optimistic atmosphere had pervaded his temporary headquarters.

Financial Statement on Senator Nixon's $18,235 Expense Fund

Special to THE NEW YORK TIMES.

LOS ANGELES, Sept. 23—Following is the text of the Nixon financial statement issued tonight:

Price Waterhouse & Co., Los Angeles, Sept. 23, 1952.

Honorable Sherman Adams
Eisenhower Headquarters
New York, New York
Dear Sir:

In accordance with your instructions received through Messrs. Gibson, Dunn & Crutcher, your attorneys in Los Angeles, Calif., we have examined the accompanying statement of Richard M. Nixon expense fund, Dana C. Smith trustee, for the period from Nov. 15, 1950 (date of opening account) to Aug. 20, 1952 (date of last disbursement of funds collected prior to nomination of Richard M. Nixon for office of Vice President of the United States of America), showing recorded contributions of $18,235.00, payments of $18,168.87 and unexpended balance of $66.13.

Our examination was confined to these particular funds and did not extend to any other funds held by Mr. Smith.

However, we noted from the file furnished us by Mr. Smith that since July 21, 1952, some $11,000.00 has been deposited in the Dana C. Smith trust account which Mr. Smith informed us will be accounted for as campaign contributions and that $347.78 had been disbursed to Richard M. Nixon in reimbursement of expenses of his Washington, D. C. office.

The recorded contributions of $18,235.00 were traced to bank statements and copies of deposit slips. In support of the payments directly to persons other than Richard M. Nixon aggregating $12,876.72, we have examined canceled checks, approved invoices and other supporting documents.

We also have examined canceled checks and other documents in support of the reimbursement to Richard M. Nixon of the $190.00 cost of copies of testimony taken in California.

In support of the payments aggregating $5,102.15 to Richard M. Nixon as reimbursement for expenses of his Washington, D. C., office, we have examined statements and correspondence from his office and the canceled trust fund checks in payment thereof.

In addition, we have inspected in the Washington office of Richard M. Nixon canceled checks, approved invoices or other documents in support of $3,559.58 of these expenditures.

We also inspected office memoranda covering the remaining $1,542.57 of these expenditures, indicating that this amount was spent: for postage $1,092.24, salaries to extra office staff $270.00, reimbursement of members of the office staff for their expenses in entertaining visitors $85.45, and office expenses, including the purchase of documents and publications for constituents, and cab fares to personnel working overtime, $94.88.

While these memoranda did not permit us to independently confirm these expenditures totaling $1,542.57, our auditing tests disclosed nothing to indicate that these expenditures are not correctly shown on the accompanying statement.

The time within which this report was required did not permit us to investigate these items further, but if you wish us to do so, we shall be pleased to receive your instructions.

In our opinion, with the foregoing explanation, the accompanying statement shows correctly the payments of $18,168.87 from the fund and the $66.13 unexpended balance.

Yours very truly,

PRICE WATERHOUSE & CO.

STATEMENT OF RICHARD M. NIXON EXPENSE FUND

DANA C. SMITH, TRUSTEE
FROM NOV. 15, 1950, TO AUG. 20, 1952

Recorded contributions	$18,235.00
Payments by Dana C. Smith, trustee, directly to persons other than Richard M Nixon	974.00
Payments to airlines and hotels for expenses of Mr. and Mrs. Richard M. Nixon principally in connection with trips in, to and from California, and the balance for similar items and automobile expenses at 5 cents per mile of or incurred by Bernard Brennan (California manager) and	
Murray Chotiner (Los Angeles publicity consultant)	2,306.54
Refundable deposit with American Airlines	425.00
Joint Senate and House recording facility for recordings for radio presentation, including shipping charges	1,878.84
Newspaper and other advertising, including publicity photographs of Richard M. Nixon and Pat Nixon	771.12
Keeper of stationery, United States Senate, for 24,518 addressograph plates for mailing list	1,281.07
Capital Engraving Company for Christmas cards: 16,500 for 1950 and 25,000 for 1951	4,237.54
Murray M. Chotiner and Bernard Brennan for telephone, telegraph and messenger expense, plus $61.00 paid directly to utilities	763.89
Meetings and luncheons at California hotels	610.00
Murray M. Chotiner and associates for index cards, files and supplies	390.42
Reimbursement of Washington office staff for meals, taxicab fares and parking charges paid for visitors	382.52
Postage, insurance and check book	29.78
Payment by Dana C. Smith, trustee, to Richard M. Nixon, reimbursement of cost of copies of testimony taken in California	190.00
Payments by Dana C. Smith, trustee, to Richard M. Nixon, as reimbursement for certain expenses of his Washington, D. C. office:	
Reprints of speeches	493.62
Recordings for radio presentation	489.60
Stationery in excess of allowance	815.56
Telephone and telegraph in excess of allowance	225.38
Postage in excess of allowance	1,202.30
Salaries paid to extra office staff	920.55
Typing of letters	157.51
Freight to Los Angeles for Christmas cards	92.66
Meals, taxicab, fare and parking charges paid by office staff for visitors	255.06
Publicity photographs	89.35
Other office expenses, including purchase of documents and publications for constituents and cab fares to office staff working overtime	361.66
Total disbursements	$18,168.87
Balance remaining from recorded contributions	66.13

Text of Senator Nixon's Broadcast Explaining Supplementary Expense Fund

New York Times

EXPLAINS SPECIAL EXPENSE FUND: Senator Richard M. Nixon, Republican Vice Presidential nominee, as seen on television screens here.

Following is the text of the nationwide broadcast from Los Angeles last night by Senator Richard M. Nixon in explanation of his $18,235 trust fund, as recorded by THE NEW YORK TIMES:

My Fellow Americans:

I come before you tonight as a candidate for the Vice Presidency and as a man whose honesty and integrity have been questioned.

The usual political thing to do when charges are made against you is to either ignore them or to deny them without giving details.

I believe we've had enough of that in the United States, particularly with the present Administration in Washington, D. C. To me the office of the Vice Presidency of the United States is a great office, and I feel that the people have got to have confidence in the integrity of the men who run for that office and who might obtain it.

I have a theory, too, that the best and only answer to a smear or to an honest misunderstanding of the facts is to tell the truth. And that's why I'm here tonight. I want to tell you my side of the case.

I am sure that you have read the charge and you've heard it that I, Senator Nixon, took $18,-000 from a group of my supporters.

Was It Wrong?

Now, was that wrong? And let me say that it was wrong—I'm saying, incidentally, that it was wrong and not just illegal. Because it isn't a question of whether it was legal or illegal, that isn't enough. The question is, was it morally wrong?

I say that it was morally wrong if any of that $18,000 went to Senator Nixon for my personal use. I say that it was morally wrong if it was secretly given and secretly handled. And I say that it was morally wrong if any of the contributors got special favors for the contributions that they made.

And now to answer those questions let me say this:

Not one cent of the $18,000 or any other money of that type ever went to me for my personal use. Every penny of it was used to pay for political expenses that I did not think should be charged to the taxpayers of the United States.

It was not a secret fund. As a matter of fact, when I was on "Meet the Press," some of you may have seen it last Sunday—Peter Edson came up to me after the program and he said, "Dick, what about this fund we hear about?" And I said, Well, there's no secret about it. Go out and see Dana Smith, who was the

administrator of the fund. And I gave him his address, and I said that you will find that the purpose of the fund simply was to defray political expenses that I did not feel should be charged to the Government.

And third, let me point out, and I want to make this particularly clear, that no contributor to this fund, no contributor to any of my campaign, has ever received any consideration that he would not have received as an ordinary constituent.

I just don't believe in that and I can say that never, while I have been in the Senate of the United States, as far as the people that contributed to this fund are concerned, have I made a telephone call for them to an agency, or have I gone down to an agency in their behalf. And the record will show that, the records which are in the hands of the Administration.

What for and Why?

But then some of you will say and rightly, "Well, what did you use the fund for, Senator? Why did you have to have it?"

Let me tell you in just a word how a Senate office operates. First of all, a Senator gets $15,000 a year in salary. He gets enough money to pay for one trip a year, a round trip that is, for himself and his family between his home

and Washington, D. C.

And then he gets an allowance to handle the people that work in his office, to handle his mail. And the allowance for my State of California is enough to hire thirteen people.

And let me say, incidentally, that that allowance is not paid to the Senator—it's paid directly to the individuals that the Senator puts on his payroll, that all of these people and all of these allowances are for strictly official business. Business, for example, when a constituent writes in and wants you to go down to the Veterans Administration and get some information about his GI policy. Items of that type for example.

But there are other expenses which are not covered by the Government. And I think I can best discuss those expenses by asking you some questions. Do you think that when I or any other Senator makes a political speech, has it printed, should charge the printing of that speech and the mailing of that speech to the taxpayers?

Do you think, for example, when I or any other Senator makes a trip to his home state to make a purely political speech that the cost of that trip should be charged to the taxpayers?

Do you think when a Senator makes political broadcasts or political television broadcasts, radio or television, that the expense of those broadcasts should be charged to the taxpayers?

Well, I know what your answer is. The same answer that audiences give me whenever I discuss this particular problem. The answer is, "no." The taxpayers shouldn't be required to finance items which are not official business but which are primarily political business.

But then the question arises, you say, "Well, how do you pay for these and how can you do it legally?"

And there are several ways that it can be done, incidentally, and that it is done legally in the United States Senate and in the Congress.

The first way is to be a rich man. I don't happen to be a rich man so I couldn't use that.

Another way that is used is to put your wife on the payroll. Let me say, incidentally, my opponent, my opposite number for the Vice Presidency on the Democratic ticket, does have his wife on the payroll. And has had her on his payroll for the ten years—the past ten years.

Now just let me say this. That's his business and I'm not critical of him for doing that. You will have to pass judgment on that particular point. But I have never done that for this reason. I have found that there are so many deserving stenographers and secretaries in Washington that needed the work that I just didn't feel it was right to put my wife on the payroll.

My wife's sitting over here. She's a wonderful stenographer. She used to teach stenography and she used to teach shorthand in high school. That was when I met her. And I can tell you folks that she's worked many hours at night and many hours on Saturdays and Sundays in my office and she's done a fine job. And I'm proud to say tonight that in the six years I've been in the House and the Senate of the United States, Pat Nixon has never been on the Government payroll.

There are other ways that these finances can be taken care of. Some who are lawyers, and I happen to be a lawyer, continue to practice law. But I haven't been able to do that. I'm so far away from California that I've been so busy with my Senatorial work that I have not engaged in any legal practice.

And also as far as law practice is concerned, it seemed to me that the relationship between an attorney and the client was so personal that you couldn't possibly represent a man as an attorney and then have an unbiased view when he presented his case to you in the event that he had one before the Government.

And so I felt that the best way to handle these necessary political expenses of getting my message to the American people and the speeches I made, the speeches that I had printed, for the most part, concerned this one message—of exposing this Administration, the communism in it, the corruption in it—the only way that I could do that was to accept the aid which people in my home state of California who contributed to my campaign and who continued to make these contributions after I was elected were glad to make.

No Special Favors

And let me say I am proud of the fact that not one of them has ever asked me for a special favor. I'm proud of the fact that not one of them has ever asked me to vote on a bill other than as my own conscience would dictate. And I am proud of the fact that the taxpayers by subterfuge or otherwise have never paid one dime for expenses which I thought were political and shouldn't be charged to the taxpayers.

Let me say, incidentally, that some of you may say, "Well, that's all right, Senator; that's your explanation, but have you got any proof?"

And I'd like to tell you this evening that just about an hour ago we received an independent audit of this entire fund.

I suggested to Gov. Sherman Adams, who is the chief of staff of the Dwight Eisenhower campaign, that an independent audit and legal report be obtained. And I have that audit here in my hand.

It's an audit made by the Price, Waterhouse & Co. firm, and the legal opinion by Gibson, Dunn & Crutcher, lawyers in Los Angeles, the biggest law firm and incidentally one of the best ones in Los Angeles.

I'm proud to be able to report to you tonight that this audit and this legal opinion is being forwarded to General Eisenhower. And I'd like to read to you the opinion that was prepared by Gibson, Dunn & Crutcher and based on all the pertinent laws and statutes, together with the audit report prepared by the certified public accountants.

"It is our conclusion that Senator Nixon did not obtain any financial gain from the collection and disbursement of the fund by Dana Smith; that Senator Nixon did not violate any Federal or state law by reason of the operation of the fund, and that neither the portion of the fund paid by Dana Smith directly to third persons nor the portion paid to Senator Nixon to reimburse him for designated office expenses constituted income to the Senator which was either reportable or taxable as income under applicable tax laws. (signed) Gibson, Dunn & Crutcher by Alma H. Conway."

Now that, my friends, is not Nixon speaking, but that's an independent audit which was requested because I want the American people to know all the facts and I'm not afraid of having independent people go in and check the facts, and that is exactly what they did.

But then I realize that there are still some who may say, and rightly so, and let me say that I recognize that some will continue to smear regardless of what the truth may be, but that there has been understandably some honest misunderstanding on this matter, and there's some that will say:

"Well, maybe you were able, Senator, to fake this thing. How can we believe what you say? After all, is there a possibility that maybe you got some sums in cash? Is there a possibility that you may have feathered your own nest?"

The Family Store

And so now what I am going to do—and incidentally this is unprecedented in the history of American politics—I am going at this time to give to this television and radio audience a complete financial history; everything I've earned; everything I've spent; everything I owe. And I want you to know the facts. I'll have to start early.

I was born in 1913. Our family was one of modest circumstances and most of my early life was spent in a store out in East Whittier. It was a grocery store—one of those family enterprises. The only reason we were able to make it go was because my mother and dad had five boys and we all worked in the store.

I worked my way through college and to a great extent through law school. And then, in 1940, probably the best thing that ever happened to me happened, I married Pat—sitting over here. We had a rather difficult time after we were married, like so many of the young couples who may be listening to us. I practiced law; she continued to teach school. I went into the service.

Let me say that my service record was not a particularly unusual one. I went to the South Pacific. I guess I'm entitled to a couple of battle stars. I got a couple of letters of commendation but I was just there when the bombs were falling and then I returned. I returned to the United States and in 1946 I ran for the Congress.

When we came out of the war, Pat and I—Pat during the war had worked as a stenographer and in a bank and as an economist for a Government agency—and when we came out the total of our savings from both my law practice, her teaching and all the time that I was in the war—the total for that entire period was just a little less than $10,000. Every cent of that, incidentally, was in Government bonds.

Well that's where we start when I go into politics. Now what have I earned since I went into politics? Well here it is—I jotted it down, let me read the notes. First of all I've had my salary as a Congressman and as a Senator. Second, I have received a total in this past six years of $1,600 from estates which were in my law firm at the time that I severed my connection with it.

Saved to Buy House

And, incidentally, as I said before, I have not engaged in any legal practice and have not accepted any fees from business that came into the firm after I went into politics. I have made an average of approximately $1,500 a year from non-political speaking engagements and lectures. And then, fortunately, we've inherited a little money. Pat sold her interest in her father's estate for $3,000 and I inherited $1,500 from my grandfather.

We live rather modestly. For four years we lived in an apartment in Park Fairfax, in Alexandria, Va. The rent was $80 a month. And we saved for the time that we could buy a house.

Now, that was what we took in. What did we do with this money? What do we have today to show for it? This will surprise you, because it is so little, I suppose, as standards generally go, of people in public life. First of all, we've got a house in Washington which cost $41,000 and on which we owe $20,000.

We have a house in Whittier, Calif., which cost $13,000 and on which we owe $3,000. My folks are living there at the present time.

I have just $4,000 in life insurance, plus my G. I. policy which I've never been able to convert and which will run out in two years. I have no life insurance whatever on Pat. I have no life insurance on our two youngsters, Patricia and Julie. I own a 1950 Oldsmobile car. We have our furniture. We have no stocks and bonds of any type. We have no interest of any kind, direct or indirect, in any business.

What Do We Owe?

Now, that's what we have. What do we owe? Well, in addition to the mortgage, the $20,000 mortgage on the house in Washington, the $10,000 one on the house in Whittier, I owe $4,500 to the Riggs Bank in Washington, D. C., with interest 4½ per cent.

I owe $3,500 to my parents and the interest on that loan which I pay regularly, because it's the part of the savings they made through the years they were working so hard, I pay regularly 4 per cent interest. And then I have a $500 loan which I have on my life insurance.

Well, that's about it. That's what we have and that's what we owe. It isn't very much but Pat and I have the satisfaction that every dime that we've got is honestly ours. I should say this—that Pat doesn't have a mink coat. But she does have a respectable Republican cloth coat. And I always tell her that she'd look good in anything.

One other thing I probably should tell you, because if I don't they'll probably be saying this about me too, we did get something—a gift—after the election. A man down in Texas heard Pat on the radio mention the fact that our two youngsters would like to have a dog. And, believe it or not, the day before we left on this campaign trip we got a message from Union Station in Baltimore saying they had a package for us. We went down to get it. You know what it was.

Disagrees With Mitchell

It was a little cocker spaniel dog in a crate that he sent all the way from Texas. Black and white spotted. And our little girl—Trisha, the 6-year-old—named it Checkers. And you know the kids, love the dog and I just want to say this right now, that regardless of what they say about it, we're gonna keep it.

It isn't easy to come before a nation-wide audience and air your life as I've done. But I want to say some things before I conclude that I think most of you will agree on. Mr. Mitchell, the chairman of the Democratic National Committee, made the statement that if a man couldn't afford to be in the United States Senate he shouldn't run for the Senate.

And I just want to make my position clear. I don't agree with Mr. Mitchell when he says that only a rich man should serve his Government in the United States Senate or in the Congress.

I don't believe that represents the thinking of the Democratic party, and I know that it doesn't represent the thinking of the Republican party.

I believe that it's fine that a man like Governor Stevenson who inherited a fortune from his father can run for President. But I also feel that it's essential in this country of ours that a man of modest means can also run for President. Because, you know, remember Abraham Lincoln, you remember what he said: 'God must have loved the common people—he made so many of them.'

And now I'm going to suggest some courses of conduct.

First of all, you have read in the papers about other funds now. Mr. Stevenson, apparently, had a couple. One of them in which a group of business people paid and helped to supplement the salaries of state employes. Here is where the money went directly into their pockets.

And I think that what Mr. Stevenson should do should be to come before the American people as I have, give the names of the people that have contributed to that fund; give the names of the people who put this money into their pockets at the same time that they were receiving money from their state government, and see what favors, if any, they gave out for that.

Urges Sparkman Statement

I don't condemn Mr. Stevenson for what he did. But until the facts are in there there is a doubt that will be raised.

And as far as Mr. Sparkman is concerned, I would suggest the same thing. He's had his wife on the payroll. I don't condemn him for that. But I think that he should come before the American people and indicate what outside sources of income he has had.

I would suggest that under the circumstances both Mr. Sparkman and Mr. Stevenson should come before the American people as I have and make a complete financial statement as to their financial history. And if they don't it will be an admission that they have something to hide. And I think that you will agree with me.

Because folks, remember, a man that's to be President of the United States, a man that's to be Vice President of the United States must have the confidence of all the people. And that's why I'm doing what I'm doing, and that's why I suggest that Mr. Stevenson and Mr. Sparkman since they are under attack should do what they are doing.

Now, let me say this: I know that this is not the last of the smears. In spite of my explanation tonight other smears will be made; others have been made in the past. And the purpose of the smears, I know, is this—to silence me, to make me let up.

Well, they just don't know who they're dealing with. I'm going to tell you this: I remember in the dark days of the Hiss case some of the same columnists, some of the same radio commentators who are attacking me now and misrepresenting my position were violently opposing me at the time I was after Alger Hiss.

But I continued the fight because I knew I was right. And I can say to this great television and radio audience that I have no apologies to the American people for my part in putting Alger Hiss where he is today.

And as far as this is concerned, intend to continue the fight.

Why do I feel so deeply? Why do I feel that in spite of the smears, the misunderstandings, the necessities for a man to come up here and bare his soul as I have? Why is it necessary for me to continue this fight?

And I want to tell you why. Because, you see, I love my country. And I think my country is in danger. And I think that the only man that can save America at this time is the man that's running for President on my ticket—Dwight Eisenhower.

Attacks State Department

You say, "Why do I think it's in danger?" and I say look at the record. Seven years of the Truman-Acheson Administration and what's happened? Six hundred million people lost to the Communists, and a war in Korea in which we have lost 117,000

American casualties.

And I say to all of you that a policy that results in a loss of 600,000,000 to the Communists and a war which costs us 117,000 American casualties isn't good enough for America.

And I say that those in the State Department that made the mistakes which caused that war and which resulted in those losses should be kicked out of the State Department just as fast as we can get 'em out of there.

And let me say that I know Mr. Stevenson won't do that. Because he defends the Truman policy and I know that Dwight Eisenhower will do that, and that he will give America the leadership that it needs.

Take the problem of corruption. You've read about the mess in Washington. Mr. Stevenson can't clean it up because he was picked by the man, Truman, under whose Administration the mess was made. You wouldn't trust a man who made the mess to clean it up—that's Truman. And by the same token you can't trust the man who was picked by the man that made the mess to clean it up—and that's Stevenson.

And so I say, Eisenhower, who owes nothing to Truman, nothing to the big city bosses, he is the man that can clean up the mess in Washington.

Take communism. I say that as far as that subject is concerned, the danger is great to America. In the Hiss case they got the secrets which enabled them to break the American secret State Department code. They got secrets in the atomic bomb case which enabled 'em to get the secret of the atomic bomb, five years before they would have gotten it by their own devices.

And I say that any man who called the Alger Hiss case a "red herring" isn't fit to be President of the United States. I say that a man who like Mr. Stevenson has pooh-poohed and ridiculed the Communist threat in the United States—he said that they are phantoms among ourselves; he's accused us that have attempted to expose the Communists of looking for Communists in the Bureau of Fisheries and Wildlife—I say that a man who says that isn't qualified to be President of the United States.

And I say that the only man who can lead us in this fight to rid the Government of both those who are Communists and those who have corrupted this Government is Eisenhower, because Eisenhower, you can be sure, recognizes the problem and he knows how to deal with it.

Now let me say that, finally, this evening I want to read to you just briefly excerpts from a letter which I received, a letter which, after all this is over, no one can take away from me. It

reads as follows:

"Dear Senator Nixon,

"Since I'm only 19 years of age I can't vote in this Presidential election but believe me if I could you and General Eisenhower would certainly get my vote. My husband is in the Fleet Marines in Korea. He's a corpsman on the front lines and we have a two-month-old son he's never seen. And I feel confident that with great Americans like you and General Eisenhower in the White House, lonely Americans like myself will be united with their loved ones now in Korea.

"I only pray to God that you won't be too late. Enclosed is a small check to help you in your campaign. Living on $85 a month is all I can afford at present. But let me know what else I can do."

Folks, it's a check for $10, and it's one that I will never cash.

And just let me say this. We hear a lot about prosperity these days but I say, why can't we have prosperity built on peace rather than prosperity built on war? Why can't we have prosperity and an honest government in Washington, D. C., at the same time. Believe me, we can. And Eisenhower is the man that can lead this crusade to bring us that kind of prosperity.

And, now, finally, I know that you wonder whether or not I am going to stay on the Republican ticket or resign.

Let me say this: I don't believe that I ought to quit because I'm not a quitter. And, incidentally, Pat's not a quitter. After all, her name was Patricia Ryan and she was born on St. Patrick's Day, and you know the Irish never quit.

But the decision, my friends, is not mine. I would do nothing that would harm the possibilities of Dwight Eisenhower to become President of the United States. And for that reason I am submitting to the Republican National Committee tonight through this television broadcast the decision which it is theirs to make.

Let them decide whether my position on the ticket will help or hurt. And I am going to ask you to help them decide. Wire and write the Republican National Committee whether you think I should stay on or whether I should get off. And whatever their decision is, I will abide by it.

But just let me say this last word. Regardless of what happens I'm going to continue this fight. I'm going to campaign up and down America until we drive the crooks and the Communists and those that defend them out of Washington. And remember, folks, Eisenhower is a great man. Believe me. He's a great man. And a vote for Eisenhower is a vote for what's good for America.

PRAISE BY GENERAL

He Commends Senator for 'Magnificent' Talk on His Finances

STUMPS OHIO WITH TAFT

Then Discards Cleveland Text to Laud Running Mate as a Courageous Person

By JAMES RESTON
Special to THE NEW YORK TIMES.

CLEVELAND, Sept. 23—Gen. Dwight D. Eisenhower listened to Senator Richard M. Nixon's explanation of his defense fund tonight and immediately indicated that he would retain the Senator as his Vice Presidential running mate.

In an extraordinary evening that started with a defense of Senator Nixon's honesty and developed into a Hollywood-type story of the Senator's life, General Eisenhower told a roaring crowd of 15,000 in the Cleveland Public Auditorium that his personal admiration and affection for the Californian were "undiminished."

The Republican Presidential nominee, who watched the Nixon telecast while the audience in the Public Auditorium listened to it over a loudspeaker, withheld final judgment on the case, but he praised Senator Nixon's courage and left no doubt that, unless some wholly new element were introduced into the controversy, Senator Nixon would receive his endorsement. He also called the Senator to a personal meeting with him.

'Affection' Is Undiminished

General Eisenhower wired Mr. Nixon tonight as follows:

"Your presentation was magnificent. While technically no decision rests with me, yet you and I know that the realities of the situation will require a personal pronouncement, which so far as the public is concerned, will be considered decisive.

"In view of your comprehensive presentation, my personal decision is going to be based on a personal conclusion. To complete the formulation of that personal decision, I feel the need of talking to you and would be most appreciative if you could fly to see me at once. Tomorrow night I shall be at Wheeling, W. Va.

"I cannot close this telegram without saying that whatever personal admiration and affection

I have for you, and they are very great, are undiminished."

The general had prepared a speech on inflation, but his first announcement to the audience was that he had thrown it away. He then said he liked a courageous man and had seen one tonight.

He also said it was clear in his mind what the test of his own judgment would be when the chairman of the Republican National Committee, Arthur E. Summerfield, called on him for his decision—whether or not to keep the Senator as his running mate.

First, the general said, it would not be decided by his idea of what would get the most votes or what would serve administrative convenience.

Second, his test would be whether he believed that this man, Senator Nixon, was the kind of man America would want as its Vice President.

The general left no doubt in anybody's mind here about what his judgment would be. By his manner, by his praise of Senator Nixon before this audience, he appeared to be saying clearly that, so far as he was concerned, Senator Nixon was "in."

At the same time the general was aware of the proprieties in the matter. His judgment was that this was not a decision for him to take on his own, but a decision for his party to take through its National Committee.

Accordingly, he did not pass judgment, but he made clear that he expected his judgment to be listened to, and he left no doubt that he would make up his mind on his own.

He said that he had been forced in his lifetime to make many tough decisions about men: Whether they had the qualities to command a regiment, a division, an Army corps, even that most solemn of all decisions—whether to order an execution or send men into battle.

The general, however, was not able to conceal his admiration for the report made to the people by his running-mate.

General Eisenhower drew a parallel between the Nixon case and his support of the late Gen. George S. Patton Jr. during the war. At one period during the war, General Patton was widely criticized because he had slapped a soldier in an Army hospital, and there was a great outcry against him because of the incident. But in the end, General Eisenhower, though he reproved General Patton, backed him up.

Scorns 'Pussyfooters'

General Eisenhower recalled this tonight and said that General Patton had committed an error, "a definite error," but, he added:

"I believe that the work of that man was too great to sacrifice. He made his amends for his error. He has gone before the highest judge of all, but certainly George Patton justified my faith."

Then General Eisenhower added this:

"I happen to be one of those people who, when I get in a fight, would rather have a courageous and honest man by my side than a whole box car full of pussyfooters."

The audience roared.

The general's political speeches have been widely criticized as cold and stilted, but tonight he was on

his own, without script, without worries about timing for the television cameras, facing a new situation, and acting quickly and forcefully.

He was more relaxed than he had been at any time in this campaign trip. He stood erect at the podium.

"I have been a warrior," he said, "and I like courage. Tonight I saw an example of courage."

The crowd roared and waved thousands of small flags, high up into the galleries.

"I have seen brave men in tough situations," he continued. "I have never seen any come through in better fashion than Senator Nixon did tonight.

'He Is a Courageous Man'

"I do not mean to say that there will not be some who will find new items on which they will want further explanations, possibly. But I do say this, that when a man in furtherance of what he believes to be correct and right stands up in front of all the American people and bares his soul, brings his family with him and tells the truth, and brings with him every bit of evidence that he can get hold of to substantiate his story, to bare the secrets of his economic and financial life, he is a courageous man."

The general indicated two things—first that he was going to recommend the retention of Senator Nixon, and second, that he thought the Senator had committed an error of judgment.

He pointed out, however, that in his mind there was a great difference between the kind of thing Mr. Nixon was accused of doing and the "corruption issue" that, in the Presidential campaign, he was leveling against the Democratic Administration.

"Between that and whatever error of judgment may have been committed by Senator Nixon there is a gulf as wide as the Pacific."

Technically, the general said, he has no decision to make in this matter, but that, as the standard bearer of the Republican party, he must form a conclusion. This conclusion, he emphasized, probably would be decisive in the public mind.

"I'm not intending to duck any responsibility that falls upon me in connection with the great task I have undertaken to be the standard bearer of the Republican party," he said.

The general added that it was entirely possible that some of his best friends would disagree with him, but that as he saw it, it had been given to him to reach a decision, and he added, "I shall do it."

The general ended on this note:

"Ladies and gentlemen, it has been a dramatic evening. I have failed you in the type of presentation you should like from me, I offer you my apologies, but I have given you exactly what has been in my heart."

The audience showed the Republican nominee that his apologies were unnecessary, and unlike other audiences who have responded without much enthusiasm to his prepared addresses, this crowd roared its approval.

As a matter of fact, the judgment of his aides was that this was the most exciting political meeting that the general had had on this

trip, and the feeling among those traveling with him was that the Nixon incident, which has been an immense embarrassment for the last seventy-two hours, had been turned into a political advantage.

One of the regrets of the general's advisers was that this particular extemporaneous speech was not one of the many television and radio broadcasts sent across the country. Because it was regarded as a particularly important political development, arrangements were made immediately to rebroadcast it tonight and tomorrow.

The dramatic effect of this evening's performance was heightened by the fact that this great audience had sat intently listening to Senator Nixon's broadcast from beginning to end. From time to time there were outbursts of applause, and when the Senator had finished, women all over the audience were seen weeping openly. When the broadcast was completed, the audience, openly sympathetic, applauded enthusiastically.

General Eisenhower watched the television broadcast of the Senator's presentation. Between the time the Senator finished and the time General Eisenhower reached the hall, someone in the gallery started shouting: "We want Nixon." This was immediately picked up by the crowd and carried on for a minute or so, but it was nothing to compare with the endorsement that came for the Senator a few minutes later.

Asked by a reporter to ascertain the opinion of the audience after hearing the Nixon broadcast, Representative George Bender, Republican of Ohio, the chairman of the meeting, put the question: "Are you in favor of retaining Senator Nixon as the Republican party's Vice Presidential nominee?"

A tumultuous "yes" immediately filled the hall.

When he put the opposite question, there were perhaps twenty or thirty "no's" in the audience of 15,000. He then put the question again, and "aye" responded through the rafters once more.

In the speech he had prepared for tonight's appearance, the general had charged that the inflation of the nation's currency was not an accident but a calculated policy devised by the Administration to keep itself in power.

This was the highlight of a full day of campaigning that carried the general and Senators Robert A. Taft and John W. Bricker of Ohio all the way from the Ohio River in Cincinnati to Lake Erie in the north. The Republican candidate made back-platform talks at Middletown, Dayton, Springfield, Columbus, Delaware, Galion and Wellington, all in Ohio. At most of these places he discussed the high cost of living and the fiscal policies of the Administration, which he blamed for present prices.

Signs For and Against

The general was well received in most towns by crowds ranging in the smaller places from 1,500 to 4,000; a large but unenthusiastic audience of 30,000 crowded onto the lawn of the state Capitol in Columbus to hear him and he received a noisy reception when he arrived in Cleveland this evening.

At Columbus signs for and against Senator Nixon appeared in the audience for the first time since the controversy over the Californian's private expense fund arose. Some signs read: "Nixon's Okay, Nixon's Okay."

Several larger signs also appeared reading as follows: "Nixon fooled America before he got a good hold—Send Nixon to the grand jury for an accounting—The people will get it straight."

Senator Taft and Senator Bricker were introduced at most of the whistle stops. In Springfield, Senator Taft made a short speech and promised the general that Ohio would do its very best to give him a large majority in the November election.

In most places however the crowd was more enthusiastic in its applause for Mr. Taft than for General Eisenhower, indicating that the disappointment of Mr. Taft's supporters over his loss of the Republican nomination had not yet vanished.

Senator Taft, before the Cleveland audience tonight, said that General Eisenhower had expressed a philosophy in Ohio today "which I've been preaching for fourteen years in the Congress of the United States."

Representative Bender had introduced Senator Taft in the following manner: "Now I introduce the man we all came—one of the two men we all came to hear, one of the outstanding statesmen of the world, Senator Bob Taft."

Here was how General Eisenhower phrased his central attack on the fiscal policy of the Administration in his prepared text:

"The resort to 'cheap money,' like the resort to cheap politics, is not new. It is one of the oldest, most standard devices of a regime dedicated to perpetuating itself in power.

"It is the mark of an Administration that cares more for the next election than for the next generation."

The general then laid down a three-point program for dealing with the inflation:

1. Drop the present Administration's maxim that, he averred, says "inflation is the best policy." In other words, end the policy of "cheap money."
2. Unify the policies of the various economic agencies of the Government so that they are working together and not fighting against one another.
3. Introduce an "intelligent planned attack on the spending program of our Federal Government.

General Eisenhower was scheduled to continue his twelve-state whistle-stop tour in southern Ohio and in West Virginia tomorrow. He will speak in Chillicothe, Portsmouth and Ironton, Ohio, and in Kenova, Huntington, Parkersburg and Wheeling, W. Va.

September 24, 1952

G. O. P. HEADS RALLY TO NIXON'S SUPPORT

Summerfield Asserts Attack Has 'Backfired'—Senator's Position Held Stronger

Before the announcement by Gen. Dwight D. Eisenhower last night that the Republican National Committee had voted 107 to 0 to retain Senator Robert M. Nixon on the ticket, a survey by THE NEW YORK TIMES showed the committee overwhelmingly in favor of the Senator.

The backers of the Republican Vice Presidential nominee included Arthur E. Summerfield, chairman of the committee.

On Tuesday night, at the end of Senator Nixon's half-hour broadcast explanation of the $18,235 expense fund donated to him by California supporters, he declared he was submitting the question whether he should stay in the race to the committee and would abide by its decision.

He made it clear that his own inclination was to remain, that his conduct was fully justified.

Mr. Summerfield declared in Cleveland that attacks on Senator Nixon because of the fund had "backfired." He predicted that Senator Nixon's speech would prove "the turning point of the campaign."

His views were echoed throughout the country by Republican officials as they attempted to dig themselves clear of the thousands of messages they were receiving from rank-and-file Republicans who listened to the Senator's explanation of his personal finances.

In Montpelier, Vt., the biennial State Republican Convention unanimously adopted a resolution pledging Senator Nixon its "continued and hearty support."

In New Orleans John Minor Wisdom, National Committeeman, asserted that Senator Nixon "probably won millions of votes by that single speech which explained so much and summed up so much—not only about his own case but the campaign issues generally."

J. Russell Sprague, National Committeeman for New York, voiced the opinion that Senator Nixon had made himself "a national hero" by his speech. In Corpus Christi, Tex., Mrs. Walter Groce, a former Republican leader, reported that she had received several anonymous telephone calls calling her "a disgrace to womanhood," "a detriment to the party" and a Communist because she had sent Senator Nixon a telegram describing his speech as "tearful but no soap."

Before General Eisenhower and the Senator met in Wheeling, W. Va., last night, national committeemen from thirty-seven states had publicly declared themselves in favor of retaining the Californian on the ticket. Not a single committeeman from any of the eleven others had voiced any contrary opinion.

Mr. Sprague disclosed at his offices in Mineola that Mr. Summerfield had polled the fifteen members of the National Executive Committee by telephone before the speech and that all fifteen had declared at that time that Senator Nixon should remain.

Sinclair Weeks, National Committeeman for Massachusetts and chairman of the Republican Finance Committee, telegraphed Mr. Summerfield that there was no need for a meeting of the National Committee to decide whether Senator Nixon should drop out or stay on the ticket. He said it would be "unthinkable" not to carry on with the Californian.

"Let's put the show on the road and get going," he declared.

In San Francisco, former President Herbert Hoover said the tumult over the fund was a "smear" that would leave the "Republican party 'firmer in the hearts and confidence of the American people."

Robert K. Goodwin of Iowa, director of the Republican farm division, reported that a contribution for $100 had been enclosed with one letter urging that Mr. Nixon be retained. J. P. Langan of West Orange, N. J., announced he was sending $100 to Dana C. Smith of Pasadena, Calif., trustee of the Nixon fund, to encourage the establishment of similar endowments. Former State Senator William H. Lee of Lockport, N. Y.,

announced he was sending $100 to Republican National Headquarters to help finance the printing of Senator Nixon's address.

Several Democrats likewise came to Senator Nixon's defense. Senator Estes Kefauver of Tennessee, who had been one of the contenders for the Democratic Presidential nomination, said on his return from Europe that he was not familiar with the charges and therefore could not express a considered opinion but added:

"I've known Mr. Nixon both in the Senate and the House and I'd be very much surprised if he did anything wrong."

T. James Tumulty, secretary to Mayor John V. Kenny of Jersey City, made public the following telegram he had sent to General Eisenhower:

"American sense of fair play requires Nixon stay in race. After tonight's speech any fair-minded Democrat believes as I do in his integrity. Let's fight on the issues."

Upwards of 6,000 telegrams and uncounted telephone calls were received during the day at General Eisenhower's personal headquarters in the Hotel Commodore, most of which urged Senator Nixon to stay on the ticket. Other thousands of telegrams and messages to the same effect were received at the headquarters of the National Citizens for Eisenhower and Nixon at the Hotel Marguery, according to Walter Williams, national chairman of the citizens' organization.

John R. Crews, Brooklyn Republican leader, said he never had received such an avalanche of telegrams and telephone calls in his years in politics. The sentiment in favor of Senator Nixon that they conveyed was overwhelming, he declared.

John J. Dickerson, New Jersey Republican State Chairman, said the response to Senator Nixon's defense assured him of a hearty welcome when he came to New Jersey Oct. 4. Senator Nixon is scheduled to enter the state from Delaware and visit as many of its population centers as he can.

In Oklahoma, too, Republican leaders were confident that Senator Nixon would get a heartier welcome than would have been the case if the fund incident had not arisen.

Thomas J. Curran, New York County Republican Chairman, estimated that the reaction to Senator Nixon's address was so favorable that "if the election were held today, he would win in a sweep on that one speech alone."

NIXON IS ACCLAIMED BY AIRPORT CROWDS

Response Is Reassuring as He Crosses Country—He Says He Has 'Not Begun to Fight'

By GLADWIN HILL
Special to THE NEW YORK TIMES.

WHEELING, W. Va., Sept. 24—Senator Richard M. Nixon broke off his Western campaign tour today for a 2,400-mile cross-country trip in his chartered airliner to meet his running-mate, Gen. Dwight D. Eisenhower, and receive from him formal word of the Republican party's full acceptance of his public defense of his integrity.

Greeted with great cordiality by the general aboard his DC-6 as it touched down here, the Republican Vice-Presidential candidate drove twenty miles into town and appeared with him at a large rally at the city's Island Stadium.

The rendezvous was worked out in an overnight series of long-distance telephone conversations.

It was expected in the Nixon camp to serve the main purpose of betokening the solidarity of the Republicans' November election ticket, in the wake of allegations from both Democratic and Republican sources that the California Senator's past use of a privately contributed $18,235 "supplementary expenditures" fund ethically disqualified him as a candidate.

Dropping an itinerary that called for him to spend today stumping Montana and South Dakota by plane, Senator Nixon, with an entourage of some thirty persons, left Missoula, Mont., in his chartered DC-6 at eleven A. M., mountain standard time, for the 2,400-mile trip to Wheeling. The trip was broken only by a stop to change crews at Denver.

From indirect communications with the Eisenhower campaign train, bound from Ohio to West Virginia, with the Republican National Chairman, Arthur Summerfield, in Cleveland, acting as go-between, Nixon aides drew the definite conclusion that the Republican high command considered the Senator had vindicated himself by his detailed explanation of his personal and professional finances over a nation-wide radio and television hookup from Los Angeles last night.

Eisenhower Requested Meeting

Immediately after the broadcast, General Eisenhower wired the Senator of his desire for a meeting as soon as possible.

In his talk, Senator Nixon maintained that the fund, contributed by seventy-six Southern California supporters over the two-year period between his election to the Senate and his present nomination, had been used for political traveling, speeches and mailings not properly covered by regular Senatorial allowances.

He said that he never had benefited personally from the fund and that he never had granted, nor had the donors sought, any political favors in return for the contributions. He bolstered his statement with reports from a law firm and an accounting concern pronouncing the arrangement legitimate.

He asked his listeners to wire and write the Republican National Committee, as the chief authority over his candidacy, whether they thought he should be dropped or retained.

Telegraph circuits into Los Angeles and telephone lines into his temporary headquarters at the Ambassador Hotel there immediately were jammed with messages, virtually all of which, his aides said, expressed approval of his continued candidacy.

Western Union officials assisting with the tour communications said that up to midnight last night, Los Angeles and suburban offices of the company had received about 5,200 incoming telegrams addressed to the Senator. They could not recall when any other public issue had evoked such an outpouring of opinion.

Crowds Are at Airport

The Senator was greeted warmly by the first crowds he encountered after the talk. Approximately 200 persons, cheering and waving partisan placards, were waiting at the Los Angeles International Airport when he arrived about 11 o'clock last night to take off for Missoula, continuing the ten-day tour of Western and Southern States he broke off Monday to return to Los Angeles for the broadcast.

The candidate planned to resume the hour by flying back to Salt Lake City, tomorrow, after his meeting with General Eisenhower.

At the Los Angeles Airport, the Senator clambered onto a car and thanked his well-wishers briefly, and made two more brief statements for newsreels, in each proclaiming the slogan "we haven't begun to fight."

Arriving at Missoula at 3 A. M. Senator Nixon was met by about seventy-five persons, led by Mayor Ralph L. Starr, who presented a "key to the city" to the candidate and Mrs. Nixon, remarking:

"We're proud of you—the whole country is proud of you — after your speech tonight."

After barely three hours' sleep in the Florence Hotel, Senator Nixon arose and took a walk by himself to collect his thoughts for a 9:30 A. M. address on the city's main street in front of the hotel.

His staff said that despite his assured manner on the air, the talk had made him so tense that at the end he had broken down and wept for a few moments before leaving the Hollywood television studio.

About one-fifth of Missoula's 23,000 inhabitants, according to the estimate of Police Chief Dan Rice, turned out this morning to hear his speech, from a decorated truck in the middle of Higgins Avenue.

'I Love My Country' Theme

Speaking unusually slowly, and departing from his usual repertoire of remarks, the Senator took as his theme the comment "I love my country," which he had interjected in his television talk. Among the nation's imposing qualities, he said, there stood foremost its Constitution and the freedoms guaranteed under it.

These freedoms, he said, encompassed the fact that "a person from a humble family can run for office; for the Senate—even the Vice Presidency.

"And when enemies attack him," he added, "he can go on television and the radio, and all he has to do is tell the truth."

He said the fact that politics was "a dirty game" should not deter any of his youthful auditors from entering the field.

"The thing to do," he said, "is go in and clean it up."

At Denver, 500 to 1,000 persons were at the airport, even though there had been no great publicity about the stop there. How many were normal airline passengers and how many were Nixon boosters could not be determined, but they cheered him enthusiastically when, standing on a loading ramp, he declared again "we have not begun to fight."

CANDIDATES MEET

Airport Greeting Warm— General Calls Senator a 'Man of Honor'

TICKET HARMONY ASSURED

Californian Now 'Stands Higher Than Ever,' Eisenhower Says of His Explanation

By JAMES RESTON
Special to The New York Times.

WHEELING, W. Va., Sept. 24—Gen. Dwight D. Eisenhower said tonight that his Vice Presidential running mate, Senator Richard M. Nixon of California, had been "completely vindicated" of charges in connection with a privately raised expense fund.

Speaking before a cheering and enthusiastic crowd here, the Republican Presidential nominee announced that the 107 members of the Republican National Committee who could be reached had all voted for retaining Mr. Nixon on the ticket. There are 138 members on the full committee.

General Eisenhower declared he believed Senator Nixon "had been subjected to an unfair and vicious attack."

"He is not only completely vindicated as a man of honor but, as far as I am concerned, he stands higher than ever before," said the general.

Thus it was plain that, although there had been no official statement sealing the California Senator's place on the ticket, the general's statement taken with the report on the national committee, made it certain that Mr. Nixon would remain the Republican party's Vice Presidential nominee.

'A Man of Honor'

General Eisenhower's remarks were:

"Ladies and gentlemen, my colleague in this political campaign has been subject to a very unfair and vicious attack. So far as I am concerned, he has not only vindicated himself, but I feel that he has acted as a man of courage and honor and so far as I am concerned, stands higher than ever before.

"I am going to ask Senator Nixon to speak a few words to you this evening, but before he comes to this podium, let me read to you two messages. The first one is a tribute. This is a telegram to me:

"'Dear General: I am trusting that the absolute truth may come out concerning this attack on Richard and when it does I am sure you will be guided right in your decision to place implicit faith in his integrity and honesty. Best wishes from one who has known Richard longer than anyone else. His mother.'

"Now, as I waited on him at the plane this evening, I received a telegram from the Republican National Committee signed by the chairman. It reads:

"'This is to advise you that as of 9:00 this evening, 107 of the 138 members of the Republican National Committee who could be reached, either by telephone or telegram, have been asked for their reaction to the Senator's suggestion that the committee decide if it wants him to stay on the Republican ticket as the Vice Presidential candidate.

"'I am proud to inform you that the results were 107 to 0 in support of Senator Nixon.

"'The comment accompanying their unanimous response was overwhelmingly enthusiastic. Their telegrams reflected a deep conviction that Richard M. Nixon not only deserved the support of every American, but is worthy of the highest public trust.

"'As a member of the Republican National Committee, it gave me great satisfaction to join with my colleagues in this stirring tribute to a truly great American who walked unafraid through the valley of despair and emerged unscathed and unbowed.

"'Let there be no doubt about it, America has taken Dick Nixon to its heart. Every Republican is proud to have him on the ticket. (Signed) Arthur E. Summerfield, Chairman Republican National Committee.'"

The general met the Senator at 10 o'clock when his special plane arrived from the West. A crowd of about 3,000 was on hand at the airport when the Republican Presidential nominee reached the field.

The general went aboard the plane and stayed for a couple of minutes, then reappeared and shook hands warmly with Mr. Nixon for the photographers.

The pair had a chance to visit together during the twenty-minute drive from the airport to the City Island Stadium, where about 6,000 were gathered to meet him.

Senator Nixon, who flew here from Montana, listened to the general's brief statement and then, in a short speech said:

"I want you to know that this is probably the greatest moment of my life. The man whom I think will make the best President we have had in many, many years has stood before this audience and has said, 'We are going to fight for the principles in which all Americans have believed.'"

Senator Nixon criticized Gov. Adlai E. Stevenson of Illinois, the Democratic nominee, for refusing to disclose the names of the men who contributed to and benefited from the Illinois fund raised to encourage good men to remain in the Illinois Government.

If the Governor insisted on this position, he said, it would prove he had something to hide and it would cost him the election.

September 25, 1952

Crowds Cheer Nixon

The vindication meeting was held after General Eisenhower had toured up the Ohio River Valley from Portsmouth, Ohio, to Wheeling. During the day he had concrete evidence that the Nixon incident, which three days ago looked like a serious handicap to the Republican ticket, had actually increased the party's popularity.

The crowds today were larger, considering the size of the towns than at any time since the start of the twelve-day tour of the Middle West and border states. The people were more boisterous in their applause, and every mention of Senator Nixon brought roaring applause.

Senator Nixon was completely at his ease when General Eisenhower called on him to address the crowd. He started by saying that there were two times in his life when he was prouder to be an American than at any other time.

The first time, he said, was when General Eisenhower was hailed in a great ticker-tape parade after VE-Day and the Senator, just back from the South Pacific, watched the general ride by from Navy Headquarters on Church Street in New York.

"The other time when I think when I have had this feeling most deeply," the young Senator said, "was today."

Mr. Nixon said that after his nation-wide television broadcast last night, in which he explained how he had received an $18,235 expense fund from his followers in California and what he had done with it, his train stopped today at Denver, Colo., and there and in Wheeling he had an exciting experience.

"As we went through these places and saw the facts we heard them say both to Pat [his wife] and to me: 'Keep it up, keep fighting, we believe in you.'"

Mr. Nixon said that this made him realize that all you have to do in this country is to tell the people the truth and not try to hide anything from them.

Senator Nixon had praised General Eisenhower for the way he had handled the case. A lesser man, he said, would have treated the charges merely as a "smear" and would have refused to listen to the evidence about them.

Fortunately, the Senator declared, General Eisenhower had not done that.

"There has been too much of that in the present Administration * * * to much of this business of covering * * * clamming up whenever charges are made against those in high places," he said.

Praise for Eisenhower

The Senator said that if General Eisenhower would do that for him "just think what he is going to do when he becomes President—it is going to be the cleanest, the most honest Administration this country has ever had."

A great deal of the Senator's speech was a eulogy of General Eisenhower and the general's wife.

"What I want to tell you folks," he said in conclusion, "and this comes from the depths of a man's heart: This man Eisenhower is a great American and America needs him * * * So remember this folks: What is good for America, that is what Eisenhower stands for. And what is good for America, believe me, is good for you."

In his speech here this evening General Eisenhower criticized those who had condemned him for trying to unify the divergent elements in the Republican party.

He said that in Europe, where he had served as Supreme Commander of the North Atlantic Treaty Organization, there had been a tendency for minorities within political parties to break away and form competitive splinter parties.

"This splinter-party system of Europe is what the Democrats recommend for us Republicans," he continued. "They most generously advise me which Senators I should work with and which I should disown. Just what kind of people do these Administration Democrats think we are?

"To hear them talk you would think that the Republican party was something that I invented and they own—that they can dictate to me a course of action and Republican candidates will fall in line. Well, let us be thankful that Republicans think for themselves."

For Tolerance in Party

It was the expectation of the founding fathers, the general observed, that political leaders would bring men of different points of view into a workable combination for the good of all. He added that in his judgment membership in the Republican party did not necessarily mean mutual agreement or approval, other than on basic objectives and principles.

This line of reasoning, which the general is expected to develop in greater detail in a major speech at Baltimore tomorrow night, was directed at those who had criticized him because he had announced his support of all Republican candidates for Congress, including Senators Joseph R. McCarthy of Wisconsin and William E. Jenner of Indiana, and others who had opposed policies favored by General Eisenhower.

He said there was general agreement within the Republican party:

¶To seek a just and lasting peace for the United States and the rest of the free world. He added that it was essential that the nation be strong in order to achieve peace.

¶To maintain prosperity in America but to do so without war.

¶To achieve a true equality of opportunity for all men in America. "I have no patience with the idea of second class citizenship," he added.

¶To seek in the United States "a government close to the people and responsive to their needs."

The atmosphere on the campaign train was different today than it had been heretofore. At the beginning of the week it seemed to the Eisenhower supporters on board that Senator Nixon was trapped behind his own goal line and the spectators on the Eisenhower side were gloomy and silent.

But, as sometimes happens in football and politics, the man with the ball suddenly got loose and now seems to be racing down the sidelines, to the astonishment of many and the cheers of the multitude.

The change was manifest in many ways. The general was visibly more confident. The farther the train traveled, the broader became his Kansas accent, the more he dropped into the vernacular, the more he talked about "Dick Nixon," the happier he looked.

At every mention of Senator Nixon the crowds whooped with delight. At every stop, stacks of telegrams addressed to "Ike" and "the Eisenhower train" were heaved aboard. There were so many of them that they were not even counted, let alone read.

Hesitancy Disappears

Long before the general met his running mate, it was obvious that he had made up his mind.

Last night in Cleveland, he withheld his decision and indicated that he would go over the facts in greater detail after he had talked with Senator Nixon before making up his mind, but he did not sound very juridical or hesitant at the stops this morning.

At Point Pleasant, W. Va., where he was introduced as "here's the fighting son-of-a-gun Ike Eisenhower". The general appealed to the crowd not to send him any more telegrams.

Previously, General Eisenhower had appeared worried about the criticism of Senator Nixon's actions, especially since much of it had come from newspapers supporting his candidacy.

Indeed, he had had two private meetings with reporters on the train in which he had indicated his opposition to the idea of private expense funds. But after last night's television talk by Senator Nixon and this morning's reaction to it he left no doubt that he now felt that he had a political asset on his hands.

After Point Pleasant, though the crowds kept appearing at the stations along the way, the train didn't even slow down at Ravenswood, W. Va. There must have been 2,000 persons, accompanied by a scarlet coated high school band, along the track waving and crying, "We want Ike!" but by that time he was already behind schedule and kept rolling.

Tomorrow, General Eisenhower continues his tour of the border states. He will be in West Virginia in the morning, and will tour Maryland in the afternoon, with his major speech scheduled for Baltimore tomorrow night.

Donor of Puppy to Nixons Says It Had 'No Price Tag'

By The United Press

BELTON, Tex., Sept. 24—A salesman who identified himself as "a fighting Texas Republican" sent to Senator Richard M. Nixon's daughter the black and white cocker spaniel that Mr. Nixon mentioned in his speech last night.

Lewis L. Carrol said he had sent the puppy the day after Labor Day—"with no strings attached and no price tag."

He said he had done it because he was an "Ike-Nixon" man and had read that Mr. Nixon wanted a puppy. Mr. Carrol said the dog was about five months old, pedigreed and registered.

MESSAGES POUR IN BACKING NOMINEE

Wires at Rate of 4,000 an Hour Overwhelmingly in Favor of Retaining Californian

By CLAYTON KNOWLES
Special to The New York Times

WASHINGTON, Sept. 24—A flood of telegrams, pouring in on the Republican National Committee at the rate of 4,000 an hour, appeared tonight to have assured Senator Richard M. Nixon's retention on the Republican national ticket even before he met with Gen. Dwight D. Eisenhower in West Virginia.

With more than 75,000 messages tallied by 5 P. M., sentiment was running overwhelmingly in favor of the Californian's remaining as his party's Vice Presidential candidate.

Samplings both by the committee and by individual reporters who had free access to the great piles of telegrams showed that by a margin of about 200 to 1 voters wiring headquarters felt that Mr. Nixon's Los Angeles speech last night had put him in the clear on the controversial $18,235 "supplementary expenditures" fund put at his disposal by a group of California supporters.

Republican leaders were elated by the reaction to the Nixon speech.

White House Is Silent

There was no comment at the Democratic National Committee or at the White House. Senator Clinton P. Anderson, Democrat of New Mexico, interviewed as he left the White House after a visit with the President, said that, as a Democrat, he felt any advantage arising from the incident would "be our way."

The impact of the Nixon talk also was apparent in editorial comment in the capital.

The Washington Post, supporting General Eisenhower, which last Saturday called upon the Senator to withdraw from the ticket, will say in an editorial to be printed in tomorrow morning's editions that Mr. Nixon's public report has "confirmed our belief that he has done nothing 'involving moral turpitude'—to quote the phrase he used in urging the resignations of William Boyle and Guy Gabrielson." The editorial continued:

"But we remain of the conviction that he has committed an error of judgment, however unwittingly * * *. Many people will continue to view the Nixon episode as evidence that the Eisenhower crusade is overtolerant of missteps within its own membership.

"For that reason, Senator Nixon has added a burden to the Eisenhower candidacy by his decision not to withdraw. He has lessened that burden by his public avowal of his good intentions. He could lessen it further by re-examining the inherent evil in such private funds and by announcing that he will no longer avail himself of them."

As telegrams poured in on Washington from every state and territory in the union, while thousands of others went to New York, Los Angeles and other Republican regional headquarters, Western Union called on every facility to try to keep abreast of the messages.

George T. Harris, Western Union supervisor for the Washington area, said the flood of messages was far greater than that which followed the dismissal of General of the Army Douglas MacArthur by President Truman last year. On that occasion 125,000 telegrams were directed to Washington over a three-day period.

In an effort to keep up with the messages, Mr. Harris began calling in operators from New York, Philadelphia and Baltimore last night. He estimated that forty to fifty had been added to the normal central office force in this way. With every possible circuit open, he said, there still was a large backlog of messages waiting to be received.

Many of the messages were signed by groups or families and a large number of those with single signatures were from women. The great majority strongly urged Mr. Nixon's retention, and some said they would vote Republican only if the Californian were kept on the ticket.

"For God's sake, keep Senator Nixon on the ticket," said a cablegram signed by the master and officers of the American ship Sea Gallant, off the Japanese coast. Thousands of others were in similar vein.

An occasional message left some doubt as to the sender's intentions. One simply said: "Keep Senator Nixon." It was signed: "Cocker Spaniel Lover."

The largest number of messages were telegraphed from New York State but no actual count was kept on a state-by-state basis. For a time, the National Committee, bringing in every spare worker possible, sought to keep an accurate tally pro and con. It abandoned the effort when the first 4,000 telegrams revealed only twenty-one opposed to Mr. Nixon.

Gov. Arthur B. Langlie of Washington, continuing the Republican Governors' radio series on "Choosing the Right President," charged that Gov. Adlai E. Stevenson of Illinois, the Democratic Presidential nominee, was not the one to right the nation's finances on the basis of his record at home.

He said that Mr. Stevenson had inherited a state surplus of $150,000,000 when he took office in 1949 and "now that has all been spent and he has a deficit of $37,000,000 as well."

Contributions Mailed In

PASADENA, Calif., Sept. 24 (AP)—Letters supporting Senator Nixon and containing contributions ranging from 1 cent to $250 were piled high on the desk of Dana Smith today.

Mr. Smith is the trustee of the controversial Nixon expense fund and the letters were those mailed before the Republican Vice Presidential nominee made his nationwide radio and television address last night.

"This spontaneous response has taken me somewhat by surprise," said Mr. Smith, who announced the total received in three days totaled slightly more than $2,000.

"More than one-half the contributions were less than $5," he said. "In one envelope obviously addressed by a child there was a penny.

September 25, 1952

G.O.P. Officially Closes Book On Nixon Expense Fund Case

Summerfield Goes Through Formality of Notifying Senator He Will Stay on Ticket—Messages Still Pour In

By CLAYTON KNOWLES
Special to THE NEW YORK TIMES.

WASHINGTON, Sept. 25—Arthur E. Summerfield, Republican National Chairman, went through the formality today of telegraphing Senator Richard M. Nixon of California to tell him that "the combined decision" of Gen. Dwight D. Eisenhower and the Republican National Committee assured his continuance on the ticket.

"They not only want you to remain on the ticket as the party's Vice Presidential candidate, but they demand it," the telegram said.

The message marked an official end to the controversy within the Republican party since Mr. Nixon, in making a public statement on his personal finances and the "supplementary expenditures" fund set up for him by a group of Californians, had left it up to the national committee to decide whether he should remain on the ticket.

In making the telegram public, Mr. Summerfield said that he ceased polling the 138 members of the committee when the first 112 responses showed unanimous approval of Mr. Nixon's retention.

The text of the Summerfield telegram was as follows:

"Realizing the agonizing ordeal to which you have been so unjustly subjected, it is my great privilege to say to you that the combined decisions of Dwight D. Eisenhower and an overwhelming majority of the Republican National Committee members remove any doubt whatsoever about your status. They not only want you to remain in the ticket as the party's Vice Presidential candidate, but they demand it.

"I am certain that these have been trying days for your wife, your mother and your father, but I know that like all of us, they are prouder today of you than ever before.

"Therefore, as chairman of the Republican National Committee, permit me to congratulate you and assure you that not only every Republican, but I believe the vast majority of the American people intend to put their shoulder to the wheel to make certain that the great team of Eisenhower and Nixon is elected next Nov. 4."

President Truman refused all comment at his news conference today on the Nixon episode, and there was no comment from the Democratic National Committee. Yet it was apparent that, despite the large and favorable reaction to the Senator's country-wide appeal for confidence, the issue was not dead in this campaign.

John B. Dunlap, Commissioner of Internal Revenue, declined to discuss a published report that the Treasury Department had started a full-scale investigation here, as well as in California, of tax returns of both Mr. Nixon and the contributors to his fund.

"We never have discussed and never will discuss investigations of taxpayers' returns," he said. This statement, he added, applied equally to any persons who might have contributed or benefited from the fund Gov. Adlai E. Stevenson, the Democratic Presidential candidate, has admitted existed in Illinois.

The flood of telegrams supporting Mr. Nixon that descended on the Republican National Committee yesterday continued today, if at an abated rate. At 5 P. M., 126,522 telegrams had been received, and Western Union said that there were another 25,000 in the process of transmission.

As the flow of telegrams lessened, however, letters by the tens of thousands began reaching headquarters. Eighteen big mail sacks were delivered before noon. The National Committee, reporting that the letters, too, overwhelmingly backed Mr. Nixon, estimated the number at 110,000.

Mr. Summerfield, who is having these messages carefully catalogued, examined them today with Senator Karl Mundt of South Dakota, chairman of the Republican Senatorial Campaign Committee, and Representative W. Leonard Hall of New York, Republican House campaign chairman. It was apparent that they planned to seek to use this list of obvious supporters either in fund raising or campaign work.

"We plan to make use of these letters, but just how I cannot say yet" was all Mr. Summerfield would say.

Gov. Walter J. Kohler of Wisconsin continued tonight the Republican attack on the record of Mr. Stevenson as Governor of Illinois. He asserted that the crime rate in Illinois had increased at a rate "far more than the national average," while scandals, a number of them involving state officials, cropped up recurrently.

Speaking over a country-wide radio hook-up, Mr. Kohler said that no one could question "the high standards of personal integrity and morality displayed by General Eisenhower, or the vigor of his opposition to the corrupt and sordid elements in our national Administration."

Funds Flow in for Nixon
Special to THE NEW YORK TIMES.

LOS ANGELES, Sept. 25—Two days after Senator Nixon made his personal appeal to the people for endorsement, Western Union here reported its circuits to Washington still overloaded with telegrams to the Republican National Committee.

Among the messages were more than 100 money orders ranging from $1 to $1,000 addressed to the Nixon campaign fund. The total message count here will run well above 20,000.

Meanwhile, a "crusading dollars" fund inspired by the controversy over Senator Nixon's privately contributed political expense fund of $18,235 grew unexpectedly.

John Krehbiel, an insurance executive of Pasadena who announced the movement a week ago, said that he had received more than $1,000 in contributions.

Dana Smith, trustee of the controversial Nixon expense fund, said that letters supporting the Senator and containing contributions from one penny to $250 were piled in his office. Mr. Smith said that the total received in three days was slightly more than $1,000, with "more than half of it in sums less than $5."

Western Union said here that it had handled more than 150,000 telegrams up to noon yesterday, as a result of the television and radio speech of Senator Nixon Tuesday night. The company added that thousands of other telegrams, many of a congratulatory nature, were arriving in Washington, addressed to the Republican National Committee.

Additional thousands of telegrams have been delivered to the Eisenhower headquarters in New York, to Republican state headquarters and to General Eisenhower and Senator Nixon, who received about 6,000 telegrams at Wheeling, W. Va.

Western Union estimated that its operators had sent more than 5,000,000 words in transmitting telegrams arising from disclosure of the Nixon expense fund.

NIXON TELLS HOW TO WIN TV FRIENDS

Citing '52 Speech, He Says Talks Should Be Prepared Well, but Not Seem So

Vice President Richard M. Nixon, widely regarded as an accomplished television artist, took the position yesterday that good off-the-cuff broadcasts take far more time to prepare than do formal speeches. He came out against written texts or the use of prompters in airwave campaigning.

That was one of a number of secrets for his own TV success that he made public yesterday at a luncheon of the Radio and Television Executives Society of New York. On hand at the Roosevelt Hotel were 600 executives and their friends.

Among those who had declined invitations to hear Mr. Nixon were four notable Democrats, Mayor Wagner, Governor Harriman, Gov. Abraham A. Ribicoff of Connecticut and Gov. Robert B. Meyner of New Jersey.

Mr. Nixon said his advice would be equally nourishing for Republicans and Democrats, and added that "there isn't any such thing as a nonpolitical speech by a politician."

Disapproves Cheap Air Time

"Sell him the best time for drawing an audience, even if it costs twice as much," the Vice President recommended. "Candidates should be prepared to spend as much money on building up a program, through advertisements and organization work, as they do on air time.

"Now, how to hold that audience? This is a serious problem. One can broadcast at political rallies, on question-and-answer forums, or by the intimate fireside technique. Rallies aren't effective, except as a show intended to arouse the organization members."

Mr. Nixon indicated a preference for the intimate approach with plenty of audience participation. Problems were outlined thus:

¶Be sure the candidate is at his best, not worn out after a breathless day's campaigning.

¶Do not tie him down with canned news releases, for once a candidate is committed to a statement, it must be read.

¶Stick to a subject he knows, never use television to bring up something new.

¶Remember that once he gets before the cameras, he will be worried enough as it is; so let him alone for a reasonable time before he goes on the air.

Mr. Nixon illustrated his points by recalling the famous broadcast he delivered on Sept. 23, 1952. It was his reply to the disclosure that he had received $18,000 from a group of Californians to pay political expenditures.

That speech, in the middle of a Presidential campaign, was described both as "a masterpiece" and as "soap opera."

"This is what really happened," said Mr. Nixon. The broadcast was put off from Sunday until Tuesday night for two reasons, to give him time to prepare thoroughly and to build up the audience—"we wanted to create suspense."

There was no rehearsal, because "when you rehearse you lose in spontaneity what you gain in smoothness." Mr. Nixon arrived, fairly fresh, only twenty minutes before the broadcast, without a prompter or script other than five pages of notes.

An efficient "off-the-cuff" appearance on television, creating the illusion of intimacy so desirable to win the viewers, according to Mr. Nixon, entails many hours of preparatory work. He implied that there was, in fact, very little done or said that could be termed genuinely impromptu.

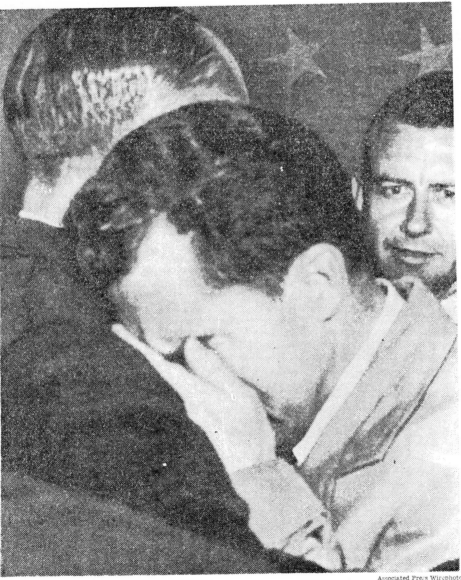

Associated Press Wirephoto

OVERWHELMED: Senator Richard M. Nixon breaks down on the shoulder of Senator William F. Knowland after finishing his speech before the rally in Wheeling, W. Va., on Wednesday night. Gen. Dwight D. Eisenhower, Republican Presidential candidate, declared then that the Senator had cleared himself of blame in accepting private help on expenses.

September 26, 1952

September 15, 1955

Cases in Point—3: The Age of the Debate

N.B.C. Plans to Present Debates by Candidates

The National Broadcasting Company said yesterday that it would present a series of debates between Democratic and Republican presidential nominees on television and radio if Congress should pass legislation easing equal time requirements.

Robert W. Sarnoff, chairman of the network's board, outlined the plan in a message to Speaker Sam Rayburn, Texas Democrat, urging him to hasten approval of such a measure by the House of Representatives. It has already been passed by the Senate.

The special series, "The Great Debate," would offer eight hours a week. Four would consist of discussions between the nominees. The other four would present them under questioning by journalists.

LINCOLN DEBATES EASILY ARRANGED

He and Douglas Needed Only 4 Letters to Agree on Plans for 1858 Contest

By LLOYD B. DENNIS
Special to The New York Times.

WASHINGTON, Sept. 25—"Will it be agreeable to you to make an arrangement for you and myself to divide time, and address the same audiences during the present canvass?"

So wrote Abraham Lincoln to Stephen A. Douglas on July 24, 1858. What came to pass was the Lincoln-Douglas debates, the most famous face-to-face encounter in American political history.

For four exciting months, Lincoln, "the first and only choice of the Republicans," and Douglas, the Democratic incumbent, campaigned up and down the state for the honor of representing Illinois in the United States Senate.

One hundred and two years later, another Republican, Vice President Nixon, will engage in a face-to-face political debate with another Democrat, Senator John F. Kennedy. But the series of debates starting tomorrow night will be seen by millions of Americans, thanks to television.

Political historians at the Library of Congress cannot recall any other occasion when nominees for the Presidency have met in face-to-face debate.

In recent times, however, there have been several debates between men seeking their party's Presidential nomination.

In 1948, two leading contenders for the Republican nomination—Gov. Thomas E. Dewey of New York and Harold E. Stassen—met in Portland, Ore.,

and debated whether the Communist party should be outlawed in the United States.

On May 21, 1956, Senator Estes Kefauver of Tennessee and Adlai E. Stevenson, contenders for the Democratic Presidential nomination, discussed campaign issues in a national telecast debate in Miami.

This year, two of the Democratic contenders for the nomination, Senator Lyndon B. Johnson of Texas and Senator Kennedy, debated the issues at the Los Angeles convention on July 12. Today Senator Johnson is Senator Kennedy's running mate.

On May 4, during the primary campaigns, Senator Kennedy debated with another contender, Senator Hubert H. Humphrey of Minnesota, at Charleston, W. Va.

To arrange the Nixon-Kennedy debates, negotiations have been going on since invitations were first extended in July by the three major television networks and the four major radio networks.

Plenty of Arranging

It has taken ten conferences of the candidates' staffs, letters from the heads of networks and letters from the candidates, and numberless phone calls and telegrams between political headquarters in Washington and the television officials in New York to arrange the coming four broadcasts.

By contrast, arranging the debates of 1858 was easy. Four letters passed between Lincoln and Douglas within one week, and the debates were on.

Lincoln's proposal in 1858 was for "joint discussions" on the issues of the day. Douglas accepted this and, in his reply, listed Ottawa, Freeport, Jonesboro, Galesburg, Quincy, Charleston and Alton as the cities where they would meet.

In the entire campaign the two candidates traveled nearly

10,000 miles by rail, packet boat and horses and made speeches to nearly 80,000 persons in more than seventy-five towns. However, they met on the same platform in only the seven towns. All of Illinois was watching and much of the country was reading about the campaign.

Leading newspapers of the day told their readers that by shorthand writing, newly invented then, reporters would give them "full phonographic verbatim reports."

At the first debate in Ottawa, 12,000 persons sat in the public square under a broiling summer sun. For three hours they listened. Seventeen railroad passenger cars came from Chicago, while boats and buggies brought flag-waving voters.

The pro-Lincoln Chicago Tribune commented:

"The Ottawa debate gave great satisfaction to our side. Mr. Lincoln, we thought, had the better of the argument, and we all came away encouraged also."

The pro-Douglas Chicago Times also had its say. In headline style, it told its readers:

THE CAMPAIGN
Douglas Among the People.
Joint Discussion at Ottawa!
Lincoln Breaks Down.
Enthusiasms of the People!
Lincoln's Heart Fails Him!
Lincoln's Legs Fail Him!
Lincoln's Tongue Fails Him!
Lincoln's Arms Fail Him!
Lincoln Fails All Over!
The People Refuse to Support Him!
The People Laugh at Him!
Douglas the Champion of the People!

That was how it was in Chicago on Aug. 22, 1858, the day after the first debate.

At one point during the debates, Douglas told a crowd that Lincoln had been a storekeeper who sold whisky at one time. Lincoln replied:

"But the difference between Judge Douglas and myself is

From the Collections of the Library of Congress

HISTORIC PROPOSAL: Letter written by Abraham Lincoln to Stephen A. Douglas in 1858, proposing that the two candidates for the Senate from Illinois share the same platform during their campaign. Suggestion resulted in the famous series of debates.

just this, that while I was behind the bar he was in front of it."

Later at Freeport, a torchlight parade greeted Douglas, while Lincoln rode up to the speaker's platform in a covered wagon drawn by six white horses.

In Galesburg, a crowd of 20,000 stood listening for three hours while a raw wind tore flags and banners and forced everyone to button coats to the neck.

On Oct. 15, the steamboat City of Louisiana docked at 5 A. M. at Alton with both candidates aboard. They were to face each other for the last time. Although they had debated over a period of many weeks, and had split on many issues, they were not enemies, only rivals.

Lincoln summed it up this way:

"I have said and I repeat it here, that if there be a man amongst us who does not think that the institution of slavery is wrong in any one of the aspects of which I have spoken, he is misplaced and ought not be with us. Has anything ever threatened the existence of this Union save and except this very institution of slavery? This is the real issue. This is the issue that will continue in this country when these poor tongues of Judge Douglas and myself shall be silent. It is the eternal struggle between these two principles—right and wrong—throughout the world."

JOHNSON STRIVES TO HALT KENNEDY

They Meet in a TV 'Debate' —Texan Criticizes Rival on Senate Absenteeism

By JOHN D. MORRIS
Special to The New York Times.

LOS ANGELES, July 12 -- Senator Lyndon B. Johnson seized the headlines momentarily today in what was widely regarded as a last-ditch bid to slow the bandwagon of Senator John F. Kennedy.

The Texas candidate arranged a nationally televised face-to-face "debate" with his front-running opponent from Massachusetts and sought to take him to task for Senate absenteeism and for his voting record on the farm issue and natural resources.

However, more compliments than brickbats were exchanged. And the brickbats themselves, if any struck home, failed to do any visible damage.

The two leading candidates for the Democratic Presidential nomination wound up the performance by exchanging promises to campaign vigorously for the winner.

Senator Kennedy had the last word. Even at this stage of the contest, he said, "I strongly support him [Senator Johnson] for majority leader" of the Senate.

The face-to-face exchange of views was the second and milder of two "debates" in which the Massachusetts and Texas Senators engaged today.

The first took place at arms length through much of the day as telegrams were shuttled back and forth between the ninth-floor Biltmore Hotel suite of Mr. Kennedy and the seventh-floor suite of Mr. Johnson.

The issue was whether an invitation by Senator Johnson to "debate the issues" was to take place before a joint meeting of the Texas and Massachusetts delegations to the convention or before the Texas delegation alone.

It was settled only a moment before the 3 P. M. camera-time by a characteristic Johnsonian compromise. The Texas delegation was present in full force. The Massacusetts delegation was represented by about twenty volunteers. Senator Johnson accepted the token Massachusetts representation as meeting the condition he had laid down for the meeting—that it take place before both delegations.

In the televised part of the show, the issues between the two were somewhat obscure, but the main one seemed to be Mr. Kennedy's Senate absenteeism during round-the-clock debate on the civil rights bill this year.

It was raised by Senator Johnson and produced cheers and applause from the Texans present. As majority leader, he said, he answered all fifty quorum calls in the six-day nonstop session and voted in all forty-five roll-calls on the bill and amendments. But "some Senators," he asserted, answered none of the quorum calls and missed thirty-four of the voting roll-calls. He obviously was referring to only one —Senator Kennedy.

Senator Kennedy listened, smiling, and when his turn came merely remarked that he assumed Mr. Johnson had been talking about "some of the other candidates."

Senator Johnson opened the proceedings as chairman of the host Texas delegation, which had reserved the Biltmore Hotel ballroom for the occasion. The Texans had given him a standing ovation when he arrived. They cheered and applauded almost as long and loud for Senator Kennedy when Senator Johnson introduced him.

The Texan presented Mr. Kennedy as "a man of unusually high character" and "great intellect" and "a dedicated and devoted public citizen."

Senator Kennedy set a nonpartisan tone in his opening speech of about ten minutes. He praised Texas and the Democratic party, invited Senator Johnson to address the Massachusetts delegation and predicted that the winner of the nomination, whoever he might be, would leave the convention with the party's "united support."

He suggested that some Texans might not agree with him on the civil rights issue, but promised nevertheless to support the Democratic platform, "as I am confident Senator Johnson will do."

He recalled that he had backed a strong price-support farm policy for the last four or five years and was a firm believer in development of the country's natural resources. He called the maintenance of peace "the great problem" of the times.

Senator Johnson opened a twenty-minute speech by saying he agreed with "every word" Senator Kennedy had uttered.

Still predicting his own nomination, he declared that the party would not "veto a man or choose a man" because of his religion or the region from which he came.

Then he aimed some barbs in Senator Kennedy's general direction. He said he had shared the Senator's views on the farm problem of the last four or five years "for twenty-four years, since I went to Congress under the F. D. R. Administration." And he said he had never voted against flood control, power and rural telephone legislation.

Although Senator Johnson did not say so, Senator Kennedy's voting record on these issues is regarded by some critics as spotty.

Senator Johnson did not mention the stiff civil rights plank that went before the convention tonight. At a news conference this morning he said he had not read it but believed "we will have a good platform plank in that regard."

In the televised "debate," he classed the religious issue with civil rights. He said Mr. Kennedy had proved in the West Virginia primary that Protestants would vote for a Roman Catholic.

"What we want," he declared, "is equal proof that a Catholic state will go for a Protestant, and I have not the slightest doubt but what this convention tomorrow is going to prove it."

Senator Kennedy wound up the proceedings with a five-minute response in a light vein. He praised Senator Johnson's "wonderful record" of answering Senate quorum calls. Looking out at the roomful of Texans, he said he was glad the "issues" they had discussed would not be put to a vote there.

The hastily arranged affair was the upshot of routine telegram in which Senator Kennedy asked all convention delegations, including Texas's, for the opportunity to talk to them. Senator Johnson seized upon it as an opportunity to challenge Mr. Kennedy to a television debate before a joint session of the Texas and Massachusetts delegations.

Excerpts From Debate by Johnson and Kennedy

Following are excerpts of the statements by Senators Lyndon B. Johnson and John F. Kennedy in their debate before the Texas delegation at the Democratic National Convention yesterday, as recorded by The New York Times:

SENATOR JOHNSON — Senator Kennedy in a telegram delivered to the * * * hotel to Lyndon Johnson * * * requested an opportunity to appear before the Texas delegation.

I suggested that we both appear together before a joint meeting of our two home-state delegations to discuss and debate the issues before us, before our nation, before our party, rather than talking solely on regional or sectional lines.

Senator Kennedy accepted. * * *

A United Party

SENATOR KENNEDY — * * * I sent a wire to the Texas delegation and to every delegation at this convention because I believe that the Democratic party is a national party. I do not think it's divided by geography or region. * * *

I hope that before this convention ends, as John McCormack, our chairman, has said, * * * that Senator Johnson will * * * speak to the Massachusetts caucus, not because we're going to get delegate votes, but because whoever wins this convention, whether it be Senator Johnson or myself or another candidate, I hope he's going to go out from this convention with the united support of the Democratic party.

The purpose of this convention is not an end in itself. It is to win in November, and that is to win in Texas as well as in Massachusetts. So therefore I hope I come to you today as a colleague in your party, as one who shares your desire to win, as one who is not coming to you for support in this convention, but who is coming to join you today in an association which I hope will bring success in November.

Senator Johnson, in his wire, suggested that we might debate the great issues which face our party and country. If by debate he means argument, I don't think I will, because I don't think Senator Johnson and I disagree on the great issues that face us.

I have supported him for the majority leadership on every time his name has come to a vote in the United States Senate, and as you know on every occasion his choice has been unanimous, and if I am kept in the Senate by popular demand at this convention, if I continue to represent Massachusetts in the Senate, I shall continue to vote for him as President, if he's nominated, and as majority leader, if he shares my fate. * * *

Some of you may disagree with my views on civil rights, but I'm sure that you realize that I say the same thing in this state as I said in Georgia, as I said in Michigan, as I say in Massachusetts.

I will support the Democratic platform in all of its particulars, as I'm confident Senator Johnson will, if he is nominated.

I think the great issues, in many ways, are to continue the progress which was written into the statute books during the Administrations of Franklin Roosevelt, and many of those provisions were written in by the speaker of the House, Mr. Rayburn, and in the Administration of Mr. Truman, and also to recognize that in many ways the problems are entirely new, entirely undreamt-of in the Administrations of Franklin Roosevelt and Harry Truman.

Challenge to Doctrine

We never expected to see directly a challenge to the Monroe Doctrine in the days of Franklin Roosevelt. Our relations with Latin America in those days were nearly paternalistic. Now we are being challenged on every front and in every way, and I think our great task as a party is to demonstrate that we can make a free society work, that we can develop economic policies which will prevent a slide into recession which I think the high interest rate policies, hard money policies of this Administration are going to bring about in the next twelve months unless there's a change in Administration.

Secondly, I hope that in addition to changing administrations and changing the Secretary of Agriculture, that we can change the domestic agricultural policies of this Administration.

For myself, though I come from an urban section of the United States, I have supported for the past four or five years a policy of a strong-support prices, of parity for agriculture, of a balance between supply and demand and a fair price for the farmer in the marketplace. * * *

Thirdly, I think we should develop the resources of the United States. I don't think they're Western resources, I think they're American resources. * * *

Problem of Peace

The great problem, I will say in conclusion, of course, is the maintenance of peace. How can we live on the same globe as the Soviet Union? How can we prevent the outbreak of war? How can we protect our security? How can we maintain the peace?

How these problems will test the best of all of us. * * *

The problems and the responsibilities will dwarf the talents of any American. But nevertheless I think the job must be done. I have great confidence in this country. I think we can set up in this country the kind of society that will serve as a beacon to a watching world which stands now on the razor edge of decision to determine which road they shall take. I think they should come with us.

I think that is the responsibility of our party—to help build in this country a society which serves our people and serves as an attraction to those who determine which road they shall take. * * *

If Senator Johnson is nominated, I will stump all over Massachusetts with him to make sure that Massachusetts supports him in November. And I am confident that if I am nominated in this convention Senator Johnson will take me by the hand through the length and breadth of Texas for the same purpose.

Thank you very much.

SENATOR JOHNSON— * * * I can agree with every word that Senator Kennedy said. * * *

And I plan to spend all the energy and talents, if any, I possess to the end that the nominee of this convention of this convention not only carries Texas and Massachusetts but sweeps the entire nation. * * *

Among the delegates from all sections of the nation I find serious consideration being given the problem of national leadership. Our party is not going to veto a man, or vote for a man, because of his religion.

Our party is not going to veto a man, or vote for a man, because of the region from which he comes. * * *

All of us in this room know, and the Senator and I have had it emphasized upon us in the last few weeks, that we're only minutes away from Mr. Khrushchev's missiles. Just as Mr. Khrushchev knows, and I never want him to forget, that he's only missiles away—minutes away from our missile deterrent.

In the past two weeks, two of America's airplanes have been shot down by the Russians. Four American boys will never come home again— they're dead.

Puppet State Cited

In the past forty-eight hours, Mr. Khrushchev, who was demanding an apology from our President in Paris, has threatened to support a Communist puppet state in Cuba. And I'm sad to observe, that some of our most treasured neighbors, and at least their unofficial spokesmen in our Republic to the south, have lent encouragement to Mr. Castro's efforts.

This is not a day or time or age of press agentry and hoopla. This is the age of ultimate decision for mankind. Through panic and foolish policies and lack of judgment, we could, in a matter of moments, destroy all of our centuries of civilization.

Mankind's destiny is upward. It's upward with the progress of freedom. It's not downward to the dismal end of a hydrogen war.

My place in the months and years ahead will be at my country's service; at the service of the cause of the free world. Where my office shall be is a matter for this convention to decide. And I do, heer and now, solicit the votes of every delegate present in this room or the sound of my voice. * * *

You must select the voice of leadership who has encountered the trials and the problems of bringing men together, bringing sections together, bringing countries together, because this is one of our most trying hours.

I share Senator Kennedy's views of the last four or five years on the farm program. I've shared them for twenty-four years, since I first went to Congress under the FDR Administration.

And I want to remember and I hope that you will never forget that I have never at any time during my public career embraced any of the policies of Ezra Taft Benson and his farm program.

I have never voted against damming our streams or harnessing our rivers, or increasing our Southwest Power Administration to serve our REA. * * *

Now we do have differences. * * *

Civil Rights

So now we'll talk about civil rights.

There are two things about civil rights. One is the platform, one is doing something about the platform.

First of all, I feel no superiority because of my race or religion or my region to anyone. And I hope and pray that no member of my delegation, or no delegate supporting me, will ever say that Senator Kennedy can't be elected because he's an Easterner. Or because of his religion. * * *

Because of those that talk too much and studied too little, we passed a series of civil rights bills following the reconstruction period that we've been repealing for the last eighty or ninety years.

At every convention since I have been an adult, we have talked about the protection of civil liberties and the civil rights of all of our people. And I say here and now, that when I took my oath of office I intended to live up to it.

And when I take the oath of office as President next January, I assure every American and everyone interested everywhere that no person in this nation will be discriminated against by me because of his race or his religion or his region. And I shall see to it if it's within the power of the President to see that every person's full constitutional rights are protected, regardless of his color. * * *

Two Civil Rights Bills

For eighty years we talked about it and we never put one statute on the books. As leader of the Democrats in the Senate we have passed two civil rights bills in the last three years. They weren't all that I wanted or all I asked for. They didn't include some of the most basic and important strengths that I wanted to see. But they were acceptable to the author of the bills, Mr. Celler from Brooklyn, and to the Attorney General who must enforce them.

And we are protecting every person's right to vote in this country, and if you protect a person's right to vote, he'll protect himself better than you can.

KENNEDY ACCEPTS NIXON TV DEBATE

Vice President Is Agreeable but Bars Reading Notes —8 Hours Proposed

A series of television debates this fall between the Republican and Democratic candidates for President became a likelihood last evening.

In Hyannis Port, Mass., Senator John F. Kennedy accepted an invitation by the National Broadcasting Company to appear on eight one-hour evening programs with his opponent.

In Chicago, Herbert G. Klein, Vice President Nixon's press secretary, said Mr. Nixon was "willing to debate a rival candidate, including Senator Kennedy, if this is the desire of the networks and the public."

However, Mr. Klein said, the Vice President wants to examine the format of such debates, "as Senator Kennedy is doing."

"To have a really effective debate," he added, "it should be one in which the candidates speak without notes or text. It should be a debate, as opposed to two people reading notes. It should be a free contest — an opportunity for each to examine the other's mind."

Sent By Sarnoff

The N. B. C. invitation was tendered in telegrams by Robert W. Sarnoff, chairman. It proposed that the two candidates meet in face-to-face debate for four hour-long programs. These would be followed by four panel discussions during which they would face questioning by newsmen.

"I wholeheartedly accept your invitation to meet on television with Vice President Nixon dur-ing the coming campaign," Senator Kennedy said in a telegram to Mr. Sarnoff. "I believe you are performing a notable public service in giving the American people a chance to see the candidates of the two major parties discuss the issues face to face."

Later last evening, the Columbia Broadcasting System and the American Broadcasting Company also offered prime evening time to the top candidates.

Dr. Frank Stanton, president of C. B. S., extended the invitation to the Vice-Presidential nominees as well. He suggested a series of eight broadcasts, with the Presidential candidates sharing the opening and closing ones, and "intervening programs devoted to discussions between opposing Presidential and Vice-Presidential candidates and press interviews."

Leonard H. Goldenson, president of American Broadcasting-Paramount Theatres, Inc., sent telegrams to Mr. Nixon and Mr. Kennedy proposing that the three networks alternate in giving them prime time one evening a week for nine weeks.

All three networks specified that their invitations were contingent upon passage of pending legislation that would excuse them from the need to give equal time to candidates of minor parties. The legislation has been approved by the Senate, but awaits action by the House of Representatives.

Section 315 of the Federal Communications Act has been interpreted as requiring a broadcaster to extend to all candidates for a public office, upon request, air time equal to that granted any one candidate.

Senator Kennedy designated J. Leonard Reinsch, his radio-television aide, to work out arrangements with N. B. C. for what Mr. Sarnoff had called "The Great Debate."

This was, however, before the rival networks had made their own bids. It appeared likely that negotiations would have to be held between representatives of the candidates and the networks before the final form of the debate could be arranged.

Debate Audience Yields Wide Range of Reaction

A nation-wide audience listened last night to the debate between Vice President Nixon and Senator John F. Kennedy on political philosophies. Most of the audience apparently made one of two basic decisions: their vote preferences remained unchanged, or they were still very much undecided.

A sampling of opinions among those in the city and near-by areas who tuned in on the debate showed a wide range of reactions, but perhaps the most typical of the responses was given by Patrick Lally, a maintenance man who lives at 142 Park Place and was questioned in a Brooklyn bar.

"I don't think these debates will change anyone's mind who has already decided on the candidates. It's more for people who haven't made up their mind."

He said his vote was still for Senator Kennedy.

The hour-long exchange, which began at 9:30 P. M. New York time, was carried by all major television and radio networks.

Some Viewers Fret

Some of the listeners and viewers were nettled because they were unable to flip on a favorite dramatic show or such bits of fare as an "Adventures in Paradise" repeat, which was canceled to make way for the political presentation. But the end-of-summer hiatus in the studios, with many of the winter programs not opening until next week, lessened the debate's impact on the entertainment habits of most radio and television fans.

One man in the same bar as Mr. Lally, Callahan's Bar at 235 Flatbush Avenue, refused to give his name but declared emphatically:

"So far neither one of these guys has said anything."

Mr. and Mrs. John F. Kennedy, of Stuyvesant Town—and no relation to the Democratic candidate—said they did not watch the debate.

"What show you talking about?" asked Mrs. Kennedy when asked for a comment. "Oh, the television show. We didn't get around to it. We were out visiting."

Many of the first, quick samplings showed that a considerable number of voters were apparently far from making any vote decision yet.

Teacher "Unconvinced"

"For tonight, I'd say Senator Kennedy was the better TV performer," said Louis Votino, a teacher of 215 Pierson Avenue, Hempstead, L. I. "Would he be a better president? I don't know. I don't think either one was too articulate. The debate has not changed my mind at all. I'm still unconvinced."

"The program was very upsetting," said Virginia Lichtner, of 331 West 19th Street. "Nixon seemed more interested in presenting a pleasant facade; everytime he spoke he seemed to end it with a little smile. He seemed to say, 'Yes, I want more education,' but he wouldn't say how he was going to get it. Kennedy seemed to have a quicker mind."

Dan Rosenbloom of 65-81 Parsons Boulevard, Flushing, Queens, said:

"I think Mr. Nixon did a very good juggling act. He made it sound as if the Administration was doing everything the people want. Mr. Kennedy impressed me as someone who is just trying to get across some of the things he failed to help get through the Congress. Neither impressed me too much."

A partisan group of about 400 persons called by the Citizens for Kennedy, was gathered in the Delmonico Hotel at Park Avenue and Fifty-ninth Street to watch the debate. The audience of Democrats was restrained, but when some of them thought that Mr. Nixon looked uncomfortable or pressed by Senator Kennedy in the political exchange they would cheer or applaud.

Even there, however, there was a general satisfaction that the debate was showing the voters both candidates in a face-to-face challenge.

Mrs. Nona Dowd of 5410 Netherlands Avenue, Riverdale, called it a "wonderful program for both of them" and said that she thought they were both pretty close to each other on ideas.

Alvin Hellerstein, an attorney at 61 Broadway, watched with the same group. He said he thought that Mr. Kennedy had given an appearance of great vigor and seriousness but that Mr. Nixon had seemed to be talking down to the people.

Cheers and applause Mr. Nixon echoed at the Federal Republican Club, 237 East Seventh Street, where about 125 party members had gathered. General silence greeted Mr. Kennedy when he was in view on the screen.

Bernard Newman, New York County Republican leader, said:

"Mr. Nixon's maturity and experience showed through clearly and unmistakeably while Mr. Kennedy seemed to want to be all things to all men on all issues."

To Nicholas Atlas, former Assistant United States Attorney, of 141 East Third Street, Senator Kennedy appealed to nostalgia.

"He was talking to the generation that was gone," Mr. Atlas said. "The New Deal is behind us."

Both candidates appeared well-informed in the opinion of Mrs. Anne J. Mathes, a lawyer, of 274 First Avenue.

"But Kennedy was emotional and seemed scared," she said, "while Nixon struck to the point and was logical."

Mrs. Jesse Lehman of 19 Hickory Drive, Great Neck, L. I., said:

"I was surprised at Mr. Nixon's very defensive attitude. He seemed to justify his position on the basis of the fact that Mr. Kennedy agreed with him. Mr. Nixon said very little effectively. Mr. Kennedy was very forthright. I was pleasantly surprised at the way he handled himself. I thought he was outspoken, clear and to the point."

Not everyone was satisfied with last night's political substitute for the usual fare of entertainment. One woman reached by telephone in Queens said she watched the first half of the program, and then fell sound asleep.

A rubbish collector, John Marrone, of 334 East Twenty-Fourth Street, was sold on Senator Kennedy after the television show.

"I like his stand on old-age pension, and all that stuff," he said. "And I don't like Nixon. Those Republicans don't live up to their promises."

There was some disappointment over the absence of oratorical fireworks. Some viewers said they had not been expecting so much politeness between the two candidates.

Jerome I. Levine of 2411 East Third Street, Brooklyn, said:

"There wasn't much said. They kept repeating over and over that 'it's a matter of means.' They were both very impressive and seemed to have firm convictions. But there were too many generalizations. It seems they were just being very nice to each other."

Other viewers were disappointed that the two candidates mostly restricted themselves to domestic issues. Later debates are scheduled to go into other fields, including foreign relations.

"I thought that Nixon was more effective," said Mrs. Thomas Madigan of 225 East Seventy-third Street.

"He wants to keep the Federal Government out of the affairs of state government. Yet I think they both talked too much about local issues, and should have talked more about the international situation and about Russia and the U. N. Maybe they'll do that the next time."

Mrs. Henry Mason of 523 East Seventy-Eighth Street liked the show and thought there should

be more like it, but she offered no estimate of which of the two candidates had impressed her the most.

"I wouldn't want to commit myself," she said.

Florence Mervis of 2665 Grand Concourse, the Bronx, thought the debate was "very good" and that "Kennedy showed up much better than Nixon." However, she doubted that it had added anything to her understanding of the issues. She declined to say how she would vote.

At Frank and John's Grill at 136 Flatbush Avenue in Brooklyn there were ten customers who obviously preferred juke-box polkas to the political debate. But at Paddy's Bar a few doors away on Flatbush Avenue several patrons asked for the debate and turned off the juke-box. About half-way through the debate one patron began saying some unkind things about Mr. Kennedy. He was thrown out.

A housewife with two children in high school thought the program and the others to follow would have a definite influence on her vote.

"The personality of the men showed through," said Mrs. Jerome Gilbert of 21 Oak Street, Elmont, L. I. "They could reach me where they never could have otherwise."

Three quarters of the people at a listening house party in Montclair, N. J., felt that Senator Kennedy had the better of the debate.

Many thought the Vice President seemed nervous, but there were some who thought that this was a deliberate affectation.

Party's Consensus

Most of the group at the party felt that Senator Kennedy ot only introduced most of the concrete points of the program in his presentation but also accounted best in the give and take.

"Kennedy looked less like Henry Aldrich," said one of the guests, a Columbia University professor.

"I resent the fact that Nixon has lost his jowls and Kennedy seems to have picked them up," said a housewife, a member of the League of Women Voters.

"I think Nixon showed up remarkably well in the question and answer period," said one housewife. "He looked particularly well when he was asked to comment on what he had contributed in the way of concrete program to the achievements of the Eisenhower Administration in the last eight years."

Lazar Engelberg of 329 East Eighty-third Street said:

"I'm a Democrat, so my side is Kennedy. I think he did very well."

Debate's TV Audience Estimated at 60 Million

The American Research Bureau estimated early this morning that 60,000,000 persons had watched the televised debate between Vice President Nixon and Senator John F. Kennedy.

The rating concern said that in seven cities an average of 53.5 per cent of the entire television audience watched the debate. The cities were New York, Chicago, Detroit, Philadelphia, Baltimore, Cleveland and Washington.

The Nielsen rating concern said that 54 per cent of all the homes with television sets in the New York metropolitan area were tuned to the debate. Since there are 4,150,000 homes with at least one television set in the area, about 2,241,000 sets were tuned to the debate.

September 27, 1960

NIXON AND KENNEDY CLASH IN TV DEBATE

By RUSSELL BAKER
Special to The New York Times.

CHICAGO, Sept. 26—Vice President Nixon and Senator John F. Kennedy argued genteelly tonight in history's first nationally televised debate between Presidential candidates.

The two men, confronting each other in a Chicago television studio, centered their argument on which candidate and which party offered the nation the best means for spurring United States growth in an era of international peril.

The candidates, without ever generating any real heat in their exchanges, clashed on the

following points:

¶Mr. Nixon's farm program, which Senator Kennedy said was merely another version of policies that had been tried and had failed under Ezra Taft Benson, Secretary of Agriculture.

¶The Republican and Democratic performance records on efforts to increase the minimum wage of $1 an hour and broaden its coverage, school construction legislation and medical-care for the aged. Mr. Kennedy charged that the Republican record on these measures showed the party gave only "lip service" to them.

The New York Times (by John Orris)

KENNEDY VS. NIXON ON THE HOME SCREEN: On the left, the Democratic Senator; on the right, the Republican Vice President. The moderator is Howard K. Smith of C. B. S. and the panelists shown are Robert Fleming, left, A. B. C.; Stuart Novins, C. B. S.

The comparative records of the Truman and Eisenhower Administrations on fiscal security, Mr. Nixon asserted that in school and hospital construction the Republican years had seen an improvement over the previous seven Democratic years. Moreover, he said, wages had risen "five times as much" in the Eisenhower Administration as during the Truman Administration, while the rise in prices has been only one-fifth of that in the Truman years.

In one of the sharper exchanges of the hour-long encounter, Mr. Nixon charged that the Democratic domestic program advanced by Senator Kennedy would cost the taxpayer from $13,200,000,000 to $18,000,000,000.

This meant, Mr. Nixon contended, that "either he will have to raise taxes or you have to unbalance the budget."

Unbalancing the budget, he went on, would mean another period of inflation and a consequent "blow" to the country's aged living on pension income.

"That," declared Senator Kennedy, in one of the evening's few shows of incipient heat, "is wholly wrong wholly in error." Mr. Nixon, he said, was attempting to create the impression that he was "in favor of unbalancing the budget."

In fact, Mr. Kennedy contended, many of his programs for such things as medical care for the aged, natural resources development, Federal assistance to school construction and teachers salaries could be financed without undue burden on the taxpayer if his policies for increasing the rate of economic growth were adopted.

"I don't believe in big government, but I believe in effective government," Mr. Kennedy said. "I think we can do a better job. I think we are going to have to do a better job."

Continuing his portrayal of the Eisenhower years as a period of stagnation, he asserted that the United States last year had the lowest rate of economic growth of any industrial state in the world. Steel production, he noted, was only 50 per cent of capacity. The Soviet Union, he said, is "turning out twice as many engineers as we are."

At the present rate of hydro-electric-power construction, he went on, the Soviet Union would be "producing more power than we are" by 1975.

"I think it's time America started moving again," he declared.

Nixon Disagrees

Mr. Nixon replied that he had no quarrel with Mr. Kennedy's goal of increasing the rate of national growth. But, he said, Mr. Kennedy's statistics showing a slow growth rate last year were misleading because they were based on activity in a recession year. This year, by contrast, the rate is 6.9 per cent—"one of the highest rates in the world," he said.

In other areas of debate, these were the major points:

¶Mr. Nixon asserted that Senator Kennedy's failure to get any significant part of his program enacted at the August session of Congress was not due to President Eisenhower's threatened vetoes but to lack of national support for items in the program. It was "not because the President was against them," Mr. Nixon said. "It was because the people were against them. They were too extreme."

¶Mr. Kennedy answered Mr. Nixon's frequently repeated campaign assertion that he was too immature for the Presidency by asserting that Abraham Lincoln had come out of obscurity, as an inexperienced Congressman, to the White House. He and Mr. Nixon had "both come to Congress together" in the same year — 1946, Mr. Kennedy noted.

"Our experience in government is comparable." And, he contended, "there is no certain road to the Presidency. There is no guarantee that if you take one road or the other you will be a successful President."

¶Mr. Nixon, using the only language heard all evening that bordered on the colorful, contrasted the Republican program for national growth with Mr. Kennedy's in these terms. Mr. Kennedy's, he said, "seem to be simply retreads of programs of the Truman Administration."

For the most part, the exchanges were distinguished by a suavity, earnestness and courtesy that suggested that the two men were more concerned about "image projection" to their huge television audience than about scoring debating points.

Senator Kennedy, using no television makeup, rarely smiled during the hour and maintained an expression of gravity suitable for a candidate for the highest office in the land.

Mr. Nixon, wearing pancake makeup to cover his dark beard, smiled more frequently as he made his points and dabbed frequently at the perspiration that beaded out on his chin.

The debate was carried simultaneously by all three major television networks, the American Broadcasting Company, the National Broadcasting Company and the Columbia Broadcasting System. It was also carried by the radio networks of all three and that of the Mutual Broadcasting System.

The first debate, produced by C. B. S., took place in a big studio at the C. B. S. Chicago outlet, Station WBBM-TV. Studio One, in which they met, was sealed off from the hundreds who swarmed through its corridors and sat in adjoining studios to watch the show on station monitors.

When the debate was over, the two candidates were spirited out of the studio through a freight driveway.

Nixon Noncommittal

At his hotel later, Mr. Nixon was noncommittal about how well he thought he had done. "A debater," he said, "never knows who wins. That will be decided by the people Nov. 8."

Mr. Kennedy was not available for comment, but his advisers said they were elated over his performance.

The only persons permitted in the studio besides television crewmen were two wire service reporters, three photographers and one aide to each candidate.

When the show ended each man was asked how he felt about the outcome.

"A good exchange of views," said Mr. Nixon.

"We had an exchange of views," Mr. Kennedy agreed.

Under the rules agreed upon by the candidates, each man opened with an eight-minute exposition of his general position on domestic affairs.

This was followed by about thirty-five muntes of question-and-answer with the questions being put by four television newsmen selected by each of the four networks. This was followed by three minute closing statements by each candidate.

The television news representatives on the panel were Sander Vanocur of N. B. C., Robert Fleming of A. B. C., Charles Warren of Mutual and Stuart Novins of C. B. S. Howard K. Smith of the C. B. S. Washington staff acted as moderator, but except for introducing the two, had a quiet evening.

Nixon Arrives First

Mr. Nixon arrived first at the studio on Chicago's Near North Side near the lakefront. His car entered the building through a freight driveway and pulled up by a receiving line of network executives.

Mr. Nixon made small talk for a few moments, then entered the studio accompanied by his press secretary, Herbert G. Klein.

Senator Kennedy arrived eight minutes later, accompanied by several of his campaign aides.

After working the broadcasting executives reception line, he entered the studio where Mr. Nixon was waiting. The two men smiled and shook hands.

"Good to see you. I heard you had a big audience in Cleveland," Mr. Nixon told Mr. Kennedy. The Senator's reply was lost in the hubhub as the photographers worked.

Outside the building several hundred demonstrators with printed placards demonstrated at the curb for Mr. Kennedy. There was no evidence of any Nixon rooting section.

Text of the Debate Between Kennedy and Nixon Held on Television in Chicago

Following is the text of the Kennedy-Nixon debate in Chicago last night, televised and broadcast nationally, as recorded by The New York Times:

HOWARD K. SMITH, Moderator:

Good evening. The television and radio stations of the United States and their affiliated stations are proud to provide facilities for a discussion of issues in the current political campaign by the two major candidates for the Presidency. The candidates need no introduction. The Republican candidate, Vice President Richard M. Nixon, and the Democratic candidate, Senator John F. Kennedy.

According to the rules set by the candidates themselves, each man shall make an opening statement of approximately eight minutes' duration and a closing statement of approximately three minutes' duration. In between the candidates will answer, or comment, upon answers to questions put by a panel of correspondents. In this, the first discussion in a series of four joint appearances, the subject-matter, it has been agreed, will be restricted to internal or domestic American matters.

And now for the first opening statement by Senator John F. Kennedy.

SENATOR KENNEDY—In the election of 1860 Abraham Lincoln said the question was whether this nation could exist half-slave or half-free.

In the election of 1960, and with the world around us, the question is whether the world will exist half-slave or half-free, whether it will move in the direction of freedom, in the direction of the road that we are taking, or whether it will move in the direction of slavery.

I think it will depend in great measure upon what we do here in the United States, on the kind of society that we build, on the kind of strength that we maintain.

We discuss tonight domestic issues, but I would not want that to be any implication to be given that this does not involve directly our struggle with Mr. Khrushchev for survival.

Mr. Khrushchev is in New York and he maintains the Communist offensive throughout the world because of the productive power of the Soviet Union itself.

Calls Chinese Dangerous

The Chinese Communists have always had a large population, but they are important and dangerous now because they are mounting a major effort within their own country. The kind of country we have here, the kind of society we have, the kind of strength we build in the United States will be the defense of freedom.

If we do well here, if we meet our obligations, if we're moving ahead, then I think freedom will be secure around the world. If

we fail, then freedom fails.

Therefore, I think the question before the American people is: Are we doing as much as we can do, are we as strong as we should be, are we as strong as we must be if we're going to maintain our independence, and if we're going to maintain and hold out the hand of friendship to those who look to us for assistance, to those who look to us for survival?

I should make it very clear that I do not think that we're doing enough, that I am not satisfied as an American with the progress that we're making.

This is a great country, but I think it could be a greater country; and this is a powerful country, but I think it could be a more powerful country.

I'm not satisfied to have 50 per cent of our steel-mill capacity unused. I'm not satisfied when the United States had last year the lowest rate of economic growth of any major industrialized society in the world, because economic growth means strength and vitality; it means we're able to sustain our defenses, it means we're able to meet our commitments abroad.

I'm not satisfied when we have over $9,000,000,000 worth of food, some of it rotting, even though there is a hungry world and even though 4,000,000 Americans wait every month for a food package from the Government, which averages 5 cents a day per individual.

I saw cases in West Virginia, here in the United States, where children took home part of their school lunch in order to feed their families because I don't think we're meeting our obligations toward these Americans.

Voices Dissatisfaction

I'm not satisfied when the Soviet Union is turning out twice as many scientists and engineers as we are.

I'm not satisfied when many of our teachers are inadequately paid, or when our children go to school in part-time shifts. I think we should have an educational system second to none.

I'm not satisfied when I see men like Jimmy Hoffa in charge of the largest union in the United States still free.

I'm not satisfied when we are failing to develop the natural resources of the United States to the fullest.

Here in the United States, which developed the Tennessee Valley and which built the Grand Coulee and the other dams in Northwest United States. At the present rate of hydropower production — and that is the hallmark of an industrialized society—the Soviet Union by 1975 will be producing more power than we are.

These are all the things, I think, in this country that can make our society strong, or can mean that it stands still.

I'm not satisfied until every American enjoys his full constitutional rights. When a Negro baby is born—and this is true also of Puerto Ricans and Mex-

icans in some of our cities—he has about one-half as much chance to get through high school as a white baby. He has one-third as much chance to get through college as a white student. He has about one-third as much chance to be a professional man, about half as much chance to own a house. He has about four times as much chance that he'll be out of work in his life as the white baby.

I think we can do better. I don't want the talents of any American to go to waste. I know that there are those who say that we want to turn everything over to the Government. I don't at all. I want the individuals to meet their responsibilities. And I want the states to meet their responsibilities. But I think there is also a national responsibility.

The argument has been used against every piece of social legislation in the last twenty-five years. People of the United States individually cannot have developed the Tennessee Valley —collectively, they could have. A cotton farmer in Georgia or peanut farmer or a dairy farmer in Wisconsin and Minnesota, he cannot protect himself against the forces of supply and demand in the market place, but working together in effective governmental programs he can do so.

Seventeen million Americans who live over 65, on an average Social Security check of about $78 a month, they are not able to sustain themselves individually, but they can sustain themselves through the social security system.

I don't believe in big government.

But I believe in effective governmental action. And I think that's the only way that the United States is going to maintain its freedom. It's the only way we're going to move ahead.

Must Do 'Better Job'

I think we can do a better job. I think we're going to have to do a better job if we are going to meet the responsibilities which time and events have placed upon us.

We cannot turn the job over to anyone else. If the United States fails, then the whole cause of freedom fails. And I think it depends in great measure on what we do here in this country.

The reason Franklin Roosevelt was a good neighbor in Latin America was because he was a good neighbor in the United States. Because they felt that the American society was moving again.

I want us to recapture that image.

I want people in Latin America and Africa and Asia to start to look to America. To see how we're doing things. To wonder what the President of the United States is doing, and not to look to Khrushchev, or look at the Chinese Communists.

That is the obligation upon our generation.

In 1933, Franklin Roosevelt said in his inaugural that this generation of Americans has a rendezvous with destiny.

I think our generation of Americans has the same rendezvous.

The question now is: Can freedom be maintained under the most severe attack it has ever known? I think it can be.

And I think, in the final analysis, it depends upon what we do here.

I think it's time America started moving again.

MR. SMITH—And now the opening statement by Vice President Richard M. Nixon.

MR. NIXON—

Mr. Smith. Senator Kennedy. The things that Senator Kennedy has said many of us can agree with. There is no question but that we cannot discuss our internal affairs in the United States without recognizing that they have a tremendous bearing on our international position. There is no question but that this nation cannot stand still because we are in a deadly competition, a competition not only with the men in the Kremlin but the men in Peking.

Ahead in Competition

We're ahead in this competition, as Senator Kennedy, I think, has implied, but when you're in a race, the only way to stay ahead is to move ahead. And I subscribe completely to the spirit that Senator Kennedy has expressed tonight, the spirit that the United States should move ahead.

Where, then, do we disagree?

I think we disagree on the implication of his remarks tonight and on the statements that he has made on many occasions during his campaign to the effect that the United States has been standing still.

We heard tonight, for example, the statement made that our growth in national product last year was the lowest of any industrial nation in the world. Now last year, of course, was 1958. That happened to be a recession year. But when we look at the growth of G. N. P. this year, a year of recovery, we find that it's 6.9 per cent and one of the highest in the world today. More about that later.

Looking then to this problem of how the United States should move ahead and where the United States is moving, I think it is well that we take the advice of a very famous campaigner. Let's look at the record. Is the United States standing still? Is is true that this Administration, as Senator Kennedy has charged, has been an Administration of retreat, of defeat, of stagnation?

Is it true that, as far this country is concerned in the field of electric power, in all of the fields that he has mentioned, we have not been moving ahead?

Well, we have a comparison we can make. We have the record of the Truman administration of seven and a half years and the seven and a half years of the Eisenhower Administration.

When we compare these two records in the area that Senator Kennedy has discussed tonight, I think we find that America has been moving ahead.

Let's take schools. We have built more schools in these last seven and a half years than we built in the previous seven and a half, for that matter in the previous twenty years.

Let's take hydroelectric power. We have developed more hydroelectric power in these seven and a half years than was developed in any previous administration in history.

Let us take hospitals. We find that more have been built in this Administration than in the previous administration.

The same is true of highways.

Let's put it in terms that all of us can understand. We often hear gross national product and in that respect may I say that when we compare the gross in this Administration with that of the previous administration that then there was total gross of 11 per cent over seven years. In this Administration there has been a total gross of 19 per cent over seven years.

That shows that there has been more gross in this Administration than in its predecessor.

Example of Average Family

But let's not put it there. Let's put it in terms of the average family.

What has happened to you?

We find that your wages have gone up five times as much in the Eisenhower Administration as they did in the Truman Administration.

What about the prices you pay? We find that the prices you pay went up five times as much in the Truman Administration than they did in the Eisenhower Administration.

What's the net result of this? It means that the average family income went up 15 per cent in the Eisenhower years as against 2 per cent in the Truman years.

Now this not standing still. But good as this record is, may I emphasize it isn't enough.

A record is never something to stand on. It's something to build on. And in building on this record, I believe that we have the secret for progress. We know the way to progress, and I think, first of all, our own record proves that we know the way.

Senator Kennedy has suggested that he believes he knows the way. I respect the sincerity in which he makes that suggestion. But, on the other hand, when we look at the various programs that he offers, they do not seem to be new. They seem to be simply retreads of the programs of the Truman Administration which preceeded. And I would suggest that during the course of the evening he might indicate those areas in which his programs are new, where they will

Associated Press Wirephoto

KENNEDY'S TURN: The Democratic Senator offers his side in debate with Vice President Nixon in Chicago television studio. The two panelists shown are Charles Warren, left, of M. B. C. and Sander Vanocur of N. B. C. Moderator is Howard K. Smith of C. B. S.

mean more progress than we had then.

What kind of programs are we for? We are for programs that will expand education opportunities, that will give to all Americans their equal chance for education for all of the things which are necessary and dear to the hearts of our people. We are for programs, in addition, which will see that our medical care for the aged is much better handled than it is at the present time.

Cites Spending Plans

Here again, may I indicate that Senator Kennedy and I are not in disagreement as to the aims. We both want to help the old people. We want to see that they do have adequate medical care. The question is the means.

I think the means that I advocate will reach that goal better than the means that he advocates. I could give better examples, but for whatever it is, whether it's in the field of housing, or health, or medical care, or schools, or the development of electric power, we have programs which we believe will move America, move her forward and build on the wonderful records made over these past seven and a half years.

Now, when we look at these programs, might I suggest that in evaluating them we often have a tendency to say that the test of a program is how much you're spending.

I will concede that in all the areas to which I have referred Senator Kennedy would have the Federal Government spend more than I would have it spend.

I counted out the cost of the Democratic platform. It runs a minimum of $13,200,000,000 a year more than we are presently spending to a maximum of $18,000,000,000 a year more than we're presently spending.

Now the Republican platform will cost more too. It will cost a minimum of $4,000,000,000 a year more, a maximum of $4,900,000,000 a year more than we're presently spending.

Now, does this mean that his program is better than ours? Not at all. Because it isn't a question of how much the Federal Government spends. It isn't a question of which Government does the most. It's a question of which administration does the right thing.

And in our case, I do believe that our programs will stimulate the creative energies of 180,000,000 free Americans.

I believe the programs that Senator Kennedy advocates will have a tendency to stifle those creative energies.

I believe, in other words, that his programs would lead to the stagnation of the motive power that we need in this country to get progress.

The final point that I would like to make is this: Senator Kennedy has suggested in his speeches that we lack compassion for the poor, for the old, and for others that are unfortunate.

Let us understand throughout this campaign that my motives and mine are sincere. I know what it means to be poor. I know what it means to see people who are unemployed. I know that Senator Kennedy

feels as deeply about these problems as I do, but our disagreement is not about the goals for America but only about the means to reach those goals.

MR. SMITH—Thank you, Mr. Nixon.

ROBERT FLEMING OF A. B. C.—Senator, the Vice President in his campaign has said that you were naive and at times immature. He has raised the question of leadership. On this issue, why do you think people should vote for you rather than the Vice President?

MR. KENNEDY—The Vice President and I came to the Congress together in 1946. We both served in the Labor Committee. I've been there now for fourteen years, the same period of time that he has, so that our experience in government is comparable.

Secondly, I think the question is what are the programs that we advocate, what is the party record that we lead? I come out of the Democratic party, which in this century has produced Woodrow Wilson, and Franklin Roosevelt and Harry Truman, and which supported and sustained these programs which I've discussed tonight.

Mr. Nixon comes out of the Republican party. He was nominated by it. And it is fact that through most of these last twenty-five years the Republican leadership has opposed Federal aid for education, medical care for the aged, development of the Tennessee Valley, development of our natural resources.

I think Mr. Nixon is an effective leader of his party. I hope he would grant me the same.

The question before us is which point of view and which party do we want to lead the United States?

MR. SMITH — Mr. Nixon would you like to comment or that statement? [Mr. Nixon would not comment.]

MR. SMITH—The next question, Mr. Novins.

STUART NOVINS OF C. B S.—Mr. • Vice President, your campaign stresses the value of your eight-year experience, and the question arises as to whether that experience was as an observer or as a participant or as an initiator of policy-making. Would you tell us please specifically what major proposals you have made in the last eight years that have been adopted by the Administration?

Recalls Trips Abroad

MR. NIXON—It would be rather difficult to cover them in two and a half minutes. I would suggest that these proposals could be mentioned. First, after each of my foreign trips I have made recommendations that have been adopted.

For example, after my first trip abroad I strongly recommended that we increase our

Blue and Gray Clothes Chosen by Candidates

Vice President Nixon and Senator John F. Kennedy chose blue and gray clothes for their television debate last night.

Mr. Nixon wore a blue-gray suit, a pale blue shirt and a dark blue tie.

The Senator was dressed in an oxford gray single-breasted suit in the narrow Ivy League cut. He wore a non-telegenic white shirt.

exchange programs particularly as they related to exchange of persons, of leaders in the labor field and in the information field. After my trip to South America, I made recommendations that a separate inter-American lending agency be set up which the South American nations would like much better than to participate in the lending agencies which treated all the countries of the world the same.

I have made other recommendations after each of the other trips. For example, after my trip abroad to Hungary I made some recommendations with regard to the Hungarian refugee situation which were adopted, not only by the President but some of them were enacted into law by the Congress.

Within the Administration, as a chairman of the President's Committee on Price Stability and Economic Growth, I have had the opportunity to make recommendations which have been adopted within the Administration and which, I think, have been reasonably effective.

I know Senator Kennedy suggested in his speech at Cleveland yesterday that that committee had not been particularly effective. I would only suggest that while we do not take the credit for it. I would not presume to, that since that committee has been formed the price

line has been held very well within the United States.

Comparison on Growth

MR. KENNEDY — Well, I would say in the latter that the, —and that's what I found somewhat unsatisfactory about the figures, Mr. Nixon, that you used in your speech, when you talked about the Truman administration.

Mr. Truman came to office in 1944 [the date was April 12, 1945] and at the end of the war and difficulties that were facing the United States during that period of transition, and 1946 when price controls were lifted, so it is rather difficult to use an overall figure taking those seven and a half years and comparing them to the last eight years.

I prefer to take the over-all percentage record of the last twenty years of the Democrats and the eight years of the Republicans to show an overall period of growth.

In regard to price stability, I'm not aware that that committee did produce recommendations that ever were certainly before the Congress from the point of view of legislation in regard to controlling prices.

In regard to the exchange of students and labor unions I am chairman of the subcommittee on Africa and I think that one of the most unfortunate phases of our policy towards that country is the very minute number of exchanges that we had.

I think it's true of Latin America also. We did come forward with a program of students for the Congo of over 300 which was more than Federal Government had for all of Africa the previous year, so that I don't think that we have moved at least in those two areas with sufficient vigor.

CHARLES WARREN of M. B. S.—Senator Kennedy, during your brief speech a few minutes ago you mentioned farm surpluses. I'd like to ask this: It's a fact, I think, that Presidential candidates traditionally make promises to farmers. Lots of people, I think, don't understand why the Government pays farmers for not producing certain crops or paying farmers if they over-produce for that matter.

Asks About Farmers

Let me ask, sir, why can't the farmer operate like the business man who operates a factory? If an auto company overproduces a certain model car Uncle Sam doesn't step in and buy up the surplus.

Why this constant courting of the farmer?

MR. KENNEDY — Well, because I think that if the Federal Government moved out of the program and withdrew its support, then I think you'd have complete economic chaos.

The farmer plants in the spring and harvests in the fall. There are hundreds of thousands of them. They really don't— they are not able to control their market very well. They bring their crops in or their livestock in, many of them about the same time. They have only a few purchases. They buy their milk or their hogs. The farmer

is not in a position to bargain very effectively in the marketplace.

I think the experience of the Twenties has shown what a free market could do to agriculture. And if the agricultural economy collapses, then the economy of the rest of the United States sooner or later will collapse.

The farmers are the No. 1 market for the automobile industry of the United States. The automobile industry is the No. 1 market for steel. So if the farmers' economy continues to decline as sharply as it has in recent years, then I think you would have a recession in the rest of the country.

So I think the case for the Government intervention is a good one.

Secondly, my objection to present farm policy is that there are no effective controls to bring supply and demand into better balance.

The dropping of the support price in order to limit production does not work, and we now have the highest surpluses — $9,000,000,000 worth. We've had a higher tax load from the Treasury for the farmer in the last few years with the lowest farm income in many years.

I think that this farm policy has failed. In my judgment the only policy that will work will be for effective supply and demand to be in balance.

And that can only be done through governmental action.

I, therefore, suggest that in those basic commodities which are supported that the Federal Government, after endorsement by the farmers in that commodity, attempt to bring supply and demand into balance. Attempt effective production controls. So that we won't have that 5 or 6 per cent surplus which breaks the price 15 or 20 per cent.

Says Benson Failed

I think Mr. Benson's program has failed. And I must say, after reading the Vice President's speech before the farmers, as he read mine, I don't believe that it's very much different from Mr. Benson's. I don't think it provides effective governmental controls.

I think the support prices are tied to the average market price of the last three years, which was Mr. Benson's theory. I therefore do not believe that this is a sharp enough breach with the past, to give us any hope of success for the future.

MODERATOR: Mr. Nixon. comment?

MR. NIXON — I, of course, disagree with the Senator inso far as his suggestion as to what should be done on the farm program. He has made the suggestion that we need is to move in the direction of more Government controls, a suggestion that would also mean raising prices that the consumers pay for products and imposing upon the farmers controls on acreage even far more than they have today.

I think this is the wrong direction. I don't think this has worked in the past. I do not think it will work in the future.

The program that I have advocated is one which departs from the present program that

we have in this respect. It recognizes that the Government has a responsibility to get the farmer out of the trouble he presently is in because the Government got him into it. And that's the fundamental reason why we can't let the farmer go by himself at the present time.

The farmer produces these surpluses because the Government asked him to through legislation during the war.

Now that we have these surpluses, it's our responsibility to indemnify the farmer during that period that we get rid of the surpluses.

Until we get the surpluses off the farmer's back, however, we should have a program such as I announced, which will see that farm income holds up. But I would propose holding that income up not through a type of program that Senator Kennedy has suggested that would raise prices, but one that would indemnify the farmer, pay the farmer in kind from the products which are in surplus.

Kennedy-Nixon Debate First of Four Meetings

Senator John F. Kennedy and Vice President Nixon are scheduled for three more joint appearances on television. On two they will meet face-to-face, but on the third they will be a continent apart—thus necessitating the split screen, or electronic togetherness, technique.

The Presidential candidates will be questioned by a panel of news reporters on the next two one-hour programs, which will forgo debates. According to present indications, the program on Oct. 7 at 7:30 P. M. will originate in Cleveland. The split-screen program on Oct. 13 at 7:30 P. M. will find Mr. Nixon in Los Angeles and Mr. Kennedy in New York.

The modified debate format will be resumed by the candidates on Oct. 21 at 10 P. M., when they meet in a television studio here to discuss foreign affairs.

SANDER VANOCUR, of N. B. C.—Mr. Vice President, since the question of Executive leadership is a very important campaign issue, I'd like to follow Mr. Novins' question. Now, Republican campaign slogans—you'll see them on signs around the country as you did last week—say it's experience that counts. That's over a picture of yourself, sir, implying that you've had more governmental executive decision-making experience than your opponent. Now, in his news conference on Aug. 24, President Eisenhower was asked to give one example of a major idea of yours that he adopted. His reply was, and I'm quoting: "If you give me a week I might think of one. I don't remember."

Asks for Clarification

Now that was a month ago, sir, and the President hasn't brought it up since, and I'm wondering, sir, if you can clarify which version is correct—the one put out by Republican campaign leaders or the one put out by President Eisenhower?

MR. NIXON—Well, I would suggest, Mr. Vanocur, that if you know the President, that was probably a facetious remark. I would also suggest that insofar as his statement is concerned, that I think it would be improper for the President of the United States to disclose the instances in which members of his official family had made recommendations, as I have made them through the years to him, which he has accepted or rejected.

The President has always maintained and very properly so that he is entitled to get what advice he wants from his Cabinet and from his other advisers without disclosing that to anybody including as a matter of fact the Congress.

Now I can only say this. Through the years I have sat in the National Security Council. I have been in the Cabinet. I have met with the legislative leaders. I have met with the President when he made the great decisions with regard to Lebanon, Quemoy and Matsu, other matters. The President has asked for my advice. I have given it.

Sometimes my advice has been taken. Sometimes it has not. I do not say that I have made the decisions. And I would say that no President should ever allow anybody else to make the major decisions. The President only makes the decisions. All that his advisers do is to give counsel when he asks for it.

As far as what experience counts and whether that is experience that counts, that isn't for me to say. I can only say that my experience is there for the people to consider. Senator Kennedy's is there for the people to consider. As he pointed out, we came to the Congress in the same year.

His experience has been different from mine. Mine has been in the Executive Branch. His has been in the Legislative Branch. I would say that the people now have the opportunity to evaluate his as against mine and I think both he and I are going to abide by whatever the people decide.

MR. SMITH—Senator Kennedy.

MR. KENNEDY — Well, I'll just say that the question is of experience and the question also is what our judgment is of the future, and what our goals are for the United States, and what ability we have to implement those goals.

Abraham Lincoln came to the Presidency in 1860 after a rather little known session in the House of Representatives and after being defeated for the Senate in '58 and was a distinguished President.

'Road to Presidency'

There's no certain road to the Presidency. There are no guarantees that if you take one road or another that you will be a successful President. I have been in the Congress for fourteen years. I have voted in the

last eight years, and the Vice President was presiding over the Senate and meeting his other responsibilities.

I have met decisions over 800 times on matters which affect not only the domestic security of the United States but as a member of the Senate Foreign Relations Committee.

The question really is which candidate and which party can meet the problems the United States is going to face in the Sixties.

MODERATOR — The next question to Senator Kennedy from Mr. Novins.

MR. NOVINS—Senator Kennedy, in connection with these problems of the future that you speak of, and the program that you enunciated earlier in your direct talk, you call for expanding some of the welfare programs for schools, for teacher salaries, medical care, and so forth; but you also call for reducing the Federal debt. And I'm wondering how you, if you're President in January, would go about paying the bill for all this. Does this mean —

MR. KENNEDY—I did not advocate reducing the Federal debt. Because I don't believe that you're going to be able to reduce the Federal debt very much in 1961, 2 or 3. I think you have heavy obligations which affect our security, which we're going to have to meet. And, therefore, I've never suggested we should be able to retire the debt substantially, or even at all in 1961 or 2.

Q.—Senator, I believe, in one of your speeches.

MR. KENNEDY—No, never.

Q.—you suggested that reducing the interest rate would help toward —

MR. KENNEDY—No. No. Not reduce the interest.

Q.—A reduction of the Federal debt.

MR. KENNEDY — Reducing the interest rate. In my judgment, the hard money, tight money policy, fiscal policy of this Administration has contributed to the slow-down in our economy, which helped bring the recession of '54; which made the recession of '58 rather intense, and which has slowed, somewhat, our economic activity in 1960.

What I have talked about, however, the kind of programs that I talk about, in my judgment, are fiscally sound. Medical care for the aged I would put under Social Security.

The Vice President and I disagree on this.

The program—the Javits-Nixon or the Nixon-Javits program—would have cost, if fully used, $600,000,000 by the Government per year, and $600,000,000 by the state.

The program which I advocated, which failed by 5 votes in the United States Senate, would have put medical care for the aged in Social Security. And would have been paid for through the Social Security System and the Social Security tax.

Secondly, I support Federal aid to education and Federal aid for teachers' salaries. I think that's a good investment. I think we're going to have to do it.

And I think to keep the burden further on the property tax,

which is already strained in many of our communities, will provide, will make—insure, in my opinion—that many of our children will not be adequately educated, and many of our teachers not adequately compensated.

There is no greater return to an economy or to a society than an educational system second to none.

On the question of the development of natural resources, I would pay as you go in the sense that they would be balanced and the power revenues would bring back sufficient money to finance the projects, in the same way as the Tennessee Valley.

I believe in the balanced budget. And the only conditions under which I would unbalance the budget would be if there was a grave national emergency or a serious recession. Otherwise, with a steady rate of economic growth—and Mr. Nixon and Mr. Rockefeller, in their meeting, said a 5 per cent economic growth would bring by 1962 $10,000,000,000 extra in tax revenues. Whatever is brought in, I think we can finance essential programs within a balanced budget, if business remains orderly.

MODERATOR — Mr. Nixon, your comment?

MR. NIXON—I think what Mr. Novins was referring to was not one of Senator Kennedy's speeches, but the Democratic platform, which did mention cutting the national debt. I think, too, that it should be pointed out that, of course, it is not possible, particularly under the proposals that Senator Kennedy has advocated, either to cut the national debt or to reduce taxes. As a matter of fact it will be necessary to raise taxes. As Senator Kennedy points out that as far as his one proposal is concerned—the one for medical care for the aged—that that would be financed out of Social Security.

Sees Alternate Roads

That, however, is raising taxes for those who pay Social Security. He points out that he would make pay-as-you-go be the basis for our natural resources development. Well, our natural resources development, which I also supported, incidentally — however, whenever you appropriate money for one of these projects, you have to pay now and appropriate the money.

While they eventually do pay out, it doesn't mean the Government doesn't have to put out the money this year. And so I would say that in all of these proposals Senator Kennedy has made, they will result in one of two things: Either he has to raise taxes or he has to unbalance the budget.

If he unbalances the budget, that means you have inflation, and will be, of course, a very cruel blow to the very people—the older people—who we've been talking about. As far as aid for school construction is concerned, I favor that, as Senator Kennedy did, in January of this year, when he said he favored that rather than aid to teacher salaries.

I favor that because I believe that is the best way to aid our schools without running any

risk whatever of the Federal Government telling our teachers what to teach.

MODERATOR — The next question to Vice President Nixon from Mr. Warren.

MR. WARREN — Mr. Vice President, you mentioned schools and it was just yesterday I think you asked for a crash program to raise education standards, and this evening you talked about advances in education. Mr. Vice President, you said it was back in 1957 that salaries paid to school teachers were nothing short of a national disgrace. Higher salaries for teachers, you added, were important and if the situation wasn't corrected it could lead to a national disaster. Yet, you refused to vote in the Senate in order to break a tie vote when that single vote, if it had been yes, would have granted salary increases to teachers. I wonder if you could explain that, sir.

MR. NIXON: I'm awfully glad you got that question because as you know I got into it at the last of my other question and wasn't able to complete the argument.

I think that the reason that I voted against having the Federal Government pay teacher's salaries was probably the very reason that concerned Senator Kennedy when in January of this year, in his kick-off press conference, he said that he favored aid for school construction, but at that time did not feel that theer should be aid for teachers salaries. At least that's the way I read his remarks.

Now, why should there be any question about the Federal Government aiding teachers salaries. Why did Senator Kennedy take that position then? Why do I take it now?

We both took it then, and I take it now, for this reason. We want higher teachers' salaries. We need higher teachers' salaries. But we also want our education to be free of Federal control. When the Federal Government gets the power to pay teachers, inevitably, in my opinion, it will acquire the power to set standards and to tell the teachers what to teach. I think this would be bad for the country, I think it would be bad for the teaching profession.

For Higher Salaries

There is another point that should be made. I favor higher salaries for teachers. But, as Senator Kennedy said in January of this year, in this same press conference, the way that you get higher salaries for teachers is to support school construction, which means that all of the local school districts in the various states then have money which is freed to raise the standards for teachers' salaries.

I should also point out this: once you put the responsibility on the Federal Government for paying a portion of teachers' salaries, your local communities and your states are not going to meet the responsibility as much as they should. I believe, in other words, that we have seen the local communities and the state assuming more of that responsibility.

Teachers' salaries very fortunately have gone up 50 per cent in the last eight years as against only a 34 per cent rise for other salaries. This is not enough. It should be more.

But I do not believe that the way to get more salaries for teachers is to have the Federal Government get in with a massive program. My objection here is not the cost in dollars. My objection here is the potential cost in control and eventual freedom for the American people by giving the Federal Government power over education, and that is the greatest power

MODERATOR—Senator Kennedy's comment?

MR. KENNEDY—When the Vice President quotes me in January '60 I do not believe the Federal Government should pay directly teachers' salaries, but that was not the issue before the Senate in February. The issue before the Senate was that the money would be given to the state. The state then could determine whether the money would be spent for school construction or teacher salaries.

On that question the Vice President and I disagreed. I voted in favor of that proposal and supported it strongly because I think that that provided assistance to our teachers for their salaries without any chance of Federal control and it is on that vote that Mr. Nixon and I disagreed, and his tie vote defeated, his breaking the tie defeated the proposal.

I don't want the Federal Government paying teachers' salaries directly. But if the money will go to the states and the states can then determine whether it shall go for school construction or for teachers' salaries, in my opinion you protect the local authority over the school board and the school committee. And therefore I think that was a sound proposal and that is why I supported it and I regret that it did not pass.

Defends Party Plaform

Secondly, there have been statements made that the Democratic platform would cost a good deal of money and that I am in favor of unbalancing the budget. That is wholly wrong, wholly in error, and it is a fact that in the last eight years the Democratic Congress has reduced the requests for the appropriations by over $10,000,-000,000.

That is not my view and I think it ought to be stated very clearly on the record. My view is that you can do these programs — and they should be carefully drawn—within a balanced budget if our economy is moving ahead.

MODERATOR — The next question to Senator Kennedy from Mr. Vanocur.

MR. VANOCUR — Senator, you've been promising the voters that if you are elected President you'll try and push through Congress bills on medical aid to the aged, a comprehensive minimum hourly wage bill, Federal aid to education. Now, in the August post-convention session of the Congress when you at least held the possibility that you could one day be President and when you had overwhelming majorities, especially in the Senate, you could not get action on these bills. Now, how do you feel that you'll be able to get them in January

if you weren't able to get them in August?

MR. KENNEDY — If I may take the bills we did pass, the Senate a bill to provide a $1.25 minimum wage. It failed because the House did not pass it and House failed by eleven votes. And I might say that two-thirds of the Republicans in the House voted against $1.25 minimum wage and a majority of the Democrats sustained it. Nearly two-thirds of them voted for the $1.25.

We were threatened by a veto if we passed $1.25. Its extremely difficult with the great power that the President has to pass any bill when the President is opposed to it. All the President needs to sustain his veto of any bill is one-third plus one in either the House or the Senate.

Second, we passed a Federal aid to education bill in the Senate. It failed to come to the floor of the House of Representatives. It was killed in the Rules Committee. And it is a fact in the August session that the four members of the Rules Committee who were Republicans—joining with two Democrats voted against sending the aid to education bill to the floor of the House. Four Democrats voted for it. Every Republican on the Rules Committee voted against sending that bill to be considered by the members of the House of Representatives.

Offered Amendment

Thirdly, on medical care for the aged, this is the same fight that's been going on for twenty-five years of Social Security. We wanted to tie it to Social Security. We offered an amendment to do so. Forty-four Democrats voted for it, one Republican voted for it. And we were informed at the time it came to a vote that if it was adopted the President of the United States would veto it.

In my judgment, a vigorous Democratic President supported by a Democratic majority in the House and Senate can win the support for these programs. But if you send a Republican President and a Democratic majority and a threat of a veto hangs over the Congress, in my judgment you will continue what happened in the August session, which is a clash of parties and inaction.

MODERATOR — Mr. Nixon.

MR. NIXON—Well, obviously, my views are a little different. First of all I don't see how it's possible for a one-third of a body, such as the Republicans have in the House and Senate, to stop two-thirds if the two-thirds are adequately led.

I would say, too, that when Senator Kennedy refers to the action of the House Rules Committee, there are eight Democrats on that committee and four Republicans. It would seem to me that it is very difficult to blame the four Republicans for the eight Democrats' not getting something through that particular committee.

I would say further that to blame the President in his veto power for the inability of the Senator and his colleagues to get action in this special session misses the mark. When the President exercises his veto power, he has to have the peo-

ple behind him, not just a third of the Congress.

Because lets consider it. If the majority of the members of the Congress felt that these particular proposals were good issues—the majority of those who were Democrats — why didn't they pass them and send them to the President and get a veto and have an issue?

The reason why these particular bills in these various fields were not passed was not because the President was against them, it was because the people were against them. It was because they were too extreme. And I am convinced that the alternate proposals that I have, that the Republicans have in the field of health, in the field of education, in the field of welfare, because they are not extreme, because they will accomplish the ends without too great cost in dollars or in freedom, that they could get through the next Congress.

MODERATOR — The next question to Vice President Nixon from Mr. Fleming.

MR. FLEMING — Mr. Vice President, do I take it then you believe that you could work better with Democratic majorities in the House and the Senate than Senator Kennedy could work with Democratic majorities in the House and Senate?

MR. NIXON—I would say this: That we, of course, expect to pick up some seats in both the House and the Senate. We would hope to control the House, to get a majority in the House, in this election. We cannot, of course, control the Senate.

I would say that a President will be able to lead. A President will be able to get his program through to the effect that he has the support of the country, the support of the people.

Sometimes we get the opinion that in getting programs through the House or the Senate it's purely a question of legislation finagling, and all that sort of thing. It isn't really that.

Actions by Congress

Whenever a majority of the people are for a program, the House and the Senate responds to it. And whether this House and Senate, in the next session, is Democratic or Republican, if the country will have voted for the candidate for the Presidency and for the proposals that he has made, I believe that you will find that the President, if it were a Republican, as it would be in my case, would be able to get his program through that Congress.

Now, I also say that as far as Senator Kennedy's proposals are concerned, that, again, the question is not simply one of a Presidential veto stopping programs. You must always remember that a President can't stop anything, unless he has the people behind him.

And the reason President Eisenhower's vetoes have been sustained; the reason the Congress does not send up bills to him which they think will be vetoed is because the people and the Congress, the majority of them, know the country is behind the President.

MODERATOR—Senator Kennedy.

MR. KENNEDY—Well, now lets look at these bills that the Vice President suggests were too extreme.

One was a bill for $1.25 an hour for anyone who works in a store or company that has a $1,000,000 a year business. I don't think that's extreme at all and yet nearly two-thirds to three-fourths of the Republicans in the House of Representatives voted against that proposal.

Secondly was the Federal aid to education bill. It was a very —because of the defeat of teacher salaries, it was not a bill that met in my opinion the needs. The fact of the matter is it was a bill that was less than you recommended, Mr. Nixon, this morning in your proposal.

'Not an Extreme Bill'

It was not an extreme bill and yet we could not get one Reepublican to join, at least I think four of the eight Democrats voted to send it to the floor of the House—not one Republican—and they joined with those Democrats who were opposed to it.

I don't say the Democrats are united in their support of the program. But I do say a majority are. And I say a majority of the Republicans are opposd to it.

The third is medical care for the aged which is tied to Social Security, which is financed out of Social Security funds.

It does not put a deficit on the Treasury. The proposal advanced by you and by Mr. Javits would have cost $600,-000,000. Mr. Rockefeller rejected it in New York. He said he didn't agree with the financing at all, said it ought to be on Social Security.

So these are three programs which are quite moderate. I think it shows the diference between the two parties. One party is ready to move in these programs. The other party gives them lip service.

MR. SMITH—Mr. Warren's question for Senator Kennedy.

MR. WARREN — Senator Kennedy, on another subject, communism is so often described as an ideology or a belief that exists somewhere other than in the United States. Let me ask you, sir, just how serious a threat to our national security are these Communist subversive activities in the United States today?

MR. KENNEDY—Well, I think they're serious. I think it's a matter that we should continue to give great care and attention to. We should support the laws which the United States has passed in order to protect us from those who would destroy us from within. We should sustain the Department of Justice in its efforts in the F.B.I. and we should be continually alert.

I think if the United States is maintaining a strong society here in the United States, I think that we can meet any internal threat. The major threat is external and will continue.

MODERATOR — Mr. Nixon, comment?

MR. NIXON—I agree with

Senator Kennedy's appraisal generally in this respect. The question of communism within the United States has been one that has worried us in the past. It is one that will continue to be a probem for years to come.

We have to remember that the cold war that Mr. Khrushchev is waging and his colleagues are waging is waged all over the world and it's waged right here in the United States. That's why we have to continue to be alert. It is also essential in being alert that we be fair. Fair because by being fair we uphold the very freedoms that the Communists would destroy. We uphold the standards of conduct which they would never follow.

And, in this connection, I think that we must look to the future having in mind the fact that we fight communism at home not only by our laws to deal with Communists, the few who do become Communists and the few who do become fellow travelers, but we also fight communism at home by moving against those various injustices which exist in our society which the Communists feed upon.

And in that connection I again would say that while Senator Kennedy says we are for the status quo I do believe that he would agree that I am just as sincere in believing that my proposals for Federal aid to education, my proposals for health care are just as sincerely held as his. The question again is not one of goals. We're for those goals. It's one of means.

MODERATOR — Mr. Vanocur's question for Vice President Nixon.

MR. VANOCUR: Mr. Vice President, in one of your earlier statements you said we've moved ahead, we've built more schools, we built more hospitals. Now, sir, isn't it true that the building of more schools is a local matter for financing. Now, you claiming that the Eisenhower Administration was responsible for the building of these schools or is it the local school districts that provide for it?

MR. NIXON: Not at all. As a matter of fact your question brings out a point that I'm very glad to make.

Too often in appraising whether we are moving ahead or not we think only of what the Federal Government is doing. Now that isn't the test of whether America moves. The test of whether America moves is whether the Federal Government, plus the state government, plus the local government, plus the biggest segment of all — individual enterprise.

We have for example a gross national product of approximately $500,000,000,000. Roughly $100,000,000, to $125,000,000,000 of that is the result of government activity. $400,000,000,000 parroximately is a result of what individuals do.

Cites Economy Expansion

Now the reason the Eisenhower Administration has moved, the reason that we've had the funds, for example, locally to build the schools, and the hospitals, and the highways, to make the progress that we have is because this Administration has encouraged individual en-

terprise and it has resulted in the greatest expansion of the private sector of the economy that has ever been witnessed in an eight-year period. And that is growth, that is the growth that we are looking for, it is the growth that this Administration has supported and that its policies has stimulated.

MODERATOR—Senator Kennedy.

MR. KENNEDY — Well, I must say that the reason that the schools have been constructed is because the local school districts were willing to increase the property taxes to a tremendously high figure, in my opinion, almost to the point of diminishing returns in order to sustain these schools.

Secondly, I think we have a richer country. And I think we have a powerful country. I think what we have to do, however, is have the President and the leadership set before our country exactly what we must do in the next decade, if we are going to maintain our security, in education, in economic growth, in development of natural resources.

The Soviet Union is making great gains. It isn't enough to compare what might have been done eight years ago, or ten years ago, or fifteen years ago, or twenty years ago, I want to compare what we're doing with what our adversaries are doing, so that by the year 1970 the United States is ahead in education, in health, in building, in homes, in economic strength. I think that's the big assignment, the big task, the big function of the Federal government.

MODERATOR—Now the summation time, please. We've completed our questions and our comments, and in just a moment, we'll have the summation time.

VOICE—This will allow three minutes and twenty seconds for the summation by each candidate.

MODERATOR — Three minutes and twenty seconds for each candidate. Mr. Nixon, will you make the first summation?

MR. NIXON — Thank you, Mr. Smith, Senator Kennedy.

First of all, I think it is well to put the perspective where we really do stand with regard to the Soviet Union in this whole matter of growth.

The Soviet Union has been moving faster than we have. But the reason for that is obvious. They start from a much lower base.

Although they have been moving faster in growth than we have, we find, for example, today that their total gross national product is only 44 per cent of our total gross national product. That's the same percentage that it was twenty years ago.

And as far as the absolute gap is concerned, we find that the United States is even further ahead than it was twenty years ago.

Is this any reason for complacency? Not at all.

Because these are determined men. They are fanatical men. And we have to get the very most out of our economy.

I agree with Senator Kennedy completely on that score.

Where we disagree is in the means that we would use to get the most out of our economy.

I respectfully submit that Senator Kennedy too often would rely too much on the Federal Government, on what it would do to solve our problems, to stimulate growth.

Takes Up Health

I believe that when we examine the Democratic platform, when we examine the proposals that he has discussed tonight, when we compare them with the proposals that I have made, that these proposals that he makes would not result in greater growth for this country than would be the case if we followed the program that I have advocated.

There are many of the points that he has made that I would like to comment upon. The one in the field of health is worth mentioning.

Our health program, the one that Senator Javits and other Republican Senators, as well as I, supported, is one that provides for all people over 65 who want health insurance, the opportunity to have it if they want it.

It provides a choice of having either Government insurance or private insurance. But it compels nobody to have insurance who does not want it.

His program, under Social Security, would require everybody who had Social Security, to take Government health insurance whether he wanted it or not. And it would not cover several million people who are not covered by Social Security at all.

Here is one place where I think that our program does a better job than his. The other point that I would make is this: This downgrading of how much pened when during the Truman Administration the Government was spending more than it took in. We found savings over a lifetime eaten up by inflation. We found the people who could least afford it, people on retired incomes, peoples on fixed incomes, we found them unable to meet their bills at the end of the month. It is essential that a man who is President of this country certainly stand for every program that will mean growth. And I stand for programs that will mean growth and progress. But it is also essential that he not allow a dollar spent that could be better spent by the people themselves.

MODERATOR: Senator Kennedy, your conclusion.

MR. KENNEDY: The point was made by Mr. Nixon that the Soviet production is only 44 per cent of ours. I must say that 44 per cent and that Soviet country is causing us a good deal of trouble tonight. I want to make sure that it stays in that relationship. I don't want to see the day when its 60 per cent of ours, 70 and 75, 80 and 90 per cent of ours, with all the force and power that it could bring to bear in order to cause our destruction.

Secondly, the Vice President mentioned medical care for the aged. Our program was an amendment to the Kerr bill. The Kerr bill provided assistance to all those who were not on Social security. I think it's a very clear contrast.

In 1935, when the Social Security Act was written, ninety-four of ninety-five Republicans voted against it. Mr. Landon ran in 1936 to repeal it.

In August of 1960, we tried to get it again, but this time for medical care we received the support of one Republican in the Senate on this occasion.

Thirdly, I think the question before the American people is, as they look at this country and as they look the world around them, the goals are the same for all Americans. The means are a question. The means are an issue.

If you feel that everything that is being done now is satisfactory, the relative power and prestige and strength of the United States is increasing in relation to that of the Communists, if we are gaining more security, that we are achieving everything as a nation that we should achieve, that we are achieving a better life for our citizens and greater strength, then I agree I think you should vote for Mr. Nixon.

But if you feel that we have to move again in the Sixties, that the function of the President is to set before the people the unfinished business of our society, as Franklin Roosevelt did in the Thirties, the agenda for our people is what we must do as a society to meet our needs in this country and protect our security and help the cause of freedom.

As I said at the beginning, the question before us all, facing all Republicans and all Democrats, is: Can freedom in the next generation conquer, or are the Communists going to be successful? That's the great issue.

And if we meet our responsibilities I think freedom will conquer. If we fail, if we fail to move ahead, if we fail to develop sufficient military and economic and social strength here in this country, then I think that the tide could begin to run against us.

And I don't want historians, ten years from now, to say these were the years when the tide ran out for the United States. I want them to say these were the years when the tide came in; these were the years when the United States started to move again.

That's the question before the American people, and only you can decide what you want, what you want this country to be, what you want to do with the future.

I think we're ready to move. And it is to that great task, if we're successful, that we will address ourselves.

MODERATOR — Thank you very much, gentlemen. This hour has gone by all too quickly. Thank you very much for permitting us to present the next President of the United States on this unique program.

I've been asked by the candidates to thank the American networks and the affiliated stations for providing time and facilities for this joint appearance. Other debates in this series will be announced later and will be on different subjects.

This is Howard K. Smith. Good night from Chicago.

September 27, 1960

NIXON AND KENNEDY CLASH ON TV OVER ISSUE OF QUEMOY'S DEFENSE; U-2 'REGRETS' AND RIGHTS ARGUED

REPUBLICAN: Vice President Nixon as he appeared last night on TV screen.

The New York Times (by John Orris)

DEMOCRAT: Senator John F. Kennedy taking part in telecast from Washington.

Kennedy Protests Lighting And Cold and Wins on Both

By W. H. LAWRENCE
Special to The New York Times.

WASHINGTON, Oct. 7—Short-lived disagreements over blinding lights and a frigid studio developed tonight just before Vice President Nixon and Senator John F. Kennedy made their second joint nation-wide television appearance.

Democrats were the complainants in both instances, contending that steps taken to improve Mr. Nixon's television appearance were unfair to Senator Kennedy.

The studio had been chilled to 64 degrees to relieve Mr. Nixon's heavy perspiration problem that contributed to his generally unsatisfactory physical appearance on television last week.

Senator Kennedy tested the flood lighting from both his own lectern and Mr. Nixon's before the show began. He complained that four bright lights shone directly into his eyes from his own position but only one bright light hit him directly when he stood in Mr. Nixon's spot.

Adjustments Made

After the complaints, network officials adjusted the lighting to Senator Kennedy's satisfaction, and an engineer turned up the thermostat to a 70-degree temperature in the studio.

At the end of an hour-long show, the consensus among studio observers was that Mr. Nixon's make-up artist and lighting experts had done a better job for him than last time and that the physical image projected by the cameras was a vast improvement over the debate from Chicago on Sept. 26.

The Vice President wore what was described as "a mild amount of make-up."

Senator Kennedy, as before, declined all make-up assistance and appeared before the nation without applying powder.

While partisans for both sides claimed victory, the two Presidential candidates avoided any claims themselves. Each was asked, "Who won," and each responded:

"We'll know the answer to that on Nov. 8."

As Mr. Nixon drove away from the National Broadcasting Company studio in northwest Washington, a friend approached his limousine and shouted:

"You really clobbered him tonight."

The Kennedy camp agreed that Mr. Nixon was a better performer tonight than in the Chicago debate.

"But the Vice President had no way to go but up," said one Kennedy staff member. "If he hadn't improved tonight, the campaign would have been all over."

Both candidates appeared less tense than during the first joint appearance, but Senator Kennedy still seemed more at ease than did Mr. Nixon, and he showed more fluidity in gestures.

Both felt the question-and-answer panel form, without opening and closing statements, and a less austere stage setting were improvements over the first debate.

They shot partisan criticism back and forth during the show, but relaxed and engaged in friendly small talk as they posed for photographers at the end of the show.

There was some joshing back and forth about "crowdsmanship," by which one supporter attempts to claim bigger audiences for his candidate than for his rival in the same city or area. But the Vice President brought that discussion to a close by saying, "Let's stipulate that both of us have had good crowds."

Appearance Important

The lighting controversy underlined the great importance both candidates attach to their physical appearance and the impression that may be made on the viewing audience.

Last week, Mr. Nixon appeared to many to be nervous and haggard. Even some of his most ardent supporters agreed that the physical impression he made was not a good one.

The Nixon appearance was laid to improper make-up and lighting. There were published reports, subsequently denied by Mr. Nixon's own aides, that a Democrat might have made up the Vice President in order to create a bad impression.

Tonight, the Vice-Presidential make-up was certified by a card-carrying Republican, Stan Lawrence, a long-time associate of Mr. Nixon. It was applied at the Nixon home even before he reached the studio.

One of the factors in Mr. Nixon's appearance last week was that he perspired heavily and rivulets of perspiration collected on his chin, causing the make-up to show through.

Senator Kennedy was the first on the scene of tonight's discussion—the big N. B. C. studio near Massachusetts and Nebraska Avenues in northwest Washington. He arrived at 6:28 P. M., an hour and two minutes before air time, accompanied by his brother, Robert, who is his campaign manager.

Mr. Nixon arrived at 6:52 P. M., accompanied by one of his staff aides, Don Hughes.

Mr. Nixon was wearing a gray suit and a blue shirt. Senator Kennedy had on a black suit and a blue shirt. The Massachusetts Senator forgot television's demand for a blue shirt last week and had to send back for one after he reached the Chicago studio.

Tonight's studio design was markedly different from the stark and cold setting set up by the Columbia Broadcasting System for the first discussions, which caused many complints from viewers. Tonight's set was described as one that gave a greater feeling of warmth and comfort.

Behind the set tonight stood two American flags. There were no flags last week, and many persons wrote and telegraphed to object.

Just before tonight's show began, both candidates were unsmiling and obviously tense as they stood for voice and camera checks.

The panel of four questioners was in full camera view tonight, whereas last week the faces of a similar panel were visible only during a brief over-the-shoulder introduction.

The candidates, who dash with happy abandon into unfamiliar street crowds of hundreds of thousands during their campaigning, whent behind a radio-TV iron curtain as soon as they reached the broadcasting studio tonight. They were fenced off from a few hundred reporters and invited guests of the candidates' own choosing, and the security was extremely tight.

Even ninety minutes before the show began and long before the principals were on the scene, reporters were not allowed a glimpse of the studio set.

JOHNSON AND LODGE REJECT TV DEBATE

WASHINGTON, Oct. 7 (UPI) —The two major Vice-Presidential candidates have rejected proposals that they confront each other on television, Dr. Frank Stanton, president of the Columbia Broadcasting System, said today.

He said both Senator Lyndon B. Johnson and Henry Cabot Lodge had rejected the idea without explanation. There was speculation that the candidates had felt they would be handicapped by reason of their special backgrounds. Mr. Lodge is identified primarily with international affairs and Mr. Johnson with domestic affairs.

Mr. Stanton's network produced the first Nixon-Kennedy television confrontation in Chicago.

Associated Press Wirephoto

IN WASHINGTON STUDIO: Senator John F. Kennedy, left, and Vice President Nixon just before their debate. Moderator is Frank McGee. Questioners are in the foreground.

EXCHANGES SHARP

Senator Is Accused of 'Woolly Thinking'— He, Too, Is Tough

By RUSSELL BAKER
Special to The New York Times.

WASHINGTON, Oct. 7—Vice President Nixon and Senator John F. Kennedy raised the campaign temperature tonight, clashing sharply on foreign policy and civil rights in the second of their nation-wide television debates.

The question of who won will have to await the surveys of voters, but the equally nagging question for Republicans — of how Mr. Nixon would "project" after his unhappy appearance in the first debate—was answered immediately. The Vice President did not have the thin, emaciated appearance that worried Republicans across the nation during the first debate.

One of the high points of tonight's debate was a direct conflict between the Presidential candidates over policy for dealing with the islands of Quemoy and Matsu off the Chinese mainland.

Criticizes Vagueness

Mr. Kennedy took the position that the islands were militarily worthless and, lying virtually in a harbor on the Communist mainland, were indefensible.

Moreover, he said, Administration vagueness about whether the islands would be defended in case of Communist attack created a dangerous uncertainty for the Chinese about this country's intentions. While Taiwan (Formosa) should certainly be defended, he indicated, he favored a pull-back from Quemoy and Matsu by the Chinese Nationalists.

Mr. Nixon denounced this as "the same kind of woolly thinking that led to disaster in Korea." He insisted that the islands should be held. "These two islands are in the area of freedom," he said. To give them up, he argued, would only encourage the Communists to press their drive on Taiwan.

The question was not of "two tiny pieces of real estate," he said, but a matter of principle.

Johnson Is Nixon Target

In a long running exchange over civil rights, Mr. Nixon denounced the Democratic Vice-Presidential candidate, Senator Lyndon B. Johnson of Texas, as a man who had voted against most of the civil rights proposals in the Democratic platform and "who opposes them at the present time."

Although Mr. Johnson contends that, as Democratic Senate leader, he is responsible for the only two civil rights bills to be enacted since the Reconstruction period after the Civil War, Mr. Kennedy did not expand on this issue.

Instead, Mr. Kennedy charged that the Republican Administration had given no leadership to enforce the Supreme Court's school-desegregation decision of 1954. He also accused the Administration of lacking "vigor" in ending job discrimination.

The two men also clashed on the Administration's handling of the U-2 espionage flight over the Soviet Union on May 1. Mr. Kennedy charged that the Vice President had "distorted" his comment that this Government might have expressed "regrets" to Moscow if such action could have saved the Paris summit meeting of May 16.

In fact, Mr. Kennedy said, diplomatic "regrets" were accepted practice on such occasions. They were routinely sent to Cuba last winter and to the Soviet Government after an American plane flew over Russian territory two years ago, he declared.

Mr. Nixon replied that Senator Kennedy was "wrong on three counts." He was wrong in suggesting that an expression of official "regrets" might have saved the summit, Mr. Nixon said. Mr. Khrushchev, he asserted, was determined to destroy the conference and merely used the U-2 case as a pretext to do so.

Calls Analogy Wrong

Second, he went on, Mr. Kennedy was "wrong in the analogy he makes." When this country did "something that is wrong, we can express regrets," he said. But the U-2 flight had been "right" because its purpose was to defend the country against surprise attack, and it should not apologize for doing what is "right," he said.

Third, he said, "we all remember Pearl Harbor." The lesson was that "we cannot afford an intelligence gap," Mr. Nixon said. Therefore, intelligence operations had to be continued without apology, he concluded.

The two candidates divided over the Eisenhower Administration's policies toward Cuba. Mr. Nixon insisted that Cuba was not lost and that the Administration was following the proper course to see that the Cuban people "get a chance to realize their aspirations of progress through freedom."

He described Senator Kennedy's assertions that Cuba was lost as "defeatist talk." In fact, he said, if Mr. Kennedy wanted to compare the number of dictators bred under the Truman and Eisenhower Administrations in Latin America, he would find that eleven were ruling in Latin America under President Truman while only three remained today.

Senator Kennedy replied that he had "never suggested that Cuba was lost, except for the present." He criticized the Administration for not using "its great influence to persuade the Cuban Government to hold free elections." In 1957 and 1958, he said, he expressed the hope that Cuba would rise, but "I don't think it will rise if we continue the same policies toward Cuba that we did in recent years."

To what extent substantive points of debate affect a huge viewing audience like tonight's is a moot point among politicians, but all were intensely interested in the battle of "images."

The question as the show opened was how the two candidates would "project." That is, would television distort one man to the advantage of the other?

Mr. Nixon's advisers have argued for two weeks that the camera distorted his appearance during the first debate in Chicago Sept. 26. Great pains were taken to improve the "image" he would project tonight.

Nixon More Aggressive

In addition, Mr. Nixon, whose Chicago appearance was criticized by many Republicans as too agreeable toward Mr. Kennedy's policies, was consciously more aggressive tonight.

The result was a considerably different television "image" of the Vice President than was projected from Chicago. Mr. Kennedy, whose advisers regarded the Chicago show as a triumph of "image" projection, maintained the style he used so successfully there.

Neither man smiled at any time during the hour-long show. Each repeatedly accused the other of distorting the record and resorting to inaccuracies.

Both men were earnest. Mr. Kennedy seemed to start off with more assurance. Mr. Nixon appeared slightly tense at the start and stumbled on a few of his early sentences.

But as the debate progressed he seemed to gather assurance. Toward the close he went after Mr. Kennedy with gusto on the issue of Quemoy and Matsu.

Tonight's debate was held in Studio A of Station WRC-TV, the National Broadcasting Company's Washington outlet. N. B. C. produced this, the second in the series, for simultaneous broadcast on all three major television networks and the four major radio networks.

At that time, each candidate received eight minutes at the start for opening statements and three minutes at the end to close. The interval was spent answering newsmen's questions.

Tonight's program consisted entirely of answers to questions from a panel of four newsmen. As in Chicago, the questions were rotated between the candidates. Each man had two-and-one-half minutes to answer and his opponent had a minute and a half to rebut.

The newsmen of tonight's panel were Alvin Spivak of United Press International, Harold P. Levy of Newsday, Paul Niven of the Columbia Broadcasting System and Edward P. Morgan of the American Broadcasting Company. The moderator was Frank McGee of N. B. C.

Thirteen questions were posed to the candidates. Eight dealt with foreign policy and five with domestic affairs or campaign tactics. Two of the domestic questions concerned civil rights.

Mr. Nixon listed three civil rights areas that he considered acute—jobs, school integration and the sit-in demonstrations to end discrimination at lunch counters in privately owned stores.

On jobs, he said, the President's Committee for Equality of Employment Under Government Contracts—now operating under Presidential appointment—should be given statutory authority by Congress.

On schools, he said, Congress should provide Federal assistance for school districts desiring to make the transition from segregated to integrated facilities.

On sit-ins, he said, "we have to look to Presidential leadership." Lunch-counter discrimination in stores that sell Negroes other merchandise over the counter "is wrong, and we have to do something about it," he said.

"Mr. Nixon hasn't discussed the two basic questions," Mr. Kennedy countered.

Cites Court Decision

These, he said, were what the President would do to enforce the Supreme Court's school-desegregation decision of 1954 and how he would end job discrimination. President Eisenhower, he noted, had consistently refused to say whether he even thought the court decision was right.

And, he added, though Mr. Nixon now heads the President's Committee on Government Contracts, only two actions have been successfully brought in its lifetime to end discrimination by employers under Federal contract.

Mr. Nixon struck back hard with a personal blow at Senator Johnson, with a sarcastic reference to a Kennedy campaign song, "High Hopes."

"Senator Kennedy has expressed some high hopes in this field," he said. "But let's look at the performance. When he selected his Vice-Presidential running mate he selected a man who had voted against most of these proposals and a man who opposes them at the present time."

Transcript of the Second Nixon-Kennedy Debate on Nation-Wide Television

REMAINS AGGRESSIVE: Senator Kennedy in TV debate   **GETS TOUGHER:** Vice President Nixon makes his reply

Following is a transcript of the Nixon-Kennedy broadcast debate last night, as recorded by The New York Times:

FRANK McGEE—Good evening. This is Frank McGee, N. B. C. News, in Washington.

This is the second in a series of programs unmatched in history. Never have so many people seen the major candidates for President of the United States at the same time, and never, until this series, have Americans seen the candidates in face-to-face exchange.

Tonight, the candidates have agreed to devote the full hour to answering questions on any issue of the campaign.

And here tonight are the Republican candidate, Vice President Richard M. Nixon, and the Democratic candidate, Senator John F. Kennedy.

Now, representatives of the candidates and of all the radio and television networks have agreed on these rules. Neither candidate will make an opening statement or a closing summation. Each will be questioned in turn. Each will have an opportunity to comment upon the answer of the other; each reporter will ask only one question in turn. He is free to ask any question he chooses. Neither candi-

date knows what questions will be asked, and only the clock will determine who will be asked the last question.

These programs represent an unprecedented opportunity for the candidates to present their philosophies and programs directly to the people, and for the people to compare these, and the candidates.

2 Selected by Lot

The four reporters on tonight's panel include a newspaper man and a wire service representative. These two were selected by lot by the press secretaries of the candidates from among the reporters traveling with the candidates. The broadcasting representatives were selected by their respective companies.

The reporters are: Paul Niven of CBS, Edward P. Morgan of ABC, Alvin Spivak of United Press International, and Harold R. Levy of Newsday.

The first question is from Mr. Niven and is for Vice President Nixon.

MR. NIVEN—Mr. Vice President, Senator Kennedy said last night that the Administration would take responsibility for the loss of Cuba.

Would you compare the validity of that statement with the

validity of your own statements in previous campaigns that the Truman Administration was responsible for the loss of China to the Communists?

MR. NIXON—Well, first of all, I don't agree with Senator Kennedy that Cuba is lost and certainly China was lost when this Administration came into power in 1953.

As I look at Cuba today, I believe that we are following the right course, a course which is difficult but a course which under the circumstance is the only proper one which will see that the Cuban people get a chance to realize their aspirations of progress through freedom and that they get that with our cooperation with the other states in the Organization of American States.

Now Senator Kennedy has made some very strong criticisms of my part or alleged part in what has happened in Cuba.

He points to the fact that I visited Cuba while Mr. Batista was in power there. I can only point out that if we are going to judge the Administrations in terms of our attitude toward dictators we're glad to have a comparison with the previous administration. There were eleven dictators in South Amer-

ica and in Central America when we came in in 1953.

Today there are only three left, including the one in Cuba. We think that's pretty good progress.

Senator Kennedy also indicated with regard to Cuba that he thought that I had made a mistake when I was in Cuba in not calling for free elections in that country.

Now, I'm very surprised at Senator Kennedy who is on the Foreign Relations Committee would have made such a statement of this kind.

Cites Kennedy's Book

As a matter of fact in his book, "The Strategy for Peace," he took the right position and that position is that the United States has a treaty—a treaty with all of the Organization of American states—which prohibits us from interfering in the internal affairs of any other state and prohibits them as well.

For me to have made such a statement would have been in direct opposition to that treaty.

Now with regard to Cuba, let me make one thing very clear. There isn't any question but that we will defend our rights there.

There isn't any question but that we will defend Guantanamo if it's attacked.

There also isn't any question but that the free people of Cuba —the people who want to be free—are going to be supported and that they will attain their freedom.

No, Cuba is not lost, and I don't think this kind of defeatist talk by Senator Kennedy helped the situation one bit.

MR. McGEE—Senator Kennedy, would you care to comment?

SENATOR KENNEDY — In the first place, I never suggested that Cuba was lost except for the present. In my speech last night, I indicated that I thought that Cuba one day again would be free.

Where I've been critical of the Administration's policy and where I criticized Mr. Nixon was because in his press conference in Havana in 1955, he praised the competence and stability of the Batista dictatorship — that dictatorship that killed over 20,000 Cubans in seven years.

Secondly, I did not criticize him for not calling for free elections.

What I criticized was the failure of the Administration to use its great influence to persuade the Cuban Government to hold free elections—particularly in 1957 and 1958.

Thirdly, Arthur Gardner, a Republican Ambassador, Earl Smith, a Republican Ambassador, in succession, both have indicated in the past six weeks that they reported to Washington that Castro was a Marxist; that Raul Castro was a Communist, and that they got no effective results. Instead, our aid continued to Batista, which was ineffective; we never were on the side of freedom, we never used our influence when we could have used it most effectively— and today Cuba is lost to freedom.

I hope some day it will rise. But I don't think it will rise if we continue the same policies toward Cuba that we did in recent years, and in fact toward all of Latin America — when we've almost ignored the needs of Latin America. We beamed not a single Voice of America program in Spanish to all of Latin America in the last eight years, except for the three months of the Hungarian Revolution.

MR. McGEE—Mr. Morgan, with a question for Senator Kennedy.

MR. MORGAN—Senator, last May in Oregon, you discussed the possibilities of sending apologies or regrets to Khrushchev over the U-2 incident. Do you think now that that would have done any good? Did you think so then?

MR. KENNEDY—Mr. Morgan, I suggested that if the United States felt that it could save the summit conference it would have been proper for us to express regrets.

In my judgment that statement has been distorted by Mr. Nixon and others, in their debates around the country and in their discussions.

Mr. Lodge, on "Meet the Press" a month ago, said if there was ever a case when we did not have law on our side it was in the U-2 incident.

The U-2 flights were proper from the point of view of protecting our security. But they were not in accordance with international law.

Deplores Lie-Telling

And I said that I felt that rather than tell the lie which we told, rather than indicate that the flights would continue—in fact, I believe Mr. Nixon himself said on May 15 that the flights would continue, even though Mr. Herter testified before the Senate Foreign Relations Committee that they had been canceled as of May 12, that it would have been far better if we had expressed regrets—if that would have saved the summit.

And if the summit is useful— and I believe it is.

The point that is always left out is the fact that we expressed regrets to Castro this winter; that we expressed the regrets— the Eisenhower Administration expressed regrets for a flight over Southern Russia in 1958. We expressed regrets for a flight over Eastern Germany under this Administration.

The Soviet Union in 1955 expressed regrets to us over the Bering Sea incident.

The Chinese Communists expressed regrets to us over a plane incident in 1956. That is the accepted procedure between nations and my judgment is that we should follow the advice of Theodore Roosevelt: "Be strong. Maintain a strong position. But also speak softly."

I believe that in those cases where international custom calls for the expression of a regret; if that would have kept the summit going in my judgment it was a proper action.

It's not appeasement. It's not soft. I believe we should be stronger than we now are. I believe we should have a stronger military force. I believe we should increase our strength all over the world.

But I don't confuse words with strength and in my judgment if the summit was useful; if it would have brought us closer to peace, that rather than the lie that we told, which has been criticized by all responsible people afterwards it would have been far better for us to follow the common diplomatic procedure of expressing regret and then trying to move on.

MR. McGEE—Mr. Vice President.

MR. NIXON—I think Senator Kennedy is wrong on three counts. First of all he's wrong in thinking or even suggesting that Mr. Khrushchev might have continued the conference if we had expressed regrets. He knew these flights were going on long before and that wasn't the reason that he broke up the conference.

Second, he's wrong in the analogies that he makes. The United States is a strong country. Whenever we do anything that's wrong, we can express regrets. But when the President of the United States is doing something that's right, something that is for the purpose of defending the security of this country against surprise attack, he can never express regrets or apologize to anybody, including Mr. Khrushchev.

Now in that connection, Senator Kennedy has criticized the President on the ground not only of not expressing regrets but because he allowed this flight to take place while the summit conference or immediately before the summit conference occurred. This seems to me criticism that again is wrong on his part.

We all remember Pearl Harbor. We lost 3,000 American lives. We cannot afford an intelligence gap. And I just want to make my position absolutely clear with regard to getting intelligence information.

Won't Express Regrets

I don't intend to see to it that the United States is ever in a position where while we're negotiating with the Soviet Union that we discontinue our intelligence effort. And I don't intend ever to express regrets to Mr. Khrushchev or anybody else if I'm doing something that has the support of the Congress and that is right for the purpose of protecting the security of the United States.

MR. McGEE: Mr. Spivak with a question for Vice President Nixon.

MR. SPIVAK — Mr. Vice President, you have accused Senator Kennedy of avoiding the civil rights issue when he has been in the South and he has accused you of the same thing. With both North and South listening and watching, will you sum up your own intentions in the field of civil rights if you become President?

MR. NIXON—My intentions in the field of civil rights have been spelled out in the Republican platform. I think we have to make progress first in the field of employment, and there we would give statutory authority to the Committee on Government Contracts, which is an effective way of getting real progress made in this area, since about one out of every four jobs is held by, and is alloted by, people who have Government contracts.

Certainly, I think all of us agree that when anybody has a Government contract, certainly the money that is spent under that contract ought to be disbursed equally without regard to the race, or creed, or color of the individual who is to be employed.

Second, in the field of schools, we believe that there should be provisions whereby the Federal Government would give assistance to those districts who do want to integrate their schools. That, of course, was rejected, as was the Government contracts provision by the special session of the Congress in which Mr. Kennedy was quite active.

And then as far as other areas are concerned, I think that we have to look to Presidential leadership. And when I speak of Presidential leadership, I refer, for example, in our attitude on the sit-in strikes. Here, we have a situation which causes all of us concern—causes us concern because of the denial of the rights of people to the equality which we think belongs to everybody.

Talked to Negro Mothers

I have talked to Negro mothers. I've heard them explain —try to explain—how they tell their children how they can go into a store and buy a loaf of bread but then can't go into that store and sit at the counter and get a Coca-Cola. This is wrong and we have to do something about it.

So, under the circumstances, what do we do?

Well, what we do is what the Attorney-General of the United States did under the direction of the President: call in the owners of chain stores and get them to take action.

Now there are other places where the Executive can lead, but let me just sum up by saying this:

Why do I talk every time I'm in the South on civil rights? Not because I'm preaching to the people of the South because this isn't just a Southern problem. It's a Northern problem and a Western problem. It's a problem for all of us.

I do it because it's the responsibility of leadership. I do it because we have to solve this problem together. I do it right at this time particularly because when we have Khrushchev in this country—a man who has enslaved millions, a man who has slaughtered thousands —we cannot continue to have a situation where he can point the finger at the United States of America and say that we are denying rights to our citizens.

And so I say both the candidates and both the Vice-Presidential candidates, I would hope as well, including Senator Johnson, should talk on this issue at every opportunity.

MR. McGEE—Senator Kennedy:

MR. KENNEDY—Well, Mr. Nixon hasn't discussed the two basic questions: What is going to be done and what will be his policy in implementing the Supreme Court decision of 1954. Giving aid to schools technically that are trying to carry out the decision is not the great question.

Secondly, what's he going to do to provide fair employment. He's been the head of the Committee on Government Contracts that's carried out two cases—both in the District of Columbia. He has not indicated his support of an attempt to provide fair employment practices around the country, so that everyone can get a job regardless of their race or color. Nor has he indicated that he will support Title 3 which would give the Attorney General additional powers to protect constitutional rights.

These are the great questions: Equality of education in school. About 2 per cent of our population of white people is illiterate —10 per cent of our colored population. Sixty to 70 per cent of our colored children do not finish high school.

These are the questions in these areas that the North and the South, East and West are entitled to know. What will be the leadership of the President in these areas to provide equality of opportunity for employment? Equality of opportunity in the field of housing, which could be done in all Federal-supported housing by a stroke of the President's hand.

What will be done to provide equality of education in all sections of the United States? Those are the questions to which the President must establish a moral tone and moral leadership. And I can assure you that if I'm elected President we will do so.

MR. McGEE—Mr. Levy with a question for Senator Kennedy:

Mr. LEVY—Senator, on the same subject, in the past you have emphasized that the President's responsibility as a moral leader as well as an executive on civil rights questions—what specifically might the next President do in the event of an occurrence such as Little Rock or the lunch-counter sit-ins?

MR. KENNEDY—Let me say that I think the President operates in a number of different areas. First, as a legislative leader, and as I just said that I believe that the passage of the so-called Title 3, which gives the Attorney General the power to protect constitutional rights in those cases where it's not possible for the person involved to bring a suit.

Secondly, as an executive leader. There had been only six cases brought by this Attorney General under the voting bill passed in 1957 and the voting bill passed in 1960. The right to vote is basic. I do not believe that this Administration has implemented those bills which represent the will of the majority of the Congress on two occasions with vigor.

Thirdly, I don't believe the Government contracts division is operated with vigor. Everyone who does business with the Government should have the opportunity to make sure that they do not practice discrimination in their hiring. And that's in all sections of the United States.

And then, fourthly, as a moral leader. There is a very strong moral basis for this concept of equality before the law; not only equality before the law but also equality of opportunity. We are in a very difficult time. We need all the talent we can get. We sit on a conspicuous stage. We are a goldfish bowl before the world. We have to practice what we preach.

We preach a very high standard for ourselves. The Communists do not. They set a low standard of materialism. We preach in the Declaration of Independence and in the Constitution, in the statement of our greatest leaders we preach very high standards and if we're not going to be charged before the world with hypocrisy we have to meet those standards.

I believe the President of the United States should indicate this.

Now lastly, I believe in the case of Little Rock. I would have hoped that the President of the United States would have been possible for him to indicate it clearly that the Supreme Court decision was going to be carried out. I would have hoped it would have been possible to use marshals to do so but it—evidently under the handling of the case—it was not. I would hope an incident like that would not happen. I think if the President is responsible, if he consults with those involved, if he makes it clear that the Supreme Court decision is going to be carried out in a way that the Supreme Court planned with deliberate speed, then in my judgment, providing he's behind action, I believe we can make progress.

Now, the present Administration—the President—has never indicated what he thought of the 1954 decision. Unless the President speaks, then of course the country doesn't speak. As Franklin Roosevelt said: "The Presidency of the United States is, above all, a place of moral leadership." And I believe on this great moral issue he should speak out and give his views clearly.

MR. McGEE—Mr. Vice President.

MR. NIXON—Senator Kennedy has expressed some high hopes in this field—hopes which I think all Americans would share who want some progress in this area. But let's look at the performance.

When he selected his Vice-Presidential running mate he selected a man who had voted against most of these proposals and a man who opposes them at the present time. Let me look also at what I did. I selected a man who stands with me in this field and who will talk with me and work with me on it.

Now the Senator referred to the Committee on Government Contracts. And yet that very committee of which I am chairman has been handicapped by the fact that we have not had adequate funds; we have not had adequate powers; we haven't had an adequate staff. Now in the special session of Congress and in the session that preceded it—the Democratic Congress in which there's a 2-1 Democratic majority—was asked by the President to give us the funds and give us the power to do a job and they did nothing at all.

And in the special session in which Senator Kennedy was calling the signals along with Senator Johnson they turned it down and he, himself, voted against giving us the power, despite the fact that the bill had already been considered before; it had already had hearings on and the Congress already knew what it had before it.

All that I can say is that: What we need here are not just high hopes. What we need is action.

And in the field of executive leadership, I can say that I believe it's essential that the President of the United States not only set the tone but he also must lead; he must act as he talks.

MR. McGEE—Mr. Morgan, with a question for Vice President Nixon.

MR. MORGAN — Mr. Vice President, in your speeches you emphasized that the United States is doing basically well in the "cold war." Can you square that statement with a considerable mass of bipartisan reports and studies, including one prominently participated in by Governor Rockefeller, which almost unanimously concludes that we are not doing nearly so well as we should?

MR. NIXON—Mr. Morgan, no matter how well we're doing in the "cold war," we're not doing as well as we should. And that will always be the case as long as the Communists are on the international scene, in the aggressive tendencies that they presently are following.

Now as far as the present situation is concerned, I think it's time that we nail a few of these distortions about the United States that have been put out.

First of all, we hear that our prestige is at an all-time low. Senator Kennedy has been hitting that point over and over again. I would just suggest that after Premier Khrushchev's performance in the United Nations, compared with President Eisenhower's eloquent speech, that at the present time Communist prestige in the world is at an all-time low and American prestige is at an all-time high.

'Significant' Factor

Now that, of course, is just one factor—but it's a significant one. When we look, for example, at the vote on the Congo—we were on one side, they were on the other side. What happened? There were seventy votes for our position and none for theirs.

Look at the votes in the United Nations over the past seven and a half years. That's a test of prestige. Every time the United States has been on one side and they've been on the other side, our position has been sustained.

Now, looking to what we ought to do in the future:

In this "cold war" we have to recognize where it is being fought and then we have to develop programs to deal with it. It's being fought primarily in Asia, in Africa and in Latin America.

What do we need? What tools do we need to fight it?

Well we need, for example, economic assistance. We need technical assistance. We need exchange. We need programs of diplomatic and other character which will be effective in that area.

Now, Senator Kennedy a moment ago referred to the fact that there was not an adequate Voice of America program for Latin America. I'd like to point out that in the last six years, the Democratic Congresses, of which he'd been a member, have cut $20,000,000 off of the Voice of America programs. They also have cut $4,000,000,000 off of mutual security in these last six years. They also have cut $2,000,000,000 off of defense.

Now when they talk about our record here, it is well that they recognize that they have to stand up for their record as well.

So let me summarize by saying this: I'm not satisfied with what we're doing in the "cold war" because I believe we have to step up our activities and launch an offensive for the minds and hearts and souls of men. It must be economic, it must be technological. Above all, it must be ideological.

But we've got to get help from Congress in order to do this.

MR. McGEE—Senator Kennedy.

MR. KENNEDY—Of course Mr. Nixon is wholly inaccurate when he says that the Congress has not provided more funds in fact than the President recommended for national defense.

Nineteen Fifty-three, we tried to put an appropriation of $5,000,000,000 for our defenses. I was responsible for the amendment with Senator Monroney in 1954 to strengthen our ground forces.

The Congress of the United States appropriated $677,000,000 more than the President was willing to use up till a week ago.

Secondly, on the question of our position in the United Nations we all know about the vote held this week—of the five neutralists—and it was generally regarded as a defeat for the United States.

Thirdly, in 1952, there were only seven votes in favor of the admission of Red China into the United Nations.

Strengthening of Position

Last year there were twenty-nine and tomorrow when the preliminary vote is held you will see a strengthening of that position or very close to it.

We have not maintained our position and our prestige. A Gallup poll taken in February of this year asking—in eight out of nine countries—they asked the people who do they think would be ahead by 1970 militarily and scientifically and a majority in eight of the nine countries said the Soviet Union would by 1970.

Governor Rockefeller has been far more critical in June of our position in the world than I have been.

The Rockefeller Brothers report, General Ridgway, General Gavin, the Gaither report, various reports of Congressional committees all indicate that the relative strength of the United States both militarily, politically, psychologically and scientifically and industrially—the relative strength of United States compared to that of the Soviet Union and the Chinese Communists together has deteriorated in the last eight years and we should know it and the American people should be told the facts.

MR. McGEE—Mr. Spivak, with a question for Senator Kennedy.

MR. SPIVAK—Senator, following this up—how would you go about increasing the prestige you say we're losing and could the programs you've devised to do so be accomplished without absolutely wrecking our economy?

MR. KENNEDY—Yes. We have been wholly indifferent to Latin America until the last few months.

The program that was put forward this summer, after we broke off the sugar quota with Cuba, really was done because we wanted to get through the O. A. S. meeting a condemnation of Russian infiltration of Cuba. And therefore we passed an authorization, not an aid bill, which was the first time, really, since the Inter-American Bank, which was founded a year ago, was developed, that we really have looked at the needs of Latin America; that we associated ourselves with those people.

Secondly, I believe that in the case—that it's far better for the United States, instead of concentrating our aid, particularly in the under-developed world, on surplus military equipment— we poured $300,000,000 of surplus military equipment into Laos; we paid more military aid, more aid into Laos per person than in any country in the world, and we know now that Laos is moving from neutralism in the direction of the Communists.

Long-Term Loans

I believe instead of doing that we should concentrate our aid in long-term loans, which these people can pay back either in hard money or in local currency. This permits them to maintain their self-respect. It permits us to make sure that the projects which are invested in are going to produce greater wealth.

And I believe that in cases of India and Africa and Latin America, that this is where our emphasis should be. I would strengthen the Development Loan Fund. And Senator Fulbright, Senator Humphrey and I tried to do that. We tried to provide an appropriation of a billion and a half for five years, on a long-term loan basis, which this Administration opposed.

Well, unless we're ready to carry out programs like that in the Sixties, this battle for economic survival, which these people are waging, are going to be lost. And if India should lose her battle, with 35 per cent of the people of the under-developed world within her borders, then I believe that the balance of power could move against us.

I think the United States can afford to do these things. I think that we could not afford not to do these things.

This goes to our survival. And here, in a country which is moving ahead, if it's developing its economy to the fullest— which we are not now— in my judgment, we'll have the resources to meet our military commitments and also our commitments overseas.

I believe it's essential that we do it because in the next ten years the balance of power is going to begin to move in the world from one direction or another—towards us or towards the Communists, and unless we

begin to identify ourselves not only with the anti-Communist fight but also with the fight against poverty and hunger, these people are going to begin to turn to Communists as an example. I believe we can do it.

If we build our economy the way we should, we can afford to do these things, and we must do it.

MR. McGEE—Mr. Vice President.

MR. NIXON — Senator Kennedy has put a great deal of stress on the necessity for economic assistance. This is important. But it's also tremendously important to bear in mind that when you pour in money without pouring in technical assistance as well that you have a disastrous situation.

We need to step up exchange we need to step up technical assistance so that trained people in thee newly developing countries can operate the economies.

We also have to have in mind something else with regard to this whole situation in the world, and that is that as America moves forward, we not only must think in terms of fighting communism, but we must also think primarily in terms of the interests of these countries.

We must associate ourselves with their aspirations. We must let them know that the great American ideals of independence of the right of people to be free and the right to progress, that these are ideals that belong not to ourselves alone, but they belong to everybody.

Adequate Funds

This we must get across to the world, and we can't do it unless we do have adequate funds for, for example, for information, which has been cut by the Congress; adequate funds for technical assistance.

The other point that I would make with regard to economic assistance and technical assistance is that the United States must not rest its case here alone. This is primarily an ideological battle—a battle for the minds, and the hearts, and the souls of men. We must not meet the Communists purely in the field of gross atheistic materialism. We must stand for our ideals.

MR. McGEE—Mr. Levy, with a question for Vice President Nixon.

MR. LEVY—Mr. Vice President: the Labor Department today added five more major industrial centers to the list of areas with substantial unemployment. You said in New York this week that as President you would use the full powers of the Government, if necessary, to combat unemployment. Specifically, what measures would you advocate and at what point?

MR. NIXON—To combat unemployment we first must concentrate on the very areas to which you refer—the so-called depressed areas.

Now in the last Congress— the special session of the Congress — there was a bill — one by the President, one by Senator Kennedy and members of his party. Now the bill that the

President had submitted would have provided more aid for those areas that really need it— areas like Scranton and Wilkes-Barre and the areas of West Virginia, than the ones that Senator Kennedy was supporting.

On the other hand we found that the bill got into the legislative difficulties and consequently no action was taken. So point one, at the highest priority we must get a bill for depressed areas through the next Congress. I have made recommendations on that and I have discussed them previously and I will spell them out further in the campaign.

Second, as we consider this problem of unemployment, we have to realize where it is. In analyzing the figures we will find that our unemployment exists among the older citizens. It exists also among those who are inadequately trained—that is, those who do not have an adequate opportunity for education. It also exists among minority groups.

If we're going to combat unemployment then, we have to do a better job in these areas. That's why I have a program for education, a program in the case of equal job opportunities and one that would also deal with our older citizens.

Now, finally, with regard to the whole problem of combating recession as you call it, we must use the full resources of the Government in these respects.

1. We must see to it that credit is expanded as we go into any recessionary period—and understand: I do not believe we're going into a recession. I believe this economy is sound and that we're going to move up.

2. In addition to that, if we do get into a recessionary period we should move on the part of the economy which is represented by the private sector—and I mean stimulate that part of the economy that can create jobs—the private sector of the economy. This means through tax reform and if necessary, tax cuts that will stimulate more jobs.

I favor that rather than massive Federal spending programs which will come into effect usually long after you've passed through the recessionary period. So we must use all of these weapons for the purpose of combatting recession if it should come. But I do not expect it to come.

MR. McGEE—Senator Kennedy.

MR. KENNEDY: Well, Mr. Nixon has stated the record inaccurately in regard to the depressed area bill. I'm very familiar with it. It came out of the committee of which I was the chairman—the labor subcommittee, in '55. I was the floor manager.

We passed an area development bill far more effective than the bill the Administration suggested on two occasions, and the President vetoed it both times.

We passed a bill again this year in the Senate and it died in the rules committee of the House of Representatives.

Let me make it very clear that the bill that Mr. Nixon talked about did not mention Wilkes-Barre or Scranton, it did not mention West Virginia. Our bill was far more effective. The bill introduced and sponsored by Senator Douglas was far more effective in trying to stimulate the economy of those areas.

Secondly, he has mentioned the problem of our older citizens. I cannot still understand why this Administration and Mr. Nixon oppose putting medical care for the aged under social security to give them some security.

Third, I believe we should step up the use of our surplus foods in these areas until we are able to get the people back at work. Five cents a day is what the food package averages per person.

Fourthly, I believe we should stimulate the economy. I believe we should not carry out a hard-money, high-interest-rate policy which helped intensify certainly the recession of 1958 and I think helped bring the slowdown of 1960. If we move into a recession in '61 then I would agree that we have to put more money into the economy, and it can be done by either one of the two methods discussed. One is by a program such as aid to education, the other would be to make a judgment of what's the most effective tax program to stimulate our economy.

MR. McGEE — Mr. Niven with a question for Senator Kennedy.

MR. NIVEN—Senator, while the main theme of your campaign has been this decline of American power and prestige in the last eight years, you've hardly criticized President Eisenhower at all. In a speech last week-end you said you had no quarrel with the President. Now isn't Mr. Eisenhower and not Mr. Nixon responsible for any such decline?

MR. KENNEDY—I understood that this was the Eisenhower-Nixon Administration, according to all the Republican propaganda that I've read. The question is what we're going to do in the future. I've been critical of this Administration and I've been critical of the President. In fact, Mr. Nixon discussed that a week ago in a speech.

I believe that our power and prestige in the last eight years has declined.

Now what is the issue is what we are going to do in the future. And that's the issue between Mr. Nixon and myself.

He feels that we're moving ahead; we're not going into a recession in this country, economically; he feels that our power and prestige is stronger than it ever was relative to that of the Communists, that we're moving ahead.

I disagree. I believe the American people have to make the choice on Nov. 8 between the view of whether we have to move ahead faster or that what we're doing now is not satisfactory, whether we have to build greater strength at home and abroad and Mr. Nixon's view. That's the great issue.

President Eisenhower moves

from the scene on Jan. 20 and the next four years are the critical years. And that's the debate. That's the argument between Mr. Nixon and myself and on that issue the American people have to make their judgment and I think it's an important judgment.

I think in many ways this election is more important than any since 1932 or certainly almost any in this century.

Disagree Fundamentally

Because we disagree very fundamentally on the position of the United States and if his view prevails then I think that's going to bring an important result to this country in the Sixties. If our view prevails—that we have to do more; that we have to make a greater national and international effort; that we have lost prestige in Latin America—the President of Brazil, the new incumbent running for office called on Castro during his campaign because he thought it was important to get the vote of those who were supporting Castro in Latin America.

In Africa: the United States has ignored Africa. We gave more scholarships to the Congo this summer than we've given to all of Africa the year before. Less than 200 for all the countries of Africa and they need trained leadership more than anything.

We've been having a very clear decision in the last eight years. Mr. Nixon has been part of that Administration. He's had experience in it. And I believe this Administration has not met its responsibilities in the last eight years; that our power relative to that of the Communists is declining; that we're facing a very hazardous time in the Sixties, and unless the United States begin to move here, unless we start to go ahead, I don't believe that we're going to meet our responsibilities to our own people or to the cause of freedom. I think the choice is clear and it involves the future.

MR. McGEE—Mr. Vice President.

MR. NIXON—Well, first of all I think Senator Kennedy should make up his mind with regard to my responsibility. In our first debate he indicated that I had not had experience or at least had not participated significantly in the making of the decisions. I'm glad to hear tonight that he does suggest that I have had some experience. Let me make my position clear.

I have participated in the discussions leading to the decisions of this Administration. I'm proud of the record of this Administration. I don't stand on it because it isn't something to stand on but something to build on.

Now looking at Senator Kennedy's credentials: he is suggesting that he will move America faster and further than I will.

But what does he offer? He offers retreads of programs that failed. I submit to you that as you look at his programs, his program for example, with regard to the Federal Reserve and free money or loose money, low interest rates, his programs in the economic field generally are the programs that were adopted and tried during the Truman Administration.

And when we compare the economic progress of this country in the Truman Administration with that of the Eisenhower Administration we find that in every index there has been a great deal more performance and more progress in this Administration than in that one.

I say the programs and the leadership that failed then is not the program and the leadership that America needs now. I say that the American people don't want to go back to those policies.

And incidentally if Senator Kennedy disagrees he should indicate where he believes those policies are different from those he's advocating today.

Mr. McGEE—Mr. Spivak with a question for Vice President Nixon.

MR. SPIVAK—Mr. Vice President. According to news dispatches Soviet Premier Khrushchev said today that Prime Minister Macmillan had assured him that there would be a summit conference next year after the Presidential elections. Have you given any cause for such assurance and do you consider it desirable or even possible that there would be a summit conference next year if Mr. Khrushchev persists in the conditions he's laid down?

MR. NIXON—No. Of course, I haven't talked to Prime Minister Macmillan. It would not be appropriate for me to do so. The President is still going to be President for the next four months and he, of course, is the only one who could commit this country in this period.

As far as the summit conference is concerned, I want to make my position absolutely clear. I would be willing as President to meet with Mr. Khrushchev or any other world leader if it would serve the cause of peace.

I would not be able—would be willing to meet with him however unless there were preparations for that conference which would give us some reasonable certainty—some reasonable certainty—that you were going to have some success.

We must not build up the hopes of the world, and then dash them as was the case in Paris. There, Mr. Khrushchev came to that conference determined to break it up. He was going to break it up because he knew that he wasn't going to get his way on Berlin and on the other key matters with which he was concerned at the Paris conference.

Now, if we're going to have another summit conference, there must be negotiations at the diplomatic level, the ambassadors, the Secretaries of State, and others at that level, prior to that time, which will delineate the issues and which will prepare the way for the heads of state to meet, and make some progress.

Otherwise, if we find the heads of state meeting and not making progress, we will find that the cause of peace will have been hurt rather than helped.

So under these circumstances I, therefore, strongly urge, and

I will strongly hold, if I have the opportunity to urge or to hold, this position, that any summit conference would be gone into only after the most careful preparation and only after Mr. Khrushchev, after his disgraceful conduct at Paris, after his disgraceful conduct at the United Nations, gave some assurance that he really wanted to sit down and talk and to accomplish something, and not just to make propaganda.

MR. McGEE—Senator Kennedy.

MR. KENNEDY—I have no disagreement with the Vice President's position on that. It—my view is the same as his.

Let me say there is only one point I would add.

Before we go into the summit, before we ever meet again, I think it's important that the United States build its strength—that it build its military strength, as well as its own economic strength.

Decision on Berlin

If we negotiate from a position where the power balance or wave is moving away from us, it's extremely difficult to reach a successful decision on Berlin, as well as the other questions.

Now, the next President of the United States in his first year is going to be confronted with a very serious question on our defense of Berlin, our commitment to Berlin.

It's going to be a test of our nerve and will. It's going to be a test of our strength. And because we're going to move in '61 and '62, partly because we have not maintained our strength with sufficient vigor in the last years, I believe that before we meet the crisis, that the next President of the United States should send a message to Congress asking for revitalization of our military strength—because, come spring or late in the winter, we're going to be face-to-face with the most serious Berlin crisis since 1949 or '50.

On the question of the sum-

====

Debate Hits Business; Some Gain, Some Lose

The Nixon-Kennedy television debate last night affected business in the midtown area, but it was a question of just which theatre or restaurant was concerned.

Those restaurants and bars with television drew well, while those without said business was better after the debate ended at 8:30 P. M.

With the theatres, heavy advance sales for Broadway attractions ensured capacity audiences. The movie theatres showing film with muscles and mass appeal were sold out. However, the foreign film houses reported a falling off of business.

====

mit, I agree with the position of Mr. Nixon. I would not meet Mr. Khrushchev unless there were some agreements at the secondary level—foreign ministers or ambassadors—which would indicate that the meeting would have some hope of success, or useful exchange of ideas.

MR. McGEE—Mr. Levy with a question for Senator Kennedy.

MR. LEVY—Senator, in your acceptance speech at Los Angeles, you said that your campaign would be based not on what you intend to offer the American people, but what you intend to ask of them. Since that time you have spelled out many of the things that you intended to do but you have made only vague reference to sacrifice and self-denial. A year or so ago, I believe, you said that you would not hesitate to recommend a tax increase if you considered it necessary.

MR. KENNEDY — That's right.

MR. LEVY—Is this what you have in mind?

MR. KENNEDY: Well, I don't think that in the winter of '61, under present economic conditions, a tax increase would be desirable. In fact, it would be deflationary; it would cause great unemployment; it would cause a real slowdown in our economy. If it ever becomes necessary, and is wise economically and essential to our security, I would have no hesitancy in suggesting a tax increase or any other policy which would defend the United States.

I have talked in every speech about the fact that these are going to be very difficult times in the Nineteen Sixties and that we're going to have to meet our responsibility as citizens.

I'm talking about a national mood. I'm talking about our willingness to bear any burdens in order to maintain our own freedom and in order to meet our freedom around the globe.

We don't know what the future's going to bring. But I would not want anyone to elect me as President of the United States or vote for me under the expectation that life would be easier if I were elected.

Now, many of the programs that I'm talking about—economic growth, development of our natural resources—build the strength of the United States. That's how the United States began to prepare for its great actions in World War II and in the post-war period. If we're moving ahead, if we're providing a viable economy, if our people have sufficient resources so that they can consume what we produce, then this country's on the move, then we're stronger, then we set a better example to the world.

So we have the problem of not only building our own military strength and extending our policies abroad. We have to do a job here at home.

So I believe that the policies that I recommend come under the general heading of strengthening the United States. We're using our steel capacity 55 per cent today. We're not able to consume what we're able to produce at a time when the Soviet Union is making great economic gains.

And all I say is I don't know what the Sixties will bring—except I think they will bring hard times in the international sphere. I hope we can move ahead here at home in the United States. I'm confident we can do a far better job of mobilizing our economy and resources in the United States.

And I merely say that if they elect me President, I will do my best to carry the United States through a difficult period, but I would not want the people to elect me because I promise them the easy, soft life. I think it's going to be difficult. But I'm confident that this country can meet its responsibilities.

MR. McGEE—Mr. Vice President.

MR. NIXON—Well, I think we should be under no illusions whatever about what the responsibilities of the American people will be in the Sixties.

Our expenditures for defense, our expenditures for mutual security, our expenditures for economic assistance and technical assistance are not going to get less.

In my opinion, they're going to be greater.

I think it may be necessary that we have more taxes. I hope not. I hope we can economize elsewhere so that we don't have to.

But I would have no hesitation to ask the American people to pay the taxes even in 1961 if necessary to maintain a sound economy and also to maintain a sound dollar because when you do not tax and tax enough to pay for your outgo, you pay it many times over in higher prices and inflation and I simply will not do that.

Platform Attacked

I think I should also add that as far as Senator Kennedy's proposals are concerned, if he intends to carry out his platform, the one adopted in Los Angeles, it is just impossible for him to make good on those promises without raising taxes or without having a rise in prices or both.

The platform suggests that it can be done through economic growth, that it can be done, in effect, with mirrors. But it isn't going to be working that way.

You can't add billions of dollars to our expenditures and not pay for it. After all, it isn't paid for by my money, it isn't paid for by his, but by the people's money.

MR. McGEE—Mr. Niven with a question for Vice President Nixon.

MR. NIVEN—Mr. Vice President, you said that while Mr. Khrushchev is here, Senator Kennedy should talk about as well as what's wrong with the country. In the 1952 campaign, when you were Republican candidate for Vice President, we were at war with the Communists, did you feel a similar responsibility to talk about what was right with the country?

MR. NIXON—I did. And as I pointed out in 1952, I made it very clear that as far as the Korean War was concerned, that I felt that the decision to go into the war in Korea was right and necessary.

What I criticized were the policies that made it necessary to go to Korea.

Now, incidentally, I should point out here that Senator Kennedy has attacked our foreign policy. He said that it's been a policy that has led to defeat and retreat. And I'd like to know where have we been defeated and where have we retreated.

In the Truman Administration, 600,000,000 people went behind the Iron Curtain, including the satellite countries of Eastern Europe and Communist China. In this Administration, we've stopped them at Quemoy and Matsu. We've stopped them in Indochina. We've stopped them in Lebanon. We've stopped them in other parts of the world.

I would also like to point out that as far as Senator Kennedy's comments are concerned, I think he has a perfect right and a responsibility to criticize this Administration whenever he thinks we're wrong. But he has a responsibility to be accurate, and not to misstate the case.

I don't think he should say that our prestige is at an all-time low. I think this is very harmful, at a time when Mr. Khrushchev is here—harmful, because it's wrong. I don't think it was helpful when he suggested, and I'm glad he's corrected this to an extent, that 17,000,000 people go to bed hungry every night in the United States. Now this just wasn't true.

Now, there are people who go to bed hungry in the United States—far less, incidentally, than used to go to bed hungry when we came into power at the end of the Truman Administration. But the thing that is right about the United States, it should be emphasized, is that less people go to bed hungry in the United States than in any major country in the world. We're the best fed. We're the best clothed, with a better distribution of this world's goods to all of our people than any people in history.

America's Strength

Now, in pointing out the things that are wrong, I think we ought to emphasize America's strength. It isn't necessary to run America down in order to build her up.

Now, just so that we get it absolutely clear, Senator Kennedy must, as a candidate—as I, as a candidate in '52—criticize us when we're wrong. And he's doing a very effective job of that, in his way.

But on the other hand, he has the responsibility to be accurate. And I have a responsibility to correct him every time he misstates the case. And I intend to continue to do so.

MR. McGEE: Senator Kennedy.

MR. KENNEDY: Well, Mr. Nixon, I'll just give you the testimony of Mr. George Aiken—Senator George Aiken, the ranking minority member, Republican member and former chairman of the Senate Agricultural Committee testifying in 1950 — who said there were 26,000,000 Americans who did not have the income to afford a decent diet. Mr. Benson, testifying on the food stamp plan in 1957, said there were 25,000,000 Americans who could not afford an elementary low-cost diet. And he defined that as someone who uses beans in place of meat.

Now, I've seen a good many hundreds of thousands of people who are not adequately fed. You can't mean that a surplus food distribution of 5 cents per person and that nearly 6,000,000 Americans receiving that is adequate. You can't tell me anyone who uses beans instead of meat in the United States—and there are 25,000,000 of them, according to Mr. Benson—is well fed, or adequately fed.

I believe that we should not compare what our figures may be to India or some other countries that has serious problems but to remember that we are the most prosperous country in the world and that these people are not getting adequate food. And they're not getting in many cases adequate shelter. And we ought to try to meet the problem.

Secondly, Mr. Nixon has continued to state—and he stated it last week—these fantastic figures of what the Democratic platform would cost. They're wholly inaccurate.

I said last week I believed in a balanced budget. Unless there was severe recession—and after all the worst unbalanced budget in history was in 1958; $12,000,000,000, larger than in any Administration in the history of the United States. So that I believe that on this subject we can balance the budget unless we have a national emergency or unless we have a severe recession.

MR. McGEE: Mr. Morgan with a question for Senator Kennedy.

MR. MORGAN: Senator, Saturday on television you said that you had always thought that Quemoy and Matsu were unwise places to draw our defense line in the Far East. Would you comment further on that and also address to this question: Couldn't a pull-back from those islands be interpreted as appeasement?

MR. KENNEDY—Well, the United States has on occasion attempted—mostly in the middle Fifties—to persuade Chiang Kai-shek to pull his troops back to Formosa. I believe strongly in the defense of Formosa. These islands are a few miles—five or six miles—off the coast of Red China, within a general harbor area and more than 100 miles from Formosa. We have never said flatly that we will defend Quemoy and Matsu if attacked. We say we will defend it if it's part of a general attack on Formosa. But it's extremely difficult to make that judgment.

Mr. Herter in 1958 when he was Under Secretary of State, said they were strategically undefensible. Admirals Spruance and Collins in 1955 said that we should not attempt to defend these islands in their conference in the Far East. General Ridgway has said the same thing.

I believe that if you're going to get into war for the defense of Formosa it ought to be on a clearly defined line. One of the problems, I think, at the time of South Korea was the question of whether the United States would defend it if it were attacked. I believe that we should defend Formosa. We should come to its defense. We leave this rather in the air— "that we would defend it under some conditions but not under other." I think is a mistake.

Secondly, I would not suggest the withdrawal at the point of the Communist gun. It is a de-cision finally that the Nationalists should make and I believe that we should consult with them and attempt to work out a plan by which the line is drawn at the Island of Formosa.

It leaves 100 miles between the sea. But with General Ridgway, Mr. Herter, General Collins, Admiral Spruance and many others, I think it's unwise to take the chance of being dragged into a war which may lead to a world war over two islands which are not strategically defensible, which are not, according to their testimony, essential to the defense of Formosa [Taiwan].

I think that we should protect our commitments. I believe strongly we should do so in Berlin. I believe strongly we should do so in Formosa and I believe we should meet our commitments to every country whose security we guaranteed.

But I do not believe that that line in case of a war should be drawn on those islands but instead on the Island of Formosa.

And as long as they are not essential to the defense of Formosa it's been my judgment ever since 1954 at the time of the Eisenhower Doctrine for the Far East that our line should be drawn in the sea around the island itself.

MR. McGEE: Mr. Vice President.

MR. NIXON: I disagree completely with Senator Kennedy on this point.

I remember in the period immediately before the Korean War. South Korea was supposed to be indefensible as well. Generals testified to that, and Secretary Acheson made a very famous speech at the Press Club early in the year that the Korean War started indicating in effect that South Korea was beyond the defense zone of the United States.

I suppose it was hoped when he made that speech that we wouldn't get into a war. But it didn't mean that. We had to go in when they came in.

Principle Cited

Now, as far as Quemoy and Matsu are concerned that the question is not one two little pieces of real estate—they are unimportant. It isn't the few people who live on them—they are not too important. It's the principle involved.

These two islands are in the area of freedom. The Nationalists have these two islands. We should not force our Nationalist allies to get off of them and give them to the Communists.

If we do that we start a chain reaction because the Communists aren't after Quemoy and Matsu. They're after Formosa. In my opinion, this is the same kind of woolly thinking that led to disaster for America in Korea. I'm against it. I would never tolerate it as President of the United States, and I will hope that Senator Kennedy will change his mind if he should be elected.

MR. McGEE: Gentlemen, we have approximately four minutes remaining. May I ask you to make your questions and answers as brief as possible consistent with clarity. And Mr. Levy has a question for Vice President Nixon.

413

MR. LEVY—Mr. Vice President, you are urging voters to forget party labels and vote for the man. Senator Kennedy says that in doing this you are trying to run away from your party on such issues as housing and aid to education by advocating what he calls a me-too program. Why do you say that party labels are not important?

MR. NIXON—Because that's the way we elect a President in this country, and it's the way we should.

I'm a student of history as is Senator Kennedy, incidentally, and I have found that in the history of this country, we've had many great Presidents. Some of them have been Democrats and some of them have been Republicans.

The people, someway, have always understood that at a particular time a certain man was the one the country needed.

Now, I believe that in an election when we are trying to determine who should lead the free world—not just America—perhaps, as Senator Kennedy has already indicated—the most important election in our history—it isn't the label that he wears or that I wear that counts. It's what we are. It's our whole lives. It's what we stand for. It's what we believe.

And consequently, I don't think it's enough to go before Republican audiences — and I never do—and say "Look, vote for me because I'm a Republican." I don't think it's enough for Senator Kennedy to go before the audiences on the Democratic side and say "Vote for me because I'm a Democrat." That isn't enough.

What's involved is the question of leadership for the whole free world.

Now that means the best leadership. It may be Republican, it may be Democratic. But the people are the ones that determine it. The people have to make up their minds.

And I believe the people, therefore, should be asked to make up their minds. Not simply on the basis of 'Vote the way your grandfather did,' 'vote the way your mother did.' I think the people should put America first, rather than party first.

Now, as far as running away from my party is concerned, Senator Kennedy has said that we have no compassion for the poor, that we are against progress—the enemies of progress, is the term that he's used, and the like—all that I can say is this:

We do have programs in all of these fields—education, housing, defense—that will move America forward. They will move her forward faster, and they will move her more surely than his programs.

This is what I deeply believe. I'm sure he believes just as deeply that his will move that way.

I would suggest, however, that in the interest of fairness that he could give me the benefit of also believing, as he believes.

MR. McGEE—Senator Kennedy.

MR. KENNEDY — Well, let me say I do think that parties are important in that they tell something about the program and something about the man. Abraham Lincoln was a great President of all people but he was selected by his party at a key time in history because his party stood for something.

The Democratic party in this century has stood for something. It has stood for progress. It has stood for concern for the people's welfare. It has stood for a strong foreign policy and a strong national defense and as a result produced Wilson, President Roosevelt and President Truman.

The Republican party has produced McKinley and Harding, Coolidge, Dewey and Landis. They do stand for something. They stand for a whole different approach to the problems facing this country at home and abroad.

That's the importance of party—only if it tells something about the record.

And the Republicans in recent years, not only the last twenty-five years but in the last eight years, have opposed housing, opposed care for the aged, opposed Federal aid to education, opposed minimum wage. And I think that record tells something.

MR. McGEE — Thank you gentlemen. Neither the questions from the reporters nor the answers you heard from Senator John Kennedy or Vice President Richard Nixon were rehearsed.

By agreement neither candidate made an opening statement or a closing summation. They further agreed that the clock alone would decide who would speak last and each has asked me to express his thanks to the networks and their affiliated stations.

Another program similar to this one will be presented Thursday, Oct. 13, and the final program will be presented Friday, Oct. 21. We hope this series of radio and television programs will help you toward a fuller understanding of the issues facing our country today and that on Election Day, Nov. 8, you will vote for the candidate of your choice.

This is Frank McGee.

Goodnight from Washington.

The preceding program has been produced and presented by the N. B. C., A. B. C. and C. B. C. networks, the Mutual Broadcasting System and their affiliated stations throughout the United States.

Join us once again on Thursday, Oct. 13th at this same time for the third program in this series of joint appearances by Vice President Richard M. Nixon and Senator John F. Kennedy.

The Second Debate

By JAMES RESTON

Special to The New York Times.

WASHINGTON, Oct. 7—The general feeling in the capital tonight was that the second Presidential debate was a great improvement on the first: more informative, more aggressive, and more personal.

Vice President Nixon clearly made a comeback after his disappointing showing in the first

News Analysis

debate. He had obviously taken the advice of his supporters to be assertive, and he pressed the initiative most of the way.

He was more composed this time, and much more political in his answers to the reporters' questions. At the end of the first debate, his supporters were discouraged; tonight when the lights went out, they were pleased and even delighted.

In a quick survey of the reporters at the studio, eleven thought the Vice President had come out ahead tonight, eleven thought it was a stand-off and five thought Senator John F. Kennedy had won.

This performance helped clarify the essential difference between the two candidates for the Presidency. Senator Kennedy rested his case on the proposition that this is a time for innovation in both foreign and domestic policy. To go on as we now are, he argued, would produce stagnation abroad and a steady deterioration of America's position in the world.

Concession by Nixon

Vice President Nixon did not argue for the status quo. He conceded that it was essential to do more in the fields of collective security overseas and Social Security at home, but he concentrated on what was right with present policies while Senator Kennedy emphasized what was wrong and what needed to be done to correct present deficiencies.

This has been the basic issue between the two men in the hustings in the first month of the campaign. It is still the main issue at the half-way point, a month from Election Day. But it is an issue that gives the Vice President several fundamental advantages in debate and he exploited them to the full tonight.

He presented Senator Kennedy as selling the country short while Premier Khrushchev was in the United States. He blamed the Democrats for the Korean war. He insisted that they had been responsible for letting China and eastern Europe go Communist. And he asserted that it was the Soviet Union and not the United States that was losing prestige in the world.

Senator Kennedy had the weight of informed opinion on his side in their discussion of the U-2 spy plane over the summit and on the catalogue of reports by experts on the state of the nation's foreign policy and its defenses.

Accordingly, he was arguing that the nation was doing badly in Cuba, that its rate of growth was insufficient, that its programs for the old people and the depressed areas were inadequate.

Mr. Nixon's tactic was to deny everything except that the Communists were wicked and formidable adversaries and that he had the experience and the programs that would deal with them.

Politically, this is an effective position. It appeals to the voters' pride in country, to their desire to feel that the nation is doing all right, and that, if things are wrong, the fault lies not with Washington but with Moscow.

Accordingly, these arguments come down to a question of personal judgment about which of the two candidates is nearer to the truth in his analysis of the present situation in the world.

Mr. Kennedy is arguing the disagreeable unpleasant side of the case. He is crying Churchillian gloom, calling for new exertions, new programs, new approaches to old and complex and dangerous problems.

Presentation by Nixon

It is, in a way, the ancient political and philosophical debate between the ins and the outs. Mr. Kennedy is trying to win by dispelling what he believes to be the popular illusion of security. Mr. Nixon in denying that there is any illusion in his assertion that if we go on patiently and steadily all will be well.

In dealing with this problem tonight, Mr. Nixon seemed at least to this observer to have scored the most telling political debating points, but he is presenting a picture of the nation's position that is definitely not supported by most well-informed observers either in this capital or in the United Nations.

There was a great deal of sharp disagreement on facts in tonight's debate that never got clarified. Indeed, both repeatedly charged the other with inaccuracies, and it was left to the viewer to decide for himself who was right and who was wrong.

Senator Kennedy did, however, state the main issue of the debate and the election quite clearly and put it to the voters to decide.

"The issue," he said, "is what we are going to do in the future, and that is an issue between Mr. Nixon and myself. He feels that we are moving ahead, that we are not going into a recession in this country economically. He feels that our power and prestige is stronger than it ever was relative to that of the Communists; that we are moving ahead.

"I disagree, and I believe the American people have to make the choice on Nov. 8 between the view of whether we have to move ahead faster, whether we have to build greater strength at home and abroad; and Mr. Nixon's view. That is the great issue."

414

NIXON AND KENNEDY RENEW FIGHT OVER QUEMOY IN HEATED DEBATE; ALSO CLASH ON LABOR PROGRAMS

AT START OF DEBATE: Vice President Nixon and Senator John F. Kennedy as they appeared on the television screen. Mr. Nixon was in Los Angeles and Mr. Kennedy here.

The New York Times

EXCHANGE BITTER

Vice President Takes a Softer Position on Defending Islands

By RUSSELL BAKER

Senator John F. Kennedy and Vice President Nixon bitterly accused each other before a national television audience last night of advocating policies on Quemoy and Matsu that would lead to war.

While the rhetorical temperature of the third debate was torrid, the actual policy difference between the two Presidential candidates appeared to have narrowed considerably. Mr. Nixon pulled back from the strong position he took last week.

Debate over Quemoy and Matsu, which both candidates have decided to make a major issue of the campaign, dominated the program.

It was not entirely a foreign policy fight, however. In other exchanges the candidates clashed on such domestic issues as labor legislation, farm policy, spending, the costs of their respective proposals, economic growth and the 27½ per cent depletion allowance given oil and gas producers.

Arbitration Disputed

The clash on labor arose from Mr. Nixon's assertion that Senator Kennedy favored compulsory arbitration of major disputes. Mr. Kennedy denied vehemently that this was his position.

Last week the Vice President said that defending the two islands, situated four and five miles off the Chinese mainland, was a matter of "principle" because no territory "in the area of freedom" should be surrendered.

In last night's hour-long debate he was much less categorical. He suggested that Quemoy and Matsu would be defended if an attack upon them were "a prelude to an attack on Formosa [Taiwan]." This is essentially the position taken by the Eisenhower Administration since 1954.

Senator Kennedy sought to remind the audience that this was not the position that Mr. Nixon took in their television debate last Friday. Mr. Kennedy, who favors defending Taiwan against Communist attack, said "Mr. Nixon suggests the United States should go to war if these two islands are attacked."

If a Communist attack were aimed at Taiwan, Mr. Kennedy said, the question of Quemoy and Matsu would be academic because the country would be at war in any event, honoring its commitment to Taiwan.

'Extending Commitment'

"He's indicating that we should fight for these islands come what may, because they are, to quote his words, 'in the area of freedom,' " Mr. Kennedy said. "He didn't take that position on Tibet. He didn't take that position on Hungary * * * He's extending the Administration's commitment."

Throughout the hour, the candidates reached a pitch of acrimony unmatched in either of their two previous encounters. Time and again the nation's living rooms were filled with such phrases as "I resent," "He simply doesn't know what he's talking about" and "that's untrue."

At one point, in a voice oozing sarcasm, Mr. Kennedy said:

"I always have difficulty recognizing my positions when they're stated by the Vice President."

Mr. Nixon, countering the Senator's complaints of misrepresentation, announced that he would issue a "white paper" after the program documenting Mr. Kennedy's position in Mr. Kennedy's own language.

Claims Misrepresentation

Senator Kennedy accused Mr. Nixon of misrepresenting or distorting his positions on compulsory arbitration, the cost of his farm program, its effect on food prices and his stand on depletion allowances for oil producers.

For last night's debate, although the candidates were arguing with a continent between them, both men appeared free of the electronic troubles that had plagued Mr. Nixon in the debate from Chicago Sept. 26. At that time he was widely regarded as having looked "tired," "gaunt" or "haggard."

Last night both appeared robust and combative. Unsmiling throughout, each appeared intent on seizing the aggressive position, and neither was reluctant to punish the other during rebuttal.

Vice President Nixon was in the American Broadcasting Company's television center in Hollywood, Calif. Mr. Kennedy was at A. B. C.'s television here at 7 West Sixty-sixth Street. A panel of newsmen was in Hollywood in a studio apart from Mr. Nixon.

Schedule Brought Change

The arrangement was necessitated by the candidates' campaign schedules, which put them on opposite coasts at this stage of the campaign. A. B. C. produced the program for simultaneous television showing on the Columbia Broadcasting System, the National Broadcasting system and its own network, plus the radio networks of all three and the Mutual Broadcasting System.

In the two previous debates, the candidates appeared together in the same studio. They will do so again in the fourth in New York next Friday.

The panel consisted of S. Douglass Cater of The Reporter magazine, Roscoe Drummond of The New York Herald

Tribune, Frank McGee of N. B. C. and Charles von Fremd of C. B. S.

The moderator was Bill Shadel of the A. B. C. news department.

Quemoy Aired Repeatedly

The Quemoy-Matsu issue, first developed in last Friday's debate and sharpened by both men during the last week, was brought up again and again. Mr. Kennedy sought to deprive Mr. Nixon of the "peace" issue and Mr. Nixon sought to depict Mr. Kennedy as a man dangerously ignorant of the ways of dictators.

Last week Mr. Kennedy stated that Taiwan and the related Pescadores Islands should be defended but that Quemoy and Matsu, deemed indefensible by nonpartisan military authorities, created the danger of a new war.

Administration policy is ambiguous about their defense, he noted, holding that they would be defended if an attack upon them were considered part of an attack on Taiwan.

The ambiguity of this position, he declared, might tempt the Communists to adventures that could lead this country to war. Because the islands have no military value—"two rocks off the coast of China," he called them Monday—this country should induce the Chinese Nationalists to abandon them rather than continue the risk of occupying them, he said.

Mr. Nixon denounced this as "the same kind of woolly thinking" that had led to "disaster" in Korea. The islands, he declared, should be held on the "principle" that no territory lying inside "the area of freedom" should be surrendered, regardless of its strategic unimportance.

Last Wednesday, in a speech here, Mr. Kennedy suggested that this kind of policy offered the country "trigger-happy leadership."

Resents Comment

At the start of last night's debate, Mr. Nixon began by saying:

"I resent that comment. I resent it because it's an implication that Republicans have been trigger-happy and would lead this nation into war."

In fact, he said, during the last fifty years, Democratic Presidents have led the country three times into war, but no Republican President had taken it to war.

Mr. Nixon was asked if, sitting in the White House, he would "launch the United States into a war" by resisting a Communist attack on the islands and what weapons he would use to defend them.

"It would be completely irresponsible for a candidate for the Presidency or for the President himself to indicate the course of action and the weapons he would use in the event that such an attack occurred," the Vice President said.

"In the event the attack was a prelude to an attack on Formosa, which would be the indication today, * * * there isn't any question but that the United States would * * * honor our treaty obligation and stand by our ally, Formosa."

'Whets Their Appetite'

He continued:

"If you surrender or indicate in advance that you're not going to defend any part of the free world, and you figure that's going to satisfy them, it doesn't satisfy them. It only whets their appetite."

Mr. Kennedy replied that the Formosa Resolution of 1955, which he supported, had been backed by a letter from President Eisenhower to the chairman of the Senate Foreign Relations Committee, Senator Theodore Francis Green, Democrat of Rhode Island.

"Neither you nor any other American need feel that the United States will be involved in military hostilities merely in the defense of Quemoy and Matsu," the letter said. The commitment, Mr. Kennedy continued, was to defend Taiwan and the Pescadores, and "does not include these two islands."

Mr. Kennedy went on:

"What Mr. Nixon wants to do is commit us, as I understand him, so that we can be clear if there is a disagreement. He wants us to be committed to the defense of these islands merely as the defense of these islands as free territory, not as part of the defense of Formosa."

Mr. Nixon, however, was not going this far last night.

Attaches Conditions

He denied that the late Secretary of State, John Foster Dulles, had ever suggested that the islands should not be defended "in the event that they were attacked and that attack was a preliminary to an attack on Formosa."

Here again, Mr. Nixon attached conditions to the islands' defense.

He hoped Mr. Kennedy would change his position, he said, for "he is only encouraging the aggressors * * * to press us to the point where war is inevitable."

"I don't think it's possible for Mr. Nixon to state the record in distortion of the facts with more precision than he just did," Mr. Kennedy shot back.

Mr. Dulles had said that the Formosa Resolution excluded Quemoy and Matsu, Mr. Kennedy said. "Therefore that treaty does not commit the United States to defend anything except Formosa and the Pescadores and to deal with acts against that treaty area." He completely supported that position, he said.

Refers to Treaty

"I believe that we should meet our commitments and if the Chinese Communists attack the Pescadores and Formosa, they know that it will mean a war," he went on. "I would not hand over these islands under any point of gun. But I merely say that the treaty is quite precise and I sustain the treaty."

Mr. Nixon, he said, "would add a guarantee to islands five miles off the coast" of China "when he's never really protested the Communists seizing Cuba, ninety miles off the coast of the United States."

Answering other questions, Mr. Kennedy hammered away in an effort to break Mr. Nixon's grip on the "peace" issue. In 1954, he charged, Mr. Nixon had "talked" about "putting American boys into Indo china" during the war between the Communist Viet Minh and the French Army.

At the time of the U-2 espionage plane incident, he added Mr. Nixon said on May 15 that he favored continuing the

flights, although President Eisenhower three days earlier had ordered them suspended.

On economic matters, Mr. Kennedy said he favored a balanced Federal budget at all times, except during periods of "serious recession" and "national emergency."

The two men then fell to quarreling about each one's estimates of the cost of the other's programs. Mr. Kennedy said his farm program would cost $2,000,000,000 less than the present Administration farm program, while Mr. Nixon's would cost $1,000,000,000 more.

Mr. Nixon retorted that Mr. Kennedy's was the "worst program for the farmers America has ever foisted upon it" and would cost the consumer a 25 per cent rise in food costs.

Scores Interest Policy

Mr. Kennedy said he could reduce the budget by $1,000,000,000 by abandoning the high-interest policy. This policy, he said, has added $3,000,000,000 a year to the cost of funding the debt.

"What he's saying there is, 'We're going to have inflation,'" Mr. Nixon replied.

Mr. Kennedy said the Eisenhower program of medical care for the aged would cost Federal and state governments $2,000,000,000 in taxes. His own program would be financed through Social Security at a cost of "less than 3 cents per day per person," he said.

Mr. Kennedy, Mr. Nixon replied, was indulging in "a mirror game—here it is—here it isn't." A rise in Social Security costs was the same as a tax increase, he said.

On a question about the 27½ per cent depletion allowance for oil and gas producers, neither candidate favored reducing it. Mr. Kennedy noted that there were 104 commodities that enjoyed depletion allowances of some sort.

He favored reviewing all to see their merits as part of a general tax revision program to close "loopholes," he said.

Mr. Nixon came out flatly for maintaining the oil and gas allowance, "not because I want to make a lot of oil men rich, but because I want to make America rich."

TV Rating for Nation As High as 2d Debate's

Sixty million persons were estimated to have watched last night's third television debate between Vice President Nixon and Senator John F. Kennedy, according to the American Broadcasting Company.

This was the same as watched last Friday's second debate, and compared with 66,000,000 viewers for the Presidential candidates' first joint telecast Sept. 26, the network said. This was based on a Trendex reading in twenty-five cities, projected to estimate that 50.7 per cent of the nation's television sets were turned in on some program—and of these, 50.4 per cent watched the candidates.

In the New York metropolitan area, the A. C. Nielsen Company, another rating agency, said 38 per cent of sets were tuned in to the program. This compared with 54 per cent for the first debate, and 39 per cent for the second.

ORIGINATOR OF DEBATES

Blair Moody Jr., son of the late Democratic Senator from Michigan, thanked Robert Sarnoff yesterday for crediting his father with originating the idea for television debates between Presidential candidates.

In a letter to Mr. Sarnoff, chairman of the board of National Broadcasting Company, Mr. Moody said:

"I recall very vividly the time that this suggestion was made by my father, and it was very gracious of you to remember him and bestow upon him the credit for this idea."

Senator Moody died in 1954. Mr. Sarnoff cited his suggestion in a talk before the San Francisco Advertising Club.

October 14, 1960

Associated Press

JUST BEFORE THE DEBATE: Mrs. John F. Kennedy, at door of her husband's dressing room, views TV stage.

Nixon Hints a Fifth Debate, But It Depends on Schedule

By DOUGLAS DALES

Vice President Nixon indicated last night that he would accept Senator John F. Kennedy's proposal for a fifth nation-wide television and radio debate. But the Republican Presidential candidate said it would depend "solely on my schedule" and suggested he might make a debate of two hours' length a condition of his acceptance.

Questioned after his fourth debate last night at the American Broadcasting Company studios, he said he had always wanted debates of two hours.

As to his preference for a format for another meeting on the air waves with Mr. Kennedy, the Vice President said he preferred a program confined to questioning rather than having part of the time consumed by opening and closing statements, as was the case in the first and fourth meetings.

Kennedy Protests Gap

Senator Kennedy began pressing ten days ago for a fifth debate, arguing that the eighteen-day gap between last night's meeting and Election Day, Nov. 8, was too long.

As Mr. Nixon was making his comments on another debate, Senator Kennedy's press aide, Pierre Salinger, was telling reporters that his group was renewing its appeal.

Earlier in the day, the Democratic nominee had sent a telegram to Mr. Nixon urging him to tell the national television audience that he would accept other debates, and suggesting there might be more than five.

"I again strongly urge you to join me in discussing the issues in this election in a fifth debate to be held shortly before the election," the telegram stated.

"Only in this way," it continued, "will the American people be able to evaluate the arguments and issues which are raised in the closing days of the campaign. In fact, I believe that more than five debates would be helpful if the record were to be corrected properly.

"If you should relent in your opposition to further debates, and I invite you to do so in tonight's debate, I hope your representatives can contact mine to work out one or more dates at the earliest opportunity."

Until last night, Mr. Nixon had objected to a further encounter on the ground it would throw his campaign schedule out of kilter.

Kennedy aides, meanwhile, have implied that the Vice President was "afraid" to meet his opponent beyond the originally scheduled four debates.

Position May Change

There were indications earlier in the day that the Vice President might be changing his position on the Kennedy demand.

It was understood that Mr. Nixon met with several friends and advisers on Thursday night at the Waldorf-Astoria Hotel to discuss the question. Among those present were former President Herbert Hoover and Thomas E. Dewey, the Republican Presidential candidate in 1944 and 1948.

Mr. Nixon reportedly was told that his refusal of a fifth debate might be dangerous politically. For the last week Mr. Kennedy has been ridiculing Mr. Nixon's position with the argument that the Vice President boasted about "standing up to Mr. Khrushchev," but was unwilling to "stand up to" his opponent in this country.

Mr. Nixon remained in seclusion in his suite at the Waldorf-Astoria during the day, preparing and resting for the debate.

He arrived at the A. B. C. studios at 9:02 P. M., going unrecognized by a group of 150 of his supporters and about 350 Kennedy rooters, who shared the south side of the sidewalk on West Sixty-sixth Street. His car was driven down a ramp that took him inside the building.

Nixon Wears Make-Up

Mr. Nixon went directly to one of the two-room cottage-type dressing rooms that had been constructed for the nominees, and underwent a fifteen-minute test before the cameras before the program started. He wore make-up for the debate, although Mr. Kennedy rejected it.

Mrs. Nixon remained at the hotel and watched the program with a group of friends.

The studio temperature was reported at just over 71 degrees when the program started. In Mr. Nixon's dressing room, it was 56 degrees.

Two glasses of water were placed on the podium during the program, but he was not observed to take a drink. Although Mr. Kennedy rarely looked at his rival, Mr. Nixon turned half way around and watched as the Senator spoke. Neither used notes.

The candidates shook hands briefly immediately after the program.

"It's interesting," Mr. Kennedy said.

"I'll answer your wire," Mr. Nixon called after his Democratic opponent as Mr. Kennedy left the set.

Asked for his comment on the debate, Mr. Nixon said: "It was a good exchange and the voters will determine it."

Mr. Nixon's press secretary, Herbert G. Klein, said last night that the Republican candidate won "a clear-cut victory" in the fourth debate with Senator Kennedy.

NIXON AND KENNEDY DEBATE CUBA; ALSO CLASH OVER QUEMOY ISSUE, ATOM TESTING AND U.S. PRESTIGE

Associated Press

FACE TO FACE: Senator John F. Kennedy turns toward Vice President Nixon during their fourth debate, in a scene photographed as it appeared on the TV screen last night.

CHARGES TRADED

Most Heated Dispute Concerns Methods of Dealing With Castro

By RUSSELL BAKER

Vice President Nixon and Senator John F. Kennedy clashed before a national television audience last night over United States policy toward Cuba and the Chinese offshore islands of Quemoy and Matsu.

In one of the sharpest exchanges of their fourth debate, which seemed comparatively tepid after the last two meetings, Mr. Nixon called Senator Kennedy's proposals for dealing with Premier Fidel Castro's regime in Cuba "probably the most dangerously irresponsible that he's made in the course of this campaign."

If carried out, the Vice President said, his rival's policies would probably cost this country "all our friends in Latin America," lead to its condemnation in the United Nations and produce a "civil war" in Cuba, with the Soviet Union probably involved.

Mr. Kennedy replied that the Nixon proposal for "quarantining" Cuba through economic sanctions would be useless because the Administration did not have the cooperation of other Latin-American and European states in the effort to put economic pressure on the Castro Government.

Debate Nuclear Tests

These were the other major points as the candidates discussed foreign policy in the hour-long program:

¶Nuclear testing. Mr. Nixon proposed making a decision before Jan. 1 for resuming nuclear testing underground unless Moscow indicated it was ready to move toward agreement. Senator Kennedy proposed "one last effort" after the next President

takes office to reach a testing agreement with the Russians. If that failed, he said, tests should be resumed underground or in outer space.

¶United States prestige. Mr. Nixon, accusing Senator Kennedy of contributing to a decline in American prestige, said his opponent was "dead wrong" in picturing the country as "standing still." Diplomatically, in relative military strength and in economic strength, Mr. Kennedy replied, this country is "standing still."

¶Summit meetings. Mr. Nixon said that there should be no further meetings with Premier Khrushchev unless there was reasonable assurance that the Premier was willing to negotiate seriously on agenda points on which there was some likelihood of agreement. Mr. Kennedy said he would not participate in a summit conference unless there was some indication that agreement was possible on Berlin, outer space, general disarmament or nuclear testing.

In response to one question,

each man declined to give any indication of whom he might nominate as Secretary of State

Mr. Nixon, asked about a United States Information Agency report purportedly showing a drop in this country's world prestige, said it applied only to the period immediately following the Soviet Union's first sputnik success in 1957, and that he had no objection to having it made public. Immediately after the program Pierre Salinger, Mr. Kennedy's press secretary, said Mr. Kennedy had asked the State Department to release the document.

Mr. Kennedy, in another of the sharper exchanges of the night, challenged Mr. Nixon to deny that President Eisenhower had sent missions to Chiang Kai-shek to persuade the Chinese Nationalists to withdraw their forces from Quemoy and Matsu.

At this point on the television screen, Mr. Nixon's mouth was seen to move, but the sound was off and his reply was not heard. Opportunity for further questioning ended at this time and neither man returned to the point in his statement of summation.

Last night's debate was conducted in the American Broadcasting Company's television center here for simultaneous showing on three television networks and broadcasting on four radio networks.

Few new points of controversy were developed. For much of the time the candidates restated positions already laid out on the stump or in previous television appearances. In terms of conflict, it was probably the tamest since the first debate from Chicago on Sept. 26.

For last night's debate, the candidates went back to the format they used for their first meeting in Chicago. Each made eight-minute opening statements and three-minute closing statements. The time between was used to answer questions from a panel of four television newsmen.

Four Panelists

The questioners were John Edwards of the American Broadcasting Company, Walter Cronkite of the Columbia Broadcasting System, Frank Singiser of the Mutual Broadcasting System and John Chancellor of the National Broadcasting Company.

Each was selected by his network. In the second and third programs, panels of newsmen had used the entire hour to put questions to the candidates. Opening and closing statements were not permitted.

The moderator for last night's debate was Quincy Howe of A. B. C.

The two principal points of conflict last night were Cuba and the offshore islands.

On Cuba, Mr. Nixon said his policies were "very different" from Mr. Kennedy's. On Thursday Mr. Kennedy proposed, among other things, helping opponents of the Castro regime, within and without Cuba, to work to overthrow it.

Fears Civil War

Mr. Nixon said that this country's treaty commitments with Latin America and its obligations under the United Nations Charter specifically forbade it to intervene in the internal affairs of another state.

If Mr. Kennedy's suggestion were followed, he said, "we'd lose all our friends in Latin America, we'd probably be condemned in the United Nations and we wouldn't accomplish our objective."

The result would probably be "civil war" in Latin America with the Soviet Union engaged on one side, he declared. The correct policy, he said, was the course that has been taken→ that is, to "quarantine" Cuba economically.

This course was condemned by Mr. Kennedy Thursday as "useless" on the ground the action was unilateral on the part of the United States and did not involve the cooperation of other states trading with Cuba.

Mr. Kennedy restated this argument last night. Replying to Mr. Nixon's argument against helping anti-Castro elements, he said most of the arms that had helped Dr. Castro to overthrow the regime of Fulgencio Batista had been supplied from sources inside the United States.

The Quemoy-Matsu issue was first raised when Mr. Nixon, in his opening statement, suggested that Mr. Kennedy favored "slicing off a piece of free territory and, in effect, abandoning it to the Communists."

This was an issue that had flared through the two previous debates and has become progressively fuzzier as the two candidates have modulated their positions.

Basically, Mr. Kennedy first suggested that Chiang Kai-shek should be urged to withdraw from the islands because they are indefensible and of no strategic value.

Mr. Nixon at first said that this was "the same kind of woolly thinking" that produced the Korean War, that no territory "in the area of freedom" should be abandoned, as a matter of "principle."

Subsequently, Mr. Kennedy said he would defend the islands against Communist attack if that attack were part of a Communist attack on Taiwan and Penghu. Mr. Nixon modified his first stand to say he would defend the islands if an attack were a "prelude" to an attack on Taiwan.

Mr. Kennedy said Mr. Nixon had "retreated" to Mr. Kennedy's position and proposed that the debate on the issue be ended.

Sees 'Fundamental Error'

Last night, however, Mr. Nixon declared that Senator Kennedy was persisting in a "fundamental error." In the Senate in 1955, and subsequently, the Vice President said, Mr. Kennedy supported the proposal that a line should be drawn that would specifically exclude Quemoy and Matsu from the area of United States defense.

"If he will retract," Mr. Nixon said, "then this will be right out of the campaign."

But, he went on, "the minute you draw a line, you encourage the Communists to attack." This, parenthetically, was at variance with the doctrine of the late John Foster Dulles, who insisted that the Communists be given clear notice of what territory this country would defend to prevent the possibility of war by miscalculation.

Mr. Kennedy replied that President Eisenhower had sent a mission to Chiang Kai-shek to persuade Chiang to withdraw from the islands. The mission consisted of Admiral Arthur W. Radford, former chairman of the Joint Chiefs of Staff, and Walter S. Robertson, former Assistant Secretary of State for Far Eastern Affairs, he said.

Chiang refused to withdraw, leaving this country "in a difficult position," Mr. Kennedy said. But the first position taken by the Administration was "that we should draw this line," Mr. Kennedy said.

"I challenge you to deny that."

At that point the camera switched to Mr. Nixon but his words were lost.

The opening and closing statements by both candidates were essentially abbreviated versions of the basic campaign speeches they have been delivering six times daily for the last six weeks.

Transcript of the Fourth Kennedy-Nixon Debate

Flolowing is the transcript of last night's television debate between Vice President Nixon and Senator John F. Kennedy, as recorded by The New York Times.:

QUINCY HOWE—I'm Quincy Howe of A. B. C. News saying good evening from New York where the two major candidates for President of the United States are about to engage in their fourth radio-television discussion of the present campaign.

Tonight these men will confine that discussion to foreign policy.

Good evening, Vice President Nixon.

MR. NIXON—Good evening, Mr. Howe.

MR. HOWE—And good evening, Senator Kennedy.

MR. KENNEDY—Good evening, Mr. Howe.

MR. HOWE: Now let me read the rules and conditions under which the candidates themselves have agreed to proceed. As they did in their first meeting, both men will make opening statements of about eight minutes each and closing statements of equal time running three to five minutes each.

During the half-hour between the opening and closing statements, the candidates will answer and comment upon questions from a panel of four correspondents chosen by the nation-wide networks that carry the program. Each candidate will be questioned in turn with opportunity for comment by the other. Each answer will be limited to two and one-half minutes, each comment to one and one-half minutes.

The correspondents are free to ask any questions they choose in the field of foreign affairs. Neither candidate knows what questions will be asked. Time alone will determine the final question.

Reversing the order in their first meeting, Senator Kennedy will make the second opening statement and the first closing statement. For the first opening statement, here is Vice President Nixon.

MR. NIXON — Mr. Howe, Senator Kennedy, my fellow Americans:

Since this campaign began I have had a very rare privilege.

I have traveled through forty-eight of the fifty states and in my travels I have learned what the people of the United States are thinking about.

There is one issue that stands out above all the rest, one in which every American is concerned, regardless of what group he may be a member and regardless of where he may live.

And that issue, very simply stated, is this:

How can we keep the peace—keep it without surrender?

How can we extend freedom—extend it without war?

Now, in determining how we deal with this issue, we must find the answer to a very important but simple question: Who threatens the peace? Who threatens freedom in the world?

Cites Threat to Peace

There is only one threat to peace and one threat to freedom—that is presented by the international Communist movement. And, therefore, if we are to have peace, if we are to keep our own freedom and extend it to others without war we must know how to deal with the Communists and their leaders.

I know Mr. Khrushchev. I also have had the opportunity of knowing and meeting other Communist leaders in the world. I believe there are certain principles we must find in dealing with him and his colleagues—principles, if followed, that will keep the peace and that also can extend fredom.

First we have to learn from the past, because we cannot afford to make the mistakes from the past.

In the seven years before this Administration came into power in Washington we found that 600,000,000 people went behind the Iron Curtain.

And at the end of that seven years we were engaged in a war in Korea which cost over 30,000 American lives.

In the past seven years, in President Eisenhower's Administration, this situation has been reversed.

We ended the Korean war. By strong, firm leadership we have kept out of other wars and we have avoided surrender of principle or territory at the conference table.

Lists 'Fatal Error'

Now why were we successful, as our predecessors were not successful?

I think there's several reasons. In the first place, they made a fatal error in misjudging the Communists; in trying to apply to them the same rules of conduct that you would apply to the leaders of the free world. One of the major errors they made was the one that led to the Korean war. In ruling out the defense of Korea, they invited aggression in that area. They thought they were going to have peace—it brought war.

We learned from their mistakes. And so, in our seven years, we find that we have been firm in our diplomacy; we have never made concessions without getting concessions in return.

We have always been willing to go the extra mile to negotiate for disarmament or in any other area. But we have never been willing to do anything that, in effect, surrendered freedom any place in the world.

That is why President Eisenhower was correct in not apologizing or expressing regrets to Mr. Khrushchev at the Paris conference, as Senator Kennedy suggested he could have done.

That is why Senator—President Eisenhower was also correct in his policy in the Formosa Straits, where he declined, and refused to follow the recommendations — recommendations which Senator Kennedy voted for in 1955; again made in 1959; again repeated in his debates that you have heard—recommendations with regard to—again—slicing off a piece of free territory, and abandoning it, in effect, to the Communists.

Why did the President feel this was wrong and why was the President right, his critics wrong? Because again this showed a lack of understanding of dictators, a lack of understanding particularly of Communists, because every time you make such a concession it does not lead to peace. It only encourages them to blackmail you. It encourages them to begin a war.

And so I say that the record shows that we know how to keep the peace, to keep it without surrender.

Let us move now to the future.

It is not enough to stand on this record because we are dealing with the most ruthless, fanatical leaders that the world has ever seen.

That is why I say that in this period of the Sixties, Americans must move forward in every area.

First of all, although we are today, as Senator Kennedy has admitted, the strongest nation in the world militarily, we must increase our strength, increase it so that we will always have enough strength that regardless of what our potential opponents have—if they should launch a surprise attack—we will be able to destroy their war-making capability.

'National Suicide'

They must know, in other words, that it is national suicide if they begin anything.

We need this kind of strength because we're the guardians of the peace.

In addition to military strength, we need to see that the economy of this country continues to grow. It has grown in the past seven years. It can and will grow even more in the next four.

And the reason that it must grow even more is because we have things to do at home and also because we're in a race for survival—a race in which it isn't enough to be ahead.

It isn't enough simply to be complacent. We have to move ahead in order to stay ahead.

And that is why, in this field, I have made recommendations which I am confident will make the American economy ahead move it firmly and soundly so that there will never be a time when the Soviet Union will

be able to challenge our superiority in this field.

Firmness, Not Belligerance

And so we need military strength, we need economic strength, we also need the right diplomatic policies. What are they? Again we turn to the past. Firmness but no belligerence, and by no belligerence I mean that we do not answer insult by insult. When you are proud and confident of your strength, you do not get down to the level of Mr. Khrushchev and his colleagues. And that example that President Eisenhower was set we will continue to follow.

But all this by itself is not enough. It is not enough for us simply to be the strongest nation militarily, the strongest economically, and also to have firm diplomacy. We must have a great goal. And that is not just to keep freedom for ourselves but to extend it to all the world, to extend it to all the world because that is America's destiny. To extend it to all the world because the Communist aim is not to hold their own but to extend communism. And you cannot fight a victory for communism or a strategy for victory for communism with the strategy simply of holding the line.

And so I say that we believe that our policies of military strength, of economic strength, of diplomatic firmness first will keep the peace and keep it without surrender. We also believe that in the great field of ideals that we can lead America to the victory for freedom, victory in the newly developing countries, victory also in the captive countries, provided we have faith in ourselves and faith in our principles.

MR. HOWE—Now the opening statement of Senator Kennedy.

SENATOR KENNEDY—Mr. Howe, Mr. Vice President. First, let me again try to correct the record on the matter of Quemoy and Matsu.

I voted for the Formosa [Taiwan] resolution in 1955. I have sustained it since then. I've said that I agree with the Administration policy. Mr. Nixon earlier indicated that he would defend Quemoy and Matsu even if the attack on these islands, two miles off the coast of China, were not part of a general attack upon Formosa and the Pescadores [Penghu].

I indicated that I would defend those islands if the attack were directed against Pescadores and Formosa, which is part of the Eisenhower policy. I've supported that policy.

So that really isn't an issue in this campaign. It isn't an issue with Mr. Nixon, who now says that he also supports the Eisenhower policy. Nor is the

question that all Americans want peace and security an issue in this campaign.

The question is: Are we moving in the direction of peace and security? Is our relative strength growing? Is, as Mr. Nixon says, our prestige at an all-time high, as he said a week ago, and that of the Communists at an all-time low? I don't believe it is. I don't believe that our relative strength is increasing.

And I say that not as the Democratic standard-bearer, but as a citizen of the United States who is concerned about the United States.

I look at Cuba, ninety miles off the coast of the United States. In 1957 I was in Havana. I talked to the American Ambassador there. He said that he was the second most powerful man in Cuba. And yet even though Ambassador Smith and Ambassador Gardner, both Republican ambassadors, both warned of Castro, the Marxist influences around Castro, the Communist influences around Castro, both of them have testified in the last six weeks, that, in spite of their warnings to the American Government, nothing was done.

Our security depends upon Latin America. Can any American looking at the situation in Latin America feel contented with what's happening today, when a candidate for the Presidency of Brazil feels it necessary to call not on Washington during the campaign but on Castro in Havana, in order to pick up the support of the Castro supporters in Brazil?

At the Inter-American Conference this summer, when we wanted them to join together in the denunciation of Castro and the Cuban Communists, we couldn't even get the Inter-American group to join together in denouncing Castro. It was rather a vague statement that they finally made.

Do you know today that the Russians broadcast ten times as many programs in Spanish to Latin-America as we do? Do you know we don't have a single program sponsored by our Government to Cuba to tell them we are their friends; that we want them to be free again?

Africa is now the emerging area of the world. It contains 25 per cent of all the members of the General Assembly. We didn't even have a Bureau of African Affairs until 1957.

In the Africa south of the Sahara, which is the major new section we have less students from all of Africa in that area studying under government auspices today than from the country of Thailand.

If there's one thing Africa needs it's technical assistance. And yet last year we gave them less than 5 per cent of all the technical assistance funds that we distributed around the world.

We relied in the Middle East on the Baghdad Pact, and yet when the Iraqi Government was changed, the Baghdad Pact broke down. We relied on the Eisenhower Doctrine for the Middle East, which passed the

Senate.

There isn't one country in the Middle East that now endorses the Eisenhower Doctrine.

We look to Asia because the struggle is in the under-developed world.

Which system, communism or freedom, will triumph in the next five or ten years? That's what should concern us, not the history of ten, or fifteen, or twenty years ago. But are we doing enough in these areas? What are freedom's chances in those areas?

By 1965 or 1970, will there be other Cubas in Latin America? Will Guinea and Ghana, which have now voted with the Communists frequently as newly independent countries of Africa—will there be others?

Will the Congo go Communist? Will other countries? Are we doing enough in that area?

And what about Asia? Is India going to win the economic struggle? Or is China going to win it? Who will dominate Asia in the next five or ten years? Communism? The Chinese? Or will freedom?

The question which we have to decide as Americans—are we doing enough today? Is our strength and prestige rising? Do people want to be identified with us? Do they want to follow the United States leadership?

I don't think they do, enough. And that's what concerns me.

In Africa—these countries that have newly joined the United Nations. On the question of admission of Red China, only two countries in all of Africa voted with us—Liberia and the Union of South Africa. The rest either abstained or voted against us.

More countries in Asia voted against us on that question than voted with us.

I believe that this struggle is going to go on, and it may be well decided in the next decade. I have seen Cuba go to the Communists. I have seen Communist influence and Castro influence rise in Latin America. I have seen us ignore Africa. There are six countries in Africa that are members of the United Nations. There isn't a single American diplomatic representative in any of those six.

When Guinea became independent, the Soviet Ambassador showed up that very day. We didn't recognize them for two months. The American Ambassador didn't show up for nearly eight months.

I believe that the world is changing fast. And I don't think this Administration has shown the foresight, has shown the knowledge, has been identified with the great fight which these people are waging to be free, to get a better standard of living to live better. The average income in some of those countries is $25 a year. The Communists say, "Come with us; look what we've done." And we've been, on the whole, uninterested.

I think we're going to have to do better.

Mr. Nixon talks about our being the strongest country in the world. I think we are today. But we were far stronger relative to the Communists five years ago, and what is of great concern is that the balance of power is in danger of moving with them.

They made a breakthrough in missiles, and by 1961-2-3 they will be outnumbering us in missiles. I'm not as confident as he is that we will be the strongest military power by 1963.

He talks about economic growth as a great indicator for freedom. I agree with him. What we do in this country, the kind of society that we build, that will tell whether freedom will be sustained around the world.

And yet, in the last nine months of this year, we've had a drop in our economic growth rather than a gain. We've had the lowest rate of increase in economic growth in the last nine months of any major industrialized society in the world.

I look up and see the Soviet flag on the moon.

The fact is that the State Department polls on our prestige and influence around the world have shown such a sharp drop that up till now the State Department has been unwilling to release them.

And yet they were polled by the U. S. I. A. The point of all this is, this is a struggle in which we're engaged. We want peace. We want freedom. We want security. We want to be stronger. We want freedom to gain.

But I don't believe in these changing and revolutionary times this Administration has known that the world is changing—has identified itself with that change.

I think the Communists have been moving with vigor—Laos, Africa, Cuba—all around the world they're on the move.

I think we have to revitalize our society. I think we have to demonstrate to the people of the world that we're determined in this free country of ours to be first—not first if, and not first but, not first when—but first, and when we are strong and when we are first, then freedom gains.

Then the prospects for peace increase and the prospects for our security gain.

MR. HOWE—That completes the opening statements. Now the candidates will answer and comment upon questions put by these four correspondents — Frank Singiser of Mutual News, John Edwards of A. B. C. News, Walter Cronkite of C. B. S. News, John Chancellor of N.B.C. News. Frank Singiser has the first question for Vice President Nixon.

MR. SINGISER — Mr. Vice President: I'd like to pin down the difference between the way you would handle Castro's regime and prevent the establishments of Communist governments in the Western Hemisphere and the way that Senator Kennedy would proceed. Vice President Nixon, in what important respect do you feel there are differences between you, and why do you believe your policy is better for the peace and security of the United States in the Western Hemisphere?

MR. NIXON — Our policies are very different. I think that Senator Kennedy's policies and recommendations for the handling of the Castro regime are probably the most dangerously irresponsible recommendations that he has made during the course of this campaign.

In effect, what Senator Kennedy recommends is that the United States Government should give help to the exiles and to those within Cuba who oppose the Castro regime—provided they are anti-Batista.

Now let's just see what this means. We have five treaties with Latin America, including the one setting up the Organization of American States in Bogotá in 1948 in which we have agreed not to intervene in the internal affairs of any other American country—and they as well have agreed to do likewise.

The charter of the United Nations, its Preamble, Article I and Article II also provide that there shall be no intervention by one nation in the internal affairs of another. Now I don't know what Senator Kennedy suggests when he says that we should help those who oppose the Castro regime, both in Cuba and without.

But I do know this, that if we were to follow that recommendation, that we would lose all of our friends in Latin America, we would probably be condemned in the United Nations, and we would not accomplish our objective.

I know something else. It would be an open invitation for Mr. Khrushchev to come in, to come in to Latin America and to engage us in what would be a civil war, and possibly even worse than that.

This is the major recommendation that he's made. Now, what can we do? Well, we can do what we did with Guatemala. There was a Communist dictator that we inherited from the previous Administration.

We quarantined Mr. Arbenz. The result was that the Guatemalan people themselves eventually rose up and they threw him out.

We are quarantining Mr. Castro today. We're quarantining him diplomatically by bringing back our Ambassador; economically by cutting off trade, and Senator Kennedy's suggestion that the trade we cut off is not significant is just 100 per cent wrong. We are cutting off the significant items that the Cuban regime needs in order to survive. By cutting off trade, by cutting off our diplomatic relations as we have, we will quarantine this regime so that the people of Cuba themselves will take care of Mr. Castro.

But for us to do what Senator Kennedy has suggested would bring results which I know he would not want, and certainly which the American people would not want.

MR. KENNEDY—Mr. Nixon shows himself misinformed. He surely must be aware that most of the equipment and arms and resources for Castro came from the United States, flown out of Florida and other parts of the United States to Castro in the mountains.

There isn't any doubt about that—No. 1.

No. 2, I believe that if any economic sanctions against Latin America are going to be successful they have to be multilateral. They have to include the other countries of Latin America. The very minute effect of the action which has been taken this week on Cuba's economy—I believe Castro can replace those markets very easily through Latin America, through Europe and through Eastern Europe.

If the United States had stronger prestige and influence in Latin America it could persuade, as Franklin Roosevelt did in 1940, the countries of Latin America to join in an economic quarantine of Castro. That's the only way you can bring real economic pressure on the Castro regime. And also the countries of Western Europe, Canada, Japan and the others.

No. 3, Castro is only the beginning of our difficulties throughout Latin America. The big struggle will be to prevent the influence of Castro spreading to other countries—Mexico, Panama, Brazil, Bolivia, Colombia.

We're going to have to try to provide closer ties; to associate ourselves with the great desire of these people for a better life if we're going to prevent Castro's influence from spreading throughout all of Latin America.

His influence is strong enough today to prevent us from getting the other countries of Latin America to join with us in economic quarantine.

His influence is growing mostly because this Administration has ignored Latin America.

You, yourself, said, Mr. Vice President, a month ago, that if we had provided the kind of economic aid five years ago that we are now providing we might never have had Castro. Why didn't we?

MR. HOWE—John Edwards has his first question for Senator Kennedy.

MR. EDWARDS — Senator Kennedy, one test of a new President's leadership will be the caliber of his appointments. It's a matter of interest here and overseas as to who will be the new Secretary of State. Now, under our rules, I must ask this question of you, but I would hope that the Vice President also would answer it. Will you give us the names of three or four Americans, each of whom, if appointed, would serve with distinction, in your judgment, as Secretary of State?

MR. KENNEDY—Mr. Edwards, I don't think it's a wise idea for a Presidential candidate to appoint the members of his Cabinet prospectively, or to suggest four people or indicate that one of them should be appointed.

This is a decision that the President of the United States must make. The last candidate who indicated that he knew who his Cabinet was going to be was Mr. Dewey in 1948

This is a race between the Vice President and myself for the Presidency of the United States. There are a good many able men who could be Secretary of State.

I've made no judgment about who should be the Secretary of State. I think that judgment could be made after election, if I'm successful.

The people have to make a choice between Mr. Nixon and myself, between the Republican party and the Democratic party; between our approach to the problems which now disturb us as a nation and disturb us as a world power.

The President bears the constitutional responsibility, not the Secretary of State, for the conduct of foreign affairs. Some Presidents have been strong in foreign policy; others have relied heavily on the Secretary of State.

I've been a member of the Senate Foreign Relations Committee; I run for the Presidency with full knowledge that his great responsibility, really, given to him by the Constitution and by the force of events, is in the field of foreign affairs.

I'm asking the people's support as President. We will select the best men we can get. But I've not made a judgment, and I have not narrowed down a list of three or four people, among whom would be the candidate.

MR. HOWE—Mr. Vice President, do you have a comment?

NIXON—Well, Mr. Edwards, as you probably know, I have consistently answered all questions with regard to who will be in the next Cabinet by saying that that is the responsibility of the next President, and it would be inappropriate to make any decisions on that or to announce any prior to the time that I had the right to do so. So that was my answer to this question.

If you don't mind, I'd like to use the balance of the time to respond to one of the comments that Senator Kennedy made on the previous question.

He was talking about the Castro regime and what we had been doing in Latin America. I would like to point out that when we look at our programs in Latin America, we find that we have appropriated five times as much for Latin America as was appropriated by the previous Administration; we find that we have two billion dollars more for the Export-Import Bank, that we have a new bank for Latin America alone of a billion dollars. We have the new program which was submitted at the Bogotá Conference—this new program that President Eisenhower submitted, approved by the last Congress for $500,000,000. We have moved in Latin America very effectively, and I'd also like to point this out:

Senator Kennedy complains very appropriately about our inadequate radio broadcasts for Latin America. Let me point out again that his Congress—the Democratic Congress—has cut $80,000,000 off of the Voice of America appropriations. Now, he has to get a better job out of his Congress if he's going to get us the money that we need to conduct the foreign

421

affairs of this country in Latin America or any place else.

MR. HOWE—Walter Cronkite, you have your first question for Vice President Nixon.

Q.—Mr. Vice President, Senator Fulbright and now, tonight, Senator Kennedy maintain that the Administration is suppressing a report by the United States Information Agency that shows a decline in United States prestige overseas. Are you aware of such a report, and if you are aware of the existence of such a report, should not that report, because of the great importance this issue has been given in this campaign, be released to the public?

MR. NIXON—Mr. Cronkite, I naturally am aware of it, because I, of course, pay attention to everything Senator Kennedy says, as well as Senator Fulbright. Now, in this connection I want to point out that the facts simply aren't as stated.

First of all the report to which Senator Kennedy refers is one that was made many, many months ago and related particularly to the period immediately after Sputnik.

Second, as far as this report is concerned, I would have no objection to having it made public.

Third, I would say this with regard to this report, with regard to Gallup Polls of prestige abroad and everything else that we've been hearing about "what about American prestige abroad."

America's prestige abroad will be just as high as the spokesmen for America allow it to be. Now, when we have a Presidential candidate, for example, Senator Kennedy—stating over and over again that the United States is second in space and the fact of the matter is that the space score today is 28-to-8—we've had twenty-eight successful shots, they've had eight—when he states that we're second in education, and I have seen Soviet education and I've seen ours, and we're not, that we're second in science because they may be ahead in one area or another, when over-all we're way ahead of the Soviet Union and all other countries in science; when he says as he did in January of this year that we have the worst slums, that we have the most crowded schools; when he says that 17,000,000 people go to bed hungry every night; when he makes statements like this, what does this do to American prestige?

Well, it can only have the effect certainly of reducing it. Let me make one thing clear. Senator Kennedy has the responsibility to criticize those things that are wrong, but he has also responsibility to be right in his criticism.

Every one of these iter , that I have mentioned he's been wrong—dead wrong. And for that reason he has contributed to any lack of prestige.

Finally, let me say this:

As far as prestige is concerned, the first place it would show up would be in the United Nations.

Now Senator Kennedy has referred to the vote on Communist China. Let's look at the vote on

Hungary. There we got more votes for condemning Hungary and looking into that situation than we got the last year.

Let's look at the reaction to Khrushchev and Eisenhower at the last U. N. session. Did Khrushchev gain because he took his shoe off and pounded the table and shouted and insulted?

Not at all.

The President gained. America gained by continuing the dignity, the decency that has characterized us and it's that that keeps up the prestige of America up, not running down America the way Senator Kennedy has been running her down.

MR. HOWE—Comment, Senator Kennedy?

MR. KENNEDY—I really don't need Mr. Nixon to tell me about what my responsibilities are as a citizen.

I've served this country for fourteen years in the Congress and before that in the service. I've just as high a devotion, just as high an opinion.

What I downgrade, Mr. Nixon, is the leadership the country is getting, not the country. Now I didn't make most of the statement that you said I made.

I believe the Soviet Union is first in outer space.

We may have made more shots but the size of their rocket thrust and all the rest—you yourself said to Khrushchev, "you may be ahead of us in rocket thrust but we're ahead of you in color television" in your famous discussion in the kitchen.

I think that color television is not as important as rocket thrust.

Secondly, I didn't say we had the worst slums in the world. I said we had too many slums.

And that they are bad, that we ought to do something about them, that we ought to support housing legislation which this Administration has opposed.

Denies Statement

I didn't say we had the worst education in the world. What I said was that ten years ago, we were producing twice as many scientists and engineers than the Soviet Union and today they're producing twice as many as we are and this affects our security around the world.

And fourth, I believe that the poll and other studies and votes in the United Nations and anyone reading the paper and any citizen of the United States must come to the conclusion that the United States no longer carries the same image of a vital society on the move with its brightest days ahead as it carried a decade or two decades ago.

Part of that is because we stood still here at home, because we haven't met our problems in the United States, because we haven't had a moving economy.

Part of that, as the Gallup Polls show, is because the Soviet Union made a breakthrough in outer space.

Mr. George Allen, head of your Information Service, has said that that made the people of the world begin to wonder whether we were first in science.

We're first in other areas of science but in space, which is the new science, we're not first.

MR. HOWE—John Chancellor, your first question for Senator Kennedy.

MR. CHANCELLOR—Senator, another question in connection with our relations with the Russians. There have been stories from Washington from the Atomic Energy Commission hinting that the Russians may have resumed the testing of nuclear devices.

Now, sir, if this is true, should the United States resume nuclear testing, and if the Russians do not start testing, can you perceive any circumstances in 1961 in which the United States might resume its own series of tests?

MR. KENNEDY—Yes, I think the next President of the United States should make one last effort to secure an agreement on the cessation of tests.

Number one, I think we should go back to Geneva, whoever is elected President, Mr. Nixon or myself, and try once again. If we fail then, if we're unable to come to an agreement—and I hope we can come to an agreement, because it does not merely involve now the United States, Britain, France and the Soviet Union as atomic powers, because of new breakthroughs in atomic energy technology there's some indication that by the time the next President's term of office has come to an end, there may be ten, fifteen or twenty countries with an atomic capacity; perhaps that many testing bombs with all the effect that it could have on the atmosphere and with all the chances that more and more countries will have an atomic capacity, with more and more chance of war. So one more effort should be made.

I don't think that even if that effort fails that it will be necessary to carry on tests in the atmosphere which pollute the atmosphere. They can be carried out underground, they could be carried on in outer space. But I believe the effort should be made once more by whoever is elected President of the United States. If we fail, it's been a great serious failure for everyone—for the human race.

I hope we can succeed. Then if we fail responsibility will be clearly on the Russians and then we'll have to meet our responsibilities to the security of the United States, and there may have to be testing underground. I think the Atomic Energy Committee is prepared for it. There may be testing in outer space.

I hope it will not be necessary for any power to resume testing in the atmosphere. It's possible to detect those kind of tests. The kind of tests which you can't detect are underground or perhaps in outer space. So that I'm hopeful that we can try once more. If we fail then we must meet our responsibilities to ourselves.

But I'm most concerned about the whole problem of the spread of atomic weapons. China may have it by 1963, Egypt. War has been the constant companion of mankind, so to have these weapons disseminated

around the world, I believe means that we're going to move through a period of hazard in the next few years. We ought to make one last effort.

Any comment, Mr. Vice President?

Negotiations Cited

MR. NIXON—Yes. I would say first of all that we must have in mind the fact that we have been negotiating to get tests inspected and to get an agreement for many, many months.

As a matter of fact, there's been a moratorium on testing as a result of the fact that we have been negotiating.

I've reached the conclusion that the Soviet Union is actually filibustering. I've reached the conclusion, too, based on the reports that have been made, that they may be cheating. I don't think we can wait until the next President is inaugurated and then selects a new team and then all the months of negotiating that will take place before we reach a decision.

I think that immediately after this election we should set a timetable—the next President, working with the present President, President Eisenhower—a time-table to break the Soviet filibuster. There should be no tests in the atmosphere.

That rules out any fall-out. But as far as underground tests are concerned and particularly underground tests for developing peaceful uses of atomic energy, we should not allow this Soviet filibuster to continue.

I think it's time for them to fish or to cut bait. I think that the next President immediately after his election should sit down with the President, work out a timetable and get a decision on this before January of next year.

MR. HOWE—Our second round of questions begins with one from Mr. Edwards for the Vice President.

MR. EDWARDS—Mr. Nixon, carrying forward this business about a timetable; as you know, the pressures are increasing for a summit conference. Now, both you and Senator Kennedy have said there are certain conditions which must be met before you would meet with Khrushchev. Will you be more specific about these conditions?

MR. NIXON—Well, the conditions I laid out in one of our previous television debates—and it's rather difficult to be much more specific than that.

First of all, we have to have adequate preparation for a summit conference. This means at the Secretary of State level and at the Ambassadorial level.

By adequate preparation I mean that at that level we must prepare an agenda, an agenda agreed upon with the approval of the heads of state involved.

Now this agenda should delineate those issues on which there is a possibility of some agreement or negotiation. I don't believe we should go to a summit conference unless we have such an agenda, unless we have some reasonable assurance from Mr. Khrushchev that he intends seriously, to negotiate on the points.

Now this may seem like a

rigid, inflexible position. But let's look at the other side of the coin.

If we build up the hopes of the world by having a summit conference that is not adequately prepared and, then, if Mr. Khrushchev finds some excuse for breaking it up—as he did this one—because he isn't going to get his way, we'd set back the cause of peace. We could not help it.

We can, in other words, negotiate many of these items of difference between us without going to the summit. I think we have to make a greater effort than we have been making at the Secretary of State level, at the Ambassadorial level, to work out the differences that we have.

And so as far as the summit conference is concerned, it should only be entered upon, it should only be agreed upon if the negotiations have reached a point that we have some reasonable assurance that something is going to come out of it, other than some phony spirit—a spirit of Geneva, or Camp David, or whatever it is.

When I say "phony spirit," I mean phony, not because the spirit is not good on our side, but because the Soviet Union simply doesn't intend to carry out what they say.

Now, these are the conditions that I can lay out. I can not be more precise than that, because, until we see what Mr. Khrushchev does and what he says, we cannot indicate what our plans will be.

MR. HOWE—Any comments, Senator Kennedy?

Refers to Summit

MR. KENNEDY — Well, I think the President of the United States last winter indicated that before he'd go to the summit in May, when he did last fall, he indicated that there should be some agenda, that there should be some prior agreement. He hoped that there would be an agreement in part in disarmament. He also expressed the hope that there should be some understanding of the general situation in Berlin.

The Soviet Union refused to agree to that, and we went to the summit and it was disastrous. I believe we should not go to the summit until there is some reason to believe that a meeting of minds can be obtained on either Berlin, outer space, or general disarmament —including nuclear testing.

In addition, I believe the next President in January and February should go to work in building the strength of the United States. The Soviet Union does understand strength.

We arm to parley, Winston Churchill said ten years ago. If we are strong, particularly as we face a crisis over Berlin, which we may in the spring, or in the winter, it's important that we maintain our determination here, that we indicate we're building our strength, that we are determined to protect our position, that we are determined to protect our commitments.

And then I believe we should indicate our desire to live at peace with the world.

But until we're strong here, until we're moving here, I believe a summit could not be successful. I hope that before we do meet, there will be preliminary agreements on those four questions, or at least two of them, or even one of them, which would warrant such a meeting. I think if we had stuck by that position last winter, we would have been in a better position in May.

MR. HOWE—We have time for only one or two more questions before the closing statements. Now Walter Cronkite's question for Senator Kennedy.

MR. CRONKITE — Senator, the charge has been made frequently that the United States for many years has been on the defensive around the world, that our policy has been one of reaction to the Soviet Union rather than positive action on our own. What areas do you see where the United States might take the offensive in a challenge to communism over the next four to eight years?

MR. KENNEDY—One of the areas, and of course the most vulnerable, I have felt, has been Eastern Europe. I've been critical of the Administration's failure to suggest policies which would make it possible for us to establish, for example, close relations with Poland, particularly after the '55-'56 period and the Hungarian revolution.

We indicated at that time that we were not going to intervene militarily. But there was a period there when Poland demonstrated a national independence and even the Polish Government moved some distance away from the Soviet Union.

I suggested that we amend our legislation so that we could enjoy closer economic ties. We received the support first of the Administration and then not. We were defeated by one vote in the Senate. We passed the bill in the Senate this year but it didn't pass the House.

I would say Eastern Europe is the area of vulnerability of the Soviet Union.

Secondly, the relations between Russia and China. They are now engaged in a debate over whether war is the means of communizing the world or whether they should use subversion, infiltration, economic struggles and all the rest. No one can say what that course of action will be, but I think the next President of the United States should watch it carefully. If those two powers should split, it could have great effects throughout the entire world.

Thirdly, I believe that India represents a great area for affirmative action by the free world.

India started from about the same place that China did. Chinese Communists have been moving ahead the last ten years.

India Making Progress

India under a free society has been making some progress. But if India does not succeed with her 450,000,000 people, if she can't make freedom work, then people around the world are going to determine—particular-

ly in the under-developed world —that the only way that they can develop their resources is through the Communist system.

Fourth, let me say that in Africa, Asia, Latin America, Eastern Europe, the great force on our side is the desire of people to be free.

This has expressed itself in the revolts in Eastern Europe. It's expressed itself in the desire of the people of Africa to be independent of Western Europe. They want to be free.

And my judgment is that they don't want to give their freedom up to become Communists. They want to stay free, independent, perhaps, of us, but certainly independent of the Communists.

And I believe that if we identify ourselves with that force, if we identify ourselves with it as Lincoln, as Wilson, did, as Franklin Roosevelt did, if we become known as the friend of freedom, sustaining freedom, helping freedom, helping these people in the fight against poverty, and ignorance and disease, helping them build their lives, I believe in Latin America, Africa, Asia, eventually in the Eastern Europe and the Middle East, certainly in Western Europe, we can strengthen freedom. We can make it move. We can put the Communists on the defensive.

MR. HOWE—Your comment, Mr. Vice President?

MR. NIXON—First, with regard to Poland, when I talked to Mr. Gomulka, the present leader of Poland, for six hours in Warsaw last year I learned something about their problems and particularly his.

Right under the Soviet gun, the Soviet troops there, he is in a very difficult position in taking anything independent, a position which would be independent of the Soviet Union.

And yet let's just see what we've done for Poland.

A half a billion dollars worth of aid has gone to Poland, primarily economic, primarily to go to the people of Poland.

This should continue and it can be stepped up to give them hope and to keep alive the hope for freedom that I can testify they have so deeply within them.

In addition we can have more exchange with Poland or with any other of the Iron Curtain countries which show some desire to take a different path than the path that has been taken by the ones that are complete satellites of the Soviet Union.

Questions Time Factor

Now as far as the balance of the world is concerned—I, of course, don't have as much time as Senator Kennedy had.

I would just like to add this one point.

If we are going to have the initiative in the world, we must remember that the people of Africa and Asia and Latin America don't want to be pawns simply in a struggle between two great powers—the Soviet Union and the United States.

We have to let them know that we want to help them, not because we're simply trying to save our own skin, not because we're simply trying to fight

communism, but because we care for them, because we stand for freedom, because if there were no communism in the world, we would still fight poverty and misery and disease and tyranny.

If we can get that across to the people of these countries, in this decade of the Sixties, the struggle for freedom will be won.

MR. HOWE—John Chancellor, another question for Vice President Nixon.

MR. CHANCELLOR—Sir, I'd like to ask you another question about Quemoy and Matsu. Both you and Senator Kennedy say you agree with the President on this subject and with our treaty obligations. But the subject remains in the campaign as an issue. Now, sir, is this because each of you feels obliged to respond to the other when he talks about Quemoy and Matsu, and if that's true, do you think an end should be called to this discussion, or will it stay with us as a campaign issue?

MR. NIXON—I would say that the issue will stay with us as a campaign issue just as long as Senator Kennedy persists in what I think is a fundamental error. He says he supports the President's position. He says that he voted for the resolution.

Well, just let me point this out. He voted for the resolution in 1955 which gave the President the power to use the forces of the United States to defend Formosa and the offshore islands. But he also voted then for an amendment—which was lost, fortunately—an amendment which would have drawn a line and left off those islands and denied the right to the President to defend those islands if he thought that it was an attack on Formosa.

He repeated that error in 1959 in a speech that he made. He repeated it again in a television debate that we had. Now, my point is this: Senator Kennedy has got to be consistent here. Either he's for the President and he's against the position that those who opposed the President in '55 and '59 — and the Senator's position itself was stated the other day in our debate—either he is for the President and against that position or we simply have a disagreement here that must continue to be debated.

Now if the Senator in his answer to this question will say "I now will depart, or retract my previous views, I think I was wrong in 1955, I think I was wrong in 1959, and I think I was wrong in our television debate to say that we should draw a line leaving out Quemoy and Matsu—draw a line in effect abandoning these islands to the Communists" then this will be right out of the campaign because there will be no issue between us.

Supports President

I support the President's position. I have always opposed drawing a line. I have opposed drawing a line because I know that the moment you draw a line that is an encouragement for the Communists to attack— to step up their blackmail and to force you into the war that none of us want. And so I would hope that Senator Kennedy in his answer today would clear it up.

It isn't enough for him to say "I support the President's position, that I voted for the resolution.". Of course, he voted for the resolution—it was virtually unanimous. But the point is, what about his error in voting for the amendment, which was not adopted, and then persisting in it in '59, persisting in it in the debate.

It's very simple for him to clear it up. He can say now that he no longer believes that a line should be drawn leaving these islands out of the perimeter of defense. If he says that, this issue will not be discussed in the campaign.

Mr. KENNEDY—Well, Mr. Nixon, go back to 1955. The resolution commits the President in the United States, which I supported, to defend Formosa, the Pescadores, and, if it was his military judgment, these islands.

Then the President sent a mission, composed of Admiral Radford and Mr. Robertson, to persuade Chiang Kai-shek in the spring of '55 to withdraw from the two islands, because they were exposed. The President was unsuccessful! Chiang Kai-shek would not withdraw.

I refer to the fact that in 1958, as a member of the Senate Foreign Relations Committee, I'm very familiar with the position that the United States took in negotiating with the Chinese Communists on these two islands.

General Twining, in January, 1959, described the position of the United States. The position of the United States has been that this build-up, in the words of the President, has been foolish.

Mr. Herter has said these islands are indefensible. Chiang Kai-shek will not withdraw. Because he will not withdraw, because he's committed to these islands, because we've been unable to persuade him to withdraw, we are in a very difficult position.

And therefore, the President's judgment has been that we should defend the islands if, in his military judgment and the judgment of the commander in the field, the attack on these islands should be part of an overall attack on Formosa.

I support that. In view of the difficulties we've had with the islands, in view of the difficulties and disputes we've had with Chiang Kai-shek, that's the only position we can take.

That's not the position you took, however. The first position you took, when this matter first came up, was that we should draw the line and commit ourselves, as a matter of principle, to defend these islands. Not as part of the defense of Formosa and the Pescadores. You showed no recognition of the Administration program to try to persuade Chiang Kai-shek for the last five years to withdraw from the islands.

And I challenge you tonight to deny that the Administration has sent at least several missions to persuade Chiang Kai-shek's withdrawal from these islands.

MR. NIXON—I'll do better.

MR. KENNEDY—That's the testimony of General Twining and the Assistant Secretary of State in '58.

MR. HOWE: Under the agreed rules, gentlemen, we've exhausted the time for questions. Each candidate will now have four minutes and thirty seconds for his closing statement. Senator Kennedy will make the first closing statement.

MR. KENNEDY: I said that I've served this country for fourteen years. I served it in the war. I'm devoted to it. If I lose this election, I will continue in the Senate to try to build a stronger country.

But I run because I believe this year the United States has a great opportunity to make a move forward, to make a determination here at home and around the world, if it's going to re-establish itself as a vigorous society.

My judgment is that the Republican party has stood still here in the United States, and it has also stood still around the world. We're using about 50 per cent of our steel capacity today. We had a recession in '58. We had a recession in '54.

We're not moving ahead in education the way we should. We didn't make a judgment in '57 and '56 and '55 and '54 that outer space would be important.

Loss of Influence Feared

If we stand still here, if we appoint people to ambassadorships and positions in Washington who have a status quo outlook, who don't recognize that this is a revolutionary time, then the United States does not maintain its influence. And if we fail, the cause of freedom fails. I believe it incumbent upon the next President of the United States to get this country moving again, to get our economy moving again, to set before the American people its goals, its unfinished business.

And then throughout the world appoint the best people we can get, ambassadors who can speak the language—not merely people who made a political contribution but who can speak the language—bring students here. Let them see what kind of a country we have.

Mr. Nixon said that we should not regard them as pawns in the "cold war," we should identify ourselves with them. If that were true, why didn't we identify ourselves with the people of Africa.

Why didn't we bring students over here? Why did we suddenly offer the Congo 300 students last June when they had their tremendous revolt? That was more than we had offered to all of Africa the year before from the Federal Government.

Says G. O. P. Stood Still

I believe that this party—Republican party—has stood still really for twenty-five years—its leadership has. It has opposed all the programs of President Roosevelt and others—the minimum wage and for housing and economic growth and development of our natural resources, the Tennessee Valley and all the rest.

And I believe that if we can get a party which believes in movement, which believes in going ahead, then we can re-establish our position in the world—strong defense, strong in economic growth, justice for our people, guarantee of constitutional rights, so that people will believe that we practice what we preach, and then around the world, particularly to try to reestablish the atmosphere which existed in Latin America at the time of Franklin Roosevelt.

He was a good neighbor in Latin America because he was a good neighbor in the United States, because they saw us as a society that was compassionate, that cared about people, that was moving this country ahead.

I believe it my responsibility as the leader of the Democratic party in 1960 to try to warn the American people that in this crucial time we can no longer afford to stand still. We can no longer afford to be second best.

I want people all over the world to look to the United States again, to feel that we're on the move, to feel that our high noon is in the future.

I want Mr. Khrushchev to know that a new generation of Americans who fought in Europe and Italy and the Pacific for freedom in World War II have now taken over in the United States, that they're going to put this country back to work again.

I don't believe that there is anything this country cannot do. I don't believe there is any burden, any responsibility, that any American would not assume to protect his country, to advance the cause of freedom.

And I believe it incumbent upon us now to do that.

Franklin Roosevelt said in 1936 that that generation of Americans had a rendezvous with destiny. In 1960 and '61 and '62 and '63 we have a rendezvous with destiny. And I believe it incumbent upon us to be the defenders of the United States and the defenders of freedom, and to do that, we must give this country leadership and we must get America moving again.

MR. HOWE—Now, Vice President Nixon, your closing statement.

MR. NIXON—Senator Kennedy has said tonight again what he has said several times in the course of these debates and in the campaign, that America is standing still.

America is not standing still. It has not been standing still. And let's set the record straight right now by looking at the record, as Al Smith used to say.

He talks about housing. We built more houses in the last seven years than in any Administration and 30 per cent more than in the previous Administration.

We talk about schools—three times as many classrooms built in the past Administration—and Eisenhower—than under the Truman Administration.

Let's talk about civil rights. More progress in the past eight years than in the whole eighty years before.

He talks about the progress in the field of slum clearance and the like. We find four times as many projects undertaken and completed in this Administration than in the previous one.

Traveling in America

Anybody that says America has been standing still for the last seven and a half years hasn't been traveling in America. He's been in some other country. Let's get that straight right away.

Now the second point we have to understand is this, however.

America has not been standing still. But America cannot stand pat. We can't stand pat for the reason that we're in a race, as I've indicated. We can't stand pat because it is essential that we have around the world the conflict that we have, that we not just hold our own, that we not keep just freedom for ourselves.

It is essential that we extend freedom, extend it to all the world and this means more than what we've been doing.

It means keeping America even stronger militarily than she is. It means seeing that our economy moves forward even faster than it has. It means making more progress in civil rights than we have so that we can be a splendid example for all the world to see a democracy in action at its best.

Now, looking at the other parts of the world, South America, talking about our record and the previous one. We had a good neighbor policy, yes.

Looks at Dictators

It sounded fine but let's look at it. There were eleven dictators when we came into power in 1953 in Latin America.

There are only four left.

Let's look at Africa. Twenty new countries in Africa during the course of this Administration. Not one of them selected a Communist Government. All of them voted for freedom a free type of government.

Does this show that communism has the bigger pull, or freedom has the bigger pull?

Am I trying to indicate that we have no problems in Africa or Latin America or Asia? Of course not.

What I am trying to indicate is that the tide of history's on our side, and that we can keep it on our side, because we're on the right side.

We're on the side of freedom. We're on the side of justice against the forces of slavery, against the forces of injustice.

Winning The Struggle

But we aren't going to move America forward and we aren't going to be able to lead the world to win this struggle for freedom if we have a permanent inferiority complex about American achievements, because we are first in the world in space, as I've indicated; we are first in science; we are first in education, and we're going to move even further ahead with the kind of leadership that we can provide in these years ahead.

One other point I would make: What can you do?

Senator Kennedy and I are candidates for the Presidency

of the United States. In the years to come it will be written that one or the other of us was elected and that he was or was not a great President.

What will determine whether Senator Kennedy or I, if I am elected, was a great President? It will not be our ambition that will determine it, because greatness is not something that is written on a campaign poster.

It will be determined to the extent that we represent the deepest ideals, the highest feelings and faith of the American people.

In other words, the next President, as he leads America and the free world, can be only as great as the American people are great.

And so I say in conclusion, keep America's faith strong. See that the young people of America, particularly, have faith in the ideals of freedom and faith in God, which distinguishes us from the atheistic materialists who oppose us.

MR. HOWE — Thank you, gentlemen. Both candidates have asked me to express their thanks to the networks for this opportunity to appear on this discussion. May I repeat that all those concerned in tonight's discussion have, sometimes reluctantly, followed the rules and conditions read at the outset and agreed to in advance by the candidates and the networks.

The statements ran eight minutes each. The closing statements ran four minutes, thirty seconds.

The order of speaking was reversed from their first joint appearance, when they followed the same procedure.

A panel of newsmen questioned each candidate alternately. Each had two and a half minutes to reply. The other had a minute and a half to comment.

But the first discussion dealt only with domestic policy. This one dealt only with foreign policy.

One last word. As members of a new political generation, Vice President Nixon and Senator Kennedy have used new means of communication to pioneer a new type of political debate.

The character and courage with which these two men have spoken sets a high standard for generations to come.

Surely, they have set a new precedent. Perhaps they have established a new tradition.

This is Quincy Howe. Good night from New York.

The Fourth Debate

Feeling in Washington Is That Kennedy and Nixon Went Past National Interests

By JAMES RESTON

Special to The New York Times.

WASHINGTON, Oct. 21—The Nixon - Kennedy debates are probably over, and the general feeling here tonight was that it is none too soon.

The one this evening was highly repetitive. For the most part, both candidates for the Presidency went over old arguments, often with the same tired and familiar phrases of the last month. Washington would be glad to see them end, too, because they have been drifting more and more into discussion of strategic plans for dealing with Cuba and Quemoy and Matsu, and few observers here think this is in the national interest.

News Analysis

The Vice President's criticism of Senator Kennedy's program for assisting the anti-Castro forces to regain power in Cuba was approved by well-informed people here tonight. They have been saying today that while it may be all right to do that, it is not the sort of thing to discuss publicly, especially in the face of the nation's treaties with Latin America, which specifically forbid economic or political interference in the internal affairs of the American Republics.

Drift to Communism

For example, the Eisenhower Administration did intervene to prevent the drift of Guatemala toward communism, and Vice President Nixon referred to this tonight. But public promises of intervention in advance of the event are generally opposed here. As a result, the feeling here was that the Vice President scored on this point.

On the other hand, the Vice President's opening and closing statements were not only a collection of points he has made repeatedly in the past, but seemed here to lack much of the fire of his statements in the past.•

Mr. Kennedy, in contrast, finished stronger tonight than he began, and his statement on the nuclear testing issue had a balance and even eloquence that he seldom matched in the three other debates.

The question now, of course, is: Which of the two men gained by this experiment in television campaigning? And here, on balance, the feeling among the political pros is that Mr. Kennedy came out on top, primarily because he started these broadcasts far behind.

The Vice President was better known than the Senator a month ago. Though many Americans had seen the Democratic nominee during his travels across the nation in the past four years, many more seemed to have the impression that he was merely a handsome young magazine "cover boy" who somehow had managed to get the Democratic nomination with the aid of his good looks and his family's fortune.

By comparison, the Vice President went into the debate a month ago widely regarded as an experienced official and a skillful debater who was taking on what the Republicans and some prominent Democrats, including former President Truman and Senator Lyndon B. Johnson, had described as an "immature" and inexperienced opponent.

Mr. Kennedy's achievement in the last month is that he has shattered this impression for a great many voters. On the same screen with Mr. Nixon, he managed to reduce the "age issue" and the "immaturity" charge. He spoke with great assurance. He had a grasp of specific detail that came as a surprise even to many of his supporters. And, particularly in the first nation-wide discussion, he more than held his own with the Vice President.

Beyond this, the debates are subject to endless controversy over who won what points, but the general impression seems to have been that Mr. Kennedy was a much more experienced and competent man than most

people thought before the debate began, and in this sense he has certainly gained in the conflict.

In the perspective of all four discussions, both men have probably gained in public esteem. Despite the immense pressures of the largest audiences ever to watch and listen to political debate in America, they have been relatively calm. Despite the emotions of the period, they have been relatively fair and courteous to each other.

In the process, the experiment has been a service in public education. Though there has been much criticism of the format, primarily because it has forced the candidates to jump quickly from one topic to another, and thus encouraged short and often superficial answers, nevertheless the candidates have provoked considerable discussion of their personalities and policies.

Teachers See Results

Teachers, for example, are now testifying that never before can they remember their students' participating so eagerly in debates of their own as a result of these four discussions. And the example of the Presidential candidates has led simultaneously to many useful debates across the nation by candidates for other Federal, state and local offices.

Both men ended tonight as they began the first broadcast. The Vice President's main argument is that the nation is doing well in the "cold war" and that, as a result of his experience, it will do even better in the future.

Senator Kennedy's argument is that we are not doing well enough, that we must do better and that this requires new leadership and new policies provided by the Democratic party.

It is not the policies or the parties that have come through in these debates, however, so much as the personalities and the qualities of the men themselves. Mr. Kennedy was confident from the start that if he could get on the same screen with the Vice President, he could deal with the problem of his comparative youth and the charge of immaturity, and the general impression here is that he has succeeded in this objective.

Nixon Proposes Debate on Cuba; Kennedy Objects to Limitation

Vice President Caustic

By HARRISON E. SALISBURY
Special to The New York Times.

WASHINGTON, Oct. 23 — Vice President Nixon accepted conditionally tonight Senator John F. Kennedy's challenge to a fifth television debate. His condition was that it be limited to the question:

"What should the United States Government do about Castro?"

The Vice President made his suggestion in the form of a tentative proposal. But he said that if Mr. Kennedy agreed to the idea he would have his representatives meet with those of the Democratic nominee and "discuss possible arrangements for a debate in depth of this subject of paramount importance."

Senator Kennedy has been making a campaign issue of the fifth debate and s been stressing the Vice President's apparent reluctance to agree to a meeting. Thus the Nixon suggestion tonight was in effect a counter-proposal.

Mr. Nixon coupled his proposal with sharp aspersions upon Mr. Kennedy's stand with respect to Cuba. He also attacked Mr. Kennedy for charging that the Vice President was "afraid" to meet him in debate. This statement, Mr. Nixon said, "is sophomoric and not worthy of one who is running for the highest office in this land."

It was the second time in twenty-four hours that Mr. Nixon had used the appellation "sophomoric" with respect to Mr. Kennedy. He used that word last night to describe Mr. Kennedy's position on Cuba.

The Nixon proposal for a Cuban debate was in line with the new stepped-up vigor of the Vice President's campaign. The new phase opened last night with Mr. Nixon's charge that Mr. Kennedy's Cuban notions raised the possibility of a third world war. Mr. Nixon repeated that theme tonight in his statement on the debate.

Mr. Nixon also suggested that his running-mate, Henry Cabot Lodge, and the Democratic Vice-Presidential nominee, Senator Lyndon B. Johnson, appear on the program before the debate.

He asked that each "discuss in turn his concept of the office to which he aspires and how it might continue to be employed in support of the struggle for peace and freedom."

Mr. Nixon's proposal, in the form of a telegram to Senator Kennedy, was not a flat proposition for a fifth debate. The Vice President said that he had commitments for all the campaigning days between Oct. 21 and Nov. 8.

He said that the opinion of unbiased observers was that in the last two of the television debates some ground had been covered repetitiously and that, in some respects, the meetings had not been debates but "merely interrogations on some of the issues of the day."

Now, however, Mr. Nixon said a clear-cut issue between the two candidates had developed.

He said that Mr. Kennedy has specifically stated: "We must attempt to strengthen the non-Batista Democratic anti-Castro forces in exile and in Cuba itself who offer eventual hope of overthrowing Castro."

This, Mr. Nixon said, clearly means that the Massachusetts Senator is calling for Government aid to overthrow the Castro regime in violation of the Inter-American Treaty prohibition against intervention in the internal affairs of the hemispheric republics.

The Vice President, boarding his train at Union Station tonight, had this to say to a crowd of supporters:

"This is a Diesel train but we are going to pour on coal from now on. Whatever has happened up to now, you haven't seen anything yet. This train will take us into the states that will decide the election. We intend to win every one of them."

Rival for Full Agenda

By W. H. LAWRENCE
Special to The New York Times.

MILWAUKEE, Oct. 23—Senator John F. Kennedy declined tonight to accept Vice President Nixon's proposed limitation on a fifth television debate. Mr. Nixon would confine the debate to what the United States should do about Fidel Castro's pro-Communist regime in Cuba.

The Democratic Presidential nominee said a limitation to a single subject and a single country would "subvert" the purposes of the debate, "gag" press representatives' questioning the candidates and deprive the people of a full and free discussion of many domestic and foreign issues.

As the challenger for a fifth debate, Senator Kennedy said he welcomed the Vice President's acceptance of it in principle. The Senator called another exchange essential to keeping the record straight and "correcting any distortions made in the closing days of the campaign."

Mr. Kennedy's reply came after a day of campaigning in Wisconsin. Thousands cheered him and top party leaders were confident that the state's twelve electoral votes were his.

Canceling all rest days from now until the Nov. 8 election, the Democratic Presidential nominee kept to a heavy schedule that took him from a Green Bay breakfast to a noon airport rally in LaCrosse, an afternoon speech at the University of Wisconsin and a major speech here this evening.

In this predominantly agricultural state, Mr. Kennedy struck at Vice President Nixon as a follower of the much-criticized farm programs of Ezra Taft Benson, Secretary of Agriculture.

He accused his rival of having told Midwesterners that the Democratic farm program would do them no good and having warned Easterners that the same program would raise food prices 25 per cent.

"This is an old Nixon tactic —attempt to divide and conquer, setting farmers against the city consumer, their best customer," the Bostonian charged in a statement. "I say this is dangerous divisive political trickery, and I say it won't work."

Senator Kennedy mostly stuck to his theme that his fight with Mr. Nixon was not between individuals for the Presidency, nor between opposing parties, but was a "contest between two political philosophies, between the comfortable and the contented and the concerned, between those who look to the future and those who stand still." This theme was a crowd-pleaser everywhere.

He charged that the Eisenhower-Nixon-Benson farm program had brought farmers "close to ruin, and Mr. Nixon proposes to continue it."

"Mr. Nixon went to New Jersey the other day," he continued, "and in one of those speeches for which he has become famous, he said that the proposals that I put forward for increasing farm income would increase food prices 25 per cent.

"Then he comes out here to LaCrosse and says that my farm plan would not mean a thing for the farmers. He should make up his mind. He should say the same thing in LaCrosse as he does in New Jersey.

"The fact is he should say the same thing in the North that he says in the South, the same thing that he says in the East that he says in the West."

Party leaders, led by Gov. Gaylord Nelson, assured Senator Kennedy his indicated lead over Mr. Nixon in this state was so large he could not lose it in the final weeks of the campaign.

Even in strongly Republican communities, such as Green Bay and LaCrosse, the crowds that turned out were encouraging to Democratic leaders.

For the breakfast in Green Bay, which voted 2-to-1 Republican in the two previous Presidential elections, the Brown County Veterans Memorial Arena was jammed to its 8,000-seat capacity.

The LaCrosse airport crowd was estimated by the police at 15,000, but others thought this figure to be high.

A shouting, stamping crowd estimated at 12,500 jammed the Wisconsin field house. This surprised and relieved Kennedy campaign aides, who earlier had opposed engaging such a large hall on a Sunday afternoon in fear they might not fill it.

Derisively the nominee said Mr. Nixon had sent Senator Barry Goldwater of Arizona, conservative spokesman, to the South "in an old Confederate uniform" to say that Republican civil-rights pledges meant nothing, and Senator Hugh Scott of Pennsylvania across the North to say all rights promises would be carried out.

In Milwaukee Mr. Kennedy reviewed his position on disarmament by saying:

"Mr. Nixon and I both want peace, but we disagree fundamentally on the nature of the effort and leadership which the pursuit of peace demands."

The night audience in the Milwaukee Arena, which seats 13,000, fell about 3,000 short of capacity, but exceeded that for Mr. Nixon's one appearance here.

Nixon Telegram to Kennedy on Debate

Special to The New York Times.

WASHINGTON, Oct. 23— *Following is the text of a telegram sent by Vice President Nixon tonight to Senator John F. Kennedy concerning a fifth television debate:*

As I told you Friday evening, your wire with regard to asking for a fifth debate was delivered to me just prior to our going on the air.

In view of the fact that I told you on that occasion that I was preparing an answer to your wire and have since indicated a willingness to meet with you on television again if I am convinced it would be constructive and in the public interest, I find it difficult to understand your continued public statements to the effect that "I am afraid to meet you in debate." Such a statement is sophomoric and not worthy of one who is running for the highest office in this land. Furthermore, you know it is untrue.

Just to set the record straight with regard to our debates up to this point, it was first agreed that we should have three debates. And that at your request we would attempt to work out the terms for a fourth debate, which I did. At that time it was definitely agreed that we could go forward with planning our campaign appearances on the assumption that this would be the total number during the campaign. As a result, I have made commitments for all the campaigning days between Oct. 21 and Nov. 8.

The record should also show that when you suggested a fifth debate, I agreed provided we could do it by adding an extra hour on the same evening we had the fourth debate. Your representatives at first refused to accept this proposal and when you finally announced you would accept it, the networks were unable to arrange it.

Looking to the future, let me state my position clearly so you will understand it.

I will try to rearrange my schedule to fit in a fifth meeting, if I believe it would serve a constructive public purpose.

Unbiased observers agree that in our last two debates some of the same ground has been covered and that the questions in some instances have become repetitious. For four hours we have discussed on television many questions —how to keep the peace and extend freedom — the state of our military and moral strength — our economic growth — and the problems of providing for the human needs of our people. However, in one sense, these meetings have not been debates but merely interrogations on some of the issues of the day.

Comparing these meetings with the Lincoln-Douglas debates, as some have done, is not an accurate analogy. What made those debates significant and memorable is that they dealt with one subject of great immediate public interest on which the candidates completely disagreed with each other. Such an issue has developed in this campaign during the last several days as a result of my speech before the American Legion on Wednesday and your response issued in New York on Thursday, and the brief discussion which we had concerning it during our television appearance on Friday. The question can be stated this way: "What should the United States Government do about Castro?" I favor an economic and political quarantine as outlined in my American Legion speech. Specifically you state that "we must attempt to strengthen the non-Batista democratic anti-Castro forces in exile, and in Cuba itself who offer eventual hope of overthrowing Castro. Thus far these fighters for freedom have had virtually no support from our Government."

This clearly means, as The New York Times Washington correspondent, James Reston, reported in today's paper: "His statement this week on Cuba publicly calling for Government aid to overthrow Castro is a clear violation of the Inter-American Treaty prohibition against intervention in the internal affairs of the hemisphere republics."

Thus it is clear that you and I are diametrically opposed in a matter of great public interest and one which the next President may have to deal with as soon as he assumes the office.

It is my firm belief that the course of action proposed by you is recklessly dangerous because:

1. It clearly violates the United States Government's solemn commitments to the United Nations and the Organization of American States not to intervene in the internal affairs of other members of these organizations. It would, in fact, violate a total of five treaties to which the United States has pledged itself.

2. It would, as we have seen from the immediate response of shock and dismay in Latin America, alienate every one of our sister American republics whose friendship you have acknowledged is of vital importance to our effort against Communism.

3. It would give Mr. Khrushchev a valid excuse to intervene in Cuba on the side of the Castro Government, saying that the United States had intervened in violation of its treaty obligations in trying to overthrow the existing government. If this happened, your policy could lead to World War III.

Here we have a clear-cut difference of opinion involving policy considerations of the highest importance and involving a decision that the next President may have to make early in his term. The people are entitled to know why each of us holds the views that we do so that they can make an intelligent choice between us.

I will be glad to have my representative meet with yours at any convenient time to discuss possible arrangements for a debate in depth on this subject of paramount importance.

In addition, I believe it would be in the public interest, and the fifth debate would afford a good opportunity, for each of the Vice-Presidential candidates to discuss, in turn, his concept of the office to which he aspires and how it might continue to be employed in support of the struggle for peace and freedom. I would suggest that each of the Vice-Presidential candidates might speak on that subject as a preliminary to our final debate.

Kennedy's Reply to Nixon

Special to The New York Times.

MILWAUKEE, Wis., Oct. 23 —*Following is the text of a telegram from Senator John F. Kennedy to Vice President Nixon concerning a possible fifth television debate:*

With regard to your telegram of today, I am glad you have finally accepted my challenge to participate in this debate. I suggested a fifth debate close to the election as a means of keeping the record straight, face-to-face, and correcting any distortions made in the closing days of the campaign.

Your telegram to me tonight clearly indicates I was right in calling for such a debate, for the distortions of the record concerning my position on Cuba exceed any others you have made during this campaign. You have developed the technique of having your writers rewrite my statements, using those rewritten statements and attacking me for things I have never said or advocated. This is certainly the record with regard to the speeches you have been making in the past forty-eight hours on Cuba.

I have never advocated, and I do not advocate, intervention in Cuba in violation of our treaty obligations, and, in fact, stated in Johnstown, Pa., that whatever we did with regard to Cuba should be within the confines of international law.

What I have advocated is that we use all available communications—radio, TV and the press—and the moral power of the American Government to let the forces of freedom in Cuba know that we believe that freedom will again rise in that country.

I will be pleased to discuss the whole record of Cuba with you—how this island, only ninety miles from our borders, fell into Communist hands and the sorry record of Administration inaction with regard to Cuba.

I cannot understand, however, why you wish to place a gag on the press in this final debate. Cuba is important, but so are our relations with the Soviet Union, the problems of Latin America, Africa and Asia. Equally important are the domestic issues which you and the Republican party seem to wish to bury during this campaign —minimum wage, medical care for the aged, aid to education and the rising rate of unemployment.

Only a week ago you stated you were going to talk about Quemoy and Matsu every day for the final three weeks of the campaign. Now it is Cuba. These latter two are important issues, but I think the American people want and deserve to hear us discuss all the important problems which face our country, and to limit the subject of the fifth debate to one country would be to subvert the purpose of such a debate.

I have instructed Mr. Leonard Reinisch of my staff to meet with your staff and attempt to further work out details for this important fifth debate.

NOMINEES ARGUE OVER NEW DEBATE

Kennedy Asks for a Meeting on All Questions—Nixon Sees Rival Reneging

Special to The New York Times.

PEORIA, Ill., Oct. 24 —Senator John F. Kennedy charged today that his Republican rival, Vice Presidential Nixon, "would rather debate with mimeograph machines and telegrams than face to face."

This was the Democratic nominee's response to another telegram from Mr. Nixon concerning terms and conditions of a projected fifth and final televised debate.

Once again Senator Kennedy insisted that the debate should be held without limitations on subjects. He rejected the Vice President's proposal that this final debate be limited to the single subject of "what should the United States Government do about" Fidel Castro's regime in Cuba.

Senator Kennedy said he would appear at the fifth debate ready to answer any questions raised by a panel of reporters and that he hoped the Vice President would do the same thing. Where and when they would appear, or whether still wasn't decided.

Nixon Sends Telegram

PITTSBURGH, Oct. 24 (AP) —Mr. Nixon sent another telegram to Mr. Kennedy today or the snarled issue of a fifth television-radio debate.

The Vice President said he could not understand from Mr Kennedy's reply to his wire yesterday whether the Democratic candidate accepted Mr. Nixon's proposals for such an encounter

But Mr. Nixon said he still would be glad to have his representative. Under Secretary of the Treasury Fred Scribner meet with Mr. Kennedy's staff to try to work out arrangements for the fifth meeting.

The Vice President said his plans for the final campaign week were somewhat up in the air because of the uncertainty over the debate.

Mr. Nixon asked yesterday that a fifth debate be devoted largely to Cuba and that the Vice Presidential nominees also participate.

In today's telegram Mr. Nixon suggested that Mr. Kennedy was trying to back out of the implications of his statement last Thursday on Cuba.

But Mr. Nixon said virtually all major newspapers were agreed that the Senator's comment clearly implied direct United States Government support of anti-Castro forces in Cuba. Mr. Kennedy has declared he never advocated such direct intervention.

First Steps Taken

Special to The New York Times.

WASHINGTON, Oct. 24— Representatives of the two Presidential candidates took steps toward a fifth televised debate today, but settled none of the issues involved.

An announcement from the office of J. Leonard Reinsch, the television negotiator for Senator Kennedy, said he had talked with Fred Scribner, Vice President Nixon's representative.

The announcement said the two were "assembling the facts necessary for a complete discussion which will probably take place Tuesday afternoon."

Mr. Kennedy, the Democratic nominee, has made a series of talks accusing Mr. Nixon of dodging a fifth televised discussion. Mr. Nixon replied at first that the meeting could not be worked into his schedule.

Yesterday, however, he proposed that a fifth debate be held and that Cuban policy be the topic.

Mr. Kennedy accepted but said the debate should be open to discussion on all the issues of the campaign. Both candidates instructed their representatives to begin negotiations on this and other details.

Candidates' Statements on Fifth Debate

Following are the text of a telegram by Vice President Nixon to Senator John F. Kennedy on the question of a fifth television debate and the text of a statement by Senator Kennedy:

Nixon Telegram

My telegram to you yesterday contained exact language from your mimeographed statement issued in New York on Thursday, Oct. 20. Do you now contend that the quotation is inaccurate?

Your language clearly means what James Reston of The New York Times said it means, as I quoted in my telegram to you, as follows:

"His [Mr. Kennedy's] statement this week on Cuba publicly calling for Government aid to overthrow Castro is a clear violation of the inter-American treaty prohibition against intervention in the internal affairs of the hemisphere republics."

Virtually every major newspaper which has commented on the subject understood your remarks as Mr. Reston did and as I did—that you were advocating direct Government support of the anti-Castro forces both in exile and in Cuba.

This is another case of your speaking first and thinking afterwards—a habit which is a very dangerous one for a man who is asking the American people to select him as commander-in-chief of all the armed forces of this nation.

If your original statement on Cuba has been intended only to cover what you now claim in your telegram, to the effect that we should "let the forces of freedom in Cuba know that we believe that freedom will again arise in their country," you would have been advocating what has been the policy which the Administration has been following for months. Apparently you are under the impression that when attention is called to your mistakes you can confuse people by immediately claiming that you were misquoted or that what you said was distorted. I will cite two other examples of this technique.

1. When a report came out about what you said in Oregon, to the effect that President Eisenhower could have expressed regrets to Khrushchev, you claimed that your remarks had been distorted. You will recall that your present running mate took the lead in ridiculing your claim that your remarks had been distorted. Finally, when you were forced to put your remarks in the Congressional Record, it was clear that you had not been misquoted and that what you said had not been distorted.

2. You claimed distortion when I said that you advocated in 1955 that the free world should abandon Quemoy and Matsu and that in our second television debate you advocated the same policy. However, your vote favoring the resolution excluding Quemoy and Matsu from the Formosa defense perimeter, which would mean abandonment, is a matter of record which you cannot deny. Your language during the second television debate clearly indicates that you still favor that policy.

Now you cry distortion about your remarks on Cuba even though every major newspaper understood it the way I did— as did those most directly affected and with the most knowledge of the situation, the ambassadors to the United Nations from the Latin American countries, many of whom expressed shock and dismay at your proposal.

'Greater Blunder' Seen

It is true, as you stated in your telegram, that I said that I intended to talk about Quemoy and Matsu every day for the final three weeks of the campaign. When I said that, I had no idea that you would make even a greater blunder about Cuba.

Consequently, I will talk about not only Quemoy and Matsu but also about Cuba every day during the next two weeks—I will do this because I am deeply concerned about the policies you advocate in those two areas of the world which might well lead to abandoning free territory in the Far East, and loss of all of our Latin American allies in this hemisphere or worse. The United States in these critical times cannot risk a President who makes mistakes of this magnitude.

Your telegram does not make it clear whether you accept my proposal or not. However, I will be glad to have Fred Scribner meet with your staff to discuss the matter. I assume from your silence that you accept my proposal concerning the Vice-Presidential candidates and have instructed Mr. Scribner accordingly.

Kennedy Statement

I have asked Mr. Nixon to participate in a fifth debate which I think should cover the question of Cuba and other important problems facing the American people.

I still find it impossible to understand why Mr. Nixon wants to limit the debate to one subject where there are so many important problems facing the American people. I think the fifth debate should include all questions which the members of the press [panel] feel are of importance.

As to Mr. Nixon's latest lengthy telegram today, I think the American people will well be able to judge which candidate has been guilty of distortions in this campaign. They will render their decision on Nov. 8 and I have the greatest confidence in that decision.

Mr. Nixon's message is another indication of the fact that he would rather debate with mimeograph machines and telegram than face to face.

I plan to appear at the fifth debate prepared to answer any questions which the panel may wish to ask me. I hope he will appear prepared to do the same thing.

TV'S CAMPAIGN CONTRIBUTION

The Medium, Freed of Inhibiting Restrictions, Finds It Can Play a Major Role in Covering Canddates

By JACK GOULD

ONE of the benefits from the series of joint appearances by Vice President Nixon and Senator John F. Kennedy has been largely overlooked: the political revolution inherent in the willingness of the three television networks and four radio chains to grant many hours of free time to the Republican and Democratic candidates.

By this move the broadcasting industry has taken a giant stride in reducing the traditional political advantage enjoyed by the nominee whose party has the most money to spend, a matter of historic concern in American politics. More especially, the broadcasters, by their initiative in affording equal opportunity to both candidates, have altered fundamentally the old-fashioned concept about the relative prominence of candidates.

Format

Necessarily, the format of the debates has tended to receive primary attention and no one would want to suggest that they have been ideal. Surely, the confrontations have stimulated an awareness of the two men and their opinions, which in itself is progress of a high order. But much also can be said against off-the-cuff responses on delicate matters of foreign affairs, excessive repetition, a frequent lack of substantive depth and a preoccupation with picking a winner in each so-called "debate."

But such problems of execution, all of which are readily susceptible to improvement or modification as experience dictates, should not be allowed to obscure the deeper implications of what has happened in this campaign, namely, the assumption by TV of a positive rather than a passive role in the political arena.

In previous campaigns the TV industry essentially offered itself to politicians as a platform for hire. This was because of two factors: first, the Federal communications law dictated that if free time were offered the two major candidates, the same privilege had to be accorded to dozens of minor candidates. Such a course was economically absurd, and the net effect was for TV to curtail coverage on its own. Second, the broadcasters were not overly conscious of their public-service requirements and even if there were no legal barriers, there was strong resistance to waiving revenue from regular commercial attractions.

The major consequence of these conditions was that politicians rather than broadcasters largely controlled the medium during a campaign. The party with the biggest purse could buy all the time it wanted, the law merely requiring a station to offer to sell similar time to others who could afford the price. The national committees and their advertising agencies to a substantial degree dictated the form and extent of TV's coverage.

Last summer, partly as a result of inter-network rivalry to don the mantle of virtue, Congress finally eased the ridiculous all-candidate provision of the law and the way was paved for the much publicized "great debates," an idea that had the virtue of novelty in the context of Presidential politics.

But whether the "great debates" have materialized or not the role of television in politics would have been greatly changed in any case. With the freedom and the will to jump into the controversial political arena the world of TV was bound to contribute a new influence to the 1960 campaign —and one that will extend to future years.

Reportage

Television for the first time is doing its own extensive reporting and assessment of the campaign. The week-end interview programs have been host to a procession of candidates and campaign advisers, and the networks have been offering their own roundup in choice evening time. These free hours are in addition to the night-time hours assigned to the debates.

While paid political broadcasts and five-minute announcements still exist in profusion, the broadcasters, in a sense, have recaptured control of their medium and now can assure an essentially even break for two candidates in using the medium. By removing a major part of the financial burden of TV from the backs of the candidates and the parties, TV itself has gained in serving the voting viewer. Whatever the faults of the debates, they have established vividly the principle of equality of opportunity in gaining access to a public-owned medium, something long needed in video and politics.

What might be accurately described as the economic and legal liberation of TV to perform its independent news function largely makes academic the argument that Vice President Nixon only "builds up" Mr. Kennedy in agreeing to the debates and that an incumbent President seeking re-election would never so allow his prestige to rub off on a lesser-known aspirant to his office.

The faulty reasoning behind these contentions is that politicians will be able to manipulate video to "hide" a rival from public view and appraisal. In the past this was true; but so long as TV assigns without charge many hours of good evening time to a Presidential contest, both men are going to become extremely well-known under video's normal laws of exposure. Debates constitute something of a ready-made "equalizer," to be sure, but even without debates the video medium of its own accord would match up the positions of candidates on major issues.

Promise

In many respects the possibilities of much fuller independent coverage by the TV networks outweighs in promise the debates themselves. Too much of the debates has revolved around controversies over what the candidates allegedly said elsewhere. Greater first-hand coverage of speeches on TV tape could be illuminating, especially brought together in hour-long summaries that would show up inconsistencies and contradictions.

In 1964 the networks should take a stronger initiative in insisting on formats that suited the problems under discussion. Live pickups of half-hour public speeches on the same subject would seem a possible alternative to a studio presentation; a more systematic selection of topics, so that no major area would be omitted, would be desirable. Clarification of disputed facts similarly would be in order.

But the dominant gain of the 1960 campaign is that TV has been freed from unrealistic restrictions and that by assuming as never before the cost responsibility of bringing the campaign into the home it has contributed substantially to fairness in politics and to a greater interest in the outcome of the election. There is no question that hereafter TV and politics will be inseparable as never before: the importance of the 1960 experience is how to make that relationship even more fruitful in the future. October 30, 1960

Poser for Pundits

The political avant garde is thinking about 1964 already— not who's going to run for the big prize (that's kid stuff), but will the candidates meet on television?

Some think television debates are inevitable henceforth. No candidate could refuse. He would be running away from the fight, they argue.

But others note that, in all likelihood, one of the candidates in 1964 will be the President of the United States, seeking re-election. As a practical matter, twin billing on television would let the opponent share in the advantageous spotlight that falls naturally on a President. As a philosophical matter, the President might be overexposing himself and his mighty office.

November 7, 1960

429

Kennedy Agreeable To 1964 TV Debate

By TOM WICKER
Special to The New York Times.

WASHINGTON, Feb. 1—President Kennedy declared today his willingness to engage in a televised debate with a contender for his office in 1964.

To a reporter who raised the question at his news conference today, Mr. Kennedy said flatly: "I would, yes."

Mr. Kennedy's victory over Richard M. Nixon in the Presidential election last year has been attributed by some to his performance in four televised discussions with the Republican candidate.

Shortly after his election on Nov. 8, Robert F. Kennedy, his brother's campaign manager and now the Attorney General, speculated that an incumbent President might be unwilling to give a challenger the opportunity to question him before a national audience.

Since then it has been widely doubted that President Kennedy would agree to debate in 1964. The doubters pointed out that he had benefited last year from appearing on equal terms with the better-known Vice President and might not wish to give a 1964 opponent the same privilege.

Others speculated that a functioning President could not afford to put himself in a position where he might have to decline an answer or disclose information injurious to the nation or to his Administration.

President Kennedy, by his unequivocal stand today, appeared to have committed himself, however, to enter such debates in 1964—provided he is the Democratic nominee and provided the Republican challenger is willing.

In another question about politics, the President was asked what his philosophy was.

He replied:

"I don't call myself anything except a Democrat who's been elected President of the United States, and I hope I am a responsible President."

Meanwhile, developments on Capitol Hill indicated probable modification of the equal time requirement for radio and television political broadcasts. That would make possible a broadcast debate between Presidential candidates.

A temporary suspension of the equal time requirement for President and Vice-Presidential candidates only permitted last year's Nixon-Kennedy debates as well as several interview and documentary programs.

Ordinarily, the equal time requirement, a part of the law governing political broadcasting since 1934, makes it mandatory for broadcasters to provide the same amount of free time to all candidates for an office that they give to any one candidate.

Since there are many minor-party Presidential candidates, this provision had to be suspended before the television and radio networks could give the major party candidates free time for joint or separate appearances.

Representatives of the American Broadcasting Company and the Mutual Broadcasting System told a Senate subcommittee today that they supported a bill offered by Senator Warren G. Magnuson of Washington, the Democratic chairman of the Interstate and Foreign Commerce Committee. It would make the 1960 suspension permanent.

Alfred R. Beckman, vice president, represented A. B. C. Stephen J. McCormick, also a vice president, spoke for Mutual.

Mr. Beckman's position was more restricted than that taken by Mr. McCormick or those of Dr. Frank Stanton, president of the Columbia Broadcasting System; Robert E. Kintner, president of the National Broadcasting Company, and Leroy Collins, president of the National Association of Broadcasters, all of whom testified yesterday.

These witnesses advocated the outright repeal of the equal time requirement, an action that would eliminate it for all political candidates, national, state and local.

Repeal has the personal support of Senator John O. Pastore of Rhode Island, the Democratic chairman of the subcommittee. Senator Magnuson's bill, however, is considered likelier to win Congressional approval.

It would not remove the obligation imposed on broadcasters to operate "in the public interest" and thus to deal objectively and fairly with all candidates for an office, and with all sides of an issue.

KENNEDY TERMED DEBATES' WINNER

Sociologists Hear a Report on 22 Studies of Response

By DONALD JANSON
Special to The New York Times.

ST. LOUIS, Sept. 2—The debate over the "great debates" of last year's Presidential campaign has been settled, at least to the satisfaction of the sociologists.

A study of twenty-two surveys of public response to the four televised encounters indicates that President Kennedy was the over-all winner.

The study also indicates that the debates contributed to Mr. Kennedy's close victory at the polls over Richard M. Nixon.

These conclusions were reached although, according to the study, Mr. Kennedy clearly won only the first debate and his greatest gain in winning it was to nail down the support of doubting Democrats.

The study was made by Prof. Elihu Katz of the University of Chicago and Jacob J. Feldman of the National Opinion Research Center. Their findings were presented today at a panel discussion at the annual meeting of the American Sociological Association.

Issues and Images

Eleven of the twenty-two surveys involved sought to determine who won the debates. Each gave the first encounter to Mr. Kennedy. The second and fourth were found to be very close. The third, on foreign policy, was given to Mr. Nixon.

The study said that foreign policy was the paramount issue in the campaign and that it increased in importance following the second, third and fourth debates. Therefore, the study suggested, Mr. Nixon "surely ought to have won" the debates if issues had been decisive.

But issues were not decisive, the analysts concluded.

"There is no doubt," they said, "that the debates were more effective in presenting the candidates than the issues."

They found a consensus that Mr. Kennedy did "far better" than his opponent in suggesting a positive image.

Public interest in the debates was found to have decreased noticeably after the first one.

"The first debate," the analysts decided, "apparently made most of the difference."

They said that Mr. Kennedy had strengthened his Democratic support and converted a few Republicans in the first encounter.

It was found that "a sizable proportion" of the voting population, especially Democrats, felt that the debates had helped them decide how to vote.

A national poll showed that the Kennedy vote had increased 5 per cent during the campaign and that the Nixon vote had fluctuated only a few percentage points.

"But these figures conceal considerable movement," the analysts reported. Some of the surveys indicated that as much as 20 per cent of the electorate changed from undecided to a candidate, or from one candidate to the other.

According to the surveys, about 70,000,000 of the 107,000,000 adults in the country, more than 65 per cent, watched the first debate, and none of the telecasts drew fewer than 55 per cent. It was estimated that more than 80 per cent of the population saw or heard at least one of the debates.

Make-Up of Audiences

The surveys indicated that the audiences contained about an equal number of Nixon and Kennedy supporters, proportionately more Roman Catholics than Protestants and proportionately more college graduates than non-college voters.

It was estimated that 80 per cent of the nation's business and professional men and women heard the debates, compared with about half of the farmers and manual workers.

Those who did not tune in to the debates heard about them quickly through discussion and newspaper reports.

"Not more than 10 per cent of the population failed to learn about the debates within twenty-four hours," the analysts said.

CHANGES URGED FOR TV DEBATES

4 Published Reports Propose Altering Present Format

By VAL ADAMS

Three political scientists and a journalist made suggestions yesterday for changes in the method of presenting televised debates by Presidential candidates.

One suggestion would have Congress enact a law calling upon the networks to allocate time for joint appearances (no more than five and not less than three) by candidates of both major parties. If either candidate failed to appear, the time should be forfeited and made available to his opponents.

Varying views on changing Presidential debates for public betterment were contained in a pamphlet issued by the Center for the Study of Democratic Institutions, which was founded by the Fund for the Republic. Four reports in the pamphlet, entitled "The Great Debates," analyzed the joint television appearances in 1960 of Senator John F. Kennedy, the Democratic candidate, and Vice President Richard M. Nixon, the Republican nominee.

The suggestion for new Federal regulations was made by Malcolm Moos, now on the staff of the Rockefeller Brothers Fund and formerly a Special Assistant to Dwight D. Eisenhower when he was President. Mr. Moos, who thinks the debates offer new hope of a more rational politics, said he could foresee a day when a candidate who is a Presidential incumbent might not want to face his lesser known opponent on television.

'President Should Appear'

"The President should appear in the debates . . . to help restore the balance that heavily favors incumbency," said Mr. Moos. "Year by year the advantage of incumbency becomes more apparent."

Harvey Wheeler, formerly Professor of Political Science at Washington and Lee University, also brought up the question of a future President who might wish to draw on the full dignity of his office and avoid direct confrontation with his challenger.

"This is what gives force to the recommendations contained in the paper by Malcolm Moos," said Mr. Wheeler.

Opposition to any proposed laws governing debates was expressed by Earl Mazo, chief of the Washington bureau of The New York Herald Tribune.

"I believe," he said, "that the broadcasting industry, the Presidential candidates and their campaign hierarchies will manage the situation very well, in view of the wisdom they usually display collectively."

In 1960 the networks made free air time available for the debates after Congress suspended equal-time regulations covering all candidates. Several bills now pending in Congress would modify or again suspend the equal-time law in Congressional and gubernatorial races this year and the Presidential election in 1964.

Changes Suggested

Format changes suggested by Mr. Mazo included restricting the first two or three debates in the series to one or two overriding issues, having the Vice Presidential candidates appear on at least one program and making the final program "a no-holds-barred verbal contest between the candidates with no one in the middle."

Mr. Wheeler said a weakness of the 1960 debates was that the candidates concentrated on projecting images instead of reality.

"What must be emphasized is not the competition between personalities but the competition between programs and policies," he said.

The most critical report on the 1960 TV debates was written by Hallock Hoffman, a staff member of the Center for Democratic Institutions and director of its study of the political process. He said the debates represented efforts by candidates to avoid offending any substantial group and appearing personally attractive to everyone.

July 16, 1962

ROCKEFELLER BIDS GOLDWATER JOIN DEBATE ON ISSUES

By JOSEPH A. LOFTUS
Special to The New York Times

EUGENE, Ore., Oct. 12—Governor Rockefeller of New York invited Senator Barry Goldwater of Arizona today to join him in a series of debates on how the Republican party could best deal with the issues of the day.

The Governor, here for a conference of Republicans from 13 western states, said he thought former Vice President Richard M. Nixon was a candidate for the Republican nomination for President in 1964.

In his prepared remarks for a conference luncheon, Governor Rockefeller said:

"I invite Senator Goldwater to join with me in a series of debates on how our party can best deal with the vital issues before the American people today, issues that so crucially affect their future, the future of their families and the future of freedom everywhere."

Drives for a Consensus

"This, in my opinion, would greatly sharpen public interest in the Republican party and what it stands for, and accelerate the achievement of a Republican consensus."

[In San Francisco. Senator Goldwater conditionally accepted holding a "discussion" with Governor Rockefeller on the party's role. The Senator, on his way to Oregon, said he would do this if both men became candidates for the Republican nomination and if Mr. Rockefeller "would spend his time discussing the Kennedy Administration," United Press International reported.]

The Governor's statement on Mr. Nixon was an answer to a news conference question. He declined to elaborate.

Mr. Rockefeller was the first prominent Republican to say publicly that he thought the former Vice President, who lost narrowly to President Kennedy in 1960, was a candidate for the nomination in 1964.

Mr. Nixon has repeatedly said in recent weeks that he was not a candidate. He has said that his answer covered all contingencies because he did not believe there could be a real draft without the connivance of the man being drafted.

In another answer, the Governor found himself interpreted as saying that Senator Goldwater would be an easier target for President Kennedy in 1964 than some other Republican nominee. But then he deftly withdrew from that position.

The Senator was also attending the conference, which filled every hotel and motel room in that area. Mr. Goldwater, in remarks prepared for a dinner meeting, confined himself to sharp attacks on the Kennedy Administration and to the alternative offered by the Republicans.

Governor Rockefeller, answering questions at his press conference, acknowledged that his divorce and remarriage had set him back politically but he said that "time will tell" whether the effect would be permanent. He also agreed that, while his personal life was not a legitimate issue, it was "rightly a concern" of every voter and delegate to the Republican National Convention.

The Governor said he was "sorry Happy [Mrs. Rockefeller] is not here, but we have been in Europe two weeks and she felt she could not leave the children."

He made this comment to an audience at French Lick, Ind., yesterday, remarking, for the first time in a speech, on Mrs. Rockefeller's children by her previous marriage. The Rockefeller staff declined to say where the children were living or how frequently Mrs. Rockefeller saw them.

The subject of Mr. Nixon arose with the question, "What do you think Mr. Nixon's role will be in 1964?"

"I think he's a candidate," was the reply. Then the following exchange took place.

Q. Why? A. You asked me what role he'd play and I said he was a candidate.

Q. If Nixon is a candidate, how do you tell who is not a candidate, since everybody denies it? A. That's a good question.

Q. Do you have an answer? A. No.

Governor Rockefeller was asked if he has an agreement with Mr. Nixon regarding 1964. He replied, "absolutely not," and the questioning continued:

Q. Do you reject the view that Senator Goldwater has 500 convention votes? A. I don't see how he could. They haven't been elected yet.

Q. The President seemed optimistic about Senator Goldwater's chances to be nominated? A. I should think he would want to be.

Q. Why? A. I suppose he would—he'd like to continue.

It seemed clear that Mr. Rockefeller was implying that Senator Goldwater would be an easier opponent for Mr. Kennedy, but the next question and answer made that fuzzy.

"Why," he was asked, "would the President prefer Senator Goldwater as the nominee?"

"Well," said the Governor, pausing at length, "I only know what I read in the newspapers."

Then he was asked whether the President could beat Senator Goldwater and he answered, "No."

Governor Rockefeller was asked if he was not implying that Senator Goldwater would be the easiest candidate for President Kennedy to beat.

"My implication," he replied, "was that that's what President Kennedy thought."

In his remarks, Senator Goldwater characterized the Kennedy Administration as "bereft of principles, barren of frankness nad bogged in doubletalk."

The Senator said Republican principles demanded that American strategy be tested by this standard: "If it advances the cause of freedom, do it. If it injures that cause, reject it."

He went on:

"What has the New Frontier to offer in that area? It has the wall in Berlin. It has the slow take-over of Laos. It has the Bay of Pigs. It has chaos in Vietnam. It has the drying shell of what was once the mightiest alliance for peace and freedom ever forged, NATO. It has new enemies and few good neighbors in Latin America. It has, in short, failure and fear where, under Republicans, we had known forthrightness, hope and confidence."

October 13, 1963

GOVERNOR GOADED BY MORGENTHAU

Democrat Challenges Him to Argue National Issues

Robert M. Morgenthau declared yesterday that he was prepared to debate Governor Rockefeller on national affairs if the Governor persisted in refusing to debate state issues.

The Democratic-Liberal candidate for Governor said it was now obvious that "the real gleam in Rockefeller's eye is the White House, not affairs here at home."

"I accept Rockefeller's challenge to make President Kennedy and his program a major issue in this campaign," he said. "I know the people will stand with Kennedy and not with Rockefeller."

Mr. Morgenthau's statement was viewed as an effort to turn New York's 1962 race in part into a Kennedy vs. Rockefeller battle.

The candidate, back on full campaign schedule after fighting off an influenza attack for 48 hours, put it almost in those words.

"If the people of New York want to help President Kennedy, then let's beat Rockefeller now," he said.

In this and another statement, Mr. Morgenthau charged the Governor was taking the New York electorate "for granted," purposely kept them uninformed on state matters and sought "to cloud the issues with happy promises and phony statistics."

Mr. Morgenthau asserted that the Governor, who has declined free television and radio time offered for debate, "even refuses to appear on the same television show even though our appear-

ances would be in separate interviews."

He said the Governor had "ducked out" on such a scheduled joint appearance on the "Today" show on WNBC, set for the morning of Oct. 29. Producers of the show, however, said late yesterday that negotiations for the Governor's appearance were still in progress.

Both Mr. Morgenthau and William H. McKeon, the Democratic state chairman, denounced the New York Republican delegation's record in Congress. Mr. Morgenthau accused the Governor of "condoning and encouraging" the delegation's overwhelming opposition to medical care for the aged, economic aid to depressed areas, housing and other Kennedy programs.

Mr. Morgenthau attacked the Rockefeller administration for failure to meet the crisis in state education at rallies before students and faculty at Columbia University and City College.

Mr. Morgenthau spent the afternoon with Controller Arthur Levitt and John J. Burns, their running mate for Lieutenant Governor, shaking hands with shopping crowds along Brooklyn's Fulton Street. Walking with them were City Controller Abraham D. Beame and Borough President Abe Stark of Brooklyn.

Hundreds surged up to shake hands with the candidates, who traveled with many on the local ticket. Despite Mr. Morgenthau's shy manner, he was warmly received and many who did not stop to shake his hand shouted, "Good luck!" or "Five votes in our house for you!"

In the evening, the candidate addressed a total of 600 persons at rallies in Oyster Bay, East Meadow and Elmont, all in Nassau County.

October 19, 1962

N.B.C. WILL SPONSOR A TV DEBATE STUDY

CHICAGO, March 5 (AP) — Robert W. Sarnoff, board chairman of the National Broadcasting Company, said tonight that a study would be made to determine the best format for television debates between the 1964 Presidential candidates.

Mr. Sarnoff told the 26th Chicago World Trade Conference that N.B.C. had made a grant for this purpose to the American Political Science Association, a professional organization devoted to the study of Government and politics.

The study will be conducted by a seven-man committee appointed by the association. The committee will be headed by Dr. Carl J. Friedrich, president of the association and Eaton professor of the science of government at Harvard University.

"By starting at this early date," Mr. Sarnoff said, "the group will be able to present its findings well in advance of the 1964 Presidential campaign. I am confident that its proposals will be a major contribution to our Democratic process."

March 6, 1963

Rockefeller Rebuts Goldwater; Senator Scorns Call to Debate

Arizonan Attacks Again
By The Associated Press

LOS ANGELES, Jan. 4 — Senator Barry Goldwater said today that Governor Rockefeller was more a Democrat than a Republican.

The conservative Arizona Senator, stopping here on his way back to Washington from Phoenix, Ariz., said he saw no sense in the face-to-face debates proposed by the New York Governor, the only other announced candidate for the Republican Presidential nomination.

"I'd rather take on President Johnson on the weaknesses of his Administration," Mr. Goldwater said.

He said in an interview at the airport here that Mr. Rockefeller advocated policies more in keeping with the Democratic platform than with Republican principles.

Mr. Goldwater, who entered the race for the Republican nomination yesterday, said the nation should have a clear choice of philosophies. But he said of Governor Rockefeller:

"Debating him would be more like debating a member of the New Frontier than like debating another Republican."

Mr. Goldwater said that if he won the nomination he wanted to debate with President Johnson. He said he thought Mr. Johnson would debate in the Presidential campaign.

"I see no sense in Republicans berating other Republicans," Mr. Goldwater said.

"If I can get the nomination, I think I can run a stronger race than any other Republican," he said. "A strong race, win, lose or draw, will strengthen the Republican party."

Mr. Goldwater said a strong showing in the Presidential election would carry with it victory for Republicans running for Governor, Congress and state legislatures across the nation.

The Senator said he thought President Kennedy would have been a more formidable opponent for the Republicans than Mr. Johnson. "He had a lot of things that President Johnson doesn't have," Mr. Goldwater said.

January 5, 1964

MILLER BELIEVES GOLDWATER LEADS

WASHINGTON, Jan. 11 (UPI) — Representative William E. Miller of New York, the Republican national chairman, said today that the race for the G.O.P. Presidential nomination was wide open but that Senator Barry Goldwater of Arizona appeared to be the strongest candidate.

He gave his appraisal after a Republican National Committee meeting that concluded four days of conferences by party leaders preparing for the 1964 campaign.

But Mr. Miller said at a news conference that no candidate was yet close to the 655 convention votes needed to win the nomination next July.

In winding up the meeting, the national committee adopted a number of resolutions, among them one calling for nationally televised debates between the Democratic and Republican candidates next fall.

debated the then Vice President Richard M. Nixon, the Republican candidate.

Noting that President Johnson had sought a debate with Mr. Kennedy in 1960, the resolution urged that there be more than four debates—the number held by Mr. Kennedy and Mr. Nixon. Mr. Johnson and Mr. Kennedy, then rival candidates for the Democratic Nomination, made a joint appearance before the Texas delegation at the party's national convention.

Another G.O.P. resolution

adopted today urged the President to name a bipartisan commission to study the problem of Presidential succession.

Former Vice President Richard M. Nixon urged today that the nation's major political parties nominate men of equal ability as President and Vice President and abandon the "politically cynical" formula of balancing the tickets.

He pointed out that 16 times in our history, for a total of 40 years, the office of Vice President had been vacant.

The office, he said, "has become necessary to the country."

"From now on it is absolutely essential that both political party conventions nominate two Presidents—candidates for both national offices, President and Vice President — who have the ability and experience to lead the nation in these perilous times."

Referring to President Kennedy's assassination, Mr. Nixon said that "we have swiftly and dramatically been reminded again that when we choose a man for Vice President, we may also be choosing a man who will become President."

He also urged that permanent formula for third-in-line successor be enacted. He suggested that the Constitution be amended to provide for the electoral college to be reconvened to choose a man to fill a Vice-Presidential vacancy.

Mr. Nixon made the remarks in an article in the current issue of The Saturday Evening Post.

January 12, 1964

The first of the Kennedy-Nixon debates in 1960. Moderator Howard K. Smith, center, faces a panel of network reporters.

"The television debates of 1960 were the most significant innovation in Presidential campaigns since popular elections began."

The Case for Political Debates on TV

A broadcaster analyzes the role of his medium in Presidential campaigns, and argues that bringing candidates face to face can only help the electorate choose wisely.

By FRANK STANTON

IN 1960, for the first time in history, the two major candidates for the Presidency of the United States met face to face on television in direct, unrehearsed discussion of the issues before the nation. More than 100 million people saw at least one of the four broadcasts. Public-opinion polls revealed that those "very much interested" in the campaign rose from 45 per cent before the debates to 57 per cent after them, compared with a rise, during a like period in 1956, from 46 per cent to only 47 per cent. And on Election Day, 1960, 64.5 per cent of eligible voters went to the polls as compared with 60.4 per cent four years earlier.

James Reston concluded that the debates were "a great improvement over

FRANK STANTON, the president of C.B.S., was instrumental in persuading Congress to suspend temporarily the "equal-time" law in 1960 and thus make possible the televised Kennedy-Nixon campaign debates that year.

the [candidates'] frantic rushing about the nation, roaring at great howling mobs. . ." Walter Lippmann called them a "bold innovation which is bound to be carried forward into future campaigns and could not now be abandoned."

Yet, as this year's Presidential campaign approaches, one hears questions of the wisdom of repeating face-to-face encounters between the candidates on television. I think the answer is plain, that the 1960 debates made clear the importance of television as a compelling means of interesting and informing the public the very foundation of democratic action. But the medium remains, as it has been from the beginning, a source of uneasy or wistful concern to many politicians and their managers.

Franklin Roosevelt had used radio so effectively from 1932 to 1945 that the far greater potential of television was instinctively both feared and coveted from the beginning. It was unrealis-

tically assumed that the new medium could "sell" the public a nonentity. A photogenic candidate, it was imagined, skillfully presented over TV, would sweep the country and result in a kind of "government by Nielsen rating."

WHAT we now know about television and elections is infinitely less sensational but far more encouraging. Surveys during the nineteen-fifties showed that television was becoming an important source of information to the voter, as the medium developed in terms of both set ownership and news production facilities. By 1960, according to a University of Michigan Survey Research Center team, 60 per cent of American voters got most of their information on national elections from television. At the same time, research into the behavioral patterns of voters influenced by radio and television dispelled fears that the new medium could sell candidates like soap.

First, it showed that there was an extremely high tuneout—even of the party faithful—during paid political broadcasts, and that there was a point beyond which candidates occupied the airwaves at their own risk. Adlai Stevenson recognized this in 1952 when, after pre-empting prime evening time, he received a telegram saying: "I like Ike and I love Lucy. Drop dead."

Second, research indicated that a massive, one-sided political advertising campaign can alienate viewers and actually prove a liability to the candidate it means to promote. British researchers investigating the impact of television in their 1959 election found respondents disliking "the absence of the other party to answer back."

Finally, it was found that one-sided election propaganda rarely converts. Rather, it merely strengthens opinions already held. Moreover, it is the interested and the decided voter who most exposes himself to campaign oratory — probably primarily to confirm his own preformed opinions.

Instinctively sensing such a situation, from the beginning of television, political managers have experimented with new techniques for inviting and holding audience interest. In the 1950 New York gubernatorial campaign, Thomas E. Dewey pioneered the television "talkathon" as a form of paid political advertising. Questions were phoned in to Mr. Dewey, who answered them on the spot. At first glance, the innovation seemed impressive. The columnist John Crosby commented that "a man thinking on his feet is likely to blurt out the truth rather than the well-rounded wind-filled phrase . . . the old-fashioned campaign speech is a dead form of oratory on television."

THIS interment of the political monolog was slightly premature. The talkathon was indeed an imaginative, attention-getting device. But in subsequent applications it developed that there was frequently less to it than met the eye. Not always as spontaneous as it seemed to be, it could be staged and even rehearsed. Carefully phrased questions, the answers to which could

be worked out in committee long before broadcast time, were often the major substance of such programs, rather than genuine questions actually phoned in by the audience.

SUCH dangers are implicit in any broadcast which is arranged and controlled by a political organization, with a skilled staff determined to "protect" its candidate and to present only a predetermined "image." It is for this reason that the cameras need the freedom, during campaigns, to play their important—and perhaps even crucial—role as objective reporters on political figures and institutions, and should not be limited to service as hired-out facilities to partisan groups.

Network television cameras were able to bring the nominating conventions into the home, and fully reveal the sometimes impressive and sometimes ludicrous proceedings of these vitally important institutions, because they were free to show everything happening on the floor as well as in committee rooms, adjacent corridors and even surrounding hotels. The viewer knew more of what went on, in many cases, than those at the scene.

Of the 1952 Democratic national convention, Philip Hamburger wrote in The New Yorker:

"In a sense, television coverage of a national convention turns the entire nation into a huge town meeting." He called the proceedings "a manifestation of the right of every delegate—and by extension, every citizen — to take a direct part in the choosing of his President."

Conversely, television dealt a fatal blow to nomination by cabal. The television camera pushed open the door of the smoke-filled room with such finality that it is unlikely ever again to take the main event away from the convention floor.

Throughout the Presidential campaigns of the nineteen-fifties, however, television was severely handicapped by the famous "equal-time law." This law prohibits broadcasters from granting free time, or selling paid time, to the Democratic and Republican candidates unless an equal amount of time is offered on the same terms to all minority candidates, who in some elections have numbered as many as 20.

The original intent of the law was simply to prevent broadcasters from giving unfair advantage to one candidate over another. But its practical effect has been to bar debates and other special broadcasts presenting the major candidates, because the cost of providing equal time for all the minor candidates would be prohibitive.

Only a temporary suspension of this law, insofar as it applied to the Presidency, made possible the debates between John F. Kennedy and Richard M. Nixon four years ago. Otherwise, television would have had to make equal time available to such candidates as those of the Prohibition party, Independent American, Industrial Government, Vegetarian, and all the other parties that can meet the very liberal legal requirements, varying from state to state, for appearing on the ballot. It does not require a computer to figure out what an unbearable

burden this would place on the broadcaster, not to mention the ordeal it would inflict on the public.

DURING the first session of the present Congress, both houses passed bills—with minor differences still to be resolved—allowing broadcasters almost the same freedom in 1964 to cover the Presidential election campaign as they were given in 1960. Whether this action will result in debates or other broadcasts in which the candidates confront each other in face-to-face discussions, or whether TV will be limited to other ways of revealing the candidates and their views, is of course not certain in view of the death of President Kennedy (he had said on no fewer than three occasions that he would debate his opponent in 1964). It is certain that debates should not be casually dismissed.

TRUE, the 1960 "debates"— or, more properly, joint appearances—were criticized by some on the basis of their format. There is no doubt that the format was far from perfect. In fact, the networks originally suggested a simpler format, which would have engaged the candidates in direct discussion without the interposition of a panel of newsmen.

The candidates, however, preferred a more cautious approach. At the time, we were dealing not with what might be the ideal thing to do, but with a practical situation. We were trying to bring about the most significant innovation in Presidential campaigns since popular elections began. Remember that these were not only the first broadcast debates between major Presidential candidates; they were also the first face-to-face discussions of any kind between Presidential candidates in the history of the Republic. (Many forget that Lincoln and Douglas were running not for the Presidency but for the Senate at the time of their famous debates.)

The networks in 1960 were understandably flexible. Indeed, we would have been less than responsible if we had insisted on doing it our way or not at all. Our clear duty was to exercise the opportunities which we sought from the Congress — to bring to the American people, in the language of the Senate Subcommittee on Communications, "the living image of the Presidential candidate — how he looks, what he believes, what is his idea of America's future and its place in the world, and how he will exercise the power of the Presidency."

DESPITE imperfections of timing and format, every one of these objectives was advanced by both the substance and the manner of the joint appearances.

There were some astonishing criticisms of the debates. A magazine editor wrote that "the very fact of arousing the interest of the millions further lowers the level of campaign oratory." Beneath the surface of this charge is the conviction that the electorate is a great mob incapable of listening intelligently to a debate on government. It seems to me this is nothing more than a declaration of the bankruptcy of democracy, and I think it is both premature and fraudulent.

Surely it is better for the candidates to be judged with-

CHAT—"F.D.R. had used radio so effectively that TV's potential was feared and coveted from the start."

in the sight and hearing of all the voters than to be peddled as myths constructed out of the political mumbo jumbo which has so often in the past reduced the Presidential office to passiveness and inaction.

A prominent historian criticized the debates on the ground that some of the great Presidents of the past might not have fared so well as their opponents — a rather useless parlor game, especially since the historian did not mention the nonentities, scarcely known to the electorate, who did get into office. Nor did he mention the pressures under which a modern President works.

FOR example, while Lincoln had months to ponder the secession issue, from his election until the attack on Fort Sumter, Kennedy had little more than days to ponder the Russian missiles in Cuba. Presidents must stand far more demanding pressures of time today, and campaigns, to be revealing of how a man responds to pressures, should be attuned to them.

I hope that the candidates this year will see their way clear to participating in direct dialogues without the interposition of a panel of newsmen to ask the questions. Since the political history of this country has always focused on a few fundamental issues, I believe that it would be most desirable to have some debates on single issues. Such discussions, in depth and at length, could be the single most powerful force in educating our citizens during the campaign, and much of the effect would hold over long after the election.

Additionally, I believe that the Vice-Presidential candidates should also engage in broadcast debates. C.B.S. has offered the major parties time for such broadcasts as well as for Presidential confrontations.

In letters to the chairmen of the Democratic and Republican National Committees—sent, it turned out unhappily, on the day before President Kennedy's assassination — I noted that "it has been truly said that the Vice President is but a heartbeat away from the Presidency." The tragic events of the following day bore somber witness to the ever-present relevancy of the Vice President's qualifications.

IT is reasonable to assume that the Republican candidate for the Presidency, under present circumstances, would want to debate his opponent. It is equally reasonable to believe that President Johnson's decision, assuming his candidacy, will be much more difficult. It has been said that President Johnson may suffer unfavorably in comparison with Mr. Kennedy's debate appearances in 1960. His advisers have been reported as urging him not to give his lesser-known opponent the opportunity to debate with him. There have been recollections of the belief prevalent in 1960 that Mr. Nixon lost the election when he consented to debate.

And yet, in 1960, many of Senator Kennedy's advisers had serious reservations about letting him debate with Vice President Nixon. The Vice President was known as a skilled debater and a forceful television personality. His famous "Checkers speech" in 1952 was supposed to have revealed him as a master of the medium. His experience in the Administration, his knowledge of inside facts and his close relationship with President Eisenhower added to his prospects. At the time, it might very well have been said that John F. Kennedy was no match for Richard M. Nixon before the camera.

There is, in my opinion, no such thing as a "telegenic" political personality. It is a myth that television can alone make or break a candidate. Television cannot "create" a personality. It can only give the personality that exists a wider audience—in effect, enlarge the meeting place where he appears before the voters.

AS a matter of fact, it was much easier in the days of the "front-porch" campaign—when nobody but a trickle of party stalwarts saw the candidates except at a few carefully staged rallies—to create a political personality out of thin air. One has to go back no farther than the Harding campaign to suggest that many an inadequate candidate in the past could not have survived the scrutiny permitted the voter by television in 1960. Far from creating synthetic personalities, television can only unmask them.

Both the style and personality of President Johnson, as revealed on television, are different from those of President Kennedy But the difference is not rooted in television; the two men are in fact different in their personalities and in their styles—off television as well as on.

President Kennedy was a man of distinctive character and characteristics—and they were clearly perceptible on television. So is President Johnson. Indeed, President Johnson seems to have captivated and strengthened the whole country and reassured the world by the warmth and earnestness of his television appearances immediately following his accession to the Presidency. These and other qualities are ones that he brings to the office and that are revealed

on television — not what he brings to television and then adapts to the office.

THE argument that it would be highly dangerous—or even imprudent, as President Eisenhower thought—for an incumbent President to debate in any forum does not seem to me persuasive. After all, the President has been televised live in news conferences and has been regularly questioned by as many as 200 correspondents on any subject they may wish to bring up. Surely, his opponent for the Presidency would be no less responsible and no less devoted to the national interest than the newsmen.

And surely any audience would recognize the need for restraint on the part of both candidates. As a matter of fact, Mr. Nixon was, in 1960, privy to the highest state secrets, and Mr. Kennedy respected his position.

As for the dangers of direct dialogue between the two candidates, they may also be more imagined than real. In many other democracies, heads of government periodically submit to questioning by the Opposition as a part of the parliamentary system. This practice is considered a distinct advantage over ours by many political scientists, who envy for instance, the Opposition's power in England to question the Prime Minister on the floor of the House of Commons.

This system depends importantly on the Opposition's maintaining the same high degree of responsibility in its questioning that we could certainly expect from a candidate running against an incumbent President. He would have little to gain — and everything to lose—by exceeding the bounds of propriety.

In the final analysis, the public should be the only touchstone to the decision of whether or not there should be debates. It may well be that, under some circumstances, more informal dialogues between candidates would be equally or even more helpful to the voters. It is not a question of what is in the best interests of the candidate. It is not a question of what is in the best interests of broadcasters or any other group. The one, the only, valid question is what is most helpful to the people in the first business of democracy the free and informed choice of its leadership.

DEBATES ON TV

TO THE EDITOR:

Frank Stanton based "The Case for Political Debates on TV" (Jan. 19) on false premises, omissions and strained logic.

His claim that "very liberal legal requirements" permit many Presidential candidates to qualify for equal time is untrue. The fact is in 1960 only four minority parties could meet these requirements in more than one state.

His contention that limiting TV opportunities to two think-alike major candidates would enlighten the electorate and enhance democracy is specious. Presenting one view exclusively, while suppressing other divergent views, fails to enlighten and is the antithesis of democracy.

The American people can pass proper judgment only if fully informed on all views. In a democracy the right to hear is as important as the right to speak.

Active, vocal minorities have often been a source of social progress as American history amply demonstrates. Accordingly, the rights and opportunities for minorities such as the Socialist Labor Party to be heard over the publicly owned airwaves should be protected and fortified, not weakened nor suppressed.

ERIC HASS,

Editor, Weekly People. New York.

March 8, 1964

Nixon Urges TV Debates

CINCINNATI, Feb. 12 (UPI) —Mr. Nixon said today he believed Presidential candidates should meet in face-to-face debates.

"National television debates should be used," Mr. Nixon said. "They are necessary and desirable."

He said he thought that the debates he had with President Kennedy in 1960 "rendered a great service." Millions of persons, he said, watched and "the American people won."

He acknowledged that the four debates might have played a decisive part in his narrow loss to Mr. Kennedy, but he said he still favored debates.

APPROVAL NEARS FOR TV DEBATES

Congressional Accord on Equal Time Is Reached

By CABELL PHILLIPS
Special to The New York Times

WASHINGTON, May 7—The prospect of televised debates between the Presidential candidates moved an important step toward realization today.

House and Senate conferees agreed on a compromise version of bills already passed by each body permitting the Federal Communications Commission to suspend temporarily its equal-time provision for broadcasts by political candidates.

The proposal duplicates a measure enacted in 1960 under which the historic campaign debates between John F. Kennedy and Richard M. Nixon took place.

The House approved such a bill for the 1964 campaign last June and the Senate followed suit in October. The House version called for suspension of the F. C. C. regulations in the last 75 days of the campaign and the Senate bill for a suspension of 60 days.

Today's conference report is based on the Senate's 60-day version. The bill may now be brought up in each chamber at any time, and passage seems assured.

Legislation was necessary to set aside a provision of the communications act of 1934. This provision requires broadcasting companies allowing free time to any political candidate to "afford equal opportunities to all other candidates for that office," including minor and splinter parties.

TV DEBATES HELD USEFUL TO PUBLIC

But Great Caution Is Urged if a President Participates

By ROBERT B. SEMPLE Jr.
Special to The New York Times

WASHINGTON, July 12 — A special commission of the American Political Science Association said today that televised debates between Presidential candidates added a useful dimension to American public life—with one important exception.

The commission said that such debates should be approached with great care whenever one of the opposing candidates already occupies the Presidency.

As a result, the commission's 43-page report, which is generally favorable in its tone and its conclusions to the principle of televised debates, may reinforce the misgivings about such debates expressed privately by both President Johnson and his probable Republican opponent, Senator Barry Goldwater of Arizona.

Reservations Indicated

Neither Mr. Johnson nor Mr. Goldwater has publicly announced a refusal to participate in debates similar to those between Vice President Richard M. Nixon and Senator John F. Kennedy in 1960. But both are said to have deep reservations, based largely on the fear that the debates might confront an incumbent President with an unhappy choice between divulging classified information or adopting a false position to conceal it.

Mr. Johnson's confidence in his own ability to perform successfully before the television cameras has grown in the eight months he has been in office. Despite this, however, his aides are known to fear not only that he might be placed in a position where he would have to deal with classified information or adopt a position to conceal it, but also that he should not engage in any encounter that might lessen the prestige of his office.

As for Mr. Goldwater, he has refused an invitation to debate Pennsylvania's Governor, William W. Scranton, but has said that he would debate Democrats. Mr. Goldwater has also told associates, however, that he thinks the President of the United States can create great misunderstandings at home and abroad by impromptu remarks, and on this ground would probably oppose any debates between Mr. Johnson and himself.

Appears to Agree

In its report, the commission appeared to agree with these views. "Extraordinary situations," it wrote, "may be created by the exigencies of the world situation and the international position of the United States. In some of these situations it may be contrary to our national interest for the President to engage in debates. The Cuban invasion and the missile crisis are recent examples. It is possible to imagine even more perilous situations."

The report was compiled partly on the basis of the committee's own readings and partly on the basis of replies to a letter asking for the views of all members of Congress, all state governors, the Republican and Democratic National Chairmen, and the chairmen of both parties in all 50 states.

A substantial number of those replying, the report said, questioned the advisability of the President's participating in televised debates.

Headed by Professor

The commission, appointed in the spring of 1963, was headed by Carl J. Friedrich, professor at Harvard University's Graduate School of Public Administration, and included Evron M. Kirkpatrick, executive director of the American Political Science Association; Harold D. Lasswell, professor of law and political science at Yale; Richard E. Neustadt, professor of government at Columbia University; Peter H. Odegard, professor of political science at the University of California; Elmo Roper of Elmo Roper and Associates, a public-opinion firm; Telford Taylor of the Columbia Law School; Charles A. H. Thompson of the Rand Corporation; and Gerhart D. Wiebe, dean of Boston University's School of Public Communication.

The commission said that debates, "properly conducted, are a desirable extension of traditional campaigning now that television is a settled feature of our national communications."

But it took pains to point out that not only its members but also those interviewed had criticized aspects of the Kennedy-Nixon debates. The most frequent criticism was that the format of those debates had turned them into a personality contest rather than a rational discussion of the issues. To that end, the commission made a number of suggestions for changes in format and procedure, among them these:

¶Encounters should consist not only of the Presidential debates, but also of discussions and other presentations, including perhaps debates between Vice-Presidential candidates and leading members of both parties.

¶The debates should take place weekly between Labor Day and Election Day, and should last for at least one hour.

¶The issues to be discussed should be clearly defined in advance and the debates should be sharply focused on particular topics.

¶Interviewers should be broadly representative of the American people, and not chosen from the press alone.

Goldwater 'Ready' To Debate Johnson In Campaign on TV

By E. W. KENWORTHY
Special to The New York Times

WASHINGTON, July 28 — Senator Barry Goldwater told a group of House Republicans today that he was "ready, willing and able" to debate the campaign issues with President Johnson on television.

Representative Jack Westland of Washington disclosed the Senator's readiness to face the President in debate after emerging from an hour-long meeting between the Republican nominee and 70 to 80 Republican members of the House.

The meeting was arranged by Mr. Westland for those House members who supported Senator Goldwater before the balloting began at San Francisco.

Debates of 1960 Recalled

Mr. Westland said Senator Goldwater had told the House group that he would like Congress to complete action before adjournment on legislation that would suspend the present so-called "equal-time" law.

Under the present law, candidates of minor parties can demand and get "equal time" if the broadcasting companies have given time to candidates of the major parties.

This law was suspended in 1960 by Congressional resolution. The suspension made possible the four debates between John F. Kennedy and Richard M. Nixon.

In June, 1963, the House passed a bill that would again suspend the "equal-time" requirement, and in October, 1963, the Senate passed a somewhat different version.

Last May 7, a conference committee of the two Houses agreed on a compromise. The conference report was filed in the House that month, but was not filed in the Senate until June 3 and nothing more has been done.

At his news conference last week, President Johnson dismissed a question on whether he would favor debates with his opponent by saying he would cross that bridge when he got to it.

Senator Goldwater himself has expressed doubts about the wisdom of an incumbent President's engaging in campaign debate. Last Feb. 12 in Portland, Ore., he said:

"I don't think a President of the United States should debate anybody. He . . . could very well disclose secrets that only he knows."

May 8, 1964

July 13, 1964

436

And on Jan. 31, he said:

"I think it's kind of dangerous to subject a President of the United States to questioning and debate. . . . After all, his is the most responsible job in the world and he just might slip and say something inadvertently that might change the course of history."

Administration Dubious

There is reason to believe that some Administration officials are reluctant to have the President engage Senator Goldwater for fear the Senator might be tempted in the heat of the contest to disclose something that would affect national security or relations with foreign countries.

As a member of the Senate Armed Services Committee and as a major general in the Air Force Reserve, Senator Goldwater has access to much classified information, particularly on military affairs.

Last April President Johnson publicly offered intelligence briefings to the candidates for the Republican nomination. Governor Rockefeller, Gov. William W. Scranton of Pennsylvania and Senator Margaret Chase Smith of Maine accepted the offer. Senator Goldwater rejected it as "an off-hand political gesture" that was "basically unwise."

According to informed sources, Secretary of State Dean Rusk, who relayed the first invitation under instructions of the President, wrote a second letter to Senator Goldwater in May renewing the invitation. These sources say that Mr. Rusk has not received a reply.

McCarthy's View

Last Sunday on the National Broadcasting Company's "Meet the Press" program, Senator Eugene J. McCarthy, Democrat of Minnesota, gave the following description of his experience in debating Senator Goldwater:

"The problem in debating with Senator Goldwater is that he really kind of steps outside of history, you see. He moves off into a kind of another world in which different standards prevail. He declares for himself a kind of immunity, really, from history, and it is extremely difficult to debate when the terms of the dialogue and the terms of correspondence have somehow been changed."

After today's meeting with House Republicans, Senator Goldwater held a peripatetic conference with reporters on the way to his black sports roadster.

He said the meeting last Friday afternoon with President Johnson to discuss how to avoid increasing racial tensions during the campaign had been amicable.

In San Francisco, Senator Goldwater had questioned the President's sincerity on civil rights, saying he was "the biggest faker in the United States" and "the phoniest individual who ever came around."

When a reporter asked today if there had been "any roasting of anybody's hide" at last Friday's meeting, Senator Goldwater replied:

"No, we're good friends. We're old political friends."

Asked if any subject other than racial tensions had come up, Senator Goldwater said:

"He warned me never to pull my dog's ears."

Sources close to the White House, however, give a somewhat different story.

One said today that the President was "chilly" toward Senator Goldwater; another said he gave him "the frigid treatment," and a third described the President's demeanor as neither friendly nor cold, but rather distant.

White House Cool To Debates on TV

By TOM WICKER
Special to The New York Times

WASHINGTON, July 29—President Johnson began something like a cat-and-mouse game with Senator Barry Goldwater today on the question of televised debates in the coming campaign.

George E. Reedy, the White House press secretary, made the President's move by using Senator Goldwater's words. He cited statements the Senator made last winter to the effect that a President in office was not obligated to debate his opponent.

Mr. Reedy declined to say, however, whether Mr. Johnson took the same view. And he said the question of debating the Republican Presidential candidate would be decided by "the Democrats" after the campaign had begun.

The White House statements were made in response to reports yesterday that Senator Goldwater had told a Congressional group that he was "ready, willing and able" to debate Mr. Johnson.

The net effect of the response was to leave the President free to enter a debate if he chooses, but also to lay the groundwork for refusing.

Informed sources insisted today that the President had made no decision on the debate question, and that in fact little thought had been given to the matter by him or by his advisers.

It was conceded, however, that a number of Mr. Johnson's associates are opposed to his participation in televised debates.

One reason for the opposition is the feeling that a President of the United States should not debate directly with anyone, even with a challenger for his office.

A more practical political consideration is that a Johnson-Goldwater political debate would tend to place Senator Goldwater more nearly in a status of equality with the President, thus lessening an immense campaign asset of any incumbent.

In addition, by appearing on the same television program with the President, Senator Goldwater would be given more public "exposure" than he might be able to get by appearing alone.

Another reason advanced by some of those opposed to a debate is that the campaign might become centered in the public mind on the single question of who scores the most points in a direct confrontation. Again, that might dissipate many of the advantages an incumbent President takes with him into a campaign.

All these factors, to some extent, worked to the advantage of Senator John F. Kennedy in his four campaign debates with Vice-President Richard M. Nixon in 1960.

He was less well known than the Vice President when the campaign opened, he was considered less experienced and, as the candidate of an incumbent party, Mr. Nixon had some of the assets of an incumbent President.

Most political observers agree that Senator Kennedy appeared to better advantage than Mr. Nixon in their first debate, however. He gained, as a result, wide public exposure and an equal footing with the Vice President.

No Johnson Decision

Mr. Johnson was pictured today as having no fear of debating Senator Goldwater but as having made no decision on the advantages and disadvantages involved.

The major argument against refusing to debate is that, after the pattern set by the Nixon-Kennedy confrontation, the public expects Presidential campaign debates and would tend to resent it if there were none in 1964.

Senator Goldwater also would be enabled to make the argument that the President feared or was in too weak a position to debate.

The Goldwater statements referred to today by Mr. Reedy would tend to weaken the Senator's ability to make that argument.

On Jan. 31, he said, "I think it's kind of dangerous to subject a President of the United States to questioning and debate. After all, his is the most responsible job in the world and he just might slip and say something inadvertently that might change the course of history."

He also said, on Feb. 12, as Mr. Reedy pointed out:

"I don't think a President of the United States should debate anybody. He could very well disclose secrets that only he knows."

Questions Challenge

Mr. Reedy also raised the question whether Senator Goldwater really had challenged the President to debate. He said the White House had had no formal word from the Senator and "all we've seen so far is the reported accounts of what Senator Goldwater has said, either directly or through an intermediary."

Senator Goldwater's remarks yesterday were given to the press by Representative Jack Westland, Republican of Washington. The Senator's office confirmed Mr. Westland's version of the remarks today.

But Mr. Reedy said that as a result of the Senator's statements last winter, and the apparently contradictory eagerness to debate he expressed yesterday, "we're not certain what he intends."

In any case, he said, carefully avoiding characterizing Mr. Johnson as a candidate for re-election, "the Democrats" would decide what to do about debates after the campaign begins in the fall.

Other sources insisted that little thought as yet had been

July 29, 1964

given to the question of Mr. Johnson's participation in the debates, and that the President had not expressed himself firmly, even to his aides.

But one Johnson supporter conceded:

"The more we get to thinking about the campaign, the more we'll have to think about the debates."

One factor that might influence that thinking was the recent report of a special commission of the American Political Science Association, which concluded that Presidential debates were useful but possibly dangerous when an incumbent was involved.

In some situations, the commission said, "It may be con- trary to our national interest for the President to engage in debates. The Cuban invasion and the missile crisis are recent examples. It is possible to imagine even more perilous situations."

Young-Taft Debate

WASHINGTON, July 29 (AP) —Senator Stephen M. Young, a Democrat, and Representative Robert Taft Jr., his Republican oppenent in this year's Ohio Senatorial election, have agreed to debate in Cleveland.

"I have accepted the invitation of the City Club of Cleveland to debate with my opponent," Mr. Young said in a statement.

An aide said Mr. Taft also had accepted the invitation.

July 30, 1964

A Presidential TV Debate?

The first debate of the Presidential campaign is over whether President Johnson should agree to a nationwide television debate with Senator Barry Goldwater.

The Republican nominee is reported "ready, willing and able" to debate. But he seems to have fashioned an escape-hatch for the President if Mr. Johnson wishes one by saying earlier: "I don't think a President of the United States should debate anybody. He could very well disclose secrets that only he knows."

There are some hazards to TV debate, of course, as Richard M. Nixon discovered to his lasting regret when he took on the late John F. Kennedy. But these are more political than they are dangers to the security of secret information. Every time a President subjects himself to questioning on a live TV and radio transmission of a press conference he incurs the identical peril of unwise disclosure. The nation has survived many such sessions.

As for the political risks, neither the President nor Mr. Goldwater can refuse television debate without inviting the charge of being "afraid" to face the opponent. However unjustified, this is hard to live down, and has to be endured. President Johnson handles himself adeptly and forcefully in the give-and-take of the press conference, and presumably would do at least as well in debate. The strategy question he and his advisers would have to answer would be whether he was doing his opponent a political favor by giving him the opportunity for wider public exposure.

The winner of a TV debate does not necessarily make the best President. But the good sense of the American people is the best assurance that they will give debate the right weight, no more no less than deserved, in the scales of decision on a President. They have now come to expect such debate. It will, we believe, become a permanent fixture of the American campaign, and a highly useful one for enabling the public to judge candidates and the merits of what they stand for. A Johnson-Goldwater debate— or debates—should be had, and it would be a good show.

July 31, 1964

Candidates' Debate on TV

C.B.S. Head Says Law's Equal-Time Provision Bars Broadcasts

To the Editor:

Tom Wicker's comprehensive news article in The New York Times July 30 concerning the possibility of radio and television debates between President Johnson and Senator Goldwater omits a basic fact. As a practical matter, broadcasters cannot carry such debates under the present law.

Section 315 of the Communications Act—the so-called equal-time provision—is still on the books, requiring that minor-party candidates, of which in each recent election there have been more than a dozen, would have to be given equal time. Only by the temporary suspension of Section 315 were the Kennedy-Nixon broadcast debates made possible. That suspension by the Congress in 1960 expired by its own terms after the 1960 election.

Pending Bill

This year, in order to make such debates possible again in the 1964 Presidential campaign, both the House and the Senate, by huge majorities, passed another suspension. But there was a slight variation between the House and Senate versions —one providing that the suspension would be effective beginning 60 days before Election Day, the other providing for 75 days.

After considerable delay, a conference committee resolved this difference. But the conference committee bill has not yet been reported out to, or voted on by, the Senate and the House. And there the matter stands.

On Nov. 21, 1963, I wrote the chairman of the Democratic National Committee and the chairman of the Republican National Committee, stating that, assuming the final passage of the Section 315 suspension, the Columbia Broadcasting System offers, over its television and radio networks, prime time for an extended series of joint appearances of the major parties' Presidential candidates and of their Vice-Presidential candidates during the eight-week period from Labor Day to Election Day. And I noted in the letters that we hoped very much that the candidates would see their way clear to appear in direct dialogues, where there could be an exchange of views and questions between them, without reliance upon a panel to put the questions or to determine the course of the discussion.

Single Issues

In the letter I also suggested that the candidates give serious consideration to the possibility of debates on single issues—such as civil rights, defense policies, the economy, relations with our allies and the containment of our adversaries. I suggested that for the initial and concluding joint appearances it would be greatly helpful for the candidates to discuss their over-all approach to the sum of the problems facing the nation.

And I emphasized that time would also be available for joint appearances of the major-party candidates for the Vice-Presidency.

I reaffirmed my strong view that the issue of whether the law should be suspended is not a question of what is in the interest of a particular candidate or of the broadcasters. The one, the only, valid standard is whether the public is served.

The offer we made in that letter of Nov. 21 and our views and hopes for the suspension of the law still stand. But until the conference committee reports the matter out to the House and Senate, and the House and Senate act, the question of broadcast debates between the Presidential candidates remains academic.

FRANK STANTON,
President, Columbia Broadcasting System.
New York, July 30, 1964.

August 1, 1964

SENATE G.O.P. EAGER TO CLEAR TV DEBATE

Special to The New York Times

WASHINGTON, Aug. 4—Senator Everett McKinley Dirksen indicated today that Republicans would force a vote on legislation to clear the way for debates by the Presidential candidates if they agree to debate.

A law now on the books requires that candidates of minor parties get time equivalent to that made available by the radio and television networks to the major party candidates.

In 1960, Congress voted to suspend the application of the law for the candidates for President and Vice President. This made possible the debates between John F. Kennedy and Richard M. Nixon.

A similar suspension bill has been agreed on by the Commerce committees of both houses. The conference report has been on the Senate table since June 3, but has not been called up. Since the Senate must act first, nothing has been done.

But since the report is a privileged matter, any member can call it up, and Senator Dirksen intimated he might do so Thursday.

Senator Dirksen's eagerness for action stems from an apparent change in attitude by Senator Goldwater. Earlier this year the Republican Presidential nominee said he thought an incumbent President should not participate in such debates. But last week Senator Goldwater said he was "ready, willing and able" to debate President Johnson.

August 5, 1964

If the President Debates

Gilbert Seldes Points to Restrictions Incumbent Faces

TO THE EDITOR:

Tom Wicker's news dispatch (July 30) from Washington is a comprehensive index of the problems involved in "the great debate" which have long concerned students of the mass media. I cannot be sure that any of my colleagues agree with my own solutions, but they all do agree that the decisions should be based on some general principle of action. Mr. Wicker's story indicates that all principles may be sacrificed to give a temporary advantage to either side.

One aspect of the situation is accepted: that the conditions of the debate differ when the conditions of the candidates are different. Four years ago we had two men equal in one respect, that neither was President of the United States.

This year we will have an incumbent President as one candidate. It is assumed that the other is at a disadvantage.

In practice, the President is in the difficult position of not being able to ask all sorts of questions and certainly of not being free to answer certain questions because of his position. He cannot, moreover, dodge, evade or even hesitate without giving the impression that something of grave importance cannot be divulged. A single troubled look before the TV cameras may start a panic—if not in the chancelleries of Europe, in Wall Street.

Not Extempore

The simple working rule should be that the President-as-candidate does not confront his rival in extempore debate. The consequence of this rule is that he is never challenged to that kind of debate so that he cannot be accused of being afraid of his rival.

This does not in the slightest degree limit the public "right to know." There are other ways of making known what needs to be known. There are other ways of asking the right and even the wrong questions.

The one thing we will not find out is how well the President-candidate handles himself before the cameras—how quick his responses are, how well he can box his rival, how skillful he is at dissembling.

These are indeed virtues in a man who must deal with politicians as well as statesmen. But it is possible to conceive of a man supremely well-fitted for the office who has these qualities in a very low degree, who prefers to speak only after he has done the fundamental brainwork of thinking, who is not a mental gymnast but understands the needs of his country, who does not shy away from appearing before the public and stating his position clearly, who can listen and argue, but isn't as effective as the man who has such a fast answer that one hardly stops to wonder whether the answer is right. GILBERT SELDES.

Truro, Mass., July 30, 1964.

The writer is Professor Emeritus of Communications, University of Pennsylvania.

August 6, 1964

For All Parties' TV Debate

Socialist Labor Party Candidate Backs Equal-Time Provision

TO THE EDITOR:

Your July 31 editorial urging a Presidential TV debate failed to mention a crucial factor on which the networks' concurrence in holding such debates hinges—namely, the suspension for Presidential candidates of Section 315a of the Communications Act. This is the law discussed by Frank Stanton, president of the Columbia Broadcasting System, in his letter to The Times published Aug. 1. Under this law all qualified candidates for public office are entitled to equal opportunity in the use of the publicly owned air waves.

Ironically, when the broadcasters and their friends urge the suspension of this law, they invariably argue that it would be in the interest of extending and enhancing democracy. I say "ironically" because it is a strange kind of "democracy" that is extended and enhanced by restricting free speech.

That, of course, is what the suspension of Section 315a would accomplish, for it would in effect confer a monopoly of the publicly owned air waves on the major-party candidates to the exclusion of the minor parties. It would deprive the candidates of the 74-year-old Socialist Labor party, for example, of freedom of speech.

Right to Hear

But it would also deprive the American people of freedom to hear all sides in the discussion of the grave issues of the campaign. The right to hear is as important as the right to speak.

Your news columns and editorials are witness to the multiplicity of the evils afflicting society. They range from abrasive poverty, race tensions and chronic unemployment to war, the anarchy of urban growth and the deadly pollution of air and water.

Few would deny that the roots of all these evils lie deep in the social and economic system. And those who really believe in democracy would, I think, agree that it is of crucial importance that light be thrown upon them from all angles and in the freest possible discussion.

A great deal is being said nowadays about the alleged differences between President Johnson and Senator Goldwater. But whatever differences there are, the two gentlemen are in basic agreement on the proposition that capitalism is the best of all possible systems and that the system of private ownership of the socially operated industries should be preserved at all costs.

Examination of Capitalism

Therefore, in any so-called debate between them, they could not objectively examine this system, nor could they logically indict it as the cause of unnecessary poverty, unemployment and war, etc., no matter how conclusive the evidence pointing in that direction.

In the interest of real democracy and the freest possible discussion of social issues, Section 315a (or what is left of it after the emasculating amendments of 1959) should be preserved even at the cost of forgoing what you describe as a "good show."

ERIC HASS,
Socialist Labor Party Candidate for President, 1964.
New York, Aug. 3, 1964.

August 7, 1964

439

RIGHTIST PLEDGES TO AID GOLDWATER

Christian Crusade Director Bids Candidates Debate

By DONALD JANSON
Special to The New York Times

DALLAS, Aug. 7 — The Rev. Billy James Hargis, founder and director of the Christian Crusade, endorsed Senator Barry Goldwater for President today.

He said in an interview on the opening day of the ultraconservative group's annual convention that he would do "everything in my power to help him."

The fundamentalist preacher is heard regularly over 400 radio stations in the United States, many of them in the South and Southwest.

He demanded that televised debates between the nominees of the two major parties be held.

Cites Democratic 'Excuse'

"The American people have a right to see these two candidates facing each other in public debate," he said.

Mr. Hargis said Democratic hesitation because of fear that President Johnson might reveal classified information was an invalid "excuse" to hide fear of losing the debates.

He said it was his impression, after traveling in several states this summer, that each candidate now had a 50-50 chance of election.

"The outcome will not be decided," he asserted, "by the work of right-wing and left-wing organizations such as the Christian Crusade, John Birch Society, Americans for Democratic Action and the National Association for the Advancement of Colored People.

"It will be decided," he said, "by the philosophies of the candidates themselves. The man who is the most convincing spokesman for his viewpoint will win."

He declared that conservatives "could not find a better spokesman for their cause than Barry Goldwater."

He said he might also add "waggishly" that he was "glad" President Johnson would be the spokesman for the "liberal" cause.

"Conversatives have greater reason for hope than we have ever had," the Oklahoman said.

He said the opportunity for a clear choice between the two philosophies, long sought by the right wing, was "the healthiest situation that could exist."

Mr. Goldwater's chances are greatly enhanced, he said, because the assassination of President Kennedy "by a Communist" had "exploded the liberal myth that there is no danger of internal Communist subversion."

Sees Party Realignment

Mr. Hargis said the campaign would hasten the process of realigning political party affiliation. He said he hoped to see the day when the "phony facades" of Democratic and Republican would be dropped and the nation would have only liberal and conservative groupings as in Britain.

For example, he said, having Governor Rockefeller and Senator Strom Thurmond of South Carolina on sides aligned with philosphies contrary to their views makes no sense.

Mr. Hargis said Senator Goldwater was right in renouncing support of the Ku Klux Klan yesterday. He said both the Klan and the Northern civil rights "invaders" now working on voter registration in Mississippi were "anarchists" and that "we must disavow anarchy."

He also supported the Arizonan's refusal to renounce the John Birch Society.

"Senator Goldwater would be very foolish to disavow the members of the John Birch Society and other conservative groups," he said, "because they include some of the best patriots in the country."

Johnson-Goldwater Debate Is Ruled Out by Senate Vote

By MARJORIE HUNTER
Special to The New York Times

WASHINGTON, Aug. 18 — Brushing aside Republican taunts that they were "chicken," Senate Democrats succeeded tonight in ruling out chances for televised debates between the Presidential candidates this fall.

Administration leaders rolled up a narrow three-vote majority to kill a compromise proposal suspending equal-time provisions of the Federal Communications Act. The vote was 44 to 41 to table the bill.

The motion to table the conference report was made by the Senate majority leader, Mike Mansfield of Montana. Republicans, solidly opposing the move, were joined by 12 Democrats.

The action ruled out hope for any "great debates," as they were called in 1960. Those debates between John F. Kennedy and Richard M. Nixon were made possible by Congressional suspension of the equal time provision.

By failing to suspend the equal-time provision, the Senate action would appear to limit the television industry to functioning solely within the framework of existing TV news programs except for paid political time.

Senator Urged Debate

If a network undertook any special reporting of candidates, it could leave itself liable to having to offer costly air time to all other candidates, including those from minor parties.

Thus far, there has been no test before the Federal Communications Commission on whether news conferences by Presidential or Vice-Presidential candidates would entitle minor candidates to equal time.

A loud, almost rowdy, debate preceded tonight's action.

Senator Hugh Scott, Republican of Pennsylvania, accused Democratic leaders of "taking orders from higher up."

Senator Scott suggested that the Democrats were being chicken by being afraid to allow President Johnson to face the Republican candidate, Senator Barry Goldwater.

Senator Goldwater has urged the President to debate him this fall. President Johnson has said, in effect, that he would cross that bridge when he came to it.

Senator Scott suggested that the Democrats should change their ballot symbol from a rooster to a chicken.

Senator John O. Pastore, Democrat of Rhode Island, jumped to his feet and shook his fist as he shouted:

"Don't let the Senator from Pennsylvania call us chicken. The chickens were hatched at the Cow Palace in San Francisco."

Senator Goldwater was nominated at the Cow Palace convention, despite efforts of some Republican party leaders, including Senator Scott. Since then, Senator Scott has said he will support Mr. Goldwater.

Senator Pastore, glancing toward Senator Scott, asked:

"Why didn't Mr. Goldwater debate with Mr. Scranton? Mr. Scranton said to Mr. Goldwater, 'Let's debate.'"

Senator Scott supported Gov. William W. Scranton of Pennsylvania for the Republican nomination.

Waving his arms as he paced around the Senate chamber, Senator Pastore said:

"No, they aren't playing politics. Who are they kidding?"

Joining Senator Scott in leading the Republican fight against the Democratic move to kill the proposal, Senator Norris Cotton, Republican of New Hampshire, said:

"Some who led the fight four years ago for this same thing have now turned their back on it."

He pointed out that 14 splinter parties would have been able to demand equal time in 1960 if Congress had not temporarily suspended the equal-time provision.

Tonight's showdown came 14 months after the House had passed a bill to suspend the equal-time provision for 75 days before the 1964 general election.

The Senate, last October, amended the bill to cut the suspension time to 60 days. But no efforts were made to hurry the bill off to conference, since the election was then a year away.

The compromise agreed on by conferees would have suspended the time for 60 days before the election—that is, from Sept. 4 to Nov. 2.

Roll-Call Vote in Senate On Equal-Time Measure

WASHINGTON, Aug. 18 (AP) —Following is the roll-call by which the Senate tonight killed, by tabling, a bill that would have suspended the equal-time provision of the Communications Act to permit Presidential debates. The vote was 44 to 41.

FOR THE MOTION—44

Democrats

Anderson (N. M.)   Long (La.)
Bartlett (Alaska)   Mansfield (Mont.)
Bayh (Ind.)   McCarthy (Minn.)
Bible (Nev.)   McClellan (Ark.)
Byrd (Va.)   McGee (Wyo.)
Byrd (W. Va.)   McGovern (S. D.)
Church (Idaho)   McIntyre (N. H.)
Clark (Pa.)   McNamara (Mich.)
Dodd (Conn.)   Metcalf (Mont.)
Douglas (Ill.)   Moss (Utah)
Edmondson (Okla.)   Muskie (Me.)
Fulbright (Ark.)   Neuberger (Ore.)
Gore (Tenn.)   Randolph (W. Va.)
Gruening (Alaska)   Ribicoff (Conn.)
Hart (Mich.)   Robertson (Va.)
Hayden (Ariz.)   Russell (Ga.)
Holland (Fla.)   Salinger (Calif.)
Humphrey (Minn.)   Smathers (Fla.)
Inouye (Hawaii)   Stennis (Miss.)
Johnston (S. C.)   Symington (Mo.)
Lausche (Ohio)   Talmadge (Ga.)
Long (Mo.)   Walters (Tenn.)

AGAINST THE MOTION—41

Democrats—12

Ellender (La.)   Pastore (R.I.)
Ervin (N.C.)   Pell (R.I.)
Jackson (Wash.)   Proxmire (Wis.)
Jordan (N.C.)   Sparkman (Ala.)
Monroney (Okla.)   Thurmond (S.C.)
Morse (Ore.)   Young (Ohio)

Republicans—29

Aiken (Vt.)   Keating (N.Y.)
Allott (Colo.)   Kuchel (Calif.)
Beall (Md.)   Mechem (N.M.)
Bennett (Utah)   Miller (Iowa)
Boggs (Del.)   Morton (Ky.)
Carlson (Kan.)   Mundt (S.D.)
Case (N.J.)   Prouty (Vt.)
Cotton (N.H.)   Saltonstall (Mass.)
Curtis (Neb.)   Scott (Pa.)
Dirksen (Ill.)   Simpson (Wyo.)
Dominick (Colo.)   Smith (Me.)
Fong (Hawaii)   Tower (Tex.)
Hruska (Neb.)   Williams (Del.)
Javits (N.Y.)   Young (N.D.)
Jordan (Idaho)

Paired were Hill, Democrat of Alabama, for, and Nelson, Democrat of Wisconsin, against; and Burdick, Democrat of North Dakota, for, and Hartke, Democrat of Indiana, against.

Dirksen Indifferent

WASHINGTON, Aug. 18 (UPI)—The Senate Republican leader, Everett McKinley Dirksen, told a news conference today he could "understand the argument on both sides" of the debate issue and the outcome made no difference to him.

Asked if he thought the Democratic move meant President Johnson was "afraid" to face Mr. Goldwater in television debates, the Illinois Republican replied:

"Maybe he's reluctant. Maybe he feels the dignity of his office is such he oughtn't to go out that way—that, being human, maybe his tongue would slip."

Setback Is Seen

Dr. Frank Stanton, president of the Columbia Broadcasting System, said last night: "This rejection of a previous overwhelming affirmative vote by both the House and the Senate represents a disturbing step backward in the progressive effort toward a better-informed electorate."

A spokesman for the National Broadcasting Company declined to comment on the Senate vote.

August 19, 1964

JOHNSON ASSAILED ON TV-DEBATE BILL

By JOSEPH A. LOFTUS
Special to The New York Times

WASHINGTON, Aug. 19— Senator Barry Goldwater's forces accused President Johnson today of ordering the death of a bill on free time that would have permitted a television debate between the two candidates for President.

Dean Burch, the Republican national chairman, who made the accusation, challenged the President to meet the issue by debating Senator Goldwater, the Republican Presidential nominee, on paid time and splitting the costs.

A half-hour program plus production expenses on one network would cost about $125,000.

Mr. Burch also said that the accounting of President Johnson's personal holdings, released today, was pointless, because present worth, not original cost was the pertinent point.

The President's method of listing his assets, Mr. Burch said is "like the City of New York listing the value of Manhattan Island as $24."

Says Public Should Know

The bulk of Mr. Johnson's wealth, he said was made in areas of Federal control-communication. The public has a right to know the fair market value of these assets, he said.

Mr. Burch refrained from a charge of wrongdoing but said a public officer must be not only above evil but also above the appearance of evil.

"Homicide" was Mr. Burch's word for the Senate's tabling yesterday of a bill that would have suspended the equal-time requirements of the Federal Communications Act.

The law provides that when a broadcast station gives a candidate free time it must afford all rival candidates equal opportunity to use the same facilities free. The problem flowing from this provision is the demand of splinter parties for time equal to any given the candidates of the two major parties.

Bill Aimed at Suspension

The bill tabled by the Senate Democrats would have suspended the provision.

The equal-time requirement does not apply to the appearances of candidates in connection with bona fide newscasts, bona fide news interviews, bona fide documentary broadcasts, and on-the-spot coverage of news events.

Mr. Burch said he had Senator Goldwater's assurance that he was willing to debate the President.

The decision to exploit President Johnson's reluctance to engage in TV debates is a switch in tactics. Last Feb. 12 in Portland, Ore., the Arizona Senator said:

"I don't think a President of the United States should debate anybody. He . . . could very well disclose secrets that only he knows."

Mr. Burch said that he did not want to do anything to imperil national security and that he would be glad to accept reasonable ground rules that would keep the debaters out of sensitive areas.

Mr. Burch, in his news conference, remarked:

"I can understand President Johnson's position, having seen him on television." Mr. Johnson, while in the Senate, did not oppose the bill suspending equal time, Mr. Burch said.

The chairman insisted that the President had "instructed" the Democratic Senators to table the bill.

"I don't think there is any other conclusion," he said.

Miller Sees 'Integrity' Issue
By EARL MAZO
Special to The New York Times

ROSLYN, L. I., Aug. 19 — Representative William E. Miller of upstate New York, the Republican candidate for Vice President, said yesterday that President Johnson's personal wealth could become a major "integrity" issue in the national campaign.

At a news conference before a Republican rally on the Winston C. Guest estate, Mr. Miller declared:

"I would hope always that integrity in office — morality in office — is an issue in campaigns."

Then he said "there should be some question of integrity" when a full-time public official for more than 30 years "accumulates in course of that time a fortune [of about] $14 million" mostly in what he said was in property subject to regulation by a Government agency.

Mr. Miller was referring to Mr. Johnson, and noted that "experts" at evaluating the worth of television property "told me the Johnson holding [in television stations alone] are worth over $10,000,000."

During the second day of a two-day visit in the New York area Mr. Miller also did these things:

¶Attacked Johnson Administration policy in Vietnam.

¶Said that neither he nor Senator Goldwater was being briefed by Government intelligence chiefs, as was the case with Presidential and Vice-Presidential candidates in past national campaigns. Mr. Johnson offered briefings to Mr. Goldwater and other Republican contenders for the Republican nomination last spring, and Mr. Goldwater rejected the offer.

Mr. Miller's formal campaign is scheduled to begin Sept. 5 at a rally in Lockport, N.Y., his home town. Mr. Goldwater and other Republican figures will also speak.

The Vice-Presidential candidate's activities in the New York area yesterday and today were, in effect, a trial run. Mr. Miller and his staff will make another trip next week in the Jamestown and Olean, N.Y., areas and in the Bradford, Pa., area.

The highlight of Mr. Miller's campaigning today was the rally on the Guest estate, attended by more than 3,000 well-wishers who overflowed a huge green-striped revival tent to hear Mr. Miller and others, including Assembly Speaker Joseph F. Carlino, the Republican chairman in Nassau county.

Mr. Carlino, a political lieutenant of Governor Rockefeller and leader of the anti-Goldwater moderates at the Republican National Convention last month, predicted that the Goldwater-Miller ticket "will carry Nassau County by one of the biggest majorities in history."

N.B.C. Invites Johnson and Goldwater to Appear on TV Programs

By VAL ADAMS

President Johnson and Senator Barry Goldwater were invited yesterday to appear on a series of one-hour "Meet the Press" programs on television and radio.

They would not debate but would be questioned by newsmen in accordance with the regular format of "Meet the Press."

Robert W. Sarnoff, chairman of the board of the National Broadcasting Company, proposed six programs. He suggested that Mr. Johnson and Mr. Goldwater appear on four and that their Vice-Presidential candidates appear on the others.

But he said N. B. C. was prepared to adjust the number of broadcasts and their distribution between the candidates.

Mr. Sarnoff's invitation was extended a day after the Senate, by a three-vote margin, rejected a compromise proposal for temporarily suspending equal-time provisions of the Federal Communications Act. This ruled out chances for televised debates between the major Presidential candidates.

Under Section 315 of the Communications Act, if station licensees provide time for a debate by two candidates, equal time must be offered all other candidates. The section was temporarily suspended in 1960 and the networks televised debates by Senator John F. Kennedy and Vice President Richard M. Nixon.

Mr. Sarnoff said "Meet the Press" was exempt from the equal-time requirement. He referred to a bill signed by President Eisenhower in 1959 that exempted radio and television news programs from equal-time demands by political candidates.

The exempted categories are bona fide newscasts, news interviews, news documentary presentations and on-the-spot coverage of bona fide news events. Mr. Sarnoff classified "Meet the Press" as a "bona fide news interview program."

The telegrams to President Johnson and Senator Goldwater said:

"Under the present circumstances where broadcast appearances of candidates are limited, N.B.C. respectfully invites you and the [other major party] Presidential nominee to appear in a series of one-hour weekly 'Meet the Press' broadcasts to be scheduled at 6 to 7 P.M. Eastern time Sundays over the N.B.C. national television and radio networks in the period between early September and election day.

"These could be joint appearances, or if you and the opposing candidate prefer, the hour broadcast could be divided into two half-hour segments, with one candidate appearing individually in one half-hour segment and the other appearing individually in the adjacent half-hour segment, the order of appearances to rotate from week to week.

"The format would be identical with the present 'Meet the Press' format, based on well-informed and unrehearsed questions by impartial, trained journalists designed to bring forward the candidates' views on the basic issues in the campaign. Each program could range over the various issues, or if the candidates preferred, a broad area could be agreed upon by them in advance as the general subject of questions for each particular broadcast."

The White House had no comment last night on the invitation. A spokesman recalled that in the past when President Johnson was asked about the possibility of his appearing on televised debates he said he would make no formal decision until after the Democratic National Convention, which begins Monday in Atlantic City.

Mr. Sarnoff said N. B. C. would make the programs available to other networks "if they judge that they are legally able to broadcast them under the present provisions of the law." When asked why it might not be legal for all networks if it was for N. B. C., Mr. Sarnoff said "Meet the Press" was a regularly scheduled program on N. B. C. but not on other networks.

No Debate

The decision of President Johnson to avoid a television debate with Senator Goldwater is poor public policy, whether or not it is wise politics. The Senate Democrats were clearly deferring to the President's assessment of his own political interests when they voted to table the bill which would have suspended the equal-time requirement and thus cleared the way for a direct confrontation before a nationwide audience.

It is in the public's interest that a Presidential campaign should approach as nearly as possible a coherent and responsive dialogue between the two candidates. The televised debates, as our experience of 1960 demonstrated, are valuable in developing that dialogue. They could have been especially useful this year in view of the Republican candidate's apparent determination to avoid press conferences and his propensity for repudiating or reinterpreting his previous remarks.

President Johnson is not a man given to underconfidence in his own persuasiveness. His reticence in this instance has put an unfortunate limit on the evidence available to the voters in judging which nominee is better qualified to act as spokesman for this nation before the world.

Goldwater Lists Terms for TV Panel

By CHARLES MOHR
Special to The New York Times

WASHINGTON, Aug. 20 — Senator Barry Goldwater said today that he might agree to joint television press conferences with President Johnson, but he added, "I would want the right to pick at least half of the newsmen."

Mr. Goldwater was commenting on a proposal by Robert W. Sarnoff, National Broadcasting Company president, that the two Presidential candidates appear on special, hour-long versions of the network's "Meet the Press" program.

The White House said it had no comment on Mr. Sarnoff's offer.

Meantime, Dean Burch, Republican National Chairman, sent a letter to the Democratic National Chairman, John M. Bailey, offering to pay one-half of the cost of purchasing television air time for a debate between the two candidates.

On Tuesday the Senate killed a bill which would have suspended the provisions of the so-called "equal time" law as was done in 1960 and would have made it possible for the three television networks to grant free air time for a debate.

Republican spokesman have charged that President Johnson directed the Senate Democrats to kill the legislation to try to prevent the possibility of a debate.

Yesterday at Springfield, Ill., Mr. Goldwater said that he wanted to debate Mr. Johnson and that, "I am willing to pay for the time." He later explained that the Republicans would pay for all of the air time needed for a debate.

This contrasted with Mr. Burch's letter today, which offered to pay half the cost. Paul Wagner, Mr. Goldwater's press secretary, was asked to explain the contrast and said:

"We think it's reasonable that we should pay half. If the Democrats can't afford to pay their half, we'd go all the way."

Mr. Goldwater was questioned by newsmen about the Sarnoff proposal earlier in the day. The Senator has often said that he dislikes the idea of a debate format that would include a panel of newsmen to question the two candidates. He reiterated that feeling today.

He was first asked for his reaction to Mr. Sarnoff's idea and he said he had none, adding, "We want to wait and see what the reaction of the President is."

But then he added that he did not like the "Meet the Press" format in a debate.

He said, however, "But if the President wanted to do it, I would be perfectly glad to do it with our own ground rules."

He also said, "if it's the only way, but I would want the right to pick at least half of the newsmen."

President Johnson recently said that he would wait until after the Democratic National Convention next week to make a final decision on a television debate.

Mr. Burch's letter to Mr. Bailey blamed Mr. Johnson for killing the bill to suspend the equal time law, and offered to share payment for purchased time.

Mr. Bailey is an Atlantic City preparing for the Democratic convention and made no comment immediately.

Meantime, it was announced that Mr. Goldwater would go to New York City Monday to meet, in private social circumstances, "with members of industry, banking and commerce."

Mr. Goldwater will attend an invitational reception at the University Club Monday afternoon and a private dinner at another club that evening.

Ralph J. Cordiner, the retired chairman of the General Electric Company who is now finance chairman for the Republican National Committee, arranged the meetings.

A statement from Mr. Cordiner's office said the Senator "has expressed an interest in stating first-hand his positions on domestic and international problems, and this informal dinner will also enable the guests and the Senator to become better acquainted with each other and afford the opportunity for two - way communication through questions and answers."

The statement said it was "not a fund-raising activity" and that no funds would be "accepted."

However, another source very close to the Senator said that the original purpose of the two affairs had been "to have Barry meet some men who are a bit cool to the idea of contributing to the campaign and to help warm them up."

JOHNSON IS CHIDED BY G.O.P. SENATORS

WASHINGTON, Aug. 21 (AP) —Republican Senators asked in a campaign document today whether President Johnson was afraid to debate Senator Goldwater.

The Senate Republican Memo commented on the 44-41 Senate vote Tuesday that killed a bill to permit television and radio networks and stations to provide free time for debates or appearances of the Presidential and Vice-Presidential candidates of the two major parties this fall.

The Memo is published by the Senate Republican Policy Committee, headed by Senator Bourke B. Hickenlooper of Iowa. With support of President Kennedy, both the House and Senate passed bills that would have authorized the campaign TV-radio exchanges as was done four years ago, suspending a rule that would have saddled the networks with providing equal time for minor candidates.

A compromise on these bills lacked only final Congressional approval when the Senate Democratic leader, Mike Mansfield of Montana, moved to table and thus kill the proposal.

August 22, 1964

JOHNSON IS PRODDED BY MILLER ON DEBATE

OLCOTT, N.Y., Aug. 27 (AP)– Representative William E. Miller said today that he was willing to engage Senator Hubert H. Humphrey in a debate of Vice-Presidential candidates "if President Johnson will debate Senator Goldwater."

"Maybe a sort of package deal could be arranged," covering all four nominees, "but any debate would have to include the Presidential candidates."

He said he thought the Democrats would "try to take the sting out of no debate between the two principals" by promoting one between himself and Mr. Humphrey.

"That won't satisfy the American public," Mr. Miller said. "It's not good enough for them. The President and Senator Goldwater are the candidates."

Mr. Miller said the selection of Mr. Humphrey would give the voters a clear choice between the party tickets. "I'd define us as moderately conservative and the other side as moderately liberal," he said.

Mr. Miller was released from Buffalo General Hospital yesterday after a three-day physical checkup.

August 28, 1964

GOLDWATER SAYS PRESIDENT AVOIDS CAMPAIGN ISSUES

Senator, in North Carolina, Asks to Meet Johnson 'Before the World'

DEBATES ARE DEMANDED

Administration Is Denounced as Believing Government Is 'Master of People'

By FENDALL W. YERXA
Special to The New York Times

CHARLOTTE, N. C., Sept. 21—Senator Barry Goldwater of Arizona accused President Johnson tonight of avoiding the issues of the campaign, and "dared" the President to face him in debate "before the world."

He accused the Administration of holding the belief that government is "master, not servant of the people," and of operating through a centralized authority "that has even given you a number to replace your name."

"We want to give you your freedom and your names back again," Mr. Goldwater, the Republican Presidential candidate, said in a speech before a capacity crowd of 17,000 at a campaign rally in the Charlotte Coliseum. He continued:

"We want to give the Government of this nation back to the people of this nation. An administration that understands, rather than one that tries to wreck the balances of constitutional power, can do the job."

Coliseum Is Packed

The Senator's plane from Washington, landing under a full moon, was greeted by a few hundred persons at the airport, and there was apparently no effort to turn out a crowd along the motor-caravan route through the city to the splendid new glass-and-concrete coliseum.

But in the domed stadium, it was different. The place was packed with applauding, yelling Republicans.

Strom Thurmond, the South Carolina Senator who recently shifted from the Democratic to the Republican party, received an ear-splitting ovation when he was introduced and told the gathering:

"I didn't leave the Democratic party—it left me."

It was Mr. Goldwater's third trip into North Carolina in six days. This state, with 13 electoral votes, was once solidly Democratic, but the Republicans have received nearly half of its votes in the last two Presidential elections.

North Carolina gave 58 per cent of its vote to President Truman in 1948, but this margin was cut to 50.7 for Adlai E. Stevenson in 1956. John F. Kennedy won 52.1 per cent of the state's votes in 1960.

This morning the Senator was in Gettysburg, Pa., with former President Dwight D. Eisenhower. Then he flew to Charlotte, and back to Washington to open a week of vigorous campaigning, which will take him to the Southwest, including Texas, the Midwest, New England and upstate New York.

The Senator began his speech with an attack on Mr. Johnson, saying that the President "will not face the issues, he will not face me, he will not face you."

"Instead," he said, "he sends forth his curious crew of camp followers to speak for him. Some are socialistic radicals like his running mate, Hubert Horatio."

"Some are bosses of big cities, big unions and big business. Some are bureaucratic lackeys. Some are even buildings. We keep hearing that the White House announces or that the Pentagon says such-and-such.

"The Pentagon talks so much that I've suggested it be given a name—like Peter Pentagon. It is an interesting thing, a building with five sides and a hole in the middle. It ought to be able to talk.

"Can my opponent talk? What does my opponent have to say? I challenge my opponent, the interim President Lyndon Baines Johnson, to face the issues. I dare him to face me before the world. I ask of him, debate."

"We do not want oppressive powers in the hand of the executive branch, or the Supreme Court," he continued. "We don't want oppressive powers in the hands of Congress or the states. But we do want proper powers restored to the Congress and to the states. We do want the proper balance between all branches and all levels."

In the past, Mr. Goldwater has expressed doubt about whether an incumbent President should debate his opponent.

"I don't think a President of the United States should debate anybody," he said in Portland, Ore., on Feb. 12. "He . . . could very well disclose secrets that only he knows."

And on Jan. 31, the Senator said:

"I think it's kind of dangerous to subject a President of the United States to questioning and debate. . . ."

The Supreme Court, he said, until recently exercised restraint in striking down acts of Congress.

"But not the Supreme Court of today," he said. "I weigh my words carefully when I say that, of all three branches of Government, today's Supreme Court is least faithful to the constitutional tradition of limited government, and to the principle of legitimacy in the exercise of power."

Tapes TV Film

Senator Goldwater spent the day today with General Eisenhower at the general's farm in Gettysburg. Early this morning, he flew from Washington to Gettysburg for a strategy session with the general, and to tape with him a half-hour television program.

He flew to Charlotte this evening, drove in a motorcade to the Coliseum for his speech, and returned immediately to Washington. He takes off in the morning for Tulsa, Okla., on a swing through the Southwest.

The Senator's headquarters in Washington announced today the formation of two groups to assist in his campaign. The first was a Peace Through Preparedness task force, headed by Neil H. McElroy, Secretary of Defense under President Eisenhower.

Senator Goldwater said in a statement that the seven-member panel would review and evaluate the nation's defense programs and their relationship to foreign policy and domestic economy.

The task force will also have in it Prescott S. Bush, partner in Brown Brothers, Harriman & Co. of New York, who is a former Senator from Connecticut; James H. Douglas of Chicago, former Secretary of the Air Force and Deputy Secretary of Defense; Representative Gerald R. Ford of Michigan, ranking Republican of the House Defense Appropriations subcommittee; Wilfred J. McNeil, president of Grace Lines and former controller of the Defense Department; Adm. Arthur W. Radford (ret.), former Chairman of the Joint Chiefs of Staff; Gen. Nathan F. Twining (ret.), former Air Force Chief of Staff and Chairman of the Joint Chiefs of Staff.

This is the third such group of experts established by Mr. Goldwater's campaign forces. The others are on foreign policy, headed by former Vice President Richard M. Nixon; and one on fiscal and economic policy, headed by former Treasury Secretary George M. Humphrey.

The Citizens for Goldwater-Miller Committee also announced the formation of an executive committee of 450 businessmen backing the Republican ticket. Among them are Mr. Humphrey and Vivien Kellems, Connecticut businesswoman. Clifton White, national director of the citizens group, said the business committee represented "the overwhelming majority of the nation's responsible businessmen."

Named as co-chairmen of the committee were Charles M. White, honorary chairman of the Republic Steel Corporation, Cleveland; George C. Montgomery, chairman of the Kern County Land Company, San Francisco; and Mrs. Russell Stover, chairman of Russell Stover Candies, Kansas City, Mo.

Mr. White said the committee members came from all 50 states and from large, middle-sized and small companies. The list includes the heads of big corporations listed on the New York Stock Exchange, such as L. G. Porter, president of the Borg-Warner Corporation, and local proprietors, such as John Hitt, identified as "General Store, Powder River, Wyo."

Among the better-known men on the committee were these:

Calvin Fentress Jr., chairman of the Allstate Insurance Company; F. K. Weyerhauser, chairman of the Weyerhauser Company; William L. McKnight, chairman of the Minnesota Mining & Manufacturing Company; Thomas E. Millsop, chairman of the National Steel Corporation; G. P. MacNicol, chairman of the Libby-Owens - Ford Glass Company; Barry T. Leithead, president of Cluett Peabody & Company; Merritt D. Hill, president of the J. I. Case Company.

Also, Robert W. Galvin, president of Motorola, Inc.; Alwin F. Franz, honorary chairman of the Colorado Fuel and Iron Corporation; Bennett S. Chappel Jr., administrative vice president of the United States Steel Corporation; H. Stephen Chase, executive vice president of the Wells Fargo Bank, San Francisco; Harrison Chandler, vice president of The Los Angeles Times-Mirror; Sinclair Weeks, who was President Eisenhower's first Secretary of Commerce; Hugh L. White, a former Governor of Mississippi; Harry H. Timken Jr., chairman of Timken Roller Bearing Company, Canton, Ohio.

Also, Edwin L. Ramsey, a vice president of the Rexall Drug and Chemical Company; John Redding, president of Pinehurst Textiles, Ashboro, N. C.; Nicholas Peterson, president of Peterson House of Fudge, Inc., Wilmington, Del.; R. P. Price, director of the Hazard Coal Operators Association, Lexington, Ky.; Daniel A. Parker, president of the Parker Pen Company; Edward Lyman, president of the United States National Bank, Omaha; Henry Bubb, chairman of the Capital Federal Savings and Loan Association, Topeka, Kan.

Wallace Bennett was listed simply as "chairman of the board, Bennett's, Salt Lake City, Utah." Mr. Bennett, a Republican, is the senior Senator from Utah. The family-owned company is in the paint business, an aide said.

Nixon Favors TV Debates in 1968

But He Wants G.O.P. Strategy to Be Different From His Own Campaign in '60

By WARREN WEAVER Jr.
Special to The New York Times

WASHINGTON, Nov. 27 — Richard M. Nixon said tonight that the Republican Presidential candidate and President Johnson should engage in televised political debates during the campaign in 1968.

Only last week, the former Vice President had said that his appearance in debate with John F. Kennedy, in the 1960 campaign had played a major part in his losing that election. He attributed it to bad make up on television.

Interviewed on the National Educational Television network, Mr. Nixon urged that next year's Republican candidate conduct "quite a different campaign" than he himself did in 1960, with one exception. The interview was taped in New York on Nov. 20 for showing tonight.

"I believe there should be debates," he declared. "I believe that the debates of 1960 served a great cause in creating tremendous interest in the campaign, also in educating people about the great issues.

Quotes Kennedy

"And I would hope that President Johnson would reverse his stand of '64 and do what President Kennedy said he would have done just before he died, when he said, 'Of course, I'll debate my opponent,' because President Johnson then will give the nation a good choice, President Johnson and his Republican opponent debating the great issues on television."

Mr. Nixon hopes to be that opponent. He has been organizing a campaign for the Re-

publican Presidential nomination for the better part of a year and is expected to make the formal announcement of his candidacy in mid-January.

In response to questions by Paul Niven, an N.ET. correspondent, the former Vice President said he believed that the Republican position on Vietnam should shift to something "quite different" at the end of President Johnson's term, assuming a Republican victory in November.

Aid for Rest of Team

Mr. Nixon said to the Republicans that, despite disagreements with President Johnson, "we for the balance of his term are going to support the commitment in Vietnam so that the enemy will not be encouraged to hang on with the idea that after the election he's going to get concessions, appeasement from the Republicans."

"Now I don't mean that after, the Republican position should not be different — it should be quite different," he continued, "in terms of the conduct of the war, because I believe this war has gone much longer than it needed to. I believe we've never had so much military and economic and diplomatic power used so ineffectively."

Mr. Nixon also reported that he had changed his previous view that politicans should absorb what they regard as unfair newspaper or television treatment in silence. During the 1960 campaign and his entire Washington career, he said, he never complained about a reporter to his superior or publisher.

"I don't think it is healthy for the press and the television producers to feel that they have an absolutely free hand," he observed. "And perhaps the political man, now and then, without perhaps the heat I displayed in 1962, if he thinks he is being put upon, he should say so."

Kennedy Willing to Debate McCarthy and Humphrey

LOS ANGELES, April 25 (AP) —Spokesmen for Senator Robert F. Kennedy's California campaign said today the New York Senator would accept offers to debate Senator Eugene I. McCarthy only if Vice President Humphrey participated.

Offers to debate on television before the June 4 California primary have been issued by the Columbia Broadcasting System and the American Broadcasting Company to both Senators.

A spokesman for Mr. McCarthy said last night the Minnesota Senator had accepted the offer from C.B.S.

John Campbell, general manager of KABC-TV in Los Angeles, said McCarthy spokesmen had told him Senator McCarthy accepted the A.B.C. offer as well.

TV NETWORKS SHAPE PLAN FOR DEBATES

WASHINGTON, May 24 (UPI) —The three major television networks have worked out a tentative plan for 1968 Presidential campaign debates that would include George C. Wallace along with the nominees of the Republican and Democratic parties, Senate sources said Friday.

The network proposal was discussed during a secret and often stormy session yesterday between presidents of the National Broadcasting Company, the Columbia Broadcasting System and the American Broadcasting Company, and members of the Senate Commerce Committee.

According to Senate sources, Frank Stanton of C.B.S. presented the plan. Basically, Mr. Wallace, as a third party candidate — American Independent party—and the major party contenders would be given network time to present their views in a three-part series.

The proposal, which could have a substantial impact on this year's Presidential election, hinges on Congressional approval of a bill suspending equal time provisions of the Federal Communications Act. A committee vote on the bill was put off last night and rescheduled for consideration next week.

KENNEDY PLEDGES TO QUIT IF BEATEN IN CALIFORNIA BID

Agrees to TV Debate This Weekend With McCarthy After Oregon Defeat

By JOHN HERBERS
Special to The New York Times

LOS ANGELES, May 29 — Senator Robert F. Kennedy acknowledged today that his defeat in the Oregon Presidential primary was a "setback I could ill afford" and promised to withdraw as a candidate unless he won in California next Tuesday.

"I will abide by the results of that test," the New York Democrat said in a news conference held at the Los Angeles International Airport this morning upon his arrival from Portland, Ore.

Takes New Stands

Senator Kennedy also took the following stands:

¶Agreed to debate Senator Eugene J. McCarthy, the winner in yesterday's Oregon Democratic primary, on national television, a reversal of his previous position that he would agree to such an encounter only if Vice President Humphrey were included.

¶Said unequivocally for the first time since he entered the race on March 16 that he would support the Democratic Presidential nominee in the general election, whoever that might be.

¶Repeated, with added emphasis, that "under no circumstances" would he accept the nomination for Vice President.

¶Said if Mr. Humphrey and Richard M. Nixon are the Presidential nominees of the two major parties the American political system would have failed "to offer the people a chance to move in a new and more hopeful direction" in both foreign and domestic policy.

Welcomed in Los Angeles

After the news conference, Senator Kennedy drove through downtown Los Angeles and received one of the largest and most demonstrative welcomes in his six weeks of campaigning for the White House.

Thousands lined the streets, showered his motorcade with confetti and swarmed around his car during the tour that lasted more than one hour.

At the end of the demonstration the tired, weather-beaten candidate said:

"After last night in Oregon I'm going to call Los Angeles Resurrection City."

Senator Kennedy received the news of his Oregon defeat last night aboard his chartered jet after a day of campaigning in Santa Barbara, Calif.

For several days he had appeared strained by his inability to move Oregon audiences and attract enthusiastic crowds in that state of the kind that turned out in Los Angeles today.

The blow was made even worse by the fact that no member of his immediate family had ever lost an election and by the fact that he had said that unless he won all of the primaries he entered, he would no longer be a "viable candidate" for the Presidency.

The Senator said it several times before college audiences. He also said it on a television interview taped Sunday night, at a time when his advisers were saying the Kennedy campaign in Oregon was in trouble.

But there was no public display of his disappointment. He and his wife, Ethel, smiled broadly when they arrived at Kennedy headquarters in Portland. He acknowledged in a telegram of congratulation to Senator McCarthy that the victory was a significant one for the Minnesotan.

Setback Conceded

This morning, Senator Kennedy, looking a little more rested and relaxed, opened his news conference by saying the Oregon vote "represents a setback to my prospects for obtaining the Presidential nomination of my party—a setback, as I have previously stated, which I could ill afford."

"However, many Presidential nominees have lost the primary and won both the nomination and election," he said. "The Oregon primary, although a personal loss, clearly shows that the citizens who make up the Democratic party wish to select their own nominee, since they gave more than 80 per cent of their vote to candidates willing to enter the primaries and anxious for a change."

He made it clear that he still considered his candidacy as that best able to offer alternatives and said it was "time for the Vice President to confront the forces of progress and change within the Democratic party."

He continued:

"Vice President Humphrey is the leading contender for the Democratic nomination, even

Associated Press
BACK IN ACTION: Senator Robert F. Kennedy, standing on back of car, moves slowly through Los Angeles crowd.

though he has been unwilling to present his views to the voters in a single state. I have worked with the Vice President in the past and he is a fine man.

"He has spoken out for virtually every policy and program of the past five years. And the fervor and expression of his views leaves little doubt of the sincerity of his convictions."

But then he added:

"If the Vice President is nominated to oppose Richard Nixon, there will be no candidate who has opposed the course of escalation of the war in Vietnam.

"There will be no candidate committed to the kinds of programs which can remedy the conditions which are transforming our cities into armed camps.

"There will be no candidate committed to return government to the people, or returning to the economic policies which gave us rising prosperity without destructive inflation."

After the Senator finished reading his prepared statement, he was asked about his remarks that a defeat in any primary would make him no longer a "viable candidate."

"Well, I've slept on it," he said with a small laugh. "I'm just going to try to ask that I be tested before the voters of California."

Asked if he would consider California the ultimate test of his candidacy, he said, "that would be very close to describing how I feel."

Asked about his change of position on debating Senator McCarthy, he replied:

"I'm not the same candidate I was before Oregon and I can't claim that I am."

He had ignored Senator McCarthy and declined to enter such a debate, his advisers said, because such appearances would only acknowledge that the Minnesotan was a serious contender and help him to become better known among voters.

But the Oregon primary clearly established Senator McCarthy as a strong competitor, they said, and almost everywhere Senator Kennedy had gone he had been taunted by McCarthy supporters accusing him of running out on an exchange of opinions. It had become a chief issue of the campaign.

The Kennedy forces attribute their Oregon defeat to a combination of factors, partly that the electorate contained few of the ethnic or racial groups where the Senator is strong.

But chiefly, they said, he was never able to establish a rapport with the voters of the kind he did in Nebraska and to some extent in Indiana.

There was a consensus in Portland today that Oregon voters felt that Senator Kennedy was dealing too lightly with the issues.

"Oregon voters like to be treated seriously and like a detailed discussion of the issues and that is what Senator Kennedy failed to provide here," said one prominent Democrat.

May 30, 1964

TV DEBATE LIKELY DURING. WEEKEND

Kennedy, McCarthy Agree —Humphrey Unavailable

By ROBERT E. DALLOS

Senator Robert F. Kennedy and Senator Eugene J. McCarthy, who are on the ballot in the California Democratic primary on Tuesday, agreed yesterday to hold a live television debate over the weekend.

Vice President Humphrey, the other contender for the Democratic Presidential nomination, though not on the ballot in California, indicated he would not join in a debate with his two opponents.

The time of the debate, the site of the studio in which it would be held and its format had not been worked out by late last night. All three of the major networks invited the three candidates to take part in a debate.

The American Broadcasting Company said it had set aside Saturday at 9:30 P.M. The Columbia Broadcasting System invited the candidates for a debate on Sunday at 7 P.M. The National Broadcasting Company said it was ready to televise a debate on Friday at 10 P.M., Saturday at 7:30 P.M. or Sunday at 6:30 P.M. All of the debates would last one hour and would be carried simultaneously on radio, the networks said.

The possibility of a television debate among the Democratic hopefuls was opened early yesterday morning after Mr. Kennedy's defeat in the Oregon primary. The American Broadcasting Company, at that time, received word from Pierre Salinger, press consultant to Mr. Kennedy, that Mr. Kennedy would be willing to accept the network's earlier invitation for a debate on the Sunday news show, "Issues and Answers," which is normally scheduled at 1:30 P.M.

Mr. McCarthy, who like Mr. Kennedy and the Vice President had been invited by A.B.C. to a debate in April, had agreed immediately to a face-to-face meeting on television with his opponents.

But the New York Senator had insisted up until yesterday that Mr. Humphrey must take part in any debate. With Mr McCarthy's victory in Oregon Mr. Kennedy agreed to debate Mr. McCarthy alone, but expressed the hope that the Vice President would join, too.

Mr. Kennedy said yesterday that he was setting no conditions for the debate and would appear for the encounter whether or not the Vice President also was involved.

Norman Sherman, the Vice President's press secretary, said in a telephone interview yesterday that Mr. Humphrey's schedule for the weekend, which called for visits in Arkansas and Minnesota, would not allow him to take part in the debate.

The Vice President, it is known, has not been in favor of a debate with other contenders for the Democratic nomination, though he said in a television interview in St. Louis recently, that he did favor debates between Presidential candidates of the two major parties once they had been chosen.

Mr. McCarthy, who had a commitment to appear on C.B.S.'s "Face the Nation" program on Sunday at 12:30 P.M., told A.B.C. that he would be willing to debate any time except Sunday. William Sheehan, vice president for television news, said that an invitation for Saturday night was then extended. Immediately thereafter, similar invitations were sent out by the other networks

Mr. Salinger indicated in a telephone interview from California last night that Mr. Kennedy would want to take part in one debate only and that this might be accomplished by a pool arrangement of the three networks.

An official at McCarthy headquarters in California, who asked not to be identified, also said that he "could not conceive of three debates," but added that it could not be "totally ruled out." He said that "since A.B.C. had been the first to offer time, careful consideration would be given to that."

M'CARTHY DEBATE WITH KENNEDY SET

Candidates Will Appear on A.B.C.-TV Tomorrow

Senators Robert F. Kennedy and Eugene J. McCarthy will hold a televised debate tomorrow night on the American Broadcasting Company network.

The one-hour debate, originating in California, will be shown live in the East at 9:30 o'clock, in the Central time zone at 8:30 and in the Mountain time zone at 7:30. It will be taped for viewing on the West Coast at 9:30.

The A.B.C. television outlet in New York is Channel 7.

Though Mr. McCarthy was also willing to hold similar debates on the Columbia Broadcasting System and National Broadcasting Company, Mr. Kennedy agreed to accept only one network invitation.

Mr. McCarthy and Mr. Kennedy are seeking the Democratic Presidential nomination. They are opponents in the California Presidential primary next Tuesday.

Their rival for the nomination, Vice President Humphrey, who is not a contestant in California, declined to take part in the debate.

Mr. Kennedy had previously refused to debate Mr. McCarthy unless Mr. Humphrey also participated. But he changed his stand after his defeat by Mr. McCarthy in the Oregon primary last Tuesday.

Explanation by Salinger

Mr. Kennedy's aide Pierre Salinger explained in a telephone interview from Los Angeles yesterday why Mr. Kennedy wanted only one television confrontation. He said:

"There's no need for more than one debate. Studies of the 1960 debates between John F. Kennedy and Richard M. Nixon clearly showed that the only one that anybody paid any attention to was the first.

"The others were widely watched. But the people had made up their minds on the first and watched the other three to root for their man."

In informing C.B.S. and N.B.C. of his decision, Mr. Kennedy said he had accepted the A.B.C. invitation because that network had extended the first invitation.

All three candidates had been invited by A.B.C. to debate during April. Only Mr. McCarthy accepted immediately.

The TV-radio debate will originate in the studios of KGO-TV in San Francisco, an A.B.C.-owned station. The format will be that of the network's Sunday public affairs program "Issues and Answers."

A.B.C. said the two Senators would answer questions from three A.B.C. newsmen, Frank Reynolds, Robert Clark and William Lawrence. Neither Senator will make a formal opening or closing statement.

After one Senator answers a question, the other will be given a chance to comment.

Mr. Reynolds will be moderator. There will be no studio audience and no commercials. The split screen technique will not be used.

In Los Angeles yesterday, Senator McCarthy said he was not completely satisfied with the format.

"We're just going to sit around a table and be nice to each other," he said. "It isn't what we [the McCarthy forces] were talking about when we asked for a debate."

May 30, 1968

May 31, 1968

Kennedy Criticizes Humphrey In Asking Him to Join Debate

By JOHN HERBERS
Special to The New York Times

FRESNO, Calif. May 30 — Senator Robert F. Kenned, asked Vice President Humphrey today to join him and Senator Eugene J. McCarthy in a nationally televised debate Saturday night to "assure a serious discussion of the issues within the Democratic party."

The request was made in a telegram that the New York Democrat read to a cheering crowd of several thousand as he began a whistle-stop tour of the San Joaquin Valley.

Mr. Humphrey had already declined to join in the debate when the telegram was sent but Senator Kennedy used the telegram to point up his opposition to the foreign and domestic policies of the Johnson Administration and Mr. Humphrey's commitment to those policies.

Senator Kennedy, in his campaign speeches for the California Presidential primary next Tuesday, has become increasingly critical of the Vice President, both for his positions on issues and his avoidance of public appearances in the primary states.

Agreement Reached

After his loss to Senator McCarthy in the Oregon primary Tuesday, Senator Kennedy agreed to debate the Minnesotan. They will appear on the American Broadcasting Company network Saturday night.

In his telegram to the Vice President, Senator Kennedy said:

"I hope very much that you will decide to join with us on this occasion.

"One great issue of contention within our party has been the continued escalation of the war in Vietnam. In recent weeks, even since President Johnson's speech of March 31,

the intensification of the war has meant an increase in American deaths. In one recent week more American troops were killed in Vietnam than in all the years from 1961 through 1964.

"You have supported, and I have opposed the continued escalation of the war. There are also disagreements between us on the somber question of our national future—especially the racial injustices in our society and the violence to which injustice has led."

Senator Kennedy pointed out that he had called for an implementation of the recommendations of the President's National Advisory Commission on Civil Disorders, made earlier this year.

"The Administration of which you are the second highest official has opposed this," Senator Kennedy said. "My experience as Attorney General has convinced me of the urgent need for strong and compassionate action.

"I feel that our party and our country would be enlightened by discussion between us regarding the commission report and regarding your Administration's failure to fight poverty effectively and to humanize our cities."

Despite Senator Kennedy's loss in Oregon, he has continued to attract large, enthusiastic crowds in California

Today he stopped at small towns along the Southern Pacific railroad—Madera, Merced, Turlock, Modesto, Stockton and Lodi — where he told audiences ranging from several hundred to several thousand that new directions in American policy were needed and attacked Mr. Humphrey's "politics of happiness and joy."

May 31, 1968

KENNEDY DISPUTES M'CARTHY ON WAR IN TV DISCUSSION

Rivals Differ Over Whether Peace Parleys Should Urge a Coalition Government

AGREE ON MOST ISSUES

High - Level Confrontation Is First of Their Campaign for Democratic Nomination

By R. W. APPLE Jr.

Senators Robert F. Kennedy and Eugene J. McCarthy met last night in the first face-to-face confrontation of their campaign for the Democratic Presidential nomination. It was a high-level discussion of issues in which they rarely disagreed.

The two Senators disputed one key point relating to the Vietnam peace negotiations. Mr. McCarthy urged the Administration to state now that it would accept a coalition Government in Saigon while Mr. Kennedy opposed such a declaration at this time.

After the Minnesotan had made his point, Senator Kennedy said he opposed "what I understand [to be] Senator McCarthy's position of forcing a coalition Government on the Government of Saigon, a coalition with the Communists."

Subtle Disagreements

Mr. McCarthy replied that that was not what he meant. He said that "if the South Vietnamese want to continue the fight, work out their own negotiation, that's well and good," but that the United States should take a stand.

There were other subtle disagreements in the hour-long discussion, which was nationally televised by the American Broadcasting Company from a studio in San Francisco. But the two contenders for the nomination agreed on a wide range of political, economic, civil rights and foreign policy questions.

Senator McCarthy mounted an unusually strong attack on Secretary of State Dean Rusk, whom he has said he would oust. Mr. Kennedy said he

would prefer not to indulge in personalities, but, as the discussion progressed, he commented that he would not be likely to retain Mr. Rusk if elected President in view of their sharp differences of opinion on Vietnam

"I happen to disagree with the policy he's espousing . . . but he's served the country in the way he thinks is most fitting." Senator Kennedy said.

"I think we give Cabinet members too much protection," Senator McCarthy replied.

Mr. Kennedy and Mr. McCarthy agreed that a massive effort to rebuild the slums was needed, although they disagreed slightly as to procedure. They joined in condemning Negro rioting in the cities, took the same approach to what they called the overextension of the United States abroad, and agreed that a tax increase was needed.

The two Senators, both dressed in business suits and wearing striped ties, sat around a circular table in the television studio. They were questioned by three A.B.C. correspondents: Frank Reynolds, the moderator; Robert Clark and William H. Lawrence.

Senator McCarthy had been pressing for a "debate" for many weeks. Senator Kennedy had refused to appear jointly until he was upset by Mr. McCarthy in last Tuesday's Oregon primary election.

Vice President Humphrey, the third major contender for the nomination, was invited to appear but declined to join Mr. McCarthy and Mr. Kennedy.

Their meeting recalled the series of four television debates between John F. Kennedy, Senator Kennedy's brother, and Richard M. Nixon during the 1960 Presidential campaign. John Kennedy's showing in those confrontations—particularly the first one, in Chicago on Sept. 26—was later described as a major factor in his victory.

Last night, Senator Kennedy gestured with his right hand throughout the discussion in a manner associated with his brother. He emphasized his membership on the National Security Council when he was Attorney General, his experience in handling civil rights crises and his record on crime.

Mr. McCarthy's performance was in a lower key. He used less vivid gestures, spoke more slowly than Mr. Kennedy and appeared a bit more relaxed. He, too, stressed experience, describing his Congressional service.

The direct goal of the Senators' appeals was the California primary Tueday in which 174 votes at the Democratic National Convention will be at stake. But in a broader sense they were attempting to sell their candidacies to the public and, through the public, to the still uncommitted delegates chosen in states without primaries.

Only One Spirited Exchange

Only at one point in the program was there a spirited exchange between Mr. Kennedy and Mr. McCarthy. That came when they discussed a newspaper advertisement placed in California by the McCarthy forces.

Senator McCarthy said the advertisement, which put part of the blame for American involvement in Vietnam and the Dominican Republic on Mr. Kennedy, was designed to raise the question of "who decides, who is responsible" for policy-making.

This byplay followed:

KENNEDY: Could I just say . . .

McCARTHY: That ad ran only one day and I . . .

KENNEDY: It also said that I intervened in the Dominican Republic. How did they get that?

McCARTHY: Well, I think that they did, I . . .

KENNEDY: I hadn't even been in Government at the time.

McCARTHY: Well, you weren't out very long.

KENNEDY: But it said —— and then it ran again today.

"In any case, I had not seen the ad," Senator McCarthy said after more discussion. "When I saw it, I said 'stop it.' And they stopped it as soon as they could."

Mr. Kennedy again refused to say directly whether he had approved, as Attorney General, a tap on the telephone of the late Rev. Dr. Martin Luther King Jr. He said he was forbidden by law to do so, but he described Dr. King as a great and loyal American.

Senator McCarthy expressed reservations about Federal wiretapping practices and the director of the Federal Bureau of Investigation, J. Edgar Hoover. He said "we ought to have another look at it with a new director because there are enough indications of practices here that I think should be challenged."

The question of a tap on Dr. King's phone was raised by the columnist Drew Pearson in an article published a week ago.

Discussing the civil rights

and urban problems in a larger context, Mr. McCarthy proposed that industry be introduced into the slums and some of the inhabitants of the slums be moved to outlying areas. Otherwise, he contended, the United States will continue to have a kind of de facto apartheid.

Senator Kennedy also urged a massive effort to rehabilitate the slums, but argued that it was impractical to relocate their residents now. In better areas, he said, they would not be able to afford housing, would not be able to compete for jobs and would find their children unable to meet school standards.

Of the Johnson Administration's reaction to urban rioting, Mr. Kennedy said "we said a prayer and we appointed a commission"—the National Advisory Commission on Civil Disorders, headed by former Gov. Otto Kerner of Illinois.

War Diverts Funds

"There hasn't been anybody from the Administration that's come in and said 'this is what we should do, these are the steps that we need to take,'" the Senator continued. "All we know is the welfare handout, and that's not satisfactory and it hasn't been adequate and it won't ever be."

Mr. McCarthy said the war had diverted needed funds from housing and other urban programs, and agreed that the Administration "didn't seem to have a sense of real need."

When the program ended, the two Senators shook hands, Mr. Kennedy extending both hands to grasp Mr. McCarthy's right hand. They smiled at each other, as they had done repeatedly during their discussion.

Senator McCarthy told reporters later that the confrontation had been "kind of a no-decision bout with three referees." But he said it had given him a chance to point up several differences with Senator Kennedy. He mentioned the Cabinet issue, the slum problems, and Federal wiretapping.

Mr. Kennedy said: "I thought it was fine."

Senator Kennedy's wife, Ethel, said of her husband: "I always think he wins."

Excerpts From the Kennedy-McCarthy Televised Discussion

Following are excerpts from yesterday's television discussion of the issues by Senators Eugene J. McCarthy of Minnesota and Robert F. Kennedy of New York as recorded by The New York Times from San Francisco through the facilities of A.B.C. News. Other participants were Robert Clark, William H. Lawrence and Frank Reynolds, the moderator.

Q. For both Senators, really. You are presenting yourself tonight to the American people and to the voters of California as candidates for the Presidency. If in fact you were President, what would you do at this time that President Johnson is not doing in order to bring peace in Vietnam?

McCARTHY. There are two or three things that I would be doing, or at least recommending, if I were President at this time. I would be de-escalating the war in Vietnam, drawing back from some of our advanced positions while still holding strength in Vietnam. I would not have the Secretary of State making statements about how we would have no coalition government come out of the conference in Paris; nor have someone say that the Vice President made a slip of the tongue when he talked about involving the National Liberation Front.

I think these are the important positions that have to be taken; one, a de-escalation of the war, and secondly, recognition that we have to have a new government in South Vietnam. I'm not particularly concerned whether it's called a coalition or a fusion or a new government of some kind.

And we have to recognize that the government would include the National Liberation Front. I think this is prerequisite to any kind of negotiations that may move on to talk about what the nature of that new government might be.

We've not really made any significant changes that I can see in terms of our activities or our words. We're calling up more troops, we say we're going to send more troops, we have intensified the bombing. Taken all together, I don't see either in action or in words any significant change on the part of the Administration since the negotiations began.

Pursue Negotiations

KENNEDY—Well, I'd pursue the negotiations in Paris at the same time and make it quite clear that we would expect Saigon, the Government in Saigon, to begin their own negotiations with the National Liberation Front. I would be opposed to what I understand is Senator McCarthy's position to be of forcing a coalition government on the Government of Saigon, a coalition with the Communists, even before we begin the negotiations.

I would make it quite clear that we are going to the negotiating table not with the idea that we want them to unconditionally surrender but —and that we expect that the National Liberation Front and the Vietcong have a place somewhere in the future political process of South Vietnam — but that should be determined by the negotiators and particularly by those people in South Vietnam.

I think that's terribly important that we accept that, because without accepting that what we're really asking for is unconditional surrender, and they're not going to turn over their arms—lay down their arms—live in peace if the Government is going to be run by General Ky and General Thieu.

End of Corruption

The next point: I would demand privately and publicly an end of public corruption, the official corruption that exists in Vietnam; a land reform program that's meaningful so that they can gain the support of the people themselves; I would pull back from the Demilitarized Zone—I think that's an important area — but I would permit the troops of South Vietnam to remain there— rather than American troops —where a third of our casualties have occurred—half really—and I would end the search and destroy missions by American troops and American marines and let the South Vietnamese soldiers and troops carry that burden of the conflict.

I would make it clear as we went along that the South Vietnamese are going to carry more and more of the burden of the conflict — I'm not going to accept the idea that we can draft the young man from the United States, send him to South Vietnam to fight and maybe to die while at the same time a

AT THE DEBATE'S END: Senator Eugene J. McCarthy and Frank Reynolds, of the American Broadcasting Company,

Senator Robert F. Kennedy shake hands after broadcast. the moderator, is between them in San Francisco studio.

Associated Press

young man, if he's wealthy enough, can buy his way out of the draft in South Vietnam.

McCARTHY. I didn't say I was going to force a coalition government on South Vietnam. I said we should make clear that we're willing to accept that. Now if the South Vietnamese want to continue the fight, work out their own negotiation, that is well and good. But I don't think there's much point in talking about reform in Saigon or land reform, because we've been asking for that for at least five years and it hasn't happened.

Q. Senator Kennedy, last week at his, this week at his press conference in Texas, the President indicated he was not closing any of his options. Indeed, he was considering perhaps resuming bombing farther north around Hanoi and Haiphong if something didn't happen in Paris pretty soon. Was this a wise move? In the interest of peace?

A. Well, I think that escalating the conflict again is not going to be a wise move. I think that the decision as I read about it in the newspapers as to why they de-escalated and went to the conference table was made on the basis that the bombing hadn't been successful.

I think that the reports of the intelligence community show quite clearly that rather than having been successful it strengthened the will of the people of North

Vietnam to resist the United States and resist the outside, as they described it, the outside aggressor. So I think that to resume the bombing in that fashion is not going to be any more successful now than it has been in the past.

Will to Fight

Third, Secretary McNamara has already testified before Congressional committees that the bombing of the North does not stop the North from sending whatever men and materials they need into the South. What, in the last analysis, is needed in South Vietnam is for the people themselves to have the will to fight

If they don't have that will, no matter how many men we send over there, how many bombs we drop—and we're dropping more now than we dropped in the Second World War—no matter how much we do with that, if they don't have the will and desire themselves, no matter what we do, we can't instill that in them.

And that's why I want to make it clear, if I was President of the United States, and why I was critical back in 1965 because I felt we were making it America's war, we were militarizing the conflict, that this is the South Vietnamese war. I'm opposed to unilaterally withdrawing from there, but they have to carry the major burden of this conflict. It can't be carried by American soldiers.

Q. Well, Senator McCarthy, in commenting on Senator Kennedy's answer, would you also take into account the charge made by some critics of the Administration, who are more hawkish, that we give the North Vietnamese a rather clear berth by telling them exactly what we're not going to do and that this doesn't increase the pressure for peace?

Intensity of Bombing

A. Well I don't think it makes much difference because we are really doing enough to them in any case and we say we're not going to do more in this particular area doesn't really change the ratio, it seems to me, of force to any significant degree. As far as the bombing is concerned, for example, the question of what area you bomb is not as important, it seems to me, as how intensely you bomb the areas that you are bombing.

I look upon the bombing question really as one that has to be considered in relation to what we are doing with reference to other troop movements in South Vietnam. Where to resume or not to resume, I think, has now become really a tactical question that—since negotiations have started, and also a practical question because we've had through the years testimony from many experts saying that it was wasteful, that it wasn't accomplishing anything, that we were losing planes and spending money and not breaking—I remem-

ber Secretary McNamara telling us in early '66 that if we resume the bombing and intensify it he said they will be able to infiltrate up to 4,500 men a month and supply them and then we can wear them down in South Vietnam.

By June of that year, the report was they were infiltrating up to 7,000 a month after the bombing had been intensified. His explanation was that the number they could infiltrate had always been "X"—that's what it has been.

Commitment in Asia

Q. Senator Kennedy, President Johnson has been emphasizing to the world in general and particularly to foreign leaders, such as the leader of South Korea and the Australian Prime Minister, his view that no matter who is the next President, the United States will keep its commitments in Asia. Now, is the President speaking for you as a potential next President?

A. I would have to have an outline of what those commitments . . .

Q. Say Korea, for example.

A. I expect that we're going to remain in Korea. I think that we have a position around the world that we cannot ignore. I don't think that position rests on military power so much as what our moral leadership is—what we do here within the United States and what we stand for around the rest of the globe.

Q. Well, how would we react, for example, to a renewal of aggression from North Korea into South Korea?

A. Well, I think that that aggression would be against the United Nations, which is still the power within South Korea, which is still nominal head of the armed forces within South Korea. So that I would expect the United Nations would act. I think that's far more advisable than what we're doing at the moment, which is we're acting ourselves.

I do think that we have some commitments around the globe. I think we have a commitment to Israel, for instance, that has to be kept. But what I don't think is that we can be the policeman of the world, and go in all over the rest of the globe and settle every internal dispute with American soldiers or American arms. And that is the tendency that I sensed over the period of the last two or three years.

Early in Campaign

Q. Senator McCarthy.

A. Bill, early in my campaign there were people who said this was the new kind of Midwestern isolationism, and some of the columnists said this is a retreat from responsibility. I was quick to say then that I have been a strong defender of President Truman and his intervention in Korea. I gave rather a serious paper justifying what he was doing.

I think we have clear obligations to the Chinese in Formosa and Taiwan; we have clear obligations to the Japanese by virtue of the treaty ending that war in which we demilitarized Japan; we have clear obligations to India, to speak only about Asia.

We have the responsibility, as the Senator said, clear moral and legal responsibilities in the Middle East and Israel and, also, I think, a strong obligation to maintain strength in NATO. As to the other areas of Southeastern Asia, Thailand, Malaysia and Indonesia Cambodia, we have a very limited commitment there, I think, one which we have to balance against what good can come out of what we might do there and also balanced against our responsibilities in other parts of the world. But it is not the kind of almost complete commitment in an area where success is very unlikely and which would drain off our resources, physical and moral, from attending to our other responsibilities.

Q. Well, Senator, you said that we have a very limited commitment in Southeast Asia, and you ticked off the countries. But it seems to me that, at the moment at any rate, we have kind of an overwhelming commitment there and that really what you're talking about is scaling down the commitment the Johnson Administration has made.

A. Well, I don't think we've had a legal or moral commitment to do what we're doing in Vietnam.

Q. If we don't have a legal or moral commitment, then why don't we just get out?

A. Well, you don't do it because there are other complications than just pull out. You've got some responsibilities that come in consequence of what we've done, and it's a residual kind of moral responsibility and political responsibility, too, that we have to carry on.

Commitment to Israel

Q. Do I gather that . . .

A. As I say if we didn't have the obligation to put a half-million men into that country to do what we're doing in that country where we spend $30-billion, whatever the objective is, and no one anticipated when we went in, no one said we had this kind of an obligation.

Q. Do I gather that aside from Vietnam, though, that there's not really any basic disagreement between you two and the President?

KENNEDY. I think that there's a difference between external aggression and internal aggression.

Q. Well, explain that.

A. If there was external aggression, for instance, against India or Pakistan, if China came across the border, I think that would be an entirely different kind of situation than if you have some turmoil within northeast Thailand.

Whether we should assist a country that has this internal difficulty or internal trouble or struggle between two groups, I think depends, on analysis of the situation, would depend on whether the Government had the support of the people, such as Israel, again as an example, whether they are making an effort themselves to develop the political and social and economic reforms that are so necessary to gain the support of their people, or whether it's just a society that lives on a strata that has no contact with the people and is just attempting to keep its control by yelling Communism to try to get American soldiers in there.

I'm opposed, under those circumstances, to sending American soldiers in, because I don't think we can be the police of the world and straighten out every problem all over the globe.

A Question on Riots

Q. Senator Kennedy, if we can move on here to some of our domestic problems which we want to cover—you've been telling campaign audiences that if you become

President you're going to do away with riots and violence in this country, that they simply won't be tolerated. What specific methods are you going to use to accomplish this, and I mean aside from the long-range efforts to improve life in the nation's ghettos?

A. Well I think what I've said is that as Attorney General I was the chief law enforcement officer, and I know how important it is we abide by the law, and violence and rioting and lawlessness cannot be tolerated in the United States. A high Administration official said a short time ago that we can expect rioting summer after summer. I don't think that's acceptable in the United States.

I would help police departments through funds, I would help them in the experience we've gained over the period of the last several years. When I was Attorney General of the United States, we had a riot at the University of Mississippi, and yet no one fired a gun—the marshals or the troops that came into that area. We kept a mob under control at the University of Alabama. We did it at the same time on the Freedom Riders. I therefore have some experience in dealing with these kind of problems.

The second part of it, which I think is terribly important, is the fact that we had some communication with those who feel that they are suffering from injustices. I have gone into the ghettos. I've gone and talked to the Indians or Mexican-Americans or whatever group and said we can't solve these problems overnight, they cannot be solved by violence and lawlessness.

But what we can do is to start at least providing jobs and employment for people, and people look at the statistics across the United States and say there is only 3½ per cent unemployed. In some of these areas the unemployment is 30, 40 per cent; in some parts of the United States it goes up to 80 per cent. I've been to Indian villages where it is 100 per cent.

I think we've got to provide jobs, with the Government being the employer as a last resort, and then bringing the private sector in in a major way and hiring people, doing away as much as possible with the welfare system, the handout of the dole, and getting people jobs by giving the private sector tax incentives and tax credits.

Q. Senator McCarthy.

A. Well I think I'm in general agreement. I think everyone feels that we need better police forces now, that there ought to be more Federal money given to the state and local authorities so that

we could have more policemen and more patrolmen, that use of either Federal troops or National Guard should be a very reserved use.

I think the way in which they responded generally in the riots following the assassination of Martin Luther King was entirely commendable on the side of restraint without shooting and without violence. This must be; also we must have interim programs if there is a threat of violence before we get around to doing the things that have to be done.

I think that critical to all of this is our really giving genuine hope to the people who live in the ghettos or who live in poverty. In my judgment, the principal cause of the riots—and this is as old as the history really of riots—is this, that with the passage of civil rights legislation and the kind of new spirit that moved in this country and around the world, Negroes particularly, but also other minorities in this country, have been kept really as a kind of colonial nation living in our midst, and they quite suddenly said, we are going to be free, and we said, that's fine, we're going to pass civil rights legislation that's going to set you free.

And then having done that, they went back to the same old miserable house, they went back to the same old job, they went back to the same poverty and the same ill health they'd known before, the rats than they talked about; and what we have to do is to begin to build a million houses a year for the low income people. Our housing is worse now than it was in 1948. The congestion in the ghettos is worse than it was. But we have to open it up so that you could say to people, well, in two years or three years or five years, all of you will somehow be set free from at least these physical conditions.

Unless we do that, then I think we have to face the prospect that no matter how many police we have, no matter how much repression we have, there will be protests, there will be some violence.

Tax Increase

Q. While we're talking about taxes, as Senator McCarthy was a moment ago—the President has again made a very strong appeal for this 10 per cent surcharge. Yet both of you gentlemen are opposed to it, if I understand you correctly.

KENNEDY. Well, I have said that I would take an increase in taxes. I think the 10 per cent is too high and I think it's too unfair to middle-income groups in the United States. It puts the heaviest burden on the lower

and the middle-income groups, so therefore I have reservations about that.

Secondly, I would like a tax reform program—and a real tax reform program. There are dozens of people in the United States who make more than $200,000 a year who pay no taxes at all. There are dozens of people who make more than a million dollars a year who pay no taxes at all. But a person, on the average, who makes $200,000 a year in this country pays the same percentage in taxes as the person who makes between $11,000 and $12,000 a year. I think that's unfair. I think it's unjust and unreasonable.

Q. Senator McCarthy, are you for people paying their just share?

A. I think everyone is for that — the question of eliminating inequities. And so it was — these real loopholes are the things we should have attacked in the big tax cut of '64 when we were cutting everyone's taxes.

We did make a slight move in that year on oil depletion allowances — the only thing we've been able to do in roughly 20 years that I've been in Congress, during which we've been trying to do something about oil depletion allowances. I think we got a $40-million increase that year.

Statements on Presidency

Insofar as the specific question of the surtax is concerned, I recommended early that they use other taxes — that they use credit controls and some selective excise instead of the surtax. They've not done that, and we may be down to the point now where it's a choice of forcing the President to cut the budget or expenditures by $6-billion, or to have a greater increase even in the surtax.

Q. I'd like to give each of you a couple of minutes to speak to the country and to say why you should be the next President of the United States. Senator Kennedy.

A. I've had the, as I've mentioned, the experience in the executive branch of the Government, the National Security Council. As Attorney General of the United States I was involved in the three great questions that affect our country—the problems of peace, the problems of races getting along together and the problems of the development of — the problems of riots and violence in this country.

I think that based on that experience and the work that I've done in the Senate of the United States as well as in the executive branch of the Government that — and experience I've had the test-ban treaty and the Cuban missile crisis — that perhaps

there is something that I can contribute in the cause of peace and trying to end the conflict that now exists in Vietnam and, as Thomas Jefferson said, standing for the last best hope of mankind, which we are in this country.

We dealt with the problems of riots while I was Attorney General of the United States and we also dealt with the problems of equal justice.

I think it's very easy to talk in generality. But I've sponsored specific pieces of legislation.

In the last analysis, however, it's up to the people of California and it's up to the people of the United States to make their judgment and determination about any of us. I'm going to dedicate myself no matter what happens to the betterment and improvement of the country and the people. And the choice really is up to you, and I'm glad to have it that way.

Q. Senator McCarthy.

Record in Congress

A. I've served in the Congress for 20 years—10 years in the House and 10 years in the Senate. In that time, I think I've served on nearly every one of the critical committees—I've served on Agriculture, I think I know something of the problems of rural America.

I've served on the Committee on Interior, and I think, therefore, I know something about the problems of the resources of this country.

I've served on the Banking and Currency Committee, and also my background is economic, so therefore, I think really fully qualified to deal with the very complicated economic problems, both domestic ones and also the international trade problems and the balance of payments. I've served on both the Ways and Means Committee of the House and the Finance Committee of the Senate, which I think gives me a full familiarity with the tax problems of this country. And on Foreign Relations for some five years.

In addition to that, since 1949, I've been involved in the problem of civil rights. Not only that, but with the problems of migratory workers. I was the first—back in '52—to begin to raise the question about them. And whereas I may not get the same kind of immediate response from them, I think that when they begin to look at my record they will say here is someone who has been concerned about us for a long, long time. He may not have received any publicity, but he saw what our needs were and he began to anticipate that something had to be done about those things.

450

And I believe that on that basis the problem of reconciliation with the races will be no particular problem.

Secondly, I think that in this year I sensed what the country needed. Namely, that it needed and wanted a challenge to the President of the United States on the policies of Vietnam and priority for America.

And I think there's something to be said for a President or a Presidential candidate who can somehow anticipate what the country wants, especially when what they want is on the side of good and justice, and to provide—not real leadership in the sense of saying you've got to follow me—but at least to be prepared to move out ahead, somewhat, so that the people of the country can follow.

And thirdly, I think that I sense what the young people of this country needed. As young students were dropping out and were saying the establishment was no good, we've had a genuine reconciliation of old and young in this country, and the significance of that is, I think, that through the whole country now there's a new confidence in the future of America. It's a projection of this country in trust, which has always been the character of this country, and it's in that mood and that spirit that I would act as President of the United States.

CALIFORNIA VOTE TO TEST IMPACT OF VIDEO DEBATE

Primary Campaign Resumed by Kennedy and McCarthy After Confrontation on TV

BOTH SIDES CLAIM GAIN

But Concede Main Question Is Effect on Viewers and the Voters Tomorrow

By TOM WICKER
Special to The New York Times

SAN FRANCISCO, June 2—Senators Eugene J. McCarthy and Robert F. Kennedy resumed campaigning today in the California Presidential primary, after an apparently inconclusive debate last night on a national television network.

Both sides claim to have won on points but both conceded privately that the questions and answers mattered less than the impact on the millions of viewers who watched the American Broadcasting Company program —and particularly the impact on the three million or more Californians who are expected to vote in the Democratic primary Tuesday.

1960 Reaction Recalled

What that impact was, no one in either candidate's camp could be sure. Neither contestant stumbled obviously, neither appeared at a physical disadvantage, neither sprang a surprise, both appeared calm from start to finish—at least as far as studio viewers could tell.

It was being freely recalled, however, that it was several days after the celebrated debate between John F. Kennedy and Richard M. Nixon in 1960 before it became clear that the general public considered Mr. Kennedy the winner.

John Kennedy's greatest gain from that encounter, most political analysts believe, was that he was given equal exposure and debated on equal terms with Mr. Nixon, then the Vice President and a better-known candidate.

Mr. McCarthy undoubtedly gained a similar advantage,

which the Kennedy forces had steadfastly denied him during three previous primary contests.

On the other hand, the initial reaction of many in the press and staff entourages of both candidates was that the debate had disclosed few significant differences between the two men.

If the viewing public shared that impression, it could prove costly to Mr. McCarthy. He has worked hard to differentiate his campaign from Mr. Kennedy's and is believed to have won in Oregon primarily because of his claim to have been first to oppose President Johnson on the war in Vietnam—a war for which he charged Mr. Kennedy with a share of the responsibility.

Mr. McCarthy did not turn his caustic wit on Mr. Kennedy during the hours of questions and answers broadcast from a virtually empty sound stage at KGO-TV, the A.B.C. outlet here.

The format—questions were asked by three A.B.C. reporters, William H. Lawrence, Frank Reynolds and Robert Clark—did not allow for many direct exchanges between the candidates. Each answered questions from the reporters, then each had the opportunity to comment on the other's answer.

Officials of the network said the candidates spoke for total amounts of time that were only four seconds apart.

The only thing approaching a general exchange — or a heated one—came when Mr. Kennedy accused Mr. McCarthy of publishing an advertisement charging him with participating in the decision to intervene militarily in the Dominican Republican in 1965.

Movement From Slums

Mr. McCarthy conceded that Mr. Kennedy had resigned from the Cabinet before that decision was taken by President Johnson, called the ad a mistake and said he had ordered its publication stopped.

That, he said, was more than Mr. Kennedy had done about ads that Mr. McCarthy said had distorted his voting record in Congress.

"I don't know to what he is referring," Mr. Kennedy said.

Ads that Mr. McCarthy says misrepresent his voting record have been widely published in the college press. They have been sponsored by groups supporting Mr. Kennedy. The same material has appeared in numerous direct mailings.

There were few California references in the debate, but at one point Mr. Kennedy did raise a local matter, the political effect of which remains to be seen.

Mr. McCarthy had criticized Mr. Kennedy for overconcentration on improving living

conditions in the Negro slums and had advocated the dispersal of those living in the slums to avoid "a kind of apartheid in this country."

Mr. Kennedy replied:

"When you say you are going to take 10,000 black people and move them into Orange County . . . putting them in suburbs where they can't afford the housing, where their children can't keep up with the schools, and where they don't have the schools or the jobs, it's just going to be catastrophic. I don't want to have them moved."

Some observers speculated that these remarks might cause alarm about Mr. McCarthy's views in Orange County, a largely white suburban community in Southern California that he had not mentioned. Others contended that Negro groups might resent Mr. Kennedy's words, and some felt that both effects might be forthcoming.

Generally speaking, the Negro vote in California is considered highly favorable to Mr. Kennedy, while Mr. McCarthy is thought to be stronger in the white suburbs.

Under questioning by Mr. Lawrence, Mr. Kennedy evaded a direct response to allegations that, as Attorney General, he had authorized a telephone tap on the Rev. Dr. Martin Luther King Jr.

Mr. McCarthy seized this opportunity to criticize wire-tapping generally, as well as the retention by the Federal Bureau of Investigation of irrelevant material gleaned from wiretapping. He called once again for the resignation of F.B.I. Director J. Edgar Hoover.

Even though the debate produced little excitement, it was in many ways the climax of the California campaign, in which Mr. Kennedy is a somewhat uneasy favorite.

Mr. McCarthy's victory in Oregon last Tuesday helped him considerably, and most analysts now consider the California race close.

Some point to the presence of a considerable number of "undecided" voters (as disclosed by the candidates' canvassing operations) as a threat to Mr. Kennedy, since in Oregon most of those who had been "undecided" voted ultimately for Mr. McCarthy.

Nevertheless, the Kennedy forces believe that the large minority group and urban vote in California will deliver a victory to them, and keep their candidate in the race for the Democratic Presidential nomination.

More than California's 174 convention votes are at stake. Mr. Kennedy needs to win here by a large margin to redeem his Oregon loss and to be able to present himself to Democratic leaders in the nonprimary states—particularly to the influential Mayor Richard J. Daley of Chicago—as the party's best vote-getter.

Without such a smashing victory in California, most analysts give Mr. Kennedy little chance in the nonprimary states. Vice President Humphrey appears at the moment to be collecting most of the delegates from those states.

Mr. McCarthy, by winning California with even a small

Debate Participants

Senator Eugene J. McCarthy

Associated Press
Senator Robert F. Kennedy

margin, could go to the convention with impressive credentials as a giant-killer. He could claim to have eliminated both President Johnson and Mr. Kennedy—who has said he will withdraw if he loses here—and to have established his ability to win Republican and independent votes as well as Democratic votes.

Mr. Humphrey is untested in any primary, except for relatively unimpressive write-ins A third delegate slate, headed by California's Attorney Gen-

Following are highlights of the television discussion Saturday night between Senators Robert F. Kennedy and Eugene J. McCarthy. The face-to-face confrontation was the first of their campaign for the Democratic Presidential nomination

VIETNAM

McCarthy: Favored de-escalation of the war, a pullback from advanced positions while maintaining strength in Vietnam, and formation of a new Government in the south along with recognition that this Government would include the National Liberation Front, the political arm of the Vietcong. Urged the Administration to state now that it would accept a coalition Government in Saigon.

Kennedy: Opposed such a statement at this time, but said the United States should make clear an expectation that the Saigon Government will begin its own negotiations with the National Liberation Front as the United States pursues talks with North Vietnam in Paris. Favored a demand for an end to official corruption in Vietnam. Favored a meaningful program of land reform, a pullback from the demilitarized zone and shifting of the burdens of fighting from United States to South Vietnamese troops.

Asked about bombing of the North, both Senators indicated strongly that they considered it to have been unsuccessful.

WORLD COMMITMENTS

Kennedy: Recognized a global position that he declared could not be ignored, but said that it rested more on moral leadership than military power and that he did not think "we can be the policeman of the world." Recognized a commitment in North Korea through the United Nations, a commitment to Israel. Made a distinction between response to external aggression and to internal struggles and cautioned against United States intervention in cases where the foreign Government lacked support of the populace.

McCarthy: Said he did not recognize a moral or legal commitment for the United States' present role in Vietnam. Recalled his support for United States intervention in Korea, said he recognized obligations to the Chinese on Formosa, to the Japanese, to Israel and the Middle East and to NATO.

But said the United States' commitment in Southeast Asia was "very limited." He said it must be balanced against the good "we might do there" and "our responsibilities in other parts of the world."

SECRETARY OF STATE RUSK

McCarthy: Attacked Mr. Rusk, whom he has said he would oust if elected President.

Kennedy: Said he would prefer not to indulge in personalities, but indicated later that he would not be likely to retain Mr. Rusk in his Cabinet if elected.

RACE, CRIME, LAW ENFORCEMENT

Kennedy: Said violence, rioting and lawlessness could not be tolerated. Favored funding for heightened training of local police. Said he was forbidden by law to say whether he had approved, as Attorney General, a tap on the telephone of the late Rev. Dr. Martin Luther King Jr., whom he described as a great and loyal American. Said welfare was an inadequate answer to the problems of the poor, urged provision of jobs through the Government and private enterprise. Urged massive effort to rehabilitate slums.

McCarthy: Favored a replacement for J. Edgar Hoover as Director of the Federal Bureau of Investigation. Favored Federal funds for more state and local policemen and "very reserved use" of Federal troops or National Guardsmen in riots. Favored massive new housing for low-income groups, proposed introduction of industry into the slums and some movement of slum dwellers to outlying areas. Urged interim programs "if there is a threat of violence before we get around to doing the things that have to be done."

TAXES

Kennedy: Termed the 10 per cent surcharge proposed by President Johnson "too high" and said its heaviest burdens would fall on middle- and lower-income groups. Urged a major tax reform program that would spread the burdens of taxation in a just and reasonable fashion.

McCarthy: Also favored elimination of inequities and loopholes in the tax laws. With respect to the proposed surcharge, he noted that he had recommended alternatives in the form of credit controls and selective excise taxes.

---

eral, Thomas C. Lynch, is generally considered favorable to the Humphrey candidacy and is expected to receive a sizable vote here Tuesday.

There are 7.9 million registered voters in California, including 4,347,406 Democrats and 3,197,185 Republicans. About two-thirds of the total are expected to vote.

Crossovers are not permitted. That is, a voter registered in one party cannot vote in the primary of the other.

Polling hours vary from place to place. The earliest opening is at 7 A.M. The latest closing is at 8 P.M. (11 P.M., Eastern daylight time).

Paper ballots are used throughout 26 of the 58 counties. The rest use, for the most part, either voting machines or a new system of computer cards.

Size of Audience

The debate between Senator Kennedy and Senator McCarthy was viewed by 38 per cent of the available national TV audience, according to the American Broadcasting Company.

The national Arbitron ratings, A.B.C. said yesterday, showed that the audience averaged 25.5 million during the hour-long program and that 32 million persons viewed the program at some time during its presentation.

June 3, 1968

M'CARTHY CALLS DEBATE STANDOFF

Says That Neither He Nor Kennedy Gained Much

By E. W. KENWORTHY
Special to The New York Times

SAN FRANCISCO, June 2 — Senator Eugene J. McCarthy was of the opinion today that neither he nor Senator Robert F. Kennedy had gained much out of last night's "debate."

In two television appearances here this morning and in an interview later, the Minnesotan said he thought he had opened some significant differences between himself and his rival for the Democratic Presidential nomination but had been unable to exploit them effectively because of the format of the joint appearance before reporters of the American Broadcasting Company.

He had little hope of making much use of the differences in the two days remaining before the California primary on Tuesday.

June 3, 1968

June 3, 1968

"If we had debated two weeks ago," he said in an interview, "we would have known what his position was."

The areas of difference with the New Yorker, Mr. McCarthy said, were negotiations on Vietnam, the shift of Negro workers into white suburbs, the financing of housing and rehabilitation projects in the slums and the question of electronic surveillance by the Federal Bureau of Investigation.

'Coalition' Debated

In the debate last night Mr. Kennedy said he was opposed to "forcing a coalition government" in South Vietnam and Mr. McCarthy replied, "I didn't say I was going to force a coalition government over South Vietnam; I said we should make sure we are willing to accept that."

Today, however, in a panel discussion on Station KRON-TV, Mr. McCarthy said:

"He [Mr. Kennedy] said he wouldn't force a coalition. I feel that, directly or indirectly, that's what we have to do."

Earlier on the Columbia Broadcasting System's "Face the Nation" program, Mr. McCarthy said that to leave to the South Vietnamese Government the decision on a coalition regime would simply "put us right back where we are."

On the problem of the slums, Senator McCarthy's position was that the location of industry there and the construction of new housing and the improvement of education were necessary in the short run but in the long run many Negro workers would have to be moved into the suburbs, where most of the new jobs were.

Senator Kennedy said that Negroes could not be moved to the suburbs while they were not educated to hold jobs there and could not afford the homes there. He asked whether Senator McCarthy was "going to take 10,000 black people

and move them into Orange County."

Today on "Face the Nation," Mr. McCarthy said under questioning that he would not immediately concentrate on moving Negroes out of the slums but that there had to be a program for letting them out.

In a statement issued later, Mr. McCarthy charged that Mr. Kennedy had "injected scare tactics into the campaign" by his suggestion about moving Negroes into Orange County. This, he said, was "a crude distortion of my proposals" that could "increase suspicion and mistrust among the races."

June 3, 1968

Kennedy-McCarthy Dialogue

The hour-long television panel discussion in which Senators Eugene J. McCarthy and Robert F. Kennedy participated on Saturday evening was a model of civilized political discourse. It was a conversation rather than a debate and it demonstrated that the two rivals are in substantial agreement on every major issue. The one unfortunate note was the obfuscation created around the question of forcing Saigon to accept a postwar coalition regime in South Vietnam.

If there was no dramatic conflict, the show was nevertheless informative on a wide range of public problems. The only significant omission was the failure to explore the opinions of the two men regarding the Communist superpowers, Russia and China. Otherwise both Senators proved that they have a strong grasp of the facts and an impressive keenness and lucidity in setting forth their views.

On questions of substance the two men are proved to be evenly matched, but in the over-all impression each made Mr. McCarthy was ahead on points because he was his natural urbane self while Mr. Kennedy, a man of more sharply varying moods, was less at ease because he seemed to be reining in his native aggressiveness and trying deliberately to be low-keyed.

Although this confrontation was not a decisive political event like the first Kennedy-Nixon debate of 1960, it was so obviously useful to the voters in understanding and judging Senators Kennedy and McCarthy that it is unfortunate Vice President Humphrey refused to take part.

He owes it to the people to cease pretending that his rivals for the nomination do not exist and to join with them in some future discussion of the nation's needs. Similarly, a discussion among former Vice President Nixon and Governors Rockefeller and Reagan would contribute to the Republican party's search for the best man.

June 3, 1968

TV: Viewing Candidates

Perhaps an Earnest Hunt for Pertinence Would Be More Helpful Than Debates

By JACK GOULD

THE television world's quadrennial yearning for political debates may need fresh appraisal after Saturday night's electronic tennis game, in which Senators Robert F. Kennedy and Eugene J. McCarthy played on the same side of the net.

The chief effect of the hour on the American Broadcasting Company was to remind the set owner of the missing man, Vice President Humphrey. Mr. Humphrey's decision to stay out of the San Francisco studio left video with only half a story.

Saturday night's program clearly raises the question of whether television is deluding itself and the viewer by placing such a high priority on debates over which the medium really does not have any control. For pragmatic political reasons President Johnson avoided debates in 1964. On Saturday night Vice President Humphrey made the point again, that one way to be a winner is to detect the political value of a well-timed absence. In championing debates, TV may be encouraging a candidate to exercise a power of veto that suits his convenience. There are other methods of political reporting open to TV and they should be explored.

Major segments of the TV industry have incessantly declared that Section 315 of the Federal Communications Act must be suspended after the Presidential conventions, if the networks are not to be handicapped in giving adequate time to the principal candidates. Without such suspension, they note, they would be legally required to accord equal time to perhaps a score of marginal candidates, a ludicrous situation in which fringe aspirants would outnumber the two candidates of importance.

Saturday night the A.B.C. lawyers deftly slipped in a precautionary wrinkle, which went virtually unnoticed on the screen but could have formidable pertinency between now and November. Regularly scheduled newscasts are exempt from the restrictive provisions of Section 315, so the meeting between Senator Kennedy and Senator McCarthy was discreetly billed as "a special edition" of the regular A.B.C. program entitled "Issues and Answers."

If regularly scheduled news programs, such as the National Broadcasting Company's "Meet the Press" and its Frank McGee weekend presentation or the Columbia Broadcasting System's "Face the Nation" and its Tuesday night hour, can be shifted at will under the guise of a special edition, then why all the years of argument over Section 315? Free time in prime hours can be allocated by the networks now, if just putting a regular title on such presentations obviates any legal problem. The maneuver of the A.B.C. News Department could have interesting applications.

The stratagem of rescheduling regular news programs to meet the journalistic needs of a Presidential political year also holds the advantage of coping with the problem of a candidate who may not choose to show up for a studio debate, with all its attendant tensions and perennial arguments over ground rules. Ideally, to be sure, there is extra drama in seeing two rivals sit side-by-side and respond to each other's remarks.

But television is not solely dependent on a joint studio appearance to achieve the larger objective of showing where and how candidates may differ. The networks normally follow the candidates in their wanderings, and by sensible selection of filmed excerpts they could easily put together a special edition of a regular show to compare the similarities, differences or evasions of candidates on the day's prime issues. This documentary approach has been used before, and it may be more truly revealing of the postures of candidates than either interviews or debates, particularly in illustrating how aspirants may adjust their views to different sections of the country.

Such independent political reporting in the field, with no candidate exempt from proportionate coverage, as was the case with Vice President Humphrey on Saturday night, may not appease television's excessive preoccupation with making headlines in newspapers. But for the viewer at home it could be more useful and educational, and would avoid the demeaning ritual of television's asking Congress for special concessions to do its job.

June 3, 1968

453

ROCKEFELLER ASKS DEBATE WITH NIXON

LOS ANGELES, June 12 (AP) —Governor Rockefeller of New York said today that he would welcome a nationally televised debate with Richard M. Nixon, his opponent for the Republican Presidential nomination.

Asked if he would challenge the former Vice President to a debate, Mr. Rockefeller replied: "If one of the national television networks invite us to debate, I'd accept immediately. I'm ready."

He also said he would be happy to meet with Mr. Nixon in different parts of the country to discuss major issues.

He made the comments in an interview with a local television station, KNBC, which taped it for release Sunday.

In New York, Mr. Nixon turned down the Governor's challenge.

A spokesman said that Mr. Nixon believed such a debate "would only serve the Democrats by promoting divisive tendencies among Republicans."

Mr. Nixon returned to New York from a brief vacation in the Bahamas.

ROCKEFELLER PRODS NIXON TO DEBATE

Challenges Rival on Coast to Appear on Television

By R. W. APPLE Jr.
Special to The New York Times

SAN FRANCISCO, June 13— Governor Rockefeller intensified his pressure on former Vice President Richard M. Nixon today in his reinvigorated bid for the Republican Presidential nomination.

Speaking at a news conference, the Governor formally challenged Mr. Nixon to a series of television debates, as proposed by the networks. He had said several times previously that he was willing to debate, but he has never issued a challenge.

Mr. Nixon, who was considered the odds-on favorite to win the nomination, rejected the proposal for a debate yesterday with the assertion that it "would only serve the Democrats by promoting divisive tendencies among Republicans."

"I'd like to see three or four debates in different parts of the country," Mr. Rockefeller said. "I want people to get a taste of the issues."

Asked why he thought Mr. Nixon was reluctant, the Governor alluded to the former Vice President's experience in 1960. His televised confrontations with John F. Kennedy in that year were credited with helping to elect the Democratic nominee.

"Maybe he's got a conditioned reaction to debates," Mr. Rockefeller said, smiling. "I'd hope he'd change his mind."

In the question-and-answer period following a speech to the Commonwealth Club here, the Governor again suggested that Mr. Nixon welcomed the support of segregationists.

He quoted Howard Callaway, Mr. Nixon's Southern regional campaign manager, as having said in Jackson, Miss., on June 1:

"Perhaps we can get George Wallace on our side; that's where he belongs."

"Dick Nixon has got to de-nounce that statement," Mr. Rockefeller said.

In still another phase of his attack on his rival, the Governor sent a telegram to Price Daniel, assistant to the President for Federal-state relations, proposing a series of gun-control measures.

He urged support for President Johnson's gun control program, but also asked that Congress establish standards for state and local licensing of the owners of all firearms and registration of all hand guns. He recommended that interstate shipment of arms and ammunition in states without licensing systems be banned if they did not adopt systems in two years.

Mr. Rockefeller's proposal tied in with the second of a series of full-page newspaper advertisements, which was published this morning in The New York Times, The San Francisco Chronicle, The Los Angeles Times, The Washington Post, The Wall Street Journal and approximately 45 other major papers.

"Our cities can be saved but they will not be saved by a gospel of do-nothing," the ad said.

"They will not be saved by men who read rousing speeches about crime control—and say not a word about gun control.

"They will not be saved by men who choke hope in the name of law and order—and then turn to undermine our highest court of law."

Said To Refer To Nixon

The "men" referred to in the text in the advertisement was in fact only one man, Mr. Nixon, according to Rockefeller aides.

It is expected that Mr. Rockefeller's advertising campaign will cost several million dollars before the Republican National Convention opens Aug. 5 in Miami Beach, Fla. He conceded today that it "obviously isn't cheap," but he provided no estimate.

However, it is known that the Rockefeller organization plans to insert seven full-page ads in 41 newspapers in 35 cities — and two this week and one a week for the next five weeks.

The Chronicle's rate is $6,653.44 a page; that of The New York Times is $6,960. Some other newspapers have considerably lower rates.

Nixon Declines Debate
Special to The New York Times

CHICAGO, June 20 — Former Vice President Nixon refused again today to respond to Governor Rockefeller's challenge to debate the issues.

He told a crowded news conference in a fifth-floor lobby of the Sheraton Blackstone Hotel, where he was surrounded by Secret Service men, that he thought he could win a debate. But he said that the main winner would be Vice President Humphrey, the leading Democratic candidate, if a debate divided Republicans.

He said that his victories in the primaries were sufficient evidence that he was the popular choice among Republican voters.

Senator Charles H. Percy appeared at the news conference, as he had earlier in the day here with Governor Rockefeller. In both cases he maintained neutrality and spoke of the two candidates as the most qualified for the Presidency.

Presidential TV Debates _Before_ the Conventions

By HERBERT MITGANG

About a century ago, in September of 1960, Richard M. Nixon and John F. Kennedy met in the first of a series of Presidential debates that showed the American people their personalities, styles and programs. This remarkable confrontation, seen each time by an estimated 65 million television viewers, took place _after_ the nominating conventions.

It's a different political ball game—not to mention a different United States and world—less than eight years later. The state primaries have left no doubt that large numbers of Americans are outraged at the whole course of foreign and domestic policy. They will be even more outraged if the national conventions strip them of any real opportunity to force a change by their votes next November.

The real question now is: Shall the months of July and August up to each party's convention be filled only with paid political commercials and dead political air? Will prime evening time be devoted to the usual TV stuff or will the public get a chance to see the real contenders of both parties—Nixon vs. Rockefeller and Humphrey vs. McCarthy—debate _before_ the conventions? Watchmen (and women), what of the night?

At this stage of the game, whom the convention delegates will vote for rather than whom the country will vote for is all-important. The delegates can be convinced by the pollsters, whose educated guess work is based on samplings of a few thousand "weighted" opinions that profess to speak for tens of millions of unclassifiable Americans. They can be convinced by the regular politicians who can control the machinery so effectively that any effort to open the conventions will be frustrated.

Prime Time Debates

Or, they can be convinced by a series of major prime time debates that it is their obligation to study the candidates in close-up, respond to the reaction of the national constituency, and do what the conventions do not always do—choose the best man for party and country.

The decision is up to the networks and the candidates, not Congress and the Federal Communications Commission. All three networks have expressed a willingness to provide free political time for debates between Labor Day and Election Day, as they did in 1960. Since they are always interested in underscoring the fact that they come within the First Amendment freedom despite F.C.C. licensing of stations, they might well be willing in the public interest to extend the offer for TV debates to include the period between Independence Day and convention time.

The Senate, by a voice vote on May 29, suspended the equal-time requirement (to be accurate, Section 315 of the Communications Act calls it "equal opportunities," which is more flexible), meaning that no-hope candidates like Harold Stassen would not have to be given free reply hours on the air. The Senate resolution was sent to the House Committee on Interstate and Foreign Commerce, where it now is. The committee chairman, Representative Staggers, holds the key to that lock.

Whether or not he turns it, this joint resolution to suspend in 1968 would not take effect until Aug. 31—after the candidates have been picked and too late to have any effect on the delegates. Ideally, the joint resolution necessary to defuse Section 315 would open the airwaves right after the Fourth of July.

But even if the ideal is too much to hope for, the three networks can proceed boldly on their own to exercise journalistic initiative and courage. A precedent was established before the California primary when Senators Kennedy and McCarthy appeared jointly on A.B.C.'s "Issues and Answers." Although it was not a full-fledged debate, it was an enlightening confrontation that could be amplified without breaching the present law.

For there are several exceptions allowed under Section 315 even if Congress does not suspend at all. Equal opportunities need not be given to minor candidates if the major candidates appear on "bona fide news interview" broadcasts. That is what occurred on "Issues and Answers." The other networks also have similar regularly scheduled "bona fide news interview" programs—C.B.S.'s "Face the Nation" and N.B.C.'s "Meet the Press."

Let the Candidates Appear

Between July 4 and the conventions, the three networks could invite Vice President Humphrey and Senator McCarthy to appear with each other and Mr. Nixon and Governor Rockefeller to appear with each other. The format could be worked out by the networks and the candidates to include statements, cross talk, and the normal "bona fide" questioning by newsmen.

Governor Rockefeller and Senator McCarthy are willing to debate their rivals on television. The front runners have only to say yes. If the word "debates" makes the networks queasy, call them "joint discussions." That was good enough for Lincoln and Douglas, before pancake make-up and inglorious living color, over a century ago.

HERBERT MITGANG is a member of the editorial board of The Times.

McCarthy Seeks to Debate Humphrey on 'Crucial Issues'

Special to The New York Times

CHICAGO, June 30—Senator Eugene J. McCarthy challenged Vice President Humphrey today to meet him in public debate "on the crucial issues facing America."

"If the Vice President feels that he is not free to discuss these issues, Mr. McCarthy said, "let him be set free."

"Let the President release him to speak his full mind and to defend or reject the policies of this Administration," Senator McCarthy said. "Let the Vice President take part in public debate with me on the issues which have been troubling the American people for so long."

Senator McCarthy issued his challenge in a speech at a fund-raising affair in the Auditorium Hotel in Chicago after a flight from Lansing, Mich., where he spoke to the Michigan delegates to the Democratic Convention.

Humphrey Bars Pre-Convention Debate With Rival

By WARREN WEAVER Jr.
Special to The New York Times

CLEVELAND, July 2—Vice President Humphrey rejected today Senator Eugene J. McCarthy's challenge to meet him in television debate prior to the Democratic National Convention next month.

"I'm saving up my ammunition for Richard Nixon, and I intend to use it on him," Mr. Humphrey said in response to a question after a speech to the Cleveland City Club at the Cleveland Sheraton Hotel.

On Sunday in Chicago, Senator McCarthy called on the Vice President to debate with him "the crucial issues for America" and implied that President Johnson was restricting Mr. Humphrey's availability for such a confrontation.

"If the Vice President feels he is not free to discuss the issues," Mr. McCarthy said at that time, "let him be set free. Let the President release him to speak his full mind, to defend or reject the policies of this Administration."

Separate Appearances

Mr. Humphrey said today there was "no problem about presenting the issues" between the two Presidential candidates since he and Senator McCarthy had appeared "together" at four Democratic state conventions in recent days.

The two Democratic Presidential candidates made separate speeches during the last 10 days to the Minnesota, North Dakota, Oklahoma and Iowa conventions, usually only a short time apart, but they never appeared on the platform together or engaged in any public exchange before the delegates.

Mr. Humphrey recalled that in 1960 when he was an underdog he had not profited from a debate challenge to John F. Kennedy and said facetiously of Senator McCarthy: "I'm warning him. I may have to accept him."

Race as Independent

The Cleveland City Club did not present one of the Vice President's more successful audiences. More than 1,000 luncheon guests did not interrupt his 47-minute speech on urban problems once for applause, and three of the four questions afterward were clearly pro-McCarthy.

He received a standing ovation at the end, however, and spirited applause on each of his replies to the hostile questions.

Asked if he would unite the party behind Mr. McCarthy if

the Senator should win the Democratic Presidential nomination, Mr. Humphrey said that unlike some of his colleagues, "I am a Democrat and I will support the nominee of my party."

There has been increasing speculation that Senator McCarthy might run as an independent candidate if he failed to obtain the Democratic nomination.

"I look forward to his support in August after I get the nomination," Mr. Humphrey said of his fellow Minnesotan, "just as he would look for my support if he gets the nomination, which I doubt he's going to get."

In his formal speech to the City Club, the Vice President amplified his earlier proposal to establish a National Urban Development Bank, which would help finance business, housing and rehabilitation programs in the slums, with an initial Government investment but largely with borrowed private funds.

'Say No to Hu-Bird'

Humphrey aides estimated that this proposal could make $150-billion to $300-billion available over the next 10 years for nonprofit neighborhood development corporations, loans to small businesses, technical assistance and housing development in such "inner cities" as Cleveland's Hough.

While the Vice President spoke and answered questions in the Sheraton Cleveland ballroom, more than 150 pickets marched outside the hotel, carrying signs like "The Happy Warrior of Vietnam," "Say No to Hu-Bird" and "Stokes Yes, Humphrey No."

Mayor Carl B. Stokes, a strong Humphrey supporter, accompanied the Vice President this morning to a community center in the Hough neighborhood, where Mr. Humphrey announced the allocation of a $1.6-million poverty grant for an economic development program in that area of the city's worst racial rioting.

Mr. Stokes, in the manner of the late Senator Robert F. Kennedy, tried to get his audience of 300 to give the Vice President full political credit in choral replies to his questions.

"How much are we getting?" he asked.

"A million and a half dollars," a few voices answered raggedly.

"Who brought it here?" the Mayor inquired. "Humphrey," said a few more people.

"Who's going to handle it?" the Negro Mayor asked. "We are," a strong response came back.

Candidate Debates—Now

The value of public debates on television between the leading Presidential candidates prior to the conventions would be twofold: An opportunity would be given to the American public to see the men and pinpoint the issues; an opportunity would be given to the delegates to judge the candidates away from the circus atmosphere of the conventions.

The American Broadcasting Company has extended an invitation to the two leading candidates of each party to appear together on "Issues and Answers," a regularly scheduled news program, before the conventions. This program broke the ice before the California primary when Senators McCarthy and Kennedy appeared jointly and responded to questions by newsmen. The result was a unique and valuable opportunity for voters to see and hear them discuss the same issues at the same moment.

The A.B.C. invitation could be fortified if the Columbia Broadcasting System and the National Broadcasting Company also asked the candidates to appear together on their "Face the Nation" and "Meet the Press." If all three networks devoted merely one hour of night time confrontations to the two pairs of leading Democratic and Republican candidates, commercial television would be performing a public service.

It would be useful if, as Mr. Stanton of C.B.S. suggests in a letter published today, the House voted to suspend Section 315 of the Communications Act so that debates like those in 1960 could take place. However, simply suspending Section 315 would not come to grips with the immediate realities of the election campaign of 1968. For the necessary joint resolution would not take effect until September—after the conventions were over.

In this respect, Mr. Stanton's reasoning fails to mention what A.B.C.'s "Issues and Answers" proved in California—that a network can bring candidates face to face on an exempt program without violating the equal-time law. That program format did not change; newsmen were included then and could be included again to interrogate candidates. The F.C.C. did not take away the exempt status of "Issues and Answers" nor did it insist that Vegetarian and other minor candidates get equal time.

The networks—and the candidates—can show their ingenuity and courage by giving the delegates and the American electorate this opportunity to make an independent judgment.

TWO DEMOCRATS AGREE ON TV TALK

Vice President Humphrey announced through an aide last night that he had accepted the idea of a discussion of campaign issues on network television with Senator Eugene J. McCarthy.

The Vice President said that he had accepted the idea in telegrams to all three networks.

Earlier last night, Senator McCarthy said he had accepted an offer by the Columbia Broadcasting System to appear with the Vice President on an hour-long, prime-time show and had instructed his campaign manager to enter into "immediate negotiations" with representatives of Mr. Humphrey and C.B.S.

Offer by 3 Networks

A spokesman for Senator McCarthy said early this morning that the Senator had seen only the telegram with the C.B.S. offer. "He has not said no to the other two [networks]," he reported.

Until his action yesterday, Vice President Humphrey had taken the position that he would not discuss the issues with a fellow Democrat before the convention. He had indicated he was saving his ammunition for the Republican candidate in the fall.

The Vice President's aide, Ted Van Dyk, said that he had been in touch by telephone last night with Blair Clark, Mr. McCarthy's campaign manager, and Thomas Finney, another McCarthy campaign official, and reported they had said they saw no problem concerning the television discussion.

No definite date or format has been set for the program. However, Mr. Van Dyk said the Vice President wanted the discussion with his rival to take place during the week of Aug. 18, the week before the Democratic National Convention.

Details Still to Be Set

On the other hand, Mr. Clark said, "The debate should happen sooner rather than later—the sooner the better, so that the Democratic delegates and the constituencies they represent can have ample time to consider the views on the issues of the Vice President and of Senator McCarthy."

All three television networks had extended separate invitations yesterday for a discussion between the candidates. They apparently issued the invitations after the publication yesterday morning of a report in The Washington Post that the Vice President had tentatively expressed interest in such a discussion.

Mr. Van Dyk said that Mr. Humphrey was agreeing to the discussion at this time because this was the first official invitation by the networks to the two candidates. He said that the Vice President had received earlier "feelers" concerning a discussion with his rival for the Democratic Presidential nomination from the National Broadcasting Company.

Senator McCarthy's acceptance of the C.B.S. offer came after his attention was called during a news conference in Nashville to the dispatch in The Washington Post. The Post reported that the Vice President had said in an interview: "It may be desirable to have such a discussion before the convention."

In a telegram to C.B.S., Senator McCarthy said:

"I accept the offer of C.B.S. News to meet with Vice President Humphrey in a joint televised appearance. I am pleased to see published reports that the Vice President is also agreeable to such a meeting.

"I have instructed my campaign manager to enter into immediate negotiations with representatives of both the Vice President and the network to arrange the details of such a meeting."

In Washington, Mr. Clark reported that he had been in touch with Richard Salant, C.B.S. News president, and said that the Senator would be ready to appear either this Sunday or the following Sunday.

Mr. Van Dyk said that the Vice President wanted the discussion to take place the week before the convention—because his schedule is fairly full until then and because he believes the discussion would have more impact at that time.

The American Broadcasting Company asked them to debate dates to meet "in an hour-long, prime-time, face-to-face TV and radio discussion on Vietnam and other issues."

A.B.C. asked them to debate for 90 minutes on Saturday, Aug. 24 from 9:30 to 11 P.M. Eastern daylight time with a format to be decided on by representatives of the candidates and the network.

N.B.C. said it had issued an invitation for the candidates to appear on "Meet the Press."

It seemed likely that, if Senator McCarthy agreed to the invitations of the two other networks, the result might be a pool arrangement.

McCarthy Challenges Humphrey to Debate Now

By ROBERT E. DALLOS

Senator Eugene J. McCarthy challenged Vice President Humphrey yesterday to submit to immediate face-to-face confrontations on national television instead of waiting until the eve of the Democratic National Convention.

Mr. McCarthy also asked his opponent for the Democratic Presidential nomination to submit to a series of three debates —one on foreign policy, another on domestic and economic policy and the third on the two candidates' conceptions of the office of the Presidency and the conduct of government.

More Time on N.B.C.

The possibility of any debate between the two men developed late Saturday when the Vice President announced through an aide that he had accepted the idea of a discussion on network TV with the Minnesota Senator. Before that he had declined to agree to a discussion with a fellow Democrat before the convention.

The possibility of heightened political activity on network television this fall increased still more yesterday with the announcement by the National Broadcasting Company that it would make available an extra minute of advertising time for political spots on one hour and on 90-minute programs. N.B.C. also said it would cut to 50 per cent of rate card prices the cost of political sponsorship between Aug. 1 and election day.

Mr. McCarthy's challenge was made yesterday in a statement released in Washington by Blair Clark, his campaign manager.

It read in part: "Senator McCarthy has from the beginning of his campaign sought to discuss the issues before the public with the other candidates for the Democratic nomination.

"Yesterday he accepted the Columbia Broadcasting System offer of a discussion with the Vice President for the 21st or 28th of July. We understand that the Vice President is willing to have a discussion, but only in the week before the convention, which starts in five weeks.

"That means a four-week delay in presenting his discussion to the public. We regret this delay and would urge that the date be advanced so that the Democratic delegates and the constituency they represent can have ample time to consider the views of the Vice President and Senator McCarthy."

The statement went on to suggest the three separate topics for discussions "if there is to be a serious public discussion of the issues confronting and dividing the nation and party."

Talks May Begin Today

Ted Van Dyk, an aide to the Vice President, said in a telephone interview last night that "the idea is interesting but we are a little surprised that it was given out by press release rather than discussed in talks with us."

He said that the "Vice President's preference remains for a discussion a week before the convention" but added that "both candidates are committed to the idea of a debate and we have to sit down and talk about it."

Talks between representatives of the two candidates will begin either today or tomorrow, both sides indicated.

All three networks extended separate invitations Saturday for a discussion between the candidates.

The American Broadcasting Company said it would provide time on Aug. 24 from 9:30 to 11 P.M. N.B.C. issued an invitation for the candidates to appear on "Meet the Press." C.B.S. offered an hour of prime time for last night or next Sunday.

The N.B.C. action was announced by Ernest Lee Jahncke Jr., vice president, political broadcast unit. He said the step was being taken to meet the unexpected requirements of candidates. He said that politicians were placing greater emphasis on television and that the TV business was so good generally that in a few weeks all advertising time for the fall would be sold out.

The extra minute—a seventh for hour-long programs and a 10th for 90-minute programs—will make time available for politicians.

So as not to "gain a windfall" from the extra time, Mr. Jahncke said yesterday, the price cut is being instituted for all political minute spots, while N.B.C. affiliate stations will continue to be compensated as before.

There will be no price cuts for political TV time of more than a minute. Since even minute spot prices vary, it is difficult to determine what savings would be. A minute on the Dean Martin Show on N.B.C., for instance, is listed at $63,000. It would go to the politician for $31,500.

One informed source said yesterday that by cutting 50 per cent of the rate card list prices, N.B.C. was not actually giving half price to politicians, since commercial advertising is more often than not sold for lower than the rate card price.

HUMPHREY SCORES M'CARTHY ON WAR

Says He Complains but Has No Peace Plan — Terms Issues at Home Ignored

By CLAYTON KNOWLES

Vice President Humphrey sharply criticized Senator Eugene J. McCarthy yesterday, contending he did not discuss "crucial issues" on the home front and limited himself to "complaint" about Vietnam rather than developing a peace plan.

The attack on the Minnesota Senator and his Presidential campaign, possibly the strongest Mr. Humphrey has yet made, came in response to the renewed McCarthy challenge to engage in a series of debates before the Democratic National Convention, which opens in Chicago on Aug. 26.

Without ruling out the series, the Vice President hinted broadly that he might limit televised confrontations to one in the week before the convention.

Mr. Humphrey declared he would feel more interested in broader discussions if Senator McCarthy were to spell out his position on the issues at home and abroad.

"I am for peace," the Vice President said. "He has not said how he will get it. We believe the way to get it is at the Paris peace conference. We have a program. The opposition has a complaint."

On domestic issues, Mr. Humphrey said he would like "to find out where the Senator stands on the education of our people, the rebuilding of our cities, training the jobless, urban affairs, the whole health program and fiscal matters."

Stating he had addressed himself to all these issues, Mr. Humphrey suggested that debates could become a "monologue" unless the position of both candidates for the Democratic Presidential nomination were known.

"I will not get caught up like a broken record," he said. "As yet I have not been able to find out what the Senator stands for."

At a news conference upon his arrival at La Guardia Airport, the Vice President ruled out in equally blunt language any "deal" with former Gov. George C. Wallace of Alabama that would help Mr. Humphrey get nominated or elected.

"I would rather not be President, I would rather not be nominated as the Presidential candidate than depend on a racist vote to get the nomination or the election," he said.

With Mr. Wallace waging a vigorous third-party bid for the Presidency, the election could be thrown into the House of Representatives for decision if no one of the three nominees could win a majority of the electoral votes. Each state delegation in the House would cast one ballot, thereby heightening the influence of the South in the final choice.

Mr. Humphrey came to New York City for two days of campaigning, the first he has undertaken since he recovered from a 10-day bout of influenza. The high point of his stay will be a $500-a-plate dinner at the Waldorf-Astoria Hotel tonight set up by his supporters.

He met with reporters yesterday morning just off the airstrip at La Guardia Airport's Marine Terminal, looking cheerful, confident and completely fit.

He parried some questions but answered most of them fully and forcefully. On one involving the most recent Harris poll, published yesterday, showing him doing less well against Richard M. Nixon than did Senator McCarthy, he said:

"The polls since May have indicated—every poll—that I was ahead. One little dip does not bother me. I hope to see that corrected shortly. We're doing well with the delegates and the delegates pretty well represent the views of the people."

He noted that his illness had kept him from campaigning and that he had refrained from campaigning also during the two weeks following the death of Senator Robert F. Kennedy on June 6.

When asked about his chances of a first-ballot nomination, the Vice President looked at the bright skies over the airfield and said:

"My chances are as good as this day is beautiful."

He conceded he saw "a cloud here and there representing the opposition." He continued the analogy when asked if he did not fear the McCarthy cloud.

Looking skyward again, he replied: "Not if it doesn't get any bigger than that one over there that floats off first to the left and then to the right."

He rather lightly dismissed a suggestion by Gov. Phillip H. Hoff of Vermont that he resign to show he was his own man as a candidate. He said he doubted Governor Rockefeller had ever thought about such a move, then added:

"We'd have a lot of resignations. About the only one who wouldn't have to resign is Mr. Nixon, and I refuse to let him have an open field."

Asked about the possibility of Senator Edward M. Kennedy's becoming his running mate, he said there were "a number of good men in the Democratic party" and added that he felt complimented reporters thought he would "have something to say about the question."

Mr. Humphrey also observed that there was "a season for all things, and this is the season for baseball, for picnicking and for vacations."

Mr. Humphrey, after his arrival, went to recording studios to tape campaign spots for use on radio and television.

Last night he attended a reception of Hispanic-Americans for Humphrey at the Waldorf-Astoria.

Mrs. Humphrey accompanied her husband to the reception. During the afternoon she spent a relaxed hour with a group of women, nearly all of them friends, at a tea given in her honor in the home of Mollie Parnis (Mrs. Leon J. Livingston), the dress designer, at 812 Park Avenue.

July 23, 1968

Politics in the Air

Call them joint discussions, regularly scheduled news interview programs, or debates, the semantics are less important than the fact that at last two of the leading Presidential contenders from the same party — Vice President Humphrey and Senator McCarthy — have consented to appear together before a television audience of what will undoubtedly be several millions.

We have urged such a confrontation on the twofold ground that it would give the candidates an unusual opportunity to clarify the issues and that it would permit the delegates to evaluate the two men apart from the "circus atmosphere" of the conventions. It would also be desirable if the two principal Republican candidates would follow the Democrats' example. Mr. Nixon's previous refusal to do so on grounds that he does not wish to argue with a fellow Republican ignores the fact that there are genuine differences between the men and their approaches to national and foreign problems.

The more guidance the delegates get, the better will be their knowledge—and their independence of choice. These public confrontations can help to open up the conventions.

July 23, 1968

Debates Without Delay

The issues between Vice President Humphrey and Senator McCarthy are at last being joined—which makes it all the more urgent that they confront each other openly in public debate instead of sniping through spokesmen or between courses at fund-raising dinners.

The full-scale presentation of their views and differences can best be achieved by several face-to-face meetings on television evenings over the course of the next weeks. These should take place as soon as possible.

Senator McCarthy's spokesmen seek three separate hours to debate foreign policy; domestic and economic policy; and the role and responsibilities of the President. This amount of time does not seem too much, considering the gravity of the issues. All three networks have now offered their facilities for the debates, and they could share hour-long confrontations. The American Broadcasting Company's proposal of three Saturdays—July 27, Aug. 10 and Aug. 24—seems reasonable.

And it is still not too late for Mr. Nixon to accept the invitation of the networks, as Governor Rockefeller has, for a television discussion between them. The Republican delegates, and voters in general who may do much crossing-over from their regular parties, deserve to know as much as they can about the men and the issues.

July 25, 1968

McCarthy's Aides Press for Debate

By E. W. KENWORTHY
Special to The New York Times

BOSTON, July 25 — Aides of Senator Eugene J. McCarthy said today that Vice President Humphrey had refused to meet him in a debate unless it was held the week before the Democratic National Convention.

In a news conference immediately following one by Senator McCarthy, Richard Goodwin, a principal adviser, said that he and the Minnesota Senator's campaign manager, Blair Clark, met yesterday with Norman Sherman, the Vice President's press secretary, and Theodore Van Dyk, a Humphrey speech writer, to discuss arrangements for a television debate between the contenders for the Democratic Presidential nomination.

Last weekend Senator McCarthy accepted offers from the television networks for a debate and an aide of Mr. Humphrey said that the Vice President was interested in the idea.

Mr. Clark and Mr. Goodwin, in a statement read by Mr. Goodwin, said that Mr. McCarthy had accepted the network proposals for a series of debates "to begin on the 27th or 28th of July."

"The Vice President has rejected these suggestions and has said he will only debate in the week immediately before the Democratic convention," the statement said.

If the Vice President stands by his position, the McCarthy aides said, "we suggest that it would be more effective to debate in front of the assembled delegates at the convention itself than to hold a debate at so late a date."

Mr. Goodwin said that this had not been discussed with Mr. Humphrey's representatives.

Mr. Clark and Mr. Goodwin charged that the Vice President wanted to delay the debate until it was too late for the public response to be registered in the polls and thus transmitted to convention delegates and party leaders.

Senator McCarthy said at his news conference that he would like three debates—one on foreign policy with emphasis on Vietnam, one on economic pol-

icy and the problem of inflation and one on "the processes of government and the concept of the Presidency."

The Senator said, in response to a question, that he would not say that the Vice President's campaign had "peaked." But, he added, the polls did show Mr. Humphrey's strength declining "for some time."

Whether this will continue, Mr. McCarthy would not predict.

"But we're not much of an underdog, and I would rather be in my position than in the position of the Vice President right now," he said.

'An Open Fight'

Mr. Goodwin said:

"It is now clear that nobody will enter the convention with a majority. It is an open fight."

Mr. McCarthy said that he had not decided whether to make a trip to Europe, but if he did go, he doubted whether he would talk with North Vietnamese representatives at the Paris negotiations.

He also said that he had reservations about the proposal of Representative Morris K. Udall, Democrat of Arizona, for an agreement by the two major parties to thwart former Gov. George C. Wallace of Alabama by casting all the votes of state Congressional delegations for the candidate getting the largest popular vote if the election were thrown into the House of Representatives.

Tonight at Fenway Park Senator McCarthy drew the largest crowd since he began his campaign last Nov. 30. Every seat in the Red Sox ball park—a total of 33,000—was sold out several days ago. Outside the park a crowd estimated at more than 6,000 saw the rally over 200 TV sets.

Reporters who had followed the late Senator Robert F. Kennedy and Vice President Humphrey were agreed that this was the biggest rally so far of the 1968 campaign.

As the crowd roared, Senator McCarthy said that his campaign "was not something new in America but something old that has come back."

"It is as old as the Boston Tea Party," he said, and embodied what President John

Adams called the public happiness—"a delight in taking upon one's self the burdens of citizenship."

Humphrey Aides Respond

WASHINGTON, July 25 (AP) —Humphrey headquarters responded tonight to the assertions by Senator McCarthy's aides with the following statement:

"We don't intend to issue any press releases criticizing Senator McCarthy or members of his staff concerning the proposed TV discussion. Our meeting was held in good faith and we thought in a cooperative spirit. It was our feeling following the meeting that agreement would be reached quite soon on the timing and format of the discussion.

"We favor one discussion the week preceding the Democratic convention. We think this is a good time for it—to summarize the candidates' position and to give the public and the Democratic delegates a final summing-up prior to the convention.

"There are some factual and other errors in the statement released by Mr. Clark and Mr Goodwin, but we are not going to be contentious. We still want to work this out and we think we can."

July 26, 1968

Arthur M. Schlesinger Jr., historian and aide to President Kennedy, and a group of distinguished educators called upon Vice President Humphrey and Richard M. Nixon yesterday to accept the invitations of their opponents to debate on major issues.

"As educators and observers of the political scene, we believe that the 1968 election will leave this country and especially its young people with profound feelings of frustration and disillusion with the Democratic process unless these issues are fully and candidly debated before the conventions," the group said in a statement issued in New York.

Among the 175 signers, in addition to Mr. Schlesinger, were Prof. Alexander M. Bickel of the Yale Law School, Prof. John Morton Blum of the Aspen Institute for Humanistic Study, Prof Paul Doty of Harvard University, Prof. Seymour E. Harris, Dr. Reinhold Neibuhr, and Prof. Richard Wade of the University of Chicago, and Dean Jerome D. Wiesner of the Massachusetts Institute of Technology.

July 26, 1968

Those TV Debates

A number of well-known educators and historians have now banded together to urge Vice President Humphrey and former Vice President Nixon to appear in joint discussions with their respective principal opponents for the Presidential nomination. An agreement in principle has already been reached for a Humphrey-McCarthy television debate, but important details are still in dispute.

The time and length of the confrontation are crucial. It is very late for Mr. Nixon to accept the challenge of Governor Rockefeller, but there could still be at least one or two prime-time meetings on the air before the Republican convention. The Humphrey-McCarthy meeting should not dissolve into a single debate on the eve of the Democratic convention, when it would be too late for what the candidates say to be properly evaluated by the delegates and voters.

"As educators and observers of the political scene," said the 175 signers from Yale Law School, M.I.T., University of Chicago and other institutions, "we believe that the 1968 election will leave this country and especially its young people with profound feelings of frustration and disillusion with the democratic process unless these issues are fully and candidly debated before the conventions."

No one can say who will gain the most ground from these face-to-face discussions. The only certainty is that the American electorate stands in need of them if it is to be adequately prepared for its responsibility at the ballot box—and so do the delegates at the conventions.

July 27, 1968

NIXON ACCEPTS BID TO DEBATE ON TV

Richard M. Nixon accepted yesterday an offer by the Columbia Broadcasting Company for a series of televised debates with the Democratic candidate in the Presidential campaign.

Shortly after Mr. Nixon's nomination early yesterday morning in Miami Beach, Frank Stanton, the president of C.B.S., sent the Republican candidate a telegram extending "facilities and prime time" for "broadcast discussions."

Herbert G. Klein, Mr. Nixon's press secretary accepted the invitation.

Mr. Klein observed, however, that Congress had not yet acted to suspend the equal-time provision of the Federal Communications Act. He echoed Mr. Nixon's frequent statements during the primaries that mentioned debates only with the Democratic candidate and not with former Gov. George C. Wallace of Alabama, an independent candidate for President.

The American Broadcasting Company and the National Broadcasting Company said that they would also make time available for debates but that they had made no formal invitation since the Nixon nomination.

August 9, 1968

M'CARTHY CANCELS HUMPHREY TV DUEL

Special to The New York Times

WASHINGTON, Aug. 19—Senator Eugene J. McCarthy withdrew today from a scheduled television appearance Sunday with Vice President Humphrey.

A top aide to the Senator said the reason was that Mr. McCarthy was "skeptical" about the program because "it could be used to say a debate had occurred when none had."

The National Broadcasting Company announced in New York that Senator McCarthy had withdrawn from the planned one-hour special on "Meet the Press' scheduled a day before the convention opens in Chicago.

WASHINGTON, Aug. 19 (AP) —Norval Reece, a spokesman for Senator McCarthy, said today it was "ridiculous and completely unfounded" to say he had withdrawn from a scheduled appearance with Mr. Humphrey on "Meet the Press."

"I was unable to clear the necessary time for this special show," Mr. Reece said. "We had never committed Senator McCarthy to the show but had tried hard to work out a mutually convenient time."

August 20, 1968

Humphrey-McCarthy Debate

If Vice President Humphrey and Senator McCarthy do not stand on ceremony and the television networks devise a format for a real debate, the two major candidates for the Democratic nomination will finally carry out what the leading Republican candidates failed to achieve—a joint preconvention appearance to discuss the issues openly, frankly and face-to-face.

At the moment, a tentative three-network "debate" is in the works for next Friday, from 7:30 to 8:30 P.M. Network news executives this weekend will shape the program. Ideally, it should include a head-on debate (possibly followed by questioning) on foreign and domestic affairs and the role of the Presidency. The networks are proceeding with circumspection, since they have an obligation to provide "equal opportunities" for legally qualified candidates.

All three networks have boldly offered this evening time for a joint Humphrey-McCarthy appearance. In doing so, they have shown commendable awareness of the precedent set before the California primary when the late Robert F. Kennedy and Senator McCarthy appeared together on a broadcast.

Their joint appearance brought no challenge from the Federal Communications Commission that it violated Section 315 of the Communications Act requiring "equal opportunities" for all candidates. Exemptions are provided under the law for bona fide newscasts, spot coverage, documentaries and regularly scheduled news interview programs.

A stumbling-block to the Humphrey-McCarthy confrontation has now been raised by Senator McGovern's last-minute entry into the Presidential race. He has requested that any debate be a three-way affair. We hope he will not press his claim to the point where it kills all chances for a joint appearance by the two chief contenders. Rather than be cast in a spoiler role, Senator McGovern could appear on his own. C.B.S. and A.B.C. have both offered him a free and separate half-hour. News interview programs by the three networks as well as the National Educational Television network (N.E.T.) have been fair in giving various candidates free time.

The more time the delegates—and the electorate—get to see and hear the two leading candidates, the better will they be able to decide fairly and wisely. The Humphrey-McCarthy confrontation should be arranged and announced without further delay.

August 17, 1968

Humphrey-McCarthy TV Debate Plan Snarled

By BEN A. FRANKLIN
Special to The New York Times

WASHINGTON, Aug. 20—Plans for Vice President Humphrey and Senator Eugene J. McCarthy to debate on national television Friday night became entangled today in a four-way equal time dispute with the two other declared candidates for the Democratic Presidential nomination.

One network executive said the demands of Senator George S. McGovern of South Dakota and Gov. Lester G. Maddox of Georgia to be included in what was planned as a confrontation of the two front-runners might well cause a cancellation of the intricately negotiated debate. All sides said a decision would come tomorrow.

Representatives of the Vice President and Senator McCarthy said late last night that they had agreed—subject to a number of caveats about the format of their debate—to confront each other for one hour before television cameras feeding all three networks at 7:30 P.M. Eastern daylight time on Friday.

The television offers came from the Columbia Broadcasting System, the National Broadcasting Company and the American Broadcasting Company.

The Vice President and the Minnesota Senator had not agreed then—and were still not in agreement tonight—on the rules for the debate.

The Vice President's representatives were said to be holding out for a three-segment format, with about 20 minutes each devoted to domestic affairs, foreign policy and concepts of the Presidency.

Senator McCarthy's negotiators want an open, uncategorized debate for the full hour, they said.

There were also suggestions,

Demands for the Inclusion of McGovern and Maddox May Imperil Program

principally by exasperated network officials, that neither candidate was really very eager for the debate.

Blair Clark, Senator McCarthy's campaign manager, made that contention openly tonight about the Vice President when Mr. Humphrey's representative, Ted Van Dyke, canceled an 8 P.M. negotiating session with Mr. Clark and network executives.

The Vice President's office here said that meeting would be held tomorrow.

But the prospects of a Friday night debate took another complex and pessimistic turn this afternoon. Senator McGovern, having been denied a place in the Humphrey-McCarthy debate by Richard S. Salant, president of C.B.S. News, the pool producer of the debate for all three networks, filed a formal, five-page complaint alleging equal-time infractions with the Federal Communications Commission.

In addition, Governor Maddox, who declared his candidacy for the Presidential nomination only three days ago, made a polite demand for an invitation from the networks today—an action short of filing an F.C.C. complaint.

In a telegram to Mr. Salant, the Georgia Governor said, "I would appreciate being offered an opportunity of appearing on any debate."

And there remained the threat of Senator McGovern's lawyers to seek a Federal court injunction, barring the television transmission of a Humphrey-McCarthy debate, should the F.C.C. reject his demand that the agency force the networks to seat him in the debating studio.

Senator McGovern has already labeled as unsatisfactory the networks' offer of a separate half-hour of television time on his own.

Mr. McGovern's complaint cited the equal-time provision of the Federal Communications Act of 1934—a provision known as Section 315.

He charged that in excluding him the television networks were illegally "discriminating between the candidates," "subjecting the excluded candidate to prejudice and disadvantage," and "permitting some qualified candidates to broadcast to the exclusion of another legally qualified candidate for the same office."

Mr. Salant, who is in Chicago to supervise his network's coverage of the Democratic convention, which will convene Monday, denied that there had been any violation of Senator McGovern's equal-time rights.

"We refused Senator McGovern [a place in the Friday night debate] because we're not required by law to put him in it,' Mr. Salant said in a telephone interview.

But in addition, in the telephone conversation and in nearly identical telegrams he sent today to Senator McGovern and Governor Maddox, Mr. Salant pointed out that the agreement for a Humphrey-McCarthy debate, itself, was fragile and might not survive the weight of the late-starting Senator from South Dakota and/or Governor of Georgia.

"We have every reason to believe, based on indications from the first two candidates themselves. [Mr. Humphrey and Senator McCarthy] and from their representatives, that insistence on added participants at this late date would preclude any debate at all," Mr. Salant declared.

August 21, 1968

Humphrey Calls Off TV Debate With McCarthy

By FRED P. GRAHAM
Special to The New York Times

WASHINGTON, Aug. 21 — Vice President Humphrey called off today the proposed televised debate with Senator Eugene J. McCarthy, citing the tense international situation and the demands by other candidates to participate.

Senator McCarthy's campaign manager, Blair Clark, immediately issued a statement saying:

"Senator McCarthy has always been ready to debate the Vice President . . . The Vice President now, for reasons of his own, does not want the debate.

"I regret that the public has lost an opportunity to view and judge the two candidates on the issues of this election."

The proposed face-to-face televised discussion between the two candidates for the Democratic Presidential nomination had been placed in doubt by demands made yesterday by Senator George S. McGovern of South Dakota and Gov. G. Maddox of Georgia, two recently announced candidates, that they be included.

Humphrey's Statement

Mr. Humphrey's statement, which was given out by Norman Sherman, his press secretary, said:

"After discussions with Senator McCarthy's staff, we have notified Richard Salant of C.B.S.—representing the three television networks—that it will not be possible to undertake the proposed television discussions on Friday night.

"This notification has been made in light of the sensitive international situation, the requests of Senator McGovern and Governor Maddox that they participate and Senator McGovern's expressed intent to seek a Federal court injunction against the debates."

The television networks had offered both Mr. Maddox and Mr. McGovern a half-hour of television time in lieu of appearing on the confrontation Friday night, but both had declared this inadequate.

Mr. McGovern filed a petition yesterday with the Federal Communications Commission, demanding to be permitted to take part in the broadcast Friday. He said that he would take the matter to court if the agency failed to act. The agency is now expected to dismiss the petition as moot.

Under Section 315 of the Communications Act of 1934, if a broadcaster gives you time to one candidate he must accord the same privilege to all candidates for the same office.

This is generally called the "equal-time" provision, but Senator McGovern insisted that it requires an equal opportunity to appear before the viewers. He charged that his candidacy would be downgraded and that he would not get an equal audience if he was barred from the other candidates' debate.

The "equal-time" requirement also raised questions today in connection with tentative plans of the Columbia Broadcasting System to televise the nominating convention of former Alabama Gov. George C. Wallace's American Independent party.

The date and place for the convention have not yet been set, but C.B.S. informed the communications commission tonight that it planned to televise Mr. Wallace's convention speech if it could be assured that the dozen or so major and minor Presidential candidates could not demand and get equal time.

A. H. Dwyer, the network's general attorney, said in a telegram to the commission that the network considered Mr. Wallace "a significant factor in the Presidential campaign," and that it wished to telecast his speech.

Under the communications act, the commission does not have to grant equal time for on-the-spot coverage of news events, including political nominating conventions. However, since Mr. Wallace is already established as his party's nominee and is expected to name his running mate before the convention, there will be no voting for party nominees at the convention.

August 22, 1968

Debating the Presidency

Vice President Humphrey has deprived the Democratic delegates and the American electorate of the opportunity to see him and Senator McCarthy in a televised debate. Mr. Humphrey notified the three networks that he was pulling out of the debate, which had been arranged for tonight, because of the "sensitive international situation" and the requests of Senator McGovern and Governor Maddox to appear on the same program.

But Czechoslovakia (not to mention Vietnam, which hasn't gone away) is all the more reason to discuss the Presidency and foreign affairs. As for the other Democratic candidates, the networks had offered them separate time. To have two rear-running candidates ruin the chances of a confrontation between the main contenders is merely another indication of how Section 315 of the Federal Communications Act can be used as a convenient excuse to have less instead of more "equal time" on the American political air. Trying to suspend the law always puts Congress under pressure from the party in power in the White House. Section 315 has once again proved to be a roadblock instead of an opportunity for free discussion in the public interest.

August 23, 1968

HUMPHREY AIDE HITS FOE ON DEBATE MOVE

Special to The New York Times

WASHINGTON, Aug. 23 — An aide to Vice President Humphrey has accused Blair Clark, Senator Eugene McCarthy's campaign manager, of a "gross misrepresentation" in contending that a television debate between the two candidates had been called off unilaterally by Mr. Humphrey.

Ted Van Dyk, the Humphrey aide, said that to the contrary, the first suggestion thta the debate be canceled had come from the McCarthy camp.

The debate had been tentatively scheduled for tonight.

"On Wednesday," Mr. Van Dyk said in a statement, "I received a telephone call from a senior member of Senator McCarthy's staff suggesting that the debate be canceled in light of the complications which had arisen around it. After staff discussions with both candidates, it was jointly agreed to follow this course."

Parker Donham, a press aide in the McCarthy headquarters, said today he did not know whether the McCarthy camp had agreed to a joint cancellation of the debate. "I think we didn't want to be a party to calling it off, but we wanted to let them off the hook," Mr. Donham said.

August 24, 1968

461

Why Not Debate With Wallace?

By JACK GOULD

THE prospect of televised debates between former Vice President Richard M. Nixon and the nominee of the Democratic National Convention are not notably bright. The legislation necessary to make the confrontations possible will not come up in Congress before mid-September and there does not appear to be undue enthusiasm in the House to implement such a move.

But what appears a reasonable certainty is that if the major contenders should be Vice President Hubert H. Humphrey and Mr. Nixon, there is scant likelihood that they would relish a joint appearance with George C. Wallace, former Governor of Alabama, who is running for the Presidency on his own American Independent party ticket.

Indeed, a social argument could be raised against such a three-way meeting on the home screen. With all the latent domestic tensions of the hour, would it be wise to elevate Mr. Wallace, a man with strong appeal to racial segregationists, to a level of electronic parity with the two principal candidates who have disavowed him? As dispassionate political observers have noted, Mr. Wallace's versatility on a platform also might overshadow the performances of his rivals—if only in his adroit use of emotionalism, which can register so strongly on the TV screen.

The strongest argument for amending Section 315 of the Federal Communications Act, which calls for the allocation of equal time to candidates outside a regularly scheduled newscast, is that the nation will be the biggest loser if the two men with the largest followings cannot be heard because of the obvious impracticality of simultaneously accommodating perhaps a couple of dozen other aspirants who appear to be marginal or frivolous entries.

But Mr. Wallace may well have thrown a political monkey wrench into this theory. Thus far the networks have fielded the problem by indicating that Mr. Wallace would receive proportionate time on the air but would be unwelcome in the debates themselves, if only because his mere presence, in effect, would probably wash out the face-to-face dialogues.

Yet from a dispassionate legal and journalistic standpoint, Mr. Wallace may have a case that outmodes a great deal of previous thinking on the subject of Section 315. He is certainly not a fringe candidate in the usual meaning of the phrase.

As of this writing, Mr. Wallace is likely to appear on the ballots in at least 40 states. Virtually all of the electronic and printed journalistic media, moreover, have speculated that he might conceivably carry enough states to throw the selection of the next President into the House of Representatives. In short, the importance of Mr. Wallace puts all the usual philosophical discussions about debates into a different context. For those who disagree with his views most, would it really be wise to lock him out of participation?

The irony of the years of debate over Section 315 is that chief protests against its suspension have come from small groups of liberal persuasion, excluding perhaps the likes of vegetarians or prohibitionists. By a quirk of the political fates, however, the real challenge now comes not from such corners of the political spectrum but from an avowed rightist.

But if the cause of genuine liberalism in free speech is to have its honest meaning, must it not be extended with equal force to those with whom one most strongly disagrees? Mr. Wallace, like it or not, has succeeded in establishing that he is a third political force that must be reckoned with.

It is a privilege, of course, of the Democratic and Republican candidates to accept or reject TV invitations as they wish, but it becomes a somewhat different matter when they can exercise veto power over the involvement of a figure they would prefer to disown. But the substantial crowds attracted by Mr. Wallace, the outpouring of small campaign gifts, and his own unflagging confidence, suggest that perhaps several million people will support him, not only in the South but in segregationist areas in the North.

On the remote chance that TV debates come to pass after the conventions, there is at least a conceivable possibility that making Mr. Wallace ineligible could backfire. His supporters are co-owners of the national airwaves just as much as those who reject him. The Republican and Democratic candidates may feel the wisest course is to ignore Mr. Wallace. But to foreclose on a man who will be running in an overwhelming majority of the states seems a strange concept of full discussion and recognition of a minority. The way to handle Mr. Wallace is not to sidestep the man, but to give exposure to his views and then answer them, which is all too rarely done on national TV. There should be greater trust in the judgment of the voting viewer, whose capability for seeing through demagoguery has always been underestimated. Keeping Mr. Wallace off the debating screen conceivably could better serve his goals than putting him on. The ventilation of prejudices is to be preferred to bottling them up.

Whether the format of debates, with all the interminable backing and filling over ground rules, is really the best way of encouraging interest in government perhaps itself is becoming debatable. Admittedly, the prospect of two candidates speaking to each other on specific issues arouses an audience interest exceeding a unilateral speech or interview. But if events in Washington preclude debates, the networks are not left without an option, which they have already used, to present the candidates in sequence addressing themselves to identical issues.

*

With both the Republicans and Democrats obviously concerned over political trends in the South, Mr. Wallace, on journalistic grounds alone, deserves more adequate TV reportage than he has received. Television exposure in the form of searching inquiry could be a major help in understanding the causes of a divided country. Mr. Wallace's anticipated defeat in a popular vote would acquire added meaning if, through television, his supporters knew that he had a fair opportunity to make his case. The conservative Southerner should have a sense of participation no less than that of the liberal Northerner.

TV: California Gets 3
Candidates on Air Together

Unruh Solves Problem
Networks Could Not

By JACK GOULD

TELEVISION'S coverage of the Democratic National Convention has been a striking study in extremes. Thanks to the political leverage of Jesse M. Unruh, leader of the large California delegation, there was presented unexpectedly yesterday what many have long sought—a face-to-face confrontation involving Vice President Humphrey, Senator Eugene J. McCarthy and Senator George McGovern.

The debate, which the networks taped in installments and then sent by motorcycle couriers to their control points in the international amphitheater, was a thoroughly civilized and often good-humored exchange. The appearance of the three major candidates for the Democratic nomination truly afforded a viewer an opportunity to compare the men and their opinions.

Mr. Unruh achieved what the networks alone had been unable to do by themselves: He persuaded the candidates to speak to the same points at the same time. If there was a winner, it appeared to be Senator McGovern, both for the specific clarity of his remarks, and probably because he was a late starter in the campaign, and had the novelty factor working in his favor.

After so much backing and filling on the question of televised debates, Mr. Unruh and the California delegation removed any lingering doubts of their value in helping a viewer reach individual assessments of political contestants. The ground rules were simple: opening statements, an opportunity for questions to specific members of the trio, a chance for a reply to one another's remarks, and closing summations.

Mr. Unruh was able to arrange this debate because the three major candidates want to collect the 174 votes of the California delegation. It was an inducement in practical politics that the television networks by themselves could not offer. Hopefully, Mr. Unruh has established a precedent to future conventions.

●

The networks had to tape the confrontations because of the strike of telephone work-

ers. But the time lag was not terribly substantial, and a viewer had a feeling that the program was live. It was carried by the American Broadcasting Company, Columbia Broadcasting System and National Broadcasting Company.

They did not have to worry about the equal opportunity provisions of the Federal Communications Act. The California delegation did not invite Gov. Lester G. Maddox of Georgia, the fourth candidate, so the TV networks were free to cover a topical news event as it was arranged by others.

The Californians not only performed a service for voters of all affiliations, but simultaneously showed that there is more than one way to stage a debate. Repercussions of the session within the TV world conceivably might be formidable.

●

The complaints of the television networks that they were going to be hobbled in their convention coverage by strikes and other limitations were not evident on the home screen. By means of peripheral cameras above the camera floor, both N.B.C. and C.B.S. were able to zero in on their full quotas of floor reporters during a Monday session that began as torturous tedium and built to chaos and demonstrations over the issue of credentials of the Georgia delegation. At times the TV chains were trying to cover three stories at once, all within the convention.

Two ladies put the confusion and undertone of gloom at the Democratic National Convention into prompt focus on the home screen. Aretha Franklin sang what to many ears, notably those of a thoroughly rattled orchestra, was the first soul version of "The Star-Spangled Banner." Musically, the generation gap was never so wide.

Shirley MacLaine, the actress, spoke a few words which on TV carried more personal impact than all the tape and pictures of Mayor Richard J. Daley's armored columns, barbed wire and temporary fences shielding delegates from the sight of ugly ghettos. To gain entrance to the International Amphitheatre to participate in democracy, she said simply, she had to let her pocketbook be thoroughly searched.

●

As had been widely forecast, the Democrats themselves provided enough of a show so that the contribu-

tions of the floor reporters, while helpful at times, did not rank as the national priority of the week. In alert choice of shots, C.B.S. had an editorial edge over N.B.C. But all anchormen should learn the rule of shutting up immediately when a contest is in progress. A viewer does not need to be constantly reminded of what he has watched, is watching and will be watching.

It was going on toward 4 A.M. yesterday when excitement peaked over rejection of the bid of the Julian Bond integrated delegation to be the sole representatives of Georgia, a decision that was followed by the first emotional outburst from the floor. To join in the procedures of government these days it is not enough to be 21 and registered; citizenship also entails being a night owl with a stash of benzedrine.

Once again the A.B.C. network outdrew each of its rivals in the early popularity ratings, by offering entertainment from 7:30 to 9:30 P.M., when nothing was happening in Chicago. If experience from the Republican National Convention is a guide, this lead will subside as the Chicago convention nears its nominating climax. Some of A.B.C.'s rivals darkly hinted that the chain's early evening audience is comprised mostly of nonvoting children. N.B.C. contends that the adult audience for its convention summary has risen dramatically from four years ago.

●

The networks, incidentally, did achieve film coverage of the disturbances and arrests outside the convention hall. How crucial — or desirable — live coverage of such disorders might be in itself is the subject of some debate in the TV industry.

Eric Sevareid of C.B.S. observed that the Democratic convention reflected more realistically than the Republican parley the frustrations and divisions besetting the country as a whole. But as the deliberations in Fortress Chicago proceed this week, a viewer cannot wholly forget that the scenes and details of the police and military precautions are being relayed on TV screens around the world. That the world's most vibrant and expansive democracy must select a Presidential nominee under almost warlike circumstances is the lingering and disheartening Chicago story. That image may be difficult to erase.

August 28, 1968

HUMPHREY TERMS NIXON 'A WIGGLER' ON CRUCIAL ISSUES

CHANGES DEBATE STAND

By MAX FRANKEL
Special to The New York Times

FLINT, Mich., Sept. 11— Vice President Humphrey attacked Richard M. Nixon today as "a wiggler and a wobbler" on the most crucial issues and the creator of doubts that he said were aggravating the international situation.

In a change of heart and tactics, Mr. Humphrey offered to include George C. Wallace, if necessary, to get Mr. Nixon into a direct debate, on or off television.

He said that he would then try to force the Republican off his "sort of in-between" positions on the nuclear nonproliferation treaty, the nomination of Associate Justice Abe Fortas to be Chief Justice of the United States and many questions raised by the issue of "law and order."

House Committee Acts

Meanwhile, in Washington, the House Commerce Committee approved a Senate bill to suspend the equal-time provisions of the Federal Communications Act for this year's Presidential campaign, thus improving the chances of television debates between Mr. Humphrey and Mr. Nixon.

The Vice President set out in some detail his own views on law and order in an address to the American Legion convention in New Orleans, stressing the need to attack the root causes of crime and insisting that law enforcement would cost money that the Federal Government had to provide.

He charged Mr. Nixon with an "unpardonable" undermining of law and order by criticizing the Supreme Court and some of its rulings.

Speaks at Shopping Center

And in his first suburban shopping center rally here this evening, he waited out several hundred noisy college demonstrators in a crowd of 4,000 to 5,000 persons to obtain the chance to defend his own passionate interest in peace and to continue his attacks on what he called the Nixon-Agnew-

Strom Thurmond reactionary coalition.

But in a day that took him from Houston to Flint, Mich., Mr. Humphrey was eager above all to seize the offensive and to overcome the bad political breaks and omens that he had encountered in his first week of jetborne touring as the Democratic candidate for President.

Despite Mr. Humphrey's stout defense of President Johnson and the Administration's policy in Vietnam, and despite his conciliatory overtures to moderate Southern leaders, most of the leaders of Mr. Johnson's native Texas snubbed his visit to Houston.

After the sting of that affront, the Vice President then indicated erroneously that a withdrawal of American troops from Vietnam had begun, causing consternation and confusion all around him.

After a mere five hours' sleep, however, he came out fighting again, taking a vigorous half-hour stroll around downtown Houston and escalating the assault on his opponent in a television taping session with a group of students.

Informed this morning that the House of Representatives might be delayed in acting to suspend the equal-time rule—the action would permit televised Humphrey-Nixon debates without Mr. Wallace—the Vice President said that he wanted to engage his oponents on television or off, at a county fair, rodeo or even in a hotel lobby.

Hitherto, Mr. Humphrey had refused to include Mr. Wallace in the debates because he regarded him as a demagogue with whom orderly discussion was not possible. But when asked about debating the third-party challenger, he said that he would take on any man who sought the Presidency.

Mr Humphrey's staff, which had not been informed of his change of position, said later that it was a deliberate switch and a serious offer.

The Vice President then gave the student questioners an indication of some of the major questions he would put to Mr. Nixon.

"He has not been very specific," he said. "He has concerns, he has doubts, but he doesn't come down foursquare."

The doubts that Mr. Nixon expressed about the treaty to prevent the proliferation of nuclear weapons "are going to injure" its chances for ratification by the Senate, Mr. Humphrey said.

Greater Danger Seen

"I want to say that is not an act of peace," he said. "I think that that aggravates the international situation. I think it precipitates greater danger in the world situation."

Mr. Nixon has also failed to tell anybody "where you are" on the Fortas nomination, Mr. Humphrey said.

"He says Mr. Fortas is a fine man, and yet his own Republicans in the Congress, joined by conservative Southern Democrats, are blocking the confirmation of that nomination," he added.

For the third or fourth time in this campaign, the Vice President said, he is asking the Republican candidate:

"Are you for his confirmation or are you not? Are you going to ask your Republican leadership in the Senate to confirm that nomination or are you going to permit them, by your silence, to engage in the undemocratic practice called a filibuster?"

Then, linking the treaty and the Fortas question, Mr. Humphrey said that he wished to ask whether Mr. Nixon intended to "weasel and wiggle and wobble."

"This country doesn't need a wiggler and a wobbler," he asserted. "It needs a leader."

The higher pitch of Mr. Humphrey's rhetoric persisted right through his address to the American Legion convention, which heard Mr. Wallace this morning and will hear Mr. Nixon tomorrow. The reactions to Mr. Wallace and Mr. Humphrey were said to have been mixed, moving from polite warmth to moderate enthusiasm.

Shopping Center Rally

On his arrival at the Dort Mall Shopping Center in Flint, Mr. Humphrey had to be wedged through a dense throng of shoppers, political fans and collegiate detractors who crowded into the indoor shopping arcade of this city, 60 miles northwest of Detroit.

The demonstrators carried signs reading "Heil Hubert Humphrey" and "Build America, Not Bombs." They chanted long and loud on the Vice President's arrival and when he tried to begin his speech.

They were shouted down by sympathizers and also quieted by Mr. Humphrey's calm lecture to them on the blessings of free assembly and free speech, which he said should be denied neither by government nor by mob.

Flint's Negro Mayor, Floyd McCree, and Mr. Humphrey told the demonstrators that there was no one in the hall or indeed around the country who did not want peace and that the mere shouting of it would not bring it any nearer.

Mr. Humphrey returned to the capital late tonight. He will resume campaigning tomorrow morning, setting out on a three-day trip to Delaware, New Jersey and Pennsylvania.

September 12, 1968

3 Candidates Invited To Metromedia Debate

Metromedia, the broadcasting network, has invited the three major Presidential candidates to participate in a 90-minute debate next month.

The network, which owns WNEW-TV (Channel 5) here, sent telegrams yesterday to Vice President Humphrey, Richard M. Nixon and George C. Wallace inviting them to appear in a live broadcast in mid-October or late October at a time of their own choosing.

Metromedia officials said the debate would be carried on all the network's owned stations and would be made available, live or on tape, to all radio and television stations in the country.

The offer was made contingent upon the waiver of Section 315 of the Federal Communications Act, which grants equal time to all candidates for the same office.

September 13, 1968

Wallace Accepts a Bid To Meet Rivals on TV

LEXINGTON, Ky., Sept. 14 (UPI)—the third-party candidate for President, announced today after a visit to the University of Kentcky that he had accepted an invitation by Metromedia News of New York City to debate the Republican candidate, Richard M. Nixon, and the Democratic candidate, Hubert H. Humphrey, in a 90-minute program in October.

Mr. Wallace said that the telegram from Metromedia had informed him that the program would be carried on Metromedia's radio and television stations and their affiliates from coast to coast.

Special to The New York Times

WASHINGTON, Sept. 14—A Humphrey aide said tonight the Vice President had accepted the way debate in principal but had not yet responded to the Metromedia invitation. Mr. Humphrey plans to do so as soon as possible, the aide said. There was no indication of Mr. Nixon's plans.

September 15, 1968

Campaign on TV

To the Editor:

It is unfortunate that the bill which would permit TV debates between Vice President Humphrey and Mr. Nixon seems to be irretrievably bottled up in the Congress. There is, however, a plan which would allow these two major candidates to be seen in debate.

According to Jack Gould, during the Democratic convention Speaker [Jesse] Unruh of California did what the TV networks had been unable to do and brought the three major Democratic candidates together before the California caucus. It was Mr. Unruh and the California delegates who determined the ground rules. The networks, according to Mr. Gould, quite properly covered the confrontation as a major news item.

In line with this example, a university, a civic group or some national organization could invite Humphrey and Nixon under mutually agreed-upon ground rules to engage in one or more debates. The networks would then be free to make a determination of the news value of such confrontations and cover or not cover them as they might wish.

Given the importance of this year's election, it will be most unfortunate if television is not given every opportunity to bring the campaign into millions of Americans' homes in every appropriate way.

DONALD G. HERZBERG
Director
Eagleton Institute of Politics
Rutgers, The State University
New Brunswick, N. J.
Sept. 9, 1968

September 17, 1968

WALLACE TAUNTS NIXON TO DEBATE

Says He Will Tell the Nation of Republican's 'Record'

By ROY REED
Special to The New York Times

KANSAS CITY, Mo., Sept. 18 —George C. Wallace taunted Richard M. Nixon tonight to debate him and Vice President Humphrey.

"My advice to you is not to accept," he said sarcastically, "because if you do I'm going to tell the American people your record."

Mr. Wallace has accused the Republican nominee of saying different things in different parts of the country.

Mr. Nixon has said he would not enter a Presidential debate if Mr. Wallace were involved. Mr. Humphrey has said he was willing to debate both opponents.

Mr. Wallace made the statement before an almost unruly crowd of 10,000 persons at a rally at the American Royal Exposition Hall here.

Hecklers disrupted the rally repeatedly. The police hustled dozens of anti-Wallace persons from the hall.

The rally was one of the most tumultuous of the Wallace campaign, but there was little physical violence.

Police Quell Fight

One fist fight was broken up by the police. Wallace supporters threw crushed cold-drink cups at one group of hecklers. But most of the disruption was caused by the deafening noise of thousands of shouting people, some for Wallace and some against him.

Mr. Wallace cautioned the crowd at one point, when his supporters seemed ready to move in on a group of hecklers. "Let's let the police handle it," he said.

He added, speaking from behind his bullet-proof rostrum: "These are the kind of people that the American people are sick and tired of."

He was not dismayed. He sees such disruptions as benefitting his candidacy.

Earlier today, at a rally at Cape Girardeau, Mo., he derided both his opponents as latecomers to the cause of "law and order."

"They ought to help bring about law and order," he told 3,500 persons at a stock-car race track. "they helped to destroy it by kowtowing to a group of anarchists that folks like you and me said we ought to do something about."

He said the foreign policy of the two major parties had been equally disastrous and had resulted in "Communists running wild in the United States."

Mr. Wallace, noting that a large number of farmers were in his audience, said farm prices should be supported at 85 to 90 per cent parity, rather than at 73 per cent as is done now.

Foreign policy under recent Republican and Democratic Administrations has pushed American farmers into perhaps worse conditions than they suffered during the Depression of the nineteen-thirties, he declared.

Referring to the civil rights movement and civil disobedence, Mr. Wallace said, "Mr. Humphrey and Mr. Nixon, back in '60 when it started, you ought to read the statements they made."

"Mr. Nixon said, 'It's a great movement. It's constitutional, yessiree,'" he said. "Mr. Humphrey said, 'I'd lead a revolt.' and now they all stand saying, 'We've got to have law and order in this country.'"

With a tight grin, he took note of the worry he is causing both major parties this year.

"At least, they're beginning to say, 'Well, Governor Wallace's strength is going to decline,'" he said. "They used to say we didn't have any strength."

The audience, which included well-dressed townfolk from this Mississippi River city of 30,000 as well as khaki-dressed farmers, stood and shouted approvingly when he said, "We together, by standing up for our great country and standing up for the state of Missouri, we will shake the eyeteeth of the liberals in both parties."

He said his opponents had belittled the strength of his movement by saying he had no Governors or Senators behind him. That is not true, he said, but even if it were, it would make no difference because he has "the people" behind him.

Claiming broad support from "the people," has become a major theme of his campaign. He was asked by newsmen today about a remark yesterday by A. B. (Happy) Chandler, former Governor of Kentucky, whom Mr. Wallace discarded as a possible running mate last

week. Mr. Chandler said Mr. Wallace had been persuaded to drop him by southwest oil interests and specifically by an unnamed "Mr. Big".

Mr. Wallace declared: "Mr. Big are the people of the country, and they are very big."

Mr. Wallace has begun to mention foreign policy more frequently in his speeches, apparently to try to broaden the appeal of his candidacy and move beyond his reputation as a one-issue candidate concerned only with race and violence.

He does not offer many foreign policy ideas, but depends mainly on ridicule of his opponents.

He told his Cape Girardeau audience that the major party leaders had dismissed him along with people like those listening to him by saying, "What foreign policy does that group of folks that support Wallace — what do they know about foreign policy?"

"Well, I ask you," he said, "what do the Republicans and Democrats know about it? They've been in charge of the Government for the last 50 years and we've had four wars, we've spent $122-billion of our money, we're about broke and we've got less friends than we've ever had and we've got the Communists running wild in the United States."

The denunciatory reference to Communists brought loud applause, as almost any mention of Communists in his speeches does.

He got a similarly big applause when he denounced as "pure and simple treason" the practice of some antiwar demonstrators of chanting "Ho—Ho—Ho Chi Minh."

He generally lumps together as equally undesirable Communists, anarchists and "free speech folks." He delighted a large audience at Tulsa, Okla., last night by saying of free speech advocates who used four-letter words in public demonstrations: "I know two four-letter words they don't know how to spell—w-o-r-k, work and s-o-a-p, soap."

Mr. Wallace declared in a brief interview on his plane today that he thought his candidacy was hurting Vice President Humphrey, the Democratic nominee, more than Richard M. Nixon, the Republican nominee.

That was in reply to Mr. Nixon's suggestion yesterday that Mr. Humphrey might be in collusion with Mr. Wallace to deny Southern votes to the Republican ticket.

HUMPHREY PRODS NIXON TO ENGAGE IN DIRECT DEBATE

By MAX FRANKEL
Special to The New York Times

LOUISVILLE, Ky., Sept. 20 —With ever more bite and passion, Vice President Humphrey pursued Richard M. Nixon across mid-America today, exhorting his rival to join in direct debate and bitterly accusing him of compromise and evasion on all issues, especially human rights.

Mr. Humphrey stood on the steps of Abraham Lincoln's home in Springfield, Ill., and gave his Republican opponent a Trumanesque tongue-lashing for avoiding an open forthright face-to-face meeting.

Then, in an even more impassioned presentation to a rally of Democrats here tonight, the Vice President said it was time for him to give Mr. Nixon some talcum powder because he "must be getting saddle sore from straddling all those issues."

Alleges Contradictions

Reciting what he said were contradictions in Mr. Nixon's approach to law and order, civil rights, Federal aid to education, health and the elderly, the nuclear nonproliferation treaty and many other questions, Mr. Humphrey remarked in Springfield:

"Mr. Nixon is having his own debate. And I have a feeling, my good friends, that the new Nixon and the old Nixon are going to go at it for some time and you're going to find out who is the real Nixon and you're not going to like it."

The Vice President said he was going to keep asking the questions until the entire country knew that Mr. Nixon was not answering and thus force him to try to reply.

And "when he gives us the answers," Mr. Humphrey said in Louisville this evening, "that'll be the end of Mr. Nixon because the answers will be wrong."

Invokes Lincoln's Spirit

Then, on an issue that he himself has treated with great circumspection, Mr. Humphrey sought new words in both places to suggest that he could and would find peace in Vietnam. Invoking the spirit of Lincoln, he said that the nation had to be "emancipated from the yesterdays, where they were wrong," and from the fears and doubts that now paralyze it.

He was not specific about Vietnam but emphasized his concern with his position by noting that the Vice-Presidential seal bore "only one little sprig of olive branch" while the eagle on the Presidential seal carried a whole cluster.

"How can you expect me to be the No. 1 peace man with just one little sprig of olive branch?" Mr. Humphrey asked. "You let me have a handful and, believe me, you'll have peace."

But the campaign for him in Illinois, he discovered, has barely begun and different factions of Kentucky Democrats have barely begun to speak to each other.

In response, the Vice President evinced a new, hard-driving spirit as though he had decided he could salvage victory this year only by the force of his attacks on Mr. Nixon and by the force of his own efforts and arguments.

Appropriately enough to the new mood, Mr. Humphrey and his running mate, Senator Edmund S. Muskie, arranged tonight to meet in Independence, Mo., tomorrow with former President Harry S. Truman, the master of the "give 'em hell" technique that won the 1948 election for the Democrats.

Much of this new spirit seems to have been inspired by the remarkable day Mr. Humphrey spent yesterday with Senator Edward M. Kennedy in Boston and Senator George S. McGovern in Sioux Falls, S. D.

Pleads With Farmers

The day brought him more tough news of voter resistance. It brought him new conflict with an angry crowd of anti-war demonstrators. It brought new urgings that he move away from President Johnson on the war.

And it showed him that even Middle Western farm audiences would cheer more for one brief promise of peace than for an hour of promises of fuller stomachs.

The Springfield crowd applauded warmly, too, for the pledges of peace in Vietnam, and the Louisville crowd, as if it had witnessed the reaction in South Dakota, also reserved its first standing ovation for the Vice President's vigorous assertion that the war had to be ended "so we can get on with business here at home."

Mr. Humphrey spent last night pleading to know why farmers did not prefer one of their own—himself—to look after their interests. And today he pleaded to know why the voters would not entrust national unity to a man who had proved his lifelong interest in equality and full opportunity for every American.

"I do not come to you saying the Federal Government has the solution to everything," Mr. Humphrey said in Springfield. "I come to tell you that this Government will be no better than the people who inspire it."

He accused both Mr. Nixon and George C. Wallace, the third-party challenger for President, of dealing with extremists in seeking solutions in "slogans and bumper stickers." Recognizing the appeal of slogans to the voters, Mr. Humphrey said he intended to put these questions before the nation over and over until November:

"Are we better than some of our pollsters and our commentators and our politicians give us credit for being? Are we strong enough, I ask you, to bear the responsibilities of power?"

"And power is no privilege or luxury, my dear friends; it's an awesome responsibility," he said. "The task of statesmanship is not merely the exercise of power, but it is the restraint of the use of power in a powerful age."

Presidents do not need to be popular but Presidents and candidates must stand on principle, the Vice President asserted, adding:

"An America of equal justice and equal opportunity, you know as well as I do, has been the guiding principle of my life. It's been a principle that's caused me pain and suffering on occasion, but in the main

it has made me feel cleaner and better.

"I shall not under any circumstances compromise with the principle of equal justice, equal rights and equal treatment for every American."

Mr. Humphrey predicted he would win the election only in the hearts of the people, when the American people knew that "pettiness" and "bitterness" were traits of a weak and lost people and that only "goodness can produce greatness."

"Help me unite this America," he pleaded.

To confront Mr. Nixon in a direct televised debate has become one of the central purposes of the Humphrey campaign. The Vice President said again today that, to obtain that debate, he would agree to include Mr. Wallace, whom Mr. Nixon—and until recently Mr. Humphrey, too—did not want to dignify as a major candidate.

In an attempt to bait Mr. Nixon into the debate, Mr. Humphrey accused the Republican candidate of speaking differently on civil rights to the South and to the North and of keeping the country guessing as to his position on the nuclear nonproliferation treaty and many other issues.

"I want him to answer," Mr. Humphrey said. "Mr. Nixon, where do you stand on the feed grain program? Mr. Nixon, where do you stand on Federal aid to education? Mr. Nixon, where do you stand on expanded medical care? Mr. Nixon, where do you stand on aid to higher education? Mr. Nixon, where do you stand on the wheat program? Where you stand on Justice Fortas? Where do you stand? Where DO you STAND?"

The Republican candidate has said he has taken firm positions on 167 issues, Mr. Humphrey noted, commenting, "I want to tell you, Mr. Nixon's firm position would make an ad for jell-o look like concrete."

Nixon Restates Position

PHILADELPHIA, Sept. 20 (UPI) — Mr. Nixon reiterated today his position that he would not enter a three-way television debate with Mr. Humphrey and Mr. Wallace.

Agnew Says He and Nixon Won't Debate Humphrey

ANNAPOLIS, Md., Sept. 25 (UPI) — Gov. Spiro T. Agnew, back from a nine-day campaign trip through Hawaii and the Western states, said tonight that he and the Republican Presidential candidate, Richard M. Nixon, were not interested in debating Vice President Humphrey.

Mr. Agnew addressed a fund-raising dinner for Representative Rogers C. B. Morton, Republican of Maryland, at the National Guard Armory here.

The Republican Vice Presidential candidate said: "If Hubert Humphrey wants to debate anyone, he should debate Lyndon Johnson first, and if that doesn't work he should debate himself."

O'Brien Bids Nixon Debate With Humphrey on Vietnam

WASHINGTON, Oct. 1 AP) — Lawrence F. O'Brien, the Democratic National Chairman, challenged Richard M. Nixon tonight to meet Hubert H. Humphrey in a nationwide television debate on Mr. Humphrey's proposals for peace in Vietnam.

"If Mr. Nixon really needs a 'clarification' from the Vice President," Mr. O'Brien said, "there would be no more effective way than for him to pose his questions directly in a televised confrontation—or preferably in a series of televised debates."

Pay Offer for Debates

WASHINGTON, Oct. 5 (UPI) —Vice President Humphrey has offered to pay all or half of the estimated $300,000 cost for three televised debates with Richard M. Nixon, it was disclosed today.

Democratic campaign officials have told aides of Mr. Nixon the Republican party should pay half the cost involved.

"We believe, however, the importance of a debate between the two major Presidential candidates is so important and so vital to the voters we would find a way to pay the entire cost," said Alvin Spivak, director of public affairs for the Democratic National Committee.

G.O.P. Stalls House In TV Debate Battle

By MARJORIE HUNTER
Special to The New York Times

WASHINGTON, Wednesday, Oct. 9—Bleary-eyed but determined, House Democrats battled into the early hours today in an effort to break Republican delaying tactics that threatened to block televised debates by the Presidential candidates.

The Democrats accused the Republicans of stalling to protect Richard M. Nixon from face-to-face debate with Vice President Humphrey.

The Republicans, in turn, accused Democrats of blocking bills for election reforms and Congressional reorganization.

The marathon session, which began at noon yesterday, shattered all previous records for roll-calls of members—the principal device used by the Republicans to stall action on the bill paving the ay for televised debate.

Cheered on by happy democrats convinced that the Republicans had unwittingly pulled a campaign boner, Vice President Humphrey rushed to Capitol Hill late yesterday.

There, almost within earshot of the House floor, Mr. Humphrey accused Republicans of stalling tactics and challenged Mr. Nixon to end the snarl.

"I didn't think Mr. Nixon needed that kind of protection," Mr. Humphrey said. "All he needs to do is pick up a phone and say, 'Let's pass that bill.',"

The phone call, he went on, "could even be collect—I'd pay the bill."

Mr. Humphrey has repeatedly urged legislation to permit televised debates with both his opponents, Mr. Nixon, the Republican nominee, and George C. Wallace, the candidate of the American Independent party.

Mr. Nixon has indicated he would be willing to debate with Mr. Humphrey, but has ruled out a three-way debate involving Mr. Wallace.

Mr. Humphrey appeared in the office of House Speaker John W. McCormack, just a few feet from the House floor, in late afternoon.

Outside, members were wearily trudging onto the floor for the 10th quorum call of the day, as a band of young Republicans sought to block action on the so-called "equal time suspension" bill that would clear the way for debates.

Democrats Are Happy

Hours later, as the filibuster entered its 11th hour, other Republicans, obviously worried, sought to end the marathon session by adjournment. But the Democrats gleefully blocked the move:

"Hell, they've given us the campaign break we've been waiting for," one Democrat said happily. "Let's see them get out of this one."

As the session dragged on into the early hours today, the roll of members had to be called a record total of 26 times, each quorum call taking at least 25 minutes. The previous record for roll-calls in a single day's session was 22.

Tired members stretched out on sofas in the cloakroom as midnight approached. Others sat yawning on the House floor. On the balcony, just off the Speaker's lobby, Representative Del Clawson, Republican of California, softly played "My Buddy" on the saxophone.

Earlier, the Republicans explained they were holding the equal-time bill as leverage in an effort to force the Democratic leadership into scheduling action on Congressional reorganization and election reform bills, passed by the Senate but long stalled in the House.

"Mr. Humphrey wants this [equal time suspension] bill," Representative Donald Rumsfeld, Republican of Illinois, said. "What better leverage do we have to get what we want?"

Democratic leaders, in turn, accused the Republicans of attempting to block the bill that would clear the way for televised debates.

Lawrence F. O'Brien, Democratic National Chairman, issued a statement last night contending that "the Republicans not only are trying to prevent a debate between Humphrey and Nixon, they have even resorted to stalling tactics to prevent a debate about the debate."

And the House majority leader, Carl Albert of Oklahoma, said: "The argument that this was to force action on Congressional and election reforms falls flat on its face."

He pointed out that a discharge petition, seeking to force House action on Congressional reorganization, "has been resting on the Speaker's desk for nearly three weeks."

To date, the petition has been signed by less than 70 persons, far short of the required 217 names needed. Only a few Republicans have signed.

The Senate already has passed legislation permitting TV debates between the Republican and Democratic candidates, with the networks given discretion on how they will arrange for appearances by Mr. Wallace. The House has a different version of the legislation that would authorize debates between all "qualified" Presidential candidates—a term designed to include Mr. Wallace.

From noon on, the Republicans successfully stalled action on the equal-time bill by demanding a reading of the previous day's journal of the House and by demanding quorum calls—that is, a roll-call of House members.

After answering their names, the members would drift away, only to be summoned back by clanging bells announcing another roll-call.

Speaker Exasperated

Exasperated by the disappearing quorum between roll-calls, Speaker McCormack finally demanded that all doors into the chamber be closed and guarded, and that no members, once on the floor, be allowed to leave.

However, at the completion of each roll-call, members drifted away again, and the whole process began all over again.

With regard to the impasse over the televised debate legislation, Mr. Humphrey wrote a letter and personally delivered it to the Speaker in late afternoon.

"I urge the enactment of the legislation," he wrote, "as a matter of overriding public interest."

Asked if he thought Mr. Nixon was behind the Republican move to stall the bill, Mr. Humphrey replied, "I don't know." He remarked that Mr. Nixon "can read the [wire service] tickers as well as I can."

Mr. Humphrey said the nominees "could have as many debates as we want, even one a week until election day."

He said he did not think that "the Presidency is for sale." "It shouldn't go to the candidate with the biggest advertising budget," he said.

And he said he felt that the American people "have had enough of the circus atmosphere of the campaign and now they want a serious discussion of issues."

HOUSE APPROVES DEBATES OVER TV

By MARJORIE HUNTER
Special to The New York Times

WASHINGTON, Oct. 9 — Choking off a round-the-clock Republican filibuster, fiercely determined Democrats won House approval today of a bill that could open the way for a televised Humphrey-Nixon Wallace debate.

The noisy 27-hour filibuster, the second longest in House history, came to a quiet halt after 45 roll-calls, a record number.

The vote for final passage was surprisingly lopsided, 280 to 35.

Accusing Republicans of trying to shield their Presidential nominee, Richard M. Nixon, from face-to-face debates with his opponents, jubilant Democrats contended that the action could be the turning point in the Presidential campaign.

Vice President Humphrey, the Democratic nominee, has repeatedly sought to debate both other major nominees.

But Mr. Nixon, while hinting that he would debate Mr. Humphrey, has balked at a three-way debate involving George C. Wallace, the candidate of the American Independent party.

Within minutes after House passage, Frank Stanton, president of Columbia Broadcasting System, sent telegrams to all three candidates, offering peak viewing time on the four Sunday nights remaining before the Nov. 5 election.

Mr. Stanton suggested that three hours could be used for Humphrey-Nixon-Wallace debates and a fourth for a debate by their running mates—Edmund S. Muskie, Democrat; Spiro T. Agnew, Republican; and Curtis E. LeMay, American Independent.

The times offered were 8 to 9 P.M., Oct. 13; 10 to 11 P.M. Oct. 20; 7 to 8 P.M., Oct. 27; and 9 to 10 P.M., Nov. 3.

The Senate majority leader Mike Mansfield of Montana predicted today that the Senate would accept the House version of the bill making three-way debates possible

The Senate earlier passed a bill permitting televised denates between the Republican and Democratic candidates, with the television networks given discretion as to how they would arrange for appearances by Mr. Wallace.

Both the Senate and House versions would temporarily suspend current law to free the networks from having to offer equal time to lesser party candidates for President.

Records tumbled and tempers flared as the partisan House free-for-all over televised debates continued into the morning hours today.

In carrying out their filibuster, a small band of young Republicans demanded a full reading of the 66-page Journal of proceedings of the previous day. And whenever members drifted from the floor, in search of food or sleep, the Republicans demanded time-consuming quorum calls — roll-calls of members, each lasting about 25 minutes.

Taft Slips Outside

Shortly before dawn, the still sleepless Speaker, 76-year-old John W. McCormack, ordered members locked in the House chamber for two and one-half hours in order to maintain a quorum and complete reading of the Journal.

Representative Robert Taft Jr., Republican of Ohio, protested. He slipped out an unlocked door, opened to allow another member to go to the men's room under escort.

Outside, Mr. Taft scuffled with the sergeant-at-arms, Zeake Johnson, and a door guard. He challenged Mr. Johnson to arrest him.

Speaker McCormack quickly sent word not to arrest him. Instead, the Speaker warned that Mr. Taft could be censured for violating House rules. Mr. Taft returned to the chamber.

The last previous House lock-up occurred Feb. 14, 1917, in a debate over a home for disabled volunteer soldiers.

Even before midnight, the House toppled its previous record of 22 consecutive roll-calls in a single day's session.

The 27-hour filibuster was second in length only to a debate in 1854, lasting two full days and nights, over repeal of the Missouri Compromise.

'Sweet Sue' on Clarinet

Slumped in their seats, or draped over tiny benches in the back of the chamber, members dozed fitfully in the pre-dawn hours.

A few wandered out onto the darkened Speaker's lobby balcony, where Representative Del Clawson, Republican of California, was playing such old favorites as "Sweet Sue" and "Red Sails in the Sunset" on a clarinet.

There were barbershop quartets, too, on the balcony, while in the chamber two hoarse reading clerks spelled each other in the endless drone of the roll-calls: "Abbitt . . . Abernethy . . . Adair . . ."

Unlike the Senate, where a debate can last indefinitely if two-thirds of the Senators are not willing to vote to end it, the end of the debate in the House was inevitable. For once the Journal had been read, the filibuster was certain to die as soon as a majority of representatives were on the floor.

The Journal was completed, and the filibuster ended, shortly before noon, and the House plunged into debate on the bill.

Accusing networks of wanting to stage "a three-way circus," Republicans charged that some television reporters "try to make fools of Congress."

And Republicans charged that "two Democrats," Mr. Humphrey and Mr. Wallace, were "trying to gang up" on Mr. Nixon.

Little Fire in Debate

Democrats, in turn, taunted Republicans for allegedly trying to keep Mr. Nixon "under wraps until Election Day."

But unshaven and bleary-eyed, their suits rumpled and their voices hoarse with fatigue, the groggy Democrats and Republicans showed little fire as the debate droned on.

Republicans sought to substitute "separate but equal" debates, but failed. Lesser amendments, too, were handily rejected.

In the end, 98 Republicans joined 182 Democrats in voting for passage. Opposed were 35 Republicans.

Republicans contended from the start that their stalling had been aimed not to block television debates but to try to force House action on Congressional reorganization and election reforms, passed by the Senate but long dormant in the House.

Bars Wallace Debate

CHICAGO, Oct. 9 (UPI)—Mr. Nixon is ready to debate Mr. Humphrey but not Mr. Wallace, John N. Mitchell, Mr. Nixon's national campaign manager, said today.

Nixon Role Denied

LOS ANGELES, Oct. 9 (UPI) —A spokesman for Mr. Nixon said today that the candidate had "absolutely nothing" to do with the Republican efforts to delay the legislation.

Ronald Ziegler, Mr. Nixon's press aide, said that the House Republicans were "acting independently."

N.B.C. and A.B.C. Comment

The National Broadcasting Company has invited representatives of the three Presidential candidates to begin discussions immediately on the possibility of debates.

An American Broadcasting Company spokesman said, "If Congress completes the action on the legislation and accepts the House version of the bill, A.B.C. will reaffirm its offer to Vice President Humphrey and Mr. Nixon and will extend an invitation to Governor Wallace to appear on the same platform."

October 10, 1968

Debates at Last?

It is now up to the Presidential candidates to give the nation a television debate.

The House of Representatives, following the lead of the Senate, has voted to suspend Section 315 of the Communications Act. By removing the "equal time" obstacle that has proved so legally burdensome for the networks and so politically convenient for some of the candidates this year the way is cleared at last for a series of debates comparable to those between John Kennedy and Richard Nixon in 1960, the last time the law was suspended.

The three networks have offered their time and facilities. N.B.C. and A.B.C. have expressed their willingness to cooperate. C.B.S. has come forward with a specific plan for four Sunday discussions.

In recent weeks Mr. Nixon has expressed unwillingness to appear on the same platform with Mr. Wallace; Mr. Humphrey has been willing to do so in order to confront both Mr. Nixon and Mr. Wallace.

It is time now for the candidates—preferably all three (House and Senate versions of the suspension bill differ on this point)—to speak jointly so that the electorate can see them together and make direct comparisons. There soon should no longer be any excuse to evade this opportunity.

October 10, 1968

Candidates' Debate

To the Editor:

For one reason or another it seems unlikely that we shall have the opportunity to judge the Presidential candidates in a nationwide debate. I have another suggestion (which will probably fare no better) which I believe has merit.

I propose a Vice-Presidential candidate debate.

In these badly divided and tumultuous times we certainly need to know how the man who could become President stands. (Mrs.) BETSY OLSON
Scarsdale, N. Y., Sept. 28, 1968

October 10, 1968

Humphrey Seeking a Way To Force Nixon to Debate

By MAX FRANKEL

Vice President Humphrey rode yesterday through the artificial storms of Wall Street confetti and around the turmoil in his New York political organization. All the while he promoted Senator Edmund S. Muskie as his "greatest asset" and mapped new ways to force Richard M. Nixon into televised debates.

Thus, what outwardly looked like a conventional day of New York campaigning actually turned on some very unconventional tactics.

Mr. Humphrey gathered some warm but unemotional crowds downtown, and he visited two banquets and dozens of potential financial contributors that his Democratic organization had failed to tap in midtown.

But all around the town, and apparently around the country, he was planning to focus the rest of the campaign on Mr. Nixon's allegedly inadequate choice of a running mate and the Republican Presidential candidate's alleged refusal to go before the voters in candid debate.

To Address Empty Chair

"I'm going to start talking to that empty chair down there," Mr. Humphrey exclaimed at a dinner here last night in emphasis of this issue.

Between campaign appearances here, Mr. Humphrey met at the Waldorf Towers with Mr. Muskie, his Vice-Presidential candidate, and with Lawrence F. O'Brien, their campaign manager.

After mapping tactics for the final month of the campaign, they said that they would make a special statement on the debate issue this morning. Speculation around the Humphrey party was that they would offer to pay part or all of the cost of a television debate.

Mr. Humphrey argued again yesterday for a three-man discussion that would include George C. Wallace, the third-party challenger. But he may meet Mr. Nixon's objection to that by proposing two-man debates as an alternative.

To press the other current feature of his campaign, Mr. Humphrey is also expected to demand a television confrontation that pits Mr. Muskie against the Republican and third-party Vice-Presidential candidates, Gov. Spiro T. Agnew of Maryland, and General Curtis E. LeMay, retired.

"When you vote in this election in November, you are not only voting for one man," Mr. Humphrey told the crowd that filled the two long blocks at Wall and Broad Streets at noon. It was the second consecutive day that he had emphasized this argument around New York.

"You are indeed voting for the stewardship of your country as a team," Mr. Humphrey said. "I ask you to consider that team. I ask you to remember whether or not, in light of the history of the last half century, where the odds are one out of every three Presidents have failed to live out his term—I ask you to consider the possibility of a President LeMay; the possibility if you please, of a President Agnew."

After praising the crowd for its derisive reaction to this, he asked it to consider by contrast "the great possibility of a President Ed Muskie."

Finds Trust Big Issue

Mr. Muskie, sharing a platform later with Mr. Humphrey and some supporters in the entertainment world at the Waldorf, gave a calm and concise definition of the message that the Vice President has tried to deliver around the country at much greater length.

He was delighted to be running even on an "underdog ticket," Mr. Muskie said, because of the rare opportunity to confront a great issue that many preachers as well as politicians seem to have missed."

"The great issue in this election is whether or not Americans can trust each other," the Maine Senator remarked, speaking without a text. "Not simply trust between friends or trust between neighbors, or citizens of the same town, but the kind of trust that will risk injury at the hands of those trusted in order to make possible a free society.

"It isn't an issue of who will be President and Vice President, but whether after Nov. 5 the people of America will be moving toward a united country in which people will try to learn to trust each other or moving toward a divided America in which they will fear each other. I think it's that kind of a watershed election."

Mr. Humphrey sat admiringly through these remarks and led the applause of the screen and stage stars.

Drives to Wall Street

No such discussion was possible at the noontime street rally in the financial district, which seemed, despite all the noise, like a strange, almost pantomime re-enactment of the political ritual of another era.

Mr. Humphrey drove under gray skies at noon to City Hall, where he met briefly with City Council President Frank D. O'Connor and other Council members, many of whom are hardly on speaking terms with still other Democrats in the New York Humphrey organization.

From there, the Vice President drove in an open car down Broadway through lunchtime crowds that gradually grew behind the police barricades from two deep on either side to five and six deep as the car turned the corner into Wall Street.

From the steps of the Subtreasury Building, the Vice President could see at once that he had outdrawn Miss Francine Gottfried, the buxom sweater girl who set a standard for crowds at the corner of Wall and Broad last month when more than 10,000 persons assembled in vain for a glimpse of her 43-25-31 figure.

Mr. Humphrey measures 42½-37-40, but he had considerably better advance work, a band, entertainers and dozens of confetti throwers to attract the throng that filled Wall Street for a block to Broadway and almost to William Street

Associated Press

DOWNTOWN: Vice President Humphrey waves to supporters as he rides through a storm of confetti on the way to speak from steps of the Subtreasury Building on Wall Street.

to the east. The estimates ranged from 20,000 persons to an implausible 65,000.

Addresses Garmentmakers

The Vice President spoke last night to a campaign dinner sponsored by the Apparel Industries Committee at the Americana Hotel and later to Queens County Democrats at the Commodore Hotel.

After again berating Mr. Nixon for not debating him, Mr. Humphrey turned his speech to about 600 persons at the garmentmakers' fund-raising affair to a plea that much more, not less, needed to be done by the Federal Government to help the city's and the nation's poor.

He pleaded guilty to what he called Mr. Nixon's "charge" that a Humphrey administration would increase the poverty program and invest "millions, perhaps billions, of dollars in our cities, in education and in health."

After a morning television appearance and the statement on televised debates today, Mr. Humphrey plans to answer the questions of policemen at the John Jay College of Criminal Justice in downtown Manhattan.

He will then fly to Cincinnati for an afternoon of campaigning before returning here for a busy Saturday schedule. It will include the Columbus Day parade, a tour of Negro and Puerto Rican sections of Harlem, a visit to the Bronx and a nationwide television address on the subject of law and order.

October 11, 1968

Senate Democrats Give Up Fight to Clear TV Debates

Drop Bid for Confrontation of 3 Nominees as G.O.P. Bars Quorum With 'Sit-Out' —Issue Appears Dead for 1968

By MARJORIE HUNTER
Special to The New York Times

WASHINGTON, Oct. 10 — Bowing to Republican demands, Senate Democratic leaders quickly abandoned today the fight for legislation opening the way for televised debates by Presidential candidates.

With Congress expected to adjourn this weekend, the so-called "great debate" issue now appears dead for this Presidential campaign.

By staging a "sit-out" and threatening further delaying moves, Senate Republicans succeeded where House Republicans had failed in a marathon 27-hour session earlier this week.

The Senate, some months ago, passed a bill that would have permitted networks to provide free time for debates between the two major party nominees, Richard M. Nixon and Hubert H. Humphrey.

The House bill passed just yesterday would have opened the way for three-way debates, involving Mr. Nixon, Mr. Humphrey and George C. Wallace, the candidate of the American Independent party.

Mr. Nixon has said he would debate Mr. Humphrey, but not Mr. Wallace. Mr. Humphrey has pushed for debates with Mr. Nixon, but has said he would agree to three-way debates, too. And Mr. Wallace, now trailing the two front-runners, is said to be willing to debate either or both.

Noting that Mr. Nixon has already ruled out an appearance on the same platform, or same program, with Mr. Wallace, Senate Republicans argued that the House version would be unfair to their Presidential nominee.

"This bill doesn't give equal time," the Senate minority leader, Everett McKinley Dirksen of Illinois, protested. "This gives equal time on the condition that you throw them all on the platform at the same time. That's the hooker."

Under the House version, networks could provide free time for Humphrey-Wallace debates if Mr. Nixon refused to participate. But in refusing to take part, Mr. Nixon would forfeit any claim to free equal time from the networks.

Mr. Dirksen said he had not discussed the televised debate with Mr. Nixon, but had talked "to others" in the Nixon campaign.

Minutes after the Senate convened today at 10 A.M., two hours earlier than usual, the Republican strategy for blocking the legislation was unveiled.

Senator Dirksen demanded a live quorum, which meant that at least 51 members would have to answer the roll-call for Senate business to proceed.

Pages and doorkeepers were instructed by Senator Dirksen to inform all Republicans approaching the chamber not to appear.

While Democrats control the Senate—63 Democrats to 37 Republicans—many members of both parties are away campaigning for re-election. Thus, a substantial number of Republicans would be needed for a quorum.

The Republican "sit out" succeeded. Nearly an hour after beginning of the roll-call, only three Republicans had appeared.

Later, other Republicans drifted into the chamber to make up the quorum. But by that time, the Senate majority leader, Mike Mansfield, had agreed to abandon the fight.

"After some conversation with the distinguished minority leader," Senator Mansfield announced, "it appears to be in the best interests of all concerned that the pending legislation be set aside."

Senator Dirksen noted that Democrats, including then-Senator Humphrey, opposed similar legislation four years ago to permit debates between President Johnson and the Republican nominee, Barry Goldwater.

"If it was fish then, it ought to be fish now," Senator Dirksen said. "If it was fowl then, it ought to be fowl now."

Senator John O. Pastore, Democrat of Rhode Island, floor leader for the bill, reluctantly conceded defeat.

"They [the Republicans] know they can stop it," he told the Senate. "And they know I know they can do it."

But he predicted that "these debates will be held" on a commercially paid basis. He said, pacing the floor, "I'd be the first to contribute $5, and a lot of other people would be willing to put up $5 to see much an important confrontation."

Senator Hugh Scott, Republican of Pennsylvania, said he was still anxious for a Nixon-Humphrey debate, but questioned whether "we ought to dignify the most blatant of demagogues, a racist, a bigot, one of the most irresponsible candidates in our history" by including Mr. Wallace in the debates.

Meanwhile, House Democratic leaders, who had kept the House in session for 27 hours to defeat Republican delaying tactics over the debate issue, expressed disappointment over the Senate action.

Representative James G. O'Hara of Michigan, chairman of a band of liberal House Democrats called the Democratic Study Group, said this evening that he might lead a "sit-out" himself to block adjournment until the Senate voted on the debate bill. He said he had talked to 50 other Democrats who were willing to participate with him.

Both the House and Senate must adjourn at the same time, and, if Mr. O'Hara could keep a quorum off the House floor, adjournment would be impossible. Observers here, however, believed it highly doubtful that the adjournment would be delayed.

The Democratic minority leader, Carl Albert of Oklahoma, said of the Senate action: "It shows once and for all what the Republicans are up to. They're trying to shield Nixon."

The House speaker, John W. McCormack of Massachusetts, also accused Republicans of trying to protect Mr. Nixon.

Representative Richard Bolling, Democrat of Missouri, commented tersely: "I've been saying all along that Dirksen runs the Senate."

Mr. Nixon and the Television Debates

By JAMES RESTON

The Republicans have managed to scuttle the Congressional bills to arrange television debates between Richard Nixon and Vice President Humphrey, and this tells us quite a lot about the Republican party's confidence in Mr. Nixon and Mr. Nixon's confidence in himself.

He is running ahead in the campaign for the Presidency. He is exploiting the grievances of the voters against the blunders and misfortunes of the Administration at home and abroad. Also, he lost the Presidency in 1960 against John F. Kennedy by a mere 113,000 votes—at least partly and probably mainly because Mr. Kennedy got him into a television studio and beat him in fair and open debate.

Expediency or Morality

Against this background it could be said that the Republicans on Capitol Hill, operating in accordance with Mr. Nixon's wishes, were merely following the line of expedient politics, and were in fact being very clever, which is true. The only trouble with it is that the last thing the country needs in its present political crisis is more "expedient politics" and more "clever politicians."

This is precisely why President Johnson was driven out of the Presidential campaign. He carried the nation into a big war in Asia almost by stealth. He was remarkably "clever" and "expedient," and if these are the qualities we want in this election, maybe we should have kept him in the race. But why trade one clever politician for another—an amateur for a professional?

The Main Objective

The main objective in this election is to get a man of character and integrity. Nobody in the race has the answer to the problems of peace abroad and civil order at home; therefore, we have to rely on faith and trust in the man in the White House. Mr. Nixon and Mr. Humphrey have different political arguments and different policy tendencies on questions of arms control and welfare, but in the end the main problem is personal and the issue before the voter is how to judge the character of the three men in the race.

October 11, 1968

This is what the battle in Congress over the television debates was all about. The point of changing the Federal Communications Act to permit debates among the candidates was to allow the voters to see them together and judge how they reacted under pressure. It is, admittedly, a brutal test, but so is the Presidency, and the test of TV debate is undoubtedly better than the tests we now have.

Mr. Nixon is now operating, wherever he can, in a controlled situation. So is Mr. Humphrey, for that matter, but Mr. Nixon is doing it better, with better financing. He has analyzed and mastered the techniques of the big-city rally and the television interview.

Humphrey wants to get down to a debate on the issues. Part of this obviously is self-serving; he is behind. Nixon, who is ahead, is satisfied to rely on the new political techniques. He has calculated the political problem much better than Humphrey. He knows precisely where to talk about Vietnam and where to avoid talking about Vietnam, where to talk about inflation or emphasize crime; whether to do it on radio or television. This is another kind of "new politics." It is the art of computerizing prejudice, and if this is the test of the election, Nixon should be chosen without delay.

Nevertheless, it would be interesting to put the candidates to Ernest Hemingway's test of courage, which is "grace under pressure," and the defeat of the Congressional effort to arrange debate need not be decisive.

Mr. Nixon says he is perfectly willing to debate Mr. Humphrey but not Mr. Wallace, which is understandable because Mr. Wallace's appeal to prejudice is even greater than Mr. Nixon's. But the failure of the TV networks to arrange free national debates need not end the matter.

Why Not Newspapers?

If Mr. Nixon is really eager to debate Mr. Humphrey, as he says, he need not be blocked by Section 315 of the Federal Communications Act. The newspapers of the country would undoubtedly be willing to hire Madison Square Garden, the Houston Astrodome, and the Hollywood Bowl for a direct personal discussion of the major issues of the campaign by the candidates in the last three weekends of the election.

The newspapers are not bound by the F.C.C. Act. They can provide the forum, the networks can cover it as a news event or ignore it as they like; but the question is whether Mr. Nixon is really interested. If he is really sorry that the Congress could not arrange a debate with Mr. Humphrey, no doubt it could be arranged; for whatever the candidates want, it is fairly clear that the voters want some honest plain discussion of the issues between the candidates before Nov. 5.

October 11, 1968

Debate Blackout

In an about-face utterly contemptuous of the American electorate, the Republican leadership in the Senate has wrecked the chances of a television debate among the three Presidential candidates.

The House had overwhelmingly approved a change in the law to permit a Nixon-Humphrey-Wallace debate. The Senate had previously endorsed the idea of a Nixon-Humphrey debate. In both cases, Section 315 of the Communications Act necessitating "equal time" for other minor candidates had been suspended. But the Senate's delaying action yesterday, engineered by the Republican leader Everett M. Dirksen, virtually killed the chances for any sort of joint discussion, with or without Mr. Wallace.

Does anyone believe that the Republican Senators would have behaved this way had not Mr. Nixon wanted them to? Senator Dirksen was clearly doing Mr. Nixon's negative work for him. The Republican candidate, who has been as evasive on the debates as on more vital matters, no longer has to search for a convenient excuse to avoid sharing a TV platform with Vice President Humphrey.

October 11, 1968

MUSKIE ASSAILS NIXON ON DEBATES

By WARREN WEAVER Jr.

TRENTON, N.J., Oct. 10—Senator Edmund S. Muskie asserted today that Richard M. Nixon was unqualified to serve as President because he did not trust the American people to judge a debate between the three national candidates.

Reacting indignantly to the news that Republican pressure had forced Congress to abandon debate legislation, the Democratic Vice-Presidential candidate told a street rally that "as far as I'm concerned, it ought to be a requirement of law that Presidential candidates debate each other."

"How else can we penetrate the fog of deception and rhetoric and Madison Avenue propaganda to get at the truth?" he asked.

Senator Muskie pulled a slip of paper out of his pocket and read this quotation from Mr. Nixon: "Let's suppose Nixon, Humphrey and Wallace each said what he would do to end the war. I doubt if the American people would have the ability to make a judgment."

"A man who believes that is unqualified to be President of the United States," Mr. Muskie shouted, and the crowd of 1,500 applauded.

During a day of motorcade campaigning through New Jersey, the Democrat from Maine shifted his fire back to Mr. Nixon after three days of attacks on George C. Wallace. Most politicians believe Mr. Nixon enjoys a substantial lead in this state.

Mr. Muskie also attacked Senator Everett McKinley Dirksen for threatening to filibuster against the debate bill if it came back to the Senate floor.

"Imagine the Senate leader of one of our great political parties using the right of unlimited debate in the Senate to cut off debate in the countryside among the Presidential candidates for our country. Can you imagine that?" he asked.

Earlier at a party breakfast in Camden, Mr. Muskie sought to contrast Vice President Humphrey to Mr. Nixon by comparing their relations with Senator Strom Thurmond of South Carolina.

He said Mr. Humphrey "drove" Mr. Thurmond, then a Democrat, out of the party convention of 1948 by leading the fight there for a strong civil rights platform. Now, he said, Mr. Nixon has "embraced the same Strom Thurmond, one of the symbols of distrust among people."

Mr. Muskie got a full-dress reception from New Jersey Democrats, headed by Gov. Richard J. Hughes and including Senator Harrison A. Williams, the state chairman; Robert J. Burkhardt, and Representative Frank Thompson.

October 11, 1968

CONGRESS DEFERS PLAN TO ADJOURN; NEW SNAG ARISES

Liberals in House Protest Senate G.O.P.'s Blocking of TV Debate Measure

By MARJORIE HUNTER
Special to The New York Times

WASHINGTON, Oct. 11—Plagued by House absenteeism and faced with a boycott by Democratic liberals angered over the scuttling of a television debate bill, Congress abandoned plans to adjourn tonight.

With the Senate in recess until Monday, hopes for adjournment this weekend collapsed.

Earlier, with the Congressional decks virtually cleared of pending legislation, the Senate signaled the House shortly after dusk that it was ready to adjourn.

But unable to raise a quorum—a minimum of 217 members—the House recessed at 8 P.M. until noon tomorrow.

The Senate, too, was caught in the squeeze. It cannot adjourn sine die (end the session) without the House having done so first. Almost certain that the House will be unable to raise a quorum tomorrow, the Senate, after recessing at 6:17 P.M., reconvened at 10 P.M. and immediately voted to recess until Monday.

Treaty Action Put Off

Earlier, the Senate Democratic leadership postponed the consideration of the nuclear nonproliferation treaty despite an appeal from President Johnson for immediate action.

The first indication of adjournment problems came at noon when a group of House Democratic liberals announced that they would boycott the adjournment vote that had been scheduled for tonight.

Protesting a Republican "sit-out" yesterday that blocked Senate action on a bill to permit television debates by Presidential candidates, the liberals threatened to keep Congress in session until the debate bill cleared the Senate.

Because of heavy absenteeism on both sides of the aisle, the walkout by liberals was certain to hold up an adjournment resolution in the House.

471

Quorum Call Demanded

The final breakdown in adjournment plans was caused by a Republican, Representative Delbert L. Latta of Ohio, who demanded a quorum call just as the House majority whip, Representative Hale Boggs of Louisiana, rose to make a speech accusing oil company executives of seeking to "bribe" him.

The slow roll-call of members began. Two and a half hours later, 189 members had answered to their names, 28 short of a quorum, and leaders reluctantly recessed the House.

Many of those planning the adjournment boycott had already left the Capitol. Some had left the city for their home districts.

Earlier, House Democratic leaders sought to persuade the liberals not to block adjournment.

"I tried to talk them out of it," the harried majority leader, Representative Carl Albert of Oklahoma, said.

But the leader of the adjournment boycott, Representative James G. O'Hara of Michigan, said that his group would persist.

"It is our intention to hold out for the public right to see and hear these candidates," he said.

The O'Hara forces charged that Senate Republicans, by blocking action on the television debate bill, had confirmed "that Mr. Nixon is a candidate in hiding, and the Republican party wants to keep him there."

The bill clearing the way for networks to provide free time for a debate among Vice President Humphrey, Richard M. Nixon and George C. Wallace cleared the House earlier this week after Democrats broke Republican delaying tactics that lasted 27 hours.

But Democratic leaders in the Senate shelved the bill yesterday when Republicans boycotted a quorum vote and threatened further delaying moves.

Mr. Humphrey, the Democratic Presidential nominee, has stepped up his demands for debates with Mr. Nixon, the Republican nominee, and Mr. Wallace, the American Independent party candidate.

Mr. Nixon has said that he would debate Mr. Humphrey, but would refuse to appear on the same platform or program with Mr. Wallace.

Meanwhile, both houses the decks of pending

roved a
se

Kuchel Asserts Humphrey Has Shifted on TV Debate

The Republican "truth squad" said yesterday that Vice President Humphrey had had "a complete change of heart on the issue of televised campaign debates."

Senator Thomas Kuchel of California noted at a news conference here that on Aug. 18, 1964, Mr. Humphrey, as a Senator, voted to kill a proposal that would have permitted debate between candidates of the two major parties.

"It is clear," Mr. Kuchel said, "the Vice President has been converted on this issue because he realizes how far behind he is in the Presidential race."

Humphrey Offers to Purchase Time for 3-Way Debate on TV

Suggests Hour Oct. 20
By MAX FRANKEL

Vice President Humphrey offered yesterday to buy an hour of television time Sunday evening, Oct. 20, for a debate with his rivals for the Presidency, Richard M. Nixon and George C. Wallace.

Mr. Humphrey said that purchasing the time would get around a law forbidding the networks to give the leading candidates free time without also offering it to all minor party contenders.

Some broadcasters have expressed doubt that even this approach would prevent application of the equal-time rule, but a source at the Federal Communications Commission in Washington, who did not wish to be quoted by name, sided with Mr. Humphrey's view. He said that the Democratic Vice President could buy time for any purpose and that the only obligation of the networks would then be to sell equal amounts of time to other candidates.

Wallace Is Willing

For the moment, in any case, the question remained academic. Mr. Wallace was expected to agree to debate under any circumstances, but Mr. Nixon, the Republican nominee, has taken the position that he will not dignify the third-party challenger by joining a three-way discussion.

Mr. Humphrey said that he would decide later whether to face Mr. Wallace alone if Mr. Nixon declines all invitations to debate. His main interest, he explained, is in "smoking out" Mr. Nixon and holding him to past commitments to debate.

He asked his rivals and the general public to help pay for the broadcast, which could cost more than $200,000.

The Columbia Broadcasting System said that Mr. Humphrey had approached it about the possibility of obtaining an hour for the debate from 10 to 11 P.M. Oct. 20.

The Vice President made his proposal in two appearances early yesterday before he canceled most of his other engagements in Cincinnati yesterday and in New York today because of what he called "a touch of stomach flu."

Dr. Edgar F. Berman, the Vice President's personal physician, said it was a mild gastro-intestinal disturbance that had not incapacitated the Vice President but had left him feeling "achey and dragged out from a loss of fluids." He was given intestinal antibiotics and was ordered to rest in his room at the Waldorf Towers.

Mr. Humphrey's schedule was canceled gradually through the day and selectively for this afternoon. He first pulled out from a question-and-answer session with policemen at the John Jay College of Criminal Justice here. He then withdrew from two speaking dates in Cincinnati.

Last evening it was still not clear whether he would tour today through Negro and Spanish sections of Harlem and the south Bronx. He may also participate briefly in the Columbus Day parade.

He also plans to tape a nationwide address on law and order that is to be shown on the Columbia Broadcasting System at 9:30 P.M. today.

It was the second time in the campaign this year that the 57-year-old Vice President had canceled election activities for reason: of health. He was bedridden i or a week last June with a respiratory grippe.

Only yesterday, however, in reporting on the candidate's general physical condition, Dr. Berman pronounced him as being "in really very good shape."

Pressing hard his contention that Mr. Nixon was evading the issues and afraid to risk his lead in the campaign by debating, Mr. Humphrey proposed two one-hour discussions among the three Presidential candidates and a third session among their running mates, Senator Edmund S. Muskie, of Maine, the Democrat; Gov. Spiro T. Agnew of Maryland, the Republican, and Gen. Curtis E. LeMay, retired, of the American Independent party.

Mr. Humphrey and Senator Muskie appeared together before reporters at the Waldorf-Astoria Hotel to announce their move and to note that both had always agreed to debate their opponents in Senate races as a matter of principle, even when the opinion polls showed them running far ahead.

The Vice President said that he could not recall whether he and other Democrats had opposed a change in the law in 1964 so as to avoid a television debate between President Johnson and his challenger, Barry Goldwater. If he did oppose it, as charged this week by Republicans, "it was a mistake," Mr. Humphrey said.

On Aug. 18, 1964, Mr. Humphrey voted to kill a proposal to suspend the equal-time rule for that year. The motion, tabling the bill, was passed, 44 to 41.

Until Thursday, the Democratic candidates had hoped to overcome Republican resistance in Congress for a change in the law this year to permit the networks to grant free time for the top three Presidential Candidates. They prevailed in the House but were outmaneuvered in the Senate.

Southern Democrats, yielding to Wallace sentiment among

their constituents, had refused to accommodate Mr. Nixon's request that the third-party challenger be excluded.

By including Mr. Wallace in his proposal, though he knows it to be unacceptable to the Republicans, Mr. Humphrey appeared to be trying to undermine whatever attraction Mr. Nixon might have to Wallace supporters. Some private reports from the Southern and border states have suggested to the Vice President that the debate issue is hurting Mr. Nixon.

The calculation of Democratic strategists is that, if they cannot win marginal Southern states, they wish at the least to keep them from giving pluralities to Mr. Nixon. At the same time, Mr. Humphrey is prepared to confront Mr. Wallace directly to try to reduce his appeal to normally Democratic voters in the key Northern states.

The way to "expose" Mr. Wallace's candidacy is not by denying him a public forum but by facing him squarely, Mr. Humphrey said. He remarked that, though he did not like it, Mr. Wallace had become a "very serious" candidate who could not be denied recognition.

October 12, 1968

Nixon Stand Unchanged

By E. W. KENWORTHY
Special to The New York Times

DALLAS, Oct. 11—An aide to Richard M. Nixon said today that, so far as the Republican Presidential nominee was concerned, the question of a debate with Vice President Humphrey "is closed."

Mr. Nixon did not himself make any comment on the offer by Mr. Humphrey today to purchase television time on Sunday, Oct. 20, so that the major party candidates and George C. Wallace, the third-party candidate, could debate the issues of the campaign.

But Ron Ziegler, Mr. Nixon's traveling press aide, told reporters after consultation with the candidate that Mr. Humphrey's offer was "just a phony deal." He termed it "a campaign gimmick" designed to build up Mr. Wallace in the desperate hope that the Alabamian would get enough electoral votes to throw the election into the House of Representatives and thus deny victory to Mr. Nixon.

Mr. Ziegler said that Mr. Nixon's position remained what it had been all along, and was adamant. Mr. Nixon has said that he is quite ready to debate Mr. Humphrey but was not going to build up Mr. Wallace or impair the two-party system by engaging in a three-way debate.

Federal law prohibits television stations from making free time available to any candidate without making equal time available to all candidates for the same office. The stations have declined to give time to major party candidates for fear that they will be flooded with demands for time from candidates of many minor parties.

Congress, Mr. Ziegler went on, has refused to amend the equal-time law to permit a debate between the candidates of the major parties. He said it was now obvious from Mr. Humphrey's offer that the Vice President simply wanted "to develop a debate about a debate" and that Mr. Nixon would not get involved in such an exchange.

When Mr. Zeigler was asked what Mr. Nixon's response would be if Mr. Humphrey offered to buy time for a two-man debate, he replied; "But he has not bought the time."

"This is an obvious strategy for a guy in his position," Mr. Ziegler said.

Many observers on the Nixon campaign trail tend to agree with Mr. Nixon's reading of the Humphrey offer — that Mr. Humphrey does not want to debate Mr. Nixon alone and that he insists on including Mr. Wallace for the very reasons assigned by Mr. Nixon.

On the other hand, these observers give very little credence to Mr. Nixon's reasons for refusing to engage in a three-way debate. They believe Mr. Nixon has no desire to meet Mr. Humphrey, alone or in company with Mr. Wallace, for the simple reason that the polls show him ahead and he sees no point in risking any diminution of that lead.

For the second time since he began his campaign, Mr. Nixon came into President Johnson's territory last night in search of the electoral votes that went to Dwight D. Eisenhower in 1952 and 1956 but were denied Mr. Nixon by a narrow margin in 1960.

The race is deemed very close at the moment, with Mr. Humphrey not more than 2 or 3 points ahead of Mr. Nixon.

The outcome may hinge on Mr. Nixon's ability to woo Wallace voters and even some conservative Democrats who have had difficulty breaking their old party allegiance.

The Nixon campaign has been making a great effort in the last month to get young people out to his rallies, and the effort has been increasingly successful.

One of the largest turnouts was at Moody Coliseum of Southern Methodist University in Dallas this noon. The floor and galleries of the huge basketball court were jammed with a crowd estimated at 11,000 persons, and there were several hundred more outside. When Mr. Nixon asked that all those under 30 stand up, virtually the whole audience rose.

October 12, 1968

SENATOR SCORES NIXON ON DEBATES

Recalls His Underdog Race for Governor of Maine

By WARREN WEAVER Jr.
Special to The New York Times

PRESQUE ISLE, Me., Oct. 11
The traditional landing applause was a little more fervent than usual, and there were cheers from the staff as the Down East Yankee touched down on the rutted tarmac here at midday. Senator Edmund S. Muskie was home.

Maine is the spiritual if not geographical base of the Muskie campaign. It provides the candidate's dialect, a series of deadpan anecdotes about local rustics and the currently welcome story of how a Democratic underdog can upset Republican odds to win.

It did not matter to Senator Muskie today that the skies were overcast, the temperature near freezing and a chilling rain in the air. He was so moved by the airport welcome of some 600 loyal State of Mainers that he had to stop in the middle of the speech to regain his composure.

"I didn't realize what a heart-warming experience it would be to come home again," observed Mr. Muskie, who had not been back to his native state since just after the Democratic convention nominated him for Vice President.

'Old Friends and Neighbors'

"When I came down the ramp and saw so many old friends and good neighbors. . ."
His deep voice broke, his eyes misted over and he filled the gap with a drink of water. Resuming with an apologetic smile, he said: "The press has been asking whether my accent would be the same at home. Well, of course it is."

Senator Muskie was not so overcome with sentiment, however, that he failed to renew the Democrats' running battle with Richard M. Nixon for his refusal to engage in televised debates, using his strongest language yet.

The Democrat recalled how, in his underdog campaign for Governor of Maine in 1954, he had challenged his opponent, Gov. Burton Cross, to debate him and had been refused.

"That was the beginning of the end for Governor Cross," he said. "Governor Cross is history, but we have exactly the same kind of situation on a national basis here today.

"What is Mr. Nixon afraid of?" he continued. "He's seeking the Presidency, a job that calls for a man of courage, a man who is willing to face tough problems, a man who can stand up under pressure, a man who has the courage of his convictions.

"Now, is a Presidential candidate who runs away from a debate with his opponents in a year like this that kind of a man?" Senator Muskie asked. "What is he afraid of? Is he so afraid of his own views, of his own position, that he fears that to expose them might cost him his lead?

"We can't afford a President who plays it safe, we can't afford a President who can't stand up under pressure, we can't afford a President who can't look his opponent in the eye. Mr. Nixon remembers the 1960 debates. He doesn't want the country to see those Nixon qualities again."

The Senator then flew to Bangor, where he pressed his attack on Mr. Nixon still more vigorously, insisting that "the American people want a Presidential candidate who has the guts to stand up to his opponents."

At a hurried news conference in the Bangor airport, the Senator declined to say whether his ticket was currently leading in Maine, insisting that "I never fancied myself as a prophet, only as a fighter."

October 12, 1968

NIXON WEIGHING HIS FINAL MOVES

By ROBERT B. SEMPLE Jr.
Special to The New York Times

KEY BISCAYNE, Fla., Oct. 12
—Buoyed by the public opinion polls and by a routinely successful week of campaigning, Richard M. Nixon arrived on this narrow, sunswept peninsula early this morning for three days of rest and strategy meetings with his key advisers.

Planes converging from California, Texas and New York reunited the candidate with most of the men who have guided him since his early primary campaigns.

These included his campaign manager, John N. Mitchell; his national political director, Robert J. Ellsworth; Senator Thruston B. Morton of Kentucky; his media advisers, Leonard Garment and Frank J. Shakespeare, and perhaps a half-dozen speechwriters.

These are two major questions confronting Mr. Nixon's entourage. One is whether he

473

can gracefully withstand the pressure of Vice President Humphrey's repeated challenges to debate the issues on national television, especially if Mr. Humphrey offers to pay the cost.

The answer among the majority of his staff already seems to be that a confrontation should be avoided. They are acutely aware of what happened to Mr. Nixon in the 1960 debates with John F. Kennedy. They believe that the public is not as interested in debates as the commentators and the media are, and they are convinced that the risks of a direct confrontation are far greater than the temporary embarrassment and minor political damage the candidate might sustain should he continue to avoid it.

The second question is whether any substantial changes should be made in the candidate's rhetoric and schedule in the last three weeks.

It is a very good bet at this stage that Mr. Nixon's basic speech—a recitation of the alleged blunders and misfortunes of the last eight years combined with a general pledge for new leadership—will undergo some changes in tone but not in substance.

In his primary campaigns earlier this year, Mr. Nixon tended to escalate his rhetorical denunciations of the Johnson Administration as voting day neared.

Watching Wallace Threat

The Republican nominee's schedule for next week is firmly established. He will spend the first half in several states that he thinks are winnable but where the threat from George C. Wallace is particularly acute—Florida, North Carolina, Tennessee, and Missouri.

Later in the week he will campaign in New York, Massachusetts and Illinois. The last two weeks of the campaign are being reserved for extended forays into the larger states.

Correspondents covering the former Vice Pdesident's campaign have rarely seen him in a better mood. He seemed relaxed and radiantly happy as he moved down the aisle of his campaign plane last night, and when the plane landed at Miami International Airport at 2:30 A.M. he spent several minutes under the floodlights

tossing a football back and forth with a newsman.

His confidence is reflected in other ways: In his well-rehearsed platform performances and in his generous self-appraisals in the last week.

He has identified himself as an "expert" or "something of an expert" on demonstrations in Latin America, world history, tax reform, law and order and maybe a half-dozen other issues.

The only small cloud on the candiate's Florida horizon was the arrival this afternoon of Richard Tuck, the prankster of the 1960 campaign whose practical jokes bedeviled Mr. Nixon and his entourage.

Mr. Tuck, a former associate of both John F. and Robert F. Kennedy, promised some merriment during his stay here but confessed that he did not see much hope of upsetting Mr. Nixon's bandwagon.

"Larry O'Brien asked me how much time I would need," he said, referring to the Democratic National Chairman. "I told him about six weeks," Mr. Tuck said.

Using Smathers's Home

As the candidate conferred with aides and puttered about today—in a seaside house owned by Democratic Senator George A. Smathers—his staff released statements on Cuba and air pollution.

The Cuba statement charged the Administration with "inattention and inaction which has encouraged adventurism" by the Castro Government. He pledged that a new Administration would "bring into office a new awareness" of the Cuban problem.

The statement on pollution—representing Mr. Nixon's first extended comments on the subject in eight months of campaigning—likewise accused the Administration of "failure" and promised a six-point program.

The program involves efforts to "perfect and expand" regional approaches to water and air pollution, Federal aid to accelerate development of pollution control devices, new research efforts, the development of new, effective and fair enforcement procedures, the consolidation of related Federal programs, and the elimination of pollution by the Federal Government.

Mr. Nixon also recommended the use of tax credits to encourage industry to speed up the installation of new pollution equipment.

To Debate or Not?

On an October day exactly 110 years ago, the most celebrated debate in American political annals took place. This October, despite the experience of a century and the wonders of instantaneous national communication, the voices of the Presidential candidates in joint discussion are stilled. In terms of a debate, the giant tongue of television lies dumb.

When Lincoln and Douglas debated six times during their Illinois Senatorial contest, lung-power plus the press enabled them to speak to tens of thousands. Speaking in front of a flag with 32 stars, Lincoln set forth the essential issue in a memorable phrase — that whoever says the Negro has no share in the fundamental freedoms is "blowing out the moral lights around us."

With 50 stars in that flag now, and the opportunity to be seen and heard simultaneously by tens of millions in New York and California and the states in-between, the American public may be denied the chance to study the candidates face-to-face. Then war was on the horizon. Now a foreign war exists. Then the issue of Negro freedom was tearing the country apart. Now it still does.

Why, therefore, cannot the enormous power of television be used to inform the electorate in 1968? The answer is two-fold: First, Congressional roadblocks and commercial network fears of violating the law stand in the way; second, the candidates are perfectly free to seek—or avoid—a debate and Richard M. Nixon, at least, does not seem wildly enthusiastic about the idea of a TV confrontation.

For one day last week, the outlook was good for a television series that would smoke out the candidates and the issues. By an overwhelming vote of 280 to 35 in the House of Representatives, Section 315 of the Communications Act was suspended to allow a debate among Vice President Hubert H. Humphrey, George C. Wallace and Richard M. Nixon without giving all the minor candidates an equal opportunity on the air. The Senate earlier in the political year had agreed to suspend and allow a debate between

Humphrey and Nixon, with Wallace getting separate time.

When it came time for the Senate to follow through on the House plan for a three-way debate, the Republican leadership last week prevented the Senate from acting. Senator Everett McKinley Dirksen, the Minority Leader, simply declared that the Republicans were against suspension and prevented a quorum. Senator Mike Mansfield, the Majority Leader, was forced to give up the effort to suspend Section 315.

Few observers of the Washington and broadcasting scene doubted that when Dirksen told his fellow - Republicans to use "the means at their command" to block suspension, he was doing Nixon's work for him.

What is behind the debate over the debates is not simply suspension of the burdensome section of the Communications Act, about which the candidates couldn't care less. Rather, it is the political risks and opportunities behind a public confrontation at this time, with less than a month remaining to Election Day.

Vice President Humphrey has everything to gain and very little to risk because he is trailing in polls, crowds and finances. He is desperately looking for a campaign turning-point. From Humphrey's viewpoint, the debate could pin the new Nixon to the issues specifically and possibly cause him to lose his cool and show the old Nixon under stress.

What Nixon Risks

Nixon, still bearing the electronic wounds from his losing encounter with John Kennedy in 1960 does not want to debate Humphrey and perhaps risk breaking his winning stride. In this respect, he is following President Johnson's avoidance of a debate with Barry Goldwater in 1964 and even Humphrey's failure to have his spokesman work out a debate with Senator Eugene McCarthy in the primary contests this year. It has become axiomatic that front-runners won't debate while candidates trying to catch up are willing.

Nevertheless, Congress's refusal to suspend the equal time requirements of the Communications Act may only have given Nixon a temporary reprieve from the debate issue.

The reason was that Humphrey offered last week to subsidize all or part of the cost of a TV debate, which would circumvent the equal-time provision. It may be very embarrassing for Nixon to reject such an offer, since he has repeatedly said that he would engage Humphrey in a two-way confrontation. All along, his stated objection to a debate has been that he does not want to appear on a platform with Wallace.

His unwillingness to do that is undoubtedly genuine but not necessarily for the reason he has given—that he does not want to dignify and give more exposure to the Wallace viewpoint. Rather, Nixon's tactics are to cut into the Wallace vote without antagonizing Wallace and his present supporters. If they shared a platform, Nixon would have to dispute the racist candidate openly on the law-and-order issue—or sound like Wallace.

The 1960 Nixon-Kennedy debate seems almost as ancient history as the 1858 Lincoln-Douglas debate. For the American electorate, watching but not seeing or hearing in 1968, television appears not as an instrument of public education but a White House laugh-in.

—HERBERT MITGANG

Humphrey Asserts He Reserved Time For 3-Way Debate

WASHINGTON, Oct. 13 (UPI)—Vice President Humphrey sent telegrams today to Richard M. Nixon and George C. Wallace saying he had reserved an hour's time on the Columbia Broadcasting System next Sunday from 10 to 11 P.M. for a three-way debate.

"The cost of presenting this debate should be shared among us, but if you are not willing to share the cost I will secure funds to pay for the time myself providing you [Mr. Nixon and Mr. Wallace] both accept my invitation," Mr. Humphrey said in the telegrams.

The Democratic candidate asked Mr. Nixon, the Republican nominee, and Mr. Wallace, the American Independent party candidate, for replies by 5 P.M. Tuesday "because we must make a final decision on programing" so that "appropriate arrangements can be made."

Mr. Nixon has repeatedly said he would be willing to debate Mr. Humphrey, but would have no part of any debate involving Mr. Wallace. A Humphrey spokesman said that if Mr. Nixon turned down the latest Humphrey debate offer on this basis, the Vice President would offer to pay for a two-way debate between him and Mr. Nixon.

October 14, 1968

WALLACE AGREES TO 3-WAY DEBATE

Will Accept Humphrey Offer if Nixon Does, Too

By ROY REED
Special to The New York Times

FRESNO, Calif., Oct. 14—George C. Wallace said today he would accept Vice President Humphrey's offer to debate on television if Richard M. Nixon, the Republican nominee, also accepted. He added he doubted that Mr. Nixon would agree.

Mr. Wallace said his headquarters in Montgomery would reply to Mr. Humphrey's telegram of invitation and tell him that he would be willing to share the cost of the one-hour program if Mr. Nixon also agreed to pay a share.

Mr. Humphrey sent telegrams to both his opponents yesterday saying that he had reserved an hour on the Columbia Broadcasting System's national television network next Sunday evening for a three-way debate. He said he would pay for it if his opponents were unwilling to pay a portion.

Mr. Nixon has steadfastly refused to debate Mr. Humphrey if Mr. Wallace was included.

Crowd Is Unresponsive

Mr. Wallace encountered an unexpected pocket of apathy here today. The central California area has many Southerners who moved here to find work and might be expected to support the former Alabama Governor.

The American Independent party candidate drew about 3,500 persons to the lawn of the modern Fresno County Courthouse at noon, but they were unenthusiastic.

Men in shirtsleeves at the edge of the crowd listened to the entire Wallace speech without applauding. They grinned approvingly when he spoke of "weaning" anarchists from lying down in front of Presidential limousines, but they did not take their hands from their pockets.

Signs of Exhaustion Appear

The crowd did not bother to hiss or boo when a young anti-Wallace couple, a Negro man and a white girl, danced on a raised platform while the Wallace string band played "Your Cheatin' Heart." Such antics at other stops, have brought shouts of disapproval from whites in the crowds.

Even a small band of hecklers here was weak-voiced. Mr. Wallace had to taunt them repeatedly to raise an uneven chorus of "Sieg Heil."

Mr. Wallace responded, as he always does to that salute, by saying he had fought the Nazis and Fascists before the young hecklers were born.

He used the same line later in the speech, apparently having forgotten that he had already said it.

He has repeated lines in speeches elsewhere in recent days and his standard speech, a collection of catch-phrases delivered in no particular order, has seemed, by his standards, unusually disordered.

The 49-year-old candidate has confided to numerous persons in recent days that he is severely tired.

Between stops on his travels, he has taken to sitting slumped in his airplane seat almost motionless, speaking to no one and staring at the wall of the cabin.

October 15, 1968

AGNEW RIDICULES A 3-WAY DEBATE

Tells a Conservative Dinner It Would Be a 'Circus'

Spiro T. Agnew, the Republican candidate for Vice President, told a Conservative party audience last night that a debate among all the Presidential candidates would be a "three-way circus."

In a loudly applauded 23-minute speech to a party that is running a candidate against the Republican candidate for Senator, Mr. Agnew criticized Yippies and those who practiced civil disobedience.

Mr. Agnew never mentioned the New York Senate race, and he declined to talk to reporters after his speech. But his press secretary, Herb Thompson, when asked about the apparent incongruity of the Agnew appearance at a Conservative party function, said that it constituted "no endorsement" of James L. Buckley, the Conservative candidate for the Senate.

If Mr. Agnew lived in New York, he said, he would vote for the Republican incumbent, Senator Jacob K. Javits, and he would be "very happy" to campaign for Mr. Javits.

Mr. Agnew's plan to visit the annual Conservative dinner had stirred considerable political controversy.

The Maryland Governor did not get to the Conservative dinner in the Waldorf Astoria until 10:54 P.M., but the party leadership on the dais was delighted to pad out its speeches waiting for him.

The usual star performer at these Conservative dinners, William F. Buckley Jr., the editor, television personality and younger brother of the party's Senate candidate, was absent last night. He was said to be "becalmed off Bermuda" in a boat that had run out of gas.

In his speech, Mr. Agnew expressed scorn at Vice President Humphrey's call for a debate among Presidential candidates.

"Dick Nixon's not going to get involved with any kind of a sideshow to confuse them [the voters] with George Wallace," he declared.

Before the dinner, Conservative leaders said that arrangement for Mr. Agnew's visit had been made during the discussions that resulted in the Conservative decision to forgo naming Presidential electors in opposition to the Republican slate.

This was not a "deal," these Conservatives said, adding that the two arrangements simply had been discussed at the same time.

Mr. Agnew addressed the $25-a-plate dinner after James L. Buckley.

According to party leaders, the invitation to have Mr. Agnew or the Republican Presidential nominee, Richard M. Nixon at the dinner—and acceptance of the invitation — came as party leaders were discussing with leaders of the national Republican party a Conservative offer to have a joint slate of Presidential electors in New York.

State Republican leaders rejected this. The Conservatives, after trying to put up a separate Nixon-Agnew elector slate, decided to bow to the Republican decision and, in effect, leave the top line of their Row C on the ballot blank.

The party members heard a letter of thanks from Mr. Nixon read by J. Daniel Mahoney, Conservative chairman, before deciding to give up their plan for a separate elector slate.

Reached for comment, Senator Javits said through a spokesman that he knew nothing about the discussions.

Last night's dinner, party leaders said, produced $20,000 for the party.

For the six-year-old Conservative party, these annual dinners have been "family" affairs of a sort, but Mr. Buckley, their Senatorial candidate, suggested in his text that the party had outgrown its modest beginnings.

"It is an awesome fact," he said, "that in six short years the Conservative party has grown from a small brotherhood of pragmatic idealists into a very real power in the public affairs of this state."

Press Club Would Sponsor A Humphrey-Nixon Debate

WASHINGTON, Oct. 14 (UPI)—The National Press Club has invited Vice President Humphrey and Richard M. Nixon to debate under its auspices, the club president, Allen W. Cromley, announced today.

He said that telegrams were sent Friday to both the Democratic and Republican Presidential candidates proposing at a time agreeable to them. He said that no replies had been received.

Mr. Humphrey has accepted an invitation by the Overseas Press Club in New York to debate Mr. Nixon under the club's auspices, the club said last night.

October 15, 1968

F.C.C. Rejects a Plan For Two-Way Debate

WASHINGTON, Oct. 15 (AP)—The Federal Communications Commission rejected today a proposal by the National Press Club to stage a debate between two major Presidential candidates without including the third.

A commission spokesman, advised of the move to get Richard M. Nixon and Vice President Humphrey on the same platform, said equal time must be afforded the third-party candidate, George C. Wallace, if the event were to be covered by television and radio.

The club's president, Allan Cromley, in announcing yesterday that he had sent telegrams inviting Mr. Nixon and Mr. Humphrey to debate, said he could see no problem arising with the F.C.C. on the equal time statute.

But the commission official said the invitation to the Republican and Democratic candidates "would be evading the whole purpose" of that section of the F.C.C. act containing the equal time clause.

The Great Debate Debate

House minority leader Gerald Ford of Michigan has accused Vice President Humphrey, who is currently seeking a TV confrontation with Mr. Nixon, of changing his mind about the desirability of TV debates between Presidential candidates. Even if the charge is true, Mr. Humphrey isn't alone.

Mr. Nixon, who has been avoiding a direct encounter with the Vice President, said in a television interview on Nov. 27, 1967:

"I believe there should be debates. I believe that the debates of 1960 served a great cause in creating a tremendous interest in the campaign, also in educating people about the great issues.

"And I would hope that President Johnson would reverse his stand of '64 and do what President Kennedy said he would have done just before he died, when he said, 'Of course, I'll debate my opponent,' because President Johnson then will give the nation a good choice, President Johnson and his Republican opponent debating the great issues on television."

Mr. Nixon was so right—then. Why not now?

October 17, 1968

HUMPHREY AND NIXON GET C.B.S. DEBATE BID

The Columbia Broadcasting System sent telegrams last night to Vice President Humphrey and Richard M. Nixon, inviting them to appear jointly in a debate to be televised on Sunday.

The offer was made after George C. Wallace said last night in Roanoke, Va., that he would be willing to make a separate television appearance if it would lead to a Nixon-Humphrey debate.

C. B. S. also sent a telegram last night to Mr. Wallace offering him a half hour on Sunday, Nov. 3. There was no immediate reaction from him or from the other candidates.

Mr. Nixon has repeatedly said he would be willing to debate Mr. Humphrey, but would have no part of a debate involving Mr. Wallace.

Ron Ziegler, an aide to Mr. Nixon, said that the Republican candidate was standing by his earlier position that he would do nothing to build up a third-party candidate, which would be the effect, he said, if C.B.S. gave Mr. Wallace a half-hour of television time.

The question of the debate is further complicated by Federal regulations that would still require any radio and television station giving free time to a Nixon-Humphrey debate to provide equal time for all candidates of the various minor parties.

The TV Debates: Mr. Nixon Then and Now

By JAMES RESTON

"The hardest thing about any political campaign," Adlai Stevenson once said, "is how to win without proving that you are unworthy of winning."

It is a sad remark, but when you read Richard Nixon's evasive ambiguities about Vietnam, and his appeals to the emotions and prejudices of the voters in the name of "law and order," and his excuses for not debating Hubert Humphrey on television, the Stevenson remark seems all too true.

Nature of the Beast

Politics, of course, is not a charitable occupation, and nobody would blame Mr. Nixon if he merely said that he lost one Presidential election debating John F. Kennedy and thought that was enough. But first he said he was all for debating, and then he was for debating Mr. Humphrey but not George Wallace, and finally when Mr. Wallace offered to withdraw from the same program, the last word from Mr. Nixon's headquarters was that the issue was "closed."

The irony of this is that Mr. Nixon is winning largely on the reaction in the country against President Johnson's own brand of slippery politics. And another irony is that the best argument we know for Presidential television debates was made by Mr. Nixon himself.

"Television debates," he wrote in The Saturday Evening Post in June of 1964, "were not designed to serve a candidate for office; they were designed to serve the public. ... I believe that television debates contribute significantly to four major objectives which are in the public interest: a bigger vote, better informed voters, lower campaign costs and, in the end, a better President. ..."

Now, of course, he has other things in mind. A bigger vote, and better-informed voters are not in his interest, but in Mr. Humphrey's, and lower campaign costs are not now one of Mr. Nixon's major objectives, since he has a fatter kitty than the Vice President.

"I believe," he wrote in that same article, "the strongest argument for debates is that they make candidates put on a better campaign, with the result that the man who wins becomes a better President.

"As Professor Harvey Wheeler pointed out," Mr. Nixon added, "(1) Debates prevent a candidate from waging a campaign on the basis of special interest appeals—no longer can he say one thing when addressing labor and something else when addressing business. (2) Debates force a candidate to present a systematic program. ... Voters also have the opportunity to see the real man, not the synthetic product of public relations experts. ..."

Oh, real man, where are you now? Where is that "better campaign," those "systematic programs," those consistent themes for the whole electorate? They are obviously lost most of the time behind "the synthetic product of public relations experts. ..."

The Important Symbols

Hubert Humphrey, of course, has his own special interest groups, and the big buses ride up and down the streets of New York proclaiming "Humphrey Is a Man You Can Trust," which is a Madison Avenue trick for suggesting that the same cannot be said about Mr. Nixon. Still, the Vice President has at least been willing to stand up and be questioned on the record by all comers, while Mr. Nixon has picked his questioners and stacked his audiences whenever he could.

Also, Mr. Humphrey may go down with President Johnson around his neck, but at least he stuck with him, which may have been silly but was at least loyal. When a President picks a Vice President, he gives him some cards he must never play: that is the rule of the game, and the Vice President has been faithful to it, even if he has not quite been faithful to himself.

The television debate issue was not momentous in itself. Winners seldom give up the ball to the opposition in the last five minutes of the game. But the TV issue is not really "closed," because it opens up again the much larger issue of the campaign—the character of the candidates under pressure—and underscores Mr. Nixon's tendency to play the game by his own rules.

Maybe Adlai Stevenson merely proves he was right, for Adlai specialized in defeat, though in retrospect he almost makes defeat seem glorious, "A campaign," he once said, "addressed not to men's minds and to their best instincts but to their passions, emotions and prejudices, is unworthy at best. Now, with the fate of the nation at stake, it is unbearable."

October 25, 1968

Nixon Rejects Debate Offer

HOUSTON, Oct. 25 (UPI)—Free use of the Houston Astrodome was offered today for a debate between Richard M. Nixon and Vice President Humphrey. Roy Hofheinz, president of the Houston Sports Association, said that Mr. Humphrey had accepted. But a Nixon aide in New York turned down the bid as "just another gimmick."

October 26, 1968

Nixon Permits a Protest, Then Replies to Students

By ROBERT B. SEMPLE Jr.
Special to The New York Times

SYRACUSE, Oct. 29—In perhaps the most dramatic political rally of his campaign, Richard M. Nixon sat quietly tonight on the stage of the War Memorial Auditorium here and permitted some 1,100 Syracuse University students to sing a song of protest against him.

"I'm delighted to hear these differences," he told the students. "The floor is yours."

He then sat down while the students, massed in the rear of the auditorium, sang Simon and Garfunkel's "The Sounds of Silence" in protest against what they declared was Mr. Nixon's refusal to debate the issues, his "Madison Avenue image" and his "non-stances" on the issues.

Supporters Silenced

At one point during the song the Republican partisans in an overflow crowd of some 12,000 persons started to chant "we want Nixon" in an effort to drown out their youthful antagonists. But Mr. Nixon rose and ordered them into silence.

"They have indicated that if they are allowed to sing they will listen to me, so let them sing," he said.

When the students had finished, Mr. Nixon rose and began his speech by answering four specific complaints that they had lodged against his campaign in a statement that reached him shortly before his motorcade left the Hotel Syracuse for the auditorium.

The students alleged that he had wavered between support of student dissenters and assertions that they should be expelled; that he had not made clear whether he wanted a military or a negotiated settlement in Vietnam; that he opposed Social Security and Medicare, and that his position on the treaty to halt the spread of nuclear weaponry remained unclear.

Devoting five minutes to each question, the Republican candidate said that he supported "legitimate" dissent that did not break the law.

He asserted that he would wholeheartedly support the nuclear treaty when the Soviet Union "normalized" its relations with Czechoslovakia.

He insisted, as he has throughout the campaign, that he supported both Social Security and Medicare. And he declared that he would seek a negotiated settlement in Vietnam.

Voice Appreciation

In the course of his Vietnam answer, he asserted that he would broaden the negotiations to admit the Soviet Union to the conference table."

Aides explained, however, that Mr. Nixon did not mean that he would admit the Soviet Union immediately to the peace

477

negotiations in Paris. He was simply suggesting, they said, that the Russians should be enlisted generally in the effort to secure peace in Southeast Asia. This is a point that Mr. Nixon has made many times in his campaign.

Student leaders later expressed their appreciation that Mr. Nixon had attempted to address himself to their questions. But they complained still of his refusal to debate Vice President Humphrey and of what some felt was "smugness" in answering the questions.

Under questioning, they admitted that they were largely devoted to the Humphrey candidacy, and they suggested that their real grievance against Mr. Nixon was his refusal to confront the Democratic nominee.

The confrontation ended a day in which the Republican candidate visited two highly industrialized states, drumming on what he considers the crucial choice in this year's Presidential campaign.

During a motorcade tour of three Detroit suburbs this morning and a rally this evening in Syracuse, the Republican candidate offered himself as a man who could bring a durable peace abroad, a sense of direction and stability at home and reconciliation between business and labor, white and black and young and old in an economy of prosperity without inflation.

At the same time, he sought to portray Mr. Humphrey as the candidate of a divided party and a disruptive convention in Chicago, incapable of unifying the nation, naive in his approach to the delicate business of arms negotiations with the Soviet Union and "cheap" and personal in his political attacks.

Mr. Nixon refused, despite what he regards as Mr. Humphrey's attempts to portray him as a champion of an accelerated arms race, to soften his view that successful arms reduction negotiations with the Soviet Union would depend on America's military credibility

"In the next four years," he declared, "we will see a period in which we have the greatest danger of world war that could destroy the world. Due to what I think was a mistake in American military policy, the Soviet Union will acquire equality and perhaps superiority over the United States in certain critical areas. This does not necessarily mean that there will be war. But it does mean that the

United Press International

Richard M. Nixon, Senator Jacob K. Javits, center, and unidentified man with them on the podium during a rally in Syracuse listening as students sang a song in protest.

diplomatic requirements for the United States must be infinitely greater if we are to avoid it."

He went on to assert that "what has kept the peace" for the last two decades "has been the immense superiority—the fact that President Eisenhower could speak with authority whenever he met with the other nations of the world, the fact that President Kennedy at the time of the Cuban confrontation knew that he had the immense edge that General Eisenhower left him. That avoided world war at that time."

Asserting ever more emphatically that firmness and consistency are the proper guides to peace, Mr. Nixon insisted that his rival had yet to display the temperament to assure world stability. In Michigan he said:

"At this time, the voters of Michigan must think not in terms of Republican vs. Democrat, not in terms of the cheap party attacks which are being made by the other side on me and my running mate. That isn't what is involved. What you must think of now are the men and their records. What you must think of is this nation and whether one man or the other has the ability to keep the peace.

"Yesterday, Hubert Hum-

phrey, making a speech, charged that he thought that I might endanger peace. All right let's be quite candid about it. I trained for eight years under General Eisenhower. He's trained for four years under Lyndon Johnson. In the four years of his Administration, we've never had a moment of peace. In the eight years of our Administration, we ended one war and maintained eight years of peace, and I think that's what the American people want.

The former Vice President kept up his attack on Mr. Humphrey as he jumped from rally to rally in Livonia, Warren, and Southfield, largely white suburbs of Detroit.

In each place, George C. Wallace is said to have a considerable following. Accordingly, Mr. Nixon sought to stress the differences between himself and Mr. Humphrey and thereby portray the Republican party as an acceptable way-station between both of his opponents—more positive than Mr. Wallace, more responsible than Mr Humphrey.

At each stop, he urged his devoted listeners to spread their enthusiasm to other voters —"if each of you persuade five voters," he declared, "we'l win"—and he tried to provide them with the rationale for doing so.

Debates Rejected
To the Editor:

The assumption by James Reston *et al.* appears to be that Mr. Nixon has sinned by his reluctance to engage in a debate spectacular with Vice President Humphrey because such an encounter would enlighten the voters on the character of the candidates and the issues they are supposed to represent.

Actually it is difficult to imagine a worse method of achieving such a desirable result. At the least, the contestants score cute, Harvard-Yale-type debating points off each other after arduous research into supposedly damning and probably indiscreet past utterances by the opposition. At the worst, they are trapped into making irresponsible pledges and unredeemable promises which could limit their options for future action.

Why the Republican leaders should be so coy in stating their opposition to these rhetorical orgies, when the objections are so obvious, is beyond me. The experience of 1960, when Nixon won the debate on logic but couldn't match the Kennedy "charisma," should be sufficient to indicate the futility of such a match.   FREDERIC NELSON

Truro Mass.. Oct. 12. 1968

October 30, 1968

October 31, 1968

Libel Suit by Barry Goldwater Against Magazine Due for Trial

A $2-million libel suit by Barry Goldwater against the now-defunct Fact Magazine comes to trial in Federal Court here tomorrow.

Mr. Goldwater, the 1964 Republican Presidential candidate, is expected to testify on his charge that the magazine attacked him with "actual malice" in its issue of September-October, 1964, when it ran a 41-page article headlined, "1,189 Psychiatrists Say Goldwater Is Psychologically Unfit to Be President."

The suit also names as defendants the magazine's publisher, Ralph Ginzburg, and its managing editor, Warren Boroson. They had tried unsuccessfully to get a summary dismissal of the suit by the United States Court of Appeals.

Fact was a bimonthly magazine that first appeared in February, 1964. In July of that year, it sent questionnaires to 12,356 psychiatrists across the country, asking them to comment on the question, "Is Barry Goldwater psychologically fit to be President of the United States?"

Of the 2,417 who replied, according to the magazine, 1,189 said he was unfit, 657 said he was fit, and 571 said they did not know enough about him to answer. Fact published excerpts from the psychiatrists' replies.

Soon thereafter, the American Psychiatric Association assailed the poll as "a hodge-podge" of personal political opinion rather than professional diagnosis, and the American Medical Association called it an example of yellow journalism.

The Fair Campaign Practices Committee cited the article as one of the few incidents that both the Democratic and Republican parties had reported during the campaign.

Advertisements by the magazine before the appearance of the article asked:

"What do psychiatrists think of Goldwater's fitness to keep his finger on the atomic trigger? Of his tendency to view issues and people from extremes, as either all good or all bad? Of his veneration of the military, his aversion to compromise, his mistrust of strangers and the impulsive statements he later modifies or denies?"

Mr. Goldwater, whose term as a Senator from Arizona ran out in 1964, in seeking the Senate seat now held by Carl Hayden. Mr. Hayden, who is 90 years old, is to announce his retirement tomorrow.

Goldwater Never Mentally Ill, Wife Testifies at Libel Trial

By EDWARD C. BURKS

The wife of Barry M. Goldwater testified yesterday at the beginning of his $2-million libel action against Ralph Ginzburg, the publisher, in Federal Court here.

Mrs. Peggy Goldwater, whose husband was the 1964 Republican Presidential candidate, smilingly but firmly denied a claim in a 1964 issue of Mr. Ginzburg's Fact Magazine that her husband had suffered from mental illness.

Mr. Goldwater's attorney, Roger Robb of Washington, asked if the plaintiff had ever suffered any mental illness.

"No, never," she replied.

Had he ever consulted a psychiatrist or taken psychiatric treatment?

"No."

Rights of Press an Issue

One major point at issue in the suit has to do with the rights a publication is entitled to under the Consitution in criticizing a public figure.

Mr. Goldwater contends that Mr. Ginzburg and his co-defendant, Warren Boroson, Fact's managing editor published false, scandalous and defamatory statements knowing them to be false or "recklessly not caring if they were true or not."

Harris Steinberg, counsel for the 38-year-old publisher, said in his opening statement to the jury of nine men and three women:

"I'm going to show you there's nothing false in that magazine. It was good journalism, although racy and tough and not for the old lady from Dubuque."

He argued that the material and the quotations in the articles had been used by the defendants in the belief that they were "true and proper."

The suit is based on the October, 1964, issue of Fact, dated one month before the election, which was billed as a "special issue on the mind of Barry Goldwater."

In addition to a long lead article by Mr. Ginzburg describing Mr. Goldwater as "paranoid" and comparing him to Hitler, the edition featured the results of a questionnaire that had been mailed to psychiatrists across the country.

The cover bore the legend in big type: "1,189 Psychiatrists Say Goldwater Is Unfit to Be President!"

Mr. Goldwater, looking in ruddy, good health, sat quietly in the small, dark-paneled courtroom.

Mrs. Goldwater cheerful

The plaintiff's wife, dressed in a navy blue suit and a white blouse, was cheerful and calm during an hour of testimony and cross-examination.

Led by Mr. Robb, she denied comments in the magazine that she was "weepy," that her husband was not close to his family and that he had been very businesslike in his proposal of marriage.

Mr. Steinberg said the only relevant issue was whether the defendants published the articles in good faith, with no intention to lie, and in the belief that they were making a rightful, responsible contribution to predicting how a candidate might perform if elected.

Fact was discontinued last January and merged into another Ginzburg publication, Avant-Garde.

The trial is to resume at 10 A.M. today before Judge Harold R. Tyler Jr.

GOLDWATER SEEKS LIBEL PRECEDENT

By EDWARD C. BURKS

Barry Goldwater said yesterday that his $2-million libel action against Ralph Ginzburg, the publisher, sought a precedent-making decision against false and scurrilous attacks in print.

Testifying in Federal Court here, the ruddy-faced 1964 Republican Presidential candidate denounced a 1964 issue of Mr. Ginzburg's now-defunct magazine Fact as producing a "totally dishonest" picture of him.

"This kind of thing should never be permitted in American journalism," the 59-year-old former Arizona Senator testified. He described the 64-page issue devoted to his "fitness" as filled with quotations out of context, falsehoods and statements with no substance, all of which he said, added up to a "ton" of scurrilous matter.

Asked by his lawyer, Robert Robb, if the attack in the magazine on his mental state and on his masculinity had caused him mental suffering, Mr. Goldwater replied:

"It did and it still does. Even today when people smile at me on the street I don't know whether they're thinking, 'There goes that queer, that homosexual, that fears for his masculinity and hates his wife.' I worry not so much for myself but for my children."

Mr. Robb kept the former Senator on the stand all day as he pressed his attempt to prove malice and reckless disregard of the truth on the part of Mr. Ginzburg and his codefendant, Warren Boroson, who was Fact's managing editor.

With no outward show of anger, Mr. Goldwater heard quotations from the magazine about his "sadistic childhood," his "cruel practical jokes," his "uncontrolled outbursts," his "paranoia" and his "paralyzing, deep-seated, irrational fear."

The quotations were from a 22-page leading article by Mr. Ginzburg, who also accused Mr. Goldwater of being the type who would brandish nuclear weapons.

Origins of Charges

In calm tones, the Arizonan replied: "I've never advocated the use of atomic weapons in Vietnam or any place else." He said, however, that he had urged that the United States "should get along with planning the use of such weapons" as a defense measure because otherwise enemy nations would have a great advantage.

There were moments of laughter in the long day as Mr. Goldwater explained in detail the origin of some of the charges in the magazine.

The Ginzburg article carried a statement that Mr. Goldwater had rigged up a microphone and loudspeaker so he could talk to anyone in the bathroom of his house, and that he would use the system to frighten young women visitors.

Not so, said Mr. Goldwater. He said it was true that he enjoyed working with communications equipment, but the speaker he had wired up for a joke was in the 18th hole of an Arizona golf course during a tournament.

The article told of his frightening a salesgirl in one of his Arizona department stores by sending mice through pneumatic tubes. Mr. Goldwater explained that the woman cashier there enjoyed practical jokes and once put a dead scorpion in his desk drawer, knowing that they "scared me worse than a rattlesnake."

He retaliated, he said, by dumping a dead mouse into the pneumatic tube leading to her desk. "When she saw it she chased me all over the place and finally threw it at me."

During the day Mr. Goldwater denied charges in the magazine that he hated his wife, had beaten his son, had a bad relationship with his Jewish father, had repudiated his Jewish heritage, and had been trigger-happy.

His father, he said, was married in the Episcopal church because there was no synagogue in Phoenix in those days. Mr. Goldwater, an Episcopalian, added: "I was quite young — one year old — when my religion was determined for me at my christening in the Episcopal church."

For the first time in his life Mr. Goldwater heard his military efficiency ratings as Mr. Robb quoted at length from them in order to deny Mr. Ginzburg's charge that he had been a "society soldier." The reports, both when he was on active duty in the war years and later as a reserve Air Force officer and general, were uniformly "excellent" or "superior."

A large part of the disputed issue of Fact was given over to quotations, signed and unsigned, from psychiatrists who described Mr. Goldwater as unfit psychologically to be President.

Mr. Robb read one from an unidentified Stamford, Conn., psychiatrist, who said of Mr. Goldwater: "He is a mass-murderer at heart. A dangerous lunatic!" The psychiatrist had appended a postscript: "Any psychiatrist who does not agree with the above is himself psychologically unfit to be a psychiatrist."

The trial resumes before Judge Harold R. Tyler, at 10:30 this morning, with Mr. Goldwater to be on the stand again.

DEFENSE ATTACKS CALM GOLDWATER

Pleads 'Truth' to Charges of Mental Instability

By EDWARD C. BURKS

The defense began a barbed cross-examination of Barry Goldwater in Federal Court yesterday on the fourth day of his $2-million libel action against Ralph Ginzberg, the publisher.

"We plead truth," Harris declared. He sought to establish that Mr. Ginzburg's Fact magazine was in no way libelous in its October, 1964, issue in picturing the 1964 Republican Presidential nominee as psychologically unfit — in fact, a menace.

"Senator," asked Mr. Steinberg, "didn't you hear rumblings among the American people during the campaign that you were a nut?"

After Mr. Goldwater had demurred with a smile, Mr. Steinberg jokingly came back to the theme later: "Nobody's ever looked at you like you're nuts?"

The former Arizona Senator responded with a quip: "Well, I've had some looks that I've had my suspicions about."

Psychological Issue Raised

While the two exchanged frequent sallies that led to laughter in the crowded courtroom, Mr. Steinberg was completely serious in pressing a main contention: The "psychological makeup" of a Presidential candidate — his "subconscious," his fitness to make awesome decisions in the nuclear age—are vital matters for the public to know of and to debate.

Lean, and with an outdoors look about him, the former Arizona Senator and retired Air Force general remained calm as he heard allegations that he had a medical history, 20 years ago, of emotional upsets.

Mr. Steinberg quoted from records of the plaintiff's private physician, mentioning "emotional upsets" in 1946 and injections of testosterone, a male sex hormone, on four occasions in 1947-48, when Mr. Goldwater complained of feeling tired.

Mr. Goldwater replied: "I've never had emotional upsets. That's the doctor's own phraseology."

He also told Judge Harold R. Tyler Jr. and the jury of nine men and three women that he had never had any psychological difficulties in his life.

Denounced in Magazine

Fact, now defunct, devoted its entire October, 1964, issue to Mr. Goldwater, describing him in scathing terms as trigger-happy, paranoid, mean and anxious about his masculinity. He was likened to Hitler. These conclusions were in a leading article by Ginzburg, the publisher.

The magazine also carried a large number of sharp judgments on Mr. Goldwater made by psychiatrists who had answered a questionnaire sent out by Mr. Ginsburg's managing editor and co-defendant, Warren Boroson. Among the judgments, many unsigned, were some referring to Mr. Goldwater as "emotionally unstable," "grossly psychotic" and "schizophrenic."

On the witness stand Mr. Goldwater said that he had certainly never seen any of those psychiatrists professionally — nor any psychiatrist, for that matter—and doubted he had ever met one of them socially.

It was a day of contrasts. Before the cross-examination, with its emphasis on his medical history, Mr. Goldwater, at the request of his attorney, Roger Robb, told of the outdoor pursuits he still enjoyed with his wife and grown children—boating, camping, fishing, hunting, swimming and target-shooting. Mr. Robb also read long letters that Mr. Goldwater had written during World War II to his young children while he was an Air Corps pilot.

Letters Are Cited

The letters, often with drawings, expressed a warm fatherly interest and included much advice about following the "golden rule" and experiencing the beauties of nature.

In one he wrote: "It's the person who doesn't pray and doesn't believe in God who lives a sad and lonely life." In another he said of Hitler in 1943: "He is one of the bad snakes God put on earth, a bad mistake God made once. He doesn't make many, but when He does, they are loo loos."

Mr. Goldwater summed up his feelings about Fact's strongest comments: "These are nothing but out and out lies."

He said that if anyone could "sit down and plan something like this," then good men would no longer run for public office. On cross-examination, Mr. Steinberg accused Mr. Goldwater of failing to tell military doctors of previous "emotional upsets."

On the subject of testosterone, Mr. Steinberg asked: "Do you know it comes from the sex glands of a bull? Was this some kind of treatment to bolster your masculinity or potency?"

Mr. Goldwater replied that he did not know but would certainly ask his physician, Dr. Leslie Kober. Then he said, "Can I ask you a medical question: Does it have anything to do with mental illness?"

The cross-examination continues today.

DEFENSE ATTACKS GOLDWATER AGAIN

But the Ex-Senator Remains Calm Under Questioning

By EDWARD C. BURKS

Former Senator Barry Goldwater, undergoing cross-examination yesterday in his $2-million libel suit, was called on by the defense to explain matters ranging from right-wing political backing to how he treated his pet bulldog.

Harris Steinberg, defense counsel in the suit brought by Mr. Goldwater in Federal Court against Ralph Ginzburg, the publisher, conducted an all-day counterattack.

In effect, Mr. Steinberg accused the 1964 Republican Presidential nominee of singling out Mr. Ginzburg and his Fact magazine for the suit because they were weaker than other critics.

"Why didn't you sue The New York Times?" Mr. Steinberg asked. Why didn't you sue C.B.S.?" He was referring to Mr. Goldwater's complaints in 1964 that both the newspaper and the network had put out dishonest stories about him.

Mr. Goldwater responded that those stories had been "grains of sand" compared with Fact's attack.

Mr. Goldwater is seeking damages from Mr. Ginzburg on the ground that the October, 1964, issue of the now defunct Fact carried no fewer than 40 deliberately "false, scandalous and defamatory statements" about him.

He agreed that he had made some sharp comments in 1964 about unfair press criticism, but he added: "Newspapers don't print things like you print in this magazine."

Mr. Steinberg tried to show that Mr. Goldwater had never repudiated right-wing extremist, anti-Semitic support in 1964, and named among those supporters Robert Welch of the John Birch Society, the Ku Klux Klan, and Gerald L. K. Smith.

Repudiated Welch

Mr. Goldwater retorted, "I've publicly repudiated Robert Welch many times." He referred to Gerald L. K. Smith as an extremist "of the worst kind," but he had not repudiated his support because he never knew that he had it.

The defense attorney appeared somewhat surprised that Mr. Goldwater had never heard of a New York Times report telling of Smith's support. "Where were you?" he snapped, "fishing?"

"Yes," said Mr. Goldwater, "at the time I was fishing for votes."

The defense argues that sharp verdicts on Mr. Goldwater's fitness made by psychiatrists and a highly critical article by Mr. Ginzburg in the disputed issue in no way libelled the plaintiff, even though such words as "paranoid" and mental instability were used.

Mr. Goldwater contended yesterday that in at least three instances the magazine attempted to give the impression that he was a "queer" or "homosexual." He added that the 64-page issue was a "compilation" of innuendoes, suggestions, quotes out of context and "out-and-out lies" that added up to a "filthy thing" in American politics.

Just before adjournment until Monday Mr. Steinberg asked: "Didn't you and a dentist pull your dog's tooth out one night after a few drinks?"

Mr. Goldwater answered that the dog had broken the tooth, that it was not pulled, but that the dentist put a gold cap on it.

Law

Problem Is to Prove Malice

WASHINGTON — When Barry Goldwater was a boy, his mother once told him "never enter a race you can't win." In 1964, Mr. Goldwater violated that rule and was buried under the Johnson landslide in the Presidential race. Now he is putting that rule to another stern test in his $2,000,000 libel suit against Ralph Ginsburg and the defunct magazine "Fact."

In a special edition in the fall of 1964 the magazine said that Senator Goldwater suffered from paranoia, likened him to Hitler, asserted that he felt "intense anxiety about his manhood," called him a "cruel" practical joker and made a host of other charges. It cited a poll of psychiatrists to back up its accusations.

It is not impossible for Mr. Goldwater to win a judgment from the jury of 9 men and 3 women who are hearing the case in New York, but he will have to overcome formidable odds to prevail. His lawyers' task is not simply to convince the jury that the charges are false; they will also have to show that the libel was with malice.

For in 1964, the United States Supreme Court held that anyone could make defamatory remarks about the public life of officials —and get away with it—as long as malice was not proved. And malice, the court said, was limited to the calculated lie or reckless disregard of truth.

Ever since then the courts have struck down libel judgment after libel judgment on finding that there was no malice. In the landmark case in which the new libel rule was promulgated, the Supreme Court held that The New York Times had not "recklessly disregarded truth" even though its advertising department failed to check the accuracy of an advertisement with news stories that showed that charges against officials of Montgomery, Ala., were false.

While many readers might think the charges in the Goldwater article wild, the Supreme Court, in its latest libel decision last month, made clear that "reckless conduct is not measured by whether a reasonably prudent man would have published, or would have investigated before publishing."

"There must be," the Court went on, "sufficient evidence to permit the conclusion that the defendant in fact entertained serious doubts as to the truth of his publication. Publishing with such doubts shows reckless disregard for truth or falsity and demonstrates actual malice."

Quip

One exchange that drew laughs during Barry Goldwater's $2-million libel action against Fact magazine came last Thursday when Mr. Goldwater was being cross-examined by attorney Harris Steinberg.

Mr. Steinberg: "Nobody's ever looked at you like you're nuts?"

Mr. Goldwater: "Well, I've had some looks that I've had my suspicions about."

Then, Justice Bryon R. White, who wrote the decision, tossed in a sentence that seemed to open up a wider possibility of proving malice. Professions of good faith will not be likely to prevail, he said, "when the publisher's allegations are so inherently improbable that only a reckless man would have put them in circulation."

In only one case has the Supreme Court found actual malice present. That was in upholding a $460,000 judgment for Wallace Butts, former athletic director of the University of Georgia, who was accused in a Saturday Evening Post article of giving away his football team's secrets to fix a game.

The Post did check the charge of Mr. Butts' fix of a football game with a number of persons, but many quotations were disputed, credibility of the key source for the story was thrown into doubt, and an appeal to withhold publication was rejected. The mass of evidence made the Post story look to the jury as if it had been fabricated.

Lawyers for Mr. Ginzburg are banking on the poll of psychiatrists and articles from books and magazines as the basis of their charges that Mr. Goldwater was "psychologically unfit to be President." Whether this will prove convincing in court may provide another guide to how far the press may go in criticizing public figures.

—ROBERT A. PHELPS

GOLDWATER CALLS ARTICLE 'GARBAGE

Says Ginzburg's Conclusion Is Malicious and False

By EDWARD C. BURKS

Barry Goldwater, after hearing himself described in Federal Court yesterday as having the "courage of a cowardly juvenile delinquent," testified that such "garbage" had prompted him to press his libel suit.

The 1964 Republican Presidential candidate is suing Ralph Ginzburg, the publisher, for $2-million for alleged character assassination in a pre-election 1964 issue of the defendant's now defunct Fact magazine.

After three days of cross-examination by the defense lawyer, Harris Steinberg, and with more to come, Mr. Goldwater was still relaxed and frequently able to make a joke that caused laughter in the small, crowded courtroom.

The statement about his "courage" was one of many made by Mr. Ginzburg in a 20-page article in the Fact issue of October, 1964.

At Mr. Steinberg's suggestion, a "true and false box score" was kept on a blackboard while he read line by line through most of the article. As of yesterday, despite some haggling between the lawyer and Mr.

Goldwater, the "box score" showed 114 "true" statements, 75 "false," 37 "false but accurately quoted," 10 "unimportant," 2 "false opinions," one "inaccurate," and one "true but inaccurately quoted."

Likened to Garbage

Mr. Goldwater accused the writer of putting together a collection of unsubstantiated, malicious conclusions, out-of-context quotations and lies to imply that he was homosexual and paranoid, when the author had no competence in medical or psychological questions. Some of the alleged distortions were relatively minor standing alone, according to Mr. Goldwater, but he gave this summary:

"I don't object to one little orange peel, or maybe an egg shell, a banana peel, a bottle cap or an empty oatmeal box, but when it becomes a pile of garbage, then I'm concerned." The jury laughed when he added: "While I wasn't here during the garbage strike, I think most New Yorkers would understand what I'm talking about."

Mr. Steinberg argued that Mr. Ginzburg's article was well-researched and included the opinions of a large number of sources, and that the conclusions were "a kind of summary" of those opinions.

The former Arizona Senator also attacked the cartoons used in Fact's issue, describing them as far exceeding the satire of the usual political lampoon.

One he described as "pornographic" and "the worst cartoon I've ever seen." It portrayed him clad only in diapers

and holding them open. Mr. Goldwater said that the obvious intent of the cartoon was to have him looking to determine what sex he was.

Father Called Effeminate

Another Ginzburg conclusion, described by Mr. Goldwater as "malicious," was this one:

"This is a man who obviously identifies with a masculine mother rather than an effeminate father, and is victim to all the ambivalence that such identification must create."

In earlier testimony it was brought out that the former Senator is an outdoors man, and he testified that his father was anything but effeminate, being a man who played baseball, boxed and played cards.

Still another quotation from the article attacked by Mr. Goldwater said, "Goldwater's 'masculine' facade fools many people."

In another section the author spoke of Mr. Goldwater's "inner conviction that everybody hates him" and "that is why the theme of betrayal—so typical of the paranoiac—is recurrent in Goldwater's utterances."

Mr. Steinberg, seeking to establish that the plaintiff had "not had one important bill passed" during his 12 years in the Senate, was given a list by Mr. Goldwater.

"You must have been a little surprised after your research," Mr. Steinberg commented, "to find you only had 12 passed that weren't just junk bills. Wouldn't you say this is a very, very low output?"

Mr. Goldwater disagreed that sponsoring bills was that important.

Goldwater Lawyer Reads Letters to Show the Intent to Libel

By EDWARD C. BURKS

Counsel for Barry Goldwater argued in Federal Court yesterday that Fact magazine had maliciously set out to libel him in 1964 while pretending to publish an impartial analysis.

The 1964 Republican Presidential nominee is suing Ralph Ginzburg, publisher of the now defunct magazine for $2-million, because of its October, 1964, issue "on the mind of Barry Goldwater."

The plaintiff offered evidence intended to show that Mr. Ginzburg and his managing editor, Warren Boroson, had decided what their article on his "psychological fitness" to be President would say well before they conducted a poll of psychiatrists.

More than a week before questionnaires were mailed to the nation's 12,356 psychiatrists, Mr. Boroson, a co-defendant in the suit, had written to Walter Reuther, head of the United Automobile Workers and a Goldwater critic, for help.

That letter, read to the jury of nine man and three women, said in part:

"I'm writing an article for Fact about an old enemy of yours — Barry Goldwater. It's going to be a psychological profile, and will say, basically, that Goldwater is so belligerent, suspicious, hot-tempered and rigid because he has deep-seated doubts about his masculinity. We're surveying psychiatrists and psychologists to find out what they think of Goldwater; a few are already giving me guidance on writing the article.

"Now, you yourself have said that Goldwater 'is mentally unstable and needs a psychiatrist.' Can you tell me of any personal incidents — either on the record or off the record—that led you to say that? Times he lost his temper, episodes that demonstrate his suspiciousness and so on."

Mr. Boroson said in a long deposition read to the court that Mr. Reuther had never responded.

In another deposition, Mr. Ginzburg was quoted as saying that the 20-page article under his byline, which led to the suit, "was the mutual creation of Warren Boroson and myself," adding, "He obtained all of the source material. I did all of the writing."

Mr. Ginzburg went on to say that he had approved the letter that was sent with the questionnaire to the psychiatrists. The letter over Mr. Boroson's signature asked for a "yes" or "no" answer on Mr. Goldwater's psychological fitness, but also welcomed remarks, signed or unsigned, on these questions: Was he prone to aggressive behavior and destructiveness? Was he callous to the downtrodden? Did his two "nervous breakdowns" have any bearing on his fitness?

Mr. Ginzburg conceded in the deposition that he had already made up his mind about Mr. Goldwarter's "aggressive behavior" and said that most people regarded a nervous breakdown as a sign of mental illness. But he argued that the letter was a fair statement.

Mr. Goldwater has denied any nervous breakdowns or mental disorders, and described Fact's characterization of him as "garbage." Fact had called him "paranoid" and unsure of his masculinity.

Mr. Goldwater's attorneys, Roger Robb and Peter Corbett, spent the day reading the depositions taken in 1966, as well as some comments from psychiatrists who had objected strenuously to Fact's type of survey.

Fact had reported that 1,189 psychiatrists of 2,417 who responded found Mr. Goldwater "psychologically unfit"; 571 did not know and 657 pronounced him fit. Although it printed comments criticizing its survey, it left out a sharp one by Walter E. Barton, medical director of the American Psychiatric Association, promising to take all measures "to disavow its validity."

Other psychiatrists whose comments were not published described the Fact survey as "contemptible," "filthy," "made for the purposes of character assassination," "the most malicious use of polling," a blackmark against honest journalism."

Goldwater Rests Libel Suit, Charging Malicious Editing

By EDWARD C. BURKS

Barry Goldwater rested his libel case against Fact magazine yesterday after his attorney alleged that material gathered for a Goldwater issue had been maliciously edited and distorted.

The trial of Mr. Goldwater's $2-million suit against Ralph Ginzburg, the publisher, before Judge Harold R. Tyler Jr. in Federal Court here will go into its third week Monday when the defense presents its side.

In a deposition, Mr. Ginzburg gave this description of the 1964, issue, which found Mr. Goldwater psychologically unfit for the Presidency: "I am indeed proud of it."

Goldwater's Allegations

The plaintiff offered evidence to sustain these claims:

¶ That Fact tampered with comments sent in by psychiatrists on Mr. Goldwater's fitness, either through omitting qualifying sentences or rewriting entire sentences.

¶ That Fact while claiming to be a nonpartisan magazine, brought suits in California and New Jersey in unsuccessful attempts to keep Mr. Goldwater off the ballot.

¶ That favorable matter about Mr. Goldwater was trimmed away before an isolated quotation out of context was used to present a harsh view of him in a 20-page article by Mr. Ginzburg.

In the deposition read to the jury, Mr. Ginzburg was quoted as saying he had edited letters from psychiatrists for his special issue "on the mind of Barry Goldwater" so as to produce a "distillation."

One unsigned letter from a psychiatrist said, according to the deposition: "This is a frightened, sick man." Mr. Ginzburg was quoted as admitting that he rewrote the sentence to read for publication: "Barry Goldwater is a sick man who is to be pitied and feared."

'Nervous Breakdowns'

Another short, unsigned letter in the magazine spoke of Mr. Goldwater's being too risky after having "suffered two nervous breakdowns."

Mr. Goldwater's attorney, Roger Robb, produced the original letter in court to show that in condensing it Mr. Ginzburg had added the part about "nervous breakdowns" for there was no mention of them in the letter, although it was highly critical. Mr. Ginzburg's quoted response was: "I think that the condensation is an accurate distillation."

Psychiatrists across the nation had received a questionnaire from Fact, and the gist of the special issue was that most who responded found Mr. Goldwater psychologically unfit. Mr. Ginzburg conceded that he had "plucked" material from one anonymous letter to add it to another in at least one instance.

Since the 38-year-old defendant will not take the stand until the defense presents its case, Mr. Robb has spent two full days reading the deposition made by Mr. Ginzburg in 1966, after Mr. Goldwater brought suit.

In the deposition, Mr. Ginzburg said that Fact, through the lawyer Melvin Belli in California and with the sister of its managing editor in New Jersey, had brought the suits to get Mr. Goldwater off the ballot.. They alleged that Mr. Goldwater did not meet the constitutional requirement of native birth since Arizona had not attained statehood at the time of his birth there in 1912.

Fear of War Raised

In a 1964 press release, which was read into the record, Mr. Ginzburg said that Mr. Goldwater's proposed policies could only lead to nuclear war. The suits, therefore, were not against him as an individual, the statement said, but because he was "undesirable" for the Presidency.

Evidence showed that Fact spent $80,000 in buying full-page advertisements in ten newspapers, including The New York Times, to announce its special Goldwater issue and that 14,582 subscriptions resulted from the ads. The paid circulation of the Goldwater issue was 160,000.

Defendant Denies Intent to Libel as Goldwater Trial Enters Third Week

By EDWARD C. BURKS

The 1964 issue of Fact magazine, which led to a $2-million libel action by Barry Goldwater, was an honest effort to appraise his fitness for the Presidency, the defense contended yesterday.

Warren Boroson, who at the time was managing editor of Fact, now defunct, took the stand in Federal Court to explain the decision to publish a special issue on "the mind" and "psychological fitness" of the 1964 Republican candidate.

The slight, 33-year-old editor said that in July of that year he had suggested having an article done by a psychiatrist on Mr. Goldwater's mental stability.

According to Mr. Boroson, the things that he had read about Mr. Goldwater suggested "rather extreme" variations of mood and "rather extreme" political viewpoints.

"Mr. Goldwater's mental stability was becoming more and more discussed," he said.

As the trial before Judge Harold R. Tyler Jr. went into the thiird week yesterday, the defense began its case. The first two weeks were taken up with Mr. Goldwater's case. He charged that Fact, its publisher, Ralph Ginzburg, and Mr. Boroson maliciously defamed him.

Specifically he contended that an article by Mr. Ginzburg had pictured him as a paranoid, a latent homosexual, an anal character and a Hitler-like character. Mr. Ginzburg will take the stand today.

Yesterday Mr. Boroson explained that his extensive readings in psychological studies raised a concern in his mind about the effect of tensions on men in high office, especially men prone to instability.

His idea, he continued, had been to produce an issue in which Mr. Goldwater would be compared with the "authoritarian personality," which he described as a person who "had to continually prove to himself he was tough and super-maculine, therefore, who couldn't sympathize with the weak."

Mr. Boroson, a bespectacled soft-spoken man with wavy dark hair, had to be told several times to raise his voice. He testified that Mr. Ginzburg had accepted his basic idea but had decided to poll all of the nation's psychiatrists instead of having the article done by a single psychiatrist.

As it turned out, Mr. Boroson researched books, magazines and newspapers giving "an insight into the Goldwater personality," he said, and then produced a research draft for Mr. Ginzburg.

It was Mr. Ginzburg, he said, who wrote the 20-page lead article that preceded 40 pages of comments by psychiatrists, the majority of them extremely critical of Mr. Goldwater.

Mr. Boroson's attorney, Stanley S. Arkin, asked:

"Did you seek to create a false impression of Senator Goldwater?" "Did you knowingly try to defame him?" "Did you knowingly say anything false about him?"

Each time the witness responded, "No."

He testified that he had written a three-paragraph introduction to the comments by the psychiatrists but had had no part whatsoever in selecting or editing those statements.

Mr. Boroson is presently an editor of Transaction, a university-sponsored magazine dealing with sociological, psychological and political subjects, published in St. Louis.

Mr. Boroson testified that he had no reason not to believe published accounts that Mr. Goldwater had suffered "two nervous breakdowns" in the late 1930's.

A questionnaire and letter sent out to the nation's psychiatrists over his signature had asked them to rate Mr. Goldwater's "psychological fitness" and also to comment on such matters as his "two nervous breakdowns."

Mr. Goldwater has denied flatly on the witness stand ever having had a nervous breakdown or any mental difficulty.

Before Mr. Boroson testified, the defense read pretrial depositions of five doctors who took part in Fact's poll. Each stated that his comment on Mr. Goldwater's fitness was "a personal and political opinion" rather than a professional diagnosis.

One psychiatrist, G. Templeton of Locust Valley, N.Y., had been quoted in Fact as writing: "If Goldwater wins, both you and I will be among the first into concentration camps."

Asked by Mr. Goldwater' counsel if he really meant that the psychiatrist responded in the deposition: "It was written more as a quip. If I really believed it, I would be somewhat paranoid."

Another psychiatrist, Dr. Leonard R. Sillman of Westport, Conn., and with an office here, was quoted as accusing Mr. Goldwater's attorneys of trying to "badger" him and "intimidate" him from exercising his right of free speech.

"Are you intimidated?" Roger Robb, the attorney asked.

"Yes, I am," Dr. Sillman responded.

Dr. Sillman's comment published in Fact referred to Mr. Goldwater as a "gray-haired man with the social comprehension of a 4-year-old."

GINZBURG LIKENS 'FACT' TO CRUSADE

Defends Goldwater Article as 'Historical Contribution'

By EDWARD C. BURKS

Ralph Ginsburg was subjected to a searing, five-hour cross-examination of his motives and fairness yesterday as Barry Goldwater's $2-million libel action against him neared a conclusion.

The publisher said defiantly that he had made a "historic contribution" to crusading journalism with the October, 1964, issue of his now-defunct Fact magazine on Mr. Goldwater's psychological fitness to be President.

In fact, Mr. Ginzburg revealed during his long day on the witness stand in Federal Court, his successor magazine, Avant-Garde, had planned a similar psychological study on President Johnson's mental and emotional fitness.

The issue of Fact, describing Mr. Goldwater as a menace and carrying numerous sharp judgments against him by psychiatrists, led to the present suit. Both sides have now completed their cases, and summations will be made today before the jury of nine men and three women.

■ Mr. Ginzburg said that the special study on Mr. Johnson was dropped after the President decided not to run again. Both the Goldwater and Johnson studies were based on a poll of the nation's psychiatrists.

Called Character Assassination

■ The thrust of yesterday's cross-examination by Roger Robb, Mr. Goldwater's lawyer, was that the defendant had conducted a rigged poll in 1964 and also written a 20-page article which was simply a character assassination.

■ The two men jabbed at each other throughout the day. Mr. Robb, a soft-spoken Washingtonian, with a way of conveying an impression of controlled outrage, would go over one passage after another from the magazine and ask quietly: "Do you think that was fair?"

■ Mr. Ginzburg's temper flared several times as Mr. Robb suggested that he sent a letter to the psychiatrists that was grossly slanted against Mr. Goldwater and then tampered with the replies to picture the candidate in the worst light.

● While Mr. Goldwater listened quietly, Mr. Ginzburg in a loud voice made these points: He was a conscientious journalist; he bore the plaintiff no malice; he had tried to give an honest presentation of what psychiatrists and respected journalists were saying about the Goldwater personality; he was nonpartisan in having planned a similar survey on Mr. Johnson, who incidentally, had won a favorable verdict from a majority of psychiatrists.

Mr. Robb, armed with the original letters from the psychiatrists, which he obtained by a court order, countered with these claims: The defendant had thrown out letters questioning the ethics of the poll or remarking that psychiatrists are generally biased in favor of liberal candidates. He had recklessly used letters calling Mr. Goldwater a "mass murderer at heart" and a "latent homosexual," Mr. Robb argued.

Eros Brought Up

Mr. Ginzburg is free in $10,000 bail while seeking a reduction of a five-year sentence or sending obscene matter—his now defunct magazine Eros—through the mails.

"Do you exhibit these magazine to your children?" Mr. Robb asked.

The defendant, who has two daughters, 14 and 7, and a son, 10, snapped: "You and your ilk may not understand, but an ability to face up to sex is a healthy attitude." He added that his children could freely consult all of his publications, as they would an encyclopedia, but that generally they had ignored Eros.

"Only dirty-minded people" might construe that as evil, Mr. Ginzburg went on. Mr. Robb, referring to a Supreme Court decision upholding the publisher's conviction in the Eros case, replied, "You mean like the Supreme Court."

In a vehement reply, Mr. Ginzburg said: "I didn't call the Supreme Court a body of jackasses, like your client did."

Mr. Robb argued that the defendant had been reckless in not caring whether the statements by the psychiatrists, who had never seen Mr. Goldwater in person, were true or not. He also argued that Mr. Ginzburg was deliberately malicious through use of "twisted" facts. For example, the article said that Mr. Goldwater was widely regarded as a "man' man," had shot the Colorado River rapids six times, had donated 90 pints of blood and flown 75 different kinds of aircraft. But that was all summed up, Mr. Robb said, as a "constant irrational and unnecessary show of strength," as a "masculine facade that "fools many people."

May 23, 1968

GOLDWATER SAYS HE IS VINDICATED

Barry Goldwater said yesterday he had been vindicated as a Federal Court jury awarded the former Republican Presidential candidate $75,000 in punitive damages in his libel suit against Fact magazine and its publisher, Ralph Ginzburg.

Mr. Ginzburg, who swiftly announced that he would appeal the verdict, asserted that the "decision precludes the possibility of a vigorous, robust, and no-holds-barred debate in the upcoming election."

After 13 hours' deliberation, the jury of nine men and three women reported at 12:40 A.M. its decision that Mr. Goldwater had been subjected to deliberate character assassination in the October, 1964, issue of Fact magazine. The issue of the now-defunct publication, which was devoted to "The Mind of Barry Goldwater," sold 160,000 copies.

Mr. Goldwater, who expressed pleasure at the jury decision, is expected to announce his intention to run for the United States Senate in Phoenix, Ariz., tomorrow. His previous service as Senator ended in 1964, when he ran for the Presidency.

Commenting on the outcome of the case later at a news conference in the offices of Avant Garde Magazine, 110 West 40th Street, Mr. Ginzburg said it would make the 1968 Presidential campaign "probably the most inhibited in American history."

The publisher, who wore a blue Nehru jacket over a white turtleneck sweater, said:

"To a greater degree than ever before, the American people will be forced to choose a leader on the basis of only those facts that the candidates themselves wish to have known."

The jury asssesed punitive damages of $50,000 against Fact Magazine, Inc., of which Mr. Ginzburg was the sole owner and $25,000 against Mr. Ginzburg as the publisher; and "compensatory damages" of $1 against Mr. Ginzburg, Fact and the magazine's managing editor, Warren Boroson, who was a co-defendant in the case.

Mr. Goldwater's original request in his suit, charging deliberate character assassination, was for $2-million damages.

The three-week trial followed with great attention by politician, lawyers and the press because it ws considered a potential landmark case that might lead to the elaboration of new guidelines for libel cases involving public personages.

In yesterday's news conference, Mr. Ginzburg criticized the jury's decision as "completely illogical . . . a complete put-down ofb everything and everyone involved in the case."

He said he had $75,000 although he was "not a rich publisher."

Although it would be "a whole lot cheaper for me to make a settlement with Mr. Goldwater," he would appeal yesterday's decision, the publisher declared, because "the question is whether a man can still get up on a soapbox and speak his mind about a presidential candidate without fear of being dragged off in manacles or wiped out financially."

May 26, 1968

Court Allows Goldwater Judgment to Stand

By ROBERT H. PHELPS
Special to The New York Times

WASHINGTON, Jan. 26 — The Supreme Court denied today a request by Ralph Ginzburg, the publisher, for a review of a $75,000 libel judgment won by Senator Barry Goldwater.

The Court made the decision in a one-line order backed by a 5-to-2 vote. Justice Hugo L. Black filed a dissent, in which Justice William O. Douglas joined, asserting that the review should have been granted and the Court of Appeals upholding of the judgment reversed "summarily."

Chief Justice Warren E. Burger took no part in the case.

The Arizona Republican had sued Mr. Ginzburg, Fact magazine, and Warren Boroson, managing editor of Fact, for $2-million.

The suit cited the September-October 1964 issue of Fact that said that Mr. Goldwater, who was then the Republican candidate for President, suffered from paranoia, likened him to Adolph Hitler, asserted that he felt "intense anxiety about his manhood," called him a "cruel" practical joker and made a host of other charges. To back up its accusations Fact printed comments from a poll of psychiatrists.

A Federal district court in New York awarded Mr. Goldwater $1 in compensatory damages and $75,000 in punitive damages. The Court of Appeals for the Second Circuit upheld the judgment.

Since the Supreme Court wrote no opinion in the case, it did not make new law. But Justice Black said that it confirmed his fears that the present rules of the libel law were not sufficient to guarantee uninhibited debate of public issues.

Under a 1964 decision in a case involving The New York Times, the court held that false charges of fact could be published about public officials if malice was not present. It defined malice as calculated falsity or reckless disregard of the truth.

In only one other case, a suit by Wallace Butts, former athletic director of the University of Georgia, against the Saturday Evening Post, has the Supreme Court upheld a libel verdict under The New York Times rule.

Mr. Goldwater's lawyer, John J. Wilson of Washington, argued that Fact was malicious because Mr. Ginzburg had decided that the Senator was paranoid and then picked "bits and pieces" to support the charges, that the American Psychiatric Association had denied the validity of the poll before the article was published but its view had not been run in the magazine and that some of the quotations had actually been "melded" from various letters.

Justice Black agreed that the jury was justified in finding that the articles had been prepared with reckless disregard of truth, but added:

"The grave dangers of prohibiting or penalizing the publication of even the most inaccurate and misleading information seem to me to more than outweigh any gain, personal or social, that might result from permitting libel awards such as the one before the Court today. I firmbly believe it is precisely because of these considerations that the First Amendment bars in absolute, unequivocal terms any abridgement by the Government of freedom of speech and press."

In 1966, in urging a prohibition against all libel judgments, Mr. Black had warned that the New York Times rule was "little portection against high emotions and deep prejudices which frequently pervade local communities where libel suits are tried."

Mr. Black also said that Goldwater judgment shoulnt not have been upheld because the Senator suffered little if any actual harm.

Mr. Ginzburg issud a statement asserting that "this is a black day for the Constitution." Fact magazine has not published since July, 1967. Its staff now publishes Avant Garde.

Mr. Ginzburg was represented by David H. Mariln, Helen Stern and Harold Cohn of Philadelphia.

January 27, 1970

AGNEW CHARGES 'BLOOPER' BY TIMES

By HOMER BIGART
Special to The New York Times

HOUSTON, Oct. 28—Spiro T. Agnew today accused The New York Times of "having pulled the major blooper of the campaign" by making what he termed inaccurate charges and false statements and libeling him in an editorial declaring him unfit to be Vice President.

Governor Agnew characterized the editorial, which appeared last Saturday, in a statement distributed by one of his press aides in Houston.

In the statement, the Republican Vice-Presidential candidate said:

"Everyone knows that The Times endorsed Vice President Humphrey and is actively supporting him. The fact that The Times waited until a week before the election to distort the facts and make its inaccurate charges against me compounds the libel.

"Before the editorial was written The Times was advised by my campaign manager that its information was inaccurate."

Expects Retraction

After Governor Agnew's statement was issued, his campaign manager, George W. White Jr., was made available for questions. Mr. White was asked, "Are you taking it to court?"

He replied: "It'll depend on the circumstances. We expect them [The Times] to print a retraction."

Mr. White, who is also Governor Agnew's lawyer, declared the editorial "absolutely libelous," said he would recommend that Mr. Agnew sue The Times and, when asked why The Times might, as he charged, distort the facts, replied: "Because they want Humphrey elected."

Mr. Agnew's statement declared "completely false" a charge or inference in the editorial that his financial worth had "risen sharply" while in office because of favorable treatment given friends.

He accused The Times of distorting his dealings in land on the probable approach route of a new span of the Chesapeake Bay Bridge. He declared "untrue" an allegation that he approved the route of the bridge and said it had been approved and recommended by the State Roads Commission under a Democratic Governor prior to his administration.

To a charge that Governor Agnew's association with the Chesapeake National Bank, whose letterhead lists him as a director, involves "clear and repeated conflicts of interest," Mr. Agnew said: "Everyone in Maryland has known since 1964 that I was a director of the bank."

The Times editorial said that Mr. Agnew was responsible for the enforcement of the state banking laws and the state had public funds on deposit with the bank.

Denies Inheritance Statement

In his statement, Governor Agnew denied that he voted to deposit funds in the bank when he was a county executive and he also said that the state of Maryland did not have an account in the bank. He said the state had bought a certificate of deposit with the bank in 1964 and added: "At no time during my term in office were any additional state funds deposited in this bank or any state accounts opened."

He described as "untrue in its entirety" a part of the editorial that said that he had explained that his stock in the bank had been inherited from his father. He said that he had never made such a statement to anyone.

The editorial also stated that Mr. Agnew was still a partner in a Virgin Islands land venture with some of the same businessmen with whom he joined in the Chesapeake Bay Bridge route deal. Governor Agnew, in his statement, said the Virgin Islands venture to date had shown a loss and added that he had purchased a vacation apartment in this condominium.

"There is nothing improper in having such an investment," he declared.

He asserted: "The Times has stated that if it finds its editorial to be inaccurate, it will write a retraction in its editorial columns. There is documentary proof of what I say and I assume that The New York Times will keep its word."

Meanwhile, speaking at a rally attended by about 1,000 people at the Pasadena High School auditorium here, Mr. Agnew made no reference to his finances. It was his standard speech for rallies, to which he added an endorsement for the NASA manned spacecraft center here.

He said a Nixon-Agnew Administration "would not tolerate America becoming second-best" in the conquest of space.

In New York, John N. Mitchell, national campaign manager for the Nixon-Agnew ticket, released a statement similar to that of Mr. Agnew. It called The Times editorial "such a distortion of the true facts that it raises fundamental questions of fairness and responsibility."

Times Replies to Nixon Charge On the Sale of Land By Agnew

The New York Times has responded to a charge by Richard M. Nixon that it had been guilty of "gutter journalism" in an editorial about his running mate, Spiro T. Agnew. The reply appears in an editorial on Page 46.

Mr. Nixon said Sunday night that "the charges" in an editorial about Mr. Agnew that appeared in Saturday's issue of The Times "are inaccurate in one major respect."

At that time, in response to further questioning on the Columbia Broadcasting System's TV program, "Face the Nation," Mr. Nixon refused to elaborate. He said, "A retraction will be demanded at The Times legally tomorrow."

Yesterday, Everett I. Willis, a partner in the law firm of Dewey, Ballantine, Bushby, Palmer & Wood, of 140 Broadway, met with Louis M. Loeb and James C. Goodale, lawyers for The Times.

According to Harding F. Bancroft, the executive vice president of The Times, Mr. Willis criticized one statement in the editorial. It dealt with the sale by Mr. Agnew of his share of a tract of land on the probable approach route of a new span of the Chesapeake Bay Bridge.

Mr. Bancroft said that Mr. Willis had criticized a sentence that said: "In response to public criticism, Governor Agnew later sold his share of the land."

According to Mr. Bancroft, Mr. Willis contended that the sentence gave the impression that Mr. Agnew sold the land after he became Governor of Maryland.

In today's editorial, which includes the text of Saturday's editorial, The Times states that Mr. Agnew's share of the land was sold while he was Governor, although it had been placed in trust for sale by a bank the previous year, before his election as Governor.

The editorial says that the land was sold for the price Mr. Agnew had paid for it and adds: "The only (and successful) bidder was a lawyer representing Mr. Agnew's former partners in the investment."

Mr. Willis was not immediately available for comment. Benjamin F. Holme, who described himself as a spokesman for the Dewey, Ballantine firm, said that it was not representing any candidate or committee. He said that Mr. Willis was working "in an individual capacity" for the Nixon-Agnew campaign.

A statement on Saturday's editorial was issued by Governor Agnew in Houston yesterday. It was received by The Times after the editorial replying to Mr. Nixon had appeared in today's first edition. Mr. Agnew's statement will be discussed editorially in tomorrow's editions.

Text of Agnew Statement in Rebuttal to The Times

Special to The New York Times

HOUSTON, Oct. 28—Following is a statement issued tonight by Gov. Spiro T. Agnew of Maryland, Republican candidate for Vice President:

It is unfortunate that The New York Times, long considered one of the leading publications in this country, should find itself in the embarrassing position of having pulled the major blooper of the campaign.

Everyone knows that The Times endorsed Vice President Humphrey and is actively supporting him. The fact that The Times waited until a week before the election to distort the facts and make its inaccurate charges against me compounds the libel.

Before the editorial was written The Times was advised by my campaign manager that its information was inaccurate.

Denies He Aided Friends

Specifically, The Times charged or inferred that because of favorable treatment given friends of mine while I was in office that my financial worth has "risen sharply." This is a completely false statement. No improper treatment was given friends of mine while I was in office. Moreover, if you eliminate some $35,000 to $40,000 that I inherited or was given by my parents, my net worth is considerably less than that of any other of the Presidential or Vice-Presidential candidates. My total net worth is $111,084.44. Eliminating the monies received from my parents, my net worth would be approximately $74,000.

The second charge is that in 1965 I joined with these same friends in purchasing a tract of land on the probable approach route of a new parallel span of the Chesapeake Bay Bridge in Maryland—that as Governor I approved the route and in response to public criticism I later (and I underscore later) sold my share of the land.

The following facts clearly reveal the distortion:

When I ran for Governor of Maryland in 1966, so that there could be no misunderstanding, I voluntarily disclosed that I had a one-ninth interest in a piece of land that could possibly involve an approach to the Bay Bridge.

On Sept. 16, 1966, before my election as Governor of Maryland (and I underscore before) I deeded my interest in this land in trust, under the terms of which trust my interest was to be sold and any profit was to go to charity. This was an irrevocable trust which could not be changed. The Maryland National Bank in Baltimore was the trustee.

Sold at Public Auction

After Sept. 16, 1966, I no longer had any control over this property. The trust required that if the property was not sold privately by the trustees within a year, it would be sold at public auction. This was done after proper public notification of the auction by newspaper advertisement. The allegation that I approved the route by the Bay Bridge is untrue. The route was approved and recommended by the State Roads Commission under a Democratic Governor prior to my Administration. The State Roads Commission was controlled by the Democratic party and the route was selected after employing engineering consultants. The Governor has no authority to approve or disapprove any route. By law, the State Roads Commission is an autonomous body of the state and the commission and its chairman-director are the body empowered to select and determine all state road routes. The route was already selected and it has been considered for years. All state road maps prior to my election showed these routes.

Virgin Islands Venture

The next charge is that I am a partner in a Virgin Islands land venture. I do have a $1,600 interest in a condominium venture in the the Virgin Islands which to date has shown a loss. I later purchased a vacation apartment in this condominium. There is nothing improper in having such an investment.

The next charge is that as a director of the Chesapeake National Bank, I am involved in "clear and repeated conflict of interest" as it is charged that I am responsible for the enforcement of the state banking laws and the state has funds on deposit with the bank.

Everyone in Maryland has known since 1964 that I was a director of the bank.

The bank is a national bank and not a state bank. The Comptroller of the Currency of the United States has jurisdiction over all national banks.

The same article alleges that as County Executive of Baltimore County, I voted to deposit funds in the bank. This is untrue. The selecting of banks and the amounts to be deposited are determined by the County Director of Finance (orginally appointed by the previous Democratic administration). He will verify that I adopted his recommendations in entirety.

No State Account

The state does not have an account in Chesapeake National Bank. On March 18, 1964, shortly after the bank opened its doors, a certificate of deposit, dated April 1, 1964, in the amount of $200,000 was purchased by the State of Maryland. This certificate was purchased by the Democratic State Treasurer, John Leutmeyer, while Governor [Millard J.] Tawes, a Democrat, was in office.

This certificate requires the bank to purchase compensatory U. S. Treasury notes in a like amount as security for the certificate. This certificate has remained with the bank since its inception and is currently yielding the State of Maryland 5 per cent per annum in interest. At no time during my term in office were any additional state funds deposited in this bank or any state accounts opened.

The last charge is that in my gubernatorial campaign two years ago, I explained that I inherited bank stock from my father but it was subsequently learned that my father died a year before the bank opened, and that I, in fact, purchased the shares.

The allegation is untrue in its entirety. I never stated to anyone that the Chesapeake National Bank stock was inherited from my father. I did previously state that I sold stock inherited from my father and purchased the Chesapeake National Bank stock. My father died in March, 1963, owning $10,000 debenture note in the Koontz Creamery in Baltimore, which was in both my mother's and father's name.

In May of 1963, my mother placed the debenture note in her name and mine. In December of 1963, she and I sold the debenture and received a check in the amount of $10,000 payable to her and to me from the Koontz Creamery, which check we endorsed over to the Chesapeake National Bank in exchange for bank stock which my mother then insisted be placed in my name alone.

Creamery Has Canceled Check

The Koontz Creamery still has the original canceled check showing the transaction and the endorsement to the Chesapeake National Bank.

The Times has stated that if it finds its editorial to be inaccurate, it will write a retraction in its editorial columns. There is documentary proof of what I say and I assume that The New York Times will keep its word.

Unfortunately, when someone is libeled in this fashion, a retraction does not reach all the persons who read the original libel. In addition, other newspapers and news media pick up the original libel and repeat it before the retraction appears, thus compounding the situation.

The reporter who made the investigation for The Times reported to it that the above charges are old allegations and that his investigation "turned up little hard fact that is new."

The Times knew of these old charges and had a complete file on me in 1966 when it endorsed me for Governor of Maryland, and I quote two of its statements:

"As Executive of Baltimore County Agnew has gained the experience to be a competent Governor."

"Both the State of Maryland and the cause of modern-minded Republicans in the nation will benefit if the voters elect him."

Agnew Presses Times to Retract
Critical Editorials

The campaign manager of Gov. Spiro T. Agnew of Maryland, the Republican Vice-Presidential candidate, charged yesterday that The New York Times had shown a "wanton, reckless disregard" of Mr. Agnew's reputation by reprinting yesterday an editorial critical of the candidate.

A lawyer here for the Nixon-Agnew Campaign Committee, Everett I. Willis, also disputed a statement in yesterday's Times that Mr. Agnew's complaint against the editorial, entitled "Mr. Agnew's Fitness," involved only one sentence. "This is inaccurate," Mr. Willis declared.

Both Mr. Willis and George W. White Jr., Mr. Agnew's campaign manager, reiterated yesterday their demands for a "full retraction" of charges contained in the editorial, originally printed last Saturday. The editorial said that the Republican Vice-Presidential nominee had been involved in "clear and repeated conflicts of interest."

The editorial elicited from Richard M. Nixon, the Republican candidate for President, the comment that The Times's editors had resorted to "the lowest kind of gutter politics that a great newspaper could possibly engage in." Mr. Nixon made his remarks during a nationally televised interview Sunday night.

The editorial was reprinted as part of an editorial that appeared in yesterday's Times. In today's Times there is an editorial discussing a statement by Mr. Agnew replying to the original editorial and demanding a retraction.

Mr. Agnew's statement, which was made Monday night after the first edition of yesterday's Times had appeared, accused The Times of having "pulled the major blooper of the campaign" in the editorial, which declared that the Governor was "not fit to stand one step away from the Presidency."

In a speech last night in Staunton, Va., Mr. Agnew announced that he was sending Mr. White to New York today "to see if they are big enough at The Times to swallow their pride and accept their wrong."

"Newspapers expect politicians to admit their mistakes—and I'm ready and willing to admit mine—but some of them just can't stand to admit when they blunder and are caught in error," Governor Agnew declared to about 2,500 persons in Staunton's Robert E. Lee High School.

He continued:

"We all say a few things that need correction from time to time. The way you separate the men from the boys is when a man admits his mistakes, while a boy might try to find an easier way out. I say to the editorial board of The Times, 'Act with decency, act like men, act with intellectual honesty, let in the fresh air.'"

Mr. Agnew said two leading Democrats in Maryland "who are backing Hubert Humphrey for the Presidency came to my rescue today."

The reference was to John A. Leuktemeyer, State Treasurer, and Dale Anderson, Baltimore County Executive. Both issued statements earlier yesterday saying The Times was mistaken in its charges against Mr. Agnew.

Both Mr. White, representing Governor Agnew, and Mr. Willis, for the Nixon-Agnew Campaign Committee, were to resume today conferences with editors and lawyers of The Times.

Referring to the original editorial, Mr. Willis said that he had been "startled" to read in yesterday's Times "a report quoting me as saying that the sole factual point under challenge was a single sentence. This is inaccurate."

In a letter sent to The Times and released for publication by the Nixon-Agnew Campaign Committee, Mr. Willis said:

"I reiterate my request of yesterday for a full public retraction of the charges and refer you to the public statements of the facts issued by Gov. Agnew and Mr. [John N.] Mitchell."

Mr. Mitchell is Mr. Nixon's national campaign manager.

One of the charges in the original editorial was based on a news article printed in The Times Oct. 22. The article involved Mr. Agnew's election as a director of the Chesapeake National Bank in Towson, Md., in which the Governor also owns 400 shares of stock valued at about $11,000.

Mr. Agnew served as a director of the bank, an office he still holds as Governor, at the same time he was the elected county executive of suburban Baltimore County, which deposited funds in the bank.

In his detailed statement of rebuttal Monday, Mr. Agnew said that the Chesapeake National Bank "is a national bank and not a state bank." He said that at no time has he exercised any administrative control over the bank, either as county executive or Governor.

Mr. White's statement yesterday said that "a newspaper that can't tell the difference between a state bank and a national bank when the word 'national' is part of its name can't tell the difference between right and wrong."

The typewritten statement of Governor Agnew's campaign manager, Mr. White, who is also the candidate's personal lawyer, was distributed to newsmen yesterday on Mr. Agnew's chartered campaign plane, on the way from Houston, Tex., to appearances yesterday afternoon in South Carolina.

TEXT OF STATEMENT

The New York Times has again clearly demonstrated that it is guilty of 'gutter politics,' as charged by Richard Nixon, in reprinting its false and libelous editorial on Governor Agnew.

On Monday morning The Times stated it would investigate the matter and print a retraction if the facts proved it wrong. Instead, on Tuesday morning, it reprinted the libel. They have now published two separate and distinct libels.

A newspaper that can't tell the difference between a state bank and a national bank when "national" is part of its name can't tell the difference between right or wrong.

Every allegation it made against Governor Agnew is false and there is documentary proof to establish the falsity of its editorial.

The Times has become so powerful and arrogant that it thinks it can do as it pleases.

The republishing of the libel in today's paper establishes the malice in its action and its wanton, reckless disregard of the rights and reputations of others.

A newspaper is supposed to fairly and impartially report the news. The Times has violated this code of ethics and in its desire to elect its chosen candidate, Hubert Humphrey, has become an "advocate" and lost all sense of decency. There are a number of fine reporters with The Times. The fact that its editorial staff is so reckless must be a matter of great concern to these men.

October 30, 1968

Points in the Agnew-Times Dispute Are Clarified

Gov. Spiro T. Agnew of Maryland, the Republican nominee for Vice President, who criticized The New York Times in a statement this week for printing "distorted," "inaccurate" and allegedly "libelous" editorial comments about his fitness as a candidate, raised three substantial objections to the editorials.

Mr. Agnew's detailed criticism, and demand for a retraction, of the Times editorials was printed in late editions of the newspaper last Tuesday and in the first edition on Wednesday.

His statement contended that The Times, in editorials published on Oct. 26 and 29, falsely "charged or inferred" to him actions involving conflicts of interest between his official duties and his role as a private citizen.

Governor Agnew also said the editorials contained errors of fact. The editorials were based on a news article that appeared in The Times on Oct. 22. The Governor raised no complaint against the news article.

Demand Rejected

Executives of The Times and the editor of the editorial page rejected earlier this week the Governor's demand for a "full retraction" of the original editorial charge that Mr. Agnew had been involved in "clear and repeated conflicts of interest" as Governor of Maryland and the elected chief executive of suburban Baltimore County.

In a statement last Wednesday, George W. White Jr., Governor Agnew's campaign chief of staff and his personal lawyer, asserted that in a third editorial, printed that day, "The Times did indirectly admit . . . that Governor Agnew had not been guilty of any wrongdoing."

Mr. White said he had hoped that The Times would "have the honesty and courage" to acknowledge openly the editorial errors he alleged. Because of the newspaper's "arbitrary action" in rejecting his demand for a retraction, Mr. White declared, he will recommend that Mr. Agnew file a libel suit against The Times.

The Wednesday editorial that Mr. White criticized said that "nowhere in our [earlier] editorial comment did we accuse him [Mr. Agnew] of violating the law."

Governor Agnew has made no public comment on his at-torney's recommendation that he file a libel suit against The Times.

Issue of Bank Funds

Several points in the record of the dispute have remained unclear. What follows is a clarification of these points.

1. The editorial of Oct. 26 said that, as County Executive, Mr. Agnew had "voted to deposit county funds" in the Chesapeake National Bank of Towson, Md. He has disclosed in voluntary campaign financial statements that he owns 400 shares of stock in the bank valued at $11,000.

Mr. Agnew has been a director of the bank since it was chartered in January, 1964, during his term as County Executive.

The statement in the editorial that he had "voted" was erroneous. As County Executive, Mr. Agnew occupied a position analogous to that of a chief executive, with largely administrative powers. He had no vote on the Baltimore County Council, a legislative body.

The council by resolution on Feb. 3, 1964, authorized the deposit of county tax collections in the Chesapeake National Bank. Mr. Agnew was not empowered to vote on the resolution and did not vote.

The language of the resolution, approved at a public meeting, disclosed Mr. Agnew's connection with the bank and declared that "the interest of said County Executive in the aforesaid Chesapeake National Bank does not violate the public interest."

But Mr. Agnew's rebuttal statement printed by The Times asserts that "the selecting of banks and the amounts to be deposited are determined by the County Director of Finance (originally appointed by the previous Democratic administration). He will verify that I adopted his recommendations in entirety."

Powers of Director

Section 516 of the Baltimore County Charter says that "the Director of Finance shall have the following specific powers and duties: to deposit funds of the county in such banks or trust companies as the County Executive may designate subject to such adequate requirements as to security and interest as may be provided by law."

Thus, by law, Mr. Agnew was empowered to instruct the Di-rector of Finance as to which banks were to receive county funds.

The Director of Finance at the time of the 1964 resolution was Norman W. Wood. Mr. Wood served under the Democratic administration of Mr. Agnew's predecessor as County Executive, as Mr. Agnew stated in his rebuttal. He was reappointed by Mr. Agnew in 1963.

2. In his rebuttal statement, Governor Agnew also asserted that The Times's editorial "allegation that I approved the route by the Bay Bridge is untrue."

This concerns The Times's editorial comment on Mr. Agnew's role in a nine-man partnership that purchased a 106-acre tract in 1963 near the proposed approach road of a new, parallel span of the Chesapeake Bay Bridge at Annapolis. Two main issues are involved.

One is Mr. Agnew's contention that there could be no conflict of interest since he placed his share in the land for sale by disinterested trustees before he was elected Governor in 1966 and given administrative powers, at least indirectly, over the state road system. This was reported in a news article in The Times on Oct. 22.

Appointed by Agnew

"By law, the State Roads Commission is an autonomous body of the state and the commission and its chairman-director are the body empowered to select and determine all state road routes," Mr. Agnew declared in criticizing the Times editorials.

The present chairman-director of the State Roads Commission, Jerome Wolff, a Democrat who serves at the pleasure of the Governor, was appointed by Mr. Agnew after his inauguration as Governor in January, 1967. Mr. Wolff was an official of the Baltimore County Department of Public Works during Mr. Agnew's administration there as County Executive, and later became a private engineering consultant to the county.

After placing his share in the Bay Bridge land parcel in trust to be sold, Mr. Agnew voted as Governor on the approval of engineering and design con-tracts for the bridge approach road, still owned by seven of his friends and business associates in other ventures.

Records of the Board of Public Works show that Mr. Agnew joined with the two other board members on Oct. 12, 1967, in voting unanimous approval of design and engineering supervision contracts for the bridge approach roads.

His vote Oct. 12, 1967, was cast in a telephone poll of members of the Board of Public Works on the same day the Maryland National Bank, the trustee assigned to sell his one-ninth share in the land, announced a public auction of his share of the tract to be held Oct. 31, 1967. Mr. Agnew's share was then sold to the sole bidder, representing the remaining partners in the original venture. The only bid was $34,-200, exactly Mr. Agnew's purchase price.

Tract Rezoned

The tract was rezoned last summer by the zoning commissioner of Anne Arundel County from an agriculture classification to a light industrial classification, enhancing its value.

3. The Governor described as "untrue" a report both in the Times news article and in the Oct. 26 and 29 editorials that he had said in 1966 that he had inherited the Chesapeake National Bank stock from his father, who died in 1963. The bank was not chartered until 1964.

An article published in The Baltimore Sun in 1966 reported that Mr. Agnew, in disclosing his personal net worth, had told newsmen then that the stock was an inheritance from his father. The Governor's aides have since described the Sun account as "mistaken."

The files of The Baltimore Sun, however, include a published letter to the editor from Mr. Agnew dated July 14, 1966, in which he corrected and clarified another portion of the newspaper's report on his financial statement but did not challenge the same article's statement attributing to him the explanation that he had inherited the bank stock from his father.

In his rebuttal statement this week, Mr. Agnew said that he had inherited other securities from his father that he sold to pay for the bank stock, purchased by himself.

The Times Replies to Mr. Agnew's Advertisement

In an advertisement attacking The Times today, the forces behind Gov. Spiro T. Agnew carry to its climax in this campaign one of the oldest of political strategies: When criticized, deny everything, cry "Foul," capitalize on a posture of injured innocence and denounce your critic in the wildest terms. This is the course set by Mr. Nixon a week ago last Sunday when confronted with The Times editorial commenting on Mr. Agnew's involvement in conflict-of-interest situations in Maryland.

It is the course that has been followed since then by Mr. Agnew, who has sought to give the impression by means of a propaganda blitz that he is the innocent victim of a vicious and irresponsible newspaper attack.

Sequence of Events

After the editorial of Oct. 26, The Times had no intention of reverting to the question of Mr. Agnew's conflicts of interest, but Mr. Nixon's and Mr. Agnew's subsequent statements required replies, which were given editorially on Oct. 29 and 30. The renewed misrepresentations in today's advertisement now oblige us to discuss this distasteful subject once again. We enumerate below a few of these misrepresentations, followed by the facts.

Misrepresentation No. 1: The implication that Mr. Agnew, as Governor, had no beneficial interest in a tract of land whose value would be enhanced by a proposed Chesapeake Bay bridge route.

Fact: Although Mr. Agnew had, as he says, placed his interest in the land in trust before his election, it was actually sold, for the price he had paid for it, after he had become Governor and after he had helped push approval of the bridge route through the 1967 Legislature. The purchasers were his former associates in the original deal; and the land has subsequently been rezoned to the enhancement of its value and of their investment.

Misrepresentation No. 2: As Governor of Maryland, he has no authority over the route selection of state roads.

Fact: The present chairman-director of the State Roads Commission was appointed by Mr. Agnew and holds office at his pleasure. Records of the Board of Public Works show that Gov. Agnew joined with the two other board members on Oct. 12, 1967, in voting approval of the engineering and design contracts for the Bay Bridge approach road.

Misrepresentation No. 3: As County Executive Mr. Agnew had no responsibility for the deposit of county funds in the Chesapeake National Bank.

Fact: Section 516 of the Baltimore County Charter states that "the Director of Finance shall have the following specific powers and duties: to deposit funds of a county in such banks or trust companies as the County Executive may designate." The Times erred in stating that Mr. Agnew had "voted" to deposit the funds, but under the law he had ultimate responsibility for designation of the banks—whether or not he exercised it.

Denials Published

There are other statements in today's advertisement which we question, but the above examples are sufficient to demonstrate the misleading character of Mr. Agnew's denials, which have been fully published in The Times. For further detailed discussion, we refer our readers to the news story of Oct. 22 on which the original editorial was based, and to a follow-up news story of Nov. 2.

The Fundamental Issue

In his comments on a variety of subjects during this campaign, Spiro T. Agnew has amply proved his inadequacy for the high office to which he aspires. But he has proved it in no case more convincingly than in his attitude toward the conflict-of-interest situations in which he had involved himself in Maryland. The fundamental issue is not over the details of shades of meaning, or the omission of relevant facts; the fundamental issue is Mr. Agnew's apparent failure to comprehend the importance of the special standards of propriety that are rightly demanded of any holder of public office. It is his insensitivity to this problem of ethics of public servants that now stands revealed and reinforces our belief that he is a poor choice to be placed one step away from the Presidency of the United States.

Agnew Says TV Networks Are Distorting the News

Accuses Some Commentators of Bias and Calls on Viewers to Complain— Criticizes Harriman's Paris Role

By E. W. KENWORTHY
Special to The New York Times

WASHINGTON, Nov. 13—Vice President Agnew accused the television networks tonight of permitting producers of news programs, newscasters and commentators to give the American people a highly selected and often biased presentation of the news.

In a speech released here and delivered in Des Moines, Iowa, before the Mid-West Regional Republican Committee, the Vice President called upon the American people to "let the networks know that they want their news straight and objective."

Mr. Agnew urged television viewers to register "their complaints" by writing to the networks and phoning to local stations.

Thousands of Americans immediately responded to the Vice President's invitation by calling the networks and many newspapers and venting their views on the media's handling of the news.

The Vice President's speech was vigorously defended and denounced. In some cities, such as Dallas, television stations reported that most callers supported Mr. Agnew's views. In other cities, such as New York, the reaction was more mixed.

In addition to attacking the networks, the Vice President also denounced the Johnson Administration and W. Averell Harriman, the former United States peace negotiator in Paris, for the "concessions" that he asserted had been made to the North Vietnamese.

During the 10 months that Mr. Harriman was chief negotiator, Mr. Agnew said, "the United States swapped some of the greatest military concessions in the history of warfare for an enemy agreement on the shape of a bargaining table."

Mr. Agnew did not say what the "concessions" were.

Negotiations over the shape of the table took place after the end of the bombings of North Vietnam, Nov. 1, 1968, and were completed in mid-January.

The Vice President's press secretary, Herbert Thompson, said that he did not know what concessions the Vice President had in mind. He contended that Mr. Agnew would not have made the statement without substantive information to back up his charges.

Mr. Agnew said that Mr. Harriman, who had commented on the President's Vietnam speech two weeks ago over the American Broadcasting Company's network, was apparently under "heavy compulsion to justify his failures to anyone who will listen," and "the networks have shown themselves willing to give him all the time he desires."

At the conclusion of his speech, Mr. Agnew seemed to challenge the networks to carry his speech nationally. He said that every elected leader depended on the television media and yet "whether what I have said to you tonight will be heard and seen at all by the nation is not my decision, it is not your decision, it is their decision."

The three networks accepted the challenge. They all carried the speech live. In New York their regular news programs moved up to clear time for Mr. Agnew's address.

In an interview in the current U.S. News & World Report, Mr. Agnew sharply criticized the press, saying that he sometimes thought those writing for the papers, especially the "big-city liberal media, were "about the most superficial thinkers I've ever seen."

In his Des Moines speech, Mr. Agnew said that the American people would be right in refusing to tolerate in Government the kind of concentration of power that had been allowed in the hands "of a tiny and closed fraternity of privileged men, elected by no one, and enjoying a monopoly sanctioned and licensed by Government."

As a particularly flagrant

example of what he called the biased reporting of "self-appointed analysts," the Vice President cited the treatment of the President's speech on Vietnam two weeks ago.

Most of the commentators, he said, expressed "in one way or another, their hostility to what he had to say," and "it was obvious that their minds were made up in advance."

Expanding his criticism to cover also the producers of the programs, the Vice President said:

"To guarantee in advance that the President's plea for national unity would be challenged, one network trotted out Averell Harriman for the occasion."

"When the President concluded," Mr. Agnew went on, "Mr. Harriman recited perfectly. He attacked the Thieu Government as unrepresentative; he criticized the President's speech for various deficiencies; he twice issued a call for the Senate Foreign Relations Committee to debate Vietnam once again; he stated his belief that the Vietcong or North Vietnamese did not really want a military takeover of South Vietnam . . ."

"Every American," Mr. Agnew declared, "has a right to disagree with the President of the United States, and to express publicly that disagreement. But the President of the United States has a right to communicate directly with the people who elected him, and the people of this country have the right to make up their own minds and form their own opinions about a Presidential address without having the President's words and thoughts characterized through the prejudices of hostile critics before they can even be digested."

In recent weeks Mr. Agnew has drawn both criticism and praise for the pungency of his language as he has characterized Vietnam war critics as "an effete corps of impudent snobs" and demonstrations against the war as "a carnival in the streets."

There has been much speculation here on whether the President has encouraged, or at least not disapproved, the Vice President's recent speeches.

There were some who thought that the President was encouraging Mr. Agnew to play the "point of the spear," as Mr.

Nixon did in the early years of the Eisenhower Administration.

There were others who believed that Mr. Agnew was acting on his own.

But there seemed little question that in his attack on the networks Mr. Agnew was expressing the resentments of the White House. Several White House officials have made no secret of their anger at the way at least one network handled the commentary after the President's speech.

Gerald Warren, the assistant White House press secretary, said that neither the President nor the press office had seen the text of Mr. Agnew's speech. Mr. Warren said that there would be no immediate comment from the White House.

Asked for comment tonight on Mr. Agnew's criticism of him, Mr. Harriman said:

"I don't think that the statement deserves serious comment. All I can say is that I'm glad to be included with the television news media, which I feel, by and large are trying to do a conscientious job of keeping the American public informed on many subjects of national interest."

An examination of what Mr. Harriman said as a guest commentator for A.B.C. suggests that he was not explicitly critical of the President.

He began by saying, "I'm sure you know that I wouldn't be [so] presumptuous [as] to give a complete analysis of a very carefully thought-out speech by the President of the United States. I'm sure he wants to end this war and no one wishes him well any more than I do."

Not Seeking Censorship

Mr. Harriman went on to say that his approach to the problem differed in some ways from that of the President, and gave his reasons. But he concluded by saying: "There are so many things we've got to know about this, but I want to end this by saying I wish the President well, I hope he can lead us to peace. But this is not the whole story that we've heard tonight."

Mr. Agnew said that he was not asking for Government censorship of the networks. He was, he said, simply asking whether the commentators themselves were not censoring

the news.

"The views of this fraternity," he said, "do not represent the views of America. That is why such a great gulf existed between how the nation received the President's address – and how the networks reviewed it."

While not proposing censorship of television commentary, Mr. Agnew seemed to suggest that the networks had not the same claim to First Amendment rights as the newspapers.

The situations were not identical, Mr. Agnew said, because television has more impact than the printed page, and because the networks have a near monopoly and the viewers have little selection, whereas a man who does not like a newspaper's views or news handling can switch to another paper.

The Public Responds

By JOSEPH P. FRIED

Thousands of Americans accepted last night Vice President Agnew's invitation to express their views on the television networks' handling of the news.

In phone calls to the networks and to many newspapers that began just after the Vice President's speech was broadcast, Mr. Agnew's remarks were both defended and denounced.

In some cities, such as Dallas, most callers supported Mr. Agnew's views, according to The Associated Press. In New York and other cities, the reaction appeared to be more mixed.

But there was no doubt, from the emotional response on both sides , that Mr. Agnew had touched a sensitive nerve in the American people.

Mary Procter, a Brooklyn clerk, said in a phone call to The New York Times:

"I'm heartily in favor of everything that he said.

"I think the entire speech exactly the way it should have been and I'm neither a Bircher or a right winger—I just want to be a good American."

Sidney Unger of New Rochelle, president of the Kord Manufacturing Company in the Bronx, said in a call to The

Times:

"I was horrified by the Agnew speech. It reminded me of speeches of Hitler before he got into power and he was brainwashing the German people against opinions that were against him." '

'I'm No Kook'

Another pro-Agnew statement came from a caller who identified himself as Joseph Ercolano of Ozone Park in Queens.

"I'm no kook," he said. "I'm against the war and for the moratorium. But I do not believe there is a broad representative viewpoint either in the newspapers or on TV. There is only the extreme right of The Daily News and the extreme left of The Times and The Post."

Another anti-Agnew response was voiced by a caller who identified herself as Mrs. Milton Jucovy of Great Neck. "I'm terribly distressed at the speech and frightened," she said. "It seems that totalitarian government is taking over here.

Generally, pro-Agnew callers lauded the Vice President for speaking out against what they described as slanted news by a small group of broadcasters and newspaper writers who, the callers contended, did not represent the true views of most Americans.

And many critics of the Vice President asserted that his views were more suited to an official of a dictatorship that would control broadcasters than to a leader of democracy.

About 40 calls came to The Times in the three hours after Mr. Agnew's speech was broadcast. About half supported him and half opposed him.

The National Broadcasting Company reported that, in the first hour after the broadcast of the speech ended here, it had received 614 calls favoring Mr. Agnew's views and 554 opposing them.

Both the American Broadcasting Company and the Columbia Broadcasting System reported receiving hundreds of calls at their New York offices after the broadcast of the speech, but said they had no immediate tally on the number for and against the Vice President.

Transcript of Address by Agnew Criticizing Television on Its Coverage of the News

Following is a transcript of an address last night by Vice President Agnew to the Mid-West Regional Republican Committee at Des Moines, Iowa, as recorded by The New York Times:

Tonight I want to discuss the importance of the television news medium to the American people. No nation depends more on the intelligent judgment of its citizens. No medium has a more profound influence over public opinion. Nowhere in our system are there fewer checks on vast power. So, nowhere should there be more conscientious responsibility exercised than by the news media. The question is, Are we demanding enough of our television news presentations? And are the men of this medium demanding enough of themselves?

Monday night a week ago, President Nixon delivered the most important address of his Administration, one of the most important of our decade. His subject was Vietnam. His hope was to rally the American people to see the conflict through to a lasting and just peace in the Pacific. For 32 minutes, he reasoned with a nation that has suffered almost a third of a million casualties in the longest war in its history.

Weeks of Preparation

When the President completed his address — an address, incidentally, that he spent weeks in the preparation of— his words and policies were subjected to instant analysis and querulous criticism. The audience of 70 million Americans gathered to hear the President of the United States was inherited by a small band of network commentators and self-appointed analysts, the majority of whom expressed in one way or another their hostility to what he had to say.

It was obvious that their minds were made up in advance. Those who recall the fumbling and groping that followed President Johnson's dramatic disclosure of his intention not to seek another term have seen these men in a genuine state of nonpreparedness. This was not it.

One commentator twice contradicted the President's statement about the exchange of correspondence with Ho Chi Minh. Another challenged the President's abilities as a politician. A third asserted that the President was following a Pentagon line. Others, by the expression on

United Press International

ASSAILS NETWORKS: Vice President Agnew before Mid-West Regional Republican Committee in Des Moines, Iowa.

their faces, the tone of their questions and the sarcasm of their responses, made clear their sharp diapproval.

About Mr. Harriman

To guarantee in advance that the President's plea for national unity would be challenged, one network trotted out Averell Harriman for the occasion. Throughout the President's message, he waited in the wings. When the President concluded, Mr. Harriman recited perfectly. He attacked the Thieu Government as unrepresentative; he criticized the President's speech for various deficiencies; he twice issued a call to the Senate Foreign Relations Committee to debate Vietnam once again; he stated his belief that the Vietcong or North Vietnamese did not really want a military takeover of South Vietnam; and he told a little anecdote about a "very, very responsible" fellow he had met in the North Vietnamese delegation.

All in all, Mr. Harriman offered a broad range of gratuitous advice challenging and contradicting the policies outlined by the President of the United States. Where the President had issued a call for unity, Mr. Harriman was encouraging the country not to listen to him.

A word about Mr. Harriman. For 10 months he was America's chief negotiator at the Paris peace talks—a period in which the United States swapped some of the greatest military concessions in the history of warfare for an enemy agreement on the shape of the bargaining table. Like Coleridge's Ancient Mariner, Mr. Harriman seems to be under some heavy compulsion to justify his failure to anyone who will listen. And the networks have shown themselves willing to give him all the air time he desires.

Now every American has a right to disagree with the President of the United States and to express publicly that disagreement. But the President of the United States has a right to communicate directly with the people who

elected him, and the people of this country have the right to make up their own minds and form their own opinions about a Presidential address without having a President's words and thoughts characterized through the prejudices of hostile critics before they can even be digested.

When Winston Churchill rallied public opinion to stay the course against Hitler's Germany, he didn't have to contend with a gaggle of commentators raising doubts about whether he was reading public opinion right, or whether Britain had the stamina to see the war through.

Sole Source of News

When President Kennedy rallied the nation in the Cuban missile crisis, his address to the people was not chewed over by a roundtable of critics who disparaged the course of action he'd asked America to follow.

The purpose of my remarks tonight is to focus your attention on this little group of men who not only enjoy a right of instant rebuttal to every Presidential address, but, more importantly, wield a free hand in selecting, presenting and interpreting the great issues in our nation.

First, let's define that power. At least 40 million Americans every night, it's estimated, watch the network news. Seven million of them view A.B.C., the remainder being divided between N.B.C. and C.B.S.

According to Harris polls and other studies, for millions of Americans the networks are the sole source of national and world news. In Will Rogers's observation, what you knew was what you read in the newspaper. Today for growing millions of Americans, it's what they see and hear on their television sets.

Now how is this network news determined? A small group of men, numbering perhaps no more than a dozen anchormen, commentators and executive producers, settle upon the 20 minutes or so of film and commentary that's to reach the public. This selection is made from the 90 to 180 minutes that may be available. Their powers of choice are broad.

They decide what 40 to 50 million Americans will learn of the day's events in the nation and in the world.

We cannot measure this

power and influence by the traditional democratic standards, for these men can create national issues overnight.

They can make or break by their coverage and commentary a moratorium on the war.

They can elevate men from obscurity to national prominence within a week. They can reward some politicians with national exposure and ignore others.

For millions of Americans the network reporter who covers a continuing issue—like the ABM or civil rights—becomes, in effect, the presiding judge in a national trial by jury.

It must be recognized that the networks have made important contributions to the national knowledge — for news, documentaries and specials. They have often used their power constructively and creatively to awaken the public conscience to critical problems. The networks made hunger and black lung disease national issues overnight. The TV networks have done what no other medium could have done in terms of dramatizing the horrors of war. The networks have tackled our most difficult social problems with a directness and an immediacy that's the gift of their medium. They focus the nation's attention on its environmental abuses—on pollution in the Great Lakes and the threatened ecology of the Everglades.

But it was also the networks that elevated Stokely Carmichael and George Lincoln Rockwell from obscurity to national prominence.

Nor is their power confined to the substantive. A raised eyebrow, an inflection of the voice, a caustic remark dropped in the middle of a broadcast can raise doubts in a million minds about the veracity of a public official or the wisdom of a Government policy.

One Federal Communications Commissioner considers the powers of the networks equal to that of local state and Federal Governments all combined. Certainly it represents a concentration of power over American public opinion unknown in history.

Now what do Americans know of the men who wield this power? Of the men who produce and direct the network news, the nation knows practically nothing. Of the commentators, most Americans know little other than that they reflect an urbane and assured presence seemingly well-informed on every important matter.

We do know that to a man these commentators and producers live and work in the geographical and intellectual confines of Washington, D.C., or New York City, the latter of which James Reston terms

the most unrepresentative community in the entire United States.

Provincialism Charged

Both communities bask in their own provincialism, their own parochialism.

We can deduce that these men read the same newspapers. They draw their political and social views from the same sources. Worse, they talk constantly to one another, thereby providing artificial reinforcement to their shared viewpoints.

Do they allow their biases to influence the selection and presentation of the news? David Brinkley states objectivity is impossible to normal human behavior. Rather, he says, we should strive for fairness.

Another anchorman on a network news show contends, and I quote: "You can't expunge all your private convictions just because you sit in a seat like this and a camera starts to stare at you. I think your program has to reflect what your basic feelings are. I'll plead guilty to that."

Less than a week before the 1968 election, this same commentator charged that President Nixon's campaign commitments were no more durable than campaign balloons. He claimed that, were it not for the fear of hostile reaction, Richard Nixon would be giving into, and I quote him exactly, "his natural instinct to smash the enemy with a club or go after him with a meat axe."

Had this slander been made by one political candidate about another, it would have been dismissed by most commentators as a partisan attack. But this attack emanated from the privileged sanctuary of a network studio and therefore had the apparent dignity of an objective statement.

The American people would rightly not tolerate this concentration of power in Government.

Fair and Relevant

Is it not fair and relevant to question its concentration in the hands of a tiny, enclosed fraternity of privileged men elected by no one and enjoying a monopoly sanctioned and licensed by Government?

The views of the majority of this fraternity do not—and I repeat, not—represent the views of America.

That is why such a great gulf existed between how the nation received the President's address and how the networks reviewed it.

Not only did the country receive the President's address more warmly than the networks, but so also did the Congress of the United States.

Yesterday, the President was notified that 300 individual Congressmen and 50 Senators of both parties had endorsed his efforts for peace.

As with other American institutions, perhaps it is time that the networks were made more responsive to the views of the nation and more responsible to the people they serve.

Now I want to make myself perfectly clear. I'm not asking for Government censorship or any other kind of censorship. I'm asking whether a form of censorship already exists when the news that 40 million Americans receive each night is determined by a handful of men responsible only to their corporate employers and is filtered through a handful of commentators who admit to their own set of biases.

The questions I'm raising here tonight should have been raised by others long ago. They should have been raised by those Americans who have traditionally considered the preservation of freedom of speech and freedom of the press their special provinces of responsibility.

They should have been raised by those Americans who share the view of the late Justice Learned Hand that right conclusions are more likely to be gathered out of a multitude of tongues than through any kind of authoritative selection.

Advocates for the networks have claimed a First Amendment right to the same unlimited freedoms held by the great newspapers of America.

Situations Not Identical

But the situations are not identical. Where The New York Times reaches 800,000 people, N.B.C. reaches 20 times that number on its evening news. [The average weekday circulation of The Times in October was 1,012,-367; the average Sunday circulation was 1,523,558.] Nor can the tremendous impact of seeing television film and hearing commentary be compared with reading the printed page.

A decade ago, before the network news acquired such dominance over public opinion, Walter Lippman spoke to the issue. He said there's an essential and radical difference between television and printing. The three or four competing television stations control virtually all that can be received over the air by ordinary television sets. But besides the mass circulation dailies, there are weeklies, monthlies, out-of-town newspapers and books. If a man doesn't like his newspaper, he can read another from

House Report Cited

The newspapers of mass out of town or wait for a

weekly news magazine. It's not ideal, but it's infinitely better than the situation in television.

There if a man doesn't like what the networks are showing, all he can do is turn them off and listen to a phonograph. Networks he stated which are few in number have a virtual monopoly of a whole media of communications.

circulation have no monopoly on the medium of print.

Now a virtual monopoly of a whole medium of communication is not something that democratic people should blindly ignore. And we are not going to cut off our television sets and listen to the phonograph just because the airways belong to the networks. They don't. They belong to the people.

As Justice Byron White wrote in his landmark opinion six months ago, it's the right of the viewers and listeners, not the right of the broadcasters, which is paramount.

Now it's argued that this power presents no danger in the hands of those who have used it responsibly. But, as to whether or not the networks have abused the power they enjoy, let us call as our first witness former Vice President Humphrey and the city of Chicago. According to Theodore White, television's intercutting of the film from the streets of Chicago with the current proceedings on the floor of the convention created the most striking and false political picture of 1968—the nomination of a man for the American Presidency by the brutality and violence of merciless police.

If we are to believe a recent report of the House of Representatives Commerce Committee, then television's presentation of the violence in the streets worked an injustice on the reputation of the Chicago police. According to the committee findings, one network in particular presented, and I quote, "a one-sided picture which in large measure exonerates the demonstrators and protesters." Film of provocations of police that was available never saw the light of day while the film of a police response which the protesters provoked was shown to millions.

Another network showed virtually the same scene of violence from three separate angles without making clear it was the same scene. And, while the full report is reticent in drawing conclusions, it is not a document to inspire confidence in the fairness of the network news.

Serious Questions Raised

Our knowledge of the impact of network news on the national mind is far from complete, but some early returns are available. Again, we have enough information to raise serious questions about its effect on a democratic society. Several years ago Fred Friendly, one of the pioneers of network news, wrote that its missing ingredients were conviction, controversy and a point of view. The networks have compensated with a vengeance.

And in the networks' endless pursuit of controversy, we should ask: What is the end value — to enlighten or to profit? What is the end result — to inform or to confuse? How does the ongoing exploration for more action, more excitement, more drama serve our national search for internal peace and stability.

Gresham's Law seems to be operating in the network news. Bad news drives out good news. The irrational is more controversial than the rational. Concurrence can no longer compete with dissent.

One minute of Eldridge Cleaver is worth 10 minutes of Roy Wilkins. The labor crisis settled at the negotiating table is nothing compared to the confrontation that results in a strike — or better yet, violence along the picket lines.

Normality has become the nemesis of the network news. Now the upshot of all this controversy is that a narrow and distorted picture of America often emerges from the televised news.

A single, dramatic piece of the mosaic becomes in the minds of millions the entire picture. And the American who relies upon television for his news might conclude that the majority of American students are embittered radicals. That the majority of black Americans feel no regard for their country. That violence and lawlessness are the rule rather than the exception on the American campus.

We know that none of these conclusions is true.

Perhaps the place to start looking for a credibility gap is not in the offices of the Government in Washington but in the studios of the networks in New York.

Quiet Men Less Known

Television may have destroyed the old stereotypes, but has it not created new ones in their places?

What has this passionate pursuit of controversy done to the politics of progress through local compromise essential to the functioning of a democratic society?

The members of Congress or the Senate who follow their principles and philosophy quietly in a spirit of compromise are unknown to many Americans, while the loudest and most extreme dissenters on every issue are

TV Networks' Response to Agnew

Following are statements by the presidents of the three major television networks regarding Vice President Agnew's criticism of TV news coverage:

A. B. C.

Leonard H. Goldenson

In our judgment, the performance of A.B.C. news has always been and will continue to be fair and objective. In the final analysis, it is always the public who decides on the reliability of any individual or organization. We will continue to report the news accurately and fully, confident in the ultimate judgment of the American public.

C. B. S.

Dr. Frank Stanton

No American institution, including network news organizations, should be immune to public criticism or to public discussion of its performance. In a democracy this is entirely proper. We do not believe,

however, that this unprecedented attempt by the Vice President of the United States to intimidate a news medium which depends for its existence upon Government licenses represents legitimate criticism. The public, according to opinion polls, has indicated again and again that it has more confidence in the credibility of television news than in that of any other news medium.

Our newsmen have many times earned commendations for their enterprise and for their adherence to the highest professional standards. Since human beings are not infallible, there are bound to be occasions when their judgment is questioned.

Whatever their deficiencies, they are minor compared to those of a press which would be subservient to the executive power of Government.

N. B. C.

Julian Goodman

Vice President Agnew's at-

tack on television news is an appeal to prejudice. More importantly, Mr. Agnew uses the influence of his high office to criticize the way a Government-licensed news medium covers the activities of Government itself. Any fair-minded viewer knows that the television networks are not devoted to putting across a single point of view but present all significant views on issues of importance.

It is regrettable that the Vice President of the United States would deny to television freedom of the press.

Evidently, he would prefer a different kind of television reporting—one that would be subservient to whatever political group was in authority at the time.

Those who might feel momentary agreement with his remarks should think carefully whether that kind of television news is what they want.

known to every man in the street.

How many marches and demonstrations would we have if the marchers did not know that the ever-faithful TV cameras would be there to record their antics for the next news show?

We've heard demands that Senators and Congressmen and judges make known all their financial conections so that the public will know who and what influences their decisions and their votes. Strong arguments can be made for that view.

But when a single commentator or producer, night after night, determines for millions of people how much of each side of a great issue they are going to see and hear, should he not first disclose his personal views on the issue as well?

In this search for excitement and controversy, has more than equal time gone to the minority of Americans who specialize in attacking the United States—its institutions and its citizens?

Tonight I've raised questions. I've made no attempt to suggest the answers. The answers must come from the media men. They are challenged to turn their critical powers on themselves, to direct their energy, their talent and their conviction toward improving the quality and objectivity of news presentation.

They are challenged to structure their own civic ethics to relate their great sponsibilities they hold.

And the people of America are challenged, too, challenged to press for responsible news presentations. The people can let the networks know that they want their news straight and objective. The people can register their complaints on bias through mail to the networks and phone calls to local stations. This is one case where the people must defend themselves; where the citizen, not the Government, must be the reformer; where the consumer can be the most effective crusader.

By way of conclusion, let me say that every elected leader in the United States depends on these men of the media. Whether what I've said to you tonight will be heard and seen at all by the nation is not my decision, it's not your decision, it's their decision.

In tomorrow's edition of The Des Moines Register, you'll be able to read a news story detailing what I've said tonight. Editorial comment will be reserved for the editorial page, where it belongs. Should not the same wall of separation exist between news and comment on the nation's networks?

Now, my friends, we'd never trust such power, as I've described, over public opinion in the hands of an elected Government. It's time we questioned it in the hands of a small and unelected elite.

The great networks have dominated America's airwaves for decades. The people are entitled to a full accounting of their stewardship. November 14, 1969

KENNEDY CRITICIZES SPEECH AS DIVISIVE

WASHINGTON, Nov. 13 (UPI) —Senator Edward M. Kennedy, Democrat of Massachusetts, said today that Vice President Agnew's speech criticizing television news operations was "an attack designed to pit American against American."

In a statement, the Senate Democratic whip said Mr. Agnew's Des Moines speech constituted "an attack with the ultimate aim of dividing this country into those who support and those who do not support our President's position in Vietnam."

"If it is allowed to go on," Senator Kennedy said, "this will be tragic. Our nation has passed through such a period of recrimination before with much hurt and much regret."

The Senator took strong issue with Vice President Agnew's remarks about former Ambassador W. Averell Harriman, who negotiated with the North Vietnamese in Paris under the Johnson Administration.

"Any man aware of Ambassador Harriman's service to America cannot remain silent while he is made the subject of thoughtless remarks," Senator Kennedy said.

November 14, 1969

3 Networks Reply To Agnew Attack

By PAUL L. MONTGOMERY

The television networks reacted quickly and sharply last night to Vice President Agnew's assertions that their news coverage of national policy on the Vietnam war and other sensitive matters was parochial, biased and monopolistic.

The presidents of the three major networks, who received advance texts of the Vice President's address early in the afternoon, all issued answering statements before they broadcast Mr. Agnew's discourse.

"It is regrettable that the Vice President of the United States would deny to television freedom of the press," said Julian Goodman, president of the National Broadcasting Company.

"Evidently," Mr. Goodman said, "he would prefer a different kind of television reporting—one that would be subservient to whatever political group was in authority at the time."

Dr. Frank Stanton, president of the Columbia Broadcasting System, said that Mr. Agnew had made "an unprecedented attempt to intimidate a news medium." Dr. Stanton noted that a broadcasting station needed a license issued by the Federal Government in order to function.

"The performance of A.B.C. News has always been, and will continue to be, fair and objective," said Leonard H. Goldenson, president of the American Broadcasting Companies. "We will continue to report the news accurately and fully, confident in the ultimate judgment of the American public."

C.B.S. broadcast the statements of all three network officials as an addendum to Mr. Agnew's attack. N.B.C. issued its statement to the press and also broadcast it on its 11 P.M. news show. A.B.C., whose statement was by far the mildest of the three, issued a press release, which was not broadcast.

Part of Mr. Agnew's attack against television news was that network commentators enjoyed the privilege of "instant rebuttal" to speeches their stations carried.

Steve McCormick, vice president of the Mutual Broadcasting Company, a radio network, disagreed with his television colleagues. He said that he "heartily endorsed" what he said was Mr. Agnew's "call for fairness, balance responsibility and accuracy in news presentation.

The Vice President's criticisms also drew response from groups connected with broadcasting.

"Agnew's disgraceful attack tonight against network television news officially leads us as a nation into an ugly era of the most fearsome suppression and intimidation," said Thomas P. F. Hoving, chairman of the National Citizens Committee for Broadcasting.

"Should the people believe Agnew's ignorant, base attack on the only regularly worthwhile arm of American broadcasting, it is the beginning of the end for us as a nation," Mr. Hoving went on. "Agnew's terrible and fraudulent evaluation is the most shocking use ever of political power against all of the people whom he and his running mates were ostensibly elected to serve last November."

Victor Wasilewski, president of the National Association of Broadcasters, said "All broadcasters become concerned when any high Government official singles out for censure news policies, procedures or conduct with which he disagrees."

J. W. Roberts, president of the Radio, Television News Directors Association, said that his group "cannot accept the concept of managed news advocated by the Vice President tonight." He declared, "Broadcast journalists are not and will not be a propaganda agency for any Government's policies or for any Government officials."

In his address, Mr. Agnew noted the power of selection exercised by the networks. "Whether what I've said to you tonight will be heard and seen at all by the nation is not my decision, it's not your decision, it's their decision."

Spokesmen for the networks, discussing their decision, said they had had no trouble determining that the Vice President's address was a newsworthy event that should be broadcast live. Arrangements were made in Des Moines to pick up the speech and stations were advised three hours in advance that it was available.

The Public Responds
By JOSEPH P. FRIED

Thousands of Americans accepted last night Vice President Agnew's invitation to express their views on the television networks' handling of the news.

In phone calls to the networks and to many newspapers that began just after the Vice President's speech was broadcast, Mr. Agnew's remarks were both defended and denounced.

In some cities, such as Dallas, most callers supported Mr. Agnew's views, according to The Associated Press. In New York and other cities, the reaction appeared to be more mixed.

But there was no doubt, from the emotional response on both sides, that Mr. Agnew had touched a sensitive nerve in the American people.

Mary Procter, a Brooklyn clerk, said in a phone call to The New York Times:

"I'm heartily in favor of everything that he said.

"I think the entire speech exactly the way it should have been and I'm neither a Bircher or a right winger—I just want to be a good American."

Sidney Unger of New Rochelle, president of the Kord Manufacturing Company in the Bronx, said in a call to The Times:

"I was horrified by the Agnew speech. It reminded me of speeches of Hitler before he got into power and he was brainwashing the German people against opinions that were against him."

Another pro-Agnew statement came from a caller who identified himself as Joseph Ercolano of Ozone Park in Queens.

"I'm no kook," he said. "I'm against the war and for the moratorium. But I do not believe there is a broad representative viewpoint either in the newspapers or on TV. There is only the extreme right of The Daily News and the extreme left of The Times and The Post.

Another anti-Agnew response was voiced by a caller who identified herself as Mrs. Milton Jucovy of Great Neck. "I'm terribly distressed at the speech and frightened," she said. "It seems that totalitarian government is taking over here."

Generally, pro-Agnew callers lauded the Vice President for speaking out against what they described as slanted news by a small group of broadcasters and newspaper writers who, the callers contended, did not represent the true views of most Americans.

And many critics of the Vice President asserted that his views were more suited to an official of a dictatorship that would control broadcasters than to a leader of democracy.

About 40 calls came to The Times in the three hours after Mr. Agnew's speech was broadcast. About half supported him and half opposed him.

The National Broadcasting Company reported that, in the first hour after the broadcast of the speech ended here, it had received 614 calls favoring Mr. Agnew's views and 554 opposing them.

Both the American Broadcasting Company and the Columbia Broadcasting System reported receiving hundreds of calls at their New York offices after the broadcast of the speech, but said they had no immediate tally or the number for and against the Vice President.

Nixon Aide Says Agnew Stand Reflects White House TV View

By E. W. KENWORTHY
Special to The New York Times

WASHINGTON, Nov. 15—Vice President Agnew's speech charging the television networks with biased news reporting "reflected the views of the Administration," Clark R. Mollenhoff, special counsel to President Nixon, said today.

Controversy meanwhile, continued to swirl over the Vice President's remarks, both in the United States and abroad. Six former Government officials and 11 law school deans signed a statement expressing alarm over the "inflammatory" remarks attributed to Mr. Agnew and other high officials.

Mr. Mollenhoff said there had been discussion within the White House staff "for a long time" about the way network reporters and news commentators had dealt with various issues.

Mr. Mollenhoff was responding to questions about a Washington dispatch in today's issues of The Des Moines Register, for which Mr. Mollenhoff worked before he joined the President's staff. In the dispatch, Nick Kotz wrote that Mr. Mollenhoff had told him in an interview that the Vice President's speech "was developed by various White House aides."

At another point, Mr. Kotz wrote that Mr. Mollenhoff said the Agnew speech "was developed in the White House" and represented the Administration's concern "that it is not being fairly treated by the news media."

Asked about this statement today, Mr. Mollenhoff said, "If you are asking me, 'does it reflect the Administration's views,' the evidence is abundant that it does."

That the Administration has felt that it had problems with television reporting and commentaries, Mr. Mollenhoff said, is obvious from the fact that he himself in recent speeches in Iowa had pointed out "false allegations" by the press of "impropriety and unethical conduct" by Judge Clement R. Haynsworth, the President's nominee for Supreme Court Justice.

Mr. Mollenhoff said also that it was obvious from the Vice President's speech that other areas where the Administration believed there had been distortions of its position included the antiballistic missile program, Vietnam policy and the peace demonstrations.

However, Mr. Mollenhoff said that he had no knowledge that the Vice President's speech had actually been written by the President's own speechwriters, or other staff aides.

"I can say that I did not work on the speech that Mr. Agnew gave," he said.

Herbert Klein, the President's Director of Communications, said in another telephone interview that he believed the speech was "an Agnew staff production," and that it was probably written by Cynthia Rosenwald, Mr. Agnew's regular speechwriter, and that the Vice President had also done some of the writing.

In still another telephone interview, Ronald L. Ziegler said, "The President didn't discuss this subject with the Vice President."

Mr. Ziegler also said. "The President has great confidence in his Vice President and he supports his Vice President in the office." But he added, the President thought the Vice President had expressed himself "with great candor."

In November, 1962, after he had been defeated for Governor of California, Mr. Nixon gave a news conference in which he complained bitterly of the unfairness with which he believed the newspapers had treated him.

At that time he said: "I think that it's time that our great newspapers have at least the same objectivity, the same fulness of coverage, that television has. And I can only say thank God for television and radio for keeping the newspapers a little more honest."

There is a feeling among some members of Congress that Mr. Agnew would have not stirred up such a storm if he had simply raised the question whether the networks, with all their power to influence opinion, were keeping a critical eye on their news reports and commentaries.

Where Mr. Agnew went astray and aroused fears, these critics believe, was in putting his criticism in political context.

What these critics took exception to was Mr. Agnew's statements that "the views of this fraternity do not represent the views of America," and "perhaps it is time that the networks were made more responsive to the views of the nation and to the people they serve."

Mr. Mollenhoff, a former Washington reporter for The Des Moines Register, said both he and Herbert Klein, the President's director of communications, had made similar criticisms of the news media, but that the Agnew speech "was the most direct confrontation" by the Nixon Administration.

Mr. Mollenhoff's statement that the White House was responsible for the speech differed from the view presented by the White House press secretary, Ronald Ziegler.

Mr. Ziegler said Mr. Nixon had not discussed the speech with the Vice President, but that the President thought Mr. Agnew had expressed himself "with great candor."

"The Vice President is entitled to express his own views," Mr. Ziegler said.

November 16, 1969

Dispute Over Agnew's Speech Keeps On Boiling

By THOMAS F. BRADY

Controversy over Vice President Agnew's attack on television news reporting and analysis continued to echo across the nation yesterday.

The American Civil Liberties Union said that Mr. Agnew had voiced a "clear and chilling threat" of censorship.

John de V. Pemberton Jr., the union's executive director, sent a telegram to the Vice President saying that the First Amendment ensured his right to rebut television commentators just as it protected their right to criticize the Nixon Administration.

"But," Mr. Pemberton said, "by joining your reaction to the commentators' criticism with the demand that 'the networks be made more responsive to the views of the nation' you have made a clear and chilling threat of Government measures

to penalize those criticisms. That threat is inherently a threat of censorshhip."

'Audiences Are Earned'

Mr. Pemberton denied that the networks' choice of commentators was an exercise of arbitrary power by television executives, as Mr. Agnew contended. Commentators, like news columnists, "must earn their audiences," Mr. Pemberton said.

The national convention of Sigma Delta Chi, the journalistic society, in San Diego, passed a resolution yesterday rejecting "any effort" by Mr. Agnew or other Government officials to "control or impede the flow of legitimate comment or analysis of the news."

Gov. Lester G. Maddox of Georgia said in a speech in Atlanta that the Vice President had not gone far enough. In a

comment Friday, Mr. Maddox said:

"The handful of men with this dreadful power of opinion-making also come from areas other than the TV networks. This unprecedented concentration of power also comes from the White House, some members of the Supreme Court, the Department of Health, Education and Welfare, other news media, some members of Congress and some big shot leaders in education and religion."

Dean Burch, chairman of the Federal Communications Commission; George Romney, Secretary of Housing and Urban Development, and Gov. Ronald Reagan of California had previously voiced their agreement with Mr. Agnew.

Senator Barry Goldwater, Republican of Arizona, said yesterday that he agreed com-

pletely with the Vice President's criticism and added that there was a group of persons and major newspapers trying to "break" President Nixon.

"When the President doesn't do exactly as they think he should do," the Senator said at a news conference before addressing a Republican rally in Houston, "they start telling the people what the President should do."

Mr. Goldwater said that The New York Times, The Washington Post, The St. Louis Post-Dispatch and the Boston newspapers were in this group.

Hugh Scott, Republican leader in the Senate, said, however:

"Congress recently raised the Vice President's salary. Now we're paying him by the word." Speaking in Boston, the Senator said: "I am against all forms of Government censorship or control, but I would hope that when broadcasters are reporting the news they say so. When they're editorializing, they should say so, so that people aren't misled."

Newton N. Minow, the former chairman of the Federal Communications Commission who in 1961 characterized television as "a vast wasteland", said he disagreed with many of the Vice President's conclusions.

Mr. Minow, who was reached by telephone at the Rand Corporation in Santa Monica, Calif., said that he had always believed that news was one of the program areas in which television conducted itself with honesty and forthrightness.

The former F.C.C. chairman said he believed Mr. Agnew had underestimated the intelligence of American viewers in assuming that they could not distinguish between President Nixon's formal speech and the informal discussion among network correspondents that followed.

Mr. Minow said he believed that Government was entering upon a new era in its relationship to the communications world and that noncommercial television had reasons for apprehension fully as much as commercial television.

In Phoenix, Ariz., Eric Sevareid, Columbia Broadcasting System commentator, said that if television newsmen used the "invective, epithets and demagoguery the Vice President has recently resorted to" they "would soon be off the air."

Speaking Friday night at Phoenix College, Mr. Sevareid said the Nixon administration was trying to intimidate and isolate the critics of the Vietnam war by making it a patriotic issue.

Andrew Jacobs, Democratic Representative from Indiana, said, "Balanced news coverage requires that broadcasters indiscriminately report the good news, the bad news and the Agnews."

Stratton Backs Agnew

But Representative Samuel S. Stratton, Democrat of upstate New York and a strong supporter of the President's war policy, endorsed Mr. Agnew's views and said the subject had "long desperately needed to be brought into the open."

Mr. Stratton specifically criticized Chet Huntley, David Brinkley and Sander Vanocur of the National Broadcasting Company, Walter Cronkite of the Columbia Broadcasting System, and Martin Agronsky of the C.B.S. affiliate in Washington.

In London the authoritative newspaper, The Guardian, commented editorially that Mr. Agnew's views were "amusingly similar to what the Czechoslovak Government has been saying about the news media in its country."

Alistair Cooke, the Guardian's correspondent, said Mr. Agnew had objected to what he called "instant analysis and querulous criticism" by network commentators. "This, of course," Mr. Cooke added, "is standard practice on every television station in countries not run by Communists, Fascists or military juntas."

Telephone calls to The New York Times yesterday were about evenly divided between supporters and critics of Mr. Agnew. The C.B.S. television network news desk had about the same division, with a slight majority favoring the network's handling of the news. The A.B.C. news desk said calls had slowed down to about 25 a night after an initial flood and that "a very heavy majority" favored the Vice President. N.B.C. had no approximate count last night.

David Schoenbrun of Columbia University, a former Paris and Washington bureau chief of C.B.S., called Mr. Agnew's speech "partisan and political." Speaking at the Cincinnati chapter of Sigma Delta Chi, Mr. Schoenbrun also criticized the networks for broadcasting the Vice President's speech and a speech by Senator Edward M. Kennedy in July on "prime time."

He said both speeches should have been handled through "normal news channels."

Mr. Schoenbrun said also that he agreed with Mr. Agnew's objection to "instant analysis" of televised Presidential speeches. "I see no reason," Mr. Schoenbrun said, "for a major event to be analyzed five seconds after it happens." He said analysis should wait at least three days and then should be done by a panel of experts.

NIXON AIDE WIDENS CRITICISM ON NEWS

Klein Says All Media Need to Re-examine Coverage —Disclaims Any Threat

By RICHARD HALLORAN
Special to The New York Times

WASHINGTON, Nov. 16 — President Nixon's director of communications, Herbert G. Klein, widened the Administration's criticism of news coverage today to include all news media, not just television.

Referring to Vice President Agnew's censure of news commentators on television networks Thursday night, Mr. Klein said:

"I think you can go beyond that. All of the news media needs to re-examine itself in the format it has and its approach to problems of news, to meet the current issues of the day."

Mr. Klein, interviewed on the C.B.S. program "Face the Nation," said: "I include the newspapers very thoroughly in this, as well as the networks —if you look at the problems you have today and you fail to continue to examine them, you do invite the Government to come in. I would not like to see that happen."

Reached by telephone later, Mr. Klein said that any industry failing to examine itself "opens the door for unscrupulous politicians to move in." He said the Nixon Administration had no intention to do so and that his remarks were an observation, not a threat. He said he did not have a specific method of Government intervention in mind.

On the television program, Mr. Klein said, "I think there is a legitimate question to be debated within the industry, and I would be opposed to Government participation in it, but within the industry, as to whether we are doing a good enough job, whether we are being objective enough, and whether we ought not to spend more time in self-examination."

Mr. Klein, a former reporter and editor, said in the telephone interview that this was part of a theme he had expounded at various times over the past six years .

Mr. Klein also said that Vice President Agnew was speaking on his own when he criticized television news commentators Thursday, but that the Vice President's speech reflected a widely held view in the top levels of the Nixon Administration.

Mr. Klein also said that the Vice President had informed the President that he was going to make the speech and told Mr. Nixon what the subject would be.

Time magazine reported last night that the President had ordered Mr. Agnew to make the speech and had assigned Patrick Buchanan, one of the President's speech writers, to write it.

White House sources said last night that they believed that Cynthia Rosenwald, who writes speeches for Mr. Agnew, had drafted the speech and that the Vice President himself had done considerable work on it.

On the Columbia Broadcasting System program, Mr. Klein reiterated Mr. Agnew's criticism of W. Averell Harriman, who had been President Johnson's chief negotiator at the Paris peace talks.

Mr. Klein said "it was obvious that he was the first voice and the only public voice which came on immediately after the President's speech, that it would be a form of rebuttal, that if you look at any statement he made, none have been in favor of policies that the President has had."

Mr. Klein was asked to specify what military concessions the Vice President had in mind when he said Thursday that the period while Mr. Harriman was the chief negotiator in Paris was one "in which the United States swapped some of the greatest military concessions in the history of warfare for an enemy agreement on the shape of the bargaining table." Mr. Klein replied that he had not discussed the speed with the Vice President.

Scott Joins in Criticism

Senator Hugh Scott, the Republican leader from Pennsylvania, appeared on A.B.C.'s "Issues and Answers" with more criticism of the news media and Mr. Harriman.

Senator Scott said of Mr. Harriman that "having been Ambassador at the time when peace efforts did not work and the war was escalated, it is very important for him, as a public official, somehow to convince the public that he really was more successful than in fact he was."

The Senator said, however, that he did not know what the Vice President was talking about in his charge of swapping military concessions for the shape of the bargaining table.

"He may have referred to the suspension of the bombing,

for example," Senator Scott said.

Senator Scott generally supported Mr. Agnew's criticism of television news.

"What he said was firm," the Senator said. "It opened up a dialogue, it found the television networks very defensive on the issue. There are people who say, in a rustic way, that it is the pig that is caught under the fence that squeals."

He said, however, that "I don't think the networks or the press should be responsive to anybody's views and to that degree I disagree" with the Vice President, who had called on television to reflect more accurately the views of the American public.

White House Conciliatory On Protests and the Press

By R. W. APPLE Jr.

Special to The New York Times

WASHINGTON, Nov. 17—Former Vice President Hubert H. Humphrey accused the Nixon Administration today of a concerted effort to suppress dissent in the United States—an effort that he said could "open a Pandora's box of reaction, backlash and repression."

Mr. Humphrey characterized Vice President Agnew's attack on television commentators and similar remarks by other Administration officials as "an obvious and calculated appeal to our people's lesser or baser instincts."

Speaking between sessions of the first meeting of the Democratic Policy Council, which was organized two months ago to speak for the party on national issues, the former Vice President stopped short of a direct attack on Mr. Nixon. But he said that either the President was coordinating the assault on the media and on antiwar demonstrators "or it's one of the most unusual coincidences within the memory of man."

"When you have the chairman of the Federal Communications Commission, Cabinet officials, the Vice President and the National Committee of the Republican party all working the same line," he asserted, "this isn't as if the Vice President just had a lost weekend."

The council, composed of 72 party leaders headed by Mr. Humphrey, later passed a resolution deploring "efforts to stif criticism of Government officia by dissenting citizens and responsible newsmen." The resolution said that speeches by Mr. Agnew; Dean Burch, chairman of the Federal Communications Commission; Herbert G. Klein, the Administration's Director of Communications, and others "alarm those who believe in the right of dissent and in a free press."

In a speech in Des Moines, Iowa, last Tuesday, the Vice President upbraided what he called the "small and unelected" elite of television commentators for remarks critical of President Nixon's Nov. 3 Vietnam policy speech. Mr. Klein and Mr. Burch expanded on that theme, and other Administratio spokesmen have attacked participants in this weekend's antiwar demonstrations here.

"I believe the Nixon Administration is not really trying to bring us together," said Mr. Humphrey, leading the Democratic counterattack by turning one of Mr. Nixon's favorite slogans to his own use. "It is engaged, knowingly or unknowingly, in a polarization process."

"I, for one, want to make it clear that I disagree with those who would create an atmosphere of suppression and call it patriotism," Mr. Humphrey said.

At Mr. Humphrey's side in a conference room at the Watergate Hotel was W. Averell Harriman, whose televised commentary on the President's speech was singled out by Mr. Agnew for condemnation. Mr. Harriman has been selected as the chairman of the council's committee on international affairs.

The 78-year-old diplomat joined in the rebuttal to Mr. Agnew's remarks, commenting that they "smacked of a totalitarianism which I don't like at all."

Mr. Humphrey also spoke more harshly of President Nixon's Vietnam policy than at any time since he said, after a visit to the White House on Oct. 10, that Mr. Nixon was "proceeding along the right path" in Vietnam.

This afternoon, he praised certain aspects of the President's policy—including troop withdrawals, more restricted American offensive operations and plans for greater "Vietnamization" of the war—and again promised to refrain from partisanship.

But he also said that the Nixon policy's "weakness" was the degree to which it depended upon the actions of the gvernments in Hanoi and Saigon. Mr. Nixon said in his policy statement that troop withdrawals depended in part on South Vietnamese ability to take over the burden of combat and North Vietnamese restraint on the battlefield.

"I want to make sure," said Mr. Humphrey, "that we don't leave American policy in the hands of a rather weak government in Suth Vietnam or an intemperate and stubborn government in North Vietnam. Otherwise we can be held there forever by either the pleas of the south or the sporadic attacks of the north."

Mr. Humphrey added that he believed that only if troop withdrawals were both rapid and systematic would the President's policy be successful. He repeatedly emphasized that American actions must be linked to "out national interests" and nothing else.

His comments were remarkably similar to those made after Mr. nixon's speech by foes of the war, including Representative Allard K. Lowenstein, Democrat of Nassau County, L.I.

JOHNSON DISMAY AT TV DISCLOSED

But Secretary Says He Did Not Contemplate Attack

By ROBERT D. McFADDEN

George Christian, who served as President Johnson's press secretary, says that Mr. Johnson and some of his key aides held misgivings over television news coverage similar to those expressed in the last week by Vice President Agnew and other members of the Nixon Administration.

Nevertheless, Mr. Christian said, Mr. Johnson "never considered making a broad, frontal attack" on the mass media during his tenure in the White House.

Mr. Christian gave his views by telephone from his home in Austin, Tex., this week following the publication of an interview in the current issue of TV Guide, in which he discussed the treatment of news by television during Mr. Johnson's term in office.

One reason for the President's restraint, he said, was a belief that such criticism would be interpreted as an attack on the First Amendment guarantees of freedom of the press

Not His Style

In addition, Mr. Christian said, it was not Mr. Johnson's style to level harsh public criticisms against individuals or particular institutions

"It's in the nature of the way he did business," he said. "On occasion, his feelings of anger [at news media] were every bit as strong as those of the present Administration. After all, we did get some punishing treatment.

"But he chose to make his feelings known to reporters and networks personally, on a sort of man-to-man approach. He never considered making a broad, frontal attack. It never got to the nationwide TV speech level."

Mr. Christian noted that all Presidents have, in their time, been at odds with the news media, but few Administrations have made public criticisms of the press.

Mr. Agnew opened the Nixon Administration's criticism last Thursday night with the speech in Des Moines, Iowa, accusing the television networks of offering a highly selected and often biased presentation of the news.

Defended By Agnew

On Friday, Dean Burch, the chairman of the Federal Communications Commission, defended Mr. Agnew's speech and said he saw no suggestion of intimidation against the networks in the Vice President's remarks.

November 17, 1969

November 18, 1969

On Sunday, Herbert G. Klein, President Nixon's director of communications, widened the Administration's criticisms to include all news media, not just television, and warned that failure of the media to re-examine itself would "invite Government to come in."

Mr. Christian noted that President Johnson's strongest public comments on responsibility in television news coverage were offered only after he announced he would not be a candidate for reelection.

On April 1, 1968—the day after his announcement — Mr. Johnson, in an address to the National Association of Broadcasters in Chicago, said:

"You, the broadcast industry, have enormous power in your hands. You have the power to clarify. And you have the power to confuse. But I did not come here this morning to sermonize in matters of fairness and judgment. All I mean to do—what I'm trying to do—is to remind you where there's great power there must also be great responsibility."

Causes for Distress

According to Mr. Christian, the moderation of the President's tone in that speech reflected a belief that harsher criticisms "would not serve any useful purpose."

Presidential aides, accordingly, also felt restrained in their public comments on the news media, aware that criticisms might be interpreted as reflecting Mr. Johnson's views. he said.

"It was a personal feeling of [Mr. Johnson's] that the President ought to be very, very careful about public criticism," he said.

Mr. Johnson and others in his Administration were "distressed by the coverage of the Vietnam war, the [Presidential election] campaign and the [1968 Democratic National] Convention," Mr. Christian said.

And Mr. Johnson did react, he said, adding: "There were many newsmen who he talked to when he thought they had done something to injure him."

In addition, he added, Mr. Johnson was "not loath to talk to the networks" about his misgivings, and occasionally made "one-liner" public criticisms at his news conferences.

However, he declined to "make a concerted issue out of it," Mr. Christian said. "He felt he could achieve fairness ir other ways."

The former press secretary is now the president of Christian-Miller-Honts, Inc., a public relations concern with offices in Washington and Austin.

TV Dispute Seen Aiding Bill to Protect Licensees

By CHRISTOPHER LYDON
Special to The New York Times

WASHINGTON, Nov. 19 — Senator John O. Pastore said today that the criticism of the television industry by Vice President Agnew and other Administration figures had increased the urgency — and improved the chances — of protective legislation for broadcasters.

The Rhode Island Democrat, chairman of the Senate Subcommittee on Communications, is the principal sponsor of a bill that would give broadcasters a virtually permanent grip on their stations by banning competitive license applications unless an established broadcaster had first been found to have violated his public trust.

In hearings earlier this year, Senator Pastore advocated the bill principally on the ground that the growing number of license challenges threatened the economic stability of the broadcast industry.

But in an interview today, he said that what he views as a threat of political pressure on television news and of politically motivated license awards by the Federal Communications Commission was an even more compelling reason.

Opposition to the Pastore bill has focused on the contention that it would freeze the present concentration of media ownership and would diminish broadcasters' responsiveness to local audiences.

Senator Pastore expects fresh support for his bill, particularly among liberals.

"People have a new understanding," he said, "of the fundamental issue: How do you promote independence and freedom of thought and expression when the sword of Damocles is hanging over every broadcaster's head?"

Senator Pastore indicated he had no evidence that White House complaints had inspired Dean Burch, the new chairman of the F.C.C., to call the network presidents for transcripts of their commentaries on President Nixon's Nov. 3 speech on Vietnam.

But he described Mr. Burch's action as "unprecedented" and "out of bounds" and said he feared that the F.C.C. would become a political instrument when President Nixon's appointees form a majority of the seven-member regulatory commission.

"There's tremendous power in the hands of the F.C.C.," he said, "to bring pressure on the industry—and now I'm talking on the question of ideology."

The Vice President's speech last Thursday, which Mr. Burch has endorsed, "has split us all into two schools—those who are for the Administration and those who are against the Administration," Senator Pastore said.

"Apparently the liberals have

now become sensitive to the implications. The former Vice President [Hubert H. Humphrey] has called the Agnew speech an attempt to stifle expression and thought. Now those are the things that were on my mind in this bill," he said.

He continued: "How are we going to preserve the independence of this industry so that, within the bounds of morality and decency, they can think as they like and say what they think?

"Certainly, if you put these stations in fear for their licenses, you'll find they are going to want to please the Administration, and the F.C.C. Don't forget, when Dean Burch called the networks for those transcripts, he got them, didn't he?"

Fred W. Friendly, former president of the Columbia Broadcasting System's news division, who is now a professor of journalism at Columbia University, reiterated his opposition to the Pastore bill here today.

The F.C.C.'s traditional authority to review broadcasters' performance every three years against the challenge of competitors is "the last best hope we[the public] have for controlling television," Mr. Friendly said in response to questions at the World Mental Health Assembly.

Editor Says Nixon Seeks To Muzzle News Media

By JERRY M. FLINT
Special to The New York Times

ANN ARBOR, Mich., Nov. 19 —The Nixon Administration seeks to intimidate and muzzle the American press and television, Norman Issacs, president of the American Society of Newspaper Editors, charged today.

He implied that the Administration was trying to whip the news media into a Soviet-style system, one that "says that you support the Government or you go."

In a speech and at a news conference on the campus of the University of Michigan here, Mr. Issacs, who is executive editor of The Courier-Journal and Louisville Times, said that the press and TV news had their faults and there was "a

germ of truth" in charges that New York and Washington dominate the news.

But, he said, any Government threat against television station licenses goes far beyond fair criticism and "smacks of intimidation and control." It is, he said, an attempt to "shut off the voices of dissent."

Cites Media Rivalry

"The newspaper and broadcast arms of communications are rivals," he said. "For years they have been openly contemptuous of each other. Yet whatever their differences, they are now driven together as the co-targets of what can only be described as an open campaign by the national Administration to discredit them—and, more importantly, to seek to bring

theit under some form of covert control."

Vice President Agnew, who attacked television news in a speech last week, "was the spear-bearer of this attack," Mr. Isaacs said.

He said that Clark Mollenhoff, a White House aide, and Attorney General John N. Mitchell "would seem to be working together," that George Romney, Secretary of Housing and Urban Development, "looks like he's a Johnny-come-lately," and that Dean Burch's "role I can't quite figure out," unless it was "to make the intimidation" clear.

Mr. Burch, chairman of the Federal Communications Commission, "ought to be fired," Mr. Isaacs said, because he is acting as both prosecutor and judge in criticizing television.

'Muzzling' Effort Seen

Mr. Isaacs said: "The Vice President's text disclaimed any intent to legislate against the communications media. But he did appeal openly for public control — and what other interpretation can be drawn than Administration support for such challenges? And with a chairman of the F.C.C. who openly adopts a welcoming stance to such challenges?

"You have one of two options in analysis of the motives. One is intimidation, the other is control. But is there any essential difference, so long as you succeed? The end result is muzzling of some kind."

And he said of Mr. Agnew and Mr. Burch: "I cannot help but wonder what the substantive difference is between their position and that in practice in the Soviet Union?"

In his speech the editor was critical of the press and television, and some of his complaints were close to those of the Government officials.

There are "arrogant" publishers and editors who refuse to see that their papers are not performing adequate public service and "shrug away protests about errors and misstatement."

And young newsmen, he said, "so often seem determined to do precisely what the national Administration charges us with doing — advancing their own ideas in print or on the TV screen."

He complained that there was too much emphasis on the "scoop" in both the press and on television and not enough clear-cut separation between news and interpretation.

He emphasized, however, tha he thought the complaints by Mr. Agnew and others were intimidation and not fair criticism.

AGNEW ATTACKS PRESS AS UNFAIR; NAMES 2 PAPERS

Cites New York Times and The Washington Post— They Dispute Charges

By CHRISTOPHER LYDON
Special to The New York Times

MONTGOMERY, Ala., Nov. 20 — Vice President Agnew broadened his attack on the communications media tonight to include newspapers, particularly The New York Times and The Washington Post.

A week after he accused the three national television networks of abusing their power over public opinion, the Vice President challenged the news judgment and the fairness of the press.

Where he had previously addressed himself to "a small band of network commentators," he spoke this time, without reference to personalities of the diminishing choice of newspapers and the growing concentration of corporate media control.

More Power, Fewer Hands

"The American people should be made aware," he said, "of the trend toward the monopolization of the great public information vehicles and the concentration of more and more power in fewer and fewer hands."

"Many, many strong independent voices have been stilled in this country in recent years," he said, speaking of defunct newspapers. "And lacking the vigor of competition, some of those that have survived have—let's face it—grown fat and irresponsible."

He spoke specifically of the decline of newspaper competition in Washington and New York.

"When The Washington Times-Herald died in the nation's capital, that was a political tragedy," he said. "And when The New York Journal-American, The New York World-Telegram and Sun, The New York Mirror and The New York Herald Tribune all collapsed within this decade, that was a great, great political tragedy for the people of New York."

"The New York Times," he said, "was a better newspaper when they were all alive than it is now that they are gone."

[In New York, Arthur Ochs Sulzberger, president and publisher of The New York Times, said that Mr. Agnew was inaccurate in some of his statements. Mrs. Katharine Graham, president of the Washington Post Company, said that the Vice President's remarks about the company were not supported by the facts.]

The Vice President delivered his address before the Alabama Chamber of Commerce in the State Capitol where former Gov. George C. Wallace often attacked The Times and The Post as symbols of "Eastern establishment" thinking.

The two daily newspapers here, The Montgomery Advertiser and The Alabama Journal are owned by Multimedia, Inc., a conglomerate communications corporation, but maintain separate and competing news staffs. Both papers subscribe to The New York Times News Service.

The Vice President stated, as the Administration has repeatedly affirmed in the last week, that he was "opposed to censorship of television or the press in any form."

As an example of "the growing monopolization of the voices of public opinion," he cited The Washington Post Company, which publishes The Post and Newsweek magazine and owns the WTOP radio and television station in Washington.

"I'm not recommending the dismemberment of the Washington Post Company," he said. "I'm merely pointing out that the public should be aware that these four powerful voices harken to the same master."

WTOP Television and Radio carried the address live, as did WINS Radio. None of the networks carried it.

His speech included three criticisms of news coverage and editorials in The New York Times.

First, he charged that The Times, which he said "considers itself America's paper of record," did not carry "a word" about the endorsement of President Nixon's Vietnam policy by 300 Congressmen and 59 Senators.

"If a theology student in Iowa should get up at a P.T.A. luncheon in Sioux City and attack the President's Vietnam policy, my guess is that you'd probably find it reported somewhere the next morning in The New York Times," he said.

"But when 300 Congressmen endorse the President's Vietnam policy, the next morning it's apparently not considered news fit to print."

Second, he complained that last Tuesday, when Pope Paul

Speech Brings Spate Of Calls to The Times

Vice President Agnew's speech prompted a flood of telephone calls to The New York Times and The Washington Post last night.

By midnight, 140 calls had been received at The Times's New York office. Eighty-one callers disagreed with the Vice President, 58 agreed with him and one man said, "I have my own thing against the media, but dig, anything he says immediately turns me off."

The Washington Post reported that by 12:30 A.M. today it had received more than 200 calls, 129 supporting Mr. Agnew's views and 87 supporting The Post.

VI "endorsed" the way President Nixon was proceeding in Vietnam, The Times reported the news on page 11.

"The same day," he commented, "a report about some burglars who broke into a souvenir shop at St. Peter's and stole $9,000 worth of stamps and currency—that story made Page 3. How's that for news judgment?"

Third, he quoted a recent Times editorial, written in response to his remarks about young demonstrators that "American youth today is far more imbued with idealism, a sense of service, and a deep humanitarianism than any generation in recent history, including particularly Mr. Agnew's generation."

The editorial, he said, "seems a peculiar slur on a generation that brought America out of the great Depression without resorting to the extremes of communism or fascism.

"Whatever freedom exists today in Western Europe and Japan," he continued, "exists because hundreds of thousands of young men in my generation are lying in graves in North Africa and France and Korea and a score of islands in the Western Pacific.

"This might not be considered enough of a 'sense of service' or a 'deep humanitarianism' for the 'perceptive critics' who write editorials for The New York Times, but it's good enough for me. And I'm content to let history be the judge."

Mr. Agnew devoted a substantial part of his speech to the harsh criticism, from Congress and the media of his speech concerning television in Des Moines last week.

He referred to the criticism as "classic examples of overreaction" and stated that he had not been intimidated.

"I'm not asking any immunity from criticism," he said. "This is the lot of a man in politics—we wouldn't have it any other way in a democratic society."

He added, however, that "the network commentators and even the gentlemen of The New York Times" would not be immune from counterattack.

"When they go beyond fair comment and criticism they will be called upon to defend their statements and their positions just as we must defend ours," he said. "And when their criticism becomes excessive or unjust, we shall invite them down from their ivory towers to enjoy the rough and tumble of the public debate.

"I don't seek to intimidate the press or the networks or anyone else from speaking out. But the time for blind acceptance of their opinions is past. And the time for naive belief in their neutrality is gone."

Comment by Ziegler
Special to The New York Times

WASHINGTON, Nov. 20 — Ronald L. Ziegler, the White House press secretary, said tonight that President Nixon had not seen the text of Mr. Agnew's speech. The spokesman declined to accept further questions on the subject.

Following is a transcript of Vice President Agnew's address last night to the Montgomery Chamber of Commerce, as recorded by The New York Times:

Governor and Mrs. Brewer, Postmaster General and Mrs. Blount, Congressman Dickinson and the other distinguished members of the Alabama Legislature in the audience, officers, members of the board of directors and members of the Alabama Chamber of Commerce and my Alabama friends all—I want to first express my very sincere appreciation to the people of Alabama for the very warm welcome which they have given to me and to my wife on our arrival here today.

And I particularly want to thank Governor Brewer for that very gracious and warm introduction. Governor Brewer and I never got to know each other as well as perhaps I would have liked because after he became Governor of this state, I didn't stay Governor much longer.

But I want you to know one thing—that I did have a chance to serve with him and to be with him at a Southern Governors Conference, and I was tremendously impressed with the sincerity and the depth and the dedication of Governor Brewer, and I think the state of Alabama is very fortunate to have him.

As for the Postmaster General and his lovely wife, what can I say? He's taken us in Washington by storm, with his very perceptive feeling for people and his very warm concern about the problems of the country and, above all, his courage. Who else would dare to take on the monumental problems of reforming the postal division of the United States singlehanded, other than Red Blount.

And to Red and Mary Kaye, also, a very, very warm thank you for opening your home to us and making us feel so welcome. I'm sorry we can't try that tennis court, but there just isn't time and the weather doesn't seem too conducive to that right now, anyhow.

Warmth of Welcome

I am really pleased that, included in the warmth of the welcome of the people of Alabama today was something that struck me as particularly significant and that was the fact that the young people at the airport were so enthusiastic. And it showed me beyond any doubt that young people, just as old people, refuse to be conformed and patterned into a specific mold and they have a right and a privilege and an obligation to think

Associated Press

CHALLENGES FAIRNESS OF THE PRESS: Vice President Agnew at Alabama Chamber of Commerce, Montgomery.

for themselves, and I'm glad to see how the young people of Alabama are thinking.

One week ago tonight I flew out to Des Moines, Iowa, and exercised my right to dissent.

This is a great country—in this country every man is allowed freedom of speech, even the Vice President.

Of course, there's been some criticism of what I said out there in Des Moines. Let me give you a sampling.

One Congressman charged me with, and I quote, "a creeping socialistic scheme against the free enterprise broadcast industry." Now this is the first time in my memory that anyone ever accused Ted Agnew of having socialist ideas.

On Monday, largely because of that address, Mr. Humphrey charged the Nixon Administration with a "calculated attack" on the right of dissent and on the media today. Yet it's widely known that Mr. Humphrey himself believes deeply that the unfair coverage of the Democratic convention in Chicago, by the same media, contributed to his defeat in November.

'Rugged Dissent'

Now his wounds are apparently healed, and he's casting his lot with those who were questioning his own political courage a year ago. But let's leave Mr. Humphrey to his own conscience. America already has too many politicians who would rather switch than fight.

There were others that charged that my purpose in that Des Moines speech was to stifle dissent in this country. Nonsense. The expression of my views has produced enough rugged dissent in the last week to wear out a whole covey of commentators and columnists.

One critic charged that the speech was disgraceful, ignorant and base; that leads us as a nation, he said, into an ugly era of the most fearsome suppression and intimidation.

One national commentator, whose name is known to everyone in this room, said: "I hesitate to get in the gutter with this guy."

Another commentator charges that "it was one of the most sinister speeches that I've ever heard made by a public official."

The president of one network said that it was an unprecedented attempt to intimidate a news medium which depends for its existence upon Government licenses. The president of another charged me with an appeal to prejudice, and said that it was evident that I would prefer the kind of television that would be subservient to whatever political group happened to be in authority at the time.

And they say I have a thin skin.

Here indeed are classic examples of overreaction. These attacks do not address themselves to the questions I raised. In fairness, others, the majority of the critics and commentators, did take up the main thrust of my address.

And if the debate that they have engaged in continues, our goal will surely be reached, our goal which of course is a thorough self-examination by the networks of their own policies and perhaps prejudices. That was my objective then, and that's my objective now.

Opposes Censorship

Now let me repeat to you the thrust of my remarks the other night and perhaps make some new points and raise a few new issues.

I'm opposed to censorship of television, of the press in any form. I don't care whether censorship is imposed by government or whether it results from management in the choice and presentation of the news by a little fraternity having similar social and political views. I'm against, I repeat, I'm against media censorship in all forms.

But a broader spectrum of national opinion should be represented among the commentators in the network news. Men who can articulate other points of view should be brought forward and a high wall of separation should be raised between what is news and what is commentary.

And the American people should be made aware of the trend toward the monopolization of the great public information vehicles and the concentration of more and more power in fewer and fewer hands.

Should a conglomerate be formed that tied together a shoe company with a shirt company, some voice will rise up righteously to say that this is a great danger to the economy and that the conglomerate ought to be broken up.

But a single company, in the nation's capital, holds control of the largest newspaper in Washington, D. C., and one of the four major television stations, and an all-news radio station, and one of the three major national news magazines—all grinding out the same editorial line—and this is not a subject that you've seen debated on the editorial pages of The Washington Post or The New York Times.

For the purpose of clarity, before my thoughts are obliterated in the smoking typewriters of my friends in Washington and New York, let me emphasize that I'm not recommending the dismemberment of the Washington Post Company. I'm merely pointing out that the public should be aware that these four powerful voices hearken to the same master.

Voices of Opinion

I'm raising these questions so that the American people will become aware of—and think of the implications of—the growing monopoly that involves the voices of public opinion, on which we all depend for our knowledge and for the basis of our views.

When The Washington Times-Herald died in the nation's capital, that was a political tragedy; and when The New York Journal-American, The New York World-Telegram and Sun, The New York Mirror and The New York Herald Tribune all collapsed within this decade, that was a great, great political tragedy for the people of New York. The New York Times was a better newspaper when they were all alive than it is now that they are gone.

And what has happened in the city of New York has happened in other great cities of America.

Many, many strong, independent voices have been stilled in this country in recent years. And lacking the vigor of competition, some of those who have survived have — let's face it — grown fat and irresponsible.

I offer an example: When 300 Congressmen and 59 Senators signed a letter endorsing the President's policy in Vietnam, it was news —and it was big news. Even The Washington Post and The Baltimore Sun — scarcely house organs for the Nixon Administration—placed it prominently in their front pages.

Yet the next morning The New York Times, which considers itself America's paper of record, did not carry a word. Why? Why?

If a theology student in Iowa should get up at a P.T.A. luncheon in Sioux City and attack the President's Vietnam policy, my guess is that you'd probably find it reported somewhere in the next morning's issue of The New York Times. But when 300 congressmen endorse the President's Vietnam policy, the next morning it's apparently not considered news fit to print.

Just this Tuesday when the Pope, the spiritual leader of half a billion Roman Catholics, applauded the President's effort to end the war in Vietnam and endorsed the way he was proceeding, that news was on Page 11 of The New York Times. The same day a report about some burglars who broke into a souvenir shop at St. Peter's and stole $9,000 worth of stamps and currency—that story made Page 3. How's that for news judgment?

A few weeks ago here in the South I expressed my views about street and campus demonstrations. Here's how The New York Times responded:

"He [that's me] lambasted the nation's youth in sweeping and ignorant generalizations, when it's clear to all perceptive observers that American youth today is far more imbued with idealism, a sense of service and a deep humanitarianism than any generation in recent history, including particularly Mr. Agnew's generation."

That's what The New York Times said.

'A Peculiar Slur'

Now that seems a peculiar slur on a generation that brought America out of the Great Depression without resorting to the extremes of Communism or Fascism. That seems a strange thing to say about an entire generation that helped to provide greater material blessings and more personal freedom—out of that Depression—for more people than any other nation in history. We have not finished the task by any means—but we are still on the job.

Just as millions of young Americans in this generation have shown valor and courage and heroism fighting the longest, and least popular, war in our history, so it was the young men of my generation who went ashore at Normandy under Eisenhower, and with MacArthur into the Philippines.

Yes, my generation, like the current generation, made its own share of great mistakes and great blunders. Among other things, we put too much confidence in Stalin and not enough in Winston Churchill.

But, whatever freedom exists today in Western Europe and Japan exists because hundreds of thousands of young men of my generation are lying in graves in North Africa and France and Korea and a score of islands in the Western Pacific.

This might not be considered enough of a sense of service or a deep humanitarianism for the perceptive critics who write editorials for The New York Times, but it's good enough for me. And I'm content to let history be the judge.

Now, let me talk briefly about the younger generation. I have not and I do not condemn this generation of young Americans. Like Edmund Burke, I wouldn't know how to draw up an indictment against a whole people. After all, they're our sons and daughters. They contain in their numbers many gifted, idealistic and courageous young men and women.

'The Efficacy of Violence'

But they also list in their numbers an arrogant few who march under the flags and portraits of dictators, who intimidate and harass university professors, who use gutter obscenities to shout down speakers with whom they disagree, who openly profess their belief in the efficacy of violence in a democratic society.

Oh, yes, the preceding generation had its own breed of losers and our generation dealt with them through our courts, our laws and our system. The challenge is now for the new generation to put its house in order.

Today, Dr. Sydney Hook writes of "storm troopers" on the campus: that "fanaticism seems to be in the saddle." Arnold Beichman writes of "young Jacobins" in our schools who "have cut down university administrators, forced curriculum changes, halted classes, closed campuses and set a nationwide chill of fear all through the university establishment." Walter Laqueur writes in Commentary that "the cultural and political idiocies perpetuated with impunity in this permissive age have gone clearly beyond the borders of what is acceptable for any society, however liberally it may be constructed."

George Kennan has devoted a brief, cogent and alarming book to the inherent dangers of what's taking place in our society and in our universities. Irving Kristol writes that our "radical students find it possible to be genuinely heartsick at the injustice and brutalities of American society, at the same time they are blandly approving of injustice and brutality committed in the name of 'the revolution.'" Or, as they like to call it, "the movement."

Now those are not names drawn at random from the letter head of an Agnew-for-Vice President committee. Those are men more eloquent and erudite than I, and they raise questions that I've tried to raise.

For we must remember that among this generation of Americans there are hundreds who have burned their draft cards and scores who have deserted to Canada and Sweden to sit out the war. To some Americans, a small minority, these are the true young men of conscience in the coming generation.

Voices are and will continue to be raised in the Congress and beyond asking that amnesty—a favorite word—amnesty should be provided for these young and misguided American boys. And they will be coming home one day from Sweden and from Canada and from a small minority of our citizens they will get a hero's welcome.

They are not our heroes. Many of our heroes will not be coming home; some are coming back in hospital ships, without limbs or eyes, with scars they shall carry for the rest of their lives.

Having witnessed firsthand the quiet courage of wives and parents receiving posthumously for their heroes Congressional Medals of Honor, how am I to react when people say, "Stop speaking out, Mr. Agnew, stop raising your voice?"

Finds War Vilified

Should I remain silent while what these heroes have done is vilified by some as "a dirty, immoral war" and criticized by others as no more than a war brought on by the chauvinistic anti-Communism of Presidents Kennedy, Johnson and Nixon?

These young men made heavy sacrifices so that a developing people on the rim of Asia might have a chance for freedom that they obviously will not have if the ruthless men who rule in Hanoi should ever rule over Saigon. What's dirty or immoral about that?

One magazine this week said that I'll go down as the "great polarizer" in American politics. Yet, when that large group of young Americans marched up Pennsylvania Avenue and Constitution Avenue last week, they sought to polarize the American people against the President's policy in Vietnam. And that was their right. And so it is my right, and my duty, to stand up and speak out for the values in which I believe.

How can you ask the man in the street in this country to stand up for what he believes if his own elected leaders weasel and cringe.

It's not an easy thing to wake up each morning to learn that some prominent man or some prominent institution has implied that you're a bigot or a racist or

a fool.

I'm not asking immunity from criticism. This is the lot of a man in politics; we wouldn't have it any other way in a democratic society.

But my political and journalistic adversaries sometimes seem to be asking something more—that I circumscribe my rhetorical freedom while they place no restriction on theirs.

As President Kennedy observed in a far more serious situation: This is like offering an apple for an orchard.

'Immunity . . . Is Over'

We do not accept those terms for continuing the national dialogue. The day when the network commentators and even the gentlemen of The New York Times enjoyed a form of diplomatic immunity from comment and criticism of what they said is over.

Yes, gentleman, that day is passed.

Just as a politician's words —wise and foolish—are dutifully recorded by press and television to be thrown up at him at the appropriate time, so their words should be likewise recorded and likewise recalled.

When they go beyond fair comment and criticism they will be called upon to defend their statements and their positions just as we must defend ours. And when their criticism becomes excessive or unjust, we shall invite them down from their ivory towers to enjoy the rough and tumble of public debate.

I don't seek to intimidate the press, or the networks or anyone else from speaking out. But the time for blind acceptance of their opinions is past. And the time for naive belief in their neutrality is gone.

As to the future, each of us could do worse than to take as our own the motto of William Lloyd Garrison who said, and I'm quoting: "I am in earnest. I will not equivocate. I will not excuse. I will not retreat a single inch. And I will be heard."

Response to Vice President's Attack

Following are the texts of replies to Vice President Agnew's speech on the press yesterday by Arthur Ochs Sulzberger, president and publisher of The New York Times, and Mrs. Katharine Graham, president of the Washington Post Company, and of statements by Reuven Frank, president of N.B.C. News; Dr. Frank Stanton, president of the Columbia Broadcasting System, and Leonard H. Goldenson, president of the American Broadcasting Companies, Inc.:

Mr. Sulzberger's Reply

Vice President Agnew is entitled to express his point of view, but he is in error when he implies that The New York Times ever sought or enjoyed immunity from comment and criticism. Indeed, all American institutions from the press to the Presidency should be the subjects of free and open debate.

It would be wise, however, for those involving themselves in such a discussion to be certain of their facts. Some of Mr. Agnew's statements are inaccurate.

The Vice President has accused us of avoiding the issue of monopoly journalism. Quite the opposite. In fact in an editorial on March 13, 1969, headed "Competition Not Monopoly," The Times stated: "The constitutional guarantee of freedom of the press provides the press with no warrant for seeking exemption from the laws prohibiting monopoly. If anything, the sanctity attached to press freedom by the First Amendment makes it the special obligation of the press to fight for the broadest extension of that freedom."

This is a sentiment that The New York Times has expressed repeatedly and still holds.

Mr. Agnew is again mistaken when he says that The Times did not "carry a word" on the story about the Congressmen and Senators signing a letter endorsing the President's policy in Vietnam. The New York Times printed the story. Unfortunately, it failed to make the edition that reached Washington but was carried in a later edition of The Times. Moreover, The Times has given considerable attention to that story as it developed. In the paper of Nov. 6, there was a story on Page 11. In the paper of Nov. 7, there was a front page story that the House Foreign Affairs Committee had approved a

resolution endorsing President Nixon's "efforts to negotiate a just peace in Vietnam." In the paper of Nov. 13, there was the story to which the Vice President referred. In the paper of Nov. 14, President Nixon's visit to the House and the Senate to convey his appreciation to those who supported his Vietnam policy was the lead story. That story again reported the fact that more than 300 Congressmen and 59 Senators had signed the resolution.

As to the assertion that the story about the Pope appeared on Page 11 while a less important story was printed on Page 3, the Vice President unfortunately does not understand some of the complicated problems of making up a newspaper. Many important stories have to appear on pages other than Page 1 and a story that appears on Page 3 or Page 6 is not necessarily considered more important than a story that appears on Page 11 or 13.

It is the basic credo of The Times that news and editorial opinion are kept separate and that opinion should appear only on the editorial page. We shall continue to follow that credo.

Mrs. Graham's Reply

Vice President Agnew's remarks about the Washington Post Company are not supported by the facts.

The Washington Post, Newsweek, WTOP-TV, and WTOP Radio decidedly do not "grind out the same editorial line."

It is long-standing policy of the Post Company to enlist in each of its enterprises the best professional journalists we can find and give them a maximum of freedom in which to work. Each branch is operated autonomously. They compete vigorously with one another. They disagree on many issues. We think that the result is journalism of a high caliber that is notable for a diversity of voices on a wide range of public issues.

As to the voices of public opinion in the Washington area, they are plentiful and diverse. Washington is one of the most competitive communications cities in America by any objective standards. It is one of only three cities left with three major newspapers under separate ownership, all of them first rate.

In addition to the four major television stations, there are three ultra-highfrequency stations. Radio is even more competitive in the area with some 35 outlets.

Mr. Goldenson's Statement

As I said last week, after the Vice President's first speech, I firmly believe that in our free society the ultimate judges of the reliability of our news presentation will be the viewing public.

Again I leave it to the public to determine whether the Vice President's renewed attack today is an attempt to intimidate and discredit not only television news reporting but other major news media. Personally, I believe it is.

I hope we are not facing a period in the history of our nation when high Government officials try to act both as judge and jury on the issue of a free press.

Mr. Frank's Statement

In Vice President Agnew's second speech on the press, he seems to have lowered his voice, but is seeking new targets.

His first speech concentrated on the news operations of the television networks. He said that because they reached many more people than The New York Times, they were not entitled to the protection of press freedom.

His current attack is aimed primarily at The Washington Post and The New York Times and particularly at the "news judgment" of The Times. We do not welcome this sort of Government intervention directed against newspapers any more than we relish it when it strikes at broadcast news.

Dr. Stanton's Statement

Apparently the Vice President is embarked upon a campaign, despite his rhetoric to the contrary, to intimidate the news media into reporting only what he wants to hear. We repeat what we said in reference to his attack last week: Whatever the deficiencies of a free press, they are minor compared to those of a press which would be subservient to the executive power of Government.

Washington: Mr. Agnew and the Commentators

By JAMES RESTON

WASHINGTON, Nov. 20—In his speech to the Montgomery, Ala., Chamber of Commerce, Vice President Agnew said his criticism of network and newspaper commentators had two objectives: (1) to make the American people aware of "the growing monopolization of the voices of public opinion on which we all depend . . ." and (2) to encourage a "thorough self-examination by the networks [and presumably the newspapers] of their own policies, and perhaps prejudices."

If this were all he had in mind, it is fair enough. The number of daily newspapers in this country has declined from 1,944 in 1929 to 1,752 in 1969 and the number of cities with newspapers owned by one company has greatly increased in these forty years. So that it is accurate to say that a great many more Americans have fewer sources of daily newspaper information now than then.

The Liberal Commentators

It is also a fair generalization that a majority of the nationally syndicated columnists and network commentators are more for progressive domestic legislation and more critical of the Vietnam war than Mr. Agnew, but these generalizations have to be qualified.

Actually, with the rise of television and radio broadcasting stations, the sources of information in the United States have dramatically increased in recent decades, breaking the monopoly of the printing press. There were only 69 television stations in 1949 and 869 today, and the number of radio stations has increased from 2,777

in 1949 to 6,717 in 1969.

The One-Party Press?

Out of this vast network of stations and newspapers now pours night and day the greatest flow of information and the loudest clash of divergent opinion ever inflicted on a long-suffering people in the history of the written and spoken word. But the Vice President has a point: most of the *national* commentary by individuals and national columnists is more "liberal," if Mr. Agnew will permit the word, than the Vice President.

And this is interesting. Not so long ago, Adlai Stevenson was complaining, as Truman and Roosevelt had before him, about the development of what he called "a one-party press [meaning Republican] in a two-party country." What Lyndon Johnson had to say about the owners of the papers made Mr. Agnew sound like the president of the American Society of Newspaper Editors.

The Vice President says the day when commentators enjoyed "a form of diplomatic immunity from comment and criticism—that day is over!"

But when did that day ever dawn in America? "We have some infamous papers," President Washington complained, "calculated for disturbing, if not absolutely intended to disturb, the peace."

Mr. Jefferson wrote Thomas McKean in 1803 that "even the least informed of the people have learnt that nothing in a newspaper is to be believed."

Andrew Jackson criticized in 1837 some editors "who appear to fatten on slandering their neighbors, and hire writers to lie for them." And Woodrow

Wilson actually considered setting up a Federal publicity bureau to give the people "the real facts." Playing up differences of opinion and predicting difficulties, he said, impede "the public business."

The Power Watchers

It is a very long story. Watchful commentators from the beginning of the Republic have tended to be critical of the party in power, and the greater the power in the Presidency, particularly the power to make war, the greater the skepticism and the harder the criticism.

How odd of a Republican Vice President to miss that point. It has of course often been abused, but it is at the very heart of the First Amendment. Mr. Agnew is right that we tend to play up the unusual and the contentious, which, incidentally, is why he is being played up now.

'I Will Be Heard'

It is strange, however, that he should argue his case in high moral tones, as if continuing the war were somehow more "moral" than speeding its end, as if his critics were indifferent to the "heavy sacrifices" of the young soldiers and the suffering of the Vietnamese when in fact his critics are crying out in pity for them.

Mr. Agnew invited us all to a debate. We should, he suggested, follow him in repeating William Lloyd Garrison's motto: "I am in earnest. I will not equivocate. I will not excuse. I will not retreat a single inch. And I will be heard."

We're right behind you Mr. Vice President. This is the best offer we've had since the Newspaper Guild got us up to $20 a week back in 1933.

Agnew on the News

To the Editor:

I believe the American public is a better judge of what the news media are reporting than Vice President Agnew's overly suspicious characterization before a captive audience. He has indeed used his high office to create an atmosphere of fright —and hate—when none really exists. HARRY M. LESSIN
Norwalk, Conn., Nov. 14, 1969

●

Vice President Backed

To the Editor:

It was with great interest and total agreement that my husband and I heard Vice President Agnew's speech concerning TV news coverage.

We hope that the media will heed this challenge. As Americans we want the news in its entirety exactly as it happens, not the biased presentation of some newsmen.

We are of the opinion that so much attention has been focused on the sometimes treasonous action of the so-called peace groups in this country that the very freedoms (freedom of press for instance) on which this country was founded are in great jeopardy.

This sort of coverage presented with apparent sympathetic overtones for these groups at times is giving the Communists victories they might not otherwise realize.

Lest this type of coverage eventually lead to censorship, we hope the news media in all fields will be more exacting in their presentation in the future.

(Mrs.) HOUSTON F. WHEELER
Rome, Ga., Nov. 17, 1969

Burch's Letter Appears to Rebuff Critics of TV

By CHRISTOPHER LYDON
Special to The New York Times

WASHINGTON, Nov. 21— Dean Burch, the new chairman of the Federal Communications Commission, appeared today to have answered his own doubts about the fairness of television network news and also to have warned the Nixon Administration against further criticism of the media.

Mr. Burch's views, endorsed by a unanimous vote of the seven-member commission, were stated in a letter to a Houston woman who had complained about the network commentaries that followed President Nixon's Nov. 3 speech on Vietnam.

Mr. Burch himself called each of the three major network presidents on Nov. 5, requesting transcripts of their commentators' remarks about the President's address. But in his letter to Mrs. J. R. Paul, he said, in effect, that his inquiry had been unwarranted.

The commission, he wrote, "cannot properly investigate to determine whether an account or analysis of a news commentator is 'biased' or 'true.'"

The Chill of Censorship

While Vice President Agnew was expanding his indictment of television and newspapers, Mr. Burch's letter said, "No Government agency can authenticate the news, or should try to do so. Such an attempt would cast the chill of omnipresent government censorship over the newsmen's independence in news judgment."

Mr. Burch previously conceded that his personal request for network transcripts was a departure from the routine staff handling of public complaints. But the response to Mrs. Paul, adopted by the full commission and signed by Mr. Burch, was even more conspicuously a special reaction to the widening discussion of news coverage.

The letter noted that, in addition to complaints of "bias and distortion of news by the television networks," fear had been expressed "regarding possible Government intimidation or censorship of the networks' news operation." Mr. Burch stated that the commission wanted to "use this opportunity" to restate its proper role.

Open Forum on Issues

The fundamental requirement under the commission's "fairness doctrine," he said, is simply that broadcasters must keep their facilities open as forums on controversial issues.

The doctrine does not require that every commentator be neutral, or that every program present both sides of an issue, but rather that broadcasters "devote substantial amounts of time for contrasting viewpoints," he said.

The limit of the commission's authority, he wrote, is to assure that broadcasters air the different sides of a public argument. Beyond that, the commission is "not the arbiter of the 'truth' of a news event," Mr. Burch wrote. He continued:

"Indeed, the drafters of the First Amendment to our Constitution knew that the way to preserve truth was not through government surveillance or censorship (for that government may also be wrong), but by giving all persons with views the freedom to express them."

Mr. Burch noted with emphasis that in two recent cases the commission invoked the same limits on its power when Democrats complained of network news coverage.

The commission ruled that neither the coverage of the Democratic National Convention in Chicago last year nor the Columbia Broadcasting System's documentary "Hunger in America" warranted investigations because of allegations of distortion. From the latter decision, Mr. Burch quoted the commission's judgment that the Government's intervention to prove such distortion would likely constitute "a worse danger than the possible rigging itself."

2 Papers Still Getting Calls on Agnew Speech

The New York Times and The Washington Post continued to receive calls yesterday from persons responding to Vice President Agnew's criticisms of the papers.

As of 6 P.M., The Times received 377 calls yesterday, 198 expressing support of the paper and 179 seconding the Vice President's speech of Thursday night.

The Washington Post reported that the number of calls it received from Thursday through last evening totaled 537, with 332 favoring the Vice President and 205 supporting The Post.

On Capitol Hill today there were mixed reactions to Mr. Agnew's speech last night in Montgomery, Ala., which cited The New York Times and The Washington Post as prime examples of what the Vice President called the "growing monopolization of the voices of public opinion."

Senator Thomas J. Dodd, Democrat of Connecticut, said that a "first-class inquiry" into the power of the press might be in order. He said that The Times had used its power to overthrow governments friendly to the United States and had brought unfriendly governments to power. He offered no examples.

Senator Mike Mansfield of Montana, the majority leader, rose in the Senate immediately after Mr. Dodd finished and said, "I would hope none of us become so concerned that we feel we couldn't stand the heat once we reached the kitchen."

"I think th t the radio, television, news magazines and newspapers have on the whole done a very competent and fair job informing the people just what the issues are," Mr. Mansfield said.

Fred W. Friendly, the Edward R. Murrow Professor of Broadcast Journalism at Columbia University, noted in a California speech this evening that the Democratic Presidents who preceded Mr. Nixon had also been subjected to the immediate, critical analysis by television commentators, of which Mr. Agnew complained.

"The Vice President has forgotten history," said Mr. Friendly, former president of C.B.S. News, "when he criticized the American Broadcasting Company's journalistic enterprise in arranging for Ambassador Harriman to participate in the broadcast that followed Mr. Nixon's speech on Nov. 3.

"I don't think President Kennedy rejoiced in having Senator Homer Capehart, an Indiana Republican, critique his Berlin crisis speech of 1961, or Ladd Plumley, president of the National Chamber of Commerce, pursuing him after his controversial 1962 speech on the state of the economy."

"How many times," Mr. Friendly asked, "did President Johnson have to listen to the cutting remarks of Minority Leaders Dirksen and Ford? It was all part of the democratic process."

"After all," he said, "the President had prime time on all three networks and a small measure of counterfire from the loyal opposition was hardly stacking the deck."

November 21, 1969

U.S.I.A. Chief Sees Ideology as Factor in TV Jobs

By TAD SZULC

Special to The New York Times

WASHINGTON, Nov. 22—Vice President Agnew's criticism of the political fairness of television networks' was preceded seven weeks ago by the suggestion by an Administration official that the networks might wish to consider "a man's ideology" before hiring him as a newsman.

This suggestion was made by Frank J. Shakespeare Jr., director of the United States Information Agency, in a speech last Sept. 26, in which he stated that "TV news, as it exists in the country today, is rather clearly liberally oriented."

The speech attracted no national attention at the time, but its text was made available by the U.S.I.A. here today in response to a request. Mr. Agnew criticized the networks in a nationally televised speech Nov. 13.

Mr. Shakespeare, who is 44 years old, once served as senior vice president of the Columbia Broadcasting System-Television and later as president of the C.B.S.-TV Service Division, which deals with the network's foreign operations.

During the Presidential campaign last year, he was Mr. Nixon's television adviser and was named U.S.I.A. director early this year.

Some of the agency's activities have recently become the subject of a controversy after it produced and sent to 104 foreign countries a television film, "The Silent Majority."

The film, which appears to deride domestic dissent from the Administration's Vietnam policies, was criticized as "unbalanced" this week by some members of the House Subcommittee on Government Information, which acts as a watchdog over the agency.

While Mr. Shakespeare's speech last September appeared to be a forerunner of Mr. Agnew's comments on television, a spokesman for the Vice President said the U.S.I.A. director had no role in preparing the Agnew address.

Addressing the annual Paul White Awards dinner of the RadioTelevision News Directors' Association in Detroit, Mr. Shakespeare argued that, because of the networks' liberal orientation, they cannot be objective even though "you sweat blood trying to be decent, objective and fair."

"I suppose that you could say that it would be shocking to take into account a man's ideology when you hire him. You want to hire a man because he is the best writer that there is, or he's the best reporter, or he's the best scenic designer, or director or news editor and not because he is a Republican, or a Democrat, or for Wallace, or a member of the John Birch Society, or the A.D.A., or whatever he is. Those are his private views and he is entitled to them."

"But," Mr. Shakespeare continued, "if out of 50 or 100 men that you hire purely on the basis of ability you are going to end up with a tremendous number on one side of the ideological fence rather than the other, then you are going to end up in a box. How are you going to handle it?"

Mr. Shakespeare then suggested that television "might consider taking a leaf from the newspapers." He cited The New York Post, which he described as being "completely oriented on the Democratic side," as an example because it publishes a column by William F. Buckley Jr. along with what Mr. Shakespeare described as "a brilliant stable of liberal writers."

Mr. Shakespeare said that The Post publishes the Buckley column because "it represents the other point of view."

Addressing the Detroit audience, Mr. Shakespeare asked:

"Do you do that? Do the networks do that? Do you purposely put a man in there because he represents the other point of view that could come into discussion?

"In any event," he continued, "I think the responsibility that you have is greater than that of the press because the press in this country is completely private enterprise. You have that terrible dilemma of licensing. Because you use the airways, your moral responsibility is greater."

"If you take 50 people who go into business, those men, by and large, would tend to be conservative," Mr. Shakespeare said.

"The overwhelming number of people who go into the creative side of television and the news side of television tend by their instincts to be liberally oriented," Mr. Shakespeare asserted.

Mr. Shakespeare cited the networks' coverage of the 1964 and 1968 Republican Presidential conventions as examples of a "certain unfairness" and "bad judgment."

He told a C.B.S. news executive in 1964 that the network was erroneously reporting that Gov. William Scranton of Pennsylvania had a chance of being nominated instead of Senator Barry Goldwater.

"I think that it was such anathema, to the TV people who were calling the shots, that Goldwater could in fact be nominated, that it affected their judgment," Mr. Shakespeare added.

At the Miami convention last year, he said "many of the television commentators . . . were giving more emphasis to [Governor] Rockefeller than it was due."

"As a result," he said, "the judgments were wrong and the people of this country and the Western world were misled."

Mr. Shakespeare cited the network coverage this year of an incident involving a United States Army company that allegedly refused to fight North Vietnamese troops as another example of what he termed a lack of objectivity.

"I suppose that happened 50 or 100 or 1,000 times in World War II and Korea but it happened this once in Vietnam or maybe a lot more, and this once it was focused on," he said, adding that this "was totally misleading the American public."

Mr. Shakespeare suggested that this incident occurred because the networks "were totally opposed to our involvement in Vietnam and they almost wanted to believe that maybe the American Army would refuse to fight."

McCarthy Says Press Wasn't Detached in '68

Senator Eugene J. McCarthy, Democrat of Minnesota, said yesterday that the press in Washington did not cover his 1968 campaign for the Presidential nomination "in a detached or objective way." He was questioned on the subject in the wake of criticisms of the news media by Vice President Agnew.

"I think the Washington press has set itself up as being expert on campaigns," Senator McCarthy said. He said that when his campaign did not fit the news media's preconceptions, the press "almost rewrote the story."

He praised European reporters covering his campaign, saying they "didn't take the standard judgments."

Washington: Are You an Agnewstic?

By JAMES RESTON

WASHINGTON, Nov. 22 — The big new cult in Washington now is Agnewsticism. To be in the inner, inner circle of the Administration, you have to be an Agnewstic, which is defined as one who disbelieves anything printed or broadcast East of the Ohio River.

It is a modern adaptation of the ancient Greek word "gnostic" — meaning know-it-all: i.e. Walter Cronkite—and also from "agnostic," the doctrine that neither the existence nor the nature of god, nor the ultimate origin of the universe, is known or knowable. Thus:

Agnewsticism (ăg-nūs′tĭ sĭz′m)

1. The doctrine that truth is safer in the hands of politicians than of television commentators or newspaper columnists. 2. Any doctrine which affirms that vast power in the possession of any small group of men, particularly in New York or Washington, is dangerous and should be watched and criticized. 3. A theory that patriots back the Government in war, even if they think it is wrong. 4. In some minds, a symbol of pressure by politicians to cover their blunders and muffle their critics.

The cult of Agnewsticism was named for Spiro Theodore Agnew, the Vice President of the United States, which is to say, the President in charge of stamping out vice. In the autumn of 1969 he discovered a "small and unelected élite" who decided every night in New York what 40 or 50 million Americans should hear and see on the television networks.

Among these city slickers or "effete snobs" were the aforementioned Cronkite from St. Joseph, Mo., David Brinkley of Wilmington, N. C., Chester Huntley of Cardwell, Mont., Howard K. Smith of Ferriday, La., Eric Sevareid of Velva, N.D., and others from "big cities," most of whom analyzed the news from left of center.

Mr. Agnew argued that commentators ought to reflect majority opinion rather than their own best judgment, and at least, that the other, or Agnewstic side, ought to have a wider hearing. At that moment, the cult of Agnewsticism was born.

Its members are a large and divergent company: People who have some grievance against television, which includes almost everybody; listeners who just don't understand how a few commentators and columnists can be so darn smart about so many things on such short notice; haters of singing commercials; card-carrying Republicans who just naturally chase commentators, as dogs chase cats.

Other Agnewstics are moderate people who simply think the critics are giving the President a hard time when he's in trouble; American Legionnaires, who think most liberal commentators are soft boiled eggs; and even some people who think "the small group of men" who are directing the war are less of a menace than the other "small group of men" in television and newspapers who are passing judgment on it.

The difference between an agnostic and an Agnewstic is critical.

Agnosticism is the principle, as defined by Thomas Huxley, "that it is wrong for a man to say that he is certain of the objective truth of any proposition unless he can produce evidence which logically justifies that certainty . . ."

Agnewsticism, as outlined by Mr. Agnew, is that it is okay for the President to assert he is "right" about Vietnam, even if he cannot "produce evidence which logically justifies that certainty," but it is *not* okay for New York commentators to doubt him unless they can prove their point and reflect majority opinion, whatever that is.

Like most theological and doctrinal controversies, however, this one divided the common allies at home and diverted them from the common enemy abroad, and raised a prophet whose disciples were more zealous than their leader or their leader's leader.

Mr. Agnew and his doctrine thus became a force of unexpected proportions. He had zeal, courage, presence, and, unlike most of the other Republican disciples, something plain to say, which he said directly and even with a certain elegance.

He set out, not to persuade the unbelievers, but to overwhelm them. His goal was merely to arouse the "silent majority" but he got them in full cry and in language which would make even a Chicago Democrat blush.

This is not a fable, and it is not entirely a joke. Agnew created a cult and dealing with the violent Agnewstics will not be easy.

November 23, 1969

Exercise in Folly

Vice President Agnew has now emerged as the bare-knuckled defender of the Nixon Administration against its critics in television and press. As such, he is acting in the tradition of American politicians who have excoriated the press when they believed it to be unfair, and who believed it to be unfair when it was against them. There is nothing new in attacks on the press, and there is nothing new in the press's criticism of an Administration in office.

But the context of Mr. Agnew's two recent speeches and the tenor of his remarks carry his comments beyond the give-and-take of normal political debate, and lend to some of his words ugly implications that he himself may not fully appreciate.

When the Vice President of the United States charges the television networks with ganging up on the Administration by employing uniformly unfriendly commentators, such a charge—however ill-founded—cannot be disassociated from the inherent power of the Government to control the airwaves through the licensing process.

When the Vice President suggests that a "growing monopoly" of irresponsible manipulators is controlling the organs of public opinion—demonstrably untrue though such a charge may be—there is a clear undertone of intimidation despite his explicit disclaimers.

When Mr. Agnew indicates that the press or the networks seek "immunity from comment and criticism" or "blind acceptance of opinions," he is conjuring up a fictitious picture of a conspiratorial, monolithic, sinister communications structure that bears no relation to reality. When with abrasive phrases, the Vice President focuses his bitter attack on those who oppose the Administration's present policy in Vietnam, he is only exacerbating the divisions in this country, and making a mockery of the President's evidently forgotten plea for reasoned discourse among the great majority of moderate, patriotic but not necessarily silent Americans.

While we reject Mr. Agnew's sweeping denunciations as ill-informed and potentially dangerous—coming as they do from one in his high office and with obvious if tacit approval of the President—we also recognize that he touched on certain points that have long been of concern to thoughtful newspapermen. The question of monopoly control can be serious; but the fact is that some of the best of American newspapers are published in "monopoly" towns, and the two cities—Washington and New York—singled out for special mention enjoy keen competition and sharp differences of editorial opinion among their respective newspapers. The "high wall of separation" between news and opinion is indeed an ideal not always achieved, and if the Vice President's strictures can help attain it so much the better.

Everyone, particularly newspaper and television professionals, realizes that the quality both of American newspapers and of television programing falls far short of the ideal. This newspaper among others has not hesitated to be critical of the failings of the communications media.

But the main thrust of the Vice President's criticism has not been directed to the genuine faults in the television and newspaper professions. The main thrust has been an attack squarely against the political opposition, an attack composed of implied threats, veiled intimidation and inflammatory language that can only further divide the American people and deflect their attention from the genuine issues of war and peace, of domestic and foreign policy, that now confront the country. Perhaps that is the reason for Mr. Agnew's exercise in folly.

Press Defended

To the Editor:

Vice President Agnew's attack on The New York Times and The Washington Post is in the worst tradition of demagoguery.

The Administration is violating the basic tenets of American democracy by the utilization of its power to intimidate the press and TV. God bless America. May it survive such totalitarian actions.

WILLIAM R. KITTAY
Roslyn Heights, L. I.
Nov. 21, 1969

November 24, 1969

AGNEW EXPLAINS: 'I'D HAD ENOUGH

He Writes in Life About Why He Decided to Speak Out

By WILLIAM BORDERS

Vice President Agnew decided to speak out against antiwar demonstrators, he says, not at the prompting of the President but because, "like the great, silent majority, I had had enough."

"I had endured the didactic inadequacies of the garrulous in silence, hoping for the best but witnessing the worst for many months. And because I am an elected official, I felt I owed it to those I serve to speak the truth," he said in an article published yesterday in Life magazine.

Besides denying that he had been speaking for President Nixon in his controversial speech in New Orleans last Oct. 19, Mr. Agnew took another look in the magazine article at "the frightening forces set in motion" by demonstrators.

"Perpetual street and campus demonstrating can erode the fabric of American democracy," the Vice President said in the two-page article, which he wrote early last week at the invitation of the magazine.

'Brutally Counterproductive'

In the widely quoted New Orleans address, while discussing antiwar protests, he said:

"A spirit of national masochism prevails, encouraged by an effete corps of impudent snobs who characterize themselves as intellectuals."

Elaborating in Life, Mr. Agnew said:

"The Vietnam Moratorium is not only negative in content but brutally counterproductive.

"It encourages the North Vietnamese Government to escalate the fighting and fortifies their recalcitrance at the bargaining table in Paris. It undermines the policies of the President of the United States."

'Emotion-Provoking Tactics'

The Vice President said that peaceful picketing and demonstrations "which interfere with no law nor any individual's rights are clearly protected by the Constitution."

"But this does not necessarily mean that such emotion-provoking tactics are justified to marshal opinion for every dispute," he continued.

Since making the speech on the protests, Mr. Agnew has stirred controversy again by two other speeches: first criticizing television news presentation and then the print news media.

Newsweek magazine, reporting on those more recent speeches in the issue that comes out this week, quotes an unnamed aide as having said that the assault on television and the press was "a campaign, and carefully organized."

Newsweek also quotes Mr. Agnew, after having denied any attempt to intimidate the news media, as countering in an interview: "The Vice President has a right to dissent, too. If anybody is intimidated, it should be me. I don't have the resources the networks have."

Mr. Agnew's office said yesterday that he had written the Life essay at the same time he was preparing the speech, delivered Thursday, in which he criticized The New York Times and The Washington Post.

But the article was devoted largely to the antiwar protesters, not to the news media.

November 24, 1969

508

Attack on Agnew

To the Editor:

As usual, Vice President Agnew's speech criticizing the major networks for reportorial bias on specific occasions was met by the various media with no serious attempt really to rebut the statements and several instances recited by Mr. Agnew. Rather, it brought forth a barrage of generalized demeaning comments, plus loud wails of threats to freedom of the press and the First Amendment.

One must conclude, therefrom, that the major networks plus a goodly portion of the daily press consider themselves above criticism yet will not hesitate to take the low road subtly to malign those who would take issue with their treatment of events that concern us all.

Freedom of the press evidently means freedom to distort and emotionalize the news as they so see fit, freedom to brainwash the public with one-sided opinions and analyses, and freedom to attribute to those critics motives which they themselves do not hesitate to employ.

By the very nature of this combined assault on Vice President Agnew are they not, in effect, attempting to stifle criticism and dissent?

Are these the standards the news media constantly self-congratulate themselves for trying to uphold?   A. FINN
Bronx, Nov. 19, 1969

Reply to Intimidation

To the Editor:

Vice President Spiro Agnew's attempt to silence TV and newspaper critics of the Nixon Administration should dispel forever the perennially naive illusions about the "New Nixon."

Nixon remains the same old demagogue, the genteel Joe McCarthy who used Communist-style innuendo to smear his political foes.

As James Reston so aptly put it, Agnew "has the courage of Nixon's convictions."

The most alarming thing about this Nixon-Agnew attempt to intimidate journalistic critics is the response of the victims. Many have acted as if this totalitarian rubbish deserved a serious reply. McCarthy similarly jolted his victims off balance. Instead of attacking that cowardly buffoon as a liar, his victims whined and pleaded innocent to McCarthy's insane accusations, issuing ridiculous appeals to fair play.

Like McCarthy, Nixon and Agnew aren't interested in fair play. They want power over a docile press and citizenry. The answer to their brazen effort at intimidation is a renewed attack on their disastrous economic, racial, and international policies.

Liberals should have learned from Joe McCarthy that the best defense against totalitarianism is a good offense.
C. W. GRIFFIN JR.
Denville, N. J., Nov. 21, 1969

Issue Discussed on TV

Walter Cronkite, the C.B.S. newsman, said last night that Mr. Agnew's speech was "a clear effort at intimidation."

Herbert Klein denied that any intimidation was meant or that Mr. Agnew had cleared the speech with President Nixon.

Bill D. Moyers, publisher of Newsday, who was President Johnson's press secretary, said that when Hubert H. Humphrey was Vice President, he was always expressing Administration policy.

Those three views, and the opinions of a number of other television commentators, were expressed in a taped hour-long C.B.S. television program, "60 Minutes."

David Brinkley the N.B.C. newsman, said that politicians have always complained of their treatment by the media.

'All that's new is that this time, this time, it's in the form of a threat," Mr. Brinkley said.

Mr. Cronkite said there was more than a hint of intimidation in that Mr. Agnew "recalled rather pointedly that the radio and television stations of this country are federally licensed." Mr. Cronkite said he felt that rather than overreacting, the networks did not react enough.

Howard K. Smith, A.B.C. newsman, said American journalism has a "negative" tradition, and that it fails to tell enough about what is right with the country.

"I think we should welcome criticism. We need it. But I think we can insist that it stop well short of intimidation," he said.

Eric Sevareid, C.B.S. commentator, said that anyone who wants the media to stress agreeable news "has only to visit Moscow or Castro's Cuba."

"Mr. Agnew would like those privileged to speak and write on these matters to reflect the majority mood of the country," Mr. Sevareid said. "Not only do majority moods change, but the public mood of the moment is not necessarily in the long-range public interest."

Mr. Moyers said, "The press should be neither a cheerleader nor a collaborator. I have yet —I have not yet decided what it is President Nixon wants the press to do."

Mr. Klein, former editor of The San Diego Union, said Mr. Nixon "would like it to be more favorable, and it's just a natural, human thing."

"But I think over a long period of time, as someone who has been in the public arena, he recognizes that the adversary relationship is going to be there, and will be there, and it is right now."

New Attacks Doubted

WASHINGTON, Nov. 25 (AP) — Vice President Agnew has no desire to keep up his attacks on the news media, a spokesman said today, and very likely will let the matter drop.

Mr. Agnew is described as believing he has made his point and stimulated discussion and self-examination among the press and television. He attacked both in nationally broadcast speeches in the last two weeks.

"I don't think he wants to harp on it," said Herbert Thompson, Mr. Agnew's press secretary.

Function of the Press

As a reader of The Times for nearly forty years, I find myself in complete agreement with Vice President Spiro Agnew regarding the one-sided presentation and the crusading spirit of The Times, especially in the last few years.

It appears that The Times is not interested in reporting events, but rather in presenting its interpretation of the events which reflects its political and social philosophy. I do not believe this is the function of a newspaper.

This problem of control over men's minds by an oligarchy of articulate individuals with no responsibility to anyone except to sell their wares, is one which should be examined thoroughly and resolved in such a way as to protect the public. Hiding behind the First Amendment is one of the facets that should be examined. Is it really freedom of the press or freedom for the press?

ALAN L. BENOSKY
New Hyde Park, L. I.
Nov. 23, 1969

November 27, 1969

Accord With Agnew

To the Editor:

I am in absolute accord with the statements made by the Vice President of the United States, Spiro T. Agnew, in his speeches of Nov. 13 and Nov. 20. Is that sensitivity on one hand and your insensitivity on the other, conflict with the basic traditions and principles of the news media. I think the Vice President has made his point quite well. You fail to convince me as to your objectivity in the presentation of the news.

ALBERT KLEVAN
Baltimore, Md., Nov. 21, 1969

Washington: The Voices of the Silent Majority

By JAMES RESTON

WASHINGTON — The efforts of the President and the Vice President to arouse support for the Administration's Vietnam policy and discredit the critics of that policy have produced a remarkable response from the people. In fact, the public reaction may very well be more violent, and even vicious, than the Administration intended.

It is hard to generalize about public opinion from letters coming into newspapers or TV networks in this part of the country, but the letters coming into The New York Times are overwhelmingly favorable to Mr. Nixon and Mr. Agnew and sharply, even savagely, critical of the press and networks.

Most of these letter writers are saying that they are with the President and Vice President, and they are charging the press and networks with embarrassing the Administration and helping the enemy. But quite a few of them go beyond this into a general indictment of reporters and commentators —often lumped together as if their assignments were the same—for "stirring up trouble" among the poor, the blacks, and the rebellious young on the university campuses.

Many of these letters come from obviously sincere people who are troubled by the turmoil of the time—by the war, the uproar in the cities, and the colleges; by the cost of living, the inflation, the alarming incidence of drug addiction, and the decline of authority in the family, the schools, and the churches.

What is clear from many of these private correspondents, however, is that press and television, particularly the "liberal" commentators of the East, are being blamed for supporting the social revolution of the last two generations, for backing the growth of the welfare state, for dramatizing the plight of the Negroes, and for prolonging the war they have sought to end.

In short, the press is now being charged by the conservatives for advocating the turmoil it is reporting — which sometimes it does and sometimes it doesn't — and the paradox of this is that the press is also being attacked almost as violently by the militant radicals of the left for being an instrument of "the establishment" and the status quo.

It is not hard to understand why the President authorized this campaign against his critics on the war. They were dominating the comment on Vietnam and no doubt giving the impression, which was probably never true, that they represented the feelings of most of the American people.

When Mr. Nixon speeded up the process of withdrawal from Vietnam and changed the battlefield orders to minimize the casualties and the search-and-destroy tactics, he thought he would get support from his critics in the East, but he got very little. Accordingly he set out to energize his natural supporters in the middle and on the right. One doubts that he intended to arouse the old backlash extremists on the right, but with the help of the Vice President, he has apparently done so.

For the appeal against the "Eastern" snobs has not only aroused support for his Vietnam policy, but revived the always latent anti-New York feelings in the country, and this in turn has produced some ugly anti-Negro and anti-Semitic, and anti-Communist reactions which neither Mr. Nixon nor Mr. Agnew could have intended.

This is not a major theme in the letters coming into this office, but it is clearly an element in the controversy. Critics of the war are addressed as "Communists" who are helping Hanoi, the blacks, the unions, the young, and "all the other troublemakers."

It is not only that we are "unfair" and "inaccurate"—as God knows we sometimes are — but that we are "subversives." A column that supports a reader's opinion is usually characterized as "objective" and "fair," while one that disagrees is "subjective," "opinionated," and even pro-Communist.

Typical of the extreme comments from the right is one from a reader in Texas: "You are the clique that are polarizing the country. The typical Communist reverse psychology doesn't work with those of us who work for a living. Keep trying there in the slums. You made them, and buddy, you keep telling them I'm going to pay for them. Just keep it up. They believe you? Regards to the rest of the Jewish businessmen."

Nevertheless, the Administration has clearly mobilized a lot of support that is now attacking its critics. The President's popularity has soared in the polls since the counterattack started, and now all he has to prove is his assertion that this support can really help him end the war.

November 28, 1969

Agnew's Attack

To the Editor:

I heartily agree with Vice President Agnew's speech and sentiments on TV news coverage. This speech on the subject is long overdue. He showed great courage in his attack for now he will be at their mercy.

I feel somewhat the same way about your fine newspaper. The Times has so many wonderful departments but some of its news coverage is definitely slanted and biased.

Advertising is so very expensive, but so much of it is given free to causes, situations and people who really don't deserve it.

ROBERT F. CARNEY
New Rochelle, N. Y.
Nov. 14, 1969

●

Disagrees With Agnew

To the Editor:

Please accept my vote of confidence in regard to your editorial policy. I disagree completely with Vice President Agnew's remarks.

We need frank, honest and objective reporting which media like The Times and Washington Post have been giving the American public.

Please don't be intimidated.

(Rev.) MATTHEW COSTELLO
O.S.B.
Newton, N. J., Nov. 21, 1969

November 28, 1969

November 29, 1969

Power of the Media

To the Editor:

Nobody likes to make enemies with the town crier, but it is important that the Vice President's excessive partisanship not be permitted to cloud the thrust of his comments on the serious problems posed for our democracy by the concentration of power in the media.

Power is not in itself anathema to democracy if it is accompanied by proper restraints. Restraints against the enormous power of the communications media are inadequate and becoming more so.

It is axiomatic that a mutual nonaggression pact is the best one can hope for in the relationship of public officials to journalists. The facts, however, are that the media not only have a credibility gap with public officials but also with the public as a whole. Unfortunately, newspapers have long been criticized for emphasizing sensationalism. Over the years, the public has come to depend more on television for its news and to believe television more than newspapers. But with the new trend in television journalism which seeks to introduce opinion and controversy, it is now clear that television is moving toward the same presentation of images that distort reality. It is not easy to define the meaning of news precisely, but it obviously is not the equivalent of the aberrational.

These problems are particularly troublesome with the absence of professionalism as an effective form of self-restraint. Most of Washington's newsmen seek to be professionals in the best sense of the word. But there is no such requirement. Neither professional training nor specific education are prerequisites for their employment.

Once a newsman is on a payroll, he is answerable only to himself and his editors. Doctors can and do lose their licenses for malpractice. There is a procedure for disbarring irresponsible lawyers. Even stockbrokers can be barred from selling to the public if they violate established ethical codes. But the newsman can, with impunity, sell wares which poison the wells from which democracy must drink. There are no accepted ethical codes available to guide him or by which to judge him.

These questions must be raised without introducing the ominous threat of Government censorship. Unrestrained power in a democratic society is a highly dangerous phenomenon. To propose that the media come up with procedures to discipline and contain the awesome power it possesses is reasonable.

Our country boasts some of the best journalists in the world. The quality and competence represented in the profession should be capable of tackling the questions raised and supplying answers worthy of a responsible fourth estate.

MAX M. KAMPELMAN
Washington, Nov. 18, 1969

●

Agnew's Campaign

To the Editor:

Out of 1,752 daily newspapers in the United States, with a total circulation of 62.5 million, the Agnew antibias campaign has fingered The Times and The Washington Post, with a combined daily circulation of less than two million.

It is well that our national leaders express concern for the ideal of informed citizens with access to all shades of opinion. The Times and The Post do have a mild liberal bias, although liberal often means being better informed and not viewing the world in black-and-white simplifications. However, the Vice President should also consider the other sixty million front pages that are read daily.

Indeed, it might be found that the silent American is silent because most U.S. newspapers—each controlled by a handful of editorial decision-makers—provide skimpy and slanted information on national and international affairs, and many of these papers are marked by a blatant right-wing bias.

Perhaps Mr. Agnew can grow into a champion of an informed citizenry. But this may be too much to hope for. It is far easier simply to manipulate the ignorant.

MICHAEL MARIEN
Research Associate
Educational Policy Research Center, Syracuse University
Syracuse, Nov. 24, 1969

Music

Agnew: Like a Producer When His Show Is Panned?

By HAROLD C. SCHONBERG

SHOW business is show business, whether on Broadway or in Washington. It was with a certain amount of amusement that I listened to, and later read, the speech by Vice President Agnew about the news broadcasts on television. He was so much in the position of a producer whose show had been panned by the critics. Those miserable wretches even had the temerity to criticize his leading man, President Nixon. So the Vice President exploded, much as David Merrick has exploded over certain (to him) cretinous reviews, and in much the same manner that President Truman once took pen in hand to tell off Paul Hume, the music critic of the Washington Post.

How often have critics in all fields come across the parallel argument to the one the Vice President made! "When the President completed his address — an address, incidentally, that he spent weeks in the preparation of—his words and policies were subjected to instant analysis and querulous criticism." Substitute a play, or a recital, or a new piece of music. We have spent years preparing for this event, runs the complaint, and those critics destroy us in ten minutes. Those self-appointed critics, yet. Everybody knows critics are self-appointed. Like me, for instance. I walked into the managing editor's office one day and said I wanted to appoint myself music critic of The New York Times. "Yes, of course, by all means. Take it. Is there anything else I can do for you?"

＊

And, continued the Vice President, the self-appointed pundits "can make or break by their coverage and commentary . . ." Sound familiar? "They can elevate men from obscurity to national prominence within a week." Yet they are at bottom parochial, reflecting the narrow views of Washington or (shudder) New York. They are not objective. The Vice President made a great deal of this lack of objectivity.

The problem of objectivity has bedeviled historians, critics, analysts and editors ever since speech was invented. George Bernard Shaw once said, in effect, "Who am I to be objective?" He added that the only one in the universe who could be objective was God. Critics, newspapermen, editors, vice presidents — all reflect their own mind and their own backgrounds, else they would not be men. The New York Times some years ago started "news analysis" columns, as opposed to straight news, so that the reader would be warned. People who plead loudest for objectivity are generally the ones whose own interests are involved. Vice President Agnew, perhaps not the most objective person in the country, tried to offer one suggestion: that the analysts or critics, and the networks, be "made more responsive to the views of the nation and more responsible to the people they serve."

But that is not criticism. It would put a critic in the position merely of reflecting a majority point of view. It may be that the Vice President has a point when he claims that the dissemination of news on television is controlled by too few men. But he has no point at all when he criticizes analysts, such as the group who came on the air directly after President Nixon's speech on Vietnam. Those men were not there in a news function. They were specifically there as analysts, to discuss the meaning and implications of the speech. They happen to be very well-trained men, with long experience in politics and the Washington scene. One does not have to agree or disagree with their opinions, but surely they are worth listening to.

And that introduces the old, old subject of what the Vice President called "instant criticism." If his logic can be followed, he was saying that since President Nixon took weeks in preparing his address to the nation, the analysts should have spent equal time thinking about it. We get that in music criticism all the time. "It took me three years to compose that opera, and the critic, who has heard it only once . . ." The older critics had an answer to that one. As soon as you crack an egg, they would say, you know if it is good or rotten. The point is that experienced music critics, like experienced drama critics or political analysts, are not writing snap judgments. They are bringing years of background to their "instant" opinion. Musicians are apt to be hypocrites on the subject. When a professional musician goes, say, to a piano recital, he knows within five minutes whether or not the pianist is good or bad. But he will be the first to raise a howl at an "instant" review criticizing an artist. He can do it, but the critic shouldn't.

But nobody has come up with an alternative—nobody, at least, in a free society. The Communists have solved the problem, and so have the dictators of the Right. There the press and other communications media reflect only one point of view. Presumably we do not want that in the United States. Yet Herbert Klein, praising the Agnew speech, said that he hoped — he *hoped!*—that the Government would not have to step in and do something about it. The exact words of his not so veiled threat were: "If you look at all the problems you have today and you fail to examine them, you do invite the Government to come in. I would not like to see that happen." Those words should have caused a thrill of fear in anybody who cherishes American institutions.

It was an implied threat to Constitutional liberty. Yet there was no great public outcry. Are we approaching the point where our own Government is going to tell critics what to write and analysts what to say? Only three weeks ago, in Greece, a law was passed providing prison terms and fines for "press offenses." Deputy Premier Stylianos Patakos rationalized it very well. "Severity," he said, "is the mother of justice and freedom." Or, in more direct English, you write what we tell you to write, or else.

*

In an open society, there has to be a free exchange of ideas, and it is the critic who most often carries ideas. That does not mean that critics—or analysts, or anybody else engaged in a critical function—should themselves be immune from criticism. Many of them should be criticized and, indeed, are constantly being criticized. Bernard Haggin thinks that I am a disgrace to American music criticism, and I think that he is a sour, pedantic old maid of a critic who was left at the altar many years back and has since been taking it out on everybody else. He wants to substitute his set of values for mine, just as John Simon wants the world to accept his values rather than Clive Barnes's and just as Vice President Agnew wants his set of values considered juster than those of the "self-appointed" David Brinkley. Fine. And it will remain fine as long as opponents joust with ideas, trying to convince the world one way or another through the strength of their ideas. But when talk of thought control enters the picture, then severity indeed will be the mother of justice and freedom.

Biased News Charge

To the Editor:

I agree with Vice President Agnew that The Times slants its news against the Administration.

But this is no new thing. You angled it that way all through President Nixon's campaign before he was elected.

It is true too The Times has become a monopoly newspaper. As my sister-in-law, actress June Havoc says, The Times has the power alone to make or kill a play by the review of one man. This is an awesome power.
CARLETON L. SPIER
Scarsdale, N.Y., Nov. 24, 1969

Agnew on Garrison

To the Editor:

One wonders whether Vice President Spiro Agnew, his speechwriters and his enraptured audience of Alabamians on Nov. 20 have any idea of who William Lloyd Garrison actually was and what the circumstances were under which Garrison uttered those words with which Mr. Agnew concludes his denunciation of the Eastern press: "I am in earnest—I will not equivocate—I will not excuse—I will not retreat a single inch —and I will be heard."

Garrison was probably the most radical newspaper editor in the annals of American journalism. He was the leader of the extreme militant wing of the abolitionist movement and made a profession of denouncing the United States Government in his famous Liberator, founded in 1831. The first issue of that paper contained a ringing manifesto from which Mr. Agnew quoted. Among other inflammatory statements and acts that followed in Garrison's thirty-year campaign of civil and sometimes not so civil disobedience, he declared that the Constitution of the United States (because it recognized slavery as legal) was "a covenant with death and an agreement with hell"; and on the Fourth of July in 1854, at Framingham, Mass., he publicly burned the Constitution of the United States, crying: "So perish all compromises with tyranny!"

Extremism sometimes brings strange yokefellows together.
L. H. BUTTERFIELD
Cambridge, Mass., Nov. 21, 1969
The writer, a historian, edited The Adams Papers.

December 3, 1969

Agrees With Agnew

To the Editor:

Another voice from the silent majority. Vice President Agnew is absolutely right in what he says about your paper, and I sincerely hope you do get the message.
HAYDEN PRESTON
Fort Lee, N. J., Nov. 22, 1969

TV: N.E.T.'s 'Middle America' Answers Agnew

By JACK GOULD

TELEVISION'S first acceptance of Vice President Agnew's challenge that the public hears too many liberal viewpoints from New York and Washington and not enough conservative opinions from the Midwest was heard from Chicago last night on "News in Perspective" over Channel 13.

To the extent that a small panel of journalists can reflect regional differences the ideological conclusions seemed very nearly divided, but it was refreshing to see and hear new faces besides the familiar network.

M. Stanton Evans, editor of The Indianapolis News; Clayton Kirkpatrick, editor of The Chicago Tribune; Mark Ethridge Jr., editor of The Detroit Free Press, and Seth King, Midwest correspondent of The New York Times, were questioned for an hour by Clifton Daniel, associate editor of The Times. "News in Perspective" is jointly produced by The Times and National Educational Television.

On the program, entitled "Middle America," Mr. Evans held the strongest view that the television networks were too liberally slanted but later agreed that the peace movement did seem to be growing in the Midwest. Together with others, he drew the distinction between general support for President Nixon's Vietnam policy and the nonpartisan yearning for the war's end.

Mr. Kirkpatrick saw no threat of intimidation in Mr. Agnew's speeches because,

he said, a newspaper should be accustomed to criticism. Mr. Ethridge felt Mr. Agnew might have unwisely polarized opinion because disagreement on national policy suddenly had become shriller since his speeches and he thought this a dangerous trend.

Mr. King said that one could detect in the Midwest a deeper feeling for "family, flag and church" than in the East but observed that while covering the frst peace moratorium in Minneapolis the police there reported a record crowd. Concerning the alleged massacre at Songmy, Mr.

Kirkpatrick defended a Chicago Tribune editorial expressing the hope the incident would not be used to whip up emotion against national policy.

As moderator, Mr. Daniel did not let his ugests off the hook on questions that might have been embarrassing and Mr. King wryly cited two polls by Chicago newspapers that resulted in diametrically opposed results.

But the main virtue of "News in Perspective," which was televised at WTTW-TV Chicago, was to open airwaves to a larger section of opinion and not always hear-

ing the same people on the same programs. In due course similar presentations from the Deep South and the West Coast might be of value. Last night's program registered well as an example that the so-called "silent majority" west of the Hudson is just as concerned with contemporary issues as the East.

"News in Perspective" was supplemented by man-in-the-street interviews, which constituted the only opportunity for youth to be heard very briefly. This is one point that the formal discussion could have covered more fully.

December 4, 1969

Agnew's a Hit at Wife's Party

Special to The New York Times

WASHINGTON, Dec. 4— Vice President Agnew crashed his wife's party today and stole the spotlight.

In the course of his visit, the Vice President (1) played the piano; (2) discussed his musical tastes; (3) had some kind things to say about the press, and (4) indicated that he may visit Vietnam during the three-week trip to the Far East that he and his wife

Judy will make starting Dec. 26.

Mr. Agnew walked in on a coffee party that his wife was giving for 75 women reporters to show off the refurbished Blair House. His timing couldn't have been better, since it came moments after Mrs. Agnew mournfully noted that he was out of practice now that their piano is in storage.

"I must get it unpacked and put into our apartment,"

commented Mrs. Agnew, who looked trim in an easy-skirted black dress with a green and white scarf tied around the neck. She no sooner had finished speaking than Mr. Agnew walked in and, after first demurring, gave in to the insistent reporters and sat down at Blair House's spinet piano.

The Vice President played a free-form version of "Sophisticated Lady," said he has always liked Duke Ellington, who wrote the piece, and revealed that "for the first time" he had found a young rock group that he liked. It was the Fifth Dimension, which played at the White House last night.

The Vice President, whose earlier comments about the nation's press have been on the abrasive side, suavely commented that he thought "the women of the press are prettier and more objective than the men."

First Trip Abroad

Mr. Agnew didn't go into detail about his trip to the Far East, but Mrs. Agnew did. She said it would be her first trip out of the country and that she still hadn't planned her wardrobe for it.

Before leaving, the Agnews plan to celebrate Christmas at home with their children and grandchild. Mrs. Agnew said she is doing needlepoint pillows ("a blue elephant") for her grandchild, Michele.

On the way out ("I have got to get back to the Senate," he explained) Mr. Agnew paused long enough to order his evening meal. "Have steak for dinner," he said to his wife. She nodded and he left.

Associated Press

Vice President Agnew playing the piano yesterday at wife's party for women reporters.

December 5, 1969

GOODELL URGES TV NOT TO EASE VIEWS

Says He's Troubled by Tone of Agnew's Criticism

By RICHARD L. MADDEN
Special to The New York Times

WASHINGTON, Dec. 4 — Senator Charles E. Goodell urged the broadcasting networks today not to react to Vice President Agnew's criticism "by compromising in any way their responsibility to offer informative and provocative news analysis and comment."

In a 4,600-word speech on the Senate floor, the New York Republican said he was "deeply troubled" by the tone and implications of Mr. Agnew's recent criticism of the communications media.

The Senator said that the Vice President had raised important questions about the television industry but had discussed those questions "in a manner that was not particularly conducive to rational debate."

Mr. Goodell said that Mr. Agnew had let "bad rhetoric drive out good sense," and declared:

"He seems to have fallen victim to the very same failing of which he accuses the networks: stressing confrontation at the expense of reasoned argument."

Noting that Mr. Agnew had insisted that he had no intent to propose Government censorship of television, Mr. Goodell said:

"The question remains, however, whether the Vice President has attempted to use the prestige of his high office to place pressure upon the networks to report the news in a manner more favorable to the Administration."

Mr. Agnew was not presiding over the Senate when Mr. Goodell delivered his speech criticizing the Vice President. Many members of Mr. Goodell's staff watched from the gallery as the speech touched off a brisk but brief debate among the few other Senators on the floor at the time.

Senator Russell B. Long, Democrat of Louisiana, said that many persons approved of Mr. Agnew's views. Mr. Long criticized a television commentator, whom he did not identify ("some fellow I never heard of"), who appeared on camera right after President Nixon's speech on Vietnam last month and said, as Mr. Long recalled, "The public will be disappointed." Mr. Long said of the commentator:

"He probably couldn't be elected dogcatcher in his own home town, that's probably why he's in New York."

Mr. Long also attacked what he called the "slanted and unfair" coverage of the Democratic National Convention in Chicago last year and said: "It helped to elect a Republican."

Supporting Mr. Goodell was his Republican colleague from New York, Senator Jacob K. Javits. "Nobody's trying to muzzle the Vice President," Mr. Javits said. He said Mr. Goodell's speech assured the networks that "they have champions and need not be inhibited" by Mr. Agnew's criticism.

At one point in the debate, the Senate majority leader, Mike Mansfield of Montana, opened a book and read the First Amendment to the Constitution, which provides for freedom of speech and the press. "That applies to every American," he said. "I hope we never forget it."

About the time he was being discussed in the Senate Mr. Agnew dropped in at Blair House, where his wife was meeting over coffee with a group of women reporters.

The Vice President disclosed that he would make a "major speech" later this month before he leaves Dec. 26 with his wife on a 22-day trip to the Pacific and the Far East. He said only: "I'll have something rather interesting to say in December."

In his speech, Mr. Goodell said that "sanitized television news, made to appeal to the lowest common denominator in the name of appealing to some elusive consensus, will make Americans stop using their intelligence about politics."

Referring to Mr. Agnew's speech of Nov. 20, in which the Vice President criticized the growing concentration of corporate control and The New York Times and The Washington Post, Mr. Goodell said that Mr. Agnew "suggests that he only objects to concentration when the media involved opposes the policies that he supports." Mr. Goodell said:

"The criticized the Washington Post Company for owning both a radio and television station, but omitted any reference whatsoever to The Washington Star, which also owns a radio and television station but tends to favor the positions of the Administration.

"He had harsh words for The New York Times, but no criticism of The New York Daily News, which boasts a circulation two and a half times that of The Times, controls television station WPIX, and is owned by the largest paper in mid-America, The Chicago Tribune."

In Midwest, the Media Must 'Make Sense

By JAMES T. WOOTEN
Special to The New York Times

GRAND ISLAND, Neb. — Mrs. Morris Z. Niedenheim loves Walter Cronkite.

She said so near the produce section of the Hinky Dinky supermarket, where she disclosed a similar fondness for The Omaha World Herald, Paul Harvey, Chet Huntley, U. S. News & World Report, David Lawrence and the Grand Island Independent.

"But it doesn't make any difference where I read it or who says it," the 56-year-old grandmother added a few days ago as she guided her cart toward the meat counter. "If it doesn't make sense to me, I just don't believe it."

In the distance between the lettuce and the lamb chops she had articulated the news perspective embraced by many of her neighbors here in this prairie town of 30,000. It is an attitude that has come under close scrutiny in this country since Vice President Agnew's recent attacks on the news media.

Where do the people of Grand Island get their news? What is the source of their opinions?

According to Mr. Agnew, "a small band of self-elected men" in Washington and New York controls the news and manipulates the opinions of the American people. While Grand Islanders are obviously not "the American people," they may be considered at least representative of a substantial portion of the populace of the heartland.

"He may be right. I don't know," John D. Kinzie conceded as he tinkered beneath the hood of a car in his service station. "But if the press is trying to 'snow' the country, they'd have a hell of a time doing it in Grand Island. We're just too independent."

Many of his fellow Grand Islanders would probably agree, for in their daily regimen is a healthy strain of the rugged individualism for which the vast, Midwestern region of this country is noted.

This is the land of Willa Cather's "O Pioneers," of homesteads and Pawnees, of land rushes and buffalos, of William Jennings Bryan, and a one-house state legislature that has always insisted on pay-as-you-go government.

The people work hard, pay their bills, go to church, spank their children when they think they deserve it, live longer than most Americans, love football, and generally believe their way of life is better than any other.

Core of Economy

Their town was born a century ago as the child of hardy pioneers and the expanding Union Pacific Railroad, and although the years have wrought inevitable changes the soul of Grand Island has remained intact.

Agriculture is still, as it has always been, the core of Grand Island's economy. The flat land stretches for miles, irrigated expertly from the Platte River and other sources, and planted in corn, milo and soybeans.

But the industrial revolution is creeping into the city. A farm implement manufacturing plant, a meat packing company and a Government ammunition factory employ hundreds of local residents.

"I'd rather work than play," Richard D. Spelts Jr. boasted in his office, from which he runs a highly successful combine of construction and construction supply companies interspersed with a variety of other companies, all of which began with the $2,000 he saved as a Navy officer during World War II. "I think you'll find most of us around here like that."

The emphasis on work is at the heart of the city's existence and nearby is an affection is selective isolationism that began when the railroads and the Conestoga wagons lumbered through on their way West.

"All types of folks came through here back then," said Bud Berry, who, at 36, is the youngest train master on the Union Pacific. "I think that was when the people who lived here —the ones who stayed behind when the trains pulled out— they realized that they could pick up and choose from the ideas and opinions and whatever else the people brought with them from the East."

The passenger service, once a booming part of the life of the city, has waned considerably and the dusty, dingy old depot, creaking with ghosts of nearly forgotten days, is open only at night when the only two trains come roaring in and out of Grand Island. Still, the lessons learned by their ancestors are practiced by the people here today.

Now, the ideas of the East are channeled into the city by television and the newspapers and news magazines. But, like Mrs. Neidenheim and their grandfathers and grandmothers, the people of Grand Island ask that they meet their stand-

The New York Times (by Gary Settle)

Keith O'Neil, a disk jockey at radio station KRGI in Grand Island, Neb., offers American flags for sale to listeners. This is done by KRGI and KMMJ, the other local station. They also support National Unity Week and other causes.

ards of reason and common sense or they reject them.

Despite the fact that Grand Island residents seem generally immune to the moods that capture many other Americans in many other places, they are neither unaware nor uninformed.

And despite their claim to independence they are to some extent at least dependent on the traditional sources of news for the basis of their independent opinions.

A glance at their immediate news sources may provide a clue, to their independence.

Two local radio stations, both with New York City network affiliations, offer a diet of music and news and occasional comment that probably does have an impact on the thought processes of their listeners.

On KRGI, mid-morning listeners hear the familiar, "Hello America? This is Paul Harvey!" and the now famous, sometimes sarcastic, always provocative, habitually conservative news commentary that follows, usually from Chicago.

Throughout the day, both KRGI and KMMJ, the older of the two stations, frequently air patriotic, public service announcements promoting the purchase and display of American flags, support for National Unity Week and similar causes.

In the evenings, news from all three major television networks is available both before and after local news programs on stations broadcasting from Lincoln, the Nebraska capital, nearby Hastings and Kearney.

In addition to its own daily newspaper, The Grand Island Independent, local residents regularly read The Lincoln Star or The Omaha World Herald, or both—and all three publications are traditionally Republican-oriented.

Their columnists are, day by day, more attuned to the virtues than to the alleged vices of the present Administration, and their editorials generally applaud or support steps taken or recommended by Republicans both locally and in Washington.

Counter Sales Brisk

The Denver Post and The Kansas City Star both enjoy brisk counter sales at Ruby's news shop where Time, Newsweek, U. S. News & World Report, The New York Times Sunday edition and The Chicago Tribune run far behind the regional publications.

The Grand Island Independent is owned by Stauffer Newspapers, Inc., with headquarters in Topeka, Kan., and among some of the more outspoken community leaders is regarded more or less as an innocuous shopping guide.

That view, however, is somewhat misleading since The Independent provides Grand Islanders with a mixture of local, state, national and international news and well-written editorial comment.

Following the recent controversy over the nomination of Judge Clement F. Haynsworth to the Supreme Court, The Independent editorially refused to approve or disapprove of the Senate's rejection of Judge

Haynsworth, but did criticize all public officials whose personal insensitivity to the appearance of impropriety "brings distrust and suspicion to the minds of the electorate."

Soon after Veterans Day last month, The Independent spoke out on the prospects of the shutdown of the Cornhusker Army Ammunition Plant, four miles from Grand Island, and the source of many thousands of dollars for the city's economy.

While recognizing that any cutback of its workload would have a substantial impact on the rest of the community, The Independent said that "like all other Nebraskans we want this war to end."

"I think we're well-informed out here, and I wouldn't want to discount the subjective powers of the press, especially television," the 50-year-old Mr. Spelts said. "But what is important to remember is that we are deliberate people who depend on our own instincts and judgment."

William H. Riley, a young bank vice president, agreed. "Television and the rest of the press have a tremendous influence on the country," he said. "But not politically. At least not around here."

The 36-year-old Mr. Riley is a Roman Catholic Democrat, "because my Dad was one, I suppose—but I still make my own decisions regardless of that."

According to Mr. Riley, the attitudes of many Grand Is-

landers can occasionally result in a failure to understand or relate to the world around them. "Omaha could go to hell but we would still be all right," he said, only half in jest. "A lot of people here actually believe that's true."

"Sometimes I think I even believe it," he laughed, shooting the cuffs of his blue, button-down shirt and flicking a speck of lint from the front of his finely cut, wool plaid suit.

"Sure, we're influenced by what everybody calls the Eastern Establishment," he continued. "We pick up the styles of dress, the class entertainment, the quality books — but those are really rather insignificant areas of life."

For Mr. Riley then, the threat of a subliminal move to capture his mind and those of his fellow Grand Islanders is "at most rather minimal and, very frankly speaking, fairly absurd."

Upstairs, above the bank, Richard L. DeBacker sat in his book-lined office and considered the same subject. "As an attorney," he said. "I deal with all sorts of people—people in trouble, people with money, people without money, people about to get money. I'd say that if they have anything in common, it is their stubborn independence."

Grand Island, Mr. DeBacker believes, "would be the last place in the world to try to put something over on somebody." As a "liberal Democrat" who once served as county attorney, an elective office, he has had considerable practical experience in local politics. "They are really sort of predictable here," he said. "I don't think there have been any surprises in several years."

The political structure of the community is evenly divided between Democrats and Republicans and the willingness of Grand Island voters to move across their party's lines may be observed in the last three Presidential elections.

In 1960, Richard M. Nixon defeated John F. Kennedy in the city by a margin of approximately 3 to 1.

In 1964, Lyndon B. Johnson emerged victorious in the city's precincts by a similar margin, and last November, while the state of Nebraska was giving Mr. Nixon his largest margin of victory, Grand Islanders were also endorsing him at a ratio of nearly 4 to 1.

It was, of course, no surprise to Mr. DeBacker or anyone else in the town that Mr. Nixon was the biggest votegetter last year, just as he had been in 1960.

"George Wallace's showing was really rather laughable," Mr. DeBacker recalled. "Something less than 5 per cent of the votes.

The Wallace candidacy, according to Mr. Spelts, was a source of local humor from the moment it began until the election. "We'd see him on television and listen to him and we all knew what he was up to and we all laughed because we knew this kind of stuff just didn't make sense," Mr. Spelts said.

The fact that nearly 10 million Americans did not consider the Wallace candidacy a laughing matter only mildly disturbed Mr. Spelts, a man of considerable wealth who has been active in state and national Republican affairs for several years.

He was the leader of the Goldwater Truth Squad in 1964, a team of Republicans that followed the Democratic candidates around the country and tried to rebut their own campaign statements.

"Politics is a matter of emotions, and around here one of the chief emotions, strangely, is what the people believe to be their own common sense," Mr. Spelts said. "Nobody around here, regardless of their gripes and their passions, is going to give Wallace and his type of candidates any serious thought at all."

Once again, as it had in conversations at the supermarket, the service station, the bank and in the law office, the emphasis on reason and common sense was given new voice.

Down the street from the bank, Mr. I. J. Matthews settled into the chair at Darrell's Barber Shop and applied his 81 years of experience to the same topic. "The news folks got power, that's true, all right, and they do need to watch what they do with it, like Agnew says," he growled. "But anybody with power has to watch what they do with that power, don't you think?"

Not many years before Mr. Matthews was born, during the Reconstruction Era, two men who had fought on opposite sides in the Civil War took the Overland Trail westward to find new lives.

They settled in Grand Island and became close friends, because, as a local historian has recorded, "they were reasonable gentlemen who forgot the past, paid small mind to the sorry temper of the country, and ignored Eastern politics."

After nearly a century, their logic still prevails and no one here is really very worried about the same things that worry Mr. Agnew.

Transcript of the President's News Conference

...s ...to ...if they did ...ear the ...cent men that ...one to Vietnam in a very, in ...pinion, important cause.

3. Agnew Speeches

Q. Mr. President, Vice President Agnew in recent weeks has made two speeches in which he has criticized the news media—broadcasting in particular.
A. Yes, I know.

Q. What, if anything, in those speeches is there with which you disagree?

A. Before this audience? The Vice President does not clear his speeches with me, just as I did not clear my speeches with President Eisenhower. However, I believe that the Vice President rendered a public service in talking in a very dignified and courageous way about a problem that many Americans are concerned about, and that is the coverage by news media—and particularly television news media—of public figures.

Now let me be quite precise. He did not advocate censorship. On the contrary, he advocated that there should be free expression. He did not oppose bias. On the contrary, he recognized—as I do—that there should be opinion.

Let me say on that score that I don't want a bunch of intellectual eunuchs either writing the news or talking about the news. I like excitement in the news, whether it's on television or whether it's in the columns.

He did say, and perhaps this point should be well taken, that television stations might well follow the practice of newspapers of separating news from opinion. When opinion is expressed, label it so, but don't mix the opinion in with the reporting of the news.

It seems to me these were useful suggestions. Perhaps the networks disagreed with the criticisms, but I would suggest that they should be just as dignified and just as reasonable in answering the criticisms as he was in making them.

4. Tax Veto

Q. Sir, if the final version ... reform bill now ... inclu... th...

Nixon Reaffirms Stand on Dissent and Defends Agnew

By JAMES M. NAUGHTON
Special to The New York Times

WASHINGTON, Dec. 8 — President Nixon said tonight that he would not permit dissent in America to dissuade him from following the path he believes will lead to a "just peace" in Vietnam.

In his first full-dress news conference since Sept. 26, Mr. Nixon dealt at length with dissent—from the news media and from citizens voicing opposition to his policies.

He said he had "no complaints" about the way the media had treated his Administration. But he defended Vice President Agnew's criticism of the media, calling it "a public service."

Asked if he and Mr. Agnew were purchasing support for Vietnam policy at the risk of polarizing the country, Mr. Nixon said that one of the problems of leadership is that it involves taking positions.

"I like to be liked," the President said. "I don't like to say things that everybody doesn't agree with."

It would be easy, he noted, to greet peace marchers in Washington and agree to do what they demand.

"But a President has to do what he considers to be right—right for the people, right, for example, in pursuing a just peace, not just peace for our time, for a little time," he added.

Reminded that his Administration had been criticized for failing to reach young people, Mr. Nixon said he believed that "you reach the young people more by talking to them as adults than talking to them as young people."

He added that he was pleased that many young people wrote to him expressing opinions about his Vietnam speech last month, noting that "they didn't all agree, but at least they had listened, they had paid attention."

The televised news conference was the first that the President has held since mass antiwar dmonstrations near the White House in October and November.

It also was his first meeting with the media since Vice President Agnew criticized the television networks and later, The New York Times and The Washington Post.

"I believe that the Vice President rendered a public service in talking in a very dignified and courageous way," Mr. Nixon said, "about a problem that many Americans are concerned about, and that is the coverage by news media—and particularly television news media—of public figures."

Although Mr. Agnew and other Administration officials have contended that news media sometimes dramatize negative aspects of American life rather than report on what the majority feels or does, Mr. Nixon said he likes "excitement in the news."

It would not be appropriate, the President added, for "a bunch of intellectual eunuchs" to write the news or relate it over broadcast outlets.

But he said that Mr. Agnew's point should be "well taken, that television stations might well follow the practice of newspapers of separating news from opinion."

The President said, nonetheless, that he felt the media had been generally fair in coverage of his actions and those of the Vice President and others in his Administration.

He said that he would have no complaints "just so long as the news media allows—as it does tonight—an opportunity for me to be heard directly by the people, and then the television commentators to follow me," adding that "I'll take my chances."

December 9, 1969

POWER OF THE 'FEW' IN PRESS DEPLORED

AUSTIN, Tex., Dec. 13 (AP) — Too few have too much power in the press as well as broadcasting, an authority on communications law says.

Prof. James Barron of the George Washington University Law School said Wednesday that he agreed with Vice President Agnew that "media power" was too concentrated. But he disagreed with what he said was Mr. Agnew's approach to the problem.

Professor Barron gave the eighth annual Lecture on Law and the Free Society at the University of Texas Law School.

Professor Barron said the resolution of the problem "is not that henceforth networks and famous newspapers should strive to please Vice Presidents, but rather by the creation of machinery for dialogue.

"Resolution should be sought by evoking mechanisms which permit the various segments of opinion to avail themselves of the opinion-making process."

Professor Barron said the situation of newspapers was "starkly different" from that of broadcasters.

"Unlike broadcasters, newspaper publishers are totally without any legal objection to reply," he said.

He said a "necessary step" to securing free debate "should have been to require newspapers to provide the subjects of their attacks with an opportunity to reply."

December 14, 1969

FORTAS DECLARES AGNEW STIRS FEAR

WASHINGTON, Dec. 15 (UPI) — Former Supreme Court Justice Abe Fortas said today that Vice President Agnew had generated fears that the Government might retaliate when the press criticized United States officials.

He did not say that was the intention of Mr. Agnew's recent attacks on news media, but he said that it was the "inevitable" effect because the Government licenses television stations and newspapers' television stations.

"The owners of television properties cannot escape the gnawing and corrosive fear that official criticism of their news reporting may be reflected in the F.C.C. [Federal Communications Commission] proceedings either by encouraging competitive applications, or even in a refusal to renew their licenses," Mr. Fortas said in a speech at the National Press Club.

Mr. Fortas resigned from the high court early this year because of widespread criticism of his financial links to a family foundation controlled by Louis Wolfson, a financier who was convicted of charges of illegal stock dealings.

Bill of Rights Stressed

Mr. Fortas's prepared text to the press club was devoted to the Bill of Rights. He said, apparently alluding to Mr. Agnew: "Holders of high political office must be exceptionally careful when they assail newscasters and the press for engaging in political criticism.

"They should realize that those who hold positions at the summit of Government do not —they do not—have the same freedom to criticize that an ordinary citizen has; because their words, however well-intentioned, necessarily are intimidating in those regrettable circumstances where freedom of the press is inextricably dependent upon short-term Government licenses."

December 16, 1969

Agnew's Rights

To the Editor:

The First Amendment is not the special privilege of the networks and the newspapers. Everyone—including Vice President Agnew—has as much right to express his opinions as C.B.S., N.B.C., The Times and The Washington Post without being falsely accused of "McCarthyism" and "intimidation." You censor and manage the news by the items you put in your paper, and by the items you choose to omit.

In this advanced age of mass communications, a deluge of words and ideas are poured out daily by the networks and newspapers which sway and influence the public mind. So let's be thankful for the Spiro Agnews who help keep the all-powerful news media on an even keel.

I am still waiting for the American Civil Liberties Union to leap to the defense of Mr. Agnew who, as an American citizen, is entitled to his basic right of freedom of expression.

NATHAN BERDINGER
Elmhurst, N. Y., Dec. 7, 1969

'Media Have Been Fair'

To the Editor:

In his Dec. 8 televised news conference President Richard Nixon acknowledged "the news media have been fair" to him.

Spiro Agnew's current attacks on the news media obviously are much ado about nothing. HARRY A. BLACHMAN
Cleveland, Dec. 9, 1969

December 11, 1969

December 13, 1969

517

BALTIMORE PAPER ACCUSES AGNEW

By JAMES M. NAUGHTON
Special to The New York Times

WASHINGTON, Dec. 17—Vice President Agnew was accused today by one of his hometown newspapers, The Baltimore Sun, of having excluded its reporter from his forthcoming Asian goodwill trip because he disliked that newspaper's editorial policies. ·

The Vice President's office confirmed that Mr. Agnew did not see eye to eye with the newspaper, but said that was not the reason its reporter would not be aboard the Air-Force jet leaving Dec. 26.

"We had 10 spaces and 32 requests," said Herbert L. Thompson, Mr. Agnew's press secretary. "There was no room for The Sun or for some other publications."

Among other news publications denied seats on the Vice President's plane were Time magazine, The Washington Post and The Christian Science Monitor.

Those getting seats were: The New York Times, The Associated Press, Hearst News Service, The Chicago Tribune, The Los Angeles Times, U. S. News & World Report, the three television networks and The Nashville Banner.

United Press International did not request a seat.

In an editorial published today, The Sun said that Mr. Thompson had told one of its reporters the Vice President did not like the newspaper.

'It Hurts Him'

In an accompanying news article, Mr. Thompson was quoted as saying that The Sun did not like Mr. Agnew and "make it clear in their editorials."

"It hurts him," Mr. Thompson is quoted. "He feels he is a hometown boy, and instead of taking pride in him, it [The Sun] acts like it is ashamed of him. He's not going out of his way to do something for The Sun."

Mr. Thompson said in an interview that he was quoted accurately but that his comments did not reflect the reason The Sun was not among the 10 news media granted seats on Mr. Agnew's plane.

The Vice President made the final decisions on filling the seats. According to Mr. Thompson, they went to "major newspapers with news services, or wire services, or representatives of a group of newspapers

and correspondents of the television networks."

He added that his comments were in response to statements made by Philip Potter, The Sun's Washington bureau chief, who was quoted by Mr. Thompson as saying that "his newspaper had been a strong supporter of the Vice President and was from his hometown and should receive special consideration."

The Sun endorsed Mr. Agnew for Governor of Maryland in 1966 and supported the Republican ticket in 1968. It said, however, that the choice of Mr. Agnew as a running mate to President Nixon last year was the one "major flaw" in the campaign.

In support of his statement that editorial policy had not been considered in filling the 10 press seats, Mr. Thompson said that Mr. Agnew "has been known to disagree with certain editorial policies of The New York Times." He said that The Times had been granted a seat because its news service, with 210 clients in the United States, would "make a wide distribution of stories on the trip."

Those selected to accompany Mr. Agnew represent news media with major circulation and broad geographic distribution, Mr. Thompson said.

Mr. Thompson confirmed that he had been criticized for including the Nashville newspaper but said that it was the only representative of the South and its correspondent would also represent at least five other Southern newspapers.

Protests Made Privately

Representatives of Time magazine, The Washington Post and The Christian Science Monitor protested privately to Mr. Thompson that they had been cut from the trip.

Mr. Thompson said that Time had been eliminated because U.S. News & World Report, another news weekly, had been chosen. The Washington Post was excluded, he said, because it shares a news service with The Los Angeles Times, which will accompany the Vice President.

On trips made by the President, a charter aircraft commonly carries the large White House press corps. ·

Mr. Thompson said that he had explored the possibility of a charter for Mr. Agnew's trip but had been told it would not be economically possible unless about 60 correspondents signed up. Reporters accompanying Mr. Agnew will be charged about $3,200.

Mr. Agnew will represent the United States at the inauguration of President Ferdinand E. Marcos of the Philippines on Dec. 30 and will continue on a good will mission to Taiwan, Thailand, Nepal, Afghanistan, Malaysia, Singapore, Indonesia, Australia and New Zealand.

Agnew Offers to Charter Extra Plane if Press Pays

WASHINGTON, Dec. 19 (UPI)—Vice President Agnew's office, which had said there would be only 10 seats for newsmen on his plane during his coming Far East tour, offered today to charter a special press plane—for $178,000.

About 30 news organizations, including the Baltimore Sun, in Mr. Agnew's home town, were turned down for seats on his own plane because of limited space, according to the Vice President's office.

The cost of the Boeing 707 charter for newsmen would be distributed equally among those who made the trip.

Mr. Agnew's press secretary, Herbert L. Thompson, said that 30 organizations had expressed an interest to send a man on the trip. If all sent a man the cost would be $6,000 apiece, Mr. Thompson said.

Press Institute Calls Criticism by Agnew Major Threat in '69

Special to The New York Times

GENEVA, Dec. 31—Vice President Agnew's attacks on newspapers and television were 1969's "most serious threat to the freedom of information in the Western World," the International Press Institute said today.

The Zurich-based institute represents 1,600 newspaper editors in 58 non-Communist countries. Its annual survey of press freedom was prepared by its director, Ernest Meyer.

The institute's statement referred to Mr. Agnew's criticism of television networks' "immediate analysis" of President Nixon's nationwide address last May 14, in which Mr. Nixon stated his Administration's policy on the war in Vietnam. In his remarks, at a Republican party meeting in Iowa on Nov. 13, the Vice President reminded broadcasters that they were licensed by the Federal Government.

On Nov. 20, he similarly criticized the handling of news by newspapers and magazines, specifically mentioning The Washington Post and The New York Times.

The survey commented that normally the Vice President's office carried little weight. For this reason, it found that the most serious aspect of Mr. Agnew's remarks was that they might have been inspired by the office of President Nixon.

Reviewing the 1960's, the survey said that the underdeveloped nations of the world were falling further behind in press freedom.

Television

A Few Ripples From Mr. Agnew's Stone

By JACK GOULD

WHEN all the repercussions of Vice President Agnew's attack on the television medium are collected in a doctoral thesis a few years hence, its outcome may be seen as materially different from current judgments. At this juncture, however, several developments are worth noting. For one thing, Vice President Agnew may have rallied the "silent majority" to the side of President Nixon. In consequence, the networks were left open to some legitimate criticism for failure to give any live coverage to the massive peace march in Washington. If one of the largest crowds in the country's history turned out to disagree with the White House, what more was required to make the demonstration qualify as news on TV? What was clearly an event was virtually converted by television into a non-event.

On the other hand, if the Vice President succeeded in persuading some individual stations to adopt a more neutral position in covering the controversy over the Vietnamese war, he and President Nixon are learning that, in many instances, the networks are leaning over backward to see that they are not immune to a sustained assault by comedians and their guests. Vice President Agnew is now a running gag on many segments of TV and the President himself is coming in for barbs as pointed as those which were directed at former President Johnson.

*

A recent incident on the Merv Griffin show illustrated how the Agnew controversy is carrying over into regular TV programing. Comedienne Carol Burnett and actress Elke Sommer were allowed by CBS to be critical of the handling of the Vietnamese war, but when they asked viewers to write in and support "People for Peace" their remarks were deleted. A CBS spokesman said it was a standard network rule not to allow appeals for support of specific organizations without any advance check on a particular group's merit. Some such inquiry is not totally alien to journalistic practice, but CBS had 10 days to learn about "People for Peace," which is headed by Mrs. Martin Luther King. It was understandable, therefore, that Miss Burnett took umbrage at the ruling. If the Vice President, maintaining the somewhat ridiculous position that he was just a private citizen and not an arm of the Administration, could ask viewers to support a cause, why shouldn't Miss Burnett, as a laywoman, lay claim to equal rights of outspokenness? CBS almost has a duty now to make a study of "People for Peace" and let viewers know the outcome.

In another publicized incident, National Educational Television, which 10 days ago had the attractive idea of commissioning samplings of programs from different affiliate stations, found itself entangled with poet Lawrence Ferlinghetti over a reading of his new poem, "Tyrannus Nix," an anti-Nixon work which originally was presented at length on the liberal and controversial outlet KQED-TV in San Francisco. KQED agreed to cut the work to 10 minutes to fit NET's needs. Subsequently, an additional cut of 1 minute 40 seconds was made for reasons of time, as were parts of other segments of the program entitled "Thoughts of the Artist on Leaving the Sixties."

According to reliable reports, Ferlinghetti did not see the edited version in advance, but nonetheless the trade papers cried censorship. The overtone of opportunistic publicity was not lacking, but the episode was symptomatic of what television is facing: If Vice President Agnew prefers that life be reported more his way, the peace militants are going to be just as insistent that they, too, have their full hearing. The more progressive stations and networks, with-

out making a fuss about it, propose to stick to their middle course, and if they have overlooked the silent majority they have no intention of ignoring the articulate minority. There is no other way.

*

From a completely informal and admittedly incomplete survey of telecasts heard only in New York City, the Agnew uproar seems to have had little effect on the content of recent programs, although a viewer cannot tell what goes on behind the scenes. And, in addition to the national network programs, there is growing competition locally between Channel 11, Channel 9 and Channel 13 to pursue different points of view.

Thoughtful journalists continue to remain appalled that Vice President Agnew, with the obvious passive concurrence of President Nixon, would subject a Federally licensed medium to selective attack. His argument that there should always be self-examination of one's performance is about as novel as urging the wisdom of a periodic physical check-up.

But in arguing that there are two sides to the Vietnamese controversy, each of which should be fairly scrutinized, Mr. Agnew may have elevated the tensions without being altogether sure of his strength with the silent majority. TV by its very presence may on occasion have provoked incidents designed for the camera's consumption, but over the long run it has been a conscientious mirror of our society's difficulties. The picture tube played no part in America's entry into Vietnam, where the attainment of withdrawal will be duly reflected on the home screen. Men in high office, not a sprinkling of producers, editors and commentators, have to make the decisions to which 50 million-odd viewing homes will respond with, one hopes, lessened acrimony.

Agnew's Speeches

To the Editor:

With the Vice President abroad, it may now be appropriate to discuss his two famous speeches with some perspective. He holds a frustrating post, a fact testified to by all who have held it, from John Adams to Hubert Humphrey. He is not a powerful figure; in The Times he was referred to as "the guffaw of 1968" and "a household joke." Neither office nor man could intimidate.

He did not speak for "the Government." Save on some phases of foreign policy no one can; constitutional checks and balances guarantee that. He could not speak for "the Administration," which has many voices except where the President takes personal responsibility.

The agency to implement supposed threats is "independent," not directly part of "the Administration." The Federal Communications Commission can take away station licenses, but only after such protracted procedures that it is almost a paper tiger. The networks are not subject to licenses and the commentators are not employed by vulnerable stations but by giant corporations, a division of which is "solely responsible" for all in the broadcasts, an effective shield against intimidation.

Amid the uproar, Congress was seldom mentioned. That a Democratic Congress would stand idle while a Republican Administration gagged opinion is ridiculous.

The episode highlights two current tendencies in the media: overdramatization of ephemeral episodes, and refusal to deal with a speech as a whole. Instead, one part is seized upon for overemphasis. The factual statements in the speeches went virtually unnoticed. His rejection of all censorship was brushed off.

He suggested "self-examination"—surely legitimate. As for the "wall of separation" between fact and opinion, several stations now broadcast "editorials," recognizing the propriety of the wall. The speeches contained regrettable passages, which were properly rebuked, but they also showed some admirable candor, seldom mentioned.

One must conclude that the reaction of men both better known and vastly more powerful was out of proportion to alleged "intimidation."

HENRY M. WRISTON
New York, Jan. 6, 1970

Mrs. Agnew Backs Speeches

WASHINGTON, Feb. 3 (UPI) — Mrs. Spiro T. Agnew said today that her husband "speaks for himself" when he makes his speeches. But she added, "I usually agree with him." The Vice President's wife also told newswomen in the Agnews' Sheraton Park Hotel apartment here that the controversy surrounding her husband's pronouncements about the news media and antiwar protesters did not bother her.

Goldwater Accuses Television Industry Of 'Biased Attitude'

WASHINGTON, March 12 (AP)—Senator Barry Goldwater accused segments of the television industry today of having a biased attitude, which he said was earning it disrespect from the American people.

"If the TV industry is seriously worried about the freedom of the press," Senator Goldwater said, "I suggest it look to its own performance. Because I believe the most serious threat to freedom of the press is the media's own biased attitude."

The Arizona Republican, addressing a Young Republican Leadership Training School here, said: "Liberal comments about the Nixon Administration have taken on an edge of desperation and hysteria since Vice President Agnew has begun to give voice to some of the pet peeves of the silent majority."

Senator Goldwater singled out a speech by Julian Goodman, president of the National Broadcasting Company, calling recent criticism of the news media the greatest threat to press freedom since the Sedition Act of 1798. Mr. Goodman also asked Federal and state officials to quit serving subpoenas on the news media.

Senator Goldwater termed this "one of the most ridiculous statements of the new decade."

"I think it's time to ask just who these TV news people think they are," Mr. Goldwater continued.

"If one of their employes has information or material that would be useful to grand jury or a district attorney in legal proceedings, why shouldn't he be asked to produce the items requested? Are we to take Mr. Goodman's word for the fact that the news media is above the law?" he asked.

Mr. Goodman answered the Senator in a letter, in which the N.B.C. official said that in charging a threat to press freedom, he "was referring to subpoenas that compromise news sources or prejudice further news access."

"I base this view on the constituional guarantee of press freedom," he said, "and I suggested that constitutional self-restraint should discourage Government from 'the broad use of subpoena powers.' I did not and do not suggest that the news media should be above the law."

Agnew Criticizes Press on Coverage Of Conflict in Laos

CHARLOTTE AMALIE, V. I., (AP)—Vice President Agnew again criticized the press tonight, this time on its coverage of recent events in Laos.

"In Laos we have 1,000 men —military and civilian contract personnel," he said. "But how much do you read about the North Vietnamese there? They have 67,000 troops attempting to overthrow a prime minister who was their choice in a coalition government."

"I'll admit that Pulitzers are not won as quickly exposing the evils of Communism as they are by discrediting an American public official," he said.

But Mr. Agnew told 291 guests at a $100-a-plate fund-raising dinner given by Virgin Islands Republicans that "innuendos and smears" against public official s appear in the American news media every day.

"Some of this effort should be directed to the threats we face on the outside," he said.

The Vice President, his wife, Judy, and their daughter Kim are in the Virgin Islands for a week's vacation. The Agnews flew to St. Croix, largest of the United States Virgin Islands, yesterday. They and many old friends from Baltimore have condominiums on the island. Mr. Agnew is a former Governor of Maryland.

The Agnews flew from St. Croix to St. Thomas tonight for the dinner but were delayed almost two hours when their plane developed engine trouble. A replacement was flown from the Roosevelt Roads Naval Station in Puerto Rico

AGNEW LINKS VOTE TO 'LIBERAL MEDIA'

Assails Rights Groups and Unions for 'Pressure'

Special to The New York Times

WASHINGTON, April 10 — Vice President Agnew charged today that the Senate had rejected the nomination of G. Harrold Carswell to the Supreme Court on the basis of "subjective judgements" after its members had been "snowed" by material in "the liberal media" and subjected to "formidable, almost incredible pressures from organized labor and civil rights activists.

Mr. Agnew made his comments in a television interview with Roger Mudd, the Columbia Broadcasting System Correspondent.

Mr. Mudd asked the Vice President whether President Nixon had been politically motivated in lashing out yesterday at the Senate for rejecting Judge Carswell. "I don't believe the President made the statement with a political view in mind," Mr. Agnew replied.

The Vice President said that Mr. Nixon "was simply reacting to what was certainly a very serious disappointment relative to the Carswell nomination."

Asked if he thought the President's statements would have a political effect, Mr. Agnew said, "Everything the President does has a political impact in the final analysis."

Regional Bias Alleged

The President yesterday denounced the Senators who rejected the nomination and declared that the Senate "as presently constituted" would not approve a Southern conservative. He said he would therefore look outside the South for a candidate to fill the vacancy on the Court.

In words that conveyed bitterness and anger, Mr. Nixon accused the Senate opponents of the nomination of Mr. Cars-

well and, earlier of Clement F. Haynsworth Jr. of "vicious" tactics and "regional discrimination" against Southerners.

In the television interview, Mr. Agnew said that the two nominees had been put to "subjective judgments." The charges of mediocrity, the charge of insensitivity," he said, "what do these terms mean? Who is a judge of mediocrity of any person? Or of insensitivity? These are simply ways to say that this man is not compatible with my thinking, and therefore I'll have nothing to do with him."

"You can't prove mediocrity," Mr. Agnew continued. "Among a bunch of lawyers, it would seem to me, that you'll find 100 who admire and respect a particular judge, and a hundred who think he's terrible. Maybe they lost a case before him."

Mr. Agnew said that pressures had been brought on the Senate by "organized lobbies" of "organized labor, on the one hand, and the civil rights activists, on the other." He said that he would not blame anybody in the Senate for the defeats and "certainly would not single out any Senator for an act of retribution."

'Terrific Liberal Pressure'

"The reprehensible part of the case against these two men," the Vice President said, "is that it was contrived from outside."

"The liberal community saw fit to engage in what I consider to be a very calculated effort to affect, through terrific pressures of all types, the Senate of the United States. Some Senators were affected by this."

There have been several reports from Capitol Hill that White House aides applied considerable pressure to Senators whose votes were crucial in the Carswell debate to support the President's nominee.

Mr. Agnew said that he thought the Senate had received "the worst snow job of any legislative body in history."

"I assume," he continued, "they read the proliferation of material that descended on them each morning from the liberal media, and I think they were affected by it; I think they were snowed, to use a common phrase."

Agnew Assails Songs and Films That Promote a 'Drug Culture'

By JAMES M. NAUGHTON
Special to The New York Times

LAS VEGAS, Nev., Sept. 14— Vice President Agnew said tonight that American youths were being "brainwashed" into a "drug culture" by rock music, movies, books and underground newspapers. He called these part of "a depressing life style of conformity that has neither life nor style."

After describing himself as a "bumpkin" earlier today in San Diego, the Vice President came to the capital of American gambling to lecture against "creeping permissiveness" and urge the election of "square" Republicans.

Mr. Agnew said in a speech to 1,000 Republicans at the Space Center Auditorium of the Sahara Hotel that popular songs such as the Beatles' "With a Little Help From My Friends" or the Jefferson Airplane's "White Rabbit" were a message of drug use.

'Pill-Popping' Parents

He placed part of the blame on "pill-popping" parents and "growing adult alcoholism" that were setting examples for younger citizens "to do some experimenting on their own."

The Vice President urged Nevadans to "open your eyes and your ears" to the drug culture, "establish authority with compassion" in their families and elect William Raggio, the Reno District Attorney, who is the Republican senatorial candidate against Senator Howard W. Cannon, a Democrat.

He told the Republicans who paid $100-a-couple to attend the rally and those who saw it on a statewide telecast that he "may be accused of advocating 'song censorship' for pointing this out, but have you really heard the words of some of these songs?"

The Beatles' tune, he said, included these lines:

"I get by with a little help from my friends, I get high with a little help from my friends. . . ."

A Catchy Tune

Mr. Agnew said that it was, like many of the rock songs, "a catchy tune, but until it was pointed out to me, I never realized that the 'friends' were assorted drugs."

He charged that a recent movie, which he did not name but which apparently was "Easy Rider," promoted as heroes "two men who are able to live a carefree life off the proceeds of illegal sales of drugs."

Although the Nixon Administration is taking steps to curtail the spread of drugs and to advise against their use, and

some news media are also warning against drug abuse, the Vice President said, "far too many producers and editors are still succumbing to the temptation of the sensational and playing right into the hands of the drug culture."

Mr. Agnew said that "those who close their eyes to the pernicious influence of any form of drug—for fear of being out of step with the times— are dismally failing their own sons and daughters." If such an attitude brings down on him and others the label "squares," he added, "then we will just have to live with it."

Wave of the Future

His message here was part of the general Republican campaign theme. As Mr. Agnew rephrased it in a short speech to 1,000 persons, mostly schoolchildren, at the Las Vegas Airport, "You need a Congress that will see to it that the wave of permissiveness, the wave of pornography and the wave of moral pollution never become the wave of the future in our country."

The Vice President, his wife, Judy, and their 14-year-old daughter, Kim, who wore a gray minidress, traveled to the Frontier Hotel from the airport past signs that read "All You Can Drink, $2.25."

One hotel marquee advertised: "Welcome Vice President Spiro Agnew. Keno. Poker." Another declared: "The NOW Year. Folies Bergère. Welcome Vice President Agnew." A gas station sign said: "Free aspirin. Ask us anything."

Nevada Democrats were asking the Republicans to explain why schoolchildren had been bused to the airport to greet the Agnews. Republican state employes were given time off to take part in the reception and, according to the Democratic State Chairman, Philip Carlino, pressure was put on casinos to sell tickets to the rally.

Before flying here, the Vice President told interviewers in San Diego:

"Speeches are of limited effect on the American people. Speeches and rallies and demonstrations, I think, have been grossly overrated as a way of appealing to the people to designate the kind of leadership they want to represent them."

He said that citizens were sophisticated, "even those of us who are described as the ordinary bumpkins throughout the countryside and may not be card-carrying members of the so-called intellectual community."

Agnew Says He Is Victim of 'Hate' Campaign

By ROBERT B. SEMPLE JR.
Special to The New York Times

CHICAGO, Oct. 19 — Vice President Agnew portrayed himself today as the victim of a "hate" campaign, abetted by the nation's press.

Mr. Agnew also accused the Democratic senatorial candidate in Illinois, Adlai E. Stevenson 3d, of besmirching the "great name" of his father, the late Adlai Stevenson, former Presidential candidate and Ambassador to the United Nations.

Appearing before a large crowd at a $250-a-plate fund-raising dinner here, the Vice President said his opponents had reacted to his criticisms by calling him everyting from "an emissary of hate" to a "racist."

He said that, whereas his own utterances had been examined and cross-examined at every turn, the nation's press had failed to subject the "libelous mouthings" of his opponents to equally strict standards.

Charges Listed

Mr. Agnew contended that Representative Richard L. Ottinger of Westchester, the Democratic candidate for the Senate in New York, had called him an "emissary of hate"; that Dr. Benjamin Spock, the pediatrician and antiwar activist, had labeled him a "racist"; that officials of the Americans for Democratic Action had charged him with dispensing "the politics of hate," and that, here in Illinois, Mr. Stevenson had called him a "peddler of hate."

"These charges are not reported as demagoguery, not name-calling, not ethnic slurs, not divisiveness, not 'escalation of the rhetoric,'" the Vice President said. "We hear no whimpering about polarization' from this mudslinging. And why not? Because we are led to believe radical liberals just never stoop to scurrility."

Mr. Agnew went on to say that he found it "meaningful" that the press had given what he called "radical liberals" a "free throw with their charges of malevolence and racism. No quotations, no facts — only libelous mouthings, which are faithfully broadcast by the media."

Renews Attack

The Vice President, who has been subjected to mounting criticism, both editorially and by the targets of his own rhetoric, then renewed an attack on Mr. Stevenson that he started in Springfield, Ill., at the beginning of his campaign in September. Mr. Stevenson is thought to be ahead of his opponent, incumbent Senator Ralph T. Smith, a Republican, who sat next to Mr. Agnew at the head table tonight.

Mr. Agnew again recalled Mr. Stevenson's portrayal of Chicago policemen after the Democratic National Conven-

The New York Times (by Gary Settle)

AT FUND-RAISING DINNER IN CHICAGO: H. Clement Stone, Republican fund-raiser, chats with Senator Ralph T. Smith, left, and Vice President Agnew at Conrad Hilton Hotel.

tion in 1968 as "storm troopers in blue." The Vice President called the policemen "sentinels in blue" and thanked them for their "friendly escort into this great city."

But Mr. Agnew criticized Mr. Stevenson less for his alleged sins of the past than for what the Vice President said Mr. Stevenson's efforts to erase the stigma of his earlier mistakes.

Mr. Agnew contended that the Democratic candidate had engaged in "pathetic contortions" designed to camouflage his earlier criticism of the Chicago police and "becloud his liberalism." Mr. Agnew was apparently referring to Mr. Stevenson's recent addition to his staff of Thomas Foran, former United States Attorney and prosecutor of the Chicago Seven.

'Demeaned His Name'

Mr. Agnew also accused Mr. Stevenson of refusing to seek peace by working "wholeheartedly with America's allies" and said he had instead regularly denounced the Saigon regime. The Vice President added:

"By putting vote-mongering ahead of long-held leftist convictions, by placing a yen for publicity ahead of the nation's striving for an honorable peace, by 'smearing others in public life, I say that Adlai 3d has demeaned his great name, and the people of Illinois will drive that home on Nov. 3."

Mr. Agnew went on to say that there was hope for economic stability if the voters would throw "political profligates" out of Congress, and hope for progress in the war on crime "if you and your countrymen join in stopping the permissiveness that has sheltered

and cultivated social weeds in America."

Mr. Agnew also touched on what he termed "social permissiveness" when he drew a distinction between the press coverage given a right-wing attack on Lyndon B. Johnson when he was a Vice-Presidential candidate during the 1960 campaign in Texas, and the coverage given a rock-throwing incident involving President Nixon in Vermont last Saturday.

'Shower of Rocks'

He said the press had responded to the attack on Mr. Johnson with heavy coverage and moral outrage, but had either buried or failed to mention the fact that, last Saturday, "the President of the United States was the target of a shower of rocks thrown by young radical thugs."

Most reporters who witnessed the incident were able to establish that only two or three rocks had been thrown, and could not identify those who threw them. There were apparently no arrests.

The Vice President did not directly criticize the press for its alleged failure to report the incident properly, reserving his contempt for those who had helped "create the atmosphere of permissiveness" that he said had made such behavior possible.

"Any public man, of any party, who has helped to create the atmosphere of permissiveness—where this kind of obscene outrageous conduct has become so commonplace that it is no longer news—that public man should go down to humiliating political defeat in the election on Nov. 3," Mr. Agnew said.

Agnew Divides Missouri City's Voters

By STEVEN V. ROBERTS
Special to The New York Times

ST. CHARLES, Mo.—Mr. and Mrs. William Cannon were out for a Sunday stroll when a reporter asked them what they thought of Spiro T. Agnew.

"I like him," replied Mr. Cannon. A salesman of automotive supplies. "He's a man who speaks his mind. And the fact that he does goof up makes him human. We all do that."

Peg Cannon smiled sweetly at her husband and said, "It makes him a clod."

This middle-class suburb of 28,000 about 20 miles northwest of St. Louis is the Cannons' home town. Its new industry, housing tracts and shopping centers more and more typify today's middle America.

What do the people of this town, in a Border state that swings regularly between the two parties, think of Spiro Agnew? Dozens of random interviews indicate that in St. Charles, as in many areas across the country, the Vice-President provokes deep and often angry disagreement—even between husband and wife.

Need for Restraint

Some voters who agree with what Mr. Agnew is saying worry about the way he says it. They tend to feel that as a national leader, he should be more restrained and dignified. "He says what a lot of us feel about the students and the courts," said Barry Fondaw, an electrician. "But he could say things a lot better without insulting people. He doesn't think. Sometimes I feel embarrassed for him."

"He strikes me favorably," said Bob Zelmer, a young engineer, as he wheeled his daughter in a grocery cart. "Sometimes when you watch, though, it's more like watching a comedian than a public official. There are so many antics. I wouldn't want him to be President or anything, but at least he's open and honest."

At the same time, the Vice President clearly has broad support in St. Charles. A. P. Farr, a young engineer at the huge McDonnel-Douglas aircraft plant here, made a typical comment: "He's for law and and order and no foolishness and I think that's great."

"He's like my old man used to be." said Gene Shuler, a refrigerator mechanic, "When I did something wrong he whacked me across the house. Today they say, "Look, honey, don't do it again.'"

Several people compared the Vice President to former President Truman. They feel he speaks plainly and honestly and "gives 'em hell." As John Heppler, an accountant, put it: "He doesn't double talk you like a lot of those politicians. When a lot of them finish you don't know what they're said. You know with Agnew."

A Yearning for Absolutes

Mr. Agnew seems to fill a yearning for moral absolutes. Roy Booker, an electrical contractor, put it this way:" I think somebody in this country has to speak out. What's right is right and what's wrong is wrong."

Most people in St. Charles feel the Vice President has re-enforced their old beliefs but has not persuaded them to hold new ones. One thing he has influenced, however, is their view of the media.

"He changed my ideas about newspapers," said Mr. Farr, "Maybe they have more sway over the American public than I thought."

Harold Demien, another aerospace worker, added: "One thing he says is that the papers and TV publicize violence too much. When someone burns down a building they make him look like a hero. I never stopped to think about that until he brought it to light."

Called Divisive

If many voters like Mr. Agnew's vigorous and sweeping statements, others find them offensive and even dangerous.

A teacher in a religious school here declared: "He's a terribly divisive force in the country and lacks any sensitivity to the real feelings of thinking people. Life is just not black and white. He's trying to make a name for himself by bombastic statements but he's really displaying his own ignorance. He's a terrible detriment to the country, because he puts people in two warring camps."

"He's doing the opposite of bringing us together, he's driving us apart," said Earl Favor, a toolmaker. "When we talk politics at work we're just asg head-on as we could be, and that's not good."

"I dislike his lambasting of the students and the academic community," said Don Bergman, a railroad employe, "Sure, there's a lot of foment on the campuses, but it's probably a good thing. There's a lot wrong in this country, and God help us if we can't criticize our own society."

Gallup Rating High
Special to The New York Times

PRINCETON, N.J., Oct. 24—Vice President Agnew has achieved fairly high popularity with a wide range of voters during the 1970 campaign, according to the Gallup Poll.

Citing a survey of 1,507 people in 336 locations between Oct. 7 and 11, the poll reports that Mr. Agnew has achieved a level of popularity among Republicans, particularly conservative ones, reached only by Republican Presidents in recent years.

The comparable figures among voters who describe themselves as independent are 24 per cent and 16 per cent.

Among Democrats outside the South, the poll says, the Vice President is the most unpopular man holding high office in the last decade. Only 14 per cent give him a "highly favorable" rating, and 26 per cent the opposite. The sentiment is reversed among Southern Democrats, however — 23 per cent highly favorable and 13 per cent highly unfavorable. cent years. Forty-eight per cent give him a "highly favorable" rating and only four per cent give "highly unfavorable."

October 25, 1970

AT NAVY LEAGUE DINNER: Vice President Agnew after his speech at the Waldorf-Astoria Hotel last night.

The New York Times (by Mike Lien)

...said that the had contributed about million to Senate candidates since 1962.

Mr. Agnew flew to New York from Raleigh, N. C., where yesterday morning he accused the "big media" of not investigating "highly inflammatory" statements made against him while requiring him to document everything he said.

He specifically criticized The New York Times for using "purple prose of exaggerated rhetoric" in an editorial supporting Senator Goodell.

He said in an interview for a local television station in Raleigh: "Just listen to this, this is the lead in this New York Times editorial: 'A nation starved for political leadership heard last night the moving voice of a public official determined to keep freedom from being assassinated by the ruthless night riders of the political right.' How's that for rhetoric?"

October 28, 1970

Agnew Says His Jabs at Media Have Achieved Goal

By JAMES M. NAUGHTON
Special to The New York Times

HONOLULU, Nov. 20 — If there is any censorship of news in the United States it is done by the media and not by the Government, Vice President Agnew told a group of editors here today.

"No matter how much I or anyone else may be accused of trying to bulldoze the press, you and I know perfectly well that you can't be intimidated," the Vice President told the annual conference of the Associated Press Managing Editors' Association at lunch in the Ilikai Hotel.

He said that his speeches criticizing the media during the last year had been aimed at encouraging the profession to look critically at itself, a goal he said had been accomplished. He declared that censorship by government or anyone was "totally repugnant" to him.

"If a broader look is in fact being taken," Mr. Agnew said, "it is due to the public response to those speeches, not to the speeches themselves." An outpouring of criticism by readers and viewers who agreed with his views and added some of their own "came as a revelation to media officials," he contended.

In a question period following his speech, Mr. Agnew defended his political rhetoric when asked whether it ran counter to President Nixon's inaugural theme, "Bring us together."

He said that he did not believe Mr. Nixon intended the theme to mean that everyone should agree on issues.

"It's unrealistic to say 'bring us together to a single point of view,'" the Vice President added, saying that would represent a situation too similar to what is found in a Communist society.

Faced with an audience of several hundred newspaper executives and their wives, Mr. Agnew said he wanted to discuss both strong and weak points of their efforts.

"It may surprise you to learn," he added, "that I believe there are far more strengths than weaknesses."

He praised the media for what he termed swift and detailed interpretation of political events—a contrast to his complaint last year that television commentators had been too quick to analyze President Nixon's Nov. 3, 1969, address to the nation on Vietnam.

"I have not the least doubt," he went on, "that the United States has the most self-demanding, least self-satisfied, most ingenious, least inhibited, best informed, least controlled, most professional, least subjective, most competitive, least party-line, fairest and finest journalistic complex in the entire world."

Criticizes Hypersensitivity

But the Vice President quickly added that he still had some gripes. For one, he said, "I wish the media would overcome their hypersensitivity to being challenged in return. It is a knee-jerk reaction that I feel ill becomes a proud profession that is guaranteed freedom by the Constitution and that ought to be eager to police itself."

He praised efforts within the journalistic profession to develop moral and ethical standards for self-regulation. But he said he could not specifically endorse the establishment of a press council such as exists in Britain because his endorsement "would surely kill the idea."

As he had before, Mr. Agnew urged the news executives to make a greater effort to present balanced coverage of controversial issues. He said there was a pressing need for balance because only 45 of the 1,500 cities in America with daily newspapers had two or more competing, separately owned dailies.

Although newspapers have generally done a credible job of clearly separating factual news from opinion—an effort Mr. Agnew said was not made as well by radio, television and news magazines — he complained that "still we see slanted stories, whether or not the tilt is deliberate."

He urged editors to guard against the less obvious forms of bias, such as selecting a photograph or determining the size and content of a headline to place a particular slant on the news.

He recalled a letter from a young journalist at a major newspaper who reportedly protested that his editors objected to printing a public opinion poll showing Mr. Agnew's popularity on the rise and played up an errant golf shot by the Vice President that hit Doug Sanders, the professional golfer, in the head.

Joking before his speech, Mr. Agnew said: "Any rumors that Richard Nixon will not be on the ticket with me in 1972 are totally without foundation."

Mr. Agnew and his wife, Judy, their daughters, Susan and Kim, and Mrs. Agnew's mother, Mrs. Lee Judefind, accompanied him here for a five-day rest. They will fly to Palm Springs, Calif., on Monday and spend Thanksgiving Week there.

November 21, 1970

524

C.B.S. Is Challenged by Agnew To Admit 'Errors' in 3 TV Films

WASHINGTON, March 20 (UPI) — Vice President Agnew challenged the Columbia Broadcasting System tonight to admit or deny his charges of "error and propagandistic manipulation" in three C.B.S. television documentaries.

In a statement issued by his office, Mr. Agnew said that Frank M. Stanton, president of C.B.S., had made "a typical nonrejoinder" in reply to a critical speech the Vice President delivered against the network last Thursday in Boston.

By stating that "my indictment is mistaken," Mr. Agnew said, "he cleverly avoids an encounter with the direct evidence of C.B.S. error and propagandistic manipulation."

In New York, a spokesman for C.B.S. said that "there would be no further comment" on Mr. Agnew's statement.

'Propaganda Attempt'

The Vice President contended that the C.B.S.-TV documentary "The Selling of the Pentagon," which was broadcast on Feb. 23, "was a clever propaganda attempt to discredit the defense establishment of the United States." He accused the network of assembling military officers' remarks out of context "to create a false impression" and of obtaining interviews with "leading public figure un-

der false pretenses."

Mr. Agnew also contended that, in the documentary "Hunger in America," C.B.S. told an "untruth" when it said a premature baby was dying of starvation when it actually died of injuries resulting from a fall by its mother prior to delivery.

The Vice President added that the network had "recklessly stimulated an attempt to forcibly overthrow a foreign government" by financing a taged invasion of Haiti for the documentary "Project Nassau," which was never broadcast.

In a related development today, Senator Mike Mansfield, the majority leader, defended television coverage of Southeast Asia and urged newsmen not to be "intimidated" by Republican charges of bias.

The Montana Democrat, who met with newsmen in his office, took issue with Mr. Agnew, Senator Robert J. Dole of Kansas. the Republican National Chairman, and others who have contended that the networks have distorted coverage of American and South Vietnamese operations in Laos.

"I disagree," Senator Mansfield said. "All the networks have been doing a good job, as has the press, and I hope that this constant criticism will not have the effect of intimidating the networks."

Agnew Challenges C.B.S. To Let Him Edit Remarks

WASHINGTON, March 22 (UPI) — Vice President Agnew challenged the Columbia Broadcasting System television network today to allow him to edit personally his own critical remarks that will appear tomorrow night following the repeat showing of the documentary "The Selling of the Pentagon."

C.B.S. had said it would run 15 minutes of edited criticism by three officials unhappy with the program — Mr. Agnew, Defense Secretary Melvin R. Laird and Representative F. Edward Hébert, Louisiana Democrat who is chairman of the House Armed Services Committee.

But Mr. Agnew challenged the network, "in the interest of real and not simulated fairness, to permit the critics themselves to participate in the selection of whatever film footage of their remarks will be shown by the network tomorrow night." A C.B.S. spokesman in New York said the network would have "no comment" on Mr. Agnew's request.

AGNEW CRITICISM OF C.B.S. RENEWED

Network Edited Rebuttal, He Charges in St. Louis

ST. LOUIS, March 24 (UPI)— Vice President Agnew aimed more criticism at Columbia Broadcasting System television today, accusing the network of "deliberately publishing untruths." He also attacked a Newsweek magazine report that a new image was being created for the Vice President.

He said he was "totally dissatisfied with what C.B.S. characterized as a rebuttal on the part of Administration officials, including myself," to the network's documentary, "The Selling of the Pentagon."

Mr. Agnew's original criticism, made last week in Boston, was broadcast by C.B.S. last night after a rebroadcast of the documentary. Richard S. Salant, president of C.B.S. News, also went on the air and said the network "can refute every charge" leveled by Mr. Agnew, Secretary of Defense Melvin Laird and Representative F. Edward Hébert, chairman of the House Armed Services Committee.

Mr. Agnew, interviewed by an editorial board panel of the St. Louis area's top news executives, said: "It's rather unusual to give you the right of rebuttal and not allow you to decide what you're going to say in rebuttal. They edited some of my previous remarks and [remarks of] two other Administration people and showed the ones they wanted to show."

He termed the Newsweek article about his image "a sloppy piece of journalism." He prefaced his remarks by saying that Newsweek is "not one of my favorite magazines."

The Vice President said: "The media are big boys now and they are subject to being criticized just as I, as a public official, have to be criticized."

Dole Doubts Fairness

COLUMBUS, Ohio, March 24 (AP) — Senator Robert Dole, Republican of Kansas, said today that he felt the Administration "definitely has a hard time getting its views across in the nation's televised medium."

He said a survey of C.B.S. News reports concerning the United States involvement in the Laos campaign showed that of 106 comments, "all but 16 were critical or suggested criticism."

The Senator added: "I'm not suggesting we should sit around for 30 minutes praising Richard Nixon on a TV program. Wouldn't that be dull?"

AGNEW DEPLORES MEDIA 'PARANOIA'

Sees Peril to Credibility in 'Frenzy' Over Criticism

Special to The New York Times

WASHINGTON, June 1—Vice President Agnew said today that "attempts to portray the Government as anxious to control or suppress the news media in the United States can only backfire," compounding the "credibility problem" faced by journalists.

The news industry, not the Nixon Administration, is beset by a "wave of paranoia," the Vice President asserted in a speech to radio executives.

Mr. Agnew, in one of his periodic critiques of the media, said the "constructive" criticism he and others voiced in the last 18 months had been met by a "frenzy about intimidation and repression" in the media, among "those in Congress who would like to curry favor with the media" and in "an occasional voice from academe."

Speech to Broadcasters

His assessment was contained in a speech to the National Advisory Board of the Mutual Broadcasting System, a group that represents the 550 independent radio affiliates, at its annual meeting on Paradise Island in the Bahamas. The text was made available here.

The Vice President, at the close of his address, said the United States had "the best, most professional news fraternity in the world."

Most of his comments, however, supported his theme that the news media could guarantee this strength by turning their critical powers on themselves "rather than screaming 'intimidation' every time [they are] criticized by a public official."

On a single day last week, Mr. Agnew said, in three separate news articles, a television executive charged that the Administration was engaged in a "most formidable" challenge to a free press; the president of Sigma Delta Chi, a journalism fraternity, said the media welcomed Administration criticism but not "threats," and Senator Frank E. Moss, Democrat of Utah, spoke of "thought control by an Administration paranoid with fear, suspicion and loathing of a free and undomesticated press."

Fear and Suspicion

These articles and "hundreds of others" indicate, Mr. Agnew went on, that "if anyone is 'paranoid with fear, suspicion and loathing,' it is not the Administration but rather those who keep voicing fear, suspicion and loathing."

The Vice President made light of a charge, reported in The New York Times May 11, that freedom of information in this country was undergoing "its most formidable challenge" since colonial times. The charge was made by Dr. Morris Forkosch of the Brooklyn Law School.

"There's no question we have a wave of paranoia today," Mr. Agnew said. "The question is which direction it's coming from. And the comments that I have cited to you, including those of a scholar, leave no doubt in my mind about the direction."

The Vice President said criticism of the media was neither new nor partisan. He said it was significant that it was a "Democrat-controlled Congressional subcommittee" of the House Commerce Committee that was investigating editing techniques used in the Columbia Broadcasting System's documentary, "The Selling of the Pentagon."

What the Administration has done, Mr. Agnew said, is to urge the free press to "police itself against excesses that on occasion have been so blatant they have undermined the confidence of the public."

In that vein, he contended that journalism "fell short" in April during capital protests by Vietnam Veterans Against the War. He said "scant" attention was paid to discoveries that one of the group's leaders was a sergeant posing as a captain and had never been to Vietnam and that another leader whose testimony impressed the Senate Foreign Relations Committee had material prepared by a speech writer for the late Senator Robert F. Kennedy.

Rather than respond constructively to notations of "distortions or inaccuracies," the media tend to "yell 'intimidation'" or to defend the fault, Mr. Agnew said. He particularly objected to the Emmy award given to C.B.S. for the Pentagon documentary.

"If the judges honestly thought that program merited an Emmy and didn't award it out of spite then I'm surprised," Mr. Agnew said. "They didn't vote an Emmy for costume design to the producers of 'Oh, Calcutta!'"

AGNEW CRITICIZES MEDIA ON ATTICA

Says 'Radical Left' Seeks Another Cause Celebre

By JAMES M. NAUGHTON
Special to The New York Times

WASHINGTON, Sept. 27—Vice President Agnew accused the "radical left" and news media today of seeking to transform the Attica Prison revolt into "yet another cause célèbre in the pantheon of radical revolutionary propaganda."

The Vice President praised Governor Rockefeller for "the courageous action he took in ending the confrontation at Attica after exhausting all practicable alternatives."

Mr. Agnew thus took issue with critics who have blamed Mr. Rockefeller for complicity in the deaths of 29 inmates and nine hostages who died as a result of the armed assault Sept. 13 on sections of the prison held by the inmates. There were 42 deaths in all stemming from the five-day uprising at the maximum security prison.

633 Law Officials Killed

Instead of paying homage to 633 law enforcement officials killed in the United States in 10 years, there has been "inordinate attention focused on the self-declared and proven enemies of our society," the Vice President declared in a speech to the International Association of Chiefs of Police in Anaheim, Calif. Copies of the speech were made available here.

"Now the name 'Attica' joins the list of geographic place names and slogans whose very utterance, in the litany of anti-American hate preached by radical propagandists, is a dagger at the heart of our country's free institutions," Mr. Agnew said.

Some members of an observer committee of legislators, lawyers, newsmen and former Attica inmates have criticized Governor Rockefeller for refusing to visit the prison when they sought to mediate an end to the uprising.

Demands Are Scored

"A Governor of a state cannot allow himself to be peremptorily summoned into the presence of outlaws to meet their demands," the Vice President said. "Had he gone, and still refused to surrender the state, the next demand might have been for the President of the United States to demean himself in their presence."

Although he said no citizen could ignore the real need for prison reform, Mr. Agnew said that was not the primary issue of Attica.

"Only by the total inversion of all civilized values can those among the militant inmates who killed a guard and slashed the throats of fellow inmates during the period of their holdout be termed heroes in a struggle for human life and dignity," he said.

Cases in Point—6: "The Selling of the Pentagon"

A C.B.S. Rerun Adds Agnew-Laird View

By LINDA CHARLTON

The Columbia Broadcasting System, caught in a controversy over its documentary, "The Selling of the Pentagon," showed the film again last night, adding the criticism of three Nixon Administration officials and a defense of the film by the president of C.B.S. News.

The documentary, which deals with the public relations efforts of the Department of Defense, and details the time, money and enthusiasm devoted to these efforts, provoked a widespread response after its initial showing Feb. 23. The network says that the response was "predominantly favorable," but the response of the Nixon Administration and other public officials was sharply critical.

After rebroadcasting the documentary, the network last night presented interviews with three of the most prominent critics, Vice President Agnew, Melvin R. Laird, the Secretary of Defense, and Representative F. Edward Hébert, the Louisiana Democrat who heads the House Armed Services Committee.

The interviews were followed by a statement from Richard S. Salant, the president of C.B.S. News, who began by stating that "no one has refuted the essential accuracy" of the documentary, and went on to reply to a number of specific charges made by Mr. Agnew and Mr. Hébert.

The specific allegations to which Mr. Salant replied were one by Mr. Hébert that C.B.S. had obtained film used in the documentary under false pretenses, and that the statement of one person had been edited before being used. Those by Mr. Agnew were a charge that C.B.S. had financed a secret and illegal invasion to overthrow Haiti for filming purposes, and that a contention made in an earlier C.B.S. documentary, "Hunger in America," concerning the alleged death of a baby from malnutrition was untrue.

Mr. Salant said that the network had "an answer for every one of the criticisms you've heard" but that he would restrict himself to "only a few charges" because of time.

He ended his statement by saying:

"Finally, let me sum up our position regarding all those charges against C.B.S. News: We can refute every charge. We are proud of 'The Selling of the Pentagon,' and C.B.S. News stands behind it. We are confident that when passions die down, it will be recognized as a vital contribution to the people's right to know."

A Challenge by Agnew

Mr. Agnew, on Monday, challenged the network to allow him to edit his own critical remarks, a challenge to which the network replied with a "no comment." Mr. Agnew has attacked the documentary on several occasions as containing inaccuracies and backing up its contention of a Pentagon "propaganda barrage" with, in his words, "alleged facts which are untrue."

Mr. Hébert, saying that he saw nothing wrong in the Pentagon "trying to sell the best bill of goods it can," called the documentary "one of the most un-American things I've ever seen . . . on the tube."

Mr. Laird, in the interview broadcast last night, said that he felt "there probably could have been a little more professionalism shown in putting the show together." He said that the documentary had evoked increased Congressional support. "Well, we've had a tremendous response from it," he said.

Army TV in Saigon Airs 'Selling of the Pentagon'

Special to The New York Times

SAIGON, South Vietnam, March 26—The official Army television station here aired the Columbia Broadcasting System's "The Selling of the Pentagon" twice—last Saturday at 6 P.M. and yesterday at 5 P.M.

The broadcast was the original version of the hour-long show, and did not include the comments by Vice President Agnew that were added to the repeat broadcast in the United States. A spokesman for the American Forces Network said the later version with the Vice President's criticisms would be broadcast "if they send it to us."

Agnew, Pentagon and C.B.S.

To the Editor:

I see from the reports of Vice President Agnew's speech to a Republican club in Boston that he is playing golf with the facts again. I refer to his attack on the recent Columbia Broadcasting System documentary entitled "The Selling of the Pentagon." Without offering a significant example of misrepresentation or inaccuracy, he castigated the documentary as a severe example of bias and distortion.

I beg to suggest that Mr. Agnew has hit the wrong ball. To one who has enjoyed more than a passing acquaintance with the way Washington works, the documentary rings true from start to finish; and if it were to be faulted, it should be for the reason that in the time at hand C.B.S. could throw the light on only a part of the story of the Defense Department's mighty propaganda engine.

For those who might care to assay the Vice President's charges, I suggest a reading of Chapters thirteen and fourteen in the recently published book, "The Military Establishment," a Twentieth Century Fund Study by Adam Yarmolinsky and a team of contributors. I hope that Mr. Agnew, at least, will read the material.

ROBERT MANNING
Boston, March 19, 1971

TV's 'Pentagon' Divides the Media

By JACK GOULD

The controversy over the Columbia Broadcasting System's controversial documentary, "The Selling of the Pentagon," continues unabated, and in due course undoubtedly will be the subject of a Congressional inquiry. The latest twist in the Washington cause célèbre is not merely the program itself but the matter of editing procedures in the print and electronic media.

News Analysis

The latest chapter in the episode was initiated by The Washington Post followed by heated letters from Richard S. Salant, president of C.B.S. News, and Reuven Frank, president of the National Broadcasting Company news department.

Two Sides of Controversy

The Pentagon and some key members of Congress see the issue in terms of the basic credibility of the home screen; Messrs. Salant and Frank see the problem as the imposition of a double standard in journalism, one for TV and one for newspapers.

The Washington Post initiated the latest brouhaha by by criticizing C.B.S. News for rearranging and taking out of sequence the remarks of Col. John A. MacNeill of the United States Marines and allegedly misrepresenting and cutting the interview with Daniel Z. Henkin, Assistant Secretary of Defense. Moreover, The Post suggested that the subject of an interview should have the opportunity to see and approve any revision in his remarks.

Mr. Salant heatedly defended the integrity of "The Selling of the Pentagon" and charged that Colonel MacNeill, who speaks under the auspices of the Industrial College of the Armed Forces, was not above picking such remarks from an address by Premier Souvanna Phouma of Laos that bolstered his argument and omitting others. The Pentagon has charged that C.B.S. News attributed to Colonel MacNeill views actually expressed by Prince Souvanna Phouma.

Journalistic Principle

Mr. Frank, who was not involved in the program but feels a vital journalistic principle is at stake, said it was "frightening" that a major newspaper should subscribe to the theory that the editing of remarks should be left to the interested party, the man who made the speech. He charged that The Washington Post was stooping to "Agnewism."

The Post, in return, maintained that as with business, government and the Pentagon a newspaper had to examine its methods, seek improvements and not be shy about criticism. Ironically, to outside observers, The Post's television station, WTOP-TV, twice repeated "The Selling of the Pentagon" without intervention by the common ownership. The Post and WTOP-TV pride themselves on their separate autonomies.

The kernel of the controversy lies in editing. The nature of TV is such that to a viewer a program may appear as a continuously unfolding narrative, though the quick film cutting is apparent to more discerning set owners.

Newspapers, for their part, also may pluck the newsworthy nuggets out of a protracted interview and they also are regular targets of complaints on that score. But the emotional impact and number of persons involved are far smaller.

Thus far the controversy over "The Selling of the Pentagon" has centered on complex and specific details rather than the larger debate over whether the military was trying to impose its views of the world on civilians. Last night several Washington communications lawyers posed what they felt was the overriding dilemma: Can foreign affairs and military operations any longer be separated?

Several members of the House of Representatives have already referred the dispute to the Federal Communications Commission, an action that almost assures a running dialogue between the print media and TV. The broadcasters observe that unlicensed newspapers can make mistakes or offend individuals without the implied possibility of economic reprisal. Licensed broadcasting stations, on the other hand, are required to appear either before the F.C.C. or Congress when complaints are made against them.

HOUSE PANEL BIDS C.B.S. YIELD FILMS

But Network Won't Provide Material Not Broadcast in Pentagon Documentary

By JACK GOULD

The House Interstate and Foreign Commerce Committee served a subpoena yesterday on the Columbia Broadcasting System to obtain all televised and untelevised materials pertaining to the network's controversial documentary "The Selling of the Pentagon."

Dr. Frank Stanton, president of the network, replied that the House of Representatives was welcome to material that had actually been broadcast but that the network would not make available unused films, textual matter or notes that were not shown on the home screen.

The exchange set the stage for what could be a running battle between Congress and the television industry over the journalistic independence of a broadcasting entity that operates under a Federal license.

Seeks to 'Get Facts'

Representative Harley O. Staggers, chairman of the Commerce Committee and of its Special Subcommittee on Investigations, said that, with the dispute over the Pentagon show still raging, the sensible course was "to get the facts."

"Matters can only grow worse without the facts," he said from his home in Keyser, W. Va. "We are not blaming anyone and we have not reached any decisions. After the inquiry we hope to issue a statement that will be factual."

Asked if the accuracy and preparation of television documentaries had not become an issue in Washington, the West Virginia Democrat agreed they had and said that a purpose of the inquiry was to try to shed constructive light on the issue.

Dr. Stanton said that the House committee's subpoena appeared to be designed to help the committee make the news judgments of C.B.S. News subject to legislative surveilance.

"The subpoena raises an unprecedented issue in the history of the relationship between the Federal Government and the press in this nation," he said. "No newspaper, magazine or other part of the press could be required constitutionally to comply with such a subpoena with respect to material gathered by reporters in the course of a journalistic investigation but not published.

Cites First Amendment

"The fact that television and radio stations are licensed by the Government does not deprive the press of First Amendment protection, and the courts have so held. That protection does not depend on whether the Government believes we are right or wrong in our news judgments.' '

The next legal question, according to the network, is whether the committee will ask the full House to hold the network in contempt for not fully answering the subpoena. If the House should so vote, it was said, the network is prepared for a legal battle up to the United States Supreme Court.

Meanwhile, the investigating subcommittee served a subpoena on the National Broadcasting Company in connection with the inclusion of old film in "Say When," a documentary stressing the balance of nature and decrying the indiscriminate shooting of a mother polar bear.

N.B.C. Drafts Guidelines

But both Washington political circles and New York television circles agreed that the committee was primarily concerned with the C.B.S. documentary, detailing purported propaganda activities of the Pentagon and charging officers with defying directives not to discuss matters of foreign affairs.

It was said that N.B.C. had been included so as to avert allegations that the committee was "picking on" one network. N.B.C. refrained from comment yesterday but was drafting new guidelines to avoid any viewer misunderstanding as to what he is seeing.

The C.B.S. subpoena, returnable on April 20, calls for film prints and the transcript of "The Selling of the Pentagon" as initially broadcast on Feb. 23 and the repeat performance on March 23, to which were added edited criticisms of the program by Vice President Agnew and Secretary of Defense

Melvin R. Laird, and a rebuttal by Richard S. Salant, president of C.B.S. News.

The parts of the subpoena that Dr. Stanton rejected call for the following:

¶All film, workprints, outtakes, sound tape recordings and transcripts, whether they were used on the air or not.

¶The names and address of all persons appearing on "The Selling of the Pentagon," other than members of Congress, military personnel and persons who were regular C.B.S. employes as of Jan. 1, 1970.

¶A statement of all disbursements of money, things of value or legal considerations of any kind to these persons.

¶Copies or descriptions of any contracts, agreements or releases that may have been negotiated with these persons, whether written or oral.

The second subpoena involved both N.B.C. and David Wolper, a package producer. Mr. Wolper's program was designed to demonstrate that nature preserved a balance of species through its own design. To make the point that a hunter killing a mother bear could disturb the balance, he used footage of a bear seemingly killed. Actually, the bear had been shot with a tranquilizing gun for purposes of tagging.

Mr. Wolper defended his documentary reconstruction on the ground the segment did not violate truth—mother bears are killed by hunters, he said—and the sequence was hardly something he could "stage" or hope to encounter with a cameraman on the spot.

The Federal Communications Commission, which regulates stations under "the fairness doctrine," held its commission membership meeting yesterday but took no action on the controversy over documentaries.

A case testing the scope of a Congressional committee's power to subpoena a news medium is now before the United States Court of Appeals for the District of Columbia. The case involves Black Politics of Berkeley, Calif., a now-defunct underground periodical that published articles on revolutionary tactics by a writer who used a pseudonym. The Senate Permanent Investigations Subcommittee subpoenaed an editor of Black Politics, Tom Sanders, in an effort to determine the name of the writer.

The appeals court has stayed the issuance of the subpoena pending a decision on the newspaper's contention that such action would violate the First Amendment's guarantee of freedom of the press.

A Diversionary Program

The effort by a Congressional committee to subpoena the film and records of C.B.S. News has the effect of turning "The Selling of the Pentagon" into a new show that could be called "The Unmaking of a Documentary." This counterattack, which continues the pressure brought against the network by the Vice President and Secretary of Defense, is a diversionary move that overlooks the substance of the program and instead investigates the bearer of bad news.

The program, which certainly had a point of view but did not materially distort the facts, was presented mainly in the words and pictures of the Defense Department itself. Public relations colonels were photographed touring the country and telling civilians what policies they should support in Indochina and elsewhere—a direct violation of the laws and traditions prohibiting the military from engaging in political propaganda.

The dragnet subpoena against C.B.S. is properly being resisted by the network, which is willing to cooperate to the extent of supplying information about what has been seen by the public. Forcing a broadcaster or filmmaker to supply his "outtakes" — the discarded matter that winds up on the cutting-room floor—is the equivalent of searching the unfinished notes of a reporter.

Most of the facts brought out in the program can be found in Government records and in Senator J. W. Fulbright's book, "The Pentagon Propaganda Machine." Instead of attacking the documentary, Congress would be better advised to study the Pentagon's practice of selling the Vietnam war to the civilian populace by men in uniform.

April 10, 1971

Pentagon Says C.B.S. Program Led to Public Relations Reforms

WASHINGTON, April 9 (UPI) —The Defense Department acknowledged today that the Columbia Broadcasting System's documentary "The Selling of the Pentagon," which the department has criticized as distorted and unfair, has resulted in some beneficial reforms in the military's public information program.

"Times do change and we try to learn from them," the Pentagon spokesman, Jerry W. Friedheim, told reporters, "and from time to time we learn something from suggestions that you make."

He said that the television program had led Daniel Z. Henkin, Assistant Defense Secretary for Public Affairs, to order commanders to stop glamorizing judo and other types of hand-to-hand combat in open house demonstrations on military bases.

Mr. Friedheim said that Mr. Henkin had also ordered a review of films that the Pentagon makes available to the public to weed out those reflecting outdated foreign policy concepts.

The C.B.S. documentary, first broadcast in February and again televised last month, has drawn sharp criticism from Vice President Agnew, Defense Secretary Melvin R. Laird and Representative F. Edward Hébert, Democrat of Louisiana who is chairman of the House Armed Services Committee They termed the program a biased assault on the military

Mr. Friedheim said that both the reforms grew out of scenes in the documentary, including one showing Army Green Berets demonstrating judo before children at a New Jersey base.

Mr. Friedheim said that the services "should take another look and be sure those events presented — and those narrations involved, and the activities shown — where children will be present, will be appropriate for youngsters to view."

He said that all base commanders had been advised to use "good judgment" but that no type of demonstration was specifically banned.

The review of films grew out of another segment of the document, which showed part of a 1952 movie, "Red Nightmare," about a man who dreams the Russians have taken over his town.

"That particular film was produced during the cold war period at a time when the nation's foreign policy was different, at a time when we regarded the Communist bloc as a monolith," Mr. Friedheim said.

C.B.S. Gains Support for Defiance of Subpoena

By JACK GOULD

The American Civil Liberties Union and Elie Abel, dean of the Columbia University Graduate School of Journalism, supported yesterday the Columbia Broadcasting System's refusal to respond to portions of a Congressional subpoena that demanded details on matters not broadcast.

The liberties union, in a statement, urged Dr. Frank Stanton, the network president, to continue to resist efforts of the House Interstate and Foreign Commerce Committee to obtain untelevised film or textual materials bearing on the network's controversial documentary "The Selling of the Pentagon."

On Thursday, Dr. Stanton agreed to supply only such film and text as had been shown on the home screen.

The liberties union, which volunteered legal aid to the network, cited Federal court decisions in the case of Earl Caldwell, a reporter for The New York Times. It said the courts held that the Government could not impose unreasonable restraints on a journalist in the performance of his duties or, by subpoenaing his personal notes, jeopardize his opportunities for independent inquiry.

Alan Reitman, associate director of the union, said that his group was deeply concerned over governmental intrusion into the operations of the news media, including television, and possible circumvention of the First Amendment. A fresh policy review is now in progress, he said.

Mr. Abel said that Dr. Stanton "was right" and had a true understanding of the efforts of a groups of politicians to impose on the media a "Federal standard of truth." He said that such efforts varied with the party in power and added that he regretted "many newspapers don't see the issue as clearly as they should."

The Columbia dean reported that he had made an exhaustive review of the controversy over "The Selling of the Pentagon" and did not feel the Department of Defense or the House Armed Services Committee had succeeded in refuting the program's central charge that the Pentagon was spending millions to propagandize civilians.

Instead, he said the argument had become sidetracked by a debate over taking quotations out of their original sequence, a practice followed by newspapers and news agencies without protest.

Richard P. Kleeman, chairman of the Freedom of Information Committee of Sigma Delta Chi, professional journalistic fraternity, telegraphed a protest to Representative Harley O. Staggers, chairman of the House committee, protesting the C.B.S. subpoena as representing unwarranted harassment.

Indicative of the broad range of response prompted by the subpoena was the disclosure of a petition by the National Citizens Committee for Broadcasting, usually one of the sharpest critics of commercial broadcasting practices.

The petition, filed March 29, asked the Federal Communications Commission to promulgate a firm ruling that "a broadcaster's criticisms of the Government will in no way jeopardize his license to operate over the public airwaves." The committee is headed by Thomas P. F. Hoving, director of the Metropolitan Museum of Art.

Broadcasters Protest

The National Association of Broadcasters, in Washington, challenged the constitutionality of the subpoena on C.B.S. and protested any infringement on electronic journalism.

It was understood that, in the controversy over "The Selling of the Pentagon," the network believed it had found a clear-cut issue warranting an appeal to the United States Supreme Court, if necessary. Other television cases have been complicated by suggestions of possible violations of criminal law and have not been confined solely to the journalistic right of voicing an opinion.

Last night C.B.S. announced that it would present an hour's panel discussion by supporters and critics of "The Selling of the Pentagon" at 10 P.M. Sunday, April 18. A spokesman said that the participants had not yet been selected.

The Federal Communications Commission, which licenses stations, may ask the network to respond to a two-page letter reporting complaints of alleged unfairness and inaccuracy in the program. A tentative draft of the commission's letter circulated in Washington yesterday.

At a recent meeting of C.B.S. affiliated stations in Chicago, the owners of several outlets strongly indicated a lack of sympathy with the policies of C.B.S. News. One broadcaster in Texas quoted Herbert G. Klein, director of communications for the executive branch, as saying that the local station was doing an excellent news job and asking why it relied on C.B.S. News.

Guidelines by Mitchell

Special to The New York Times

WASHINGTON, April 9—Last August Attorney General John N. Mitchell announced guidelines designed to reduce the volume of subpoenas that had been issued from Federal grand juries to obtain tapes and notes of reporters and film takeouts of television newsmen.

The guidelines ordered Justice Department lawyers who were investigating suspected lawbreakers to make all reasonable efforts to get information elsewhere before resorting to subpoenas of newsmen.

Furthermore, they stated that the Justice Department would not authorize its lawyers to subpoena newsmen unless the information was essential to a successful investigation. Even then, confidential communications between newsmen and their sources are ordinarily not to be subpoenaed.

These guidelines apply only to lawyers in the Justice Department, and no Congressional investigating committee has suggested that it would voluntarily abide by them.

Also, the Attorney General's guidelines are designed to avoid using newsmen as unwilling investigative agents of the Government in criminal investigations of third parties. Thus, they are not precisely applicable to an investigation of the news media itself.

However, the United States Court of Appeals for the Ninth Circuit adopted the principle of the Attorney General's guidelines last year when it dissolved a subpoena that was served, before the guidelines were announced, upon Earl Caldwell, a reporter for The New York Times in San Francisco.

The Ninth Circuit held that under certain circumstances the First Amendment's free press guarantee shields news reporters from having to answer such subpoenas, if the result would be to frighten away news sources and reduce the public's access to full news coverage of controversial issues.

Clash Over Question Of 'Free Press'

"If our freedom as a nation is to continue, then the guarantee of journalistic freedom must be maintained." That was the reaction of Vincent T. Wasilewski, president of the National Association of Broadcasters, to the latest salvo last week in the war between the Federal Government and the news media.

The salvo was a subpoena served by the House Interstate and Foreign Commerce Committee on the Columbia Broadcasting System to obtain all televised and unused materials relating to the network's documentary, "The Selling of the Pentagon," which dealt with the public relations efforts of the Department of Defense.

The documetary, broadcast on Feb. 23 and March 23, stirred a storm of criticism from officials in Washington, including Vice President Spiro T. Agnew who has been attacking the media for what he regards as unfair anti-Nixon Administration positions. Representative F. Edward Hébert of Louisiana, who heads the House Armed Services Committee called the program "one of the most un-American things I've ever seen . . . on the tube."

Representative Harley O. Staggers, chairman of the House committee's Subcommittee on Investigations, said the purpose of the subpoena was "to get the facts" in the controversy. Dr. Frank Stanton, president of C.B.S., replied that the House was welcome to materials broadcast but not to films, textual matter or notes not used on the program. The protection of the First Amendment "does not depend on whether the Government believes we are right or wrong in our news judgments," Dr. Stanton said.

The subpoena is returnable on April 20. If C.B.S. continues to refuse to provide the requested material, and if the House should vote a contempt citation, there could be a major court test of broadcast journalism's freedom.

Suppose 'The Selling of the Pentagon' Had Been a Newspaper Article

By JOHN J. O'CONNOR

IN the fracas over "The Selling of the Pentagon," there is one curious fact that tends to get lost in the giant shuffle. As television journalism, the Columbia Broadcasting System news documentary was undoubtedly strong television. But, in the over-all context of the mass media, it was relatively tame journalism.

If precisely the same story had appeared in a newspaper or magazine, it might have stirred a small ripple of public response and perhaps a letter to the editor from a predictably irate Government official. Investigative journalism has a long, respectable tradition in the print media. And, by its very nature, that tradition is not noted for its balanced objectivity.

When an editor or reporter decides to investigate an individual or a situation, he proceeds on the premise that somewhere in the background there lurks something that should be exposed. If nothing is found, he has no story. If something is found and it doesn't provoke shrieks about distortion and prejudice from the object under attack, he hasn't written much of a story.

*

"The Selling of the Pentagon" concentrated on the military's giant apparatus for distributing information, contending that much of the data constantly being fed to the public was really propaganda for military policy. Defenders of the military and military policy lost no time in objecting long and loudly. Yet, assuming for the moment that there is at least some substance to one or two of their technical objections, not one critic has disproved the over-all thesis of the program.

Meantime CBS and the rest of the television industry wind up in the middle of a heated controversy that promises to go on for months, if not years. Why? There are interesting reasons on either side of the question.

Both sides recognize the incredible power of television, in its immediate emotional impact on the viewer and in the size of its total audience. The research department of the National Broadcasting Company recently reported that the number of people watching television during the average prime-time minute rose to a record of more than 77 million between October 1970 and February 1971.

Then there is the key difference between television and the print media. Newspapers, magazines and books have long fought for their rights under the First Amendment, and over the decades have solidly established those rights in the courts. Government officials are likely to think more than twice before jumping into battle with the print media. This doesn't rule out Government criticism, of course, but it does take the edge off Government threats.

*

Broadcasting stations, however, are licensed by the Federal Communications Commission, and licensed stations are required to appear before the FCC or Congress when complaints are lodged against them. As the number of broadcast frequencies and channels is limited, it is up to the Government agency to decide who will get to use them.

The basic danger was pinpointed by Clifton Daniel, associate editor of this newspaper, on the WQXR program "Insight": "The exercise of that authority carries with it the temptation to decide not only *who* may broadcast but *what* may be broadcast. If we are to preserve freedom of speech and of the press, that temptation must be resisted."

But that temptation is not being resisted, neither in certain Government quarters nor in the print media, where some militantly right-wing publications are calling for the outright dumping of CBS from the airwaves. All of this stridency is being stimulated by a program that appears hard-hitting only in the context of the bland fare that usually overwhelms TV scheduling.

It is understandable, though. An alternate title for the CBS documentary might have been "The Selling of the Vietnam War." And while there is increasing, if not unanimous, recognition that the war has been disastrous for everyone concerned, the reflex policy in official quarters is to man the defensive barriers against any criticism: No matter what the immediate facts are, judgment should be suspended. Leave analysis to the experts. President Nixon began a recent address to the nation with the observation. "Over the past several weeks you have heard a number of reports on TV, radio and in your newspapers on the situation in Southeast Asia. I think the time has come for me as President, and as Commander in Chief of our armed forces to put these reports in perspective . . ."

Earlier, in his interview with ABC's Howard K. Smith, the President referred to the Laos "incursion" and argued that "we cannot judge it before it is concluded. We cannot judge it even after it is concluded. We can only see it in perspective."

Seeing it in perspective, however, is often not that easy, as was made apparent in a special television-news report on correspondents covering the Laos story. As it happens the report was part of the April 1 edition of the "ABC Evening News with Howard K. Smith and Harry Reasoner." Reporter Don Farmer concluded:

"When they say things like, 'We now have cut the Ho Chi Minh Trail,' you and I know that that's absurd. And that's the kind of statements we're getting and they're so unbelievable that I think sometimes we're getting slightly paranoid, you know. We start looking for lies where maybe they don't exist. And I think it's a natural human failing, that—partly our fault, but there's a reason for it. And that is we've been lied to so many times that you begin to suspect that no one tells you the truth."

The "credibility gap" has long been with us, and evidently is not yet quite ready to fade from the scene. It hasn't however, sprung full-blown from the head of a paranoid journalist. There is much more substance than shadow in its appearance.

*

The best journalism on the Vietnam war has been produced by those reporters who, with the best will in the world, couldn't see "the light at the end of the tunnel," couldn't comprehend the inherent virtues of "pacification." They mightn't have contributed much to the power of positive thinking but then journalists are notorious for their negative approach. That's what makes them valuable for keeping matters in perspective.

Television, however, is under attack and there is nothing like even the hint of a threat to station licenses to give broadcasters a severe case of the jitters. Good investigative reporting had already been cut back drastically in recent years. Many of the critics of "The Selling of the Pentagon" know this, and want to keep it that way. And instead of getting a valuable dialogue between the investigators and their critics, the viewer probably will wind up with a few more harmless situation comedies.

The solution to the problem of controversial television is more of the same, not less. As Mr. Daniel observed, "Freedom and fairness on the airwaves can best be preserved, not by attempting to dictate the tone, tenor and content of news programs, documentaries and commentary, but by encouraging a multiplicity of voices in the community."

That multiplicity will not be encouraged by re-runs of "I Love Lucy."

April 18, 1971

C.B.S. Sees Recovery

By ROBERT A. WRIGHT
Special to The New York Times

LOS ANGELES, April 21—The most vocal dissent at the annual meeting of the Columbia Broadcasting System here today came from top management. Frank Stanton, president of the network, dispensed with his customary report on operations to reassert the company's stand against a Congressional subpoena that it feels violates freedom of the press.

Mr. Stanton reviewed C.B.S.'s refusal to provide the House Interstate and Foreign Commerce Committee with unbroadcast materials gathered in preparation for the controversial television program "The Selling of the Pentagon." The program dealt with expenditures for military public relations.

The executive said that a company officer presented the committee yesterday with film prints and the transcript of the materials that had been broadcast. C.B.S. was given 10 days to reconsider its withholding of material that had been deleted in editing.

Addressing himself to financial matters, William S. Paley, chairman, said that the company had expected the sharp drop in first-quarter sales and earnings reported last week because of the loss of cigarette advertising on television. Profits fell to 22 cents a share from 47 cents in the 1970 period.

A Surge of Business

But Mr. Paley said that television operations experienced "a dramatic surge of business" in March, providing a momentum that gave "promise of a significant recovery for the second half of the year." If that is realized, he said, earnings for 1971 should equal those of 1970.

The corporation took extra security measures, hiring eight off-duty plainclothes men from the Los Angeles police department to supplement its regular security force at the C.B.S.

Studio Center, where 600 stockholders gathered in the scoring studio. But the meeting was businesslike and orderly, although nonmanagement nominations were made for directors.

Today's meeting was in sharp contrast with last year's in San Francisco. Then, an angry group of women protested alleged discrimination by the company against women.

Today, the issue was raised again, but calmly, by Dr. Carlton Goodlett, chairman of the California Black Leadership Conference and publisher of The Sun-Reporter, a San Francisco newspaper of largely Negro circulation. Dr. Goodlett nominated Mrs. Aileen Hernandez, president of the National Organization of Women.

He also nominated Willie L. Brown, California State Assemblyman from San Francisco. Mr. Paley, who ruled that Dr. Goodlett's nominations could be admitted without seconding, defended the company's record in hiring minority groups and women.

The question and answer period was orderly. One stockholder and former employe deplored the use of certain television cameras by the local C.B.S. station because, he said, they broke down repeatedly and were costly to operate.

Another stockholder inquired about how the company had arrived at the name Viacom International for one of the company's operations. And Robert S. Lewine, a stockholder and president of the National Academy of Television Arts and Sciences, rose to commend the network's stand on press freedom and pledged his organization's support.

The management slate of directors was overwhelmingly reelected, and a "performance share unit plan" to replace the company's stock option plan was approved with no discussion. A proposal by Evelyn Y. Davis to limit the company's charitable contributions, contained in the proxy statement, was offered by a company executive in Mrs. Davis's absence and defeated.

C.B.S. 'PENTAGON' GETS EMMY AWARD

Peter Davis's Documentary Scored Military Spending

The Columbia Broadcasting System's documentary, "Selling of the Pentagon," won an Emmy award last night for outstanding achievement in news documentary programing.

The producer, Peter Davis, accepted the award at a dinner at the New York Hilton Hotel and said "great pressure has been put upon us in television news and particularly us at C.B.S. News and this helps to ease that pressure."

The documentary has come under attack from the Nixon Administration figures. The House Special Subcommittee on Investigations has subpoenaed material used in putting the documentary together. C.B.S. has refused to provide any material except what was broadcast and the network has defended the program.

Other Emmy awards in news documentaries presented by the National Academy of Television Arts and Sciences went to C.B.S.'s "The World of Charlie Company" and to its correspondent, John Laurence, and to the National Broadcasting Company's "Pollution Is a Matter of Choice" and to its writer and producer, Fred Freed.

In magazine-type programing, Emmys were presented to "The Great American Dream Machine" of the Public Broadcasting Service, to Mike Wallace of C.B.S.'s "60 Minutes" and to the Gulf of Tonkin Segment of "60 Minutes," produced by Joseph Wershba.

The "Today" program on N.B.C. received an Emmy as the outstanding daytime program and Emmys for children programing went to "Sesame Street" for the second year and to Burr Tillstrom, of "The Kukla, Fran and Ollie" series on P.B.S.

Conductor Leopold Stokowski received an Emmy for the National Educational Television festival series as the outstanding classical music program.

"The Selling of the Pentagon," first aired on Feb. 23 and rebroadcast with comment and criticism March 23, said the military establishment was spending at least $30-million and possibly as much as $190-million on public relations.

C.B.S. News suggested in the documentary that the Pentagon was using its public relations funds not only to inform, but also to persuade the public on vital issues of war and peace.

Stanton Bars C.B.S. Data

By CHRISTOPHER LYDON
Special to The New York Times

WASHINGTON, June 24—Dr. Frank Stanton, president of the Columbia Broadcasting System, refused again today to show Congress either the raw materials or the editing procedures that produced the television documentary "Selling of the Pentagon" last winter.

The program dealt critically with the Defense Department's large-scale public relations activities.

Representative Harley O. Staggers, Democrat of West Virginia, promptly told the network executive, "In my opinion, you are in contempt," and threatened to press a contempt citation before the full House.

Mr. Staggers is chairman of the House Commerce Committee and of the Investigations Subcommittee that had subpoenaed all the film, scripts and recordings that contributed to the program.

Both men described their showdown this morning as the start of a historic test.

For Mr. Staggers, who said that television networks already were the most powerful institution in America, the issue is whether a Government-licensed broadcaster could be held answerable against charges of "deceit."

For Mr. Stanton, and many other leaders of the broadcast industry, the case represents a landmark fight for full freedom-of-the-press privileges under the First Amendment.

"There can be no doubt in anyone's mind that the First Amendment would bar this subpoena if directed at the editing of a newspaper report, a book or a magazine," Dr. Stanton said.

"We're not interested in the First Amendment, we're interested in deceit," responded Representative William L. Springer of Illinois, the ranking Republican on the Commerce Committee.

Media Difference Seen

In addition, Mr. Staggers, Mr. Springer and the committee staff all insisted that television journalism was crucially different from the print media, with respect to its power, its constitutional and legal standing and its techniques — including the splicing of interview film that drew such sharp criticism in "The Selling of the Pentagon."

The charge most frequently repeated against that program today was that C.B.S. had altered the meaning of remarks by Assistant Defense Secretary Daniel Z. Henkin by rearranging his answers and the questions addressed to him.

C.B.S. officials have previously denied that they distorted Mr. Henkin's statements. But under questioning today, Dr. Stanton said only that he considered the program "fair" and declined to discuss or defend the editing techniques used in the Henkin interview in any detail.

"While responsible journalists may reasonably differ considering particular practices in particular cases," Dr. Stanton said, "we do not intend to ignore these differences or to shrink from continuing self-examination of our own practices. What we do object to is being subjected to compulsory questioning in a government inquiry, expressly intended to determine whether this or any other C.B.S. news report meets government standards of truth."

Justice Burger Quoted

Daniel Minelli, counsel to the investigation subcommittee, invoked Supreme Court opinions to support the distinction between electronic and printed journalism. He quoted Chief Justice Warren E. Burger as stating that "a newspaper can be operated at the whim or caprice of its owners; a broadcast station cannot"; and "a broadcast license is a public trust subject to termination for breach of duty."

Dr. Stanton acknowledged the "trustee or fiduciary" role of the broadcaster but added, "We also have an obligation to uphold the First Amendment," which guarantees freedom of expression.

Underlying the legal issues, Mr. Staggers suggested, is a practical issue of power.

"You talk about 'chilling effects,'" Mr. Staggers said, quoting Dr. Stanton's warning about the impact of Government inspection on journalism, "but your power sends chills up and down the spine of many men in this country."

Where is the check, he asked, on the networks, which he said are the nation's most powerful instruments of public opinion? "They can ruin every President, and every member of Congress.

"This is a turning point," he said. "If this kind of practice isn't stopped, it will go on and on and on."

House Unit Accuses C.B.S. Head

Special to The New York Times

WASHINGTON, June 29—The Special Investigations Subcommittee of the House Commerce committee voted today, 5 to 0, to seek a contempt of Congress citation against Dr. Frank Stanton, president of the Columbia Broadcasting System, for refusing to turn over to it the unedited film that went into the documentary "The Selling of the Pentagon."

The subcommittee also voted to cite the network itself for contempt.

Dr. Stanton, who views the subcommittee's demands as a violation of the freedom of the press, said in New York, "We will take every step necessary and open to us to resist this unwarranted action and to keep broadcast journalism free of Government surveillance."

Representative Harley O. Staggers, Democrat of West Virginia, who is chairman of the Commerce Committee, regards his inquiry into the documentary of last winter as an equally vital test of Congress's subpoena power and its authority to keep what he calls "deceit" off the airwaves. He said he would press for a contempt citation by the full committee and the full House.

Full Panel to Meet

The prospects of sustaining the contempt action in the 43-member Commerce Committee, which will meet on the matter Thursday morning, or in the 435-member House were considered uncertain.

Representative Torbert H. Macdonald, a Massachusetts Democrat who ranks second to Mr. Staggers on the committee and heads the Communications subcommittee, has not yet taken a position on the issue.

The House leadership, which would prefer to avoid the legal and political risks in such a direct confrontation with the broadcasting industry, was reportedly trying to help Mr. Staggers find some accommodation with the network.

There was no evidence of any compromising spirit on either side today, however.

Voting with Mr. Staggers to cite Dr. Stanton for contempt were Representatives William L. Springer of Illinois and Richard G. Shoup of Montana, both Republicans, and J. J. Pickle of Texas and Ray Blanton of Tennessee, both Democrats.

At a public hearing last Thursday, in which Dr. Stanton repeatedly refused to discuss the editing of the hour-long program critical of the Pentagon's

United Press International
Harley O. Staggers

public relations, Mr. Staggers insisted on the right to investigate charges that the splicing of interviews had misled the television audience.

The network said today that it was continuing a year-old review of its standards and practices and welcomed "professional" criticism of its procedures. It declared again, however, that the First Amendment's guarantee of a free press "bars the Government from compelling the production of outtakes [unused film and tape recordings] for the purpose of setting official standards of newsgathering, news editing or news broadcasting."

Julian Goodman, president of the National Broadcasting Company, said in New York in response to press queries, "The subcommittee's action is a matter of grave concern to all who believe in a free press and a free society. We hope the other members of the House who will have an opportunity to vote on this critical issue, will, upon thoughtful consideration, recognize the principle involved—maintaining freedom of expression—and reject the subcommittee recommendation."

New Rules From C.B.S.

By JACK GOULD

The Columbia Broadcasting System issued yesterday new rules governing news documentaries that meet some criticisms voiced against "The Selling of the Pentagon."

Under the general heading of editing news presentations, Dr.

Stanton, the network president, said that if the answer to one question asked of an interviewed person was taken from a reply to another question, the viewer must be so advised.

A second proviso is that excerpts from speeches or statements must be presented in the same sequence as originally delivered unless the viewer is advised to the contrary.

Daniel Z. Henkin, Assistant Secretary of Defense for Public Affairs, had charged "doctoring" of an interview he gave to Roger Mudd, network Washington correspondent, for "The Selling of the Pentagon." He raised the matters of transposed answers and words taken out of sequence.

These rules were added to a number of C.B.S. standards and practices in broadcast journalism that have been in operation for some years. The action, as Dr. Stanton faces possible charges of contempt of Congress, had the incidental effect of drawing attention to possible hazards in electronic journalism.

One practice previously restricted is the "reverse question." The network said it must not be used if its effect is in any way misleading.

The technique of the "reverse question" is employed where a single camera may be focused on the interviewed person and then at a later time a shot is made of the interviewer asking the question. The use of two cameras, one aimed at the interviewer and the other at the interviewed person, eliminates the problem, which generally arises when only a single camera is employed.

The interviewed person has a right to watch the process of making the "reverse question," which cannot be invoked "to clean up a poorly phrased or poorly stated original question," the network said. It also made it mandatory hereafter that an interviewed person receive a complete transcript of a broadcast interview upon request.

Another stipulation is that the audience cannot be misled into assuming that a correspondent is actually on the scene of an event when in reality he may dub in questions from a studio while an unidentified aide initially asks the questions on location. The technique of such dubbing without disturbing a star commentator's usual routine was not uncommon many years ago.

House Unit, 25-13, Votes to Cite C.B.S., Stanton for Contempt

By CHRISTOPHER LYDON
Special to The New York Times

WASHINGTON, July 1—The House Commerce Committee voted today to press a contempt of Congress citation against the Columbia Broadcasting System and its president, Dr. Frank Stanton, for refusing to cooperate with a Congressional investigation of the controversial documentary "The Selling of the Pentagon." The vote was 25 to 13.

The committee action opened the way for a House floor fight on the issues of freedom and accountability in broadcast journalism.

If the House cites Dr. Stanton and C.B.S. for contempt, the Justice Department would be authorized to initiate a criminal prosecution as well as a constitutional test that both sides in the dispute have said they welcome.

Dr. Stanton had refused to supply the Congressional investigators with film that was not used in the documentary, which dealt critically with the extensive publicity efforts of the armed services.

The House committee's vote to press for a contempt citation was backed by 14 Democrats and 11 Republicans.

Some observers saw room for a compromise that would avoid a vote of the full House. Representative Harley O. Staggers, the West Virginia Democrat who had subpoenaed the C.B.S. film that went into the documentary, had made the issue a test of his leadership as chairman of the Commerce Committee.

Although Dr. Stanton refused to supply film that was shot but not broadcast in the program, Pentagon sources long ago supplied the unedited transcripts of interviews, disclosing the process by which C.B.S. had abridged and, in some instances, reversed the questions and answers.

Mr. Staggers, again insisting that he was not trying to censor the network, said that broadcasters, licensed by the Government to operate in the public interest, were not entitled to newspapers' freedom from regulation and Government inquiry.

"It might be good," he told reporters today, "to clear the air and show the American people that their elected representatives are trying to get at the truth." The issue, he said, "is whether the American people have the right to know if they are being deceived by the electronic media."

In New York, Dr. Stanton deplored the committee's vote. He said it was "in disappointing contrast to the Supreme Court's ringing reaffirmation yesterday of the function of journalism in a free society," a reference to the case involving The New York Times and The Washington Post.

"If broadcasters must submit to Government surveillance of news judgments," he said, "broadcast journalism can never perform the independent and robust role which the Constitution intended for the American press in preserving freedoms."

Representative Torbert H. Macdonald, Democrat of Massachusetts, who is chairman of the Commerce Subcommittee on Communications, voted in favor of the contempt citation on the ground, he said, that Dr. Stanton had refused to answer the committee subpoena.

Representative Brock Adams, a Washington Democrat, opposed the citation as "a dangerous precedent—the first step down the path to Government censorship of the press."

Representative Clarence J. Brown, Republican of Ohio, attacked C.B.S. but also defended it under the First Amendment's guarantee of press freedom.

"C.B.S. has a right to lie, and does so frequently," he said. "It is not up to me to decide what's untruthful, biased and slanted, but if Frank Stanton doesn't wake up to the fact that he has a tremendous power and responsibility to the American people, the people will take care of him—or we will take care of him some other way."

On Tuesday, the Special Investigations subcommittee of the House Commerce Committee voted to seek the contempt citation against Dr. Stanton and cite his network for contempt of Congress.

The same day, the network issued new rules governing news documentaries. One requires that, if the answer to one question asked of an interviewed person is taken from a reply to another question, the viewer must be so advised. A second rule requires that excerpts from speeches or statements be presented in the same sequence as originally delivered unless the viewer is advised to the contrary.

Contempt for the Constitution

First Amendment guarantees of press freedom, reaffirmed this week by the Supreme Court, have again come under governmental attack—this time by a committee of Congress.

Following the lead of its Special Subcommittee on Investigations, the House Commerce Committee has voted to recommend a contempt of Congress citation for the Columbia Broadcasting System and its president, Dr. Frank Stanton. Dr. Stanton has quite properly refused to turn over to the subcommittee material gathered for, but not used in, the provocative C.B.S. documentary, "The Selling of the Pentagon."

The original subcommittee demand for Dr. Stanton's appearance was itself "wrong and an infringement of the freedom of the press," as White House Communications Director Herbert G. Klein observed at the time. A contempt citation would compound the outrage and put Congress in contempt of the Constitution. The committee's recommendation should be vigorously rejected by the House.

Rep. Broyhill Scores Panel On Censure of C.B.S. Head

WASHINGTON, July 4 (AP) — Representative James T. Broyhill, Republican of North Carolina, said today that the pending House action against the Columbia Broadcasting System sets a dangerous precedent by seeking to establish Congress as the final judge of editorial content.

Mr. Broyhill opposed the action by the House Commerce Committee last week that recommended that the C.B.S. president, Dr. Frank Stanton, be held in contempt of Congress for refusing to turn over some unused film clips to Congress.

In a statement, Mr. Broyhill, a member of the Commerce panel, said that the action "has drastic implications of abridging the freedom of the press guaranteed by the First Amendment to the Constitution."

Minority on House Panel Issues a Report on C.B.S.

WASHINGTON, July 10 (AP) —A minority of the members of the House Commerce Committee believe it is unnecessary as well as unconstitutional to require the Columbia Broadcasting System to submit to the committee untelevised material it gathered for its documentary "The Selling of the Pentagon."

The committee has voted, 25 to 13, in support of a demand by the chairman, Harley O. Staggers, Democrat of West Virginia, that the network and its president, Dr. Frank Stanton, be cited for contempt for refusing to supply the unused material.

Ten Democrats and three Republicans said yesterday in a minority report that Congress already had a tape of the program as well as a transcript of statements made by persons interviewed.

C.B.S. Stands Up

By TOM WICKER

WASHINGTON, July 12—Two well-established operating rules of legislative life are at work against C.B.S. News in its struggle against chairman Harley Staggers and the House Commerce Committee:

1. Legislators are reluctant to offend or oppose powerful leaders whose favor they may later need.

2. Those who think they have the votes always want to vote as soon as possible.

If it were not for these two factors, Mr. Staggers probably would not stand a chance to get the House of Representatives to vote tomorrow to hold C.B.S. News in contempt of Congress. He knows well, however, that never in contemporary history—not even to forestall some of the worst excesses of the Communist-hunters of the 1950's—has the House failed to uphold one of its committees and its chairman when they have recommended a contempt citation. And Mr. Staggers has shown that he knows exactly how to play upon the legislators' reluctance to vote against their own institutions and leaders.

Beginning with this head start, Mr. Staggers has taken further advantage of the parliamentary privilege the House rules give him to bring the issue to a vote any time he chooses. He gave opponents just five days, from the time the committee voted the contempt recommendation, to organize their support. This is haste indeed, measured by the usual stately pace of Congressional proceedings, particularly since Mr. Staggers' committee acted last week despite a request for delay by about half its members and despite the fact that it did not yet have a transcript of subcommittee hearings on the matter.

IN THE NATION

The House Democratic leadership apparently wants Mr. Staggers to delay his headlong rush to a vote, but he can hardly be in much doubt that delay would work against him. His case is so weak that the more time he allows C.B.S. News and its supporters to explain their case, the more likely he would be to suffer unprecedented humiliation on the House floor.

The contempt issue arises from Mr. Staggers' demand that C.B.S. News turn over its notes, transcripts and particularly its "out-takes"—unused film—from the production of the documentary "The Selling of the Pentagon." When Dr. Frank Stanton of C.B.S. refused to do so' on First Amendment grounds, the contempt recommendation was voted.

Yet the committee can establish no practical or legislative need for this material. In the case of the film's most controversial passage — an interview with Assistant Secretary of Defense Dan Henkin—it already has Mr. Henkin's own undisputed transcript of what he actually said. This would be enough to establish that C.B.S. doctored or perverted Mr. Henkin's remarks, if it did; and in any case, as a result of the controversy, Dr. Stanton has issued new internal rules for editing taped interviews. Mr. Staggers' subcommittee has conceded that its inquiry would have been unnecessary had these rules been in effect at the time "The Selling of the Pentagon" was filmed.

Thus, the committee cannot show that it needs the materials it demanded in order to pass a law; it cannot even show that it needs to pass a law, which is supposed to be the basis of

its investigative power; and it certainly cannot show that if it did pass a Federal law regulating television interviews the result would be fairer or more complete or more objective news than the public gets under the networks' own rules.

But even if all of that were not true, Mr. Staggers surely would not be proceeding in this manner against a newspaper—which would mean subpoenaing reporters' notes, tapes, unused story drafts and minutes of editorial conferences, all with the intent to legislate. That would be so clearly unconstitutional that even the Staggers subcommittee fell back on the assertion that broadcast news could not be equated with printed news because of Government regulatory authority over television and radio licenses.

That is soggy constitutional ground; as recently as last month, the Supreme Court in a libel case reaffirmed First Amendment protection for broadcast news. Is Congress really to take the position that although it cannot regulate the news that appears in the printed press, it can regulate the news that appears on television and is heard on the radio?

If that proposition were true, the air waves would quickly become a propaganda medium. Even the kind of witch hunt to which C.B.S. News so far has been subjected, if often repeated, would have an inhibiting effect on television reporters and their sources. So far, however, the network's stand deserves the salute of news colleagues and of the public; because whatever happens in the House tomorrow, C.B.S. and Dr. Stanton will also have to go right on dealing with Harley Staggers and the Commerce Committee.

July 13, 1971

The First Reaffirmed

The rights guaranteed to the American people by the First Amendment were reaffirmed once more yesterday when the House sent back to the Commerce Committee a proposed contempt-of-Congress citation against the Columbia Broadcasting System and its president, Dr. Frank Stanton. The 226-181 vote was a deserved if unusual rebuff to Commerce chairman Harley O. Staggers, Democrat of West Virginia, for his misbegotten effort to compel C.B.S. to turn over unused material compiled for its documentary, "The Selling of the Pentagon." The merits of that controversial production were not at issue. The House has recognized, as Mr. Staggers did not, the very clear constitutional prohibition against such interference with freedom of the press as applied to electronic journalism.

July 14, 1971

U.S. ASSURES PANEL ON VIETNAM NEWS

WASHINGTON, May 24 (UPI) — The Government assured a House Information subcommittee today that it was doing all that it could to arrange a free flow of news from South Vietnam.

Ironically, the Government's account was given at a secret session of the subcommittee which never before in its eight years of existence had closed its doors to the press.

The subcommittee's chairman, Representative John E. Moss, Democrat of California, said the closed session had been ordered with regret and only because it was expected that questions and answers would bear on matters of military security.

The panel later made public a prepared statement by Roger Hilsman, Assistant Secretary of State for Far Eastern Affairs. Mr. Hilsman said that the Vietnamese had "authoritative traditions" going back 2,000 years and that it had taken a while to develop mutually responsible relations between their Government and the American press during the anti-Communist struggle there.

Americans Vexed By Inability to Act In Vietnam Dispute

By DAVID HALBERSTAM
Special to The New York Times

SAIGON, Vietnam, June 9 — The conflict between the South Vietnamese Government and Buddhist priests is sorely troubling American officials here.

It has brought to the surface American frustrations over the apparently limited influence of the United States here despite its heavy investment in troops, economic aid and prestige to help South Vietnam block Communism.

The feeling today was that the situation might get worse. One official described his feeling as "watching something slowly slipping through your fingers."

For a variety of reasons Americans wish to dissociate themselves from the Saigon Government's role in the religious crisis. Any public disavowal, however, would contrast so sharply with the previous American policy of all-out support that it would be interpreted as heralding a change in the United States' attitude toward the Government of President Ngo Dinh Diem. Thus any expression would be a far-reaching policy statement.

It is reported that Washington has already told its officials here to express extreme concern over the developments and the Government's handling of them, and to press for a solution to the religious strife.

Americans are deeply embarrassed by the events, and frustrated in the face of persistent questioning by individual Vienamese, who ask:

"Why does your Government allow this to go on? Why don't you Americans say or do something?"

Americans are not at all pleased to have the world see Vietnamese troops with American arms and training putting down Buddhist riots in Hue, or modern M-113 armored amphibious personnel carriers guarding the streets.

The situation became more distasteful this week when the Government asked for United States Air Force planes to fly special troops into Hue. The Americans refused, so the Vietnamese used their own air force transports. These are former United States Air Force transports, which came here under earlier aid agreements. To the Vietnamese these planes still look like American aircraft.

Cooperation on News Ends

The American military is extremely sensitive over developments. American officials have stopped flying American newsmen into Hue. The American Military Information Office which customarily forwards messages to correspondents in the interior, has stopped the practice as far as Hue is concerned. Col. Basil Lee Baker, head Public Information officer, said:

"We don't want the Vietnamese to think we are participating in this."

The religious dispute, as other Americans have pointed out, is a Vietnamese internal matter. But then, as Americans here have also noted, the political nature of the civil war in South Vietnam gives international implications to all internal matters.

American political officials here are worried about the effect of the crisis on the war effort in a country where an estimated 70 per cent of the population considers itself Buddhist. Since President Ngo Dinh Diem and most of his close associates are Roman Catholics, it is almost impossible to maintain the Government's stand that it is only interested in keeping order, and that the struggle has no religious overtones.

Some feel that already deep damage has resulted, and that even if the Ngo Dinh Diem Government were able to end the Buddhist demonstrations, there would remain a great risk that a large section of the population would quietly disengage itself from the war effort. In a political war like this one a disengaged population would help the rebel Vietcong.

There is also a feeling here that the Government's over-all handling of the month-long crisis, and particularly yesterday's strong attacks on Buddhists by a women's group led by the President's sister-in-law, has made a casualty of Washington's attempt to portray the Government as leading a broad national movement to which the population is constantly rallying. Rather the picture of the Government, even among its most recent supporters here, is one of a regime aloof and inflexible.

G.I.'s Told Not to Criticize Vietnam

By DAVID HALBERSTAM
Special to The New York Times

SAIGON, Vietnam, June 23 — United States servicemen coming to South Vietnam are now being told by their officers to give a more positive picture of events here to American reporters. They have been told to avoid "gratuitous criticism."

An official Army directive on the subject says "As songwriter Johnny Mercer put it you've got to accentuate the positive and eliminate the negative."

The written directive was prepared in the United States to be read by officers to their troops. It reflects a growing concern over both recent reporting from South Vietnam and the attitude of many of the 12,000 American servicemen estimated to be here in support and advisory roles.

Troops' Attitude Criticized

The directive quotes a team of senior officers just back from a tour of South Vietnam as having said: "The majority of the team was impressed by the careless and frequently erroneous subjective interpretation of fact, rumor and fancy by a large number of U.S. military personnel . . . these individuals quickly and gratuitously drew gross generalizations as to what was wrong with the country, the Government and its leaders and almost any allied subject."

"The bitter truth is that critical comments by indiscreet or uninhibited advisers are producing 'bad' stories which adversely affect public understanding of American policy in Vietnam. Continuation of this trend would unjustifiably weaken public support of that policy," the directive says.

The directive was prepared this month by the headquarters of the United States Continental Army Command at Fort Monroe, Va., as a briefing to be given to all servicemen going to South Vietnam. It has been sent to commanders in charge of men going overseas by Col. B. Miller, Deputy Adjutant General.

A letter from Colonel Miller says, "Indoctrination of military personnel on the importance of suppressing irresponsible and indiscreet statements is necessary."

The orientation speech outlined in the directive emphasizes that soldiers should not discuss major matters because "it is difficult for you to see the big picture."

As a bad reporting, it cites a recent dispatch by a United

States correspondent about deterioration of the military situation in the Mekong delta region, where, in the view of high American military advisers, a virtual stalemate prevails.

A check showed that Army officials had taken the references cited out of context. Qualifying phrases were omitted to make it appear that the dispatch had been written about all of South Vietnam instead of the delta region alone.

The orientation speech comments:

These quotations were not the result of a briefing or interview with a spokesman who knew the whole picture of our activities in Vietnam." It said the information had come from military advisers "who, though they may have been very knowledgeable about their particular patch of terrain and their own particular Vietnamese unit, were necessarily limited on the knowledge of overall conditions."

The speech refers to "well-meaning but nonetheless indiscreet advisers who no doubt failed to appreciate their uninhibited views would be widely published in this critical fashion."

Actually, the report about the Mekong delta that was cited was thoroughly detailed and documented specific troubles. The sources for the information knew what the reaction would be but felt the seriousness of the situation there warranted giving the information.

The orientation speech adds: "Your approach to the questions of the press should emphasize the positive aspects of your activities and avoid gratuitous criticism. Emphasize the feeling of achievement, the hopes for the future, and the instances of outstanding individual or unit performance and optimism in general, but don't destroy your personal credibility by gilding the lily."

June 24 1963

Washington

On Suppressing the News Instead of the Nhus

By JAMES RESTON

WASHINGTON, Sept. 10—President Kennedy has asked the American people to be "patient" about Vietnam, but it would be nice to know what we are being asked to be patient about.

The truth is that the country does not know what the situation is in Vietnam because of the censorship imposed by the Diem Government.

Some censored dispatches are coming through direct from Saigon, but nobody but the correspondents knows what is cut out, and communication with them is neither free nor prompt.

Most dispatches are getting out by travelers leaving Vietnam for Manila in the Philippines or Hong Kong, but again it is hard for anybody here to know what didn't get out and, of course, the whole process of communications is slow and unreliable.

Obviously, this censorship is not directed at the Communists or the Buddhists. It is aimed primarily at preventing the American people, who are paying most of the bill, from knowing the details of the internal struggle in the Vietnamese capital.

Those American Guns

President Kennedy is undoubtedly right in his advice. He has been clumsy in his handling of the crisis but he has kept his eye on the main thing—fighting the Communists.

He has tried to change the Diem Government on television and so far he has failed. He has not let his failure divert him from the main objective. But there are some things he might do, short of changing the personnel of the Diem Government, which would make it easier to tolerate a disagreeable situation, and one of these would be to get the censorship lifted.

Another might be to try to persuade the Diem Government not to use American equipment to carry out anti-Buddhist policies that are offensive to the American people.

It would also help if we had a little more information about the activities of the Central Intelligence Agency in Vietnam. The President has assured the country that the C.I.A. is not operating on its own there and that it "coordinates its efforts with the State Department and the Defense Department."

Nevertheless, the impression persists that the C.I.A., which was created to get rid of bad guys, is in this case cooperating with them and financing them, and part of the reason for this impression is that the C.I.A. has not taken the trouble to explain the facts.

Apparently, the facts are not as ominous as the C.I.A.'s silence has made them appear. The "special forces" under Ngo Dinh Nhu that raided the Buddhist temples are apparently still being paid by the U.S. Government, but these "special forces" are not only carrying out internal political raids but are also fighting Communists in the fortified Vietnam villages.

This helps explain why it is difficult to cut the special forces fund, but the C.I.A. refuses to make the explanation and is visibly annoyed by any questions about it.

This lack of information and candor, then, is adding to the impatience President Kennedy deplores. The American correspondents in Saigon have done a remarkable job under the circumstances. They have been in physical danger more than is realized. They have been working under the power of a hostile Government which seems at times more interested in what they write than what the Communists do. And all correspondents in Saigon have been working with one another to get the news out in the face of military forces which at times have threatened their personal security.

The Kennedy Administration has recognized this problem and has been trying, for example, to give physical protection to David Halberstam, the brilliant young New York Times correspondent in Saigon, and his colleagues; but what Halberstam and the other correspondents there are pleading for, even more than physical protection, is freedom to get the news and get it back to their newspapers and radio and television networks.

Unless this greater freedom for American correspondents in Saigon is granted, the impatience is likely to grow both in the country and on Capitol Hill. Senator Frank Carlson, Republican of Kansas, one of the most patient men in Congress, announced today that he would support a move to cut off all further aid to South Vietnam as long as the regime of Ngo Dinh Diem remains in power. This, of course, is precisely what the Communists would like, and, if carried out, could lead to the loss of the whole Vietnamese peninsula and more.

'No Nhus Is Good News'

Yet unless the lines of communication are opened and the American people can learn what they are getting there for their million dollars a day, even President Kennedy may not be able to prevent the Congress from making cuts that could cripple the whole war effort.

Ambassador Lodge has apparently made this point, but without any success. He has asked for suppression of the Nhus and has merely got suppression of the news; and to try our patience even more, Madame Nhu is apparently coming here to tell us, in her own sweet way, how wrong we are about the whole thing.

September 11, 1963

Dodd Says Misinformation Led to Diem's Overthrow

WASHINGTON, Feb. 23 (UPI)—South Vietnam's Ngo Dinh Diem regime was overthrown as a result of serious misinformation given to the American public about last year's Buddhist persecutions, Senator Thomas J. Dodd said today.

The charge by Senator Dodd, a Connecticut Democrat, came in a letter accompanying the report of the United Nations fact-finding mission to South Vietnam, which was reproduced by the Senate subcommittee on internal security at the Senator's request.

President Diem and one of his brothers, Ngo Dinh Nhu, were killed following the coup d'état last November.

"We were told that the Diem Government was guilty of such brutal religious persecution that innocent Buddhist monks had been driven to commit suicide in protest," Senator Dodd's letter said.

"Now it turns out that the persecution was either nonexistent or vastly exaggerated and that the agitation was essentially political."

February 24, 1964

537

TV: Nation Now Eyewitness to Vietnam Debate

Hearings Are Shown by C.B.S. and N.B.C.

By JACK GOULD

THE hearings of the Senate Foreign Relations Committee were carried live yesterday by the Columbia Broadcasting System and National Broadcasting Company, and the two networks planned to continue their extensive coverage next week. In effect, the debate over Vietnam has now begun and television will enable the mass audience to be an eyewitness.

•

The desirability of televising the hearings was clearly demonstrated in the six hours of questioning of David E. Bell, administrator of the Agency for International Development. Also, the session indicated the difficulty of maintaining a sense of proportion in covering a national controversy, a matter that reportedly was giving the White House some measure of concern.

It was not only Mr. Bell's direct answers to the leading questions of the Senators that were of interest in the home. Of equal value to the layman was the recital of the scope and nature of the A.I.D. efforts to strengthen the economic and social structure of South Vietnam.

Some of the detail that Mr. Bell offered admittedly may not have been especially newsworthy by the standards of the Washington press corps, but it is not to be forgotten that viewers, so many of whom rely on TV rather than the press for their news, cannot be expected to enjoy their expertise.

In answering the extraordinarily wide range of questions asked by Senator J. W. Fulbright, Democrat of Arkansas, committee chairman, and his colleagues, Mr. Bell gave a lucid picture of the exceptional complexity of the Asian war. Seldom on television has there been such a full primer on the endless economic ramifications of the Vietnam conflict, both in Saigon and here at home.

That the Senators and the spokesmen for the Johnson Administration disagreed much of the day added to the viewer interest, but the larger gain was the set owner's sense of greater familiarity with the over-all agonizing problem.

•

It is in pursuit of that basic informational end that TV can render a distinct service. With no end to the conflict in sight after the collapse of the "peace offensive" and the prospects for escalation so strong, the Vietnam war is now a local story for viewing families, to whom increased draft calls are an intensely personal and overriding concern.

The television networks cannot escape censure for their inexcusable action last week in only giving routine summaries of the appearance before the committee of Secretary of State Dean Rusk; he should have been carried in full to assure balanced coverage. But if on the home screen an automatic theatrical advantage falls to the questioner of a witness, the answer to the problem lies in responses that are complete and convincing. The influence of television, which plays a greater role in White House strategy than is often realized, may turn out to be the catlyst that brought about a coast-to-coast debate that now cannot be avoided by Administration leaders.

•

The C.B.S. network carried yesterday's proceedings in their entirety; N.B.C. was on hand for all but a half-hour of soap opera. The American Broadcasting Company gave regular bulletins but otherwise adhered to its normal daytime schedule.

With President Johnson's sudden announcement that he would fly to Hawaii and the first still pictures of the Soviet soft landing on the moon it was a busy news day for television. Hopes that there might be live coverage of the President's conference in Honolulu, via the Pacific satellite Syncom 3, appeared dashed last night with the disclosure that there was no ground station to receive signals from Hawaii. The West Coast station that picked up the Olympic Games in Tokyo has been dismantled, it was reported.

The first pictures of the moon landing were of remarkable quality considering the circumstances under which they were shown. British scientists composed the pictures from signals coming from the moon. The British Broadcasting Corporation showed the result. The news wire services then took pictures off the British television screen and relayed them by facsimile to this country. Finally, American television showed pictures of those pictures.

Of equal interest was the extraordinary strength of the signals as aurally recorded in Britain and rebroadcast here. They sounded like a moon beep-o-phone.

Schneider and Friendly Split On Vietnam-Hearing Telecasts

By JACK GOULD

A policy conflict between John A. Schneider, newly appointed head of the Columbia Broadcasting System's broadcasting activities, and Fred W. Friendly, president of C.B.S. News, broke out yesterday on the issue of live television coverage of the hearings of the Senate Foreign Relations Committee.

Mr. Schneider, who on Wednesday was appointed to the No. 3 post in the company, said that he had decided against live televising of yesterday's testimony of George F. Kennan, former United States Ambassador to Moscow, on United States policies in Vietnam.

He explained that he thought relatively few persons sat at home for the prolonged hearings of the committee and that a greater service was rendered by extracting the hard news and presenting it in compact evening newscasts enjoying far larger audiences.

Mr. Friendly remained incommunicado throughout the day but Mr. Schneider readily agreed that the C.B.S. News executive had a different point of view. It was learned that Mr. Friendly appealed repeatedly to Mr. Schneider to cancel regular programing, as C.B.S. did last week for other witnesses before the committee.

N.B.C. Carried Sessions

Mr. Friendly was known to feel that the telecasts of the extended hearings had proved their worth in familiarizing viewers with the intricacies of the Vietnam problem.

The National Broadcasting Company carried Mr. Kennan's statements during the morning and afternoon.

The cleavage between Mr. Schneider and Mr. Friendly assumed such proportions as to prompt rumors that Mr. Friendly might resign on a point of principle. Staff members of C.B.S. informally agreed "the next day or two will have to be interesting."

Until Wednesday's announcement that Mr. Schneider had been named C.B.S. group vice president — broadcasting, Mr. Friendly reported directly to Dr. Frank Stanton, president. Under the executive realignment he will deal with Mr. Schneider, who, in turn, will report to Dr. Stanton.

It is an accepted maxim in TV journalism that the head of a news division is on the strongest ground if he has direct access to the chief executive officer, a role that Dr. Stanton is expected to assume fully in coming weeks. Mr. Friendly reportedly feels he is now one step removed from that authority.

In effect, however, management interprets the realignment as meaning that Dr. Stanton has delegated a portion of his authority to Mr. Schneider and that Mr. Schneider will be exercising virtual presidential powers over the television, radio, news and station divisions of the company.

At 10 A.M., 'I Love Lucy'

The first visible hint of internal stresses at C.B.S. came at 10 A.M., when the Senate committee meeting opened. While N.B.C. posted an announcement of its special coverage from the caucus room, C.B.S. went into its scheduled rerun of "I Love Lucy," starring Lucille Ball and Desi Arnez.

C.B.S. had not formally committed itself to presenting the hearing but from last week's performance had invited the assumption that it would do so. It was learned that C.B.S. affiliated stations in Hartford and in Louisville, Ky., called C.B.S. in New York to inquire why the live coverage was not on the air.

Mr. Schneider said that his decision on Mr. Kennan's testimony was prompted in part by the experience of covering Tuesday's appearance of Lieut. Gen. James M. Gavin before the committee.

The general was on the live screen for hours, Mr. Schneider said, but C.B.S. News had no difficulty in condensing his opinions into a 20-minute summary that same evening.

"There is a question whether the greatest service is rendered by putting a hearing on whole or distilling the essence of a hearing," the C.B.S. executive noted.

Cost Said to Be no Factor

Mr. Schneider maintained that it required an "enormous commitment," far beyond that held by the average viewer, to sit for six hours in order to get the gist of a witness's position. He suggested that knowledgeable selection of hard news was part of the function of an able editor.

The cost of pre-empting a day's regular commercial schedule, which in C.B.S.'s case reportedly runs to about $175,000, is not the determining factor, Mr. Schneider said.

"With space shoots and other events we've learned to live with that problem," he said.

He went on to observe that while those who followed all-day hearings might be very enthusiastic, extensive research showed that the over-all number of viewers dropped substantially. A majority of the country's opinion-makers, Mr. Schneider said, are busy at work while the hearings are being conducted and get a chance to see only evening news programs.

Friendly's Position

Mr. Friendly's over-all position is that the full live coverage of the hearings has contributed to a fruitful national debate over the issues of Vietnam and Asia and that the educational value of the full hearings cannot be conveyed in spot news bulletins.

He thinks that the extensive detail elicited at the hearings is essential to understanding of the complexity and delicacy of the war and the attendant problems.

Network rivalry is also a factor in the apprehensions voiced by members of the C.B.S. News staff. They said that in recent days C.B.S. had taken some of news initiative away from N.B.C. and noted that yesterday N.B.C. was coming closer to the format that C.B.S. had employed earlier in the week, notably in providing background commentary.

Efforts to conciliate the differences between Mr. Schneider and Mr. Friendly were reportedly under way in some C.B.S. circles last night, but this could not be confirmed.

February 11, 1966

Friendly Quits C.B.S. News Post In Dispute Over Vietnam Hearing

By JACK GOULD

Fred W. Friendly resigned yesterday as president of the Columbia Broadcasting System News Division in protest against working under a new superior who canceled live coverage of last Thursday's hearing of the Senate Foreign Relations Committee.

Mr. Friendly charged that John A. Schneider, newly appointed to the No. 3 post in the C.B.S. hierarchy, lacked adequate experience in national and international affairs to have a veto power over the news department.

Mr. Friendly, who first achieved renown as co-editor with the late Edward R. Murrow of the controversial "See It Now" documentaries, said that Mr. Schneider's cancellation of Thursday's hearing was "a business, not a news, judgment." He argued that the autonomy of the news department had suffered a "form of emasculation."

C.B.S. management vigorously supported Mr. Schneider's qualifications as group vice president — broadcasting, the post in which he will have responsibility for the news, television, radio and station divisions.

The over-all C.B.S. record in news deserves to be remembered,

Associated Press Wirephoto
Fred W. Friendly at airport in Washington yesterday.

an official of the broadcasting organization said, and he added that both William S. Paley, chairman, and Dr. Frank Stanton, president, were as interested now as before in thorough reporting.

The network announced last night that C.B.S. would carry live the testimony of Gen. Maxwell D. Taylor, former chairman of the Joint Chiefs of Staff at tomorrow's hearing of the Senate committee and Secretary of State Dean Rusk's appearance on Friday. The National Broadcasting Company, which carried last Thursday's hearing, had announced similar plans on Monday.

A summary of testimony by witnesses before the Senate hearing also will be carried on C.B.S. television from 10 to 11 P.M. Friday, pre-empting "Trials of O'Brien."

Mr. Friendly's resignation came as a climax to five days of corporate drama that showed no signs of subsiding last night.

Sixteen news producers at C.B.S. sent a joint telegram to Mr. Paley, Dr. Stanton and Mr. Schneider urging that new efforts be initiated to reconcile the intracorporation differences. Walter Cronkite, the network's star commentator on its evening news show, voiced regret over Mr. Friendly's departure and said it meant the loss of his "brilliant, imaginative and hard-hitting guidance."

The three vice-presidents working directly under Mr. Friendly—David Klinger, Bill Leonard and Gordon Manning—joined in the appeal to find "some means to make it possible for Mr. Friendly to resume his leadership."

Prospects of a successful appeal are not considered bright because reinstatement of Mr. Friendly would mean a lessening of the stature of Mr. Schneider, according to TV officials familiar with the industry's periodic shake-ups.

After his resignation, Mr. Friendly addressed the assembled members of the New York staff of C.B.S. News and then flew to Washington to apprise reporters in the capital of his decision.

Late last night reports circulated that Mr. Manning was the leading contender for Mr. Friendly's job. A management spokesman said, however, there was "nothing definite."

Last week's realignment of the top C.B.S. executive structure carried the approval of the board of directors and Mr. Paley.

It was reported last night that in the last few days a number of prominent persons in Washington had voiced hopes to C.B.S. that Mr. Friendly would be retained.

Mr. Friendly first offered his retirement on Thursday when he watched N.B.C. present the testimony of George F. Kennan, former Ambassador to Moscow, while C.B.S. was carrying a rerun of "I Love Lucy." A showdown over the weekend was postponed, but yesterday Dr. Stanton announced acceptance of the resignation.

The text of his statement follows:

"It is with deep regret that I accept the resignation of Fred W. Friendly as president of the C.B.S. News Division. Mr. Friendly feels that he is unable to continue in his post as a result of a decision made by the recently appointed Group Vice President, Broadcasting, John A. Schneider, not to schedule live television coverage of the testimony of George F. Kennan before the Senate Foreign Relations Committee last week.

"Fred Friendly has been an outstanding leader of broadcast journalism. His contributions to the public, to his profession and to C.B.S. have been great indeed. My associates, his colleagues and I will miss him."

Mr. Friendly, who has always displayed a fierce dedication to the journalistic potential of TV, released a four-page letter in which he asserted the failure to carry Thursday's hearing made a "mockery" of the crusade by Mr. Paley, Dr. Stanton and the Columbia News Division to obtain access to Congressional debates.

But the heart of Mr. Friendly's thesis, echoed in his quotations from a 1958 speech by Mr. Murrow, was directed at Mr. Schneider's qualifications. For eight years the new head of the broadcasting divisions worked in the sales end of the television business and then became a station general manager in Philadelphia and New York. As president of the C.B.S. television network until last week, he was chiefly concerned with entertainment matters.

Mr. Friendly noted that historically, final decisions on news matters were rendered either by Mr. Paley or Dr. Stanton.

"Mr. Schneider, because of his absolute power, would have more authority than William Paley or Frank Stanton have exercised in the past two years," Mr. Friendly said. "This, in spite of the fact that Mr. Schneider's news credentials were limited in the past to local station operations, with little experience in national or international affairs."

Mr. Friendly's resignation stunned the broadcasting industry more than any other executive upheaval in recent years because his letter raised the question over TV content, probably the most perennially debated aspect of the medium. In addition, his association with Mr. Murrow has made him a symbol of provocative journalism.

The 50-year-old Mr. Friendly's height and broad shoulders have earned him the nickname of "the big bear." Within the industry the passion of his commitment to video journalism is legendary and it has been especially pronounced in the current Vietnam crisis.

Mr. Friendly said he had no immediate future plans but it was known that he would not entertain an N.B.C. bid lest it force him to compete with the C.B.S. News department that he has tried to strengthen.

In the "See It Now" series with Mr. Murrow, his most spectacular production was the documentary on the late Senator Joseph R. McCarthy; before becoming C.B.S News president on March 2, 1964, he was executive producer of "C.B.S. Reports."

The Columbia management said it was perplexed by Mr. Friendly's concern about reporting to Mr. Schneider since the news head still would have access to Dr. Stanton either informally or through regular weekly meetings of the company's news executive committee.

Text of Friendly's Letter of Resignation to C.B.S.-TV Executives

Following is the text of the letter of resignation sent yesterday by Fred W. Friendly, president of C.B.S. News, to William S. Paley, chairman of the Columbia Broadcasting System, and Dr. Frank Stanton, president:

Dear Bill and Frank:

This is the third time since last Thursday that I have asked you to accept my resignation as president of C.B.S. News, and this time you have an obligation to accept it.

It is important that you and my colleagues in the News Division know that I am not motivated by pique or change of status in a table of organization, or lack of respect for Jack Schneider. He is, as you have both recalled, someone I had asked to join the News Division in an administrative role more than a year ago, when he was station manager of WCAU-TV.

I am resigning because C.B.S. News did not carry the Senate Foreign Relations Committee hearings last Thursday, when former Ambassador George Kennan testified on Vietnam. It was the considered news judgment of every executive in C.N.D. [Columbia News Division] that we carry these Vietnam hearings as we had those of the other witnesses. I am convinced that the decision not to carry them was a business, not a news, judgment.

I am resigning because the decision not to carry the hearings makes a mockery of the Paley-Stanton C.N.D. crusade of many years that demands broadest access to Congressional debate. Only last year, in a most eloquent letter, you petitioned the Chief Justice for the right to televise live sessions of the Supreme Court. We cannot, in our public utterances, demand such access and then, in one of the crucial debates of our time, abdicate that responsibility. What happens to that sense of fairness and balance so close to both of you, when one day's hearings, and perhaps the most comprehensive, are omitted? How can we return on Thursday and Friday of this week without denying Schneider's argument that "the housewife isn't interested?" Why were N.B.C.'s housewives interested? What would have happened to those housewives if the Supreme Court had said "Yes" to your plea for live coverage? Where would broadcast journalism have been last Thursday if N.B.C.

John A. Schneider, executive who is in charge of all broadcasting of Columbia Broadcasting System.

had elected not to carry the U.S. Senate hearings on the war?

When last Thursday morning at 10 o'clock I looked at the monitors in my office and saw the hearings on Channel 4 (pool production, by the way, via C.B.S. News crews) and saw a fifth rerun of "Lucy," then followed by an eighth rerun of "The Real McCoys," I wanted to order up an announcement that said: "Due to cricumstances beyond our control the broadcast originally intended for this time will not be seen." It was not within C.N.D.'s control because the journalistic judgment had been by a sudden organizational act transferred to a single executive. Mr. Schneider, because of his absolute power, would have more authority than William Paley or Frank Stanton have exercised in the past two years. This, in spite of the fact that Mr. Schneider's news credentials were limited in the past to local station operations, with little experience in national or international affairs.

The concept of an autonomous news organization responsible only to the chairman and the president was not a creation of mine. It is a concept almost as old as C.B.S. News, and is a tradition nurtured by the Ed Klaubers, the Ed Murrows, the Paul Whites, and rigidly enforced by both of you. The dramatic change in that con-

cept is, to my mind and that of my colleagues, a form of emasculation.

Actually, it is the second step of the emasculation that began when C.B.S. News was shorn of its responsibility in the news operation at WCBS-TV here in New York. Had I been in my current position at the time of this change, I should have resisted it as I do the current weakening. It denied C.B.S. News a highly professional outlet in New York, a competitive position with the other networks, and the training apparatus for the Sevareids, the Cronkites, the Reasoners of the future.

My departure is a matter of conscience. At the end of the day it is the viewer and the listener who have the biggest stake in all this. Perhaps my action will be understood by them. I know it will be understood by my colleagues in news and I know Ed Murrow would have understood. A speech he delivered to the Radio Television News Directors Association in 1958 spelled it all out:

"One of the basic troubles with radio and television news is that both instruments have grown up as an incompatible combination of show business, advertising, and news. Each of the three is a rather bizarre and demanding profession. And when you get all three under one roof, the dust never settles. The top management of the networks, with a few notable exceptions, has been trained in advertising, research, sales, or show business. But, by the nature of the corporate structure, they also make the final and crucial decisions having to do with news and public affairs.

"Frequently they have neither the time nor the competence to do this. It is not easy for the same small group of men to decide whether to buy a new station for millions of dollars, build a new building, alter the rate card, buy a new Western, sell a soap opera, decide what defensive line to take in connection with the latest Congressional inquiry, how much money to spend on promoting a new program, what additions or deletions should be made in the existing covey or clutch of vice presidents and, at the same time—frequently on the same long day — to give mature, thoughtful consideration to the manifold problems that confront those who are charged with the responsibility for news and public affairs . . ."

Such a day was last Thursday when a non-news judgment was made on the Kennan broadcast.

Murrow went on to say: "Upon occasion, economics and editorial judgment are in conflict. And there is no law which says that dollars will be defeated by duty. Not so long ago the President of the United States delivered a television address to the nation. He was discoursing on the possibility or probability of war between this nation and the Soviet Union and Communist China—a reasonably compelling subject. Two networks — C.B.S. and N.B.C. —delayed that broadcast for an hour and 15 minutes. If this decision was dictated by anything other than financial reasons, the networks didn't design to explain those reasons. That hour-and-15-minute delay, by the way, is about twice the time required for an I.C.B.M. to travel from the Soviet Union to major targets in the United States. It is difficult to believe that this decision was made by men who love, respect and understand news."

In that speech Ed also said: "There is no suggestion here that networks or individual stations should operate as philanthropies. I can find nothing in the Bill of Rights or the Communications Act which says that they must increase their net profits each year, lest the republic collapse."

I now leave C.B.S. News convinced, ironically, that my leaving will help insure the integrity and independence of the news operation. I believe that the Senate hearings next Thursday and Friday will be televised live because of circumstances within the control of the man you choose to succeed me. For the kind of news executive who would warrant the trust of the two recipients of this letter would insist upon such a mandate. Senator George Norris, quoted in John Kennedy's "Profiles in Courage," says, "Whatever use I have been has been accomplished in the things I failed to do rather than in the things I actually did do."

I now leave C.B.S. News after 16 years, believing that the finest broadcast journalists anywhere will yet have the kind of leadership they deserve. I know that I take with me their respect and affection as, indeed, I hope I do yours.

Faithfully,
Fred.

New York: Say It Isn't So, Fred

By JAMES RESTON

Something is going on these days behind the glassy square eye of television news broadcasting. David Brinkley came out publicly the other day against "star" newscasters — which is a little like Lyndon Johnson attacking Texas—and Fred W. Friendly, the president of C.B.S. News, quit because some advertising man cut his copy.

Part of this is old stuff. Brinkley was brought up in the low-pay, hard-work school of Carolina newspapers and is simply too honest to adjust easily to the high-pay and theatrical opulence of telecasting. In short, a nice guy.

Friendly never has adjusted to the obvious fact that television is essentially an entertainment business that happens to run news on the side. "I hate war," said he, proposing to televise the Senate hearings on Vietnam. "I Love Lucy," said C.B.S., whereupon Lucy won and Friendly quit.

The New Problems

All this adds to the gossip of New York, but behind the gossip are one or two issues of public importance, not connected with the Friendly resignation but not likely to be resolved without men of Friendly's stature and conviction.

This is the first American war, for example, fought with the television cameras right on the battlefield. The advantages are obvious. These nightly television scenes of our men under fire are taking some of the silly romance out of war, but inevitably they portray only one side of the story.

The cameras, of course, are only on our side of the lines. They record mainly our casualties and the pathetic scenes of the South Vietnamese refugees overrun by our troops. This is one problem.

The Magnified Distortion

Another problem is the cumulative effect of the Cronkite and Huntley - Brinkley half - hour news shows on the viewers. Thoughtful newspapermen have been concerned for years about the tendency of newspapers to transfer to the world the habits of police court and county court house reporting, which is the reporting of violence, of division, of trouble, of the unusual rather than the usual.

The news on television has inflated this problem because the picture is more vivid than the word, and if you watch a solid hour of Huntley-Brinkley and Cronkite, it is easy to conclude that nothing is happening in the world except trouble. Somehow the entire Continent of Europe has vanished from the TV screens and most of the front pages because it is quiet and prosperous.

It was to correct all this and get a little more perspective into television reporting that the late Edward R. Murrow, Fred Friendly, Eric Sevareid, Walter Cronkite, Howard K. Smith, Edward P. Morgan, Huntley and Brinkley, and many others of this remarkable generation of TV and radio reporters fought for the documentary reports of great public issues. They have made great progress, but it has been hard going against the advertisers and the entertainers, who bring in more money.

Friendly was getting at the same thing in his fight to televise the Fulbright hearings on Vietnam. Instead of the usual one-minute summaries on the news shows, he wanted the Senate debate to be run in full, and resigned when he lost the battle.

It is too bad. For the choice before the networks surely is not limited to an inadequate trickle of news or a torrent. Given the capacity of our legislators for verbosity and banality, an hour's summary of six hours of debate on Vietnam in the evening could be an improvement over an all-day marathon. Why do we have to choose between Lucy and Dean Rusk?

The Continuing Fight

Also, if the networks are going to follow the bad habits of the newspapers, they might consider some of our few good habits and give us a really detailed News Review of the Week on Sundays. This might get in the way of Wilt Chamberlain, but even so.

This is the kind of thing Friendly has fought for over the years. He was particularly upset this time because the Vietnam hearings are the first major public inquiry into our wandering foreign policy since before the Kennedy Administration, but why quit?

The big problems of public education about Asia are just coming up, and producing new problems for the networks and the newspapers in the process, and without the Friendlys and other public spirited characters in the business, they are not likely to be solved.

February 18, 1966

Topics: *Let's Put It on the Train to Hanoi*

By DAVID VIENNA

It is apparent that President Johnson is having a hard time convincing the North Vietnamese that he would rather quit than fight. Maybe what is needed is an advertising agency to help the State and Defense Departments sell the idea of peace to the Communists.

Since he took office the President has been fighting the advertising agencies and he's lost every battle.

He asks Americans to travel in their own country rather than abroad so that the outflow of gold can be slowed. An agency places pictures of little cars with the caption "Beetle" in magazines and newspapers across the country, and Americans begin seeing the U.S.A.— in cars made overseas.

Harmless Weapons

One of the President's advisers suggests that cigarette smoking may not be the healthiest practice. An advertising agency promptly sticks a cigarette in a cowboy's mouth and makes him wear a hat just like the one the President wears. Before you know it more people are smoking now — and maybe enjoying it less—than they were before they were warned about smoking.

An agency may be the means to a solution in Vietnam. The campaigns it could provide are undoubtedly the most peaceful way to end the war. The weapons are harmless but effective: washing machines that are ten feet tall; white tornadoes, armored knights on horseback — the list is a long one.

A New Image

Now if Mr. Johnson were to seek the help that only Madison Avenue specialists can provide, the first thing nine out of ten advertising men would do is make him more appealing to the Orientals. A new image — even a new name.

Nationwide, worldwide, you can depend on men to be more friendly to other men with names they trust. Lyndon Baines Johnson is the enemy, but "Lin din" could be a friend.

Then there would be a campaign to send a dove flying into Ho Chi Minh's kitchen. Everybody knows that a dove is a sign of peace. And the Madison Avenue dove is a special kind of bird; it'll get Ho out of his kitchen fast. He'll move even faster when he hears the Jolly Green Giant in the dining room calling "Ho! Ho! Ho!"

In this carefully planned advertising campaign, Ho would, of course, be surprised to see Lin at his dining-room table. The President would stand to greet the leader and as a sign of friendship he might say: "Ho, mah friend, how 'bout lettin' me send your sinuses tah Arizona?"

Think Younger

Impressed with the gesture, the Vietnamese leader would sit down at the conference table with the President. They might sip an American soft drink that would help them think younger or livelier. And while they're both there thinking lively, they just might call a truce.

But in case Ho continued to believe that coups do more for him, there must be an alternative campaign.

The President would suggest that Vietcong brush their teeth for one year with a leading Communist brand and the Americans would do the same with a United States toothpaste. The group with 21 per cent fewer cavities at the end of the year wins the war.

Or they could try something different for a change — something with more spirit to it. A race in cars from Hanoi to Saigon.

"Let me put you in the driver's seat of this fine new convertible," the President might offer. No doubt Ho would refuse, choosing a weapon with which he is more familiar: a Soviet model. Mistakenly believing that the tiger in LBJ's tank is a paper one, Ho would feel like a Giant Killer. But the President, driving an American car that combined the best features of a Barracuda, a Fury, a Marlin and a Mustang, would win the economy run to Hanoi with miles to spare.

Or an advertising campaign could get the Vietcong asking themselves, "Do capitalists have more fun?" Even though they can never be certain because only their accountants know for sure, they can be convinced that they will be in good hands with the United States.

It is too early for President Johnson to despair about Vietnam. A man who has gone as far as he has with the slogan "All the way with LBJ" should realize that he has not mobilized America's full resources as long as the advertising agencies remain unused.

Mr. Vienna is a free-lance writer.

May 7, 1966

Stratton Criticizes Press As Biased on Vietnam War

SENECA FALLS, N. Y., May 21 (AP)—Representative Samuel S. Stratton, Democrat of New York, said tonight that "the American press has grievously failed in giving the American people an accurate and unbiased account of the progress of the war in Vietnam."

Mr. Stratton, who recently headed a House delegation on a 10-day tour of the Vietnam front, said in a talk prepared for delivery here:

"Our upstate press has been excellent. But there is no question that important segments of the national and metropolitan press, which plays the biggest role in shaping the nation's information picture, are biased against our commitment in Vietnam and have played down reports favorable to that commitment and played up reports unfavorable to it."

This, he said, "is irresponsible reporting and irresponsible editing and is doing a grave disservice to the American people."

May 22, 1966

TV: Sevareid Speaks Out

C.B.S. Permits Commentator to Give Personal Analysis of Vietnam War

By JACK GOULD

A NOVELTY in television news commentary was introduced last night when Eric Sevareid of the Columbia Broadcasting System gave a half-hour personal analysis of the war in Vietnam. Only sparing illustrations were employed; essentially the program consisted entirely of Mr. Sevareid's own words.

●

The format itself was a welcome one. The complexity of the Vietnamese conflict often does not lend itself to pictorial treatment, and on the home screen there has been a surfeit of front-line battle scenes. Aural reportage does have its advantages, and C.B.S. News is to be commended for experimenting along such lines.

Mr. Sevareid expressed more criticism of the Pentagon than has been generally carried on TV, though characteristically he never raised his voice above a measured calm.

He questioned the accuracy of figures about American casualties and touched on the specter of a constantly expanding military establishment. He predicted that attempts to democratize a country such as Vietnam could lead to long years of instability as conflicting forces vied for power. He believed that the real issue in Southeast Asia is social and economic liberation of the individual.

Mr. Sevareid's conclusion was anything but controversial. He advanced no recommendations, but rather thought that God once again would look after America and that the country would come safely through the agony in Southeast Asia.

●

The half-hour admittedly suggested little that has not been reported in the press with considerably more vigor and incisiveness. Mr. Sevareid's essay would not seem likely to generate much discussion. But for the television medium in general and C.B.S. in particular the commentary was a step in the right direction of allowing TV correspondents more leeway in advancing their own opinions and frankly labeling them as such.

June 22, 1966

HAIPHONG REPORT ANGERS U.S. AIDES

But They Do Not Confirm or Deny Leaks on Bombing

By MAX FRANKEL
Special to The New York Times

WASHINGTON, June 28—Administration officials, apparently reflecting the feelings of President Johnson, described themselves today as angry and upset by recent reports that the United States was about to bomb oil storage depots near Haiphong, which is the port for Hanoi.

They did not confirm or deny such a decision to extend the bombing raids on North Vietnam closer than ever before to a major population center. Nor did they comment on a new report that the attack was postponed because of the news leaks.

It appeared to observers here that, if an attack had actually been scheduled, it had been delayed until American planes could strike with some surprise. The indications over the last week have been that President Johnson has decided to extend the list of targets and is waiting only for the right moment.

Security investigators here believed to be looking for the sources of leaks in Washington and Saigon. No one would discuss the situation in definite terms and officials appeared to be under even stricter orders than usual not to speculate about military operations.

Johnson Made Statement

President Johnson himself alerted many newsmen to the likelihood of new types of air attacks with a statement on June 18. A review of tactics persuaded him, he said, that "we must continue to raise the cost of aggression at its source."

The word "source" clearly meant in North Vietnam. In view of the known recommendations of the Joint Chiefs of Staff, many assumed that the Haiphong oil depots would soon be among the targets.

Moreover, the suppression of political turmoil in South Vietnam is believed to have reopened the subject of new targets.

More severe air attacks would be designed to damage the will of the North Vietnamese as well as their means of waging further war against the South.

A Washington dispatch in The New York Times last Friday reported that the end of political demonstrations in Saigon had revived discussion of new air strikes.

The same day, the Dow-Jones news service carried a dispatch from Washington saying that the decision was made Thursday to expand the bombing to include the oil depots at Haiphong and that the attacks were expected to begin within a few days.

On Saturday morning, the Columbia Broadcasting System carried a report from Saigon saying that such an attack was actually scheduled for that day. The C.B.S. correspondent, Murray Fromson, reported today that the scheduled raids were called off because of "flagrant security leaks in Washington."

Some officials said they were most upset by the C.B.S. report. Others singled out the Dow-Jones report, a brief line of which was carried yesterday by the Dow-Jones newspaper, The Wall Street Journal, together with a White House denial. Still other officials were critical of all the reports.

June 29, 1966

Washington:
Vietnam and the Press

By JAMES RESTON

WASHINGTON, June 28 — President Johnson is reported to be furious about several recent disclosures in the press about his military plans in Vietnam, and this time he has some reason to complain.

In recent days the papers have been full of speculation that the bombing of the enemy's oil refineries and power plants in the Hanoi and Haiphong regions was imminent, and this goes beyond the proper bounds of public military information.

Public discussion of the wisdom or stupidity of extending the bombing to the populous areas of these two cities is fair enough, but public disclosure of the timing of operational military plans is not.

Inevitably, it puts the enemy on tactical alert for a military exercise that depends largely for its success on tactical surprise, and if the carrier-based pilots and bombardiers have protested this disclosure, they are well within their rights.

Most of the North Vietnamese antiaircraft equipment, supplied by the Soviets, is mobile. With a few days' advance notice, it can be moved into position to defend the critical targets around Hanoi and Haiphong, thus raising the risk to the American planes, which have had enough trouble with the enemy's ground-to-air missiles, and particularly its radar-controlled antiaircraft guns, in the past.

Ironically, President Johnson himself started the speculation in the press by the statement in his last news conference that "We must continue to raise the cost of aggression." This could mean only one thing - that the long campaign by the Joint Chiefs of Staff to hit the refineries and the power plants had finally succeeded, and it was so interpreted in most papers.

War always raises delicate and even dangerous complications in the relations between officials and reporters, but Vietnam has raised more than most. The normal restraints of a declared war have not always been present in this conflict. The private conferences between Gen. George C. Marshall with the Washington bureau chiefs in the last World War which did so much to keep this problem under control, have not been repeated as regularly or effectively in this one.

Also, the Administration's relations with reporters in the Vietnam war have been poisoned by a long record of misleading statements by generals in the field and officials in Washington about how well the war was going, how well the various Saigon Governments were doing, etc. The result is that there is now little faith here in the press about the official pronouncements on the war.

Finally, the policy of raising the level of the bombing and extending it to targets around Hanoi and Haiphong has been bitterly contested here and in other world capitals for months, and those who have been advocating such a policy have not been able to conceal their satisfaction that the President has apparently now agreed to take the larger risk.

The question of printing a good story has been a problem ever since the beginning of the cold war. Allen Dulles, former head of the Central Intelligence Agency, illustrates it in his book "The Craft of Intelligence." "I recall," he wrote, "the days when the intelligence community was perfecting plans for various technical devices to monitor Soviet missile-testing and space operations. The technical journals exerted themselves to give the American public, and hence the Soviet Union, the details of radar screens and the like, which for geographic reasons, to be effective, had to be placed on the territory of friendly countries close to the Soviet Union.

"These countries," Mr. Dulles continued, "were quite willing to cooperate as long as secrecy could be preserved. This whole vital operation was threatened by public disclosure. . . . Except for a small number of technically minded people, such disclosures added little to the welfare or happiness or even to the knowledge of the American people. Certainly this type of information did not fall in the 'need to know' category for the American public."

The same is undoubtedly true of the actual battlefield plans of the Government in Vietnam. Some of us think it is a tragic blunder to extend the bombing to Hanoi and Haiphong, but the right of dissent does not extend to publishing operational plans that help the enemy and increase the risk to our own fliers.

June 29, 1966

F.B.I. OPENS INQUIRY IN 'LEAK' ON BOMBING

WASHINGTON, June 29 (AP)—The Federal Bureau of Investigation, on President Johnson's orders, has opened an intensive inquiry into whether United Sattes officials informed newsmen in advance about the decision to expand the bombing in North Vietnam to oil facilities in the Haiphong-Hanoi area.

Neither the F.B.I. nor Administration sources would comment. But other sources said the investigation was under way, spurred by a concern at the highest levels over the possibility that word of today's bombing had been given out in advance.

The general rule within the Administration is to refuse comment on any specific future military operation. The stated reason is to avoid giving advance plans to the enemy and thus endangering the lives of United States servicemen.

It was understood that a prime purpose of the current inquiry is to guard against future "leaks."

Mr. Johnson said at a news conference June 18 that in attacking North Vietnam military targets "we must continue to raise the cost of aggression at its source."

The following week a number of news stories pointed toward bombing of the oil depots outside Hanoi and Haiphong.

June 30, 1966

In The Nation: The Words That Sprung the 'Leak'

By ARTHUR KROCK

WASHINGTON, June 29 — Until President Johnson, at a White House news conference on June 18, used the carefully chosen words "we must continue to raise the cost of aggression at its source," the official explanation for not bombing the major war-making facilities at Hanoi and Haiphong was the unbroken Administration line. Its spokesmen had repeatedly justified this limitation on two grounds: (1) The bombing would imperil the civilian population mass in the immediate vicinity of these facilities; and (2) make Americans and South Vietnamese in Saigon the special targets of retaliation by Hanoi and the Vietcong.

The Locus of the Cost

But when the President identified "the source" of North Vietnamese "aggression" as the locus of the increased "cost" to be inflicted, it logically followed that a change of the official policy with respect to bombing the Hanoi and Haiphong facilities was in prospect, if not already decided on. For his news conference audience knew perfectly well what Secretary of Defense McNamara certified today: that "At Haiphong . . . is the only existing North Vietnamese facility for off-loading petroleum from ocean-going tankers"; and at Hanoi is the petroleum "main storage and distribution facility."

A Careful Draft

This implication of the President's phraseology was plain. It was also clear from Mr. Johnson's text that it had been drafted with great care and deliberation in which every word was weighed on the scale of the general purpose. The certain consequences were a news conference inquiry whether the President meant to forecast the change of policy he strongly implied; and a press alert in Washington and in Vietnam for evidences of this change and its timing.

The news conference question was: "Does the statement imply or mean there may be a step-up in the air strikes in North Vietnam?" To which the President replied that he didn't want to be "boxed in" on a "commitment" he "would do this or that," and "the country" thereby denied "some flexibility in case our interests required it." The alerted press soon began to find the signs of solid basis for the spec-

ulation Mr. Johnson's words inevitably had evoked, and was confirmed by today's bombing of the major petroleum facilities on the edge of the crowded urban areas.

These were the events leading up to the "leak" which came very near to disclosing to the world—the American people, those of enemy, allied and uncommitted nations—the precise timing of the air attacks. In this instance, the normally useful competition of public communications media to be first with the news overcame the higher obligation of the press to the public interest that, in the particular circumstances, involved the lives of United States airmen and the essential element of enemy surprise. But, since the chain reaction began with a deliberately planned and composed Presidential public statement, the thinking behind it has become a subject of intense though inconclusive speculation - in this political community.

Was the President's purpose in making the statement ten days beforehand, and in choosing its significant phraseology, to prepare the American people and those of friendly nations for the attack, thereby softening the impact of the policy change? Was the purpose also or only, to assure Moscow and Peking in advance that the attack on the facilities did not represent a change of policy to unlimited war? (The stress on "continued limited objectives" in the June 18 statement could have been the vehicle designed to carry this assurance.)

Allies Were Notified

The mere ritual denunciation of the attack by the Soviet Union suggests that, if this was the objective of that caveat, it was comprehended and accepted. And the polished diction of Prime Minister Wilson's comment "dissociating" the United Kingdom from expanding the air war in any degree while at the same time expressing a sympathetic understanding of its provocations, leaves no doubt the British Government was notified in advance, as were other allies.

In view of the fact that, as Republican comment noted, all the reasons McNamara gave for the policy shift have existed for some time, there is another speculative assignment here for its timing. This is that the internal troubles of the Peking Government have removed any risk there may ever have been of a military response.

June 30, 1966

Up and Down on Vietnam

Capital, Both Optimistic and Pessimistic, Charges the Press Habitually Overreacts

By MAX FRANKEL
Special to The New York Times

WASHINGTON, July 18—After three months of pessimism and two weeks of optimism about the war in Vietnam, the Johnson Administration now insists that it never indulges in anything but realism.

Realism, of course, does not preclude considerable and genuine fluctuations of hope. But the White House and State Department contend that all reports of significant changes of mood here have been false, the concoctions of an ignorant or sensational press that habitually "overreacts."

News Analysis

The record does not support the complaints, for it shows a good number of authoritative statements of optimism after the bombings at Hanoi and Haiphong June 29, until high officials realized, last week, that they had stimulated dangerous and possibly false expectations among the American people.

But the complaints have raised even deeper questions than the accuracy of the press.

A Series of Questions

There are questions here about the haste with which the President's subordinates rush to support what they take to be his deliberate propaganda line. There are questions about the Administration's use of words to influence opinion at home and abroad. And there are questions about how, after all, it really assesses the course of the war.

To take the pulse of this Administration, it is never enough to rely upon its words. Since the bombing at Hanoi, for instance, President Johnson has said that we have "begun to turn the tide" of war, to which Secretary of State Dean Rusk added, "We are not over the hump yet."

The President's Special Assistant, Walt W. Rostow, said two weeks ago that the Vietcong had been "tactically defeated." Mr. Rusk, however, found 10 days later that "We haven't begun to see the end of this thing."

Under Secretary of State George W. Ball was "encouraged" but not "overly optimistic" and two days later Defense Secretary Robert S. McNamara was "cautiously optimistic."

Contacting Always Shifting

President Johnson's consistent warnings that only North Vietnam can determine when the war will end and what it will cost have always had to be read in a context that is now grim, now hopeful.

When the Administration hints at secret reports that Hanoi knows it is losing, the meaning is clearly different from when it deplores political strife in Saigon as a costly diversion from the war.

To those who have watched the Administration from up close over the last six months, there has been little doubt about its real moods.

In February and March, after the resumption of bombings of North Vietnam, there was real encouragement about the ground war in South Vietnam. The Vietcong were felt to be taking a severe beating, suffering losses of men and supplies and morale that they were held incapable of sustaining alone for much more than a year, especially in the face of increasing American pressure.

In April, May and June, however, the political turmoil in South Vietnam seemed to threaten not only these gains but, also all chances of success. Washington was overcome by dismay, almost despair. There was not only grave political damage but also a serious military disruption. Even if hurt, Hanoi was bound to draw comfort and encouragement from events.

As soon as Saigon's military junta put down the Buddhist challenge, therefore, Washington weighed in with its Sunday punch, the air strike at the oil depots. The South Vietnamese army, to everyone's surprise, snapped back into reasonable shape. The enemy air

defenses proved ineffective. The Chinese Communists were beset by more internal difficulties than usual. Still more American, Korean and Filipino troops sailed to war, and spirits here soared.

In the first week of July, Administration officials took their cue from a tough but buoyant President, talking of "steady gains" and the beginnings of a "win," and of faint signs that the North Vietnamese were wearing down, and, in Vice President Humphrey's phrase, "looking for a way out."

Tactics and Politics Conceded

These appeared to be genuine expectations. They were eagerly exposed to dispel the springtime gloom, to bolster the sagging morale of the American people and to enhance the intimidating effect of the more intense bombing. Good tactics and good politics seemed to coincide, because support — from the governor's meeting in California and from the opinion polls — was expected to help dash hopes in Hanoi that domestic opposition would stay the President's hand.

But a week ago, after the results of the polls and the return of Secretary Rusk from Asia, the White House suddenly began to accuse the press of having misinterpreted determination as optimism.

The polls showed a remarkable jump in support for the President, by 10 points to 52 per cent, and 5-to-1 support for the new bombings. But they also showed 86 per cent of the people of the opinion that the bombings would hasten the end of the war.

Mr. Rusk, who has always foreseen a long war of attrition not subject to quick solutions by either diplomacy or militancy, undoubtedly added a warning against rousing insatiable hopes.

"One can be encouraged without believing the war is over," was the gracious way in which he chided his colleagues while scolding the press for having misled the public. "It may last a long time," the President added the same day.

The indications are that the Administration is very encouraged militarily and vaguely hopeful politically. It thinks the North Vietnamese have little reason to fight on without much outside help against ever more American power, but it honestly does not know how long they will do so.

July 20, 1966

U.S. NEWS POLICIES IN SAIGON SCORED

Defense Department information policies and press briefings in Vietnam were sharply criticized by four American correspondents there in a television program last night.

The correspondents, whose remarks were taped in Saigon, said briefings by United States military spokesmen were often colorless, late and inaccurate. The daily briefings are called "The 5 o'clock Follies" by many correspondents, Dean Brelis of the National Broadcasting Company said.

Malcolm Browne, a former Associated Press reporter and a Pulitzer Prize-winner now doing free lance work in Vietnam, said on the National Educational Television program on WNDT that the briefing officers often lied.

Charles Mohr, a New York Times correspondent, said the information officers in Saigon were "more interested in policy than facts" and "the effect of a story—rather than its accuracy."

He said the Administration was reluctant for correspondents to write abut napalm or antipersonnel bombs. "They want to make it a sanitary war," he said.

Mr. Browne criticized the Pentagon's news policies, which, he said prevented reporters from getting first-hand information about American military activity in Laos and Thailand. "As far as the command is concerned publicly," said the writer, "Laos doesn't exist. Neither does Thailand."

He said Arthur Sylvester, Assistant Secretary of Defense for Public Affairs, was "one of the great practitioners" of the "art" of news management.

He said the Administration, and "particularly Secretary [of Defense Robert S.] McNamara, have deliberately misled American public opinion." An example of this, he said, is "the continual harping on the North Vietnamese aggression." Mr. Browne said the war in Vietnam was basically a civil war. The three other correspondents agreed.

Jack Foisie, a reporter for The Los Angeles Times, said he would prefer "formal censorship" to news management "that squashes information at the roots."

There was sympathy for the briefing officers, though. Mr. Mohr said they often "give a distorted picture, not out of either bad motive or viciousness, but simply because they themselves don't have a clear idea of what happened."

The correspondents agreed with a statement by Mr. Brelis that no one could cover the war adequately from Saigon. "You've got to go out there," he said.

No Comment in Washington

WASHINGTON, Aug. 1 — There was no immediate comment today from the Defense Department on the correspondents' criticism.

August 2, 1966

The Inevitable Credibility Gap

By TOM WICKER

WASHINGTON, Aug. 11—A number of Republican candidates, seeking a way to exploit the Vietnamese issue in the coming campaign, are planning to emphasize the so-called "credibility gap." They are likely to turn up some votes, too, because most political observers believe that a good part of the public does believe there is a suspicious gap between the Administration's statements and the facts of the war.

Some Justification

Some of this feeling is justified. The records of both the Kennedy and Johnson Administrations are sprinkled with overoptimistic and unwarranted claims, wrong or changed assumptions and justifications, and misleading simplifications, as well as with seemingly contradictory positions — for instance, landing a large American force in South Vietnam during the January bombing pause, then later using the fact that North Vietnam had increased its infiltration of the South in the same period as one reason for resuming the bombing of the North.

On the other hand, Administration officials — particularly the President and Secretary of State Rusk — have frequently complained about what they called untrue, misleading, or ill-informed press reporting of the war, from both Saigon and Washington.

Yet neither Administration sins nor those it attributes to the press entirely explain the gap. This week, for instance, a number of newspapers including The New York Times carried authoritative stories from Saigon saying that Pentagon "studies" showed that at its present pace the war would last for eight years.

The next day at his news conference, President Johnson denied any knowledge of such studies. Other high officials even more sweepingly claimed that no such studies existed. The best explanation available here is that the story emanated from a meeting of reporters in Saigon with Gen. Wallace Greene, the Marine Corps Commandant.

General Greene is believed here to have said substantially what the press reported. One version is that he was expressing a personal or Marine view not unconnected with the Marines' desire for a bigger corps and a bigger role in Vietnam. Another is that he discussed contingencies loosely enough to appear to be posing a concrete

prospect. But the highest officials here insist that there is no official study or conclusion that supports General Greene's reported view.

Thus neither bad reporting nor Administration skulduggery is responsible for an incident almost certain to dig the "gap" a little deeper in the public mind.

Another report in this newspaper this week said that intelligence sources in South Vietnam estimated that North Vietnamese infiltration had risen sharply, despite the bombing attacks, so that the total of enemy troops in the South is now 52,000 more than it was in January. In that period, 31,571 enemy personnel were officially reported as killed in action; yet there were only about 34,000 known infiltrators and no more than 54,000 counting the "possibles."

Thus—although there is no official confirmation here of any of the infiltration figures—either the infiltration and enemy force estimates are far off, or the officially reported casualties are exaggerated, or both. Numbers games of this kind, in fact, while obviously made available to reporters by supposedly responsible sources, are dangerous indeed.

The Administration, even if it does no figure juggling, would stand less chance of later embarrassment if it did not disclose such estimates, certainly of infiltrators and probably even of casualties. But public clamor for knowledge of what is happening makes it inevitable that some kind of figures and progress reports have to be given.

In an illuminating discussion on the educational television network of the problems of reporting the war, four correspondents in Saigon recently gave the Administration bad marks for exaggerated claims and trying to "sanitize" the war.

Charles Mohr of The Times, nevertheless, pointed out that information officers often "give a distorted picture of what happened in a given action, but not out of either bad motive or viciousness, but simply because they themselves don't have a clear idea of what happened."

Thus, while the Administration obviously has sought on occasion to picture the war in self-serving terms, and while no one associated with the press would claim infallibility for it, it is just as well to remember that few more complicated, confusing and emotionally distressing matters ever have confronted either. And some "credibility gap" is probably inevitable.

August 12, 1966

Inquiry on Vietnam News Set

WASHINGTON, Aug. 15 (UPI) — Senator J. W. Fulbright, Democrat of Arkansas, announced today that the Senate Foreign Relations Committee, which he heads, will hold hearings on news coverage of Vietnam. He called Leonard H. Marks, director of the United States Information Agency, as the chief witness when the hearings open Wednesday.

August 16, 1966

Fulbright Is Critical of U.S.I.A. For Flying Newsmen to Vietnam

By M.S. HANDLER
Special to The New York Times

WASHINGTON, Aug. 17— Senator J. W. Fulbright suggested today that newspapers and correspondents who accepted Government transportation to Vietnam might be in a conflict of interest with their readers.

Mr. Fulbright, chairman of the Foreign Relations Committee, raised the question during a hearing at which Leonard H. Marks, director of the United States Information Agency, testified. Mr. Marks was questioned about the advisability and propriety of the agency's payment for the transportation of 30 to 35 European and Asian correspondents who flew to Vietnam during the last year.

Senator Fulbright pointed out that The Toronto Star and The Globe and Mail of Toronto, two of Canada's leading newspapers, had refused the information agency's offer of free transportation, and he asked Mr. Marks why. Mr. Marks said he did not know and would ask the head of the agency in Canada.

Selection Process Criticized

Senator Fulbright, Democrat of Arkansas, and other members of his committee, including Senator Albert Gore, Democrat of Tennessee, suggested that the correspondents who made the free trips had been chosen because the agency hoped their reports would counterbalance the unfavorable and frequently hostile views in many countries about United States military activities in Vietnam. The Senators contended that the selection process indicated that this was the intention.

Mr. Marks rejected the suggestion. He argued that many European and Asian newspapers could not afford to send correspondents to Vietnam and that it was the agency's hope that once in the area the reporters would determine the facts for themselves and report accordingly.

Senator Fulbright, as well as Senator Eugene J. McCarthy, Democrat of Minnesota, and Senator Clifford P. Case, Republican of New Jersey, pressed

Associated Press Wirephoto

Leonard H. Marks, the U.S. Information Agency head, before Senate committee.

Mr. Marks on the problem as a whole and the refusal of the Canadian newspapers in particular.

Mr. Fulbright asked: "Doesn't this point to a possible conflict of interest that might compromise the objectivity newspapers owe their readers?"

When Mr. Marks asserted repeatedly that the information agency did not operate within the United States and did not transport American reporters to Vietnam, Senator McCarthy said that The Washington Post had declined Pentagon offers of transportation to Vietnam — a practice followed by other newspapers, including the New York Times — and he asked Mr. Marks if he could explain this.

He replied that he did not know, but assumed that The Washington Post was a rich newspaper and could afford to pay for transportation.

Senator Fulbright asked whether there might be a reason other than money to explain The Washington Post's refusal to accept free transportation.

Mr. Marks repeated his assertion that the newspaper's policy could be explained by its wealth. Mr. Fulbright's rejoinder implied that the newspaper was motivated by the wish to protect its readers from a conflict of interest that would compromise the objectivity of its correspondents.

In defense of his program, Mr. Marks insisted that the correspondents his agency transported could report on any events they wished and were given all the facilities available to the information agency. Mr. Marks said

SYLVESTER FACES SENATORS TODAY

By E. W. KENWORTHY
Special to The New York Times

WASHINGTON, Aug. 30—Arthur Sylvester, Assistant Secretary of Defense for Public Affairs, is expected to be questioned closely on Defense Department news policies regarding Vietnam when he appears tomorrow before the Senate Committee on Foreign Relations.

It was Mr. Sylvester who stirred a tempest in 1962 in the aftermath of the Cuban missile crisis when he said:

"It's inherent in Government's right, if necessary, to lie to save itself when it's going up into nuclear war. This to me seems basic."

Senator J. W. Fulbright of Arkansas, the committee chairman, announced yesterday that Mr. Sylvester had been summoned.

Some committee members attribute to Mr. Sylvester's application of his news philosophy much of the "credibility gap" they purport to find in the Pentagon's information on the Vietnam war.

Discussion in Saigon

What some members, it is understood, wish to question Mr. Sylvester about tomorrow s the conflict in accounts of a session he had with several reporters in Saigon on July 17, 1965, at the home of Barry Zorthian, minister-counselor of the United States Embassy.

According to an article by Morley Safer, former Vietnam correspondent for the Columbia Broadcasting System, in Dateline 1966, a publication of the Overseas Press Club of America, Mr. Zorthian set up the meeting for a discussion of mutual problems by Mr. Sylvester and the reporters.

One of the problems, Mr. Safer wrote, arose from a loose rule of self-censorship on reporting battles and casualties —a rule that the military complained was frequently broken.

Another problem arose from what the reporters regarded as, at times, an incomplete fulfillment on the part of civilian

that the agency was interested only in objective reporting of facts and recognized that reporters might have opinions.

Compares Articles

In this connection, Mr. Marks waved copies of articles on the same subject published in The New York Times and The Washington Post to illustrate his contention that two reputable reporters could report the same facts in different ways.

The dispatches, from Tokyo, reported former Ambassador Edwin O. Reischauer's opinions about the Vietnam situation. The headline on The Washington Post dispatch, published Aug. 11, read: "Reischauer Backs U.S. Viet Policy." The dispatch published Aug. 10 in The Times, an Associated Press

and military officials of Mr. Zorthian's promised policy of "total candor."

In his article, Mr. Safer, who was at the meeting, quoted Mr. Sylvester as saying:

"I can't understand how you fellows can write what you do while American boys are dying out here."

Mr. Safer then continued:

"Then he went on to the effect that American correspondents had a patriotic duty to disseminate only information that made the United States look good.

"A network television correspondent said, 'Surely, Arthur, you don't expect the American press to be handmaidens of Government.'

"'That's exactly what I expect,' came the reply.

"An agency man raised the problem that had preoccupied Ambassador [Maxwell D.] Taylor and Barry Zorthian — about the credibility of American officials. Responded the Assistant Secretary of Defense for Public Affairs:

"'Look, if you think any American official is going to tell you the truth, then you're stupid. Did you hear that? — stupid.'

"One of the most respected of all the newsmen in Vietnam — a veteran of World War II, the Indochina War and Korea — suggested that Sylvester was being deliberately provocative. Sylvester replied:

"'Look, I don't even have to talk to you people. I know how to deal with you through your editors and publishers back in the States.'"

In a later letter to Bulletin, another publication of the Overseas Press Club, Mr. Sylvester wrote it was "utterly untrue" that he had said he expected reporters to be "hand-maidens of Government."

And Malcolm W. Browne, former Associated Press correspondent in Saigon, supplied to Bulletin a memo on the meeting by his colleague Ed White, which said in part:

"Sylvester engaged specific correspondents in near name-calling, twice telling Jack Langguth [of The New York Times] he was stupid. At one point Sylvester actually made the statement he thought press should be 'handmaiden' of Government."

report, appeared under the headline "Reischauer Critical of Vietnam Policy."

In the dispatches, which reported an interview with Mr. Reischauer in Tokyo, the departing Ambassador said that the United States must find a better way to handle the Vietnamese problem, based on local nationalism and broader international support. He asserted that though he supported and would continue to support United States policy in Vietnam, the situation there was not satisfactory.

Mr. Fulbright asserted that he had read the two dispatches, and despite their different headlines, they were not far apart in reporting Mr. Reischauer's views.

August 18, 1966

Senate Committee to Study Pentagon War News Policy

WASHINGTON, Aug. 29 (AP)—The Senate Foreign Relations Committee announced today that it would conduct a hearing Wednesday on Pentagon news policies relating to the war in Vietnam.

The committee chairman, Senator J. W. Fulbright, Democrat of Arkansas, said the committee planned to question the Defense Department's chief public information official, Assistant Secretary Arthur Sylvester.

August 30, 1966

Pentagon's News Chief

Arthur Sylvester

Special to The New York Times

WASHINGTON, Aug. 30—The tables have turned for Arthur Sylvester. When he was chief of the Washington bureau of The Newark Evening News he was known as an aggressive reporter who took no guff from Government officials. In the five years he has been in charge of public information at the Pentagon, he has acquired a reputation as a caustic critic of the reporters he once worked with.

Man in the News

The quiet, gray-haired Mr. Sylvester sees no conflict. The flare of temper, the barbed remark, the wisecrack, he says, are only an act he puts on to dramatize a point he is trying to make.

Whether the quick temper is affected or real, members of the Foreign Relations Committee will be watching for it tomorrow when the Assistant Secretary of Defense for Public Affairs testifies on Vietnam news policies.

But reporters who are most critical of Mr. Sylvester's views — he once suggested that public officials sometimes had a right to lie— agree that he has opened up the Pentagon to a wider flow of information. Officials who once would not be interviewed have been made to answer questions.

And the same Sylvester temper that grates on newsmen has been known to be turned on the brass, especially in his early days in the Pentagon.

On one such occasion Mr. Sylvester ended the argument by shouting: "All right, General, if you say so, I'll take your word for it—but I don't believe it!"

Wants the Last Word

But whether he is arguing with a newspaperman or a general Mr. Sylvester seems to be compelled to have the last word—even if it hurts him.

Away from the caverns of the Pentagon, however, he is known as a charming companion, who will go out of his way to be gracious, even to those most critical of his policies.

Mr. Sylvester has lasted a long time at the Pentagon because of his knowledge of the news. He also has a fast friendship with his chief—Defense Secretary Robert S. McNamara.

Arthur Sylvester did not aim at public service, or even newspapering, when he went to school in Montclair, N. J., where he was born on Oct. 21, 1901. His goal was as an English major at Princeton University was to write creatively. To this day his failure to write the Great American Novel, or at least a novel, is his great disappointment.

He started as a shipping clerk and salesman with the Macmillan Company, the publishers, but soon joined the staff of The Newark News as a suburban news reporter. He quickly moved up the ladder and became city editor. Old-timers still remember his kindnesses to cub reporters.

Mr. Sylvester was passed over twice in selecting an editor for The News, but he was made Washington correspondent in 1944.

Secretary McNamara flew to New York in 1961 to offer him the job of information chief. Mr. Sylvester says he "walked the streets for three days" before deciding to accept.

Aside from baiting reporters and generals, Mr. Sylvester's favorite hobby now is walking—he tries to circle the Pentagon every day—about a mile.

He and his wife live in an apartment in Arlington. Their son, Tony, is a White House correspondent for WTOP-TV news; their daughter, Mrs. Anthony Scarola, is a book designer in New York.

August 31, 1966

Is TV Hardening Us to the War in Vietnam?

By FREDRIC WERTHAM, *prominent psychiatrist and author of "A Sign for Cain: An Exploration of Human Violence"*

AT a recent panel discussion held by the International Writers Guild, James C. Hagerty, former press secretary to President Eisenhower and now an ABC executive, praised the television treatment of the war in Vietnam. The Vietnam war films, he said, show us war as it is and thereby help to advance the cause of peace. The daily exposure to the rigors of the battlefield, which for the first time in history everyone can experience in his home, will "convince people that war is the least sensible way of settling disputes." In other words, the mass coverage of the Vietnam war represents, in his view, a kind of electronic pacifism.

＊

My observations are different. They are based on the reactions of teen-agers in individual and group sessions, when discussing war and its representation on the screen. I have also studied adult audiences. The conclusion became inescapable that if you want to condition people to *accept* war and violence, the present TV treatment is excellent. Our channels of communication are hardening us to war rather than educating us against it.

Bertolt Brecht has said that the truth can be concealed in many ways and can be told in many ways. That is certainly true. How can we get people used to the bombing of the countryside? The best way is evidently to show it to them all the time. In the Vietnam war this is supplemented by an occasional comment like that made by a high-ranking government official who said that our bombing is "miraculously accurate" and does not hurt civilians. One cumulative result of the war coverage has been that it has helped to transform us from Nervous Nellies into placid participants.

The effect of the war films cannot be evaluated in isolation. They hit a generation well prepared. No generation growing up in any epoch of history or in any place has had to face such a deluge of violence as modern American youth, now old enough to make history itself. The deluge begins in the nursery with the "kill toys" — as the children call them — guns and elaborate warfare weapons advertised as suitable for even the pre-school child. These toys teach that it is fun to play killing and that war is a good thing.

The education progresses to sadistic bubblegum cards, violent crime comic books, brutal movies and rough TV shows, crudely illustrated booklets like "Sin and Pain" sold under the counter to teen-agers, gorily presented murder news, etc. The audience so conditioned from childhood on finds the Vietnam fighting pictures really tame stuff and is easily manipulated with regard to violence by the huge public relations establishment that has been constructed at the top of the military set-up. And the well-accomplished task of these public relations experts is to teach us not revulsion against war and violence, but receptivity to it. Practically every TV newscast now has some war pictures. In effect, these really are war commercials.

The endless repetition of fragmented and fragmentary battle scenes, without indication of an over-all design, gives them a cliché-like character. What could be most moving scenes if presented in a sufficiently severe frame and with proper reverence for human life becomes a mere backdrop for violence and the expectation of violence. Our senses are being dulled. Big things become small.

What we are given is a hawk's-eye view of life and death. We have seen so many villages burn, so many soldiers going single file into the jungle, so many wounded being interviewed, so many helicopters taking off on desperate missions, that war is becoming routine and the corrosion of war commonplace. We claim to be concerned. But we view these scenes self-indulgently for their entertainment value and add them up subconsciously not to a yearning for peace but to a total belief in the morality of force.

＊

The network news programs offer ever-increasing battle coverage. At the same time, more than a third of the new season's television series rely on physical violence as the climactic point of each story. In the minds of many, the war news films merge with the fictional action movies, especially Westerns. Teen-agers have called Lyndon Johnson "the fastest gun in the West." Some have told me: "We have to kill the gooks - all the gooks!" Adults call that escalation.

Interspersed between fighting scenes are visual reports of benevolent efforts in Vietnam: "pacification in the countryside," programs for health, education and social rehabilitation, attempts to provide low-cost housing, efforts "to stimulate democratic institutions" among the peasants, construction of schools. Aline Saarinen reports our training of Vietnamese so that they can make "the thousands of artificial limbs needed." A small band of U.S. soldiers entertains Vietnam women and children with music.

In the midst of all the destruction, devastation and suffering, these minor politico-philanthropic endeavors seem incongruous. They remind one of the rich old lady who invited groups of wounded veterans for dinner. She asked the hospital to select as her guests those most severely wounded. Then she would tell friends: "Last night I had 12 veterans for dinner. And all together there were only 20 arms, 18 legs and 19 eyes!" French psychiatrists call that *philanthropie hysterique*.

＊

The number of our troops in Vietnam has steadily increased. The Vietnam war reports on television do not as a rule announce these increases very forthrightly. Sometimes they are buried among other, much less important facts or they are given out as an aside "upon inquiry." Early in 1965 there were 30,000 U.S. troops in Vietnam. A little later 75,000 soldiers seemed a very large number. Now it is "more than 331,000" (only a few days ago it was 328,000). As feelers for the future, 600,000 and even three-quarters of a million are mentioned. It seems that when a "peace offensive" is loudly proclaimed it is accompanied or followed by a military expansion. We are being conditioned -- like Pavlovian dogs — so that when the "peace offensive" bells ring we won't expect peace but accept an acceleration of bombing and an increase in the strength of the army.

Communication is the opposite of violence. Where communication ends, violence begins. When we do not communicate with one another, we cannot know one another; when we do not know one another, we can be stirred up to hate; when we hate, we are apt to resort to violence.

If we want to understand the effect of the Vietnam films, we must realize that over the years the mass media, of which television is the most potent, have helped to create the present international communication gap. There exists, in fact, what amounts to a vast machinery of hate. Any country that is regarded as a potential opponent, or any country that gets into the power orbit of a potential opponent, is vilified. No notice is taken of any good thing about it whatever and everything possibly bad is emphasized. Suspicion and denigration rule. Every utterance by its leaders is interpreted in the worst possible light. Special experts see to that. We have become so used to this that we are not even aware of it any more. In this way a warlike attitude is created. The peaceful messages get lost, the hostile ones get priority.

Suppose, as an experiment, that I were to send a script of the Sermon on the Mount to a broadcasting station, suggesting that it be read on the air, with special attention to the passages about not killing and not being "angry with your brothers." The station would probably reply that it would have to give equal time to the opposite view.

But can't it be argued that the networks are just supplying the public with the kind of war coverage it wants? I do not think so. Nobody has expressed better what the audience expects than Truman Capote. "Watch," he writes. "You can see it on their faces. . . . It says: tell us truth, give us an answer, give us something which is not a smoke ring, but an emblem against our time." Surely we have had some very frank reporting. But frankness, as Katherine Mansfield said, is "truth's ugly and stupid half-sister." We need more. For Vietnam may be the prologue to a much bigger war which no television screen will be able to show at all.

A VISITOR TO HANOI INSPECTS DAMAGE LAID TO U.S. RAIDS

A Purposeful and Energetic Mood in Embattled Capital Found by a Times Man

2 RECENT ATTACKS CITED

Witnesses Certain American Bombs Dropped Inside City Dec. 13 and 14

The writer of the following dispatch is an assistant managing editor of The New York Times, who reached Hanoi Friday.

By HARRISON E. SALISBURY

Special to The New York Times

HANOI, North Vietnam, Dec. 24—Late in the afternoon of this drizzly Christmas Eve the bicycle throngs on the roads leading into Hanoi increased.

Riding sidesaddle behind husbands were hundreds of slender young Hanoi wives returning to the city from evacuation to spend Christmas with their families. Hundreds of mothers had small children perched on the backs of bicycles—children being returned to the city for reunions during the Christmas cease-fire.

In Hanoi's Catholic churches mass was celebrated, and here and there in the small foreign quarter there were more elaborate holiday observances. Five Canadian members of the International Control Commission had a fat Christmas goose brought in specially for them from Vientiane, Laos, on the I.C.C. flight into Hanoi yesterday.

Visitors Have a Party

And in Hanoi's rambling, old high-ceilinged Thongnhat (Reunification) Hotel (formerly the Metropole), there was a special Christmas party for a handful of foreign visitors who chanced to be here.

But this random evidence of Christmas spirit did not convey the mood of North Vietnam's capital, at least not as it seemed to an unexpected observer from the United States.

The mood of Hanoi seemed much more that of a wartime city going about its business briskly, energetically, purposefully. Streets are lined with cylindrical one-man air-raid shelters set in the ground at 10-foot intervals.

The shelters are formed of prestressed concrete with concrete lids left ajar for quick occupancy—and they are reported to have been occupied quite a bit in recent days with the sudden burst of United States air raids. There is damage, attributed by officials here to the raids, as close as 200 yards from this hotel.

Hanoi was laid out by French architects with broad boulevards over which arch leafy trees, and with squares, public gardens and pleasant lakes. Today it seems a bit like a mixture of the Moscow and Algiers of World War II. There are khaki and uniforms everywhere and hardly a truck moves without its green boughs of camouflage. Even pretty girls camouflage their bicycles and conical straw hats.

Christmas Eve found residents in several parts of Hanoi still picking over the wreckage of homes said to have been damaged in the United States raids of Dec. 13 and 14. United States officials have contended that no attacks in built-up or residential Hanoi have been authorized or carried out. They have also suggested that Hanoi residential damage in the two raids could have been caused by defensive surface-to-air missiles that misfired or fell short.

[Although American authorities have said that they were satisfied no bombs fell inside Hanoi and that only military targets were attacked, the State Department said Thursday that "the possibility of an accident" could not be ruled out. A spokesman said that if the bombing had caused civilian injury or damage, the United States regretted it.]

This correspondent is no ballistics specialist, but inspection of several damaged sites and talks with witnesses make it clear that Hanoi residents certainly believe they were bombed by United States planes, that they certainly observed United States planes overhead and that damage certainly occurred right in the center of town.

Large, Sprawling City

Hanoi is a very large, sprawling city. The city proper has a population of 600,000, and the surrounding metropolitan area brings the total to 1,100,000.

The built-up, densely populated urban area extends for a substantial distance in all directions beyond the heavy-lined city boundaries shown on a map by the State Department and published in The New York Times of Dec. 17.

For instance, the Yenvien rail yard, which was listed as one of the targets in the raids Dec. 14 and 15, is in a built-up area that continues south west to the Red River with no visible breaks in residential quarters. Much the same is true of the Vandien truck park south of the city, which was another listed target.

Oil tanks between Yenvien and Gialam, listed as another target, are in a similarly populated region. It is unlikely that any bombing attack on such targets could be carried out without civilian damage and casualties.

The location of two of the damaged areas inspected today suggests that the western approaches to the Paul Doumer Bridge may have been aimed for.

Both damaged areas lie in the Hoankiem quarter of Hanoi. Other administrative quarters of the city are Badinh, Haiba and Dongda. All have suffered some damage.

The first area inspected was Pho Nguyen Thiap Street, about a three-minute drive from the hotel and 100 yards from the central market. Thirteen houses were destroyed—one-story brick and stucco structures for the most part. The Phuc Lan Buddhist pagoda in the same street was badly damaged.

Five persons were reported killed and 11 injured, and 39 families were said to be homeless.

Says Bomb Exploded

Tuan Ngoc Trac, a medical assistant who lived at 46 Pho Nguyen Thiep Street, said he was just going to the clinic where he works when an air alert sounded, indicating planes 25 kilometers (about 15 miles) from Hanoi. He had stepped to the street with his medical bag in his hand when he heard a plane and flung himself to the ground.

He said that the next instant a bomb exploded just over a row of houses, collapsing nine on the other side of the street. Tuan Ngoc Trac displayed an American leaflet, which he said he had found in the street, warning Hanoi residents not to remain in the vicinity of military objectives.

The North Vietnamese say that almost simultaneously—also about 3 P.M. Dec. 13—about 300 thatch and brick homes and huts along the Red River embankment, possibly a quarter of a mile from Pho Nguyen Thiep Street and equally distant from the Thongnhat Hotel, were

hit. The principal damage was again done by a burst just above the houses, but there were also three ground craters caused either by rocket bursts or small bombs.

This area, 200 by 70 yards, was leveled by blast and fire. Four persons were reported killed and 10 injured, most of the residents having been at work or in a large well-constructed shelter.

Another damage site inspected was in the Badinh quarter which is Hanoi's diplomatic section. There, on Khuc Hao Street lies the rear of the very large Chinese Embassy complex backing on the Rumanian Embassy. Minor damage was done to the roofs of the Chinese and Rumanian Embassies by what was said to have looked like rocket fire. Both embassies produced fragments, which they said had come from United States rocket bursts.

House Is Inspected

Also examined was a house on Hue Lane in the Haiba quarter. It was reported hit Dec. 2, with the death of one person and the wounding of seven others, including two children.

Contrary to the impression given by United States communiqués, on-the-spot inspection indicates that American bombing has been inflicting considerable civilian casualties in Hanoi and its environs for some time past.

The North Vietnamese cite as an instance the village of Phuxa, a market gardening suburb possibly four miles from the city center. The village of 24 houses was reported attacked at 12:17 P.M. Aug. 13 by a United States pilot trying to bomb a Red River dike. The village was destroyed and 24 people were killed and 23 wounded. The pilot was shot down.

A crater 25 feet deep was reported blasted in the dike, but it was said to have been filled within three hours. The village has now been completely rebuilt, and has a small museum of mementos of the attack. In the museum is the casing of a United States fragmentation bomb, which bears the legend, "Loaded 7/66." A month after that date it was said to have fallen on Phuxa village, releasing 300 iron spheres, each about the size of a baseball and each loaded with 300 steel pellets about the size and shape of bicycle bearings. Those missiles are reported to have caused most of the Phuxa casualties.

It is the reality of such casualties and such apparent byproducts of the United States bombing policy that lend an atmosphere of grimness and foreboding to Hanoi's Christmas cease-fire. It is fair to say that, based on evidence of their own eyes, Hanoi residents do not find much credibility in United States bombing communiqués.

December 25, 1966

TV: Exposing the False Glory of War

By JAMES C. HAGERTY, *an ABC vice-president and former press secretary to President Eisenhower.*

RECENTLY in these columns, Fredric Wertham, the prominent psychiatrist, expounded his side of a panel discussion he and I had about television coverage of the war in Vietnam. In our original confrontation, the basic differences between Dr. Wertham and myself were these:

I contended (and still do) that the coverage of the sight and sound of the war in Vietnam by American television was exposing the false glory of war by showing its utter savageness, wastefulness and uselessness. By doing so, such coverage was contributing, slowly but inevitably, to a growing public consciousness that war should no longer be tolerated as a way to settle disputes among peoples and nations.

Dr. Wertham disagreed, asserting that I did not understand the psychological effects on the national audience of such daily television coverage. He declared that we in television were "conditioning" our viewers, particularly those of the younger generation, to accept war as a part of modern life.

Normally, the dialogue between us, as far as I was concerned, would have ended with the panel discussion. I would have been content to let our audience on that occasion form their own opinion as to our respective arguments. But in his article on this page, Dr. Wertham chose to broaden considerably his points of view and raised several new areas for disagreement between us that I cannot let stand unanswered.

At the outset, let me readily admit that I do not pose as an expert in psychology or psychiatric study and research. Indeed, I couldn't even qualify as a rank amateur in the field. Consequently, it would be an exercise in futility for me to attempt to refute Dr. Wertham's professional opinions on the basis of my psychiatric knowledge.

*

Instead, all I can say is that there is a great difference of professional opinion in his field. Particularly is this true in the many studies that have been made which seek to discover the relationship between anti-social behavior and violence as presented in fictional television programs, in horror movies and violent literature. It may be ascertainable; again it may not be clearly established. There seem to be valid arguments on both sides by the psychiatric professional experts and I merely point that out to Dr. Wertham.

But in his article, Dr. Wertham devoted much of his comment to, what for him, was a series of non-professional charges against television's coverage of the Vietnam War. In doing so, he projected himself into the business of news reporting — of news integrity — of the basic right of the news media to present, comment on, and interpret the news developments of our times. When he does so, I think I can appropriately take definitive issue with him.

Let's take a look at some of Dr. Wertham's latest statements:

"One cumulative result of the war coverage has been that it has helped to transform us from Nervous Nellies into placid participants."

"The audience so conditioned from childhood now finds the Vietnam fighting pictures really tame stuff and is easily manipulated with regard to violence by the huge public relations establishment that has been constructed at the top of the military set-up."

"What we are given is a hawk's-eye view of life and death . . . war is becoming routine and the corrosion of war commonplace."

Frankly, these assertions puzzle me. I don't know what television news presentations Dr. Wertham has been watching. Certainly they can't be those of any of the three American television networks. Or maybe — as I suspect sometimes happens with critics — his viewing has been infrequent or at least not constant.

It would seem as if Dr. Wertham is suggesting that some mysterious propaganda machine, operated by equally mysterious and sinister individuals "at the top of the military set-up," can control and "manipulate" the news departments of ABC, CBS and NBC. Indeed, the thrust of his contention appears to be that a gigantic conspiracy exists between the television news departments and a military cabal to transform the entire population of the nation into robots or "placid participants" for their own designs. This, of course, is downright preposterous.

It insults the integrity of all news media personnel as well as the devotion to country of the many dedicated members of the military who hate war the most because they know war the most. Further, it violates the very basic principles of our form of government by suggesting that the military has assumed power over civilian control. And it completely overlooks innumerable statements by our government that they desire to bring an end to the fighting and settle differences through negotiation — if only the other side will agree to act like civilized human beings and come to the conference table to discuss it.

But, as long as the war in Vietnam continues, television has an obligation, a duty, to cover it in all its aspects — the fighting and the pacification efforts in Vietnam, the political developments in that nation, the controversy here at home concerning Administration policies, and the reaction to the war abroad by friends and allies, by the neutral nations and by the Communist world. And television will continue to do just that — honestly and fairly, presenting many different points of view.

*

The continuing coverage of the war through the sight and sound of television is really unique in the history of mass communications. Never before has any news media brought war and the controversy that surrounds it so vividly into the living rooms of our people.

Television war coverage does not, as Dr. Wertham stated, "give a hawk's-eye view of life and death." Between them, the three American networks have nearly 100 news people in Vietnam. These people are responsible newsmen, trained and skilled in their profession. Their reports and analyses are not subjected to influence from any group or any source. They, like their colleagues in the newspaper and magazine news field, are rightly proud of their profession and fiercely protective of their rights and obligations as independent reporters and interpreters of the news of our times.

The situation in Vietnam and its worldwide ramifications are not being glorified or propagandized by anyone that I know of — including television. The glory has gone out of battle. The age of grand military parades, stirring marches, pretty girls kissing the boys goodbye has passed forever. And the coverage by television is increasing this realism.

A prime example is the public attitude toward the Vietcong and the infiltrating North Vietnamese forces. They are not vilified and despised as were the Japanese in World War II. Instead, they are increasingly recognized by our military forces and the civilian population as tough opponents with whom we must, as soon as possible, find an equitable and honorable solution to the war — a sane alternative to the battlefield.

In television's coverage of the war, the battlefield, of course, has been pictured and discussed and will continue to be shown. It is there, it is happening, and it must be covered. But, other important developments are also fully reported: the battle to help the South Vietnamese establish a workable government, a functioning and stable economy and a safer and peaceful life for the people of the land. Whenever they are obtainable, films from the other side, carefully identified as such, are shown on all the networks.

Here at home, opponents of the Administration policy on Vietnam are given consistent hearing. The list is too long to enumerate, but spokesmen of the opposition — from Senator Fulbright to student leaders — are presented in detail on news programs and on special presentations. Leaders and "men-in-the-street" from nations who oppose our presence in Vietnam, including spokesmen for the Vietcong, have been interviewed. Highlights from "Viet Rock," an off-Broadway play with music satirizing and protesting the war, have been shown nationally. The whole range of opposition, both here and abroad, has been conscientiously reported — and listened to.

We at ABC have found that our viewing public is vitally interested in all phases of the Vietnam War. The public also reacts positively to our reporting of the war. Last September, after our Peter Jennings feature of a film report of the plight of a South Vietnamese orphanage, over 1,000 viewers called and wrote offering their help and contributions. Surely this was not the response of people hardened to war and its effects.

Our people are, despite detractors, a people whose history is based on freedom and the rights of the individual. We are not imperialists and never have been. We wish to live in peace and have always been willing to help others to resist aggression and win a peaceful way of life for themselves.

I cannot believe that with our national background, we, as a people and a nation, would make an about-face and become a country of "placid participants" in a war in which we are so intimately involved. That is not our nature. We have hawks and doves and in-betweens. Dictated acceptance of any event — even war, unless we are attacked — has never been a weakness of our national character, and I am confident it never will be.

Our people are traditionally the best informed people in the world. They expect the news media to present all the news — the good and the bad, the pros and the cons — and then, on the basis of such information, they form their opinions. This is what we, in television, are doing with the Vietnam War. I contend that we are contributing through that coverage to a growing public consciousness that war is an anachronism, not a condition, of modern life.

Hanoi During an Air Alert: Waitresses Take Up Rifles

By HARRISON E. SALISBURY
Special to The New York Times

HANOI, North Vietnam, Dec. 27—Just before 2:25 P.M. yesterday, there was a muffled distant roar, 10-foot windows in this old French-built hotel rattled and heavy gray curtains gently swayed inward.

At the count of three there was another tremendous distant rumble and again the windows shook and the curtains swayed. Moments later came a third.

The wail of a siren then sounded the alert, and the hotel's defense staff scrambled for tin hats and rifles.

Guests emerged from their rooms and hurried down the great marble staircase, through the long lounge with its slightly bedraggled tropical Christmas tree, its bar with a remarkable collection of liquors of all lands—including Stolichnaya vodka from Moscow, rice wine from Peking and Gordon's gin from London—and out across the interior courtyard where shelters are situated.

By the time the guests had begun to descend into the sturdy concrete bunker, little waitresses in their black sateen trousers and white blouses stood ready with rifles to fire at any low-flying planes.

Inside the shelter, by curious coincidence, Americans found themselves in the majority — four members of an American peace delegation, Mrs. Grace Newman of New York; Mrs. Joe Griffith, whose husband is a Cornell instructor; Mrs. Diane Bevel, associated with the Student Nonviolent Coordinating Committee, and Miss Barbara Deming of Liberation magazine, and this correspondent.

But it was a widely international group, including the deputy director of Tass, Aleksandr A. Vishnevsky, who chanced to be in town; a correspondent of the Italian Communist newspaper L'Unita, members of a Soviet trade-union delegation, two Cubans and an East German. There were no Chinese.

The foreigners chatted a little excitedly about what was to most a new thrill. But to the Vietnamese air alerts and air raids are no novelty and no thrill; they are deadly serious business.

The pretty waitresses with rifles are part of this serious business. It is unlikely that

United States planes are brought down by rifle fire, but the population is trained to man posts and throw up a hurricane of small-arms fire in support of conventional antiaircraft and missile defenses.

The small-arms fire has two purposes.

First, it is designed to make United States low-level attacks increasingly hazardous. According to Hanoi residents, low-level bombing is frequently employed by United States planes in an effort to circumvent the radar and missile system.

Second, the firing of rifles gives the populace a feeling of participation and of fighting back—important in maintaining morale and counteracting the feelings of helplessness and defenselessness that civilian populations often experience.

Alert of 6 or 7 Minutes

The alert yesterday was only six or seven minutes long. It was caused, the authorities said, by the appearance of a pilotless American reconnaissance craft near the city. The three tremendous blasts presumably were SAM surface-to-air missiles. The same kind of robot plane, it was disclosed, caused Hanoi's Christmas alert at almost the same hour.

Today the foreign press corps was taken to see where the drone that appeared on Christmas was shot down. They went in a convoy of half a dozen cars, most of them covered with camouflage fishnet, which quickly slides over the roof and hood and into which leaves and greenery can be slipped.

Hardly a car or truck moves outside Hanoi without camouflage, and most cars in the city are permanently bedecked. So, for that matter, are many people, who wear sprays of leaves and branches in their helmets or straw hats. This too is part of an organized, well-designed effort to reduce bombing hazards.

The caravan made its way northeast across the Paul Doumer Bridge. It appeared, from this trip across the bridge, that bombing on Dec. 14 was directed at its approaches and

fell short in each case, striking residential quarters. The bombs dropped in the Hoan Kiem and Gialem and Yenvien quarters.

Describing the Yenvien attack, an American communiqué said the target was rail yards. Some bombs certainly fell along the railroad. But there are large numbers of apartment houses close by, and one after another was blasted out.

Because of the highly organized repair facilities, rail traffic is moving normally, but residents who were not casualties have been compelled to leave their destroyed homes.

The drone downed on Christmast Day fell 12 or 13 miles northeast of the city in the Tienson district of Habac Province. It proved to be a Ryan model with a wingspread of about 18 feet that the Americans call the Firebee.

The wing and fuselage, somewhat crumpled, lay in a pile. Eight or nine girls dug in muck about seven feet deep for the engine, which was gradually being recovered.

The robot plane, which was shot down adjacent to the main rail line linking Hanoi to China, presumably had been dispatched to transmit photographic intelligence on rail conditions and traffic movements. According to the girls digging out the engine, the drone was at an altitude of only about a mile when downed.

The seriousness with which the North Vietnamese take the air threat has undoubtedly kept civilian casualties lower than might be expected in comparison with the vast damage said to have been done to ordinary living quarters and the destruction reported in small towns and villages.

The key to this is the manhole concrete shelter, which seems to be a North Vietnamese invention. There are hundreds of thousands of them along every highway and every city street, and they are still being put in place by the thousands.

At 5 o'clock the other morning I saw one lonely man patiently digging one in. They are made with concrete exteriors like drain pipes, largely by hand. With their two-inch-thick concrete covers they are impervious to anything but a direct or very close hit.

The other factor reducing casualties and loss is dispersion. Everything dispersible has been dispersed. The countryside is strewn with dispersed goods and supplies. The same is true of the people.

Two-thirds of the machinery and workers at the big textile plant near Gialem have been sent to the countryside. The wisdom of the precaution was demonstrated, it was said, when the plant suffered damage from United States rocket fire Dec. 13 and 14.

U.S. GETS PRAISE ON HANOI REPORTS

Times Articles Seen Abroad as Indication of Freedom

Special to The New York Times

WASHINGTON, Jan. 17 — The United States system of democracy has recently been praised by European newspapers as a result of a series of reports in North Vietnam by Harrison E. Salisbury, an assistant managing editor of The New York Times.

According to recent surveys of the world press by the United States Information Agency, Mr. Salisbury's articles, telling of civilian casualties attributed by the North Vietnamese to United States bombing, have been "widely reported and generally accepted as true."

British, French and Austrian newspapers, for example, have lauded the American system of democracy for permitting the press "to investigate and publish reports that run counter to official statements" and for allowing officials "to openly admit that mistakes have been made."

Comment in 2 Nations

The Paris mass-circulation newspaper France Soir was quoted as having said that the "Americans are playing fair" and "proving that American democracy is not a mere word." The Independent Scotsman of Edinburgh was said to have commented:

"It is admirable that The New York Times should send a reporter to Namdinh and that official spokesmen should openly admit mistakes by American troops in the South."

Mr. Salisbury visited Namdinh, the third largest city in North Vietnam, and described extensive damage to residential areas.

The reference to "mistakes" made by American troops in South Vietnam and openly admitted by official spokesmen had to do with accidental bombing of United States forces and accidental killing of Vietnamese civilians, officials here said.

In reporting on its press surveys, the Government's information agency said that as a result of the Salisbury articles "further doubt has been cast on the veracity of official U. S. statements."

It noted that the articles had been the springboard for extensive press comment—mostly in Europe—and cited a widespread belief that the loss of civilian life and property, as reported by Mr. Salisbury, indicated that "U. S. bombing is not as accurate as it claims to be."

December 28, 1966

The articles were said to have led to foreign editorial conclusions that there was now even more reason to stop the bombing of North Vietnam and that Communist countries would never permit one of their editors to make such reports.

That was the gist of an examination of world press comment as of Dec. 30, a few days after Mr. Salisbury's first dispatches from Hanoi.

The survey said the New Year found many West Europeans "steeped in gloom" over the prospect of continued bombings of North Vietnam. Opinion in the Far East was said to have fastened primarily on the forthcoming lunar New Year truce and on seeking "clues to future moves which could lead to negotiations."

Observers here have noted the candor with which an official United States Government agency has reprinted—and has made available to the American press—excerpts from a wide variety of foreign editorials and newspaper commentaries, many of which are highly critical of alleged lack of candor by high United States officials.

The information agency's report also contained editorial praise of the United States policy in Vietnam, notably from the highly respected Economist of London, which observed in early January:

"The American task in Vietnam is to prevent Vietnam from becoming either a Munich or a Sarajevo. President Johnson has steered this increasingly difficult course in 1966 with superb individual courage; and it is right to say that a realization of this in Britain has also been more widespread and sensible than we had apprehended."

Television

A Critic of the Vietnam War Offers a Challenge to All TV

By JACK GOULD

IN some respects the most intriguing broadcaster of the current season is Stimson Bullitt, who operates major TV stations in Seattle, Spokane and Portland. As far as available records show, he is the first video station owner to go on the air with an editorial challenging President Johnson's conduct of the Vietnamese war and urging a cessation of the bombing of North Vietnam.

Mr. Bullitt said he was motivated by two considerations, among others. First, he felt that the United States was digging itself deeper into a hole in Southeast Asia and that, on balance, the possible gains to this country did not outweigh the cost in lives and world influence. Second, he suggested that the national networks had failed in their regular evening newscasts to give responsible and balanced coverage to critics of the United States involvement in Vietnam, and that newsreels of draft card burners and pictures of protests by "beatniks in sandals and beards" tended to implant the thought that dissent on the war was limited to youthful excesses that invited easy dismissal.

Mr. Bullitt is president of the King Broadcasting Company, which owns Station KING-TV in Seattle; KREM-TV in Spokane and KWG-TV in Portland. The Bullitt family is one of the more prominent in the Northwest. His mother, Mrs. Dorothy Stimson Bullitt, is a leader in business, cultural and civic affairs in Seattle.

Mr. Bullitt's editorial was carried on the three stations just prior to Christmas and, since then, he has commissioned other critics of the Administration's policies to prepare broadcasts which, he believes, would contribute to a more rounded perspective on Asian events.

The most obvious importance of Mr. Bullitt's action, of course, is to focus attention on editorializing over the air. The wisdom of broadcast editorializing has been a subject of debate for years, but the Federal Communications Commission finally has specifically encouraged the practice as long as the station makes a genuine effort to see that contrary opinions are also offered.

Among local television stations, the practice has grown substantially but is still far from general. In New York, for example, it is only WABC-TV and WCBS-TV that offer editorials with regularity. The drawback to these editorializing policies is the limitation of expression to local or state issues. Not that such editorials are either unimportant or may not have beneficial effect. But to editorialize without touching on the overriding international concern of the moment or without digging into Washington developments is to create the illusion of speaking out without raising one's voice in the areas of dominant interest.

There is a reason. Television may be unhesitatingly bold and hard-hitting when it comes to reporting a crisis in Outer Mongolia, but when it comes to Washington the kid gloves are often put on. As a licensed medium not immune to real or imagined pressures from politicians, there is a disinclination to stir up Washington tempers. Before editorials are to be expected, the straight reportage of the Washington scene requires far more vigor and incisiveness.

It is pertinent that Mr. Bullitt, in discussing network coverage, stressed the importance of the nightly newscasts as opposed to special documentaries or occasional coverage of specific hearings. He noted that the nightly newscasts are what most people see with consistency and that it is within the body of this service that the need for sustained depth and balance is most essential.

Yet the format of the half-hours, with their emphasis on the brevity of individual items and pictorial considerations, can lead to problems. Because of the normal public interest in the well-being of American servicemen in Vietnam and the vivid pictures that are an inevitable sequel to war, the greatest amount of air-time is accorded the newsreels coming from Saigon.

But, as James Reston, associate editor of The New York Times, remarked in a recent appearance on National Educational Television, the central issue in Washington, at the moment, may well be the so-called credibility gap, the mood of public skepticism in the search for hidden motives behind Administration pronouncements and actions. Within the context of TV's half-hours, the running story on the national uneasiness certainly has not been elucidated with compelling thoroughness and regularity. The independent candor and realism that has distinguished some of TV's coverage in Saigon needs equal application in Washington. Merely giving equal time to Republicans and Democrats in interview roundups is no substitute for vigorous nonpartisan interpretation and background on the swirling currents in the capital.

The challenge to TV is all the greater because such stories may have to be developed outside the range of cameras. Whether a viewer chances to agree or disagree with Mr. Bullitt's views on the conduct of the Vietnamese war is one thing. But in speaking up as he has, he is now one member of the broadcasting fraternity who has sounded a timely warning that the TV medium may wish to review its procedures in nightly newscasting, which is the front page of electronic journalism. The agonies of the battle in Vietnam will, of course, need continued diligent coverage. But the soul-searching on the home-front over America's long-range role in world affairs assuredly is no less a story. Mr. Bullitt's criticism and admonition is completely constructive.

PRESIDENT DENIES RIFT ON BOMBING; DEFENDS POLICIES

Replies at News Conference to Senate Panel's Call for Wider War in Air

DIFFERENCES BELITTLED

Johnson Blames the Press for Reports of Division Among His Advisers

By ROY REED

Special to The New York Times

WASHINGTON, Sept. 1 — President Johnson defended today his policy of controlled bombing of North Vietnam and denied the existence of any serious rift between his military and civilian advisers.

Speaking at an unscheduled news conference in his office, the President offered a low-key, cautiously worded reply to those who have demanded that he widen the air war.

The Senate Preparedness Investigating Subcommittee, headed by Senator John Stennis of Mississippi, urged him yesterday to expand the air war, abandon "carefully controlled" bombing and pay more attention to his top-level military advisers in selecting targets.

Calls Policy Sound

Mr. Johnson said he did not want to argue with the subcommittee Then he added:

"I believe our policy is a sound one. It is based on the best judgment that we have. Every decision is going to be made after we get all the facts and then we are going to do what we think is in the national interest. I am sure the committee wants to do the same thing."

Mr. Johnson conceded that the military and civilian chiefs running the war did not agree on everything, but he said there were "no deep divisions."

"There are no quarrels, no antagonisms," he said.

He said that in his 36 years in Washington, he had never seen "more harmony, more general agreement and a more cooperative attitude" from the armed services.

Right Is Defended

Responding to a later question, the President defended the right of the military commanders to take their case to the public, even when it conflicted with their civilian chiefs.

Once again, Mr. Johnson cautioned against seeing too great a conflict between the military and civilian spokesmen of the Government. He suggested that the current conflict was mainly the work of an over-zealous press.

"I think you would be doing the country a disservice if you felt for a moment that there were any deep divisions between us," he said.

"I think you make a little copy out of it and you blow it up," he said, directly addressing the 50 or so reporters around his desk. "I don't detect any fire, except from what I read."

The differences of opinion that the President sought to minimize have existed for some time. They came to light again during nearings on the bombing conducted by the Stennis subcommittee during the last several weeks.

The Joint Chiefs of Staff, testifying individually, told the subcommittee that United States planes should close the port of Haiphong, strike all meaningful military targets in North Vietnam and increase interdiction of the lines of communication from Communist China.

Secretary of Defense Robert S. McNamara, while calling his differences with the Joint Chiefs "very narrow," told the subcommittee during the same hearings that he saw no reason to believe that North Vietnam could be "bombed to the negotiating table."

Senator Mike Mansfield, the Democratic leader in the Senate, and George Christian, White House press secretary, said Mr. McNamara was speaking for the Administration.

Still In Charge

Mr. Johnson left no doubt that if any controversy existed between military and civilian thinkers, then, he, as the No. 1 civilian, was still in charge.

Asked if he saw a challenge of civilian control in the recommendation of the generals and the Stennis subcommittee, Mr. Johnson replied:

"No, we have gone through these things in every period of hostility that this nation has engaged in. We speak our minds freely. We have differences and we express them.

"But as President Truman used to say, in the last analysis, decisions will have to be made, and are made."

He jabbed his green-topped desk with his right hand to show precisely where the decisions finally were made.

"I try to give proper weight to the recommendations made to me and than do what I think is best for our country," he said.

Mr. Johnson replied to a question prompted by a Columbia Broadcasting System report that friends of Secretary McNamara had contended that he has considered resigning over expansion of the air war in Vietnam.

Asked if Mr. McNamara had suggested that he would resign if the bombing were stepped up, Mr. Johnson said:

"Absolutely not. That is the most ridiculous, nonsensical report that I have seen, I think, since I have been President. Anyone who knows Secretary McNamara would know that on the face that was not true. He doesn't go around threatening anything or anyone."

Without commenting directly on demands for a widened air war, Mr. Johnson noted that he already had authorized the bombing of about 300 of some 350 targets listed by the Joint Chiefs.

"The 50 left are in very strategic areas, primarily the port of Haiphong, Hanoi and the buffer zone," he said. "The decisions to bomb those other 50 targets have not been made.

Consider the Views

"Before the President acts on them he will carefully consider the views of his principal military advisers, such as the Joint Chiefs, and his principal political advisers, the Secretary of State, his principal deputy in military matters, the Secretary of Defense."

The President emphasized that bombing strategy was worked out by a number of military and civilian officials. Noting that they sometimes have varying opinions, he said:

"Some of them don't have the viewpoint on how it might affect our over-all political situation in the world, and so forth. All of those things are considered."

The President was asked if he agreed with a statement by Gen. Harold K. Johnson, Army Chief of Staff, that the United States might be able to begin slowly withdrawing troops from Vietnam in 18 months if present progress continued.

"That is General Johnson's opinion," the President said. "I have made no prediction and wouldn't care to at this time. General Johnson is a very competent military officer and he has been out there and reached some conclusions. He expreseed those to me. But I haven't made any prediction."

SWITCHES BY PRESS ON WAR REPORTED

7 Papers More Critical of U.S.—4 More Hawkish

Special to The New York Times

BOSTON, Feb. 17 — Seven major newspapers in the nation have shifted in the last few months from general support of the Administration on Vietnam to criticism of recent military escalation, according to a survey by The Boston Globe.

In a report appearing in tomorrow's editions of The Sunday Globe, the newspaper also found that four dailies had moved in an opposite direction by favoring stronger military measures and criticizing the Administration for not escalating fast enough.

The survey was taken last month among 39 major United States newspapers with a circulation of 22 million. The Globe mailed questionnaires to 45 newspapers.

The seven that moved to a more dovish position or one critical of escalation were The Charlotte Observer, The Cleveland Plain Dealer, The Detroit Free Fress, The Kansas City Star, The Los Angeles Times, The Minneapolis Star and Tribune and The Richmond Times-Dispatch.

Four More Hawkish

The four that moved to a more hawkish position away from the Administration because they favored a more militant policy were The Chicago Tribune, The Cincinnati Enquirer, The New York Daily News and the St. Louis Globe-Democrat.

The newspapers were asked to submit editorials, but some, including The New York Times, The Washington Post and The Washington Star, gave evidence of their positions through background interviews or by written statements.

The questionnaires asked the newspapers to state whether they had been for, against or unstated editorially on 20 positions ranging from unconditional withdrawal to an invasion of North Vietnam.

The newspapers also were asked to identify their general editorial positions and to say whether they had shifted editorial policy in the last two years.

Among the editorial suggestions for ending the conflict were demands for an all-out military effort, by four newspapers; various plans for de-escalation and a bombing pause, and a number of negotiation formulas and hints at unilateral withdrawal.

September 2, 1967

Other findings drawn from The Globe's survey were these:

¶Of the 39 newspapers surveyed, 16 generally supported the Administration on Vietnam and 19 supported the American commitment but were critical of the President's military and peace efforts.

¶Of 31 that answered the questionnaires fully, all but one said they favored—or have not spoken editorially against — some type of Geneva settlement. [The 1954 Geneva Conference partitioned Vietnam along the 17th parallel, banned new troops or bases, created the International Control Commission and scheduled reunification elections. The United States and South Vietnam did not sign the accords].

¶There was unanimous opposition to unconditional withdrawal at this time. None of the newspapers favored invasion of North Vietnam.

¶None wanted a formal declaration of war.

¶All but three asked for increased pacification efforts; the remaining three said they did not oppose such efforts.

¶One paper favored bombing the Red River dikes. The rest were against or uncommitted on that position.

¶Two favored invasion of the northern section of the demilitarized zone; the remainder were against or uncommitted.

¶Fifteen opposed additional troop commitments; four dailies favored further manpower buildups.

President Johnson was criticized by many of the newspapers for what they considered creating a credibility gap, stifling public debate, evading the issues, crushing peace overtures, hiding facts and clumsy timing.

February 18, 1968

State Conservative Party Hails Curb on Battle News

The New York Conservative party last night cheered the report that the United States command in Vietnam was going to tighten restrictions on the reporting of military information.

In a telegram to President Johnson, Kieran O'Doherty, chairman of the party's national affairs committee, called the move "a long-overdue essential measure."

"The New York Times and the national TV and radio news networks have been most conspicuous, even to the extent of endangering the lives of fighting men, by publicizing information of major intelligence value to the enemy," the telegram said.

February 27, 1968

War Stand of the Times-Dispatch

To the Editor:

The story carried on Feb. 18 by John H. Fenton under a Boston dateline correctly quoted The Boston Globe's listing of the Richmond Times-Dispatch as "dovish" on Vietnam, but The Globe was in error.

In answering the Globe's questionnaire, I stated that we were suggesting that ships be sunk in the channel to the port of Haiphong to cut off vital shipments to North Vietnam. This proposal, which certainly is not "dovish," The Globe overlooked.

We are "more critical" of the Johnson Administration's policy than we were, as correctly stated by The Globe. And yet I wouldn't say that we are "hawkish." All of which shows the difficulty of applying labels in one's discussion of this miserable war, which we never should have entered.

VIRGINIUS DABNEY
Editor
Richmond Times-Dispatch
Richmond, Va., Feb. 21, 1968

February 28, 1968

PENTAGON DEFENDS INFORMATION POLICY

WASHINGTON, March 15 (UPI)—The Defense Department's information chief said today that total United States casualties and equipment losses in Vietnam would continue to be announced, although some details were being withheld for security reasons.

Phil G. Goulding, Assistant Secretary of Defense for Public Affairs, defended the policy recently announced by United States commanders in Vietnam of withholding exact information on the number of enemy rounds, American casualties and damage to aircraft or other equipment from enemy fire against fixed United States installations in South Vietnam.

The policy, announced Feb. 26, is based on the ground that such detailed information helps the enemy improve artillery, mortar and rocket fire against American bases.

Mr. Goulding said that United States casualties at the Marine outpost at Khesanh would be included in the figures for Operation Scotland, of which the Khesanh operation is a part.

March 16, 1968

AMERICAN FORCES LEAVING KHESANH FOR NEARBY POSTS

Changes in Military Situation Cited in Withdrawal From Base Once Held Vital

By The Associated Press

SAIGON, South Vietnam, Thursday, June 27—The United States Marines are pulling out of the combat base at Khesanh, where they withstood a bitter North Vietnamese siege for 77 days last winter, the United States command said today.

In announcing the withdrawal from a base once described as vital to allied defenses near the demilitarized zone, the United States command said that enemy pressure was part of the reason. In an official statement, the command said:

"There have been two significant changes in the military situation in Vietnam since early this year—an increase in friendly strength, mobility and firepower and an increase in the enemy's threat due to both a greater flow of replacements and in a change in tactics."

Defense Was Determined

Khesanh is the first major base abandoned under such circumstances in the war.

During the long winter siege, senior United States officers here and in the United States said the base would be held at all costs. However, when a relief force finally was sent to break the siege in April, the decision to pull out apparently had already been made.

The disclosure of the withdrawal came two days after The Baltimore Sun, in a dispatch sent from Khesanh on Monday, reported the withdrawal and said that United States forces were building up their strength at nearby combat bases a few miles to the east.

John S. Carroll, the correspondent who wrote the dispatch, was disaccredited by the United States military command yesterday on the ground that he had violated security regulations.

Military regulations forbid the reporting of troop movements in advance of official announcements. The disac-

creditation means that Mr. Carroll will be unable to travel on United States military planes or attend military briefings or news conferences.

The Khesanh combat base was originally set up as a Special Forces camp to check infiltration along Route 9 from Laos seven miles to the west, and across the western part of the demilitarized zone 14 miles to the north.

The marines were sent to reinforce Khesanh in 1967 because of increasing enemy pressure.

The force, according to senior officers' private estimates, was unable either to check or effectively monitor infiltration that flowed past the base.

The siege, which opened on Jan. 20, was the result of an apparent attempt by the North Vietnamese command to overrun the base. The big assault never came, but during the 11 weeks thousands of artillery rounds exacted a heavy toll in American casualties. About 100 died and hundreds more were wounded.

The new western anchor of the American base system along the DMZ apparently was to be Landing Zone Stud about 10 miles to the east along Route 9. The landing zone has been used for all resupply and support of the eight battalions that were operating around Khesanh since the siege was lifted.

The base has a landing strip capable of handling medium-size transport planes. Its big advantage is that it is out of range of the North Vietnamese artillery dug into Coroc mountain in Laos that severely punished Khesanh.

The official statement said: "Mobile forces tied to specific terrain must be used to the utmost to attack, intercept, reinforce or take whatever action is most appropriate to meet enemy threats. Therefore, we have decided to continue the mobile posture we adopted in western Quangtri Province with Operation Pegasus in April.

"The decision makes occupation of the base at Khesanh unnecessary.

"In I Corps tactical zone there has also been a net increase in enemy strength. In January the enemy had at least the equivalent of six divisions, today he has at least the equivalent of eight. This gives him the capability of mounting several sizable attacks concurrently.

"To meet this significantly increased threat, friendly forces must make maximum advantage of their superior firepower and mobility."

30-Day Suspension Indicated

SAIGON, June 26—Brig. Gen. Winant Sidle, the chief of information, who announced the suspension of the Baltimore Sun correspondent John Carroll today because of Mr. Carroll's dispatch on the Khesanh withdrawal, said the suspension was of indefinite duration. However, he indicated that it would be lifted after 30 days.

During the war in Vietnam, only a handful of correspondents have lost their accreditation, generally for 30 days. In the last year, no correspondent from a major newspaper, network or magazine had been suspended.

Mr. Carroll, who is 26 years old, is the son of Wallace Carroll, the editor and publisher of The Winston-Salem Journal and Sentinel.

Commenting today on his report of the Khesanh withdrawal, Mr. Carroll said: "The Marine privates knew about it, the North Vietnamese knew about it and the only ones who didn't know about it were the people in the United States."

U.S. 'Ground Rules' Keep Rein on War Reporting

By GENE ROBERTS
Special to The New York Times

SAIGON, South Vietnam, July 1 — This morning, as they do every morning, representatives of the United States command placed a hefty stack of mimeographed press statements on a table in a Government building in downtown Saigon.

One item told of a battle 46 miles north of Saigon in which two United States infantrymen were killed and four wounded. Although the battle took place at 9 A.M. yesterday, news correspondents — including any who might have witnessed it— were forbidden to say how many had been killed and wounded until the statement appeared on the table.

The battle was only a routine notice in a routine report, but it illustrated how the military's "ground rules" for press coverage apply. The ground rules set forth 15 categories of information — including United States casualties — that cannot be reported until a formal announcement is made in Saigon.

Last week the ground rules were dramatized when John Carroll, The Baltimore Sun's correspondent, wrote that the United States was in the process of abandoning its garrison at Khesanh after successfully defending it for three months earlier this year against the longest enemy siege of the war.

Brig. Gen. Winant Sidle, chief of information for the military command, ruled that Mr. Carroll had violated a rule that forbids discussion of troop movements until they have been "cleared" by the military. He suspended Mr. Carroll's military accreditation card for an indefinite period, effectively preventing him from talking with military and embassy officials and barring him from military transportation.

How sweeping are the ground rules? Do they prevent the press from relaying facts a reader in the United States would need to reach a solid opinion on the conduct of the war? Do they prevent the enemy from getting information that would jeopardize the lives of allied troops?

In broad terms, the rules are designed to deny the enemy information about tactics, troops movements, air strikes, supply levels, future plans, and casualties and damage caused by enemy attack.

The commanders here reason, for example, that if the enemy forces knew that rocket attacks on a base had seriously hurt the allies, they might order a ground attack in an effort to overrun the base while it was at its weakest. On the other hand, if they found out that the attack had done little

damage, they might cancel a planned assault that would have pitted them against a superior force.

Before a newsman can become accredited by the United States command, he has to sign a statement that he will abide by the rules. Few if any correspondents object to signing. For the most part they look upon the rules as a reasonable alternative to censorship, which has not been imposed in this war.

"An army has a right to protect itself," says a French reporter who is not in sympathy with the American position here. "I think the ground rules are fair. They may delay you a bit in telling the story to your readers, but you can tell it eventually. If there were censorship, the censors could edit out anything embarrassing to the United States."

Most of the more than 500 accredited correspondents here appear to share that assessment.

"The ground rules work pretty well," General Sidle says. "The press, as a whole, tries to abide by them."

"Ground rules are common sense," he adds. "All a reporter has to do is ask himself, 'will this help the enemy?'"

Although reporters have little quarrel with the rules, there are sporadic objections to the way they are applied. The loudest complaints came in April, when the Americans moved into the Ashau Valley in one of the war's major operations but refused to let newsmen say they were there until the operation was 11 days old. Normally, the military announce an operation after the second or third day.

Several newsmen suspected the command of having embargoed the operation to avoid "embarrassing" the United States while it was trying to get peace talks under way. Still others maintained that there was no valid military reason for not writing that the Americans were in Ashau inas much as the enemy was shooting at them.

Last week Mr. Carroll made much the same argument after reporting the Khesanh withdrawal. He went to Khesanh and saw marines disassembling the metal runway and dynamiting bunkers. He said he became convinced that enemy troops could see all this from nearby positions, so that there was no valid military reason for withholding the report.

Information officers counter that they are in a better position than newsmen to decide when information will benefit the enemy. One high-ranking information officer conceded that there was at least a 90

per cent chance that Mr. Carroll was right, but added that when there was even the slightest chance that the enemy did not know, it was best not to tell him.

Vulnerable to Attack

The command contends that troops are especially vulnerable to attack when withdrawing. At the time of the Ashau operation, it maintained that the enemy had no way of knowing how many men the United States would ultimately commit.

The command's position was that the tone of press reports might indicate that more troops were on their way and that the operation was to become a major one. It ultimately involved two United States divisions, plus several South Vietnamese batallions.

The command agreed to publication on the 11th day of the operation only because Joseph Alsop, the columnist, announced it from Washington. A strong advocate of United States involvement in Vietnam, he was never disciplined for having broken the embargo.

Military men contend that for the most part they have tended to give reporters the benefit of the doubt in enforcing the ground rules. General Sidle says that accreditation cards have been suspended only four times since 1966 when the rules were written, and that it is customary to reaccredit after 30 days.

"An awful lot of odds and ends get out that are helpful to the enemy," according to General Sidle, "but you can't have ground rules for everything."

Although he believes the enemy is assisted unwittingly by newspapers, he has not advocated censorship, saying:

"I don't see how it would work. How do you keep a guy from going to Hong Kong to file his story? And if the United States imposed censorship, this wouldn't affect foreign newsmen. How are you going to censor television films?"

For its part, the press corps is less concerned over not reporting all it knows at the earliest possible moment than it is over the possibility that it may not be getting all pertinent battle information. Reporters often guess wrong in trying to anticipate looming battles, so they depend on the daily military communiqué.

The communiqué is often sketchy, in the opinion of most newsmen, and official briefing officers frequently say they have no further information.

Military men contend that it is impossible in a war situation to get reporters complete information as fast as they want it. The reporters insist that it could be done.

War Correspondent Is Barred 6 Months By U.S. Command

By BERNARD WEINRAUB
Special to The New York Times

SAIGON, South Vietnam, July 27—The military accreditation of John S. Carroll, correspondent of The Baltimore Sun, was lifted for six months today by the United States Command. It was the first time in the war that the credentials of a correspondent for a major publication had been lifted for more than 30 days.

Mr. Carroll was suspended "indefinitely" last month after having written that the Marines were abandoning their longheld outpost at Khesanh. Although the article was later confirmed by the military, Mr. Carroll was suspended for violating a ground rule that forbids public discussion of pending troop operations.

Brig. Gen. Winant Sidle, the chief of information, said today that the "indefinite" suspension had been "reduced" to six months.

The move surprised Mr. Carroll and the sizable Saigon press corps. General Sidle had indicated earlier that the suspension would not last beyond 30 days.

"No one ever said 30 days," General Sidle said today. "The original suspension was indefinite."

"For a major violation of this type, 30 days seems awfully light," he added. "Our position is that a flat 30-day suspension should not encompass all violations. The suspension must fit the violation."

General Sidle said that the decision had been approved by Gen. Creighton W. Abrams, the United States commander in Vietnam.

The suspension of Mr. Carroll's credentials prevents him from taking military transport around the country, attending United States mission briefings and conferring with military officials. He can remain in Vietnam.

Mr. Carroll said today that the move by the military command was "extraordinarily vindictive."

"Some sort of ground rules are necessary, but this arbitrary system of penalties could very well be abused to stem the flow of honest and accurate reporting," he added.

Mr. Carroll, 26, is the son of Wallace Carroll, the editor and publisher of The Winston-Salem Journal and Sentinel

July 28, 1968

Credentials of U.P.I. Editor In Vietnam Are Suspended

Special to The New York Times

SAIGON, South Vietnam, Sept. 24—The press accreditation of Bert W. Okuley, a news editor in the Saigon bureau of United Press International, was suspended today for 30 days by the United States command.

Brig. Gen. Winant Sidle, chief of information, said Mr. Okuley had broken the command's ground rules by writing a report last Friday about an operation by United States marines in the demilitarized zone before the news had been officially made public by his office.

A spokesman for the U.P.I. bureau said that the transmission of the report had been inadvertent.

September 25, 1968

NEWSWEEK CRITICAL OF JOHNSON ON WAR

Newsweek magazine said yesterday in an editorial on the Vietnam war that President Johnson had failed to provide "the firm, clear leadership expected of the man in the White House."

The editorial, appearing as part of an eight-page section on Vietnam in the March 18 issue, advocates a military stalemate leading to negotiations in which "both Washington and Hanoi are willing to make substantial compromises."

"After three years of gradual escalation," the editorial says, "President Johnson's strategy for Vietnam has run into a dead end. Only the chronic optimist can now see the 'light at the end of the tunnel' that used to illuminate the rhetoric of the military briefing officers."

The recent offensive by the enemy on South Vietnamese cities, the magazine holds, "exposed the utter inadequacy of the Administration's war policy."

This was the second time in the magazine's 35-year-history that it had taken an editorial stand. The first was in its "Negro in America" issue of Nov. 2, 1967, in which it made recommendations to help the Negro achieve full equality.

March 11, 1968

Gen. Walt Revisits Vietnam; Finds 'Nothing but Optimism'

DANANG, South Vietnam, Nov. 22 (Reuters)—Gen. Lewis W. Walt, Assistant Commandant of the United States Marine Corps, said today that he had found "nothing but confidence and optimism" after a five-day visit to South Vietnam.

He accused American news media of failing to present a more positive picture of the war.

"The amount of time this war is going to last from here on out is going to depend in lots of respects on how good treatment it gets from our news media," he said at a news conference.

General Walt, who commanded the United States Marines in Vietnam from 1965 to 1967, said the impatience of the American people about the war stemmed primarily from the lack of understanding about its complexities.

"Another thing that makes this war so difficult for our people to understand," General Walt said, "is the Communist propaganda thrown habitually at them in order to confuse them. The news media have got to help us out."

November 23, 1969

Army 'Censorship'

To the Editor:

As a public relations officer for the XIV Army Corps in the Pacific in World War II and deputy information officer of United States forces in Korea for a time during the war there, I feel impelled to comment on the story concerning Army Specialist 5 Robert Lawrence and his charge that radio news is being censored by the Army in Vietnam.

During World War II enlisted men who were editors of camp newspapers now and then would write editorials criticizing the commanding officer or the generals. As pointed out in your story, these editors were part of the military concerned primarily with keeping up, the morale by providing news and information.

A similar situation prevails in businesses which have internal publications with which to communicate with their employes. It would be unrealistic for the editor of one of these publications to disagree with the way the chief executive is operating the company.

The Armed Forces Radio, the unit and camp newspapers and others are primarily morale factors and the principal business is fighting the war. Incidentally, in your story of Jan. 5, you say there was press censorship during the Korean War. There was no formal censorship although correspondents checked their copy with public relations officers for security. If there was something considered objectionable or giving comfort to the enemy, it was suggested to the correspondent that he delete it, but if he persisted he could still send his story to his agency or to his newspaper.

Specialist 5 Lawrence should realize he is willingly or unwillingly working for the Army. [Editorial Jan. 6.] What would happen to correspondents for newspapers, radio and television stations and magazines if they started to criticize in writing or broadcasting the people for whom they work?

REGINALD S. JACKSON
Toledo, Ohio, Jan. 8, 1970

January 18, 1970

CENSORSHIP DENIED BY U.S. COMMAND

SAIGON, South Vietnam, Jan. 28 (AP)—The United States command today denied charges that unfavorable news reports were censored by the Armed Forces Vietnam Network.

In a summary of an investigation of the charges, the command said the only reports prohibited from the network's programming were those that would give information of value to the enemy or offend the South Vietnamese Government.

The command opened its inquiry after a network newscaster, Specialist 5 Robert E. Lawrence, accused the military of censorship. During a televised broadcast earlier this month Specialist Lawrence charged that network newscasters were being "suppressed" and were "not free to tell the truth." He was then removed from his job.

The command said the prohibition of material of value to the enemy or offensive to Saigon does not preclude the use of items unfavorable to South Vietnam, the United States or the armed forces. Such items have been used, it said.

The command said the investigators had looked into 23 cases of alleged censorship cited by Specialist Lawrence and other network staffers over a six-month period.

"The investigation concluded that this small percentage of contested news items did not constitute a pattern of censorship," it said.

Vast Review of War Took a Year

By HEDRICK SMITH

In June, 1967, at a time of great personal disenchantment with the Indochina war and rising frustration among his colleagues at the Pentagon, Secretary of Defense Robert S. McNamara commissioned a major study of how and why the United States had become so deeply involved in Vietnam.

The project took a year to complete and yielded a vast and highly unusual report of Government self-analysis. It was compiled by a team of 30 to 40 Government officials, civilian and military, many of whom had helped to develop or carry out the policies that they were asked to evaluate and some of whom were simultaneously active in the debates that changed the course of those policies.

While Mr. McNamara turned over his job to Clark M. Clifford, while the war reached a military peak in the 1968 Lunar New Year offensive, while President Johnson cut back the bombing of North Vietnam and announced his plan to retire, and while the peace talks began in Paris, the study group burrowed through Government files.

The members sought to probe American policy toward Southeast Asia from the World War II pronouncements of President Franklin D. Roosevelt into the start of Vietnam peace talks in the summer of 1968. They wrote nearly 40 book-length volumes backed up by annexes of cablegrams, memorandums, draft proposals, dissents and other documents.

Many Inconsistencies

Their report runs to more than 7,000 pages—1.5 million words of historical narratives plus a million words of documents—enough to fill a small crate.

Even so, it is not a complete or polished history. It displays many inconsistencies and lacks a single all-embracing summary. It is an extended internal critique based on the documentary record, which the researchers did not supplement with personal interviews, partly because they were pressed for time.

The study emerged as a middle-echelon and official view of the war, incorporating material from the top-level files of the Defense Department into which flow papers from the White House, the State Department, the Central Intelligence Agency and the Joint Chiefs of Staff.

Some important gaps appear in the study. The researchers did not have access to the complete files of Presidents or to all the memorandums of their conversations and decisions.

Moreover, there is another important gap in the copy of the Pentagon study obtained by The New York Times: It lacks the section on the secret diplomacy of the Johnson period.

But whatever its limitations, the Pentagon's study discloses a vast amount of new information about the unfolding American commitment to South Vietnam and the way in which the United States engaged itself in that conflict. It is also rich in insights into the workings of government and the reasoning of the men who ran it.

Throughout the narrative there is ample evidence of vigorous, even acrimonious, debate within the Government —far more than Congress, the press and the public were permitted to discover from official pronouncements.

But the Pentagon account and its accompanying documents also reveal that once the basic objective of policy was set, the internal debate on Vietnam from 1950 until mid-1967 dealt almost entirely with how to reach those objectives rather than with the basic direction of policy.

The study related that American governments from the Truman Administration onward felt it necessary to take action to prevent Communist control of South Vietnam. As a rationale for policy, the domino theory — that if South Vietnam fell, other countries would inevitably follow—was repeated in endless variations for nearly two decades.

Confidence and Apprehensions

Especially during the nineteen-sixties, the Pentagon study discloses, the Government was confident that American power—or even the threat of its use—would bring the war under control.

But the study reveals that high officials in the Johnson Administration were troubled by the potential dangers of Chinese Communist intervention and felt the need for self-restraint to avoid provoking Peking, or the Soviet Union, into combat involvement.

As some top policy makers came to question the effectiveness of the American effort in mid-1967, the report shows, their policy papers began not only to seek to limit the military

556

strategies on the ground and in the air but also to worry about the impact of the war on American society.

"A feeling is widely and strongly held that 'the Establishment' is out of its mind," wrote John T. McNaughton, Assistant Secretary of Defense, in a note to Secretary McNamara in early May, 1967. Mr. McNaughton, who three years earlier had been one of the principal planners of the air war against North Vietnam, went on to say:

"The feeling is that we are trying to impose some U.S. image on distant peoples we cannot understand (any more than we can the younger generation here at home), and that we are carrying the thing to absurd lengths. Related to this feeling is the increased polarization that is taking place in the United States with seeds of the worst split in our people in more than a century."

At the end of June, 1967, Mr. McNamara—deeply disillusioned with the war—decided to commission the Pentagon study of Vietnam policy that Mr. McNaughton and other high officials had encouraged him to undertake.

Mr. McNamara's instructions, conveyed orally and evidently in writing as well, were for the researcher to pull together the Pentagon's documentary record and, according to one well-placed former official, to produce an "objective and encyclopedic" study of the American involvement.

Broadest Possible Interpretation

The Pentagon researchers aimed at the broadest possible interpretation of events. They examined not only the policies and motives of American administrations, but also the effectiveness of intelligence, the mechanics and consequences of bureaucratic compromises, the difficulties of imposing American tactics on the South Vietnamese, the governmental uses of the American press, and many other tributaries of their main story.

The authors reveal, for example, that the American intelligence community repeatedly provided the policy makers with what proved to be accurate warnings that desired goals were either unattainable or likely to provoke costly reactions from the enemy. They cite some lapses in the accuracy of reporting and intelligence, but give a generally favorable assessment of the C.I.A. and other intelligence units.

The Pentagon researchers relate many examples of bureaucratic compromise forged by Presidents from the conflicting proposals of their advisers.

In the mid-fifties, they found, the Joint Chiefs of Staff were a restraining force, warning that successful defense of South Vietnam could not be guaranteed under the limits imposed by the 1954 Geneva accords and agreeing to send in American military advisers only, on the insistence of Secretary of State John Foster Dulles.

In the nineteen-sixties, the report found, both Presidents Kennedy and Johnson chose partial measures, overriding advice that some military proposals were valid only as packages and could not be adopted piecemeal.

In examining Washington's constant difficulties with the governments in Saigon, the study found the United States so heavily committed to the regime of the moment and so fearful of instability that it was unable to persuade the South Vietnamese to make the political and economic reforms that Americans deemed necessary to win the allegiance of the people.

Though it ranges widely to explain events, the Pentagon report makes no summary effort to put the blame for the war on any single administration or to find fault with individual officials.

The writers appear to have stood at the political and bureaucratic center of the period, directing their criticisms toward both left and right.

In one section, Senator Eugene J. McCarthy, the antiwar candidate for the 1968 Democratic Presidential nomination, is characterized as "impudent and dovish," and as an "upstart challenger." At another point in the same section the demands of Adm. U.S. Grant Sharp, commander of Pacific forces, for all-out bombing of North Vietnam, are characterized as "fulminations."

For the most part, the writers assumed a calm and unemotional tone, dissecting their materials in detached and academic manner. They ventured to answer key questions only when the evidence was at hand. They found no conclusive answers to some of the most widely asked questions about the war, including these:

¶Precisely how was Ngo Dinh Diem returned to South Vietnam in 1954 from exile and helped to power?

¶Who took the lead in preventing the 1956 Vietnam elections required under the Geneva accords of 1954—Mr. Diem or the Americans?

¶If President Kennedy had lived, would he have led the United States into a full-scale ground war in South Vietnam and an air war against North Vietnam as President Johnson did?

¶Was Secretary of Defense McNamara dismissed for opposing the Johnson strategy in mid-1967 or did he ask to be relieved because of disenchantment with Administration policy?

¶Did President Johnson's cutback of the bombing to the 20th Parallel in 1968 signal a lowering of American objectives for the war or was it merely an effort to buy more time and patience from a war-weary American public?

The research project was organized in the Pentagon's office of International Security Affairs—I.S.A., as it is known to Government insiders—the politico-military affairs branch, whose head is the third-ranking official in the Defense Department. This was Assistant Secretary McNaughton when the study was commissioned and Assistant Secretary Paul C. Warnke when the study was completed.

'It Remained McNamara's Study'

In the fall of 1968, it was transmitted to Mr. Warnke, who reportedly "signed off" on it. Former officials say this meant that he acknowledged completion of the work without endorsing its contents and forwarded it to Mr. Clifford.

Although it had been completed during Mr. Clifford's tenure, "in everyone's mind it always remained Mr. McNamara's study," one official said.

Because of its extreme sensitivity, very few copies were reproduced—from 6 to 15, by various accounts. One copy was delivered by hand to Mr. McNamara, then president of the World Bank. His reaction is not known, but at least one other former policy maker was reportedly displeased by the study's candor.

Other copies were said to have been provided to President Johnson, the State Department and President Nixon's staff, as well as to have been kept for Pentagon files.

The authors, mostly working part-time over several months, were middle-level officials drawn from I.S.A., Systems Analysis, and the military staffs in the Pentagon, or lent by the State Department or White House staff. Probably two-thirds of the group had worked on Vietnam for the Government at one time or another.

Both the writing and editing were described as group efforts, through individuals with academic qualifications as historians, political scientists and the like were in charge of various sections.

For their research, the Pentagon depended primarily on the files of Secretary McNamara and Mr. McNaughton. William P. Bundy, former Assistant Secretary of State for Far Eastern Affairs, provided some of his files.

For extended periods, probably the most serious limitation of the Pentagon study is the lack of access to White House archives. The researchers did possess the Presidential decision papers that normally circulated to high Pentagon officials, plus White House messages to commanders or ambassadors in Saigon. These provide insight into Presidential moods and motives, but only intermittently.

An equally important handicap is that the Pentagon researchers generally lacked records of the oral discussions of the National Security Council or the most intimate gatherings of Presidents with their closest advisers, where decisions were often reached.

As the authors themselves remark, it is common practice for the final recommendations drafted before a key Presidential decision to be written to the President's spoken specifications on the basis of his reactions to earlier proposals. The missing link is often the meeting of the Administration's inner circle.

Also, because the Pentagon study draws almost entirely on internal Government papers, and primarily papers that circulated through the Defense Department, the picture of so important a figure as Secretary of State Dean Rusk remains shadowy. Mr. Rusk was known as a man who rarely committed himself to paper and who, especially during the Johnson Administration, saved his most sensitive advice for solitary talks with the President.

In the late months of the Johnson Administration, the lack of records of such meetings is a considerable weakness because, as the survey comments, Mr. Johnson operated a split-level Government. Only his most intimate advisers were aware of the policy moves he was contemplating, and some of the most important officials at the second level of government—Assistant Secretaries of State and Defense—were late to learn the drift of the President's thinking.

The Pentagon account notes that at times the highest Administration officials not only kept information about their real intentions from the press and Congress but also kept secret from the Government bureaucracy the real motives for their written recommendations or actions.

"The lesson in this," one Pentagon analyst observes, "is that the rationales given in such pieces of paper (intended for fairly wide circulation among the bureaucracy, as opposed to tightly held memoranda limited to those closest to the decision maker), do not reliably indicate why recommendations were made the way they were." The words in parentheses are the analyst's.

Another omission is the absence of any extended discussion of military or political responsibility for such matters as civilian casualties or the restraints imposed by the rules of land warfare.

Necessarily Fragmented Account

The approach of the writers varies markedly from section to section. Some of the writers are analytical and incisive. Others offer narrative compendiums of the most important available documents for their periods, with little comment or interpretation.

As a bureaucratic history, this account is necessarily fragmented. The writers either lacked time or did not choose to provide a coherent, integrated summary analysis for each of the four administrations that became involved in Vietnam from 1950 to 1968.

The Pentagon account divides the Kennedy period, for example, into five sections—dealing with the key decisions of 1961, the strategic-hamlet programs, the buildup of the American advisory mission in Vietnam, the development of plans for phased American withdrawal, and the coup d'état that ousted President Diem.

In the Johnson era, four simultaneous stories are told in separate sections—the land war in South Vietnam, the air war against the North, political relations with successive South Vietnamese governments and the secret diplomatic search for negotiations. There is some overlapping, but no single section tries to summarize or draw together the various strands.

The overall effect of the study, nonetheless, is to provide a vast storehouse of new information—the most complete and informative central archive available thus far on the Vietnam era.

Vietnam Archive: Pentagon Study Traces 3 Decades of Growing U. S. Involvement

By NEIL SHEEHAN

A massive study of how the United States went to war in Indochina, conducted by the Pentagon three years ago, demonstrates that four administrations progressively developed a sense of commitment to a non-Communist Vietnam, a readiness to fight the North to protect the South, and an ultimate frustration with this effort—to a much greater extent than their public statements acknowledged at the time.

The 3,000-page analysis, to which 4,000 pages of official documents are appended, was commissioned by Secretary of Defense Robert S. McNamara and covers the American involvement in Southeast Asia from World War II to mid-1968—the start of the peace talks in Paris after President Lyndon B. Johnson had set a limit on further military commitments and revealed his intention to retire. Most of the study and many of the appended documents have been obtained by The New York Times and will be described and presented in a series of articles beginning today.

Though far from a complete history, even at 2.5 million words, the study forms a great archive of government decision-making on Indochina over three decades. The study led its 30 to 40 authors and researchers to many broad conclusions and specific findings, including the following:

¶That the Truman Administration's decision to give military aid to France in her colonial war against the Communist-led Vietminh "directly involved" the United States in Vietnam and "set" the course of American policy.

¶That the Eisenhower Administration's decision to rescue a fledgling South Vietnam from a Communist takeover and attempt to undermine the new Communist regime of North Vietnam gave the Administration a "direct role in the ultimate breakdown of the Geneva settlement" for Indochina in 1954.

¶That the Kennedy Administration, though ultimately spared from major escalation decisions by the death of its leader, transformed a policy of "limited-risk gamble," which it inherited, into a "broad commitment" that left President Johnson with a choice between more war and withdrawal.

¶That the Johnson Administration, though the President was reluctant and hesitant to take the final decisions, intensified the covert warfare against North Vietnam and began planning in the spring of 1964 to wage overt war, a full year before it publicly revealed the depth of its involvement and its fear of defeat.

¶That this campaign of growing clandestine military pressure through 1964 and the expanding program of bombing North Vietnam in 1965 were begun despite the judgment of the Government's intelligence community that the measures would not cause Hanoi to cease its support of the Vietcong insurgency in the South, and that the bombing was deemed militarily ineffective within a few months.

¶That these four succeeding administrations built up the American political, military and psychological stakes in Indochina, often more deeply than they realized at the time, with large-scale military equipment to the French in 1950; with acts of sabotage and terror warfare against North Vietnam beginning in 1954; with moves that encouraged and abetted the overthrow of President Ngo Dinh Diem of South Vietnam in 1963; with plans, pledges and threats of further action that sprang to life in the Tonkin Gulf clashes in August, 1964; with the careful preparation of public opinion for the years of open warfare that were to follow; and with the calculation in 1965, as the planes and troops were openly committed to sustained combat, that neither accommodation inside South Vietnam nor early negotiations with North Vietnam would achieve the desired result.

The Pentagon study also ranges beyond such historical judgments. It suggests that the predominant American interest was at first containment of Communism and later the defense of the power, influence and prestige of the United States, in both stages irrespective of conditions in Vietnam.

And it reveals a great deal about the ways in which several administrations conducted their business on a fateful course, with much new information about the roles of dozens of senior officials of both major political parties and a whole generation of military commanders.

The Pentagon study was divided into chronological and thematic chapters of narrative and analysis, each with its own documentation attached. The Times —which has obtained all but one of nearly 40 volumes—has collated these materials into major segments of varying chronological length, from one that broadly covers the two decades before 1960 to one that deals intensively with the agonizing debate in the weeks following the 1968 Tet offensive.

The months from the beginning of 1964 to the Tonkin Gulf incident in August were a pivotal period, the study makes clear, and The Times begins its series with this phase.

The Covert War

The Pentagon papers disclose that in this phase the United States had been mounting clandestine military attacks against North Vietnam and planning to obtain a Congressional resolution that the Administration regarded as the equivalent of a declaration of war. The papers make it clear that these far-reaching measures were not improvised in the heat of the Tonkin crisis.

When the Tonkin incident occurred, the Johnson Administration did not reveal these clandestine attacks, and pushed the previously prepared resolution through both houses of Congress on Aug. 7.

Within 72 hours, the Administration, drawing on a prepared plan, then secretly sent a Canadian emissary to Hanoi. He warned Premier Pham Van Dong that the resolution meant North Vietnam must halt the Communist-led insurgencies in South Vietnam and Laos or "suffer the consequences."

The section of the Pentagon study dealing with the internal debate, planning and action in the Johnson Administration from the beginning of 1964 to the August clashes between North Vietnamese PT boats and American destroyers—portrayed as a critical period when the goundwork was laid for the wider war that followed—also reveals that the covert military operations had become so extensive by August, 1964, that Thai pilots flying American T-28 fighter planes apparently bombed and strafed North Vietnamese villages near the Laotian border on Aug. 1 and 2.

Moreover, it reports that the Administration was able to order retaliatory air strikes on less than six hours' notice during the Tonkin incident because planning had progressed so far that a list of targets was available for immediate choice. The target list had been drawn up in May, the study re-

---

The accompanying article, as well as the rest of the series on the Pentagon's study of the Vietnam war, was a result of investigative reporting by Neil Sheehan of The New York Times Washington bureau. The series has been written by Mr. Sheehan, Hedrick Smith, E. W. Kenworthy and Fox Butterfield. The articles and documents were edited by Gerald Gold, Allan M. Siegal and Samuel Abt.

---

ports, along with a draft of the Congressional resolution—all as part of a proposed "scenario" that was to build toward openly acknowledged air attacks on North Vietnam.

Simultaneously, the papers reveal, Secretary McNamara and the Joint Chiefs of Staff also arranged for the deployment of air strike forces to Southeast Asia for the opening phases of the bombing campaign. Within hours of the retaliatory air strikes on Aug. 4 and three days before the passage of the Congressional resolution, the squadrons began their planned moves.

'Progressively Escalating Pressure'

What the Pentagon papers call "an elaborate program of covert military operations against the state of North Vietnam" began on Feb. 1, 1964, under the code name Operation Plan 34A.

President Johnson ordered the program, on the recommendation of Secretary McNamara, in the hope, held very faint by the intelligence community, that "progressively escalating pressure" from the clandestine attacks might eventually force Hanoi to order the Vietcong guerrillas in Vietnam and the Pathet Lao in Laos to halt their insurrections.

In a memorandum to the President on Dec. 21, 1963, after a two-day trip to Vietnam, Mr. McNamara remarked that the plans, drawn up by the Central Intelligence Agency station and the military command in Saigon, were "an excellent job."

"They present a wide variety of sabotage and psychological operations against North Vietnam from which I believe we should aim to select those that provide maximum pressure with minimum risk," Mr. McNamara wrote. [See text.]

President Johnson, in this period, showed a preference for steps that would remain "noncommitting" to combat, the study found. But weakness in South Vietnam and Communist advances kept driving the planning process. This, in turn, caused the Saigon Government and American officials in Saigon to demand ever more action.

Through 1964, the 34A operations ranged from flights over North Vietnam by U-2 spy planes and kidnappings of North Vietnamese citizens for intelligence information, to parachuting sabotage and psychological-warfare teams into the North, commando raids from the sea to blow up rail and highway bridges and the bombardment of North Vietnamese coastal installations by PT boats.

These "destructive undertakings," as they were described in a report to the President on Jan. 2 1964, from Maj. Gen. Victor H. Krulak of the Marine Corps, were designed "to result in substantial destruction, economic loss and harassment." The tempo and magnitude of the strikes were designed to rise in three phases through 1964 to "targets identified with North Vietnam's economic and industrial well-being."

The clandestine operations were directed for the President by Mr. McNamara through a section of the Joint Chiefs organization called the Office of the Special Assistant for Counterinsurgency and Special Activities. The study says that Mr. McNamara was kept regularly informed of planned and conducted raids by memorandums from General Krulak, who first held the position of special assistant, and then from Maj. Gen. Rollen H. Anthis of the Air Force, who succeeded him in February, 1964. The Joint Chiefs themselves periodically evaluated the operations for Mr. McNamara.

Secretary of State Dean Rusk was also informed, if in less detail.

The attacks were given "interagency clearance" in Washington, the study says, by coordinating them with the State Department and the Central Intelligence Agency, including advance monthly schedules of the raids from General Anthis.

The Pentagon account and the documents show that William P. Bundy, the

Assistant Secretary of State for Far Eastern Affairs, and John T. McNaughton, head of the Pentagon's politico-military operations as the Assistant Secretary of Defense for International Security Affairs, were the senior civilian officials who supervised the distribution of the schedules and the other aspects of interagency coordination for Mr. McNamara and Mr. Rusk.

The analyst notes that the 34A program differed in a significant respect from the relatively low-level and unsuccessful intelligence and sabotage operations that the C.I.A. had earlier been carrying out in North Vietnam.

Air Raids Were Planned Jointly

The 34A attacks were a military effort under the control in Saigon of Gen. Paul D. Harkins, chief of the United States Military Assistance Command there. He ran them through a special branch of his command called the Studies and Observations Group. It drew up the advance monthly schedules for approval in Washington. Planning was done jointly with the South Vietnamese and it was they or "hired personnel," apparently Asian mercenaries, who performed the raids, but General Harkins was in charge.

The second major segment of the Administration's covert war against North Vietnam consisted of air operations in Laos. A force of propeller-driven T-28 fighter-bombers, varying from about 25 to 40 aircraft, had been organized there. The planes bore Laotian Air Force markings, but only some belonged to that air force. The rest were manned by pilots of Air America (a pseudo-private airline run by the C.I.A.) and by Thai pilots under the control of Ambassador Leonard Unger.

Reconnaissance flights by regular United States Air Force and Navy jets, code-named Yankee Team, gathered photographic intelligence for bombing raids by the T-28's against North Vietnamese and Pathet Lao troops in Laos.

The Johnson Administration gradually stepped up these air operations in Laos through the spring and summer of 1964 in what became a kind of preview of the bombing of the North. The escalation occurred both because of ground advances by the North Vietnamese and the Pathet Lao and because of the Administration's desire to bring more military pressure against North Vietnam.

As the intensity of the T-28 strikes rose, they crept closer to the North Vietnamese border. The United States Yankee Team jets moved from high-altitude reconnaissance at the beginning of the year to low-altitude reconnaissance in May. In June, armed escort jets were added to the reconnaissance missions. The escort jets began to bomb and strafe North Vietnamese and Pathet Lao troops and installations whenever the reconnaissance planes were fired upon.

The destroyer patrols in the Gulf of Tonkin, code-named De Soto patrols, were the third element in the covert military pressures against North Vietnam. While the purpose of the patrols was mainly psychological, as a show of force, the destroyers collected the kind of intelligence on North Vietnamese warning radars and coastal defenses that would be useful to 34A raiding parties or, in the event of a bombing campaign, to pilots. The first patrol was conducted by the destroyer Craig without incident in February and March, in the early days of the 34A operations.

Separate Chain of Command

The analyst states that before the August Tonkin incident there was no attempt to involve the destroyers with the 34A attacks or to use the ships as bait for North Vietnamese retaliation. The patrols were run through a separate naval chain of command.

Although the highest levels of the Administration sent the destroyers into the gulf while the 34A raids were taking place, the Pentagon study, as part of its argument that a deliberate provocation was not intended, in effect says that the Administration did not believe that the North Vietnamese would dare to attack the ships.

But the study makes it clear that the physical presence of the destroyers provided the elements for the Tonkin clash. And immediately after the reprisal air strikes, the Joint Chiefs of Staff and Assistant Secretary of Defense McNaughton put forward a "provocation strategy" proposing to repeat the clash as a pretext for bombing the North.

Of the three elements of the covert war, the analyst cites the 34A raids as the most important. The "unequivocal" American responsibility for them "carried with it an implicit symbolic and psychological intensification of the U.S. commitment," he writes. "A firebreak had been crossed."

The fact that the intelligence community and even the Joint Chiefs gave the program little chance of compelling Hanoi to stop the Vietcong and the Pathet Lao, he asserts, meant that "a demand for more was stimulated and an expectation of more was aroused."

Warning by the Joint Chiefs

On Jan. 22, 1964, a week before the 34A raids started, the Joint Chiefs warned Mr. McNamara in a memorandum signed by the Chairman, Gen. Maxwell D. Taylor, that while "we are wholly in favor of executing the covert actions against North Vietnam . . . it would be idle to conclude that these efforts will have a decisive effect" on Hanoi's will to support the Vietcong.

The Joint Chiefs said the Administration "must make ready to conduct increasingly bolder actions," including "aerial bombing of key North Vietnam targets, using United States resources under Vietnamese cover," sending American ground troops to South Vietnam and employing "United States forces as necessary in direct actions against North Vietnam."

And after a White House strategy meeting on Feb. 20, President Johnson ordered that "contingency planning for pressures against North Vietnam should be speeded up."

"Particular attention should be given to shaping such pressures so as to produce the maximum credible deterrent effect on Hanoi," the order said.

The impelling force behind the Administration's desire to step up the action during this period was its recognition of the steady deterioration in the positions of the pro-American governments in Laos and South Vietnam, and the corresponding weakening of the United States hold on both countries. North Vietnamese and Pathet Lao advances in Laos were seen as having a direct impact on the morale of the anti-Communist forces in South Vietnam, the primary American concern.

This deterioration was also concealed from Congress and the public as much as possible to provide the Administration with maximum flexibility to determine its moves as it chose from behind the scenes.

The United States found itself particularly unable to cope with the Vietcong insurgency, first through the Saigon military regime of Gen. Duong Van Minh and later through that of Gen. Nguyen Khanh, who seized power in a coup d'état on Jan. 30, 1964. Accordingly, attention focused more and more on North Vietnam as "the root of the problem," in the words of the Joint Chiefs.

Walt W. Rostow, the dominant intellectual of the Administration, had given currency to this idea and provided the theoretical framework for escalation. His concept, first enunciated in a speech at Fort Bragg, N.C., in 1961, was that a revolution could be dried up by cutting off external sources of support and supply.

Where North Vietnam was concerned, Mr. Rostow had evolved another theory —that a credible threat to bomb the industry Hanoi had so painstakingly constructed out of the ruins of the French Indochina War would be enough to frighten the country's leaders into ordering the Vietcong to halt their activities in the South.

'No Longer a Guerrilla Fighter'

In a memorandum on Feb. 13, 1964, Mr. Rostow told Secretary of State Rusk that President Ho Chi Minh "has an industrial complex to protect: he is no longer a guerrilla fighter with nothing to lose."

The Administration was firmly convinced from interceptions of radio traffic between North Vietnam and the guerrillas in the South that Hanoi controlled and directed the Vietcong. Intelligence analyses of the time stated, however, that "the primary sources of Communist strength in South Vietnam are indigenous," arising out of the revolutionary social aims of the Communists and their identification with the nationalist cause during the independence struggle against France in the nineteen-fifties.

The study shows that President Johnson and most of his key advisers would not accept this intelligence analysis that bombing the North would have no lasting effect on the situation in the South, although there was division — even among those who favored a bombing campaign if necessary—over the extent to which Vietcong fortunes were dependent on the infiltration of men and arms from North Vietnam.

William Bundy and Mr. Rusk mentioned on several occasions the need to obtain more evidence of this infiltration to build a case publicly for stronger actions against North Vietnam.

COURT STEP LIKELY

Return of Documents Asked in Telegram To Publisher

By MAX FRANKEL
Special to The New York Times

WASHINGTON, June 14—Attorney General John N. Mitchell asked The New York Times this evening to refrain from further publication of documents drawn from a Pentagon study of the Vietnam war on the ground that such disclosures would cause "irreparable injury to the defense interests of the United States."

If the paper refused, another Justice Department official said, the Government would try to forbid further publication by court action tomorrow.

The Times refused to halt publication voluntarily.

The Justice Department's request and intention to seek a court enjoinder were conveyed by Robert C. Mardian, Assistant Attorney General in charge of the internal security division, to Harding F. Bancroft, executive vice president of The Times.

Spoke by Telephone

They spoke by telephone at about 7:30 P.M., which was some two hours before tomorrow's first edition of the paper was scheduled to go to press with the third installment of the articles about the Pentagon study.

An hour later, a telegram from Mr. Mitchell asked that The Times halt further publication of the material and return the documents to the Pentagon.

The Times then issued the following statement:

"We have received the telegram from the Attorney General asking The Times to cease further publication of the Pentagon's Vietnam study.

"The Times must respectfully decline the request of the Attorney General, believing that it is in the interest of the people of this country to be informed of the material contained in this series of articles.

"We have also been informed of the Attorney General's intention to seek an injunction against further publication. We believe that it is properly a matter for the courts to decide. The Times will oppose

any request for an injunction for the same reason that led us to publish the articles in the first place. We will of course abide by the final decision of the court."

Telegram From Mitchell

The telegram from Attorney General Mitchell, addressed to Arthur Ochs Sulzberger, president and publisher of The Times, said:

"I have been advised by the Secretary of Defense that the material published in The New York Times on June 13, 14, 1971, captioned 'Key Texts From Pentagon's Vietnam Study' contains information relating to the national defense of the United States and bears a top secret classification.

"As such, publication of this information is directly prohibited by the provisions of the Espionage Law, Title 18, United States Code, Section 793.

"Moreover, further publication of information of this character will cause irreparable injury to the defense interests of the United States.

"Accordingly, I respectfully request that you publish no further information of this character and advise me that you have made arrangements for the return of these documents to the Department of Defense."

Espionage Law Cited

The section cited by the Attorney General is labeled "gathering, transmitting or losing defense information."

The laws governing the disclosure of secret documents were described earlier in the day by a Pentagon spokesman as containing "certain ambiguities" about whether they apply to publications or only to their sources of information. Government lawyers were divided on the matter, the spokesman indicated, because there appeared to be no precedent for application of the law to a publication.

Both Mr. Mitchell and the Pentagon spokesman, Jerry W. Friedheim, cited sections of the Espionage and Censorship Chapter of the Federal criminal code. Mr. Friedheim mentioned Section 798, entitled "Disclosure of Classified Information." The Attorney General mentioned Section 793, headed "Gathering, Transmitting or Losing Defense Information."

Much of Section 793 refers to spying on defense installations and to obtaining code books, blueprints, maps or other defense-related documents.

Selections From Section

It goes on to state that "whoever having unauthorized possession of, access to, or control over any document, writing,

code book . . . or information relating to the national defense which information the possessor has reason to believe could be used to the injury of the United States or to the advantage of any foreign nation, willfully communicates, delivers, transmits . . . the same to any person not entitled to receive it, or willfully retains the same and fails to deliver it to the officer or employee of the United States entitled to receive it . . . shall be fined not more than $10,000 or imprisoned not more than ten years, or both."

The Justice Department's request conveyed by Mr. Mardian was the first direct contact between the Government and The Times about the publication of the Pentagon papers.

The first group of materials, published in the Sunday issue of the paper, dealt with the clandestine warfare carried on against North Vietnam before the Tonkin Gulf incident in August, 1964. The second installment, in this morning's issue, covered the Johnson Administration's decision to begin open bombing of North Vietnam in February, 1965.

Before Mr. Mardian's call, the Administration had said only that the Justice Department was investigating the disclosures, at the request of the Defense Department.

Laird Sees 'Violation'

Secretary of Defense Melvin R. Laird said the disclosure "violated the security regulations of the United States."

The Secretary implied a difference between the violation of security regulations—by officials subject to these regulations—and violation of law. He said he had asked the Justice Department to determine the legal implications.

This morning, a formal Pentagon statement expressed concern about "this violation of security" but left determination of legal action to the Justice Department.

At the Justice Department this afternoon, a spokesman said the subject was still under consideration by Attorney General Mitchell. "We have yet to determine whether or not there is something to investigate," the spokesman added, explaining that Mr. Mitchell was dealing during the day with a statement on housing discrimination and had not yet considered the matter fully.

As of that time, there was said to have been no order for any Justice investigation, but other agencies of government reported intensive inquiries into the affair.

Authority Unchallenged

Mr. Mitchell, Secretary Laird and White House officials began to confer on Sunday on the disclosures in The Times.

No official here challenged the authenticity of the account of the Pentagon study and of the documents printed in The

Times. Only a few members of Congress commented on their content.

The White House referred to the Pentagon all questions on the circumstances of the disclosure. Under vigorous questioning about the documents, it chose to emphasize that President Nixon had developed a "new Vietnam policy" and decided when he took office in 1969 "not to engage ourselves in a continuation or justification" of the policies of earlier administrations, which are the subject of the Pentagon papers.

Ronald L. Ziegler, the President's press secretary, said that a copy of the 1967-68 Pentagon study was brought to the White House this morning from the Defense Department.

Although Mr. Nixon and his aides were said to be unfamiliar with this "internal" archive, Mr. Ziegler stressed that the basic documents and information contained in them had been available to the new Administration and were fully considered in its own policy review in early 1969.

Asked whether The Times had informed the White House of its publishing plans, Mr. Ziegler said the newspaper "did not at any time check with us." Asked whether the President was concerned about the publication of secret documents, he replied:

"I'm not going to build up, by White House comment, the exposure of classified information."

The only formal public statement was that by the Pentagon referring the matter to the Justice Department. This came after Secretary Laird was drawn into a discussion of the affair by Senator Stuart Symington, Democrat of Missouri, at a hearing of the Senate Foreign Relations Committee on foreign aid.

Data Called Still 'Sensitive'

Senator Symington announced his intention to propose a "full examination of the origins of the war" for the benefit of future generations. Mr. Laird opposed the idea, arguing that a debate of the past "would not serve the interests of the country and would not help us disengage from Vietnam."

Stating a theme that he apparently hoped would dominate the reaction to The Times' disclosures, Mr. Laird said that "the divisions caused by debate of the past actions would not serve a useful purpose today." He has been trying to shift focus away from "Why Vietnam?" to the means of disengaging in an honorable way, he declared.

Mr. Laird said the disclosure of the Pentagon papers was "unauthorized" and "violates the security regulations of our Government." Although the study covers information only to 1968, he added, the information "remains sensitive" and its publication does not serve "a useful purpose." The Secretary

561

said the documents would remain classified and would not be made available to the Foreign Relations Committee.

Senator Symington observed that the committee had tried several times to obtain the material, on a confidential basis. He said it was "shocking" that Congress had been kept ignorant of the materials and that even now he had to read about them in the newspapers.

Asked whether he knew who might have passed the materials to The Times, Mr. Laird said, "No, I don't yet know." But since there were so few copies, he added, "it won't be hard to track down whoever was responsible.

"This is highly sensitive information and should not have been made public," he declared.

Legal Distinction Implied

Shortly afterward, Mr. Friedheim, the Pentagon briefing officer, read a statement that had been worked out after a full day of consultation among Mr. Mitchell, Mr. Laird, some White House officials and lawyers of the Defense and Justice Departments. Inferentially, the statement made a distinction between violation of Government security regulations and possible violations of law. It said:

"The Department of Defense must be and is concerned about the disclosure of publication of highly classified information affecting national security.

"The material remains classified and sensitive despite the fact that it covers a period that ended in 1968.

"It is our responsibility to call this violation of security to the attention of the Justice Department. We have done so.

"The Government has the responsibility to determine what individual or individuals, if any, violated the laws relating to national security information by unauthorized disclosure of classified material."

Mr. Friedheim said officials of the Justice and Defense De-

partments had had various discussions of the matter, face to face and also by telephone, since Sunday, when The Times began publication of its series of articles.

He said the relevant law was Title 18 of the United States Code, Section 798, noting that it contained "certain ambiguities" as to whether it applies to publications or only to their sources of secret information.

"Some lawyers are of the opinion that the publication is liable to prosecution as well as the official [source]," the spokesman said. "but there appears no precedent to establish that point. Justice is studying the whole matter to decide who, if anyone, to charge with law violation."

Classified Data Defined

The section that he cited states: "Whoever knowingly and willfully communicates, furnishes, transmits, or otherwise makes available to an unauthorized person, or publishes, or uses in any manner prejudicial to the safety or interest of the United States or for the benefit of any foreign government to the detriment of the United States any classified information . . . shall be fined not more than $10,000 or imprisoned not more than 10 years, or both."

The section contains a list and definition of classified information as bearing on codes, weapons and materials, intelligence activities and material obtained from the communications of foreign governments.

Mr. Friedheim said the Pentagon had determined that there were "a dozen or so" copies of the papers and that half of these, at the Defense Department, "have remained under extremely tight control." He said he did not believe the Pentagon's copies had either been duplicated or shown to unauthorized persons. He refused to say where the other copies had been kept.

7,000 Pages of Material

There is a possibility, the spokesman remarked, that unauthorized duplicate copies were made at some point, "or even that a set of the study was stolen at some point." The materials run to about 7,000 pages of analysis and documentation.

As a practical matter, Mr. Friedheim said, the Pentagon regards individuals with authorized clearance to handle classified information as primarily responsible for the protection of such information.

He said Secretary Laird had been aware of the secret Pentagon study since he came into office in 1969 and had even once referred to its existence in public testimony before the Senate Foreign Relations Committee.

The spokesman then emphasized again Mr. Laird's "philosophical" conviction that it was more important to consider ways of disengaging from Vietnam than to "rake over the coals" of past policies.

At the State Department, a spokesman said he could not comment "on the accuracy of —or make any useful comment on the substance of — these papers until we have had an opportunity to check the original."

Checking was difficult, the spokesman, Charles W. Bray 3d, said this morning, because the department had not had time to locate its copy of the report, or even to determine whether it had one.

Several hours later, according to Mr. Bray, the papers were found in personal files that had been left behind by William P. Bundy, who served as Assistant Secretary of State for East Asian and Pacific Affairs during the Johnson Administration.

Secretary of State William P. Rogers had no comment on the matter today, but he is likely to be asked about the materials at a news conference scheduled for tomorrow.

In Congress, there were only a few other comments on the matter and no indication that disclosure of the Vietnam materials would significantly influence the Senate vote Wednesday on legislation that would require withdrawal of American forces from the war zone by the end of this year.

Materials Called 'Instructive'

Senator George S. McGovern of South Dakota, a cosponsor of that measure and candidate for the Democratic Presidential nomination, said the documents told a story of "almost incredible deception" of Congress and the American people by the highest officials in Government, including the President. He said that he did not see how any Senator could ever again believe it was safe to permit the executive branch to make foreign policy alone, and added:

AT VIETNAM HEARING: Secretary of Defense Melvin R. Laird and Senator Stuart Symington at Foreign Relations Committee session held yesterday.

"We would make a serious mistake to assume the kind of deception revealed in these documents began and ended with the Johnson Administration."

Senator Hugh Scott of Pennsylvania, the Republican leader, said that the "release" of the documents was "a bad thing, it's a federal crime." But he described their content as "very instructive and somewhat shocking."

"I think the American people have never been told as much as they could digest about the war until President Nixon assumed office," he added. "He has been more than candid. This President has taken the people into his confidence more than anyone else."

Asked whether The Times should continue publication of its articles, Senator Scott said the paper would have to decide "on its good judgment."

PRINTING OF PAPERS ASSESSED: Senator George S. McGovern, left, South Dakota Democrat, said Vietnam documents told story of "deception." Senate Minority Leader Hugh Scott called "release" of study a "crime."

Representative Paul N. Mc Closkey Jr. of California, who has talked of challenging Mr Nixon for the Presidency in th Republican primaries next year discussed The Times article and underlying Pentagon paper on the floor of the House.

Deception Is Charged

He said "the issue of truthfulness in Government is a problem as serious as that of ending the war itself." He also complained of "deceptive," "incomplete" and "misleading" briefings given to him during a recent visit to Southeast Asia, often, he said, with officers who knew the statements to be incorrect standing mute in his presence.

"This deception is not a matter of protecting secret information from the enemy," Mr. McCloskey said. "The intention is to conceal information from the people of the United State as if we were the enemy."

Robert S. McNamara, the former Secretary of Defense, who commissioned the Pentagon study in 1967, was reported to have sent the copy later delivered to him to the National Archives.

Mr. McNamara turned down several invitations to make a public comment today on the ground that this was inappropriate to his present duties as President of the International Bank for Reconstruction and Development—the World Bank.

Goldwater Says He Knew of War Plan

By RICHARD HALLORAN
Special to The New York Times

WASHINGTON, June 14— Senator Barry Goldwater, the Republican Presidential candidate in 1964, said today that he had known one month before the clashes in the Gulf of Tonkin that President Johnson was planning to widen the war in Vietnam.

"I did not know the exact details," the Senator said in a television interview, "but I knew that a scenario was written that would give an excuse for war."

He also said that he knew during his Presidential campaign that Mr. Johnson was planning to bomb North Vietnam and to send American soldiers to fight in South Vietnam.

"See, I was being called trigger - happy, warmonger, bomb-happy, and all the time Johnson was saying he'd never send American boys," the Senator said. "I knew damn well he would."

The Senator was interviewed by Marvin Kalb for the Columbia Broadcasting System and by Paul Duke for the National Broadcasting Company.

Mr. Goldwater was asked to comment on articles being published in The New York Times on a secret study, made in the Pentagon, on American participation in the Vietnam war.

Mr. Goldwater, who was re-

Associated Press
Senator Barry Goldwater

elected to the Senate in 1968, was asked whether he thought the Johnson Administration had lied to the American people. "I would have to say yes," the Senator replied.

"It was too bad that the President would not level with the American people," Mr. Goldwater added. "It would have been better for the American people to have known about it."

A spokesman for the Senator, in response to inquiries after the television interview, said

that Mr. Goldwater had had access to some information as a member of the Armed Services Committee. He was also then a brigadier general in an active reserve unit and had many friends in the military who gave him bits of information, the spokesman said.

Security Involved

One unit commander, for instance, called the Senator to tell him that he was being ordered to Southeast Asia but that his command was not properly equipped. The spokesman said that the Senator was asked whether he could do something about it.

The spokesman said that Senator Goldwater was convinced that other members of the Armed Services Committee had come to the same conclusions that he had. He did not name them.

The spokesman said that Mr. Goldwater did not use the information in the Presidential campaign because he felt he did not have sufficient credibility to stand up to the Commander in Chief on such a serious charge.

Moreover, the spokesman said, the Senator knew that the security of American military forces was involved. He said that the Senator believes in a certain amount of secrecy when a strategic military operation is being mapped.

June 15, 1971

Court Here Refuses to Order Return of Documents Now

By FRED P. GRAHAM

United States District Judge Murray I. Gurfein yesterday ordered The New York Times to halt publication of material from a secret Pentagon study of the Vietnam war for four days. Argument on publication thereafter will be heard Friday.

The judge granted a request by the Justice Department for temporary relief, but he gave no hint as to how he would eventually rule. He also refused to order The Times to return the massive report immediately to the Government.

Declaring that the case could be an important one in the history of relations between the Government and the press, Judge Gurfein said that any temporary harm done to The Times by his order "is far out-

weighed by the irreparable harm that could be done to the interests of the United States" if more articles and documents in the series were published while the case was in progress.

The Times, in a statement issued after the hearing, said:

"The Times will comply with the restraining order issued by Judge Murray I. Gurfein. The Times will present its arguments against a permanent injunction at the hearing scheduled for Friday."

Lawyers for The Times and the Justice Department told the judge, at the proceedings in the Federal District Court House at Foley Square, that this appeared to be the first time in the nation's history that a newspaper was being restrained by a court from publishing an article.

Meanwhile, the Justice Department disclosed in Washington that the Federal Bureau of Investigation was investigating possible violations of

federal criminal laws in connection with publication of the secret documents.

The bureau was known to be checking all who had access to the document, of which Justice Department sources said there were 15 copies.

Judge Gurfein, in his first day on the bench after having taken his oath of office last week, acted upon the Justice Department's argument that the publication of further articles by The Times would cause serious injury to the nation's international relations.

The 63-year-old judge deferred until Friday's hearing a decision on the Government's request that The Times be ordered immediately to return the voluminous documents from which its Vietnam series has been drawn.

Order Expires Saturday

The temporary restraining order issued by Judge Gurfein yesterday expires at 1 P.M. Saturday.

His action came a day after Attorney General John N. Mitchell had requested that The Times cease publishing the documents and The Times had refused to do so voluntarily.

Yesterday afternoon, the Justice Department filed a civil suit

seeking to permanently enjoin The Times and 22 of its officers, editors and reporters from going forward with the series of articles and documents on the origins of the Indochina war. Three installments had been published and The Times had said that the series was to continue.

Word filtered through the city's legal community yesterday that the Government had

Associated Press
Murray I. Gurfein, Federal judge, issued order.

563

requested an afternoon hearing on a temporary restraining order against The Times, and the courtroom was packed—mostly with young lawyers and spectators — when the mustached judge took his seat in Room 605 of the United States Court House.

The arguments pitted a 30-year-old staff member of the United States Attorney's office, Michael D. Hess, against Prof. Alexander M. Bickel of the Yale Law School, a 46-year-old constitutional authority who has been mentioned as a possible Supreme Court nominee. Prof. Bickel represented The Times and its personnel.

The gist of the Government's argument was that The Times had violated a statute that makes it a crime for persons having "unauthorized possession" of Government documents to disclose their contents under circumstances that "could be used to the injury of the United States or to the advantage of any foreign nation."

In his argument, Mr. Hess asserted that "serious injuries are being inflicted on our foreign relations, to the benefit of other nations opposed to our form of government." He told the judge that Secretary of State William P. Rogers had said that several friendly nations had expressed concern over the disclosures in the articles.

With the Government facing the prospect of "irreparable injury" in its international relations, Mr. Hess said, The Times should be required to suffer a "slight delay" in its publication schedule until the case could be heard on Friday.

Otherwise, he said, the case would be mooted by publication of the material before a decision could be reached.

Professor Bickel, a tanned,

dapper man in a brown suit and blue shirt, replied that this was a "classic case of censorship" that is forbidden by the First Amendment's free-press guarantee. He also insisted that the statute being invoked by the Government was an anti-espionage law that had never been intended by Congress to be used against the press.

The law, Title 18 of the United States Code, Section 793, provides for a maximum punishment of 10 years' imprisonment and a $10,000 fine against:

"Whoever having unauthorized possession of, access to, or control over any document . . . relating to the national defense, or information relating to the national defense which information the possessor has reason to believe could be used to the injury of the United States or to the advantage of any foreign nation, willfully communicates . . . the same to any person not entitled to receive it, or willfully retains the same and fails to deliver it to the officer or employe of the United States entitled to receive it."

Mr. Bickel contended that to rely upon this wording to bar a newspaper from publishing certain matter "for the first time in this history of the republic" would set an unfortunate precedent. "A newspaper exists to publish, not to submit its publishing schedule to the United States Government," he argued.

During a final discussion in his chambers, Judge Gurfein heard brief statements from two civil liberties groups that asked to be heard as friends of the court. Norman Dorsen, general counsel of the American Civil Liberties Union, and Kristin Booth Glen of the Emergency Civil Liberties Committee made

the statements and asked to be heard again on Friday.

Judge Gurfein instructed them to file briefs and reserved judgment on their request to be heard.

He urged The Times to consent to a restraining order, but Mr. Bickel refused, saying that to do so would invite future Government efforts to curb news publications. The order was issued over Mr. Bickel's objections.

Order Not Appealed

The Times could have attempted to appeal the order to the United States Court of Appeals for the Second Circuit. However, such extraordinary appeals of temporary restraining orders are rarely granted, and The Times elected to have the issue tried on its merits before Judge Gurfein.

Mr. Bickel was accompanied in court by Floyd Abrams, a partner in the New York law firm of Cahill, Gordon, Sonnett, Reindel and Ohl.

The Justice Department named the following defendants in addition to The New York Times Company in today's injunction: Arthur Ochs Sulzberger, president and publisher, who will return today from a trip to London; Harding F. Bancroft and Ivan Veit, executive vice presidents; and Francis A. Cox, James C. Goodale, Sydney Gruson, Walter Mattson, John McCabe, John Mortimer and James Reston, vice presidents.

Also, John B. Oakes, editorial page editor; A. M. Rosenthal, managing editor; Daniel Schwarz, Sunday editor; Clifton Daniel and Tom Wicker, associate editors; Gerald Gold and Allan M. Siegal, assistant foreign editors; Neil Sheehan, Hedrick Smith, E. W. Kenworthy and Fox Butterfield, reporters; and Samuel Abt, a foreign desk copy editor.

Times's Vietnam Series Circulating in Pentagon

Special to The New York Times

WASHINGTON, June 15—The first three installments of The New York Times series on the Defense Department's secret study on Vietnam have been circulating in the Pentagon after having been routinely reproduced in an internal news publication.

The publication, Current News, is circulated six days a week to about 2,000 senior officials of the Defense Department.

An official of Executive Agency Services, an Air Force agency that publishes Current News under the jurisdiction of the Assistant Secretary of Defense for public affairs, said that he had received no orders not to reproduce the articles.

"We had to leave out a lot of other stories in order to get that stuff in," the official said.

Neither the United States Information Agency nor the armed forces radio and television network reproduced or broadcast any of the classified information contained in the news articles, officials at both Government agencies said.

Moscow Terms Documents Record of Official Duplicity

MOSCOW, June 15 (AP)—The Soviet press agency Tass said today that the secret Defense Department documents published by The New York Times were a "record of official duplicity."

The documents, the agency said in a dispatch from New York, "confirm that the United States deliberately escalated and broadened the war in Indochina and misled the American public in giving its reasons for doing so."

The Soviet Government newspaper Izvestia said: "The publication completely undermines the basis of the Vietnam policy of Johnson's Administration and his successors in the White House."

United States policy has "always been presented as an American defense of 'Saigon democracy' from 'Communist aggression,'" it said.

Texts of Government Papers in Complaint Against The Times and Judge's Order

Following are the texts of a United States Government complaint and a United States District Court temporary restraining order served on The New York Times Company, its officers and several of its employes yesterday in connection with a series of articles and documents on the Vietnam war that The New York Times has been publishing. Also included is the text of a memorandum of law submitted by the Government in support of its petition for the restraining order.

Complaint

UNITED STATES OF AMERICA, Plaintiff

v.

NEW YORK TIMES COMPANY, ARTHUR OCHS SULZBERGER, HARDING F. BANCROFT, IVAN VEIT, FRANCIS A. COX, JAMES C. GOODALE, SYDNEY GRUSON, WALTER MATTSON, JOHN McCABE, JOHN MORTIMER, JAMES RESTON, JOHN B. OAKES, A. M. ROSENTHAL, DANIEL SCHWARZ, CLIFTON DANIEL, TOM WICKER, E. W. KENWORTHY, FOX BUTTERFIELD, GERALD GOLD, ALLAN M. SIEGAL, SAMUEL ABT, NEIL SHEEHAN and HEDRICK SMITH, Defendants

The United States of America, by its attorney, Whitney North Seymour Jr., United States Attorney for the Southern District of New York, at the direction of the Attorney General of the United States, brings this action against the defendants and alleges as follows:

[1]

This Court has jurisdiction over the subject matter of this action pursuant to Title 28, United States Code, Section 1345.

[2]

This is a civil action to obtain an order enjoining the dissemination, disclosure or divulgence without authority by the defendants of official information classified "Top Secret" or "Secret" in the interests of the national defense under the authority and pursuant to the requirements of Executive Order 10501 entitled "Safeguarding Classified Information."

[3]

Defendant New York Times Company is a corporation with its principal place of business in the City and State of New York and which publishes a daily newspaper under the title of The New York Times. The individual defendants are employees and/or officers of the aforementioned company, serving in the following capacities: Arthur Ochs Sulzberger, President and Publisher; Harding F. Bancroft, Executive Vice President; Ivan Veit, Executive Vice President; Francis A. Cox, Vice President; James C. Goodole, Vice President; Sydney Gruson, Vice President; Walter Mattson, Vice President; John McCabe, Vice President; John Mortimer, Vice President; James Reston, Vice President; John B. Oakes, Editorial Page Editor; A. M. Rosenthal, Managing Editor; Daniel Schwarz, Sunday Editor; Clifton Daniel, Associate Editor; Tom Wicker; Associate Editor. Defendants Neil Sheehan, Hedrick Smith, E. W. Kenworthy, Fox Butterfield, Gerald Gold, Allan M. Siegal and Samuel Abt are employees and/or reporters for the aforementioned publication.

[4]

At a time and place and in a manner unknown to the plaintiff the defendants without lawful authority obtained a copy of certain documents consisting of 47 volumes entitled "History of U.S. Decision-Making Process on Vietnam Policy", covering the period 1945-1967, prepared in 1967-1968 at the direction of then Secretary of Defense Robert McNamara and which is and at all times material herein has been classified "Top Secret-Sensitive," and the internal documents from which the said study was drawn are variously classified as "Top Secret" and "Secret," pursuant to the aforementioned Executive Order 10501 as evidenced by the attached affidavit of J. Fred Buzhardt, General Counsel of the United States Department of Defense.

[5]

Also, at a time and place and in a manner unknown to the plaintiff the defendants without lawful authority obtained a copy of a document described as a "one-volume command and control study of the Gulf of Tonkin incident" dated Feb. 26, 1965, prepared for the Joint Chiefs of Staff by the Weapons Systems Evaluation Group of the United States Department of Defense which is and at all times material herein has been classified "Top Secret" pursuant to the aforementioned Executive Order 10501, as evidenced by the aforementioned attached affidavit.

[6]

As defined in Executive Order 10501 "Top Secret" information is ". . . that information or material the defense aspect of which is paramount, and the unauthorized disclosure of which could result in exceptionally grave damage to the nation such as leading to a definite break in diplomatic relations affecting the defense of the United States, an armed attack against the United States or its allies, a war, or the compromise of military or defense plans, or intelligence operations, or scientific or technological developments vital to the national defense," and "Secret" information is defined as ". . . defense information or material the unauthorized disclosure of which could result in serious damage to the nation, such as by jeopardizing the international relations of the United States, endangering the effectiveness of a program or policy of vital importance to the national defense, or compromising important military or defense plans, scientific or technological developments important to national defense, or information revealing important intelligence operations."

[7]

On June 13, 1971, The New York Times published an article entitled "Vietnam Archive: Pentagon Study Traces Three Decades of Growing U.S. Involvement," authored by defendant Sheehan, and an article entitled "Vast Study of War Took a Year," authored by defendant Smith. These articles were represented to be the initial articles in a series written by defendants Sheehan, Smith, defendant E. W. Kenworthy and defendant Fox Butterfield. The series was represented to be one reporting on [a history of] the United States' decision making process on Vietnam policy for the period 1945-1967. The articles in the series and the classified documents upon which they are based were edited by defendants Gold, Siegal, and Abt. In the aforementioned article, authored by the defendant Sheehan, it is asserted that "most of the study (described in the article as 'a massive study of how the United States went to war in Indochina, conducted by the Pentagon three years ago') and many of the appended documents have been obtained by The New York Times and will be described and presented in a series of articles beginning today." It was also asserted in the June 13 issue of The New York Times with respect to the aforementioned "one-volume command and control study" that the Times had obtained a summary of that study.

[8]

On June 13 and 14, the defendants have without authority intentionally and knowingly published excerpts and other portions of the aforementioned classified defense information knowing that such information had been classified "Top Secret" or "Secret" pursuant to the authority of Executive Order 10501. At the time of such publication the said defendants, and each of them, knew, or had reason to believe, that such information could be used to the injury of the United States and to the advantage of a foreign nation and notwithstanding such knowledge and belief did willfully communicate, deliver and transmit said information by the publication thereof, to persons not entitled to receive such information.

[9]

The publication of the information published as aforesaid on June 13 and June 14, 1971, has prejudiced the defense interests of the United States and the publication of additional excerpts from the documents hereinbefore referred to would further prejudice the defense interests of the United States and result in irreparable injury to the United States.

[10]

The defendants have publicly announced their avowed determination to continue publishing excerpts and other portions of the aforementioned "Top Secret" or "Secret" documents relating to the national defense and unless the defendants, and all persons in active concert and participation with the defendants are enjoined from such, the national defense interests of the United States and the nation's security will suffer immediate and irreparable harm, for which injury plaintiff has no adequate remedy at law.

WHEREFORE, the plaintiff, the UNITED STATES OF AMERICA, prays:

[1]

That this Court enter its order enjoining the defendants, their agents, servants and employees and all persons acting in concert with them from further dissemination, disclosure or divulgence of the information heretofore described in paragraphs 4 and 5 of this complaint, or any excerpt, portion or summary thereof.

[2]

That the Court order the defendants and each of them having possession of the documents referred to in the complaint to deliver said documents and any copies, excerpts, duplications or other tangible evidence of such documents to the plaintiff herein.

[3]

That this Court, pending the final determination of this cause, issue a preliminary injunction, restraining and enjoining the defendants in the manner and form aforesaid.

[4]

That, pending the issuance of the aforesaid preliminary injunction, this Court issue forthwith a temporary restraining order restraining and enjoining the defendants in the manner and form aforesaid and further ordering said defendants to deliver to this Court all the documents and materials referred to in paragraph 2 of the prayer herein to be held by this Court in camera pending a final order of this Court.

[5]

That this Court grant such other, further, and different relief as the Court may deem just and equitable.

JOHN N. MITCHELL
Attorney General
of the United States

WHITNEY NORTH SEYMOUR Jr.
United States Attorney

By: MICHAEL D. HESS
Chief, Civil Division

Temporary Restraining Order

#71 Civ. 2662

UNITED STATES OF AMERICA, Plaintiff

v.

NEW YORK TIMES COMPANY, ARTHUR OCHS SULZBERGER, HARDING F. BANCROFT, IVAN VEIT, FRANCIS A. COX, JAMES C. GOODALE, SYDNEY GRUSON, WALTER MATTSON, JOHN McCABE JOHN MORTIMER, JAMES RESTON, JOHN B. OAKES, A. M. ROSENTHAL, DANIEL SCHWARZ, CLIFTON DANIEL, TOM WICKER, E. W. KENWORTHY, FOX BUTTERFIELD, GERALD GOLD, ALLAN M. SIEGAL, SAMUEL ABT, NEIL SHEEHAN and HEDRICK SMITH, Defendants

MEMORANDUM

The United States seeks a temporary restraining order and a preliminary injunction against The New York Times, its publisher and other officers and employes to restrain them from further dissemination or disclosure of certain alleged top secret or secret documents of the United States referred to in a verified complaint filed herewith. I have granted the order to show cause as to why a preliminary injunction against the defendants should not be entered and have made it returnable Friday morning, June 18.

Preliminary thereto the Government has requested a temporary restraining order and also a direction from this Court to require the defendants to deliver to the Court certain documents and other tangible evidence to be held by the Court pending final determination of the cause. At this stage of the proceedings I do not direct The New York Times or the other defendants to produce the documents pending the outcome of the litigation. I do not believe that The New York Times will wilfully disregard the spirit of our restraining order. I am restraining The New York Times and the other defendants, however, from publishing or further disseminating or disclosing the documents consisting of 47 volumes entitled "History of United States Decision-Making Process on Vietnam Policy," covering the period 1945-67, prepared in 1967-68 at the direction of the then Secretary of Defense, Robert McNamara, the internal documents from which the aforesaid documents were prepared, and a one-volume "Command and Control Study of the Tonkin Gulf Incident," prepared in 1965 for the Joint Chiefs of Staff by the Weapon System Evaluation Group of the United States Department of Defense, pending the hearing of the Government's application for a preliminary injunction.

The questions raised by this action are serious and fundamental. They involve not only matters of procedure, but matters of substance and presumptively of constitutional implication as well. I have, in effect, been asked by the parties to pass on the merits of the litigation upon the arguments made on the order to show cause. I believe that the matter is so important and so involved with the history of the relationship between the security of the Government and of a free press that a more thorough briefing than the parties have had an opportunity to do is required. I have granted the restraining order because in my opinion any temporary harm that may result from not publishing during the pendency of the application for a preliminary injunction is far outweighed by the irreparable harm that could be done to the interests of the United States Government if it should ultimately prevail. I have intentionally expressed no opinion on the merits, but I believe this matter is brought in good faith by the United States and that on the balancing of interests mentioned, both parties deserve a full consideration of the issues raised.

Accordingly, the restraining order will be in effect until Saturday afternoon at 1 o'clock unless the Court directs otherwise.

The parties are requested to brief as thoroughly as possible the points adverted to in the oral arguments by 5 P.M. Thursday, June 17, 1971.

M. I. GURFEIN
U.S.D.J.

Dated: June 15, 1971.

Memorandum of Law

PRELIMINARY STATEMENT

This action has been commenced to preliminarily and permanently enjoin defendants and their agents from further disseminating documents consisting of 47 volumes entitled "History of U.S. Decision-Making Process on Vietnam Policy." Plaintiff further seeks to gain the recovery of the aforementioned documents from defendants. This memorandum is submitted in support of plaintiff's application for an order temporarily restraining the defendants from further disseminating the aforementioned documents and requiring the delivery of the documents to this court pending the determination of plaintiff's motion for a preliminary injunction.

STATUTE RELIED UPON

Section 793 (d) of Title 18 of the United States Code provides as follow: "Whoever, lawfully having possession of, access to, control over, or being entrusted with any document, writing, code book, signal book, sketch, photograph, photographic negative, blueprint, plan, map, model, instrument, appliance, or note relating to the national defense, or information relating to the national defense which information the possessor has reason to believe could be used to the injury of the United States or to the advantage of any foreign nation, willfully communicates, delivers, transmits or causes to be communicated, delivered, or transmited or attempts to communicate, deliver, transmit or cause to be communicated, delivered or transmitted the same to any person not entitled to receive or willfully retains the same and fails to deliver it upon demand to the officer or employe of the United States entitled to receive it. . . ."

ARGUMENT

Defendants are in possession of a 47-volume study entitled "History of the United States Decision-Making Process on Vietnam Policy." This study is currently classified as "Top Secret-sensitive"* pursuant to the provisions of Executive Order 10501. As defined in the Executive Order, top-secret information is "that information or material the defense aspect of which is paramount, and the unauthorized disclosure of which could result in exceptionally grave damage to the nation. . . ."

On June 13, 14 and 15, 1971, defendants published documents contained in the study. By telegram dated June 14, 1971, defendants were advised by the Attorney General of the United States that further publication of the contents of the study will cause irreparable injury to the defense interests of the United States. In the telegram, defendants were requested to cease publication of the contents of the study and to return the study to the Department of Defense. Defendants have expressed the intention to continue to publish documents contained in the study until they are restrained from doing so by an order of this Court.

Section 793 (d) of Title 18 of the United States Code provides for criminal penalties against a person who, while lawfully in possession of information relating to the national defense which could be used to the injury of the United States, willfully communicates that information to persons not en-

*In determining whether information properly has been classified top secret, the test to be applied by the court is whether the classifying authority acted capriciously. Epstein v. Resor, 296 F. Supp. 214 (N. D. Calif. 1969).

titled to receive it or willfully fails to deliver it, on demand, to the officer of the United States entitled to receive it. The applicability of Section 793 (d) has not been restricted to criminal actions. *Dubin v. United States,* 289 F. 2d 651 (Ct. Cl. 1961).

Further publication of the contents of the study and defendants' continued refusal to return all of the papers to the Department of Defense will constitute a violation of Section 793 (d). Moreover, such publication will result in irreparable injury to the interests of the United States, for which there is no adequate remedy at law. An injury is deemed irreparable when it cannot be adequately compensated in damages due to the nature of the injury itself or where there exists no pecuniary standard for the measurement of the damages. *Luckenbach S. S. Co. v. Norton,* 12 F. Supp. 707,709 (E. D. Pa. 1937). Irreparable injury also means "that species of damage, whether great or small, that ought not to be submitted to on the one hand or inflicted on the other." *Anderson v. Sooza,* 38 Cal. 2d, 825,243 P. 2d 497,503 (1952). The inadequacy of a remedy at law exists where the circumstances demand preventive relief. *Cruikshank v. Bidwell* 176 U.S. 73,81 (1900).

In the instant case, defendants will suffer no injury if they cease to publish the contents of the study in their possession pending the determination of plaintiff's motion for a preliminary injunction. On the other hand, the national interest of the United States may be seriously damaged if the defendants continue to publish the contents of the study. Under circumstances in which no injury will result to defendants from the cessation of publication of the study in their possession and irreparable injury may result to the United States, the granting of a temporary restraining order is appropriate.

CONCLUSION

For the foregoing reasons, the plaintiff's application for a temporary restraining order pending the determination of its motion for a preliminary injunction should be granted. Plaintiff's application for an order temporarily restraining the further publication of the contents of the study in defendant's possession should be granted.

Dated: New York, New York
June 15, 1971
Respectfully submitted,

WHITNEY NORTH SEYMOUR Jr.
United States Attorney for
the Southern District of
New York, Attorney for the
plaintiff, United States
of America.

MICHAEL D. HESS
HOWARD S. SUSSMAN
MILTON SHERMAN
Assistant United States
Attorneys, United of Counsel.

The Vietnam Documents

In an unprecedented example of censorship, the Attorney General of the United States has temporarily succeeded in preventing The New York Times from continuing to publish documentary and other material taken from a secret Pentagon study of the decisions affecting American participation in the Vietnam War.

Through a temporary restraining order issued by a Federal District judge yesterday, we are prevented from publishing, at least through the end of the week, any new chapters in this massive documentary history of American involvement in the war. But The Times will continue to fight to the fullest possible extent of the law what we believe to be an unconstitutional prior restraint imposed by the Attorney General.

What was the reason that impelled The Times to publish this material in the first place? The basic reason is, as was stated in our original reply to Mr. Mitchell, that we believe "that it is in the interest of the people of this country to be informed. . . ." A fundamental responsibility of the press in this democracy is to publish information that helps the people of the United States to understand the processes of their own government, especially when those processes have been clouded over in a hazy veil of public dissimulation and even deception.

As a newspaper that takes seriously its obligation and its responsibilities to the public, we believe that, once this material fell into our hands, it was not only in the interests of the American people to publish it but, even more emphatically, it would have been an abnegation of responsibility and a renunciation of our obligations under the First Amendment not to have published it. Obviously, The Times would not have made this decision if there had been any reason to believe that publication would have endangered the life of a single American soldier or in any way threatened the security of our country or the peace of the world.

The documents in question belong to history. They refer to the development of American interest and participation in Indochina from the post-World War II period up to mid-1968, which is now almost three years ago. Their publication could not conceivably damage American security interests, much less the lives of Americans or Indochinese. We therefore felt it incumbent to take on ourselves the responsibility for their publication, and in doing so raise once again the question of the Government's propensity for over-classification and mis-classification of documents that by any reasonable scale of values have long since belonged in the public domain.

We publish the documents and related running account not to prove any debater's point about the origins and development of American participation in the war, not to place the finger of blame on any individuals, civilian or military, but to present to the American public a history—admittedly incomplete—of decision-making at the highest levels of government on one of the most vital issues that has ever affected "our lives, our fortunes and our sacred honor"—an issue on which the American people and their duly elected representatives in Congress have been largely curtained off from the truth.

It is the effort to expose and elucidate that truth that is the very essence of freedom of the press.

June 16, 1971

Vietnam: Pentagon Study

To the Editor:

If the "Pentagon Study" of the Vietnam war is to be believed—and sadly I think there is more there to believe than to disbelieve—it is evident that the American people have been lied to and distrusted by their own leaders and representatives.

In the study we have many famous Americans presented to us as planning for the bombing and accepting the resulting killing of human beings in an almost too casual manner. Such a manner of life, of decision-making in an almost amoral manner, does little to differentiate the American policymaker from any one of history's other tyrants.

It is again clear, as it was to such men as Jefferson in the days of our Revolution, that unless we return to basic morality and elect moral representatives, we will witness the sad decline of whatever advantages America has to offer.

LOUIS F. LOMBARDI
Richmond, Va., June 13, 1971

The Endless Tragedy

By JAMES RESTON

For the first time in the history of the Republic, the Attorney General of the United States has tried to suppress documents he hasn't read about a war that hasn't been declared. This is one of the final ironies of this tragic Vietnam war, but it won't work for long.

The constitutional issue can be left to the courts. They need time. The issue is complicated: there is clearly a conflict between the Government's desire to preserve the privacy of its internal communications, which everybody recognizes, and its attempt to extend this procedure to old historic documents, which analyze the blunders of the past.

But in practical terms, the documents will not be suppressed. The New York Times will abide by the final decision of the courts, but too many copies of the McNamara Papers are around, and too many fundamental issues are involved to suppose that this official record of the war can be censored for long.

It is easy to get lost in the legalities, ambiguities and politics of this controversy, but the central issue is what former Secretary of Defense McNamara had in mind when he ordered this analysis of the war in the first place.

McNamara was a principal actor in the drama, deeply involved and even incriminated in the struggle, but near the end he insisted, on his own responsibility, that outside and objective minds should look at the record and try to find out what went wrong and why. This involved many people—around thirty—all of whom have knowledge of critical parts of the Pentagon investigation, some of whom have some of the documents, and a few of whom have copies or access to copies of most of the whole.

McNamara is clearly not alone in feeling that the basic questions—how did we really get involved, how did we lose our way?—should be made clear in order to avoid similar mistakes in the future. And at least some of these men are not going to be silenced by temporary or even permanent court injunctions against publications of the facts.

The Attorney General, by seeking for the first time a court injunction before publication, has dramatized the issue. He has transformed an academic monograph, with a very limited audience of politicians, bureaucrats, journalists and scholars, into a world issue on the American war and the First Amendment of the American Constitution on the freedom of the press. And his efforts at suppression, while they may prevail for a short time, will almost certainly fail in the long run.

For the men who know most about these documents do not believe that publication involves national security or would cause, in the Attorney General's words, "irreparable injury to the defense interests of the United States."

In fact, many of them in possession of the facts, and a few of them in possession of the documents, believe that the security argument is being used to cover up the blunders and deceptions of the past in Vietnam, and would gladly go to jail rather than submit to the suppression of their information.

Mr. Mitchell, consciously or not, has raised a fundamental question: What causes "irreparable damage" to the Republic? Publication of documents that expose the weaknesses and deceptions of the Government on issues of war and peace? Or the censorship of these documents in the name of "national security"?

This is the central issue. The Attorney General and the Secretary of Defense have a respectable argument; they have the right to private communication. The Secretary of State, William Rogers, also has a point: other nations cannot do business with Washington if their communications are going to end up in the headlines of the American press. But beyond that, and even above it, there is the question of the integrity of the American Executive in its dealings with the American people and their representatives in the Congress.

These documents are in the possession of the principals. President Johnson has a copy. Clark Clifford and Robert McNamara are reported to have copies, and other interested parties have copies or access to parts of them, and all are writing their own versions of history. So the legal injunction, as it now stands, is only against making the main documents available to disinterested scholars and the general public.

This is the main point about these documents, and why the documents themselves had to be published. For they demonstrate beyond question, not reporters' opinions or speculations about Presidential action, but obvious and even calculated deception in the words of the officials themselves.

It will be interesting to see how the courts, and even the principal personalities react to this tangle of legal and philosophical questions. But however they react, the objective of the McNamara inquiry is going to be achieved. The basic facts of the American involvement in Vietnam, many of them idealistic and many of them tragic, are going to be revealed, no matter what the Attorney General says, and in the end, we may be a little nearer to the truth.

Opponents of War In Congress Decry U.S. Suit on Study

By DAVID E. ROSENBAUM
Special to The New York Times

WASHINGTON, June 16—Congressional opponents of the war in Indochina criticized the Nixon Administration today for having sought and obtained a court order temporarily preventing The New York Times from publishing further material from a secret Pentagon study on Vietnam.

In Los Angeles, however, Vice President Agnew questioned the judgment of The Times in publishing the material for three days before the court order was issued yesterday.

Two members of Congress —Senator J. W. Fulbright, Democrat of Arkansas, the chairman of the Foreign Relations Committee, and Representative Paul N. McCloskey Jr., Republican of California—asked The Times to turn over to them copies of unpublished material, since the Administration has refused Congressional access to the documents. The Times refused both requests.

At the White House, Ronald L. Ziegler, President Nixon's press secretary, said that no consideration was being given to declassifying—removing the official secrecy from—the documents published by The Times.

Asked why the Administration had moved against The Times when it had never before attempted to prevent publication of information, Mr. Ziegler said, "I don't know that there are other cases . . . where a publication stated that it intended to publish highly classified material."

A major figure in the Pentagon study, Gen. Maxwell D. Taylor, who was Ambassador to South Vietnam from the summer of 1964 to the summer of 1965 said in a television interview tonight that The Times had initiated "a practice of betrayal of Government secrets."

Response by Taylor

Asked on the Columbia Broadcasting System's evening news program how his position squared with "the people's right to know," General Taylor responded:

"I don't believe in that as a general principle. You have to talk about cases. What is a citizen going to do after reading these documents that he wouldn't have done otherwise? A citizen should know those things he needs to know to be a good citizen and discharge his functions, but not to get into secrets that damage his Government and indirectly damage the citizen himself."

The Times's disclosures General Taylor said, were "laying a foundation for bad history."

The requests to The Times for copies of the unpublished material were made by letter.

Senator Fulbright, writing to Arthur Ochs Sulzberger, president and publisher of The Times, said the information that had been printed had not breached the national security and that it was within The Times's right under the First Amendment to publish it. The Senator, who was in London, added, "Too often national security has been invoked solely to prevent personal embarrassment."

Representative McCloskey made his request in a letter to A. M. Rosenthal, managing editor of The Times. He said that if he were given copies of the unpublished secret material he would have it printed in the Congressional Record.

The disclosures in The Times series published on Sunday, Monday and Tuesday and the temporary court order that was issued yesterday were major topics of discussion on Capitol Hill today.

Sixty-two members of the House of Representatives, nearly all of them liberal Democrats, signed letters to Secretary of Defense Melvin R. Laird and Attorney General John N. Mitchell, asking Mr. Laird to make the Pentagon study available to Congress and protesting to Mr. Mitchell about what they termed his "harassment" of The Times. The letters were initiated by Representative Jonathan B. Bingham, Democrat of the Bronx.

Senator Hugh Scott of Pennsylvania, the minority leader, said that both the publication of the classified documents and the contents of the documents damaged public confidence in the Government.

The public must question the Government's security now, Mr. Scott said, but he added that it was "perfectly clear that American people were not told things [about the war in Indochina] that they should have been told."

In the House, the Information subcommittee of the Government Operations Committee announced hearings next week on the Government's classification procedures and on the policies of withholding data from Congress and the public on the ground of "executive privilege."

Representative Ogden R. Reid of Westchester County, the subcommittee's ranking Republican member, said he hoped to call officials from the State, Defense and Justice Departments and the White House staff.

'To Save Some Red Faces'

The subcommittee is headed by Representative William S. Moorhead, a Pennsylvania Democrat. He said that the classification of the Pentagon study "was done not so much to save the security of the United States but to save some red faces."

Vice President Agnew, the highest Administration official to comment on the disclosures, was interviewed by reporters after he discussed the Administration's revenue-sharing program at a meeting of the Los Angeles County Board of Supervisors.

"In my opinion, what is the proper amount of classified information that should be released is a matter for professional judgment," the Vice President, a frequent critic of the press, said.

A reporter asked his opinion about the judgment of American officials in withholding information about the war from the public. Mr. Agnew replied, "The Nixon Administration has a great deal more confidence in the judgment of elected officials than it does in The New York Times."

'Secretive and Clandestine'

Mr. Agnew said that The Times knew that the material was classified but had "proceeded to publish it in a secretive and clandestine fashion."

Among the few public statements from Congressmen critical of The Times was one from Senator John G. Tower, Republican of Texas.

He said that the published information had been "particularly interesting," but he questioned whether "the publication of classified documents remains within the excellent and responsible motto of which The New York Times prides itself— 'All the news that's fit to print.'"

Another piece of criticism came from W. Averell Harriman, who served as President Johnson's delegate to the Paris peace talks. At a breakfast meeting with newsmen, Mr. Harriman said that he believed that the public had been "misled by the publication of a lot of miscellaneous documents."

Another member of the Johnson Administration, Senator Hubert H. Humphrey of Minnesota, the former Vice President, discounted reports that McGeorge Bundy and Walt W. Rostow, Mr. Johnson's assistants for national security affairs, had been the men closest to the President on war matters. Senator Humphrey said that "day in and day out" Secretary of State Dean Rusk and Secretary of Defense Robert S. McNamara had been the key officials.

Gen. Earle G. Wheeler, who was chairman of the Joint Chiefs of Staff for six years during the war, said by telephone today from his retirement home in Martinsburg, W. Va., that his office had asked for a copy of the Vietnam study but had not been given it. He said he had never seen the report.

Most members of Congress who commented publicly today are, like Mr. Harriman, now critics of the war.

Senator George S. McGovern, Democrat of South Dakota, said in a statement that the Justice Department's use of espionage laws to "harry The New York Times" not only violates the constitutional principle of freedom of the press "but also shuts off a free flow of vital information to the public."

In Manchester, N. H., where he was speaking to a Republican group, Gov. Ronald Reagan of California told newsmen said there might be a "real threat to security" in the disclosures. The news media, he said, had an obligation to review material before publication in light of national security interests.

Fulbright Sees 'Deception'

Special to The New York Times

LONDON, June 16—Senator Fulbright said tonight that publication of the documented Vietnam war history would help restore the American constitutional balance.

He said the articles had confirmed "deliberate and flagrant deception" on the part of President Johnson. That deceit, he said, had done "serious injury" to the ability of Congress and the public to deal with issues of war and peace.

Mr. Fulbright, who has been traveling in England since receiving an honorary degree at Cambridge last week, made his comments in an interview. He has long been critical of the statements made by President Johnson and his aides after the Tonkin Gulf incident in August, 1964.

The executive branch spoke of a "barbaric, unprovoked attack on the high seas," Senator Fulbright said tonight, and on that basis got Congress to give President Johnson openended war authority in Vietnam.

"I feel strongly because I played a part personally," Senator Fulbright said.

"I told my colleagues that they should vote for the Tonkin Gulf resolution, without amendment, because I had the President's assurance of its purpose. That was to prevent enlargement of the war.

"The President told me that if the Congress showed united support for his policy, our strength and determination would persuade North Vietnam to stop supporting the Vietcong. Then the American role could be limited.

"But we now know from these documents that the experts inside the executive

569

branch at that very time had no belief in the North Vietnamese reacting that way.

"It all seems terribly naive now, that we would believe it. But the President, you know, had us down to the White House, and there was this fever of excitement."

REPORTS SAY TEXTS MIGHT HELP SOVIET

Special to The New York Times

WASHINGTON, June 16—The Defense Department declined to comment tonight on anonymous reports that Government officials feared that the Soviet Union could break United States codes of the 1960's by studying the texts of diplomatic cables published by The New York Times.

The departmental spokesman, Jerry R. Friedheim, said that the law precluded him from making any comment whatsoever on any aspect of codes or ciphers.

The reports, citing unnamed Government sources, said that the codes might be broken by comparing the texts with encoded messages intercepted and believed taped by Soviet intelligence. Any information obtained might be used to decode other messages sent during that period, the reports said.

The reports noted that military and diplomatic codes are changed frequently to thwart deciphering. It was said to be almost certain that no codes used by the United States during the period when the published messages were sent are still in use today.

The New York Times/Barton Silverman

PUBLISHER RETURNS FROM LONDON: Arthur Ochs Sulzberger, president and publisher of The New York Times, answering queries at news session at Kennedy Airport.

Sulzberger Terms Documents 'History'

Arthur Ochs Sulzberger, president and publisher of The New York Times, said yesterday that the documents on the origins of the Vietnam war whose publication has been curbed by court order are "a part of history that should have been made available long ago."

Mr. Sulzberger made the comment at a news conference at John F. Kennedy International Airport just after he arrived on a flight from London. He had been in England on a business trip since Monday

In reply to a question asking whether he felt that national security could be endangered by the publication of the Pentagon report, Mr. Sulzberger replied:

"I certainly do not. This was not a breach of the national security. We gave away no national secrets. We didn't jeopardize any American soldiers or marines overseas. These papers, I think, as our editorial said this morning, are a part of history."

Mr. Sulzberger said he thought that governments often "stamp secret on too many things because they don't want people to find out things that are embarrassing to them."

He was then asked if his newspaper "should be the arbiter of whether or not particular documents threaten the security of the United States?"

"No," he replied. "You see, we can't read through all the Government documents. I suppose it's up to the Government; I wish the Government used its head a little bit more.

"There are tons of documents —even from World War II, which has been over 25 years now—that are still classified secret. And, I think, that it's a wonderful way if you've got egg on your face to prevent anybody from knowing it, stamp it secret and put it away."

In response to a question asking what political impact the publication might have on President Nixon, Mr. Sulzberger answered: "I hope it will have an impact on the President. I don't know that it will be a political impact. I think it'll open a lot of people's eyes as to what happened during those years when all the people in the press were apparently being told one story, and the Government, the people close to the Government, were having something else told to them."

Laird Refused '69 Fulbright Request For the Pentagon Study on Vietnam

By JAMES M. NAUGHTON
Special to The New York Times

WASHINGTON, June 16—Eighteen months ago, in a letter to Senator J. W. Fulbright, the Secretary of Defense, Melvin R. Laird, described a secret Pentagon study of American involvement in Vietnam as a "compilation of raw materials to be used at some unspecified, but distant, future date."

Mr. Laird declined in the letter to give the study to the Senate Foreign Relations Committee, which Mr. Fulbright heads. The Secretary said that to do so "would clearly be contrary to the national interest."

The letter offered no specific reason why the national interest might be jeopardized. Mr. Laird contended that the material was sensitive because contributors to the study had been guaranteed confidentiality.

The Pentagon spokesman, Jerry W. Friedheim, declined today to expand on the meaning of Mr. Laird's remarks in the letter, dated Dec. 20, 1969.

Mr. Friedheim said that he assumed that Secretary Laird had stated "what he means" in the letter and that "it sounds to me like he thought it was a historical document."

The Justice Department obtained a Federal Court order yesterday, temporarily halting publication of parts of the Pentagon study in The New York Times.

Secretary Laird said Monday that publication of the documents "violated the security regulations of the United States." He emphasized, in testimony before the Senate Foreign Relations Committee, that he thought it served no useful purpose to make public sensitive information.

In his 1969 letter to Mr. Fulbright, the Defense Secretary similarly stressed the sensitivity of the subject rather than its potential impact on national security.

He said the study had been commissioned in 1967 by Secretary of Defense Robert S. McNamara.

"It was conceived as a compilation of raw materials to be used at some unspecified, but distant, future date," the letter said. "On the basis of the understanding that access and use would be restricted, the documents were designed to contain an accumulation of data of the most delicate sensitivity, including N.S.C. [National Security Council] papers and other Presidential communications which have always been considered privileged.

"In addition, the papers included a variety of internal advice and comments central to the decision-making process. Many of the contributions to this total document were provided on the basis of an expressed guarantee of confidentiality."

Access Highly Limited

Mr. Laird's letter continued: "As intended from the start, access to and use of this document has been extremely limited. It would clearly be contrary to the national interest to disseminate it more widely. However, the Department of Defense is naturally prepared to provide the committee information with respect to executive branch activities in Vietnam for any portion of the period covered by this compendium."

Mr. Friedheim said today in response to a telephone request for clarification that "it is obviously what Laird thought at that time." The spokesman for the Secretary said that he could not "add any words to what the letter says."

He expressed surprise that the correspondence had been made public. It was part of a series of written exchanges between Senator Fulbright and Secretary Laird that was inserted in the committee's record by Senator Stuart Symington of Missouri following the hearing Monday.

Senator Fulbright first asked for a copy of the Pentagon study in a letter to Mr. Laird on Nov. 11, 1969. In another letter, on Jan. 19, 1970, the Senator urged that Mr. Laird reconsider his refusal to provide the material.

After one of Mr. Laird's assistants had replied that the Secretary was studying the matter, Mr. Fulbright wrote in April and again in July of last year to ask what Mr. Laird's response was.

On July 21, 1970, Mr. Laird again rejected the request.

"My letter of Dec. 20, 1969, indicated that access to and use of this document, as intended from the start, has been and remains extremely limited," Mr. Laird wrote. "For the reasons expressed in that letter, I have again concluded that it would be clearly contrary to the national interest to disseminate the compendium more widely."

Last April 30, Senator Fulbright again asked for the study in a letter to Mr. Laird and asked whether "executive privilege is being invoked by the President" as authority for withholding the study and other requested documents.

Along with the letter the Senator sent Mr. Laird a copy of a Presidential memorandum dated March 24, 1969, in which Mr. Nixon said his policy was "to comply to the fullest extent possible with Congressional requests for information" unless, "in the most compelling circumstances" it was necessary to invoke executive privilege. Even then, the memorandum stipulated, the privilege would not be invoked "without specific Presidential approval."

Secrecy and Passage Into the Quagmire

To the Editor:

A sense of outrage, like a poor knife, gets dulled by use, and such has been the effect for many of us of Vietnam. But mine has been usefully sharpened again by the Pentagon Study, and, as usual, personal experience helped.

In 1964, with numerous others, I campaigned across the country for the Johnson-Humphrey ticket. I was, by then, considerably concerned over our Vietnam involvement. I spoke principally of the need for military restraint, of the irresponsibility of Senator Goldwater's talk about unleashing the Air Force.

All this became an unpleasant matter for reflection a few weeks later when, as it then seemed, the Administration changed its mind. One now discovers that the plans for the bombing already existed and were awaiting an excuse that would, if necessary, be manufactured.

It follows that, to the knowing, those of us who were making the speeches were patsies serving usefully because of our ignorance. I do not reflect on such trickery with relish. I hope that all who were similarly involved have a like reaction.

But if one can contain his personal anger, there are further lessons. What we have learned is that a small group of professionally assured, morally astigmatic and—a point to be emphasized—intellectually myopic men had undertaken deliberately to mislead the Congress, the public and the people of the world at large as to their intentions and, so far as might be possible, as to their actions.

They would largely have escaped criticism if The Times, in an action which belies much that is said about the modern institutionalized press, had not ripped away the protecting shroud. Whatever the plea, the primary effect of the present court action is to protect what is still undisclosed of this mendacity and duplicity.

But this is not all. The further lesson is that we can no longer afford the secrecy which protects such conduct of our public affairs, for against whom is such secrecy employed? It was not employed against the Government of North Vietnam. The papers are replete with references to our desire to make clear our intentions to that Government, and the worse our intentions seemed, the better.

Professor Walt Rostow is associated with more signals than an old-time telegrapher. Much consideration was given to informing the Soviets and the Chinese.

It was for protection from the Congress, our own people and our friends that this secrecy was employed, as the most casual reading of the papers will make clear. And the thing it protected, above all, was the freedom to make catastrophic mistakes.

June 17, 1971

For if the public had known that the Administration was seeking a Gulf of Tonkin Resolution in the spring of 1964, or had plans to bomb North Vietnam that autumn, or intended putting in large numbers of troops with a combat mission in the spring of 1965, there would have been a vigorous and bruising debate.

Foreseeing and fearing such a debate, the Administration might well have reconsidered the action. Or, in the wake of the debate, it might have been forced to do so. And in the course of the debate the very great question which—as the papers show, none of the strategists (George Ball apart) ever sought to ask—would have been asked. That is: Where does this policy lead us? It was secrecy that made possible our silent and unhampered passage into the quagmire.

It was part of our founding wisdom that public power, whether guided by good sense or, as in this case, by stupidity, must be subject to the hard test of public discussion. In these last years we've allowed soldiers and civilian strategists—the most bizarre of authorities to entrust with such a matter—to divert us with the doctrine that because the Communist countries do not have public debate on public decisions, neither should we.

Let us now accept the lesson. What may work for the Communists works disaster for us. The worst policy is one made in secrecy by the experts. Our safety lies, and lies exclusively, in making public decision subject to the test of public debate. What cannot survive public debate—as the experience of Vietnam shows—we must not do.   JOHN KENNETH GALBRAITH
. Cambridge, Mass., June 16, 1971

The 'Irreparable Injury'

By TOM WICKER

The Government has alleged that The New York Times, in publishing the Defense Department's own record of the nation's involvement in Vietnam, "has prejudiced the interests of the United States and the publication of additional excerpts . . . would further prejudice the defense interests of the United States and result in irreparable injury to the United States." That is a travesty of fact and common sense.

Is it alleged by the Government that these appalling documents are not genuine? No.

Is it alleged by the Government that The Times is in any way distorting or manipulating this historical record to its own ends? No.

Is it alleged by the Government that these documents bear in any way on current or future military operations? No.

Is it alleged by the Government that these historical documents recount any of the confidential deliberations concerning Vietnam of the present Administration? No; the compilation of the record was completed in 1968, before President Nixon's election.

There remain two ways in which The Times might be charged with having damaged the nation's "defense interests" by publishing historical documents. One is by the mere act of publication, since the Pentagon study was "classified."

Aside from the fact that newspapers publish and Government officials "leak" classified information every day —Presidents and Cabinet officers have been known to do it — the statute that The Times is alleged to have violated is one adopted to guard against espionage, not against a free press in pursuit of its duty to publish. Nor can a wartime emergency be invoked to justify supression of information about public business, since the Government in its wisdom has never seen fit to declare war on North Vietnam or any other entity with which it may be at odds in Southeast Asia.

Since the documents in the Pentagon record go back to the Truman Administration, since they were collected in 1967 and 1968 expressly for historical purposes, and since they bear on present diplomatic and military operations only in a historical sense, for any newspaper or scholar to concede that they can properly be "classified" and kept from the public would be to concede that history itself can be classified and suppressed.

It must be, therefore, that the Government believes further publication would "result in irreparable injury to the United States" because of the

IN THE NATION

content—because the documents themselves form an almost incredible record of subterfuge, deception, shortsightedness, mistakes, wrong assumptions and arrogant disregard of truth. Moreover, these are not the creation of that devil-press Vice President Agnew likes to denounce; nor are they the fantasies of "peaceniks." This is the factual record of what happened, compiled within the Pentagon itself, often by men who bore the responsibility for much of that record.

But no statute exists that says Government officials must be protected from the exposure of their follies or misdeeds. Indeed, the great lesson of the Pentagon record is that the ability to operate in secrecy breeds contempt for that very public in whose name and interest officials claim to act. It often is argued that government cannot function if its officers cannot deal with one another in confidence; but seldom if ever has it been so graphically demonstrated that when men are relieved of the burden of public scrutiny, uncomfortable as it may be, no other form of accountability can effectively take its place.

Although it may be long past the point when the tragedy might have been averted, and although it may now be too late to hold anyone effectively accountable for the blunders and deceptions of the past, one thing is apparent: reading this sad record can teach every American something about the nation, the world, the past—and therefore about the future. Can anyone maintain that the public will be less enlightened and the future of the nation more endangered if these documents are made available for study and reflection? On the other hand, can anyone conceivably suggest that the people of the United States would be better off and the interests of the nation further advanced if this dark chapter of its history were locked away in the vaults of the Pentagon?

To advance the latter argument would be to assert that truth has less value than deception, and that in a democracy the people ought not to know. Yet that is essentially what the Government is asking the courts to rule; and in the legal ground upon which it tries to base its case, it is also asking that the self-serving security classifications of the Defense Department take precedence over the First Amendment to the Constitution.

That is the only "irreparable injury" that can be done, in this painful matter, to the real interests of the United States, and it is not The New York Times that can perpetrate it.

Freedom and Security

By JAMES RESTON

*"Here various news we tell, of love
    and strife,*

*Of peace and war. health, sickness,
    death and life . . .*

*Of turns of fortune, changes in the
    State,*

*The falls of favorites, projects of the
    great,*

*Of old mismanagements, taxations
    new,*

*All neither wholly false, nor wholly
    true."*

—New London, Conn., Bee,
        March 26, 1800.

Great court cases are made by the
clash of great principles, each formidable standing alone, but in conflict
limited, "all neither wholly false nor
wholly true."

The latest legal battle, *"The United
States v. The New York Times,"* is such
a case: The Government's principle of
privacy and the newspaper's principle
of publishing without Government
approval.

This is not essentially a fight between Attorney General Mitchell and
Arthur Ochs Sulzberger, publisher of
The New York Times. They are merely
incidental figures in an ancient drama.
This is the old cat - and - dog conflict
between security and freedom.

It goes back to John Milton's pamphlet, *Areopagitica,* in the seventeenth
century against Government censorship, or as he called it: "for the liberty
of unlicenc'd printing." That is still
the heart of it: the Government's claim
to prevent, in effect to license, what
is published ahead of publication,
rather than merely to exercise its right
to prosecute after publication.

Put another way, even the title of
this case in the U.S. District Court is
misleading, for the real issue is not
The New York Times versus the United
States, but whether publishing the
Government's own analysis of the
Vietnam tragedy or suppressing that
story is a service to the Republic.

It is an awkward thing for a reporter to comment on the battles of
his own newspaper, and the reader
will make his own allowances for the
reporter's bias, but after all allowances are made, it is hard to believe
that publishing these historical documents is a greater threat to the security of the United States than suppressing them, or, on the record, as
the Government implies, that The
Times is a frivolous or reckless paper.

The usual charge against The New
York Times, not without some validity, is that it is a tedious bore, always
saying on the one hand and the
other, and defending, like The Times
of London in the thirties, "the Government and commercial establishment."

During the last decade, it has been
attacked vigorously for "playing the
Government game." It refused to print
a story that the Cuban freedom fighters were going to land at the Bay
of Pigs "tomorrow morning." It agreed
with President Kennedy during the
Cuban missile crisis that reporting the
Soviet missiles on that island while
Kennedy was deploying the fleet to
blockade the Russians was not in the
national interest.

Beyond that, it was condemned for
not printing what it knew about the
U.S. U-2 flights over the Soviet Union,
and paradoxically, for printing the
Yalta Papers and the Dumbarton Oaks
papers on the organization of the
United Nations.

All of which suggests that there
is no general principle which governs
all specific cases, and that, in the
world of newspapering, where men
have to read almost two million words
a day and select 100,000 to print, it
comes down to human judgments
where "all [is] neither wholly false nor
wholly true."

So a judgment has to be made when
the Government argues for security,
even over historical documents, and
The Times argues for freedom to publish. That is what is before the court
today. It is not a black and white
case—as it was in the Cuban missile
crisis when the Soviet ships were approaching President Kennedy's blockade in the Caribbean.

It is a conflict between printing or
suppressing, not military information
affecting the lives of men on the
battlefield, but historical documents
about a tragic and controversial war;
not between what is right and what is
wrong, but between two honest but
violently conflicting views about what
best serves the national interest and
the enduring principles of the First
Amendment.

June 18, 1971

Appeals Court Reverses Decision Favoring Paper

By JAMES M. NAUGHTON
Special to The New York Times

WASHINGTON, Saturday, June
19—In a 2-to-1 decision this
morning the United States Court
of Appeals reversed the ruling
of a lower court and ordered
The Washington Post to stop
publication of a series of articles, based on classified information, on the history of the
nation's involvement in the
Vietnam war.

The court, however, permitted
The Post to continue publication
of its Saturday editions containing the second of the articles.
Lawyers for the newspaper said
they would decide later today
what course to take in seeking
to continue with the series.

The court overturned an earlier ruling by District Court
Judge Gerhard A. Gesell that
had permitted the newspaper to
publish the second article in a
series based on secret Pentagon
documents.

Judges Spottswood Robinson
3d and Roger Robb agreed with
the Justice Department that
The Post should not be permitted to continue the articles
until hearings were completed
on the Government's request
for a permanent injunction
against the use of the classified
information.

The judges made their ruling
known at 1:20 A.M., about five
hours after Judge Gesell ruled
that there was no evidence that
the articles represented a threat
to national security.

No Statement by Dissenter

Judge J. Skelly Wright dissented, but did not issue a separate statement.

Judges Robinson and Robb
said in a brief order that the
Government had supported its
argument that the articles could
lead to "irreparable" damage to
national security.

The judges set a deadline of
5 P.M. Monday for a decision
by the lower court on the Justice Department's request for a
permanent injunction. The ruling stipulated that the articles
could not continue.

Judge Gesell had ruled, a
little more than two hours before The Post went to press,
that the Government had no
right to seek prior restraint of
the articles. He said that the
Government's proper recourse,
if the publication violated security laws, was to bring criminal action against the newspaper and those responsible.

At the same time, Judge
Gesell said it was unfortunate
that The Post had refused to
cooperate with the Justice Department's request for a voluntary postponement of the series
so that the constitutional clash
of free press and security
classification could be argued
at length in court.

The heart of the Justice Department's complaint—that the
publication of the sensitive information jeopardized national
security—was disregarded by
Judge Gesell. He said in his
three-page written ruling that
"the court has before it no precise information suggesting in
what respects, if any, the publication of this information will
injure the United States."

The Justice Department and
the newspaper repeated before
the three Appeals Court judges
the arguments that they had
presented earlier in the evening before Judge Gesell. The
appellate hearing lasted about
50 minutes.

During the proceeding, The
Post's attorney's warned that
the newspaper was scheduled
to print its first Saturday edition at 10:15 P.M. and that
within 10 minutes it would be
unable to recall the issue.

At 10:20 P.M. the judges recessed.

"We're going, boy, we're
going," said Benjamin C. Bradlee, the executive editor, when
he learned of the decision.

The Government moved to
halt The Post's series as it had
acted against The Times articles four days ago, after The
Post refused today to stop publication of the articles voluntarily.

Times Proceedings Cited

In a key paragraph in his
ruling, Judge Gesell declared:
"What is presented is a raw
question of preserving the freedom of the press as it confronts
the efforts of the Government
to impose a prior restraint on
publication of essentially historical data. The information
unquestionably will be embarrassing to the United States,
but there is no possible way
after the most full and careful
hearing that a court would be
able to determine the implications of publication on the conduct of Government affairs or
to weigh these implications
against the effects of withholding information from the
public."

Judge Gesell said that the Government's determination, announced earlier in court, to proceed against The Post regardless of the outcome of the case against The Times, together with The Post's stated determination to publish the material last night, required that he act.

Suppression Held Impossible

He warned, at the same time, that the newspaper had placed itself "in serious jeopardy of criminal prosecution" by making the material public.

In an earlier hearing on the Government's request, Judge Gesell had said that The Post would not agree to his request for a delay over the weekend to weigh carefully the issue of prior restraint of a free press.

Roger A. Clark, the attorney for The Washington Post Company, insisted that the court would be "treading on dangerous ground if it tries to determine what is news."

In seeking both a temporary restraining order against continuation of the series and a permanent injunction against the use of material from the Pentagon documents, the Justice Department asserted that to continue the articles would cause "irreparable injury" to the national security of the United States.

Kevin T. Maroney, a deputy assistant attorney general, argued in court last night that The Post, in printing the material, was taking the position that its judgment was superior to that of the Government. "Their judgment cannot prevail over the judgment of the Secretary of Defense," Mr. Maroney said.

History has shown that information of this sort cannot be suppressed, Mr. Clark argued

If the Post were restrained, he continued, "the irreparable injury, in my judgment, would be to the system that has worked for 200 years."

The relationship between the Government's action against the Post articles and its earlier court action against The New York Times was argued in the courtroom last night.

Judge Gesell had stated earlier in the day that the principle of comity—courtesy as between equals—should apply and that he believed The Post would suffer no irreparable injury if it were delayed in publication while the Times was under a restraining order. He said that to deny the Government's request for a similar order against The Post would be to decide the case in New York, because The Times could then argue that it had been damaged by the restraint.

Mr. Clark contended that persons who had made the sensitive documents available to the two newspapers out of a "moral fervor" were likely to make them available to others.

Obviously there has been "a leak in the dike" that cannot be plugged, The Post's lawyer said.

When Judge Gesell asked whether the Government knew if any publications other than The Times and The Post had obtained access to the information, Mr. Maroney said he had no information that they might, but he added: "It was news to us to see it in The Post this morning."

Asked what position the Justice Department might take if The Times were permitted to publish its articles today, Mr. Maroney said the case against The Post would continue because different publications might print different parts of the massive Pentagon study.

Mr. Maroney said that the Government was not seeking to impose prior restraint on The Post but to secure the return of top secret documents that the newspaper had "in unlawful possession."

Mr. Bradlee had vowed since receiving a midafternoon telephone call from the Justice Department seeking a voluntary halt in the series to proceed with the articles and to "fight" the request for a court injunction.

Earlier Mr. Bradlee said in an interview that The Post welcomed the court challenge on the issue of prior restraint.

"It seems to me that they've got two people to tangle with now," he said. "It helps the cause. The issue is more joined and more important than ever."

The Post was understood to have received copies of some of the Pentagon study documents through the mail on Monday and to have obtained another group of the Pentagon papers later this week. The newspaper's editors would not disclose the source of their documents, nor did they allude to the method of their receipt in the article yesterday.

The article did not appear in the first two editions of The Post. Mr. Bradlee said that was attributable to lengthy discussions with the newspaper's lawyers. Other employes said that The Post had also taken into account the possibility that if the article had appeared in its early editions, available at 10:30 o'clock Thursday night, the Justice Department might have been alerted to seek to halt the publication of the information between editions.

About half-a-dozen Post reporters were said to have been assigned to the study of the Pentagon documents, working under Chalmers M. Roberts. Other reporters working on the material included Murray Marder, Marilyn Berger and Bernard C. Nossiter. They were said to be preparing a series of six or seven articles, although one Post editor said privately that there was enough material in the documents to publish articles "all year."

Mr. Bradlee said that the decision to publish the first article in a series, while The Times was under a temporary order

restraining it from continuing with its account of the documents, had been reached after extensive discussion.

One Post editor said that a desire to demonstrate to the Justice Department that silencing The Times would not kill the story was "one of the reasons" for publishing the start of The Post's series.

In an advisory notice to editors of some 345 publications that subscribe to the Washington Post-Los Angeles Times News Service, the point was underlined.

Drawing attention to the Justice Department's proceedings against The Times in New York for its use of the same materials, the message said: "In the judgment of the editors, nothing in this article could be used to the injury of the United States."

Unlike the first three installments of The Times's series, the article yesterday in The Post was not accompanied by

separate reproduction of the classified documents, although the article quoted extensively from 15 of the classified papers and from the classified study itself.

The defendants in the civil suit against The Post were all those officers named on the newspaper's masthead plus Mr. Roberts.

The others were Frederick S. Beebe, chairman of The Washington Post Company; John W. Sweeterman, vice chairman of the board; Katherine Graham, publisher; Paul R. Ignatius, president; Mr. Bradlee; Philip L. Beyelin, editorial page editor; Eugene C. Patterson, managing editor; James J. Daly, vice president and general manager; Gerald W. Siegel, vice president and counsel; Robert P. Thome, treasurer; Joseph Lynch, vice president-advertising; Jack F. Patterson, circulation director, and Julian J. Eberle, production operations director.

PRECEDENT SEEN

Nixon's Main Concern Over Future Leaks, High Aide Says

By MARJORIE HUNTER
Special to The New York Times

WASHINGTON, June 18—A high Administration spokesman says that President Nixon is more concerned that a precedent might be set for future disclosures of secret documents than he is over whether The New York Times endangered national security by publishing a Pentagon study.

The President's position was outlined to a small group of newsmen yesterday by Herbert G. Klein, Director of Communications for the Administration.

Mr. Klein told the newsmen that the President's principal concern in The Times case was to discourage officials opposed to the Vietnam war from giving other classified documents to the press.

Meanwhile, The Times's decision to publish the series on the Pentagon study was applauded by some — including George E. Reedy Jr., Press Secretary to former President Lyndon B. Johnson, and Senator Robert W. Packwood, Republican of Oregon—and criticized by others, including Senator Henry M. Jackson, a potential candidate for the Democratic presidential nomination.

3 Installments Published

The Administration has obtained a temporary restraining order from a court—and in seeking a permanent injunction —to prevent The Times from publishing further articles and documents of the secret Pentagon study on United States involvement in the war. Three installments of the series were published early this week.

The Klein briefing—to which The New York Times was not invited—was held on a "background basis," with those present told to attribute the remarks to "White House officials."

The dozen or so newsmen were called about noon by a member of Mr. Klein's staff and invited to a "backgrounder" on The Times case in his office in the Executive Office Building.

One newsman present said that the briefing had lasted two and a half hours, with the first part of it devoted to a discussion by Administration officials of the President's proposed antinarcotics program submitted to Congress earlier yesterday.

"After what seemed an eternity, we finally got around to what we went there for, The Times case," the newsman said.

Several of those present confirmed that Mr. Klein stressed the President's concern over encouraging future disclosures of classified documents.

Mr. Klein repeatedly described the material on which The Times based its series of stories as "stolen goods."

Later in the briefing, however, John W. Dean, counsel to the President, suggested that it might be more appropriate to say that The Times had "unauthorized possession" of the documents.

Mr. Klein told newsmen that the attempt to halt publication of the Pentagon study in The

Times should not be considered an attempt to stifle freedom of the press.

Meanwhile, Lieut. Gov. Lester G. Maddox of Georgia, in a statement yesterday, said that he felt The Times series should be resumed if it "proves that our political leaders have not been honest with the people."

He added, however, "If there is no dishonesty and the release of the information could jeopardize national security, then not another word should be printed."

Mr. Reedy, who was press secretary to President Johnson in 1964 and 1965, said yesterday: "The New York Times has not only a right but an obligation to print the story, to tell the public what is in the study."

Mr. Reedy also told Sid Davis, Washington bureau chief of Westinghouse Broadcasting, that he had been unaware of Administration plans for escalation of the war in early 1965, although he knew something was going on, and that he was told to hold the line that there was no change of policy.

"That's when I suddenly found life unbearable for me," he said in the telephone interview.

Senator Jackson, Democrat of Washington, said yesterday in Sacramento, Calif., that the publication of the Pentagon study might jeopardize the effectiveness of the nation's intelligence system.

But the Senator said that The Times case indicated a need for a review of the nation's methods of classifying and protecting secret information so that only truly sensitive information is kept secret.

Senator Packwood said yesterday that the Government's "embarrassment" over the publication of the study did not justify censoring the articles.

He termed the publication of the articles and the Government's attempt to halt it "one of the 10 biggest" events of the century.

In another development, Senator Stuart Symington, Democrat of Missouri, introduced a resolution today to authorize $250,000 for a two-year study by the Foreign Relations Committee of the policies of the United States in Southeast Asia.

In a letter to Defense Secretary Melvin R Laird, Representative John E. Moss, Democrat of California, demanded access to the 47-volume Pentagon study "in accordance with provisions of the Freedom of Information Act."

Mr. Moss said that under that act, which he helped draft, the burden for justifying withholding of government information rested "squarely on the agency seeking to withhold, and, in my opinion, your department has not offered any legitimate justification to date."

Gurfein's Decision Due Before 1 P.M. Deadline

By FRED P. GRAHAM

Federal District Judge Murray I. Gurfein refused yesterday to permit The New York Times to resume publication immediately of its material from a secret Pentagon study on Vietnam although The Washington Post began publishing a series of articles based on the study in its Friday issue.

In Washington, a Government move for a court order to halt The Post's series was initially rejected by a Federal district judge. However, this decision was reversed early this morning by an appeals court ruling, which ordered The Post to stop publication of its series.

Alexander M. Bickel, a lawyer for The Times, told the court here yesterday that "the readers of The New York Times alone in this country are deprived of this story." He asked that the temporary restraining order imposed on Tuesday be lifted so that The Times could resume publication.

The Washington Post article was distributed by The Washington Post-Los Angeles Times News Service, which has 345 publications as clients, and was also described at length in dispatches by The Associated Press and United Press International, which reach almost all the daily newspapers in the country, as well as in radio and television broadcasts.

Judge Gurfein declined to act on the motion by The Times after the Government gave assurances in open court that legal action would also be taken against The Washington Post if necessary to prevent further publication. Within hours Justice Department lawyers moved in Federal District Court in Washington to enjoin The Post.

The restraining order against The Times is scheduled to expire at 1 P.M. today, which would free the newspaper to put the next installment in the series in Sunday's issue. Before the deadline Judge Gurfein is expected to hand down his decision on the Justice Department's action to enjoin The Times indefinitely.

Three Installments

The Times published the first three installments on Sunday, Monday and Tuesday, at which time the temporary order halted publication. The articles and documents printed covered events surrounding the Tonkin Gulf incident in 1964, the decision to bomb North Vietnam and the first use of American soldiers in ground combat in South Vietnam.

The effort by The Times to dissolve the restraining order came at the beginning of a daylong series of open and secret hearings. The Government insisted on secret "in camera" testimony by three Washington officials on the ground that they would explain how further publication could damage national interests and that open testimony would itself cause harm.

The arguments in open court were held in a court chamber where every seat was filled and as many more spectators stood pressed together along the walls and in the aisles.

Whitney North Seymour Jr. the United States Attorney, had been away during the week and a 30-year-old assistant, Michael D. Hess, had handled the case. Mr. Seymour appeared yesterday to make the Government's primary argument.

At the defendants' counsel table, in addition to Mr. Bickel, there were two New York trial lawyers, Floyd Abrams and William E. Hegarty, and James C. Goodale, general counsel for The Times. All four had been given emergency security clearances by the Government so that they could participate in the secret session.

Mr. Seymour based his argument on the assertion that The Times had violated United States law and Presidential orders by illegally "declassifying" top secret documents by publishing them. That, he said, had "compromised our current military and defense plans and intelligence operations and has jeopardized our international relations."

The Times, in a legal brief and affidavits filed late last night, asserted that the Government's security classification system was a sham in which documents were routinely overclassified and that officials used it to hide embarrassing information while "leaking" other sensitive material.

In any event, The Times argued, the First Amendment forbids either the executive branch or the courts to use "national security" grounds to prevent the news media from publishing any article except in such extreme situations as threatened publication of troop movements or battle plans in wartime.

In the abbreviated open testimony by the Government's witnesses, they sought to show that the system of classifying documents "top secret" "secret" "confidential" or "restricted" was carefully administered" to avoid abuses.

Dennis J. Doolin, Deputy Assistant Secretary of Defense for Internal Security Affairs, said he had reviewed the Pentagon study on Vietnam on several occasions to decide if it should be declassified because Senator J. W. Fulbright, chairman of the Senate Foreign Relations Committee, had asked to see it.

'Entwined' Information

Mr. Doolin said that his staff considered the "universe" of security interests affected by the entire 47-volume study and concluded that it could not be declassified. It would be impractical to declassify certain nonsensitive portions, he said, because the information was "entwined."

William B. Macomber, Deputy Under Secretary of State in charge of administration, testified that the three articles already published by The Times had damaged the United States' international relations. "It is absolutely essential to the conduct of diplomacy that governments be able to deal in confidence," he said, without fear that communications will appear in print.

The Vice Chief of Naval Operations, Vice Adm. Francis J. Blouin, testified that "it would be a disaster" to publish all the documents in the 7,000-page Pentagon archive. "Any intelligence organization would derive a great deal of benefit from the articles that have already been published," he asserted.

The Government's final witness, George MacClain, holds the title of director of the Security Classification Management Division in the office of the Assistant Secretary of Defense for Administration. He explained the intricate procedures by which documents become classified and, in some cases, lose their classified status years later.

The major answer by The Times came in an affidavit by Max Frankel, the Washington correspondent of The Times and the head of its Washington bureau, who called the Government's view of secrecy "antiquated, quaint and romantic." In practice, he said, it serves to mask "traffic in secrets" in which officials peddle "secret" information for their own ends and journalists publish it in wholesale amounts.

Judge Gurfein broke off the secret testimony at about 8 P.M. yesterday and returned after dinner at 9:30 P.M. for the final arguments in open court.

Participants in the closed testimony had been told not to disclose it, but Mr. Bickel said during his closing argument that "nothing I heard 'in camera' struc. me as justifying going on in this case."

At 10:30 P.M. the final arguments were over. The judge told the lawyers to contact him at 11 A.M. today, possibly to receive his decision.

During the morning session the Judge referred repeatedly to the duty of a "patriotic press" and suggested that disputes such as the spreading legal confrontation over the Pentagon study could be avoided if journalists would clear sensitive articles with the Government "from a security point of view" before publication.

"It seems to me that a free and independent press ought to be willing to sit down with the Department of Justice," he said, "and as a matter of simple patriotism determine whether the publication of any of them [classified documents] is or is not dangerous to the national security."

Mr. Bickel, who is a professor of law at Yale, replied that the suggestion was "utterly inconsistent with the First Amendment." He said it would lead to self-censorship by the press or censorship by government.

Affidavits supporting the position of The Times were filed by Theodore C. Sorenson. who served as special counsel to President John F. Kennedy;

Sanford Cobb, president of the Association of American Publishers, Inc.; Col. Augustus McKnight, president of the American Society of Newspaper Editors; Adrian S. Fisher, former deputy director of the United States Arms Control and Disarmament Agency and dean of the Georgetown University Law Center; Francis T. P. Plimpton, former Ambassador and Deputy United States permanent representative at the United Nations and a former president of the Bar Association of New York City; James McGregor Burns, Pulitzer Prize-winning presidential biographer and historian; Eric F. Goldman, former special consultant to President Johnson and now Rollins Professor of History at Princeton University; Barbara W. Tuchman, Pulitzer Prize - winning historian; Neil Sheehan and Hedrick Smith, who are co-defendants in the suit, and Mr. Frankel, the chief of the Washington bureau of The Times, and Tad Szulc, Robert M. Smith, John W. Finney and Walter Rugaber, reporters of the Washington Bureau.

Mr. Sorensen said that during his three years as President Kennedy's special counsel he held "a top security clearance, read classified documents daily and drafted many such documents to or for the President."

He read the materials that appeared in The Times on June 13, 14 and 15, he said, and, in his judgment their publication would not embarrass foreign governments, nor did any of the "information and opinions revealed appear to have any current facets requiring continued secrecy."

Excerpts From Arguments in U.S. Case Against Times

Following are excerpts from arguments before Judge Murray I. Gurfein in United States District Court here yesterday in the case of the United · States Government against The New York Times Company and from affidavits by Max Frankel, a member of the staff of The Times, and by Theodore C. Sorensen, a former Presidential adviser:

Arguments

ALEXANDER M. BICKEL, for The Times—Your Honor, the new matter I wish to bring to your attention came to our attention first thing this morning. The Washington Post has begun publication, under a headline, and I will go into that in a moment more thoroughly, "Documents Reveal U. S. Effort in '54 to Delay Viet Election," heavily quoting from the same documents that The New York Times is alleged to possess, and publication proceeds from portions of those documents which The New York Times has not yet published. It is the first in a series.

Now, Your Honor, The Washington Post runs a news service to 345 clients, including The Washington Post among them, which has the article, "More War Secrets," and we have, if Your Honor wishes to see, what went out from The Washington Post News Service.

The New York Post in introducing the series, which it gets from The Washington Post News Service, says, "The Washington Post has obtained access to sections of the Pentagon report on the Vietnam war, part of which appeared in The New York Times before the Government got a temporary injunction to halt publication. The first in a series of articles based on previously unpublished parts of the report begins here."

These articles were published, those portions that The New York Times is under temporary restraining order not to publish. These stories have gone out on the wire services. There are three AP stories, one UPI story quoting heavily from The Post, so that I think, Your Honor, without any exaggeration, we can assume this story is out and available, those portions of it which The New York Times had not printed before are out and available and will be made

available by every news medium in the United States to the public. We suggest, Your Honor, that this radically changes the posture of the case, it radically changes the position of the temporary restraining order that Your Honor issued.

May I add, before I go on to that, the stories, as we read them in The Washington Post, quote heavily and at great length—I see no difference from what The Times itself did—from documents of exactly the same sort that The Times had, there are quotations from National Security Council documents, there are ample quotations, at length, for more than a column, with my red markings on them, and perhaps your Honor will examine it yourself, the length of these quotations, from cavils, various documents of exactly the same sort, and it is the portion of them that The Times has not yet printed.

Question About Document

THE COURT—Would The Times then voluntarily show me what you have? You still have not done anything about that and I am in the dark and I don't know whether it was the same document or another document.

MR. BICKEL—We have now given the Government a list which I think is responsive to that request.

THE COURT—But it is not responsive to an allegation that The Washington Post is publishing the same thing. I have nothing before me that indicates that.

MR. BICKEL—Your Honor has the list which we have made available to the Government of documents in the possession of The New York Times, which I think will confirm that The Washington Post, as it itself says, is publishing from the same documents and from the portion of the documents that The Times has not yet published, what The New York Times has.

May I say parenthetically that your Honor is aware, of course, that this is a different issue for us because— this is a separate issue for us because there is a separate Constitutional ground that The Times relies on, the Caldwell ground, essentially, which disables The Times, in its view, from making available the copies of the documents that it has.

The Government is in a perfect position to confirm what The Washington Post stories are and I think, from the list, so is your Honor.

Times Readers Deprived

It seems to us that the radical change in the situation is that there is now a situation which the readers of The New York Times alone in this country are deprived of this story. This is a degree of irreparable damage which varies, is different, it seems to me, altogether from the situation that confronted your Honor on Tuesday last when you granted the temporary restraining order.

The Washington Post, I simply want to say, is in our view doing exactly what is its right to do and, indeed, is doing, in our view, its duty as a newspaper.

But the fact is that the readers of The New York Times, probably by afternoon the single newspaper in the country of which it can be said, are being deprived and thus The Times and they are irreparably damaged, are being deprived of access to a story which every other medium in the country now has, or will have, 345 papers directly from The Washington Post News Service, and as Your Honor knows there is also a question under an order such as Your Honor issued whether The Times is free or in what position The Times is free to report the story as it is appearing elsewhere.

From the Government's point of view, the situation is equally radically changed. We suggest to Your Honor that the case is simply, in the simplest terms, moot, that there is no national security consideration, if there ever was one, which we don't concede, left in this case, there is nothing for Your Honor to protect with a temporary restraining order.

Issue of Permanent Injunction

I will add only that it seems to us also that the possibility of prevailing and getting a permanent injunction, which is of course relevant on the hearing this morning and relevant as well on the temporary restraining order in an attenuated fashion — that possibility, it seems to us, has vanished.

It seems to us quite clear that if there was any further reason to demonstrate that all The Times did is what every newspaper in the country would do given the opportunity, that The Times acted within the well-understood usages of the newspaper profession and this proves it and in our view of the case that defeats the Government's case, that makes it impossible to speak of this within the First Amendment as an unauthorized or unlawful publication within 793-E.

So, Your Honor, I am moving now for an order to vacate your temporary restraining order and if Your Honor desires, we are having papers prepared and will hand them up to the bench as soon as they become available. But I move orally now that the order be vacated.

MICHAEL D. HESS, for the Government—Pursuant to Your Honor's suggestion, the parties got together yesterday after court to discuss the possibility of our obtaining a list from The Times. The list that we got then was just four pages long. The items on those four pages were stated in very broad terms, and, frankly, Your Honor, they did not help us as much as we had hoped.

THE COURT—What I am really asking you is, does the Government intend to move against The Washington Post, if you know?

MR. HESS—I do not know at this moment, Your Honor, but we will show you that the case is certainly not moot and that there are serious problems of foreign relations that will result if The Times does publish, and that issue still remains in the case this morning. They are the defendants here, Your Honor. They are the only ones before Your Honor, and we wish to proceed as planned.

THE COURT—In denying interventions I said that The Times could adequately represent the interests of the reading public, and I meant it. Now Professor Bickel makes the point that in the present situation the readers of The New York Times are the only readers who cannot read this material.

Position Called Unique

MR. HESS—Your Honor, I would say that The Times put themselves, in a way, in this position by opening the subject, being the first to announce that they were going to publish and coming into this Court and asking this Court to decide. They said they would agree that the Court should decide. We would say that they put themselves in this unique position.

MR. BICKEL—First of all, Your Honor, we are not in this Court because we came into this Court seeking its approval of our publishing enterprise. We are in this Court because the Government brought us in this Court. The Government obtained from your Honor a temporary restraining order on the basis that there was relatively no damage, no injury, to The Times in imposing a temporary restraint on publication, and, on the other hand, that there was serious damage impending to the Government.

We suggest to Your Honor that the position has changed radically on both sides. There is now damage to The Times and from the Government's point of view the security interest is not visible with the naked eye any longer. These things are coming out.

The Government says it may move against The Washington Post. It may move against The Washington Post —when?

We are talking about a publication of maybe two, three days, a series, and The Times's story is gone. That is simply not sufficient, your Honor, at this stage to outweigh the interest of The Times.

The Government's position in this court, Your Honor, was that grave danger to the national security would occur if another installment of a story that The Times had were published. Another installment of that story has been published. The republic stands and it stood the first three **days.**

We don't see how the national interest can now remain in danger in the Government's view of this case which prevailed with Your Honor on Tuesday last. This story is out. We have information that Congressman McCloskey has a copy and is about to put it in the Congressional Record. Every news medium in the United States has access to exactly what The Times is alleged to have. How can it be said that The Times is in a special position of being the only one in the media under a restraining order and how can the damage that is thus done to the readership of The Times be supportable?

THE COURT—You pose a very difficult problem. The question is still, so far as the United States security is concerned, that a free and independent press ought to be willing to sit down with the Department of Justice and screen these documents that you have or The Washington Post has or anybody else has as a matter of simple patriotism to determine whether the publication of any of them is or is not dangerous to the national security.

If you disagree, then surely you would have the right and the Government has the right equally to go into a court and ask a court to make that decision. I am concerned about things that come right to the surface. The lack of perhaps paraphrase of code messages, I use that as one illustration, I am concerned about material sent by foreign governments which do not belong to the United States under the rules of international law, as I know them, they are merely in our custody, and a few other limited categories of that type or perhaps the revelation of methods of intelligence gathering, all of which as patriotic citizens I think the press as well as anybody else agrees should be kept sacrosanct, not to deprive anybody of a right to express an opinion, mind you, but in order to protect what is dear to all of us, the security of the country.

Explanation Requested

I say that only preliminary to my asking you again in good faith whether The Times cannot supply us, supply the Court—and I can order it, you know, I am trying to stay so closely within the ambit of your Constitutional protection that if I can do it without an order, I would rather do it—I don't understand, though, frankly, why a patriotic press should not be willing to subject these papers not to censorship of any kind, except from a limited security point of view. I wish you would answer that because it is troubling me.

MR. BICKEL—We are prepared, if Your Honor so wishes, to expand the list that we have handed the U. S. Attorney. Beyond that, I think we can assume we are all, as the light is given to us to see, equally interested in the national security and equally interested in the First Amendment.

THE COURT — I assume that and that is why I made the suggestion.

MR. BICKEL — Precisely. We know of no allegation in any of the Government's papers of nothing that is substantial and specific that suggests that anything that The Times put in print broke a code, compromised a code, came within five miles of an existing code that the United States is interested in the security of.

THE COURT—With all due respect, I may say that neither you nor I nor The New York Times is competent to pass on that subject as to what will lead to the breaking of a code.

WHITNEY NORTH SEYMOUR Jr., for the Government—As we see it, the issue in this proceeding is a very simple one, and that is whether, when an unauthorized person comes into possession of documents which have been classified under lawful procedures, that person may unilaterally declassify those documents in his sole discretion.

The position of the Government in the proceeding is equally simple. These are stolen documents. They are classified. They compromise our current military and defense plans and intelligence operations and jeopardize our international relations.

Contrary to some of the suggestions in counsel's argument, and in the brief, that what this amounts to is a bald attempt at suppression and censorship, we have attempted to approach the matter with the highest regard for the Constitutional rights of all concerned and in an orderly, lawful process.

As your Honor will recall, the proceeding began with the sending of a very polite telegram from the Attorney General to The Times asking them if they would, voluntarily cease publication and return the documents. The Times in its discretion refused to do so.

We then, with as much notice as we could under the circumstances, approached the Court to have the matter decided judicially under our system, and again, during the course of those preliminary proceedings, Your Honor, also asked The Times if they would voluntarily suspend publication so that the matter could be considered reasonably by the Court, and again The Times refused to do so, and it was only in those circumstances that the temporary restraining order was signed.

We are now at the point where we are presenting the matter on the merits, and I think it is important to recognize at the outset that our sole purpose here is to present the evidence to the Court so that the matter can be decided impartially and objectively on the facts and on the merits and in accordance with the law.

We are prepared, in fact, to do what we believe the defendants should have done in reverse—that is, to submit to the Court, under appropriate protections, the classified documents so your Honor yourself can make the determination as to whether the Government's position is sound.

In doing so, we remind Your Honor that the Congress in its wisdom has enacted the Freedom of Information Act, which was precisely designed to take care of the problems of access to Government documents, that there in fact has been a specific test under that act and under the Congressional intention about the declassification of documents, and that the present law is that only if the classification has been arbitrary or unsupportable will the documents be declared to be declassified and available for unauthorized distribtuion.

THE COURT—That is a statutory matter, Mr. Seymour.

MR. SEYMOUR—Yes, sir.

THE COURT—But we are talking of the Constitutional matter beyond that. I think that the question then would be whether, assuming that in the guise of security—you must face that question — a government wishes to suppress matters that might be embarrassing to it domestically, the Government has the right to do that under the First Amendment.

Mr. SEYMOUR — I think that is very fair statement of the issue, and we are prepared to meet it head-on.

Suppression Charge Denied

Contrary, again, to counsel's allegations both in the brief and in the argument that this is an attempt by the Government to suppress the publication of historical data, or as I think he just said censorship to avoid matters which might cause discomfiture, the concern of the United States in this proceeding is a very fundamental one and it deals directly on the merits with the security of the United States, military matters, defense matters, intelligence matters, international relations, and we intend to show by live witnesses and documentary evidence that some of these matters may have occurred a few years ago, some going back beyond that, that interwoven in the materials which have been the subject of these presentations are documents which still have current vitality, whose disclosure would currently adversely affect the military alliances, diplomatic efforts relating to a number of sensitive matters, including military matters, and present and future military and defense plans and strategy.

Obviously we approach this proceeding on the assumption that The Times acted in complete good faith and had no knowledge itself of these potential consequences, or indeed, if they had, they would have forebore from publishing it. We wish we had had an opportunity to discuss it with them under less tense circumstances, but this was the only option that was ultimately left open to us when they refused to voluntarily suspend.

That good faith, however, does not alter the fundamental fact that the defendants had in their possession material that was classified, that they were not authorized to have that material, and they decided on their own to declassify it and to operate as if it were not protected under the Executive order and the statutes, without making any effort to determine whether there could be any objection to doing so.

The starting point in the Government's proof today,

your Honor, will of course be the Executive orders, Executive Order 1051 as amended, promulgated by Presidents Eisenhower and Kennedy, and the Government will offer proof, first of all, that The Times has already published verbatim texts of classified documents; secondly, that although it may not be obvious to the layman, to the trained intelligence man there are already disclosures which are harmful to the interests of the United States;· that the international relations of the United States have already been impaired; and that we are not dealing with matters of closed history but matters which have very current vitality and significance.

Witnesses Described

The proof we will offer will be documents and live witnesses. And I should point out, your Honor, that the witnesses that you will hear are career officers of the military and diplomatic services.

After preliminary testimony by the first witness, about the nature of the documents in question and the procedures that were followed, we will then move to have testimony that relates to the specific classified material heard en camera and the documents received en camera under appropriate protections that maintain the classification of the documents.

Obviously, as we approach the task, it is more difficult because we have only this list as to what The Times has in its possession. And so, on the basis of that, we are going to have to speculate to some extent as to precisely what they do have. But to get the issue properly before your Honor, we are left with little alternative.

Affidavit by Frankel

The Government's unprecedented challenge to The Times in the case of the Pentagon papers, I am convinced, cannot be understood, or decided, without an appreciation of the manner in which a small and specialized corps of reporters and a few hundred American officials regularly make use of so-called classified, secret and top-secret information and documentation. It is a cooperative, competitive, antagonistic and arcane relationship.

Without the use of "secrets" that I shall attempt to explain in this affidavit, there could be no adequate diplomatic, military and political reporting of the kind our people take for granted, either abroad or in Washington, and there could be no mature system of communication between the Gov-

ernment and the people. That is one reason why the sudden complaint by one party to these regular dealings strikes us as monstrous and hypocritical—unless it is essentially perfunctory, for the purpose of retaining some discipline over the Federal bureaucracy.

Rarely Just for Public

Presidents make "secret" decisions only to reveal them for the purposes of frightening an adversary nation, wooing a friendly electorate, protecting their reputations. The military services conduct "secret" research in weaponry only to reveal it for the purpose of enhancing their budgets, appearing superior or inferior to a foreign army, gaining the vote of a Congressman or the favor of a contractor. High officials of the Government reveal secrets in the search for support of their policies, or to help sabotage the plans and policies of rival departments. Middle-rank officials of government reveal secrets so as to attract the attention of their superiors or to lobby against the orders of those superiors. Though not the only vehicle for this traffic in secrets—the Congress is always eager to provide a forum—the press is probably the most important.

In the field of foreign affairs, only rarely does our Government give full public information to the press for the direct purpose of simply informing the people. For the most part, the press obtains significant information bearing on foreign policy only because it has managed to make itself a party to confidential materials, and of value in transmitting these materials from government to other branches and offices of government as well as to the public at large. This is why the press has been wisely and correctly called The Fourth Branch of Government.

Consistent Violations

I turn now in an attempt to explain, from a reporter's point of view, the several ways in which "classified" information figures in our relations with government. The Government's complaint against The Times in the present case comes with ill-grace because government itself has regularly and consistently, over the decades, violated the conditions it suddenly seeks to impose upon us—in three distinct ways:

First, it is our regular partner in the informal but customary traffic in secret information, without even the pretense of legal or formal "declassification." Presumably, many of the "secrets" I cited above, and all the

The New York Times/Neal Boenzi

AT U.S. COURT HOUSE: Alexander M. Bickel, left, and Floyd Abrams, with sunglasses, lawyers for The Times, arriving for session yesterday. Behind them are, from left: Max Frankel, the Washington correspondent; Tom Wicker, associate editor; Harding F. Bancroft, executive vice president, and James C. Goodale, vice president.

"secret" documents and pieces of information that form the basis of the many newspaper stories that are attached hereto, remain "secret" in their official designation.

Regular Misuse of Data

Second, the Government and its officials regularly and customarily engage in a kind of ad hoc, de facto "declassification" that normally has no bearing whatever on considerations of the national interest. To promote a political, personal, bureaucratic or even commercial interest, incumbent officials and officials who return to civilian life are constantly revealing the secrets entrusted to them. They use them to barter with the Congress or the press, to curry favor with foreign governments and officials from whom they seek information in return. They use them freely, and with a startling record of impunity, in their memoirs and other writings.

Third, the Government and its officials regularly and routinely misuse and abuse the "classification" of information, either by imposing secrecy where none is justified or by retaining it long after the justification has become invalid, for simple reasons of political or bureaucratic convenience. To hide mistakes of judgment, to protect reputations of individuals, to cover up the loss and waste of funds, almost everything in Government is kept secret for a time and, in the foreign policy field, classified as "secret" and "sensitive" beyond any rule of law or reason. Every minor official can testify to this fact.

Affidavit by Sorensen

I believe the national security interests of the United States will be irreparably injured if these documents are suppressed from public and Congressional view; if the United States is thereby prevented as a nation from learning the true history of what went wrong in Vietnam; if the same policies of concealment and deception which prevented debate and produced mistakes in this nation's approach to Vietnam are thereby judicially encouraged to continue.

June 19, 1971

PANEL WILL RULE

Government's Plea to Be Heard by Three Judges Tomorrow

By FRED P. GRAHAM

United States District Judge Murray I. Gurfein refused yesterday to enjoin The New York Times from publishing further articles based upon a secret Pentagon study of the origins of the Vietnam war.

However, Judge Irving R. Kaufman of the United States Court of Appeals for the Second Circuit blocked The Times from resuming publication of the material in today's issue.

He restrained further publication until noon tomorrow, to allow time for a three-judge panel of the Court of Appeals to consider Judge Gurfein's ruling before the series resumes. The panel will meet tomorrow morning at the United States Court House on Foley Square.

Explains Action

Judge Kaufman explained in a brief opinion that the law required decisions by the Court of Appeals to be made by three-judge panels, not single judges. For him to let The Times publish the material before a three-judge court could be convened, he said, would be tantamount to deciding the case alone.

The series, documenting the American involvement in Vietnam, appeared in the Sunday Monday and Tuesday issues last week before it was halted by a temporary restraining order.

Judge Gurfein temporarily broke the tension of the four-day legal struggle between the United States Government and The Times in midafternoon when he issued a 16-page opinion that rejected the Justice Department's assertion that the publication would severely damage the national interest.

Stresses Press Freedom

Insisting that the most important concern was "the free flow of information so that the public will be informed," he declared that the press must be free to print sensitive matter even if it embarrassed the Government.

"If there be some embarrassment to the Government in security aspects as remote as the general embarrassment that flows from any security breach, we must learn to live with it," he declared. "The security of the nation is not at the ramparts alone. Security also lies in the value of our free institutions."

The heart of Judge Gurfein's decision was his finding that the Government had failed to show that the disclosure of what he referred to as "historic" documents would harm the national interest enough to justify a "prior restraint" on a publication.

7,000-Page Study

The First Amendment's free-press guarantee prevents any such restraint, he said, unless the Government can show that it is "absolutely vital to current national security." He noted that this appeared to have been the first time in the nation's history that the Government had attempted to do so in the name of "national security."

The Times articles were drawn from a 7,000-page study, prepared at the direction of Secretary of Defense Robert S. McNamara, which traces the American involvement in Vietnam until early 1968.

Following Judge Gurfein's decision, Arthur Ochs Sulzberger, president and publisher of The Times, said:

"Judge Gurfein's opinion reaffirms the basic principles on which a free press must be based. This reaffirmation is what The Times sought in the court proceedings, and we are heartened that the great Constitutional issues involved have been faced and resolved in favor of the citizen's right to know."

At the injunction hearing on Friday, three Washington officials testified before Judge Gurfein at an "in camera" hearing, in order to support the Government's claims of threatened peril to the national security.

He declared in the opinion that this secret testimony "did not convince this court that the publication of these historical documents would seriously breach the national security."

"It is true, of course, that any breach of security will cause the jitters in the security agencies" and among foreign governments, he said. But he concluded that "no cogent reasons were advanced as to why these documents except in the general framework of embarrassment previously mentioned, would vitally affect the security of the nation."

Thus the Government failed to establish the threat of "irreparable injury" that is necessary to obtain a preliminary injunction, Judge Gurfein said. He added that he considered it unlikely that the Government could succeed in its case later, if more evidence were taken in a permanent injunction proceeding.

In his opinion, Judge Gurfein rejected the Government's assertion that various provisions of the espionage laws could be used as a basis to block newspaper publication of classified matter.

Referring to Title 18 of the United States Code, section 793 (d), which was a major provision cited by the Government, Judge Gurfein termed it "truly an espionage section" aimed at "secret or clandestine communications" to foreign agents.

This section makes it a crime for anyone having unauthorized possession of secret documents, code books or other secret material to communicate them to others with the belief that they might be used to harm the country.

Even if this law might be held by a higher court to apply to newspapers, he said, it would not apply to The Times' publication. "There is no reasonable likelihood of the Government successfully proving that the actions of The Times were not in good faith," he said. "This has been an effort on the part of The Times to vindicate the right of the public to know."

These findings could substantially reduce the possibility that the Justice Department will bring criminal action against the newsmen who participated in the publication. Justice Department officials have said that an investigation is in progress to determine if any criminal laws were violated.

The opinion traced many of the legal arguments advanced in the brief and oral argument of The Times's lawyer, Prof. Alexander M. Bickel of the Yale Law School. The judge concluded, as Mr. Bickel had argued, that Congress had considered statutes to censor the press, and that—even under the stress of wartime—had always refused to enact them.

The New York law firm of Cahil, Gordon also represented The Times. Two of its partners, Floyd Abrams and William E. Hegarty, participated in the trial.

Judge Gurfein concluded with the observation that in his view the Justice Department had not attempted to "stifle criticism." But he said that the Government's efforts could result in precensorship, "the primary evil to be dealt with in the First Amendment."

When the temporary restraining order that he had issued on Tuesday lapsed at 1 P.M. yesterday, Judge Gurfein had not announced his decision and tension mounted among the lawyers, newsmen and spectators that gathered at the Foley Square Court House.

The Times, having notified the court that the deadline for its first Sunday edition was 4:30 P.M., withheld any publication action as the 1 P.M. deadline passed. Finally it was decided that the next installment of the series would be withheld from The Times's news service wires.

Judge Gurfein's decision finally came down from his 29th floor office at 2:30 P.M. While he ruled for the newspaper, he restrained it from publishing until the Government asked the Court of Appeals for a stay.

Whitney North Seymour Jr., the United States Attorney, went promptly to the Court of Appeals chambers. Judge Kaufman was on duty to handle emergency matters in the absence of the other judges, and he heard arguments from Mr. Seymour and Mr. Bickel in open court.

Mr. Seymour noted that The Washington Post had also been restrained from publishing materials from the secret study, and that the order would lapse at 5 P.M. tomorrow, after hearings before a three-judge panel. He asked for a similar order, so that both newspapers would be subject to the same time schedule.

Judge Kaufman told Mr. Bickel that the judge's colleagues could say that he had "usurped power" if he alone settled the matter by allowing publications to resume. He left the courtroom briefly and returned at 3:43 P.M. to read his brief decision.

Sydney Gruson, a vice president of The Times, announced later that The Times would not attempt to take the matter to the Supreme Court over the weekend, but would ask the Court of Appeals to lift the stay at the hearing scheduled for tomorrow morning. The normal meeting time for the Court of Appeals is 10:30 A.M.

Text of Court of Appeals Opinion Restraining The Washington Post From Publishing Articles

Special to The New York Times

WASHINGTON, June 19—Following is the text of the opinion by the United States Court of Appeals for the District of Columbia today in The Washington Post case; as well as the text of the dissenting opinion by Judge J. Skelly Wright.

Court's Opinion

UNITED STATES COURT OF APPEALS
FOR THE DISTRICT OF CO-LUMBIA CIRCUIT No. 71-1478
UNITED STATES OF AMER-ICA
v.
THE WASHINGTON POST COMPANY, et al on motion for summary reversal of the order of the District Court denying a temporary restraining order.

Per Curiam: Very early this morning, we entered an order in this case summarily reversing an order of the District Court denying appellant, the Government, a temporary restraining order. We now summarize the reasons for the action we deemed necessary in the unusual circumstances with which we were confronted.

Appellees, the Washington Post Company and certain of its officers, are in possession of portions of a 47-volume "top secret" document known as the "History of U.S. Decision-Making Process on Vietnam Policy." Yesterday they published information derived from that document, and admittedly intend to publish more. The Government filed in the District Court a complaint and affidavits of responsible officials claiming that publication of material from the document has prejudiced and will prejudice the conduct of the nation's military efforts and diplomatic relations, and will result in irreparable harm to the national defense. Appellees claim that the material is historical in character, that its publication, therefore, cannot reasonably be expected to prejudice defense interests, though it may embarrass both governments and individuals, and that the First Amendment protects their right to publish it.

About 8 P.M. yesterday,

the District Court denied the Government's request for a temporary restraining order to prevent further publication of this material by appellees. In its memorandum opinion, the Court expressed the views that the Supreme Court's opinion in Near v. Minnesota, 283 U.S. 697 (1931), supported total freedom of the press, and that criminal sanctions were the Government's only remedy for publication of classified information. The Court also said that it had no precise indication of how publication of the material would injure the United States; it felt that other parties may also have copies of the document and may divulge its contents to other sources, so that judicial intervention might ultimately be futile. The Court was also concerned that even after a full hearing, it might not be able to weight the conflicting private, public and governmental interests in secrecy and freedom of the information.

We have concluded that the District Court's action was improper. In the first place, freedom of the press, as important as it is, is not boundless. The Near case relied on so heavily by the District Court involved a broad scheme for injunctions against "obscene, lewd and lascivious" or "malicious, scandalous and defamatory" publications. In the Supreme Court's opinion, that scheme was clearly a prior restraint on the press prohibited by the. First Amendment. But Near recognized a narrow area, embracing prominently the national security in which a prior restraint on publication might be appropriate. See 283 U.S. At 715-16. We think the instant case may lie within that area.

Second, the District Court placed questionable reliance on the traditional rule that equity will not enjoin conduct amounting to crime. The principle is a corollary of the more general principle that equitable relief is inappropriate where there is an adequate remedy at law. The Supreme Court has recognized exceptions to the rule against injunctions to prevent crimes in cases where an important public interest was threatened with irreparable

harm. See, e.g., Hecht Co. v. Bowles, 321 U.S. 321 (1944); in re Debs, 158 U.S. 564 (1895). Section 1(B) of the Internal Security Act of 1950 indicates that the criminal sanctions the act provides for dissemination of classified information are not to be construed as establishing military or civilian censorship. 64 Stat. 987; see 18 U.S.C. graf 793 (1964). But it is hardly clear that Congress thereby meant to foreclose all possible resort to injunctive relief to protect such information in such exceptional circumstances as would justify prior restraints under Near.

Thus we think the law permits an injunction against publication of material vitally affecting the national security. In this case, the Government makes precisely that claim—that publication by appellees will irreparably harm the national defense. The District Court, nevertheless, found that the Government had not advanced even a basis for a temporary restraint to determine whether there is any merit to its claim. Under the circumstances, we think that the District Court erred in that ruling.

We are aware that the Government has not set forth particular elements of prejudice to the national defense, and that the document in question covered a period which ended over four years ago. But we also recognize that the Government may not have been able to make specific allegations without knowing precisely what parts of the document are held by appellees, and that there is an interest in avoiding disclosure of classified information even in court where such disclosure is not crucial to the court's decision. See United States v. Reynolds, 345 U.S. 1, 8-10 (1953). The document is admittedly a review of the conduct of military and diplomatic affairs with respect to a war which continues into the present. And the Government did present affidavits of officials in a position to know what sort of harm might result from publication of material derived from the documents. These circumstances do not provide a sufficient basis

for determining, one way or the other, whether all of the document is essentially historical in character or whether any of it has a present impact on vital matters affecting national security. We do not understand how it can be determined without a hearing and without even a cursory examination of the material that it is nothing but "historical data" without present vitality.

While we are advertent to the heavy burden the Government bears to demonstrate ample justification for any restraint on publication, we are unable to escape the conclusion that the denial of a temporary restraining order may possibly threaten national security. Judicial responsibility, in our view, cannot properly be discharged without some inquiry into the matter. The Government does not ask us to accept its allegations, but only to afford it an opportunity to prove them. While appellees will be delayed by a grant of relief, and while courts should always hesitate to restrain free expression, the injury to appellees from a brief pause in publication is clearly outweighed by the grave potentiality of injury to the national security.

Under these circumstances, we felt compelled to reverse the decision of the District Court, and to restrain publication for the shortest possible period consistent with an opportunity for the Government to substantiate its claims at a hearing on its request for a preliminary injunction.
REVERSED

Dissenting Opinion

Wright, Circuit Judge, dissenting: This is a sad day for America. Today, for the first time in two hundred years of our history, the Executive Department has succeeded in stopping the presses. It has enlisted the judiciary in the suppression of four most precious freedoms. As if the long and sordid war in Southeast Asia had not already done enough harm to our people, it now is used to cut out the heart of our free institutions and system of government. I decline to follow my colleagues down this road and I must forcefully state my dissent.

The Executive Department has sought to impose a prior restraint on publication of a series of articles by The Washington Post. The District Court refused to cooperate. Very basic constitutional principles support the District Court's decision.

In Near v. Minnesota, 283 U. S. 713 (1931), Mr. Chief Justice Hughes spoke for the Supreme Court and stated that imposition of prior restraints upon publishing is "the essence of censorship." ID. At 713. He quoted Blackstone, the father of our common-law liberties, and Madison, the father of our Constitution, to the effect that prior restraints on speech and press constitute the most heinous encroachment on our freedom. In the early days, Americans such as Madison had hoped that their country would not follow the repressive course of England. "Here, as Madison said, 'the great and essential rights of the people are secured against legislative as well as executive ambition. They are secured, not by laws paramount to prerogative, but by constitutions paramount to laws. This security of the freedom of the press requires that it should be exempt not only from previous restraint by the Executive, but from legislative restraint also.'" ID. At 714.

Under the First Amendment of our Constitution, prior restraints upon speech and press are even more serious than subsequent punishment. There is no question as to the extent of the deterrent effect. A restraining order imposed by a court, applies directly against a particular individual or newspaper and carries very specific and very severe penalties for contempt. It is imposed before the speech at issue has even seen the light of day. As in this case, it is imposed even before the judges have read the offending material—imposed quite literally in the dark. The weapon of the prior injunction is a weapon long unused, but potentially deadly.

It is said that a temporary restraining order suppresses free speech only for a few days, and what is the hurry? That argument, in my opinion, cheapens the First Amendment. All of the presumptions must run in favor of free speech, not against it. It is the Government, not the newspapers, which should be asked, "What is the hurry?"

Thus, we arrive at the key issue here. The burden is on the Government. Clearly, there are some situations in which a prior restraint on speech or press might conceivably be allowable. But those situations are very exceptional and must be very convincingly established by the party seeking an injunction. The Near court recognized as much and said:

The protection even as to previous restraint is not unlimited. But the limitation has been recognized only in exception cases:.... No one would question but that a government might prevent actual obstruction to its recruiting service or the publication of the sailing dates or transports or the number and location of troops. On similar grounds, the primary requirements of decency may be enforced against obscene publications. The securing of the community life may be protected against incitements to acts of violence and the overthrow by force of orderly government. The constitutional guarantee of free speech does not 'protect a man from an injunction against uttering words that may have all the effect of force.' ID. At 716

In this case, the executive department has made no allegations—to say nothing of convincing showings — that troop movements or recruitment are threatened. Neither obscenity nor overthrow of the Government is at issue. All that is at issue is what the District Court termed "essentially historical data." It is at least three years old and as much as twenty years old. It records the plans and policies of bygone days; it does not reveal the current plans of the present Administration, which, by its own account, is pursuing a different policy.

Since we are dealing with "essentially historical data," the Executive Department has an even greater burden to suggest what specific sort of harm may result from its publication. Yet it seeks to suppress history solely on the basis of two very vague allegations:

(1) The data has been classified as "top secret," because (2) the data is said to adversely affect our national security.

With the sweep of a rubber stamp labeled "top secret," the Executive Department seeks to abridge the freedom of the press. It has offered no more. We are asked to turn our backs on the First Amendment simply because certain officials have labeled material as unfit for the American people and the people of the world. Surely, we must demand more. To allow a Government to suppress free speech simply through a system of bureaucratic classification would sell our heritage far, far too cheaply.

It is said that it is better to rely on the judgment of our Government officials than upon the judgment of private citizens such as the publishers of The Washington Post. Again, that misses the point. The First Amendment is directed against one evil: suppression of the speech of private citizens by Government officials. It embodies a healthy distrust of governmental censorship. More importantly, it embodies a fundamental trust of individual Americans. Any free system of government involves risks. But we in the United States have chosen to rely in the end upon the judgment and true patriotism of all the people, not only of the officials.

This case would seem to be a good illustration. As the District Court said, a detailed account of our initiation and prosecution of the War in Vietnam "unquestionably will be embarrassing to the United States." But that is due to the nature of the history, not to the nature of the account. Surely, mere "embarrassment" is not enough to defeat First Amendment rights. Indeed, it may be a necessary part of democratic self-government. At a time when the American people and their Congress are in the midst of a pitched debate over the war, the history of the war, however disillusioning, is crucial. The Executive Department, which brought us into the war and which would be primarily "embarrassed" by publication of the material in question, must not be allowed to bury that history at such a time. Democracy works only when the people are informed.

Whatever temporary damage may come to the image of this country at home and abroad from the historical revelations in these Pentagon papers is miniscule compared to the lack of faith in our Government engendered in our people from their suppression. Suppression breeds suspicion and speculation. I suggest the truth is not nearly so devastating as the speculation following suppression. We are a mature people. We can stand the truth.

Thus, in my view, the Government faces a very great burden of justification in this case. It has sought to meet that burden with general allegations about national security and "top secret" classifications. It suggests that it may have more specific allegations, but refuses even to hint at them until we bend to its will and grant a temporary restraining order. I refuse to act on such a basis. I believe that the Government has not met its burden —it has not even come close. In that circumstance, I feel duty- and honor-bound to vote to affirm the decision of the District Court.

I respectfully dissent.

Decided: June 19, 1971

APPEARANCES

KEVIN T. MARONEY, attorney, Department of Justice, with whom Robert C. Mardian, assistant attorney general; Thomas A. Flannery, United States attorney; Joseph M. Hannon, John A. Terry and Daniel J. McAuliffe, assistant United States attorneys, were on the pleadings for appellant.

ROGER A. CLARK, with whom Anthony F. Essaye and William C. Potter Jr. entered appearances on behalf of appellees.

BEFORE:
WRIGHT
ROBINSON
ROBB,
Circuit Judges.

Text of Gurfein Opinion Upholding The Times and Kaufman Order Extending Ban

Following is the text of the opinion of United States District Judge Murray I. Gurfein yesterday denying the Justice Department's request for a permanent injunction to prohibit The New York Times from publishing further articles and documents in its Vietnam series, as well as the text of the order by Judge Irving I. Kaufman of the Court of Appeals extending the temporary restraining order against The Times:

Judge Gurfein's Opinion

UNITED STATES DISTRICT COURT
SOUTHERN DISTRICT OF NEW YORK
71 Civ. 2662
UNITED STATES OF AMERICA,
Plaintiff,

v.

NEW YORK TIMES COMPANY, et al, Defendants.

GURFEIN, D. J.

On June 12, June 13 and June 14, 1971, The New York Times published summaries and portions of the text of two documents—certain volumes from a 1968 Pentagon study relating to Vietnam and a summary of a 1965 Defense Department study relating to the Tonkin Gulf incident. The United States sues to enjoin The Times from "further dissemination, disclosure or divulgence" of materials contained in the 1968 study of the decision-making process with respect to Vietnam and the summary of the 1965 Tonkin Gulf study. In its application for a temporary restraining order the United States also asked the Court to order The Times to furnish to the Court all the documents involved so that they could be impounded pending a determination. On June 15 upon the argument of the order to show cause the Court entered a temporary restraining order against The New York Times in substance preventing the further publication until a determination by the Court upon the merits of the Government's application for a preliminary injunction. The Court at that time, in the absence of any evidence, refused to require the documents to be impounded.

The Government contends that the documents still unpublished and the information in the possession of The Times involves a serious breach of the security of the United States and that the further publication will cause "irreparable injury to the national defense."

The articles involved material that has been classified as Top-Secret and Secret, although the Government concedes that these classifications are related to volumes rather than individual documents and that included within the volumes may be documents which should not be classified in such high categories. The documents involved are a 47-volume study entitled "HISTORY OF UNITED STATES DECISION-MAKING PROCESS ON VIETNAM POLICY" and a document entitled "THE COMMAND AND CONTROL STUDY OF THE TONKIN GULF INCIDENT DONE BY THE DEFENSE DEPARTMENT'S WEAPONS SYSTEM EVALUATION GROUP IN 1965." There is no question that the documents are in the possession of The Times.

Reviews Security Aspects

The issue of fact with respect to national security was resolved in the following manner. In view of the claim of the Government that testimony in support of its claim that publication of the documents would involve a serious security danger, would in itself be dangerous, the Court determined that under the "Secrets of State" doctrine an *in camera* proceeding should be held at which only the attorneys for each side, witnesses for the Government and two designated representatives of The New York Times would be present. It was believed that this would enable the Government to present its case forcefully and without restraint so that the accommodation of the national security interest with the rights of a free press could be determined with no holds barred. It was with reluctance that the Court granted a hearing from which the public was excluded, but it seemed that there was no other way to serve the needs of justice. My finding with respect to the testimony on security will be adverted to below.

1. This case is one of first impression. In the researches of both counsel and of the Court nobody has been able to find a case remotely resembling this one where a claim is made that national security permits a prior restraint on the publication of a newspaper. The Times in affidavits has indicated a number of situations in which classified information has been "leaked" to the press without adverse governmental or judicial action. It cites news stories and the memoirs of public officials who have used (shortly after the events) classified material in explaining their versions of the decision making process. They point out that no action has ever been taken against any such publication of "leaks." The Government on the other hand points out that there has never been an attempt to publish such a massive compilation of documents, which is probably unique in the history of "leaks." The Vietnam study had been authorized by Secretary of Defense McNamara, continued under Secretary Clifford and finally delivered to the present Secretary of Defense Laird. The White House was not given a copy. The work was done by a group of historians, including certain persons on contract with the Government. It is actually called a "history." The documents in the Vietnam study relate to the period from 1945 to early 1968. There is no reference to any material subsequent to that date. The Tonkin Gulf incident analysis was prepared in 1965, six years ago. The Times contends that the material is historical and that the circumstance that it involves the decision-making procedures of the Government is no different from the descriptions that have emerged in the writings of diarists and memoirists. The Government on the other hand contends that by reference to the totality of the studies an enemy might learn something about United States methods which he does not know, that references to past relationships with foreign governments might affect the conduct of our relations in the future and that the duty of public officials to advise their superiors frankly and freely in the decision-making process would be impeded if it was believed that newspapers could with impunity publish such private information. These are indeed troublesome questions.

Good Faith of U.S. Is Noted

This case, in the judgment of the Court, was brought by the Government in absolute good faith to protect its security and not as a means of suppressing dissident or contrary political opinion. The issue is narrower—as to whether and to what degree the alleged security of the United States may "chill" the right of newspapers to publish. That the attempt by the Government to restrain The Times is not an act of attempted precensorship as such is also made clear by the historic nature of the documents themselves. It has been publicly stated that the present Administration had adopted a new policy with respect to Vietnam. Prior policy must, therefore, be considered as history rather than as an assertion of present policy the implementation of which could be seriously damaged by the publication of these documents.

2. The Times contends that the Government has no inherent power to seek injunction against publication and that power of the Court to grant such an injunction can be derived only from a statute. The Government has asserted a statutory authority for the injunction, namely, the Act of June 25, 1948, c. 645, 62 Stat. 736; Sept. 23, 1950, c. 1024, Tit. I, Sec. 18, 64 Stat. 1003 (18 U.S.C. 793). The Government contends moreover, that it has an inherent right to protect itself in its vital functions and that hence an injunction will lie even in the absence of a specific statute.

There seems little doubt that the Government may ask a Federal District Court for injunctive relief even in the absence of a specific statute authorizing such relief.

The Supreme Court has held that "(o)ur decisions have established the general rule that the United States may sue to protect its interests. . . . This rule is not necessarily inapplicable when the particular governmental interest sought to be protected is expressed in a statute carrying criminal penalties for its violation." *Wyandotte Co. vs. U. S.*, 389 U. S. 191, 201-2 (1967).

In recent times the United States has obtained an injunction against the State of Alabama from enforcing the miscegenation laws of that State. *U. S. vs. Britain*, 319 F. Supp. 1058, 1061. The United States has been held entitled to restrain a collection of a tax because "the interest of the national government in the proper implementation of its policies and programs involving the national defense such as to vest in it the non-statutory right to maintain this action. *U. S. vs. Arlington County*, 326 F. 2d 929, 932-33 (4th Cir. 1964). Recently in *U. S. vs. Brand Jewelers, Inc.*, 318 F. Supp. 1293, 1299, a decision by Judge Frankel of this Court collects the authorities illustrating the various situations in which the classic case of *In re Debs*, 158 U. S. 564 (1895) has been cited. Accordingly, even in the absence of statute the Government's inherent right to protect itself from breaches of security is clear.

That however, is only the threshold question. Assuming the right of the United States and, indeed, it's duty in this case to attempt to restrain the further publication of these documents, the Government claims and the Times denies that there is any statute which proscribes such publication. The argument requires an analysis of the various sections (792-799) contained in Chapter 37 of Title 18 of the U. S. Criminal Code entitled "ESPIONAGE AND CENSORSHIP." The statute seems to be divided into two parts. The first, which for lack of a better term may be considered simple espionage, and the second, the publication of information. The Government relies upon Section 793. There are two subsections concerning which the question of interpretation has arisen. Subsection (d) deals with persons with lawful possession..."whoever lawfully having possession of any document, writing, code book, etc...relating to the national defense or information relating to the national defense which information the possessor has reason to believe could be used to the injury of the United States or to the advantage of any foreign nation..." It seems clear that neither The Times nor the Government now claim that subsection (d) applies, since it is fairly obvious that "lawful" possession means the possession of Government officials or others who have authorized possession of the documents. The Government, however, relies on subsection (e) which reads as follows:

"(e) Whoever having unauthorized possession of, access to, or control over any document, writing, code book, signal book, sketch, photograph, photographic negative, blueprint, plan, map, model, instrument, appliance, or note relating to the national defense, or information relating to the national defense which information the possessor has reason to believe could be used to the injury of the United States or to the advantage of any foreign nation, willfully communicates, delivers, transmits or causes to be communicated, delivered, or transmitted, or attempts to communicate, deliver, transmit or cause to be communicated, delivered, or transmitted the same to any person not entitled to receive it, or willfully retains the same and fails to deliver it to the officer or employee of the United States entitled to receive it; or"

'Publication' Is Not Mentioned

It will be noted that the word "publication" does not appear in this section. The Government contends that the word "communicates" covers the publication by a newspaper of the material interdicted by the subsection. A careful reading of the section would indicate that this is truly an espionage section where what is prohibited is the secret or clandestine communication to a person not entitled to receive it where the possessor has reason to believe that it may be used to the injury of the United States or the advantage of any foreign nation. This conclusion is fortified by the circumstance that in other sections of Chapter 37 there is specific reference to publication. The distinction is sharply made in Section 794 entitled "Gathering or Delivering Defense Information to Aid Foreign Governments." Subsection (a) deals with peace-time communication of documents, writings, code books, etc. relating to national defense. It does not use the word "publication." Subsection (b) on the other hand which deals with "in time of war" does punish anyone who "publishes" specific information "with respect to the movement, numbers, description, condition or disposition of any of the Armed Forces, ships, aircraft or war materials of the United States or with respect to the plans or conduct, or supposed plans or conduct of any naval or military operations, or with respect to any works or measures undertaken for or connected with, or intended for the fortification or defense of any place, or any other information relating to the public defense, which might be useful to the enemy...."

Similarly, in Section 797, one who publishes photographs, sketches, etc. of vital military and naval installations or equipment is subject to punishment. And finally, in Section 798 which deals with "Disclosure of Classified Information" there is a specific prohibition against one who "publishes" any classified information. This classified information is limited to the nature, preparation, or use of any code, cipher, or cryptographic system of the United States or any foreign government; or the design, construction, use, maintenance, or repair of any device, apparatus, or appliance used or prepared or planned for use by the United States or any foreign government for cryptographic or communication intelligence purposes; or the communication intelligence activities of the United States or any foreign government; or obtained by the processes of communications of any foreign government, knowing the same to have been obtained by such processes.

The Government does not contend, nor do the facts indicate, that the publication of the documents in question would disclose the types of classified information specifically prohibited by the Congress. Aside from the internal evidence of the language in the various sections as indicating that newspapers were not intended by Congress to come within the purview of Section 793, there is Congressional history to support the conclusion. Section 793 derives from the original espionage act of 1917 (Act of June 15, 1917, Chap. 30, Title I, Sections 1, 2, 4, 6, 40 Stat. 217, 218, 219). At that time there was proposed in H.R. 291 a provision that "during any national emergency resulting from a war to which the United States is a party, or from threat of such a war, the President may, by proclamation, prohibit the publishing or communicating of, or the attempting to publish or communicate any information relating to the national defense, which in his judgment is of such character that it is or might be useful to the enemy." This provision for prior restraint on publication for security reasons limited to wartime or threat of war was voted down by the Congress. In the debate Senator Ashhurst in a scholarly speech stated the problem as follows:

"Freedom of the press means simply, solely, and only the right to be free from a precensorship, the right to be free from the restraints of a censor. In other words, under the Constitution as amended by Amendment No. 1, 'freedom of the press' means nothing except that the citizen is guaranteed that he may publish whatever he sees fit and not be subjected to pains and penalties because he did not consult the censor before doing so."*

Notes Congressional Refusal

It would appear, therefore, that Congress recognizing the Constitutional problems of the First Amendment with respect to free press, refused to include a form of precensorship even in wartime.

In 1957 the report of the United States Commission on Government Security, in urging further safeguards against publication of matters affecting national security, recognized that "any statute designed to correct this difficulty must necessarily minimize constitutional objections by maintaining the proper balance between the guarantee of the First Amendment, on one hand, and required measures to establish a needed safeguard against any real danger to our national security." Report of the United States Commission on Government Security 619-20 (1957).

Senator Cotton, a sponsor of the bill, recognized in debate that "it should be made crystal clear that at the present time penalties for disclosure of secret information can only be applied against those employed by the Government. The recommendation extended such control over those outside the Government." The bill proposed was never passed. The significance lies, however, in the awareness by the Congress of the problems of prior restraint and its determination to reject them except in the limited cases involved in Section 794 and Section 798 involving codes, communication intelligence, and the like.

The injunction sought by the Government must, therefore, rest upon the premise that in the absence of statutory authority there is inherent power in the Executive to protect the national security. It was conceded at the argument that there is Constitutional power to restrain serious security breaches vitally affecting the interests of the Nation. This Court does not doubt the right of the Government to injunctive relief against a newspaper that is about to publish information or documents absolutely vital to current national security. But it does not find that to be the

---

*The First Amendment reads:
"Congress shall make no law respecting an establishment of religion, or prohibiting the free exercise thereof; or abridging the freedom of speech, or of the press; or the right of the people peaceably to assemble, and to petition the Government for a redress of grievances."

case here. Nor does this Court have to pass on the delicate question of the power of the President in the absence of legislation to protect the functioning of his prerogatives—the conduct of foreign relations, the right to impartial advice and military security, for the responsibility of which the Executive is charged—against private citizens who are not Government officials. For I am constrained to find as a fact that the in camera proceedings at which representatives of the Department of State, Department of Defense and the Joint Chiefs of Staff testified, did not convince this Court that the publication of these historical documents would seriously breach the national security. It is true, of course, that any breach of security will cause the jitters in the security agencies themselves and indeed in foreign governments who deal with us. But to sustain a preliminary injunction the Government would have to establish not only irreparable injury, but also the probability of success in the litigation itself. It is true that the Court has not been able to read through the many volumes of documents in the history of Vietnam, but it did give the Government an opportunity to pinpoint what it believed to be vital breaches to our national security of sufficient impact to contravert the right of a free press. Without revealing the content of the testimony, suffice it to say that no cogent reasons were advanced as to why these documents except in the general framework of embarrassment previously mentioned, would vitally affect the security of the Nation. In the light of such a finding the inquiry must end. If the statute (18 U.S.C. 793) were applicable (which I must assume as an alternative so that this decision may be reviewed by an appellate court) it is doubtful that it could be applied to the activities of The New York Times. For it would be necessary to find as an element of the violation a willful belief that the information to be published "could be used to the injury of the United States or to the advantage of any foreign nation." That this is an essential element of the offense is clear. Gorin v U.S., 312 U.S. 19 (1941).

I find that there is no reasonable likelihood of the Government successfully proving that the actions of The Times were not in good faith, which is here irreparable injury to the Government. This has been an effort on the part of The Times to vindicate the right of the public to know. It is not a case involving an intent to communicate vital secrets for the benefit of a foreign government or to the detriment of the United States.

3. As a general matter we start with the proposition that prior restraint on publication is unconstitutional. Near v. Minnesota, 283 U.S. (1931). As the Supreme Court observed in Grosjean v. American Press Co. Inc., 297 U.S. 233:

"The predominant purpose of the . . . (First Amendment) was to preserve an untrammeled press as a vital source of public information. The newspapers, magazines and other journals of the country, it is safe to say, have shed, and continue to shed, more light on the public and business affairs of the nation than any other instrumentality of publicity; and since informed public opinion is the most potent of all restraints upon misgovernment, the sup-

pression or abridgement of the publicity afforded by a free press cannot be regarded otherwise than with grave concern." (297 U.S. at 250.)

Yet the free press provision of the First Amendment is not absolute. Near v. Minnesota, Supra. In the Near case the Court said that "no one would question but that a government might prevent actual obstruction to its recruiting service or the publication of the sailing of transports or the number or location of troops." The illustrations accent how limited is the field of security protection in the context of the compelling force of First Amendment right. The First Amendment concept of a "free press" must be read in the light of the struggle of free men against prior restraint of publication. From the time of Blackstone it was a tenet of the founding fathers that precensorship was the primary evil to be dealt with in the First Amendment. Fortunately, upon the facts adduced in this case there is no sharp clash such as might have appeared between the vital security interest of the Nation and the compelling Constitutional doctrine against prior restraint. If there be some embarrassment to the Government in security aspects as remote as the general embarrassment that flows from any security breach we must learn to live with it. The security of the Nation is not at the ramparts alone. Security also lies in the value of our free institutions. A cantankerous press, an obstinate press, a ubiruitous press must be suffered by those in authority in order to preserve the even greater values of freedom of expression and the right of the people to know. In this case there has been no attempt by the Government at political suppression. There has been no attempt to stifle criticism. Yet in the last analysis it is not merely the opinion of the editorial writer, or of the columnist, which is protected by the First Amendment. It is the free flow of information so that the public will be informed about the Government and its actions.

These are troubled times. There is no greater safety valve for discontent and cynicism about the affairs of Government than freedom of expression in any form. This has been the genius of our institutions throughout our history. It has been the credo of all our Presidents. It is one of the marked traits of our national life that distinguish us from other nations under different forms of government.

For the reasons given the Court will not continue the restraining order which expires today and will deny the application of the Government for a preliminary injunction. The temporary restraining order will continue, however, until such time during the day as the Government may seek a stay from a Judge of the Court of Appeals for the Second Circuit.

The foregoing shall constitute the Court's findings of fact and conclusions of law under Rule 52 (a) of the Federal Rules of Civil Procedure.

SO ORDERED.

(s.) M. I. GURFEIN, U.S.D.J.

Dated: June 19, 1971.

APPEARANCES

WHITNEY NORTH SEYMOUR, JR., United States Attorney for the South-

ern District of New York. Attorney for Plaintiff United States of America
By: Michael D. Hess
Joseph D. Danas
Daniel Riesel
Michael I. Saltzman
Milton Sherman
Howard S. Sussman,
Assistant United States Attorneys
United States Courthouse
New York, N. Y. 10007
CAHILL, GORDON, SONNETT, REINDEL & OHL Attorneys for Defendant
New York Times Company
By: Alexander M. Bickel
Floyd Abrams
William E. Hegart,
Of Counsel.
80 Pine Street
New York, N. Y. 10005.
AMICI CURIAE:
AMERICAN CIVIL LIBERTIES UNION
NEW YORK CIVIL LIBERTIES UNION
By: Norman Dorson
Melvin L. Wulf
Osmond K. Fraenkel
Burt Neuborne
NATIONAL EMEGENCY CIVIL LIBERTIES COMMITTEE
BY: Victor Rabinowitz,
Kristin Booth Glen

The Government has moved for a stay pending appeal from an order of the District Court denying a preliminary injunction and I have heard brief oral argument.

A serious question has been presented concerning the right of the Government to restrain prior to publication certain information and reproductions of specific documents relating to the past conduct of hostilities in Vietnam. It is apparent that Judge Gurtein has been and this court will be presented with factual, statutory, and constitutional questions of immediate practical moment and involving fundamental rights guaranteed by the First Amendment of the Constitution.

It appears likely that unless the status quo is maintained for a further brief period, the jurisdiction of this court over this proceeding will, in practical effect, be defeated.

The ultimate disposition of this appeal must be made by a panel of at least three judges. For the purpose of preserving the jurisdiction of this court in this matter, it is necessary that I, sitting as a single judge of this multi-judge court, do not by my sole action permit this case to become moot before other members of this court have had an opportunity to pass on this application or to consider the issues raised. Institutional considerations compel my action.

Therefore, and emphatically intending to intimate no views as to the merits of the Government's appeal nor as to whether I would have granted a temporary restraining order in the first instance, I am required to extend the temporary restraining order issued by Judge Gurfein dated June 15, 1971, until a full panel of this court can meet to consider this application. A panel will convene in regular session on Monday morning.

Accordingly, I extend the temporary restraining order until this application is presented to and passed upon by a full panel of this court. In any event, this extension will expire on June 21 at 12 noon. So ordered.

(S) IRVING R. KAUFMAN
U. S. C. J.

June 20, 1971

Letters on War Documents

To the Editor:

For many years I have been a faithful reader of The Times. I appreciated your paper's role as the "newspaper of record," printing "all the news that's fit to print."

However, in the last few years I have been dismayed by the appearance of yellow-tinged journalism in your good gray pages: editorializing and slanting of news have been evident in your news stories; frivolous feature stories have appeared on page one; Tom Wicker seems to have become a hippie; a gossip column graces your pages; and the generally "hip" liberal attitudes that characterized the last days of The New York Herald Tribune seem to have been adopted as your editorial policy.

Despite these disheartening signs I remained a daily Times buyer and reader—but no longer. Your publication of an admittedly "secret" Government report seems to me utterly unethical, if not treasonable.

When the American people elect a Government, it is given the responsibility for conduct of foreign affairs and national security matters. By what mandate does The Times act? Who has given your paper the right to put our national security in possible jeopardy? Who elected you? (Or is the press above democratic institutions?) Your circulation may rise for a while as a result of such irresponsible journalism, but your moral position is permanently damaged. I will no longer spend fifteen cents a day for a publication I cannot respect; but I mourn the passing of the great tradition of the Good Gray Times.
> J. P. DAVIS
> Teaneck, N. J., June 14, 1971

•

To the Editor:

When I was a boy in California, my father was then President of the California Bankers Association and in this capacity he stumped the state for McKinley in the McKinley-Bryan election. Returning from his speaking engagements, he used to tell me that there was one thing he wanted me never to forget—if an issue was fairly presented to the American people, they could be counted on to reach a sound conclusion. This, after all, was fundamental to the democratic process as he understood it.

I grew up in this belief until in recent years I found that issues were no longer fairly presented. In fact, they were often misrepresented, and under these circumstances a fundamental aspect of the democratic process as we knew it was in danger of being undermined.

The recent publication by The Times of excerpts from the Pentagon-Vietnam study affords striking evidence of the extent to which this process has proceeded. I can only hope that this disclosure will serve to awaken the American public to the threat to our democratic process which is involved in the substitution by Government of deceit for the frank presentation to the electorate of the issues with which it is confronted.

Only an aroused public opinion, to which The Times has made a notable contribution, can insure a return to the integrity of the democratic process in which we have been brought up to believe.
> FRANK ALTSCHUL
> New York, June 16, 1971

•

To the Editor:

The intended balance of power between branches of our Government can be badly upset, perhaps fatally, by an imbalance of information. For one branch can enforce its prejudices and will on another by withholding facts and distorting events, the knowledge of which it is privy to.

I refer of course to the war in Vietnam and to the specific facts and intelligence estimates withheld by the Executive from the Congress and the public. Two outstanding examples are the Tonkin Gulf incident and the C.I.A. report that the Vietcong was largely

indigenous. If these items had been presented honestly, it is doubtful that the Executive would have rallied the support it did for our warlike actions.

Another related point—the majority of people in any nation, be it Germany, Russia or the U.S. or Vietnam, will believe what its government tells it about dangers from outside and will dutifully kill the men, women and children of "the enemy" in the name of patriotism. Thus the government plays the dual role of creator of an attitude and user of the attitude.

When the public attitude is based on lies and distortions, its use as a justification for actions or policy is contrary to the basic principles of our form of society, and dangerous. Where I find fault with the "silent majority" approach of our present Administration is in its use, with the knowledge that the majority has been deceived.

The Times is to be congratulated for its true patriotism and conformance with our ideals in bringing the facts of our Vietnam interference to light. You are correctly carrying out the role of a free press in our system, and there is no substitute for this necessary function.
> MILLARD M. BRENNER
> Philadelphia, June 16, 1971

•

To the Editor:

It is hardly a source of satisfaction, but it should serve as a lesson, that everything the radical left has said about the Vietnam war finds support in the Pentagon study published by The Times. In fact, as in so many other aspects of American politics (government surveillance, for example) things turn out to be substantially worse than the left imagined.

In this case, the Vietnam escalation was planned even earlier than the summer of 1964, and the "preparation" of public opinion was even more consummate, the reliance on military force to destroy an admittedly popular, mass-based peasant movement even more cynical, and the torpedoing of possibilities for a negotiated settlement even more deliberate than the dissenting writers on Vietnam assumed.

I wonder what impact all of this will have on "objective" social scientists who dismiss leftist critiques of American society as "paranoid" and excessively oriented toward "conspiracy" theories.
> RICHARD B. DU BOFF
> Associate Professor of Economics
> Bryn Mawr College
> Bryn Mawr, Pa., June 14, 1971

•

To the Editor:

It is with great sadness that I have been reading your paper while back here for a brief visit.

I find your slanting of the news in The Herald Tribune in Europe difficult to read, but your recent articles in The Times on Vietnam are not only irresponsible, but detrimental to our country, in my opinion.

When we move back to Greenwich I can assure you The Times will no longer be our newspaper.

DOROTHY B. MOORE
Greenwich, Conn., June 15, 1971

●

To the Editor:

Perhaps if the television networks would have done what you are now doing, in regard to your carrying the story of the Vietnam war and what went on behind the scenes, the Bill of Rights, especially the First Amendment, would be alive and well and undisputed in the United States.

The Times is pursuing its usual course in publishing, in full, important documents and speeches. This is surely the most important story you have done in my memory, and the most worthwhile. The people of this country owe you a debt of gratitude, which they will only realize in years to come.

Permit me to quote from the Russian poet, Yevtushenko:

*"One day posterity will remember
This strange era, these strange
times,
When honesty was called courage."*

BETTY FRIER
Kingston, Pa., June 15, 1971

To the Editor:

Although it is disturbing to see documents with a current classification of "Top Secret" published in The Times, a reading of them reveals that the "Top Secret" and "Secret" stamp is being used in many instances for the purpose of keeping facts from the American people—facts which the enemy is well aware of.

Documents should not be classified for the sole purpose of preventing embarrassment of an Administration, and the laws regulating disclosure should be subordinate to laws regulating the purposes which compel classification.

EDWARD EARLY
Stamford, Conn., June 15, 1971

●

To the Editor:

Your publication of apparently stolen secret Government documents concerning United States military action in Vietnam appears to be aimed at supporting your own conclusions that our Government is morally at fault, is the aggressor, and is guilty of massive deception of the American people concerning the war.

The documents themselves do not support such broad generalizations or conclusions, and do not, in fact, contain very much substantive material not previously known.

Your efforts appear to be directed toward the slander of the United States Government and stampeding the United States out of Vietnam by means of internal political pressure and the fomenting of public hysteria.

United States citizens will not be stampeded by such tactics. The Government is, and always has been, morally right in fighting Communist aggression in Southeast Asia, and the Communists are, and always have been, morally wrong. Your actions and your conclusions are a discredit to the people and to the Government of the United States, and, for the record, are hereby totally rejected by the undersigned.

JOHN R. WILLIAMS
West Palm Beach, Fla., June 16, 1971

●

The New York Times/George Tames

To the Editor:

This letter is in protest against your publishing classified documents of the United States.

Whatever may be the legal ramparts behind which you seek to secure yourselves in this matter, this is clearly violative of all the force and obligations of good citizenship. To attempt to set yourselves up as arbiters of what is and is not aid and comfort to the enemy is perfectly outrageous. This is an exercise which, if pursued to its fullest, would lead everyone to make his own determination of law, which is anarchy. To say that freedom of the press is the issue is not valid; freedom of the press cannot be freedom to be irresponsible.

This is an issue which is quite aside from the question of whether we should or should not be involved in the war in Vietnam. At issue is a direct assault on the security of the United States.

JOHN B. RICHTER
Philadelphia, June 16, 1971

To the Editor:

Thank you for printing the material from the Pentagon study of the history of the Vietnam war.

Not a year in Vietnam in the military, not the antiwar certainty of my youthful peers, not the moral outrage of much of the American press and not the heavy-handedness of former President Johnson nor the political morality of President Nixon had accomplished what you have done for me.

After reading the material I have finally been personally touched by the sense of this war's tragedy. That the President would not only cruelly deceive the American people but that he would do this for his own vanity and power—at the cost of millions of lives—literally made me ill.

And now, like others, I believe the time for rhetoric has passed. There is no light at the end of this tunnel. We must free ourselves from this tunnel and breathe the air and see the sunlight again.

GENE CUDWORTH
New York, June 16, 1971

●

The Secret Glut; or, Pentagon Surplus

By RUSSELL BAKER

In Washington classified documents are piling up in the corridors of the Pentagon, the State Department and the White House, and the men who are supposed to leak them to the press are in despair.

At the Pentagon yesterday, for example, reporters and famous syndicated columnists were going out of their way to avoid the Office of Overt Graduated Document Leakage. The man in charge there, whose code name is Bill, was standing in the hall buttonholing complete strangers.

"Listen to this," Bill said, flipping open the classified document which he was trying to leak. "This is the latest secret report about the Russian missile buildup. I'm willing to leak it right away. It's all yours, my friend, in the national security."

"Not a chance."

"If this document isn't published by tomorrow afternoon," Bill argued, "we won't possibly be able to panic the Congress in time to get it to vote us another $5 billion for an American missile buildup, and then there will be a missile gap."

"That would be bad."

"It certainly would," Bill said. "You wouldn't want to be responsible for damaging the national security by not taking a little leaked document, would you?"

His lower lip was trembling. It was hard to give him the truth straight out, perhaps because this was the Pentagon. Still——.

"I'm not a reporter, Bill."

"That's all right," Bill said. "You must know somebody who is a reporter. Give it to him."

He was still holding out the document for leaking when two strong men approached him pushing wheelbarrows loaded with the latest classified documents.

"These are to be leaked immediately," the first wheelbarrow pusher told Bill.

"In the national security," the other explained.

"What do they reveal?" Bill asked. He was near collapse.

"That America's enemies everywhere are moving ahead in every conceivable kind of armament and that Congress should therefore vote us more money at once," said the first wheelbarrow pusher.

"In the national security," said the other.

Bill was weeping now. "What am I going to do?" he cried. "Since the Justice Department started taking people to court for possession of leaked documents, the press won't take them any more."

"Why don't you declassify them and issue them as press releases?"

"Don't talk nonsense at a time like this," Bill blubbered. "No editor in his right mind would believe any of this stuff if we didn't put 'classified' labels on it."

Suddenly, down a mile-long corridor, Bill recognized a famous syndicated columnist, scooped up an armful of documents and ran full speed to intercept him.

"Moe, baby," he laughed. "Look what I've got for you. A whole truckload of captured documents from North Vietnam proving once again that there is a wind-down at the end of the tunnel."

The famous syndicated columnist winced. "Not interested, old boy," he told Bill.

"But they're classified, Moe! Classified! Look at these labels! Secret. Super-secret. Hyper-secret. Feel them, Moe. The ink is still wet."

"Out of the question," said the famous syndicated columnist. "If the Justice Department takes me into court next week I won't be able to get away on my summer vacation."

Back at his office Bill's phone was ringing. It was a very loud general. "Why haven't you leaked those documents yet proving that Communism will take over Samoa if Congress doesn't buy me a new jet?" the general was demanding.

In front of the White House special assistants for White House leaks were trying to hustle documents among the sightseeing buses.

"Classified, you say?" asked a woman tourist.

"Hush-Hush and Upper-Level Secret," the document leaker replied. "Proves indisputably that nothing can save the country but the re-election of the present Administration in 1972. Take it and pass it on to a friend who knows a reporter."

The woman refused. She said it would be treasonous to be a party to publishing a document labeled "Hush-Hush and Upper-Level Secret." The bus took her away while the special assistant for leaks was explaining the difference between good leaks, which were patriotic, and bad leaks, which let people in on what was going on in Washington.

June 20, 1971

Secrecy vs. Security

By C. L. SULZBERGER

PONT-SAINTE-MAXENCE, France—One blazing difference between free government and government by restraint comes in their contrasting views of the press. Authoritarian regimes insist on deciding themselves what is proper for the people to know.

Lenin wrote: "Just as the army cannot fight without arms, so the party cannot carry out its ideological mission without that efficient and powerful weapon, the press . . . . We cannot put the press into unreliable hands."

There has never been a press problem in the Soviet Union. Lee Hills, when president of the American Society of Newspaper Editors, observed several years ago: "Manipulation of the news is the Soviet way of manipulating people, and this manipulation of human beings is the biggest difference between Communism and our system."

Free government accepts the principle of press freedom but seeks to insure that such freedom doesn't impinge upon national security. This has produced legal restrictions which never quite seem to work.

Articles 99 and 100 of the West German Penal Code ban publication of information deemed prejudicial to "the interest of the Federal Republic," a vague concept already successfully challenged by one magazine. The French Penal Code (Article 78) prohibits disclosure of "military information which has not been made public by the competent authority and whose disclosure is manifestly of a nature to prejudice national defense."

The French have been rather successful in making this stick and one consequence has been periodic complaints about government interference with the information media. The British Official Secrets Act (comprising three separate laws of 1911, 1920 and 1939) bans information "prejudi-

FOREIGN AFFAIRS

cial to the safety or interests of the state" and publication or even retention of an official document by anyone who "has no right to retain it."

But the British have had trouble reconciling law and liberty. Long before the secrets legislation, William Howard Russell of The Times of London horrified the Government when he wrote of the "incompetency, lethargy, aristocratic hauteur, official indifference, favor, routine, perverseness and stupidity" on the Crimean battlefront.

The concept of official secrets was grossly misused when the whole world knew the story of King Edward VIII's impending abdication but Englishmen had to glean what they could from foreign reports. This year The London Sunday Telegraph won an action brought against it by the Government for publishing a classified report that manifestly should not have been classified. The British law is both too broad in its application and too feeble in its authority.

For its part, the United States tried twice (1798 and 1918) to legislate against security infringements as "sedition." The first shortlived effort banned "scandalous and malicious writing or writings against the Government." The second, enacted under Wilson during World War I, aimed at Socialists and pacifists — and also failed.

In 1788 James Madison warned against "gradual and silent encroachments" against liberties, including that of the press. Every President since Hoover — except Eisenhower — had sharp disputes with that institution. The Kennedy, Johnson and Nixon Administrations sought in various ways to manage the news as (quoting a Pentagon official) "part of the arsenal of weaponry."

This is the philosophical, legal and political background to the specific argument between The New York Times and the Government over publication of classified reports. It is a sour note that the U.S. legal structure is so confused that Federal action must be pressed under the espionage law.

Once I asked Eisenhower whether he thought an official secrets act desirable and he indignantly rejected the idea, saying he would never muffle the press. This might not necessarily be the case with a well-drafted statute providing for impartial referees who could be consulted by private and public media but the implied dangers are frightening.

Certainly there is risk in the absence of some such machinery, as demonstrated during World War II when a newspaper disclosed that the U.S.A. had broken the Japanese naval code. But there is also risk in even contemplating legal blockage of leaks if such blockage can ever be used to accomplish "gradual and silent encroachments."

Moreover it is ridiculous to consider steps against press publication of classified documents while Government officials are permitted to rush into print with memoirs quoting secret papers. The spate of books following President Kennedy's death, to say nothing of Lyndon Johnson's forthcoming recollections, are notable examples.

Trunkloads of highly classified documents have been removed from official files in recent years by American officials planning to write about them. It is ridiculous to even consider press violations of security when a free hand is allowed the officials who themselves make the policy of secrecy.

June 20, 1971

Back to the Congress

By JAMES RESTON

"A cantankerous press, an obstinate press, a ubiquitous press must be suffered by those in authority in order to preserve the even greater values of freedom of expression" — U.S. District Judge M. L. Gurfein in U.S.A. vs The New York Times.

The press is still riding the tide of tradition in the courts against the rising power of the Presidency, but even when it prevails in its conflicts with the White House, its power is limited. It can expose but cannot correct error. It can oppose executive power and on great issues find the judiciary on the side of free dissent, but even when it wins in court, it is no substitute for the Congress as an effective instrument of investigation. It is "suffered" but not followed. Accordingly, a very strong case has now been made for a thorough Congressional investigation of the war, going far deeper and far beyond anything the press has been able to do. The integrity of the Government, the judgment and even the honor of many officials are at issue. The cost has been appalling and the confusion over how it all happened and where it is all leading remain. In short, the issues are too important to be evaded any longer, or to be left to the Department of Justice and the press.

It was only when Secretary of Defense Laird refused to decontaminate and declassify the documents for the Foreign Relations Committee that men who had worked on the papers and reporters who had heard about them set out to expose the blunders and the cover-up.

This conflict between the Government and the press is only a symbol of a much larger and more serious problem. There has always been a certain amount of deception between the executive and legislative branches, but it has been much worse under Presidents Johnson and Nixon and suspicion grows on itself. For years now, we have not had that feeling of honest differences openly faced and plainly discussed which is essential even in adversary proceedings. Almost everybody in Washington is looking for the other motive or the dirty trick.

This case has done more to revive the muckraker tradition of the American press than anything since the days of Lincoln Steffens. The evidence already published demonstrates the capacity of the President to expand this war, deceive the public and intimidate even the most intelligent of men in the civil service, the Cabinet and the White House staff, but by disclosing the evidence, the press cannot cure the problem.

What it can do and has done in this case is to get the facts of the Pentagon Papers to the official representatives

WASHINGTON

of the people, and they will have to take it from here. They are better able than the press to discriminate between documents that may really do damage to the security or diplomatic relations of the nation and documents which expose the blunders of officials or the errors in the decision-making process.

All the documents in the Pentagon Papers are marked "top secret"—the documents that cover military maneuvers long ago, the documents that cover sensitive diplomatic problems that still exist, and the documents that expose the most calculated deception by the President and the most arrogant misjudgments by his staff.

The press cannot sort all this out. It is a blunt but limited instrument of democracy. For example, when The Times got the Pentagon Papers, it could not do what it normally does—double-check its facts, go to the men mentioned in the papers for their side of the story—it could not do this in advance without inviting legal action and blocking the facts it was trying to disclose.

But the Congress can deal with these important distinctions. It has the power of subpoena. It can bring in legally the men who wrote the Pentagon Papers, if they want to come, without subjecting them to criminal penalties. It can hear testimony in private about secret codes and sensitive diplomatic exchanges with other nations—that is to say, it can do all these useful things, which are part of its duty, if it has the facts and a decent and fair relationship with the White House and the Cabinet.

This, however, is precisely the problem. There is no such relationship today. The political game, as it is now played in Washington, is like a football game without boundaries, rules or officials. All the men in the press box can do is report the shambles. Who elected The New York Times to get into the game? some people ask, and the answer is nobody but the men who wrote the First Amendment to the Constitution.

The reporter—in the Pentagon case a handsome, pugnacious Irishman named Neil Sheehan of The Times, half cop, half idealist, respected by the men who knew him best, hated and vilified by his subjects in the Pentagon and the war hawks in the press—have liberated the Government's own official Vietnam indictment of itself. But they cannot do much more than that.

The facts have to be sifted and analyzed much more carefully than the press can do, and this is now a job for the Congress or for some outside commission of respected and experienced citizens.

RULING IN CAPITAL

Appellate Judges Still Restrain Paper to Allow U.S. Move

By JAMES M. NAUGHTON
Special to The New York Times

WASHINGTON, June 23—The United States Court of Appeals ruled tonight that The Washington Post had a Constitutional right to publish articles based on a secret Pentagon study of how the United States became involved in Vietnam, but restrained the newspaper from continuing its series until Friday night to allow a Government appeal.

In a ruling by seven of the nine judges, the Court said that the "vitality of the principle that any prior restraint on publication comes into court under a heavy presumption against its Constitutional validity" had been established by the Supreme Court.

The judges ruled that the Government had failed to prove its contention that continued publication of material in the secret study would jeopardize national security.

Friday Deadline Set

Two judges wrote dissenting opinions, although one of them, Malcolm R. Wilkey, said he dissented only from "blanket, total affirmance" of the district court's decision Monday in favor of The Post.

An appeal to the Supreme Court by the Justice Department had been pledged before the decision, but the Court of Appeals gave the Government until 6 P.M. Friday to make the appeal.

Also today, the Justice Department announced that it did not plan to take legal action against The Chicago Sun-Times, which yesterday published a story that it said was based on Government documents. The material, the department said, "was taken from documents which were declassified by President Johnson in 1968."

Globe Wins Modification

Still barred by court orders from publication of material based on the Pentagon study, however, was The Boston Globe. But The Globe obtained a modification of an earlier order that all documents in its possession be turned in to the court. The Globe was allowed

to place the material in a safe deposit box.

Meanwhile, the Knight newspaper group published in at least eight of its 11 papers, a major article that was said to have been based on the Pentagon study. The Los Angeles Times also published an article it said was based on the study.

In the ruling involving The Washington Post, the opinion which was unsigned and in the name of the Court of Appeals for the District of Columbia, said that the Government had failed to prove its argument that national security required the prevention of publication of articles based on the Pentagon study.

"Our conclusion to affirm the denial of injunctive relief is fortified," the court said, "by the consideration [of] the massive character of the 'leak' which has occurred."

The decision was issued on behalf of the Chief Judge, David L. Bazelon, and Circuit Judges J. Skelly Wright, Carl Mc-Gowan, Edward Allen Tamm, Harold Leventhal, Spottswood W. Robinson 3d and Roger Robb.

The opinion referred to the several newspapers that have published material based on the study and said that the proliferation of newspapers involved raised "substantial doubt that effective relief of the kind sought by the Government can be provided by the judiciary."

The two judges suggested in their dissent that they would have liked to have seen further examination by the lower court of The Post's right to publish an undisclosed number of "specific documents" that the Government had apparently said in a secret session would be specifically harmful to the national interest if they were made public.

Judge Wilkey wrote that he had not seen any of the original documents. But he said he had seen affidavits citing documents that, if possessed and published by The Post, "could clearly result in great harm to the nation."

He said that by "harm" he meant "the death of soldiers, the destruction of alliances, the greatly increased difficulty of negotiation with our enemies, the inability of our diplomats to negotiate as honest brokers between would-be belligerents."

Judge Wilkey said that since neither the appellate judges nor the district judge had seen these documents he would prefer to remand the case to the district court for further consideration. The district court had rejected the United States plea for an injunction but had restrained the paper until an appeal could be heard.

Judge Wilkey suggested that the Government could thus identify those documents it objected to having published and thus release the remainder for publication.

At the same time Judge Wilkey made it clear that he had no objection to the lower court's refusal to prevent publication of "the vast majority of these documents."

Judge George E. MacKinnon said in his dissent that the court unfortunately faced a "blind record" regarding the documents. He also complained that the court's ability to deal with the case was "complicated" by the release of the entire study to Congress, "where the problem of disclosure may be compounded."

He said that the widespread nature of the publications — in The New York Times, then The Post and The Boston Globe —would minimize the value of any restraining order.

Even so, Judge MacKinnon said, "at the very least I would remand to the District Court for a more precise ruling by the trial court" on those documents the Government does not want to see in print.

"I would not reward the theft of these documents by a complete declassification," he stated.

The decision by the Appeals Court came several hours after a secret, unannounced hearing by the nine judges.

Justice Department officials said that they understood the court was receiving an affidavit from the Government stipulating additional materials that it believed ought to be examined by the lower court to determine whether publication might jeopardize national security.

Lawyers for The Post and the hearing in the United States Government were closeted more than four hours before the Court House at Constitution Avenue and John Marshall Place.

Both sides made it evident that they would appeal the eventual verdict of the Court of Appeals to the Supreme Court. Kevin T. Maroney, Deputy Assistant Attorney General in the internal security division, said that the Government would seek a stay of execution, if necessary, from Chief Justice Warren E. Burger.

The Appeals Court received the case Monday night, after Judge Gerhard A. Gesell of the District Court for the District of Columbia ruled that the Government had not proved that there would be irreparable injury to the national security if The Post were permitted to continue its series of articles.

A 5-TO-3 DECISION

Court Here Orders Gurfein to Weigh Security Issue

By FRED P. GRAHAM

The United States Court of Appeals here ordered a further delay yesterday in the publication by The New York Times of material from Pentagon papers on the American involvement in the Vietnam war.

The Appellate Court's brief 5-to-3 decision contained two major provisions.

It held that after Friday, June 25, The Times could resume publication of its series but could not use any material that the Government contended was dangerous to national security.

Secret Hearings Ordered

It also instructed Federal District Judge Murray I. Gurfein to hold secret hearings next week and to determine by Saturday, July 3, which portions of the study "pose such grave and immediate danger to the security of the United States as to warrant their publication being enjoined."

Arthur Ochs Sulzberger, publisher of The Times, said that the newspaper would appeal to the United States Supreme Court as soon as possible. He said he had instructed the counsel to The Times to prepare the necessary papers for immediate application.

Court to Recess Monday

The Times's lawyers were scheduled to fly to Washington this morning and to immediately file appeal papers with Justice John M. Harlan, who has jurisdiction over the judicial circuit that includes New York.

The Supreme Court is due to hold its final public session next Monday and then to recess for the summer. In the past, when emergency relief such as The Times's appeal have reached the court so late in its term, it has frequently either acted without hearing arguments or has scheduled eleventh-hour ar-

guments before the Justices left for the summer recess.

A crucial item in the decision here by the full bench of the Circuit Court was a sealed list filed last Monday by the United States Attorney here, Whitney North Seymour Jr. The document, called a "special appendix," contained a lengthy list of items in the 47-volume Pentagon study that the Government said would cause grave national danger if disclosed.

Alexander M. Bickel, counsel to The Times, objected to this, asserting that at the trial before Judge Gurfein the Government had cited only half a dozen items as being dangerous. He protested that to add to the list at the appeals level was tantamount to inserting testimony there.

But the Court of Appeals ruled yesterday that the Government must be given an opportunity to prove in secret testimony that the items on the list, plus any additions that the Government makes between now and Friday, do pose a sufficiently grave threat so that they should be barred from publication.

The effect of the Court of Appeals decision would be to require Judge Gurfein to consider these items one-by-one and to hear testimony from Government witnesses as to how each item might prejudice the national security.

The Times series, which included the publication of documents accompanying the study, appeared on June 13, 14 and 15 before it was halted by Judge Gurfein pending his consideration of the Government's suit to enjoin further publication.

The trial was held before Judge Gurfein last Friday. It began at 10 A.M. and continued throughout the day in open and secret session.

The next day, Judge Gurfein held that the Government had proved that the articles caused "embarrassment" but not damage to the national security. The Justice Department appealed, and the Second Circuit Court of Appeals decided to hear the case in an "en banc" session of the entire bench. There is one vacancy on the nine-man panel.

Breakdown on Decision

The unsigned opinion issued yesterday was supported by Chief Judge Henry J. Friendly and Judges J. Edward Lumbard, J. Joseph Smith, Paul R. Hays and Walter R. Mansfield.

Judges Irving R. Kaufman, Wilfred Feinberg and James L.

Oakes signed a brief dissent. It said: "We dissent and would vacate the stay and affirm the judgment of the court below."

By implication the majority opinion accepted the finding of Judge Gurfein that matter cannot be banned from publication essentially because it is classified "top secret" by the executive branch.

Judge Gurfein also rejected the Government's assertion that it could rely on the Espionage Act of 1917 to enjoin publication of any document "relating to the national defense" that it had reason to believe could harm the United States, and the Court of Appeals did not dispute that decision.

However, by accepting Judge Gurfein's ruling that courts can bar publication of any matter that poses "grave and immediate danger" to the national security, the Court of Appeals opened the possibility that resumption of The Times series could be delayed for months while the various courts combed through the massive study to consider items singled out by the Government.

Yesterday's ruling by the Court of Appeals would permit suppression of material in the Pentagon study if the threat was grave enough, without requiring that the disclosure violated law.

TEXT OF THE OPINION

Following is the text of the majority opinion handed down by the Appeals Court:

Upon consideration by the court en banc, it is ordered that the case be remanded to the District Court for further in camera proceedings to determine, on or before July 3, 1971, whether disclosure of any of those items specified in the special appendix filed with this Court on June 21, 1971, or any of such additional items as may be specified by the plaintiff with particularity on or before June 25, 1971, pose such grave and immediate danger to the security of the United States as to warrant their publication being enjoined, and to act accordingly, subject to the condition that the stay heretofore issued by this court shall continue in effect until June 25, 1971, at which time it shall be vacated except as those items which have been specified in the special appendix as so supplemented and shall continue in effect as to such items until disposition by the district court.

RESTRAINT HOLDS

In Dissent, 4 Justices Support Publication Without a Hearing

By FRED P. GRAHAM
Special to The New York Times

WASHINGTON, June 25 — The Supreme Court agreed today to hear arguments tomorrow on the Government's effort to enjoin The New York Times and The Washington Post from publishing material from the Pentagon papers on Vietnam.

In two brief orders signed by Chief Justice Warren E. Burger, the Court also placed both The Times and The Post under equal publication restraints, based upon the restrictions imposed upon The Times by the United States Court of Appeals for the Second Circuit.

Four Justices — Hugo L. Black, William O. Douglas, William J. Brennan Jr. and Thurgood Marshall — declared in a dissent that they favored freeing both newspapers to print, without hearing arguments.

Lists Required From U.S.

The Justice Department was required to file with the Court and the newspapers' lawyers by 5 P.M. today lists of any portions of the 47-volume Pentagon archive that the Government asserted would inflict "grave and immediate danger" to the nation's security if disclosed.

The Justices' order was issued in the early afternoon, and the call for the list by 5 P.M. touched off feverish activity in the Justice Department's Internal Security Division, which is handling the efforts to suppress the articles — and in other Government agencies, including the Defense Department. Justice Department lawyers had filed a 22-page typed list of "dangerous" documents at an earlier stage, and by the 5 P.M. deadline it added a further list of items that reportedly swept vast portions of the Pentagon papers into the dangerous" category.

Awaits Court Decision

Under the order issued today, both newspapers are free to publish in their Saturday issues any other information in the study. But they may not print any items on the Government's "dangerous" list until the Supreme Court decides the cases.

The New York Times said that it would not resume the series on the Pentagon archive on Saturday because the matter was before the Court, and that printing an article whose content was dictated by Government officials would amount to submitting to censorship.

The Times series on the origins of the Vietnam war, which included publication of documents accompanying the study, appeared on June 13, 14 and 15 before it was halted by the litigation that is now before the Supreme Court.

The Washington Post said that it likewise would not resume publication of material from the archive.

Justices Black, Douglas, Brennan and Marshall also dissented from the part of the order that restrained the newspapers from publishing certain material.

Today's order was issued after the justices met in conferences this morning, and communicated by telephone with Justice Douglas, who is vacationing at Goose Prairie, Wash.

Justice Douglas's office announced that he was flying back to Washington.

The importance of the case was underscored by the Court's decision to schedule a rare Saturday session to hear arguments. Solicitor General Erwin N. Griswold has been granted one hour to argue for the Government. Alexander M. Bickel, a Yale law professor who represents The Times, and William R. Glendon of Washington, The Post's lawyer, will argue for 30 minutes each.

No mention was made in the Supreme Court's order of an "in camera" hearing, the kind that was conducted by the lower courts. The order did say that secret briefs or sealed portions of the lower court records could be submitted to the Justices.

As soon as the order was issued, Court officials were besieged with requests from journalists, lawyers, scholars and the curious for seats in the chamber. It seats about 300 people.

No hint was given as to when the Court's decision would come. In similar emergency situations in the past, the Justices have sometimes issued their decision quickly, with written opinions to follow.

However, in this instance, some delay seems likely because of the task of checking the Justice Department's lengthy "dangerous" list against the 7,000-page study. The Court is scheduled to hold its final decision-making session Monday morning, but it has been known to issue decisions during a weekend.

Today's terse orders broke legal ground. The Supreme Court had never before restrained a newspaper's publication of an article, and had not previously ruled on a case involving an attempted "prior restraint" by the courts of a newspaper article.

The major benchmark for the courts has been a statement that the Supreme Court made in a 1931 libel decision, Near v Minnesota. In it, the Court said in passing that under certain circumstances of extreme emergency — the opinion mentioned the publication of a troopship's sailing date or of battle plans—courts could block publication, despite the First Amendment's guarantee of press freedom.

TWO-HOUR DEBATE

Justices Leave for Day Without Disclosing Their Decision

By FRED P. GRAHAM
Special to The New York Times

WASHINGTON, June 26 — The Supreme Court heard two hours of arguments today and then took under advisement the Government's effort to enjoin The New York Times and The Washington Post from publishing material from the Pentagon papers on Vietnam.

After the arguments were completed, the Justices spent the afternoon in conference and left the Supreme Court building at 6 P.M. without announcing a decision. The final scheduled meeting of the Court's 1970-71 term is on Monday morning, and no decision was expected to be made public before then.

No part of the hearing was held in secret, after the Court rejected by a 6 to 3 vote the Government's request to give "in camera" the reasons why it believed that publication of the study would damage the national security. The dissenters were Chief Justice Warren E. Burger and Justices Harry A. Blackmun and John M. Harlan.

No Wavering by Dissenters

During the argument, there was no sign of wavering by any of the four Justices who announced in a dissent when the hearing was granted that they favored freeing both newspapers to resume publication of the Vietnam articles immediately, without a Supreme Court hearing. The four were Hugo L. Black, William O. Douglas, William J. Brennan Jr. and Thurgood Marshall.

This focused attention upon Justices Potter Stewart and Byron R. White, who questioned Solicitor General Erwin N. Griswold closely on his arguments for the Government. Either one could apparently swing the case in favor of the newspapers.

At one point late in the argument, Justice Stewart and Mr. Griswold virtually compressed the issues in the cases into a single exchange. It came after Mr. Griswold complained that there had not been enough time in the lower courts to fully explore the possible security breaches in the 47-volume study. He said no harm would come from continuing to restrain the newspapers from further publications, while more Court hearings were held.

"Unless the Constitution has been changed," Justice Stewart said, "a prior restraint is presumptively unconstitutional."

Mr. Griswold assured him that the Government considered the First Amendment "very important—but so is the national security."

Justice Stewart expressed his own concern about "security" later in the argument when he pressed lawyers for the newspapers to say whether the Supreme Court should not intervene if the Justices find something in the documents "that absolutely convinces us that its disclosure would result in the sentencing to death of 100 young men whose only offense had been that they were 19 years old and had low draft numbers."

The answer was that this was a very hard question.

Justice White also seemed concerned at the Government's request that the two cases be sent back to the lower courts for more litigation, now that 11 days have passed since The Times was halted from printing further articles. The series on the origins of the Vietnam war appeared on June 13, 14 and 15 before it was restrained while the courts considered whether it should be permanently enjoined.

In his oral argument and in the Government's brief, Mr. Griswold de-emphasized the Justice Department's earlier arguments that the newspaper's publication of documents that had been stamped "Top Secret" could be barred as violations of the espionage laws and of the statutes and executive orders that give the President the sole authority to control classified material.

He said he could not abandon these assertions, which "some responsible officers of the Government feel are proper." But he relied basically upon the claim that the courts may block the publication of secrets that pose a "grave and irrevocable"

threat to the national security.

Stresses Peril to Diplomacy

He stressed, as the Government has throughout its efforts to suppress the Pentagon papers, the injury to future United States diplomatic moves that might result because foreign nations would fear to speak confidentially to American officials.

Mr. Griswold urged the Supreme Court to adopt a standard that would permit Federal courts to halt any publication if "it will affect lives, it will affect the termination of the war, it will affect the process of recovering our prisoners of war."

Mr. Griswold was asked what effect a Supreme Court decision in favor of The Times would have on possible future prosecutions of The Times or its personnel under the espionage laws. He replied that in his view such a prosecution would be unsupportable, because the high court would have already held that the material disseminated by The Times was not damaging to the national security.

Mr. Griswold was accompanied by the United States Attorney for the Southern District of New York, Whitney North Seymour Jr.

Yesterday, the Supreme Court had ordered the Government to list by 5 in the afternoon all of the portions of the 7,000-page Pentagon archive that might harm the national security if disclosed. At the beginning of today's hearing, Mr. Griswold told the Court that the list, compiled by others in the Department of Justice, was "entirely too broad."

In its place, he submitted in a sealed envelope what he described as "further descriptive material" from Defense and State Department officials pointing out reasons why certain documents "would really cause trouble" if disclosed. Mr Griswold said this narrower list contained "10 items," but noted that one "item" alone encompassed four of the 47 volumes.

Alexander M. Bickel, a Yale professor of Constitutional law who argued for The New York Times, asserted that if the President had any "inherent power" to obtain injunctions against the press, it must only

be used under extraordinary circumstances. He proposed a standard whereby "prior restraints" could be imposed only when publication of an article would have the "direct, immediate and visible" result of causing a grave harm to the nation.

Mr. Bickel insisted that the dangers cited by the Government — that future diplomatic initiatives might suffer or the course of the war might be lengthened — were too remote from the publications to warrant their suppression.

Justice William O. Douglas, who flew yesterday from his mountain retreat in the state of Washington to attend the hearing, scribbled busily throughout most of the argument, as is his custom.

Justice Douglas, who is a leading adherent of the school that considers the First Amendment an absolute shield to the press, perked up when Mr. Bickel argued that the courts might have the power to restrain the press if Congress passed a law specifically authorizing it. Professor Bickel is known for his scholarly articles arguing against Constitutional absolutism.

"The First Amendment provides that Congress shall make no law abridging the freedom of the press," Justice Douglas said. "Do you read that to mean that Congress can make some laws abridging freedom of the press?" He concluded that "that is a very strange argument for The Times to be making."

William P. Glendon, a Washington lawyer who argued for The Washington Post, called the Government's cases one of "broad claims and narrow proof." He insisted that "the hypothesis that diplomatic negotiations would be jeopardized does not warrant stopping the presses."

He said the only portion in the material held by The Post that could remotely affect future military fortunes was one document that set forth "certain options" for the future course of the Vietnam war. He added that "any high school boy" could list the same options if he was told to state the contingency plans available to the United States.

A Troubled Friend

BY JAMES RESTON

WASHINGTON, June 26—A troubled friend wants to know why the newspapers don't leave the questions of secret documents and national security to the President. Let us suppose that we did.

Presidential power is now greater than at any other time in the history of the Republic. Ever since the invention of atomic weapons and intercontinental ballistic missiles, it is clear that the nation could be mortally wounded before the Congress could ever be assembled on Capitol Hill.

Accordingly, the balance of decisive power in the foreign field—but not over internal policy—has passed from the Congress, where it lay before the two world wars, to the White House. This may or may not have been what we wanted but it was clearly what we had to do.

Other inventions tipped the balance of political power toward the President, especially nationwide television. It is at his disposal whenever he likes, with a studio in the White House. He has instant communications with the people and the world, all of which is necessary. The Congress cannot compete with him in the use of these modern instruments in the conduct of public policy.

But these unavoidable facts raise serious questions. Should such power not be subject to review by the representatives of the people? Should the Congress not know what is going on? Should the executive be free to use the power it needs to deal with the threat of nuclear war in undeclared wars like Vietnam? Should the press shut its eyes to any documents, even old historical documents, the executive chooses to mark top secret?

The fuss over the Pentagon Papers is only a symbol of a much larger problem. It is true that these papers raise questions of "national security," but the greatest threat to national security in this time is the division of the people over a war they have had to fight in accordance with decisions of governments that didn't tell them the truth. The nation is seething with distrust, not only of the Government but of the press, and the issue of the Pentagon Papers is merely whether we should get at the facts and try to correct our mistakes, or suppress the whole painful story.

Fundamentally, this is not a fight between the Government and the press. It is not even a fight over the President's decisive power to defend the nation in an age of nuclear missiles. Congress has submitted to the scientific facts on the ultimate questions of nuclear war.

But now it has been asked, in the name of "security," not even to look at a historical analysis of a war it has financed but not declared, not to question the unelected members of the White House staff, who had access to the papers Congress could not see, and to respect the Administration's right to stamp "secret" on any documents it likes, and to keep them secret years after the event, when officials long out of office are writing their own versions of history out of the "secret documents."

My "troubled friend" has good cause for anxiety. He is right to wonder whether the press knows enough and is responsible enough to publish things the Attorney General wants suppressed. He is right to concern himself with the security of the nation.

But what is being exposed here is not primarily some Government documents that might cause "irreparable damage" to the defense of the nation, but a system of secrecy, of Presidential presumption, of influential staff advice by men who cannot be questioned, of concealment and manipulation, all no doubt with the best motives, but nevertheless a system which has got out of hand and could really cause "irreparable damage" to the Republic.

No doubt the press itself is often poorly informed and clumsy in its efforts to expose the dangers of this system, but the greater the power in the hands of the executive, the greater the need for information and skepticism on the part of the Congress and the press.

My anxious friend might be careful about weakening the instruments of information and review at such a time. No doubt they are blunt instruments, often misused, but in this case of the Pentagon Papers, or so it seems here, the greater danger is the system of executive secrecy, and the greater danger to the security of the nation is the mistrust this system of secrecy and contrived television propaganda has caused.

James Madison summed up the problem at the beginning of the Republic:

"Among those principles deemed sacred in America, among those sacred rights considered as forming the bulwark of their liberty, which the Government contemplates with awful reverence and would approach only with the most cautious circumspection, there is no one of which the importance is more deeply impressed on the public mind than the liberty of the press.

"That this liberty is often carried to excess; that it has sometimes degenerated into licentiousness, is seen and lamented, but the remedy has not yet been discovered.

"Perhaps it is an evil inseparable from the good with which it is allied; perhaps it is a shoot which cannot be stripped from the stock without wounding vitally the plant from which it is torn. However desirable those measures might be which might correct without enslaving the press, they have never yet been devised in America."

The Common Interest

By TOM WICKER

WASHINGTON—In publishing the highly classified "Pentagon Papers," wasn't The New York Times setting itself up to judge the national interest? What gave The Times either the right or the standing to make such a judgment? And anyway, isn't the national interest properly the Government's to define?

That, roughly, is the line of argument most frequently advanced by those who question The Times' decision to print these important documents.

This argument rests on two assumptions—that "national interest" is primarily a matter of "national security," and that only the most skilled, experienced and informed Government officials know anything about it. Both are false.

In the latter case, the truth is that most legitimate "secrets" are not involved, technical, specialized matters —arcane weaponry details, for instance. Instead, they are policy and procedural questions on which secrecy must be temporarily imposed to give the Government some necessary freedom of action.

It was such questions of what to do and how to do it that the Johnson Administration was secretly debating in 1964 and 1965, as the situation deteriorated in Vietnam. The partial documentary record of that debate, and its evident consequences in the years since, is proof enough that even the most skilled and experienced Government officials can sadly miscalculate the "national interest."

Nor is it necessarily true that the Government has more and better information than anyone else. Subordinates reporting to their chiefs are always under pressure to report greater achievements than exist; officials who have shaped a policy have an interest in justifying it, no matter what the actual results; and preconceived policy convictions are likely to be held despite contrary facts. Sometimes the best available information can be ignored; the Pentagon Papers show that the C.I.A. repeatedly warned against overcommitment in Vietnam, and when a long-experienced State Department official advocated withdrawal from what he saw as the hopeless situation in that country in 1963, Secretary Rusk is said to have insisted that it was a basic premise of American policy not to pull out of Vietnam until the war was won. What good is even precise information in the face of such fixed attitudes?

Moreover, governments always have their own political self-interest to consider as they weigh questions of national interest. High officials' ability to discuss and decide in secrecy tends

to isolate them from disinterested criticism and fresh insights. The institutional, impersonal nature of national power is likely to diminish the sense of personal responsibility; members of the National Security Council do not personally drop napalm on villages.

A brilliant editorial in the Washington Post has pointed out that even the bureaucratic language disclosed in the Pentagon Papers—the repetitive jargon of "scenario" and "option" and "orchestration" and "crescendo" and "signal" and "limited action"—was so much "in flight from and in defense against reality" that those who spoke and wrote it need never have acknowledged its meaning in an actual world of falling bombs and scorched earth and terrified children.

As for the assumption that "national interest" and "national security" are somehow synonymous, it can be justified, if at all, only in some dark hour of national crisis, when survival is at stake. At any other time, "national security" can be only one important part of a democracy's "national interest"—which might be better understood as what it really is, the "common interest."

If, for example, the ultimate check on government is the people's right to vote, the exercise of it and the outcome of elections depend heavily upon how much the people know, and how accurate their knowledge is. Therefore, the press acts as much on behalf of the people in trying to inform them about what government is doing and why, and how well it works, as government does in trying to manage the people's affairs and protect their security.

That is why The Times had not only the right but the duty to judge whether the national interest required it to print the Pentagon Papers when they came to hand. If The Times — or any news organization in the same circumstances —had no such right, then only the Government could judge the common interest, even on the question of what the people should know about the Government.

In that case, the Government need never fear public scrutiny nor account for its actions. Honest men may conclude that The Times judged incorrectly, that "national security" would have been better served by keeping the Pentagon Papers secret. But if so, the damage done by this bad judgment is minor compared to the blow that would have been struck against the "common interest" had The Times abdicated its right to judge, without Government direction, what that interest is.

BURGER DISSENTS

First Amendment Rule Held to Block Most Prior Restraints

By FRED P. GRAHAM

Special to The New York Times

WASHINGTON, June 30 — The Supreme Court freed The New York Times and The Washington Post today to resume immediate publication of articles based on the secret Pentagon papers on the origins of the Vietnam war.

By a vote of 6 to 3 the Court held that any attempt by the Government to block news articles prior to publication bears "a heavy burden of presumption against its constitutionality."

In a historic test of that principle — the first effort by the Government to enjoin publication on the ground of national security — the Court declared that "the Government has not met that burden."

The brief judgment was read to a hushed courtroom by Chief Justice Warren E. Burger at 2:30 P.M. at a special session called three hours before.

Old Tradition Observed

The Chief Justice was one of the dissenters, along with Associate Justices Harry A. Blackmun and John M. Harlan, but because the decision was rendered in an unsigned opinion, the Chief Justice read it in court in accordance with long-standing custom.

In New York Arthur Ochs Sulzberger, president and publisher of The Times, said at a news conference that he had "never really doubted that this day would come and that we'd win." His reaction, he said, was "complete joy and delight."

The case had been expected to produce a landmark ruling on the circumstances under which prior restraint could be imposed upon the press, but because no opinion by a single Justice commanded the support of a majority, only the unsigned decision will serve as precedent.

Uncertainty Over Outcome

Because it came on the 15th day after The Times had been restrained from publishing further articles in its series mined from the 7,000 pages of material—the first such restraint

in the name of "national security" in the history of the United States—there was some uncertainty whether the press had scored a strong victory or whether a precedent for some degree of restraint had been set.

Alexander M. Bickel, the Yale law professor who had argued for The Times in the case, said in a telephone interview that the ruling placed the press in a "stronger position." He maintained that no Federal District Judge would henceforth temporarily restrain a newspaper on the Justice Department's complaint that "this is what they have printed and we don't like it" and that a direct threat of irreparable harm would have to be alleged.

However, the United States Solicitor General, Erwin N. Griswold, turned to another lawyer shortly after the Justices filed from the courtroom and remarked: "Maybe the newspapers will show a little restraint in the future." All nine Justices wrote opinions, in a judicial outpouring that was described by Supreme Court scholars as without precedent. They divided roughly into groups of three each.

The first group, composed of Hugo L. Black, William O. Douglas and Thurgood Marshall, took what is known as the absolutist view that the courts lack the power to suppress any press publication, no matter how grave a threat to security it might pose.

Justices Black and Douglas restated their long-held belief that the First Amendment's guarantee of a free press forbids any judicial restraint. Justice Marshall insisted that because Congress had twice considered and rejected such power for the courts, the Supreme Court would be "enacting" law if it imposed restraint.

The second group, which included William J. Brennan Jr., Potter Stewart and Byron R. White, said that the press could not be muzzled except to prevent direct, immediate and irreparable damage to the nation. They agreed that this material did not pose such a threat.

The Dissenters' Views

The third bloc, composed of the three dissenters, declared that the courts should not refuse to enforce the executive branch's conclusion that material should be kept confidential — so long as a Cabinet-level officer had decided that it should—on a matter affecting foreign relations.

They felt that the "frenzied train of events" in the cases before them had not given the courts enough time to determine those questions, so they concluded that the restraints upon publication should have been retained while both cases

were sent back to the trial judges for more hearings.

The New York Times's series drawn from the secret Pentagon study was accompanied by supporting documents. Articles were published on June 13, 14 and 15 before they were halted by court order. A similar restraining order was imposed on June 19 against The Washington Post after it began to print articles based on the study.

Justice Black's opinion stated that just such publications as those were intended to be protected by the First Amendment's declaration that "Congress shall make no law . . . abridging the freedom of the press."

Paramount among the responsibilities of a free press, he said, "is the duty to prevent any part of the Government from deceiving the people and sending them off to distant lands to die of foreign fevers and foreign shot and shell."

"In my view, far from deserving condemnation for their courageous reporting, The New York Times, The Washington Post and other newspapers should be commended for serving the purpose that the Founding Fathers saw so clearly," he said. "In revealing the workings of government that led to the Vietnam war, the newspapers nobly did precisely that which the founders hoped and trusted they would do."

Justice Douglas joined the opinion by Justice Black and was joined by him in another opinion. The First Amendment's purpose, Justice Douglas argued, is to prohibit "governmental suppression of embarrassing information." He asserted that the temporary restraints in these cases "constitute a flouting of the principles of the First Amendment."

Justice Marshall's position was based primarily upon the separation-of-powers argument that Congress had never authorized prior restraints and that it refused to do so when bills were introduced in 1917 and 1957.

He concluded that the courts were without power to restrain publications. Justices Brennan, Stewart and White, who also based their conclusions on the separation-of-powers principle, assumed that under extreme circumstances the courts would act without such powers.

Justice Brennan focused on the temporary restraints, which had been issued to freeze the situation so that the material would not be made public before the courts could decide if it should be enjoined. He continued that no restraints should have been imposed because the Government alleged only in general terms that security breaches might occur.

Justices Stewart and White, who also joined each other's opinions, said that though they had read the documents they felt that publication would not be in the national interest.

But Justice Stewart, a former chairman of The Yale Daily News, insisted that "it is the duty of the executive" to protect state secrets through its own security measures and not the duty of the courts to do it by banning news articles.

He implied that if publication of the material would cause "direct, immediate, and irreparable damage to our nation or its people," he would uphold prior restraint, but because that situation was not present here, he said that the papers must be free to publish.

Justice White added that Congress had enacted criminal laws, including the espionage laws, that might apply to these papers. "The newspapers are presumably now on full notice," he said, that the Justice Department may bring prosecutions if the publications violate those laws. He added that he "would have no difficulty in sustaining convictions" under the laws, even if the breaches of security were not sufficient to justify prior restraint.

The Chief Justice and Justices Stewart and Blackmun echoed this caveat in their opinions — meaning that one less than a majority had lent their weight to the warning.

Chief Justice Burger blamed The Times "in large part" for the "frenetic haste" with which the case was handled. He said that The Times had studied the Pentagon archives for three or four months before beginning its series, yet it had breached "the duty of an honorable press" by not asking the Government if any security violations were involved before it began publication.

He said he found it "hardly believable" that The Times would do this, and he concluded that it would not be harmed if the case were sent back for more testimony.

Justice Blackmun, also focusing his criticism on The Times, said there had been inadequate time to determine if the publications could result in "the death of soldiers, the destruction of alliances, the greatly increased difficulty of negotiation with our enemies, the inability of our diplomats to negotiate." He concluded that if the war was prolonged and a delay in the return of United States prisoners result from publication, "then the nation's people will know where the responsibility for these sad consequences rests."

In his own dissenting opinion, Justice Harlan said: "The judiciary must review the initial executive determination to the point of satisfying itself that the subject matter of the dispute does lie within the proper compass of the President's foreign policy relations power.

"The judiciary," he went on, "may properly insist that the determination that disclosure of that subject matter would

595

'DELIGHTED' WITH COURT RULING: Arthur Ochs Sulzberger, president and publisher of The New York Times, at conference on Vietnam papers with A. M. Rosenthal, left, managing editor; James C. Goodale, right, general counsel.

irreparably impair the national security be made by the head of the executive department concerned—here the Secretary of State or the Secretary of Defense—after actual personal consideration.

"But in my judgment, the judiciary may not properly go beyond these two inquiries and redetermine for itself the probable impact of disclosure on the national security."

The Justice Department initially sought an injunction against The Times on June 15 from Federal District Judge Murray I. Gurfein in New York.

Judge Gurfein, who had issued the original temporary restraining order that was stayed until today, ruled that the material was basically historical matter that might be embarrassing to the Government but did not pose a threat to national security. Federal District Judge Gerhard A. Gesell of the District of Columbia came to the same conclusion in the Government's suit against The Washington Post.

The United States Court of Appeals for the Second Circuit, voting 5 to 3, ordered more secret hearings before Judge Gurfein and The Times appealed. The United States Court of Appeals for the District of Columbia upheld Judge Gesell, 7 to 2, holding that no injunction should be imposed. Today the Supreme Court affirmed the Appeals Court here and reversed the Second Circuit.

The Supreme Court also issued a brief order disposing of a few other cases and adjourned until Oct. 4, as it had been scheduled to do Monday.

Arthur Ochs Sulzberger, president and publisher of The New York Times, said yesterday that his reaction to the Supreme Court's decision was "one of complete joy and delight."

Mr. Sulzberger held a news conference with A. M. Rosenthal, managing editor of The Times, and James C. Goodale, the newspaper's general counsel, about 20 minutes after the decision was announced.

The publisher said that he had "never really doubted that this day would come and that we'd win," adding that "sometimes it seems like it was going to be a little longer waiting than I had hoped." The Times had been under court orders to suspend publication of its series on the Pentagon papers since June 15.

When asked, "Knowing what you know about what happened, would you do this again if someone came to you with what you considered to be an equally important discovery?" Mr. Sulzberger replied that he would.

'A Joyous Day . . .'

Mr. Rosenthal, asked for his reaction, said: "Well, I think it's a joyous day for the press and for American society. And I thought this was the way it would turn out. I prayed it would."

He said also that "there will be no changes in the presentation of the articles" as a result of the Government's action and the delay. "We will present them exactly as we planned." He added:

"Obviously, I'm not filled with joy that other newspapers have had pieces of this story, but I really do not think it dilutes it. Quite the contrary— I think that an enormous amount of interest has been built up in these papers, and I think that the job we intend to do will demonstrate that they are a matter of enormous historical interest."

Mr. Rosenthal was asked if he felt the decision would "open up channels of information to the news media that may heretofore have been closed?"

"Yes, I do, really," he replied. "I think this whole case will have done that. I think that people in the press, people in government and people in the public will see as the result of this whole case that a great deal of information is classified for no real national security interest and I think the move will be in the direction of more information rather than less."

Press Freedom 'Upheld'

He said also that he thought the Court, in its decision, "upheld the freedom of the press and that is a matter for great joy."

A great deal of the material, Mr. Rosenthal said, had been "a rather profound surprise" to him. "Not individual decisions . . . but the rationale or lack of rationale, the government planning or lack of government planning," he said.

Mr. Goodale, asked if he thought there was "a new kind of antagonism between First Amendment rights and the Nixon Administration," said: "I don't really know if that's the case. I sometimes suspect it to be the case. But . . . I can't really answer that, I don't know."

Mr. Rosenthal, asked the same question, said that he felt there was "a tendency to . . . try to take legal action that is more pronounced in this Administration than in others." And in reply to the succeeding question, as to whether such antagonism between the press and government might not be "a sign of good health in both parties," he said:

"To a great extent I think it is. I don't think we'll ever see the day, nor should we see the day, when we're in bed together."

Toward the end of the 30-minute news conference, the questioning returned to Mr. Sulzberger, who was asked if he felt the motto of The Times — "All the News That's Fit to Print" — had been upheld.

"Yes, sir," Mr. Sulzberger said, "I think it was very much upheld."

Texts of the Supreme Court Decision, Opinions and Dissents in Times-Post Case

Special to The New York Times

WASHINGTON, June 30—Following is the text of the decision by the United States Supreme Court upholding The New York Times and The Washington Post against an effort by the Federal Government to halt publication of articles and documents based on the Pentagon study of the Vietnam war and the texts of the concurring and dissenting opinions:

Decision

New York Times Company, Petitioner, v. United States
United States, Petitioner, v. The Washington Post Company et al.

Per curiam.

We granted certiorari in these cases in which the United States seeks to enjoin The New York Times and The Washington Post from publishing the contents of a classified study entitled "History of U.S. Decision-Making Process on Viet Nam Policy" (1971).

"Any system of prior restraints of expression comes to this court bearing a heavy presumption against its constitutional validity." Bantam Books, Inc. v. Sullivan, 372 U.S. 58, 70 (1963); see also Near v. Minnesota, 283 U.S. 697 (1931). The Government "thus carries a heavy burden of showing justification for the enforcement of such a restraint." Organization for a Better Austin v. Keefe (1971). The District Court for the Southern District of New York in The New York Times case and the District Court for the District of Columbia and the Court of Appeals for the District of Columbia Circuit in The Washington Post case held that the Government had not met that burden.

We agree.

The judgment of the Court of Appeals for the District of Columbia Circuit is therefore affirmed. The order of the Court of Appeals for the Second Circuit is reversed and the case is remanded with directions to enter a judgment affirming the judgment of the District Court for the Southern District of New York. The stays entered June 25, 1971, by the court are vacated. The mandates shall issue forthwith.

So ordered.

Concurring Opinions

Mr. Justice Douglas, with whom Mr. Justice Black joins, concurring.

While I join the opinion of the Court I believe it necessary to express my views more fully.

It should be noted at the onset that the First Amendment provides that "Congress shall make no law ... abridging the freedom of speech or of the press." That leaves, in my view, no room for governmental restraint on the press.

There is, moreover, no statute barring the publication by the press of the material which The Times and Post seek to use. 18 U.S.C. Section 793 (e) provides that "whoever having unauthorized possession of, access to, or control over any document, writing, ... or information relating to the national defense which information the possessor has reason to believe could be used to the injury of the United States or to the advantage of any foreign nation, wilfully communicates ... the same to any person not entitled to receive it ... shall be fined not more than $10,000 or imprisoned not more than 10 years or both."

The Government suggests that the word "communicates" is broad enough to encompass publication.

There are eight sections in the chapter on espionage and censorship, Sections 792-799. In three of those eight, "publish" is specifically mentioned: Section 794 (b) provides, "Whoever in time of war, with the intent that the same shall be communicated to the enemy, collects records, publishes, or communicates ... [the disposition of armed forces]."

Section 797 prohibits "reproduces, publishes, sells, or gives away" photos of defense installations.

Section 798 relating to cryptography prohibits: "communicates, furnishes, transmits, or otherwise makes available ... or publishes." Thus it is apparent that Congress was capable of and did distinguish between publishing and communication in the various sections of the Espionage Act.

The other evidence that Section 793 does not apply to the press is a rejected version of Section 793. That version read: "During any national emergency resulting from a war to which the U.S. is a party or from threat of such a war, the President may, by proclamation, prohibit the publishing or communicating of, or the attempting to publish or communicate, any information relating to the national defense, which in his judgment is of such character that it is or might be useful to the enemy." During the debates in the Senate the First Amendment was specifically cited and that provision was defeated. 55 Cong. Rec. 2166.

Judge Gurfein's holding in The Times case that this act does not apply to this case was therefore pre-eminently sound. Moreover, the act of Sept. 23, 1950, in amending 18 U.S.C. Section 793, states in Section 1 (b) that:

"Nothing in this act shall be construed to authorize, require, or establish military or civilian censorship or in any way to limit or infringe upon freedom of the press or of speech as guaranteed by the Constitution of the United States and no regulation shall be promulgated hereunder having that effect." 64 Stat. 987.

Thus Congress has been faithful to the command of the First Amendment in this area.

So any power that the Government possesses must come from its "inherent power."

The power to wage war is "the power to wage war successfully." See Hirabayashi v. United States, 320 U.S. 81, 93. But the war power stems from a declaration of war. The Constitution by Article I, Section 8, gives Congress, not the

President, power "to declare war." Nowhere are Presidential wars authorized. We need not decide therefore what leveling effect the war power of Congress might have.

These disclosures may have a serious impact. But that is no basis for sanctioning a previous restraint on the press. As stated by Chief Justice Hughes in Near v. Minnesota, 283 U.S. 697, 719-720:

"...While reckless assaults upon public men, and efforts to bring obloquy upon those who are endeavoring faithfully to discharge official duties, exert a baleful influence and deserve the severest condemnation in public opinion, it cannot be said that this abuse is greater, and it is believed to be less, than that which characterized the period in which our institutions took shape. Meanwhile, the administration of government has become more complex, the opportunities for malfeasance and corruption have multiplied, crime has grown to most serious proportions, and the danger of its protection by unfaithful officials and of the impairment of the fundamental security of life and property by criminal alliances and official neglect, emphasizes the primary need of a vigilant and courageous press, especially in great cities. The fact that the liberty of the press may be abused by miscreant purveyors of scandal does not make any the less necessary the immunity of the press from previous restraint in dealing with official misconduct."

As we stated only the other day in Organization for a Better Austin v. Keefe, "any prior restraint on expression comes to this court with a 'heavy presumption' against its constitutional validity."

The Government says that it has inherent powers to go into court and obtain an injunction to protect that national interest, which in this case is alleged to be national security.

Near v. Minnesota, 283 U.S. 697, repudiated that expansive doctrine in no uncertain terms.

The dominant purpose of the First Amendment was to prohibit the widespread practice of governmental suppression of embarrassing information. It is common knowledge that the First Amendment was adopted against the widespread use of the common law of seditious libel to punish the dissemination of material that is embarrassing to the powers-that-be. See Emerson, "The System of Free Expressions," C. XIII (1941). The present cases will, I think, go down in history as the most dramatic illustration of that principle. A debate of large proportions goes on in the nation over our posture in Vietnam. That debate antedated the disclosure of the contents of the present documents. The latter are highly relevant to the debate in progress.

Secrecy in government is fundamentally antidemocratic, perpetuating bureaucratic errors. Open debate and discussion of public issues are vital to our national health. On public questions there should be "open and robust debate." New York Times, Inc. v. Sullivan, 376 U.S. 254, 269-270.

I would affirm the judgment of the Court of Appeals in The Post case, vacate the stay of the Court of Appeals in The Times case and direct that it affirm the District Court.

The stays in these cases that have been in effect for more that a week constitute a flouting of the principles of the First Amendment as interpreted in Near v. Minnesota.

Mr. Justice Brennan, concurring.

I

I write separately in these cases only to emphasize what should be apparent: that our judgment in the present cases may not be taken to indicate the propriety, in the future, of issuing temporary stays and restraining orders to block the publication of material sought to be suppressed by the Government. So far as I can determine, never before has the United States sought to enjoin a newspaper from publishing information in its possession. The relative novelty of the questions presented, the necessary haste with which decisions were reached, the magnitude of the interests asserted, and the fact that all the parties have concentrated their arguments upon the question whether permanent restraints were proper may have justified at least some of the restraints heretofore imposed in these cases. Certainly it is difficult to fault the several courts below for seeking to assure that the issues here involved were preserved for ultimate review by this Court. But even if it be assumed that some of the interim restraints were proper in the two cases before us, that assumption has no bearing upon the propriety of similar judicial action in the future. To begin with, there has now been ample time for reflection and judgment; whatever values there may be in the preservation of novel questions for appellate review may not support any restraints in the future. More important, the First Amendment stands as an absolute bar to the imposition of judicial restraints in circumstances of the kind presented by these cases.

II

The error which has pervaded these cases from the outset was the granting of any injunctive relief whatsoever, interim or otherwise. The entire thrust of the Government's claim throughout these cases has been that publication of the material sought to be enjoined "could," or "might" or "may" prejudice the national interest in various ways. But the First Amendment tolerates absolutely no prior judicial restraints of the press predicated upon surmise or conjecture that untoward consequences may result. Our cases, it is true, have indicated that there is a single, extremely narrow class of cases in which the First Amendment's ban on prior judicial restraint may be overridden. Our cases have thus far indicated that such cases may arise only when the nation "is at war," Schenck v. United States, 249 U.S. 47, 52 (1919), during which times "no one would question but that a government might prevent actual obstruction to its recruiting service or the publication of the sailing dates of transports or the number and location of troops." Near v. Minnesota, 283 U.S. 697, 716 (1931). Even if the present world situation were assumed to be tantamount to a time of war, or if the power of presently available armaments would justify even in peacetime the suppression of information that would set in motion a nuclear holocaust, in neither of these actions has the Gov-

ernment presented or even alleged that publication of items from or based upon the material at issue would cause the happening of an event of that nature. "The chief purpose of [the First Amendment's] guarantee [is] to prevent previous restraints upon publication." Near v. Minnesota, supra, at 713. Thus, only governmental allegation and proof that publication must inevitably, directly and immediately cause the occurrence of an event kindred to imperiling the safety of a transport already at sea can support even the issuance of an interim restraining order. In no event may mere conclusions be sufficient: for if the executive branch seeks judicial aid in preventing publication, it must inevitably submit the basis upon which that aid is sought to scrutiny by the judiciary. And, therefore, every restraint issued in this case, whatever its form, has violated the First Amendment—and none the less so because that restraint was justified as necessary to afford the Court an opportunity to examine the claim more thoroughly. Unless and until the Government has clearly made out its case, the First Amendment commands that no injunction may issue.

Mr. Justice Stewart, with whom Mr. Justice White joins, concurring.

In the governmental structure created by our Constitution, the executive is endowed with enormous power in the two related areas of national defense and international relations. This power, largely unchecked by the legislative and judicial branches, has been pressed to the very hilt since the advent of the nuclear missile age. For better or for worse, the simple fact is that a President of the United States possesses vastly greater constitutional independence in these two vital areas of power than does, say, a prime minister of a country with a parliamentary form of government.

In the absence of the governmental checks and balances present in other areas of our national life, the only effective restraint upon executive policy and power in the areas of national defense and international affairs may lie in an enlightened citizenry — in an informed and critical public opinion which alone can here protect the values of democratic government. For this reason, it is perhaps here that a press that is alert, aware, and free most vitally serves the basic purpose of the First Amendment. For without an informed and free press there cannot be an enlightened people.

Yet it is elementary that the successful conduct of international diplomacy and the maintenance of an effective national defense require both confidentiality and secrecy. Other nations can hardly deal with this nation in an atmosphere of mutual trust unless they can be assured that their confidences will be kept. And within our own executive departments, the development of considered and intelligent international policies would be impossible if those charged with their formulation could not communicate with each other freely, frankly and in confidence. In the area of basic national defense the frequent need for absolute secrecy is, of course, self-evident.

I think there can be but one answer to this dilemma, if dilemma it be. The responsibility must be where the power is. If the Constitution gives the executive a large degree of unshared power in the conduct of foreign affairs and the maintenance of our national defense, then under the Constitution the executive must have the largely unshared duty to determine and preserve the degree of internal security necessary to exercise that power successfully. It is an awesome responsibility, requiring judgment and wisdom of a high order. I should suppose that moral, political and practical considerations would dictate that a very first principle of that wisdom would be an insistence upon avoiding secrecy for its own sake.

If Everything, Then Nothing

For when everything is classified, then nothing is classified, and the system becomes one to be disregarded by the cynical or the careless, and to be manipulated by those intent on self-protection or self-promotion. I should suppose in short, that the hallmark of a truly effective international security system would be the maximum possible disclosure, recognizing that secrecy can best be preserved only when credibility is truly maintained. But be that as it may, it is clear to me that it is the constitutional duty of the executive —as a matter of sovereign perogative and not as a matter of law as the courts know law—through the promulgation and enforcement of executive regulations, to protect the confidentiality necessary to carry out its responsibilities in the fields of international relations and national defense.

This is not to say that Congress and the courts have no role to play. Undoubtedly Congress has the power to enact specific and appropriate criminal laws to protect Government property and preserve Government secrets. Congress has passed such laws, and several of them are of very colorable relevance to the apparent circumstances of these cases, and if a criminal prosecution is instituted, it will be the responsibility of the courts to decide the applicability of the criminal law under which the charge is brought. Moreover, if Congress should pass a specific law authorizing civil proceedings in this field, the courts would likewise have the duty to decide the constitutionality of such a law as well as its applicability to the facts proved.

But in the cases before us we are asked neither to construe specific regulations nor to apply specific laws. We are asked, instead, to perform a function that the Constitution gave to the executive, not the judiciary. We are asked, quite simply, to prevent the publication by two newspapers of material that the executive branch insists should not, in the national interest, be published. I am convinced that the executive is correct with respect to some of the documents involved. But I cannot say that disclosure of any of them will surely result in direct, immediate and irreparable damage to our nation or its people. That being so, there can under the First Amendment be but one judicial resolution of the issues before us.

I join the judgments of the court.

Mr. Justice Marshall, concurring.

The Government contends that the only issue in this case is whether in a suit by the United States, "the First Amendment bars a court from prohibiting a newspaper from publishing material whose disclosure would pose a grave and immediate danger to the security of the United States." Brief of the Government, at 6. With all due respect, I believe the ultimate issue in this case is even more basic than the one posed by the Solicitor General. The issue is whether this Court or the Congress has the power to make law.

In this case there is no problem concerning the President's power to classify information as "secret" or "top secret." Congress has specifically recognized Presidential authority, which has been formally exercised in Executive Order 10501, to classify documents and information. See, e.g., 18 U.S.C. Section 798; 50 U.S.C. Section 783. Nor is there any issue here regarding the President's power as Chief Executive and Commander in Chief to protect national security by disciplining employes who disclose information and by taking precautions to prevent leaks.

The problem here is whether in this particular case the executive branch has authority to invoke the equity jurisdiction of the courts to protect what it believes to be the national interest. See In Re Debs, 158 U.S. 564, 584 (1895). The Government argues that in addition to the inherent power of any government to protect itself, the President's power to conduct foreign affairs and his position as Commander in Chief give him authority to impose censorship on the press to protect his ability to deal effectively with foreign nations and to conduct the military affairs of the country. Of course, it is beyond cavil that the President has broad powers by virtue of his primary responsibility for the conduct of our foreign affairs and his position as Commander in Chief. Chicago & Southern Air Lines, Inc., v. Waterman Corp., 333 U. S. 103 (1948); Hirabayashi v. United States, 320 U. S. 81, 93 (1943); United States v. Curtiss-Wright Export Co., 299 U. S. 304 (1936). And in some situations it may be that under whatever inherent powers the Government may have, as well as the implicit authority derived from the President's mandate to conduct foreign affairs and to act as Commander in Chief there is a basis for the invocation of the equity jurisdiction of this Court as an aid to prevent the publication of material damaging to "national security," however, that term may be defined.

It would, however, be utterly inconsistent with the concept of separation of power for this Court to use its power of contempt to prevent behavior that Congress has specifically declined to prohibit. There would be a similar damage to the basic concept of these co-equal branches of government if when the executive has adequate authority granted by Congress to protect "national security," it can choose instead to invoke the contempt power of a court to enjoin the threatened conduct. The Constitution provides that Congress shall make laws, the President execute laws, and courts interpret law. Youngs-

stown Sheet & Tube Co. v. Sawyer, 343 U. S. 579 (1952). It did not provide for government by injunction, in which the courts and the executive can "make law" without regard to the action of Congress. It may be more convenient for the executive if it need only convince a judge to prohibit conduct rather than to ask the Congress to pass a law, and it may be more convenient to enforce a contempt order than seek a criminal conviction in a jury trial. Moreover, it may be considered politically wise to get a court to share the responsibility for arresting those who the executive has probably cause to believe are violating the law. But convenience and political considerations of the moment do not justify a basic departure from the principles of our system of government.

In this case we are not faced with a situation where Congress has failed to provide the executive with broad power to protect the nation from disclosure of damaging state secrets. Congress has on several occasions given extensive consideration to the problem of protecting the military and strategic secrets of the United States. This consideration has resulted in the enactment of statutes making it a crime to receive, disclose, communicate, withhold and publish certain documents, photographs, instruments, appliances and information The bulk of these statutes are found to Chapter 37 of U.S.C., Title 18, entitled "Espionage and Censorship." In that chapter, Congress has provided penalties ranging from a $10,000 fine to death for violating the various statutes.

Thus it would seem that in order for this Court to issue an injunction it would require a showing that such an injunction would enhance the already existing power of the Government to act. See Bennett v. Laman, 277 N. Y. 368, 14 N. E. 2d 439 (1938). It is a traditional axiom of equity that a court of equity will not do a useless thing just as it is a traditional axiom that equity will not enjoin the commission of a crime. See Z. Chaffe & E. Re, Equity 935-954 (5th ed. 1967); H. Joyce, injunctions sections 58-60A (1909). Here there has been no attempt to make such a showing. The Solicitor General does not even mention in his brief whether the Government considers there to be probable cause to believe a crime has been committed or whether there is a conspiracy to commit future crimes.

If the Government had attempted to show that there was no effective remedy under traditional criminal law, it would have had to show that there is no arguably applicable statute. Of course, at this stage this Court could not and cannot determine whether there has been a violation of a particular statute nor decide the constitutionality of any statute. Whether a good-faith prosecution could have been instituted under any statute could, however, be determined.

Relevant Statute Noted

At least one of the many statutes in this area seems relevant to this case. Congress has provided in 18 U.S.C. Section 793 (e) that whoever "having unauthorized possesion of, access to, or control over any document, writing, code book, signal book . . . or note relating to the national defense, or information relating to the national defense which information the possessor has reason to believe could be used to the injury of the United States or to the advantage of any foreign nation, willfully communicates, delivers, transmits . . . the same to any person not entitled to receive it, or willfully retains the same and fails to deliver it to the officer or employe of the United States entitled to receive it . . . shall be fined not more than $10,000 or imprisoned not more than 10 years, or both." 18 U.S.C. Section 793 (e). Congress has also made it a crime to conspire to commit any of the offenses listed in 18 U.S.C. Section 793 (e).

It is true that Judge Gurfein found that Congress had not made it a crime to publish the items and material specified in Section 793 (e): He found that the words "communicates, delivers, transmits . . ." did not refer to publication of newspaper stories. And that view has some support in the legislative history and conforms with the past practice of using the statute only to prosecute those charged with ordinary espionage. But see 103 Cong. Rec. 10449 (remarks of Senator Humphrey). Judge Gurfein's view of the statute is not, however, the only plausible construction that could be given. See my brother White's concurring opinion.

Even if it is determined that the Government could not in good faith bring criminal prosecutions against The New York Times and The Washington Post, it is clear that Congress has specifically rejected passing legislation that would have clearly given the President the power he seeks here and made the current activity of the newspapers unlawful. When Congress specifically declines to make conduct unlawful it is not for this Court to redecide those issues —to overrule Congress. See Youngstown Sheet & Tube v. Sawyer, 345 U.S. 579 (1952).

On at least two occasions Congress has refused to enact legislation that would have made the conduct engaged in here unlawful and given the President the power that he seeks in this case. In 1917 during the debate over the original Espionage Act, still the basic provisions of Section 793, Congress rejected a proposal to give the President in time of war or threat of war authority to directly prohibit by proclamation the publication of information relating to national defense that might be useful to the enemy. The proposal provided that:

"During any national emergency resulting from a war to which the United States is a party, or from threat of such a war, the President may, by proclamation, prohibit the publishing or communicating of, or the attempting to publish or communicate any information relating to the national defense which, in his judgment, is of such character that it is or might be useful to the enemy. Whoever violates any such prohibition shall be punished by a fine of not more than $10,000 or by imprisonment for not more than 10 years, or both: provided, that nothing in this section shall be construed to limit or restrict any discussion, comment or criticism of the acts or policies of the Government or its representatives or the publication of the same." 55 Cong. Rec. 1763.

No Request of Congress

Congress rejected this proposal after war against Germany had been declared even though many believed that the threat of security leaks and espionage were serious. The executive has not gone to Congress and requested that the decision to provide such power be reconsidered. Instead, the executive comes to this Court and asks that it be granted the power Congress refused to give.

In 1957 the United States Commission on Government Security fund that "airplane journals, scientific periodicals and even the daily newspaper have featured articles containing information and other data which should have been deleted in whole or in part for security reasons." In response to this problem the commission, which was chaired by Senator Cotton, proposed that "Congress enact legislation making it a crime for any person willfully to disclose without proper authorization, for any purpose whatever, information classified 'secret' or 'top secret,' knowing, or having reasonable grounds to believe, such information to have been so classified." Report of Commission on Government Security 619-620 (1957). After substantial floor discussion on the proposal, it was rejected. See 103 Cong. Rec. 10447-10450. If the proposal that Senator Cotton championed on the floor had been enacted, the publication of the documents here would certainly have been a crime. Congress refused, however, to make it a crime. The Government is here asking this Court to remake that decision. This court has no such power.

Either the Government has the power under statutory grant to use traditional criminal law to protect the country or, if there is no basis for arguing that Congress has made the activity a crime, it is plain that Congress has specifically refused to grant the authority the Government seeks from this Court. In either case this Court does not have authority to grant the requested relief. It is not for this Court to fling itself into every breach perceived by some Government official, nor is it for this Court to take on itself the burden of enacting law, especially law that Congress has refused to pass.

I believe that the judgment of the United States Court of Appeals for the District of Columbia should be affirmed and the judgment of the United States Court of Appeals for the Second Circuit should be reversed insofar as it remands the case for further hearings.

Mr. Justice Black, with whom Mr. Justice Douglas joins, concurring.

I adhere to the view that the Government's case against The Washington Post should have been dismissed and that the injunction against The New York Times should have been vacated without oral argument when the cases were first presented to this Court. I believe that every moment's continuance of the injunctions against these newspapers amounts to a flagrant, indefensible and continuing violation of the First Amendment. Furthermore, after oral arguments, I agree completely that we must affirm the judgment of the Court of Appeals for the District of Columbia and reverse the judgment of the Court of Appeals for the Second

Circuit for the reasons stated by my brothers Douglas and Brennan. In my view it is unfortunate that some of my brethren are apparently willing to hold that the publication of news may sometimes be enjoined. Such a holding would make a shambles of the First Amendment.

Our Government was launched in 1789 with the adoption of the Constitution. The Bill of Rights, including the First Amendment, followed in 1791. Now, for the first time in the 182 years since the founding of the Republic, the Federal courts are asked to hold that the First Amendment does not mean what it says, but rather means that the Government can halt the publication of current news of vital importance to the people of this country.

In seeking injunctions against these newspapers and in its presentation to the Court, the executive branch seems to have forgotten the essential purpose and history of the First Amendment. When the Constitution was adopted, many people strongly opposed it because the document contained no bill of rights to safeguard certain basic freedoms. They especially feared that the new powers granted to a central government might be interpreted to permit the government to curtail freedom of religion, press, assembly and speech. In response to an overwhelming public clamor, James Madison offered a series of amendments to satisfy citizens that these great liberties would remain safe and beyond the power of government to abridge. Madison proposed what later became the First Amendment in three parts, two of which are set out below, and one of which proclaimed: "The people shall not be deprived or abridged of their right to speak, to write, or to publish their sentiments; and the freedom of the press, as one of the great bulwarks of liberty, shall be inviolable." The amendments were offered to curtail and restrict the general powers granted to the executive, legislative and judicial branches two years before in the original Constitution. The Bill of Rights changed the original Constitution into a new charter under which no branch of government could abridge the people's freedoms of press, speech, religion and assembly.

'Perversion of History'

Yet the Solicitor General argues and some members of the Court appear to agree that the general powers of the Government adopted in the original Constitution should be interpreted to limit and restrict the specific and emphatic guarantees of the Bill of Rights adopted later. I can imagine no greater perversion of history. Madison and the other framers of the First Amendment, able men that they were, wrote in language they earnestly believed could never be misunderstood: "Congress shall make no law . . . abridging the freedom of the press." Both the history and language of the First Amendment support the view that the press must be left free to publish news, whatever the source, without censorship, injunctions or prior restraints.

In the First Amendment the Founding Fathers gave the free press the protection it must have to fulfill its essential role in our democracy. The press was to serve the governed, not the governors. The Government's power to censor the press was abolished so that the press would remain forever free to censure the Government. The press was protected so that it could bare the secrets of government and inform the people. Only a free and unrestrained press can effectively expose deception in government. And paramount among the responsibilities of a free press is the duty to prevent any part of the Government from deceiving the people and sending them off to distant lands to die of foreign fevers and foreign shot and shell. In my view, far from deserving condemnation for their courageous reporting, The New York Times, The Washington Post and other newspapers should be commended for serving the purpose that the Founding Fathers saw so clearly. In revealing the workings of government that led to the Vietnam war, the newspapers nobly did precisely that which the founders hoped and trusted they would do.

The Government's case here is based on premises entirely different from those that guided the framers of the First Amendment. The Solicitor General has carefully and emphatically stated: "Now, Mr. Justice [Black], your construction of . . . [the First Amendment] is well known, and I certainly respect it. You say that no law means no law, and that should be obvious. I can only say, Mr. Justice, that to me it is equally obvious that 'no law,' and I would seek to persuade the Court that that is true . . . [t]here are other parts of the Constitution that grant power and responsibilities to the executive and . . . the First Amendment was not intended to make it impossible for the executive to function or to protect the security of the United States."

Government Stand Rebutted

And the Government argues in its brief that in spite of the First Amendment, "the authority of the executive department to protect the nation against publication of information whose disclosure would endanger the national security stems from two interrelated sources: the constitutional power of the President over the conduct of foreign affairs and his authority as Commander in Chief."

In other words, we are asked to hold that despite the First Amendment's emphatic command, the executive branch, the Congress and the judiciary can make laws enjoining publication of current news and abridging freedom of the press in the name of "national security." The Government does not even attempt to rely on act of Congress. Instead it makes the bold and dangerously far-reaching contention that the courts should take it upon themselves to "make" a law abridging freedom of the press in the name of equity, Presidential power and national security, even when the representatives of the people in Congress have adhered to the command of the First Amendment and refused to make such a law. See concurring opinion of Mr. Justice Douglas, Post.

To find that the President has "inherent power" to halt the publication of news by resort to the courts would wipe out the First Amendment and destroy the fundamental liberty and security of the very people the Government hopes to make "secure." No one can read the history of the adoption of

the First Amendment without being convinced beyond any doubt that it was injunctions like those sought here that Madison and his collaborators intended to outlaw in this nation for all time.

The word "security" is a broad, vague generality whose contours should not be invoked to abrogate the fundamental law embodied in the First Amendment. The guarding of military and diplomatic secrets at the expense of informed representative government provides no real security for our Republic.

The framers of the First Amendment, fully aware of both the need to defend a new nation and the abuses of the English and colonial Governments, sought to give this new society strength and security by providing that freedom of speech, press, religion and assembly should not be abridged. This thought was eloquently expressed in 1937 by Mr. Chief Justice Hughes—great man and great Chief Justice that he was—when the Court held a man could not be punished for attending a meeting run by Communists.

"The greater the importance of safeguarding the community from incitements to the overthrow of our institutions by force and violence, the more imperative is the need to preserve inviolate the constitutional rights of free speech, free press and free assembly in order to maintain the opportunity for free political discussion, to the end that government may be responsive to the will of the people and that changes, if desired, may be obtained by peaceful means. Therein lies the security of the Republic, the very foundation of constitutional government."

Mr. Justice White, with whom Mr. Justice Stewart joins, concurring.

I concur in today's judgments, but only because of the concededly extraordinary protection against prior restraints enjoyed by the press under our constitutional system. I do not say that in no circumstances would the First Amendment permit an injunction against publishing information about Government plans or operations. Nor, after examining the materials the Government characterizes as the most sensitive and destructive, can I deny that revelation of these documents will do substantial damage to public interests. Indeed, I am confident that their disclosure will have that result. But I nevertheless agree that the United States has not satisfied the very heavy burden which it must meet to warrant an injunction against publication in these cases, at least in the absence of express and appropriately limited Congressional authorization for prior restraints in circumstances such as these.

The Government's position is simply stated: The responsibility of the executive for the conduct of the foreign affairs and for the security of the nation is so basic that the President is entitled to an injunction against publication of a newspaper story whenever he can convince a court that the information to be revealed threatens "grave and irreparable" injury to the public interest; and the injunction should issue whether or not the material to be published is classified, whether or not publication would be lawful under relevant criminal statutes enacted by Congress and regardless of the circum-

stances by which the newspaper came into possession of the information.

At least in the absence of legislation by Congress, based on its own investigations and findings, I am quite unable to agree that the inherent powers of the executive and the courts reach so far as to authorize remedies having such sweeping potential for inhibiting publications by the press. Much of the difficulty inheres in the "grave and irreparable danger" standard suggested by the United States. If the United States were to have judgment under such a standard in these cases, our decision would be of little guidance to other courts in other cases, for the material at issue here would not be available from the Court's opinion or from public records, nor would it be published by the press. Indeed, even today where we hold that the United States has not met its burden, the material remains sealed in court records and it is properly not discussed in today's opinions. Moreover, because the material poses substantial dangers to national interests and because of the hazards of criminal sanctions, a responsible press may choose never to publish the more sensitive materials. To sustain the Government in these cases would start the courts down a long and hazardous road that I am not willing to travel, at least without Congressional guidance and direction.

'Not Easy to Deny Relief'

It is not easy to reject the proposition urged by the United States and to deny relief on its good-faith claims in these cases that publication will work serious damage to the country. But that discomfiture is considerably dispelled by the infrequency of prior restraint cases. Normally, publication will occur and the damage be done before the Government has either opportunity or grounds for suppression. So here, publication has already begun and a substantial part of the threatened damage has already occurred. The fact of a massive breakdown in security is known, access to the documents by many unauthorized people is undeniable and the efficacy of equitable relief against these or other newspapers to avert anticipated damage is doubtful at best.

What is more, terminating the ban on publication of the relatively few sensitive documents the Government now seeks to suppress does not mean that the law either requires or invites newspapers or others to publish them or that they will be immune from criminal action if they do. Prior restraints require an unusually heavy justification under the First Amendment; but failure by the Government to justify prior restraints does not measure its constitutional entitlement to a conviction for criminal publication. That the Government mistakenly chose to proceed by injunction does not mean that it could not successfully proceed in another way.

When the Espionage Act was under consideration in 1917, Congress eliminated from the bill a provision that would have given the President broad powers in time of war to proscribe, under threat of criminal penalty, the publication of various categories of information related to the national defense. Congress at that time was unwilling to clothe the President with such far-reaching powers to monitor the press, and those opposed to this part of the legislation assumed that a necessary concomitant of such power was the power to "filter out the news to the people through some man." 55 Cong. Rec. 2008 (1917) (remarks of Senator Ashurst). However, these same members of Congress appeared to have little doubt that newspapers would be subject to criminal prosecution if they insisted on publishing information of the type Congress had itself determined should not be revealed. Senator Ashurst, for example, was quite sure that the editor of such a newspaper "should be punished if he did publish information as to the movements of the fleet, the troops, the aircraft, the location of powder factories, the location of defense works and all that sort of thing." 55 Cong. Rec. 2009 (1917).

The Criminal Code contains numerous provisions potentially relevant to these cases. Section 797 makes it a crime to publish certain photographs or drawings of military installations. Section 798, also in precise language, proscribes knowing and willful publications of any classified information concerning the cryptographic systems or communication intelligence activities of the United States as well as any information obtained from communication intelligence operations. If any of the material here at issue is of this nature, the newspapers are presumably now on full notice of the position of the United States and must face the consequences if they publish. I would have no difficulty in sustaining convictions under these sections on facts that would not justify the intervention of equity and the imposition of a prior restraint.

Under 'a Wider Net'

The same would be true under those sections of the Criminal Code casting a wider net to protect the national defense. Section 798 (e) makes it a criminal act for any unauthorized possessor of a document "relating to national defense" either (1) willfully to communicate or cause to be communicated that document to any person not entitled to receive it or (2) willfully to retain the document and fail to deliver it to an officer of the United States entitled to receive it. The subsection was added in 1950 because pre-existing law provided no penalty for the unauthorized possessor unless demand for the documents was made. "The dangers surrounding the unauthorized possession of such items are self-evident, and it is deemed advisable to require their surrender in such a case, regardless of demand, especially since their unauthorized possession may be unknown to the authorities who would otherwise make the demand." S. Rep. No. 2369, 81st Cong., 2d Sess., 9 (1950). Of course, in the cases before us, the unpublished documents have been demanded by the United States and their import has been made known at least to counsel for the newspapers involved. In Gorin v. United States, 312 U. S. 19, 28 (1941), the words "national defense" as used in a predecessor of Sec. 793 were held by a unanimous court to have "a well-understood connotation"—a "generic concept of broad connotations, referring to the military and naval establishments and the related activities of national preparedness"—and to be "sufficiently definite to apprise the public of prohibited activities" and to be consonant with due

process. 312 U. S., at 28. Also, as construed by the Court in Gorin, information "connected with the national defense" is obviously not limited to that threatening "grave and irreparable" injury to the United States.

It is thus clear that Congress has addressed itself to the problems of protecting the security of the country and the national defense from unauthorized disclosure of potentially damaging information. Cf. Youngstown Sheet & Tube Co. v. Sawyer, 343 U. S. 579, 585-586 (1952): see also id., at 593-628 (Frankfurter, J., concurring). It has not, however, authorized the injunctive remedy against threatened publication. It has apparently been satisfied to rely on criminal sanctions and their deterrent effect on the responsible as well as the irresponsible press. I am not, of course, saying that either of these newspapers has yet committed a crime or that either would commit a crime if they published all the material now in their possession. That matter must await resolution in the context of a criminal proceeding if one is instituted by the United States. In that event, the issue of guilt or innocence would be determined by procedures and standards quite different from those that have purported to govern these injunctive proceedings.

Dissents

Mr. Chief Justice Burger, dissenting.

So clear are the constitutional limitations on prior restraint against expression, that from the time of Near v. Minnesota, 283 U. S. 697 (1931), until recently in Organization for a Better Austin v. Keefe, (1971), we have had little occasion to be concerned with cases involving prior restraints against news reporting on matters of public interest. There is, therefore, little variation among the members of the Court in terms of resistance to prior restraints against publication. Adherence to this basic constitutional principle, however, does not make this case a simple one. In this case, the imperative of a free and unfettered press comes into collision with another imperative, the effective functioning of a complex modern government, and specifically the effective exercise of certain constitutional powers of the executive. Only those who view the First Amendment as an absolute in all circumstances—a view I respect, but reject—can find such a case as this to be simple or easy.

This case is not simple for another and more immediate reason. We do not know the facts of the case. No District Judge knew all the facts. No Court of Appeals Judge knew all the facts. No member of this Court knows all the facts.

Why are we in this posture, in which only those judges to whom the First Amendment is absolute and permits of no restraint in any circumstances or for any reason, are really in a position to act?

I suggest we are in this posture because these cases have been conducted in unseemly haste. Mr. Justice Harlan covers the chronology of events demonstrating the hectic pressures under which these cases have been processed and

I need not restate them. The prompt setting of these cases reflects our universal abhorrence of prior restraint. But prompt judicial action does not mean unjudicial haste.

Here, moreover, the frenetic haste is due in large part to the manner in which The Times proceeded from the date it obtained the purloined documents. It seems reasonably clear now that the haste precluded reasonable and deliberate judicial treatment of these cases and was not warranted. The precipitous action of this court aborting a trial not yet completed is not the kind of judicial conduct which ought to attend the disposition of a great issue.

'The Public Right to Know'

The newspapers make a derivative claim under the First Amendment; they denominate this right as the public right to know; by implication, The Times asserts a sole trusteeship of that right by virtue of its journalist "scoop." The right is asserted as an absolute. Of course, the First Amendment right itself is not an absolute, as Justice Holmes so long ago pointed out in his aphorism concerning the right to shout of fire in a crowded theater. There are other exceptions, some of which Chief Justice Hughes mentioned by way of example in Near v. Minnesota. There are no doubt other exceptions no one has had occasion to describe or discuss. Conceivably such exceptions may be lurking in these cases and would have been flushed had they been properly considered in the trial courts, free from unwarranted deadlines and frenetic pressures.

A great issue of this kind should be tried in a judicial atmosphere conducive to thoughtful, reflective deliberation, especially when haste, in terms of hours, is unwarranted in light of the long period The Times, by its own choice, deferred publication.

It is not disputed that The Times has had unauthorized possession of the documents for three to four months, during which it has had its expert analysts studying them, presumably digesting them and preparing the material for publication. During all of this time, The Times, presumably in its capacity as trustee of the public's "right to know," has held up publication for purposes it considered proper and thus public knowledge was delayed. No doubt this was for a good reason; the analysis of 7,000 pages of complex material drawn from a vastly greater volume of material would inevitably take time and the writing of good news stories takes time.

But why should the United States Government, from whom this information was illegally acquired by someone, along with all the counsel, trial judges, and appellate judges be placed under needless pressure? After these months of deferral, the alleged right to know has somehow and suddenly become a right that must be vindicated instanter.

Would it have been unreasonable, since the newspaper could anticipate the Government's objections to release of secret material, to give the Government an opportunity to review the entire collection and determine whether agreement could be reached on publication? Stolen or not, if security was not in fact jeopardized, much of the material could no doubt have been declassified, since it spans a period ending in 1968.

'Duty of Honorable Press'

With such an approach—one that great newspapers have in the past practiced and stated editorially to be the duty of honorable press—the newspapers and Government might well have narrowed the area of disagreement as to what was and was not publishable, leaving the remainder to be resolved in orderly litigation if necessary. To me it is hardly believable that a newspaper long regarded as a great institution in American life would fail to perform one of the basic and simple duties of every citizen with respect to the discovery or possession of stolen property or secret Government documents. That duty, I had thought—perhaps naively—was to report forthwith, to responsible public officers. This duty rests on taxi drivers, justices and The New York Times. The course followed by The Times, whether so calculated or not, removed any possibility of orderly litigation of the issues. If the action of the judges up to now has been correct, that result is sheer happenstance.

Our grant of the writ before final judgment in The Times case aborted the trial in the District Court before it had made a complete record pursuant to the mandate of the Court of Appeals, Second Circuit.

The consequences of all this melancholy series of events is that we literally do not know what we are acting on. As I see it we have been forced to deal with litigation concerning rights of great magnitude without an adequate record, and surely without time for adequate treatment either in the prior proceedings or in this court. It is interesting to note that counsel in oral argument before this Court were frequently unable to respond to questions on factual points. Not surprisingly they pointed out that they had been working literally "around the clock" and simply were unable to review the documents that give rise to these cases and were not familiar with them. This Court is in no better posture. I agree with Mr. Justice Harlan and Mr. Justice Blackmun but I am not prepared to reach the merits.

I would affirm the Court of Appeals for the Second Circuit and allow the District Court to complete the trial aborted by our grant of certiorari, meanwhile preserving the status quo in The Post case. I would direct that the District Court on remand give priority to The Times case to the exclusion of all other business of that court but I would not set arbitrary deadlines.

I should add that I am in general agreement with much of what Mr. Justice White has expressed with respect to penal sanctions concerning communication or retention of documents or information relating to the national defense.

We all crave speedier judicial processes, but when judges are pressured as in these cases the result is a parody of the judicial process.

Mr. Justice Harlan, with whom the Chief Justice and Mr. Justice Blackmun join, dissenting.

These cases forcefully call to mind the wise admonition of Mr. Justice Holmes, dissenting in Northern Securities Co. v. United States, 193 U. S. 197, 400-401 (1904):

"Great cases like hard cases make bad law. For great cases are called great, not by reason of their real importance in shaping the law of the future, but because of some accident of immediate overwhelming interest which appeals to the feelings and distorts the judgment. These immediate interests exercise a kind of hydraulic pressure which makes what previously was clear seem doubtful, and before which even well settled principles of law will bend."

With all respect, I consider that the Court has been almost irresponsibly feverish in dealing with these cases.

Both the Court of Appeals for the Second Circuit and the Court of Appeals for the District of Columbia Circuit rendered judgment on June 23. The New York Times's petition for certiorari, its motion for accelerated consideration thereof, and its application for interim relief were filed in this Court on June 24 at about 11 A.M. The application of the United States for interim relief in The Post case was also filed here on June 24, at about 7:15 P.M. This Court's order setting a hearing before us on June 26 at 11 A.M., a course which I joined only to avoid the possibility of even more peremptory action by the Court, was issued less than 24 hours before. The record in The Post case was filed with the clerk shortly before 1 P.M. on June 25; the record in The Times case did not arrive until 7 or 8 o'clock that same night. The briefs of the parties were received less than two hours before argument on June 26.

This frenzied train of events took place in the name of the presumption against prior restraints created by the First Amendment. Due regard for the extraordinarily important and difficult questions involved in these litigations should have led the Court to shun such a precipitate timetable. In order to decide the merits of these cases properly, some or all of the following questions should have been faced:

1. Whether the Attorney General is authorized to bring these suits in the name of the United States. Compare In Re Debs, 158 U.S. 564 (1895), with Youngstown Sheet & Tube Co. v. Sawyer, 343 U.S. 479 (1952). This question involves as well the construction and validity of a singularly opaque statute—the Espionage Act, 18 U.S.C. Section 793 (e).

2. Whether the First Amendment permits the Federal Courts to enjoin publication of stories which would present a serious threat to national security. See Near v. Minnesota, 283 U.S. 697, 716 (1931) (dictum)

3. Whether the threat to publish highly secret documents is of itself a sufficient implication of national security to justify an injunction on the theory that regardless of the contents of the documents harm enough results simply from the demonstration of such a breach of secrecy.

4. Whether the unauthorized disclosure of any of these particular documents would seriously impair the national security.

5. What weight should be given to the opinion of high officers in the executive branch of the Government with respect to questions 3 and 4.

6. Whether the newspapers are entitled to retain and use the documents notwithstanding the seemingly uncontested facts that the documents, or the original of which they are duplicates, were purloined from the Government's possession and that the newspapers received them with the knowledge that they had been feloniously acquired. Cf. Liberty Lobby, Inc., v. Pearson, 390 F. 2d 489 (CADC 1968).

7. Whether the threatened harm to the national security or the Government's possessory interest in the documents justifies the issuance of an injunction against publication in light of—

A. The strong First Amendment policy against prior restraints on publication;

B. The doctrine against enjoining conduct in violation of criminal statutes; and

C. The extent to which the materials at issue have apparently already been otherwise disseminated.

'Difficult Questions of Fact, Law'

These are difficult questions of fact, of law and of judgment; the potential consequences of erroneous decision are enormous. The time which has been available to us, to the lower courts and to the parties has been wholly inadequate for giving these cases the kind of consideration they deserve. It is a reflection on the stability of the judicial process that these great issues—as important as any that have arisen during my time on the Court—should have been decided under the pressures engendered by the torrent of publicity that has attended these litigations from their inception.

Forced as I am to reach the merits of these cases, I dissent from the opinion and judgments of the Court. Within the severe limitations imposed by the time constraints under which I have been required to operate, I can only state my reasons in telescoped form, even though in different circumstances I would have felt constrained to deal with the cases in the fuller sweep indicated above.

It is a sufficient basis for affirming the Court of Appeals for the Second Circuit in The Times litigation to observe that its order must rest on the conclusion that because of the time elements the Government had not been given an adequate opportunity to present its case to the District Court. At the least this conclusion was not an abuse of discretion.

In The Post litigation the Government had more time to prepare; this was apparently the basis for the refusal of the Court of Appeals for the District of Columbia Circuit on rehearing to conform its judgment to that of the Second Circuit. But I think there is another and more fundamental reason why this judgment cannot stand—a reason which also furnishes an additional ground for not reinstating the judgment of the district court in The Times litigation, set aside by the Court of Appeals. It is plain to me that the scope of the judicial function in passing upon the activities of the executive branch of the Government in the field of foreign affairs is very narrowly restricted. This view is, I think, dictated by the concept of separation of powers upon which our constitutional system rests.

In a speech on the floor of the House of Representatives, Chief Justice John

Marshall, then a member of that body, stated:

"The President is the sole organ of the nation in its external relations, and its sole representative with foreign nations." Annals, 6th Cong., Col. 613 (1800).

From that time, shortly after the founding of the nation, to this, there has been no substantial challenge to this description of the scope of executive power. See United States v. Curtiss-Wright Export Corp., 299 U.S. 304, 319-321 (1936), collecting authorities.

From this constitutional primacy in the field of foreign affairs, it seems to me that certain conclusions necessarily follow. Some of these were stated concisely by President Washington, declining the request of the House of Representatives for the papers leading up to the negotiation of the Jay Treaty:

"The nature of foreign negotiations requires caution, and their success must often depend on secrecy; and even when brought to a conclusion a full disclosure of all the measures, demands, or eventual concessions which may have been proposed or contemplated would be extremely impolitic; for this might have a pernicious influence on future negotiations, or produce immediate inconveniences, perhaps danger and mischief, in relation to other powers." J. Richardson, "Messages and Papers of the Presidents" 194-195 (1899).

Need for Judicial Review Seen

The power to evaluate the "pernicious influence" of premature disclosure is not, however, lodged in the executive alone. I agree that, in performance of its duty to protect the values of the First Amendmen against political pressures, the judiciary must review the initial executive determination to the point of satisfying itself that the subject matter of the dispute does lie within the proper compass of the President's foreign relations power. Constitutional considerations forbid "a complete abandonment of judicial control." Cf. United States v. Reynolds, 345 U.S. 1, 8 (1953). Moreover, the judiciary may properly insist that the determination that disclosure of the subject matter would irreparably impair the national security be made by the head of the executive department concerned — here the Secretary of State or the Secretary of Defense — after actual personal consideration by that office. This safeguard is required in the analogous area of executive claims of privilege for secrets of state. See United States v. Reynolds, supra, at 8 and N. 20; Duncan v. Cammell, Laird & Co., (1942) A. C. 624, 638 (House of Lords).

But in my judgment the judiciary may not properly go beyond these two inquiries and redetermine for itself the probable impact of disclosure on the national security.

"The very nature of executive decisions as to foreign policy is political, not judicial. Such decisions are wholly confided by our Constitution to the political departments of the Government, executive and legislative. They are delicate, complex, and involve large elements of prophecy. They are and should be undertaken only by those directly responsible to the people whose welfare they advance or imperil. They are decisions of a kind for which the judiciary has neither aptitude, facilities nor responsibility and which has long been held to belong in the domain of political power not subject to judicial intrusion or inquiry." Chicago & Southern Air Lines v. Waterman Steamship Corp., 333 U.S. 103, 111 (1948) (Jackson, J.).

Even if there is some room for the judiciary to override the executive determination, it is plain that the scope of review must be exceedingly narrow. I can see no indication in the opinions of either the District Court or the Court of Appeals in The Post litigation that the conclusions of the executive were given even the deference owing to an administrative agency, much less that owing to a coequal constitutional prerogative.

Accordingly, I would vacate the judgment of the Court of Appeals for the District of Columbia Circuit on this ground and remand the case for further proceedings in the District Court. Before the commencement of such further proceedings, due opportunity should be afforded the Government for procuring from the Secretary of State or the Secretary of Defense or both an expression of their views on the issue of national security. The ensuing review by the District Court should be in accordance with the views expressed in this opinion. And for the reasons stated above I would affirm the judgment of the Court of Appeals for the Second Circuit.

Pending further hearings in each case conducted under the appropriate ground rules, I would continue the restraints on publication. I cannot believe that the doctrine prohibiting prior restraints reaches to the point of preventing courts from maintaining the status quo long enough to act responsibly in matters of such national importance as those involved here.

Mr. Justice Blackmun.

I join Mr. Justice Harlan in his dissent. I also am in substantial accord with much that Mr. Justice White says, by way of admonition, in the latter part of his opinion.

At this point the focus is on only the comparatively few documents specified by the Government as critical. So far as the other material — vast in amount—is concerned, let it be published and published forthwith if the newspapers once the strain is gone and the sensationalism is eased, still feel the urge so to do.

But we are concerned here with the few documents specified from the 47 volumes. Almost 70 years ago Mr. Justice Holmes, dissenting in a celebrated case, observed:

"Great cases like hard cases make bad law. For great cases are called great, not by reason of their real importance in shaping the law of the future, but because of some accident of immediate overwhelming interest which appeals to the feelings and distorts the judgment. These immediate interests exercise a kind of hydraulic pressure. . . ." Northern Securities Co. v. United States, 193 U.S. 197, 400-401 (1904).

The present cases, if not great, are at least unusual in their posture and implications, and the Holmes observation certainly has pertinent application.

The New York Times clandestinely devoted a period of three months examining the 47 volumes that came into its unauthorized possession. Once it had begun publication of material from those volumes, the New York case now before us emerged. It immediately assumed, and ever since has maintained, a frenetic pace and character. Seemingly, once publication started, the material could not be made public fast enough. Seemingly, from then on, every deferral or delay, by restraint or otherwise, was abhorrent and was to be deemed violative of the First Amendment and of the public's "right immediately to know." Yet that newspaper stood before us at oral argument and professed criticism of the Government for not lodging its protest earlier than by a Monday telegram following the initial Sunday publication.

The District of Columbia case is much the same.

'Pressed Into Hurried Decision'

Two Federal District Courts, two United States Courts of Appeals, and this Court—within a period of less than three weeks from inception until today —have been pressed into hurried decision of profound constitutional issues on inadequately developed and largely assumed facts without the careful deliberation that, hopefully, should characterize the American judicial process. There has been much writing about the law and little knowledge and less digestion of the facts. In the New York case the judges, both trial and appellate, had not yet examined the basic material when the case was brought here. In the District of Columbia case, little more was done, and what was accomplished in this respect was only on required remand, with The Washington Post, on the excuse that it was trying to protect its source of information, initially refusing to reveal what material it actually possessed, and with the District Court forced to make assumptions as to that possession.

With such respect as may be due to the contrary view, this, in my opinion, is not the way to try a lawsuit of this magnitude and asserted importance. It is not the way for Federal Courts to adjudicate, and to be required to adjudicate, issues that allegedly concern the nation's vital welfare. The country would be none the worse off were the cases tried quickly, to be sure, but in the customary and properly deliberative manner. The most recent of the material, it is said, dates no later than 1968, already about three years ago, and The Times itself took three months to formulate its plan of procedure and, thus, deprived its public for that period.

The First Amendment, after all, is only one part of an entire Constitution. Article II of the great document vests in the executive branch primary power over the conduct of foreign affairs and places in that branch the responsibility for the nation's safety.

Each provision of the Constitution is important, and I cannot subscribe to a doctrine of unlimited absolutism for the First Amendment at the cost of downgrading other provisions.

First Amendment absolutism has never commanded a majority of this court. See, for example, Near v. Minnesota, 283 U.S. 697, 708 (1931), and Schenck v. United States, 249 U.S. 47, 52 (1919). What is needed here is a weighing, upon properly developed standards, of the broad right of the press to print and of the very narrow right of the Government to prevent. Such standards are not yet developed. The parties here are in disagreement as to what those standards should be. But even the newspapers concede that there are situations where restraint is in order and is constitutional. Mr. Justice Holmes gave us a suggestion when he said in Schenck:

"It is a question of proximity and degree. When a nation is at war many things that might be said in time of peace are such a hindrance to its effort that their utterance will not be endured so long as men fight and that no court could regard them as protected by any constitutional right." 249 U.S., at 52.

'Better Quality' of Presentation

I therefore would remand these cases to be developed expeditiously, of course, but on a schedule permitting the orderly presentation of evidence from both sides, with the use of discovery, if necessary, as authorized by the rules, and with the preparation of briefs, oral argument and court opinions of a quality better than has been seen to this point. In making this last statement, I criticize no lawyer or judge. I know from past personal experience the agony of time pressure in the preparation of litigation. But these cases and the issues involved and the courts, including this one, deserve better than has been produced thus far.

It may well be that if these cases were allowed to develop as they should be developed, and to be tried as lawyers should try them and as courts should hear them, free of pressure and panic and sensationalism, other light would be shed on the situation and contrary considerations, for me, might prevail. But that is not the present posture of the litigation.

The Court, however, decides the cases today the other way. I therefore add one final comment.

I strongly urge, and sincerely hope, that these two newspapers will be fully aware of their ultimate responsibilities to the United States of America. Judge Wilkey, dissenting in the District of Columbia case, after a review of only the affidavits before this Court, (the basic papers had not then been made available by either party), concluded that there were a number of examples of documents that, if in the possession of The Post, and if published, "could clearly result in great harm to the nation," and he defined "harm" to mean "the death of soldiers, and destruction of alliances, the greatly increased difficulty of negotiation with our enemies, the inability of our diplomats to negotiate. . . ." I, for one, have now been able to give at least some cursory study not only to the affidavits, but to the material itself. I regret to say that from this examination I fear that Judge Wilkey's statements have possible foundation. I therefore share his concern. I hope that damage already has not been done.

If, however, damage has been done, and if, with the Court's action today, these newspapers proceed to publish the critical documents and there results therefrom "the death of soldiers, the destruction of alliances, the greatly increased difficulty of negotiation with our enemies, the inability of our diplomats to negotiate," to which list I might add the factors of prolongation of the war and of further delay in the freeing of United States prisoners, then the nation's people will know where the responsibility for these sad consequences rests.

July 1, 1971

Airing of Pentagon Data Backed in Poll

A Gallup Poll made public today indicates that, even before the Supreme Court ruled in favor of newspapers' right to publish the Pentagon papers, a majority of Americans familiar with the issue thought publication of the articles was "the right thing."

The poll's findings, according to George Gallup, head of the Princeton, N. J. organization, were based on interviews with 1,326 persons over 18 years old throughout the country.

Each was asked, first, whether he had "heard or read about the articles first published in The New York Times about how we got involved in the Vietnam war?" Only about 55 per cent said they were familiar with the articles.

Those who had given an affirmative reply were then asked whether the newspapers had done "the right thing or the wrong thing in publishing these articles."

58 Pct. Favored Publication

The results were, according to Dr. Gallup, that 58 per cent of the sample thought publication was "the right thing"; 30 per cent thought it was "the

wrong thing," and 12 per cent had no opinion either way.

The comments from those questioned, Dr. Gallup said, show that "few issues of recent times have provoked such deeply-felt opinions."

Most of those who favored publication stressed the people's right to know. Dr. Gallup cited this remark from a 40-year-old New York City mechanic:

"People should know what the hell is going on in this country. Why do things always have to be so hush-hush? The Pentagon's not worried about national security, they're afraid of being embarrassed."

A 66-year-old retired tool-and-die maker from Evansville. Ind., said:

"If the newspapers don't publish the true facts, how are we going to know? I think the public is being kept in the dark too much."

The most frequent position of those who indicated they felt it was "the wrong thing" to publish the Pentagon papers was that the information was secret. A Virginia banker, 59, was quoted as having said:

"Those papers were stolen. It's a case of treason pure and simple—"

A 58-year-old farmer from Iowa said:

"This is top secret material. The Government hasn't changed that classification and it certainly isn't up to the newspapers to change it on their own."

Disclosure Criticized

A gas-station manager from Colorado, 64, expressed what the report indicated was another common viewpoint among those critical of the papers being published:

"Other nations must be laughing at us. We splash top-secret international documents across the front page as if they were comic strips."

The June 30 ruling by the Supreme Court of the United States was split 6-3. The report notes that public opinion, as shown in these "near final returns" from a survey of "more than 1,500 persons," was divided in approximately the same ratio.

The Gallup Poll, the report said, was completed June 28.

The report said also that the results of a survey designed to assess the impact of the Pentagon papers on President Nixon's popularity were now being tabulated.

Mrs. Mitchell Suggests Press May Be Silenced

WASHINGTON, July 4 (Reuters) — Mrs. Martha Mitchell suggested today that the American press might be suppressed if it continued to reveal Government secrets.

Mrs. Mitchell, the often outspoken wife of Attorney General John N. Mitchell, was referring to the secret Pentagon study of the Vietnam war, which the Supreme Court has ruled can be published.

"I resent, regret and abhor that the news media has taken upon itself to interfere with possible lines of communication with the Vietcong," Mrs. Mitchell said in a telephone call to The Washington Star, which reported her comment today.

"I deplore the indiscreet judgment, that smells of political implications, on the part of the press. which has reached such an extent that it may result in complete suppression of the press—in which event it will have caused its own death," she continued.

Mrs. Mitchell added that her remarks were not an assault on freedom of the press. "I think the greatest thing going for this country is freedom of the press, and I don't want to see them destroy themselves."

July 5, 1971

The Purloined Papers

By DEAN ACHESON

WASHINGTON—More than a century ago Alexis de Tocqueville told us: "Scarcely any political question arises in the United States that is not resolved, sooner or later, into a judicial question."

Here the question, both political and ethical—whether a newspaper may properly receive and publish papers illegally taken from the Government—merges into the question whether judges must let the would-be publisher get away with publishing by virtue of the freedom-of-the-press provision of the First Amendment. In this case the ethical question disappeared and the political question became hopelessly simplified into whether publication would give aid and comfort to some enemy. The Solicitor General agreed that his case required him to show that publication of the Pentagon Papers would result in an immediate grave threat to the security of the United States of America.

Justice Stewart: "However it was acquired, and however it was classified?"

The Solicitor General: "Yes, Mr. Justice, but I think the fact that it was obviously acquired improperly is not irrelevant in the consideration of that question. I repeat, obviously acquired improperly."

But he never discussed how that fact was relevant or what conclusions should be drawn from it.

The Chief Justice, however, in his dissenting opinion did so:

"To me it is hardly believable that a newspaper long regarded as a great institution in American life would fail to perform one of the basic and simple duties of every citizen with respect to the discovery or possession of stolen property or secret Government documents. That duty, I had thought—perhaps naively—was to report forthwith to responsible public officers. This duty rests on taxi drivers, justices and The New York Times. The course followed by The Times, whether so calculated or not, removed any possibility of orderly litigation of the issues."

Later, counsel for The Washington Post was asked by Justice Stewart: "Mr. Glenden, wouldn't you be making the same argument if your client had stolen the papers?"

Mr. Glenden: "I don't think the source of how we obtained them features in this case."

But the ethical issue, or its ghost, continued to haunt The Times. Exorcism by incantation was tried. Thus Mr. Neil Sheehan:

"This history is public property, not the property of Lyndon Johnson or Robert McNamara or the Bundy brothers or any other public figure involved in the Vietnam war. The story belongs to the people. They paid for it with their lives and treasure. As far as I am concerned, they own it and have the right to know of its contents."

Oratory aside, the Pentagon Papers belong to the United States of America as clearly as does the battleship Missouri or the White House silver. To jump from the assertion that the papers do not belong to any public figure to the conclusion that they do belong to

Saul Steinberg

all the two hundred million inhabitants of the United States violates Mr. Johnson's advice to Boswell not "to think foolishly."

The issue between the newspapers and the Government became narrowed by the frenetic conduct of the case to the nature, degree, and immediacy of the danger threatened to the security of the United States and how directly it would follow from the publication. The newspapers insisted that it must be such danger as the breaking of diplomatic relations, war, sinking of ships, attack on military units, or disclosure of war plans and weapons. The Government would have included a wider range of dislocation of diplomatic ne-

gotiations relating to security. Both are practically impossible for the Government to prove or judges to apply with proper regard to the complexity of the problems involved. Two of the six majority judges believed that the public interest would be harmed by publication and that there might be room for a statute to provide some relief.

Here is a supreme example of the problems we pose for ourselves by turning every political question—and some ethical questions—into judicial questions. In my lifetime it has been done with the question of monopolistic practices, labor relations, control of alcoholic beverages, race discrimination, control of pornography, determination of election districts, qualifications for voters. All of these questions are too complicated for judicial solution under the formal procedures of courts and the guidance of sibylline phrases such as "contracts and combinations in restraint of trade," "liberty of contract," "equal protection of the laws," "interstate commerce," and so on. Nearly all of these judicial experiments have failed and driven us through painful experience to use—as we should have done in the first place—all the devices of government and the means of social control outside of government.

So it is with freedom of the press. Judges cannot spin from that phrase a solution of the situation resulting from the purloining of the Pentagon Papers. We need a severe Official Secrets Act to prevent irresponsible or corrupt transfer of secret papers from the Government to publishers, a commission of the quality of the Royal Commission recently created in Britain under the chairmanship of Lord Franks, to determine how this present disclosure came about and what laws and procedures we need to prevent its repetition and for the faster declassification and release of most papers.

Finally, the creation of a self-governing body for the press, as in Britain, might be very helpful, headed by a universally respected public figure, past the age of ambition, to stimulate more ethical professional relations with the Government and self-restraint in publishing material ethically undesirable.

In short, what is needed now is more than prohibitions, punishments, or Pulitzer Prizes. Far-reaching improvement of public health in the relations between press and Government is called for.

Dean Acheson was Secretary of State in the Truman Administration.

Thinking Foolishly

By TOM WICKER

WASHINGTON, July 7 — Former Secretary of State Dean Acheson has entered the controversy over publication of the Pentagon Papers, suggesting that an "ethical issue, or its ghost" has continued to "haunt" The New York Times. More specifically, he called for a "severe official secrets act" and a self-governing body for the press "to stimulate more ethical professional relations with the Government."

Mr. Acheson's so-called "ethical question" rests on his notion that the Pentagon Papers were simply stolen items and that, as Chief Justice Burger put it, "a duty rests on taxi drivers, justices and The New York Times" to report such thefts to "responsible public officers." Mr. Acheson drew a further comparison; the Pentagon Papers, he said, were property that belong "to the United States of America as clearly as does the battleship Missouri or the White House silver."

Now it may seem strange to consider the duties of a justice, a taxi driver and a newspaper as one and the same, at that crucial moment when any one of them comes into possession of the Pentagon Papers. It may seem downright frivolous to compare these documents to tangible items of determinable value, like a battleship or the White House silver. But according to Mr. Acheson it is Neil Sheehan of The Times who has violated Samuel Johnson's advice to Boswell not "to think foolishly."

Mr. Sheehan is thus dismissed for having said that the history contained in the Pentagon Papers "belongs to the people . . . they own it and have the right to know of its contents." Aside from the question whether there is not some considerable sense in which the people also own the Missouri and the White House dinner knives, the people having paid for

IN THE NATION

them, the real issue here, political and ethical, is the publication of information; and the real cant is to try to suggest that the issue is instead a matter of stolen items.

Former Secretary McNamara ordered this history compiled, according to its authors, so that it might be seen where and how errors had been made and so that others might therefore profit by those errors—perhaps even avoid them. But who was to study the record—the Johnson Administration? Virtually all its high officials went out of office, like Secretary Rusk, not knowing that the Pentagon Papers existed.

The Nixon Administration? The record is clear that few of its high officials even knew the record existed, and none had studied it; it took the State Department a day or two even to locate its copy.

Congress? Senator Fulbright's request for the study was rejected by a low-level official in the Pentagon who testified in court that he had not known the study existed until the Senator asked for it.

There remain, of course, the same people who paid for the Missouri, the White House silver and Vietnam. They now know most of what was in the Pentagon record, and even their Congressmen and Senator Fulbright—as a result of the papers' publication—have been given limited access to this historical matter.

So how foolishly was Mr. Sheehan thinking after all? As a practical matter, the people who read these documents in The Times were the first to study them; and as a theoretical matter, they are the ones for whom the history was intended in the first place. Mr. McNamara himself sought to de-

classify and publish them, but was overruled at the White House.

As for an official secrets act, no doubt such a law would have effectively prevented publication of the Pentagon Papers. It is not likely that comparable documents would have been published in Britain, for instance, where there is an Official Secrets Act as severe as the one Mr. Acheson wants.

But assuming such an act could be squared with the First Amendment— a long assumption — Mr. Acheson's final point is remarkable. The press, he says, should police itself into "more ethical professional relations with the Government." But who, pray, in that case, is going to police the Government into more ethical professional relations with the people?

However the words "deceit" and "misled" may be deplored, even cursory examination of the Pentagon Papers discloses how little successive Administrations told the public. From the U-2 incident to Cambodia, the record of those Administrations is replete with dissembling, sophistries and outright lies. As far back as 1949, even Mr. Acheson "propagated myths" about Chinese-American relations, according to recent testimony before the Foreign Relations Committee by Allen Whiting of the Center for Chinese Studies at the University of Michigan.

Yet, here is a formula that would give the Government immensely greater power to make and keep secrets, while the press was policing itself against "publishing material ethically undesirable." Samuel Johnson would know what to say to *that:* "The mass of every people must be barbarous where there is no printing."

July 8, 1971

Free Press, Free People

By OGDEN R. REID

Our democracy does not work well in secret. The Pentagon Papers illuminate the arrogance of those in high places and the serious erosion, if not breakdown, of our constitutional system of checks and balances.

At least two Administrations, if not three, believed that they were not accountable to the Congress and the American people for watershed decisions taken about Indochina.

The present Administration has gone even further and launched the most serious attack on the press in our

history: subpoenaing reporters' notes, threatening reprisals against television and radio stations under the power to license, and, for the first time nationally, invoking prior restraint against the right to publish.

This precensorship was claimed to be justified because of an "immediate grave threat to national security." Critical national security touching our very survival is not in fact at issue here—nor is cryptographic intelligence.

While the Kennedy and particularly the Johnson Administrations' failure to inform Congress is a shocking example of unilateral executive decision-making,

the attempted effort by the Nixon Administration to prevent what is essentially past history reaching Congress or being published is hardly more reassuring.

After six days of hearings before the Government Information Subcommittee of the House of Representatives, certain remedies are clearly called for if the Congress is to reassert its constitutional role.

First, the Congress must enact a new statute governing classified documents. This law must sharply limit that which should be labeled secret and it must provide for automatic de-

BRAD HOLLAND

Brad Holland

classification and Congressional oversight. If a matter should remain secret after a stated period, there should be an affirmative, positive finding as to why continued secrecy is necessary.

The Congress should explicitly reserve the right to make public material improperly classified by the executive contrary to statute when its classification is not a matter of national security and is simply a device to avoid governmental embarrassment. Equally, no Executive order on classification should be issued that subverts the intent of the Congress. Above all, there must be a vast reduction in the corps of 8,000 Defense Department officers who now have authority to originate top secret and secret designations.

Second, the Freedom of Information Act should be tightened in two respects. The types of information now permitted to be withheld must be sharply limited, and time permitted for Government response to a court suit must be reduced from the present 60 days.

Third, the Congress must come to grips with executive privilege. Here we are dealing with a collision between the executive and the Congress that has been going on since George Washington assumed office. It should be subject to accommodation, but that will never happen if the Congress does not assert the powers and responsibilities given to it by the Constitution.

Fourth, legislation may well be required to protect the Fourth Estate. The press often serves as a coordinate branch of our democracy, especially when a breakdown occurs between the other three. Specifically, we need a national Newsmen's Privilege Act — now law in six states—protecting the confidentiality of sources, absent a threat to human life, espionage, or foreign aggression. Legislation should be enacted to prohibit the issuance by the courts of injunctions against publication, thereby removing prior restraint from the reach of the executive.

Congressional legislation and assertion of appropriate initiatives can help redress the current situation. If need be, the power of the purse can be more resolutely used vis-à-vis an unresponsive executive. But more fundamentally, what we need is government with faith in the American people and in their right to participate in the great decisions. If we do not see this now, after the Bay of Pigs, the Dominican Republic intervention and the whole tragic history of Indochina, then as a nation we do not really understand democracy.

Ogden R. Reid, Republican, is member of Congress for the 26th New York district.

Letters to the Editor

More on the Pentagon Papers

To the Editor:

Tom Wicker's almost savage reply to Dean Acheson's remarks on The Times' publication of the Pentagon papers suggests that Mr. Acheson has struck a nerve when he wonders why the papers weren't returned to their owner as stolen goods.

While this is really a nasty bag to open, I was struck while reading Mr. Wicker's article by the similarities between the action taken by The Times and that taken by the student rioters: Both had grievances and both chose to settle them beyond the law claiming justification in the theory of individual ethics. It would appear that we are in for a lot of chaos if the country's leading newspaper begins to advocate such procedures.

One of the tests to which any action is commonly put is to examine the effect it has had and to see who has gained by it. In the case of publishing the Pentagon papers, while it is clearly premature, it appears that the principal beneficiary is The Times itself. If we are to accept the Machiavellian view of government suggested by The Times in its recent series, it becomes doubly confusing since these papers must then have been released surreptitiously by the Government, which The Times is then aiding while making an issue of its opposition.

Whether The Times is being altruistic or not, it is difficult to see how the people benefit. While the real problems remain unsolved and in many cases untouched, The Times shows us that, contrary to popular thought, the judicial system is not dead and can, in fact, spring to life and respond to the call of The Times in a matter of days. In the meantime the poor rot in jail waiting for years to be heard.

In closing, Mr. Wicker gives us Samuel Johnson in defense of stealing. This has the distinct odor of Kenneth Galbraith, who suggests quoting Churchill when cornered since Churchill has at one time or another advocated every possible point of view.

W. R. SPILLERS
Professor of Civil Engineering
Columbia University
New York, July 10, 1971

•

To the Editor:

We regard the news media's handling of the Pentagon papers as weak, inconclusive and confusing to the public. Granted, the media have shown courage and solidarity in defending the freedom of the press in America. However, apart from the admirable efforts of The Times, they have displayed, on the whole, little initiative or incisiveness in clarifying for the public the significance of the information contained in the report.

For example, we have found very little discussion so far of the most important and most scandalous disclosure in the archives: namely, that the United States planned and executed an aggressive war against North Vietnam in 1964-65. An informed and truly courageous press would have quickly recognized that such an aggressive war violates the Nuremberg principles and the U.N. Charter and constitutes a crime against peace.

Furthermore, alert journalism would have called attention to the inescapable conclusion that the disclosures of the report eliminate any pretense of a legal basis for our continued presence in Indochina.

The television networks have been particularly negligent and shallow in their discussion of the report. With instinctive reverence for authority, they have sought out Gen. Maxwell Taylor, Walt Rostow and Dean Rusk, and have afforded these suspect individuals an opportunity to compound their original deceptions and prevarications of 1964-65 with new deceptions and prevarications.

We do not criticize the procedure of the networks in offering these men —whose conduct and reputations have been (or ought to have been) severely damaged by the Pentagon papers— a chance to defend themselves. However, we question whether sheer declarations by discredited officials, without commentary, without comparison with the Pentagon report, and without an opposing viewpoint, can be responsible journalism.

Statements by men of authority and power presented without comment have the effect of network endorsement, and confuse the public about the veracity of the Pentagon papers themselves.

At the same time, the media as a whole and the TV networks in particular have made little effort to consult the other side: the numerous scholars who have long maintained that the war was and is aggressive, illegal and criminal.

The systematic exclusion of a whole range of antiwar scholars from the national networks at this timely juncture suggests that the networks are either surprisingly ignorant, or in unconscious complicity with the Government in its continuing effort to keep the ugly truth about the criminality of the war from the American public.

We call upon all media to educate the public now with a searching and thorough inquiry into the unlawful origins and the ongoing illegitimacy of the war.

MARK SACHAROFF, RICHARD FALK
RICHARD BARNET, SEYMOUR MELMAN
PETER WEISS, EDWARD S. HERMAN
Philadelphia, July 9, 1971

Letters to the Editor

Press Freedom and Responsibility

To the Editor:

Neither the decision of the Supreme Court in the cases of the purloined Pentagon papers nor that of the House of Representatives in the case of the C.B.S. documentary has resolved the fundamental conflict between press freedom, on which the preservation of our democracy rests, and national security, on which the preservation of our nation rests.

It is undeniable that the right of classification has been severely abused and that more realistic procedures must be devised. But neither the Court nor the Congress has denied either that criminal penalties may be assessed against those who improperly use classified documents or that there may be situations in which press freedom is not absolute but must yield to the requirements of national security. In the great debate which will continue, the press must realize that its freedom can be destroyed by its own irresponsibility.

It must therefore give pause to the publication of classified documents improperly obtained when the national security is involved; eschew the publication of the exact text of coded messages without paraphrasing — to avoid endangering the security of every coded message sent up to and perhaps even after the date of first publication—and refrain from analyses that improperly treat position papers and contingency plans as Presidential decisions.

Unless these principles are followed, the press will destroy its own credibility and perhaps even its freedom for it is extremely doubtful that a majority of an enlightened citizenry will long permit any and all journalists to be absolute arbiters of our security.

Nor can the press continue to demand a double standard for itself. It cannot successfully maintain on the one hand that it is free to publish any Government document regardless of its sensitivity to national security and on the other that it can with impunity falsify documents and interviews even to the point of presenting answers to one question as though they had been directed to a totally different question.

The public has as much right to know about press machinations as it does about Government machinations, and journalism carries heavy responsibilities, not the least of which is not to destroy freedom of the press by abusing that freedom.

BENJAMIN H. OEHLERT JR.
Palm Beach, Fla., July 16, 1971

Suggested Reading

Books, Articles and Pamphlets on the Relationship Between the Mass Media and Politics

Agee, Warren K. (ed). *Mass Media in a Free Society*. University of Kansas Press, 1969.

Aronson, James. *The Press and the Cold War*. Bobbs-Merrill, 1970.

Berdes, George R. *Friendly Adversaries: The Press and Government*. Marquette University, 1969.

"Big Push for Campaign Ceilings." *Broadcasting*, Vol. 80, No. 14, April 5, 1971, pp. 58-60.

"Blanket Political Spending Limits Asked." *Broadcasting*, Vol. 80, No. 4, January 25, 1971, pp. 43-44.

Blumler, Jay G. and McQuail, Denis. *Television in Politics: Its Uses and Influences*. University of Chicago Press, 1969.

"Campaign Management: Expertise Brings Dollars: Who the Media Producers and Political Consultants Are." *Congressional Quarterly Weekly Report*, Vol. 27, No. 18, May 1, 1970, pp. 1183-1191.

Cater, Douglass. *The Fourth Branch of Government*. Vintage, 1965.

Chafee, Zechariah Jr. *Government and Mass Communications*. Archon Books, 1965.

Chester, Edward W. *Radio, Television and American Politics*. Sheed & Ward, 1970.

Cohen, Bernard C. *The Press and Foreign Policy*. Princeton University Press, 1963.

Cranberg, Gilbert. "Is 'Right of Access' Coming?" *Saturday Review*, Vol. 53, No. 32, August 8, 1970, pp. 48-49+.

"Crunch Coming on Campaign Reforms." *Broadcasting*, Vol. 80, No. 10, March 8, 1971, pp. 22-27.

Dunn, Delmer D. *Public Officials and the Press*. Addison-Wesley, 1969.

Gimlin, Hoyt. "First Amendment and Mass Media." *Editorial Research Reports*, Vol. 1, No. 3, January 21, 1970, pp. 43-60.

Goldstein, Abraham S. "Newsmen and Their Confidential Sources." *New Republic*, Vol. 162, No. 12, March 21, 1970, pp. 13-15.

Goodman, Julian. "TV: Formulas Won't Bring Fairness." *Wall Street Journal*, Vol. 176, No. 24, August 3, 1970, p. 8.

"Government vs. the Press: Pentagon Study of the War in Vietnam." *Newsweek*, Vol. 68, No. 1, July 5, 1971, pp. 17-19.

Kimball, Penn T. "Congressional Candidates and the Broadcast Media in the 1968 Campaign." Grosset & Dunlap, 1966, pp. 83-95. (Chapter in Barrett, Marvin [ed]. *The Alfred I. DuPont-Columbia University Survey of Broadcast Journalism, 1968-1969*).

Lang, Kurt and Gladys E. *Voting and Nonvoting: Implications of Broadcasting Returns Before Polls Are Closed*. Ginn and Co., 1968.

Lazarsfeld, Paul, *et al. People's Choice: How the Voter Makes Up His Mind in a Presidential Campaign*. Columbia University Press, 1948.

McGinniss, Joe. *The Selling of the President, 1968*. Trident Press, 1969.

Mendelsohn, H. A. and Crespi, I. *Polls, Television, and the New Politics*. Chandler Publishing Co., 1970.

"Opening TV to the Political Outs." *Broadcasting*, Vol. 78, No. 26, June 29, 1970, pp. 32-34.

"Sedulus." "Frank Merriwell's Way: Equal Time for Political Parties and Political Minorities." *New Republic*, Vol. 162, No. 25, June 20, 1970, pp. 30-32.

Seifert, William. "Local Broadcast Coverage of the 1968 Political Campaign." Grosset & Dunlap, 1969, pp. 96-104. (Chapter in Barrett, Marvin [ed]. *The Alfred I. DuPont-Columbia University Survey of Broadcast Journalism, 1968-1969*.)

Smith, Hendrick. "When the President Meets the Press." *Atlantic*, Vol. 226, No. 2, August, 1970, pp. 65-67.

Thomson, Charles A. H. *Television and Presidential Politics*. Brookings Institution, 1956.

Thorp, Bruce E. "Fairness Doctrine Raises Hopes—and Questions—About Access to Air Time." *National Journal*, Vol. 2, No. 45, November 7, 1970, pp. 2463-2469.

Tobin, R. L. "When Newspapers Do Their Thing." *Saturday Review*, Vol. 54, No. 28, July 10, 1971, pp. 37-8.

Watkins, Arthur V. *Enough Rope*. (Original title: *Censure of Senator McCarthy*.) Prentice-Hall, 1969.

Whale, John. *The Half-Shut Eye: Television and Politics in Britain and America*. St. Martin's Press, 1969.

Wyckoff, Gene. *Image Candidates: American Politics in the Age of Television*. Macmillan, 1968.

—Compiled by Madeline Greenleaf

Index

Note: In cases where closely related stories from a single issue of *The New York Times* are reprinted, the date reference appears only below the last story. However, the index references are to the page number of the first story.

Abrams, Creighton W., 555
Abrams, Floyd, 563
Abt, Samuel, 563
Acheson, Dean, 16, 308, 366, 606, 607, 609
Adams, Brock, 534
Adams, John Quincy, 36
Adams, Morgan, Jr., 370
Adams, Paul L., 172
Adams, Sherman, 145, 166, 366, 381
Adonis, Joe, 8
Advertisers, control of the media by, 76, 353
Advertising, political:
    Agencies' relations with candidates, 44, 46, 146, 158, 159, 161, 163, 164, 172
    Cost of TV-radio campaigns, 4, 18, 25, 46, 59, 161, 163, 164, 171, 186, 194, 204, 205, 206, 207, 208, 209, 213, 214, 216, 217, 223, 225, 226, 230, 249, 277, 280, 284, 392, 457
        Proposals for reduction of rates, 225, 226, 227, 228, 229, 230, 245
        Spending limitations proposed, 194, 285
    General, 44, 46, 102, 111, 141, 147, 161, 163, 164, 171, 172, 217, 223, 327
    Newspaper, 162, 163
        Rates, 454
    Spending limits, 227, 228, 229, 231, 232, 233, 234, 235, 236, 237, 238, 240, 241, 242, 243, 245
    TV, effectiveness, 194
    TV-radio spots, 141, 147, 163, 164, 171, 172, 194, 204, 217, 223, 226, 227, 233, 234, 236, 251, 283, 284, 457
    TV ratings, 164
AFL-CIO, 235
Agar, Herbert, 63
Agnew, Spiro T., 186, 283
    Criticisms of newspapers, 104, 105, 500, 526
        Effect on Washington press corps, 192, 199
        Seen as part of administration strategy, 193
    Criticisms of TV news policies, 52, 53, 104, 105, 188, 189, 190, 490-526
        N. Johnson comment, 196

    Letter to the editor, 200
    Maryland gubernatorial election (1966), 88
    Pentagon Papers, 569
    Presidential election (1968), 51
        Campaign debates on television, proposed, 466, 467, 469, 475
        Campaign expenditures, 227
        Dispute with *The New York Times,* 486-490
    "Selling of the Pentagon", 527, 528, 529, 530
    Standing in opinion polls, 523
Agnew, Mrs. Spiro T., 520
Agronsky, Martin, 22, 496
Ahlgren, Frank R., 343
Aiken, George D., 238
Albert, Carl, 466, 470, 471
Alexander, Archibald S., 254
Alexander, Herbert E., 218, 222, 223, 244
Allen, Herbert A., 244
Allen, James B., 238
Allen, Robert E., 102
Allen, Steve, 90
Alsop, Joseph, 80, 138, 164
Alsop, Stewart, 80, 138, 170, 338
Altschul, Frank, 586
America, 75
American Broadcasting Company, 75, 80, 170, 182, 190, 224, 251, 332, 354, 358
    Civil Disorders, National Advisory Commission on, 94
    Convention coverage
        1952, 251
        1968, 89, 92, 95
        Cost to network, 207
    Convention facilities (1960), 74
    Election returns:
        Pool coverage of, 79, 84
        Vote projection, 72, 83, 88, 94, 172
    Equal time, 255, 261, 263, 265, 266, 273, 276, 283, 327, 355, 430
    Merger with ITT, proposed, 344
    Political advertising, 226, 227, 230, 243

"The Political Obituary of Richard M. Nixon", 76
TV debates:
    1968 California primary, 444, 446-451, 453
    1960 Presidential election, 396, 397, 406, 415, 417
    1968 Presidential election, 458, 460, 467
  White House TV studio, 81, 191
"American Forum of the Air", 63
American Independent Party, 182, 461
American Telephone and Telegraph Company, 344
Ampex Corporation, 73
Anderson, Clinton P., 390
Anderson, Dale, 488
Anderson, John B., 240
Anderson, Paul, 320
Andrews, Bert, 320
Annenberg, Walter H., 190
Archibald, Samuel J., 348
Arkin, Stanley S., 484
Armstrong, J. Sinclair, 316
Arrowsmith, Martin, 149
Assassinations, media coverage of, 51, 94, 103
Associated Press, 78, 79, 84, 166, 169, 266, 294, 327
Associated Press Association, N. Y., 75
Associated Press Broadcast Association, 358
Associated Press Managing Editors' Association, 16, 306, 313, 314, 319, 358, 524
Attlee, Clement, 29
Aubrey, James T., 341
Auerbach, Carl S., 81
Austin, Warren, 8
Authors League of America, 358
Automobile Workers, United, 235, 483
Autrey, Gene, 244
Avant-Garde, 479, 484, 485
Avnet, Lester, 244
Ayers, Eben, 301
Ayers, Harry M., 316
Aylesworth, Merlin H., 204

Babbridge, Homer D., Jr., 358
Bacall, Lauren, 130
Bahmer, Robert H., 348
Bailey, Deardourff and Bown, 194
Bailey, John M., 442
Baillie, Hugh, 133
Baker, Basil Lee, 536
Baker, James, 206
Baker, Richard T., 103, 187
Baker, Robert G., 347
Baker, William W., 176
Baldwin, Hanson W., 65
Ball, George W., 25, 174, 544, 571
Baltimore Sun, 518, 553, 555
Bancroft, Harding F., 354, 486, 563
Banghart, Kenneth, 72
Bankhead, William B., 292
Bar Association, American, 347, 348
Bar Association, Philadelphia, 341
Barceloneta Shoe Corp., 349
Barkely, Alben W., 23

Barnes, Clive, 510
Barnet, Richard, 609
Barnum, Jerome D., 290
Barrett, Edward W., 103, 311, 319
Barron, James, 517
Barron, Jerome A., 105
Bartlett, Charles Leffingwell, 338
Bartley, Robert T., 261, 273, 316, 344, 355
Barton, Walter E., 483
Baruch, Steven H., 91
Bassett, James, 379, 380, 381
Bates, Ted, Co., 147
Batten, Barton, Durstine and Osborn, 44
Bay of Pigs, 39, 75, 76, 85, 338
Bayh, Birch, 104, 188
Bazelon, David L., 590
Beale, William L., 72
Beame, Abraham D., 432
Beatty, Frank, 294
Beckman, Alfred R., 430
Beebe, Frederick S., 573
"Behind the News", 263
Belafonte, Harry, 352
Bell, David E., 538
Bell, Howard H., 76
Belli, Melvin, 483
Bender, George, 383
Ben-Gurion, David, 363
Bennett, James Gordon, 64
Bennett, John B., 270
Bennett, Rawson, 142
Benny, Jack, 255
Benosky, Alan L., 510
Benson, Ezra Taft, 397, 426
Benton, William, 11, 126, 184, 209, 309
Benton and Bowles, 46
Berdinger, Nathan, 517
Berger, Marilyn, 573
Bernbach, William, 46
Berns, William A., 137
Bernstein, Robert L., 358
Berrigan, Daniel J., 358
Berrigan, Phillip F., 358
Beveridge, Albert J., 191
Beyelin, Philip L., 573
Bickel, Alexander M., 358, 459, 563, 591, 592, 595
Biddle, George, 225
Birch Society, John, 440, 481
Birmingham News, 101
Bishop, Jim, 343
Blachman, Harry A., 517
Black, Hugo L., 344, 485, 592, 595
Black Politics (underground newspaper), 528
Blackmun, Harry A., 592, 595
Blake, Walter, 322
Blanton, Ray, 533
Blaustein, Jacob, 244
Bliss, Ray C., 172
Bloom, Marshall I., 143, 145
Blough, Roger, 168

Bluedorn, Victor E., 318
Blum, John Morton, 459
Bogart, Humphrey, 130
Boggs, Hale, 208, 213, 214
Bolling, Richard, 470
Bolton, Oliver P., 79
Boroson, Warren, 479, 480, 483, 484, 485
Boston Globe, 192, 552, 553, 590
Boyle, William, 379, 390
Bradlee, Benjamin C., 573
Brandt, Irving, 63
Brandt, Raymond P., 337
Branzburg, Paul M., 358
Bray, Charles W., 3d, 561
Brecht, Bertolt, 547
Brelis, Dean, 544
Brennan, William J., Jr., 592, 595
Brenner, Millard M., 586
Bricker, John W., 297, 307, 313, 314, 385
Brigham, William H., 265
Brinkley, David, 53, 71, 72, 100, 274, 334, 507, 509, 511, 541
Broadcast Institute, International, 178
Broadcast journalism, survey of, 103, 187
Broadcast Laboratory, Public, 91
Broadcast technique (makeup, orientation of candidates, etc.), 3, 6, 17, 18, 20, 24, 25, 74, 91, 108, 136, 137, 141, 234, 405
Broadcasters, National Association of, 8, 76, 79, 179, 180, 254, 255, 259, 260, 269, 273, 286, 290, 291, 299, 316, 326, 332, 352, 495, 498, 529, 530
Broadcasting, 79
Broadcasting, freedom of, 71, 105, 188, 283
Broadcasting, National Citizens Committee for, 178, 495, 529
Broadcasting Union, International, 4
Broderick, Raymond, 194
Broger, John C., 353
Brookings Institution, 253, 268, 341
Brown, Clarence J., 208, 213, 534
Brown, Edmund G. (Pat), 72, 81, 153, 272
Brown, John Paulding, 208
Brown, Willie L., 532
Browne, Malcolm W., 544, 546
Browne, Millard, 348
Brownell, Herbert, Jr., 191
Browning, James, 354
Broyhill, James T., 534
Brucker, Herbert, 325
Brucker, Wilber A., 318
Bryan, John Stewart, 290
Bryan, William Jennings, 3, 11, 36
Bryant, Farris, 81
Bucci, E. John, 216
Buchanan, Patrick J., 189
Buckley, James L., 475, 524
Buckley, William F., 506
Bulganin, Nikolai, 139, 143
Bullitt, Stimson, 551
Bundy, McGeorge, 59, 178, 193, 569
Bundy, William P., 46, 223

Burch, Dean
    Chairman, F.C.C., 103, 187, 189, 196, 285, 287, 351, 352, 355, 356, 357, 496, 498, 499, 501
    Chairman, Republican National Committee, 163, 441, 442
    Member, Twentieth Century Fund's commission on campaign costs, 186
Burdick, Quentin N., 194
Burger, Warren E., 532, 592, 595, 606, 607
Burnett, Carol, 519
Burnett, Leo, Company, 44, 158, 159, 161, 163
Burns, John A., 81
Burns, John J., 217, 432
Burr, Aaron, 191
Bush, Earl, 95
Bush, George, 194
Business Executives Move for Peace in Vietnam, 283
Business Week, 348
Butler, Paul M., 71, 72, 252, 327
Butterfield, Fox, 563
Butterfield, L. H., 512
Butts, Wallace, 481, 485
Byrnes, James F., 376

Cahill, Gordon, Sonnett, Reindel and Ohl, 563
Cahn, Edgar S., 348
Cahn, Jean Camper, 348
Caldwell, Earl, 95, 354, 358, 529
Califano, Joseph A., Jr., 173, 218, 280, 282, 283
Calkins, Robert D., 341
Callaway, Howard, 454
Cameron, Bruce, 257
Campaign debates, *see* Elections: TV-radio coverage
Campbell, John, 444
Cannon, Howard W., 521
Capehart, Homer, 505
Capote, Truman, 547
Carlino, Joseph F., 441
Carlino, Philip, 521
Carlson, Frank, 366, 374, 536
Carnegie Endowment for International Peace, 178
Carney, Robert F., 510
Carpenter, Elizabeth, 51
Carpenter, Frank E., 131
Carrington, Elsworth T., 244
Carrol, Lewis, 389
Carroll, John S., 553, 554, 555
Carroll, Wallace, 553, 555
Carswell, G. Harrold, 521
Carter, Don E., 524
Cartoonists, American Association of, 166
Case, Clifford, 236, 545
Castle, Latham, 277
Castro, Fidel, 39, 415, 417, 426, 428
Cater, S. Douglass, 173, 415
Catledge, Turner, 72, 75, 85, 267, 306, 311
Celler, Emmanuel, 255, 319, 327, 335
Censorship by media, 59, 64, 327, 330, 336, 340, 344, 519
Cerf, Bennett, 334

Chafee, Zechariah H., 301
Chambers, Lenoir, 316
Chancellor, John, 95, 417
Chandler, A. B. (Happy), 465
Chandler, Otis, 96
Chapman, Oscar L., 16
Chavez, Dennis, 140
Checkers affair (1952), 25, 133, 365-392, 433
Cherne, Leo, 178
Chiang Kai-shek, 417
Chicago Daily News, 358
Chicago Journalism Review, 99
Chicago Sun-Times, 358, 590
Childs, Marquis, 80
Chiles, Lawton, 194
China, 37, 406, 415, 417, 428
Chotiner, Murray M., 198, 369, 379, 381
Christian, George B., 31, 173, 186, 192, 343, 498, 552
Christian Science Monitor, 518
Church, Frank, 327
Churchill, Winston, 199
Citizen's Advocate Center, 348
Citizens Research Foundation (Princeton), 218, 241, 244
Civic Education by Radio, Committee on, 3
Civil disturbances, media coverage, 51, 93, 94, 95, 100, 101, 103, 104, 177, 344
Civil Liberties Committee, Emergency, 563
Civil Liberties Union, American, 177, 252, 254, 266, 319, 496, 529, 563
Clark, Blair, 276, 457, 459, 460, 461
Clark, Joseph S., 221
Clark, Ramsey, 345
Clark, Robert, 446, 451
Clark, Roger A., 573
Clawson, Del, 467
Clayton, Charles C., 316
Clements, S. E., 142
Clifford, Clark M., 183, 349, 556, 568
Clynes, Manfred, 244
Cochran, Ron, 274
Cohen, Arthur G., 244
Cohn, Harold, 485
Cohn, Roy, 28
"College News Conference", 264
Collins, Leroy, 79, 332
Colson, Charles W., 198
Columbia Broadcasting System, 7, 17, 19, 80, 91, 274, 332, 354, 358
    Awards, 526, 532
    Civil Disorders, National Advisory Commission on, 94
    Convention coverage:
        1952, 22, 68, 251
        1956, 71, 88, 141
        1968, 89, 92, 95, 101
        Cost to network, 207
    Convention facilities (1952), 18
    Election coverage:
        1966, 88
        1968, 51

Election returns:
    Pool coverage of, 78, 79, 84
    Vote projection, 72, 81, 83, 88, 94, 172
Equal time, 246, 253, 255, 257, 258, 259, 261, 262, 263, 265, 266, 271, 272, 273, 274, 276, 277, 278, 280, 283, 327, 355, 357
Judicial proceedings, coverage of, 341
News policies, 162, 193
Political advertising, 205, 226, 227, 230, 243, 251, 327
Roosevelt inauguration (1936), 5
"Selling of the Pentagon", 286, 358, 525, 526, 527-535, 610
TV debates:
    1956, 252
    1960 Presidential election, 396, 397, 406, 415, 417
    1968 California primary, 444, 446
    1968 Presidential election, 475, 476
White House TV studio, 81, 191
Columbia University:
    Columbia College, 224
    DuPont-Columbia University Survey of Broadcast Journalism, 103, 187
    Graduate School of Journalism, 177
Commager, Henry Steele, 225
Common Cause, 235, 237, 240, 245
Commonwealth Club of California, 275
Congress, National Committee for an Effective, 59, 225-228, 231, 232, 233, 235, 241, 285
Conlisk, James B., 95
Connally, John B., 173
Conniff, Frank, 160
Conrad, Frank, 2
Conroy, Jack, 172
Conservative Party, N. Y., 553
Constitution Party, 266
Consumers Union, 348
Convention coverage, radio:
    1936 Democratic convention, 112, 204
    1936 Republican convention, 111, 112, 204, 246
Convention coverage, TV-radio, 19, 20, 22, 23, 65, 67, 70, 71, 72, 92, 103, 112, 113, 169, 433
    1952 Democratic convention, 433
    1952 Republican convention, 68, 251
    1956 Democratic convention, 71, 141
    1956 Republican convention, 72, 215
    1960 Democratic convention, 99, 264
    1960 Republican convention, 264
    1964 Republican convention, 506
    1968 American Independent Party, 182
    1968 Democratic convention, 51, 89, 92, 95, 96, 99, 101, 354, 463, 505, 514
    1968 Republican convention, 89, 92, 99, 506
    Commercial sponsorship of, 2, 67, 70, 169, 207
    Cost to broadcasters, 207, 230
Convention programs, tax-deductible advertising, 224, 225
Cony, Edward R., 178
Cook, Fred J., 188
Cook, Marlow W., 104

Cooke, Alistair, 496
Coolidge, Calvin, 5, 29, 31, 36, 40, 45
Coolidge, Charles A., 142, 318
Cooper, Kent, 306
Corbett, Peter, 483
Corcoran, Thomas G., 186
Cordiner, Ralph J., 442
Cormier, Frank, 170
Corn, Herbert F., 313, 314
Cornish, George, 316
Correa, Alfred, 74
Costello, Frank, 8, 20
Costello, Matthew, 510
Cott, Ted, 331
Cotton, Norris, 272, 440
Coughlin, Charles E., 4, 108, 246
Counts, George S., 370
Court proceedings, media coverage of, 101, 279, 341, 342, 347
Cowles, John, 330
Cowles Publications, 166
Cox, Edward E., 250
Cox, Francis A., 563
Cox, James M., 31
Cox, Kenneth A., 273, 344, 355
Coy, Wayne, 250, 299, 300, 304
Craig, May, 40
Cramer, William C., 194, 268
Cranston, Alan, 78
Craven, T.A.M., 261, 291
Crews, John R., 387
Cromley, Allan, 476
Cronkite, Walter, 53, 194, 357, 417, 496, 507, 509
    CBS convention coverage
        1952, 22, 68
        1956, 71, 88
        1968, 95
    CBS election coverage (1966), 88
    CBS Evening News, 91, 274
Crosby, John, 433
Cross, Harold, 325
Cross, John S., 261
Cuban missile crisis, 336, 337, 338, 339, 573
Cudworth, Gene, 586
Cunningham, Glenn, 258
Curran, Thomas J., 387
Cushing, Ned, 267
Cutler, Robert, 145

Dabney, Virginius, 325, 553
Daily Newspapers Association, Texas, 105
Daley, John P., 142
Daley, Richard J., 95, 101, 257, 259, 260, 261, 262, 264, 265, 451, 463
Daly, James J., 573
Daly, John, 22, 71, 72, 255, 260, 261
Daly, Lar, 257, 258, 259, 260, 261, 262, 263, 264, 265
Daniel, Clifton, 85, 364, 513, 531, 563
Daniel, Price, 454

Danzig, Jerry, 161
Davies, John Paton, 28
Davis, Clifford, 268
Davis, Elmer, 23
Davis, Evelyn Y., 532
Davis, H. P., 2
Davis, Howard, 290
Davis, J. P., 586
Davis, Peter, 532
Davis, Rennie, 95
Davis, Richard Harding, 144
Dawson, William L., 350
Dear, Joseph A., 81
DeBerry, Clifton, 81
Dedmon, Emmett, 99, 192
Deerlin, Lionel Van, 269
Democratic Action, Americans for, 440, 522
Democratic Digest, 147
Democratic Institutions, Center for the Study of, 431
Democratic National Committee, 243, 254, 280, 282, 283, 347, 355, 357
    1936 radio plans, 205
    1952 campaign expenditures, 208, 214
Democratic Society, Students for a, 354
Dempsy, John P., 81
Dennis, Bruce, 276
Dennison, Robert L., 300
Denny, Charles M., 298
Dent, H. K., 297
Dent, Harry S., 198
Des Moines Register, 496
DeSapio, Carmine, 257
Desautels, Claude, 152
Devoto, Bernard, 64
Dewey, Ballantine, Bushby, Palmer and Wood, 486
Dewey, Thomas E., 11, 82, 147, 234, 297, 378, 393, 433
Dickerson, John J., 387
Dilliard, Irving, 316
Dillon, C. Douglas, 338, 363
Dirkson, Everett McKinley, 163, 224, 281, 439, 440, 470, 471, 505
Dobbs, Farrell, 253
Dodd, Thomas J., 238, 346, 505, 537
Doerfer, John C., 259, 260, 261
Dole, Robert J., 188, 355, 525
Dominick, Peter H., 238
Donaldson, Sam, 182
Donham, Parker, 461
Donovan, Hedley, 96, 354
Dorfman, Ronald, 99
Dorn, William, 269
Dorsen, Norman, 563
Doty, Paul, 459
Douglas, Helen Gahagan, 381
Douglas, James H., 322
Douglas, John W., 354
Douglas, Paul H., 222, 366
Douglas, Stephen A., 37, 393
Douglas, William O., 485, 592, 595

Dow Jones Publishing Co., 358
Dowling, Robert W., 244
Downey, Sheridan, 250, 381
Doyle Dane Bernbach, Inc., 46, 158, 159, 161, 163, 164
Drewry, John E., 334
Dreyer, Thorne, 96
Dreyfus, Jack, Jr., 244
Drummond, Roscoe, 80, 415
Dryfoos, Orvil, 85
Du Boff, Richard B., 586
Dudley, Guilford, Jr., 244
Duffey, Joseph D., 194
Dulles, Allen, 542
Dulles, John Foster, 28, 31, 50, 70, 135, 139, 143, 145, 415
Dunbar, Ernest, 354
Dunlap, John B., 391
DuPont-Columbia U. Survey of Broadcast Journalism, 103, 187
Duram, Arthur E., 102
Dutton, Frederick G., 330
Dwight, William, 319
Dwyer, A. H., 461
Dwyer, Florence P., 350

Eagleton, Thomas F., 178
Eames, William, 79
Early, Edward, 586
Early, Robert, 267
Early, Stephen P., 31, 48, 116, 294
Eastern Educational Network, 91, 93, 278
Eastland, James O., 188, 238, 316, 317
Eberle, Julian J., 573
Editor and Publisher, 100
Editorial Association, National, 142, 313
Editorial endorsements, 100, 116, 131, 270
    Effectiveness of, 153
Editorials, *New York Times, see New York Times, editorials*
Editorials by broadcasters, 31, 38, 235, 253, 258, 259, 260, 269, 270, 271, 277, 293, 303, 333, 334, 341, 343, 345, 551
Edson, Peter, 365
Educational Network, Eastern, 91, 93, 278
Educational TV Network, National, 93, 168, 519
Edwards, India, 141
Edwards, John, 417
Ehrlich, Aaron, 46
Ehrlichman, John D., 201
Eisenhower, Dwight David, 28, 48, 76, 77, 224, 256, 257, 260, 261, 264, 265, 268, 363, 431
    Government information policies, 142, 146, 318, 319, 320, 325, 327
    Presidential election, 1952, 17, 20, 25, 36, 69, 130, 147, 159
        Republican convention, 251
    Presidential election, 1956, 141, 147, 253
        Media coverage of health issue, 138, 140, 143, 144, 191, 338, 363
    Presidential election, 1960, 147

Presidential election, 1964, 80, 443
    Press conferences, 22, 27, 28, 29, 31, 40, 45, 59, 75, 133, 134, 135, 137, 143, 144, 145, 149
    Press relations, 40, 133, 134, 159, 199
Eisenhower, Milton S., 51, 147, 366
Elections: costs
    1960, 69
    1962, 223
    1966, 223
    1968, 223, 227, 231, 232, 233, 234, 235, 236, 237, 238, 239, 240, 241, 242
    1970, 237, 244, 245
    See also specific party
Elections: finances
    Disclosure of contributions, 242
    General, 207, 208, 215
    Minority parties, 218, 229
    N.Y. gubernatorial election (1966), 217
    Pennsylvania gubernatorial election (1966), 216
    Proposals for government financing, 218, 221, 222, 223, 228, 240, 242, 243, 245
    Proposals for tax-deductible contributions, 207, 214, 243, 245
Elections: general
    Effect of TV-radio on voter registration, 25, 38
    Proposals for uniform poll closing, 91
Elections: Presidential
    1948, 65
    1952
        Campaign expenditures, 206, 208, 209, 213, 214
        Television coverage, 18, 25, 130, 147
    1956
        TV-radio coverage, 72
    1960
        Campaign expenditures, 216, 223
        TV-radio coverage, 36
    1964
        Campaign expenditures, 223
        Intelligence briefings for Republican candidates, 436
        Proposed Goldwater-Rockefeller debate, 431
        TV coverage, 38
    1968, 51
        Campaign expenditures 244, 454
    Proposals for shortening campaigns, 222, 236, 268
        Campaign expenditures, 227, 229, 230, 231, 232, 233, 235, 236, 238, 244
    See also Elections: TV-radio coverage
Elections: primary
    California (1968), 444-453, 455, 456, 460
    N. H. preferential primary
        1952, 17
        1964, 161
Elections: returns
    Broadcast of, 2, 172
    Pool coverage, 78, 79, 83, 84, 100
    Vote projection, 72, 79, 80, 81, 82, 83, 88, 89, 91, 94, 100, 172, 277
Elections: TV-radio coverage
    1948, 65

1952, 18, 25, 130, 147
1956, 72
1958, 72
1966, 88, 172
Broadcast of returns, 2, 172
Effect on voter registration, 25, 38
Campaign Broadcast Reform Act (1970), 227, 228, 229, 230, 231, 232, 233, 234, 235, 237, 238, 239, 240, 241, 242
Televised campaign debates, 37, 46, 51, 59, 147, 171, 227, 229, 231, 236, 239, 241, 252, 256, 257, 266, 268, 269, 272, 273, 274, 277, 278, 286, 341
  California Democratic Presidential primary (1968), 444, 445, 446-451, 452, 453, 355, 356, 460
Presidential elections:
  1960, 393, 396, 397, 405, 406, 415, 417, 426, 428, 429, 430, 431, 432, 433, 435, 436, 437, 438, 439, 440, 444, 446, 451, 453, 454, 455
  1964 (Proposed), 38, 59, 171, 229, 272, 273, 274, 429, 430, 431, 432, 433, 435, 436, 437, 439, 440, 441, 443, 444
  1968, 229, 278, 285, 444, 445, 453, 454, 455, 456, 457, 458, 459, 460, 461, 462, 463, 464, 465, 466, 467, 468, 469, 470, 471, 472, 473, 474, 475, 476, 477, 478
See also Convention coverage
Ellender, Allen J., 239
Elliott, George Fielding, 292
Elliott, Osborn, 354
Ellsworth, Robert J., 473
Engle, Clair, 264, 340
Enthoven, Alain, 197
Equal newspaper space proposed, 266, 267
Equal time, 171, 188, 191, 327
  Application to TV newscasts, 257, 258, 259, 260, 261, 262, 263, 264, 265, 273, 274, 276
  Discussion of, 17, 38, 204-287, 324, 333, 334, 355
  Minority parties, 182, 227, 239, 252, 253, 254, 256, 257, 262, 263, 264, 265, 266, 278, 285, 433, 435, 436, 439, 440, 461, 472
  Proposals for repeal of, 252, 259, 286
  Requests for, Presidential Election (1968), 460, 461
  Supreme Court reorganization controversy (1937), 248
  Suspension of,
    1960 Presidential election, 393, 396, 397, 429, 431, 433
    1964 Presidential election (proposed), 430, 431, 436, 438, 439, 440, 441, 442
    1968 Presidential election, 444, 453, 456, 460, 461, 462, 463, 464, 467, 468, 469, 470, 471, 472
    Proposals for, 214, 227, 229, 230, 231, 236, 239, 253, 254, 265, 266, 268, 269, 272, 273, 274, 277, 278, 341
Erickson, Frank, 8
Erlick, Everett H., 276
Eros, 484
Ervin, Sam J., Jr., 108, 358
Estes, Billie Sol, 156, 339
Etheridge, Mark, Jr., 176, 513
Evans, M. Stanton, 513
Eyerly, Frank, 319

"Face the Nation", 159, 262, 263, 264, 274, 352, 446, 452, 453, 455, 456, 497
Fact, 479-485
Factor, John (Jake the barber), 244
Fair Campaign Practices Committee, 479
Fairness doctrine, 345, 355, 356, 357, 490
  "Personal attack" provisions, 344, 347
  Proposals for application to newspapers, 355
Falk, Richard, 609
Farbstein, Leonard, 355
Faris, Barry, 70
Farley, James A., 204
Farmer, Don, 531
Feinberg, Wilfred, 591
Feldman, Jacob J., 430
Feliz, David H. H., 303
Fellows, Harold E., 254, 259
Fenton, John H., 553
Feree, Mark, 330
Fernhead, Jock, 255
Field, Marshall, 119
Field Foundation, 348
Finletter, Thomas K., 225
Finley, Robert, 145
Finn, A., 509
Finney, Thomas, 457
Fireside chats, *see* Roosevelt, Franklin D.
Flanders, Ralph Edward, 28
Fleeson, Doris, 138
Fleischmann, Manly, 313
Fleming, Robert H., 49, 170, 174, 397
Fletcher, Henry P., 204, 246, 247
Fly, James Lawrence, 294, 298, 352
Flynn, Joe, 90
Flynn, Edward J., 206
Foisie, Jack, 544
Foley, Louis, 118
Foran, Thomas, 522
Ford, Frederick W., 38, 261, 273, 332
Ford, Gerald R., 505
Foreign Policy Association, 178
Forkosch, Morris, 526
Forrest, Wilbur, 292
Fortas, Abe, 517
Foss, Joe, 255
Frandsen, Julius, 72
Frank, Reuven, 95, 99, 100, 190, 503, 528
Frantz, John C., 358
Free time, proposals for, 214, 224, 226, 230, 245, 249, 252, 254, 266, 274, 275, 276, 277, 327
Freedom House, 178
Freedom of broadcasting, 71, 105, 188, 283
"Freedom of Information", 347, 526
Freedom of the press, *see* Press, freedom of
Freeman, Mrs. Frankie, 46
Freeman, Orville L., 262
Fremd, Charles von, 415
Friedheim, Jerry W., 529, 561, 569
Friedrich, Carl J., 432, 436
Friendly, Edwin S., 66

Friendly, Fred W., 79, 80, 83, 334, 499, 505, 538, 539, 541
Friendly, Henry J., 591
Frier, Betty, 586
Fromson, Murray, 542
Fry, Kenneth D., 19, 121
Fulbright, J. William, 53, 529
    Pentagon Papers, 529, 569, 607
    Proposes "equal access" to TV for Congress, 280, 281, 282, 283
    Reconstruction Finance Corp. investigation, 375
    Vietnam hearings (1966), 538, 541, 545, 546, 549
Fuller and Smith and Ross, 102, 158, 159, 161
Furman, Feiner and Co., 172
Furness, Betty, 72
Fyfe, Hamilton, 6

Gable, Clark, 130
Gabrielson, Guy George, 206, 375, 390
Gage, Robert, 46
Galbraith, John Kenneth, 571, 609
Gallagher, Wes, 79
Gallup Poll, 236, 523, 605
Gannett Newspapers, 75
Gardner, John W., 235, 237, 240, 245
Gardner, Trevor, 318
Garment, Leonard, 473
Garrison, William Lloyd, 7, 504, 512
Gavin, James M., 538
Georgia, University of, School of Journalism, 334
Gesell, Gerhard A., 573, 590, 595
Ghost writing, 526
Gibson, Dunn and Crutcher, 381
Gideonse, Harry D., 178
Giegerich, Carl R., 161
Gilbert, Ben W., 224
Gilbert, Milton, 244
Gilligan, John J., 194
Ginsburg, David, 280
Ginzburg, Ralph, 479-485
Glen, Kristin Booth, 563
Glendon, William R., 592, 606
Glenn, John, 230
Gold, Gerald, 563
Goldberg, Arthur, 49, 168, 171, 185
Goldenson, Leonard H., 96, 226, 282, 396, 503
Goldfine, Bernard, 145
Goldman, Ralph, 131
Goldwater, Barry M., 351, 496, 520, 522
    Criticism of press and TV, 153
    Libel suit against *Fact*, 479-485
    Presidential elections
        1956, 140
        1960, 426
        1964, 44, 46, 79, 81, 83, 102, 156, 158, 159, 161, 163, 164
            Campaign debates on TV, 229, 272, 273, 431, 432, 436-438, 439-443, 506
    Press relations, 80, 162, 164, 171

Goldwater, Peggy, 479
Goodale, James C., 486, 563
Goodell, Charles E., 235, 280, 514, 524
Gooding, Gladys, 18
Goodlet, Carlton, 532
Goodman, Julian B., 96, 226, 282, 357, 495, 520, 533
Goodwin, Richard, 459
Goodwin, Robert K., 387
Gordon, Milton, 244
Gordon, Sherwood R., 269
Gore, Albert, 194, 221, 545
Gould, H. E., 244
Gould, Jack, 257
Gould, Leslie, 316
Goulding, Phil G., 177, 343, 553
Governors' Conference, National, 81
Grace, D. L., 255
Graham, James H., 46, 164
Graham, Katherine, 96, 500, 503, 573
Grant Advertising, 159
Gravel, Mike, 240, 243
Gray, Gordon, 145
Gray, Robert A., 208
Greenberg, Bradley S., 100
Greene, Wallace, 545
Griffin, Robert P., 189, 282
Griswold, Erwin N., 592, 595, 606
Groce, Mrs. Walter, 387
Gross, H. R., 185
Gross, Nelson C., 194
Gruson, Sydney, 563
Gubser, Charles S., 145
Guggenheim, Charles, 194
Guggenheim, Harry F., 173
Guild, Bascom and Bonfigli, Inc., 158
Gumbinner-North, Inc., 158
Gurfein, Murray I., 563, 580, 590, 591, 595
Guylay, L. Richard, 216

Haddad, William F., 172
Hagerty, James C., 29, 40, 48, 59, 75, 76, 91, 134, 135, 138, 140, 143, 146, 190, 224, 254, 260, 320, 378, 547
Halberstamm, David, 536
Haley, Sir William, 103
Hall, Durward G., 79, 269
Hall, Leonard W., 72, 141, 215, 216, 391
Halley, Rudolph, 8, 11
Hamburger, Philip, 433
Hamilton, George, 170
Hammarskjold, Dag, 139
Hampson, Eugen F., 176
Hansen, Clifford P., 81, 357
Hanson, Elisha, 114
Hard, William, 204
Harding, Warren G., 31, 36, 40, 45
Hardy, Ralph W., 208
Hargis, Billy James, 188, 440
Harlan, John M., 592, 595
Harness, Forest A., 250, 299, 300

Harr, Karl G., 145
Harriman, W. Averell, 16, 20, 23, 72, 190, 255, 363, 490, 494, 497, 498, 505, 517
Harris, Fred R., 280
Harris, George T., 390
Harris, George W., 3
Harris, Louis, 79
Harris, Oren, 252, 264, 268
Harris, Seymour E., 459
Harrison, Walter M., 315
Hart, Philip A., 194, 224, 228, 229, 233, 234
Hass, Eric, 81, 435, 439
Hastings, Harold K., 362
Hatcher, Andrew T., 152
Hatfield, Mark O., 81, 235
Havoc, June, 512
Hayakawa, S. I., 104
Hayden, Carl, 479
Hayden, Thomas, 95
Haynesworth, Clement F., Jr., 188, 496, 521
Hays, Paul R., 591
Haywood, Alan S., 370
Heald, Don Elliot, 352
Healy, Robert, 192
Heard, Alexander, 186
Hearst, William Randolph, 4
Hearst, William Randolph, Foundation, 160
Hearst, William Randolph, Jr., 160, 330
Heatter, Gabriel, 204
Heaton, Leonard, 138
Hebert, F. Edward, 263, 525, 527, 529
Hefferman, John W., 185
Hefferman, Joseph V., 251
Heller, Walter H., 49
Hemenway, Russell D., 225, 230, 233
Hemphill, Robert W., 269
Henkin, Daniel Z., 528, 529, 532, 533, 535
Hennings, Thomas C., Jr., 214, 325
Hennock, Frieda, 303
Henry, Bill, 22, 68
Henry, E. William, 269, 270, 273, 275, 344
Herding, Andrew H., 146
Herling, John, 348
Herman, Edward S., 609
Hernandez, Aileen, 532
Herrick, Robert C., 176
Hershey, Lewis B., 350
Herter, Christian A., 146, 363
Herzberg, Donald G., 464
Hess, Leon, 244
Hess, Michael D., 563
Hickenlooper, Bourke B., 443
Hicks, George, 23
Hill, Edwin C., 204
Hill, Virginia, 8
Hilliard, David, 354
Hillings, Patrick J., 381
Hillman, William, 362
Hilsman, Roger, 536

Hiss, Alger, 369, 380
Hitler, Adolf, 6
Hobby, Oveta Culp, 28
Hoff, Phillip H., 458
Hoffa, James R., 259, 262, 263
Hoffman, Clare E., 324
Hoffman, Hallock, 431
Hofheinz, Roy, 477
Holloway, Harrison, 247
Holman, Benjamin, 177
Holme, Benjamin F., 486
Hooper, C. E., Inc., 14, 25
Hoover, Herbert, 3, 5, 29, 31, 36, 45, 62, 77
Hoover, J. Edgar, 195, 451
Hope, Peter, 146
Horwitz, Solis, 349
Hoving, Thomas P. F., 175, 495, 529
Howard, Bailey K., 96
Howe, Quincy, 417
Hoyt, Palmer, 330
Hruska, Roman L., 105, 188
Hughes, Charles Evans, 5, 31
Hughes, Richard J., 134
Hull, Cordell, 31
Hume, Paul, 31, 130
Humphrey, George M., 28
Humphrey, Hubert H., 168, 189, 498, 499, 509, 544
    Democratic convention, 1948, 471
    Pentagon Papers, 569
    Presidential elections:
        1960, 262, 263, 393
        1964, 46, 159, 163, 443
        1968, 231, 454
            California primary, 444, 445, 446, 447, 453
            Campaign debates on TV, 460, 462, 463, 464, 465, 466, 467, 468, 469, 470, 471, 472, 473, 474, 475, 476, 477, 478
            Debate with Eugene McCarthy, 455, 456, 457, 459, 460, 461, 463
            Democratic convention, 51, 94, 95
            Newspaper endorsements, 100
Humphreys, Robert H., 147
Hungate, William L., 346
"Hunger in America", (CBS TV), 525
Huntley, Chet, 37, 53, 71, 72, 274, 496, 507, 541
Hurd, Peter, 185
Hurja, Emil, 112
Hyde, Rosel M., 226, 261, 273, 303, 352

Ickes, Harold L., 16, 63
Ignatius, Paul R., 573
Indianapolis Star, 267
Industrial Organizations, Congress of, 299
Industrial Relations Research Association, 175
Ingle, Edward T., 19
Inouye, Daniel K., 228, 233
International News Service, 70
International Press Institute, 518
International Telephone and Telegraph Corp., 344

Interview programs, *see under* Radio; Television
Isaacs, Norman E., 105, 318, 499
"Issues and Answers" (ABC TV), 159, 274, 276, 453, 455

Jackson, Donald, 380
Jackson, Henry M., 216
Jackson, Reginald S., 555
Jackson, William H., 319
Jacobs, Andrew, 496
Jacobsen, Jake, 173
Jahncke, Ernest Lee, Jr., 457
Javits, Jacob K., 44, 183, 217, 322, 475, 477, 514
Jefferson, Thomas, 191, 199, 304, 307, 504
Jencks, Richard W., 280
Jenkins, Walter, 166
Jenner, William E., 366, 375, 388
Jennings, Mabelle, 204
Jewish Committee, American, 177
Johnes, R. Robert L., 160
Johnson, Edwin C., 300
Johnson, Harold K., 552
Johnson, Hillis A., 344
Johnson, Lady Bird, press secretary, 51
Johnson, Louis, 362
Johnson, Lyndon Baines, 538
    Government information policies, 179, 184, 186, 191, 258, 262, 542
    Majority leader, U.S. Senate, 214, 244
    Presidential appointments, 344
    Presidential elections:
        1960, 73, 147, 262, 265, 406
            Debate with JFK, 393, 394, 432
        1964, 159, 432, 433, 435, 436, 437, 438, 439, 440, 441, 442, 443
            Advertising campaign, 161, 162, 163
            Campaign debates on TV, 59, 171, 229, 272, 273, 274
        1968, 46, 83
    Press conferences, 45, 46, 49, 59, 158, 160, 167, 168, 185, 192, 273, 543, 552
    Press relations, 49, 51, 53, 80, 127, 157, 165, 166, 167, 168, 170, 171, 176, 185, 186, 193
    Press secretary, 48, 49, 174
    Proposal for government financing of presidential election campaigns, 218, 221, 223
    Vietnam, 556, 569
Johnson, Nicholas, 189, 196, 226, 283, 344, 352, 355, 357
Johnson, Stuart H., Jr., 335
Johnson, Zeake, 467
Joint Committee Against Toll TV, 352
Jones, Alexander F., 306, 315
Jones, Jesse H., 294
Jones, Robert F., 303
Jordan, Absalom, 283
Jordan, Frank, 79
Jordan, Max, 4

Kaltenborn, H. V., 23, 71, 134, 204, 260
Kampelman, Max M., 511

Kastor, Hilton, Chesley and Clifford, 146
Katcher, Leo, 376
Katz, Elihu, 430
Katzenbach, Nicholas deB., 165
Kaufman, Irving R., 355, 580, 591
KBUZ radio, Phoenix, Ariz., 269
KDKA radio, Pittsburgh, Pa., 2
KECA radio, Los Angeles, Calif., 247
Kefauver, Estes W., 8, 11, 20, 23, 67, 141, 251, 327, 366, 393
Kelly, Walt, 101
Kem, James P., 374
Kennan, George F., 538, 539
Kennecott Copper Corp., 348
Kennedy, Edward M., 95, 101, 105, 194, 278, 458, 494, 496
Kennedy, Jacqueline, 40
Kennedy, John F.:
    Assassination, news coverage of, 94
    Bay of Pigs, 85
    Cuban missile crisis, 336, 337, 338, 339, 573
    Government information policies, 151, 327, 330, 331, 336, 337, 338
    Presidential elections:
        1960, 73, 82, 147, 216, 262, 264, 393, 443
            Campaign debates on TV, 36, 37, 91, 229, 269, 272, 278, 393, 396, 397, 405, 406, 415, 417, 426, 428, 429, 430, 431, 433, 435, 436, 437, 440, 451, 454, 455
            Pre-convention debates, 393, 394
        1964 campaign debates on TV, 38, 430, 432, 444
    Press conferences, 40, 44, 45, 59, 147, 149, 150, 152, 160, 331, 337, 430
    Press relations, 40, 49, 151, 152, 159, 193
    Press secretary, 48
    Religion, 75, 394
    Senate campaign (1952), 209
    Special TV appearances, 268
    Vietnam war, 556
Kennedy, Robert F.:
    Assassination, 51, 94
    TV debate with McCarthy (1968), 444, 445, 446, 447, 451, 452, 453, 455, 456
    U.S. Attorney General, 156, 430
    Vietnam war, 167
Kennedy Family, 40, 348
Kenny, John V., 387
Kenworthy, E. W., 563
Kenyon and Eckhardt, 158, 159
Keogh, Eugene J., 327
Kerner Commission, *see* United States: Civil Disorders, National Advisory Commission on
KFI radio, Los Angeles, Calif., 247
Khrushchev, Nikita S., 73, 139, 146
Kiker, Douglas, 170
Kiley, Roger J., 277
Killian, James R., 178
King, Cy, 181
King, Martin Luther, Jr., 51, 153, 447, 451
King, Mrs. Martin Luther, 519
King, Seth, 513

King, Susan, 245
King, William Henry, 248
Kinney, A. J., 322
Kintner, Robert E., 265, 430
Kirchofer, A. H., 316
Kirkpatrick, Clayton, 513
Kirkpatrick, Evron M., 436
Kirkpatrick, William H., 303
Kissinger, Henry A., 183, 192, 193
"Kitchen debate", 73
Kittay, William R., 508
Klapper, Joseph T., 100
Kleeman, Richard P., 529
Klein, Herbert G.:
    Director of Information, Nixon administration, 182,
        183, 184, 189, 190, 192, 193, 196, 496, 497,
        498, 509, 511, 534
    Press secretary, R. M. Nixon, California gubernatorial
        election (1962), 153
    Press secretary, Vice-President Nixon, 267, 396, 460
Klein, Julius, 529
Klevan, Albert, 510
Klinger, David, 539
KNBC-TV, Los Angeles, Calif., 187
Knight, Goodwin J., 255
Knight, John S., 138, 140, 179
Knight Newspaper Group, 590
Knowland, William F., 28, 137, 140, 214, 392
Knox, Frank, 249
Kober, Leslie, 480
Koenig, Julian, 44
Kohler, Walter J., 391
KOOL TV, Phoenix, Ariz., 162
Kotz, Nick, 496
KQED TV, San Francisco, Calif., 187
Kraft, John, 172
Krajewski, Henry, 263
Krassner, Paul, 96
Krehbiel, John, 391
Krim, Arthur B., 162
Krock, Arthur, 63, 113, 292, 320
KSCO radio, San Diego, Calif., 269
Kuchel, Thomas, 228, 472
Ku Klux Klan, 440, 481
KWTX-AM-TV, Waco, Tex., 265

LaGuardia, Fiorello H., 4, 7, 64
Lahey, Edward, 31
Laird, Melvin R., 525, 527, 528, 529, 561, 568, 569, 590
Landon, Alfred M., 3, 62, 111, 206, 247
Langan, J. P., 387
Langguth, Jack, 546
Langlie, Arthur B., 390
Lasky, Victor, 156
Lasswell, Harold D., 436
Latta, Delbert L., 471
Laurence, William L., 65
Lawrence, David, 334
Lawrence, Robert E., 555, 556
Lawrence, Stan, 405

Lawrence, William H., 150, 172, 446, 451
Leary, Timothy, 96
Lee, H. Rex, 355
Lee, Robert E., 261, 273, 355
Lee, Stanley, 46
Lee, William H., 387
Leeds Advertising, Inc., 172
Leeney, Robert J., 181
Leggieri, Peter, 96
Lehman, Herbert H., 37
Lehman, Orin, 225
LeMay, Curtis E., 467, 469
Lenin, Nikolai, 7, 589
Leonard, William, 79, 89, 539
Lessin, Harry M., 505
Leuhman, Arno H., 322
Leuktemeyer, John A., 488
Leventhal, Harold, 590
Levien, Francis S., 244
Levitt, Arthur, 432
Levy, Harold P., 406
Lewine, Robert S., 532
Lewis, Fulton, Jr., 292, 333, 334
Lewis, Opal, 522
Libel suits, 324, 326, 485
    Barry Goldwater vs. *Fact* magazine, 479-485
    Proposals to exempt political broadcasters, 214, 250,
        299, 300, 316, 535
"Liberty at the Crossroads" (1936), 204
Life, 142, 198, 346, 508
Lightburn, Joseph, 81
Lincoln, Abraham, 37, 199, 393
Lincoln, Gould, 316
Lincoln-Douglas Debates (1858), 37, 393, 455, 474
Lindsay, John Vliet, 168, 170, 179
Lippmann, Walter, 80, 138, 164, 204, 334
Lipscomb, Glen, 365
Livable World, Council for a, 524
Lloyd, David, 362
Lockhart, Jack H., 306
Lodge, Henry Cabot, 105, 130, 147, 166, 209, 251, 405
Loeb, John, 244
Loeb, Louis M., 486
Loeb, William, 267
Loevinger, Lee, 273
Lohr, Lenox R., 204
Lomakin, Jacob M., 301
Lombardi, Louis F., 568
Long, Earl K., 263
Long, Edward V., 342, 345, 346, 350
Long, Huey, 108
Long, Russell B., 171, 218, 221, 222, 222, 281, 415
Look, 96, 222, 354
Los Angeles Times, 78
Lovett, Robert A., 16
Lowenstein, Allard K., 498
Lower, Elmer, 100, 169, 182
Luce, Clare Booth, 297
Luce, Henry R., 142
Lucey, Charles, 316

Luevano, Daniel M., 46
Lumbard, Edward, 591
Lynch, Joseph, 573
Lynch, Thomas C., 451
Lyon, George R., 161

McAndrew, William R., 79, 89, 169, 273, 276, 331
MacArthur, Douglas, 20, 29, 390
McCabe, John, 563
McCall's, 343
McCann, Marshalk, 159
McCarthy, Eugene J.:
    "Humphrey for President Committee" (1960), 262
    Presidential election (1968), 276, 347, 457, 458, 459,
      460, 461, 463
      California primary, 444-453, 455-456
      Campaign costs, 244
      Vietnam war, 543, 556
McCarthy, Joseph R., 22, 133, 252, 362, 366, 374, 375,
    376, 380, 388
McCauslin, Daniel, 96
McClellan, John L., 215, 238
McClendon, Sarah, 144, 185
McClosky, Paul N., Jr., 561, 569
McCone, John A., 165, 338
McConnaughey, George C., 252, 253
McCormack, John W., 467, 470
McCormick, Kenneth D., 358
McCormick, Stephen J., 430, 495
McCrary, Tex, 130
McDermott, Michael, 126
McDevitt, James L., 208
MacDonald, Torbert H., 225, 230, 243, 533, 534
McElroy, Neil H., 325
McFarland, Ernest W., 316
McGannon, Donald H., 270
McGee, Frank, 146, 406, 415
McGee, Gale W., 238, 333
McGhee, George, 177
McGhee, Michael A., 177
McGill, Ralph, 224
McGovern, George S., 243, 460, 461, 463
McGowan, Carl, 590
McGranery, James P., 208
McGrath, Howard, 16
McKean, Thomas, 504
McKelway, Benjamin M., 306, 311, 330
McKeon, William H., 432
McKinley, William, 11, 36
MacKinnon, George E., 590
McLean, Robert, 294, 312
Macmillan, Harold, 146
McNamara, Pat, 140
McNamara, Robert Strange, 46, 168, 177, 201, 338, 340,
    343, 347, 543, 544, 546, 552, 556, 561, 568, 569,
    607
McNaughton, John T., 81, 556
MacNeil, John A., 528
McNinch, Frank R., 250, 291
McPherson, Harry C., 173

Macy, John, 174
Maddox, Lester G., 89, 460, 461, 496
Madison, James, 592
Magnuson, Warren G., 233, 327, 430
Mahaffey, John Q., 316
Mahoney, George P., 88
Mahoney, J. Daniel, 475
Mahoney, Walter J., 331
Malin, Patrick Murphy, 266, 319
Manatos, Mike, 152
Manchester (N.H.) *Union-Leader*, 267
Mann, Thomas, 81
Mannes, Marya, 103
Manning, Gordon, 539
Manning, Robert J., 338, 339, 527
Manoff, Richard K., 172
Manoff, Richard K., Inc., 217
Mansfield, Mike, 144, 208, 235, 241, 443, 470, 505,
    514, 525, 552
Mansfield, Walter R., 591
Manson, Charles, 59, 191
Marder, Murray, 573
Mardian, Robert C., 561
Marien, Michael, 511
Mariln, David H., 485
Maris, Albert B., 303
Marks, Leonard H., 545
Maroney, Kevin T., 573, 590
Marshall, George C., 542
Marshall, Thurgood, 592, 595
Martin, Joseph W., Jr., 381
Mathias, Charles McC., Jr., 241
Mattson, Walter, 563
Maurer, Fleisher, Zon and Associates, 162
Maurer, Robert S., 162
Mazo, Earl, 156, 431
Meade, William F., 303
Meaney, Donald, 89
Meany, George, 49
Media mergers, 335, 344
Medical Association, American, 479
Meerloo, Joost A.M., 44
"Meet the Press", 27, 85, 159, 186, 263, 264, 274, 327,
    441, 442, 453, 456, 457
Mellett, Lowell, 294
Melman, Seymour, 609
Menninger, W. Walter, 100, 104
Merman, Ethel, 72
Metromedia, 464
Metzenbaum, Howard M., 230
Meyer, Agnes, 140
Meyer, Ernest, 518
Meyer, Sylvan H., 181
Meyers, Tedson J., 335
Meyner, Robert B., 392
Mickelson, Sig, 19, 72, 257, 259
Miller, Alan, 244
Miller, B., 536
Miller, Herbert J., 354
Miller, Jack, 238

Miller, James, 147
Miller, Paul, 75
Miller, William E., 46, 163, 432, 441
Mills, J. S., 142
Mills, Wilbur D., 201
Minelli, Daniel, 532
Minow, Newton N., 153, 331, 332, 334, 344, 496
Mitchell, John N.:
    Attorney General, Nixon administration, 59, 105, 189, 191, 486, 488, 499, 516, 517, 518
    Nixon campaign manager (1968), 467, 473
Mitchell, Stephen A., 208, 214, 365, 369, 375
Mohr, Charles, 544, 545
Mollenhoff, Clark R., 76, 496, 499
Monroney, A. S. Mike, 142, 251, 327
Montgomery Ward and Co., 118
Moody, Blair, 309, 415
Moore, Charles F., Jr., 161
Moore, Dorothy, 586
Moos, Malcolm, 431
Moranda, George E., 177
Morgan, Edward P., 91, 541
Morgan, John, 172
Morganthau, Hans, 225
Morganthau, Robert M., 432
Morgen, Edward P., 406
Morgen, Gerald D., 319
Morris, Thomas D., 177
Morse, Howard Newcomb, 257
Morse, Wayne, 166
Mortimer, John, 563
Morton, Rogers C. B., 232, 466
Morton, Thruston B., 80, 223, 473
Moses, Robert, 331
Moss, Frank E., 526
Moss, John E., 76, 142, 264, 270, 271, 316, 317, 318, 319, 320, 322, 323, 324, 325, 337, 338, 339, 342, 343, 350, 351, 536
Mott, Steward R., 225, 244
Moyers, Bill D., 46, 49, 91, 166, 167, 168, 169, 170, 173, 174, 184, 509
Mudd, Roger, 278, 521
Mundt, Karl E., 80, 235, 238, 370, 391
Mungo, Raymond A., 96
Munn, Earl H., 81
Murphy, Adrian, 251
Murphy, Arthur S., 244
Murphy, George, 194, 234
Murphy, Robert T., 297, 363
Murray, J. Edward, 181
Murrow, Edward R., 17, 23, 71, 72, 539, 541
Muskie, Edmund S., 198, 282, 465, 469, 471, 472, 473
Mutual Broadcasting System, 205, 263, 333, 526
    Kennedy-Nixon debate (1960), 397
    Suspension of equal time, 430
Myers, Sidney, 46

Napolitan, Joseph, 194, 216
National Broadcasting Company, 332, 358
    Awards, 187

Civil Disorders, National Advisory Commission on, 94
Convention coverage:
    1952, 251
    1968, 89, 92, 95, 101
    Cost to network, 207
Election returns:
    Pool coverage, 78, 79, 84
    Vote projection, 83, 88
Equal time, 253, 255, 261, 262, 263, 265, 266, 273, 276, 277, 280, 327
Political advertising, 205, 243, 251
TV debates:
    1960, 393, 396, 397, 406, 415, 417
    Sponsors study of, 432, 436
White House TV studio, 81, 191
National Observer, 40
Neibuhr, Reinhold, 459
Nelson, Frederic, 477
Nelson, Gaylord, 426
Network Election Service, 79, 83, 84
    See also News Election Service
Neuberger, Richard L., 136
Neustadt, Richard, 436
Nevard, Jacques, 344
New Hampshire preferential primary:
    1952, 17
    1964, 161
New York Daily News, 192
New York Daily Worker, 317
New York Herald Tribune, 152, 170
New York Post, 331, 370, 371, 376, 380
New York Stock Exchange, 348
New York Times, The, 40, 50, 51, 65, 75, 76, 78, 80, 85, 113, 139, 142, 146, 150, 162, 175, 179, 224, 276, 302, 316, 317, 348, 349, 356, 545, 553
    Dispute with Agnew, 486-490, 496, 500, 514, 517, 518, 524
    Earl Caldwell subpoena case, 95, 354, 358, 529
    Editorials, 4, 7, 24, 39, 62, 67, 69, 82, 89, 131, 184, 205, 208, 221, 225, 226, 227, 228, 232, 236, 240, 242, 260, 271, 299, 307, 322, 336, 346, 351, 371, 438, 442, 453, 456, 458, 459, 460, 461, 468, 471, 507, 529, 534, 567
    Harrison Salisbury, Hanoi reports (1966), 548, 550
    Libel suits against, 485
    Opinion Surveys, 9, 11, 14, 188, 209, 371, 372, 387
    Pentagon Papers, 358, 534, 556-610
New Yorker, 433
News Directors Association, Radio and TV, 254, 277, 316, 495
News Election Service, 151
    See also Network Election Service
Newsday, 173
Newsom, Phil, 343
Newspaper Editors, American Society of, 69, 105, 135, 160, 176, 181, 286, 306, 308, 309, 315, 316, 325, 358, 499
Newspaper Editors, New York Society of, 94, 292, 318, 348
Newspaper Enterprise Association Syndicate, 365
Newspaper Guild, American, 358

Newspaper Publishers Association, American, 66, 76, 85, 114, 290, 317, 327, 330, 337
Newspaper Syndicate, National, 348
Newspapers:
    Accused of biased reporting, 63, 69, 118, 119, 131, 138, 142, 162, 188, 264, 266, 267
    Alleged intimidation of reporters, 156
    Coverage held inadequate, 126, 170, 175, 177
    Criticized for stressing "bad", 178, 179
    Equal space proposed, 266, 267
    Fairness doctrine, 355
    Libel suits, 485
    Self-censorship urged, 327, 330, 337, 340, 344
    Underground press, 96, 528
    Washington Press corps, 170
    See also Agnew, Spiro T.; *specific newspaper, publisher*
Newspapers Association, Arizona, 179
Newsweek, 354, 358, 508, 555
Newton, Carroll P., 44
Newton, V. M., Jr., 318, 319
Ngo Dinh Diem, 364, 536, 537, 556
Ngo Dinh Nhu, 537
Ngo Dinh Nhu, Mme., 537
Niven, Paul, 168, 406, 444
Nixon, Richard M., 232, 283, 363
    Agnew-TV network news dispute, 496, 497, 499, 508, 509, 510, 516, 517
    Appointments, 351
    California gubernatorial election, 1962, 40
    Checkers affair (1952), 25, 133, 365-392, 433
    Government information policies, 184, 190, 191, 192, 193, 196, 197
    Manson case, 59, 191
    Presidential elections:
        1956, 252
        1960, 82, 90, 91, 151
            Campaign costs, 69
            TV debates, 36, 37, 393, 396, 397, 405, 406, 415, 417, 426, 428, 429, 430, 431, 433, 435, 436, 437, 440, 451, 454, 455
        1964, 46, 159, 161, 269, 272, 431, 432, 435
        1968, 51, 59, 100
            Campaign costs, 227, 231, 232, 233, 234, 235, 236, 237, 238, 239, 240, 241, 242
            Newspaper endorsements, 100
            Republican convention, 99
            TV debates, 229, 278, 445, 453, 454, 455, 458, 459, 460, 462, 463, 464, 465, 466, 467, 471, 472, 473, 474, 475, 476, 477, 478
    Press conferences, 52, 59, 105, 141, 147, 153, 156, 191, 192, 193, 195, 197, 199
    Press criticisms, 444
    Press relations, 51, 52, 80, 153, 156, 182, 184, 193, 195, 198, 199
    Vice-Presidency, 135, 138
    "Kitchen debate" with Khrushchev, 73
    Special TV appearances, 201
    State of the Union message, 191
    "The Political Obituary of Richard M. Nixon", 76
    Vietnam, 531

Nobleman, Eli E., 313, 314
Nolan, Lloyd, 147
Norman, Craig and Kummel, 158
Northwestern University, 305
Nossiter, Bernard C., 573
Novins, Stuart, 397

Oakes, James L., 591
Oakes, John B., 175, 319, 563
Oatis, William N., 306
O'Brien, Lawrence F., 233, 238, 280, 282, 357, 466, 467, 469
O'Connor, Basil, 362
O'Connor, Frank D., 172, 217, 275, 469
O'Connor, Patrick, 244
Odegard, Peter H., 436
O'Doherty, Kieran, 553
O'Donnell, John, 31
O'Donnell, Kenneth, 59
O'Dwyer, William, 11, 370
Oehlert, Benjamin H., Jr., 610
O'Hara, James G., 470, 471
O'Keefe, John, 294
Okuley, Bert W., 555
Olson, Betsy, 468
Olson, Kenneth E., 305
O'Meara, Andrew P., 177
Opinion Research Center, National, 430
Oppenheimer, J. Robert, 28, 135, 136
Orange, Adam M., 263
Oswald, Lee Harvey, 82
Ottinger, Richard L., 194, 230, 231, 522
Overseas Press Club of America, 175, 546
Owens, John W., 63

Pachios, Harold C., 167
Painter, Ralph, 162
Paley, William S., 19, 27, 89, 204, 246, 304, 532, 539
Papert, Koenig, Lois, Inc., 44
Parker, Barrington D., 245
Parker, Everett C., 187
Pastore, John O., 327, 499
    Equal time, 264, 269, 272, 280, 282, 283, 285, 430, 440, 470
    Proposal for government financing of campaigns, 242
    Proposal for reduced cost air time, 226-230, 240, 241
    Sponsors Senate bill on broadcast licenses, 103, 187
Patterson, Alicia, 173
Patterson, Eugene C., 573
Patterson, Jack F., 573
Patton, George S., Jr., 381
Paul, Mrs. J. R., 505
Paul, Weiss, Rifkind, Wharton & Garrison, 277
Paulucci, Jeno, 244
Payne, George H., 250
Payne, John, 147
Payzs, Tibor, 147
Peabody Award, George Foster, 334
Peabody Coal Co., 348
Pearson, Drew, 31, 40, 64, 140, 447

Pearson, James B., 188, 235, 240
Pearson, Robert B., 225, 228, 229
Pegler, Westbrook, 130
Pemberton, John deV., Jr., 496
Pen and Pencil Club, 116
Pentagon Papers, The, 358, 534, 556-610
Pepper, Thomas, 96
Percy, Charles H., 454
Peretz, Martin, 244
Performing artists, political activity, 130, 147, 519
Person, W. Theodore, 282
Phillips, Warren, 176
Phillips, Wayne, 169
Phillips, Z. B., 5
Picker, Arnold M., 244
Pickle, J. J., 533
Pierson, W. Theodore, 299
"Plate-side chat", 116
Plumley, Ladd, 505
Police, International Association of Chiefs of, 526
"Political Obituary of Richard M. Nixon, The", 76
Political parties, Minority:
    Campaign finances, 218, 229
    Equal ti..ne for, 227, 239, 252, 253, 254, 256, 257,
        262, 263, 264, 265, 266, 285, 433, 435, 436,
        439, 440, 472
    Free time for, 275
Political rally, effect of mass communications on, 108
Political Science Association, American, 146, 432, 436
Polk, James H., 177
Pollard, James E., 16
Pollock, James K., 147, 208
Pollock, John C., 324
Poole, Cecil, 354
Poor Richard Club, 27
Pope, James S., 306
Porter, Paul A., 25
Post, Robert, 31
Potter, Philip, 518
Powell, Adam Clayton, 175, 346
President's Club, 162
Press, freedom of, 7, 16, 39, 49, 75, 76, 118, 139, 179,
    188, 200, 290, 292, 297, 304, 534, 535, 567, 586,
    589, 592, 593, 595, 606, 610
Press Association, Inter-American, 305, 327
Press Club, National, 476, 517
Press Club, Women's National, 339
Press Club of America, Overseas, 175, 546
Press Conference, Inter-American (1950), 305
Press conferences, 117, 272
    See also specific President
Press Photographers Association, National, 358
Press Telecommunications Committee, International, 178
Preston, Hayden, 512
Price, Byron, 336, 340
Price, Robert, 186
Price, Waterhouse and Co., 381
Prouty, Winston L., 238
Psychiatric Association, American, 479, 483, 485
Public affairs programming, TV-radio, 188

Public Opinion Surveys, Princeton, N.J., 216
Publications, reduced rate postage, 258
Publishers, Association of American, 358
Publishers Auxiliary, Chicago, 131

Quarles, Donald A., 318
Quayle, Oliver, 206
Quemoy-Matsu issue (1960), 37, 406, 415, 417, 428

Radio:
    Competition from TV, 23
    Coverage of court proceedings, 101, 342, 348
    Expected to shorten political speeches, 247
    First use for election returns, 2
    First use at nominating conventions (1924), 204
    First use for political campaign, 108
    Free time proposals, 214, 223, 226, 245, 249, 252,
        254, 275, 276, 277
    Interview programs, 111
    Mass audience for public events, 108, 111, 113
        Roosevelt inauguration (1937), 5
    News commentators, 333, 334
    Presidential criticism of, 118
    Self-censorship urged, 64, 336
    See also Advertising, political; Equal time; specific
        network, station
Radio, Committee on Civic Education By, 3
Radio and Television Executives Society, 392
Radio and Television Society, International, 170, 190,
    287, 352
Radio Corporation of America, 65
Radio Institute of Audible Arts, 3
Radio-TV stations, Licensing of, 103, 105, 188, 248,
    257, 271, 286, 293, 298, 299, 316, 344, 352, 357,
    499, 517, 520
Rafferty, Max, 228
Raggio, William, 521
Rambert, Maurice, 4
Rand Corporation of California, 268
Randolph, Jennings, 104
Raskin, A. H., 175
Rather, Dan, 91
Rayburn, Sam, 322, 393
Reader's Digest, 163
Reagan, Ronald, 59, 88, 90, 453, 496, 569
Reardon, Paul C., 101
Reasoner, Harry, 531
Reece, Carroll, 251
Reece, Norval, 460
Reed, Thomas H., 3
Reedy, George E., 48, 165, 166, 167, 184, 437
Reeves, Rosser, 147
Reid, Ogden R., 350
Reid, Ralph W., 145
Reinsch, J. Leonard, 254, 396, 428
Reis, Harold F., 354
Reischauer, Edwin O., 545
Reitman, Alan, 529
"Report to the People", 49
Reporters:
    Alleged intemidation of, 156

Subpoena of notes by gov't., 286, 354, 358, 520, 528, 529, 530, 532, 533, 534, 535, 607
"Reporters Round-Up," 263
Republican National Committee, 268, 282, 355, 379, 380, 381, 388, 390, 391
    1936 Presidential election, 205, 207, 246, 247
    1952 campaign expenditures, 208, 214
    1956 campaign expenditures, 215
Reston, James, 50, 76, 85, 100, 139, 142, 276, 279, 339, 353, 428, 433, 563
Reuss, Henry, 76, 339
Reuther, Walter, 483
Reynolds, Frank, 53, 446, 451
Reynolds, R. J., 206
Rhodes, James A., 183
Ribicoff, Abraham A., 95, 392
Richmond *Times-Dispatch,* 553
Richter, John B., 586
Riesel, Victor, 175
Robb, Gene, 76
Robb, Roger, 479, 480, 483, 484, 573, 590
Roberts, Chalmers M., 573
Roberts, Roy A., 316
Robertson, Walter S., 417
Robinson, Hubbell, Jr., 259, 332
Robinson, Joseph T., 5
Robinson, Spotswood W., 3d, 573, 590
Rockefeller, Mrs. John D., Jr., 244
Rockefeller, Nelson A., 44, 73, 81, 526
  New York gubernatorial elections:
    1958, 118
    1962, 432
    1966, 88, 171, 172
      Campaign costs, 217, 227, 275
    1970 campaign costs, 59, 194, 232
  Presidential elections:
    1960, 263, 267
    1964, 156, 158, 159, 161, 431, 432, 436, 440
      California primary, 79
    1968, 453, 454, 455, 458, 459
      Campaign costs, 244, 454
Rockefeller, Winthrop, 2nd, 194
Rockefeller Foundation, 348
Rogers, Ginger, 147
Rogers, Lawrence H., 2d, 341
Rogers, Walter E., 271
Rogers, Will, 236
Rogers, William P., 192, 260, 261, 325, 379, 381, 561, 563, 568
Rolfson, John, 80
Romney, George W., 81, 159, 175, 496
Roosevelt, Franklin D., 4, 116
  Criticisms of the press, 63, 114
  Fireside chats, 3, 4, 6, 28, 159, 169, 247
  Government information policies, 296
  Health, a campaign issue, 140
  "Microphone technique", 3, 6, 62, 108
  Political use of radio, 5, 40, 204, 206, 247
  Presidential election (1936), 5, 62, 110, 246
  Press conferences, 16, 29, 31, 40, 115, 117, 119, 144, 292
  Press relations, 113, 116, 291, 292
Roosevelt, Franklin D., Jr., 171, 217, 275
Roosevelt, Theodore, 29, 31, 36, 40, 199
Root, Elihu, 62
Roper, Elmo, 436
Rosenfeld, Stephen, 348
Rosenthal, A. M., 224, 563, 569
Rosenwald, Cynthia, 497
Ross, Charles G., 29, 126, 127, 130, 300, 301
Ross, David, 179
Ross, Robert Tripp, 318
Rostow, Eugene, 352
Rostow, Walt W., 193, 544, 569, 571, 609
Roth, William V., 351
Rowan, George, 370
Rowan, Robert, 370
Rowe, Charles S., 76
Rowley, James, 300
Royster, Vermont, 181, 316
Rubin, William B., 297
Ruby, Jack, 82
Rumsfeld, Donald, 467
Rusk, Dean, 48, 49, 59, 186, 192, 436, 447, 538, 539, 544, 545, 569, 594, 607, 609
Russell, Margery F., 244
Russell, Richard, 20, 23
Rutstein, David B., 140

Sacharoff, Mark, 609
Safer, Morley, 546
St. John, Jill, 90
St. Louis Post-Dispatch, 49
Salant, Richard S., 51, 89, 95, 100, 169, 190, 252, 257, 357, 460, 461, 527, 528
Salinger, Pierre, 91, 171
  California senatorial election (1964), 78
  Press consultant, RFK (1968), 94, 184, 446
  Press secretary, JFK administration, 40, 48, 75, 149, 151, 152, 216, 267, 330, 339
  Press secretary, LBJ administration, 158, 166
Salisbury, Harrison E., 358, 548, 550
San Francisco Chronicle, 162
Sanders, Doug, 524
Sarnoff, David, 65
Sarnoff, Robert W., 81, 259, 261, 262, 268, 331, 393, 396, 415, 432, 441, 442
Saturday Evening Post, 485
Sawyer, Charles, 16
Sawyer, Grant, 81
Saxbe, William B., 238
Schafer, Roy A., 266, 267
Scherr, Max, 96
Scheubel, Miss Reggie, 158
Schick Safety Razor Company, 76
Schine, Gerald D., 28
Schlesinger, Arthur M., Jr., 59, 85, 459
Schneider, John A., 538, 539
Schoenbrun, David, 224, 496

Schorr, Daniel, 80, 162
Schultz, Chiz, 352
Schultz, George P., 201
Schwarz, Daniel, 563
Scott, Hugh, 216, 231, 238, 240, 241, 242, 281, 333, 426, 440, 470, 497, 561, 569
Scranton, William W., 81, 159, 161, 216, 436, 440
Scribner, Frederick C., 145, 428
"Searchlight" (WNBC-TV), 179
Seaton, Fred, 366, 369, 376, 378
"See It Now" (CBS), 539
Seldes, Gilbert, 439
"Selling of the Pentagon", 286, 358, 525-526, 527-535, 610
Seltzer, Louis B., 316
Sevareid, Eric, 71, 72, 94, 95, 195, 200, 347, 463, 496, 507, 509, 541, 542
Seymour, Whitney North, 358
Seymour, Whitney North, Jr., 591, 592
Shadel, Bill, 74, 415
Shafer, Raymond P., 216
Shakespeare, Frank J., Jr., 506
Shapp, Milton J., 194, 216
Shapshak, Rene, 363
Shaw, George Bernard, 511
Sheehan, Neil, 563, 590, 606, 607
Sheehan, Timothy P., 257
Sheehan, William, 446
Shell Oil Company, 348
Shelton, Robert M., 182
Shepilov, Dmitri T., 139
Sherman, Norman, 446, 459
Shero, Jeff, 96
Shockley, William, 323
Short, Joseph, 306, 314, 315
Short, Robert E., 244
Shoup, Richard G., 533
Shriver, Sargent, 159, 174
Sidle, Winant, 553, 554, 555
Siegal, Allan M., 563
Siegel, Gerald, W., 573
Sigma Delta Chi, 72, 105, 267, 316, 318, 358, 496, 526
    Freedom of Information Committee, 347, 529
Sillman, Leonard R., 484
Simon, John, 511
Singiser, Frank, 417
Sisco, Joseph, 192
Smart, William B., 181
Smathers, George A., 473
Smith, Alfred E., 31, 36, 110
Smith, Dana C., 365, 366, 369, 370, 376, 379, 387, 391
Smith, Frank L., 209
Smith, Gerald L. K., 481
Smith, Gerard, 145
Smith, Harmon Dunlap, 208, 213
Smith, Hedrick, 563
Smith, Howard K., 76, 88, 159, 201, 397, 433, 507, 509, 531, 541
Smith, Howard W., 268
Smith, J. Joseph, 591

Smith, Kingsbury, 70
Smith, Malcolm E., Jr., 261
Smith, Margaret Chase, 159, 161, 238, 436
Smith, Merriman, 138
Smith, Preston, 194
Smith, Ralph T., 522
Smith, Tony, 164
Smith, W. Bedell, 121, 125, 126
Snyder, Al, 190
Snyder, Arnold, 79
Snyder, John W., 16
Snyder, Murray, 140, 322, 323, 325
Socialist Labor Party, 257, 435, 439
Socialist Party, 334
Sociological Association, American, 430
Sommer, Elke, 519
Sorensen, Theodore C., 45, 59, 104, 166, 277
Sparkman, John J., 131, 238, 365, 381
Spier, Carleton L., 512
Spillers, W. R., 609
Spivak, Alvin A., 406
Spivak, Lawrence E., 159
Spock, Benjamin, 522
Sprague, J. Russell, 387
Sprague, Mansfield, 145
Sprague, William B., 268
Springer, William L., 532, 533
Staebler, Neil, 147, 208
Staggers, Harley O., 343, 528, 530, 532, 533, 534, 535
Staley, Austin L., 303
Stamler, Joseph, 74
Stanley, Edward, 255
Stanton, Frank, 162, 171, 331, 354
    Congress, television coverage of, 104, 282
    Cost of political advertising, 226
    Democratic convention (1956), 71
    Democratic convention (1968), 96
    Dispute with Agnew, 495, 503, 525, 538, 539
    Editorials by broadcasters, 270, 271
    Election returns, delayed reporting, 81, 91
    Equal time, 258, 263, 265, 266, 268, 272, 273, 276, 277
        Proposes suspension of, 430, 433, 435, 438, 439, 440, 444, 456
    Free time for political candidates, 327
    Judicial proceedings, media coverage of, 341
    Letters to the editor, 230
    Offers debate time (1968), 467
    "Selling of the Pentagon", 528, 529, 532, 533, 534, 535
    TV debates (1960), 396, 405
Stark, Abe, 432
Stars and Stripes, 177
Starzel, Frank J., 266
Stassen, Harold E., 20, 72, 161, 393
State legislatures, broadcast of proceedings, 11
Stein, Howard, 244
Steinberg, Harris, 479, 480, 481, 482
Steinkraus, Herman W., 8
Steiwer, Frederick, 111

Stennis, John, 238, 320, 552
Sterling, George E., 303
Stern, Helen, 485
Stevenson, Adlai E., 159, 362, 477, 522
    Checkers affair, 366, 374, 378, 381, 388, 390, 391
    Cuban missile crisis, 338
    Presidential election (1952), 20, 25, 131
        Democratic convention, 23
    Presidential election (1956), 141, 252, 443
        Debate with Kefauver, 393
    Press criticisms, 69
Stevenson, Adlai E., 2nd, 194, 235, 522
Stewart, Potter, 592, 595, 606
Stokes, Carl B., 456
Stone, W. Clement, 522
Stone, Walker, 306
Storer Broadcasting Company, 49
Stratton, Samuel S., 496, 542
Strother, Randal, 131
Sugarman, Norman A., 208
Sullivan, Barry, 90
Sullivan, Ed, Show, 255
Sullivan, Frank J., 95
Sullivan, Mark, 292
Sullivan, William H., 192
Sulzberger, Arthur Hays, 290
Sulzberger, Arthur Ochs, 96, 354, 500, 503, 561, 563, 569, 573, 580, 591, 595
Sulzberger, C. L., 201
Summerfield, Arthur E., 208, 366, 376, 379, 380, 385, 387, 388, 391
Surrey, Stanley, 218
Surveys
    Gallup Poll, 236, 523, 605
    National Opinion Research Center, 430
    New York Times, 9, 11, 14, 188, 209, 371, 372, 387
    Of broadcast journalism, 103, 187
    Of Vietnam editorials (1968), 552, 553
    Public Opinion Surveys, N.J., 216
Sweeterman, John W., 573
Swygert, Luther M., 277
Sylvester, Arthur, 76, 336, 339, 340, 343, 544, 546
Symington, Stuart, 157, 188, 262, 265, 561

Taft, Robert A., 11, 17, 20, 22, 251, 257, 307, 374, 376, 378, 385
Taft, Robert, Jr., 437, 467
Taft, William H., 31
Tamm, Edward Allen, 590
Tananbaum, Martin, 275
Tannenbaum, Percy, 100
Taylor, Davidson, 72
Taylor, E. B., 322
Taylor, Maxwell D., 166, 539, 546, 569, 609
Taylor, Telford, 225, 436
Tebbel, John, 142
Television:
    Comparisons with publications, 19, 153
    Competition between networks, 538
    Coverage of court proceedings, 101, 341, 342, 348

Effects on:
    Motion pictures, 9
    Radio, 14, 23
Free time proposals, 214, 223, 226, 230, 245, 252, 254, 266, 274, 275, 276, 277, 327
Image of candidates, 20
Interview programs, 73, 91, 159, 168, 169, 198, 262, 263, 264, 274
    As surrogates for campaign debates, 453, 455, 456, 460
Licensing, *see* Radio-TV stations, licensing of
Mass audience for public events, 17, 36, 37, 38, 67
    Congressional hearings, 8, 11
News commentators, 53, 68, 73, 196, 542
Newscasts, 53, 178, 189, 257, 275
Public affairs programming, 188
Self-censorship urged, 59, 336, 344, 519
Toll TV, Joint Committee Against, 352
See also Advertising, political; Agnew, Spiro T., Equal time; *specific network, program, station*
Television Arts and Sciences, National Academy of, 91
Temple, Shirley, 90
Templeton, G., 484
Theater Owners, National Association of, 352
Thomas, Charles S., 318
Thomas, Helen, 158
Thomas, Lowell, 23, 118, 180, 204
Thome, Robert P., 573
Thompson, Charles A. H., 253, 268, 436
Thompson, Dorothy, 204
Thompson, Herbert L., 475, 490, 509, 518
Thurmond, Strom, 269, 440, 443, 463, 471
Tilt, Albert, 163
Time, 189, 497, 518
Time, Inc., 354
Tinker, Jack, and Partners, 172, 217
Tobey, Charles W., 206
"Today Show" (WNBC TV), 75, 262, 263
"Tonight Show" (WNBC TV), 91
Tonkin Gulf Resolution, 569, 571, 586
Tower, John G., 183, 569
Townley, A. C., 326
Transaction, 484
Trealeaven, Harry, 194
Treibel, Charles O., 145
Treyz, Oliver, 327, 332
Triangle Publications, Inc., 190
Trout, Robert, 23, 141
Trujillo Molina, Rafael Leonidas, 363
Truman, Harry S., 11, 17, 130, 134
    Government information policies, 305, 308, 310, 313, 314, 315, 318
    Presidential elections:
        1948, 36
        1952, 25
        1956, 71, 141
        1960, 73, 265
    Press conferences, 29, 31, 40, 59, 120, 127, 131, 133, 144
    Press relations, 40, 127, 129, 138, 300, 315
    Walking, 361-364

Truman, Margaret, 362, 363, 364
Tubby, Roger, 325
Tuchman, Barbara, 225
Tuck, Richard, 473
Tumulty, T. James, 387
Tunney, John V., 194
Twentieth Century Fund, 186, 226, 245, 527
Twining, Nathan F., 139
Tyler, Harold R., Jr., 479, 480, 483, 484

Udall, Morris K., 459
Underground press, 96, 528
Underground Press Service, 96
Uniform poll closing, proposals for, 91
Union Carbide Corp., 348
United Nations, proposed convention on news gathering (1949), 302
United Press International, 266, 272, 327, 343, 555
United States:
    Administrative Procedure Act, 342
    American Military Information Office, Vietnam, 536
    Archives, National, 348, 561
    Armed Forces publications and broadcasting facilities, 177, 222, 223, 299, 353, 527
    Army, Dep't. of, Censorship of military personnel, 536
    Campaign Broadcast Reform, 227, 228, 229, 230, 231, 232, 233, 234, 235, 237, 238, 239, 240, 241, 242
    Civil Disorders, National Advisory Commission on, 94, 95, 224, 447
    Civil Service Commission, 330
    Communications Act, Federal (1934), 253, 257, 263, 264, 277, 284
    Communications Commission, Federal, 38, 51, 79, 81, 91, 101, 178, 187, 188, 190, 196, 204, 207, 214, 223, 227, 229, 248, 250, 252, 253, 254, 255, 256, 257, 258, 259, 260, 261, 262, 263, 264, 265, 268, 269, 271, 273, 274, 276, 277, 280, 282, 283, 285, 287, 290, 291, 293, 297, 298, 299, 300, 303, 316, 327, 331, 335, 344, 345, 351, 352, 355, 357, 528, 529, 531
        Survey of Political Broadcasting (1968), 225, 226
    See also Burch, Dean (F.C.C. Chairman)
    Congress: General
        Broadcast of proceedings:
            Hearings, 8, 11, 28, 141, 269, 348, 538, 539, 541
            Other proceedings, 31, 79, 250, 279, 280, 281, 282
    Congress: House of Representatives
        Campaign expenditures, special committee to investigate, 208, 209, 213, 214
        Commerce Committee, 343, 526
        Freedom of Information and Government Operations Subcommittee, 349, 351
        Government Information, Subcommittee on, 76, 142, 325
        Government Information and Foreign Operations Subcommittee, 338, 339, 342, 343
        Government Operations Committee, 151, 350
        Interstate and Foreign Commerce Committee, 51, 268, 269, 270, 528, 530, 532, 533, 534, 535
        Judiciary Committee, 335
        Un-American Activities, Committee on, 369

Congress: Senate
    Administrative Practice and Procedure Subcommittee, 350
    Black Committee, 290
    Campaign Expenditures, Committee on, 206, 297
    Commerce Committee, 91, 261, 272
        Subcommittee on Communications, 226, 227, 229, 269, 499
    Constitutional Rights, Subcommittee on, 105
    Crime Investigating Committee, 8, 11
    Declines to seat members due to campaign financing, 209
    Elections Subcommittee, 18
    Foreign Relations Committee, 146, 151, 538, 539, 545, 546, 561, 590
    Freedom of Communications, Subcommittee on, 333, 334
    Internal Security Subcommittee, 316, 317
    Judiciary Committee, 104, 188, 341
    Standards and Conduct, Select Committee on, 179
Corrupt Practices Act (1925), 25, 224, 231, 240
Crime and Violence, President's Commission on, 51
Defense, Department of, 348, 351
    Information policies and press briefings, Vietnam, 544, 545, 546, 553, 554, 555
    Public relations, 527, 529
Economic Advisers, President's Council of, 49
Emergency Planning, Office of, 254
Federal Agencies, disclosures under Freedom of Information Act, 348
Federal Reserve Board, 348
Federal Trade Commission, 348, 351
Freedom of Information Act, 345, 346, 347, 348, 350, 351, 607
Government information policies, 49, 52, 53, 134, 171, 176, 177, 182, 184, 190, 192, 195, 196, 199, 200, 248, 279, 317, 324, 326, 339, 341, 342, 343, 345, 346, 347, 348, 542
    Censorship, 544
        By Defense Department, 326, 343, 347, 349, 353
        Of Government officials, 186
        Of newspapers, 171, 177, 189, 294, 300, 301, 304, 327, 330, 335
        Of newsreels, 301
        Of TV-radio, 51, 81, 177, 189, 190, 297, 331, 332, 335, 340, 352
    Central clearing house urged, 351
    "Credibility gap", 49, 174, 176, 181, 182, 184, 531, 545, 550
    "Freedom of information", 49, 105, 166
    Lies, 184, 186, 544, 590
    National security, 75, 171, 186, 321, 322, 327, 336, 337, 561, 569, 571, 586, 589, 592, 594, 610
    "News leaks", 49, 85, 120, 134, 135, 136, 142, 151, 165, 182, 318, 319, 320, 322, 323, 330, 340, 343, 347, 349, 542, 543, 544
    "News management", 76, 151, 156, 176, 177, 186, 248, 308, 325, 336, 337, 338, 339, 343, 347, 544
    Official briefings, 146, 184, 192, 193
    Presidential press secretary, 29, 48, 49, 59, 75, 91, 165, 166, 167, 173, 174, 184

Press conferences:
    Cabinet members, 16, 28, 105, 146, 175
    Presidential, 200, 301
       Political uses, 160, 192, 193, 196, 197, 273, 274
       TV-radio coverage, 19, 27, 31, 45, 46, 52, 59, 141, 149, 150, 152, 158, 167, 192, 195, 199, 292
       See also specific President
    Press releases, 31, 53, 143, 192, 316, 554
    Propaganda, 66, 70, 114, 117, 140, 292, 297, 301
    Public relations, 8, 249, 292
    Secrecy, 75, 151, 308, 309, 318, 319, 322, 324, 325, 327, 331, 339, 571, 593
    Security classification, 142, 305, 306, 307, 308, 309, 311, 312, 313, 314, 316, 319, 572, 586, 588, 589
    "Trial balloons", 135
    TV appearances, special Presidential, 347
    White House, Office of Telecommunications, 287
Government Security, Commission on, 319, 320, 321, 322, 323
Health, Education and Welfare, Dep't. of, 348
Information Agency, 506, 545, 550
Intelligence Agency, Central, 85, 536, 586, 594
Interior, Dep't. of the, 348
International Television, Office of (proposed), 335
International Development, Agency for, 538
Investigation, Federal Bureau of, 543, 563
Justice Department, 344
Labor Relations Board, National, 348
Public Health Service, 348
Radio Act (1927), 204
Secretary of Communications, Proposal for, 352
Securities and Exchange Commission, 345
Subversive Activities Control Board, 358
Supreme Court, 591, 592, 595
    Proposals for broadcast of proceedings, 279
Veterans Administration, 348
Violence, National Commission on the Causes and Prevention of, 51, 100, 104

Unruh, Jesse, 463, 464
Urban Coalition, 237
U.S. News and World Report, 346, 490, 518
U-2 incident, 39, 76, 338, 406, 415

Vandenberg, Arthur H., 374
Van Dyk, Theodore, 457, 459, 460, 461
Vanocur, Sander, 397, 496
Vare, William S., 209
Veit, Ivan, 563
Vietnam war, media coverage, 536-609
    Criticism of, 498, 506, 524, 536, 542, 543, 544, 547, 552, 555
    Defense of, 525, 549
Vincent, Scott, 74
Vinson, Fred, 300
Voege, Roy, 91
Voght, John W., Jr., 192
Voice of America, 66, 121, 125, 126, 311

Volpicelli, Lou, 74
Voter registration, effect of TV-radio on, 25, 38
"Voters' time", 186, 245

WAAB radio, Boston, Mass., 293
Wade, Richard, 459
Wagner, Robert F., Jr., 392
Walker, Paul A., 208, 214, 303
Wall Street Journal, 40, 178
Wallace, George C., 364
    Criticisms of news media, 51, 53, 500
    Presidential election, 1968, 100, 101, 227, 444, 454, 458, 459
       Aide charged with seizure of film, 182
       Asks "equal coverage" for American Independent Party convention, 182
       Campaign debates on television, 460, 462, 463, 464, 465, 467, 469, 471, 472
       Equal time, 278, 285, 461
    Presidential election, 1972, 229
Wallace, Henry A., 119
Wallace, Mike, 91
Wallace, Tom, 305
Walrus, John, 96
Walt, Lewis W., 555
Walter, Francis E., 322
Walter, Wilmer J., 362
Walters, Barbara, 201
Waring, Fred, 130
Warnke, Paul C., 556
Warren, Charles, 397
Warren, Earl, 20
Warren, Gerald, 490
Warren Commission, 82
Wasey, Ruthrauf & Ryan, Inc., 163, 164
Washington, George, 16, 324
Washington Post, 78, 80, 130, 235, 348, 349, 358, 370, 371, 390, 457, 534, 545
    Dispute with Agnew, 496, 500, 514, 517, 518
    Pentagon Papers, 573, 590, 592, 594, 595
Washington press corps, 192, 199
Washington Star, 192, 349
Wasilewski, Vincent T., 285, 352, 495, 530
Wasserman, Lou, 244
Watson, W. Marvin, 173
Watts, Alan, 96
WBBM TV, Chicago, Ill., 85, 257
WDAY TV, Fargo, N.D., 324, 326
Weaver, Sylvester L. (Pat), 72
Webster, Edward M., 303
Wechsler, James, 224, 370, 380
Weeks, Sinclair, 207, 208, 209, 387
Weicker, Lowell P., 194
Weisl, Edwin L., 244
Weiss, Peter, 609
Welch, Robert, 481
Wells, Robert, 351, 355
Wendt, Lloyd, 99
Wertham, Frederic, 549
Western States Democratic Conference, 90

Westinghouse Broadcasting Co., 357
Westinghouse Radio Stations Inc., 303
Westland, Jack, 436, 437
Westmoreland, William C., 349
WGAR TV, Cleveland, Ohio, 25
WGCB, Red Lion, Pa., 188, 239
WGO TV, San Francisco, Calif., 451
Wheeler, Burton K., 248, 291
Wheeler, Earle G., 349
Wheeler, Harvey, 431, 477
Wheeler, Mrs. Houston F., 505
White, Byron R., 238, 481, 592, 595
White, Ed, 546
White, George W., Jr., 486, 488, 489
White, Harry Dexter, 191
White, Kevin H., 194
White, Lincoln, 66
White, Paul Dudley, 138
White, Paul W., 7
White, Wallace H., Jr., 298
White, William Allen, 160
White House broadcasting studio, 81, 191
Whitebrook, Lloyd G., 146
Whitehead, Clay T., 287
Whitney, John Hay, 152
Whitten, Thomas E., 208
WHLS radio, Pt. Huron, Mich., 299
Wicker, Tom, 438, 439, 563, 609
Wiebe, Gerhart D., 436
Wiegand, Harold J., 116
Wiesner, Jerome D., 459
Wiggins, James Russell, 31, 306
Wiley, W. Bradford, 358
Wilkey, Malcolm R., 590
Wilkins, Roger W., 344
Wilkinson, James, 191
Williams, Harrison A., Jr., 194
Williams, John J., 169, 222, 238
Williams, John R., 586
Williams, Paul, 96
Williams, Walter, 208
Willis, Everett I., 486, 488
Wilson, Charles E., 137, 142, 318, 322, 323

Wilson, John J., 485
Wilson, Woodrow, 29, 31, 36, 45, 82, 140
Winchell, Walter, 64
Wirtz, W. Willard, 168, 175, 178
Wisdom, John Minor, 387
WLW radio, Cincinnati, Ohio, 5
WMCA radio, New York, 334
WNDT TV, New York, 91
WNHC TV, New Haven, Conn., 190
WNYC radio, New York, 331
Wolff, Jerome, 489
Wolfson, Louis, 517
Women, National Organization of, 532
Women in Radio and Television, American, 277
Wood, Norman W., 489
Woods, Jack, 265
Woods, Mark, 64
Woodside, Byron D., 316
Working Press in Chicago, Association of the, 99
World Peace Foundation, 178
WRCA TV, New York, 137
Wright, J. Skelly, 573, 590
Wright, Lloyd, 46, 163, 320, 321, 322, 323
Wriston, Henry M., 520
WRKL radio, Mount Ivy, N.Y., 187
WSB TV, Atlanta, Ga., 187, 188
WTOP radio, Washington, D.C., 283, 500
WXYZ TV, Detroit, Mich., 147

Yarborough, Ralph W., 333
Yarmolinsky, Adam, 527
Young, Milton R., 238
Young, Robert, 147
Young, Stephen M., 437
Young Democratic Clubs, 266, 267
Young Republican National Federation, 267

Zassoursky, Yessen N., 353
Zenger Award, John Peter, 179
Ziegler, Ronald L., 183, 186, 189, 191, 193, 197, 238, 467, 500, 561, 569
Zorthian, Barry, 546
Zutter, Henry de, 99

Byline Index

Acheson, Dean, 606

Adams, Val, 68, 94, 172, 182, 254, 255, 258, 259, 334, 341, 430

Apple, R. W., Jr., 95, 244, 280, 447, 454, 498

Baker, Russell, 149, 214, 316, 397, 406, 415, 417, 588

Bart, Peter, 44, 158, 159

Belair, Felix, Jr., 144, 260, 350

Bendiner, Robert, 25

Benjamin, Philip, 74

Bigart, Homer, 486, 524

Blair, William M., 342

Borders, William, 508

Brady, Thomas F., 496

Brown, Francis, 108

Burks, Edward C., 497, 480, 481, 482, 483, 484

Charlton, Linda, 527

Dales, Douglas, 209, 255, 331

Dallos, Robert E., 217, 446, 447, 457

Davies, Lawrence E., 275, 323, 369, 379

Dennis, Lloyd B., 393

Dougherty, Philip H., 102, 172

Drury, Allen, 142, 326

Dunlap, Orrin E., Jr., 2, 3, 5, 6, 62, 113, 204

Ferretti, Fred, 103, 187, 190, 225, 226, 352

Finney, John W., 231

Flint, Jerry M., 499

Frankel, Max, 173, 182, 184, 195, 463, 465, 469, 472, 542, 544, 561

Franklin, Ben A., 216, 333, 460

Fried, Joseph P., 495

Galbraith, John Kenneth, 50

Gans, Herbert J., 53

Gardner, John W., 237, 245

Gent, George, 93, 99

Gould, Jack, 8, 9, 11, 14, 17, 18, 19, 20, 22, 23, 27, 51, 64, 71, 72, 73, 78, 79, 81, 83, 88, 91, 92, 94, 95, 100, 130, 150, 171, 178, 188, 239, 252, 253, 256, 261, 265, 266, 271, 272, 274, 278, 279, 284, 287, 331, 334, 344, 352, 357, 429, 453, 462, 463, 513, 519, 528, 529, 533, 538, 539, 541, 551

Graham, Fred P., 344, 461, 563, 580, 591, 592, 595

Gwertzman, Bernard, 185

Hagerty, James A., 549

Halberstam, David, 536

Halloran, Richard, 192, 497

Hamill, Pete, 46

Handler, M. S., 545

Herbers, John, 346, 445

Hill, Gladwin, 90, 153, 164, 365, 380, 381, 387

Hunter, Marjorie, 440, 467, 470, 471

Hurd, Charles W., 115

Huston, Luther, 117

Janson, Donald, 99, 347, 430, 440

Kennedy, Paul P., 370

Kenworthy, E. W., 152, 276, 320, 436, 452, 459, 472, 490, 496, 546

Kihss, Peter, 177

Klein, Herbert G., 197

Kluckhohn, Frank L., 296

Knowles, Clayton, 208, 213, 390, 391, 458

Krock, Arthur, 37, 48, 66, 67, 118, 119, 120, 134, 136, 165, 166, 167, 248, 304, 310, 314, 321, 337, 338, 375, 543

Lawrence, William H., 199, 262, 405, 426

Leo, John, 96

Leviero, Anthony, 127, 131, 300, 301, 307, 311

Lewis, Anthony, 80, 273

Lissner, Will, 84, 224

Loftus, Joseph A., 156, 348, 431, 435, 441

Lubasch, Arnold H., 159

Lydon, Christopher, 194, 196, 227, 230, 280, 282, 283, 355, 356, 357, 499, 500, 505, 534

McCormick, Anne O'Hare, 112

McFadden, Robert D., 498

Madden, Richard L., 514

Mallon, Winifred, 299

Middleton, Drew, 125

Minow, Newton N., 186

Mitgang, Herbert, 455, 474

Mohr, Charles, 442
Montgomery, Paul L., 495
Morris, John D., 394
Naughton, James M., 189, 198, 517, 518, 521, 524, 526, 573, 590
Nuccio, Sal, 161, 164
O'Connor, John J., 531
Phelps, Robert A., 481, 485
Phillips, Cabell, 29, 36, 339, 436
Phillips, Wayne, 363
Pomfret, John D., 49
Porter, Paul A., 298
Porter, Russell, 267, 317, 327
Raymond, Jack, 82, 139
Raymont, Henry, 89, 158, 358
Reed, Roy, 465, 475, 552
Reid, Ogden R., 607
Reston, James, 16, 28, 31, 38, 40, 46, 51, 77, 126, 133, 135, 137, 138, 143, 144, 145, 146, 150, 151, 156, 160, 168, 174, 191, 234, 251, 286, 308, 320, 322, 338, 347, 366, 374, 378, 385, 388, 470, 477, 504, 507, 510, 537, 541, 542, 568, 573, 590, 593
Roberts, Gene, 554
Roberts, Steven V., 523
Robinson, Douglas, 275
Ronan, Thomas P., 170
Salinger, Pierre, 59
Salisbury, Harrison E., 301, 426, 548, 550
Schonberg, Harold C., 512
Semple, Robert B., Jr., 167, 168, 183, 193, 201, 436, 454, 473, 477, 522

Sevareid, Eric, 199
Shanahan, Eileen, 223
Shanley, J. P., 70, 331
Shepard, Richard F., 75, 137, 257, 263
Sloane, Leonard, 163
Smith, Hedrick, 556
Spielvogel, Carl, 146
Stanton, Frank, 433
Stern, Philip M., 243
Stetson, Damon, 175
Sullivan, Ronald, 76
Sulzberger, C. L., 589
Szulc, Tad, 506
Teltsch, Kathleen, 302
Toth, Robert C., 76
Trussell, C. P., 254, 269, 324, 335
Vienna, David, 541
Weart, William G., 312
Weaver, Warren, Jr., 101, 188, 227, 232, 233, 235, 238, 240, 241, 285, 444, 456, 471, 473
Wehrwein, Austin C., 153
Weinraub, Bernard, 555
Welles, Benjamin, 177, 550
Wertham, Fredric, 547
Wicker, Tom, 38, 40, 45, 52, 59, 157, 166, 198, 218, 222, 241, 245, 281, 430, 437, 451, 535, 545, 572, 594, 607
Wolters, Larry, 19
Wood, Lewis, 303
Wooten, James T., 514
Wright, Robert A., 532
Yerxa, Fendall W., 443